D0902255

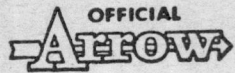

OFFICIAL

U.S. POSTAL ZIP CODE

DIRECTORY

COVERING ALL FIFTY STATES

- Detailed ZIP Code maps of principal cities

- Special Mail Services

- Alphabetical list of all Cities & Towns

- Latest Postal Rates — Domestic & Foreign

- Detailed street listings for Atlanta, Chicago, Detroit, New York City, and Metropolitan Boston

International Standard Book Number: 0-913450-87-1
Copyright © 1986 by Arrow Publishing Co., Inc.
All rights reserved

Published by Arrow Publishing Company, Inc.
1020 Turnpike Street
Canton, Massachusetts 02021
(Not affiliated with U.S. Postal Service)

First Edition © Arrow Street Guides, Inc., 1972
Second Edition © Pathfinder Publications, Inc. 1974
Second Printing, 1979
Third Printing, April, 1983
Fourth Printing, October, 1983
Fifth Printing, December, 1983
Sixth Printing, February, 1984
Seventh Printing, April, 1984
Third Edition © Arrow Publishing Co., Inc. 1984
Fourth Edition © Arrow Publishing Co., Inc. 1985
Second Printing, June, 1985
Fifth Edition © Arrow Publishing Co., Inc. 1986

Printed in the United States of America

CONTENTS

ZIP Code Map List vii

Introduction ix

Index to State Lists and
    City Appendices xi

Postal Rates xiii

Atlanta Street List 104

Chicago Street List 161

Boston Street List 259

Detroit Street List 351

New York Street List 465

Two-Letter State Abbreviations

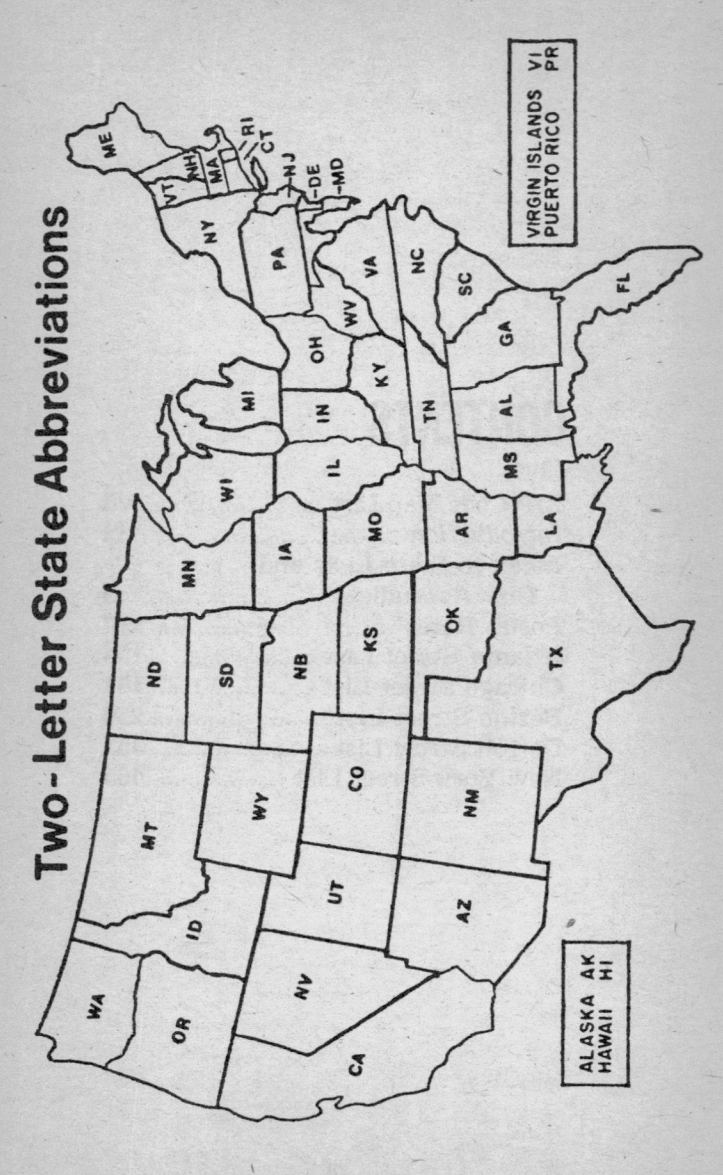

ZIP CODE MAP LIST

CITY	PAGE
Albuquerque, NM	436
Atlanta, GA	101
Baltimore, MD	248
Boston, MA	270
Boston Abbreviations	257
Bronx, NY	451
Brooklyn, NY	452
Charleston, SC	567
Chicago, IL	156
Cincinnati, OH	503
Dallas, TX	597
Des Moines, IA	210
Detroit, MI	350
Hartford, CT	67
Honolulu, HI	144
Indianapolis, IN	200
Kansas City, MO	400
Little Rock, AR	15
Los Angeles, CA	58
Manhattan, NY	461
Miami, FL	89
Milwaukee, WI	653
Minneapolis, MN	386
New Orleans, LA	234
Newark, NJ	428
Philadelphia, PA	543
Portland, ME	241
Portland, OR	523
Providence, RI	561
St. Louis, MO	404
San Francisco, CA	58
Tucson, AZ	15
Washington, D.C.	72

INTRODUCTION

WHAT IS ZIP CODE?

ZIP Code is a five-digit geographic code that identifies areas within the United States and its possessions for purposes of simplifying the distribution of mail by the U.S. Post Office Department.

In devising the ZIP Code, the United States and its possessions were divided into 10 large geographic areas. Each area consists of three or more States or possessions and is given a number between 0 and 9.

ZIP CODE NATIONAL AREAS

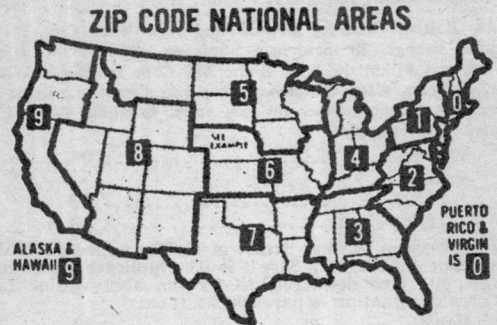

Because of favorable transportation facilities, key post offices in each area are designated as Sectional Centers. Each Sectional Center post office receives and transmits mail moving between post offices within its section. It also receives and transmits all mail moving into or out of the section.

WHAT YOUR ZIP CODE MEANS

• Together, the first three digits of any ZIP Code number stand for either a particular Sectional Center or a metropolitan city.

• The last two digits of a Sectional Center ZIP Code number stand for one of the associated post offices served by the Sectional Center.

• The last two digits of a metropolitan city ZIP Code stand for one of the delivery areas served by the city post office, its branches and stations.

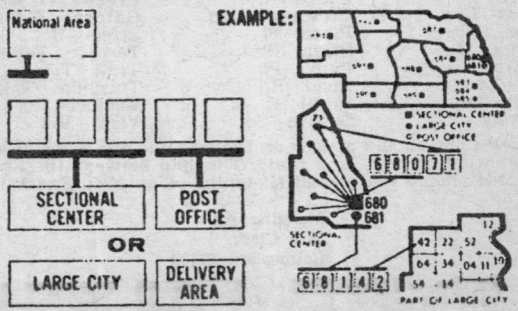

FINDING THE ZIP CODE IN THIS BOOK

Each State contains two parts, a STATE LIST containing all post offices in that State and all named stations and branches, and an APPENDIX, breaking down major cities that are multi-coded. The appendix section immediately follows the regular state listing, is in alphabetical order, and includes, if applicable, the following: Post Office Boxes, Rural Routes, Stations, Branches, and Units, Principal buildings, Hospitals, Colleges, and Universities. In the appendix section and street lists, the zip code is determined by copying the three digits at the top of the first column followed by the two digits beside the entry.

For Atlanta, Boston, Chicago, Detroit, and New York City, there are complete street listings. In these lists, where no house number is shown, the entire street is within the area of the ZIP Code indicated. When the word "out" appears after a number, it signifies that particular house number and any higher number on that street is within the ZIP Code area indicated. For example:

Walnut 06
Valley
    1-1399 09
    1400 — out 03

Thus, any address on Walnut Street is 06. The address 138 Valley Street is 09, but 1650 Valley Street is 03. Duplicate street names in the same city are distinguished by the abbreviation of the branch or area designation in parenthesis, thus:

Velvet 10
Velvet (T) 11

(The listing of postal facilities at the beginning of that city's appendix will give the full name of the branch.)

NOTE: The notation "(1st)" is used to identify First Class Post Offices as an assistance to Parcel Post mailers. The class of a particular post office determines the size and weight of parcels that may be mailed from it.

In addition, the following abbreviations are used:

Alley—Aly	Causeway- Cswy	Drive- Dr
Arcade- Arc	Center -Ctr	Expressway Expy
Avenue Ave	Circle -Cir	Extended- Ext
Boulevard Blvd	Court- Ct	Extension- Ext
Branch Br	Courts- Cts	Freeway -Fwy
Bypass- Byp	Crescent Cres	Gardens- Gdns
Grove -Grv	Place -Pl	Street--St
Heights Hts	Plaza- Plz	Terrace- Ter
Highway Hwy	Point- Pt	Trail Trl
Lane- Ln	Road--Rd	Turnpike- Tpke
Manor- Mnr	Rural- R	Viaduct —Via
Parkway--Pky	Square—Sq	Vista - Vis

The ZIP Code should appear on the last line of all postal addresses, following the city and State. The gap between the State and ZIP Code should not exceed six-tenths of an inch. Example:

Mr. Eric Allen
3850 Clark
Boston, MA 02109

INDEX to STATE LISTS and CITY APPENDICES

	Page		Page		Page
ALABAMA	1	Santa Rosa	55	Peoria	191
Birmingham	5	Stockton	56	Rockford	192
Gadsden	6	Sunnyvale	56	Springfield	192
Huntsville	6	Thousand Oaks	56	**INDIANA**	193
Mobile	6	Torrance	56	Anderson	198
Montgomery	7	Van Nuys	56	Evansville	198
ALASKA	9	Ventura	57	Fort Wayne	199
Anchorage	10	Walnut Creek	57	Gary	199
ARIZONA	11	West Covina	57	Hammond	201
Glendale	13	Whittier	57	Indianapolis	201
Mesa	13	Wilmington	57	Lafayette	202
Phoenix	13	**COLORADO**	59	Muncie	202
Scottsdale	14	Arvada	62	South Bend	202
Tempe	14	Boulder	62	Terre Haute	203
Tucson	14	Colorado Springs	62	**IOWA**	204
ARKANSAS	16	Denver	62	Cedar Rapids	209
Little Rock	20	Littleton	64	Davenport	209
North Little Rock	20	Pueblo	64	Des Moines	211
CALIFORNIA	21	**CONNECTICUT**	65	Sioux City	212
Alhambra	32	Bridgeport	68	Waterloo	213
Anaheim	32	Hartford	68	**KANSAS**	214
Bakersfield	33	New Britain	68	Kansas City	218
Berkeley	33	New Haven	69	Shawnee Mission	218
Beverly Hills	34	Norwalk	69	Topeka	218
Buena Park	34	Stamford	69	Wichita	219
Burbank	34	Waterbury	70	**KENTUCKY**	220
Canoga Park	34	**DELAWARE**	71	Covington	227
Chula Vista	34	Wilmington	71	Lexington	227
Compton	34	**DISTRICT OF**		Louisville	228
Concord	34	**COLUMBIA**	73	Newport	229
Costa Mesa	34	Washington	73	**LOUISIANA**	230
Daly City	34	**FLORIDA**	79	Baton Rouge	233
Downey	35	Bradenton	85	Metairie	235
El Cajon	35	Clearwater	85	New Orleans	235
El Monte	35	Daytona Beach	85	Shreveport	237
Escondido	35	Fort Lauderdale	85	**MAINE**	238
Fremont	35	Fort Myers	86	Portland	242
Fresno	35	Hialeah	86	**MARYLAND**	243
Fullerton	36	Hollywood	86	Annapolis	246
Gardena	36	Jacksonville	87	Baltimore	247
Garden Grove	37	Lakeland	88	Ellicott City	251
Glendale	37	Melbourne	88	Hyattsville	252
Hayward	37	Miami	90	Rockville	252
Huntington Beach	38	Orlando	91	Silver Spring	252
Inglewood	38	Pensacola	92	**MASSACHUSETTS**	253
Laguna Beach	38	Pompano Beach	92	Ayer	255
Lakewood	38	St. Petersburg	93	Boston	255
La Puente	38	Sarasota	93	Brockton	340
Long Beach	38	Tallahassee	94	Chicopee	340
Los Angeles	39	Tampa	94	Fall River	340
Modesto	44	West Palm Beach	95	Falmouth	340
Mountain View	44	**GEORGIA**	96	Lawrence	341
Newport Beach	44	Albany	102	Lowell	341
North Hollywood	44	Atlanta	102	Lynn	341
Oakland	45	Augusta	138	New Bedford	341
Ontario	46	Columbus	139	North Attleboro	341
Orange	46	Decatur	140	Plymouth	341
Palo Alto	46	Macon	141	Springfield	341
Pasadena	46	Savannah	142	Worcester	342
Pomona	47	**HAWAII**	143	**MICHIGAN**	342
Redondo Beach	47	Honolulu	145	Ann Arbor	348
Redwood City	47	**IDAHO**	146	Battle Creek	348
Richmond	47	Boise	148	Birmingham	349
Riverside	48	**ILLINOIS**	149	Dearborn	349
Sacramento	49	Arlington Heights	157	Detroit	349
San Bernardino	50	Aurora	157	Flint	376
San Diego	50	Belleville	157	Grand Rapids	377
San Fernando	51	Chicago	157	Jackson	378
San Francisco	52	Decatur	190	Kalamazoo	378
San Gabriel	53	Des Plaines	190	Lansing	378
San Jose	53	East Saint Louis	190	Livonia	378
San Leandro	53	Evanston	190	Muskegon	379
San Mateo	54	Joliet	191	Pontiac	379
San Pedro	54	Melrose Park	191	Royal Oak	379
San Rafael	54	Oak Lawn	191		
Santa Ana	54	Oak Park	191		
Santa Barbara	55				
Santa Clara	55				
Santa Monica	55			(Continued)	

MICHIGAN
(Continued)

	Page
Saginaw	379
Southfield	379
St. Clair Shores	379
Sterling Heights	380
Warren	380
Wyandotte	380

MINNESOTA ... 380

Duluth	385
Minneapolis	387
St. Paul	388

MISSISSIPPI ... 389

| Biloxi | 393 |
| Jackson | 393 |

MISSOURI ... 394

Florissant	401
Hazlewood	401
Independence	401
Kansas City	401
Saint Joseph	403
Saint Louis	405
Springfield	408

MONTANA ... 409

| Billings | 411 |
| Great Falls | 411 |

NEBRASKA ... 412

| Lincoln | 415 |
| Omaha | 415 |

NEVADA ... 417

| Las Vegas | 417 |
| Reno | 418 |

NEW HAMPSHIRE ... 418

| Manchester | 420 |

NEW JERSEY ... 420

Atlantic City	424
Camden	425
Cherry Hill	425
Clifton	426
East Orange	426
Elizabeth	426
Englewood	427
Hackensack	427
Jersey City	427
Montclair	429
Newark	429
New Brunswick	430
Orange	430
Passaic	430
Paterson	430
Perth Amboy	430
Plainfield	431
Rahway	431
Ridgewood	431
Rutherford	431
Trenton	431
Westfield	432

NEW MEXICO ... 432

| Albuquerque | 435 |

NEW YORK ... 437

Albany	448
Babylon	449
Binghamton	449
Bronx	449
Brooklyn	450
Buffalo	454
Elmira	456
Far Rockaway	456
Floral Park	457
Flushing	457
Great Neck	458
Hempstead	458
Hicksville	458
Jamaica	459
Long Island City	459

	Page
Mount Vernon	460
New Rochelle	460
New York	460
Niagara Falls	471
Poughkeepsie	471
Rochester	472
Rockville Centre	473
Schenectady	473
Staten Island	474
Syracuse	475
Troy	476
Utica	476
Valley Stream	476
White Plains	477
Yonkers	477

NORTH CAROLINA ... 478

Asheville	483
Charlotte	484
Durham	485
Fayettteville	486
Greensboro	487
High Point	488
Raleigh	488
Winston-Salem	489

NORTH DAKOTA ... 491

OHIO ... 494

Akron	501
Canton	501
Cincinnati	502
Cleveland	505
Columbus	507
Cuyahoga Falls	509
Dayton	509
Elyria	509
Hamilton	509
Lima	510
Lorain	510
Mansfield	510
Springfield	510
Toledo	511
Warren	511
Youngstown	512

OKLAHOMA ... 513

| Oklahoma City | 517 |
| Tulsa | 518 |

OREGON ... 519

Eugene	522
Portland	522
Salem	524

PENNSYLVANIA ... 525

Allentown	538
Altoona	538
Bethlehem	538
Chester	538
Erie	538
Harrisburg	539
Johnstown	540
Lancaster	540
Levittown	541
McKeesport	541
Media	541
New Castle	541
Norristown	542
Philadelphia	542
Pittsburgh	546
Pittston	552
Reading	552
Scranton	552
Upper Darby	553
Wilkes-Barre	553
York	554

PUERTO RICO ... 555

| San Juan | 557 |

RHODE ISLAND ... 559

| Pawtucket | 560 |
| Providence | 560 |

	Page
Wakefield	560
Warwick	562

SOUTH CAROLINA ... 563

Charleston	566
Columbia	568
Greenville	569
Spartanburg	570

SOUTH DAKOTA ... 571

| Sioux Falls | 573 |

TENNESSEE ... 574

Chattanooga	578
Kingsport	579
Knoxville	579
Memphis	579
Nashville	581

TEXAS ... 583

Abilene	593
Amarillo	593
Arlington	994
Austin	594
Beaumont	595
Corpus Christi	595
Dallas	596
El Paso	598
Fort Worth	600
Garland	601
Houston	601
Irving	603
Lubbock	603
Pasadena	604
San Antonio	604
Waco	606
Wichita Falls	606

UTAH ... 608

| Ogden | 610 |
| Salt Lake City | 610 |

VERMONT ... 612

VIRGINIA ... 614

Alexandria	621
Arlington	621
Charlottesville	622
Chesapeake	622
Falls Church	622
Hampton	623
Lynchburg	623
Newport News	623
Norfolk	624
Portsmouth	625
Richmond	625
Roanoke	627
Springfield	627
Virginia Beach	627

WASHINGTON ... 628

Bellevue	632
Everett	632
Olympia	633
Seattle	633
Spokane	634
Tacoma	635
Vancouver	636
Yakima	636

WEST VIRGINIA ... 638

| Charleston | 644 |
| Huntington | 644 |

WISCONSIN ... 646

Green Bay	651
Madison	651
Milwaukee	652
Racine	654

WYOMING ... 655

PACIFIC ISLANDS—
VIRGIN ISLANDS ... 657

DOMESTIC FIRST-CLASS RATES
(Effective February 17, 1985)

FIRST-CLASS

LETTER RATES:

1st ounce...22¢
Each additional ounce.................................17¢

For Pieces Not Exceeding (oz.)	The Rate Is	For Pieces Not Exceeding (oz.)	The Rate Is
1..................	$0.22	7..................	$1.24
2..................	0.39	8..................	1.41
3..................	0.56	9..................	1.58
4..................	0.73	10................	1.75
5..................	0.90	11................	1.92
6..................	1.07	12................	2.09

FOR PIECES OVER 12 OUNCES SEE FIRST-CLASS ZONE RATED (PRIORITY) MAIL RATES

CARD RATES:

Single postal cards sold by the post office.... 14¢ each.
Double postal cards sold by the post office... 28¢ (14¢ each half)
Single post cards....................................... 14¢ each.
Double post cards (reply-half of
double post card does not have to bear
postage when originally mailed)............. 28¢ (14¢ each half)
Presort rate.. Consult Postmaster
Business reply mail.................................. Consult Postmaster

Note: To qualify for *card rates*, a card may not be larger than 4¼ by 6 inches, nor smaller than 3½ by 5 inches. The thickness must be uniform and not less than 0.007 of an inch.

FIRST-CLASS ZONE RATED (PRIORITY) MAIL

Weight over 12 ounces and not exceeding—pound(s)	Local zones 1, 2, and 3	Zone 4	Zone 5	Zone 6	Zone 7	Zone 8
1	$2.40	$2.40	$2.40	$2.40	$2.40	$2.40
2	2.40	2.40	2.40	2.40	2.40	2.40
3	2.74	3.16	3.45	3.74	3.96	4.32
4	3.18	3.75	4.13	4.53	4.92	5.33
5	3.61	4.32	4.86	5.27	5.81	6.37
6	4.15	5.08	5.71	6.31	6.90	7.66
7	4.58	5.66	6.39	7.09	7.80	8.67
8	5.00	6.23	7.07	7.87	8.68	9.68
9	5.43	6.81	7.76	8.66	9.57	10.69
10	5.85	7.39	8.44	9.44	10.45	11.70
11	6.27	7.97	9.12	10.22	11.33	12.71
12	6.70	8.55	9.81	11.01	12.22	13.72
13	7.12	9.12	10.49	11.79	13.10	14.73
14	7.55	9.70	11.17	12.57	13.99	15.74
15	7.97	10.28	11.86	13.36	14.87	16.75
16	8.39	10.86	12.54	14.14	15.75	17.75
17	8.82	11.44	13.22	14.92	16.64	18.76
18	9.24	12.01	13.90	15.70	17.52	19.77
19	9.67	12.59	14.59	16.49	18.41	20.78
20	10.09	13.17	15.27	17.27	19.29	21.79

For rates on items greater than 20 lbs. and over 84 inches in girth, consult your local post office.

* Be sure to obtain from your local post office the "Official Zone Chart" for your city in order to determine the proper zone.

INTERNATIONAL FIRST-CLASS RATES

A. *Regular Surface Mail* - Letters and Post Cards (Countries except Canada and Mexico)

    37 cents for the first ounce;

    20 cents for each additional ounce up to 8 ozs;

    $3.40 for 9 ozs. up to 16 ozs;

    $4.66 for 17 ozs. up to 24 ozs;

    $5.92 for 25 ozs. up to 32 ozs;

    $6.84 for 33 ozs. up to 40 ozs;

    $7.76 for 41 ozs. up to 48 ozs;

    $8.68 for 49 ozs. up to 56 ozs;

    $9.60 for 57 ozs. up to 64 ozs;

    25 cents each for post cards.

Weight limit: 4 pounds.

B. *Air Mail* - Letters , Aerogrammes and Post Cards

To Central America, Colombia, Venezuela, the Caribbean Islands, the Bahamas, Bermuda, and the Islands of St. Pierre and Miquelon. Also from American Samoa to Western Samoa and from Guam to the Philippines.

    39 cents for each ½ ounce up to and including 2 ozs. and

    33 cents each additional ½ ounce up to and including 32 ozs.

    33 cents each additional ounce over 32 ozs.

All other countries (except Canada and Mexico)

    44 cents for each ½ ounce up to and including 2 ozs. and

    39 cents for each additional ½ ounce up to and including 32 ozs.

    39 cents for each additional ounce over 32 ozs.

    36 cents each for aerogrammes.

    33 cents each for post cards.

Weight limit: 4 pounds.

C. *Canada and Mexico* - Surface Rates For Letters, Letter Packages and Post Cards

    22 cents for the first ounce;

    18 cents for each additional ounce up to 12 ozs;

    64 cents for 13 ozs. to 16 ozs;

    64 cents for each additional ½ pound (8 ozs.) up to 4 pounds;

    14 cents each for post cards.

Weight limit: 4 pounds.

NOTE: Letter class mail to Canada and Mexico receives First-Class service in the United States and airmail service in Canada and Mexico.

DOMESTIC PARCEL POST

Service by the U.S. Postal Service

Rates for parcel post are governed by a zone structure. You must request the 'Official Zone Chart' and the table of rates from your local post office. There are eight zones, each with sixty-nine rate steps.

U.P.S. MAILING INFORMATION

Service by the United Parcel Service (UPS)

This organization, a private company, offers a service in the parcel delivery field which competes favorably with the U.S. Postal Service. UPS distinctive brown vans are seen almost as often in metropolitan areas as those of the U.S. Postal Service.

UPS is very competitive on both rates and service, particularly if the destination is within 500 miles. They also handle expeditiously parcels outside the U.S. Postal Service's weight and size regulations.

Call your local UPS office for further information.

ALABAMA
(Abbreviation: AL)

Abbeville............................36310
Abernant............................35440
Acmar...............................35004
Adamsville..........................35005
Addison.............................35540
Adger...............................35006
Akron...............................35441
Alabama City, Sta. Gadsden..35904
Alabaster (1st)....................35007
Alberta.............................36720
Albertville (1st)..................35950
Alden...............................35008
Alexander City (1st)...............35010
Alexandria..........................36250
Aliceville..........................35442
Allen...............................36419
Allgood.............................35013
Alma................................36501
Alpine..............................35014
Alton...............................35015
Altoona.............................35952
Andalusia (1st)....................36420
Anderson............................35610
Annemanie...........................36721
Anniston (1st).....................36201
Ansley..............................36001
Arab (1st).........................35016
Ardmore Highway, Sta.
  Huntsville........................35805
Ariton..............................36311
Arkadelphia, R. Br. Bremen..35033
Arley...............................35541
Arlington...........................36722
Armstrong...........................36002
Ashford.............................36312
Ashland.............................36251
Ashville............................35953
  Whitney, R. Sta..................35991
Athens (1st).......................35611
Atmore (1st).......................36502
  Canoe, R. Br.....................36514
Attalla (1st)......................35954
Auburn (1st).......................36830
Autaugaville........................36003
Avondale, Sta. Birmingham..35222
Axis................................36505
Baileyton...........................35019
Baker Hill..........................36004
Banks...............................36005
Bankston............................35542
Barlow Bend.........................36506
Barton..............................35614
Bates Field, R. Br. Mobile..36608
Bay Minette (1st)..................36507
Bayou La Batre......................36509
Bear Creek..........................35543
Beatrice............................36425
Beaverton...........................35544
Bel Air, Sta. Mobile...............36606
Belk................................35545
Bellamy.............................36901
Belle Mina..........................35615
Bellwood............................36313
Benton, R. Br. Tyler...............36785
Berry...............................35546
Bessemer (1st).....................35020
Bexar...............................35547
Bigbee..............................36510
Billingsley.........................36006

BIRMINGHAM (1st) (see
  appendix)
Black...............................36314
Bladon Springs......................36902
Blountsville........................35031
Blue Mountain, Br. Anniston..36201
Blue Spring, Sta. Huntsville
  (see appendix)
Bluff Park, Br. Birmingham..35226
Boaz (1st).........................35957
Boligee.............................35443
Bolinger............................36903
Boling..............................36007
Bon Air.............................35032
Bon Secour..........................36511
Booth...............................36008
Borden Springs......................36252
Boykin..............................36723
Boyleston, Br. Montgomery..36110
Boys Ranch, R. Br. Minter..36761
Brantley............................36009
Bremen..............................35033
Brent...............................35034
Brewton (1st)......................36426
Bridgeport..........................35740
Brierfield..........................35035
Brighton, Br. Bessemer..35020
Brilliant...........................35548
Brooklyn............................36429
Brookside...........................35036
Brookwood...........................35444
Browns..............................36724
Brownsboro..........................35741
Brownville, R. Br. Northport..35445
Brundidge...........................36010
Bryant..............................35958
Bucks...............................36512
Buena Vista.........................36430
Buhl................................35446
Burkville...........................36725
Burnt Corn..........................36431
Burnwell............................35038
Butler (1st).......................36904
  Choctaw, R. Br..................36905
Bynum...............................36253
Cahaba Heights, Br.
  Birmingham........................35243
Calcis, R. Br. Vincent..35039
Calera..............................35040
Calhoun.............................36012
Calvert.............................36513
Camden (1st).......................36726
Camp Hill...........................36850
Campbell............................36727
Canoe, R. Br. Atmore...............36514
Capitol Heights, Sta.
  Montgomery........................36107
Capps...............................36315
Capshaw.............................35742
Carbon Hill.........................35549
Cardiff.............................35041
Carlton, R. Br. Jackson..36515
Caroline Avenue, Sta.
  Mobile............................36604
Carolyn, Sta. Montgomery..36106
Carrollton..........................35447
Castleberry.........................36432
Catherine...........................36728
  Flatwood, R. Br................36739
Cecil...............................36013
Cedar Bluff.........................35959
Center Point, Br.
  Birmingham (see appendix)

Central.............................36014
Centre..............................35960
Centreville.........................35042
Chance..............................36729
Chancellor..........................36316
Chapman.............................36015
Chase...............................35743
Chatom..............................36518
Chelsea.............................35043
Cherokee............................35616
Chickasaw, Br. Mobile..36611
Childersburg........................35044
Choccolocco.........................36254
Choctaw, R. Br. Butler..36905
Chrysler............................36520
Chunchula...........................36521
Citronelle..........................36522
  Seaboard, R. Br................36573
Claiborne, R. Br. Frisco City..36434
Clanton (1st)......................35045
Clay................................35048
Clayton.............................36016
Cleveland...........................35049
Clinton.............................35448
Clio................................36017
Clopton.............................36317
Cloverdale..........................35617
Cloverland, Sta.
  Montgomery........................36105
Coalburg............................35050
Coaling.............................35449
Coatopa.............................35450
Coden...............................36523
Coffee Springs......................36318
Coffeeville.........................36524
Coker...............................35452
Collinsville........................35961
Columbia............................36319
Columbiana..........................35051
Comer...............................36018
Cooks Springs.......................35052
Coosa Pines, Br.
  Childersburg......................35044
Coosada.............................36020
Cordova.............................35550
Cottage Grove, R. Br.
  Kellyton..........................35088
Cottage Hill, Sta. Mobile
  (see appendix)
Cottondale..........................35453
Cottonton...........................36851
Cottonwood..........................36320
  Madrid, R. Br...................36348
Courtland...........................35618
Cowarts.............................36321
Coy.................................36435
Cragford............................36255
Craig A F B, Br. Selma..36701
Crane Hill..........................35053
Creola..............................36525
Crestline Heights, Br.
  Birmingham........................35213
Crichton, Sta. Mobile..36607
Cromwell............................36906
Cropwell............................35054
Crossville..........................35962
Cuba................................36907
Cullman (1st)......................35055
Cullomburg, R. Br. Silas..36920
Cusseta.............................35454
Cypress.............................36426
Dadeville...........................36853
Daleville (1st)....................36322

Danville................................35619
Daphne................................36526
   Spanish Fort, R. Br.........36527
Darlington............................36730
Dauphin Island.....................36528
Daviston..............................36256
Dawson...............................35963
Dayton................................36731
De Armanville.......................36257
Deatsville............................36022
Decatur (1st)........................35601
Deer Park.............................36529
Delmar................................35551
Delta...................................36258
Demopolis (1st)....................36732
Detroit.................................35552
Dickinson.............................36436
Dixiana................................35059
Dixons Mills.........................36736
Docena................................35060
Dolomite..............................35061
Dora....................................35062
Dothan (1st).........................36301
Double Springs.....................35553
Douglas...............................35964
Downtown, Sta. Tuscaloosa....35401
Dozier.................................36028
Drewry................................36438
Duke...................................36259
Duncanville..........................35456
Dutton................................35744
East Brewton, Br. Brewton....36426
East Gadsden, Sta.
   Gadsden.........................35903
East Lake, Sta. Birmingham....35206
East Side, Sta. Tuscaloosa....35401
East Tallassee.......................36023
Eastaboga...........................36260
Eastbrook, Sta. Montgomery....36109
Eastern Valley, Br.
   Bessemer........................35020
Echola.................................34557
Eclectic................................36024
Edwardsville.........................36261
Eight Mile, Br. Mobile............36613
Elba (1st).............................36323
Elberta................................36530
Eldridge...............................35554
Elkmont...............................35620
Elliotsville, R. Br. Siluria.........35144
Elmore.................................36025
Elrod...................................35458
Elting, Sta. Florence..............35630
Emelle.................................35459
Empire.................................35063
Ensley, Sta. Birmingham.......35218
Enterprise (1st).....................36330
Eoline, R. Br. Centreville.......35042
Epes....................................35460
Equality...............................36026
Estillfork..............................35745
Ethelsville............................35461
Eufaula (1st)........................36027
Eutaw..................................35462
Eva.....................................35621
Evergreen (1st).....................36401
Excel...................................36439
Fabius.................................35965
Fackler................................35746
Fairfax.................................36854
Fairfield (1st)........................35064
Fairford, R. Br. Mc Intosh......36531
Fairhope (1st).......................36532

Fairview, Sta. Birmingham....35208
Falkville...............................35622
Farley, Sta. Huntsville (see
   appendix)
Farmersville.........................36737
Faunsdale.............................36738
Fayette (1st).........................35555
Fernbank..............................35558
Finchburg.............................36440
Fitzpatrick............................36029
Five Points...........................36855
Flat Rock..............................35966
Flatwood, R. Br. Catherine....36739
Flomaton..............................36441
Florala.................................36442
Florence (1st).......................35630
Foley (1st)............................36535
Forest Home.........................36030
Forestdale, Br. Birmingham....35214
Forkland...............................36740
Fort Davis............................36031
Fort Deposit.........................36032
Fort Mc Clellan, Br.
   Anniston.........................36201
Fort Mitchell.........................36856
Fort Payne (1st)....................35967
Fort Rucker, Br. Ozark..........36360
Fosters................................35463
Fountain..............................36443
Franklin...............................36444
Frankville.............................36538
Frisco City............................36445
   Claiborne, R. Br...............36434
Fruitdale..............................36539
Fruithurst.............................36262
Fulton..................................36446
Fulton Road, Sta. Mobile.......36605
Fultondale............................35068
Furman................................36741
Fyffe....................................35971
GADSDEN (1st) (see
   appendix)
Gainestown...........................36540
Gainesville............................35464
Gallant................................35972
Gallion................................36742
Gantt...................................36038
Gantts Quarry.......................35069
Garden City..........................35070
Gardendale...........................35071
Garland...............................36448
Gastonburg..........................36743
Gaylesville...........................35973
Geneva (1st).........................36340
Georgiana.............................36033
Geraldine..............................35974
Gilbertown............................36908
Glen Allen............................35559
Glencoe, Br. Gadsden............35905
Glendean, Sta. Auburn..........36830
Glenwood.............................36034
Golden Springs, Sta.
   Anniston.........................36201
Goodsprings..........................35560
Goodwater............................35072
Goodway..............................36449
Gordo..................................35466
Gordon................................36343
Goshen................................36035
Gosport, R. Br. Whatley.........36450
Grady..................................36036
Graham................................36263
Grand Bay............................36541

Grant...................................35747
Grayson...............................35562
Graysville.............................35073
Green Lantern, Sta.
   Montgomery....................36111
Green Pond...........................35074
Greensboro...........................36744
Greenville (1st).....................36037
Grove Hill.............................36451
Groveoak.............................35975
Guin....................................35563
Gulf Shores..........................36542
Gunter A F B, Br.
   Montgomery (see
   appendix)
Guntersville (1st)...................35976
Gurley.................................35748
Hackleburg...........................35564
Haleyville (1st)......................35565
Halsell.................................36909
Hamilton (1st).......................35570
Hanceville............................35077
Hardaway.............................36039
Harpersville..........................35078
Hartford...............................36344
Hartselle (1st).......................35640
Harvest................................35749
Hatchechubbee......................36858
Havana................................35467
Hayden................................35079
Hayneville............................36040
Hazel Green..........................35750
Headland..............................36345
Heflin..................................36264
Helena.................................35080
Henagar...............................35978
Higdon.................................35979
Highland Home......................36041
Hillsboro..............................35643
Hissop.................................35081
Hodges................................35571
Hokes Bluff, R. Br. Gadsden....35903
Hollins.................................35082
Holly Pond...........................35083
Hollytree..............................35751
Hollywood............................35752
Holt, Br. Tuscaloosa..............35401
Holy Trinity...........................36859
Homewood, Br. Birmingham....35209
Honoraville...........................36042
Hoover, Br. Birmingham........35226
Hope Hull.............................36043
Horton.................................35980
Houston...............................35572
Hueytown, Br. Bessemer.......35020
HUNTSVILLE (1st) (see
   appendix)
Hurtsboro............................36860
Huxford...............................36543
Hybart.................................36452
Hytop..................................35753
Ider.....................................35981
Irondale, Br. Birmingham.......35210
Irvington..............................36544
Jachin..................................36910
Jack....................................36346
Jackson (1st)........................36545
   Carlton, R. Br..................36515
Jacksons Gap........................36861
Jacksonville (1st)...................36265
Jamestown............................35982
Jasper (1st)...........................35501
Jefferson..............................36745

Jemison	35085
Joe Wheeler Dam	35644
Johns	35086
Jones	36749
Jonesboro, Sta. Bessemer	35020
Joppa	35087
Kansas	35573
Kellerman	35468
Kellyton	35089
Cottage Grove, R. Br.	35088
Kennedy	35574
Kent	36045
Killen	35645
Kimberly	35091
Kimbrough, R. Br. Pine Hill	36746
Kinston	36453
Knoxville	35469
Laceys Spring	35754
Lafayette	36862
Lamison	36747
Lanett	36863
Langdale	36864
Langston	35755
Lapine	36046
Lavaca	36911
Lawley	36793
Leeds (1st)	35094
Leesburg	35983
Leighton	35646
Lenlock, Br. Anniston	36201
Lenox	36454
Leroy	36548
Lester	35647
Letohatchee	36047
Lexington	35648
Lillian	36549
Lincoln	35096
Linden	36748
Lineville	36266
Lipscomb, R. Br. Bessemer	35020
Lisman	36912
Pushmataha, R. Br.	36917
Little River	36550
Littleville, R. Br. Russellville	35654
Livingston	35470
Loachapoka	36865
Lockhart	36455
Locust Fork	35097
Logan	35098
Loop, Sta. Mobile	36606
Louisville	36048
Lower Peach Tree	36751
Lowndesboro	36752
Loxley	36551
Luverne (1st)	36049
Lynn	35575
Madison	35758
Madrid, R. Br. Cottonwood	36348
Magazine	36554
Magnolia	36754
Magnolia Springs	36555
Magnolia Terminal	36755
Malcolm	36556
Malvern	36349
Mantua	35472
Maplesville	36750
Marbury	36051
Margaret	35112
Marion (1st)	36756
Marion Junction	36759
Marshall Space Flight Center, Br. Huntsville	35812
Marvel	35113

Mathews	36052
Maxwell A F B, Sta. Montgomery (see appendix)	
Maylene	35114
Mc Calla	35111
Mc Cullough	36552
Mc Farland, Sta. Tuscaloosa	35401
Mc Intosh	36553
Fairford, R Br.	36531
Mc Kenzie	36456
Mc Shan	35471
Mc Williams	36753
Megargel	36457
Melvin	36913
Mentone	35984
Meridianville	35759
Mexia	36458
Midfield, Br. Birmingham (see appendix)	
Midland City	36350
Midway	36053
Miles, Sta. Fairfield	35064
Millbrook	36054
Millers Ferry	36760
Millerville	36267
Millport	35576
Millry	36558
Minter	36761
MOBILE (1st) (see appendix)	
Monroeville (1st)	36460
Montevallo (1st)	35115
Underwood, R. Br.	35174
MONTGOMERY (1st) (see appendix)	
Montrose	36559
Mooresville	35649
Morgan City, R. Br. Laceys Spring	35754
Morris	35116
Morvin	36762
Moulton (1st)	35650
Moundville	35474
Mount Hope	35651
Mount Meigs	36057
Mount Olive	35117
Mount Vernon	36560
Mountain Brook, Br. Birmingham (see appendix)	
Mountain Creek	36056
Mulga	35118
Munford	36268
Muscadine	36269
Muscle Shoals, Br. Sheffield	35660
Myrtlewood	36763
Nanafalia	36764
Napier Field, R. Br. Dothan	36301
Natural Bridge	35577
Nauvoo	35578
Needham	36915
New Brockton	36351
New Castle	35119
New Dora, R. Sta. Dora	35062
New Hope	35760
New Market	35761
New Site, R. Br. Alexander City	35010
Newbern	36765
Newell	36270
Newton	36352
Newville	36353
Nixburg	36058

Normal	35762
North Birmingham, Sta. Birmingham	35207
North Florence, Sta. Florence	35630
Northport (1st)	35476
Brownville, R. Br.	35445
Northside, Sta. Dothan	36301
Notasulga	36866
Oak Grove, R. Br. Adger	35006
Oakhill	36766
Oakman	35579
Oakwood College, R. Br. Huntsville	35806
Odenville	35120
Ohatchee	36271
Oneonta (1st)	35121
Opelika (1st)	36801
Opp (1st)	36467
Orange Beach	36561
Orrville	36767
Owassa	36468
Owens Cross Roads	35763
Oxford, Br. Anniston	36201
Ozark (1st)	36360
Paint Rock	35764
Palmerdale	35123
Panola	35477
Pansey	36370
Parkland, Sta. Jasper	35501
Parrish	35580
Paul	36469
Pelham	35124
Pell City (1st)	35125
Pennington	36916
Pepperell, Sta. Opelika	36801
Perdido	36562
Perdido Beach, R. Br. Elberta	36530
Perdue Hill	36470
Perote	36061
Peterman	36471
Peterson	35478
Petrey	36062
Phenix City (1st)	36867
Phil Campbell	35581
Piedmont	36272
Pigeon Creek	36063
Pike Road	36064
Pinckard	36371
Pine Apple	36768
Pine Hill	36769
Kimbrough, R. Br.	36746
Pope, R. Br.	36770
Yellow Bluff, R. Br.	36789
Pine Level	36065
Pinson	35126
Pisgah	35765
Pittsview	36871
Plantersville	36758
Plateau, Br. Mobile	36610
Pleasant Grove	35127
Point Clear	36564
Pope, R. Br. Pine Hill	36770
Powderly, Sta. Birmingham	35221
Powhatan	35128
Praco	35129
Prairie	36771
Pratt City, Sta. Birmingham	35214
Prattville (1st)	36067
Prestwick	36566
Prichard, Br. Mobile	36610
Princeton	35766

3

Pushmataha, R. Br. Lisman	36917	
Putnam	36772	
Quinton	35130	
Ragland	35131	
Rainbow City, Br. Gadsden	35901	
Rainsville	35986	
Ralph	35480	
Ramer	36069	
Ranburne	36273	
Randolph	36792	
Range	36473	
Red Bay	35582	
Red Level	36474	
Redstone Arsenal, Br.		
Huntsville (see appendix)		
Reform	35481	
Remlap	35133	
Repton	36475	
Riderwood	36918	
River Falls	36476	
River View	36872	
Riverside	35135	
Roanoke (1st)	36274	
Roba	36070	
Robertsdale	36567	
Seminole, R. Br.	36574	
Robinwood, R. Br.		
Birmingham	35217	
Rock Mills, R. Br. Roanoke	36274	
Rockford	35136	
Rogersville	35652	
Roosevelt, R. Sta. Bessemer	35020	
Russellville (1st)	35653	
Littleville, R. Br.	35654	
Rutledge	36071	
Rutledge, Br. Birmingham	35228	
Ryland	35767	
Safford	36773	
Saginaw	35137	
Saint Bernard	35138	
Saint Clair	36774	
Saint Elmo	36568	
Saint Stephens	36569	
Salem	36874	
Salitpa	36570	
Samantha	35482	
Samford University, Br.		
Birmingham	35209	
Samson	36477	
Saraland	36571	
Sardis	36775	
Satsuma	36572	
Sawyerville	36776	
Sayre	35139	
Scottsboro (1st)	35768	
Seaboard, R. Br. Citronelle	36573	
Seale	36875	
Searles	35483	
Section	35771	
Sellers	36072	
Selma (1st)	36701	
Seminole, R. Br.		
Robertsdale	36574	
Semmes	36575	
Shady Grove	36074	
Shannon	35142	
Shawmut	36876	
Sheffield (1st)	35660	
Shelby	35143	
Shorter	36075	
Shorterville	36373	
Silas	36919	
Cullomburg, R. Br.	36920	

Siluria	35144	
Silverhill	36576	
Sims Chapel	36577	
Sipsey	35584	
Skipperville	36374	
Slocomb	36375	
Smiths	36877	
Snead, R. Br. Altoona	35952	
Snow Hill	36778	
Somerville	35670	
South Guntersville, Sta.		
Guntersville	35976	
South Highlands, Sta.		
Birmingham	35205	
Southside, R. Br. Gadsden	35901	
Spanish Fort, R. Br. Daphne	36527	
Sprague	36076	
Spring Garden	36275	
Spring Hill, Sta. Mobile (see appendix)		
Springville	35146	
Sprott	36779	
Spruce Pine	35585	
Standing Rock	36878	
Stanton	36790	
Stapleton	36578	
Steele	35987	
Sterrett	35147	
Stevenson	35772	
Stewart	35484	
Stockton	36579	
Sulligent	35586	
Sumiton	35148	
Summerdale	36580	
Sumterville	35485	
Sunflower	36581	
Sunny South	36780	
Suttle	36781	
Sweet Water	36782	
Sycamore	35149	
Sylacauga (1st)	35150	
Sylvania	35988	
Talladega (1st)	35160	
Talladega Springs, R. Br. Sylacauga	35150	
Tallassee	36078	
Tanner	35671	
Tarrant, Br. Birmingham	35217	
Theodore	36582	
Thomaston	36783	
Thomasville (1st)	36784	
Thorsby	35171	
Three Notch	36079	
Tibbie	36583	
Tillmans Corner, Br. Mobile	36619	
Titus	36080	
Toney	35773	
Town Creek	35672	
Townley	35587	
Toxey	36921	
Trafford	35172	
Trenton	35774	
Trinity	35673	
Troy (1st)	36081	
Trussville (1st)	35173	
Tunnel Springs	36479	
Tuscaloosa (1st)	35401	
Tuscumbia (1st)	35674	
Tuskegee (1st)	36083	
Tuskegee Institute (1st)	36088	
Tyler	36785	
Underwood, R. Br.		
Montevallo	35174	

Union Grove	35175	
Union Springs (1st)	36089	
Uniontown	36786	
University (1st)	35486	
Uptown, Sta. Bessemer	35020	
Uriah	36480	
Valhermoso Springs	35775	
Valley Head	35989	
Vance	35490	
Vandiver	35176	
Verbena	36091	
Vernon	35592	
Vestavia Hills, Br.		
Birmingham (see appendix)		
Veterans Administration Fac, Br. Tuskegee	36083	
Veterans Hospital, R. Sta. Tuscaloosa	35401	
Village Springs	35177	
Vina	35593	
Vincent	35178	
Calcis, R. Br.	35039	
Vinegar Bend	36584	
Vinemont	35179	
Vredenburgh	36481	
Wadley	36276	
Wagarville	36585	
Walker Springs	36586	
Walnut Grove	35990	
Ward	36922	
Warrior	35180	
Waterloo	35677	
Watson	35181	
Wattsville	35182	
Waverly	36879	
Weaver	36277	
Webb	36376	
Wedowee	36278	
Wellington	36279	
Weogufka	35183	
West, Sta. Huntsville (see appendix)		
West Blocton	35184	
West End, Sta. Birmingham	35211	
West Greene	35491	
West Side, Sta. Montgomery	36108	
Westover	35185	
Wetumpka (1st)	36092	
Whatley	36482	
Gosport, R. Br.	36450	
Whistler, Br. Mobile	36612	
Whitfield	36923	
Whitney, R. Sta. Ashville	35991	
Wilmer	36587	
Wilsonville	35186	
Wilton	35187	
Winfield	35594	
Wing	36483	
Woodland	36280	
Woodlawn, Sta. Birmingham	35212	
Woodstock	35188	
Woodville	35776	
Woodward	35189	
Wylam, Sta. Birmingham	35224	
Yantley	36924	
Yellow Bluff, R. Br. Pine Hill	36789	
Yellow Pine	36588	
York	36925	

BIRMINGHAM 352

POST OFFICE BOXES

Box Nos.

1-116	Powderly Sta	21
1-2514	Main Office	01
2521-2799	Main Office	02
2801-2999	Woodlawn Sta	12
3201-3499	South Highlands Sta	05
3501-3799	West End Sta	11
3801-3999	Fairview Sta	08
4001-4699	East Lake Sta	06
5001-5199	Pratt City Sta	14
5201-5599	North Birmingham Sta	07
5701-6194	Homewood Br	09
6201-6599	Tarrant Br	17
6601-6899	Irondale Br	10
7001-7299	Wylam Sta	24
7301-7699	Mountain Brook Br	23
7701-7937	Midfield Br	28
8001-8374	Ensley Sta	18
8901-9274	Crestline Heights Br	13
9501-9999	Center Point Br	15
10001-11112	Main Office	02
20001-20260	Vestavia Hills Br	16
26001-26499	Bluff Park Br	26
2801A-2899A	Woodlawn Sta	12
30001-31399	Avondale Sta	22
3201A-3499A	South Highland Sta	05
39001-39076	Fairview Sta	08
43001-43499	Cahaba Heights Br	43
57001-58099	Homewood Br	09
7301A-7572A	Mountain Brook Br	23
DRAWER A-F	Fairview Sta	08
DRAWER A-F	Pratt City Sta	14
DRAWER A-H	Ensley Sta	18
DRAWER A-H	Midfield Br	28

RURAL ROUTES

1	11
2	17
3	14
4	10
5	15
6	17
7	15
8	24
10	28
11	10
12	15
13	43
14,15,16	24
17	11

STATIONS, BRANCHES AND UNITS

Avondale Sta	22
Bluff Park Br	26
Cahaba Heights Br	43
Crestline Heights Br	13
East Lake Sta	06

Birmingham (Con.) 352

Ensley Sta	18
Fairview Sta	08
Forestdale Br	14
Homewood Br	09
Hooper Br	26
Irondale Br	10
Midfield Br	28
Mountain Brook Br	23
North Birmingham Sta	07
Powderly Sta	21
Pratt City Sta	14
Robinwood Rural Br	17
Rutledge Br	28
Samford University Br	09
South Highlands Sta	05
Tarrant Br	17
West End Sta	11
Woodlawn Sta	12
Wylam Sta	24
General Delivery	
Postmaster	03

APARTMENTS, HOTELS, MOTELS

A G Gaston Motel, 1510 5th Ave N	02
Airport Motel, Municipal Airport	06
Altamont Apts, 2831 Highland Ave	05
Bankhead, 2300 5th Ave N	01
City Center Motel, 424 No 23rd	03
Colony Motor Hotel, 2840 Highland Ave	05
Dinkler, 2005 5th Ave	01
Downtowner Mtr Inn, 2224 5th Ave N	01
Essex House Apts, 605 No 21st	03
Guest House Mtr Inn, 951 18th S	05
Holiday Inn, 1313 No 3rd Ave	03
Molton, 507 N 20th	03
Parliament House, 420 20th S	01
Redmont, 2101 5th Ave N	01
Ridgely Apts, 608 No 21st	03
Sheration Motor Inns, 2040 Highland Ave	05
Thomas Jefferson, 1631 2nd Ave N	02
Town House Apts, 2008 8th Ave So	33
Tutwiler, 2005 5th Ave	01

BUILDINGS

Alabama Power, 600 N 18th	02
American Life, 2308 4th Ave N	03
Bank For Savings, 1919 Morris Ave	03
Brown Marx, 2000 1st Ave N	03
Chamber Commerce, 1914 6th Ave No	03
City Federal, 2026 2nd Ave N	03
City Hall, 710 No 20th	03
City National Bank, 1928 1st Ave N	03

Birmingham (Con.) 352

County Court House, 716 No 21st	03
Farley, 1929 3rd Ave No	03
Federal Reserve Bank	02
Federal, 1800 5th Ave N	03
First National, 17 N 20th	03
Frank Nelson, 205 N 20th	03
Jackson, 215 N 21st	03
Liberty Building, 301 So 20th	02
Massey, 2025 3rd Ave N	03
Municipal Auditorium, 1926 8th Ave No	03
Protective Life, 2027 1st Ave N	03
Seventeen Ten, 1710 1st Ave N	03
Stallings, 1829 1st Ave N	03
Title, 2030 3rd Ave No	03
United States Post Office 351 North 24th Street	03
Watts, 2008 3rd Ave N	03
Woodward, 1927 1st Ave N	03
2121 Building, 2121 8th Ave N	03

HOSPITALS

Babtist Medical Center, 800 Montclair Rd	13
Birmingham Baptist, 701 Princeton Ave S. W.	11
Carraway Methodist, 2506 16th Ave N	34
Childrens, 1501 6th Ave S	33
Crippled Childrens Clinic, 620 19th S	33
East End Memorial, 7916 2nd Ave S	06
Saint Vincents, 2701 9th Ct S	01
Salvation Army, 6001 Crestwood Blvd	12
South Highlands Infirmary, 1127 S 12th	05
University, 619 S 19th	33
Veterans Administration, 720 S 19th	33

UNIVERSITIES AND COLLEGES

Alverson-Draughn Business College 2110 1st Ave N	01
B'Ham Baptist	11
B'Ham School Of Law	03
B'Ham Southern, 800 8th Ave W	04
Booker T Washington Business College, 1527 5th Ave N	02
Massey, 2024 1/2 3rd Ave No	03
Medical College Of Ala, 1919 7th Ave So	33
Miles College, Vinesville	08
Samford University, 800 Lakeshore Dr	09
Southern Business College, Clark Bldg	03
University of Ala (B'Ham Center), 720 So 20th	33

5

GADSDEN   359

POST OFFICE BOXES

Box Nos.

A-R	Alabama City Sta	04
1-539	Glencoe Br	05
1-1920	Gadsden	02
2001-2596	East Gadsden Sta	03
4001-4410	Alabama City	04

RURAL ROUTES

1	01
2	03
3	01
4	04
5	03
6	01
7	03
8	04
9	05
10	01

STATIONS, BRANCHES AND UNITS

Alabama City Sta	04
East Gadsden Sta	03
Glencoe Br	05
Hokes Bluff Rural Br	03
Rainbow City Br	01
Southside Rural Br	01
General Delivery	01
Postmaster	01

BUILDINGS

Medical Arts Building, 303 Bay St	01

HUNTSVILLE   358

POST OFFICE BOXES

Box Nos.

1-999	Main Office	04
1000-1999	West Sta	07
2000-2999	Main Office	04
3000-3999	Blue Spring Sta	10
4000-49..	Farley Sta	02
5000-5999	Ardmore Highway Sta	05
6000-6999	Contract Station 04	06

RURAL ROUTES

1	10
2	11
3	06
4	03
5	11

STATIONS, BRANCHES AND UNITS

Ardmore Highway Sta	05
Blue Spring Sta	10
Farley Sta	02
Marshall Space Flight Center Br	12

Huntsville (Con.)   358

Oakwood College Rural Br	06
Redstone Arsenal, Br	08
West Sta	05
General Delivery	04
Postmaster	04

APARTMENTS, HOTELS, MOTELS

Russell Erskine, 125 Clinton Ave W	04

BUILDINGS

Boeing Company, 220 Wynn Dr, N W	07
Brown Engineering Company, 300 Sparkman Dr NW	07
Chrysler Corp, 102 Wynn Dr, N W	07
Clinton Bldg, 2109 Clinton Ave, W	05
Dunnavants Mall Shopping Center	01
Five Points Shopping Center, 5 Points E	01
Haysland Square Shopping Center	02
Heart Of Huntsville Shopping Center, S Memorial Pkwy	01
Holiday Office Center, 3322 S Memorial Pkwy	01
Holiday Plaza Shopping Center, Patton Rd-Bob Wallace	05
Huntsville West Shopping Center 4700 University Dr NW	05
International Business Machines Corporation	07
Jetport, Highway 20 West	06
National Aeronautics & Space Agency	12
North Memorial Plaza Shopping Center	10
Northside Plaza Shopping Center, 3300 Memorial Pkwy NW	10
Parkway City Shopping Center, S Memorial Pkwy NE	01
Pearsall Shopping Center, 2400 Memorial Pkwy NW	10
Sahara Office Center, 3313 Memorial Pkwy SW	01
South Memorial Plaza Shopping Center	02
State National Bank Bldg., East Side Square	01
Terry-Hutchens, 102 Clinton Ave W	01
Times, 226 Holmes Ave E	01

GOVERNMENT OFFICES

City Hall, Gallatin & Fountain Rw	01
Court House, Square	01
United States Court House, 101 Holmes Ave E	04
United States Post Office, 101 Holmes Ave E	04

Huntsville (Con.)   358

HOSPITALS

Crestwood Hospital, Mc Callister Dr SW	05
Fifth Ave Hospital, 107 Governors Dr SW	01
Huntsville Clinic, Lowell Dr	01
Huntsville Hospital, 910 Madison S	01
Medical Center Hospital Inc., 911 Big Cove Rd SE	01

MILITARY INSTALLATIONS

Marshall Space Flt Ctr Br	12
Redstone Arsenal, Redstone Arsenal, Al	09

UNIVERSITIES AND COLLEGES

Oakwood College, Oakwood Rd NW	06
University Of Alabama Huntsville C, 4701 University Dr NW	07

MOBILE   366

POST OFFICE BOXES

Box Nos.

A-K	Mobile	01
1-2748	Mobile	01
4000-4999	Caroline Avenue Sta	04
5000-5599	Fulton Road Sta	05
6000-6999	Loop Sta	06
7000-7999	Crichton Sta	07
8000-8599	Spring Hill Sta	08
8901-8949	Bates Field R Br	08
9000-9999	Cottage Hill Sta	09
10000-10699	Prichard Br	10
10800-10900	Plateau	10
11000-11428	Chickasaw	11
12000-12250	Whistler	12
13000-13599	Eight Mile	13
16000-16999	Bel Air	16

RURAL ROUTES

1	05
2	09
3	08
4	09
5	08
6	13
7,8	08
9	13
10	09

STATIONS, BRANCHES AND UNITS

Bates Field Rural Br	08
Bel Air Sta	06
Caroline Avenue Sta	04
Chickasaw Br	11

Mobile (Con.)	366
Crichton Sta	07
Eight Mile Br	13
Fulton Road Sta	05
Loop Sta	06
Plateau Br	10
Prichard Br	10
Tillmans Corner Br	19
Whistler Br	12
American National Bank	29
G M & O Railroad	24
G M A C General Motors Accep	31
Gayfer S Bel-Air	26
General Delivery	01
Hammels	23
Merchants National Bank	22
Mobile Press Register	30
Morrison S Cafeteria	25
Postmaster	01
U S Engineers	28

APARTMENTS, HOTELS, MOTELS

Admiral Semmes	01
Admiral Semmes Motor	01
Battle House	01
Downtown Hotel Courts	04
Mobile Travelodge	01
Roadway Inn 1500 Government St	04
Saint Francis Motor Courts, 2501 Government Blvd	06
Town House Motor, 1061 Government St	04

BUILDINGS

American National Bank, 30 St Joseph	02
E A Roberts Bldg 61 St Joseph	02
Federal, 109 St Joseph	02
First Federal Towers, Bel-Air	06
First Federal, 100 St Joseph	02
First National Bank, 31 N Royal St	02
Government Street Office, 951 Government	04
Merchants Bank, 58 St Joseph	02
Milner, 118 N Royal	02
Mobile Public Library, 701 Government	02
Office Park Bldg, 273 Azalea Rd	09
Van Antwerp, 103 Dauphin	02

GOVERNMENT OFFICES

City Auditorium, 401 Auditorium Dr	02
County Court House, 109 Government	02
Police Station, 51 Government	02

HOSPITALS

Doctors Hospital	01
Mobile General, 2451 Fillingim	17

Mobile (Con.)	366
Mobile Infirmary	07
Providence Hospital, 1504 Springhill Ave	04
Sixth District Tuberculosis, 800 St Anthony	03

UNIVERSITIES AND COLLEGES

Carver State Technical School	07
Catholic Schools Office	01
Mobile College, Kali-Oka Rd	13
Mobile Public Schools Office	01
Mobile State Jr College 351 N Broad	03
Southwest State Technical Institute	05
Spring Hill College, 4307 Old Shell Rd	08
University Of South Alabama 307 Gaillard Dr	88

MONTGOMERY   361

POST OFFICE BOXES

Box Nos.		
A-Q	Cloverland Sta	05
1-711	Main Office	01
721-1671	Main Office	02
1681-2271	Main Office	03
2501-2830	Cloverland Sta	05
3001-3417	Eastbrook Sta	09
4001-4327	Main Office	04
6001-6250	Carolyn Sta	06
7001-7504	Capitol Heights Sta	07
8001-8296	Boylston Br	10
9001-9432	West Side Sta	08
11001-11432	Green Lantern	11

RURAL ROUTES

1	05
2	08
3	10
4	09
5	08
6	09
7	08
8	09
9	09
10	11

STATIONS, BRANCHES AND UNITS

Boyleston Br	10
Capitol Heights Sta	07
Carolyn Sta	06
Cloverland Sta	05
Eastbrook Sta	09
Green Lantern Sta	11
West Side Sta	08
General Delivery	04
Postmaster	04

APARTMENTS, HOTELS, UNITS

Camelot Mcgehee Rd	11
Capitol Towers 7 Clayton	04

Montgomery (Con.)	361
Carriage Hills 5605 Calmar Dr	11
Exchange, 5 Commerce	01
Holiday Inn East, Eastern Blvd	09
Holiday Inn Midtown, 924 Madison Ave	04
Holiday Inn So. West, 4231 Mobile Hwy	08
Howard Johnson Motor Lodge, 1108 Eastern Bypass	09
Howard Johnson Motor Lodge, 995 W. South Blvd	05
Jefferson Davis, 348 Montgomery	01
Red Lion Narrow Lane Rd	11
Richardson Terrace 1301 Adams Ave	04
Richlieu 555 So Mcdonough	04
Sheraton Motor Inn, 1100 W. South Blvd	05
Spanish Gardens 4017 Beth Manor Dr	09
Spanish Quarters 5700 Calmar Dr	11
Travelodge Motel, 1550 Federal Dr	09
Vieux Carre 3551 Carter Hill Rd	11
Whitley, 231 Montgomery	01
Woodley Square East, South, Boulevard	11

BUILDINGS

Alabama National Bank, 32 Commerce	01
Aronov, 474 So. Court	04
Associations, 660 Adams	04
Bartlett, 48 Clayton	04
Bell, 207 Montgomery	04
Burkhart, 137 South Court	04
City Hall, 127 N Perry	02
County Court House, 142 Washington	02
Davis, 136 Catoma	04
Executive Building	04
First National Bank, 8 Commerce	01
Government Office, 474 S Court	04
Hill, 73 Washington	04
Leu, 79 Commerce	04
Moore, 217 South Court	04
Reese, 145 Molton	04
State Capitol	04
Town House, 238 S Decatur	04
Tyson, 41 South Lawrence	04
Union Bank & Trust, 100 Commerce	03
Washington, 125 Washington	04
10 High, 10 High St	04

GOVERNMENT OFFICES

Aronov, 474 So. Court	04
City Hall, 127 North Perry	02
County Court House, 142 Washington	02
State Capitol	04
United States Post Office, 15 Lee	04

7

ALASKA

(Abbreviation: AK)

Akhiok, R. Br. Kodiak	99615
Akiachak	99551
Akiak	99552
Akutan	99553
Alakanuk	99554
Aleknagik	99555
Alitak, R. Br. Kodiak	99615
Allakaket	99720
Ambler	99786
Amchitka, R. Br. Anchorage	99541
Anaktuvuk Pass	99721
Anchor Point	99556
ANCHORAGE (1st) (see appendix)	
Angoon	99820
Aniak	99557
Annette	99920
Anvik	99558
Arctic Village	99722
Auke Bay	99821
Baranof	99822
Barrow	99723
Beaver	99724
Bethel	99559
Kongiganak, R. Br.	99559
Napaskiak, R. Br.	99559
Newtok, R. Br.	99559
Nightmute, R. Br.	99690
Toksook Bay, R. Br.	99637
Tuluksak, R. Br.	99679
Tuntutuliak, R. Br.	99680
Bettles Field	99726
Border, R. Br. Tok	99780
Brevig Mission	99785
Buckland	99727
Cantwell	99729
Cape Yakataga	99560
Central	99730
Chalkyitsik, R. Br. Fort Yukon	99788
Chatanika	99731
Chefornak	99561
Chevak	99563
Chicken	99732
Chignik	99564
Chignik Lagoon	99565
Chignik Lake, R. Br. Anchorage	99502
Chitina	99566
Chugiak	99567
Circle	99733
Clam Gulch	99568
Clarks Point	99569
Clear, MOU, Fairbanks	99704
Cohoe	99570
Cold Bay	99571
College, Br. Fairbanks	99701
College Village, Br. Anchorage	99504
Cooper Landing	99572
Copper Center	99573
Cordova	99574
Craig	99921
Crooked Creek	99575
Deering	99736
Delta Junction	99737
Dillingham	99576
Dot Lake, R. Br. Delta Junction	99737

Douglas	99824
Eagle	99738
Eagle River	99577
Eastchester, Sta. Anchorage (see appendix)	
Eek	99578
Egegik	99579
Eielson A F B, Br. Fairbanks	99702
Ekwok	99580
Elfin Cove	99825
Elim	99739
Elmendorf A F B, Br. Anchorage	99506
Emmonak	99581
Ester	99725
Fairbanks (1st)	99701
Clear, MOU	99704
College, Br	99701
Eielson A F Br.	99702
Federal, Sta	99707
Fort Wainright, Br.	99703
Hogatza, R. Br	99744
Mckinley Park, R. Br.	99755
North Pole, Br.	99705
University, Br.	99701
False Pass	99583
Federal, Sta. Fairbanks	99707
Federal, Sta. Anchorage	99501
Flat	99584
Fort Richardson, Br. Anchorage	99505
Fort Wainwright, Br. Fairbanks	99703
Fort Yukon	99740
Chalkyitsrk, R. Br.	99788
Fortuna Ledge	99585
Gakona	99586
Galena	99741
Gambell	99742
Girdwood	99587
Glennallen	99588
Golovin, R. Br. Nome	99762
Goodnews Bay.	99589
Grayling	99590
Gustavus	99826
Haines	99827
Halibut Cove, R. Br. Homer	99603
Healy	99743
Usibelli, R. Br.	99787
Hogatza, R. Br. Fairbanks	99744
Holy Cross	99602
Homer	99603
Hoonah	99829
Hooper Bay	99604
Hope	99605
Hughes	99745
Huslia	99746
Hydaburg	99922
Hyder	99923
Iguigig, R. Br. King Salmon	99613
Iliamna	99606
Kokhanok, R. Br.	99606
Pedro Bay, R. Br.	99647
Indian, R. Br. Anchorage	99540
Ivanof Bay, R. Br. Anchorage	99502
Juneau (1st)	99801
Kake	99830
Kaktovik	99747
Kalskag	99607
Kaltag	99748
Karluk	99608
Kasaan	99924

Kasigluk	99609
Kasilof	99610
Kenai (1st)	99611
Ketchikan (1st)	99901
Meyers Chuck, R. Br.	99903
Kiana	99749
King Cove	99612
King Salmon	99613
Kipnuk	99614
Kivalina	99750
Klatt Road, R. Br. Anchorage	99501
Klawock	99925
Kobuk	99751
Kodiak (1st)	99615
Akhiok, R. Br.	99615
Alitak, R. Br.	99615
Kokhanok, R. Br. Iliamna	99606
Koliganek, R. Br. Dillingham	99576
Kongiganak, R. Br. Bethel	99559
Kotlik	99620
Kotzebue	99752
Koyuk	99753
Koyukuk	99754
Kwethluk	99621
Kwigillingok	99622
Lake Minchumina	99623
Larsen Bay	99624
Levelock	99625
Little Diomede, R. Br. Nome	99762
Lower Kalskag	99626
Manley Hot Springs	99756
Manokotak	99628
Mc Grath	99627
Nikolai, R. Br.	99691
Mckinley Park, R. Br. Fairbanks	99755
Medfra	99629
Mekoryuk	99630
Metlakatla	99926
Meyers Chuck, R. Br. Ketchikan	99903
Miller House, R. Br. Central	99730
Minto	99758
Moose Pass	99631
Mount Edgecumbe, Br. Sitka	99835
Mountain View, Sta. Anchorage	99504
Mountain Village	99632
Naknek	99633
Napakiak	99634
Napaskiak, R. Br. Bethel	99559
Nenana	99760
New Stuyahok	99636
Newtok, R. Br. Bethel	99559
Nightmute, R. Br. Bethel	99690
Nikolai, R. Br. Mc Grath	99691
Nikolski	99638
Ninilchik	99639
Noatak	99761
Nome	99762
Nondalton	99640
Noorvik	99763
North Kenai, R. Br. Kenai	99611
North Pole, R. Br. Fairbanks	99705
Northway	99764
Nulato	99765
Nunaka Valley, Br. Anchorage	99504
Nunapitchuk	99641
Old Harbor	99643
Ouzinkie	99644

Palmer (1st)	99645	Savoonga	99769	Tenakee Springs	99841
Pauloff Harbor	99646	Scammon Bay	99662	Tetlin, R. Br. Tok	99779
Paxson, R. Br. Delta		Selawik	99770	Togiak	99678
Junction	99737	Seldovia	99663	Tok	99780
Pedro Bay, R. Br. Hiamna	99647	Seward	99664	Border, R. Br.	99780
Pelican	99832	Shageluk	99665	Tanacross, R. Br.	99776
Perryville	99648	Shaktoolik	99771	Tetlin, R. Br.	99779
Petersburg	99833	Sheldon Point, R. Br.		Toksook Bay, R. Br. Bethel	99637
Pilot Point	99649	Emmonak	99666	Tuluksak, R. Br. Bethel	99679
Pilot Station	99650	Shishmaref	99772	Tuntutuliak, R. Br. Bethel	99680
Pitka'S Point, R. Br. Saint		Shungnak	99773	Tununak	99681
Marys	99658	Sitka (1st)	99835	Tyonek	99682
Platinum	99651	Skagway	99840	Ugashik	99683
Point Baker	99927	Skwentna	99667	Unalakleet	99684
Point Hope	99766	Sleetmute	99668	Unalaska	99685
Port Alsworth	99653	Soldotna (1st)	99669	University, Br. Fairbanks	99701
Port Ashton	99654	South Naknek	99670	Usibelli, R. Br. Healy	99787
Port Lions	99550	Spenard, Sta. Anchorage	99503	Valdez	99686
Portage Creek, R. Br.		Stebbins	99671	Venetie	99781
Dillingham	99576	Sterling	99672	Wainwright	99782
Quinhagak	99655	Stevens Village	99774	Wales	99783
Rampart	99767	Sutton	99674	Ward Cove	99928
Red Devil	99656	Takotna	99675	Wasilla	99687
Ruby	99768	Talkeetna	99676	White Mountain	99784
Russian Mission	99657	Tanacross, R. Br. Tok	99776	Whittier, R. Br. Anchorage	99501
Saint Marys	99658	Tanana	99677	Willow	99688
Saint Michael	99659	Tatitlek	99677	Wrangell	99929
Saint Paul Island	99660	Teller	99778	Yakutat	99689
Sand Point	99661				

ANCHORAGE   995

POST OFFICE BOXES

Box Nos.		
1-2999	Federal	10
4A-4ZZZ	Spenard Sta	09
8A-8AF	Mountain View	
	Sta	08
3000-3999	Eastchester	
	Sta	01
6000-6999	Main Office Br	02

7000-7999	Federal Sta	01
8000-8999	Mountain View	
	Sta	08
10000-10999	Klatt Road Br	02
4-001-4-2200	Spenard Sta	09

STATIONS, BRANCHES AND UNITS

Amchitka Rural Br		41
Chignik Lake Rural Br		02
College Village Br		04

Eastchester Sta		01
Elmendorf A F B Br		06
Federal Sta		01
Fort Richardson Br		05
Indian Rural Br		40
Ivanof Bay Rural Br		02
Klatt Road Rural Br		01
Mountain View Sta		04
Nunaka Valley Br		04
Spenard Sta		03
Whittier Rural Br		01
General Delivery		01
Postmaster		02

ARIZONA

(Abbreviation: AZ)

Agua Fria, R. Br. Prescott......86301
Aguila......85320
Ajo......85321
Alpine......85920
Amado, R. Br. Tumacacori......85640
Apache Junction (1st)......85220
  Florence Junction, R. Br......85233
  Queen Valley, R. Br......85220
Arcadia, Sta. Phoenix......85018
Arivaca......85601
Arizona City, R. Br. Casa
  Grande......85223
Arlington......85322
Ash Fork......86320
Avondale......85323
Bagdad......86321
Bapchule......85221
Bellemont, R. Br. Flagstaff......86001
Benson......85602
Benson Highway, Br. Tucson......85076
Bisbee (1st)......85603
Black Canyon City......85324
Blue......85922
Bouse......85325
Bowie......85605
Boys Ranch, R. Br.
  Chandler......85224
Buckeye (1st)......85326
Buckhorn, R. Br. Mesa......85201
Bullhead City (1st)......86430
  Mohave Valley, R. Br......86440
  Riviera, R. Br......86442
Bumble Bee......85327
Bylas......85530
Cameron......86020
Camp Verde......86322
Capitol, Sta. Phoenix (see
  appendix)
Carefree, R. Br. Cave Creek......85331
Casa Grande (1st)......85222
  Arizona City, R. Br......85223
  Eleven Mile Corner, R.
  Br......85222
Casas Adobes, R. Br.
  Tucson......85704
Cashion......85329
Cave Creek......85331
Central......85531
Chambers......86502
Chandler (1st)......85224
Chandler Heights......85227
Chinle......86503
Chino Valley......86323
Chloride......86431
Cibecue, R. Br. Show Low......85901
Clarkdale......86324
Clay Springs......85923
Claypool......85532
Clifton......85533
Cochise......85606
College, Sta. Tucson......85719
Colorado City......86021
Commerce, Sta. Phoenix......85030
Concho......85924
Congress......85332
Coolidge (1st)......85228
Copper Queen, Sta. Bisbee......85603
Cornville......86325

Coronado, Sta. Tucson......85711
Cortaro......85230
Cottonwood......86326
Crown King, R. Br. Mayer......86333
Dateland......85333
Davis Monthan A F B, Br.
  Tucson (see appendix)
Desert Sage, Br. Mesa......85201
Dewey......86327
Dinosaur City, R. Br. Peach
  Springs......86434
Dolan Springs, R. Br.
  Kingman......86441
Douglas (1st)......85607
Downtown, Sta. Phoenix (see
  appendix)
Downtown, Sta. Tempe......85281
Dragoon......85609
Duncan......85534
Eagar......85925
East Fork, R. Br. Whiteriver......85941
Eden......85535
Ehrenberg......85334
El Mirage......85335
Eleven Mile Corner, R. Br.
  Casa Grande......85222
Elfrida......85610
Elgin......85611
Eloy......85231
Emery Park, Sta. Tucson
  (see appendix)
Fairbank......85612
Flagstaff (1st)......86001
  Bellemont, R. Br......86001
  Gray Mountain, R. Br......86001
  Happy Jack, R. Br......86024
  Mormon Lake, R. Br......86038
  Mountainaire, R. Br......86001
  Munds Park, R. Br......86001
  N A U, Sta......86001
  Parks, R. Br......86001
  Two Gun Town, R. Br......86001
Florence......85232
Florence Junction, R. Br.
  Apache Junction......85233
Fort Apache......85926
Fort Defiance......86504
Fort Grant, R. Br. Willcox......85643
Fort Huachuca (1st)......85613
Fort Thomas......85536
Franklin, R. Br. Duncan......85534
Fredonia......86022
Gadsden......85336
Ganado......86505
Gila Bend......85337
Gilbert......85234

GLENDALE (1st) (see appendix)

Globe (1st)......85501
Goodyear......85338
Grand Canyon (1st)......86023
Gray Mountain, R. Br.
  Flagstaff......86001
Greasewood, R. Br. Ganado......86505
Green Valley......85614
Greenway, Sta. Tucson......85713
Greer......85927
Guadalupe, R. Br. Tempe......85281
Hackberry, R. Br. Kingman......86401
Happy Jack, R. Br. Flagstaff......86024
Hawley Lake, R. Br. Mc
  Nary......85930
Hayden......85235

Heber......85928
Hereford......85615
Higley......85236
Holbrook (1st)......86025
  Indian Wells, R. Br......86031
  Petrified Forest National
  Pk, R. Br......86025
  Sun Valley, R. Br......86025
Hotevilla......86030
Houck......86506
  Lupton, R. Br......86508
Huachuca City......85616
Hualapai, R. Br. Kingman......86401
Humboldt......86329
Indian School, Sta. Phoenix
  (see appendix)
Indian Wells, R. Br.
  Holbrook......86031
Inspiration......85537
Iron Springs, R. Br. Prescott......86330
Jacob Lake, R. Br. Fredonia......86022
Jerome......86331
Joseph City......86032
Kaibito, R. Br. Tonalea......86044
Kayenta......86033
Keams Canyon......86034
Kearny......85237
Kingman (1st)......86401
  Dolan Springs, R. Br......86441
  Hackberry, R. Br......86401
  Hualapai, R. Br......86401
  Temple Bar Marina, R.
  Br......86443
Kino, Sta. Tucson......85705
Kirkland......86332
Klondyke, R. Br. Willcox......85643
Kofa, Sta. Yuma......85364
Kohls Ranch, R. Br. Payson......85538
Lake Havasu City (1st)......86403
Lake Montezuma, R. Br.
  Sedona......86336
Lakeside......85929
Laveen......85339
Leupp......86035
Litchfield Park......85340
Littlefield......86432
Lowell, Sta. Bisbee......85603
Lukachukai......86507
Luke A F B, Br. Glendale......85301
Lukeville......85341
Lupton, R. Br. Houck......86508
Mammoth......85618
Many Farms, R. Br. Chinle......86503
Marana......85238
Marble Canyon, R. Br. Page......86036
Maricopa......85239
Marine Corps Air Station, Br.
  Yuma......85364
Martinez Lake, R. Br. Yuma......85364
Maryvale, Sta. Phoenix (see
  appendix)
Mayer......86333
Mc Dowell, Sta. Phoenix (see
  appendix)
Mc Nary......85930
Mc Neal......85617

MESA (1st) (see appendix)

Miami......85539
Miller Valley, R. Sta.
  Prescott......86301
Miracle Valley, R. Br. Sierra
  Vista......85645

Mohave Valley, R. Br.
　Bullhead City 86440
Morenci 85540
Mormon Lake, R. Br.
　Flagstaff 86038
Morristown 85342
Mount Lemmon 85619
Mountainaire, R. Br.
　Flagstaff 86001
Munds Park, R. Br.
　Flagstaff 86001
N A U. Sta. Flagstaff 86001
Naco 85620
Navajo 86509
Nogales (1st) 85621
North Rim, R. Br. Fredonia .. 86022
Northeast, Sta. Phoenix 85016
Northwest, Sta. Phoenix (see
　appendix)
Nutrioso 85932
Oatman 86433
Oracle 85623
Oraibi 86039
Overgaard 85933
Page 86040
　Marble Canyon, R. Br. 86036
Palo Verde 85343
Papago, Sta. Scottsdale 85257
Paradise Valley, Br.
　Scottsdale 85253
Parker (1st) 85344
　Poston, R. Br. 85371
Parks, R. Br. Flagstaff 86001
Patagonia 85624
Paulden 86334
Payson 85541
　Kohls Ranch, R. Br. 85538
Peach Springs 86434
Pearce 85625
Peoria 85345
Peridot 85542
Petrified Forest National Pk.
　R. Br. Holbrook 86025
PHOENIX (1st) (see
　appendix)
Picacho 85241
Pima 85543
Pine 85544
Pinedale 85934
Pinetop 85935
Pinon 86510
Pirtleville 85626
Pisinemo, R. Br. Sells 85634
Polacca 86042
Pomerene 85627
Portal, R. Br. San Simon 85632
Poston, R. Br. Parker 85371
Prescott (1st) 86301
　Agua Fria, R. Br. 86301
　Iron Springs, R. Br. 86330

Milter Valley, R. Sta 86301
　Whipple, Sta. 86301
Quartzsite 85346
Queen Creek 85242
Queen Valley, R. Br. Apache
　Junction 85220
Randolph 85243
Red Rock 85245
Rillito 85246
Rimrock 86335
Rincon, Sta. Tucson (see
　appendix)
Riverside Stage Stop, R. Br.
　Kearny 85237
Riviera, R. Br. Bullhead City . 86442
Roll 85347
Roosevelt 85545
Sacaton 85247
Safford (1st) 85546
Sahuarita 85629
Saint David 85630
Saint Johns 85936
Saint Michaels 86511
Salome 85348
San Carlos 85550
San Luis 85349
San Manuel 85631
San Simon 85632
Sanders 86512
Sasabe 85633
Sawmill, R. Br. Fort
　Defiance 86504

SCOTTSDALE (1st) (see
　appendix)
Second Mesa 86043
Sedona (1st) 86336
Seligman 86337
Sells 85634
Sherwood, Sta. Mesa 85201
Shonto, R. Br. Tonalea 86044
Show Low 85901
Sierra Vista (1st) 85635
　Miracle Valley, R. Br. 85645
Silver Bell 85270
Skull Valley 86338
Snowflake 85937
Solomon 85551
Somerton 85350
Sonoita 85637
South Central, Sta. Phoenix
　(see appendix)
South Tucson, Br. Tucson ... 85713
Speedway, Sta. Tucson 85716
Springerville 85938
Stanfield 85272
Student Union, Sta. Tucson . 85720
Sun City (1st) 85351
Sun Valley, R. Br. Holbrook . 86025
Sunnyslope, Sta. Phoenix
　(see appendix)

Supai 86435
Superior 85273
Surprise, R. Br. Peoria 85345
Tacna 85352
Taylor 85939
Teec Nos Pos. 86514
TEMPE (1st) (see appendix)
Temple Bar Marina, R. Br.
　Kingman 86443
Thatcher 85552
Tolleson 85353
Tombstone 85638
Tonalea 86044
Tonopah 85354
Tonto Basin 85553
Topawa 85639
Topock 86436
Tortilla Flat 85290
Tuba City 86045
Tubac, R. Br. Tumacacori 85640
TUCSON (1st) (see appendix)
Tumacacori 85640
Two Gun Town, R. Br.
　Flagstaff 86001
University, Sta. Tucson (see
　appendix)
Vail 85641
Valentine 86437
Valley Farms 85291
Vernon 85940
Waddell 85355
Warren, Sta. Bisbee 85603
Wellton 85356
Wenden 85357
West Sedona, R. Br. Sedona . 86340
Whipple, Sta. Prescott 86301
White Mountain Lake, R. Br.
　Show Low 85901
Whiteriver 85941
Why, R. Br. Ajo 85321
Wickenburg (1st) 85358
Wide Ruins, R. Br.
　Chambers 86502
Wikieup 85360
Willcox (1st) 85643
Williams 86046
Williams A F B, Br.
　Chandler 85224
Window Rock 86515
Winkelman 85292
Winslow (1st) 86047
Wittmann 85361
Woodruff 85942
Yarnell 85362
Young 85554
Youngtown (1st) 85363
Yucca 86438
Yuma (1st) 85364
Yuma Proving Ground, Br.
　Yuma 85364

GLENDALE   853

POST OFFICE BOXES

Box Pos.
1-1762   Main Office 11

RURAL ROUTES

1,2,3 01

STATIONS, BRANCHES AND UNITS

Luke A F B Br	01
General Delivery	01
Main Office	01
Postmaster	01

GOVERNMENT OFFICES

County Offices 7115 N 57 Dr.	01
Municipal 7022 N 58 Dr.	01

MILITARY INSTALLATIONS

Luke A F B	09

UNIVERSITIES AND COLLEGES

Thunderbird Graduate School
Of International
Management 06

MESA   852

POST OFFICE BOXES

Box Nos.
A-R	Main Office	01
1-1999	Main Office	01
2000-2699	Sherwood Sta	04
3900-3999	Desert Sage Sta.	07
4000-4999	Main Office	01

STATIONS, BRANCHES AND UNITS

Buckhorn Rural Br	01
Desert Sage Br	01
Sherwood Sta	01
General Delivery	01
Postmaster	01

BUILDINGS

Valley National Bank, 66 W
Main 01

HOSPITALS

Mesa General, 515 N Mesa Dr.	01
Mesa Lutheran, 501 W 10th Pl.	01
Southside, 21 S Hibbert...........	02

PHOENIX   850

POST OFFICE BOXES

Box Nos.
1-2199	Downtown............	01
2200-2599	Downtown............	02
2900-2999	Main Office	36
2900-2999	Main Office	62
5000-5999	Mc Dowell Sta......	10
6000-6999	Capitol Sta..........	05
7000-7999	Indian School Sta...............	11
8000-8999	South Central Sta...............	40
9000-9999	Sunnyslope Sta...............	68
10000-10999	Northeast Sta......	16
11000-11999	Northwest Sta......	61
13000-13999	Downtown............	02
14000-14999	Maryvale Sta........	31
15000-15999	Arcadia	60
16000-16999	Indian School Sta...............	11
19000-19999	Capitol Sta..........	09
20000-21999	Main Office	36
22000-22999	Sta 24	28

RURAL ROUTES

1	40
3	09
4	31
5	09

STATIONS, BRANCHES AND UNITS

Arcadia Sta.	18
Capitol Sta.	05
Commerce Sta.	30
Downtown Sta.	04
Indian School Sta....................	31
Maryvale Sta.	31
Northeast Sta.	16
Northwest Sta.	16
South Central Sta.	40
Sunnyslope Sta.	20
Black Canyon Star Route........	20
Cave Creek Star Route...........	20
General Delivery	26
Postmaster	26

BUILDINGS

Arizona Bank, 34 W Monroe	03
Arizona Title Annex, 135 N 2nd Ave..............................	03
Arizona Title, 111 W Monroe....	03
Central Towers, 2727 N Central Ave.......................	04
Del Webb, 3800 N Central Ave.	12
Del Webb'S Townhouse, 100 W Clarendon Ave	13
Executive Towers, 207 W Clarendon Ave	13
Financial Center, 3443 N Central Ave.......................	12
First Federal Savings, 3003 N Central Ave..................	12
First National Bank Plaza 100 W Washington	03
Ford Law. 11 N 2nd Ave	03

Phoenix (Con.)   850

Goodrich, 14 N Central Ave.....	04
Greater Arizona Savings, 112 N Central Ave	04
Greyhound Towers 111 W Clarendon Ave	13
Luhrs Central, 132 S Central Ave.	04
Luhrs Tower, 45 W Jefferson....	03
Luhrs, 11 W Jefferson.............	03
Mayer Central, 3033 N Central Ave.......................	12
Park Central, 550 W Thomas Rd	13
Phoenix Public Library, 12 E Mcdowell Rd	04
Phoenix Towers, 2201 N Central Ave.......................	04
Professional, 15 E Monroe.......	04
Rosenzweigs Center, 3814 N Central Ave.......................	12
Security Center, 222 N Central Ave.......................	04
Security, 234 N Central Ave	04
State Highway, 1739 W Jackson	07
Terminal, 218 S 4th.................	04
Transamerica Title, 114 W. Adams	03
United Bank Of Arizona, 3550 N Central Ave..........	12
Arizona Public Service 411 N Central Ave	04

GOVERNMENT OFFICES

Arizona State Capitol, 1700 W Washington.................	07
Arizona State Office, 1632 W Adams	07
County Court House, 125 W Washington	03
County Office, 101 W Jefferson	03
Federal, 230 N 1st Ave...........	25
Municipal, 251 W Washington	03

HOSPITALS

Arizona State Hospital, 2500 E Van Buren	08
Baptist Hospital Of Phoenix, 6025 N 20th Ave...............	15
Camelback Hospital, 5055 N 34th	18
Crippled Childrens 1825 E Garfield	06
Doctor'S, 1947 E Thomas Rd...	16
Franklin, 367 N 21st Ave.........	09
Good Samaritan, 1033 E Mc Dowell Rd.	06
Lincoln John C, 9111 2nd........	20
Maricopa County 2601 E Roosevelt	08
Maryvale Community, 5102 W Campbell Ave	31
Memorial, 1200 S 5th Ave.......	03
North Mountain, 48 E Foothill Dr	20
Phoenix General, 1950 W Indian School Rd	15

Phoenix (Con.) 850

Phoenix Phs Indian 4212 N
16th 16
Saint Josephs Hospital, 350
W Thomas Rd 13
Saint Lukes Hospital, 1820 E
Polk 06
Veterans Administration, 650
E Indian School Rd 12

UNIVERSITIES AND COLLEGES

City School Administration,
125 E Lincoln 04
Grand Canyon College, 3300
W Camelback Rd 17
Phoenix Union High Sch
System 2225 N 16th 2526
W Osborn Rd 17

SCOTTSDALE 852

POST OFFICE BOXES

Box Nos.
A-Z   Main Office 52
1-2999   Main Office 52
3001-3599   Papago Sta 57

RURAL ROUTES

1 56

STATIONS, BRANCHES AND UNITS

Papago Sta 57
Paradise Valley Br 53
General Delivery 51
Postmaster 51

TEMPE 852

POST OFFICE BOXES

Box Nos.
A-Z   Downtown Sta 81
1 3189   Downtown Sta 81
AA-UF   Downtown Sta 81
2A 2U   Main Office 82
26001-28999   Main Office 82

RURAL ROUTES

1 2 82

STATIONS, BRANCHES AND UNITS

Downtown Sta 81
Guadalupe Rural Br 81
General Delivery 82
Postmaster 82

UNIVERSITIES AND COLLEGES

Arizona State University 81

TUCSON 857

POST OFFICE BOXES

Box Nos.
1-3069   Main Office 02
3301-3744   College Sta 22
3901-4999   University Sta ... 17
5001-5987   Kino Sta 03
6001-6809   Speedway Sta 16
7001-7897   South Tucson
              Br 25
8001-8416   Greenway Sta 23
9001-10999   Student Union
              Sta 20
11001-11727   Emery Park
              Sta 06
12001-13499   Coronado Sta 11
15001-15177   Davis Monthan
              A F B 08
17001-17960   Rincon Br 10
20001-21110   Student Union ... 20
49001-49337   University Sta ... 17
50001-50895   Kino Sta 03
80001-83958   Davis Monthan
              A F B
              Military 07

RURAL ROUTES

1 04
2 15
3 06
4 18
5 04
6 14
7 10
8 05
9 18
10 05
11 16
12 15
13 05
14 15
15 15
16 06

STATIONS, BRANCHES AND UNITS

Benson Highway Br 06
Casas Adobes Rural Br 04
College Sta 19
Coronado Sta 11
Emery Park Sta 06
Greenway Sta 13
Kino Sta 05
Rincon Sta 10
South Tucson Br 16
Speedway Sta 16
Student Union Sta 20
General Delivery 02

Tuscon (Con.) 857

Postmaster 26

APARTMENTS, HOTELS, MOTELS

Arizona Inn, 2200 East Elm 19
Arizona, 35 North 6th Ave 01
Congress, 311 East
Congress 01
El Presidio, 245 East
Broadway 01
Pioneer, 80 North Stone Ave ... 01
Roskruge, 57 South Scott 01
Santa Rita, 109 South Scott 01
Westerner, 63 South Stone
Ave 01

BUILDINGS

Arizona Bank, Alameda &
Stone 01
Garden Plaza, 201 North
Stone 01
Lawyers Title, 199 North
Stone 01
Pima Plaza, 2030 East
Broadway 19
Pima, 151 North Stone 01
Transamerica Title, 177
North Church 01
Tucson Federal Savings
Tower, 32 North Stone 01
Tucson Title, 45 West
Pennington 01
Valley National Bank, 2 East
Congress 01

HOSPITALS

Carl Hayden Memorial, 402
West Congress 01
Pima County, 2900 South 6th
Ave 13
Saint Josephs, 350 North
Wilmot Rd 11
Saint Marys, 1700 West St.
Marys Rd 05
Tucson General, 3838 North
Campbell Ave 19
Tuscon Medical Center E
Grant And Beverly Blvd 16
Veterans Adm., 3601 South
5th Ave 23

MILITARY INSTALLATIONS

Davis Monthan AFB 07

UNIVERSITIES AND COLLEGES

Arizona Medical Center 24
Pima College 09
University Of Arizona 21

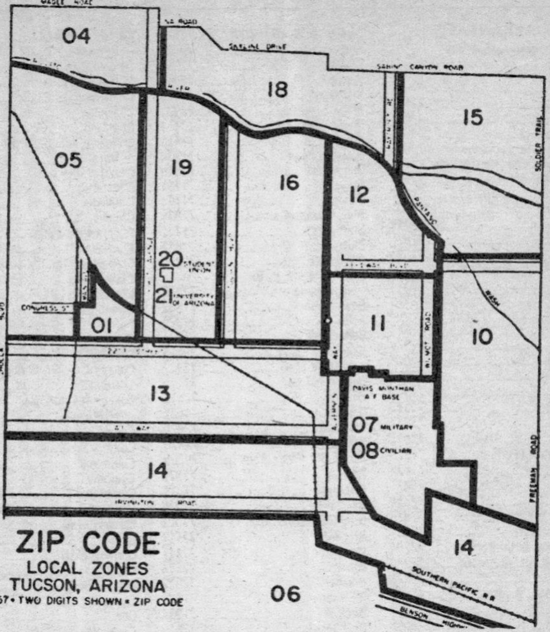

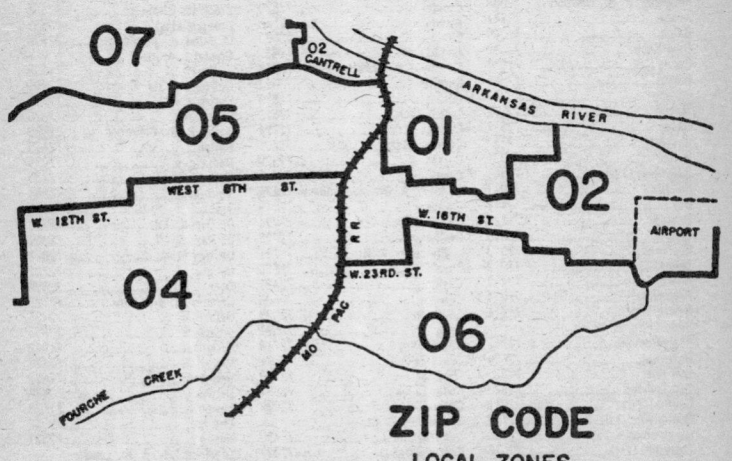

ZIP CODE
LOCAL ZONES
TUCSON, ARIZONA
857 • TWO DIGITS SHOWN • ZIP CODE

ZIP CODE
LOCAL ZONES
LITTLE ROCK, ARK.
722 + TWO DIGITS SHOWN = ZIP CODE

ARKANSAS
(Abbreviation AR)

Abbott 72929
Adona 72001
Agnes 72510
Air Base, Sta. Jacksonville ... 72076
Alberi Prke, Sta. Hot Springs
   National Park 71901
Alco 72612
Alexander 72002
Alicia 72410
Alix 72820
Alleene 71820
Allison, R. Br. Mountain
   View 72511
Alma 72921
Almyra 72003
Alpena 72611
Alpine 71920
Altheimer 72004
Altus 72821
Amagon 72005
Amity 71921
Antoine 71922
Appleton, R. Br. Atkins 72822
Arkadelphia (1st) 71923
Arkansas City 71630
Arkinda 71821
Armorel 72310
Ash Flat 72513
Ashdown (1st) 71822
Asher, Sta. Little Rock 72204
Athens, R. Br. Glenwood 71927
Atkins 72823
   Appleton, R. Br. 72822
Aubrey 72311
Augusta 72006
Austin 72007
Auvergne, R. Br. Newport 72008
Avoca 72711
Balch 72009
Bald Knob 72010
Banks 71631
Barber 72922
Barling 72923
Barton 72312
Bass 72612
Bassett 72313
Bates 72924
Batesville (1st) 72501
Bauxite 72011
Bay 72411
Bearden 71720
Beaver 72613
Bee Branch 72013
Beebe 72012
Beech Grove 72412
Beedeville 72014
Beirne 71721
Bella Vista, R. Br.
   Bentonville 72712
Belleville 72824
Ben Hur 72825
Ben Lomond 71823
Benton (1st) 72015
Bentonville (1st) 72712
Bergman 72615
Berryville (1st) 72616
Bexar 72515
Bigelow 72016

Bigflat, R. Br. Marshall 72617
Biggers 72413
Birdeye 72314
Biscoe 72017
Bismarck 71929
Black Fork 72925
Black Oak 72414
Black Rock 72415
Black Springs 71930
Blackwell 72019
Blakely 71931
Blevins 71825
Blue Mountain 72826
Bluff City 71722
Bluffton 72827
Blytheville (1st) 72315
Blytheville A F B, Br.
   Blytheville 72315
Board Camp 71932
Boles 72926
Bonnerdale 71933
Bono 72416
Booneville (1st) 72927
Boston 72715
Boswell 72516
Boydell 71632
Bradford 72020
Bradley 71826
Brady Sta. Little Rock 72205
Branch 72928
Brickeys 72320
Briggsville 72828
Brinkley (1st) 72021
Brockwell 72517
Brookland 72417
Bruno 72618
Bryant 72022
Buckner 71827
Buckville 71934
Bull Shoals 72619
Burdette 72321
Busch 72620
Byron 72518
Cabot 72023
Caddo Gap 71935
Calamine, R. Br. Strawberry 72418
Caldwell 72322
Cale 71828
Calico Rock 72519
Calion 71724
Camden (1st) 71701
Camp 72520
Canehill 72717
Canfield, R. Br. Lewisville 71829
Caraway 72419
Carlisle 72024
Carthage 71725
   Princeton, R. Br. 71761
Casa 72025
Cash 72421
Casscoe 72026
Cauthron 72929
Cave City 72521
Cave Springs 72718
Cavecreek 72621
Cecil 72930
Cedar Creek 72931
Cedarville 72932
Center Hill, R. Br.
   Paragould 72450
Center Ridge 72027
Centerton 72719
Centerville 72829

Central Baptist College, Sta.
   Conway 72032
Central City, Br. Hot Springs
   National Park 71901
Charleston 72933
Charlotte 72522
Chatfield 72323
Cherokee Village, R. Br.
   Hardy 72542
Cherry Valley 72324
Chester 72934
Chidester 71726
Chimes 72622
Choctaw 72028
Clarendon 72029
Clarkedale 72325
Clarkridge 72623
Clarksville (1st) 72830
Cleveland 72030
Clifty 72720
Clinton 72031
Coal Hill 72832
College City, Br. Walnut
   Ridge 72476
College Heights, Br.
   Monticello 71655
Collins 71634
Colt 72326
Columbus 71831
Combs 72721
Compton 72624
Concord 72523
Conway (1st) 72032
Cord 72524
Corning (1st) 72422
Cotter 72626
Cotton Plant 72036
Cove 71937
Coy 72037
Cozahome 72627
Crawfordsville 72327
Crocketts Bluff 72038
Crossett (1st) 71635
Crumrod 72328
Crystal Springs, R. Br.
   Royal 71938
Cullendale, Sta. Camden 71701
Curtis 71728
Cushman 72526
Daisy, R. Br. Glenwood 71939
Dalton 72423
Damascus 72039
Danville 72833
Dardanelle 72834
Datto 72424
De Queen (1st) 71832
De Valls Bluff 72041
De Witt (1st) 72042
Decatur 72722
Deer 72628
Delaney, R. Br. Elkins 72723
Delaplaine 72425
Delaware 72835
Delight 71940
Dell 72426
Dennard 72629
Denver 72630
Dermott 71638
Des Arc 72040
Desha 72527
Diamond City, R. Br. Lead
   Hill 72644
Diaz 72543

16

Dierks	71833	
Doddridge	71834	
Dogpatch	72648	
Dollarway, Br. Pine Bluff	71601	
Dolph	72528	
Donaldson	71941	
Dover	72837	
Dowdy	72529	
Drasco	72530	
Driver	72329	
Dumas (1st)	71639	
Dutton	72726	
Dyer	72935	
Dyess	72330	
Eagle Mills	71729	
Earle	72331	
East Camden, Br. Camden	71701	
Edgemont	72044	
Edmondson	72332	
Egypt	72427	
El Dorado (1st)	71730	
El Paso	72045	
Elaine	72333	
Elizabeth	72531	
Elkins	72727	
Delaney, R. Br.	72723	
Elm Springs	72728	
Emerson	71740	
Emmet	71835	
England	72046	
Enola	72047	
Ethel	72048	
Etowah	72428	
Eudora (1st)	71640	
Eureka Springs	72632	
Evansville	72729	
Evening Shade	72532	
Everton	72633	
Fair Oaks, R. Br. Wynne	72397	
Fairfield Bay, R. Br. Shirley	72153	
Fargo	72049	
Farmington	72730	
Fayetteville (1st)	72701	
Ferndale, R. Br. Little Rock	72208	
Fiftysix, R. Br. Mountain View	72533	
Fisher	72429	
Flippin	72634	
Floral	72534	
Fordyce (1st)	71742	
Foreman	71836	
Forest Park, Sta. Little Rock	72207	
Forrest City (1st)	72335	
Fort Smith (1st)	72901	
Forty Four	72535	
Forum	72731	
Fouke	71837	
Fountain Hill	71642	
Fox	72051	
Franklin	72536	
Frenchmans Bayou	72338	
Friendship	71942	
Fulton	71838	
Gamaliel	72537	
Garfield	72732	
Garland	71839	
Garner	72052	
Gassville (1st)	72635	
Gateway	72733	
Genevia	72053	
Genoa	71840	
Gentry	72734	
Georgetown, R. Br. Searcy	72054	

Gepp	72538	
Gilbert	72636	
Gillett	72055	
Gilliham	71841	
Gilmore	72339	
Glencoe	72539	
Glenwood	71943	
Athens, R. Br.	71927	
Daisy, R. Br.	71939	
Goodwin	72340	
Goshen	72735	
Gould	71643	
Grady	71644	
Grand Glaise	72056	
Grandview	72637	
Grannis	71944	
Grapevine	72057	
Gravel Ridge, R. Br. Jacksonville	72076	
Gravelly	72638	
Gravette	72736	
Green Forest	72638	
Greenbrier	72058	
Greenland	72737	
Greenway	72430	
Greenwood	72936	
Gregory	72059	
Griffithville	72060	
Grubbs	72431	
Guion	72540	
Gurdon	71743	
Guy	72061	
Hackett	72937	
Hagarville	72839	
Hamburg	71646	
Hampton	71744	
Hanover	72541	
Hardy (1st)	72542	
Harrell	71745	
Harriet	72639	
Harrisburg	72432	
Harrison (1st)	72601	
Hartford	72938	
Hartman	72840	
Harvey	72841	
Haskell	72062	
Hasty	72640	
Hatfield	71945	
Hattieville	72063	
Hatton	71946	
Havana	72842	
Haynes	72341	
Hazen	72064	
Heber Springs	72543	
Hector	72843	
Helena (1st)	72342	
Henderson	72544	
Henderson College, Sta. Arkadelphia	71923	
Hendrix College, Sta. Conway	72032	
Hensley	72065	
Hermitage	71647	
Ingalls, R. Br.	71648	
Heth	72346	
Hickory Plains	72066	
Hickory Ridge	72347	
Higden	72067	
Higginson	72068	
Hillcrest, Sta. Little Rock	72205	
Hindsville	72738	
Hiwasse	72739	
Holly Grove	72069	

Holly Springs, R. Br. Sparkman	71746	
Hon	72939	
Hope (1st)	71801	
Horatio	71842	
Horseshoe Bend, R. Br. Franklin	72536	
Hot Springs National Park (1st)	71901	
Houston	72070	
Howell	72071	
Hoxie	72433	
Huff	72545	
Hughes	72348	
Hulbert, Sta. West Memphis	72301	
Humnoke	72072	
Humphrey	72073	
Hunt	72844	
Hunter	72074	
Huntington	72940	
Huntsville	72740	
Huttig	71747	
Ida	72546	
Imboden	72434	
Industrial, Sta. Little Rock	72209	
Ingalls, R. Br. Hermitage	71648	
Ivan	71748	
Jacksonport	72075	
Jacksonville (1st)	72076	
Jamestown	72547	
Jasper	72641	
Jefferson	72079	
Jennie	71649	
Jerome	71650	
Jersey	71651	
Jerusalem	72080	
Jessieville	71949	
Johnson	72741	
Joiner	72350	
Jones Mill, R. Br. Malvern	72105	
Jonesboro (1st)	72401	
Jordan	72548	
Judsonia	72081	
Junction City	71749	
Keiser	72351	
Kensett	72082	
Keo	72083	
Kingsland	71652	
Kingston	72742	
Kirby	71950	
Knobel	72435	
Knoxville	72845	
La Crosse	72549	
La Grange	72352	
Lafe, R. Br. Marmaduke	72436	
Lake Catherine, R. Br. Hot Springs National Park	71901	
Lake City	72437	
Lake Hamilton	71951	
Lake Village	71653	
Lakeview	72642	
Lamar	72846	
Lambert, R. Br. Bismarck	71929	
Lambrook	72353	
Landis	72643	
Laneburg	71844	
Langley	71952	
Larue	72743	
Lavaca	72941	
Lawson	71750	
Leachville (1st)	72438	
Lead Hill	72644	
Leola	72084	

17

Lepanto 72354
Leslie 72645
Letona 72085
Lewisville 71845
  Canfield, R. Br. 71829
Lexa 72355
Light, R. Br. Paragould 72439
Limestone 72646
Lincoln 72744
LITTLE ROCK (1st) (see appendix)
Lockesburg 71846
Locust Grove 72550
London 72847
Lonoke 72086
Lonsdale 72087
Louann 71751
Lowell 72745
Luber 72551
Luxora 72358
Lynn 72440
Mabelvale 72103
Macks, R. Br. Newport 72113
Madison 72359
Magazine 72943
Magness 72553
Magnolia (1st) 71753
Main Street, Sta. North Little Rock 72119
Malvern (1st) 72104
  Jones Mill, R. Br. 72105
Mammoth Spring 72554
Manila 72442
Manning 71757
Mansfield 72944
Marble 72746
Marcella 72555
Marianna (1st) 72360
Marion 72364
Marked Tree 72365
Marmaduke 72443
  Lafe, R. Br. 72436
Marsena 72649
Marshall 72650
  Bigflat, R. Br. 72617
  Snowball, R. Br. 72676
Marvell 72366
Mayflower 72106
Maynard 72444
Maysville 72747
Mc Caskill 71847
Mc Crory 72101
Mc Dougal 72441
Mc Gehee (1st) 71654
Mc Hue 72552
Mc Nab 71849
Mc Neil 71752
Mc Rae 72102
Melbourne 72556
Mellwood 72367
Mena (1st) 71953
Menifee 72107
Midland 72945
Midway 72651
Mineral Springs 71851
Minturn 72445
Moko 72557
Monette 72447
Monroe 72108
Monticello (1st) 71655
Montrose 71658
Moreland 72849
Morganton 72109

Moro 72368
Morrilton (1st) 72110
Morriston, R. Br. Salem 72559
Moscow 72749
Moscow 71659
Mossville 72652
Mount Holly 71758
Mount Ida 71957
Mount Judea 72655
Mount Pleasant 72561
Mount Vernon 72111
Mountain Home (1st) 72653
Mountain Pine 71956
Mountain Top 72850
Mountain View 72560
  Allison, R. Br. 72511
  Fiftysix, R. Br. 72533
  Newnata, R. Br. 72657
  Saint James, R. Br. 72574
Mountainburg 72946
Mulberry 72947
Murfreesboro 71958
Nail 72656
Nashville (1st) 71852
Natural Dam 72948
Nettleton, Sta. Jonesboro 72401
New Blaine 72851
New Edinburg 71660
Newark 72562
Newburg 72563
Newhope 71959
Newnata, R. Br. Mountain View 72657
Newport (1st) 72112
  Auvergne, R. Br. 72008
  Macks, R. Br. 72113
  Shofner, R. Br. 72154
  Weldon, R. Br. 72177
Nimmons 72448
Norfork 72658
  Old Joe, R. Br. 72659
Norman 71960
Norphlet 71759
North Cedar, Sta. Pine Bluff 71601
NORTH LITTLE ROCK (1st) (see appendix)
North Rural Branch, R. Br. Crossett 71635
O'Kean 72449
Oakgrove 72660
Oakland 72661
Oark 72852
Oden 71961
Ogden 71853
Oil Trough 72564
Okay 71854
Okolona 71962
Ola 72853
Old Joe, R. Br. Norfork 72659
Olmstead, R. Br. North Little Rock 72116
Olyphant, R. Br. Bradford 72020
Omaha 72662
Oneida 72369
Onia 72663
Opal 71963
Osage 72664
Osceola (1st) 72370
Ouachita College, Sta. Arkadelphia 71923
Oxford 72565
Ozan 71855
Ozark (1st) 72949

Ozone 72854
Palestine 72372
Pangburn 72121
Paragould (1st) 72450
  Center Hill, R. Br. 72450
  Light, R. Br. 72439
Paris 72855
Park Hill, Sta. North Little Rock 72116
Parkdale 71661
Parkin 72373
Parks 72950
Paron 72122
Parthenon 72666
Patmos 71856
Patrick 72250
Patterson 72123
Payneway, R. Br. Trumann 72472
Pea Ridge 72751
Peach Orchard 72453
Pearcy 71964
Peel 72668
Pelsor 72856
Pencil Bluff 71965
Perla 72124
Perry 72125
Perrytown, R. Br. Hope 71801
Perryville 72126
Pettigrew 72752
Philander Smith College, Sta. Little Rock 72203
Pickens 71662
Piggott 72454
Pindall 72669
Pine Bluff (1st) 71601
Pine Ridge 71966
Pinecrest, Br. Pine Bluff 71601
Pineville 72566
Plainview 72857
Pleasant Grove 72567
Pleasant Plains 72568
Plumerville 72127
Pocahontas (1st) 72455
  Warm Springs, R. Br. 72478
Pollard 72456
Ponca 72670
Poplar Grove 72374
Portia 72457
Portland 71663
Postelle 72375
Pottsville 72858
Poughkeepsie 72569
Powhatan 72458
Poyen 72128
Prairie Grove 72753
Prairie View, R. Br. Scranton 72859
Prattsville 72129
Prescott (1st) 71857
Prim 72130
Princeton, R. Br. Carthage 71761
Proctor 72376
Pruitt 72671
Pyatt 72672
Quitman 72131
Ratcliff 72951
Ravenden 72459
Ravenden Springs 72460
Reader, R. Br. Chidester 71726
Readland 71664
Rector 72461
Redfield 72132
Reed, R. Br. Tillar 71670

Reydell 72133
Reyno 72462
Rison 71665
Rivervale 72577
Rockwell, R. Br. Hot Springs
    National Park 71901
Rodney 72570
Roe 72134
Rogers (1st) 72756
Rohwer 71666
Roland 72135
Rolla 71967
Romance 72136
Rose Bud 72137
Rose City, Sta. North Little
    Rock 72117
Roseland 72463
Rosie 72571
Rosston 71858
Round Pond 72378
Rover 72860
Royal 71968
    Crystal Springs, R. Br. 71938
Rudy 72952
Rule 72673
Russell 72139
Russellville (1st) 72801
Saffell 72572
Sage 72573
Saint Charles 72140
Saint Francis 72464
Saint James, R. Br.
    Mountain View 72574
Saint Joe 72675
Saint Paul 72760
Salado 72575
Salem 72576
    Morriston, R. Br. 72559
Salus 72861
Saratoga 71859
Scotland 72141
Scott 72142
Scottsville 72862
Scranton 72863
    Prairie View, R. Br. 72859
Searcy (1st) 72143
Sedgwick 72465
Sheridan (1st) 72150
Sherrill 72152
Sherwood, Br. North Little
    Rock 72116
Shirley (1st) 72153
Shoffner, R. Br. Newport 72154
Sidney 72577
Sidon 72155
Siloam Springs (1st) 72761
Sims 71969
Smackover 71762
Smithville 72466
Snow Lake 72379
Snowball, R. Br. Marshall 72676
Solgohachia 72156
South Fort Smith, Sta. Fort
    Smith 72901
South Side, Sta. Little Rock .. 72206
Southern State College, Sta.
    Magnolia 71753

Sparkman 71763
    Holly Springs, R. Br. 71746
Springdale (1st) 72764
Springfield 72157
Springtown 72767
Stamps 71860
Star City (1st) 71667
State Capitol, Sta. Little
    Rock 72201
State College Of Arkansas,
    Sta. Conway 72032
State Hospital 72158
State University 72467
Stephens 71764
Steprock 72159
Steve 72864
Stonewall 72468
Story 71970
Strawberry 72469
    Calamine, R. Br. 72418
Strong 71765
Sturkie 72578
Stuttgart (1st) 72160
Subiaco 72865
Success 72470
Sulphur Rock 72579
Sulphur Springs 72768
Summers 72769
Summit 72677
Sweet Home 72164
Swifton 72471
Tamo, R. Br. Grady 71644
Taylor 71861
Tech, Br. Russellville 72801
Texarkana (1st) 75501
Thida 72165
Thornton 71766
Tichnor 72166
Tillar 71670
Tilly 72679
Tilton 72380
Timbo 72680
Tinsman 71767
Tomato 72381
Tontitown 72770
Traskwood 72167
Trumann (1st) 72472
Tucker 72168
Tuckerman 72473
Tull, R. Br. Benton 72015
Tulot 72483
Tumbling Shoals 72581
Tupelo 72169
Turner 72383
Turrell 72384
Twist 72385
Tyronza 72386
Ulm 72170
Umpire 71971
Union 72582
Uniontown 72955
Urbana 71768
Urbanette 72681
Valley Springs 72682
Van 72172
Van Buren (1st) 72956
Vandervoort 71972

Vanndale 72387
Vendor 72683
Veterans Administration Fac,
    Br. North Little Rock 72114
Victoria 72388
Village 71769
Vilonia 72173
Viola 72583
Violet Hill 72584
Wabash 72389
Wabbaseka 72175
Walcott 72474
Waldenburg 72475
Waldo 71770
Waldron 72958
Walnut Ridge (1st) 72476
Ward 72176
Warm Springs, R. Br.
    Pocahontas 72478
Warren (1st) 71671
Washington 71862
Watson 71674
Waveland 72867
Wayton 72684
Weathers 72772
Weiner 72479
Weldon, R. Br. Newport 72177
Wesley 72773
West Fork 72774
West Helena (1st) 72390
West Memphis (1st) 72301
West Point 72178
West Ridge 72391
Western Grove 72685
Wheatley 72392
Wheeler 72775
Whelen Springs 71772
White Hall, Br. Pine Bluff 71601
Wickes 71973
Wideman 72585
Widener 72394
Wilburn 72179
Williford 72482
Willisville 71864
Wilmar 71675
Wilmot 71676
Wilson 72395
Wilton 71865
Winchester 71677
Wing 72868
Winslow 72959
Winthrop 71866
Wiseman 72587
Witter 72776
Witts Springs 72686
Wolf Bayou 72588
Woodson 72180
Wooster 72181
Wright 72182
Wrightsville 72183
Wynne (1st) 72396
    Fair Oaks, R. Br. 72397
Yellville 72687
Yorktown 71678
Zinc 72688
Zion 72589

LITTLE ROCK   722

POST OFFICE BOXES

Box Nos.

1-3864	Main Office	03
4001-4584	Asher Sta	04
5001-5199	Hillcrest Station	05
5200-5999	Brady Station	05
6001-6319	South Side Sta.	06
7201-7594	Forest Park Sta.	07
9001-9999	Industrial Sta.	09

RURAL ROUTES

1		04
2		05
3		05
4		06
5		07

STATIONS, BRANCHES AND UNITS

Asher Sta.	04
Brady Sta.	05
Ferndale Rural Br.	08
Forest Park Sta.	07
Hillcrest Sta.	05
Industrial Sta.	09
Philander Smith College Sta.	03
South Side Sta.	06
State Capitol Sta.	01
General Delivery	01
Postmaster	01

BUILDINGS

Adkins, 115 E Capitol	0
Albert Pike Memorial Temple, 700 Scott	01
Arkansas Education Association, 1500 W 4th	01
Baptist Medical Arts, 1120 Marshall	02
Baptist, 525 W. Capitol	01
Boyle, 103 W Capitol	01
Commercial National Bank, 200 Main	01
Commercial Warehouse, 1800 E 26th	06

Little Rock (Con.)   722

Cotton Exchange, 202 E 2nd	01
Doctors, 500 So University St	05
Donaghey, 103 E 7th	01
Dyke, 309 Center	01
Elrock, 1015 Louisiana St	02
Exchange, 106 E Capitol	01
Farm Bureau, 7th & High	02
Fausett, Markham & University	05
First Federal Savings, 312 Louisiana	01
Gazette, 118 W 3rd	01
Hall, 209 W Capitol	01
Justice, Capitol Grounds	01
Little Rock Public Library, 7th & Louisiana	01
Mart, Cantrell & Cedar Hill	02
National Investors-Life, 2nd & Broadway	01
National Old Line, Capitol & Woodlane	01
Pulaski Federal Savings, 410 W 3rd	01
Pyramid, 221 W 2nd	01
Rector, 409 W 3rd	01
Reed, 112 E 7th	01
Southern Equitable, 3rd & Center	01
State Capitol, 5th & Woodlane	01
Stephens, 114 E Capitol	01
Terminal Warehouse, 500 E Markham	01
Tower, 4th & Center	01
Union Life, 212 Center	01
Union National Bank, 124 W. Capitol	01
Union Station, Markham & Victory St	01
University Tower, 1200 So University St	04
Waldon, 110 E 7th	01
Wallace, 105 S Main	01
Worthen Bank, 200 W. Capitol	01
Worthen Motor Bank, 4th & Scott	01

GOVERNMENT OFFICES

City Hall, Markham & Broadway	01

Little Rock (Con.)   722

County Court House, 405 W Markham	01
Federal Offices Building, 700 W. Capitol	01
Police Department, 700 W Markham	01
U.S. Post Office & Court House Building, 600 W. Capitol	01

NORTH LITTLE ROCK   721

POST OFFICE BOXES

Box Nos.

1-277	Levy Sta	18
1-1189	North Little Rock	15
3001-3114	Rose City Sta	17
4001-4220	Park Hill Sta	16
5001-5851	Main St Sta	19
6001-6115	Sherwood	13

RURAL ROUTES

1		17
2		18
3		16
4		17
6		18

STATIONS, BRANCHES AND UNITS

Main Street Sta.	19
Olmstead Rural Br.	16
Park Hill Sta.	16
Rose City Sta	17
Sherwood Br	16
Veterans Administration Fac Br	14
General Delivery	14
Postmaster	14

APARTMENTS, HOTELS, MOTELS

Campus Towers	14
East Gate Ter	14
Heritage House	14
Lakewood House	16
Shorter College Gardens	14
Willow House, 2500 Willow	14

20

CALIFORNIA
(Abbreviation: CA)

Acampo..................................95220
Acton....................................93510
Adelanto...............................92301
Adin......................................96006
Agnew, Sta. Santa Clara.......95054
Agoura..................................91301
Agua Caliente Springs, R.
  Br. Julian............................92036
Agua Dulce, R. Br. Saugus....91350
Aguanga................................92302
Ahwahnee.............................93601
Airport, Sta. Ontario..............91761
Airport, Br. San Francisco......94128
Airport, Sta. Oakland.............94614
Al Tahoe, Sta. South Lake
  Tahoe.................................95705
Alameda (1st).......................94501
Alamo (1st)...........................94507
Albany, Br. Berkeley (see
  appendix)
Albion..................................95410
Alderpoint............................95411
ALHAMBRA (1st) (see
  appendix)
Alisal, Sta. Salinas................93901
All American, Sta. Cupertino...95014
Alleghany..............................95910
Almanor, R. Br. Greenville.....95911
Alondra, Br. Gardena.............90249
Alpaugh................................93201
Alpine...................................92001
Alta......................................95701
Alta Loma..............................91701
Altadena (1st).......................91001
Altaville................................95221
Alturas (1st)..........................96101
Alvarado, Sta. Union City.......94587
Alviso...................................95002
Amador City..........................95601
Ambassador, Sta. Los
  Angeles..............................90070
Amboy..................................92304
American Canyon, Br.
  Vallejo................................94590
Amphibious Base, Br. San
  Diego.................................92155
ANAHEIM (1st) (see
  appendix)
Anderson (1st).......................96007
Andrew Jackson, Sta. San
  Diego.................................92115
Angels Camp..........................95222
Angelus Oaks.........................92305
Angwin (1st)..........................94508
  Deer Park, Br.......................94576
Annapolis..............................95412
Antelope...............................95602
Antioch (1st).........................94509
Anza.....................................92306
Apple Valley (1st)..................92307
Applegate..............................95703
Aptos (1st)............................95003
Arbuckle...............................95912
Arcade, Sta. Los Angeles........90052
Arcadia (1st).........................91006
Arcata (1st)...........................95521
Arden, Br. Sacramento...........95825
Argus, Br. Trona.....................93562
Arlanza Village, Sta.
  Riverside............................92505

Arleta, Sta. Pacoima..............91331
Arlington, Sta. Riverside.........92503
Armona.................................93202
Army Terminal, Sta.
  Oakland..............................94626
Arnold...................................95223
  Bear Valley, R. Br................95223
  Camp Connell, R. Br............95223
  Lake Alpine, R. Br...............95235
Aromas..................................95004
Arroyo, Sta. Walnut Creek......94598
Arroyo Grande (1st)...............93420
Artesia (1st)..........................90701
Artois...................................95913
Arvin (1st).............................93203
Ashlan Park, Sta. Fresno........93726
Asti.......................................95413
Atascadero (1st)....................93422
Atherton, Br. Menlo Park........94025
Atwater (1st).........................95301
Atwood..................................92601
Auberry.................................93602
Auburn (1st)..........................95603
Avalon...................................90704
Avenal...................................93204
Avery.....................................95224
Avila Beach............................93424
Azusa (1st)............................91702
Baden, Sta. South San
  Francisco............................94080
Badger, R. Br. Miramonte.......93603
Bailey, Sta. Whittier (see
  appendix)
Baker.....................................92309
BAKERSFIELD (1st) (see
  appendix)
Balboa, Sta. Newport Beach....92661
Balboa Island, Sta. Newport
  Beach.................................92662
Baldwin Park (1st).................91706
Balhco...................................95303
Ballroad, Sta. Cypress...........90630
Bangor...................................95914
Banning (1st).........................92220
Banta, Br. Tracy.....................95304
Bard......................................92222
Barrington, Sta. Los
  Angeles..............................90049
Barstow (1st).........................92311
Barton, Sta. Fresno................93702
Base Line, Sta. San
  Bernardino..........................92410
Bass Lake...............................93604
Bassett, Br. La Puente...........91746
Baxter....................................95704
Bay, Sta. Big Bear Lake..........92315
Bay View, Sta. San
  Francisco............................94124
Bay-Osos, Br. San Luis
  Obispo................................93401
Bayliss, R. Br. Glenn..............95943
Bayside..................................95524
Beach Center, Sta.
  Huntington Beach................92648
Beale A F B, Br. Marysville......95903
Bear River Lake, R. Br.
  Pioneer...............................95666
Bear Valley, R. Br. Arnold.......95223
Beaumont (1st)......................92223
Beckwourth, R. Br. Portola......96129
Belden...................................95915
Bell (1st)...............................90201
Bell, Sta. Merced...................95340

Bell Gardens, Br. Bell............90201
Bella Vista.............................96008
Bellflower (1st)......................90706
Belmont (1st).........................94002
Belvedere-Tiburon (1st).........94920
Ben Lomond...........................95005
Bendix, Sta. North
  Hollywood...........................91605
Benicia (1st)..........................94510
Benton...................................93512
BERKELEY (1st) (see
  appendix)
Bermuda Dunes, R. Br.
  Indio...................................92201
Bernal, Sta. San Francisco......94110
Berry Creek............................95916
Berwick, Br. Carmel...............93921
Bethel Island.........................94511
BEVERLY HILLS (1st) (see
  appendix)
Bieber...................................96009
Big Bar..................................96010
Big Basin, R. Br. Boulder
  Creek..................................95006
Big Bear City..........................92314
  Sugarloaf, R. Br...................92386
Big Bear Lake (1st)................92315
Big Bend................................96011
Big Creek...............................93605
  Cedar Crest, R. Br...............93605
  Huntington Lake, R. Br........93629
Big Oak Flat...........................95305
Big Pine.................................93513
Big Sur..................................93920
Biggs.....................................95917
Biola.....................................93606
Birds Landing.........................94512
Bishop (1st)...........................93514
Bixby, Sta. Long Beach..........90807
Blairsden...............................96103
  Cromberg, R. Br..................96103
  Graeagle, R. Br...................96103
  Sloat, R Br..........................96127
Blocksburg.............................95514
Bloomington (1st)..................92316
Blossom Hill, Sta. San Jose....95123
Blossom Valley, Sta.
  Mountain View.....................94040
Blue Jay................................92317
Blue Lake..............................95525
Blythe (1st)...........................92225
Bodega..................................94922
Bodega Bay...........................94923
Bodfish.................................93205
Bolinas..................................94924
Bolsa, Sta. Westminster.........92683
Bonita...................................92002
Bonsall..................................92003
Boonville...............................95415
Boron....................................93516
Borrego Springs.....................92004
Bostonia, Sta. El Cajon..........92021
Boulder Creek........................95006
Boulevard..............................92005
Bowman, Br. Auburn..............95603
Boyes Hot Springs..................95416
Boyle, Sta. Los Angeles.........90033
Boys Republic, R. Br. Chino....91710
Bradbury, Br. Duarte..............91010
Bradford, Sta. Hayward..........94541
Bradley..................................93426
Brandeis, R. Br. Simi Valley....93064
Branscomb.............................95417

Brawley (1st) 92227
　Glamis, R. Br. 92248
Brea (1st) 92621
Brentwood (1st) 94513
Bridgeport 93517
Bridgeville 95526
Briggs, Sta. Los Angeles 90048
Brisbane (1st) 94005
Bristol, Sta. Santa Ana 92703
Broadway, Sta. Sacramento 95818
Broadway Manchester, Sta.
　Los Angeles 90003
Broderick 95605
Brookdale 95007
Brookhurst Center, Sta.
　Anaheim 92804
Brooks 95606
Browns Valley 95918
Brownsville 95919
Bryant, Sta. Long Beach 90815
Bryn Mawr 92318
Bryte, Br. Broderick 95605
Buellton 93427
BUENA PARK (1st) (see
　appendix)
BURBANK (1st) (see
　appendix)
Burlingame (1st) 94010
Burney 96013
Burnt Ranch 95527
　Denny, R. Br. 95535
Burrel 93607
Burson 95225
Butte City 95920
Butte Meadows, R. Br.
　Chico 95921
Buttonwillow 93206
Byron 94514
Cabazon 92230
Cabrillo, Sta. Long Beach 90810
Cachuma, R. Br. Santa
　Barbara 93101
Cadiz 92319
Calabasas (1st) 91302
Calabasas Park, Br.
　Calabasas 91302
Calexico (1st) 92231
Caliente 93518
California City, Br. Mojave 93501
California Hot Springs 93207
California Valley, R. Br.
　Santa Margarita 93453
Calimesa (1st) 92320
Calipatria 92233
Calistoga 94515
Callahan 96014
Calpella, Br. Ukiah 95418
Calpine, R. Sta. Sattley 96124
Calwa, Br. Fresno (see
　appendix)
Camarillo (1st) 93010
Cambria 93428
Cambrian Park, Br. San Jose
　(see appendix)
Camellia Station, Sta.
　Sacramento 95819
Camino 95709
Camp Connell, R Br. Arnold ..95223
Camp Kaweah, Br. Sequoia
　National Park 93262
Camp Meeker 95419
Camp Nelson, R. Br.
　Springville 93208

Camp Pendleton, Br.
　Oceanside 92055
Camp Richardson, R. Br.
　South Lake Tahoe 95705
Campbell (1st) 95008
Campo 92006
Campo Seco, R. Br. Valley
　Springs 95226
Camptonville 95922
Canby 96015
Canoga Annex, Sta. Canoga
　Park 91304
CANOGA PARK (1st) (see
　appendix)
Cantil 93519
Cantua Creek 93608
Canyon 94516
Canyon Country, Br. Saugus ...91350
Canyon Crest, Sta.
　Riverside 92507
Canyondam 95923
Capay 95607
Capistrano Beach, Br. San
　Clemente 92624
Capitola (1st) 95010
Cardiff By The Sea 92007
Cardwell, Sta. Fresno (see
　appendix)
Caribou, R. Br. Belden 95915
Carlotta 95528
Carlsbad (1st) 92008
Carmel (1st) 93921
Carmel Rancho, Br. Carmel ..93921
Carmel Valley 93924
Carmichael (1st) 95608
Carnelian Bay 95711
Carpinteria (1st) 93013
Carson, Br. Wilmington 90746
Carson, Br. Wilmington 90745
Cartago 93520
Caruthers 93609
Carwood, Sta. Lakewood 90713
Casa Blanca, Sta. Riverside 92504
Casa Correo, Sta. Concord 94521
Casmalia 93429
Caspar, R. Br. Fort Bragg 95420
Cassel 96016
Castaic 91310
Castella 96017
Castle A F B, Br. Merced 95342
Castro Valley, Br. Hayward 94546
Castroville 95012
Catalina, Sta. Pasadena 91106
Cathedral City (1st) 92234
Catheys Valley 95306
Cayucos 93430
Cazadero 95421
Cecilville 96018
Cedar, Sta. Lancaster 93534
Cedar Crest, R. Br. Big
　Creek 93605
Cedar Glen 92321
Cedar Ridge 95924
Cedarpines Park 92322
Cedarville 96104
Central District, Sta.
　Pomona (see appendix)
Central Valley 96019
Centre, Br. Sacramento 95860
Century City, Sta. Los
　Angeles (see appendix)
Ceres (1st) 95307
Cerritos, Br. Artesia 90701

Challenge 95925
Charter Oak, Br. Covina 91722
Chatsworth (1st) 91311
Cherry Valley, R. Br.
　Beaumont 92223
Chester 96020
Chicago Park 95712
Chico (1st) 95926
　Butte Meadows, R. Br. 95321
　Midtown, Sta. 95926
　Richardson Springs, R.
　Br. 95973
Chilcoot 96105
Childrens Fairyland, Sta.
　Oakland 94622
China, Sta. San Francisco 94108
China Lake, Br. Ridgecrest ..93555
Chinese Camp 95309
Chino (1st) 91710
Chiriaco Summit, R Br.
　Indio 92201
Cholame 93431
Chowchilla (1st) 93610
Chualar 93925
CHULA VISTA (1st) (see
　appendix)
Cima 92323
Cimarron, Sta. Los Angeles 90018
Citrus Heights (1st) 95610
City Hall, Sta. San
　Francisco 94102
City Of Commerce, Sta. Los
　Angeles (see appendix)
City Of Industry, Br. La
　Puente 91744
City Terrace, Sta. Los
　Angeles (see appendix)
Civic Center, Br. San Rafael ..94903
Civic Center, Sta. Oakland 94604
Claremont (1st) 91711
Clarksburg 95612
Clayton 94517
Clearlake Highlands 95422
Clearlake Oaks 95423
Clearlake Park 95424
Clements 95227
Clinter, Sta. Fresno 93703
Clio 96106
Clipper Mills 95930
Cloverdale (1st) 95425
Clovis (1st) 93612
Coarsella, Sta. 92236
Coalinga (1st) 93210
Coarsegold 93614
Cobb 95426
　Hobergs, R. Br. 95496
　Loch Lomond, R. Br 95426
Coddingtown, Sta. Santa
　Rosa 95406
Cole, Br. Los Angeles 90046
Coleville 96107
Colfax 95713
College Center, Br.
　Bakersfield 93306
College City 95931
College Grove Center, Sta.
　San Diego 92115
Collier, Br. Canoga Park 91304
Colma, Sta. Daly City 94014
Coloma 95613
Colonial, Sta. Sacramento
　(see appendix)

Colton (1st) 92324
Columbia 95310
Colusa (1st) 95932
Commonwealth, Sta.
  Fullerton 92632
Comptche 95427
COMPTON (1st) (see
  appendix)
CONCORD (1st) (see
  appendix)
Cool 95614
Copperopolis 95228
Corcoran (1st) 93212
Cornell, R. Sta. Agoura 91301
Corning (1st) 96021
  Flournoy, R. Br. 96029
Corona (1st) 91720
Corona Del Mar (1st) 92625
Coronado, Br. San Diego ..92118
Corralitos, Br. Watsonville 95076
Corte Madera (1st) 94925
COSTA MESA (1st) (see
  appendix)
Cotati (1st) 94928
Cottonwood 96022
  Manzanita Lake, R. Br. ..96060
Coulterville 95311
Court, Sta. Martinez 94553
Courtland 95615
Covelo 95428
Covina (1st) 91722
Coyote 95013
Crenshaw, Sta. Los Angeles
  (see appendix)
Crenshaw Imperial, Sta.
  Inglewood (see appendix)
Crescent City (1st) 95531
Crescent Mills 95934
Cressey 95312
Crest Park 92326
Cresta Blanca, R. Br.
  Livermore 94550
Crestline 92325
Creston 93432
Crockett (1st) 94525
Cromberg, R. Br. Blairsden 96103
Crows Landing 95313
Cucamonga (1st) 91730
Cudahy, Br. Bell 90201
Culver City (1st) 90230
Cummings, R. Br. Wilits. ...95477
Cupertino (1st) 95014
Curry Village, Br. Yosemite
  National Park 95389
Cutler 93615
Cutten 95534
Cuyama 93214
Cypress (1st) 90630
Daggett 92327
Dairy Farm, R. Br. Vallejo .94590
DALY CITY (1st) (see
  appendix)
Dana Point (1st) 92629
Danville (1st) 94526
Dardanelle, R. Br. Pinecrest 95314
Darwin 93522
Davenport 95017
Davis (1st) 95616
  El Macero, R. Br. 95618
  U C D, Br. 95616
Davis Creek 96108
Death Valley 92328
Death Valley Junction, R. Br.

Death Valley 92328
Deer Park, Br. Angwin 94576
Del Mar (1st) 92014
Del Mar Heights, R. Sta.
  Morro Bay 93442
Del Monte Park, Br. Pacific
  Grove 93950
Del Paso Heights, Sta.
  Sacramento 95838
Del Rey 93615
Del Rey Oaks, Br. Monterey 93940
Del Rosa, Br. San
  Bernardino 92404
Del Valle, Sta. Los Angeles 90015
Delano (1st) 93215
Delevan, R. Br. Willows 95988
Delhi 95315
Delkern, R. Br. Bakersfield 93309
Delta, Sta. Stockton (see
  appendix)
Denair 95316
Denny, R. Br. Burnt Ranch 95535
Descanso 92016
Desert Center 92239
Desert Hot Springs (1st) ...92240
Di Giorgio 93217
Diablo 94528
Diamond, Sta. Santa Ana ..92704
Diamond Bar, Br. Pomona ..91765
Diamond Heights, Sta. San
  Francisco 94131
Diamond Springs 95619
Dillon Beach 94929
Dimond, Sta. Oakland 94602
Dinkey Creek, R. Br. Shaver
  Lake 93617
Dinuba (1st) 93618
Dixon (1st) 95620
Dobbins 95935
Dockweiler, Sta. Los
  Angeles 90007
Dollar Ranch, Sta. Walnut
  Creek 94595
Domingues Hills, Br
  Gardena 90247
Dorris 96023
Dos Palos (1st) 93620
Dos Rios, R Br. Willits 95429
Douglas, Sta. Santa Monica 90405
Douglas City 96024
Douglas Flat, R. Br. Vallecito 95229
DOWNEY (1st) (see
  appendix)
Downieville 95936
Downtown, Sta. Burbank 91503
Downtown, Sta. San
  Bernardino 92403
Downtown, Sta. Redwood
  City 94063
Downtown, Sta. Manhattan
  Beach 90266
Doyle 96109
Drytown, R. Br. Sutter Creek 95699
Duarte (1st) 91010
Dublin, Br. Pleasanton 94566
Ducor 93218
Dulzura 92017
Duncans Mills 95430
Dunlap 93621
Dunnigan 95937
Dunsmuir 96025
Durham 95938
Dutch Flat 95714

Dutch Village, Sta.
  Lakewood 90713
Eagle Mountain 92241
Eagle Rock, Sta. Los
  Angeles (see appendix)
Eagleville 96110
Earlimart 93219
Earp 92242
East Compton, Sta.
  Compton 90220
East Fresno, Br. Fresno 93727
East Highlands 92329
East Irvine 92650
East Long Beach, Sta. Long
  Beach 90804
East Los Angeles, Br. Los
  Angeles (see appendix)
East Lynwood, Sta. Lynwood 90262
East Nicolaus 95622
East Palo Alto, Sta. Palo
  Alto (see appendix)
East Pasadena, Sta.
  Pasadena 91107
East San Diego, Sta. San
  Diego 92105
East Santa Cruz, Sta. Santa
  Cruz 95060
East Stockton, Sta. Stockton 95205
East Ventura, Sta. Ventura 93003
Eastgate, Sta. Fresno 93702
Eastmont, Sta. Oakland 94605
Easton, Br. Fresno 93706
Eastside, Sta. San
  Bernardino 92410
Echo Lake, R. Br. Little
  Norway 95721
Edendale, Sta. Los Angeles
  (see appendix)
Edgemont, Br. Riverside 92508
Edgewood, R Br Weed 96094
Edison 93220
Edwards (1st) 93523
Edwards Air Force Base,
  Sta. Edwards 93523
EL CAJON (1st) (see
  appendix)
El Camino College, Br.
  Torrance 90506
El Centro (1st) 92243
  Plaster City, R. Br. 92269
El Cerrito (1st) 94530
El Dorado 95623
El Dorado Hills, R. Br.
  Folsom 95630
El Granada 94018
El Macero, R Br Davis 95618
El Modena, Sta Orange 92667
EL MONTE (1st) (see
  appendix)
El Nido 95317
El Portal 95318
El Segundo (1st) 90245
El Sereno, Sta. Los Angeles
  (see appendix)
El Sobrante, Br. Richmond .94803
El Toro (1st) 92630
El Toro Marine Corp Air Sta,
  Br. Santa Ana 92709
El Verano 95433
El Viejo Sta. Modesto (see
  appendix)
Eldridge 95431

Elk 95432
Elk Creek 95939
Elk Grove (1st) 95624
Elmhurst, Sta. Oakland 94603
Elmira 95625
Elmwood, Sta. Berkeley (see
   appendix)
Elsinore (1st) 92330
Elverta 95626
Emeryville, Br. Oakland 94608
Emigrant Gap 95715
Empire 95319
Encanto, Sta. San Diego
   (see appendix)
Encinal, Sta. Sunnyvale 94087
Encinitas (1st) 92024
Encino, Br. Van Nuys 91316
Enterprise, Br. Redding 96001
Escalon (1st) 95320
ESCONDIDO (1st) (see
   appendix)
Esparto 95627
Essex 92332
Estudillo, Sta. San Leandro 94577
Etiwanda 91739
Etna 96027
Eureka (1st) 95501
   A, Sta. 95501
   Henderson, Sta. 95501
   Myrtletowne, Br. 95501
Evergreen, Br. Santa Maria 93454
Exeter (1st) 93221
Fair Oaks (1st) 95628
Fairfax (1st) 94930
Fairfield (1st) 94533
   Travis A F B. Sta 94535
Fairmount, Sta. El Cerrito 94530
Fairview, Br. Goleta 93017
Fall River Mills 96028
   Glenburn, R. Br. 96036
Fallbrook (1st) 92028
Fallen Leaf, R. Br. South
   Lake Tahoe 95716
Fallon, R. Br. Tomales 94932
Fancher, Br. Fresno 93702
Farmers Market, Sta. Los
   Angeles 90036
Farmersville 93223
Farmington 95230
Fawnskin 92333
Feather Falls 95940
Federal, Sta. Covina 91722
Federal, Sta. Anaheim 92805
Federal Annex, Sta. Oxnard 93030
Federal Terrace, Br. Vallejo 94590
Fellows 93224
Felton (1st) 95018
Fenner 92334
Fernbridge, R. Br. Fortuna 95540
Ferndale 95536
Fiddletown 95629
Fields Landing 95537
Fig Garden Village, Br.
   Fresno 93704
Figueroa, Sta. Altadena 91001
Fillmore (1st) 93015
Finley 95435
Firebaugh 93622
Firestone, Sta. South Gate 90280
First Street, Sta Oceanside 92054
Fish Camp 93623
Fisk, Sta. San Francisco 94122

Fitchburg, Sta. Oakland 94621
Five Points 93624
Fleet, Sta. San Diego 92132
Fleetwood Annex, Br. Covina 91722
Fletcher Hills, Sta. El Cajon 92020
Florence, Br. Los Angeles
   (see appendix)
Florin, Br. Sacramento (see
   appendix)
Floriston 96111
Flournoy, R. Br. Corning 96029
Folsom (1st) 95630
Fontana (1st) 92335
Foothill Center, Sta. Azusa 91702
Foothill Farms, Br.
   Sacramento (see
   appendix)
Forbestown 95941
Forest Falls 92339
Forest Glen, R. Br. Hayfork 96030
Forest Knolls 94933
Forest Ranch 95942
Foresthill 95631
Forestville 95436
Forks Of Salmon 96031
Fort Baker, Br. Sausalito 94965
Fort Bidwell 96112
Fort Bragg (1st) 95437
   Caspar, R. Br. 95420
Fort Dick 95538
Fort Irwin, Br. Barstow 92311
Fort Jones 96032
Fort Mac Arthur, Sta. San
   Pedro 90731
Fort Ord, Br. Monterey 93941
Fort Seward 95438
Fort Sutter, Sta.
   Sacramento 95816
Fortuna (1st) 95540
Foster City, Br. San Mateo 94404
Fountain Valley, Br. Santa
   Ana 92708
Fowler 93625
Foy, Sta. Los Angeles 90017
Franklin, Sta. Napa 94558
Frazier Park 93225
Freedom (1st) 95019
Freestone, R. Br. Sebastopol 95472
FREMONT (1st) (see
   appendix)
French Camp 95231
French Gulch 96033
FRESNO (1st) (see appendix)

Friant 93626
Frontera, R. Br. Corona 91720
Fruitvale, Sta. Oakland 94601
FULLERTON (1st) (see
   appendix)
Fulton 95439
Gabilan, Sta. Salinas 93901
Galt (1st) 95632
Garberville 95440
GARDENA (1st) (see
   appendix)
GARDEN GROVE (1st) (see
   appendix)
Garden Valley 95633
Gasquet 95543
Gateway, Sta. Culver City 90230
Gaviota, R. Br. Goleta 93017
Gazelle 96034
Geary, Sta. San Francisco 94108

George A F B. Br. Victorville 92392
George Washington, Sta.
   San Diego 92102
Georgetown 95634
Gerber 96035
Geyserville 95441
Giant Forest, R. Sta.
   Sequoia National Park 93262
Gilman Hot Springs 92340
Gilroy (1st) 95020
Glamis, R. Br. Brawley 92248
Glassell, Sta. Los Angeles 90065
Glen Ellen 95442
Glenburn, R. Br. Fall River
   Mills 96036
Glencoe 95232
GLENDALE (1st) (see
   appendix)
Glendora (1st) 91740
Glenhaven 95443
Glenn 95943
Glennville 93226
Glenoaks, Sta. Burbank (see
   appendix)
Gold Run 95717
Goleta (1st) 93017
Gonzales 93926
Goodyears Bar 95944
Gorman, R. Br. Lancaster 93534
Goshen 93227
Graeagle, R Br Blairsden 96103
Granada Hills, Br. San
   Fernando 91344
Grand Avenue, Sta. Elsinore 92330
Grand Central, Sta.
   Glendale 91201
Grand Lake, Sta. Oakland 94510
Grand Terrace, Br. Colton 92324
Grantville, Sta San Diego
   (see appendix)
Grass Valley (1st) 95945
   Penn Valley, R. Br. 95946
Graton 95444
Green, Sta. Los Angeles 90037
Green Valley, R. Br. Saugus 91350
Green Valley Lake 92341
Greenacres, R Br.
   Bakersfield 93308
Greenbrae, Br. San Rafael 94904
Greenfield 93927
Greenmead, Sta. Los
   Angeles 90059
Greenview 96037
Greenville 95947
   Almanor, R. Br. 95911
Greenwood 95635
Grenada 96038
Gridley (1st) 95948
Griffith, Sta. Los Angeles 90039
Grimes 95950
Grizzly Flats 95636
Groveland 95321
   Mather, R. Br. 95339
Grover City 93433
Guadalupe 93434
Gualala 95445
Guasti 91743
Guatay 92031
Guerneville 95446
   Guernewood Park, R. Br. 95446
   Rio Nido, R. Br. 95471
Guernewood Park, R. Br.
   Guerneville 95446

Guinda 95637
Gustine 95322
Hacienda Heights, Br. La
   Puente 91745
Malcyon, Br Arroyo Grande ..93420
Half Moon Bay 94019
Hamilton Air Force Base
   (1st) 94934
Hamilton City 95951
Hancock, Sta. Los Angeles ..90044
Hanford (1st) 93230
Happy Camp 96039
Harbor City (1st) 90710
Harder Annex, Sta. Hayward
   (see appendix)
Hardman Center, Sta.
   Riverside 92504
Harmony 93435
Harris 95447
Hat Creek 96040
Hathaway Pines 95233
Havasu Lake, R. Br.
   Needles 92363
Hawaiian Gardens, Br.
   Lakewood (see appendix)
Hawthorne (1st) 90250
Hayfork 96041
   Forest Glen, R. Br. 96030
HAYWARD (1st) (see
   appendix)
Hazard, Br Los Angeles 90063
Heald-burg (1st) 95448
Heber 92249
Helena, R Br. Weaverville ..96042
Helendale 92342
Helm 93627
Heiner (1st) 92343
Henderson, Sta. Eureka 95501
Herald 95638
Hercules 94547
Herlong 96113
Hermosa Beach, Br.
   Redondo Beach 90254
Herndon, R. Br. Fresno 93721
Hesperia (1st) 92345
Heyer, Br. Hayward 94541
Hickman 95323
Highgrove, Br Riverside 92507
Highland (1st) 92346
Highland Park, Sta. Los
   Angeles (see appendix)
Highway City, Br. Fresno 93705
Hillcrest, Sta. San Diego 92103
Hillcrest Center, Br.
   Bakersfield 93306
Hillsborough, Br.
   Burlingame 94010
Hillsdale, Sta. San Mateo ..94403
Hilmar 95324
Hilt 96043
Hinkley 92347
Hobergs, R. Br. Cobb 95496
Hollister (1st) 95023
Hollydale, Sta. South Gate ..90280
Hollywood, Sta. Los Angeles
   (see appendix)
Holt 95234
Holtville 92250
Holy City 95026
Homeland 92348
Homestead, Sta Stockton ..95206
Homewood 95718
Honeydew 95545

Hood 95639
Hoopa 95546
Hope Valley, R. Br.
   Markleeville 96139
Hopland 95449
Hornbrook 96044
Hornitos 95325
Horse Creek 96045
Hub City, Sta. Compton 90220
Hudson, Sta. Modesto 95354
Hughson 95326
Hume, R. Br. Miramonte 93628
Hunter Liggett, MOU. Jolon ..93928
Hunters Point, Sta. San
   Francisco 84135
HUNTINGTON BEACH (1st)
   (see appendix)
Huntington Lake, R. Br. Big
   Creek 93629
Huntington Park (1st) 90255
Huron 93234
Hyampom 96046
Hydesville 95547
Idna 95027
Idyllwild 92349
Ignacio, Sta. Novato 94947
Igo 96047
Imola, Br. Napa 94558
Imperial (1st) 92251
Imperial Beach (1st) 92032
Independence 93526
Indian Wells, Br. Palm
   Desert 92260
Indio (1st) 92201
Industrial, Sta. Santa Ana ..92705
INGLEWOOD (1st) (see
   appendix)
Institute, Sta. Riverside 92503
Inverness 94937
Inyokern 93527
Ione 95640
Iowa Hill, R. Br. Colfax 95713
Irvine, Br. Newport Beach ..92664
Irvington, Sta. Fremont 94538
Irwindale, Br. Baldwin Park ..91706
Isla Vista, Br. Goleta 93017
Island Mountain, R. Br.
   Willits 95478
Isleton 95641
Italian Swiss Colony, R. Br.
   Madera 93638
Ivanhoe 93235
Jackson (1st) 95642
Jacumba 92034
Jamestown 95327
Jamul 92035
Janesville 96114
   Wendel, R. Br. 96136
Jenner 95450
Johannesburg 93528
John Adams, Sta. San Diego ..92116
Johnsondale 93236
Jolon 93928
Joshua Tree 92252
Julian 92036
Junction City 96048
June Lake 93529
Kaiser Center, Sta. Oakland ..94612
Kaweah 93237
Kearny, Sta. Los Angeles ..90011
Keddie, R. Br. Quincy 95952
Keeler 93530

Keene 93531
Kelsey 95643
Kelseyville 95451
Kelso 92351
Kensington, Br. Berkeley
   (see appendix)
Kentfield, Br. San Rafael 94904
Kenwood 95452
Kerman (1st) 93630
Kern City, R. Br. Bakersfield..93309
Kernville 93238
Kester, Sta. Van Nuys (see
   appendix)
Kettleman City 93239
Keyes 95328
King, Sta. Santa Ana 92706
King City (1st) 93930
Kings Beach 95719
Kings Canyon National Park,
   R. Br. Miramonte 93633
Kingsburg (1st) 93631
Kit Carson, R. Br. Pine
   Grove 95644
Klamath 95548
Klamath River 96050
Kneeland 95549
Knights Ferry, R. Br.
   Oakdale 95361
Knights Landing 95645
Knightsen 94548
Korbel 95550
Kyburz 95720
La Canada (1st) 91011
   Mount Wilson, R. Br. 91023
La Costa, Sta Malibu 90265
La Crescenta, Sta. Glendale ..91214
La Grange 95329
La Habra (1st) 90631
La Honda 94020
La Jolla (1st) 92037
La Mesa (1st) 92041
La Mirada (1st) 90638
La Palma, Br. Buena Park ..90620
La Porte, R. Br. Strawberry
   Valley 95981
LA PUENTE (1st) (see
   appendix)
La Quinta 92253
La Selva Beach, R. Br.
   Watsonville 95076
La Sierra, Sta. Riverside 92505
La Tijera, Sta. Los Angeles ..90043
La Verne (1st) 91750
La Vina, Sta. Altadena 91001
Ladera, Br. Menlo Park 94025
Ladera Heights, Sta. Los
   Angeles 90045
Lafayette (1st) 94549
LAGUNA BEACH (1st) (see
   appendix)
Laguna Hills, Br. Laguna
   Beach 92653
Laguna Niguel, Br. Laguna
   Beach 92677
Lagunitas 94938
Lake Alpine, R. Br. Arnold ..95235
Lake Arrowhead 92352
Lake City 96115
Lake Hughes 93532
Lake Isabella 93240
Lake Kirkwood, R. Br.
   Pioneer 95646

Lake San Marcos, Br. San
  Marcos..................................92069
Lake View Terrace, Br. San
  Fernando..............................91342
Lakehead................................96051
  O'Brien, R. Br.......................96070
Lakeport (1st)........................95453
Lakeshore..............................93634
  Mono Hot Springs, R. Br...93642
Lakeside (1st)........................92040
Lakeview................................92353
LAKEWOOD (1st) (see
  appendix)
Lamont (1st)..........................93241
Lancaster (1st).......................93534
Land Park, Sta. Sacramento
  (see appendix)
Landers, R. Br. Yucca
  Valley...................................92284
Landscape, Sta. Berkeley
  (see appendix)
Larkfield, Br. Santa Rosa....95401
Larkspur................................94939
Lathrop (1st).........................95330
Laton.....................................93242
Laurel, Sta. Oakland............94619
Lawndale (1st).......................90260
Laytonville.............................95454
Le Grand...............................95333
Lebec....................................93243
Lee Vining.............................93541
Leggett..................................95455
Lemon Grove (1st)...............92045
Lemoncove.............................93244
Lemoore (1st)........................93245
Lennox, Br. Inglewood..........90304
Lenwood, R. Br. Barstow......92311
Leona Valley, R. Br.
  Palmdale..............................93550
Letterman, Sta. San
  Francisco..............................94129
Leucadia, Br. Encinitas.........92021
Lewiston................................96052
Liberty Farms........................95647
Likely....................................96116
Lincoln..................................95648
Lincoln Acres, Br. National
  City.....................................92047
Lincoln Heights, Sta. Los
  Angeles (see appendix)
Lincoln Village, Br. Stockton...95207
Linda Vista, Sta. San Diego
  (see appendix)
Linden...................................95236
Linden Avenue, Sta. South
  San Francisco.......................94080
Lindsay (1st)..........................93247
Linnell, R. Br. Visalia............93277
Litchfield...............................96117
Little Lake.............................93542
Little Norway.........................95721
Little Valley, R. Br. Mc
  Arthur..................................96053
Littleriver..............................95456
Littlerock...............................93543
Live Oak................................95953
Livermore (1st).......................94550
Livingston..............................95334
Llano.....................................93544
Loch Lomond, R. Br. Cobb....95426
Lockeford...............................95237

Lockheed S C T B, R. Br.
  Santa Cruz...........................95060
Lockwood..............................93932
Lodi (1st)...............................95240
Loleta....................................95551
Loma, Sta. Long Beach (see
  appendix)
Loma Linda (1st)....................92354
Loma Mar..............................94021
Lomita (1st)...........................90717
Lompoc (1st)..........................93436
  Vandenberg A F B, Br.........93437
London, R. Br. Dinuba..........93618
Lone Pine..............................93545
Long Barn.............................95335
LONG BEACH (1st) (see
  appendix)
Lookout.................................96054
Loomis..................................95650
Loop, Sta. South Gate..........90280
Los Alamitos (1st).................90720
Los Alamos............................93440
Los Altos (1st).......................94022
Los Altos Hills, Br. Los
  Altos....................................94022
Los Amigos, Sta. Downey......90240
LOS ANGELES (1st) (see
  appendix)
Los Banos (1st)......................93635
Los Feliz, Sta. Los Angeles....90027
Los Gatos (1st)......................95030
Los Molinos............................96055
Los Nietos, Br. Whittier.........90606
Los Olivos..............................93441
Los Serranos, R. Br. Chino....91710
Lost Hills...............................93249
Lost Lake, R. Br. Blythe.........92225
Lotus.....................................95651
Lower Lake............................95457
Loyalton................................96118
Lucerne.................................95458
Lucerne Valley.......................92356
Ludlow...................................92357
Lugo, Sta. Los Angeles..........90023
Lynwood (1st).........................90262
Lytle Creek............................92358
Macdoel.................................96058
Maclay, Sta. San Fernando....91340
Mad River..............................95552
Madeline................................96119
Madera (1st)..........................93637
  Italian Swiss Colony, R.
  Br..93638
Madison.................................95653
Magalia..................................95954
Magnolia Center, Sta.
  Riverside..............................92506
Magnolia Park, Sta.
  Burbank................................91505
Malaga, Br. Fresno................93725
Malibu (1st)...........................90265
Mammoth Lakes.....................93546
Manchester............................95459
Manhattan Beach (1st)..........90266
Manteca (1st).........................95336
Manton..................................96059
Manzanita Lake, R. Br.
  Cottonwood..........................96060
Mar Corps Rct Dep, Sta.
  San Diego............................92140
Mar Vista, Sta. Los Angeles
  (see appendix)
Marcelina, Sta. Torrance......90501

March A F B, Br. Riverside....92508
Mare Island, Sta. Vallejo......94592
Maricopa...............................93252
Marin City, Br. Sausalito.......94965
Marina, Sta. San Francisco....94123
Marina (1st)...........................93933
Marina Del Rey, Br. Venice...90291
Marine Corps Base, Br.
  Twentynine Palms................92278
Marine Corps Supply Center,
  Br. Barstow..........................92311
Mariposa...............................95338
Market, Sta. Los Angeles......90021
Markleeville...........................96120
  Hope Valley, R. Br..............96139
  Woodfords, R. Br................96120
Marshall.................................94940
Martell...................................95654
Martinez (1st).........................94553
Marysville (1st).......................95901
  Beale A F B, Br...................95903
Mather, R. Br. Groveland......95339
Mather A F B, Br.
  Sacramento..........................95655
Maxwell.................................95955
Maywood (1st)........................90270
Mc Arthur..............................96056
  Little Valley, R. Br..............96053
Mc Clellan A F B, Br.
  Sacramento..........................95652
Mc Cloud...............................96057
Mc Farland.............................93250
Mc Henry Village, Sta.
  Modesto................................95350
Mc Kinleyville, Br. Arcata.....95521
Mc Kittrick.............................93251
Mc Laren, Sta. San
  Francisco..............................94134
Mead Valley, R. Br. Perris.....92370
Meadow Valley.......................95956
Meadow Vista.........................95722
Mecca...................................92254
Meeks Bay, R. Br. Tahoe
  City......................................95723
Meiners Oaks, R. Br. Ojai.....93023
Mendocino.............................95460
Mendota................................93640
Menlo Park (1st)....................94025
Mentone.................................92359
Merced (1st)...........................95340
  Bell, Sta..............................95340
  Castle A F B, Br.................95342
  Red Top, R. Br...................95340
Meridian.................................95957
Merrill, Br. Fontana...............92335
Mesa Center, Sta. Costa
  Mesa....................................92627
Metro Main, Sta.
  Sacramento..........................95801
Metropolitan, Sta. Los
  Angeles (see appendix)
Mi-Wuk Village......................95346
Mid City, Sta. Stockton.........95202
Middlefield Road, Br.
  Redwood City.......................94061
Middletown.............................95461
Midpines................................95345
Midtown, Sta. Chico..............95926
Midway City (1st)...................92655
Milford..................................96121
Mill Creek..............................96061
Mill Valley (1st).....................94941
Millbrae (1st).........................94030

Mills, Sta. San Francisco......94104
Mills College, Sta. Oakland...94613
Millsdale, Sta. Burlingame....94010
Millville........................96052
Milpas, Sta. Santa Barbara...93103
Milpitas (1st)...................95035
Mineral............................96063
Mineralking, R. Br. Three
   Rivers.........................93253
Mira Loma......................91752
Mira Vista, Sta. Richmond....94805
Miracle Hot Springs, R. Br.
   Bakersfield....................93301
Miraleste, Br. San Pedro.....90732
Miramar, Br. San Diego......92145
Miramonte.......................93641
   Badger, R. Br................93603
   Hume, R. Br.................93628
   Kings Canyon National
   Park, R. Br..................93633
Miranda..........................95553
Missile View, Br. Santa
   Maria..........................93454
Mission, Sta. Santa Clara....95051
Mission Hills, Br. San
   Fernando (see appendix)
Mission Rafael, Sta. San
   Rafael.........................94901
Mission San Jose, Sta.
   Fremont.......................94538
Mission Viejo, Br. San Juan
   Capistrano....................92675
Moccasin.........................95347
MODESTO (1st) (see
   appendix)
Moffett Field (1st)............94035
Mojave (1st)....................93501
Mokelumne Hill.................95245
Mono Hot Springs, R. Br.
   Lakeshore....................93642
Monolith.........................93548
Monrovia (1st)..................91016
Monta Vista, Br. Cupertino...95014
Montague.........................96064
Montalvo, Br. Ventura.........93003
Montara..........................94037
Montclair (1st).................91763
Monte Rio.......................95462
Monte Sereno, Br. Los Gatos..95030
Montebello (1st)...............90640
Montecito, Br. Santa
   Barbara.......................93103
Monterey (1st).................93940
   Del Rey Oaks, Br...........93940
   Fort Ord, Br................93941
   Presidio Of Monterey,
   Sta.............................93940
   U S N Postgraduate
   School, Sta...................93940
Monterey Bay Academy, R.
   Br. Watsonville..............95076
Monterey Park (1st)...........91754
Montgomery Creek...............96065
Montgomery Village, Sta.
   Santa Rosa...................95405
Montrose (1st)..................91020
Mooney, Sta. Visalia..........93277
Moorpark.........................93021
Mora Villa, Sta. Santa
   Barbara.......................93104
Moraga (1st)....................94556
Moreno...........................92360
Morgan Hill (1st)..............95037

Morningside Park, Sta.
   Inglewood....................90305
Morongo Valley..................92256
Morro Bay (1st)................93442
Moss Beach......................94038
Moss Landing....................95039
Mount Baldy.....................91759
Mount Eden (1st)...............94557
Mount Hamilton, R. Br. San
   Jose...........................95140
Mount Hebron....................96066
Mount Hermon....................95041
Mount Laguna....................92048
Mount Shasta (1st)............96067
Mount Wilson, R. Br. La
   Canada........................91023
Mountain Center.................92361
Mountain Mesa, R. Br. Lake
   Isabella......................93240
Mountain Pass, R. Br.
   Nipton........................92366
Mountain Ranch..................95246
Mountain View (1st)...........94040
Mt. Aukum.......................95656
Murphys..........................95247
Murrieta.........................92362
Muscoy, Br. San Bernardino...92405
Myers Flat.......................95554
Myrtletowne, Br. Eureka......95501
Napa (1st)......................94558
National City (1st)............92050
   Lincoln Acres, Br...........92047
Naval, Sta. San Diego.........92136
Naval, Sta. Port Hueneme.....93043
Naval Air Station, Br. San
   Diego..........................92135
Naval Air Station, Br.
   Alameda.......................94501
Naval Air Station, Br.
   Lemoore.......................93245
Naval Hospital, Sta. San
   Diego..........................92134
Naval Hospital, Sta.
   Oakland.......................94627
Naval Supply Center, Sta.
   Oakland.......................94625
Naval Training Center, Sta.
   San Diego....................92133
Navarro, R. Br. Philo.........95463
Needles (1st)...................92363
Nelson...........................95958
Nestor...........................92053
Nevada City (1st)..............95959
New Almaden.....................95042
New Cuyama......................93254
Newark (1st)....................94560
Newberry Springs................92365
Newbury Park, Br. Thousand
   Oaks...........................91320
Newcastle.......................95658
Newhall (1st)...................91321
Newman...........................95360
NEWPORT BEACH (1st) (see
   appendix)
Nicasio..........................94946
Nice.............................95464
Nicolaus.........................95659
Niland...........................92257
Niles, Sta. Fremont...........94536
Nipomo...........................93444
Nipton...........................92364
Noe Valley, Sta. San
   Francisco.....................94114

Norco (1st).....................91760
Norden...........................95724
North Annex, Br. San
   Fernando......................91342
North Beach, Sta. San
   Francisco.....................94133
North Berkeley, Sta.
   Berkeley......................94709
North Downey, Sta. Downey...90240
North Edwards, R. Sta.
   Edwards.......................93523
North Fork.......................93643
North Gardena, Br. Gardena...90247
North Glendale, Sta.
   Glendale (see appendix)
North Highlands (1st).........95660
North Hills, Br. San
   Fernando......................91344
NORTH HOLLYWOOD (1st)
   (see appendix)
North Inglewood, Sta.
   Inglewood (see appendix)
North Long Beach, Sta. Long
   Beach.........................90805
North Palm Springs.............92258
North Park, Sta. San Diego...92104
North Redondo Beach, Sta.
   Redondo Beach...............90278
North San Juan.................95960
North Seal Beach, Sta.
   Seaside.......................90740
North Shore, R. Br. Mecca....92254
North Torrance, Sta.
   Torrance......................90504
Northridge (1st)...............91324
Norton A F B, Sta. San
   Bernardino....................92409
Norwalk (1st)...................90650
Norwalk Manor, Br. Norwalk..90650
Norwood Center, Br. San
   Fernando......................91343
Novato (1st)....................94947
Nubieber.........................96068
Nuevo............................92367
Number Fifty Seven, Sta.
   San Francisco................94101
Number Forty, Sta. San
   Francisco.....................94101
Number Forty Four, Sta. San
   Francisco.....................94101
Number Twenty Three, Sta.
   San Francisco................94101
Nut Tree, R Sta. Vacaville...95688
O'Brien, R. Br. Lakehead.....96070
O'Neals..........................93645
Oak Knoll, Sta. Redwood
   City...........................94061
Oak Park, Sta. Sacramento...95817
Oak Run..........................96069
Oak Valley, Br. Agoura.......91301
Oak View.........................93022
Oakdale (1st)...................95361
Oakhurst.........................93644
OAKLAND (1st) (see
   appendix)
Oakley...........................94561
Oaks, Sta. Arroyo Grande.....93420
Oakville.........................94562
Oakwood, Sta. Los Angeles...90004
Occidental.......................95465
Ocean Beach, Sta. San
   Diego..........................92107

27

Ocean Park, Sta. Santa
  Monica 90405
Jceano.....................................93445
Oceanside (1st)........................92054
  Camp Pendleton, Br. 92055
  First Street, Sta. 92054
&cotillo...................................92259
Oildale, Br. Bakersfield....93308
Ojai (1st)..................................93023
Olancha....................................93549
Old San Diego, Sta. San
  Diego 92110
Old Station..............................96071
Olema......................................94950
Olinda, R. Br. Anderson........96007
Olive, Sta. Orange..................92665
Olive View, Br. San
  Fernando............................91330
Olivehurst..............................95961
Olivenhain, R. Br. Encinitas...92024
Olympic, Sta. Beverly Hills....90212
Olympic Valley, Er. Tahoe
  City......................................95730
Omo Ranch..............................95661
Ono; R Br. Redding................96072
ONTARIO (1st) (see
  appendix)
Onyx..93255
Opal Cliffs, Sta. Santa Cruz...95060
ORANGE (1st) (see
  appendix)
Orange Cove 93646
Orangehurst, Sta. Fullerton...92632
Orangevale (1st)......................95664
Orcutt, Br. Santa Maria..........93463
Ordbend, R. Br. Glenn............95942
Oregon House..........................95962
Orick..95555
Orinda (1st)..............................94563
Orland (1st)..............................95963
Orleans....................................95556
Oro Grande..............................92368
Orosi..93647
Oroville (1st)............................95965
  Pulga, R. Br 95965
  Storrie, R. Br...................95980
Osbourne, Sta. Los Angeles...90028
Oval, Sta. Visalia....................93277
Oxnard (1st)............................93030
Pacheco, Br. Martinez............94553
Pacific, Sta. Long Beach........90806
Pacific Beach, Sta. San
  Diego..................................92109
Pacific Grove (1st)..................939:)
Pacific House............................95725
Pacific Palisades (1st)............90272
Pacifica (1st)............................94044
Pacoima (1st)..........................9135?
Paicines..................................95043
Pala..92059
Palermo....................................95968
Palm City, Br. Palm Desert....92260
Palm Desert (1st)....................92260
Palm Springs (1st)..................92262
Palmdale (1st)..........................93550
Palms, Sta. Los Angeles
  (see appendix)
PALC ALTO (1st) (see
  appendix)
i >lo Cedro................................96073
Palo Verde................................92266
Palomar Mountain....................92060
Palos Verdes Estates, Br.

Palos Verdes Peninsula 90274
Palos Verdes Peninsula
  (1st)....................................90274
Panorama City, Sta. Van
  Nuys (see appendix)
Paradise (1st)..........................95969
Paramount (1st)......................90723
Parcel Post, Sta. Berkeley....94710
Park, Sta. Berkeley................94702
Parker Dam..............................92267
Parkside, Sta. San
  Francisco............................94116
Parkway, Br. Sacramento
  (see appendix)
Parlier......................................93648
PASADENA (1st) (see
  appendix)
Paskenta..................................96074
Paso Robles (1st)....................93446
Patterson (1st)........................95363
Patton (1st)..............................92369
Pauma Valley............................92061
Paynes Creek............................96075
Pearblossom............................93553
Pebble Beach (1st)..................93953
Pedley, Br. Riverside..............92509
Peninsula Village, R. Br.
  Westwood............................96137
Penn Valley, R. Br. Grass
  Valley..................................95946
Penngrove................................94951
Penryn......................................95663
Perkins, Br. Sacramento (see
  appendix)
Permanente, R. Br.
  Cupertino............................95014
Perris (1st)..............................92370
Perry, Sta. Whittier (see
  appendix)
Pescadero................................94060
Petaluma (1st)........................94952
Petrolia....................................95558
Phelan......................................92371
Phillipsville..............................95559
Philo..95466
  Navarro, R. Br..................95463
Pico, Sta. Pico Rivera............90660
Pico Heights, Sta. Los
  Angeles (see appendix)
Pico Rivera (1st)......................90660
Piedmont, Sta. Oakland (see
  appendix)
Piedra......................................93649
Piercy......................................95467
Pilot Hill..................................95664
Pine Grove................................95665
  Kit Carson, R. Br. 95644
Pine Valley..............................92062
Pinecrest..................................95364
  Dardanelle, R. Br. 95314
  Strawberry, R. Br. 95375
Pinedale..................................93650
Pinole (1st)..............................94564
Pinon Hills................................92372
Pioneer......................................95666
  Bear River Lake, R. Br. ...95666
  Lake Kirkwood, R. Br. 95646
Pioneertown............................92268
Piru..93040
Pismo Beach (1st)..................93449
Pittsburg (1st)..........................94565
Pixley......................................93256
Placentia (1st)..........................92670

Placerville (1st)........................95667
Plainview, R. Br. Strathmore..93267
Planada....................................95365
Plaster City, R. Br. El
  Centro................................92259
Platina......................................96076
Playa Del Rey, Sta. Venice....90291
Plaza, Sta. Orange..................92666
Plaza Center, Sta. Ontario....91762
Pleasant Grove........................95668
Pleasant Hill, Br. Concord....94523
Pleasanton (1st)......................94566
Plymouth..................................95669
Point Arena..............................95468
Point Loma, Sta. San Diego...92106

Point Mugu, Br. Port
  Hueneme............................93042
Point Reyes Station................94956
Point Richmond, Sta.
  Richmond............................94807
Points, Sta. El Monte............91732
Pollock Pines............................95726
POMONA (1st) (see
  appendix)

Pond, R. Br. Ware co 93100
Pondosa....................................:6027
Pope Valley..............................94567
Poplar, R. Br. Porterville........93257
Port Costa................................94569
Port Hueneme (1st)................93041
Porterville (1st)........................93257
Portola......................................96122
  Beckwourth, R. Br...........96129
Portola Valley, Br. Menlo
  Park....................................94025
Portuguese Bend, R. Br.
  Palos Verdes Peninsula ...90274
Posey..93260
Potrero......................................92063
Potter Valley............................95469
Poway (1st)..............................92064
Prather......................................93651
Presidio, Sta. San Francisco...94129
Presidio Of Monterey, Sta.
  Monterey............................93940
Preuss, Sta. Los Angeles
  (see appendix)
Princeton..................................95970
Proberta..................................96078
Project City..............................96079
Prunedale, R. Br. Salinas......93901
Pulga, R. Br. Oroville............95965
Pumpkin Center, R. Br.
  Bakersfield........................93309
Quail Valley, R. Br. Sun City..92380
Quartz Hill, R. Br. Lancaster..93534
Quincy (1st)..............................95971
  Keddie, R. Br...................95952
  Spring Garden, R. Br.......95971
Rackerby..................................95972
Rail Road Flat..........................95248
Rainbow Valley, R. Br.
  Fallbrook............................92028
Raisin......................................93652
Ramirez, Sta. Los Angeles....90037
Ramona (1st)............................92065
Ranchita..................................92066
Rancho California, R. Br.
  Temecula............................92390
Rancho Cordova (1st)............95670
Rancho Del Rey, Br. Chula
  Vista 92011

Rancho La Costa, R Br
  Carlsbad 92008
Rancho Mirage (1st) 92270
Rancho Park, Sta. Los
  Angeles (see appendix)
Rancho Santa Fe (1st) 92067
Randsburg 93554
  Red Mountain, R. Br. 93558
Ravendale 96123
Raymond 93653
Red Bluff (1st) 96080
Red Mountain, R. Br.
  Randsburg 93558
Red Top, R. Br. Merced ..95340
Redcrest 95569
Redding (1st) 96001
  Enterprise, Br. 96001
  Ono, R. Br. 96072
  Wildwood, R. Br. 96001
Redlands (1st) 92373
REDONDO BEACH (1st) (see
  appendix)
Reds Meadow, R. Br.
  Mammoth Lakes 93546
Redway 95560
REDWOOD CITY (1st) (see
  appendix)
Redwood Estates. 95044
Redwood Valley 95470
Reedley (1st) 93654
Refugio Beach, R Br
  Goleta. 93017
Rescue 95672
Reseda (1st) 91335
Rheem Valley 94570
Rialto (1st) 92376
Richardson Grove, R. Br
  Garberville 95440
Richardson Springs R Br.
  Chico. 95973
Richgrove 93261
RICHMOND (1st) (see
  appendix)
Richvale 95974
Ridgecrest (1st) 93555
Rimforest 92378
Rimpau, Sta. Los Angeles
  (see appendix)
Rincon Annex, Sta. San
  Francisco (see appendix)
Rio Dell 95562
Rio Linda (1st) 95673
Rio Nido, R. Br Guerneville ..95471
Rio Oso 95674
Rio Vista (1st). 94571
Ripley 92272
Ripon (1st) 95366
River Pines 95675
Riverbank (1st) 95367
Riverdale 93656
RIVERSIDE (1st) (see
  appendix)
Robbins 95676
Rocket Test Site. Br.
  Edwards 93523
Rocklin. 95677
Ruckridge. Sta. Oakland ..94618
Rodeo 94572
Rohnert Park, Br. Cotati ..94928
Rohnerville. Br Fortuna ..95540
Rolling Hill Estates, R. Br.
  Palos Verdes Peninsula ..90274
Rolling Hills, R Br Palos

Verdes Peninsula. 90274
Rome Lane, Sta. Salinas ..93901
Romoland, Br. Sun City ..92380
Roosevelt, Sta. Modesto ..95350
Roosevelt Corner. R. Br
  Lancaster 93534
Rosamond 93560
Rose Bowl, Sta. Pasadena ..91103
Roseland, Br Santa Rosa ..95401
Rosemead (1st) 91770
Roseville (1st) 95678
Ross 94957
Rossmoor, Br. Los Alamitos ..90720
Rough And Ready 95975
Round Mountain. 96084
Rowland Heights, Br. La
  Puente 91745
Rubidoux, Br. Riverside ..92509
Ruby Valley, R. Br. Redway ..95560
Rumsey 95679
Running Springs 92382
Ruth, R. Br Bridgeville ..95526
Rutherford 94573
Ryde 95680
SACRAMENTO (1st) (see
  appendix)
Saint Helena (1st) 94574
Saint James Park, Sta. San
  Jose 95113
Saint Matthew, Sta. San
  Mateo 94401
Salida 95368
Salinas (1st) 93901
Salton City, R. Br. Thermal. ..92274
Salyer. 95563
Samoa 95564
San Andreas (1st). 95249
  Sheepranch, R. Br. 95250
San Anselmo (1st) 94960
San Ardo. 93450
SAN BERNARDINO (1st) (see
  appendix)
San Bruno (1st) 94066
San Carlos (1st) 94070
San Clemente (1st) 92672
SAN DIEGO (1st) (see
  appendix)
San Dimas (1st) 91773
SAN FERNANDO (1st) (see
  appendix)
SAN FRANCISCO (1st) (see
  appendix)
San Gabriel (1st) 91776
San Geronimo 94963
San Gregorio 94074
San Jacinto (1st). 92383
San Joaquin 93660
SAN JOSE (1st) (see
  appendix)
San Juan Bautista 95045
San Juan Capistrano (1st) ..92675
SAN LEANDRO (1st) (see
  appendix)
San Lorenzo (1st) 94580
San Lucas 93954
San Luis Obispo (1st) 93401
San Luis Rey 92068
San Luis Rey Downs, Br.
  San Luis Rey 92068
San Marcos (1st) 92069
San Marino, Br. Pasadena ..91108
San Martin 95046
SAN MATEO (1st) (see

appendix)
San Miguel. 93451
San Pablo, Br. Richmond. ..94806
SAN PEDRO (1st) (see
  appendix)
San Quentin 94964
SAN RAFAEL (1st) (see
  appendix)
San Ramon 94583
San Roque, Sta. Santa
  Barbara 93105
San Simeon 93452
San Tomas, Br. Campbell. ..95008
San Ysidro (1st) 92073
Sand City, Br. Seaside 93955
Sanford, Sta. Los Angeles ..90005
Sanger (1st) 93657
SANTA ANA (1st) (see
  appendix)
SANTA BARBARA (1st) (see
  appendix)
SANTA CLARA (1st) (see
  appendix)
Santa Cruz (1st) 95060
Santa Fe Springs (1st) 90670
Santa Margarita 93453
Santa Maria (1st) 93454
SANTA MONICA (1st) (see
  appendix)
Santa Nella, R. Br. Gustine ..95322
Santa Paula (1st) 93060
Santa Rita Park 93661
SANTA ROSA (1st) (see
  appendix)
Santa Susana, Sta. Simi
  Valley 93063
Santa Western, Sta. Los
  Angeles 90072
Santa Ynez 93460
Santa Ysabel 92070
Santee (1st) 92071
Saratoga (1st) 95070
Sather Gate, Sta. Berkeley ..94704
Saticoy, Br. Ventura 93003
Sattley 96124
Saugus (1st) 91350
  Agua Dulce, R. Br. 91350
  Canyon Country, Br. 91350
  Green Valley, R. Br. 91350
  Val Verde Park, R. Br ..91350
  Valencia, R. Br. 91355
Sausalito (1st) 94965
Saviers Annex, Sta. Oxnard ..93030
Sawyers Bar, R. Br. Etna. ..96027
Scenic Center, Br. Modesto. ..95350
Scotia 95565
Scott Bar 96085
Scotts Valley, R. Br. Santa
  Cruz 95060
Seabright, Sta. Santa Cruz ..95060
Seal Beach (1st) 90740
Seaside (1st) 93955
Sebastopol (1st) 95472
Seeley 92273
Seiad Valley 96086
Selma (1st) 93662
Sepulveda, Br. San
  Fernando 91343
Sequoia National Park ..93262
Serra Mesa, Sta. San Diego
  (see appendix)
Shafter (1st) 93263
Shandon 93461

Shasta 96087
Shaver Lake 93664
   Dinkey Creek, R. Br. 93617
Sheepranch, R. Br. San
   Andreas 95250
Shell Beach, Sta. Pismo
   Beach 93449
Sheridan 95681
Sherman Oaks, Sta. Van
   Nuys (see appendix)
Shingle Springs 95682
Shingletown 96088
Shore Acres, Br. Pittsburg 94565
Shoshone 92384
Sierra, Sta. Fresno 93703
Sierra City 96125
Sierra Madre (1st) 91024
Sierraville 96126
Signal Hill, Br. Long Beach ... 90806
Silver Lake, R. Br. Jackson ... 95642
Silverado 92676
Simi Valley (1st) 93065
Skyforest 92385
Sloat, R. Br. Blairsden 96127
Sloughhouse 95683
Smartville 95977
Smith River 95567
Smithflat 95727
Smoke Tree, Sta. Palm
   Springs 92262
Snelling 95369
Soda Springs 95728
Solana Beach (1st) 92075
Soledad (1st) 93960
Solvang (1st) 93463
Somerset 95684
Somesbar 95568
Somis 93066
Sonoma (1st) 95476
Sonora (1st) 95370
Soquel (1st) 95073
Soto, Sta. Huntington Park ... 90255
Soulsbyville 95372
South, Sta. Van Nuys 91404
South, Sta. Los Angeles 90061
South Alhambra, Sta.
   Alhambra 91803
South Berkeley, Sta. Berkeley
   (see appendix)
South Dos Palos 93665
South Downey, Sta. Downey ... 90242
South El Monte, Br. El
   Monte 91733
South Gardena, Sta.
   Gardena 90247
South Gate (1st) 90280
South Laguna, Br. Laguna
   Beach 92677
South Lake Tahoe (1st) 95705
   Al Tahoe, Sta. 95705
   Camp Richardson, R. Br. ... 95705
   Fallen Leaf, R. Br. 95716
   Stateline, Sta. 95705
   Tahoe Paradise, R. Br. 95705
   Tahoe Valley, Sta. 95705
South Main, Sta. Santa Ana ... 92707
South Modesto, Br. Modesto ... 95350
South Pasadena (1st) 91030
South San Francisco (1st) 94080
South San Gabriel, Sta.
   Rosemead 91770
South San Leandro, Sta. San
   Leandro 94578

South Shore, Sta. Alameda ... 94501
South Whittier, Br. Whittier ... 90605
Southeastern, Sta. San
   Diego 92113
Southland, Sta. Hayward 94545
Spanish Flat, R. Br. Napa 94558
Spreckels 93962
Spring Garden, R. Br.
   Quincy 95971
Spring Valley (1st) 92077
Springstowne, Sta. Vallejo ... 94590
Springville 93265
   Camp Nelson, R. Br. 93208
Spurgeon, Sta. Santa Ana 92702
Spyrock, R. Br. Willits 95479
Squaw Valley, R. Br. Orange
   Cove 93646
Standard 95373
Standish 96128
Stanford, Br. Palo Alto 94305
Stanton (1st) 90680
State Capitol, Sta.
   Sacramento 95814
State Street, Sta. Huntington
   Park 90255
Stateline, Sta. South Lake
   Tahoe 95705
Station A, Sta. Walnut
   Creek 94596
Steele Park, R. Br. Napa 94558
Stevinson 95374
Stewarts Point 95480
Stinson Beach 94970
Stirling City 95978
STOCKTON (1st) (see
   appendix)
Stonestown, Sta. San
   Francisco 94132
Stonyford 95979
Storrie, R. Br. Oroville 95980
Stratford 93266
Strathmore 93267
Strawberry, R. Br. Pinecrest ... 95375
Strawberry Valley 95981
Studio City, Sta. North
   Hollywood 91604
Subway, Sta. Los Angeles 90052
Sugarloaf, R. Br. Big Bear
   City 92386
Suisun City (1st) 94585
Sultana 93666
Summerland 93067
Summit 92387
Summit City 96089
Sun City (1st) 92381
   Quail Valley, R. Br. 92380
   Romoland, Br. 92380
Sun Valley (1st) 91352
Sunkist, Sta. Anaheim 92806
Sunland (1st) 91048
Sunny Hills, Sta. Fullerton ... 92632
Sunnymead (1st) 92388
Sunnyside 92079
SUNNYVALE (1st) (see
   appendix)
Sunol 94586
Sunset, Sta. San Francisco ... 94122
Sunset Beach 90742
Sunset Whitney Ranch, R.
   Sta. Rocklin 95677
Surfside 90743
Susana Knolls, R. Br. Simi
   Valley 93063

Susanville (1st) 96130
Sutter 95982
Sutter Creek 95685
   Drytown, R. Br. 95699
Sylmar, Br. San Fernando 91342
Taft (1st) 93268
Tahoe City (1st) 95730
   Meeks Bay, R. Br. 95723
   Olympic Valley, Br. 95730
Tahoe Paradise, R. Br. South
   Lake Tahoe 95705
Tahoe Valley, Sta. South
   Lake Tahoe 95705
Tahoe Vista 95732
Tahoma 95733
Talmage 95481
Tamal, Sta. San Quentin 94964
Tarzana (1st) 91356
Taylorsville 95983
Tecate 92080
Tecopa 92389
Tehachapi (1st) 93561
Tehama 96090
Temecula 92390
Temescal, Sta. Oakland 94609
Temple City (1st) 91780
Templeton 93465
Terminal Annex, Sta. Los
   Angeles 90054
Terminal Island, Sta. San
   Pedro 90731
Termo 96132
Terra Bella 93270
Terra Linda, Sta. San
   Rafael 94901
Textile, Sta. Los Angeles 90015
The Sea Ranch, R. Br.
   Gualala 95497
Thermal (1st) 92274
Thornton 95686
THOUSAND OAKS (1st) (see
   appendix)
Thousand Palms 92276
Three Rivers 93271
   Mineralking, R. Br. 93253
Tipton 93272
Todos Santos, Sta. Concord ... 94522
Tollhouse 93667
Toluca Lake, Sta. North
   Hollywood 91602
Tomales 94971
   Fallon, R. Br. 94932
Toms Place, R. Br. Bishop ... 93514
Topanga 90290
Topaz 96133
TORRANCE (1st) (see
   appendix)
Tower, Sta. Fresno (see
   appendix)
Town And Country Village,
   Br. Sacramento 95821
Trabuco Canyon 92678
Tracy (1st) 95376
Tranquillity 93668
Traver 93673
Travis A F B, Sta. Fairfield ... 94535
Treasure Island, Sta. San
   Francisco 94130
Tres Pinos 95075
Trinidad 95570
Trinity Center 96091
Trona 93562

Tropico, Sta. Glendale (see appendix)
Trowbridge................................95687
Truckee....................................95734
Tujunga (1st)............................91042
Tulare (1st)..............................93274
Tulelake...................................96134
Tuolumne..................................95379
Tuolumne Meadows, Sta.
   Yosemite National Park...95389
Tupman....................................93276
Turlock (1st).............................95380
Tustin (1st)...............................92680
Tuxedo Park, Sta. Stockton....95204
Twain......................................95984
Twain Harte..............................95383
Twentynine Palms (1st).............92277
   Marine Corps Base, Br....92278
Twin Bridges............................95735
Twin Peaks...............................92391
U C D, Br. Davis......................95616
U S N Postgraduate School,
   Sta. Monterey.................93940
U S Naval Hospital, Br. Long
   Beach.............................90801
Ukiah (1st)...............................95482
Union City (1st).........................94587
Univ Of Santa Clara Sta.
   Santa Clara....................95053
Universal City, Br. North
   Hollywood.......................91608
University, Br. Santa
   Barbara..........................93107
University City, Sta. San
   Diego.............................92122
University Park, Sta. Los
   Angeles..........................90007
Upland (1st).............................91786
Upper Lake...............................95485
Uptown, Sta. San Bernardino
   (see appendix)
Vacaville (1st)...........................95688
Val Verde Park, R. Br.
   Saugus..........................91350
Valencia, R. Br. Saugus...........91355
Valinda, Br. La Puente..............91744
Vallecito...................................95251
   Douglasflat, R. Br...........95229
Vallejo (1st).............................94590
   A, Sta...........................94590
   American Canyon, Br.......94590
   Dairy Farm, R. Br..........94590
   Federal Terrace, Br........94590
   Mare Island, Sta............94592
   Springstowne, Sta...........94590
Valley Center...........................92082
Valley Fair, Sta. San Jose........95128
Valley Ford..............................94972
Valley Home..............................95384
Valley Plaza, Sta. North
   Hollywood.......................91606
Valley Springs...........................95252
   Campo Seco, R. Br..........95226
Valley Village, Sta. North
   Hollywood.......................91607
Valleydale, Br. Azusa...............91702
Valyermo..................................93563
Van Duzen, R. Br.
   Bridgeville.......................95526
VAN NUYS (1st) (see
   appendix)
Vandenberg A F B, Br.
   Lompoc...........................93437

Vanowen, Sta. Van Nuys.........91407
Venice (1st)..............................90291
VENTURA (1st) (see
   appendix)
Verdugo City (1st).....................91046
Vermont Avenue, Sta. Los
   Angeles..........................90029
Vernalis...................................95385
Vernon, Br. Los Angeles (see
   appendix)
Veterans Administration, Br.
   Los Angeles....................90073
Veterans Administration
   Hosp, Br. Long Beach......90801
Veterans Bureau Hospital,
   Sta. Palo Alto................94304
Veterans Home, Sta.
   Yountville.......................94599
Victor......................................95253
Victorville (1st)..........................92392
Victory Center Annex, Sta.
   North Hollywood (see
   appendix)
Vidal.......................................92280
Viking, Sta. Long Beach...........90808
Villa Grande.............................95486
Villa Park, R. Br. Orange.........92667
Village, Sta. Los Angeles.........90024
Vina..96092
Vineburg..................................95487
Vinton.....................................96135
Visalia (1st).............................93277
Visitacion, Sta. San
   Francisco........................94134
Vista (1st)................................92083
Vista Grande, Sta. Daly City...94016
Vista Park, Br. Bakersfield......93307
Volcano...................................95689
Wagner, Sta. Los Angeles........90047
Waite, Sta. Los Angeles...........90018
Wallace....................................95254
Walnut (1st).............................91789
WALNUT CREEK (1st) (see
   appendix)
Walnut Grove............................95690
Walteria, Sta. Torrance............95505
Warm Springs, Sta. Fremont....94538
Warner Springs.........................92086
Wasco (1st)..............................93280
Washington...............................95986
Washington Manor, Sta. San
   Leandro..........................94579
Waterford.................................95386
Waterman, Br. San
   Bernardino.......................92408
Watsonville (1st).......................95076
Watts, Sta. Los Angeles (see
   appendix)
Waukena..................................93282
Wawona, Sta. Yosemite
   National Park..................95389
Weaverville...............................96093
   Helena, R. Br.................96042
Webster Street, Sta.
   Alameda.........................94501
Weed.......................................96094
Weimar....................................95736
Weldon....................................93283
Wendel, R. Br. Janesville........96136
Weott......................................95571
West, Br. Los Angeles..............90069
West Adams, Sta. Los
   Angeles (see appendix)

West Arcadia, Sta. Arcadia ...91006
WEST COVINA (1st) (see
   appendix)
West Garden Grove, Sta.
   Garden Grove..................92641
West Los Angeles, Sta. Los
   Angeles (see appendix)
West Menlo Park, Br. Menlo
   Park..............................94025
West Orange, Sta. Orange ...92668
West Pittsburg, Br.
   Pittsburg........................94565
West Point................................95255
West Portal, Sta. San
   Francisco........................94127
West Sacramento (1st).............95691
Westchester, Sta. Los
   Angeles (see appendix)
Westend....................................93564
Western Avenue, Br. San
   Pedro.............................90732
Westgate, Sta. San Jose...........95129
Westhaven, R. Br. Trinidad......95570
Westlake, Sta. Daly City...........94015
Westlake Village, Br.
   Thousand Oaks...............91360
Westley....................................95387
Westminster (1st).......................92683
Westmorland.............................92281
Westport...................................95488
Westside, Sta. Modesto............95351
Westvern, Sta. Los Angeles......90062
Westwood.................................96137
Wheatland.................................95692
Wheeler Ridge...........................93284
Whiskeytown.............................96095
Whispering Pines, R. Br.
   Middletown......................95461
White Pines..............................95256
White Water..............................92282
Whitethorn................................95489
Whitmore..................................96096
WHITTIER (1st) (see
   appendix)
Wilcox, Sta. Los Angeles..........90038
Wildomar..................................92395
Wildwood, R. Br. Redding........96001
Will Rogers, Sta. Santa
   Monica...........................90401
William Howard Taft, Sta.
   San Diego (see appendix)
Williams...................................95987
Willits (1st)..............................95490
   Cummings, R. Br............95477
   Dos Rios, R. Br.............95429
   Island Mountain, R. Br...95478
   Spyrock, R. Br...............95479
Willow Brook, Br. Compton......90222
Willow Creek.............................95573
Willow Ranch.............................96138
Willows (1st).............................95988
Wilmington (1st)........................90744
Wilseyville................................95257
Wilshire-La Brea, Sta. Los
   Angeles..........................90036
Wilton.....................................95693
Winchester................................92396
Windsor....................................95492
Winnetka, Sta. Canoga Park....91306
Winterhaven..............................92283
Winters....................................95694
Winton.....................................95388
Wishon....................................93669

Witter Springs	95493
Wofford Heights	93285
Wondacre	94973
Woodbridge	95258
Woodfords, R. Br.	
Markleeville	96120
Woodlake	93286
Woodland (1st)	95695
Woodland Hills (1st)	91364
Woodside, Br. Redwood City	94062
Woodville, R. Br. Porterville	93257
Woody	93287

Worldway Postal Center, Sta. Los Angeles (see appendix)	
Wrightwood	92397
Yermo	92398
Yermo Annex, Br. Barstow	92311
Yettem	93670
Yolo	95697
Yorba, Sta. Pomona	91767
Yorba Linda (1st)	92686
York, Sta. Los Angeles	90050
Yorkville	95494

Yosemite Lodge, Br. Yosemite National Park	95389
Yosemite National Park (1st)	95389
Yountville	94599
Yreka (1st)	96097
Yuba City (1st)	95991
Yucaipa (1st)	92399
Yucca Valley (1st)	92284
Zamora	95698
Zenia	95495

ALHAMBRA 918

POST OFFICE BOXES

Box Nos.
1-1311	Alhambra	02
2001-2344	South Alhambra Sta.	03

STATIONS, BRANCHES AND UNITS

South Alhambra Sta.	03
General Delivery	02
Postmaster	02

ANAHEIM 928

POST OFFICE BOXES

Box Nos.
1-999	Federal Sta.	05
2001-2999	Brookhurst Center Sta.	04
3001-4709	Main Office	03
5000-5215	Brookhurst Center Sta.	04
6000-6579	Sunkist Sta.	06

RURAL ROUTES

1	06

STATIONS, BRANCHES AND UNITS

Brookhurst Center Sta.	04
Federal Sta.	05
Sunkist Sta.	06
General Delivery	03
Postmaster	03

APARTMENTS, HOTELS, MOTELS

Broadway Village, 801 N Loara	01
Charterhouse, 1700 S Harbor Blvd.	02

City Center, 610 N Anaheim Blvd.	05
Commons, 425 N Magnolia	01
Desert Inn, 1600 S Harbor Blvd.	02
Disneyland Hotel, 1441 S West	02
Dunes, 1326 S West	02
El Coco Palms, 1919 E Center	05
French Quarter, 2001 S Haster	02
Frontier, 933 S Harbor Blvd.	05
Grand Hotel, 7 Freedman Way	05
Jolly Roger Inn, 640 W Katella	02
Kettle, 1760 W Lincoln	01
Lincoln Arms, 145 S Westchester Dr.	04
Mauna Loa Apartments, 1541 E La Palma	05
Musketeer, 733 W Katella, Ave.	02
Palm Gardens, 629 W Vermont.	05
Peter Pan Motor Lodge, 2029 S Harbor Blvd.	02
Pickwick, 225 S Anaheim Blvd.	05
Pleasant, 306 W Lincoln	05
Rose Marie Apartments, 309 W Lincoln	05
Saga Motor, 1650 S Harbor Blvd.	02
Sandman, 1248 E Lincoln	05
Shellstone Apartments, 613 W Lincoln	05
Tops, 909 S Harbor Blvd	05
Twilight, 1050 W Katella	02
Valencia, 182 W Lincoln	05
Wanderlust, 1701 S West	02
Water Wheel Lodge, 1144 N Euclid	01

BUILDINGS

Anaheim Bulletin, 232 S Lemon	05
Anaheim Stadium, 2000 S State College	06
Autonetics, 3370 Miraloma	06
Broadway, 444 N Euclid	01
California Federal Savings, 1695 W Crescent	01
Convention Center, 800 W Katella	02
Disneyland, 1313 S Harbor	02
Kraemer Bldg, 106 N Claudina	05
Medical Arts, 1120 W La Palma	01
Pacific Telephone, 217 N Lemon	05
Palomar, 800 S Brookhurst	04
Robinsons, 530 N Euclid Ave.	01
Wilshire Towers, 280 N Wilshire	01

GOVERNMENT OFFICES

Anaheim City Hall, 204 E Lincoln	05
Anaheim Fire Dept, 500 E Broadway	05
Anaheim Police Department, 425 S Harbor Blvd.	05
Municipal Court, 1170 N Anaheim Blvd	01

HOSPITALS

Anaheim General Hospital, 3350 W Ball Rd.	04
Anaheim Memorial Hospital, 1111 W La Palma.	01
Broadway Clinic Hospital, 1660 W Broadway.	02
Buena Vista Hospital, 1682 W Buena Vista	02

Anaheim (Con.) 928

Garden Park General
Hospital, 9922 Gilbert 04
Hillhaven Convalescent
Hospital, 1130 W La
Palma................. 01
Lutheran Home Convalescent
Hospital, 1303 W Ball Rd .. 02
Martin Luther Hospital, 1825
W Romneya Dr............. 01
Parkview Convalescent
Hospital, 1514 E Lincoln.... 05
West Anaheim Community,
3033 W Orange............. 04

BAKERSFIELD 933

POST OFFICE BOXES

Box Nos.
1-149	Del Kern R. Sta.............	07
1-288	Pumpkin Center R. Sta.	07
1-926	Miracle Hot Springs R. Sta.............	01
1-1799	Main Office	02
1800-2999	Main Office	03
3000-3499	Station A	05
4001-4288	Station B	07
5001-5749	Oildale Br	08
6001-6446	Hillcrest Center Br...........	06
9000-9458	Kern City R. Sta.............	09

RURAL ROUTES

1	08
2,3,4,5,6,7,8	07

STATIONS, BRANCHES AND UNITS

College Center Br............	06
Delkern Rural Br.............	09
Greenacres Rural Br.........	08
Hillcrest Center Br	06
Kern City Rural Br..........	09
Miracle Hot Springs Rural Br.	01
Oildale Br	08
Pumpkin Center Rural Br....	09
Vista Park Br...............	07
General Delivery	02
Postmaster	02

BUILDINGS

Bakersfield Savings, 1730 Chester.............	01
Civic Center, 1601 H	01
Great Western Savings 1730 Chester.............	01
Haberfeld, 1706 Chester......	01
Hay, 1612 19th...............	01
Moronet, 1522 18th	01
Sill, 1508 18th..............	01

GOVERNMENT OFFICES

City Hall 1501 Truxtun........ 01

Federal Offices, 800 Truxton... 01
Kern County Courts &
Adminisrative, 1415
Truxtun................. 01
Social Security Admin (H E
W) 2619f................. 01

HOSPITALS

Bakersfield Memorial, 420
34th..................... 01
Kern County General, 1830
Flower................... 05
Mercy, 2215 Truxton.......... 01
Physicians, 901 Olive Dr...... 08
San Joaquin, 2628 I St....... 01

UNIVERSITIES AND COLLEGES

Bakersfield Junior, 1801
Panorama................. 05
Calif. State College, 9001
Stockdale Highway......... 09

BERKELEY 947

POST OFFICE BOXES

Box Nos.
1-1999	Main Office	01
2000-2999	A Sta	02
3000-3999	South Berkeley Sta.............	03
4000-4999	Sather Gate Sta.............	04
5000-5999	Elmwood Sta	05
6000-6999	Albany Br	06
7000-7999	Landscape Sta .	07
9000-9999	North Berkeley..	09

STATIONS, BRANCHES AND UNITS

Albany Br...................	06
Elmwood Sta.................	05
Kensington Br...............	07
Landscape Sta...............	07
North Berkeley Sta	09
Parcel Post Sta.............	10
Park Sta	02
Sather Gate Sta.............	04
General Delivery	01
Postmaster	04

APARTMENTS, HOTELS, MOTELS

Amherst, 2231 Shattuck Ave... 04
Bel Air Hotel, 1330
University Ave........... 02
Berkeley Hotel, 2039
Shattuck Ave............. 04
Berkeley House, 920
University Ave........... 10
Berkeley Inn, 2501 Haste..... 04
Berkeley Motel, 2001
Bancroft Way............. 04
Bonanza Motel, 1720 San
Pablo Ave................ 02
Cal Hotel, 2008 Shattuck
Ave..................... 04
California Motel, 1461
University Ave........... 02
Campanile Hotel, 2070
University Ave........... 04

Campus Motel, 1619
University Ave........... 03
Capri Motel, 1512 University
Ave..................... 03
Carlton, 2338 Telegraph Ave.. 04
Claremont, Ashby &
Claremont................ 05
Durant, 2600 Durant Ave...... 04
Flamingo Motel, 1761
University Ave........... 03
Golden Bear Motel, 1620 San
Pablo Ave................ 02
Marina Lodge, 975 University
Ave..................... 10
Marriott Inn 200 Marina
Blvd.................... 10
Nash House, 2045 University
Ave..................... 04
Oxford Hall, 2140 Oxford 04
Plaza Motel, 1175 University
Ave..................... 02
Stark, 2024 University Ave 04
Travelodge Motel, 1820
University Ave........... 03
U C Hotel, 1040 University
Ave..................... 10
University Hotel 2057
University Ave........... 04
Villa Motel, 1155 San Pablo
Ave..................... 06
Ymca, 2001 Allston Way........ 04

BUILDINGS

Acheson, 2131 University
Ave..................... 04
Berkeley Center Bldg., 2000
Center................... 04
Berkeley Professional, 2975
Sacramento............... 02
Cal-Farm Bureau, 2855
Telegraph Ave............ 05
Central Berkeley Medical,
3031 Telegraph Ave....... 05
Farm Credit Administration,
2180 Milvia.............. 04
Great Western Savings Bldg.,
2150 Shattuck Ave........ 04
Koerber, 2054 University Ave.. 04
Medical-Dental, 2490
Channing Way............. 04
Milvia Center, 2118 Milvia ... 04
Physicians, 2131 University
Ave..................... 04
Shattuck, 2171 Shattuck Ave.. 04
Stead, 1960 Addison.......... 04
Tioga, 2020 Milvia 04
Wells Fargo Bldg., 2140
Shattuck Ave............. 04
Woolsey, 2168 Shattuck Ave... 04
Wright, 2161 Shattuck Ave..... 04

GOVERNMENT OFFICES

City Hall, Allston & Grove....... 04
State Department Of Public
Health, 2151 Berkely Way.. 04
Western Regional Laboratory,
800 Buchanan............. 10

33

**Berkeley — Beverly Hills — Buena Park
Burbank — Canoga Park — Chula Vista — Compton
Concord — Costa Mesa — Daly City CALIFORNIA**

Appendix

Berkeley (Con.)   947

HOSPITALS

Albany Hospital, 1247 Marin Ave.	06
Alta Bates Community Hospital, 3000 Regent	05
Cowell Memorial Hospital, Univ Of California	20
Herrick Memorial Hospital, 2001 Dwight Way	04

UNIVERSITIES AND COLLEGES

American Baptist Seminary Of The West, 2606 Dwight Way	04
Armstrong College, 2222 Harold Way	04
Berkeley Baptist Divinity School, 2606 Dwight Way	04
Blind School Of California, 3001 Derby	05
California School Of Deaf, 2601 Warring	04
Church Divinity School Of The Pacific, 2451 Ridge Road	09
Franciscan School Of Theology, 1712 Euclid Ave.	09
Graduate Theological Union, 2465 Le Conte Ave.	09
Jesuit School Of Theology, 1735 Le Roy Ave.	09
Pacific Lutheran Theological Seminary, 2770 Marin Ave.	08
Pacific School Of Religion, 1798 Scenic Ave.	09
University Of California	20
Williams College 1960 San Antonio Ave.	07

BEVERLY HILLS   902

POST OFFICE BOXES

Box Nos.		
A-Z	Main Office	13
1-2090	Main Office	13
AA-AH	Main Office	13
AA-HH	Main Office	13
3001-3799	Olympic Sta	12
5001-5399	Maple Annex	10

STATIONS, BRANCHES AND UNITS

Olympic Sta	12
General Delivery	13
Postmaster	13

BUENA PARK   906

POST OFFICE BOXES

Box Nos.		
6441-6570	Main Office	22

STATIONS, BRANCHES AND UNITS

La Palma Br.	20
Postmaster	22

HOSPITALS

Beach Community Hospital 5742 Beach Blvd.	21

BURBANK   915

POST OFFICE BOXES

Box Nos.		
1-911	Downtown Sta.	03
1000-1714	Magnolia Park Sta.	05
3001-3399	Glenoaks Sta.	03
4000-4440	Downtown Sta.	03
6001-7277	Main Office	05

STATIONS, BRANCHES AND UNITS

Downtown Sta	03
Glenoaks Sta	04
Magnolia Park Sta	05
General Delivery	05
Postmaster	05

CANOGA PARK   913

POST OFFICE BOXES

Box Nos.		
1-632	Main Office	05
1000-1599	Canoga Park Annex Sta	04
2000-2399	Winnetka Sta	06

STATIONS, BRANCHES AND UNITS

Canoga Annex Sta	04
Collier Sta	04
Winnetka Sta	06
General Delivery	03
Postmaster	03

CHULA VISTA   920

POST OFFICE BOXES

Box Nos.		
1-1749	Main Office	12
3001-3866	Rancho Del Rey Br	11

STATIONS, BRANCHES AND UNITS

Rancho Del Rey Br	11
General Delivery	10
Postmaster	10

COMPTON   902

POST OFFICE BOXES

Box Nos.		
1-1199	Hub City Sta	23
2000-2999	East Compton Sta.	23
3000-3999	Willowbrook Br.	23
4000-5999	Compton	24

STATIONS, BRANCHES AND UNITS

East Compton Sta.	20
Hub City Sta.	20
Willow Brook Br.	22
General Delivery	20
Postmaster	20

CONCORD   945

POST OFFICE BOXES

Box Nos.		
1-1134	Todos Santos Station	22
2101-21419	Casa Correo	21
2301-23666	Pleasant Hill Br	23
5001-6094	Main Office	24
20-300-1-0203108	Station A	20

STATIONS, BRANCHES AND UNITS

Casa Correo Sta	21
Pleasant Hill Br.	23
Todos Santos Sta	22
General Delivery	20
Postmaster	20

COSTA MESA   926

POST OFFICE BOXES

Box Nos.		
1-1049	Mesa Center Sta.	27
1101-2299	Main Office	26

STATIONS, BRANCHES AND UNITS

Mesa Center Sta	27
General Delivery	26
Postmaster	26

DALY CITY   940

POST OFFICE BOXES

Box Nos.		
A-M	Main Office	17
1-0000360	Vista Grande Sta.	16
301-1799	Colma Sta	14
501-979	Main Office	17
3001-3645	Westlake Sta	15

STATIONS, BRANCHES AND UNITS

Colma Sta	14
Vista Grande Sta	16
Westlake Sta	15
General Delivery	15
Postmaster	17

Daly City (Con.)   940

HOSPITALS

Junipero Serra Emergency Center	14
Marys Help	15
Skyline Convalescent	15
Villa Sanitarium	14

DOWNEY   902

POST OFFICE BOXES

Box Nos.

A-Z	Main Office	41
1-999	Main Office	41
1001-1999	North Downey Sta.	40
2001-2999	South Downey Sta.	42
3001-3999	Los Amigos Sta.	42
4000-4999	Main Office	41

STATIONS, BRANCHES AND UNITS

Los Amigos Sta.	40
North Downey Sta.	40
South Downey Sta.	42
General Delivery	41
Postmaster	41

GOVERNMENT OFFICES

California St Bd Of Equalization, 11229 Woodruff	41
California St Dept Of Agriculture, 8635 Firestone Blvd.	41
Los Angeles Municipal Court, 8206 3rd	41
United States Revenue Service, 8524 Firestone Blvd.	41

HOSPITALS

Downey Community, 11500 Brookshire Ave.	41
Rancho Los Amigos, 7601 Imperial Hwy.	42
Rio Hondo Memorial, 8300 Telegraph Rd.	40

El CAJON   920

POST OFFICE BOXES

Box Nos.

1-1494	Main Office	22
2001-2596	Bostonia Sta.	21
3001-3244	Fletcher Hills	20

STATIONS, BRANCHES AND UNITS

Bostonia Sta.	21
Fletcher Hills Sta.	20

General Delivery	20
Postmaster	20

EL MONTE   917

POST OFFICE BOXES

Box Nos.

1-1999	Main Office	34
2000-2999	Points Sta.	32
3000-3999	South El Monte Br.	33

STATIONS, BRANCHES AND UNITS

Points Sta.	32
South El Monte Br.	33
General Delivery	34
Postmaster	31

ESCONDIDO   920

	25
	26
	27

FREMONT   945

POST OFFICE BOXES

Box Nos.

A-T	Main Office	37
1-999	Main Office	37
M-1-M-50	Main Office	37
1000-1999	Irvington Sta.	38
2000-2999	Niles Sta.	36
3000-3999	Mission San Jose Sta.	38
4000-4999	Warm Springs Sta.	38

STATIONS, BRANCHES AND UNITS

Irvington Sta.	38
Mission San Jose Sta.	38
Niles Sta.	36
Warm Springs Sta.	38
General Delivery	36
Postmaster	36

FRESNO   937

POST OFFICE BOXES

Box Nos.

A-K	Cardwell	55
1-192	Main Office	07
201-432	Main Office	08
441-672	Main Office	09
681-872	Main Office	12
881-1112	Main Office	14
1121-1352	Main Office	15
1361-1592	Main Office	16
1601-1832	Main Office	17
1841-2072	Main Office	18
2081-2194	Main Office	19
2201-2314	Main Office	20
2321-2499	Main Office	23
2501-2999	Caiwa Br.	45
3001-3499	G Street Sta.	66
4001-4757	Tower Sta.	44
5001-5999	Cardwell	55
6001-6999	Clinter	03
7701-8999	E Fresno Br.	27
10001-10187	Caiwa Br.	45

RURAL ROUTES

2	27
3,4,5	25
6,7,8	06
9,10,11	05
12	06

STATIONS, BRANCHES AND UNITS

Ashlan Park Sta.	26
Barton Sta.	02
Caiwa Br.	25
Cardwell Sta.	04
Clinter Sta.	03
East Fresno Br.	27
Eastgate Sta.	02
Easton Br.	06
Fancher Br.	02
Fig Garden Village Br.	04
Herndon Rural Br.	21
Highway City Br.	05
Malaga Br.	25
Sierra Sta.	03
Tower Sta.	44
General Delivery	21
Postmaster	21
Star Route	21

APARTMENTS, HOTELS, MOTELS

Airport Marine Hotel, 5155 Mckinley Ave. E.	27
Alhambra Trailer Lodges, 1898 E Gettysburg Ave.	26
Americana 205 N Blackstone Ave	01
Ashcroft, 4415 N Clark	26
Avalon Motel, 3621 N U S Hwy 99.	05
Ayres Motel, 2710 S. Orange Ave.	25
Balmoral, 1741 W Clinton	05
Bel Air Motel, 740 W Olive Ave	28
Blackstone Motel 5577 N Blackstone Ave	10
Brix, 2311 Fresno	21
Broadway Motel, 1840 Broadway	21
Brooks Manor, 1558 N Brooks Ave	28
Calaveras Gardens, 150 N Calveras	01
Californian, Van Ness & Kern	21
Carousel Motel 1444 W White	28
City Motel, 2309 S G	21
Del Mar Motel, 1849 N Motel Dr	28
Del Webb Towne House, 2220 Tulare St.	21
Desert Inn 2445 W Whites Bridge Rd.	06

35

El Capitan Motel, 4850 N
Blackstone Ave............... 26
El Grande Motel, 1425 N
Motel Dr........................ 28
El Rancho Motel 1265 N
Motel Dr........................ 28
Fresno Mill Motel, 2835 E.
Church Ave.................... 21
Fresno Motor Lodge Motel,
1587 N Motel Dr............ 28
Fresno, 1257 Broadway....... 21
Golden Key Motel, 2425
Merced........................... 21
Hacienda Motel, 2515 N Hwy
99.................................. 05
Hillcrest Arms, 2964 E
Mckenzie....................... 01
Holiday Motel, 1409 N Motel
Dr.................................. 28
Imperial 400 Motel, 2127
Inyo............................... 21
Kings Canyon Motel 4770 E
Kings Canyon Rd............ 02
London Motel, 797 N Pkwy
Dr.................................. 28
Manchester Manor, 2147 E
Shields.......................... 26
Manchester Motel 3844 N
Blackstone Ave.............. 26
Millbrook Garden, 3384 N
Millbrook....................... 26
Motel Fresno, 1325 N Motel
Dr.................................. 28
Motel 6, 4245 N Blackstone
Ave................................ 26
Motel 6, 949 N Parkway Dr... 28
Nordic Inn, 949 N Pkwy Dr.... 28
Normandie Apartments,
Osage 635 E Belmont Ave.... 01
Palm Motel, 1515 N Motel
Dr.................................. 28
Palms, 104 N Calaveras........ 01
Park Cedar, 522 S Cedar....... 02
Park Motel, 327 W Belmont
Ave................................ 28
Park Terrace, 1040 S........... 21
Parkview Mobile Lodge, 1719
W Olive Ave.................. 28
Parkway Motel, 6239 N
Blackstone Ave.............. 10
Plaza Motel, 1940 Broadway... 21
Ramada Inn 324 E Shaw
Ave................................ 10
Ranch-O-Tel Motel, 1487 N
Motel Dr........................ 28
Ritz Motor, 1557 N Motel Dr... 28
Sahara Motel, 530 N Weber
Ave................................ 28
Sands Motel, 1441 N Motel
Dr.................................. 28
Sequoia Motel, 4707 E Kings
Canyon Rd..................... 02
Talsness Terrace, 2039 E
Simpson......................... 03
Tower. Motel, 3353 N U S
Hwy 99.......................... 05
Town House Motor, 1383 N
Motel Dr........................ 28
Towne & Country Lodge,
3093 N Hwy 99.............. 05
Travelodge Motel, 888
Broadway....................... 21
Tropicana Lodge, 4061 N

Blackstone......................... 26
Valeria Arms, 248 Valeria....... 01
Villa Motel, 817 N Pkwy Dr.... 28
Virginia 2125 Kern................ 21

BUILDINGS

Bank Of America, 1015
Fulton............................ 21
Brix, 1221 Fulton................. 21
Caplan-Lowe, 1715 Fulton....... 21
Crocker Citizens, 2135
Fresno........................... 21
Del Webb, 2220 Tulare St........ 21
Fresno Guarantee Savings,
1171 Fulton................... 21
Helm, 1111 Fulton............... 21
Mason, 1044 Fulton.............. 21
New Bank Of America Bldg,
1011 Van Ness,.............. 21
Pacific Gas & Electric, 1401
Fulton............................ 21
Patterson, 2014 Tulare.......... 21
Rowell, 2100 Tulare.............. 21
Security Bank, 1060 Fulton..... 21
United California Bank Bldg,
1177 Van Ness................ 21

GOVERNMENT OFFICES

Federal Bldg, 1130 O............. 21
Fresno City Hall, 2326
Fresno........................... 21
Fresno County Courthouse,
1100 Van Ness Ave......... 21
Fresno County Hall Of
Records 2281 Tulare....... 21
Fresno I R S Center, 5045
Butler Ave. E................. 30
Law Enforcement Admin.
Bldg., 2200 Fresno......... 21
State Building, 2550
Mariposa....................... 21

HOSPITALS

Fresno Community, 2823
Fresno........................... 21
Fresno County Tuberculois,
435 S Cedar Ave............ 02
Saint Agnes, 530 W
Floradora....................... 28
Sierra, 2025 E Dakota Ave...... 26
U.s. Government Veterans
Admin., 2615 Clinton Ave
E.................................... 03
Valley Childrens Hospital &
Guidance Clinic.............. 03
Valley Medical Center 445
So. Cedar Ave................ 02

UNIVERSITIES AND COLLEGES

California Christian College,
4481 E. University Ave.... 03
Central California
Commercial, 1921
Tuolumne....................... 21
Fresno City, 1101 E
University....................... 04

Fresno State University 5241
N. Maple Ave.................. 18

FULLERTON 926

POST OFFICE BOXES

Box Nos.
1-672   Commonwealth
                        Sta................... 32
800-899   Contest Mail...... 38
20AA-20JK   Orangehurst
                        Sta................... 33
2001-2849   Orangehurst
                        Sta................... 33
3001-4372   Main Office........ 34
5001-5534   Sunny Hills
                        Sta................... 35

STATIONS, BRANCHES AND UNITS

Commonwealth Sta............... 32
Orangehurst Sta.................. 33
Sunny Hills Sta................... 32
General Delivery.................. 31
Postmaster.......................... 31

APARTMENTS, HOTELS, MOTELS

Fullerton Continental, 400 N
Acacia............................ 31
Holiday Inn, 1500 S
Raymond........................ 31
Hyatt Lodge, 1009 S Harbor
Blvd............................... 32
International Hotel, 1830 W
Commonwealth................ 33
Meredith Man: 1500 S
Pomona.......................... 32
Orange Gardens, 400 N
Orangethorpe.................. 32
Othrys Hall, 601 & 651 N
Titan.............................. 31

HOSPITALS

Fullerton Community, 100 E
Valley View Dr............... 35
St Jude, 101 E Valencia
Mesa Dr......................... 34

UNIVERSITIES AND COLLEGES

Cal State Fullerton, 800 N
State College.................. 34
Fullerton Junior College, 321
E Chapman..................... 34

GARDENA 902

POST OFFICE BOXES

Box Nos.
A-F   Main Office....... 47
1-472   South Gardena
                        Sta................... 47

Gardena (Con.) 902

1001-1647	Alondra Br	49
2001-2550	Main Office	47

STATIONS, BRANCHES AND UNITS

Alondra Br	49
Domingues Hills Br	47
North Gardena Br	47
South Gardena Sta	47
General Delivery	47
Postmaster	47

BUILDINGS

California Highway Patrol, 18220 S Broadway	47
Gardena City Hall, 1700 W 162 Nd St	47
Gardena Fire Dept, 1650 W 162 Nd St	47
Gardena Y M C A, 1700 Redondo Bch Blvd	47
Los Angeles County Public Library, 1731 Gardena Blvd	47
Masonic Temple, 1250 W 155 Th St	47
U S Selective Service, 14911 Crenshaw Blvd	49

HOSPITALS

Community Hospital, 1246 W 155 Th St	47
Gardena Medical Center, 2315 Compton Blvd	49
Memorial Hospital Of Gardena, 1145 W Redondo Bch Blvd	47

GARDEN GROVE 926

POST OFFICE BOXES

Box Nos.

1-1647	Main Office	42
AA-FR	Main Office	42
5000-5600	West Garden Grove Station	45

STATIONS, BRANCHES AND UNITS

West Garden Grove Sta	41
General Delivery	40
Postmaster	40

GLENDALE 912

POST OFFICE BOXES

Box Nos.

1-2074	Main Office	09
4001-0004689	North Glendale Sta	02
5001-5245	Grand Central Sta	01

0003001-0003985	Grand Central Sta	01
0006001-6999	Tropico Sta	05
0008001-8694	La Crescenta	14
0010001-0010880	Main Office	09

STATIONS, BRANCHES AND UNITS

Grand Central Sta	01
La Crescenta Sta	14
North Glendale Sta	02
Tropico Sta	04
General Delivery	09
Postmaster	09

APARTMENTS, HOTELS, MOTELS

Bell Motor, 1126 E Colorado	05
English Garden, 1227 S Central Ave	04
Gainsborough, 1003 S Central Ave	04
Gene Louise, 140 N Jackson	06
Glendale, 701 E Broadway	05
Golden Key, 123 W Colorado	04
Golden State, 214 E Chestnut	05
Jackson, 115 N Jackson	06
Mackenzie, 339 N Brand Blvd	03
Maryland, 202 E Wilson Ave	06
Orange Grove, 700 Orange Grove Ave	05
Park Lane, 309 W Colorado	04
Ragalodge, 200 W Colorado	04
Regent Annex, 315 W Lomita Ave	04
Regent, 445 S Central Ave	04
Ritz, 721 N Brand Blvd	03
Vagabond, Motor Hotel, 120 W Colorado	04
Woodlands, 1756 N Verdugo Rd	08

BUILDINGS

Bank Of America, 110 W Broadway	04
Central, 111 E Broadway	05
Federal, 313 E Broadway	05
Fidelity Federal, 225 E Broadway	05
Forest Lawn Memorial Park, 1712 S Glendale	05
Glendale Federal Savings, 401 N Brand Blvd	03
Glendale News-Press, 111 N Isabel	06
Grandview Memorial Park, 1341 Glenwood Rd	01
Hahn, 103 N Brand Blvd	03
Jensen, 203 E Broadway	05
Library, 319 E Harvard	05
Professional, 229 N Central Ave	03
Public Service, 119 N Glendale Ave	06
Salvation Army, 320 W Windsor Rd	04

Security, 102 N Brand Blvd	03

GOVERNMENT OFFICES

Chamber Of Commerce, 200 S Louise	05
City Hall Annex, 111 Howard	06
City Hall, 613 E Broadway	05
Police, 600 E Wilson Ave	06

HOSPITALS

Behrens Memorial, 446 Piedmont	06
Broadway Medical, 660 W Broadway	04
Glendale Adventist Hospital, 1509 E Wilson Ave	06
Glendale Community, 800 S Adams	05
Memorial, 1420 S Central Ave	04
North Glendale, 1401 W Glenoaks Blvd	01
Pacific Glen, 712 S Pacific Ave	04

UNIVERSITIES AND COLLEGES

Board Of Education, 411 E Wilson	06
Glendale Business, 120 S Glendale Ave	05
Glendale, 1500 N Verdugo Rd	08
Los Angeles Chiropractic, 920 E Broadway	05

HAYWARD 945

POST OFFICE BOXES

Box Nos.

1-1999	Bradford Sta	43
2000-2999	Castro Valley Br	46
3000-5999	Main Office	40
6000-6999	Southland Sta	45

RURAL ROUTES

1	46

STATIONS, BRANCHES AND UNITS

Bradford Sta	41
Castro Valley Br	46
Harder Annex Sta	44
Heyer Br	41
Southland Sta	45
General Delivery	41
Postmaster	44

UNIVERSITIES AND COLLEGES

California State College, 25800 Hillary	42
Chabot College, 25555 Hesperian Blvd	45

37

HUNTINGTON BEACH 926

POST OFFICE BOXES

Box Nos.
A-Q	Beach Center Sta	48
1-899	Beach Center Sta	48
1001-2557	Main Office	47

STATIONS, BRANCHES AND UNITS

Beach Center Sta	48
General Delivery	47
Postmaster	47

BUILDINGS

Huntington Center 7777 Edinger Ave.	47
Mc Donnell Douglas Corp. 5301 Bolsa Ave.	47

HOSPITALS

Huntington Intercommunity Hospital, 17772 Beach Blvd.	47

UNIVERSITIES AND COLLEGES

Goldenwest College	47

INGLEWOOD 903

POST OFFICE BOXES

Box Nos.
1-459	Main Office	06
ANY	Main Office	06
461-999	Main Office	07
1000-1999	Main Office	08
2000-2999	Morningside Park Sta	05
3000-3999	Lennox Br	04
4000-4999	North Inglewood Sta	09
5000-5999	Crenshaw Sta	10

STATIONS, BRANCHES AND UNITS

Crenshaw Imperial Sta	03
Lennox Br	04
Morningside Park Sta	05
North Inglewood Sta	01
General Delivery	06
Postmaster	06

GOVERNMENT OFFICES

Department Of Veterans Affairs, 830 N La Brea Ave	09
Social Security Administration, 608 E Manchester	06
State Board Of Equalization, 630 N La Brea Ave	09
State Department Of	

Employment, 4546 W Century Blvd | 04
State Department Of Motor Vehicles, 150 W Florence | 01

HOSPITALS

Brierwood Territory Convalescent, 301 Centinela	02
Centinela Valley Community, P O Box 720	07
Daniel Freeman Memorial, P O Box 100	06
Imperial, 11222 Inglewood	04
Inglewood Bassinette, 9619 S Inglewood	01
Inglewood Convalarium, 100 S Hillcrest Blvd	01
Inglewood Hospital, 426 E 99th	01
Kaiser Foundation Extended Care, 3425 W. Manchester	05
Manchester, 401 W Manchester	01

UNIVERSITIES AND COLLEGES

Northrop Institute Of Technology, P O Box 260	06

LAGUNA BEACH 926

POST OFFICE BOXES

Box Nos.
A-D	Laguna Hills Br	53
1-758	South Laguna	77
1-1649	Finance Station A	52
2001-2367	Laguna Hills	53

STATIONS, BRANCHES AND UNITS

Laguna Hills Br	53
Laguna Niguel Br	77
South Laguna Br	77
General Delivery	52
Postmaster	51

LAKEWOOD 907

POST OFFICE BOXES

Box Nos.
A-P	Main Office	14
1-719	Main Office	14
1301-1896	Hawaiian Gardens Br	16

STATIONS, BRANCHES AND UNITS

Carwood Sta	13
Dutch Village Sta	13
Hawaiian Gardens Br	16
General Delivery	14
Postmaster	14

LA PUENTE 917

POST OFFICE BOXES

Box Nos.
A-Z	Main Office	47
1-1099	Main Office	47
2001-2488	Bassett Br	46
3000-3746	City Of Industry Br	44

STATIONS, BRANCHES AND UNITS

Bassett Br	46
City Of Industry Br	44
Hacienda Heights Br	45
Rowland Heights Br	45
Valinda Br	44
General Delivery	47
Postmaster	47

LONG BEACH 908

POST OFFICE BOXES

Box Nos.
1-2919 –	Main Office	01
3001-3999	Sta B	03
4000-4535	East Long Beach Sta	04
5001-5736	North Long Beach Sta	25
6001-6448	Pacific Sta	06
6501-6796	Bryant Sta	15
7000-7996	Bixby Sta	07
8000-8659	Viking Sta	08
9001-9355	Cabrillo Sta	10
14351-14799	Loma Sta	14
15001-15415	Bryant Sta	15
16001-16184	Pacific Sta	06
17001-17148	Bixby Sta	07
20001-20900	Main Office	01

STATIONS, BRANCHES AND UNITS

Bixby Sta	07
Bryant Sta	15
Cabrillo Sta	10
East Long Beach Sta	04
North Long Beach Sta	05
Pacific Sta	06
Signal Hill Br	06
U S Naval Hospital Br	01
Veterans Administration Hosp Br	01
Viking Sta	08
General Delivery	01
Postmaster	01

APARTMENTS, HOTELS, MOTELS

Bixby Knolls Towers, 3737 Atlantic Ave	07
Blackstone, 330 W Ocean Blvd	02
Brethren Manor, 3333 N Pacific Place	06
Buffum, 210 E 3rd	12
Edgewater Inn Marina Hotel, 6400 E Pacific Coast Hwy.	03
Golden Sails Inn, 6285 E Pacific Coast Hwy.	03

Huntington Vista, 1290 E
　Ocean Blvd 02
International Tower, 666 E
　Ocean Blvd 02
Lafayette, 140 Linden Ave 02
New Robinson Hotel & Apts,
　334 E Ocean Blvd 02
Pacific Holiday Apartments 02
Portofino Marina Apts, 5400
　E The Toledo 03
Schuyler, 117 W Ocean Blvd .. 02
Six Hundred Ocean Bldg, 600
　E Ocean Blvd 02
The Breakers, 210 E Ocean
　Blvd 02
The Galaxy Condominium,
　2999 E Ocean Blvd 03

BUILDINGS

Andrus, 215 N Long Beach
　Blvd 02
Armed Services Ymca, 151
　Queens Way 02
Bank Of California, 444 W
　Ocean Blvd 02
Edison, 100 N Long Beach
　Blvd 02
F & M, 320 Pine Ave 12
Fidelity Federal Plaza, 525 E
　Ocean Blvd 02
Harbor Administrative, 925 S
　Harbor Plaza 02
Heartwell, 19 Pine Ave 02
Insurance Exchange, 205 E
　Broadway 02
Jergins Trust, 100 E Ocean
　Blvd 02
Kennebec, 141 W Ocean
　Blvd 02
Kress, 122 W 5th 12
Labor Temple, 1231 Locust
　Ave 13
Municipal Auditorium, 270 E
　Seaside Way 02
Municipal Utilities, 215 W
　Broadway 02
Ocean Center, 110 W Ocean
　Blvd 02
One-Fifteen Pine Avenue, 115
　Pine Ave 02
Press-Telegram, 604 Pine
　Ave 01
Professional Annex, 812 Pine
　Ave 13
Professional Center, 125 E
　8th 13
Professional, 117 E 8th 13
Security, 110 Pine Ave 02
Veterans Memorial, 245 W
　Broadway 02
Ymca, 600 N Long Beach
　Blvd 12
Ywca, 550 Pacific Ave 12

GOVERNMENT OFFICES

City Hall, 205 W. Broadway 02
County Court, 415 W Ocean
　Blvd 02
Federal, 300 N Long Beach
　Blvd 01

Public Safety, 400 W
　Broadway 02

HOSPITALS

Community, 1720 Termino
　Ave 01
Long Beach El Cerrito, 1401
　Chestnut Ave 13
Long Beach General, 2597
　Redondo Ave 06
Los Altos, 3340 Los Coyotes
　Diagl 08
Magnolia, 2101 Magnolia
　Ave 06
Memorial Hospital Of Long
　Beach, 2801 Atlantic Ave.. 01
Pacific Hospital Of Long
　Beach, 2776 Pacific Ave .. 01
Saint Marys, 509 E 10th 01
US Naval, 7500 E Carson 01
Veterans Administration,
　5901 E 7th 01
Woodruff Community, 3800
　Woodruff Ave 08

UNIVERSITIES AND COLLEGES

California State, 6101 E 7th.. 01

LOS ANGELES　900

POST OFFICE BOXES

Box Nos.
A-L　　　　Ambassador
　　　　　　Sta 70
1-210　　　Ambassador
　　　　　　Sta 70
1-3431　　Main Office 53
1-4164　　Terminal Annex
　　　　　　Box Sta 51
1-4220　　Hollywood Sta.. 28
5001-6647　Metropolitan
　　　　　　Sta 55
6651-7327　East Los
　　　　　　Angeles Br .. 22
8051-8999　Crenshaw Sta.. 08
11001-11599　Kearny Sta .. 11
15001-15544　Del Valle Sta.. 15
17001-17899　Foy Sta 17
18000-18994　Cimarron Sta.. 18
19391-19999　Rimpau Sta .. 19
20501-20999　Pico Heights
　　　　　　Sta 06
21001-21999　Market Sta .. 21
22001-22300　East Los
　　　　　　Angeles Br .. 22
23001-23646　Lugo Sta 23
24001-24999　Village Sta .. 24
25001-25999　West Los
　　　　　　Angeles Sta.. 25
26001-26600　Edendale Sta.. 26
27001-27999　Los Feliz Sta.. 27
29001-29920　Vermont
　　　　　　Avenue Sta .. 29
30001-30099　Terminal Annex
　　　　　　Sta 30
31001-31999　Lincoln Heights
　　　　　　Sta 31
32001-32999　El Sereno Sta.. 32
33101-33549　Boyle Sta 33

34001-34877　Palms Sta 34
35001-35999　Preuss Sta .. 35
36001-36694　Wilshire La
　　　　　　Brea Sta 36
37001-37999　Green Sta 37
38001-38999　Wilcox Sta .. 38
39601-39999　Griffith Sta .. 39
41001-41999　Eagle Rock
　　　　　　Sta 41
42001-42499　Highland Park
　　　　　　Sta 42
42501-42999　York Sta 50
43001-43546　La Tijera Sta.. 43
44451-44914　Hancock Sta.. 44
45000-45999　Westchester
　　　　　　Sta 45
46001-46714　Cole Br 46
47601-47999　Wagner Sta .. 47
48301-48999　Briggs Sta .. 48
49001-49999　Barrington Sta. 49
54001-54999　Terminal Annex
　　　　　　Sta 54
55001-55999　Metropolitan
　　　　　　Sta 55
57001-57999　Flint Sta 57
58001-58767　Vernon Br .. 58
59001-59999　Greenmead
　　　　　　Sta 59
60001-60999　Terminal Annex
　　　　　　Sta 60
61001-61999　South Sta 61
62001-62999　Westvern Sta.. 62
63001-63999　Hazard Sta .. 63
64151-64799　Rancho Park
　　　　　　Sta 64
65551-65978　Glassell Sta.. 65
66001-66578　Mar Vista Sta.. 66
67001-67572　Century City
　　　　　　Sta 67
69581-69995　West Br 69
71401-71998　Florence Br.... 01
72001-72419　Watts Sta 02
73101-73644　Broadway-
　　　　　　Manchester
　　　　　　Sta 03
74151-74999　Oakwood Sta.. 04
75001-75999　Sanford Sta .. 75
76000-76999　Sanford Sta.. 76
77001-77999　Dockweiler Sta. 67
78001-78598　West Adams
　　　　　　Sta 16
80000-81000　World Way Sta.. 80
84001-84599　Veterans
　　　　　　Ad-
　　　　　　ministration Br　73
85001-85449　Santa Western
　　　　　　Sta 72
90001-95999　World Way
　　　　　　Sta. 09

STATIONS, BRANCHES AND UNITS

Ambassador Sta. 79
Arcade Sta. 52
Barrington Sta. 49
Boyle Sta. 33
Briggs Sta. 48
Broadway Manchester Sta. 03
Central City Sta. 67
Cimarron Sta. 18
City of Commerce Sta. 22
City Terrace Sta. 63

39

Los Angeles (Con.)   900

Cole Br. 46
Crenshaw Sta. 08
Del Valle Sta. 15
Dockweiler Sta. 67
Eagle Rock Sta. 41
East Los Angeles Br. 22
Edendale Sta. 26
El Sereno Sta. 32
Farmers Market Sta. 36
Florence Br. 01
Foy Sta. 17
Glassell Sta. 65
Green Sta. 37
Greenmead Sta. 59
Griffith Sta. 39
Hancock Sta. 44
Hazard Br. 63
Highland Park Sta. 42
Hollywood Sta. 28
Kearny Sta. 11
La Tijera Sta. 43
Ladera Heights Sta. 45
Lincoln Heights Sta. 31
Los Feliz Sta. 27
Lugo Sta. 23
Market Sta. 21
Mar Vista Sta. 66
Metropolitan Sta. 14
Oakwood Sta. 04
Osbourne Sta. 28
Palms Sta. 34
Pico Heights Sta. 06
Preuss Sta. 35
Ramirez Sta. 37
Rancho Park Sta. 64
Rimpau Sta. 19
Sanford Sta. 05
Santa Western Sta. 72
South Sta. 61
Subway Sta. 52
Terminal Annex Sta. 54
Textile Sta. 15
University Park Sta. 07
Vermont Avenue Sta. 29
Vernon Br. 58
Veterans Administration Br. 73
Village Sta. 24
Wagner Sta. 47
Waite Sta. 18
Watts Sta. 02
West Br. 69
West Adams Sta. 16
Westchester Sta. 45
West Los Angeles Sta. 25
Westvern Sta. 62
Wilcox Sta. 38
Wilshire-La Brea Sta. 36
Worldway Postal Center Sta. 09
York Sta. 50
General Delivery. 53
Postmaster. 52

APARTMENTS, HOTELS, MOTELS

Admiral, 840 S Serrano Ave 05
Alexandria, 210 W 5th 13
Alvarado, 847 S Alvarado 57
Ambassador, 3400 Wilshire
   Blvd. 10

Ancelle, 701 S Gramercy Pl 05
Ansonia, 2505 W 6th 57
Ardmore, 1850 Whitley Ave 28
Asbury Apartment, 2505 W
   6th 57
Ashley Arms, 10490 Wilshire
   Blvd. 24
Bel Air Sands, 11461 Sunset
   Blvd. 49
Bel Air, 701 Stone Canyon
   Rd 24
Beverly Comstock, 10300
   Wilshire Blvd 24
Biltmore, 515 S Olive. 13
Blair House, 445 N Rossmore
   Ave 04
Bresner Towers, 8440 Sunset
   Blvd. 69
Bryson Apartment, 2701
   Wilshire Blvd 57
Bunker Hill Towers, 222 S
   Figueroa 12
Bunker Hill Towers, 234 S
   Figueroa 12
Bunker Hill Towers, 800 W
   1st 12
Canterbury, 1746 N
   Cherokee 28
Cavalier, 10724 Wilshire
   Blvd. 24
Cecil, 640 S Main 14
Chalfonte, 720 S Normandie 05
Chancellor, 1842 N Cherokee .. 28
Chancellor, 3191 W 7th 05
Chapman Park, 615 S
   Alexandria Ave 05
Chateau Marmont, 8221
   Sunset Blvd 46
Churchill Towers, 10450
   Wilshire Blvd 24
Clark International, 426 S
   Hill 13
Coliseum, 457 W Santa
   Barbara Av 37
Commodore, 1203 W 7th 17
Cordingly, 10401 Wilshire
   Blvd. 24
Crescent Heights, 6301
   Orange 48
Del Capri, 10587 Wilshire
   Blvd. 24
Doheny Towers, 838 N
   Doheny Dr 69
Dracker, 10824 Lindbrook Dr .. 24
Du Barry, 458 S Catalina 05
El Royale, 450 N Rossmore
   Ave 04
Elaine, 1245 N Vine 38
Embassy, 851 S Grand Ave 17
Fifield Wilshire, 2619
   Wilshire Blvd 57
Figueroa, 939 S Figueroa. 15
Fireside Manor, 7070
   Franklin Ave 28
Garden Court, 7021
   Hollywood Blvd. 28
Gates, 830 W 6th 17
Gaylord, 3355 Wilshire Blvd 10
Gene Autrys Continental,
   8401 Sunset Blvd 69
Harvey, 5640 Santa Monica

Blvd. 38
Hastings, 6162 Hollywood
   Blvd 28
Hayward, 206 W 6th 14
Hermoyne, 569 N Rossmore
   Ave 04
Hollywood Astoria, 7100
   Hillside Ave 46
Hollywood Biltmore, 1745 N
   Orange Dr 28
Hollywood Inn, 6724
   Hollywood Blvd. 28
Hollywood Landmark, 7055
   Franklin Ave 28
Hollywood Plaza, 1637 Vine 28
Hollywood Roosevelt, 7000
   Hollywood Blvd. 28
Hollywood Tower, 6200
   Franklin Ave 28
Hyatt House, 5547 W Century
   Blvd. 45
Langham, 715 S Normandie
   Ave 05
Lankershim, 230 W 7th 14
Leighton, 2127 W 6th 57
Lido, 6500 Yucca 28
Los Altos, 4121 Wilshire
   Blvd. 05
Los Angeles Hilton, 930
   Wilshire Blvd. 17
Marie Antoinette Towers,
   10787 Wilshire Blvd. 24
Marie Antoinette, 10795
   Wilshire Blvd. 24
Mayan, 3049 W 8th 05
Mayfair, 1256 W 7th 17
Mayflower, 535 S Grand Ave 17
Miramar, 2000 Miramar. 45
Montecito, 6650 Franklin Ave. .. 28
Oliver Cromwell, 418 S
   Normandie Ave 20
Olympian, 1903 W Olympic
   Blvd. 06
Padre, 1961 N Cahuenga
   Blvd. 28
Palms Wilshire, 626 S
   Alvarado. 57
Park La Brea Towers, 6200 W
   3rd 36
Park Sunset, 8462 Sunset
   Blvd. 69
Park Westwood Towers, 969
   Hilgard Ave 24
Park Wilshire Apartment,
   2424 Wilshire Blvd 57
Ravenswood, 570 N
   Rossmore Ave 04
Rex Arms, 945 Wilshire Blvd 17
Rosslyn, 111 W 5th. 13
Saint Paul, 1021 W 6th. 13
San Carlos, 527 W 5th 13
Sands Of Hollywood, 7220
   Hollywood Blvd. 46
Sands Sunset, 8775 Sunset
   Blvd. 69
Savoy Plaza, 601 W 6th. 17
Sheraton-West, 2961 Wilshire
   Blvd 10
Sheraton-West, 639 S
   Commonwealth Ave 05
Sir Francis Drake, 841 S
   Serrano. 05

Los Angeles (Con.)　　　　　900

Sunset Terrace, 11783
　　Sunset Blvd 49
Sunset Towers West, 8400
　　Sunset Blvd 69
Talmadge, 3276 Wilshire
　　Blvd 05
Teris, 1254 W 6th 17
Thunderbird Inn, 8300
　　Sunset Blvd 69
Tiverton Terrace, 1052
　　Tiverton Ave 24
Towers, 10941 Strathmore
　　Dr 24
Twilighter Doric, 4300
　　Wilshire Blvd 10
Versailles, 614 S St Andrews
　　Pl 05
Westchester, 1275
　　Westchester Pl 19
Westwood Manor, 10527
　　Wilshire Blvd 24
Westwood Sovereign, 10776
　　Wilshire Blvd 24
Westwood Towers, 10717
　　Wilshire Blvd 24
William Penn, 2208 W 8th 57
Wilshire Ardmore, 1129
　　Westwood Blvd 24
Wilshire Carlton, Blvd & 875
　　Comstock Av 24
Wilshire Carlton, 10635
　　Wilshire Blvd 24
Wilshire Holmby, 10437
　　Wilshire Blvd 24
Wilshire Manor, 620 S St
　　Andrews Pl 05
Wilshire Terrace, 10375
　　Wilshire Blvd 24
Wilshire Terrace, 850 S
　　Beverly Glen Bd 24
Wilshire Westwood, 10530
　　Whilshire Blvd 24
Wilshire, 10620 Wilshire
　　Blvd 24
Windsor, 3198 W 7th 05

BUILDINGS

A G Bartlett, 215 W 7th 14
A P Giannini, 649 S Olive 14
Adams Plaza, 1541 Wilshire
　　Blvd 17
American Cement, 2404
　　Wilshire Blvd 57
Apparel Mart, 112 W 9th 15
Atlantic Richfield Plaza 505
　　S Flower 71
Atlantic Richfield Plaza 525
　　S Flower 71
Atlantic Richfield Plaza 555
　　S Flower 71
Bank Of America, 650 S
　　Spring 14
Bank Of California, 550 S
　　Flower 17
Bankers Life, 6400 Wilshire
　　Blvd 48
Bankers, 629 S Hill 14
Banks Huntley, 634 S Spring . 14
Barrington Plaza, 11700
　　Wilshire Blvd 25
Bendix, 1206 Maple Ave 15

Brack Shops, Broadway
　　Arcade, 542 S Broadway 13
Brack Shops, 527 W 7th 14
Broadway-Hill, 233 S
　　Broadway 12
Broadway-Third, 306 W 3rd ... 13
Brockman, 520 W 7th 14
Buckeye, 9225 Sunset Blvd ... 69
Builders Exchange, 656 S
　　Los Angeles 14
Cahuenga Sunset, 6430 W
　　Sunset Blvd 28
Cairns, 108 W 6th 14
California Federal Plaza,
　　5670 Wilshire Blvd 36
California Highway, 120 S
　　Spring 12
California State Office, 107 S
　　Broadway 12
California State, 217 W 1st ... 12
Canadian, 432 S Main 13
Capitol Tower, 1750 N Vine .. 28
Casualty National 600 S
　　Commonwealth Ave 05
Century City, 1801 Ave Of
　　The Stars 67
Chapman, 756 S Broadway 14
Chester Williams, 215 W 5th .. 13
Citizens National Bank, 453
　　S Spring 13
City Health, 111 E 1st 12
City National Bank, 9229
　　Sunset Blvd 69
Civic Center, 205 S
　　Broadway 12
Coast Federal, 315 W 9th 15
Commercial Exchange, 416 W
　　8th 14
Consolidated, 607 S Hill 14
Continental Bank, 8730
　　Sunset Blvd 69
Continental, 408 S Spring 13
Cooper, 860 S Los Angeles ... 14
Corporation, 724 S Spring 14
Cotton Exchange, 106 W 3rd .. 13
Crocker Citizens Plaza, 611
　　W 6th 14
Douglas Oil, 530 W 6th 14
Douglas, 257 S Spring 12
Edison, 601 W 5th 17
Equitable Life, 411 W 5th 13
Equitable, 6253 Hollywood
　　Blvd 28
F P Fay, 326 W 3rd 13
Faiabrino Giannini, 3400 W
　　6th 20
Farmers And Merchants
　　Bank, 124 W 4th 13
Farmers And Merchants
　　Bank, 401 S Main 13
Fashion Design Center, 117
　　W 9th 15
Federal, 11000 Wilshire Blvd.. 24
Federal, 300 N Los Angeles ... 12
Financial Center, 704 S
　　Spring 14
First Federal, 1717 N
　　Highland Ave 28
First Western Bank, 548 S
　　Spring 13
Folb, Stanley, 6464 W Sunset
　　Blvd 28
Foreman, 707 S Hill 14

Franklin Life, 3780 Wilshire
　　Blvd 05
Garfield, 403 W 8th 14
Garland, 740 S Broadway 14
Guaranty, 6331 Hollywood
　　Blvd 28
H W Hellman, 354 S Spring ... 13
Halliburton, 1709 W 8th 17
Harris Newmark, 127 E 9th... 15
Hass, 219 W 7th 14
Havenstrite Oil, 811 W 7th ... 17
Hollywood Center, 1655 N
　　Cherokee Ave 28
Hollywood First National,
　　6777 Hollywood Blvd 28
Hollywood Pantages, 6233
　　Hollywood Blvd 28
Hollywood Security, 6381
　　Hollywood Blvd 28
Hollywood Western, 5504
　　Hollywood Blvd 28
Hollywood, 6404 Hollywood
　　Blvd 28
Holmby, 921 Westwood Blvd... 24
Home Furnishings Mart, 1933
　　S Broadway 67
Home Savings, 307 W 8th 14
James Oviatt, 617 S Olive 14
Jewelry Trades, 220 W 5th ... 13
Jewish Community, 590 N
　　Vermont Ave 04
Judson C Rives, 424 S
　　Broadway 13
Kirkeby Center, 10889
　　Wilshire Blvd 24
Knickerbocker, 643 S Olive ... 14
Lane Mortgage, 208 W 8th 14
Latin American, 430 S
　　Broadway 13
Laughlin Homer, 315 S
　　Broadway 13
Lee Tower, 5455 Wilshire
　　Blvd 26
Liberty Mutual, 6006 Wilshire
　　Blvd 36
Lissner, 524 S Spring 13
Los Angeles Home Furnishing
　　Mart, 1933 S Broadway 67
M B Scott, 8721 Sunset
　　Blvd 69
M J Connell, 746 S Los
　　Angeles 14
Maxfield, 819 Santee 14
Mc Comas, 120 E 8th 14
Mc Kinley, 3757 Wilshire
　　Blvd 10
Mercantile Center, 122 E 7th . 14
Merchandise Mart, 712 S
　　Olive 14
Merchants Exchange, 719 S
　　Los Angeles 14
Metropolitan, 315 W 5th 13
Mid Wilshire Medical, 6317
　　Wilshire Blvd 48
Mirror, 145 S Spring 12
Mobil, 612 S Flower 17
Mortgage Guarantee, 626 S
　　Spring 14
Mutual Of Omaha, 5225
　　Wilshire Blvd 36
National Oil, 609 S Grand
　　Ave 17

Los Angeles (Con.)   900

National Title, 3540 Wilshire Blvd................... 05
New Orpheum, 846 S Broadway................... 14
Ninth And Broadway, 850 S Broadway................... 14
Occidental Center, 1150 S Olive................... 15
Occidental Life, 1151 S Broadway................... 15
One Park Plaza 3250 Wilshire Blvd................... 10
Pacific Electric, 610 S Main.. 14
Pacific Employers Group, 4050 Wilshire Blvd........ 10
Pacific Finance, 621 S Hope.. 17
Pacific Indemnity, 3200 Wilshire Blvd................ 05
Pacific Mutual, 523 W 6th.... 14
Pacific Southwest, 215 W 6th................... 14
Park Central, 412 W 6th....... 14
Park Wilshire Professional, 2412 W 7th................... 57
Patroitic Hall, 1816 S Figueroa................... 15
Pershing Square, 448 S Hill.. 13
Petroleum, 714 W Olympic Blvd................... 15
Pioneer Savings & Loan, 4243 Wilshire Blvd........ 05
Professional, 1052 W 6th..... 17
Quinby, 650 S Grand Ave..... 17
Radio Center, 1509 Vine...... 28
Roosevelt, 727 W 7th.......... 17
Rowan, 458 S Spring........... 13
San Fernando, 108 E 4th...... 13
San Fernando, 406 S Main.... 13
Santa Fe, 121 E 6th............ 14
Sassony, 356 S Broadway..... 13
Security, 510 S Spring......... 13
Shell Oil, 1008 W 6th.......... 17
Signal Oil & Gas, 1010 Wilshire Blvd................ 17
Spreckels, 714 S Hill.......... 14
Spring Arcade, 541 S Spring.. 13
Spring Street, 621 S Spring... 13
Standard Oil, 615 W Olympic Blvd................... 15
Statler Center, 675 S Figueroa................... 17
Statler Center, 900 Wilshire Blvd................... 17
Stauffer Chemical, 500 S Virgil Ave................. 05
Stock Exchange, 618 S Spring................... 14
Sunset Doheny West, 9255 Sunset Blvd................ 69
Taft, 1680 Vine................. 28
Taul, 312 E 1st.................. 12
Texaco, 3350 Wilshire Blvd.. 10
Third And Broadway, 306 W 3rd................... 13
Tidewater, 4201 Wilshirebldg.. 05
Time Oil, 5150 Wilshire Blvd.. 36
Times Mirror, 202 W 1st...... 12
Tishman, 3400 Wilshire Bd.... 10
Title Insurance, 433 S Spring................... 13
Transport Indemnity, 3670

Wilshire Blvd................... 05
Travelers Insurance, 3600 Wilshire Blvd............ 10
Union Bank Center, 3810 Wilshire Blvd............ 05
Union Bank, 325 W 8th....... 14
Union Bank, 742 S Hill........ 14
Union Federal, 426 S Spring.. 13
Union Oil Center, 461 S Boylston................... 17
United California Bank, 600 S Spring................. 14
United Of America, 4055 Wilshire Blvd............ 10
United States Borax, 3075 Wilshire Blvd............ 05
United States Courthouse, Temple & Spring.......... 12
United, 707 S Broadway....... 14
Van Nuys I N, 210 N 7th...... 14
Walter P Story, 610 S Broadway................... 14
Western Federal, 606 S Hill St................... 14
Western Pacific, 1031 S Broadway................... 15
Westlake Park, 2024 W 6th... 57
Westrade, 420 S San Pedro... 13
Wilcox, 206 S Spring.......... 14
Wilflower, 515 S Flower....... 17
William Fox, 608 S Hill....... 14
Wilshire Center Company, 5371 Wilshire Blvd........ 36
Wilshire Center, 3055 Wilshire Blvd............ 10
Wilshire Central, 3723 Wilshire Blvd............ 05
Wilshire Grand, 611 Wilshire Blvd................... 17
Wilshire Professional, 3875 Wilshire Blvd............ 10
Wilshire Tower, 5514 Wilshire Blvd................... 36
Wilshire West, 10880 Wilshire Blvd................... 24
Wilshire Westlake, 2007 Wilshire Blvd............ 57
Wilson, 132 W 1st............. 12
Wright And Callender, 405 S Hill................... 13
Yellow Pages, 3636 Beverly Blvd................... 04
Yucca Vine, 6305 Yucca....... 28

GOVERNMENT OFFICES

California State Office, 107 S Broadway................... 12
California State, 217 W 1st... 12
City Hall, 200 N Spring........ 12
City Health, 111 E 1st......... 12
Civic Center, 205 S Broadway................... 12
County Court House, 110 N Grand Ave................ 12
County Engineering, 108 W 2nd................... 12
Hall Of Administration, 500 Temple................... 12
Hall Of Justice, 211 Temple ... 12
Hall Of Record New, 320 Temple................... 12
Hall Of Record Old, 220 N

Broadway................... 12
Los Angeles City Police Administration, 150 N Los Angeles................... 12
United States Courthouse, Temple & Spring.......... 12
United States Post Office, 300 N Los Angeles....... 12

HOSPITALS

Baldwin Hills, 5525 W Slauson Ave................ 56
Bel Air Chateau, 2311 Roscomare Rd............ 24
Bella Vista, 5425 E Pomona Blvd................... 22
Belvedere, 127 S Utah......... 33
Beverly Glen, 10361 W Pico Blvd................... 64
Beverly Hills Doctors, 10390 Santa Monica Bd......... 25
Beverly Sunset Medical, 9201 Sunset Blvd................ 69
Brentwood Veterans Administration Facility....... 25
California Babies & Childrens, 1415 S Grand Ave................... 15
California Lutheran, 1414 S Hope................... 15
California Medical, 1401 S Hope................... 15
Childrens, 4614 W Sunset Blvd................... 27
City Of Hope Administration Office, 208 W 8th.......... 14
City View, 3711 Baldwin...... 31
Community Of Los Angeles, 4081 E Olympic Blvd...... 23
Crenshaw Center, 3831 Stocker................... 08
Crenshaw Medical Arts Center, 3756 Santa Rosalta Dr................. 08
Crenshaw Medical Center, 3701 Stocker.............. 08
Crippled Childrens, 3160 Geneva................... 05
Doctors, 325 W Jefferson Blvd................... 07
Eastside General, 4056 Whittier Blvd.............. 23
Edgemont, 4841 Hollywood Blvd................... 27
Eye & Ear, 1314 N Vermont Ave................... 27
French, 531 W College......... 12
Gateway, 1891 Effie........... 26
General Hospital, 1200 N State................... 33
Good Samaritan, 1212 Shattoo................... 17
Hollywood Community, 6245 Delongpre Ave............ 28
Hollywood Medical Center, 6755 Hollywood Blvd...... 28
Hollywood West, 1233 N La Brea Ave................ 38
Japanese, 101 S Fickett....... 33
John Wesley, 2826 S Hope..... 07

Los Angeles (Con.) — 900

Hollywood West, 1233 N La Brea Ave	38
Japanese, 101 S Fickett	33
John Wesley, 2826 S Hope	07
Kaiser Foundation, 4867 Sunset Blvd	27
Lincoln, 443 S Soto	33
Linde Medical, 10921 Wilshire Blvd	24
Medical Office, 1136 W 6th	17
Medico Dental, 947 W 8th	17
Monte Sano, 2834 Glendale Blvd	39
Morningside, 8711 S Harvard Blvd	47
Mount Sinai General, 8720 Beverly Blvd	48
Oak Park Community, 369 W Manchester Ave	03
Olmsted Memorial, 1322 N Vermont Ave	27
Optical, 314 W 6th	14
Park View, 1021 N Hoover	29
Queen Of Angels, 2301 Bellevue Ave	26
Rose, 3858 W 54th	43
Saint Annes, 155 N Occidental Blvd	26
Saint Vincents, 2131 W 3rd	57
San Vincente, 6000 San Vincente Blvd	36
Santa Fe, 610 S St Louis	23
Santa Marta, 328 N Humpreys Ave	22
Shriners	20
South Hoover, 5700 S Hoover	37
Southern California, 3261 Overland Ave	34
Stephan A Seymour, 3324 Sunset Blvd	26
Sunset Boulevard, 4670 Sunset Blvd	27
Sunset Medical, 6642 W Sunset Blvd	28
U C L A Medical Center, 10833 Le Conte Ave	24
University, 3787 S Vermont Ave	07
View Park, 5035 Coliseum	16
Wadsworth General Veterans Administration Facility	25
Washington, 12101 W Washington Bd	66
West Wilshire Medical Center, 11600 Wilshire Blvd	25
Westlake Medical, 1913 Wilshire Blvd	57
Westlake, 644 S Alvarado	57
Weyburn Medical, 10911 Weyburn Ave	24
White Memorial, 1720 Brooklyn Ave	33
Wilshire Carthay Medical, 6333 Wilshire Blvd	48
Wilshire La Jolla Medical, 6360 Wilshire Blvd	48
Wilshire Medical Arts, 6221 Wilshire Blvd	48
Wilshire Medical, 1930 Wilshire Blvd	57

UNIVERSITIES AND COLLEGES

East Los Angeles, 5357 Brooklyn Ave	22
George Pepperdine, 8035 S Vermont Ave	44
Immaculate Heart, 2021 N Western Ave	27
Loma Linda University, 1720 Brooklyn Ave	33
Los Angeles City, 855 N Vermont Ave	29
Los Angeles College Of Optometry, 950 W Jefferson Blvd	07
Los Angeles Pacific, 625 Coleman Ave	42
Los Angeles Trade-Technical, 400 W Washington Blvd	15
Loyola University School Of Law, 1137 S Grand Ave	15
Loyola University, 7101 W 80th	45
Marymount, 10643 Sunset Blvd	24
Metropolitan College Of Business, 1601 S Olive	15
Mount Saint Marys, 12001 Chalon Rd	49
Occidental, 1600 Campus Rd	41
Pacific States University, 1516 S Western Ave	06
Southwestern University, 1121 S Hill	15
State College At Los Angeles, 5151 State College Dr	32
U C L A Extension Division, 813 S Hill	14
U C L A Medical Center, 10833 Le Conte Ave	24
U S C School Of Medicine, 2025 Zonal Ave	33
U S C School Of Public Administration, 145 S Spring	12
U S C University College, 3551 University Ave	07
U S C University Park, 3551 University Ave	07
University Of California At Los Angeles, 405 Hilgard Ave	24
Van Norman University, 1001 N Vermont Ave	29
West Coast University, 3006 W 7th	05
Wilshire Medical Arts, 6221 Wilshire Blvd	48
Woodbury, 1017 Wilshire Blvd	17

MODESTO — 953

POST OFFICE BOXES

Box Nos.		
1-1532	El Viejo Sta	53
1601-2145	Hudson Sta	54
2201-2546	Westside Sta	51
3001-3489	El Viejo Sta	53
3501-4445	Main Office	52

RURAL ROUTES

1	55
2	50
3,4,5	51
6	50
7,8,9	51
10	50

STATIONS, BRANCHES AND UNITS

Hudson Sta	54
Mc Henry Village Sta	50
Roosevelt Sta	50
Scenic Center Br	50
South Modesto Br	50
Westside Sta	51
General Delivery	53
Postmaster	50

MT VIEW — 940

STATIONS, BRANCHES AND UNITS

Blossom Valley Sta	40

NEWPORT BEACH — 926

POST OFFICE BOXES

Box Nos.		
1-537	Balboa Island Sta	62
501-999	Balboa Sta	61
1001-2346	Main Office	63
4001-5050	Irvine	64

STATIONS, BRANCHES AND UNITS

Balboa Sta	61
Balboa Island Sta	62
Irvine Br	64
General Delivery	60
Postmaster	60

NORTH HOLLYWOOD — 916

POST OFFICE BOXES

Box Nos.		
1-999	Main Office	03
1000-1778	Studio City Sta	04
2001-2540	Toluca Lake Sta	02
3000-3297	Victory Center Annex Sta	09
4001-4917	Valley Village Sta	07
5001-5099	Bendix Sta	05
6000-6099	Main Office	03
8001-8699	Universal City Br	0R
9151-9747	Victory Center Annex	09

STATIONS, BRANCHES AND UNITS

Bendix Sta	05
Studio City Sta	04

North Hollywood (Con.) 916

Toluca Lake Sta	02
Universal City Br	04
Valley Plaza Sta	06
Valley Village Sta	07
Victory Center Annex Sta	05
General Delivery	03
Postmaster	03

APARTMENTS, HOTELS, MOTELS

Aloha Garden, 6227 Craner Ave	06
Aqua Vista, 11022 Aqua Vista	02
Biltmore Palms, 5017 Bakman Ave	01
Chandler Pines, 12541 Chandler Blvd	07
Coral Gables, 3874 Willowcrest Ave	04
Denny Plaza, 6737 Denny Ave	06
Diplomat, 12360 Riverside Dr	07
Fulton Plaza, 7144 Fulton Ave	05
Glenn Valley, 12933 Ventura Blvd	04
Lankershim Gardens, 5110 Bakman Ave	01
Mayers Apartments, 10920 Ventura Blvd	04
New Frontier, 7130 Ethel Ave	05
North Hollywood, 6724 Tujunga Ave	06
Oxnard Dunes, 12524 Oxnard	06
Park Village, 11563 Magnolia Blvd	01
Parkmoor Gardens, 11308 Moorpark	02
Sans Souci, 5045 Whitsett Ave	06
Sheraton Universal Hotel, 30 Universal City Plz	08
Sherman, 11439 Sherman Way	05
Sportsmen's Lodge Hotel, 12825 Ventura Blvd	04
Tahitienne, 4616 Cahuenga Ave	02
Toluca Isle, 4604 Cahuenga Ave	02
Toluca Lake, 4258 Cahuenga Ave	02
Toluca Lanai, 4130 Cahuenga Ave	02
Toluca Tropics, 10250 Camarillo	02
Twin Palms, 11456 Burbank Blvd	01
Valley Heart Terrace, 12958 Valleyheart Dr	04
Valley Terrace, 6706 Laurel Grove Ave	06
Valli Sahara, 4020 Arch Dr	04
Victory Plaza, 11601 Victory Blvd	06
Villa Nova, 7125 Fulton Ave	05
Villi Sands, 4040 Arch Dr	04
Whipple Pine, 10869 Whipple	02
Wilson, 4918 Cahuenga Ave	01

HOSPITALS

Colonial Convalescent, 10830 Oxnard	06
Community, 6421 Coldwater Canyon Ave	06
Toluca Lake, 10425 Magnolia Blvd	01
Valley Doctors, 12629 Riverside Dr	07

OAKLAND 946

POST OFFICE BOXES

Box Nos.		
1-2099	Civic Center Station	04
2101-2299	Fitchburg Sta	21
2301-2699	Airport Sta	14
2701-2799	Dimond Sta	02
2801-2999	Rockridge Sta	18
3001-3999	Temescal Sta	09
5001-5999	Eastmont Sta	05
6001-6999	Elmhurst Sta	03
7001-7999	Fruitvale Sta	01
8001-8999	Emeryville Br	62
9001-9999	Mills College Sta	13
10001-10999	Grand Lake	10
11001-11999	Piedmont Sta	18
12001-12999	Civic Center Station	04
13001-13999	Station E	11
19001-19999	Laurel Station	19
23001-24999	Main Office	23

STATIONS, BRANCHES AND UNITS

Airport Sta	14
Army Terminal Sta	26
Childrens Fairyland Sta	22
Civic Center Sta	04
Dimond Sta	02
Eastmont Sta	05
Elmhurst Sta	03
Emeryville Br	08
Fitchburg Sta	21
Fruitvale Sta	01
Grand Lake Sta	10
Kaiser Center Sta	12
Laurel Sta	19
Mills College Sta	13
Naval Hospital Sta	27
Naval Supply Center Sta	25
Piedmont Sta	11
Rockridge Sta	18
Temescal Sta	09
General Delivery	17
Postmaster	15

APARTMENTS, HOTELS, MOTELS

Claremont, Po Box 2807	18
Cori-Ramsey, 1445 Harrison	12
Harrison, 1415 Harrison	12
Hill Castle Apartments, 1431 Jackson	12
Lake Merritt, 1800 Madison	12
Leamington, 1814 Franklin	12
Menlo, 344 13th	12
Saint Mark, 394 12th	07
San Pablo, 1955 San Pablo Ave	12
Touraine, 559 16th	12

BUILDINGS

Bank Of America, 1212 Broadway	12
Bermuda, 2150 Franklin	12
Broadway, 1419 Broadway	12
California, 1736 Franklin	12
Cathedral, 1615 Broadway	12
Central, 436 14th	12
Chamber Of Commerce, 1320 Webster	12
El Dorado, 360 22nd	12
Financial Center, 405 14th	12
First Savings, 1706 Broadway	12
Fox Oakland, 1815 Telegraph Ave	12
Franklin, 1624 Franklin	12
Fruitvale Professional, 3124 East 14th	01
Insurance, 1404 Franklin	12
Jules, 364 14th	12
Kaiser Center, 300 Lakeside Dr	12
Labor Temple, 2315 Valdez	12
Latham Square, 508 16th	12
Ludar, 2030 Franklin	12
Mc Mullen, 1305 Franklin	12
Medical, 1904 Franklin	12
Morgan, 512 16th	12
Ordway, 2150 Valdez	12
Pacific, 610 16th	12
Plaza, 506 15th	12
Popper Bernheim, 414 13th	12
Press, 408 12th	07
Tribune Tower, 409 13th	12
Union Bank, 344 San Pablo	12
Union Trust, 428 13th	12
United California Bank, 1330 Broadway	12
Wakefield, 426 17th	12
Webster, 1956 Webster	12
1440 Broadway, 1440 Broadway	12
1916 Broadway, 1916 Broadway	12
1924 Broadway, 1924 Broadway	12

GOVERNMENT OFFICES

City Hall, 14th & Washington	12
County Administration, 1221 Oak	12
County Of Alameda Health Department, 499 5th	07
Court House, 1225 Fallon	12
Federal, 201 13th	12
Main Post Office, 1675 7th	07
Oakland Hall Of Justice, 600 Washington	07
State, 1111 Jackson	07

Oakland (Con.)   946
HOSPITALS

Booth Memorial, 2794 Garden	01
Childrens Of East Bay, 5105 Dover	09
Civic Center, 390 40th	09
Highland-Alameda County, 2701 14th Ave	06
Kaiser Foundation, 280 West Macarthur Bd	11
Merritt, 3321 Webster	09
Oakland, 2648 East 14th	01
Peralta, 450 30th	09
Providence, 3012 Summit	09

UNIVERSITIES AND COLLEGES

California College Of Arts & Crafts, 5212 Broadway	18
College Of The Holy Names, 3500 Mountain Blvd	19
Grove Street College 5714 Grove	09
Laney College 900 Fallon	07
Merritt College 12500 Campus Dr	19
Mills College, Seminary Av & Macarthur	13

ONTARIO   917
POST OFFICE BOXES

Box Nos.		
1-999	Main Office	61
1001-1999	Plaza Center Sta	62

RURAL ROUTES

1	61

STATIONS, BRANCHES AND UNITS

Airport Sta	61
Plaza Center Sta	62
General Delivery	61
Postmaster	61

ORANGE   926
POST OFFICE BOXES

Box Nos.		
1-999	Plaza Sta	66
1000-1999	West Orange Sta	68
2000-2999	El Modeno Sta	69
3000-3999	Olive Sta	65
5000-6999	Main Office	67

STATIONS, BRANCHES AND UNITS

El Modena Sta	67
Olive Sta	65
Plaza Sta	66
Villa Park Rural Br	67
West Orange Sta	68
General Delivery	67

Postmaster | 67
Star Route | 67

BUILDINGS

Orange Mall	65
The City	68
Town And Country	68
Union Bank Square	68

HOSPITALS

Chapman General Hosp 2601 E Chapman	69
Childrens Hosp.,1109 W.la Veta	68
Orange Co. Med. Center.,101 S. Manchester	68
St. Joseph Hosp., 1100 W. Stewart	68

UNIVERSITIES AND COLLEGES

Chapman College., 333 N. Glassell	66

PALO ALTO   943
POST OFFICE BOXES

Box Nos.		
1-1505	Main Office	02
V-1-V-30	Veterans Hosp Br	04
2001-9680	Stanford Br	05
10000-10999	East Palo Alto Sta	04
11001-11806	A Sta	06

STATIONS, BRANCHES AND UNITS

East Palo Alto Sta	0.
Stanford Br	05
Veterans Bureau Hospital Sta	04
General Delivery	02
Postmaster	02

APARTMENTS, HOTELS, MOTELS

Alma Terrace, 3039 Alma	06
Amarillo Apartments, 2570 W Bayshore	03
Cabana, 4290 El Camino	06
Casa Real, 360 Forest	01
Channing House, 850 Webster	01
Craig, 164 Hamilton	01
Escondido Village, Stanford University	05
Everett House Community, 360 Everett	01
Forest Towers, 501 Forest	01
Galantine Apartments, 724 Arastradero Rd	06
Laning Chateaux, 345 Forest	01
Midtown Gardens, 2727 Midtown Ct	03
Oak Creek Apartments, 1600 Willow	04
Palo Alto Apartment, 101 Alma	01

Palo Alto Town House Apartments, 2721 Midtown Ct	03
President, 488 University	01
Rickeys Studio Inn, 4219 El Camino	06
Stanford Villa, 3351 Alma	06
Tan Plaza Continental, 580 Arastradero	06
Tan Plaza International, 565 Arastradero	06
Tan Village, 1094 Tanland Dr	03
Villa Capri, 3085 Middlefield	06
Villa Capri, 750 University Ave	01
Willow Creek, 1850 Willow	04

BUILDINGS

Palo Alto Office Center, 525 University Ave	01
Palo Alto Square 3000 El Camino	04
Stanford Shopping Center, 150 El Camino	04
Town & Country Village, 855 El Camino	01

HOSPITALS

Stanford Medical Center, 300 Pasteur	04
Veterans Admin Hosp. 3801 Miranda	04

UNIVERSITIES AND COLLEGES

Stanford University	05

PASADENA   911
POST OFFICE BOXES

Box Nos.		
A-Z	Main Office	09
1-50	Arroyo Annex	09
1-200	C Sta	04
1-1199	Main Office	02
1200-1999	Main Office	09
2000-2999	D Sta	05
3000-3999	Rose Bowl	03
4000-4999	Catalina Sta	06
5000-5999	East Pasadena Sta	07
8001-8384	San Marino Br.	08

STATIONS, BRANCHES AND UNITS

Catalina Sta	06
East Pasadena Sta	07
Rose Bowl Sta	03
San Marino Br	08
General Delivery	09
Postmaster	09

APARTMENTS, HOTELS, MOTELS

Green, 50 E Green	05
Huntington Sheraton, 1401 S Oak Knoll	09

46

Pasadena (Con.)   911

Pasadena Hilton 150 South
Los Robles Avenue............... 01
Sage Motor Lodge, 1633 E
Colorado............................ 06

BUILDINGS

Citizens Bank 01
First Western 01
Mutual 01
Oak Knoll Bank 01
Professional 01
Security 01
Union Bank 01

GOVERNMENT OFFICES

City Hall 09

HOSPITALS

California Emergency, 536 S
Arroyo Pkwy........................ 85
City Of Pasadena Emergency
Hospital, 142 N Arroyo
Pkwy................................... 03
Huntington Memorial, 100
Congress 05
Las Encinas, 2900 Del Mar
Blvd.................................... 07
Pasadena Community, 1845
N Fair Oaks........................ 03
St.luke, 2632 E Washington
Blvd.................................... 07

UNIVERSITIES AND COLLEGES

Ambassador College, Box
1250................................... 09
Cal Tech, 1201 E Calif Blvd... 09
Fuller Theological Seminary,
135 N Oakland 01
Highland College, 450 Ave
64....................................... 85
Pasadena City College, 1570
E Colorado Blvd................... 06
Pasadena College, 1539 E
Howard............................... 04

POMONA   917

POST OFFICE BOXES

Box Nos.
A-J   Pomona 66
1-1372   Central District
Sta 69
2001-2815 Pomona 66
4001-4146 Diamond Bar
Br 65

STATIONS, BRANCHES

Central District Sta.............. 66
Diamond Bar Br 65
Yorba Sta 67
General Delivery 66
Postmaster 66

HOSPITALS

Pacific State Hospital, 3530
Pomona Blvd........................ 68
Pomona Valley Community
Hospital, 1798 N Garey
Ave...................................... 67

UNIVERSITIES AND COLLEGES

Calif State Polytechnic
College, 3801 W Temple
Ave...................................... 68

REDONDO BEACH   902

POST OFFICE BOXES

Box Nos.
1-513   Main Office 77
1-746   Hermosa Beach
Br 54
1000-1389 North Redondo
Beach Sta 78

STATIONS, BRANCHES AND UNITS

Hermosa Beach Br 54
North Redondo Beach Sta...... 78
General Delivery Hermosa
Bea.................................... 54
General Delivery Redondo
Bea.................................... 77
Postmaster 77

APARTMENTS, HOTELS, MOTELS

Plush Horse Inn, 1700 S.
Pacific Coast Hwy................. 77
Portofino Inn, 260 Portofino
Way.................................... 77

BUILDINGS

T R W, Inc., 1 Space Park...... 78

HOSPITALS

South Bay Hospital, 514 N.
Prospect Ave........................ 77

REDWOOD CITY   940

POST OFFICE BOXES

Box Nos.
1-2180   Downtown
Finance
Section 64
5001-5598 Main Office 63

STATIONS, BRANCHES AND UNITS

Downtown Sta 63
Middlefield Road Br 61
Oak Knoll Sta 61
Woodside Br 62
General Delivery 63
Postmaster 64

RICHMOND   948

POST OFFICE BOXES

Box Nos.
1-476   Point
Richmond
Sta................. 07
1-807   San Pablo Br... 06
150-647   A Sta............... 08
691-988   El Sobrante Br . 03
1001-1872   Main Office...... 02

STATIONS, BRANCHES AND UNITS

El Sobrante Br...................... 03
Mira Vista Sta...................... 05
Point Richmond Sta.............. 07
San Pablo Br........................ 06
General Delivery 02
Postmaster 02

APARTMENTS, HOTELS, MOTELS

Aztec Apartments, 2677
Rollingwood Dr.................... 06
Bond, 334 2nd St 01
Brookside Apartments, 1230
Brookside Dr....................... 06
Casa Del Sol Apartments,
5017 San Pablo Dm Rd 03
Chancelet Apartments, 225
16th.................................... 01
De Anza Sands Apartments,
4670 San Pablo Dm Rd 03
Denver, 621 Mac Donald Ave. 01
Don, 10th & Nevin Ave.......... 01
Frazier, 56 Gertrude Ave 01
John L Davis, 430 Mac
Donald Ave......................... 01
Johnson, 1514 Mac Donald
Ave..................................... 01
Leo, 275 16th St.................... 01
Mac, 50 Washington Ave....... 01
Metropolitan, 208 23rd St 04
Monson Apartments, 4017
Garvin Ave.......................... 05
Montoya Garden Apartments,
5005 Montoya Ave............... 05
Nichol Court Apartments, 226
28th.................................... 04
Richmond Hacienda, 1300
Roosevelt............................ 01
Richmond, 1214 Mac Donald
Ave..................................... 01
Ricks, 335 1st St................... 01
Sun Garden Apartments,
4231 San Pablo Dm Rd 03
Travelers, 521 Mac Donald
Ave..................................... 01
Travelodge, 425 24th St 04

BUILDINGS

American Trust, 1001 Mac
Donald Ave......................... 01
Standard Oil, Po Box 1272 02

GOVERNMENT OFFICES

County Building, 100 37th...... 05

Richmond (Con.)   948

Richmond City Hall, Civic Center & Mac Donald 04

HOSPITALS

Convalescent Church Lane Branch, Dover & Church Lane 06
Greenvale Convalescent, 2140 Vale Rd 06
Kaiser, S 14th & Cutting Blvd 04
Richmond Convalescent, 955 23rd St 04
Richmond, 23rd & Gaynor 04
Shields & Terrell Convalescent, 1919 Cutting Blvd 04
Ventura Sanitarium, 1520 Ventura 06
Walkers Convalescent, 955 23rd St 04

MILITARY INSTALLATIONS

Pt. Molate Naval Fuel Depot 04

UNIVERSITIES AND COLLEGES

Contra Costa 06

RIVERSIDE   925

POST OFFICE BOXES

Box Nos.
1-1799   Main Office 02
2000-2999   Magnolia Center Sta 06
3000-3999   Rubidoux Br 09
4000-4999   Hardman Center Sta 04
5000-5999   Canyon Crest Sta 07
7000-7999   Arlington Sta 03
8000-8999   La Sierra Br 05

RURAL ROUTES

1 83
3 04
8 09

STATIONS, BRANCHES AND UNITS

Arlanza Village Sta 05
Arlington Sta 03
Canyon Crest Sta 07
Casa Blanca Sta 04
Edgemont Br 08
Hardman Center Sta 04
Highgrove Br 07
Institute Sta 03
La Sierra Sta 05
Magnolia Center Sta 06
March A F B Br 08
Pedley Br 09
Rubidoux Br 09
General Delivery 02
Postmaster 82

APARTMENTS, HOTELS, MOTELS

Ace, 3593 Wallace 09
Aloha, 905 La Cadena Dr 01
Alvord Heights Trailer Village, 12149 Indiana Ave 03
Ambler, 10900 Magnolia Ave 05
Arcadia Acres, 3720 Crestmore Rd 09
Arlington, 11011 Magnolia Ave 09
Aurea Vista, 3480 8th 01
Avalon Trailer Village, 3319 Avalon 09
Bahia, 7450 Mt Vernon 04
Bel-Air Mobile Estates, 6154 Mission Blvd 09
Box Springs Canyon, Box Springs Grade 07
Braemar Co-Op, 4600 Braemar Pl 01
California Mobile Estates, 3695 Avalon 09
Caravan Inn, 1860 8th 01
Colonial, 4221 Brockton Ave 01
Cottonwood, 5171 Mission Blvd 09
Country Club, 2005 Linden 07
Crescent, 3474 8th 01
Dale, 11848 Revena Ave 05
De Anza Motel & Apartments, 3425 Market 01
De Luxe Madison, 7490 Magnolia Ave 04
Edgemont, 13810 Highway 395 08
El Camino, 1616 8th 07
Elm, 5741 Mission Blvd 09
Farm House, 1393 8th 07
Franklin Square, 4160 Ottawa Ave 07
Glen Avon Mobile Estates, 9861 Mission Blvd 09
Harmony Motel And Trailer Park, 6045 Mission Blvd 09
Hi-Ho, 2055 8th 07
Highgrove Trailer Court, 220 La Cadena Dr 01
Holiday House, 13931 Ellsworth Ave 08
Imperial 400, 3225 Main 01
Imperial, 2045 Linden 07
Iowa Motel, 3735 Iowa Ave 07
Jefferson Arms, 3742 Jefferson 04
La Cadena, 219 La Cadena Dr 01
La Casa Contenta, 1435 8th 07
Las Palmas, 5943 Palm Ave 06
Magnolia Palms, 6979 Palm Ave 06
Magnolia, 6555 Brockton Ave 06
Major House, 2032 Linden 07
Mark Allison, 4575 Jurupa Ave 06
Market House Motel & Apartments, 1077 La Cadena Dr 01
Mission Inn Garden, 3649 7th 01
Mission, 5687 Mission Blvd 09

Mount Vernon Manor, 7432 Mt Vernon 04
Mountain View Trailer Court, 5479 34th 09
Mowrys Motel & Apartments, 9646 Magnolia 03
Orange Tract, 6353 Mission Blvd 09
Palm Rose Garden, 6684 Palm Ave 06
Palm View, 6038 Mission Blvd 09
Palms, 9245 Mission Blvd 09
Paradise Manor, 4206 Tyler Ave 03
Park Terrace, 9452 California Ave 03
Plaza Lane, 4572 Plaza Lane 09
Plaza, 3824 8th 01
Poolside, 9442 Hayes 03
Riverside Motor Inn, 5115 Mission Blvd 09
Riverside Town House, 3412 5th 01
Riverside Travelodge, 1911 8th 07
Riverside, 3401 8th 01
Roosevelt, 3772 Roosevelt 03
Ross, 983 La Cadena Dr 01
Rubidoux Trailer Village, 3661 Pacific Ave 09
Rubidoux, 4296 8th 01
Sage And Sand, 1971 8th 07
Shady Grove Trailer Terrace, 5803 Mission Blvd 09
Shady Rest, 7721 Mission Blvd 09
Shady Terrace, 4146 Melrose Dr 04
Sierras, 3766 8th 01
Sixty-Nine Palms Motel, 5887 Mission Blvd 09
Skylark, 2140 E 8th 07
Spring Garden, 1175 Spring 07
Stagecoach, 6050 Mission Blvd 09
Swiss Inn, 3210 Main 01
Thunderbird Lodge, 2711 8th 07
Town And Country, 1910 8th 07
Town Lodge, 4045 8th 01
Twin Palms, Box Springs Grade 07
Wagon Wheel, 10299 Magnolia Ave 03
Walnut Grove Mobile Estates, 5925 Mission Blvd 09
Western Village, 10513 Magnolia Ave 05

BUILDINGS

Bonnett, 3820 Orange 01
Central, 3859 Main 01
Health And Finance Bldg, 4080 Lemon 01
Law, 3972 Main 01
Lerner, 3631 10th 01
Loring, 3691 Main 01
Magnolia Professional, 5896 Magnolia Ave 06
Masonic Temple, 3650 11th 01
Mile Square, 3500 13th 01
Mission Inn, Nevada, 8616 Main 01

Riverside (Con.)　　925
Pritchard, 3514 9th..................... 01
Security Bank Rooms in 200-
300 Series, 6363 De Anza
Ave................................. 06
Security Bank Rooms in 400
Series, 3800 Main................. 01
Security Title Insurance,
3610 8th........................... 01
Shacker................................ 01

GOVERNMENT OFFICES

Court House Annex, 3998
Orange............................. 01
Court House, 4050 Main............. 01
Federal, 3890 Orange................ 01

HOSPITALS

Community, 4445 Magnolia
Ave................................. 01
General 9851 Magnolia Ave....... 03
Hillhaven Convalescent, 8487
Magnolia Ave...................... 04
Knollwood, 5900 Brockton
Ave................................. 06
Medical Square, 4033
Brockton Ave...................... 01
Medico Dental, 4177
Brockton Ave...................... 01
Permanente Medical Group,
3951 Van Buren................... 03
Riverside Convalescent, 4768
Palm Ave........................... 01
Riverside Medical Clinic,
3660 Arlington Ave................ 06

MILITARY INSTALLATIONS

March AFB Calif...................... 08

UNIVERSITIES AND COLLEGES

California Baptist College,
8432 Magnolia..................... 04
La Sierra, Pierce And Sierra
Vsta................................ 05
Loma Linda University-La
Sierra Campus..................... 05
University Of California............ 02

SACRAMENTO　　958

POST OFFICE BOXES

Box Nos.
A-Z　　　Main Office 13
1-231　　Metro Main
Sta................ 01
241-471　Metro Main
Sta................ 02
481-711　Metro Main
Sta................ 03
721-959　Metro Main
Sta................ 04
961-1139　Metro Main
Sta................ 05
1141-1379　Metro Main
Sta................ 06
1381-1619　Metro Main
Sta................ 07

1621-1799　Metro Main
Sta................ 08
1801-2038　Metro Main
Sta................ 09
2041-2271　Metro Main
Sta................ 10
2281-2511　Metro Main
Sta................ 11
2521-3027　Metro Main
Sta................ 12
4401-4999　Arden Br........... 25
5001-5599　Oak Park Sta....... 17
6001-6499　Centre Br.......... 60
7001-7499　Perkins Br........ 26
9001-9499　Fort Sutter Sta.... 16
9501-9999　Parkway Br........ 23
13001-13999　Main Office....... 13
15001-15999　Main Office....... 13
16001-16999　Fort Sutter Sta... 16
18001-18499　Broadway Sta..... 18
19001-19999　Camellia Sta 19
20001-20999　Colonial Sta 20
22001-22999　Land Park Sta.... 22
26001-26999　Perkins Br 26
28001-28999　Florin Br........ 28
38001-38999　Del Paso
Heights Sta 38
41001-41999　Foot Hill Farms
Br 41
214001-
215099　　Town &
Country Br...... 21

RURAL ROUTES

2 26
3 15
8 23

STATIONS, BRANCHES AND UNITS

Arden Br............................. 25
Broadway Sta........................ 18
Camellia Station Sta................ 19
Centre Br............................ 60
Colonial Sta......................... 20
Del Paso Heights Sta................ 38
Florin Br............................ 28
Foothill Farms Br................... 41
Fort Sutter Sta...................... 16
Land Park Sta........................ 22
Mather AFB Br........................ 55
McClellan AFB Br.................... 52
Metro Main Sta....................... 01
Oak Park Sta......................... 17
Parkway Br........................... 23
Perkins Br........................... 26
State Capitol Sta.................... 14
Town and Country Village Br...... 21
General Delivery..................... 14
Postmaster........................... 13

APARTMENTS, HOTELS, MOTELS

Aloha Manor, 2421 Marconi........ 21
Arden Fair, 2229 Royale Rd...... 15
Berry, 725 L......................... 14
Bohemian Gardens, 2900
Calderwood La..................... 21
California, 800 I St................. 14
Capitol Towers, 530 N............. 14
Carriage House Apts, 2724
Elvyra Way........................ 21

Castle Hill, 2725 Elvyra Way.. 21
Charlotte Manor, 5488
Carlson Dr........................ 19
Club, 3401 Balmoral Dr.......... 21
Clunie, 805 K....................... 14
Coralaire, 2545 Fulton Ave...... 21
Cosmopolitan El Mirador,
1230 N............................ 14
Country Club Town House,
2833 El Camino Ave.............. 21
Crisler, 2425 I..................... 16
Cypress Arms, 2909 Marconi
Ave............................... 21
Del Mar, 3821 Annandale
Lane.............................. 21
Edison Estates, 2501 Edison
Ave............................... 21
Fountain Garden, 2227 N 16
Freeport Manor, 5942
Freeport Blvd..................... 22
Holiday Inn North, 1900
Canterbury Rd.................... 15
Holiday Inn South, 4390 47th
Ave............................... 24
Imperial 400 Motel, 1319
30th.............................. 16
Jamaica Plaza, 2251 Watt
Ave............................... 25
Lake Crest Manor, 5949 Lake
Crest Wy.......................... 22
Lewis, 1100 N....................... 14
Mansion Inn, 728 16th............ 14
Morris, 2900 Marconi Ave 21
Palm, 3909 Watt Ave.............. 21
Park Hills Place, 6050 South
Land Park Dr..................... 22
Park Vista, 1326 N 14
Park, 1121 9th...................... 14
Parkfair Garden, 431 Parkfair
Dr................................ 25
Ramona, 1007 6th.................. 14
Rigsby Arms, 1100 39th.......... 16
Rosemont Gardens, 9216
Kiefer Blvd....................... 26
Sacramento Inn, 1501 Arden
Way.............................. 15
Sacramento Manor, 7300
24th St By-Pass................. 22
Senator, 12th & L................. 14
Sequoia, 911 K..................... 14
Sunset Garden, 3836 Auburn
Blvd.............................. 21
Thayer, 1228 N...................... 14
The Royal Villa, 4900 Royal
Villa Dr.......................... 41
Town & Country Garden,
2927 Marconi Ave................ 21
Travelodge, 1101 H................ 14
Vanguard Village, 1055
Fairlake Ave...................... 25
Village Oaks, 2839 Marconi
Ave............................... 21
Whitney Arms, 3525 Whitney
Ave............................... 21
Woodlake Inn, 500 Leisure
Lane.............................. 15

BUILDINGS

Anglo Bank, 1007 7th............. 14
Arcade Square, 3333 Watt
Ave............................... 21
Bank Of America, 900 8th....... 14

Sacramento (Con.)   958
California Fruit, 1006 4th.......   14
Eleventh & L, 1127 11th.......   14
Forum, 1107 9th.......   14
I B M Office Bldg, 520
   Capitol Mall.......   14
Medical Arts, 2720 Capitol
   Ave.......   16
Nine Twenty Six Jay, 926 J.....   14
St. Lukes Medical, 2600
   Capitol Ave.......   16
Wright, 1209 8th.......   14

GOVERNMENT OFFICES

Chamber Of Commerce, 919
   7th.......   14
City Hall, 915 I St.......   14
City School Administration,
   1619 N.......   14
County Administration, 827
   7th.......   14
County Courthouse, 720 9th
   St.......   14
Federal & Crthse Bldg, 650
   Capitol Mall.......   14
Federal Bldg, 2800 Cottage
   Wy.......   25
Federal Bldg, 805 I St.......   14
Motor Vehicle, 2570 24th.......   18
Post Office, 2000 Royal Oaks
   Dr.......   15
Resources Bldg, 1416 9th.......   14
State Agricultural, 1220 N.....   14
State Board Of Education,
   721 Capitol Mall.......   14
State Capitol, 10th At L & N..   14
State Department Of Public
   Works, 1120 N.......   14
State Dept. Of Employment,
   800 Capitol Mall.......   14
State Office 01, 915 Capital
   Mall.......   14
State Office Bldg No 8, 714
   P.......   14
State Office Bldg No 9, 744
   P.......   14
State Personnel Bd, 801
   Capitol Mall.......   14
State Prof. & Vocational
   Stds., 1020 N.......   14

HOSPITALS

Community Memorial, 2251
   Hawthorne.......   15
Kaiser Foundation, 2025
   Morse Ave.......   25
Mercy General, 40th & Jay..   19
Sacramento Medical Center,
   2325 Stockton Blvd.......   17
Sutter General, 2820 L St.......   16
Sutter Memorial, 52nd & F......   19
Woodside Community, 3201
   Del Paso Blvd.......   15

UNIVERSITIES AND COLLEGES

American River College E,
   4700 College Oak Dr.......   41
Cosumnes River College,
   8400 Center Pky.......   23

Sacramento City, 3835
   Freeport Blvd.......   22
Sacramento Nursing, 2325
   Stockton Blvd.......   17
Sacramento State, 6000 J.....   19

SAN BERNARDINO   924

POST OFFICE BOXES

Box Nos.
1-1318   Downtown Sta...   02
2001-2968   Uptown Sta...   06
3001-3689   Del Rosa Br....   04
4001-4569   Norton Air
                Force Base
                Sta.......   09
5001-6472   Main Office.....   12

STATIONS, BRANCHES AND UNITS

Base Line Sta.......   10
Del Rosa Br.......   04
Downtown Sta.......   03
Eastside Sta.......   10
Muscoy Br.......   09
Norton A F B Sta.......   09
Uptown Sta.......   05
Waterman Br.......   08
General Delivery.......   03
Postmaster.......   03

BUILDINGS

Andreson, 320 N E St.......   01
Arrowhead, 515 Arrowhead
   Ave.......   01
Blackstone, 362 N Arrowhead
   Ave.......   01
Katz, 315 N E.......   01
Law, 560 Arrowhead Ave.....   01
Platt, 491 5th.......   01
Professional, 481 W Church..   01
State Office, 303 Third.......   01

GOVERNMENT OFFICES

City Hall, 426 W 3rd Street.....   01
Civic Center, 157 W 5th.......   01
County Court House, 351 No
   Arrowhead Ave.......   01
Federal Bldg., 390 W 5th.......   01
Hall Of Justice, 453 No
   Arrowhead Ave.......   01
Hall Of Records, 172 W 3rd...   01

HOSPITALS

Community, 1500 17th.......   01
County, 780 E Gilbert.......   04
Saint Bernardine'S, 2101
   Waterman Ave.......   04

UNIVERSITIES AND COLLEGES

Cajon High, 1200 Hill Dr.......   07
City Schools Administration,
   799 N F.......   10
San Bernardino State
   College, 5500 State
   College Pky.......   07
San Bernardino Valley
   College, 701 S Mt Vernon..   10

SAN DIEGO   921

POST OFFICE BOXES

Box No.
1-578   Coronado Br.....   18
1-2999   Main Office....... 12
01-0199   College Grove
                Center Sta....... 15
3001-3994   Hillcrest Sta..... 03
4001-4519   North Park Sta..   04
5001-5727   East San Diego
                Sta.......   05
6001-6599   Point Loma
                Sta.......   06
7001-7539   Ocean Beach
                Sta.......   07
8001-8447   George
                Washington
                Sta.......   02
9001-9999   Pacific Beach
                Sta.......   09
10001-10775   Old San Diego
                Sta.......   10
11011-11299   Linda Vista
                Sta.......   11
12001-12389   Main Office....... 13
13001-13294   Southeastern
                Sta.......   12
14001-14294   Encanto Sta.....   14
15001-15594   Andrew
                Jackson Sta..   15
16001-16118   John Adams
                Sta.......   16
17001-17446   William H Taft
                Sta.......   17
19001-19147   Navajo Sta....... 19
20001-20866   Grantville Sta... 20
22001-22230   University City
                Station.......   22
23001-23448   Serra Mesa.....   23
45001-45089   Miramar Sta....   45
80000-82999   Main Office....... 38
99001-99240   Pacific Beach
                Sta.......   09

STATIONS, BRANCHES AND UNITS

Amphibious Base Br.......   55
Andrew Jackson Sta.......   15
College Grove Center Sta......   15
Coronado Br.......   18
East San Diego Sta.......   05
Encanto Sta.......   14
Fleet Sta.......   32
George Washington Sta.......   02
Grantville Sta.......   20
Hillcrest Sta.......   03
John Adams Sta.......   16
Linda Vista Sta.......   11
Mar Corps Rct Dep Sta.......   40
Miramar Br.......   45
Naval Sta.......   36
Naval Air Station Br.......   35
Naval Hospital Sta.......   34
Naval Training Center Sta.......   33
North Park Sta.......   04
Ocean Beach Sta.......   07
Old San Diego Sta.......   10
Pacific Beach Sta.......   09
Point Loma Sta.......   06

San Diego (Con)   921
Serra Mesa Sta. 23
Southeastern Sta. 13
University City Sta. 22
William Howard Taft Sta. 17
General Delivery 01
Postmaster 10

APARTMENTS, HOTELS, MOTELS

Bahia Motor, 998 Ventura
  Blvd. 09
Catamaran Motor, 3999
  Mission Blvd. 09
Churchill, 827 C 12
El Cortez, 702 Ash 12
Embassy, 3645 Park Blvd. 03
Golden West, 720 4th 12
Grant, 326 Broadway 12
Half Moon Inn, 1180 Yacht
  Harbor Dr 06
Hanalei, 2270 West Hotel
  Circle 08
Islandia, 1441 Quivira Rd 09
Kings Inn, 1333 West Hotel
  Circle ....
Maryland, 630 F 12
Master Hosts Inn, 950 Hotel
  Circle 08
Mission Valley Inn, 875 West
  Hotel Circle 08
Mission Valley Travelodge,
  1201 West Hotel Circle. 08
New Palace, 480 Elm 01
New Plaza, 1037 4th Ave 01
New Saint James, 830 6th
  Ave 12
Pickwick, 132 W Broadway 01
Point Loma Inn, 2930
  Fenelon 06
San Diego, 339 West
  Broadway 01
Sands, 5550 Kearny Mesa
  Road 11
Shelter Island Inn, 950 Yacht
  Harbor Dr 06
Town And Country, 500 Hotel
  Circle 08
Travolator Motor, 719 Ash 01
Villa Fontana Hotel, 2101
  South Hotel Circle. 08
Westgate Plaza Hotel, 1055
  2nd Avenue 01

BUILDINGS

Armed Services Ymca, 500
  West Broadway 01
Bank Of America, 625
  Broadway 01
California State, 1350 Front 01
California Theatre, 1122 4th
  Ave 01
Central Federal Savings And
  Loan, 640 C 01
Chamber Of Commerce, 233
  A 01
Chamberlain, 1551 4th Ave. 01
Channel 8 Tv, 1405 5th Ave 01
Charter Oil, 110 West C 01
Cosgrove, 411 Broadway 01
Crabtree, 303 A 01

Driver Insurance, 400 Cedar 01
Fifth Avenue Financial
  Center, 2550 5th Ave 03
First National Bank, 1201
  5th Avenue 01
Fox, 770 B 01
Frank Hope, 1475 6th
  Avenue 01
Granger, 964 5th Avenue 01
Home Tower, 707 Broadway 01
Imperial Corporation, 1010
  2nd Ave 01
Lawyers Professional, 1140
  Union 01
Pacific Center, 1017 1st
  Avenue 01
Park Plaza, 333 Plaza 01
Robinson, 520 E 01
San Diego Gas & Electric,
  101 Ash 01
San Diego Trust & Savings
  Ba, 530 Broadway 01
Scripps, 525 C 01
Security First National Bank,
  233 A 01
Spreckels, 121 Broadway 01
Telephone Company, 1188-
  6th Ave 01
Time Savings, 1023 2nd
  Avenue 01
Travelator, 1430 7th Avenue 01
Union Tribune, 940 3rd
  Avenue 01
United States National Bank,
  1010 2nd Ave 01
Ymca, 1115 8th Ave 01
Ywca, 1012 C 01

GOVERNMENT OFFICES

City Concourse 01
County Administration
  Center, 1600 Pacific Hwy 01
County Court House, 210
  West Broadway 01
US Customs, 1415 6th Ave 01

HOSPITALS

Childrens Hospital, 8001
  Frost 23
Clairemont General, 5255 Mt
  Etna Dr 17
College Park, 6666
  Montezuma Rd 15
County University, 225 W
  Dickenson 10
Doctors, 3475 Kenyon 01
Hillside, 1940 El Cajon Blvd 04
Mercy, 4099 Hillcrest Dr 03
Mesa Vista, 7850 Vista Hill. 12
Naval Hospital 34
Sharp Memorial, 7901 Frost 23
Veterans Hospital 3350 La
  Jolla Village Dr 61
Villa View, 4095 55th 15

MILITARY INSTALLATIONS

Anti-Submarine Warfare
  School 47
Coast Guard Air Station,
  2710 Harbor Dr 01

Commander Training Pacific .. 47
Fleet Anti-Air Warfare
  Training Center 47
Fleet Anti-Submarine Warfare
  School 47
Fleet Station 32
Fleet Training Group 47
Fort Rosecrans 06
Marine Corps Recruit Depot. 40
Miramar Naval Air Station 45
Naval Air Station 35
Naval Amphibious Base 55
Naval Electronics Laboratory . 52
Naval Hospital 34
Naval Radio Station, Chollas
  Heights 15
Naval Receiving Station 36
Naval Station 36
Naval Supply Depot 32
Naval Training Center 33
Naval Underseas Warfare
  Center 32
Naval Underwater Research
  And Development Center ... 32
Submarine Development
  Group 1 And 3 32
United States Quarantine
  Station, Point Loma 06
11th Naval District, Foot Of
  Broadway 32

UNIVERSITIES AND COLLEGES

California Western University,
  3902 Lomaland Dr 06
San Diego City College, 1425
  Russ Blvd 01
San Diego Mesa College,
  7250 Artillery Dr 11
San Diego State College,
  5402 College Avenue 15
U S International Unversity
  8655 E. Pomerado Rd 24
University Of San Diego,
  Alcala Park 10

SAN FERNANDO   913

POST OFFICE BOXES

Box Nos.
1-1272   Main Office 31
2001-2864   Sepulveda Br 43
3001-3524   Granada Hills
                Br 44
4001-4588   North Annex
                Sta. 42
5001-5591   Mission Hills
                Br 40

STATIONS, BRANCHES AND UNITS

Granada Hills Br 44
Lake View Terrace Br 42
Maclay Sta 40
Mission Hills Br 40
North Annex Br 42
North Hills Br 44
Norwood Center Br 43
Olive View Br 39
Sepulveda Br 43
Sylmar Br 42

51

San Fernando (Con.)   913
General Delivery 40
Postmaster 40

BUILDINGS

Bendix Corporation 42
Farmers Insurance Group 42
General Telephone Co Of
   California 42
I T & T 42
Metropolitan Life Insurance 40
Spectrolab 42
Warwick Electronics, Inc 43

HOSPITALS

Holy Cross Hospital 40
Pacoima Lutheran Hospital 42
San Fernando Hospital 40
Sepulveda Veterans Hospital 43

SAN FRANCISCO   941

POST OFFICE BOXES

Box Nos.
1-1899   Main Office 01
2001-2999   B Sta 26
3000-3999   Rincon Sta 19
4001-6200   Main Office 01
7000-7999   Rincon Sta 20
8000-8099   Airport Sta 28
9000-9099   Presidio Sta 29
12000-12296   F Sta 12
14000-14287   G Sta 14
15000-15446   A Sta 15
16000-16099   Parkside Sta 16
18000-18099   M Sta 18
22000-22099   Sunset Sta 22
24000-24539   Bayview
                 Station 24
26000-26499   B Sta 26
27000-27428   West Portal 27
31000-31099   Diamond
                 Heights Sta 31
34000-34499   Visitacion Sta 34
36000-36099   Federal
                 Building Sta 02
37000-37999   Rincon Sta 37
38000-38999   Rincon Sta 38
39000-39999   Rincon Sta 39
40000-40999   C Sta 40
42000-42999   Main Office 42
44000-44999   Rincon Sta 44
45000-45999   Rincon Sta 45
77000-77099   E Sta 07
99001-99580   O Sta 09

STATIONS, BRANCHES AND UNITS

Airport Br 28
Bay View Sta 24
Bernal Sta 18
China Sta 08
City Hall Sta 02
Diamond Heights Sta 31
Fisk Sta 22
Geary Sta 08
Hunters Point Sta 35
Letterman Sta 29
Marina Sta 23

Mc Laren Sta 34
Mills Sta 04
Noe Valley Sta 14
North Beach Sta 33
Number Fifty Seven Sta 61
Number Forty Sta 61
Number Forty Four Sta 61
Number Twenty Three Sta 61
Parkside Sta 16
Presidio Sta 29
Rincon Sta 19
Stonestown Sta 32
Sunset Sta 22
Treasure Island Sta 30
Visitacion Sta 34
West Portal Sta 27
General Delivery 61
Postmaster 01

APARTMENTS, HOTELS, MOTELS

Bellevue, 505 Geary 61
Californian, 405 Taylor 61
Cartwright, 524 Sutter 61
Chancelior, 433 Powell 61
Clift, 495 Geary 61
Del Webb'S Towne House,
   1185 Market 61
Drake-Wiltshire, 340
   Stockton 06
Fairmont, 950 Mason 06
Fielding, 386 Geary 61
Golden State, 114 Powell 61
Jack Tar, 1101 Van Ness
   Ave 61
Manx, 225 Powell 61
Mark Hopkins, 999
   California 06
Olympic, 230 Eddy 61
Oxford, 16 Turk 61
Plaza, 310 Post 06
Saint Francis, 335 Powell 19
San Franciscan, 1231
   Market 19
San Francisco Hilton Inn 28
San Francisco Hilton, 333
   O'Farrell 61
Sheraton Palace, 637 Market 19
Sir Francis Drake, 450
   Powell 01
Stewart, 351 Geary 61

BUILDINGS

Adam Grant, 114 Sansome 04
Aetna Life And Casualty
   Bldg, Crocker Plaza 1
   Post 04
Alaska Commercial, 310
   Sansome 04
Alcoa, 1 Maritime Plz 11
Alexander, 155 Montgomery 04
American International, 206
   Sansome 04
American Savings, 690
   Market 04
Anglo Bank, 830 Market 02
Appraisers, 630 Sansome 11
Balboa, 593 Market 05
Bank Of America Plaza, 555
   California 04
Bank Of America, 300
   Montgomery 04

Bankers Investment, 742
   Market 02
Bechtel, 50 Beale 05
Board Of Trade, 444 Market 11
Brooks Hall, 99 Grove 02
California Commercial Union,
   315 Montgomery 04
California Pacific, 105
   Montgomery 04
Call, 74 New Montgomery 05
Central Tower, 703 Market 03
Chronicle, 905 Mission 03
Columbus Towers, 916
   Kearny 33
Commercial, 833 Market 03
Crocker Plaza, 1 Post 04
Crocker-Anglo National Bank,
   1 Montgomery 04
Crown Zellerbach, 1 Bush 04
Custom House, 555 Battery 11
Equitable Life, 120
   Montgomery 04
Exchange Block, 369 Pine 04
Executive Towers, 503
   Market 05
Federal Office, 50 Fulton 02
Federal Reserve Bank, 400
   Sansome 20
Federal, 450 Golden Gate
   Ave 02
Ferry, Foot Of Market 11
First Savings, 401 California 04
Fitzhugh, 384 Post 08
Flood, 870 Market 04
Foremost, 111 Pine 11
Fox Plaza, 1390 Market 02
Fox Warfield, 988 Market 02
Fremont, 341 Market 05
Golden Gate, 25 Taylor 02
Grant, 1095 Market 03
Hall Of Justice, 850 Bryant 03
Hartford, 650 California 08
Hearst, 5 3rd 03
Hobart, 582 Market 04
Holbrook, 58 Sutter 04
Hong Kong Bank, 160
   Sansome 04
Humboldt Bank, 785 Market 03
Industrial Indemnity, 255
   California 11
Insurance Center, 450
   Sansome 11
Insurance Exchange, 433
   California 04
Insurance Securities, 100
   California 11
International, 601 California 08
J. Harold Dollar, 351
   Sansome 04
Kohl, 400 Montgomery 04
Matson, 100 Mission 05
Medico-Dental, 490 Post 02
Merchants Exchange, 465
   California 04
Mills Tower, 220 Bush 04
Mills, 220 Montgomery 04
Monadnock, 681 Market 05
Mutual Benefit Life, 1
   California 11
Pacific Mutual, 600 - 610
   California 08
Pacific, 821 Market 03
Phelan, 760 Market 02

52

San Francisco (Con.)   941
Rialto, 116 New Montgomery..   05
Robert Dollar, 311 California.. 04
Royal Insurance, 201
  Sansome..................... 04
Russ, 235 Montgomery.........   04
S F Civic Auditorium, 99
  Grove......................   02
Sheldon, 9 1st...............   05
Shell Oil, 100 Bush..........   04
Southern Pacific, 1 Market...   05
Standard Oil, 225 Bush.......   04
Standard Oil, 555 Market.....   20
State Annex, 455 Golden
  Gate Ave...................   02
State, 350 McAllister........   02
Tidewater, 55 New
  Montgomery.................   05
Transport, Foot Of Mission..   05
Underwood, 525 Market........   05
United California Bank, 405
  Montgomery.................   04
Van Ness Post Center, 1255
  Post......................   09
Wells Fargo, 44 Montgomery...   04
West Coast Life, 605 Market..   05
Western Merchandise Mart,
  1355 Market................   03
World Trade Center, Foot Of
  Market....................   11

GOVERNMENT OFFICES

Main Post Office, 99 7th.....   03
Rincon Annex Post Office, 99
  Mission...................   19
San Francisco City Hall, 400
  Van Ness Ave..............   02
United States Mint, 133
  Herman....................   02
Veterans Administration, 49
  4th.......................   03

HOSPITALS

Callison Memorial, 1055
  Pine......................   09
Children&s, 3700 California .. 18
Chinese, 835 Jackson.........   33
Elizabeth'S..................   18
Franklin, 2 Noe..............   14
French, 4131 Geary Blvd......   19
Garden, 2750 Geary Blvd......   18
Golden Gate, 1065 Sutter.....   09
Hahnemann, 3698 California...   18
Harkness Memorial, 1400
  Fell.......................   17
Joseph'S....................   17
Kaiser Foundation, 2425
  Geary Blvd.................   15
Laguna Honda, 375 Laguna
  Honda Blvd.................   16
Langley Porter Clinic,
  Parnassus Ave & Arguello
  Blvd......................   22
Letterman General, Presidio
  Of San Francisco..........   29
Luke'S......................   10
Mary'S......................   17
Mount Zion, 1600 Divisadero..   19
Notre Dame, 1590 Broadway...   09
Presbyterian Medical Center,

2351 Clay...................   15
Saint Francis Memorial, 900
  Hyde......................   09
San Francisco Eye & Ear,
  1801 Bush.................   09
San Francisco General, 1001
  Potrero Ave...............   10
Shriners Hospital For
  Crippled Children, 1651
  19th Ave..................   22
United States Public Health,
  2 14th Ave................   18
University Of Calif Medical
  Center, 551 Parnassus
  Ave.......................   22
Veterans Administration,
  4150 Clement..............   21

UNIVERSITIES AND COLLEGES

City College Of San
  Francisco, 50 Phelan Ave..   12
Golden Gate College, 536
  Mission...................   05
Hastings College Of Law,
  198 McAllister............   02
Lone Mountain College.......   18
San Francisco State, 1600
  Holloway Ave..............   32
University Of California
  Extension Center, 55
  Laguna....................   02
University Of California
  Medical Center, 551
  Parnassus Av.............   22
University Of San Francisco,
  2130 Fulton...............   17
University Of The Pacific,
  2155 Webster..............   15

SAN GABRIEL   917

POST OFFICE BOXES

Box Nos.
A-P   Main Office 78
1-0001195   Main Office 78

STATIONS, BRANCHES AND UNITS

General Delivery.............   76
Postmaster...................   76

SAN JOSE   951

POST OFFICE BOXES

Box Nos.
1-511   Saint James
               Park Sta   03
521-910   Saint James
               Park Sta   06
911-1300   Saint James
               Park Sta   08
1301-1799   Saint James
               Park Sta   09
3001-3999   B Sta........... 16
4001-4999   C Sta........... 26
5001-7999   Main Office..... 50

8001-8999   B Sta..........   25
9001-9999   Westgate Sta...   29
21001-21999   Hillview Sta...   51
23001-23999   Blossom Hill
               Sta...........   53
24001-24999   Cambrian Park
               Sta...........   54

RURAL ROUTES

2............................   31
3............................   21

STATIONS, BRANCHES AND UNITS

Blossom Hill Sta.............   23
Cambrian Park Br.............   24
Mount Hamilton Rural Br......   40
Saint James Park Sta.........   13
Valley Fair Sta.............   26
Westgate Sta.................   29
General Delivery.............   13
Postmaster...................   25

GOVERNMENT OFFICES

City Hall, 801 N 1 St........   10
Court House, 139 N 1st.......   13
Post Office, 105 N 1st.......   13
Santa Clara County Offices,
  70 W Hedding St...........   10

HOSPITALS

Agnew State, Mauvais Ln.....   14
Alexan Bros, 225 N Jackson
  Ave.......................   16
Alum Rock Sanitarium,
  Crothrs RdOpo Box 71).....   63
Doctors, 976 Lenzen Avenue..   26
Good Samaritan, 15825
  Samaritan Dr.............   24
O'Connor, 2105 Forest Ave...   14
San Jose 14th And Santa
  Clara St.................   12
Santa Clara Valley Medical
  Center, 751 S Bascom
  Ave......................   28

UNIVERSITIES AND COLLEGES

Heald Business, 10 Notre
  Dame Ave.................   13
San Jose City, 2060 Kingman
  Ave......................   14
San Jose State, Washington
  Square...................   14

SAN LEANDRO   945

POST OFFICE BOXES

Box Nos.
1-999   Estudillo Sta ... 77
1500-2999   Main Office 77
3000-3499   South San
               Leandro Sta....   78
5000-5599   Main Office.....   77

San Leandro (Con.) 945

STATIONS, BRANCHES AND UNITS

Estudillo Sta..................................... 77
South San Leandro Sta................... 78

Washington Manor Sta.................... 79
General Delivery............................... 77
Postmaster.. 77

SAN MATEO 944

POST OFFICE BOXES

Box Nos.
1-812   Saint Matthews
                   Sta..................... 01
901-1198   A Sta.................. 03
1201-2091 Saint Matthews
                   Sta..................... 01
3001-3355 Hillsdale Sta........ 03
4001-4299 Foster City............ 04
5001-5550 San Mateo............ 02
6001-6299 A Sta.................. 03

STATIONS, BRANCHES AND UNITS

Foster City Br.................................. 04
Hillsdale Sta..................................... 03
Saint Matthew Sta........................... 01
General Delivery............................... 02
Postal Data Center.......................... 49
Postmaster.. 02

BUILDINGS

City Hall, 330 W 20th Ave...... 03

HOSPITALS

Mills Memorial Hospital, 100
  S San Mateo Dr................ 01
Mills Square Extended Care
  Hospital, 101 S San Mateo
  Dr.. 01
Rehabilitation Center, 35
  Tower Rd............................ 02
San Mateo County General
  Hospital, 222 W 39th Ave.. 03

UNIVERSITIES AND COLLEGES

College Of San Mateo, 1700
  W Hillsdale Blvd................ 02

SAN PEDRO 907

POST OFFICE BOXES

Box Nos.
1-1999   Main Office 33
2601-2728 Fort Mac
                   Arthur Sta 31
3001-3432 Terminal Island
                   Sta 31

STATIONS, BRANCHES AND UNITS

Fort Mac Arthur Sta...................... 31
Miraleste Br..................................... 32

Terminal Island Sta......................... 31
Western Avenue Br.......................... 32
General Delivery............................... 31
Postmaster.. 31

BUILDINGS

Consolidated Marine
  Terminal.............................. 31
Fidelity Federal Savings &
  Loan..................................... 32
Harbor.. 31
Los Angeles County Court
  House................................... 31
Pacific Trade Center....................... 31
San Pedro City Hall........................ 31

GOVERNMENT OFFICES

Federal Bldg...................................... 31
Federal Correctional
  Institution, Box 7, Term Is,
  Ca... 31
U S Customs House........................ 31
U. S. Immigration And
  Naturalization Service........ 31

HOSPITALS

Los Palos Convalescent 32
San Pedro Community...................... 32
Seacrest Convalescent 32

MILITARY INSTALLATIONS

Fort Macarthur 31
U. S. Coast Guard Base.................. 31

SAN RAFAEL 949

POST OFFICE BOXES

Box Nos.
1-689   Kentfield Br........ 04
1-1380   Mission Rafael
                   Sta..................... 02
2000-3799 Main Office........ 02
4001-4430 Civic Center
                   Br...................... 03
6000-6399 Terra Linda
                   Sta..................... 03

STATIONS, BRANCHES AND UNITS

Civic Center Br................................ 03
Greenbrae Br.................................... 04
Kentfield Br...................................... 04
Mission Rafael Sta.......................... 01
Terra Linda Sta............................... 01
General Delivery............................... 02
Postmaster.. 01

HOSPITALS

Marin General Hospital, 250
  Bon Air Rd.......................... 02

UNIVERSITIES AND COLLEGES

College Of Marin, Kentfield..... 04
Dominican College &
  Convent, 1520 Grand Ave .. 01

SANTA ANA 927

POST OFFICE BOXES

Box Nos.
1-1999   Spurgeon Sta ... 02
2000-2999   South Main
                     Sta................... 07
4000-4999   Spurgeon Sta ... 02
5000-5999   Diamond Sta ... 04
8000-8999   Fountain Valley
                     Br.................... 08
10000-11999 Main Office 11
15000-15399 Industrial Sta ... 05
0006000-
  -0006999   King Sta 06

RURAL ROUTES

2 05

STATIONS, BRANCHES AND UNITS

Bristol Sta.. 03
Diamond Sta..................................... 04
El Toro Marine Corp Air Sta
  Br... 09
Fountain Valley Br........................... 08
Industrial Sta................................... 05
King Sta.. 06
South Main Sta................................ 07
Spurgeon Sta.................................... 02
General Delivery............................... 11
Postmaster.. 11

APARTMENTS, HOTELS, MOTELS

Bali Hi, 432 S Harbor................. 04
Bit O'Home, 5002 W Mc
  Fadden................................. 04
California, 2901 W 1st................ 03
Caravana, 306 S Sullivan........... 04
Contempo Mobilehome Park,
  4080 W 1st.......................... 03
Continental, 2804 W 1st............. 03
Country Club Mobile Manor,
  518 S Sullivan...................... 04
Fairview, 206 S Sullivan.......:..... 04
Gardners, 2424 W 1st................ 03
Kellogg, 2613 Arnett.................. 06
Kona Kai, 4117 W Mcfadden..... 04
Liberty, 329 S Harbor................ 04
New Holiday Mobile Estates,
  3424 W Washington.............. 03
Quiet Village, 3126 W Bolsa...... 04
Rainbow, 12062 Edinger............ 04
Royal Coach, 215 So
  Sullivan............................... 04
Sahara, 1517 N Newhope........... 03
Sandlewood Mobil Homes,
  507 S Euclid......................... 04
Santa Ana Trailer Park, 1669
  E 1st.................................... 01
Standard Avenue Mobile
  Homes, 1527 S Standard ... 07
Taggin Wagon, 2767 W 1st..... 03
The Meadows, 14851 Jeffrey
  Rd.. 05
Town & Country, 3928 W 5th.. 03

Santa Ana (Con.)   927

BUILDINGS

Arcade, 515 N Main	01
Bank Of America, 801 N Main	01
Commercial, 514 Main	01
Community Center, 1104 W 8th	01
Duncan, 1905 E 17th	01
First Western Bank, 102 W 4th	01
Grand Central, 116 N Sycamore	01
Great American Of Dallas, 1525 E 17th	01
Hall Of Records, 212 W 8th	01
Library, 502 W 8th	01
Marsile, 1833 E 17th	01
Muckenthaler, 325 N Broadway	01
New Arcade, 1740 S Main	07
Otis, 408 N Main	01
Pacific, 225 W Broadway	01
Pan American Medical, 1206 E 17th	01
Ramona, 118 W 5th	01
Santa Ana Medical Arts Center, 1125 E 17th	01
Santiago, 206 N Main	01
Second & Broadway, 207 N Broadway	01
Segerstrom Center, 1010 N Main	01
Social Welfare, 601 N Ross	01
Spurgeon, 206 W 4th	01

GOVERNMENT OFFICES

City Hall, 217 N Main	01
County Jail, 550 N Flower	03
Court House, 700 W 8th	01
Police, 511 W 6th	01

HOSPITALS

Community, 600 E Washington	01
Doctors, 1901 College	06
Riverview, 1901 Berrydale	06

MILITARY INSTALLATIONS

Marine Corps Air Station	09
Station (H)	10

UNIVERSITIES AND COLLEGES

Santa Ana Junior College, 1530 W 17th	06

SANTA BARBARA 931

POST OFFICE BOXES

Box Nos.		
A-Z	Santa Barbara	02
1-1999	Santa Barbara	02
3000-39999	San Roque Sta.	05
4000-4999	Milpas Sta	03

5000-5999	Montecito Br	08
9000-9999	Cachuma Rural Sta	09
11101-15260	University Of California Br	07
0006000-0006999	Magnolia Branch	11

STATIONS, BRANCHES AND UNITS

Cachuma Rural Br	01
Milpas Sta	03
Montecito Br	03
Mora Villa Sta	04
San Roque Sta	05
University Br	07
General Delivery	02
Postmaster	02

APARTMENTS, HOTELS, MOTELS

Biltmore	02
California, 35 State	01
Carrillo, 31 W Carrillo	01
El Encanto	02
Miramar, 1555 S Jameson Ln	02
San Ysidro Ranch, 900 San Ysidro Lane	08

BUILDINGS

Balboa, 735 State St	01
El Paseo, 813 Anacapa St	01
Federal, 836 Anacapa St	01
Granada, 1216 State St	01
Howard Canfield, 831 State St	01
La Arcada, 1114 State St	01
La Rinconada, 205 E Carillo St	01
State, 411 E Canon Perido St	01

GOVERNMENT OFFICES

City Hall, De La Guerra Plaza	01
Court House, 1120 Anacapa St	01

HOSPITALS

Cottage Hospital	02
County General Hospital	05
Goleta Valley Community Hospital, 351 S Patterson Ave	11
Saint Francis Hospital, 601 E Micheltorena St	03
Sansum Medical Clinic	02
Santa Barbara Medical Clinic, 215 Pesetas L(	02

UNIVERSITIES AND COLLEGES

Santa Barbara City, 721 Cliff Dr	09
University Of California, Santa Barbara Cal	06

Westmont College, 955 La Paz Rd	08

SANTA CLARA 950

POST OFFICE BOXES

Box Nos.		
1-629	Agnew Station	54
1-805	Main Office	52
2001-2854	Mission Station	51

STATIONS, BRANCHES AND UNITS

Agnew Sta	54
Mission Sta	51
Univ Of Santa Clara Sta	53

SANTA MONICA 904

POST OFFICE BOXES

Box Nos.		
1-1999	Main Office	06
3001-3999	Will Rogers Sta	03
5001-5999	Ocean Park Sta	05

STATIONS, BRANCHES AND UNITS

Douglas Sta	05
Ocean Park Sta	05
Will Rogers Sta	01
General Delivery	06
Postmaster	06

SANTA ROSA 954

POST OFFICE BOXES

Box Nos.		
A-Z	Santa Rosa	02
1-1199	Santa Rosa	02
AZ ZZ	Santa Rosa	03
1201-1999	Santa Rosa	03
2001-2999	Montgomery Village Sta	05
3001-3400	Santa Rosa	03
6001-6999	Coddingtown Sta	06
7001-7999	Roseland Sta	01
9000-9999	Montgomery Village Sta	05
11000-11999	Coddingtown Sta	06

RURAL ROUTES

3,4	04

STATIONS, BRANCHES AND UNITS

Coddingtown Sta	06
Larkfield Br	01
Montgomery Village Sta	05
Roseland Br	01
General Delivery	02
Postmaster	02

Santa Rosa (Con.)   954

HOSPITALS

Santa Rosa General, 7 & A	01
Santa Rosa Memorial, 1165 Montgomery Dr	02
Sonoma County Community, 3325 Chanate Rd	02
Warrack, 2457 Summerfield Rd	05

UNIVERSITIES AND COLLEGES

Los Guilocos School For Girls, 7501 Sonoma Hwy	05
Santa Rosa Junior College, 1501 Mendocino Ave	02
Ursuline School, Angela Ave	01

STOCKTON   952

POST OFFICE BOXES

Box Nos.

A-Z	Delta Sta	01
1-2169	Delta Sta	01
4001-4698	Tuxedo Park Sta	04
5001-5294	East Stockton Sta	05
6000-6700	Homestead Sta	06
2001-7358	Lincoln Village Br	07
8000-9200	Main Office	04

STATIONS, BRANCHES AND UNITS

Delta Sta	02
East Stockton Sta	05
Homestead Sta	06
Lincoln Village Br	07
Mid City Sta	02
Tuxedo Park Sta	04
General Delivery	02
Postmaster	04

BUILDINGS

Bank Of America, 343 East Main	02
Bank Of Stockton, 311 East Main	02
Belding, 110 North San Joaquin	02
California, 11 South San Joaquin	02
Center, 7 West Acacia	02
City Hall, 425 North El Dorado	02
Eden Square Medical Center, 127 East Acacia	02
Elks, 42 North Sutter	02
Exchange, 142 North California	02
Federal, 401 North San Joaquin	02
Five Forty, 540 North California	02

Hunter, 407 North San Joaquin	02
Medico Dental, 242 North Sutter	02
San Joaquin County Court House, 222 East Weber	02
San Joaquin Farm Bureau, 145 South American	02
State, 31 East Channel	02
Wells Fargo, 305 North El Dorado	02

GOVERNMENT OFFICES

City Hall, 425 North El Dorado	02
Federal, 401 North San Joaquin	02
San Joaquin County Courthouse, 222 E Weber	02
State Building, 31 East Channel	02

HOSPITALS

Dameron, 525 W. Acacia	03
Oak Park Community, 2510 N California	04
Saint Josephs, 1800 North California	04
San Joaquin General, Box 1020	01
Stockton State, 510 East Magnolia	02

MILITARY INSTALLATIONS

Nav. Com. Sta	03

UNIVERSITIES AND COLLEGES

Humphreys, 6650 Inglewood Ave	07
San Joaquin Delta, 3301 Kensington Way	04
University Of The Pacific, 3601 Pacific Ave	04

SUNNYVALE   940

POST OFFICE BOXES

Box Nos.

A-J	Encinal Sta	87
1-1536	Main Office	88
2001-2417	Encinal Sta	87

STATIONS, BRANCHES AND UNITS

Encinal Sta	87
General Delivery	88
Postmaster	86

THOUSAND OAKS   913

POST OFFICE BOXES

Box Nos.

1-800	Station A	60

1000-1999	Main Office	60

RURAL ROUTES

1	60

STATIONS, BRANCHES AND UNITS

Newbury Park Br	20
Westlake Village Br	60
Gen Delivery	60
Postmaster	60

BUILDINGS

California Luthern College, Olsen Rd	60
Capitol Records, 1050 Rancho Conejo Blvd	60

TORRANCE   905

POST OFFICE BOXES

Box Nos.

A-X	Marcelina Sta	07
1-328	Marcelina Sta	07
AA-VV	Marcelina Sta	08
331-629	Marcelina Sta	08
1001-1466	Walteria Sta	05
2900-2999	Main Office	09
3001-4299	Main Office	10
6001-6509	North Torrance Sta	04

STATIONS, BRANCHES AND UNITS

El Camino College Br	06
Marcelina Sta	01
North Torrance Sta	04
Walteria Sta	05
General Delivery	03
Postmaster	10

HOSPITALS

Harbor General	09
Little Company Of Mary, 4101 Torrance Blvd	03
Riviera Community Hospital, 4026 W 226th	05
Torrance Memorial Hospital 3330 Lomita Blvd	09

UNIVERSITIES AND COLLEGES

El Camino College, 16007 Crenshaw Blvd	06

VAN NUYS   914

POST OFFICE BOXES

Box Nos.

1-599	Main Office	08
1-787	Encino Br	16
1681-1797	Encino Br	16
2000-2999	South Sta	04
3001-3594	Van Owen Sta	07
4001-4999	Panorama City Sta	12

Van Nuys (Con.) 914

5001-5999	Sherman Oaks Sta.	13
7000-7999	Valley Annex Sta.	09
44000-44999	Panorama City Sta.	12
55001-55999	Sherman Oaks.	13

STATIONS, BRANCHES AND UNITS

Encino Br.	16
Kester Sta.	05
Panorama City Sta.	03
Sherman Oaks Sta.	04
South Sta.	04
Vanowen Sta.	07
General Delivery	08
Postmaster	08

APARTMENTS, HOTELS, MOTELS

A Kingston, 5401 Sepulveda Blvd.	01
Ace, 16008 Arminta.	06
Birmingham, 7740 Balboa Blvd.	06
C Horace Heidt, 14155 Magnolia Blvd.	03
C Magnolia Biltmore, 15101 Magnolia Blvd.	03
Central Valley, 16741 Saticoy.	06
Homestead, 8009 Haskell Ave	06
Metropolitan, 16823 Saticoy.	06
Park Royale, 7650 Balboa Blvd.	06
Shady Grove, 16811 Saticoy.	06
Strathern, 15927 Strathern.	06
Valencia, 7800 Balboa Blvd.	06
Van Nuys Y M T, 7625 Hayvenhurst Ave	06
Youngs, 15460 Erwin.	01
Youngs, 7647 Hayvenhurst Ave	06

BUILDINGS

County, 14401 Delano.	01
Panorama Towers, 8155 Van Nuys Blvd.	02
Titus, 14547 Titus.	02
Union Bank, 14530 Roscoe Blvd.	02

GOVERNMENT OFFICES

City Hall, 14410 Sylvan	01

HOSPITALS

Balowen Convalescent, 16955 Van Owen.	06
Kaiser Foundation, 13652 Cantara.	02
Mid-Valley Community, 7533 Van Nuys Blvd.	05
Presbyterian, 15107 Van Owen.	05
Sher Wood 13524 Sherman Way.	05
Sherman Oaks Community 4929 Van Nuys Blvd.	03
Valley, 14500 Sherman Cw.	05
Van Nuys Golden Cross, 7447 Sepulveda Blvd.	05

UNIVERSITIES AND COLLEGES

Valley, 5800 Fulton Ave.	01

VENTURA 930

POST OFFICE BOXES

Box Nos.		
A-Z	Main Office	01
1-2117	Main Office	01
AA-DG	Main Office	01
3001-3504	East Ventura Sta.	03
4001-4599	Saticoy Br.	03
5001-5312	Montalvo Br.	03

STATIONS, BRANCHES AND UNITS

East Ventura Sta.	03
Montalvo Br.	03
Saticoy Br.	03
General Delivery	01
Postmaster	01

WALNUT CREEK 945

POST OFFICE BOXES

Box Nos.		
236-359	Station A	97
2001-2200	Dollar Ranch Station	95
4000-5999	Main Office	96

STATIONS, BRANCHES AND UNITS

Arroyo Sta.	98
Dollar Ranch Sta.	95
Station A Sta.	96
General Delivery	96
Postmaster	96

WEST COVINA 917

POST OFFICE BOXES

Box Nos.		
A-M	Main Office	90
1-999	Main Office	93

STATIONS, BRANCHES AND UNITS

General Delivery	90
Postmaster	90

WHITTIER 906

POST OFFICE BOXES

Box Nos.		
1-999	Bailey Sta.	08
1000-1999	Perry Sta.	09
2000-2999	Los Nietos Br.	06
3000-3999	South Whittier Br.	05
4000-4999	Whittier	07

STATIONS, BRANCHES AND UNITS

Bailey Sta.	01
Los Nietos Br.	06
Perry Sta.	03
South Whittier Br.	05
General Delivery	07
Postmaster	05

WILMINGTON 907

STATIONS, BRANCHES AND UNITS

Carson Br.	45
Carson Br.	46

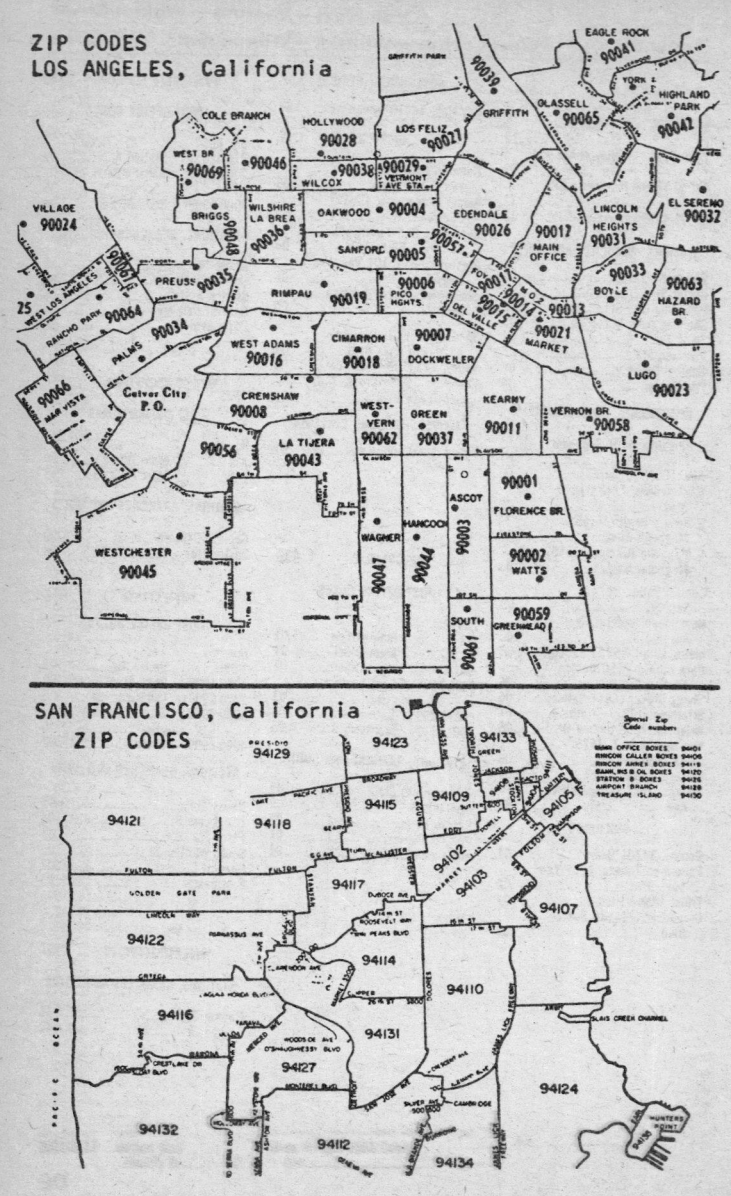

ZIP CODES
LOS ANGELES, California

SAN FRANCISCO, California
ZIP CODES

COLORADO
(Abbreviation: CO)

Alameda, Br. Denver 80226
Alamosa (1st) 81101
Alcott, Sta. Denver 80212
Allenspark 80420
Alma 80420
Almont 81210
Altura, Br. Aurora 80010
Amherst 80721
Anton 80801
Antonito 81120
Arapahoe 80802
Arboles 81121
Arlington 81021
Arriba 80804
Arvada (1st) see appendix
Aspen (1st) 81611
Aspen Gerbaz, R. Br. Aspen..81611
Association Camp, R. Br.
  Estes Park 80511
Atwood 80722
Ault 80610
Aurora (1st) 80010
Austin 81410
Avon 81620
Avondale 81022
Bailey 80421
Basalt 81621
Bayfield 81122
Bedrock 81411
Bellvue 80512
Belmar, Br. Denver (see
  appendix)
Belmont, Sta. Pueblo 81001
Bennett 80102
Berthoud 80513
Bethune 80805
Beulah 81023
Black Forest, R. Br. Colorado
  Springs 80908
Black Hawk 80422
Blanca 81123
Boncarbo 81024
Bond 80423
Boone 81025
BOULDER (1st) (see
  appendix)
Boyero 80806
Brandon, R. Br. Eads 81026
Branson 81027
Breckenridge 80424
Briggsdale 80611
Brighton (1st) 80601
Bristol 81028
Broadmoor, Br. Colorado
  Springs (see appendix)
Brookridge, Sta. Englewood ..80110
Broomfield (1st) 80020
Brush (1st) 80723
Buena Vista 81211
  Granite, R. Br. 81228
Buffalo Creek, R. Br. Pine 80425
Burlington (1st) 80807
Burns 80426
Byers 80103
Cadet, Sta. U S A F
  Academy 80840
Cahone 81320
Calhan 80808

Campo 81029
Canon City (1st) 81212
  Royal Gorge, R. Br. 81246
Capitol Hill, Sta. Denver 80218
Capulin 81124
Carbondale 81623
Carr 80612
Cascade 80809
  Chipita Park, R. Br. 80811
Castle Rock 80104
Cedaredge 81413
Centennial, Sta. Englewood ..80110
Center 81125
Central City 80427
Chama 81126
Cheraw 81030
Cherry Creek, Sta. Denver 80226
Cheyenne Wells 80810
Chimney Rock, R. Br.
  Pagosa Springs 81127
Chipita Park, R. Br.
  Cascade 80811
Chivington 81031
Chromo 81128
Cimarron 81220
Clark 80428
Clifton 81520
Climax 80429
Coal Creek 81221
Coaldale 81222
Coalmont 80430
Cokedale 81032
Collbran 81624
College, Sta. Greeley 80631
College Heights, Sta.
  Durango 81301
Colorado City, R. Br. Pueblo ..81004
COLORADO SPRINGS (1st)
  (see appendix)
Commerce City (1st) 80022
Como, R. Br. Fairplay 80432
Conejos 81129
Conifer 80433
Cope 80812
Cortez (1st) 81321
Cory 81414
Cotopaxi 81223
Cowdrey 80434
Craig (1st) 81625
  Elk Springs, R. Br. 81633
  Lay, R. Br. 81625
Crawford 81415
Creede 81130
Crescent, R. Br. Golden 80401
Crested Butte 81224
Crestone 81131
Cripple Creek 80813
Crook 80726
Crowley 81033
Cuchara, R. Br. La Veta 81055
Dacono 80514
Dayton, Sta. Aurora 80010
De Beque 81630
Deer Trail 80105
Del Norte 81132
Delhi 81034
Delta (1st) 81416
DENVER (1st) (see appendix)
Deora 81035
Dillon 80435
Dinosaur 81610
Divide 80814
Dolores 81323

Dove Creek 81324
Downtown, Sta. Englewood ..80110
Drake 80515
Dumont 80436
Dupont 80024
Durango (1st) 81301
Eads 81036
  Brandon, R. Br. 81026
Eagle 81631
Eastlake 80614
Eaton 80615
Eckert 81418
Eckley 80727
Edgemont, Br. Golden 80401
Edgewater, Br. Denver 80214
Edwards 81632
Egnar 81325
El Rancho, R. Br. Golden 80401
Elbert 80106
Eldora, R. Br. Nederland 80437
Eldorado Springs 80025
Elizabeth 80107
Elk Springs, R. Br. Craig 81633
Empire 80438
Englewood (1st) 80110
Ent A F B, MOU. Colorado
  Springs 80912
Erie 80516
Estes Park (1st) 80517
  Association Camp, R. Br. ..80511
Evans 80620
Evergreen (1st) 80439
Fairplay 80440
  Como, R. Br. 80432
  South Park City, Sta. 80440
Farisita 81037
Federal Heights, Br. Denver ..80221
Firestone 80520
Fitzsimons, Br. Denver 80240
Flagler 80815
Fleming 80728
Florence 81226
Florissant 80816
Fort Carson, Br. Colorado
  Springs 80913
Fort Collins (1st) 80521
Fort Garland 81133
Fort Logan, Br. Denver 80236
Fort Lupton 80621
Fort Lyon 81038
Fort Morgan (1st) 80701
Fountain 80817
Fountain Valley School, R.
  Br. Colorado Springs 80911
Fowler 81039
Foxton 80441
Franktown 80116
Fraser 80442
Frederick 80530
Frisco 80443
Fruita 81521
Galeton 80622
Garcia, R. Br. San Luis 81134
Gardner 81040
Garfield, R. Br. Salida 81227
Gateway 81522
Genoa 80818
Georgetown 80444
Gilcrest 80623
Gill 80624
Gilman 81634
Gilsonite, R. Br. Fruita 81521
Glade Park 81523

59

Glen Haven	80532	
Glendale, Br. Denver (see appendix)		
Glendevey, R. Br. Walden	80485	
Glenwood Springs (1st)	81601	
Golden (1st)	80401	
Goodrich	80625	
Gould	80445	
Granada	81041	
Granby	80446	
Grand Junction (1st)	81501	
Grand Lake	80447	
Grand Valley	81635	
Granite, R. Br. Buena Vista	81228	
Grant	80448	
Greeley (1st)	80631	
Green Mountain, Br. Denver (see appendix)		
Green Mountain Falls	80819	
Greystone	81636	
Grover	80729	
Guffey	80820	
Gulnare	81042	
Gunnison (1st)	81230	
Sapinero, R. Br.	81247	
Gypsum	81637	
Hale	80730	
Hamilton	81638	
Hartman	81043	
Hartsel	80449	
Hasty	81044	
Haswell	81045	
Haxtun	80731	
Hayden	81639	
Heeney, R. Br. Kremmling	80459	
Henderson	80640	
Hereford	80732	
Hesperus	81326	
Hideaway Park	80450	
High Mar, Sta. Boulder	80303	
Highlands, Sta. Denver	80211	
Hillrose	80733	
Hillside, R. Br. Salida	81232	
Hoehne	81046	
Hoffman Heights, Sta. Aurora	80010	
Holly	81047	
Holyoke	80734	
Homelake, R. Br. Monte Vista	81135	
Hooper	81136	
Hot Sulphur Springs	80451	
Hotchkiss	81419	
Howard	81233	
Hoyt	80641	
Hudson	80642	
Hugo	80821	
Hygiene	80533	
Idaho Springs	80452	
Idalia	80735	
Idledale	80453	
Ignacio	81137	
Iliff	80736	
Indian Hills	80454	
Jamestown	80455	
Jansen	81048	
Jaroso	81138	
Jefferson	80456	
Joes	80822	
Johnstown	80534	
Julesburg	80737	
Karval	80823	
Keenesburg	80643	

Keota	80738	
Kersey	80644	
Kim	81049	
Kiowa	80117	
Kirk	80824	
Kit Carson	80825	
Kittredge	80457	
Knob Hill, Sta. Colorado Springs (see appendix)		
Kremmling	80459	
Heeney, R. Br.	80459	
Radium, R. Br.	80472	
La Garita	81139	
La Jara	81140	
La Junta (1st)	81050	
La Salle	80645	
La Veta	81055	
Lafayette	80026	
Laird	80739	
Lake City	81235	
Lake George	80827	
Lakeside, Br. Denver (see appendix)		
Lakewood, Br. Denver (see appendix)		
Lamar (1st)	81052	
Laporte	80535	
Virginia Dale, R. Br.	80548	
Larkspur	80118	
Las Animas	81054	
Lay, R. Br. Craig	81625	
Lazear	81420	
Leadville (1st)	80461	
Lewis	81327	
Limon	80828	
Lindon	80740	
LITTLETON (1st) (see appendix)		
Livermore	80536	
Loma	81524	
Longmont (1st)	80501	
Loretto, Sta. Denver (see appendix)		
Louisville	80027	
Louviers	80131	
Loveland (1st)	80537	
Lowry A F B, Sta. Denver	80230	
Lucerne	80646	
Lycan	81056	
Lyons	80540	
Mack	81525	
Maher	81421	
Manassa	81141	
Mancos	81328	
Manitou Springs	80829	
Manzanola	81058	
Marvel	81329	
Masonville	80541	
Matheson	80830	
Maybell	81640	
Mc Clave	81057	
Mc Coy	80463	
Mead	80542	
Meadowlark, Br. Denver (see appendix)		
Meeker	81641	
Meredith	81642	
Merino	80741	
Mesa, Sta. Pueblo	81005	
Mesa	81643	
Mesa Verde National Park	81330	
Mesita	81142	
Milliken	80543	

Milner, R. Br. Steamboat Springs	80477	
Minturn	81645	
Model	81059	
Moffat	81143	
Molina	81646	
Montclair, Sta. Denver	80220	
Monte Vista (1st)	81144	
Homelake, R. Br.	81135	
Montezuma	80454	
Montrose (1st)	81401	
Monument	80132	
Morrison	80465	
Mosca	81146	
Mountain Park, R. Br. Golden	80401	
Nathrop	81236	
Naturita	81422	
Nederland	80466	
Eldora, R. Br.	80437	
New Castle	81647	
New Raymer	80742	
Niwot	80544	
North Avondale, R. Br. Pueblo	81061	
North End, Sta. Colorado Springs (see appendix)		
North Pecos, Br. Denver	80221	
North Pole, R. Br. Colorado Springs	80901	
Northglenn, Br. Denver (see appendix)		
Norwood	81423	
Nucla	81424	
Number Five, Sta. Denver	80202	
Number One, Sta. Denver	80202	
Nunn	80648	
Oak Creek	80467	
Ohio	81237	
Olathe	81425	
Olney Springs	81062	
Ophir	81426	
Orchard	80649	
Orchard Plaza, Br. Littleton	80121	
Ordway	81063	
Otis	80743	
Ouray	81427	
Ovid	80744	
Padroni	80745	
Pagosa Springs	81147	
Chimney Rock, R. Br.	81127	
Palisade	81526	
Palmer Lake	80133	
Paoli	80746	
Paonia	81428	
Paradox	81429	
Park Hill, Sta. Denver (see appendix)		
Parker	80134	
Parlin	81239	
Parshall	80468	
Peetz	80747	
Penrose (1st)	81240	
Peoples, Sta. Aurora	80010	
Peterson Field, Br. Colorado Springs	80914	
Peyton	80831	
Phippsburg	80469	
Pierce	80650	
Pine	80470	
Buffalo Creek, R. Br.	80425	
Pinecliffe	80471	
Pitkin	81241	

Placerville 81430
Platteville 80651
Pleasant View 81331
Poncha Springs 81242
Powderhorn 81243
Pritchett 81064
Pryor 81065
PUEBLO (1st) (see appendix)
Pueblo West, R. Br. Pueblo 81007
Radium, R. Br. Kremmling 80472
Ramah 80832
Rand 80473
Rangely 81648
Red Feather Lakes 80545
Red Wing, R. Br.
   Walsenburg 81066
Redcliff 81649
Redvale 81431
Rico 81332
Ridgway 81432
Rifle 81650
   Rio Blanco, R. Br. 81651
Rio Blanco, R. Br. Rifle 81651
Rockvale 81244
Rocky Ford (1st) 81067
Roggen 80652
Rollinsville 80474
Romeo 81148
Royal Gorge, R. Br. Canon
   City 81246
Rush 80833
Rye 81069
Saguache 81149
Salida (1st) 81201
   Garfield, R. Br. 81227
   Hillside, R. Br. 81232
San Acacio 81150
San Luis 81152
   Garcia, R. Br. 81134
San Pablo 81153
Sanford 81151
Santa Fe Drive, Sta. Denver 80204
Sapinero, R. Br. Gunnison 81247
Sargents 81248
Security, Br. Colorado
   Springs 80911
Sedalia 80135
Sedgwick 80749
Segundo 81070
Seibert 80834
Severance 80546
Shawnee 80475
Sheridan Lake 81071
Silt 81652

Silver Cliff 81249
Silver Plume 80476
Silverthorne, R. Br. Dillon 80435
Silverton 81433
Simla 80835

Slater 81653
Slick Rock 81333
Snowmass 81654
Snyder 80750
Somerset 81434
South Denver, Sta. Denver
   (see appendix)
South Fork 81154
South Park City, Sta.
   Fairplay 80440
Spivak, Br. Denver 80214
Springfield 81073
Starkville 81074
Steamboat Springs (1st) 80477
Sterling (1st) 80751
Stockyards, Sta. Denver 80216
Stoneham 80754

Stonington 81075
Strasburg 80136
Stratton 80836

Sugar City 81076
Swink 81077
Tabernash 80478
Telluride 81435
Terminal Annex, Sta. Denver 80217
Texas Creek 81250
Thatcher 81078
Thornton, Br. Denver (see
   appendix)
Timnath 80547
Toponas 80479
Towaoc 81334
Towner 81080
Trinchera 81081

Trinidad (1st) 81082
Twin Lakes 81251
Two Buttes 81084
U S A F Academy (1st) 80840
University Park, Sta. Denver 80210
Uravan 81436
Utleyville 81086
Vail 81657

Vernon 80755
Victor 80860
Vilas 81087
Villa Grove 81155
Villegreen 81088
Virginia Dale, R. Br. Laporte 80548
Vona 80861
Walden 80480
   Glendevey, R. Br. 80485

Walsenburg 81089
   Red Wing, R. Br. 81066
Walsh 81090
Ward 80481
Watkins 80137
Weldona 80653
Wellington 80549
Wellshire, Sta. Denver (see
   appendix)
West End, Sta. Colorado
   Springs 80904
West Village, Br. Aspen 81611
Westcliffe 81252
Westminster (1st) 80030
Weston 81091
Westwood, Sta. Denver (see
   appendix)
Wetmore 81253

Wheat Ridge (1st) 80033
Whitewater 81527
Wiggins 80654
Wild Horse 80862
Wiley 81092
Windsor 80550
Windsor Gardens, Sta.
   Denver 80222
Winter Park 80482
Wolcott 81655
Woodland Park 80863
Woodrow 80757
Woody Creek 81656
Wray 80758
Yampa 80483
Yellow Jacket 81335
Yoder 80864
Yuma 80759

ARVADA   800

STATIONS, BRANCHES AND UNITS

General Delivery	01
Postmaster	01

GOVERNMENT OFFICES

City Of Arvada	02

BOULDER   803

POST OFFICE BOXES

Box Nos.

A-Z	Main Office	02
1-2999	Main Office	02
3000-3999	High-Mar Sta	03

RURAL ROUTES

1	03
2	01
3	03

STATIONS, BRANCHES AND UNITS

High Mar Sta	03
Flagstaff Star Route	02
General Delivery	02
Jamestown Star Route	02
Nederland Star Route	02
Postmaster	02
Salina Star Route	02
Sugarloaf Star Route	02

APARTMENTS, HOTELS, MOTELS

Williams Village	02

GOVERNMENT OFFICES

Environmental Science Services Administration	02
National Bureau Of Standards	02
National Center For Atmospheric Research	02

HOSPITALS

Boulder Memorial Hospital, 250 Maxwell Ave	02
Community Hospital, 1100 Balsam Ave	02

UNIVERSITIES AND COLLEGES

University Of Colorado	02

COLORADO SPRINGS 809

POST OFFICE BOXES

Box Nos.

1-2999	Main Office	01
4000-4999	Knob Hill Sta	09

5000-5999	Security Br	31
6001-6999	West End Sta	04
7000-7999	North End Sta	33
9000-9999	Station A	32
14000-14999	Peterson Field Br	14

RURAL ROUTES

1	07
2	09
3,4	08
5	07
6	09
7,8	04
10	16
12	07

STATIONS, BRANCHES AND UNITS

Black Forest Br	08
Broadmoor Br	06
Fort Carson	13
Fountain Valley School Br	11
Knob Hill Sta	09
North End Sta	07
North Pole Br	01
Peterson Field Br	14
Security Br	11
West End Sta	04
General Delivery	01
Postmaster	01

APARTMENTS, HOTELS, MOTELS

Acacia, 104 E Platte Ave	02
Albany, 228 N Tejon	02
Antlers Plaza, 130 Chase Stone Ctr	02
Broadmoor, Broadmoor	06
Holiday Inn, 8th & Cimarron	05
Mayfair, 120 E Platte Ave	02

BUILDINGS

Burns, 23 E Pikes Peak Ave	02
Colorado Commercial Bank, 104 S Tejon	02
Colorado Springs National Bank, 31 N Tejon	02
El Paso County Office, 27 E. Vermijo	02
Exchange National Bank, 6 S Tejon	02
First Natiooal Bank, 6 N Tejon	02
Holly Sugar, 100 Chase Stone Center	02
Independence, 121 E Pikes Peak Ave	02
Mining Exchange, 8 S Nevada Ave	02

GOVERNMENT OFFICES

City Hall, 107 N Nevada Ave	02
Courthouse, 215 S Tejon	02

HOSPITALS

Emory John Brady, 401 Southgate Rd	06

Mamie Doud Eisenhower Osteopathic, 33 Barnes Ave	09
Memorial, 1400 E. Boulder	09
Penrose, 2215 N Cascade Ave	07
Saint Francis, 800 E Pikes Peak Ave	03

MILITARY INSTALLATIONS

Ent Afb, 1500 E Boulder	12
Federal Aviation Agency, Peterson Field	14
Fort Carson, South Of Colorado Sprg	13
Headquarters Air Defense Command, 1500 E Boulder	12
Headquarters Commander Naval Forces Norad	12
Headquarters United States Army Air Defense Command	12
North American Air Defense Command, 1500 E Boulder	12
Peterson Field Administrative Offices	16
Peterson Field Air Terminal Of Colorado Springs	16
Peterson Field, E Of Colorado Springs - Military	14
United States Naval Reserve Training Center, Lake & Logan	10

UNIVERSITIES AND COLLEGES

Blair Business College, 10 N Farragut	09
Colorado College	03
University Of Colorado Extension, Cragmor Rd	07

DENVER   802

POST OFFICE BOXES

Box Nos.

1-388	Ft Logan Brch	36
1-3199	Main Office Sta	01
4001-4999	Santa Fe Dr Sta	04
5001-5999	Terminal Annex Sta	17
6001-6418	Fitzsimons Br	40
6001-6999	Cherry Creek Sta	06
7001-7999	Park Hill Sta	07
9001-9999	South Denver Sta	09
10001-10999	University Park Sta	10
11001-11999	Highlands Sta	11
12001-12999	Alcott Sta	12
14001-14999	Edgewater Br	14
15001-15999	Lakewood Br	15
16001-16999	Stockyards Sta	16

Denver (Con.)   802

17001-17999 Terminal Annex
          Sta............................. 17
18001-18999 Capitol Hill
          Sta............................. 18
19001-19999 Westwood Sta..... 19
20001-20999 Montclair Sta...... 20
21001-21999 North Pecos Br..... 21
22001-22999 Wellshire Sta....... 22
26001-26999 Belmar Br............ 26
29001-29999 Thornton Br......... 29
30001-30999 Lowry Air Force
          Base........................... 30

RURAL ROUTES

1.. 29
2.. 22

STATIONS, BRANCHES AND UNITS

Alameda Br................................. 26
Alcott Sta................................... 12
Belmar Br................................... 26
Capitol Hill Sta.......................... 18
Cherry Creek Sta........................ 06
Edgewater Br.............................. 14
Fitzsimons Br............................. 40
Fort Logan Br............................. 36
Glendale Br................................. 22
Green Mountain Br...................... 28
Highlands Sta.............................. 11
Lakeside Br................................. 12
Lakewood Br............................... 15
Loretto Sta.................................. 36
Lowry AFB Sta............................ 30
Meadowlark Br............................ 15
Montclair Sta.............................. 20
Northglenn Br............................. 33
North Pecos Br........................... 21
Number One Sta......................... 02
Number Five Sta......................... 02
Park Hill Sta............................... 07
Santa Fe Drive Sta..................... 04
South Denver Sta........................ 09
Spivak Br.................................... 14
Stockyards Sta............................ 16
Terminal Annex Sta.................... 17
Thornton Br................................. 29
University Park Sta...................... 10
Wellshire Sta.............................. 22
Westwood Br............................... 19
Windsor Gardens Sta.................. 22
General Delivery.......................... 01
Postmaster.................................. 02

APARTMENTS, HOTELS, MOTELS

Albany, 1720 Stout..................... 02
Ambassador, 130 Pearl............... 03
Americana, 1121 Albion.............. 20
Argonaut, 233 E Colfax Ave....... 03
Avondale Village, 3295 W
     Avondale Dr............................ 04
Bahama, 1180 Sherman.............. 03
Bermuda, 1080 Logan................. 03
Brown Palace, 321 17th.............. 02
Buchtel Grove, 2105 Buchtel
     Blvd....................................... 10
Cheesman Towers, 1201
     Williams................................. 18

Cherry Creek Towers, 3100
     Cherry Creek S Dr................... 09
Colburn Apts, 250 Grant St........ 09
Colburn Hotel, 980 Grant St....... 03
Cosmopolitan, 1780
     Broadway................................ 02
Country Club Gardens, 1100
     E Ellsworth Ave....................... 09
Denver Downtowner Mtr Inn,
     303 W Colfax Ave.................... 04
Denver-Hilton, 1550 Court Pl...... 01
Eight-Eighty-Eight Logan, 888
     Logan..................................... 03
Eleven Hundred Cheesman
     Pk, 1111 Race......................... 06
Grosvenor Arms, 333 E 16th
     Ave.. 03
Holiday Central, 1975 Bryant
     St.. 04
Holiday So Colo, 1475 So
     Colo Blvd................................ 22
La Fontana, 4570 E Yale
     Ave.. 22
Lanai, 800 Washington............... 03
Lido, 790 Washington................. 03
Lion Gate, 90 Corona.................. 18
Mayflower Motel, 1710 Grant...... 03
Olin Hotel & Apts, 1420
     Logan St................................. 83
Park Lane Towers, 480 S.
     Marion St Pky......................... 09
Penn Vii, 700 Pennsylvania........ 03
Polo Club, 3131 E Alameda
     Ave.. 09
Radisson-Denver, 1790 Grant..... 03
Ramada Inn, 455 S Colo
     Blvd....................................... 22
Regency Roadway Inn, 3900
     Elati....................................... 16
Roger Williams Manor, 101
     Grant..................................... 03
Rossonian, 2642 Welton............. 05
Sherman Plaza, 901
     Sherman.................................. 02
Skyline, 1801 Arapahoe.............. 03
Skyways Motor, 3855 Quebec..... 07
Travelodge North, 200 W
     Warner Pl................................ 16
Twelve-Hundred Vine, 1200
     Vine....................................... 06
Versailles, 789 Clarkson............. 18
Wellshire Arms, 2499 S Colo
     Blvd....................................... 22
Windsor Gardens, 600 S
     Clinton.................................... 31
Writers Manor, 1730 S Colo
     Blvd....................................... 22
Ymca, 25 E 16 Th Ave................. 02
Ywca Colorado Hotel, 406
     17th.. 02

BUILDINGS

American National Bank, 818
     17th.. 02
Boston, 828 17th........................ 02
Brooks Tower, 1020 15th St....... 02
C A Johnson, 509 17th............... 02
Capitol Life Center, 225 E
     16th Ave.................................. 03
Central Bank, 1108 15th............. 02
Colorado Bldg, 1615
     California St............................ 02

Colorado State Bank, 1600
     Broadway................................ 02
Continental Oil 1755
     Glenarm Pl.............................. 02
Denham Bldg, 1812
     California................................ 02
Denver Center 1776 Lincoln....... 03
Denver Club Bldg, 518 17 Th
     St.. 02
Denver Merchandise Mart,
     451 E. 58th Ave....................... 16
Empire, 430 16th........................ 02
Equitable, 730 17th.................... 02
Executive Club........................... 10
First National Bank, 621
     17th.. 02
Guaranty Bank, 817 17th............ 02
Hilton Office, 1515 Cleveland
     Pl.. 02
Ideal Cement, 821 17 Th St........ 02
Insurance Exchange, 910
     15th.. 02
Insurance, 831 14 Th St.............. 02
Kittredge, 511 16th.................... 02
Lincoln Tower Office, 1860
     Lincoln................................... 03
Livestock Exchange, 4701
     Marion.................................... 16
Majestic, 209 16th...................... 02
Metropolitan, 1612 Court Pl....... 02
Midland Savings, 444 17th.......... 02
One-O-One University, 101
     University Blvd........................ 06
Park Central, 1515 Arapahoe...... 02
Patterson, 555 17th.................... 02
Petroleum, 110-16th................... 02
Prudential Plaza, 1050 17th........ 02
Republic, 1612 Tremont Pl......... 02
Security Life, 1616 Glenarm
     Pl.. 02
Security, 650 17th....................... 02
Symes, 820 16th......................... 02
Three-Thirty-Three, 333 W
     Colfax Ave.............................. 04
Title, 909 17 Th St..................... 02
Tower, 1700 Broadway................ 02
United Bank Of Denver, 1740
     Broadway................................ 02
University, 910 16th.................... 02
Western Federal Savings, 718
     17th.. 02

GOVERNMENT OFFICES

City & County, 1437
     Bannock.................................. 02
Denver Chamber Of
     Commerce, 1301 Welton......... 04
Denver Convention
     Complex, 1323 Champa........... 04
Denver Federal Center................ 25
Federal Office Building, 1961
     Stout...................................... 02
Hall Of Justice, 1929 Stout......... 02
Post Office, 1823 Stout.............. 02
State Capitol Annex, 1375
     Sherman.................................. 03
State Capitol, 200 E. Colfax
     Ave.. 03
State Museum, 200 E. 14th
     Ave.. 03
State Office, 201 E Colfax
     Ave.. 03
State Service, 1525 Sherman..... 03

Denver (Con.)　　　　802

State Social Services, 1575
　Sherman............................... 03
United States Customs
　House, 721 19th.................... 02

HOSPITALS

American Medical Center, (U
　C R S) 6401 W Colfax
　Ave..................................... 14
Beth Israel, 1601 Lowell
　Blvd..................................... 04
Childrens Asthma ,3401 W
　19th Ave.............................. 04
Childrens Hospital
　Association, 1056 E 19th
　Ave..................................... 18
Colorado General, 4200 E 9th
　Ave..................................... 20
Denver General, 301 W 7th
　Ave.....................................
Fitzsimons General, 12101 E
　Colfax Ave........................... 40
Fort Logan Mental Health,
　3520 W Oxford Ave............... 36
General Rose Memorial, 1050
　Clermont.............................. 20
Life Center, 5775 E 8th Ave.... 20
Mercy, 1619 Milwaukee.......... 06
National Jewish Hospital in
　Denver, 3800 E Colfax
　Ave..................................... 06
Porter Memorial Hospital,
　2525 S Downing.................... 10
Presbyterian Medical Center,
　1719 E 19th Ave................... 18
Rocky Mountain Osteopathic
　4701 E 9th Ave..................... 20
Saint Anthonys, 4231 W 16th
　Ave..................................... 04
Saint Josephs, 1835 Franklin.. 18
Saint Lukes, 601 E 19th Ave... 63
Spears Chiropractic
　Santarium & Hospital, 927
　Jersey.................................. 20
Valley View, 8451 Pearl......... 29
Veterans Administration,
　1055 Clermont..................... 20

MILITARY INSTALLATIONS

Air Force Acct & Finance
　Center, 3800 York St............ 05
Lowry AFB.............................. 30
Martin Company...................... 01
Rocky Mountain Arsenal......... 40
Stapleton International Airp..... 87

UNIVERSITIES AND COLLEGES

Barnes School O₂ Commerce,
　1410 Glenarm Pl................... 02
Central Business, 1177
　Grant................................... 03

Community College Of
　Denver, 1001 E. 62nd
　Ave..................................... 16
Iliff School Of Theology, 2201
　S University Blvd................... 10
Loretto, 3001 S Federal Blvd... 36
Metro State, 250 W 14th Ave.. 04
Regis, 3539 W 50th Ave......... 21
Temple Buell, 1800 Pontiac
　St....................................... 20
University Of Colorado School
　Of Medicine, 4200 E 9th
　Ave..................................... 20
University Of Colorado,denver
　Center, 1100 14 Th St.......... 02
University Of Denver, 2115 S
　University Blvd..................... 10

LITTLETON　　801

POST OFFICE BOXES

Box Nos.
1-1999　　　　Main Office...... 20
1-1999　　　　Main Office...... 20

RURAL ROUTES

1,2,3,3................................... 20

STATIONS, BRANCHES AND UNITS

Orchard Plaza Br...................... 21

PUEBLO　　810

POST OFFICE BOXES

Box Nos.
1-1999　　　　Pueblo.......... 02
2000-2999　　A Sta............ 04
3000-3999　　Mesa Sta....... 05
4000-4999　　Parel Post
　　　　　　　Annex............ 03
11000-11999　Belmont Sta.... 01

RURAL ROUTES

1,2,3,4................................... 04

STATIONS, BRANCHES AND UNITS

Belmont Sta............................ 01
Colorado City Rural Br............. 04
Mesa Sta................................. 05
North Avondale Rural Br.......... 61
Pueblo West Rural Br.............. 07
General Delivery...................... 02
Postmaster............................. 03

APARTMENTS, HOTELS, MOTELS

B T C Tower House, 1111
　Bonforte Blvd....................... 01
Chilton Inn, 800 Highway 50
　W.. 08
Continental, 1021 Ruppel........ 01
Presbyterian Towers, 220 W
　15th.................................... 03
Ramada Inn, E Hwy 50
　Bypass & N Hudson Ave........ 01
Town House Motor Hotel, 8th
　& Santa Fe........................... 03

BUILDINGS

Bon Durant Bldg, 5th &
　Court St............................... 03
City Hall, 100 N Union............. 03
Colorado Bldg, 407 N Main...... 03
Federal Building 5th & Main..... 03
Judicial 10th & Grand.............. 03
Pueblo Clinic, 702 N Main....... 03
Pueblo County Court House,
　10th & N Grand.................... 03
St Mary-Corwin Medical Arts,
　1925 E Orman Ave................ 04
Thatcher Bldg, 5th & Main
　St....................................... 03

GOVERNMENT OFFICES

Government Printing Office,
　Pueblo Industrial Park........... 09

HOSPITALS

Colorado State Hospital,
　1600 W 24th......................... 03
Parkview Episcopal, 400 W
　16th.................................... 03
St Mary Corwin, 1008
　Minnequa............................. 04

MILITARY INSTALLATIONS

Pueblo Army Depot................. 01
Pueblo Memorial Airport.......... 04
US High Speed Ground Test
　Center................................. 01

UNIVERSITIES AND COLLEGES

Belmont Campus, 2200
　Bonforte Blvd....................... 01
Southern Colorado State
　College, 900 W Orman
　Ave..................................... 05

CONNECTICUT
(Abbreviation: CT)

Abington 06230
Amity, Sta. New Haven 06525
Amston 06231
Andover 06232
Ansonia (1st) 06401
Avon (1st) 06001
Balouville 06233
Baltic 06330
Bantam 06750
Barnum, Sta. Bridgeport 06605
Barry Square, Sta. Hartford 06114
Beacon Falls 06403
Beardsley, Sta. Bridgeport 06606
Belden, Sta. Norwalk 06850
Berlin, Br. Kensington 06037
Bethel (1st) 06801
Bethlehem 06751
Bishops Corner, Br. Hartford ..06117
Bissell, Sta. South Windsor 06074
Bloomfield (1st) 06002
Blue Hills, Sta. Hartford 06112
Bolton, Br. Manchester 06040
Borough, Sta. Groton 06340
Botsford 06404
Branford (1st) 06405
BRIDGEPORT (1st) (see
   appendix)
Bridgewater 06752
Bristol (1st) 06010
Broad Brook 06016
Brookfield (1st) 06804
Brookfield Center 06805
Brooklyn 06234
Buckland, Sta. Manchester 06040
Burlington, R. Br. Unionville ..06085
Byram, Br. Port Chester, N
   Y 10573
Canaan (1st) 06018
Candlewood Isle, Br.
   Danbury 06810
Canterbury 06331
Canton 06019
Canton Center 06020
Center, Br. Bridgeport 06611
Centerbrook 06409
Centerville-Mount Carmel,
   Br. New Haven (see
   appendix)
Central, Sta. Hartford 06103
Central Village 06332
Chaplin 06235
Cheshire (1st) 06410
Chester (1st) 06412
Clinton (1st) 06413
Cobalt 06414
Colchester (1st) 06415
Colebrook 06021
Collinsville 06022
Columbia 06237
Corbins Corner, Br. Hartford ..06110
Cornwall 06753
Cornwall Bridge 06754
Cos Cob (1st) 06807
Coventry (1st) 06238
Cromwell (1st) 06416
Danbury (1st) 06810
Danielson (1st) 06239
Darien (1st) 06820
Dayville 06241
Deep River (1st) 06417
Derby (1st) 06418

Devon, Sta. Milford 06460
Durham 06422
East Berlin 06023
East Canaan 06024
East Derby, Sta. Derby 06418
East End, Sta. Waterbury 06705
East Glastonbury 06025
East Granby 06026
East Haddam 06423
East Hampton (1st) 06424
East Hartford, Br. Hartford
   (see appendix)
East Hartland 06027
East Haven, Br. New Haven ..06512
East Killingly 06243
East Lyme 06333
East Windsor Hill 06028
East Woodstock 06244
Eastford 06242
Easton 06425
Ellington 06029
Elmwood, Br. Hartford 06110
Enfield (1st) 06082
Essex (1st) 06426
Fabyan 06245
Fair Haven, Sta. New Haven ..06513
Fairfield (1st) 06430
Falls Village 06031
Farmington (1st) 06032
Fitchville 06334
Forestville, Sta. Bristol 06010
Gales Ferry (1st) 06335
   Ledyard, Sta. 06339
Garden, Br. Bridgeport 06611
Gaylordsville 06755
Georgetown (1st) 06829
Gilman 06336
Glasgo 06337
Glastonbury (1st) 06033
Glenbrook, Sta. Stamford 06906
Glenville, Sta. Greenwich 06830
Goshen 06756
Granby 06035
Grand Street, Sta.
   Waterbury 06701
Greens Farms 06436
Greenwich (1st) 06830
Grosvenor Dale 06246
Groton (1st) 06340
Groton Long Point, Sta.
   Groton 06340
Guilford (1st) 06437
Haddam 06438
Hadlyme 06439
Hamden, Br. New Haven
   (see appendix)
Hampton 06247
Hanover 06350
HARTFORD (1st) (see
   appendix)
Harwinton, Br. Torrington 06790
Hawleyville 06440
Hazardville, Sta. Enfield 06082
Hebron 06248
Higganum 06441
Hillside, Sta. Bridgeport 06610
Hotchkiss School, Sta.
   Lakeville 06039
Huntington, Sta. Shelton 06484
Ivoryton 06442
Jewett City (1st) 06351
Kensington (1st) 06037
Kent 06757
Kilby, Sta. New Haven 06519

Lakeside 06758
Lakeville (1st) 06039
Lebanon 06249
Ledyard, Sta. Gales Ferry 06339
Lisbon, R. Br. Jewett City 06351
Litchfield (1st) 06759
Madison (1st) 06443
Manchester (1st) 06040
Mansfield Center 06250
Mansfield Depot 06251
Maple Hill, Br. Hartford 06111
Marble Dale 06761
Marion 06444
Mechanicsville 06252
Melrose 06049
Meriden (1st) 06450
Merrow 06253
Middle Haddam 06456
Middlebury (1st) 06762
Middlefield (1st) 06455
Middletown (1st) 06457
Milford (1st) 06460
Milldale 06467
Monroe (1st) 06468
Montville 06353
Moodus 06469
Moosup 06354
Morris 06763
Mystic (1st) 06355
Naugatuck (1st) 06770
NEW BRITAIN (1st) (see
   appendix)
New Canaan (1st) 06840
New Fairfield, Br. Danbury 06810
New Hartford (1st) 06057
NEW HAVEN (1st) (see
   appendix)
New London (1st) 06320
New Milford (1st) 06776
New Preston 06777
Newfield, Sta. Bridgeport 06607
Newington, Br. Hartford 06111
Newtown (1st) 06470
Niantic (1st) 06357
Noank, Sta. Groton 06340
Noble, Sta. Bridgeport 06608
Norfolk 06058
Noroton, Sta. Darien 06820
Noroton Heights, Sta.
   Darien 06820
North Branford (1st) 06471
North Canton 06059
North End, Sta. Waterbury 06704
North Franklin 06254
North Granby 06060
North Grosvenordale 06255
North Haven (1st) 06473
North Stonington 06359
North Westchester 06474
North Windham 06256
North Woodstock 06257
Northfield 06778
Northford 06472
NORWALK (1st) (see
   appendix)
Norwich (1st) 06360
Oakdale 06370
Oakville (1st) 06779
Old Greenwich (1st) 06870
Old Lyme (1st) 06371
Old Mystic 06372
Old Saybrook (1st) 06475
Oneco 06373
Orange (1st) 06477

65

Oxford, R. Br. Seymour	06483
Parcel Post. Sta.	
Manchester	06040
Parcel Post, Sta. Milford	06460
Parcel Post Annex, Sta.	
Waterbury	06704
Pawcatuck, Br. Westerly, R I.	02891
Pequabuck	06781
Pine Meadow	06061
Pine Rock Park, R. Sta.	
Shelton	06484
Plainfield	06374
Plainville (1st)	06062
Plantsville (1st)	06479
Pleasant Valley	06063
Plymouth	06782
Pomfret	06258
Pomfret Center	06259
Poquonock	06064
Portland (1st)	06480
Prospect, Br. Waterbury	06712
Putnam (1st)	06260
Quaker Hill	06375
Quinebaug	06262
Redding	06875
Redding Ridge	06876
Ridgefield (1st)	06877
Ridgeway, Sta. Stamford	06905
Riverside (1st)	06878
Riverton	06065
Rockfall	06481
Rocky Hill (1st)	06067
Rogers	06263
Rowayton, Sta. Norwalk	06853
Roxbury	06783
Salisbury	06068
Samp Mortar, Sta. Fairfield	06430
Sandy Hook	06482
Saugatuck, Sta. Westport	06880
Scotland	06264
Seymour (1st)	06483
Sharon	06069
Shelton (1st)	06484
Sherman	06784
Short Beach, Sta. Branford	06405
Simsbury (1st)	06070
Somers	06071
Somersville	06072
South Britain	06487

South Glastonbury	06073
South Kent	06785
South Lyme	06376
South Meriden, Sta. Meriden	06450
South Wilington	06265
South Windham	06266
South Windsor (1st)	06074
South Woodstock	06267
Southbury (1st)	06488
Southington (1st)	06489
Southport (1st)	06490
Springdale, Sta Stamford	06907
Stafford	06075
Stafford Springs (1st)	06076
Staffordville	06077
STAMFORD (1st) (see appendix)	
Sterling	06377
Stevenson	06491
Stonington (1st)	06378
Stony Creek, Sta. Branford	06405
Storrs (1st)	06268
Submarine Base, Sta.	
Groton	06340
Suffield (1st)	06078
Taconic	06079
Taftville (1st)	06380
Tariffville	06081
Terminal, Sta. New Haven	06511
Terryville (1st)	06786
Thomaston (1st)	06787
Thompson	06277
Tolland (1st)	06084
Torrington (1st)	06790
Harwinton, Br.	06790
Trumbull, Br. Bridgeport	06611
Uncasville (1st)	06382
Union City, Sta. Naugatuck	06770
Unionville (1st)	06085
Vernon (1st)	06086
Versailles	06383
Voluntown	06384
Wallingford (1st)	06492
Warehouse Point (1st)	06088
Warren, R. Br. Cornwall	
Bridge	06754
Warrenville	06278
Washington	06793
Washington Depot	06794

WATERBURY (1st) (see appendix)	
Waterford (1st)	06385
Watertown (1st)	06795
Waterville, Sta Waterbury	06714
Wauregan	06387
Weatogue	06089
Wesleyan, Sta. Middletown	06457
West Cornwall	06796
West Granby	06090
West Hartford, Br Hartford (see appendix)	
West Hartland	06091
West Haven, Br. New Haven	06516
West Mystic	06388
West Putnam Avenue, Sta.	
Greenwich	06830
West Redding	06896
West Simsbury	06092
West Suffield	06093
West Willington	06279
Westbrook (1st)	06498
Weston, Br. Westport	06880
Westport (1st)	06880
Westville, Sta. New Haven	06515
Wethersfield, Br Hartford	06109
Whitneyville, Br. New Haven (see appendix)	
Wildemere Beach, Sta.	
Milford	06460
Willimantic (1st)	06226
Wilson, Sta. Windsor	06095
Wilton (1st)	06897
Winchester Center, R. Sta.	
Winsted	06094
Windham	06280
Windsor (1st)	06095
Windsor Locks (1st)	06096
Windsorville	06097
Winsted (1st)	06098
Winchester Center, R. Sta.	06094
Wolcott, Br. Waterbury	06716
Woodbury (1st)	06798
Woodmont, Sta. Milford	06460
Woodstock	06281
Woodstock Valley	06282
Yale, Sta. New Haven	06520
Yalesville, Sta. Wallingford	06492
Yantic	06389

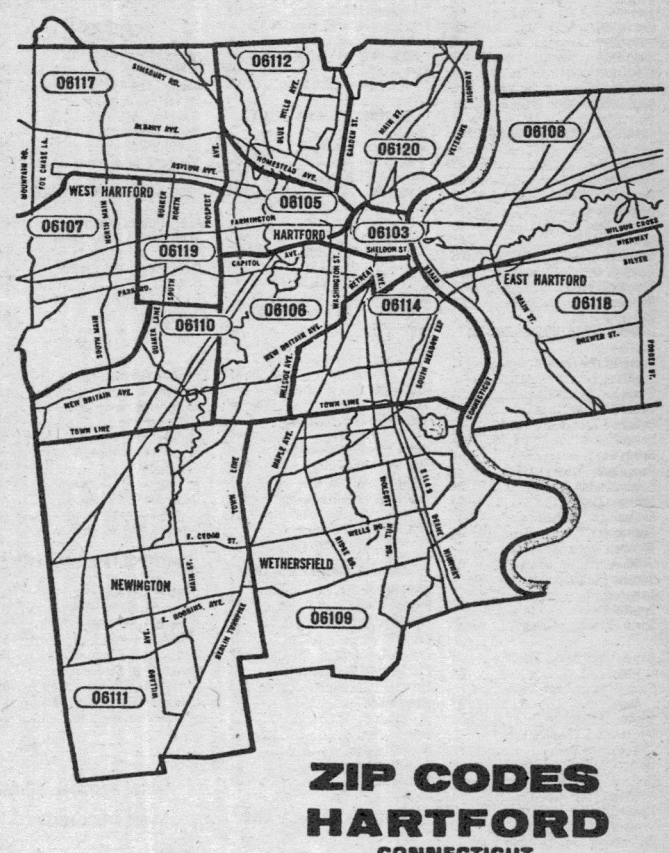

ZIP CODES
HARTFORD
CONNECTICUT

BRIDGEPORT 066

POST OFFICE BOXES

Box Nos.
1-400	Trumbull Br	11
1-1999	Main Office	01
2001-2999	Noble Sta	08
3000-3999	Barnum Sta	05
4000-4999	Newfield Sta	07
5000-5999	Hillside Sta	10
6000-6999	Beardsley Sta	06
9000-9200	Main Office	01

STATIONS, BRANCHES AND UNITS

Barnum Sta	05
Beardsley Sta	06
Center Br	11
Garden Br	11
Hillside Sta	10
Newfield Sta	07
Noble Sta	08
Trumbull Br	11
General Delivery	01
Postmaster	02

APARTMENTS, HOTELS, MOTELS

Barnum, 140 Fairfield Ave	03
Beardsley Terrace, Trumbull Ave	06
Canaan Village	10
Charles F Greene, Highland Ave	04
Father Panik Village	08
Harbor View Towers, 376 E Washington Ave	08
Marina Village	
P T Barnum, Taylor Dr	05
Pequonnock, Broad & Allen	04
Stratfield Motor Inn, 1241 Main	03
Success Park, Granfield & Success Av	10

BUILDINGS

City Savings Bank, 948 Main	03
Conn National Bank 886 Main	03
Jayson, 181 Middle	03
Mechanics & Farmers Bldg., 114 State St	03
Medical Center, 2660 Main	06
Medical, 144 Golden Hill	03
Newfield, 1188 Main	03
Peoples Saving Bank, 855 Main	03
Professional, 881 Lafayette Blvd	03
Raffel, 240 Fairfield Ave	03
Security, 1115 Main	03
Underwood-Commerce, 527 Broad	04
Warner, 83 Fairfield Ave	03

GOVERNMENT OFFICES

State Court House, 172 Golden Hill	04

US Court House & Federal Office Building 915
Lafayette Blvd	03

HOSPITALS

Bridgeport, 267 Grant	02
Emergency, 835 Washington Ave	04
Hillside Hospital, 540 Bond	10
Park City, 695 Park Ave	04
Saint Vincents, 2820 Main	06

UNIVERSITIES AND COLLEGES

Sacred Heart University, 5229 Park Ave	04
University Of Bridgeport, 285 Park Ave	02

HARTFORD 061

POST OFFICE BOXES

Box Nos.
1-2580	Main Office	01
3001-3999	Central Sta	03
6001-6999	Station A	06
7001-7999	West Hartford Br	07
8001-8999	East Hartford Br	08
9001-9999	Wethersfield Br	09
10001-10999	Elmwood Br	10
11001-11999	Newington Br	11
12001-12999	Blue Hills Sta	12
14001-14999	Barry Square Sta	14
17001-17999	Bishops Corners Br	17

STATIONS, BRANCHES AND UNITS

Barry Square Sta	14
Bishops Corner Br	17
Blue Hills Sta	12
Central Sta	03
Corbins Corner Br	10
East Hartford Br	08
Elmwood Br	10
Maple Hill Br	11
Newington Br	11
West Hartford Br	07
Wethersfield Br	09
General Delivery	01
Postmaster	01

APARTMENTS, HOTELS, MOTELS

Ambassador, 206 Farmington Ave	05
Briarcliff, 7 May	05
Hampshire House, 887 Farmington Av	19
Kingswood Court, 877 Farmington Ave	19
Packard, 745 Farmington Av	19
Shoreham, 440 Asylum	03
Sonesta, Constitution Plz	03
Statler-Hilton, 10 Ford	01

Westgate, Wickham Gardens, Woodland (column 3)

Westgate, 1248 Farmington	07
Wickham Gardens, 1267-1299 Burnside Ave	08
Willoughby, 330 Laurel	05
Woodland House, 31 Woodland	05

BUILDINGS

American Industrial, 983 Main	03
Capitol, 410 Asylum	03
Medical, 85 Jefferson	06
Municipal, 550 Main	03
Woodland Medical Center, 140 Woodland	05
100 Constitution Plaza	03

GOVERNMENT OFFICES

Federal Office, 450 Main	03
State Capitol, 210 Capitol Ave	15
State Office, 165 Capitol Ave	15
United States Post Office, 135 High	01

HOSPITALS

Hartford Hospital, 80 Seymour	15
Institute of Living, 200 Retreat Ave	02
Mt Sinai, 500 Blue Hills Ave	12
Newington Childrens'S Hospital	
St Francis, 114 Woodland St	05
University Of Connecticut Hospital - Mccook Div	12
Veterans, 555 Willard Ave	11

UNIVERSITIES AND COLLEGES

Hartford Seminary Foundation, 55 Elizabeth	05
Saint Josephs College, 1687 Asylum Ave	17
Trinity College, Summit	06
University Of Connecticut, 1280 Asylum Ave	05
University Of Hartford, 200 Bloomfield Ave	17

NEW BRITAIN 060

POST OFFICE BOXES

Box Nos.
1-1328	Main Office	50

STATIONS, BRANCHES AND UNITS

General Delivery	50
Postmaster	50

HOSPITALS

New Britain General, 100 Grand St	50

Appendix

New Britain (Con.)   060

New Britain Memorial, 2150
  Corbin Ave 50

UNIVERSITIES AND COLLEGES

Central Connecticut State
  College, 1615 Stanley St 50

NEW HAVEN   065

POST OFFICE BOXES

Box Nos.
1-210	Main Office	01
1-320	East Haven Br. ...	12
1-325	Fair Haven Sta.	13
1-392	West Haven Br. ..	16
1-3440	Yale Sta	20
211-506	Main Office	02
511-806	Main Office	03
811-1106	Main Office	04
1111-1406	Main Office	05
1411-1630	Main Office	06
1631-1810	Main Office	07
1811-1900	Main Office	08
1901-1970	Main Office	09
2901-3131	Westville Sta ...	25
3601-3994	Amity Br	15
4001-4380	Hamden Br.	14
5001-5548	Mount Carmel Br. ...	18
6001-6206	Whitneyville Br.	17
7001-7447	Kilby Sta.	19

RURAL ROUTES

1,2,3,4,5,6,7 25

STATIONS, BRANCHES AND UNITS

Amity Sta.	25
East Haven Br.	12
Fair Haven Sta.	13
Kilby Sta.	19
Terminal Sta.	11
West Haven Br	16
Westville Sta.	15
Yale Sta.	20
General Delivery	01
Postmaster	01

APARTMENTS, HOTELS, MOTELS

Crown Towers, 123 York	11
Duncan, 1151 Chapel	11
Holiday Inn O 1, 1605 Whalley Ave.	15
Holiday Inn O 2, 30 Whalley Ave.	11
Madison Towers, 111 Park	11
Midtown Motor Inn, 1157 Chapel.	11
Park Plaza, 155 Temple	10
Taft Hotel, 265 College	10

University Towers, 100 York.... 11
Ymca, 52 Howe.................... 11
Ywca, 42 Howe................... 11

BUILDINGS

Chapel Square, 900 Chapel...	10
Community Services Bldg. 1 State.	11
Knights Of Columbus Supr Hdg. Church.	07
Maltey, 2 Church	10
Medical Bldg, 2 Church So....	19
Penn. Central R.r. New Haven Dist.	06
Southern New England Telephone Co. 300 George.	06
US Post Office & Federal Bldg. 141 Church	10

HOSPITALS

Hospital Of Saint Raphael, 1450 Chapel	10
Physician & Surgeons, 198 Sherman Ave.	11
U. S. Veterans Hospital, West Spring	16
Yale-New Haven Community Hospital, 789 Howard Ave.	04

UNIVERSITIES AND COLLEGES

Albertus Magnus, 700 Prospect.	11
Quinnipiac College, Mt. Carmel Avenue	18
Southern Conn State College, 501 Crescent	15
Stone, 54 Wall.	07
University Of New Haven	05

NORWALK   068

POST OFFICE BOXES

Box Nos.
A-J	Rowayton Sta. ...	53
1-192	Rowayton Sta. ...	53
1-761	Norwalk Main Office.	56
1-940	Belden Sta.	52

RURAL ROUTES

1	51
2,3	50

STATIONS, BRANCHES AND UNITS

Belden Sta.	50
Rowayton Sta.	53
General Delivery	56
Postmaster	56

APARTMENTS, HOTELS, MOTELS

Admiral Motel, 377 Main Ave.	51
Carlton Court, Monterey Pl	54

Carver Apts, 43 Butler St 50
Clarmore, 1 Clarmore Dr.... 50
Dreamy Hollow, 41 Wolfpit
  Ave. 51
Elmcrest, 8 Elmcrest Tr.... 50
Flax Hill, 208 Flax Hill Rd ... 54
General Putman Inn, 1 Park
  St 51
Kingsley Garden, 11 Bedford
  Ave. 50
Meadow Garden, Meadow St... 54
Nor-West, 80 County St.... 51
Norwalk Motor Inn, 99 East
  Ave. 51
Overlook Terrace, 45 Maple
  St 50
Park Towers, 9-11 Park...... 51
Town House, 25 Monroe 54
Trinity, 17 Fairfield Ave 54

BUILDINGS

Executive House Bldg, 83 East Ave.	51
Frost Bldg, 520 West Ave.	50
W N L K Building, 64 Wall St.	50
50 Washington St Bldg.	54

GOVERNMENT OFFICES

Dept Of Internal Revenue, 83
  East Ave. 52

HOSPITALS

Norwalk Hospital, 24 Stevens
  St 56

UNIVERSITIES AND COLLEGES

Norwalk Community College,
  Highland Ave. 56

STAMFORD   069

POST OFFICE BOXES

Box Nos.
1-1999	Main Office	04
2000-2999	Glenbrook Sta.	06
3000-3999	Ridgeway Sta.	05
4000-4999	Springdale Sta.	07

STATIONS, BRANCHES AND UNITS

Glenbrook Sta.	06
Ridgeway Sta	05
Springdale Sta	07
General Delivery	04
Postmaster	04

APARTMENTS, HOTELS, MOTELS

Mayflower Gardens, Summer..	05
Morgan Manor, 83 Morgan St.	05
Roger Smith, 65 River	01

Stamford (Con.)   069

St John'S Towers, South & Willow	01
Stamford Motor, Main St & Seaside Ave	02
Woodside Village, Bridge St	05

BUILDINGS

Gurley, 322 Main	01
State National Bank Of Connecticut, 1 Atlantic	01
Union Trust Co, 300 Main	01
Washington Plaza 65 Washington Ave	02

GOVERNMENT OFFICES

Municipal Offices, 429 Atlantic St	01
Town Hall, Atlantic Square	01

HOSPITALS

Saint Josephs, 128 Strawberry Hill Ave	04
Stamford Hospital, 190 W Broad	02

UNIVERSITIES AND COLLEGES

Saint Basils, 14 Peveril Rd	02
University Of Connecticut, Scofieldtown Rd	03

WATERBURY   067

POST OFFICE BOXES

Box Nos.

1-2600	Main Office	20
3000-3999	East End Sta	05
4000-4999	Waterville Sta	14
5000-5999	North End Sta	04
6000-6999	Wolcott Br	16
7000-7200	Prospect Br	12

RURAL ROUTES

1	12

STATIONS, BRANCHES AND UNITS

East End Sta	05
Grand Street Sta	01
North End Sta	04
Parcel Post Annex Sta	04
Prospect Br	12
Waterville Sta	14
Wolcott Br	16
General Delivery	20
Postmaster	01

APARTMENTS, HOTELS, MOTELS

Alma, 32 Willow	10
Bernard, 174 Willow	10
Cables, 43 Prospect	02
Carroll, 44 Willow	10
Carrollton, 80 Willow	10
Glen Ridge, 7 Glenridge	10
Gloria, 261 Grove	10
Grove Hall, 38 Grove	10
Grove Manor, 145 Grove	10
Hitchcock, 164 W Main	02
Holiday Inn 82 South Elm Street	02
Howard Johnson'S Motor Lodge 2640 South Main Street	06
Kingsbury Incorporated, 44 Center	02
Northrop, 182 W Main	02
Palace, 94 E Main	20
Plaza, 365 Willow	10
Quality Motel Schraffts Drive	05
Ridgewood, 51 Ridgewood	10
Saint Regis, 330 E Main	02
Trinity, 41 Prospect	02
Waterbury Motor Inn Scott Road	05
Waterbury, 364 W Main	02
Watorian, 144 Grove	10

BUILDINGS

Apothecaries Hall, 63 Bank	02
Bergins Block, 246 E Main	02
Boys Club	05
Brown, 1 S Main	02
Brown, 20 E Main	02
Camps Block, 33 Center	02
Cassidy Patrick, 33 Leavenworth	02
Castle Memorial, 30 Central Ave	02

Chipman, 49 Center	02
Cowell-Guifoile, 186 Grand	02
Cowell-Guifoile, 65 Leavenworth	02
Farrington, 131 W Main	02
Fox-Poli, 84 E Main	02
G L D, 95 N Main	02
Garden, 162 E Main	02
Hampson, 91 W Main	02
Howland-Hughes Company, 110 Bank	20
Jefferson Sq., 1 Jefferson Sq.	06
Johnson Block, 111 Bank	02
Jones-Morgan, 96 Bank	02
Lilley, 103 W Main	02
Lincoln House, 35 Field	02
Masonic Temple, 156 W Main	02
Palomba, 100 Grand	02
Platt Irving, 1 E Main	02
Prichard, 187 Bank	02
Professional, 43 Central Ave	02
Russell, 73 & 230 Bank	02
Steele, 51 W Main	02
Telephone, 348 Grand	20
Telephone, 65 State	20
Waterbury National Bank, 193 Grand	02
Waterbury Trust Company, 132 Grand	02
Ymca, 136 W Main	02
Ywca, 80 Prospect	02

GOVERNMENT OFFICES

Court House, 7 Kendrick Ave	02
Federal Building 14 Cottage Pl	02
Post Office, 135 Grand	01

HOSPITALS

Saint Marys, 56 Franklin	02
Waterbury, 64 Robbins	20

UNIVERSITIES AND COLLEGES

Mattatuck Community College, 236 Grand	02
Mattatuck Community College, 411 Highland Ave	08
Post College, 800 Country Club Rd	08
University Of Connecticut, 32 Hillside Ave	10

DELAWARE
(Abbreviation: DE)

Bear	19701
Bellefonte, Br. Wilmington	19809
Bethany Beach	19930
Bethel	19931
Bridgeville	19933
Brookside, Br. Newark	19711
Camden-Wyoming (1st)	19934
Cannon	19935
Cheswold	19936
Christiana	19702
Clarksville	19937
Claymont (1st)	19703
Clayton (1st)	19938
Crossroads, Br. New Castle	19720
Dagsboro	19939
Delaware City	19706
Delmar	19940
Dewey Beach, R. Br. Rehoboth Beach	19971
Dover (1st)	19901
Dover A F B, Br. Dover	19901
Ellendale	19941
Farmington	19942
Federal, Sta. Newark	19711
Felton	19943
Fenwick Island, R. Br. Selbyville	19944

Frankford	19945
Frederica	19946
Georgetown (1st)	19947
Greenville, Br. Wilmington	19807
Greenwood	19950
Hamilton Park, Br. New Castle	19720
Harbeson	19951
Harrington (1st)	19952
Hartly	19953
Hockessin	19707
Houston	19954
Kenton	19955
Kirkwood	19708
Laurel (1st)	19956
Lewes (1st)	19958
Lincoln	19960
Little Creek	19961
Magnolia	19962
Manor, Br. New Castle	19720
Marshallton, Br. Wilmington	19808
Meadowood, Br. Newark	19711
Middletown	19709
Milford (1st)	19963
Millsboro (1st)	19966
Millville	19967
Milton	19968
Montchanin	19710
Nassau	19969
New Castle (1st)	19720

Newark (1st)	19711
Newport, Br. Wilmington	19804
Ocean View	19970
Odessa	19730
Ogletown, Br. Newark	19711
Polly Drummond, Br. Newark	19711
Port Penn	19731
Rambleton Acres, Br. New Castle	19720
Rehoboth Beach (1st)	19971
Rockland	19732
Rodney Village, Br. Dover	19901
Saint Georges	19733
Seaford (1st)	19973
Selbyville (1st)	19975
Fenwick Island, R. Br.	19944
Smyrna (1st)	19977
Stanton, Br. Wilmington	19804
Talleyville, Br. Wilmington	19803
Townsend	19734
Union Street, Sta. Wilmington	19805
Viola	19979
WILMINGTON (1st) (see appendix)	
Winterthur, R. Br. Wilmington	19735
Woodside	19980
Yorklyn	19736

Appendix

WILMINGTON   198

POST OFFICE BOXES

Box Nos.
1-2499	Main Office	99
2501-2999	Union Street Sta.	05
3001-3499	Newport Br	04
3501-4499	Greenville Br	07
5001-5499	Marshallton Br	08
6001-6499	Stanton Br	04
7001-7499	Talleyville Br	03

STATIONS, BRANCHES AND UNITS

Bellefonte Br	09
Greenville Br	07
Marshallton Br	08
Newport Br	04
Stanton Br	04
Talleyville Br	03
Union Street Sta.	05
Winterthur Rural Br	19735
General Delivery	99
Postmaster	99

APARTMENTS, HOTELS, MOTELS

Brandywine Hundred Apts.	03
Cedar Tree Apts	10
Clifton Park	02
Darling Court	06
Denbigh Hall	06
Devon	06
Dorset	06
Du Pont	99
Electra Arms	02
Foster Park	05
Fourteen-O-One	06
Kynlyn	09
Lancaster Court	99
Lord De La Warr	99
Mayfair	06
Monroe Park	07
Parklyn	05
Plaza	06
Rockford Park	06
Rockford Tower	06
Rodney Court	06
Stratford Apts.	10
Towne House	06
Woodland	05

BUILDINGS

Bank Of Delaware	01
Continental American	01
Delaware Trust	01
Di Sabatino	01
Du Pont	01
E I Du Pont De Nemours & Company Incorporated	98
Farmers Bank	01
Federal	01
Market Twr	01
Municipal	01
Nemours	01
Wilmington Trust	01
Wilmington Twr	01

HOSPITALS

A I Du Pont Institute	99
Delaware	99
Emily P Bissell	08
Eugene Du Pont Memorial	07
Memorial	99
Riverside	99
Saint Francis	05
Veterans Administration	05
Wilmington General	99

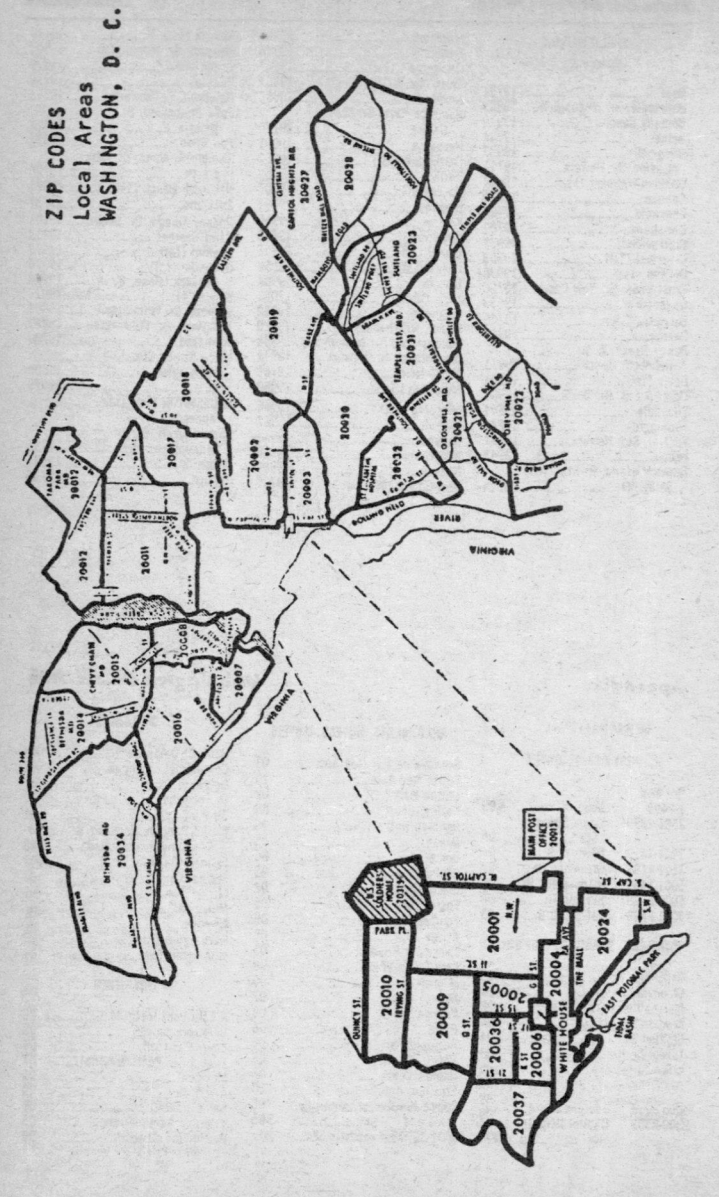

ZIP CODES
Local Areas
WASHINGTON, D. C.

DISTRICT OF COLUMBIA
(Abbreviation: DC)

Anacostie, Sta. Washington...20020
Benjamin Franklin, Sta.
  Washington...................20044
Benning, Sta. Washington....20019
Bolling A F B, Sta.
  Washington...................20332
Brightwood, Sta.
  Washington...................20011
Brookland, Sta. Washington...20017
Calvert, Sta. Washington.....20007
Cardinal, Sta. Washington....20017
Central, Sta. Washington......20005
Cleveland Park, Sta.
  Washington...................20008
Columbia Heights, Sta.
  Washington (see
  appendix)
Congress Heights, Sta.
  Washington...................20032
Customs House, Sta.
  Washington...................20018

Eagle, Sta. Washington........20016
F Street, Sta. Washington.....20004
Fort Davis, Sta. Washington...20020
Fort Mc Nair, Sta.
  Washington...................20315
Friendship, Sta. Washington...20016
Georgetown, Sta.
  Washington...................20007
Hoya, Sta. Washington........20007
Kalorama, Sta. Washington...20009
Kendall Green, Sta.
  Washington...................20002
Mid City, Sta. Washington....20005
National Airport, Sta.
  Washington...................20001
Naval Research Laboratory,
  Sta. Washington............20390
Naval Station, Sta.
  Washington...................20390
Northeast, Sta. Washington...20002
Northwest, Sta. Washington...20015
Palisades, Sta. Washington...20016
Park View, Sta. Washington...20010

Petworth, Sta. Washington....20011
Randle, Sta. Washington 20020
Southeast, Sta. Washington...20003
Southwest, Sta. Washington...20024
State Department, Sta.
  Washington...................20520
T Street, Sta. Washington.....20009
Temple Heights, Sta.
  Washington...................20009
Treasury, Sta. Washington....20220
Truxton Circle, Sta.
  Washington...................20002
Twentieth Street, Sta.
  Washington (see
  appendix)
Walter Reed, Sta.
  Washington...................20012
WASHINGTON (1st) (see
  appendix)
Watergate, Sta. Washington...20037
West End, Sta. Washington...20037
Woodley Road, Sta.
  Washington...................20008
Woodridge, Sta. Washington...20018

Appendix

Washington

WASHINGTON	200

POST OFFICE BOXES

Box Nos.
1-999	Benjamin Franklin Sta	44
1000-2999	Main Office	13
3000-3499	Columbia Heights Sta	10
3500-3999	Georgetown Sta	07
4000-4199	Chevy Chase Br	15
4200-4399	Takoma Park Br	12
4400-4599	Brookland Sta	17
4600-4799	Anacostia Sta	20
4800-4999	Cleveland Park Sta	08
5000-5199	Benning Sta	19
5200-5499	Seat Pleasant Br	27
5500-5699	Friendship Sta	16
5700-5999	Bethesda Br	14
6000-6099	Mid City Sta	05
6100-6199	Benjamin Franklin Sta	44
6200-6399	Northwest Sta	15
6400-6699	T Street Sta	09
6700-6899	Fort Davis Sta	20
6900-7099	Congress Heights Sta	32
7100-7999	Benjamin Franklin Sta	44
8000-8299	Southwest Sta	24
8300-8599	Capitol Heights Br	27

8600-8799	Brightwood Sta	11
8801-9099	Southeast Sta	03
9100-9299	Suitland Br	23
9300-9399	Mid City Sta	05
9401-9599	Calvert Sta	07
9600-9799	Friendship Sta	16
9800-9999	Chevy Chase Br	15
10000-10299	Woodridge Sta	18
10301-10499	Oxon Hill Br	21
11001-11999	Cleveland Park Sta	08
12001-12999	Mid City Sta	05
13001-13999	T Street Sta	09
14001-14999	Benjamin Franklin Sta	44
16001-16999	Suitland Br	23
17001-17999	Dulles International Airport br	41
18001-18999	Oxon Hill Br	21
19001-19999	Twentieth Street Sta	36
21001-21999	Kalorama Sta	09
22001-22999	Northeast Sta	02
26001-26999	Truxton Circle Sta	02
28001-28999	Central Sta	05
29001-29052	Brookland Sta	17
30001-30399	Bethesda Br	14
31001-31252	Temple Hills Br	31
33001-33499	District Heights Br	28
34001-34999	West Bethesda Br	34
38001-38999	Anacostia Sta	20

39001-39999	Friendship Sta	16
40001-40999	Palisades Sta	16

STATIONS, BRANCHES AND UNITS

Anacostia Sta	20
Andrews A F B Br	20331
Andrews Air Force Hospital Br	20331
Benjamin Franklin Sta	44
Benning Sta	19
Bethesda Br	14
Bolling A F B Sta	20332
Brightwood Sta	11
Brookland Sta	17
Calvert Sta	07
Camp Springs Br	31
Capitol Heights Br	27
Cardinal Sta	17
Central Sta	05
Chevy Chase Br	15
Cleveland Park Sta	08
Columbia Heights Sta	09
Congress Heights Sta	32
Customs House Sta	18
District Heights Br	28
Dulles International Airport Br	41
Eagle Sta	16
F Street Sta	04
Fort Davis Sta	20
Fort Mc Nair Sta	20315
Friendship Sta	16
Georgetown Sta	07
Hoya Sta	07
Kalorama Sta	09
Kendall Green Sta	02
Marlow Heights Br	31
Mid City Sta	05
National Airport Sta	01

Washington, D.C. (Con.)   200

National Naval Med Center
Br.................................... 14
Naval Air Facility Br............20390
Naval Research Laboratory
Sta..................................20390
Naval Station Sta................20390
Navy Annex Br....................20370
Northeast Sta...................... 02
Northwest Sta...................... 15
Oxon Hill Br........................ 21
Palisades Sta...................... 16
Park View Sta...................... 10
Pentagon Br........................20301
Petworth Sta........................ 11
Randle Sta.......................... 20
Seat Pleasant Br.................. 27
Southeast Sta...................... 03
Southwest Sta...................... 24
State Department Sta............20520
Suitland Br........................ 23
T Street Sta........................ 09
Takoma Park Br.................... 12
Temple Heights Sta.............. 09
Temple Hills Br.................... 31
Treasury Sta........................20220
Truxton Circle Sta................ 02
Twentieth Street Sta............ 06
U S Naval Communications
CtrBr................................20390
Walter Reed Sta.................. 12
Watergate Sta...................... 37
West Bethesda Br................ 34
West End Sta........................ 37
Woodley Road Sta................ 08
Woodridge Sta...................... 18
General Delivery.................. 13
Postmaster.......................... 13

APARTMENTS, HOTELS, MOTELS

Aberdeen Hall, Mclean
Gardens, 3415 38th N. W. . 16
Alban Towers, 3700
Massachusetts Ave NW 16
Albermarle House, 4501
Connecticut Ave NW 08
Albert Pick Motor Inn, 1201
K, NW................................ 05
Ambassador, 1412 K NW...... 05
Annapolis, 1111 H, NW........ 05
Army Navy Club, 1627 I, NW 06
Bay State, 1701
Massachusetts Ave NW 36
Bellevue, 15 E NW................ 01
Benning Hall, Mclean
Gardens, 3445 38th N. W. 16
Berkshire, 4201
Massachusetts Ave NW 16
Boston House, 1711
Massachusetts Ave N. W. .. 36
Brandywine, 4545
Connecticut Ave NW 08
Brighton, 2123 California
NW.................................... 08
Brittany, 5432 Connecticut
Ave NW.............................. 15
Broadmoor, 3601 Connecticut
Ave NW.............................. 08
Brunswick, 1414 17th
NW.................................... 36

Burlington, 1120 Vermont
Ave NW.............................. 05
Cairo, 1615 Q NW................ 09
Calvert Woodley, 2601
Woodley Place NW............ 08
Cambridge, 921 19th NW...... 06
Capitol Park, 800 4th SW..... 24
Carillon, 2500 Wisconsin Ave
NW.................................... 07
Carlyn, 2500 Q NW.............. 07
Cathedral Mansions............ 08
Cavalier, 3500 14th NW........ 10
Chalfonte, 1601 Argonne Pl
NW.................................... 09
Chancery, 3130 Wisconsin
Ave NW.............................. 16
Chanute Hall, Mclean
Gardens, 3800 Porter N W. 16
Chase Plaza, 5406
Connecticut Ave NW 15
Chastleton, 1701 16th NW.... 09
Chesapeake, 4607
Connecticut Ave NW 08
Chesterfield, 3315 Wisconsin
Ave NW.............................. 16
Chillum Manor, 5320 Rock
Creek Church Rd NE.......... 11
Clifton Terrace, 1300-1350
Clifton NW.......................... 09
Commodore, 520-530 North
Capitol.............................. 01
Conard, 1228 I NW.............. 05
Congressional, 300 New
Jersey Ave SE.................... 03
Connecticut House, 4500
Connecticut Av NW............ 08
Coronet, 200 C SE................ 03
Cosmos Club, 2121
Massachusetts Ave NW 08
Crestwood, 3900 16th NW.... 11
Croydon, 1815 17th NW........ 09
Davenport Terrace, 3511
Davenport NW.................... 08
Davenport Terrace, 4817
36th NW.............................. 08
Delano, 2745 29th NW.......... 08
Devans Hall, Mclean
Gardens, 20 Plattsburg Ct
NW.................................... 16
Devonshire Courts,
4105&4115 Wisconsin Ave
NW.................................... 16
Diplomat, 2420 16th NW...... 09
Dodge, 20 E NW.................. 01
Dorchester House, 2480 16th
NW.................................... 09
Drake, 2119 H NW................ 37
Dresden, 2126 Connecticut
Ave NW.............................. 08
Dunbar, 2105 15th NW.......... 09
Dupont Plaza, 1500 New
Hampshire Ave NW............ 36
Ebbitt, 10 & H NW................ 01
Elise, 825 New Hampshire
Ave NW.............................. 37
Embassy, 1613 Harvard N W. 09
Empire, 2000 F NW.............. 06
Envoy Towers, 2400 16th NW. 09
Envoy, 2144 California NW.... 08
Essex, 4740 Connecticut Ave
NW.................................... 08

Eustis Hall, Mclean Gardens,
3831 Porter NW.................. 16
Evangeline, 1330 L NW........ 05
Everglades, 2223 H NW........ 37
Executive House, 1515 Rhode
Island Ave NW.................... 05
Fairfax, 2100 Massachusetts
Ave NW.............................. 08
Frankford Hall, Mclean
Gardens, 40 Plattsburg Ct
N W.................................... 16
Frontenac, 4550 Connecticut
NW.................................... 08
Gadsden Hall, Mclean
Gardens, 30 Plattsburg Ct
NW.................................... 16
Garfield, 5410 Connecticut
NW.................................... 15
Gelmarc Towers, 1930
Columbia Rd NW................ 09
General Scott, 1 Scott Cir
NW.................................... 36
Governor Shepherd, 2121
Virginia Ave NW................ 37
Gramercy Inn, 1616 Rhode
Island Ave NW.................... 36
Granite State, 1731 New
Hampshire Ave NW............ 09
Greenbrier, 4301
Massachusetts Ave NW 16
Greystone, 815 18th NW...... 06
Guthridge, 2115 F NW.......... 37
Greenwood, 1020 19th NW.... 36
Hamilton, 1001 14th NW...... 05
Hampshire Gardens, 4900
New Hampshire Ave NW 11
Hampton Court, 2013 New
Hampshire Ave NW............ 09
Hancock Hall, Mclean
Gardens, 3665 38th N W.... 16
Harrington, 11th & E NW...... 04
Hartnett Hall, 1426 21st NW. 36
Harvard Hall, 1650 Harvard
NW.................................... 09
Hay Adams House, 800 16th
NW.................................... 06
Hotel Sonesta, 10 Thomas
Cir NW.............................. 05
Huntington, 5225
Connecticut Ave NW 15
Idaho Terrace, 3040 Idaho
Ave NW.............................. 16
Jefferson Hall, Mclean
Gardens, 3685 38th N W.... 16
Jefferson, 1200 16th NW...... 36
John Paul Jones, 1717 G NW. 06
Kenesaw, 3060 16th NW...... 09
Kenmore, 5415 Connecticut
Ave NW.............................. 15
Kennedy-Warren, 3133
Connecticut Ave NW 08
Kenwood House, 5100 Dorset
Ave (Md)............................ 15
Kew Gardens, 2700 Q NW.... 07
La Reine, 5425 Connecticut
Ave NW.............................. 15
La Salle, 1028 Connecticut
Ave NW.............................. 36
Le Bourget, 2127 California
NW.................................... 08
Lenshire House, 3140
Wisconsin Ave NW............ 16

Washington, D.C. (Con.)   200

Lombardy, 2019 I NW 06
Madison, 1177 15th NW 05
Majestic, 3200 16th NW 10
Marcheta, 1121 New
   Hampshire Ave NW 37
Marlyn, 3000 39th NW 16
Marriott Key Bridge Motor
   Hotel, Key Bridge 07
Marriott Motor Hotel, Twin
   Bridges On US 1 01
Maryland Courts, 518 9th
   NE 02
Maryland Courts, 816 E NE 02
Mayflower, 1127 Connecticut
   Ave NW 36
Mclean Gardens, 3811 Porter
   N W 16
Melwood, 1803 Biltmore NW 09
Meridian Hill, 2601 16th NW ... 09
Metropolitan Club, 1700 H
   NW 06
Metropolitan, 200 Rhode
   Island Ave NE 02
Milton Hall, 2222 I NW 37
Miramar, 1301 15th NW 05
New Amsterdam, 2701 14th
   NW 09
Normandie, 6817 Georgia Ave
   NW 12
North Brook Courts, 3426
   16th NW 10
Ogden Gardens, 1445 Ogden
   NW 10
Ontario, 2853 Ontario Rd
   NW 09
Pall Mall, 1112 16th NW 36
Park Central, 705 18th NW 05
Park Lane, 2025 I NW 06
Park Plaza, 1629 Columbia
   Rd NW 09
Pennsylvania Hotel, 20 F NW .. 05
Pick-Lee House, 15th & L
   NW 05
Potomac Plaza, 2475 Virginia
   Ave NW 37
President, 2141 I NW 37
Presidential Apts, 1026 16th
   NW 36
Presidential Hotel, 900 19th
   NW 06
Quebec House North, 2801
   Quebec NW 08
Quebec House South, 2800
   Quebec NW 08
Rhode Island Plaza, 2705
   13th NE 18
Rittenhouse, 6101 16th NW 11
Roger Smith, 18th &
   Pennsylvania Ave NW 06
Roosevelt, 2101 16th NW 09
Saxony, 1801 Clydesdale Pl
   NW 09
Schenley, 2121 H NW 37
Schuyler Arms, 1954
   Columbia Rd NW 09
Sedgewick Gardens, 3726
   Connecticut Ave NW 08
Sheraton Carlton, 923 16th
   NW 06

Sheraton Park, 2660 Woodley
   Rd NW 08
Shoreham, 2500 Calvert NW 08
South Brook Courts, 3420
   16th NW 10
State House, 2122
   Massachusetts Ave NW 08
Statler Hilton, 16th & K NW ... 36
Stratford, 25 E NW 01
Tilden Gardens, 3900
   Connecticut Ave NW 08
Touraine, 1630 R NW 09
Town House, 601 19th NW 06
Trinity Towers, 3023 14th
   NW 09
University Club, 1135 16th
   NW 36
Valley Vista, 2032 Belmont
   Rd NW 09
Wakefield Hall, 2101 New
   Hampshire Ave NW 09
Washington Circle, 2430
   Pennsylvania Ave NW 37
Washington Hilton, 1919
   Connecticut Ave NW 09
Washington Hotel, 15th &
   Pennsylvania Ave NW 04
Washington House, 2120
   16th NW 09
Watergate East, 2500
   Virginia Ave., N.w. 37
Watergate Hotel, 2650
   Virginia Ave., N.w. 37
Watergate South, 700 New
   Hampshire Ave., N.w. 37
Watergate West, 2700
   Virginia Ave., N.w. 37
Westchester, 3900 & 4000
   Cathedral Ave NW 16
Willard, 14th & Pennsylvania
   Ave NW 04
Wiltshire Crescent, 3801
   Connecticut Ave NW 08
Wiltshire Parkway, 3701
   Connecticut Ave NW 68
Windemere, 1825 New
   Hampshire Ave NW 09
Windsor Park, 2300
   Connecticut Ave NW 08
Winthrop House, 1727
   Massachusetts Ave NW 36
Woodley Park Towers, 2737
   Devonshire Pl NW 08
Woodner, 3636 16th NW 10
Wyoming, 2022 Columbia Rd
   NW 09
York, 532 20th NW 06
Young Men'S Christian
   Association, 1726-1736 G
   NW 06

BUILDINGS

A F Of L-C I O, 16th NW 06
Acacia Life Insurance, 51
   Louisiana Ave NW 01
Adams, 1333 F NW 04
Air Rights, 7315 Wisconsin
   Ave (Md) 14
Ajax, 1107 19th NW 36
Albee, 1426 G NW 05

Altimont, 4929 Bethesda Ave
   (Md) 14
American Council On
   Education, 1785
   Massachusetts Ave NW 36
American Security, 730 15th
   NW 05
American, 1317 F NW 04
Andrew Jackson, 806
   Connecticut Ave NW 06
Appeals, 426 5th NW 01
Associations, 1145 19th NW ... 36
Atlas, 527 9th NW 04
Baker, 1320 F NW 04
Barlow, 5454 Wisconsin Ave
   (Md) 15
Barnabas, 4400 Stamp Rd
   SE (Md) 31
Barr, 910 17th NW 06
Barrister, 635 F NW 04
Becker, 1314 F NW 04
Bender, 1120 Connecticut
   Ave NW 36
Bethesda (The), 4725
   Bethesda Ave (Md) 14
Bethesda Bank, 7500
   Wisconsin Ave (Md) 14
Bethesda Bradley, 6900
   Wisconsin Ave (Md) 15
Bond, 1404 New York Ave
   NW 05
Boss & Phelps, 1417 K NW 05
Bowen, 815 15th NW 05
Bragg, 705 12th NW 05
Brawner, 888 17th NW 06
Brookings, 1775
   Massachusetts Ave NW 36
Cafritz, 1625 I NW 06
Carpenters, 1003 K NW 01
Carry, 927 15th NW 05
Central National Bank, 631
   Pennsylvania Ave NW 04
Central, 805 G NW 01
Century, 412 5th NW 01
Chamber Of Commerce, U. S.
   1615 H N W 06
Chandler, 1427 I NW 05
City Bank, 1612 K NW 06
City Post Office, N Capital &
   Mass Ave 13
Coal, 1130 17th NW 36
Colonial, 923 15th NW 05
Colorado, 1341 G NW 05
Columbia Medical, 1835 I
   NW 06
Columbian, 416 5th NW 01
Commerce, 1700 K NW 06
Commonwealth, 1625 K NW 06
Communications, 710 14th
   NW 05
Continental, 1012 14th NW 05
Daily News, 1013 13th NW 05
De Moll, 700 12th NW 05
De Sales, 1741 De Sales NW ... 36
Denrike, 1010 Vermont Ave
   NW 05
District National Bank, 1406
   G NW 05
District Of Columbia National
   Bank, 1812 K NW 06
District, 14th & Pennsylvania
   NW 04

Dupont Circle, 1344-1346 Connecticut Ave NW 36
Duryea, 1101 Connecticut Ave NW 36
Editors, 1729 H NW 06
Edmonds, 917 15th NW 05
Electrical Workers, 1200 15th NW 05
Engineers, 921 17th NW 05
Enterprise, 1718 I NW 06
Equitable Life Insurance, 3900 Wisconsin Ave NW 16
Evans, 1420 New York Ave NW 05
Executive, 1030 15th NW 05
Farragut, 900 17th NW 06
Federal, 1522 K NW 05
Federation, 817 14th NW 05
Fleming, 800 17th NW 05
Folger, 725 15th NW 05
Franklin Square North, 1325 K NW 05
Franklin, 1327 F NW 04
Georgetown, 2233 Wisconsin Ave NW 07
Glover & Flather, 1508 H NW 05
Headquarters, 2002 P NW 36
Heurich, 1627 K NW 06
Hibbs, 723 15th NW 05
Hill, 839 17th NW 06
Homer, 601 13th NW 04
Hyde, 7979 Old Georgetown Rd (Md) 14
Indiana, 633 Indiana Ave NW 04
International Telephone & Telegraph, 1707 L NW 05
International, 1319 F NW 04
Investment, 1511 K NW 05
Jefferson, 1225 19th NW 36
Jordan, 1301 G NW 05
Judiciary, 601 Indiana Ave NW 04
Le Droit, 802 F NW 04
Lenox, 1523 L NW 05
Lewis, 2001 11th NW 01
Lincoln, 514 10th NW 04
Machinist, 1300 Connecticut Ave NW 05
Madison, 1155 15th NW 05
Marlo - Edgemoor, 4801 Montgomery Ln (Md) 14
Marsh, 1832 M NW 36
Mather, 916 G NW 01
Mc Gill, 910 G NW 01
Mc Kim, 1311 G NW 05
Mc Lachlen, 666 11th NW 01
Medical Science, 1029 Vermont Ave NW 05
Mercury, 1925 K NW 06
Methodist, 100 Maryland Ave NE 02
Metropolis, 201 Pennsylvania Ave SE 03
Metropolitan Bank, 613 15th NW 05
Mills, 1700 Pennsylvania Ave N W 06
Montgomery, 4720 Montgomery Ln (Md) 14
Municipal, 300 Indiana Ave NW 01
Munsey, 1329 E NW 04

Mutual, 1309 L NW 05
N A D A, 2000 K NW 06
National Assoc Of Letter Carriers, 100 Indiana Ave NW 01
National Bank, 6917 Arlington Rd (Md) 14
National Grange, 1616 H NW 06
National Press, 529 14th NW 04
National Savings & Trust, 719 15th NW 05
National Union, 918 F NW 04
Naval Lodge Hall, 328 Pennsylvania Ave SE 03
New Medical, 1726 I NW 06
Northwestern, 1800 G NW 06
Occidental, 1411 Pennsylvania Ave NW 04
Ocean Sciences, 4905 Del Ray Ave (Md) 14
Octagon, 1741 New York Ave NW 06
Operations Engineers, 1125 17th NW 36
Oriental, 600 F NW 04
Otis, 810 18th NW 06
Parkwood Medical, 1746 K 06
Pennsylvania, 425 13th NW 04
Peoples Life Insurance, 601 New Hampshire Ave NW 37
Perpetual, 1111 E NW 04
Philips, 4915 Saint Elmo Ave (Md) 14
Premier, 1725 I NW 06
Professional Arts, 1722 I NW 06
Prudential Bank, 1334 G NW 05
Public Employee Union, 815 Mount Vernon Pl NW 01
Public National Bank, 1430 K NW 05
R C A, 1725 K NW 06
Realty, 1424 K NW 05
Richards (The), 6935 Arlington Rd (Md) 14
Riddell, 1730 K NW 06
Riggs National Bank, 1503 Pennsylvania Ave NW 05
Ring, 1200 18th NW 36
Rust, 1001 15th NW 05
Saint Albans, 1419 H NW 05
Saul, 925 15th NW 05
Securities, 729 15th NW 05
Semmes Riggs, Dupont Cir NW 36
Sheraton, 711 14th NW 05
Shoreham, 806 15th NW 05
Solar, 1000 16th NW 36
Southern Railroad, 920 15th NW 05
Southern, 1425 K NW 05
Taft, 1603 K NW 06
Tivoli, 3313 14th NW 10
Tower, 1403 K NW 05
Trades Unionist, 720 5th NW 01
Trailways, 1200 I NW 05
Trans-Lux, 724 14th NW 05
Trans-World Airline, 1026 17th NW 36
Transporation, 815 17th NW 06
Union Trust, 740 15th NW 05
United Assn, 901 Massachusetts Ave NW 01

Universal, North, 1875 Connecticut Ave NW 09
Universal, 1825 Connecticut Ave NW 09
Vanguard, 1111 20th NW 36
Vermont, 1100 Vermont Ave NW 05
Victor, 724 9th NW 01
Walker, 734 15th NW 05
Warner, 501 13th NW 04
Washington Evening Star, 225 Virginia Avenue SE 03
Washington Gas Light, 740 11th NW 01
Washington Loan & Trust, 9th & F NW 04
Washington Medical, 1801 I NW 06
Washington Post, 1150 15th N.w. 05
Washington, 15th & New York Ave NW 05
Wender, 2026 I NW 06
Western Union, 1405 G NW 05
Westory, 605 14th NW 05
Whitfield Professional, Branch Ave & Colebrook Dr SE (Md) 31
Whitford, 424 5th NW 01
Wilico, 7824 Eastern Ave NW 12
Wire, 1000 Vermont Ave NW 05
Wiscon, 7550 Wisconsin Ave (Md) 14
Woodward, 733 15th NW 05
World Center, 918 16th NW 06
Wyatt, 777 14th NW 05

GOVERNMENT OFFICES

Administrative Office, U S Courts 20544
Advisory Commission On Intergovermental Relations 20575
Agency For International Development (A I D) 20523
Agriculture, Dept Of (Offices At Headquarters) 20250
Agriculture, Dept Of (Other Offices) 20251
Air Force, Dept Of (Offices At Headquarters-Pentagon) 20330
Air Force, Dept Of (Offices In Forrestal Bldg) 20314
Air Force, Dept Of (Other Offices) 20333
American Revolution Bicentennial Commission 06
Architect Of The Capitol 20515
Arlington Annex, Marines Headquarters 20388
Arlington Annex, Navy 20378
Arms Control And Disarmament Agency, U S (Field Oper Off) 20451
Army-Air Force Recruiting Station 04
Army, Dept Of (Offices At Headquarters-Pentagon) 20310
Army, Dept Of (Offices In Forrestal Bldg) 20314
Army, Dept Of (Other Offices) 20315

Washington, D.C. (Con.) 200

Atomic Energy Commission,
U S................................20545
Board Of Governors Of The
Federal Reserve System.....20551
Bureau Of Employees
Compensation (Labor) 20211
Bureau Of Standards,
National 20234
Capitol Building, Architect......20515
Capitol Building, House Of
Representatives.................20519
Capitol Building, United
States Senate 20510
Census Bureau 20233
Central Intelligence Agency
(C I A).............................20505
Civil Aeronautics Board 20428
Civil Service Commission, U
S.................................20415
Coast Guard, U S 20591
Commerce, Dept Of (Offices
At Headquarters)...............20230
Commerce, Dept Of (Other
Offices) 20235
Commerce, Dept Of, Bureau
Of Census 20233
Commerce, Dept Of, National
Bureau Of Standards..........20234
Commerce, Dept Of, Patent
Office 20231
Commission On Civil Rights...20425
Court Of Customs And Patent
Appeals, U S....................20439
Court Of Military Appeals, U
S.................................20442
Defense, Dept Of (Offices At
Headquarters-Pentagon) 20301
Defense, Dept Of (Other
Offices) 20305
Environmental Protection
Agency...........................20460
Equal Employment
Opportunity Commission.....20506
Exec Offices Of The President
C I A 20505
Exec Offices Of The
President, (Other
Organizations)..................20506
Exec Offices Of The
President, Mgmt, Budget
Off................................20503
Exec Offices Of The
President, N. A. S. C..........20502
Exec Offices Of The
President, Office Of Emerg
Prep'Dness 20504
Exec Offices Of The
President, The White
House Office 20500
Export Import Bank Of
Washington 20571
Farm Credit Administration ...20578
Federal Aviation
Administration..................20590
Federal Bureau Of
Investigation (F B I)...........20535
Federal Communications
Commission 20554
Federal Deposit Insurance
Corporation 20429

Federal Home Loan Bank
Board 20552
Federal Housing
Administration,
Comptroller (H U D)........20412
Federal Housing
Administration, Main, (H U
D)...............................20411
Federal Maritime
Commission, U S............20573
Federal Mediation And
Conciliation Service 20427
Federal Metal And Non-
Metallic Safety Board Of
Review 09
Federal National Mortgage
Association (H U D)........... 05
Federal Power Commission ...20426
Federal Records Center (G S
A).............................20409
Federal Reserve System,
Board Of Governors 20551
Federal Trade Commission ...20580
Food And Agriculture
Organization Of The
United Nations................20437
Food And Drug
Administration (H E W)......20204
Foreign Claims Settlement
Commission, U S............20579
Foreign Service Posts And
Mail Room (State Dept).....20521
General Accounting Office 20548
General Services
Administration (G S A
Headquarters).................20405
General Services
Administration, Crystal
Mall Bldg. 4..................20406
General Services
Administration, Federal
Records Ctr 20409
General Services
Administration, National
Archives 20408
General Services
Administration, Region 3 ...20407
Government Printing Office.....20401
Government Printing Office,
Field Service Division 20403
Government Printing Office,
Superintendent Of
Documents 20402
H E W, Food And Drug
Administration................20204
H E W, National Institutes Of
Health 14
H E W, Office Of Education ...20202
Harry Diamond Laboratories ...20438
Health, Education And
Welfare, Dept Of
(Headquarters)................20201
Health, Education And
Welfare, Dept Of (Other
Offices) 20203
House Of Representatives
And Office Buildings 20515
Housing And Urban
Development, Dept Of
(Headquarters)................20410
Housing Assistance
Administration (H U D).....20413
Immigration And
Naturalization Service.......20536

Inter American Defense
Board 20441
Inter American Development
Bank 20577
Interior, Dept Of
(Headquarters)...............20240
Interior, Dept Of (Other
Offices) 20242
Internal Revenue Service
(Int'L) Treasury Dept 20225
Internal Revenue Service,
Treasury Dept 20224
International Bank For
Reconstruction And
Development 20433
International Joint
Commission - U S And
Canada 20440
International Monetary Fund ...20431
Interstate Commerce
Commission 20423
J F Kennedy Center For
Performing Arts..............20566
Justice, Dept Of
(Headquarters)...............20530
Justice, Dept Of (Other
Offices) 20537
Justice, Dept Of Immigration
And Naturalization Service.20536
Justice, Dept Of, Federal
Bureau Of Investigation ...20535
Labor, Dept Of
(Headquarters)...............20210
Labor, Dept Of (Other
Offices) 20212
Labor, Dept Of, Bureau Of
Employees Compensation ...20211
Lib Of Congress, Div Of
Blind 20542
Library Of Congress 20548
Library Of Congress, Card
Division 20541
Marine Corps Headquarters,
Arlington Annex..............20380
National Academy Of
Sciences And Research
Council 20418
National Aeronautics And
Space Administration (N A
S A)...........................20548
National Aeronautics And
Space Council.................20502
National Archives And
Records Service (G S A)....20408
National Bureau Of
Standards.....................20234
National Capitol Housing
Authority......................20430
National Capitol Planning
Commission 05
National Credit Union
Administration................20456
National Gallery Of Art........20565
National Institutes Of Health .. 14
National Labor Relations
Board 20570
National Library Of Medicine.. 14
National Mediation Board.....20572
National Naval Medical
Center 14
National Science Foundation .20550
Naval Hospital................... 14

Washington, D.C. (Con.) 200

Navy Dept Of Offices At
  Crystal City Complex 20360
Navy Ship Research And
  Development Center 34
Navy-Marine Recruiting
  Station 04
Navy, Dept Of (Arlington
  Annex) 20370
Navy, Dept Of (Other Offices
  Located Out Of H Q) 20390
Navy, Dept Of, (Offices At H
  Q-Pentagon) 20350
Navy, Dept Of, Main Navy
  Building 20360
Navy, Dept Of, Marine
  Headquarters, Arlington
  Annex 20380
Office Of Economic
  Opportunity 20506
Office Of Education (H E W) ...20202
Office Of Emergency
  Preparedness 20504
Office Of Management,
  Budget 20503
Oversea'S Private Investment
  Corp 20527
Passport Office, State Dept ...20524
Patent Office 20231
Pay Board And Price
  Commission 20508
Pentagon, Dept Of Air Force...20330
Pentagon, Dept Of Army 20310
Pentagon, Dept Of Defense..... 20301
Pentagon, Dept Of Navy 20350
Postal Rate Commission, U
  S 20268
Postal Service U S
  (Headquarters) 20260
Postal Service U S Regional
  Office 20269
President Of The United
  States 20500
President'S Committee Equal
  Opportunity Armed Forces ...20453
President'S Committee On
  Status Of Women 20210
Renegotiation Board 20446
Renegotiation Board, Eastern
  Region 20447
Securities And Exchange
  Commission 20549
Selective Service System, U
  S 20435
Senate, U S And Office
  Buildings 20510
Small Business
  Administration 20416
Smithsonian Institution 20560
Soldiers Home, U. S. 20315
State, Dept Of
  (Headquarters) 20520
State, Dept Of (Other
  Offices) 20525
State, Dept Of, Agency For
  International Development...20523
State, Dept Of, Foreign
  Service Posts And Mail
  Room 20521

State, Dept Of, Passport
  Office 20524
Subversive Activities Control
  Board 37
Superintendent Of
  Documents, Government
  Printing Office 20402
Supreme Court Of The U S ...20543
Tariff Commission, U S 20436
Tax Court Of The U S 44
Tennessee Valley Authority ...20444
Transportation, Dept Of
  (Headquarters) 20590
Transportation, Dept Of
  (Other Offices) 20591
Treasury, Dept Of
  (Headquarters) 20220
Treasury, Dept Of Internal
  Revenue, International ...20225
Treasury, Dept Of, (Other
  Offices Located Out Of H
  Q) 20226
Treasury, Dept Of, Internal
  Revenue (Main) 20224
United States Coast Guard ...20591
United States House Of
  Representatives 20515
United States Information
  Agency (U S I A) 20547
United States Postal Service
  Hq 20260
United States Senate 20510
United States Supreme Court .20543
United States Tariff
  Commission 20436
Veterans Administration
  (Central) 20420
Veterans Administration,
  Benefits Office 20421
Veterans Administration, New
  Veterans Hospital 20422
Vice President Of The U S ...20501
Vice President Of The U S At
  U S Senate 20510
Walter Reed Army Medical
  Center (Hospital) 12
White House, The 20500

HOSPITALS

Cafritz Memorial, 1310
  Southern Ave. 32
Childrens, 2125 13th NW 09
Columbia, 2425 L NW 37
D C General, 19th & C SE...... 03
Doctors, 1815 I NW 06
Freedmans, 6th & Bryant
  NW 01
George Washington
  University, 901 23rd NW 37
Georgetown, 3800 Reservoir
  Rd NW 07
Hadley Memorial, 4601
  Nichols Ave SW 32
Metropolitan, 1143 New
  Hampshire Ave., N.w. 37
Providence, 1150 Varnum NE. 17
Rogers Memorial, 708
  Massachusetts Ave, NE 02

Saint Elizabeth, 2690-2698
  Ave SE M.I. King Jr 32
Sibley, 5255 Loughboro Rd
  NW 16
Suburban, 8600 Old
  Georgetown Rd (Md) 14
United States Naval,
  Bethesda Md. 14
Upshur Street, 14th &
  Upshur NW 11
Veterans Hospital, 50 Irving
  NW 20422
Walter Reed Army Medical
  Cen, 6825 16th NW 12
Washington Hospital Center,
  110 Irving NW 18
Washington Sanitarium,
  Takoma Park Md. 12

MILITARY INSTALLATIONS

Andrews AFB 20331
Bolling AFB. 20332

UNIVERSITIES AND COLLEGES

American University,
  Massachusetts &
  Nebraska Ave NW 16
Benjamin Franklin University,
  1100 16th NW 36
Catholic University, 620
  Michigan Ave NE 17
Columbus University, 620
  Michigan Ave N. E. 17
D C Teachers, Wilson Bldg.,
  11th & Harvard NW 09
Dunbarton, 2935 Upton
  Street NW 08
Federal City College, 425 2nd
  NW 01
Gallaudet, Florida Avenue At
  7th NE 02
George Washington University
  Medical School, 1335 H
  NW 05
George Washington
  University, 2029 G NW 06
Georgetown University Law
  School, 506 E St NW 01
Georgetown University, 37th
  & O NW 07
Howard University, 2401 6th
  NW 01
Marjorie Webster Junior, 7775
  17th N W 12
Montgomery Junior, Takoma
  Park, M D 12
Mount Vernon Seminary,
  2100 Foxhall Rd NW 07
Potomac University, 6830
  Laurel NW 12
Southeastern University,
  1736 G NW 06
Strayers Business, 601 13th
  NW 05
Trinity, Michigan Av &
  Franklin NE 17
Washington Missionary,
  Takoma Park, Md. 12

FLORIDA
(Abbreviation: FL)

Air Mail Facility, Br. Miami.....33159
Airgate, Br. Sarasota.............33578
Airport, Br. Saint Petersburg...33732
Alachua.................................32615
   Sante Fe, R. Br.................32616
Alford...................................32420
Allandale, Br. Daytona
   Beach.................................32023
Aliapattah, Sta. Miami...........33142
Altamonte Springs.................32701
Altha....................................32421
Altoona.................................32702
Alturas.................................33820
Alva.....................................33920
Anna Maria............................33501
Anthony................................32617
Apalachicola..........................32320
Apollo Beach, R. Br. Ruskin...33570
Apopka (1st)..........................32703
Arcadia (1st)..........................33821
Archer..................................32618
Argyle..................................32422
Aripeka................................33502
Arlington, Sta. Jacksonville
   (see appendix)
Astatula...............................32705
Astor....................................32002
Astronaut Trail, Sta.
   Titusville...........................32780
Atlantic Beach, Br.
   Jacksonville.......................32233
Auburndale (1st)....................33823
Audubon, Br. Merritt Island...32952
Auxiliary Field Nine, Br.
   Eglin A F B.........................32544
Avon Park (1st)......................33825
Azalea Park, Br. Orlando........32807
Babson Park...........................33827
Bagdad.................................32530
Bahia Mar, Sta. Fort
   Lauderdale.........................33316
Baker...................................32531
Bal Harbour, Br. Miami..........33154
Baldwin, Br. Jacksonville.......32234
Balm....................................33503
Barberville............................32005
Barry College, Br. Miami........33161
Barth....................................32532
Bartow (1st)..........................33830
Bascom.................................32423
Basinger...............................33428
Bay Pines.............................33504
Bay Vista, Sta. Saint
   Petersburg.........................33705
Bayard, R. Sta. Jacksonville...32224
Bayshore Gardens, Br.
   Bradenton..........................33505
Beach, Sta. Vero Beach.........32960
Beacon Light, Br. Pompano
   Beach.................................33064
Bean City.............................33429
Bee Ridge, Br. Sarasota........33578
Bell.....................................32619
Belle Glade (1st)....................33430
Belleair Bluffs, Br. Largo.......33540
Belleview.............................32620
Benbow, R. Br. Clewiston......33440
Bens Lake, Sta. Eglin A F B...32542
Betty Lane, Sta. Clearwater...33515

Big Bayou, Sta. Saint
   Petersburg.........................33739
Big Bend Farm, R. Br.
   Tallahassee........................32311
Big Pine Key, Br.
   Summerland Key................33043
Biscayne Annex, Sta. Miami...33152
Blind Pass, Br. Saint
   Petersburg.........................33706
Blountstown..........................32424
Boca Grande..........................33921
Boca Raton (1st)....................33432
Bokeelia...............................33922
Bonifay................................32425
Bonita Springs.......................33923
Bostwick...............................32007
Boulevard, Sta. Clearwater....33515
Bowling Green........................33834
Boynton Beach (1st)...............33435
Braden Castle, R. Sta.
   Bradenton..........................33505
Bradenton (1st)......................33505
Bradenton Beach (1st)............33510
   Holmes Beach, R. Br.........33509
Bradfordville, R. Br.
   Tallahassee........................32301
Bradley.................................33835
Brandon (1st).........................33511
Branford...............................32008
Brent, Br. Pensacola..............32505
Bright, Sta. Hialeah...............33013
Bristol..................................32321
Bronson................................32621
Brooker................................32622
Brooks Plaza, Sta. Fort
   Walton Beach.....................32548
Brooksville (1st).....................33512
Brookview, Sta. Jacksonville...32211
Bruce, R. Br. Ponce De Leon...32455
Bryant, R. Br. Canal Point.....33439
Bryceville.............................32009
Buena Vista, Sta. Miami
   (see appendix)
Bunnell.................................32010
Bushnell................................33513
Callahan...............................32011
Calloway, R. Br. Panama
   City...................................32401
Campbellton..........................32426
Canal Point...........................33438
   Bryant, R. Br....................33439
   Pelican Lake, R. Br...........33491
Candler................................32624
Cantonment...........................32533
Cape Canaveral (1st)..............32920
Cape Coral, Br. Fort Myers.....33904
Captiva................................33924
Carl Fisher, Br. Miami...........33139
Carlton, Br. Clearwater.........33515
Carrabelle.............................32322
   Lanark Village, R. Br.........32323
Carver, Sta. Jacksonville......32209
Caryville..............................32427
Cassadaga............................32706
Casselberry...........................32707
Cecil Field, MOU.
   Jacksonville.......................32215
Cedar Key.............................32625
Center Hill.............................33514
Century.................................32535
Charlotte Harbor, Br. Punta
   Gorda................................33950
Chattahoochee (1st)...............32324

Chiefland..............................32626
Chipley (1st)..........................32428
Chipola, R. Br. Marianna........32450
Chokoloskee..........................33925
Christmas..............................32709
Chuluota, R. Br. Oviedo........32766
Citra....................................32627
Citrus Tower, Sta. Clermont...32711
Clair Mel City, Br. Tampa.......33619
Clarcona...............................32710
Clarksville.............................32430
Clearview, Br. Saint
   Petersburg.........................33714
CLEARWATER (1st) (see
   appendix)
Clearwater Beach, Sta.
   Clearwater.........................33515
Clermont (1st)........................32711
Cleveland Street, Sta.
   Clearwater.........................33517
Clewiston (1st).......................33440
Cocoa (1st)............................32922
   Five Points, Sta.................32922
   Patrick A F B, Br..............32925
Cocoa Beach (1st)..................32931
Coconut Grove, Sta. Miami.....33133
Colee, Sta. Fort Lauderdale....33303
Coleman................................33521
College Park, Sta. Orlando......32804
Coloniatown, Sta. Orlando......32803
Compass Lake, R. Br.
   Marianna...........................32448
Congress Avenue, Br. Lake
   Worth................................33460
Cooper City, Br. Fort
   Lauderdale.........................33314
Copeland..............................33926
Coral Gables, Br. Miami (see
   appendix)
Coral Ridge, Sta. Fort
   Lauderdale.........................33306
Coral Springs, R. Br.
   Pompano Beach.................33060
Cornwell, R. Br. Lorida..........33836
Coronado, Sta. New Smyrna
   Beach................................32069
Cortez..................................33522
Cortez Plaza, Br. Bradenton....33505
Cottage Hill, R. Br.
   Cantonment.......................32533
Cottondale............................32431
Country Club, R. Br. Fort
   Pierce...............................33450
Country Club Estates, Br.
   Lakeland............................33801
Cove, Sta. Panama City.........32401
Coytown, Sta. Orlando...........32803
Crawfordville.........................32327
Crescent Beach, Br.
   Sarasota............................33578
Crescent City.........................32012
Crestview (1st).......................32536
   Lakewood, R. Br...............32566
   Milligan, R. Br..................32537
   Paxton, R. Br....................32538
Cross City.............................32628
Crossroads, Sta. Saint
   Petersburg.........................33710
Crystal Beach........................33523
Crystal Lake, R. Br. Wausau...32463
Crystal River.........................32629
Crystal Springs......................33524
Cutler Ridge, Br. Miami..........33157

Cypress...32432
Cypress Gardens, R. Br. Winter Haven...33880
Dade City (1st)...33525
Dania (1st)...33004
Davenport...33837
Davie, Br. Fort Lauderdale...33314
Day...32013
DAYTONA BEACH (1st) (see appendix)
Daytona Beach Shores, Br. Daytona Beach...32016
De Bary...32713
De Funiak Springs (1st)...32433
Mossy Head, R. Br....32434
De Land (1st)...32720
Glenwood, R. Br....32722
De Leon Springs...32028
Deerfield Beach (1st)...33441
Delray Beach (1st)...33444
Deltona, R. Br. Orange City...32763
Destin...32541
Dinsmore, R. Sta. Jacksonville...32219
Disston Plaza, Sta. Saint Petersburg...33710
Dixie Village, Sta. Orlando...32806
Dixieland, Sta. Lakeland...33803
Doctors Inlet...32030
Dona Vista, R. Br. Umatilla...32784
Dover...33527
Dover Shores, Sta. Orlando...32806
Dowling Park, R. Br. Live Oak...32060
Downtown, Sta. Orlando...32802
Downtown, Sta. Tampa...33602
Driftwood, Sta. Hollywood...33024
Dundee...33838
Dunedin (1st)...33528
Dunfawton, Br. Daytona Beach...32019
Dunn Avenue, Sta. Jacksonville...32218
Dunnellon...32630
Durant...33530
Eagle Lake...33839
Earleton...32631
East Avenue, Sta. Sarasota...33578
East Hill, Sta. Pensacola (see appendix)
East Palatka...32031
Eastgate, Sta. Winter Park...32789
Eastlake Weir...32632
Eastpoint...32328
Eaton Park...33840
Eatonville, R. Br. Maitland...32751
Eau Gallie, Sta. Melbourne...32935
Ebro...32437
Edgar, R. Br. Interlachen...32049
Edgewater...32032
Edgewater Gulf Beach, R. Br. Panama City...32401
Edison Center, Sta. Miami...33151
Eglin A F B (1st)...32542
Auxiliary Field Nine, Br....32544
Bens Lake, Sta....32542
U S A F Hospital, Sta....32542
El Jobean, R. Br. Punta Gorda...33927
Elfers...33531
Elkton...32033
Ellenton...33532

Ellinor Village, Sta. Ormond Beach...32074
Ellyson Field, Br. Pensacola...32509
Eloise, Br. Winter Haven...33880
Englewood (1st)...33533
Ensley, Br. Pensacola...32504
Enterprise, R. Br. Orange City...32763
Estero...33928
Esto, R. Br. Bonifay...32425
Euclid, Sta. Saint Petersburg (see appendix)
Eustis (1st)...32726
Everglades City...33929
Evinston...32633
Fairfield...32634
Fairvilla, Br. Orlando...32804
Fedhaven, R. Br. Lake Wales...33854
Felda...33930
Fellsmere...32948
Fern Park (1st)...32730
Fernandina Beach (1st)...32034
Ferndale...32729
Five Points, Sta. Cocoa...32922
Flagler, Sta. Key West...33040
Flagler Beach...32036
Flamingo, R. Br. Homestead...33030
Florahome...32635
Floral City...32636
Florence Villa, Sta. Winter Haven...33880
Florida City, Br. Homestead...33030
Florida Southern College, Sta. Lakeland...33802
Forest City, R. Br. Maitland...32751
Forest Hills, Sta. Tampa (see appendix)
Forest Ridge, Br. Hollywood...33023
Fort George Island, R. Sta. Jacksonville...32226
Fort Green, R. Br. Bowling Green...33834
FORT LAUDERDALE (1st) (see appendix)
Fort Mc Coy...32637
Fort Meade...33841
FORT MYERS (1st) (see appendix)
Fort Myers Beach (1st)...33931
Fort Ogden...33842
Fort Pierce (1st)...33450
Fort Pierce Beach, Br. Fort Pierce...33450
Fort Walton Beach (1st)...32548
Fort White...32038
Forty Ninth Street, Br. Saint Petersburg...33707
Fountain...32438
Four Points, Br. West Palm Beach...33406
Freeport...32439
Frostproof...33843
Fruitland Park...32731
Fruitville, Br. Sarasota...33578
Gainesville (1st)...32601
Garden City, R. Sta. Jacksonville...32218
Gateway Mall, Sta. Saint Petersburg...33702
Geneva...32732
Georgetown...32039

Gibson Plaza, Sta. Fort Walton Beach...32548
Gibsonton...33534
Gifford, Br. Vero Beach...32960
Glen Saint Mary...32040
Glenwood, R. Br. De Land...32722
Golden Beach, Br. Miami...33160
Golden Gate, R. Br. Naples...33940
Golden Glades, Br. Opa Locka...33054
Goldenrod...32733
Gonzalez...32560
Goodland...33933
Gotha...32734
Goulds...33170
Graceville...32440
Graham...32042
Grand Crossing, Sta. Jacksonville...32205
Grand Island...32735
Grand Ridge...32442
Grandin...32638
Grant...32949
Gratigny, Br. Miami (see appendix)
Green Cove Springs (1st)...32043
Greenacres City, Br. Lake Worth...33460
Greensboro...32330
Greenville...32331
Greenwood...32443
Gretna...32332
Grove City, R. Br. Englewood...33533
Grove Park, Sta. Lakeland...33803
Groveland...32736
Gulf Breeze (1st)...32561
Gulf Hammock...32639
Gulfport, Br Saint Petersburg (see appendix)
Haines City (1st)...33844
Hallandale (1st)...33009
Hamilton, Sta. Pompano Beach...33062
Hampton...32044
Harbour Heights, R. Br. Punta Gorda...33950
Harlem, R. Br. Clewiston...33440
Harlem Heights, R. Sta. Winter Garden...32787
Harold...32563
Hastings...32045
Havana...32333
Hawthorne...32640
Hernando...32642
Herndon, Sta. Orlando...32814
HIALEAH (1st) (see appendix)
Hialeah Lakes, Sta. Hialeah (see appendix)
High Springs...32643
Highland Beach, R. Br. Delray Beach...33444
Highland City...33846
Highland Terrace, Sta. Pensacola...32503
Hiland Park, Br. Panama City...32401
Hilldale, Sta. Tampa (see appendix)
Hilliard...32046
Hobe Sound...33455
Holder...32645

Holiday, Br. Tarpon Springs....33589
Holiday Plaza, Br. Panama
  City..32401
Holley, R. Br. Gulf Breeze......32561
Hollister.....................................32047
Holly Hill, Br. Daytona
  Beach....................................32017
HOLLYWOOD (1st) (see
  appendix)
Hollywood Hills, Sta.
  Hollywood...........................33021
Holmes Beach, R. Br.
  Bradenton Beach.................33509
Holt..32564
Homeland.................................33847
Homestead (1st)......................33030
Homestead A F B, Br.
  Homestead...........................33030
Homosassa...............................32646
Homosassa Springs..................32647
Horseshoe Beach......................32648
Hosford....................................32334
  Sumatra, R. Br.....................32335
Howey In The Hills...................32737
Hudson, R. Br. Port Richey......33568
Immokalee................................33934
Indialantic, Br Melbourne.......32903
Indian Harbor Beach, Br.
  Melbourne...........................32937
Indian Lake Estates, R. Br.
  Lake Wales..........................33855
Indian River City, Sta.
  Titusville.............................32780
Indian Rocks Beach (1st)........33535
Indiantown...............................33456
Indrio-Saint Lucie, Br. Fort
  Pierce..................................33450
Inglis.......................................32649
Interbay, Sta. Tampa...............33611
Intercession City......................33848
Interlachen..............................32048
  Edgar, R. Br.........................32049
International Airport, Br.
  Miami..................................33148
Inverness (1st).........................32650
Inwood, Br. Winter Haven.......33880
Irvine.......................................32653
Islamorada...............................33036
Island Grove............................32654
Istachatta................................33536
JACKSONVILLE (1st) (see
  appendix)
Jacksonville A M F, Sta.
  Jacksonville.........................32229
Jacksonville Beach, Br.
  Jacksonville.........................32250
Jacksonville Nas. Sta.
  Jacksonville.........................32212
Jacksonville University, Sta.
  Jacksonville.........................32211
Jasper......................................32052
Jay..32565
Jennings..................................32053
Jensen Beach (1st).................33457
Johns Pass, Br. Saint
  Petersburg...........................33708
Jupiter (1st).............................33458
Kathleen..................................33849
Kenansville..............................32739
Kendall Br Miami.....................33156
Kennedy Space Center, Br
  Orlando (see appendix)

Kenneth City, Br. Saint
  Petersburg...........................33709
Key Biscayne, Br. Miami..........33149
Key Colony Beach, R. Br.
  Marathon.............................33051
Key Largo................................33037
  Upper Key Largo, R. Br........33038
Key West (1st).........................33040
Keystone Heights......................32656
Keysville, R. Br. Lithia.............33547
Killarney..................................32740
Kinard, R. Br. Marianna...........32449
Kissimmee (1st).......................32741
La Belle....................................33935
La Crosse.................................32658
Lacoochee................................33537
Lady Lake................................32659
Lafayette, R. Br.
  Tallahassee..........................32308
Laguna Beach, R. Br.
  Panama City.........................32401
Lake Alfred..............................33850
Lake Butler..............................32054
Lake City (1st).........................32055
Lake Como...............................32057
Lake Forest, Sta.
  Jacksonville (see
  appendix)
Lake Geneva.............................32660
Lake Hamilton..........................33851
Lake Harbor.............................33459
Lake Helen...............................32744
Lake Jem, R. Br Mount
  Dora....................................32745
Lake Lucina, Sta.
  Jacksonville.........................32211
Lake Mary................................32746
Lake Monroe............................32747
Lake Panasoffkee......................33538
Lake Park, Br. West Palm
  Beach..................................33403
Lake Placid (1st)......................33852
Lake Shore, Sta. Jacksonville
  (see appendix)
Lake Tarpon, Br. Palm
  Harbor.................................33563
Lake Wales (1st)......................33853
  Fedhaven, R. Br...................33854
  Indian Lake Estates, R
  Br..33855
  Nalcrest, R. Br.....................33856
Lake Worth (1st)......................33460
LAKELAND (1st) (see
  appendix)
Lakewood, R. Br. Crestview.....32566
Lamont.....................................32336
Lanark Village, R. Br.
  Carrabelle............................32323
Land O'Lakes...........................33539
Lantana, Br. Lake Worth..........33460
Largo (1st)...............................33540
Lauderdale-by-the-Sea, Br.
  Fort Lauderdale...................33308
Lauderhill, Br. Fort
  Lauderdale...........................33313
Laurel......................................33545
Laurel Hill................................32567
Lawtey.....................................32058
Lecanto....................................32661
Lee..32059
Leesburg (1st)..........................32748
Lehigh Acres (1st)....................33936

Leisure City, Br. Homestead....33030
Lelyland, R. Br Naples.............33940
Lemon City, Sta. Miami...........33137
Leon, Sta. Tallahassee.............32303
Leonia, R. Br. Westville...........32464
Lighthouse Point, Br.
  Pompano Beach....................33064
Lincoln, Br. Miami...................33139
Lithia.......................................33547
Little River, Sta. Miami (see
  appendix)
Live Oak (1st)..........................32060
Lloyd.......................................32337
Lochloosa.................................32662
Lockhart, Br. Orlando..............32810
Lockwood Ridge, Sta.
  Sarasota...............................33578
Long Key..................................33001
Longboat Key...........................33548
Longwood................................32750
Lorida......................................33857
  Cornwell, R. Br....................33836
Loughman................................33858
Loveridge Heights, Sta.
  Melbourne...........................32935
Lowell......................................32663
Loxahatchee.............................33470
Ludlam, Br. Miami...................33155
Lulu..32061
Lutz...33549
Lynn Haven..............................32444
Mac Dill A F B, Br. Tampa......33608
Macclenny................................32063
Madeira Beach, Br. Saint
  Petersburg (see appendix)
Madison (1st)...........................32340
Mainland, Sta. Ormond
  Beach..................................32074
Maitland (1st)..........................32751
Malabar...................................32950
Malone.....................................32445
Manatee, Sta. Bradenton........33505
Mandarin, Sta. Jacksonville.....32217
Mango.....................................33550
Marathon (1st).........................33050
  Key Colony Beach, R. Br......33051
  Marathon Shores, Br............33052
Marathon Shores, Br.
  Marathon.............................33052
Marco......................................33937
Margate, Br. Pompano
  Beach..................................33063
Marianna (1st).........................32446
  Chipola, R. Br.....................32450
  Compass Lake, R. Br...........32448
  Kinard, R. Br.......................32449
  Round Lake, R. Br...............32447
  West End, Sta......................32446
Mary Esther.............................32569
Masaryktown, R. Br.
  Brooksville..........................33512
Mascotte..................................32753
Matlacha, R. Br. Fort Myers....33901
Maxville, R. Sta.
  Jacksonville.........................32265
Mayo.......................................32066
Mayport, Sta. Jacksonville.......32267
Mayport Naval Station, Sta.
  Jacksonville (see
  appendix)
Mc Alpin..................................32062
Mc Coy A F B, MOU.
  Orlando...............................32812

Mc David	32568
Mc Intosh	32664
Melbourne (1st)	32901
Melbourne Beach, Br. Melbourne	32951
Melrose	32666
Merritt Island (1st)	32952
Mexico Beach, R. Br. Panama City	32410
MIAMI (1st) (see appendix)	
Miami Beach, Br. Miami (see appendix)	
Miami Gardens, Br. Opa Locka	33054
Miami Shores, Br. Miami	33153
Miami Springs, Br. Miami (see appendix)	
Micanopy	32667
Miccosukee, R. Br. Tallahassee	32309
Middleburg	32068
Midway	32343
Milligan, R. Br. Crestview	32537
Milton (1st)	32570
Mims	32754
Minneola	32755
Mintons Corner, Br. Melbourne	32901
Miracle Mile, Sta. Fort Myers	33901
Miramar, Br. Hollywood	33023
Miramar Beach, R. Br. Destin	32541
Mobile Home Park, Sta. Sarasota	33578
Mobile Manor, R. Br. Longwood	32750
Molino	32577
Monticello (1st)	32344
Montverde	32756
Moore Haven	33471
Morriston	32668
Mossy Head, R. Br. De Funiak Springs	32434
Motel Row, Br. Miami	33160
Mount Dora (1st)	32757
Lake Jem, R. Br.	32745
Triangle, Sta.	32757
Mount Pleasant, R. Br. Quincy	32352
Mulberry (1st)	33860
Murdock	33938
Murray Hill, Sta. Jacksonville (see appendix)	
Myakka City	33551
Myrtle Grove, Br. Pensacola	32506
Nalcrest, R. Br. Lake Wales	33856
Naples (1st)	33940
Naranja, Br. Homestead	33030
Naval, Sta. Key West	33040
Naval Comm Training Center, Br. Pensacola	32511
Naval Hospital, Sta. Jacksonville	32214
Naval Station, Br. Pensacola	32508
Naval Training Center, Sta. Orlando	32813
Neptune Beach, Br. Jacksonville	32233
New Port Richey (1st)	33552
New Smyrna Beach (1st)	32069
Newberry	32669

Newport, R. Br. Saint Marks	32355
Newtown Heights, Sta. Sarasota	33578
Niceville	32578
Nichols	33863
Nobles, Sta. Pensacola	32504
Nobleton	33554
Nocatee	33864
Nokomis (1st)	33555
Noma	32452
Norland, Br. Miami	33169
Normandy, Br. Miami	33141
North Babcock, Sta. Melbourne	32901
North Bay Village, Br. Miami	33141
North Fort Myers, Br. Fort Myers	33903
North Miami, Br. Miami	33161
North ami Beach, Br. Miami (see appendix)	
North Palm Beach, Br. West Palm Beach	33403
North Port Charlotte, R. Br. Venice	33595
Northeast Park, Sta. Saint Petersburg	33704
Northside, Sta. Sarasota	33578
Northside Center, Br. Miami	33147
Northwest, Br. Miami	33147
Northwood, Sta. West Palm Beach	33407
Nova Road, Br. Ormond Beach	32074
O'Brien	32071
Oak Hill	32759
Oakland	32760
Oakland Park, Br. Fort Lauderdale (see appendix)	
Ocala (1st)	32670
Ocean Ridge, R. Br. Delray Beach	33444
Ocean View, Br. Miami	33140
Oceanway, Sta. Jacksonville (see appendix)	
Ochopee	33943
Ocoee	32761
Odessa	33556
Ojus, Br. Miami	33163
Okahumpka	32762
Okeechobee (1st)	33472
Okeelanta, R. Br. South Bay	33493
Oklawaha	32679
Old Town	32680
Oldsmar	33557
Olustee, R. Br. Sanderson	32072
Olympia Heights, Br. Miami	33165
Ona	33865
One Hundred Sixty Third St, Br. Miami	33162
Oneco (1st)	33558
Opa Locka (1st)	33054
Open Air, Sta. Saint Petersburg (see appendix)	
Orange Blossom, Sta. Orlando	32805
Orange City (1st)	32763
Orange Lake	32681
Orange Park (1st)	32073
Orange Springs	32682
ORLANDO (1st) (see appendix)	

Orlando Naval Hospital, Sta. Orlando	32813
Orlovista, Br. Orlando	32811
Ormond Beach (1st)	32074
Ormond By The Sea, Br. Ormond Beach	32074
Ortega, Sta. Jacksonville	32210
Osprey	33559
Osteen	32764
Otter Creek	32683
Overstreet	32453
Oviedo	32765
Chuluota, R. Br.	32766
Oxford	32684
Ozona	33560
Pace, Br. Milton	32570
Pahokee (1st)	33476
Paisley	32767
Palatka (1st)	32077
Palm Bay, Br. Melbourne	32905
Palm Beach (1st)	33480
Palm City	33490
Palm Harbor	33563
Palm River, Br. Tampa	33619
Palm Shores, R. Br. Melbourne	32935
Palm Springs, Br. Lake Worth	33460
Palm Village, Sta. Hialeah	33012
Palma Ceia, Sta. Tampa	33609
Palma Sola, R. Br. Bradenton	33505
Palmdale	33944
Palmetto (1st)	33561
Panacea	32346
Panama City (1st)	32401
Calloway, R. Br.	32401
Cove, Sta.	32401
Edgewater Gulf Beach, R. Br.	32401
Hiland Park, Br.	32401
Holiday Plaza, Br.	32401
Laguna Beach, R. Br.	32401
Mexico Beach, R. Br.	32410
Panama City Beach, Br.	32401
Parker, Br.	32401
Saint Andrews, Sta.	32401
Southport, R. Br.	32409
Springfield, Br.	32401
Tyndall A F B, Br.	32401
U S Navy Mine Defense Lab, Br.	32401
West Panama City Beach, Br.	32401
Westbay, R. Br.	32401
Panama City Beach, Br. Panama City	32401
Parker, Br. Panama City	32401
Parrish	33564
Pass-a-Grill Beach, Br. Saint Petersburg	33741
Patrick A F B, Br. Cocoa	32925
Paxon, Sta. Jacksonville	32205
Paxton, R. Br. Crestview	32538
Pelican Lake, R. Br. Canal Point	33491
Pembroke	33866
Pembroke Pines, Br. Hollywood	33023
Peninsula, Sta. Daytona Beach	32018
Peninsula, Sta. Tampa	33609
Penney Farms	32079

PENSACOLA (1st) (see
appendix)
Pensacola Beach, Br. Gulf
Breeze 32561
Perrine, Br. Miami (see
appendix)
Perry (1st) 32347
Pierce 33867
Pierson 32080
Pine Castle, Br. Orlando 32809
Pine Hills, Br. Orlando 32808
Pinecraft, Br Sarasota 33578
Pineland 33945
Pinellas Park (1st) 33565
Pinetta 32350
Placida 33946
Plant City (1st) 33566
Plantation, Br. Fort
Lauderdale (see
appendix)
Plaza, Sta. Ocala 32670
Plymouth 32768
Point Washington 32454
Polk City 33868
Pomona Park 32081
POMPANO BEACH (1st) (see
appendix)
Pompano Isles, Sta.
Pompano Beach 33062
Ponce, Br. Miami 33134
Ponce De Leon 32455
Ponte Vedra Beach 32082
Port Charlotte, Br. Punta
Gorda 33950
Port Everglades, Sta. Fort
Lauderdale 33316
Port Orange, Br. Daytona
Beach 32019
Port Richey (1st) 33568
Port Saint Joe (1st) 32456
Port Saint Lucie, Br. Fort
Pierce 33450
Port Salerno 33492
Port Tampa City, Sta.
Tampa (see appendix)
Pottsburg, Sta. Jacksonville
(see appendix)
Princeton 33171
Produce, Sta. Tampa (see
appendix)
Punta Gorda (1st) 33950
Charlotte Harbor, Br. 33950
El Jobean, R. Br. 33927
Harbour Heights, R. Br. 33950
Port Charlotte, Br. 33950
Tropic Heights, R. Br. 33950
Putnam Hall 32685
Quincy (1st) 32351
Mount Pleasant, R. Br. 32352
Raiford 32083
Rainbow Lakes, R. Br.
Dunnellon 32630
Redbay, R. Br. Ponce De
Leon 32455
Reddick 32686
Redington Beach, Br. Saint
Petersburg 33708
Ridge Manor, R. Br. Dade
City 33525
Ritta, R. Br. Clewiston 33440
River Junction, Sta.
Chattahoochee 32324

Riverside, Sta. Miami (see
appendix)
Riverview 33569
Riviera Beach, Br. West
Palm Beach 33404
Rockledge (1st) 32955
Roseland 32957
Rotonda West, R. Br.
Placida 33946
Round Lake, R. Br.
Marianna 32447
Rubonia, R. Br. Palmetto 33561
Ruskin (1st) 33570
Safety Harbor 33572
Saint Andrews, Sta. Panama
City 32401
Saint Armands, Sta.
Sarasota 33578
Saint Augustine (1st) 32084
Saint Augustine Beach, Br.
Saint Augustine 32084
Saint Catherine 33573
Saint Cloud (1st) 32769
Saint James City 33956
Saint Leo 33574
Saint Marks 32355
SAINT PETERSBURG (1st)
(see appendix)
Saint Petersburg Beach, Br.
Saint Petersburg (see
appendix)
Salem 32356
Samoset, Br. Bradenton 33505
San Antonio 33576
San Mateo 32088
Sanderson 32087
Olustee, R. Br. 32072
Sanford (1st) 32771
Sanibel 33957
Santa Rosa Beach 32459
Sante Fe, R. Br. Alachua 32616
SARASOTA (1st) (see
appendix)
Sarno Plaza, Sta. Melbourne ..32935
Satellite Beach, Br.
Melbourne 32937
Satsuma 32089
Saufley Field, Br. Pensacola ..32510
Scottsmoor 32775
Seabreeze, Sta. Daytona
Beach 32020
Searstown, Sta. Lakeland 33801
Sebastian 32958
Sebring (1st) 33870
Sebring Southgate, Br.
Sebring 33870
Seffner 33584
Seminole, Br. Largo 33540
Seminole Annex, Sta. Fort
Lauderdale (see
appendix)
Seminole Heights, Sta.
Tampa 33603
Seville 32090
Shackleford, Sta. Pensacola ..32503
Shady Grove 32357
Shalimar 32579
Sharpes 32959
Shell Land, Br. Clearwater 33516
Shenandoah, Sta. Miami
(see appendix)
Siesta, Br. Sarasota 33578

Silver Springs 32688
Singer Island, Br. West Palm
Beach 33404
Sipes, R. Br. Sanford 32771
Skycrest, Sta. Clearwater 33515
Sneads 32460
Sopchoppy 32358
Sorrento 32776
Soutel, Sta. Jacksonville 32208
South Andrews, Sta. Fort
Lauderdale (see
appendix)
South Bay 33493
South Daytona, Br. Daytona
Beach 32021
South Fort Myers, Sta. Fort
Myers 33901
South Jacksonville, Sta.
Jacksonville 32207
South Miami, Br. Miami 33143
South Pasadena, Br. Saint
Petersburg 33707
South Patrick, Br.
Melbourne 32937
South Trail, Br. Sarasota 33578
South Venice, Br. Venice 33595
Southboro, Sta. West Palm
Beach 33405
Southeast, Sta. Winter
Haven 33880
Southgate, Sta. Sarasota 33579
Southport, R. Br. Panama
City 32409
Southshore, R. Br.
Clewiston 33440
Southside, Sta. Sarasota 33578
Sparr 32690
Spring Hill, Br. Brooksville 33512
Spring Park, Sta.
Jacksonville 32207
Springfield, Br. Panama
City 32401
Starke (1st) 32091
Steinhatchee 32359
Stuart (1st) 33494
Sugar Loaf Shores, R. Br.
Summerland Key 33044
Sulphur Springs, Sta.
Tampa 33604
Sumatra, R. Br. Hosford 32335
Summerfield 32691
Summerland Key 33042
Big Pine Key, Br. 33043
Sugar Loaf Shores, R. Br. ..33044
Sumterville 33585
Sun City 33586
Sun City Center, Br. Ruskin ...33570
Sunny Isles, Br. Miami 33160
Sunnyside 32461
Sunrise, Sta. Fort
Lauderdale (see
appendix)
Sunrise Golf Village, Br. Fort
Lauderdale 33313
Sunshine, Br. Tampa 33615
Surfside, Br. Miami 33154
Suwannee 32692
Sydney 33587
T B Hospital, Sta. Tampa 33614
Taft, R. Br. Orlando 32809
TALLAHASSEE (1st) (see
appendix)

Tallevast.............................33588
Tamarac, Br. Fort
  Lauderdale.......................33313
Tamiami, Sta. Miami (see
  appendix)
TAMPA (1st) (see appendix)
Tangerine.............................32777
Tarpon Springs (1st).............33589
Tavares (1st)........................32778
Tavernier..............................33070
  Vacation Village, & Br....33071
Telogia.................................32360
Temple Terrace, Br. Tampa..33617
Tequesta, Br. Jupiter............33458
Terra Ceia............................33591
The Village, R. Br. Odesse..33556
Thonotosassa........................33592
Tice, Br. Fort Myers.............33905
Tierra Verde, R. Br. Saint
  Petersburg.......................33715
Tildenville, R. Br. Winter
  Garden.............................32787
Titusville (1st)......................32780
Towers, Sta. Winter Park......32789
Town And Country Plaza, Br.
  Pensacola..........................32505
Trailer City, R. Br.
  Tallahassee......................32301
Trailer Estates, Br.
  Bradenton.........................33505
Trailer Haven, Sta.
  Melbourne.........................32901
Treasure Island, Br. Saint
  Petersburg.......................33740
Trenton................................32693
Triangle, Sta. Mount Dora....32757
Trilby...................................33593
Tropic Heights, R. Br. Punta
  Gorda................................33950
Twin Lake, Br. Tampa...........33604
Tyndall A F B, Br. Panama
  City....................................32401
U S A F Hospital, Sta. Eglin
  A F B................................32542
U S Navy Mine Defense Lab.
  Br. Panama City................32401
Uleta, Br. Miami...................33164
Umatilla................................32784
Union Park, R. Br. Orlando..32807
University, Sta. Gainesville...32601

University Of Miami, Br.
  Miami.................................33124
University Of Tampa, Sta.
  Tampa...............................33606
University Of West Florida,
  R. Br. Pensacola................32504
Upper Key Largo, R. Br. Key
  Largo.................................33038
Vacation Village, R. Br.
  Tavernier...........................33071
Valparaiso (1st)....................32580
Valrico.................................33594
Venice (1st)..........................33595
Venus..................................33960
Vernon.................................32462
Vero Beach (1st)..................32960
Village Green, Sta.
  Rockledge..........................32955
Wabasso...............................32970
Wacissa...............................32361
Wahneta, Br. Winter Haven..33880
Wakulla Springs, R. Br.
  Tallahassee......................32305
Waldo..................................32694
Walnut Hill, R. Br. Mc
  David.................................32568
Warm Mineral Springs, R.
  Br. Venice.........................33595
Warrington, Br. Pensacola....32507
Wauchula (1st).....................33873
Wausau................................32463
Waverly................................33877
Webbs City, Sta. Saint
  Petersburg.......................33701
Webster................................33597
Weeki Wachee, R. Br.
  Brooksville........................33512
Weirsdale.............................32695
Welaka.................................32093
Wellborn..............................32094
Wesconnett, Sta.
  Jacksonville......................32210
Wesley Manor, R. Br.
  Jacksonville......................32223
West Bay Annex, Sta.
  Jacksonville......................32203
West Central, Sta. Saint
  Petersburg.......................33707
West Eau Gallie, Br.
  Melbourne.........................32935

West End, Sta. Marianna.....32446
West Hollywood, Br.
  Hollywood (see appendix)
West Lantana, Br. Lake
  Worth................................33460
WEST PALM BEACH (1st)
  (see appendix)
West Palmetto Park, Sta.
  Boca Raton.......................33432
West Panama City Beach,
  Br. Panama City................32401
West Pensacola, Br.
  Pensacola..........................32505
West Tampa, Sta. Tampa....33607
Westbay, R. Br. Panama
  City....................................32401
Westgate, Br. Bradenton.....33505
Westville..............................32464
Westwood, Br. Hollywood....33024
Wewahitchka........................32465
Whispering Palms, Sta. Lake
  Worth................................33460
White Springs.......................32096
Whitehouse, R. Sta.
  Jacksonville......................32220
Wildwood..............................32785
Williston...............................32696
Wilton Manors, Br. Fort
  Lauderdale........................33305
Wimauma.............................33598
Windermere..........................32786
Winter Beach........................32971
Winter Garden (1st)..............32787
Winter Haven (1st)...............33880
Winter Park (1st)..................32789
Woodville..............................32362
Woodward Avenue, Sta.
  Tallahassee......................32304
Worthington Springs.............32697
Wright, Br. Fort Walton
  Beach................................32548
Yalaha.................................32797
Yankeetown..........................32698
Ybor City, Sta. Tampa (see
  appendix)
Youngstown..........................32466
Yukon, Sta. Jacksonville.....32230
Yulee...................................32097
Zellwood...............................32798
Zephyrhills (1st)...................33599
Zolfo Springs........................33890

BRADENTON 335

POST OFFICE BOXES

Box Nos.		
1 143	Braden Castle Rural Sta.	05
1-2489	Main Office	06
P33-P78	Palma Sola Rural Sta.	05
2001-3147	Manatee Sta.	05
4001-4199	Cortez Plaza Br	07
5001-6999	Trailer Estates Br	07
7001-7599	Samoset Br	05
8000-8999	Bayshore Gardens Br	07

RURAL ROUTES

1,2,3		05

STATIONS, BRANCHES AND UNITS

Bayshore Gardens Br	05
Braden Castle Rural Sta.	05
Cortez Plaza Br	05
Manatee Sta.	05
Palma Sola Rural Br	05
Samoset Br	05
Trailer Estates Br	05
Westgate Br	05
General Delivery	06
Myakka Star Route	05
Postmaster	06

CLEARWATER 335

POST OFFICE BOXES

Box Nos.		
A-Q	Main Office	18
1-1880	Cleveland St Sta.	17
3001-3477	Clearwater Beach Sta	15
4001-5309	Main Office	18

RURAL ROUTES

1		18
2		15

STATIONS, BRANCHES AND UNITS

Betty Lane Sta	15
Boulevard Sta.	15
Carlton Sta	15
Clearwater Beach Sta.	15
Cleveland Street Sta	17
Shell Land Br	16
Skycrest Sta	15
General Delivery	15
Postmaster	18

APARTMENTS, HOTELS, MOTELS

Ambassador, 432 Bay Ave.	16
Bayview Gardens, 2855 Gulf To Bay Blvd.	15

Belleview Biltmore P O Box 1430	17
Belvedere, 300 N. Osceola Ave.	15
Betty Drew, 200 N. Betty Lane	15
Clearwater Point Apts, 825 Gulfview Br	15
Continental Towers, 668 S Gulfview Blvd.	15
Dearborn Towers, 223 Island Way	15
Fleetwood, 1200 S Greenwood Ave.	16
Golfview, 1280 E. Druid Road	16
Gray Moss Inn, P O Box 1328	17
Greenwood, N Greenwood Ave 1/2 Palmetto St	15
Horizon House, 31 Island Way	15
Imperial Court, 1425 S Blecher Road	16
Imperial Cove, 1433 U S Hwy 19 S	16
Imperial Gardens, 2100 Nursery Road	16
Jack Tar Harrison, P O Box 1049	17
Kalmia, 1227 S Highland Ave	18
Lindru, 711 S. Lincoln Ave.	16
Mandalay Shores, 880 Mandalay Ave.	15
Seville, 999 US Hwy 19 S.	16
Spanish Villas, State Route 60	15
Yacht Basin, 501 Mandalay Ave.	15

BUILDINGS

City Building, 112 S Osceola Ave.	16
Pinellas County Court House, 315 Haven	16
Professional Building, 301 Pierce	16

HOSPITALS

Clearwater Community	16
Morton F Plant, P O Box 210	17

DAYTONA BEACH 320

POST OFFICE BOXES

Box Nos.		
1-792	Holly Hill Br	17
1-1287	Port Orange Br.	19
1-0002767	Main Office	18
3001-3999	Peninsula Sta	18
4001-4655	South Daytona Br	21
5001-5897	Seabreeze Sta	20
6001-6369	A Sta	22
7001-7527	Datona Beach Shores Br	16

8001-8999	Allandale Br	23

RURAL ROUTES

1		14
2,3		19

STATIONS, BRANCHES AND UNITS

Allandale Br	23
Daytona Beach Shores Br	16
Dunlawton Br	19
Holly Hill Br	17
Peninsula Sta	18
Port Orange Br	19
Seabreeze Sta	20
South Daytona Br	21
General Delivery	15

FORT LAUDERDALE 333

POST OFFICE BOXES

Box Nos.		
A-Z	South Andrews.	15
1-1782	Fort Lauderdale	02
2000-2999	Colee Sta	03
3000-3999	Bahia-Mar Sta.	16
4000-4999	Sunrise Sta	04
6500-6999	Station 9	16
7000-7999	Sunrise Sta	04
8000-9999	Seminole Annex Sta.	10
10000-10999	Wilton Manors Br	05
11000-11999	Coral Ridge Sta	06
12000-12999	Plantation Br	14
13000-13999	Port Everglades Sta.	16
22000-22999	South Andrews Sta.	15
23000-24500	Oakland Park Br	07

RURAL ROUTES

1		14

STATIONS, BRANCHES AND UNITS

Bahia Mar Sta.	16
Colee Sta	03
Cooper City Br	14
Coral Ridge Sta.	06
Davie Br	14
Lauderdale-by-the-Sea Br	08
Lauderhill Br	13
Oakland Park Br	08
Plantation Br	14
Port Everglades Sta.	16
Seminole Annex Sta.	10
South Andrews Sta.	15
Sunrise Sta.	04
Sunrise Golf Village Br	13
Tamarac Br	13
Wilton Manors Br	05
General Delivery	19
Postmaster	10

Fort Lauderdale (Con.)   333

APARTMENTS, HOTELS, MOTELS

Atlantic Towers, 1920 S Ocean Dr	16
Birch Tower, 3003 Terramar	04
Breakwater Towers, 1900 S Ocean Dr	16
Broward, 304 S Andrews Ave	01
Caribe, 4050 N Ocean Dr	08
Casa Glamoretta, 435 N Bayshore Dr	04
Coral Ridge Towers, 3233 NE 34th	08
Coral Sands, 1224 E Las Olas Blvd	01
Doctor Kennedy Homes, 1004 W Broward Blvd	12
Dorset House, 2881 NE 32nd	06
Edgewater Arms, 3600 Galt Ocean Dr	08
Escape, 2900 Riomar	04
Everglades House, 2000 S Ocean Dr	16
Fountain Head, 3900 N Ocean Dr	08
Galt Ocean Mile, 3200 Galt Ocean Dr	08
Holiday, 1250 Mayan Dr	16
Karen Club, 1943 Karen Dr	04
Lago Mar, 1700 S Ocean Dr	16
Lauderdale Beach, 101 S Atlantic Blvd	16
Marie Anntoinette, 2222 N Atlantic	05
Maybury Mansions, 5200 NE 24 Ter	06
Ocean Manor, 4040 Galt Ocean Dr	08
Ocean Summit, 4010 N Ocean Dr	08
Park View, 907 NE 15th Ave	04
Pier 66, 2301 SE 17th	16
Riverside, 620 E Las Olas Blvd	01
Riverview Gardens, 1000 SE 4th	01
Royal Admiral, 3800 Galt Ocean Dr	08
Sea Tower, 2840 N Ocean Blvd	08
Sheraton, 303 N Atlantic Blvd	04
Sky Harbor East, 2100 S Ocean Dr	16
Springlide, 345 N Atlantic Blvd	04
Sunrise Tower, 888 Intracostal	04
Trade Winds, 1 N Atlantic Blvd	04
Versailles, 215 N Birch Rd	04
Yankee Clipper Beachside, 1136 Holiday Dr	16
Yankee Clipper, 1140 Seabreeze Blvd	16

BUILDINGS

Anaconda, 1766 E Sunrise Blvd	04

86

Atlantic Federal, 1750 E Sunrise Blvd	04
Bayview, 1040 Bayview Dr	04
Blount, 25 E Las Olas Blvd	01
Broward Bank, 25 S Andrews Ave	01
Coral Center, 30 108	06
Coral Ridge, 3350 N Federal Hwy	06
Court House Square, 200 SE 6th	01
First Federal, 301 E Las Olas Blvd	01
First National Bank, 1 Financial Plaza	94
Gateway, 1800 E Sunrise Blvd	04
Grandway, 3901 W Broward Blvd	12
Kenann, 3101 N Federal Hwy	06
Las Olas, 305 S Andrews Ave	01
Plaza, 3900 W Broward Blvd	12
Professional, 915 Middle River Dr	04
Romark, 3521 W Broward Blvd	12
Sunrise Plaza, 2501 E Sunrise Blvd	04
Sweet, 305 S Andrews Ave	01
Times Square Professional, 3042 N Federal Hwy	06
Tropical Arcade, 224 S Andrews Ave	01

GOVERNMENT OFFICES

Broward County Courthouse, 221 SE 6th	01
City Hall, 100 N. Andrews Ave	01
Internal Revenue, 2309 N Federal Hwy	05
Social Security, 308 N 3rd Ave	01

HOSPITALS

Beach, 125 N Birch Rd	04
Broward General, 1600 S Andrews Ave	16
Doctors General, 6701 W Sunrise Blvd	13
Holy Cross, 4701 N Federal Hwy	08
Las Olas, 1516 E Las Olas Blvd	01
Plantation General, 401 NW 42nd Ave	13

UNIVERSITIES AND COLLEGES

Broward Community College, 3600 SW 70th Ave	14
Drake, 1401 E Broward Blvd	01
Nova, College Ave	14

FORT MYERS   339

POST OFFICE BOXES

Box Nos.		
A-Z	Cape Coral	04

A-Z	Main Office	02
1-697	Matlacha R. Sta	01
1-898	Tice Br	05
1-1379	Cape Coral Br	04
1-2415	Main Office	02
AA-ZZ	Cape Coral	04
AA-ZZ	Main Office	02
AB-AZ	Cape Coral	04
BA-BP	Cape Coral	04
CE-CP	Cape Coral	04
AAA-BBB	Main Office	02
3001-3317	North Fort Myers Br	03
5001-5148	South Fort Myers Sta	01
6001-7192	Miracle Mile Br	01

RURAL ROUTES

1	05
2	03
3	01
4	05
5	01
6	03
7	05
8	01
9	04

STATIONS, BRANCHES AND UNITS

Cape Coral Br	04
Matlacha Rural Br	01
Miracle Mile Sta	01
North Fort Myers Br	03
South Fort Myers Sta	01
Tice Br	05
General Delivery	02
Postmaster	02

HIALEAH   330

POST OFFICE BOXES

Box Nos.		
1-1999	Main Office	11
2000-2999	Palm Village Sta	12
3000-3999	Bright Sta	13
4000-4999	Hialeah-Lakes Sta	14

RURAL ROUTES

1	10

STATIONS, BRANCHES AND UNITS

Bright Sta	13
Hialeah Lakes Sta	14
Palm Village Sta	12
General Delivery	10
Postmaster	10

HOLLYWOOD   330

POST OFFICE BOXES

Box Nos.		
A-HHH	Main Office	22

Hollywood (Con.)   330

1-2454	Main Office	22
3551-4455	West Hollywood	
	Br	23
5000-5294	Driftwood Br	24
6001-7075	Hollywood Hills	
	Sta	21

STATIONS, BRANCHES AND UNITS

Driftwood Sta	24
Forest Ridge Br	23
Hollywood Hills Br	21
Miramar Br	23
Pembroke Pines Br	23
West Hollywood Br	23
Westwood Br	24
General Delivery	22
Postmaster	22

JACKSONVILLE   322

POST OFFICE BOXES

Box Nos.

A-Z	West Bay	
	Annex Sta	03
1-38	Ft George	
	Island Sta	26
1-88	Grand Crossing	
	Sta	05
1-108	Maxville Rural	
	Sta	65
1-114	Ortega Sta	10
1-148	Bayard Rural	
	Sta	24
1-225	Neptune Beach	
	Sta	33
1-298	Whitehouse R	
	Sta	20
1-313	Dinsmore R	
	Sta	19
1-360	Mayport Sta	67
1-467	Oceanway Sta	18
1-746	Baldwin Br	34
1-1148	Atlantic Beach	
	Br	33
1-1999	Main Office	01
138-276	Ft George	
	Island Sta	26
2000-2999	West Bay	
	Annex Sta	03
3000-3999	Station F	06
4000-4999	Main Office	01
5000-5999	South	
	Jacksonville	
	Sta	07
6000-6999	Murray Hill	
	Sta	05
7000-7999	Lake Shore	
	Sta	10
8000-8999	Arlington Sta	11
9000-9999	Lake Forest	
	Sta	08
10000-10999	South	
	Jacksonville	
	Sta	07
11000-11999	Arlington Sta	11
12000-12999	Carver Sta	09
13000-13999	Station F	06

14000-14999	Lake Shore	
	Sta	10
16000-17999	Pottsburg Sta	16
18000-18999	Air Mail	
	Facility Sta	29
26000-26999	Oceanway Sta	18
27000-27999	Station 19	05
30000-31999	Yukon Sta	30
35000-35999	Main Office	02
36000-36999	Garden City R	
	Sta	18
37000-37999	Murray Hill	
	Sta	05
38000-38999	Station G	02
50000-51999	Jacksonville	
	Beach Br	50

RURAL ROUTES

1	11
2,3	18
4	10
5	05
6	17
7	05
8	16
9	08
SR	29
10	05
11	18
12	18
13	05
14	08
15	34
16	08
17	17
18	16
19	10

STATIONS, BRANCHES AND UNITS

Arlington Sta	11
Atlantic Beach Br	33
Baldwin Br	34
Bayard Sta	24
Brookview Sta	11
Carver Sta	09
Cecil Field MOU	15
Dinsmore Sta	19
Dunn Avenue Sta	18
Fort George Island Sta	26
Garden City Rural Sta	18
Grand Crossing Sta	05
Jacksonville AMF Sta	29
Jacksonville Beach Br	50
Jacksonville NAS Br	12
Jacksonville University Sta	11
Lake Forest Sta	08
Lake Lucina Sta	11
Lake Shore Sta	10
Maxville Rural Sta	65
Mayport Sta	67
Mayport Naval Station Sta	28
Mandarin Sta	17
Murray Hill Sta	05
Naval Hospital Sta	14
Neptune Beach Br	33
Oceanway Sta	18
Ortega Sta	10
Paxon Sta	05
Pottsburg Sta	16
Soutel Sta	08
South Jacksonville Sta	07
Spring Park Sta	07

Wesconnett Sta	10
Wesley Manor Rural Br	23
West Bay Annex Sta	03
Whitehouse Rural Sta	20
Yukon Sta	30
General Delivery	01
Postmaster	01

APARTMENTS, HOTELS, MOTELS

Adrian, 118 Clay	02
Amelia, 1308 Willowbranch Ave	05
Aragon	01
Commander, 3946 St Johns Ave	05
Durkeeville Project, 1601 N Myrtle Ave	09
Floridan	01
Hilton, 565 S Main	07
Johnson Terrace, 33 E Monroe	02
Joseph H Blodgett Homes, 1207 Davis	09
Martha Washington, 1636 King	04
Mayflower	01
Park Lane, 1846 Margaret	04
Pickwick, 521 N Main	02
Place By The Sea, 901 Ocean Blvd	33
Ramada Inn Airport, 1351 Airport Rd	18
Ramada Inn Downtown, 510 Lane Ave S	05
Riverton Towers, 5353 Mathews Expy	11
Robert Meyer	01
Rollins, 312 W Forsyth	02
Tahitian Village, 1100 Seagate	33
Talleyrand, 720 Talleyrand Ave	02
Thunderbird Motor Hotel, 5865 Mathews Expy	11

BUILDINGS

American Heritage Life, 13 E Forsyth	02
American National Bank Of Jacksonville, 2031 Hendricks	07
Atlantic Bank, 121 W Forsyth	02
Barnett, 112 W Adams	02
Baymar, 233 E Bay	02
Bugbee, 1143 Mary	07
Carpenters, 920 N Main	02
Clara White Mission, 613 W Ashley	02
Coffey, 404 W Monroe	02
Daniel, 325 N Main	02
Exchange, 218 W Adams	02
Federal, 400 W Bay	02
Fidelity Federal, 16 N Laura	02
First Bank & Trust Company, 231 E Forsyth	02
First Federal Savings, 306 W Adams	02
Florida Bank, 223 W Adams	02
Florida Baptist, 1230 Hendricks Ave	07
Florida State Office, 300 E Monroe	02

Jacksonville (Con.)   322

Florida Title, 108 W Forsyth..... 02
Graham Title, 108 W Forsyth.. 02
Greenleaf Annex, 111 W
  Adams................................. 02
Greenleaf, 208 N Laura........ 02
Guaranty Life, 137 E Forsyth.. 02
Hamby, 325 W Forsyth........... 02
Hemming Park, 46 W Duval.... 02
Hildebrandt, 306 W Adams.... 02
Independent Life, 233 W
  Duval................................... 02
J C Lanier, 107 N Market....... 02
Jacksonville National Bank
  Annex, 117 Laura................ 02
Jacksonville National Bank,
  45 W Forsyth....................... 02
Law Exchange, 238 E
  Forsyth............................... 02
Nasrallah, 2720 Park............. 05
Oreilly, 237 W Forsyth........... 02
Professional, 127 W Adams.... 02
Prudential 841 Prudential Dr.. 07
Saint James, 117 W Duval..... 02
Schultz, 118 W Adams........... 02
Seminole, 122 W Forsyth....... 02
Slappey, 317 W Forsyth......... 02
Smith, 211 E Forsyth............. 02
Suwannee, 424 W Forsyth...... 02
Title & Trust, 200 E Forsyth.. 02
Trout, 28 E Bay.................... 02
Union Terminal Warehouse,
  700 E Union......................... 06
Universal-Marion, 21 W
  Church............................... 02
Williams, 7 W Forsyth........... 02

GOVERNMENT OFFICES

City Hall, 220 E Bay.............. 02
City Utilities, 34 S Laura....... 02
County Court House, 330 E
  Bay..................................... 02
Criminal Court, 330 E Bay..... 02
United States Court House,
  311 W Monroe...................... 02
United States Federal Bldg,
  400 W Bay........................... 02

HOSPITALS

Baptist, 800 Prudential Dr..... 07
Doctor Millers Sanitarium,
  2460 Atlantic Blvd............. 07
Doctors, 2821 Riverside Ave.. 05
Duval Medical Center, 2000
  Jefferson........................... 06
Five Points Medical Center,
  800 Lomax........................... 04
Hope Haven Association,
  5721 Atlantic Blvd............. 07
Jacksonville Convalescnet,
  131 E 7th........................... 06
Medical Dental, 225 W
  Ashley............................... 02
Memorial Hospital, 3625
  University Blvd., S............. 16
Methodist, 1640 Jefferson.... 09
Riverside Hospital, 2033
  Riverside Ave..................... 04
Saint Lukes, 1900 Boulevard.. 04
Saint Vincents, Foot Of
  Barrs................................. 04

University Hospital, 655 W
  8th...................................... 09

UNIVERSITIES AND COLLEGES

Edward Waters College,
  Kings Rd............................. 09
Jacksonville University,
  University Blvd N................ 11

LAKELAND   338

POST OFFICE BOXES

Box Nos.		
A-BW	Main Office	02
1-1999	Main Office	02
2001-2736	Dixieland Sta.	03
3000-3520	Main Office	02

RURAL ROUTES

1 09
2,3 01
4 03
5,6,7 01
8 03
9,10,11 01

STATIONS, BRANCHES AND UNITS

Country Club Estates Br........ 01
Dixieland Sta....................... 03
Florida Southern College Sta.. 02
Grove Park Sta..................... 03
Searstown Sta...................... 01
General Delivery................... 02
Postmaster.......................... 02

MELBOURNE   329

POST OFFICE BOXES

Box Nos.		
1-837	Palm Bay Br....	05
1-957	Melbourne	
	Beach Br....	51
1-1569	Eau Gallie Sta..	35
1-2316	Melville Br...	01
2001-2875	Satellite Beach	
	Br........	37
3001-3599	Indialantic Br...	03

RURAL ROUTES

1 35
2 01
3 51
STAR................................... 01

STATIONS, BRANCHES AND UNITS

Eau Gallie Sta...................... 35
Indialantic Br....................... 03
Indian Harbor Beach Br......... 37
Loveridge Heights Sta........... 35
Melbourne Beach Br.............. 51
Mintons Corner Br................ 01
North Babcock Sta................ 01

Palm Bay Br......................... 05
Palm Shores Rural Br............ 35
Sarno Plaza Sta.................... 35
Satellite Beach Br................. 37
South Patrick Br................... 37
Trailer Haven Sta.................. 01
West Eau Gallie Br................ 35

APARTMENTS, HOTELS, MOTELS

Apollo Apartments 650 Palm
  Dr...................................... 37
Eau Gallie Imperial Hotel
  1477 Pineapple Ave............ 35
Holiday Inn Of Melbourne
  440 So Harbor City Blvd..... 01
Holiday Inn West, 10900
  West New Haven Ave.......... 01
Host Of America 420 So
  Harbor City Blvd............... 01
Hotel Melbourne 1960 So
  Harbor City Blvd............... 01
Howard Johnson Motor Lodge
  1515 So Harbor City Blvd.. 01
Ocean View Apartments 2642
  A-1-A Hwy.......................... 37
Orange Court Apartments
  2100 So Melbourne Court.. 01
Parkway Palms Apartments
  201 Harbor City Parkway.. 37
Pentagon Apartments 21 E
  Strawbridge Ave................ 01
Pines Motel 1894 So Patrick
  Drive................................. 37
Royal Motor Lodge 1423 So
  Harbor City Blvd............... 01
Sandpiper Towers 205 A-1-A
  Hwy.................................... 37
Shore View Apartments 50
  Berkeley St........................ 37
Southgate Blvd Apartments
  50 E Southgate Blvd........... 01
Trinity Towers Apartments
  East 700 E Strawbridge
  Ave....................................
Trinity Towers Apartments
  West 632 E Strawbridge
  Ave.................................... 01
Wickham Oaks Apartments
  1432 Parkway Drive............ 35

GOVERNMENT OFFICES

Chamber Of Commerce 657
  Eau Gallie Blvd.................. 35
County Court House South
  Brevard Branch 55 So
  Neiman Ave......................... 01

HOSPITALS

Brevard Crippled Childrens
  Clinic 450 E Sheridan Rd... 01
Brevard Hospital 1350 S
  Hickory St.......................... 01
Carnegie Gardens Nursing
  Home 1415 S Hickory St.... 01
Florida Convalescent Home
  Of Melbourne 516 E
  Sheridan Rd....................... 01
Medic Home Health Center
  1420 S Oak St..................... 01

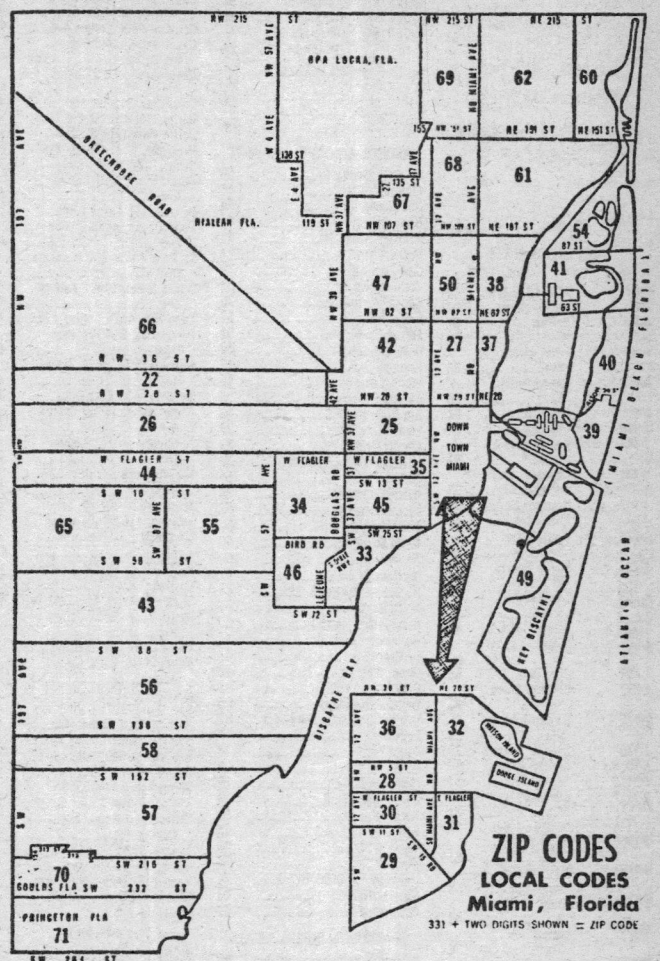

ZIP CODES
LOCAL CODES
Miami, Florida
331 + TWO DIGITS SHOWN = ZIP CODE

Melbourne (Con.)   329

MILITARY INSTALLATIONS

Armed Forces Reserve Center
   1889 Stewart Rd 35
Naval Reserve Training
   Facility 1889 Stewart Rd.... 35

UNIVERSITIES AND COLLEGES

Florida Institute Of
   Technology 7901 S
   Country Club Rd 01

MIAMI   331

POST OFFICE BOXES

Box Nos.
A-G   Allapattah Sta..... 42
A-M   Northwest Br....... 47
A-T   Perrine Br.......... 57
A-Y   Kendall Br.......... 56
A-Y   Little River
            Sta.............. 38
A-Y   Miami Beach
            Br............... 39
A-Y   Ufeta Br........... 64
J-379   Ufetz Br........... 64
1-444   Edison Center
            Sta.............. 51
1-444   Olympia
            Heights Br...... 65
1-597   Gratigny Br........ 68
1-697   Allapattah Sta.... 42
1-729   North Miami
            Beach Br........ 60
1-734   Miami Shores
            Br............... 53
1-759   Shenandoah
            Sta.............. 45
1-829   Tamiami Sta 44
1-846   Miami Springs
            Br............... 66
1-894   Ojus Br............ 63
1-897   Coconut Grove
            Sta.............. 33
1-912   Biscayne Annex
            Sta.............. 52
1-975   Riverside Sta..... 35
1-1014   Kendall Br......... 56
1-1110   Perrine Br......... 57
1-1112   Buena Vista
            Sta.............. 37
1-1115   Northwest Br..... 47
1-1405   North Miami
            Br............... 61
1-1444   International
            Airport Br...... 48
1-1546   South Miami
            Br............... 43
1-1782   Little River
            Sta.............. 38
1-1800   Miami Beach
            Br............... 39
1-1918   Coral Gables
            Br............... 34
161-5222 Main Office 01
2001-2617 Airport Mail
            Facility Br...... 56

2001-2899 Ocean View Br . 40
3001-3742 Norland Br...... 69
4001-4890 Normandy Br ... 41
6001-6447 B Sta........... 23
6001-6787 Surfside Br..... 54
7001-7597 Ludlam Br...... 55
8001-9194 University Of
             Miami Br....... 24

RURAL ROUTES

1 44
2 57
4 56

STATIONS, BRANCHES AND UNITS

Air Mail Facility Br............. 59
Allapattah Sta................ 42
Bal Harbour Br................ 54
Barry College Br.............. 61
Biscayne Annex Sta.......... 52
Buena Vista Sta.............. 27
Carl Fisher Br................ 39
Coral Gables Br............... 34
Coconut Grove Sta........... 33
Cutler Ridge Br............... 57
Edison Center Sta............ 51
Golden Beach Br.............. 60
Gratigny Br................... 67
International Airport Br....... 48
Kendall Br.................... 56
Key Biscayne Br............... 49
Lemon City Sta............... 37
Lincoln Br.................... 39
Little River Sta............... 38
Ludlam Br.................... 55
Miami Beach Br............... 39
Miami Shores Br.............. 53
Miami Springs Br............. 66
Motel Row Br................. 60
Norland Br................... 69
Normandy Br................. 41
North Bay Village Br.......... 41
North Miami Br............... 61
North Miami Beach Br........ 60
Northside Center Br.......... 47
Northwest Br................. 47
Ocean View Br............... 40
Ojus Br...................... 63
Olympia Heights Br.......... 65
One Hundred Sixty Third St Br. 62
Perrine Br.................... 57
Ponce Br..................... 34
Riverside Sta................. 25
Shenandoah.................. 29
South Miami Br............... 43
Suney Isles Br................ 54
Surfside Br................... 54
Tamiami Sta.................. 26
Ufeta Br...................... 64
University of Miami Br......... 24
General Delivery.............. 01
Postmaster................... 01

APARTMENTS, HOTELS, MOTELS

Alcazar, 500 Biscayne Blvd 32
Algiers, 2555 Collins Ave....... 40
Alhambra, 119 SE 2nd St....... 31
Americana, 9701 Collins Ave.. 54
Balmoral, 9801 Collins Ave.... 54
Beau Rivage, 9955 Collins
   Ave...................... 54

Biltmore Way, 713 Biltmore
   Way...................... 34
Biscayne Terrace, 340
   Biscayne Blvd............. 32
Cadillac, 3925 Collins Ave 40
Caribbean, 3737 Collins Ave.. 40
Carillon, 6801 Collins Ave..... 41
Casablanca, 6345 Collins
   Ave...................... 41
Castaways, 16375 Collins
   Ave...................... 60
Columbus, 312 NE 1st....... 32
Cortez, 241 NE 1st Ave...... 32
Dallas Park, 111 SE 3rd...... 31
Deauville, 6701 Collins Ave... 41
Delano, 1685 Collins Ave.... 39
Desert Inn, 17201 Collins
   Ave...................... 60
Di Lido, 155 Lincoln Rd...... 39
Doral Beach, 4833 Collins
   Ave...................... 40
Du Pont Plaza, 300 Biscayne
   Blvd Way................. 31
Dunes Motel, 17001 Collins
   Ave...................... 60
Eden Roc, 4525 Collins Ave... 40
Everglades, 244 Biscayne
   Blvd...................... 32
Fontainebleau, 4441 Collins
   Ave...................... 40
Gateway, 656 East Dr....... 66
Golden Gate, 19400 Collins
   Ave...................... 60
Kenilworth, 10201 Collins
   Ave...................... 54
Key Biscayne & Villas, 300
   Ocean Dr................. 49
Leamington, 307 NE 1st.... 32
Lucerne, 4101 Collins Ave.... 40
Mc Allister, 10 Biscayne
   Blvd...................... 32
Miami Colonial, 146 Biscayne
   Blvd...................... 32
Miami Gateway, 656 East Dr. 66
Monte Carlo, 6551 Collins
   Ave...................... 41
Patricia, 312 SE 2nd Ave.... 31
Roney Plaza, 2301 Collins
   Ave...................... 39
Royalton, 131 SE 1st....... 31
San Souci, 3101 Collins Ave.. 40
Saxony, 3201 Collins Ave.... 40
Sea Isle, 3001 Collins Ave.... 40
Sea View, 9909 Collins Ave.. 54
Seville, 2901 Collins Ave..... 40
Sherry Frontenac, 6565
   Collins Ave............... 41
Thunderbird Motel, 18401
   Collins Ave............... 60
Towers, 332 SE 2nd Ave.... 31
Urmey, 34 SE 2nd Ave..... 31
Versailles, 3425 Collins Ave.. 40
Whispering Palms, 18901
   Collins Ave............... 60

BUILDINGS

Aladdin, 1213 Lincoln Rd.... 39
American Bankers Insurance
   Company, 600 Brickell
   Ave...................... 31
American Title, 901 N E 2nd
   Ave...................... 32

Miami (Con.)   331

Biscayne Towers, 100
  Biscayne Blvd................ 32
Calumet, 10 NE 3rd Ave...... 32
Capital Bank, 117 NE 1 Ave... 32
Chamber Of Commerce, 141
  NE 3 Ave.................... 32
Congress, 111 N E 2nd Ave..... 32
Coral Gables First National
  Bank, 100 Coral Way........ 34
Dade Commonwealth, 139 NE
  1st........................... 32
Dinner Key Exposition, 3360
  Dinner Key Dr............... 33
Du Pont-Plaza, 300 Biscayne
  Blvd Way.................... 31
Fashion Mart, 127 NW 2nd.... 28
Federal Office 51 SW 1 Ave..... 30
First Federal, 100 NE 1st
  Ave.......................... 31
First National Bank Miami,
  100 Biscayne Blvd S........ 31
First National Bank Miami,
  350 SE 1st.................. 31
First National Bank Miami,
  351 SE 2nd St.............. 31
First National Bank-Miami
  Beach....................... 39
Five-Fifty, 550 Brickell Ave...... 31
Flagler........................... 31
Flagler Federal Savings &
  Loan 111 NE 1st St........ 32
Florida National Bank Coral,
  159 Miracle Mile............ 34
Huntington Medical, 168 SE
  1 St......................... 31
Ingraham, 25 SE 2nd Ave...... 31
Insurance Exchange, 901 NE
  2nd Ave..................... 32
Langford, 121 SE 1st........... 31
Lincoln Medical, 541 Lincoln
  Rd........................... 39
Lincoln, 350 Lincoln Rd........ 39
Mercantile Natl Bank, 420
  Lincoln Rd.................. 39
Meridian Medical Center,
  1680 Meridian Ave.......... 39
Merrick, 5300 University Dr.... 46
Miami Beach Federal, 407
  Lincoln Rd.................. 39
Municipal, 1700 Washington
  Ave.......................... 39
Northeast Airlines, 150 SE
  2ave......................... 31
Number One Miami, 300
  Biscayne Blvd Way.......... 31
Olympia, 174 Flagler St......... 31
One Lincoln Road, 169
  Lincoln Road................ 39
Pan American Bank, 150 SE
  3rd Ave..................... 31
Plaza, 245 SE 1st.............. 31
Professional, 216 NE 2nd
  Ave.......................... 32
Roper, 20 SE 3rd Ave.......... 31
Seybold, 36 NE 1st............ 31
Shoreland, 119 E Flagler St.... 31
Six-Hundred-Five Lincoln
  Road, 605 Lincoln Road..... 39
Sterling, 927 Lincoln Rd....... 39

Three Thirty, 330 Biscayne
  Blvd.......................... 32
Three-Fifty Lincoln Road,
  1643 Washington Ave........ 39
Two-Twenty, 220 Miracle
  Mile......................... 34
Y M C A, 40 NE 3 Ave........ 32

GOVERNMENT OFFICES

Chamber Of Commerce, 141
  NE 3rd Ave................. 32

HOSPITALS

Baptist, 8900 N Kendall Dr.... 56
Cedars Of Lebanon, 1321 NW
  14 St........................ 25
Christian, 4700 NW 32 Ave.... 42
Dade County, Hospital Rd...... 56
Doctors, 5000 University Dr.... 46
Jackson Memorial, 1000 NW
  17 St........................ 36
Mercy, 3663 So Miami Ave..... 33
Miami Heart Institute 4701
  N. Meridian Ave............. 40
Mt Sinai, 4300 Alton Rd....... 40
National Childrens Cardiac,
  1475 NW 12 Ave............ 36
North Dade General, 16951
  NW 2 Ave................... 69
North Miami General, 1701
  NE 127 St.................. 61
North Shore, 9200 NW 11
  Ave.......................... 50
Northwest, 1060 NW 79....... 50
Osteopathic Genl, 1750 N E
  167.......................... 62
Pan American, 5959 NW 7
  St........................... 26
Saint Francis, 250 W 63 St.... 41
South Coral Gables, 3100
  Douglas Rd................. 34
South Miami, 7400 SW 62
  Ave.......................... 43
South Shore Hospital &
  Medical Center.............. 39
United States Veterans, 1201
  NW 16 St.................. 25
Variety Childrens, 6125 SW
  31 St........................ 55
Victoria, 930 NW 4 St......... 28
Westchester Genl, 2500 S W
  75 Ave...................... 55

UNIVERSITIES AND COLLEGES

Barry, 11300 NE 2nd Ave...... 61
Dade Junior North Campus
  11380 NW 27th Ave......... 67
Dade Junior South Campus
  11011 SW 104th St......... 56
Florida International 11200
  SW 8th St.................. 44
University Of Miami, Cgab..... 24

ORLANDO   328

POST OFFICE BOXES

Box Nos
1-3833   Downtown Sta.... 02
M-1-M-2099   Mc Coy A F B
                Sta........... 12

5000-5999   Orange
             Blossom Sta... 05
6000-6999   Colonialtown
             Sta........... 03
7000-7999   College Park
             Sta........... 04
8000-8999   Dixie Village
             Sta........... 06
9000-9999   Union Park
             Rural Br...... 07
10000-10999 Taft Rural Br.. 09
11000-11999 Coytown Sta... 03
13000-13999 Pinecastle Br.. 09
14000-14999 Azalea Park Br.. 07
15000-15999 Pine Hills Br.. 08
16000-16999 Orlovista Br.... 11
17000-17999 Lockhart Br.... 10
20000-20999 Herndon Sta... 14
21000-21999 Kennedy Space
             Center Br..... 15
22000-24999 Lake Buena
             Vista Br...... 30
25000-26999 Fla Tech
             University.... 16

RURAL ROUTES

1.................................. 09
2.................................. 10
3.................................. 11
4,5,6............................. 07
7.................................. 05

STATIONS, BRANCHES AND UNITS

Azalea Park Br.................. 07
College Park Sta............... 04
Colonialtown Sta............... 03
Coytown Sta.................... 03
Dixie Village Sta............... 06
Dover Shores Sta.............. 06
Downtown Sta.................. 02
Fairvilla Br..................... 04
Herndon Sta.................... 14
Kennedy Space Ctr Br........ 15
Lockhart Br.................... 10
Mc Coy A F B MOU............ 12
Naval Training Center Sta..... 13
Orange Blossom Sta........... 05
Orlando Naval Hospital Sta.... 13
Orlovista Br................... 11
Pine Castle Br................. 09
Pine Hills Br................... 08
Taft Rural Br.................. 09
Union Park Rural Br........... 07
General Delivery............... 02
Postmaster..................... 02

APARTMENTS, HOTELS, MOTELS

Angebilt, 37 Orange Ave N.... 02
Baptist Terrace, 414 Pine E.... 01
Central Towers, 350 E
  Jackson...................... 01
Downtowner, 264 Orange Ave
  S............................. 02
Executive House, 1200
  Holden Ave.................. 09
Georgetown Apts, 5500 Silver
  Star Rd..................... 08
Gurtler Lake Ivanhoe, 1701
  Gurtler Ct................... 04
Kinneret 515 Delaney Ave..... 01

Orlando (Con.) — 328

Lake Fairview Apts, 4328 Edgewater Dr ... 04
Lake Lucerne Plaza, 545 Delaney Ave S ... 01
Lake Mann Homes, Bethune Dr ... 05
Lucerne Towers, 20 Lucerne Cir W ... 01
Magnolia Towers, 100 Anderson E ... 01
Orlando Reeves Terrace, 1607 South E ... 01
Park Plaza, 431 Central Blvd E ... 02
Robert Meyer Inn, 151 Washington E ... 02
San Juan, 32 Orange Ave N ... 01

BUILDINGS

Bradshaw 14 Washington E ... 01
Citizens National Bank, 240 Orange Ave N ... 01
Cna, 255 Orange Ave S ... 01
Columbia Professional, 61 Columbia W ... 06
Executive, 2520 Orange Ave N ... 04
Federal 26 Robinson E ... 01
First Federal, 109 Church E ... 01
First National Bank, 200-228 Orange Ave S ... 01
Hartford 200 Robinson E ... 01
Metcalf, 102 Orange Ave S ... 01
One North Orange, 1-7 Orange Ave N ... 01
Rosalind, 160 Washington E ... 01
Summerlin Center, 618 South E ... 01

GOVERNMENT OFFICES

Chamber Of Commerce Building, 75 Ivanhoe Blvd E ... 04
County Court House & Annex, 65 Central Blvd E ... 01
Orlando City Hall 400 Orange Ave S ... 01

HOSPITALS

Florida Hospital, 601 Rollins E ... 02
Holiday, 92 Miller W ... 06
Mercy Medical Center, 1800 Mercy Dr ... 08
Orange Memorial, 1416 Orange Ave S ... 01
Orlando General, 7727 Lake Underhill Rd ... 07
Sunland Training Center, Hiawassa Rd ... 02

MILITARY INSTALLATIONS

Finance Unit 1 Recruit Trng Command ... 13
Kennedy Space Center ... 15
Mc Coy A F B ... 12
N A S A ... 99
Naval Training Ctr ... 13

Naval Training Device Ctr ... 13
Navy Research Lab Underwater Sound Reference Div ... 06

UNIVERSITIES AND COLLEGES

Fla Tech Univ, Alafaya Trail ... 16
Mid Florida Technical Institute, 2908 Oak Ridge Rd W ... 09
Valencia Jr College, 2908 Oak Ridge Rd W ... 09

PENSACOLA — 325

POST OFFICE BOXES

Box Nos.		
1-1999	Main Office	02
2000-2999	East Hill Sta	03
3000-3999	Myrtle Grove Br	06
4000-4999	Warrington Br	07
5000-5999	West Pensacola Br	05
6000-6999	Brent Br	03
7000-7999	Ensley Br	04
8000-8999	Town & Country Plaza Br	05
10000-10999	Nobles Sta	04
11000-11999	Naval Hospital Br	12
12000-12999	Main Office	02
14000-14999	Naval Communications Training Ctr Br	11
19000-19999	Shackleford Sta	03
31000-31999	University Of West Florida Br	04

RURAL ROUTES

1	07
2	06
3,4	03
6	07
7,8	06
9	03
10	06
11	03

STATIONS, BRANCHES AND UNITS

Brent Br ... 05
East Hill Sta ... 03
Ellyson Field Br ... 09
Ensley Br ... 04
Highland Terrace Sta ... 03
Myrtle Grove Br ... 06
Naval Comm Training Center Br ... 11
Naval Station Br ... 08
Nobles Sta ... 04
Saufley Field Br ... 10
Shackleford Sta ... 03

Town And Country Plaza Br ... 05
University Of West Florida Rural Br ... 04
Warrington Br ... 07
West Pensacola Br ... 05
General Delivery ... 02
Postmaster ... 02

MILITARY INSTALLATIONS

Fort Barrancas National Cemetary ... 08
Naval Air Station ... 08
Naval Air Station Ellyson Field ... 09
Naval Air Station Saufley Field ... 10
Naval Communications Training Ctr ... 11
Naval Hospital ... 12

UNIVERSITIES AND COLLEGES

Pensacola Junior College ... 04
University Of West Florida ... 04

POMPANO BEACH — 330

POST OFFICE BOXES

Box Nos.		
A-X	Main Office	61
1-2499	Main Office	61
2501-3288	Hamilton Sta	62
4000-4999	Margate Br	63
5000-6034	Light House Point Br	64
6000-6999	1 Sta	60
7000-7499	2 Sta	60
8000-0009244	Coral Springs Rural Br	65
10001-10059	Main Office	61

RURAL ROUTES

1,2	60

STATIONS, BRANCHES AND UNITS

Beacon Light Br ... 64
Coral Springs Rural Br ... 60
Hamilton Sta ... 62
Lighthouse Point Br ... 64
Margate Br ... 63
Pompano Isles Sta ... 62
General Delivery ... 60
Postmaster ... 60

HOSPITALS

Cypress Community Hospital 600 SW 3rd ... 60
Margate General Hospital 5850 Margate Blvd ... 63
North District Hospital, 201 E Sample Rd ... 64
Pompano Beach Hospital & Clinic, 155 E Atlantic Blvd ... 60

SAINT PETERSBURG 337

POST OFFICE BOXES

Box Nos.

A-Z	Open Air Sta	31
1-4192	Open Air Sta	31
5001-5236	Gulfport Br	37
6001-6999	Saint Petersburg Beach Br	36
7000-7999	Euclid Sta	34
8001-8999	Madeira Sta	38
9000-9999	Treasure Island Br	40
10000-14999	Saint Petersburg	33
20000-20999	Gateway Mall Sta	42
46341-46999	Pass-A-Grille Beach	41
54691-54749	Big Bayou	39

STATIONS, BRANCHES AND UNITS

Airport Br	32
Bay Vista Br	05
Big Bayou Sta	39
Blind Pass Br	06
Clearview Br	14
Crossroads Sta	10
Disston Plaza Sta	10
Euclid Sta	02
Forty Ninth Street Br	07
Gateway Mall Sta	02
Gulfport Br	37
Johns Pass Br	08
Kenneth City Br	09
Madeira Beach Br	08
Northeast Park Sta	04
Open Air Sta	01
Pass-a-Grill Beach Br	41
Redington Beach Br	08
Saint Petersburg Beach Br	06
South Pasadena Br	07
Tierra Verde Rural Br	15
Treasure Island Br	40
Webbs City Sta	01
West Central Sta	07
General Delivery	33
Postmaster	30

APARTMENTS, HOTELS, MOTELS

Albermarle, 115 3rd Ave NE	31
Carleve, 357 2nd N	31
Central, 119 2nd N	31
Colonial, 126 2nd Ave NE	31
Concord, 100 2nd Ave N	31
Cordova, 253 2nd Ave N	31
Dennis, 326 1st Ave N	31
Detroit, 215 Central Ave	31
Edge Park, 256 1st No	31
Edward James, 11750 Gulf Blvd	06
Hilton 333 1 S	31
Hollander, 421 4th Ave N	31
Martha Washington, 234 3rd Ave N	31
Moulton, 342 3rd Ave N	31
Park House, 335 2nd Ave N	31
Pennflora, 443 2nd Ave N	31
Pennsylvania, 300 4th N	31

Poinsettia, 460 Central Ave	31
Ponce De Leon, 95 Central Ave	31
Priness Martha, 401 1st Ave N	31
Randolph, 200 4th N	31
Soreno, 100 Beach Dr NE	31
Suwannee, 501 1st Ave N	31
Ten Eyck, 132 Mirror Lake Dr	31
The Madison, 424 Central Ave	31
Toffenetti, 25 2nd N	31
Vinoy Park, 325 5th Ave NE	31

BUILDINGS

First Federal, 11 4th N	01
First National Bank, 9 4th S	01
Florida National Bank, 700 Central Ave	01
Florida Office, 472 Central Ave	01
Florida, 2201 4th No	04
Hall, 4 4th S	01
Legal, 447 3rd Ave N	01
Medical Square, 666 6 Th S	01
Saint Peterburg Medical Clinic, 501 11 Th N	05
Suncoast Medical Clinic, 500 7 Th S	01
300, 300 31st N	13

GOVERNMENT OFFICES

County, 150 5 Th N	01
Federal, 144 1st Ave S	01

HOSPITALS

All Childrens Hospital, 801 6th S	01
Apollo 400 30th Ave S	05
Bayfront Medical Center, 701 6st St S	31
Doctors, 401 15 Th N	05
Palms Of Pasadena, 1501 Pasadena Ave So	36
Saint Anthony, 601 12th No	33
Saint Petersburg General, 6500 38 Ave N	33

UNIVERSITIES AND COLLEGES

Eckerd College 5401 34th So	33
Saint Petersburg Junior, 6605 5th Ave N	33
Stetson University College Of Law, 1401 61st S	07
University South Florida, 830 1 St S	01

SARASOTA 335

POST OFFICE BOXES

Box Nos.

1-4322	Main Office	78
5001-5717	Southgate Sta	79
6001-6284	Saint Armands Sta	78
7001-7799	Pinecraft Br	78

8001-8724	Mobile Home Park Sta	78
9001-9337	Newtown Sta	78
10121-10237	Fruitville Br	78
11601-11895	Bee Ridge Br	78
12001-12291	East Avenue Sta	78
13001-13095	Airgate Br	78
15001-15452	Southgate Sta	79

RURAL ROUTES

1,2	77
3	80
4	77

STATIONS, BRANCHES AND UNITS

Airgate Br	78
Bee Ridge Br	78
Crescent Beach Br	78
East Avenue Sta	78
Fruitville Br	78
Lockwood Ridge Sta	78
Mobile Home Park Sta	78
Newtown Heights Br	78
Northside Sta	78
Pinecraft Br	78
Saint Armands Sta	78
Siesta Br	78
South Trail Br	78
Southgate Sta	79
Southside Sta	79
General Delivery	78
Postmaster	78

BUILDINGS

Azar 3800 So. Tamiami Trail	79
Doctors Garden 1880 Arlington	79
Marina Mar, 2 Marina Mar Drive	77
Medical Arts 1950 Arlington	79
Palmer Bank 1405 Main	77
Sarasota Bank 1605 Main	77
1900 Bldg. 1900 Main	77

GOVERNMENT OFFICES

City Hall 1565 1st	77
County Court House 2000 Main	77
Federal Building 111 So. Orange Ave	77

HOSPITALS

Doctors 2750 Bahia Vista	79
East Manor 1524 East Ave. So	79
Extendicare 1650 Osprey Ave. So	79
Geri-Care 3250 12th	80
Hill Haven 1625 Qsprey Ave. So	79
Memorial 1901 Arlington	79
Sunnyside Haven, 5201 Bahia Vista	80

Sarasota (Con.)   335

UNIVERSITIES AND COLLEGES

New College Administrative
  Po Box 1898   78
New College Students Po Box
  1958................................   78

TALLAHASSEE   323

POST OFFICE BOXES

Box Nos.
1-1999	Main Office	02
2001-2999	Woodward	
	Avenue Sta.....	04
3001-3999	Leon Sta	03

RURAL ROUTES

1......................................	03
2......................................	01
3......................................	03
4,5,6.................................	01
7......................................	03
8......................................	01
9......................................	03
10....................................	04
11....................................	03

STATIONS, BRANCHES AND UNITS

Big Bend Farm Rural Br........	11
Bradfordville Rural Br...........	01
Lafayette Rural Br.................	08
Leon Sta	03
Miccosukee Rural Br.............	09
Trailer City Rural Br.............	01
Wakulla Springs Rural Br.......	05
Woodward Avenue Sta...........	04
General Delivery...................	02
Postmaster...........................	02
Star Routes..........................	04

APARTMENTS, HOTELS, MOTELS

Berkshire Manor, Continental	
Ave & Ocala Rd.............	04
Chateau Deville, 2020	
Continental Ave.............	04
Colony Inn, 2191 Tennessee	
W......................................	04
Floridan, Monroe & Call.........	02
Holiday Inn Downtown...........	01
Holiday Inn, 1302 Apalachee	
Pky..................................	01
Howard Johnson, Brevard W	
& Tennessee....................	04
Howard Johnson, 722	
Apalachee Pky.................	01
Osceola Hall, 500 Chapel Dr..	04
Southernaire, Brevard W &	
Tennessee........................	04
Town & Campus, 940	
Brevard W.......................	04
Travelodge, 691 Tennessee	
W......................................	04
W. T. Cash Hall, 700	
Woodward Ave N............	04

BUILDINGS

Bloxham...............................	04
Bryant..................................	04
Burns...................................	04
Caldwell...............................	04
Capitol.................................	04
Carlton.................................	04
City Hall..............................	04
Collins.................................	04
County Courthouse..............	01
Holland................................	04
Johns...................................	04
Knott...................................	04
Larson.................................	04
Mayo....................................	04
Midyette-Moor......................	01
Supreme Court.....................	04
Tallahassee..........................	03
Tallahassee Bank & Trust.....	01
Whitfield..............................	04

HOSPITALS

Suntand................................	04
Tallahassee Convalescent.....	03
Tallahassee Memorial..........	04

UNIVERSITIES AND COLLEGES

Florida A & M University........	07
Florida State University........	06
Tallahassee Jr. College..........	04

TAMPA   336

POST OFFICE BOXES

Box Nos.
1-3500	Downtown........	01
4000-4708	West Tampa	
	Sta.............	07
5000-5999	Ybor City Sta..	05
6000-6999	Macdill Air	
	Force Base -	
	Br.............	08
7001-7299	Seminole	
	Heights Sta	03
8000-9999	Sulphur	
	Springs Sta	04
10001-10999	Peninsula Sta..	09
11001-11844	Produce Sta....	10
13000-13999	Interbay Sta....	11
14000-14999	Palma Ceia	
	Sta.............	09
15000-15999	Hilldale Sta	14
16001-16200	Temple Terrace	
	Br.............	17
17000-17999	Forest Hills	
	Sta.............	12
18000-18999	Peninsula Sta..	09
19000-19999	Port Tampa	
	City Sta	16
0022000-		
-0023999	Main Office	22

RURAL ROUTES

1......................................	12
2......................................	10
3......................................	19

4......................................	15
5......................................	14
6......................................	17

STATIONS, BRANCHES AND UNITS

Clair Mel City Br.................	19
Downtown Sta......................	02
Forest Hills Sta....................	12
Hilldale Sta	14
Interbay Sta	11
Mac Dill A F B Br.................	08
Palm River Br.......................	19
Palma Ceia Sta.....................	09
Peninsula Sta	09
Port Tampa City Sta.............	16
Produce Sta..........................	10
Seminole Heights Sta............	03
Sulphur Springs Sta..............	04
Sunshine Br.........................	15
T B Hospital Sta...................	14
Temple Terrace Br................	17
Twin Lake Br........................	04
University of Tampa Sta........	06
West Tampa Sta....................	07
Ybor Sta...............................	05
General Delivery...................	02
Postmaster...........................	02

APARTMENTS, HOTELS, MOTELS

Bay View 208 Jackson	02
Bayshore Royal 2109	
Bayshore Blvd.................	06
Bayshore Towers 4015	
Bayshore Blvd.................	11
Davis Island Towers 84 Davis	
Blvd................................	06
Florida Motor Hotel 905	
Florida Ave.....................	02
Harbor House 2401 Bayshore	
Blvd................................	09
Hyde Park Towers 406 Azeele..	06
Manager Motor Inn 200	
Ashley Dr.......................	02
Morrison Court 2311 Morrison	
Ave.................................	09
Sheraton Tampa Motor 515	
E. Cass...........................	02
University Apartments 4314	
E. Fletcher......................	12

BUILDINGS

Citizens 706 N. Franklin........	02
Exchange National Bank -	
610 N. Florida Ave...........	02
First National Bank 215 E.	
Madison..........................	02
Legal Center 725 J F	
Kennedy Blvd E...............	02
Marine Bank 315 E. Madison..	02
Medical 1 Davis Blvd.............	06
Ross 112 E Cass...................	02
Stovall Professional 305 N	
Morgan...........................	02
Tampa Theatre 709 N	
Franklin..........................	02
Wallace S 608 Tampa.............	02
Western Union 501 Twiggs......	02

Tampa (Con.)   336

GOVERNMENT OFFICES

City Hall 315 J F Kennedy
  Blvd E 02
County Court House 401
  Pierce 02
Federal 500 Zack 02
State Office 800 Twiggs..... 02

HOSPITALS

Centro Asturiano 21st Ave
  13th 05
Centro Espanol 4801 N
  Howard Ave. 03
Edwards W T Tuberculosis
  4001 Tampa Bay Blvd..... 14
Saint JosephOs 3001 W
  Buffalo Ave 07
Tampa General Davis Island .. 06
University Community 13505
  N 31st 12

UNIVERSITIES AND COLLEGES

Florida College N Glen Arven
  Ave 17
University Of South Florida -
  4202 E Fowler Ave. 20
University Of Tampa 401 J F
  Kennedy Blvd W 06

WEST PALM BEACH   334

POST OFFICE BOXES

Box Nos.
1-3451   Main Office 02
6001-6894   Southboro Sta .. 05
8001-8428   Northwood Sta.. 07
9001-10729   Riviera Beach
              Br.............. 04
12001-12687   Lake Park Br..... 03
14001-14577   North Palm
              Beach.......... 08
15001-16144   Four Points...... 06

RURAL ROUTES

1 06

STATIONS, BRANCHES AND UNITS

Four Points Br...................... 06
Lake Park Br......................... 03
North Palm Beach Br 03
Northwood Sta 07
Riviera Beach Br.................. 04
Singer Island Br.................. 04
Southboro Sta 05
General Delivery 01
Postmaster 01

APARTMENTS, HOTELS, MOTELS

Alma, 534 Datura St 01
Andover Century Village....... 01
Augusta Bldg Royal Palm
  Beach 06
Barclay, 120 Celestial Way... 08
Bedford Century Village........ 01
Berkshire, Century Village..... 01
C Royal Palm Beach 06
Cambridge, Century Village 01
Camden, Century Village 01
Canterbury, Century Village.... 01
Colonnades, 101 Ocean Ave ... 04
Coventry, Century Village....... 01
Doolin, Doolin Ct 08
Dorchester, Century Village.... 01
Easthampton, Century
  Village 01
Elcid, 315 Almeria Rd.......... 05
Firestone Bldg Royal Palm
  Beach 06
Flagler Manor, 3705 S
  Flagler Dr 05
Flagler Towers, 1401 S
  Flagler Dr 01
Flagler, 214 Trinity Pl.......... 02
Garden Lane, 1809 N Flagler
  Dr 07
GolfOS Edge, Century Village... 01
Granada, 500 N Congress
  Ave 01
Greenbrier, Century Village 01
Greenbrier, 50 Celestial Way .. 08
Harbor Point, 5000 Ocean Dr.. 04
Hastings, Century Village 01
Hibiscus Garden, 619
  Hibiscus St........................ 02
Holiday Inn Town House, 100
  Datura St........................... 01
Kingswood, Century Village..... 01
La Fontana, 2800 N Flagler
  Dr..................................... 07
Lake Hotel, 201 Flagler Dr..... 01
Lincoln Plaza, 564 15th St..... 01
Marine Harbor, 100 Le Hane
  Ter.................................... 08
Monterey, 635 Clematis St 01
Norton Park Towers, 1501 S
  Flagler Dr 01
Norwich, Century Village......... 01
Old Westbury Bldg Royal
  Palm Beach 06
Oxford Century Village 01
Palm Beach Cooperative, 33
  Ocean Ave 04
Parklane, 1701 N Flagler Dr... 07
Patio, 323 Almeria Rd 05
Pebble Beach Bldg Royal
  Palm Beach 06
Plymouth Century Village 01
Portofino South, 3800
  Washington Rd 05
Portofino, 2600 N Flagler Dr .. 07
Ramada Inn, 1800 P B.
  Lakes Blvd 01
Rapallo, 1701 S Flagler Dr..... 01
Regence Club, 4500 N Dixie.. 07

Salisbury, Century Village....... 01
Sandpiper, 120 Le Hane Ter.... 08
Sea Spray, 123 Ocean Ave 04
Seminole, 40 Celestial Way 08
Sheffield Century Village 01
Shore, Shore Ct 08
South Bridge, 3915 S Flagler
  Dr 05
Spanish Courts, 1124
  Broadway 04
St Andrews Bldg Royal Palm
  Beach 06
St Andrews Residence 208
  Fern St 01
Stratford, Century Village 01
The Pennsylvania 208
  Evernia 1
Villas, 3600 Ocean Dr........... 04
Waltham, Century Village 01
Warrington Bldg Royal Palm
  Beach 06
Wellington Century Village...... 01
Windsor, Century Village 01
Woodhaven Villa, 4000 Forest
  Hill Blvd 06
Yacht Harbor Landing, 37
  Yacht Club Dr 08

BUILDINGS

Citizens, 105 S Narcissus
  Ave 01
Comeau, 319 Clematis St........ 01
Commerce, 324 Datura St....... 01
Court House, 300 N Dixie
  Hwy 01
Datura, 205 Datura St........... 01
Flagler Court, 601 Flagler
  Drive Ct............................ 01
Guaranty, 120 S Olive Ave..... 01
Harvey, 224 Datura St........... 01
Lakeview, 515 U S Highway
  1 08
Pan-A, 307 N Dixie Hwy........ 01
Professional, 531 U S
  Highway 1 08

GOVERNMENT OFFICES

Internal Revenue, 421 Iris...... 01
Social Security, 715 S Dixie
  Hwy 02

HOSPITALS

Good Samaritan, 1300 N
  Dixie Hwy 02
P B County, 1200 45th........... 07
St Marys, 900 49th................ 07

UNIVERSITIES AND COLLEGES

Palm Beach Atlantic College,
  1101 S Olive Ave 01
Rosarian Academy, 807 N
  Flagler Dr 01
University Of Palm Beach,
  660 Fern 02

GEORGIA
(Abbreviation: GA)

Abac, R. Sta. Tifton 31794
Abbeville 31001
Acworth (1st)....................... 30101
Adairsville 30103
Adel (1st) 31620
Adrien 31002
Agnes Scott College, Sta.
  Decatur 30030
Ailey 30410
Airport Mail Facility, Br.
  Atlanta 30320
Alamo 30411
Alapaha 31622
ALBANY (1st) (see appendix)
Alexander, R. Br.
  Waynesboro 30801
Allenhurst 31301
Allentown 31003
Alma (1st) 31510
Alpharetta 30201
Alps Road, Sta. Athens 30604
Alston 30412
Alto 30510
Alvaton 30202
Ambrose 31512
Americus (1st) 31709
Amsterdam, R. Br. Climax 31734
Andersonville 31711
Appling 30802
Arabi 31712
Aragon 30104
Arco, Br. Brunswick 31520
Argyle 31623
Arlington 31713
Armuchee 30105
Arnoldsville 30619
Arrowhead, Br. Jonesboro 30236
Ash Mor, Sta. Forest Park 30050
Ashburn 31714
Athens (1st) 30601
  Alps Road, Sta. 30604
  Campus, Sta. 30601
  Gaines Community, Br. 30601
  Georgia University, Sta. 30601
  Navy Supply Corps
    School, Sta. 30601
  Timothy, Br. 30601
ATLANTA (1st) (see
  appendix)
Attapulgus 31715
Auburn 30203
AUGUSTA (1st) (see
  appendix)
Austell (1st) 30001
Avera 30803
Avondale Estates (1st) 30002
Axson 31624
Bacon Park, Sta. Savannah 31406
Baconton 31716
Bainbridge (1st) 31717
Baker Village, Sta.
  Columbus 31903
Baldwin 30511
Ball Ground 30107
Barnesville (1st) 30204
Barnett 30804
Barney 31625
Bartow 30413
Berwick 31720

Battey State Hospital, Br.
  Rome 30161
Baxley (1st) 31513
Bealiwood, Sta. Columbus 31904
Bellville, R. Br. Claxton 30414
Belvedere Plaza, Br.
  Decatur 30032
Bemiss, R. Br. Valdosta 31601
Ben Hill, Sta. Atlanta 30331
Benevolence 31721
Berlin 31722
Berryton, R. Br. Summerville 30748
Bethlehem 30620
Bibb City, Br. Columbus 31904
Bishop 30621
Blackshear 31516
Blair Village, Sta. Atlanta 30354
Blairsville 30512
Blakely (1st) 31723
Bloomfield, Sta. Macon. 31206
Bloomingdale 31302
Blue Ridge 30513
  Hemp, R. Br. 30515
Bluffton 31724
Blythe 30805
Bogart 30622
Bolingbroke 31004
Bolton, Sta. Atlanta 30318
Bonaire 31005
Boneville 30806
Boston 31626
Bostwick 30623
Bowdon 30108
Bowdon Junction 30109
Bowersville 30516
Bowman 30624
Box Springs 31801
Boys Estate, R. Br.
  Brunswick 31520
Bradley, R. Br. Gray 31032
Braselton 30517
Bremen (1st) 30110
Briarcliff, Br. Atlanta 30329
Briarwood, Br. Atlanta 30344
Bridgeboro, R. Br. Albany 31701
Brinson 31725
Bristol 31518
Bronwood 31726
Brookfield 31727
Brooklet 30415
Brooks 30205
Broxton 31519
Brunswick (1st) 31520
  Arco, Br. 31520
  Boys Estate, R. Br. 31520
  Glynco, Br. 31520
  Jekyll Island, Br. 31520
  Lanier Plaza, Sta. 31520
  Saint Simons Island, Br. 31522
  Sterling, R. Br. 31520
Buchanan 30113
Buckhead 30625
Buena Vista 31803
Buford (1st) 30518
Butler 31006
Byromville 31007
Byron 31008
Cadwell 31009
Cairo (1st) 31728
Calhoun (1st) 30701
Calvary 31729
Camak 30807

Camilla (1st) 31730
Campton, R. Br. Monroe 30626
Campus, Sta. Athens 30601
Canon 30520
Canoochee 30416
Canton (1st) 30114
Canton Plaza, Br. Marietta 30060
Capitol Hill, Sta. Atlanta 30334
Carl, R. Br. Auburn 30203
Carlton 30627
Carnesville 30521
Carrollton (1st) 30117
Carters 30704
Cartersville (1st) 30120
Cascade Heights, Sta.
  Atlanta 30311
Cassville 30123
Castle Park, Sta. Valdosta 31601
Cataula 31804
Cave Spring 30124
Cecil 31627
Cedar Springs 31732
Cedartown (1st) 30125
Centerville, R. Br. Warner
  Robins 31093
Chamblee, Br. Atlanta 30341
Charing 31010
Chatillon, Br. Rome 30161
Chatsworth (1st) 30705
Chattahoochee, Sta. Atlanta 30321
Chauncey 31011
Cherrylog 30522
Chester 31012
Chestnut Mountain, R. Br.
  Gainesville 30502
Chickamauga 30707
Chicopee, Br. Gainesville 30501
Chula 31733
Cisco 30708
Civic Center, Sta. Atlanta 30308
Clarkdale 30020
Clarkesville (1st) 30523
Clarkston 30021
Claxton (1st) 30417
  Bellville, R. Br. 30414
Clayton (1st) 30525
Clem 30128
Clermont 30527
Cleveland 30528
Climax 31734
Clinchfield 31013
Cloudland 30709
Clyattville, R. Br. Valdosta 31604
Clyo 31303
Cobb 31735
Cobb County Center, Sta.
  Smyrna 30080
Cobbtown 30420
Cochran (1st) 31014
  Empire, R. Br. 31026
Cogdell 31628
Cohutta 30710
Colbert 30628
Coleman 31736
College, Sta. Fort Valley 31030
College Heights, Sta.
  Columbus 31907
College Park, Br. Atlanta 30337
Collins 30421
Colquitt 31737
COLUMBUS (1st) (see
  appendix)

Comer 30629
Commerce (1st) 30529
Concord 30206
Conley 30027
Conyers (1st) 30207
Coolidge 31738
Coosa 30129
Cordele (1st) 31015
Cornelia (1st) 30531
Cotton 31739
Court Square, Sta. Dublin 31021
Covena 30422
Covington (1st) 30209
Crandall 30711
Crawford 30630
Crawfordville 30631
Crescent 31304
Cross Keys, Sta. Macon 31201
Culloden 31016
Cumming (1st) 30130
Cusseta 31805
Custer Terrace, Br.
   Columbus 31905
Cuthbert 31740
Dacula 30211
Dahlonega 30533
Daisy 30423
Dallas 30132
Dalton (1st) 30720
Damascus 31741
Danburg 30632
Danielsville 30633
Danville 31017
Darien 31305
Desher, R. Br. Valdosta 31601
Davisboro 31018
Dawson (1st) 31742
Dawsonville 30534
De Kalb Airport, Br. Atlanta ..30341
De Lowe, Br. Atlanta 30344
De Soto 31743
Dearing 30808
DECATUR (1st) (see
   appendix)
Deepstep, R. Br.
   Sandersville 31082
Demorest 30535
   Habersham, R. Br. 30544
Denton 31532
Devereux, R. Br. Sparta 31087
Dewy Rose 30634
Dexter 31019
Dillard 30537
Dixie 31629
Dobbins A F B, Br. Marietta ..30060
Doerun 31744
Donalsonville (1st) 31745
Doraville, Br. Atlanta 30340
Douglas (1st) 31533
Douglasville (1st) 30134
Dover 30424
Dry Branch 31020
Du Pont 31630
Dublin (1st) 31021
   Court Square, Br. 31021
   East Dublin, Br. 31021
   Lovett, R. Br. 31053
   Scott, R. Br. 31095
Dudley 31022
Duluth 30136
Dunaire, Br. Decatur 30032
Dunwoody, Br. Atlanta 30338

East Atlanta, Sta. Atlanta 30316
East Dublin, Br. Dublin 31021
East Ellijay 30539
East Point, Br. Atlanta 30344
East Side, Sta. Dalton 30720
East Stone Mountain, R. Br.
   Stone Mountain 30083
Eastanollee 30538
Eastman (1st) 31023
Eastwood, Sta. Atlanta 30317
Eatonton (1st) 31024
Eden 31307
Edgewood, Sta. Columbus ..31907
Edison 31746
Elberton (1st) 30635
Eldorendo, R. Br.
   Bainbridge 31717
Elizabeth, Br. Marietta 30060
Elko 31025
Ellabell 31308
Ellaville 31806
Ellenton 31747
Ellenwood 30049
Ellerslie 31807
Ellijay (1st) 30540
Elmodel, R. Br. Newton 31748
Embry Hills, Br. Atlanta 30341
Emerson 30137
Emory University, Br. Atlanta
   (see appendix)
Empire, R. Br. Cochran 31026
Enigma 31749
Epworth 30541
Esom Hill 30138
Eton 30724
Evans 30809
Everett 31536
Experiment 30212
Fair Oaks, Br. Marietta 30060
Fairburn 30213
Fairmount 30139
Fargo 31631
Farmington 30638
Farrar 31027
Fayetteville (1st) 30214
   Inman, Br. 30232
   Peachtree City, Br. 30269
Federal Annex, Sta. Atlanta
   (see appendix)
Federal Reserve, Sta.
   Atlanta 30303
Felton 30140
Fender, R. Br. Tifton 31794
Fitzgerald (1st) 31750
Fleming 31309
Flintstone 30725
Flippen, R. Br. Mc Donough ..30215
Flovilla 30216
Flowery Branch 30542
Folkston 31537
Forest Park (1st) 30050
Forsyth (1st) 31029
Fort Benning, Br. Columbus ..31905
Fort Gaines 31751
Fort Gordon, Br. Augusta 30905
Fort Mc Pherson, Sta.
   Atlanta 30330
Fort Oglethorpe, Br.
   Rossville 30741
Fort Screven, R. Sta.
   Savannah Beach 31311
Fort Stewart, Br. Hinesville ..31313
Fort Valley (1st) 31030

Fortson 31808
Four Points, Br. Albany 31705
Fowlstown 31752
Franklin 30217
Franklin Springs 30639
Fry, R. Br. Copperhill, T N ..37317
Funston 31753
Gabbettville 31809
Gaines Community, Br.
   Athens 30601
Gainesville (1st) 30501
   Chestnut Mountain, R.
    Br. 30502
   Chicopee, Br. 30501
   New Holland, Br. 30501
   Park Hill, Sta. 30501
   Westside, Br. 30501
Garden City, Br. Savannah ..31408
Garfield 30425
Gate City, Sta. Atlanta 30312
Gay 30218
Geneva 31810
Georgetown 31754
Georgia Southern, Sta.
   Statesboro 30458
Georgia Southwestern
   College, R. Sta. Americus ..31709
Georgia University, Sta.
   Athens 30601
Gibson 30810
Gillsville 30543
Girard 30426
Glenn 30219
Glennville 30427
Glenwood 30428
Glynco, Br. Brunswick 31520
Godfrey, R. Br. Madison 30650
Good Hope 30641
Gordon 31031
Gordon Road, Sta. Atlanta ..30310
Gough, R. Br. Keysville 30811
Gracewood 30812
Grantville 30220
Graves 31755
Gray 31032
Grayson 30221
Graysville 30726
Greenbriar, Sta. Atlanta 30331
Greensboro 30642
Greenville 30222
Gresham, Br. Atlanta 30316
Griffin (1st) 30223
Grovetown 30813
Guyton 31312
Habersham, R. Br.
   Demorest 30544
Haddock 31033
Hagan 30429
Hahira 31632
Hamilton 31811
Hampton 30228
Hapeville, Br. Atlanta 30354
Haralson 30229
Hardwick 31034
Harlem 30814
Harrison 31035
Hartsfield 31756
Hartwell (1st) 30643
Hawkinsville (1st) 31036
Hazlehurst (1st) 31539
Helen 30545
Helena 31037
Hemp, R. Br. Blue Ridge 30515

Hephzibah	30815
Herndon	30430
Hi Way Eighty, Br. Savannah	31408
Hiawassee	30546
Higgston, R. Br. Ailey	30410
High Shoals	30645
Hill City, R. Br. Resaca	30735
Hillsboro	31038
Round Oak, R. Br.	31080
Hilltonia, R. Br. Sylvania	30467
Hilton	31758
Hinesville (1st)	31313
Hinsonton, R. Br. Pelham	31779
Hiram	30141
Hoboken	31542
Hogansville	30230
Holly Springs	30142
Hollywood, R. Br. Clarkesville	30523
Homer	30547
Homerville	31634
Hortense	31543
Hoschton	30548
Howard	31039
Huber	31040
Hull	30646
Hunter Army Airfield, Br. Savannah	31409
Hurst, R. Br. Morganton	30561
Ideal	31041
Ila	30647
Indian Springs	30231
Industrial, Br. Atlanta	30336
Inman, R. Br. Fayetteville	30232
International Office Park, Br. Atlanta	30354
Iron City	31759
Irwinton	31042
Irwinville	31760
Isle Of Hope, Br. Savannah	31406
Jackson (1st)	30233
Jacksonville	31544
Jakin	31761
Jasper	30143
Jefferson (1st)	30549
Jeffersonville	31044
Jekyll Island, Br. Brunswick	31520
Jenkinsburg	30234
Jersey	30235
Jesup (1st)	31545
Jewell	31045
Jonesboro (1st)	30236
Juliette	31046
Junction City	31812
Juniper	31813
Juno	30551
Kathleen	31047
Kelly	31048
Kennesaw	30144
Kensington, R. Br. La Fayette	30727
Keysville	30816
Gough, R. Br.	30811
Kibbee	30431
Kingsland	31548
Kingston	30145
Kite	31049
Knoxville	31050
La Fayette (1st)	30728
Kensington, R. Br.	30727
La Grange (1st)	30240
La Vista, Br. Atlanta	30329

Lake Park	31636
Lakeland	31635
Lakemont	30552
Lakeview Estates, R. Br. Conyers	30207
Lakewood, Sta. Atlanta	30315
Lanier Plaza, Sta. Brunswick	31520
Lavonia	30553
Lawrenceville (1st)	30245
Leary	31762
Lebanon	30146
Leesburg	31763
Lenox	31637
Lenox Square, Sta. Atlanta	30326
Leslie	31764
Lexington	30648
Lexsy, R. Br. Swainsboro	30432
Lilburn	30247
Lilly	31051
Lincolnton	30817
Lindale	30147
Lindsay Creek, Sta. Columbus	31907
Lithia Springs	30057
Lithonia (1st)	30058
Lizella	31052
Locust Grove	30248
Loganville	30249
Lollie	30433
Louisville (1st)	30434
Louvale	31814
Lovejoy	30250
Lovett, R. Br. Dublin	31053
Ludowici	31316
Lula	30554
Lumber City	31549
Lumpkin	31815
Luthersville	30251
Luxomni	30252
Lyerly	30730
Lyons	30436
Mableton (1st)	30059
MACON (1st) (see appendix)	
Madison (1st)	30650
Madras	30254
Manassas	30438
Manchester (1st)	31816
Manor	31550
Mansfield	30255
Marblehill	30148
Marietta (1st)	30060
Marshallville	31057
Martech, Sta. Atlanta	30318
Martin	30557
Martinez, Br. Augusta	30907
Matthews	30818
Mauk	31058
Maxeys, R. Br. Union Point	30671
Mayfield	31059
Maysville	30558
Mc Caysville	30555
Mc Donough (1st)	30253
Flippen, R. Br.	30215
Mc Intosh	31317
Mc Intyre	31054
Mc Rae (1st)	31055
Meansville	30256
Meigs	31765
Meldrim	31318
Menlo	30731
Meridian	31319
Mershon	31551

Mesena	30819
Metter (1st)	30439
Midland	31820
Midville	30441
Midway	31320
Milan	31060
Milledgeville (1st)	31061
Millen (1st)	30442
Millwood	31552
Milner	30257
Milstead, Br. Conyers	30207
Mineral Bluff	30559
Mitchell	30820
Molena	30258
Monroe (1st)	30655
Campton, R. Br.	30626
Montezuma (1st)	31063
Monticello	31064
Montrose	31065
Moody A F B, MOU. Valdosta	31601
Moreland	30259
Morgan	31766
Morganton	30560
Hurst, R. Br.	30561
Morris	31767
Morris Brown, Sta. Atlanta	30314
Morrow (1st)	30260
Morven	31638
Moultrie (1st)	31768
Mount Airy	30563
Mount Berry	30149
Mount Vernon	30445
Mount Zion	30150
Mountain City	30562
Mountain View	30070
Mountville	30261
Mulberry Street, Sta. Macon (see appendix)	
Murrayville	30564
Musella	31066
Mystic	31769
Nahunta	31553
Nashville (1st)	31639
Navy Supply Corps School, Sta. Athens	30601
Naylor	31641
Nelson	30151
New Holland, Br. Gainesville	30501
Newborn	30262
Newington	30446
Newnan (1st)	30263
Newton	31770
Elmodel, R. Br.	31748
Nicholls	31554
Nicholson	30565
Norcross (1st)	30071
Norman Park	31771
Norristown	30447
North Atlanta, Br. Atlanta	30319
North Decatur, Br. Decatur	30033
North Druid Hills, Br. Decatur	30033
North Side, Sta. Atlanta (see appendix)	
Northeast Plaza, Br. Atlanta	30329
Northwoods, Br. Atlanta	30340
Norwood	30821
Nunez	30448
Oak Park, R. Br. Swainsboro	30401
Oakdale, Br. Smyrna	30080
Oakfield	31772
Oakland Park, Sta. Columbus	31903

Oakman	30732
Oakwood	30566
Ochlocknee	31773
Ocilla	31774
Oconee	31067
Odum	31555
Offerman	31556
Ogeechee Road, Br. Savannah	31405
Oglethorpe, Br. Savannah	31406
Oglethorpe	31068
Okefenokee, R. Br. Waycross	31501
Oliver	30449
Omaha	31821
Omega	31775
Orchard Hill	30266
Oxford	30267
Palmetto	30268
Park Hill, Sta. Gainesville	30501
Parrott	31777
Patterson	31557
Pavo	31778
Peach Orchard, Br. Augusta	30906
Peachtree Center, Sta. Atlanta	30343
Peachtree City, Br. Fayetteville	30269
Pearson	31642
Pelham	31779
Pembroke	31321
Pendergrass	30567
Penfield	30658
Perkins	30822
Perry (1st)	31069
Perry Homes, Sta. Atlanta	30318
Philomath	30659
Pine Lake	30072
Pine Log	30152
Pine Mountain	31822
Pine Mountain Valley	31823
Pinehurst	31070
Pineview	31071
Pio Nono, Sta. Macon (see appendix)	
Pitts	31072
Plainfield	31073
Plains	31780
Plainville	30733
Plaza, Sta. Forest Park	30050
Pooler	31322
Port Wentworth, Br. Savannah	31407
Portal	30450
Porterdale	30270
Poulan	31781
Powder Springs	30073
Powersville	31824
Preston	31824
Pulaski	30451
Putney	31782
Quitman (1st)	31643
Rabun Gap	30568
Ranger	30734
Ray City	31645
Rayle	30660
Raymond	30271
Rebecca	31783
Red Oak	30272
Redan	30074
Register	30452
Reidsville	30453
Remerton, R. Br. Valdosta	31601
Rentz	31075

Resaca	30735
Rex	30273
Reynolds	31076
Rhine	31077
Riceboro	31323
Richland	31825
Richmond Hill	31324
Ridgeville, R. Br. Townsend	31325
Rincon	31326
Ringgold (1st)	30736
Rising Fawn	30738
Riverdale	30274
Riverside, Sta. Macon	31204
Roberta	31078
Robins A F B, Br. Warner Robins	31093
Robinson	30661
Rochelle	31079
Rock Spring	30739
Rockledge	30454
Rockmart (1st)	30153
Rocky Face	30740
Rocky Ford	30455
Rome (1st)	30161
Roopville	30170
Rose Hill, Sta. Columbus	31904
Rosemont, Sta. Columbus	31904
Rossville (1st)	30741
Roswell (1st)	30075
Round Oak, R. Br. Hillsboro	31080
Royston	30662
Rupert	31081
Rutledge	30663
Rydal	30171
Saint George	31646
Saint Marys	31558
Saint Simons Island, Br. Brunswick	31522
Sale City	31784
Sand Town, Br. Marietta	30060
Sandersville (1st)	31082
Sandy Springs, Br. Atlanta	30328
Sapelo Island	31327
Sardis	30456
Sargent	30275
Sasser	31785
Sautee-Nacoochee	30571
SAVANNAH (1st) (see appendix)	
Savannah Beach	31328
Fort Screven, R. Sta.	31311
Scotland	31083
Scott, R. Br. Dublin	31095
Scottdale	30079
Screven	31560
Sea Island	31561
Senoia	30276
Seville	31084
Shady Dale	31085
Shannon	30172
Sharon	30664
Sharpsburg	30277
Shellman	31786
Shiloh	31826
Shurlington, Sta. Macon	31201
Siloam	30665
Silver Creek	30173
Silvertown, Br. Thomaston	30286
Six Flags Over Georgia, R. Br. Atlanta	30336
Skyland, Br. Atlanta	30319
Smarr	31086
Smithville	31787

Smyrna (1st)	30080
Snellville	30278
Social Circle	30279
Soperton	30457
South Base, Br. Warner Robins	31093
South Cobb, Br. Austell	30001
South De Kalb, Br. Decatur	30034
South Decatur, Br. Decatur (see appendix)	
South Macon, Sta. Macon (see appendix)	
Southern Tech, Sta. Marietta	30060
Sparks	31647
Sparta	31087
Spring Place, R. Br. Chatsworth	30705
Springfield	31329
Springvale	31788
Stapleton	30823
Starrsville	30280
State College, Br. Savannah	31404
Statenville	31648
Statesboro (1st)	30458
Statham	30666
Stephens	30667
Sterling, R. Br. Brunswick	31520
Stevens Pottery	31088
Stillmore	30464
Stilwell	31330
Stilson, R. Br. Brooklet	30415
Stockbridge	30281
Stockton	31649
Stone Mountain (1st)	30083
Stonewall	30282
Stovall	30283
Suches	30572
Sugar Hill, Br. Buford	30518
Sugar Valley	30746
Summertown, R. Br. Swainsboro	30466
Summerville (1st)	30747
Berryton, R. Br.	30748
Sumner	31789
Sunny Side	30284
Surrency	31563
Suwanee	30174
Swainsboro (1st)	30401
Lexsy, R. Br.	30432
Oak Park, R. Br.	30401
Summertown, R. Br.	30466
Sycamore	31790
Sylvania (1st)	30467
Sylvester (1st)	31791
Talbotton	31827
Talking Rock	30175
Tallapoosa	30176
Tallulah Falls	30573
Talmo	30575
Tarrytown	30470
Tate	30177
Taylorsville	30178
Tazewell	31828
Temple	30179
Tennga	30751
Tennille	31089
The Hill, Sta. Augusta	30904
The Rock	30285
Thomaston (1st)	30286
Thomasville (1st)	31792
Thomson (1st)	30824
Thunderbolt, Br. Savannah	31404

Tifton (1st) 31794
Tiger 30576
Tignall 30668
Timothy, Br. Athens 30601
Toccoa (1st) 30577
Toccoa Falls, R. Br. Toccoa ...30577
Toco Hills, Br. Atlanta 30329
Toomsboro 31090
Town And Country, Sta.
     Marietta 30060
Townsend 31331
     Ridgeville, R. Br. 31325
Trenton 30752
Trion 30753
Tucker (1st) 30084
Tunnel Hill 30755
Turin 30289
Turnerville 30580
Twin City 30471
Twin Lakes, R. Br. Valdosta ...31605
Ty Ty 31795
Tyrone 30290
U S M C Supply Center, Br.
     Albany 31704
U S Naval Air Station, Br.
     Albany 31703
Unadilla 31091
Union City 30291
Union Point 30669
     Maxeys, R. Br. 30671
     Woodville, R. Br. 30670
University, Sta. Macon 31207
Upatoi 31829
Uvalda 30473
Vada, R. Br. Climax 31734
Valdosta (1st) 31601
     Bemiss, R. Br. 31601
     Castle Park, Sta. 31601
     Clyattville, R. Br. 31604

Basher, R. Br. 31601
Moody A F B, MOU 31601
Remerton, R. Br. 31601
     Twin Lakes, R. Br. 31605
Valona 31332
Vanna 30672
Varnell 30756
Veterans Hospital, Sta.
     Augusta 30904
Vidalia (1st) 30474
Vienna 31092
Villa Rica 30180
Vinings, R. Br. Smyrna 30080
Vista Grove, Br. Decatur 30033
Waco 30182
Wadley 30477
Waleska 30183
Walnutgrove, R. Br.
     Covington 30209
Walthourville 31333
Waresboro 31564
Warm Springs 31830
Warner Robins (1st) 31093
Warrenton 30828
Warthen 30829
Warwick 31796
Washington (1st) 30673
Watkinsville 30677
Waverly 31565
Waverly Hall 31831
Waycross (1st) 31501
Waynesboro (1st) 30830
     Alexander, R. Br. 30801
Waynesville 31566
Wayside, R. Br. Gray 31032
Wesleyan, Sta. Macon 31201
West Bainbridge, Sta.
     Bainbridge 31717
West End, Sta. Rome 30161

West Green 31567
West Point (1st) 31833
Westgate, Sta. Macon 31206
Weston 31832
Westside, Br. Gainesville 30501
Whigham 31797
White 30184
White Oak 31568
White Plains 30678
Whitesburg 30185
Whitestone 30186
Wildwood 30757
Wiley 30581
Willacoochee 31650
Williamson 30292
Wilmington Island, R. Br.
     Savannah 31404
Wilson Airport, R. Br. Macon ..31201
Winder (1st) 30680
Windsor Forest, Br.
     Savannah 31406
Windsor Park, Br. Columbus ..31904
Winston 30187
Winterville 30683
Woodbine 31569
Woodbury 30293
Woodland 31836
Woodstock 30188
Woodville, R. Br. Union
     Point 30678
Woolsey 30294
Wray 31798
Wrens 30833
Wright Square, Sta.
     Savannah 31402
Wrightsville 31096
Wynnton, Sta. Columbus 31906
Yatesville 31097
Young Harris 30582
Zebulon 30295

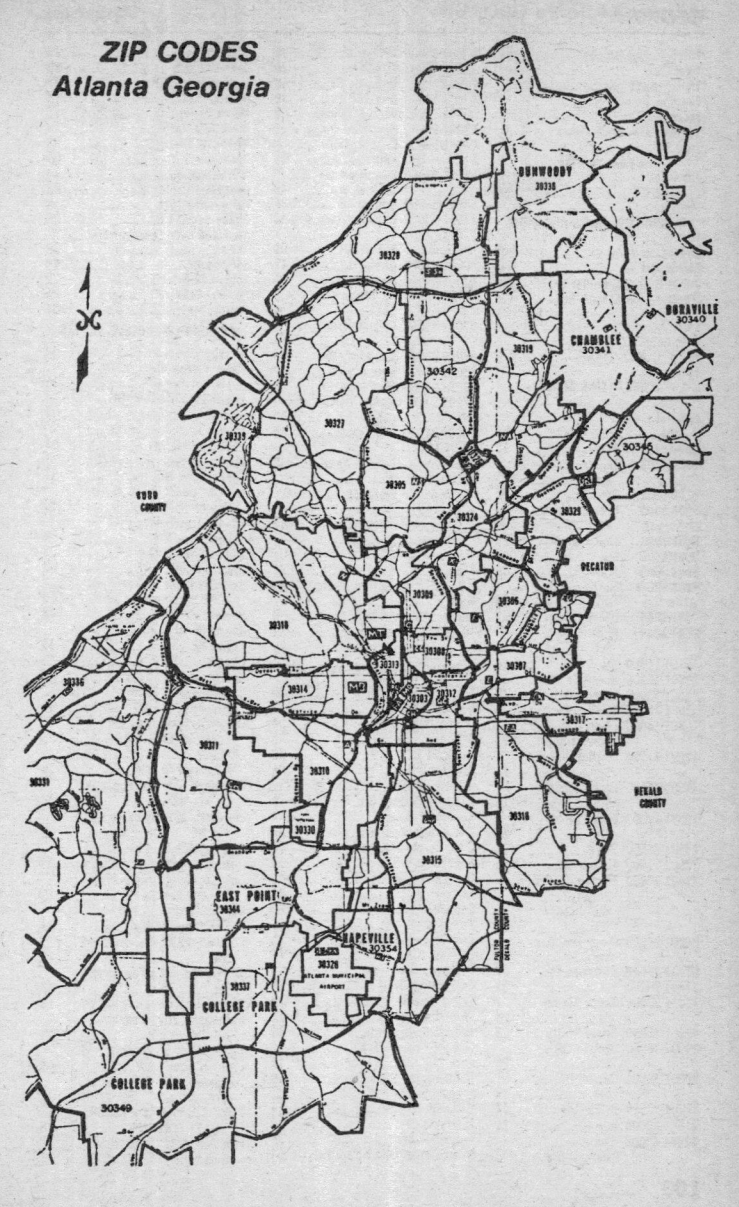

ZIP CODES
Atlanta Georgia

ALBANY 317

POST OFFICE BOXES

Box Nos.
1-2054   Main Office 02

RURAL ROUTES

1,2,3,4,5,6,7 01

STATIONS, BRANCHES AND UNITS

Bridgeboro Rural Br	01
Four Points Br	05
U S M C Supply Center Br	04
U S Naval Air Station Br	03

ATLANTA 303

POST OFFICE BOXES

Box Nos.
1-2214	Main Office	01
2301-3100	Martech Sta	18
3101-5200	Federal Annex Sta	02
5201-6000	Sta E	07
6001-6500	Civic Center Sta	08
6501-7000	Lakewood Sta	15
7001-8000	Sta C	09
8001-9000	Sta F	06
9001-9300	Morris Brown Sta	14
9301-9600	Ben Hill Sta	31
9601-10490	North Atlanta Br	19
10491-11500	Sta A	10
11501-12500	Northside Sta	05
12501-13000	Lakewood Sta	15
13001-15000	Sta K	24
15001-17000	Emory University Br	33
17001-17500	Chattahoochee Sta	21
17501-18500	East Atlanta Sta	16
18501-19500	Lenox Square Sta	26
19501-20500	Sta N	25
20501-21000	Airport Sta	20
21001-26000	Emory University Mail Room Sta	22
26001-27000	Grady Hospital Sta	03
27001-27500	Eastwood Sta	17
27501-28000	Sta No 7	27
28001-29000	Sandy Springs Br	28
29001-30000	Briarcliff Sta	29
30001-38000	Georgia Tech Sta	32
38001-38500	Capitol Hill Sta	34
39001-39500	Bolton Sta	18
41001-42000	Ben Hill	31
42001-43000	Cascade Heights Sta	11

43001-45000	Industrial	36
45001-47000	Airport	20
47001-49000	Doraville Br	40
49001-50000	Briarcliff Br	29
50001-52000	Federal Annex	02
52001-54000	Northside	05
54001-56000	Civic Center Sta	08
56001-58000	Peachtree Center Sta	43
58001-59000	Station 18	37
73001-74000	Federal Annex	50
77001-0078000	Sta C	09
80001-82000	Chamblee Br	41
82001-84000	Hapeville Br	54
84001-86000	Int Office Park Br	54
87001-88000	College Park Br	37
88001-89000	Dunwoody Br	38
89001-90000	Gate City Sta	12
90001-92000	East Point Br	44
92001-93000	Morris Brown Sta	14
93001-95000	Martech Sta	18
100001-105000	Federal Annex	48
720001-721000	Perimeter Center Station	46

RURAL ROUTES

1	31
2,3	40
4,5,6,7	37
8,9	38
10	27
13	45

STATIONS, BRANCHES AND UNITS

Airport Mail Facility Br	20
Ben Hill Sta	31
Blair Village Br	54
Bolton Sta	18
Briarcliff Br	29
Briarwood Br	44
Capitol Hill Sta	34
Cascade Heights Sta	11
Chamblee Br	41
Chattahoochee Sta	21
Civic Center Sta	08
College Park Br	37
De Kalb Airport Br	41
De Lowe Br	44
Doraville Br	40
Dunwoody Br	38
East Atlanta Sta	16
East Point Br	44
Eastwood Sta	17
Embry Hills Br	41
Emory Univ Br	22
Federal Annex Sta	02
Federal Reserve Sta	03
Fort Mc Pherson Sta	30
Gate City Sta	12
Gordon Road Sta	10
Greenbriar Sta	31
Gresham Br	16
Hapeville Br	54
Industrial Br	36
International Office Park Br	54

La Vista Br	29
Lakewood Sta	15
Lenox Square Sta	26
Martech Sta	18
Morris Brown Sta	14
North Atlanta Br	19
Northeast Plaza Br	29
North Side Sta	05
Northwoods Br	40
Peachtree Center Sta	43
Perry Homes Sta	14
Sandy Springs Br	28
Six Flags Over Georgia Rural Br	36
Skyland Br	19
Toco Hills Br	29
General Delivery	01
Postmaster	04

APARTMENTS, HOTELS, MOTELS

Air Way, Carrol Rd NW	36
Alamo Plaza Courts, 2370 Stewart Ave SW	15
Argonne, 339 Luckie NE	13
Arlington, 126 Ellis NE	03
Atlanta Americana Motor, 160 Spring NW	03
Atlanta Cabana Motor, 870 Peachtree NE	83
Atlanta Towers, 1270 W Peachtree NW	09
Atlanta Travelodge, 1641 Peachtree NW	09
Atlantan, 11 Luckie NW	03
Avon, 5 Houston NE	03
Barbizon Plaza Of New York, 1000 Peachtree NE	09
Bentley, 72 Pryor SW	03
Briarcliff, 1050 Ponce De Ln Ave NE	83
Capitol, 73 Pryor NE	03
Capri, 1152 Spring NW	09
Carlton House, 2030 Peachtree Rd NW	09
Cherokee Motor Inn, 310 Ponce De Ln Ave NE	83
Cherokee Rose Court, 1387 Northside Dr NW	18
Chestatee Inn, 580 Ponce De Ln Ave NE	08
Clermont, 789 Ponce De La Ave NE	83
Colonial Homes, 214 Colonial Hms Dr NW	09
Colonial Motor Lodge, 2720 Stewart Ave SW	15
Colonial Terrace, 2140 Peachtree Rd NW	09
Cotillion, 2200 Reynolds Dr SW	15
Cox Carlton, 683 Peachtree NE	03
Danzig, 345 Chappell Rd NW	18
Darlington, 2025 Peachtree Rd NW	09
Dinkler Mtr., 98 Forsyth, N W.	03
Dixie, 72 Baker NW	08
Downtown, 330 W Peachtree NW	08
Duke, 420 Piedmont Ave NE	08
Emory, 17 Baker NW	08
Five Acre Auto Court, 2056 Buford Hwy NE	24

Atlanta (Con.)   303

Flamingo Courts, 2766
 Stewart Ave SW 15
Frances, 1865 Buford Hwy
 NE 24
Garys, 2275 Stewart Ave SW .. 15
Georgia, 114 Luckie NW 03
Georgian Terrace, 659
 Peachtree NE 83
Georgian, 4300 Buford Hwy
 NE 29
Gordon, 211 Mitchell SW 03
Greenwood, 2160 Stewart Ave
 SW 15
Hampton, 35 Houston NE 03
Heart Of Atlanta, 225
 Courtland NE 03
Henry Grady, 210 Peachtree
 NW 03
Holiday Inn, 175 Piedmont
 Ave NE 03
Holiday Inn, 1810 Howell Mill
 Rd NW 18
Holiday Inn, 1944 Piedmont
 Cir, N E 24
Hopkins, 2865 Old Hapevl Rd
 SW 54
Howard Johnsons Motor
 Lodge, 1701 Northside Dr
 NW 18
Howard Johnsons Motor
 Lodge, 2090 N Druid Hills
 Rd NE 29
Howard Johnsons Motor
 Lodge, 745 Washington
 SW 15
Howel House, 710 Peachtree
 NE 08
Imperial, 355 Peachtree NE 83
Ivy, 195 Ivy NE 03
Jefferson, 87 Pryor SW 03
Lenox, 4 Porter Pl NE 03
Luckie, 180 Luckie NW 03
Mark Inn, 1848 Howell Mill
 Rd NW 18
Mark Inn, 2750 Forrest Hill
 Dr SW 15
Mark Inn, 277 Moreland Ave
 SE 16
Marriott Motor Hotel, 165
 Cain St NE 03
Miller, 155 Ivy NE 03
Oaks Motor Court, 1650
 Stewart Ave SW 10
Old South, 331 Cleveland
 Ave SW 15
Paces Ferry Tower, 374 E
 Paces Ferry Rd NE 05
Park, 70 Cain NE 03
Parliment House Motor Inn,
 70 Houston St NE 03
Paschal Mtr. Hotel, 830
 Hunter, N W 14
Pavilion, 14 17th NE 09
Peachtree Manor, 826
 Peachtree NE 83
Peachtree North Ave, 620
 Peachtree NE 08
Peachtree Towers, 300 W
 Peachtree NW 08
Pershing, 1428 Peachtree NE ... 83

Ponce De Leon, 551 Ponce
 De Ln Ave NE 83
Ponce De Leon, 75 Ponce De
 Leon Av NE 83
Regency Hyatt House, 265
 Peachtree NE 03
Ritz, 103 Luckie NW 03
Riviera Of Atlanta, 1630
 Peachtree NW 09
Rodeway Inn, 144 14th NW 18
Royal, 214 Auburn Ave NE 03
Savoy, 239 Auburn Ave NE 03
Scoville, 225 Mitchell SW 03
Shelton, 304 W Peachtree
 NW 08
Sheraton Biltmore, 817 W
 Peachtree NW 83
Sidney, 87 Harris NW 03
Skyline, 1375 Northside Dr
 NW 18
Southland, 825 Ponce De Ln
 Ave NE 83
Stafford, 2640 Stewart Ave
 SW 15
Starlight, 1450 Memorial Dr
 SE 17
Sylvan, 233 Mitchell SW 03
Tech, 120 North Ave NW 13
Three Thirty Peachtree, 330
 Peachtree NE 08
Tower, 374 E Paces Ferry Rd
 NE 05
Town & Country Courts, 2380
 Stewart Ave SW 15
Travelers, 139 Luckie NW 03
University, 55 Northside Dr
 NW 14
Vesta, 265 Williams NW 03
Waluhaje, 239 W Lake Ave
 NW 14

BUILDINGS

Agriculture Laboratory, 19
 Hunter SW 34
American Savings Bank, 140
 Peachtree NW 03
Archetects & Engineers
 Institute, 230 Spring NW 03
Atlanta Federal Savings, 22
 Marietta NW 03
Atlanta Joint Terminal, 104
 Central Ave SW 03
Atlanta Merchandise Market,
 240 Peachtree NW 03
Atlanta National, 50
 Whitehall SW 03
Atlanta Public Library, 126
 Carnegie Way NW 03
Auditorium, 30 Courtland SE 03
Bankers Fidelity, 2045
 Peachtree Rd NE 09
Baptist Professional, 340
 Boulevard NE 12
Baptist, 291 Peachtree NE 03
Belle Isle, 105 Pryor NE 03
Bolling Jones, 20 Ivy SE 03
Bona Allen, 133 Luckie NW 03
Candler, 127 Peachtree NE 03
Carnegie, 133 Carnegie Way
 NW 03
Citizens & Southern National
 Bank, 35 Broad NW 03

Communicable Disease
 Center, 1600 Clifton Rd N
 E 33
Continental Insurance, 165
 Peachtree St NE 03
Crumley, 70 Fairlie NW 03
Cyrus R Strickler, 1293
 Peachtree NE 09
Electrnc, 270 Peachtree NW 03
Exchange Pl, 41 Exchange Pl
 SE 03
Federal Annex, 77 Forsyth
 SW 03
Federal Office, 275 Peachtree
 NE 03
First Federal, 40 Marietta
 NW 03
First National Bank, 2
 Peachtree NW 03
First National Bank, 615
 Peachtree NW 08
Five Points Center, 15
 Peachtree NE 03
Forsyth, 86 Forsyth NW 03
Fulton Federal, 11 Pryor SW 03
Fulton National Bank, 55
 Marietta NW 03
Gas Light Tower, 235
 Peachtree St N E 83
Georgia Life Health Insurance
 Company, 66 Luckie NW 03
Georgia Power, 15 Forsyth
 SW 03
Georgia Savings Bank, 84
 Peachtree NW 03
Glenn, 120 Marietta NW 03
Haas Howell, 77 Poplar NW 03
Hartford, 100 Edgewood Ave
 SE 03
Healey, 57 Forsyth NW 03
Henry Grady, 26 Cain NW 03
Herndon, 239 Auburn Ave NE ... 03
Hickey, 81 Walton NW 03
Highway, 2 Capitol Sq SW 34
Home Savings, 75 Forsyth
 NW 03
Hurt, 45 Edgewood Ave SE 03
John Hancock, 230 Houston
 NE 03
Journal, 10 Forsyth NW 03
Labor, 254 Washington SW 34
Lenox Towers, 3390
 Peachtree Rd NE 26
Life Of Georgia, 600 W
 Peachtree St NW 08
Luftwater, 441 Peachtree NE 08
Mark, 48 Alabama SW 03
Methodist, 155 Forrest Ave
 NE 03
National Bank Of Ga, 34
 Peachtree NW 03
New Title, 30 Pryor SW 03
Palmer, 41 Maritta NW 03
Peachtree Ctr, 230 Peachtree
 NW 03
Peachtree Medical, 401
 Peachtree NE 08
Peachtree Palisades, 1819
 Peachtree St NE 09
Peachtree Seventh, 50
 Seventh St NE 23
Plaza, 5 Plaza Way SW 03

Atlanta (Con.)   303

Red Rock, 187 Spring NW 03
Rhodes Haverty, 134
   Peachtree St NW 03
Richardson, 160 Peachtree
   NW 03
Sheffield Memorial, 1938
   Peachtree NW 09
Southern Bell Telephone, 51
   Ivy NE 03
Standard Federal Savings, 44
   Broad NW 03
Standard, 95 Fairlie NW 03
State Capitol, Capitol Sq SW.. 34
State Office, 12 Capitol Sq
   SW 34
Toco Hills Shopping Center,... 29
Trust Company Of Georgia,
   36 Edgewood Ave NE 03
Walton, 87 Walton NW 03
Western Union, 56 Marietta
   NW 03
William Oliver, 32 Peachtree
   NW 03
Y W C A, 72 Edgewood Ave
   NE 03

GOVERNMENT OFFICES

Civil Criminal Court, 160
   Pryor SW 03
Court House, 130 Pryor SW 03
Fulton County Adminstration,
   165 Central Ave SW 03
Fulton County Health, 99
   Butler, S E 03
Fulton County Juvenile Court,
   445 Capitol Ave SW 15
Post Office Main, 56 Forsyth
   NW 03
Union Station, 2 Forsyth NW.. 03

HOSPITALS

Atlanta Sanitorium, 774 W
   Peachtree NW 08
Battle Hill Haven, 1821
   Anderson Ave W SW 14
Doctors Memorial Hospital,
   573 West Peachtree St.,
   N.w. 08
Doctors North Annex, 490
   Peachtree NE 08
Doctors, 478 Peachtree NE 08
Elks Aidmore, 600 Aidmore
   Dr NE 07
Emory University, 1364
   Clifton Rd NE 22
Frank K Medical Boland, 101
   3rd NE 08
Fulton, 907 Edgewood Ave
   NE 07
Georgia Baptist, 300
   Boulevard NE 12
Georgian Clinic, 1260
   Briarcliff Rd NE 06
Grady Memorial, 80 Butler
   SE 03
Happy Haven, 1821 Anderson
   Ave W SW 14

Henderson, 567 Courtland
   NE 08
High View Nursing Home,
   2800 Springdale Rd SW 15
Holy Family, Sewell &
   Fairburn SW 31
Jesse Parker Williams, 542
   Peachtree NE 08
Mc Lendon, 1370 Sharon NW.. 14
Medical Arts, 384 Peachtree
   NE 08
Our Lady Of Perpetual Care,
   760 Washington SW 15
Peachtree Medical, 401
   Peachtree NE 08
Piedmont, 1968 Peachtree Rd
   NW 09
Ponce De Leon Infirmary, 144
   Ponce De Leon Ave 08
Saint Joseph Infirmary, 265
   Ivy NE 03
Sky Ranch Rest Home, 3700
   Cascad-Palmto SW 11
Spalding Hughes Pavilion, 35
   Butler SE 03
United States Veterans, 1670
   Clairmont Rd N E 29

UNIVERSITIES AND COLLEGES

Atlanta Christian, 2775 Ben
   Hill Rd SW 11
Atlanta Law School, 134
   Peachtree NW 03
Atlanta University, 223
   Chestnut SW 14
Clark, 240 Chestnut SW 14
Emory University School Of
   Dentistry, 106 Forrest Ave
   NE 03
Emory University School Of
   Medicine, 1364 Clifton Rd
   NE 22
Emory University, 1364
   Clifton Rd NE 22
Gammon Theological
   Seminary, 9 Mcdonough
   Blvd SE 15
Georgia Institute Of
   Technology, 225 North
   Ave, NW 32
Greenleaf School Of
   Business, 193 Peachtree
   NE 03
John Marshall Law School,
   105 Forrest Ave NE 03
Marist, 3790 Ashford-Dunwdy
   NE 19
Marsh Business, 322 Ivy NE.. 03
Massey Business, Henry
   Grady Square 03
Mercer University School Of
   Pharmacy, 223 Walton St
   NW 03
Morehouse, 223 Chestnut
   SW 14
Morris Brown, 643 Hunter
   NW 14
Oglethorpe University, 4484
   Peachtree Rd NE 19
Sacred Heart, 335 Ivy NE 03

Southern Business University,
   417 Peachtree NE 08
Southern College Of
   Pharmacy, 223 Walton
   NW 03
Spelman, 350 Leonard SW 14
State University, 33 Gilmer
   SE 03
The Westminster Schools,
   1424 W Pace Ferry Rd NW.. 27

NAMED STREETS

Aaron NW 14
Abbey NW 14
Abbey Rd (EP) 44
Abbott (CP) 37
Abbott SW
   1-250- 14
   251-OUT 10
Abby Ct (DOR) 40
Abby Ln NE 45
Aberdeen Dr NW 18
Aberdeen NE 07
Aberdeen Dr & Ln NE 28
Abernathy Rd NE & NW 28
Abington Dr NE 28
Abner Ct, Pl & Ter NW 18
Academy Ct NE 45
Acadia (EP) 44
Acapulco Way (EP) 44
Acl Terminal NW 13
Acorn Ave NE 05
Acres Mill Rd NW, NW 39
Acuba Ln N NE 45
Ada Ave NW 18
Adair SW 14
Adair Ave NE 06
Adair Ave SE 15
Adams (CP) 37
Adams Dr NW 18
Adams Dr SW 11
Adams St & Ave SW 15
Adams St & Rd (CHA) 41
Adamson SW 15
Adamson Ave (HAP) 54
Adamsville Dr NW 31
Addie NW 18
Addington SW 10
Addison Dr (DOR) 40
Addison Pl NW 18
Adele Ave SW 14
Adelia Pl NE 14
Areline Ave NW 14
Adelie SE 03
Adena Ln E & W (CP) 49
Adevholdt Ferry Rd SW 31
Adina Dr NE 24
Adkins Rd NW 18
Admiral Dr & Way (CHA) 41
Adolphus Ave NE 07
Adrian Pl NW 27
Aero Ct (EP) 44
Afond Ct (CHA) 41
Afton Ln NE 29
Aidmore Dr NE 07
Aiken Dr NE 19
Aikens SW 15
Aircond Way SE 16
Airline Pl SE 12
Airline St NE & SE 12
Ajax Dr NW 18
Akers Mill Rd NW 39

Atlanta (Con.)   303

Albert NW ... 18
Alberta Dr & Ter NE ... 05
Albion Ave NE ... 07
Alco NE ... 24
Alcoa Ct (CHA) ... 41
Alcott Pl (CP) ... 37
Alden Ave NW ... 09
Alden Green Trl (EP) ... 44
Alder Ct SE ... 17
Alder Ln SW ... 11
Alderbrook Ct NE ... 45
Alderbrook Rd NE
  1597-OUT ... 45
Aldredge Blvd SW ... 36
Aldredge Rd SW ... 31
Ale Cir (EP) ... 44
Alexa SE ... 17
Alexander NE ... 08
Alexander NW
  1-100 ... 08
  101-OUT ... 13
Alexander Dr (CP) ... 37
Alexander Dr NE ... 05
Alexandria Way (CP) ... 37
Alfred Rd NW ... 31
Alice SW ... 12
Alice Ln SE ... 49
Aline Dr NW ... 18
Alison Ct SW ... 11
Allaire Ln NE ... 45
Allegheny SW ... 10
Allegro Dr NW ... 18
Allen Ct NE ... 28
Allen Dr (CP) ... 37
Allen Dr (DOR) ... 40
Allen Ln SE ... 54
Allen Rd NE
  1-300 ... 28
  301-OUT ... 24
Allen Way NE
  1-300 ... 28
  301-OUT ... 24
Allen Temple Ct NW ... 11
Allendale Dr SE ... 17
Allene Ave SW ... 10
Allison Dr (DOR) ... 40
Allison Dr NE ... 42
Alloway Pl SE ... 16
Alma NW ... 18
Alma SW ... 11
Almetta Ave NE ... 07
Almond Dr (CP) ... 37
Almond Rd SE ... 16
Almont Dr SW ... 10
Alpine Rd NE ... 05
Alston Dr SE
  1-2964 ... 17
Alta Ave NE ... 07
Alta Pl NW ... 18
Alta Vis Dr NE ... 11
Altadena Pl SW ... 19
Altaview Dr SE ... 54
Alton Rd (CHA) ... 41
Alton Rd NW ... 05
Altoona Pl SW
  1-280 ... 14
  281-OUT ... 07
Alva NE ... 03
Alvarado Ter SW ... 10
Alverstone Dr (HAP) ... 54
Alvin Dr NW ... 18

Amal Dr SW ... 15
Amanda NE ... 07
Amber Pl & Rd NW ... 31
Amberglades Ln NW ... 28
Amberly Ct N & S (DOR) ... 40
Amberly Ct, Dr & Way (DOR) ... 40
Amberridge Trl NW ... 28
Amberwood Dr & Way NE ... 45
American Dr (CHA) ... 41
American Ind Blvd & Way (CHA) ... 28
Amherst Ct NE ... 24
Amherst Pl NW ... 27
Amhurst Dr NW ... 18
Ami SE
  1-650 ... 12
  651-OUT ... 15
Amsterdam Ave NE ... 06
Amwiler Rd (DOR) ... 40
Amy Ct (CP) ... 37
Anchor Ter SW ... 10
Andalusia Ter (DOR) ... 40
Anderson Ave NW & SW ... 11
Andover Ct & Dr (DOR) ... 40
Andover Dr NW ... 27
Andrews NW ... 14
Andrews Cir NE ... 14
Andrews Dr NE ... 07
Angelo Ct & Dr NE ... 19
Angier Ave NE
  1-420 ... 12
  421-OUT ... 08
Angier Pl NE ... 08
Angier Springs Rd NE ... 06
Angus Trl NE & NW ... 28
Anita Pl NE ... 06
Aniwaka Ave SW ... 11
Anjaco Rd NW ... 09
Ann St & Ct (CHA) ... 41
Annapolis Ct NE ... 45
Anne NW ... 18
Anne Ave SE ... 15
Annelaine Dr SW ... 11
Annie NE ... 18
Anniston Ave SE ... 17
Ansley Ct & Ln NE ... 24
Ansley Dr NE ... 09
Ansley Forest Dr NE ... 24
Ansted Ln (CP) ... 49
Anthony NW ... 18
Antioch Dr NE ... 19
Antone NW ... 18
Antwerp Dr SE ... 15
Apache Trl SE ... 16
Apache Trl SW ... 31
Appalachee Dr NE ... 19
Apple Orchard Dr (CHA) ... 41
Apple Valley Rd NE ... 19
Applewood Ct NE ... 45
Appling Cir, Ct, Dr & Way (CHA) ... 41
Aragon Way NE ... 19
Arbor Ave SE ... 11
Arbor Vis Dr NE ... 29
Arc Way NE ... 05
Arcadia Cir NW ... 14
Archcrest Dr (HAP) ... 54
Archer SW ... 14
Archer Way NW ... 14
Archway Dr (CHA) ... 41
Archwood Dr (DOR) ... 40
Ard Pl NW ... 31
Arden Ave SW ... 10

Arden Rd NW
  1-2924 ... 27
  2925-OUT ... 05
Arden Way NE ... 42
Arden At Argonne NW ... 05
Ardley Rd SW ... 11
Ardmore Cir & Rd NW ... 09
Argo Dr (HAP) ... 54
Argonne Ave NE
  1-870 ... 08
  871-OUT ... 09
Argonne Dr NW ... 05
Argonne Way NE ... 24
Argus Cir NW ... 31
Argyle Dr NW ... 18
Arizona Ave NE ... 07
Arkose Dr SW ... 16
Arkwright Pl SE ... 17
Arlene Rd (CP) ... 37
Arlene Way NE ... 05
Arlington Ave SW ... 10
Arlington Ave & Pky NE ... 24
Arlington Cir NW ... 18
Arlington Dr (DUN) ... 38
Arlington Dr NW ... 11
Arlington Pl NE ... 06
Arlington Rd (EP) ... 44
Armand Ct & Rd NE ... 24
Armour Cir, Dr & Pl NE ... 24
Armstrong SE ... 03
Amand Ct (DUN) ... 38
Arno Ct & Dr NW ... 18
Arnold (HAP) ... 54
Arnold NE ... 08
Arnold Ave NE ... 24
Arrow Cir (CHA) ... 41
Arrow Creek Dr (CHA) ... 41
Arrowhead Trl NE ... 45
Arrowwood Dr SW
  1-3000 ... 44
  3001-OUT ... 31
Arthur SW ... 10
Artwood Rd NE ... 07
Aruba Cir NE ... 28
Arundel Dr NW ... 27
Arundel Rd (CP) ... 37
Asbury Ln SW ... 31
Ascent NE ... 19
Ascot Ct (CHA) ... 41
Ascot Dr NE ... 19
Ash NW ... 40
Ashburn Ln (CHA) ... 41
Ashburton Ave SE ... 17
Ashby NW
  1-560 ... 14
  561-OUT ... 18
Ashby SW
  1-300 ... 14
  301-OUT ... 10
Ashby Cir & Ter NW ... 14
Ashby Grv & Pl SW ... 14
Ashentree Ct & Dr (CHA) ... 41
Ashford Rd NE ... 19
Ashford Dunwoody Rd NE
  1-4150 ... 19
  4151-4665 ... 46
  4666-OUT ... 38
Ashland Ave & Dr NE ... 07
Ashley Ave NE ... 12
Ashley Oaks Ct & Dr NE ... 45
Ashmont Ct (DUN) ... 38
Ashton Woods Dr NE ... 19
Ashwood Ave SW ... 15

Atlanta (Con.) 303

Ashwoody Ct & Trl NE 19
Aspen Dr NE
  1-1955 45
Astor Ave SW 10
Athens Ave SW 10
Atkins (HAP) 54
Atkinson Dr NE 54
Atlanta (CP) 37
Atlanta (EP) 44
Atlanta Ave (HAP) 54
Atlanta Ave N (CP) 37
Atlanta Ave SE
  1-600 15
  601-OUT 12
Atlanta Ave SW 15
Atlantic Dr NW 18
Atlantis Ave NE 07
Atwood SW 10
Atwood Rd NE 05
Auburn Ave NE
  1-338 03
  339-OUT 12
Auditorium Dr (CP) 37
Audrey Pl NW 18
Audubon Cir SW 11
Audubon Dr NE 29
Augusta Ave & Pl SE 15
Aurora Ave NW 14
Austell Way NW 05
Austin Ave NE 07
Austin Dr (CP) 49
Austin Rd SW 31
Autumn Dr (DOR) 40
Autumn Ln SW 10
Avalon Pl NE 06
Awebury (EP) 44
Avenida SW 10
Avenue Of Redwoods (CP) 49
Avery Dr NE 09
Avery Rd SW 15
Avon Ave SW
  1-1480 10
  1481-OUT 11
Avondale Ave SE 12
Avonwood Cir SW 11
Ayrshire Cir NW 18
Azalia SW 18
Azlee Pl NW 18
Aztec Rd (DOR) 40
Bachelor (EP) 44
Bader Ave SW 10
Bagley Dr (CHA) 41
Bagwell Dr NW 15
Bailey SW 14
Bailey Dr SE 16
Baker (DOR) 40
Baker NE
  1-100 03
  101-OUT 12
Baker NW
  1-100 08
  101-OUT 13
Baker Cir, Rd & Ter NW 18
Baker Dr SW 54
Baker Ridge Dr NW 18
Bakers Ferry Rd SW
  1-4675 31
  4676-5650 36
  5651-OUT 31
Baldwin St & Pl SW 10

Ball Mill Ct & Rd (DUN) 38
Balmoral Dr (CHA) 41
Balmoral Rd NE 19
Baltimore Pl NW 08
Banberry Dr SE 15
Bankhead Ave NW
  1-3200 18
  3201-OUT 31
Bankhead Ct NW, NW 31
Bankhead Hwy NW
  1-3200 18
  3201-OUT 31
Banks SW 15
Banks Cir 37
Banks Pl NE 03
Banner Rd (CP) 49
Barbara Ln NW 27
Barcelona Ct (CP) 49
Barclay Pl NE 06
Barfield Ave SW 10
Barfield Rd NE 28
Barge Rd SW 31
Barksdale Cir (EP) 44
Barksdale Dr NE 09
Barkside Ct (CHA) 41
Barkston Ct (CHA) 41
Barnes NW 18
Barnesdale Way NE 09
Barnett St & Cir (HAP) 54
Barnett St & Pl NE 06
Barret Dr NW 18
Barret Rd NW 31
Barrett Ave & Way (EP) 44
Barron Ct NW 27
Barrow Pl SW 31
Barryln Dr (DOR) 40
Barton Dr (HAP) 54
Barton Woods Rd NE 07
Bartow SW 10
Bass SE 15
Bass SW
  1-330 15
  331-OUT 10
Bassetthall Pl NW 18
Batavia (EP) 44
Bates Ave NE & SE 17
Bates Ct NE 19
Battery Pl NE 07
Battery Way NE 44
Battle Dr NE 45
Battle Overlook NW 27
Battlefield Ave SE 17
Battleford Ct (CHA) 41
Battleview Dr NW 27
Baxter Rd SW 15
Bayard St & Cir (EP) 44
Bayberry Dr SW 11
Baylor NW 10
Baywood Dr SE 15
Beach Way SE 42
Beachland Dr NE 40
Beacon Dr (DOR) 40
Beacon Dr (CP) 49
Beacon Hill Blvd NE 29
Beard NE 12
Beatie Ave SW 10
Beauprie SW 10
Beauregard Ave SE 16
Beaver Rd NE 45
Beaverbrook Dr NW 18
Beck NW 18
Becket Dr NE 19
Beckwith St & Ct SW 14

Bedford NW 18
Bedford Pl NE
  1-490 12
  491-OUT 08
Beech Dr (EP) 44
Beech Hill Dr (DOR) 40
Beech Valley Rd & Way NE 06
Beechcliffe Dr NE 29
Beecher SW
  1-1990 10
  1991-OUT 11
Beecher Cir & Ct SW 11
Beecher Rd SW
  1-1990 10
  1991-OUT 11
Beechhaven Rd NE 24
Beechview Dr SE 16
Beechwood Ave (DOR) 40
Beechwood Ave SW 10
Beechwood Blvd SW 11
Beechwood Dr NW 27
Beeler Dr SW 31
Belaire Cir (DOR) 40
Belfast SW 10
Belfort Rd SE 54
Belgarde Pl SE 54
Belgrade Ave NE 06
Belhaven Ln SE 15
Belingham Dr NE 45
Bell (EP) 44
Bell (CP) 37
Bell NE 03
Bell SE
  1-100 03
  101-OUT 12
Bellaire Dr NE 19
Bellburn Rd (CP) 49
Belle Isle Cir NE 29
Belleau Ln SE 16
Bellemeade Ave NW 18
Bellevue Dr NE 06
Bellingrath NW 18
Bellview NW 18
Belmont Ave SW 10
Belvedere Ave SW 11
Belvedere Dr NW 18
Ben Hill Ave & Rd (EP) 44
Ben Hill Rd (CP) 49
Ben Hill Rd NE
  2013-OUT (EP) 44
  2201-2400 11
Bencal Dr SE 16
Bench Mark Dr (CP) 49
Bend Creek Ct, Rd & Way
  (DUN) 38
Bender SW 10
Bennett NW 09
Benning Pl NE 07
Bent Brook Ct & Dr (DOR) 40
Bent Creek Way SW 11
Benteen Ave SE
  1-1200 12
  1201-OUT 15
Benteen St & Way SE 15
Benton Pl NW 27
Benton Woods Dr NE 42
Benwell Dr (DUN) 38
Berean Ave SE
  1-300 16
  301-OUT 12
Berkford Cir & Ct NE 19
Berkle SW 10
Berkley Ave NW 18

Atlanta (Con.)　　　　　303

Berkley Ln NE.................................. 29
Berkley Ridge Dr (DUN)................. 38
Berkley Tarn (DUN)......................... 38
Berkshire Rd NE
　1-1000... 24
　1001-OUT..................................... 06
Bernadette Ln NE............................ 29
Bernard NW..................................... 14
Bernard Rd NW................................ 18
Berne SE
　1-770... 12
　771-OUT....................................... 16
Bernice SW...................................... 10
Bernina Ave NE............................... 07
Berwick Ave NE............................... 06
Berwick Dr NE................................. 28
Beryl SW.. 10
Best Rd (CP)................................... 37
Best Friend Rd (DOR)..................... 40
Besto Dr NW.................................... 18
Bethel Dr NW.................................. 14
Bethesda Ct & Trl (CHA)................. 41
Betsy Ave SW................................. 10
Beutell NW...................................... 14
Beverly Dr (CHA)............................ 41
Beverly Ln NE................................. 42
Beverly Rd NE................................. 09
Beverly Hills Dr (CHA).................... 41
Beverly Woods Ct (CHA)................. 41
Beya Way (DOR).............................. 40
Bicknell Dr SW................................ 15
Biggers St....................................... 12
Biglin SW... 10
Bill Cook Rd (CP)............................ 37
Billings Ave SE............................... 15
Billups SW....................................... 10
Biltmore Dr NE................................ 29
Biltmore Pl NW................................ 08
Binder Pl NE.................................... 07
Binford Pl SW.................................. 31
Binghamton Ct & Dr (DOR)............. 40
Birch (HAP)..................................... 54
Birch SW.. 10
Birchwood Dr NE............................. 05
Bisbee Ave SE................................. 15
Biscayne Dr NW.............................. 09
Bishop Aly NE................................. 08
Bishop St & Pl NW.......................... 18
Bishop Hollow Ct (CHA)................. 41
Bishop Hollow Run (CHA)............... 41
Bismark Rd NE................................ 24
Bixby St & Ter SE........................... 17
Black Forrest Tr SW....................... 31
Black Fox Dr NE.............................. 45
Black Fox Trl (EP)........................... 44
Black Oak Dr SE............................. 16
Blackberry Ln (CHA)....................... 41
Blackburn Way (CHA)..................... 41
Blackland Dr & Rd NW................... 42
Blackwater Trl NW.......................... 28
Blackwater Cove NW...................... 28
Blair Cir NE..................................... 19
Blair Villa Dr (HAP)........................ 54
Blake Ave SE.................................. 16
Blakely Dr NE................................. 24
Blalock (HAP).................................. 54
Blanche NW..................................... 18
Blanton Ave SW.............................. 31
Blanton Rd NW................................ 42
Blashfield SE................................... 15
Blayton Cir NW................................ 14

Blossom SW..................................... 10
Blossom Ln (EP).............................. 44
Blount St & Pl (EP).......................... 44
Blue Ridge Ave & Ct NE................. 06
Bluefield Dr SW............................... 10
Bluestone Rd NE............................. 28
Bluff SW... 10
Blyss Ave NW.................................. 18
Boat Rock Blvd SW, SW.................. 36
Boat Rock Rd SW............................ 31
Bob White Dr SW............................ 11
Bobolink Cir SW.............................. 11
Bocage Walk NW............................. 05
Bohler Ct NW................................... 27
Bohler Rd NW
　1-2200... 18
　2201-OUT..................................... 27
Boland Dr NE.................................. 19
Bolero Dr (CHA).............................. 41
Bolfair Dr NW.................................. 31
Bolissa Dr (DOR)............................ 40
Bolling Rd & Way NE...................... 05
Bolling Brook Dr SW....................... 11
Bolton Rd NW.................................. 18
Bolton Pt NW................................... 31
Bolton Rd NW
　1-1600... 31
　1601-OUT..................................... 18
Bon Echo Dr (CP)........................... 49
Bonair SW.. 14
Bonaventure Ave NE....................... 06
Bond Dr SW..................................... 15
Bonn SE... 15
Bonner Rd (EP)............................... 44
Bonneville Ter NW.......................... 31
Bonnevit Ct NE................................ 45
Bonnie Ave (DOR).......................... 40
Bonnie Ln NE & NW........................ 28
Bonnie Ln SE................................... 54
Bonnie Brae Ave SW...................... 10
Bonnington Ct (CHA)...................... 41
Bonnview SW................................... 10
Bonnybrook Dr & Way SW............. 11
Bonnybrook Way (EP)..................... 44
Bonview Ln NE................................ 24
Booker NW
　1-100... 14
　101-500... 15
　501-OUT....................................... 18
Booker SW
　1-100... 14
　101-300... 15
　501-OUT....................................... 18
Booker Ave NW
　1-100... 14
　101-500... 15
　501-OUT....................................... 10
Booker Ave SW
　1-100... 14
　101-500... 15
　501-OUT....................................... 10
Booker Washington Dr NW............. 14
Booth NW... 18
Bordeau Ct (DUN)........................... 38
Boston Dr (CP)................................ 37
Boulder Rd SE................................. 16
Boulder Way (EP)............................ 44
Boulder Park Dr Dr SW
　1-3300... 11
　3301-OUT..................................... 31
Bouldercliff Ct & Way SE............... 16
Bouldercrest Dr SE
　1-2846... 16

Boulderview Dr SE.......................... 16
Boulderwoods Dr SE....................... 16
Boulevard NE
　1-380... 12
　381-OUT....................................... 08
Boulevard SE
　1-1250... 12
　1251-OUT..................................... 15
Boulevard Dr NE
　1001-2930..................................... 17
Boulevard Dr SE
　1001-2930..................................... 17
Boulevard Pl NE.............................. 08
Boulevard Granada SW.................. 11
Boulevard Lorraine SW................... 11
Bowen NW.. 18
Bowen Ave SE................................. 15
Bowen Cir SW.................................. 15
Bowers SW....................................... 31
Bowling Green Way (DOR)............. 40
Box NE... 08
Boxwood Ct & Dr NE...................... 45
Boyce Ct & Dr SE........................... 16
Boyd Ave NW.................................. 18
Boykin SW.. 15
Boyleston Dr NE.............................. 28
Boynton Ave SW............................. 15
Bradbury SW................................... 13
Bradcliff Ct & Dr NE....................... 45
Braddock SW................................... 10
Bradley SE
　1-500... 16
　501-OUT....................................... 12
Bradley St & Aly NE....................... 12
Brady Ave NE.................................. 18
Braeburn Cir & Dr SE..................... 16
Braemar Ave SW............................. 11
Bragg (CHA).................................... 41
Braithwood Ct & Dr NE.................. 45
Bramble Rd NE................................ 29
Bramblewood Dr NE....................... 29
Branch Ave NE................................ 05
Branch Dr SW.................................. 31
Branchwood (EP)............................. 44
Brandon Rd (CP)............................. 37
Brandon Mill Rd NW....................... 28
Brandon Ridge Dr NE..................... 28
Brandy Tuck Way (DOR)................. 40
Brandywine SW............................... 10
Branham NE..................................... 16
Brannen Rd SE................................ 17
Brantley NE..................................... 07
Brantley NW.................................... 18
Brantley Pl NW................................ 14
Brantley Rd (DUN).......................... 38
Bratton SW....................................... 09
Brawley Cir, Dr & Way NE............. 19
Breckenridge Ct, Dr & Way
　NE... 45
Breezy Ln NE.................................. 29
Brendon Dr (DUN).......................... 38
Breningham Dr (CP)....................... 37
Brenmar Way (DOR)....................... 40
Brennan Ln SW............................... 10
Brenton Ct (DUN)........................... 38
Brenton Dr & Way NE.................... 19
Brentwood Dr & Ter NE................. 05
Brentwood Rd (CP)......................... 49
Breton Cir & Ct NE......................... 19
Brevard Ave SW.............................. 15
Brewer Blvd SW.............................. 10
Brewster SW.................................... 10
Briar Ct (EP).................................... 44

Atlanta (Con.)　　　303

Briar Glade Way (DOR) 40
Briar Park Ct Ct NE 06
Briar Ridge Cir (DOR) 40
Briar Wood Ind Ct NE 29
Briarcliff Ct, Pl & Ter NE 06
Briarcliff Ln, Trl & Way NE .. 45
Briarcliff Rd NE
　1-1799 06
　1800-3250 29
Briarcliff Rd NE, NE
　3251-4850 45
Briarcrest Trl NE 45
Briardale Ln NE 06
Briarhills Dr NE 06
Briarlake Rd NE
　1-2900 45
Briarlake Woods Way NE 45
Briarlyn Ct NE 45
Briarmill Rd NE 29
Briarmoor Rd NE 45
Briarvista Ter NE 24
Briarwillow Dr NE 45
Briarwood Blvd (EP) 44
Briarwood Ct NE 45
Briarwood Dr NE 06
Briarwood Rd NE
　1-1700 19
　1701-OUT 29
Briarwood Way NE 19
Briarwood Hills Dr NE 19
Briarwood Ind Ct NE 29
Brick Plant Rd NW 18
Bridgeport Dr NE 29
Bridgeport Dr NW 29
Bridges Ave SW 10
Bridges Creek Trl NE 28
Bridgewater SW 28
Bridgewater Dr NE 28
Bridgewood Valley Rd NW 28
Brier Glen Ct & Dr (DOR) 40
Brier Green Ct (DOR) 40
Brighton NW 18
Brighton Rd NE & NW 09
Brinkley Ln NE 42
Bristol Dr NE 29
Brittain Dr NW 13
Brittamy Trl (CP) 49
Brittley Ter (CP) 49
Brixham Ct NE 28
Broad (CHA) 41
Broad Ave (EP) 44
Broad St NW & SW 63
Broadland Ct NW 42
Broadland Rd NW
　1-520 42
　521-OUT 27
Broadview Plz NE 24
Broadwell NW 10
Bromack Rd SE & SW 15
Brompton Ct (DUN) 38
Bronx NW 14
Brook Dr NE 28
Brook Way SW 31
Brook Forrest Dr NE 24
Brook Hollow Dr NW 27
Brook Park Way (DOR) 40
Brook Valley Ln NE 24
Brookcliff Way NE 45
Brookdale Dr (EP) 44
Brookdale Dr NE
　1-2529 45

2530-ONLY 05
2531-2535 45
2536-OUT 05
Brookdale Dr NW
　1-2529 29
2530-ONLY 29
2531-2535 29
2536-OUT 05
Brookdale Dr SW 15
Brookfield Dr NE 42
Brookgreen Rd NE 28
Brookhaven Dr NE 19
Brookhurst Dr (CHA) 41
Brooklawn Ct & Rd NE 19
Brookline SW 10
Brookline Cir & Ct (DUN) 38
Brooklyn Ave NW 09
Brookridge Dr NE 06
Brooks Ave NE 07
Brooks Ave NW 18
Brooks Ave SW 10
Brookshire Ln NE 15
Brookview Dr NW
　1-3000 18
　3000-OUT 39
Brookwood Dr NE
　1-1000 09
　1001-OUT 05
Brookwood Dr NW
　1-1000 09
　1001-OUT 05
Broughton Ct (DUN) 38
Brown Ave NW 18
Brown Ave SE 15
Brown Dr (HAP) 54
Brown Pl SE 16
Brown Pl & Rd (CP) 37
Browning NE 17
Browhing SW 14
Brownlee Pl & Ter SW 31
Brownlee Rd SW
　1-293 31
　294-ONLY 11
Brownlee Rd, SW
　295-320 31
　321-OUT 11
Browns Mill Rd SE
　1-2430 15
　2431-OUT 54
Brownsville Rd NW 15
Browntown Rd NW 18
Brownwood Ave SE 16
Broyles SE 12
Bruce (DOR) 40
Bruce Cir SE 16
Bruce Pl SW 31
Bruce Rd NE 29
Brunswick Ave SE 17
Bry-Mar Dr NE 45
Bryan SE 12
Bryan Ave & Cir (EP) 44
Bryant (HAP) 54
Bryant Dr (EP) 44
Brynmawr Cir & Ln NW 27
Bubbling Creek Rd NE 19
Buchanan NE 18
Buchanan NW 15
Buchanan Ln SE 15
Buckeye SW 10
Buckeye Rd (CHA) 41
Buckhead Ave & Way NE 05
Buckhorn (DUN) 38
Buckhorn E (DUN) 38

Buckingham Cir NW 27
Buckley Ct (CHA) 41
Buckline Cir & Ct (DUN) 38
Bucknell Dr SW 36
Bucktrout Pl (CHA) 41
Buena Vista Ave (DOR) 40
Buena Vista Ave Ave SW 15
Buff Dr NE 42
Buffington Rd (CP) 49
Buford Dr (CHA) 41
Buford Hwy NE
　1-2800 24
　2801-3920 29
　3921-4310 45
　4311-5054 41
Buford Hwy NE, NE
　5055-6106 40
Buford Rd NE
　1-2800 24
　2801-3920 29
　3921-4310 45
　4311-5054 41
Buford Rd NE
　5055-6106 40
Buford Hwy
　4141-5791 (GC) 40
Bullock SW 15
Bunker Hill Dr SW 31
Burbank Dr NW & SW 14
Burch Cir NE 19
Burchill SW 10
Burden NW 18
Burdett Dr NW 28
Burdett Rd (CP) 37
Burdett Rd NE 27
Burks Ct 49
Burke Dr (CHA) 41
Burke NE 05
Burlingame Dr (DOR) 40
Burlington Pl & Rd NE 07
Burnham Ct (DOR) 40
Burns SE 16
Burns Dr SW 10
Burnt Hickory Dr SW 11
Burroughs St & Ave SE 15
Burton Dr 29
Burton Rd NW 11
Burton Plaza Ln Ln NE 19
Burton Plaza Way Way NE 19
Burtz NW 18
Bussey NW 18
Butler NE
　1-200 03
　201-400 12
　401-OUT 08
Butler SE 03
Butler Way NW 18
Butner Rd SW
　1-3600 31
　3601-OUT 49
Button Rd NE 24
Button Gwinnett Rd (DOR) ... 40
Bynum Rd NE 19
Byrd SE 15
Byrere Ter SW 10
Byron Dr SW 10
Byway NE 06
Bywood Ln SW 10
Cadillac Dr NE 45
Cadiz Ln N & W (CP) 49
Cahaba Dr SW 11
Cahoon SW 10

Atlanta (Con.)	303
Cain NE	
1-300	03
301-OUT	12
Cain NW	03
Cains Hill Pl NW	05
Cairo NW	14
Caladium Dr NE	45
Caldwell Rd NE	19
Calhoun NW	18
Calhoun Ave (EP)	44
Calhoun Ter SW	14
Callahan NW	18
Callan Cir SW	07
Calloway Dr NW	14
Calmer Cir (EP)	44
Calvert Ln NE	18
Calvin Ave (EP)	44
Cambria NW	18
Cambridge Ave (EP)	44
Cambridge Ave (CP)	37
Cambridge Dr (DUN)	38
Cambridge Dr NE	31
Camden Rd NE & NW	09
Cameron SE	12
Cameron Ct NE	06
Camfield Ct SW	10
Camilla SW	14
Camille Dr NE	19
Camp Creek Pky	
1-3000 (CP)	37
3001-OUT (EP)	44
Camp Creek Pky SW	31
Camp Ground Rd SW	31
Campbell SE	17
Campbell Cir (HAP)	54
Campbell Rd (CP)	49
Campbellton Cir SW	31
Campbellton Pl SW	10
Campbellton Rd SW	
1-1400	10
1401-3400	11
3401-OUT	31
Camrose Way NW	31
Canaan Ct & Dr SE	16
Candace Dr & Ln SE	16
Candlelight Ln SW	31
Candler NE	07
Candler Rd NE	
1-100	17
Candler Rd SE	
1-375	17
Candler Lake Cir & Ct NE	19
Candler Park Dr Dr NE	07
Candlewood Dr (EP)	44
Canfield Dr (CHA)	41
Canmont Rd NE	19
Canna Ridge Cir NE	45
Cannon St & Ct (CP)	37
Cannon Farm Hills Rd NE	29
Cannon Farm Meadows Rd NE	29
Canoochee Dr NE	19
Canova SW	11
Canter Rd NE	24
Canterbury Rd NE	24
Cantey Pl NW	27
Cantrell Rd NE	19
Canyon Creek Trl NE	45
Capehart Cir & Pl NE	45
Capitol Ave SE	
1-400	34
401-650	12
651-OUT	15
Capitol Ave SW	
1-400	34
401-650	12
651-OUT	15
Capitol Pl & Sq SW	34
Capitol View Ave NW	18
Capri Ct & Ter (EP)	44
Captain Dr (CHA)	41
Cardera Ct (CP)	49
Cardigan Cir NE	28
Cardinal Way SW	11
Cardine Pl NW	05
Cardo Dr NW	18
Cardova Dr NE	24
Carey Dr SE	15
Careygate NW	05
Caribea Trl SE	16
Carlile Ct NE	16
Carlington Ct NE	45
Carlisle NW	18
Carlo Ct & Ter SW	31
Carlo Woods Dr SW	31
Carlton Dr (CHA)	41
Carlton Dr NE	42
Carlton Pl NE	19
Carmain Dr NE	42
Carmel Ave NE	07
Carmel Dr NE	44
Carmel Dr & Rd (CHA)	41
Carmel Ln (CP)	37
Carnaby Ct (DUN)	38
Carnegie Ave (EP)	44
Carnegie Way NW	03
Carol Ct (EP)	44
Carol Ln NE	06
Carol Ln & Way NW	27
Carole Dr (DOR)	40
Caroline NE	07
Carolwood Ln NE	42
Carolyn NW	18
Carolyn SW	31
Carolyn Dr NE	29
Caron Cir NW	18
Carpenter Dr NE	28
Carr NW	18
Carriage Ct, Ln & Way (CP)	49
Carriage Dr NE	28
Carriage Way (EP)	44
Carriage Way NW	27
Carriage House Ct (EP)	44
Carrol Ave & Cir (CHA)	41
Carroll SE	12
Carroll Ave SW	31
Carroll Rd NW	
1-1350	36
1351-OUT	31
Carroll St, Ave & Dr NW	18
Carson Pass SW	31
Cartecay Dr NE	19
Carter NW	14
Carter Ave SE	
1-260	17
Carter Cir (EP)	44
Carter Dr NE	19
Carter Rd SE	
1-260	17
Carver Cir (DOR)	40
Carver Cir & Dr NW	14
Carver Hill Dr (DOR)	40
Cascade Ave SW	
1-822	10
823-3500	11
3501-OUT	31
Cascade Cir & Ter SW	11
Cascade Pl SW	10
Cascade Rd SW	
1-822	10
823-3350	11
3351-OUT	31
Cascade Palmetto Hwy SW	31
Cascade Springs Rd SW	36
Casplan SW	
1-650	15
651-OUT	10
Casplan Ct SW	10
Cassanova SE	15
Casson NE	07
Castaway Ct & Ln (CHA)	41
Castle Falls Dr NE	29
Castleberry SW	03
Castlegate Dr NW	27
Castleridge Dr NE	42
Castleton Dr NW	28
Castleway Dr & Ln NE	45
Castlewood (EP)	44
Castlewood Dr NW	27
Catalina Cir (EP)	44
Catalina Dr (CHA)	41
Cates Ave NE	19
Catherine SW	10
Cativo Dr SW	11
Cato NW	18
Cavanaugh Ave SE	16
Cave NE	27
Cecelia Dr SE	16
Cecil Ct SE	17
Cecile Ave SE	16
Cedar (DOR)	40
Cedar Ave (EP)	44
Cedar Ave NW	18
Cedar Brook Ct SE	16
Cedar Canyon Ct & Dr NE	45
Cedar Island Dr SW	11
Cedarhurst Ct, Trl & Way (CP)	49
Cedarhurst Dr (DUN)	38
Cedarwood Ct, Dr & Trl (CP)	49
Celeste Dr (HAP)	54
Center NW	18
Center Ave (EP)	44
Center Hill Ave NW	18
Centra Villa Dr SW	11
Central Ave (EP)	44
Central Ave (HAP)	54
Central Ave (DOR)	40
Central Ave SW	
1-350	03
351-650	12
651-OUT	15
Central Dr NW	14
Century Blvd & Pky NE	45
Century Ct (DOR)	40
Cerro SW	14
Cerro Vista Dr Dr SE	16
Chadwell Ct & Ln (DUN)	38
Chaise Rd (CHA)	41
Chalet Ct (DOR)	40
Chalmers Dr NW	18
Chalmette Dr NE	06
Chamberlin SE	12
Chambers Ave (EP)	44
Chamblee Dunwoody Rd	
1-4920 (CHA)	41

Atlanta (Con.)　　　303

Chamblee Tucker Rd
  1-3792 (CHA)............... 41
  3793-4317 (DOR)........... 40
Chambord Way NE............. 19
Champa Ave NW................ 18
Chancery Ln (CHA)............ 41
Channing Dr & Pl NW......... 18
Chantilly Dr NE................. 24
Chantilly Ter (CP)............. 49
Chaparral Dr & Pl (DUN)..... 38
Chapel SW....................... 13
Chapman Ave (EP)............. 44
Chapman Springs Rd (CP)... 37
Chappel Cir & Ln (DOR)...... 40
Chappell Rd NW
  1-300........................ 14
  301-OUT.................... 14
Chappell Rd SW................ 14
Charity Dr NE................... 16
Charles Ct SE................... 17
Charles Dr (EP)................ 44
Charles Pl NW.................. 18
Charles Allen Dr NE
  1-920........................ 08
  921-OUT.................... 09
Charleston Ave SE............. 15
Charlestown Dr (CP).......... 37
Charline Ln NE.................. 06
Charlotte Pl NW................ 18
Charmant Pl (DOR)............ 40
Charter Oak Dr SW............ 31
Chase Rd (CHA)................ 41
Chaseland Rd NE.............. 28
Chastain SE..................... 12
Chateau Blvd (EP)............. 05
Chateau Ct & Dr NW.......... 05
Chateaugay Ln NE............. 42
Chatham Ave SW............... 11
Chatham Dr (DOR)............ 40
Chatham Rd NW................ 05
Chatham Way NW.............. 14
Chattahoochee Ave & Cir NW. 18
Chattahoochee Dr SW......... 31
Chattahoochee Pl (EP)........ 44
Chatterton Rd (CP)............ 49
Chatworth Ct NE............... 42
Chaucer Dr SW................. 11
Chaucer Ln NE.................. 19
Chaumont Sq NW.............. 27
Cheateau Ct & Dr (CHA)..... 41
Chelsea Cir NE
  301-OUT.................... 07
Chelsea Cres NE............... 19
Cheminde Vie NW............. 42
Chenault Pl NW................ 14
Cheney (EP)..................... 44
Cherie Ct & Ln (CP)........... 49
Cherokee (DUN)................ 38
Cherokee Ave SE
  1-650........................ 12
  651-OUT.................... 15
Cherokee Cir (CP)............. 49
Cherokee Ct & Rd (DOR)..... 40
Cherokee Pl SE................. 12
Cherokee Rd NW............... 05
Cherokee Trl SW............... 31
Cherring Dr & Ln (CHA)...... 41
Cherry (EP)...................... 44
Cherry NW
  1-800........................ 13

801-OUT..................... 18
Cherry SE........................ 15
Cherry Blossom Dr SW....... 31
Cherry Blossom Ln (EP)...... 44
Cherry Hill (DOR).............. 40
Cherry Laurel Ln (EP)......... 44
Cherry Laurel Ln SW.......... 11
Cherry Tree Ln NE............. 28
Cherry Valley Cir & Dr SE.... 16
Cherrywood Ct NE............. 45
Cherrywood Ln NE............. 42
Cheryl Dr (EP).................. 44
Cheryl Lynne Ln (CP)......... 49
Chesapeake Pt NW............ 44
Chesapeake Way (EP)........ 44
Cheshire Way NE............... 19
Cheshire Bridge Rd NE....... 24
Chesson Ct NE.................. 19
Chester Ave SE................. 16
Chesterfield Ct (CP)........... 49
Chesterfield Dr (DOR)........ 45
Chestnut (HAP)................. 54
Chestnut NW
  1-430........................ 14
  431-OUT.................... 18
Chestnut SW.................... 14
Chestnut Aly, Ave & Way NE. 17
Chestnut Dr (EP)............... 44
Chestnut Dr (DOR)............ 40
Chestnut Pl NW................ 14
Chestnut Forest Ct & Ln
  (DOR)...................... 40
Chestnut Hall Dr NW.......... 27
Chestnut Oak Ct NW.......... 27
Chevelle Ln SE
  1001-2930.................. 17
Cheviot Glen (EP)............. 44
Chevron Dr & Way (DUN).... 38
Chicago Ave NW................ 18
Chicamauga Ave & Pl SW.... 11
Chicopee Dr (DOR)............ 40
Childerlee Ln NE............... 29
Childers Rd NE................. 24
Childress Dr SW................ 11
Childs Dr NW................... 14
Chilton Dr NW.................. 18
Chinaberry Way SW........... 11
Chipley NE....................... 07
Chippewa Rd NE............... 19
Chivers NW...................... 18
Chowning Way (CHA)......... 41
Christian City (CP)............. 49
Christman SW................... 10
Christmas Ln NE............... 29
Christopher Ct (DOR)......... 40
Christophers Walk NW........ 27
Chrysler Dr & Ter NE.......... 45
Church (EP)...................... 44
Church (DOR)................... 40
Church NW....................... 18
Churchill Downs Dr NE....... 19
Circle NE......................... 07
Circle 85 (CP)................... 49
Circlewood Rd NE.............. 45
Citadel Dr (HAP)............... 54
Clair Dr NE
  1-300........................ 15
  301-OUT.................... 07
Claire Dr SE
  1-300........................ 15
  301-OUT.................... 07
Claire Dr SW

1-100......................... 15
101-OUT..................... 10
Clairmont Ct, Ln, Pl & Way
  NE........................... 29
Clairmont Rd NE
  2201-3390.................. 29
  3391-3620.................. 19
  3621-OUT.................. 41
Clairmont Ter NE.............. 45
Clairview Dr (CHA)............ 41
Clairwood Ter (CHA).......... 41
Claremont NW.................. 18
Clarendale Dr NW............. 27
Claridge Ct (DOR)............. 40
Clarissa Dr NW................. 18
Clark NW......................... 18
Clark Dr (EP).................... 44
Clark Howell Hwy (EP)....... 49
Clark Howell Hwy (HAP)..... 54
Clark Howell Pl NW........... 13
Clarke........................... 12
Claude NW....................... 18
Clay Dr (DOR).................. 40
Clay Dr (DUN).................. 38
Clay St NE & SE................ 17
Clayton Ct SE................... 17
Clearbrook Dr NW............. 11
Clearview Ave, Dr, Pky & Pl
  (DOR)...................... 40
Clearview Dr NE............... 19
Clearvue Ter SW............... 11
Clearwater Dr (CP)............ 49
Clearwater Rd SW............. 31
Cleburne Ave SE............... 07
Cleburne Ter NE
  1-500........................ 07
  601-OUT.................... 06
Clement Dr & Way SW........ 31
Clementstone Dr NE.......... 42
Clemont Dr NE................. 06
Clemson Dr (CHA)............. 41
Cleremont Ave & Ct (EP).... 44
Cleveland Ave (EP)............ 44
Cleveland Ave SE............. 16
Cleveland Ave SE
  1-130........................ 15
  131-OUT (HAP)........... 54
Cleveland Ave SW
  1-1000...................... 15
  1001-OUT.................. 44
Cleveland Cir SW.............. 15
Cliff Valley Way NE
  1-1500...................... 19
  1501-OUT.................. 29
Clifford Ave NE................. 17
Cliffway Dr (CHA).............. 41
Clifton NE
  1-100........................ 17
  101-1350................... 07
  1351-1363.................. 33
  1364-1364.................. 22
  1365-1404.................. 33
  1405-1405.................. 22
  1406-1450.................. 33
  1451-1461.................. 29
  1462-ONLY................. 33
  1463-1599.................. 29
  1600-1600.................. 33
  1601-OUT.................. 29
Clifton SE
  1-350........................ 17
  351-OUT.................... 16
Clifton Ct NE................... 29

Atlanta (Con.)　　　　　　303

Clifton Ct Cir NE 29
Clifton Pl NE 12
Clifton Rd NE
　1-100 17
　101-1350 07
　1351-1450 22
　1451-1461 29
　1462-ONLY 33
　1463-1599 29
　1600-ONLY 33
　1601-OUT 29
Clifton Rd SE
　1-350 17
　351-OUT 16
Clifton Ter NE 07
Clifton Way NE
　1-1000 29
　1001-OUT 16
Clifton Way SE
　1-1000 29
　1001-OUT 16
Clifton Church Rd SE 16
Cliftondale Pl (CP) 49
Cliftwood Dr NE 28
Climax SE 15
Climax Pl SW 15
Clipper Trl NW 28
Cloudland Dr NW 27
Clover SW 10
Clover Ln NE 08
Cloverdale Dr SE 16
Cloverhurst Cir & Dr (EP) 44
Cloverleaf Dr SE 16
Clovis Ct NW 31
Club Cir, Dr, Ln & Ter NE 19
Club Pl SE 17
Club Valley Dr NE 19
Clyde Dr (CHA) 41
Cobble Ln (CHA) 41
Coca Cola Pl SE 03
Cochise Dr NW 39
Cochran Dr NW 27
Cochran Rd (CP) 49
Cochran Rd SW 31
Cofield Dr (HAP) 54
Coggins Dr SE 12
Cohen SW 10
Coldsprings Ln (CHA) 41
Coldstream Ct NW 28
Coldstream Dr (DOR) 40
Colebridge Rd NW 28
Colebrook Ct NW 27
Colegate Dr SW 36
Coleman (HAP) 10
Coleman SW 10
Colewood Ct & Way NW 28
Colina Ct (CP) 49
Colland Dr NW 18
College (HAP) 54
College (CP) 37
College Ave NE 17
College Ave & Pl SW 15
College Park Rd (HAP) 54
College Park Rd (CP) 49
Collier Ct NW 31
Collier Dr NW
　1-3300 18
　3301-OUT 31
Collier Pl NW 18
Collier Rd NW
　1-460 09

461-OUT 18
Collier St NW & SW 14
Collier Ridge Dr NW 18
Collingswood Ter (CP) 49
Collins SE 03
Collins Dr (EP) 44
Collins Dr & Rd NW 18
Collum NW 14
Colmer SE 17
Cologne Dr SE 54
Colonial Dr (CP) 37
Colonial Dr NE 19
Colonial Way (CHA) 41
Colonial Homes Dr NW 09
Colony Sq NE 09
Colorado Ave (HAP) 54
Colorado Pl & Trl SW 31
Colquitt Ave NE 07
Colquitt Dr (DUN) 38
Colquitt Dr (DOR) 40
Colt Dr (CHA) 41
Colton Dr NE 42
Columbia Ave (CP) 37
Columbia Ave E & W (CP) 37
Columbia Ave NE 09
Colville Ave (HAP) 54
Commander Dr (CHA) 09
Commerce Cir SW 36
Commerce Dr NW
　1-2000 18
　2001-OUT 36
Commerce Dr SW
　1-2000 18
　2001-OUT 36
Commerce Way (HAP) 54
Commercial Ave NW 18
Commodore Ct, Dr & Ln
　(CHA) 41
Commodore Dr NW 18
Commodore Way NE 45
Compton Dr SE 15
Concord Ct (EP) 44
Cone NW 03
Confederate Ave SE
　1-990 12
　991-OUT 16
Confederate Ct SE 12
Congress Cir & Ct (CHA) 41
Conifer Cir NE 42
Conley (CP) 37
Conley S
　100-299 (CP) 37
Conley Cir (HAP) 54
Conley Rd SE 54
Conley Old N
　100-590 (CP) 37
Connally (CP) 37
Connally SE
　1-650 12
　651-OUT 15
Connally Ave SW 10
Connally Ct (EP) 44
Connally Dr SW
　1-2700 44
　2701-OUT 11
Connally Pl SE 12
Connecticut Ave NE 07
Connell Ave SW 15
Connell Rd (CP) 49
Conover Dr (DUN) 38
Conrad SE 15
Constance (EP) 44

Constitution Rd SE
　1-1200 15
　1201-OUT 16
Continental Dr NE 45
Continental Colony Pky SW 31
Converse Dr NE 24
Convoy Dr (HAP) 54
Conway NW
　1-1250 27
　1551-OUT 27
Conway Dr NW, E
　1-1200 27
　1551-OUT 27
Conway Dr NW, W
　1-1200 27
　1551-OUT 27
Conway Pl NW 18
Conway Pl SE 12
Conway Rd NW, E
　1-1250 27
　1551-OUT 27
Conway Rd NW, W
　1-1250 27
　1551-OUT 27
Conway Forrest Dr NW 27
Conway Valley Ct & Rd NW 27
Cook NW 18
Cook Rd (CP) 49
Cooks Aly SE 12
Cooledge Ave NE 06
Coolridge Cir (CHA) 41
Cooper SW
　1-650 12
　651-OUT 15
Coosawatte Dr NE 19
Copeland Ave SW 10
Copeland Rd NE 42
Copenhill Ave NE 07
Coral Dr SE 16
Coral Pl NW 18
Coral Way (CHA) 41
Corando Way (CHA) 41
Corbally Pl SW 12
Cordell Dr (CP) 49
Cordoba Sq NW 05
Cordova SW 10
Corley NE 12
Cornelia SE 12
Cornell Blvd SW 31
Cornell Rd NE 06
Coronado Dr NW 27
Coronation Ct & Dr NE 28
Coronet Way NW 18
Corporate Sq NE 29
Corporate Sq Blvd NE 29
Corporate Sq Mall Sq Mall
　NE 29
Corral Dr SE 16
Cortez Ln & Way NE 19
Corvair Dr SE 54
Cosmos Ct & Dr NE 45
Cotillion Dr (CHA) 41
Cotswold Dr NE 19
Cottage Grv Ave SE 17
Cottage Ln NW 18
Cottonwood Dr SE 16
Council Bluff Ct & Dr NE 45
Country Ln NE 24
Country Club Dr & Ln SW 11
County Line Rd SW 31
Courtenay Dr NE 06
Courtland NE
　1-400 03

Atlanta (Con.) 303

Courtland SE ... 03
Courtleigh Dr (DUN) ... 38
Cove Cir NE ... 19
Cowley Ave SW ... 14
Cox Ave SW
 1-500 ... 11
 501-OUT ... 10
Cox Dr SW
 1-500 ... 11
 501-OUT ... 10
Craggy Point NW ... 39
Crane Rd NE ... 24
Cranton Ct NE ... 19
Cravendge Dr NE ... 19
Cravey Dr NE ... 45
Creek Valley Ct SW ... 31
Creek View Cir (CP) ... 49
Creel Cir (CP) ... 37
Creel Rd (CP) ... 49
Creighton Rd SW ... 31
Crescendo Dr NW ... 18
Crescent Ave NE ... 09
Crest Ave NE ... 24
Crest Valley Dr NW ... 27
Crestdale Cir SE ... 16
Cresthill Ave NE ... 06
Crestline Ct & Dr NE ... 45
Crestline Rd NE ... 28
Crestline Valley Cir NE ... 28
Crestmont Ln SW ... 11
Crestridge Dr NE ... 06
Crestwood Cir (CP) ... 49
Crestwood Dr (CP) ... 37
Crestwood Dr SE ... 16
Crestwood Ln NW ... 39
Crew SW
 1-650 ... 12
 651-OUT ... 15
Crocus Ave, NW ... 14
Croft Pl NW ... 31
Crogman SE ... 15
Cromwell Rd NE ... 28
Crosby Dr NW ... 31
Cross NW ... 18
Cross Rd SE ... 54
Cross Creek Pky NW ... 27
Cross Gate Ct NW ... 27
Cross Keys Dr NE ... 19
Crown Rd ... 54
Crumley Pl SW ... 12
Crumley Row SW ... 10
Crumley St SE & SW ... 12
Crystal Ln (CP) ... 49
Crystal Lake Rd (CP) ... 49
Culberson SW ... 18
Culpepper NW ... 18
Cumberland Cir & Rd NE ... 06
Cumberland Dr & Rd (CHA) ... 41
Cumberland Pky NW ... 39
Cumberland Rd (EP) ... 44
Cumberland Club Cir & Dr NW ... 39
Cumming Dr SW ... 11
Cummings SE ... 16
Cunningham Pl SW ... 10
Curran NW ... 18
Currier NE
 1-300 ... 08
 301-OUT ... 12
Currier Pl NE ... 12

Curtis Dr NE SW ... 19
Cushman Cir SW ... 11
Custer (HAP) ... 54
Custer Ave SE
 1-800 ... 15
 801-OUT ... 16
Cynthia Dr NE ... 19
Cypress NE
 1-870 ... 08
 871-OUT ... 09
Dabney Ter (EP) ... 44
Dahlgreen SE ... 17
Dahlia Ave NW ... 14
Dale Dr NE ... 05
Dale Dr SE ... 15
Dale Ln SW
 1-3400 ... 11
 3401-OUT ... 31
Dale Creek Dr NW ... 18
Daleview Dr SE ... 15
Dalewood Dr NE ... 29
Dallas NE ... 08
Dalmer Rd NE ... 42
Dalney NW ... 18
Dalon Rd NE ... 06
Dalrymple Rd NE ... 28
Dalton SE ... 15
Dalvigney NW ... 18
Dameron Cir SW ... 11
Damon Ct & Pl (DUN) ... 38
Dan Ln NE ... 24
Dan Johnson Rd NE ... 07
Danbury Ln NW ... 27
Danby Ct (DOR) ... 40
Danbyshire Ct NE ... 45
Danforth Rd SW ... 31
Daniel SE ... 12
Daniel Ave NE & SE ... 17
Daniel Rd SW ... 31
Danner SE ... 16
Danny Rd SW ... 31
Dantzler St, Ct & Dr NE ... 29
Danube Rd NE ... 42
Dargan Pl SW ... 10
Darlington Cir & Rd NE ... 05
Darlington Oak Dr (DOR) ... 40
Darrah Dr SW ... 31
Dartford Dr (DUN) ... 38
Dartmoor Cir NE ... 28
Dartmouth Dr SW ... 31
Datona Dr SW ... 31
Dauphine (EP) ... 44
Davage SW ... 15
Daventry Ct & Dr (DUN) ... 38
David Rd (CHA) ... 41
Davidson Dr NE ... 19
Davis (HAP) ... 54
Davis NW
 1-380 ... 14
 381-OUT ... 18
Davis SW ... 13
Davis Ave (EP) ... 18
Davis Cir & Pl NW ... 18
Davis Ct & Rd (CP) ... 37
Davis Dr NW ... 27
Dawn View Ln NW ... 27
Daws Ave SW ... 17
Day SW ... 10
Dayton Pl NE ... 08
De Clair Dr NE ... 29
De Foor Ave, Cir & Pl NW ... 18
De Foor Ferry Rd NW ... 18

De Foor Hills Rd NW ... 18
De Gress Ave NE ... 07
De Kalb Ave NE ... 07
De Lowe Dr SW
 1-2010 ... 11
 2011-OUT (EP) ... 44
De Lowe Pl SW ... 11
Deacon Ave (HAP) ... 54
Deacon Ln (CHA) ... 41
Dean Dr NW ... 18
Dearborn SE ... 17
Dearborn Plz (HAP) ... 54
Dearwood Dr SW ... 15
Deauville Ct NW ... 18
Deborah Dr (DOR) ... 40
Deborah Dr NE ... 45
Decatur SE
 1-310 ... 03
 311-OUT ... 12
Deckner Ave SW ... 10
Deer Park Rd NE ... 45
Deer Run Trl (CP) ... 49
Deere Dr (CHA) ... 41
Deerfield Ct & Ln (CP) ... 49
Deerfield Tr (CP) ... 49
Deering Rd NW ... 09
Dejarnette Dr (EP) ... 44
Del Mar Ln NW
 1-3250 ... 11
 3251-OUT ... 31
Delano Dr NE ... 17
Delaware Ave NE ... 07
Delaware Ave SE ... 16
Delbridge NW ... 14
Delevan SW
 1-314 ... 15
 315-OUT ... 10
Dellwood Dr NW
 1-2150 ... 09
 2151-OUT ... 05
Delmar Ave SE
 1-800 ... 12
 801-OUT ... 16
Delmar Ct SE ... 16
Delmar Ln NW
 1-3250 ... 11
 3251-OUT ... 31
Delmont Dr NE ... 05
Delmoor Ct & Dr NW ... 11
Delray Dr NW ... 18
Delta Dr (EP) ... 44
Delta Pl NE ... 07
Delverton Dr (DUN) ... 38
Demooney Rd (CP) ... 49
Demorest Ave SW ... 05
Denise Dr (CP) ... 37
Denny Dr (CP) ... 49
Depauw Dr SW ... 36
Derby Dr SW ... 11
Deren Way NE ... 45
Dering Cir & Ct NE ... 45
Derrick Rd (CP) ... 49
Derrick Jones Rd (CP) ... 49
Derry Ave SW ... 10
Desert Dr (EP) ... 44
Desoto NW ... 14
Desoto Ave SW ... 10
Detroit Ave & Ct NW ... 14
Devereaux Ct (DUN) ... 38
Devilla Trce (CP) ... 49
Devin Cir NE ... 19
Devinney Cir NE ... 19

Atlanta (Con.) 303

Devonshire Ct, Rd & Way
(DUN) 38
Devonwood Dr NE 28
Dewberry Ln SW 44
Dewey SW 10
Dewey Ave (EP) 44
Diamond Ave SE 16
Diana Dr SW 15
Diane Ct SE 16
Diane Dr (DOR) 40
Dickson NE 19
Dickson Pl NW 09
Dilbeck Pl NW 42
Dill Ave SW 10
Dillon NE 18
Dimmock SW 10
Division NW 14
Division Pl SW 10
Dixie SE 17
Dixie Ave NE 07
Dixie Hills Cir NW 14
Dixon NE 19
Doane SW 15
Dobbs Cir NW 27
Dobbs Dr SE 15
Dobbs Way (EP) 44
Dodd Ave NE 15
Dodge NE 12
Dodson (HAP) 54
Dodson Dr SW
  1-2100 11
  2101-OUT 10
Dodson Ter (EP) 44
Dodson Ter SW 11
Dodson Connector Dr (EP) 44
Dodson Lee Dr (EP) 44
Dogwood (CP) 37
Dogwood Dr (EP) 44
Dogwood Ln (CP) 49
Dogwood Ln NE 45
Dogwood Ter NE 15
Dogwood Valley Dr NE 42
Dollar Mill Ct, Rd & Way SW 31
Dolphin Dr SW 11
Don Juan Cir (CHA) 41
Donaldson Ct NE 19
Donaldson Dr NE
  1-3750 19
  3751-OUT 41
Doncaster Dr NE 09
Donnalee SE 16
Donnebrook Ln SE 54
Donnelly Ave SW 10
Donzi Ln SE 16
Dora SW 14
Doral Cir, Ct & Dr (DOR) 40
Dorchester Ave NW 18
Doreen Ct NE 45
Doroco Ct, Dr & Way (DOR) 40
Dorothy SE 15
Dorsey SW 10
Dorsey Ave (EP) 44
Dorsey Rd (HAP) 54
Dot Rd (EP) 49
Douglas SE 17
Douglas SW 14
Douglas Dr (EP) 44
Douglas Rd NE 42
Dove Dr SW 31
Dover Blvd & Ct SW 31
Dover Rd NW 27

Doverhill Pl NE 45
Dovers Aly SW 10
Dowdell Dr (CHA) 41
Dower SW 10
Downey Dr (CP) 49
Downs Dr SW 11
Downwood Cir NW 27
Doyle SE 17
Drake Dr SW 36
Draper Dr (CP) 37
Dresden Ct & Way (CHA) 41
Dresden Dr NE
  1-1960 19
  1961-OUT 41
Dresden Trl (EP) 44
Drew Dr & Pl NW 18
Drew Valley Rd NE 19
Drewry NE 06
Drexel Ln (EP) 44
Druid Cir & Pl NE 07
Druid Valley Dr & Rd NE 29
Drummond SW 14
Drury Ct (DOR) 40
Duberry Ct NE 19
Dublin Dr SW 31
Dudley Ct & Ln NW 27
Duffield Dr NW 18
Duke Rd (CHA) 41
Duke Of Gloucester (EP) 44
Duke Of Windsor (EP) 44
Dumbarton Ct & Rd NW 27
Dummereland Ct & Ter (CP) 49
Dunbar SW 10
Dunbritton (CP) 49
Duncan (CP) 49
Duncan Dr (CHA) 41
Duncannon Ct (CHA) 41
Duncourtney Dr NE 28
Dundee Ave NE 07
Dunedin Dr, SW 31
Dunex Hill Ln NE 24
Dunhaven Ct, Dr & Rd (CHA) 41
Dunhill Ct NW 28
Dunhill Ter NE 28
Dunkerrin Ln (DOR) 40
Dunlap Ave (EP) 44
Dunn SW 10
Dunning SE 15
Dunnington Cir (CHA) 41
Dunover Cir (DOR) 40
Dunridge Ct (DUN) 38
Dunseath Ave NW 18
Dunwoody Ln NE 17
Dunwoody Ln NE 19
Dunwoody Park (CHA) 41
Dunwoody Pl & Rd (DUN) 38
Dunwoody Pl & Trl NE 24
Dunwoody Rd NE 28
Dunwoody-Club Dr
  1-2700 (DUN) 38
  2701-3100 (DOR) 40
  3101-4000 (DUN) 38
  4001-OUT (DOR) 40
Dunwoody Village Rd (DUN) 38
Dupont Ave NW 18
Dupont Ave SE 17
Dupree Ave NW 18
Dupree Dr NW 27
Durand Dr NE 07
Durango Rd SW 31
Durant Pl NE
  1-870 08
  871-OUT 09

Durden Dr NE 19
Dutch Valley Pl & Rd NE 24
Dyer Cir (CHA) 41
Dykes Dr NW 42
Dyson Dr NE
  1-1770 07
Eaglerock Dr (DOR) 40
Earle NW
  1-2000 13
  2001-OUT 18
Earlhurst Ln (CP) 49
Earlston Dr NE 28
Early NW 05
Eason NW 14
East Ave NE 12
East Ave NW 18
East Dr NE 05
East Park Ln NE 09
East Andrews Dr NW 05
East Anthony NW 18
East Beechwood Dr NW 27
East Belle Isle Rd NE 42
East Brookhaven Dr NE 19
East Cedar Ln SW 11
East Clifton Rd NE 07
East Club Dr & Ln NE 19
East Confederate Ave SE
  1-800 12
  801-OUT 16
East Conway Dr NW
  1-1250 27
  1551-OUT 27
East Conway Rd NW
  1-1250 27
  1551-OUT 27
East Deckner Ave SW 10
East Hampton Ct (CP) 49
East Handy Dr NW 18
East Kildare Ave NW 18
East Lake Blvd, Dr, Rd & Ter
  SE 17
East Lake Dr (DOR) 40
East Lake Dr NE
  1-100 17
  1101-2291 07
East Lake Rd NE
  1-100 17
  1101-2291 07
East Lindmont Ct NE 24
East Nancy Creek Dr NE
  1-1675 19
  1676-OUT 41
East Northbrook Ct (DOR) 40
East Ontario Ave SW 10
East Osborne Rd NE 19
East Paces Ferry Rd, NE
  1-800 05
  801-OUT 26
East Park Ln NE 09
East Pine Valley Rd NW 05
East Point (EP) 44
East Side Ave SE 16
East Simon Ter NW 18
East Sussex Rd NE 06
East Tupelo SE 17
East Wesley Ave NE
  1-600 05
  601-OUT 24
East Wesley Rd NE
  1-600 05
  601-OUT 24
East Wesley Ter NE 24

Atlanta (Con.)   303

East Wood Valley Rd NW 27
Eastbrook Ct (DOR) 40
Eastland Rd SE 16
Easton Dr SW 31
Eastport Ter SE 17
Eastridge Rd SW 11
Eastwood Ave SE 16
Eaton Pl (CHA) 41
Eberhart Dr (HAP) 54
Echo NW 18
Echo Dr & Trl NE 45
Echo Hills Cir NE 45
Echo W NW 18
Echocliff Ct NE 45
Echoto Ct NW 18
Ector Ct NE 45
Eddie Ave SE 12
Eden Ave SE 16
Eden Roc Ln NW 42
Edenton Ct NE 19
Edgefield Dr SW 10
Edgehill Ave NW 18
Edgemore Dr SE 16
Edgewater Ct, Dr & Trl NW ... 28
Edgewater Dr SW 11
Edgewood Ave NE
   1-300 03
   301-670 12
   671-OUT 07
Edgewood Ave SE
   1-300 03
   301-670 12
   671-OUT 07
Edinboro Dr & Rd NW 27
Edinburg Ter NE 07
Edison Ave NE 05
Edison Dr (CP) 37
Edison Rd (DOR) 40
Edith NE 08
Edwards (DOR) 40
Edwards NW 14
Edwards Dr NW 18
Edwin St & Pl NW 18
Edwina Ln SW 31
Egleston SW 10
Eisenhower Cir, Ct & Rd SE ... 54
El Paso Rd SW 31
Elaine Ave NW 18
Elbert SW 10
Elbridge Dr NW 18
Elden Dr NE 42
Eldorado Dr NE 45
Eleanor SE 17
Eleanor Ct & Ter NW 14
Electric Ave NW 14
Elinor Pl NW 18
Elinwood Ct & Dr (EP) 44
Elixir Ave SW 10
Elizabeth NE 07
Elizabeth Ave SW 10
Elizabeth Ln (EP) 44
Elizabeth Pl NW 19
Elizabeth Ann Ln NE 24
Elkins (HAP) 54
Elkmont Dr NE 06
Elks Dr SW 31
Elleby Rd SE 15
Ellen NW 18
Ellendale Ln NW 18
Ellery Dr (HAP) 54
Ellijay Dr NE 19

Ellington SE 17
Elliott NW
   1-200 13
   201-1000 14
   1001-OUT 18
Elliott SW 13
Elliott Cir (CHA) 41
Elliott Cir NE 05
Ellis St NE & NW 03
Ellisbury Dr (CHA) 41
Ellsworth Dr NW 18
Ellsworth Industrial Dr NW ... 18
Ellwood Dr NE 05
Ellwyn Dr (CHA) 41
Elm (EP) 44
Elm (HAP) 54
Elm (CP) 37
Elm NW
   1-416 14
   417-OUT 18
Elm SW 14
Elm St Ct SW 14
Elmco Rd SW 31
Elmhurst Cir SE 16
Elmira Pl NE 07
Elmtree Dr SW 11
Elmwood Dr NE 06
Elmwood Rd NW 18
Eloise St & Ct SE 12
Elrod (DOR) 40
Elsinor (EP) 44
Elva Dr SW 31
Elvira SE 15
Elysian Way NW 27
Embry Cir N (CHA) 41
Embry Cir & Ct (CHA) 41
Embry Hills Dr (CHA) 41
Emerald Ave SE 16
Emerald Ave SW 10
Emerson Ave SE 16
Emery NW 18
Emery Pl NE 17
Emily Pl NW 18
Emily Way (CP) 49
Emma Ln NE 42
Emmanual Dr SW 36
Emmett NW 18
Emory Cir, Ct & Dr NE 07
Emory Rd NE 06
Emory Court Annex NE 07
Empire (EP) 44
Empire Blvd & Way SW 54
Engle Rd NW 18
Englewood SE 15
Englewood Dr (EP) 44
English Cir & Dr SW 31
English Ln (CP) 37
English St & Ave NW 18
English Oak Dr (DOR) 40
Ennis Aly NW 18
Enoch Dr (CP) 37
Enon Rd (CP) 49
Enon Rd SW 31
Enota Pl NW 10
Ensign Ct & Dr (CHA) 41
Enterprise Blvd SW 36
Epping Forest Dr NE 19
Eppington Dr NW 27
Epworth SW 10
Eric SE 15
Ericson SE 34
Erin Ave SW 10
Erin Rd SW 31

Ernest NW 18
Essex Ave SW 11
Essie SE 16
Estelle (HAP) 54
Esten SE 16
Estes Dr (CP) 49
Estes Dr SW 10
Estoria SE 16
Ethan Allen Ct & Dr (CP) ... 49
Ethel NW 18
Etheridge St & Dr NW 18
Eton Ct NE 19
Etowah (DUN) 38
Etowah Dr NE 19
Eubanks Ave (EP) 44
Euclid Ave & Ter NE 07
Eugenia SW 12
Eugenia Pl NW 18
Euharlee SW 14
Eula Cir (DOR) 40
Eulalia Rd NE 19
Eureka Dr NE 05
Eustace SE 15
Eva Dr NW 18
Evans (HAP) 54
Evans Dr (CP) 37
Evans Ln SE 17
Evans Rd
   1-3550 (CHA) 41
   3551-OUT (DOR) 40
Evans St & Dr SW 31
Evans Dale Cir & Dr (DOR) ... 40
Evans Wood Dr (DOR) 40
Evelyn Pl & Way NW 18
Evelyn St NE 06
Everett Pl SW 10
Evergreen Dr NE 19
Evergreen Ln NW 18
Everhart SW 10
Ewing SW 31
Ewing Dr NE 19
Ewing Pl SW 10
Exchange Pl SE 03
Executive Park NE, E 29
Executive Park NE, S 29
Executive Park NE, W 29
Executive Park Dr NE 29
Exeter Close NW 27
Ezra Church Dr NW 14
Ezzard SE 12
Fabin NW 18
Fair NW
   1-370 63
   371-510 13
   511-OUT 14
Fair Dr SW 15
Fair Oaks Mnr NW 27
Fairbanks SW 10
Fairburn Ave & Rd SW 31
Fairburn Cir, Pl & Rd NW ... 31
Fairfax Ave (EP) 44
Fairfield Pl NW 14
Fairfield Rd NW 27
Fairhaven Cir NE 05
Fairhill Ln NE 19
Fairlane Cir, Ct & Dr NW ... 31
Fairlane Dr (DOR) 40
Fairlane Dr SE 54
Fairlie NW 03
Fairlock Ln NW 31
Fairmont NW 18
Fairview Rd NE 06
Fairway Cir NE 19

Fairway Cir SW 31
Fairway Dr (CP) 49
Fairway Hill Dr SE 17
Fairwood Ln NE 45
Faith Ave SE 16
Fala Pl NE 19
Falcon Dr SW 11
Falkirk Pl NE 45
Fallview Ter (EP) 44
Fama Dr NE 29
Fargo Pl SE 16
Farley Ave SW 31
Farley St & Ct (EP) 44
Farmington Ct, Dr & Ter NW 39
Farmington Ln NE 19
Faronview Dr (DOR) 40
Farrington Ave & Pl SE 44
Farris Ave (EP) 24
Faulkner Rd NE 28
Faunsworth Dr NE 16
Fay SE 16
Fayetteville Ct SE 16
Fayetteville Rd NE
   1-500 17
   501-OUT 16
Fayetteville Rd SE
   1-500 17
   501-OUT 16
Fayetteville Rd W
   4525-5008 (CP) 37
   5096-OUT (CP) 49
Feagin Dr NE 19
Fearn Cir NE 19
Federal Ter SE 15
Fedora Way NW 31
Fellwood Pl & Rd (CP) 49
Felton Dr (EP) 44
Felton Dr NE
   1-500 12
   501-OUT 08
Felton Way NE 08
Fenwood SW 14
Ferguson St 07
Fermi Dr SW 36
Fern Ave SE 15
Fern Creek Ln NE 29
Fern Valley Cir & Rd SW 31
Fern Valley Ct & Dr (EP) 44
Fernbank Dr SW 31
Ferncliff Pl & Rd NE 24
Fernleaf Cir & Ct NW 18
Ferno Dr NW 18
Fernwood Cir NE 19
Fernwood Dr (EP) 44
Fernwood Rd NW 18
Ferris SW 10
Ferry Dr NE 28
Ferry Landing NW 28
Field SE 18
Field Rd NW 18
Fielder NW 18
Fielding Ct & Ln SW 11
Finch Dr SE 15
Finchley Ct NW 28
Finistere Ct NE 19
Finley NE 07
Finley Ave NW 18
Firth Ln (DOR) 40
Fisher SE
   1-1600 16
   1601-OUT 15
Fisher Ave NW 18

Fisher Rd SE
   1-1600 16
   1601-OUT 15
Fisher Trl NE 45
Fisk Dr, SW 36
Fitzgerald SE 12
Flagler Ave NE 09
Flagstone Ct & Dr SW 31
Flagstone Dr SE 16
Flair Knoll Ct & Dr NE 45
Flamingo Dr (EP) 44
Flamingo Dr SW 11
Flat Rock Rd
   1-1300 (CP) 49
Flat Shoals Ave SE
   1-2373 16
Flat Shoals Rd
   1-4630 (CP) 49
Flat Shoals Rd SE
   1-2373 16
Flat Shoals Way SE 16
Fleet SW 10
Fleetwood Cir & Ct SW 11
Fleetwood Dr SE 16
Flemington Rd NE 45
Flemish Ct (CP) 49
Fletcher SW
   1-312 15
   313-OUT 10
Fleur De Lis Ct, Pl & Way
   (DOR) 40
Flindt Ct (CHA) 41
Flintlock Rd NW 27
Flintshire Ct (CHA) 41
Flintwood Dr SE 16
Flora Ave NE 07
Florence NE 12
Florence Pl NW 18
Florida Ave (DOR) 40
Florida Ave SE 16
Florida Ave SW 10
Flowerland Dr NE 19
Flowers Dr (CP) 49
Flowers Dr, S. 36
Flowers Pl NW 41
Flowers Rd (CHA) 41
Flowers Rd (DOR) 40
Flynn NW 31
Flynn Rd SE 54
Folkstone Rd NE 29
Fontainbleau Ct & Dr (DOR) 40
Fontaine Ave SW 11
Fontainebleau SW 31
Foote St & Row NE 07
Ford NW 18
Ford Pl NE 06
Ford St & Pl SE 16
Fordham Ct NE 06
Forest Ave (HAP) 54
Forest Trl (EP) 44
Forest Hills Dr (HAP) 54
Forest Park Rd SE
   1-2790 15
   2791-OUT 54
Forest Valley Ct & Rd NE 42
Forest Valley Dr SE 16
Foresta Ct (CHA) 41
Forestdale Dr NE 42
Forestwood Ln NE 28
Formwalt SW
   1-650 12
   651-OUT 15
Forrest Ave (FP) 44

Forrest Ave NE
   1-160 03
   161-OUT 12
Forrest Cir, Dr & Ter SE 54
Forrest Ct (CHA) 41
Forrest Rd NE
   1-800 12
   801-OUT 06
Forrest St, Ave, Pl & Trl NW 18
Forrest Way NE
   1-1000 08
   1001-OUT 05
Forrest Green Dr NE 29
Forrest Hills Dr NE
   1-1000 42
   1001-OUT 15
Forrest Hills Dr SW
   1-1000 42
   1001-OUT 15
Forrest Lake Dr NW 27
Forrest Ridge Dr NW 18
Forrestal Dr (CHA) 41
Forsyth St NW & SW 03
Fort NE 12
Fort Valley Dr (EP) 44
Fort Valley Dr SW 11
Fortingale Dr (CHA) 41
Fortner (EP) 44
Fortress Ave SW 15
Fortune St & Pl NE 12
Foster St & Pl NW 18
Foster Ridge Ct & Rd NE 45
Foundry NW
   1-260 03
   261-470 13
   471-OUT 14
Fountain Dr SW 14
Fowler NE 17
Fowler NW
   1-850 13
   851-OUT 18
Fox NW 18
Fox Creek Ct (DOR) 40
Fox Glen Ct NE 19
Fox Hollow Ct (DOR) 40
Fox Hunt Ln (EP) 44
Foxcroft Rd NW 27
Foxford Ct & Dr (DOR) 40
Foxhall Ln (CP) 49
Foxhall Ln SE 16
Foxlair Dr & Ln (CP) 49
Foxwood Ct (DOR) 40
Fradon Ct (CP) 49
Framons Ct (DUN) 38
Frances Ave SE 12
Francis NE 19
Francis St, Ave & Pl NW 18
Francona Dr NW 36
Frank SW 14
Franklin Cir NE 24
Franklin Rd NE 42
Fraser SE
   1-650 12
   651-OUT 15
Fredell Cir (EP) 44
Frederica NE 06
Frederick Ct & Dr SW 36
Fredicksburg Dr (CP) 37
Freeman Ct (CP) 37
Fremont SE 15
Friair Tuck Way (DOR) 40
Friar Tuck Rd NE 09
Frisco NW 18

Atlanta (Con.)   303

Front Royal Ct (CHA).......... 41
Frontac Way NW.............. 05
Frontage Rd (CP).............. 49
Frontenac Ct NE.............. 19
Frontier Ct & Trl (CHA)....... 41
Fulford Dr (HAP).............. 54
Fuller Rd NE.................. 19
Fulton Ave
   1-3000 (EP)............... 44
   3001-OUT (HAP).......... 54
Fulton St SE & SW............ 12
Fulton Ter SE................. 16
Fulton Industrial Blvd SW
   1-5400................... 36
   5400-OUT................ 31
Fulton Industrial Blvd NW,
NW
   1-1350................... 36
   1351-OUT................ 31
Funston Ave SE............... 15
Gail Dr NE................... 19
Gainer Rd SW................. 15
Gainsborough Dr (CHA)....... 41
Gaither Cir NE............... 24
Galahad Dr NE................ 45
Galengale Way (DOR)......... 40
Gammon Ave SE............... 15
Garber Dr NE................. 28
Garden Ln NW................ 09
Gardenia St & Dr NW......... 14
Gardenside Ct NE............. 19
Gardner SW.................. 10
Garfield Way SE (HAP)....... 54
Garibaldi SW
   1-660.................... 12
   661-OUT................. 10
Garland SW.................. 15
Garmon Rd NW............... 27
Garnett SW.................. 03
Garrett Cir (DOR)............ 40
Garrison Dr SW............... 31
Carroux Rd NW............... 27
Garson Dr NE................. 24
Gartrell St & Pl SE........... 12
Gary Ave, Ct & Rd NW........ 18
Gaskill SE................... 16
Gaspero NE.................. 12
Gaston SW.................. 10
Gatewood Ct NW.............. 27
Gatewood Rd NE............. 29
Gault SE.................... 15
Geary Dr NW................. 09
General Truman NW.......... 18
Geneva (HAP)................ 54
Gentilly Pl (DOR)............. 40
George NW................... 18
George SE................... 12
George Wythe Pl NW.......... 18
Georgetown Ct & Way (CHA).. 41
Georgia Ave (DOR)........... 40
Georgia Ave (EP)............. 44
Georgia Ave (HAP)........... 54
Georgia Ave SE & SW......... 12
Georgia Ave, Cir & Dr (CP)... 37
Georgian Dr E & W (CHA)..... 41
Georgian Ter (CHA).......... 41
Georgiana Dr NE............. 29
Geraldine Ct (DOR).......... 40
Gerry Ln NE................. 28
Gertrude Pl NW.............. 18
Giben Rd SW................. 15

Gibson SE................... 16
Gideons Dr SW............... 14
Gift Ave SE.................. 16
Gilbert SE................... 16
Gilbert Rd SE................ 54
Gilbert Way (HAP)........... 54
Gillem Dr (EP).............. 44
Gillette Ave SW.............. 10
Gilmer SE................... 03
Givens NW................... 18
Glace Rd (CP)............... 49
Glade Springs Ct NE.......... 45
Gladney Dr
   1-3850 (CHA)............ 41
   3851-OUT (DOR)......... 40
Gladstone Rd NW............. 18
Glass NW................... 18
Glaze Dr (DOR).............. 40
Glen Arden Dr & Pl NW....... 05
Glen Arden Way NE.......... 06
Glen Bonnie Ct & Dr (DOR)... 40
Glen Castle Dr NW........... 27
Glen Devon Dr NW........... 27
Glen Echo Dr NW............ 11
Glen Errol Rd NW............ 27
Glen Forrest Rd NE........... 28
Glen Iris Dr NE
   1-370................... 12
   371-OUT................ 08
Glen Lake Dr NW............. 27
Glen View Cir, Dr & Ter SW... 31
Glenairy Ct & Dr NE.......... 28
Glenald Way NW............. 27
Glenbriar Dr NW............. 45
Glenbrook Dr NW............ 27
Glencourtney Dr NE.......... 28
Glencove Ave SE............. 17
Glenda Dr (CP).............. 37
Glenda Way (DOR)........... 40
Glendale Ave NE............. 07
Glendale Ct & Dr (EP)....... 44
Glendale Ter NE
   1-880................... 08
   881-OUT................ 09
Glendalough Pl SW........... 10
Glengary Dr NE.............. 42
Glenn SE................... 12
Glenn SW
   1-620................... 12
   621-OUT................ 10
Glenn Ave NW............... 18
Glenrich Ct & Dr (DUN)...... 38
Glenridge Dr NE
   1-5700.................. 42
   5701-OUT............... 28
Glenrock Dr NW............. 18
Glenrose Cir & Ct SW......... 54
Glenway Dr (EP)............. 44
Glenwood Ave SE
   1-750................... 12
   751-2330................ 16
   2331-2944............... 17
Glenwood Dr NE............. 05
Glenwood Pl SE.............. 16
Glenwood Rd SE
   1-750................... 12
   751-2330................ 16
   2331-2944............... 17
Glidden NW.................. 18
Glynn Dr SE................. 16
Godby Pl & Rd (CP).......... 49
Goddard SE.................. 15
Godfrey Dr NW............... 18

Golden Dr (EP)............... 44
Golden Dawn Dr SW.......... 11
Golden Gate Dr NW.......... 09
Goldsboro Rd NE............. 07
Golf Cir NE................. 09
Golf View Dr & Rd NW........ 09
Goodson Rd (CP)............. 49
Goodwin Rd NE.............. 24
Gordon SW
   1-2320.................. 10
   2321-3300............... 11
   3301-3815............... 31
   3816-OUT............... 36
Gordon Ave NE............... 07
Gordon Cir N & S (HAP)...... 54
Gordon Pl SW................ 10
Gordon Rd
   1-2320.................. 10
   2321-3300............... 11
   3301-3815............... 36
Gordon Rd SW
   3816-OUT............... 36
Gordon Ter SW............... 14
Gotham Way NE.............. 24
Gould SE................... 15
Grace SE................... 15
Grace Dr (HAP).............. 54
Gracewood Ave SE........... 16
Grady Pl (HAP).............. 54
Grady Pl SE................. 16
Graham SE.................. 10
Graham Cir SE............... 16
Granada Pl (EP)............. 44
Grand Ave NW
   1-2000.................. 18
   2001-OUT............... 15
Grand Ave SW
   1-2000.................. 18
   2001-OUT............... 15
Grand De Ct (CP)............ 49
Grand Prix Ct & Dr NE........ 45
Grandview Ave NE
   1-2500.................. 18
   2501-OUT............... 05
Grandview Ave NW
   1-2500.................. 18
   2501-OUT............... 05
Grandview Cir SE............ 16
Grange Ct & Dr SE........... 15
Granger Ct & Dr (CHA)....... 41
Grant SE
   1-660................... 12
   661-OUT................ 15
Grant Cir SE................. 15
Grant Dr NE................. 19
Grant Dr & Rd SW............ 31
Grant Pl NE................. 08
Grant St & Ave SW........... 15
Grant Park Pl Pl SE.......... 15
Grant Valley Rd NE.......... 05
Grape NE................... 12
Grape SE................... 15
Grass Valley Rd SW.......... 11
Graves NW.................. 14
Gray NW
   1-380................... 14
   381-OUT................ 18
Graymont Dr SW............. 10
Graywall St & Ct (EP)........ 44
Great Southwest Pky SW...... 36
Green NW................... 18
Green Hill Pl & Rd NE........ 42
Green Ind Way (CHA)........ 41
Green Meadows Ln NE........ 19

Atlanta (Con.)   303

Green Mountain Trl (CP) 49
Green Oak Cir NE 45
Green Oak Ct NW 27
Green Oak Dr (DOR) 40
Green Pines Dr NE 42
Green Rock Ct & Trl (DOR) 40
Green Trail Dr (CP) 49
Green Tree Ln (CP) 49
Green Valley (EP) 44
Green Valley Dr (CP) 37
Greenbriar Pky & Trl SW 31
Greenbriar Rd NE 28
Greenbrook Trl & Way NE 45
Greenbush Pl NE 45
Greencove Ave NE 06
Greencove Ln SE 16
Greencrest Dr NE 45
Greendale Dr NW 27
Greendale Dr SE 15
Greenfield NW 18
Greenfield Ave SE 15
Greenglade Rd NE 45
Greenhill Dr (CHA) 41
Greenland Dr NE 06
Greenland Rd NE 42
Greenleaf Cir SW 31
Greenleaf Rd SE 36
Greensboro Dr SE 36
Greensferry Ave SW
    1-770 14
    771-OUT 18
Greensprings Rd (CP) 37
Greensward Dr NE 49
Greentree Trl (CP) 49
Greenview Ave NE 05
Greenway (DUN) 38
Greenwich SW 10
Greenwillow Dr NE 45
Greenwood Ave NE
    1-600 08
    601-OUT 06
Greenwood Cir (EP) 44
Gregg SW 22
Grenoble Ct (DOR) 40
Grenock Cir NE 28
Gresham Ave & Rd SE 10
Gress Ave SE 12
Graystone Rd NW 18
Griffin NW
    1-410 14
    411-OUT 18
Griggs NW 14
Grossmont Dr SW 36
Grove Ave (EP) 44
Grove Cir (HAP) 54
Grove St & Dr NE 19
Grove Park Pl Pl NE 09
Groveland Ave NW 18
Guilford Ln (CP) 49
Gun Club Rd NW 14
Gunby SE 12
Gwendolyn Dr (CP) 49
Haas Ave SE 16
Habersham Rd NE & NW 05
Habersham Way NW 05
Haddon Hall Rd NW 27
Hadlock SW 11
Halcyon Dr (CP) 49
Haldane Rd NW 11
Hale NE 07
Hall SW 10

Hall Ave SE 16
Hall St & Pl NW 18
Hallcrest Dr NE 19
Hallie Ln (CP) 49
Hallie Mill Ln (CP) 49
Hallman NE 17
Hallman Ave NW 16
Hallmark Ct SE 15
Ham Dr (CHA) 41
Hambrick Dr (CP) 49
Hamilton (HAP) 54
Hamilton Ave (EP) 44
Hamilton Ave SE 12
Hamilton Blvd SW 54
Hamlin Cir & Rd (CHA) 41
Hammarskjold Dr (EP) 44
Hammock Pl SE 12
Hammond SW 10
Hammond Dr NE 18
Hampton NW 14
Hampton Ter NE 08
Hampton Way NE 24
Hampton Hall Dr & Way NE 15
Hancock Dr NE 06
Handley Ave SW 10
Handy Dr NW 18
Hanford Dr NE 15
Hannah SE 16
Hannah Rd (CP) 49
Hanover SE 16
Hanover West Ct, Dr, Ln &
    Ter NW 27
Hansell SE 12
Hapeville Rd SW
    1-2700 15
    2701-OUT 54
Happy Hollow Ct (CP) 49
Happy Hollow Rd (DOR) 40
Happy Valley Cir SW 31
Happy Valley Tr Trl SE 47
Haralson Ave NE 07
Harber Valley (DOR) 40
Harbin Rd SW 11
Hardee NE
    1-1490 07
    1491-OUT 17
Hardee Ave (CHA) 41
Hardee Ave W (CHA) 41
Hardee Cir NE 17
Hardeman Rd NE 42
Harden SE 16
Harden Dr NW 31
Harden Rd NW 15
Hardendorf Ave NE 07
Hardin Ave (EP) 44
Hardin Ave (CP) 49
Harding Ave (HAP) 54
Hardman Ct NE 42
Hardwick SE 15
Hargis SE 15
Harlan Dr (EP) 44
Harlan Rd NW 11
Harleston Rd NE 28
Harmony Way (EP) 44
Harold Ave SE
    1-700 07
    701-OUT 16
Harold Ave SE
    1-700 07
    701-OUT 16
Harper NW 18
Harper Rd SE 15

Harper Valley Dr (CP) 49
Harriett SE 15
Harrington Pl, SW 11
Harris NE
    1-100 03
    101-OUT 12
Harris NW
    1-100 03
    101-166 13
    167-OUT 03
Harris Cir (DUN) 38
Harris Dr (CP) 37
Harris St & Dr (EP) 44
Harris Manor Dr NW 11
Harris Tr (CHA) 27
Harris Valley Rd NW 27
Harrison Ct & Rd (CP) 37
Harrison Pl SW 14
Harrison Pl Ct SW 14
Harrison Rd (EP) 44
Harrogate Dr NW 27
Harrogate Ln NE 28
Harrow Dr (CHA) 41
Harte Dr NW 10
Hartford Ave & Pl SW 10
Harts Mill Ct (CHA) 41
Harts Mill Rd NE
    1-1700 19
    1701-OUT 41
Harts Mills Ln NE 19
Harvard Ave (CP) 37
Harvard Rd NE 06
Harvel Dr NW 18
Harvest Ln SE 17
Harvester Rd (EP) 44
Harwell NW 14
Harwell Pl NW 18
Harwell Rd NW
    1-100 11
    101-470 31
    471-OUT 18
Harwood Dr (EP) 44
Mascall Rd NW 09
Hasty Ct NE 19
Hasty Pl NW 18
Hatcher Ave SW 15
Hatfield Cir SE 16
Hathaway Ct (CHA) 41
Hathburn Ct (DUN) 38
Hathcock Rd (CP) 37
Havalyn Ln (DOR) 40
Haven SE 15
Haven Ridge Dr NW 05
Haverhill Dr NE 42
Havermill Way NE 45
Haverstraw Ct & Dr (CHA) 41
Havilon Dr SW 11
Hawick Dr NW 27
Hawkins NW 14
Hawthorne NE 07
Hawthorne Ave (CP) 37
Hawthorne Ave NW 09
Hawthorne Dr NE 45
Hawthorne Way (EP) 44
Hawthorne Pl NE 45
Hayden NW 13
Hayden Dr (EP) 44
Haygood Ave SE & SW 15
Haygood Dr NE 07
Haynes NW
    1-180 13
    181-OUT 14
Haynes SW 13

Atlanta (Con.)   303

Hazel Dr SE	16
Hazelrig Dr SE	15
Hazelwood Ct & Dr NE	45
Hazelwood Dr SW	11
Head Rd SW	11
Headland Dr SW	
1826-2900	44
2901-OUT	11
Headland Ter (EP)	44
Heard Pl SW	10
Heards Dr NW	
1-800	27
801-OUT	28
Heards Creek Trl NW	28
Heards Ferry Rd NW	28
Hearst Cir & Dr NE	42
Heartwood Ln (DOR)	40
Heather Ct SW	11
Heather Dr (EP)	44
Heather Ln (CP)	49
Heatherdale Ln (DOR)	40
Heatherland Dr SW	11
Heatherly Dr (CP)	49
Heatherwood Dr SW	31
Heathfield Dr NW	28
Heaton Dr (EP)	44
Heaton Park Dr NE	
1-195	07
Hedden Rd NE	42
Hedgewood Dr & Ln NW	11
Helen Dr NE	06
Helen Ln SW	31
Helena SE	15
Helena Ave NW	
1-50	10
51-OUT	14
Helmsdale Dr NE	45
Hemlock Cir SE	16
Hemperley Rd (CP)	49
Hemphill	37
Hemphill Ave NW	18
Hemphill Rd NW	31
Hemphill School Rd NW	31
Henderson Creek Rd (CHA)	
Henderson Mill Ct NE	45
Henderson Mill Rd NE	
1-2610	45
2611-OUT	41
Hendon Rd SE	54
Hendrix Ave (EP)	44
Hendrix Ave SW	15
Henry Ave SW	10
Henry Thomas Dr SE	15
Hensley Dr (DUN)	38
Heritage Ter SE	27
Heritage Dr NE	45
Heritage Way NE	28
Heritage Valley Rd SW	31
Hermance Dr NE	19
Hermer Cir NW	11
Herndon NW	18
Herring Rd SW	11
Herrington Dr NE	42
Herschel Pl (CP)	49
Herschel Rd (CP)	37
Hewlett Rd (DUN)	38
Hiawassee Dr SW	11
Hickman Dr NW	11
Hickory Ln (DOR)	40
Hickory Rd (CHA)	41
Hickory Wood Ln (DOR)	40

Hidden Ct (CP)	49
Hidden Acres Dr (DOR)	40
Hidden Branches Ct, Dr &	
Way (DUN)	38
Hidden Branches Close	
(DUN)	38
Hidden Brook Ct, Dr & Trl	
(CP)	49
Hidden Forest Ct SE	16
Hidden Valley Ct & Dr (CP)	49
Higgins SW	10
High Court Rd NW	27
High Haven Ct NE	29
High Point Dr & Pl NE	06
High Point Ln & Rd NE	42
High Point Trl, SW	31
High Tarn (DUN)	38
Highbrook Dr NE	42
Highbury Trl SW	54
Highland Ave NE	12
Highland Dr NE	05
Highland Ter NE	06
Highland View NE	05
Hightower Ct & Pl NW	18
Hightower Rd NW	
1-100	11
101-OUT	18
Hightower Trl (DUN)	38
Highview Rd SW	11
Highway 85 (CP)	49
Highwood Dr SW	31
Hilderbrand Dr NE	28
Hildon Cir & Rd (CHA)	41
Hill NW	18
Hill SE	
1-660	12
661-OUT	15
Hill Acres Rd SW	31
Hillandale Dr (CP)	49
Hillburn Dr SE	16
Hillcrest Ave NE & SE	17
Hillcrest Dr (EP)	44
Hillcrest Dr SE	16
Hilliard St NE & SE	12
Hillpine Dr NE	06
Hills Ave SW	13
Hills Ave & Pl NW	15
Hillsdale Dr SW	15
Hillside Ave SE	15
Hillside Dr (DOR)	40
Hillside Dr NW	42
Hillside Dr SW	15
Hillstone Ct NE	16
Hillswick Ct NE	28
Hilltop Cir NW	14
Hilltop Dr (CHA)	41
Hilltop Dr (CP)	37
Hilltop Dr, Pl & Way SW	15
Hilltop Rd SW	31
Hillview Ave NE	19
Hillwood Ct SE	16
Hillwood Ter NE	19
Hipp SW	15
Hirsch NW	18
Hitching Post Trl NE	42
Hobart Ave SE	12
Hobart Dr NW	18
Hobson St & Cir SW	10
Hogan Rd SW	
1 3000	44
3001-OUT	31
Hogue NE	12
Hoke NW	18

Holcomb St & Ct (EP)	44
Holderness SW	
1-270	14
271-OUT	10
Holiday Ave NE	07
Holiday Pl (DOR)	40
Holley NW	18
Holley Rd NW	
1-300	14
301-OUT	18
Hollis Ter NW	11
Holliston Ct & Rd (DOR)	40
Holly NW	18
Holly Ct (EP)	44
Holly Dr SE	54
Holly Ln NE	29
Holly Bank Cir (DUN)	38
Holly Oaks Dr (DUN)	38
Hollydale Ct NW	42
Hollydale Dr SW	11
Hollywood Ct, Dr & Rd NW	18
Holmes NW	18
Holtzclaw SE	16
Home Ave SE	12
Home Park Ave Ave NW	18
Homeland Dr (DOR)	40
Homestead Ave NE	06
Honeysuckle Ln (DOR)	40
Honeysuckle Ln (CP)	49
Honeysuckle Ln SW	11
Honour Ave & Cir NW	05
Hood SW	12
Hood Ave (CHA)	41
Hood Ave NW	18
Heods Dr SW	10
Hooper NE	
1-100	18
101 500	17
501-1800	07
2001-OUT	18
Hooper NW	
1-100	18
101-500	17
501-1800	07
2001-OUT	18
Hooper SE	
1-500	17
501 OUT	07
Hooper Ave NE	
1-100	18
101 500	17
501 1800	07
2001-OUT	18
Hooper Ave NW	
1-100	18
101-500	17
501 1800	07
2001-OUT	18
Hooper Ave SE	
1-100	18
101 500	17
501-1800	07
2001-OUT	18
Hope (HAP)	54
Hope Rd (DUN)	38
Hope St & Dr SW	10
Hopewell Rd (CP)	37
Hopkins SE	15
Hopkins SW	
1-300	14
301 OUT	10
Hopkins Ter NE	24
Hornady NW	18

Atlanta (Con.)   303

Horseshoe Dr SE	16
Hortense St, Pl & Way NW	18
Horton Dr (CF)	37
Hospital Ave W (CHA)	41
Houghton Ct (DUN)	38
Houghton Ct N (DUN)	38
Houston NE	
1-300	03
301-OUT	12
Houston Mill Rd NE	29
Hovey Ct (CP)	49
Howard NW	14
Howard Cir NE	07
Howard Dr (CP)	37
Howard St NE & SE	17
Howell Dr SE	16
Howell Dr & Ter SW	31
Howell Pl SW	10
Howell St NE & SE	12
Howell Mill Rd NW	
1-2570	18
2571-OUT	27
Howland Ct (DUN)	38
Hubbard SW	10
Huber NW	18
Hudgens Rd (CP)	49
Hudgins Aly SW	12
Hudson Dr NE	06
Huff Rd NW	18
Hugh SW	10
Hughes NW	31
Hugo SW	15
Hull NW	13
Humility Dr & Ln NE	19
Humming Bird Ln NE	07
Humphries (EP)	44
Humphries SW	
1-660	12
661-OUT	10
Humphries Dr SE	54
Humphries Way (DOR)	40
Hunnerkoff NW	18
Hunnicutt NW	
1-100	08
101-OUT	13
Hunt NE	08
Hunt Ct (CP)	37
Huntcliff St & Pt (DUN)	38
Huntcliff Lake Ct (DUN)	38
Huntcliff Trace (DUN)	38
Hunter NW	
1-20	34
21-300	03
301-470	13
471-OUT	14
Hunter SE	
1-3	34
4-ONLY	03
5-12	34
13-OUT	12
Hunter SW	
1-20	34
21-300	03
301-470	13
471-OUT	14
Hunter Pl NW	14
Hunter Rd (CP)	49
Hunters Pt NE	28
Hunters Branch St, Clse, Dr & Ln NE	28

Hunters Glen Ct NE	28
Hunters Trace Cir NE	28
Hunting Creek Rd NE	28
Huntington Cir (CHA)	41
Huntington Rd NE & NW	09
Huntington Trl (DUN)	38
Huntley Dr NE	05
Hurst Dr NE	05
Hurt NE	07
Hutchens Rd SE	54
Hutchinson NE	07
Hutton Pl NW	18
Hyacinth Ave NW	14
Hyde Mnr Dr NW	27
Idlewild Ct & Trl NE	28
Idlewild Dr (EP)	44
Idlewood Oaks Ct NE	19
Illinois Ave NE	14
Impala Dr NE	45
Imperial Dr NE	05
Indale Pl SW	10
Independence Pl NW	18
Indian Ln (DOR)	40
Indian Trl NE	27
Indian Rock Rd SW	31
Indian Valley Trl (CHA)	41
Indiana Ave NE	07
Indigo Ln NE	18
Industrial Blvd SW	
1-5400	36
5401-OUT	30
Industrial Cir SW	36
Ingersoll Rand Dr (CHA)	41
Ingledale Dr NW	31
Inman SW	10
Inman Ave NE	08
Inman Cir NE	06
Inman Dr NE	19
Innsbruck Dr (DUN)	38
Innwood Rd NE	29
Interchange Dr SW	36
Interlochen Dr NE	42
International Blvd (HAP)	54
Interstate Pkwy NW	39
Interstate Pl NW, NW	39
Interstate North NW	39
Inverness Ave NE	06
Inwood Ct NE & NW	09
Iona Dr SE	16
Ira SW	
1-660	12
661-OUT	10
Irby Ave NW	05
Ireland Pl NW	18
Iron Bound Pl NW	18
Iroquois Path NE	19
Irvindale Dr (CHA)	41
Irwin NE	12
Isa Dr SE	15
Island Ferry Rd (DUN)	38
Ison Dr (DUN)	38
Iswald SE	16
Ivan Hill Cir & Dr SW	11
Ivanhoe Dr NW	27
Iverson NE	07
Ivy Ln, Pky, Rd, Sq & Trl NE	42
Ivy Pl NE	07
Ivy St NE & SE	03
Ivy Gates NE	42
Ivy Ridge NE	42
Ivydale (EP)	44
Ivydale Dr SW	11
Ivywood Dr SW	31

Jackson (CP)	37
Jackson (HAP)	54
Jackson Dr (EP)	44
Jackson Pl SW	11
Jackson St NE & SE	12
Jacolyn Pl NE	29
Jailette Rd (CP)	49
Jamaica Rd NW	18
James Dr NW	18
James Jackson Pky NW	18
Jan Dr (CP)	37
Jan Hill Ln NE	29
Jane Rd (DOR)	40
Janellen Dr NE	45
Janes Ln NE	24
Janice Cir & Ct (CHA)	41
Janice Dr (EP)	44
Janice Dr (CP)	37
Jasmine Ct NE	45
Jasper NE	14
Jay Pl SE	15
Jefferson (CP)	37
Jefferson (CHA)	41
Jefferson NW	18
Jefferson Ave SW	
1-850	15
851-OUT	44
Jefferson Ter (EP)	44
Jeffrey Dr (CP)	49
Jenkins SW	15
Jenny Wren Ln NW	11
Jeptha SW	14
Jernigan Dr & Pl SE	15
Jerome Rd (CP)	49
Jersey Rd (EP)	44
Jesup (EP)	44
Jetal Pl NW	18
Jett NW	
1-870	18
871-OUT	14
Jett Dr (DOR)	40
Jett Rd NW	27
Jett Ferry Ct & Rd (DUN)	38
Jettridge Rd NW	27
Jewell (EP)	44
Joan Of Arc Pl (CP)	49
Jobeth SE	16
Jody Ln NE	29
Joe Louis Dr NW	14
Joel Ct, Ln & Pl (DOR)	40
John NW	
1-390	14
391-OUT	18
John Calvin Ave (CP)	37
John Freeman Way (EP)	44
John Glen Dr (CHA)	41
John Hope Ct & Dr SW	14
John Wesley Ave (CP)	37
Johnny's Ln (DOR)	40
Johns Way NE	08
Johnson NW	14
Johnson Ave NE	12
Johnson Cir E & W (CHA)	41
Johnson Dr (DOR)	40
Johnson Rd NE	
1-1910	06
1911-OUT	45
Johnson Rd NW	18
Johnson Ferry Rd NE	
1-800	28
801-1100	42
1101-2320	19
2321-2600	41

Atlanta (Con.)   303

Johnson Ferry Rd NW 28
Jolly Rd (CP) 49
Jolyn Pl NE 42
Jonathon Ln NE 19
Jones Aly SW 12
Jones Ave (EP) 44
Jones Ave NW
  1-1000 14
  1001-OUT 18
Jones Cir & Rd (CP) 49
Jones Rd NW 42
Jones Ferry Dr (CP) 40
Jones Mill Rd (CP) 40
Jonesboro Rd (CP) 49
Jonesboro Rd SE
  1-2600 15
  2601-3900 54
Jordan SE 15
Jordan Ter NE 45
Josephine (CP) 49
Josephine NE 07
Josephine Ave SE 16
Josephine Rd (DOR) 40
Journal Way NW 03
Joyce SW 14
Joylan Pl SW 15
Joyland Ave SW 15
Judith Way NE 24
Judson (EP) 44
Judy Ln SW 15
Judy Lynn (CP) 49
Julian NW 18
Juniper NE
  1-870 08
  871-OUT 09
Kadleston Way NE 19
Kalb SE 12
Kammeyer Ln (CHA) 41
Karen Rd (CP) 37
Karland Dr NW 05
Katherwood Dr SW 10
Kathryn Cir SW 31
Kathryn Ct (EP) 44
Katomarick Dr SE 54
Kay Ln NE 06
Kayron Dr NE
  1-5620 42
  5621-OUT 28
Keats Dr NW 11
Keenan Ct, Ln & Rd (CP) 49
Keiths Cir NE 05
Kelden Cir & Ct (CP) 49
Kelley St & Pl SE 12
Kellog Cir (DUN) 38
Kellog Springs Dr (DUN) 38
Kelso Dr SW 11
Kemper Way NE 42
Kenbrook Dr & Way NW 27
Kendall NE 12
Kendall Ct NE 42
Kendrick Ave SE 15
Kendrick Rd NE 19
Kenelworth Dr (EP) 44
Kenilworth Dr SW 10
Kenlock Pl NE 05
Kenmore SW 11
Kennedy St & Ct NW 18
Kennesaw Ave NE 08
Kennesaw Dr NW 18
Kennett SE 15
Kenney Ct (EP) 44

Kenneys Aly SW 63
Kennington Ct NE 19
Kenny Rd SW 31
Kenolia Dr SW 18
Kenora Dr SW 31
Kensington NE 07
Kent SE 12
Kent Rd (CP) 37
Kenton Pl SE 16
Kentucky Ave NE 06
Kentucky Ct (EP) 44
Kenway Dr (HAP) 54
Kenwood Ave NW 09
Kenwood Dr (HAP) 54
Kenyon SE 16
Kerry Cir NW, NW 18
Kerry Dr & Pl NW 18
Keswick Ct & Dr (CHA) 41
Kevin Ct (CP) 37
Kevin Ct NW 31
Key Rd SE 16
Keystone Dr (HAP) 54
Kilburn Dr NE 24
Kilby Pl NW 27
Kildare Ave NW 18
Kilgore NW 18
Kilgore Rd (CP) 49
Killian SE
  1-800 12
  801-OUT 16
Kilt Ct (DOR) 40
Kim Ct (DOR) 40
Kimball Rd SW 31
Kimball Way NE 03
Kimberly Ct (DOR) 40
Kimberly Ct SW, SW 11
Kimberly Ln NE 06
Kimberly Rd SW 31
Kimberly St & Cir (CP) 49
Kimberly Mill Ln & Rd (CP) .. 49
Kimblewick Cove (DUN) 38
Kimmeridge Dr (EP) 44
Kimsey Dr (CP) 37
King (DOR) 40
King SE 12
King Rd (HAP) 54
King Rd NW 42
King Alfred Dr SW 31
King Arnold (HAP) 54
King Arthur Cir & Ct NE 45
King Arthur Rd SW 31
King Charles Rd SW 31
King Edward Trl SW 31
King George Ln SW 31
King Henry Rd SW 31
King James Dr SW 31
King Richard Dr SW 31
King Smith Rd SE 54
Kings Cir NE 05
Kings Ct NE 06
Kings Walk NE 07
Kings Way NW 27
Kings Down Cir, Ct, Rd &
  Way (DUN) 38
Kings Grant Dr NW 18
Kings Point Cir E (CHA) 41
Kings Point Cir, Ct & Dr
  (CHA) 41
Kingsboro Rd NE
  1-3500 26
  3501-OUT 19
Kingscliff Dr & Way NE 45
Kingsdale Dr SW 11

Kingsfield Ct (CHA) 41
Kingsgate Ct & Dr (CHA) 41
Kingsglenn Ct & Dr (DOR) ... 40
Kingslake Ct NE 45
Kingsland Ct & Dr (DOR) 40
Kingsley Cir NE 24
Kingstavern Pl NW 18
Kingston Ct & Dr NE 42
Kingston Rd NW 18
Kingston Ter (EP) 44
Kingswood Cir (CP) 49
Kingswood Ln NW 05
Kinlock NW 27
Kinnard (DOR) 40
Kinsey Ct NE 05
Kipling Dr NW 18
Kipling St & Cir SE 15
Kirkland Dr NE 18
Kirkwood Ave SE 16
Kirkwood Rd NE 17
Kittredge Ct & Dr NE 29
Kittredge Park Rd NE 29
Kittrell Dr SW 31
Kitty Hawk Dr & Pl NE 42
Knight Ct SE 16
Knighton Cir & Dr (CP) 49
Knob Hill Ct & Dr NE 29
Knob Hill Dr NW 39
Knollwood Dr NW 05
Knollwood Trl (EP) 44
Knott SE 16
Knotts Ave (EP) 44
Knox NE 17
Knox Ave (CHA) 41
Knox Dr SE 15
Kodiak Cir & Dr NE 45
Kowetta Rd & Trl (CP) 49
Krog NE 07
La Chona Ct NE 29
La Dawn Ln NW 18
La Fayette Dr NE 09
La Fayette Rd & Way NW 27
La France NE 07
La Rue Pl NW 27
La Salle Way SW 31
La Verne Dr NW 18
La Vista Rd
  1-1500 24
La Vista Rd NE
  1501-2460 29
Lacey Cir (HAP) 54
Ladd St & Pl SW 10
Ladovia Ln NE 45
Lady Marion Ln NE 09
Lafayette Ave NW 27
Lafayette Ln (CP) 37
Lagrange Blvd SW 36
Lajean Dr (CP) 49
Lake Ave NE 07
Lake Ave SW 11
Lake Ave & Dr (HAP) 54
Lake Cir & Dr SE 15
Lake Dr (CP) 37
Lake Dr (DOR) 40
Lake Ter (EP) 44
Lake Allen Ln NE 28
Lake Brook Ct (DOR) 40
Lake Flair Cir & Ct NE 45
Lake Forrest Ct & Ln NE 42
Lake Forrest Dr NE
  1-5750 42
  5751-OUT 28

Atlanta (Con.)　　303

Lake Forrest Dr NW
　1-5750 42
　5751-OUT 28
Lake Hearn Ct, Dr & Pl NE 19
Lake Island Dr NW 27
Lake Mirror Rd (CP) 49
Lake Placid Dr NE 42
Lake Valley Rd NW 31
Lakehaven Dr NE 19
Lakeland Dr NE & NW 05
Lakemont Dr
　1-4000 (EP) 44
　4001-OUT (CP) 37
Lakemoore Dr NE 42
Lakeridge Cir SW 31
Lakeshore Cir NE 24
Lakeshore Dr (CP) 37
Lakeshore Dr NE
　1-200 24
　201-OUT 07
Lakeshore Dr At Crystal Lake
　(CP) 49
Lakeside Dr (DOR) 40
Lakeside Dr NE 26
Lakeview Ave NE
　1-500 05
　501-OUT 68
Lakeview Dr (CP) 37
Lakeview Dr NE & SE 17
Lakeview Ln (DOR) 40
Lakewood Ave (EP) 44
Lakewood Ave SW, SE
　1-2930 15
　2931-OUT 10
Lakewood Ter SE 15
Lakewood Way SW 15
Lamar SE 15
Lamar Ave SW
　1-50 10
　51-OUT 14
Lambert Dr NE 24
Lambeth Cir & Ln (DOR) 40
Lamon Ave SE 16
Lampkin NE 12
Lamsden Ln NW 27
Lanark Dr SW 31
Lancaster Dr (EP) 44
Lancaster Loop NE 28
Land Olakes Ct & Dr NE 42
Landmark Dr NE 11
Landrum Dr SW 42
Landsdowne Dr NW 28
Lanes Ln NE 17
Lang Ave (HAP) 54
Lang Dr SW 15
Langford Ln NW 27
Langhorn SW 15
Langland Ct NE 45
Langston Ave SW 10
Langston Dr SW 15
Lanier NW 18
Lanier Blvd & Pl NE 06
Lanier Dr NE 19
Lanier Dr SW 15
Lannon Ave NE 17
Lansbury Dr NE 42
Lansbury Village Dr (CHA) 41
Lansing SE 15
Lansol Rd (DOR) 40
Lantera Ln (CP) 49

Lanvale Dr SW 10
Laquita Dr SE 15
Laramie Dr NW 39
Larchmont Cir, Ct & Dr NW 18
Larchwood SW 10
Laren SW 11
Largo Ln SW 10
Larkfield Dr NE 28
Larkin SW
　1-530 13
　531-OUT 14
Larkin Ct SW
　1-530 13
　531-OUT 14
Larkin Pl SW 13
Larkspur Dr SE 16
Larosa Ter SW 10
Larose (EP) 44
Latham SW 10
Lathrop SE 15
Latimer NW 13
Latona Dr SW 54
Lauderdale Dr NE 45
Laurel Ave NW 18
Laurel Ave SW
　1-280 14
　281-OUT 15
Laurel Dr NE 42
Laurel Forrest Cir NE 42
Laurel Oak Ct (DOR) 11
Laurelmont Dr SW 11
Laurelwood Dr SW 11
Laurelwood Rd (DOR) 40
Laurens Cir, Dr & Way SW 11
Lavender Dr NW 10
Laventure Dr & Rd (CHA) 41
Lavista Cir & Dr (HAP) 54
Law NW 18
Lawn NW 10
Lawrence Dr SW 31
Lawrence St & Ave (EP) 44
Lawshe SW 14
Lawshe St SW 14
Lawson Way (CHA) 41
Lawton SW
　1-270 14
　271-OUT 10
Lawton Ave & Pl SW 10
Layton Ave NW 18
Le Baron Dr NE 45
Le Brun Rd NE 42
Le Conte Ave NE 19
Le Conte Hwy SW 31
Leach NW 14
Leathers Cir NW 14
Leavens (EP) 44
Lebanon Dr NE 24
Ledgewood Dr (CHA) 41
Lee (EP) 44
Lee Cir NE 24
Lee St & Pl SW 10
Lee Andrews Ave SE 15
Leeds Ct & Way (DUN) 38
Lees Mill Rd (CP) 49
Leesburg Ct SW 31
Legion Way (EP) 44
Leila Ln SE 15
Leisure Ct, Dr & Ln (DOR) 40
Leisure Ln (CP) 49
Leisure Lake Dr (DOR) 40
Leith (EP) 44

Leland Pl SW 31
Leland Ter NE 17
Lena NW 14
Lenox Cir NE 06
Lenox Pl & Way NE 24
Lenox Rd NE
　1-2020 06
　2021-3290 24
　3291-OUT 26
Lenox Sq Shopping Center 26
Leonard SW
　381-OUT 13
Leonardo Ave NE 07
Leonardo Dr SW 31
Lesley Dr (CP) 37
Leslie NE 07
Leslie SE 17
Leslie Ave (HAP) 54
Leslie Ct, Dr & Ln NE 45
Lester (EP) 44
Lester NW 14
Lester Rd (CP) 49
Lethea SE 15
Level Ridge Rd SE 54
Lewfield Cir SE 16
Lewis Cir (CP) 37
Lewis Rd SE 15
Lexington Ave (EP) 44
Lexington Ave SW 10
Liawen Ct NE 29
Liberty (CP) 37
Liberty Ave SE 17
Liddell Dr NE 24
Light House Pt NW 28
Lilla Cir & Dr SW 10
Lillian SW 10
Limerick Dr SW 31
Limey Dr NW 18
Linam Ave SE 15
Lincoln Ave SW 17
Lincoln Ct & Dr NW 18
Lincoln St, Ave, Dr & Pl SW 15
Linda Ln SE 15
Linda Way SW 10
Lindberg Way NE 24
Lindbergh Cir NE 24
Lindbergh Dr NE
　1-450 05
　451-OUT 24
Linden Ave NE & NW 08
Linden Ln (DOR) 40
Linden Garden Dr (CP) 49
Lindenwood Ln NE 19
Lindmont Cir & Ct NE 24
Lindridge Dr & Way NE 24
Lindsay NW
　1-560 14
　561-OUT 18
Lindsay Pl NW 14
Lindsey Dr SE 15
Line Rd SW 31
Lingo Way SW 12
Linkwood Pl NW 18
Linkwood Rd NW
　1-160 11
　161-OUT 18
Linwood Ave (EP) 44
Linwood Ave NE 06
Lisa Ct & Dr SW 11
Lisa Ln (DUN) 38
Lisbon Dr SW 10
Little St SE & SW 15
Little John Trl NE 09

Atlanta (Con.)   303

Little John Way (DOR) 40
Live Oak Dr (DOR) 40
Lively Trl NE 45
Lively Ridge Rd NE 29
Livermore SE 15
Livesy Ct (DOR) 40
Loch Lomond Tr Trf SW 31
Lochland Rd SE 16
Locke Dr SE 16
Lockhaven Cir SW 11
Locklear Ct & Way (DOR) 40
Lockridge Dr (DOR) 40
Lockwood Dr SW 11
Locust NE 17
Locust Ln SE 15
Lofton Rd NW 09
Logan SE 12
Logan Cir NE
   1-1500 18
   1501-OUT 19
Logan Cir NW
   1-1500 18
   1501-OUT 19
Logan Pl (HAP) 54
Loghaven Dr NW 18
Lois Ln SE 15
Lois Pl NW 18
Loma Linda SW 10
Lombardy Way NE 09
Lomita Rd SE 16
London Dr NW 27
London Rd (CHA) 41
Londonberry Rd NW 27
Lone Oak Ave SW 54
Lone Star Trl (DOR) 40
Lonetia SE 12
Long (EP) 44
Long Acres Dr NW 28
Long Branch Ct NE 19
Long Island Ct NE & NW 28
Long Island Dr NE
   1-4900 42
   4901-5800 27
   5801-OUT 28
Long Island Dr NW
   1-4900 42
   4901-5800 27
   5801-OUT 28
Long Island Pl NE & NW 28
Long Island Rd & Way NW 27
Long Island Ter NE 42
Long Leaf Dr NE 42
Longchamps Rd NE 19
Longley Ave NW 18
Longmeadow Ln (CP) 49
Longmire Way (DOR) 40
Longview (EP) 44
Longview Ave SE 12
Longview Dr & Way (CHA) 41
Longwood Dr NW 05
Lookout Ave NW 18
Lookout Pl NE 05
Loomis Ave SE 12
Loraine Dr NW 19
Lorell Ter NE 28
Lorenzo Dr SW 10
Lori Ln (DOR) 40
Loridan Cir & Dr NE 42
Loring SE 16
Loring Dr NW 09
Los Angeles Ave NE 06

Los Olas Dr (CP) 49
Lost Mine Trl (DOR) 40
Lottie Pl (CP) 37
Lotus Ave NW 18
Louden Dr NE 45
Louis Xiv Ln (CP) 49
Louise (HAP) 54
Louise Aly NW 13
Louise Pl NW 18
Love St SE & SW 15
Lovejoy NW 13
Loveless Ave NW 18
Lovridge Dr SW 31
Lowe (CP) 37
Lowe NW 18
Lowergate Dr NW 07
Lowes Aly SW 13
Lowndes (CP) 37
Lowndes (EP) 44
Lowndes Ave SW 10
Lowry NE 07
Loyd SW 03
Loyola Dr SW 36
Lu-Jan Dr (CHA) 41
Lucile Ln (EP) 44
Lucile Ave SW 10
Luckie NW 18
   1-234 03
   235-OUT 13
Luckie Ln NE 29
Lucy SE 12
Lullwater Pky, Pl & Rd NE ... 07
Lumpkin (EP) 44
Luray Ct & Dr (CHA) 41
Luther SE 15
Luther Cir & Dr (EP) 44
Lydia Dr SE 15
Lyle Ave
   1-1500 (EP) 44
   1501-OUT (CP) 37
Lyle Pl NW 18
Lyle Rd & Ter (CP) 37
Lynch Ave NW 18
Lyndale Dr SE 16
Lynfield Ct & Dr (CP) 49
Lynfield Dr SW 11
Lynford Dr SW 10
Lynhaven Dr SW 10
Lynhurst Cir & Dr SW 11
Lynmoor Dr NE 19
Lynn Cir & Dr SW 11
Lynn Dr (CP) 37
Lynn Valley Rd NW 11
Lynnray Dr (DOR) 40
Lynray Ln & Pl (DOR) 40
Lynway Ln SW 11
Lynwood SE 12
Lynwood Ave (CP) 37
Lynwood Dr NE 19
Lynwln SE 16
Lyons Ave NE 12
Lyric Ct & Ln (HAP) 54
Lyric Way NW 18
Lytle Ave SE 16
Mabry Ln NE 19
Mabry Rd NE
   1-1000 28
   1001-OUT 19
Mac Dougall Dr SW 36
Macaw SW 18
Macedonia Rd SW 54
Mack Dr NW 18
Macklone NE 07

Maco NW 18
Macon Dr SE
   1-2700 15
   2701-OUT 54
Macon Dr SW
   1-2700 15
   2701-OUT 54
Macon Pl SE 54
Macon Ter SW 54
Maddox Aly SE 12
Maddox Dr NE 09
Maderia Ave NE 07
Madison (EP) 37
Madison Ave NE 19
Madronah NW 18
Magic Pac Way SW 54
Magna Carta Dr NW 18
Magnolia (EP) 44
Magnolia NW
   1-470 13
   471-OUT 14
Magnolia Pl NW 13
Mailing Ave SE 15
Main (HAP) 54
Main (EP) 44
Main (EP) 37
Main NW 18
Main St E & S (EP) 44
Main At Crystal Lake (CP) 49
Maison Pl NW 27
Malabar Dr NE 45
Maldo Dr NW 18
Mallard NW 18
Mallory Rd (CP) 49
Malone Dr (CHA) 41
Manchester Rd NE 24
Maney Ln 10
Manford Rd SW
   1-300 15
   301-OUT 10
Manget Ct & Way (DUN) 38
Mango Cir NW 18
Mangum NW
   1-180 13
   181-OUT 14
Mangum SW 13
Mangum Ln SW 11
Manhasset Dr (DUN) 38
Manhasset Cove (DUN) 38
Manigault SE 16
Manning (DOR) 40
Manor (EP) 44
Manor Pl SW 10
Manor Ridge Dr NW 05
Mansfield Ave NE 07
Manson Ave SW 10
Mantissa NW 18
Manville Dr (CHA) 41
Maple (EP) 44
Maple (HAP) 54
Maple Dr NE 05
Maple St, Aly & Pl NW 14
Mapledale Ln (CP) 49
Marann Dr NE 45
Marbury Cir NW 27
Marbut Ave SE 16
Marcell Ave SW 11
Marchman Dr NW 42
Marco Dr NW 18
Marcus SE 16
Marcy SE 15
Margaret (HAP) 54
Margaret SE 15

Atlanta (Con.) 303

Margaret Cir (CP)	49
Margaret Pl NW	18
Margaret Mitchell Ct & Dr NW	27
Margavera Ter (CHA)	41
Marian Rd NE	24
Maribeau Sq NW	27
Marie Ave NW	14
Marie Head Ter (EP)	44
Marietta NW	
1-245	03
246-666	13
667-OUT	18
Marietta Blvd, Pl & Rd NW	18
Marina (HAP)	54
Marion SE	
1-1060	12
1001-OUT	15
Marion Ave SE	
1-1000	12
1001-OUT	15
Marion St, Ave & Pl NE	07
Marjan St, Ct & Dr (DOR)	40
Mark Pl NW	31
Mark Two NW	18
Markan Ct & Dr NE	06
Market Dr (HAP)	54
Market Sq Pl NW	18
Markham SW	13
Markone NW	18
Marktray NW	18
Marlborough Cir (CP)	49
Marlbrook Dr NE	07
Marlin Cir, Dr & Way (CHA)	41
Marne Dr NW	05
Marona NE	07
Marray Dr (CHA)	41
Marstevan Dr NE	06
Martell Dr (EP)	44
Martha Ave NE	17
Martin (EP)	44
Martin SE	
1-650	12
651-OUT	15
Martin Ave SE	15
Martina Dr (DUN)	38
Martina Dr NE	05
Marvin NW	18
Marvin Ln SW	11
Marvin Miller Dr SW	36
Mary SW	18
Mary Briggs Ct (DOR)	40
Mary Dell Dr SE	18
Mary George Ave NW	18
Mary Lou Ln SE	16
Maryeanna Dr NE	42
Maryland (EP)	44
Maryland Ave NE	06
Maryland Dr (DOR)	40
Mason Rd (CP)	49
Mason Mill Rd NE	
1-1730	29
Mason Woods Dr NE	29
Massachusetts Blvd (CP)	37
Matador Ct (EP)	44
Mathews NE	19
Mathews SW	18
Mathews Ave NE	07
Mathewson Pl SW	
1-280	14
281-OUT	10

Mathieson Dr, Pl & Rd NE	05
Matilda Pl NW	18
Mauldin NW	18
Mauldin SE	16
Maxwell Dr SW	11
May Ave NE	19
May Ave SE	16
Mayes NW	14
Mayfair Dr NE	11
Mayflower Ave SW	11
Mayflower Rd (CP)	37
Mayland Ave & Cir SW	10
Maynard Ct & Rd NW	31
Maynard Ter SE	16
Mayo Pl SW	11
Mayson NE	24
Mayson Ave NE	
1-70	17
71-OUT	07
Mayson Turner Ave & Rd NW	14
Maywood Pl NW	18
Mc Alee NW	18
Mc Alee NW	13
Mc Alister SW	16
Mc Callie Blvd NW	18
Mc Clatchey Cir NE	42
Mc Clure Ave NW	14
Mc Cully Ct & Dr NE	45
Mc Daniel SW	
1-400	13
401-660	12
661-OUT	10
Mc Donald SE	18
Mc Donough Blvd SE	16
Mc Dougall Dr SW	36
Mc Griff NW	18
Mc Jenkins Dr NE	45
Mc Kay Dr SE	15
Mc Kenzie Dr NE	12
Mc Kinley Rd NW	18
Mc Lain NE	07
Mc Lendon Ave NE	07
Mc Lendon Cir NW	18
Mc Lynn Ave NE	06
Mc Millan NW	18
Mc Murray Dr SW	11
Mc Pherson Ave & Pl SE	16
Mc Veigh Ln SW	10
Mc Williams Ave SE	16
Mc Williams Rd SE	15
Mcalpine Ter (EP)	44
Mcarthur Blvd NW	18
Mcbaine Ln (DOR)	40
Mccall Dr & Pl (DOR)	40
Mcclaren Cir (DOR)	40
Mcclave Dr (DOR)	40
Mcclelland Ave (EP)	44
Mcconnell Dr (DOR)	40
Mccree Dr (CP)	37
Mcdaniel (CHA)	41
Mcdonald (CP)	37
Mcdonald Dr SE	15
Mcdonald Trl (CP)	49
Mcelroy (CP)	49
Mcelroy Rd (DOR)	40
Mcgaw Dr (CHA)	41
Mcghee Way (EP)	44
Mckenzie Ct SW	11
Mckenzie Dr (EP)	44
Mcmullin Ter (EP)	44
Mcpherson Dr (EP)	44
Mead SE	
1-580	15

581-OUT	12
Meador Ave & Way SE	15
Meadow Rd (HAP)	54
Meadow Lane Rd (DUN)	38
Meadow Park Dr & Ln SW	15
Meadow Valley Dr NE	42
Meadowbrook Dr NE	42
Meadowcliff Dr NE	45
Meadowdale Ave NE	06
Meadowlake Dr SE	17
Meadowlake Dr & Ln (DUN)	38
Meadowlane Dr SW	11
Meadowlane Pl SW	
1-3400	11
3401-OUT	31
Meadowlark Dr & Ln (EP)	44
Meadowood Ln (CHA)	41
Meadowridge Dr SW	31
Meadowvale Dr NE	45
Meadowview Dr & Ln SE	16
Means NW	18
Mecaslin NW	
1-1400	18
1401-OUT	09
Mechanic NW	13
Mechanicsville Rd (DOR)	40
Medfield Tr NE	45
Medinah Ct (CHA)	41
Meeting Rd NE	19
Melanie Ln (CP)	49
Melante Dr NE	24
Melbenan Dr SW	11
Meldon Ave SE & SW	15
Meldrum NW	18
Melinda Ct & Dr NE	45
Mell Ave NE	07
Mellrich Ave NE	17
Mellview Ave NE	10
Mellwood Ave SW	31
Melrose Dr SE	16
Melrose Dr SW	10
Melvin Dr SW	31
Memorial Dr SE	
1-670	12
671-1272	16
1273-3150	17
Memorial Dr SW	03
Memorial Ter SE	19
Mendell Cir NE	19
Mendell Ct & Dr SW	36
Mendenhall Dr (CHA)	41
Menlo Dr NW	
1-3400	18
3401-4050 (DOR)	40
Menlo Way (DOR)	40
Mentelle Dr NE	08
Mercedes Ct & Dr NE	45
Mercer (EP)	44
Mercer SE	
1-850	12
851-OUT	16
Mercer Ave (CP)	37
Merck Rd SW	31
Mercury Dr NW	31
Meredith Dr NW	18
Meridian SE	17
Merlendale Ct & Dr NW	27
Merlin Ave SE	17
Merrick Dr NE	24
Merrill Ave SW	10
Merrimac Ct NE	29
Merriman Ln NE	24
Merritts Ave NE	08

Atlanta (Con.)   303

Merritts Ave NW 13
Merry Ln NE 29
Merton Rd NE 06
Mesa Dr SE 16
Metal Rd NE 24
Metropolitan Ave & Pl SE 16
Miami Cir NE 24
Michael NE 29
Michael Dr (CP) 49
Michael Pl 10
Michelle Cir NW 42
Michigan Ave NW 14
Middle SW 10
Middle Plantation Rd NW 18
Middleburg Dr (CP) 49
Middlebury Ln NW 27
Middlesex Ave NE 06
Middleton SW 15
Middleton Dr & Rd NW 11
Midvale Dr NE 42
Midvale Rd NE
  1-3400 45
Midway SE 15
Mifflin Pl NE 24
Milam Ave SW 15
Milan Dr (CP) 49
Mildred SW 14
Mildred Pl NW 14
Miles Cir (EP) 44
Miles Rd (CP) 49
Mill Ct (DOR) 40
Mill Acres Dr SW 11
Mill Brook Dr (DUN) 38
Mill Creek Rd NE 19
Mill Gate Dr (DUN) 38
Mill Glen Ct & Dr (DUN) 38
Mill Race Ct (DUN) 38
Mill Shire Ln (DUN) 38
Mill Stream Ct (DUN) 38
Mill Trace Ct & Dr (DUN) 38
Mill Vale Ct (DOR) 40
Mill Valley Rd SW 31
Millboro Ln (CP) 49
Millbrook Dr NW 27
Milledge Ave SE
  1-1000 12
  1001-OUT (EP) 44
Milledge Ct SE 12
Milledge Pl NE 29
Millege Ave 44
Miller Ave NE 07
Miller Cir & Dr SW 18
Miller Ct (DOR) 40
Miller Dr (CHA) 41
Miller Rd (CP) 49
Miller Reed Ave SE 15
Millirons Dr SW 15
Mills NW
  1-100 08
  101-OUT 13
Mills Pl SW 36
Milmar Dr NW 27
Milowyn Pl NE 19
Milton SW 14
Milton Ave & Ter SE 15
Milton Pl SE 16
Mims SW 14
Mirror Ln SE 17
Mission Ridge Cir, Ct, Ln &
  Rd NW 39

Mitchell SW
  1-250 63
  251-470 13
  471-OUT 14
Mitchell Rd NW 28
Mobile NW 14
Mobile Ave NE 05
Mobile Ave SW 15
Mobley Ct & Dr SE 15
Mocking Bird Ln SW 11
Mollie SE 16
Monarch Rd SE 16
Monica Ct SW 11
Monroe Cir NE 08
Monroe Dr (CP) 37
Monroe Dr NE
  1-1000 08
  1001-1320 06
  1321-OUT 24
Monroe Pl NE 24
Montana Rd NW 27
Montclair Dr NW 09
Monte Sq NW 27
Monte Carlo Dr NW 27
Montecello Ct & Dr (DUN) 38
Monteel Dr NW 14
Montego Bay Dr (CP) 49
Monterey Dr NW 18
Montevallo Dr NE 42
Montevista SW 14
Montford Dr (CHA) 41
Montgomery NE 07
Montgomery SE 17
Montgomery Ferry Dr NE
  1-450 09
  451-OUT 24
Montgomery Ferry Rd NE
  1-450 09
  451-OUT 24
Monticello Way (CP) 37
Montilly Cir & Pl (CP) 49
Montreat Ave SW
  1-1500 10
  1501-OUT 11
Montreat Pl SW 11
Montrose Ave SW 11
Montrose Dr (EP) 44
Montvallo Ter SE 16
Montview Dr NW 05
Monument Ave SE 16
Moody Dr SW 15
Moore SW 18
Moore SE
  1-200 63
  201-OUT 12
Moore Dr (CHA) 41
Moores Mill Rd NW
  1-600 65
  601-1700 27
  1701-OUT 18
Moray SW 11
Morehouse Dr NW 14
Moreland Ave NE
  1-660 07
  661-OUT 06
Moreland Ave SE
  1-2070 16
  2071-2910 15
Moreland Dr SE 15
Moreland Pl SE 16
Moreland Way (HAP) 54
Morgan NE 08
Morgan Pl SE 17

Morgan Rd (DOR) 40
Morgan Falls Rd (DUN) 38
Morley Ave SE 12
Morning Trl (CP) 49
Morning Creek Cir & Dr (CP) .. 49
Morningside Dr NE
  1-850 24
  851-OUT 06
Mornington Dr NW 27
Morosgo Ct, Dr, Pl & Way NE.. 24
Morris (HAP) 54
Morris NE
  1-4000 18
Morris NW, NW
  4001-OUT 42
Morris Ave (EP) 44
Morris Ave NE
  1-4000 18
Morris Ave NE, NE
  4001-OUT 42
Morris Rd NW
  1-4000 18
Morris Rd NW, NW
  4001-OUT 42
Morris Brown Ave NW 14
Morris Brown Dr SW 14
Morris Landers Dr NE 45
Mortimer St & Pl SE 17
Morton Ave SW 15
Mosey Vale Way NW 28
Moss Oak Dr (DOR) 40
Motors Ind Way (DOR) 40
Moughorn NW 14
Mount Airy Dr SW 14
Mount Brian Rd NE 29
Mount Gilead Pl SW 11
Mount Gilead Rd SW
  1-3000 31
  3001-3350 11
  3351-OUT 31
Mount Mariah Pl & Rd NE 29
Mount Paran Pky & Rd NW 27
Mount Paran Rd NE 42
Mount Royal Dr NE 29
Mount Vernon Hwy NE
  1-1000 28
  1001-2380 38
  2381-2900 (EVEN) 40
  2381-2900 (ODD) 40
  2901-OUT 40
Mount Vernon Hwy NW
  1-400 28
  401-OUT 27
Mount Vernon Pky NW 27
Mount Vernon Rd NW
  1-400 28
  401-OUT 27
Mount Zion Rd SE 54
Mount Zion Rd SW
  1-280 54
Mountain Dr & Way NE 29
Mountain Brook Ln & Way
  NW 28
Mountain Creek Rd NE 28
Mountain Creek Trl NW 28
Moury SE 15
Moury Ave SW 14
Morley Dr & Pl SW 44
Mt Olive Rd (EP) 44
Mt Vernon Dr (EP) 44
Mt Vernon Pl & Way (DUN) ... 38
Mt Vernon Way (CP) 37

Atlanta (Con.)   303

Mt Vernon Forest Ct (DUN) 38
Mulberry St & Ct (EP) 44
Mundy Dr (CHA) 41
Mural Dr (CHA) 41
Muriel Ave NE 07
Murphy Ave & Cir SW 10
Murphy Candler Ct NE 19
Murray SE 15
Murray Hill Ave NE 17
Muscogee Ave NW 05
Muse SW 10
Musket Ridge NW 27
Myrtle (HAP) 54
Myrtle NE
   1-870 08
   871-OUT 09
Myrtle Dr SW 11
Myrtle St & Ln (CP) 37
Mystic Dr & Pl NE 42
N Powers Ferry Rd NW 27
N Stratford Rd NE 42
Nabel (EP) 44
Nacoochee Dr NW 05
Nancy Ln NE 45
Nancy Creek Rd NW 27
Nancy Creek Way NE 27
Nancy Creek Bluffs NW 27
Nandina Ln (DUN) 38
Nantahalla Ct NE 29
Napier SE 16
Napoleon (NEWCP) 37
Napoleon (OLDCP) 37
Napoleon Dr SW 14
Narmore Dr NE 19
Narron Ct SW, SW 31
Narron Dr SW, NW 31
Narrow Ave SE 12
Nash Ave SE 16
Nash Rd NW 31
Nassau NW 03
Natham Dr SE 15
Nathan Rd SW 31
Navaho Trl (CP) 49
Navajo Pl & Trl NE 19
Navajo Trl SW 31
Nawench Dr NW 27
Neal NW
   1-860 18
   861-OUT 14
Neal Pl NW 14
Neely Ave (EP) 44
Nehoma NW 18
Helms Ave NE 07
Helms Dr SW 15
Nelson SW
   1-300 03
   301-OUT 13
Neola Ln (CP) 49
Neptune Pl NW 31
Nerene Cir (DUN) 38
Nesbit Dr NE 19
Nesbit Ferry Rd (DOR) 40
Neveis Rd (CP) 49
New (EP) 44
New NE 07
New Hope Rd SW 31
New Jersey Ave NW 14
New London Trace NW 27
New Macon Hwy SE
   1-2910 15

New Paces Ferry Rd NW............ 39
New Peachtree Rd
   1-5715 (CHA) 41
   5716-OUT (DOR) 40
New South Pryor Rd SW 15
New York Ave NE 07
Newborn Dr (CP) 49
Newcastle NW 14
Newman Cir & Pl NW 18
Newnan Ave (EP) 44
Newport NW
   1-430 14
   431-OUT 18
Newport Pl NW 18
Newton Ave NW 14
Newton Ave SE 16
Newton Dr (DOR) 40
Newton Dr SW 31
Niles Ave NW 18
Niskey Lake Cir, Rd & Trl
   SW 31
Noble Dr NE 06
Noel Ave NW 18
Noel Dr NE 19
Noland SE 15
Norcross SW 10
Norfleet Rd NW 05
Norfolk NW 14
Norman Blvd & Dr (CP) 49
Norman Berry Blvd (EP) 44
Normandy Dr NE
   1-2000 06
   2001-OUT 05
Normandy Dr NW
   1-2000 06
   2001-OUT 05
North (EP) 44
North Ave NE
   1-700 08
   701-1070 06
   1071-1462 07
North Ave NW
   1-100 08
   101-400 13
   225-225 32
   401-OUT 18
North Dr SW 31
North St & Ave (HAP) 54
North Akin Dr NE 45
North Amanda Cir NE 29
North Angier Ave NE 08
North Blackland Rd NW 27
North Boundary Pl NW 18
North Broadland Rd NW 42
North Camp Creek Pky SW,
   SW 31
North Circle Dr NW 18
North Cliff Valley Way NE
   1-1500 19
   1501-OUT 29
North Close SW 31
North Colonial Homes Cir
   NW 09
North Decatur Rd NE
   1-1500 06
   1501-2049 07
North Dekalb Dr (DOR) 40
North Druid Hills Rd NE
   1-2000 19
   2001-3050 29
North East Expressway (CHA) . 41
North East Expressway
   Access (CHA) 41

North Ellington SE 17
North Emory Pl NE 06
North Fulton Dr NE 05
North Garden Ln NW 09
North Gatewood Rd NE 29
North Green Dr & Rd NW 28
North Hampton Dr NE 28
North Harbor Ct & Dr NW 28
North Haven Ln (DOR) 40
North Highland Ave NE
   1-610 07
   611-OUT 06
North Hills Dr NE 05
North Holly Ln NE 29
North Howard NE 17
North Island Dr & Ter NW 27
North Island Ferry Rd (DUN) ... 38
North Ivy Rd NE 42
North Kimberly Dr (DOR) 40
North Lake Dr, Trl & Way
   (DOR) 40
North Mill Ct & Rd NW 28
North Muscogee Ave NW 05
North Paces Ferry Rd NW 39
North Peachtree Rd
   1-4825 (CHA) 41
   4826-5050 (DOR) 40
   5051-OUT (DUN) 38
North Peachtree Way (DUN) 38
North Pelham Rd NE 24
North Pharr Ct NW 05
North Piper Cir SE 16
North Ponce De Leon Ave NE .. 07
North Powers Ferry Rd NW 27
North Rhodes Center NW 09
North Ridgeway Rd NE 45
North River Dr (DUN) 38
North Shore Dr SW 11
North Spring Ct NW 28
North Springs Dr (DUN) 38
North Star Trl SW 31
North Stratford Rd NE 42
North Thompson Rd NE 19
North Umberland Dr (DOR) 40
North Virginia Ave NE 06
North Warren NE 17
North Wood Valley Rd NW 27
North Woodland Cir & Dr
   (DOR) 40
North Woods Pl (HAP) 54
Northbrook Ct (DOR) 40
Northbrook Dr
   1-3050 40
   3051-3255 (CHA) 41
   3256-OUT (DUN) 40
Northchester Ct (DUN) 38
Northcliffe Dr NW 18
Northcrest Rd (DOR) 40
Northeast Fwy NE
   1-1900 29
   1901-2850 45
   2851-3500 41
Northeast Fwy, NE
   3501-OUT 40
Northeast Plz NE 29
Northeast Shopping Center
   NE 29
Northern Ave NE 16
Northfield Blvd & Ct (CP) 49
Northland Ct & Dr NE 42
Northridge Dr (DUN) 38
Northrope Dr NE 24
Northside Cir NW 09

Atlanta (Con.)   303

Northside Dr (HAP) 54
Northside Dr NW
  1-340 14
  341-2020 18
  2021-3850 05
  3851-4240 42
  4241-5500 27
  5501-OUT 28
Northside Dr SW
  1-450 13
  451-500 03
  501-600 10
Northside Pky NW 27
Northside 75 NW 18
Northview Ave NE 06
Northway Dr & Ln NE 42
Northwest (HAP) 54
Northwest (CP) 37
Northwest Dr NW
  1-1514 18
  1515-ONLY 31
  1516-1550 18
  1551-OUT 31
Northwood Ave NE & NW 09
Norwalk Rd (CHA) 41
Norwich Cir NE 24
Norwood Ave NE 17
Norwood Rd SE 15
Nottaway Ct (CHA) 41
Nottingham Way NE 09
Nutting NE 08
Oak (EP) 44
Oak (CP) 37
Oak NW 18
Oak SW 10
Oak Dr SE & SW 54
Oak Ln NE 29
Oak Rd (DOR) 40
Oak St & Dr (HAP) 54
Oak Forest Dr (HAP) 54
Oak Forrest Ct & Dr NE 19
Oak Grove Ave SE 16
Oak Grove Rd NE
  1806-OUT 45
Oak Knoll Cir & Ter SE 15
Oak Ridge Ave (HAP) 54
Oak Ridge Ln (EP) 44
Oak Tree Ct (EP) 44
Oak Valley Rd NE 26
Oakawana Dr NE 45
Oakcliff Ct NW 31
Oakcliff Rd (DOR) 40
Oakcliff Rd NW
  1-3200 11
  3201-OUT 31
Oakcliff Ind Ct (DOR) 40
Oakcliff Industrial (DOR) 40
Oakcrest Dr SW 11
Oakdale NW 18
Oakdale Rd (HAP) 54
Oakdale Rd NE 07
Oakfield Dr SE 16
Oakhill Ave SW 10
Oakhill Dr (CP) 37
Oakland Ave SE
  1-650 12
  651-OUT 15
Oakland Dr, Ln & Ter SW 10
Oaklawn Ave NE 19
Oakleigh Dr (EP) 44
Oakley Rd (CP) 49

Oakmont Ave (DOR) 40
Oakmont Dr NW 14
Oakridge Ave NE & SE 17
Oakside Dr SW 31
Oakview Rd NE & SE 17
Oana SW 10
Ocala Ave SW 11
Ocean Valley Dr (CP) 49
Oconee Pass NE 19
Octavia SE 15
Octavia Pl (DOR) 40
Odd Fellows Pl SE 12
Ogden SW 14
Ogilvie Dr NE 24
Oglethorpe Ave (CP) 37
Oglethorpe Ave NE 19
Oglethorpe Ave SW 10
Ohara Pl SE 15
Ohenry SW 15
Ohoopee Dr NE 19
Old Alabama SW 03
Old Bolton Rd NW 27
Old Briarcliff Rd NE 06
Old Cabin Rd NW 28
Old Cambellton Rd SW 31
Old Chamblee Tucker Rd
  (DOR) 40
Old Chattahoochee Ave NW ... 18
Old College Way NE 28
Old Colony (EP) 44
Old Conley Rd SW 54
Old Creek Rd NE 42
Old Creek Trl NW 28
Old Decatur Rd NE 05
Old Dixie Rd (HAP) 54
Old Dominion Dr (DUN) 38
Old Fairburn Rd (CP) 49
Old Fairburn Rd SW
  1-4100 31
  4101-OUT 49
Old Fairburn Close SW 31
Old Farm Rd (CP) 49
Old Field Rd (CP) 49
Old Flat Shoals Rd SE 12
Old Gordon Rd NW
  1-3815 31
  3816-OUT 36
Old Hapeville Rd SW
  1-2700 15
  2701-OUT 54
Old Harbor Dr NW 28
Old Hickory Pt NW 28
Old Highway 41 (HAP) 54
Old House Trl NE 42
Old Ivy Ln & Rd NE 42
Old Johnson Ferry Rd NE 19
Old Jonesboro Rd SW
  1-3073 15
  3074-OUT 54
Old Lawrenceville Rd
  1-2700 (DUN) 38
  2701-OUT (DOR) 40
Old Maine Pl NE 28
Old Marietta Rd NW 18
Old Mcdonough Rd SE 15
Old National Fhwy
  1-4990 (CP) 37
  4991-OUT (CP) 49
Old Orchard Ct (CHA) 41
Old Peachtree Rd (DOR) 40
Old Planatation Rd NW 27
Old Post Rd NW 28
Old Powers Ferry Rd NW 27

Old Pryor SW 03
Old Rough & Ready Rd SE 54
Old Settlement Rd NW 27
Old Spanish Trl (CP) 49
Old Spring House Ct & Ln
  (CHA) 41
Old Village Run (CHA) 41
Old Wheat NE 12
Old Winters Chapel Rd
  (DOR) 40
Old Woodbine Rd NE 19
Old 10th NE 09
Olde Village Ct & Ln (CHA) 41
Oldfield Ct (CP) 49
Oldfield Rd NW 27
Oldknow Dr NW 18
Oleander NW 14
Olive SE 15
Olive SW 10
Oliver NW
  1-560 14
  561-OUT 18
Oliver Dr & Rd SW 31
Ollie St & Cir NW 14
Ollinger Way NE 08
Olympian Cir, Dr & Way SW ... 10
Omaha NW 31
Ontario Ave SW 10
Oostanaula Dr NE 19
Ora Ave SW 31
Orange Dr SW 31
Orange Blossom Trl SE 16
Orchard (HAP) 54
Orchard Ln SE 15
Orchard Rd (CP) 49
Orchard Knob Dr & Rd NW 39
Orchard Lake Rd NW 39
Oriole Dr SW 11
Orkney Ln SW 11
Orlando St & Pl SW 11
Orleans SE 12
Orleans Ct, Dr & Way (CHA) .. 41
Orly Ter (CP) 49
Orme Cir NE 06
Ormewood Ave SE
  1-830 12
  831-OUT 16
Ormewood Ter SE 16
Ormond St SE & SW 15
Orr NW 18
Orr Dr (EP) 44
Ortega Way (CHA) 41
Osborne (EP) 10
Osborne Rd NE 19
Osner Dr NE 42
Ottley Dr NE 24
Overbrook Dr NW 18
Overhill Ct NW 28
Overland Ter SE 17
Overlook Dr SW 44
Overlook Dr & Way NE 45
Overton NW 18
Ovidia Cir SW 11
Owens SW 15
Oxford Ave (CP) 37
Oxford Cres NE 19
Oxford Pl NE 07
Oxford Rd NE
  1-1310 06
  1311-OUT 07
Ozark Trl SW 31
Ozburn Rd NW 18
Ozone NE 14

Atlanta (Con.)   303

Peachtree Battle Cir NW 27
Peachtree Dunwoody Cir NE 42
Peachtree Dunwoody Ct NE 28
Peachtree Dunwoody Rd NE
   1-5850 42
   5851-OUT 28
Peachtree Hills Ave NE 05
Peachtree Ind Blvd
   1-6000 (CHA) 41
   6001-OUT (DOR) 40
Peachtree Ind Ct (CHA) 41
Peachtree Memorial Dr NW 09
Peachtree North Ct (DOR) 40
Peachtree Shopping Center
   NE 29
Peachtree Valley Rd NE &
   NW 09
Peachtree View NE 19
Peachtree Village Plaza NE ... 29
Peachwood Cir NE 45
Pear SE 15
Pearce SW 10
Pearl (EP) 44
Pearl SE 16
Pearl Ln (CHA) 41
Pearl Ln (DOR) 40
Pearl Lane Ct (CHA) 41
Pebble Dr (EP) 44
Pebble Beach Dr (EP) 49
Pecan Dr SW 15
Peeks Rd NW 18
Peeler Rd
   1-2500 (CHA) 41
   2501-OUT (DOR) 40
Peeler Mill Ct & Rd (CHA) 41
Peeples SW 10
Pegg Rd SW 15
Pegg Rd & Ter (EP) 44
Pelham NW 18
Pelham Rd NE 24
Pelot Dr (EP) 44
Pelton Pl NW 18
Pemberton Rd SW 31
Pembroke Pl NE
   1-2000 09
   2001-OUT 24
Pembrook Pl NE
   1-2000 09
   2001-OUT 24
Pendleton SE 16
Pendley (DOR) 40
Penelope St, Dr, Pl & Rd NW .. 14
Penfield Cir (HAP) 54
Penn Ave NE
   1-870 08
   871-OUT 09
Penn Ct SE 15
Pennington Cir SW 54
Pennington Pl SE 16
Pennsylvania (EP) 44
Penny Ln (EP) 44
Penrose Dr (EP) 44
Perdue NW 18
Perimeter Ctr NE, E. 46
Perimeter Ctr NE, W. 46
Perimeter Park S (CHA) 41
Perimeter Parkway (CHA) 41
Perkerson Rd SW
   1-2100 18
   2101-OUT. 15

Perkins (HAP) 54
Perkins Aly NE 12
Perkins Dr (CP) 37
Permalume Pl NW 18
Pernoshall Ct (CHA) 41
Perry Blvd NW 18
Pershing Ave & Pl SE 12
Pete NW 18
Peters SW 13
Peyton Ave & Rd NW 18
Peyton Pl & Rd SW 18
Peyton Woods Trl SW 11
Pharr Ro NE
   1-1000. 05
   1001-OUT 17
Pharr Rd NW 05
Philadelphia Ave SW 11
Philadelphia Pl (EP) 44
Phillips Ave & Ct (EP) 44
Phillips Dr & Pl SE 15
Phillips-Lee Rd SW 36
Phipps Plz NE 26
Phoenix Blvd, Ctr & Pky (CP) . 49
Pickens SE 16
Pickett SE 16
Pickfair Ave SW 15
Piedmont Ave NE
   1-200 83
   201-350. 12
   351-870 08
   871-1500 09
   1501-2680 24
   2681-OUT 05
Piedmont Ave SE 03
Piedmont Cir & Way NE 24
Piedmont Rd NE
   1-200 83
   201-350. 12
   351-870 08
   871-1500 09
   1501-2680 24
   2681-OUT 05
Pierce (CP) 37
Pierce NW 18
Pierce Dr NE
   1-3000 67
   3001-OUT 41
Pierce Rd (CP) 49
Pike Ave NW 14
Pin Oak Cir & Way (DOR) 40
Pine (HAP) 54
Pine NW
   1-100 08
   101-500 13
   501-1500 09
   1501-OUT 18
Pine Ave (EP) 44
Pine Cir NE 05
Pine Dr (CP) 49
Pine Grv Ave NE 19
Pine Grv Dr NW 19
Pine Grv Ter NE 19
Pine Mnr Ct SE 16
Pine St & Pl NE 08
Pine St & Rd (DOR) 40
Pine Trl SE 16
Pine Bark Cir, Clse, Ct & Ln
   (DUN) 38
Pine Branches Clse (DUN) 38
Pine Castle Dr & Way (DUN) ... 38
Pine Cone Dr SW 31
Pine Cone Ln NE 19

Pine Forest Dr SE 54
Pine Forest Rd NE
   1-1000 42
   1001-OUT 45
Pine Forrest Dr NE
   1-1000 42
   1001-OUT 45
Pine Haven Ln NE 42
Pine Knoll Ave NE 31
Pine Lake Dr NW 27
Pine Meadow Rd NW 27
Pine Mill Ln NE 28
Pine Needle Ct, Dr & Ter
   (EP) 44
Pine Oak Dr SW 10
Pine Ridge Dr & Rd NE 24
Pine Tree Cir NE 29
Pine Tree Dr NE
   1-1000 05
   1001-OUT 24
Pine Tree Rd NE
   1-1000 05
   1001-OUT 24
Pine Valley Dr (CP) 37
Pine Valley Ln (EP) 44
Pine Valley Rd NW 05
Pinebrook Rd NE 28
Pinecliff Dr NE 45
Pinecrest Dr (CP) 37
Pinecrest Rd NE 42
Pinedale Dr NW 14
Pinehill Pl NW 42
Pinehurst Dr (EP) 44
Pinehurst Dr (HAP) 54
Pinehurst Dr SW 11
Pinehurst Ter SW 10
Pineland Ave (DOR) 40
Pineland Rd NW 42
Pinella Dr SW 31
Pineside Dr (CP) 49
Pinestream Rd NW 27
Pinevalley Cir & Ct (EP) 44
Pineview Dr (CP) 49
Pineview Ter SW 11
Pineway Dr NE 24
Piney Fork Ln (CP) 49
Piney Wood Dr, Ln & Ter
   (EP) 44
Pioneer Ct (CHA) 41
Piper Cir SE 16
Pitman Rd (CP) 49
Pittman NW 18
Pitts Rd (DUN) 38
Plainville Dr SW 31
Plant (EP) 44
Plantation Dr (EP) 44
Plantation Ln (CHA) 41
Plasamour Dr NE 24
Plaster Ave NE
   1-2200 24
   2201-OUT 05
Plaster Rd NE 45
Plaster Bridge Rd NE
   1-2200 24
   2201-OUT 05
Play Lane NW 14
Plaza Ave SW 10
Plaza Ln SW 11
Plaza Way (CHA) 41
Plaza Way SW 63
Pleasant Hill Rd (CP) 49
Pleasant Valley Rd & Trl
   (DOR) 40

Atlanta (Con.)   303

Pleasantdale Rd (DOR) 40
Plum NW
  1-660 13
  661-OUT 18
Pluma Dr SE 16
Plymouth Ave & Rd NW 18
Plymouth Rd NE 06
Plymstock Ln NW 27
Pointer Ct & Rd (CP) 49
Pointview Dr (EP) 44
Polar Rock Ave, Dr, Pl, Rd &
  Ter SW 15
Pollard Dr (EP) 44
Pollard Dr SW 11
Polo Dr NE 09
Pomona Cir SW 15
Pompey Dr SW 31
Ponce De Leon Ave NE
  1-74 08
  75-75 83
  76-319 08
  320-320 83
  321-550 08
  551-551 83
  552-700 08
  701-788 83
  789-789 83
  790-824 06
  825-825 83
  826-1049 06
  1050-1050 83
  1051-1400 06
  1401-2177 07
Ponce De Leon Cir (DOR) 44
Ponce De Leon Ct NE 08
Ponce De Leon Mnr NE 07
Ponce De Leon Pl & Ter NE 06
Pond NW 14
Ponder Aly SW 03
Ponders Aly NE 08
Ponders Ave NW 18
Ponders Way (EP) 44
Pontiac Cir (DOR) 40
Pontiac Pl SE
  1-1500 16
  1501-OUT 15
Poole Dr & Rd SW 11
Poole Pl SW 10
Poole Creek Rd (HAP) 54
Pope SW 15
Poplar (EP) 44
Poplar NW 03
Poplar Cir NE 07
Poplar Grv Dr NE 06
Poplar St, Dr & Rd (DOR) 40
Poplar Springs Dr NE 19
Poplarcrest Cir SE 15
Porter Dr NW 14
Porter Pl NE 14
Porter Glade Ct (DOR) 40
Portland Ave SE 16
Postell NW 14
Potomac Ave NE 05
Potomac Ct, Dr & Ter (EP) 44
Potomac Way (DUN) 38
Powderhorn Rd NE 12
Powell St & Ct SE 16
Powers Ferry Rd NW
  1-4300 42
  4301-6590 27
  6591-OUT 39

Prado NE 09
Prairie View Dr & Pl SW 11
Prescott NE 08
Prescott Walk NE 07
Presley Way NE 17
Prestwood Ct (DUN) 38
Primrose SE
  1-650 12
  651-OUT 15
Primrose Cir SE 15
Prince George (EP) 44
Princess Ave 3W 10
Princess Cir NE 45
Princeton Ave E & W (CP) 37
Princeton Ave & Dr (CP) 37
Princeton Pl SW 31
Princeton Trce NE 28
Princeton Way NE 07
Pritchard Way NE 26
Proctor (HAP) 54
Proctor NW 14
Produce Pl & Row SW 03
Prospect Ave SE 16
Prospect Pl NE 12
Pryor SW
  1-350 03
  351-660 12
  661-OUT 15
Pryor Rd SW
  1-350 03
  351-660 12
  661-OUT 15
Pryor St & Pl NE 03
Pueblo Dr SW 31
Pullen Ln (CP) 49
Pulham SW
  1-650 12
  651-OUT 15
Putnam Cir NE 42
Putnam Dr NW 42
Pylant NE 06
Pyrenees Ct (DOR) 40
Pyrite Cir SW 31
Quaker SW 15
Queen NW 18
Queen NW 10
Queen Anne Pl NW 18
Queen Elizabeth (EP) 44
Queens Way (CHA) 41
Queensborough Dr NE 28
Queensbury Ln NW 05
Quillian SE 17
Rabun SW 11
Rachael SE 15
Racine SW 14
Radar Dr (HAP) 54
Radar Rd NE 45
Radcliffe Dr NW 18
Ragley Hall Rd NE 19
Railroad Ave NE 26
Rainbow Ridge NW 28
Rainey Ave (HAP) 54
Rainier Falls Dr NE 29
Rains Ct NE 19
Raintree Ct & Dr NE 45
Raintree Ln NW 27
Ralph Rd NE 24
Ramsgate St & Ct NE 05
Ramundo Dr (DOR) 40
Ranchwood Dr NE 45
Randall (EP) 44
Randall Rd NW 39
Randall Farm Rd NW 39

Randall Hall NW 27
Randall Mill Rd NW 27
Randall Ridge Rd NW 27
Randee NW 18
Rando Ln NW 18
Randolph NE 12
Randolph Ct & Rd NE 45
Rangewood Ct & Dr NE 45
Ranier Dr NE 27
Ranier Pl NE 06
Rankin St & Pl NE 08
Ranlo Dr (DOR) 40
Rantin Dr (EP) 44
Raspberry Aly NE 03
Raven Ave NW 18
Raven Hill Dr NE 19
Ravencliff Ln (CP) 49
Ravenwood Dr (CP) 49
Ravenwood Dr & Way NE 29
Rawlins SE 15
Rawson St SE & SW 12
Raymond Dr (DOR) 40
Raymond St NW & SW 14
Read Ln NE 28
Rebecca Dr NE 11
Rebel Trl NW 27
Rebel Forest Dr SE 15
Rector Dr SW 11
Red Oak Dr (DOR) 40
Red Oak Rd (CP) 49
Red Valley Rd NW 05
Redbud Ln NE 11
Redcliff Ct & Way (DUN) 38
Redding Rd & Way NE 15
Redford Dr SE 15
Redland Rd NW 09
Redwine (CP) 37
Redwine Ct & Rd (EP) 44
Redwine Rd (CP) 49
Redwine Rd SW 31
Redwood (DOR) 40
Reed (CP) 37
Reed SE
  1-646 12
  647-OUT 15
Reed Ave (EP) 44
Reeder Cir NE 06
Reeves (CHA) 41
Reeves Cir NW 11
Regalwoods Dr (DOR) 40
Regency Rd NW 27
Regent SE 10
Regina Dr NW 18
Regis Rd SE 15
Reid Ln NW 27
Reindeer Dr NE 29
Reinhardt SE 12
Rembrandt Rd NW 27
Remington (EP) 44
Remington Rd (CHA) 41
Rena Cir SW 11
Renault Ln NE 45
Renault Rd SE 54
Renfrew Ct SW 31
Renfro Dr NW 18
Renfroe St & Aly SE 16
Rennes Ct & Dr NE 19
Reservoir Dr NW 18
Revere Ct (EP) 44
Revere Dr NW 18
Revere Rd SW 31
Reville Cir SW 16
Rex Ave SW 31

Atlanta (Con.) 303

Rey NW	18
Reynolds Ave NW	18
Reynolds Dr SW	
1-1980	31
1981-OUT	15
Reynolds Rd SW	
1-1980	31
1981-OUT	15
Rhinehill Rd SE	15
Rhineland Ct NE	45
Rhodenhaven Dr NW	27
Rhodes (CP)	37
Rhodes NW	
1-470	13
471-OUT	14
Rhodes Ctr NW	09
Rhodesia Ave SE	15
Rhomboid NW	18
Rhondo Rd (HAP)	54
Riada Dr NW	05
Rice NW	18
Richards NW	18
Richardson Rd NW	14
Richardson St SE & SW	12
Richland Rd SW	
1-1500	16
1501-OUT	11
Richmond SE	12
Richmond Ave & Cir SE	15
Richwood Dr NE	19
Rickenbacker Dr NE	42
Rickenbacker Way NE	42
Ridge Ave NW	18
Ridge Ave SE	15
Ridge Mill Ln NE	28
Ridge Tarn (DUN)	38
Ridge Valley Ct & Rd NW	27
Ridgecrest Ct & Rd NE	07
Ridgecrest Ln (EP)	44
Ridgedale Rd NE	17
Ridgeland Way NE	05
Ridgelock Ct (DOR)	40
Ridgemont Rd (DUN)	38
Ridgemore Dr (DOR)	40
Ridgemore Pl & Rd NW	18
Ridgeside Ct (CHA)	41
Ridgeview Rd (DUN)	38
Ridgeview Trl NE	28
Ridgeway Ave NW	18
Ridgeway Dr (DOR)	40
Ridgeway Dr (CP)	37
Ridgewood Ave NE	
1-2320	07
2321-2600	18
2601-OUT	27
Ridgewood Ave NW	
1-2320	07
2321-2600	18
2601-OUT	27
Ridgewood Cir NW	27
Ridgewood Dr NE	
1-2320	07
2321-2600	18
2601-OUT	27
Ridgewood Dr NW	
1-2320	07
2321-2600	18
2601-OUT	27
Ridgewood Ln SW	11
Ridgewood Rd NE	
1-2320	07

2321-2600	18
2601-OUT	27
Ridgewood Rd NW	
1-2320	07
2321-2600	18
2601-OUT	27
Ridgewood Ter NW	18
Rigdon Pl NW	14
Riggs Dr (EP)	44
Rilman Dr & Rd NW	27
Rimell Ln (CP)	49
Ringle Rd (CHA)	41
Ringsmith Rd NE	45
Rio Grande Rd SW	31
Ripplewater Dr SE	16
River Clse (DUN)	38
River Pky E, N & W (DUN)	38
River Court Pky NW	28
River Crest Ct NW	28
River Forest Rd NW	27
River Gate Dr (DUN)	38
River Hill Dr NW	28
River North Cir, Ct, Dr, Pky & Run NW	28
River North Walk NW, NW	28
River Overlook Ct & Dr NW	28
River Park Dr NE	28
River Ridge Dr SE	54
River Ridge Rd (DUN)	38
River Run (DUN)	38
River Shore Ct & Pky NW	28
River Springs Ct, Ln & Rd NW	28
River Valley Rd NW	28
Riverchase Cir & Pt NW	28
Riverchase Ridge NW	28
Rivercliff Dr NW	28
Riverdale Rd	
1-5100 (CP)	37
5101-OUT (CP)	49
Riveredge Dr & Ln NW	28
Riverglen Cir (CHA)	41
Riverglen Trce NW	28
Riverly Rd NW	27
Rivermeade Dr, Ln & Way NW	27
Rivers Rd NW	05
Riverside Dr NW	
1-5900	27
5901-OUT	28
Riverside Dr SW	31
Riverside Pky, Trce & Way NW	28
Riverview Rd NW	27
Riverwood Dr NW	28
Roach SW	14
Roanoke Ave NE	05
Robert NW	18
Roberta Dr NW	27
Roberts (HAP)	54
Roberts Dr SE	
1-1500	15
1501-OUT	38
Roberts Way NE	19
Robin Ln (CP)	49
Robin Ln NE	06
Robin Pl (CP)	37
Robin Hood Rd NE	09
Robinson Ave (HAP)	54
Robinson Ave SE	
1-580	15
581-OUT	12
Robson Pl NE	17

Rochelle Ct & Dr (CHA)	41
Rochelle Dr SW	10
Rochelle Way (CP)	49
Rock NW	14
Rock Hill Dr	49
Rock Hill Rd (CP)	37
Rock Springs Cir, Ct & Ter NE	06
Rock Springs Rd NE	
1-850	24
851-1600	06
1601-OUT	24
Rockbridge Rd (DOR)	40
Rockcliff Pl & Rd SE	24
Rockhaven Cir NE	24
Rockingham Dr NW	27
Rockland Dr SE	16
Rockledge Rd NE	24
Rockmart NW & SW	14
Rockmont Dr NE	24
Rockport Pl SW	31
Rockridge Trl NW	39
Rockwell SW	
1-300	54
301-OUT	10
Rockwood NW	18
Rockwood Rd (EP)	44
Rockyford Rd NE & SE	17
Rodeo Ct SE	16
Rodney Dr SW	11
Rogerette Dr NE	29
Rogers Ave SW	10
Rogers St NE & SE	17
Rolling Brook Trl (EP)	44
Rolling Green Ridge SW	31
Rolling Hill Rd SW	31
Rollingwood Ct, Dr & Ln SE	16
Romain Way (EP)	44
Rome Dr NW	14
Romelie Dr (DOR)	40
Roosevelt (CP)	37
Roosevelt Dr SE	54
Roosevelt Hwy	
1941-3040 (CP)	37
3041-4900 (CP)	49
Rosaire Pl NW	27
Rosalia SE	12
Rosalind Dr NE	29
Rose Cir SW	10
Rose Ter (HAP)	54
Roseclair Dr SE	17
Rosedale Ave SE	12
Rosedale Dr & Rd NE	06
Rosehaven Ter SW	10
Rosemary Ave SW	11
Rosemary Dr NW	18
Rosemont Dr SE	17
Roses Of Picardy (CP)	49
Rosewood Dr NE	06
Ross (CP)	37
Ross SW	
1-1000	15
1001-OUT	54
Ross Dr (EP)	44
Ross Rd (DOR)	40
Rosser SW	14
Roswell SW	31
Roswell Ct NE	05
Roswell Rd NE	
1-3652	05
3653-5750	42
5751-7450	28
7451-OUT	38

Atlanta (Con.)   303

Roswell Rd NW
  1-3652........................... 05
  3653-5750...................... 42
  5751-7450...................... 28
  7451-OUT...................... 38
Rou Royal Ave SW................ 31
Roxboro Cir NE................... 26
Roxboro Dr NE.................... 24
Roxboro Rd NE
  1-3400........................... 24
  3401-OUT...................... 26
Roy SW............................... 10
Royal Ct (CHA).................... 41
Royervista Dr NE................. 42
Rufus Pl (DOR).................... 40
Rugby Ave
  1-1600 (EP)................... 44
  1601-2440 (EP).............. 37
  2441-OUT (EP)............... 44
Rugby Cir, Ln & Ter (CP)...... 37
Rumson Rd & Way NE.......... 05
Runnemede NW.................... 27
Runnymeade Ln (EP)............ 44
Runnymeade Rd NE.............. 19
Rupley Dr NE...................... 06
Rushton NE......................... 07
Russell (HAP)...................... 54
Russell NE.......................... 17
Russian River Dr (CP).......... 49
Rustic Ridge Dr NE.............. 19
Rustlewood Ln (DOR).......... 40
Rutgers Dr SW.................... 31
Ruth NW............................. 18
Rutherford NW.................... 18
Rux Rd SW.......................... 31
Ruzelle Dr SE & SW............ 54
Ryan SW............................. 10
Rycroft Way NW.................. 05
Ryefield Ct & Dr (DUN)........ 38
Ryland Trl SW..................... 31
Ryne NW............................. 18
Saffron Ct, Dr & Way (DUN)... 38
Sagamore Dr NE
  1-2000........................... 45
  2001-OUT...................... 05
Sagamore Dr NW
  1-2000........................... 45
  2001-OUT...................... 05
Sage (DOR).......................... 40
Sage Ln SE.......................... 16
Sahara Dr SE....................... 16
Sahara Dr SW...................... 31
Saint Andrews Ct NE............ 45
Saint Andrews Dr SW........... 31
Saint Augustine Pl NE........... 06
Saint Charles Ave NE
  1-600............................. 08
  601-OUT........................ 06
Saint Charles Pl NE.............. 06
Saint Charles Way NE........... 08
Saint Clair Ct NE................. 19
Saint George Ave NE............ 12
Saint James Dr & Pl NW....... 18
Saint Johns Ave & Cir SW..... 15
Saint Joseph Ave NW........... 18
Saint Louis Pl NE................. 06
Saint Patrick St................... 17
Saint Paul Ave NW............... 18
Saint Paul Ave SE................. 12
Saint Peters Ave NW............ 18
Salmon Ave SE.................... 17

Sam NW............................. 18
Sample Way (EP)................. 44
Sampson NE........................ 12
Seaborn Rd NW................... 18
San Antonio Dr NE.............. 06
San Marino Ct (CP)............. 49
Sancroft Ct (DUN).............. 38
Sandell Ct (DUN)................ 38
Sanders Ave SE................... 16
Sanderson NE...................... 07
Sandgate Rd (CP)................ 49
Sandiewood Ln (CHA).......... 41
Sandpiper Cir SW................ 11
Sandringham Dr SW............. 11
Sandtown Rd SW
  1-1000........................... 31
  1001-OUT...................... 11
Sandy Creek Dr NW
  1-3500........................... 31
  3501-OUT...................... 36
Sandy Creek Rd NW
  1-3500........................... 31
  3501-OUT...................... 36
Sandy Springs Cir, Dr & Pl
  NE................................. 28
Santa Barbara Dr NW........... 18
Santa Fe Trl (DOR).............. 40
Santa Fe Trl SW.................. 31
Santa Lucia Ter NW............. 18
Santa Monica Dr NW............ 18
Santa Rosa Dr SW............... 31
Saramac (HAP).................... 54
Sargent Ave SE.................... 16
Sargent Dr & Pl SE.............. 15
Sarnia Ln SW...................... 31
Saturn Dr NW..................... 31
Saunders NE........................ 17
Savannah SE........................ 16
Savoy Dr (CHA).................. 41
Sawtell Ave SE.................... 15
Saxon (HAP)....................... 19
Saybrook Dr NE.................. 19
Scarborough Rd (CP)........... 49
Scarlett Oak Ct & Dr (DOR).. 40
Scenic Cir & Dr (EP)........... 44
Schell Rd SE....................... 15
Schoen SE........................... 15
School NE........................... 08
School Dr (CHA)................. 41
School Dr
  1-3000 (DOR)................. 40
  3001-OUT (CHA)............ 41
School Dr NW...................... 27
School Dr SE....................... 54
Schooner Cir NW................. 28
Schuyler Ave SE.................. 12
Sciple Ter NW..................... 14
Scofield Rd (CP)................. 49
Scott NW
  1-500............................. 14
  501-OUT........................ 18
Scott SW
  1-100............................. 15
  101-1000........................ 11
  1001-3000...................... 15
  3001-OUT...................... 11
Scott Valley Rd NW............. 28
Scottland Pl NW.................. 18
Scottridge NW..................... 18
Scout (HAP)........................ 54
Screven NE......................... 07
Sea Marsh Ct NW................ 28
Seaboard Ave NE................. 07
Seaboard Ave & Pl NW......... 18

Seaboard Industrial Blvd NW.. 18
Seaborn Pl (CP).................. 49
Seaborn Rd NW................... 18
Seal Pl NE.......................... 08
Seaman Cir & Way (CHA)..... 41
Seaton Dr (DUN)................ 38
Second Ave (CP)................. 37
Selig Dr SW........................ 36
Selkirk Dr NE..................... 28
Sells Ave SW...................... 10
Selman SE........................... 16
Selwin SW........................... 10
Seminole Ave NE................. 07
Semmes (EP)....................... 44
Sentinel Post Rd NW............ 27
Sentinel View NW................ 27
Sentry Hill Trl NE............... 28
Sequoia Dr NE
  1-2840........................... 19
  2841-OUT...................... 27
Sequoia Rd NE
  1-2840........................... 19
  2841-OUT...................... 27
Sequoyah Dr NW
  1-2840........................... 19
  2841-OUT...................... 27
Sequoyah Rd NW
  1-2840........................... 19
  2841-OUT...................... 27
Serpentine Dr NE................ 45
Service Rd (CP)................... 49
Settle Cir SE....................... 16
Seven Oaks Ln (EP)............. 44
Seville Ln (EP).................... 44
Sewanee Ave NE.................. 14
Sewell Rd SW
  1-3400........................... 11
  3401-OUT...................... 31
Sexton Woods Dr (CHA)....... 41
Shadecrest Dr NE................ 19
Shadow Ln NE..................... 19
Shadowlawn Ave E & W........ 05
Shadowlawn Plain NE........... 05
Shadowood Pky NW............. 39
Shadowridge Dr SE.............. 16
Shadromat Way (CHA)......... 41
Shady Oak Ct & Dr (DOR).... 40
Shady Valley Dr NE............. 24
Shadydale Ave SE................ 15
Shalimar Dr NE................... 45
Shallowford Rd N (CHA)....... 41
Shallowford Rd NE
  1-2650........................... 45
  2651-3372...................... 41
  3373-3600 (ODD)........... 40
  3374-3600 (EVEN)......... 41
  3601-OUT...................... 40
Shallowford Ter (CHA)......... 41
Shancey Ln (CP).................. 49
Shannon Dr SW................... 10
Shannon Mill Rd NE............ 19
Shannonlore Dr (CP)........... 49
Shanter Trl SW.................... 11
Sharon NE.......................... 14
Sharon Valley Ct
  1-4625 (CHA)................. 41
  4626-OUT (DOR)............ 40
Sharondale Cir, Ct & Dr NE... 05
Shasta Way NE.................... 45
Shaw SW............................ 15
Shawnee Ln NE................... 19
Sheffield Dr NE................... 29
Sheffield Dr SW................... 11

Atlanta (Con.)   303

Sheffield Pl & Rd (CP) 49
Shelborne Dr (CHA) 41
Shelby Pl SE 16
Sheldon Dr NE 42
Shell Rd SE 15
Shelly Dr SW 11
Shelton Ave SW 10
Shenandoah Ave NE 05
Shenandoah Valley Rd NE 45
Shepherd Cir SW 11
Shepherd Ln NE 24
Sheppard Pl NE 07
Sherbrook Ct & Dr (CP) 49
Sherbrooke Ct & Dr NE 45
Sherbrooke Way SW 31
Sheridan Dr NE 05
Sheridan Rd NE 24
Sheriff Rd (CP) 49
Sherman Rd (HAP) 54
Sherrell Dr NE 42
Sherwood Cir & Dr (CP) 37
Sherwood Rd NE 24
Sheryl Pl NW 09
Shirley NW
   1-1900 18
   1901-OUT 11
Shirley Dr SW 36
Shirley Pl NW 14
Shoppers Ln (CP) 49
Shore Dr SW 11
Shoreham Ct (CP) 37
Shorehain Dr (CP) 49
Shoreland Dr SW 31
Short (EP) 44
Short SE 16
Shorter Ter NW 18
Shoshonee Dr (CP) 49
Shurfine Dr (CP) 37
Sidis Ct (DOR) 40
Silvapine Trl NE 45
Silvastone Dr NE
   1976-OUT 45
Silver Ln NE 28
Silver Lake Dr NE 19
Silver Springs Cir W 18
Silverdale Rd (CP) 49
Silverwood Rd NE 42
Simca SE 54
Simmons NW 18
Simmons Ave (CP) 37
Simmons Cir (DOR) 40
Simon SE 54
Simon Ter NW 18
Simpson NW
   1-100 08
   101-330 13
   331-OUT 14
Simpson Cir NE 19
Simpson Ter NW 18
Sims (HAP) 54
Sims SW 18
Sims Ave NW 18
Sims Cir NE 05
Sims Ct (CP) 37
Sinclair Ave NE 07
Sir Henry (EP) 44
Sirron Dr (DUN) 38
Sisk NW 18
Sisson Ave NW 17
Sizemore Ave NW 18

Skipper Dr, Ln & Pl NW 18
Sky Haven Rd SE 16
Skyland Dr NE
   1-2780 19
   2781-4300 41
   4301-OUT 42
Skyland Plz, Rd, Ter, Trl &
   Way NE 19
Skyland Shopping Center NE 19
Skyline Dr (CP) 37
Skyview Dr SW 31
Slaton Dr NW 05
Sloan (CP) 37
Sloan Ave 18
Sloan Cir SE 16
Sloop Way (CP) 49
Smith NW 18
Smith SE 16
Smith SW
   1-660 12
   661-OUT 18
Smoketree Ct & Rd NE 45
Snow Rd SW 11
Snyder NW 18
Solomon SE 12
Sombrero Way SE 16
Somerled Trl (CP) 49
Somerset Cir & Trl SW 31
Somerset Dr NW 27
Somerset Ter NE 06
Sommers Pl NW 08
Sorrento Cir SW 31
South (HAP) 54
South (CP) 49
South Ave SE 15
South Akin Dr NE 45
South Alvarado Ter SW 11
South Bamby Ln NE 45
South Bend Ave SE 15
South Colonial Homes Cir
   NW 09
South Expressway (HAP) 54
South Gordon SW 10
South Hampton Rd (CP) 49
South Howard SE 17
South Johnson Ferry Rd NE 19
South Olympian Way SW 10
South Peachtree Rd
   1-5715 (CHA) 41
   5716-OUT (DOR) 40
South Perimeter Hwy (CP) 49
South Pharr Ct NW 05
South Piper Cir SE 16
South Prado NW 09
South Pryor Cir SW 15
South Rhodes Center NW 09
South River Industrial Blvd
   SE 15
South Warren SE 17
South Woodland Dr (DOR) 40
Southerland Ter NE 07
Southern NW 18
Southland Cir NW 18
Southland Ct (EP) 44
Southland Vis Ct NE 29
Southwest (HAP) 54
Southwick Ct (CP) 49
Spad Ave NW 18
Spain Dr (EP) 44
Spain Pl NW 18
Spalding Cir, Ct & Ln NE 28
Spalding Dr NE

1-1300 28
1301-3670 38
3671-3900 40
3901-4038 28
4039-4045 40
4046-4050 28
4051-OUT 40
Spanish Oak Dr (DOR) 40
Spanish Tr (EP) 44
Sparks SW 10
Spellman NW 14
Spelman Ln SW 14
Spence Ave NE & SE 17
Spencer NW 14
Spencer Ave (EP) 44
Spinks NW 18
Spinks Aly NW 13
Spinning House Pl NW 14
Spreading Oak Dr SW 11
Spring (HAP) 44
Spring (CHA) 41
Spring (HAP) 54
Spring (CP) 49
Spring NW
   1-282 03
   283-920 08
   921-2000 09
   2001-OUT 18
Spring SW 03
Spring Ave, Cir & Rd NW 18
Spring Dr (DOR) 40
Spring Grv Ave NW 18
Spring Ln Dr NW 14
Spring Garden Dr & Ln SW 15
Spring Green Pl NW 18
Spring Lake Dr NW 05
Spring Lake Rd (CP) 49
Spring Mill Cove (DOR) 40
Spring Mill Ct & Ln NE 19
Spring Valley Blvd, Cir, Ct,
   Pky, Rd & Way (CP) 49
Spring Valley Ln NE 06
Spring Valley Rd NW 18
Spring Valley Trace (CP) 49
Springdale Cir & Pl SW 15
Springdale Cir & Rd (EP) 44
Springdale Dr NE 05
Springdale Rd NE 06
Springdale Rd SW
   1-3000 15
   3001-OUT 54
Springer NW 18
Springfield Ct (CP) 49
Springfield Ct & Dr (DUN) 38
Springhaven (HAP) 54
Springside Dr (CP) 49
Springside Dr SE & SW 54
Springside Pl SE 54
Springside Ter SW 54
Springview Rd NW 14
Spruce NE 07
Spruce Point Rd (CP) 49
Spruill Springs Rd NE 42
Spurgeon Rd (CP) 49
Squire Pl. NE 24
St Francis (EP) 44
St Joseph (EP) 44
St Lo Ln (CP) 49
St Michael (EP) 44
St Tropez Way (DUN) 38
St. Johns Dr (EP) 44
Stacks Rd (CP) 49
Stafford Pl (DOR) 40

Atlanta (Con.)   303

Stafford St NW & SW 14
Stallings Ave SE 16
Stamford Rd SW 31
Stancil Rd (CP) 19
Standard Dr NE 19
Standish Ave NW 09
Stanhope Cir NW 14
Stanley Way SE 16
Stanton Cir & Ct (EP) 44
Stanton Rd SW
   1-1799 11
   1800-OUT 44
Stantondale Dr (CHA) 41
Stanwood Ave SE 17
Star Dr NE 11
Star Mist Dr SW 39
Starcross Ct (DUN) 38
Starfire Dr NE 45
Stark Ln (CHA) 41
Starlight Cir, Ct, Dr & Ln NE . 42
State NW
   1-778 19
   779-OUT 18
Statewood Rd NE 42
Steele Ave SW 15
Steele Dr NW 09
Stella Dr NW 27
Stephanie Dr SW 05
Stephen Long Ave & Dr NE 31
Stephens SW 10
Stephens Dr NE 29
Sterling NE 07
Sterling SE 15
Stetson Pl NW 18
Steve Dr (DOR) 40
Steve Dr SW 15
Stevens NW 18
Stewart Ave SW
   1-1655 10
   1656-3000 15
   3001-OUT 54
Stewart Dr NE 42
Stewart Rd (DOR) 40
Stiff NW 15
Stillman SE 18
Stillwood Dr (HAP) 54
Stillwood NW 06
Stirrup Ln SE 16
Stockbridge Dr SE 16
Stokes Ave SW 10
Stokeswood Ave SE 18
Stoland Dr NE 19
Stone Rd SW
   1-3150 44
   3151-OUT 31
Stone Hogan Rd Connector
   SW 31
Stone Mill Trl NE 28
Stone Mountain Rd (CHA) 41
Stonecrest Ct (CHA) 41
Stonegate Ct, Dr, Trl & Way
   (DOR) 40
Stoneham Ct (CP) 49
Stonehill Dr SW 36
Stonehurst Pl NW 11
Stoneview Ter (EP) 44
Stonewall SW
   1-500 13
   501-OUT 14
Stonewall Dr SE 15
Stonewall Tell Rd (CP) 49

Stonewall Tell Rd SW 31
Stonington Cir & Rd (CHA) 41
Stonington Dr NW 28
Stonybrook Dr SE 16
Stovall SE 19
Stovall Blvd NE
   1-900 42
   901-OUT 19
Stovall Ter NE 42
Strait (DOR) 40
Strasburg Ct (CHA) 41
Stratfield Cir & Dr NE 19
Stratford Dr NW 11
Stratford Rd NE 19
Stratford Arms Dr (CHA) 41
Stratham Dr (DUN) 38
Strathmore Dr NE 24
Street De Ville NE 45
Strong NW 18
Stubbs Rd (CP) 49
Sturbridge Way (CP) 49
Suber Rd SW 31
Sudbury Ct E & W (DOR) 40
Sudbury Rd
   1-1000 (DOR) 28
Sudbury Rd NE
   1-1000 28
   1001-OUT (DOR) 40
   1001-OUT (DOR) 40
Sugar Creek Pl SE 16
Sugarplum Ct & Rd (CP) 49
Sulene Dr (CP) 49
Sullivan Rd
   1-1015 (CP) 49
   1016-OUT (CP) 37
Sumac Dr (DOR) 40
Sumlin Ave NW 18
Summerford Ct & Dr (DUN) 38
Summit NE 42
Summit Ave NW 18
Summitridge Dr (DOR) 40
Sumter NW 18
Sun Valley Blvd (EP) 44
Sunbury Pl NE 45
Suncrest Ln NE 18
Sunderland Cir, Ct & Way
   NE 19
Sundown Dr NE 45
Sunland Dr NW 18
Sunny Hill Dr SE 16
Sunnybrook Dr (DUN) 38
Sunnybrook Ln & Pl NE 28
Sunridge Ave SE 15
Sunrise Ct & Trl (CP) 49
Sunrise Dr NE 45
Sunset Ave NW
   1-410 14
   411-OUT 18
Sunset Dr (HAP) 54
Sunset Dr NE 45
Sunset Dr SW 31
Sunset Ln (CP) 44
Sunset Ridge NE 19
Sunshine Dr SW 54
Surrey Cir & Ln (CHA) 41
Surrey Ln (CP) 37
Surrey Trl (CP) 49
Surry County Pl NW 18
Susaleen Ct NE 45
Susan Ln (DOR) 40
Susan Ln SW 31
Sussex Rd NE 06
Susy Griffin Rd SE 54

Sutton SE 17
Suzanne Way (CP) 37
Swallow Cir SE 15
Swann Dr SE 15
Swansea Ct (CP) 49
Swathmore Dr NW 27
Sweat Rd NW 18
Swims Valley Dr NW 27
Sydney SE 12
Sylvan Cir NE 19
Sylvan Cir, Pl & Way SW 10
Sylvan Rd SW
   1-2100 18
   2101-3000 44
   3001-OUT 54
Sylvan Ter (EP) 44
Sylvan Ramble Rd NE 45
Sylvan Ridge Dr SW 10
Sylvester Cir SE 16
Symphony Ln NW 18
Tacoma Dr NW 18
Taft Ave NE 09
Taft St & Pl SW 15
Tahoe Dr (CP) 49
Taliaferro NW 14
Talisman Ct NE 45
Tall Oaks Dr NE 42
Tall Pines Ct & Dr NW 27
Tall Tree Dr NE 24
Talley Dr (CHA) 41
Tallulah NE 18
Tallulah Dr NE 19
Tally Ho Dr SE 16
Tamassee Ct (DOR) 40
Tamerlane NW 27
Tampa Trl SW 31
Tamworth Dr NE 28
Tanacrest Cir, Ct & Dr NW 28
Tanbark Ct NE 19
Tanglewood Cir NE 45
Tanglewood Ct & Trl NW 27
Tanglewood Dr NW 39
Tanglewood Trl (EP) 44
Tanner SE 12
Tanner Rd (CP) 37
Tara Cir SE 54
Tara Trl NW 27
Tartan Ln SW 31
Tarver Ter (CP) 49
Tate Rd (CP) 49
Tatnall SW
   1-470 13
   471-OUT 14
Taylor NW 18
Taylor Ave (EP) 44
Tazor NW 14
Teal Rd (CHA) 41
Techwood Dr NW
   1-100 83
   101-900 13
   901-OUT 18
Tee Ln NE 11
Tejas Trl SW 31
Telfair Ln SW 11
Telford Pl NE 19
Telhurst SW 10
Tell Rd SW 31
Temple NW 14
Temple Ave (CP) 37
Templewood Dr NE 19
Tennelle SE 12
Tennessee Ave SW 15
Tennyson Dr NW 18

Atlanta (Con.)　303

Terian Pl (EP).... 44
Terminal NW.... 13
Terrace Ave NE.... 87
Terrace Dr NE.... 05
Terrace Way SE.... 15
Terrell NW.... 18
Terrell Dr (CHA).... 41
Terrell Mill Rd (CP).... 49
Terry SE
　1-650.... 12
　651-OUT.... 15
Terry Mill Rd SE.... 16
Teton Ave SE.... 12
Teton Dr NW.... 39
Thackery Pl NW.... 11
Thames Rd (CP).... 49
Thaxton Dr & Pl SE.... 15
Thaxton Rd SW
　1-4000.... 31
　4001-OUT.... 49
Thayer Ave SE.... 15
The Ascent NE.... 19
The Byway NE.... 06
The Cottage (CHA).... 41
The Falls Ct NE.... 87
The Fountainebleau SW.... 31
The Meadow's Way (CP).... 49
The Prado NE.... 09
The Savoy (CP).... 49
The 16th Fairway (DUN).... 38
The 5th Green (DUN).... 38
Thirkield Ave SE & SW.... 18
Thomas Rd NW.... 18
Thomasville Ct & Dr SE.... 15
Thompson Ave (EP).... 44
Thompson Dr NW.... 31
Thompson Rd (CP).... 49
Thompson Rd NE.... 19
Thoms Dr NW.... 18
Thorn Briar Dr (DOR).... 40
Thornberry Ln SW.... 31
Thornburg Way (CP).... 49
Thorncliff Dr NE.... 45
Thorne Ave SW.... 18
Thornhill Ct (DUN).... 38
Thornhill Ln NE.... 28
Thornridge Dr & Way (DOR).... 40
Thornton Dr (CP).... 49
Thornton St & Pl SW.... 15
Thornwell Dr NE.... 45
Thornwood Dr (DOR).... 40
Thornwood Dr NE.... 18
Thurgood SW.... 14
Thurman Rd (CP).... 49
Thurmond NW
　1-300.... 13
　301-OUT.... 14
Tichnor Ct (DUN).... 38
Tift St & Ave SW.... 15
Tiger Flowers Cir & Dr NW.... 14
Tilden NW.... 18
Tilly Mill Rd (DOR).... 40
Tilson Dr SE.... 17
Tilton Ln (DOR).... 40
Timber Ln Ter NE.... 28
Timber Trl NE.... 42
Timber Oak Dr (DOR).... 40
Timber Valley Rd NE.... 42
Timberland Dr NE
　1-1000.... 42
　1001-OUT.... 45

Timberland Rd NE
　1-1000.... 42
　1001-OUT.... 45
Timms Cir SE.... 16
Timms Valley Rd NE.... 05
Timothy Dr NE.... 29
Timothy Dr SW.... 11
Tobey Rd (CHA).... 41
Tocoma Trl (CP).... 49
Todd SE.... 12
Todd Rd NE.... 06
Toll House Ln SW.... 31
Tolleson Ct (DUN).... 38
Tonawanda Dr SE.... 15
Toni Pl SE.... 15
Topaz Ln SW.... 31
Torrence NW.... 14
Towanda Cir & Dr (CP).... 49
Tower Hill Rd NW.... 18
Towerview Dr NE.... 24
Town Country Dr NE.... 16
Townly Cir & Ct (DOR).... 40
Toxaway Ct (CHA).... 41
Trabert NW
　1-600.... 09
　601-OUT.... 18
Trabert Ave NW
　1-600.... 09
　601-OUT.... 18
Trafalgar Way (CHA).... 41
Trafalger Ct NW.... 27
Trail Ridge Ln (DUN).... 38
Trammell Dr (HAP).... 54
Trapnall Ct & Dr (DUN).... 38
Travis NW.... 18
Treadwell Cir SW.... 31
Tree Haven Dr NE.... 42
Tremont Dr NW.... 14
Trenholm SW.... 13
Trenton SE.... 16
Trentwood Pl NE.... 14
Tribble Dr NW.... 18
Tribble Ln NW.... 11
Trilby SE.... 16
Trimble Rd NE.... 42
Trinity Ave SW
　1-70.... 34
　71-OUT.... 03
Tripple Creek Ct NE.... 19
Tristan Cir & Way NE.... 45
Triumph Cir SE.... 54
Trotti NE.... 17
Troup SW.... 14
Trowbridge Dr (DUN).... 38
Troy NW.... 14
Troy SE.... 15
Truitt SW.... 10
Trumbull Ct & Dr (DUN).... 38
Trusco Way SW.... 10
Tryon Pl & Rd NE.... 19
Tuckawanna Dr SW.... 11
Tucker St, Ave & Pl SW.... 10
Tucson Trl SW.... 31
Tudor SE.... 15
Tugaloo Dr NE.... 19
Tula NW.... 09
Tulane Dr SW.... 36,
Tully Cir & Rd NE.... 29
Tumlin NW.... 18
Tupelo SE.... 17
Turman Ave SE.... 15
Turner (CP).... 49
Turner (EP).... 44

Turner Dr (DOR).... 40
Turner Rd SE.... 15
Turpin Ave SE.... 12
Tuskegee SE
　1-1000.... 15
　1001-OUT.... 54
Tuskegee Ave SE
　1-1000.... 15
　1001-OUT.... 54
Tuxedo Ave NE.... 07
Tuxedo Pky NW.... 05
Tuxedo Rd NW
　1-3830.... 05
Tuxedo Rd NW, NW
　3831-OUT.... 42
Tuxedo Ter NW.... 42
Twiggs SW.... 15
Twilley Dr NW.... 18
Twin Branch Ct, Ln & Rd NE.... 28
Twin Branches Way (DUN).... 38
Twin Branches Close (DUN).... 38
Twin Brooks Rd NE.... 19
Twin Springs Rd NW.... 27
Tycoon Sq (CHA).... 41.
Tye SE.... 15
Tyewood Ln (EP).... 44
Tyler NW.... 14
Tyndall Ct (DUN).... 38
Tynecastle Dr & Way (DUN).... 38
Umberland Dr (DOR).... 40
Underground Atlanta SW.... 03
Underwood Ave SE.... 16
Underwood Dr NW.... 18
Union Ave (HAP).... 54
Union Rd SW
　1-3500.... 31
　3501-OUT.... 49
University Ave SW
　1-270.... 15
　271-OUT.... 10
University Dr NE.... 06
University Pl NW.... 14
University Plz SE.... 03
Upshaw NW.... 18
Upton Rd NW.... 15
Utoy Cir & Ct SW.... 31
Utoy Springs Rd SW.... 31
Valante Ter (EP).... 44
Valcouri Sq NW.... 05
Valeland Ave SW.... 31
Valiant Dr NE.... 05
Valley Cir & Rd NW.... 05
Valley Dr (EP).... 44
Valley Ln NE.... 28
Valley Trl Dr NW.... 39
Valley Bend Dr (CP).... 49
Valley Bluff Dr (DOR).... 40
Valley Brook Dr NE.... 42
Valley Creek Dr NW.... 39
Valley Green Dr NE.... 42
Valley Hall Dr (DUN).... 38
Valley Heart Dr NW.... 18
Valley Lake Rd & Ter (CP).... 49
Valley Ridge Dr & Ter SW.... 31
Valley Stream Dr (DOR).... 40
Valley Tarn (DUN).... 38
Valley View Ct & Rd (DUN).... 38
Valley View Dr (EP).... 44
Valley View Rd NE.... 15
Valleydale Dr SW.... 11
Vallo Vis Ct NE.... 42
Valmar Dr (DOR).... 40
Valvedere Dr NE.... 19

Atlanta (Con.)   303

Van Buren SW 10
Van Epps Ave SE 16
Van Fleet Cir (DOR) 40
Van Heusen Blvd NW 18
Van Vleck Ave SE 16
Vance SW 14
Vance Ave NE 06
Vance Dr (EP) 44
Vance Dr NE 45
Vanderbilt Ct & Ln NW 18
Vanderlyn Dr (DUN) 38
Vandiver Rd SW
    1-4000 10
    4001-OUT 31
Vanet Rd (CHA) 41
Vanetta Pl NW 18
Vanira SE 15
Vannoy SE 15
Vanse Dr (EP) 44
Varner Dr NE 45
Vassar SW 15
Vassar Ave (CP) 37
Vaud Ave NE 07
Vaughn SE 17
Vedado Way NE 08
Velma SE 11
Veitre Cir & Pl SW 11
Venable NW 13
Venetian Dr SW 11
Venice Dr SE 17
Venus Pl NW 31
Vera SE 16
Verbena NW 14
Verdon Ct & Dr (DUN) 38
Verdun Dr NW 05
Verlaine Pl NW 27
Vermack Rd (DUN) 38
Vermont Rd NE 18
Verner NW 18
Vernon N (DUN) 38
Vernon Ave SE 16
Vernon Pl NE 12
Vernon Rd NW 05
Vernon Lake Dr (DUN) 38
Vernon Oaks Dr (DUN) 38
Vernon Ridge Ct & Dr (DUN) 38
Vernon Springs Ct, Dr & Trl
    NW 27
Vernon Springs Dr (DUN) 38
Vernon Way Ct (DUN) 38
Vernon Woods Dr NE 28
Vesta Ave (CP) 37
Vesta Ave NW 14
Vesta Ave & Ter (EP) 44
Veterans (EP) 44
Vicar Rd (DOR) 40
Vickers SE 16
Vickers Dr NE 07
Vicki Ln SE 16
Victor Cir NW 14
Victor Rd NE 24
Victoria (CP) 37
Victoria NE 19
Victoria NW 14
Victoria Dr (EP) 44
Victoria (HAP) 54
Victoria St N & S (CP) 37
Victoria Falls Dr NE 29
Victory Cir (DOR) 40
Victory Dr SW 10
Vienah Ln NE 07

Villa Cir (HAP) 54
Villa Dr NE 06
Villa Esta Dr (CHA) 41
Village Dr SW 31
Village Creek Ct & Dr (CHA) 41
Village Green Dr (CP) 49
Village Mill Ct & Rd (CHA) 41
Villanova Dr SW 36
Ville SE 15
Vine NW
    1-416 18
    417-OUT 14
Vine SW 14
Vinson Dr SE 15
Vinson Pl SW 15
Vintage Ln (CHA) 41
Violet Ave NW 18
Violet Ave SE 15
Violet Ave SW 10
Virgil NE 07
Virginia Ave (DOR) 40
Virginia Ave (CP) 37
Virginia Ave (EP) 44
Virginia Ave & Cir NE 06
Virginia Ave & Pl (HAP) 54
Virginia Pl NE 05
Vista Sq NW 27
Vista Trl NE 24
Vista Valley Dr NE 29
Vivian Ln NE 05
Volberg NW 18
Wabash Ave NE 12
Waddell NE 07
Waddeston Way NE 19
Wade NE 07
Wade Ave NE 17
Wadley NW 14
Wadley Ave (EP) 44
Wadsworth Dr NW 18
Weinwright Dr SE 41
Waits Ave SW 31
Wake Robin Trl (CHA) 41
Wakefield Dr NE & NW 09
Walden SE 12
Waldo SE 18
Wales Ave NW 18
Waleska Way (EP) 44
Walker (HAP) 54
Walker SE 13
Walker Ave (EP) 44
Walker Ave (CP) 37
Walker Ave SE 16
Walker Rd (CP) 49
Walker Ter NE 09
Walker View Ct SE 16
Wall St E & W 03
Wall Plain SW 03
Wallace Ave & Rd SW 31
Wallace Cir NW 39
Wallace Dr (CHA) 41
Wallace Dr SW 54
Walnut (HAP) 54
Walnut NW
    1-400 14
    401-OUT 18
Walnut SW 14
Walnut Hill Pl NW 18
Walthall NE 07
Walthall SE
    1-50 17
    51-OUT 16
Walthall Ct & Dr SE 18
Waltham Pl SE 16

Walton NW 03
Walton Ln SE 17
Wanda Cir SW 15
Wandawood Rd (DOR) 40
Ward Dr SE & SW 54
Ward St & Cir (EP) 44
Ware Ave (EP) 44
Warfield NW 18
Warfield Ct (CP) 49
Warlick Pl NE 17
Warner SW 10
Warren Ct & Rd NW 18
Warren Pl SE 03
Warren St NE & SE 17
Warren Way (EP) 44
Warrenhall Ln NE 19
Warrington Pl (CP) 49
Warwick SE 16
Warwick Cir NE 45
Wascanna Rd (HAP) 54
Washington (CP) 37
Washington NW 18
Washington SW
    1-230 03
    231-270 34
    271-300 03
    301-650 12
    651-OUT 15
Washington Ave
    900-4485 (EP) 44
    4486-OUT (CP) 49
Washington Cir (EP) 44
Washington Hts Ter NW 14
Washington Pl SW 14
Washington Rd
    900-4485 (EP) 44
    4486-OUT (CP) 49
Washita Ave NE 07
Water Front Dr & Rd SW 36
Water Oak Way (DOR) 40
Waterbury Dr NW 14
Waterford Rd NW 18
Waters Dr SW 10
Waters Rd SW 54
Waterton Ct (DUN) 38
Watkins Pl NE 19
Watkins St & Dr NW 18
Watson NE 07
Watson Cir SE 17
Watson Dr (DOR) 40
Watts Rd NW 18
Waverly Way NE 07
Wawona Dr & Ter NE 19
Wayland Cir NE 19
Wayne Ave NE 06
Wayne Pl SW 10
Wayside Dr NE 19
Weatherby SE 16
Weatherly Dr & Ln NE 28
Weaver Way (DOR) 40
Webster SW 14
Wedgeway (DUN) 38
Wedgewood Dr NW 18
Wee Kirk Rd SE 16
Weems Dr (CP) 49
Weigelia Rd NE 45
Welborn Ct (CP) 49
Welch SW 15
Welch SW 10
Welcome All Rd SW
    1-3850 31
    3851-OUT 49
Welcome All Ter (CP) 49
Weldon Pl NE 12

Atlanta (Con.)   303

Weldstone Ct & Ter NE	28
Welland Ave SE	16
Wellborn SW	10
Wellbourne Dr NE	24
Wellesley Dr NW	05
Wellington SW	
1-280	14
281-OUT	10
Wellona Pl NE	45
Wells Dr	
1-620	12
621-OUT	10
Wells Ave (CP)	37
Wells Ct SW	12
Wells Dr SW	11
Wellswood Dr SE	15
Wendell Dr NW & SW	36
Wendell Dr SE	15
Wendland Dr NE	45
Wendover Dr NE	19
Wenlock Ave NW	18
Wentworth Dr NE	45
Wesco Way NW	18
Wesley Ave NE	07
Wesley Dr NW	05
Wesley Pky NW	27
Wesley Oaks Rd NW	28
Wesleyan Dr SW	36
Wessyngton Rd NE	06
West Ave NE	14
West Ave SW	15
West Mnr Cir SW	11
West Mnr Ln SW	11
West Rd NE	24
West Anderson Ave SW	14
West Andrews Dr NW	05
West Anthony NW	18
West Ashland Ave NE	07
West Belle Isle Rd NE	42
West Brookhaven Dr NE	19
West Candler Lake Ct NE	19
West Caribea Trl SE	16
West Cedar Ln SW	11
West Chester Blvd NW	14
West Club Dr & Ln NE	19
West Conway Dr NW	
1-1250	27
1551-OUT	27
West Conway Rd NW	
1-1250	27
1551-OUT	27
West Druid Hills Dr NE	29
West Echo NW	18
West End Ave & Pl SW	10
West Fontainbleau Ct & Dr (DOR)	48
West Garmon Rd NW	27
West Handy Dr NW	18
West Kildare Ave NW	18
West Kimberly Rd SW	31
West Kingston Ct & Dr NE	42
West Lake Ave NW	
1-300	14
301-OUT	18
West Lake Ave SW	14
West Lake Ct & Dr NW	14
West Lane Dr NW	18
West LeeOs Mill Rd (CP)	49
West Lindmont Ct NE	24
West Main NW	18
West Marietta NW	18

West Moreland Cir NW	18
West Muscogee Ave NW	05
West Nancy Creek Ct NE	19
West Nancy Creek Dr NE	
1-1750	19
1751-OUT	41
West Northbrook Ct (DOR)	40
West Ontario Ave SW	10
West Paces Ferry Rd NW	
1-600	05
601-OUT	27
West Peachtree NW	
1-816	08
817-817	83
818-870	08
871-OUT	09
West Peachtree Pl NW	
1-100	08
101-OUT	13
West Pine Valley Rd NW	05
West Point Ave & Rd (CP)	37
West Roxboro Rd NE	24
West Simon Ter NW	18
West Sussex Rd NE	06
West Wesley Rd NW	
1-600	05
601-OUT	27
West Whitehall SW	10
West Wieuca Rd NE & NW	42
Westboro Dr SW	10
Westchester Dr (EP)	44
Westerhall Ct NE	28
Western Ave NW	14
Westfalia Ct NE	42
Westfield Ct NE	42
Westfield Trl (CP)	49
Westford Cir & Ct (CP)	49
Westhaven Dr SW	11
Westhill Cir (CP)	49
Westland Blvd NW	11
Westmart Ln (DOR)	40
Westmeath Dr NW	18
Westminster Cir NW	27
Westminster Dr NE	
1-500	09
501-OUT	24
Westminster Way NE	07
Westmont Dr (DOR)	40
Westmont Rd SW	11
Westmoor Dr NW	14
Westover Dr (EP)	44
Westover Dr NW	05
Westover Plantation Rd NW	18
Westridge Rd SW	11
Westshire Pl NW	18
Westview Dr SW	10
Westview Pl SW	14
Westwood Ave (EP)	44
Westwood Ave SW	18
Westwood Dr (DOR)	40
Wetzel Dr SW	11
Wexford Dr & Rd (CP)	49
Weyman Ave SW	15
Weyman Ct NW	27
Wharton Dr SW	36
Whatley SE	15
Wheaton Dr SW	36
Wheeler (HAP)	54
Wheeler NW	18
Wheeler Dr (DOR)	40
Wheeler Dr SW	10
Whipple Ave (HAP)	54
Whipple Ave (EP)	44

Whispering Ln, Trl & Way NE	28
Whispering Hills Ct & Dr (CHA)	41
Whisperwood Trl (EP)	44
Whitaker NW	18
Whitaker Cir NW	14
Whitam Dr (DUN)	38
Whitby Dr (DOR)	40
White (CP)	37
White NW	18
White SW	10
White City Rd (CP)	37
White Oak Ave NW	18
White Oak Ave SW	18
White Oak Hollow NE	24
White Water Creek Rd NW	27
Whiteford Ave NE	07
Whiteford Ave SE	17
Whitehall SW	
1-620	03
621-OUT	10
Whitehall Ter SW	
1-430	03
431-OUT	12
Whitehouse Dr SW	10
Whiteleigh Ct & Dr NE	45
Whites Aly & Pl SW	10
Whiteway (EP)	44
Whitewood Ct (DUN)	38
Whitfield Dr (DUN)	38
Whiting NW	18
Whitmore Dr NW	05
Whitner Dr NW	27
Whitney Ave (HAP)	54
Whittier Ave NW	18
Whittington Ct & Dr NE	42
Whitworth Dr SW	31
Wichita Dr SW	11
Wickcliff Ct (CHA)	41
Wickersham Dr (CP)	37
Wickersham Dr NW	27
Wickford Way (DUN)	38
Wieuca Rd & Ter NE	42
Wilbur Ave SE	16
Wilcox SW	15
Wild Creek Trl NE	24
Wilder Ct (DUN)	38
Wildwood Pl NE	
1-930	24
931-1800	06
1801-OUT	24
Wildwood Rd NE	
1-930	24
931-1800	06
1801 OUT	24
Wildwood Lake Dr SW	31
Wilford Dr NE	19
Wilkerson Dr SE	17
Wilkes Cir NW	18
Will Lee Pl & Rd (CP)	49
Will Rogers Pl SE	16
Will Ross Ct (CHA)	41
Willard Ave SW	10
Williams NW	
1-284	03
285-500	08
501-700	13
701-900	08
901-OUT	09
Williams Ave (EP)	44
Williams Pl NW	18
Williams Mill Rd NE	06
Williamsburg Dr (CP)	37

Atlanta (Con.)　　　　303

Willingham Dr
　1-1565 (EP)............ 44
　1566-OUT (CP)........ 37
Willis NW.................. 14
Willis Mill Rd SW........ 11
Willoughby Way NE...... 12
Willow NW................. 08
Willow Ave NE............ 05
Willow Pl SE.............. 16
Willow Trl SW............ 11
Willow Bend Dr NE...... 28
Willow Cove Dr SW...... 31
Willow Creek Dr NE...... 28
Willow Heights Dr NE.... 28
Willow Lake Dr NE....... 29
Willow Oak Way (DOR)... 40
Willowbrook Dr NE....... 11
Willowdale Cir SE........ 16
Willowwood Cir SE....... 17
Willowwood Ct NE........ 45
Wilmer NE................. 08
Wilmington SW........... 10
Wilmont Dr NE............ 29
Wilmont Ln SW............ 10
Wilson Ave NW
　1-100................... 10
　101-OUT............... 14
Wilson Dr SW............. 11
Wilson Rd (CP)........... 49
Wilson Rd NW
　1-3000.................. 18
　3001-OUT.............. 54
Wilson Rd SE
　1-3000.................. 18
　3001-OUT.............. 54
Wilson James Rd SW..... 31
Wilson Mill Rd SW........ 31
Wilton Ave (DOR)......... 40
Wimberly Rd NE.......... 19
Wimbledon Rd NE........ 24
Winall Down Rd NE....... 19
Winburn Dr & Ter (EP)... 44
Winchester Trl (CHA)..... 41
Windemere Dr NE......... 24
Windhaven Trl SW, SW.... 31
Winding Ln NE............ 19
Winding Branch Cir, Ct, Dr &
　Ln (DUN)............... 38
Winding Creek Ct & Trl NW. 28
Winding Ridge Ct (DUN).. 38
Winding River Dr (DUN).. 38
Windsor SW
　1-660................... 12
　661-760................ 10
　761-870................ 15
　871-OUT............... 10
Windsor Dr SW........... 11
Windsor Pky NE
　1-250................... 19
　251-1000.............. 42
　1001-OUT.............. 19
Windsor Forest Dr (CHA). 41
Windsor Oak Dr (DOR).... 40
Windwood Ct, Dr & Ln (DOR). 40
Windy Ridge Dr NE....... 42
Windy Rush Dr (EP)....... 44
Winfield Ave SE
　1-1500.................. 16
　1501-OUT.............. 17
Winfred Ter (EP).......... 44
Wing (DUN)............... 38

Wingate SW............... 18
Wingate Dr & Rd (CHA)... 41
Wingedfoot Dr (DUN)..... 38
Winslow Dr NE............ 05
Winstead Ct (CP)......... 49
Winter Ave NE............ 17
Winter Crest Ct (DOR)... 40
Winters Chapel Rd (DOR). 40
Winterthur Dr & Ln NW.. 28
Winterthur Ridge NW..... 28
Winthrop Dr SE........... 16
Winthrop Rd (CP)......... 37
Winton Ter NE............ 08
Wise Way NE.............. 19
Wisteria Ln SW........... 31
Wisteria Way (EP)........ 44
Wisteria Way NE.......... 17
Withers Pl SW............ 15
Withrow St & Dr (DOR) ... 40
Wolfe Ave NE............. 26
Wolf Creek Cir & Dr SW... 31
Womack Ave (EP)......... 44
Womack Ct & Dr (DOR)... 40
Womack Rd
　1-2800 (DUN)......... 38
　2801-OUT (DOR)...... 40
Wood St & Ave NW....... 18
Wood Acres Rd NE....... 45
Wood Hollow Dr (DOR)... 40
Wood Valley Ct NE....... 19
Wood Valley Dr NE....... 27
Wood Valley Rd NW...... 27
Woodall Way (DOR)....... 40
Woodall Ferry (DOR)...... 40
Woodberry St & Dr SW.... 11
Woodbine Ave NE & SE... 17
Woodbine Cir SE.......... 17
Woodbine Ter NE......... 29
Woodbourne Dr SW....... 31
Woodbury Ave (EP)....... 44
Woodbury St & Dr SW.... 11
Woodcastle Ln SE........ 16
Woodcliffe Dr NE......... 28
Woodcliffe Ter NE........ 24
Woodcrest Ave NE & NW. 09
Wooddale Dr NE.......... 26
Woodgreen Dr (CHA)..... 41
Woodham Way SE........ 16
Woodhaven Cir (EP)...... 44
Woodhaven Dr NE........ 24
Woodhaven Rd NW....... 05
Woodhill Cir & Ln (EP).... 44
Woodlake Dr NE.......... 29
Woodland Ave (CP)....... 49
Woodland Ave NE......... 24
Woodland Ave SE
　1-1650.................. 16
　1651-OUT.............. 15
Woodland Cir (EP)........ 44
Woodland Cir SE.......... 16
Woodland Ct & Way (DOR). 40
Woodland Dr (HAP)....... 54
Woodland Park Dr NE..... 45
Woodland Ter SW......... 11
Woodland Brook Dr NW... 39
Woodland Hills Ave NW... 18
Woodland Hills Dr NE.... 24
Woodlawn Ave NW....... 18
Woodley Dr NW........... 18
Woodlynne Way (DOR).... 40
Woodmere Dr NW......... 18
Woodmere Sq NW........ 27
Woodmont Ln NW......... 18
Woodrow NW............. 18

Woodrow SW.............. 10
Woodrow Ave (HAP)...... 54
Woodrow Way NE......... 19
Woods Cir NE............. 24
Woods Dr NE
　1-1500.................. 18
　1501-OUT.............. 19
Woods Dr NW
　1-1500.................. 18
　1501-OUT.............. 19
Woods Rd NE
　1-1500.................. 18
　1501-OUT.............. 19
Woods Rd NW
　1-1500.................. 18
　1501-OUT.............. 19
Woods St & Ave NW...... 18
Woodsdale Rd NE......... 24
Woodsey Way SE.......... 15
Woodside Way (CHA)..... 41
Woodson SE............... 15
Woodsong Ct, Dr & Trl (DUN). 38
Woodstock Dr SW......... 31
Woodstock Rd SE......... 16
Woodstream Cir NE...... 19
Woodvale Dr NW......... 27
Woodvalley Dr (EP)....... 44
Woodward Ave SE........ 12
Woodward Dr (CP)........ 49
Woodward Way NW
　1-600................... 05
　601-800................ 27
　801-OUT............... 05
Woodwardia Rd NE....... 45
Woodwin Ct & Rd (DOR).. 40
Woody Trl NE............. 19
Worchester Dr NE........ 06
Worth Dr NW............. 27
Wortham Ave NW......... 11
Wrenwood Dr & Pl NE.... 07
Wright NE
　1-1000.................. 26
　1001-OUT.............. 24
Wright Ave NE
　1-1000.................. 26
　1001-OUT.............. 24
Wright Cir & Rd NE....... 28
Wright Dr SW............. 11
Wyatt (HAP).............. 54
Wycherly Ct NE.......... 19
Wycliff Rd NW............ 09
Wycombe Rd NE.......... 28
Wye Ln (CHA)............ 41
Wyland Dr SW............ 10
Wylie SE
　1-1195.................. 16
　1196-OUT.............. 17
Wyman St NE & SE....... 17
Wyncourtney Dr & Ln NE. 28
Wyndale Ct (CHA)........ 41
Wyndham Dr NW......... 28
Wyngate NW.............. 05
Wynhill Dr NE............ 28
Wynnton Dr NE........... 19
Wynwood Dr NE.......... 19
Xavier Dr SW............. 36
Yale Ave (CP)............ 37
Yale Pl SW............... 15
Yarmouth Ct (DUN)...... 38
Yates Dr NW............. 18
Yates Rd (CP)............ 37
Yonah Dr NE............. 09
Yonge St NE & SE........ 12

Atlanta (Con.)   303

Yonkers Ave NW	14
York Ave SW	10
York Rd (CP)	37
Yorkshire Rd NE	06
Young SE	16
Young Dr (CP)	37
Young Dr (EP)	44
Young Rd (CHA)	41
Yukon Ct SE	16
Zachery SW	10
Zane Grey Dr SE	16
Zelda Dr NE	45
Zimmer Dr NE	06
Zip Industrial Blvd SE	54
Zone Ave SW	31
Zonolite Pl & Rd NE	06

NUMBERED STREETS

1st NE	
1-1000	14
1001-1500	18
1501-2400	07
2401-2500	18
1st NW	
1-1000	14
1001-1500	18
1501-2400	07
2401-2500	18
1st SW	
1-1000	14
1001-1500	18
1501-2400	07
2401-2500	18
1st Ave (CP)	37
1st Ave NE & SE	17
1st Ave NW	18
1st Ave SW	15
1st thru 6th St (EP)	44
2nd Ave (DOR)	40
2nd Ave NE & SE	17
2nd St & Ave NW	18
3rd (DOR)	40
3rd NW	
1-6	18
7-100	08
101-400	13
401-OUT	18
3rd Ave NE & SE	17
3rd St & Ave SW	15
3rd thru 6th St NE	08
4th NW	
1-100	08
101-300	13
301-1000	32
1001-OUT	18
4th Ave NE & SE	17
4th thru 5th St SW	15
4th thru 6th St (CHA)	41

5th (HAP)	54
5th (DOR)	40
5th NW	
1-100	08
101-200	13
201-OUT	18
5th Ave NE	17
6th NW	
1-200	13
201-OUT	18
7th NW	
1-49	08
50-50	23
51-OUT	08
7th thru 8th St SW	15
7th thru 9th St NW	18
8th (EP)	44
8th NW	
1-450	09
451-OUT	08
8th thru 9th St (CHA)	41
9th thru 12th St NE	09
10th NW	
1-150	09
151-OUT	18
11th NW	
1-300	09
301-OUT	18
12th NW	09
13th St NE & NW	09
14th NW	
1-130	09
131-OUT	18
14th St & Pl NE	09
15th NW	18
15th thru 17th St NE	09
16th NW	
1-100	09
101-OUT	18
18th NW	09
25th thru 26th St NW	09
28th NW	09

AUGUSTA   309

POST OFFICE BOXES

Box Nos.		
1-1999	Main Office	03
2701-3999	The Hill Sta	04
4001-4999	Martinez Br	07
5001-5999	Peach Orchard Br	06
7001-7999	Fort Gordon Br	05

RURAL ROUTES

1	06
2	04
3	08
4,5	07
6	06

STATIONS, BRANCHES AND UNITS

Fort Gordon Br	05
Martinez Br	07
Peach Orchard Br	06
The Hill Sta	04
Veterans Hospital Sta	04
General Delivery	03
Postmaster	01

APARTMENTS, HOTELS, MOTELS

Alamo Plaza, Gordon Hwy	01
Augusta Homes, 100 Telfair Extension	01
Aumond Villa, W Lake Forrest Dr	04
Bon Air, Walton Way	04
Broadway, 335 Broad	01
Calcutta 1011 River Ridge Rd	04
Charlestowne South, 2119 Lumpkin Rd	06
Colonial Court, 2549 Walton Way	04
Continental Airport, Bush Field	06
Country Club, Milledge Rd	04
East Gate, Gwinnett	01
Fairway Village, 2910 Richmond Hill Rd	06
Forest Hills, 2801 Walton Way	04
Gateway, 110 3rd	01
George Walton, 2068 Walton Way	04
Georgetown Court, Walton Way	04

Augusta (Con.)   309

Georgian Arms, 2440 Damascus Rd	04
Gilbert Manor, 1300 Railroad Ave	01
Golf Park, 156 Damascus Rd	04
Heritage, Wrightsboro & Jackson Rd	04
Hickman Arms, Hickman Rd	04
Holiday Inn, 1602 Gordon Hwy	06
Hornes Motor Lodge, 1520 Gordon Hwy	06
Howard Johnson Motor Lodge, 1238 Gordon Hwy	01
James, Po Sq	02
Keystone, 1927 Central Ave	04
Magnolia Villa, Walton Way	04
Mcdonald, Wrightsboro Rd & Baker	04
Medical Terrace, 1105 15 Th St	01
Miles, 2077 Old Savannah Rd	01
Monte Sano, 801 Monte Sano Ave	04
Peachtree Gardens, Wrightsboro Rd	04
Pine Hill, Henry	04
Ramada Inn 1365 Gordon Highway	01
Richmond 744 Broad	02
Royal Palms, 2904 Peach Orchard Rd	06
Town Towers, 444 Broad St	02
University, 1410 Gwinnett	02
Valley Park, 3100 Wrightsboro Rd	04
Warrick, 441 Broad	02
Waverly Villa, 500 Norwich Rd	04
Williamsburg South	04

BUILDINGS

Augusta Aviation	04
Augusta Medical Park, 1021 15 Th St	01
Bush Field	06
Campbell, 102 8th	02
Commerce, 666 Broad St	02
Daniel Village, Wrightsboro Rd	04
First Federal, 958 Broad	02
First National, 801 Broad St	02
Georgia Railroad Bank, 699 Broad St	02
Johnson, 208 8th	02
Marion, 739 Broad	02
Medical Arts, 1467 Harper St	02
Mid South, 360 Bay St	01
National Hills, 2701 Washington Rd	04
News, 725 Broad	02
Peach Orchard Plz	06
Seaboard Coast Line, 120 Gwinnett	01
Southern Finance, 753 Broad	02
Southgate Plaza, Gordon Hwy	06

The 500, 501 Greene St	02
Union Savings Bank, 142 8th	02

GOVERNMENT OFFICES

City-County Municipal, 530 Greene St	02

HOSPITALS

Andress Nursing Home, 2121 Scott Rd	06
Bayvale Rest Home, 3212 Milledgeville Rd	04
Beverly Manor 1600 Anthony Rd	04
Blair Nursing Home, 2541 Milledgeville Rd	04
Georgia War Veterans Nursing Home, 1101 15th	01
Leisure Homes, 3235 Deans Bridge Rd	04
Maroni Convalescent Home, 409 Pleasant Home Rd	07
Medical College Of Georgia, 1459 Gwinnett St	01
Medicenter, 1355 Nelson	01
Myers Rest Home, 2622 Milledgeville Rd	04
Saint Josephs Hospital, 1600 Winter	04
Talmadge Memorial Hospital, 1120 15th	02
University Hospital, University Pl	02
Vetrans Administration Hospital, Forest Hills	04
Virginias Convalescent Home, 717 Bohler Ave	04

UNIVERSITIES AND COLLEGES

Augusta College, 2500 Walton Way	04
Medical College Of Georgia, 1459 Gwinnett St	02
Paine College, 1235 15th	01

COLUMBUS   319

POST OFFICE BOXES

Box Nos.		
1-2872	Main Office	02
1400-2386	Fort Benning Br	05
3000-3277	Baker Village Sta	03
4000-4246	Beallwood Sta	04
5000-5399	Wynnton Sta	06
6001-6592	Lindsey Creek	07

RURAL ROUTES

1	04
2	07

STATIONS, BRANCHES AND UNITS

Baker Village Sta	03
Beallwood Sta	04
Bibb City Br	04
College Heights Sta	07
Custer Terrace Br	05
Edgewood Sta	07
Fort Benning Br	05
Lindsey Creek Sta	07
Oakland Park Sta	03
Rose Hill Sta	04
Rosemont Sta	04
Windsor Park Br	01
Wynnton Sta	06
General Delivery	02
Postmaster	02

APARTMENTS, HOTELS, MOTELS

Baker Village	03
Baker Village Annex	03
Booker T Washington	04
Buena Vista Estates	06
Camelia Motel Apts	03
Cardinal Hotel	01
Central Court	01
Chase	04
Cherokee	06
Coronado	03
Cusseta Place	03
Delmar	06
Diane	06
Eliz F Canty	03
Elliot	03
Gateway	03
Glendale Arms	01
Grady	04
Haralson	04
Highland Court	06
Hilton Arms	03
Hieges Road Apartments	06
Impalla Apartments	04
Ladelle	06
Lincoln Court	04
Luther C Wilson	04
Manor Arms	01
Mirada	01
Peabody	04
Pine Terrace	03
Prince	01
Ralston	02
Rankin	02
Stripling Terrace	03
Victory	03
Warren Williams	06
Waverly	01

BUILDINGS

Biggers	01
Bush	01
Columbus Bank & Trust Company	01
Commerce	01
Edge	04
Empire	01
First National Bank	01
Flowers	01
Fourth National Bank	01
Hill	04
Interstate	01

Columbus (Con.) 319

Martin............................ 61
Professional...................... 01
Swift Kyle....................... 01
416............................. 01

HOSPITALS

Martin Army Hospital, Ft
Benning.......................... 05
Medical Center, 710 Center
St............................... 02
Saint Francis, Expressway....... 04

UNIVERSITIES AND COLLEGES

Columbus College, Algonquin
Dr............................... 07
Meadows Business College........ 02
Phillips College................. 02

DECATUR 300

POST OFFICE BOXES

Box Nos.
A-H   South Decatur... 32
1-1875   Main Office..... 31
32001-32499 South Decatur... 32
33001-33299 North Decatur... 33

RURAL ROUTES

1,2.............................. 34

STATIONS, BRANCHES AND UNITS

Agnes Scott College Sta.......... 30
Belvedere Plaza Br............... 30
Dunaire Br....................... 32
North Decatur Br................. 33
North Druid Hills Br............. 33
South Decatur Br................. 32
South De Kalb Br................. 34
Vista Grove Br................... 33
General Delivery................. 30
Postmaster....................... 30

APARTMENTS, HOTELS, MOTELS

Adair Oaks, 222 Adair Ct........ 30
Alexandria Fairington Pky....... 34
Alpine, 2571 Candler Rd......... 30
Ambridge Arms, 1031 Scott
Blvd............................. 30
Belvedere Medical Center,
3300 Memorial Dr................ 32
Belvedere Motel, 3480
Memorial Dr..................... 32
Belvedere Park, 1593 1/2
1592 Line Cir................... 32
Belvedere Park, 1642 1/2
1584 Line....................... 32
Brittany, 3320 Covington Dr..... 32
Camellia Ct, 4082 1/2 4108
Glenwood Rd..................... 32
Candler East, 2423 & 2425
Candler Rd...................... 32
Candler Hotel, 150 E. Ponce
De León......................... 30

Casa Rio, 3850 Memorial Dr...... 32
Catalina, 4371 Glenwood Rd...... 32
Cedar Brook Village, Cedar
Brook Dr........................ 33
Cedar Creek Village Cedar
Creek Pky....................... 33
Charter Square, Town
Houses, I-24 Charter
Square.......................... 30
Chateau-Belvedere, 1668
Welika Dr....................... 32
Christian Towers, 1438
Church.......................... 30
Cindy Ct 4120 Glenwood Rd....... 32
Columbia Heights, 1221
Forest Blvd..................... 30
Country Estates, 2505
Columbia Dr..................... 34
Crescent Court, 1021 Scott
Blvd............................. 30
Decatur Inn, 921 Church......... 30
Decatur Townhouses 317
Adair St........................ 30
Dekalb Towers 02, 1501
Clairmont Road.................. 33
Dekalb Towers, Farnell Ct...... 33
Dekalb-Cambridge, 3661 N.
Decatur Rd...................... 33
Eagle 212 Adair St.............. 30
East Lake, 746 East Lake Dr..... 30
Eastwyck Village, Candler
Rd.............................. 32
Emory Gardens, 1111
Clairmont Ave................... 30
Emory Woods, North Decatur
Rd.............................. 33
Fairington, Fairington Ct, Dr,
Pky............................. 34
Fontain, Rue Fontaine........... 34
Four Forty 1/2 nine, 449
Clairmont Ave................... 30
Gateway Manor, 421 W.
Trinity Pl...................... 30
Glen Hollow, Glen Hollow Cir.... 34
Glen Hollow, Glen Hollow Dr..... 34
Glen Hollow, Glen Hollow Ln..... 34
Glen Point, Highcourt Pl........ 32
Glenshire Townhouses, Glen
Acres Ct........................ 32
Glenwood Springs, 3481 1/2
3513 Glenwood Rd................ 32
Gray Manor, 2825-2853
Belvedere Ln.................... 32
Green Acres, 3937 Glenwood
Rd.............................. 32
Gresham Park, 2520 - 2548
Flat Shoals Rd.................. 32
Grovenor House, 2517
Columbia Dr..................... 34
Habitat, Habitat Cir............ 34
Habitat, Habitat Ct............. 34
Habitat, Habitat Pl............. 34
Habitat, Habitat Way............ 34
Harbour Oaks, 2503
Lawrenceville Hwy............... 33
Heart Of Decatur Motel, 245
E Trinity Pl.................... 30
Hearthstone, Ember Dr........... 34
Hillcrest, 351 Hillcrest St..... 30
Hillyer Square, Hillyer Sq...... 34
Kandy Court, 3975 Covington
Hwy............................. 32

Kenco-Decatur, 1175 & 1225
Church St....................... 30
Kenco-Memorial, 3754 - 3766
Memorial Dr..................... 32
Lin-Del, 1575 Line St........... 32
Medical Surgical Plaza, 365
Winn Way........................ 30
Medlock Pines, 773 1/2 813
Scottdale Rd.................... 33
Midway Manor, 3626 Midway
Rd.............................. 32
Misty Waters Misty Waters
Dr.............................. 32
Montclair, 1272 - 1378
Clairmont Rd.................... 33
Montville, 1760 Clairmont
Rd.............................. 33
Mountain Trace, 3360
Mountain Dr..................... 30
North Decatur Gardens, 1384
Lawrenceville Hwy............... 33
North Decatur Manor, 3757 -
3805 North Decatur Rd........... 33
North Decatur Office Center,
3796 N Decatur Rd............... 33
North Dekalb, 2326 1/2 2340
Lawrenceville Hwy............... 33
Old South Gardens, 135 East
Hill St......................... 30
One West Court Square, W
Court Sq........................ 30
Phillips Towers, 218 E Trinity
Pl.............................. 30
Pinewood, Treeview Ct........... 34
Pinewood, Treeview Dr........... 34
Pinewood, Treeview Ln........... 34
Plantation Oaks, 1043
Holcomb Rd...................... 32
President Park, 1231
Clairmont Ave................... 30
Province-East, 3800 Flat
Shoals Rd....................... 34
Rainbow Forest, Rainbow
Forest Cir...................... 34
Robin Hood Villa, 2427
Lawrenceville Hwy............... 33
Rodeway Inn, 1706 Clairmont
Rd.............................. 33
Scott Pines, 927 Scott Blvd..... 30
Scott-Landover, 1020 Scott
Blvd............................ 30
Sharwell, 1111 1/2 1219 &
1301 1/2 1321 Oakview
Rd.............................. 30
Snapfingerwoods, Snapfinger
Woods Dr........................ 32
Spanish Trace, 2929
Panthersville Rd................ 34
Susan Court, 3961 Covington
Hwy............................. 32
Sycamore Square, Town
Houses, I-26 Sycamore
Sq.............................. 30
Tower Gardens, 4015
Covington Hwy................... 32
Tregoney, Tregoney Dr........... 34
Twin Oaks, Twin Oaks Dr......... 30
University, Williams Ln.,
Shoupe Ct., & O'Neal Pl......... 33
Venetian Club, 510 Coventry
Rn.............................. 30

Decatur (Con.) 300

Villa, 2812 - 2870 Villa Cir	30
Wellington Wellington Ct	34
Westchester Square, Westchester Sq	30
Whispering Pines, 2784 1/2 2800 Kelly Lake Rd	32
Williamsburg Medical Center, Mcconnell Dr	32
Williamsburg, Blackshear & North Jamestown	33
Willowick, Willowick Ct	34
Willowick, Willowick Dr	34
Winston Manor, 2420 Candler Rd	32
Woodlake, Clubhouse, Gatehouse, Whitepine	32

BUILDINGS

Court House, Court Sq	30
Decatur Federal, 250 E Ponce De Leon	30
Decatur Professional North, 755 Columbia	30
Dekalb Administration, 556 N Mcdonough	30
Dekalb County Federal, 116 Clairmont Ave	30
Dekalb Professional, 2754 N Decatur Rd	33
Dekalb, 430 N Mc Donough	30
Executive Square, 4277-79 Memorial Dr	32
Executive, 125 Trinity Pl	30
Federal, 141 Trinity Pl	30
First National Bank, 315 W Ponce De Leon	30
Hooper, 525 Marshall	30
Law, 103 Beaumont Pl	30
Masonic Temple, 108 E Ponce De Leon	30
Professional, 235 E Ponce De Leon	30
Trinity, 118 Trinity Pl	30
Trust, 545 N Mc Donough	30
Watkins, 112 E Ponce De Leon	30
Weeks, 140 Sycamore	30

HOSPITALS

Dekalb General, 2701 N Decatur Rd	33
Georgia Regional Hospital, 3073 Panthersville Rd	34
V A, 1660 & 1670 Clairmont Rd	33

UNIVERSITIES AND COLLEGES

Agnes Scott, E College Ave	30
Columbia Seminary, 701 Columbia	30

MACON 312

POST OFFICE BOXES

Box Nos.		
A-U	Mulberry Street Sta	02
1-999	Mulberry Street Sta	02
1-1539	University Sta	07
101-942	Wesleyan Sta	01
2001-2999	Pio Nono Sta	03
3001-3999	South Macon Sta	05
4001-6999	Macon	08
7001-7354	Riverside Sta	04

RURAL ROUTES

1,2	04
3	06
4,5,6	02
7,8	06
9	01
10	06

STATIONS, BRANCHES AND UNITS

Bloomfield Sta	06
Cross Keys Sta	01
Mulberry Street Sta	01
Pionono Sta	03
Riverside Sta	04
South Macon Sta	05
Shurlington Sta	01
University Sta	07
Wesleyan Sta	01
Westgate Sta	06
Wilson Airport Rural Br	01
General Delivery	01
Postmaster	01

APARTMENTS, HOTELS, MOTELS

Alpine Lodge, 1900 Riverside Dr	02
Ambassador Motel, 2772 Riverside Dr	04
Azalea Motel, 5797 Houston Rd	06
Belmont, 625 Walnut	01
Biltmore, 811 Poplar	01
Bowden Homes, 2250 Cedar	06
Brooks, 165 5th	01
Brookwood, 3111 Brookwood Dr	04
Brown House Motor, 589 Broadway	01
Buckingham Court, 111 Buckingham Pl	04
Capitol, 580 Plum	01
Central, 310 Broadway	02
College Hill, 464 College	01
Colonial, 544 Orange	01
Courtesy Court Incorporated, 2240 Gray Hwy	01
Dempsey Motor, 387 3rd	02
Douglas, 373 Broadway	01
Drills Motel, 1232 Jeffersonville Rd	01
Ellisonian, 478 College	01
Felton Homes, 2035 Felton Ave	01
Fireproof Courts, 4168 Broadway	06

Franklin, 1131 Broadway	01
Fredonia, 1007 Bond	01
Georgian Terrace, 1061 Georgia Ave	01
Georgian, 683 Mulberry	02
Georgian, 819 Poplar	01
Gilman, Smith, 2281 Vineville Ave	04
Glenwood Terrace, Ricemill Road	06
Grace, 233 Corbin Ave	01
Grady, 301 Cherry	02
Heart Of Georgia, 561 Broadway	01
Heritage Motel, 2690 Riverside Dr	04
Holiday Inn Of America, 1044 Riverside Dr	08
Inglewood, 2484 Ingleside Ave	04
J & J, 1112 Broadway	01
J Clay Murphy Homes, 2499 B Street	06
Jacksons Motor Court, 4670 Houston Rd	06
Katherine Court, 855 Mulberry	01
Knox, 333 Cherry	02
Lafayette, 233 College	01
Lake Terrace Apartments	04
Lake Terrace Court	04
Laurine, 635 Orange	01
Leonard Court, 575 Virgin	01
Macon Homes, 2850 Cherry Ave	04
Macon Motor Court, 4057 Houston Ave	06
Macon Plaza Motel, 759 Orange Ter	01
Macon, 389 Mulberry	01
Magnolia Court & Grill, 4739 Houston Rd	06
Married Students & Faculty Apartments, Stadium Dr	01
Massee, 347 College	01
Middle Street, 425 Middle	01
Miller, 601 3rd	01
Monroe, 633 Monroe	01
Nevarro, 551 Orange	01
New Street Apartments, 363 New	01
Normandy, 2416 Vineville Ave	04
North Garden, 833 North Ave	01
North Napier Apartment, Napier Ave	04
Oglethorpe Homes, 1130 Oglethorpe	01
Old South, 1034 Georgia Ave	01
Palisades, 643 Orange	01
Park, 506 Poplar	01
Peach State Motel, 5417 Houston Rd	06
Pendleton Homes, 3401 Houston Ave	06
Pinebrook Inn & Courts, 4420 Forsyth Rd	04
Plaza, 518 Mulberry	01
Pursley, 455 Pursley	01
Rembert, 1605 Rembert Ave	01
Riverdale, 1080 Nottingham Dr	01

Macon (Con.) 312

Rushin, 397 College 01
Siesels, 619 College 01
Simmons, 578 College 01
Skyline Grill & Court, Clinton
Rd 01
South Winds Motel, 3010
Riggins Mill Rd 01
Terrace, 876 Mulberry 01
Tindall Heights Homes, 985
Plant 01
Town House Apartments,
Rogers Ave 04
Town Pavilion, 205
Broadway 01
Twin Pine, 1585 Hawthorne
Rd 01
Vineville Court, 1975
Vineville Ave 01
Vineville Gardens, 2020
Vineville Ave 04
Walnut, 931 Walnut 01
Welchs Lounge, 361
Mulberry 01
Williamson Terrace,
Williamson Road 06
Winship Gardens, 2140
Ingleside Ave 04

BUILDINGS

Chandler, 154 Broadway 01
Cochran Field 01
Colonnade, 1073 Georgia
Ave 01
Federal, 475 Mulberry 01
First National Bank, 425
2nd 01
Georgia Power, 595 Mulberry .. 01
Hardeman, 305 Cotton Ave 01
Hart, 348 Cotton Ave 01
Mc Cowen Plaza, 2110
Ingleside Ave 04
One Sixty Five First 01
One Sixty Two First 01
Persons, 544 Mulberry 01
Robert E Lee, 830 Mulberry 01
Schwartz, 653 2nd 01
Seven Forty Hemlock 01
Southern Trust, 682 Cherry 01
Southern United, 407 Cherry .. 01
United States Post Office,
451 College 01
Walker & Meadows, 828
Riverside Dr 01
Walton, 591 Cotton Ave 01
Washington Block, 590
Mulberry 01
Westgate Shopping Center,
2525 Pio Nono Ave 06

GOVERNMENT OFFICES

Bibb County Courthouse, 275
2nd 01
City Hall, 718 Poplar 01
Macon Municipal Airport 01
United States Federal
Building & Courthouse,
475 Mulberry 01
United States Federal, 451
College 01

HOSPITALS

Coliseum Hospital, 350
Hospital Dr 01
College Street Hospital 685
College 01
Doctors, 700 Spring 01
Macon Hospital, 777
Hemlock 08
Medical Center Office, 724
Hemlock 01
Middle Georgia Hospital, 746
Spring 01
Parkview Private Hospital,
1429 Oglethorpe 01
Physicians & Surgeons, 729
Pine 01
Riverside Clinic, 577 Walnut .. 01
Saint Luke Hospital, 853
Tatnall 08

UNIVERSITIES AND COLLEGES

Business Training Institute,
Box 144 02
Crandall Business College,
555 Mulberry 01
G A B School Of Commerce,
556 First 01
Georgia Beauty Academy,
524 Mulberry 01
Macon Junior College, 5357 06
Macon University Of
Cosmetology, 1248
Oglethorpe 01
Mercer University, 1400
Coleman Ave 07
Wesleyan College, 4760
Forsyth Rd 01

SAVANNAH 314

POST OFFICE BOXES

Box Nos.
1-399   Thunderbolt Br. 04
1-2792   Main Office 02
3000-3499   A Sta 03
3500-3999   B Sta 04
4000-4999   Port Wentworth
Br. 07
5001-5194   C Sta 03
6000-6999   C Sta 05
7000-7399   Garden City Br. 08
8001-10999 Wright Square
Sta. 02
13001-13607 Oglethorpe Br. 06
20001-20840 Savannah
State College 04

RURAL ROUTES

1 01
2 08
3 06
4 05
5 01
6,7 04
8 05

STATIONS, BRANCHES AND UNITS

Bacon Park Sta 06
Garden City Br 08
Hi Way Eighty Br 08
Hunter Army Airfield Br 09
Isle Of Hope Br 06
Ogeechee Road Br 05
Oglethorpe Br 06
Port Wentworth Br 07
State College Br 04
Thunderbolt Br 04
Wilmington Island Rural Br 04
Windsor Forest Br 06
Wright Square Sta 02
General Delivery 02
Postmaster 01

APARTMENTS, HOTELS, MOTELS

Alamo Plaza, 1600 W Bay 01
Chatham City, 4309 Augusta
Rd 08
Chatham, 609 Abercorn 01
Chelsea, 11-B Chelsea Dr 04
Clark Terrace, Cedar Ave &
Metts Dr 04
Continental Inn, 412 W. Bay .. 01
Court, 1712 Abercorn 01
De Renne, 24 E Liberty 01
Desoto, 15 E Liberty 01
Drayton Arms, 102 E Liberty .. 01
Forsyth, 106 W Gwinnett 01
Fort Wayne, 36 E Broad 01
Franklin, 1800 E 38th 04
Graham, 210 E State 01
Heart Of Savannah, 300 W
Bay 01
Holiday Inn, 121 W Boundary .. 01
John Wesley, 29 Abercorn 01
Lamara, De Renne Ave &
Habershm 05
Nelson, De Renne Ave &
Reynolds 05
Savannah Club, 1800 E
38th 04
Savannah Inn & Country
Club 612, Wilmington
Island Rd 04

BUILDINGS

A C L, 601 E Liberty 01
American Bldg, 7 Drayton St .. 01
Arcade, 105 E Bay 01
Board Of Education, 208
Bull 01
Central Of Georgia, 233 W
Broad 01
Citizens And Southern Bank
Bldg, 300, Bull St 01
Georgia State Bank, 136
Bull 01
Industrial Bank, 35 Bull 01
Liberty National Bank, 41
Bull 01
Morel, 5 Bull 01
Realty, 24 Drayton 01
Savannah Bank, 2 E Bryan 01
Western Union, 15 Drayton 01

Savannah (Con.)   314

Saint Josephs 11705 Mercy
 Blvd 06
United States Public Health
 Service, 115 E York 01

GOVERNMENT OFFICES

Chatham County Court, 130
 Bull 01
U S Post Office Bldg 01
United States Custom, 1 E
 Bay 01

Candler General, 601
 Abercorn 01
Candler-Central, 3025 Bull 05
Candler, 17 E Park Ave 01
Georgia Infirmary, 1900
 Abercorn 01
Georgia Regional Hospital
 1915 Eisenhower Drive 06
Memorial Medical Center,
 4700 Waters Ave 04

UNIVERSITIES AND COLLEGES

Armstrong State College,
 11935 Abercorn 06
Savannah State College,
 Georgia 04

State List of Post Offices

HAWAII
(Abbreviation: HI)

Aiea (1st) 96701
Aina Haina, Sta. Honolulu
 (see appendix)
Airport, Sta. Honolulu 96820
Ala Moana, Sta. Honolulu 96814
Anahola 96703
C C H, Sta. Laie 96762
Captain Cook 96704
Chinatown, Sta. Honolulu 96817
Eleele 96705
Ewa, Sta. Ewa Beach 96706
Ewa Beach (1st) 96706
Ford Island, Sta. Honolulu 96818
Fort Shafter, Sta. Honolulu 96823
Haiku 96708
Haina 96709
Hakalau 96710
Halaula, Br. Kapaau 96711
Haleiwa 96712
Haliimaile, Br. Makawao 96787
Hana 96713
Hanalei 96714
Hanamaulu 96715
Hanapepe 96716
Hauula 96717
Hawaii National Park 96718
Hawaiian Village, Sta.
 Honolulu 96813
Hawi 96719
Hickam A F B, Sta.
 Honolulu 96824
Hilo (1st) 96720
Holualoa 96725
Honaunau 96726
Honokaa 96727
HONOLULU (1st) (see
 appendix)
Honomu 96728
Hoolehua 96729
Kaaawa 96730
Kahuku 96731
Kahului (1st) 96732

Kailua (1st) 96734
Kailua Kona (1st) 96740
Kaimuki, Sta. Honolulu 96816
Kalaheo 96741
Kalaupapa 96742
Kalihi, Sta. Honolulu 96817
Kamuela (1st) 96743
Kaneohe (1st) 96744
Kaneohe M C A S, Br.
 Kailua 96734
Kapaa 96746
Kapaau 96755
Kaumakani 96747
Kaunakakai 96748
Kawaihae, R. Sta. Kamuela 96743
Keaau 96749
Kealakekua 96750
Kealia 96751
Kekaha 96752
Kihei 96753
Kilauea 96754
Koloa 96756
Kualapuu 96757
Kukuihaele 96758
Kula 96790
Kunia 96759
Kurtistown 96760
Lahaina (1st) 96761
Laie 96762
Lanai City 96763
Laupahoehoe 96764
Lawai 96765
Lihue (1st) 96766
Makaha Valley, Br. Waianae 96792
Makakilo, Br. Ewa Beach 96706
Makawao 96768
 Haiimaile, Br. 96787
 Pukalani, R. Br. 96788
Makaweli 96769
Maunaloa 96770
Mililani Town Area, Sta.
 Wahiawa 96789
Moilihi, Sta. Honolulu 96814
Mountainview 96771
Naalehu 96772
Nanakuli, Br. Waianae 96792

Napili, R. Br. Lahaina 96761
Naval Air Station, Sta. Ewa
 Beach 96706
Naval Communication
 Station, Sta. Wahiawa 96786
Navy Cantonment, Sta.
 Honolulu 96818
Navy Terminal, Sta.
 Honolulu 96818
Ninole 96773
Ookala 96774
Paauhau 96775
Paauilo 96776
Pahala 96777
Pahoa 96778
Paia 96779
Papaaloa 96780
Papaikou 96781
Pawaa, Sta. Honolulu (see
 appendix)
Pearl City (1st) 96782
Pepeekeo 96783
Puhi, R. Br. Lihue 96766
Pukalani, R. Br. Makawao 96788
Puunene 96784
Schofield Barracks, Sta.
 Wahiawa 96786
Submarine Base, Sta.
 Honolulu 96818
Tripler Army Hospital, Sta.
 Honolulu 96819
Ulupalakua, R. Br. Kula 96790
University, Sta. Honolulu 96825
Volcano 96785
Wahiawa (1st) 96786
 Mililani Town Area, Sta. 96789
 Naval Communication
  Station, Sta. 96786
 Schofield Barracks, Sta. 96786
Waialae Kahala, Sta.
 Honolulu 96816
Waialua 96791
Waianae (1st) 96792
Waikiki, Sta. Honolulu 96815
Wailuku (1st) 96793
Waimanalo 96795
Waimea 96796
Waipahu (1st) 96797

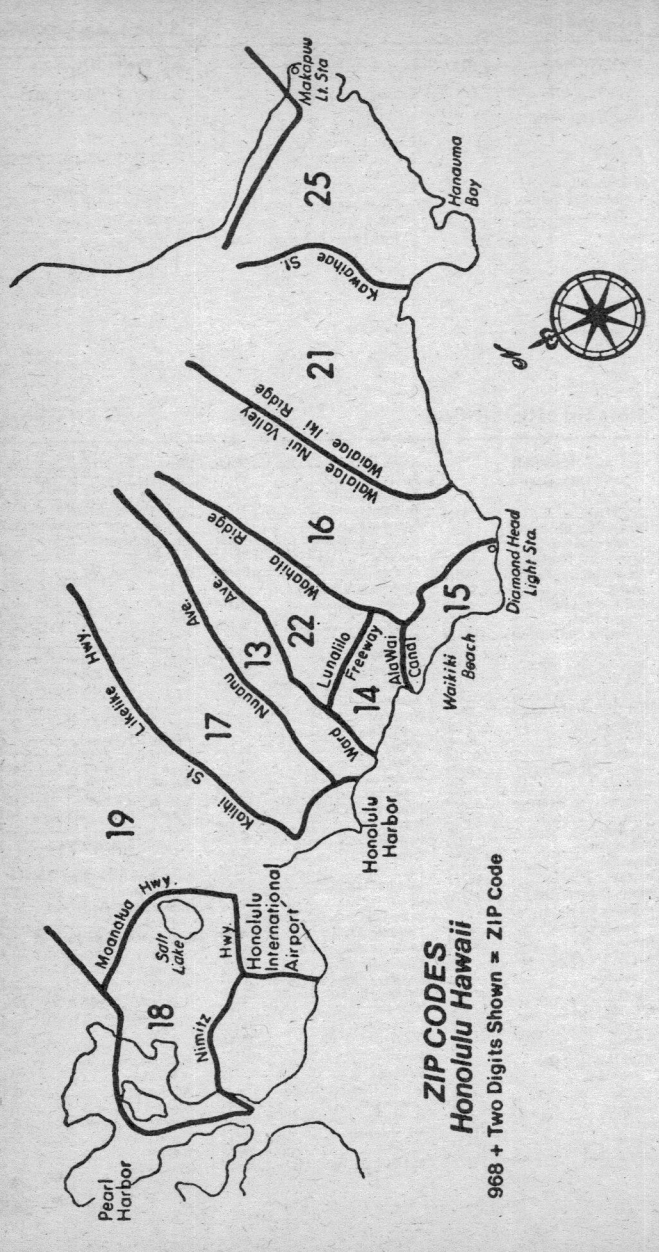

**ZIP CODES
Honolulu Hawaii**

968 + Two Digits Shown = ZIP Code

HONOLULU 968
POST OFFICE BOXES

Box Nos.

A-Z	Waikiki Sta	15
A-CD	Waikiki Sta	15
A-AAB	Waikiki	15
1-230	Main Office	10
10A-10Q	Waialae-Kahala	16
231-701	Main Office	09
711-1101	Main Office	08
1111-1410	Main Office	07
1411-1801	Main Office	06
1811-2201	Main Office	05
2211-2561	Main Office	04
2571-2870	Main Office	03
2871-3170	Main Office	02
3171-3470	Main Office	01
3473-3710	Main Office	11
3713-3950	Main Office	12
3953-4545	Main Office	13
5000-5999	Pawaa Sta	14
6000-6999	Navy Cantonment Sta	18
7000-7499	Aina Haina Sta	21
7500-7999	Hawaii Kai Sta	25
8000-8999	Waikiki Sta	15
9000-9999	Airport Sta	20
10000-10999	Waialae-Kahala	16
11000-11999	Moiliili Sta	14
17001-17934	Kapalama Sta	17
88001 88149	Waikiki Sta	15

STATIONS, BRANCHES AND UNITS

Airport Sta	20
Aina Haina Sta	16
Ala Moana Sta	14
Chinatown Sta	17
Ford Island Sta	18
Fort Shafter Sta	23
Hawaiian Village Sta	15
Hickam A F B Sta	24
Kaimuki Sta	16
Kalihi Sta	17
Moiliili Sta	14
Navy Cantonment Sta	18
Navy Terminal Sta	14
Pawaa Sta	14
Submarine Base Sta	18
Tripler Army Hospital Sta	19
University Sta	25
Waialae-Kahala Sta	16
Waikiki Sta	15
General Delivery	13
Postmaster	13

APARTMENTS, HOTELS, MOTELS

Ainahau Apartments, 334 Seaside Ave	15

Ala Wai Terrace, 1547 Ala Wai Blvd	15
Alexander Young, 1077 Bishop	13
Atkinson Towers, 419 A Atkinson Dr	14
Breakers, 250 Beach Walk	15
Colony Surf, 2895 Kalakaua Ave	15
Diamond Head Ambassador, 2957 Kalakaua Ave	15
Diamond Head Apartments, 2969 Kalakaua Ave	15
Edgewater, 2168 Kalia Rd	15
Foster Tower, 2500 Kalakaua Ave	15
Halekulani, 2199 Kalia Rd	15
Hawaiiana, 260 Beach Walk	15
Hilton Hawaiian Village, 2005 Kalia Rd	15
Islander, 351 Seaside Ave	15
Kalia, 425 Ena Rd	15
Moana, 2365 Kalakaua Ave	15
Oahuan Tower, 1710 Makiki Ave	22
Park Terrace, 509 University Ave	14
Polynesian, 314 Beach Walk	15
Princess Kaiulani, 120 Kaiulani Ave	15
Reef Tower, 227 Lewers	15
Reef, 2169 Kalia Rd	15
Rosalei Apartments, 445 Kaiolu	15
Royal Hawaiian, 2259 Kalakaua Ave	15
Sans Souci, 2877 Kalakaua Ave	15
Seaside Towers, 435 Seaside Ave	15
Surfrider, 2365 Kalakaua Ave	15
Town House, 1415 Victoria	22
Tradewinds Apartments, 1720 Ala Moana Blvd	15
Waikiki Biltmore, 2424 Kalakaua Ave	15
Waikiki Cadillac, 411 Kuamoo	15
Waikiki Shores, 2161 Kalia Rd	15
Waikikian, 1811 Ala Moana Blvd	15

BUILDINGS

Aina Haina Shopping Center, 820 Hind Dr	21
Ala Moana Shopping Center, 1450 Ala Moana Blvd	14
Ala Moana, 1441 Kapiolani Blvd	14
Alexander & Baldwin, 141 Merchant	13

Alexander Young, 1015 Bishop	13
Aliiolani Hale, 417 S King	13
Boston 1037 Fort St Mall	13
Capital Investment, 850 Richard	13
Continental, 1521 S King	14
Damon, 919 Bishop	13
Dillingham Transportation, 735 Bishop	13
Federal, 335 Merchant	13
Finance Factor, 195 S King	13
Financial Plaza Of The Pacific 111 S King	13
First Hawaiian Bank, 161 S King St	13
Gasco, 1060 Bishop	13
Hawaiian Life, 1311 Kapiolani Blvd	14
Honolulu Merchandise Mart, 198 S Hotel	13
Kahala Mall, 4211 Waialae	16
Kalihi Shopping Center, 2295 N King	19
Kamamalu, 250 S King St	13
King Center, 1451 S King	14
Marine Finance, 1109 Bethel	13
Moanalua Shopping Center	18
Professional Center, 1481 S King	14
Queen Street Corporation, 235 S Queen	13

HOSPITALS

Childrens, 226 N Kuakini	17
Convalescent Nursing, 5113 Maunalani Cir	16
Emergency, 1027 Hala Dr	17
Kaiser Foundation Medical Center, 1697 Ala Moana Blvd	15
Kapiolani Maternity, 1611 Bingham	14
Kuakini, 347 N Kuakini	14
Leahi, 3675 Kilauea Ave	16
Maluhia, 1027 Hala Dr	17
Queens Medical Center, 1301 Punchbowl	13
Saint Francis, 2260 Liliha	17
Shriners, 1310 Punahou	14

UNIVERSITIES AND COLLEGES

Chaminade, 3140 Waialae Ave	16
Hawaii Pacific College, 1149 Bethel	13
Honolulu Christian, 829 Pensacola	14
University Of Hawaii, 1801 University Ave	22

IDAHO
(Abbreviation: ID)

Aberdeen...........................83210
Acequia............................83310
Ahsahka...........................83520
Air Base, MOU, Mountain
    Home...........................83648
Alameda, Sta. Pocatello...83201
Albion..............................83311
Almo................................83312
American Falls..................83211
Arbon..............................83212
Arco................................83213
Arimo..............................83214
Ashton.............................83420
Athol...............................83801
Atlanta.............................83601
Atomic City.......................83215
Avery...............................83802
Baker...............................83461
Bancroft............................83217
Banida, R. Br. Preston......83264
Banks...............................83602
Bannock, Sta. Pocatello...83201
Basalt..............................83218
Bayview............................83803
Bear, R. Br. Council..........83603
Bellevue............................83313
Bennington, R. Br.
    Montpelier.....................83219
Bern.................................83220
Blackfoot (1st)..................83221
    Springfield, R. Br...........83277
Blanchard..........................83804
Bliss................................83314
Bloomington.......................83223
BOISE (1st) (see appendix)
Bonners Ferry.....................83805
Borah, Sta. Boise (see
    appendix)
Bovill..............................83806
Bridge, R. Br. Malta..........83315
Bruneau.............................83604
Buhl (1st)..........................83316
Burke, R. Br. Wallace.......83807
Burley (1st)........................83318
Calder..............................83808
Caldwell (1st)....................83605
Cambridge..........................83610
Carey...............................83320
Careywood, R. Br.
    Sandpoint......................83809
Carmen.............................83462
Cascade............................83611
    Warm Lake, R. Br...........83611
    West Mountain, R. Br......83611
Castleford..........................83321
Cataldo.............................83810
Challis.............................83226
Chester.............................83421
Chubbuck, R. Br. Pocatello...83201
Clark Fork..........................83811
Clarkia.............................83812
Clayton.............................83227
Clearwater.........................83521
Cliften..............................83228
Cobalt..............................83229
Cocolalla...........................83813
Coeur D' alene (1st).........83814
Colburn, R. Br. Sandpoint...83865
Collister, Sta. Boise.........83703
Conda...............................83230

Coolin...............................83821
Copeland............................83822
Corral, R. Br. Fairfield.......83322
Cottonwood.........................83522
    Keuterville, R. Br............83538
Council.............................83612
    Bear, R. Br...................83603
Craigmont..........................83523
Culdesac............................83524
Darlington..........................83231
Dayton..............................83232
Deary...............................83823
Declo...............................83323
Denton, Br. Boise.............83704
Desmet..............................83824
Dietrich.............................83324
Dingle...............................83233
Dixie, R. Br. Elk City........83525
Donnelly............................83615
Dover...............................83825
Downey.............................83234
Driggs...............................83422
Dubois..............................83423
Eagle................................83616
Eagle Rock, Sta. Idaho Falls...83401
Eastport.............................83826
Eden.................................83325
Elba.................................83326
Elk City.............................83525
Elk River............................83827
Ellis................................83235
Emida, R. Br. Saint Maries...83828
Emmett (1st).......................83617
Enaville.............................83829
Fairfield.............................83327
    Corral, R. Br.................83322
Farragut, Br. Bayview.......83803
Felt..................................83424
Fenn, R. Br. Grangeville.....83531
Ferdinand............................83526
Fernwood............................83830
Filer................................83328
Firth................................83236
Fish Haven, R. Br. Paris....83261
Fort Hall, R. Br. Pocatello...83203
Franklin.............................83237
Fruitland............................83619
Fruitvale............................83620
Garden City, Br. Boise.....83704
Garden Valley......................83622
Gardena.............................83621
Genesee.............................83832
Geneva..............................83238
Georgetown.........................83239
Gibbonsville.......................83463
Glenns Ferry........................83623
Gooding (1st)......................83330
Grace...............................83241
    Thatcher, R. Br..............83283
Grand View.........................83624
Grangeville (1st).................83530
    Fenn, R. Br..................83531
Grasmere............................83625
Greencreek..........................83533
Greenleaf............................83626
Grouse..............................83242
Hagerman............................83332
    Tuttle, R. Br.................83354
Hailey...............................83333
Hamer...............................83425
Hammett.............................83627
Hansen..............................83334
Harrison.............................83833

Medimont, R. Br...............83842
Harvard.............................83834
Hayden Lake........................83835
Hazelton............................83335
Headquarters.......................83534
Heyburn.............................83336
Hill City............................83337
Hillview, Br. Idaho Falls......83401
Holbrook............................83243
Homedale............................83628
Hope.................................83836
Horseshoe Bend...................83629
    Sweet, R. Br.................83670
Howe................................83244
Huston..............................83630
Idaho City..........................83631
    Placerville, R. Br............83666
Idaho Falls (1st)................83401
Indian Valley.......................83632
Inkom...............................83245
Iona.................................83427
Irwin................................83428
Island Park.........................83429
Jerome (1st).......................83338
Juliaetta............................83535
Kamiah..............................83536
Kellogg (1st)......................83837
Kendrick............................83537
Ketchum.............................83340
Keuterville, R. Br.
    Cottonwood....................83538
Kimberly............................83341
King Hill............................83633
Kingston............................83839
Kooskia.............................83539
Kootenai, R. Br. Sandpoint...83840
Kuna................................83634
Laclede.............................83841
Lake Fork...........................83635
Lamont..............................83430
Lapwai..............................83540
Lava Hot Springs.................83246
Leadore.............................83464
Lemhi...............................83465
Lenore..............................83541
Leslie...............................83249
Letha...............................83636
Lewiston (1st).....................83501
Lewisville...........................83431
Lorenzo.............................83432
Lowman, R. Br. Boise........83637
Lucile...............................83542
Mackay..............................83251
Macks Inn..........................83433
Malad City..........................83252
Malta...............................83342
Marsing.............................83639
May..................................83253
Mc Call.............................83638
Mc Cammon.........................83250
Meadows, R. Br. New
    Meadows........................83640
Medimont, R. Br. Harrison...83842
Melba...............................83641
Menan...............................83434
Meridian (1st).....................83642
Mesa................................83643
Middleton...........................83644
Midvale.............................83645
Minidoka............................83343
Monteview..........................83435
Montour.............................83646
Montpelier..........................83254
    Bennington, R. Br...........83219

Moore..................................83255
Moreland.............................83256
Moscow (1st).......................83843
Mountain Home (1st)............83647
  Air Base, MOU..................83648
  Mountain Home A F B.
  Br. 83648
Mountain Home A F B, Br.
  Mountain Home................83648
Mountain View, Sta. Boise...83704
Moyie Springs.....................83845
Mullan................................83846
Murphy...............................83650
Murray, R. Br. Wallace.......83874
Murtaugh............................83344
Naf, R. Br. Malta.................83345
Nampa (1st)........................83651
Naples................................83847
New Meadows.....................83654
  Meadows, R. Br. 83640
New Plymouth......................83655
Newdale..............................83436
Nezperce.............................83543
Nordman.............................83848
North Fork...........................83466
  Shoup, R. Br. 83469
Notus.................................83656
Oakley................................83346
Obsidian..............................83259
Ola.....................................83657
Oreana................................83659
Orofino (1st).......................83544
Osburn...............................83849
Ovid...................................83260
Page, R. Br. Pinehurst.........83850
Palisades.............................83437
Paris...................................83261
Parker.................................83438
Parma.................................83660
Paul....................................83347
Payette (1st).......................83661
Peck...................................83545
Picabo................................83348
Pierce.................................83546
Pinehurst............................83850
Pingree...............................83262
Placerville, R. Br. Idaho City...83666
Plummer..............................83851
Pocatello (1st).....................83201
  Alameda, Sta. 83201
  Bannock, Sta. 83201

Chubbuck, R. Br. 83201
Fort Hall, R. Br. 83203
Pollock...............................83547
Ponderay............................83852
Porthill...............................83853
Post Falls...........................83854
Potlatch..............................83855
Preston...............................83263
  Banida, R. Br. 83264
Priest Lake, R. Br. Priest
  River..............................83856
Priest River........................83856
Princeton............................83857
Rathdrum............................83858
Reubens..............................83548
Rexburg (1st)......................83440
  Thornton, R. Br. 83453
Richfield.............................83349
Rigby..................................83442
Riggins...............................83549
Ririe...................................83443
Roberts...............................83444
Rockland.............................83271
Rogerson, R. Br. Twin Falls...83302
Rupert (1st).........................83350
Sagle..................................83860
Saint Anthony......................83445
Saint Charles.......................83272
Saint Maries........................83861
  Emida, R. Br. 83828
Salmon (1st).......................83467
Samaria, R. Br. Malad City...83252
Samuels..............................83862
Sanders...............................83863
Sandpoint (1st)....................83864
  Careywood, R. Br. 83809
  Colburn, R. Br. 83865
  Kootenai, R. Br. 83840
Santa..................................83866
Shelley................................83274
Shoshone............................83352
Shoup, R. Br. North Fork......83469
Silverton.............................83867
Skyline, Sta. Idaho Falls......83401
Smelterville.........................83868
Soda Springs.......................83276
South Gate Plaza, Br.
  Lewiston..........................83501
Southside, Sta. Boise...........83706
Southwick...........................83550
Spalding..............................83551

Spencer..............................83446
Spirit Lake..........................83869
Springfield, R. Br. Blackfoot...83277
Squirrel..............................83447
Stanley................................83278
Star....................................83669
Sterling...............................83279
Stites.................................83552
Stone.................................83280
Sugar City..........................83448
Sun Valley..........................83353
Swan Valley........................83449
Swanlake............................83281
Sweet, R. Br. Horseshoe
  Bend...............................83670
Tendoy...............................83468
Tensed...............................83870
Terreton..............................83450
Teton..................................83451
Tetonia...............................83452
Thain Road, R. Br. Lewiston...83501
Thatcher, R. Br. Grace.........83283
Thornton, R. Br. Rexburg.....83453
Troy...................................83871
Tuttle, R. Br. Hagerman.......83354
Twin Falls (1st)...................83301
  Rogerson, R. Br. 83302
Ucon..................................83454
University, Sta. Moscow.......83843
Ustick, R. Br. Boise.............83702
Victor.................................83455
Viola..................................83872
Wallace (1st).......................83873
  Burke, R. Br. 83807
  Murray, R. Br. 83874
Wardner..............................83875
Warm Lake, R. Br. Cascade...83611
Warren................................83671
Wayan................................83285
Weippe...............................83553
Weiser (1st)........................83672
Wendell..............................83355
West Mountain, R. Br.
  Cascade...........................83611
Weston...............................83286
White Bird...........................83554
Whitney, Sta. Boise.............83705
Wilder................................83676
Winchester..........................83555
Worley................................83876
Yellow Pine.........................83677

BOISE 837

POST OFFICE BOXES

Box Nos.

1-80	Main Office	07
81-2999	Borah Sta	01
3000-3999	Collister Sta	03
5000-5899	Whitney Sta	05
7000-8599	Main Office	07

RURAL ROUTES

1,2	02
3	05
4	02
5	05

STATIONS, BRANCHES AND UNITS

Borah Sta	02
Collister Sta	03
Denton Br	04
Garden City Br	04
Lowman Rural Br	83637
Mountain View Sta	04
Southside Sta	06
Ustick Rural Br	02
Whitney Sta	05
General Delivery	01
Postmaster	07

APARTMENTS, HOTELS, MOTELS

Baxter, 303 N 2nd	02
Belgravia, 100 S 5th	02
Belgravia, 415 Main	02
Boise Courtel, 3525 Chinden Blvd	04
Boise, 800 Bannock	01
Boisean, 1300 S Capitol Blvd	06
Boulevard, 1121 S Capitol Blvd	06
Cabana, 1618 Main	06
Cambridge Square, 303 S Straughn	02
Capital, 1009 S 9th	06
Capri, 2600 Fairview Ave	06
Chalet, 1300 S Capitol Blvd	06
Cole, 112 E Idaho	02
Colorado, 959 Federal Way	05
Columbia, 1006 1/2 Main	02

Crescent Rim, 3011 Crescent Rim Dr	04
Desert Skies, 3636 Chinden Blvd	04
Dorchester Apts, 300 S Straughn	02
Downtowner, 1901 Main	07
East Side, 2519 Federal Way	05
Evergreen Motor Court, 1315 S Capitol Blvd	06
Garden City, 4509 Chinden Blvd	04
Grandview, 1315 Federal Way	05
Green Gables, 6608 Fairview Ave	04
Hiway 30 Motel, 7121 Fairview Ave	05
Holiday Inn, 3300 Vista	05
Holiday, 5416 Fairview Ave	04
Home, 105 N 11th	01
Idan-Ha, 928 Main	07
Imperial Plaza Apts, 200 N 3rd	02
Jim Dandy, 6727 Fairview Ave	04
Lakeside, 6911 State	03
Magnolia, 702 Hays	02
Magnolia, 708 Hays	02
Manitou	02
Mitchell, 235 S 10th	06
Olympic, 1009 1/2 Main	02
Overland, 213 S 9th	01
Owyhee Motor Inn, 1109 Main	07
Park View Apts, 3110 Crescent Rim Dr	04
Plaza Inn, 1025 S Capitol Blvd	06
Raffroy, 2223 Federal Way	05
Rim Crest Apts, 3701 Crescent Rim Dr	04
Riverview, 1070 Leadville Ave	06
Rose Hill, 2709 Rose Hill	05
Sands, 1111 State	02
Seek Rest, 3349 Federal Way	05
Seven K, 3633 Chinden Blvd	04
Skyline, 3209 Federal Way	05
Sunliner, 3433 Chinden Blvd	04
Sunset Cottages, 6713 Fairview Ave	04

Town And Ranch, 4902 Fairview Ave	04
Travelers, 5620 Fairview Ave	04
Travelodge, 1314 Grove	06
University Village, 538 Hale	06
Valencia, 612 Idaho	02
Vista Courts, 415 Vista	05
Wellman, 500 Franklin	02
White Savage, 1307 Washington	02
White Savage, 521 N 13th	02
Whitney, 402 Vista	05

BUILDINGS

Bank Of Idaho	02
Broadbent	02
Continental Life	06
Eastman	02
Equitable Life, 501 N 5th	02
Fidelity	02
First National Bank	02
First Security Bank	02
Gem	02
Idaho	02
Jefferson	02
Owyhee Plaza	02
Provident S & L Bldg	02
Simplot	02
Sonna	02
Sun	02

GOVERNMENT OFFICES

City Hall	02
County Courthouse	02
Federal Bldg Borah Sta	02
Federal Bldg U S Court House	02

HOSPITALS

Booth Memorial, 1617 N24	07
Elks Rehabilitation Center, 204 Fort	02
Saint Alphonsus, 506 N 5th	02
Saint Lukes, 130 E Bannock	02
Veterans	07

UNIVERSITIES AND COLLEGES

Boise State College	07

ILLINOIS
(Abbreviation: IL)

Abbott Park, Br. North
  Chicago................................60064
Abingdon...................................61410
Adair...61411
Addieville..................................62214
Addison (1st)............................60101
Adrian.......................................62310
Akin..62805
Albany.......................................61230
Albers..62215
Albion.......................................62806
Alden, R. Br. Harvard.............60001
Aledo (1st)...............................61231
Alexander..................................62601
Alexis..61412
Algonquin (1st)........................60102
Alhambra...................................62001
Allendale....................................62410
Allenville, R. Br. Sullivan.......61901
Allerton......................................61810
Alma..62807
Alpha..61413
Alsey...62610
Alsip, R. Br. Chicago (see
  appendix)
Alta, R. Br. Peoria...................61608
Altamont....................................62411
Alto Pass..................................62905
Alton (1st)................................62002
Altona.......................................61414
Alvin..61811
Amboy.......................................61310
Anchor.......................................61720
Ancona, R. Br. Streator..........61311
Andalusia...................................61232
Andover.....................................61233
Anna (1st).................................62906
Annapolis...................................62413
Annawan....................................61234
Antioch (1st)............................60002
Apple River................................61001
Arcola.......................................61910
Arenzville..................................62611
Argenta......................................62501
Argo (1st)..................................60501
Argonne, Br. Lemont...............60439
Arlington....................................61312
ARLINGTON HEIGHTS (1st)
  (see appendix)
Armington...................................61721
Armstrong..................................61812
Aroma Park...............................60910
Arrowsmith.................................61722
Arthur...61911
Ashburn, Sta. Chicago.............60652
Ashkum......................................60911
Ashland......................................62612
Ashley.......................................62808
Ashmore.....................................61912
Ashton..61006
Assumption.................................62510
Astoria.......................................61501
  Summum, R. Br....................61566
Athens.......................................62613
Atkinson....................................61235
Atlanta......................................61723
Atwater......................................62511
Atwood.......................................61913
Auburn.......................................62615

Auburn Park, Sta. Chicago.....60620
Augusta.....................................62311
AURORA (1st) (see
  appendix)
Austin, Sta. Chicago...............60644
Ava...62907
Aviston......................................62216
Avon..61415
Baileyville..................................61007
Baldwin......................................62217
Bardolph....................................61416
Barnhill......................................62809
Barrington (1st).......................60010
Barry...62312
Barstow.....................................61236
Bartelso.....................................62218
Bartlett (1st).............................60103
Bartonville, Br. Peoria.............61607
Basco...62313
Batavia (1st)............................60510
Batchtown..................................62006
Bath...62617
Baylis...62314
Beardstown (1st)......................62618
Beason.......................................62512
Beaverville.................................60912
Beckemeyer................................62219
Beecher......................................60401
Beecher City..............................62414
Belknap......................................62908
Belle Rive..................................62810
Belleview....................................62008
BELLEVILLE (1st) (see
  appendix)
Bellflower...................................61724
Bellmont.....................................62811
Bellwood (1st)..........................60104
Belmont Road, Sta. Downers
  Grove.....................................60515
Belvidere (1st)..........................61008
Bement.......................................61813
Benld...62009
Bensenville (1st)......................60106
Benson.......................................61516
Bentley.......................................62315
Benton (1st).............................62812
Berwick......................................61417
Berwyn (1st).............................60402
Bethalto.....................................62010
Bethany......................................61914
Bible Grove................................62813
Big Rock....................................60511
Biggsville...................................61418
Bingham.....................................62011
Birds...62415
Bishop Hill.................................61419
Bismarck.....................................61814
Blackstone..................................61313
Blandinsville...............................61420
Bloomingdale..............................60108
Bloomington (1st).....................61701
Blue Island (1st).......................60406
Blue Mound................................62513
Bluff Springs..............................62622
Bluffs...62621
Bluford.......................................62814
Bogota.......................................62416
Boles...62909
Bolingbrook, R. Br. Lemont....60439
Bondville....................................61815
Bone Gap...................................62815
Bonfield......................................60913

Bonnie.......................................62816
Boody...62514
Boulder Hill, Br.
  Montgomery...........................60538
Bourbonnais (1st)....................60914
Bowen..62316
Braceville...................................60407
Bradford.....................................61421
Bradley (1st).............................60915
Braidwood..................................60408
Breese..62230
Brettwood, Sta. Decatur..........62526
Bridgeport..................................62417
Bridgeview, Br. Oak Lawn......60455
Brighton.....................................62012
Brimfield....................................61517
  Oak Hill, R. Br.....................61518
Bristol..60512
Broadlands..................................61816
Broadview, Br. Maywood.........60153
Broadway, Sta. Rockford..........61106
Broadwell...................................62623
Brocton......................................61917
Brookfield (1st)........................60513
Brookport....................................62910
Broughton...................................62817
Brownfield..................................62911
Browning....................................62624
Browns.......................................62818
Brownstown.................................62418
Brussels......................................62013
Bryant..61519
Buckingham.................................60917
Buckley......................................60918
Buckner......................................62819
Buda..61314
Buffalo.......................................62515
Buffalo Grove, Br. Wheeling....60090
Buffalo Prairie.............................61237
Bulpitt..62517
Buncombe...................................62912
Bunker Hill.................................62014
Burbank, Br. Oak Lawn............60459
Bureau.......................................61315
Burlington...................................60109
Burnside.....................................62318
Burnt Prairie...............................62820
Bushnell.....................................61422
Butler...62015
Byron...61010
Cabery.......................................60919
Cache...62913
Cahokia, Br. East Saint
  Louis......................................62206
Cairo (1st)................................62914
Caledonia...................................61011
Calhoun......................................62419
Calumet City (1st)....................60409
Calumet Park, Br. Chicago
  (see appendix)
Camargo.....................................61919
Cambria.....................................62915
Cambridge...................................61238
Camden.......................................62319
Cameron.....................................61423
Camp Grove................................61424
Camp Point................................62320
Campbell Hill..............................62916
Campus.......................................60920
Canton (1st).............................61520
Cantrall......................................62625
Capitol, Sta. Springfield...........62706
Capron.......................................61012

Carbon Cliff	61239
Carbondale (1st)	62901
Carlinville (1st)	62626
Carlock	61725
Carlyle (1st)	62231
Carman	61425
Carmi (1st)	62821
Carpentersville (1st)	60110
Carriers Mills	62917
Carrollton	62016
Carterville	62918
Carthage (1st)	62321
Fountain Green, R. Br.	62337
Cary (1st)	60013
Casey	62420
Caseyville (1st)	62232
Castleton	61426
Catherine Avenue, Br. La Grange	60525
Catlin	61817
Cave In Rock	62919
Cazenovia	61522
Cedar Point	61316
Cedarville	61013
Centralia (1st)	62801
Centreville, Br. East Saint Louis	62206
Cerro Gordo	61818
Chadwick	61014
Chambersburg	62323
Champaign (1st)	61820
Chana	61015
Chandlerville	62627
Channahon	60410
Chanute A F B, Sta. Rantoul	61868
Chapin	62628
Charleston (1st)	61920
Chatham	62629
Chatsworth	60921
Chebanse	60922
Chenoa	61726
Cherry	61317
Cherry Valley	61016
Chester (1st)	62233
Chesterfield	62630
Chesterville	61923
Chestnut	62518
Chestnut Street, Sta. Chicago	60610
CHICAGO (1st) (see appendix)	
Chicago Heights (1st)	60411
Chicago Lawn, Sta. Chicago	60629
Chicago Ridge (1st)	60415
Chillicothe (1st)	61523
Chrisman	61924
Christopher	62822
Cicero, Br. Chicago	60650
Cisco	61830
Cisne	62823
Cissna Park	60924
Clare	60111
Claremont	62421
Clarence	60925
Clarendon Hills (1st)	60514
Clay City	62824
Clayton	62324
Claytonville	60926
Clearing, Sta. Chicago	60638
Clifton	60927
Clinton (1st)	61727
Coal City	60416

Coal Valley	61240
Coatsburg	62325
Cobden	62920
Coello	62825
Coffeen	62017
Colchester	62326
Coleta, R. Br. Sterling	61017
Colfax	61728
Collinsville (1st)	62234
Collison	61831
Colmar	62327
Colona	61241
Colp	62921
Columbia (1st)	62236
Columbus, R. Br. Quincy	62328
Colusa	62329
Compton	61318
Concord	62631
Congerville	61729
Congress Park, Sta. Brookfield	60513
Cooksville	61730
Cordova	61242
Cornell	61319
Cornland	62519
Cortland	60112
Cottage Hills	62018
Coulterville	62237
Country Club Hills Br. Tinley Park	60477
Country Fair, Sta. Champaign	61820
Cowden	62422
Cragin, Sta. Chicago	60639
Creal Springs	62922
Crescent City	60928
Crest Hill, Br. Joliet	60435
Creston	60113
Crete (1st)	60417
Creve Coeur, Br. Peoria	61611
Cropsey	61731
Crossville	62827
Crystal Lake (1st)	60014
Cuba	61427
Cullom	60929
Curran, R. Br. New Berlin	62632
Custer Park	60418
Cutler	62238
Cypress	62923
Dahinda	61428
Dahlgren	62828
Dakota	61018
Dale	62829
Dallas City	62330
Dalton City	61925
Dalzell	61320
Dana	61321
Danforth	60930
Danvers	61732
Danville (1st)	61832
Darien, Br. Westmont	60559
Davis	61019
Davis Junction	61020
Dawson	62520
De Kalb (1st)	60115
De Land	61839
De Soto	62924
DECATUR (1st) (see appendix)	
Deer Creek	61733
Deer Grove	61243
Deerfield (1st)	60015
Delavan	61734

Dennison	62423
Denver	62331
Depue	61322
DES PLAINES (1st) (see appendix)	
Detroit	62332
Dewey	61840
Dewitt	61735
Dieterich	62424
Divernon	62530
Division Street, Sta. Chicago	60651
Dix	62830
Dixon (1st)	61021
Dolton (1st)	60419
Dongola	62926
Donnellson	62019
Donovan	60931
Dorchester, R. Br. Gillespie	62020
Dorsey	62021
Dover	61323
Dow	62022
Dowell	62927
Downers Grove (1st)	60515
Downey, Br. North Chicago	60064
Downs	61736
Downtown, Sta. Springfield (see appendix)	
Du Quoin (1st)	62832
Dubois	62831
Dundas	62425
Dundee (1st)	60118
Dunfermline	61524
Dunlap	61525
Dunning, Sta. Chicago	60634
Dupo	62239
Durand	61024
Dwight (1st)	60420
Eagarville	62023
Earlville	60518
East Alton (1st)	62024
East Carondelet	62240
East Dubuque	61025
East Galesburg	61430
East Lynn	60932
East Moline (1st)	61244
East Peoria, Br. Peoria	61611
East Rockford, Sta. Rockford (see appendix)	
EAST SAINT LOUIS (1st) (see appendix)	
Easton	62633
Eddyville	62928
Edelstein	61526
Eden, R. Br. Hanna City	61527
Edgebrook, Sta. Chicago	60646
Edgemont, Sta. East Saint Louis	62203
Edgewood	62426
Edinburg	62531
Edison Square, Sta. Waukegan	60085
Edwards	61528
Edwardsville (1st)	62025
Effingham (1st)	62401
Egan	61026
El Dara	62333
El Paso	61738
El Vista, Sta. Peoria	61604
Elburn	60119
Elco	62929
Eldena	61324
Eldorado (1st)	62930

Eldred 62027
Elroy 61027
Elgin (1st) 60120
Elizabeth 61028
Elizabethtown 62931
Elk Grove Village, Br.
　Arlington Heights 60007
Elkhart 62634
Elkville 62932
Ellery 62833
Elliott 60933
Ellisgrove 62241
Ellisville 61431
Ellsworth 61737
Elmhurst (1st) 60126
Elmwood 61529
Elmwood Park, Br. Chicago
　(see appendix)
Elsah 62028
Elsdon, Sta. Chicago 60632
Elvaston 62234
Elwin 62532
Elwood 60421
Emden 62635
Emington 60934
Emma 62834
Energy 62933
Enfield 62835
Englewood, Sta. Chicago ...60621
Eola 60519
Equality 62934
Erie 61250
Esmond 60129
Essex 60935
Eureka (1st) 61530
EVANSTON (1st) (see
　appendix)
Evansville 62242
Evergreen Park, Br. Chicago
　(see appendix)
Ewing 62836
Fairbury (1st) 61739
Fairfield (1st) 62837
Fairmount 61841
Fairview 61432
Fairview Heights, Br.
　Caseyville 62232
Fairview Heights, Br. East
　Saint Louis 62208
Fancy Prairie 62637
Farina 62838
Farmer City 61842
Farmersville 62533
Farmington 61531
　Middlegrove, R. Br. 61549
Fenton 61251
Ferris 62336
Fiatt 61433
Fidelity 62030
Fieldon 62031
Fillmore 62032
Filson 61926
Findlay 62534
Fireworks, Br. East Saint
　Louis 62207
Fisher 61843
Fithian 61844
Flanagan 61740
Flat Rock 62427
Flora (1st) 62839
Flossmoor (1st) 60422
Foosland 61845
Forest City 61532

Forest Park (1st) 60130
Forrest 61741
Forreston 61030
Forsyth 62535
Fort Dearborn, Sta. Chicago ...60611
Fort Sheridan, Br. Highland
　Park 60037
Fountain Green, R. Br.
　Carthage 62337
Fowler 62338
Fox Lake (1st) 60020
Fox River Grove 60021
Frankfort 60423
Frankfort Heights 62840
Franklin 62638
Franklin Grove 61031
Franklin Park (1st) 60131
　Schiller Park, Br. 60176
Frederick 62639
Freeburg 62243
Freeman Spur 62841
Freeport (1st) 61032
　Scioto Mills, R. Br. 61076
Fulton (1st) 61252
Fults 62244
Gages Lake, Br. Grayslake ...60030
Galatia 62935
Gale 62936
Galena (1st) 61036
Galesburg (1st) 61401
Galt 61037
Galva 61434
Garden Prairie 61038
Gardner 60424
Garfield Park, Sta. Chicago ...60624
Garrett 61927
Gays 61928
Geff 62842
Geneseo (1st) 61254
Geneva (1st) 60134
Genoa 60135
Georgetown 61846
Gerlaw 61435
German Valley 61039
Germantown 62245
Gibson City (1st) 60936
Gifford 61847
Gilberts 60136
Gillespie 62033
　Dorchester, R. Br. 62020
Gilman 60938
Gilson 61436
Girard 62640
Gladstone 61437
Glasford 61533
Glen Carbon 62034
Glen Ellyn (1st) 60137
Glenarm 62536
Glencoe (1st) 60022
Glendale 62937
Glenview (1st) 60025
　Naval Air Station, Br. 60026
Glenwood (1st) 60425
Godfrey (1st) 62035
Golconda 62938
Golden 62339
Golden Eagle 62036
Goldengate 62843
Golf 60029
Golf Mill, Br. Chicago 60648
Good Hope 61438
Goodfield 61742
Goodwine 60939

Goreville 62939
Gorham 62940
Grafton 62037
Grand Chain 62941
Grand Crossing, Sta.
　Chicago 60619
Grand Ridge 61325
Grand Tower 62942
Granite City (1st) 62040
Grant Park 60940
Grantsburg 62943
Granville 61326
Graymont 61743
Grayslake (1st) 60030
Grayville 62944
Great Lakes, Br. Waukegan ...60088
Green Valley 61534
Greenfield 62044
Greenup (1st) 62428
　Hazel Dell, R. Br. 62430
Greenview 62642
Greenville (1st) 62246
Gridley 61744
Griggsville 62340
Groveland 61535
Gurnee (1st) 60031
Hagarstown 62247
Hamburg 62045
Hamel 62046
Hamilton (1st) 62341
Hamletsburg 62944
Hammond 61929
Hampshire 60140
Hampton 61256
Hanna City 61536
　Eden, R. Br. 61527
Hanover 61041
Hanover Park-Ontarioville,
　Br. Bartlett 60103
Hardin 62047
Harmon 61042
Harrisburg (1st) 62946
Harristown 62537
Hartford 62048
Hartsburg 62643
Harvard (1st) 60033
　Alden, R. Br. 60001
Harvel 62538
Harvey (1st) 60426
Harwood Heights, Br.
　Chicago (see appendix)
Havana (1st) 62644
Hawthorne, Sta. Chicago ...60623
Haymarket, Sta. Chicago ...60606
Hazel Crest (1st) 60429
Hazel Dell, R. Br. Greenup ...62430
Hebron (1st) 60034
Hecker 62248
Hegewisch, Sta. Chicago ...60633
Henderson 61439
Hennepin 61327
Henning 61848
Henry (1st) 61537
Herald 62845
Herod 62947
Herrick 62431
Herrin (1st) 62948
Herscher 60941
Hersman, R. Br. Mount
　Sterling 62342
Hettick 62649
Heyworth 61745
Hickory Hills, Br. Oak Lawn ...60457

Hidalgo 62432
Highland (1st) 62249
Highland Park (1st) 60035
   Fort Sheridan, Br. 60037
   Ravinia, Sta. 60035
Highwood (1st) 60040
Hillcrest, Sta. East Moline ...61244
Hillsboro (1st) 62049
Hillsdale 61257
Hillside-Berkeley, Br. Melrose
   Park (see appendix)
Hillview 62050
Hinckley 60520
Hindsboro 61930
Hines (1st) 60141
Hinsdale (1st) 60521
Hodgkins, Br. La Grange 60525
Hoffman 62250
Hoffman Estates, Br.
   Roselle 60172
Holcomb 61043
Holder 61746
Homer 61849
Hometown, Br. Oak Lawn 60456
Homewood (1st) 60430
Hoopeston (1st) 60942
Hoopple 61258
Hopedale 61747
Hopkins Park 60944
Hoyleton 62803
Hubbard Woods, Sta.
   Winnetka 60093
Hudson 61748
Huey 62252
Hull 62343
Humboldt 61931
Hume (1st) 61932
Huntley (1st) 60142
Huntsville 62344
Hurst 62949
Hutsonville 62433
Hyde Park, Sta. Chicago
   (see appendix)
Illinois City 61259
Illiopolis 62539
Ina 62846
Indianola 61850
Industry 61440
Ingleside 60041
Ingraham 62434
Iola 62847
Ipava 61441
Iroquois 60945
Irving 62051
Irving Park, Sta. Chicago 60641
Irvington 62848
Island Lake 60042
Itasca (1st) 60143
Iuka 62849
Ivesdale 61851
Jackson Park, Sta. Chicago ...60637
Jacksonville (1st) 62650
Jacob 62950
Janesville 62435
Jefferson, Sta. Chicago 60630
Jerseyville (1st) 62052
Jewett 62436
Johnsonville 62850
Johnston City 62951
JOLIET (1st) (see appendix)
Jonesboro 62952
Joppa 62953
Joy 61260

Junction 62954
Junction City, Sta. Peoria 61614
Kampsville 62053
Kane 62054
Kaneville 60144
Kankakee (1st) 60901
Kansas 61933
Karbers Ridge 62955
Karnak 62956
Kasbeer 61328
Kedzie Grace, Sta. Chicago ...60618
Keenes 62851
Keensburg 62852
Keithsburg 61442
Kell 62853
Kemper 62055
Kempton 60946
Kenilworth (1st) 60043
Kenney 61749
Kent 61044
Kewanee (1st) 61443
Keyesport 62253
Kilbourne 62655
Kincaid 62540
Kinderhook 62345
Kings, R. Br. Rochelle 61045
Kingston 60145
Kingston Mines 61539
Kinmundy 62854
Kinsman 60437
Kirkland 60146
Kirkwood 61447
Kishwaukee, Br. Rockford 61109
Knoxville 61448
La Clede 62437
La Fayette 61449
La Grange (1st) 60525
La Grange Highlands, Br. La
   Grange 60525
La Grange Park, Br. La
   Grange 60525
La Harpe 61450
La Hogue 60947
La Moille 61330
La Place 61936
La Prairie 62346
La Rose 61541
La Salle (1st) 61301
Lacon 61540
Ladd 61329
Lafox 60147
Lake Bluff (1st) 60044
Lake City 61935
Lake Forest (1st) 60045
Lake Fork 62541
Lake Villa (1st) 60046
Lake Zurich (1st) 60047
Lakeview, Sta. Chicago 60613
Lakewood 62438
Lanark 61046
Lancaster 62855
Lane 61750
Langleyville 62542
Lansdowne, Sta. East Saint
   Louis 62204
Lansing (1st) 60438
Latham 62543
Laura 61451
Lawndale 61751
Lawrenceville (1st) 62439
Le Roy 61752
Leaf River 61047
Lebanon 62254

Lee 60530
Lee Center 61331
Leland 60531
Lemont (1st) 60439
Lena 61048
Lenzburg 62255
Leonore 61332
Lerna 62440
Lewistown 61542
Lexington 61753
Liberty 62347
Libertyville (1st) 60048
Lima 62348
Limestone, Br. Peoria 61607
Lincoln (1st) 62656
Lincoln Park, Sta. Chicago ...60614
Lincolns New Salem 62659
Lincolnwood, Br. Chicago
   (see appendix)
Lindenhurst, Br. Lake Villa ...60046
Lindenwood 61049
Lisle (1st) 60532
Litchfield (1st) 62056
Literberry 62660
Little York 61453
Littleton 61454
Liverpool 61543
Livingston 62058
Loami 62661
Lockport (1st) 60441
Loda 60948
Logan 62856
Logan Square, Sta. Chicago ...60647
Lomax 61454
Lombard (1st) 60148
London Mills 61544
Long Grove, R. Br. Lake
   Zurich 60047
Long Point 61333
Longview 61852
Loogootee 62857
Loraine 62349
Lostant 61334
Louisville 62858
Lovejoy 62059
Loves Park, Br. Rockford 61111
Lovington 61937
Lowder 62662
Lowpoint 61545
Ludlow 60949
Lyndon 61261
Lynn Center 61262
Lyons (1st) 60534
Macedonia 62860
Mackinaw 61755
Macomb (1st) 61455
Macon 62544
Madison (1st) 62060
Madison Park, Br. Peoria 61604
Maeystown 62256
Magnolia 61336
Mahomet 61853
Main Post Office, Sta.
   Chicago 60680
Makanda 62958
Malden 61337
Malta 60150
Manchester 62663
Manhattan 60442
Manito 61546
Manlius 61338
Mansfield 61854
Manteno 60950

Manville.................................61339
Maple Park............................60151
   Virgil, R. Br.....................60182
Mapleton..............................61547
Maquon.................................61458
Marblehead............................62350
Marengo (1st).........................60152
Marietta................................61459
Marine.................................62061
Marion (1st)...........................62959
Marissa.................................62257
Mark....................................61340
Markham, Br. Harvey.................60426
Maroa..................................61756
Marseilles.............................61341
Marshall (1st).........................62441
Martinsville...........................62442
Martinton..............................60951
Maryville..............................62062
Mascoutah (1st)......................62258
Mason..................................62443
Mason City............................62664
Matherville...........................61263
Matteson (1st).........................60443
Mattoon (1st).........................61938
Maunie.................................62861
Maywood (1st).........................60153
Mazon..................................60444
Mc Clure..............................62957
Mc Connell............................61050
Mc Cook, Br. La Grange.............60525
Mc Gaw Park, Br.
   Waukegan.........................60085
Mc Henry (1st)........................60050
Mc Lean................................61754
Mc Leansboro.........................62859
Mc Nabb...............................61335
Meadow Mart, Br. Rockford.........61111
Meadows Avenue, Br. Peoria.......61611
Mechanicsburg........................62545
Media..................................61460
Medinah...............................60157
Medora................................62063
MELROSE PARK (1st) (see
   appendix)
Melvin..................................60952
Menard.................................62259
Mendon................................62351
Mendota (1st).........................61342
Meppen.................................62064
Merchandise Mart, Sta.
   Chicago...........................60654
Merchants, Sta. Alton................62002
Meredosia.............................62665
Merna..................................61758
Metamora..............................61548
Metcalf................................61940
Metropolis (1st).......................62960
Michael.................................62065
Mid-West, Sta. Chicago.............60612
Middlegrove, R. Br.
   Farmington.......................61549
Middletown............................62666
Midlothian (1st).......................60445
Milan (1st).............................61264
Milford 60953
Mill Shoals............................62862
Millbrook...............................60536
Millcreek...............................62961
Milledgeville...........................61051
Miller City.............................62962
Millington.............................60537
Millstadt...............................62260

Milmine................................61855
Milton..................................62352
Mineral.................................61344
Minier..................................61759
Minonk.................................61760
Minooka................................60447
Mitchell, Br. Granite City...........62040
Mode...................................62444
Modesto................................62667
Modoc, R. Br. Prairie Du
   Rocher............................62261
Mokena.................................60448
Moline (1st)............................61265
Momence (1st)........................60954
Monee..................................60449
Monica, R. Br. Princeville...........61559
Monmouth (1st).......................61462
Monroe Center........................61052
Montgomery (1st).....................60538
Monticello (1st).......................61856
Montrose...............................62445
Mooseheart (1st)......................60539
Morgan Park, Sta. Chicago.........60643
Moro....................................62067
Morris (1st)............................60450
Morrison (1st).........................61270
Morrisonville...........................62546
Morton (1st)...........................61550
Morton Grove (1st)...................60053
Mossville...............................61552
Mound City............................62963
Mounds.................................62964
Mount Auburn.........................62547
Mount Carmel (1st)..................62863
Mount Carroll.........................61053
Mount Clare...........................62068
Mount Erie.............................62446
Mount Greenwood, Sta.
   Chicago...........................60655
Mount Morris (1st)...................61054
Mount Olive...........................62069
Mount Prospect (1st)................60056
Mount Pulaski.........................62548
Mount Sterling........................62353
   Hersman, R. Br.................62342
Mount Vernon (1st)..................62864
Mount Zion............................62549
Moweaqua.............................62550
Mozier.................................62070
Muddy.................................62965
Mulberry Grove......................62262
Mulkeytown...........................62865
Muncie.................................61857
Mundelein (1st).......................60060
Murdock................................61941
Murphysboro (1st)...................62966
Murrayville.............................62668
Nachusa................................61057
Nameoki, Sta. Granite City.........62040
Naperville (1st)........................60540
Naples..................................62669
Nashville...............................62263
Nason..................................62866
National Stock Yards (1st)..........62071
Nauvoo.................................62354
Naval Air Station, Br.
   Glenview..........................60026
Nebo...................................62355
Nelson, R. Br. Rock Falls...........61058
Neoga 62447
Neponset..............................61345
New Athens...........................62264
New Baden............................62265

New Bedford...........................61346
New Berlin.............................62670
   Curran, R. Br....................62632
New Boston............................61272
New Burnside.........................62967
New Canton...........................62356
New Douglas..........................62074
New Haven.............................62867
New Holland..........................62671
New Lenox (1st)......................60451
New Liberty...........................62968
New Memphis.........................62266
New Minden...........................62804
New Salem............................62357
New Windsor.........................61465
Newark.................................60541
Newman................................61942
Newton (1st)..........................62448
   Rose Hill, R. Br.................62457
Niantic.................................62551
Niles, Br. Chicago (see
   appendix)
Nilwood................................62672
Nineteenth Avenue, Sta.
   Melrose Park.....................60160
Niota....................................62358
Noble...................................62868
Nokomis................................62075
Nora....................................61059
Normal (1st)...........................61761
Normandy.............................61347
Norris..................................61553
Norris City.............................62869
North, Sta. Evanston.................60201
North Aurora (1st)....................60542
North Chicago (1st)...................60064
North Henderson.....................61466
North Riverside, Br.
   Riverside.........................60546
North Town, Sta. Chicago..........60645
Northbrook (1st)......................60062
Northfield, Br. Winnetka.............60093
Northlake, Br. Melrose Park.........60164
Norwood Park, Sta. Chicago......60631
O Hare Airport, Sta.
   Chicago...........................60666
O'Fallon (1st).........................62269
Oak Brook, Br. Hinsdale............60521
Oak Forest (1st)......................60452
Oak Hill, R. Br. Brimfield............61518
OAK LAWN (1st) (see
   appendix)
OAK PARK (1st) (see
   appendix)
Oak Street, Sta. Danville...........61832
Oakdale................................62268
Oakford................................62673
Oakglen, Sta. Lansing..............60438
Oakland................................61943
Oakley.................................62552
Oakton, Sta. Des Plaines..........60018
Oakwood...............................61858
Oblong.................................62449
Oconee................................62553
Odell...................................60460
Odin....................................62870
Ogden..................................61859
Ogden Park, Sta. Chicago.........60636
Oglesby................................61348
Ohio....................................61349
Ohlman................................62076
Okawville..............................62271
   Venedy, R. Br...................62296

Old Orchard, Sta. Skokie.........60076
Old Post Office, Sta.
  Chicago (see appendix)
Olive Branch.........................62969
Olivet...................................61860
Olmsted...............................62970
Olney (1st)............................62450
Olympia Fields.......................60461
Omaha..................................62871
Onarga.................................60955
Oneida.................................61467
Opdyke................................62872
Opheim................................61468
Oquawka..............................61469
Orangeville...........................61060
Oraville................................62971
Orchardville..........................62873
Oreana.................................62554
Oregon (1st).........................61061
Orient...................................62874
Orion....................................61273
Orland Park (1st)...................60462
Osco.....................................61274
Oswego................................60543
Ottawa (1st).........................61350
Owaneco...............................62555
Ozark...................................62972
Palatine (1st)........................60067
Palestine...............................62451
Palmer..................................62556
Palmyra................................62674
Paloma.................................62359
Palos Heights (1st).................60463
Palos Hills, R. Br. Palos
  Park...................................60465
Palos Park (1st).....................60464
  Palos Hills, R. Br..................60465
Pana (1st).............................62557
Panama.................................62077
Papineau...............................60956
Parcel Post, Sta. East Saint
  Louis..................................62205
Paris (1st).............................61944
Park Forest (1st)....................60466
Park Ridge (1st).....................60068
Parkersburg...........................62452
Patoka..................................62875
Patterson..............................62078
Pawnee.................................62558
Pawpaw................................61353
Paxton (1st)..........................60957
Payson..................................62360
Pearl.....................................62361
Pearl City..............................61062
Pecatonica.............................61063
Pekin (1st)............................61554
Penfield................................61862
PEORIA (1st) (see appendix)
Peoria Heights, Br. Peoria.......61614
Peotone................................60468
Percy....................................62272
Perks....................................62973
Perry.....................................62362
Peru (1st).............................61354
Pesotum................................61863
Petersburg (1st).....................62675
Philo.....................................61864
Piasa....................................62079
Pierron..................................62273
Pierson Station.......................61947
Pilsen, Sta. Chicago...............60608
Pinckneyville (1st)..................62274

Pinkstaff...............................62453
Piper City..............................60959
Pittsburg...............................62974
Pittsfield (1st)........................62363
Plainfield (1st).......................60544
Plainview...............................62676
Plainville...............................62365
Plano (1st)............................60545
Plato Center..........................60170
Plaza, Sta. Belleville..............62223
Plaza, Sta. Chicago................60607
Pleasant Hill..........................62366
Pleasant Plains.......................62677
Plymouth...............................62367
Pocahontas............................62275
Polo.....................................61064
Pomona.................................62975
Pontiac (1st).........................61764
Pontoosuc.............................62368
Poplar Grove.........................61065
Port Byron............................61275
Posen...................................60469
Potomac...............................61865
Prairie City............................61470
Prairie Du Rocher...................62277
  Modoc, R. Br......................62261
Prairie View..........................60069
Preemption............................61276
Princeton (1st).......................61356
Princeville..............................61559
Prophetstown.........................61277
Prospect Heights (1st)............60070
Prudential Plaza, Sta.
  Chicago..............................60601
Pulaski..................................62976
Putnam..................................61560
Quad City Airport, R. Br.
  Moline.................................61265
Quincy (1st)..........................62301
  Columbus, R. Br..................62328
  Quinsippi, R. Sta..................62301
  Soldiers Home, Sta...............62301
Quinsippi, R. Sta. Quincy.......62301
Radom...................................62876
Raleigh..................................62977
Ramsey..................................62080
Rankin...................................60960
Ransom..................................60470
Rantoul (1st).........................61866
Rapids City............................61278
Rardin...................................61948
Raritan..................................61471
Ravenswood, Sta. Chicago......60625
Ravinia, Sta. Highland Park.....60035
Raymond................................62560
Red Bud................................62278
Red Oak................................61066
Reddick.................................60961
Redmon.................................61949
Renault..................................62279
Reynolds................................61279
Richmond (1st).......................60071
Richton Park..........................60471
Richview................................62877
Ridge Farm............................61870
Ridgway................................62979
Ridott...................................61067
Riggston................................62680
Rinard...................................62878
Ringwood..............................60072
Rio.......................................61472
River Forest, Br. Oak Park......60305

River Grove (1st)...................60171
Riverdale, Br. Chicago (see
  appendix)
Riverside (1st).......................60546
Riverton................................62561
Roanoke................................61561
Robbins.................................60472
Robbs...................................62980
Roberts.................................60962
Robinson (1st).......................62454
Rochelle (1st)........................61068
  Kings, R. Br.........................61045
Rochester..............................62563
Rock City..............................61070
Rock Falls (1st).....................61071
  Nelson, R. Br.......................61058
Rock Island (1st)...................61201
Rockbridge............................62081
Rockdale, Br. Joliet................60436
ROCKFORD (1st) (see
  appendix)
Rockport................................62370
Rockton (1st).........................61072
Rockwood..............................62280
Rogers Park, Sta. Chicago......60626
Rolling Acres, Sta. Peoria.......61614
Rolling Meadows, Br.
  Arlington Heights.................60008
Rome....................................61562
Roodhouse............................62082
Rosamond..............................62083
Roscoe..................................61073
Rose Hill, R. Br. Newton........62457
Rosebud................................62981
Roseland, Sta. Chicago...........60628
Roselle (1st)..........................60172
Rosemont, Br. Des Plaines......60018
Roseville...............................61473
Rosewood, Br. East Alton.......62024
Rosiclare...............................62982
Rossville................................60963
Round Grove..........................61280
Round Lake (1st)...................60073
Roxana..................................62084
Royal....................................61871
Royalton................................62983
Rushville................................62681
Russell..................................60075
Rutland.................................61358
S I U, Br. Edwardsville...........62025
Sadorus................................61872
Sailor Springs.........................62879
Saint Anne.............................60964
  Wichert, R. Br.....................60965
Saint Augustine......................61474
Saint Charles (1st).................60174
Saint David............................61563
Saint Elmo.............................62458
Saint Francisville.....................62460
Saint Jacob............................62281
Saint Joseph..........................61873
Saint Libory...........................62282
Saint Peter............................62880
Sainte Marie..........................62459
Salem (1st)...........................62881
San Jose................................62682
Sandoval...............................62882
Sandwich (1st).......................60548
Sauget, Br. East Saint
  Louis..................................62201
Sauk Village, Br. Chicago
  Heights...............................60411
Saunemin..............................61769

Savanna (1st) 61074
Savoy 61874
Sawyerville 62085
Saybrook 61770
Scales Mound 61075
Schaumburg, Br. Roselle ...60172
Scheller 62883
Schiller Park, Br. Franklin
   Park 60176
Sciota 61475
Scioto Mills, R. Br. Freeport...61076
Scott A F B, Br. Belleville...62225
Scottville 62683
Seaton 61476
Seatonville 61359
Secor 61771
Seneca 61360
Serena 60549
Sesser 62884
Seward 61077
Seymour 61875
Shabbona 60550
Shannon 61078
Shattuc 62283
Shawneetown 62984
Sheffield 61361
Shelbyville (1st) 62565
Sheldon 60966
Sheridan 60551
Sheridan Village, Sta.
   Peoria 61614
Sherman 62684
Sherrard 61281
Shipman 62685
Shirland 61079
Shirley 61772
Shobonier 62885
Shorewood, R. Br. Joliet...60436
Shumway 62461
Sibley 61773
Sidell 61876
Sidney 61877
Sigel 62462
Silvis (1st) 61282
Simpson 62985
Sims 62886
Skokie (1st) 60076
Smithboro 62284
Smithfield 61477
Smithshire 61478
Smithton 62285
Soldiers Home, Sta. Quincy...62301
Solon Mills 60080
Somonauk 60552
Sorento 62086
South, Sta. Evanston 60202
South Beloit (1st) 61080
South Bridgeview, Br. Oak
   Lawn 60455
South Central, Sta. Chicago...60605
South Chicago, Sta.
   Chicago 60617
South Chicago Heights, Br.
   Chicago Heights 60411
South Elgin 60177
South Holland (1st) 60473
South Jacksonville, Br.
   Jacksonville 62650
South Oak Park, Sta. Oak
   Park 60304
South Pekin 61564
South Roxana 62087
South Shore, Sta. Chicago...60649

South Standard 62686
South Stickney, Br. Oak
   Lawn 60459
South Wilmington 60474
Sparland 61565
Sparta (1st) 62286
Speer 61479
Spring Grove 60081
Spring Valley (1st) 61362
Springerton 62887
SPRINGFIELD (1st) (see
   appendix)
Standard 61363
Stanford 61774
Staunton 62088
Steeleville 62288
Steger (1st) 60475
Sterling (1st) 61081
   Coleta, R. Br. 61017
Steward 60553
Stewardson 62463
Stickney, Br. Berwyn 60402
Stillman Valley 61084
Stock Yards, Sta. Chicago...60609
Stockland 60967
Stockton 61085
Stone Park, Br. Melrose
   Park 60165
Stonefort 62987
Stonington 62567
Stoy 62464
Strasburg 62465
Strawn 61775
Streamwood, Br. Bartlett...60103
Streator (1st) 61364
   Ancona, R. Br. 61311
Stronghurst 61480
Sublette 61367
Sugar Grove 60554
Sullivan (1st) 61951
   Allenville, R. Br. 61901
Summer Hill 62372
Summerfield 62289
Summit, Sta. Argo 60501
Summum, R. Br. Astoria...61566
Sumner 62466
Sunnyland, Br. Washington...61571
Sutter 62373
Swansea, Br. Belleville...62221
Swanwick 62290
Sweet Water 62687
Sycamore (1st) 60178
Table Grove 61482
Taft, Br. Melrose Park...60163
Tallula 62688
Tamaroa 62888
Tamms 62988
   Unity, R. Br. 62993
Tampico 61283
Taylor Ridge 61284
Taylor Springs 62089
Taylorville (1st) 62568
Techny (1st) 60082
Temple Hill 62989
Tennessee 62374
Teutopolis 62467
Texico 62889
Thawville 60968
Thayer 62689
Thebes 62990
Thomasboro 61878
Thompsonville 62890
Thomson 61285

Thornton 60476
Tilden 62292
Timewell 62375
Tinley Park (1st) 60477
Tioga, R. Br. Mendon...62351
Tiskilwa 61368
Toledo 62468
Tolono 61880
Toluca 61369
Tonica 61370
Topeka 61567
Toulon 61483
Tovey 62570
Towanda 61776
Tower Hill 62571
Tremont 61568
Trenton 62293
Trilla 62469
Triumph 61371
Trivoli 61569
Troy 62294
Troy Grove 61372
Tunnel Hill 62991
Tuscola (1st) 61953
Twenty Second Street, Sta.
   Chicago 60616
Ullin 62992
Union 60180
Union Hill 60969
Unity, R. Br. Tamms 62993
University, Sta. Urbana...61801
Upper Alton, Sta. Alton...62002
Uptown, Sta. Chicago...60640
Urbana (1st) 61801
Ursa 62376
Utica 61373
Valier 62891
Valmeyer 62295
Van Orin 61374
Vandalia (1st) 62471
Varna 61375
Venedy, R. Br. Okawville...62296
Venice 62090
Vergennes 62994
Vermilion 61955
Vermont 61484
Vernon 62892
Verona 60479
Versailles 62378
Victoria 61485
Vienna 62995
Villa Grove 61956
Villa Park (1st) 60181
Villa Ridge 62996
Viola 61486
Virden 62690
Virgil, R. Br. Maple Park...60182
Virginia 62691
Waddams Grove, R. Br.
   Lena 61048
Wadsworth 60083
Waggoner 62572
Walnut 61376
Walnut Grove 61487
Walnut Hill 62893
Walsh 62297
Walshville 62091
Waltonville 62894
Wapella 61777
Warren 61087
Warrensburg 62573
Warrenville 60555
Warsaw 62379

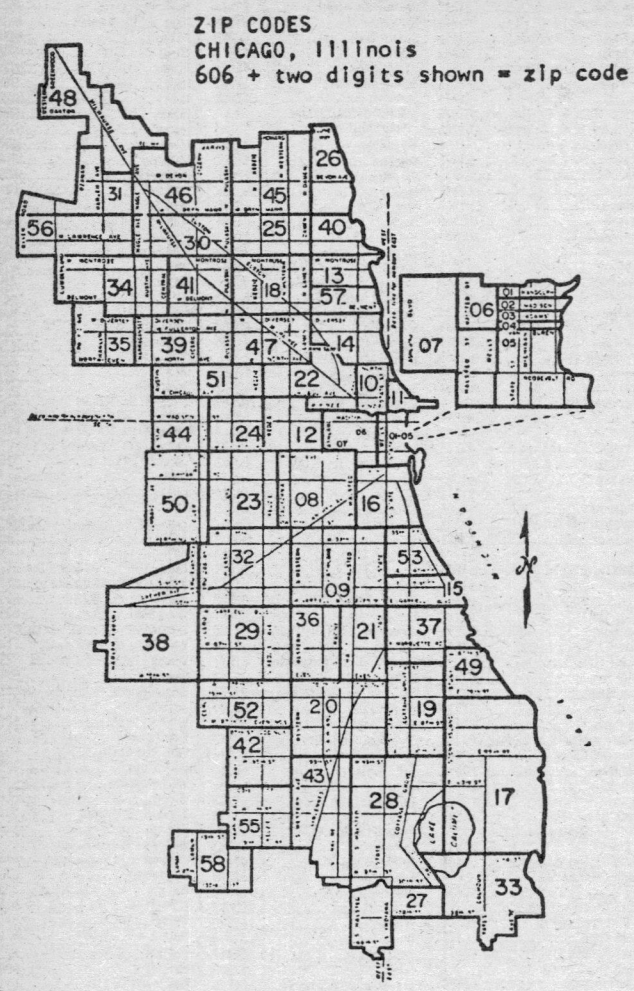

ZIP CODES
CHICAGO, Illinois
606 + two digits shown = zip code

Wasco............................60183
Washburn........................61570
Washington (1st)................61571
Washington Park, Br. East
    Saint Louis..................62204
Wataga..........................61488
Waterloo (1st)..................62298
Waterman........................60556
Watseka (1st)...................60970
Watson..........................62473
Wauconda (1st)..................60084
Waukegan (1st)..................60085
    Edison Square, Sta..........60085
    Great Lakes, Br.............60088
    Mc Gaw Park, Br.............60085
Waverly.........................62692
Wayne...........................60184
Wayne City......................62895
Waynesville.....................61778
Wedron..........................60557
Weldon..........................61882
Welge...........................62299
Wellington......................60973
Wenona..........................61377
Wentworth Woods, Sta.
    Calumet City................60409
West Brooklyn...................61378
West Chicago (1st)..............60185
West Frankfort (1st)............62896
West Gate, Sta. Joliet (see

appendix)
West Glen, Sta. Peoria..........61614
West Liberty....................62475
West Point......................62380
West Salem......................62476
West Union......................62477
West York.......................62478
Westchester, Br. Maywood........60153
Western Springs (1st)...........60558
Westervelt......................62574
Westfield.......................62474
Westmont (1st)..................60559
Westville.......................61883
Wheaton (1st)...................60187
Wheeler.........................62479
Wheeling (1st)..................60090
White Hall......................62092
White Heath.....................61884
Whittington.....................62897
Wichert, R. Br. Saint Anne......60965
Wicker Park, Sta. Chicago.......60622
Wildwood, Br. Grayslake.........60030
Williamsfield...................61489
Williamsville...................62693
Willisville.....................62997
Willow Hill.....................62480
Willow Springs (1st)............60480
Wilmette (1st)..................60091
Wilmington (1st)................60481
Wilsonville.....................62093

Winchester......................62694
Windsor.........................61957
Windsor Square, Sta. Peoria.....61614
Winfield (1st)..................60190
Winnebago.......................61088
Winnetka (1st)..................60093
Winslow.........................61089
Winthrop Harbor.................60096
Witt............................62094
Wolf Lake.......................62958
Wonder Lake.....................60097
Wood Dale (1st).................60191
Wood River (1st)................62095
Woodhull........................61490
Woodland........................60974
Woodlawn........................62898
Woodridge, Br. Downers
    Grove.......................60515
Woodson.........................62695
Woodstock (1st).................60098
Woosung.........................61091
Worden..........................62097
Worth (1st).....................60482
Wrights.........................62098
Wyanet..........................61379
Wyoming.........................61491
Xenia...........................62899
Yale............................62481
Yates City......................61572
Yorkville.......................60560

Appendix

ARLINGTON HEIGHTS 600

POST OFFICE BOXES

Box Nos.
ANY   Arlington
             Heights..........06

STATIONS, BRANCHES AND UNITS

Elk Grove Village Br............07
Rolling Meadows Br..............08
General Delivery................04
Postmaster......................04

AURORA   605

POST OFFICE BOXES

Box Nos.
1-1612   Main Office.......07

RURAL ROUTES

1,2,3..........................04

STATIONS, BRANCHES AND UNITS

General Delivery................07
Postmaster......................07

BELLEVILLE   622

POST OFFICE BOXES

Box Nos.
A-Z   Main Office.......22
1-690   Main Office.......22
1-790   Scott Air Force
             Base Sta.........25
800-999   Plaza Sta........23

RURAL ROUTES

1,2,3..........................21

STATIONS, BRANCHES AND UNITS

Plaza Sta......................23
Scott A F B Br.................25
Swansea Br.....................21
General Delivery...............20
Postmaster.....................20

CHICAGO   606

POST OFFICE BOXES

Box Nos.
A-Z   Downtown Sta..   90
1-2000   Downtown Sta..   90
AA-ZZ   Downtown Sta   90

2000-2999   Downtown Sta..   90
3000-4230   Merchandise
             Mart.........   54
4301-8687   Chicago.....   80
9000-9999   Downtown Sta..   90
09000-09199 Stock Yards...   09
11000-11999 Fort Dearborn
             Sta........   11
16000-16999 Twenty Second
             Street Station.   16
17001-17599 South Chicago... 17
24001-24999 Garfield Park... 24
27001-27179 Riverdale.....   27
35001-35270 Elmwood Park...   35
42601-42999 Evergreen Park.   42
45001-45375 Northtown.....   59
48001-48329 Niles........   48
50001-50397 Cicero.....   50
56001-56239 Harwood
             Heights....   56
66001-66518 O Hare
             International
             Airport.....   66
91000-97899 Bank Boxes....   90

RURAL ROUTES

1..............................58

STATIONS, BRANCHES AND UNITS

Alsip Br.......................58
Ashburn Sta....................52
Auburn Park Sta................20

Chicago (Con.)   606

Austin Sta................................ 44
Calumet Park Br...................... 43
Chestnut Street Sta................. 10
Chicago Lawn Sta.................... 29
Cicero Br................................. 50
Clearing Sta............................. 38
Cragin Sta............................... 39
Division Street Sta.................. 51
Dunning Sta............................ 34
Edgebrook Sta......................... 46
Elmwood Park Br..................... 35
Englewood Sta......................... 21
Evergreen Park Br.................... 42
Fort Dearborn Sta.................... 11
Garfield Park Sta...................... 24
Golf Mill Br............................. 48
Grand Crossing Sta.................. 19
Harwood Heights Br................. 56
Hawthorne Sta......................... 23
Haymarket Sta......................... 06
Hegewisch Sta......................... 33
Hillside-Berkley Br................... 62
Hyde Park Sta.......................... 15
Irving Park Sta......................... 41
Jackson Park Sta...................... 37
Jefferson Sta........................... 30
Kedzie Grace Sta..................... 18
Lakeveiw Sta........................... 13
Lincoln Park Sta....................... 14
Logan Square Sta..................... 47
Main Post Office Sta................. 80
Merchandise Mart Sta.............. 54
Mid-West Sta............................ 54
Mid-West Sta............................ 12
Morgan Park Sta....................... 43
Mount Greenwood Sta.............. 55
Niles Br.................................... 60
Nineteenth Avenue Sta............. 19
North Town Sta........................ 45
Norwood Park Sta.................... 31
O Hare Airport Sta.................... 66
Ogden Park Sta........................ 36
Old Post Office......................... 02
Pilsen Sta................................ 08
Plaza Sta.................................. 07
Prudential Plaza Sta................. 01
Ravenswood Sta....................... 25
Riverdale Br............................. 27
Rogers Park Sta....................... 26
Roseland Sta............................ 28
South Central Sta..................... 05
South Chicago Sta.................... 17
South Shore Sta....................... 49
Stock Yards Sta........................ 09
Twenty Second Street Sta......... 16
Uptown Sta.............................. 40
Wicker Park Sta........................ 22
General Delivery....................... 07
Postmaster............................... 07

APARTMENTS, HOTELS, MOTELS

Allerton, 701 N Michigan......... 11
Ambassador West, 1300 N
    State................................... 10
Ambassor East, 1301 N State
    St.. 10

Belden Stratford, 2300 N
    Lincoln Park W................... 14
Belmont, 3156 N Sheridan...... 57
Berkshire, 15 E Ohio............... 11
Bismarck, 171 W Randolph...... 01
Cass, 640 N Wabash................ 11
Civic Center, 167 W
    Washington........................ 02
Congress, 520 S Michigan....... 05
Conrad Hilton, 720 S
    Michigan............................. 05
Continental, 909 N Michigan.... 11
Croydon, 616 N Rush............... 11
Del Prado, 5307 S Hyde Park... 15
Devonshire, 19 E Ohio............. 11
Drake, 140 E Walton................ 11
East End Park, 5240 S Hyde
    Park.................................... 15
Eastgate, 162 E Ontario........... 11
Executive House, 71 E
    Wacker Dr........................... 01
Flamingo, 5520 S South
    Shore.................................. 37
Fort Dearborn, 117 W Van
    Buren.................................. 05
Harrison, 65 E Harrison............ 05
Knickerbocker, 163 E Walton... 11
La Salle, 12 N La Salle............. 02
Lake Shore Drive, 181 Lake
    Shore.................................. 11
Maryland, 900 N Rush.............. 11
Midland, 172 W Adams............. 03
New Lawrence, 1020 W
    Lawrence............................ 40
Oxford House, 225 N
    Wabash............................... 01
Palmer House, 17 E Monroe..... 90
Parkway, 2100 N Lincoln
    Park W................................ 14
Pearson, 190 E Pearson........... 11
Planters, 19 N Clark................. 02
Plaza, 1555 N Clark.................. 10
Saint Clair, 162 E Ohio St......... 11
Seneca, 200 E Chestnut........... 11
Sheraton Blackstone, 636 S
    Michigan............................. 05
Sheraton-Chicago, 505 North
    Michigan Ave....................... 11
Sherman, 112 W Randolph....... 01
Sherry, 1725 E 53rd................. 15
Shoreland, 5454 S South
    Shore.................................. 15
Somerset, 5009 N Sheridan...... 40
Southmoor, 6646 S Stony
    Island................................. 37
Sovereign, 6200 N Kenmore..... 26
Water Tower Inn, 800 N
    Michigan............................. 11
Webster, 2150 N Lincoln Park
    W.. 14
Windermere, 1642 E 56th......... 37
Y M C A, 826 S Wabash St........ 05

BUILDINGS

Adams & Franklin, 222 W
    Adams................................. 06
Adams & Wabash, 207 S
    Wabash............................... 02
American Dental Assoc, 211
    E Chicago St....................... 11
American National Bank, 33
    N La Salle........................... 02

Apollo Savings, 430 N
    Michigan Ave....................... 11
Art Institute, S Michigan & E
    Adams................................. 03
Association, 19 S La Salle........ 03
Bankers, 105 W Adams............ 03
Barrister Hall, 29 S La Salle
    St.. 03
Bay State, 140 N State............. 02
Bell Savings, 79 W Monroe...... 03
Bell Telephone, 208 W
    Washington........................ 06
Bentley-Murray, 511 S
    Plymouth Ct....................... 05
Blum, 624 S Michigan.............. 05
Board Of Trade, 141 W
    Jackson............................... 04
Borg-Warner, 200 S
    Michigan............................. 04
Borland Manufacturing, 636
    S Federal............................ 05
Borland, 105 S La Salle............ 03
Boyce, 510 N Dearborn............ 10
Brooks, 223 W Jackson............ 06
Brunswick, 623 S Wabash........ 05
Brunswick, 69 W Washington... 02
Builders, 228 N La Salle........... 01
Butler, 162 N State................... 01
Canterbury, 173 W Madison..... 02
Carbide & Carbon, 230 N
    Michigan............................. 01
Central Station, 135 E. 11th
    Pl....................................... 05
Champlain, 37 S Wabash.......... 03
Chicago Burlington & Quincy,
    547 W Jackson.................... 06
Chicago Daily Defender, 2400
    Michigan............................. 16
Chicago Federal Savings,
    108 N State......................... 02
Chicago Garment Center, 337
    S Franklin.......................... 06
Chicago Mercantile
    Exchange, 308 W
    Washington........................ 06
Chicago Motor Club, 66 E
    South Water St.................... 01
Chicago Northwestern, 500 W
    Madison.............................. 06
Chicago Park District
    Burnham Park, 425 E.
    McIetridge Dr..................... 05
Chicago Real Estate Board,
    105 W Madison.................... 02
Chicago Stadium, 1800 W
    Madison St.......................... 12
Chicago Temple, 77 W
    Washington........................ 02
Chicago Title & Trust, 111 W
    Washington........................ 02
Chicago Today, 445 N.
    Michigan Ave....................... 11
Chicago Tribune, 435 N
    Michigan............................. 11
Chicago-Clark, 800 N Clark...... 10
Chicago, 7 W Madison.............. 02
Civic Center, 50 W
    Washington........................ 02
Congress Bank, 506 S
    Wabash............................... 04
Consumers Company, 220 S
    State................................... 04

Chicago (Con.)   606

Continental Illinois Bank, 231 S La Salle St...... 04
Continental Illinois Bank, 231 S. La. Salle St...... 93
Converse, 618 W Jackson...... 06
Corn Products, 201 N Wells. 06
Coronet, 65 E South Water. 01
County, 118 N Clark...... 02
Crane, 836 S Michigan...... 05
Cuneo, 151 N Michigan...... 01
Daily News, 401 N Wabash. 11
Daily Sun Times, 401 N Wabash...... 11
Dearborn Station, 47 W Polk St...... 05
Delaware, 36 W Randolph..... 01
Distributors, 236 N Clark..... 01
Donohue, 711 S Dearborn.... 05
Douglas, 20 E Jackson...... 04
Dwight, 626 S Clark...... 05
Edison, 72 W Adams...... 03
Eiger, 1255 S Wabash...... 04
Electrical, 625 W Jackson.... 06
Engineering, 205 W Wacker Dr...... 06
Enterprise, 311 N Desplaines. 06
Equitable, 401 N Michigan St...... 11
Esquire, 65 E South Water.... 01
Everett Mckinley Dirksen, 219 S. Dearborn...... 04
Exchange, Union Stock Yards. 09
Exhibitors, 325 N Wells...... 10
Fairbanks-Morse, 600 S Michigan...... 05
Farwell, 664 N Michigan...... 11
Fashion Trades, 318 W Adams...... 06
Federal Reserve Bank, 230 S La Salle...... 04
Federal, 536 S. Clark...... 05
Federation, 175 W Madison... 04
Finchley, 23 E Jackson...... 04
Findlay, 320 S Michigan...... 04
Fine Arts, 410 S Michigan.... 05
First Federal, 7 S Dearborn... 03
First National Bank, One First National Plaza...... 70
Fisher, 343 S Dearborn...... 04
Flomor, 1018 S Wabash...... 05
Frank J Lewis, 25 E Jackson.. 04
Franklin, 525 S Dearborn..... 05
Fulton Market Cold Storage, 1000 W Fulton...... 07
Furniture Mart, 666 N Lake Shore Dr...... 11
Garland, 111 N Wabash...... 02
Goddard, 27 E Monroe...... 03
Great Lakes, 180 N Wacker Dr...... 06
Greyhound, 71 W Lake St...... 01
Harris Bank, 111 W Monroe... 03
Harrison-Clark, 85 W Harrison...... 05
Hearst, 326 W Madison...... 06
Hertz, 218 S Wabash St...... 04
Heyworth, 29 E Madison...... 02
Hull House, 800 S Halsted St...... 07

I.b.m. Plaza, 1 E. I.b.m. Plaza...... 11
Illinois Central Station, 135 E 11 Th Pl...... 05
Industry, 117 N Wells St...... 06
Inland Steel, 30 W Monroe..... 03
Insurance Center, 330 S Wells...... 06
Insurance Exchange Annex, 166 W Van Buren...... 04
Insurance Exchange, 175 W Jackson...... 04
International Harvester, 180 N Michigan...... 01
Isabella, 21 E Van Buren..... 05
Jackson-Franklin, 309 W Jackson...... 06
Jewelers, 19 S Wabash...... 03
Joel Hunter, 123 W Madison.. 02
John Crerar Library, 35 W 33rd St...... 16
John Hancock, 875 N. Michigan...... 11
Kemper Insurance, 20 N Wacker Dr...... 06
Kiwanis International, 101 E Erie...... 11
L B Knight, 549 W Randolph.. 06
La Salle Bank, 135 S Lasalle...... 03
La Salle Station, 139 W Van Buren St...... 05
La Salle-Wacker, 221 N La Salle...... 01
Lake View, 116 S Michigan St...... 03
Lawyers, 166 W Washington... 02
Le Moyne, 180 N Wabash...... 01
Lees, 19 S Wells...... 06
Lincoln Towers, 75 E Wacker Dr...... 01
Lions, 209 N Michigan...... 01
Loop End, 177 N State...... 01
Lundington, 1104 S Wabash... 05
Lyon & Healy, 64 E Jackson... 04
Lytton, 14 E Jackson...... 04
Machinery Hall, 549 W Washington...... 06
Machinery Sales, 565 W Washington...... 06
Madison Terminal, 9 S Clinton...... 06
Magill Weinsheimer, 1332 S Wabash...... 05
Majestic, 22 W Monroe...... 03
Mallers, 5 S Wabash...... 03
Manhattan, 431 S Dearborn... 05
Maremont, 168 N Michigan... 01
Marina City, 300 N State St... 10
Market Exchange, 1440 S Racine...... 08
Marlennan Plaza, 222 S. Riverside Plaza...... 06
Marquette, 140 S Dearborn... 03
Marshall Field Annex, 25 E Washington...... 02
Marycrest, 120 S State...... 03
Masonite, 29 N Wacker Dr..... 06
Mc Cormick Place Chicago Exposition, 23 Rd & S Lake Shore Dr...... 16
Mc Cormick, 332 S Michigan. 04

Mc Graw Hill, 520 N Michigan St...... 11
Mc Kinlock, 209 W Jackson ... 06
Memorial Hall, 85 E Randolph...... 01
Mentor, 6 E Monroe...... 03
Merchandise Mart, 222 Merchandise Mart Plaza.... 54
Metropolitan, 134 N La Salle.. 02
Michigan Boulevard, 30 N Michigan...... 02
Michigan Square, 540 N Michigan...... 11
Midland, 176 N Adams...... 03
Midway Airport Terminal, 5700 S Cicero St...... 38
Millinery Mart, 323 S Franklin...... 06
Monadnock Block, 53 W Jackson...... 04
Monroe, 104 S Michigan...... 03
Morton Salt, 110 N Wacker Dr...... 06
Moser, 621 S Plymouth Ct..... 05
Moses, 234 S Wells...... 05
Mossner, 108 W Lake...... 01
National Cash Register, 223 N Michigan...... 01
National Republic, 134 S La Salle...... 03
North American Life, 35 E Wacker St...... 01
North American, 36 S State.... 03
Northern Trust Company, 50 S La Salle...... 03
Northwestern, 500 W Madison...... 06
Oakes, 658 S Clark...... 05
Occidental, 109 N Wacker Dr.. 06
Ogden, 192 N Clark...... 01
Ohio, 509 S Wabash...... 05
Old Colony, 407 S Dearborn... 05
Old Republic, 307 N Michigan...... 01
One La Salle Street, 1 N La Salle...... 02
One-Sixty-Two, 162 N State St...... 01
Orchestra Hall, 220 S Michigan...... 04
Otis Elevator, 600 W Jackson. 03
Otis, 10 S La Salle...... 03
Outer Drive East, 400 E Randolph St...... 01
Patten, 161 W Harrison...... 05
Pelouze, 230 E Ohio...... 11
Peoples Gas, 122 S Michigan...... 03
Peterson, 523 S Plymouth Ct.. 05
Pittsfield, 55 E Washington... 02
Playboy Club 919 Michigan Ave. N...... 11
Plymouth-Polk, 731 S Plymouth Ct...... 05
Pontiac, 542 S Dearborn...... 05
Pope, 633 S Plymouth Ct...... 05
Printers, 732 S Sherman...... 05
Prudential, 130 E Randolph... 01
Railway Exchange, 80 E Jackson St...... 04
Randolph Towers, 188 W Randolph...... 01
Randolph-Wells, 130 N Wells.. 06

Chicago (Con.)   606

Riverside Plaza, 2 N
  Riverside Plaza 06
Roanoke, 11 S La Salle 03
Rookery, 209 S La Salle 04
Roosevelt, 179 W
  Washington 02
Science Research, 259 E
  Erie 11
Security, 189 W Madison 02
Shops, 17 N Wabash 02
Silversmiths, 10 S Wabash
  St 03
Socony Vacuum, 59 E Van
  Buren 05
Standard Oil, 910 S
  Michigan 05
Stark, 234 S Wabash 04
State & Lake, 190 N State 01
State & Randolph, 6 W
  Randolph 01
State-Madison, 22 W
  Madison 02
Steger, 28 E Jackson 04
Stevens, 17 N State 02
Stone Container, 360 N
  Michigan 01
Sun-Times Sun-Times Daily
  News Plaza, 401 N
  Wabash 11
Telephone, 230 W
  Washington 06
Terminals, 537 S Dearborn 05
The Canterbury, 173 W
  Madison 02
Thirty Five East Wacker 01
Thirty North La Salle 02
Thirty Three East Congress
  Parkway, 33e. Congress
  Pkwy 05
Transportation, 608 S
  Dearborn 05
Tribune Tower, 435 N
  Michigan 11
Tuttle, 6 E Lake 01
Union Station, 516 W
  Jackson St 06
Union Tank, 111 Jackson
  Blvd 04
United Insurance, 1 E
  Wacker 01
United States Gypsum, 101 S
  Wacker 06
Utilities, 327 S La Salle 04
Van Buren, 210 W Van
  Buren 07
Wall Street Journal, 711 W.
  Monroe 90
Western Union, 427 S La
  Salle 05
Westminster, 110 S
  Dearborn 03
Williams, 59 E Monroe 03
Wilkamson, 605 W
  Washington 03
Willoughby, 8 S Michigan 03
Woods, 54 W Randolph 01
Wrigley Annex, 410 N
  Michigan 11
Wrigley, 400 N Michigan 11

GOVERNMENT OFFICES

Chicago Police Dept, 1111 S
  State St 05
Chicago Public Library, 78 E
  Washington St 02
City Hall, 121 N La Salle St 02
Main Post Office, 433 W Van
  Buren 07
State Of Illinois Office, 160
  N La Salle 01
United States Courthouse,
  219 S Dearborn 04

HOSPITALS

Alexian Brothers, 1200 W
  Belden 14
American, 850 W Irving Park 13
Augustana, 409 W Dickens 14
Belmont, 4058 W Melrose 41
Bethany Home & Hospital Of
  The Methodist, 5015 N
  Paulina 40
Bethany, 3420 W Van Buren 24
Bethesda, 2451 W Howard 45
Billings, 950 E 59 Th St 37
Bobs Roberts, 920 E 59th 37
Central Community, 5701 S
  Wood 36
Chicago Eye Ear Nose &
  Throat, 231 W
  Washington 66
Chicago Lying-In, 5845 S
  Maryland 37
Chicago Osteopathic, 5200 S
  Ellis 15
Chicago State, 6500 W Irving
  Park Rd 34
Children Department Michael
  Reese, 29th & Ellis 16
Childrens Memorial, 2300
  Children'S Plaza 14
Columbus, 2520 N Lakeview 14
Contagious Disease, 3026 S
  California 08
Cook County, 1835 W
  Harrison 12
Covenant, 5145 N California 25
Cuneo Frank, 750 W
  Montrose St 13
Doctors General, 6970 N
  Clark 26
Dunning, 6500 W Irving Park
  Rd 34
Edgewater, 5700 N Ashland 60
Englewood, 6001 S Green 21
Evangelical, 5421 S Morgan 09
Forkosh, 2544 W Montrose 16
Franklin Boulevard
  Community, 3240 W
  Franklin Blvd 24
Friend Pavillion, 3001 S Ellis 16
Garfield Park, 3821 W
  Washington 24
Grant, 551 W Grant 14
Henrotin, 939 N La Salle 10
Holy Cross, 2700 W 69th 29
Ida Mae Scott, 5027 S
  Prairie 15
Illinois Central, 5800 S Stony
  Island 37
Illinois Eye & Ear Infirmary
  904 W Adams 07

Illinois Masonic, 834 W
  Wellington 57
Illinois State Pediatric, 1640
  W Roosevelt Road 68
Illinois State Psychiatric
  Institute, 1601 W Taylor 12
Jackson Park, 7531 S Stony
  Island 49
La Rabida, 6501 So
  Promontory Dr 49
Little Company Of Mary,
  2800 W 95th 42
Loretto, 625 S Central 44
Louis A Weiss Memorial,
  4646 N Marine Drive 40
Louise Burg, 225 W Cermak
  Rd 16
Lutheran Deaconess, 1138 N
  Leavitt 22
Martha Washington, 2318 W
  Irving Park 18
Mary Thompson, 140 N
  Ashland 07
Mercy Hospital, 2510 S King
  Dr 16
Michael Reese, E 29th &
  Ellis 16
Misericordia, 2916 W 47th 32
Mount Sinai, 2750 W 15th
  Pl 68
Municipal Tuberculosis
  Sanitarium, 5601 N
  Pulaski Rd 46
North Avenue, 1625 W North
  St 22
Northwest, 5645 W Addison 34
Norweigian American, 1044 N
  Francisco 22
Passavant Memorial, 303 E
  Superior 11
Presbyterian Saint Lukes 12
Provident, 426 E 51st 15
Ravenswood, 1917 W Wilson 40
Resurrection, 7435 W Talcott 31
Roosevelt Memorial, 426 W
  Wisconsin 14
Roseland Community, 45 W
  111th 28
Saint Annes, 4950 W
  Thomas 81
Saint Anthony De Padua,
  2875 W 19th 28
Saint Bernards, 6337 S
  Harvard 21
Saint Elizabeths, 1435 N
  Claremont 22
Saint Francis X Cabrini, 811
  S Lytle St 07
Saint Georges, 449 W
  Winneconna 20
Saint Josephs, 2900 N
  Lakeshore Dr 57
Saint Marys Of Nazareth,
  1120 N Leavitt 22
Saint Vincents Infant, 721 N
  La Salle 10
Sarah Morris, 29th & Ellis 16
Shriners, 2211 N Oak Park
  Ave 35
South Chicago Community,
  2320 E 93rd 17
South Shore, 8015 S Luella 17

Chicago (Con.)   606

Swedish Covenant, 5145 N
   California 25
University Of Illinois General,
   840 S Wood 12
University Of Illinois
   Neuropsychiatric, 912
   Wood St 12
Veterans Administration
   Research, 333 E Huron 11
Veterans Administration, 820
   S Damen 12
Walther Memorial, 1116 N
   Kedzie 51
Wesley Memorial, 250 E
   Superior 11
Woodlawn, 6060 S Drexel 37

UNIVERSITIES AND COLLEGES

Chicago Kent College Of Law,
   10 N Franklin 06
De Paul University, 2322 N
   Kenmore 14
Illinois Institute Of
   Technology, 3300 S
   Federal 16
John Marshall Law, 315 S
   Plymouth Ct 04
Lewis Towers, 820 N
   Michigan 11
Loyola University, 6525 N
   Sheridan Rd 26
Mundelein, 6363 N Sheridan .. 26
North Park, 5125 N
   Spaulding 25
Northwestern University
   Chicago Camp Us, 301 E
   Chicago Av. 11
Roosevelt University 430
   Michigan Ave. S. 05
Saint Xavier, 103rd &
   Central Park 55
University Of Chicago,
   Downtown Center, 65 E.
   South Water 01
University Of Chicago, 5801
   S Ellis 37
University Of Ill Cir Campus .. 80
University Of Illinois Medic,
   1853 W Polk 12

NAMED STREETS

Abbott Ave S 20
Aberdeen N
   1-399 07
   400-OUT 22
Aberdeen S
   1-1199 07
   1200-3499 08
   4700-5499 09
   5500-7499 21
   7500-9499 20
   9500-13199 43
Achsah Bond Dr 05
Acme Ave W 27
Ada N
   1-399 07
   400-OUT 22
Ada S
   600-999 07
   1600-1799 08
   4700-5499 09

   5500-7499 36
   7500-9499 20
   9500-13199 43
Adams E 03
Adams W
   1-199 03
   200-799 06
   800-1599 07
   1600-3199 12
   3200-4599 24
   4600-5999 44
Addison W
   500-1999 13
   2000-3999 18
   4000-5599 41
   5600-8399 34
Agatite Ave W
   800-999 40
   2100-3999 25
   4000-6399 30
   6400-8799 56
Ainslie W
   800-1999 40
   2000-3999 25
   4000-6399 30
   7200-8799 56
Albany Ave N
   1-799 12
   800-1599 22
   1600-2799 47
   2800-4399 18
   4400-5599 25
   5600-6399 59
   6400-7599 45
Albany Ave S
   1-1199 12
   1200-3499 23
   3500-5499 32
   5500-7499 29
   7500-8699 52
   8700-10299 42
   10300-11499 55
Albany Dr S
   11500-11899 55
Albion Ave W
   1000-1999 26
   2000-3999 45
   4000-5299 46
   6500-7299 31
Aldine Ave W 57
Alexander W 16
Algonquin Ave N 46
Allen Ave N 18
Allport S 08
Almond S 12
Alpine Dr S 58
Alta Vis Ter N 13
Altgeld W
   800-1999 14
   2000-3999 47
   4000-6399 39
   6400-7999 35
Amelia Dr W 48
Ancona W 22
Anthony Ave S
   6800-7099 37
   7100-7999 19
   8000-OUT 17
Arcade Pl W
   100-199 03
   500-799 06
   800-1599 07
   1600-OUT 12

Arch S 08
Archer Ave S
   1900-2499 16
   2500-3499 08
   3500-3699 09
   3700-5399 32
   5400-7199 38
Ardmore Ave W
   900-1999 60
   2000-3999 59
   4000-6399 46
   6400-7899 31
Argyle W
   800-1999 40
   2000-3999 25
   4000-6399 30
   6400-8799 56
Arlington Pl W 14
Armitage Ave W
   200-1499 14
   1500-1999 22
   2000-3999 47
   4000-6399 35
   6400-7999 35
Armour N 22
Armstrong E 11
Armstrong Ave W
   5200-5599 46
Artesian Ave N
   200-799 12
   800-1599 22
   1600-2799 47
   2800-4399 18
   4400-5599 25
   5600-6399 59
   6400-7599 45
Artesian Ave S
   300-399 12
   2500-3499 08
   3500-5499 32
   5500-7499 29
   7500-8699 52
   8700-10299 42
   10300-11899 55
Arthington W
   400-1599 07
   1600-3199 12
   3200-4599 24
   4600-5999 44
Arthur Ave W
   1100-1999 26
   2000-3999 45
   4000-4799 46
   6400-7199 31
Ashland Ave N
   1-399 07
   400-1999 22
   2000-2799 14
   2800-3599 57
   3600-4399 13
   4400-5599 40
   5600-6399 60
   6400-7799 26
   8800-9599 48
Ashland Ave S
   1-1199 07
   1200-3499 08
   3500-5499 09
   5500-7499 36
   7500-9499 20
   9500-12925 43
   12927-13199 (ODD) 43
Astor N 10

Chicago (Con)   606

Atlantic Ave S	27
Attrill W	47
Augusta Blvd W	
1200-3199	22
3200-5999	51
Austin Ave N	
1-799 (ODD)	44
801-1599 (ODD)	51
1600-2799	39
2800-4399	34
4400-5599	30
5600-6399	46
Austin Ave S	
1-1199 (ODD)	44
1200-3899	50
4700-7499	38
Avalon Ave S	
7600-9499	19
9500-OUT	28
Avenue A S	17
Avenue B S	
10200-12199	17
Avenue C S	
10100-12199	17
Avenue D S	
10100-12199	17
Avenue E S	17
Avenue F S	
10200-12199	17
12200-13799	33
Avenue G S	17
Avenue H S	17
Avenue J S	17
Avenue K S	33
Avenue L S	
9500-12199	17
12200-13799	33
Avenue M S	
9500-12199	17
12200-13599	33
Avenue N S	
9500-12199	17
12200-13599	33
Avenue O S	
8500-12199	17
12200-14399	33
Avers Ave N	
200-799	24
800-1599	51
1600-2799	47
2800-4399	18
4400-5599	25
5600-6399	59
6400-7399	45
Avers Ave S	
1200-3499	23
3500-5499	32
5500-7499	29
7500-8699	52
8700-10299	42
10300-11899	55
11900-13299	58
Avondale Ave N	
2900-3899	18
3900-4399	41
4400-5599	30
5600-5699	46
5700-OUT	31
Badger Dr W	58
Baker Ave S	17

Balbo Ave E	05
Ballard Rd W	48
Balmoral Ave W	
900-1999	40
2000-3999	25
4000-6399	30
6400-8399	56
Baltimore Ave S	
8300-12199	17
12200-13599	33
Banks E	10
Barber W	07
Barry Ave W	
300-1999	57
2000-3999	18
4000-5599	41
5600-7199	34
7200-7999	35
Bauwans N	22
Beach Ave W	
1600-1799	22
3200-5999	51
Beacon N	40
Belden Ave W	
300-1999	14
2000-3999	47
4000-5599	39
6400-7999	35
Bell Ave N	
1-799	12
800-1599	22
1600-2799	47
2800-4399	18
4400-5599	25
5600-6399	59
6400-7599	45
Bell Ave S	
1-1199	12
1200-3499	08
3500-5499	09
5500-7499	36
7500-9499	20
9500-11899	43
Belle Plaine Ave W	
800-1999	13
2000-3999	18
4000-5599	41
5600-8399	34
Bellefort N	48
Bellevue Pl E	11
Belmont Ave W	
300-1999	57
2000-3999	18
4000-5599	41
5600-7599	34
7600-7998 (EVEN)	35
7601-7999 (ODD)	35
8000-8398 (EVEN)	34
Belt Circle Dr S	38
Benck Dr W	58
Bennett Ave S	
6700-7899	49
7900-12199	17
Bensley Ave S	
9400-12199	17
12200-14599	33
Benson S	08
Berenice Ave W	
1800-1999	13
2000-3999	18
4000-5599	41
5600-7999	34

Berkeley Ave S	
4100-4699	53
4700-OUT	15
Bernard N	
1600-2799	47
2800-4399	18
4400-5599	25
5600-6399	59
6400-7199	45
Berry Dr S	16
Berteau Ave W	
1400-1999	13
2000-3999	18
4000-5599	41
5600-8399	34
Berwyn Ave W	
1000-1999	40
2000-3999	25
4000-6399	30
6400-8799	56
Besly Ct N	22
Betty Ter W	48
Beverly Ave S	
8700-9499	20
9500-OUT	43
Beverly Glen Pky W	43
Bingham N	47
Birchdale Ave W	35
Birchwood Ave W	
1300-1999	26
2000-3199	45
6800-7799	48
Birkhoff Ave S	20
Bishop N	
1-99	07
400-OUT	22
Bishop S	
400-999	07
1800-1899	08
4600-5499	09
5500-7499	36
7500-9499	20
9500-13199	43
Bissell N	14
Bittersweet Pl W	13
Blackhawk W	
400-799	10
800-OUT	22
Blackstone Ave S	
4800-5499	15
5500-7099	37
7100-9499	19
9500-OUT	28
Blake S	09
Blanchard Ct S	16
Bliss W	22
Bloomingdale Ave W	
1500-1999	22
2000-3999	47
4000-6399	39
6400-7999	35
Blue Island Ave S	
600-1199	07
1200-OUT	08
Bonaparte S	08
Bond Ave S	17
Bonfield S	08
Bosworth Ave N	
1200-1999	22
2300-2799	14
2800-3599	57
3600-4399	13
6400-7799	26

Chicago (Con.)   606

Boulevard Way S 23
Bowen Ave E 53
Bowler W 12
Bowmanville Ave N 25
Bradley Pl W
  800-1999 13
  2000-OUT 18
Brainard Ave S 33
Brandon Ave S
  7900-12199 17
  12200-13699 33
Brayton St E & W 28
Breen Ave W 48
Brennan Ave S 17
Brewery Ave S 16
Briar Pl W 57
Brighton Pl S 32
Broad S 08
Broadway N
  2800-3599 57
  3600-4399 13
  4400-5599 40
  5600-6399 60
Brodman Ave W 56
Brompton Ave W 57
Bross Ave W 08
Browning Ave E 53
Bruce Dr W 48
Bryn Mawr Ave W
  900-1999 60
  2000-3999 59
  4000-6399 46
  6400-8799 31
Buckingham Pl W 57
Buena Ave W 13

Buffalo Ave S
  7900-12199 17
  13000-13699 33
Burley Ave S
  7900-12199 17
  12200-13599 33
Burling N
  1200-1599 10
  1600-2699 14
  2800-2999 57
Burnham Ave S
  7600-7899 49
  7900-12199 17
  12200-14399 33
Burr Oak Ave W
  1600-1799 43
  1800-1948 (EVEN) 43
Burton Pl E & W 10
Busse Ave N 56
Butler Dr E 33
Byron W
  1000-1999 13
  2000-3999 18
  4000-5599 41
  5600-8399 34
Cable Pl E 37
Cabrini W 07
Cal-Sag Rd S 58
Caldwell Ave N
  5600-7199 46
  7200-8399 48
Calhoun Ave S
  9400-12199 17
  12200-14599 33

California Ave N
  1-799 12
  800-1599 22
  1600-2799 47
  2800-4399 18
  4400-5599 25
  5600-6399 59
  6400-7599 45
California Ave S
  1-1199 12
  1200-3499 08
  3500-5499 32
  5500-7499 29
  7500-8699 52
  8700-10299 42
  10300-11499 55
Callero Dr N 48
Calumet Ave S
  1800-3499 16
  3500-4699 53
  4700-5499 15
  5500-7099 37
  7100-9499 19
  9500-12999 28
  13000-13799 27
Calumet River S
  8900-12199 17
  12200-OUT 33
Cambridge Ave N
  800-1199 10
  2300-2399 14
  2800-3199 57
Campbell Ave N
  1-799 12
  800-1599 22
  1600-2799 47
  2800-4399 18
  4400-5599 25
  5600-6399 59
  6400-7599 45
Campbell Ave S
  1-1199 12
  1200-3499 08
  3500-5499 32
  5500-7499 29
  7500-8699 52
  8700-10299 42
  10300-11899 55
Campbell Park W 12
Canal N 06
Canal S
  1-399 06
  400-1599 07
  1600-3499 16
  3500-OUT 09
Canalport Ave S
  1700-2057 16
  2058-OUT 08
Canfield Ave N
  4400-5599 56
  5600-6399 31
Capitol Dr N 45
Carmen Ave W
  800-1999 40
  2000-3999 25
  4000-6399 30
  6400-8799 56
Carol Ave W 48
Carolyn Ln S 58
Carondolet Ave S
  10600-12199 17
  12200-13499 33

Carpenter N
  1-399 07
  400-OUT 22
Carpenter S
  400-1099 07
  1600-3499 08
  5008-5499 09
  5500-7499 21
  7500-9499 20
  9500-13199 43
Carroll Ave W
  1-399 10
  400-799 06
  800-1599 07
  1600-3199 12
  3200-4599 24
  4600-OUT 44
Carver Plz E 53
Castlewood Ter W 48
Catalpa Ave W
  900-1999 48
  2000-3999 25
  4000-6399 30
  6400-8799 56
Cathedral Sq N 11
Catherine Ave W 56
Catino Ter W 48
Caton W 47
Cedar E 11
Cedar Ln W 48
Central Ave N
  1-799 44
  800-1599 51
  1600-2799 39
  2800-4399 34
  4400-5599 30
  5600-6799 46
  6800-7198 (EVEN) 46
  7200-7599 48
Central Ave S
  1-1199 44
  1200-3899 50
  4700-7499 38
  12525-12699 (ODD) 58
Central Park Ave N
  200-799 24
  800-1599 51
  1600-2799 47
  2800-4399 18
  4400-5599 25
  5600-6399 59
  6400-7199 45
Central Park Ave S
  1-1199 24
  1200-3499 23
  3500-5499 32
  5500-7499 29
  7500-8699 52
  8700-10299 42
  10300-11899 55
  11900-13299 58
Cermak Rd E 16
Cermak Rd W
  1-799 16
  800-2799 08
  2800-4599 23
  4600-6199 50
Chalmers Pl W 14
Champlain Ave S
  4200-4699 53
  4700-5099 15
  6000-7099 37
  7100-9499 19

Chicago (Con.)	**606**
9500-12699	28
13000-13799	27
Chanay W	47
Chappel Ave S	
6700-7899	49
7900-12199	17
12200-13799	33
Charles S	
9400-9499	20
9500-OUT	43
Charleston W	47
Charmaine Rd W	56
Chase Ave W	
1200-1999	26
2000-3999	45
4000-4899	46
7100-7799	48
Chelsea Pl W	43
Cheltenham Pl E	49
Cherry Ave N	
900-OUT	22
Cherry Ave W	
6800-6899	48
Cherry Ln N	
6400-7399	45
Chester Ave N	
4400-5599	56
8100-9199	48
Chestnut E	11
Chestnut W	
1-799	10
800-OUT	22
Chicago Ave E	11
Chicago Ave W	
1-799	10
800-3199	22
3200-5999	51
Chicago Beach Dr S	15
Chicora Ave N	46
Childrens Plz W	14
Chippewa Ave S	
11600-12199	17
13800-13999	33
Christiana Ave N	
400-799	24
800-1199	51
2800-4399	18
4400-5599	25
5600-6399	59
6400-7199	45
Christiana Ave S	
300-399	24
1200-3499	23
4300-5499	32
5500-7499	29
7500-8699	52
10300-11499	55
Church S	43
Church St & Ter W	48
Churchill W	47
Churchill Ave W	
8000-8099	48
Churchill Cir N	
9000-9099	48
Cicero Ave N	
1-799	44
800-1599	51
1600-2799	39
2800-4399	41
4400-5599	30
5600-7399	46
Cicero Ave S	
1-1199	44
1200-4199	50
4200-5498 (EVEN)	38
4201-5499 (ODD)	32
5500-7099	38
7100-7499	29
7500-8299	52
8301-8699 (ODD)	52
11100-12899	58
Clara Dr W	48
Claremont Ave N	
300-799	12
800-1599	22
1600-2799	47
2800-4399	18
4400-5599	25
5600-6399	59
6400-7599	45
Claremont Ave S	
400-1199	12
1300-3499	08
3500-5499	09
5500-7499	36
7500-9499	20
9500-OUT	43
Clarence Ave W	31
Clarendon Ave N	
3900-4399	13
4400-OUT	40
Clark N	
1-149	02
150-299	01
300-1599	10
1600-2799	14
2800-3599	57
3600-4399	13
4400-5599	40
5600-6399	60
6400-7599	26
Clark S	
1-199	03
200-399	04
400-1599	05
1600-2199	16
13000-14599	27
Clark Dr W	42
Cleaver N	22
Cleveland W	
6800-7599	48
Cleveland Ave N	
800-1599	10
1600-OUT	14
Clifford Ave N	46
Clifton N	
4800-5199	56
8100-9199	48
Clifton Ave N	
1600-2799	14
2800-3599	57
3600-4399	13
4400-OUT	40
Clifton Park Ave S	42
Clinton N	06
Clinton S	
1-399	06
400-1599	07
1600-OUT	16
Clybourn Ave N	
1200-1565	10
1566-1599	22
1600-2799	14
2800-OUT	18
Clyde Ave S	
6700-7899	49
7900-12199	17
12200-13799	33
Coast Guard Dr S	49
Coles Ave S	
7100-7899	49
7900-OUT	17
Colfax Ave S	
7400-7899	49
7900-OUT	17
Columbia Ave W	
1000-1999	26
2000-3999	45
4000-4799	46
7600-7799	31
Columbus Ave W	
2400-2599	29
2600-4022	52
Columbus Dr S	
200-ONLY	03
201-399	04
400-OUT	05
Commercial Ave S	
7900-10399	17
12200-13499	33
Commons Dr N	56
Commonwealth Ave N	
2300-2399	14
2800-2999	57
Concord Ln N	48
Concord Pl W	
300-1199	14
1200-1999	22
2000-3999	47
4000-6399	39
Congress Pky E	05
Congress Pky W	
1-199	05
200-1599	07
1600-3199	12
3200-4599	24
4600-5999	44
Conrad W	48
Constance Ave S	
6700-7899	49
7900-12199	17
Coral Dr W	56
Corbett S	08
Corcoran Dr W	
(ODD)	44
Corliss Ave S	
10300-12699	28
13000-13799	27
Cornelia Ave W	
500-1999	57
2000-3999	18
4000-5599	41
5600-8399	34
Cornell Ave S	
4800-5499	15
5500-5599	37
6700-7899	49
7900-12199	17
Cortez W	
1200-3199	22
3200-5999	51
Cortland W	
1200-1429	14
1430-1999	22
2000-3999	47
4000-6399	39
6400-7799	35

Chicago (Con.)	606
Cortland Pky W	35
Cottage Grv Ave S	
2200-3499	16
3500-4699	53
4700-5499	15
5500-7099	37
7100-9499	19
9500-12999	28
13000-13799	27
Cottage Pl W	07
Couch Pl W	06
Coulter W	08
Country Club Dr S	42
Court Pl W	06
Courtland Ave N	
4400-5599	56
5600-5699	31
9000-9599	48
Courtland Ave W	
7900-8199	56
Coyle Ave W	
2400-3999	45
4000-4899	46
7200-7399	31
Crain W	48
Crandon Ave S	
6700-7899	49
7900-12199	17
12200-13799	33
Crawford Ave N	
6400-7399	46
Crawford Ave S	
8701-10299 (ODD)	42
10301-11099 (ODD)	55
11100-11499	55
11500-13299	58
Cregier Ave S	
6700-7899	49
7900-12199	17
Crescent Ave N	
4800-5599	56
5600-5699	31
Cressett Dr W	35
Crestline W	52
Crilly Ct W	14
Croissant Dr S	33
Croname Rd N	48
Crosby N	10
Crowell S	08
Crystal W	
1300-3199	22
3200-5999	51
Cullerton E	16
Cullerton W	
1-799	16
800-2799	08
2800-4599	23
Cullom Ave W	
900-1999	13
2000-3999	18
4000-5599	41
5600-8399	34
Cumberland Ave N	
4400-5299	56
5600-5999	31
5000-9199	48
Cuyler Ave W	
800-1999	13
2000-3999	18
4000-5599	41
5600-7199	34

Cyril Ct S	49
Czagany Ave N	56
Bakin W	
800-1999	13
2000-3999	18
4000-5599	41
5600-7999	34
Bamen Ave N	
1-399	12
400-1599	22
1600-2799	47
2800-4399	18
4400-5599	25
5600-6399	59
6400-7599	45
Damen Ave S	
1-1199	12
1200-3499	08
3500-5499	09
5500-7499	36
7500-9499	20
9500-10099	43
Daniel Ave, S	
13000-13199	27
Dante Ave S	
6300-7099	37
7100-OUT	19
Dauphin Ave S	
8700-9299	19
10000-OUT	28
Davis W	48
Devlin Ct N	18
Davol S	43
Dawson Ave N	18
Days Ter W	48
Dayton N	
1400-1599	22
1600-2799	14
2800-3599	57
3600-4399	13
De Koven W	07
De Saible W	09
Dean N	22
Dearborn N	
1-149	02
150-299	01
300-OUT	10
Dearborn S	
1-199	03
200-399	04
400-799	05
1200-1599	05
1600-3499	16
3500-5499	09
13800-14599	27
Dearborn Pky N	10
Delaware Pl E	11
Delaware Pl W	10
Delphia Ave N	
4400-5599	56
8100-8399	48
Deming Pl W	
400-699	14
4000-6399	39
Dempster W	
7001-7999 (ODD)	48
7700-7998 (EVEN)	48
8000-8599	48
Denal N	56
Denvir Ave S	12
Desplaines N	
1-399	06
400-OUT	10

Desplaines S	
1-399	06
400-1199	07
1600-OUT	16
Devon Ave W	
1000-1999	60
2000-3999	59
4000-6399	46
6400-7799	31
Dewitt Pl N	11
Dexter Park Ave S	09
Dickens Ave W	
300-399	14
2000-3999	47
4000-6399	39
6400-7999	35
Dickinson Ave N	41
District Blvd W	32
Diversey Ave W	
300-399	57
400-1999	14
2000-3999	47
4000-6399	39
6400-7999	35
Diversey Blvd W	
300-399	57
400-1999	14
2000-3999	47
4000-6399	39
6400-7999	35
Diversey Pky W	
300-399	57
400-1999	14
2000-3999	47
4000-6399	39
6400-7999	35
Division E	10
Division W	
1-799	10
800-3199	22
3200-5999	51
Dobson S	
6800-7599	48
Dobson Ave S	
7100-9499	19
9500-9899	28
13000-13799	27
Dominick N	14
Dorchester Ave S	
4700-5499	15
5500-7099	37
7100-9499	19
9500-OUT	28
Doty Ave S	
9500-10299	17
10300-12199	28
12200-12998 (EVEN)	28
12201-12999 (ODD)	33
Douglas Blvd W	23
Dover N	40
Dowagiac Ave N	46
Drake Ave N	
400-799	24
800-1199	51
1600-2799	47
2800-4399	18
4400-5599	25
5600-6399	59
6400-7199	45
Drake Ave S	
1400-3499	23
4300-5499	32

Chicago (Con.)   606

5500-7499	29
7500-8699	52
10300-11699	55
11900-13299	58
Draper W	14
Drew S	43
Drexel Ave S	
3900-4699	53
4700-5499	15
5500-7099	37
7100-9499	19
9500-9899	28
12700-12999	28
13000-13799	27
Drexel Blvd S	
3900-4699	53
4700-5499	15
5500-7099	37
7100-9499	19
9500-9899	28
13000-13799	27
Drexel Sq E	15
Drummond Pl W	
500-1499	14
2000-3999	47
4000-6399	39
Dunbar Ave S	19
Early Ave W	60
East Cir Ave N	31
East Brook Rd N	35
East End Ave S	
4800-5099	15
6700-7899	30
7900-12199	17
East Prairie Rd N	45
East River Rd N	
4800-5599	56
5600-5999	31
East View Park S	15
Eastlake Ter N	26
Eastman S	22
Eastwood Ave W	
800-1999	40
2000-3999	25
4000-6399	30
7000-8799	56
Eberhart Ave S	
3900-3999	53
6000-7099	37
7100-9499	19
9500-12699	28
13000-13399	27
Ebinger Dr W	48
Edbrooke Ave S	
9900-12699	28
13000-14599	27
Eddy W	
1000-1999	57
2000-3999	18
4000-5599	41
5600-7999	34
Edens Pky N	30
Edgebrook Ter N	46
Edgewater Ave W	60
Edmaire W	43
Edmunds W	14
Edward Ct N	30
Eggleston Ave S	
5900-7499	21
7500-9499	20
9500-12999	28
13400-14599	27
Elaine Pl N	57
Elbridge Ave N	18
Eleanor S	08
Elias Ct S	08
Elizabeth N	
1-399	07
400-899	22
Elizabeth S	
4700-5499	09
5500-7499	36
7500-9499	20
10000-13199	43
Elizabeth W	
8000-8399	48
Elk Grv N	22
Ellen W	22
Elliot Ave S	17
Ellis Ave S	
2800-3299	16
3500-4699	53
4700-5499	15
5500-7099	37
7100-9499	19
9500-12999	28
13000-13799	27
Ellis Park S	53
Elm E	11
Elm W	10
Elm Dr W	56
Elmdale Ave W	60
Elmgrove Dr W	35
Elmore S	48
Elmwood Pky	35
Elston Ave N	
800-1999	22
2000-2399	14
2400-2799	47
2800-4299	18
4300-4399	41
4400-5599	30
5600-6399	46
Emerald Ave S	
2400-3499	16
3580-5499	09
5500-7499	21
7500-9499	20
9500-13099	28
13800-14599	27
Emmett N	47
Engle Rd S	
4800-5499	58
12700-12799	58
Englewood Ave W	21
Entre Ave S	33
Erie E	11
Erie W	
1-799	10
800-1999	22
2000-3199	12
3200-4599	24
4600-5999	44
Ernst Ct N	11
Escanaba Ave S	
7800-7899	49
7900-12199	17
12200-13299	33
Esmond S	43
Essex Ave S	
7500-7899	49
7900-12199	17
Estes Ave W	
1300-1999	26
2000-3999	45
4000-6399	46
7200-7799	31
Euclid Ave S	
6700-7899	49
7900-12199	17
Euclid Pky S	49
Eugenie W	14
Evans Ave S	
4200-4699	53
4700-5099	15
6000-7099	37
7100-9499	19
10300-10799	28
13000-13799	27
Evelyn Ln W	56
Everell Ave W	31
Everett Ave S	
5400-5499	15
5500-OUT	37
Evergreen Ave W	
200-799	10
800-3199	22
3200-OUT	51
Evergreen Park Arc S	42
Evergreen Park Plz S	42
Ewing Ave S	17
Exchange Ave S	
7100-7899	49
7900-12199	17
12200-13399	33
Exchange Ave W	09
Executiv Ct W	56
Fair Pl W	10
Fairbanks Ct N	11
Fairfield Ave N	
200-799	12
800-1599	22
1600-2799	47
2800-3199	18
4400-5599	25
5600-6399	59
6400-7599	45
Fairfield Ave S	
900-1199	12
1200-2199	08
4100-5499	32
5500-7499	29
7500-8699	52
8700-10299	42
10300-11499	55
Fairview Ave N	
5500-5599	56
5600-5899	31
Fargo Ave W	
1300-1999	26
2000-3199	45
6800-7799	48
Farnsworth Dr N	48
Farragut Ave W	
1400-1999	40
2000-3999	25
4000-6399	30
6400-8399	56
Farrell S	08
Farwell Ave W	
1100-1999	26
2000-3999	45
4000-4899	46
7200-7399	31

Chicago (Con.)　606

Federal S
300-399............................ 04
400-1599.......................... 05
1600-3499........................ 16
3500-5499........................ 09
Felton Ct N............................ 10
Ferdinand W
1400-1999........................ 22
2000-2399........................ 12
3600-4599........................ 24
4600-OUT......................... 44
Fern Ct N.............................. 14
Fey Ln S............................... 58
Field Dr N............................ 48
Fielding Ave S....................... 20
Fillmore W
1300-1599........................ 07
1600-3199........................ 12
3200-4599........................ 24
4600-OUT......................... 44
First National Plz S................. 70
Fitch Ave W
2000-3999........................ 45
4000-4899........................ 46
5800-6399........................ 46
7200-7999........................ 31
Fletcher W
700-1999.......................... 57
2000-3999........................ 18
4000-5599........................ 41
5600-7199........................ 34
7200-7999........................ 35
Flournoy W
1200-1599........................ 07
1600-3199........................ 12
3200-4499........................ 24
4600-5999........................ 44
Ford Ave S............................ 16
Ford City Dr W....................... 52
Forest Ave S
9100-9499........................ 19
9500-11499...................... 28
13000-13799.................... 27
Forest Glen Ave N
5300-5599........................ 30
5600-6399........................ 46
Forest Preserve Ave W
6400-6699........................ 56
6700-8399........................ 34
Forest View Dr W.................... 48
Forestview Ave N.................... 56
Forrestville Ave S
4300-4699........................ 53
4700-5099........................ 15
11100-11499.................... 28
13000-13799.................... 27
Foster Ave W
900-1999.......................... 40
2000-3999........................ 25
4000-6399........................ 30
6400-9399........................ 56
9400-9998 (EVEN)............. 56
Foster Ln N W
8000-8199........................ 48
Foster Pl & Ter W................... 56
Francis Pl W.......................... 47
Francisco Ave N
1-799.............................. 12
800-1599.......................... 22
1600-2799........................ 47

2800-4399........................ 18
4400-5599........................ 25
5600-6399........................ 59
6400-7599........................ 45
Francisco Ave S
1-1199............................ 12
2400-3499........................ 23
3500-5499........................ 32
5500-7499........................ 29
7500-8699........................ 52
8760-10299...................... 42
Frank Pky N........................... 56
Franklin N
1-299.............................. 06
300-OUT.......................... 10
Franklin S
1-399.............................. 06
400-OUT.......................... 07
Franklin Blvd W
3000-3199........................ 12
3200-OUT......................... 24
Franks Ave N......................... 48
Fremont N
1400-1599........................ 22
1600-2299........................ 14
3200-3599........................ 57
3600-3999........................ 13
Front Ave S........................... 28
Frontier Ave N
1200-1599........................ 10
3900-OUT......................... 13
Fry W.................................. 22
Fuller W............................... 08
Fullerton Ave W
300-1999.......................... 14
2000-3999........................ 47
4000-6399........................ 39
6400-7999........................ 35
Fulton W
400-799............................ 06
800-1599.......................... 07
1600-3199........................ 12
3200-4599........................ 24
4600-5999........................ 44
Fulton Market W
600-799............................ 06
800-OUT.......................... 07
Gale W................................ 30
Gale Ter W............................ 48
Garfield Blvd E
1-399 (ODD)...................... 37
2-398 (EVEN).................... 15
Garfield Blvd W
1-1199 (ODD).................... 21
2-2398 (EVEN).................. 09
1201-2399 (ODD)............... 36
Garibaldi Pl S........................ 07
Garvey Ct N........................... 01
Gaslight Sq W
3700-3899........................ 58
Geneva Ter N......................... 14
Genoa Ave S
8700-9499........................ 20
9500-OUT......................... 43
George W
800-1999.......................... 57
2000-3999........................ 18
4000-5599........................ 41
5600-7199........................ 34
7200-7799........................ 35
Georgia Dr W......................... 48
Germania Pl W....................... 10

Gettysburg W......................... 30
Giddings W
2000-3999........................ 25
4000-6399........................ 30
7700-8799........................ 56
Gilbert Ct S........................... 20
Giles Ave S
3100-3499........................ 16
3500-OUT......................... 53
Givins Ct S............................ 20
Gladys Ave W
700-799............................ 06
800-1399.......................... 07
2100-2799........................ 12
3300-4599........................ 24
4600-OUT......................... 44
Glen Ln W............................. 27
Glendale Ln N........................ 48
Glenlake Ave W
900-1999.......................... 60
2000-3999........................ 59
4000-6399........................ 46
7700-7899........................ 31
Glenroy Ave S........................ 43
Glenwood Ave N
4900-5599........................ 40
5600-6399........................ 60
6400-7799........................ 26
Goethe St E & W..................... 10
Golf Rd W
8001-8499 (ODD)............... 48
8500-8599........................ 48
Goodman W........................... 30
Gordon Ter W......................... 13
Grace W
600-1999.......................... 13
2000-3999........................ 18
4000-5599........................ 41
5600-8399........................ 34
Grace Ave N........................... 48
Grady Ct S............................. 08
Graham Ct N.......................... 10
Grand N
8800-8999........................ 48
Grand Ave E........................... 11
Grand Ave W
1-799.............................. 18
800-1999.......................... 22
2000-2899........................ 12
2900-3199........................ 22
3200-4341........................ 51
4342-6399........................ 39
6400-7999........................ 35
Grand Ct N
8100-8199........................ 48
Grant Pl W............................. 14
Granville Ave W
900-1999.......................... 60
2000-3999........................ 59
4000-6399........................ 46
Gratten Ave S......................... 08
Green N
1-399.............................. 07
400-OUT.......................... 22
Green S
1-599.............................. 07
2400-3299........................ 08
4700-5499........................ 09
5500-7499........................ 21
7500-9499........................ 20
9500-13199...................... 43

Chicago (Con.)   606

Green Bay Ave S
| 8100-12199 | 17 |
| 13000-14499 | 33 |
Greendale Ave W 48
Greenleaf Ave W
1000-1999	26
2000-3999	45
4000-6399	46
7000-8399	48
7200-7499	31
Greenview Ave N
800-1699	22
2200-2799	14
2800-3599	57
3600-4399	13
4400-5599	40
5600-6399	60
6400-7799	26
Greenwood Ave N
4800-5199	56
8100-8599	48
8601-9799 (ODD)	48
Greenwood Ave S
4200-4699	53
4700-5499	15
5500-7099	37
7100-9499	19
9500-9899	28
13000-13799	27
Gregory W
1400-1999	40
2000-3999	25
4000-6399	30
6400-8799	56
Grennan Pl W 48
Grenshaw W
300-1599	07
1600-3199	12
3200-OUT	24
Gresham Ave N 18
Gross Point Rd W 48
Grove S 16
Groveland Park E 16
Grover W 30
Gunnison W
800-1299	40
2400-3099	25
4400-6399	30
6400-8399	56
Haddon Ave W
1300-3199	22
3200-5999	51
Haft W 46
Haines N
700-799	10
800-OUT	22
Hale Ave S 43
Halsted N
1-399	06
400-1599	22
1600-2799	14
2800-3599	57
3600-OUT	13
Halsted S
1-399	06
400-1599	07
1600-3499	08
3500-5499	09
5500-7499	21
7500-9499	20

9500-12299	28
12300-12698 (EVEN)	43
12301-12699 (ODD)	28
12700-12999	28
13000-14599	27
Hamlin Ave N
5600-6399	59
Hamilton Ave N
2200-2799	47
2800-4399	18
4400-4999	25
5600-6399	59
6400-7599	45
Hamilton Ave S
1-1199	12
1700-3499	08
3500-4299	09
5500-7499	36
7500-9499	20
9500-10699	43
Hamilton Dr W 48
Hamlet Ave S 43
Hamlin Ave N
1-799	24
800-1599	51
1600-2799	47
2800-4399	18
4400-5599	25
5600-6399	59
6400-7199	45
7227-7227	
Hamlin Ave S
1-599	24
1400-3499	23
3500-5499	32
5500-7499	29
7500-8699	52
8700-10299	42
10300-11899	55
11900-13299	58
Hamlin Ct S 58
Hampden Ct N 14
Harbor Ave S 17
Harding Ave N
1-799	24
800-1599	51
1600-2799	47
2800-4399	18
4400-5599	25
5600-6399	59
6400-7399	45
Harding Ave S
1200-3499	23
3500-5499	32
5500-7499	29
7500-8699	52
8700-10299	42
10300-11899	55
11900-13299	58
Harlem Ave N
1600-2999	35
3000-4399	34
4400-5599	56
5600-7199	31
7200-8799	48
Harlem Ave S
5101-7499 (ODD)	38
Harper Ave S
5000-5499	15
5500-7099	37
7100-9499	19
9500-9899	28

Harrison E 05
Harrison W
1-199	05
200-1599	07
1600-3199	12
3200-4599	24
4600-5999	44
Harrison W, W
8201-8359 (ODD)	48
Hart N 22
Hartland Ct N 22
Harts Rd W 48
Hartwell Ave S 37
Harvard W 48
Harvard Ave S
6300-7499	21
7500-9499	20
9500-13099	28
Haskins Ave N 26
Hastings W 08
Haussen Ct N 18
Hawthorne Pl W 57
Hayes Ave W 31
Hayes Dr S 49
Hayford W 52
Haynes Ct S 08
Hazel N
4200-4399	13
4400-OUT	40
Heath Ave S 08
Henderson W
1200-1999	57
2700-3999	18
4000-5599	41
5600-7199	34
Henry Ct W 47
Hermione W 46
Hermitage Ave N
1-399	12
400-1999	22
2000-2799	14
2800-3599	57
3600-4399	13
4400-5599	40
5600-6399	60
6400-7799	26
Hermitage Ave S
1-1199	12
3400-3499	08
3500-5499	09
5500-7499	36
7500-9499	20
Hermosa Ave S 43
Hiawatha Ave N 46
Hickory Ave N 22
Higgins Ave W
5400-6399	30
6400-7499	56
7500-8399	31
8401-8999 (ODD)	31
Highland Ave W
1400-1999	60
2000-3999	59
4000-6399	46
6400-7399	31
Highlawn Ave S 27
Hill W 10
Hillock Ave S 08
Hirsch W
2200-3199	22
3200-5999	51
Hobart Ave W 31
Hobbie W 10

Chicago (Con.)　　　　　606

Hobson Ave N 14
Hoey S 08
Holbrook W 46
Holden Ct S
　400-1599 05
　1600-OUT 16
Holland Rd S 20
Holly Ave N
　2000-2099 14
　2600-OUT 47
Hollywood Ave W
　900-1999 60
　2000-3999 59
　4000-6399 46
Homan Ave N
　1-799 24
　800-OUT 51
Homan Ave S
　1-1199 24
　1200-3499 23
　3500-5499 32
　5500-7499 29
　7500-8699 52
　8700-10299 42
　10300-11899 55
　11900-12699 58
Homer W
　1500-1699 22
　2000-3999 47
　4000-6399 39
Homewood Ave S 43
Honore N
　900-1999 22
　2000-2799 24
　2800-3599 57
　3600-4399 13
　5200-5299 40
　6700-7599 26
Honore S
　1-599 12
　1500-1599 08
　3500-5499 09
　5500-7499 36
　7500-9499 20
　11800-12699 43
Hood Ave W
　1200-1999 60
　2000-3999 59
　7100-7799 31
Hooker N 22
Hopkins Pl W 20
Hortense Ave W 31
Houston Ave S
　8000-12199 17
　12200-13499 33
Howard W
　1300-1999 26
　2001-3207 (ODD) 45
　5601-5999 (ODD) 48
　6000-7599 48
　7601-7799 (ODD) 48
Howdy Ln W 58
Howe N
　1100-1599 10
　1800-OUT 14
Howland Ave W 20
Hoxie Ave S
　9400-12193 17
　12200-14599 33
Hoyne Ave N
　1-799 12

800-1599 22
1600-2799 47
2800-4399 18
4400-5599 25
5600-6399 59
6400-7599 45
Hoyne Ave S
　1-1199 12
　1200-3499 08
　3500-5499 09
　5500-7499 36
　7500-9499 20
　9500-11199 43
Hoyt Ave S 08
Hubbard E 11
Hubbard W
　1-799 10
　800-1999 22
　2000-3199 12
　4600-OUT 44
Huber Ln N 48
Hudson Ave N
　600-1599 10
　1600-2199 14
　3100-3199 57
Huguelet Pl N 11
Humboldt Blvd N 47
Hunt Ave W 20
Huntington W 46
Hurlbut W 31
Huron E 11
Huron W
　1-799 10
　800-1999 22
　2000-3199 12
　3200-4599 24
　4600-5999 44
Hutchinson W
　600-1499 13
　2000-3999 18
　4000-OUT 41
Hyacinth W 46
Hyde Park Blvd
　700-1799 19
　5000-5499 15
　5500-OUT 37
Ibm Plz E 11
Ibsen W 31
Iglehart Ct S 16
Illinois E 11
Illinois S
　13700-14599 27
Illinois W 10
Imlay W 31
Independence Blvd S
　500-1199 24
　1200-OUT 23
Indian Rd N 46
Indiana Ave S
　1200-1599 05
　1600-3499 16
　3500-4699 53
　4700-5499 15
　5500-7099 37
　7100-9499 19
　9500-12999 28
　13000-14599 27
Indianapolis Ave S 17
Ingleside Ave S
　4700-5499 15
　5500-7099 37
　7100-9499 19
　9500-12999 28

13000-13799 27
Institute Pl W 10
Ionia Ave N 46
Iowa W
　500-799 10
　1800-3199 22
　3200-5999 51
Irene Ave N 18
Iron S
　3200-3499 08
　3500-OUT 09
Irving Park Rd W
　600-1999 13
　2000-3999 18
　4000-5599 41
　5600-8399 34
Isham Ave W 31
Ivanhoe Dr E 27
Ivanhoe Ter 27
Jackson E 04
Jackson W
　1-199 04
　200-799 06
　800-1599 07
　1600-3199 12
　3200-4599 24
　4600-5999 44
James W 09
Janssen Ave N
　2200-2799 14
　2800-3599 57
　3600-4399 13
　4900-4999 40
Jarlath W
　2000-3999 45
　4000-4899 46
　7200-7799 48
Jarvis Ave W
　1200-1999 26
　2000-3399 45
　3801-3999 (ODD) 45
　4001-4899 (ODD) 46
　5600-7799 48
Jasper Pl S 09
Jean W 58
Jean Ave N 46
Jefferson N
　1-399 06
　400-OUT 10
Jefferson S
　1-399 06
　400-1599 07
　1600-OUT 16
Jeffery Ave S
　6700-7899 49
　7900-12199 17
　12200-13799 33
Jerome W
　2000-3999 45
　7200-7799 48
Jersey Ave N
　5600-6399 59
Jessie Ct N 12
Joalyce Ct S
　11801-11827 (ODD) 58
Joalyce Dr S 58
Jobev Ln S 58
Joey Dr N 48
Johanna Dr W 48
Jones N 47
Jonquil Ter W
　1400-1799 26
　6800-7599 48

Chicago (Con.)   606

Jourdan Ct S	08
Julia Ct W	47
Julian W	22
Juneway Ter W	
1400-1899	26
Junior Ter W	13
Justine N	.07
Justine S	
3300-3499	08
3500-5499	09
5500-7499	36
7500-9499	20
11500-13199	43
Kamerling Ave W	51
Karlov Ave N	
1-799	24
800-1599	51
1600-2799	39
2800-4399	41
4400-5599	30
5600-7399	46
Karlov Ave S	
1-1199	24
1200-3499	23
3900-5499	32
5500-7499	29
7500-8699	52
11500-13299	58
Kasson Ave N	30
Kay W	48
Kearsarge Ave N	41
Keating Ave N	
1200-1599	51
1600-2799	39
2800-4399	41
4400-5599	30
5600-7399	46
Keating Ave S	
3900-5499	32
5500-7499	29
7500-8699	52
Kedvale Ave N	
1-799	24
800-1599	51
1600-2799	39
2800-4399	41
4400-5599	30
5600-7399	46
Kedvale Ave S	
600-899	24
1200-3499	23
3900-5499	32
5500-7499	29
7500-8699	52
11500-13299	58
Kedzie W	
7000-8599	48
Kedzie Ave N	
1-799	12
800-1599	51
1600-2799	47
2800-4399	18
4400-5599	25
5600-6399	59
6100-7599	45
Kedzie Ave S	
1-1199	12
1200-3499	23
3500-5499	32
5500-7499	29
7500-8699	52

8700-10299	42
10300-11899	55
Keefe Ave S	37
Keeler Ave N	
1-799	24
800-1599	51
1600-2799	39
2800-4399	41
4400-5599	30
5600-7399	46
Keeler Ave S	
1-1199	24
1200-3499	23
3900-5499	32
5500-7499	29
7500-8699	52
11500-13299	58
Keeley S	08
Keene Ave N	46
Keeney W	48
Kelso Ave N	30
Kemper Pl W	14
Kendall W	12
Kenmore Ave N	
1800-2799	14
2800-3599	57
3600-4399	13
4400-5599	40
5600-6399	60
Kenneth Ave N	
200-299	24
1600-2799	39
2800-4399	41
4400-5599	30
5600-7399	46
Kenneth Ave S	
600-899	24
1200-3499	23
4000-5499	32
5500-7499	29
7500-8699	52
11500-11699	58
Kennicott Ave N	30
Kennison Ave N	30
Kenosha Ave N	41
Kensington Ave E	28
Kenton Ave N	
1-799	44
1600-2799	39
2800-4399	41
4400-5599	30
5600-7399	46
Kenton Ave S	
1-1199	44
1200-3499	23
3900-5499	32
5500-7499	29
7500-8699	52
11500-11699	58
Kentucky Ave N	30
Kenwood Ave S	
4700-5499	15
5500-7099	37
7100-9499	19
9500-OUT	28
Keokuk Ave N	30
Keota Ave N	45
Kerbs Ave N	46
Kercheval Ave N	46
Kerfoot Ave S	70
Kewanee Ave N	30
Keystone Ave N	
1-799	24

800-1599	51
1600-2799	39
2800-4399	41
4400-5599	30
5600-7399	46
Kilbourn Ave N	
1-799	24
800-1599	51
1600-2799	39
2800-4399	41
4400-5599	30
5600-7399	46
Kilbourn Ave S	
1-1199	24
1200-3499	23
4100-5499	32
5500-7499	29
7500-8699	52
11500-11699	58
Kildare Ave N	
1-799	24
800-1599	51
1600-2799	39
2800-4399	41
4400-5599	30
5600-7399	46
Kildare Ave S	
1-1199	24
1200-3499	23
3900-5499	32
5500-7499	29
7500-8699	52
11500-13299	58
Kilpatrick Ave N	
1-799	44
800-1599	51
1600-2799	39
2800-4399	41
4400-5599	30
5600-7399	46
Kilpatrick Ave S	
1-1199	44
3900-5499	32
5500-7499	29
7500-8699	52
Kimball Ave N	
1600-2799	47
2800-4399	18
4400-5599	25
5600-6399	59
6400-7199	45
Kimbark Ave S	
4700-5499	15
5500-7099	37
7100-9499	19
9500-OUT	28
Kimberly Ave N	30
King (Martin Luther Jr) Dr, S	
1200-1599	05
1600-3499	16
3500-4699	53
4700-5499	15
5500-7099	37
7100-9499	19
9500-12999	28
13000-13799	27
Kingsbury N	
300-1199	10
1200-1599	22
1600-OUT	14
Kingsdale Ave N	46
Kingston Ave S	
7300-7899	49

Chicago (Con.)	606
Kinzie E	11
Kinzie W	
1-799	10
800-1999	22
2000-3199	12
3200-4599	24
4600-OUT	44
Kinzua Ave N	46
Kiona Ave N	30
Kirby Ave N	46
Kirk W	48
Kirkland Ave S	
2200-2499	23
7900-8699	52
Kirkwood Ave N	46
Knight Ave N	
4800-5199	56
8200-8399	48
Knox Ave N	
1600-2799	39
2800-4399	41
4400-5599	30
5600-7399	46
Knox Ave S	
3900-5499	32
5500-7499	29
7500-8699	52
11500-11699	58
Kolin Ave N	
1-799	24
800-OUT	51
Kolin Ave S	
1200-3499	23
4000-5499	32
5500-7499	29
7500-8699	52
11500-13299	58
Kolmar Ave N	
200-799	24
800-1599	51
1600-2799	39
2800-4399	41
4400-5599	30
5600-7399	46
Kolmar Ave S	
1-1199	24
1200-3499	23
4100-5499	32
5500-7499	29
7500-8699	52
11500-11699	58
Komensky Ave S	
1200-3499	23
3900-5499	32
5500-7499	29
7500-8699	52
11500-13299	58
Kostner Ave N	
1-799	24
800-1599	51
1600-2799	39
2800-4399	41
4400-5599	30
5600-7399	46
Kostner Ave S	
1-1199	24
1200-3499	23
3500-5499	32
5500-7499	29
7500-8699	52
11500-13299	58

Kroll Dr S	58
Kruger Ave N	30
La Crosse Ave N	
100-299	44
1600-2799	39
2800-4399	41
4400-5599	30
5600-6399	46
La Crosse Ave S	
4300-7499	38
11500-12999	58
La Salle N	
1-149	02
150-299	01
300-1599	10
1600-OUT	14
La Salle S	
1-199	03
200-399	04
400-999	05
1600-3499	16
3500-5499	09
5500-7499	21
7500-9499	20
9500-12899	28
13700-14599	27
Lacey Ave N	46
Lafayette Ave S	
5500-7499	21
7500-9499	20
9500-12799	28
Laflin N	07
Laflin S	
1-1199	07
1200-3499	08
3500-5499	09
5500-7499	36
7500-9499	20
11000-13199	43
Laflin Pl S	09
Lake E	01
Lake W	
1-199	01
200-799	06
800-1599	07
1600-3199	12
3200-4599	24
4600-5999	44
8000-8179	48
Lake Park Ave S	
2300-3499	16
3500-4699	53
4700-5499	15
5500-5699	37
Lake Park Ave S	
7100-OUT	49
Lake Shore Dr N	
100-1199	11
1200-1599	56
2800-3599	57
3600-4299	13
4400-5599	40
Lake Shore Dr S	
1200-1599	05
1600-OUT	16
Lake Shore Plz N	11
Lakeside Pl W	40
Lakeview Ave N	14
Lakewood Ave N	
2000-2799	14
2800-3599	57
3600-3999	13
5200-5599	40

5600-6399	60
6400-6999	26
Lamon Ave N	
1-799	44
800-1599	51
1600-2799	39
2800-4399	41
4400-5599	30
5601-7399 (ODD)	46
Lamon Ave S	
4300-7499	38
11500-12999	58
Landers Ave N	46
Langley Ave S	
3700-4699	53
4700-4999	15
6000-7099	37
7100-9499	19
9500-12999	28
13000-13799	27
Lansing Ave N	46
Laporte Ave N	
1-799	44
1600-2799	39
2800-4399	41
4400-5599	30
5600-6799	46
Laporte Ave S	
4300-7499	38
11900-12999	58
Laramie Ave N	
1-799	44
800-1599	51
1600-2799	39
2800-4399	41
4400-OUT	30
Laramie Ave S	
1-1199	44
1200-3899	50
4300-7499	38
11900-12799	58
Larchmont Ave W	13
Larcom Ave W	46
Larned Ave N	30
Larrabee N	
600-1599	10
1600-OUT	14
Las Casas Ave N	46
Latham Ave N	30
Latrobe Ave N	
1-799	44
800-1599	51
1600-2799	39
2800-4399	41
4400-OUT	30
Latrobe Ave S	
4700-7499	38
Lauren Ln N	48
Lavergne Ave N	
1-799	44
800-1599	51
1600-2799	39
2800-4399	41
4400-OUT	30
Lavergne Ave S	
1-1199	44
4300-7499	38
11900-12999	58
Lawler W	
7400-7599	48
Lawler Ave N	
400-799	44
800-1599	51

Chicago (Con.)   606

1600-2799 39
2800-4399 41
4400-OUT 30
Lawler Ave S
4300-7499 38
11900-12999 58
Lawndale Ave N
400-799 24
800-1599 51
1600-2799 47
2800-4399 18
4400-5599 25
5600-6399 59
6400-7199 45
Lawndale Ave S
1-1199 24
1200-3499 23
3500-5499 32
5500-7499 29
7500-8699 52
8700-10299 42
10300-11899 55
11900-13299 58
Lawrence Ave W
700-1999 40
2000-3999 25
4000-6399 30
6400-8799 56
Le Mai Ave N 46
Le Moyne W
1200-3199 22
3200-5999 51
Leader Ave N 46
Leamington Ave N
1-799 44
800-1599 51
1600-2799 39
2800-4399 41
4400-OUT 30
Leamington Ave S
1-1199 44
4300-7499 38
11900-12799 58
Leavenworth Ave N 30
Leavitt N
1-799 12
800-1599 22
1600-2799 47
2800-4399 18
4400-5599 25
5600-6399 59
6400-7599 45
Leavitt S
1-1199 12
1200-3499 08
3500-5499 09
5500-7499 36
7500-9499 20
9500-OUT 43
Leclaire Ave N
1-799 44
800-1599 51
1600-2799 39
2800-4399 41
4400-OUT 30
Leclaire Ave S
4300-7499 38
11900-12799 58
Lee W
7100-8399 48

Lee Pl W 12
Lee Rd S
11500-11699 58
Legett Ave N 46
Lehigh Ave N
6100-7199 46
7200-7999 48
Lehmann Ct N 14
Leland Ave W
700-1999 40
2000-3999 25
4000-6399 30
6800-8799 56
Lemont Ave N 46
Lenox Ave N 46
Leona Ave N 46
Leonard Ave N
5400-5599 30
5600-5999 46
Leonard Dr Dr N 56
Leonora Ln W 35
Leoti Ave N 46
Leroy Ave N 46
Lessing N 22
Lester Ave N 30
Levee W 08
Lexington W
500-1599 07
2000-3199 12
3200-4599 24
4600-5999 44
Lexington Ln N 48
Layden Ave S 27
Liano Ave N 30
Liberty W
500-799 07
1000-OUT 08
Lieb Ave N 46
Lightfoot Ave N 30
Lill W
7100-7399 48
Lill Ave W
800-1499 14
Lill Ct W
7800-7899 48
Lincoln S
12300-12699 43
Lincoln Ave N
1800-2799 14
2800-3599 57
3600-3999 13
4000-4399 18
4400-5599 25
5600-6399 59
6400-6749 45
6750-7399 46
Lincoln Ln N 48
Lincoln Park West N ... 14
Lincolnwood Dr N 14
Lind Ave N 30
Linden Ave N
5400-5599 56
Linden Pl N
1600-2599 47
Linder Ave N
1200-1599 51
1600-2799 39
2800-4399 41
4400-5599 25
5600-6399 46
Linder Ave S
4700-7499 38

Linecrest Dr W 58
Linn White Dr S 05
Lipps Ave N 30
Lister Ave N 14
Lituanica Ave S
3100-3499 08
3500-OUT 09
Livermore Ave N 46
Lloyd Ave S 08
Lock S 08
Lockwood Ave N
1-799 44
800-1599 51
1600-2799 39
2800-4399 41
4400-5599 30
5600-6799 46
Lockwood Ave S
1-1199 44
4700-7499 38
Locust W 10
Logan Blvd W 47
Loleta Ave N 46
Lomax Pl W 07
Lombard Ave S
1201-3899 (ODD) 50
Lombard Ln S 58
London Ave N 46
Long Ave N
1-799 44
800-1599 51
1600-2799 39
2800-4399 41
4400-OUT 30
Long Ave S
4700-7499 38
Longmeadow Ave N 46
Longwood Ave S
8700-9499 20
9500-11899 43
Longwood Blvd
8700-9499 20
9500-11899 43
Longwood Dr
8700-9499 20
9500-11899 43
Loomis N 07
Loomis Blvd S
7500-9499 20
Loomis Blvd S,
1-1199 07
1200-3499 08
3500-5499 09
5500-7499 36
9500-13199 43
Loomis Pl S 09
Loras Ln N 48
Loret Ave N
1-799 44
800-1599 51
1600-2799 39
2800-OUT 41
Loret Ave S
4700-7499 38
Loring Ave N 30
Loron Ave N 46
Lothair Ave S 43
Lotus Ave N
1-799 44
800-1599 51
1600-2799 39
2800-4399 41
4400-OUT 30

Chicago (Con.)   606

Lotus Ave S
1-1199 44
4700-7499 38
Louise Ave N 46
Lovejoy Ave N 30
Loveland S 58
Lowe Ave S
2400-3499 16
3500-5499 09
5500-7499 21
7500-9499 20
9500-13099 28
13100-14599 27
Lowell Ave N
1600-2799 39
2800-4399 41
4400-5399 30
5600-7399 46
Loyola Ave W
1000-1999 26
2000-3999 45
Lucerne Ave N 46
Ludlam Ave N 30
Luella Ave S
7100-7899 49
7900-12199 17
12200-13799 33
Lumber S
1200-1599 07
1600-2399 16
2400-OUT 08
Luna Ave N
1200-1599 51
1600-2799 39
2800-4399 41
4400-5599 30
5600-6399 46
Luna Ave S
4700-7499 38
Lundy Ave N 46
Lunt Ave W
1100-1999 26
2000-3999 45
4000-4899 46
5400-5599 46
7200-7799 31
Luther W 08
Lutz Pl W 10
Lyman S 08
Lynch Ave N 30
Lyndale W
2000-3999 47
4000-6399 39
Lyon Ave S 19
Lyons W 48
Lytle S 07
Mackinaw Ave S
7900-12199 17
13000-14399 33
Madison E
1-50 02
51-69 (ODD) 03
52-68 (EVEN) 02
70-OUT 02
Madison W
1-199 02
200-799 06
800-1599 07
1600-3199 12
3200-4599 24
4600-5999 44

6800-8799 48
Madison Ct W 48
Madison Park E 15
Magnet Ave N 30
Magnolia Ave N
1400-1699 22
1900-2299 14
3600-4399 13
4400-5599 40
5600-6399 60
6400-6599 26
Main W 48
Major Ave N
1600-2799 39
2800-4399 34
4400-5599 30
5600-6399 46
Major Ave S
4900-7499 38
Malden N 40
Malta S 43
Mandell Ave N 46
Mango Ave N
1600-2799 39
2800-4399 34
4400-5599 30
5600-6399 46
Manila Ave N 30
Manistee Ave S
7900-12199 17
12200-14599 33
Mankato Ave N 46
Manor Ln N 25
Manor Ln N
5400-5599 56
5600-5699 31
Manton Ave N 46
Maple W
1-199 10
3200-3599 42
Maple Ave W
8100-8399 56
Maplewood Ave N
200-799 12
800-1599 22
1600-2799 47
2800-4399 18
4400-5599 25
5600-6399 59
6400-7599 45
Maplewood Ave S
300-799 12
3200-3499 08
3500-5499 32
5500-7499 29
7500-8699 52
8700-10299 42
10300-11899 55
Marble Pl W 06
Marcey N 14
Margate Ter W 40
Marine Dr N
3900-4399 13
4400-OUT 40
Marion Ct N 22
Markham Ave N 46
Marmora Ave N
1600-2799 39
2800-4399 34
4400-5599 30
5600-6399 46
Marquette Ave S
7500-7899 49

Marquette Rd E & S 37
Marquette Rd W
1-1199 21
1200-2399 36
2400-4799 29
4800-6399 38
Marshall Blvd S 23
Marshfield Ave N
400-1399 22
2000-2799 14
2800-3599 57
3600-4399 12
7500-7799 26
Marshfield Ave S
1-1199 12
3400-3499 08
3500-5499 09
5500-7499 36
7500-9499 20
11900-12999 43
Marshfield Ave S,
11100-11199 43
Marwood Ave W 35
Mary S 08
Maryland N
8800-9599 48
Maryland Ave S
4900-5499 15
5500-7099 37
7100-9499 19
9500-10599 28
13000-13799 22
Mason Ave N
1-799 44
800-1599 51
1600-2799 39
2800-4399 34
4400-5599 30
5600-7199 46
Mason Ave S
1-1199 44
4900-7499 38
Massasoit Ave N
800-OUT 51
Massasoit Ave S
5100-7499 38
Matson Ave W 46
Maud Ave N 14
Mautene Ct N 22
Maxwell W
500-799 07
800-OUT 08
May N
1-399 07
400-OUT 22
May S
600-1199 07
1200-3499 08
3500-5499 09
5500-7499 21
7500-9499 20
9500-13199 43
Mayfield Ave N
1-799 44
800-1599 5
1600-OUT 39
Mayfield Ave S
1-1199 44
5100-7499 38
Maynard Dr N 48
Maynard Rd W 48

Chicago (Con.)   606

Maypole Ave W
1600-3199	12
3200-4599	24
4600-OUT	44

Mc Alpin Ave N	46
Mc Clellan Ave N	46
Mc Clurg Ct N	11
Mc Cook Ave N	46

Mc Cormick Blvd N
5600-6399	59
6400-7299	45

Mc Daniel S	58
Mc Dermott S	08
Mc Dowell Ave S	09

Mc Lean Ave W
1400-1999	14
2000-3999	47
4000-6399	39
6400-7999	35

Mc Leod Ave N	46

Mc Vicker Ave N
1600-2799	39
2800-4399	34
4400-5599	30
5600-6399	46
7200-7399	48

Mc Vicker Ave S
5100-7499	38

Mccarthy Dr S	16
Mcfetridge Dr E	05
Meacham Ct N	48

Meade Ave N
1600-2799	39
2800-4399	34
4400-5599	30
5600-6399	46
7200-7399	48

Meade Ave S
5100-7499	38

Meadow Ln Dr S
11500-11899	55

Meadow Ln Dr W	55
Medford Ave N	46

Medill Ave W
1200-1799	14
2000-3999	47
4000-6399	39
6400-7999	35

Medina Ave N	46

Melrose W
400-1999	57
2000-3999	18
4000-5599	41
5600-7999	34

Melvina Ave N
1600-2799	39
2800-4399	34
4400-5599	30
5600-7199	46
7200-7499	48

Melvina Ave S
5100-7499	38

Memory Ln W	56

Menard Ave N
1-799	44
800-1599	51
1600-2799	39
2800-4399	34
4400-5599	30
5600-6399	46
7500-7599	48

Menard Ave S
1-1199	44
4900-7499	38

Mendell N
1900-1999	22
2000-OUT	14

Mendota Ave N	46
Menomonee W	14
Merchandise Mart Plz	54
Meredith Ave N	46

Merrill N
8000-8999	48

Merrill Ave S
6700-7899	49
7900-12199	17
12200-13799	33

Merrimac Ave N
1600-2799	39
2800-4399	34
4400-5599	30
5600-7199	46
7600-7899	48

Merrimac Ave S
4800-7499	38

Merrion Ave S	17
Metron Dr S	33
Metropole W, W	35
Meyer Ct N	14
Miami Ave W	46

Michigan N
5200-5299	56

Michigan Ave N
1-149	02
150-399	01
400-OUT	11

Michigan Ave S
1-199	03
200-399	04
400-1599	05
1600-3499	16
3500-4699	53
4700-5499	15
5500-7099	37
7100-9499	19
9500-12699	28
13000-14599	27

Michigan Blvd N
1-149	02
150-399	01
400-OUT	11

Michigan Blvd S
1-199	03
200-399	04
400-1599	05
1600-3499	16
3500-4699	53
4700-5499	15
5500-7099	37
7100-9499	19
9500-12699	28
13000-14599	27

Midway Park W	44

Mildred Ave N
2600-2799	14
2800-2999	57

Millard Ave S
500-599	24
1200-3499	23
3500-5499	32
5500-7499	29
7500-8699	52
8700-10299	42
10300-11899	55

Miller S
600-1199	07
1200-OUT	08

Miltimore Ave N	46

Milwaukee Ave N
200-399	06
400-499	10
500-1599	22
1600-2799	47
2800-3299	18
3300-4399	41
4400-5599	30
5600-6399	46
6400-6599	31
6600-9799	48

Minerva Ave S	37
Minnehaha Ave N	46
Minnetonka Ave N	46
Mission Dr N	56

Mobile Ave N
1600-2799	39
2800-4399	34
4400-5599	30
5600-7199	46

Mobile Ave S
5100-7499	38

Moffat W
2000-3999	47
4000-6399	39

Mohawk N
800-1599	10
1600-OUT	14

Monitor Ave N
1000-1599	51
1600-2799	39
2800-4399	34
4400-5599	30
5600-6399	46

Monitor Ave S
1-1199	44
4900-7499	38

Monon Ave N	46
Monroe E	03

Monroe W
1-199	03
200-799	06
800-1599	07
1600-3199	12
3200-4599	24
4600-5999	44
7000-8399	48

Monroe Ct W
6900-7099	48

Mont Clare Ave N
2300-2799	35
2800-2999	34
4400-5599	56

Montana W
900-1699	14
2000-2399	47
4000-6399	39

Monterey Ave N	56

Monterey Ave W
1600-1999	43

Montgomery Ave S
2600-4199	32

Monticello N
6400-7199	45

Monticello Ave N
400-799	24
800-1599	51
1600-2799	47
2800-4399	18

Chicago (Con.)   606

4400-5599........................ 25
5600-6399........................ 59
6400-7199........................ 45
Montrose Ave W
600-1999......................... 13
2000-3999........................ 18
4000-5599........................ 41
5600-8399........................ ..
Montvale Ave W.................... 43
Moody Ave N
1600-2799........................ 39
2800-4399........................ 34
4400-5599........................ 32
5600-7199........................ ..
Moody Ave S
5100-7499........................ 38
Moore N.......................... 10
Moorman N........................ 22
Moreland Ave N................... 56
Morgan N
1-399............................ 07
400-OUT.......................... 22
Morgan S
1-1199........................... 07
1200-3499........................ 08
3500-5499........................ 09
5500-7499........................ 21
7500-9499........................ 20
9500-13199....................... 43
Morse Ave W
1100-1999........................ 26
2000-3999........................ 45
4000-OUT......................... 46
Moselle Ave N.................... 46
Mozart N
100-299.......................... 12
800-1599......................... 22
1600-2799........................ 47
2800-4399........................ 18
4400-5599........................ 25
5600-6399........................ 59
6400-7599........................ 45
Mozart S
300-1199......................... 12
3500-5499........................ 32
5500-7499........................ 29
7500-8699........................ 52
8700-10299....................... 42
Mulford W........................ 48
Mulligan Ave N
1600-2799........................ 39
2800-4399........................ 34
4400-5599........................ 30
5600-6399........................ 46
Mulligan Ave S
5100-7499........................ 38
Museum Dr E...................... 37
Muskegon Ave S
7700-7899........................ 49
7900-12199....................... 17
12200-13299...................... 33
Myrick W......................... 52
Myrtle Ave W..................... 31
Nagle Ave N
1600-2799........................ 35
2800-4399........................ 34
4400-4599........................ 56
4600-5599........................ 30
5600-7199........................ 46
Nagle Ave S
5100-7499........................ 38

Naper Ave N...................... 31
Naples Ave N..................... 31
Napoleon Ave N................... 31
Narragansett Ave N
1600-2799........................ 39
2800-4399........................ 34
4400-5599........................ 30
Narragansett Ave S
5100-7499........................ 38
Nashotah Ave N................... 31
Nashville Ave N
1600-2799........................ 35
2800-4399........................ 34
4400-5599........................ 56
5600-6599........................ 31
Nashville Ave S
5100-7499........................ 38
Nassau Ave N..................... 31
Natchez Ave N
1600-2799........................ 35
2800-4399........................ 34
4400-5599........................ 56
7400-7599........................ 48
Natchez Ave S
5100-7499........................ 38
National N....................... 48
Natoma Ave N
1600-2799........................ 35
2800-4399........................ 34
4400-5599........................ 56
5600-6599........................ 31
Natoma Ave S
5100-7499........................ 38
Navajo Ave N..................... 46
Navarre Ave N.................... 31
Navy Pier E...................... 11
Neenah Ave N
2800-4399........................ 34
4400-5599........................ 56
5600-6399........................ 31
Neenah Ave S
5100-7499........................ 38
Nelson W
800-1999......................... 57
2000-2999........................ 18
4000-5599........................ 17
5600-7199........................ 34
Neola Ave N...................... 31
Nettleton Ave N.................. 31
Neva Ave N
1600-2799........................ 35
2800-4399........................ 34
4400-5599........................ 56
5600-6599........................ 31
7200-8399........................ 48
Neva Ave S
5100-7499........................ 38
New England Ave N
1600-2799........................ 35
2800-4399........................ 34
4400-5599........................ 56
6400-6499........................ 31
7200-8399........................ 48
New England Ave S
5199-7499........................ 38
New Hampshire Ave N.............. 31
Newark Ave N
5600-6499........................ 31
6500-7199........................ 48
Newberry Ave S
1000-1199........................ 07
1200-OUT......................... 08
Newburg Ave N.................... 31

Newcastle Ave N
1600-2799........................ 35
2800-4399........................ 34
4400-5599........................ 56
5600-6699........................ 31
8000-8299........................ 48
Newcastle Ave S
5100-7499........................ 38
Newgard Ave N.................... 26
Newland Ave N
1600-2799........................ 35
2800-4399........................ 34
4400-5599........................ 56
6400-6599........................ 31
8000-8399........................ 48
Newland Ave S
5100-7499........................ 38
Newport Ave W
800-1999......................... 57
2000-3999........................ 18
4000-5599........................ 41
5600-7999........................ 34
Niagara Ave N.................... 31
Nickerson Ave N.................. 31
Nicolet Ave N.................... 31
Niles Ave & Ter W................ 48
Nina Ave N....................... 31
Nixon Ave N...................... 31
Noble N.......................... 22
Nokomis Ave N.................... 46
Nora Ave N
2800-4399........................ 34
7200-8099........................ 48
Nordica Ave N
1600-2799........................ 35
2800-4399........................ 34
4400-5599........................ 56
5600-6699........................ 31
7400-7999........................ 48
Nordica Ave S
5100-7499........................ 38
Norma Ct W....................... 48
Normal Ave S
1600-3499........................ 16
3500-5499........................ 09
5500-7499........................ 21
7500-9499........................ 20
9500-12999....................... 28
13000-14599...................... 27
Normal Ave W
8400-8799........................ 48
Normal Blvd S
1600-3499........................ 16
3500-5499........................ 09
5500-7499........................ 21
7500-9499........................ 20
9500-12999....................... 28
13000-14599...................... 27
Normal Pky W..................... 21
Normandy Ave N
1600-2799........................ 35
2800-4399........................ 34
4400-5599........................ 56
6200-6699........................ 31
7200-7599........................ 48
Normandy Ave S
5100-7499........................ 38
Norridge W....................... 56
North Ave W
100-799.......................... 10
800-1999......................... 22
2000-3999........................ 47
4000-5999........................ 39

Chicago (Con.)	606
North Blvd E	10
North Blvd W	
1-99	10
North Park Ave N	
1300-1599	10
1600-OUT	14
North Ter W	
8400-8799	48
North Branch N	22
North Shore Ave W	
1000-1999	26
2000-3999	45
4000-5399	46
7200-7799	31
North Water E	11
Northcott Ave N	31
Northwest Hwy N	
4800-5599	30
5600-5729	46
5730-OUT	31
Norton S	67
Norwood W	
1200-1999	60
2000-3999	59
6000-6399	46
7600-7899	31
Norwood Ct W	56
Nottingham Ave N	
2800-4399	34
4400-5599	56
5600-5799	31
7200-7799	48
Nottingham Ave S	
5100-7499	38
Nursery N	14
Oak E	11
Oak N	
4500-4599	56
Oak W	10
Oak Ave W	
8000-8599	48
Oak Ln W	48
Oak Park Ave N	
1600-2799	35
2800-4399	34
4400-5599	56
5600-6699	31
7200-7599	48
Oak Park Ave S	
5100-7499	38
Oak View N	56
Oakdale Ave W	
300-1999	57
2000-3999	18
4000-5599	41
5600-7199	34
Oakenwald Ave S	53
Oakland Cres S	53
Oakleaf Ave W	35
Oakley Ave N	
1-799	12
800-1599	22
1600-2799	47
2800-4399	18
4400-5599	25
5600-6399	59
6400-7599	45
Oakley Ave S	
1-1199	12
1200-3499	08
3500-5499	09

5500-7499	36
7500-9499	20
9500-11899	43
Oakley Blvd N	
1-799	12
800-1599	22
1600-2799	47
2800-4399	18
4400-5599	25
5600-6399	59
6400-7599	45
Oakley Blvd S	
1-1199	12
1200-3499	08
3500-5499	09
5500-7499	36
7500-9499	20
9500-11899	43
Oakton N	
6700-7999	48
8000-8398 (EVEN)	48
Oakton Ct W	
6700-7199	48
Oakwood Ave E	53
Oakwood Blvd	53
Obrien W	67
Oconto Ave N	
3000-3199	35
3200-4399	34
4400-5599	56
5600-7199	31
7200-8399	48
Octavia Ave N	
3000-3199	35
3200-4399	34
4400-5599	56
5600-7199	31
7200-8399	48
Odell Ave N	
3000-3199	35
3200-4399	34
4400-5599	56
5600-7199	31
7200-8399	48
Ogallah Ave N	31
Ogden Ave N	
1-399	67
400-1199	22
1200-1599	10
1600-OUT	14
Ogden Ave W	
1567-1599	67
1600-2299	12
2300-2799	08
2800-4599	23
4600-6199	50
Ogden Blvd W	
1567-1599	67
1600-2299	12
2300-2799	08
2800-4599	23
4600-6199	50
Oglesby Ave S	
6700-7899	49
7900-12199	17
12200-13799	33
Ohio E	11
Ohio W	
1-799	10
800-1999	22
2000-3199	12
3200-4599	24
4600-5999	44

Oketo Ave N	
3000-3199	35
3200-4399	34
4400-5599	56
5600-7199	31
7200-8799	48
Olcott Ave N	
3000-3199	35
3200-4399	34
4400-5599	56
5600-7199	31
7200-8799	48
Oleander Ave N	
3000-3199	35
3200-4399	34
4400-5599	56
5600-7199	31
7200-8799	48
Oliphant Ave N	31
Olive Ave W	
1400-1999	60
2000-3999	59
7200-7899	31
Olmsted Ave N	31
Olympia Ave N	
5000-5199	56
6000-6399	31
Onarga Ave N	31
Oneida Ave N	
5000-5199	56
6400-6799	31
Ontario E	11
Ontario W	
1-599	10
1600-1699	22
3900-OUT	24
Opal Ave N	
3200-4399	34
4400-5199	56
Orange Ave N	
3200-4399	34
4400-4999	56
5700-5799	31
Orchard N	
1200-1599	10
1600-2799	14
2800-3199	57
Orchard S	
11900-12799	58
Oriole Ave N	
3000-3199	35
3200-4399	34
4400-5599	56
5600-7199	31
7200-8799	48
Orleans N	
300-398 (EVEN)	10
301-399 (ODD)	54
400-1599	10
1700-2099	14
Osage Ave N	
3200-4399	34
4400-4799	56
5600-5799	31
Osceola Ave N	
3000-3199	35
3200-4399	34
4400-5599	56
5600-7199	31
7200-8799	48
Oshkosh Ave N	31
Oswego N	22
Otsego Ave N	31

Chicago (Con.)   606

Ottawa Ave N
3200-4399	34
4400-5599	56
5600-7199	31
7200-8799	48

Otto Ave N. 56

Overhill Ave N
3200-4399	34
4400-5599	56
5600-7199	31
7200-8799	48

Owen Ave N. 31
Oxford Ave N. 31

Ozanam Ave N
3200-4399	34
4400-5599	56
5600-7199	31
8000-8999	48

Ozark Ave N
3200-4399	34
4400-5599	56
5600-7199	31
7400-8799	48

Pacesetter Pky W. 27
Pacific Ave N. 34
Packers Ave S 09

Page S
11900-12999	43

Page Ave N
3200-3999	34

Palatine Ave W. 31
Palisades Dr W. 55

Palmer W
2000-3999	47
4000-6399	39
6400-7999	35

Panama Ave N
3200-3999	34
5400-5599	56

Paris Ave N
3200-3999	34
4400-5599	56

Park Ave W
5600-6199	50
7800-8599	48

Park Ln W. 48
Park Pl E. 37
Park Lane Dr W. 58

Parker Ave W
3000-3999	47
4000-6399	39

Parkside Ave N
1-799	44
800-1599	51
1600-2799	39
2800-4399	34
4400-5599	30
5600-6399	46

Parkside Ave S
1-1199	44
5100-7499	38

Parnell Ave S
2900-3499	16
3500-5499	09
5500-7499	21
7500-9499	20
9500-13099	28
13100-14599	27

Patterson Ave W
600-1999	13

4000-5599	41
5600-7999	34

Paulina N
1-399	12
400-1999	22
2000-2799	14
2800-3599	57
3600-4399	13
4400-5599	40
5600-6399	60
6400-7799	26

Paulina S
1-1199	12
1200-3499	08
3500-5499	09
5500-7499	36
7500-9499	20
11600-12999	43

Paxton Ave S
6700-7899	49
7900-12199	17
12200-13799	33

Pearl Ct N 14
Pearson E. 11

Pearson W
1-799	10
1500-OUT	22

Pensacola Ave W
900-1999	13
2000-3999	18
4000-5599	41
5600-8399	34

Peoria N
1-399	07
400-OUT	22

Peoria S
1-1199	07
1200-2699	08
3900-5499	09
5500-7499	21
7500-9499	20
9500-13199	43

Perry Ave S
5500-7499	21
7500-9499	20
9500-12999	28
13000-13699	27

Pershing Pl W. 09
Pershing Rd E 53

Pershing Rd W
1-2399	09
2400-4599	32
4600-OUT	50

Peshtigo Ct N 11
Peter Ter W. 48

Peterson Ave W
1600-1999	60
2000-3999	59
4000-6399	46
6400-7899	31

Phillips Ave S
7200-7899	49
7900-12199	17

Pierce Ave W
1600-3199	22
3200-OUT	51

Pine Ave N
1-799	44
800-OUT	51

Pine Grv Ave N
2700-2799	14
2800-3599	57
3600-3999	13

Pioneer Ave N
3200-4199	34
4800-5599	56

Pippin W. 52
Pitney Ct S 08

Pittsburgh Ave N
3200-4399	34
4800-5599	56

Plainfield Ave N
3200-4399	34
4400-5399	56

Pleasant Ave S. 20

Plymouth Ct S
300-399	04
400-OUT	05

Poe N. 14
Point N. 47

Polk W
1-199	05
200-1599	07
1600-3199	12
3200-4599	24
4600-5999	44

Ponchartrain Blvd N. 46

Pontiac Ave N
3200-4399	34
4400-5299	56

Poplar Ave S. 08
Portland Ave S 09
Potawatami N. 56

Potomac Ave W
1300-3199	22
3200-5999	51

Prairie Ave S
1600-3499	16
3500-4699	53
4700-5499	15
5500-7099	37
7100-9499	19
9500-12999	28
13000-13799	27

Pratt Ave W
1000-1999	26
2000-3999	45
4000-4899	46
4901-5599 (ODD)	46
7200-7799	31

Pratt Blvd W
1000-1999	26
2000-3999	45
4000-4899	46
4901-5599 (ODD)	46
7200-7799	31

Prescott Ave N. 46

Princeton Ave S
2200-3499	16
3500-5499	09
5500-7499	21
7500-9499	20
9500-12699	28

Prindiville W. 47
Proesel Ave N. 45
Promontory Dr S. 49

Prospect Ave N
4800-5599	56
5600-5799	31
8000-9599	48

Prospect Ave S
9500-11099	43

Prospect Ct W. 48
Prospect Sq S. 20
Prudential Plz E. 01
Pryor Ave W. 43

Chicago (Con.)   606

Pueblo Ave N
3200-4399................ 34
4400-4799................ 56
5300-5399................ 56
Pulaski Rd N
1-799..................... 24
800-1599................. 51
1600-2799............... 39
2800-4399............... 41
4400-5599............... 30
5600-6399............... 46
Pulaski Rd S
1-1199................... 24
1200-3899............... 23
3900-5499............... 32
5500-7499............... 29
7500-8699............... 52
8701-10299 (ODD)...... 42
10301-11099 (ODD)..... 55
11100-11499............ 55
Purple S................. 16
Quincy W
1-199.................... 04
200-799.................. 06
800-1599................. 07
1700-1799............... 12
4800-5599............... 44
Quinn S................. 08
Race Ave W
1200-1999............... 22
2000-2299............... 12
4600-5999............... 44
Racine Ave N
1-399.................... 07
400-999.................. 22
1900-2799............... 14
2800-3599............... 57
3600-4399............... 13
4400-OUT................ 40
Racine Ave S
1-1199................... 07
1200-3499............... 08
3500-5499............... 09
5500-7499............... 36
7500-9499............... 20
9500-13199.............. 43
Railroad Ave S........ 17
Ramona N.............. 46
Rance Ter W
2000-3999............... 45
Randolph E............ 01
Randolph W
1-199.................... 01
200-799.................. 06
800-1599................. 07
3100-OUT................ 12
Rascher Ave W
1400-1999............... 40
2000-3999............... 25
4000-6399............... 30
6400-8799............... 56
Raven W
6200-6399............... 46
6400-6899............... 31
Ravenswood Ave N
2800-3599............... 57
3600-4399............... 13
4400-5599............... 40
5600-6399............... 60
6400-7799............... 26
Rays Ct S............. 09

Redwood Dr N
4400-5599............... 56
5600-5799............... 31
Reilly Ter S.......... 52
Reserve Ave N......... 56
Reta Ave N............ 57
Rexford S............. 58
Rhodes Ave S
3100-3499............... 16
3500-3999............... 53
6000-7099............... 37
7100-9499............... 19
9500-10899.............. 28
13000-13399............. 27
Rice W
1800-3199............... 22
3200-5999............... 51
Richmond N
800-1599................. 22
1600-2799............... 47
2800-4399............... 18
4400-5599............... 25
5600-6399............... 59
6400-7599............... 45
Richmond S
300-399.................. 12
1100-1199............... 12
3500-5499............... 29
5500-7499............... 29
7500-8699............... 52
8700-10299.............. 42
Ridge Ave N
5600-6399............... 60
6400-6799............... 26
6800-7599............... 45
Ridge Blvd N
5600-6399............... 60
6400-6799............... 26
6800-7599............... 45
Ridge Rd N
5600-6399............... 60
6400-6799............... 26
6800-7599............... 45
Ridgeland Ave S
6700-7899............... 49
7900-12199.............. 17
Ridgeway Ave N
400-799.................. 24
800-1599................. 51
1600-2799............... 47
2800-4399............... 18
4400-5599............... 25
5600-6399............... 59
6400-7199............... 45
Ridgeway Ave S
1400-3499............... 23
3500-5499............... 32
5500-7499............... 29
7500-8699............... 52
8700-10299.............. 42
10300-11899............. 55
11900-13299............. 58
Ridgewood Ave N
4800-5099............... 56
Ridgewood Ct S....... 15
Ritchie Ct N.......... 10
River Rd N............ 56
Riverdale Ave S....... 27
Riverside Dr N
7100-7199............... 48
Riverside Plz N....... 06
Riverside Plz S
1-99..................... 06

Riverview Rd N........ 48
Robbins Ter W......... 13
Robin Rd N............ 48
Robinson S............ 08
Rochdale Pl E......... 15
Rockwell N
200-799.................. 12
800-1599................. 22
1600-2799............... 47
2800-4399............... 18
4400-5599............... 25
5600-6399............... 59
6400-7599............... 45
Rockwell S
1-1199................... 12
1200-3499............... 08
3500-5499............... 32
5500-7499............... 29
7500-8699............... 52
8700-10299.............. 42
10300-11899............. 55
Rogers Ave W
5200-5599............... 30
5600-6099............... 46
6100-6399............... 59
6400-7299............... 45
7300-7699............... 26
Ronald N.............. 56
Roosevelt Rd E........ 05
Roosevelt Rd W
1-299.................... 05
300-799.................. 07
800-2799................. 08
2800-3199............... 12
3200-4599............... 24
4600-5999............... 50
6001-6199 (ODD)........ 50
Root W................ 09
Root St & Ct N....... 48
Roscoe W
4C0-1999................ 57
2000-3999............... 18
4000-5599............... 41
5600-8399............... 34
Rose N................ 56
Rosedale Ave W
1200-1399............... 60
4000-6399............... 46
7400-7899............... 31
Rosehill Dr W......... 60
Rosemary Ln N........ 48
Rosemary Ln S
11700-11899............. 58
Rosemont Ave W
900-1999................. 60
2000-3999............... 59
4000-6399............... 46
Roseview Dr W........ 48
Roslyn Pl W........... 14
Ross Ave S............ 21
Ruble S............... 16
Rumsey Ave W......... 52
Rundell Pl W.......... 07
Rush N
400-1099................. 11
1100-OUT................ 10
Rutherford Ave N
1600-2799............... 35
2800-4399............... 34
4400-5599............... 56
Rutherford Ave S
5100-7499............... 38

Chicago (Con.) 606

Sacramento Ave N
1-799.................... 12
800-1199................ 22
1600-2799.............. 47
2800-4399.............. 18
4400-5599.............. 25
5600-6399.............. 59
6400-7599.............. 45
Sacramento Ave S
1-1199................. 12
2200-3499.............. 23
3500-5499.............. 32
5500-7499.............. 29
7500-8699.............. 52
8700-10299............. 42
10300-11499............ 55
Sacramento Dr S
11500-11899............ 55
Sacramento Sq W..... 12
Saginaw Ave S
7500-7899.............. 49
7900-12199............. 17
12200-14599............ 33
Saint Clair N........ 11
Saint Georges Ct W... 47
Saint Helen Ct W..... 47
Saint James Pl W..... 14
Saint Joseph Ave W... 56
Saint Lawrence Ave S
3200-3299.............. 16
3700-4699.............. 53
4700-5099.............. 15
6000-7099.............. 37
7100-9499.............. 19
9500-12999............. 28
13000-13799............ 27
Saint Louis Ave N
200-799................ 24
800-1599............... 51
1600-2799.............. 47
2800-4399.............. 18
4400-5599.............. 25
5600-6399.............. 59
6400-7199.............. 45
Saint Louis Ave S
1-1199................. 24
1200-3499.............. 23
3500-5499.............. 32
5500-7499.............. 29
7500-8699.............. 52
8700-10299............. 42
10300-11699............ 55
Saint Marys St & Ct W. 47
Saint Michaels Ct N... 14
Saint Paul Ave W
200-299................ 14
2000-3999.............. 47
4000-6399.............. 39
Sandburg Ter N....... 10
Sangamon N
1-399.................. 07
400-OUT................ 22
Sangamon S
1-1199................. 07
1200-2399.............. 08
3500-5499.............. 09
5500-7499.............. 21
7500-9499.............. 20
9500-13199............. 43
Sauganash Ave N...... 46

Sawyer Ave N
400-799................ 24
1600-2799.............. 47
2800-4399.............. 18
4400-5599.............. 25
5600-6399.............. 59
Sawyer Ave S
1200-3499.............. 23
3500-5499.............. 32
5500-7499.............. 29
7500-8699.............. 52
8700-10299............. 42
10300-11499............ 55
Sayre Ave N
1600-2799.............. 35
2800-4399.............. 34
4400-5599.............. 56
5600-6399.............. 31
Sayre Ave S
5100-7499.............. 38
Schick Pl N.......... 10
Schiller E........... 10
Schiller W
1-799.................. 10
1900-OUT............... 22
School N
7200-7499.............. 48
School W
900-1999............... 57
2000-3999.............. 18
4000-5599.............. 41
5600-8399.............. 34
School Ave S
13400-14599............ 27
Schorsch W........... 34
Schreiber Ave W
1400-1999.............. 26
2000-3999.............. 45
6600-7199.............. 31
Schubert Ave W
600-1799............... 14
2300-3999.............. 47
4000-6399.............. 39
6400-7999.............. 35
Scott Dr W
3600-3699.............. 58
Scott St E & W....... 10
Scottsdale Ave S..... 52
Sedgwick N
600-1599............... 10
1600-OUT............... 14
Seeley Ave N
400-499................ 12
2200-2799.............. 47
2800-4399.............. 18
4400-5599.............. 25
5600-6399.............. 59
6400-7599.............. 45
Seeley Ave S
1-1099................. 12
2300-2399.............. 08
3200-3499.............. 08
3500-5499.............. 09
5500-7499.............. 36
7500-9499.............. 20
9500-10899............. 43
Seminary W........... 52
Seminary Ave N
1900-2799.............. 14
2800-3599.............. 57
3600-4399.............. 13

Seminole W
5200-6399.............. 46
7400-8299.............. 31
Seneca N............. 11
Senior Pl W.......... 34
Senour Ave S......... 08
Seward W............. 48
Shakespeare Ave W
600-1499............... 14
2000-3999.............. 47
4000-6399.............. 39
6400-7999.............. 35
Sheffield Ave N
1500-1599.............. 22
1600-2799.............. 14
2800-3599.............. 57
3600-3899.............. 13
Shelby Ct S.......... 08
Sheridan Rd N
2800-3599.............. 57
3600-4399.............. 13
4400-5599.............. 40
5600-6399.............. 60
6400-7799.............. 26
Sheridan Rd W
600-999................ 13
1000-1199.............. 60
Sherman S
300-399................ 04
400-OUT................ 05
Shermer Rd N......... 48
Sherwin Ave W
1200-1999.............. 26
2000-3399.............. 45
3800-3999.............. 45
4000-4899.............. 46
6000-7799.............. 48
Shields Ave S
2600-3499.............. 16
3500-5499.............. 09
5500-OUT............... 21
Shirley Ln W......... 58
Short S.............. 08
Silverton Way S...... 16
Sioux Ave N.......... 46
Somerset W........... 31
South Chicago Ave S
6700-7099.............. 37
7100-7899.............. 19
7900-OUT............... 17
South Park Ln Dr W... 55
South Shore Blvd
2400-2599.............. 49
4700-5499.............. 15
5500-5599.............. 37
6700-7899.............. 49
7900-OUT............... 17
South Water E........ 01
South Water Market District.. 08
Southport Ave N
1900-2799.............. 14
2800-3599.............. 57
3600-4199.............. 13
Spaulding Ave N
400-799................ 24
800-1599............... 51
1600-2799.............. 47
2800-4399.............. 18
4400-5599.............. 25
5600-6399.............. 59
6400-7199.............. 45

Chicago (Con.)   606

Spaulding Ave S
1-1199.............................. 24
1200-3499......................... 23
3500-5499......................... 32
5500-7499......................... 29
7500-8699......................... 52
8700-10299........................ 42
10300-11499....................... 55
Spencer S........................... 58
Spokane Ave N..................... 46
Springfield Ave N
400-799............................ 24
800-1599........................... 51
1600-2799......................... 47
2800-4399......................... 18
4400-5599......................... 25
5600-6399......................... 59
6400-7399......................... 45
Springfield Ave S
1-1199............................. 24
1200-3499......................... 23
3500-5499......................... 32
5500-7499......................... 29
7500-8699......................... 52
8700-10299........................ 42
10300-11899....................... 55
11900-13299....................... 58
Stark S............................. 08
State E
2400-2998 (EVEN)................. 33
State N
1-149.............................. 02
150-299........................... 01
300-OUT........................... 10
State S
1-199............................. 03
200-399........................... 04
400-1599.......................... 05
1600-3499......................... 16
3500-5499......................... 09
5500-6299......................... 21
6300-7099......................... 37
7100-9499......................... 19
9500-12799........................ 28
12800-14599....................... 27
State Pky N........................ 10
State Line Rd S.................... 17
Stave N............................ 47
Stetson Ave N...................... 01
Steuben W.......................... 43
Stewart Ave S
1600-3499......................... 16
3500-5499......................... 09
5500-7499......................... 21
7500-9499......................... 20
9500-13099........................ 28
13100-14599....................... 27
Stockton Dr N...................... 14
Stolting Rd W...................... 48
Stone N............................ 10
Stony Island Ave S
5500-6699......................... 37
6700-7899......................... 49
7900-12199........................ 17
12200-13799....................... 33
Stratford Pl W..................... 57
Streeter Dr N...................... 11
Strong W
3900-3999......................... 25
4800-6399......................... 30
6400-8399......................... 56

Sullivan W......................... 10
Summerdale Ave W
1400-1999......................... 40
2000-3999......................... 25
6900-8799......................... 56
Summit Ave S....................... 20
Sunnyside Ave W
800-1999.......................... 40
2000-3999......................... 25
4000-6399......................... 30
6400-8699......................... 56
Sunrise Ln N....................... 56
Sunset Dr W
7600-7999......................... 35
Sunset Rd W
8600-8799......................... 48
Superior E......................... 11
Superior W
1-799............................. 10
800-1999.......................... 22
2000-3199......................... 12
4600-5999......................... 44
Surf W............................. 57
Surrey Ct N........................ 14
Susan Ct N......................... 48
Swann W............................ 09
Tahoma Ave N....................... 46
Talcott Ave W
6900-7798......................... 31
Talcott Ave W, W
6700-6899......................... 56
Talcott Rd W, W
6700-6899......................... 56
6900-7798......................... 31
Talman Ave N
1-799............................. 12
800-1599.......................... 22
1600-2799......................... 47
2800-4399......................... 18
4700-5599......................... 25
5600-6399......................... 59
6400-7599......................... 45
Talman Ave S
400-1199.......................... 12
1200-1499......................... 08
3900-5499......................... 32
5500-7499......................... 29
7500-8699......................... 52
8700-10299........................ 42
10300-11499....................... 55
Taylor W
1-199............................. 05
200-1599.......................... 07
1600-3199......................... 12
3200-4599......................... 24
4600-5999......................... 44
Terra Cotta Pl W................... 14
Thatcher Ave N
1600-1999......................... 35
4400-4799......................... 56
Thomas W
1300-3199......................... 22
3200-5999......................... 51
Thome Ave W
1400-1999......................... 60
2000-3999......................... 59
4400-OUT.......................... 46
Thorndale Ave W
900-1999.......................... 60
2000-3999......................... 59
4000-6399......................... 46
6400-7899......................... 31
Throop N
1-99.............................. 07

700-OUT............................ 22
Throop S
1-1199............................ 07
1200-3299......................... 08
4700-5499......................... 09
5500-7499......................... 36
7500-9499......................... 20
9500-13199........................ 43
Tilden S........................... 16
Todd S............................. 16
Tonty Ave N........................ 46
Tooker Pl W........................ 10
Torrence Ave S
9400-12199........................ 17
12200-14599....................... 33
Touhy Ave W
1200-1999......................... 26
2000-3999......................... 45
4000-4899......................... 46
5600-7799......................... 48
Tower Cir Dr E..................... 46
Tower Cir Dr N..................... 46
Tower Cir Dr S..................... 46
Tower Cir Dr W..................... 46
Tracy Ave S........................ 27
Transit Ave W...................... 09
Tremont W.......................... 21
Tripp Ave N
800-1599.......................... 51
1600-2799......................... 39
2800-4399......................... 41
4400-5599......................... 30
5600-7399......................... 46
Tripp Ave S
600-899........................... 24
1200-3499......................... 23
3900-5499......................... 32
5500-7499......................... 29
7500-8699......................... 52
11500-13299....................... 58
Trowbridge Pl W.................... 32
Troy N
400-799........................... 12
800-1599.......................... 22
1600-2799......................... 47
2800-4399......................... 18
4400-5599......................... 25
5600-6399......................... 59
6400-7599......................... 45
Troy S
100-1199.......................... 12
1200-3399......................... 23
4300-5499......................... 32
5500-7499......................... 29
7500-8699......................... 52
8700-10299........................ 42
10300-11499....................... 55
Troy Dr S
11500-11899....................... 55
Trumbull Ave N
400-799........................... 24
800-1199.......................... 51
5600-7199......................... 45
Trumbull Ave S
300-1599.......................... 24
1400-3499......................... 23
4300-5499......................... 32
5500-7499......................... 29
7500-8699......................... 52
8700-10299........................ 42
10300-11699....................... 55
11900-13299....................... 58

Chicago (Con.)   605

Turner Ave S	42
Union Ave N	
1-399	06
400-OUT	10
Union Ave S	
1200-1599	07
1600-3499	16
3500-5499	09
5500-7499	21
7500-9499	20
9500-13099	28
13800-14599	27
University Ave S	
4400-4699	53
4700-5499	15
5500-7099	37
7100-9499	19
9500-OUT	28
Urban Ave S	19
Utica Ave S	42
Van Buren E	05
Van Buren W	
1-165	05
166-166	04
167-199	05
200-1599	07
1600-3199	12
3200-4599	24
4600-5999	44
Van Vlissingen Rd S	17
Vanderpoel Ave S	
9200-9499	20
9500-OUT	43
Vermont Ave W	
500-799	28
800-1599	43
3400-4799	58
Vernon Ave S	
2800-3499	16
3500-4399	53
6000-7099	37
7100-9499	19
9500-12999	27
13000-13799	27
Vernon Park Pl W	07
Victoria W	
1200-1999	60
2400-3999	59
4000-4299	46
7600-7899	31
Vincennes Ave S	
3500-4699	53
4700-5099	15
6700-7499	21
7500-9499	20
9500-11899	43
Vine N	
1200-1599	10
1600-OUT	14
4800-5599	56
5600-5699	31
Vintage S	08
Virginia Ave N	
4500-5599	25
5600-6399	59
Wabansia Ave W	
1300-1999	22
2000-3999	47
4000-6399	39
6400-7999	35

Wabash Ave N	
1-149	02
150-329	01
330-OUT	11
Wabash Ave S	
1-199	03
200-399	04
400-1599	05
1600-3499	16
3500-4699	53
4700-5499	15
5500-7099	37
7100-9499	19
9500-12799	29
12800-14599	27
Wacker Dr E	01
Wacker Dr N	
1-199	06
Wacker Dr S	
1-399	06
400-OUT	07
Wacker Dr W	
1-199	01
200-399	06
Walden Pky S	43
Wallace S	
2300-3499	16
3500-5499	09
5500-7499	21
7500-9499	20
9500-13099	28
13100-14599	27
Wallen Ave N	
1600-1799	26
3700-3999	45
Waller Ave N	
1-799	44
800-OUT	51
Waller Ave S	
1-1199	44
Walnut W	
600-799	06
1600-3199	12
3200-OUT	24
Walter Ln W	58
Walton E	11
Walton W	
1-799	10
1300-3199	22
3200-5999	51
Warner Ave W	
1400-1999	13
2000-3999	18
4000-OUT	41
Warren Ave W	
600-799	06
1500-1599	07
1600-3199	12
3200-OUT	24
Warren Blvd W	
600-799	06
1500-1599	07
1600-3199	12
3200-OUT	24
Warren Rd N	48
Warwick Ave W	
4000-5599	41
5600-6399	34
Waseca Pl W	43
Washburne Ave W	08
Washington E	02
Washington N	
5300-5599	56

8000-8999	48
9000-9598 (EVEN)	48
Washington W	
1-199	02
200-799	06
800-1599	07
1600-3199	12
3200-4599	24
4600-5999	44
Washington Park Ct S	15
Washtenaw Ave N	
1-799	12
800-1599	22
1600-2799	47
2800-3399	18
4700-5599	25
5600-6399	59
6400-7599	45
Washtenaw Ave S	
1-1199	12
1200-3499	08
3500-5499	32
5500-7499	29
7500-8699	52
8700-10299	42
10300-11499	55
Waterloo Ct N	57
Watkins Ave S	43
Waukegan Rd N	48
Waukesha Ave N	46
Waveland Ave W	
600-1999	13
2000-3999	18
4000-5599	41
5600-8399	34
Wayman W	
600-799	06
800-999	07
4600-OUT	44
Wayne Ave N	
2100-2799	14
2800-3599	57
3600-3999	13
5200-5599	40
5600-6399	60
6400-6999	26
Webster N	
2400-2499	35
Webster Ave W	
300-1999	14
2000-OUT	47
Weed W	
600-799	10
800-OUT	22
Wellington Ave W	
300-1999	57
2000-3999	18
4000-5599	41
5600-7199	34
7200-7999	35
Wells N	
1-299	06
300-398 (EVEN)	54
301-399 (ODD)	10
400-1599	10
1600-OUT	14
Wells S	
1-199	06
200-398 (EVEN)	06
201-399 (ODD)	04
400-1199	07
2600-3499	16
3500-5499	09

Chicago (Con.) 606

Wendell W.	10
Wendy Way N.	48
Wentworth Ave S	
1600-3499	16
3500-5499	09
5500-7499	21
7500-9499	20
9500-12899	28
12900-14599	27
Wesley Ter N.	56
West Cir Ave N.	31
West District Blvd	32
West End Ave W	
3800-4599	24
4600-5999	44
Westbrook Rd N.	35
Western Ave N	
1-799	12
800-1599	22
1600-2799	47
2800-4399	18
4400-5599	25
5600-6399	59
6400-7599	45
8200-8399	48
Western Ave S	
1-1199	12
1200-3499	08
3500-5499	09
5500-7499	36
7500-9499	20
9500-9798 (EVEN)	42
9501-9799 (ODD)	43
Western Ave, S	
9800-11899	43
Westgate Ter W.	07
Weston Pl W	
9501-9799 (ODD)	20
Westwood Dr W.	35
Whipple N	
300-799	12
800-1599	22
1600-2799	47
2800-4399	18
4400-5599	25
5600-6399	59
6400-7599	45
Whipple S	
1-1199	12
2200-3299	23
4200-5499	32
5500-7499	29
7500-8699	52
8700-10299	42
10300-11499	55
Whipple Dr W	
3100-3199	55
Wicker Park Ave N.	22
Wieland N.	10
Wilcox W	
2300-2999	12
3800-OUT	24
Wildwood Ave N.	46
Willard Ct N	
100-199	07
700-OUT	22
Willets Ct N.	47
Williams Ave S.	19
Willow N	
300-1099	14
1400-1499	22

Willow Ln N.	48
Wilmot Ave N.	47
Wilson Ave W	
700-1999	40
2000-3999	25
4000-6399	30
6400-8799	56
Wilton Ave N	
2000-2799	14
3000-3599	57
3600-3899	13
Winchester Ave N	
400-1999	22
2000-2799	14
2800-3599	57
3600-4399	13
4400-5599	40
5600-6399	60
6400-7599	26
Winchester Ave S	
1-1199	12
1200-3499	08
3500-5499	09
5500-7499	36
7500-9499	20
9500-12299	43
12301-12699 (ODD)	43
Windsor Ave W	
800-999	40
2100-3999	25
4000-6399	30
6400-8599	56
Winnebago Ave N.	47
Winneconna Pky W.	20
Winnemac Ave W	
1200-1999	40
2000-3999	25
4000-6399	30
7200-8599	56
Winona W	
800-1999	40
2000-3999	25
4000-6399	30
6400-8599	56
Winston Ave S.	43
Winthrop Ave N	
4600-5599	40
5600-6399	60
6400-6699	26
Wisconsin W.	14
Wisner N	
8000-8999	48
Wisner Ave N	
2900-2999	18
Wolcott Ave N	
1-399	12
400-1999	22
2000-2799	14
2800-3599	57
3600-4399	13
4400-5599	40
5600-6399	60
6400-7599	26
Wolcott Ave S	
1-1199	12
1200-3499	08
3500-5499	09
5500-7499	36
7500-9499	20
11800-12699	43
Wolfram W	
800-1999	57

2300-3999	18
4000-5599	41
5600-7199	34
Wood N	
1-399	12
400-1999	22
2000-OUT	14
Wood S	
1-1199	12
1200-3499	08
3500-5499	09
5500-7499	36
7500-9499	20
9500-12699	43
Woodard N.	18
Woodland Dr N.	48
Woodland Park E.	16
Woodlawn Ave S	
4400-4699	53
4700-5499	15
5500-7099	37
7100-9499	19
9500-10399	28
13000-13799	27
Wright Ter W.	48
Wrightwood Ave W	
400-1999	14
3200-3999	47
4000-6399	39
6400-7599	35
Yale Ave S	
6300-7499	21
7500-9499	20
9500-12999	28
Yates Ave S	
7100-7899	49
7900-12199	17
12200-14599	33

NUMBERED STREETS

5th Ave W	
2800-3199	12
3200-4599	24
4600-5999	44
8th thru 14th St E.	05
11th W.	07
12th Pl W	
300-799	07
2600-3399	08
3400-3599	23
4600-4799	50
13th W	
1-299	65
300-799	07
800-2799	08
2800-4599	23
4600-6199	50
13th Pl W	
1-299	05
300-799	07
800-2799	08
2800-4599	23
4600-6199	50
14th W	
1-299	05
300-799	07
800-2799	08
2800-4599	23
4600-6199	50
14th Pl W	
1-299	05

Chicago (Con.)	606

300-799	07
800-2799	08
2800-4599	23
4600-6199	50
15th W	
1-299	05
300-799	07
800-2799	08
2800-4599	23
4600-6199	50
15th Pl W	
1-299	05
300-799	07
800-2799	08
2800-4599	23
4600-6199	50
16th W	
1-799	16
800-2799	08
2800-4599	23
4600-6199	50
16th Pl W	
1-799	16
800-2799	08
2800-4599	23
4600-6199	50
16th thru 35th St E	16
17th W	
1-799	16
800-2799	08
2800-4599	23
4600-6199	50
17th Pl W	
1-799	16
800-2799	08
2800-4599	23
4600-6199	50
18th W	
1-799	16
800-2799	08
2800-4599	23
4600-6199	50
18th Pl W	
1-799	16
800-2799	08
2800-4599	23
4600-6199	50
19th W	
1-799	16
800-2799	08
2800-4599	23
4600-6199	50
19th Pl W	
1-799	16
800-2799	08
2800-4599	23
4600-6199	50
20th W	
1-799	16
800-2799	08
2800-4599	23
4600-6199	50
20th Pl W	
1-799	16
800-2799	08
2800-4599	23
4600-6199	50
21st W	
1-799	16
800-2799	08

2800-4599	23
4600-6199	50
21st Pl W	
1-799	16
800-2799	08
2800-4599	23
4600-6199	50
22nd W	
1-799	16
800-2799	08
2800-4599	23
4600-6199	50
22nd Pl W	
1-799	16
800-2799	08
2800-4599	23
4600-6199	50
23rd W	
1-799	16
800-2799	08
2800-4599	23
4600-6199	50
23rd Pl W	
1-799	16
800-2799	08
2800-4599	23
4600-6199	50
24th W	
1-799	16
800-2799	08
4600-6199	50
24th Blvd W	
2800-2999	23
24th Pl W	
1-799	16
800-2799	08
2800-4599	23
4600-6199	50
25th W	
1-799	16
800-2799	08
2800-4599	23
4600-6199	50
25th Pl W	
1-799	16
800-2799	08
2800-4599	23
4600-6199	50
26th W	
1-799	16
800-2799	08
2800-4599	23
4600-6199	50
26th Pl W	
1-799	16
800-2799	08
2800-4599	23
4600-6199	50
27th W	
1-799	16
800-2799	08
2800-4599	23
4600-6199	50
27th Pl W	
1-799	16
800-2799	08
2800-4599	23
4600-6199	50
28th W	
1-799	16
800-2799	08

2800-4599	23
4600-6199	50
28th Pl W	
1-799	16
800-2799	08
2800-4599	23
4600-6199	50
29th W	
1-799	16
800-2799	08
2600-4599	23
4600-6199	50
29th Pl W	
1-799	16
800-2799	08
2800-4599	23
4600-6199	50
30th W	
1-799	16
800-2799	08
2800-4599	23
4600-6199	50
30th Pl W	
1-799	16
800-2799	08
2800-4599	23
4600-6199	50
31st W	
1-799	16
800-2799	08
2800-4599	23
4600-6199	50
31st Blvd W	08
31st Pl W	
1-799	16
800-2799	08
2800-4599	23
4600-6199	50
32nd W	
1-799	16
800-2799	08
2800-4599	23
4600-6199	50
32nd Pl W	
1-799	16
800-2799	08
2800-4599	23
4600-6199	50
33rd W	
1-799	16
800-2799	08
2800-4599	23
4600-6199	50
33rd Pl W	
1-799	16
800-2799	08
2800-4599	23
4600-6199	50
34th W	
1-799	16
800-2799	08
2800-4599	23
4600-6199	50
34th Pl W	
1-799	16
800-2799	08
2800-4599	23
4600-6199	50
35th W	
1-799	16
800-2399	09
2400-2799	32
2800-4599	23

Chicago (Con.) 606

4800-7199	38

56th Ave S
1200-3899	50

56th Ct S
1200-3899	50

56th Pl W
1-1199	21
1200-2399	36
2400-4799	29
4800-7199	38

56th St & Pl E ... 37

57th W
1-1199	21
1200-2399	36
2400-4799	29
4800-7199	38

57th Ave S
1200-3899	50

57th Ct S
1200-3899	50

57th Pl W
1-1199	21
1200-2399	36
2400-4799	29
4800-7199	38

57th St & Pl E ... 37

58th W
1-1199	21
1200-2399	36
2400-4799	29
4800-7199	38

58th Ave S
1200-3899	50

58th Ct S
1200-3899	50

58th Pl W
1-1199	21
1200-2399	36
2400-4799	29
4800-7199	38

58th St & Pl E ... 37

59th W
1-1199	21
1200-2399	36
2400-4799	29
4800-7199	38

59th Ave S
1200-3899	50

59th Ct S
1200-3899	50

59th Pl W
1-1199	21
1200-2399	36
2400-4799	29
4800-7199	38

59th thru 60th St E ... 37

60th W
1-1199	21
1200-2399	36
2400-4799	29
4800-7199	38

60th Ave S
1200-3899	50

60th Ct S
1200-3899	50

60th Pl E ... 37

60th Pl W
1-1199	21
1200-2399	36
2400-4799	29
4800-7199	38

61st W
1-1199	21
1200-2399	36
2400-4799	29
4800-7199	38

61st Ave S
1200-3899	50

61st Ct S
1200-3899	50

61st Pl W
1-1199	21
1200-2399	36
2400-4799	29
4800-7199	38

61st St & Pl E ... 37

62nd W
1-1199	21
1200-2399	36
2400-4799	29
4800-7199	38

62nd Pl W
1-1199	21
1200-2399	36
2400-4799	29
4800-7199	38

62nd St & Pl E ... 37

63rd W
1-1199	21
1200-2399	36
2400-4799	29
4800-7199	38

63rd Pl W
1-1199	21
1200-2399	36
2400-4799	29
4800-7399	38

63rd St & Pl E ... 37

64th E
1-1599	37
1600-OUT	49

64th, W
1-1199	21
1200-2399	36
2400-4799	29
4800-7199	38

64th Pl E
1-1599	37
1600-OUT	49

64th Pl W
1-1199	21
1200-2399	36
2400-4799	29
4800-7399	38

65th E
1-1599	37
1600-OUT	49

65th, W
1-1199	21
1200-2399	36
2400-4799	29
4800-7399	38

65th Pl E
1-1599	37
1600-OUT	49

65th Pl W
1-1199	21
1200-2399	36
2400-4799	29
4800-7399	38

66th, W
1-1199	21
1200-2399	36
2400-4799	29
4800-7399	38

66th Pl W
1-1199	21
1200-2399	36
2400-4799	29
4800-7399	38

66th St & Pl E ... 37

67th E
1-1599	37
1600-OUT	49

67th W
1-1199	21
1200-2399	36
2400-4799	29
4800-7199	38

67th Pl E
1-1599	37
1600-OUT	49

67th Pl W
1-1199	21
1200-2399	36
2400-4799	29
4800-7199	38

68th E
1-1599	37
1600-OUT	49

68th W
1-1199	21
1200-2399	36
2400-4799	29
4800-7199	38

68th Pl E
1-1599	37
1600-OUT	49

68th Pl W
1-1199	21
1200-2399	36
2400-4799	29
4800-7199	38

69th E
1-1599	37
1600-OUT	49

69th W
1-1199	21
1200-2399	36
2400-4799	29
4800-7199	38

69th Pl E
1-1599	37
1600-OUT	49

69th Pl W
1-1199	21
1200-2399	36
2400-4799	29
4800-7199	38

70th E
1-1599	37
1600-OUT	49

70th W
1-1199	21
1200-2399	36
2400-4799	29
4800-7199	38

70th Pl E
1-1599	37
1600-OUT	49

70th Pl W
1-1199	21
1200-2399	36
2400-4799	29
4800-7199	38

71st E
1-1599	19

Chicago (Con.)   605

103rd Pl E
1-1599	28
1600-OUT	17

103rd Pl W
1-799	28
800-2399	43
2400-3999	55

104th E
1-1599	28
1600-OUT	17

104th W
1-799	28
800-2399	43
2400-3999	55

104th Pl E
1-1599	28
1600-OUT	17

104th Pl W
1-799	28
800-2399	43
2400-3999	55

105th E
1-1599	28
1600-OUT	17

105th W
1-799	28
800-2399	43
2400-3999	55

105th Pl E
1-1599	28
1600-OUT	17

105th Pl W
1-799	28
800-2399	43
2400-3999	55

106th E
1-1599	28
1600-OUT	17

106th W
1-799	28
800-2399	43
2400-3999	55

106th Pl E
1-1599	28
1600-OUT	17

106th Pl W
1-799	28
800-2399	43
2400-3999	55

107th E
1-1599	28
1600-OUT	17

107th W
1-799	28
800-2399	43
2400-3999	55

107th Pl E
1-1599	28
1600-OUT	17

107th Pl W
1-799	28
800-2399	43
2400-3999	55

108th E
1-1599	28
1600-OUT	17

108th W
1-799	28
800-2399	43
2400-3999	55

108th Pl E
1-1599	28
1600-OUT	17

108th Pl W
1-799	28
800-2399	43
2400-3999	55

109th E
1-1599	28
1600-OUT	17

109th W
1-799	28
800-2399	43
2400-3999	55

109th Pl E
1-1599	28
1600-OUT	17

109th Pl W
1-799	28
800-2399	43
2400-3999	55

110th E
1-1599	28
1600-OUT	17

110th W
1-799	28
800-2399	43
2400-3999	55

110th Pl E
1-1599	28
1600-OUT	17

110th Pl W
1-799	28
800-2399	43
2400-3999	55

111th E
1-1599	28
1600-OUT	17

111th W
1-799	28
800-2399	43
4801-4899 (ODD)	58

111th, W
4001-4799 (ODD)	55

111th, W
2400-3999	55

111th Pl E
1-1599	28
1600-OUT	17

111th Pl W
1-799	28
800-2399	43
2400-3999	55

112th E
1-1599	28
1600-OUT	17

112th W
1-799	28
800-2399	43
2400-3999	55

112th Pl E
1-1599	28
1600-OUT	17

112th Pl W
1-799	28
800-2399	43
2400-3999	55

113th E
1-1599	28
1600-OUT	17

113th W
1-799	28

113th Pl E
800-2399	43
2400-3999	55

113th Pl E
1-1599	28
1600-OUT	17

113th Pl W
1-799	28
800-2399	43
2400-3999	55

114th E
1-1599	28
1600-OUT	17

114th Pl E
1-1599	28
1600-OUT	17

114th Pl W
1-799	28
800-2399	43
2400-3999	55

115th E
1-1599	28
1600-OUT	17

115th W
1-799	28
800-2399	43
2400-3999	55
4000-4799	58

115th Pl E
1-1599	28
1600-OUT	17

115th Pl W
1-799	28
800-2399	43
2400-3999	55
4000-4799	58

116th E
1-1599	28
1600-OUT	17

116th W
1-799	28
800-2399	43
2400-3999	55
4000-4799	58

116th Pl E
1-1599	28
1600-OUT	17

116th Pl W
1-799	28
800-2399	43
2400-3999	55
4000-4799	58

117th E
1-1599	28
1600-OUT	17

117th W
1-799	28
800-2399	43
2400-3999	55
4000-4899	58

117th Pl E
1-1599	28
1600-OUT	17

117th Pl W
1-799	28
800-2399	43
2400-3999	55
4000-4899	58

118th E
1-1500	28
1600-OUT	17

118th W
1-799	28

Chicago (Con.)   606

800-2399	43
2400-3999	55
4000-4899	58

118th Pl E
1-1599	28
1600-OUT	17

118th Pl W
1-799	28
800-2399	43
2400-3999	55
4000-4899	58

119th E
1-1599	28
1600-OUT	17

119th W
1-799	28
800-1899	43
1900-2398 (EVEN)	43
2400-3598 (EVEN)	55
3600-5599	58

119th Pl E
1-1599	28
1600-OUT	17

119th Pl W, W
4000-4435	58

120th E
1-1599	28
1600-OUT	17

120th W
1-799	28
800-1799	43

120th Pl E
1-1599	28
1600-OUT	17

120th Pl W
1-799	28
800-1799	43
3400-5599	58

121st E
1-1599	28
1600-OUT	17

121st W
1-799	28
800-1799	43
3400-5599	58

121st Pl E
1-1599	28
1600-OUT	17

121st Pl W
1-799	28
800-1799	43
3400-5599	58

122nd E
1-899	28
900-OUT	33

122nd W
1-799	28
800-1799	43
3400-5599	58

122nd Pl E | 28 |

122nd Pl W
1-799	28
800-1799	43
3400-5599	58

123rd W
1-799	28
800-1949	43
3400-5599	58

123rd E, E
1-999	28
1000-OUT	38

123rd Pl W
3400-5599	58

124th E
1-999	28
1000-OUT	33

124th W
1-799	28
800-1949	43
3400-5599	58

124th Pl E
1-999	28

124th Pl W
1-799	28
800-1949	43
3400-5599	58

125th E
1-1099	28
1100-OUT	33

125th W
1-799	28
800-1949	43
3400-5599	58

125th Pl E | 28 |

125th Pl W
1-799	28
800-1949	43
3400-5599	58

126th E
1-1199	28
1200-OUT	33

126th W
1-799	28
800-1949	43
3400-5599	58

126th Pl W
1-799	28
800-1949	43
3400-5599	58

126th Pl, E
1200-OUT	33

126th Pl E, E
1-1199	28

127th E
1-1199	28
1200-OUT	33

127th W
1-799	28
800-1799	43
1800-1948 (EVEN)	43
5400-5598 (EVEN)	58

127th W, W
3400-5399	58

127th Pl W
1-799	28
800-1799	43
3400-4999	58

128th E
200-1299	28
1300-OUT	33

128th Pl W
1-799	28
800-1799	43
3400-4999	58

129th E
200-1399	28
1400-OUT	33

129th W
1-799	28
800-1799	43

130th E
1-199	27
200-498 (EVEN)	28
201-499 (ODD)	27

500-1399	28
1400-OUT	33

130th W
1-799	28
800-1599	43
3400-4799	58

130th Pl E
1-1599	27
1600-OUT	33

131st E
1-1599	27
1600-OUT	33

131st W
3400-4799	58

131st Pl E
1-1599	27
1600-OUT	33

132nd E
1-1599	27
1600-OUT	33

132nd W
3400-4799	58

132nd Pl E
1-1599	27
1600-OUT	33

133rd E
1-1599	27
1600-OUT	33

133rd W
3400-4799	58

133rd Pl E
1-1599	27
1600-OUT	33

134th E
1-1599	27
1600-OUT	33

134th W
1-1599	27

134th Pl E
1-1599	27
1600-OUT	33

135th E
1-1599	27
1600-OUT	33

135th W
1-799	27

135th Pl E
1-1599	27
1600-OUT	33

136th E
1-1599	27
1600-OUT	33

136th W
1-799	27

136th Pl E
1-1599	27
1600-OUT	33

137th E
1-1599	27
1600-OUT	33

137th W
1-799	27

137th Pl E
1-1599	27
1600-OUT	33

137th Pl W
1-799	27

138th E
1-1599	27
1600-OUT	33

138th W
1-799	27

Chicago (Con.) 606

138th Pl E	
2800-OUT	33
139th E	
1-199	27
2400-OUT	33
139th W	
1-799	27
140th E	
1-199	27
2400-OUT	33
140th W	
1-799	27
140th Ct E & W	27
141st E	
1-199	27
2400-OUT	33
141st W	
1-799	27
142nd E	
1-199	27
2400-OUT	33
142nd W	
1-799	27
143rd E	
1-199	27
2400-OUT	33
143rd W	
1-799	27
144th E	
1-199	27
2400-OUT	33
144th W	
1-799	27
145th E	
1-199	27
2400-OUT	33
145th W	
1-799	27
145th Pl W	
1-799	27
146th E	
1-199	27
2400-2998 (EVEN)	33
146th W	
1-799	27

DECATUR 625

POST OFFICE BOXES

Box Nos.

1-1999	Main Office	25
2000-2999	Brettwood Sta	26

RURAL ROUTES

1	26
2	21
3	26
4,6,7	21
8	22

STATIONS, BRANCHES AND UNITS

Brettwood Sta	26
General Delivery	21
Postmaster	21

DES PLAINES 600

POST OFFICE BOXES

Box Nos.

1-281	Main Office	17
300-499	Oakton Sta	18
500-799	Rosemont	18

STATIONS, BRANCHES AND UNITS

Oakton Sta	18
Rosemont Br	18
General Delivery	16
Postmaster	16

EAST SAINT LOUIS 622

POST OFFICE BOXES

Box Nos.

1-799	Main Office	02
800-999	Edgemont Sta	03
1000-1199	Lansdowne Sta	04
1200-1399	Fireworks Br	07
1400-1599	Parcel Post Sta	05
1600-1799	Cahokia Br	06

STATIONS, BRANCHES AND UNITS

Cahokia Br	06
Centreville Br	06
Edgemont Sta	03
Fairview Heights Br	08
Fireworks Br	07
Lansdowne Sta	04
Parcel Post Sta	05
Sauget Br	01
Washington Park Br	04
General Delivery	01
Postmaster	01

APARTMENTS, HOTELS, MOTELS

Brenton Bldg, 2901 Waverly	04
John Deshields, 1235 Mc Casland	01
John Robinson, 12th & Market	01
Orr, 1300 Missouri	01
Roosevelt, 1300 N 44th	04
Ruggeri, 2901 Waverly	04
Rukavina, 2901 Waverly	04
Samuel Gompers, 6th & Ohio	01
Starnes, 2901 Waverly	04
Villa Griffin, 26th & Lincoln	04

BUILDINGS

Arcade, 112–116 Collinsville Ave	01
City Hall, 7 Collinsville	01
Coldman, 338 Missouri Ave	01
First Federal, 435 Missouri Ave	01
First National Bank, 325 Missouri Ave	01
Illinois, 417 Missouri Ave	01
Murphy, 234 Collinsville Ave	01
New Federal, 650 Missouri Ave	01
Shop City Medical, 4601 State St	05

GOVERNMENT OFFICES

U S Attorney, 750 Missouri Ave	02
U S Clerk Of The Court, 750 Missouri Ave	02
U S Internal Revenue Service, 650 Missouri Ave	01
U S Judge Of Federal Courts, 750 Missouri Ave	02
U S Marshall, 750 Missouri Ave	02
U S Railroad Retirement Board, 650 Missouri Ave	01
U S Referee In Bankruptcy, 750 Missouri Ave	02
U S Social Security Admin, 650 Missouri Ave	02

HOSPITALS

Centreville Township, 5900 Bond Ave	07
Christian Welfare, 1509 Illinois Ave	01
Saint Mary'S, 129 N 8th	01

UNIVERSITIES AND COLLEGES

Park College Of Aero Tech, Falling Springs Rd	01

EVANSTON 602

POST OFFICE BOXES

Box Nos.

1-1670	Main Office	04

STATIONS, BRANCHES AND UNITS

North Sta	01
South Sta	02
General Delivery	04
Postmaster	04

APARTMENTS, HOTELS, MOTELS

Evanshire, 860 Hinman Ave	02
Evanston Inn, 840 Forest Ave	02
Homestead, 1625 Hinman Ave	01
Library Plaza, 1637 Orrington Ave	01
North Shore, 1611 Chicago Ave	01
Orrington, 1710 Orrington Ave	01
Ridgeview, 901 Maple Ave	02

Evanston (Con.)   602

BUILDINGS

State National Bank Plaza,
1603 Orrington Ave 01

HOSPITALS

Community Hospital, 2040
Brown Ave 01
Evanston Hospital, 2650
Ridge Ave 01
Saint Francis Hospital, 355
Ridge Ave 02

UNIVERSITIES AND COLLEGES

Garrett Theological Seminary,
2121 Sheridan Rd 01
Kendall College, 2408
Orrington Ave 04
National College Of
Education, 2840 Sheridan
Rd 01
Northwestern University, 633
Clark 01
Seabury Western Theological
Seminary, 2122 Sheridan
Rd 01

JOLIET   604

POST OFFICE BOXES

Box Nos.
1-948   Main Office 34

RURAL ROUTES

1,2,3,4,5 31

STATIONS, BRANCHES AND UNITS

Crest Hill Br 35
Rockdale Br 36
Shorewood Rural Br 36
West Gate Sta 35
General Delivery 31
Postmaster 31

MELROSE PARK   601

POST OFFICE BOXES

Box Nos.
1-499   19th Ave Sta 60
600-799   Hillside-
             Berkeley Br 62
1000-1199   Main Office 61
2001-2299   Northlake 64

STATIONS, BRANCHES AND UNITS

Hillside-Berkeley Br 62
Nineteenth Avenue Sta 60
Northlake Br 64
Stone Park Br 65
Taft Br 63
General Delivery 60
Postmaster 60

OAK LAWN   604

POST OFFICE BOXES

Box Nos.
ANY   Main Office 54

RURAL ROUTES

1,2,3,4,5,6 53

STATIONS, BRANCHES AND UNITS

Bridgeview Br 55
Burbank Br 59
Hickory Hills Br 57
Hometown Br 56
South Bridgeview Br 55
South Stickney Br 59
General Delivery 54
Postmaster 54

OAK PARK   603

POST OFFICE BOXES

Box Nos.
1-314   River Forest Br. 05
1-997   Oak Park 03
1001-1179   South Oak Park
             Sta 04
2001-2117   Oak Park 03

STATIONS, BRANCHES AND UNITS

River Forest Br 05
South Oak Park Sta 04
General Delivery 03
Postmaster 01

APARTMENTS, HOTELS, MOTELS

Carleton & Motor Inn, 1110
Pleasant 02
Oak Manor, 211 N Oak Park
Ave 02
Oak Park Arms, 408 S Oak
Park Ave 02
Oak Park Chateau, 330 N
Austin Blvd 02
Oak, 855 Lake 01
Oakshire Apartment, 12
Washington Blvd 02
Plaza, 123 S Marion 02
Ymca, 255 S Marion 02

BUILDINGS

Avenue State Bank, 104 N
Oak Park Ave 01
Oak Park Federal Savings &
Loan Association, 1001
Lake 01
Oak Park National Bank, 11
Madison 02
Oak Park Trust & Savings
Bank, 1048 Lake 01
River Forest State Bank &
Trust Company, 7727 W
Lake 05

Suburban Trust & Savings
Bank, 840 S Oak Park
Ave 04
Tri City Savings & Loan
Association, 6020
Roosevelt 04
Village Hall, 655 Lake St. 01
Village Savings & Loan
Association, 810 S Oak
Park Ave 04

HOSPITALS

Oak Park Hosp., 520 S Maple
Ave 04
West Suburban Hospital, 518
N Austin Blvd 02

PEORIA   616

POST OFFICE BOXES

Box Nos.
1-99   Alta R. Sta 08
1-99   Creve Coeur
             Sta 11
1-99   Limestone Br ... 07
1-99   Peoria Heights
             Br 14
1-2000   Main Office 01
2001-2999   East Peoria Br. 11
3001-3999   West Glen Sta .. 14
4001-4999   Bartonville Br. 07

RURAL ROUTES

1 11
2 14
3 07
4 14
5,6,8 11

STATIONS, BRANCHES AND UNITS

Alta Rural Br 08
Bartonville Br 07
Creve Coeur Br 11
East Peoria Br 11
El Vista Sta 04
Junction City Sta 14
Limestone Br 07
Madison Park Br 04
Meadows Avenue Br 11
Peoria Heights Br 14
Rolling Acres Sta 14
Sheridan Village Sta 14
West Glen Sta 14
Windsor Square Sta 14
General Delivery 01
Postmaster 01

APARTMENTS, HOTELS, MOTELS

Clayton House, 5712 N
Knoxville 14
Downtown Motel, 705
Hamilton 03

Peoria (Con.) 616

Four Winds Motel, 3527
  Harmon Hwy................................. 04
Holiday Inn, 401 N Main E
  Peoria....................................... 11
Howard Johnson Motel, 225 N
  E Adams..................................... 02
Imperial 400 Hotel, 202 N E
  Washington................................. 02
Lee, 225 E State.............................. 02
Manias Manor Motel, 1501
  Knoxville.................................... 03
Pere Marquette, 501 Main.................. 02
Ramada Inn, 415 Saint
  Marks Ct.................................... 03
Sands Motel, 220 NE Adams............... 02
Vonachen'S Hyatt Lodge,
  5901 N Prospect........................... 14
Voyager Inn, 504 Hamilton................. 02

BUILDINGS

Board Of Trade, 300 S
  Washington................................. 02
Caterpillar Administration,
  100 N E Adams............................. 02
Central, 101 S W Adams.................... 02
Citizens, 225 Main........................... 02
Commercial Nat'L Bank
  Bldg... 02
First Nat'L Bank Bldg....................... 02
Insurance, 3100 N Knoxville............... 03
Jefferson, 331 Fulton........................ 02
Junction City................................. 14
Lafayette, 410 Fayette...................... 02
Lehman, 405 Main............................ 06
Madison Park................................. 04
Savings Center Tower, 411
  Hamilton.................................... 02
Savings, 111 NE Jefferson................. 02
Security Savings, 200 N E
  Adams....................................... 02
Sheridan Village.............................. 14
Stockyards, Ft Of South St............... 02
Town Hall, Junction City................... 14

GOVERNMENT OFFICES

City Hall, 419 Fulton........................ 02
County Courthouse, 300
  Main... 02
No Reg Research Lab, 1815
  N University................................ 04
U S Post Office, 100 N E
  Monroe...................................... 01
2628 N Knoxville............................. 01

HOSPITALS

Methodist, 221 NE Glen Oak.............. 02
Peoria State, 7101 S Adams.............. 07
Proctor, 5409 Knoxville..................... 14
St. Francis, 530 N.e. Glen
  Oak.. 03
Zeller Zone Clinic, 5407 N
  University................................... 14

UNIVERSITIES AND COLLEGES

Bradley University, 1502 W
  Bradley...................................... 06
Illinois Central College, 2129
  Highview Rd E Peoria H.................. 11

ROCKFORD 611

POST OFFICE BOXES

Box Nos.
1-1199   Main Office......... 05
1500-1999   East Rockford
                  Sta................ 10
2000-2999   Loves Park Br........ 10
3000-3999   Broadway Sta....... 06
4000-4999   East Rockford
                  Sta................ 10

RURAL ROUTES

1... 09
2... 03
3... 03
4... 11
5... 08
6... 03
7... 08
8... 03
9... 09
10... 11

STATIONS, BRANCHES AND UNITS

Broadway Sta................................. 06
East Rockford Sta........................... 07
Kishwaukee Br................................ 03
Loves Park Br................................. 11
Meadow Mart Br.............................. 11
General Delivery.............................. 01
Postmaster.................................... 01

BUILDINGS

American National Bank, 501
  7th.. 04
Atwood Center, 2500 N Main.............. 04
Camelot Tower, 1415 E. State
  Street....................................... 08
City National Bank, 1100
  Broadway................................... 04
Empire, 206 S Main.......................... 01
First National Bank, 401 E
  State.. 04
Gas & Electric, 303 N Main............... 01
Illinois National Bank, 226 S
  Main... 04
Labor Temple, 212 S 1st................... 04
Loves Park City Hall, 540
  Loves Park Drive.......................... 11
Nu Arcade, 125 N Church.................. 01
Nu State, 119 N Church.................... 01
Rock River Savings & Loan,
  401 W State............................... 01
Rockford Commercial
  Building, 101 Chestnut................... 01
Rockford Life, 526 W State................ 01
Rockford Professional, 1221
  E State...................................... 08
Rockford Trust, 206 W State.............. 01
Talcott, 321 W State........................ 01

GOVERNMENT OFFICES

City Hall, 425 E State....................... 04
Courthouse................................... 01

HOSPITALS

Children'S Medical, 1429
  Myott Ave................................... 01
Family Medical, 2623
  Edgemont................................... 03
Rockford Memorial, 2400 N
  Rockton..................................... 01
Saint Anthony, 5666 E State
  St.. 01
Singer Zone Center, 4402 N.
  Main... 05
Swedish American, 1316
  Charles...................................... 01

UNIVERSITIES AND COLLEGES

Rock Valley College, 3301 N
  Mulford...................................... 01
Rockford College, 5050 E
  State.. 01

SPRINGFIELD 627

POST OFFICE BOXES

Box Nos.
1-2385   Downtown Sta.... 05
2501-4500   Main Office......... 08

RURAL ROUTES

1,2,3,4,5,6,7,8............................... 07

STATIONS, BRANCHES AND UNITS

Capitol Sta.................................... 06
Downtown Sta................................ 01
General Delivery.............................. 08
Postmaster.................................... 08

APARTMENTS, HOTELS, MOTELS

A Lincoln, 2927 S 6th...................... 03
Bel-Aire Manor, 2636 S 6th............... 03
Down Towner, 400 N 9th................... 02
Governor, 418 E Jefferson................. 01
Highway, 1305 Wabash Ave............... 04
Holiday Inn, 625 E Saint
  Joseph...................................... 03
Howard Johnson Motor Lodge,
  1025 S 5th................................. 05
Lamp Liter, U S Route 66 S............... 07
Leland, 527 E Capitol....................... 05
Mansion View, 529 S 4th.................. 01
Ramada Inn, 3751 S 6th................... 03
Saint Nicholas................................ 01
Sheraton Motor Inn, 3090
  Stevenson Dr.............................. 03
State House Inn, 101 E
  Adams....................................... 01
Travelodge, 500 S 9th...................... 01

BUILDINGS

Abraham Lincoln Building................... 01

Springfield (Con.)   627

Ferguson, 522 E Monroe	01
Illinois, 601 E Adams	01
Jefferson West	02
Myers, 101 S 5th	01
Reisch, 117 S 5th	01
Ridgely, 504 E Monroe	01
Security, 516 E Monroe	01
Thrifty, 425 E Monroe	01
Washington, 531 E	

Washington	01
1st National Bank, 201 S	
5th	01

GOVERNMENT OFFICES

Centennial, State Capitol	
Complex	06
Federal, 600 E. Monroe	01
Municipal, 300 S 7th	01

Sangamon County	
Courthouse	01
State Office, State Capitol	
Complex	06

HOSPITALS

Memorial	05
Saint Johns	01

State List of Post Offices   INDIANA

INDIANA
(Abbreviation: IN)

Acton, Br. Indianapolis	46259
Adams, R. Br. Greensburg	47240
Advance	46102
Air Mail Field, Sta.	
Indianapolis	46241
Akron	46910
Alamo	47916
Albany	47320
Albion	46701
Alexandria (1st)	46001
Ambia	47917
Amboy	46911
Amo	46103
ANDERSON (1st) (see	
appendix)	
Andrews	46702
Angola (1st)	46703
Arcadia	46030
Arcola	46704
Argos	46501
Arlington	46104
Ashley	46705
Athens	46912
Atlanta	46031
Attica (1st)	47918
Atwood	46502
Auburn (1st)	46706
Aurora (1st)	47001
Austin	47102
Avilla	46710
Avoca	47420
Avon, Br. Plainfield	46168
Bainbridge	46105
Bargersville	46106
Batesville (1st)	47006
Bath	47010
Battle Ground	47920
Bedford (1st)	47421
Beech Grove (1st)	46107
Bellmore	47830
Bennington	47011
Bentonville	47322
Berne (1st)	46711
Bethlehem	47104
Beverly Shores	46301
Bicknell	47512
Bippus	46713
Birdseye	47513
Blanford	47831

Blocher, R. Br. Scottsburg	47170
Bloomfield (1st)	47424
Bloomingdale	47832
Bloomington (1st)	47401
Bluffton (1st)	46714
Boggstown	46110
Boone Grove	46302
Boonville (1st)	47601
Borden	47106
Boston	47324
Boswell	47921
Bourbon	46504
Bowling Green	47833
Bradford	47107
Branchville	47514
Brazil (1st)	47834
Bremen (1st)	46506
Bridgeport, Br. Indianapolis	46231
Bridgeton	47836
Brightwood, Sta.	
Indianapolis	46218
Brimfield	46720
Bringhurst	46913
Bristol	46507
Bristow	47515
Broad Ripple, Sta.	
Indianapolis	46220
Brook	47922
Brooklyn	46111
Brookston	47923
Brookville (1st)	47012
Brownsburg (1st)	46112
Brownstown (1st)	47220
Brownsville	47325
Bruceville	47516
Brunswick, Sta. Gary	46406
Bryant	47326
Buck Creek	47924
Buckskin	47647
Buffalo	47925
Buffaloville	47518
Buffington, Sta. Gary	46406
Bunker Hill	46914
Burket	46508
Burlington	46915
Burnettsville	47926
Burney	47227
Burns City, R. Br. Loogootee	47553
Burr Oak	46509
Burrows	46916
Butler	46721
Butlerville	47223

Cambridge City (1st)	47327
Camby	46113
Camden	46917
Campbellsburg	47108
Canaan	47224
Cannelburg	47519
Cannelton	47520
Carbon	47837
Carlisle	47838
Carlos	47329
Carmel (1st)	46032
Cartersburg	46114
Carthage	46115
Castleton, Br. Indianapolis	
(see appendix)	
Cates	47927
Cayuga	47928
Cedar Grove	47016
Cedar Lake (1st)	46303
Celestine	47521
Center	46918
Centerpoint	47840
Centerton, R. Br.	
Martinsville	46116
Centerville	47330
Central	47110
Chalmers	47929
Chandler	47610
Charlestown (1st)	47111
Charlottesville	46117
Chesterfield, Br. Anderson	46017
Chesterton (1st)	46304
Chicago Avenue, Sta. East	
Chicago	46312
Chili, R. Br Denver	46926
Chrisney	47611
Churubusco (1st)	46723
Cicero	46034
Clarks Hill	47930
Clarksburg	47225
Clarksville, Br. Jeffersonville	47130
Clay City	47841
Claypool	46510
Clayton	46118
Clear Creek	47426
Clermont	46119
Clifford	47226
Clinton (1st)	47842
Cloverdale	46120
Coal City	47427
Coalmont	47845
Coatesville	46121

193

Coesse, R. Br. Columbia
  City..............................46724
Colburn...............................47931
Colfax................................46035
Collegeville, Br. Rensselaer ...47978
Columbia City (1st)............46725
  Coesse, R. Br. 46724
Columbus (1st)...................47201
Commiskey..........................47227
Connersville (1st)................47331
Converse.............................46919
Cortland.............................47228
Corunna.............................46730
Cory..................................47846
Corydon (1st).....................47112
Covington...........................47932
Craigville...........................46731
Crandall.............................47114
Crane.................................47522
Crawfordsville (1st)..............47933
Cromwell............................46732
Cross Plains........................47017
Crothersville........................47229
Crown Point (1st).................46307
Culver (1st).........................46511
Culver Military Academy, Br.
  Culver.............................46511
Cumberland, Br.
  Indianapolis.....................46229
Cutler................................46920
Cynthiana...........................47612
Dale..................................47523
Daleville.............................47334
Dana.................................47847
Danville (1st)......................46122
Darlington..........................47940
Dayton..............................47941
Decatur (1st)......................46733
Decker...............................47524
Deedsville..........................46921
Delong...............................46922
Delphi (1st).........................46923
Demotte.............................46310
Denham.............................46925
Denver...............................46926
Depauw.............................47115
Deputy..............................47230
Derby................................47525
Desoto, R. Br. Muncie...........47302
Dillsboro............................47018
Diplomat Plaza, Sta. Fort
  Wayne (see appendix)
Donaldson...........................46513
Downtown, Sta. Muncie........47305
Dublin...............................47335
Dubois...............................47527
Dugger..............................47848
Dunkirk (1st).......................47336
Dunreith............................47337
Dupont..............................47231
Dyer.................................46311
Earl Park............................47942
  Raub, R. Br. 47976
Earlham, Sta. Richmond.........47374
East Cedar Lake, R. Br.
  Cedar Lake......................46303
East Chicago (1st)................46312
East Enterprise.....................47019
East Gary, Br. Gary..............46405
Eaton................................47338
Eckerty..............................47116
Economy............................47339
Edinburg (1st)......................46124

Edwardsport........................47528
Elberfeld.............................47613
Elizabeth............................47117
Elizabethtown......................47232
Elkhart (1st)........................46514
Ellettsville..........................47429
Elnora...............................47529
Elwood (1st)........................46036
Eminence............................46125
Emison..............................47530
English...............................47118
English Lake, R. Br. North
  Judson............................46366
Etna Green.........................46524
Evanston............................47531
EVANSVILLE (1st) (see
  appendix)
Fair Oaks............................47943
Fairbanks............................47849
Fairfield, Sta. Fort Wayne......46807
Fairland.............................46126
Fairmount...........................46928
Falmouth............................46127
Farmersburg........................47850
Farmland............................47340
Ferdinand...........................47532
Fillmore.............................46128
Finly.................................46129
Fishers..............................46038
Flat Rock...........................47234
Flora.................................46929
Florence.............................47020
Floyds Knobs.......................47119
Folsomville..........................47614
Fontanet.............................47851
Foraker, R. Br. Goshen..........46525
Forest...............................46039
Fort Benjamin Harrison, Br.
  Indianapolis.....................46216
Fort Branch.........................47648
Fort Ritner..........................47430
FORT WAYNE (1st) (see
  appendix)
Fortville.............................46040
Fountain City.......................47341
Fountaintown.......................46130
Fowler (1st).........................47944
  Templeton, R. Br. 47986
Fowlerton............................46930
Francesville.........................47946
Francisco............................47649
Frankfort (1st)......................46041
  Scircleville, R. Br. 46066
Franklin (1st).......................46131
Frankton.............................46044
Fredericksburg......................47120
Freedom.............................47431
Freelandville........................47535
Freetown............................47235
Fremont..............................46737
French Lick.........................47432
Friends, Sta. Richmond..........47374
Friendship...........................47021
Fulda................................47536
Fulton...............................46931
Galveston............................46932
Garfield, Sta. Indianapolis......46203
Garrett (1st)........................46738
GARY (1st) (see appendix)
Gas City (1st)......................46933
Gaston..............................47342
Geneva...............................46740
Gentryville..........................47537

Georgetown.........................47122
Glen Park, Sta. Gary (see
  appendix)
Glendale, Sta. Indianapolis....46220
Glenwood............................46133
Goldsmith...........................46045
Goodland............................47948
Goshen (1st)........................46526
  Foraker, R. Br. 46525
  West Side, Br. 46526
Gosport..............................47433
Grabill...............................46741
Grammer.............................47236
Grandview...........................47615
Granger..............................46530
Grantsburg..........................47123
Grass Creek, R. Br.
  Kewanna..........................46935
Graysville............................47852
Greencastle (1st)..................46135
Greenfield (1st)....................46140
Greens Fork........................47345
Greensboro..........................47344
Greensburg (1st)..................47240
Greentown...........................46936
Greenville...........................47124
Greenwood (1st)...................46142
Griffin...............................47616
Griffith (1st)........................46319
Grissom A F B, Br. Peru........46970
Grovertown..........................46531
Guilford.............................47022
Gwynneville.........................46144
Hagerstown (1st)..................47346
Hall, R. Br. Monrovia............46145
Hamilton............................46742
Hamlet...............................46532
HAMMOND (1st) (see
  appendix)
Hanna...............................46340
Hanover.............................47243
Harbor, Sta. East Chicago.....46312
Hardinsburg.........................47125
Harlan...............................46743
Harmony.............................47853
Harrodsburg........................47434
Hartford City (1st)................47348
Hartsville............................47244
Hatfield.............................47617
Haubstadt...........................47639
Hayden..............................47245
Haysville, R. Br. Jasper.........47546
Hazelton.............................47640
Hazelwood, Sta. Fort Wayne..46805
Hebron..............................46341
Helmer..............................4674
Helmsburg..........................47854
Heltonville..........................47436
Hemlock.............................46937
Henryville...........................47126
Hessville, Sta. Hammond.......46323
Highland, Br. Hammond........46322
Hillsburg............................46046
Hillsboro............................47949
Hillsdale.............................47854
Hoagland............................46745
Hobart (1st)........................46342
Hobbs...............................46047
Holland..............................47541
Holton...............................47023
Homer...............................46146
Honey Creek........................47350
Hope.................................47246

Howe	46746
Howell, Sta. Evansville	47712
Hudson	46747
Hudson Lake, R. Br. New Carlisle	46552
Huntertown	46748
Huntingburg (1st)	47542
Huntington (1st)	46750
Huron	47437
Hymera	47855
Idaho, Sta. Terre Haute	47802
Idaville (1st)	47950
Illinois Street, Sta. Indianapolis	46225
Independence Hill, Br. Crown Point	46307
Indian Springs	47544
INDIANAPOLIS (1st) (see appendix)	
Ingalls	46048
Inglefield	47618
Inwood, R. Br. Plymouth	46533
Ireland	47545
Irvington, Sta. Indianapolis	46219
Jamestown	46147
Jasonville	47438
Jasper (1st)	47546
Jeffersonville (1st)	47130
Jonesboro	46938
Jonesville	47247
Judson	47856
Kempton	46049
Kendallville (1st)	46755
Kennard	47351
Kentland	47951
Kewanna	46939
Grass Creek, R. Br.	46935
Keystone	46759
Kimmell	46760
Kingman	47952
Kingsbury	46345
Kingsford Heights	46346
Kirklin	46050
Knightstown (1st)	46148
Knightsville	47857
Knox (1st)	46534
Kokomo (1st)	46901
Koleen	47439
Kouts	46347
Kramer	47953
Kurtz	47249
Kyana	47549
La Crosse	46348
La Fontaine	46940
La Porte (1st)	46350
Otis R. Br.	46367
Parcel Post Annex, Sta.	46350
Stillwell, R. Br.	46351
Laconia	47135
Ladoga	47954
LAFAYETTE (1st) (see appendix)	
Lagrange (1st)	46761
Lagro	46941
Lake Cicott	46942
Lake Village	46349
Laketon	46943
Lakeville	46536
Lamar	47550
Landess	46944
Lanesville	47136
Laotto	46763
Lapaz	46537

Larwill	46764
Laurel	47024
Lawndale, Sta. Evansville	47715
Lawrence, Br. Indianapolis	46226
Lawrenceburg (1st)	47025
Leavenworth	47137
Lebanon (1st)	46052
Leesburg	46538
Leipsic	47440
Leiters Ford	46945
Leo	46765
Leopold	47551
Leroy	46355
Lewis	47858
Lewisville	47352
Lexington	47138
Liberty	47353
Liberty Center	46766
Liberty Mills	46946
Ligonier (1st)	46767
Lincoln City	47552
Linden	47955
Linn Grove	46769
Linton (1st)	47441
Linwood, Sta. Indianapolis	46201
Little York	47139
Lizton	46149
Logansport (1st)	46947
Loogootee (1st)	47553
Losantville	47354
Lowell (1st)	46356
Lucerne	46950
Lynn	47355
Lynnville	47619
Lyons	47443
Mackey	47654
Macy	46951
Madison (1st)	47250
Magnet	47555
Manilla	46150
Mapleton, Sta. Indianapolis	46208
Maplewood Plaza, Br. Fort Wayne	46805
Marengo	47140
Mariah Hill	47556
Marion (1st)	46952
Markle	46770
Markleville	46056
Marshall	47859
Marshfield	47956
Martinsville (1st)	46151
Centerton, R. Br.	46116
Marysville	47141
Matthews	46957
Mauckport	47142
Maxwell	46154
Mays	46155
Mc Cordsville	46055
Meadows, Sta. Terre Haute	47803
Mecca	47860
Medaryville	47957
Medora	47260
Mellott	47958
Memphis	47143
Mentone	46539
Merom	47861
Merrillville, Br. Gary	46410
Metamora	47030
Methodist Memorial Home, R. Br. Warren	46792
Mexico	46958
Miami	46959
Michigan City (1st)	46360

Michigantown	46057
Middlebury (1st)	46540
Middletown	47356
Midland	47445
Milan	47031
Milford	46542
Mill Creek	46365
Miller, Sta. Gary	46403
Millersburg	46543
Millhousen	47261
Milltown	47145
Milroy	46156
Milton	47357
Mishawaka (1st)	46544
Mitchell (1st)	47446
Modoc	47358
Mongo	46771
Monon	47959
Monroe	46772
Monroe City	47557
Monroeville	46773
Monrovia	46157
Hall, R. Br.	46145
Monterey	46960
Montezuma	47862
Montgomery	47558
Monticello (1st)	47960
Montmorenci	47962
Montpelier	47359
Mooreland	47360
Moores Hill	47032
Mooresville (1st)	46158
Morgantown	46160
Morocco	47963
Morris	47033
Morristown	46161
Mount Ayr	47964
Mount Pleasant	47559
Mount Saint Francis	47146
Mount Summit	47361
Mount Vernon (1st)	47620
Mulberry	46058
MUNCIE (1st) (see appendix)	
Munster, Br. Hammond	46321
Nabb	47147
Napoleon	47034
Nappanee (1st)	46550
Nashville	47448
Nebraska	47262
Needham	46162
New Albany (1st)	47150
New Augusta, Br. Indianapolis (see appendix)	
New Carlisle	46552
New Castle (1st)	47362
New Goshen	47863
New Harmony	47631
New Haven (1st)	46774
New Lebanon, R. Br. Sullivan	47864
New Lisbon	47366
New Market	47965
New Middletown	47160
New Palestine	46163
New Paris	46553
New Point	47263
New Richmond	47967
New Ross	47968
New Salisbury	47161
New Trenton	47035
New Washington	47162

New Waverly....................46961
New Whiteland, Br.
   Whiteland...................46184
Newberry........................47449
Newburgh........................47630
Newport..........................47966
Newton Stewart...............47450
Newtonville......................47632
Newtown..........................47969
Nineveh...........................46164
Noblesville (1st)...............46060
Nora, Br. Indianapolis (see
   appendix)
Norman............................47264
North Judson....................46366
North Liberty....................46554
North Madison, Sta.
   Madison.......................47250
North Manchester (1st)......46962
North Park, Sta. Evansville..47710
North Salem.....................46165
North Terre Haute, Br. Terre
   Haute.........................47805
North Vernon (1st).............47265
North Webster...................46555
Notre Dame (1st)...............46556
Oakford...........................46965
Oakland City....................47660
Oaklandon, Br. Indianapolis..46236
Oaktown..........................47561
Oakville..........................47367
Ober...............................46560
Ockley............................46966
Odon...............................47562
Oldenburg........................47036
Olive Street, Sta. South
   Bend...........................46619
Onward............................46967
Oolitic............................47451
Ora................................46968
Orestes...........................46063
Orland.............................46776
Orleans...........................47452
Oscenia..........................46561
Osgood............................47037
Ossian............................46777
   Tocsin, R. Br................46790
Otis, R. Br. La Porte..........46367
Otisco.............................47163
Otterbein.........................47970
Otwell.............................47564
Owensburg........................47453
Owensville........................47665
Oxford.............................47971
Palmyra............................47164
Paoli (1st)........................47454
Paragon............................46166
Parcel Post, Sta. Richmond..47374
Parcel Post Annex, Sta. Fort
   Wayne..........................46802
Parcel Post Annex, Sta.
   Lafayette......................47905
Parcel Post Annex, Sta. La
   Porte...........................46350
Parcel Post Annex, Sta.
   Michigan City................46360
Paris Crossing...................47270
Park Fletcher, Br.
   Indianapolis..................46241
Parker.............................47368
Parkmor, Sta. Elkhart.........46514
Patoka.............................47666

Patricksburg.....................47455
Patriot.............................47038
Paxton.............................47865
Pekin..............................47165
Pence..............................47973
Pendleton (1st)..................46064
Pennville.........................47369
Perrysville........................47974
Pershing...........................47370
Peru (1st).........................46970
Petersburg (1st).................47567
Petroleum.........................46778
Pierceton..........................46562
Pierceville........................47039
Pierre Moran, Sta. Elkhart...46514
Pimento............................47866
Pine Village.......................47975
Pittsboro...........................46167
Plainfield (1st)...................46168
Plainville..........................47568
Pleasant Lake....................46779
Pleasant Mills....................46780
Plymouth (1st)...................46563
   Inwood, R. Br...............46533
Poland.............................47868
Poneto.............................46781
Portage (1st).....................46368
Porter, Br. Chesterton.........46304
Portland (1st)....................47371
Poseyville........................47633
Prairie Creek.....................47869
Prairieton.........................47870
Preble.............................46782
Princeton (1st)...................47670
Putnamville......................46170
Quincy.............................47456
Radnor.............................46981
Ragsdale..........................47573
Rainbow, Sta. Indianapolis...46222
Ramsey............................47166
Raub, R. Br. Earl Park........47976
Ravenswood, Br.
   Indianapolis..................46240
Ray, R. Br. Fremont...........46737
Real Silk Hosiery Mills, Sta.
   Indianapolis..................46202
Redkey............................47373
Reelsville.........................46171
Remington.........................47977
Rensselaer (1st).................47978
Reynolds..........................47980
Richland...........................47634
Richmond (1st)..................47374
Richvalley.........................46973
Ridgeville.........................47380
Riley...............................47871
Rising Sun........................47040
River Park, Sta. South Bend
   (see appendix)
Roachdale........................46172
Roann.............................46974
Roanoke...........................46783
Roby, Sta. Hammond..........46326
Rochester (1st)..................46975
Rockfield..........................46977
Rockport..........................47635
Rockville (1st)...................47872
Rolling Prairie...................46371
Rome..............................47574
Rome City.........................46784
Romney............................47981
Rosedale..........................47874
Roselawn.........................46372

Rossville..........................46065
Royal Center.....................46978
Rushville (1st)...................46173
Russellville.......................46175
Russiaville........................46979
Saint Anthony....................47575
Saint Bernice.....................47875
Saint Croix........................47576
Saint Joe.........................46785
Saint John........................46373
Saint Louis Crossing...........47271
Saint Mary-of-the-Woods.....47876
Saint Marys, Br. Notre
   Dame...........................46556
Saint Meinrad (1st).............47577
Saint Paul........................47272
Salamonia.........................47381
Salem (1st)........................47167
San Pierre........................46374
Sandborn.........................47578
Sandford...........................47877
Santa Claus (1st)...............47579
Saratoga...........................47382
Schererville.......................46375
Schneider.........................46376
Schnellville.......................47580
Scipio..............................47273
Scircleville, R. Br. Frankfort..46066
Scotland...........................47457
Scottsburg (1st)..................47170
   Blocher, R. Br...............47170
   Underwood, R. Br...........47177
Sedalia............................46067
Seelyville..........................47878
Sellersburg (1st)................47172
Selma..............................47383
Servia.............................46980
Seventeenth Avenue, Sta.
   Gary...........................46407
Seymour (1st)....................47274
Sharpsville........................46068
Shelburn..........................47879
Shelby.............................46377
Shelbyville (1st).................46176
Shepardsville.....................47880
Sheridan..........................46069
Shipshewana.....................46555
Shirley............................47384
Shoals.............................47581
Siberia............................47582
Sidney.............................46566
Silver Lake........................46982
Sims...............................46983
Smithville.........................47458
Soldiers Home, Br. Lafayette..47901
Solsberry..........................47459
Somerset..........................46984
Somerville.........................47683
SOUTH BEND (1st) (see
   appendix)
South Calumet Avenue, Sta.
   Hammond....................46324
South Kokomo, Sta. Kokomo..46901
South Marion, Sta. Marien...46952
South Milford.....................46786
South Whitley (1st).............46787
Southport, Br. Indianapolis
   (see appendix)
Speed, R. Br. Sellersburg....47172
Speedway, Br. Indianapolis
   (see appendix)
Spencer (1st).....................47460
Spencerville......................46788

Spiceland	47385
Springport	47386
Springville	47462
Spurgeon	47584
Stanford	47463
Star City	46985
State Line	47982
State Office Building, Sta. Indianapolis	46204
Staunton	47881
Stendal	47585
Stewartsville	47636
Stilesville	46180
Stilwell, R. Br. La Porte	46351
Stinesville	47464
Stockwell	47983
Straughn	47387
Stroh	46789
Sullivan (1st)	47882
New Lebanon, R. Br.	47864
Sulphur	47174
Sulphur Springs	47388
Sumava Resorts	46379
Summitville	46070
Sunman	47041
Swayzee	46986
Sweetser	46987
Switz City	47465
Syracuse (1st)	46567
Talbot	47984
Tangier	47985
Taswell	47175
Taylorsville	47280
Tefft	46380
Tell City (1st)	47586
Templeton, R. Br. Fowler	47986
Tennyson	47637
TERRE HAUTE (1st) (see appendix)	
Thayer	46381
Thorntown	46071
Times Corner, Br. Fort Wayne	46804
Tippecanoe	46570
Tipton (1st)	46072
Tobinsport	47587
Tocsin, R. Br. Ossian	46790
Tolleston, Sta. Gary	46404
Topeka	46571

Trafalgar	46181
Troy	47588
Tunnelton	47467
Twelve Mile	46988
Twelve Points, Sta. Terre Haute	47804
Tyner	46572
Underwood, R. Br. Scottsburg	47177
Union City (1st)	47390
Union Mills	46382
Uniondale	46791
Uniontown	47589
Unionville	47468
Universal	47884
Upland	46989
Uptown, Sta. Indianapolis	46205
Urbana	46990
Vallonia	47281
Valparaiso (1st)	46383
Van Buren	46991
Veedersburg	47987
Velpen	47590
Vernon	47282
Versailles	47042
Vevay	47043
Vincennes (1st)	47591
Wabash (1st)	46992
Wadesville	47638
Wakarusa	46573
Waldron	46182
Walkerton	46574
Wallace	47988
Walton	46994
Wanamaker, Br. Indianapolis	46239
Wanatah	46390
Warren	46792
Warsaw (1st)	46580
Washington (1st)	47501
Waterloo	46793
Waveland	47989
Wawaka	46794
Waynedale, Sta. Fort Wayne (see appendix)	
Waynetown	47990
Webster	47392
Weisburg	47044

West Baden Springs	47469
West Fork	47178
West Indianapolis, Sta. Indianapolis	46221
West Lafayette, Br. Lafayette	47906
West Lebanon	47991
West Middleton	46995
West Newton	46183
West Side, Br. Goshen	46526
West Terre Haute	47885
Westfield	46074
Westphalia	47596
Westpoint	47992
Westport	47283
Westville	46391
Wheatfield	46392
Wheatland	47597
Wheeler	46393
White Swan, Br. Fort Wayne (see appendix)	
Whiteland	46184
Whitestown	46075
Whiting (1st)	46394
Wilkinson	46186
Williams	47470
Williamsburg	47393
Williamsport	47993
Willow Branch	46187
Winamac (1st)	46996
Winchester (1st)	47394
Windfall	46076
Wingate	47994
Winona Lake (1st)	46590
Winslow	47598
Wolcott	47995
Wolcottville	46795
Wolflake	46796
Woodburn	46797
Worthington	47471
Wyatt	46595
Yeoman	47997
Yoder	46798
Yorktown	47396
Young America	46998
Youngs Creek	47472
Zanesville	46799
Zionsville (1st)	46077

ANDERSON 460

POST OFFICE BOXES

Box Nos.

1-209	Chesterfield Br	17
1-1200	B Sta	15
1691-1968	A Sta	14
2000-2727	Main Office	11

RURAL ROUTES

1,2,3,4,5,6,7,8,9	11

STATIONS, BRANCHES AND UNITS

Chesterfield Br	17
General Delivery	11
Postmaster	11

APARTMENTS, HOTELS, MOTELS

Abbott Apts, 1003 - 11 East 8th	12
Anderson College Apts, 1700 East 1st	12
Anderson Motor Inn, 912 Meridian	16
Beverly Terrace Apts, 1102 Central Ave	16
Bi-Nine Motel, 3114 St Rd 9 N	12
Boulevard Apts, 802 Harter Blvd	11
Brock Apts, 23 West 11th	16
Country Charm Motel, 5015 St Rd 9 N	12
Delaware Court Apts, 128 West 10th	16
Eberhart Apts, 1412 Meridian	16
Edgewood Plaza, 2725 West 16th & 1710 Brentwood Dr	11
Empire Apts, 2800 Crystal	12
Franklin Apts, 3606 - 24 Scatterfield Rd	13
Gaslight Apts, 814 - 910 West 53rd	13
Giant Oaks Apts, 1300 - 32 West 8th	11
Hilltop Apts, 4511 Columbus Ave	14
Holiday Inn Motel, 5920 Scatterfield Rd	13
Hoosier Motor Court, R 03	11
Johnsons Motel, 3711 St Rd 9 N	12
Kings Inn, 583 Broadway	12
Kingston Greene Apts, 2505 East 10th	12
Lincolnshire Apts, 330 West 12th	16
Madison Ridge Apts, 1627-31 Madison Ave N	12
Mainview Apts, 2459 Main	14
Mar Jon Motel, 1327 East 53rd	13
Mark Motor Inn, 2400 St Rd 109 S	13
New Leigh Apts, 1324 - 26 West 11th	11

Pine Tree Village, 2801 West 28th	11
Pricewood Ct, Pricewood Ct	14
Tower Apts, 1109 Jackson	16
Town Motel, 1002 Main	16
Travelers Rest, R 08	11
Vickers Apts, 2012 East 7th & 1808 East 8th	12

BUILDINGS

Anderson Bank, 931 Meridian	16
Anderson Federal Savings, 100 West 11th	16
Citizens Bank, 1106 Meridian	16
City Hall, 708 Main	11
Delco Administration, 2401 Columbus Ave	11
First Savings And Loan, 10th And Jackson	16
Guide Lamp Administration, 2915 Pendleton Ave	11
Madison Co Court House, 8th And Meridian	16
Medical Arts, 1931 Brown	14
Professional Office, 1415 Raible Ave	11
Warner Press Administration, 1200 East 5th	11

HOSPITALS

Anderson Emergency	11
Community	12
Saint Johns	11

UNIVERSITIES AND COLLEGES

Anderson	11
Indiana Business	11

EVANSVILLE 477

POST OFFICE BOXES

Box Nos.

1-159	Main Office	01
19-ONLY	Waterworks Dept	46
161-335	Main Office	02
341-515	Main Office	03
358-ONLY	Geo Koch And Sons	44
521-695	Main Office	04
569-ONLY	Sou Ind Gas And Elec Co	41
701-875	Main Office	05
778-ONLY	Citizens Natl Bank	39
881-999	Main Office	06
1000-1199	Station C	13
2001-2999	Station D	14
3001-3119	Main Office	30
3037-ONLY	District Manager Evv Postal District	99
3121-3277	Main Office	31
3281-3397	Main Office	32

3401-3477	Main Office	33
3481-3597	Main Office	34
3601-3735	Main Office	35
3741-3855	Main Office	36
4001-4999	Station A	11
5000-5999	Lawndale Sta	15
6001-6999	Station B	12
7000-7999	Howell Sta	12

RURAL ROUTES

1,2	12
3	11
4	12
5	11
7	12
8	11
13	12

STATIONS, BRANCHES AND UNITS

Howell Sta	12
Lawndale Sta	15
North Park Sta	10
General Delivery	08
Postmaster	08

APARTMENTS, HOTELS, MOTELS

Audubon	13
Beal	13
Becker	08
Bernardin	08
Buckingham	13
Cambridge Arms	13
Claremont	08
Colonial	15
Continental	15
Deakin	13
Donaldson Arms	13
Executive Inn, 600 Walnut	08
Fabian	13
Georgetown	15
Jackson House Motel, 20 Walnut	08
Jamestown	14
Maybelle	13
Mayflower	13
Mc Curdy, 101 SE 1st	08
Plaza	13
Riviera	08
Savannah	15
Shamrock	13
Sonntag, 614 Main	08
Stratford	13
Towne Motel, 15 NW Riverside Dr	08
Washington Court	13
Wedgewood	14
Williamson	15

BUILDINGS

Citizens National Bank, 19 NW 4th St	08
Commercial, 16 SE 2nd	08
Grein, 19 NW 2nd	08
Hulman, 24 NW 4th	08
Indiana Bell Telephone Company, 133 NW 5th	08
Kinkle	08
Lawndale Shopping Center	15

Evansville (Con.)   477

Metropolitan, 9 NW 4th	08
National City Bank, 227	
Main	01
Old National Bank, 416	
Main	08
Southern Securities, 329	
Main	08
Third & Main, 11 NW 3rd	08
Washington Square Mall	15
Werner	12
Wright, 109 SE 3 Rd St	08
312, 312 NW 7th	08
320	08

GOVERNMENT OFFICES

City Hall	08
City Health Dept	08
Civic Center Complex	08
Court, 123 NW 4th St	08
Courts Bldg	08
Federal Bldg	08
Main Post Office, 800	
Sycamore	08

HOSPITALS

Clearview Sanitarium,	
Kratzville Rd	01
Evansville State, Outer	
Lincoln Ave	01
Protestant Deaconness, 600	
Mary	10
Saint Marys, 3700	
Washington Ave	15
Welborn Baptist Memorial,	
412 SE 4th	13

MILITARY INSTALLATIONS

Army Reserve Center	14
United States Naval Armory	12

UNIVERSITIES AND COLLEGES

Bramswell Business 3rd And	
Main Bldg	08
Evansville Univ, 1800 Lincoln	
Ave	01
Ind State Univ Highway 62	
W	12
Lockyears Business, 209 NW	
5th	01

FORT WAYNE   468

POST OFFICE BOXES

Box Nos.		
1-1400	Main Office	01
2600-2799	D Sta	08
5000-5999	Hazlewood Sta	05
6001-6999	Diplomat Plaza	
	Sta	02
7001-7999	Fairfield Sta	07
9000-9999	Waynedale Sta	09

RURAL ROUTES

1,2	25
3	04
4	19
5	18
6	16
7	16
8	09
9	15
13	08

STATIONS, BRANCHES AND UNITS

Fairfield Sta	07
Hazelwood Sta	05
Maplewood Plaza Br	05
Parcel Post Annex Sta	02
Times Corner Br	04
General Delivery	02
Postmaster	02

APARTMENTS, HOTELS, MOTELS

Keenan, 1006 S Harrison	02
Key Largo Motor Inn,	
Highways 30 & 33, W	08
Lincolndale Trailer Court,	
2922 Coliseum Blvd W	08
Rose Marie, 119 W Columbia	02
Sheraton Inn, 330 E	
Washington Blvd	02
Van Orman Northcrest, 505	
Coliseum Blvd E	05

BUILDINGS

Anthony Wayne Bank, 203 E	
Berry	02
Central, 203 W Wayne	02
Commerce Building 127 W	
Berry Street	02
Federal, 1302 S Harrison	02
Ft Wayne National Bank, 110	
W Berry	02
Gettle, 801-03 S Calhoun	02
Indiana Bank, 915 S Clinton	02
Kover, 124 W Wayne	02
Library, 900 Webster	02
Lincoln Tower, 114 E Berry	02
National Management, 104 W	
Main	02
Peoples Trust, 913 S	
Calhoun	02
School Administration, 1230	
S Clinton	02
Standard, 217 E Berry	02
Strauss, 809 S Calhoun	02
Utility, 116 E Wayne	02

GOVERNMENT OFFICES

City-County Bldg, One Main	02
Courthouse, Allen County	02

HOSPITALS

Irene Byron Sanitorium,	
12515 Lima Rd	08
Lutheran Hospital, 3024	
Fairfield Ave	07
Parkview Hospital, 2200	
Randalia Dr	05

Saint Joseph Hospital, 700	
Broadway	02
State School, 801 E State	05
United States Veterans, 1600	
Randalia Dr	05

UNIVERSITIES AND COLLEGES

Concordia College, 6600 N	
Clinton	25
Fort Wayne Bible College,	
800 W Rudisill Blvd	07
Indiana Institute Of	
Technology, 1600 E	
Washington	03
Indiana Univ & Purdue Univ,	
2101 Coliseum Blvd E	05
Saint Francis College, 2701	
Spring	08

GARY   464

POST OFFICE BOXES

Box Nos.		
1-899	Gary	01
1100-1699	17th Avenue	
	Sta	07
1700-2199	Glen Park West	
	Sta	08
2400-2699	Miller Sta	03
4000-4999	Tolleston Sta	04
5000-5999	East Gary Br	05
6000-6999	Brunswick Sta	06
7000-8170	Merrillville	10
9000-9267	Gary	01

STATIONS, BRANCHES AND UNITS

Brunswick Sta	06
Buffington Sta	06
Diplomat Plaza Sta	06
East Gary Br	05
Glen Park Sta	08
Merrillville Br	10
Miller Sta	03
Seventeenth Avenue Sta	07
Tolleston Sta	04
Waynedale Sta	09
White Swan Br	08
General Delivery	01
Postmaster	01

APARTMENTS, HOTELS, MOTELS

Ambassador Apartment	
Building, 574 Monroe	02
Beverly Furnished	
Apartments, 411 W 8th	
Ave	02
Boulevard, 764 Washington	02
City, 127 W 4th Ave	02
Courtview, 428 Washington	02
Dalton Apartments, 131 E	
5th Ave	02
Dobbies, 1838 Virginia	07
Dolly Madison, 529 Madison	02
Gary Travel Lodge, 6230	
Melton Rd	03
Gary, 578 Broadway	02
Gateway Apartments, 406	
Washington	02

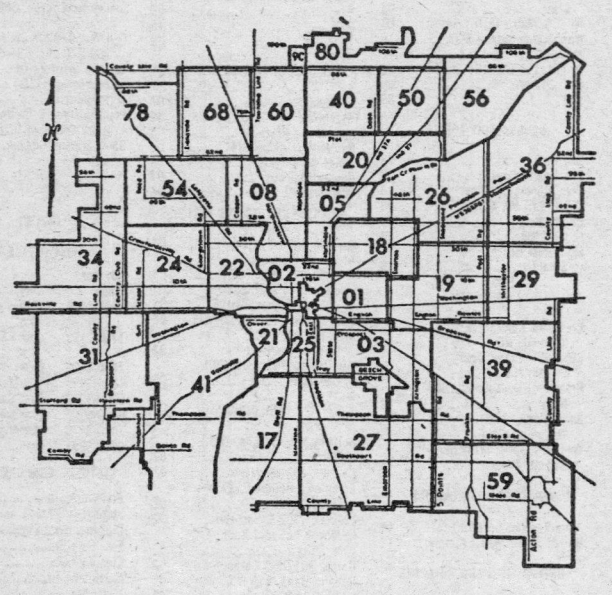

ZIP CODES
INDIANAPOLIS, Ind.
462 + two digits shown = zip code

Gary (Con.) 464

Gotham, 1235 Madison...... 07
Holiday Inn Of America, 3030
　E 8th Ave...................... 02
Holiday Inn Of America, 465
　Broadway...................... 02
Holiday Inn Of America, 800
　E 81st Ave.................... 10
Knight Of Columbus Club,
　331 W 5th Ave................ 02
Lake, 734 Washington........ 02
Madison Square Apartments,
　325 W 6th Ave................ 02
Ramada Inn, 2075 Ripley.... 05
Roosevelt, 105 E 5th Ave.... 02
Seville Court Apartments,
　1720 W 5th Ave.............. 04
Sheraton Diplomat, U S 20
　Clay St....................... 03
Toledo, 2195 Adams.......... 02
Victory Arms Apartments,
　413 Connecticut............. 02
Westbrook Apartments, 2301
　Waverly Dr................... 04

BUILDINGS

Federal, 610 Connecticut St.... 02
Gary National Bank, 504
　Broadway...................... 02
Gibralter, 1649 Broadway...... 07
Hall, 607 Broadway............ 02
Herschbach, 1085 Broadway... 02
Lake County Superior Court,
　400 Broadway................. 02
Lee, 673 Broadway............. 02
Marshall House, 31 E 5th
　Ave........................... 02
Medical Center, 2717
　Wabash....................... 04
Model, 738 Broadway.......... 02
Veterans Administration, 610
　Connecticut St............... 02

GOVERNMENT OFFICES

City Hall, 401 Broadway...... 02
County Building, 400
　Broadway...................... 02

HOSPITALS

Methodist Hospital, 1600 W
　6th Ave...................... 02
Saint Mary Mercy Hospital,
　540 Tyler.................... 02

UNIVERSITIES AND COLLEGES

Indiana University, Gary
　Center, 3400 Broadway...... 08

HAMMOND 463

POST OFFICE BOXES

Box Nos.
1-1200　　　Hammond.......... 25
1000-1999　Highland Br...... 22
2000-2999　Hessville Sta.... 23
3000-3999　Munster Br....... 21

4000-4999　South Calumet
　　　　　　Avenue Sta..... 24

STATIONS, BRANCHES AND UNITS

Hessville Sta.................... 23
Highland Br...................... 22
Munster Br....................... 21
Roby Sta......................... 26
South Calumet Avenue Sta....... 24
General Delivery................. 20
Postmaster....................... 20

INDIANAPOLIS 462

POST OFFICE BOXES

Box Nos.
1-2000　　　　　Indianapolis..... 06
11000-11999　Linwood Sta.... 01
16000-16999　Fort Benjamin
　　　　　　　Harrison Br... 16
18000-18999　Brightwood
　　　　　　　Sta.......... 18
19000-19999　Eastgate Sta... 19
20000-20999　Broad Ripple
　　　　　　　Sta.......... 20
21000-21999　West
　　　　　　　Indianapolis
　　　　　　　Sta.......... 21
22000-22999　Rainbow Sta.... 22
24000-24999　Speedway Br.... 24
26000-26999　Lawrence Br.... 26
27000-27999　Southport Br... 27
29000-29999　Cumberland
　　　　　　　Br........... 29
31000-31999　Bridgeport Br.. 31
33000-33999　Garfield Sta... 03
36000-36999　Oaklandon Br... 36
39000-39999　Wanamaker Br... 39
40000-40999　Nora Br........ 40
41000-41499　Park Fletcher
　　　　　　　Br........... 41
41501-41599　Amf Sta....... 41
44001-44999　Federal Sta.... 04
50000-50999　Castleton Sta.. 50
55000-55999　Uptown Sta..... 05
59000-59999　Acton Sta...... 59
68000-68999　New Augusta
　　　　　　　Br........... 68
88000-88999　Mapleton Sta... 08

RURAL ROUTES

1.............................. 27
2.............................. 31
3.............................. 41
4.............................. 27
5.............................. 59
7.............................. 41
8.............................. 31
9,10........................... 39
11............................. 29
12,13.......................... 36
15............................. 59
16............................. 68
17,18.......................... 24

STATIONS, BRANCHES AND UNITS

Acton Br......................... 59
Air Mail Field Sta.............. 41
Bridgeport Br................... 31

Brightwood Sta.................. 18
Broad Ripple Sta................ 20
Castleton Br.................... 50
Cumberland Br................... 29
Fort Benjamin Harrison Br...... 16
Garfield Sta.................... 03
Glendale Sta.................... 20
Illinois Street Sta............ 25
Irvington Sta................... 19
Lawrence Br..................... 26
Linwood Sta..................... 01
Mapleton Br..................... 08
New Augusta Br.................. 68
Nora Br......................... 40
Oaklandon Br.................... 36
Park Fletcher Br................ 41
Rainbow Sta..................... 22
Ravenswood Br................... 40
Real Silk Hosiery Mills Sta.... 02
•Southport Br................... 17
Speedway Br..................... 24
State Office Building Sta....... 24
Uptown Sta...................... 05
Wanamaker Br.................... 39
West Indianapolis Sta........... 21
General Delivery................ 04
Postmaster...................... 06

BUILDINGS

Architects & Builders, 333 N
　Pennsylvania.................. 04
Bankers Trust, 39 East Ohio.... 04
Big Four, 105 S Meridian....... 25
Board Of Trade, 143 N
　Meridian..................... 04
Century, 36 S Pennsylvania..... 04
Chamber Of Commerce, 320
　N Meridian................... 04
Circle Tower, 5 E Market....... 04
City-County, 200 E
　Washington................... 04
Coliseum, State Fairgrounds.... 05
Consolidated, 115 N
　Pennsylvania.................. 04
Doctors Bldg, 224 N
　Meridian..................... 04
Electric, 17 N Meridian........ 04
Empire Life, 2801 N
　Meridian..................... 08
Employment Security Division
　State Of Indian, 10 N
　Senate....................... 04
English Foundation, 615 N
　Alabama...................... 04
Farm Bureau Co-Op, 47 S
　Pennsylvania.................. 04
Farm Bureau Insurance, 130
　E Washington................. 04
Federal, Meridian & Ohio....... 04
Fidelity, 111 Monument Cir..... 04
First Federal, 11 N
　Pennsylvania.................. 04
Goodman, 40 W Washington....... 04
Guaranty, 20 N Meridian........ 04
Hornblower, 129 East Market.... 04
Hume Mansur, 23 E Ohio......... 04
I S T A Center, 150 W
　Market....................... 04
Illinois, 17 W Market.......... 04
Indiana Lumbermans Mutual,
　429 N Pennsylvania........... 04
Indiana, 120 E Market.......... 04

Indianapolis (Con.)   462

Inland, 156 E Market............ 04
Jackson, 546 S Meridian....... 25
Jefferson National, 241 N
  Pennsylvania.................. 04
Kresge, 41 E Washington..... 04
Larosa, 107 N Pennsylvania... 04
Manufacturers, State
  Fairgrounds................... 05
Merchants Bank, 11 S
  Meridian...................... 04
Morris Plan, 108 E
  Washington................... 04
Ober, 38 N Pennsylvania 04
Peoples Bank, 134 E Market .. 04
Roosevelt, 9 N Illinois......... 04
Star & News, 307 N Penn...... 06
State House, 200 W
  Washington................... 04
State Office, 100 N Senate
  Ave.......................... 04
Test, 54 Monument Cir......... 04
Underwriters, 445 N
  Pennsylvania.................. 04
Union Title, 155 E Market...... 04
120 W Market.................. 04

GOVERNMENT OFFICES

Army Finance Center............ 49

HOSPITALS

Childrens, 1040 W Michigan .. 02
Community, 1500 N Ritter
  Ave.......................... 19
Indiana University, 1100 W
  Michigan...................... 02
Larue D Carter, 1315 W
  10th.......................... 02
Marion County General, 960
  Locke......................... 02
Medical Center, 1100 W
  Michigan...................... 02
Methodist Hospital Of Ind,
  1640 N Capitol Ave........... 02
Riley, 1040 W Michigan........ 02
Robert W Long, 1100 W
  Michigan...................... 02
Saint Vincents, 120 W Fall
  Creek Pkwy.................... 08
University Heights, 3350
  Carson Ave.................... 27
Veterans Administration,
  1461 W 10th................... 02
William H Coleman, 1100 W
  Michigan...................... 02
Winona Memorial, 3202 N
  Meridian...................... 08

UNIVERSITIES AND COLLEGES

Butler University, 4600
  Sunset Ave.................... 08
Central Business, 802 N
  Meridan....................... 06
Herron Art Institute, 110 E
  16th.......................... 02
Indiana Business, 802 N
  Meridian...................... 06
Indiana Central, 4001 S
  Otterbein..................... 27

Indiana State School For The
  Blind, 7725 College Ave...... 40
Indiana State School For The
  Deaf, 1200 E 42nd............ 05
Indiana U Grad School Of
  Soccial Science, 122 E
  Michigan...................... 04
Indiana University Extension,
  518 N Delaware................ 04
Indiana University School Of
  Dentistry, 1121 W
  Michigan...................... 02
Indiana University School Of
  Law, 102 W Michigan.......... 04
Indiana University School Of
  Medicine, 1100 W
  Michigan...................... 02
Indiana University School Of
  Nursing, 1232 W
  Michigan...................... 02
Jordan College Of Music
  Branch, 3411 N
  Pennsylvania.................. 05
Jordan College Of Music Of
  Butler Univ, 4600 Sunset
  Ave........................... 08
Ladywood School, 5375
  Millersville Rd............... 26
Lein Business, 601 N
  Delaware...................... 04
Lincoln Chiropractice College
  Incorporat, 3171 N
  Meridian...................... 08
Marian, 3200 Cold Springs
  Rd............................ 22
Normal College Of American
  Gymnastic Unio, 415 E
  Michigan...................... 04
Purdue University Extension,
  1201 E 38th................... 05

LAFAYETTE   479

POST OFFICE BOXES

Box Nos.
1-1538   Lafayette......... 02
2001-2270   West Lafayette
                Br................ 06
3000-3250   Sta 11............ 06

RURAL ROUTES

1,2.............................. 06
3,4,5,6,7,8...................... 05
9,10............................. 06
11,12,13,14,15................... 06
16............................... 05
17............................... 05

STATIONS, BRANCHES AND UNITS

Parcel Post Annex Sta.......... 05
Soldiers Home Br................ 01
West Lafayette Br.............. 06
General Delivery............... 02
Postmaster..................... 01

UNIVERSITIES AND COLLEGES

Purdue University............... 07

MUNCIE   473

POST OFFICE BOXES

Box Nos.
1-1312   Downtown Sta .. 05
D1-D126   Desoto R. Sta.. 02
2001-2856   Main Office...... 02

RURAL ROUTES

1,2,3,4,5,6,7,8,9................ 02

STATIONS, BRANCHES AND UNITS

Desoto Rural Br................. 02
Downtown Sta................... 05
General Delivery............... 02
Postmaster..................... 02

APARTMENTS, HOTELS, MOTELS

Anthony Apartments Bethel 04
Canopic 215 S Jefferson....... 05
Chateau 2001 N Walnut......... 03
Cohen 110 1/2 W Seymour.... 05
Elliott 620 N Mckinley Ave..... 03
Grays Court 2000 Burlington
  Dr........................... 02
Graystone 900 E Washington.. 05
Greenbrier 720 W Centennial.. 03
Imperial 1200 S Mulberry...... 02
Jackson-Vine 209 S Vine....... 05
Kimberly Court 615 W
  Charles...................... 05
Linden House 510 Riverside... 03
Middjetown Gardens 2301 S
  Manhattan.................... 04
Munsyana Homes 800 S
  Madison...................... 02
Oakwood 326 Oakwood......... 05
Parkview Nursing Home........ 03
Rector 522 W Adams........... 05
Schiedler N Tillotson......... 02
Star 310 S Mulberry........... 05
Thomas 316 N Mulberry........ 05
Westbriar 2904 Brook.......... 04
400 Apartments 408
  Riverside.................... 03

UNIVERSITIES AND COLLEGES

Ball State Univ................. 06

SOUTH BEND   466

POST OFFICE BOXES

Box Nos.
1-1999   Main Office...... 24
2001-2499   River Park Sta.. 15
2501-2999   Station A........ 13
3001-3999   Olive Street
                Sta.............. 19

RURAL ROUTES

1............................... 14
2............................... 19
2............................... 28

South Bend (Con.)　　466

STATIONS, BRANCHES AND UNITS

Olive Street Sta	19
River Park Sta	15
General Delivery	24
Postmaster	24

APARTMENTS, HOTELS, MOTELS

Alou Motel, 52547 U S 31	37
Blackwood, 422 S 25th	15
Blue & Gold Motel, 204 Dixie Way S	37
Broadway, 104 E Broadway	18
Capitol Motel, 236 Dixie Way N	37
City Motel, 1631 Lincoln Way E	13
Drake Motel, 60971 US 31	14
Eddy Colfax, 132 N Eddy	17
Foust Motel, 23040 US 20	28
Garst Arms, 103 W Garst	18
Holiday Inn Motel, 515 Dixie Way N	37
Howard Johnson Motor Lodge, 52939 US 31	37
Ivanhoe, 1112 S 20th	15
Jefferson, 332 W Jefferson Blvd	01
Kenrose Motel, 25725 US 20	28
Kentre Motel, 25190 St Rd 2	19
Lasalle Motor Inn, 237 N Michigan	24
Lincolnwood Motel, 3300 Lincoln Way W	28
Mar Main Arms, 119-125 W Marion	01
Morningside, 413 W Colfax Ave	01
North Shore, 1405-21 North Side Blvd	15
Plaza, 628 W Western Ave	25
Ramada Inn, 52890 U S 31	37
Randalls Inn, 130 Dixie Way Blvd	37
Riverside, 1587-1683 Riverside Dr	16
Rushton, 501 W Washington	01
Shirley Motel, 60855 US 31	14
South Bend Motel, 3420 S Michigan	14
Southern, 124 W Tutt	18
Sunnyside, 1009 E Jefferson Blvd	17
The Villa, 18644 Cleveland Rd	37
Town Tower Motel, 423 N Michigan	01
Travelodge, 614 N Michigan	01
Washington Colfax, 618 W Colfax Ave	01
Westwood Motel, 25200 State Rd 2	19
Y W C A, 802 N Lafayette Blvd	01

BUILDINGS

American National Bank, 211 W Washington	01
Bendix Corporation, 401 N Bendix Dr	20
Building & Loan Tower, 216 W Washington	01
Burke, 115 N William	01
Christman, 211 N Main	01
Commerce, 105 W Wayne	01
First Bank, 205 W Jefferson Blvd	01
Hibberd, 321 S Main	01
I O O F, 104 S Main	01
J M S, 108 N Main	01
Jefferson Medical Arts, 919 E Jefferson Blvd	22
Kirk, 220 S William	25
La Salle West, 120 W La Salle Ave	01
Lafayette, 115 S Lafayette Blvd	01
Lincoln Life, 622 N Michigan	01
National Bank, 110 W Jefferson Blvd	01
Oliver Theatre, 114 N Main	01
Poledor, 102 E Colfax Ave	01
Saint Joseph Bank, 202 S Michigan	01
Sherland, 105 E Jefferson Blvd	01
South Bend Tribune, 223 W Colfax Ave	26
Tower, 216 W Washington	01
Whitcomb & Keller, 224 W Jefferson Blvd	01
Y M C A, 1201 North Side Blvd	15

GOVERNMENT OFFICES

Central Services, 701 W Sample	21
County-City, 227 W Jefferson Blvd	01
Court House 115 S Main	01
Federal, 204 S. Main	24

HOSPITALS

Healthwin, 20531 Darden Rd	37
Memorial, 615 N Michigan	01
Northern Indiana Childrens, 1234 N Notre Dame Ave	22
Saint Josephs, 811 E Madison	22
South Bend Osteopathic, 2515 E Jefferson Blvd	15

UNIVERSITIES AND COLLEGES

Indiana University Center, 1825 North Side Blvd	15

TERRE HAUTE　　478

POST OFFICE BOXES

Box Nos.		
1 1699	Main Office	08
2000-2099	Idaho Sta	02
3000-3099	Meadows Sta	03
4000-4999	Twelve Points Sta	04
5000-5099	North Terre Haute Br	05

RURAL ROUTES

21,22,23,24,25	02
31,32	03
51,52	05

STATIONS, BRANCHES AND UNITS

Idaho Sta	02
Meadows Sta	03
North Terre Haute Br	05
Twelve Points Sta	04
General Delivery	08
Postmaster	08

APARTMENTS, HOTELS, MOTELS

Albert Pick Motel, U S Hwy 41 South	02
Greenbriar Village Apts, 4961 Dixie Bee Rd	02
Heritage Apts, 3600 Poplar	03
Holiday Inn Motel, U S Hwy 41 South	02
Imperial House, Motel, 2150 N 3rd	04
Ritz Plaza Motor Lodge, 6000 Wabash Ave	03

BUILDINGS

Honey Creek Square Shopping Center, U S 41 S	02
K-Mart Plaza, 2500 Wabash Ave	03
Meadows Shopping Center, 2600 Poplar	03
Merchants Bank Bldg, 17 S 7th	07
Sycamore Bldg, 19 S 6th	07

HOSPITALS

Saint Anthony Hospital, 1021 S 6th	07
Union Hospital, 1606 N 7th	04

UNIVERSITIES AND COLLEGES

Indiana State University, 217 N 6th	09
Rose Hulman Institute Of Technology 5500 Wabash Ave	03

IOWA
(Abbreviation: IA)

Ackley 50601
Ackworth 50001
Adair .... <50002
Adel 50003
Afton 50830
Agency 52530
Ainsworth 52201
Akron 51001
Albert City 50510
Albia (1st) 52531
Albion 50005
Alburnett 52202
Alden 50006
Alexander 50420
Algona (1st) 50511
    Irvington, R. Br. 50550
Alleman 50007
Allendorf 51330
Allerton 50008
Allison 50602
Alpha 52130
Alta 51002
Alta Vista 50603
Alton 51003
Altoona 50009
Alvord 51230
Amana (1st) 52203
Amber, R. Br. Anamosa 52204
Ames (1st) 50010
Anamosa (1st) 52205
    Amber, R. Br. 52204
Andover 52701
Andrew 52030
Anita 50020
Ankeny (1st) 50021
Anthon 51004
Aplington 50604
Arcadia 51430
Archer 51231
Aredale 50605
Argyle 52619
Arion 51520
Arispe 50831
Arlington 50606
Armstrong 50514
Arnolds Park 51331
Arthur 51431
Ashton 51232
Aspinwall, R. Br. Manning 51432
Atalissa 52720
Athelstan, R. Br. Blockton 50832
Atkins 52206
Atlantic (1st) 50022
Attica, R. Br. Knoxville 50024
Auburn 51433
Audubon (1st) 50025
Aurelia 51005
Aurora 50607
Austinville 50608
Avoca 51521
Ayrshire 50515
Badger 50516
Bagley 50026
Baldwin 52207
Bancroft 50517
Barnes City 50027
Barnum 50518
Bartlett, R. Br. Thurman 51655
Batavia 52533
Battle Creek 51006

Baxter 50028
Bayard 50029
Beacon 52534
Beaconsfield 50030
Beaman 50609
Beaver 50031
Beaverdale, Sta. Des Moines .. 50310
Bedford 50833
    Conway, R. Br. 50834
Belle Plaine (1st) 52208
Bellevue 52031
Belmond (1st) 50421
Bennett 52721
Benton 50835
Bernard 52032
Berwick 50032
Bettendorf (1st) 52722
Bevington 50033
Big Rock 52725
Birmingham 52535
Blairsburg 50034
Blairstown 52209
Blakesburg 52536
Blanchard 51630
Blencoe 51523
Blockton 50836

Athelstan, R. Br. 50832
Bloomfield (1st) 52537
    Troy, R. Br. 52537
    West Grove, R. Br. 52538
Blue Grass 52726
Bode 50519
Bonaparte 52620
Bondurant 50035
Boone (1st) 50036
Booneville 50038
Boulevard, Sta. Sioux City 51109
Bouton 50039
Boxholm 50040
Boyden 51234
Braddyville 51631
Bradford 50041
Bradgate 50520
Brandon 52210
Brayton 50042
Breda 51436
Bremer 50610
Bridgewater 50837
Brighton 52540
    East Pleasant Plain, R. Br. .. 52541
Bristow 50611
Britt 50423
Bronson 51007
Brooklyn 52211
Brooks, R. Br. Corning 50838
Brunsville 51008
Bryant 52727
Buckeye 50043
Buckingham 50612
Buffalo 52728
Buffalo Center 50424
Burchinal 50425
Burlington (1st) 52601
Burnside 50521
Burr Oak 52131
Burt 50522
Bussey 50044
Calamus 52729
Call Terminal, Sta. Sioux City .. 51101
Caliender 50523

Calmar 52132
Calumet 51009
Camanche 52730
Cambria, R. Br. Corydon 50045
Cambridge 50046
Cantril 52542
Carbon 50839
Carlisle 50047
Carnarvon 51437
Carpenter 50426
Carroll (1st) 51401
Carson 51525
Cascade 52033
Casey 50048
Castalia 52133
Castana 51010
Cedar 52543
Cedar Falls (1st) 50613
Cedar Hills, Sta. Cedar Rapids .. 52405
CEDAR RAPIDS (1st) (see appendix)
Center Junction 52212
Center Point 52213
Centerville (1st) 52544
    Rathbun, R. Br. 52545
Central, Sta. Davenport 52805
Central City 52214
Central College, Sta. Pella 50219
Central Heights, R. Br. Mason City .. 50401
Chapin 50427
Chariton (1st) 50049
Charles City (1st) 50616
    Colwell, R. Br. 50620
Charlotte 52731
Charter Oak 51439
Chatsworth, R. Br. Hawarden ... 51011
Chelsea 52215
Cherokee (1st) 51012
Chester 52134
Chillicothe 52548
Churdan 50050
Cincinnati 52549
Clare 52524
Clarence 52216
Clarinda (1st) 51632
Clarion (1st) 50525
Clarksville 50619
Clear Lake (1st) 50428
Clearfield 50840
Cleghorn 51014
Clemons 50051
Clermont 52135
Climbing Hill, R. Br. Hornick ... 51015
Clinton (1st) 52732
    Lyons, Sta. 52732
    Teeds Grove, R. Br. 52771
Clio 50052
Clive, Br. Des Moines 50053
Clutier 52217
Coggon 52218
    Prairieburg, R. Br. 52219
Coin 51636
Colesburg 52035
Colfax 50054
College Springs 51637
Collins 50055
Colo 50056
Columbia 50057
Columbus City 52737

Columbus Junction	52738	Dorchester	52140	Fonda	50540

Columbus Junction...........52738
Colwell, R. Br. Charles City...50620
Conesville.......................52739
Conrad...........................50621
Conroy...........................52220
Conway, R. Br. Bedford...50834
Coon Rapids (1st)...............50058
Cooper...........................50059
Coralville, Br. Iowa City...52240
Corning (1st)...................50841
  Brooks, R. Br.............50838
Correctionville.................51016
Corwith..........................50430
Corydon.........................50060
  Cambria, R. Br...........50045
Cotter...........................52221
Coulter..........................50431
Council Bluffs (1st).............51501
Craig, R. Br. Le Mars...........51017
Cranston.........................52741
Crawfordsville..................52621
Crescent.........................51526
Cresco (1st).....................52136
Creston (1st)....................50801
Cromwell.........................50842
Crystal Lake.....................50432
Cumberland......................50843
Cumming.........................50061
Curlew...........................52527
Cushing..........................51018
Cylinder.........................50528
Dakota City......................50529
Dallas...........................50062
Dallas Center....................50063
Dana.............................50064
Danbury..........................51019
Danville.........................52623
DAVENPORT (1st) (see
  appendix)
Davis City.......................50065
  Pleasanton, R. Br........50224
Dawson..........................50066
Dayton...........................50530
De Soto..........................50069
De Witt (1st)....................52742
Decatur..........................50067
Decorah (1st)....................52101
Dedham..........................51440
Deep River.......................52222
Defiance.........................51527
Delaware.........................52036
Delhi............................52223
Delmar...........................52037
Deloit...........................51441
Delphos..........................50844
Delta............................52550
Denison (1st)....................51442
Denmark.........................52624
Denver...........................50622
Derby............................50068
DES MOINES (1st) (see
  appendix)
Dewar...........................50623
Dexter...........................50070
Diagonal.........................50845
Dickens..........................51333
Dike.............................50624
Dixon............................52745
Dolliver.........................50531
Donahue.........................52746
Donnan..........................52139
Donnellson.......................52625
Doon.............................51235

Dorchester.......................52140
Douds............................52551
Dougherty........................50433
Dow City.........................51528
Dows.............................50071
Drakesville.......................52552
Dubuque (1st)....................52001
Dumont..........................50625
Duncombe........................50532
Dundee...........................52038
Dunkerton........................50626
Dunlap...........................51529
Durango..........................52039
Durant...........................52747
Dyersville (1st)..................52040
Dysart...........................52224
Eagle Grove (1st)................50533
Earlham..........................50072
Earling...........................51530
Earlville.........................52041
Early............................50535
East Des Moines, Sta. Des
  Moines.......................50309
East Fourteenth Street, Sta.
  Des Moines (see
  appendix)
East Pleasant Plain, R. Br.
  Brighton.....................52541
Eddyville........................52553
Edgewood.......................52042
Elberon..........................52225
Eldon............................52554
Eldora (1st).....................50627
Eldorado, R. Br. West Union...52175
Eldridge.........................52748
Elgin............................52141
Elk Horn.........................51531
Elkader (1st).....................52043
Elkhart..........................50073
Elkport..........................52044
Elliott...........................51532
Elliston..........................50074
Ellsworth.........................50075
Elma.............................50628
Elwood...........................52226
Ely..............................52227
Emerson.........................51533
Emmetsburg (1st)................50536
Epworth..........................52045
Essex............................51638
Estherville (1st).................51334
Evansdale, Br. Waterloo.......50707
Everly............................51338
Exira............................50076
Exline...........................52555
Fairbank.........................50629
Fairfax...........................52228
Fairfield (1st)...................52556
Farley...........................52046
Farlin...........................50077
Farmersburg.....................52047
Farmington.......................52626
Farnhamville.....................50538
Farragut.........................51639
Fayette..........................52142
Fenton...........................50539
Ferguson.........................50078
Fertile..........................50434
Festina..........................52143
First Street, Sta. Cedar
  Rapids.......................52407
Floris...........................52560
Floyd............................50435

Fonda............................50540
  Knoke, R. Br..............50553
Fontanelle.......................50846
Forest City (1st).................50436
Fort Atkinson....................52144
Fort Dodge (1st).................50501
Fort Madison (1st)...............52627
Fostoria.........................51340
Fredericksburg...................50630
Frederika........................50631
Fremont.........................52561
Fruitland........................52749
Galt.............................50101
Galva............................51020
Garber...........................52048
Garden City......................50102
Garden Grove.....................50103
Garnavillo.......................52049
Garner...........................50438
  Hayfield, R. Br...........50445
  Miller, R. Br.............50438
Garrison.........................52229
Garwin..........................50632
Geneva...........................50633
George...........................51237
Gibson...........................50104
Gifford, R. Br. Union............50259
Gilbert...........................50105
Gilbertville......................50634
Gillett Grove.....................51341
Gilman...........................50106
Gilmore City.....................50541
Gladbrook........................50635
Glenwood.........................51534
Glidden..........................51443
Goldfield........................50542
Goodell.........................50439
Gooselake........................52750
Gowrie...........................50543
Graettinger......................51342
Grafton..........................50440
Grand, Sta Des Moines..........50309
Grand Junction...................50107
Grand Mound.....................52751
Grand River......................50108
Grandview.......................52752
Granger..........................50109
Grant............................50847
Granville.........................51022
Gravity..........................50848
Gray.............................50110
Greeley..........................52050
Green Island.....................52051
Green Mountain..................50637
Greene...........................50636
Greenfield........................50849
Greenville, R. Br. Royal.........51343
Grimes...........................50111
Grinnell (1st)....................50112
Griswold.........................51535
Grundy Center (1st).............50638
Gruver...........................51344
Guernsey, R. Br Montezuma....50172
Guthrie Center...................50115
Guttenberg.......................52052
Halbur...........................51444
Hale.............................52230
Hamburg (1st)....................51640
Hamilton.........................50116
Hamlin...........................50117
Hampton (1st)....................50441
Hancock..........................51536
Hanlontown......................50444

Hansell	50640
Harcourt	50544
Hardy	50545
Harlan (1st)	51537
Harper	52231
Harpers Ferry	52146
Harris	51345
Hartford	50118
Hartley	51346
Hartwick	52232
Harvey	50119
Hastings	51540
Havelock	50546
Haverhill	50120
Hawarden	51023
Chatsworth, R. Br.	51011
Hawkeye	52147
Hayesville	52562
Hayfield, R. Br. Garner	50445
Hazleton	50641
Hedrick	52563
Henderson	51541
Herndon, R. Br. Jamaica	50121
Hiawatha	52233
Hickman Road, Br. Des Moines	50322
Highland Center	52564
Highland Park, Sta. Des Moines	50333
Highlandville	52149
Hills	52235
Hillsboro	52630
Hinton	51024
Holland	50642
Holmes	50547
Holstein	51025
Holy Cross	52053
Homestead	52236
Honey Creek	51542
Hopkinton	52237
Hornick	51026
Climbing Hill, R. Br.	51015
Hospers	51238
Houghton	52631
Hubbard	50122
Hudson	50643
Hull	51239
Humboldt (1st)	50548
Humeston	50123
Huxley	50124
Ida Grove (1st)	51445
Imogene	51645
Independence (1st)	50644
Indianola (1st)	50125
Inwood	51240
Ionia	50645
Iowa City (1st)	52240
Iowa Falls (1st)	50126
Iowa State University, Sta. Ames	50010
Ira	50127
Ireton	51027
Irvington, R. Br. Algona	50550
Irwin	51446
Jackson Junction	52150
Jamaica	50128
Herndon, R. Br.	50121
Janesville	50647
Jefferson (1st)	50129
Jesup	50648
Jewell	50130
Johnston	50131
Joice	50446

Jolley	50551
Kalona	52247
Kamrar	50132
Kanawha	50447
Kellerton	50133
Kelley	50134
Kellogg	50135
Kensett	50448
Kent	50850
Keokuk (1st)	52632
Keosauqua	52565
Keota	52248
Kesley	50649
Keswick	50136
Keystone	52249
Killduff	50137
Kimballton	51543
Kingsley	51028
Kinross	52250
Kirkman	51447
Kirkville	52566
Kiron	51448
Klemme	50449
Knierim	50552
Knoke, R. Br. Fonda	50553
Knoxville (1st)	50138
Attica, R. Br.	50024
La Motte	52054
La Porte City	50651
Lacona	50139
Ladora	52251
Lake City	51449
Lake Mills	50450
Lake Park	51347
Lake View	51450
Lakeside, R. Br. Storm Lake	50588
Lakota	50451
Lamoni	50140
Lamont	50650
Lanesboro	51451
Langworthy	52252
Lansing (1st)	52151
Lanyon, R. Br. Harcourt	50544
Larchwood	51241
Larrabee	51029
Latimer	50452
Laurel	50141
Laurens	50554
Lawler	52154
Lawton	51030
Le Claire (1st)	52753
Le Grand	50142
Le Mars (1st)	51031
Craig, R. Br.	51017
Struble, R. Br.	51057
Le Roy, R. Br. Humeston	50123
Ledyard	50556
Leeds, Sta. Sioux City	51108
Lehigh	50557
Leighton	50143
Leland	50453
Lenox	50851
Leon	50144
Lester	51242
Letts	52754
Lewis	51544
Liberty Center	50145
Libertyville	52567
Lidderdale	51452
Lime Springs	52155
Saratoga, R. Br.	52167
Lincoln	50652
Linden	50146

Lineville	50147
Linn Grove	51033
Lisbon	52253
Liscomb	50148
Little Cedar	50454
Little Rock	51243
Little Sioux	51545
Littleport	52055
Livermore	50558
Lockridge	52635
Logan (1st)	51546
Magnolia, R. Br.	51550
Lohrville	51453
Lone Rock	50559
Lone Tree	52755
Long Grove	52756
Lorimor	50149
Lost Nation	52254
Loveland	51547
Lovilia	50150
Low Moor	52757
Lowden	52255
Lu Verne	50560
Luana	52156
Lucas	50151
Luther	50152
Luxemburg	52056
Luzerne	52257
Lynnville	50153
Lyons, Sta. Clinton	52732
Lytton	50561
Macedonia	51549
Macksburg	50155
Madrid (1st)	50156
Magnolia, R. Br. Logan	51550
Malcom	50157
Mallard	50562
Maloy	50852
Malvern	51551
Manchester (1st)	52057
Manilla	51454
Manly	50456
Manning	51455
Aspinwall, R. Br.	51432
Manson	50563
Maple Hill	50564
Mapleton	51034
Maquoketa (1st)	52060
Marathon	50565
Marble Rock	50653
Marcus	51035
Marengo	52301
Marion (1st)	52302
Marne	51552
Marquette	52158
Marshalltown (1st)	50158
Martelle	52305
Martensdale	50160
Martinsburg	52568
Mason City (1st)	50401
Masonville	50654
Massena	50853
Matlock	51244
Maurice	51036
Maxwell	50161
May City, R. Br. Ocheyedan	51349
Maynard	50655
Mc Callsburg	50154
Mc Causland	52758
Mc Clelland	51548
Mc Gregor	52157
Mc Intire	50455
Mechanicsville	52306

Mediapolis	52637	
Melbourne	50162	
Melcher	50163	
Melrose	52569	
Melvin	51350	
Menlo	50164	
Meriden	51037	
Merrill	51038	
Meservey	50457	
Middle	52307	
Middletown	52638	
Miles	52064	
Milford	51351	
Miller, R. Br. Garner	50438	
Millersburg	52308	
Millerton	50165	
Milo	50166	
Milton	52570	
Minburn	50167	
Minden	51553	
Mineola	51554	
Mingo	50168	
Missouri Valley	51555	
Mitchell, R. Br. Osage	50485	
Mitchellville	50169	
Modale	51556	
Mondamin	51557	
Moneta	51352	
Monmouth	52309	
Monona	52159	
Monroe	50170	
Montezuma (1st)	50171	
Guernsey, R. Br.	50172	
Montgomery	51353	
Monticello (1st)	52310	
Montour	50173	
Montpelier	52759	
Montrose	52639	
Moorhead	51558	
Moorland	50566	
Moravia	52571	
Morley	52312	
Morning Sun	52640	
Morningside, Sta. Sioux City		
(see appendix)		
Morrison	50657	
Moscow	52760	
Moulton	52572	
Mount Auburn	52313	
Mount Ayr	50854	
Mount Etna	50855	
Mount Pleasant (1st)	52641	
Rome, R. Br.	52642	
Mount Sterling	52573	
Mount Union	52644	
Mount Vernon (1st)	52314	
Moville	51039	
Murray	50174	
Muscatine (1st)	52761	
Mystic	52574	
Nashua	50658	
Nemaha	50567	
Neola	51559	
Nevada (1st)	50201	
Nevinville	50856	
New Albin	52160	
New Hampton (1st)	50659	
North Washington, R. Br.	50661	
New Hartford	50660	
New Haven, R. Br. Osage	50461	
New Liberty	52765	
New London	52645	
New Market	51646	

New Providence	50206	
New Sharon	50207	
New Vienna	52065	
New Virginia	50210	
Newell	50568	
Newhall	52315	
Newton (1st)	50208	
Nichols	52766	
Nodaway	50857	
Nora Springs	50458	
North Buena Vista	52066	
North English	52316	
North Liberty	52317	
North Side, Sta. Sioux City	51104	
North Washington, R. Br.		
New Hampton	50661	
Northboro	51647	
Northwest, Sta. Davenport		
(see appendix)		
Northwood	50459	
Norwalk	50211	
Norway	52318	
Numa	52575	
Oakdale	52319	
Oakland	51560	
Oakville	52646	
Ocheyedan	51354	
May City, R. Br.	51349	
Odebolt	51458	
Oelwein (1st)	50662	
Ogden	50212	
Okoboji	51355	
Olds	52647	
Olin	52320	
Ollie	52576	
Onawa	51040	
Onslow	52321	
Oran	50664	
Orange City (1st)	51041	
Orchard	50460	
Orient	50858	
Osage (1st)	50461	
Mitchell, R. Br.	50485	
New Haven, R. Br.	50461	
Osceola (1st)	50213	
Oskaloosa (1st)	52577	
Ossian	52161	
Otho	50569	
Otley	50214	
Oto	51044	
Ottosen	50570	
Ottumwa (1st)	52501	
Oxford	52322	
Oxford Junction	52323	
Oyens	51045	
Pacific Junction	51561	
Packwood	52580	
Palmer	50571	
Palo	52324	
Panama	51562	
Panora	50216	
Parkersburg	50665	
Parnell	52325	
Paton	50217	
Patterson	50218	
Paullina	51046	
Pella (1st)	50219	
Peosta	52068	
Percival	51648	
Perry (1st)	50220	
Pershing	50221	
Persia	51563	
Peru	50222	

Peterson	51047	
Pierson	51048	
Pilot Grove	52648	
Pilot Mound	50223	
Pioneer	50572	
Pisgah	51564	
Plainfield	50666	
Plano	52581	
Pleasant Valley	52767	
Pleasanton, R. Br. Davis City	50224	
Pleasantville	50225	
Plover	50573	
Plymouth	50464	
Pocahontas	50574	
Polk City	50226	
Pomeroy	50575	
Popejoy	50227	
Portsmouth	51565	
Postville	52162	
Prairie City	50228	
Prairieburg, R. Br. Coggon	52219	
Prescott	50859	
Preston	52069	
Primghar	51245	
Princeton	52768	
Prole	50229	
Promise City	52583	
Protivin	52163	
Pulaski	52584	
Quasqueton	52326	
Quimby	51049	
Radcliffe	50230	
Rake	50465	
Ralston	51459	
Randalia	52164	
Randall	50231	
Randolph	51649	
Rathbun, R. Br. Centerville	52545	
Raymond	50667	
Readlyn	50668	
Reasnor	50232	
Red Oak (1st)	51566	
Redding	50860	
Redfield	50233	
Reinbeck	50669	
Rembrandt	50576	
Remsen	51050	
Renwick	50577	
Rhodes	50234	
Riceville	50466	
Richland	52585	
Richmond, R. Br. Kalona	52247	
Ricketts	51460	
Ridgeway	52165	
Rinard, R. Br. Somers	50587	
Ringsted	50578	
Rippey	50235	
Riverside	52327	
Riverton	51050	
Robins	52328	
Rock Falls	50467	
Rock Rapids	51246	
Rock Valley	51247	
Rockford	50468	
Rockwell	50469	
Rockwell City	50579	
Rodman	50580	
Rodney	51051	
Roland	50236	
Rolfe	50581	
Rome, R. Br. Mount Pleasant	52642	

Rose Hill	52586	
Rossie	51356	
Rowan	50470	
Rowley	52329	
Royal	51357	
Greenville, R. Br.	51343	
Rubio	52587	
Rudd	50471	
Runnells	50237	
Russell	50238	
Ruthven	51358	
Rutland	50582	
Ryan	52330	
Sabula	52070	
Sac City (1st)	50583	
Saint Ansgar	50472	
Saint Anthony	50239	
Saint Charles	50240	
Saint Donatus	52071	
Saint Lucas	52166	
Saint Marys	50241	
Saint Olaf	52072	
Saint Paul, R. Br. West Point	52657	
Salem	52649	
Salix	51052	
Sanborn	51248	
Saratoga, R. Br. Lime Springs	52167	
Scarville	50473	
Schaller	51053	
Schleswig	51461	
Scotch Grove	52331	
Scranton	51462	
Searsboro	50242	
Selma	52588	
Sergeant Bluff	51054	
Sewal	52589	
Sexton	50474	
Seymour	52590	
Shambaugh	51651	
Shannon City	50861	
Sharpsburg	50862	
Sheffield	50475	
Shelby	51570	
Sheldahl	50243	
Sheldon (1st)	51201	
Shell Rock	50670	
Shellsburg	52332	
Shenandoah (1st)	51601	
Sherrill	52073	
Sibley (1st)	51249	
Sidney	51652	
Sigourney	52591	
Silver City	51571	
Sioux Center (1st)	51250	
SIOUX CITY (1st) (see appendix)		
Sioux Rapids	50585	
Slater	50244	
Sloan	51055	
Smithland	51056	
Soldier	51572	
Solon	52333	
Somers	50586	
Rinard, R. Br.	50587	
South Amana	52334	
South Des Moines, Sta. Des Moines (see appendix)		
South English	52335	
Spencer (1st)	51301	
Sperry	52650	
Spillville	52168	

Spirit Lake (1st)	51360	
Spragueville	52074	
Spring Hill	50245	
Springbrook	52075	
Springville	52336	
Stacyville	50476	
Stanhope	50246	
Stanley	50671	
Stanton	51573	
Stanwood	52337	
State Center	50247	
Steamboat Rock	50672	
Stock Yards, Sta. Sioux City	51107	
Stockport	52651	
Stockton	52769	
Storm Lake (1st)	50588	
Story City	50248	
Stout	50673	
Stratford	50249	
Strawberry Point	52076	
Struble, R. Br. Le Mars	51057	
Stuart	50250	
Sully	50251	
Sulphur Springs	50589	
Sumner	50674	
Sunbury	52770	
Superior	51363	
Sutherland	51058	
Swaledale	50477	
Swan	50252	
Swea City	50590	
Swedesburg	52652	
Swisher	52338	
Tabor	51653	
Taintor	50253	
Tama	52339	
Teeds Grove, R. Br. Clinton	52771	
Templeton	51463	
Tennant	51574	
Terril	51364	
Thayer	50254	
Thompson	50478	
Thor	50591	
Thornburg	50255	
Thornton	50479	
Thurman	51654	
Bartlett, R. Br.	51655	
Tiffin	52340	
Tingley	50863	
Tipton (1st)	52772	
Titonka	50480	
Toddville	52341	
Toeterville	50481	
Toledo	52342	
Toronto	52343	
Tracy	50256	
Traer	50675	
Treynor	51575	
Tripoli	50676	
Troy, R. Br. Bloomfield	52537	
Troy Mills	52344	
Truesdale	50592	
Truro	50257	
Turin	51059	
Udell	52593	
Ulmer	51464	
Underwood	51576	
Union	50258	
Gifford, R. Br.	50259	
Unionville	52594	
University Park	52595	
University Place, Sta. Des Moines	50311	
Urbana	52345	

Urbandale, Br. Des Moines (see appendix)		
Ute	51060	
Vail	51465	
Van Horne	52346	
Van Meter	50261	
Van Wert	50262	
Varina	50593	
Ventura	50482	
Victor	52347	
Villisca	50864	
Vincent	50594	
Vining	52348	
Vinton (1st)	52349	
Viola	52350	
Volga	52077	
Wadena	52169	
Walcott	52773	
Walford	52351	
Walker	52352	
Wall Lake	51466	
Wallingford	51365	
Walnut	51577	
Wapello	52653	
Washburn, Br. Waterloo	50706	
Washington (1st)	52353	
Washta	51061	
WATERLOO (1st) (see appendix)		
Waterville	52176	
Watkins	52354	
Waucoma	52171	
Waukee	50263	
Waukon (1st)	52172	
Waverly (1st)	50677	
Wayland	52654	
Webb	51366	
Webster	52355	
Webster City (1st)	50595	
Weldon	50264	
Wellman	52356	
Wellsburg	50680	
Welton	52774	
Wesley	50483	
West	52357	
West Bend	50597	
West Branch	52358	
West Burlington	52655	
West Chester	52359	
West Des Moines, Br. Des Moines	50265	
West Grove, R. Br. Bloomfield	52538	
West Liberty	52776	
West Point	52656	
Saint Paul, R. Br.	52657	
West Union (1st)	52175	
Westfield	51062	
Westgate	50681	
Westphalia	51578	
Westside	51467	
Wever	52658	
What Cheer	50268	
Wheatland	52777	
Whiting	51063	
Whittemore	50598	
Whitten	50269	
Whittier	52360	

William Penn College, Sta.	Winterset (1st) 52273	Wright 52596
Oskaloosa 52577	Winthrop 50682	Wyoming 52362
Williams 50271	Wiota 50274	Yale 50277
Williamsburg 52361	Woden 50484	Yarmouth 52660
Williamson 50272	Woodbine 51579	Yetter, R. Br Auburn .. 51433
Wilton 52778	Woodburn 50275	Yorktown 51656
Windsor Heights, Br. Des	Woodward 50276	
Moines 50311	Woolstock 50599	Zearing 50278
Winfield 52659	Worthington 52078	Zwingle 52079

Appendix　　　　　　　　　**Cedar Rapids — Davenport IOWA**

CEDAR RAPIDS　　524

POST OFFICE BOXES

Box Nos.
1-3999	Main Office	06
4001-5035	First Street	
	Sta.	07

RURAL ROUTES

1,2,3	01

STATIONS, BRANCHES AND UNITS

Cedar Hills Sta.	05
First Street Sta.	07
General Delivery	01
Postmaster	01

APARTMENTS, HOTELS, MOTELS

Allison, 325 1st Ave E	01
Ausadie, 845 1st Ave SE	02
Blair House, 2222 1st Ave N	
E	02
Brandywyne	04
Brown, 1234 4th Ave SE	03
Carleton, 1920 1st Ave E	01
Cedar Valley	04
Cedarwood Trace, 2040 Glass	
Rd NE	02
College, 1261 1st Ave E	02
Commonwealth Apartment,	
1400 2nd Ave SE	03
East Towne Place SE	01
Eleanor, 319 1st Ave E	01
Gateway Gardens	04
Holiday Inn	06
Iowa, 1263 1st Ave E	02
Magnus, 324 2nd Ave SE	07
Meth Wick Manor, 1224 13th	
St NW	05
Montrose, 223 3rd Ave SE	01
North Towne Place NE	02
Oakland Court, 1500 Oakland	
Rd NE	02
Oakland Gardens, 1300	
Oakland Rd NE	02
Park Towne Court NE	02
Park Towne Place NE	02

Roosevelt, 200 1st Ave E.	07
Taft, 403 2nd Ave SE	01
Town House Motor, 4747 1st	
Ave E	06
Windemere, 205 14th SE	03

BUILDINGS

American, 101 2nd SE	01
Arco, 308 3rd SE	01
Dows, 210 2nd SE	01
Executive Plaza, 4403 1st	
Ave NE	02
First Avenue, 411 1st Ave E	01
First Trust & Savings Bank,	
1201 3rd SE	01
Granby, 224 2nd SE	01
Green Engineering, 417 1st	
Ave E	01
Guaranty, 216 3rd SE	01
Higley, 118 3rd Ave SE	01
Insurance, 526 2nd Ave SE	01
Iowa Theatre, 108 3rd SE	01
Memorial Coliseum, Mays	
Island	01
Merchants National Bank,	
115 3rd SE	01
Mount Vernon Professional,	
3330 Mt Vernon Rd SE	03
Mullin, 219 2nd SE	01
Naibert, 117 3rd Ave SE	01
Namsho, 509 3rd Ave SE	01
Paramount, 305 2nd SE	01
S G A, 122 2nd SE	01
Security, 203 2nd SE	01
Town & Country, 136 36th Dr	
SE	02
Twenty Seventh Street	02

GOVERNMENT OFFICES

Chamber Of Commerce	01
City Hall, Mays Island	01
County Courthouse	01
Federal, 101 1st SE	01

HOSPITALS

Americana Nursing Home,	
1940 1st Ave NE	02
Hallmar, 835 6th Ave S E	03
Mercy, 835 6th Ave SE	03

Saint Lukes, 1026 A Ave NE	02

UNIVERSITIES AND COLLEGES

Cedar Rapids Business	
College, 128 2nd Ave S W	04
Coe College, 1220 1st Ave E	02
Kirkwood Community College,	
6301 Bowling SW	06
Mount Mercy, 1300 Elmhurst	
Dr NE	02

DAVENPORT　　528

POST OFFICE BOXES

Box Nos.
1-1240	Central Sta.	05
2001-2250	Northwest Sta	04
3001-4549	Main Office	08

RURAL ROUTES

1,2,3,4	04

STATIONS, BRANCHES AND UNITS

Central Sta	05
Northwest Sta	04
General Delivery	02
Postmaster	02

APARTMENTS, HOTELS, MOTELS

Anderson, 602 W 3rd	01
Argyle, 730 Brady.	03
Bakeris, 2935 Dubuque	03
Blackhawk, 309 Perry	01
Bronze Lantern Motel, 1661	
W Kimberly	06
Brown Motel, 4847 W	
Kimberly	06
Capitol, 224 E 6th	03
Carroll, 628 Pershing Ave	03
Century, 110 E 4th	01
Chateau, 121 W 8th	03
Clayton House, East River &	
Le Claire	01
Colonial, 839 Brady	03
Colonnades, 2016	
Rockingham Rd	02

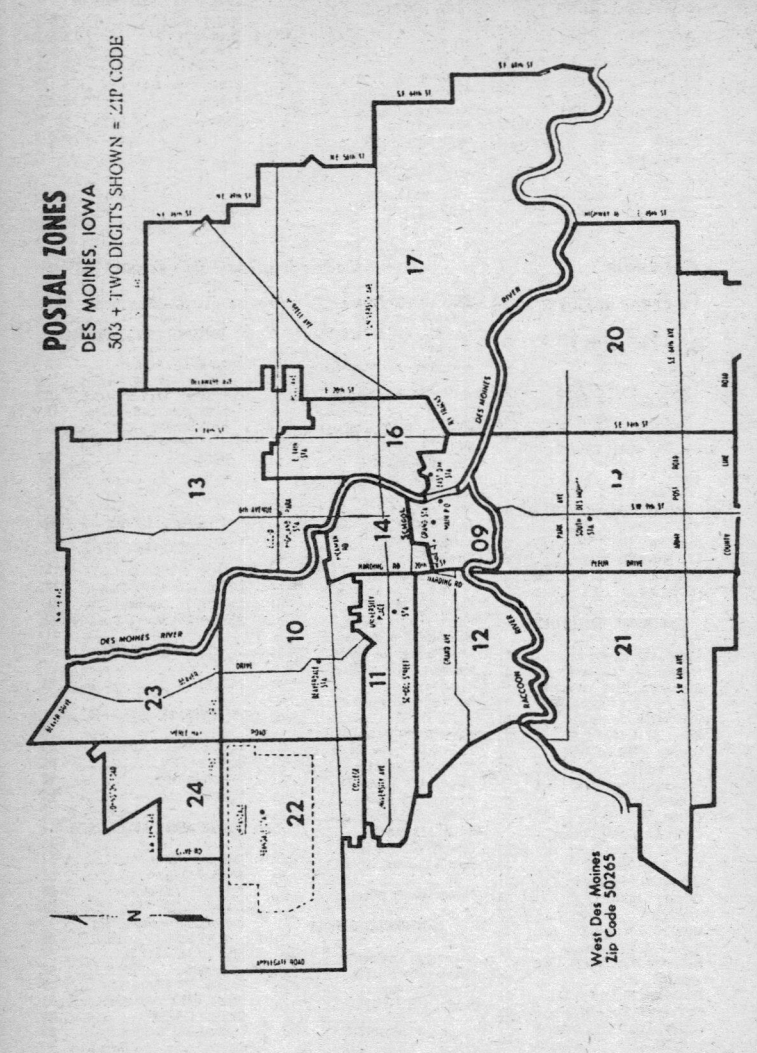

POSTAL ZONES

DES MOINES, IOWA

503 + TWO DIGITS SHOWN = ZIP CODE

West Des Moines
Zip Code 50265

Davenport (Con.)   528

Cora Lee Roy, 602 Brady	03
Courtland, 321 E 7th	03
Crest Motel, 3917 Brady	06
Crown, 805 W 2nd	02
Davenport Motel, 3202 Harrison	03
Davenport, 324 Main	01
Dempsey, 408 Main	01
Ellis & Fish, 1324 Gaines	04
Ellis & Fish, 705 W 14th	04
Fejervary, 124 W 13th	03
Fisher Crest, 223 E 35th	06
Five Seasons 5112 N Fairmount	06
Franklin, 316 Brady	01
Frey, 210 W 4th	01
Gadient, 1002 Ash	02
Geurinks, 1402 Harrison	03
Harrison Manor, 2502 Harrison	03
Holiday Inn, 5202 Brady	06
Holiday Terrace, 1935 W 40th	06
Iowa Motel, 4005 Brady	06
Janssen, 502 Perry	03
Kahl, 311 W 3rd	01
Langwith, 320 W 4th	01
Lend-A-Hand, 105 S Main	01
Linden Flats, 219 Scott	01
Maple Lane Motel, 9001 Brady	06
Mississippi, 106 E 3rd	01
Motel Six, 6111 N Brady	06
Pasadena, 1224 Main	03
Quality Motel Midtown, 226 W 6th	02
Rose Garden Motel, 4108 Hickory Grove Rd	06
Roslyn, 739 Perry	03
Scharff, 105 W 2nd	01
Schick, 120 Harrison	01
Schricker, 401 W 4th	01
Security, 217 W 4th	01
Shorey, 930 Perry	03
Standard, 712 W 2nd	02
Strahmeier, 1317 E Locust	03
Tall Corn Motor Inn, 427 W Kimberly	06
Vale, 210 E 4th	01
Van Dresky, 1003 W Locust	04
Voyager Inn, 4002 Brady	06

BUILDINGS

Bayers, 230 W 3rd	01
Brenton, 1600 Brady St	03
Citizens Federal, 218 Brady	01
Davenport Bank, 220 Main	01
Davenport Municipal Art Gallery, 1737 W 12th	04
Davenport Public Museum, 1717 W 12th	04
Eastern Office, 2212 E 12th	03
First National, 201 W 2nd	01
Insurance Exchange, 220 E 2nd	01
Kahl, 326 W 3rd	01
Kresge, 210 Main	01
Lee, 130 E 2nd	01

Midtown Plaza, 1726 Brady Street	03
Priester, 610 Brady	01
Professional Arts, 121 W Locust	03
Putnam, 215 Main	01
Union Arcade, 111 E 3rd	01
Whitaker, 230 Brady	01

GOVERNMENT OFFICES

City Hall, 226 W 4th	01
Courthouse	01
Federal Building	01

HOSPITALS

Davenport Osteopathic, 1111 W Kimberly	06
Mercy, 1326 W Lombard	04
Pine Knoll, 2504 Telegraph Rd	04
Saint Lukes, 1227 E Rusholme	03

UNIVERSITIES AND COLLEGES

American Institute Of Commerce, 617 Brady	03
Marycrest, 1607 W 12th	04
Palmer College Of Chiropractic, 1000 Brady	03
Palmer Junior College, 1000 Brady	03
Saint Ambrose, 518 W Locust	03

DES MOINES   503

POST OFFICE BOXES

Box Nos.		
A-B	East 14th Street Sta	16
A-F	So Des Moines Sta	15
C-D	East 14th Street Sta	16
E-Z	University Place Sta	11
1-147	East Des Moines Sta	09
1-300	General Post Office	01
AA-AJ	General Post Office	01
AK-AP	General Post Office	02
AQ-AZ	General Post Office	03
BA-BJ	General Post Office	04
BK-BS	General Post Office	05
BT-BZ	General Post Office	06
CA-CB	General Post Office	06
301-600	General Post Office	02

601-800	General Post Office	03
801-1000	General Post Office	04
1001-1184	University Place Sta	11
1200-1457	General Post Office	05
1461-2000	General Post Office	06
2001-2254	Beaverdale Sta	10
2501-2815	So Des Moines Sta	15
3001-3399	East 14th Street Sta	16
3501-3827	Urbandale Br	22
4000-4199	Highland Park Sta	33
4501-5199	General Post Office	06

RURAL ROUTES

1	22
3	15
4	13
5	17

STATIONS, BRANCHES AND UNITS

Beaverdale Sta	10
Clive Br	50053
East Des Moines Sta	09
East Fourteenth Street Sta	13
Grand Sta	09
Hickman Road Br	22
Highland Park Sta	33
South Des Moines Sta	15
University Place Sta	11
Urbandale Br	22
West Des Moines Br	50265
Windsor Heights Br	11
General Delivery	18
Postmaster	18

APARTMENTS, HOTELS, MOTELS

Americana Park, 2nd & University	14
Argonne, 1729 Grand Ave	09
Arlington, 1301 Locust	09
Brady, 650 16th	14
Chamberlain, 407 7th	09
Commodore, 3440 Grand Ave	12
Eddy, 1120 Polk Blvd	11
Elhott, 219 4th	09
Ewing, 917 Locust	07
Fort Des Moines, 10th & Walnut	03
Franklin Courts, 4925 Franklin Ave	10
Franklin, 5th & Locust	09
Frederick, 717 4th	09
Grand Towers, 3663 Grand	12
Hamilton, 2825 Grand Ave	12
Hampton House, 4200 Grand Ave	12
Jefferson, 1519 Grand Ave	09
Kingston, 1200 Grand Ave	09
Kirkwood, 4th & Walnut	03
Martin, 303 Locust	09
Milner, 6th & Cherry	09
Northwestern, 321 E Walnut	09

Des Moines (Con.)   503

Park Fleur, Fleur Dr & Park
 Ave 21
Randolph, 4th & Ct Ave 09
Rogers, 118 6th Ave 09
Savery, 4th & Locust 03
Thirty Six Sixty, 3660 Grand
 Ave 12
Tours, 206 11th 09
University Terrace, 3523
 University Ave 11
Wakonda Village, 1800
 Watrous Ave 15
Windsor Terrace, 3333 Grand
 Ave 12

BUILDINGS

American, 2200 Grand 06
Bankers Trust, 406 6th Ave .. 09
Capital City Bank, 431 E
 Locust 09
Central National, 317 6th
 Ave 09
City Hall, East 1st & Locust.. 07
City Library, 1st & Walnut 09
Des Moines, 405 6th Ave 09
Eastgate Shopping Center 16
Empire, 309 6th Ave 09
Equitable, 604 Locust 09
Farm Bureau, 507 10th 09
Federal Office, 210 Walnut.... 09
Fleming, 218 6th Ave 09
Hawley Welfare, 700 6th Ave.. 09
Historical, E 12th & Grand
 Ave 19
Home Federal, 601 Grand
 Ave 09
Hubbell, 904 Walnut 09
I N A, 1055 6th Ave.............. 14
Insurance Exchange, 505 5th
 Ave 09
Iowa Des Moines National
 Bank, 518 Walnut 09
James Grimes Bldg, E 14th
 & Grand 19
Jewett, 914 Grand Ave 09
Key, 518 Grand Ave 09
Kresge, 307 7th 09
Liberty, 418 6th Ave 09
Mc Kinley Plaza 15
Merle Hay Plaza 10
National Travelers Life Bldg.,
 820 Keo Way 09
Oliver Plaza 10
Paramount, 507 Grand Ave .. 09
Park Fair 13
Plymouth, 919 Walnut 09
Polk County Court House 09
Register & Tribune, 715
 Locust 09
Robert Lucas Bldg, E 12th &
 Walnut 19
Roosevelt 12
Royal Union Life, 706 Grand
 Ave 09
Savings & Loan, 206 6th
 Ave 09
Securities, 418 7th 09
Seneca Plaza 13
Sherwood Forest 22

Shoppers Fair 16
Shops, 806 Walnut................ 09
State Capitol Complex, E. 6th
 & Des Moines Street.......... 19
State Capitol, E 10 & Grand
 Ave 19
Stephens 09
Telephone, 604 9th.............. 09
Thompson Plaza 16
Travelers Insurance, 215 Keo.
 Way 09
Wakonda 21

HOSPITALS

Blank Memorial, 1200
 Pleasant 08
Broadlawns, 18th & Hickman
 Rd 14
Des Moines General, 603 E
 12th 16
Helen Powell Convalescent
 Center, 1200 Pleasant........ 08
Iowa Lutheran, 716 Parnell .. 16
Iowa Methodist Hospital,
 1200 Pleasant 08
Mercy, 5th & Ascension 14
N W Hospital, 1818 48th...... 16
Veterans, 30th & Euclid Ave .. 09
Wilden Clinic, 717 Lyon 16
Younker Memorial
 Rehabilitation Center,
 1200 Pleasant 08

UNIVERSITIES AND COLLEGES

American Institute Of
 Business, 10th & Grand
 Ave 07
College Of Automation, 3001
 Grand Ave 02
College Of Osteopathic
 Medicine & Surgery, 722
 6th Ave 09
Drake University, 25th &
 University Ave 11
Grandview, E 13th &
 Grandview Ave 16

SIOUX CITY   511

POST OFFICE BOXES

Box Nos.
1-1918   Main Office 02
1L-158L   Leeds Sta 08
2001-2128   North Side Sta . 04
2301-2468   Stock Yards
                       Sta............... 07
2501-2788   Morningside
                       Sta............... 06
3001-3455   Main Office 02

RURAL ROUTES

1 08
2 06
3 03

STATIONS, BRANCHES AND UNITS

Boulevard Sta 09
Call Terminal Sta 01
Leeds Sta 08
Morningside Sta 06
North Side Sta...................... 04
Stock Yards Sta 07
General Delivery 01
Postmaster 01

APARTMENTS, HOTELS, MOTELS

Alhambra, 801 8th St 05
Argonaut, 1103 Nebraska 05
Aventino Hotel 517-6th St...... 01
Bellevue, 2104 Summit........ 04
Biltmore Motel, 5900 Gordon
 Dr 06
Bolstein, 1626 Jackson 05
Carroll, 1101 Jackson 05
Castle, 2119 Nebraska 04
Chicago House, 807 4th St .. 01
Clifton Apts, 55 W Clifton 01
Follis, 923 Douglas St 01
Holiday Inn, 1401 Gordon Dr
 W 03
Ida, 1901 Pierce.................. 04
Imperial 400 Motel, 110 S
 Nebraska 01
Martin Apartments, 4th &
 Pierce 02
Metz, 2001 Summit.............. 04
Morningside Country Estates,
 1331 South Maple 06
Murray Apts, 823 Jackson.... 05
Palmer House Motel, 3440
 Gordon Dr 06
Parkview, 104 24th St 04
Parkwood, 4351 Lincoln Way.. 06
Pierce Plaza West, 414-11th
 St 05
River Heights Apts, 2201
 Gibson 06
Roadway Inn, 2nd &
 Nebraska St 01
Sioux, 217 19th.................... 05
Smith, 1716 Nebraska.......... 05
Stellart, 2117 Nebraska........ 04
Swanson, 1700 Jackson 05
Sydney, 1003 Pierce............ 05
Terrace, 1623 Nebraska 05
Valley Park, 3029 Park Ave .. 04
Vincent, 615 Jones.............. 05
Wirick, 402 14th St 05

BUILDINGS

Badgerow, 4th & Jackson 01
Benson, 7th & Douglas........ 01
Brown Block, 602 1/2 4th 01
Call Terminal, 4th & Court 01
Commerce, 520 Nebraska.... 01
Davidson, 505 6th St............ 01
Federal, 6th & Douglas........ 01
Frances, 503 5th St 01
Home Federal Saving And
 Loan 701 Pierce.................. 01
Insurance Exchange, 7th &
 Pierce 01
Livestock Exchange, 807
 Cunningham Dr 07

Sioux City (Con.)   511

Municipal, 114 6th 03
Northwest National Bank 500
   Jackson 01
Orpheum Electric, 6th &
   Pierce 01
Security Bank, 6th & Pierce .. 01
Sioux City Federal Plaza On
   The Mall At Jackson 01
Wright, 413 Nebraska 01

GOVERNMENT OFFICES

City Hall, 401 6th St 01
County Courthouse, 620
   Douglas St 01
Federal, 6th & Douglas St 01

HOSPITALS

Gordon Memorial, 1816 West.. 03
Saint Joseph, 2101 Court 04
Saint Vincents, 624 Jones 05
St Lukes Medical Center
   (East), 2714 Pierce.......... 04

UNIVERSITIES AND COLLEGES

Briar Cliff, 32nd & Rebecca .. 04
Morningside, 1601
   Morningside Ave 06

          WATERLOO   507

         POST OFFICE BOXES

Box Nos.
1-320   Washburn Br 06
1-1177   Main Office 04
2001-2617   A Sta 05
3001-3447   Evansdale Br 07
4000-9000   Main Office 04

         RURAL ROUTES

1,2,3,4,5 01

STATIONS, BRANCHES AND UNITS

Evansdale Br 07
Washburn Br 06
General Delivery 01
Postmaster 01

APARTMENTS, HOTELS, MOTELS

Armory, 209 E 6th 03
Belmont Court, 400 1/2 438
   Belmont 01
Brockwell Arms, 581
   Jefferson 01
Brown, 420 Commercial......... 01
Cedar 21 1/2 -27 1/2 E 5th... 03
Clayton House Motel, 300 W
   Mullan Ave................... 01
Colonial Manor Apts 425
   Allen......................... 01
Colonial, 801 1/2 811 W 4th .. 02
Drake, 933 1/2 935 W 3rd..... 01
Ellis Hotel, 705 Sycamore..... 05
Friedel, 302 Commercial....... 01
Fullerton, 533 Lime............ 03
Grand Hotel 328 W 4th......... 01
Greystone, 1306 W 3rd 01
Hileman, 617 Mulberry......... 03
Hillcrest, 309 Allen 01
Hillcrest, 833 W 2nd........... 01
Lo Dema, 222 Walnut........... 03
Martin Hotel 514 Sycamore 03
Mc Kinley, 1907 Franklin...... 03
Melrose, 618 1/2 620 W 3rd... 01
Mulberry 612 1/2 -614 1/2
   Mulberry 03
Oak Lawn Terrace, 400 1/2
   434 Oak Lawn 01
Park View, 200 1/2 255 Park
   View Blvd 02
Plaza, 1308 W 4th.............. 02
Quality Motel, W 5th &
   Jefferson.................... 01
Ramada Inn W2-Washington..... 01
Rath-Donnell, 217 1/2 E 5th .. 03

Russell Lamson Apts, 209 W
   5th 04
Star Hotel, 617 1/2
   Sycamore..................... 03
Stonewall, 614 Washington 01
Superior, 422 W 6th............ 01
Superior, 725 Washington...... 01
Walnut Court, 315 Walnut...... 03
Wellington, 505 1/2 507
   Wellington 01
Wellington, 727 W Park Ave ... 01
Windsor, 225 W 5th............. 01

BUILDINGS

Black Hawk, 206 W 4th......... 01
Black, 525 Sycamore 03
First National, 601 1/2 609
   Sycamore..................... 03
K W W L, 500 E 4th............ 03
Lafayette, 609 Lafayette...... 03
Marsh Place, 627 Sycamore 03
Repass, 604 Mulberry.......... 03
Waterloo, 531 1/2 535
   Commercial................... 01

GOVERNMENT OFFICES

City Hall, 715 Mulberry....... 05
Court House, 316 E 5th........ 03

HOSPITALS

Allen Memorial, 1825 Logan
   Ave 03
Saint Francis, 3421 W 9th 02
Schoitz Memorial, 2101
   Kimball Ave.................. 02

UNIVERSITIES AND COLLEGES

Gates College, 209 W Park
   Ave 01
Hawkeye Institute Of
   Technology, P O Box 8015.. 04

KANSAS
(Abbreviation: KS)

Abbyville	67510
Abilene (1st)	67410
Ada	67414
Admire	66830
Agenda	66930
Agra	67621
Agricola	66831
Alamota	67830
Albert	67511
Alden	67512
Alexander	67513
Aliceville	66832
Allen	66833
Alma	66401
Mc Farland, R. Br.	66501
Almena	67622
Alta Vista	66834
Altamont	67330
Alton	67623
Altoona	66710
Americus	66835
Ames	66931
Andale	67001
Andover	67002
Angola, R. Br. Coffeyville	67331
Antelope	66836
Anthony (1st)	67003
Antonino	67624
Arcadia	66711
Argentine, Sta. Kansas City	66106
Argonia	67004
Arkansas City (1st)	67005
Arlington	67514
Arma	66712
Arnold	67515
Arrington	66001
Asherville	67415
Ashland	67831
Assaria	67416
Atchison (1st)	66002
Athol	66932
Atlanta	67008
Attica	67009
Atwood	67730
Auburn	66402
Augusta (1st)	67010
Aurora	67417
Axtell	66403
Baileyville	66404
Baldwin City	66006
Barnard	67418
Barnes	66933
Bartlett	67332
Basehor	66007
Bavaria	67419
Baxter Springs (1st)	66713
Bazaar	66837
Bazine	67516
Beattie	66406
Beaumont	67012
Beaver	67517
Beeler	67518
Bellaire	66934
Belle Plaine	67013
Belleville (1st)	66935
Belmont, R. Br. Kingman	67014
Beloit (1st)	67420
Scottsville, R. Br.	67477
Belpre	67519
Belvidere	67015

Belvue	66407
Bendena	66008
Benedict	66714
Bennington	67422
Bentley	67016
Benton	67017
Bern	66408
Berryton	66409
Bethel, Sta. Kansas City (see appendix)	
Beverly	67423
Big Bow	67832
Bird City	67731
Bison	67520
Blaine	66410
Bloom	67833
Blue Mound	66010
Blue Rapids	66411
Bluff City	67018
Bogue	67625
Bonner Springs (1st)	66012
Bremen	66412
Brewster	67732
Bridgeport	67424
Bronson	66716
Brookville	67425
Brownell	67521
Bucklin	67834
Bucyrus	66013
Buffalo	66717
Buhler	67522
Bunker Hill	67626
Burden	67019
Burdett	67523
Burdick	66838
Burlingame	66413
Burlington	66839
Burns	66840
Burr Oak	66936
Burrton	67020
Bushong	66841
Bushton	67427
Byers	67021
Caldwell	67022
Cambridge	67023
Camp Funston, Br. Junction City	66442
Caney (1st)	67333
Canton	67428
Carbondale	66414
Carlton	67429
Carlyle	66718
Corona	66719
Cassoday	66842
Catharine	67627
Cawker City	67430
Cedar	67628
Cedar Point	66843
Cedar Vale	67024
Centerville	66014
Centralia	66415
Chanute (1st)	66720
Earlton, R. Br.	66731
Chapman	67431
Chase	67524
Chautauqua	67334
Cheney	67025
Cherokee	66724
Cherryvale	67335
Chetopa	67336
Chisholm, Sta. Wichita (see appendix)	
Cimarron	67835

Circleville	66416
Civic Center, Sta. Kansas City (see appendix)	
Claflin	67525
Clay Center (1st)	67432
Clayton	67629
Clearwater	67026
Clements	66844
Clifton	66937
Climax	67027
Clyde	66938
Coats	67028
Codell	67630
Coffeyville (1st)	67337
Colby (1st)	67701
Coldwater	67029
College, Sta. Pittsburg	66762
Collyer	67631
Colony	66015
Columbus (1st)	66725
Colwich	67030
Concordia (1st)	66901
Conway	67434
Conway Springs	67031
Coolidge	67836
Copeland	67837
Corbin	67032
Corning	66417
Cottonwood Falls	66845
Council Grove	66846
Courtland	66939
Coyville	66727
Crestline	66728
Crystal Springs, R. Br. Harper	67033
Cuba	66940
Culver	67435
Cummings	66016
Cunningham	67035
Damar	67632
Danville	67036
De Soto	66018
Sunflower, R. Br.	66019
Dearing	67340
Deerfield	67838
Delavan	66847
Delia	66418
Delphos	67436
Denison	66419
Dennis	67341
Densmore	67633
Denton	66017
Derby (1st)	67037
Devon	66730
Dexter	67038
Dighton	67839
Dodge City (1st)	67801
Dorrance	67634
Douglass	67039
Dover	66420
Downs	67437
Dresden	67635
Duluth	66421
Dunlap	66848
Duquoin	67040
Durham	67438
Dwight	66849
Earlton, R. Br. Chanute	66731
Easton	66020
Edgerton	66021
Edmond	67636
Edna	67342
Edson	67733

Edwardsville, Br. Kansas
City....................................66113
Effingham...............................66023
El Dorado (1st)......................67042
Elbing.....................................67041
Elgin, R. Br. Sedan................67361
Elk City..................................67344
Elk Falls.................................67345
Elkhart...................................67950
Ellinwood...............................67526
Ellis.......................................67637
Ellsworth...............................67439
Elmdale..................................66850
Elsmore..................................66732
Elwood...................................66024
Emmett...................................66422
Emporia (1st).........................66801
Englewood.............................67840
Ensign....................................67841
Enterprise..............................67441
Erie..66733
Esbon....................................66941
Eskridge.................................66423
Eudora...................................66025
Eureka (1st)...........................67045
Everest...................................66424
Fairfax, Sta. Kansas City......66115
Fairview.................................66425
Fall River...............................67047
Falun.....................................67442
Farlington..............................66734
Fellsburg...............................67048
Florence.................................66851
Fontana.................................66026
Forbes A F B, Br. Topeka......66620
Ford......................................67842
Formoso.................................66942
Fort Dodge............................67843
Fort Larned, R. Br. Larned...67550
Fort Leavenworth (1st).........66027
Fort Riley, Br. Junction City..66442
Fort Scott (1st)......................66701
Fostoria.................................66426
Fowler...................................67844
Frankfort................................66427
Franklin..................................66735
Fredonia (1st)........................66736
Freeport..................................67049
Friend....................................67845
Frontenac, Br. Pittsburg.......66762
Fulton....................................66738
Gage Center, Sta. Topeka.....66604
Galatia, R. Br. Hoisington....67528
Galena....................................66739
Galesburg..............................66740
Galva......................................67443
Garden City (1st)...................67846
Garden Plain..........................67050
Gardner (1st).........................66030
Garfield..................................67529
Garland..................................66741
Garnett (1st)..........................66032
Gas..66742
Gaylord..................................67638
Gem.......................................67734
Geneseo.................................67444
Geuda Springs........................67051
Girard (1st)............................66743
Glade.....................................67639
Glasco....................................67445
Glen Elder.............................67446
Goddard.................................67052
Goessel..................................67053

Goff.......................................66428
Goodland (1st).......................67735
Gorham..................................67640
Gove......................................67736
Grainfield...............................67737
Grantville...............................66429
Great Bend (1st)....................67530
Greeley..................................66033
Green.....................................67447
Greenleaf...............................66943
Greensburg............................67054
Greenwich..............................67055
Grenola..................................67346
Gridley...................................66852
Grinnell..................................67738
Gypsum..................................67448
Haddam..................................66944
Hallowell................................66744
Halstead.................................67056
Hamilton.................................66853
Hamlin...................................66430
Hanover..................................66945
Hanston.................................67849
Hardtner.................................67057
Harlan....................................67641
Harper....................................67058
Hartford.................................66854
Harveyville.............................66431
Havana...................................67347
Haven.....................................67543
Havensville.............................66432
Haviland.................................67059
Trousdale, R. Br............67145
Hays (1st)..............................67601
Schoenchen, R. Br........67667
Haysville (1st)........................67060
Hazelton.................................67061
Healy.....................................67850
Hepler....................................66746
Herington...............................67449
Herkimer................................66433
Herndon.................................67739
Hesston (1st).........................67062
Hewins, R. Br. Cedar Vale...67024
Hiattville................................66747
Hiawatha (1st).......................66434
Willis, R. Br.................66435
Hicrest, Sta. Topeka (see
appendix)
Highland.................................66035
Hill City.................................67642
Hillsboro (1st)........................67063
Hillsdale.................................66036
Hoisington.............................67544
Galatia, R. Br...............67528
Holcomb................................67851
Hollenberg.............................66946
Holliday, R. Br. Shawnee
Mission..........................66037
Holton (1st)...........................66436
Holyrood................................67450
Home.....................................66438
Hope......................................67451
Hopewell................................67064
Horton....................................66439
Howard...................................67349
Hoxie.....................................67740
Hoyt.......................................66440
Hudson...................................67545
Hugoton.................................67951
Humboldt...............................66748
Hunnewell, R. Br. South
Haven.............................67141

Hunter....................................67452
Huron.....................................66038
Hutchinson (1st).....................67501
Idana.....................................67453
Independence (1st).................67301
Ingalls....................................67853
Inman.....................................67546
Iola (1st)................................66749
Ionia......................................66947
Isabel.....................................67065
Iuka.......................................67066
Jamestown.............................66948
Jayhawk, Sta. Lawrence........66044
Jennings.................................67643
Jetmore..................................67854
Jewell.....................................66949
Johnson..................................67855
Junction City (1st)..................66441
Camp Funston, Br..........66442
Fort Riley, Br...............66442
Kalvesta.................................67856
Kanopolis...............................67454
Kanorado...............................67741
KANSAS CITY (1st) (see
appendix)
Kechi.....................................67067
Kelly......................................66446
Kendall...................................67857
Kensington.............................66951
Kincaid...................................66039
Kingman (1st)........................67068
Kingsdown.............................67858
Kinsley...................................67547
Kiowa.....................................67070
Kirwin....................................67644
Kismet....................................67859
La Crosse...............................67548
La Cygne................................66040
La Harpe................................66751
Labette...................................67350
Lafontaine..............................66750
Lake City................................67701
Lake Of The Forest, R. Br.
Bonner Springs..............66012
Lakin......................................67860
Lamont, R. Br. Madison........66855
Lancaster...............................66041
Lane.......................................66042
Langdon.................................67549
Lansing..................................66043
Larned (1st)...........................67550
Latham...................................67072
Lawrence (1st).......................66044
Lawton...................................66752
Le Roy...................................66857
Leavenworth (1st)..................66048
Leawood, Br. Shawnee
Mission (see appendix)
Lebanon.................................66952
Lebo......................................66856
Lecompton.............................66050
Lehigh....................................67073
Lenexa, Br. Shawnee Mission
(see appendix)
Lenora....................................67645
Leon......................................67074
Leona.....................................66448
Leonardville...........................66449
Leoti......................................67861
Leoville, R. Br. Selden..........67742
Levant....................................67743
Lewis.....................................67552
Liberal (1st)...........................67901

215

Liberty	67351	
Liebenthal	67553	
Lincoln	67455	
Lincolnville	66858	
Lindsborg	67456	
Linn	66953	
Linwood	66052	
Little River	67457	
Logan	67646	
Long Island	67647	
Longford	67458	
Longton	67352	
Lorraine	67459	
Lost Springs	66859	
Louisburg	66053	
Louisville	66450	
Lovewell	66954	
Lucas	67648	
Ludell	67744	
Luray	67649	
Lyndon	66451	
Lyons (1st)	67554	
Macksville	67557	
Madison	66860	
Lamont, R. Br.	66855	
Mahaska	66955	
Maize	67101	
Manchester	67463	
Manhattan (1st)	66502	
Mankato	66956	
Manter	67862	
Maple City	67102	
Maple Hill	66507	
Mapleton	66754	
Marienthal	67863	
Marion	66861	
Marquette	67464	
Marysville (1st)	66508	
Matfield Green	66862	
Mayetta	66509	
Mayfield	67103	
Mc Connell A F B, Br. Wichita	67221	
Mc Cracken	67556	
Mc Cune	66753	
Mc Donald	67745	
Mc Farland, R. Br. Alma	66501	
Mc Louth	66054	
Mc Pherson (1st)	67460	
Meade	67864	
Meadow Lake, Br. Shawnee Mission	66208	
Medicine Lodge	67104	
Medora	67558	
Melvern	66510	
Menlo	67746	
Mentor	67465	
Mercier	66511	
Meriden	66512	
Merriam, Br. Shawnee Mission	66203	
Midland, Sta. Wichita (see appendix)		
Milan	67105	
Mildred	66055	
Milford	66514	
Milton	67106	
Miltonvale	67466	
Minneapolis	67467	
Minneola	67865	
Mission, Br. Shawnee Mission	66222	
Modoc	67866	
Moline	67353	
Montezuma	67867	
Montrose	66957	
Monument	67747	
Moran	66755	
Morganville	67468	
Morland	67650	
Morrill	66515	
Morrowville	66958	
Moscow	67952	
Mound City	66056	
Mound Valley	67354	
Moundridge	67107	
Mount Hope	67108	
Mulberry	66756	
Mullinville	67109	
Mulvane	67110	
Muncie, Sta. Kansas City	66111	
Munden	66959	
Munger, Sta. Wichita (see appendix)		
Murdock	67111	
Muscotah	66058	
Narka	66960	
Nashville	67112	
Netoma	67651	
Navarre, R. Br. Enterprise	67469	
Neal	66863	
Nekoma	67559	
Neodesha	66757	
Neosho Falls	66758	
Neosho Rapids	66864	
Ness City	67560	
Netawaka	66516	
New Albany	66759	
New Almelo	67652	
New Cambria	67470	
Newton (1st)	67114	
Nickerson	67561	
Niles	67471	
Niotaze	67355	
Norcatur	67653	
North Newton	67117	
North Topeka, Sta. Topeka	66608	
North Wichita, Sta. Wichita (see appendix)		
Northbranch, R. Br. Burr Oak	66936	
Northwest, Sta. Kansas City	66104	
Horton (1st)	67654	
Nortonville	66060	
Norway	66961	
Norwich	67118	
Oakhill	67472	
Oaklawn, Br. Wichita	67216	
Oakley	67748	
Oberlin	67749	
Odin	67562	
Offerle	67563	
Ogallah	67656	
Ogden	66517	
Oketo	66518	
Olathe (1st)	66061	
Olivet, R. Br. Melvern	66519	
Olmitz	67564	
Olpe	66865	
Olsburg	66520	
Onaga	66521	
Oneida	66522	
Opolis	66760	
Osage City	66523	
Osawatomie (1st)	66064	
Osborne	67473	
Oskaloosa	66066	
Oswego	67356	
Otis	67565	
Ottawa (1st)	66067	
Overbrook	66524	
Overland Park, Br. Shawnee Mission (see appendix)		
Oxford	67119	
Ozawkie	66070	
Packers, Sta. Kansas City (see appendix)		
Palco	67657	
Palmer	66962	
Paola (1st)	66071	
Paradise	67658	
Park	67751	
Park City, Br. Wichita	67219	
Parker	66072	
Parsons (1st)	67357	
Partridge	67566	
Pauline, Br. Topeka	66619	
Pawnee Rock	67567	
Paxico	66526	
Peabody	66866	
Peck	67120	
Penalosa	67121	
Penokee	67659	
Perry	66073	
Peru	67360	
Pfeifer	67660	
Phillipsburg (1st)	67661	
Piedmont	67122	
Pierceville	67868	
Piper, R. Br. Kansas City	66109	
Piqua	66761	
Pittsburg (1st)	66762	
Plains	67869	
Plainville	67663	
Pleasanton	66075	
Plevna	67568	
Pomona	66076	
Portis	67474	
Potter	66077	
Potwin	67123	
Powhattan	66527	
Prairie View	67664	
Prairie Village, Br. Shawnee Mission (see appendix)		
Pratt (1st)	67124	
Prescott	66767	
Preston	67569	
Pretty Prairie	67570	
Princeton	66078	
Protection	67127	
Quenemo	66528	
Quincy	66867	
Quinter	67752	
Radium	67571	
Radley	66768	
Rago	67128	
Ramona	67475	
Randall	66963	
Randolph	66554	
Ransom	67572	
Rantoul	66079	
Raymond	67573	
Reading	66868	
Redfield	66769	
Republic	66964	
Reserve	66529	
Rexford	67753	
Rice	66965	

Richfield................67953
Richmond...............66080
Riley....................66531
Riverdale...............67130
Riverton................66770
Robinson................66532
Rock....................67131
Rolla...................67954
Rosalia.................67132
Rose Hill...............67133
Rosedale, Sta. Kansas City...66103
Rossville...............66533
Roxbury.................67476
Rozel...................67574
Rush Center............67575
Russell (1st)..........67665
Russell Springs........67755
Sabetha.................66534
Saffordville, R. Br. Strong
  City..................66869
Saint Francis..........67756
Saint George...........66535
Saint John.............67576
Saint Mary'S College, Sta.
  Leavenworth...........66048
Saint Marys............66536
Saint Paul.............66771
Salina (1st)...........67401
Satanta.................67870
Savonburg..............66772
Sawyer..................67134
Scammon.................66773
Scandia.................66966
Schoenchen, R. Br. Hays....67667
Scott City (1st).......67871
  Shallow Water, R. Br....67872
Scottsville, R. Br. Beloit...67477
Scranton...............66537
Sedan...................67361
Sedgwick...............67135
Selden..................67757
  Leoville, R. Br.......67742
Selkirk.................67873
Seneca..................66538
Severance..............66081
Severy..................67137
Seward..................67577
Shallow Water, R. Br. Scott
  City..................67872
Sharon..................67138
Sharon Springs.........67758
Shawnee, Br. Shawnee
  Mission (see appendix)
SHAWNEE MISSION (1st)
  (see appendix)
Shields.................67874
Silver Lake............66539
Silverdale, R. Br. Arkansas
  City..................67005
Simpson.................67478
Smith Center...........66967

Smolan..................67475
Soldier.................66540
Solomon.................67480
South Haven............67140
  Hunnewell, R. Br......67141
Southeast, Sta. Wichita (see
  appendix)
Spearville.............67876
Spivey..................67142
Spring Hill............66083
Stafford................67578
Stanley.................66084
Stark...................66775
State Hospital, Br.
  Osawatomie............66064
State House, Sta. Topeka...66612
Sterling................67579
Stilwell................66085
Stockton................67669
Strawn, R. Br. Burlington...66839
Strong City............66869
Studley.................67759
Stuttgart...............67670
Sublette................67877
Summerfield............66541
Sun City................67143
Sunflower, R. Br. De Soto...66019
Susank..................37580
Sycamore................67363
Sylvan Grove...........67481
Sylvia..................67581
Syracuse................67878
Talmage.................67482
Tampa...................67483
Tecumseh................66542
Tescott.................67484
Thayer..................66776
Timken..................67582
Tipton..................67485
Tonganoxie.............66086
TOPEKA (1st) (see appendix)
Toronto.................66777
Towanda.................67144
Treece..................66778
Tribune.................67879
Trousdale, R. Br. Haviland...67145
Troy....................66087
Turner, Sta. Kansas City
  (see appendix)
Turon...................67583
Tyro....................67364
Udall...................67146
Ulysses (1st)..........67880
Uniontown...............66779
University, Sta. Lawrence...66044
Utica...................67584
V A Hospital, Sta. Topeka...66622
Valley Center..........67147
Valley Falls...........66088
Vassar..................66543
Vermillion.............66544

Victoria................67671
Viola...................67149
Virgil..................66870
Vliets..................66545
Wa Keeney..............67672
Wakarusa...............66546
Wakefield..............67487
Waldo...................67673
Waldron.................67150
Walker..................67674
Wallace.................66761
Walnut..................66780
Walton..................67151
Wamego..................66547
Washburn Univ. Sta. Topeka...66621
Washington.............66968
Washington Street, Sta.
  Wichita...............67211
Waterville.............66548
Wathena.................66090
Waverly.................66871
Wayside.................67366
Webber..................66970
Weir....................66781
Welda...................66091
Wellington (1st).......67152
Wells...................67488
Wellsville.............66092
Weskan..................67762
West Mineral...........66782
Westfall, R. Br. Beverly...67489
Westmoreland...........66549
Westphalia.............66093
Wetmore.................66550
Wheaton.................66551
Wheeler.................67763
White City.............66872
White Cloud............66094
Whitewater.............67154
Whiting.................66552
WICHITA (1st) (see
  appendix)
Williamsburg...........66095
Willis, R. Br. Hiawatha...66435
Wilmore.................67155
Wilsey..................66873
Wilson..................67490
Winchester.............66097
Windom..................67491
Winfield (1st).........67156
Winifred................66553
Winona..................67764
Woodbine................67492
Woodston................67675
Wright..................67882
Yates Center...........66783
Yoder...................67585
Zenda...................67159
Zenith..................67586
Zurich..................67676

KANSAS CITY   661

POST OFFICE BOXES

Box Nos.
1000-1999   Civic Center   17
2000-2999   Main Office   18
3000-3999   Rosedale............   03
4000-4999   Northwest   04
5000-5999   Packers   19
6000-6999   Argentine...........   06
9000-9999   Bethel   09
11000-11999   Muncie............   11
14000-14999   Piper Br   14
15000-15999   Fairfax.............   15
16000-16999   Turner..............   16

RURAL ROUTES

2.................................   06
3.................................   04
4,5,6.............................   09
8,9...............................   11

STATIONS, BRANCHES AND UNITS

Argentine Sta   06
Bethel Sta   09
Civic Center Sta.................   01
Edwardsville Br..................   13
Fairfax Sta   15
Muncie Sta   11
Northwest Sta....................   04
Packers Sta   05
Piper Rural Br...................   09
Rosedale Sta......................   03
Turner Sta   16
General Delivery   01
Postmaster.......................   10

APARTMENTS, HOTELS, MOTELS

Bethany Park Plaza, 1036
Calvin............................   02
Beverly, 2030 West 39th Ave..   03
Boulevard, 1919 Olathe Blvd..   03
Casa Linda Gardens, 512
Splitlog..........................   01
Colonial, 3930 Rainbow Blvd..   03
Connelly Hall, 3101 Minn.:....   02
Eighth & Ann, 717 North 8th..   01
Fairfax Hills Gardens, 3176
W Parkwood.....................   64
Hawthorne, 3061 Parkwood   04
Hillcrest, 938 North 34th.......   02
Hillview, 448 North 18th........   02
Holiday Inn, 425 Minnesota....   17
Karloma, 1920 Olathe Blvd.....   03
Phoenix Fountain Bleau,
2330 Central......................   02
Redwood Garden, 1000 N
71st...............................   12
Roe Gardens, County Line &
Roe Ln...........................   03
Rosina, 851 Barnett.............   01
Saint Charles, 720 N 6th   01
Tally Ho   02
Terrace, 1601 Washington
Ave..............................   02
Town House   17
University, 3735 Booth..........   03
Watts, 904 Armstrong...........   01

Westheight Manor, 1201 N
18th.............................   02
Wyandotte Towers, 915
Washington Blvd...............   01
Wyandotte, 2311 Tauromee
Ave.............................   02

BUILDINGS

Brotherhood, 754 Minnesota
Ave..............................   01
City Hall, 805 N 6th............   01
Commercial Bank, 601
Minnesota Ave................   01
Fairfax Airport
Administration, 3101
Fairfax.........................   15
Fidelity, 609 Minnesota.........   01
Gateway No. 1, State At 5th...   01
Getty, 819 N 7th.................   01
Grossman, 640 Minnesota.......   01
Huron, 907 N 7th................   01
Leinbach, 721 Minnesota........   01
Library, 625 Minnesota..........   01
Medical, 155 S. 18th............   02
New Brotherhood, 745 State....   01
Public Levee Terminal, 1401
Fairfax Trfw...................   15
Security Bank, 915 N 7th.......   01
Siebers, 823 N 7th..............   01
Soldiers & Sailors Memorial,
600 N 7th.....................   01
Terrace, 1645 Washington   02
Y M C A, 900 N. 8th............   01
Y W C A, 1017 N. 6th...........   01

GOVERNMENT OFFICES

City Hall, 805 N 6th............   01
Courthouse.......................   01
Federal Building..................   01

HOSPITALS

Bell Memorial, 39th &
Rainbow........................   03
Bethany, 12th & Reynolds......   02
Douglass, 3700 N 27th..........   02
Eleanor Taylor, 311 Seminary..   03
Providence, 18th & Barnett.....   02
Saint Margaret, 8th &
Vermont........................   01
University Of Kansas Medical
Center, 39th & Rainbow
Blvd............................   03
Wesleyan Hospital, 4125
Rainbow Blvd...................   03

UNIVERSITIES AND COLLEGES

Donnelly College, 1236
Sundusky.......................   02
Kansas City Kansas Junior
College, 824 State Ave......   01

SHAWNEE MISSION   662

POST OFFICE BOXES

Box Nos.
1-999   Main Office   01

1000-1999   Mission Br......   22
2000-2999   Main Office Br .   01
3000-3999   Shawnee Br......   03
4000-4999   Overland Park
Br.............................   04
5000-5999   Lenexa Br   15
6000-6999   Leawood Br......   06
8000-9999   Prairie Village
Br.............................   08

RURAL ROUTES

1.................................   03
2.................................   15

STATIONS, BRANCHES AND UNITS

Holliday Rural Br................66037
Leawood Br......................   06
Lenexa Br   15
Meadow Lake Br.................   08
Merriam Br   03
Mission Br   22
Overland Park Br................   01
Prairie Village Br................   08
Shawnee Br......................   03
General Delivery   02
Postmaster.......................   02

HOSPITALS

Shawnee Mission Hospital,
74th & Grandview.............   04

UNIVERSITIES AND COLLEGES

Kansas City College & Bible
School, 7401 Metcalf...........   04

TOPEKA   666

POST OFFICE BOXES

Box Nos.
1-1999   Main Office   01
4000-4999   Gage Center
Sta   04
5000-5999   Hicrest Sta   05
8000-8999   North Topeka
Sta   08
19000-19999   Pauline
Branch   19

RURAL ROUTES

1.................................   19
2,3...............................   08
4.................................   05
5,6...............................   08
7,8,9.............................   04

STATIONS, BRANCHES AND UNITS

Forbes A F B Br..................   20
Gage Center Sta   04
Hillcrest Sta   05
North Topeka Sta   08
Pauline Br   19
Stale House Sta   12
V A Hospital Sta   22
Washburn Univ Sta   21

Topeka (Con.) 656

General Delivery	01
Postmaster	03

APARTMENTS, HOTELS, MOTELS

Brewster Place, 1205 W 29th	11
Capper, 918 Tyler	12
Curtis, 914 Tyler	12
Holiday Inn North	01
Holiday Inn South	01
Howard Johnson'S Motor Lodge, 3839 Topeka Ave	09
Jayhawk	01
Kansas Towers, 100 E 9th	01
Meadow Acres Motel	01
Methodist Home, 1135 College Ave	04
Mount Vernon Court, 2133 Potomac Dr	11
Presbyterian Manor, 4712 W 6th Ave	06
Ramada Inn	01
Senate, 900 Tyler	12
Town House, 635 Harrison	03
University Place, Washburn Ter	04

BUILDINGS

Capitol Federal, 700 Kansas Ave	03
Columbian, 112 W 6th Ave	03
First National Bank, 535 Kansas Ave	03
Garlinghouse, 820 Quincy	12
Insurance, 701 Jackson	03
Kansas Power & Light, 818 Kansas Ave	12
Medical Arts, 1001 Home	04
Medical Plaza, 1001 Garfield	04
Merchants National Bank, 900 Jackson	12
Mills, 109 W 9th	12
New England, 501 Kansas Ave	03
Topeka Dental, 4301 Huntoon	04
Topeka Medical Center, 918 W 10th Ave	04
V F W, 214 W 6th Ave	03

GOVERNMENT OFFICES

City Hall, 215 E 7th	03
County Courthouse, 214 E 7th St	03
Federal, 424 Kansas Ave	03
Municipal, 215 E 7th	03
State House	12
State Office	12

HOSPITALS

At & Sf, 417 E 6th Ave	07
City County Clinic, 1615 W 8th Ave	06

Kansas Neulogical Institute, 3107 W 21st	04
Menninger Foundation	04
Saint Francis, 1719 W 6th Ave	06
Stormont Vail, 845 Washburn Ave	06
Veterans, 2200 Gage Blvd	22

MILITARY INSTALLATIONS

Forbes A F B	20

UNIVERSITIES AND COLLEGES

Washburn Univ	21

WICHITA 672

POST OFFICE BOXES

Box Nos.		
2-2898	Main Office	01
4000-4999	North Wichita Sta	04
7000-7192	Main Office	01
8000-8999	Munger Sta	08
9001-9112	Delano Sta	12
11000-11999	Washington Sta	02
12001-12152	Delano Sta	12
13000-13999	West Wichita Sta	13
16000-16999	Midland Sta	16
17000-17999	Chisholm Sta	17
18000-18999	Southeast Sta	18

RURAL ROUTES

2	04
3,4	08
5	07
6	16
7	12
8	17
9	14

STATIONS, BRANCHES AND UNITS

Chisholm Sta	09
Mc Connell A F B Br	21
Midland Sta	16
Munger Sta	06
North Wichita Sta	04
Oaklawn Br	16
Park City Br	19
Southeast Sta	07
Washington Street Sta	11
West Wichita Sta	05
General Delivery	02
Postmaster	02

APARTMENTS, HOTELS, MOTELS

Allis, 200 S Broadway	02
Broadview, 101 N Waco	02
Commodore, 222 E Elm	14
Highland House, 1400 N Woodlawn	08
Hillcrest, 115 S Rutan	18
Mc Clellan, 229 E William	02
Parklane Towers, 5051 E Lincoln	18
Shirkmere, 256 N Topeka	02

BUILDINGS

Beacon	02
Bitting	02
Brown	02
Century Plaza	02
College	02
Colorado Derby	02
Commerce Plaza	02
County Court House	03
Derby	02
Farmers & Bankers	02
First National Bank	02
Fourth National Bank	02
Garvey	02
Holiday Inn Plaza	02
Insurance	02
Kaufman	02
One Twenty	02
Orpheum	02
Paige Court	02
Petroleum	02
Rule	02
Sutton Place	02
The Kiva	02
Union Center	02
Union National	02
Vickers K.s.b.&t.	02

GOVERNMENT OFFICES

United States Post Office	02

HOSPITALS

County, 1001 N Minnesota	14
Osteopathic, 2622 W Central	03
Saint Francis 929 N Saint Francis	14
Saint Joseph, 3400 Grand	18
Salvation Army, 2050 W 11th	03
Sedgwick County, 1001 N minneapolis	14
Veterans, 5500 E Kellogg	18
Wesley, 550 N Hillside	14

UNIVERSITIES AND COLLEGES

Friends University, 2000 University	13
Sacred Heart, 3100 Mccormick	13
Wichita State University, 1845 Fairmont	08

KENTUCKY
(Abbreviation: KY)

Aaron	42601
Aberdeen	42201
Acorn	42510
Adairville	42202
Adams	41201
Adolphus	42120
Aflex	41510
Ages	40801
Airport, Br. Cincinnati, O H	45275
Albany	42602
Alcalde	42511
Aleorn	40401
Alexandria	41001
Allegre	42203
Allen	41601
Allensville	42204
Allock	41710
Almo	42020
Alpha	42603
Alpine	42512
Altro	41306
Alva	40802
Alvaton	42122
Amburgey	41801
Anchorage, Br. Louisville	40223
Anco	41711
Anneta, R. Br. Leitchfield	42710
Annville	40402
Appliance Park, Br. Louisville	40225
Argillite	41121
Argo	41511
Arjay	40902
Arlington	42021
Artemus	40903
Arvel	40303
Ary	41712
Ashcamp	41512
Asher	40803
Ashers Fork	40904
Ashland (1st)	41101
Athol	41307
Auburn	42206
Augusta	41002
Ault	41122
Austin	42123
Auxier	41602
Avawam	41713
Avondale, Sta. Paducah	42001
Axtel	40103
Bagdad	40003
Baileys Switch	40905
Bakerton	42711
Balkan	40804
Bandana	42022
Banner	41603
Baptist	41308
Barbourville (1st)	40906
Baughman, R. Br.	40911
Gausdale, R. Br.	40906
Jarvis, R. Br.	40906
Kayjay, R. Br.	40906
Bardstown (1st)	40004
Bardwell	42023
Bark Camp	40720
Barlow	42024
Barnetts Creek	41202
Barrier	42604
Barterville	40304
Baskett	42402

Battletown	40104
Baughman, R. Br. Barbourville	40911
Baxter	40806
Baxter Avenue, Sta. Louisville	40204
Bays	41310
Bear Branch	41714
Bearville	41715
Beattyville	41311
Beaumont	42124
Beauty	41203
Beaver	41604
Beaver Dam	42320
Bedford	40006
Bee Spring	42207
Beech Creek	42321
Beech Grove	42322
Beechmont	42323
Beechville	42125
Beechwood, R. Br. Owenton	40359
Beetle	41123
Belcher	41513
Belfry	41514
Hatfield, R. Br.	41514
Toler, R. Br.	41569
Belknap	41312
Bell Farm	42605
Bellevue, Br. Newport	41073
Belmont, R. Br. Lebanon Junction	40105
Belton	42324
Benham	40807
Benton (1st)	42025
Berea (1st)	40403
Bernstadt, R. Br. London	40741
Berry	41003
Berrys Lick	42208
Bethanna	41401
Bethany	41313
Bethel	40306
Bethelridge	42516
Bethlehem	40007
Betsey	42606
Betsy Layne	41605
Beulah Heights	42607
Beverly	40913
Bevinsville	41606
Big Clifty	42712
Big Creek	40914
Big Laurel	40808
Big Rock	41717
Big Spring	40106
Biggs	41515
Bighill	40405
Bimble	40915
Blackey	41804
Blackford	42403
Blaine	41124
Blair, R. Br. Cumberland	40809
Blairs Mills	41402
Blandville	42026
Blaze	41403
Bledsoe	40810
Bloomfield	40008
Blue Diamond	41718
Blue River	41607
Bluehole	40917
Boaz	42027
Bond	40407
Bondville	40308
Bonnieville	42713
Bonnyman	41719

Boone	40408
Booneville	41314
Boons Camp	41204
Boston	40107
Bow	42714
Bowen	40309
Bowling Green (1st)	42101
Bradfordsville	40009
Bradley	41404
Brandenburg	40108
Breeding	42715
Bremen	42325
Bridge Street, Sta. Paducah	42001
Brightshade, R. Br. Manchester	40962
Brinkley	41805
Broad Bottom	41516
Brodhead	40409
Bronston	42518
Brooklyn	42209
Brooks	40109
Brookside	40811
Brooksville	41004
Browder	42326
Browns Fork	41720
Brownsville	42210
Bruin	41125
Brutus	40920
Bryants Store	40921
Bryantsville	40410
Buchanan, R. Br. Catlettsburg	41205
Buckhorn	41721
Buckingham	41611
Buckner	40010
Buechel, Br. Louisville (see appendix)	
Buffalo	42716
Bulan	41722
Burdine	41517
Burgin	40310
Burke	41126
Burkesville	42717
Burkhart	41315
Burlington	41005
Burna	42028
Burning Fork	41405
Burning Springs, R. Br. Manchester	40922
Burnside	42519
Burnwell	41518
Bush	40724
Buskirk	41406
Busy	41723
Butler	41006
Butterfly	41724
Bybee	40412
Bypro	41612
Cadiz	42211
Golden Pond, R. Br.	42231
Cains Store	42520
Calhoun	42327
California	41007
Callaway	40812
Calvert City (1st)	42029
Calvin	40813
Camp Dix	41127
Camp Taylor, Sta. Louisville	40213
Campbellsburg	40011
Campbellsville (1st)	42718
Campton	41301
Canada	41519
Cane Valley	42720

Caney	41407
Caneyville	42721
Canmer	42722
Cannel City	41408
Cannon	40923
Canoe	41316
Canton	42212
Carcassonne	41806
Carlisle	40311
Carpenter	40726
Carr Creek	41807
Carrie	41725
Carrollton (1st)	41008
Carrsville	42030
Carter	41128
Carver	41409
Casey Creek	42723
Catlettsburg	41129
Buchanan, R. Br.	41205
Cave City	42127
Cawood	40815
Cecilia	42724
Center	42214
Centertown	42328
Central, Sta. Louisville	40202
Central City (1st)	42330
Cerulean	42215
Chance	42725
Chaplin	40012
Chappell	40816
Charley	41207
Chavies	41727
Chenoa	40925
Cherokee	41130
Cherokee, Sta. Louisville	40205
Chesnutburg	40926
Chevrolet	40817
Cinda	41728
Cisco	41410
Clarkson	42726
Clay	42404
Clay City	40312
Clayhole	41317
Clearfield	40313
Cleaton	42332
Clementsville, R. Br. Liberty	42521
Clermont	40110
Cliff	41613
Clifford	41208
Clifty	42216
Climax	40413
Clinton (1st)	42031
Closplint	40927
Clover Bottom	40414
Cloverport	40111
Co Operative	42610
Coal Run, R. Br. Pikeville	41501
Coalgood	40818
Cobb	42405
Cobhill	40415
Cody	41808
Cold Spring-Highland Heights, Br. Newport	41076
Coldiron	40819
College, Sta. Berea	40403
College Campus, Sta. Murray	42071
College Heights, Sta. Bowling Green	42101
College Hill	40416
Colson	41809
Columbia	42728
Sparksville, R. Br.	42778

Columbus	42032
Combs	41729
Concord	41131
Confluence	41730
Conkling	41318
Conley	41411
Conrard	42523
Constance	41009
Constantine	40114
Conway	40417
Cooper	42609
Coopersville	42611
Corbin (1st)	40701
Cordell	41210
Corinth	41010
Cornettsville	41731
Cornishville	40314
Corydon	42406
Cottle	41412
Cottonburg	40418
COVINGTON (1st) (see appendix)	
Coxs Creek	40013
Coxton, R. Br. Harlan	40831
Crab Orchard	40419
Crane Nest	40928
Cranks	40820
Cranston	40315
Crayne	42033
Craynor	41614
Creekville	40929
Crescent Hill, Sta. Louisville	40206
Creston	42524
Crestwood	40014
Crittenden	41030
Crockett	41413
Crofton	42217
Cromona	41810
Cromwell	42333
Cropper	40015
Crown	41811
Crummies	40821
Crutchfield	42034
Crystal	40420
Cub Run	42729
Cubage	40822
Culver	41211
Cumberland	40823
Blair, R. Br.	40809
Cumberland College, Sta. Williamsburg	40769
Cundiff	42730
Cunningham	42035
Curdsville	42334
Curt	41319
Custer	40115
Cutshin	41732
Cutuno	41414
Cynthiana (1st)	41031
Dabolt	40421
Daisy	41733
Dalton	42407
Dana	41615
Danville (1st)	40422
Darfork, R. Br. Hazard	41701
Davella	41212
David	41616
Davisport	41213
Dawson Springs	42408
Day, R. Br. Whitesburg	41858
Dayhoit	40824
Daysboro	41320
Dayton, Br. Newport	41074

De Mossville	41033
Deane	41812
Deatsville	40016
Debord	41214
Decoy	41321
Defoe	40017
Delphia	41735
Delta	42613
Dema	41859
Democrat	41813
Denney	42614
Denniston	40316
Denton	41132
Denver	41215
Depoy	42336
Dewitt	40930
Dexter	42036
Dice	41736
Dingus	41417
Disputanta	40425
Dixon	42409
Dizney	40825
Donerail, R. Br. Lexington	40505
Dongola	41814
Dorton	41520
Dover	41034
Draffin	41521
Drake	42128
Drakesboro	42337
Dreyfus	40426
Drift	41619
Drip Rock	40427
Drum	42527
Dry Creek	41860
Dry Ridge	41035
Dryhill, R. Br. Hyden	41749
Dubre	42731
Duco	41418
Duluth	40428
Dunbar	42219
Dundee	42338
Dunmor	42339
Dunnville	42528
Dwale	41621
Dwarf	41739
Dycusburg	42037
Dyer	40116
Earlington	42410
East Bernstadt	40729
East Mc Dowell	41623
East Point	41216
Eastern	41622
Eastview	42732
Eastwood	40018
Eberle	40429
Echols	42340
Eddyville	42038
Edmonton	42129
Edna	41419
Egypt	40430
Eighty Eight	42130
Ekron	40117
Elamton	41420
Elias	40431
Elihu	42530
Elizabethtown (1st)	42701
Elizaville	41037
Elk Horn	42733
Elkatawa	41322
Elkfork	41421
Elkhorn City	41522
Elkton	42220
Elliottville	40317

Elliston	41038
Elmrock	41624
Elna	41217
Elsie	41422
Emerson	41135
Eminence	40019
Emlyn	40730
Emma	41625
Emmalena	41740
Endicott	41676
Engle	41741
Eolia	40826
Epson	41423
Erline	40931
Erlanger, Br. Covington	41018
Ermine	41815
Essie	40827
Estill	41627
Etoile	42131
Etty	41523
Eubank	42567
Evanston	41628
Evarts	40828
Verda, R. Br.	40872
Ever	41424
Ewing	41039
Ezel	41425
Fairdale	40118
Fairfield	40020
Fairplay	42735
Fairview	42221
Falcon	41426
Fall Rock	40932
Falls Of Rough	40119
Fallsburg	41218
Falmouth	41040
Fancy Farm	42039
Farler	41742
Farmers	40319
Farmington	42040
Faubush	42532
Fedscreek	41524
Felty	40933
Ferguson	42533
Fern Creek, Br. Louisville	40291
Field	40934
Fillmore	41323
Finchville	40022
Finley	42736
Firebrick	41137
Fisherville	40023
Fishtrap	41525
Fisty	41743
Fitch	41138
Flat	41325
Flat Fork	41427
Flat Lick	40935
Flatgap	41219
Flatwoods	41139
Fleming	41816
Flemingsburg	41041
Flippin, R. Br. Tompkinsville	42132
Florence (1st)	41042
Florress	41428
Fogertown	40936
Fonde	40937
Foraker	41429
Ford	40320
Fords Branch	41526
Fordsville	42343
Forest Hills	41527
Fort Campbell (1st)	42223
Fort Knox (1st)	40121
Fort Mitchell, Br. Covington	41017
Fort Thomas, Br. Newport	41075
Foster	41043
Fount	40938
Fountain Run	42133
Fourmile	40939
Foxtown	40432
Frakes	40940
Pearl, R. Br.	40975
Frankfort (1st)	40601
Franklin (1st)	42134
Frazer	42618
Fredonia	42411
Fredville	41430
Freeburn	41528
Frenchburg	40322
Frew	41744
Fritz	41431
Frozen Creek	41326
Fuget	41220
Fulton (1st)	42041
Fultz	41140
Furnace	40433
Galveston	41629
Gamaliel	42140
Gapville	41433
Gardenside, Sta. Lexington	40504
Garfield	40140
Garlin	42739
Garner	41817
Garrard	40941
Garrett	41630
Garrison	41141
Gausdale, R. Br. Barbourville	40906
Gays Creek	41745
Georgetown (1st)	40324
Germantown	41044
Ghent	41045
Gibbs	40942
Gifford	41434
Gilbertsville	42044
Gilley	41818
Gillmore	41327
Girdler	40943
Glasgow (1st)	42141
Glen Dean	40141
Glencoe	41046
Glendale	42740
Glens Fork	42741
Glenview	40025
Golden Pond, R. Br. Cadiz	42231
Goody	41529
Gooserock	40944
Gordon	41819
Goshen	40026
Grace	40945
Gracey	42232
Gradyville	42742
Graham	42344
Grahn	41142
Grand Rivers	42045
Grant	41047
Grassy Creek	41435
Gratz	40327
Gravel Switch	40328
Gray	40734
Gray Hawk	40434
Grays Knob	40829
Grayson	41143
Green Hall	41328
Green Road	40946
Greenmount, R. Br. London	40741
Greensburg	42743
Greenup	41144
Greenville (1st)	42345
Greenwood	42620
Grethel	41631
Guage	41329
Guerrant	41330
Gulnare	41530
Gulston	40830
Gunlock	41632
Guston	40142
Guthrie	42234
Gypsy	41438
Haddix	41331
Hadley	42235
Hager	41439
Hagerhill	41222
Haldeman	40329
Halfway	42150
Hall	41820
Hallie	41821
Halo	41633
Hamlin	42046
Hammond	40947
Hampton	42047
Handshoe	41634
Hanson	42413
Happy	41746
Hardburly	41747
Hardin	42048
Hardinsburg	40143
Hardshell, R. Br. Lost Creek	41348
Hardy	41531
Hardyville	42746
Harlan (1st)	40831
Coxton, R. Br.	40831
Helton, R. Br.	40840
Sunshine, Sta.	40831
Harned	40144
Harold	41635
Harper	41440
Harrods Creek	40027
Harrodsburg (1st)	40330
Hartford	42347
Hartley	41532
Hatfield, R. Br. Belfry	41514
Hatton	40332
Hawesville	42348
Hazard (1st)	41701
Hazel	42049
Hazel Green	41332
Hazel Patch	40735
Head Of Grassy	41145
Hebbardsville	42414
Hebron	41048
Hector	40948
Heidelberg	41333
Heidrick	40949
Helechawa	41334
Hellier	41534
Helton, R. Br. Harlan	40840
Henderson (1st)	42420
Hendricks	41441
Henry Clay, Sta. Lexington (see appendix)	
Herd	40435
Herndon	42236
Hestand	42151
Hi Hat	41636
Hickman	42050
Hickory	42051
Hidalgo	42622
High Bridge	40334

Highsplint	40841
Hikes Point, Sta. Louisville	40220
Hill Top	42624
Hillsboro	41049
Hima	40951
Himyar	40952
Hindman	41822
Hinkle	40953
Hippo	41637
Hisel	40436
Hiseville	42152
Hitchins	41146
Hite	41638
Hode	41223
Hodgenville	42748
Hogue	42535
Holland	42153
Hollybush	41823
Hollyhill	42625
Holmes Mill	40843
Homer	42237
Honaker	41639
Honeybee	42626
Hooker	40954
Hope	40334
Hopkinsville (1st)	42240
Horse Branch	42349
Horse Cave	42749
Hoskinston	40844
Houston	41336
Howardstown	40028
Huddy	41535
Hudson	40145
Hueysville	41640
Huff	42250
Hulen	40845
Hunter	41641
Huntsville	42251
Hustonville	40437
Hyden	41749
Dryhill, R. Br.	41749
Sizerock, R. Br.	41762
Independence	41051
Index	41442
Inez	41224
Ingle	42536
Ingram	40955
Insko	41443
Iroquois, Sta. Louisville	40214
Irvine	40336
Irvington	40146
Island	42350
Island City	41338
Isom	41824
Isonville	41149
Iuka	42052
Ivel	41642
Ivyton	41444
Jabez	42628
Jackhorn	41825
Jackson	41339
Juan, R. Br.	41339
Wilstacy, R. Br.	41392
Jacobs	41150
Jamboree	41536
Jamestown	42629
Jarvis, R. Br. Barbourville	40906
Jeff	41751
Jeffersontown, Br. Louisville	40299
Jeffersonville	40337
Jenkins	41537
Jenson	40957
Jeremiah	41826
Jeriel	41151
Jetson	42252
Jett	40338
Jinks	40438
Job	41225
Johnetta	40439
Johns Run	41152
Jonancy	41538
Jonesville	41052
Juan, R. Br. Jackson	41339
Julip	40736
Junction City	40440
Justell, R. Br. Betsy Layne	41605
Kaliopi	41752
Kayjay, R. Br. Barbourville	40906
Keaton	41226
Keavy	40737
Keene	40339
Keith	40846
Kellacey, R. Br. West Liberty	41472
Keltner	42750
Kenton	41053
Kenvir	40847
Kerby Knob	40441
Kettle	42752
Kettle Island	40958
Kevil	42053
Kidder, R. Br. Bronston	42518
Kimper	41539
Kingbee	42538
Kings Creek	41827
Kings Mountain	40442
Kirksey	42054
Kirksville	40443
Kite	41828
Kitts	40848
Knifley	42753
Knob Lick	42154
Kodak, R. Br. Vicco	41753
Kona	41829
Korea	40340
Krypton	41754
Kuttawa	42055
La Center	42056
La Fayette	42254
La Grange	40031
Lackey	41643
Lamb	42155
Lambric	41340
Lamero	40341
Lamont	41755
Lancaster (1st)	40444
Langley	41645
Langnau	40738
Larkslane	41830
Latonia, Sta. Covington	41015
Laura	41227
Lawrenceburg (1st)	40342
Lawton	41153
Leander	41228
Leatherwood	41756
Lebanon (1st)	40033
Lebanon Junction	40150
Belmont, R. Br.	40105
Leburn	41831
Ledbetter	42058
Lee City	41342
Leeco	41343
Leitchfield (1st)	42754
Anneta, R. Br.	42710
Lejunior	40849
Lenox	41447
Lerose	41344
Letcher	41832
Lewis Creek	40851
Lewisburg	42256
Lewisport	42351
LEXINGTON (1st) (see appendix)	
Liberty	42539
Clementsville, R. Br.	42521
Lick Creek	41540
Lickburg	41448
Lida	40739
Liggett	40852
Ligon	41646
Lily	40740
Lincoln	40961
Lincoln Ridge, R. Br. Simpsonville	40035
Lindseyville	42257
Linefork	41833
Littcarr	41834
Little	41346
Little Sandy	41155
Livermore	42352
Livingston	40445
Lloyd	41156
Load	41229
Lockport	40036
Locust Hill	40151
Lodiburg, R. Br. Irvington	40146
Logansport, R. Br. Morgantown	42258
Logville	41449
Lola	42059
London (1st)	40741
Lone	41347
Lone Oak, Br. Paducah	42001
Lookout	41542
Loretto	40037
Lost Creek	41348
Lothair, R. Br. Hazard	41701
Louellen	40853
Louisa	41230
LOUISVILLE (1st) (see appendix)	
Lovelaceville	42060
Lovely	41231
Lowes	42061
Lowmansville	41232
Loyall	40854
Lucas	42156
Ludlow, Br. Covington	41016
Lynch	40855
Lyndon, Br. Louisville	40222
Lynn, R. Br. Greenup	41144
Lynn Grove	42062
Lynnville	42063
Lytten	41157
Maceo	42355
Mackville	40040
Madisonville (1st)	42431
Maggard	41450
Magnolia	42757
Main Street, Sta. Pikeville	41501
Majestic	41547
Mallie	41836
Malone	41451
Maloneton	41158
Mammoth Cave	42259
Manchester	40962
Brightshade, R. Br.	40962
Burning Springs, R. Br.	40922
Mangum	42540
Manila	41233

Manitou	42436
Mannington	42260
Mannsville	42758
Manton	41648
Maple Mount	42356
Marcum	40963
Mariba	40345
Marion (1st)	42064
Marrowbone	42759
Marshallville	41452
Marshes Siding	42631
Martha	41159
Martin	41649
Martwick, R. Br. Central City	42330
Mary	41350
Mary Alice	40964
Marydell	40751
Mashfork	41453
Mason	41054
Masonic Home	40041
Matthew	41454
Maud	40042
Maulden	40449
Mayfield (1st)	42066
Mayking	41837
Mays Lick	41055
Maysville (1st)	41056
Maytown	41455
Mazie	41160
Mc Andrews	41543
Mc Carr	41544
Mc Combs	41545
Mc Daniels	40152
Mc Dowell	41647
Mc Henry	42354
Mc Kee	40447
Mc Kinney	40448
Mc Quady	40153
Mc Roberts	41835
Mc Veigh	41546
Mc Whorter	40750
Meally	41234
Means	40346
Melber	42069
Melbourne	41059
Melvin	41650
Mentor	41060
Meta, R. Br. Pikeville	41501
Middleburg	42541
Middlesboro (1st)	40965
Middletown, Br. Louisville	40243
Midway	40347
Milburn	42070
Milford	41061
Mill Springs	42632
Millard, R. Br. Pikeville	41501
Millersburg	40348
Mills	40970
Millstone	41838
Milltown	42761
Millwood	42762
Milo	41235
Milton	40045
Mima	41456
Minerva	41062
Minnie	41651
Mintonville	42542
Miracle	40856
Mistletoe	41351
Mitchellsburg	40452
Mize	41352
Monticello	42633
Montpelier	42763
Mooleyville	40154
Moon	41457
Moorefield	40350
Moores Creek	40453
Moorman	42357
Morehead (1st)	40351
Moreland	40454
Morganfield (1st)	42437
Morgantown	42261
Logansport, R. Br.	42258
Morning View	41063
Morrill	40455
Morris Fork	41353
Mortons Gap	42440
Mount Eden	40046
Mount Hermon	42157
Mount Olivet	41064
Mount Sherman	42764
Mount Sterling (1st)	40353
Mount Vernon	40456
Pine Hill, R. Br.	40364
Mount Washington	40047
Mountain Valley	41354
Mousie	41839
Mouthcard	41548
Mozelle	40858
Mud Lick	42158
Muldraugh	40155
Mummie	40457
Munfordville	42765
Murray (1st)	42071
Muses Mills	41065
Myers, R. Br. Carlisle	40311
Myra	41549
Nancy	42544
Napfor	41757
Napier	40859
Naples, R. Br. Ashland	41101
Narrows	42358
Nazareth	40048
Neafus	42766
Nebo	42441
Ned	41355
Nelse	41550
Neon	41840
Nerinx	40049
Netty	41458
Nevisdale	40754
New Castle	40050
New Concord	42076
New Haven	40051
New Hope	40052
New Liberty	40355
New Zion	40458
Newfoundland	41162
Newgarden, Sta. Fort Knox	40121
Newman	42359
NEWPORT (1st) (see appendix)	
Nicholasville (1st)	40356
Nippa	41236
Noble	41356
Noctor	41357
Noland, R. Br. Irvine	40336
North, Sta. Lexington (see appendix)	
North Middletown	40357
North Pleasureville, Sta. Pleasureville	40057
Nortonville	42442
Nuckols	42360
Oak Grove	42262
Oakland	42159
Oakton	42077
Oakville	42263
Offutt	41237
Ogle	40971
Oil Springs	41238
Okolona, Br. Louisville (see appendix)	
Olaton	42361
Old Allen, R. Sta. Allen	41601
Old Landing	41358
Oldtown	41163
Olive Hill	41164
Ollie	42264
Olmstead	42265
Olympia	40358
Omaha	41841
Oneida	40972
Onton	42443
Ophir	41459
Orkney	41652
Orlando	40460
Orville, R. Br. Pleasureville	40057
Oscaloosa	41842
Oven Fork	40861
Overlook, R. Br. Eddyville	42038
Owensboro (1st)	42301
Owenton	40359
Owingsville	40360
Owsley, R. Br. Pikeville	41501
Paducah (1st)	42001
Paint Lick	40461
Paintsville (1st)	41240
Paris (1st)	40361
Park City	42160
Parkers Lake	42634
Parksville	40464
Parrot	40465
Partridge	40862
Pathfork	40863
Patsey	40466
Paw Paw	41551
Payne Gap	41552
Payneville	40157
Peabody	40974
Pearl, R. Br. Frakes	40975
Pebworth	41359
Pellville	42364
Pembroke	42266
Pendleton	40055
Penrod	42365
Peoples	40467
Perry Park	40363
Perryville	40468
Petersburg	41080
Pewee Valley	40056
Peytonsburg	42768
Phelps	41553
Philpot	42366
Phyllis	41554
Pigeonroost	40976
Pike View	42770
Pikeville (1st)	41501
Pilgrim	41250
Pilot	40469
Pine Grove, R. Br. Winchester	40476
Pine Hill, R. Br. Mount Vernon	40364
Pine Knot	42635
Pine Mountain	40864
Pine Ridge	41360
Pine Top	41843

Pineville (1st)	40977
Pinsonfork	41555
Pippa Passes	41844
Raven, R. Br.	41861
Piso	41556
Pittsburg	40755
Plank	40978
Pleasant View, K. Br. Williamsburg	40769
Pleasure Ridge Park, Br. Louisville	40258
Pleasureville	40057
Plummers Landing	41081
Pointer	42547
Pomeroyton	40365
Poole	42444
Poplarville	42548
Port Royal	40058
Portsmouth	41361
Powderly	42367
Premium	41845
Preston	40366
Prestonsburg (1st)	41653
Price	41654
Primrose	41362
Princeton (1st)	42445
Printer	41655
Prospect	40059
Providence	42450
Provo	42267
Pryse	40471
Public	42637
Pueblo	42549
Pulaski	42550
Puncheon	41846
Putney	40865
Pyramid	41656
Quality	42268
Quicksand	41363
Quincy	41166
Raccoon	41557
Raceland, Br. Russell	41169
Radcliff (1st)	40160
Ransom	41558
Raven, R. Br. Pippa Passes	41861
Ravenna	40472
Raywick	40060
Ready	42771
Redbush	41251
Redfox	41847
Redwine	41462
Reed	42451
Regina	41559
Reidland, Br. Paducah	42001
Relief	41463
Renfro Valley	40473
Revelo	42638
Reynolds Station	42368
Rhodelia	40161
Rice Station	40474
Ricetown	41364
Riceville	41252
Richardson	41253
Richardsville	42270
Richelieu	42271
Richmond (1st)	40475
Rineyville	40162
Risner	41658
Ritchie	41758
Ritner	42639
River	41254
Riverside	42272
Roark	40979
Robards	42452
Robinson	41082
Robinson Creek	41560
Rochester	42273
Rockfield	42274
Rockholds	40759
Rockhouse	41561
Rockport	42369
Rocky Hill	42163
Rockybranch	42640
Rogers	41365
Rosine	42370
Rosslyn	40369
Roundhill	42275
Rouse, Sta. Covington	41014
Rousseau	41366
Rowdy	41367
Rowletts	42772
Roxana	41848
Royalton	41464
Rumsey	42371
Rush	41168
Russell	41169
Russell Springs	42642
Russellville (1st)	42276
Ruth	42552
Sacramento	42372
Sadieville	40370
Sadler	42773
Saint Catharine	40061
Saint Charles	42453
Saint Francis	40062
Saint Helens	41368
Saint Joseph	42373
Saint Mary	40063
Saint Matthews, Br. Louisville	40207
Saint Paul	41170
Saldee	41369
Salem	42078
Salt Gum	40980
Salt Lick	40371
Salvisa	40372
Salyersville	41465
Sample	40163
Samuels	40064
Sanders	41083
Sandgap	40481
Sandy Hook	41171
Sardis, R. Br. Maysville	41056
Sassafras	41759
Sasser	40760
Saul	40981
Sawyer	42643
Saxton, R. Br. Williamsburg	40769
Scalf	40982
Science Hill	42553
Scottsville (1st)	42164
Scranton	40373
Scuddy	41760
Se Ree	40164
Sebastians Branch	41370
Sebree	42455
Seco	41849
Sedalia	42079
Seitz	41466
Sergent	41850
Sextons Creek	40983
Sharon Grove	42280
Sharpsburg	40374
Shelbiana	41562
Shelby, Sta. Louisville (see appendix)	
Shelby Gap	41563
Shelbyville (1st)	40065
Shepherdsville (1st)	40165
Sheridan	42080
Shively, Br. Louisville	40216
Shoal	41761
Shopville	42554
Sibert	40984
Sidell	40985
Sidney	41564
Siler	40763
Silver Grove	41085
Silverhill	41467
Simpsonville	40067
Lincoln Ridge, R. Br.	40035
Sinai	40375
Sitka	41255
Sizerock, R. Br. Hyden	41762
Skyline	41851
Slade	40376
Slaughters	42456
Slavans	42645
Slemp	41763
Sloans Valley	42555
Smilax	41764
Smile	40377
Smith	40867
Smith Mills	42457
Smith Town	42646
Smithfield	40068
Smithland	42081
Smiths Creek	41172
Smiths Grove	42171
Smithsboro	41852
Soft Shell	41853
Soldier	41173
Somerset (1st)	42501
Sonora	42776
South	42777
South Carrollton	42374
South Irvine	40483
South Portsmouth	41174
South Shore	41175
South Union	42283
Southdown, R. Br. Ermine	41815
Southgate, Br. Newport	41071
Southland, Br. Lexington	40503
Sparksville, R. Br. Columbia	42778
Sparta	41086
Speight	41565
Spence, Sta. Newport	41071
Spottsville	42458
Spring Lick	42779
Spring Station	40378
Springfield	40069
Texas, R. Br.	40072
Sprule	40986
Spurlock	40987
Squib	42556
Stab	42557
Stacy Fork	41468
Staffordsville	41256
Stambaugh	41257
Stamping Ground	40379
Standiford, Sta. Louisville	40221
Stanford	40484
Stanley	42375
Stanton	40380
Stanville	41659
Stark	41176
Stay	41373
Stearns	42647
Steele	41566

Steff	42780
Stella	41469
Stephens	41177
Stephensburg	42781
Stephensport	40170
Steubenville	42648
Stinnett	40868
Stone	41567
Stoney Fork	40988
Stopover	41568
Straight Creek	40989
Strunk	42649
Sturgis	42459
Sublett	41470
Subtle, R. Br. Edmonton	42129
Sudith	40381
Sullivan	42460
Sulphur	40070
Sulphur Well, R. Br. Edmonton	42129
Summer Shade	42166
Summersville	42782
Summit	42783
Sunfish	42284
Sunnybrook	42650
Sunshine, Sta. Harlan	40831
Swamp Branch	41258
Swampton	41471
Sweeden	42285
Symbol	40764
Symsonia	42082
Talbert	41377
Talcum	41765
Tallega	41378
Tanksley	40990
Tateville	42558
Taylorsville	40071
Teaberry	41660
Tedders	40991
Teges	40992
Texas, R. Br. Springfield	40072
Thealka	41259
Thelma	41260
Thornton	41855
Thousandsticks	41766
Threeforks	41261
Tiline	42083
Tina	41768
Tinsley	40993
Toler, R. Br. Belfry	41569
Tollesboro	41189
Tolu	42084
Tomahawk	41262
Tompkinsville	42167
Flippin, R. Br.	42132
Topmost	41862
Totz	40870
Toulouse	41769
Touristville	42651
Tram	41663
Trammel, R. Br. Scottsville	42164
Trappist	40073
Tremont	40871
Trenton	42286
Tribbey	41770
Trimble	42559
Trinity	41190
Trosper	40995
Turkey	41382
Turkey Creek	41570
Turners Station	40075
Tutor Key	41263
Tuttle	40996

Tyner	40486
Typo	41771
Ulvah	41856
Ulysses	41264
Union	41091
Union City	40382
Union Star	40171
Uniontown	42461
Unity, Sta. Ashland	41101
University, Sta. Lexington	40506
Upper Tygart	41178
Upton	42784
Urban	40765
Utica	42376
Vada	41383
Valeria	41384
Valley Station, Br. Louisville	40272
Van	41857
Van Lear	41265
Vanceburg	41179
Vancleve	41385
Vanzant	40174
Varney	41571
Verda, R. Br. Evarts	40872
Verne	40766
Verona	41092
Versailles (1st)	40383
Vertrees	42785
Vest	41772
Vicco	41773
Kodak, R. Br.	41753
Victory	40767
Vincent	41386
Vine Grove	40175
Viper	41774
Virgie	41572
Volga	41266
Vortex	41387
Waco	40385
Waddy	40076
Walden	40768
Waldo	41664
Wales	41573
Walker	40997
Walkertown, Sta. Hazard	41701
Wallingford	41093
Wallins Creek	40873
Walnut Grove	42563
Walton	41094
Waneta	40488
War Creek	41388
Warbranch	40874
Warfield	41267
Warsaw	41095
Washington	41096
Water Valley	42085
Watergap	41665
Waterview	42786
Watts, R. Br. Lost Creek	41348
Waverly	42462
Wax	42787
Wayland	41666
Waynesburg	40489
Webbs Cross Roads	42652
Webbville	41180
Webster	40176
Weeksbury	41667
Welchburg	40490
Welchs Creek	42287
Wellington	40387
Wendover	41775
West Irvine	40491
West Liberty	41472

West Louisville	42377
West Paducah	42086
West Point	40177
West Prestonsburg	41668
West Somerset, Sta. Somerset	42501
West Van Lear	41268
Westbend	40388
Westport	40077
Westview	40178
Westwood, Br. Ashland	41101
Wheatcroft	42463
Wheatley	40389
Wheelersburg	41473
Wheelwright	41669
Whick	41390
White Mills	42788
White Oak	41474
White Plains	42464
Whitehouse	41269
Whitesburg	41858
Whitesville	42378
Whitley City	42653
Wiborg	42654
Wickliffe	42087
Widecreek	41391
Wilbur	41270
Wild Cat	40998
Wildie	40492
Willailla	40493
Willard	41181
Williamsburg (1st)	40769
Cumberland College, Sta.	40769
Pleasant View, R. Br.	40769
Saxton, R. Br.	40769
Wofford, R. Br.	40770
Williamsport	41271
Williamstown	41097
Willis Creek	42789
Willisburg	40078
Willow Shade	42169
Wilmore	40390
Wilstacy, R. Br Jackson	41392
Win	41272
Winchester (1st)	40391
Pine Grove, R. Br.	40470
Wind Cave	40494
Windsor	42565
Windy	42655
Wingo	42088
Winifred	41273
Winston	40495
Wittensville	41274
Wofford, R. Br. Williamsburg	40770
Wolf	41182
Wolf Coal	41393
Wolverine	41394
Wonnie	41475
Woodbine	40771
Woodburn	42170
Woodbury	42288
Woodman	41574
Woodsbend	41476
Woollum	40999
Wooton	41776
Worthington	41183
Worthville	41098
Wrigley	41477
Wurtland, R. Br. Greenup	41144
Yeaddiss	41777
Yeaman	42379

COVINGTON 410

POST OFFICE BOXES

Box Nos.

1-106	Rouse Sta	14
1-125	Fort Mitchell Br	17
1-255	Erlanger Br	18
1-1108	Main Office	12
101-399	Ludlow Br	16
802-917	Latonia Sta	15

RURAL ROUTES

1,2	17
5	15

STATIONS, BRANCHES AND UNITS

Erlanger Br	18
Fort Mitchell Br	17
Latonia Sta	15
Ludlow Br	16
Rouse Sta	14
General Delivery	11
Postmaster	11

BUILDINGS

Coppin	11
Covington Trust & Banking Co	11
First Nat Banking & Trust Co	11
Internal Revenue Service	19

HOSPITALS

Booth Memorial	11
Saint Elizabeth	14

UNIVERSITIES AND COLLEGES

Community College	11
Thomas More College	17

LEXINGTON 405

POST OFFICE BOXES

Box Nos

1-2000	Lexington	01
4001-4250	Gardenside	04
4431-5089	University Sta	06
5001-5500	North	05
7001-7300	Henry Clay Sta	02
8001-8297	Southland Br	03

RURAL ROUTES

1	03
2	04
3,4	05
5	02
6	05
7	02
8	05
9	05

STATIONS, BRANCHES AND UNITS

Donerail Rural Br	05
Gardenside Sta	04
Henry Clay Sta	02
North Sta	05
Southland Br	03
University Sta	06
General Delivery	07
Postmaster	07

APARTMENTS, HOTELS, MOTELS

Beaumont Cabana Apts., 2044 Georgian Way	04
Connie R. Griffith Manor, 540 West 2nd	08
Continental Apts, 2121 Nicholasville Road	03
Cooperstown	08
Creekside Apts., 2223 Devonport Dr	04
Hanover Towers Apts., 101 S. Hanover Ave	02
Holly Tree Manor Apts., 1435 S. Limestone St	03
Jamestown Apts, 2200 Richmond Rd	02
Lansbrook Village Apts., 3400 Lansdowne Dr	03
Lexington Hills Apts, 2150 Richmond Rd	02
Locustwood Estates, Georgetown Rd	05
Phoenix Hotel, 120 E Main	07
Rolling Ridge Apts 3525 Tates Creek Rd	02
Shawneetown Apts	03
Todds Trace Apts, 151 Todds Road	09
Wellington Arms Apts., 508 East Main Street	08

BUILDINGS

American Mutual, 496 Southland Dr	03
Bakhaus, 1500 Leestown Road	07
Bank Of Commerce, 318 E. Main	07
Bank Of Lexington, 311 E Main	07
Cardinal Valley Shopping Center, 2000 Bl Versailles Rd	04
Central Bank, 163 W Short	07
Chevy Chase Shopping Center, E High & Euclid	02
Citizens Bank Square	07
Citizens Union National Bank, 201 W Short	07
Cross Roads Shopping Center, Nicholasville Rd	03
Dunn, 288 S Limestone	08
Eastland Shopping Center, Winchester Rd	05
Exchange, 147 N Upper	07
Fayette Mall, Nicholasville Rd	03
Federal, 101 Barr	07

First Federal Savings & Loan, 134 N Limestone	07
First Security National Bank & Trust Co, 167 W Main	07
Gardenside Shopping Center, 1800 Alexandria Dr	04
General Telephone Company, 2001 Harrodsburg Rd	07
Hi-Acres Shopping Center, 1800 Bl Bryan Station Rd	05
Idle Hour Shopping Center, 2000 Richmond Rd	02
Imperial Plaza Shopping Center, 300 Waller Ave	04
Internal Revenue, 1500 Leestown Rd	05
International Business Machines Corporation	07
Kentucky Central, 200 E Main	07
Kentucky Utilities Company, 120 S Limestone	07
Lafayette Shopping Center, 1900 Harrodsbrg Rd	03
Lansbrook Village Shopping Center, 3500 Lansdowne Dr	03
Lexington Mall, 2397 Richmond Rd	02
Meadowthrope Shopping Center, 1400 Leestown Rd	05
Northland Shopping Center, 1300 N Broadway	05
Nunn, 121 Walnut	07
Romany Road Shopping Center, 300 Romany Road	02
Second National Bank & Trust Co, 123 Cheapside	07
Security Trust, 271 W Short	07
Social Security, 1500 Leestown Rd	05
Southland Shopping Center, 300 Southland Dr	03
State Office, 300 S Upper	08
Turfland Mall, 2000 Bl Harrodsburg Rd	04
Vittetow, 269 W Main	07
Zandale Shopping Center, 2200 Nichlsvlle Rd	03

GOVERNMENT OFFICES

City Hall, 136 Walnut	07
Courthouse, 201 W Main	07
Lexington Fayette County Health Departmen, 330 Waller Ave	04

HOSPITALS

Cardinal Hill Convalescent Hospital, 2050 Versailles Rd	04
Central Baptist Hospital, 1740 S Limestone	03
Eastern State Hospital, 627 W 4th	08
Good Samaritan Hospital, 310 S Limestone	08
National Institute Of Mental Health, Leestown Road	07

Lexington (Con.)   405

Saint Joseph Hospital, 1400
  Harrodsburg Rd 04
Shriners Hospital For
  Crippled Children, 1900
  Richmond Rd 02
University Hospital, 800 Rose
  St 06
Veterans Administration
  Hospital, Leestown Rd 07

MILITARY INSTALLATIONS

Lexington Blue Grass Army
  Depot 07

UNIVERSITIES AND COLLEGES

Coppertown 08
Lexington Theological
  Seminary, 631 S
  Limestone 08
Transylvania College, 201 W
  3rd 08
University Of Kentucky,
  Limestone & Euclid 06

LOUISVILLE   402

POST OFFICE BOXES

Box Nos.
1-2159	Louisville	01
4001-4336	Baxter Avenue	
	Sta	04
5001-5657	Cherokee Sta.	05
6001-6247	Crescent Hill	
	Sta	06
7001-7564	Saint Matthews	
	Br	07
8001-8434	E Sta	08
10001-10128	D Sta	10
11001-11086	H Sta	11
12001-12206	R Sta	12
13001-13321	Camp Taylor	
	Sta	13
14001-14303	Iroquois Sta.	14
16001-16374	Shively Sta	16
17001-17272	Shelby Sta	17
18001 18430	Buechel Br	18
19001-19307	Okolona Br	19
20001-20277	Hikes Point	
	Sta	20
21001-21477	Standiford Sta.	21
22001-22277	Lyndon Br	22
23001-23447	Anchorage Br	23
43001-43298	Middletown Br.	43
58001-58416	Pleasure Ridge	
	Park Br	58
72001-72386	Valley Station	
	Br	72
91001-91250	Fern Creek Br	91
99001-99398	Jeffersontown	
	Br	99

RURAL ROUTES

1	22
2,3,4	99
5,6	91
7,8	72
10	18
11,12,13,14,15,16,17.	23
18	99
19	91

STATIONS, BRANCHES AND UNITS

Anchorage Br	23
Appliance Park Br	25
Baxter Avenue Sta	04
Buechel Br	18
Camp Taylor Sta	13
Central Sta	02
Cherokee Sta	05
Crescent Hill Sta	06
Fern Creek Br	91
Hikes Point Sta	20
Iroquois Sta	14
Jeffersontown Br	99
Lyndon Br	22
Middletown Br	43
Okolona Br	19
Pleasure Ridge Park Br ...	58
Saint Matthews Br	07
Shelby Sta	17
Shively Br	16
Standiford Sta	21
Valley Station Br	72
General Delivery	02
Postmaster	01

APARTMENTS, HOTELS, MOTELS

Adams House, 512 W Ormsby	
Ave	03
Admiral Benbow Inn, 3315	
Bardstown Rd.	18
Alamo Plaza Court, 5229	
Dixie Hwy	16
Albert Pick Motel, 1620	
Arthur	17
Barkley Towers, 3201 Leith	
Ln	18
Berkeley, 664 S 4th	02
Browns, 3320 Bardstown Rd.	18
Churchill Inn, 4444 Dixie	
Hwy	16
Commodore, 2140	
Bonnycastle Ave.	05
Dartmouth Apartments, 1416	
Willow Ave	04
Executive Inn, Watterson Expy	
At Fairgrounds	13
Guthrie Coke, 411 W	
Chestnut	02
Hampton Hall, 209 York ...	03
Hillebrand House, 1235 S	
3rd	03
Holiday Inn, Central, 1921	
Bishop Ln	18
Holiday Inn, Downtown, 927	
S 2nd	03
Holiday Inn, Northeast, 4805	
Brownsboro Rd.	07

Holiday Inn, South, 3317	
Fern Valley Rd	13
Holiday Inn, Southeast, 3255	
Bardstown Rd.	05
Howard Johnsons Motor	
Lodge, 100 E Jefferson.	02
Howard Johnsons Motor	
Lodge, 4621 Shelbyville	
Rd	07
Leslies Motel, 5215 Dixie	
Hwy	16
Louisville Manor Motor Court,	
4600 Dixie Hwy.	16
Mayflower Apartments, 425	
W Ormsby Ave	03
Milner Highland, 231 W	
Jefferson	02
Motel 6, 3304 Bardstown Rd.	18
Parks Motel, 4700 Dixie Hwy.	16
Puritan Apartments, 1244 S	
4th	03
Quality Courts Motel, 735 S	
2nd	02
Ramada Inn, 9700 Bluegrass	
Pky	99
Roadway Inn, Airport, 1465	
Gardiner Ln	13
Roadway Inn, 101 E.	
Jefferson	02
Salem Square Apartments,	
521 Zorn Ave	06
Seelbach, 500 S 4th	01
Sheraton Inn, Louisville East,	
9608 Blairwood Rd	22
Southland, 1315 S 3rd	08
Standiford Motor Hotel,	
Watterson Expy At Airport.	21
Stouffers Inn, 120 W	
Broadway	02
Travelodge, 401 S 2nd	02
Trinity Towers Apartments,	
537 S 3rd	02
Watterson, 415 W Walnut..	02
Willow Terrace Apartments,	
1412 Willow Ave	04
Y M C A, 231 W Broadway.	02
Y W C A, 604 S 3rd	02
York Towers, 201 York	03
800, 800 S 4th	03

BUILDINGS

American Life, 431 W Main.	02
Brown, 321 W Broadway....	02
Center, 522 W Jefferson.....	02
Commerce, 304 W Liberty...	02
Commonwealth, 674 S 4th...	02
Cosmopolitan, 981 S 3rd.....	03
Doctors Office, 250 E Liberty..	02
Fincastle, 305 W Broadway..	02
Heyburn, 332 W Broadway...	02
Hilliard, 419 W Jefferson	02
Hoffman, 139 S 4th	02
Kentucky Home Life 239 S	
5th	02
Kenyon, 112 S 5th	02
Lincoln Federal, 600 S 4th ..	02
Lincoln Towers, 6100	
Dutchmans Ln	05
Louisville Trust, 508 S 5th..	02
Manor, E Taylor, 312 S 4th..	02
Mc Dowell, 505 S 3rd	02

Louisville (Con.) 402

Medical Arts, 1169 Eastern
  Pky 17
Medical Towers, N, 233 E
  Gray 02
Medical Towers, S, 234 E
  Gray 02
Metropolitan, 151 S 5th 02
Portland Federal, 200 W
  Broadway 02
Republic, 429 W Walnut 02
Snead, 817 W Market 02
Speed, 333 Guthrie 02
Starks, 455 S 4th 02
Theatre, 629 1/2 S 4th 02
Tyler, 319 W Jefferson 02
Washington, 136 S 4th 02
Watterson City, 1941 Bishop
  Ln 18
300, 300 W Main 02

GOVERNMENT OFFICES

City Hall, 6th & Jefferson 02
Courthouse, 531 W Jefferson .. 02
Federal, 600 Federal Pl 02
Fiscal Courts, 527 Court Pl 02
Post Office, 601 W Broadway .. 02
State Office, 600 Cedar 03

HOSPITALS

Central State, Lakeland Rd 23
Childrens, 226 E Chestnut 02
City, 323 E Chestnut 02
General, 323 E Chestnut 02
Hazelwood Sanitarium, 1800
  Bluegrass Ave 15

Jewish, 217 E Chestnut 02
Kentucky Baptist, 810 Barret
  Ave 04
Kosair Crippled Children, 982
  Eastern Pkwy 17
Louisville Memorial, 2215
  Portland Ave 12
Methodist Evangelical, 315 E
  Broadway 02
Norton Memorial Infirmary,
  231 W Oak St 03
Our Lady Of Peace, 2020
  Newburg Rd 05
Red Cross, 1436 S Shelby 01
Saint Anthony, 1313 St
  Anthony Pl 04
Saint Joseph Infirmary, 735
  Eastern Pkwy 17
Saints Mary & Elizabeth,
  4400 Churchman Ave 15
Veterans Administration,
  Mellwood Ave & Zorn Av 02

UNIVERSITIES AND COLLEGES

Bellarmine, 2009 Norris Pl 05
Presbyterian Seminary, 1042
  Alta Vista Rd 05
Southern Baptist Theological
  Seminary, 2825 Lexington
  Rd 06
Spalding, 851 S 4th 03
U Of L School Of Dentistry,
  129 E Broadway 02
U Of L School Of Medicine,
  101 W Chestnut 02
U Of L School Of Music,
  9001 Shelbyville Rd 22

University Of Louisville, 2301
  S 3rd 08
Ursuline, 3105 Lexington Rd .. 06

NEWPORT 410

POST OFFICE BOXES

Box Nos.		
1-56	Dayton Br	74
1-147	Cold Spring-Highland Heights Br	76
1-274	Fort Thomas Br	75
1-477	Main Office	72
1-539	Bellevue Br	73
1000-1199	Spence Sta	71

RURAL ROUTES

1 76

STATIONS, BRANCHES AND UNITS

Bellevue Br 73
Cold Spring-Highland
  Heights Br 76
Dayton Br 74
Fort Thomas Br 75
Southgate Br 71
Spence Sta 71
General Delivery 71
Postmaster 71

LOUISIANA
(Abbreviation: LA)

Abbeville (1st)	70510
Abita Springs	70420
Acadia Academy, R. Br.	
Eunice	70535
Acme	71316
Addis	70710
Aimwell	71401
Akers	70421
Albany	70711
Alco	71402
Alexandria (1st)	71301
Alto, R. Br. Rayville	71216
Ama	70031
Amelia	70340
Amite (1st)	70422
Anacoco	71403
Angie	70426
Angola	70712
Arabi (1st)	70032
Arcadia	71001
Archibald	71218
Arnaudville	70512
Ashland	71002
Athens	71003
Atlanta	71404
Audubon, Sta. Baton Rouge	70806
Avery Island	70513
Avondale, Br. Westwego	70094
Bains	70713
Baker (1st)	70714
Baldwin	70514
Ball	71405
Barataria	70036
Barksdale A F B, Br.	
Shreveport	71110
Basile	70515
Baskin	71219
Bastrop (1st)	71220
Batchelor	70715
BATON ROUGE (1st) (see appendix)	
Bayou Chicot, R. Br. Ville Platte	70586
Bayou Goula	70716
Bayou Pigeon, R. Br. Plaquemine	70764
Bayou Sorrel, R. Br. Plaquemine	70764
Bayou Vista, R. Br. Morgan City	70380
Bel, R. Br. Reeves	70675
Belcher	71004
Bell City	70630
Belle Chasse (1st)	70037
Belle River, R. Br. Morgan City	70380
Belle Rose	70341
Klotzville, R. Br.	70370
Belmont	71406
Benson	71005
Bentley	71407
Benton	71006
Bernice	71222
Berwick	70342
Bethany	71007
Bienville	71008
Big Bend	71318
Blanchard	71009
Blanks	70717
Bogalusa (1st)	70427

Bonita	71223
Boothville	70038
Bordelonville	71320
Bossier City (1st)	71010
Bourg	70343
Boutte	70039
Boyce	71409
Braithwaite	70040
Branch	70516
Breaux Bridge (1st)	70517
Bridge City, Br. Westwego	70094
Brittany	70718
Broadmoor, Sta. New Orleans	70125
Broadview, Sta. Baton Rouge (see appendix)	
Broussard	70518
Brownfields, Br. Baton Rouge	70807
Brusly	70719
Bryceland	71014
Buckeye	71321
Bueche	70720
Bunkie (1st)	71322
Buras (1st)	70041
Burnside, R. Br. Gonzales	70738
Bush	70431
Bywaters, Sta. New Orleans	70117
Cade	70519
Calcasieu, R. Br. Glenmora	71433
Calhoun	71225
Calvin	71410
Cameron	70631
Campti	71411
Capitol, Sta. Baton Rouge	70804
Carencro	70520
Carlisle	70042
Carrollton, Sta. New Orleans	70118
Carville	70721
Caspiana	71015
Castor	71016
Catahoula, R. Br. Saint Martinville	70582
Cecilia	70521
Cedar Grove, Sta. Shreveport	71106
Centenary, Sta. Shreveport	71104
Center Point	71323
Centerville	70522
Central City, Sta. Baton Rouge	70806
Chackbay, R. Br. Thibodaux	70301
Chalmette (1st)	70043
Charenton	70523
Chase	71324
Chataignier	70524
Chatham	71226
Chauvin	70344
Chef Menteur, Sta. New Orleans (see appendix)	
Cheneyville	71325
Chestnut	71017
Chopin	71412
Choudrant	71227
Church Point	70525
Clarence	71414
Clarks	71415
Clay, R. Br. Ruston	71228
Clayton	71326
Clinton	70722
Cloutierville	71416
Coltax	71417
College, Sta. Hammond	70401

Collinston	71229
Columbia	71418
Convent	70723
Uncle Sam, R. Br.	70792
Union, R. Br.	70723
Converse	71419
Cooper Road, Br. Shreveport	71101
Cotton Valley	71018
Cottonport	71327
Coushatta (1st)	71019
Covington (1st)	70433
Creole	70632
Creston	71020
Crowley (1st)	70526
Crowville	71230
Cullen	71021
Custom House, Sta. New Orleans	70116
Cut Off	70345
Cypress	71420
Darnell, R. Br. Pioneer	71231
Darrow	70725
Davant	70046
De Quincy	70633
De Ridder (1st)	70634
Delcambre	70528
Delhi	71232
Delta	71233
Denham Springs (1st)	70726
Derry	71421
Des Allemands	70030
Destrehan	70047
Deville	71328
Diamond	70048
Dixie	71022
Dodson	71422
Donaldsonville (1st)	70346
Donner	70352
Downsville	71234
Downtown, Sta. Morgan City	70380
Downtown, Sta. Monroe	71201
Doyline	71023
Drew, Sta. Lake Charles	70601
Dry Creek	70637
Dry Prong	71423
Dubach	71235
Dubberly	71024
Dulac	70353
Dunn	71236
Duplessis	70728
Dupont	71329
Duson	70529
East Point	71025
Easton	70530
Echo	71330
Edgard	70049
Effie	71331
Egan	70531
Elizabeth	70638
Elmer	71424
Elton	70532
Embarkation, Sta. New Orleans	70140
Empire	70050
England A F B, Br. Alexandria	71301
Enterprise	71425
Eola	71332
Epps	71237
Erath	70533
Eros	71238
Erwinville	70729
Estherwood	70534

Ethel ... 70730
Eunice (1st) ... 70535
Evangeline ... 70537
Evans ... 70639
Evergreen ... 71333
Extension ... 71239
Fair Grounds, Sta. Shreveport ... 71109
Fairbanks ... 71240
Farmerville ... 71241
Felixville ... 70731
Fenton ... 70640
Ferriday (1st) ... 71334
Fields ... 70641
Fisher ... 71426
Flatwoods ... 71427
Flora ... 71428
Florien ... 71429
Fluker ... 70436
Folsom ... 70437
Forbing ... 71026
Fordoche ... 70732
Forest ... 71242
Forest Hill ... 71430
Forked Island, R. Br. Abbeville ... 70510
Fort Necessity ... 71243
Fort Polk, Br. Leesville ... 71459
Franklin (1st) ... 70538
Franklinton (1st) ... 70438
French Settlement ... 70733
Frierson ... 71027
Frisco, R. Br. Livonia ... 70755
Frogmore ... 71335
Fullerton ... 70642
Galliano ... 70354
Garden City ... 70540
Gardner ... 71431
Garyville ... 70051
Geismar ... 70734
Gentilly, Sta. New Orleans ... 70122
Georgetown ... 71432
Gheens ... 70355
Gibsland ... 71028
Gibson ... 70356
Gilbert ... 71336
Gilliam ... 71029
Girard ... 71244
Glenmora ... 71433
Gloster ... 71030
Glynn ... 70736
Golden Meadow ... 70357
South Lafourche, R. Br. ... 70338
Goldonna ... 71031
Gonzales (1st) ... 70737
Burnside, R. Br. ... 70738
Good Hope, Br. Norco ... 70079
Good Pine ... 71337
Gorum ... 71434
Goudeau ... 71338
Grambling ... 71245
Gramercy ... 70052
Grand Cane ... 71032
Grand Chenier ... 70643
Grand Coteau ... 70541
Grand Isle ... 70358
Grant ... 70644
Gray ... 70359
Grayson ... 71435
Greensburg ... 70441
Greenwell Springs ... 70739
Greenwood ... 71033
Gretna (1st) ... 70053

Grosse Tete ... 70740
Gueydan ... 70542
Hackberry ... 70645
Hahnville ... 70057
Haile, R. Br. Marion ... 71246
Hall Summit ... 71034
Hamburg ... 71339
Hammond (1st) ... 70401
Hanna ... 71035
Narahan, Br. New Orleans ... 70123
Hardwood ... 70742
Harmon ... 71036
Harrisonburg ... 71340
Harvey (1st) ... 70058
Haughton ... 71037
Hayes ... 70646
Haynesville ... 71038
Hebert ... 71436
Heflin ... 71039
Henderson, R. Br. Breaux Bridge ... 70517
Hessmer ... 71341
Hester ... 70743
Hicks ... 71437
Highland Road, Br. Baton Rouge ... 70808
Hineston ... 71438
Hodge ... 71247
Holden ... 70744
Holly Ridge ... 71248
Homer (1st) ... 71040
Hornbeck ... 71439
Hospital, Br. Alexandria ... 71301
Hosston ... 71043
Houma (1st) ... 70360
Husser ... 70442
Iberville ... 70746
Ida ... 71044
Independence ... 70443
Industrial, Sta. Shreveport ... 71107
Innis ... 70747
International Trade Mart, Sta. New Orleans ... 70130
Intracoastal City, R. Br. Abbeville ... 70510
Iota ... 70543
Iowa ... 70647
Istrouma, Sta. Baton Rouge (see appendix)
Jackson ... 70748
Jamestown ... 71045
Jarreau ... 70749
Jeanerette (1st) ... 70544
Jefferson, Br. New Orleans ... 70121
Jefferson Island ... 70545
Jena ... 71342
Jennings (1st) ... 70546
Jewella, Sta. Shreveport ... 71109
Jigger ... 71249
Jones ... 71250
Jonesboro (1st) ... 71251
Jonesville ... 71343
Joyce ... 71440
Junction City ... 71749
Kaplan (1st) ... 70548
Keatchie ... 71046
Keithville ... 71047
Kelly ... 71441
Kenner (1st) ... 70062
Kentwood ... 70444
Kilbourne ... 71253
Killona ... 70066
Kinder (1st) ... 70648

Klotzville, R. Br. Belle Rose ... 70370
Kohn, R. Br. Alexandria ... 71301
Kraemer ... 70371
Krotz Springs ... 70750
Kurthwood ... 71443
La Place (1st) ... 70068
Labadieville ... 70372
Labarre ... 70751
Lacamp ... 71444
Lacassine ... 70650
Lacombe ... 70445
Lafayette (1st) ... 70501
Lafayette Square, Sta. New Orleans ... 70130
Lafitte ... 70067
Lake Arthur ... 70549
Lake Charles (1st) ... 70601
Lake Providence (1st) ... 71254
Lakeland ... 70752
Lakeshore, Sta. Shreveport ... 71109
Lakeside, Sta. Metairie ... 70002
Lakeview, Sta. New Orleans ... 70124
Larose ... 70373
Larto ... 71344
Lawtell ... 70550
Le Blanc ... 70651
Le Moyen ... 71347
Leander ... 71445
Lebeau ... 71345
Lecompte ... 71346
Leesville (1st) ... 71446
Fort Polk, Br. ... 71459
Post Trailer Park, Br. ... 71446
South Park Trailer Court, Br. ... 71446
Lena ... 71447
Leonville ... 70551
Lettsworth ... 70753
Libuse ... 71348
Lillie ... 71256
Linville ... 71257
Lisbon ... 71048
Livingston ... 70754
Livonia ... 70755
Lockport ... 70374
Logansport ... 71049
Longleaf ... 71448
Longstreet ... 71050
Longville ... 70652
Loranger ... 70446
Loreauville ... 70552
Lottie ... 70756
Louise Street, Sta. Baton Rouge ... 70802
Louisville, Sta. Monroe ... 71201
Lucy ... 70069
Luling (1st) ... 70070
Lutcher ... 70071
Lydia ... 70569
Madison Park, Sta. Shreveport ... 71105
Madisonville ... 70447
Mamou ... 70554
Mandeville ... 70448
Mangham ... 71259
Mansfield (1st) ... 71052
Mansura ... 71350
Many (1st) ... 71449
Maplewood, Br. Sulphur ... 70663
Maringouin ... 70757
Marion ... 71260
Haile, R. Br. ... 71246
Marksville (1st) ... 71351

Marrero (1st)	70072	Oak Grove	71263
Marthaville	71450	Oak Ridge	71264
Mathews	70375	Oakdale (1st)	71463
Maurepas	70449	Oakwood, Br. Gretna	70053
Maurice	70555	Oberlin	70655
Mayna	71352	Oil Center, Sta. Lafayette	70501
Mc Dade	71051	Oil City	71061
Meeker, R. Br. Lecompte	71346	Olla	71465
Melder	71451	Opelousas (1st)	70570
Melrose	71452	Oscar	70762
Melville	71353	Otis	71466
Mer Rouge	71261	Paincourtville	70391
Meraux	70075	Palmetto	71358
Mermentau	70556	Paradis	70080
Merrydale, Sta. Baton		Park Manor, Sta. Metairie	70003
Rouge	70805	Parks, R. Br. Saint	
Merryville	70653	Martinville	70582
METAIRIE (1st) (see		Patterson	70392
appendix)		Paulina	70763
Michoud, Sta. New Orleans	70129	Pearl River	70452
Mid City, Sta. New Orleans	70119	Pelican	71063
Mid City Annex, Sta.		Perry	70575
Shreveport	71103	Pierre Avenue, Sta.	
Midland	70557	Shreveport	71103
Milton	70558	Pierre Part	70339
Minden (1st)	71055	Pilottown	70081
Mira	71059	Pine Grove	70453
Mitchell	71453	Pine Prairie	70576
Mittie	70654	Pineville (1st)	71360
Mix	70758	Pioneer	71266
Modeste	70376	Darnell, R. Br.	71231
Moisant Airport, Sta. New		Pitkin	70656
Orleans	70141	Plain Dealing	71064
Monroe (1st)	71201	Plaquemine (1st)	70764
Montegut	70377	Plattenville	70393
Monterey	71354	Plaucheville	71362
Montgomery	71454	Pleasant Hill	71065
Montpelier, R. Br. Amite	70422	Point, R. Br. Downsville	71234
Mooringsport	71060	Point Clair, Br. Carville	70721
Mora	71455	Pointe A La Hache	70082
Moreauville	71355	Pollock	71467
Morgan City (1st)	70380	Ponchatoula (1st)	70454
Morganza	70759	Port Allen (1st)	70767
Morningside, Sta.		Port Barre	70577
Shreveport	71108	Port Sulphur	70083
Morrow	71356	Post Trailer Park, Br.	
Morse	70559	Leesville	71446
Moss Bluff, R. Br. Lake		Powhatan	71066
Charles	70601	Prairieville	70769
Mound	71262	Pride	70770
Mount Airy, R. Br. Reserve	70076	Princeton	71067
Mount Hermon	70450	Provencal	71468
Nairn	70077	Quitman	71268
Napoleonville	70390	Raceland	70394
Natalbany	70451	Ragley	70657
Natchez	71456	Rayne (1st)	70578
Natchitoches (1st)	71457	Rayville (1st)	71269
Negreet	71460	Alto, R. Br.	71216
New Iberia (1st)	70560	Reddell	70580
NEW ORLEANS (1st) (see		Reeves	70658
appendix)		Bel, R. Br.	70675
New Roads (1st)	70760	Reserve	70084
New Sarpy	70078	Mount Airy, R. Br.	70076
Newellton	71357	Rhinehart	71363
Newllano	71461	Ridgecrest, Br. Ferriday	71334
Nicholls University, Sta.		Ringgold	71068
Thibodaux	70301	Roanoke	70581
Noble	71462	Robeline	71469
Norco (1st)	70079	Robert	70455
Northeast, Sta. Monroe	71201	Rodessa	71069
Northwestern, Sta.		Rosa	71364
Natchitoches	71457	Rosedale	70772
Norwood	70761		
Roseland		70456
Rosepine		70659
Rougon		70773
Ruby		71365
Ruston (1st)		71270
Clay, R. Br.		71228
Tech, Sta.		71270
Vienna, R. Br.		71270
Saint Amant		70774
Saint Benedict		70457
Saint Bernard		70085
Saint Francisville		70775
Saint Gabriel		70776
Saint Gertrude, R. Br.		
Covington		70433
Saint James		70086
Saint Joseph		71366
Saint Landry		71367
Saint Martinville (1st)		70582
Saint Maurice		71471
Saint Rose		70087
Saline		71070
Samtown, R. Br. Alexandria		71301
Sarepta		71071
Schriever		70395
Scotlandville, Br. Baton		
Rouge (see appendix)		
Scott		70583
Shongaloo		71072
Shreve Island, Sta.		
Shreveport		71105
SHREVEPORT (1st) (see		
appendix)		
Sibley		71073
Sicily Island		71368
Sieper		71472
Sikes		71473
Simmesport		71369
Simpson		71474
Simsboro		71275
Singer		70660
Slagle		71475
Slaughter		70777
Slidell (1st)		70458
Sondheimer		71276
Sorrento		70778
South Lafourche, R. Br.		
Golden Meadow		70338
South Park, Sta. Alexandria		71301
South Park Trailer Court, Br.		
Leesville		71446
Southeast, Sta. Baton Rouge		
(see appendix)		
Southern, Br. Baton Rouge		70813
Southfield, Sta. Shreveport		71105
Southwestern, Sta.		
Lafayette		70501
Spearsville		71277
Spencer		71278
Spokane		71370
Springcreek		70461
Springfield		70462
Springhill (1st)		71075
Starks		70661
Start		71279
Sterlington		71280
Stonewall		71078
Sugartown		70662
Sulphur (1st)		70663
Summer Grove, Br.		
Shreveport		71108
Summerfield		71079

Sun	70463	Twin Cedars, Sta. Baton		Warden	71289
Sunset	70584	Rouge	70809	Washington	70589
Sunshine	70780			Waterproof	71375
Supreme, R. Br.		Uncle Sam, R. Br. Convent	70792	Watson	70786
Labadieville	70396	Union, R. Br. Convent	70723	Waverly	71290
Swartz	71281	University, Sta. Baton		Welcome	70093
Talisheek	70464	Rouge	70803	Welsh	70591
Tallulah (1st)	71282	Urania	71480	West Monroe (1st)	71291
Tangipahoa	70465	Vacherie	70090	Westlake	70669
Taylor	71080	Varnado	70467	Westport, R. Br. Pitkin	70656
Tech, Sta. Ruston	71270	Venice	70091	Westwego (1st)	70094
Temple	71476	Ventress	70783	Weyanoke	70787
Terry	71285	Verda	71481	White Castle	70788
Theriot	70397			Whiteville	71376
Thibodaux (1st)	70301	Veterans Administration		Wildsville	71377
Ticklaw	70466	Hosp. Sta. Shreveport	71101	Wilmer	70468
Tioga	71477	Vick	71372	Wilson	70789
Torbert	70781	Vidalia (1st)	71373	Winnfield (1st)	71483
Tower Park, Sta. Leesville	71446	Vienna, R. Br. Ruston	71270	Winnsboro (1st)	71295
Transylvania	71286	Vieux Carre, Sta. New		Wisner	71378
Trees	71081	Orleans	70112	Woodworth	71485
Trout	71371	Ville Platte (1st)	70586	Youngsville	70592
Tullos	71479	Vinton	70668	Zachary (1st)	70791
Tunica	70782	Violet	70092	Zion City, Br. Baton Rouge	70811
Turkey Creek	70585	Vivian	71082	Zwolle	71486
		Wakefield	70784		

Appendix

BATON ROUGE   708

POST OFFICE BOXES

Box Nos.

1-4037	Main Office	21
A-Z-PN	University	63
9201-11999	Southern	13
14501-14999	Southeast	08
15001-15999	Broadview	15
16001-32999	University	63
44001-44999	Capitol	04
52701-53999	Istrouma	05
54901-54999	Louise Street	02
64001-64999	Audubon	06
66001-66999	Central City	06
73001-73999	Scotlandville	07

RURAL ROUTES

2	15
3	08
4	05
5	87
6	15
7	07
8	08

STATIONS, BRANCHES AND UNITS

Audubon Sta.	06
Broadview Sta.	14
Brownfields Br.	07
Capitol Sta.	04
Central City Sta.	06
Highland Road Br.	08
Istrouma Sta.	05
Louise Street Sta.	02
Merrydale Sta.	05

Scotlandville Br.	07
Southeast Sta.	08
Southern Br.	13
Twin Cedars Sta.	09
University Sta.	03
Zion City Br.	11
General Delivery	21
Postmaster	21

APARTMENTS, HOTELS, MOTELS

Alamo Plaza Courts, 4242 Florida	06
Bellemont Motor Courts, 7370 Airline Highway	21
Boyd Lake Apartments, 1150 Boyd Ave	02
Capitol House, 205 Lafayette	21
College Park Apartments, 1500 Aster St	02
Continental Motor, 5180 Airline Hwy	05
Fifth Street Apartments, 439 N 5th St	01
Heidelberg, 206 Lafayette	21
Holiday Inn, 5955 Airline Highway	21
Howard Johnson, 7275 Airline Highway	15
Motor Inn, 4136 Florida Blvd.	21
Oak Manor Courts, Airline Highway	15
Oak Royale Apartments, 458 Cloud Dr.	06
Town House Motor, 7361 Airline	05
Vel Rose Motel, 4902 Airline	05

BUILDINGS

Baton Rouge Savings & Loan, 400 North Blvd	01
City National Bank, 124 N 3rd	01
Commerce, 333 Laurel	01
Courthouse Office, 233 St Ferdinand	01
Courthouse, 301 St. Louis	01
Federal Building, Florida St.	01
Fidelity Bank, 440 N 3rd	01
Guaranty Income, 929 Government	02
Kean, 207 N 4th	01
Louisiana National Bank, 451 Florida	01
Municipal, 300 North Blvd.	01
Old State Capitol, 100 St Philip	01
Post Office And Federal Bldg 700 Florida	21
Reymond, 263 Third	01
Roumain, 343 N 3rd	01
State Capitol Annex, 900 3rd.	04
State Capitol, 9th Block 3rd.	04
Taylor, 251 Florida	01
Union Federal, 500 Laurel	01
United States Courthouse	01

HOSPITALS

Baton Rouge General Hospital, 3600 Florida St.	21
Earl K Long Charity Hospital, 5825 Airline Hwy	05
Our Lady Of The Lake Hospital, 1500 N 3rd.	02

233

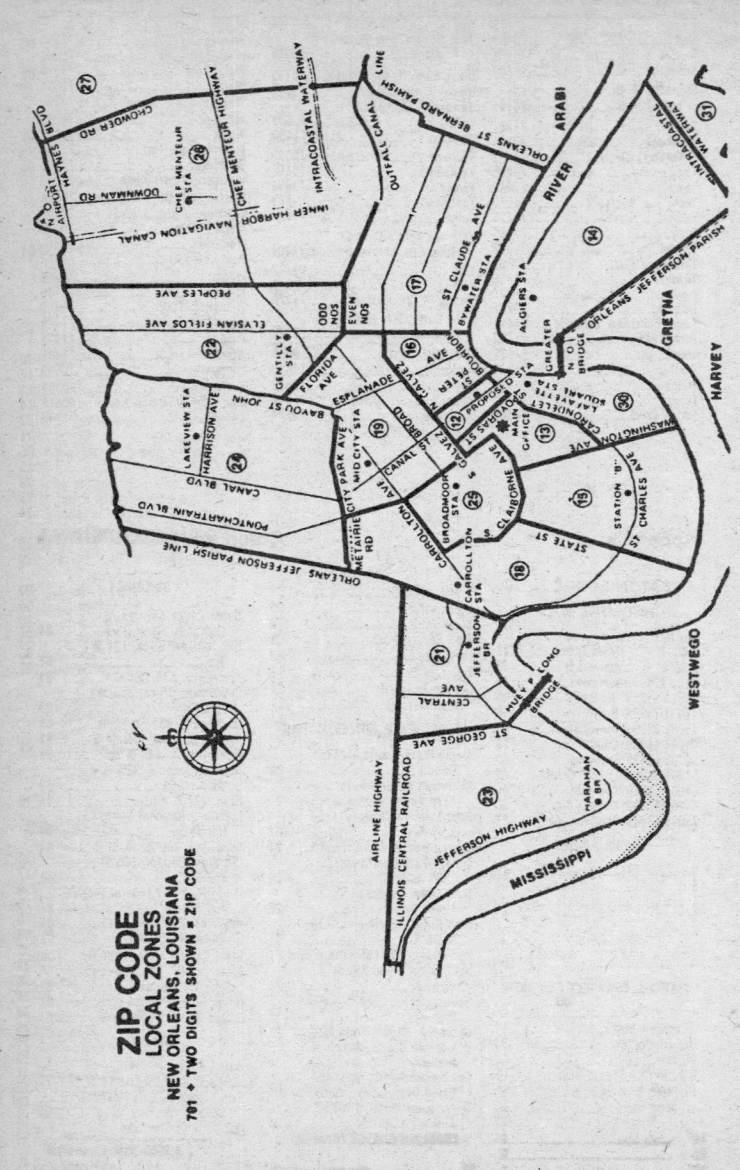

ZIP CODE
LOCAL ZONES
NEW ORLEANS, LOUISIANA
701 + TWO DIGITS SHOWN = ZIP CODE

Baton Rouge (Con.) 708

Womans Hospital, Airline
Hwy 15

UNIVERSITIES AND COLLEGES

Louisiana State University 03
Southern University 13

METAIRIE　700

POST OFFICE BOXES

Box Nos.
1-1250	Main Office	04
7001-7999	Lakeside Sta	02
9000-9450	A Sta	05
73001-73809	Park Manor Sta	03

STATIONS, BRANCHES AND UNITS

Lakeside Sta 02
Park Manor Sta 03
General Delivery 01
Postmaster 04

APARTMENTS, HOTELS, MOTELS

Adrian Arms 115 Avenue B 05
Ante Bellum 3201 Belmont
Place 02
Atlantis 2601 Metairie Lawn
Dr 02
Berkshire Apts 6300 Ackel 03
Bissonet Apts 6315 Ackel 03
Brittany Apts 3440 Edenborn ... 02
Bryn Mar Square 1035 Lake
Ave 05
Butterfly Apts 2925 Edenborn
Ave 02
Canterberry Square 3127
Transcontinental Dr 82
Causeway Apts 3505 N
Causeway Blvd 02
Charleston Apts 4110
Hessmer Ave 02
Chateau Cleary 3900 I-10
Service Rd 01
Chateau Romar 3715 Marion ... 02
Dorien Apts 3201 Richland 02
Drexel House 3340 Edenborn
Ave 02
Edgewater Apts 3901
Ridgelake Dr 02
Elmwood Plantation 6801
Veterans Blvd 03
Fernwood Apts 1010 Lake
Ave 05
Gatehouse Apts 2500
Interstate Hwy 01
Golden Key Apts 4051
Division Ave 02
Hampton Court 1168 Lake
Ave 05
Houma House 3515 Houma
Blvd 02
Imperial House, 3400 N
Causeway Blvd. 02

Jefferson Town House 1401
Lake Ave 05
Jeffersonian 3500 To 3600
Houma Blvd 02
Jeffersonian 4325
Manhattan 02
Kingston Court 3919
Hessmer 02
Labrias Apts 4021 Hessmer
Ave 02
Leesplanade Apts 3443
Edenborn Ave 02
Lafayette Square 1201 Lake
Ave 05
Lake Castle Apts 222 London
Ave 05
Lakeside Apts 01 3333
Edenborn 02
Lakeside Apts 02 3911
Hessmer 02
Lakeside Apts 03 3311
Edenborn 02
Lakeside Apts 04 3225
Ridgelake Dr 02
Lakeside Apts 3500
Edenborn 02
Lakeside Apts 810 Wilshire
Blvd 05
Malibu Apts 2935 Ridgelake
Dr 02
Marquette Square 1111 Lake
Ave 05
Metaine Plaza 1046 Lake
Ave 05
Metaine Tower Apts 401
Metairie Rd 05
Norgate Apts 3500 Division 02
Park Manor Apts 6415 Park
Manor Dr 03
Ridgelake Apts 300
Ridgelake Dr 01
Royal Arms Apts 936 Lake
Ave 05
Sena Apts 615 Sena Dr 05
Surfrider Apts 6416 Park
Manor Dr 02
Townhouse Apts 4804
Quincy 02
Villa D Orleans 01 3030
Edenborn 02
Villa D Orleans 02 3110
Edenborn 02
Village Town House 3425
Edenborn Ave 02
Westchester Apts 4217
Hessmer Ave 02
Whitney Place Apts 2400
Veterans Blvd 02
Yorkshire Arnoult 3320 N
Arnoult Rd 02
Yorkshire Edenborn 3240
Edenborn Ave 02

BUILDINGS

Causeway Interchange Bldg
2456 N Causeway Blvd. 01
East Bank Parish, 3300
Metairie Rd 01
Imperial Office, 3301 N
Causeway Blvd 02
Jefferson Bank Bldg., 3525 N
Causeway Blvd. 02

Lakeside Plaza Bldg 3425 N
Causeway Blvd 02
Security Homestead Bldg
4900 Veterans Blvd 02

HOSPITALS

East Jefferson, 4200 Houma 02
Lakeside 4700 I 10 Sen
Road 01
Metairie, 310 Codifer Blvd 05

NEW ORLEANS　701

POST OFFICE BOXES

Box Nos.
23A-23J	Harahan Br	23
2000-2999	Custom House Sta	30
3000-3999	Bywater	17
4000-4999	Carrollton Sta	18
6000-6999	A Sta	14
8000-8999	Gentilly Sta	82
10000-10999	Jefferson Br	21
13000-13999	Broadmoor Sta	25
15000-15999	B Sta	15
19000-19999	Mid City Sta	79
23000-23999	Harahan Br	23
24000-24999	Lakeview Sta	24
26000-26999	Chef Menteur Sta	26
29001-29999	Michoud Sta	29
30000-30999	Lafayette Square Sta	90
50000-50999	Main Office	50
52000-52999	Main Office	52
53000-53999	Main Office	53
60000-60999	Main Office	60
61000-61999	Main Office	61
0020000-0020099	New Orleans International Airport Moisant	41

RURAL ROUTES

6 29

STATIONS, BRANCHES AND UNITS

Broadmoor Sta 25
Bywaters Sta 17
Carrollton Sta 18
Chef Menteur Sta 26
Custom House Sta 16
Embarkation Sta 40
Gentilly Sta 22
Harahan Br 23
International Trade Mart Sta 30
Jefferson Br 21
Lafayette Square Sta 30
Lakeview Sta 24
Michoud Sta 29
Mid City Sta 19
Moisant Airport Sta 41
Vieux Carre Sta 12
General Delivery 40
Postmaster 13
Usps No Dist Office 13

New Orleans (Con.) 701

APARTMENTS, HOTELS, MOTELS

Ardens Motel, 6218 Chef
Menteur Hwy 26
Avalon Motor, 4450 Chef
Menteur Hwy 26
Brent House, 1512 Jefferson
Hwy 21
Capri Motel, 2410 Tulane
Ave 19
Carol, 2100 St Charles Ave 40
Chateau Le Moyne 303
Dauphine 12
Column Guest House, 3811
St Charles Ave 15
Congress Inn 13001 Chef
Menteur Hwy 29
De Ville, 3800 Tulane Ave 19
Del Mar Motel, 8542 Chef
Menteur Hwy 27
Fontainebleau Motor, 4040
Tulane Ave 19
French Quarter Patio, 1130
Chartres 16
Georgian, 2233 St Charles
Ave 40
Governor House Motor Hotel,
1630 Canal 12
Greystone, 3701 Canal 19
Holiday Inn 124 Royal St 30
Holiday Inn, 4861 Chef
Menteur Hwy 26
Howard Johnson 330 Loyola
Ave 12
Howard Johnson, 4300
Gentilly Road 26
John Mitchell, 637 Common
St 30
Jung, 1500 Canal St 30
Lafayette, 628 St Charles St 30
Lafitte Guest House, 1003
Bourbon St 16
Lamothe House, 621
Esplanade Ave 16
Lasalle, 1113 Canal St 12
Le Pavillon 833 Poydras 40
Le Petit Motel, 2836 Tulane
Ave 19
London Lodge Motel, 9301
Airline Hwy 18
Maison De Ville, 727
Toulouse St 30
Marriott 555 Canal St 40
Mayflower, 2203 St Charles
Ave 40
Monteleone, 214 Royal St 40
Orleanian, 1205 St Charles
Ave 30
Pontchartrain, 2031 St
Charles Ave 40
Prince Conti Motor, 830 Conti
St 12
Provincial Motel, 1024
Chartres St 16
Roosevelt, 123 Baronne St 40
Royal Orleans, 621 St Louis
St 40
Royal Sonesta Hotel 300
Bourbon.. 40
Sheraton Charles Hotel 211

St Charles...................................... 40
Sheraton Delta Motor Hotel,
1732 Canal 12
Studio Arms Iv, 200 Deckbar
Ave 21
Tamanaca Downtown Motel,
1725 Tulane Ave 12
Town House Motel, 9419
Airline Hwy 18
Tulane University Dormitory
Building, 6440 S
Claiborne Av 25
Warwick, 1315 Gravier 40
Wohl, 2111 St Charles Ave 40

BUILDINGS

Administration, New Orleans
Airport 26
American Bank, 200
Carondelet 30
American Red Cross, 2000
Tulane Ave 12
Audubon, 931 Canal 12
Balter, 403 Camp 30
Balter, 404 St Charles Ave 30
Balter, 618 Commercial Ally 30
Bank Of New Orleans 1010
Common 12
Baronne, 305 Baronne 12
Bienville Street Wharf 30
Board Of Trade Annex, 320
Board Of Trade Pl 12
California, 1111 Tulane Ave 12
Canal Lasalle 1424 Canal 12
Caribe, 2475 Canal 30
Carondelet, 226 Carondelet 30
Celeste Street Wharf 30
Cigali, 107 Camp 30
City Hall 1300 Perdido St 12
Civil Court 421 Loyola Ave 12
Commerce, 821 Gravier 12
Communications, 1215
Prytania 40
Congress Street Wharf 30
Cotton Exchange, 231
Carondelet 30
Customhouse, 423 Canal 30
Demontluzia 234 Loyola Ave 12
Desire Street Wharf 30
Dodge, 411 Bienville 30
Dumaine Street Wharf 30
Erato Street Wharf 30
Esplanade Avenue Wharf 30
Executive House, 348
Baronne.. 12
Federal Office 600 South 30
Federal Office, 701 Loyola 13
First-National Life Insurance,
1000 Howard Ave 13
First Street Wharf 30
Foreign Trade Zone Napoleon
Ave & River Allfirms................ 30
Galvez Street Wharf 17
Gateway, 124 Camp 30
Governor Nicholls Street
Wharf 30
Gravier, 535 Gravier 30
Hancock John 1055 St
Charles Ave 30
Harmony Street Wharf 30
Hibernia Bank, 812 Gravier 12
Hicks, 316 Baronne 12

Hutchinson Memorial, 143/
Tulane Ave 12
International Trade Mart, 2
Canal.. 30
International, 611 Gravier.......... 30
Julia Street Wharf 30
Louisa Street Wharf 30
Louisiana Southern Life
Insurance Building 225
Baronne St 12
Louisiana State Office, 325
Loyola Ave 12
Lowich, 2026 St Charles Ave.... 30
Maison Blanche, 921 Canal 12
Mandeville Street Wharf 30
Maritime, 203 Carondelet 30
Market Street Wharf 30
Maryland Casualty, 210
Okeefe Ave 12
Masonic Temple 333 St
Charles 30
Medallion Towers 344 Camp
St 30
Miles, 2025 Canal 12
Municipal Auditorium, 1201
St Peter 16
Nashville Ave Wharf 15
National Bank Of Commerce,
210 Baronne 12
New Orleans Public Library,
219 Loyola Ave 12
New Orleans Union
Passenger Terminal 1001
Loyola Ave 13
No 1 Shell Square 701
Poydras St 39
Norman Mayer Memorial, 211
Camp.. 30
Odeco, 1600 Canal 12
Oil & Gas 1100 Tulane Ave 12
Orange Street Wharf.................. 30
Pan American Life Insurance,
2400 Canal 19
Pauline Street Wharf 30
Pere Marquette, 150
Baronne.. 12
Pere Marquette, 837
Common 12
Physicians & Surgeons, 4500
Magnolia 15
Plaza Towers 1001 Howard
Ave 13
Plaza, 230 Loyola Ave 12
Poydras Street Wharf................ 30
Rault Center 1111 Gravier........ 12
Richards, 837 Gravier................ 12
Rivergate Exhibition &
Convention Center, 4 & 6
Canal.. 30
Robin Street Wharf 30
Saint Andrew Street Wharf 30
Saratoga, 200 Loyola Ave 12
Security Homestead, 217
Carondelet 30
Seventh Street Wharf 30
Shell 925 Common 12
Soule, 700 Lafayette 30
Stuyvesant Docks 30
Texaco, 1501 Canal 12
Thalia Street Wharf 30
Third Street Wharf 30
Toulouse Street Wharf 30
Tulane, 3308 Tulane Ave 19

New Orleans (Con.)   701

- S Postal Service 701
  Loyola Ave.................................. 13
United Fruit, 321 St Charles
  Ave... 30
Vincent, 325 Camp...................... 30
Vincent, 615 Commercial
  Alley... 30
Washington Avenue Wharf............ 30
Whitney Bank 228 St Charles
  St.. 30
Whitney Bank, 624 Common........ 30
Whitney Bank, 625 Gravier.......... 30
Wild Life & Fisheries, 400
  Royal.. 30
Wirth, 129 Marais........................ 12

GOVERNMENT OFFICES

City Hall, 1300 Perdido................ 12
Civil Court, 421 Loyola............... 12
Criminal District Court, 2700
  Tulane Ave.................................. 19
Supreme Court, 301 Loyola
  Ave... 12

HOSPITALS

Algiers General, 310
  Opelousas Ave............................ 14
Charity, 1532 Tulane Ave............. 40
Crippled Childrens, 200
  Henry Clay Ave............................ 18
De Paul Hosp 1040 Calhoun
  St.. 18
Eye Ear Nose & Throat, 145
  Elk Place.................................... 12
Flint Goodridge, 2425
  Louisiana Ave............................. 15
Hotel Dieu, 2004 Tulane Ave....... 12
Mercy 301 N Jefferson Davis
  Parkway...................................... 79
Methodist Hospital, 5620
  Read Rd...................................... 27
Montelepre Memorial, 3125
  Canal.. 19
Ochsner Foundation, 1516
  Jefferson Hwy.............................. 21
Saint Claude General, 3501
  St Claude Ave.............................. 17
Sara Mayo, 609 Jackson Ave....... 30
Southern Baptist, 2700
  Napoleon Ave.............................. 15
Touro Infirmary, 1400
  Foucher...................................... 15
United States Public Health
  Service, 210 State Street............ 18
Veterans Administration 1601
  Perdido...................................... 46

MILITARY INSTALLATIONS

Alvin Callender Field, Belle
  Chasse La.................................... 46
Army Reserve 19th Corp,
  5010 Leroy Johnson Dr............... 40
Eight Naval District, Algiers
  La.. 46
Jackson Barracks Military
  Only 6400 Dauphine St............... 46
Naval Air Station, Belle

Chasse La.................................... 46
Navy & Marine Tr Center,
  5020 Lakeshore Dr...................... 40
Navy Radio Station, 5000
  Lakeshore Dr.............................. 46
Port Of Embarkation 4400
  Dauphine St................................ 46

UNIVERSITIES AND COLLEGES

Baptist Theological Seminary,
  3939 Chef Menteur Hwy.............. 26
Dillard University, 2601
  Gentilly Blvd............................... 22
Louisiana State Univ In New
  Orleans, 2000 Lakeshore
  Dr.. 22
Louisiana State University
  Medical School, 1542
  Tulane.. 12
Loyola University, 6363 St
  Charles Ave................................ 18
Newcomb, 1229 Broadway........... 18
Saint Marys Dominican, 7214
  St Charles Ave............................ 18
Southern U. In New Orleans,
  6400 Press Dr............................. 26
Tulane University Medical
  College, 1430 Tulane Ave............ 12
Tulane University, 6823 St
  Charles Ave................................ 18
Ursuline, 2635 State................... 18
Xavier, 7325 Palmetto................ 25

SHREVEPORT   **711**

POST OFFICE BOXES

Box Nos.		
1-199	Main Office Sta.	61
200-899	Main Office Sta.	62
900-1299	Main Office Sta.	63
1300-1499	Main Office Sta.	64
1500-1699	Main Office Sta.	65
1700-1899	Main Office Sta.	66
3001-3706	Main City Annex Sta.	03
4001-4999	Centenary Sta.	04
5001-5999	Southfield Sta.	05
6001-6999	Cedar Grove Sta.	06
7001-7999	Industrial Sta.	07
8001-8999	Morningside Sta.	08
9000-9999	Jewella Sta.	09

RURAL ROUTES

1	05
2	09
3	06
4	09
5	07

STATIONS, BRANCHES AND UNITS

Barksdale A F B Br.................... 10
Cedar Grove Sta........................ 06
Centenary Sta........................... 04
Cooper Road Br......................... 01
Fair Grounds Sta....................... 09
Industrial Sta............................ 07
Jewella Sta............................... 09
Lakeshore Sta........................... 09
Madison Park Sta...................... 05
Mid City Annex Sta.................... 03
Morningside Sta........................ 08
Pierre Avenue Sta...................... 03
Shreve Island Sta...................... 05
Southfield Sta........................... 05
Summer Grove Br....................... 08
Veterans Administration
  Hosp Sta................................... 01
General Delivery........................ 02
Main Office Sta Carriers............. 01
Postmaster............................... 02

APARTMENTS, HOTELS, MOTELS

Alamo Plaza Courts 1................. 03
Alamo Plaza Courts 2................. 07
Brighton Manor.......................... 08
Caddo...................................... 01
Captain Shreve.......................... 01
Colonial Plaza........................... 05
Conquistidor.............................. 08
Cooper Road Plaza..................... 07
Downtowner.............................. 01
Evangeline................................ 06
Fairfield Oaks........................... 04
Fairway Forest Plaza, Rural
  Route 2...................................... 09
Holiday Inn Of America, 1906
  N Market.................................... 07
Holiday Inn Of America, 4900
  Greenwood................................. 09
Lincoln..................................... 01
Mid-City................................... 01
Mikado..................................... 03
Normandie Village...................... 04
Northwood................................ 07
Park Villa.................................. 05
Pinecrest Mobile Villa 6700
  Jefferson Paige Rd...................... 09
Quail Creek............................... 05
Shreveporter............................. 09
Silver Pines.............................. 08
Southside Villa.......................... 08
The Fountain............................. 01
Town House.............................. 01
Town Oak................................. 05
Town South Villa....................... 05
Villa Contessa, 7000
  Creswell St................................ 06
Villa Del Lago........................... 09
Washington-Youree..................... 01

BUILDINGS

Barnes..................................... 01
Bech.. 01
Commercial............................... 01
Commercial National Bank.......... 01
Communications........................ 01
Contl-American Bank.................. 01
Fairfield................................... 01

Shreveport (Con.)	711

First National Bank	01
Johnson	01
Lane	01
Louisiana Bank	01
Louisiana State	01
Medical Arts	01
Mid South Towers	01
Municipal Auditorium	01
Oden	01
Oil & Gas	01
Petroleum Bldg.	01
Petroleum Tower	01
Pioneer	01
Ricou-Brewster	01
Slattery	01
Texas Eastern	01

Ward	01
Western Union	01

GOVERNMENT OFFICES

Caddo Parish Courthouse	01
City Hall	01

HOSPITALS

Confederate Memorial	01
Doctors	01
Gilmers	04
Gowans	06
Highland	01
Physicians & Surgeons	01
Schumpert	01
Veterans	01

Willis-Knighton Memorial	03

MILITARY INSTALLATIONS

Barksdale Air Force Base	10
Bossier Base	10

UNIVERSITIES AND COLLEGES

Ayers School Of Business	01
Baptist Christian College	08
Centenary College	04
L S U Shreveport Branch	05
Shreveport Draughon-Norton Business College	01
Southern University Shreveport Branch	07

MAINE
(Abbreviation: ME)

Abbot Village	04406
Acton	04001
Addison	04606
Albion	04910
Alfred	04002
Alna	04535
Andover	04216
Anson	04911
Starks, R Br	04980
Ashland	04732
Masardis, R Br	04759
Ashville	04607
Athens	04912
Atlantic	04608
Auburn (1st)	04210
Augusta (1st)	04330
Aurora	04408
Bailey Island	04003
Bancroft	04409
Bangor (1st)	04401
Bar Harbor (1st)	04609
Bar Mills	04004
Baring, R Br Calais	04610
Bass Harbor	04653
Bath (1st)	04530
Bayside, R Br Belfast	04915
Bayville, R Sta Boothbay Harbor	04536
Beals	04611
Belfast (1st)	04915
Belgrade	04917
Belgrade Lakes	04918
Benedicta	04733
Benton Station	04919
Bernard	04612
Berwick	03901
Bethel	04217
Biddeford (1st)	04005
Biddeford Pool	04006
Bingham	04920
Birch Harbor	04613

Birch Island, R Br Brunswick	04011
Blaine	04734
Blue Hill	04614
Blue Hill Falls	04615
Boothbay	04537
Isle Of Springs, R Br	04549
Boothbay Harbor	04538
Bayville, R Sta	04536
Capitol Island, R Br	04538
Southport, R Br	04569
Squirrel Island, R Br	04570
Bowdoinham	04008
Bradford	04410
Bradley	04411
Brewer (1st)	04412
Bridgewater	04735
Bridgton	04009
Bristol	04539
Brooklin	04616
Brooks	04921
Brooksville	04617
Brookton	04413
Brownfield	04010
Brownville	04414
Brownville Junction	04415
Brunswick (1st)	04011
Birch Island, R Br	04011
Cundys Harbor, R Br	04011
Merepoint, R Br	04053
Bryant Pond	04219
Buckfield	04220
East Sumner, R Br	04232
Bucks Harbor	04618
Bucksport	04416
Burkettville	04560
Burlington	04417
Burnham	04922
Bustins Island, R Br South Freeport	04013
Calais (1st)	04619
Baring, R Br	04610
Milltown, Sta	04619
Cambridge	04923

Camden (1st)	04843
Hope, R Br	04847
Canaan	04924
Canton	04221
Cape Cottage, Br Portland	04107
Cape Elizabeth, Br Portland	04107
Cape Neddick	03902
Cape Porpoise, R Sta Kennebunkport	04014
Capitol Island, R Br Boothbay Harbor	04538
Caratunk	04925
Cardville	04418
Caribou (1st)	04736
Carmel	04419
Carroll	04420
Casco	04015
Castine	04421
Center Lovell	04016
Chamberlain	04541
Charleston	04422
Chebeague Island	04017
Cherryfield	04622
China	04926
Chisholm	04222
Christmas Cove, R Sta South Bristol	04542
Clayton Lake	04018
Cliff Island	04019
Clinton	04927
Columbia Falls	04623
Coopers Mills	04341
Corea	04624
Corinna	04928
Cornish	04020
Costigan	04423
Cranberry Isles	04625
Crouseville	04738
Cumberland Center	04021
Cumberland Mills, Sta Westbrook	04092
Cundys Harbor, R Br Brunswick	04011
Cutler	04626

Damariscotta (1st)	04543
Danforth	04424
Waite, R. Br.	04492
Danville	04223
Deer Isle	04627
Denmark	04022
Dennysville	04628
Derby	04425
Detroit	04929
Dexter (1st)	04930
Dixfield	04224
Dixmont	04932
Dover-Foxcroft (1st)	04426
Dresden	04342
Dryden	04225
Eagle Lake	04739
East Andover	04226
East Baldwin	04024
East Blue Hill, R. Br. Surry	04629
East Boothbay	04544
Ocean Point, R. Br.	04557
East Corinth	04427
East Dixfield	04227
East Eddington	04428
East Hampden, Br. Bangor	04401
East Holden	04429
East Lebanon	04027
East Livermore	04228
East Machias	04630
East Millinocket	04430
East Newport	04933
East Orland	04431
East Parsonfield	04028
East Peru	04229
East Poland	04230
East Sebago	04029
East Stoneham	04231
East Sullivan	04632
East Sumner, R. Br.	
Buckfield	04232
East Vassalboro	04935
East Waterboro	04030
East Waterford	04233
East Wilton	04234
East Winthrop	04343
Easton	04740
Eastport	04631
Eaton	04432
Eliot	03903
Ellsworth (1st)	04605
Ellsworth Falls	04633
Emery Mills	04031
Enfield	04433
Estcourt Station	04741
Etna	04434
Eustis	04936
Exeter	04435
Fairfield	04937
Fairmount, Sta. Bangor	04401
Falmouth, Br. Portland	04105
Farmington (1st)	04938
Farmington Falls	04940
Fayette	04344
Five Islands	04546
Forest City, R. Sta. Brookton	04413
Fort Fairfield	04742
Fort Kent	04743
Fort Kent Mills	04744
Frankfort	04438
Franklin	04634
Freedom	04941
Freeport (1st)	04032

Frenchboro	04635
Frenchville	04745
Friendship	04547
Frye	04235
Fryeburg	04037
Gardiner (1st)	04345
Garland	04939
Georgetown	04548
Glen Cove	04846
Gorham (1st)	04038
Gouldsboro	04636
Grand Isle	04746
Grand Lake Stream	04637
Gray	04039
Great Works, Sta. Old Town	04468
Green Lake	04440
Greene	04236
Greenville	04441
Greenville Junction	04442
Grove	04638
Guilford	04443
Sebec Lake, R. Br.	04482
Hallowell	04347
Hampden	04444
Hampden Highlands	04445
Hancock	04640
Hanover	04237
Harborside	04642
Harmony	04942
Harrington	04643
Harrison	04040
Hartland	04943
Haynesville	04446
Hebron	04238
Higgins Beach, R. Sta.	
Scarborough	04074
Hinckley	04944
Hiram	04041
Hollis Center	04042
Hope, R. Br. Camden	04847
Houlton (1st)	04730
Howland	04448
Hudson	04449
Hulls Cove	04644
Island Falls	04747
Isle Au Haut, R. Br.	
Stonington	04645
Isle Of Springs, R. Br.	
Boothbay	04549
Islesboro	04848
Islesford	04646
Jackman	04945
Jacksonville	04647
Jay	04239
Jefferson	04348
Jonesboro	04648
Jonesport	04649
Kenduskeag	04450
Kennebunk (1st)	04043
Kennebunk Beach, R.	
Sta.	04045
Kennebunk Beach, R. Sta.	
Kennebunk	04045
Kennebunkport	04046
Cape Porpoise, R. Sta.	04014
Kents Hill	04349
Kezar Falls	04047
Kingfield	04947
Kingman	04451
Kittery (1st)	03904
Kittery Point	03905
La Grange	04453

Lambert Lake	04454
Lee	04455
Levant	04456
Lewiston (1st)	04240
Liberty	04949
Lille	04749
Limerick	04048
Limestone (1st)	04750
Limington	04049
Lincoln	04457
Lincoln Center	04458
Lincolnville	04849
Lincolnville Center	04850
Linneus	04755
Lisbon	04250
Lisbon Center	04251
Lisbon Falls	04252
Litchfield	04350
Little Deer Isle	04650
Livermore	04253
Livermore Falls	04254
Locke Mills	04255
Long Island	04050
Lookout, R. Br. Stonington	04651
Loring A F B. Sta.	
Limestone	04750
Lovell	04051
Lubec	04652
Mac Mahan, R. Br. Bath	04530
Machias	04654
Machiasport	04655
Madawaska	04756
Madison	04950
Manchester	0435*
Manset, R. Br. Southwest	
Harbor	04656
Mapleton	04757
Maplewood	04052
Mars Hill	04758
Masardis, R. Br. Ashland	04759
Matinicus	04851
Mattawamkeag	04459
Mechanic Falls	04256
Meddybemps	04657
Medomak	04551
Medway	04460
Mercer, R. Br. Norridgewock	04957
Merepoint, R. Br. Brunswick	04053
Mexico	04257
Milbridge	04658
Milford	04461
Millinocket (1st)	04462
Milltown, Sta. Calais	04619
Milo	04463
Minot	04258
Minturn	04659
Monhegan	04852
Monmouth	04259
Monroe	04951
Monson	04464
Monticello	04760
Moody	04054
Morrill	04952
Mount Desert	04660
Mount Vernon	04352
Naples	04055
Naval Base, Br. Portsmouth,	
N H	03801
New Gloucester	04260
New Harbor	04554
Pemaquid Point, R. Br.	04561
New Limerick	04761

New Portland	84954	
New Sharon	04955	
New Sweden	04762	
New Vineyard	04956	
Newagen	04552	
Newcastle	04553	
Newfield	04056	
Newport	04953	
Newry	04261	
Nobleboro	04555	
Norridgewock	04957	
North Amity	04465	
North Anson	04958	
North Belgrade, R. Br. Oakland	04959	
North Berwick	03906	
North Bridgton	04057	
North Brooklin	04661	
North Edgecomb	04556	
North Fryeburg	04058	
North Haven	04853	
North Jay	04262	
North Leeds	04263	
North Lovell	04264	
North Lubec	04663	
North Monmouth	04265	
North New Portland	04961	
North Sebago, R. Sta. East Sebago	04029	
North Shapleigh	04060	
North Sullivan	04664	
North Turner	04266	
North Vassalboro	04962	
North Waterboro	04061	
North Waterford	04267	
North Whitefield	04353	
North Windham	04062	
Northeast Harbor	04662	
Norway (1st)	04268	
Oakfield	04763	
Oakland	04963	
North Belgrade, R. Br.	04959	
Ocean Park, R. Sta. Old Orchard Beach	04063	
Ocean Point, R. Br. East Boothbay	04557	
Ogunquit	03907	
Olamon	04467	
Old Orchard Beach (1st)	04064	
Ocean Park, R. Sta.	04063	
Old Town (1st)	04468	
Oquossoc	04964	
Orient	04471	
Orland	04472	
Orono (1st)	04473	
Orrington	04474	
Orrs Island	04066	
Otter Creek	04665	
Owls Head	04854	
Oxbow	04764	
Oxford	04270	
Palermo	04354	
Palmyra	04965	
Paris	04271	
Passadumkeag	04475	
Patten	04765	
Peaks Island, Sta. Portland	04108	
Pearl Street, Sta. Portland (see appendix)		
Pejepscot	04067	
Pemaquid	04558	
Pemaquid Beach	04559	
Pemaquid Harbor	04560	
Pemaquid Point, R. Br. New Harbor	04561	
Pembroke	04666	
Pennamaquan, R. Sta. Pembroke	04666	
Penobscot	04476	
South Penobscott, R. Sta.	04486	
Perham	04766	
Perry	04667	
Peru	04272	
Phillips	04966	
Phippsburg	04562	
Popham Beach, R. Sta.	04562	
Small Point, R. Sta.	04567	
Pittsfield (1st)	04967	
Plaisted	04767	
Pleasant Point	04563	
Plymouth	04969	
Poland	04273	
Poland Spring	04274	
Popham Beach, R. Sta. Phippsburg	04562	
Port Clyde	04855	
Portage	04768	
Porter	04068	
PORTLAND (1st) (see appendix)		
Pownal	84069	
Prentiss	04477	
Presque Isle (1st)	04769	
Princeton	04668	
Prospect Harbor	04669	
Quimby	04770	
Rangeley	04970	
Raymond	04071	
Readfield	04355	
Readfield Depot	04356	
Red Beach, R. Br. Robbinston	04670	
Richmond	04357	
Robbinston	04671	
Red Beach, R. Br.	04670	
Rockland (1st)	04841	
Rockport	04856	
Rockwood	04478	
Round Pond	04564	
Roxbury	04275	
Rumford (1st)	04276	
Rumford Center	04278	
Rumford Point	04279	
Sabattus	04280	
Saco (1st)	04072	
Saint Agatha	04772	
Saint Albans	04971	
Saint David	04773	
Saint Francis	04774	
Saint Francis College, Sta. Biddeford	04005	
Saint George	04857	
Salsbury Cove	04672	
Sandy Point	04972	
Sanford (1st)	04073	
Sangerville	04479	
Sargentville	04673	
Scarborough (1st)	04074	
Seal Cove	04674	
Seal Harbor	04675	
Searsmont	04973	
Searsport	04974	
Sebago Lake	04075	
Sebasco Estates	04565	
Sebec	04481	
Sebec Lake, R. Br. Guilford	04482	
Seboeis	04484	
Sedgwick	04676	
Shapleigh	04076	
Shawmut	04975	
Sheepscott, R. Br. Wiscasset	04566	
Sheridan	04775	
Sherman Mills	04776	
Sherman Station	04777	
Shirley Mills	04485	
Sinclair	04779	
Skowhegan (1st)	04976	
Small Point, R. Sta. Phippsburg	04567	
Smithfield	04978	
Smyrna Mills	04780	
Soldier Pond	04781	
Solon	04979	
Sorrento	04677	
South Berwick	03908	
South Bristol	04568	
Christmas Cove, R. Sta.	04542	
South Casco	04077	
South China	04358	
South Freeport	04078	
Bustins Island, R. Br.	04013	
South Gardiner	04359	
South Gouldsboro	04678	
South Harpswell	04079	
South Hiram	04080	
South Lewiston, Sta. Lewiston	04240	
South Paris	04281	
South Penobscott, R. Sta. Penobscot	04486	
South Portland, Br. Portland	04106	
South Thomaston	04858	
South Waterford	04081	
South Windham	04082	
Southport, R. Br. Boothbay Harbor	04569	
Southwest Harbor	04679	
Manset, R. Br.	04656	
Springfield	04487	
Springvale (1st)	04083	
Spruce Head	04859	
Squirrel Island, R. Br. Boothbay Harbor	04570	
Stacyville	04782	
Standish	04084	
Starks, R. Br. Anson	04980	
Steep Falls	04085	
Stetson	04488	
Steuben	04680	
Stillwater	04489	
Stockholm	04783	
Stockton Springs	04981	
Stonington	04681	
Isle Au Haut, R. Br.	04645	
Lookout, R. Br.	04651	
Stratton	04982	
Strong	04983	
Sullivan	04682	
Sunset	04683	
Surry	04684	
East Blue Hill, R. Br.	04629	
Swans Island	04685	
Temple	04984	
Tenants Harbor	04860	
Thomaston	04861	
Thorndike	04986	

ZIP CODE
PORTLAND, ME.
041 + TWO DIGITS SHOWN = ZIP CODE

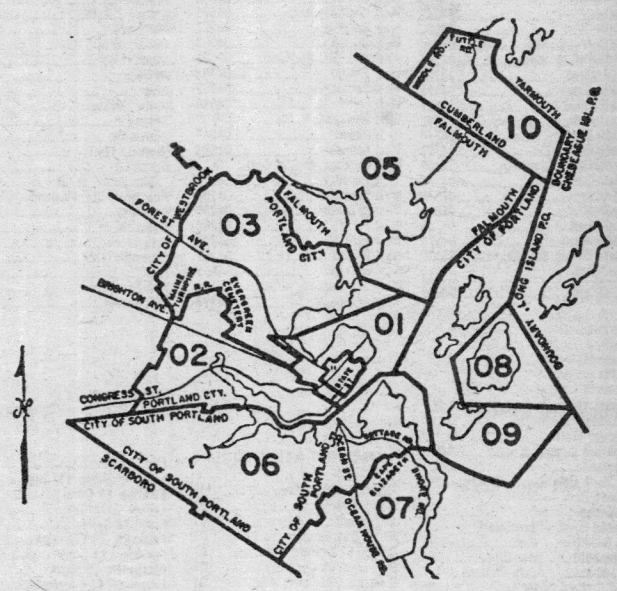

Togus, Br. Augusta	04330
Topsfield	04490
Topsham	04086
Trevett	04571
Troy	04987
Turner	04282
Turner Center, R. Sta.	
Turner	04283
Union	04862
Unity	04988
Upper Frenchville	04784
Upton, R. Br. Newry	04261
Van Buren	04785
Vanceboro	04491
Vassalboro	04989
Veazie, Br. Bangor	04401
Vienna	04360
Vinalhaven	04863
Waite, R. Br. Danforth	04492
Waldoboro	04572
Walpole	04573
Warren	04864
Washburn	04786
Washington	04574
Water Street, Sta. Augusta	04330
Waterboro	04087
Waterford	04088

Waterville (1st)	04901
Wayne	04284
Weeks Mills	04361
Weld	04285
Wellington	04990
Wells	04090
Wells Beach, R. Sta. Wells	04090
Wesley	04686
West Baldwin	04091
West Bethel	04286
West Boothbay Harbor	04575
West Bowdoin	04287
West Buxton	04093
West End, Sta. Portland	04102
West Enfield	04493
West Farmington	04992
West Forks	04985
West Jonesport, R. Sta. Jonesport	04649
West Kennebunk	04094
West Lebanon, R. Sta. East Lebanon	04027
West Minot	04288
West Newfield	04095
West Paris	04289
West Peru	04290
West Poland	04291
West Rockport	04865
West Scarborough, R. Sta. Scarborough	04074

West Southport	04576
West Sullivan	04689
West Sumner	04292
West Tremont	04690
Westbrook (1st)	04092
Westfield	04787
Weston	04494
Westpoint, R. Sta. Sebasco Estates	04565
Whitefield	04362
Whiting	04691
Whitneyville	04692
Wilsons Mills	04293
Wilton (1st)	04294
Windsor	04363
Winn	04495
Winter Harbor	04693
Winterport	04496
Winterville	04788
Winthrop (1st)	04364
Wiscasset	04578
Sheepscott, R. Br.	04566
Woodfords, Sta. Portland	04101
Woodland	04694
Woolwich	04579
Wytopitlock	04497
Yarmouth (1st)	04096
York	03909
York Beach	03910
York Harbor	03911

PORTLAND   041

POST OFFICE BOXES

Box Nos.

1-600	Pearl Street Sta.	12
601-2011	Main Office	04
2100-2599	South Portland Br	06
3000-3930	Main Office	04
4000-4368	Sta A	01
4501-4700	Pearl Street Sta.	12
5001-5149	Sta A	01

RURAL ROUTES

1,2	07
3,4	05

STATIONS, BRANCHES AND UNITS

Cape Cottage Br	07
Cape Elizabeth Br	07
Falmouth Br	05
Peaks Island Sta.	08
Pearl Street Sta.	11
South Portland Br	06
West End Sta	02
Woodfords Sta	01
General Delivery	01
Postmaster	01

APARTMENTS, HOTELS, MOTELS

Albert, 218 Park Ave	02
Alder, 40 Alder	01
Ambassador, 37 Casco	01
Arden, 314 Spring	02
Baxter, 61 Deering	01
Bellevue, 764 Congress	02
Belmead, 398 Forest Ave	01
Berkeley, 72 Park Ave	01
Berry, 88 Park	01
Beverly, 180 Danforth	02
Bowdoin, 131 Chadwick	02
Bramhall, 4 Hill	02
Brightway, 139 William	03
Bristol, 312 Congress	11
Broadview, 344 Broadway S.	06
Calvin, 24 Grant	01
Carleton, 84 Carleton	02
Carroll, 235 Brackett	02
Catir, 284 Congress	11
Chadwick, 135 Chadwick	02
Charter House Motor, 1150 Brighton Ave	02
Clarks, 291 Spring	02
Colby, 123 Sherman	01
Cope, 863 Congress	02
Copely, 485 Cumberland Ave	01
Corner Lodge, 203 Brackett	02
Court Square, 83 Market	11
Danforth, 132 B Danforth	01
Devon Court, 565 Forest Ave	01
Dora, 152 Grant	01

Dow, 17 Dow	02
Eastland Motor, 157 High	01
Eldridge, 80 Grant	01
Everett, 51 A Oak	01
Faith, 74 Spring	11
Falmouth, 19 Falmouth	03
Fenwick, 133 Grant	01
Fessenden, 15 Shepley	01
Florentine, 41 Chestnut	11
Forest Park, 1 Forest Park	01
Garfield, 505 A Washington Ave	03
Glendon Arms, 563 Cumberland Ave	01
Glendon, 549 Cumberland Ave	01
Hampden, 94 Park Ave	01
Harding, 125 Grant	01
Harlan Annex, 7 A Washington Ave	01
Harlan, 215 Congress	11
Hillside, 16 Weymouth	02
Hindscroft, 108 Noyes	03
Hindscroft, 364 Deering Ave	03
Holiday Inn, 79 Riverside St	02
Huddersfield, 197 Pine	02
John Alden House, 6 Walker	02
Jones, 116 Pine	02
Kensington, 497 Cumberland Ave	01
Kimball, 776 Congress	02
Knickerbocker, 120 Park Ave	01
Knudsen, 117 Winter	02

Portland (Con.)   041

Lafayette Town House, 638
  Congress 01
Lawler, 150 Congress 01
Lincoln, 12 Weymouth 02
Little Weymouth, 851
  Congress 02
Longfellow, 658 A Congress ... 01
Los Angeles, 419
  Cumberland Ave 01
Lynden, 407 Cumberland
  Ave 01
Macarthur Gardens, 16
  Walnut 01
Marlborough, 180 High 01
Marvin, 127 Grant 01
Marstaller, 54 Eastern
  Promenade 01
Maryland, 385 Cumberland
  Ave ....
Mc Intyre, 44 Myrtle 01
Mc Kinley, 202 Dartmouth 03
Metropolitan, 439 Congress ... 11
Miles Standish, 11 Shepley 01
Minot, 30 Preble 01
Monticello, 237 High 01
Morningside, 199 Morning 01
Nathan, 119 Sherman 01
Neal, 168 Neal 02
Northgate, 231 State 01
Oakmont, 128 Park Ave 02
Oakview, 104 Oak St 01
Ocean View, 101 Danforth 01
Oxford, 690 Congress 01
Parkview, 142 Park Ave 02
Parkway, 124 Park Ave 01
Parris, 19 Parris 01
Pilgrim, 30 West 02
Plaza Hotel 21 Preble 01
Plymouth Court, 244
  Woodfords 03
Portlander Motel, 645
  Congress 01
Raymond, 55 Morning 01
Ricker, 290 Baxter Blvd 01
Ron-Marsh, 12 Pitt 03
Roosevelt, 25 Granite 01
Saint Regis, 196 Middle 11
Shamrock, 21 1/2 Temple 11
Shepley, 18 Casco 01

Sheraton Eastland,. 157 High
  St 01
Sherman, 111 Sherman 01
Six Links, 5 Bishop 03
Somerset, 633 A Congress 01
Southcourt, 51 Park 01
Southgate, 62 State 01
Southport, 36 A S P 06
Stateway, 59 State 01
Sunnyview, 9 Cedar 11
The Oaks, 76 Park Ave 01
Thompson, 97 Emery 02
Tolman House, 6 Tolman Pl..... 01
Ulysses, 98 Grant 01
Van Brocklin, 55 William 03
Vans, 157 Grant 01
Venetian, 138 Pine 02
Victoria, 939 Congress 02
Vincent, 65 Sherman 01
Warren, 82 Park Ave 31
West View, 193 Clark 02
Whitney, 122 Neal 02
Willard, 84 Eastern
  Promenade 01
Windsor, 286 State 01
Winslow, 48 State 01
Witham, 130 Brackett 02
Withee, 22 Cedar 11
Woodbury, 111 Franklin 11

BUILDINGS

Baxter Block, 562 Congress 01
Browns Wharf 11
Canal Bank, 192 Middle......... 11
Casco Bank, 477 Congress...... 01
Central Wharf 11
City Hall, 389 Congress 01
Clapp Memorial, 443
  Congress 11
Commerce, 465 Congress 11
Congress, 615 Congress 01
Cumberland County
  Courthouse, 142 Federal 11
Custom House Wharf 11
Deakes Wharf 01
Federal, 76 Pearl 11
Gannett, 119 Exchange &
  390 Cngrs........................ 11
Holyoke Wharf 01

Libby, 10 Congress Sq 01
Maine State Armory, 772
  Stevens Ave 03
Maine State Pier 11
Masonic, 415 Congress.......... 11
Merchants Wharf 11
Merrill Wharf 11
Pinehaven, 100 1st Ave.......... 06
Portland Exposition, 239 Park
  Ave 02
Portland Pier Wharf 11
Railroad Wharf 11
Richardsons Wharf 11
South Portland Armory, 680
  Broadway 06
South Portland Municipal, 25
  Cottage Rd...................... 06
Trelawny, 655 Congress......... 01
Underwood, Underwood Rd 05
Union Mutual Life Insurance
  Company, Congress 12
Union Mutual Life Insurance
  Company, Exchange.......... 12
Union Wharf 11
United States Federal, 156
  Federal 11
United States Federal, 76
  Pearl 11
United States Post Office,
  125 Forest Ave 01
Widgery Wharf 11
Wrights Wharf 01

HOSPITALS

Maine Medical Center, 22
  Bramhall 02
Mercy, 144 State 01
Osteopathic Hospital Of
  Maine, 335 Brighton Ave.... 02

UNIVERSITIES AND COLLEGES

Northeastern Business, 97
  Danforth 01
Saint Joseph'S Academy To
  Catherine Mcauley High 03
University Of Maine, 96
  Falmouth 03
Westbrook Junior 716 Stevens
  Ave To Westbrook College... 03

State List of Post Offices

MARYLAND

(Abbreviation: MD)

A Boxes, Cumberland 21505
Abell 20606
Aberdeen (1st) 21001
Aberdeen Proving Ground
  (1st) 21005
Abingdon 21009
Accident 21520
Accokeek 20607
Adamstown 21710
Adelphi, Br. Hyattsville 20783
Allen 21810
Allentown Mall, Br. Prince
  Georges Facility........... 20748
American Cities,
  Br. Columbia 21044
Andrews AFB,
  Br. Washington, DC 20331

Andrews Air Force Hospital,
  Br. Washington, DC 20331
ANNAPOLIS, (1st) Main PO ... 21404
  (Also See Appendix)
Annapolis Junction 20701
Aquasco 20608
Arlington, Sta. Baltimore ... 21215
Arnold 21012
Asbury Methodist Home,
  R. Sta. Gaithersburg 20877
Ashton 20861
Aspen Hill,
  Br. Silver Spring 20906
Avenue 20609
Baldwin 21013
BALTIMORE (1st), Main PO .. 21233
  (Also See Appendix)
Baltimore-Washington Int'l
  Airport, Br. Baltimore ... 21240
Barclay 21607

Barnesville 20838
Barstow 20610
Barton 21521
Beallsville 20839
Bel Air (1st) 21014
Bel Alton 20611
Belcamp 21017
Beltsville (1st) 20705
Benedict 20612
Benson 21018
Bentley Springs 21019
Berlin (1st) 21811
Berwyn Hts., Sta. College Pk . 20740
BETHESDA, Main PO 20814
  (Also See Appendix)
Bethlehem 21609
Betterton 21610
Big Pool 21711
Big Spring 21722
Bishops Head 21611

Bishopville	21813	
Bittinger	21522	
Bivalve	21814	
Bladensburg (1st)	20710	
Blair, Br. Silver Spring	20910	
Bloomington	21523	
Boonsboro (1st)	21713	
Boring	21020	
Bowie (1st)	20715	
Mitchellville, Br.	20716	
West Bowie, Sta.	20715	
Boyds	20841	
Bozman	21612	
Braddock Heights	21714	
Bradshaw	21021	
Brandywine	20613	
Brentwood (1st)	20722	
Brinklow	20862	
Brookeville	20729	
Brooklandville (1st)	21022	
Brooklyn-Curtis Bay,		
Br. Baltimore	21225	
Broomes Island	20615	
Brownsville	21715	
Brunswick (1st)	21716	
Bryans Road	20616	
Bryantown	20617	
Buckeystown	21717	
Burkittsville	21718	
Burtonsville	20866	
Bushwood	20618	
Butler	21023	
Cabin John (1st)	20818	
California	20619	
Callaway	20620	
Calvert, Sta. Baltimore	21202	
Cambridge (1st)	21613	
Camp Springs, Br. Prince		
Georges Facility	20748	
Cape Saint Claire,		
R. Br. Annapolis	21401	
Capitol Heights, Br. Prince		
Georges Facility	20743	
Capitol Plaza, Br. Hyattsville	20784	
Cardiff	21024	
Carroll, Sta. Baltimore	21229	
Carrollton	21157	
Cascade	21719	
Catonsville, Br. Baltimore	21228	
Cavetown	21720	
Cecilton	21913	
Centreville (1st)	21617	
Chance	21816	
Chaptico	20621	
Charlestown	21914	
Charlotte Hall	20622	
Chase	21027	
Cheltenham	20623	
Chesapeake Beach	20732	
Chesapeake City	21915	
Chester	21619	
Chestertown (1st)	21620	
Chevy Chase, Br. Bethesda	20815	
Chewsville	21721	
Childs	21916	
Chillum, Br. Hyattsville	20783	
Church Creek	21622	
Church Hill	21623	
Churchton	20733	
Churchville	21028	
Claiborne	21624	

Clarksburg	20871	
Clarksville	21029	
Clear Spring	21722	
Clements	20624	
Clifton-East End,		
Sta. Baltimore	21213	
Clinton (1st)	20735	
Cobb Island	20625	
Cockeysville (1st)	21030	
Colesville, Br. Silver Spring	20904	
College, Sta. Westminster	21157	
College Estates,		
Sta. Frederick	21701	
College Park (1st)	20740	
Berwyn Heights, Sta.	20740	
Colora	21917	
Coltons Point	20626	
Columbia, Br. Ellicott		
City (1st)	21043	
Commerce, Sta. Baltimore	21202	
Compton	20627	
Conowingo	21918	
Cooksville	21723	
Cordova	21625	
Corriganville	21524	
Courthouse, Sta. Rockville	20850	
Crapo	21626	
Crellin, R. Br. Oakland	21525	
Cresaptown Boxes	21505	
Cresaptown, Br. Cumberland	21502	
Crisfield (1st)	21817	
Crocheron	21627	
Crofton, R. Br. Odenton	21114	
Crownsville	21032	
Crumpton	21628	
Cumberland (1st)	21502	
Damascus (1st)	20872	
Dameron	20628	
Dames Quarter	21820	
Darlington	21034	
Davidsonville	21035	
Dayton	21036	
Deal Island	21821	
Deale	20751	
Deer Park, Br. Oakland	21550	
Delmar	21875	
Denton (1st)	21629	
Derwood, Br. Rockville	20855	
Detour	21725	
Diamond Farms		
Br. Gaithersburg	20878	
Dickerson	20842	
District Hts-Forestville		
Br. Prince Georges Facility	20747	
Dowell	20629	
Drayden	20630	
Druid, Sta. Baltimore	21217	
Dundalk-Sparrows Point,		
Br. Baltimore	21222	
Dunkirk	20754	
Earleville	21919	
East End, Sta. Baltimore	21205	
East New Market	21631	
Easton (1st)	21601	
Eastport, Sta. Annapolis	21403	
Eckhart Mines	21528	
Eden	21822	
Edgewater	21037	
Edgewood (1st)	21040	
Edgewood Arsenal	21010	
Editors Park, Br. Hyattsville	20782	

Eldersburg	21784	
Elk Mills	21920	
Elkton (1st)	21921	
Ellerslie	21529	
Ellicott City (1st)	21043	
Elliott	21823	
Emmitsburg (1st)	21727	
Essex, Br. Baltimore	21221	
Eudowood, Br. Baltimore	21284	
Ewell	21824	
Fahrney Keedy Memorial Home,		
R. Br. Boonsboro	21713	
Fair Play	21733	
Fallston	21047	
Faulkner	20632	
Federalsburg (1st)	21632	
Ferndale,		
R. Br. Glen Burnie	21061	
Finksburg	21048	
Fishing Creek	21634	
Flintstone	21530	
Forest Hill	21050	
Forestville	20747	
Fork	21051	
Fort George G Meade (1st)	20755	
Fort Howard	21052	
Fort Ritchie, Br. Cascade	21719	
Fort Washington, Br.		
Prince Georges Facility	20744	
Franklin, Sta. Baltimore	21223	
Frederick (1st)	21701	
College Estates, Sta.	21701	
Hood College, Sta.	21701	
Lewistown, R. Br.	21701	
Freeland	21053	
Friendship	20758	
Friendsville	21531	
Frostburg (1st)	21532	
Fruitland	21826	
Fulton	20759	
Funkstown	21734	
Gaither	21735	
Gaithersburg (1st)	20877	
Galena	21635	
Galesville	20765	
Gambrills	21054	
Gapland	21736	
Garrett Park	20896	
Garrison	21055	
Georgetown	21930	
Germantown	20874	
Gibson Island	21056	
Girdletree	21829	
Glen Arm	21057	
Glen Burnie (1st)	21061	
Glen Echo	20812	
Glenelg	21737	
Glenn Dale	20769	
Glenwood	21738	
Glyndon	21071	
Goddard Flight Center	20771	
Goldsboro	21636	
Golts	21637	
Govans, Sta. Baltimore	21212	
Grantsville	21536	
Grasonville	21638	
Great Mills	20634	
Green Haven,		
R. Br. Pasadena	21122	
Greenbelt (1st)	20770	
Greensboro	21639	

Gunpowder, Br. Aberdeen Proving
  Ground 21010
Gwynn Oak, Sta. Baltimore . . 21207
Hagerstown (1st) 21740
Halethorpe, Br. Baltimore . . 21227
Hamilton, Sta. Baltimore 21214
Hampden, Sta. Baltimore 21211
Hampstead 21074
Hancock (1st) 21750
Hanover 21076
Harmans 21077
Harwood 20776
Havre De Grace (1st) 21078
Hebron 21830
Helen 20635
Henderson 21640
Henryton 21080
Highfield 21719
Highland 20777
Highlandtown, Sta. Baltimore . 21224
Hillsboro 21641
Hollywood 20636
Hood College, Sta. Frederick . 21701
Hoopersville 21642
Hughesville 20637
Hunt Valley, Br. Cockeysville . 21031
Huntingtown 20639
Hurlock 21643
HYATTSVILLE (1st) Main PO . . 20781
  (Also See Appendix)
Hydes 21082
Ijamsville 21754
Ilchester 21083
Indian Head (1st) 20640
Ingleside 21644
Ironsides 20643
Issue 20645
Jarrettsville 21084
Jefferson 21755
Jefferson Heights,
  Br. Hagerstown 21740
Jessup 20794
Joppa (1st) 21085
Keedysville 21756
Kenilworth, Br. Riverdale 20737
Kennedyville 21645
Kensington (1st) 20895
Keymar 21757
Kingston 21871
Kingsville 21087
Kitzmiller 21538
Knoxville 21758
La Plata 20646
La Vale, Br. Cumberland 21502
La Vale Boxes 21504
Ladiesburg 21759
Lake Shore, Br. Pasadena . . . 21122
Landover, Br. Hyattsville 20785
  (Also See Appendix)
Landover Hills, Br. Hyattsville . 20784
Langley Park, Br. Hyattsville . . 20787
Lanham-Seabrook (1st) 20706
Lantz, R. Br. Sabillasville 21760
Laurel (1st) 20707
Laytonsville,
  R. Br. Gaithersburg 20879
Leisure World,
  Br. Silver Spring 20906
Leonardtown (1st) 20650

Lewistown, R. Br. Frederick . . 21701
Lexington Park (1st) 20653
Libertytown 21762
Lincoln Avenue
  Br. Hagerstown 21740
Lineboro 21088
Linkwood 21835
Linthicum Heights (1st) 21090
Linwood 21764
Lisbon 21765
Little Orleans 21766
Lonaconing 21539
Long Green 21092
Lothian 20711
Loveville 20656
Loyola, Sta. Baltimore 21210
Luke, Br. Westernport 21540
Lusby 20657
Lutherville-Timonium (1st) . . . 21093
Lynch 21646
Maddox, R. Br. Chaptico 20621
Madison 21648
Magnolia 21101
Main Street, Sta. Salisbury . . 21801
Manchester 21102
Manokin 21836
Marbury 20658
Mardela Springs 21837
Marion Station 21838
Marriottsville,
  R. Br. Woodstock 21104
Marydel 21649
Maryland Line 21105
Massey 21650
Maugansville 21767
Mayo 21106
McDaniel 21647
McDonough, Br. Baltimore . . . 21208
McHenry 21541
Mechanicsville 20659
Middle River, Br. Baltimore . . 21220
Middleburg 21768
Middletown 21769
Midland 21542
Midlothian 21543
Millers 21107
Millersville 21108
Millington 21651
Mitchellville, Br. Bowie 20716
Monkton 21111
Monrovia 21770
Montego 21842
Montgomery Village 20879
Montpelier 20708
Morganza 20660
Mount Airy 21771
Mount Rainier (1st) 20712
Mount Savage 21545
Mount Victoria 20661
Mount Washington,
  Sta. Baltimore 21209
Mount Wilson 21208
Mountain Lake Park,
  Br. Oakland 21550
Myersville 21773
Nanjemoy 20662
Nanticoke 21840
National Naval Med Center,
  Br. Bethesda 20814

Naval Academy,
  Br. Annapolis 21402
Naval Air Facility,
  Br. Washington, DC 20390
Neavitt 21652
New Carrollton,
  Br. Hyattsville 20784
New Market 21774
New Midway 21775
New Windsor 21776
Newark 21841
Newburg 20664
Newcomb 21653
Nikep 21546
Normandy, Br. Ellicott City . . 21043
North Beach 20714
North College Park 20740
North East (1st) 21901
North Ocean City,
  Br. Ocean City 21842
Northern, Sta. Hagerstown . . 21740
Northwood 21239
Oakland (1st) 21550
  Crellin, R. Br. 21525
  Deer Park, Br. 21550
  Mountain Lake Park, Br. . . 21550
Ocean City 21842
Odenton (1st) 21113
Oldtown 21555
Olney 20832
Oriole 21853
Owings 20736
Owings Mills (1st) 21117
Oxford 21654
Oxon Hill, Br. Prince
  Georges Facility 20745
Park Hall 20667
Parkton 21120
Parkville, Br. Baltimore 21234
  (Also See Appendix)
Parsonsburg 21849
Pasadena (1st) 21122
Patapsco 21048
Patterson, Sta. Baltimore . . . 21231
Patuxent River (1st) 20670
Peninsula General Hospital . . 21801
Perry Hall (1st) 21128
Perry Point 21902
Perryman 21130
Perryville 21903
Phoenix 21131
Pike, Sta. Rockville 20852
Pikesville, Br. Baltimore 21208
Piney Point 20674
Pinto 21556
Pisgah, R. Br. Indian Head . . 20640
Pittsville 21850
Pocomoke City (1st) 21851
Point of Rocks 21777
Pomfret 20675
Poolesville 20837
Port Deposit (1st) 21904
Port Republic 20676
Port Tobacco 20677
Potomac, Br. Rockville 20854
Powellville 21852
Preston 21655
Price 21656
Prince Frederick 20678

Prince Georges Facility 20790	Secretary 21664	Tysskin 21865
Forestville 20747	Severn 21144	Tyferton 21866
Br. Camp Springs 20748	Severna Park (1st) 21146	Union Bridge 21791
Br. Capitol Heights 20743	Shady Side 20764	Uniontown,
Br. District Heights-	Sharpsburg 21782	R. Br. Westminster 21157
Forestville 20747	Sharptown 21861	Unionville 21792
Br. Ft. Washington 20744	Sherwood 21665	University of Maryland 20742
Br. Oxon Hill 20745	Sherwood Forest,	Upper Fairmount 21867
Br. Suitland 20746	R. Br. Annapolis 21405	Upper Falls 21156
Br. Temple Hills 20748	Showell 21862	Upper Hill 21868
Prince Georges Plaza,	SILVER SPRING (1st), Main PO .. 20907	Upper Marlboro (1st) 20772
Br. Hyattsville 20788	(Also See Appendix)	Upperco 21155
(Also See Appendix)	Simpsonville 21150	Valley Lee 20692
Princess Anne (1st) 21853	Smithsburg 21783	Vienna 21869
Pylesville (1st) 21132	Snow Hill (1st) 21863	Walbrook, Sta. Baltimore ... 21216
Quantico 21856	Solomons 20688	Waldorf (1st) 20601
Queen Anne 21657	South, Sta. Baltimore 21230	Walkersville 21793
Queenstown 21658	Southeast, Sta. Baltimore .. 21281	Warwick 21912
Randallstown (1st) 21133	Sparks Glencoe 21152	Washington Grove 20880
Randolph Hills, Br. Rockville .. 20852	Sperrows Point, Br. Baltimore .. 21219	Waverly, Sta. Baltimore 21218
Raspeburg, Sta. Baltimore .. 21206	Spencerville 20868	Welcome 20693
Rawlings 21557	Spring Gap 21560	Wenona 21870
Rehobeth 21857	Springfield State Hospital,	West Bethesda 20817
Reisterstown (1st) 21136	R. Br. Sykesville 21784	West Bowie, Sta. Bowie 20715
Rhodes Point 21858	Stevenson 21153	West Friendship 21794
Rhodesdale 21659	Stevensville 21666	West Hyattsville
Riderwood 21139	Still Pond 21667	Sta. Hyattsville 20782
Ridge 20680	Stockton 21864	West River 20778
Ridgely 21660	Street 21154	Westernport 21562
Rising Sun 21911	Sudlersville 21668	Westminster (1st) 21157
Rison 20658	Suitland, Br. Prince	Westover 21871
Riva 21140	Georges Facility 20746	Westwood 20613
Riverdale (1st) 20737	Sunderland 20689	Whaleysville 21872
Riviera Beach, Br. Pasadena .. 21122	Swanton 21561	Wheaton, Br. Silver Spring .. 20902
Rock Hall 21661	Sykesville (1st) 21784	White Hall 21161
Rock Point 20682	Takoma Park,	White Marsh 21162
ROCKVILLE (1st) Main PO .. 20850	Br. Silver Springs 20912	White Plains 20695
(Also See Appendix)	Tall Timbers 20690	Whiteford 21160
Rocky Ridge 21778	Taneytown 21787	Whitehaven 21873
Rohrersville 21779	Taylors Island 21669	Willards 21874
Roland Park, Sta. Baltimore .. 21210	Temple Hills, Br. Prince	Williamsburg 21643
Rosedale, Br. Baltimore 21237	Georges Facility 20748	Williamsport (1st) 21795
Royal Oak 21662	Templeville 21670	Wingate 21675
Ruxton, Br. Baltimore 21204	Thurmont (1st) 21788	Wintergreen, Sta. Rockville .. 20856
Sabillasville 21780	Tilghman 21671	Wittman 21676
Saint Inigoes 20684	Timonium 21093	Woodbine 21797
Saint James 21781	Toddville 21672	Woodmoor, Br. Silver Spring .. 20901
Saint Leonard 20685	Towson, Br. Baltimore 21285	Woodsboro 21798
Saint Marys City 20686	Towson Towne Center,	Woodstock 21163
Saint Michaels 21663	Br. Baltimore 21286	Woolford 21677
Salisbury (1st) 21801	Tracys Landing 20779	Worton 21678
Sandy Spring 20860	Trappe 21673	Wye Mills 21679
Savage 20763	Tuscarora 21790	
Scotland 20687	Twinbrook, Sta. Rockville .. 20851	

ANNAPOLIS	**214**	4,5,6	01	West End Br.	01
		7	03	General Delivery	01
POST OFFICE BOXES		8	01	Postmaster	01
Box Nos.					
1-1991 Main Office	04	**STATIONS, BRANCHES AND UNITS**		**GOVERNMENT OFFICES**	
RURAL ROUTES		Cape Saint Claire Rural Br.	01	Agriculture Department Of	
		Eastport Sta.	03	Agricultural Stabilization....	01
1,2	01	Naval Academy Br.	02	All Departments	01
3	03	Sherwood Forest Rural Br. ..	05	Ann Arundel County	
		West Annapolis Sta.	01	Agriculture Extension.......	01

| Annapolis (Con.) | 214 | BALTIMORE | 212 | 14,15,16 | 20 |

POST OFFICE BOXES

STATIONS, BRANCHES AND UNITS

Ann Arundel County Board Of
Education............................ 04
Ann Arundel County Civil
Defense.............................. 04
Ann Arundel County Clerk
Circuit Court........................ 04
Ann Arundel County County
Commissioners..................... 04
Ann Arundel County Health
Department......................... 01
Ann Arundel County Judges
Circuit Court........................ 04
Ann Arundel County Juvenile
Probation............................ 04
Ann Arundel County Liquor
License Board....................... 04
Ann Arundel County Public
Works................................ 04
Ann Arundel County Register
Of Wills.............................. 01
Ann Arundel County Sheriff....... 04
Ann Arundel County States
Attorney............................. 04
Ann Arundel County
Supervisor Of Elections.......... 04
Ann Arundel County Welfare
Board................................ 04
Bancroft Hall........................ 12
Board Of Natural Resources....... 01
Board Of Public Works............. 04
Comptroller Of Treasury........... 04
Court Of Appeals................... 04
Department Of Economic
Development........................ 01
Department Of Educational
Rehabilitation...................... 01
Department Of Employment
Security............................. 04
Department Of Forests &
Parks................................ 01
Department Of Game, Inland
Fish................................. 01
Department Research &
Education............................ 01
Department Tidewater
Fisheries............................ 01
Federal Bureau Of
Investigation....................... 04
Governor............................ 04
Land Commissioner................ 04
Selective Service System.......... 04
Soil Conservation Service.......... 01
State Library........................ 04
Treasurer............................ 04
Treasury Department Internal
Revenue Service.................... 04
Veterans Employment
Service.............................. 04
Water Pollution Control
Commission.......................... 01

Box Nos.

1-2499   Main Office...... 03
ANY   Main Office...... 33
2501-2699   Arlington Sta..... 15
2701-2899   Brooklyn-Curtis
                Bay Br........... 25
2901-3099   Carroll Sta....... 29
3101-3299   Catonsville Br.... 28
3301-3399   Clifton Sta....... 13
3401-3499   Brooklyn-Curtis
                Bay Br........... 25
3501-3699   Hamilton Sta...... 14
3701-3899   Druid Sta........ 17
3901-4099   Dundalk Br....... 22
4101-4299   East End Sta...... 05
4301-4499   Franklin Sta...... 23
4501-4699   Govans Sta....... 12
4701-4899   Hampden Sta...... 11
4901-5099   Middle River
                Br............... 20
5101-5299   Highlandtown
                Sta.............. 24
5301-5399   Mount
                Washington
                Sta.............. 09
5401-5599   Towson Br........ 04
5601-5699   Roland Park
                Sta.............. 10
5701-5999   Pikesville Br..... 08
6001-6199   Patterson Sta..... 31
6201-6299   Raspeburg Sta.... 06
6301-6499   South Sta........ 30
6501-6699   Sparrows Point
                Br............... 19
6701-6899   Towson Sta....... 04
6901-7099   Walbrook Sta..... 16
7101-7299   Waverly Sta...... 18
7301-7499   Halethorpe Br.... 27
7501-7699   Gwynn Oak Br.... 07
7701-7999   Essex Br......... 21
8001-8399   Ruxton Br........ 04
8401-8599   Parkville Br...... 34
8600-8799   Friendship
                International
                Airport Br....... 40
8801-8899   Highlandtown
                Sta.............. 24
8901-9299   Dundalk Br....... 22
9301-9499   Catonsville Br.... 28
9501-9699   Rosedale Br...... 37
9701-9899   Eudowood
                Finance Br....... 24
9901-9999   Highlandtown
                Sta.............. 24
10001-10199   Towson Br....... 04
10201-10399   Alameda
                Station.......... 39
10401-10499   Mount
                Washington
                Sta.............. 09

RURAL ROUTES

1............................. 21
2............................. 37
4............................. 27
5............................. 07
7............................. 08
10............................ 19
13............................ 21

Arlington Sta...................... 15
Brooklyn-Curtis Bay Br............. 25
Calvert Sta........................ 02
Carroll Sta........................ 29
Catonsville Br..................... 28
Clifton Sta........................ 13
Commerce Sta...................... 02
Druid Sta......................... 17
Dundalk Br........................ 22
East End Sta....................... 05
Elkridge Br........................ 27
Essex Br.......................... 21
Eudowood Br....................... 04
Fort Holabird Sta.................. 19
Franklin Sta....................... 23
Friendship Airport Br.............. 40
Govans Sta........................ 12
Gwynn Oak Sta..................... 07
Halethorpe Br..................... 27
Hamilton Sta...................... 14
Hampden Sta....................... 11
Highlandtown Sta.................. 24
Lansdowne Br...................... 27
Loch Raven Br..................... 04
Loyola Sta........................ 10
Mc Donough Br..................... 08
Merchants Sta..................... 01
Middle River Br.................... 20
Mount Washington Sta.............. 09
Overlea Br......................... 06
Parcel Post Sta.................... 33
Parkville Br....................... 34
Patterson Sta...................... 31
Pikesville Br...................... 08
Raspeburg Sta..................... 06
Roland Park Sta................... 10
Rosedale Br....................... 37
Ruxton Br......................... 04
Security Br........................ 35
South Sta......................... 30
Southeast Sta..................... 24
Southwest Sta..................... 30
Sparrows Point Br................. 19
Towson Br......................... 04
Walbrook Br....................... 16
Waverly Sta....................... 18
Westview Sta...................... 28
General Delivery................... 33
Postmaster........................ 33

APARTMENTS, HOTELS, MOTELS

Albion, 900 Cathedral............. 01
Algonquin, 704 Gladstone
Ave................................ 10
Alhambra, 825 Lake Dr............ 17
Allston, 3111 N Charles........... 18
Ambassador, 3811
Canterbury Rd................... 18
Ardmore Arms, 920 W
University Pkwy................. 10
Arlington Park, 6701 Park
Heights Ave..................... 15
Armistead, 17 Holliday............ 02
Baltimorean, 2905 N Charles...... 18
Bancroft, 6420 Park Heights
Av................................ 15
Belvedere Towers, 1190-92 W
Northern Pkwy.................. 10
Blackstone Apts 3215 N
Charles St...................... 18

HOSPITALS

Anne Arundel General
Hospital........................... 01
Naval Hospital..................... 02

UNIVERSITIES AND COLLEGES

Naval Academy..................... 02
Saint Johns College................ 04

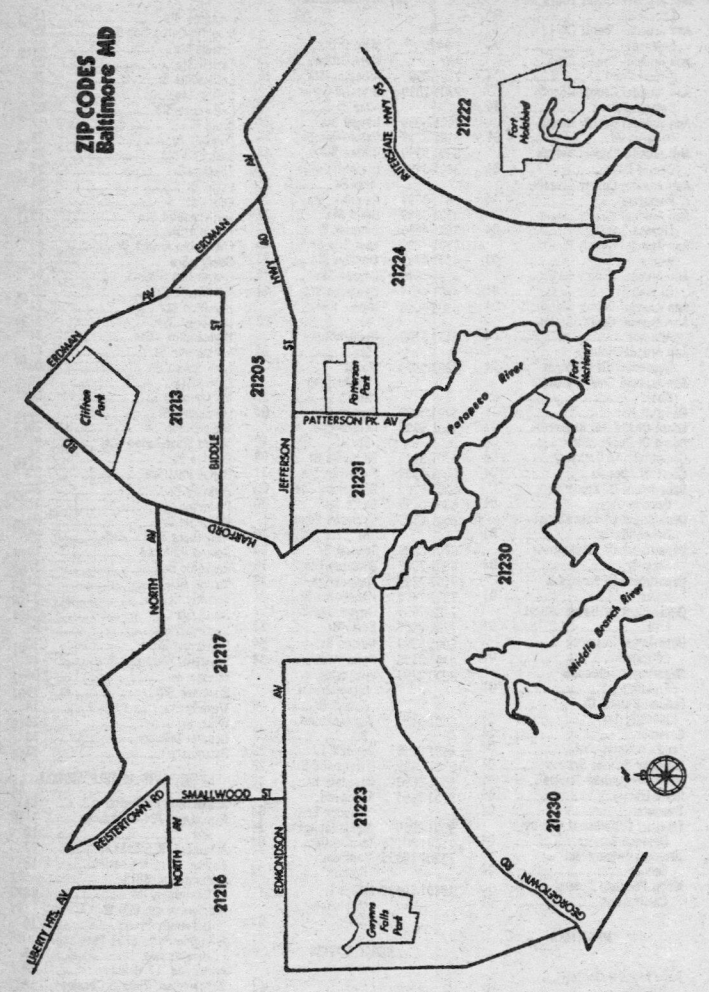

ZIP CODES
Baltimore Md

Baltimore (Con.)   212

Bradford, 3301 St Paul......   18
Broadview, 116 W University
  Pkwy..........................   10
Buckingham Arms, 3706 N
  Charles........................   18
Burford, 3209 N Charles.......   18
Calvert Court, 3024 N
  Calvert........................   18
Cambridge Arms, 3339 N
  Charles........................   18
Canterbury Hall, 100 W 39th..   10
Carlton, 3507 N Charles.......   18
Carolina, 108 W University
  Pkwy...........................   18
Carrollton, 3601 Greenway.....   10
Chadford, 909 W University
  Pkwy...........................   10
Chapelgate Apts, 5109
  Williston......................   29
Charles, 3333 N Charles   18
Charleston Hall, 4500 N
  Charles........................   10
Claremont, 1201 Brunswick....   23
Club Manor, 7302 Park
  Heights Ave...................   08
Club, 10 Club Rd................   18
Concord, 2500 W Belvedere
  Ave............................   15
Congress, 306 W Franklin......   01
Court House Square Apts 1
  Acorn Circle..................   04
De Soto, 3409 Greenway........   18
Donnybrook, 7914 Knollwood
  Rd..............................   04
Dundee Arms, 3902
  Canterbury Rd.................   18
Eden Hall, 3401 Greenway.....   18
Eleven Slade, 11 Slade Ave....   08
Emersonian, 2502 Eutaw Pl....   17
Esplanade, 2519 Eutaw Pl.....   17
Eton Hall, 5906 Park Heights
  Ave............................   15
Executive House, 7011 Park
  Heights Ave...................   15
Fordleigh, 3800 Fordleigh Rd..   15
Garden, 230 Stony Run Lane...   18
Geneva, 3405 Greenway.........   18
Georgian Court, 2516 Linden
  Ave............................   17
Gilman, 3025-43 N Calvert....   18
Goodlow House, 200 Cross
  Keys Rd........................   10
Greenbriar, 7229 Park
  Heights Ave...................   08
Greenspring Manor, 7309
  Park Heights Ave.............   08
Greenway, 3401 N Charles.....   18
Greenwich Gardens,
  Greenwich & Ol Fredk........   29
Guilford Manor, 2 W
  University Parkway...........   18
Guilford Towers, 14 W Cold
  Spring Lane...................   01
Guilford-Homewood, 300 A E
  University Pky................   18
Hamlyn, 103 W 39th...........   10
Hampton House 204 E Joppa
  Rd..............................   04
Hampton Plaza 302 E Joppa
  Rd..............................   04

Highfield House, 4000 N
  Charles........................   18
Hilton Court, 3306 N Hilton....   16
Hilton Village, 3400 Dolfield
  Ave............................   15
Holiday Inn, Howard &
  Lombard.......................   01
Homewood, 3003 N Charles....   18
Hopkins House, 110 W 39th....   10
Hopkins, 3100 St Paul.........   18
Horizon House, 1101 N
  Calvert........................   02
Ingram Hall, 7301 Park
  Heights Av....................   08
Ivy Hall, 2 E 33rd..............   18
Jefferson, 4 E 32nd............   18
Lake Court, 2517 Linden Ave..   17
Lake Drive, 903 Lake Dr.......   17
Lakeview Towers 727 Druid
  Park Lake Dr.................   17
Linkwood, 4000 Linkwood Rd..   10
Loch Bend, 8701 Raven Dr.....   34
Loch Raven, 1500 Waverly
  Way............................   39
Lochwood, 1307 E Belvedere
  Ave............................   39
Lombardy, 220 Stony Run
  Lane...........................   10
Lord Baltimore, Baltimore &
  Hanover.......................   03
Louiston Court, 2228 Mt
  Royal Ter......................   18
Madison, 817 St Paul..........   02
Marjeane, 2437 Lakeview
  Ave............................   17
Marlborough, 1701 Eutaw Pl...   17
Marylander, 3501 St Paul......   18
Melrose East, 100 E Melrose
  Ave............................   12
Memorial Apts, 301
  Mcmechen.....................   17
Mount Royal, 113 E Mt Royal
  Ave............................   01
Mount Vernon Place
  Apartment, 101 W
  Monument.....................   01
Navarre, 1700 Eutaw Pl.......   17
New Howard, 8 N Howard......   01
Normandie, 2624 St Paul......   18
Northway, 3700 N Charles.....   18
Northwood, 4230 Loch Raven
  Blvd...........................   18
Oaklee Village, 1 Oaklee
  Village........................   29
Oaklyn, 3317 Liberty Heights
  Ave............................   15
Park Lynn, 4 Upland Rd.......   10
Park Plaza, 2 W Madison.......   01
Park Regent, 6414 Park
  Heights Ave...................   15
Park Towers, 7121 Park
  Heights Ave...................   15
Pentridge, 1501 Pentridge
  Rd..............................   39
Pinkney Court, 6109 Park
  Heights Ave...................   15
Ralworth, 5702 Beechdl Ave...   39
Ramblewood, 1300 E
  Belvedere Ave................   39
Ridgemede, 221 Ridgemede
  Rd..............................   10
Riviera, 901 Lake Dr...........   17
Rochester Court, 2513 Linden

Ave.............................   17
Roland View Towers, 3939
  Roland Ave....................   11
Ruxton Towers, 8415 Bellona
  Ln..............................   04
Saint Paul Court, 3120 St
  Paul...........................   18
Samester Parkway, 7000
  Park Heights Ave.............   15
Seven Mile Lane, 3901 Seven
  Mile Ln........................   08
Shelbourne, 3801 Clarks
  Lane...........................   15
Sheraton Baltimore Inn, 400
  N Broadway....................   31
Sheraton-Belvedere, 1 E
  Chase..........................   02
Stafford, 712 N Charles.......   01
Stanley, 506 N Howard.........   01
Statler Hilton, 101 W Fayette
  St..............................   01
Strathmore Towers, 6210
  Park Heights Ave.............   15
Sutton Place Apartments,
  1111 Park Ave................   01
Temple Court, 233 E
  University Parkway...........   18
Temple Garden, 2601
  Madison Ave..................   17
The Village Of Cross Keys,
  5100 Falls Rd.................   10
The Walters 111 W Centre.....   01
Tudor Arms, 501 W University
  Parkway.......................   18
Tuscany, 221 Stony Run
  Lane...........................   10
University One, 1 E University
  Pkwy...........................   18
University, 104 W University
  Pkwy...........................   18
Victoria, 704 E Baltimore.....   02
Warren Park Apartments.......   08
Warrington, 3908 N Charles...   18
Washington, 700 N Charles....   01
Wentworth Arms, 311
  Cathedral.....................   01
Westminster House, 524 N
  Charles........................   01
Westminster, 418 W Fayette...   01
Windsor House, 6503 Park
  Heights Ave...................   15
Woodcliffe Manor, 108 W
  39th...........................   10
Wyman Park, 3915 Beech
  Ave............................   11
Wynnewood Towers, 100 W
  Cold Spring Ln...............   10

BUILDINGS

Abell, 5 South..................   02
Aerc Acres, Martin Blvd......   20
Alameda, 5600 The Alameda..   39
Alex Brown & Sons Bldg, 102
  W Penna Ave..................   04
American National, 204 N
  Liberty........................   01
American Trust, 2 Commerce   02
American, 229 E Baltimore....   02
Arbutus, 1000 Maiden Choice
  Ln..............................   29
Association Of Commerce, 22
  Light...........................   02

Baltimore (Con.)   212

Belford, Belair Rd & Frankford Av 06
Beltway Plaza, 1034 York Rd.. 04
Belvedere Gardens Belvedere Ave And Hillen 39
Blaustein, 1 N Charles 01
Broadway, Caroline & Orleans 31
Bromo Seltzer Tower, 318 W Lombard 01
Brookhill, Reistrtwn & Clarnth Rd 15
Brooklyn Park Plaza, Ritchie Hy & 11 Ave 25
Candler, 109 Market Place.. 02
Central Savings Bank, 3 E Lexington 02
Charing Cross, Baltimore Ntl Pk & Chrg Crs 29
Cherry Hill, Cherry Hill & Seabury 25
Cold Spring Lane, Cold Spring Ln & Lch Rvn..... 39
Colonial Village, Reisterstwn & Fallstlf 15
Commercial Credit, 300 St Paul Pl 02
Court Square, 200 E Lexington 02
Davison Chemical, 101 N Charles 01
Dolfield, 3500 Dolfield Av 15
Drovers & Mechanics Bank, 100 N Eutaw 01
Drumcastle, 6305 York Rd.. 12
Dulaney Plaza, 700 Dulaney Vly Rd 04
Dundalk, Commerce St & Shpg Pl 22
Eastpoint, N Point Rd & Eastern Blvd 24
Eastwood, 7500 Eastern Blvd 24
Edgemere, 7514 N Point Rd.. 19
Edgewater, 1800 Eastern Blvd 21
Edmondson Village, Edmondson & Swann Aves 29
Equitable Towson Bldg 401 Washington Ave 04
Equitable, 8 N Calvert 02
Erdman, 3901 Erdman Ave.. 13
Essex, 400 Eastern Blvd 21
Eudowood Plaza, Goucher Blvd & Joppa Rd 04
Fallstaff, Reisterstwn & Labyrnth Rds 15
Farmers Market Pulaski Hwy & Mohrs Ln 20
Federal Land Bank, 2315 St Paul 18
Fidelity, 210 N Charles 01
First National Bank, 7 E Redwood 02
Frankford, Frankford Av & Sinclair Ln 06
Frederick Avenue, 2401 Frederick Ave 23
Freedom, 4500 Erdman Ave.. 13

Garrett, 237 E Redwood 02
Gas & Electric, 39 W Lexington 01
Hamilton, 2300 E Northern Pkwy 14
Hampton Plaza Bldg 300 E Joppa Rd 04
Hawthorne, 2100 Eastern Blvd 20
Hillendale, Loch Rvn Blvd & Tylr SE 04
Hilltop, Reistrstwn Rd & Rogers 15
Ina, 301 E Fayette 02
Industrial, 501 E Preston 02
Ingleside, Baltimore Ntl Pk & Inglsd Ave 28
Jefferson 105-07 Chesapeake Ave N 04
Keyser, 207 E Redwood 02
Knickerbocker, 218 E Lexington 02
Lansdowne, 3900 Hollins Ferry Rd 27
Liberty Crest, Liberty & Croydon Rd 07
Loch Raven, Loch Raven Blvd & Northern Pkwy 39
Loch Ridge, Loch Raven Blvd & Joan Ave 34
Logan, Broening Hwy & Dundalk Ave 22
Maryland Life, 10 South 02
Maryland National Bank, 10 Light 02
Maryland Trust, 14 S Calvert 02
Mc Cormick, 414 Light 02
Medical Arts, 101 W Read St.. 01
Mercantile Towson Bldg 409 Washington Ave 04
Mercantile Trust And Bank Bldg, 2 Hopkins Plaza 01
Merritt Park, Merritt Blvd At Wise Av 22
Middle River, Eastern Blvd & Kingston Rd 20
Middlesex, Eastern Blvd & Essex Av 21
Mondawmin, Liberty Hts Ave & Tioga Pky 15
Monumental Life, Charles & Chase 02
Municipal Office, 300 E Lexington 02
Munsey, 7 N Calvert 02
National City Bank Bldg, 101 Light 02
North Point Village, 4000 North Point Blvd 22
Northwood, Loch Raven Blvd & Hvnwd Rd 18
Nottingham Bldg, 103 W. Penna Ave 04
Odonnell, Dundalk Ave & Odonnell 24
Old Town Bank, 321 Fallsway 02
One Charles Center 01
One South Calvert Bldg 1s Calvert 02
Paca-Pratt, 110 S Paca 01
Patterson Village 5/c 4100

Patterson Ave 15
Peoples Court, Fayette & Gay.. 02
Perry Hall, Belair & Joppa Rd 36
Pikesville, Reistrstwn Rd & Mchnry Ave 08
Pleasant Plains, 1000 Taylor Ave 04
Professional, 330 N Charles.. 01
Ravenwood, Loch Raven Blvd & Tylr NW 04
Reisterstown Plaza, Reistrstwn Rd & Pttrsn Ave 15
Riderwood Bldg 1107 Kenilworth Dr 04
Ritchie Highway, Ritchie Hwy & Church St 25
Satyr Hill, Joppa & Satyr Hill Rd 34
Security S/c, 6600 Security Blvd 07
Social Security, 6401 Security Blvd 35
Southview, Hmmnds Ln & Ritchie Hy 25
Standard Oil, 505 St Paul Pl.. 02
Stoney Creek, Ft Smallwood & Hilltop Rd 26
Sun Life Ins Bldg, 20 S Charles 01
Super Giant, Liberty & Milford Mill 07
The Mercantile Trust & Bank Bldg, 2 Hopkins Plaza 01
Title, 106 St Paul 02
Tower, 222 E Baltimore 02
Towson Plaza, 700 Fairmount Ave 04
U S F & G, 131 E Redwood.. 02
United States Appraisers Store, 103 's Gay 02
Vickers, 225 E Redwood 02
Victory Villa, 111 Beacon Rd.. 20
Waverly Towers, Greenmount Av & 29th 18
West Side, 2419 Frederick Ave 23
Westowne, Edmondson Ave & N Bend Rd 29
Westview, Baltimore Ntl Pk & Inglsd Ave 28
Wilkens, 3400 Wilkens Ave.. 29
Woodmoor, Liberty & Essex Rd 07

GOVERNMENT OFFICES

Baltimore Civic Center, 201 W Baltimore 01
Baltimore Municipal Court, 211 E Madison 02
County Office, 111 W Chesapeake Ave 04
Courthouse 100 N Calvert 02
Federal Bldg, 31 Hopkins Plaza 01
State Office Bldg, 301 W Preston 01
State Roads Bldg, 300 W Preston 01
The City Hall 100 Holliday 02

Baltimore (Con.) 212

United States Court House,
111 N Calvert 02
United States Customs
House, 40 S Gay.. 02

HOSPITALS

Augsburg Lutheran Home,
6811 Campfield Rd 07
Baltimore City Hospitals,
4940 Eastern Ave 24
Baltimore Eye Ear & Throat
Hospital, 1214 Eutaw Pl .. 17
Bon Secours Hospital, 2025
W Fayette 23
Childrens Hospital, 3825
Greenspring Ave 11
Church Home & Hospital,
100 N Broadway 31
Franklin Square Hospital,
9000 Franklin Sq Dr 37
General German Aged
Peoples Home, 22 S Athol
Ave 29
General German Orphan
Home, 205 Bloomsbury
Ave 28
Good Samaritan, 5601 Loch
Raven Blvd 39
Greater Baltimore Medical
Center, 6701 N Charles
St 04
Jenkins Memorial Hospital,
1000 Caton Ave 29
Johns Hopkins Hospital, 601
N Broadway 05
Kernan Hospital, Forest Park
& Windsor Mill Rd 07
Keswick Home, 790 W 40th.. 11
Levindale Hebrew Home &
Infirmary, Belvedere &
Greensprg Av 15
Lutheran Hospital Of
Maryland, 730 Ashburton .. 16
Maryland General Hospital,
Linden Ave & Madison 01
Mercy Hospital, 331 St Paul
Pl 02
Methodist Home For The
Aged, 2211 W Rogers Ave.. 09
Montebello State Hospital,
2201 Argonne Dr 18
Mount Pleasant Hospital,
Belevedere & Greenspring
Ave 15
North Charles Gen Hos. 2724
N Charles St 18
Provident Hospital 2600
Liberty Heights Ave 15
Saint Agnes Hospital, 1000
Caton Ave 29
Saint Elizabeths Home, 3725
Eifferslie Ave 18
Saint Josephs Hospital, 7620
York Rd 04
Saint Vincents Infant Home,
Reisterstown Rd 15
Seton Institute, 6400 Wabash
Ave 15
Sheppard & Enoch Pratt
Hospital, York Rd 04

Sinai Hospital, 2401 W
Belvedere Ave 15
South Baltimore General
Hospital 3⁰
Spring Grove State Hospital,
Wade Ave 28
Union Memorial Hospital, 200
E 33rd 18
United States Public Health
Service, Wyman Park Dr .. 11
University Hospital, 22 S
Greene 01
Veterans Administration
Hospital, 3900 Loch Raven
Blvd 18

UNIVERSITIES AND COLLEGES

Baltimore Hebrew College,
5800 Park Heights Ave 15
Baltimore Junior College,
2901 Liberty Heights Ave .. 15
Baltimore Polytechnic
Institute, 1400 W Cold
Spring Ln 09
Bard Avon School, 805 N
Charles 01
Bryn Mawr School, 109 W
Melrose Ave 10
Calvert Hall College High
School, 8100 La Salle Rd.. 04
Calvert School, 105 Tuscany
Rd 10
Carnegie Institute Of
Embryology, 115 W
University Pkwy 10
Catholic High School, 2810 ●
Edison Hwy 13
Catonsville Community
College, 800 S Rolling Rd.. 28
Coppin State Teachers
College, 2500 W North
Ave 16
Essex Community College 37
Friends School, 5114 N
Charles 10
Gilman School Incorporated,
5407 Roland Ave 10
Goucher College, Dulaney
Valley Rd 04
Johns Hopkins School Of
Hygiene & Health, 615 N.
Wolfe 05
Johns Hopkins University
School Of Medicine, 725 N
Wolfe 05
Johns Hopkins University,
Charles & 34th 18
Loyola College, 4501 N
Charles 10
Loyola High School, 1000
Boyce Ave 04
Maryland Institute, 1300 W
Mt Royal Ave 17
Maryland School For The
Blind, 3501 Taylor Ave 36
Maryland Training School For
Boys, 2400 Cub Hill Rd 34
Morgan College, Hillen Rd &
Cold Spring Ln 39
Mount De Sales Academy Of
The Visitation 28

Mount Saint Joseph College,
4403 Frederick Ave 29
Mount Washington School For
Boys, Smith Ave 09
Ner Israel Rabbinical College,
400 Mt Wilson Ln 08
Notre Dame College, 4701 N
Charles 10
Notre Dame Institute, 901
Aisquith 02
Notre Dame Preparatory
School, 815 Hampton
Lane 04
Peabody Dormitory, 606 St.
Paul St 02
Peabody Institute &
Conservatory, 1 E Mt
Vernon Pl 02
Roland Park Country School,
817 W University Pkwy 10
Saint Josephs Passionist
Monastery, 3800 Frederick
Ave 29
Saint Marys Seminary,
Belvedere & Roland 10
Saint Marys Seminary, 600 N
Paca 01
Samuel Ready School, 5150
Old Frederick Rd 29
Seton High School, 2800 N
Charles 18
Talmudical Academy Of
Baltimore, 4445 Old Court
Rd 08
Towson State College, 8000
York Rd 04
University Of Baltimore, 1420
N Charles 01
University Of Maryland, 522
W Lombard 01

ELLICOTT CITY 210

POST OFFICE BOXES

Box Nos.
1-399　　　　Main Office 43
401-699　　　Normandy
　　　　　　　Branch 43
801-999　　　Columbia
　　　　　　　Branch 44

STATIONS, BRANCHES AND UNITS

Columbia Br 43
Daniels Rural Br 33
Normandy Br 43
General Delivery 43
General Delivery Columbia
Br 44
Postmaster 43

APARTMENTS, HOTELS, MOTELS

Concord House 10850 Green
Mountain Cir 44
Cross Keys Inn 10207
Wincopin Cir 44

Ellicott City (Con.)   210

BUILDINGS

American Cities 10227
  Wincopin Cir 44
Awalt S 9051 Baltimore
  National Pike 43
Century Plaza 10630 Little
  Patuxent Pky 44
Columbia Mall 10300 Little
  Patuxent Pky 44
Exhibit 10215 Wincopin Cir 44
Howard County Medical
  Center 3459 St Johns La 43
Howard County Medical
  Center 3459 St Johns La 43
Normandy Shopping Center 43
Oakland Mills Shopping
  Center 45
Oakland 9042 Old Annapolis
  Rd 45
Professional 3716 Court Pl 43
Ridgely Office 5575 Sterrett
  Pl 44
Sterrett Pl 5585 Sterrett Pl.... 44
Teachers 10221 Wincopin
  Cir 44
Wilde Lake Village Green 44

GOVERNMENT OFFICES

County Court House 8360
  Court Ave 43
County Jail 1 Emory 43
County Office Building 3450
  Court House Dr 43
County Police 3676 Fells Ave .. 43
Extension Agents 3450 Court
  House Dr 43

HOSPITALS

Columbia Hospital & Clinic
  5849 Banneker Rd 44
Taylor Manor Hospital College
  Ave 43

HYATTSVILLE   207

POST OFFICE BOXES

Box Nos.
1-399   Main Office 81
700-999   Adelphi Br 83
1000-1199   Langley Park
               Br 82
1200-1499   Landover Br 85
1600-1899   Prince Georges
               Plaza Br 88
2000-2299   Capital Plaza ... 84
2300-2499   Landover Hills
               Br 84
400-699   West
               Hyattsville
               Sta 82

STATIONS, BRANCHES AND UNITS

Adelphi Br 83
Capitol Plaza Br 84
Cheverly Br..................................... 85
Chillum Br 83
Defense Highway Br 84
Editors Park Br 82
Kent Village Br 85
Landover Hills Br 84
New Carrollton Br 84
North Englewood Br 85
Palmer Park Br 85
West Hyattsville Sta 82
General Delivery 80
Postmaster 80

HOSPITALS

Prince Georges General 85

ROCKVILLE   208

POST OFFICE BOXES

Box Nos.
1-599   Court House
            Sta 50
600-799   Twinbrook Sta .. 51
1000-1799   Main Office 50
2000-2299   Pike Sta 52

STATIONS, BRANCHES AND UNITS

Courthouse Sta 50
Derwood Br..................................... 55
Pike Sta... 52
Potomac Br..................................... 54
Randolph Hills Br 53
Twinbrook Sta................................ 51
General Delivery 50
Postmaster 50

SILVER SPRING   209

POST OFFICE BOXES

Box Nos.
1-599   Main Office 07
600-899   Woodmoor Br ... 01
900-1199   Blair Br 10
1300-2299   Wheaton Br 02
4000-4499   Colesville Br 04

STATIONS, BRANCHES AND UNITS

Blair Br... 10
Colesville Br 04
Ednor Cloverly Br 04
Leisure World Br 06
Wheaton Br 02
Woodmoor Br 01
General Delivery 07
Postmaster 07

APARTMENTS, HOTELS, MOTELS

Blair House, 8201 16th 10
Blair Plaza, 1491 Blair Mill
  Rd 10
Blair Towers, 8107 Eastern
  Avenue 10

BUILDINGS

American National Bank,
  8761 Georgia Ave 10
Guardian, 8605 Cameron 10
Wheaton Plaza Office
  Building 02

MASSACHUSETTS
(Abbreviation: MA)

Abington, Sta. North
  Abington..............................02351
Accord, Br. Hingham..............02018
Acoaxet, R. Br. Little
  Compton RI.........................02701
Acton (1st)...........................01720
Acushnet, Br. New Bedford.....02743
Adams (1st)..........................01220
Agawam (1st).......................01001
Allendale, Sta. Pittsfield.........01201
Allerton, Sta. Hull.................02045
Allston, Sta. Boston (see
  appendix)
Amesbury (1st).....................01913
Amherst (1st)........................01002
Andover (1st)........................01810
  Ballardvale, Sta..................01810
  Shawsheen Village, Sta.......01810
Annisquam, Sta. Gloucester...01930
Arlington, Br. Boston..............02174
Arlington Heights, Br.
  Boston...............................02175
Ashburnham..........................01430
Ashby...................................01431
Ashfield................................01330
Ashland (1st)........................01721
Ashley Falls..........................01222
Assinippi, R. Sta. Hanover......02339
Assonet................................02702
Assumption College, Sta.
  Worcester...........................01609
Astor, Sta. Boston.................02123
Athol (1st)............................01331
  Royalston, R. Br..................01368
Attleboro (1st)......................02703
Attleboro Falls, Sta. North
  Attleboro (see appendix)
Auburn (1st).........................01501
Auburndale, Br. Boston (see
  appendix)
Avon (1st)............................02322
AYER (1st) (see appendix)
Babson Park, Br. Boston........02157
Back Back Bay Annex, Sta.
  Boston (see appendix)
Baldwinville..........................01436
Ballardvale, Sta. Andover......01810
Barnstable............................02630
Barre...................................01005
Barre Plains..........................01006
Barrowsville..........................02710
Bass River, Sta. South
  Yarmouth............................02664
Beach, Br. Boston.................02151
Becket.................................01223
Bedford (1st)........................01730
Belchertown.........................01007
Bellingham...........................02019
Belmont, Br. Boston.............02178
Berkshire.............................01224
Berlin..................................01503
Bernardston.........................01337
Beverly (1st)........................01915
Beverly Farms, Sta. Beverly...01915
Billerica (1st).......................01821
Blackstone...........................01504
Blandford............................01008
Bolton.................................01740
Bondsville...........................01009
BOSTON (1st) (see appendix)

Boston College, Br. Boston.....02167
Boston University, Sta.
  Boston...............................02215
Bourne, Sta. Buzzards Bay....02532
Boxborough, Br. Acton..........01719
Boxford................................01921
Boylston..............................01505
Bradford, Sta. Haverhill.........01830
Braintree, Br. Boston.............02184
Brant Rock...........................02020
Brewster..............................02631
Bridgewater (1st)..................02324
Brighton, Sta. Boston (see
  appendix)
Brightwood, Sta. Springfield...01107
Brimfield..............................01010
BROCKTON (1st) (see
  appendix)
Brookfield.............................01506
Brookline, Br. Boston (see
  appendix)
Brookline Village, Br.
  Boston...............................02147
Brookville..............................02326
Bryantville.............................02327
Buckland...............................01338
Burlington (1st)......................01803
Buzzards Bay (1st)..................02532
  Bourne, Sta........................02532
  Otis A F B, Br.....................02542
Byfield..................................01922
Cambridge, Br. Boston (see
  appendix)
Cambridge A, Br. Boston
  (see appendix)
Cambridge B, Br. Boston
  (see appendix)
Cambridge C, Br. Boston
  (see appendix)
Campello, Sta. Brockton........02403
Canton (1st).........................02021
Carlisle.................................01741
Carver..................................02330
Cataumet..............................02534
Cathedral, Sta. Boston...........02118
Center, Sta. Woburn..............01801
Center Street, Sta. Brockton...02401
Centerville............................02632
  Craigville, R. Br.................02636
Central Village, Sta.
  Westport............................02790
Charlemont...........................01339
Charles Street, Sta. Boston....02114
Charlestown, Sta. Boston.......02129
Charlton...............................01507
Charlton City.........................01508
Charlton Depot.......................01509
Chartley................................02712
Chatham (1st)........................02633
Chelmsford (1st)....................01824
Chelsea, Br. Boston................02150
Cherry Valley, Br. Worcester...01611
Cheshire...............................01225
Chester................................01011
Chesterfield..........................01012
Chestnut Hill, Br. Boston
  (see appendix)
CHICOPEE (1st) (see
  appendix)
Chicopee Center, Sta.
  Chicopee...........................01013
Chilmark..............................02535
Cleghorn, Sta. Fitchburg........01420

Cleveland Circle, Br. Boston...02146
Clifton, Sta. Marblehead........01945
Clinton (1st)..........................01510
Cochituate, Sta. Wayland.......01778
Cohasset (1st).......................02025
Colrain.................................01340
Concord (1st)........................01742
Conway................................01341
Cotuit..................................02635
Craigville, R. Br. Centerville....02636
Cummaquid...........................02637
Cummington..........................01026
Cushman, R. Sta. Amherst......01002
Cuttyhunk.............................02713
Dalton (1st)..........................01226
Danvers (1st)........................01923
Dartmouth............................02714
Davis, R. Sta. Acton..............01720
Dedham (1st)........................02026
Deerfield..............................01342
Dennis.................................02638
Dennis Port...........................02639
Dighton................................02715
Division Street, Sta. New
  Bedford.............................02744
Dorchester, Sta. Boston (see
  appendix)
Dorchester Center, Sta.
  Boston (see appendix)
Dover...................................02030
Dracut (1st)..........................01826
Drury...................................01343
Dudley, Br. Webster...............01570
Dudley Hill, Br. Webster.........01570
Dunstable.............................01827
Duxbury (1st)........................02332
East Arlington, Br. Boston......02174
East Boston, Sta. Boston.......02128
East Brewster........................02640
East Bridgewater (1st)............02333
East Brookfield......................01515
East Dedham, Sta. Dedham....02026
East Dennis...........................02641
East Douglas..........................01516
East Falmouth (1st)................02536
  Hatchville, R. Br................02536
  New Seabury, Br.................02536
  Popponesset Beach, R.
    Br..................................02560
  Teaticket, Sta....................02536
  Wequoit, Sta......................02536
East Freetown........................02717
East Harwich, R. Sta.
  Harwich.............................02645
East Longmeadow (1st).........01028
East Lynn, Sta. Lynn.............01904
East Mansfield.......................02031
East Northfield, Sta.
  Northfield...........................01360
East Orleans..........................02643
East Otis...............................01029
East Pembroke.......................02336
East Pepperell........................01437
East Princeton.......................01517
East Sandwich.......................02537
East Taunton..........................02718
East Templeton......................01438
East Walpole (1st).................02032
East Wareham........................02538
East Watertown, Br. Boston...02172
East Weymouth, Br. Boston
  (see appendix)
Eastham................................02642

Easthampton (1st)..............01027
Easton.............................02334
Eastondale.......................02335
Edgartown.........................02539
Elmwood...........................02337
Erving.............................01344
Essex..............................01929
Essex, Sta. Boston...............02112
Everett, Br. Boston..............02149
Fairhaven (1st)..................02719
FALL RIVER (1st) (see
  appendix)
FALMOUTH (1st) (see
  appendix)
Fayville..........................01745
Feeding Hills (1st)..............01030
Fiskdale..........................01518
Fitchburg (1st)..................01420
Flint, Sta. Fall River...........02723
Florence, Sta. Northampton...01060
Forest Park, Sta. Springfield
  (see appendix)
Forestdale........................02644
Forge Village.....................01828
Fort Devens, Sta. Ayer...........01433
Foxboro (1st).....................02035
Framingham (1st)..................01701
Framingham Center, Sta.
  Framingham.....................01701
Franklin (1st)....................02038
Gardner (1st).....................01440
Georgetown, Br. Haverhill........01833
Gilbertville......................01031
Gleasondale, R. Br. Hudson.......01749
Glendale..........................01229
Gloucester (1st)..................01930
Goshen............................01032
Grafton...........................01519
Granby............................01033
Graniteville......................01829
Granville.........................01034
Great Barrington (1st)...........01230
Green Harbor......................02041
Greenbush.........................02040
Greendale, Sta. Worcester........01606
Greenfield (1st)..................01301
Greenwood, Sta. Wakefield........01880
Griswoldville.....................01345
Groton............................01450
Grove Hall, Sta. Boston..........02121
Groveland, Br. Haverhill.........01834
Hadley............................01035
Halifax...........................02338
Hamilton..........................01936
Hampden...........................01036
Hancock, R. Br. Lanesboro........01237
Hanover (1st).....................02339
Hanover Street, Sta. Boston......02113
Hanson (1st)......................02341
Harding...........................02042
Hardwick..........................01037
Harvard...........................01451
Harwich...........................02645
Harwich Port......................02646
Harwood, Sta. Littleton..........01460
Hatchville, R. Br. East
  Falmouth.......................02536
Hatfield..........................01038
Hathorne..........................01937
Haverhill (1st)...................01830
Haydenville.......................01039
Heath.............................01346
Highland, Sta. Springfield

(see appendix)
Highlands, Sta. Lowell...........01851
Hingham (1st).....................02043
  Accord, Br.....................02018
Hinsdale..........................01235
Holbrook (1st)....................02343
Holden (1st)......................01520
Holliston (1st)...................01746
Holyoke (1st).....................01040
Hopedale (1st)....................01747
Hopkinton.........................01748
Housatonic........................01236
Hubbardston.......................01452
Hudson (1st)......................01749
Hull (1st)........................02045
Humarock..........................02047
Huntington........................01050
Hyannis (1st).....................02601
Hyannis Port......................02647
Hyde Park, Sta. Boston...........02136
Indian Orchard (1st).............01051
Inman Square, Br. Boston
  (see appendix)
Ipswich (1st).....................01938
Islington, Sta. Westwood.........02090
Jamaica Plain, Sta. Boston.......02130
Jefferson.........................01522
John Fitzgerald Kennedy,
  Sta. Boston....................02203
Kearney Square, Sta. Lowell......01852
Kendall Square, Br. Boston.......02142
Kenmore, Sta. Boston (see
  appendix)
Kingston, Br. Plymouth...........02364
Lake Pleasant.....................01347
Lakeville, R. Br. Middleboro.....02346
Lancaster.........................01523
Lanesboro.........................01237
Lanesville, Sta. Gloucester......01930
LAWRENCE (1st) (see
  appendix)
Lee (1st).........................01238
Leeds (1st).......................01053
Leicester.........................01524
Lenox (1st).......................01240
Lenox Dale........................01242
Leominster (1st)..................01453
Leverett..........................01054
Lexington, Br. Boston............02173
Lincoln (1st).....................01773
Lincoln Center, Sta. Lincoln.....01773
Linwood...........................01525
Lithia............................01055
Littleton (1st)...................01460
Long Island, Sta. Boston.........02169
Longmeadow, Br.
  Springfield....................01106
LOWELL (1st) (see appendix)
Ludlow (1st)......................01056
Lunds Corner, Sta. New
  Bedford........................02745
Lunenburg.........................01462
LYNN (1st) (see appendix)
Lynnfield (1st)...................01940
M I T, Br. Boston.................02139
Magnolia, Sta. Gloucester........01930
Malden, Br. Boston...............02148
Manchaug..........................01526
Manchester (1st)..................01944
Manomet...........................02345
Mansfield (1st)...................02048
Marblehead (1st)..................01945
Marion............................02738

Marlborough (1st).................01752
Marshfield (1st)..................02050
Marshfield Hills..................02051
Marstons Mills....................02648
Mashpee...........................02649
Mattapan, Sta. Boston............02126
Mattapoisett......................02739
Maynard (1st).....................01754
Medfield (1st)....................02052
Medford, Br. Boston..............02155
Medway (1st)......................02053
Melrose, Br. Boston..............02176
Melrose Highlands, Br.
  Boston.........................02177
Mendon............................01756
Menemsha..........................02552
Merrimac..........................01860
Merrimack College, Br.
  Lawrence.......................01845
Methuen, Br. Lawrence............01844
Middleboro (1st)..................02346
Middlefield.......................01243
Middleton (1st)...................01949
Milford (1st).....................01757
Mill River........................01244
Millbury (1st)....................01527
Millers Falls.....................01349
Millis (1st)......................02054
Millville.........................01529
Milton, Br. Boston...............02186
Milton Village, Br. Boston.......02187
Minot.............................02055
Mittineague, Sta. West
  Springfield....................01089
Monponsett........................02350
Monroe Bridge.....................01350
Monson (1st)......................01057
Montague..........................01351
Montello, Sta. Brockton..........02403
Monterey..........................01245
Monument Beach....................02553
Morningdale.......................01530
Mount Hermon......................01354
Mount Saint James, Sta.
  Worcester......................01610
Mount Tom.........................01058
Nabnasset.........................01861
Nahant, Br. Lynn..................01908
Nantucket (1st)...................02554
Natick (1st)......................01760
Needham, Br. Boston..............02192
Needham Heights, Br.
  Boston.........................02194
NEW BEDFORD (1st) (see
  appendix)
New Braintree.....................01531
New Salem.........................01355
New Seabury, Br. East
  Falmouth.......................02536
Newbury, Br. Newburyport.........01950
Newburyport (1st).................01950
Newton, Br. Boston (see
  appendix)
Newton Center, Br. Boston
  (see appendix)
Newton Highlands, Br.
  Boston (see appendix)
Newton Lower Falls, Br.
  Boston (see appendix)
Newton Upper Falls, Br.
  Boston (see appendix)
Newtonville, Br. Boston (see
  appendix)

Nonantum, Br. Boston (see appendix)

Nonquitt, R. Br New Bedford 02748

Noquochoke, Sta. Westport 02790

Norfolk 02056

North, Sta. New Bedford 02746

North Abington (1st) 02351

North Adams (1st) 01247

North Amherst Sta. Amherst.............................01059

North Andover, Br. Lawrence ..01845

NORTH ATTLEBORO (1st) (see appendix)

North Billerica (1st) 01862

North Brookfield (1st) 01535

North Carver 02355

North Chatham 02650

North Chelmsford (1st) 01863

North Cohasset, Sta. Cohasset............................02025

North Dartmouth, Br. New Bedford 02747

North Dighton (1st) 02764

North Eastham 02651

North Easton (1st) 02356

North Egremont 01252

North Falmouth 02556

Silver Beach, R. Br. 02565

North Grafton 01536

North Hatfield 01066

North Marshfield 02059

North Oxford 01537

North Pembroke 02358

North Plymouth, Sta. Plymouth...........................02360

North Quincy, Br. Boston (see appendix)

North Randolph, Sta. Randolph..........................02368

North Reading (1st) 01864

North Scituate (1st) 02060

North Truro 02652

North Uxbridge 01538

North Weymouth, Br. Boston (see appendix)

North Wilbraham (1st) 01067

North Wilmington, Sta. Wilmington........................01887

Northampton (1st)..................01060

Northborough (1st)................01532

Northbridge............................01534

Northfield...............................01360

Norton (1st)...........................02766

Norwell 02061

Norwood (1st)........................02062

Nutting Lake..........................01865

Oak Bluffs 02557

Oakdale 01539

Oakham 01068

Ocean Bluff............................02065

Ocean Grove, Sta. Swansea 02777

Onset 02558

Orange (1st) 01364

Orleans (1st) 02653

Osterville (1st) 02655

Wianno, R. Br. 02674

Otis 01253

Otis A F B, Br. Buzzards Bay 02542

Oxford 01540

Padanaram Village, Br. New Bedford 02748

Palmer (1st) 01069

Parcel Post, Sta. Worcester 01604

Parcel Post, Sta. Westfield 01085

Parcel Post, Sta. Fitchburg 01420

Paxton, Br. Worcester 01612

Peabody (1st) 01960

Pembroke 02359

Pepperell 01463

Petersham 01366

Pigeon Cove, Sta. Rockport....01966

Pinehurst 01866

Pittsfield (1st) 01201

Plainfield 01070

Plainville, Br. North Attleboro (see appendix)

Pleasant Lake.........................02656

Plum Island, Br. Newburyport.....................01950

PLYMOUTH (1st) (see appendix)

Plympton 02367

Pocasset 02559

Popponesset Beach, R. Br. East Falmouth 02560

Prides Crossing 01965

Princeton 01541

Provincetown (1st) 02657

Prudential Center, Sta. Boston 02199

Quincy, Br. Boston (see appendix)

Randolph (1st) 02368

Raynham 02767

Raynham Center.....................02768

Reading (1st) 01867

Readville, Sta. Boston 02137

Rehoboth 02769

Revere, Br. Boston 02151

Richmond 01254

Riverdale, Sta. Gloucester......01930

Rochdale 01542

Rochester 02770

Rockland (1st)........................02370

Rockport (1st) 01966

Roslindale, Sta. Boston 02131

Rowe......................................01367

Rowley (1st)...........................01969

Roxbury, Sta. Boston (see appendix)

Roxbury Crossing, Sta. Boston (see appendix)

Royalston, R. Br. Athol...........01368

Russell...................................01071

Rutland 01543

Sagamore 02561

Sagamore Beach.....................02562

Salem (1st) 01970

Salem State College, Sta. Salem...............................01970

Salisbury, Br. Newburyport.....01950

Salisbury Beach, Br. Newburyport.....................01950

Sandisfield 01255

Sandwich 02563

Saugus, Br. Lynn....................01906

Savoy 01256

Saxonville, Sta. Framingham.....................01701

Scituate (1st) 02066

Seekonk (1st) 02771

Segreganset............................02773

Sharon (1st) 02067

Shattuckville...........................01369

Shawsheen Village, Sta. Andover.............................01810

Sheffield (1st) 01257

Shelburne Falls 01370

Sheldonville 02070

Sherborn (1st) 01770

Shirley 01464

Shirley Center 01465

Shrewsbury (1st)....................01545

Shutesbury.............................01072

Siasconset 02564

Silver Beach, R. Br. North Falmouth 02565

Snug Harbor, Sta. Duxbury 02332

Soldiers Field, Sta. Boston (see appendix)

Somerset, Br. Fall River (see appendix)

Somerville, Br. Boston (see appendix)

South, Sta. Fall River.............02724

South Ashburnham...................01466

South Athol............................01372

South Attleboro, Sta. Attleboro...........................02703

South Barre 01074

South Berlin 01549

South Boston, Sta. Boston......02127

South Carver 02566

South Chatham 02659

South Chelmsford, R. Sta. Chelmsford........................01824

South Dartmouth, Br. New Bedford 02748

South Deerfield.......................01373

South Dennis 02660

South Easton 02375

South Egremont 01258

South Essex 01981

South Framingham, Sta. Framingham.....................01701

South Gardner, Sta. Gardner....01440

South Grafton 01560

South Hadley (1st) 01075

South Hadley Falls, Sta. South Hadley.....................01075

South Hamilton (1st) 01982

South Harwich 02661

South Lancaster 01561

South Lee...............................01260

South Lynnfield, Sta. Lynnfield...........................01940

South Natick, Sta. Natick.......01760

South Orleans 02662

South Postal Annex, Sta. Boston 02109

South Royalston 01374

South Swansea, Sta. Swansea...........................02777

South Walpole 02071

South Waltham, Br. Boston 02154

South Wellfleet 02663

South Westport, R. Sta. Westport...........................02790

South Weymouth, Br. Boston (see appendix)

South Yarmouth (1st) 02664

Southampton 01073

Southborough (1st) 01772

Southbridge (1st)....................01550

Southfield...............................01259

Southwick..............................01077

Spencer (1st)	01562	West Somerville, Br. Boston..02144
SPRINGFIELD (1st) (see appendix)		West Springfield (1st)	01089
Squantum, Br. Boston (see appendix)		West Stockbridge	01266
		West Tisbury	02575
State House, Sta. Boston	02133	West Townsend	01474
Sterling	01564	West Upton	01587
Sterling Junction	01565	West Warren	02576
Still River	01467	West Warren (1st)	01092
Stockbridge (1st)	01262	West Yarmouth	02673
Stoneham, Br. Boston	02180	Westborough (1st)	01581
Stoughton (1st)	02072	Westfield (1st)	01085
Stow	01775	Westford	01886
Sturbridge (1st)	01566	Westminster	01473
Sudbury (1st)	01776	Weston, Br. Boston	02193
Sunderland	01375	Westover A F B, Sta. Chicopee	01022
Swampscott, Br. Lynn	01907	Westport (1st)	02790
Swansea (1st)	02777	Westport Point	02791
Swifts Beach, R. Sta. Wareham	02571	Westwood (1st)	02090
Tapley Street Annex, Sta. Springfield	01101	Weymouth, Br. Boston (see appendix)	
Taunton (1st)	02780	Whately	01093
Teaticket, Sta. East Falmouth	02536	Wheelwright	01094
Templeton	01468	White Horse Beach	02361
Tewksbury (1st)	01876	Whitinsville (1st)	01588
Thorndike	01079	Whitman (1st)	02382
Three Rivers	01080	Wianno, R. Br. Osterville...02674
Topsfield (1st)	01983	Wilbraham	01095
Townsend (1st)	01469	Wilkinsonville	01590
Tremont, Sta. Boston	02116	Williamsburg	01096
Truro	02666	Williamstown (1st)	01267
Tufts University, Br. Boston..02153		Wilmington (1st)	01887
Turners Falls (1st)	01376	Winchendon (1st)	01475
Turnpike, Sta. Shrewsbury...01545		Winchendon Springs	01477
Twin Village, Sta. Attleboro..02703		Winchester (1st)	01890
Tyngsboro	01879	Windsor	01270
Tyringham	01264	Winter Hill, Br. Boston (see appendix)	
Uphams Corner, Sta. Boston (see appendix)		Winthrop, Br. Boston	02152
Upton	01568	Woburn (1st)	01801
Uxbridge (1st)	01569	Wollaston, Br. Boston (see appendix)	
Veterans Administration Hosp., Sta. Boston	02130	Woods Hole, Sta. Falmouth....02543
Village, Sta. Medway	02053	Woodville	01784
Vineyard Haven (1st)	02568	WORCESTER (1st) (see appendix)	
West Chop, R. Br.	02573	Woronoco	01097
Waban, Br. Boston (see appendix)		Worthington	01098
Wakefield (1st)	01880	Wrentham (1st)	02093
Wales	01081	Yarmouth Port	02675
Walpole (1st)	02081	
Waltham, Br. Boston	02154	
Waquoit, Sta. East Falmouth	02536	
Ward Hill, Sta. Haverhill	01830	
Ware (1st)	01082	
Wareham (1st)	02571	
Warren	01083	
Watertown, Br. Boston	02172	
Waverley, Br. Boston	02179	
Wayland (1st)	01778	
Webster (1st)	01570	
Webster Square, Sta. Worcester	01603	
Wellesley, Br. Boston	02181	
Wellesley Hills, Br. Boston..02181		
Wellfleet	02667	
Wendell	01379	
Wendell Depot	01380	
Wenham (1st)	01984	
West Acton, Sta. Acton	01720	
West Barnstable	02668	
West Boxford	01885	
West Boylston (1st)	01583	
West Bridgewater	02379	
West Brookfield	01585	
West Chatham	02669	
West Chesterfield	01084	
West Chop, R. Br. Vineyard Haven	02573	
West Concord, Sta. Concord..01742		
West Cummington	01265	
West Dennis	02670	
West Falmouth	02574	
West Groton	01472	
West Hanover, Sta. Hanover..02339		
West Harwich	02671	
West Hatfield	01088	
West Hyannisport	02672	
West Lynn, Sta. Lynn	01905	
West Mansfield	02083	
West Medford, Br. Boston....02156		
West Millbury	01586	
West Newbury	01985	
West Newton, Br. Boston (see appendix)		
West Peabody, Sta. Peabody..01960		
West Roxbury, Sta. Boston....02132		
West Side, Sta. Worcester....01602		

AYER	014	BOSTON	021		Sta.	14
POST OFFICE BOXES		**POST OFFICE BOXES**		9001-9188	John F Kennedy Sta.	14

Box Nos. (AYER)

Box Nos.		
A-K	Main Office	32
1-469	Main Office	32

STATIONS, BRANCHES AND UNITS

Fort Devens Sta.	33
General Delivery	32
Postmaster	32

Box Nos. (BOSTON)

Box Nos.		
1-400	Main Office	01
401-800	Main Office	02
801-1200	Main Office	03
1201-1600	Main Office	04
1601-2000	Main Office	05
2001-2200	Main Office	06
2201-2400	Main Office	07
8000-8999	John F Kennedy	

STATIONS, BRANCHES AND UNITS

Allston Sta.	34
Arlington Br.	74
Arlington Heights Br.	75
Astor Sta.	23
Auburndale Br.	66
Babson Park Br.	57
Back Bay Annex Sta.	15

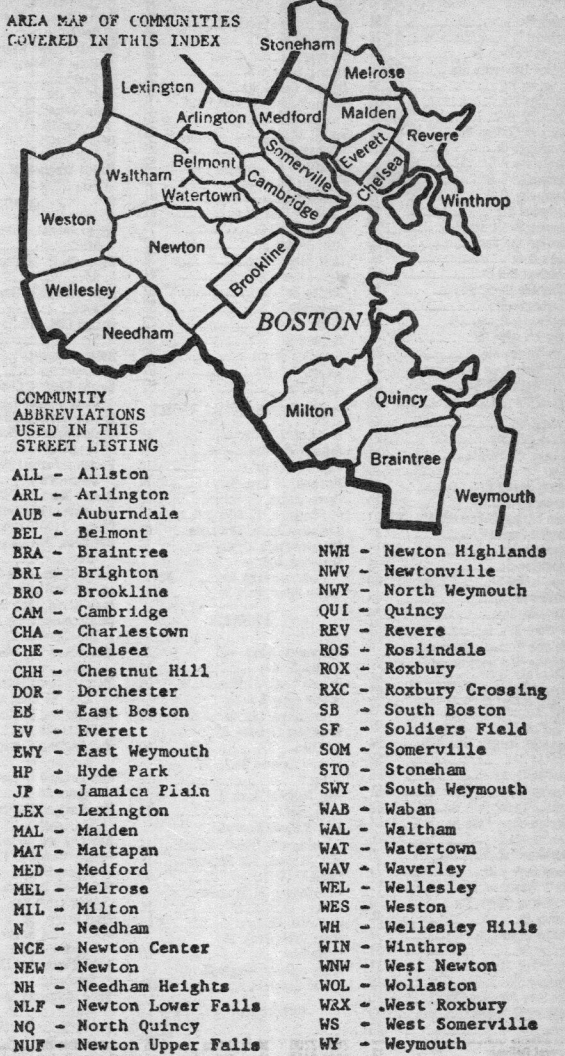

AREA MAP OF COMMUNITIES
COVERED IN THIS INDEX

COMMUNITY
ABBREVIATIONS
USED IN THIS
STREET LISTING

ALL — Allston
ARL — Arlington
AUB — Auburndale
BEL — Belmont
BRA — Braintree
BRI — Brighton
BRO — Brookline
CAM — Cambridge
CHA — Charlestown
CHE — Chelsea
CHH — Chestnut Hill
DOR — Dorchester
EB — East Boston
EV — Everett
EWY — East Weymouth
HP — Hyde Park
JP — Jamaica Plain
LEX — Lexington
MAL — Malden
MAT — Mattapan
MED — Medford
MEL — Melrose
MIL — Milton
N — Needham
NCE — Newton Center
NEW — Newton
NH — Needham Heights
NLF — Newton Lower Falls
NQ — North Quincy
NUF — Newton Upper Falls

NWH — Newton Highlands
NWV — Newtonville
NWY — North Weymouth
QUI — Quincy
REV — Revere
ROS — Roslindale
ROX — Roxbury
RXC — Roxbury Crossing
SB — South Boston
SF — Soldiers Field
SOM — Somerville
STO — Stoneham
SWY — South Weymouth
WAB — Waban
WAL — Waltham
WAT — Watertown
WAV — Waverley
WEL — Wellesley
WES — Weston
WH — Wellesley Hills
WIN — Winthrop
WNW — West Newton
WOL — Wollaston
WRX — West Roxbury
WS — West Somerville
WY — Weymouth

Boston (Con.) 021

Beach Br................................. 51
Belmont Br.............................. 78
Boston College Br...................... 67
Boston University Sta...............02215
Braintree Br............................. 84
Brighton Br.............................. 35
Brookline Br............................. 46
Brookline Village Br.................... 47
Cambridge Br............................ 38
Cambridge A Br......................... 39
Cambridge B Br......................... 40
Cambridge C Br......................... 41
Cathedral Sta............................ 18
Charles Street Sta....................... 14
Charlestown Br.......................... 29
Chelsea Br............................... 50
Chestnut Hill Br......................... 67
Cleveland Circle Br..................... 46
Dorchester Br............................ 22
Dorchester Center Sta.................. 24
East Arlington Br........................ 74
East Boston Sta.......................... 28
East Watertown Br...................... 72
East Weymouth Br...................... 89
Essex Br.................................. 12

Everett Br................................ 49
Grove Hall Sta........................... 21
Hanover Street Sta...................... 13
Hyde Park Sta........................... 36
Inman Square Br........................ 39
Jamaica Plain Sta....................... 30
John Fitzgerald Kennedy Sta.......02203
Kendall Square Br...................... 42
Kenmore Sta........................02215
Lexington Br............................. 73
Long Island Sta......................... 69
Malden Br................................ 48
Mattapan Sta............................ 26
Medford Br.............................. 55
Melrose Br............................... 76
Melrose Highlands Br.................. 77
Milton Br................................. 86
Milton Village Br....................... 87
MIT Br................................... 39
Needham Br.............................. 92
Needham Heights Br.................... 94
Newton Br............................... 58
Newton Center Br....................... 59
Newton Highlands Br................... 61
Newton Lower Falls Br................. 62
Newton Upper Falls Br................. 64
Newtonville Br.......................... 60
Nonantum Br............................ 95
North Quincy Br........................ 71
North Weymouth Br.................... 91
Prudential Center Sta................... 99
Quincy Br................................ 69
Readville Sta............................. 37
Revere Br................................ 51
Roslindale Sta........................... 31
Roxbury Sta.............................. 19
Rox bury Crossing Sta.................. 20
Soldiers Field Sta....................... 63
Somerville Br............................ 43
South Boston Sta........................ 27
South Postal Annex Sta................. 09
South Waltham Br....................... 54

South Weymouth Br..................... 90
Squantum Br............................. 71
State House Sta.......................... 33
Stoneham Br............................. 80
Tremont Sta.............................. 16
Tufts University Br...................... 53
Uphams Corner Sta..................... 25
Veterans Administration Hosp
   Sta..................................... 30
Waban Br................................. 69
Waltham Br.............................. 54
Watertown Br........................... 72
Waverley Br............................. 79
Wellesley Br............................. 81
ellesley Hills Br......................... 81
West Medford Br........................ 56
West Newton Br......................... 65
West Roxbury Sta....................... 32
West Somerville Br...................... 44
Weston Br................................ 93
Weymouth Br............................ 88
Winter Hill Br............................ 45
Winthrop Br.............................. 52
Wollaston Br............................. 70
General Delivery......................... 09
Postmaster............................... 09

APARTMENTS, HOTELS, MOTELS

Bradford, 275 Tremont................. 16
Essex, 695 Atlantic Ave................ 11
Lenox, 61 Exeter........................ 16
Madison, 76 Causeway................. 17
Parker House, 60 School............... 08
Ritz-Carleton, 15 Arlington............ 17
Sheraton-Boston, 39 Dalton........... 99
Sheraton-Plaza, Copley Sq........... 16
Somerset, 400
   Commonwealth Ave............02215
Statler-Hilton, Park Sq................. 17

BUILDINGS

Appraisers Stores, 408
   Atlantic Ave......................... 10
Beacon Trust, 31 Milk.................. 09
Boston Flour & Grain
   Exchange, 177 Milk................. 09
Employers Liability, 35
   Broad................................ 09
Federal Reserve Bank, 30
   Pearl................................. 10
First National Bank, 1
   Federal.............................. 10
John B Hynes Memorial
   Auditorium, 900 Boylston....... 15
John Hancock, 200 Berkeley.......... 16
Kimball, 18 Tremont................... 08
Park Square, 31 St James
   Ave.................................. 16
Prudential Center....................... 99
State Street Bank, 225
   Franklin............................. 10
Western Union Telegraph,
   230 Congress....................... 10

GOVERNMENT OFFICES

City Hall, Gov'T Ctr................02201
Court House, 55 Pemberton
   Square............................... 08
Custom House, 165 State.............. 09

Department Of Public Works,
   100 Nashua.......................... 14
John F Kennedy Federal Bldg,
   Gov'T Ctr........................02203
Massachusetts Registry Of
   Motor Vehicles, 100
   Nashua.............................. 14
State House.............................. 33
State Office Bldg, 100
   Cambridge........................02202
United States Court House,
   Post Office Sq....................... 09
United States Post Office,
   Post Office Sq....................... 09

HOSPITALS

Angell Animal, 180 Longwood
   Ave.................................. 15
Baker Clinic, 16 Deaconess
   Rd.................................02215
Beth Israel, 330 Brookline
   Ave.................................02215
Boston City, 818 Harrison
   Ave.................................. 18
Boston Dispensary, 25
   Bennet............................... 11
Boston Evening Clinic, 297
   Commonwealth Ave............... 15
Boston Floating, 20 Ash............... 11
Boston Hosp For Women, 221
   Longwood Ave...................... 15
Boston Industrial Medical
   Center, Fenway...................02215
Boston State, 591 Morton............. 24
Brookline, 165 Chestnut............... 46
Carney, 2100 Dorchester Ave........ 24
Childrens, 300 Longwood
   Ave.................................. 15
Joslin Clinic, Joslin Rd.............02215
Lemuel Shattuck, Circuit Dr.......... 30
Long Island, Long Island............. 69
Massachusetts Eye & Ear,
   243 Charles......................... 14
Massachusetts General, 32
   Fruit................................. 14
Massachusetts Soldiers
   Home, 91 Crest Ave................ 50
New England Baptist, 91
   Parker Hill Ave..................... 20
New England Center, 171
   Harrison Ave........................ 11
New England Deaconess, 195
   Pilgrim Rd........................02215
New England Medical Center,
   37 Bennet........................... 11
New England, Dimock................. 19
Palmer Memorial, 195
   Pilgrim Rd........................02215
Peter Bent Brigham, 721
   Huntington Ave..................... 15
Pratt Diagnostic, 30 Bennet.......... 11
Robert Breck Brigham, 125
   Parker Hill Ave..................... 20
Saint Elizabeths, 736
   Cambridge.......................... 35
Saint Margarets, 90 Cushing
   Ave.................................. 25
United States Naval, 1
   Broadway............................ 50
United States Public Health
   Service, 77 Warren................. 35
University, 750 Harrison Ave.......... 18

Boston (Con.)   021

Veterans Administration,
1400 Vfw Pkwy 32
Veterans Administration, 150
S Huntington Ave 30

MILITARY INSTALLATIONS

Army Base, 666 Summer 02210
Coast Guard, 447
Commercial 13
South Boston Annex Navy
Yard, 285 Northern Ave 02210
U S Naval Shipyard, Water 29

UNIVERSITIES AND COLLEGES

Boston College Law School,
St Thomas More 35
Boston College, 140
Commonwealth Ave 67
Boston State, 625 Huntington
Ave 15
Boston University Law
School, 11 Ashburton Pl 08
Boston University, 755
Commonwealth Ave 02215
Brandeis University, 415
South 54
Bryant & Stratton, 150
Newbury 16
Burdett, 160 Beacon 16
Emerson, 130 Beacon 16
Emmanuel, 400 Fenway 15
Franklin Technical Institute,
41 Berkeley 16
Harvard Business School, 16
N Harvard 63
Harvard Dental School, 188
Longwood Ave 15
Harvard Medical School, 25
Shattuck 15
Harvard School Of Public
Health, 55 Shattuck 15
Harvard University,
Cambridge 38
Mass Inst Of Technology, 77
Massachusetts Ave 39
Northeastern University, 360
Huntington Ave 15
Radcliffe, 10 Garden 38
Regis, 235 Wellesley 93
Simmons, Fenway 15
Suffolk University, 20 Derne 14
Tufts Medicine & Dental, 136
Harrison Ave 11
Tufts University, Medford 55
University Of Mass At
Boston, 100 Arlington 16
Wellesley, 106 Central 81
Wentworth Institute, 550
Huntington Ave 15

NAMED STREETS

A (NH) 94
A (WAV) 79
A (REV) 51
A (HP) 36
A
  1-121 (SB) (ODD) 27
  2-130 (SB) (EVEN) 27

123-OUT (ODD) 02210
132-OUT (EVEN) 02210
A Ave (WRX) 32
A Dr (EV) 49
Aaron (MEL) 76
Aaron Rd (LEX) 73
Abbey (QUI) 69
Abbey Rd (BRI) 35
Abbot (DOR) 21
Abbotsford (DOR) 24
Abbott (MAL) 48
Abbott (MED) 55
Abbott (WEL) 81
Abbott (NUF) 64
Abbott (N) 92
Abbott (SWY) 90
Abbott (BRA) 84
Abbott Ave (EV) 49
Abbott Rd (WAL) 54
Abbott Rd (WH) 81
Abbott Rd (LEX) 73
Abbottsford Rd (BRO) 46
Abdell (SOM) 43
Aberdeen (NWH) 61
Aberdeen 02215
Aberdeen Ave (WAL) 54
Aberdeen Ave & Ct (CAM) 38
Aberdeen Rd (WS) 44
Aberdeen Rd (MIL) 87
Aberdeen Rd (WES) 93
Aberdeen Rd (WEL) 81
Aberdeen Rd (ARL) 74
Aberdeen Rd (NQ) 71
Abernathy Rd (LEX) 73
Abigail Ave (QUI) 69
Abigail Adams Cir (NWY) 91
Abruzzi (REV) 51
Acacia (CAM) 38
Acacia Ave (CHH) 67
Acacia Rd (WRX) 32
Academy (ARL) 74
Academy
  1-142 (BRA) 85
  143-OUT (BRA) 84
Academy Ave
  1-107 (EWY) (ODD) 89
  2-104 (EWY) (EVEN) 89
  106-OUT (WY) (EVEN) 88
  109-OUT (WY) (ODD) 88
Academy Ct & Ter (ROX) 19
Academy Ln (MIL) 86
Academy Rd (NEW) 58
Academy Hill Rd (BRI) 35
Acadia (SB) 27
Acadia Park (SOM) 43
Access Rd (LEX) 73
Accolon Way 14
Achorn Cir (JP) 30
Ackers Ave & Ter (BRO) 46
Ackley Pl (JP) 30
Acorn (CAM) 39
Acorn (WAL) 54
Acorn 08
Acorn (LEX) 73
Acorn (BEL) 78
Acorn Dr (AUB) 66
Acorn Park (ARL) 74
Acorn Park (CAM) 40
Acorn St & Cir (BRA) 84
Acorn St & Ct (MAL) 48
Acron Rd (BRO) 46
Acton (WAL) 54

Acton (HP) 36
Acton (ARL) 74
Acton (WOL) 70
Acton (WAT) 72
Acton 18
Ada (ROS) 31
Adair Rd (BRI) 35
Adamian Park (ARL) 74
Adams (ARL) 74
Adams (MEL) 76
Adams (BEL) 78
Adams (LEX) 73
Adams (HP) 36
Adams (WIN) 52
Adams (SOM) 45
Adams (BRO) 46
Adams (MAL) 48
Adams (CHE) 50
Adams (MED) 55
Adams (BRA) 84
Adams
  1-74 (NWV) 60
  1-185 (MIL) 87
  1-773 (DOR) (ODD) 22
  2-770 (DOR) (EVEN) 22
  75-OUT (NEW) 58
  186-OUT (MIL) 86
  772-OUT (DOR) (EVEN) 24
  775-OUT (DOR) (ODD) 24
Adams Ave (EV) 49
Adams Ave (WNW) 65
Adams Ct & Ter (NEW) 58
Adams Pl (SWY) 90
Adams Pl (SB) 27
Adams Rd (STO) 80
Adams St & Ave (WAT) 72
Adams St & Ave (WAL) 54
Adams St, Cir & Ct (QUI) 69
Adams St & Ct (REV) 51
Adams St & Pl (CHA) 29
Adams St & Pl (ROX) 19
Adams Ter (DOR) 22
Adams Ter (CAM) 38
Adamson (ALL) 34
Adanac Rd (MIL) 86
Adanac Ter (DOR) 24
Adas Ct (REV) 51
Addington Cir (EWY) 89
Addington Rd (WRX) 32
Addington Rd (BRO) 46
Addison (CHE) 50
Addison (BRA) 84
Addison (EB) 28
Addison (ARL) 74
Addison Rd (WAL) 54
Adelaide Rd (SOM) 43
Adelaide St & Ter (JP) 30
Adele Rd (QUI) 69
Adeline Rd (QUI) 69
Adeline Rd (NCE) 59
Adella Ave (WNW) 65
Adena Rd (WNW) 65
Adirondack Pl (DOR) 24
Adorn (WY) 88
Adrian (SOM) 43
Adrian Rd (MIL) 86
Aerial (ARL) 74

Aerial (LEX) 73
Agassiz (CAM) 40
Agassiz Park (JP) 30
Agassiz St & Ave (WAV) 79
Agatha Ave (REV) 51

Boston (Con.) 021

Agawam (REV) ... 51
Agawam (DOR) ... 22
Agawam Rd (QUI) ... 69
Agawam Rd (WAB) ... 68
Agnes Ave (MAT) ... 26
Agneus Ave (WIN) ... 52
Agry Ter (REV) ... 51
Ainsley (DOR) ... 22
Ainsworth (ROS) ... 31
Ainsworth Pl (MEL) ... 76
Airport Rd (NQ) ... 71
Airport Rd Ext (NQ) ... 71
Airport St & Rd (EB) ... 28
Airport Service Rd (EB) ... 28
Akron (CAM) ... 38
Akron St & Pl (ROX) ... 19
Alabama (MAT) ... 26
Alachua Rd (EWY) ... 89
Alameda Rd (WRX) ... 32
Alaric St & Ter (WRX) ... 32
Alaska (ROX) ... 19
Alba Cir (NEW) ... 58
Alba Rd (WEL) ... 81
Alben (DOR) ... 24
Alban Rd (WAB) ... 68
Albano (ROS) ... 31
Albany (CAM) ... 39
Albany (WOL) ... 70
Albany
　1-199 ... 11
　200-799 ... 18
　800-OUT (ROX) ... 19
Albatross Rd (QUI) ... 69
Albemarle Ave (LEX) ... 73
Albemarle Rd (WAL) ... 54
Albemarle St & Ter ... 15
Albemarle (HP) ... 36
Albemarle (ARL) ... 74
Albemarle Rd
　1-214 (NWV) ... 60
　215-215A (NWN) ... 65
　216-OUT (NWV) ... 60
Abernathy Rd (LEX) ... 73
Albert (MEL) ... 76
Albert Ave (BEL) ... 78
Albert Ave (WIN) ... 52
Albert Ave (REV) ... 51
Albert Park (EV) ... 54
Albert Rd (WAL) ... 54
Albert Rd (AUB) ... 66
Albert Rd (EWY) ... 89
Alberta (WRX) ... 32
Alberta Rd (CHH) ... 67
Alberta Ter (CAM) ... 40
Albertina (QUI) ... 69
Albion (MEL) ... 76
Albion (HP) ... 36
Albion (EV) ... 49
Albion (MAL) ... 48
Albion (MED) ... 55
Albion (ROX) ... 19
Albion
　1-91 (SOM) ... 43
　92-OUT (WS) ... 44
Albion Ave (STO) ... 80
Albion Ct, Pl & Ter (WS) ... 44
Albion Pl (CHE) ... 50
Albion Pl (CHA) ... 29
Albion Rd (WH) ... 81
Albion Rd (WOL) ... 70
Albion St & Pl (NCE) ... 59

Albright (WRX) ... 32
Alcott (ALL) ... 34
Alcott Park (MAL) ... 48
Alcott Rd (LEX) ... 73
Alden (NCE) ... 59
Alden (MEL) ... 76
Alden (QUI) ... 69
Alden (MAL) ... 48
Alden Ave (REV) ... 51
Alden Ave (STO) ... 80
Alden Ln (MED) ... 55
Alden Pl (WNW) ... 65
Alden Rd (WH) ... 81
Alden Rd (LEX) ... 75
Alden Rd (WAT) ... 72
Alden Rd (WY) ... 68
Alden Rd (BRA) ... 85
Alden Rd (MIL) ... 86
Alden Rd (N) ... 92
Alder (ROS) ... 31
Alder St & Ter (WAL) ... 54
Aldersey (SOM) ... 43
Alderwood Rd (WAL) ... 54
Alderwood Rd (NCE) ... 59
Aldie (ALL) ... 34
Aldine ... 02210
Aldrich (ROS) ... 31
Aldrich (SOM) ... 45
Aldrich Rd (WAT) ... 72
Aldridge Rd (N) ... 92
Aldwin Rd (ROS) ... 31
Aldworth (JP) ... 30
Aletha Rd (N) ... 92
Alewife Brook Pky (SOM) ... 54
Alewife Brook Pky
　1-165 (CAM) (ODD) ... 40
　2-148 (CAM) (EVEN) ... 40
　150-OUT (CAM) (EVEN) ... 38
　167-OUT (CAM) (ODD) ... 38
Alexander (DOR) ... 25
Alexander Ave (MED) ... 55
Alexander Ave (BEL) ... 78
Alexander Rd (NWH) ... 61
Alexander Rd (BRA) ... 84
Alford (CHA) ... 29
Alfred (JP) ... 30
Alfred (SWY) ... 90
Alfred (NQ) ... 71
Alfred Rd (WAT) ... 72
Alfred Rd (ARL) ... 74
Alfred Rd (MIL) ... 86
Alfred Rd (BRA) ... 84
Alfred St & Ct (EV) ... 49
Alfred St & Ter (MED) ... 55
Alger (SB) ... 24
Algonquin (DOR) ... 25
Algonquin Rd (CHH) ... 67
Algonquin Rd (QUI) ... 69
Alhambra Rd (WEL) ... 81
Alice (REV) ... 51
Alice Rd (BRA) ... 85
Alicia Rd (DOR) ... 24
Alida St & Rd (BRA) ... 85
Alkyris Rd (WRX) ... 32
Allard Ct (RXC) ... 20
Alleghany (RXC) ... 20
Allen (HP) ... 36
Allen (CHE) ... 50
Allen (ROS) ... 31
Allen (CAM) ... 40
Allen (BRA) ... 85
Allen (N) ... 92
Allen (ARL) ... 74

Allen (LEX) ... 73
Allen Ave (WAB) ... 68
Allen Cir (MIL) ... 87
Allen Ct (MED) ... 55
Allen Pl (WNW) ... 65
Allen Pl (MEL) ... 76
Allen Rd (BRI) ... 35
Allen Rd (WH) ... 31
Allen Rd (WAL) ... 54
Allen St & Ct (SOM) ... 43
Allen Ter (NWH) ... 61
Allendale (JP) ... 30
Allendale Rd (MED) ... 55
Allendale Rd (CHH) ... 67
Allendale Rd (N) ... 92
Allenwood (WRX) ... 32
Allerton (BRO) ... 46
Allerton (QUI) ... 69
Allerton (ROX) ... 19
Allerton Rd (MIL) ... 87
Allerton Rd
　1-100 (NCE) ... 59
　101-OUT (NWH) ... 61
Alleyne (WRX) ... 32
Alleyne St & Ter (QUI) ... 69
Allison St & Park (NEW) ... 58
Allstate Rd (DOR) ... 25
Allston (DOR) ... 24
Allston (NWV) ... 60
Allston (CHA) ... 29
Allston (REV) ... 51
Allston
　1-197 (ALL) ... 34
　198-OUT (BRO) ... 46
Allston St & Ct (CAM) ... 39
Allston St, Ct & Ter (MED) ... 55
Alma Ave (WAV) ... 79
Almont (WIN) ... 52
Almont (MAT) ... 26
Almont St & Ct (MED) ... 55
Almont St & Ct (MAL) ... 48
Almquist (QUI) ... 69
Alna Pl (EB) ... 28
Alpha Rd (DOR) ... 24
Alpheus Rd (ROS) ... 31
Alpine (MAL) ... 48
Alpine (CAM) ... 38
Alpine (WS) ... 44
Alpine (MAT) ... 26
Alpine (LEX) ... 73
Alpine Ave & Rd (EV) ... 49
Alpine Dr (BRA) ... 84
Alpine Rd (EWY) ... 89
Alpine St, Pl & Ter (ROX) ... 19
Alpine St & Ter (ARL) ... 74
Alpine (N) ... 92
Alrick Rd (QUI) ... 69
Alroy Rd (SWY) ... 90
Alstead (NQ) ... 71
Alston (SOM) ... 43
Alta Rd (EWY) ... 89
Alta Crest Rd (WRX) ... 32
Altair Ave (BRA) ... 85
Altair Rd (WRX) ... 32
Altamont Ave (MEL) ... 76
Altamount Rd (QUI) ... 60
Althea (DOR) ... 22
Atther (ROX) ... 19
Alton (ARL) ... 74
Alton Ct (RXC) ... 20
Alton Ct & Pl (BRO) ... 46
Alton Rd (QUI) ... 69
Alton Ter (EWY) ... 89

Boston (Con.)   021

Altura Rd (NWY)	91
Alvah Kittredge Park (ROX)	19
Alvan Ter (DOR)	25
Alvarado Ave (HP)	36
Alves Ave (BRA)	84
Alveston St & Ter (JP)	30
Alvin Ave	
1-25 (NQ) (ODD)	71
2-108 (NQ) (EVEN)	71
27-OUT (MIL) (ODD)	86
110-OUT (MIL) (EVEN)	86
Alward Rd (ROS)	31
Alwington Rd (CHH)	67
Alwyn St, Ct & Ter (HP)	36
Amaranth Ave (MED)	55
Amasa (REV)	51
Amboy (ALL)	34
Ambrose (REV)	51
Ambrose (ROX)	19
Amelia (BEL)	78
Amelia Ave (WIN)	52
Amelia Pl (REV)	51
Amelia Rd (NH)	94
American Legion Hwy (REV)	51
American Legion Hwy	
1-250 (DOR)	24
251-OUT (ROS)	31
Ames (MED)	55
Ames (SOM)	45
Ames (CAM)	42
Ames (QUI)	69
Ames (DOR)	24
Ames Ave (LEX)	73
Amesbury (WRX)	32
Amesbury	
1-77 (NQ)	71
78-OUT (WOL)	70
Amherst (CAM)	42
Amherst (ROS)	31
Amherst (LEX)	73
Amherst (ARL)	74
Amherst Ave (WAL)	54
Amherst Rd (WAB)	68
Amherst Rd (BEL)	78
Amherst Rd (WAT)	72
Amherst Rd (WEL)	81
Amherst Rd (BRA)	85
Amor Rd (MIL)	86
Amory (BRO)	46
Amory	
1-169 (ROX)	19
170-OUT (JP)	30
Amory Ave & Ter (ROX)	19
Amory Rd (WAL)	54
Amory St & Pl (CAM)	39
Amos Ter (EV)	49
Amsden (ARL)	74
Amsterdam Ave (NQ)	71
Amy Cir (WAB)	68
Anawan Ave & Ter (WRX)	32
Andem Pl (BRO)	46
Anderson Rd (WOL)	70
Anderson Rd (BRA)	85
Anderson St & Pl.	14
Andover Rd (ROS)	31
Andrea Rd (WAL)	54
Andrew (WIN)	52
Andrew (EV)	49
Andrew (CAM)	39
Andrew (WAT)	72
Andrew (ARL)	74
Andrew (NWH)	61
Andrew Sq (SB)	27
Andrew St & Ct (MAL)	48
Andrews (MED)	55
Andrews	18
Andrews Rd (WOL)	70
Andrews Rd (MIL)	86
Andrews Rd (SWY)	90
Andria Rd (MAT)	26
Angela Rd (BRA)	85
Angell (DOR)	24
Angier Cir (AUB)	66
Angier Rd (LEX)	73
Angus (NQ)	71
Anita Cir (WAB)	68
Anita Ter (ROX)	19
Ann (LEX)	73
Ann Rd (REV)	51
Anna Rd (NWY)	91
Annabel (DOR)	25
Annafran (ROS)	31
Annapolis (DOR)	25
Annapolis Rd (MIL)	86
Annapolis Rd (WNW)	65
Annavoy (EB)	28
Annawan Rd (WAB)	66
Annese Rd (CHE)	50
Annis Rd (BEL)	78
Annunciation Rd (RXC)	20
Ansel Rd (DOR)	24
Anselm Ter (BRI)	35
Anson (JP)	30
Ansonia Rd (WRX)	32
Anthony Cir & Rd (NWV)	60
Anthony Pl	13
Anthony Rd (LEX)	73
Anthony Rd (EWY)	89
Antonellis Cir (NCE)	59
Antrim (EB)	28
Antrim (CAM)	39
Antwerp (BRI)	35
Antwerp (MIL)	86
Apache Trl (MED)	55
Apache Trl (ARL)	74
Apex (QUI)	69
Appian Dr (WEL)	81
Appian Pl (EB)	28
Appian Way (ALL)	34
Appian Way (CAM)	38
Apple Ln & Rd (MIL)	86
Apple Hill Rd (MEL)	76
Apple Tree Ln (LEX)	73
Apple Tree Ln (WY)	88
Appleby Rd (WEL)	81
Applecrest Rd (WES)	93
Applegarth (NCE)	59
Appleton (MEL)	76
Appleton (WAL)	54
Appleton (WS)	44
Appleton	16
Appleton Cir (NCE)	59
Appleton Ct (MAL)	48
Appleton Rd (N)	92
Appleton St, Ct & Ter (EV)	49
Appleton St & Pl (ARL)	74
Appleton St, Rd & Ter (CAM)	38
Appleton St & Ter (WAT)	72
April Ln (WES)	93
Apthorp (WOL)	70
Apthorp Rd (MEL)	76
Aquavia Rd (MED)	55
Aramon (EB)	28
Arapahoe Rd (WNW)	65
Arbella Rd (DOR)	24
Arbor Ln (WAL)	54
Arbor Rd (WNW)	65
Arborcrest Ter (MAT)	26
Arboretum Rd (ROS)	31
Arborfield Rd (ROS)	31
Arborough Rd (ROS)	31
Arborview Rd (JP)	30
Arborway Dr (BRA)	84
Arborway St, Ct & Ter (JP)	30
Arbroth (DOR)	22
Arbutus (DOR)	24
Arbutus Ave (BRA)	85
Arcadia (ROX)	19
Arcadia (CAM)	40
Arcadia (MAL)	48
Arcadia (WRX)	32
Arcadia (REV)	51
Arcadia Ave & Pl (WAL)	54
Arcadia Rd (WY)	88
Arcadia St, Park & Ter (DOR)	22
Arch	10
Arch (N)	92
Arch (MAL)	48
Archdale Rd (ROS)	31
Archer Ave (REV)	51
Archer Ter (ROX)	19
Arcola (JP)	30
Arcola (MAL)	48
Arcola (LEX)	73
Ardale (ROS)	31
Ardee (EB)	28
Ardell (NQ)	71
Arden (ALL)	34
Arden (N)	92
Arden Rd (MED)	55
Arden Rd (WAT)	72
Arden Rd (NWV)	60
Arden Rd (WEL)	81
Ardent (ROS)	31
Ardmore (BRA)	84
Ardmore Rd (NH)	94
Ardmore Rd (WRX)	32
Ardmore Rd & Ter (WNW)	65
Argonne (QUI)	69
Argus Pl (BRI)	35
Argyle (EV)	49
Argyle (REV)	51
Argyle (WIN)	52
Argyle	16
Argyle Ct (EWY)	89
Argyle Rd (BRA)	84
Argyle Rd (WH)	61
Argyle Rd (ARL)	74
Argyle St & Ter (DOR)	24
Arion (DOR)	25
Arizona Ter (ARL)	74
Arklow (JP)	30
Arlene Ave (STO)	80
Arlene Ter (ARL)	74
Arlington (NEW)	58
Arlington (WAT)	72
Arlington (CHE)	50
Arlington (EV)	49
Arlington (HP)	36
Arlington (MED)	55
Arlington (CAM)	40
Arlington (SOM)	45
Arlington (WY)	88
Arlington	
1-13 (NQ)	71

Boston (Con.)	021	Ash Ave (SOM)	45	75-OUT (JP)	30
		Ash St Pl (CAM)	38	Atherton Ave (ROS)	31
14-OUT (WOL)	70	Ashburton Pl (CAM)	39	Atherton Pl (NLF)	62
Arlington Ave (BRA)	85	Ashburton Pl	08	Atherton Pl (ROX)	19
Arlington Ave (REV)	51	Ashburton Pl (MEL)	76	Atherton Rd (BRO)	46
Arlington Ave (CHA)	29	Ashcroft (JP)	30	Athletic Field Rd (WAL)	54
Arlington Ave	09	Ashcroft Rd (MED)	55	Athol (ALL)	34
Arlington Rd (WAL)	54	Ashcroft Rd (MEL)	76	Atkins (BRI)	35
Arlington Rd (HH)	94	Ashcroft Rd (NWH)	61	Atkinson	18
Arlington Rd (WH)	81	Asheville Rd (CHH)	67	Atkinson Cir (WIN)	52
Arlington Rd (CHH)	67	Asheville Rd (HP)	36	Atlanta (SWY)	90
Arlington St & Ct (BRI)	35	Ashfield (ROS)	31	Atlantic (WIN)	52
Arlington St & Rd (MEL)	76	Ashford Rd (NCE)	59	Atlantic (SB)	27
Arlington St & Sq	16	Ashford St, Ct & Ter (ALL)	34	Atlantic (NQ)	71
Arlington St & Ter (MAL)	48	Ashland (WS)	44	Atlantic Ave (REV)	51
Arlmont (ARL)	74	Ashland (EV)	49	Atlantic Ave (MAL)	48
Arlo Rd (NUF)	64	Ashland (WAT)	72	Atlantic Ave	
Arlow Rd (NWH)	61	Ashland (QUI)	69	1-627 (ODD)	10
Armandine (DOR)	24	Ashland (ARL)	74	2-340 (EVEN)	10
Armington (ALL)	34	Ashland (DOR)	22	342-650 (EVEN)	02210
Armory (CHA)	29	Ashland Ave (WRX)	32	629-631 (ODD)	02210
Armory (WNW)	65	Ashland St & Pl (MAL)	48	633-OUT (ODD)	11
Armory (QUI)	69	Ashland St & Pl (MED)	55	652-OUT (EVEN)	11
Armstrong (JP)	30	Ashland St & Pl (MEL)	78	Atlantic Rd (ARL)	74
Armstrong Cir (BRA)	85	Ashley (JP)	30	Atlantis (WRX)	32
Arnold (NH)	94	Ashley St & Ave (EB)	28	Atlas Rd (BRA)	84
Arnold (REV)	51	Ashmont (EWY)	30	Atwill Rd (WRX)	32
Arnold (QUI)	69	Ashmont		Atwood (REV)	51
Arnold (ARL)	74	1-429 (DOR)	24	Atwood (WEL)	81
Arnold	18	430-OUT (DOR)	22	Atwood Ave (STO)	80
Arnold Ave & Ct (SOM)	43	Ashmont Ave		Atwood Ave (NWV)	60
Arnold Cir (CAM)	39	1-12 (NEW)	58	Atwood Sq (JP)	30
Arnold Rd (STO)	80	13-OUT (NWV)	60	Aubrey Ter (MAL)	48
Arnold Rd (WH)	81	Ashmont Ct (DOR)	24	Auburn (CHE)	50
Arnold Rd (QUI)	71	Ashmont Park (DOR)	24	Auburn (EV)	49
Arnold Rd (NCE)	59	Ashmont Rd (WAB)	68	Auburn (CAM)	39
Arnold Rd (NWY)	91	Ashmont Rd (WH)	81	Auburn (MED)	55
Arnold St & Ln (BRA)	84	Ashmont St & Park (MEL)	76	Auburn (MEL)	76
Arrow (CAM)	38	Ashton (DOR)	24	Auburn (RXC)	20
Arrow (CHA)	29	Ashton Ave & Park (NCE)	59	Auburn	
Arrowhead Ln (ARL)	74	Ashton Pl (CAM)	38	1-57 (CAM)	65
Arrowhead Rd (WES)	93	Ashton St & Pl (EV)	49	58-OUT (AUB)	66
Arsenal (WAT)	72	Ashville Rd (NLF)	62	Auburn Ave (SOM)	45
Arsenal Sq (CAM)	38	Ashwood Ter (ROS)	31	Auburn Pl (WAT)	72
Arthur (NWY)	91	Ashworth Ave (BRA)	85	Auburn Rd (WH)	81
Arthur (BRA)	84	Ashworth Park (ROX)	19	Auburn St & Ct (MAL)	48
Arthur Ave (EV)	49	Ashworth Rd (NQ)	71	Auburn St, Ct & Pl (BRO)	46
Arthur Park (CAM)	39	Aspen (ROX)	19	Auburn St, Pl, Sq & Ter	
Arthur Rd (ARL)	74	Aspen Ave (AUB)	66	(CHA)	29
Arthur Rd (BEL)	78	Aspinwall Ave (NWY)	91	Auburn St & Ter (WAL)	54
Arthur St & Ave (QUI)	69	Aspinwall Ave (BRO)	46	Auburn Ter (AUB)	66
Arthur Ter (WAT)	72	Aspinwall Rd (BRA)	85	Auburndale Ave	
Artwill (MIL)	86	Aspinwall Rd (DOR)	24	1-169 (WNW)	65
Arundel	02215	Assabet Rd (QUI)	69	170-OUT (AUB)	66
Arundel Ter (NEW)	58	Assunta Rd (REV)	51	Aucella Ct (REV)	51
Arvale Rd (DOR)	21	Aster Cir (WY)	88	Auckland (DOR)	25
Asbury (LEX)	73	Asti Ave (REV)	51	Audrey (QUI)	69
Ascenta Ter (WNW)	65	Asticou Rd (JP)	30	Audrey Ave (N)	92
Accot (BRI)	35	Aston Rd (CHH)	67	Audrey Rd (BEL)	78
Ash (CAM)	38	Astoria (MAT)	26	Audubon Ave (BRA)	P4
Ash (CHE)	50	Athelstane Rd (NCE)	59	Audubon Cir	02215
Ash (WAL)	54	Athelwold (DOR)	24	Audubon Dr (CHH)	67
Ash (MED)	55	Athenaeum (CAM)	42	Audubon Rd (WEL)	81
Ash (AUB)	66	Athens (SB)	27	Audubon Rd (LEX)	73
Ash (LEX)	73	Athens (NWY)	91	Audubon Rd (MIL)	87
Ash (NQ)	71	Athens St & Ter (CAM)	29	Augusta (REV)	51
Ash (MEL)	76	Atherstone (DOR)	24	Augusta Rd (MIL)	86
Ash (BEL)	78	Atherton (SOM)	43	Augustus (REV)	51
Ash (STO)	80	Atherton (MIL)	86	Augustus Ave (ROS)	31
Ash	11	Atherton (BRA)	84	Augustus Rd (WAL)	54
Ash (BRA)	84	Atherton (QUI)	69	Augustus Rd (LEX)	73
Ash (WES)	93	Atherton		Auriga (DOR)	22
		1-74 (ROX)	19	Austin (CHA)	29

Boston (Con.)   021

Austin (SOM)   45
Austin (MAL)   48
Austin (HP)   36
Austin (MIL)   87
Austin
  1-228 (NWV)   60
  229-OUT (WMW)   65
Austin Rd (WY)   88
Austin Rd (MED)   55
Austin St & Park (CAM)   39
Autumn (WRX)   32
Autumn (MAL)   48
Autumn (EV)   49
Autumn (SOM)   45
Autumn   02215
Autumn (BRA)   84
Autumn Ln (WAL)   54
Autumn Rd (WES)   93
Avalon (REV)   51
Avalon Ave (QUI)   69
Avalon Rd (WAB)   68
Avalon Rd (MEL)   76
Avalon Rd (MAL)   48
Avalon Rd (WRX)   32
Avalon Rd (N)   92
Avalon Rd (MIL)   87
Avenue Louis Pasteur   15
Averton (ROS)   31
Avery
  1-23   11
  24-24   12
  25-OUT   11
Avery Path (NCE)   59
Avery Pl (CHA)   29
Avery Pl   11
Avery St & Sq (RH)   94
Avila Rd (HP)   36
Avola (ARL)   74
Avon (MEL)   76
Avon (LEX)   73
Avon (STO)   80
Avon (JP)   30
Avon (EV)   49
Avon (MAL)   48
Avon (REV)   51
Avon (BRO)   46
Avon (SOM)   43
Avon (CAM)   38
Avon   11
Avon Cir (NH)   94
Avon Pl (BRA)   84
Avon Pl (CAM)   40
Avon Pl (SOM)   45
Avon Pl (CHA)   29
Avon Pl (ARL)   74
Avon Pl (NEW)   58
Avon Rd (WEL)   81
Avon Rd (WAT)   72
Avon Way (QUI)   69
Avon Hill (CAM)   40
Avondale (DOR)   24
Avondale Rd (NCE)   59
Avonis Ave (WY)   88
Ayer Rd (WEL)   81
Ayles Rc (HP)   36
Ayr Rd (BRO)   46
Azalea Rd (WAL)   54
Azel Rd (BRA)   85
B (NH)   94
B (HP)   36
B (REV)   51

B (EV)   49
B-(WAV)   79
B
  1-250 (SB)   27
  251-OUT   02210
Babbitt   02215
Babcock (MIL)   86
Babcock (QUI)   69
Babcock
  1-240 (BRO)   46
  241-OUT   02215
Babcock Ave (NWV)   91
Babson (MAT)   26
Babson Park Ave (BP)   57
Back River Rd (NWV)   91
Bacon (NEW)   58
Bacon (WH)   81
Bacon (WAT)   72
Bacon (ARL)   74
Bacon (LEX)   73
Bacon (WAL)   54
Bacon Ct (HP)   36
Bacon Pl (NUF)   64
Bacon Rd (NWV)   60
Bacon Rd (BEL)   78
Bacon Rd (NWV)   91
Badger Cir (MIL)   86
Badger Pl (CHA)   29
Badger Rd (HP)   36
Badger Rd (MED)   55
Bagnal (ALL)   34
Bailey (MED)   55
Bailey (EV)   49
Bailey (WS)   44
Bailey (QUI)   69
Bailey (DOR)   24
Bailey Ave (MIL)   86
Bailey Ave & Rd (WAT)   72
Bailey Pl (NWV)   60
Bailey Rd (ARL)   74
Bailey Rd (SOM)   45
Bainbridge (MAL)   48
Bainbridge (CHA)   29
Bainbridge (ROX)   19
Baincroft Rd (MAL)   48
Baird (DOR)   24
Baker (MAL)   48
Baker (BEL)   78
Baker Ave (QUI)   69
Baker Ave (LEX)   73
Baker Ave (BRA)   84
Baker Ave (WY)   88
Baker Ave & Ct (DOR)   25
Baker Cir (CHH)   67
Baker Pl (NLF)   62
Baker Rd (ARL)   74
Baker Rd (EV)   49
Baker St & Pl (WRX)   32
Bakers Aly   11
Bakers Hill Rd (WES)   93
Bakersfield (DOR)   25
Balcarres Rd (WMW)   65
Bald Eagle Rd (SWY)   90
Bald Knob Rd (HP)   36
Baldpate Hill Rd (NCE)   59
Baldwin (NEW)   58
Baldwin (MAL)   48
Baldwin (CHA)   29
Baldwin (REV)   51
Baldwin   02210
Baldwin Ave (MEL)   76
Baldwin Ave, Pl & Ter (EV)   49
Baldwin Cir (WES)   93

Baldwin Pl (CAM)   38
Baldwin Pl   13
Baldwin Rd (WAL)   54
Baldwin St Ct (CAM)   38
Balfour (DOR)   75
Balfour (LEX)   73
Balina Pl (DOR)   24
Ball (ROX)   19
Ball Sq (WS)   44
Ballard (NCE)   59
Ballard Pl (CAM)   39
Ballard St & Way (JP)   30
Ballard Ter (LEX)   73
Ballin Pl (JP)   30
Ballou
  1-86 (QUI)   69
  87-OUT (MIL)   86
Ballou Ave (DOR)   24
Balmoral Park (SB)   27
Balsam (DOR)   24
Banbury Ave (WAL)   54
Bancroft (WAL)   54
Bancroft (CAM)   39
Bancroft (ROX)   19
Bancroft (N)   92
Bancroft (WAT)   72
Bancroft Pl (STO)   80
Bancroft Rd (WH)   81
Bancroft Rd (MEL)   76
Banfield Ave (MAT)   26
Bangor Rd (WRX)   32
Banks (WRX)   32
Banks (CAM)   38
Banks (WAL)   54
Banks (WIN)   52
Banks (WS)   44
Banks (REV)   51
Banks (WAV)   79
Banks (NWH)   61
Banks Ave (LEX)   73
Banks Pl (MEL)   76
Banton (DOR)   24
Bantry Way (SB)   27
Baptist Walk (WAT)   72
Barbara (STO)   80
Barbara (JP)   30
Barbara Ln (MED)   55
Barbara Ln (SWY)   90
Barbara Ln (MIL)   86
Barbara Rd (N)   92
Barbara Rd (WAL)   54
Barbara Rd (BEL)   78
Barbara Rd (WNW)   65
Barbara Ter (WAT)   72
Barberry Rd (LEX)   73
Barbour Ter (QUI)   69
Barclay Rd (WRX)   32
Bard Ave (ROX)   19
Bardwell JP)   30
Barham Ave
  1-133 (NQ)   71
  134-OUT (WOL)   70
Barker (BRI)   35
Barker Rd (MAL)   48
Barlow (JP)   30
Barna Rd (DOR)   24
Barnard Ave (WAT)   72
Barnard Rd (BEL)   78
Barnard Rd (MED)   55
Barnes (WAL)   54
Barnes Ave (MAL)   48
Barnes Ave (EB)   28
Barnes Ave (SWY)   90

Boston (Con.)   021

Barnes Pl (LEX) 73
Barnes Rd (NEW) 58
Barnstable Rd (WNW) 65
Barnstable Rd (WH) 81
Barrett (N) 92
Barrett (MED) 55
Barrett (REV) 51
Barrett Ave (STO) 80
Barrett Ave (SB) 27
Barrett Rd (LEX) 73
Barrett St & Ln (MAL) 48
Barneau Ct (NWV) 60
Barrington Rd (DOR) 24
Barrows (ALL) 34
Barry (HP) 36
Barry (QUI) 69
Barry St & Park (DOR) 25
Barrymeade Dr (LEX) 73
Barstow (ALL) 34
Barstow (MAL) 48
Bartlett (MAL) 48
Bartlett (EV) 49
Bartlett (CHA) 29
Bartlett (SOM) 45
Bartlett (BRO) 46
Bartlett (QUI) 69
Bartlett (MEL) 76
Baldwin Pl (CAM) 38
Baldwin Pl 13
Baldwin Rd (WAL) 54
Baldwin St Ct (CAM) 38
Balfour (DOR) 25
Balfour (LEX) 73
Balina Pl (DOR) 24
Ball (ROX) 19
Ball Sq (WS) 44
Ballard (NCE) 59
Ballard Pl (CAM) 39
Ballard St & Way (JP) 30
Ballard Ter (LEX) 73
Ballin Pl (JP) 30
Ballou
   1-86 (QUI) 69
   87-OUT (MIL) 86
Ballou Ave (DOR) 24
Balmoral Park (SB) 27
Balsam (DOR) 24
Banbury Ave (WAL) 54
Bancroft (WAL) 54
Bancroft (CAM) 39
Bancroft (ROX) 19
Bancroft (N) 92
Bancroft (WAT) 72
Bancroft Pl (STO) 80
Bancroft Rd (WH) 81
Bancroft Rd (MEL) 76
Banfield Ave (MAT) 26
Bangor Rd (WRX) 32
Banks (WRX) 32
Banks (CAM) 38
Banks (WAL) 54
Banks (WIN) 52
Banks (WS) 44
Banks (REV) 51
Banks (WAV) 79
Banks (NWH) 61
Banks Ave (LEX) 73
Barks Pl (MEL) 76
Banton (DOR) 24
Baptist Way (SB) 27
Baptist Walk (WAT) 72

Bates Rd E (WAT) 72
Bateswell Rd (DOR) 24
Battery 09
Batterymarch
   1-21 (ODD) 09
   2-22 (EVEN) 09
   23-33 (ODD) 10
   24-OUT (EVEN) 10
   35-41 (ODD) 09
   43-OUT 10
Battle Green Rd (LEX) 73
Baxter (MEL) 76
Baxter (SB) 27
Baxter Pl & Rd (BRO) 46
Baxter St, Ave & Ln (QUI) 69
Baxter St & Ter (MED) 55
Bay (CAM) 39
Bay (WAT) 72
Bay (NQ) 71
Bay (DOR) 25
Bay 16
Bay Rd (WH) 81
Bay Rd (REV) 51
Bay State Ave (WS) 44
Bay State Pl (SB) 27
Bay State Rd (CAM) 38
Bay State Rd (WH) 81
Bay State Rd (NQ) 71
Bay State Rd (BEL) 78
Bay State Rd (MEL) 76
Bay State Rd (ARL) 74
Bay State Rd 02215
Bay State Rd (WES) 93
Bay View (REV) 51
Bay View Ave (WIN) 52
Bay View Pl (SB) 27
Bay View Rd (WH) 81
Bay View St & Ave (QUI) 69
Bayard (ALL) 34
Bayberry Ln (MIL) 86
Bayberry Ln (BRA) 84
Bayfield Rd N & S (NQ) 71
Baylee Rd (NWV) 91
Bayley Ter (SWY) 91
Bayou (WIN) 52
Bayrd St & Ter (MAL) 48
Bayside (DOR) 25
Bayside Ave (NWV) 91
Bayside Rd (NQ) 71
Bayswater (EB) 28
Bayswater Rd (QUI) 69
Bayview (NAY) 91
Beach (WOL) 70
Beach (NWV) 60
Beach 11
Beach (DOR) 22
Beach (MAL) 48
Beach (CHA) 29
Beach Ave (EWY) 89
Beach Rd (NWV) 91
Beach Rd (WIN) 52
Beach Rd (WH) 81
Beach St, Rd & Ter (REV) 51
Beacham (CHA) 29
Beacham (EV) 49
Beacham (CHE) 50
Beachland Ave (REV) 51
Beachview Ave, Pl & Ter
   (MAL) 48
Beachview Rd (EB) 28
Beacon (MAL) 48
Beacon (EV) 49

Beacon (WIN) 92
Beacon (STO) 80
Beacon (ARL) 74
Beacon
   1-99 08
   1-145 (HP) 36
   1-533 (CHH) (ODD) 67
   2-548 (CHH) (EVEN) 67
   100-400 16
   146-OUT (MIL) 86
   401-489 (ODD) 15
   402-504 (EVEN) 15
   491-997 (ODD) 02215
   506-998 (EVEN) 02215
   535-1089 (NCE) (ODD) 59
   550-1090 (NCE) (EVEN) 59
   999-2435 (BRO) 46
   1091-1199 (NWH) 61
   1200-OUT (WAB) 68
   2436-2436 (CHH) 67
   2437-2495 (BRO) 46
   2496-2496 (CHH) 67
   2497-2499 (BRO) 46
   2500-2500 (CHH) 67
   2501-OUT (BRO) 46
Beacon Cir (MIL) 86
Beacon Park (WAT) 72
Beacon St & Pl (MEL) 76
Beacon St & Pl (CHE) 50
Beacon St, Pl & Ter (SOM) 43
Beacon St & Way (QUI) 69
Beaconsfield Rd (BRO) 46
Beaconwood Rd (NWH) 61
Beal (NWY) 52
Beal Rd (WAL) 54
Beale (DOR) 24
Beale
   1-411 (WOL) 70
   412-OUT (QUI) (EVEN) 69
   413-445 (MIL) (ODD) 86
   447-OUT (QUI) (ODD) 69
Beals (NWY) 91
Beals (BRO) 46
Beals Rd (BRA) 85
Bean Ct (ROX) 19
Bear Hill Rd (WAL) 54
Bear Hill Rd (STO) 80
Bearse Ave (DOR) 24
Beatrice Cir (BEL) 78
Beatty Cir (MAT) 26
Beaudreau Ct (MAL) 48
Beaulield (DOR) 24
Beaufort Ave (N) 92
Beaufort Rd (JP) 30
Beaumont (DOR) 24
Beaumont (MEL) 76
Beaumont (LEX) 73
Beaumont Ave (NWV) 60
Beaver (WAL) 54
Beaver (HP) 36
Beaver Rd (WES) 93
Beaver St & Pl 08
Beaver Brook Rd (WAL) 54
Beck (EB) 28
Beck Rd (ARL) 74
Beckert Ave (REV) 51
Becket (NQ) 71
Becket (DOR) 24
Becket Rd (BEL) 78
Beckler Ave (SB) 27
Beckwith Cir (SOM) 43
Bedford (WAL) 54
Bedford 11

Boston (Con.)	021	Belle Ave (WRX)	32	Bemuth Rd (NWH)	61
		Belle Ave (MED)	55	Bencliffe Cir (AUB)	66
Bedford (LEX)	73	Belle Isle Ave (REV)	51	Benedict (CHA)	29
Bedford (QUI)	69	Belle Isle Ter (WIN)	52	Benedict St & Ave (SOM)	45
Bedford		Bellevue (WRX)	32	Benefit (WAL)	54
1-1 (SOM)	43	Bellevue (DOR)	25	Bengal Rd (SWY)	90
2-2 (CAM)	41	Bellevue (NEW)	58	Benham (MED)	55
3-OUT (SOM)	43	Bellevue Ave (MEL)	76	Benjamin Rd (ARL)	74
Beebe Rd (QUI)	69	Bellevue Ave (REV)	51	Benjamin Rd (BEL)	78
Beech (LEX)	73	Bellevue Ave (CAM)	40	Benjamin Rd (LEX)	73
Beech (NEW)	58	Bellevue Ave (BRA)	85	Benmore (MED)	55
Beech (WAY)	79	Bellevue Dr (N)	92	Benner (EB)	28
Beech (NH)	94	Bellevue Rd (BRA)	84	Benner Ave (MAL)	48
Beech (WES)	93	Bellevue Rd (BEL)	78	Bennet Pl (EB)	28
Beech (BRA)	84	Bellevue Rd (NQ)	71	Bennet St & Pi	11
Beech (MIL)	86	Bellevue Rd (ARL)	74	Bennett (EV)	49
Beech (WAL)	54	Bellevue Rd (WH)	81	Bennett (WAL)	54
Beech (SOM)	43	Bellevue Rd & Ter (WAT)	72	Bennett (CAM)	38
Beech (CAM)	40	Bellevue St & Ave (WAL)	54	Bennett (BRI)	35
Beech (EV)	49	Bellevue St & Ter (MED)	55	Bennett (AUB)	66
Beech		Bellevue Ter (SOM)	44	Bennett (WAT)	72
1-74 (WRX)	32	Bellevue Hill Rd (WRX)	32	Bennett Ave (LEX)	73
75-700 (ROS)	31	Bellflower (LEX)	73	Bennett Hwy	
701-OUT (HP)	36	Bellflower (DOR)	25	75-75 (MAL)	48
Beech Ave (MEL)	76	Bellingham (NWH)	61	299-299 (MAL)	48
Beech Rd (BRO)	46	Bellingham (CHE)	50	300-300 (MAL)	48
Beech Glen (ROX)	19	Bellingham Ave (EV)	49	Bennett Ln (QUI)	69
Beechcroft (BRI)	35	Bellingham Ave (REV)	51	Bennett St & Ct (SOM)	43
Beechcroft Rd (NEW)	58	Bellingham Dr & Rd (CHH)	67	Bennett St & Hwy (REV)	51
Beecher (UP)	30	Bellingham Pl	14	Bennett St & Pl (MED)	55
Beecher (EWY)	89	Bellington (ARL)	74	Bennington (REV)	51
Beecher Pl & Ter (NCE)	59	Bellington (BEL)	78	Bennington (QUI)	69
Beecher Rd (BRO)	46	Bellis Cir (CAM)	40	Bennington (NEW)	58
Beechland (ROS)	31	Bellows Pl (CHA)	29	Bennington (NH)	94
Beechmont St & Ter (HP)	36	Bellvale (MAL)	48	Bennington (EB)	28
Beechwood (QUI)	69	Bellvista Rd (BRO)	46	Bennington Rd (LEX)	73
Beechwood (DOR)	21	Belmont (CHA)	29	Benson (BRI)	35
Beechwood Ave (WAT)	72	Belmont (NEW)	58	Bent (CAM)	41
Beechwood Rd (WAL)	54	Belmont (BRA)	84	Bent Ave (MAL)	48
Beechwood Rd (BRA)	84	Belmont (WY)	88	Bent Ct (SB)	27
Beechwood Rd & Ter (WH)	81	Belmont		Bent Ter (QUI)	69
Beethoven (ROX)	19	1 68 (NQ)	71	Bentham Rd (DOR)	22
Beethoven Ave (WAB)	68	1-OUT (EV) (ODD)	49	Bentley (BRI)	35
Belair Rd (WEL)	81	1-111 (CAM) (ODD)	38	Benton (RXC)	20
Belcher Cir (MIL)	86	2-OUT (WAT) (EVEN)	72	Benton (STO)	80
Belcher St & Pi (WIN)	52	2-OUT (MAL) (EVEN)	48	Benton (WEL)	81
Belcher Gov Ln (MIL)	86	69-OUT (WOL)	70	Benton Rd (BEL)	78
Belden (DOR)	25	113-883 (BEL) (ODD)	78	Benton Rd (SOM)	43
Belfort (DOR)	25	885-OUT (WAT) (ODD)	72	Benton Rd (MED)	55
Belfry Ter (LEX)	73	Belmont Cir (WAV)	79	Benvenue	
Belgrade (REV)	51	Belmont Ct (CAM)	40	1-59 (WEL)	81
Belgrade Ave		Belmont Park (EV)	49	60-OUT (SWY)	81
1-347 (ROS) (ODD)	31	Belmont Rd (CHH)	67	Berkeley (SWY)	90
2-338 (ROS) (EVEN)	31	Belmont St & Pi (MEL)	76	Berkeley (SOM)	43
340-OUT (WRX) (EVEN)	32			Berkeley (MEL)	76
349-OUT (WRX) (ODD)	32	Belmont St, Pi, Sq & Ter		Berkeley (QUI)	69
Belgrade Ter (WRX)	32	(SOM)	43	Berkeley (WAT)	72
Belgravia Pi	13	Belmore Park (NLF)	62	Berkeley (ARL)	74
Belknap (WS)	44	Belmore Ter (JP)	30	Berkeley	16
Belknap Rd (BRA)	85	Belnap Rd (HP)	36	Berkeley Ct (BRO)	46
Belknap St & Pi (ARL)	74	Belnel Rd (MAT)	26	Berkeley Ct & Rd (WH)	81
Belknap Ter (WAT)	72	Belton (DOR)	24	Berkeley Pl (AUB)	66
Bell (QUI)	69	Belton (ARL)	74	Berkeley Rd (WAL)	54
Bell (CHE)	50	Beltran St & Ter (MAL)	48	Berkeley St & Pi (CAM)	38
Bell Ct (CAM)	39	Belvidere	15	Berkley (STO)	80
Bell Ct (SB)	27	Belvidere Pi (CAM)	39	Berkshire (DOR)	24
Bell Rd (WY)	88	Belvoir Kd (DOR)	25	Berkshire (WH)	81
Bell Rock		Belvoir Rd (MIL)	87	Berkshire Rd (NWV)	60
1-104 (MAL)	48	Bemis (WES)	93	Berkshire Rd (WAL)	54
105-OUT (EV)	49	Bemis (WAT)	72	Berkshire Rd (N)	92
Bell View Ave (EV)	49	Bemis Ave (WAL)	54	Berkshire St & Pi (CAM)	41
Bellaire Rd (ROS)	31	Bemis Rd (WH)	81	Berlin (WOL)	70
Bellamy (BRI)	35	Bemis St & Rd (NWV)	60	Berlin Ave (ML)	86

Boston (Con.)   021

Bernard (MWH) 61
Bernard (LEX) 73
Bernard (DOR) 24
Bernard Ave (EV) 49
Bernard Ln (WAB) 68
Bernard Rd (WEL) 81
Bernice (DOR) 22
Berresford Rd (CHH) 67
Berry (QUI) 69
Berry (DOR) 22
Berry (MAL) 48
Bersanie Cir (NQ) 71
Bertrand Rd (AUB) 66
Bertson Ave (WRX) 32
Bertwell Rd (LEX) 73
Berwick (BEL) 78
Berwick (WRX) 32
Berwick (SOM) 45
Berwick (BRA) 84
Berwick Ct (EV) 49
Berwick Rd (MED) 55
Berwick Rd (LEX) 73
Berwick Rd (NCE) 59
Berwick St & Pl (MEL) 76
Beryl (ROS) 31
Bess Rd (N) 92
Bestick Rd (BRA) 84
Bethel Rd (WEL) 81
Bethel Beach St & Ter (QUI) 69
Bethune (BRI) 35
Bettinson Ave & Ct (EV) ... 49
Betts Rd (BEL) 78
Betty (EV) 49
Beverly (REV) 51
Beverly (MEL) 76
Beverly (QUI) 69
Beverly 14
Beverly Ct (BRA) 84
Beverly Rd (WH) 81
Beverly Rd (NWH) 61
Beverly Rd (CHH) 67
Beverly Rd (ARL) 74
Bexley Rd (ROS) 31
Biathrow (MAL) 48
Bickford (JP) 30
Bickford Ave (REV) 51
Bickford Ave (RXC) 20
Bickford Rd (MAL) 48
Bickford Rd (BRA) 84
Bicknell (DOR) 21
Bicknell (QUI) 69
Bicknell Rd & Sq (NWY) 91
Big Blue Dr (MIL) 86
Bigelow (QUI) 69
Bigelow (SOM) 43
Bigelow (CAM) 39
Bigelow Ave & Ter (WAT) ... 72
Bigelow Rd (WMW) 65
Bigelow Rd (WAL) 54
Bigelow St & Cir (BRI) 35
Billerica 14
Billingham (WS) 44
Billings (WRX) 32
Billings (NQ) 71
Billings Ave (MED) 55
Billings Ln (JP) 30
Billings Park (NEW) 58
Billings Rd
   1-199 (NQ) (ODD) 71
   2-208 (NQ) (EVEN) 71
   201-OUT (WOL) (ODD) 70

210-OUT (WOL) (EVEN) 70
Billows (WIN) 52
Billows Ave (REV) 51
Bilts C° 15
Bilodeau Rd (DOR) 21
Biltmore (JP) 30
Biltmore (MAL) 48
Binford 02210
Binnacle Ln (QUI) 69
Binney 15
Binney
   1-340 (CAM) 42
   341-OUT (CAM) 41
Birch (NH) 94
Birch (BRA) 85
Birch (MIL) 86
Birch (NQ) 71
Birch (BEL) 78
Birch (LEX) 73
Birch (EV) 49
Birch (ROS) 31
Birch (CAM) 38
Birch Ln (MAL) 48
Birch Rd (WIN) 52
Birch Rd (WAL) 54
Birch Rd (WRX) 32
Birch Rd (WAT) 72
Birch Rd (WEL) 81
Birch Rd (STO) 80
Birch Rd (NWY) 91
Birch Hill Ln (LEX) 73
Birch Hill Rd (MEL) 76
Birch Hill Rd (BEL) 78
Birch Hill Rd (NWV) 60
Birchbrow Ave (NWY) 91
Birchcliff Rd (EWY) 89
Birchcroft Rd (BRA) 84
Birchcroft Rd (MAT) 26
Birchland Ave & Ter (WRX) . 32
Birchwood (WRX) 32
Birchwood Rd (N) 92
Bird (N) 92
Bird (CAM) 38
Bird (DOR) 25
Bird (QUI) 69
Bird Pl (WRX) 32
Bird Hill Ln & Rd (LEX) ... 73
Birds Hill Ave (N) 92
Birds Hill Rd (WH) 81
Birmingham Pky (BRI) 35
Biscayne Ave (WY) 88
Bishop (JP) 30
Bishop Rd (WAL) 54
Bishop Rd (MAL) 48
Bishop Rd (WOL) 70
Bishops Pl (SOM) 45
Bishopsgate Rd (NCE) 59
Bismarck (JP) 30
Bismarck (MAT) 26
Bispham (DOR) 22
Bither Ave (WAL) 54
Bittern Rd (QUI) 69
Bittersweet Ln (WES) 93
Bixby (REV) 51
Blaban Pl (CHA) 29
Black Hawk Rd (SWY) 90
Black Oak Rd (WES) 93
Black Rock Rd (MEL) 76
Blackfan 15
Blackinton (EB) 28
Blackman Ter (N) 92
Blacksmith Dr (N) 92
Blackstone (CAM) 39

Blackstone
   1-117 (ODD) 09
   2-122 (EVEN) 09
   119-OUT (ODD) 08
   124-OUT (EVEN) 08
Blackstone Rd (NWY) 91
Blackstone Ter (NEW) 58
Blackwell (HQ) 71
Blackwell (DOR) 22
Blackwood 15
Blagden 16
Blaine (MAL) 48
Blaine (ALL) 34
Blair Pl (CAM) 40
Blair Rd (DOR) 25
Blaisdell Rd (MED) 55
Blake (MED) 55
Blake (CAM) 40
Blake (REV) 51
Blake (MAT) 26
Blake (WOL) 70
Blake (NWV) 60
Blake (BEL) 78
Blake (N) 92
Blake Rd (WES) 93
Blake Rd (WY) 88
Blake Rd (BRA) 84
Blake Rd (LEX) 73
Blake Rd (BRO) 46
Blake Ter (EV) 49
Blakely Ave (SOM) 45
Blakely Rd (MED) 55
Blakeslee (CAM) 38
Blakeville (DOR) 21
Blanchard (CAM) 39
Blanchard Ave (EV) 49
Blanchard Ave (REV) 51
Blanchard Blvd (BRA) 84
Blanchard Rd (SWY) 90
Blanchard Rd (QUI) 69
Blanchard Rd
   1-OUT (CAM) (ODD) 38
   2-58 (CAM) (EVEN) 38
   60-OUT (BEL) (EVEN) 78
Blanche (CAM) 39
Blanche (DOR) 22
Blanche Rd (WY) 88
Blandford 02215
Blaney (REV) 51
Blantyre Rd (MAL) 48
Blanvon Rd (JP) 30
Bleachery Ct (SOM) 43
Bleakney Rd (NWY) 91
Blenford Rd (BRI) 35
Blinn Rd (LEX) 73
Blithedale (NWV) 60
Block (STO) 80
Blodgett (MAL) 48
Blodgett Rd (LEX) 73
Blomerth (MAL) 48
Bloomfield (LEX) 73
Bloomfield (NQ) 71
Bloomfield (DOR) 24
Bloomingdale (CHE) 50
Bloomington (DOR) 22
Blossom (CHE) 50
Blossom (WAL) 54
Blossom (LEX) 73
Blossom (ARL) 74
Blossom Ln (WES) 93
Blossom Ln (WY) 88
Blossom Rd (BRA) 84
Blossom St & Ct. 14

Boston (Con.)	021
Blossom Crest Rd (LEX)	73
Blue Berry Hill Rd (WES)	93
Blue Bird Rd (WH)	81
Blue Hill Ave (MAL)	48
Blue Hill Ave	
1-255 (MIL) (ODD)	87
1-279 (ROX) (ODD)	19
2-292 (ROX) (EVEN)	19
2-294 (MIL) (EVEN)	87
257-OUT (MIL) (ODD)	86
281-759 (DOR) (ODD)	21
294-760 (DOR) (EVEN)	21
296-OUT (MIL) (EVEN)	86
761-1177 (DOR)	24
1178-OUT (MAT)	26
Blue Hill Ter St (MIL)	87
Blue Hill River Rd (MIL)	86
Blue Hills Pky	
1-361 (MIL) (ODD)	87
2-406 (MIL) (EVEN)	87
363-OUT (MIL) (ODD)	86
408-OUT (MIL) (EVEN)	86
Blue Ledge Dr & Ter (ROS)	31
Blue View Cir & Rd (WRX)	32
Blueberry (WY)	88
Blueberry Dr (BRA)	84
Blueberry Ln (LEX)	73
Bluefield Ter (SWY)	90
Bluefield Ter (MAT)	26
Bluff Rd (NWY)	91
Board Aly	13
Boardman (EB)	28
Boardman Ave (MEL)	76
Boardman St & Pl (CAM)	39
Boates Ct	10
Boblink Rd (WH)	81
Bobolink (WRX)	32
Bobsled Dr (NH)	94
Bodwell (DOR)	25
Bogandale Rd (WRX)	32
Bogle (WES)	93
Boland (WAL)	54
Bolster (JP)	30
Bolster (EV)	49
Bolton (WAL)	54
Bolton (SOM)	43
Bolton (CAM)	40
Bolton (SB)	27
Bolton Pl (CHA)	29
Bolton Rd (NWV)	60
Bonad Rd (STO)	80
Bonad Rd (ARL)	74
Bonad Rd (WNW)	65
Bonad Rd (MIL)	86
Bonad Rd	
1-70 (WRX)	32
71-OUT (CHH)	67
Bonair (WRX)	32
Bonair (SOM)	45
Bonair Ave (LEX)	73
Bonaire Cir (WAB)	68
Bond (SOM)	45
Bond (CAM)	38
Bond (MAL)	48
Bond (N)	92
Bond	18
Bond Rd (LEX)	73
Bonell Ter (ROX)	19
Bonita (WNW)	65
Bonmar Cir (AUB)	66
Popner Ave (SOM)	43
Bonner Ave (MED)	55
Bonnie Rd (SWY)	90
Bonnieview Rd (BRA)	84
Bonnybrook Rd (WAB)	68
Bontempo Rd (NCE)	59
Bonwood (NWV)	60
Bonwood Rd (N)	92
Booth (NH)	94
Booth (QUI)	90
Border (WNW)	65
Border (KQ)	71
Border (EB)	28
Border Rd (N)	92
Borland (BRO)	46
Boscobel (BRA)	85
Bosson (REV)	51
Boston (SOM)	43
Boston (EV)	49
Boston (MAL)	48
Boston	
1-61 (SB)	27
62-OUT (DOR)	25
Boston Ave	
1-514 (MED)	55
515-515 (WS)	44
516-581 (MED)	55
582-OUT (WS)	44
Boston Pl	08
Boston Post Rd (WES)	93
Boston Post Rd Byp (WES)	93
Boston Rock Rd (MEL)	76
Bostonia Ave (BRI)	35
Bosworth	08
Bothfield Rd (NCE)	59
Bothwell Rd (BRI)	35
Botolph (MEL)	76
Betolph (NQ)	71
Botsford Rd (CHH)	67
Boulder (MAL)	48
Boulder Rd (NCE)	59
Boulder Rd (LEX)	73
Boulder Rd (WH)	81
Boulder Brook Rd (WH)	81
Boulevard Rd (WH)	81
Boulevard Rd (ARL)	74
Boulevard Ter (ALL)	34
Bound Brook Rd (NWH)	61
Boundary Rd (ARL)	74
Boundary Rd (MAL)	48
Bourne (AUB)	66
Bourne	
1-143 (JP) (ODD)	30
2-122 (JP) (EVEN)	30
124-OUT (ROS) (EVEN)	31
145-OUT (ROS) (ODD)	31
Bourne Rd (JP)	30
Bournedale Rd (JP)	30
Bourneside (DOR)	24
Boutwell (DOR)	22
Bow (EV)	49
Bow (MAL)	48
Bow (HP)	36
Bow (SOM)	43
Bow (CAM)	38
Bow (MED)	55
Bow (WAL)	54
Bow (ARL)	74
Bow (WH)	81
Bow (STO)	80
Bow (LEX)	73
Bow (MEL)	76
Bow Rd (BEL)	78
Bow Rd (NCE)	59
Bow St Ct (STO)	80
Bow St Pl (SOM)	43
Bowditch (BRA)	84
Bowditch Ct (ROX)	19
Bowditch Rd (JP)	30
Bowdoin (SOM)	43
Bowdoin (CAM)	38
Bowdoin (WIN)	52
Bowdoin (MED)	55
Bowdoin (MAL)	48
Bowdoin (EV)	49
Bowdoin (ARL)	74
Bowdoin (NWH)	61
Bowdoin	
1-OUT (ODD)	14
1-100 (NQ)	71
1-123 (DOR) (ODD)	14
2-98 (EVEN)	14
2-126 (DOR) (EVEN)	24
100-OUT (EVEN)	08
101-OUT (WOL)	70
125-OUT (DOR) (ODD)	22
128-OUT (DOR) (EVEN)	22
Bowdoin Ave (WAL)	54
Bowdoin Ave (DOR)	21
Bowdoin Park (DOR)	22
Bowdoin Rd (WH)	81
Bowdoin Sq	14
Bowen (SB)	27
Bowen (NCE)	59
Bowen (NH)	94
Bowen Ave (MED)	55
Bower (MED)	55
Bower (MAL)	48
Bower Rd (BRA)	84
Bower Rd (QUI)	69
Bower St, Park & Pl (ROX)	19
Bower Ter (JP)	30
Bowers (NWV)	60
Bowers Ave (MAL)	48
Bowers Ave (WS)	44
Bowes Ave (QUI)	69
Bowker (LEX)	73
Bowker (BRO)	46
Bowker St & Rd (WAL)	54
Bowman (MAL)	48
Bowman (LEX)	73
Bowman (DOR)	22
Bowman Rd (LEX)	73
Boxford Ter (WRX)	32
Boyd (DOR)	24
Boyd	
1-OUT (WAT) (ODD)	72
2-40 (WAT) (EVEN)	72
42-OUT (NEW) (EVEN)	58
Boyd Park Ter (WAT)	72
Boyden (DOR)	24
Boyle (CHA)	29
Boylston (WAT)	72
Boylston (MAL)	48
Boylston (CAM)	38
Boylston	
1-292 (CHH)	67
1-713	16
1-724 (BRO)	46
293-682 (NCE)	59
683-1102 (NWH)	61
714-878 (EVEN)	99
715-877 (ODD)	16
725-OUT (CHH)	67
879-890	16

Boston (Con.)   021

891-1049 15
1050-OUT 02215
1101-OUT (NUF) (ODD) 64
1-104-OUT (NUF) (EVEN) 64
Boylston Pl (BRO) 46
Boylston Pl & Sq 16
Boylston Rd (NWH) 61
Boylston St & Pl (JP) 30
Boylston Ter (MED) 55
Boynton (JP) 30
Boynton (WAL) 54
Boynton Rd (MED) 55
Boysen Park (BRA) 85
Bracebridge Rd (NCE) 59
Brackenbury (MAL) 48
Brackett (MED) 55
Brackett (BRI) 35
Brackett (QUI) 69
Brackett (MIL) 86
Brackett (N) 92
Brackett Ave (STO) 80
Brackett Rd (NEW) 58
Bradbury (ALL) 34
Bradbury (CAM) 38
Bradbury Ave (MED) 55
Braddock Park 16
Bradeen (ROS) 31
Bradfield Ave (ROS) 31
Bradford (MAL) 48
Bradford (WAL) 54
Bradford 18
Bradford (QUI) 69
Bradford (N) 92
Bradford Ave (MED) 55
Bradford Ave (SOM) 45
Bradford Cir (ROS) 31
Bradford Ct (NCE) 59
Bradford Park (MEL) 76
Bradford Rd (BEL) 78
Bradford Rd (WH) 81
Bradford Rd (NWH) 61
Bradford Rd (WAT) 72
Bradford Rd (WES) 93
Bradford Rd (BRA) 85
Bradford Rd (MIL) 86
Bradford Rd (SWY) 90
Bradford Rd (MAT) 26
Bradford St, Pl & Ter (EV) 49
Bradford Ter (BRO) 46
Bradlee (DOR) 24
Bradlee Rd (MED) 55
Bradlee Rd (MIL) 86
Bradlee St, Ct, Ln & Park
    (HP) 36
Bradley (SOM) 45
Bradley Ave (WEL) 81
Bradley Rd (BEL) 78
Bradley Rd (ARL) 74
Bradley Rd (BRA) 84
Bradley Rd (NWY) 91
Bradmere Way (NWY) 91
Bradshaw (WAT) 72
Bradshaw (MED) 55
Bradshaw (DOR) 21
Bradston 18
Bradstreet Ave (ROS) 31
Bradstreet Ave (REV) 51
Bradwood (ROS) 31
Bradyll Rd (WES) 93
Brae Rd (NWY) 91
Brae Rd (QUI) 69

Brae Burn Rd (AUB) 66
Braeburn Rd (MIL) 86
Braeburn Rd (HP) 36
Braeland Ave (NCE) 59
Braemore Rd (NEW) 58
Braemore Rd (MED) 55
Braemore Rd (BRO) 46
Braemore Rd (WAL) 54
Braemore Rd (BRA) 85
Braemore Ter (LEX) 73
Braeview Rd (BRA) 84
Braewood (HP) 36
Bragdon (ROX) 19
Brahms (ROS) 31
Brainard (HP) 36
Brainerd Rd (ALL) 34
Braintree (ALL) 34
Braintree Ave (QUI) 69
Bramblewood Ln (BRA) 84
Branch (QUI) 69
Branch (MAL) 48
Branch 08
Branch Ave (ARL) 74
Branch Rd (SWY) 90
Branchaud Rd (BEL) 78
Branchfield (DOR) 24
Brand (ARL) 74
Branders Cir & Rd (NCE) 59
Brandley Rd (WAT) 72
Brandon (LEX) 73
Brandon Ave (DOR) 25
Brandon Rd (MIL) 87
Brandywyne Dr (EB) 28
Brannon Harris Way 18
Branton (DOR) 22
Brantwood Rd (ARL) 74
Brastow Ave (SOM) 43
Bratley (MEL) 76
Brattle St Pl (ARL) 74
Brattle St, Cir & Sq (CAM) 38
Brattle St, Ct, Dr, Ln & Ter
    (ARL) 74
Brattle Way 14
Bray (ROX) 19
Brayton Rd (BRI) 35
Brazil (MEL) 76
Breck (MIL) 86
Breck Ave (BRI) 35
Breed (REV) 51
Breed St & Sq (EB) 28
Breedens Ln (REV) 51
Bremen St & Pl (EB) 28
Bremen Ter (JP) 30
Brennan Ave (WAL) 54
Brent (DOR) 24
Brent Rd (LEX) 73
Brenton (DOR) 21
Brenton (REV) 51
Brenton Rd (WES) 93
Brentwood (ALL) 34
Brentwood (MAL) 48
Brentwood Ave (NCE) 59
Brentwood Cir (N) 92
Brentwood Rd (STO) 80
Brettwood Rd (BEL) 78
Brewer (QUI) 69
Brewer (JP) 30
Brewer (CAM) 38
Brewster (CAM) 38
Brewster (SB) 27
Brewster Ave (WIN) 52
Brewster Ave (BRA) 85
Brewster Pl & Rd (NWY) 91

Brewster Rd (MIL) 86
Brewster Rd (WAL) 54
Brewster Rd (MED) 55
Brewster Rd (WH) 81
Brewster Rd (STO) 80
Brewster Rd (NWH) 61
Brewster Rd (ARL) 74
Brewster Ter (BRO) 46
Briar Ln (NWY) 60
Briar Ln (WES) 93
Briar Wood Trl (WY) 88
Briarcliff Ter (MAT) 26
Briarfield Rd (MIL) 87
Briarwood Cir (NH) 94
Briarwood Rd (MIL) 86
Briarwood Rd (WAL) 54
Bridge (REV) 51
Bridge (CAM) 41
Bridge (ROS) 31
Bridge (EV) 49
Bridge (HP) 36
Bridge (NH) 94
Bridge (NWY) 91
Bridge (NEW) 58
Bridge (QUI) 69
Bridge (LEX) 73
Bridge (WAT) 72
Bridge Ct 14
Bridgeham Ave (WAT) 72
Bridges Ave (NWY) 60
Bridle Path (LEX) 73
Bridle Path (EWY) 89
Bridle Trl Rd (N) 92
Brier Rd (WRX) 32
Brierfield Rd (NWH) 61
Brierwood Rd (BRA) 84
Briggs (WOL) 70
Briggs (MEL) 76
Briggs Pl 18
Briggs Rd (LEX) 73
Brigham (WAT) 72
Brigham (EB) 28
Brigham Rd (LEX) 73
Brigham Rd (WAL) 54
Bright (WAL) 54
Bright Rd (BEL) 78
Brighton (BEL) 78
Brighton (QUI) 69
Brighton (CHA) 29
Brighton Ave (ALL) 34
Brightwood Rd (WAL) 54
Brimmer 08
Brimmer (WAT) 72
Brington Rd (BRO) 46
Brinsley (QUI) 69
Brinsley (DOR) 21
Brinton (ROX) 19
Bristol 18
Bristol

1-73 (CAM) 41
74-OUT (CAM) 39
Bristol Rd (WNW) 65
Bristol Rd (WH) 81
Bristol Rd (WS) 44
Broad (QUI) 69
Broad (BEL) 78
Broad (BP) 57
Broad

1-77 (ODD) 09
1-514 (WY) 88
2-72 (EVEN) 09
74-OUT (EVEN) 10
79-OUT (ODD) 10

515-OUT (EWY) 89
Broad St Pl (WY) 88
Broad Meadows Rd (N) 92
Broad Sound Ave (REV) 51
Broadlawn Dr & Park (CHH) ... 67
Broadway (QUI) 69
Broadway (STO) 80
Broadway (WAT) 72
Broadway (ARL) 74
Broadway (REV) 51
Broadway (CHE) 50
Broadway (EV) 49
Broadway (MAL) 48
Broadway
  1-155 (CAM) 42
  1-221 (ODD) 16
  1-649 (SOM) 45
  2-218 (EVEN) 16
  156-407 (CAM) 39
  220-398 (EVEN) 11
  223-399 (ODD) 11
  400-OUT (SB) 27
  650-OUT (WS) 45
  407A-OUT (CAM) 38
Broadway Ext (SB) 27
Broadway Pl (SOM) 45
Broadway St & Ter (NWV) 60
Broadway Ter (CAM) 39
Broady Ave (QUI) 69
Brock (BRI) 35
Brockton (MAT) 26
Brockton Ave (QUI) 69
Brogan Rd (MIL) 87
Broken Tree Rd (NCE) 59
Bromfield (WOL) 70
Bromfield (WAT) 72
Bromfield 08
Bromfield Rd (WS) 44
Bromley (JP) 30
Bronsdon (BRI) 35
Bronson Ter (JP) 30
Bronx Rd (WRX) 32
Brook (ROS) 31
Brook (SOM) 45
Brook (BRO) 46
Brook (MAL) 47
Brook (CHE) 50
Brook (WOL) 70
Brook (WEL) 81
Brook (MEL) 76
Brook (LEX) 73
Brook Ave (WAL) 54
Brook Ave
  1-59 (ROX) (ODD) 19
  2-66 (ROX) (EVEN) 19
  61-OUT (DOR) (ODD) 25
  68-OUT (DOR) (EVEN) 25
Brook Rd (NH) 94
Brook Rd (WES) 93
Brook Rd (QUI) 69
Brook Rd
  1-599 (MIL) 87
  600-OUT (MIL) 86
Brook Ter (WY) 88
Brook Farm Rd (WRX) 32
Brook Hill Rd (MIL) 87
Brookdale (ROS) 31
Brookdale (BRI) 51
Brookdale Ave (WH) 81
Brookdale Rd (NWV) 60
Brookdale Rd (ARL) 74
Brookfield (ROS) 31
Brookfield Cir & Rd (WH) 81

Brookfield Rd (WIN) 52
Brookfield Rd (WAL) 54
Brookford (CAM) 40
Brookford (DOR) 25
Brookings (MED) 55
Brookledge (DOR) 21
Brookledge Rd (MEL) 76
Brookley Rd & Ter (JP) 30
Brookline (CAM) 39
Brookline (REV) 51
Brookline (WAT) 72
Brookline (N) 92
Brookline
  1-175 (CHH) 67
  176-OUT (NCE) 59
Brookline Ave
  1-549 02215
  550-OUT (BRO) 46
Brookmere Ave (WH) 81
Brookridge Rd (STO) 80
Brooks (ROS) 31
Brooks (BRI) 35
Brooks (EB) 20
Brooks Ave (ARL) 74
Brooks Ave (NWV) 60
Brooks Ave (QUI) 69
Brooks St & Park (MED) 55
Brooksdale Rd (BRI) 35
Brookside Ave (JP) 30
Brookside Ave (NWV) 60
Brookside Ave (WAV) 79
Brookside Ave (LEX) 73
Brookside Park (MIL) 87
Brookside Pky (MED) 55
Brookside Rd (N) 92
Brookside Rd (BRA) 84
Brookside Rd (WH) 81
Brookvale (DOR) 24
Brookview (DOR) 24
Brookview Rd (MED) 55
Brookway (WH) 81
Brookway Ct & Rd (WAL) 54
Brookway Rd & Ter (ROS) 31
Brookwood Rd (LEX) 73
Brow Ave (BRA) 85
Brown (WES) 93
Brown (WAV) 79
Brown (BEL) 78
Brown (MEL) 76
Brown (WAL) 54
Brown (CAM) 38
Brown (EV) 49
Brown (ROX) 19
Brown Ave (ROS) 31
Brown Rd (LEX) 73
Brown Ter (JP) 30
Brown Ter (MAL) 47
Browne (BRO) 46
Browning (WY) 88
Browning Ave (DOR) 24
Browning Rd (SOM) 45
Browning Rd (ARL) 74
Browns Ave (WAL) 54
Bruce (DOR) 24
Bruce Ln (NEW) 58
Bruce Rd (LEX) 73
Bruce Rd (WAL) 54
Brucewood Rd (WRX) 32
Bruno (REV) 51
Brunswick (NQ) 71
Brunswick (DOR) 21
Brunswick Park & Way (MEL) . 76

Brunswick Rd (ARL) 74
Brush Hill Ln (MIL) 86
Brush Hill Rd (NWH) 61
Brush Hill Rd
  1-211 (MIL) 87
  212-OUT (MIL) 85
Brush Hill Ter (HP) 36
Brushwood Cir (HP) 36
Bryant (REV) 51
Bryant (EV) 49
Bryant (MAL) 48
Bryant (CAM) 38
Bryant Ave (MIL) 86
Bryant Ave (WY) 88
Bryant Ave (QUI) 69
Bryant Rd (CHH) 67
Bryant Rd (LEX) 73
Bryant Rd (WAL) 54
Bryden Rd (WES) 93
Bryer Rd (MAL) 48
Bryn Mawr Rd (WH) 81
Bryon Rd (CHH) 67
Buchanan (WIN) 52
Buchanan Ln (SWY) 90
Buchanan Rd (ROS) 31
Buckingham (SOM) 43
Buckingham (HP) 36
Buckingham 16
Buckingham Rd (MIL) 86
Buckingham Rd (WOL) 70
Buckingham St & Pl (CAM) 38
Buckley (QUI) 69
Buckley Ave (JP) 30
Buckman Ct (ARL) 74
Buckman Dr (LEX) 73
Buckminster Rd (BRO) 46
Bucknam (EV) 49
Bucknam (RXC) 20
Bucknell (WH) 81
Buckskin Dr (WES) 93
Buckthorn Ter (WIN) 52
Buena Vista Park (CAM) 40
Buena Vista Rd (WS) 44
Buena Vista Rd (WH) 81
Buena Vista Rd (ARL) 74
Buff Cir (NCE) 59
Buick (WAT) 72
Buick 02215
Bulfinch Pl 14
Bullard (DOR) 21
Bullard Rd (WES) 93
Bullock 02210
Bullough Park (NWV) 60
Bungalow Rd (WRX) 32
Bunker (HP) 36
Bunker Ln (WNW) 65
Bunker Hill Ln (QUI) 69
Bunker Hill St & Ct (CHA) 29
Bunny Cir (NEW) 58
Bunton (MIL) 86
Burard (WRX) 32
Burbank (REV) 51
Burbank 15
Burbank Rd (MED) 55
Burch (ARL) 74
Burdean Rd (NCE) 59
Burdett Ter (MAL) 48
Burditt (EV) 49
Burgess (NQ) 71
Burgess (DOR) 25
Burget Ave (MED) 55
Burgoyne (DOR) 24

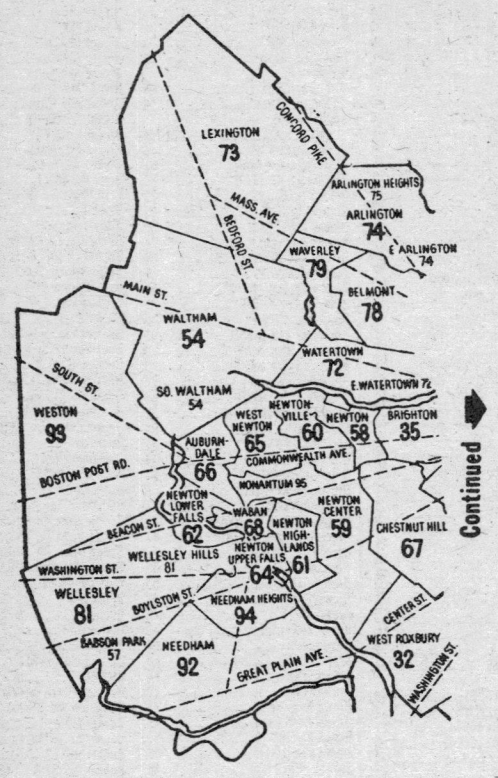

ZIP CODES
BOSTON, Massachusetts
021 + two digits shown = zip code

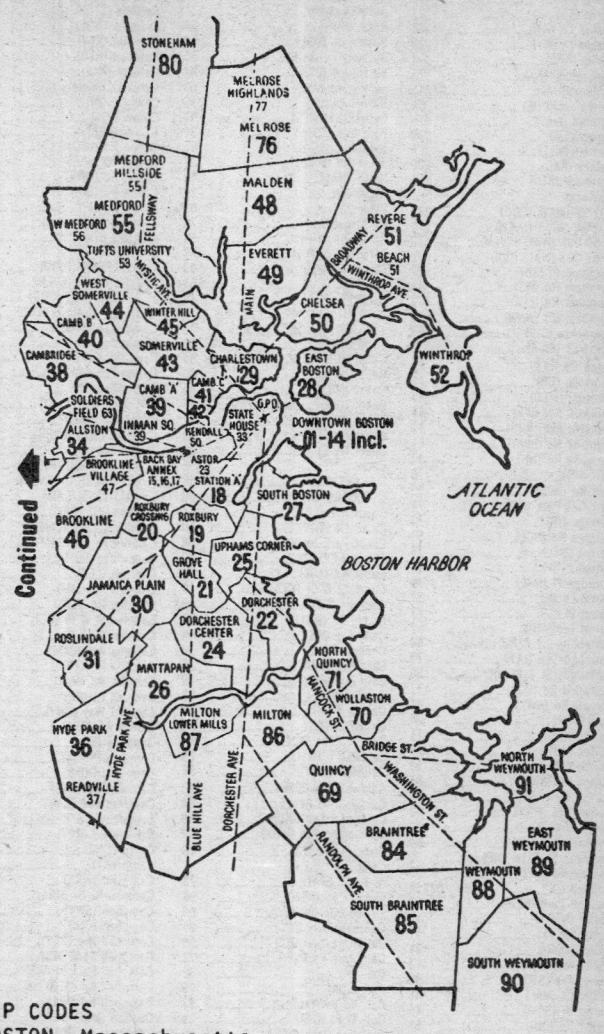

ZIP CODES
BOSTON, Massachusetts
021 + two digits shown = zip code

Burke (RXC)	20
Burke (SB)	27
Burkes Ln (WH)	81
Burkhall (SWY)	90
Burley (ROS)	31
Burlington (LEX)	73
Burlington Ave.	02215
Burma Rd (CHE)	50
Burmah (MAT)	26
Buroett (JP)	30
Burnett (MEL)	76
Burney (RXC)	20
Burnham (REV)	51
Burnham	
1-59 (WAV) (ODD)	79
2-54 (WAV) (EVEN)	79
56-OUT (WAT) (EVEN)	72
61 OUT (WAT) (ODD)	72
Burnham Pl (SB)	27
Burnham Rd (WS)	44
Burnham Rd (LEX)	73
Burnham Rd (WNW)	65
Burns Ave (QUI)	69
Burns Ct (CAM)	38
Burns Rd (LEX)	73
Burns Sq (EB)	28
Burnside (MED)	55
Burnside Ave (WS)	44
Burnside Ave (ROS)	31
Burnside Rd (NWH)	61
Burnside Rd (NH)	94
Burr (JP)	30
Burr Rd (NCE)	59
Burr Oak Park (DOR)	21
Burrage (JP)	30
Burrage Rd (NCE)	59
Burrell (MEL)	76
Burrell (ROX)	19
Burridge Pl (MAL)	48
Burrill Ln (N)	92
Burrill Pl (SB)	27
Burrill Ter (WIN)	52
Burroughs Ext & Rd (BRA)	84
Burroughs Rd (LEX)	73
Burroughs St & Pl (JP)	30
Burrwood Rd (ROS)	31
Bursely Rd (NWY)	91
Burt (DOR)	24
Burton (BRI)	35
Burton (ARL)	74
Burton Ave (ROX)	19
Burton Rd (BRA)	84
Burton Ter (SWY)	90
Burwell Rd (WRX)	32
Bushneil (DOR)	24
Bushnell Ter (BRA)	84
Business St & Ter (HP)	36
Bussell Rd (MED)	55
Buswell	02215
Buswell Park (NEW)	58
Butler (MED)	55
Butler (REV)	51
Butler (DOR)	24
Butler Ave (LEX)	73
Butler Ave (STO)	80
Butle Ct (MAL)	48
Butler Dr (SOM)	45
Butler Rd (QUI)	69
Butler Rd (BRA)	85
Butler Rd (WY)	89
Buttonwood Ln (WES)	93
Buttonwood Rd (STO)	80

Buttonwood St & Ct (DOR)	75
Buttrick (WAL)	54
Butts (NUF)	64
Buxton Ln (WAL)	54
Buzzells Ln (MED)	55
Bv French (BRA)	84
Byfield Rd (WAB)	68
Bynner (JP)	30
Bypass Rd (WES)	93
Byrd Ave (ROS)	31
Byrd Ave (WNW)	65
Byrne Rd (MIL)	87
Byron (MAL)	48
Byron (EB)	28
Byron	08
Byron Ave (LEX)	73
Byron Rd (WAL)	54
Byron Rd (WY)	88
Byron Rd (WES)	93
C (REV)	51
C (WAV)	79
C	
1-368 (SB)	27
369-OUT	02210
Cabot (NH)	94
Cabot (WY)	88
Cabot (MIL)	86
Cabot (CHH)	67
Cabot (WAL)	54
Cabot (CHE)	5C
Cabot (RXC)	20
Cabot	
1-199 (NEW)	58
200-OUT (NWV)	60
Cabot Ave (BRA)	84
Cabot Ct (NEW)	60
Cabot Park (NEW)	58
Cabot Rd (STO)	80
Cabot Rd (ARL)	74
Cabot St & Ct (EV)	49
Cadbury (CAM)	40
Caddy Rd (MAT)	26
Cady Ave (WS)	44
Cahners Pl	16
Cain Ave (BRA)	85
Cain Ave (EWY)	89
Cairn (QUI)	69
Calder (DOR)	24
Calder Pl (JP)	30
Caldon Path (NCE)	59
Caldwell (CHA)	29
Caldwell (NWY)	91
Caldwell Ave (SOM)	43
Caldwell Rd (WAL)	54
Caledonia Ave (QUI)	69
Caledonian Ave (WRX)	32
Calhoun Ave (EV)	49
California	
1-121 (WAT)	72
122-395 (NEW)	58
396-OUT (NWV)	60
California Ave (MIL)	86
California Ave (QUI)	69
California Park (WAT)	72
Call (JP)	30
Call (CHA)	29
Call Rd (NWY)	91
Call St Pl (CHA)	29
Callahan Path (NCE)	59
Callender (DOR)	24
Callender St & Pl (CAM)	39
Calnan Cir (WEY)	88
Calnan Sq (CAM)	39

Caltha Rd (BRI)	35
Calthea (STO)	80
Calumet (WOL)	70
Calumet (REV)	51
Calumet (RXC)	20
Calvary (WAL)	54
Calvary Cemetery (ROS)	31
Calvin (SOM)	43
Calvin (LEX)	73
Calvin (BRA)	84
Calvin Rd (WAT)	72
Calvin Rd (WEL)	81
Calvin Rd (NWV)	60
Calvin Ro (QUI)	69
Calvin Rd (JP)	30
Cambria (SOM)	43
Cambria	15
Cambria Rd	
1-23 (WNW) (ODD)	65
2-32 (WNW) (EVEN)	65
25-OUT (WAL) (ODD)	54
34-OUT (WAL) (EVEN)	54
Cambridge (CHA)	29
Cambridge	14
Cambridge (REV)	51
Cambridge (WAV)	79
Cambridge	
1-599 (ALL) (ODD)	34
1-1040 (ALL) (EVEN)	41
2-630 (ALL) (EVEN)	34
100-100	02202
601-OUT (BRI) (ODD)	35
632-OUT (BRI) (EVEN)	35
1041-1563 (CAM)	39
1564-OUT (CAM)	38
Cambridge Pky (CAM)	42
Cambridge Ter (CAM)	40
Cambridge Ter (ALL)	34
Camden (LEX)	73
Camden Pl (CAM)	38
Camden Rd (AUB)	66
Camden St & Pl (QUI)	69
Camden St & Pl	18
Camelia Ave (CAM)	39
Camelia Pl (LEX)	73
Camelia Rd (MAT)	26
Camelot Ct (BRI)	35
Camelot Way (SWY)	90
Cameo Rd (BRA)	85
Cameron (EV)	49
Cameron (BRO)	46
Cameron (DOR)	25
Cameron Ave (WS)	44
Cameron Ave (CAM)	40
Cameron St & Pl (WEL)	81
Camille Rd (REV)	51
Camp (CAM)	40
Camp (WY)	88
Camp Rd (WRX)	32
Campanelli Dr (BRA)	85
Campbell (SWY)	90
Campbell (QUI)	69
Campbell Ave (REV)	51
Campbell Park (WS)	44
Campbell Park Pl (WS)	44
Campbell Rd (STO)	80
Campbell Rd (ARL)	74
Canaan (MAT)	26
Canacum Rd (NWY)	91
Canal (BRA)	85
Canal	14
Canal (MAL)	48
Canal (MED)	55

Boston (Con.) 021

Canal Ln (SOM) 45
Candace Ave (WAL) 54
Candia (EWY) 89
Candia (ARL) 74
Candlewick Close (LEX) 73
Candlewood Ln (BRA) 84
Candor Pl (JP) 30
Cannell Pl (EV) 49
Cannon (RWH) 61
Canterbury
  1-250 (DOR) 24
  251-OUT (ROS) 31
Canterbury Rd (NWH) 61
Canterbury Rd (WAL) 54
Canton Ave
  1-481 (MIL) (ODD) 87
  2-474 (MIL) (EVEN) 87
  476-OUT (MIL) (EVEN) 86
  483-OUT (MIL) (ODD) 86
Canton Pl 18
Canton Rd (NQ) 71
Cantwell Rd (MIL) 87
Cape Cod Ln (MIL) 87
Cape Cod Ln (BRA) 84
Capen (MIL) 87
Capen (STO) 80
Capen (MED) 55
Capen E (MED) 55
Capen Ct (WS) 44
Capen Rd (BRA) 84
Capen St & Pl (DOR) 24
Capital (WRX) 32
Capital (NEW) 58
Capitol (WAT) 72
Cappy Cir (WNW) 65
Captain Parker Arms (LEX) 73
Captains Walk (QUI) 69
Carberry (MED) 55
Cardinal Ct (BRA) 85
Cardinal Rd (STO) 80
Cardinal Oconnell Way 14
Cardington (ROX) 19
Carey Ave (WAT) 72
Carey Pl & Rd (NH) 94
Cargill (MEL) 76
Carl (NWH) 61
Carl Rd (LEX) 73
Carl Rd (ARL) 74
Carle Rd (WOL) 70
Carleton (NEW) 58
Carleton 16
Carleton (REV) 51
Carleton (CAM) 42
Carleton Cir & Rd (BEL) 78
Carleton Rd (WEL) 81
Carleton Rd (WAL) 54
Carley Rd (LEX) 73
Carlford Rd (JP) 30
Carlida (MEL) 76
Carlida Rd (STO) 80
Carlin Rd (WAL) 54
Carlisle (CAM) 39
Carlisle (NQ) 71
Carlisle (DOR) 21
Carlisle St & Pl (NCE) 59
Carlmark (QUI) 69
Carlos (DOR) 24
Carlotta (DOR) 22
Carlow (ROX) 19
Carlson (QUI) 69

Carlson (EV) 49
Carlson Ave (REV) 51
Carlson Ave (NCE) 59
Carlson Cir (WRX) 32
Carlson Rd (MIL) 86
Carlton (SOM) 43
Carlton Rd (WEL) 81
Carlton Rd (ARL) 74
Carlton Rd (WAB) 68
Carlton St & Path (BRO) 46
Carlton Ter (WAT) 72
Carmel (CHE) 50
Carmel (RXC) 20
Carmel Cir (LEX) 73
Carmela Ln (DOR) 24
Carmen (DOR) 21
Carmen Ave (STO) 80
Carmody Ct (SB) 27
Carnegie Pl (LEX) 73
Carney (MED) 55
Carney Ct (CHA) 29
Carol (STO) 80
Carol Ave (BRO) 46
Carol Cir (WRX) 32
Carol Ln (WAL) 54
Carol Ln (LEX) 73
Carol Rd (N) 92
Carolina (MED) 55
Carolina Ave & Pl (JP) 30
Caroline (WH) 81
Caroline Park (WAB) 68
Carolyn Rd (SWY) 90
Carolyne Ave (BRA) 85
Carpenter (SB) 27
Carriage Dr (LEX) 73
Carrigg Rd (NQ) 71
Carrisbrooke Rd (WH) 81
Carroll (STO) 80
Carroll (WAT) 72
Carroll (EWY) 89
Carroll (WRX) 32
Carroll (CHE) 50
Carrolls Ln (QUI) 69
Carrolton Rd (WRX) 32
Carruth (WOL) 70
Carruth (DOR) 24
Carson (DOR) 25
Carson (WY) 88
Cart Path Rd (WES) 93
Carter (NH) 94
Carter (CHA) 29
Carter (QUI) 69
Carter (NWV) 60
Carter (CHE) 50
Carter (EV) 49
Carter (WAL) 54
Carter Rd (BRA) 85
Carter Ter (SOM) 43
Carthay Cir (NWH) 61
Cartwright Rd (WH) 81
Caruso Rd (REV) 51
Carver (CAM) 38
Carver (SOM) 43
Carver (EWY) 89
Carver 16
Carver Rd (WH) 81
Carver Rd (NWH) 61
Carver Rd (WAT) 72
Carver Rd E (WAT) 72
Carville Ave (LEX) 73
Cary Ave (LEX) 73
Cary Ave (MIL) 86
Cary Ave (REV) 51

Cary Ave (CHE) 50
Cary Pl (CHA) 29
Cary Rd (CHH) 67
Caryll (MAT) 26
Casco (QUI) 69
Case Dr (REV) 51
Caspar (WRX) 32
Caspian Way (DOR) 25
Cass (WRX) 32
Cass (MEL) 76
Cassandra Rd (EWY) 89
Cassnet (DOR) 22
Castle (WAL) 54
Castle Ct (EB) 28
Castle Pl (NH) 94
Castle Rd (EWY) 89
Castle Rd (LEX) 73
Castle St & Ct 18
Castle Rock (DOR) 25
Castlegate (DOR) 21
Castleton (JP) 30
Cataldo Dr (REV) 51
Cataumet (JP) 30
Catawba (ROX) 19
Catenaccia Way (JP) 30
Cathedral (ROX) 19
Catherine (ROS) 31
Catherine Rd (MIL) 87
Catlin (BRO) 46
Caton (MAT) 26
Caughey (WAL) 54
Caulfield Cir (NCE) 59
Causeway 14
Cavanaugh Path (NCE) 59
Cavanaugh Rd (WH) 81
Cavanaugh Rd (BRA) 84
Cavel Cir (WRX) 32
Cawfield (DOR) 25
Cazenove 16
Cazenove Pl (EV) 49
Cecelian (REV) 51
Cedar (WAL) 48
Cedar (MAL) 54
Cedar (MAT) 26
Cedar (CHA) 29
Cedar (BRA) 84
Cedar (EWY) 89
Cedar (NCE) 59
Cedar (LEX) 73
Cedar (WOL) 70
Cedar
  1-100 (SOM) 43
  1-249 (WH) 81
  101-163 (WS) 44
  164-OUT (SOM) 45
  250-OUT (NH) 94
Cedar Ave (BRA) 85
Cedar Ave (ARL) 74
Cedar Ave (SOM) 43
Cedar Ave & Way (STO) 80
Cedar Park N & S (MEL) 76
Cedar Pl (QUI) 69
Cedar Pl (DOR) 25
Cedar Rd (BEL) 78
Cedar Rd (CHH) 67
Cedar Rd (WRX) 32
Cedar Rd (MED) 55
Cedar Rd (WES) 93
Cedar St Pl (SOM) 43
Cedar St, Ct & Ter (EV) 49
Cedar St, Park & Sq (ROX) 19
Cedar St & Sq (CAM) 40
Cedar Ter (WH) 81

Boston (Con.)   021

Cedar Ter St (MIL) 86
Cedar Cliff Rd (BRA) 84
Cedar Cliff Ter (MED) 55
Cedar Croft Ln (WAL) 54
Cedar Grove (DOR) 24
Cedar Grove Cemetery (DOR) .. 24
Cedar Hill Ln (WAL) 54
Cedar Lane Way 08
Cedarbrook Rd (WH) 81
Cedarcrest Cir & Rd (WRX) ... 32
Cedarcrest Ter (WRY) 32
Cedarwood Ave (WAL) 54
Cedarwood Rd (JP) 30
Cedarwood Ter (LEX) 73
Cedric (ROX) 19
Cedric Rd (NCE) 59
Cedrus Ave (ROS) 31
Cefalo Rd (WRX) 32
Celestine Ter (STO) 80
Celia Rd (WRX) 32
Celia Rd (BRA) 85
Cemetery (ARL) 74
Cemetery Dr (CHH) 67
Cenacle Rd (BRI) 35
Centennial Ave (REV) 51
Center (WES) 93
Center (EWY) 89
Center Plz 08
Centervale Park (DOR) 24
Centola (BRI) 35
Central (WIN) 52
Central 09
Central (SWY) 90
Central (ARL) 74
Central (WEL) 81
Central
   1-112 (SOM) 43
   113-OUT (SOM) 45
Central Ave (NWV) 60
Central Ave (QUI) 69
Central Ave (MAT) 26
Central Ave (REV) 51
Central Ave (HP) 36
Central Ave (MED) 55
Central Ave (EV) 49
Central Ave (WAL) 48
Central Ave (CHE) 50
Central Ave
   1-425 (MIL) (ODD) 87
   1-763 (NH) 94
   2-434 (MIL) (EVEN) 87
   427-OUT (MIL) (ODD) 86
   436-OUT (MIL) (EVEN) 86
   764-OUT (N) 92
Central Pl (CHA) 29
Central Rd (SOM) 43
Central Sq (CAM) 39
Central Sq (EB) 28
Central St & Ave (WAL) 54
Central St & Ave (BRA) 85
Central St & Sq (STO) 80
Central St & Ter (AUB) 66
Central Ter (MEL) 76
Central Close (AUB) 66
Central Wharf 10
Centre (QUI) 69
Centre (LEX) 73
Centre (WAT) 72
Centre (WAL) 54
Centre (SOM) 43
Centre (CAM) 39

Centre (MAL) 48
Centre (WIN) 52
Centre (BRO) 46
Centre
   1-245 (DOR) 24
   1-249 (ROX) 19
   1-854 (NEW) 58
   246-OUT (DOR) 22
   250-1198 (JP) (EVEN) 30
   251-1193 (JP) (ODD) 30
   855-1457 (NCE) (ODD) 59
   856-1510 (NCE) (EVEN) ... 59
   1195-1635 (ROS) (ODD) ... 31
   1200-1634 (ROS) (EVEN) .. 31
   1459-OUT (NWH) (ODD) 61
   1512-OUT (NWH) (EVEN) ... 61
   1636-OUT (WRX) 32
Centre Ave (BEL) 78
Centre Ave (NEW) 58
Centre Ave (DOR) 24
Centre Ct (DOR) 22
Centre Ln & Ter (WRX) 32
Centre Pl (ROX) 19
Centre St Ter (ROX) 19
Centre St & Ln (MIL) 86
Century (SOM) 45
Century (MED) 55
Century Ln (MIL) 86
Century Rd (SWY) 90
Cerdan Ave (ROS) 31
Cerina Rd (JP) 30
Ceylon
   1-49 (DOR) 25
   50-OUT (DOR) 21
Chadbourne Rd (LEX) 73
Chadbourne Ter (WAT) 72
Chadwick (ROX) 19
Chadwick Rd (WES) 93
Chafee Ave (WAL) 54
Chalke (CAM) 39
Chamber (CHA) 29
Chamberlain (DOR) 24
Chamberlain Ave (WIN) 52
Chamberlain Ave (REV) 51
Chamberlain Rd (NEW) 58
Chamberlain Ter (WAL) 54
Chamblet (DOR) 25
Champa (NUF) 64
Champney (BRI) 35
Champney Pl (ROX) 19
Champney Pl 14
Chandler (WS) 44
Chandler (NEW) 58
Chandler (WAT) 72
Chandler (LEX) 73
Chandler (BEL) 78
Chandler (ARL) 74
Chandler (WY) 88
Chandler Pl (NUF) 64
Chandler Rd (MED) 55
Chandler Rd (MAL) 48
Change Ave 14
Channing (WOL) 70
Channing (NEW) 58
Channing Rd (NCE) 59
Channing Rd (WAT) 72
Channing Rd (BEL) 78
Channing Rd (BRO) 46
Channing St, Cir & Pl (CAM) . 39
Chapel (WS) 44
Chapel (BRO) 46

Chapel (NEW) 58
Chapel (QUI) 69
Chapel (N) 92
Chapel Pl (WH) 81
Chapel Rd (HP) 36
Chapin Ave (WRX) 32
Chapin Rd (NCE) 59
Chapman (WAT) 72
Chapman (WOL) 70
Chapman (ARL) 74
Chapman Pl (CAM) 38
Chapman Pl 08
Chapman St & Pl (CHA) 29
Chappie (CHA) 29
Chard (EWY) 89
Chardon Rd (MED) 55
Chardon St & Ct 14
Charger (REV) 51
Charlame St, Ct & Pl (ROX) .. 19
Charlemont (DOR) 22
Charlemont (NWH) 61
Charlemont Rd (MED) 55
Charles (WIN) 52
Charles (CAM) 41
Charles (SOM) 43
Charles (HP) 36
Charles (MAL) 48
Charles (BRO) 46
Charles (CHE) 50
Charles (WAL) 48
Charles (AUB) 66
Charles (NWH) 61
Charles (ARL) 74
Charles (WAT) 72
Charles (STO) 80
Charles (WH) 81
Charles (QUI) 69
Charles (MEL) 76
Charles (BEL) 78
Charles (LEX) 73
Charles (DOR) 22
Charles (CHA) 29
Charles (EWY) 89
Charles (NH) 94
Charles (BRA) 84
Charles
   0-ONLY 16
   1-OUT 14
Charles, S. 16
Charles Ave (REV) 51
Charles Ct E (N) 92
Charles Park Rd (WRX) 32
Charles Rd (DOR) 24
Charles St Ave (WAL) 54
Charles St Pl (MAL) 48
Charles St Pl (CHA) 29
Charles Diersh (EWY) 89
Charles E Ryan Rd (SOM) 45
Charles River (N) 92
Charles River Ave (CHA) 29
Charles River Park & Sq 14
Charles River Rd (WAL) 54
Charles River Rd (WAT) 72
Charles River Ter (NWH) 61
Charlesbank Rd & Ter (NEW) .. 58
Charlesbank Way (WAL) 54
Charlesden Park (NWV) 60
Charlesgate St E & W 02215
Charlesmount Ave (QUI) 69
Charlesview (BRI) 35
Charlotte (DOR) 21

Boston (Con.) 021

Charlotte Rd (WAL) 54
Charlotte Rd (NCE) 59
Charlton (ARL) 74
Charlton (EV) 49
Charlton (MED) 55
Charme Ave (ROS) 31
Charnwood Rd (MED) 55
Charnwood Rd (WS) 44
Charter 13
Chase (DOR) 25
Chase (NCE) 59
Chase (QUI) 69
Chase Ave (WNW) 65
Chase Ave (LEX) 73
Chase Rd (STO) 80
Chase Rd (WAL) 54
Chaske Ave (AUB) 66
Chatham (QUI) 69
Chatham (ARL) 74
Chatham (CAM) 39
Chatham Cir (WH) 81
Chatham Ln (WAL) 54
Chatham Rd (EV) 49
Chatham Rd (NWH) 61
Chatham St & Cir (BRO) 46
Chatham St & Ext (MAL) 48
Chatham St & Row 09
Chaucer (EB) 28
Chauncey (WAT) 72
Chauncy 11
Chauncy (SWY) 90
Chauncy St, Ln, Pl & Ter
    (CAM) 38
Cheever (CHE) 50
Cheever (REV) 51
Cheever (MIL) 87
Cheever Ave (NCE) 59
Cheever Ct (EB) 28
Cheever Rd (MAL) 48
Chellman (WRX) 32
Chelmsford (DOR) 22
Chelsea (CHA) 29
Chelsea St, Ct & Ter (EB) 28
Chelsea St & Pl (EV) 49
Chemical Ln (EV) 49
Chenery Ter (BEL) 78
Cheney (DOR) 21
Cheney (NH) 94
Cheney St & Ct (NUF) 64
Cheriton Rd (WOL) 70
Cheriton Rd (WRX) 32
Cherokee (RXC) 20
Cherokee Rd (ARL) 74
Cherry (BEL) 78
Cherry (MEL) 76
Cherry (QUI) 69
Cherry (LEX) 73
Cherry (CHE) 50
Cherry (EV) 49
Cherry (MAL) 48
Cherry (WS) 44
Cherry (WIN) 52
Cherry (WAL) 54
Cherry (BRA) 84
Cherry Ave (STO) 80
Cherry Ln (SWY) 90
Cherry Rd (WRX) 32
Cherry St & Ct (CAM) 39
Cherry St & Ct (MED) 55

Cherry St & Pl (WNW) 65
Cherry Brook Rd (WES) 93
Cheryl Cir & Ln (EWY) 89
Cheryl Dr (MIL) 86
Cheryl Ln (WAL) 54
Cheryl Ln (WIN) 52
Cheryl Ln (HP) 36
Chesbrough Rd (WRX) 32
Chesham Rd (BRO) 46
Cheshire (JP) 30
Chesley Ave (NWV) 60
Chesley Rd (NCE) 59
Chesley Rd (QUI) 69
Chester (*****) 61
Chester (MEL) 76
Chester (ARL) 74
Chester (WAT) 72
Chester (WOL) 70
Chester (ALL) 34
Chester
    1-18 (CAM) 40
    19-OUT (WS) 44
Chester Ave (REV) 51
Chester Ave (WIN) 52
Chester Ave (MED) 55
Chester Ave (SOM) 43
Chester Ave (CHE) 50
Chester Ave & Ln (WAL) 54
Chester Park (MAT) 26
Chester Pl (WRX) 32
Chester Pl (WS) 44
Chester Rd (BEL) 78
Chester St & Pl (MAL) 48
Chester Brook Rd (WAL) 54
Chesterfield (HP) 36
Chesterfield Rd (WNW) 65
Chesterfield Rd (MIL) 86
Chesterton (ROX) 19
Chesterton Rd (WH) 81
Chestnut (WH) 81
Chestnut (STO) 80
Chestnut (WAV) 79
Chestnut (WAT) 72
Chestnut (ARL) 74
Chestnut (QUI) 69
Chestnut 08
Chestnut (WES) 93
Chestnut (HP) 36
Chestnut (MAL) 48
Chestnut (CHE) 50
Chestnut (SOM) 43
Chestnut (CAM) 39
Chestnut (MED) 55
Chestnut
    1-400 (WNW) 65
    401-928 (WAB) 68
    929-OUT (NUF) 64
Chestnut Ave, Pl, Sq & Ter
    (JP) 30
Chestnut Pl (BRI) 35
Chestnut Rd (WRX) 32
Chestnut St, Ave, Park & Pl
    (WAL) 54
Chestnut St & Ct (CHA) 29
Chestnut St & Park (MEL) 76
Chestnut St & Pl (EV) 49
Chestnut St & Pl (BRO) 46
Chestnut St, Pl & Rd (N) 92
Chestnut Ter (NCE) 59
Chestnut Hill Ave
    1-349 (BRI) 35
    350-OUT (BRO) 46

Chestnut Hill Rd & Ter
    (CHH) 67
Cheswick Rd (AUB) 66
Cheswick Rd (ARL) 74
Chetwynd Rd (WS) 44
Chetwynd Rd (CAM) 40
Cheverus Rd (DOR) 24
Cheviot Rd (ARL) 74
Chick (WOL) 70
Chickatawbut (DOR) 22
Chickatawbut Rd (QUI) 69
Chickatawbut Rd (BRA) 84
Chickering Pl 11
Chilcott Pl (JP) 30
Child (JP) 30
Child (HP) 36
Childs Rd (LEX) 73
Chiltern Rd (WES) 93
Chilton (BEL) 78
Chilton (CAM) 38
Chilton (BRO) 46
Chilton Park (NIL) 87
Chilton Pl (NUF) 64
Chilton Rd (WRX) 32
Chinian Path (NCE) 59
Chipman (MED) 55
Chipman (DOR) 24
Chipman Ave & Ter (MEL) 76
Chisholm (EV) 49
Chisholm Ln, Rd & Ter
    (ROS) 31
Chisholm Rd (SWY) 90
Chiswick Rd
    1-99 (BRO) 46
    100-OUT (BRI) 35
Chiswick Ter (BRI) 35
Chittck Rd (HP) 36
Choate Rd (BEL) 78
Christina (NWH) 61
Christine Ave (STO) 80
Christine Rd (ARL) 74
Christine Ter (SWY) 90
Christopher (STO) 80
Christopher (DOR) 22
Christopher Dr (MIL) 86
Christopher Rd (WAL) 54
Chubbuck (QUI) 69
Church (WEL) 81
Church (WAV) 79
Church (STO) 80
Church (MEL) 76
Church (WAT) 72
Church (WAL) 54
Church (HP) 36
Church (WRX) 32
Church (EV) 49
Church (MAL) 48
Church (SOM) 43
Church (CAM) 38
Church (BRA) 84
Church (EWY) 89
Church (WES) 93
Church (DOR) 22
Church 16
Church Ave (SB) 27
Church Ct (CHA) 29
Church Pl (RXC) 20
Church St & Pl (WAV) 79
Church St & Pl (MIL) 86
Church St & Rd (NEW) 58
Church Green 10
Church Hill Ln (WAT) 72

Boston (Con.)   021

Churchill (MIL) 87
Churchill (BRO) 46
Churchill Ave (CAM) 40
Churchill Ave (ARL) 74
Churchill Ln (LEX) 73
Churchill Ln (N) 92
Churchill Rd (QUI) 69
Churchill Rd (WRX) 32
Churchill St & Ter (NWV) ... 60
Churchills Ln (MIL) 86
Cibel Path (NCE) 59
Cimino Rd (NH) 94
Cindy Ln (BRA) 84
Circle Dr (WES) 93
Circle Dr (WEY) 88
Circle Dr (WAL) 54
Circle Rd (MAL) 48
Circle Rd (LEX) 73
Circuit Ave (NWH) 61
Circuit Ave (WY) 88
Circuit Dr (JP) 30
Circuit Ln (WAL) 54
Circuit Rd (WIN) 52
Circuit Rd (SWY) 90
Circuit Rd (BRA) 84
Circuit Rd (CHH) 67
Circuit Rd (QUI) 69
Circuit St & Park (MEL) 76
Circuit St & Rd (MED) 55
Circuit St, Sq & Ter (ROX) .. 19
Citizen Pl (CAM) 41
City Sq (CHA) 29
City Hall Ave 08
City Hall Ave (CHE) 50
City Hall Mall (MED) 55
City Point Ct (SB) 27
City View Rd (BRO) 46
Claflin (BEL) 78
Claflin 02210
Claflin Path & Rd (BRO) 46
Claflin Pl (NWV) 66
Claflin Rd (WH) 81
Claflin Ter (MAL) 48
Clairemont Rd (BEL) 78
Clancy Rd (DOR) 24
Clapp (DOR) 25
Clapp (MAL) 48
Clapp (MIL) 86
Clapp Ave (WY) 88
Clare Ave
   1-85 (ROS) (ODD) 31
   2-78 (ROS) (EVEN) 31
   80-OUT (HP) (EVEN) 36
   87-OUT (HP) (ODD) 36
Claremon (WS) 44
Claremont (MAL) 48
Claremont (WAL) 54
Claremont (BRA) 84
Claremont (NEW) 58
Claremont Ave (QUI) 69
Claremont Ave & Ct (ARL) ... 74
Claremont St & Park 18
Clarence (ROX) 19
Clarence (BRO) 46
Clarence (EV) 49
Clarence Ter (MAL) 48
Clarendon (MAL) 48
Clarendon 16
Clarendon (QUI) 69
Clarendon (NWV) 60

Clarendon (MEL) 76
Clarendon (WAT) 72
Clarendon (SWY) 90
Clarendon Ave (WS) 44
Clarendon Ave (CAM) 40
Clarendon Ct & Pl (ROS) 31
Clarendon Rd (BEL) 78
Claridge Ter (DOR) 24
Clark 09
Clark (NQ) 71
Clark (NCE) 59
Clark (ARL) 74
Clark (SOM) 43
Clark (MAL) 48
Clark (EV) 49
Clark (MED) 55
Clark (BRA) 84
Clark Ave (CHE) 50
Clark Ct & Rd (BRO) 46
Clark Rd (REV) 51
Clark Rd (MIL) 86
Clark Rd (SWY) 90
Clark Rd (WH) 81
Clark Rd (WNW) 65
Clark St Pl (CAM) 39
Clark St & Ln (BEL) 78
Clark St, Ln & Ter (WAL) 54
Clarke (CAM) 39
Clarke (LEX) 73
Clarke Cir & Rd (N) 92
Clarke St Pl (CAM) 39
Clarkson (DOR) 29
Clarkson (DOR) 25
Clarkwood (MAT) 26
Claron (ROS) 31
Clary (CAM) 39
Claxton (ROS) 31
Clay (CAM) 40
Clay (MIL) 86
Clay (WOL) 70
Clay Ave (EV) 49
Claybourne (DOR) 24
Claymont Ter (DOR) 22
Claymoss Rd (BRI) 35
Clayton (MAL) 48
Clayton (DOR) 22
Clayton (WAT) 72
Clayton Ave (MED) 55
Clearview Rd (STO) 80
Clearwater Dr (WAT) 26
Clearwater Rd (CHH) 67
Clearwater Rd (NLF) 62
Clearway 15
Cleaves (ROX) 19
Cleaves (WOL) 70
Clelland Rd (LEX) 73
Clematis (DOR) 22
Clematis Ave (WY) 88
Clematis Ave & Rd (WAL) 54
Clematis Rd (MED) 55
Clematis Rd (LEX) 73
Clement (MAL) 48
Clement Ave (WRX) 32
Clement Cir (CAM) 38
Clement Ter (NQ) 71
Clementine Park (DOR) 24
Clements Rd (NEW) 58
Clements Rd (WAL) 54
Clermont (DOR) 24
Cleveland (EB) 28
Cleveland (CAM) 38
Cleveland (SOM) 43
Cleveland (MAL) 48

Cleveland (MED) 55
Cleveland (HP) 36
Cleveland (REV) 51
Cleveland (WNW) 65
Cleveland (MEL) 76
Cleveland (ARL) 74
Cleveland Ave (EV) 49
Cleveland Ave (BRA) 84
Cleveland Cir (BRO) 46
Cleveland Pl 13
Cleveland Rd (WAL) 54
Cleveland Rd (N) 92
Cleveland Rd (WAT) 72
Cleveland Rd (WH) 81
Cleveland Rd
   1-30 (BRO) 46
   31-OUT (CHH) 67
Cleveland St & Park (ROX) .. 19
Clevemont Ave (ALL) 34
Cleverly Ct (QUI) 69
Clewly Rd (MED) 55
Cliff (QUI) 69
Cliff (STO) 80
Cliff (ARL) 74
Cliff (NWY) 91
Cliff Ave (WIN) 52
Cliff Pl (ROX) 19
Cliff Rd (WAL) 54
Cliff Rd (WES) 93
Cliff Rd (BRA) 84
Cliff Rd (MIL) 87
Cliff Rd (WH) 81
Cliff Rd (NUF) 64
Cliff St, Ct & Ter (MAL) 48
Cliff St & Rd (MEL) 76
Cliffe Ave (LEX) 73
Cliffmont (ROS) 31
Clifford (HP) 36
Clifford (MEL) 76
Clifford (WEL) 81
Clifford (ROX) 19
Cliffside Ter (MAL) 48
Clifton (MAL) 48
Clifton (WS) 44
Clifton (REV) 51
Clifton (MED) 55
Clifton (CAM) 38
Clifton (BEL) 78
Clifton (QUI) 69
Clifton
   1-51 (ROX) (ODD) 19
   2-56 (ROX) (EVEN) 19
   53-OUT (DOR) (ODD) ... 25
   58-OUT (DOR) (EVEN) .. 25
Clifton Ave (STO) 80
Clifton Ave (EV) 49
Clifton Park (MEL) 76
Clifton Rd (WH) 81
Clifton Rd (NCE) 59
Clifton Rd (MIL) 86
Cliftondale (ROS) 31
Clinton (CAM) 35
Clinton (MAL) 48
Clinton (WAL) 54
Clinton (NEW) 58
Clinton 09
Clinton Path (BRO) 46
Clinton Pl (CHA) 29
Clinton Pl (NCE) 59
Clinton Rd (MEL) 76
Clinton Rd (REV) 51
Clinton Rd (EWY) 89

Boston (Con.)   021

Clinton Rd
   1-440 (BRO) 46
   441-OUT (CHH) 67
Clinton St & Ct (CHE) 50
Clinton St & Pl (EV) 49
Clive (JP) 30
Clive (NQ) 71
Cliveden (QUI) 69
Cloelia Ter (NWV) 81
Clovelly Rd (WH) 81
Clovelly Rd (CHH) 67
Clover (BEL) 78
Clover (BRA) 22
Cloverdale Rd
   1-34 (NCE) 59
   35-OUT (NWH) 61
Cluney Ct (ROX) 19
Clyde (EB) 28
Clyde (N) 92
Clyde (BEL) 78
Clyde (CHH) 67
Clyde (NWV) 60
Clyde (CHE) 50
Clyde (SOM) 45
Clyde (MAL) 48
Clyde Pl (LEX) 73
Clyde Rd ,WAT) 72
Clyde Ter (ARL) 74
Coach Rd (LEX) 73
Cobb (MED) 55
Cobb Pl (WAB) 68
Cobble Hill Rd (SOM) 43
Cobden (ROX) 19
Coburn (MAL) 48
Coburn Ct 14
Coburn Rd (WES) 93
Coburn Ter (EV) 49
Cochato (BRA) 85
Cochate Rd (BRA) 84
Cochituate Rd (NWH) 61
Cochrane (MEL) 76
Codding Ave (MED) 55
Coddington (QUI) 69
Codman Park & Pl (ROX) 19
Codman Rd (BRO) 46
Codman St & Sq (DOR) 24
Codman Hill Ave (DOR) 24
Cody Rd (SWY) 90
Coe (NQ) 71
Coffey (DOR) 22
Cogswell Ave & Pl (CAM) 40
Cohasset (ROS) 31
Coker (WAL) 54
Colasanti Rd (NWY) 91
Colberg Ave (ROS) 31
Colbert (WRX) 32
Colbert Ave (BRA) 85
Colbert Rd (WNW) 65
Colborne Rd (BRI) 35
Colbourne Cres (BRO) 46
Colburn (WAL) 54
Colburn Rd (WH) 81
Colby (BEL) 78
Colby (MED) 55
Colby (N) 92
Colby Rd (BRA) 84
Colby Rd (ROS) 31
Colby Rd (WH) 81
Colby Rd (NQ) 71
Colby Rd (AL) 74

Colby Ter (MEL) 76
Colchester (BRO) 46
Colchester (HP) 36
Colchester Rd (WES) 93
Colebrook (SB) 27
Colella Rd (NCE) 59
Coleman (DOR) 25
Coleman (HP) 36
Coleman (MAL) 48
Coleman Rd (ARL) 74
Colerain (ALL) 34
Coleridge (EB) 28
Coleus Park (DOR) 21
Colgate Park & Rd (NLF) 62
Colgate Rd (WEL) 81
Colgate Rd (ROS) 31
Colgate Rd (N) 92
Collamore (MIL) 86
College Ave (WES) 55
College Ave (ARL) 74
College Ave
   1-200 (WS) 44
   201-OUT (MED) 55
College Cir (WS) 44
College Rd (WH) 81
College Rd (CHH) 67
College Farm Rd (WAL) 54
College Hill Rd (WS) 44
Collincote (STO) 80
Collings Cir (MED) 55
Collins (HP) 36
Collins Rd (WAB) 68
Colliston Rd (BRO) 46
Colman Pl (ALL) 34
Colon (BRI) 35
Colonial Ave (WAL) 54
Colonial Ave (NWV) 60
Colonial Ave (LEX) 73
Colonial Ave (DOR) 24
Colonial Ct (STO) 80
Colonial Dr (ARL) 74
Colonial Dr (QUI) 69
Colonial Rd (REV) 51
Colonial Rd (MIL) 86
Colonial Rd (NWY) 91
Colonial Rd (N) 92
Colonial Ter (BEL) 78
Colonial Way (WES) 93
Colonial Village Dr (ARL) 74
Colony Rd (LEX) 73
Colorado (MAT) 26
Colpitts Rd (WES) 93
Columbia 11
Columbia (QUI) 69
Columbia (WH) 81
Columbia (WAT) 72
Columbia (REV) 51
Columbia (MAL) 48
Columbia
   1-279 (CAM) 39
   280-462 (CAM) (EVEN) 41
   281-459 (CAM) (ODD) 41
   461-OUT (SOM) (ODD) 43
   464-OUT (SOM) (EVEN) 43
Columbia Ave (NWH) 61
Columbia Ave (NUF) 64
Columbia Park (MIL) 87
Columbia Pl & Ter (DOR) 25
Columbia Rd (ARL) 74
Columbia Rd (MED) 55
Columbia Rd
   1-313 (DOR) (ODD) 21
   2-310 (DOR) (EVEN) 21

   312-898 (DOR) (EVEN) 25
   315-899 (DOR) (ODD) 25
   900-OUT (SB) 27
Columbia St & Ter (BRO) 46
Columbia Ter (CAM) 39
Columbia Ter (BRA) 84
Columbian
   1-595 (SWY) (ODD) 90
   2-580 (SWY) (EVEN) 90
   582-OUT (BRA) (EVEN) 85
   597-OUT (BRA) (ODD) 85
Columbine (DOR) 24
Columbine Rd (MIL) 87
Columbine Rd (WES) 93
Columbine Rd (NCE) 59
Columbus (LEX) 73
Columbus (CHE) 50
Columbus Ave (CAM) 40
Columbus Ave (SOM) 43
Columbus Ave (WAL) 54
Columbus Ave (MEL) 76
Columbus Ave (BRA) 85
Columbus Ave
   1-475 (ODD) 16
   2-472 (EVEN) 16
   474-650 (EVEN) 18
   477-649 (ODD) 18
   651-1500 (RXC) 20
   1501-OUT (ROX) 19
Columbus Pl (WNW) 65
Columbus Sq 16
Columbus St & Ter (NWH) ... 61
Colwell Ave (BRI) 35
Comeau (WH) 81
Comet Pl 18
Comins Ter (ROX) 19
Commander Shea Blvd (NQ) 71
Commerce 09
Commercial (EV) 49
Commercial (MAL) 48
Commercial (MED) 55
Commercial
   1-63 (CAM) 41
   64-OUT (CAM) 42
Commercial Sq (EWY) 89
Commercial St & Ct (BRA) ... 84
Commercial St & Ct 09
Commercial Wharf 18
Common 16
Common (CHA) 29
Common (BRA) 84
Common (WY) 88
Common (WAL) 54
Common (WAT) 72
Common (STO) 80
Common (BEL) 78
Common (QUI) 69
Commonwealth 02210
Commonwealth Ave (QUI) ... 69
Commonwealth Ave
   1-269 (WS) 16
   1-400 (CHH) 67
   2-282 (EVEN) 16
   271-393 (ODD) 15
   284-368 (EVEN) 15
   370-1110 (EVEN) 02215
   395-1123 (ODD) 02215
   401-1140 (NCE) 59
   1112-1400 (ALL) (EVEN) 34
   1125-1399 (ALL) (ODD) 34

Boston (Con.) 021

1141-1750 (WNW) 65
1401-OUT (BRI) 35
1751-OUT (AUB) 66
Commonwealth Ct (BRI) 35
Commonwealth Park (WH) 81
Commonwealth Park E & W
(NCE) 59
Commonwealth Rd (WAT) 72
Commonwealth Ter (BRO) 46
Commonwealth Pier 02210
Como (MAL) 48
Como Rd (HP) 36
Compton (ARL) 74
Compton Cir (LEX) 73
Conant (REV) 51
Conant Rd (NQ) 71
Conant Rd (WAT) 72
Conant Rd (MEL) 76
Conant Rd (CHH) 67
Conant Rd (WES) 93
Conant St & Pl (RXC) 20
Conastoga Rd (LEX) 73
Concolor Ave (NEW) 58
Concord (NLF) 62
Concord (CHA) 29
Concord (NH) 94
Concord (SWY) 90
Concord (MAL) 48
Concord Ave (SOM) 43
Concord Ave (CAM) 38
Concord Ave (MIL) 87
Concord Ave 09
Concord Ave (BEL) 78
Concord Ave & Tpke (LEX) 73
Concord Pl & Sq 18
Concord Rd (WAT) 72
Concord Rd (WES) 93
Concord Tpke
2-248 (ARL) (EVEN) 74
195-245 (CAM) (ODD) 40
250-258 (CAM) (EVEN) 40
260-398 (BEL) (EVEN) 78
554-1176 (BEL) (EVEN) 78
1178-OUT (ARL) (EVEN) 74
Condor (EB) 28
Confirmation Pl (CHA) 29
Congress (WY) 88
Congress (BRA) 85
Congress (STO) 80
Congress
1-111 (ODD) 09
2-132 (EVEN) 09
113-261 (ODD) 10
134-268 (EVEN) 10
263-OUT (ODD) 02210
270-OUT (EVEN) 02210
Congress Ave (MED) 55
Congress Ave (CHE) 50
Congress St Pl 10
Congreve (ROS) 31
Coniston Rd (ROS) 31
Conley (DOR) 22
Connecticut Ave (SOM) 45
Connell (BRA) 84
Connell (QUI) 69
Connolly Cir (BRA) 84
Conrad (BRA) 84
Conrad (QUI) 69
Conrad (DOR) 25
Conrad Rd (MEL) 76

Conry Cres (JP) 30
Considine Rd (NCE) 59
Constance (MAL) 48
Constance Rd (WRX) 32
Constitution Ave (REV) 51
Constitution Ave (SWY) 90
Constitution Rd (LEX) 73
Constitution Rd (MAT) 26
Constitution Wharf 09
Continental Rd (CHE) 50
Converse (BRI) 35
Converse Ave (MAL) 48
Converse Ave (NEW) 58
Converse Ln (MEL) 76
Conway Ct (MAL) 48
Conway Rd (MIL) 86
Conway St & Ct (ROS) 31
Conwell (SOM) 43
Conwell Ave (WS) 44
Cook (NEW) 58
Cook (CHA) 29
Cook Ave (CHE) 50
Cook Cir (MED) 55
Cook St Ct (CHA) 29
Cook St Pl (CHA) 29
Cooke Rd (LEX) 73
Cookson Ter (MAT) 26
Cooledge St & Ave (REV) 51
Coolidge (EV) 49
Coolidge (BRO) 46
Coolidge (STO) 80
Coolidge Ave (LEX) 73
Coolidge Ave (WAT) 72
Coolidge Ave (CAM) 38
Coolidge Ave (MAL) 54
Coolidge Ave (BRA) 84
Coolidge Ave (N) 88
Coolidge Ave (N) 92
Coolidge Pl (CAM) 39
Coolidge Rd (MED) 55
Coolidge Rd (ALL) 34
Coolidge Rd (MIL) 86
Coolidge Rd (NCE) 59
Coolidge Rd (BEL) 78
Coolidge Rd (MEL) 76
Coolidge Rd (ARL) 74
Coolidge Rd (DOR) 24
Coolidge Hill Rd (WAT) 72
Coolidge Hill St & Rd (CAM) 38
Cooney (SOM) 43
Cooper 13
Cooper Ln (WAL) 54
Cooper Ter (REV) 51
Copeland (WAL) 54
Copeland (WAT) 72
Copeland (QUI) 69
Copeland St, Park & Pl
(ROX) 19
Copeland Ter (MAL) 48
Copenger (RXC) 20
Copley (ROX) 19
Copley (BRO) 46
Copley (CAM) 38
Copley (WOL) 70
Copley (NEW) 58
Copley Ave (WAL) 54
Copley Sq 16
Coppersmith Way (EB) 28
Copps Hill Ter 13
Cora (WIN) 52
Coral (REV) 51
Coral (ARL) 74
Coral Ave (WIN) 52

Coral Pl (CHA) 29
Corbet (DOR) 24
Corcoran Dr (HP) 36
Corcoran Park (CAM) 38
Cordis (CHA) 29
Cordis St Ave (CHA) 29
Corey (CHA) 29
Corey (MED) 55
Corey (EV) 49
Corey (MEL) 76
Corey (SWY) 90
Corey Ln (MIL) 86
Corey Rd (MAL) 48
Corey Rd (BRO) 46
Corey St & Ter (WRX) 32
Corina Rd (WIN) 52
Corinth (ROS) 31
Corinthian Rd (WS) 44
Corliss (ROX) 19
Corliss Pl (CAM) 39
Corman Rd (MAT) 26
Cornauba (ROS) 31
Cornauba St Ext (ROS) 31
Cornelia Ct (RXC) 20
Cornell (ROS) 31
Cornell (ARL) 74
Cornell (NLF) 62
Cornell Rd (WH) 81
Corner (MEL) 76
Cornhill St & Ct 08
Cornish (EWY) 89
Cornwall (JP) 30
Cornwallis Pl (WAL) 54
Corona (DOR) 24
Coronado Rd (MAT) 26
Corporal Burns Rd (CAM) 38
Corporal Mc Ternan (CAM) 38
Corporation Way (MED) 55
Corregidor Ct (ROX) 19
Corrine Rd (BRI) 35
Corrinne Rd (MED) 55
Cortes 16
Corwin (DOR) 22
Corwood Dr (WES) 93
Cotswold Rd (BRO) 46
Cotswold Ter (NCE) 59
Cottage (BEL) 78
Cottage (WEL) 81
Cottage (STO) 80
Cottage (NUF) 64
Cottage (LEX) 73
Cottage (BRO) 46
Cottage (MED) 55
Cottage (REV) 51
Cottage (CHE) 50
Cottage (EV) 49
Cottage (EWY) 89
Cottage (EB) 28
Cottage (SB) 27
Cottage Ave (NH) 94
Cottage Ave (WIN) 52
Cottage Ave (ARL) 74
Cottage Ave & Cir (WS) 44
Cottage Ct (NEW) 58
Cottage Ct (DOR) 25
Cottage Ln (WY) 88
Cottage Park Ave (CAM) 40
Cottage Park Rd (WIN) 52
Cottage Pl (HP) 36
Cottage Pl (MIL) 86
Cottage Pl (WNW) 65
Cottage Rd (WRX) 32
Cottage St Pl (EB) 28

Boston (Con.)   021

Cottage St & Ave (QUI)............ 69
Cottage St, Ct & Row (CAM)..... 39
Cottage St & Ln (WAT)............ 72
Cottage St & Park (MEL)......... 76
Cottage St & Pl (MAL)............ 48
Cottage Farm Rd (BRO)........... 46
Cotter Rd (WAB)................. 68
Cotting (MED)................... 55
Cotton (ROS)................... 31
Cotton (NEW)................... 58
Cotton Ave (BRA)............... 84
Cuttonwood Rd (NCE)............ 59
Cottonwood Rd (WEL)............ 81
Cottrell (DOR)................. 25
Cotuit (WRX)................... 32
Coulton Park (N)............... 92
Country Dr (WES)............... 93
Country Rd (CHH)............... 67
Country Way (N)................ 92
Country Club Dr & Ln (ARL)..... 74
Country Club Ln (BEL).......... 78
Country Club Rd (MEL).......... 76
Country Club Rd (STO).......... 80
Country Club Rd (NCE).......... 59
Countryside Dr (MAT)........... 26
Countryside Rd (NCE)........... 59
County Rd (QUI)................ 69
County Rd (CHE)................ 50
County Rd (EV)................. 49
Courier (SWY).................. 90
Court (MED).................... 55
Court (NWV).................... 60
Court (ARL).................... 74
Court Rd (WIN)................. 52
Court Rd (BRA)................. 85
Court St Pl (ARL).............. 74
Court St & Sq.................. 08
Courtland (EV)................. 49
Courtland Cir (MIL)............ 86
Courtland Rd (MAT)............. 26
Courtney Rd (WRX).............. 32
Cousens Cir (NCE).............. 59
Cove (REV)..................... 51
Coventry (RXC)................. 20
Covington (SB)................. 27
Cowasset Ln (WAL).............. 54
Cowdin (BEL)................... 78
Cowdrey (STO).................. 80
Cowing (WRX)................... 32
Cowper (EB).................... 28
Cowperthwaite (CAM)............ 38
Coyne Rd (WAB)................. 68
Cozy (WAT)..................... 72
Crabtree Rd (NQ)............... 71
Craddock Ave (MED)............. 55
Craft Pl (JP).................. 30
Crafts (WAL)................... 54
Crafts
    1-409 (NWV)............... 60
    410-OUT (WNW)............. 65
Crefts Rd (CHH)................ 67
Craftsland Rd (CHH)............ 67
Cragmere Ter (MAT)............. 26
Cragmore Rd (NUF).............. 64
Craig (MIL).................... 86
Craig Ave (QUI)................ 69
Craig Ln (WAL)................. 54
Craig Pl (BRO)................. 46
Craigie St & Cir (CAM)......... 38
Craigie St & Ter (SOM)......... 43

Craigie Ter (NWV).............. 60
Craigie Bridge................. 14
Crammond Rd (CHH).............. 67
Cranberry Ln (N)............... 92
Cranberry Rd (WY).............. 88
Cranch (EWY)................... 89
Cranch (QUI)................... 69
Crandall (ROS)................. 31
Crane (MED).................... 55
Crane (HP)..................... 36
Crane Rd (QUI)................. 69
Crane Rd (MIL)................. 87
Cranmore Ln (MEL).............. 76
Cranmore Rd (WEL).............. 81
Cranmore Rd (BRA).............. 85
Cranmore Rd (HP)............... 36
Cranston (JP).................. 30
Craven Cir (WAL)............... 32
Crawford (CAM)................. 39
Crawford (MAL)................. 48
Crawford (BRA)................. 84
Crawford (NH).................. 94
Crawford (WAT)................. 72
Crawford (ARL)................. 74
Crawford (DOR)................. 21
Crawford Rd (LEX).............. 73
Crawford Rd (BRA).............. 85
Creeley Rd (WAV)............... 79
Crehore Dr (NLF)............... 62
Crehore Rd (CHH)............... 67
Creighton (CAM)................ 40
Creighton (JP)................. 30
Cremona Rd (REV)............... 51
Crescent (WIN)................. 52
Crescent (CAM)................. 38
Crescent (MED)................. 55
Crescent (EV).................. 49
Crescent (WH).................. 81
Crescent (QUI)................. 69
Crescent (WES)................. 93
Crescent
    1-50 (WNW)................ 65
    1-OUT (CHA) (ODD)......... 29
    2-OUT (SOM) (EVEN)........ 45
    51-OUT (AUB).............. 66
Crescent Ave (BRA)............. 85
Crescent Ave (STO)............. 80
Crescent Ave (NCE)............. 59
Crescent Ave (CHE)............. 50
Crescent Ave (REV)............. 51
Crescent Ave (MAL)............. 48
Crescent Ave (DOR)............. 25
Crescent Ave & Pl (MEL)........ 76
Crescent Rd (BEL).............. 78
Crescent Rd (LEX).............. 73
Crescent Rd (NH)............... 94
Crescent Rd (NWY).............. 91
Crescent Sq (NEW).............. 58
Crescent St & Park (WAL)....... 54
Crescent Hill Ave (LEX)........ 73
Crescent Hill Ave (ARL)........ 74
Crest (QUI).................... 69
Crest (WRX).................... 32
Crest Ave (WIN)................ 52
Crest Ave (REV)................ 51
Crest Ave (CHE)................ 50
Crest Ave (MEL)................ 76
Crest Ave (EWY)................ 89
Crest Rd (WEL)................. 81
Crest Rd (MEL)................. 55
Crest Hill Rd (SOM)............ 43
Cresthill Rd (BRI)............. 35
Cresto Ter. (CAM).............. 41

Creston St & Park (DOR)........ 21
Crestview Rd (WAL)............. 54
Crestview Rd (BEL)............. 78
Crestway Rd (EB)............... 28
Crestwood Dr (WH).............. 81
Crestwood Park (DOR)........... 21
Crestwood Rd (WNW)............. 65
Cricket Ln (WRX)............... 32
Cricklewood Dr (STO)........... 80
Cricklewood Ln (MEL)........... 76
Crispus Attucks (ROX).......... 19
Crocker (SOM).................. 43
Crocker Cir (WNW).............. 65
Crocker Rd (MED)............... 55
Crockers Pl (WRX).............. 32
Grockett Ave (DOR)............. 24
Croftdale Rd (NCE)............. 59
Croftland Ave (DOR)............ 24
Crofton Rd (WAB)............... 68
Cromwell Rd (HP)............... 36
Crosby (STO)................... 80
Crosby (QUI)................... 69
Crosby (ARL)................... 74
Crosby Rd (CHH)................ 67
Crosby Rd (LEX)................ 73
Crosby Sq (JP)................. 30
Cross (HP)..................... 36
Cross (MED).................... 55
Cross (CAM).................... 39
Cross (WAL).................... 54
Cross (MAL).................... 48
Cross (SOM).................... 45
Cross (CHE).................... 50
Cross (EV)..................... 49
Cross (WIN).................... 52
Cross (REV).................... 51
Cross (WNW).................... 65
Cross (ARL).................... 74
Cross (QUI).................... 69
Cross (WEL).................... 81
Cross (BEL).................... 78
Cross (WAT).................... 72
Cross (CHA).................... 29
Cross (EWY).................... 89
Cross (NH)..................... 94
Cross
    1-71 (ODD)................ 13
    2-68 (EVEN)............... 13
    70-OUT (EVEN)............. 09
    73-OUT (ODD).............. 09
Cross E (SOM).................. 45
Cross Rd (WRX)................. 32
Cross Rd (BRA)................. 85
Cross St Pl (SOM).............. 45
Cross Hill Rd (NCE)............ 59
Crossland (CAM)................ 39
Crossland Pl (BRI)............. 35
Crossman (MAT)................. 26
Crosstown Ave (WRX)............ 32
Croton (WH).................... 81
Crowell (DOR).................. 24
Crowley Ln (BRA)............... 85
Crowley Rd (MED)............... 55
Crowley Rogers Way (SB)........ 27
Crown (MAT).................... 26
Crown (SOM).................... 43
Crown (MIL).................... 87
Crown (AUB).................... 66
Crown Point Dr (HP)............ 36
Crown Ridge Rd (WEL)........... 81
Crowninshield Rd (BRO)......... 46
Croydon (MAT).................. 26
Crystal (MAL).................. 48

Boston (Con.) 021

Crystal (NCE) 59
Crystal (MEL) 76
Crystal Ave (REV) 51
Crystal Pl (CHA) 29
Crystal Cove Ave (WIN) 52
Cuba (WAT) 72
Cudworth (MED) 55
Cufflin (BRI) 35
Culbert (MAT) 26
Cumberland 15
Cumberland (EV) 49
Cumberland Ave (BRO) 46
Cumberland Rd (BEL) 78
Cumberland Rd (WNW) 65
Cummings (MED) 55
Cummings 18
Cummings Ave (REV) 51
Cummings Ave (WOL) 70
Cummings Ave (LEX) 73
Cummings Ave (SWY) 90
Cummings Rd (NCE) 59
Cummings Rd (BRO) 46
Cummington 02215
Cummins Hwy
  1-531 (ROS) 31
  532-OUT (MAT) 26
Cumner Ave (MEL) 76
Cunard (RXC) 20
Cunningham (DOR) 25
Cunningham Cir (WAL) 54
Cunningham Park (WAL) 86
Cunningham Rd (WH) 81
Curlew (WRX) 32
Curlew Rd (QUI) 69
Curley (ROS) 31
Curtis (WAL) 54
Curtis (WH) 81
Curtis (NWH) 61
Curtis (NWY) 91
Curtis (EB) 28
Curtis
  1-135 (WS) 44
  136-136 (MED) 55
  137-OUT (WS) 44
Curtis Ave (WS) 44
Curtis Rd (REV) 51
Curtis Rd (N) 92
Curtis Rd (MIL) 87
Curtis St & Ave (QUI) 69
Curtis St & Pl (MED) 55
Curve (MAL) 48
Curve (WAL) 54
Curve (WNW) 65
Curve (WEL) 81
Curve (LEX) 73
Curve (N) 92
Curve Rd (STO) 80
Cushing (LEX) 73
Cushing (RWH) 61
Cushing (WOL) 70
Cushing (SWY) 90
Cushing (WAL) 54
Cushing (MED) 55
Cushing Ave (REV) 51
Cushing Ave (BEL) 78
Cushing Ave (DOR) 25
Cushing Cir (MEL) 76
Cushing Rd (WH) 81
Cushing Rd (BRO) 46
Cushing Rd (MAL) 48

Cushing Rd (MIL) 86
Cushing St & Ct (CAM) 38
Cushman (WAT) 72
Cushman Ave (REV) 51
Cushman Rd (BRI) 35
Custer (JP) 30
Custom House 10
Cuthbert Rd (WRX) 32
Cutler (WIN) 52
Cutler (SOM) 45
Cutler Ave (CAM) 38
Cutler Ct (WAL) 54
Cutler Ct (SB) 27
Cutler Ln & Rd (CHH) 67
Cutler Rd (N) 92
Cutler Farm Rd (LEX) 73
Cutter (WAV) 79
Cutter (MEL) 76
Cutter (WAL) 54
Cutter (SOM) 45
Cutter Ave, Park, Pl & Sq
  (WS) 44
Cutter Rd (WRX) 32
Cutterhill Rd (ARL) 74
Cutting Ln (WAL) 54
Cygnet (BRI) 35
Cynthia Cir (WY) 88
Cynthia Rd (NH) 94
Cynthia Rd (NCE) 59
Cypher (SB) 27
Cypress (NCE) 59
Cypress (WAT) 72
Cypress (SWY) 90
Cypress (BRA) 84
Cypress (BRO) 46
Cypress (CAM) 38
Cypress (SOM) 43
Cypress Ct (BRI) 35
Cypress Park (MEL) 76
Cypress Rd (ARL) 74
Cypress Rd (WH) 81
Cypress Rd (MED) 55
Cypress Rd (MIL) 86
Cypress St & Ter (WRX) 32
Cyril (QUI) 69
D
  1-377 (SB) (ODD) 27
  2-350 (SB) (EVEN) 27
  352-OUT (EVEN) 02210
  379-OUT (ODD) 02210
Dabney Pl (ROX) 19
Dacia St & Ter (DOR) 25
Dacy (HP) 36
Dade (ROX) 19
Dahlgren (DOR) 24
Dahlgren (NQ) 71
Dakota (DOR) 24
Dalby (NEW) 58
Dale (NWV) 60
Dale (WH) 81
Dale (LEX) 73
Dale (CHH) 67
Dale (ROS) 31
Dale (MAL) 48
Dale (REV) 51
Dale (NH) 94
Dale Ave (QUI) 69
Dale Ct (STO) 80
Dale Rd (EWY) 89
Dale St & Cir (WAL) 54
Dalessio Ct (SB) 27

Daley St & Pl (NH) 94
Dalin Pl (DOR) 25
Dalkeith (DOR) 25
Dallas Pl (RXC) 20
Dalrymple (JP) 30
Dalton
  1-38 15
  39-39 99
  40-OUT 15
Dalton Rd (NCE) 59
Dalton Rd (BEL) 78
Daly (DOR) 22
Daly Rd (MED) 55
Damien Rd (WH) 81
Damon Ave (MEL) 76
Damon Park (ARL) 74
Damon Rd (MED) 55
Damon Rd (NH) 94
Damon St & Pl (HP) 36
Damrell (SB) 27
Dana (REV) 51
Dana (MAL) 48
Dana (BRO) 46
Dana (SOM) 45
Dana (CAM) 38
Dana Ave
  1-257 (HP) 36
  258-OUT (MIL) 86
Dana Ct (WAL) 54
Dana Pl (NH) 94
Dana Rd (WY) 88
Dana Rd (WRX) 32
Dana Rd (BEL) 78
Dana Rd (WEL) 81
Dana Rd (WNW) 65
Dana St, Ct & Pl (ROX) 19
Dana Ter (WAT) 72
Danbury Rd (MAT) 26
Danbury Rd (SWY) 90
Danby Rd (STO) 80
Dane (JP) 30
Dane (EV) 49
Dane Rd (LEX) 73
Dane St & Ave (SOM) 43
Dane Hill Rd (MWH) 61
Daney Rd (HP) 36
Danforth (JP) 30
Danforth Pl (ROX) 19
Dania St & Ter (MAT) 26
Deniel (NCE) 59
Daniel (EWY) 89
Daniel Ct (HP) 36
Daniel Rd (BRA) 85
Daniels (MAL) 48
Daniels (MED) 55
Daniels (LEX) 73
Daniels (ARL) 74
Daniels Ct (WAL) 54
Danny Rd (HP) 36
Dante Ave (WAV) 79
Dante Ter (SOM) 43
Danube (DOR) 25
Danville (WRX) 32
Darby Rd (MIL) 87
Darch Rd (WAT) 72
Darius Ct (SB) 27
Darling (RXC) 20
Darlington (DOR) 24
Darrow (QUI) 69
Dartmouth (QUI) 69
Dartmouth (WAT) 72
Dartmouth (ARL) 74
Dartmouth (WNW) 65

Boston (Con.)   021

Dartmouth (BEL)................... 78
Dartmouth (MEL).................. 76
Dartmouth (WAL)................. 54
Dartmouth (MED)................. 55
Dartmouth (MAL)................. 48
Dartmouth (SOM)................. 45
Dartmouth (EV).................... 49
Dartmouth Ave (NH).............. 94
Dartmouth St & Pl.............. 16
Dashwood (REV)................. 51
Davenport (CAM)................. 40
Davenport (RXC).................. 20
Davenport Rd (NH)............... 94
Davern Ave (DOR)................ 25
David Rd (NH)..................... 94
David Rd (JP)...................... 30
David Rd (NCE)................... 59
David Island Rd (NWY).......... 91
David's Hill Rd (NWY)........... 91
Davidson Ave (DOR)............. 25
Davis (WOL)....................... 70
Davis (REV)....................... 51
Davis (EV)......................... 49
Davis Ave & Ct (BRO).......... 46
Davis Ave & Rd (ARL).......... 74
Davis Ct (EB)..................... 28
Davis Rd (LEX)................... 73
Davis Rd (SWY)................... 90
Davis Rd (BRA)................... 84
Davis Sq (WS).................... 44
Davis St, Ave & Ct (WNW)..... 65
Davis St & Ct (CAM)............ 39
Davis St & Ct (MAL)............ 48
Davis St & Rd (WAV)........... 79
Davison (HP)...................... 36
Davitt (DOR)...................... 25
Dawes (REV)...................... 51
Dawes (WAL)..................... 54
Dawes Rd (LEX).................. 73
Dawes St & Ter (DOR).......... 25
Dawson (DOR).................... 24
Dawson Dr (N).................... 92
Day (AUB)......................... 66
Day (ARL)......................... 74
Day (MEL)......................... 76
Day (WAL)......................... 54
Day (JP)........................... 30
Day
   1-17 (CAM) (ODD)........... 40
   2-12 (CAM) (EVEN).......... 40
   14-OUT (WS) (EVEN)........ 44
   19-OUT (WS) (ODD)......... 44
Day School Ln (BEL)............ 78
Dayton (QUI)...................... 69
Dayton (DOR)..................... 24
Dayton Ave (ROX)............... 19
De Forest Rd (NLF)............. 62
De Francesco Cir (N)........... 92
De Roma Rd (WRX).............. 32
De Soto Rd (WRX)............... 32
De Stephano Rd (ROS).......... 31
De Wolf (DOR).................... 25
De Wolf St & Pl (CAM)......... 38
Deacon (CAM).................... 42
Deaconess Rd
   1-44...................02215
   45-OUT...................... 15
Dean (BRA)....................... 84
Dean (EV)......................... 49
Dean (DOR)....................... 25
Dean (BEL)....................... 78

Dean (STO)....................... 80
Dean Rd (BRO)................... 46
Dean Rd (MIL).................... 86
Dean Rd
   1-24 (WH)..................... 81
   25-OUT (WES)................ 93
Dean Way (SB)................... 52
Deane Ave (WIN)................ 52
Deane Rd (NQ)................... 71
Dearborn (WH).................... 81
Dearborn (WNW)................. 65
Dearborn (ROX).................. 19
Dearborn St & Rd (MED)....... 55
Deborah Rd (NCE)............... 59
Debra Ln (BRA).................. 84
Decatur (NWV).................... 60
Decatur (ARL).................... 74
Decatur (CAM)................... 39
Decatur (EB)..................... 28
Decatur (CHA)................... 29
Decher Ave (JP)................. 30
Deckard (DOR)................... 21
Decker (MIL)..................... 87
Dedham (WRX)................... 32
Dedham (REV).................... 51
Dedham (HP)..................... 36
Dedham
   1-300 (NWH)................. 61
   301-OUT (NCE).............. 59
Dedham Ave (N).................. 92
Dee Rd (QUI)..................... 69
Dee Rd (LEX).................... 73
Deepwater (WH).................. 52
Deer (DOR)....................... 25
Deer Path Ln (WES)............ 93
Deer Island (WIN).............. 52
Deerfield (N)..................... 92
Deerfield...................02215
Deerfield (NQ).................... 71
Deerfield Rd (WH).............. 84
Deering Ave (BRA).............. 84
Deering Ave (LEX).............. 73
Deering Rd (MAT)............... 26
Deforest
   1-99 (HP)..................... 36
   100-OUT (ROS).............. 31
Dehon (REV)...................... 51
Deigan Ave (BRA)............... 85
Delano (DOR)..................... 22
Delano Ave (REV)............... 51
Delano Ave (QUI)............... 69
Delano Ct & Park (ROS)....... 31
Delanson Cir (WEL)............ 81
Delaware (SOM).................. 45
Delaware Pl (BRI)............... 35
Deldorf (QUI)..................... 69
Delford (ROS)..................... 31
Delhi (MAT)....................... 26
Delia Walker Rd (SWY)......... 90
Dell (MAL)......................... 48
Dell (SOM)........................ 45
Dell (WH).......................... 81
Dell Ave (MEL)................... 76
Dell Ave (MED).................. 55
Dell Ave (HP).................... 92
Dell Ave & Ter (HP)........... 36
Delle Ave (RXC)................. 20
Dellmere Rd (JP)............... 30
Delmont (DOR)................... 22
Delmore Rd (NWH).............. 61
Delnore Pl (MAT)............... 26
Delore Cir (ROS)............... 31
Delorey Ave (NWY)............. 91

Delta Rd (BRA).................. 84
Demar Rd (LEX).................. 73
Demerest (WAL).................. 54
Demers Ln (EV)................... 49
Deming Rd (LEX)................. 73
Denby Rd (ALL).................. 34
Denmark Ave (MIL).............. 86
Dennis (ROX)..................... 19
Dennis Rd (MAL)................. 48
Dennis Rd (WH).................. 81
Dennison (WAL).................. 54
Dennison (ROX).................. 19
Denns Pl (NCE).................. 59
Denny (DOR)...................... 25
Denny Rd (CHH)................. 67
Densmore (NQ)................... 71
Dent (WRX)....................... 32
Denton Rd E & W (WEL)....... 81
Denton Ter (ROS).............. 31
Denver (LEX)..................... 73
Denvir (DOR)..................... 24
Depot Sq (LEX).................. 73
Derby (WNW)..................... 65
Derby (WAL)...................... 54
Derby (SOM)...................... 45
Derby (SWY)...................... 90
Derby Ln (WES).................. 93
Derby Rd (REV).................. 51
Derby Rd (WAT).................. 72
Derby Rd (MEL).................. 76
Dermody Rd (WAL).............. 54
Derne (EV)........................ 49
Derne............................. 14
Derry (EWY)...................... 89
Derry Rd (HP).................... 36
Des Moines Rd (QUI)........... 69
Desmond Ave (WAT)............ 72
Desmond Rd (MAL).............. 48
Desmond Rd (MAT).............. 26
Devens (CHA).................... 29
Devens (EV)...................... 49
Devens St Pl (CHA)............ 29
Dever (DOR)...................... 22
Devereaux (ARL)................ 74
Devine Way (SB)................ 27
Devir (MAL)....................... 48
Devon (DOR)...................... 21
Devon Rd (CHH)................. 67
Devon Rd (BRA).................. 84
Devon Rd & Ter (NCE)........ 59
Devonshire
   1-135 (ODD).................. 09
   2-100 (EVEN)................ 09
   102-OUT (EVEN)............. 10
   137-OUT (ODD).............. 10
Devonshire Rd (WAB)........... 68
Devotion (BRO).................. 46
Dewar (DOR)...................... 25
Dewey (DOR)..................... 25
Dewey (WAT)..................... 72
Dewey Ave (MED)............... 55
Dewey Ave (BRA)............... 85
Dewey Rd (BRA).................. 84
Dewey Rd (LEX)................. 73
Dewey Sq....................02210
Dewhurst (NQ)................... 71
Dewitt Rd (STO)................ 80
Dewson Rd (QUI)................ 69
Dexter (MIL)...................... 86
Dexter (MED)..................... 55
Dexter (MAL)..................... 48
Dexter (EV)....................... 49
Dexter Ave (WAT).............. 72

Boston (Con.)	021
Dexter Rd (WEL)	81
Dexter Rd (LEX)	73
Dexter Rd (NWW)	60
Dexter Rd (MEL)	76
Dexter Row (CHA)	29
Dexter St & Ave (WAL)	54
Dexter St & Pl (SB)	27
Diamond Rd (LEX)	73
Diana Ln (LEX)	73
Diane Rd (MED)	55
Dianne Rd (STO)	80
Dickens (WOL)	70
Dickens (DOR)	22
Dickens Rd (LEX)	73
Dickerman Ln (BRA)	84
Dickerman Rd (NWH)	61
Dickinson (SOM)	43
Dickinson (CAM)	39
Dickinson Rd (BRI)	35
Dickson (WS)	44
Dickson Ave (ARL)	74
Diehl Rd (LEX)	73
Dietz Ct & Rd (HP)	36
Dighton (BRI)	35
Dilworth	18
Dimick (SOM)	43
Dimmock (QUI)	69
Dimock (ROX)	19
Dinnano Rd (STO)	80
Dinsmore Ct (CAM)	38
Dinsmore Rd (WH)	81
Ditmar (NQ)	71
Ditmus Ct	18
Ditson (DOR)	22
Divinity Ave (CAM)	38
Division (CHE)	50
Division (MAL)	48
Division (NQ)	71
Division (BRA)	85
Dix (WAL)	54
Dix (WIN)	52
Dix (REV)	51
Dix (DOR)	22
Dixfield (SB)	27
Dixon (WY)	88
Dixon Park Rd (WY)	68
Dinwell (ROX)	19
Dixwell Ave (QUI)	69
Doane (QUI)	69
Doane	09
Doane (CAM)	38
Doane Ave (N)	92
Doane Rd (MED)	55
Dobbins (WAL)	54
Doble (QUI)	69
Doble Ave (MED)	55
Dobson Rd (BRA)	84
Dock (CAM)	42
Dockray (QUI)	69
Dodge (ARL)	74
Dodge (CAM)	39
Dodge (MAL)	48
Dodge Rd (HP)	36
Dogwood Ln (N)	92
Bogwood Rd (WES)	93
Dolan Ave (NWW)	65
Dolans Ct (JP)	30
Dollar Ln (MIL)	86
Dolphin (SWY)	90
Dolphin Ave (WIN)	52
Dolphin Ave (REV)	51
Dolphin Rd (NCE)	59
Don (DOR)	24
Donald (LEX)	73
Donald (WY)	88
Donald Rd (DOR)	24
Donata Rd (BRA)	85
Doncaster (ROS)	31
Donizetti (WEL)	81
Donna Rd (NCE)	59
Donna Rd (SWY)	90
Donna Rd (NH)	94
Donna Ter (HP)	36
Donnell (CAM)	38
Donnellan Cir (NWY)	91
Donnelly Sq (REV)	51
Donnybrook Rd (BRI)	35
Donoghue Pl (HP)	36
Donovan Pl (JP)	30
Donwood Ter (MAT)	26
Doonan Ave (MED)	55
Doone Ave (MAT)	26
Doran Rd (BRO)	46
Dorcar Rd	
1-56 (CHH)	67
57-OUT (NCE)	59
Dorchester (WAL)	54
Dorchester (SB)	27
Dorchester (NQ)	71
Dorchester Ave	
1-48	02210
49-74 (SB)	27
75-75	09
76-699 (SB)	27
700-1246 (DOR)	25
1247-1699 (DOR)	24
1700-OUT (DOR)	24
Doris (DOR)	25
Doris Cir (NEW)	58
Doris Dr & Rd (NWY)	91
Doris Rd (BRA)	84
Dormar Way (ARL)	74
Dorothy Rd (ARL)	74
Dorothy Rd (NCE)	59
Dorr (ROX)	19
Dorr Rd (NEW)	58
Dorrance (CHA)	29
Dorset (DOR)	25
Dorset Ln (WEL)	81
Dorset Rd (WAB)	68
Dorset Rd (BEL)	78
Dothan (ARL)	74
Doty (WAL)	54
Doublett Hill Rd (WES)	93
Douglas (REV)	51
Douglas (QUI)	69
Douglas (SB)	27
Douglas Ave (SOM)	45
Douglas Rd (WAL)	54
Douglas Rd (MED)	55
Douglas Rd (BEL)	78
Douglas Rd (LEX)	73
Douglas Rd (N)	92
Douglas St & Ct (CAM)	39
Douglass (WIN)	52
Douse Rd (WOL)	70
Dove St & Ct (DOR)	25
Dover (MED)	55
Dovers	
1-43 (CAM) (ODD)	40
2-46 (CAM) (EVEN)	40
45-OUT (WS) (ODD)	44
48-OUT (WS) (EVEN)	44
Dover Rd (WH)	81
Dow (REV)	51
Dow (WS)	44
Dow Ave (ARL)	74
Dow Rd (WRX)	32
Downer Ave (DOR)	25
Downer Ct (DOR)	22
Downey (MAL)	48
Downey (WAT)	72
Downey Ct (DOR)	25
Downing Rd (LEX)	73
Downing Rd (BRO)	46
Dowse (EV)	49
Doyle Ter (QUI)	69
Drabbington Way (WES)	93
Dracut (DOR)	24
Draelon (ARL)	73
Drake (BRA)	85
Drake Pl (EB)	28
Drake Rd (ARL)	74
Draper (DOR)	22
Draper (MED)	55
Draper Ave (ARL)	74
Drayton Ave (DOR)	25
Dresden (JP)	30
Dresden (WS)	44
Dresser (SB)	27
Drew Ave (LEX)	73
Drew Ave (EWY)	89
Drew Rd (BEL)	78
Drew Rd (CHH)	67
Driftkway Rd (NWY)	91
Driftwood Dr (WRW)	85
Driftwood Ln (WES)	93
Driftwood Rd (JP)	30
Drinkwater Ave (BRA)	84
Driscoll Dr (ARL)	24
Dromey (DOR)	25
Druce (BRO)	46
Druid (MAT)	26
Druid Hill Ave (MEL)	76
Druid Hill Rd (NWH)	61
Drumlin Rd (NCE)	59
Drumlin Rd (EB)	28
Drummond (CAM)	21
Drummond Pl (CAM)	40
Drummond Rd (STO)	80
Drury Ln (STO)	80
Drury Ln (WAL)	54
Drury Rd (HP)	36
Duane Ave (WRW)	65
Duane Rd (MED)	55
Duck Ln (EWY)	89
Duddy Ave (WAL)	55
Dudley (MED)	55
Dudley (BRO)	46
Dudley (CHE)	50
Dudley	
1-553 (ROX)	19
554-OUT (DOR)	25
Dudley Ln (MIL)	86
Dudley Rd (WH)	81
Dudley Rd (NCE)	59
Dudley Rd (LEX)	73
Dudley St Pl (ARL)	74
Dudley St & Ct (ARL)	74
Dudley St & Ct (CAM)	40
Dudley Ter (DOR)	25
Duff (WAT)	72
Duffield Rd (AUB)	66
Duffley Ct (CHH)	67
Duggan Ln (MIL)	86
Duke (MAT)	26
Duke (MAL)	48

Boston (Con.)   021

Duke Rd (WEL) ... 81
Dumas (DOR) .. 24
Dummer (BRO) .. 46
Dunbar Ave (MED) .. 55
Dunbar Ave (DOR) .. 24
Dunbar Rd (SWY) 90
Dunbarton Rd (N) 92
Dunbarton Rd (WOL) 70
Dunbarton Rd (BEL) 78
Dunboy (BRI) 35
Duncan Rd (EV) 49
Duncan Rd (WNW) 65
Duncan St, Pl & Ter (DOR) 22
Duncklee (NWH) 61
Duncklee (BRI) 35
Duncklee Ave (STO) 80
Dundee Rd (NQ) 71
Dundee Rd (ARL) 74
Dundonald Rd (BEL) 78
Dunedin Pl & Rd (WH) 81
Dunford (ROX) 19
Dunham (LEX) 73
Dunkeld (DOR) 21
Dunlap (DOR) 24
Dunlow St & Pl (RXC) 20
Dunmore (ROX) 19
Dunmore (QUI) .. 69
Dunn (DOR) 25
Dunn Rd (REV) 51
Dunning Way (JP) 30
Dunns Ct (QUI) 69
Dunns Ter (DOR) 22
Dunns Hill Rd (QUI) 69
Dunreath (ROX) 19
Dunstable (CHA) 29
Dunstable Rd (CAM) 38
Dunstan (WNW) 65
Dunster (ARL) 74
Dunster (CAM) 38
Dunster Rd (JP) 30
Dunster Rd (EV) 49
Dunster Rd (CPH) 67
Dunster Ru (NH) 94
Dunton Rd (WAT) 72
Dunwell (WRX) 32
Durant (WRX) 32
Durant (NEW) 58
Durant Rd (WH) 81
Durant Rd (SWY) 90
Durham (SOM) 43
Durham 15
Durland (BRI) 35
Durnell Ave (ROS) 31
Durso Ave (MAL) 48
Dustin (BRI) 35
Dustin (QUI) 69
Dutton (MAL) 48
Dutton Cir (MED) 55
Duval (BRI) 35
Duxbury Rd (WH) 81
Duxbury Rd (NCE) 59
Duxbury Rd (MAT) 26
Dwhinda Rd (WAB) 68
Dwight (WAT) 72
Dwight 18
Dwight (BRO) 46
Dwight Rd (N) 92
Dwinell (WRX) 32
Dwyer Cir (MED) 55
Dwyer Ln (EWY) 89
Dyer Ave (MIL) 87

Dyer Ave (BRA) 85
Dyer Ave (EV) 49
Dyer Ave (SB) 27
Dyer Ave (MEL) 76
Dyer St & Ct (DOR) 24
Dysart (QUI) 69
E
I-449 (SB) 27
450-OUT 02210
Eager Rd (MIL) 86
Eagle Sq (EB) 28
Earl (SB) 27
Earl (LEX) 73
Earl (MAL) 48
Earl Ave (MED) 55
Earle (SOM) 43
Earle (WOL) 70
Earle Rd (WH) 81
Early Ave (MED) 55
Early Path (NCE) 59
Earnshaw (WRX) 32
East (CAM) 41
East (STO) 80
East (LEX) 73
East (MEL) 76
East (DOR) 22
East 11
East (EWY) 89
East Blvd Rd (NCE) 59
East Albion (MED) 55
East Albion (SOM) 45
East Berkeley 18
East Border Rd (MAL) 48
East Border Rd (MED) 55
East Boscobel (BRA) 85
East Brookline 18
East Canton 18
East Capen (MED) 55
East Concord 18
East Cottage (DOR) 22
East Dedham 18
East Eagle (EB) 28
East Elm (EV) 49
East Elm Ave (WOL) 70
East Foster (MEL) 76
East Highland Ave (MEL) 76
East Howard (QUI) 69
East Lenox 18
East Locust (EV) 49
East Militia Hts (N) 92
East Milton Rd (BRO) 46
East Newton 18
East Quinobequin Rd (WAB) 68
East Side Pky (NEW) 58
East Springfield 18
East Squantum (NQ) 71
East Summer (EV) 49
East Wyoming Ave (MEL) 76
Eastbourne (ROS) 31
Eastbourne Rd (NCE) 59
Eastburn St, Pl & Ter (BRI) 35
Eastern Ave (CHE) 50
Eastern Ave (MAL) 48
Eastern Ave (REV) 51
Eastern Ave (LEX) 73
Eastern Ave (ARL) 74
Eastern Ave 09
Eastham Rd (NCE) 59
Eastland Rd (JP) 30
Eastman (MED) 55
Eastman (DOR) 25
Eastman Cir (WEL) 81
Eastman Pl (MEL) 76

Eastman Rd (SOM) 43
Eastmont Rd (HP) 36
Easton (ALL) 34
Easton Ave (HP) 36
Eastview Ter (STO) 80
Eastwood Ct (WRX) 32
Eastwood Circuit (WRX) 32
Easy (NWH) 61
Easy (N) 92
Easy (SWY) 90
Eaton (MIL) 86
Eaton (CAM) 39
Eaton (REV) 51
Eaton Ct (WH) 81
Eaton Rd (LEX) 73
Eaton Rd (QUI) 69
Eaton Rd & Sq (N) 92
Ebbett Ave (WOL) 70
Echo (MEL) 76
Echo (MAL) 48
Echo (ROX) 19
Echo Ave (EWY) 89
Echo Rd (WH) 81
Eddie (QUI) 69
Eddy (WNW) 65
Eddy (WAL) 54
Eden (CHE) 50
Eden (CHA) 29
Eden Ave (WNW) 65
Edenfield Ave (WAT) 72
Edgar (RXC) 20
Edgar Ave, Ct & Ter (SOM) 15
Edgar Ter (WH) 52
Edge Hill (JP) 30
Edge Hill Rd (WAL) 54
Edge Hill Rd (CHH) 67
Edge Hill Rd (QUI) 69
Edge Hill Rd (WH) 81
Edge Hill Rd (BRA) 84
Edge Hill Rd (MIL) 86
Edgebrook Rd (WRX) 32
Edgecliff Rd (WAT) 72
Edgefield Rd (QUI) 69
Edgefield Rd (WAB) 68
Edgehill Rd (ARL) 74
Edgehill Rd (WIN) 52
Edgehill Rd (BRO) 46
Edgemere (MEL) 76
Edgemere Rd (QUI) 69
Edgemere Rd (WRX) 32
Edgemont (ROS) 31
Edgemont Rd (BRA) 84
Edgemoor Ave (WH) 81
Edgemoor Rd (BEL) 78
Edgerly Pl 16
Edgerly Rd 15
Edgewater Dr (MAT) 26
Edgewater Dr (WH) 81
Edgewater Dr (QUI) 69
Edgewater Dr (N) 92
Edgewater Dr (WAL) 54
Edgewater Park (AUB) 66
Edgewood (N) 92
Edgewood Cir (QUI) 69
Edgewood Rd (WNW) 65
Edgewood Rd (LEX) 73
Edgewood St & Park (ROJ) 19
Edgeworth (CHA) 29
Edgeworth (EWY) 89
Edgeworth Rd (NQ) 71
Edinboro 11
Edinboro Rd (QUI) 69
Edinboro St, Pl & Ter (RNW) 60

Boston (Con.)   021

Edison (WY) 88
Edison Ave (MED) 55
Edison St & Park (QUI) 69
Edison Way (LEX) 73
Edison Green (DOR) 25
Edith (ARL) 74
Edith (HP) 36
Edith Ave (WAT) 72
Edith Rd (EWY) 89
Edith St & Ave (EV) 49
Edmester Ct (EV) 49
Edmonds (SOM) 45
Edmund (MAL) 48
Edmund Rd (ARL) 74
Edmunds (CAM) 40
Edmunds Rd (WH) 81
Edna (LEX) 73
Edna Rd (DOR) 24
Edson (DOR) 24
Edson St, Rd & Ter (HP) 36
Edward (WIN) 52
Edward (BEL) 78
Edward Ave (MIL) 86
Edward Rd (WAT) 72
Edward (WNW) 65
Edward St & Pl (MED) 55
Edward Cody Ln (SWY) 90
Edward Everett Sq (DOR) 25
Edward T Sullivan Rd (CAM) 38
Edward Wilson Sq (SOM) 43
Edwardel Rd (N) 92
Edwards Rd (BRA) 84
Edwards Rd (STO) 80
Edwards St & Ln (QUI) 69
Edwardson (HP) 36
Edwin (BRO) 46
Edwin (NQ) 71
Edwin (DOR) 24
Edwin Rd (WAL) 54
Egan Way (BRI) 35
Egerton Rd (ARL) 74
Egleston (JP) 30
Egleston Sq (ROX) 19
Egleton Park (WIN) 52
Egmont (BRO) 46
Egremont Rd (BRO) 46
Eighth (CAM) 41
Eighth (MED) 55
Eighth (SB) 27
Eileen Rd (MIL) 86
Eisenhower Rd (SWY) 90
Elaine Rd (STO) 80
Elba (BRO) 46
Elba Ter (DOR) 22
Elbert (ROX) 19
Elbow (EB) 28
Elcott Rd (QUI) 69
Elder (DOR) 25
Elder Rd (NH) 94
Elder Ter (ARL) 74
Eldon (DOR) 21
Eldora (RXC) 20
Eldred (LEX) 73
Eldredge (NEW) 58
Eldridge Pl (CHE) 50
Eldridge Rd (JP) 30
Eleanor (CHE) 50
Eleanor (ALL) 34
Eleanor Ct (WIN) 52
Eleanor Dr (BRA) 84
Electric Ave (BRI) 35

Electric Ave (WS) 44
Elena Rd (LEX) 73
Elene (MAT) 26
Elgin (NCE) 59
Elgin (WRX) 32
Elgin (SWY) 90
Elinor Cir (WAL) 54
Elinor Dr (BRA) 84
Elinor Rd (SWY) 90
Elinor Rd (NWH) 61
Eliot (WAT) 72
Eliot (SOM) 43
Eliot (HP) 36
Eliot (MED) 55
Eliot 16
Eliot Ave (WNW) 65
Eliot Cir & Rd (REV) 51
Eliot Ln (WES) 93
Eliot Park & Rd (ARL) 74
Eliot Rd (LEX) 73
Eliot Rd (NH) 94
Eliot Sq & Ter (ROX) 19
Eliot St, Ave & Cres (CHH) 67
Eliot St & Cir (MIL) 87
Eliot St & Pl (JP) 30
Eliot St & Sq (CAM) 38
Eliot Memorial Rd (NEW) 58
Elizabeth (MAT) 26
Elizabeth Cir (WNW) 65
Elizabeth Cir (N) 92
Elizabeth Ln (SWY) 90
Elizabeth Rd (STO) 80
Elizabeth Rd (BEL) 78
Elkins (SB) 27
Elko (BRI) 35
Ellard Rd (HP) 36
Ellen Ave (WY) 88
Ellen Rd (STO) 80
Ellen Ter (WAT) 72
Ellerton (REV) 51
Ellerton Rd (QUI) 69
Ellery (CAM) 38
Ellery (BRA) 85
Ellery (SB) 27
Ellery Rd (WAL) 54
Ellet (DOR) 22
Ellicott (N) 92
Ellington (DOR) 21
Ellington Rd (WS) 44
Ellington Rd (WOL) 70
Ellingwood (RXC) 20
Elliot (WEL) 81
Elliot 48
  1-14 (WY) 88
  1-139 (NWH) 61
  15-OUT (BRA) 84
  140-OUT (NUF) 64
Elliot Ave (NQ) 71
Elliot Pl & Ter (NUF) 64
Elliott (MEL) 76
Elliott (WIN) 52
Elliott (MAL) 48
Elliott Rd (EV) 49
Elliott Rd (BEL) 78
Ellis (NUF) 64
Ellis (QUI) 69
Ellis (LEX) 73
Ellis (MAL) 48
Ellis (HP) 36
Ellis (ROX) 19
Ellis Ave (MED) 55
Ellis Cir (SWY) 90
Ellis Ln (BRA) 84

Ellis Rd (WES) 93
Ellis Rd (WNW) 65
Ellis Farm Ln (MEL) 76
Ellison Ave (MAT) 26
Ellison Park (WAL) 54
Ellison Rd (LEX) 73
Ellison Rd (NCE) 59
Ells Ave (MEL) 76
Ells Ave (SWY) 90
Ellswood (WRX) 32
Ellsworth (MED) 55
Ellsworth (SOM) 45
Ellsworth (EV) 49
Ellsworth (CHE) 50
Ellsworth (ROX) 19
Ellsworth (DOR) 22
Ellsworth Ave (BRA) 84
Ellsworth Ave (MEL) 76
Ellsworth Ave & Park (CAM) 39
Ellsworth Rd (MIL) 86
Elhwood (CHA) 29
Elhwood Rd (MEL) 76
Elm (MEL) 76
Elm (BEL) 78
Elm (LEX) 73
Elm (QUI) 69
Elm (WAT) 72
Elm (STO) 80
Elm (WH) 81
Elm (CHA) 29
Elm (DOR) 22
Elm (MIL) 86
Elm (SWY) 90
Elm (CAM) 39
Elm (CHE) 50
Elm (BRO) 46
Elm (MED) 55
Elm (JP) 30
Elm (HP) 36
Elm (REV) 51
Elm ....
  1-53 (SOM) 43
  54-98 (WS) (EVEN) 44
  55-OUT (WS) (ODD) 44
  100-206 (CAM) (EVEN) 40
  208-OUT (WS) (EVEN) 44
Elm Ave (WOL) 70
Elm Ct (WNW) 65
Elm Ct (WS) 44
Elm Pl (SOM) 43
Elm Rd (NWV) 60
Elm St, Ave & Ct (WAL) 54
Elm St & Ct (MAL) 48
Elm St, Rd, Ter & Way (EV) 49
Elm St & Ter (BRA) 84
Elm Hill Ave & Park (DOR) 21
Elm Knoll Rd (BRA) 84
Elm Lawn (MIL) 87
Elm Lawn (DOR) 22
Elmcrest Ter (MEL) 76
Elmdale (DOR) 22
Elmer (CAM) 38
Elmer Ave (WIN) 52
Elmer Rd (DOR) 24
Elmer Rd (SWY) 90
Elmhurst (DOR) 24
Elmhurst Rd (NEW) 58
Elmhurst Rd (STO) 80
Elmhurst Rd (ARL) 74
Elmhurst Ter (WAL) 54
Elmira (BRI) 35
Elmlawn Rd (BRA) 84
Elmont (DOR) 21

Boston (Con.) 021

Elmore (ARL)	74
Elmore (NCE)	59
Elmore St & Park (ROX)	19
Elmwood (NEW)	58
Elmwood (EV)	49
Elmwood Ave (WAL)	54
Elmwood Ave (CAM)	38
Elmwood Ave (WAT)	72
Elmwood Ave (ARL)	86
Elmwood Ave (BRA)	85
Elmwood Ave & Ct (WIN)	52
Elmwood Ave & Park (WOL)	70
Elmwood Ct & Park (MAL)	48
Elmwood Park (NHV)	60
Elmwood Park (BRA)	84
Elmwood Rd (N)	92
Elmwood Rd (WH)	81
Elmwood St & Ave (REV)	51
Elmwood St, Ct & Pl (RXC)	20
Elmwood St & Ter (WS)	44
Elsie (MAL)	48
Elsie (EV)	49
Elsmere Ter (MED)	55
Elsmore Ter (BRA)	84
Elson Rd (WAL)	54
Elston (WS)	44
Elsworth Rd (NHV)	65
Elton (DOR)	25
Elton Ave (WAT)	72
Elton Rd (ARL)	86
Elva Rd (HNY)	91
Elven Rd (ROS)	31
Ehrell (MAL)	48
Ehrell Rd (JP)	30
Elvern Rd (ARL)	74
Elwood (EV)	49
Elwood Ave (STO)	80
Elwood Dr (SWY)	90
Elwood Pl (REV)	51
Elwyn Rd (DOR)	24
Ely Rd (DOR)	24
Ely Rd (ARL)	74
Emanuel (REV)	51
Embankment Rd	
1-58	14
59-OUT	08
Embassy Rd (BRI)	35
Emelia Ter (WRX)	32
Emeline Rd (EWY)	89
Emerald (MAL)	48
Emerald (BRO)	46
Emerald (MED)	55
Emerald (NEW)	58
Emerald (QUI)	69
Emerald (LEX)	73
Emerald Ave (BRA)	85
Emerald Ct (STO)	80
Emerald Ct	18
Emerson (SB)	27
Emerson (STO)	80
Emerson (NEW)	58
Emerson (BEL)	78
Emerson (MED)	55
Emerson (BRO)	46
Emerson (SOM)	43
Emerson Pl (MAL)	48
Emerson Pl (MEL)	76
Emerson Pl	14
Emerson Pl & Rd (N)	92
Emerson Rd (MIL)	86
Emerson Rd (WH)	81

Emerson Rd (LEX)	73
Emerson Rd (ARL)	74
Emerson Rd (WAT)	72
Emerson Rd (WIN)	52
Emerson Rd (WAL)	54
Emerson St E & W (MEL)	76
Emerson St & Ter (EWY)	89
Emerson Gardens (LEX)	73
Emery (WAL)	54
Emery (MED)	55
Emery (EV)	49
Emery Ct (STO)	80
Emery Rd (ALL)	34
Emily (CAM)	39
Emmeline Ave (WAL)	54
Emmet (SB)	27
Emmet Pl (EB)	28
Emmet Pl (CAM)	41
Emmet Ter (REV)	51
Emmett (HP)	36
Emmons (EB)	28
Emmons (NEW)	65
Emmons Pl (CAM)	38
Emmonsdale Rd (WRX)	32
Empire (ALL)	34
Empire (QUI)	69
Emrose Ter (DOR)	25
Emsella Ter (JP)	30
Endicott (WAL)	54
Endicott (QUI)	69
Endicott (NHV)	61
Endicott (EWY)	89
Endicott Ave (WS)	44
Endicott Ave (REV)	51
Endicott Rd (STO)	80
Endicott Rd (ARL)	74
Endicott St & Ct	13
Endicott Ter (DOR)	22
Enfield (JP)	30
Enfield Rd (WIN)	52
Englehuft Rd (MED)	55
Englewood Ave (CHE)	50
Englewood Ave (EV)	49
Englewood Ave (BRO)	46
Enmore Rd (MEL)	76
Ennis Rd (ROX)	19
Ensign (REV)	51
Enslin Rd (N)	92
Enterprise (DOR)	25
Epping (DOR)	24
Epping (EWY)	89
Epping (ARL)	74
Eric Rd (ALL)	34
Erickson (MAL)	48
Erickson (STO)	80
Erickson (BRA)	84
Ericson Rd (WY)	88
Ericsson (DOR)	22
Ericsson	
1-9 (BEL) (ODD)	78
2-OUT (BEL) (EVEN)	78
11-OUT (CAM) (ODD)	38
Erie (DOR)	21
Erie (CAM)	39
Erie Ave (NHV)	61
Erie Pl (ROX)	19
Erin Way (SWY)	90
Ernest Ave (QUI)	69
Ernest Ave (HP)	36
Ernest Rd (ARL)	74
Ernest Rd (BEL)	78
Ernest Rd (HNY)	91
Ernst (ROX)	19

Erville Ln (EWY)	89
Esmond (DOR)	21
Essex	11
Essex (WY)	88
Essex (MEL)	76
Essex (STO)	80
Essex (LEX)	73
Essex (WAT)	72
Essex (NQ)	71
Essex (MAL)	48
Essex (BRO)	46
Essex (SOM)	45
Essex (REV)	51
Essex (MED)	55
Essex Ave	04
Essex Rd (WY)	81
Essex Rd (BEL)	78
Essex Rd (CHH)	67
Essex Rd (NHV)	87
Essex St & Ct (CAM)	39
Essex St, Ct & Pl (CHE)	50
Estabrook Rd (WY)	8.
Estabrook Rd (NHV)	65
Estabrook Rd (WOL)	70
Estabrook Rd (LEX)	73
Estella (MAT)	26
Estes	2.
Estes Ave (DOR)	21
Estes Pl	02210
Estes St & Ct (EV)	49
Estey (MAL)	48
Estey (RXC)	20
Esther Rd (WRX)	32
Estrella (JP)	30
Esty Farm Rd (NCE)	59
Ethel (ROS)	31
Ethel Ct (MAL)	48
Etna (BRI)	35
Etonia (ALL)	34
Euclid (DOR)	24
Euclid Ave (QUI)	69
Eugene Rd (MED)	55
Eugenia Rd (ROS)	31
Eulita Ter (BRI)	35
Eunice (DOR)	22
Eustis (CHE)	50
Eustis (REV)	51
Eustis (LEX)	73
Eustis (WOL)	70
Eustis (STO)	80
Eustis (ARL)	74
Eustis	
1-72 (CAM)	40
73-OUT (SOM)	43
Eustis St & Pl (ROX)	19
Euston (BRO)	46
Euston Rd (BRI)	35
Eutaw Ave (BRA)	85
Eutaw St & Pl (EB)	28
Evandale Ter (DOR)	25
Evans (DOR)	24
Evans (HNY)	91
Evans (MED)	55
Evans (NQ)	71
Evans (WAT)	72
Evans Ct (MAL)	48
Evans Rd (BRO)	46
Evans Rd (STO)	80
Evans Rd (N)	92
Evans Way	15
Evelyn (MAT)	26
Evelyn Ave (MED)	55
Evelyn Ave & Pl (MAL)	48

285

Boston (Con.)   021

Evelyn Ct & Rd (EV) 49
Evelyn Ln (BRA) 85
Evelyn Pl (NQ) 71
Evelyn Rd (WAB) 68
Evelyn Rd (NH) 94
Everard (REV) 51
Everdean (DOR) 22
Everett (DOR) 22
Everett (REV) 51
Everett (MAL) 48
Everett (MED) 55
Everett (HP) 36
Everett (JP) 30
Everett (CAM) 38
Everett (SOM) 43
Everett (WAL) 54
Everett (WOL) 70
Everett (WEL) 81
Everett (STO) 80
Everett (ARL) 74
Everett (NCE) 59
Everett (MEL) 76
Everett Ave (WAT) 72
Everett Ave (SOM) 45
Everett Ave (CHE) 50
Everett Ave (DOR) 25
Everett Pl (NWY) 91
Everett St & Ave (EV) 49
Everett St, Ct & Pl (EB) 28
Everett St & Sq (ALL) 34
Evergreen (JP) 30
Evergreen Ave (SOM) 45
Evergreen Ave (WAL) 54
Evergreen Ave (WES) 93
Evergreen Ave (WH) 81
Evergreen Ave & Rd (BRA) .. 84
Evergreen Ave & Ter (AUB) .. 66
Evergreen Ln
   1-16 (LEX) 73
   17-OUT (ARL) 74
Evergreen Rd (NH) 94
Evergreen Rd (STO) 80
Evergreen Sq (SOM) 43
Evergreen Way (BEL) 78
Everton (DOR) 21
Ewell Ave (LEX) 73
Ewer (SB) 27
Exchange (MAL) 48
Exchange Ave (MED) 55
Exchange Pl 09
Exchange St, Ct & Pl (WAL) .. 54
Exeter (MED) 55
Exeter (CHE) 50
Exeter 16
Exeter (BEL) 78
Exeter (WNW) 65
Exeter (WOL) 70
Exeter (ARL) 74
Exeter Ct (CHA) 29
Exeter Park (CAM) 40
Exeter Pl 11
Exmoor Rd (NCE) 59
Export 10
F (SB) 27
Fabiano Dr (BRA) 84
Fabin 18
Fabyan (DOR) 24
Fabyan (ARL) 74
Facotry (HP) 36
Factory (EV) 49

Factory Hill (BRA) 84
Fairwood Cir (CAM) 39
Fair Oaks (CAM) 40
Fair Oaks Ave (NWV) 60
Fair Oaks Dr & Ter (LEX) ... 73
Fair Oaks Park (N) 92
Fair View (WIN) 52
Fair View Ave & Ter (MAL) .. 48
Fairbanks (BRO) 46
Fairbanks (BRI) 35
Fairbanks Ave (WH) 81
Fairbanks Rd (LEX) 73
Fairbanks Rd (MIL) 86
Fairbury (DOR) 25
Fairfax (DOR) 24
Fairfax (NWY) 91
Fairfax (WNW) 65
Fairfax (WS) 44
Fairfax Rd (WAL) 54
Fairfax Rd (MIL) 87
Fairfax Rd (N) 92
Fairfield (N) 92
Fairfield (BRA) 84
Fairfield (CAM) 40
Fairfield (REV) 51
Fairfield (MED) 55
Fairfield (NWV) 60
Fairfield (WAL) 72
Fairfield (MEL) 76
Fairfield 16
Fairfield Ave (MAL) 48
Fairfield Dr (LEX) 73
Fairfield Pl 09
Fairgreen Pl (CHH) 67
Fairhaven (NCE) 59
Fairhope Rd (WES) 93
Fairland (LEX) 73
Fairland (ROX) 19
Fairlane Rd (STO) 80
Fairlane Rd (WRX) 32
Fairlawn (MAL) 48
Fairlawn (EV) 49
Fairlawn (N) 92
Fairlawn Ave (NWY) 91
Fairlawn Ave (MIL) 87
Fairlawn Ave (MAT) 26
Fairlawn Ln (LEX) 73
Fairlee (N) 44
Fairlee Rd & Ter (WAB) 68
Fairmont (BEL) 78
Fairmont (ARL) 74
Fairmont Ave (NEW) 58
Fairmont Ave (WAL) 54
Fairmont St & Ave (CAM) ... 39
Fairmont St, Ct, Pl & Ter
   (MAL) 48
Fairmont Way (QUI) 69
Fairmount (MEL) 76
Fairmount (BRO) 46
Fairmount (EV) 49
Fairmount (MED) 55
Fairmount (DOR) 24
Fairmount Ave (WS) 44
Fairmount Ave (EWY) 89
Fairmount Ave (BRA) 84
Fairmount Ave
   1-309 (HP) 36
   310-OUT (MIL) 86
Fairmount Ct & Ter (HP) 36
Fairmount (ROS) 31
Fairview (NEW) 58
Fairview Ave (MEL) 76

Fairview Ave (ARL) 74
Fairview Ave (LEX) 73
Fairview Ave (WAT) 72
Fairview Ave (HP) 36
Fairview Ave (WAL) 54
Fairview Ave (BRA) 85
Fairview Ave
   1-15 (CAM) (ODD) 38
   2-12 (CAM) (EVEN) 38
   14-OUT (BEL) (EVEN) .. 78
   17-OUT (BEL) (ODD) ... 78
Fairview Rd (WES) 93
Fairview Rd (N) 92
Fairview Rd (QUI) 69
Fairview Rd (STO) 80
Fairview Ter (WNW) 65
Fairview Ter (SOM) 45
Fairway (WY) 88
Fairway (MAT) 26
Fairway Dr (WNW) 65
Fairway Rd (CHH) 67
Falcon (EB) 28
Falcon (N) 92
Falcon Ter (QUI) 69
Falkland (BRI) 35
Fall Rd (WRX) 32
Fall St & Park (MAL) 48
Fallgren Ln (EWY) 89
Fallon Cir (BRA) 84
Fallon Pl (CAM) 38
Falmouth (EV) 49
Falmouth (BEL) 78
Falmouth 15
Falmouth Rd (WNW) 65
Falmouth Rd (WH) 81
Falmouth Rd (WAT) 72
Falmouth Rd (ARL) 74
Falmouth Rd (WAL) 54
Falmouth Rd (WES) 93
Falmouth Rd W (ARL) 74
Faneuil (BRI) 35
Faneuil Rd (WAL) 54
Faneuil Hall Sq 09
Faraday (HP) 36
Fargo 02210
Fargo Rd (SWY) 90
Farina Rd (NCE) 59
Farlow Rd (NEW) 58
Farm (SWY) 90
Farm Rd (WES) 93
Farm Rd (BRA) 84
Farm Rd (WEL) 81
Farm Rd (BEL) 78
Farmcrest Ave (LEX) 73
Farmer Rd (ARL) 74
Farmington Rd (WNW) 65
Farmington Rd (WRX) 32
Farnham (BEL) 78
Farnham (ROX) 19
Farnsworth 02210
Farnsworth St & Ave (WAL) .. 54
Farnum (QUI) 69
Farnum Rd (WAL) 54
Farquhar (ROS) 31
Farquhar Rd (NWV) 60
Farragut (WRX) 32
Farragut Ave (WS) 44
Farragut Ave (MED) 55
Farragut Rd (SB) 27
Farrar (CAM) 38
Farrar Ave (HP) 36
Farrell (QUI) 69
Farren Rd (EWY) 89

Boston (Con.)	021
Farrington (ARL)	74
Farrington (HP)	36
Farrington	
1-56 (NQ)	71
57-OUT (WOL)	70
Farrington Ave (ALL)	34
Farview Rd (MED)	55
Farwell (WAL)	54
Farwell (NWV)	60
Farwell Ave (MEL)	76
Farwell Ave (HP)	36
Farwell Pl (CAM)	38
Father Carney Dr (MIL)	86
Father Matignon Rd (CAM)	40
Fatima Rd (STO)	80
Faulkner Pl (MEL)	76
Faulkner Pl (BRA)	84
Faulkner St & Cir (DOR)	22
Faulkner St & Sq (MAL)	48
Faun Bar Ave (WH)	52
Faunce Rd (MAT)	26
Favre (MAT)	26
Fawcett (CAM)	38
Fawndale Rd (ROS)	31
Faxon (RXC)	20
Faxon (BRA)	84
Faxon (MEL)	76
Faxon (NEW)	58
Faxon Ave & Ln (QUI)	69
Faxon Park Rd (QUI)	69
Faxon Rd (NQ)	71
Fay	18
Fay Ln (NH)	94
Fay Sq (CHE)	50
Fayerweather (CAM)	38
Fayette	16
Fayette (WAT)	72
Fayette (ARL)	74
Fayette	
1-71 (NQ) (ODD)	71
2-74 (NQ) (EVEN)	71
73-OUT (WOL) (ODD)	70
76-OUT (WOL) (EVEN)	70
Fayette Ct	11
Fayette St & Park (CAM)	39
Fayette St & Pl (NEW)	58
Fayston (DOR)	21
Faywood Ave (EB)	28
Federal (QUI)	88
Federal Ave (QUI)	69
Federal Dr (BRA)	84
Federal St & Ct	10
Federal Wharf (EB)	28
Felicia Rd (MEL)	76
Fellows (ROX)	19
Fells Ave (MED)	55
Fells Ave Ter (MED)	55
Fells Rd (WEL)	81
Fells Rd (STO)	80
Fellsmere Ave (STO)	80
Fellsmere Ave (MEL)	76
Fellsmere Rd (NCE)	59
Fellsmere Rd (MAL)	48
Fellsview Ave (MED)	55
Fellsview Rd & Ter (MEL)	76
Fellsway (MED)	55
Fellsway	
1020-1250 (MAL)	48
Fellsway E (MAL)	48
Fellsway E (MEL)	76
Fellsway W (MED)	55

Fellsway St E & W (SOM)	45
Felspa Rd (STO)	80
Felton (NQ)	71
Felton (CAM)	38
Felton (WAL)	54
Felton Pl (MEL)	76
Fencourt	15
Fendale Ave (DOR)	24
Fenelon (DOR)	21
Feneno Ter (ALL)	34
Fenley (REV)	51
Fenmere Ave (WH)	81
Fennell (CAM)	45
Fenner (ROX)	19
Fenno (ROX)	19
Fenno (REV)	51
Fenno (CAM)	38
Fenno (CHE)	50
Fenno (WOL)	70
Fenno Rd (NCE)	59
Fensmere Ave (QUI)	69
Fenton (WAL)	54
Fenton Rd (NH)	94
Fenton St & Pl (DOR)	22
Fenway	
1-55	02215
56-OUT	15
Fenway Ct	15
Fenwick (REV)	51
Fenwick (SOM)	45
Fenwick (ROX)	19
Fenwick Rd (WAB)	68
Fenwick St, Cir & Ter (MAL)	48
Fenwood Rd	15
Ferdinand (MEL)	76
Ferguson Rd (MAL)	48
Fermoy Hts Ave (DOR)	24
Fern (WAL)	54
Fern (ALL)	34
Fern (CAM)	38
Fern (AUB)	66
Fern (LEX)	73
Fern Ct (EWY)	89
Fern Rd (EWY)	90
Fern Rd (BRA)	84
Fern Rd (MED)	55
Fernald (LEX)	73
Fernald Dr (CAM)	38
Fernald Ter (DOR)	24
Fernboro (DOR)	21
Ferncroft Rd (WRX)	32
Ferncroft Rd (WAB)	68
Ferncroft Rd (BRA)	84
Ferncroft Rd (MIL)	87
Ferncroft Way (MAL)	48
Ferndale (DOR)	24
Ferndale Rd (N)	92
Ferndale Rd (WES)	93
Ferndale Rd (WOL)	70
Fernwood Ave & Pl (REV)	51
Fernwood Rd (WRX)	32
Fernwood Rd (WWN)	65
Fernwood Rd (CHH)	67
Ferrin (CHA)	37
Ferriter (QUI)	69
Ferry (CHE)	50
Ferry (EV)	49
Ferry St & Pl (MAL)	48
Fessenden (MAT)	26
Fessenden (NWV)	60
Fessenden Rd (ARL)	74
Fessenden Way (LEX)	73

Festa Rd (REV)	51
Fidelis Way (BRI)	35
Field (CAM)	38
Field (MAL)	48
Field (QUI)	69
Field	15
Field Ave (WY)	88
Field Rd (LEX)	73
Field Rd (ARL)	74
Fieldmont (HP)	36
Fieldmont Rd (BEL)	78
Fields Ct (MEL)	76
Fields Ct (DOR)	25
Fields Corner (DOR)	22
Fields Pond Rd (WES)	93
Fieldstone Dr (STO)	80
Fife Rd (WH)	81
Fifield (WAT)	72
Fifield (DOR)	22
Fifth (SB)	27
Fifth (CHE)	50
Fifth (MED)	55
Fifth	
1-199 (CAM)	41
200-OUT (CAM)	42
Fifth Ave (WAT)	72
Fifth Ave (QUI)	69
Figurehead Ln (QUI)	69
Filbert (QUI)	69
Fillmore Ter (BRO)	46
Filmore (SWY)	90
Filomena (EWY)	89
Filomena Rd (ROS)	31
Finley (ARL)	74
Fir Ave (WAL)	54
First (WRX)	32
First (MAL)	48
First (MED)	55
First (QUI)	69
First (MEL)	76
First (LEX)	73
First (WY)	88
First	
1-140 (CAM)	41
141-OUT (CAM)	42
First Ave (NH)	94
First Ave (WAL)	54
First Ave (SOM)	43
Firth Rd (ROS)	31
Fish Pier St & Rd	02210
Fisher (N)	92
Fisher Ave (BRO)	46
Fisher Ave (WEL)	81
Fisher Ave (NWH)	61
Fisher Ave (RXC)	20
Fisher Rd (ARL)	74
Fisher Rd (SWY)	90
Fisher Ter (EV)	49
Fiske (REV)	51
Fiske Ave (SOM)	45
Fiske Ave (EWY)	89
Fiske Ln (WES)	93
Fiske Pl (CAM)	39
Fiske Rd (WH)	81
Fiske Rd (LEX)	73
Fiske St & Ave (WAL)	54
Fiske Ter (ALL)	34
Fiske Wharf	09
Fitchburg (SOM)	43
Fitchburg (WAT)	72
Fitz Ter (CHE)	50
Fitz Henry Sq (REV)	51
Flagg (CAM)	38

Boston (Con.)   021

Flagg (WOL)	70
Flagg	18
Flagg Cir (WAL)	54
Flagg St Ct (CAM)	38
Flaherty Way (SB)	27
Flanders Rd (BEL)	78
Flavia (DOR)	22
Fleet (HP)	36
Fleet	
1-29 (ODD)	13
2-34 (EVEN)	13
31-OUT (ODD)	09
36-OUT (EVEN)	09
Fleming (MED)	55
Fleming Rd (MAL)	48
Fletcher (ROS)	31
Fletcher Ave (LEX)	73
Fletcher Rd (BEL)	78
Fletcher Rd (WH)	81
Fletcher Rd (N)	92
Fletcher Ter (WAT)	72
Flett Rd (WAV)	79
Flint (REV)	51
Flint (MAT)	26
Flint Ave (STO)	80
Flint Pl (SB)	27
Flint Rd (WAT)	72
Flint St & Ave (SOM)	45
Flintlock Rd (LEX)	73
Flood (WAL)	54
Flood Sq (SB)	27
Floral Ave (MAL)	48
Floral Cir (WAL)	54
Floral Pl (HP)	36
Floral St & Pl (NWH)	61
Florence (WOL)	70
Florence (MAL)	48
Florence (ROS)	31
Florence (EV)	49
Florence (CAM)	39
Florence	
1-50 (NCE)	59
51-OUT (CHH)	67
Florence Ave (REV)	51
Florence Ave & Ter (ARL)	74
Florence Cir (STO)	80
Florence Ct (NWV)	60
Florence Rd (WAL)	54
Florence St Park (MAL)	48
Florence St & Ave (MED)	55
Florence St & Ave (MEL)	76
Florence St & Ter (SOM)	45
Florence Ter (WAT)	72
Florian	
1-78 (ROS)	31
79-OUT (JP)	30
Florian Way (ROS)	31
Florida (DOR)	24
Floyd (DOR)	24
Floyd (WAL)	54
Floyd (WIN)	52
Floyd (REV)	51
Floyd (EV)	49
Flynt (NQ)	71
Foam (WIN)	52
Foam Ave (REV)	51
Foch (CAM)	40
Fogg Rd (SWY)	90
Foley (REV)	51
Foley (SOM)	45
Follen (CAM)	38

Follen Rd (LEX)	16
Follen Rd (LEX)	73
Follett (QUI)	69
Folsom (QUI)	69
Folsom (DOR)	25
Folsom (REV)	51
Folsom (ROS)	31
Folsom Ave (RXC)	20
Folsom Ct (MAL)	48
Food Mart Rd	18
Forbes (JP)	30
Forbes (CHE)	50
Forbes Rd (LEX)	73
Forbes Rd (MIL)	86
Forbes Rd (BRA)	84
Forbes Hill Rd (WOL)	70
Forbush Ave (QUI)	69
Ford (QUI)	69
Ford (REV)	51
Ford (EB)	28
Ford Rd (WAT)	72
Ford Rd (SWY)	90
Ford Ranch Rd (MIL)	86
Fordham (ARL)	74
Fordham Ct (JP)	30
Fordham Rd (ALL)	34
Fordham Rd (WNW)	65
Fore River Ave (NWY)	91
Forest (SWY)	90
Forest (MIL)	86
Forest (BRA)	85
Forest (N)	92
Forest (CHH)	67
Forest (ARL)	74
Forest (WAT)	72
Forest (MEL)	76
Forest (NWH)	61
Forest (STO)	80
Forest (MAL)	48
Forest (MFJ)	55
Forest	
1-27 (CAM)	40
1-167 (WH)	81
28-OUT (SOM)	43
168-249 (BP)	57
250-250 (WH)	81
251-OUT (BP)	57
Forest Ave (EV)	49
Forest Ave (AUB)	66
Forest Ave (WNW)	65
Forest Ave (QUI)	69
Forest Grv Rd (WAL)	54
Forest Pl (CHA)	29
Forest St & Cir (WAL)	54
Forest St & Ct (LEX)	73
Forest St & Pl (ROX)	19
Forest Hills St & Ave (JP)	30
Forestvale Rd (HP)	36
Forrest (WIN)	52
Forster (SOM)	45
Forsters Ct (CHA)	29
Forsyth	15
Forsyth (CHE)	50
Fort Ave (ROX)	19
Fort Ave Ter (ROX)	19
Fort St & Sq (QUI)	69
Fort Banks (WIN)	52
Fort Dawes (WIN)	52
Fort Heath (WIN)	52
Fort Hill Sq	10
Fort Hill Wharf	02210
Fort Point Rd (NWY)	91
Fortunato Dr (MED)	55

Forum Rd (QUI)	69
Foskett (WS)	44
Foss (MED)	55
Foss (CHA)	29
Fossdale Rd (DOR)	24
Foster (REV)	51
Foster (EV)	49
Foster (BRO)	46
Foster (QUI)	69
Foster (NWV)	60
Foster (ARL)	74
Foster Ln (MIL)	86
Foster Rd (BRA)	85
Foster Rd (LEX)	73
Foster Rd (BEL)	78
Foster St E & W (MEL)	76
Foster St & Ct	09
Foster St & Pl (CAM)	38
Foster St & Ter (BRI)	35
Foster St Ex (BRO)	46
Fosters Ct (MED)	55
Fosters Wharf	02210
Fottler Ave (LEX)	73
Fottler Rd (MAT)	26
Foundry (SB)	27
Foundry Ave (WAL)	54
Fountain (WAL)	54
Fountain (WNW)	65
Fountain (BRA)	85
Fountain Ave (SOM)	45
Fountain Pl	13
Fountain Rd (ARL)	74
Fountain St, Ct & Ter (MED)	55
Fountain St & Ln (SWY)	90
Fountain St, Pl & Sq (ROX)	19
Fountain Ter (CAM)	38
Fountain Hill (ROX)	19
Fourth (SB)	27
Fourth (MED)	55
Fourth (CHE)	50
Fourth (LEX)	73
Fourth Ave (WAL)	54
Fourth Ave (WY)	88
Fourth Ave (NH)	94
Fourth St Pl (SB)	27
Fowle (ROS)	31
Fowler (CAM)	39
Fowler (DOR)	21
Fowler (QUI)	69
Fowler Ave (REV)	51
Fox (DOR)	22
Fox Ln & Pl (NCE)	59
Fox Rd (WAL)	54
Fox Chase Ln (WES)	93
Fox Hill Ln (MIL)	86
Fox Hill Pl & Rd (NCE)	59
Fox Hill Rd (WH)	81
Fox Hill Rd (N)	92
Fox Point Rd (DOR)	25
Foxmeadow Ln (ARL)	74
Foye Ave (WY)	88
Framar Ln (WH)	81
Frances (NWH)	61
Frances Pl (CAM)	40
Frances Rd (LEX)	73
Francesca (WRX)	32
Francesca Ave (WS)	44
Francine Rd (BRA)	84
Francis (MIL)	87
Francis (N)	92
Francis (SOM)	43
Francis (WAL)	54
Francis (REV)	51

Boston (Con.)	021
Franclaire Dr (WRX)	32
Franconia (DOR)	22
Franey Rd (SOM)	45
Frank (NH)	94
Frank (WAT)	72
Frank Ave (REV)	51
Frank Rd (NWY)	91
Frankfort (EB)	28
Franklin (DOR)	22
Franklin	10
Franklin (WY)	88
Franklin (NH)	94
Franklin (MIL)	86
Franklin (BRA)	85
Franklin (WIN)	52
Franklin (ALL)	34
Franklin (EV)	49
Franklin (MED)	55
Franklin (WAT)	72
Franklin (BEL)	78
Franklin (NEW)	58
Franklin (ARL)	74
Franklin	
1-215 (STO) (ODD)	80
2-204 (STO) (EVEN)	80
206-OUT (STO) (EVEN)	76
217-1073 (MEL) (ODD)	76
1075-1075 (STO)	8C
1077-OUT (MEL) (ODD)	76
Franklin Ave & Ter (WOL)	70
Franklin Ct (DOR)	25
Franklin Gdns (DOR)	21
Franklin Park (JP)	30
Franklin Pl (ROS)	31
Franklin Pl (STO)	80
Franklin Rd (WH)	81
Franklin St & Ave (CHE)	50
Franklin St, Ave & Pl (REV)	51
Franklin St, Ave & Pl (SOM)	45
Franklin St & Ct (MAL)	48
Franklin St & Ct (BRO)	46
Franklin St & Pl (CAM)	39
Franklin St & Pl (QUI)	69
Franklin St & Ter (HP)	36
Franklin Ter (MEL)	76
Franklin Field (DOR)	24
Franklin Hill Ave (DOR)	24
Franklin Park Zoo (DOR)	21
Frano Ave (BRA)	85
Frawley	15
Frazer (DOR)	24
Frazer (HP)	36
Frazer Rd (ARL)	74
Freca Rd (QUI)	69
Fredana Rd (WAB)	68
Frederick (QUI)	69
Frederick (WAV)	79
Frederick (NWV)	60
Frederick (SB)	27
Frederick Ave (MED)	55
Frederick Park (N)	92
Frederick Rd (BRA)	85
Frederika (DOR)	24
Fredette Rd (NCE)	59
Fredith Rd (EWY)	89
Fredonia (DOR)	24
Freeland (MAT)	26
Freeman (DOR)	22
Freeman (AUB)	66
Freeman (ARL)	74
Freeman (WOL)	70

Freeman (BRO)	46
Freeman (REV)	51
Freeman Ave (EV)	49
Freeman Ave (WRX)	32
Freeman Pl	08
Freeman Pl (N)	92
Freemont (SWY)	90
Freemont (LEX)	73
Freemont Ter (WAL)	54
Freeport St & Way (DOR)	22
Fremont (MAT)	26
Fremont (WIN)	52
Fremont (WAL)	48
Fremont (SOM)	45
Fremont (NH)	94
Fremont Ave (CHE)	50
Fremont Ave (EV)	49
Fremont Ave (SOM)	45
Fremont Ave (ROX)	19
Fremont St & Ct (ARL)	74
French (NQ)	71
French (MAT)	26
French (SWY)	90
French Ave (BRA)	85
French Rd (WES)	93
French St & Ter (WAT)	72
French Ter (RXC)	20
French Bv (BRA)	85
Fresh Pond Ave, Ln & Pky (CAM)	38
Fresno (ROS)	31
Friend (REV)	51
Friend (WAL)	54
Friend (EWY)	89
Friend	14
Friendship Rd (MAT)	26
Frisbie Pl (CAM)	38
Front (CHE)	50
Front (CHA)	29
Front (BRA)	84
Front	
1-815 (WY)	88
816-OUT (SWY)	90
Frontage Rd	18
Frontenac (DOR)	24
Frost Rd	74
Frost Ave (MEL)	76
Frost Ave (DOR)	22
Frost Rd (BEL)	78
Frost St & Ter (CAM)	40
Frothingham (MIL)	87
Frothingham Ave (CHA)	29
Fruean Pl (DOR)	24
Fruit	14
Frye (REV)	51
Frye Rd (MED)	55
Fulbright (MED)	55
Fulda (ROX)	19
Fulkerson (CAM)	41
Fuller (EV)	49
Fuller (WAL)	54
Fuller (MAL)	48
Fuller (BRO)	46
Fuller (DOR)	24
Fuller (STO)	80
Fuller	
1-99 (WAB)	68
100-OUT (WNW)	65
Fuller Ave & Ter (WNW)	65
Fuller Pl (CAM)	38
Fuller Rd (WH)	81
Fuller Rd (WAT)	72
Fuller Rd (LEX)	73

Fuller Rd (NWY)	91
Fuller Rd (N)	92
Fuller Brook Rd (N)	92
Fuller Brook Rd (WEL)	81
Fullers Ln (MIL)	86
Fullerton	02215
Fulton (HP)	36
Fulton (MAL)	48
Fulton (MED)	55
Fulton Rd (LEX)	73
Fulton St & Pl	09
Fulton Spring Rd (MED)	55
Fulton Spring Rd Ext (MED)	55
Furber Ln (NCE)	59
Furbush Ave (WNW)	65
Furbush Rd (WRX)	32
Furnace Ave (QUI)	69
Furnace Brook Pky	
1-364 (QUI)	69
365-609 (WOL)	70
610-OUT (QUI)	69
Furness (REV)	51
Furnival Rd (JP)	30
G (SB)	27
Gaffney	02215
Gafford Ave (LEX)	73
Gage (N)	92
Gage Ave (REV)	51
Gail Rd (WES)	93
Gail Rd (NLF)	62
Gainsborough	15
Gale (MAL)	48
Gale (WAL)	54
Gale Ave (BRA)	84
Gale Rd (WY)	88
Gale Rd (BEL)	78
Galen (WAT)	72
Galen (MIL)	86
Galen (WAL)	54
Galena (ROX)	19
Gallivan Blvd	
1-705 (DOR) (ODD)	24
2-718 (DOR) (EVEN)	24
707-OUT (DOR) (ODD)	22
720-OUT (DOR) (EVEN)	22
Galty Ave (DOR)	24
Gambier (AUB)	66
Gammons Rd (WAB)	68
Gannett (DOR)	21
Gannett Rd (QUI)	69
Gannon Ct (WNW)	65
Garden (MEL)	76
Garden (BEL)	78
Garden (ARL)	74
Garden	14
Garden (MIL)	86
Garden (N)	92
Garden (MED)	55
Garden (EV)	49
Garden Ave (LEX)	73
Garden Cir, Ct & Ln (WAL)	54
Garden Ct (SOM)	43
Garden Ct St	13
Garden Park (BRA)	84
Garden Pl & Rd (WH)	81
Garden Rd (STO)	80
Garden Rd (NEW)	58
Garden St (CAM)	38
Garden St, Ct & Ter (CAM)	38
Garden St, Park & Ter (MAL)	48
Gardena (BRI)	35
Gardenside (ROS)	31
Gardiner Rd (QUI)	69

Boston (Con.)	021	Gay Rd (WAT)	72	Gibbs Ct (WAL)	54
		Gay Head (JP)	30	Gibbs Ct (CHA)	29
Gardner (NEW)	58	Gayland (DOR)	25	Gibson (DOR)	22
Gardner (ARL)	74	Gayland Rd (N)	92	Gibson (MAL)	48
Gardner (WAL)	54	Gaylord (DOR)	24	Gibson (MED)	55
Gardner (CHE)	50	Gellineau (MAL)	48	Gibson (N)	92
Gardner (ROX)	19	Gem Ave (BRI)	35	Gibson Rd (NWV)	60
Gardner (CHA)	29	Gene (DOR)	25	Gibson Rd (LEX)	73
Gardner Ct (EV)	49	General Putman Gdns (CAM)	39	Gibson St & Ter (CAM)	38
Gardner Rd (BRO)	46	Genesee (REV)	51	Gifford Pl (SB)	27
Gardner Rd (CAM)	39	Geneva (REV)	51	Gigante Dr (STO)	80
Gardner St & Ter (ALL)	32	Geneva (EB)	28	Gilbert (QUI)	69
Gardner St & Ter (ALL)	34	Geneva Ave		Gilbert (WAT)	72
Gardner Ter (BRA)	84	1-299 (DOR)	21	Gilbert (WNW)	65
Garey (EWY)	89	300-OUT (DOR)	22	Gilbert (WAL)	54
Garfield (N)	92	Geneva Rd (MEL)	76	Gilbert Ave (REV)	51
Garfield (CAM)	38	Genevieve Rd (EWY)	89	Gilbert Pl	02210
Garfield (QUI)	69	Genoa (REV)	52	Gilbert Rd (N)	92
Garfield (LEX)	73	George (WIN)	35	Gilbert Rd (EWY)	89
Garfield (BEL)	78	George (CAM)	40	Gilbert Rd (BEL)	78
Garfield (WAT)	72	George (SOM)	45	Gilbert St, Ct & Ter (MAL)	48
Garfield Ave (STO)	80	George (MED)	55	Gilboa Rd (ARL)	74
Garfield Ave (SOM)	45	George (EV)	49	Gile Rd (MIL)	86
Garfield Ave (CHE)	50	George (CHE)	50	Giles Park (SOM)	43
Garfield Ave (MED)	55	George (N)	92	Gilkey Ct (WAT)	72
Garfield Ave (REV)	51	George (BEL)	78	Gill Rd (WAV)	79
Garfield Ave (WY)	88	George (WAT)	72	Gill Rd	
Garfield Ave		George (ARL)	74	1-17 (WAT)	72
1-277 (HP) (ODD)	36	George (NEW)	58	18-OUT (WAL)	54
2-270 (HP) (EVEN)	36	George (STO)	80	Gillette Park (SB)	27
272-OUT (MIL) (EVEN)	86	George (MAT)	26	Gillooly Rd (CHE)	50
279-OUT (MIL) (ODD)	86	George (ROX)	19	Gilman (ROS)	31
Garfield Ave Ext (MIL)	86	George Ave (REV)	51	Gilman Rd (WAL)	54
Garfield Rd (MIL)	87	George Ln (BRO)	46	Gilman St, Sq & Ter (SOM)	45
Garfield Rd (MEL)	76	George Rd (WOL)	70	Gilmer (MAT)	26
Garfield Ter (MAL)	48	George St & Pl (MAL)	48	Gilmore (EV)	49
Garland (CHE)	50	George Aggott Rd (N)	92	Gilmore (CAM)	39
Garland (MEL)	76	George P Hassett Dr (MED)	55	Gilmore (NWY)	91
Garland Ave (MAL)	48	Georgeanna (BRA)	85	Gilmore (STO)	80
Garland Rd (NCE)	59	Georgetown Dr (HP)	36	Gilmore (WOL)	70
Garland St & Pl (EV)	49	Georgia (DOR)	21	Gilmore Rd (BEL)	78
Garner (NCE)	59	Gergia Rd (SWY)	90	Gilmore Ter (WRX)	32
Garner Rd (DOR)	22	Georgian Rd (WES)	93	Gilson Ave (MED)	55
Garnet (WAT)	72	Georgiana Rd (QUI)	69	Gilson Rd (WH)	81
Garnet (MAL)	48	Geraghty Ter (HP)	36	Gilson Rd (QUI)	69
Garnet (WRX)	32	Gerald Rd (BRI)	35	Gilson Ter (SOM)	43
Garrison (CHH)	67	Gerald Rd (STO)	80	Ginita (DOR)	22
Garrison	16	Gerald Rd (MIL)	86	Girard (MAL)	48
Garrison Ave (WS)	44	Geraldine Dr (WEL)	81	Girard Rd (STO)	80
Garrison Rd (BRO)	46	Geraldine Ln & Rd (BRA)	84	Girdlestone Rd (WIN)	52
Garrison Rd (BEL)	78	Gerard (ROX)	19	Glade Ave (JP)	30
Garrison Rd (WH)	81	Gerard Ct (WNW)	65	Gladeside Ave & Ter (MAT)	26
Garrison Rd (ARL)	74	Gerard Ter (LEX)	73	Gladstone (EB)	28
Garth Rd (WRX)	32	Germain Ave (QUI)	69	Gladstone (CAM)	40
Gartland (JP)	30	Germania (EV)	49	Gladstone (NQ)	71
Garvey (EV)	49	Germantown (QUI)	69	Gladstone St & Ter (EV)	49
Gary Rd (NH)	94	Gerrish (BRI)	35	Gladys (REV)	51
Gasbarri Ave (NCE)	59	Gerrish Ave (CHE)	50	Glastonbury Oval (WAB)	68
Gaskins Rd (MIL)	87	Gerry (CAM)	38	Glazer Rd (NCE)	59
Gaslight Dr (N)	90	Gerry Rd (CHH)	67	Gleason (WAT)	72
Gaston (MED)	55	Gerry St & Ct (STO)	80	Gleason (MAL)	48
Gaston (DOR)	21	Gerrys Landing (CAM)	38	Gleason (MED)	55
Gate House Rd (CHH)	67	Gertrose (ROX)	19	Gleason (DOR)	21
Gatehouse Ln (WES)	93	Gertrude (WAT)	72	Gleason Rd (LEX)	73
Gates (SB)	27	Gertrude Ave (QUI)	69	Gledhill Ave (EV)	49
Gatewood Rd	92	Gertrude Rd (WRX)	32	Glen (SOM)	45
Gavin (QUI)	69	Gibbens (SOM)	43	Glen (DOR)	25
Gavin Way (SB)	27	Gibbons (MEL)	76	Glen Ave (ARL)	74
Gay (RXC)	20	Gibbons (MIL)	87	Glen Ave & Rd (NCE)	59
Gay (QUI)	69	Gibbons Way (WY)	88	Glen Cir (WAL)	54
Gay (NWV)	60	Gibbs (QUI)	69	Glen Rd (BRO)	46
Gay (ARL)	74	Gibbs (NCE)	59	Glen Rd (EV)	49
Gay (N)	92	Gibbs (BRO)	46	Glen Rd (JP)	30

Boston (Con.)	021	Glide (DOR)	22	Gore (RXC)	20
		Glines Ave (ROX)	19	Gore Rd (REV)	51
Glen Rd (LEX)	73	Glines Ave (WY)	88	Gore St Pl (CAM)	41
Glen Rd (STO)	80	Globe (CHE)	50	Gorham (WS)	44
Glen Rd (BEL)	78	Gloria Rd (WRX)	32	Gorham (WAL)	54
Glen Rd (EWY)	89	Gloucester	15	Gorham (CAM)	38
Glen Rd		Gloucester (ARL)	74	Gorham (ALL)	34
1-189 (WH)	81	Glover Ave (NQ)	71	Gorham (ARL)	74
190-OUT (WES)	93	Glover Cir (WS)	44	Gorham Ave (STO)	80
Glen St, Ave & Rd (MEL)	76	Glover Ct (SB)	27	Gorham Ave (BRO)	46
Glen St & Ct (MAL)	48	Glover Pl (DOR)	22	Gorham Rd (MED)	55
Glen Cross Rd (WH)	81	Glover Rd (NH)	94	Gorham Rd (BEL)	78
Glen Gary Rd (NH)	94	Glynn Ter (QUI)	69	Gormans Ct & Ln (WAL)	54
Glen Rock Ave & Cir (MAL)	48	Goddard (QUI)	69	Goss Ave (MEL)	76
Glenarm (DOR)	21	Goddard (NWH)	61	Gothland (QUI)	69
Glenbrook (DOR)	25	Goddard Ave & Cir (BRO)	46	Gould (MEL)	76
Glenbrook Rd (WH)	81	Goden (BEL)	78	Gould (STO)	80
Glenburn Rd (ARL)	74	Godwin Pl (EV)	49	Gould (WOL)	70
Glenburne (DOR)	21	Goethe (WRX)	32	Gould (BRI)	35
Glenburnie Rd (ROS)	31	Goff (HP)	36	Gould (WRX)	32
Glencliff Rd (ROS)	31	Goff (NLF)	62	Gould (NH)	94
Glencoe (BRI)	35	Goffe Rd (LEX)	73	Gould Ave (SOM)	43
Glencoe Pl (QUI)	69	Gold (SB)	27	Gould Ave & Ter (MAL)	48
Glendale (REV)	51	Gold Star Ct, Pl & Rd (CAM)	40	Gould Rd (ARL)	74
Glendale (DOR)	25	Golden Ave (ARL)	74	Gould Rd (WAB)	68
Glendale (WY)	88	Golden Ave & Ct (MED)	55	Gould Rd (LEX)	73
Glendale Ave (MAL)	48	Golden Age Blvd & Dr (WIN)	52	Gouldville Ter (DOR)	25
Glendale Ave (WS)	44	Golden Age Cir (EV)	49	Gourley Rd (MED)	55
Glendale Ave (MEL)	76	Golden Ball Rd (WES)	93	Gove (EB)	28
Glendale Rd (BEL)	78	Goldencrest Ave (WAL)	54	Government Park (WIN)	52
Glendale Rd (QUI)	69	Goldie (REV)	51	Governor Rd (ARL)	74
Glendale Rd (STO)	80	Goldie (WAT)	72	Governor Rd (STO)	80
Glendale Rd (NCE)	59	Goldsmith Ave (MED)	55	Governor Belcher Ln (MIL)	86
Glendale Rd (N)	92	Goldsmith St & Pl (JP)	30	Governor Stoughton Ln (MIL)	86
Glendale Rd (MIL)	86	Gooch (MEL)	76	Governor Winthrop Ln (SWY)	90
Glendale Rd (BRA)	85	Goodale Rd (MAT)	26	Governor Winthrop Rd (SOM)	45
Glendale St, Ave, Pl & Ter		Goodenough (BRI)	35	Governors Ave (MED)	55
(EV)	49	Goodenough Rd (CHH)	67	Governors Rd	
Glendening Ter (SWY)	90	Goodhue (MAL)	48	1-137 (MIL) (ODD)	86
Glendon (EB)	28	Goodman Rd (CAM)	39	2-140 (MIL) (EVEN)	86
Glendoon Rd (N)	92	Goodrich Rd (JP)	30	139-OUT (QUI) (ODD)	69
Glendower Rd (ROS)	31	Goodridge Aly & Ct	13	142-OUT (QUI) (EVEN)	69
Glendower Rd (MEL)	76	Goodway Rd (JP)	30	Gowell Ln (WES)	93
Glenellen Rd (WRX)	32	Goodwin Ave (MAL)	48	Grace (SWY)	90
Glenfield E (WES)	93	Goodwin Ave (REV)	51	Grace (MAL)	48
Glenham (WRX)	32	Goodwin Ct (SB)	27	Grace (DOR)	24
Glenhaven Rd (WRX)	32	Goodwin Pl	14	Grace Ct (SB)	27
Glenhill Rd (MAT)	26	Goodwin Pl (BRO)	46	Grace Rd (MED)	55
Glenland Rd (CHH)	67	Goodwin Pl (MED)	55	Grace Rd (BRA)	85
Glenley Ter (BRI)	35	Goodwin Pl & Rd (LEX)	73	Grace Rd (QUI)	69
Glenmere Ave (MAL)	48	Goodyear Ave (MEL)	76	Grace St & Rd (NCE)	59
Glenmont Rd (BRI)	35	Gordon (NQ)	71	Gracewood Park (CAM)	38
Glenmore (MAT)	26	Gordon (QUI)	69	Gracewood Rd (STO)	80
Glenmore Ter (NWH)	61	Gordon (MAL)	48	Grady Ct (EB)	28
Glenn Ter (CAM)	39	Gordon (JP)	30	Graffam Ct (MAL)	48
Glenoe Rd (CHH)	67	Gordon (WS)	44	Grafton (DOR)	25
Glenrose Ave (BRA)	84	Gordon (WAL)	54	Grafton (NCE)	59
Glenrose Rd (DOR)	24	Gordon		Grafton (QUI)	69
Glenside Ave (JP)	30	1-75 (ALL)	34	Grafton (ARL)	74
Glenvale Ter (JP)	30	76-OUT (BRI)	35	Grafton Ave (MIL)	86
Glenview Rd (QUI)	69	Gordon Ave (HP)	36	Graham (SWY)	90
Glenville Ave & Ter (ALL)	34	Gordon Pl (CAM)	39	Graham Ct (MAL)	48
Glenway (DOR)	21	Gordon Pl (DOR)	22	Graham Rd (LEX)	73
		Gordon Rd (MED)	55	Graham St & Ter (QUI)	69
Glenwood Ave (CAM)	39	Gordon Rd (N)	92	Graham Ter (WRX)	32
Glenwood Ave (MED)	55	Gordon Rd (MIL)	86	Grahm	02215
Glenwood Ave (NCE)	59	Gordon Rd (BRA)	84	Grampian Way (WY)	88
Glenwood Ave (WH)	81	Gordon Rd (WAB)	68	Grampian Way (DOR)	25
Glenwood Ave & Pl (HP)	36	Gordon Rd (ARL)	74	Granada Ave (ROS)	31
Glenwood Rd (SOM)	45	Gordon Ter (BEL)	78	Granada Park (ROX)	19
Glenwood Rd (N)	92	Gordon Ter (NEW)	58	Granby	02215
Glenwood St, Pl & Ter (ROX)	19	Gore (CAM)	41	Grand Ave (REV)	51
Glenwood St & Ter (MAL)	48	Gore (WAL)	54	Grand Junction Wharf (EB)	28
Glenwood Way (QUI)	69				

Boston (Con.)   021

Grand View Ave (WIN) 52
Grand View Ave (REV) 51
Grand View Ave (MAL) 48
Grand View Ave (MED) 55
Grand View Ave (SOM) 43
Grand View Ave & Ter (WOL) 70
Grandview (MEL) 76
Grandview (ROS) 31
Grandview Ave (WAT) 72
Grandview Ave (LEX) 73
Grandview Ave (STO) 80
Grandview Rd (ARL) 74
Grandview Rd (CHE) 50
Grandview Rd (NWY) 91
Granfield Ave (ROS) 31
Granger (WOL) 70
Granger St & Pl (DOR) 22
Granite (WEL) 81
Granite (MEL) 76
Granite (QUI) 69
Granite (SOM) 43
Granite (CAM) 39
Granite (MAL) 48
Granite (WY) 88
Granite
   1-549 (BRA) 84
   550-OUT (BRA) 85
Granite Ave (DOR) 24
Granite Ave & Pl (MIL) 86
Granite Rd (MED) 55
Grannison Rd (WES) 93
Grant (N) 92
Grant (EWY) 89
Grant (SOM) 45
Grant (CAM) 38
Grant (DOR) 25
Grant (STO) 80
Grant (WNW) 65
Grant Ave (WH) 81
Grant Ave (WAV) 79
Grant Ave (WAT) 72
Grant Ave (NCE) 59
Grant Ave (MED) 55
Grant Pl (QUI) 69
Grant Pl (DOR) 24
Grant Rd (DOR) 21
Grant Rd (MAL) 48
Grant St, Ave & Pl (WAL) 54
Grant St & Pl (LEX) 73
Grantland Rd (WH) 81
Grantley (HP) 36
Granton Park (ARL) 74
Grants Ct (CHA) 29
Granville (DOR) 24
Granville (QUI) 69
Granville Ave (MED) 55
Granville Ave & Pl (MAL) 48
Granville Rd (CAM) 38
Grape (MAL) 48
Grapevine Ave (LEX) 73
Grasmere (NEW) 58
Grasmere Rd (NH) 94
Grassland (LEX) 73
Grassmere Rd (CHH) 67
Grassmere Rd (HP) 36
Graves Rd (REV) 51
Gray (CAM) 38
Gray (CHA) 29
Gray 16
Gray Gdns E & W (CAM) 38
Gray Rd (MEL) 76

Gray St & Cir (ARL) 74
Gray Birch Ter (NWV) 60
Gray Cliff Rd (NCE) 59
Gray Dale Cir (AUB) 66
Grayfield Ave (WRX) 32
Graylynn Rd (NCE) 59
Graymore Rd (WAL) 54
Grayson (DOR) 24
Grayson Ln (NLF) 62
Graystone Rd (STO) 80
Great Hill Dr (NWY) 91
Great Meadow Rd (NCE) 59
Great Plain Ave (WH) 81
Great Plain Ave & Ter (N) 92
Great Pond Rd (SWY) 90
Great Republic Ave (SWY) 90
Great Rock Rd (LEX) 73
Greaton Rd (WRX) 32
Greeley Cir (ARL) 74
Greeleys Ct (WAL) 54
Green (WAL) 54
Green (JP) 30
Green (REV) 51
Green (BRO) 46
Green (CAM) 39
Green (CHE) 50
Green (EV) 49
Green (STO) 80
Green (MEL) 76
Green (WOL) 70
Green (WAT) 72
Green (N) 92
Green (MIL) 86
Green (CHA) 29
Green
   1-456 (NWY) 91
   457-OUT (EWY) 89
Green Ln (WES) 93
Green Ln (NQ) 71
Green Ln (LEX) 73
Green Rd (MED) 55
Green St Ter (WAT) 72
Green St, Ct & Park (NEW) 58
Green Hill (DOR) 22
Green Hill Rd (BRO) 46
Green Hollow Ln (MIL) 86
Green River Way (WAT) 72
Greenbaum (SB) 27
Greenbrier (DOR) 24
Greenbrook Rd (HP) 36
Greendale Ave
   1-379 (NH) 94
   380-OUT (N) 92
Greendale Rd (MAT) 26
Greendale Ter (N) 92
Greene (SOM) 43
Greenfield Rd (MAT) 26
Greenhalge (MED) 55
Greenhalge Ave (EV) 49
Greenheys (DOR) 21
Greenlawn Ave (NCE) 59
Greenlawn Ave (WH) 81
Greenleaf (QUI) 69
Greenleaf 15
Greenleaf (MAL) 48
Greenleaf Ave (MED) 55
Greenleaf Pl (MEL) 76
Greenleaf Rd (MIL) 87
Greenley Pl (JP) 30
Greenmount (DOR) 25
Greenock (DOR) 24
Greenough (NH) 94

Greenough (WNW) 65
Greenough Ave (CAM) 39
Greenough Ave & Park (JP) 30
Greenough Ln 13
Greenough St & Cir (BRO) 46
Greens Block (CHA) 29
Greensbrook Way (BEL) 78
Greentree Ln (REV) 51
Greentree Ln (SWY) 90
Greenvale Ave (WY) 88
Greenview (QUI) 69
Greenview Ave (JP) 30
Greenview Rd (STO) 80
Greenville (SOM) 43
Greenville (ROX) 19
Greenway Cir (STO) 80
Greenway Ct (BRO) 46
Greenwich (DOR) 22
Greenwich Park 18
Greenwich St & Ct (RXC) 20
Greenwood (DOR) 21
Greenwood (MED) 55
Greenwood (MEL) 76
Greenwood (NCE) 59
Greenwood (LEX) 73
Greenwood Ave (WNW) 65
Greenwood Ave (WOL) 70
Greenwood Ave (EWY) 89
Greenwood Ave (N) 92
Greenwood Ave, Cir & Sq
   (HP) 36
Greenwood Ln (WAL) 54
Greenwood Park (DOR) 22
Greenwood Rd (WH) 81
Greenwood Rd (ARL) 74
Greenwood St, Ct & Ter
   (MAL) 48
Greenwood Ter (SOM) 43
Greer (WAL) 54
Gregory (WAL) 54
Grenville Rd (WAT) 72
Grenwold Rd (QUI) 69
Gretter Rd (ROS) 31
Grew Ave (ROS) 31
Grew Hill Rd (ROS) 31
Greybirch Cir & Park (BEL) 78
Greycliff Rd (BRI) 35
Greycliff Rd (EWY) 89
Greylock Rd (ALL) 34
Greylock Rd (WH) 81
Greylock Rd (NWV) 60
Greymere Rd (BRI) 35
Greystone (QUI) 69
Greystone Rd (MEL) 76
Greystone Rd (MAL) 48
Gridley (QUI) 69
Grieco A J Ter (EB) 28
Griffin (REV) 51
Griffin Ter (SWY) 90
Griffin Way (CHE) 50
Griggs Ln (MIL) 87
Griggs Rd & Ter (BRO) 46
Griggs St & Pl (ALL) 34
Grimes (SB) 27
Grimes Rd (LEX) 73
Grimshaw (MAL) 48
Grinnell (RXC) 20
Griswold (CAM) 38
Griswold (EV) 49
Griswold (REV) 51
Grogan Ave (QUI) 69
Groman Pl (MAL) 48
Groom (DOR) 25

Boston (Con.)   621

Grossman (QUI).................. 69
Grosvenor Pl (ROX)............. 19
Grosvenor Rd (BEL)............. 78
Grosvenor Rd (WAL)............. 54
Grosvenor Rd (N).............. 92
Groton (WOL).................. 70
Groton......................... 18
Grotto Glen Rd (JP)........... 30
Grouse (WRX).................. 32
Grove (MAL)................... 48
Grove (CHE).................. 50
Grove (WS)................... 44
Grove (MED)................... 55
Grove......................... 14
Grove (WAT).................. 72
Grove (QUI).................. 69
Grove (LEX).................. 73
Grove (ARL).................. 74
Grove (CHH).................. 67
Grove (MIL).................. 87
Grove (EWY).................. 89
Grove
  1-147 (BEL) (ODB)........... 78
  1-302 (AUB)................. 66
  1-379 (WEL)................. 81
  2-OUT (BEL) (EVEN)......... 78
  149-OUT (CAM) (ODD)........ 38
  303-OUT (NLF).............. 62
  380-418 (N)................ 92
  419-419 (WEL).............. 81
  420-OUT (N)................ 92
Grove Ave (CAM).............. 39
Grove St Pl (ARL)............ 74
Grove St & Cir (BRA)......... 85
Grove St & Pl (MEL).......... 76
Grove St & Rd (WAL).......... 54
Grove St & Ter (WRX)......... 32
Grove Hill Ave & Park (NWW).. 2
Groveland (AUB).............. 66
Groveland (MAT).............. 26
Groveland Ave (SWY).......... 90
Groveland Rd (MEL)........... 76
Grovenor Rd (JP)............. 30
Grover (EV).................. 49
Grover (MAL)................. 48
Grover (REV)................. 51
Grover Ave (ROS)............. 31
Grover Rd (MED).............. 55
Grover Rd Ext (MED).......... 55
Grovers Ave (WIN)............ 24
Grozier Rd (CAM)............. 38
Guam Rd (CHE)................ 50
Guernsey (ROS)............... 31
Guest (BRI).................. 35
Guild (MED).................. 55
Guild (QUI).................. 69
Guild Rd (NH)................ 94
Guild St & Row (ROX)......... 19
Guilford (ALL)............... 14
Guilford Rd (MIL)............ 86
Guinan (WAL)................. 54
Gulliver (MIL)............... 86
Gun Club La (WES)............ 93
Gun Hill (MIL)............... 86
Gurney (CAM)................. 38
Gurney (RXC)................. 20
Gussie Ter (SOM)............. 43
Gustin (SB).................. 27
Gwinnett (HP)................ 36
Gypsy Trl (WES).............. 93
H (SB)....................... 27

H St Pl (SB)................. 27
Hackensack Cir, Ct, Rd & Ter
  (CHH)...................... 67
Hadassah Way................. 16
Haddon (REV)................. 51
Hadley (CAM)................. 40
Hadley (MAL)................. 48
Hadley (EWY)................. 89
Hadley Ct (SOM).............. 45
Hadley Ct (EV)............... 49
Hadley Ct (ARL).............. 74
Hadley Rd (LEX).............. 73
Hadley St & Pl (MED)......... 55
Hadwin Way (ROS)............. 31
Hagar (JP)................... 30
Hagar (WAL).................. 54
Hagar Rd (NLF)............... 62
Hagars La (WAL).............. 54
Hagen Rd (NCE)............... 59
Hagman Rd (WIN).............. 52
Haines (MED)................. 55
Haith (REV).................. 51
Halborn (MAT)................ 26
Halcyon Rd (NCE)............. 59
Hale (NLF)................... 64
Hale (HP).................... 36
Hale (EWY)................... 89
Hale Ave (WIN)............... 52
Hale Ave (MED)............... 55
Haley (ROX).................. 19
Haley Rd (BRA)............... 84
Half Moon (DOR).............. 25
Halford Rd (WRX)............. 32
Halifax (JP)................. 30
Hall (JP).................... 30
Hall (REV)................... 51
Hall (MAL)................... 48
Hall Ave (EV)................ 49
Hall Ave (BRA)............... 84
Hall Ave (WAT)............... 72
Hall Pl (QUI)................ 69
Hall Pl (SB)................. 27
Hall Rd (STO)................ 80
Hall Rd (BRO)................ 46
Hall St Pl (REV)............. 51
Hall St & Ave (MED).......... 55
Hall St & Ave (WS)........... 44
Hall St & Pl (WAL)........... 54
Hallam (DOR)................. 25
Halleck (RXC)................ 20
Hallen Ave (MIL)............. 86
Hallet
  1-35 (DOR)................. 22
  36-OUT (DOR)............... 24
Hallet Sq (DOR).............. 24
Hallet Hill Rd (WES)......... 93
Hallet-Davis (DOR)........... 24
Halliday (ROS)............... 31
Hallowell (MAT).............. 26
Hallron (HP)................. 36
Hallron Rd (NLF)............. 62
Hallwood Rd (CHH)............ 67
Halsey Ave (WEL)............. 81
Halsey Rd (HP)............... 36
Hamblin (LEX)................ 73
Hamblin Rd (WAL)............. 54
Hamden Cir (WOL)............. 70
Hamilton (WOL)............... 70
Hamilton (NLF)............... 62
Hamilton (HP)................ 36
Hamilton (CAM).............. 39
Hamilton (MED)............... 55
Hamilton (EV)................ 49

Hamilton (BRA)............... 84
Hamilton
  1-160 (DOR)................ 25
  161-OUT (DOR).............. 22
Hamilton Ave (NQ)............ 71
Hamilton Pl (NH)............. 94
Hamilton Pl................. 08
Hamilton Rd (LEX)............ 73
Hamilton Rd (WH)............. 81
Hamilton Rd (ARL)............ 74
Hamilton Rd (BEL)............ 78
Hamilton Rd (WS)............. 44
Hamilton Rd (WAL)............ 54
Hamilton Rd (BRO)............ 46
Hamlet (SOM)................. 43
Hamlet (ARL)................. 74
Hamlet (NCE)................. 59
Hamlet (DOR)................. 25
Hamlet Pl (MAL).............. 48
Hamlin (CAM)................. 41
Hamlin (SB).................. 27
Hamlin Ave (MED)............. 55
Hamlin La (N)................ 92
Hamlin Rd (NCE).............. 59
Hammel Pl (CHH).............. 67
Hammer (WAL)................. 54
Hammett (RXC)................ 20
Hammond (WAL)................ 54
Hammond (SOM)................ 43
Hammond (CAM)................ 38
Hammond (CHH)................ 67
Hammond Ct (QUI)............. 69
Hammond Pl (MED)............. 55
Hammond Rd (BEL)............. 78
Hammond St & Ter (RXC)....... 20
Hammond Pond Pky (CHH)....... 67
Hammondswood Rd (CHH)........ 67
Hampden (WEL)................ 81
Hampden (ROX)................ 19
Hampden Ter (NCE)............ 59
Hampshire (WWW).............. 65
Hampshire (RXC).............. 20
Hampshire (EV)............... 49
Hampshire Rd (WH)............ 81
Hampshire St, Ct & Pl
  (CAM)...................... 39
Hampstead La & Rd (JP)....... 30
Hampton Ave (NH)............. 94
Hampton Rd (MEL)............. 76
Hancock (MEL)................ 76
Hancock (STO)................ 80
Hancock (AUB)................ 66
Hancock (ARL)................ 74
Hancock (WAT)................ 72
Hancock (WY)................. 88
Hancock (WS)................. 44
Hancock (CHE)................ 50
Hancock (REV)................ 51
Hancock (DOR)................ 25
Hancock......................14
Hancock
  1-487 (N).................. 71
  488-985 (WOL).............. 70
  986-OUT (QUI).............. 69
Hancock Ave (NCE)............ 59
Hancock Ct (QUI)............. 69
Hancock Rd (WES)............. 93
Hancock Rd (BRO)............. 46
Hancock St & Ave (BRA)....... 85
Hancock St & Ave (LEX)....... 73
Hancock St, Ave & Ct (MED)... 55
Hancock St, Park & Pl (CAM).. 39
Hancock St, Park & Ter (EV).. 49

Boston (Con.) 021

Hancock St & Rd (MAL) 48
Hancock St & Rd (N) 92
Hancock St & Sq (CHA) 29
Hancock Ter (WOL) 70

Hancock Vill (CHH) 67
Hanford Rd (STO) 80
Hanian Dr (EWY) 89
Hanna (QUI) 69
Hannon (DOR) 24
Hano (ALL) 34
Hanover (MAL) 48
Hanover (WY) 88
Hanover
  1-209 (ODD) 08
  2-196 (EVEN) 08
  198-OUT (EVEN) 13
  211-OUT (ODD) 13
Hanover Ave 09
Hansborough (DOR) 24
Hansford Pl (ROX) 19
Hanson 18
Hanson Ave (LEX) 73
Hanson Rd (NCE) 59
Hanson Rd (WAL) 54
Hanson St & Ave (SOM) 43
Harbell (LEX) 73
Harbell Ter (DOR) 22
Harbor 02210
Harbor View (DOR) 25
Harbor View (HQ) 71
Harbor View Ave (HWY) 91
Harbor View Ave (WIN) 52
Harbor View Park & Rd (MIL) .. 86
Harbor Villa Ave (BRA) 84
Harcourt 16
Hardan Rd (WS) 44
Harding (CAM) 41
Harding (SOM) 43
Harding (WOL) 70
Harding (WRW) 65
Harding Ave (BEL) 78
Harding Ave (WAL) 54
Harding Ave (MAL) 48
Harding Ave (EV) 49
Harding Ave (BRA) 84
Harding Ave (WY) 88
Harding Ct & Rd (MEL) 76
Harding Rd (LEX) 73
Harding Rd (N) 92
Harding Rd (ROS) 31
Hardwick (CAM) 41
Hardwick Rd (QUI) 69
Hardwick St & Ter (BRI) 35
Hardy (WAL) 54
Hardy (SB) 27
Hardy Ave (WAT) 72
Hardy Rd (WEL) 81
Hardy Pond Rd (WAL) 54
Hargrave Cir (NWH) 61
Harkins (QUI) 69
Harland (MIL) 86
Harland Rd (WY) 88
Harland Rd (WAL) 54
Harlem (DOR) 21
Harlem Rd (NWY) 91
Harley (DOR) 24
Harley Ave & Ct (EV) 49
Harlow (ARL) 25
Harlow (ARL) 74
Harmon (MAT) 26
Harmon Rd (WAL) 54

Harmony (EB) 28
Harnden Ave (WAT) 72
Harnden Rd (MAL) 48
Harold (SOM) 43
Harold (ARL) 74
Harold (MEL) 76
Harold (MIL) 87
Harold
  1-88 (ROX) 19
  89-OUT (DOR) 21
Harold Park (ROX) 19
Harold St & Rd (MED) 55
Harold Ter (WRW) 65
Harriet (BRI) 35
Harriet Ave (NQ) 71
Harriett Ave (WAV) 79
Harrington (WAT) 72
Harrington (NWV) 60
Harrington Ave (QUI) 69
Harrington Ave (ROX) 19
Harrington Cir (WY) 88
Harrington Rd (LEX) 73
Harrington Rd (CAM) 40
Harrington Rd (WAL) 54
Harrington St & Ave (REV) 51
Harrington Ter (MED) 55
Harris (REV) 51
Harris (WAL) 54
Harris (MAL) 48
Harris (BRO) 46
Harris (QUI) 69
Harris (WAV) 79
Harris 09
Harris
  1-35 (SOM) (ODD) 43
  2-30 (CAM) (EVEN) 40
  32-OUT (SOM) (EVEN) 43
  37-37 (CAM) 40
  39-OUT (SOM) (ODD) 43
Harris Ave (N) 92
Harris Ave (WH) 81
Harris Ave (EV) 49
Harris Ave (JP) 30
Harris Cir (ARL) 74
Harris Rd (WNW) 65
Harris Rd (MED) 55
Harrishof
  1-147 (DOR) 21
  148-OUT (ROX) 19
Harrison (MED) 55
Harrison (ROS) 31
Harrison (BRO) 46
Harrison (SOM) 43
Harrison (MEL) 76
Harrison (QUI) 69
Harrison (NWH) 61
Harrison Ave (CAM) 40
Harrison Ave (EV) 49
Harrison Ave (BRA) 84
Harrison Ave
  1-291 11
  292-960 18
  961-OUT (ROX) 19
Harrison Ave Ext 11
Harrison Park (DOR) 22
Harrison Rd (WS) 44
Harrow (DOR) 25
Hart (BRO) 46
Hart Ave (WY) 88
Hart Pl (SB) 27
Hartford (NWH) 61
Hartford Pl (REV) 51
Hartford Rd (ARL) 74

Hartford St, Ct & Ter (DOR) ... 25
Hartford St & Pl 10
Hartland (DOR) 25
Hartlawn Rd (WRX) 32
Hartley Rd (BEL) 78
Hartley Ter (ALL) 34
Hartman Rd (NCE) 59
Hartshorn St & Ave (MAL) 48
Hartwell (DOR) 21
Hartwell Ave (LEX) 73
Hartwell St & Pl (WAL) 54
Harvard (MAL) 48
Harvard (WIN) 52
Harvard (EV) 49
Harvard (CHE) 50
Harvard (MEL) 76
Harvard (ARL) 74
Harvard (WEL) 81
Harvard 11
Harvard (WY) 88
Harvard
  1-51 (CAM) 42
  1-100 (NQ) 71
  1-499 (DOR) 24
  52-344 (CAM) (EVEN) 39
  53-339 (CAM) (ODD) 39
  101-OUT (WOL) 70
  341-OUT (CAM) (ODD) 38
  346-OUT (CAM) (EVEN) 38
  500-OUT (MAT) 26
Harvard Ave (DOR) 21
Harvard Ave & Pl (HP) 36
Harvard Ave & Ter (ALL) 34
Harvard Park (DOR) 24
Harvard Rd (BEL) 78
Harvard Sq (CAM) 38
Harvard St, Ave, Ct, Pl & Sq
  (BRO) 46
Harvard St, Ave & Ter (MED) .. 55
Harvard St & Cir (NWV) 60
Harvard St & Pl (WAL) 54
Harvard St & Pl (SOM) 43
Harvard St, Pl & Sq (CHA) 29
Harvard Way Ext (SF) 63
Harvest St & Ter (DOR) 25
Harvester (ALL) 34
Harvey (CAM) 40
Harvey (EV) 49
Harvey Pl (WNW) 65
Harvey Steel Rd (ALL) 34
Harveys Ln (QUI) 69
Harwell Dr (CAM) 41
Harwich 16
Harwich (CHH) 67
Harwood (DOR) 24
Hasey (REV) 51
Haskell (CAM) 40
Haskell (A.L) 34
Haskell (MEL) 76
Haskell (LEX) 73
Haskell Ave (REV) 51
Haskell Ave (EV) 49
Haskins (RXC) 20
Haskins Ct (MAL) 48
Haslet (ROS) 31
Hassett George P Dr (MED) ... 55
Hastings (WRX) 32
Hastings (WH) 81
Hastings Ln (MED) 55
Hastings Rd (LEX) 73
Hastings Rd (BEL) 78
Hastings Sq (CAM) 39
Hastings St & Ave (WAL) 54

Boston (Con.) 021

Hatch (EV) 49
Hatch (SB) 27
Hatch Rd (MED) 55
Hatfield Rd (WRW) 65
Hathaway (JP) 30
Hathaway Rd (WRW) 02210
Hathaway Cir (ARL) 74
Hathaway Rd (LEX) 73
Hatherly Rd (WOL) 70
Hatherly Rd (WAL) 54
Hatherly Rd (BRI) 35
Hathon Sq (CHA) 29
Hathorn (SOM) 45
Hauman (REV) 51
Hautevale (ROS) 31
Havana (ROS) 31
Havelock (MAL) 48
Havelock (DOR) 24
Haven 18
Haven Rd (WH) 81
Haven Rd (BRA) 84
Haverford (JP) 30
Haverhill (CHA) 29
Haverhill Pl (MEL) 76
Havey (ROS) 31
Haviland (WOL) 70
Haviland 15
Havre St & Ct (EB) 28
Hawes 09
Hawes (BRO) 46
Hawes (REV) 51
Hawes Ave (MEL) 76
Hawkins (SOM) 43
Hawkins 14
Hawkins (EWY) 89
Hawley Rd (MEL) 76
Hawley St & Pl 10
Hawthorn (WAV) 79
Hawthorn (NEW) 58
Hawthorn (CAM) 38
Hawthorn (MED) 55
Hawthorn (EV) 49
Hawthorn Rd (BRO) 46
Hawthorn Rd (BRA) 84
Hawthorne (EWY) 89
Hawthorne (MAL) 48
Hawthorne (WS) 44
Hawthorne (MEL) 76
Hawthorne (WAT) 72
Hawthorne (QUI) 69
Hawthorne (ROX) 19
Hawthorne Ave (ARL) 74
Hawthorne Ave (AUB) 66
Hawthorne Ave (WRO) 52
Hawthorne Ave (N) 92
Hawthorne Ln (WES) 93
Hawthorne Park (CAM) 38
Hawthorne Pl 14
Hawthorne Rd (WAL) 54
Hawthorne Rd (MIL) 87
Hawthorne Rd (WH) 81
Hawthorne Rd (LEX) 73
Hawthorne St & Ct (CHE) 50
Hawthorne St & Ter (ROS) 31
Hay Rd (BEL) 78
Hay Rd (NCE) 59
Hayden (QUI) 69
Hayden (RXC) ....
Hayden Ave (LEX) 73
Hayden Pl (WH) 81
Hayden Rd (BRO) 46

Hayden Ter (SOM) 43
Hayden (ROS) 31
Hayes (CAM) 39
Hayes (ARL) 74
Hayes Ave (REV) 51
Hayes Ave & Ln (LEX) 73
Hayes Rd (ROS) 31
Haymarket Pl 11
Haymarket Sq 15
Haynes (EB) 28
Haynes Park (ROX) 19
Haynes Rd (NCE) 59
Hays Rd (WAL) 54
Hayward (CAM) 42
Hayward (MAL) 48
Hayward (NQ) 92
Hayward (BRA) 84
Hayward Ave (LEX) 73
Hayward Pl 11
Hazel (WAT) 72
Hazel (MIL) 86
Hazel (WAL) 54
Hazel (CAM) 38
Hazel Ln (NH) 94
Hazel Park (EV) 49
Hazel Park (ROX) 11
Hazel Rd (MED) 55
Hazel Rd (LEX) 73
Hazel Ter (ARL) 74
Hazelhurst Ave (WRW) 65
Hazelmere Rd (ROS) 31
Hazelton (MAT) 26
Hazelton Ave (N) 92
Hazelton Rd (NCE) 59
Hazelwood (ROX) 14
Hazelwood (MAL) 48
Hazelwood Ave (WRW) 65
Headland Way (MED) 30
Healey (CAM) 38
Healy Rd (WY) 88
Heard (CHE) 50
Heard (WAL) 54
Heard Rd (ARL) 74
Hearn (WAT) 72
Heath (NQ) 71
Heath (EV) 49
Heath (SOM) 45
Heath (N) 92
Heath
   1-99 (BRO) 46
   100-OUT (CHH) 67
Heath Ave (BRO) 46
Heath Ct (CHH) 67
Heath Pl (MAL) 48
Heath Rd (ARL) 74
Heath St & Sq (JP) 30
Heath Hill (BRO) 46
Heathcote (ROS) 31
Heather Ln (SWY) 90
Heather Rd (WAT) 72
Heatherland Rd (WRW) 61
Hebron (MAT) 26
Heckle (WH) 81
Hecla (DOR) 22
Hedge Rd (BRO) 46
Hedlund Ave (BRA) 84
Hefferan (ALL) 34
Held Cir (MED) 55
Heldun (WRX) 32
Helen (WAL) 54
Helen 24
Helen Rd (BRA) 84
Helen Rd (N) 92

Helena Rd (DOR) 22
Helene (QUI) 69
Helene Rd (WAB) 68
Helvic Rd (CHH) 67
Hemenway 15
Hemenway Rd (MEL) 76
Hemenway Ave & Ct (MAL) 48
Hemlock (WH) 81
Hemlock (ARL) 74
Hemlock (N) 92
Hemlock Dr (MIL) 86
Hemlock Rd (BRA) 85
Hemlock Rd (WES) 93
Hemlock Rd (NUF) 64
Hemlock Rd (WRX) 32
Hemlock Rd (CAM) 38
Hemlock Ter (WAL) 54
Hemman (ROS) 31
Henchman 13
Henderson (SOM) 45
Henderson (EV) 49
Henderson (ARL) 74
Henderson (N) 92
Henderson Ave (SB) 27
Henderson Rd (WY) 88
Henderson Rd (LEX) 73
Hendry (DOR) 22
Henley (CHA) 29
Henley (MED) 55
Henrici (MAT) 26
Henry (EB) 28
Henry (MED) 55
Henry (EV) 49
Henry (BRO) 46
Henry (CAM) 39
Henry (REV) 51
Henry (ARL) 74
Henry (BEL) 78
Henry (NQ) 71
Henry Ave (MEL) 76
Henry Ave (WS) 44
Henry St & Ct (MAL) 48
Henry Sterling Sq (SB) 27
Henshaw (BRI) 35
Henshaw St, Pl & Ter (WRW) 65
Henshaw Ter (WRX) 32
Herald 18
Herbert (DOR) 24
Herbert (WS) 44
Herbert (CAM) 40
Herbert (EV) 49
Herbert (MEL) 76
Herbert Rd (BEL) 78
Herbert Rd (NQ) 71
Herbert Rd (ARL) 74
Herbert Rd (BRA) 84
Herbertson Rd (JP) 30
Hereford 15
Hereford Rd (WAB) 68
Hereward Rd (NCE) 59
Heritage Dr & Rd (LEX) 73
Heritage Ln (BRA) 84
Heritage Ln (MIL) 86
Heritage Ln (EWY) 89
Herman (ROX) 19
Hermon (BEL) 78
Hermon (WIN) 52
Hermon Ter (NEW) 58
Heron (WRX) 32
Heron Rd (QUI) 69
Herrick (BRI) 35
Herrick Rd (NCE) 59
Hersam (STO) 80

Boston (Con.)   021

Hersey (NWH)	61
Hersey (SOM)	43
Hersey Pl (QUI)	69
Hersey Pl	11
Harsom (WAT)	72
Hersum Way (WAL)	54
Hesseltine Ave (MEL)	76
Hesston Ter (DOR)	25
Hester (BRI)	35
Hestia Park (ROX)	19
Hewes (ROX)	19
Hewett Cir (NH)	94
Hewins (DOR)	21
Hewitt Rd (NWY)	91
Hewlett (ROS)	31
Hewmason Rd (BRA)	84
Hews (CAM)	39
Heyward Ave (MEL)	76
Hiawatha Ave (WAL)	54
Hiawatha Ln & Rd (ARL)	74
Hiawatha Rd (WAT)	26
Hibbard (QUI)	69
Hibbard Rd (NEW)	58
Hibbert (ARL)	74
Hibbert (LEX)	73
Hibiscus Ave (WAL)	54
Hibiscus Ave (WY)	88
Hichborn (BRI)	35
Hichborn (REV)	51
Hickory (LEX)	73
Hickory Ave (MED)	55
Hickory Dr (WAL)	54
Hickory Ln (BEL)	78
Hickory Rd (WH)	81
Hickory Rd (BRA)	85
Hickory Rd (WES)	93
Hickory Cliff Rd (NUF)	64
Hicks Ave (MED)	55
Hidden Rd (WES)	93
Higgins (ALL)	34
Higgins (AUB)	66
Higgins (ARL)	74
Higgins Ave (MED)	55
High (MED)	55
High (CAM)	38
High (WAL)	54
High (REV)	51
High (WS)	44
High (CHE)	50
High (EV)	49
High (ARL)	48
High (BRO)	46
High (NUF)	64
High (STO)	80
High (NWH)	61
High (QUI)	69
High (NH)	94
High (MIL)	87
High (EWY)	89
High (CHA)	29
High (DOR)	22
High	10
High Rd (WRX)	32
High St N & S (MEL)	32
High St Pl (BRO)	46
High St Pl (EWY)	89
High St Ter (EV)	49
High Cliff Ter (STO)	80
High Gate (WH)	81
High Gate (N)	92
High Haith Rd (ARL)	74

High Ledge Ave (WH)	81
High Rock (N)	92
High Rock Cir (WAL)	54
High Rock Rd (MAL)	48
High Rock Ter (CHN)	67
High Rock Way (ALL)	34
High School Ave (QUI)	69
High School Ter (EWY)	89
High View Ave (WRX)	32
Highcrest Rd & Ter (ROS)	31
Highfield Cir (MIL)	86
Highfield Rd (QUI)	69
Highfield Rd & Ter (ROS)	31
Highgate (ALL)	34
Highland (HP)	36
Highland (CAM)	38
Highland (WAL)	54
Highland (CHE)	50
Highland (REV)	51
Highland (MIL)	86
Highland (WES)	93
Highland	
1-358 (WNW)	65
359-OUT (NWV)	60
Highland Ave (WH)	52
Highland Ave (STO)	80
Highland Ave (ARL)	74
Highland Ave (LEX)	73
Highland Ave (WOL)	70
Highland Ave (WAT)	72
Highland Ave	
1-220 (NWV)	60
1-228 (SOM)	43
1-1206 (NH)	94
221-OUT (WNW)	65
289-OUT (WS)	44
1207-OUT (N)	92
Highland Ave E (BRA)	84
Highland Ave E & W (WNW)	76
Highland Ave & Ct (EV)	49
Highland Ave, Ct, Park & Ter (MAL)	48
Highland Ave & Park (CAM)	39
Highland Ave & Plz (BRA)	85
Highland Ave & Ter (MED)	55
Highland Cir & Ter (NH)	94
Highland Park Ave (ROX)	19
Highland Park St (ROX)	19
Highland Park & Ter (NWV)	60
Highland Pl (N)	92
Highland Pl (SWY)	90
Highland Rd (BEL)	78
Highland Rd (WEL)	81
Highland Rd (WS)	44
Highland Rd (BRO)	46
Highland St, Ave, Pl & Ter (ROX)	19
Highview (NH)	94
Highview Ave (BRA)	85
Highview Ave (MEL)	76
Hilary (CHA)	29
Hilburn St & Pl (ROS)	31
Hilda (QUI)	69
Hildreth (DOR)	24
Hill (CHA)	29
Hill (QUI)	69
Hill (WAT)	72
Hill (LEX)	73
Hill (WRX)	32
Hill (MAL)	48
Hill (WS)	44
Hill (NH)	94
Hill (EWY)	89

Hill Ave (BRA)	84
Hill Ave (ARL)	74
Hill Rd (BEL)	78
Hill Rd (WAL)	54
Hill Top (DOR)	24
Hill St & Ct (STO)	80
Hill Top Ave (LEX)	73
Hill Top Rd (WEL)	81
Hill Top Rd (NWY)	91
Hill Top Rd (WES)	93
Hillcrest (ARL)	74
Hillcrest (WRX)	32
Hillcrest Ave (LEX)	73
Hillcrest Ave (MEL)	76
Hillcrest (WAT)	72
Hillcrest Cir (WAB)	68
Hillcrest Rd (NQ)	71
Hillcrest Rd (BEL)	78
Hillcrest Rd (N)	92
Hillcrest Rd (EWY)	89
Hillcrest Rd (MIL)	86
Hillcrest Rd (BRA)	84
Hillcrest Park (MED)	55
Hillcroft Rd (WAL)	54
Hillcroft Rd (JP)	30
Hillcroft Rd (MAL)	48
Hillcroft Rd (WH)	81
Hildale Rd (SWY)	90
Hilliard Ct (BRA)	84
Hilliard St & Pl (CAM)	38
Hillis Rd (HP)	36
Hillock (ROS)	31
Hills Ct (MAL)	48
Hillsboro (QUI)	69
Hillsboro (DOR)	25
Hillsboro Rd (MAT)	26
Hillsboro Rd (MED)	55
Hillsboro (DOR)	24
Hillsdale Rd (ARL)	74
Hillsdale Rd	
1-101 (MED) (ODD)	55
2-96 (MED) (EVEN)	55
98-OUT (WS) (EVEN)	44
103-OUT (WS) (ODD)	44
Hitlside (MIL)	86
Hitlside (RXC)	20
Hillside Ave (NH)	94
Hillside Ave (ARL)	74
Hillside Ave (WOL)	70
Hillside Ave (MED)	55
Hillside Ave (SOM)	45
Hillside Ave (JP)	30
Hillside Ave (CHE)	50
Hillside Ave (EV)	49
Hillside Ave (WIN)	52
Hillside Ave (REV)	51
Hillside Ave & Park (MEL)	76
Hillside Ave & Pl (CAM)	40
Hillside Ave & Rd (STO)	80
Hillside Ave & Rd (BRA)	84
Hillside Ave & Ter (WNW)	65
Hillside Ave & Ter (LEX)	73
Hillside Cir & Park (SOM)	43
Hillside Pl (CHA)	29
Hillside Rd (BRO)	46
Hillside Rd (WH)	81
Hillside Rd (NWH)	61
Hillside St Ext (BEL)	78
Hillside St, Ave, Park, Pl & Ter (MAL)	48
Hillside St & Rd (WAT)	72
Hillside St & Ter (BEL)	78

Boston (Con.)   021

Hillsview Rd (MIL)	86
Hilltop (MIL)	86
Hilltop (NEW)	58
Hilltop (QUI)	69
Hilltop Rd (WAT)	72
Hilltop Rd (CHH)	67
Hillview Ave (ROS)	31
Hillview Rd (BRA)	85
Hilma (NQ)	71
Hiltoq (ARL)	74
Hilton (HP)	36
Hilton (ROX)	19
Hilton Dr (SWY)	90
Hinchey Rd (LEX)	73
Hinckley (DOR)	25
Hinckley (SOM)	45
Hinckley Rd (MIL)	87
Hinckley Tar (WAB)	68
Hingham (CAM)	38
Hingham Ave (SWY)	90
Hinsdale	02215
Hinsdale (MED)	55
Hinston Rd (EWY)	89
Hitchcock Ter (QUI)	69
Hittinger (BEL)	78
Hobart (WOL)	70
Hobart (BRI)	35
Hobart Ave (BRA)	85
Hobart Rd (WEL)	81
Hobart Rd	
1-OUT (NCE) (ODD)	59
2-100 (NCE) (EVEN)	59
102-OUT (CHH) (EVEN)	67
Hobart St & Ter (BRA)	84
Hobart Ter (NCE)	59
Hobbs Ct (ARL)	74
Hobbs Rd (MED)	55
Hobbs Rd (WAL)	54
Hobbs Brook Rd (WAL)	54
Hobbs Brook Rd (WES)	93
Hobomac Rd (NWY)	91
Hobomack Rd (QUI)	69
Hobson (BRI)	35
Hobson (ROS)	31
Hodgdon Ter (WRX)	32
Hodge Rd (ARL)	74
Hodges Ave (WEL)	81
Hodges Ave & Ct (NQ)	71
Hodgkinson (QUI)	69
Hoffman (JP)	30
Hoitt Rd (BEL)	78
Holborn (MIL)	86
Holborn St, Park & Ter	
(DOR)	21
Holbrook (JP)	30
Holbrook Ave (DOR)	22
Holbrook Ave (BRA)	85
Holbrook Ct (MEL)	76
Holbrook Rd (NWY)	91
Holbrook Rd	
1-68 (WOL)	70
69-OUT (NQ)	71
Holden (DOR)	25
Holden (CAM)	38
Holden (BRO)	46
Holden (MAL)	48
Holden Ct	09
Holden Rd (BKA)	84
Holden Rd (WAV)	79
Holden Rd (WNW)	65
Holden Row (CHA)	29

Holden Green (CAM)	38
Holiday (DOR)	22
Hollace (WAL)	54
Holland (MAL)	48
Holland (WS)	44
Holland (NEW)	58
Holland (LEX)	73
Holland Rd (MEL)	76
Holland Rd (BRO)	46
Holland St & Ter (N)	92
Hollander (DOR)	21
Hollingsworth (MAT)	26
Hollingsworth Ave	
1-149 (BRA)	84
150-OUT (BRA)	85
Hollingsworth Rd (MIL)	86
Hollis (MIL)	86
Hollis (SWY)	90
Hollis	16
Hollis (NEW)	58
Hollis (WEL)	81
Hollis Ave (NQ)	71
Hollis Ave (BRA)	84
Hollis Pl (ALL)	34
Hollis St & Pl (CAM)	40
Holliston (QUI)	69
Hollow-Ridge Rd (NH)	94
Holly (WAT)	72
Holly Ave (CAM)	38
Holly Cir (WES)	93
Holly Rd (BRA)	85
Holly Rd (ROS)	31
Holly Rd (WAB)	68
Holly Hill Cir (SWY)	90
Hollywood Rd (WRX)	32
Holm Ct (MAL)	48
Holman (ALL)	34
Holman Rd (AUB)	66
Holmberg Rd (EWY)	89
Holmes (BRA)	84
Holmes (N)	92
Holmes (CAM)	38
Holmes (ALL)	34
Holmes (MAL)	48
Holmes Ave (NWY)	91
Holmes Ln (MIL)	86
Holmes Rd (MED)	55
Holmes Rd (LEX)	73
Holmes St & Pl (NQ)	71
Holmfield Ave (MAT)	26
Holt	
1-39 (WAV)	79
40-OUT (WAT)	72
Holton (MED)	55
Holton	
1-59 (ALL)	35
60-OUT (BRI)	35
Holton Rd (LEX)	73
Holts Ave (SOM)	43
Holworthy (DOR)	21
Holworthy St, Pl & Ter (CAM)	38
Holyoke (MAL)	48
Holyoke	16
Holyoke (NQ)	71
Holyoke Rd (WS)	44
Holyoke St & Pl (CAM)	38
Home (MAL)	48
Homer (BRO)	46
Homer (REV)	51
Homer (WAT)	72
Homer (NCE)	59
Homer (EB)	28
Homer (SWY)	90

Homer Cir (MED)	55
Homer Rd (QUI)	69
Homer Rd (BEL)	78
Homer Rd (ARL)	74
Homer Sq (SOM)	43
Homes Ave (DOR)	22
Homestead (DOR)	21
Homestead (LEX)	73
Homestead Ave (QUI)	69
Homestead Ave (WY)	88
Homestead Park (NH)	94
Homestead Pl (CHA)	29
Homestead Rd (ARL)	74
Homestead Rd (WEL)	81
Homestead St & Rd (WAB)	68
Homewood Rd (WRX)	32
Hommagen Pl (ROX)	19
Hood (QUI)	69
Hood (NEW)	58
Hooker (MED)	55
Hooker (ALL)	34
Hooker (BRA)	84
Hooker Ave (WS)	44
Hooper (CHE)	50
Hooper (QUI)	69
Hooper (DOR)	24
Hooten Ct (EB)	28
Hooton Way (CHE)	50
Hoover Ave (QUI)	69
Hoover Ave (BRA)	85
Hoover Rd (NH)	94
Hope (AUB)	66
Hope Ave (MIL)	86
Hope Ave (WAL)	54
Hopedale (ALL)	34
Hopedale (QUI)	69
Hopestill (DOR)	24
Hopewell Rd (MAT)	26
Hopkins (DOR)	24
Hopkins (MEL)	76
Hopkins (REV)	51
Hopkins Pl (MAT)	26
Hopkins Rd (JP)	30
Hopkins Rd (ARL)	74
Hopkinson (WH)	81
Horace (SOM)	43
Horace (MAL)	48
Horace (EB)	28
Horace (NH)	94
Horace Rd (BEL)	78
Horadan Way (RXC)	20
Horan Way (JP)	30
Horne Ave (MED)	55
Horne Rd (BEL)	78
Horsford Rd (N)	92
Horton Pl (MIL)	86
Hosmer (WAT)	72
Hosmer (EV)	49
Hosmer (MAT)	26
Hosmer (WNW)	65
Hospital Rd (ARL)	74
Hospital Rd (MAL)	48
Hotin Rd (STO)	80
Hough Rd (WAV)	79
Houghton (DOR)	22
Houghton	
1-OUT (SOM) (ODD)	43
2-4 (CAM) (EVEN)	39
6-OUT (SOM) (EVEN)	43
Houghton Rd (MIL)	86
Houghton Rd (BEL)	78
House Rock Rd (WY)	88
Houston (WRX)	32

Boston (Con.) 021

Houston Ave (MIL) 87
Houston Park (CAM) 40
Hovey (WAT) 72
Hovey (NQ) 71
Hovey (NEW) 58
Hovey Ave (CAM) 38
Hovey Rd (WAL) 54
Howard (WAL) 54
Howard (CAM) 39
Howard (WS) 44
Howard (REV) 51
Howard (NEW) 58
Howard (WAT) 72
Howard (BEL) 78
Howard (MEL) 76
Howard (ARL) 74
Howard (WNW) 65
Howard (MIL) 86
Howard (NWY) 91
Howard (ROX) 19
Howard Ave & Pl (DOR) 25
Howard Pl (CHA) 13
Howard Rd (MED) 55
Howard St & Ct (BRA) 84
Howard St & Ter (MAL) 48
Howe (SOM) 45
Howe (MIL) 86
Howe (DOR) 25
Howe (WAT) 72
Howe (WEL) 81
Howe (QUI) 69
Howe Ct (RXC) 20
Howe Rd (NCE) 59
Howe Rd (N) 92
Howell (DOR) 25
Howell Ct (CHE) 50
Howells Rd (BEL) 78
Howes (DOR) 25
Howie (MEL) 76
Howie Rd (BRA) 84
Howitt Rd (WRX) 32
Howland (CAM) 39
Howland (N) 92
Howland (DOR) 21
Howland Cir (MED) 55
Howland Rd (WNW) 65
Howley Ave (NCE) 59
Hoy Ter (MIL) 86
Hoyt (EV) 49
Hoyt (DOR) 25
Huban Ct (RXC) 20
Hubbard (JP) 30
Hubbard (MAL) 48
Hubbard (SWY) 90
Hubbard Ave (CAM) 40
Hubbard Park Rd (CAM) 38
Hubbard Rd (WES) 93
Hubbardston Rd (DOR) 25
Hubert (RXC) 20
Huckins (ROX) 19
Huckins Ave (NQ) 71
Hudson (WAT) 72
Hudson (QUI) 69
Hudson (CHA) 29
Hudson 11
Hudson (MIL) 87
Hudson
  1-92 (SOM) 43
  93-OUT (WS) 44
Hudson Rd (LEX) 73
Hudson St & Pl (CAM) 38
Hudson St & Ter (MAL) 48

Hughes (QUI) 69
Hulbert (ROX) 19
Hull 13
Hull (QUI) 69
Hull (NWV) 60
Hull (WAV) 79
Hull St Ct 13
Hull St Pl 13
Humboldt (MAL) 40
Humboldt (WAL) 54
Humboldt Ave
  1-79 (ROX) (ODD) 19
  2-90 (ROX) (EVEN) 19
  81-OUT (DOR) (ODD) 21
  92-OUT (DOR) (EVEN) 21
Humboldt Ct & Ter (ROX) 19
Humboldt Pl (SB) 27
Hume Ave (MED) 55
Humes Rd (DOR) 22
Hummock St (NQ) 71
Humphrey (EWY) 89
Humphreys St & Pl (DOR) 25
Hundreds Cir & Rd (WH) 19
Hunneman (ROX)
Hunnewell (WH)
Hunnewell Ave (NH) 76
Hunnewell Ave (MED) 55
Hunnewell Ave (BRI) 35
Hunnewell Ave & Cir (NEW) 58
Hunnewell St & Ter (NH) 94
Hunt (WY) 88
Hunt (WAT) 72
Hunt (N) 92
Hunt Ave (BRA) 84
Hunt Rd (LEX) 73
Hunter (WNW) 65
Hunter (ROS) 31
Hunter (CHA) 29
Hunter Ter (SWY) 90
Hunting (MAL) 48
Hunting (WH) 81
Hunting
  1-39 (CAM) (ODD) 41
  2-42 (CAM) (EVEN) 41
  41-OUT (SOM) (ODD) 43
  44-OUT (SOM) (EVEN) 43
Hunting Rd (NH) 94
Huntington (WAL) 54
Huntington Ave (SWY) 90
Huntington Ave
  1-85 (ROS) (ODD) 31
  1-149 16
  2-76 (ROS) (EVEN) 31
  78-OUT (HP) (EVEN) 36
  87-OUT (HP) (ODD) 36
  150-OUT 15
Huntington Rd (MIL) 86
Huntington Rd (NEW) 58
Huntington Rd (ARL) 74
Huntley Rd (QUI) 69
Huntley Rd (BRA) 84
Huntley St & Ter (MAL) 48
Huntoon (DOR) 24
Huntress (QUI)
Hunts Ter (MEL) 76
Hurd (MEL) 76
Hurd (MAL) 48
Hurd Rd (BRO) 46
Hurd Rd (BEL) 78
Hurlburt (CAM) 38
Hurlburt Ct (MAL) 48
Hurlcroft Ave (MED) 55
Hurlcroft Ave (DOR) 24

Hurlcroft Rd (MIL) 86
Hurley (CAM) 41
Hurley (BEL) 78
Hurley Rd (NCE) 59
Huron Ave (CAM) 38
Huron Cir (DOR) 24
Hutchings (DOR) 21
Hutchins Rd (MED) 55
Hutchinson (CAM) 38
Hutchinson (WIN) 52
Hutchinson (REV) 51
Hutchinson (DOR) 24
Hutchinson (MIL) 87
Hutchinson Rd (ARL) 74
Hutchinson Rd (LEX) 73
Hyde (WNW) 61
Hyde (QUI) 69
Hyde (WY) 88
Hyde (MAL) 48
Hyde Ave (NEW) 58
Hyde Park Ave
  1-336 (JP) 30
  337-749 (ROS) 31
  750-OUT (HP) 36
Hyde Sq (JP) 30
Hyde St & Pl (REV) 51
Hynes Ave (QUI) 69
Hyslop Rd (BRO) 46
Hywood (REV) 51
I (SB) 27
Ibbetson (SOM) 43
Ida (QUI) 69
Ida Rd (BRA) 84
Idaho (MAT) 26
Idlewell St & Blvd (WY) 88
Iffley Rd (JP) 32
Illinois Ave (SOM) 45
Imbaro Rd (HP) 36
Imrie Rd (ALL) 34
Ina Rd (N) 92
Incinerator Rd (CHH) 67
Independence Ave (QUI) 69
Independence Ave (LEX) 73
Independence Ave (BRA) 84
Independence Dr (CHH) 67
India
  1-20 09
  21-47 10
  48-48 09
  49-OUT 10
India Pl & Sq 10
India Wharf 10
Indian Rd (WAL) 54
Indian Hill Rd (WES) 93
Indian Hill Rd (MIL) 86
Indian Hill Rd (ARL) 74
Indian Hill Rd (BEL) 78
Indian Ridge Rd (NCE) 59
Indian Spring Rd (MIL) 86
Indian Spring Way (WH) 81
Indiana Ave (SOM) 45
Indiana Ct & Ter (NUF) 64
Industrial Pl (NUF) 64
Ingalls Ct (MEL) 76
Ingersoll Rd (WH) 81
Ingleside (DOR) 25
Ingleside Ave (MAL) 48
Ingleside Ave (WIN) 52
Ingleside Ave (CHE) 50
Ingleside Rd (WH) 81
Ingleside Rd (LEX) 73
Ingleside Rd (N) 92
Inglewood Dr (BRA) 84

Boston (Con.) 021

Ingraham Rd (WEL) 81
Ingram (QUI) 69
Ingrid Rd (WY) 88
Inis Cir (WRW) 65
Inman 02210
Inman St, Pl & Sq (CAM) 39
Inner Belt Rd (SOM) 43
Institution Ave (NCE) 55
Intervale (QUI) 69
Intervale (REV) 51
Intervale (DOR) 21
Intervale Ave (MED) 55
Intervale Rd (CHH) 67
Intervale Rd (WH) 81
Intervale Rd (ARL) 74
Intervale Rd (RE) 92
Intervale Rd (WES) 93
Intervale Rd (EWY) 89
Intervale Rd
  1-91 (NCE) 59
  92-OUT (CHH) 67
Inverness Rd (ARL) 74
Inverness Rd (WH) 81
Inwood (DOR) 25
Iola (DOR) 24
Iona (ROS) 31
Ionia (AUB) 66
Iowa (DOR) 24
Ipswich 02215
Ipswich Pl (EB) 28
Ipswich Rd (NWH) 61
Ireland Rd (NCE) 59
Irena Rd (DOR) 24
Ireson Ct (MEL) 76
Irma (DOR) 24
Irma Ave (WAT) 72
Iron Hill (EWY) 89
Iroquois (RXC) 20
Iroquois Rd (ARL) 74
Irving (ARL) 74
Irving (WAV) 79
Irving (MEL) 76
Irving (NCE) 59
Irving (STO) 80
Irving 14
Irving (MED) 55
Irving (REV) 51
Irving (WS) 44
Irving (EV) 49
Irving (BRO) 46
Irving (WAL) 54
Irving Rd (WAB) 68
Irving Rd (NWY) 91
Irving Rd (WES) 93
Irving St, Ct & Pl (MAL) 48
Irving St & Park (WAT) 72
Irving St & Ter (CAM) 38
Irvington (WAB) 68
Irvington Rd (MED) 55
Irwin (WH) 52
Irwin Ave (ROX) 19
Irwin Rd (WAB) 68
Isabella (MEL) 76
Isabella (QUI) 69
Isabella 16
Island (ROX) 19
Island Ave (QUI) 69
Island View Rd (EWY) 89
Islington Rd (AUB) 66
Islington St & Ter (ALL) 34
Itasca (MAT) 26

Ithaca Cir (NLF) 62
Ivaloo (WAL) 54
Ivaloo (SOM) 43
Ivan (LEX) 73
Ivanhoe (NEW) 58
Ivanhoe 18
Ivory (WRX) 32
Ivy (CAM) 38
Ivy (BRO) 46
Ivy Cir (ARL) 74
Ivy Cir & Rd (WEL) 81
Ivy Ln (LEX) 73
Ivy Ln (WAL) 54
Ivy Rd (MAL) 48
Ivy Rd (MED) 55
Ivy Rd (STO) 80
Ivy Rd (BEL) 78
Ivy St, Ct & Rd (SWY) 90
J Rdwy (NCE) 59
Jackson (RCE) 19
Jackson (QUI) 69
Jackson (MAL) 48
Jackson (HP) 36
Jackson (CAM) 40
Jackson (CHA) 29
Jackson Ave 13
Jackson Ave (EV) 49
Jackson Ct (LEX) 72
Jackson Gdns (CAM) 39
Jackson Rd (SOM) 45
Jackson Rd (MED) 55
Jackson Rd (BEL) 78
Jackson Rd (WH) 81
Jackson Rd & Ter (NEW) 58
Jackson Sq (EWY) 89
Jackson St & Pl (WAL) 54
Jacob (MAL) 48
Jacob (DOR) 24
Jacob Rd (BEL) 78
Jacobs Pl (EV) 49
Jacobs Ter (NCE) 59
Jaconnet (NRH) 61
Jacquelin Rd (WRX) 32
Jacqueline Rd (WAL) 54
Jacquelyn Rd (WY) 88
Jacques (SOM) 30
Jaegar Ter (JP) 30
Jaffrey
  1-114 (EWY) 89
  115-OUT (WY) 88
Jaffrey Cir (WAB) 68
Jalleison (HP) 36
Jamaica Rd (BRO) 46
Jamaica St, Pl & Way (JP) ... 30
Jamaica Way Ct (JP) 31
James (ROS) 31
James (BRO) 46
James (SOM) 45
James (MAL) 48
James (CAM) 38
James (WAL) 54
James (MED) 55
James (WWH) 65
James (LEX) 73
James (QUI) 69
James (ARL) 74
James 72
James Ave (WH) 52
James Ave (RH) 94
James Rd (EWY) 89
Jameson Rd (NEW) 58
Jamestown Ter (MAT) 26
Jane Rd (NCE) 59

Janet Rd (NCE) 59
Janet Rd (ARL) 74
Janet Rd (WOL) 70
Janice Ln (STO) 80
Janvrin Ave (REV) 51
Jarvis (REV) 51
Jarvis (CAM) 38
Jarvis Cir (RI) 92
Jarvis Pl (ROX) 19
Jason Rd (BEL) 78
Jason St, Ct & Ter (ARL) ... 74
Jason Ter (SB) 27
Jasper (SOM) 45
Jasset (NEW) 58
Jay (WS) 44
Jay (CAM) 39
Jay (BRA) 85
Jay Rd (SWY) 90
Jay St Pl (CAM) 39
Jayne Rd (RH) 94
Jean Rd (ARL) 74
Jean Rd (LEX) 73
Jeannette Ave (WAV) 79
Jeffers (ROS) 31
Jefferson (CAM) 41
Jefferson (WH) 52
Jefferson (NEW) 58
Jefferson (BRA) 85
Jefferson 16
Jefferson Ave (CHA) 29
Jefferson Ave (LEX) 73
Jefferson Ave (WAT) 72
Jefferson Ave (EV) 49
Jefferson Ave (CHE) 55
Jefferson Park (CAM) 40
Jefferson Rd (STO) 80
Jefferson Rd (WH) 81
Jefferson Rd (CHH) 67
Jeffrey Rd (ARL) 74
Jeffrey Ter (LEX) 73
Jeffries (EB) 28
Jeffts Ter (MEL) 76
Jemison (RNY) 60
Jenkins (SB) 27
Jenner (CHA) 29
Jenness (QUI) 69
Jenness Rd (BRO) 46
Jennett Ave (WRX) 32
Jennings Rd (WAL) 54
Jensen Rd (WAT) 72
Jepson Ct (WRW) 65
Jerald (WRW) 52
Jeremiah Clancy Rd (DOR) .. 24
Jericho Hill Rd (WAL) 54
Jerome (SOM) 43
Jerome (MED) 55
Jerome (DOR) 25
Jerome Ave (WRW) 65
Jerome Ct (EV) 49
Jersey 02215
Jersey Ave (BRA) 84
Jeshurun Rd (WRX) 32
Jess (JP) 30
Jewell Pl (ROX) 19
Jewett (ROS) 31
Jewett (QUI) 69
Jewett
  1-19 (WAT) 72
  20-OUT (NEW) 58
Jewett Pl (NEW) 58
Jo Anne Ter (DOR) 24
Joan (STO) 80
Joan Dr (QUI) 69

Boston (Con.) ... 021

Joan Rd (MED) ... 55
Joan Rd (HP) ... 36
Joan Ter (EWY) ... 89
Joey Rd (REV) ... 51
John (CHE) ... 50
John (WAL) ... 54
John (MAL) ... 48
John (BRO) ... 46
John (RWY) ... 91
John (NH) ... 94
John (NCE) ... 59
John (NQ) ... 71
John Ave (REV) ... 51
John A Andrew (JP) ... 30
John Alden Rd (WRX) ... 32
John Corcoran Park (CAM) ... 38
John Eliot Sq (ROX) ... 19
John F Kennedy Cir (NEW) ... 58
John James Rd (MAL) ... 48
John Mooney Rd (REV) ... 51
John Poulter Rd (LEX) ... 73
John Quincy Ln (NWY) ... 91
Johnny Ct ... 11
Johnny Rd (REV) ... 51
Johns Ct (RXC) ... 20
Johnson (WRX) ... 32
Johnson (MHL) ... 86
Johnson Ave (JP) ... 30
Johnson Ave (MED) ... 55
Johnson Ave (CHA) ... 29
Johnson Ave (QUI) ... 69
Johnson Ave & Ter (WRN) ... 52
Johnson Pl (AUB) ... 68
Johnson Rd (ARL) ... 74
Johnson Rd (NWY) ... 91
Johnson Ter (DOR) ... 24
Johnsons Ln (BRA) ... 85
Johnston Park (ROX) ... 19
Johnston Rd (DOR) ... 24
Johnswood Rd (ROS) ... 31
Joiner (CHA) ... 29
Jonathan (WAV) ... 79
Jones (EV) ... 49
Jones Ave (CHE) ... 50
Jones Ave (DOR) ... 24
Jones Ct (NEW) ... 58
Jones Rd (REV) ... 51
Jones Rd (WAL) ... 54
Jones Rd (WES) ... 93
Jordan (WOL) ... 70
Jordan Cir (BRA) ... 85
Jordan Pl (CAM) ... 42
Jordan Rd (BRO) ... 46
Jordan St & Ter (MAL) ... 48
Joseph (MAL) ... 48
Joseph (SOM) ... 43
Joseph (MED) ... 55
Joseph (QUI) ... 69
Joseph (DOR) ... 24
Joseph Rd (NWY) ... 60
Joseph Rd (LEX) ... 73
Joseph Rd (REV) ... 51
Joseph Rd (BRA) ... 84
Joseph A Fern Ct (EWY) ... 89
Josephine (DOR) ... 22
Josephine Ave (WS) ... 44
Josephine Rd (MED) ... 55
Joslin Rd ... 02215
Josselyn Ter (NWH) ... 61
Joy (SOM) ... 43
Joy (WAL) ... 54

Joy ...
1-7 ...
8-OUT ... 14
Joy Pl ... 08
Joy Ter (MAL) ... 48
Joyce Ave (WY) ... 88
Joyce Rd (WAL) ... 54
Joyce Rd (MED) ... 55
Joyce Rd (HP) ... 36
Joyce Rd (QUI) ... 69
Joyce Rd (ARL) ... 74
Joyce Hayes Way (SB) ... 27
Joyce Kilmer Rd (WRX) ... 32
Judge ... 15
Judith Rd (NCE) ... 59
Judith Rd (NWY) ... 91
Judkins (NWV) ... 60
Judkins Rd (MED) ... 55
Judson (MAL) ... 48
Judson (BRA) ... 84
Judson (DOR) ... 24
Judson Rd (WY) ... 88
Jules Ter (NCE) ... 59
Julia (MAL) ... 48
Julia Rd (NWY) ... 91
Julia Rd (N) ... 92
Julian (DOR) ... 25
Juliette (DOR) ... 22
Junction (N) ... 92
June (REV) ... 51
June Ln (NCE) ... 59
June Rd (STO) ... 80
June St & Ln (ROS) ... 31
Juniper (BRO) ... 46
Juniper Ln (NCE) ... 59
Juniper Pl & Ter (LEX) ... 73
Juniper Rd (WEL) ... 81
Juniper Rd (BEL) ... 78
Juniper Rd (WAL) ... 54
Juniper Rd (WES) ... 93
Juniper St & Ter (ROX) ... 19
Juniper Hill Rd (WAL) ... 54
Jupiter (WY) ... 88
Justin (LEX) ... 73
Justin Rd (BRI) ... 35
K (EWY) ... 89
K (SB) ... 27
K St Pl (SB) ... 27
K Way (MED) ... 55
K K Ter (EV) ... 49
Kahler Ave (MIL) ... 76
Kalada Park (DOR) ... 21
Kane (DOR) ... 25
Kaposia (AUB) ... 66
Kappius Path (NCE) ... 59
Kardon Rd (HP) ... 36
Karen Ln (WY) ... 88
Karen Rd (WAB) ... 68
Karlyn Rd (WY) ... 88
Kassul Park (CAM) ... 25
Katherine (NWY) ... 91
Katherine Rd (STO) ... 80
Katherine Rd (WAT) ... 72
Kathleen Rd (SWY) ... 90
Kays Rd (STO) ... 80
Keach (WAL) ... 54
Keane Rd (WRX) ... 32
Keaney Sq ... 14
Kearney (MAL) ... 48
Kearney Rd (NH) ... 94
Kearsarge Ave & Ter (ROX) ... 19
Keating (QUI) ... 69

Keats Rd (ARL) ... 74
Keayne (REV) ... 51
Keefe Ave (NUF) ... 64
Keenan (WAT) ... 72
Keenan Rd (BRI) ... 35
Keene (STO) ... 80
Keith (WAT) ... 72
Keith (WRX) ... 32
Keith (WY) ... 88
Keith Pl (N) ... 92
Keith Rd (MED) ... 55
Keller Path (NCE) ... 59
Kelley Ct (BRI) ... 35
Kelley Ct (CHA) ... 29
Kelley Robert E (CAM) ... 38
Kelly Rd (CAM) ... 39
Kellys Block (CHA) ... 29
Kelton (ALL) ... 34
Kelveden Rd (WAB) ... 68
Kelvin (EV) ... 49
Kemble (ROX) ... 19
Kemble Pl (SB) ... 27
Kemp (SB) ... 27
Kemper (WOL) ... 70
Kempton ... 15
Kempton Pl (WNW) ... 65
Kenberma Rd (DOR) ... 24
Kendal Ter (NEW) ... 58
Kendall ... 18
Kendall (NQ) ... 71
Kendall (WAV) ... 79
Kendall Ave (BRA) ... 85
Kendall Park (WAL) ... 54
Kendall Rd (NCE) ... 59
Kendall Rd (WH) ... 81
Kendall Rd (LEX) ... 73
Kendall Sq (CAM) ... 42
Kendall St & Pl (BRO) ... 46
Kendall Common Rd (WES) ... 93
Kendrick (NH) ... 94
Kendrick Ave (QUI) ... 69
Kenesaw Ter (RXC) ... 20
Kenilworth (ROX) ... 19
Kenilworth (MAL) ... 48
Kenilworth (NEW) ... 58
Kenilworth (EV) ... 49
Kenilworth Cir & Rd (WH) ... 81
Kenilworth Rd (ARL) ... 74
Kenilworth Rd (MIL) ... 86
Keniston Rd (MEL) ... 76
Kenmere Rd (MED) ... 55
Kenmere Rd (DOR) ... 24
Kenmore (NCE) ... 59
Kenmore Rd (MEL) ... 76
Kenmore Rd (BEL) ... 78
Kenmore Rd (MAL) ... 48
Kenmore Rd (BRA) ... 85
Kenmore Rd & Ter (WAL) ... 54
Kenmore Sq ... 02215
Kennard (MAL) ... 48
Kennard Rd (BRO) ... 46
Kennebec (MAT) ... 26
Kennedy Rd (CAM) ... 38
Kenneson Rd (SOM) ... 45
Kenneth (WRX) ... 32
Kenneth (NWH) ... 61
Kenneth Ter (STO) ... 80
Kenney (JP) ... 30
Kenney (N) ... 92
Kenney Pl (WAB) ... 68
Kenrick (BRI) ... 35
Kenrick St & Ter (NEW) ... 58
Kensington (NWV) ... 60

Boston (Con.)   021

Kensington Ave (SOM)	45
Kensington Cir (CHH)	67
Kensington Park & Rd (ARL)	74
Kensington Rd (WY)	88
Kensington St & Park (ROX)	19
Kent (RXC)	20
Kent (WAV)	79
Kent (QUI)	69
Kent Ln (ARL)	74
Kent Rd (WAB)	68
Kent Rd (WY)	90
Kent Rd (N)	92
Kent St & Ct (SOM)	43
Kent St & Sq (BRO)	46
Kenton Rd (JP)	30
Kenway (MED)	55
Kenway (CAM)	38
Kenway Ter (ROX)	19
Kenwood (DOR)	24
Kenwood (BRO)	46
Kenwood (WS)	44
Kenwood (CAM)	38
Kenwood Ave (NCE)	59
Kenwood Ave (STO)	80
Kenwood Ln (WAL)	54
Kenwood Rd (EV)	49
Kenyon (WRW)	65
Kerna Rd (WRX)	32
Kernwood (MAL)	48
Kerr Path (NCE)	59
Kerrigan Pl (BRO)	46
Kerrydale Rd (N)	92
Kershaw Rd (WRX)	32
Kerwin (DOR)	24
Keswick	02215
Kevin Rd (MIL)	86
Kevin Rd (DOR)	25
Kew Rd (BRA)	84
Kewadin Rd (WAB)	68
Keyes (QUI)	69
Keystone (WRX)	32
Kidder (QUI)	69
Kidder Ave (WS)	44
Kidney Pond Rd (WES)	93
Kiernan Rd (WRX)	32
Kilburn (REV)	51
Kilburn Rd (WRW)	65
Kilburn Rd (BFJ)	78
Kilby (QUI)	69
Kilby (SOM)	43
Kilby	09
Kiley Rd (MEL)	76
Kilgore Ave (MED)	55
Kilmarnock	02215
Kilsyth Rd (MED)	16
Kilsyth Rd & Ter (BRO)	46
Kilsythe Rd (ARL)	74
Kimball (QUI)	69
Kimball (MAL)	48
Kimball (SOM)	43
Kimball (N)	92
Kimball (DOR)	22
Kimball Ave (REV)	51
Kimball Ct (MEL)	76
Kimball Dr & Rd (STO)	80
Kimball Rd (ARL)	74
Kimball Rd (LEX)	73
Kimball Rd (WAT)	72
Kimball Rd (CHE)	50
Kimball Rd (BRA)	85
Kimball St & Ln (CAM)	40

Kimball Ter (NWV)	60
Kimlo Rd (WH)	81
Kineo (DOR)	21
King (WAT)	72
King (LEX)	73
King (ARL)	74
King (WAV)	79
King (AUB)	66
King (CAM)	40
King Ave (MED)	55
King Ave (WY)	88
King Pl (CAM)	39
King St & Sq (DOR)	22
King St & Ter (RXC)	20
King Cove Beach St & Rd (NWV)	91
King Hill Rd (BRA)	85
King Oak Ter (EWY)	89
King Phillip (SWY)	90
Kingman (WY)	88
Kingman Ave (REV)	51
Kingman Rd (SOM)	43
Kingman Rd (DOR)	24
Kingman Rd (NWH)	92
Kings Ln (QUI)	69
Kings Grant Rd (WES)	93
Kingsboro Park (JP)	30
Kingsbury (N)	92
Kingsbury (WEL)	81
Kingsbury (ROX)	19
Kingsbury Ln (WES)	93
Kingsbury Rd (CHH)	67
Kingsdale (DOR)	24
Kingsland Rd (WRX)	32
Kingsley (ALL)	34
Kingsley Ave (MEL)	76
Kingsleys Ct (WAL)	54
Kingston (WS)	44
Kingston	11
Kingston Rd (NWH)	92
Kingston Rd & Ter (WAL)	54
Kingston St & Pl (CHA)	29
Kingswood Rd (AUB)	66
Kinmouth Rd (WAB)	68
Kinnaird (CAM)	40
Kinross Rd (BRO)	46
Kinsman (EV)	49
Kipling Rd (WH)	81
Kipling Rd (ARL)	74
Kipling Rd (SWY)	90
Kippy (EV)	49
Kippy Dr (WAB)	68
Kirby (REV)	51
Kirby (BRA)	84
Kirk (WRX)	32
Kirkland	16
Kirkland Cir (WH)	81
Kirkland Rd (SWY)	90
Kirkland St, Pl & Rd (CAM)	38
Kirkstall Rd (NWV)	60
Kirkwood Rd (3RI)	35
Kirmes Rd (STO)	80
Kittredge Ave (QUI)	69
Kittredge St, Ct & Ter (ROS)	31
Klasson Ln (WY)	88
Knapp (SOM)	43
Knapp	11
Kneeland	11
Kneeland (MAL)	48
Knight (HP)	36
Knights Ct (JP)	30
Knoll (ROS)	31
Knoll (MAL)	48

Knollin (MAL)	48
Knollwood Cir (WY)	88
Knollwood Dr (WAL)	54
Knollwood Rd (MED)	55
Knollwood Rd (MQ)	71
Knowles (NCE)	59
Knowles Rd	
1-54 (WAT)	72
55-OUT (WAV)	79
Knowlton (SOM)	45
Knowlton (SB)	27
Knox	16
Knox (BEL)	78
Knox Park (EV)	49
Kodsya Rd (WAB)	68
Kondazian (WAT)	72
Kovey Rd (HP)	36
Kristen Ct (HP)	36
L (SB)	27
La Grange	16
La Grange (WRX)	32
La Grange Pl (ROX)	19
La Rose Pl (BRI)	35
La Salle Rd (NH)	94
Labadine (WOL)	70
Laban Pratt Rd (DOR)	22
Laconia	18
Laconia (LEX)	73
Ladd St & Pl (WAT)	72
Lafayette (QUI)	69
Lafayette (ARL)	74
Lafayette (MIL)	86
Lafayette (EV)	49
Lafayette (WAL)	54
Lafayette Ave (CHE)	50
Lafayette Ave (EWY)	89
Lafayette Cir (WEL)	81
Lafayette Rd (NLF)	62
Lafayette Sq (CAM)	39
Lafield (DOR)	22
Lagrange (CHH)	67
Laird Rd (MED)	55
Lake (SOM)	43
Lake (BRI)	35
Lake (MAL)	48
Lake (LEX)	73
Lake (EWY)	89
Lake (BRA)	85
Lake	
1-OUT (ARL) (ODD)	74
2-216 (ARL) (EVEN)	74
218-OUT (BEL) (EVEN)	78
Lake Ave (AUB)	66
Lake Ave (MEL)	76
Lake Ave	
1-185 (NCE)	59
186-OUT (NWH)	61
Lake Dr (N)	92
Lake Rd (WH)	81
Lake St & Rd (WAL)	54
Lake Ter (NCE)	59
Lake Shore Ct, Rd & Ter (BRI)	35
Lake Shore Dr (ARL)	74
Lake Shore Dr (EWY)	89
Lake View Ave (CAM)	38
Lakecrest St, Path & Rd (EWY)	89
Lakecroft Ct (MEL)	76
Lakehill Ave (ARL)	74
Lakehurst Ave (EWY)	89
Lakeside Ave (EWY)	89
Lakeside Ave (QUI)	69

Boston (Cont.) 021

Lakeside Ave (HP)............. 36
Lakeside Dr (BRA)............. 84
Lakeview (ARL)............. 74
Lakeview Ave (NWV)............. 60
Lakeview Ave (BRA)............. 85
Lakeview Ave (MED)............. 55
Lakeview Ave & Ter (WAL)...... 54
Lakeville Rd (JP)............. 30
Lakewood Rd (SWY)............. 90
Lakewood Rd (NWH)............. 61
Lakin Rd (NH)............. 94
Lamar Pl (ROX)............. 19
Lamartine St, Ct, Ext, Pl &
  Ter (JP)............. 30
Lambert (MED)............. 55
Lambert (CAM)............. 41
Lambert (REV)............. 51
Lambert Ave (CHE)............. 50
Lambert Ave (EWY)............. 89
Lambert Rd (BEL)............. 78
Lambert St & Ave (ROX)........ 19
Lamoine (BEL)............. 78
Lamont (RXC)............. 20
Lamont Ave (CAM)............. 38
Lamson Pl (CAM)............. 39
Lamson St & Ct (EB)............. 28
Lanark Rd (BRO)............. 46
Lanark Rd (MAL)............. 48
Lanark Rd (ARL)............. 74
Lanark Rd (WH)............. 81
Lancaster (QUI)............. 69
Lancaster (CAM)............. 40
Lancaster............. 14
Lancaster Ave (REV)............. 51
Lancaster Ln (MIL)............. 87
Lancaster Rd (BRA)............. 84
Lancaster Rd (N)............. 92
Lancaster Rd (NEW)............. 58
Lancaster Rd (ARL)............. 74
Lancaster Ter (BRO)............. 46
Landers (SOM)............. 43
Landers Rd (WOL)............. 70
Landgrane (NQ)............. 71
Landon Rd (MIL)............. 86
Landor Rd (MAT)............. 26
Landry Rd (MED)............. 55
Landseer St & Ter (WRX)........ 32
Lane (WAL)............. 54
Lane Ave (EWY)............. 89
Lane Park (BRI)............. 35
Lanesville Ter (ROS)............. 31
Langdon (NEW)............. 58
Langdon (EV)............. 49
Langdon Ave (WAT)............. 72
Langdon St & Sq (CAM)........ 38
Langdon St & Ter (ROX)........ 19
Langeley Cir (WOL)............. 70
Langford Park (ROX)............. 19
Langley Rd (ARL)............. 74
Langley Rd (NCE)............. 59
Langley Rd (BRI)............. 35
Langmaid Ave (SOM)............. 45
Lansdowne (CAM)............. 39
Lansdowne (NQ)............. 71
Lansdowne............. 02215
Lansdowne Rd (ARL)............. 74
Lansing (ROX)............. 19
Lansing Rd (NWH)............. 65
Lantern Ln (ARL)............. 74
Lantern Ln (NCE)............. 59

Lantern Ln (WH)............. 81
Lantern Ln (LEX)............. 73
Lantern Ln (WES)............. 93
Lantern Ln (WY)............. 88
Lantern Ln (MIL)............. 87
Lantern Ln (BRA)............. 84
Lantern Ln (ROS)............. 31
Lantern Rd (REV)............. 51
Lantern Rd (BEL)............. 78
Lapham (MED)............. 55
Lapland Rd (CHH)............. 67
Larch Cir (BEL)............. 78
Larch Pl (ROS)............. 31
Larch Rd (CAM)............. 38
Larch Rd (WAB)............. 68
Larch Rd (WH)............. 81
Larchmont (DOR)............. 24
Larchmont Ave (WAB)............. 68
Larchmont Ave (WAL)............. 54
Larchmont Ln (LEX)............. 73
Larchmont Rd (MEL)............. 76
Larchwood Dr (CAM)............. 38
Laredo (DOR)............. 21
Lark (SB)............. 27
Lark (QUI)............. 69
Larkhill Rd (WRX)............. 32
Larkin (REV)............. 51
Larkin Rd (MED)............. 55
Larkin Rd (CHH)............. 67
Larkin Rd (WNW)............. 65
Larkspur Rd (WAB)............. 68
Larrabee St & Pl (MEL)........ 76
Larry St & Pl (QUI)............. 69
Las Casas (MAL)............. 48
Lasell (WRX)............. 32
Lasell (AUB)............. 66
Lash (CHE)............. 50
Lathrop Pl............. 13
Lathrop Rd (WEL)............. 81
Latin Rd (WRX)............. 32
Latin Way (MED)............. 55
Lattimore Ct............. 18
Lauderdale Rd (NWV)............. 91
Laudholm Rd (NEW)............. 58
Laurel (MED)............. 55
Laurel (CHE)............. 50
Laurel (MAL)............. 48
Laurel (CAM)............. 38
Laurel (EWY)............. 89
Laurel (ROX)............. 19
Laurel (CHA)............. 29
Laurel (MEL)............. 76
Laurel (BEL)............. 78
Laurel (LEX)............. 73
Laurel (NCE)............. 59
Laurel (ARL)............. 74
Laurel (WAT)............. 72
Laurel Ave (WNW)............. 65
Laurel Ave (WAL)............. 54
Laurel Ave & Ter (WH)........ 81
Laurel Cir & Dr (N)............. 92
Laurel Path (WIN)............. 52
Laurel Rd (WES)............. 93
Laurel Rd (BRA)............. 85
Laurel Rd (MIL)............. 87
Laurel Rd (CHH)............. 67
Laurel St, Ave & Ter (SOM)... 43
Laurel St & Ct (EV)............. 49
Lauriat (DOR)............. 24
Lauriat Pl (MED)............. 55
Laurie Ave (WRX)............. 32
Lauten Pl (SB)............. 27
Laval (HP)............. 36

Lawler Rd (MED)............. 55
Lawley (DOR)............. 22
Lawleys Wharf (DOR)............. 22
Lawmarisa Rd (WAB)............. 68
Lawn (RXC)............. 20
Lawn Ave (EB)............. 28
Lawn Ave (NWV)............. 60
Lawn Ave (LEX)............. 73
Lawn Ave (QUI)............. 69
Lawn St & Ct (CAM)............. 38
Lawndale (BEL)............. 78
Lawndale Ave (WAL)............. 54
Lawndale Rd (STO)............. 80
Lawndale Rd (MIL)............. 86
Lawndale Ter (JP)............. 30
Lawnview Dr (BRA)............. 84
Lawnwood Pl (CHA)............. 29
Lawrence............. 16
Lawrence (SWY)............. 90
Lawrence (WAL)............. 54
Lawrence (CHE)............. 50
Lawrence (EV)............. 49
Lawrence (CAM)............. 39
Lawrence (MAL)............. 48
Lawrence (QUI)............. 69
Lawrence (WAT)............. 72
Lawrence Ave (DOR)............. 21
Lawrence Ave & Rd (CHH)...... 67
Lawrence Ct (SB)............. 27
Lawrence Ln (BEL)............. 78
Lawrence Ln (LEX)............. 73
Lawrence Ln (ARL)............. 74
Lawrence Rd (WEL)............. 81
Lawrence Rd (BRO)............. 46
Lawrence Rd (REV)............. 51
Lawrence Rd (MIL)............. 86
Lawrence Rd (N)............. 92
Lawrence Rd (WES)............. 93
Lawrence St & Pl (BRI)........ 35
Lawrence St & Rd (MED)....... 55
Lawrence St & Ter (CHA)...... 29
Lawry (QUI)............. 69
Lawson Ave (REV)............. 51
Lawson Ln (BRA)............. 85
Lawson Pl (EB)............. 28
Lawson Rd (SWY)............. 90
Lawson Ter (SOM)............. 43
Lawton (BRO)............. 46
Lawton Pl (WAL)............. 54
Lawton Rd (N)............. 92
Lawton Rd (QUI)............. 69
Lawton St & Ter (HP)........ 36
Le Fevre (MAT)............. 26
Leah (MEL)............. 76
Leahaven Rd (MAT)............. 26
Leahaven Rd (SWY)............. 90
Leahaven Ter (BRA)............. 85
Leamington Rd (BRI)............. 35
Lebanon (DOR)............. 25
Lebanon (MEL)............. 76
Lebanon (QUI)............. 69
Lebanon St & Ter (MAL)....... 48
Lechmere Sq (CAM)............. 41
Ledge (MEL)............. 76
Ledge (STO)............. 80
Ledge (NH)............. 94
Ledge Rd (BRA)............. 84
Ledge Rd (WAL)............. 54
Ledge Hill Rd & Ter (WY)..... 88
Ledge Ways (WH)............. 81
Ledgebrook Rd (SWY)............. 90
Ledgebrook Rd (MAT)............. 26
Ledgedale Rd (ROS)............. 31

Boston (Con.)	021
Ledgelawn Ave (LEX)	73
Ledgeriere Rd (BRI)	35
Ledges Rd (NCE)	59
Ledgeway (MIL)	86
Ledgeways (WH)	81
Ledgewood Ave (MEL)	76
Ledgewood Cir (BEL)	78
Ledgewood Rd (NWH)	61
Ledgewood Rd (BRA)	84
Ledgewood Rd (WES)	93
Ledgewood Rd (WRX)	32
Ledgewood Ter (MAL)	48
Ledyard (WH)	81
Lee (STO)	80
Lee (QUI)	69
Lee (BRO)	46
Lee (JP)	30
Lee (CAM)	39
Lee (SOM)	45
Lee (REV)	51
Lee (MED)	55
Lee (EWY)	89
Lee Rd (NH)	94
Lee Rd (CHH)	67
Lee St & Ave (LEX)	73
Lee Ter (ARL)	74
Lee Burbank Hwy (REV)	51
Lee Hill Rd (ROS)	31
Leeds (SB)	27
Leedsville St & Ct (DOR)	22
Leeland Ter (LEX)	73
Leeson Ln (NCE)	59
Leewood Rd (NWH)	61
Leewood Rd (WH)	81
Legion Pl (ROS)	31
Legion Rd (WES)	93
Lehigh (ARL)	74
Lehigh Rd (WH)	81
Leicester (BRO)	46
Leicester (BRI)	35
Leicester Rd (BEL)	78
Leighton (MED)	55
Leighton Ave (LEX)	73
Leighton Rd (WEL)	81
Leighton Rd (AUB)	66
Leighton Rd (HP)	36
Leisure Ln (STO)	80
Leisure Ter (WY)	88
Leitha Dr (WAL)	54
Leland (MAL)	48
Leland (JP)	30
Leland (SOM)	43
Leland Rd (CHH)	67
Lemoyne (BRA)	84
Lenglen Rd (NEW)	58
Leniston (ROS)	31
Lennaco Rd (JP)	30
Lennon Ct (SB)	27
Lennon Rd (ARL)	74
Lenox (NWW)	65
Lenox (QUI)	69
Lenox	18
Lenox (BRO)	46
Lenox Rd (BRA)	85
Lenoxdale Ave (DOR)	24
Leon	15
Leon (SOM)	43
Leon Cir (MED)	55
Leonard (WS)	44
Leonard (MAL)	48
Leonard (WAL)	54
Leonard (BEL)	78
Leonard Ave (NWV)	60
Leonard Ave (CAM)	39
Leonard Cir (MED)	55
Leonard Pl (SB)	27
Leonard Rd (REV)	51
Leonard Rd (MEL)	76
Leonard Rd (LEX)	73
Leonard Rd (NWY)	91
Leonard St & Ct (DOR)	22
Leonardo Ave (MAL)	48
Leroy (DOR)	22
Leroy Rd (LEX)	73
Leseur Rd (HP)	36
Lesher (ROS)	31
Lesley Ave (WS)	44
Leslie (DOR)	22
Leslie Ave (WY)	88
Leslie Park (ROX)	19
Leslie Rd (WAL)	54
Leslie Rd (WAV)	79
Leslie Rd (AUB)	66
Lester (NH)	94
Lester Pl (JP)	30
Lester Ter (WH)	44
Leston (MAT)	26
Letitia Way (BRI)	35
Letterfine Ter (DOR)	25
Levant (DOR)	22
Levbert Rd (NCE)	59
Leverett	14
Leverett (BRO)	46
Leverett Ave (REV)	51
Leverett Ave (EB)	28
Lewis (EB)	28
Lewis (SOM)	43
Lewis (MED)	55
Lewiston (N)	92
Lewis	
1-11	09
12-OUT	13
Lewis Ave (ARL)	74
Lewis Ave & Ter (WIN)	52
Lewis Pl (ROX)	19
Lewis Rd (BEL)	78
Lewis St & Pl (EV)	49
Lewis St & Ter (NEW)	58
Lewis Wharf	10
Lewiston (HP)	36
Lexington (WAV)	79
Lexington (STO)	80
Lexington (WAT)	72
Lexington (NQ)	71
Lexington (WES)	93
Lexington	
1-60 (NWW)	65
61-OUT (AUB)	66
Lexington Ave (NH)	94
Lexington Ave (HP)	36
Lexington Ave (CAM)	38
Lexington Ave (WS)	44
Lexington Ave & Rd (LEX)	73
Lexington Rd (WH)	81
Lexington St & Ave (CHA)	49
Lexington St & Park (EV)	49
Lexington St, Pl & Sq (EB)	28
Lexington St & Ter (WAL)	54
Leyden (EB)	28
Leyden St & Ave (MED)	55
Leyland (DOR)	25
Libbey (WRX)	32
Libby Rd (MIL)	86
Liberty (WAL)	54
Liberty (EV)	49
Liberty	
1-510 (BRA)	84
511-OUT (BRA)	85
Liberty Ave (MED)	55
Liberty Ave (REV)	51
Liberty Ave (LEX)	73
Liberty Ave & Rd (WS)	44
Liberty Park Ave (BRA)	85
Liberty Pl (SB)	27
Liberty Sq	09
Liberty St & Sq (SWY)	90
Liberty St & Sq (QUI)	69
Library (REV)	51
Library (CHE)	50
Life (BRI)	35
Light Guard Dr (MED)	55
Lila Ave (MED)	55
Lila Rd (JP)	30
Lilac Cir (WEL)	81
Lilac Ct (CAM)	41
Lilac Ln (WY)	88
Lilac Ter (ROS)	31
Lill Ave (NWW)	65
Lillian (EB)	28
Lillian Rd (WOL)	70
Lillian Rd (LEX)	73
Lillian Rd (MAL)	48
Lillian Rd (EWY)	89
Lillie Way (CHH)	67
Lily (MAL)	48
Lily (SB)	27
Lime	08
Lincoln	11
Lincoln (DOR)	22
Lincoln (MAL)	48
Lincoln (HP)	36
Lincoln (EV)	49
Lincoln (REV)	51
Lincoln (STO)	80
Lincoln (WAT)	72
Lincoln (MEL)	76
Lincoln (ARL)	74
Lincoln (NWH)	61
Lincoln (NWY)	91
Lincoln (BRA)	84
Lincoln (MIL)	86
Lincoln (WES)	93
Lincoln (N)	92
Lincoln	
1-199 (BRI)	35
200-OUT (ALL)	34
Lincoln Ave (WOL)	70
Lincoln Cir & Rd (WH)	81
Lincoln Ln (CAM)	38
Lincoln Pky (SOM)	43
Lincoln Pl (BRI)	35
Lincoln Rd (BRO)	46
Lincoln Rd (NEW)	58
Lincoln St, Ave & Pl (SOM)	45
Lincoln St & Pl (CAM)	41
Lincoln St & Pl (CHA)	49
Lincoln St & Rd (MED)	55
Lincoln St & Ter (WIN)	52
Lincoln St & Ter (WAL)	54
Lincoln St & Ter (LEX)	73
Lincoln Way (CAM)	40
Lincoln Wharf	09
Lind (QUI)	69
Lind Rd (NWW)	65
Linda Ln (NWH)	61
Linda Ln (DOR)	25

Boston (Con.)	021
Linda Ln (WY)	88
Linda Rd (BRA)	85
Lindale Ave (NWY)	91
Lindall (ROS)	31
Lindall Pl	14
Lindbergh Ave (WY)	88
Lindbergh Ave (MH)	94
Lindbergh Ave (WNW)	65
Lindbergh Rd (MIL)	86
Linden (BRA)	84
Linden (N)	92
Linden (NUF)	64
Linden (WOL)	70
Linden (LEX)	73
Linden (STO)	80
Linden (ARL)	74
Linden (WAT)	72
Linden (SB)	27
Linden (ALL)	34
Linden (WIN)	52
Linden (MED)	55
Linden (CAM)	38
Linden	
1-330 (WEL)	81
331-OUT (WH)	81
Linden Ave (MAT)	26
Linden Ave (RXC)	78
Linden Ave (BEL)	78
Linden Ave & Pl (MAL)	48
Linden Cir (WES)	93
Linden Ct & Pl (QUI)	69
Linden Gdns & Sq (WEL)	81
Linden Park Dr (WAL)	54
Linden Park St (RXC)	78
Linden Pl (EWY)	89
Linden Rd (WRX)	32
Linden St, Ave, Cir & Pl	
(SOM)	43
Linden St & Ct (DOR)	22
Linden St, Ct, Park, Pl & Sq	
(BRO)	46
Linden St & Pl (EV)	49
Linden St & Rd (MEL)	76
Linden St & Ter (WAL)	54
Lindenwood Rd (STO)	80
Linder Ter (NEW)	58
Lindsey (DOR)	24
Lirrdy Ln (WAL)	54
Line	
1-45 (CAM) (ODD)	38
2-120 (SOM) (EVEN)	43
47-OUT (CAM) (ODD)	39
122-OUT (CAM) (EVEN)	39
Linehurst Rd (MAL)	48
Linehurst Rd (REV)	51
Lingard (DOR)	25
Linley Ter (SB)	27
Linmoor Ter (LEX)	73
Linnaean (CAM)	38
Linnet (WRX)	32
Linsky Barry Ct (SB)	27
Linvale Ter (MAT)	26
Linway (SWY)	90
Linwood (HP)	36
Linwood (MAL)	48
Linwood (MED)	55
Linwood (ARL)	74
Linwood Ave (MEL)	76
Linwood Ave (NWY)	60
Linwood Pl (CAM)	39
Linwood Rd (WH)	81
Linwood St & Pl (SOM)	43
Linwood St & Sq (ROX)	19
Lionel Ave (WAL)	54
Lisbeth (LEX)	73
Lisbon (MAL)	48
Lisle (BRA)	84
List Pl (ROS)	31
Liszt (ROS)	31
Litchfield (BRI)	35
Lithgow (DOR)	24
Littell Rd (BRO)	46
Little Pond Rd (BEL)	78
Littledale (ROS)	31
Littlefield (QUI)	69
Littlefield Rd (NCE)	59
Littlejohn (ARL)	74
Livermore (MAT)	26
Livermore Pl (CAM)	41
Livermore Rd (WAL)	54
Livermore Rd (BEL)	78
Livermore Rd (WH)	81
Liverpool Ln (WAL)	54
Liverpool St & Ave (EB)	28
Livesey Rd (NQ)	71
Livingston Ln (WAL)	54
Livingston Rd (WH)	81
Livingstone (DOR)	24
Livingstone Cir (N)	92
Livoli Ave (BRA)	85
Llewellyn Rd (WNW)	65
Lloyd Rd (WAT)	72
Lochdale Rd (ROS)	31
Lochland (MIL)	86
Lochland Rd (HP)	36
Lochmere Ave (NWY)	91
Lochstead Ave (JP)	30
Locke (CAM)	40
Locke (CHE)	50
Locke (WAT)	72
Locke (ARL)	74
Locke Ln (LEX)	73
Locke Pl (SB)	27
Locke Rd (WAB)	93
Locke Rd (MED)	55
Lockeland Ave (ARL)	74
Locksley Rd (NCE)	59
Lockwood (HP)	36
Lockwood Dr (SWY)	90
Lockwood Rd (WNW)	65
Lockwood Rd (LEX)	73
Locust (BEL)	78
Locust (MED)	55
Locust (CHE)	50
Locust (WAL)	54
Locust Ln (N)	92
Locust Rd	
1-2 (WES)	93
3-3 (WH)	81
4-OUT (WES)	93
Locust St & Ave (LEX)	73
Locust St & Park (EV)	49
Locust St & Ter (CAM)	38
Locust St & Way (WIN)	52
Lodge (MIL)	86
Lodge Ave (MEL)	76
Lodge Rd (BEL)	78
Lodge Rd (WNW)	65
Lodgehill Rd (HP)	36
Logan (WAL)	54
Logan (ROX)	19
Logan Ave & Grv (MED)	55
Logan Rd (BRA)	85
Logan Way (SB)	27
Lois Ln (N)	92
Lois Ter (WOL)	70
Lomasney Way	14
Lombard (DOR)	24
Lombard (NEW)	58
Lombard Ct (MAL)	48
Lombard Rd & Ter (ARL)	74
London Ave (NQ)	71
London St & Ct (EB)	28
Lone Pine Path (WY)	88
Long (MED)	55
Long Ave (ALL)	34
Long Ave (BEL)	78
Long Island (QUI)	69
Long Wharf	10
Longacre Rd (N)	92
Longbow Rd (STO)	80
Longfellow (WAT)	72
Longfellow (SWY)	90
Longfellow (DOR)	22
Longfellow Park & Rd (CAM)	38
Longfellow Rd (WAL)	54
Longfellow Rd (NH)	94
Longfellow Rd (WH)	81
Longfellow Rd (MEL)	76
Longfellow Rd (ARL)	74
Longfellow Rd (LEX)	73
Longfellow Rd (NLF)	62
Longfellow Rd Ext (WH)	81
Longmeadow (ROX)	19
Longmeadow Rd (WH)	81
Longmeadow Rd (NCE)	59
Longmeadow Rd (ARL)	74
Longmeadow Rd (BEL)	78
Longmeadow Rd (WES)	93
Longview Rd (BRA)	84
Longwell Rd (NLF)	62
Longwood Ave (BRO)	46
Longwood Ave	
141-344	15
345-OUT	02215
Longwood Dr (BRA)	84
Longwood Rd (MIL)	87
Longwood Rd (WY)	88
Longwood Rd (QUI)	69
Longwood Rd (CHH)	67
Lonsdale (DOR)	24
Lookout (LEX)	73
Lookout Rd (MED)	55
Loomis (MAL)	48
Loomis (CAM)	38
Loomis (REV)	51
Loomis Ave (WAT)	72
Lopez (MAL)	39
Lopez Ave (CAM)	41
Lora (MAL)	48
Lord (WAL)	64
Lorean Ter (WIN)	52
Loren Park (EV)	49
Lorena Rd (JP)	30
Lorenzo (DOR)	22
Loretta Ave (BRA)	84
Loretta Rd (WAL)	54
Lorette (WRX)	32
Lorimer Pl (ROX)	19
Lorimer Rd (WAV)	79
Loring (WAV)	79
Loring (QUI)	69
Loring (NCE)	59
Loring (SB)	27
Loring (SOM)	43
Loring Pl (MAL)	48

Boston (Con.)   021

Loring Rd (REV) 51
Loring Rd (WIN) 52
Loring Rd (LEX) 73
Loring Rd (WES) 93
Loring St & Pl (HP) 36
Lorna Rd (NCE) 59
Lorna Rd (MAT) 26
Lorne (DOR) 24
Lorne Rd (ARL) 74
Lorraine (ROS) 31
Lorraine (EWY) 89
Lorraine Cir (WAB) 68
Lorraine Rd (MED) 55
Lorraine Ter (ALL) 34
Lorraine Ter (ARL) 74
Los Angeles (NEW) 58
Lothian Rd (BRI) 35
Lothrop (BRI) 35
Lothrop (NWV) 60
Lothrop Ave (MIL) 87
Lotus (JP) 30
Lotus Ave (STO) 80
Loud Ave (WY) 88
Louders Ln (JP) 30
Louis (CHE) 50
Louis (SB) 27
Louis Ter (DOR) 24
Louis Pasteur Ave 15
Louis Prang 15
Louisburg Pl (SOM) 45
Louisburg Sq 08
Louise (WAT) 72
Louise Ct (MAL) 48
Louise Rd (CHH) 67
Louise Rd (BEL) 78
Louise Rd (BRA) 84
Lourdes Ave (JP) 30
Love Ln (WES) 93
Lovedeed Ct (ROX) 19
Lovejoy Pl 14
Loveland Rd (BRO) 46
Lovell (WS) 44
Lovell (EB) 28
Lovell (NWY) 91
Lovell Rd (MEL) 76
Lovell Rd (WAT) 72
Lovell Rd (ARL) 74
Lovering Rd (MED) 55
Lovett Rd (NCE) 59
Lovewell Rd (WEL) 81
Lovis (SB) 27
Lowden Ave (WS) 44
Lowe (REV) 51
Lowe (QUI) 69
Lowe St Pl (REV) 51
Lowell (REV) 51
Lowell (CAM) 38
Lowell (QUI) 69
Lowell (LEX) 73
Lowell (BRA) 84
Lowell
  1-171 (SOM) 43
  172-273 (WS) 44
  274-OUT (SOM) 45
Lowell Ave (NWV) 60
Lowell Ave (WAT) 72
Lowell Cir (SOM) 43
Lowell Ct (MED) 55
Lowell Rd (WIN) 52
Lowell Rd (BRO) 46
Lowell Rd (WH) 81

Lowell St Pl (ARL) 74
Lowell St, Ave & Ter (MAL) 48
Lowell St & Pl (WAL) 54
Lowell St & Pl (ARL) 74
Lowell Ter (SOM) 45
Lowland Pl (EB) 28
Loyola (ROX) 19
Lubec (EB) 28
Lublin (ARL) 74
Lucas Ct (WRW) 65
Lucerne (DOR) 24
Lucia Ave (REV) 51
Lucille Pl (NUF) 64
Lucy (STO) 80
Ludlow (CHA) 29
Ludwig Rd (NH) 94
Lufberry (MIL) 86
Luke Rd (EV) 49
Lunar Ave (BRA) 85
Lund Rd (MED) 55
Lunda (WAL) 54
Lundquist Dr (BRA) 85
Lunt (NQ) 71
Lura (WAL) 54
Lurton (QUI) 69
Luteman Pl (RXC) 20
Luther Pl (CHE) 50
Luther Rd (MED) 55
Lyall St & Ter (WRX) 32
Lyford (DOR) 24
Lyle St & Ter (MAL) 48
Lyman Ave (NCE) 59
Lyman (MED) 55
Lyman Rd (CHH) 67
Lyman Rd (MIL) 86
Lyman Ter (WAL) 54
Lyme (MAL) 48
Lyme (EWY) 89
Lyme Rd (WRW) 65
Lynde (MAL) 48
Lynde (EV) 49
Lynde St & Ave (MEL) 76
Lynde St & Ave (CHA) 29
Lyndeboro (CHA) 29
Lyndeboro Pl 16
Lyndhurst (DOR) 24
Lyne Rd (BRI) 35
Lynn (CHE) 50
Lynn (EV) 49
Lynn (MAL) 48
Lynn Fells Pky (MEL) 76
Lynnville Ter (DOR) 21
Lynnway (REV) 51
Lyon (DOR) 22
Lyon Rd (CHH) 67
Lyons (QUI) 69
Lyons Sq (CHE) 50
Lyons St & Ct (WAT) 72
Lyra Dr (SWY) 90
M (SB) 27
M Ave (WRX) 32
M St Pl (SB) 27
Mabelle Ave (MED) 55
Mac Arthur (SOM) 45
Mac Arthur Rd (STO) 80
Mac Donald (HP) 36
Mac Dougal Ct (SWY) 90
Mac Intosh Ave (N) 92
Mace Ave (EWY) 89
Mackin (BRI) 35
Macklin Rd (MED) 55
Macks Ct (WAL) 54
Macular Rd (WRX) 32

Macy (QUI) 69
Madden (QUI) 69
Madeleine (QUI) 69
Madeline (BRI) 35
Madison (HP) 36
Madison (CAM) 38
Madison (MED) 55
Madison (SOM) 43
Madison (REV) 51
Madison (MAL) 48
Madison (BEL) 78
Madison (EWY) 89
Madison (ROX) 19
Madison Ave (QUI) 69
Madison Ave (WAT) 72
Madison Ave (NWV) 60
Madison Ave (ARL) 74
Madison Ave (LEX) 73
Madison Ave (WIN) 52
Madison Ave (CAM) 40
Madison Ave (CHE) 50
Madison Ave (EV) 49
Madison Rd (WAL) 54
Madison Rd (WH) 81
Madoc (NCE) 59
Maffa Way (CHA) 29
Magazine (ROX) 19
Magazine (CAM) 39
Magdala (DOR) 24
Magee (CAM) 39
Magee (HP) 36
Magees Cor (WIN) 52
Maggi Rd (REV) 51
Magnolia (MAL) 48
Magnolia (ARL) 74
Magnolia (MEL) 76
Magnolia (BRA) 84
Magnolia
  1-189 (DOR) 25
  190-OUT (DOR) 21
Magnolia Ave (CAM) 38
Magnolia Ave (NEW) 58
  magnolia Ct (EV) 49
Magnolia Pl & Sq (DOR) 25
Magnolia Rd (MIL) 86
Magnolia Ter (STO) 80
Magnus Ave (SOM) 43
Magoun (CAM) 40
Magoun Ave (MED) 55
Magoun Sq (SOM) 45
Mague Ave & Pl (WRW) 65
Maguire Ct (NWV) 60
Maguire Rd (LEX) 73
Mahan Pl 16
Mahler Rd (ROS) 31
Maida Ter (HP) 36
Main (SOM) 45
Main (MED) 55
Main (EV) 49
Main (MAL) 48
Main (WIN) 52
Main (WAL) 54
Main (CHA) 29
Main (STO) 80
Main (MEL) 76
Main (WAT) 72
Main (QUI) 69
Main (BRA) 85
Main
  1-385 (WY) 88
  1-505 (CAM) 42
  386-OUT (SWY) 90
  506-OUT (CAM) 39

Boston (Con.)   021

Main St Park (MAL)	48
Maine Ave & Ter (SOM)	45
Maitland (MIL)	86
Maitland	02215
Malbert Rd (BRI)	35
Malbon Pl (ROX)	19
Malcolm Rd (CAM)	38
Malcolm Rd (JP)	30
Malcomb Rd (WY)	88
Malden (REV)	51
Malden (EV)	49
Malden (MED)	55
Malden	18
Malden (QUI)	69
Malden (WAT)	72
Malden St Park (MAL)	48
Malden St & Sq (MAL)	48
Malia Ter (CHH)	67
Mall (ROX)	19
Mallard Ave (DOR)	24
Mallard Rd (QUI)	69
Mallard Rd (N)	92
Mallard Way (WAL)	54
Mallet (WS)	44
Mallet (DOR)	24
Mallon Rd (DOR)	21
Malloy Ct (SOM)	43
Malta (MAT)	26
Maltby Ln (NWY)	91
Malubar Ln (NCE)	59
Malvern (QUI)	69
Malvern (MEL)	76
Malvern (WAL)	54
Malvern (ALL)	34
Malvern Ave (WS)	44
Malvern Ter (MED)	55
Malvern Ter (AUB)	66
Malverna Rd (ROS)	31
Mamelon Cir (MAT)	26
Mamie Rd (SWY)	90
Manassas Ave (CAM)	38
Manatee Rd (EWY)	89
Manchester (MAT)	26
Manchester Rd (BRO)	46
Manchester Rd (NWH)	61
Mandalay Rd (NCE)	59
Mandalay Rd (SWY)	90
Manemet Rd (NCE)	59
Manet Ave (QUI)	69
Manet Cir & Rd (CHH)	67
Mangano Ct (WAT)	72
Mangles (SOM)	55
Manhattan Rd & Ter (WNW)	65
Manila Ave (HP)	36
Manion Rd (HP)	36
Manison (STO)	80
Manitoba Rd (WAB)	67
Manley (DOR)	22
Manley Ct (LEX)	73
Manley Ter (MAL)	48
Mann (WRX)	32
Mann (BRA)	85
Mann Ave (N)	92
Manning (ROS)	31
Manning (MED)	55
Manning (LEX)	73
Manning	
1-202 (NH)	94
203-OUT (N)	92
Manning Rd (WAL)	54
Manning Ter (EV)	49

Mannix Cir (BEL)	78
Manomet Rd (NWY)	91
Manor (DOR)	22
Manor Ave (WH)	81
Manor Rd (WAL)	54
Manor House Rd (NCE)	59
Mansfield (EV)	49
Mansfield (ALL)	34
Mansfield (SOM)	43
Mansfield Rd (WH)	81
Manson Rd (NH)	94
Mansur (JP)	30
Mansur (ROS)	31
Manthorne Rd (WRX)	32
Manton Ter (ALL)	34
Manzonetta Ave (WY)	88
Mapes (DOR)	22
Maple (MIL)	87
Maple (BRA)	84
Maple (EWY)	89
Maple (CHE)	50
Maple (BRO)	46
Maple (HP)	36
Maple (REV)	51
Maple (STO)	80
Maple (LEX)	73
Maple (QUI)	69
Maple (ARL)	74
Maple	
1-57 (WAT) (ODD)	72
2-52 (WAT) (EVEN)	72
54-OUT (NEW) (EVEN)	58
59-OUT (NEW) (ODD)	58
Maple Ave (EV)	49
Maple Ave (SOM)	45
Maple Ave (CAM)	39
Maple Ave (MED)	55
Maple Grv St (MEL)	76
Maple Park (NCE)	59
Maple Park Ave (MED)	55
Maple Pl (JP)	30
Maple Rd (WIN)	52
Maple Rd (WH)	81
Maple Rd (WES)	93
Maple St Ext (WRX)	32
Maple St, Ave, Cir & Ter (NEW)	58
Maple St & Ct (DOR)	21
Maple St, Ct, Pl & Ter (N)	92
Maple St & Park (MAL)	48
Maple St & Ter (WRX)	32
Maple St & Ter (WAL)	54
Maple St & Ter (WAV)	79
Maple St & Ter (MEL)	76
Maple St & Ter (AUB)	66
Mapleton (BRI)	35
Maplewood (WRX)	32
Maplewood (MAL)	48
Maplewood (WAT)	72
Maplewood Ave (NCE)	59
Maplewood Ave (EV)	49
Maplewood Ter (BRA)	85
Marathon (ARL)	74
Marble (STO)	80
Marble (REV)	51
Marble (RXC)	20
Marbury Ter (JP)	30
Marcella (ROX)	19
Marcella St & Ct (CAM)	41
Marcellus Dr (NCE)	59
March Ave, Ter & Way (WRX)	32
Marcia (MAT)	72
Marcia Rd (BRA)	84

Marcy Rd (MAT)	26
Mardell Cir (SOM)	43
Marden Ave (DOR)	24
Margaret	13
Margaret (ARL)	74
Margaret Dr (BRA)	85
Margaret Rd (MIL)	86
Margaret Rd (NWH)	61
Margaret Rd (STO)	80
Margaretta Dr (HP)	36
Margin (HP)	36
Marginal (CHE)	50
Marginal (EB)	28
Marginal Rd (QUI)	69
Margo Rd (BRI)	35
Marguerite Ave (WAL)	54
Maria Ln (ROS)	31
Marianne Rd (WAL)	54
Marida Way (MAL)	48
Marie (DOR)	22
Marie Ave (EV)	49
Marie Ave (CAM)	39
Marie Ave (STO)	80
Marie Ave (SWY)	90
Marieanne Ave (BRA)	85
Marietta Ave (BRA)	84
Marigold Ave (WH)	81
Marilyn Rd (MIL)	87
Marr s (SWY)	90
Marine (QUI)	69
Marine (MED)	55
Marine Rd (SB)	27
Maron (MED)	55
Marion (CAM)	41
Marion (SOM)	43
Marion (MAL)	48
Marion (WAL)	54
Marion (ROS)	31
Marion (HP)	36
Marion (WOL)	70
Marion (STO)	80
Marion (WNW)	65
Marion Ave (BRA)	85
Marion Cir & Rd (ARL)	74
Marion Rd (WAT)	72
Marion Rd (BEL)	78
Marion Rd (NWY)	91
Marion St & Pl (EB)	28
Marion St & Ter (BRO)	46
Mariposa (MAT)	26
Marisa Dr (BRA)	85
Marivista Ave (WAL)	54
Marjorie Rd (BRA)	85
Mark (JP)	30
Mark Lee Rd (NH)	94
Marked Tree Rd (N)	92
Market (BRI)	35
Market (CAM)	39
Market (EV)	49
Market (CHE)	50
Market	14
Marks Rd (EWY)	89
Marla Cir (NCE)	59
Marlboro (BEL)	78
Marlboro (WOL)	70
Marlboro (EV)	49
Marlboro (MAL)	48
Marlboro (NEW)	58
Marlboro Rd (LEX)	73
Marlboro Ter (WAT)	72
Marlborough (CHE)	50
Marlborough	
1-325	16

Boston (Con.)　　　　　　　　021

326-OUT 15
Marlborough Rd (WAL) 54
Marlin Rd (WRX) 32
Marlin Way (DOR) 22
Marlou Ter (JP) 30
Marlowe (DOR) 24
Marlton Rd (WAL) 54
Marmion (JP) 30
Marmion Rd (MEL) 76
Marney (CAM) 41
Marr Crest Dr (MIL) 86
Marrett St & Rd (LEX) 73
Marrigan (ARL) 74
Mars (WY) 88
Marsh (QUI) 69
Marsh (DOR) 24
Marsh
1-365 (BEL) (ODD) 78
2-396 (BEL) (EVEN) 78
367-OUT (WAV) (ODD) 79
398-OUT (WAV) (EVEN) ... 79
Marsh Rd (N) 92
Marshall (N) 92
Marshall (BRA) 84
Marshall 08
Marshall (WAT) 72
Marshall (NQ) 71
Marshall (NCE) 59
Marshall (SOM) 45
Marshall (MED) 55
Marshall (BRO) 46
Marshall (REV) 51
Marshall (WIN) 52
Marshall Ave (MAL) 48
Marshall Pl (CHA) 29
Marshall Rd (LEX) 73
Marshall Rd (WEL) 81
Marshall Rd (STO) 80
Marshall St Cir (SOM) 45
Marshall St & Rd (MIL) 86
Marshall Way (WES) 93
Marshfield (ROX) 19
Marshfield Rd (BRA) 85
Marshfield Rd (NCE) 59
Marston (MED) 55
Martell Rd (QUI) 69
Martensen (QUI) 69
Martha Rd 14
Marthas Ln (CHH) 67
Martin (ARL) 74
Martin (MEL) 76
Martin (MED) 55
Martin (REV) 51
Martin (WRX) 32
Martin (CAM) 38
Martin Rd (WH) 81
Martin Rd (WES) 93
Martin Rd & Ter (MIL) 86
Martin Luther King Blvd
(ROX) 19
Martinwood Rd (JP) 30
Martyn (WAL) 54
Marvin (ROX) 19
Marvin (LEX) 73
Marvin Ln (NCE) 59
Marvin Pl (CAM) 39
Marvin Rd (WEL) 81
Marvin Rd (MEL) 76
Mary (ARL) 74
Mary (QUI) 69
Mary Ann Rd (ROS) 31

Mary Ellen Rd (WAB) 68
Mary Mount Rd (AUB) 66
Maryknoll St & Ter (MAT) 26
Maryland (DOR) 25
Maryland Ave (WIN) 52
Mascoma (DOR) 21
Mascoma (WOL) 70
Mascot (DOR) 24
Mason 11
Mason (WOL) 70
Mason (LEX) 73
Mason (WS) 44
Mason (HP) 36
Mason (CAM) 38
Mason (MED) 55
Mason (MAL) 48
Mason (EV) 49
Mason (SWY) 90
Mason Ct (CHA) 29
Mason Rd (N) 92
Mason Rd (NCE) 59
Mason Rd (WAT) 72
Mason St & Ter (BRO) 46
Massachusetts Ave (MED) 55
Massachusetts Ave (LEX) 73
Massachusetts Ave (QUI) 69
Massachusetts Ave (ARL) 74
Massachusetts Ave (BRA) 85
Massachusetts Ave
1-400 15
1-975 (CAM) (ODD) 39
2-966 (CAM) (EVEN) 39
401-1099 18
968-1748 (CAM) (EVEN) ... 38
977-1737 (CAM) (ODD) 38
1100-OUT (DOR) 25
1739-OUT (CAM) (ODD) 40
1750-OUT (CAM) (EVEN) .. 40
Massapoag (SWY) 90
Massasoit (MAT) 26
Massasoit Rd (NWY) 91
Massasoit Rd (WH) 81
Massasoit St & Ct (WAL) 54
Matchett (BRI) 35
Mathaurs (MIL) 86
Mather St & Ct (DOR) 24
Matignon Rd (N) 22
Matignon Rd (CAM) 40
Mattakeeset (MAT) 26
Mattapan St & Sq (MAT) 26
Matthew (DOR) 24
Matthews 10
Mattson (QUI) 69
Maude (MAL) 48
Maude Ter (WAT) 72
Maugus Ave (WH) 81
Maugus Hill Rd (WH) 81
Maureen Rd (LEX) 73
Maurice (MAL) 48
Maurice (MED) 55
Maurice Rd (WEL) 81
Maverick (MED) 55
Maverick (CHE) 50
Maverick St & Sq (EB) 28
Max Ave (CAM) 41
Maxfield (WRX) 32
Maxim Ave (QUI) 69
Maxwell (DOR) 24
Maxwell Rd (MIL) 86
May (N) 92
May (WH) 81
May (LEX) 73
May (JP) 30

May St & Ave (BRA) 84
May Ter (SWY) 90
Mayall Rd (WAL) 54
Maybelle Ave (MED) 55
Mayberry Ave (MED) 55
Maybie (ARL) 74
Maybrook (DOR) 21
Maybury (DOR) 21
Mayfair (ROX) 19
Mayfield (DOR) 25
Mayfield (WAV) 79
Mayflower (LEX) 73
Mayflower (ALL) 34
Mayflower Ave (NWY) 91
Mayflower Dr (STG) 80
Mayflower Rd (ARL) 74
Mayflower Rd (NQ) 71
Mayflower Rd (CHH) 67
Mayflower Rd (BRA) 84
Mayflower Rd (N) 92
Mayflower Ter (NWH) 61
Mayhew (DOR) 25
Maynard (WNW) 65
Maynard (ARL) 74
Maynard (ROS) 31
Maynard (MED) 55
Maynard (MAL) 48
Maynard Pl (CAM) 38
Mayo Ave (N) 92
Mayo Rd (WH) 81
Maypole Rd (QUI) 69
Maywood St & Ter (ROX) 19
Mc Arthur Rd (WEL) 81
Mc Bride (JP) 30
Mc Bride Ct (WAL) 54
Mc Call (MED) 55
Mc Carthy Rd (CAM) 38
Mc Carthy Rd (NCE) 59
Mc Clellan Hwy (EB) 28
Mc Clure (REV) 51
Mc Coba (REV) 51
Mc Cormack (MAL) 48
Mc Cormack Ave (MED) 55
Mc Cormack Sq (EB) 28
Mc Craw (ROS) 31
Mc Culloch Rd (NH) 94
Mc Donald (QUI) 69
Mc Donald Ave (ALL) 34
Mc Donald Rd (MED) 55
Mc Donough Ct (HP) 36
Mc Donough Way (SB) 27
Mc Grath Hwy (QUI) 69
Mc Grath Hwy
1-463 (SOM) (ODD) 43
2-472 (SOM) (EVEN) 43
465-OUT (SOM) (ODD) 45
474-OUT (SOM) (EVEN) ... 45
Mc Greevey Way (RXC) 20
Mc Gregor Ave (SOM) 45
Mc Kay Pl (EB) 28
Mc Kenn (WAL) 54
Mc Kenna Ter (WRX) 32
Mc Kenzie Ave (QUI) 69
Mc Kinley (REV) 51
Mc Kinley (EV) 49
Mc Kinley Sq 09
Mc Kinnon Ave (MIL) 86
Mc Kone (DOR) 22
Mc Lean (WEL) 81
Mc Lean Pl (CAM) 40
Mc Lellan (DOR) 21
Mc Neil Way (DOR) 21
Mc Nulty Ct (CHA) 29

Boston (Con.) 021

Mc Tiernan (CAM) ... 39
Meacham (SOM) ... 45
Meacham (HP) ... 36
Meacham (MEL) ... 76
Meacham Rd
  1-25 (CAM) (ODD) ... 40
  2-28 (CAM) (EVEN) ... 40
  27-OUT (WS) (ODD) ... 44
  30-OUT (WS) (EVEN) ... 44
Mead (QUI) ... 69
Mead (CAM) ... 40
Mead (WS) ... 44
Mead (EV) ... 49
Mead (ALL) ... 34
Mead (CHA) ... 29
Mead St Ct (CHA) ... 29
Meade (SWY) ... 90
Meade Rd (WAL) ... 54
Meade St & Rd (ARL) ... 74
Meader Rd (EV) ... 49
Meadow (NQ) ... 71
Meadow Ln (WH) ... 81
Meadow Ln (WAL) ... 54
Meadow Ln (SWY) ... 90
Meadow Ln (MIL) ... 86
Meadow Ln & Rd (N) ... 92
Meadow Rd (CHE) ... 50
Meadow Rd (STO) ... 80
Meadow Way (CAM) ... 38
Meadow Brook Ave (LEX) ... 73
Meadow Brook Rd
  1-60 (CHH) ... 67
  61-OUT (BRO) ... 46
Meadowbank Ave (MAT) ... 26
Meadowbrook Rd (WES) ... 93
Meadowbrook Rd (N) ... 92
Meadowbrook Rd (BRA) ... 85
Meadowbrook Rd (WH) ... 81
Meadowbrook Rd (WOL) ... 70
Meadowbrook Rd (NCE) ... 59
Meadowview Rd (MEL) ... 76
Meadowview Rd (MIL) ... 86
Meadowview Rd (HP) ... 36
Meadowview Rd (EV) ... 49
Meagher Ave (MIL) ... 87
Mears Ave (QUI) ... 69
Mechanic (QUI) ... 69
Mechanic (NUF) ... 64
Mechanic (MIL) ... 86
Mechanic (WAL) ... 54
Mechanic St & Ct ... 13
Medfield ... 02215
Medford ... 14
Medford (CHA) ... 29
Medford (CHE) ... 50
Medford (ARL) ... 74
Medford
  1-333 (SOM) ... 43
  334-OUT (SOM) ... 45
Medford Ct ... 18
Medford St & Sq (MED) ... 55
Medford St & Ter (MAL) ... 48
Medina Way (RXC) ... 20
Mediterranean Dr (WEY) ... 88
Medway (DOR) ... 24
Medway (QUI) ... 69
Meehan St & Pl (JP) ... 30
Meeting House Cir (N) ... 92
Meeting House Ln (EWY) ... 89
Meigh Rd (CHH) ... 67
Meisel Path (BEL) ... 78

Melba Ln (STO) ... 80
Melba Way (HP) ... 36
Melbourne (DOR) ... 24
Melbourne Ave (MEL) ... 76
Melbourne Ave (NWV) ... 60
Melbourne Rd (MIL) ... 86
Melcher ... 02210
Melendy Ave (WAT) ... 72
Melina Rd (NCE) ... 59
Mellen (NH) ... 94
Mellen (DOR) ... 24
Mellen (CAM) ... 38
Mellen Rd (LEX) ... 73
Mellon Rd (WEL) ... 81
Melody Ln (WAL) ... 54
Melody Ln (SWY) ... 90
Melrose (MEL) ... 76
Melrose (ARL) ... 74
Melrose ... 16
Melrose Ave (LEX) ... 73
Melrose Ave (N) ... 92
Melrose St & Ave (AUB) ... 66
Melton Rd (BRI) ... 35
Melvern Rd (N) ... 92
Melville Ave (NWV) ... 60
Melville Ave & Ln (DOR) ... 24
Melville Rd (SOM) ... 45
Melville Ter (WAT) ... 72
Melvin (SOM) ... 45
Melvin Ave (BRO) ... 46
Melvin Rd (ARL) ... 74
Melvinside Ter (DOR) ... 25
Memorial Dr (N) ... 92
Memorial Dr (EWY) ... 89
Memorial Rd (WAT) ... 72
Memorial Dr
  1-49 (CAM) ... 42
  50-50 (CAM) ... 39
  51-218 (CAM) ... 42
  219-820 (CAM) ... 39
  821-OUT (CAM) ... 38
Memorial Rd (SOM) ... 45
Memorial Way (ARL) ... 74
Mendell Way (JP) ... 30
Mendelssohn (ROS) ... 31
Mendum (ROS) ... 31
Mendum (MEL) ... 76
Menlo (BRI) ... 35
Menotomy Rd & Way (ARL) ... 74
Menotomy Rocks Dr (ARL) ... 74
Menton (MAT) ... 26
Mercantile ... 09
Mercer (MAT) ... 26
Mercer (SB) ... 27
Mercer Cir (CAM) ... 38
Mercer Rd (NH) ... 94
Merchants Row ... 09
Merchants Row (WAT) ... 72
Mercier Ave (DOR) ... 24
Mercury (WY) ... 88
Meredith (WRX) ... 32
Meredith Ave (NWH) ... 61
Meredith Cir (MIL) ... 86
Meredith Cir (N) ... 92
Meredith Way (WY) ... 88
Meriam (LEX) ... 73
Meridian (MEL) ... 76
Meridian (EB) ... 28
Meridian St & Pky (MAL) ... 48
Merilyn Rd (SWY) ... 90
Merlin (DOR) ... 24
Mermaid Ave (WIN) ... 52
Merola Park (MAT) ... 26

Merriam (JP) ... 30
Merriam (SOM) ... 43
Merriam (WES) ... 93
Merrifield Ave (WAT) ... 72
Merrill (CAM) ... 39
Merrill (DOR) ... 21
Merrill Ave (BEL) ... 78
Merrill Ave (WOL) ... 70
Merrill Rd (WAT) ... 72
Merrill Rd (NCE) ... 59
Merrimac ... 14
Merritt Ave (BRA) ... 84
Merrow Ln (STO) ... 80
Merrymount Ave (WOL) ... 70
Merrymount Rd (SWY) ... 90
Merrymount Rd & Ter (QUI) ... 69
Merton (NEW) ... 58
Merton (WS) ... 44
Merton Pl (ROX) ... 19
Meshaka (WRX) ... 32
Messenger (REV) ... 51
Messengers Ct (MEL) ... 76
Messina (BRA) ... 85
Messinger (MAT) ... 26
Metacomet Rd (WAB) ... 68
Metcalf (ROS) ... 31
Metcalf (MED) ... 55
Metcalf Ct (JP) ... 30
Metcalf Sq (WIN) ... 52
Metropolitan Ave
  1-427 (ROS) ... 31
  428-999 (HP) ... 36
  1000-OUT (MIL) ... 86
Metropolitan Cir & Ter (ROS) ... 31
Meyer St & Ct (ROS) ... 31
Miami Ave & Ter (WRX) ... 32
Mica Ln (WH) ... 81
Michael (ARL) ... 74
Michael Ave (WAT) ... 72
Michael Rd (BRI) ... 35
Michael A Sullivan Sq (CAM) ... 38
Michelanglo ... 13
Michelle Ln (BRA) ... 84
Michigan Ave (DOR) ... 21
Michigan Ave (SOM) ... 45
Middle (NEW) ... 58
Middle (SB) ... 27
Middle (BRA) ... 84
Middle (WAT) ... 72
Middle (STO) ... 80
Middle (LEX) ... 73
Middle
  1-661 (EWY) ... 89
  662-1060 (WY) ... 88
  1061-OUT (SWY) ... 90
Middle St & Ct (WAL) ... 54
Middle Way (WES) ... 93
Middleby Rd (LEX) ... 73
Middlecot (BEL) ... 78
Middlesex (WEL) ... 81
Middlesex (NQ) ... 71
Middlesex (CAM) ... 40
Middlesex (MAL) ... 48
Middlesex (CHA) ... 29
Middlesex Ave (SOM) ... 45
Middlesex Ave (MED) ... 55
Middlesex Cir & Rd (WAL) ... 54
Middlesex Cir & Rd (CHH) ... 67
Middlesex Rd (WAT) ... 72
Middlesex Rd (STO) ... 80
Middleton (DOR) ... 24
Midland (DOR) ... 25
Midland (WAT) ... 72
Midland (BEL) ... 78

Boston (Con.)   021

Midland Ave (NEW)	58
Midland Dr (WAL)	54
Midland Rd (WEL)	81
Midvale Rd (WRX)	32
Midway	02210
Mifflin Pl (CAM)	38
Mignon Rd (WNW)	65
Milano (REV)	51
Mildred Ave (MAT)	26
Mildred Rd (NCE)	59
Miles (ROX)	19
Miles Dr (QUI)	69
Milford	18
Militia Dr (LEX)	73
Milk (LEX)	73

Milk

1-21 (ODD)	09
2-22 (EVEN)	08
23-66	09
67-67	10
68-OUT	09
Milk Pl (SOM)	43
Mill (REV)	51
Mill (CAM)	38
Mill (WY)	88
Mill (LEX)	73
Mill (QUI)	69
Mill (WAV)	79
Mill (DOR)	22
Mill (CHA)	29
Mill (EB)	28

Mill

1 160 (NCE)	59
161-OUT (NWV)	60
Mill Ct (CHE)	50
Mill Ln (BRA)	84
Mill Rd (MEL)	76
Mill St Ct (CHA)	29
Mill St Pl (CHA)	29
Mill St Pl (REV)	51
Mill St & Ln (ARL)	74
Millbrook Dr (ARL)	74
Millbrook Rd (LEX)	73
Millen Cir (MAL)	48
Miller (CHE)	50
Miller (EV)	49
Miller (SOM)	43
Miller (QUI)	69
Miller (CHA)	29
Miller (N)	92
Miller Ave (MIL)	86
Miller Ave (CAM)	40
Miller Park (ROX)	19
Miller Rd (NCE)	59
Miller St & Ave (BRA)	84
Millers Ln (DOR)	24
Millers Stile Rd (QUI)	69
Millet (DOR)	24
Millett (ARL)	74
Millett Ave (SWY)	90
Millmont (ROX)	19
Mills (ROX)	19
Mills (MAL)	48
Mills Ave (REV)	51
Mills Rd (NH)	94
Milstone Rd (HP)	36
Milner (WAL)	54

Milo

1-6 (WNW)	65
7-7 (WAL)	54
8-8 (WNW)	65

9-9 (WAL)	54
10-OUT (WNW)	65
Milton (MIL)	86
Milton (WAL)	54
Milton (MAL)	48
Milton (ARL)	74
Milton (WOL)	70
Milton (BEL)	78

Milton

1-20 (CAM)	40
21-OUT (WS)	44
Milton Ave (WNW)	65
Milton Pl	10
Milton Rd (NQ)	71
Milton Rd (BRA)	85
Milton Rd (BRO)	46
Milton St & Ave (DOR)	24
Milton St, Ave & Ter (HP)	36
Milton Hill Rd (MIL)	86
Milwood St & Ter (DOR)	24
Minden (JP)	30
Mindora (RXC)	20
Miner (SOM)	45
Miner	02215
Mingo (MIL)	86
Mingo (MAL)	48
Minihans Ln (QUI)	69
Minnesota Ave (SOM)	45
Minnie Ct (SB)	27
Minola Rd (LEX)	73
Minot (STO)	80

Minot

1-209 (DOR)	22
210-OUT (DOR)	24
Minot Park (DOR)	24
Minot Pl (NWV)	60
Minton (JP)	30
Minute Man Ln (WEL)	81
Minute Man Ln (LEX)	73
Miriam (QUI)	69
Miriam Rd (WAL)	54
Mishawum (CHA)	29
Mission	15
Mitchell (SB)	27
Mitchell (QUI)	69
Mitchell Ave (MED)	55
Moccasin Path (ARL)	74
Model Pl (EB)	28
Modena (ARL)	74
Moffat Rd (QUI)	69
Moffat Rd (WAB)	68
Mohan (EV)	49
Mohawk (SB)	27
Mohawk Rd (ARL)	74
Mokena Ave (WAL)	54
Molloy (WAT)	72
Moloney (WRX)	32
Monadnock (DOR)	25
Monadnock Rd (ARL)	74
Monadnock Rd (CHH)	67
Monadnock Rd (WH)	81
Monastery Rd (BRI)	35
Monatiquot (NWY)	91
Monatiquot Ave (BRA)	84
Mondamin Ct (SOM)	43
Monks (SB)	27
Monmouth (SOM)	43
Monmouth (NQ)	71
Monmouth Ave (MED)	55
Monmouth St & Ct (BRO)	46
Monmouth St & Sq (EB)	28
Monponset (MAT)	26
Monroe (MAL)	48

Monroe (NWV)	60
Monroe Rd (QUI)	69
Monsignor Obrien Hwy (CAM)	41
Monsignor Reynolds Way	18
Monsignor Shea Rd	11
Monson (MAT)	26
Montague (DOR)	24
Montague (CAM)	39
Montague (ARL)	74
Montana (DOR)	21
Montcalm Ave (BRI)	35
Montclair Ave (ROS)	31
Montclair Ave (WAL)	54
Montclair Ave (NQ)	71
Montclair Rd (WAB)	68
Mohtebello Rd (JP)	30
Montello (DOR)	22
Monterey Ave (MAT)	26
Montfern Ave (BRI)	35
Montfern Ave (REV)	51
Montgomery (CAM)	40
Montgomery	16
Montgomery Ave (SOM)	45
Monticello Ave (DOR)	25
Montillio (QUI)	69
Montmorenci Ave (EB)	28
Montpelier Rd (DOR)	25
Montrose (ROX)	19
Montrose (NEW)	58
Montrose (EV)	49
Montrose Ave (ARL)	74
Montrose St & Ct (SOM)	43
Montrose St & Ct (MAL)	48
Montvale (MAL)	48
Montvale (ROS)	31
Montvale (MEL)	76
Montvale (WES)	93
Montvale Ave (STO)	80
Montvale Rd (WH)	81
Montvale Rd (NCE)	59
Montview (WRX)	32
Montview Ave & Cir (WAL)	54
Monument Ct (SB)	27
Monument St, Ave, Ct & Sq (CHA)	29
Monument St & Ter (MED)	55
Moody (WAL)	54
Moody (DOR)	24
Moody (CHH)	67
Moody Ave (EV)	49
Moon	43
Moon Hill Rd (LEX)	73
Moon Island Rd (NQ)	71
Mooney (CAM)	38
Mooney Rd (REV)	51
Moore (WIN)	52
Moore (WAL)	54
Moore (CAM)	39
Moore (WS)	44
Moore (BEL)	78
Moore (QUI)	69
Moore (EB)	28
Moore	18
Moore Pl (ARL)	74
Moore Rd (EWY)	89
Mooreland Rd (MEL)	76
Mora (DOR)	24
Moraine (JP)	30
Moraine (WAY)	79
Moreland (ROX)	19
Moreland (SOM)	45
Moreland (WRX)	32
Moreland Ave (LEX)	73

Boston (Con.)   021

Moreland Ave (NCE) 59
Moreland Rd (EV) 49
Moreland Rd (QUI) 69
Moreland Rd (BRA) 84
Moreland Rd (NWY) 91
Morey Rd (ROS) 31
Morgan (SOM) 43
Morgan (MEL) 76
Morgan 16
Morgan Ave (STO) 80
Morgan Ave (MED) 55
Morgan Pl (NEW) 58
Morgan Rd (WOL) 70
Morgan Rd (LEX) 73
Morley (ROX) 19
Morley (N) 92
Morley Rd (WOL) 70
Morningside Dr (ARL) 74
Morningside Path (EWY) 89
Morningside Rd (N) 92
Morrell (NWY) 91
Morrill (WNW) 65
Morrill (DOR) 25
Morris (EB) 28
Morris (ARL) 74
Morris (LEX) 73
Morris (EV) 49
Morris (REV) 51
Morris (MAL) 48
Morrison (MAL) 55
Morrison (QUI) 69
Morrison Ave & Pl (WS) 44
Morrison Ct (CAM) 40
Morrison Rd (WAT) 72
Morrison St & Rd (BRA) 84
Morrissey Wm T Blvd
   1-620 (DOR) 25
   621-OUT (DOR) 22
Morrissey Wm T Ter (DOR) .. 25
Morrow Rd (BRI) 35
Morse (DOR) 21
Morse (WAT) 72
Morse (WOL) 70
Morse Rd (NWV) 60
Morse Pond Rd (WH) 81
Moreland Ave (NCE) 59
Mortimer Pl (SOM) 45
Mortimer Ter (QUI) 69
Morton (QUI) 69
Morton (WAT) 72
Morton (SOM) 45
Morton (WIN) 52
Morton (WAL) 54
Morton 13
Morton (NH) 94
Morton
   1-499 (JP) 30
   500-600 (DOR) (EVEN) .. 24
   501-593 (DOR) (ODD) ... 24
   595-OUT (MAT) (ODD) .. 26
   602-OUT (MAT) (EVEN) . 26
Morton Ave (MED) 55
Morton Pl (RXC) 20
Morton Pl (EB) 28
Morton Rd (ARL) 74
Morton Rd & Ter (MIL) 87
Morton St & Ave (MAL) 48
Morton St & Cir (WEL) 81
Morton St & Rd (NCE) 59
Morton Village Dr (MAT) 26
Moscow (NQ) 71

Moseley (DOR) 25
Mosely Rd (NCE) 59
Mosgrove Ave (ROS) 31
Mosley Ave (N) 92
Moss Hill Rd (JP) 30
Mossdale Rd (JP) 30
Mossfield Rd (WAB) 68
Mossland (WS) 44
Mossman (WNW) 65
Mother Julian Rd (DOR) 24
Motley (RXC) 20
Mott (ARL) 74
Moulton (NLF) 62
Moulton (CHA) 29
Moulton (CAM) 38
Moulton Ave (STO) 80
Moulton Ave (NWY) 91
Moulton Rd (ARL) 74
Moultrie (DOR) 24
Mound (QUI) 69
Mount Alvernia Rd (CHH) 67
Mount Ararat Rd (QUI) 69
Mount Auburn (WAT) 72
Mount Auburn St & Pl (CAM) . 38
Mount Bowdoin Ter (DOR) ... 21
Mount Calvary Rd (ROS) 31
Mount Cushing Ter (DOR) 25
Mount Everett (DOR) 25
Mount Hood Rd (BRO) 46
Mount Hood Ter (MEL) 76
Mount Hope (ROS) 31
Mount Hope Cemetery (MAT) . 26
Mount Ida Rd (DOR) 22
Mount Ida Rd (EWY) 89
Mount Ida St & Ter (NEW) ... 58
Mount Ida Ter (WAL) 54
Mount Pleasant (WAL) 54
Mount Pleasant (HP) 36
Mount Pleasant (CAM) 40
Mount Pleasant Ave (MAL) .. 48
Mount Pleasant Ave, Pl & Ter
   (ROX) 19
Mount Pleasant St & Ct
   (SOM) 45
Mount Tabor Rd (LEX) 73
Mount Vernon (QUI) 69
Mount Vernon (ARL) 74
Mount Vernon (STO) 80
Mount Vernon (SOM) 45
Mount Vernon (CAM) 40
Mount Vernon (WRX) 32
Mount Vernon (DOR) 25
Mount Vernon
   1-174 (NWV) 60
   175-OUT (WNW) 65
Mount Vernon Ave (N) 92
Mount Vernon Ave (WAL) 54
Mount Vernon Rd E & W
   (EWY) 89
Mount Vernon St & Ave
   (BRI) 35
Mount Vernon St & Ave
   (CHA) 29
Mount Vernon St & Ave
   (BRA) 84
Mount Vernon St & Ave
   (MEL) 76
Mount Vernon St & Park
   (MAL) 48
Mount Vernon St, Pl & Sq 08
Mount Vernon Ter (NWV) 60
Mount Walley Ave (JP) 30
Mount Walley Rd (WAL) 54

Mount Warren (ROX) 19
Mount Washington (EV) 49
Mount Washington Ave
   (MAL) 48
Mount Washington Ave 02210
Mount Washington Pl (SB) ... 27
Mount Zion Rd (MEL) 76
Mountain Ave (ARL) 74
Mountain Ave (DOR) 24
Mountain Ave (MAL) 48
Mountain Ave (SOM) 43
Mountain Ave (REV) 51
Mountain Ave E (REV) 51
Mountain Ave N & S (MEL) .. 76
Mountain Rd (LEX) 73
Mountain Rd (WAL) 54
Mountain View Rd (EWY) 89
Mountfort
   1-124 02215
   125-OUT (BRO) 46
Mountfort Rd (NWH) 61
Mountview Rd (Wil) 81
Moville (WRX) 32
Mozart (JP) 30
Mugford (WIN) 52
Muirhead (WOL) 70
Mulberry (CHE) 50
Mulberry Pl (ROX) 19
Mulberry Rd (MIL) 87
Muldoons Ct (WAL) 54
Mulford (BRO) 46
Mullen Ct (NWH) 61
Muller Ave (CAM) 40
Mullin Ave (QUI) 69
Mullins Ct (CAM) 41
Mulvey (MAT) 26
Mulvey Ter (ROX) 19
Munroe (ROX) 19
Munroe (CAM) 42
Munroe (SOM) 43
Munroe (BEL) 78
Munroe Ave (WAT) 72
Munroe Ave (WAL) 54
Munroe Rd (WH) 81
Munroe Rd (LEX) 73
Munson 02215
Munster Ter (WAL) 54
Murdock (CAM) 39
Murdock (SOM) 45
Murdock Ave (QUI) 69
Murdock St & Ter (BRI) 35
Murley Ln (NCE) 59
Murphy Ct (NEW) 58
Murphy Rd (N) 92
Murray (SOM) 43
Murray (WAL) 54
Murray (MAL) 48
Murray (CHE) 50
Murray (ARL) 74
Murray Ave (MIL) 86
Murray Ave (ROX) 19
Murray Ct (EB) 28
Murray Rd & Ter (WNW) 65
Murray Ter (DOR) 24
Murray Hill Park & Rd (MAL) . 48
Murray Hill Rd (CAM) 40
Murray Hill Rd (MED) 55
Murray Hill Rd (ROS) 31
Museum
   1-111 (CAM) 38
   112-OUT (SOM) 43
Museum Rd 15
Music Hall Ave (WAL) 54

Music Hall Pl 08
Muzzey (LEX) 73
Myers Ln (MIL) 86
Myerson Ln (NCE) 59
Myles Standish Rd (WES) 93
Myles Standish Rd (WRX) 32
Myopia Rd (HP) 36
Myopia Rd (STO) 80
Myopia Rd
  1-49 (WOL) 70
  50-OUT (QUI) 69
Myrick (ALL) 34
Myrna Rd (LEX) 73
Myrtle (LEX) 73
Myrtle (BRA) 84
Myrtle (STO) 80
Myrtle (WNW) 65
Myrtle (WAT) 72
Myrtle (NQ) 71
Myrtle (BEL) 78
Myrtle (MEL) 76
Myrtle (WAL) 54
Myrtle (MED) 55
Myrtle (EV) 49
Myrtle (EWY) 89
Myrtle 14
Myrtle (JP) 30
Myrtle Ave (BRA) 85
Myrtle Ave (CAM) 38
Myrtle Ave (WIN) 52
Myrtle Ave (AUB) 66
Myrtle Pl (ROX) 19
Myrtle St & Ct (MAL) 48
Myrtle St, Ct & Pl (SOM) 46
Myrtlebank Ave (DOR) 24
Mystic (EV) 49
Mystic (ARL) 74
Mystic Ave (MEL) 76
Mystic Ave (SOM) 45
Mystic St Ext (MED) 55
Mystic St & Ave (MED) 55
Mystic St, Ave & Pl (CHA) 29
Mystic Bank (ARL) 74
Mystic Lake Dr (ARL) 74
Mystic River Rd (MED) 55
Mystic Valley Pky (ARL) 74
Mystic Valley Pky
  1-500 (SOM) 44
  501-OUT (MED) 55
Mystic View Ter (ARL) 74
Mystic Wharf (CHA) 29
N (SB) 27
Nahant Ave (DOR) 22
Nahant Ave (WIN) 52
Nahant Ave (REV) 51
Nahanton (NCE) 59
Nahanton Ave (MIL) 86
Nanapashemet Ave (MAL) 48
Nancia (EB) 28
Nancy Rd (MIL) 86
Nancy Rd (CHH) 67
Nanset, Rd (NWY) 91
Nantasket Ave (BRI) 35
Nant... .et Rd (NWH) 61
Nantucket Rd (WH) 81
Naomi (EB) 28
Napier Park (DOR) 25
Naples Rd (BRO) 46
Naples Rd (REV) 51
Naples Rd (MEL) 76
Nardell Rd (NCE) 59
Nardone Rd (NCE) 59
Nardone Rd (N) 92

Narraganset Ave (WY) 88
Narraganset Rd (QUI) 69
Narragansett (DOR) 22
Nash (WAT) 72
Nash (MIL) 86
Nzsh Ave (QUI) 69
Nash Ln (WES) 93
Nash Ln & Rd (SWY) 90
Nash Row (CHA) 29
Nash Sq (CHA) 90
Nashua 14
Nashua (SOM) 45
Nason Dr (MEL) 76
Nassau St & Pl 11
Natalie Ave (MEL) 76
Nathan (ROX) 19
Nathan Rd (NCE) 59
Nathan Rd (WAL) 54
National (SB) 27
Naval Hwy & Ter (NQ) 71
Navarre
  1-82 (ROS) 31
  83-OUT (HP) 36
Navarre Pl (HP) 36
Navarro Cir (MED) 55
Naviens Ln (WAL) 54
Navillus Ter (DOR) 22
Nay (EB) 28
Nazing St & Ct (DOR) 21
Neal (MAL) 48
Neal (NLF) 62
Neal Ct (CHA) 29
Nearen Row (CHA) 29
Necco St, Ct & Pl 02210
Neck (NWY) 91
Needham
  1-162 (NWH) 61
  163-OUT (NUF) 64
Needham Rd (HP) 36
Needhamdale Rd (N) 92
Neframer Rd (NCE) 59
Nehoiden (N) 92
Nehoiden Rd (WAB) 68
Neighbors Ln (WAL) 54
Neillan Cres (JP) 30
Neilon Park (MAL) 48
Neilson Ave (EV) 49
Nell Rd (REV) 51
Nelson (HP) 36
Nelson (DOR) 24
Nelson (QUI) 69
Nelson (BRA) 84
Nelson Dr (CHH) 67
Nelson Rd (SWY) 90
Nelson Rd & Ter (MEL) 76
Neponset Ave (REV) 51
Neponset Ave (HP) 36
Neponset Ave & Cir (DOR) 22
Neponset Ave & Ct (ROS) 31
Neponset Rd (QUI) 69
Neponset Valley Pky (HP) 36
Neponset Valley Pky (MIL) 86
Neptune Ave (WIN) 52
Neptune Rd (EB) 28
Nerious Ave (REV) 51
Neshobe Rd (WAB) 68
Nestor Ln (WAL) 54
Netherlands Rd (BRO) 46
Nevada (WIN) 52
Nevada (NWV) 60
Nevada (DOR) 24
Nevada Ave (MAL) 48
Nevada Ave (SOM) 43

Nevada Rd (QUI) 69
Nevada Rd (NH) 94
Nevin Rd (SWY) 90
New (CAM) 38
New (EB) 28
New Park Ave (ROS) 31
New Ter Rd (BRO) 46
New Acre Rd (HP) 36
New Bedford (HP) 36
New Bert Ave (SWY) 90
New Castle Rd (BEL) 78
New Chardon 14
New Cross (SOM) 45
New England Ave (DOR) 24
New Hampshire Ave (SOM) 45
New Haven (WRX) 32
New Heath
  1-20 (ROX) 19
  21-45 (RXC) (ODD) 20
  22-30 (RXC) (EVEN) 20
  32-OUT (JP) (EVEN) 30
  47-OUT (JP) (ODD) 30
New Sudbury 14
New Woodcliff (DOR) 25
Newark (ROX) 19
Newbern (JP) 30
Newbern Ave (MED) 55
Newbern Pl 16
Newbern St & Ct (RXC) 20
Newbrne (WS) 44
Newbrook Cir (CHH) 67
Newburg (ROS) 31
Newburgh (WAL) 54
Newbury (WS) 44
Newbury (MAL) 48
Newbury (REV) 51
Newbury
  1-279 (ODD) 16
  2-282 (EVEN) 16
  284-448 (EVEN) 15
  450-OUT (ODD) 02215
  279A-449 (ODD) 15
Newbury Park (N) 92
Newbury St & Ave (NQ) 71
Newbury St & Ter (NCE) 59
Newcastle (MAT) 26
Newcastle Ct 18
Newcastle Rd (BRI) 35
Newcomb (MED) 55
Newcomb 18
Newcomb (QUI) 69
Newcomb (ARL) 74
Newcomb Rd (MEL) 76
Newcomb Ter (WY) 88
Newcroft Cir (MAT) 26
Newell Ave (N) 92
Newell Rd (AUB) 66
Newell Rd (BRO) 46
Newell St & Ter (CAM) 40
Newfield (WRX) 32
Newfield (WOL) 70
Newhall (MAL) 48
Newhall (REV) 51
Newhall St & Pl (DOR) 22
Newhill Pl (SB) 27
Newkirk (DOR) 22
Newland 16
Newland (NQ) 71
Newland (AUB) 66
Newland Rd (ARL) 74
Newland St & Ter (MAL) 48
Newman (REV) 51

Boston (Con.)   021

Newman (CAM) 40
Newman Pl (SOM) 45
Newman Rd (ROX) 19
Newman Rd (MAL) 48
Newman Way (ARL) 18
Newmarket Sq 18
Newport (DOR) 25
Newport (ARL) 74
Newport Ave (MED) 55
Newport Ave (BRA) 85
Newport Ave
   1-115 (NQ) 71
   116-OUT (WOL) 70
Newport Rd (CAM) 40
Newport Ter (WOL) 70
Newsome Park (JP) 30
Newton (QUI) 69
Newton (BEL) 78
Newton (CAM) 39
Newton (MAL) 48
Newton (BRI) 35
Newton (WAL) 54
Newton (EV) 49
Newton (WES) 93
Newton
   1-209 (BRO) (ODD) 46
   2-282 (BRO) (EVEN) 46
   211-OUT (CHH) (ODD) 67
   284-OUT (CHH) (EVEN) 67
Newton Ave (WOL) 70
Newton Rd (ARL) 74
Newton Rd (MED) 55
Newton St & Ave (BRA) 84
Newton St & Ct (NWY) 91
Newton St & Pl (SOM) 43
Newtonville Ave
   1-258 (NEW) 58
   259-OUT (NWV) 60
Newtowne Ct (CAM) 39
Nichol (QUI) 69
Nicholas Rd (BRA) 84
Nichols (EV) 49
Nichols (CHE) 50
Nichols Ave (WAT) 72
Nichols Pl (CAM) 38
Nichols Rd (MAL) 48
Nichols Rd (LEX) 73
Nichols Rd (N) 92
Nickerson Rd (LEX) 73
Nickerson Rd (BRA) 84
Nickerson Rd (CHH) 67
Nickerson Field (WES) 93
Nicod (ARL) 74
Nightingale (DOR) 24
Nightingale Ave (QUI) 69
Nightingale Path (NCE) 59
Nikisch Ave (ROS) 31
Niles (BRI) 35
Niles Rd (NWH) 61
Nilsen Ave (QUI) 69
Nina (MEL) 76
Ninth (MED) 55
Ninth (SB) 27
Nira (MAL) 48
Nira Ave (JP) 30
Nix Point Rd (SWY) 90
Nixon (DOR) 24
Nixon Ln (STO) 80
Nixon Pl (ALL) 34
Noah (MAT) 26
Noanet 11

Noanet (QUI) 69
Noanet Rd (NH) 94
Nob Hill Rd (WY) 88
Noble (WNW) 65
Noble (MAL) 48
Noble (REV) 51
Noble Ct (EB) 28
Nobscot Rd (WH) 81
Nobscot Rd (NCE) 59
Nobscot Rd (WES) 93
Nod Hill Rd (NWH) 61
Nonantum (BRI) 35
Nonantum St, Pl & Rd
   (NEW) 58
None Such Way (WES) 93
Nonquit (DOR) 25
Noonan (WAL) 54
Norcross Pl (SB) 27
Norcross St & Cir (ARL) 74
Norfolk (WOL) 70
Norfolk (ROX) 19
Norfolk (N) 92
Norfolk (WY) 88
Norfolk
   1-409 (CAM) (ODD) 39
   1-430 (DOR) 24
   2-412 (CAM) (EVEN) 39
   411-OUT (SOM) (ODD) 43
   414-OUT (SOM) (EVEN) 43
   431-OUT (MAT) 26
Norfolk Ave
   1-279 (ROX) 19
   280-OUT (DOR) 25
Norfolk Ct, Pl & Ter (CAM) 39
Norfolk Pl 11
Norfolk Rd (ARL) 74
Norfolk Rd (BRA) 84
Norfolk Rd (CHH) 67
Norfolk Ter (WEL) 81
Norfolk Ter (DOR) 24
Norma Ave (WY) 88
Norman (MIL) 86
Norman (CAM) 38
Norman (REV) 51
Norman (EV) 49
Norman Rd (QUI) 69
Norman Rd (NWH) 61
Norman Rd (MEL) 76
Normandy (DOR) 21
Normandy Ave & Ter (CAM) 38
Normandy Rd (CHE) 50
Normandy Rd (AUB) 66
Normandy Rd (LEX) 73
Norris (CAM) 40
Norris Ct (MEL) 76
Norris Rd (HP) 36
Norseman Ave (WAT) 72
North (NQ) 71
North (LEX) 73
North (NCE) 59
North (NWV) 60
North (STO) 80
North (BRA) 84
North (WS) 44
North (MED) 55
North
   1-174 09
   1-514 (NWY) 91
   175-OUT 13
   515-OUT (EWY) 89
North Ave (WES) 93
North Ave (WH) 52
North Ave (MEL) 76

North St & Ave (REV) 51
North Anderson 14
North Beacon
   1-105 (ALL) 34
   106-OUT (BRI) 35
North Beacon St & Ct (WAT) 72
North Bennet St, Ct & Pl 13
North Border Rd (STO) 80
North Bowditch (BRA) 84
North Cedar Park (MEL) 76
North Central Ave (WOL) 70
North Charlame St, Ct & Ter
   (ROX) 19
North Crescent Circuit (BRI) 35
North Forest (MEL) 76
North Gate Park (WNW) 65
North Gate Rd (WH) 81
North Hancock (LEX) 73
North Hanover Ct 13
North Harvard
   1-94 (SF) 63
   95-OUT (ALL) 34
North Hill Rd (N) 92
North Hudson 13
North Irving Park (WAT) 72
North Margin 13
North Market 09
North Mead (CHA) 29
North Mead St Ct (CHA) 29
North Milton (MAL) 48
North Munroe Ter (DOR) 22
North Park (WAT) 72
North Payne (QUI) 69
North Quincy Pl (CHA) 29
North Russell (MIL) 87
North Shore Rd (REV) 51
North Station 14
North Union (SOM) 45
North Union (ARL) 74
North Washington
   1-221 (ODD) 14
   2-198 (EVEN) 14
   200-OUT (CHA) (EVEN) 29
   223-OUT (CHA) (ODD) 29
Northam Park (DOR) 24
Northampton
   1-28 (ROX) 19
   29-OUT 18
Northampton Pl 18
Northbourne Rd (JP) 30
Northdale Rd (WRX) 32
Northdale Rd Ext (WRX) 32
Northdale Rd Ter (WRX) 32
Northern Ave .02210
Northern Ave (WY) 88
Northern Cir (REV) 51
Northern Rd (MAL) 48
Northfield Ave (QUI) 69
Northgate Rd (STO) 80
Norton (BRA) 84
Norton (HP) 36
Norton (NWY) 91
Norton
   1-68 (DOR) 25
   69-OUT (DOR) 22
Norton Ave (MED) 55
Norton Pl (CAM) 38
Norton Rd (QUI) 69
Norton Rd (LEX) 73
Norumbega (CAM) 38
Norumbega Park (AUB) 66
Norumbega Rd (WES) 93
Norumbega Ter (WAL) 54

Boston (Con.)   621

Norval Ave (STO)................ 80
Norway......................... 15
Norway Park (HP).............. 36
Norway Rd (MIL)............... 87
Norwell
  I-155 (DOR)................... 21
  156-OUT (DOR)............... 24
Norwich Cir (MED)............. 55
Norwich Rd (N)................ 92
Norwich Rd (WH).............. 81
Norwood (EV).................. 49
Norwood (DOR)................ 22
Norwood Ave (SOM)........... 45
Norwood Ave (NCE)........... 59
Norwood Ave (NWV)........... 60
Norwood St & Pl (MAL)....... 48
Notre Dame (ROX)............. 19
Notre Dame Ave (CAM)........ 40
Nott (HP)...................... 36
Nottingham (WAL)............. 54
Nottingham (DOR)............. 21
Nottingham (NCE)............. 59
Nottinghill Rd (BRI).......... 35
Nourse (ARL).................. 74
Nowell Rd (MEL).............. 76
Nowers Rd (LEX).............. 73
Noyes (N)..................... 92
Noyes Pl....................... 13
Nun Buoy Ln (QUI)............ 69
Nursery Ln (EV)............... 49
Nut Island Ave & Rd (QUI).... 69
Nutting Rd (CAM)............. 38
Nutting Rd (WAL)............. 54
Nyack (WAT).................. 72
O (SB)......................... 27
O St Pl (SB).................... 27
Oak (CHA)..................... 29
Oak (MEL)..................... 76
Oak (NUF)..................... 64
Oak (WEL)..................... 81
Oak (BRA)..................... 84
Oak (STO)..................... 80
Oak (CAM)..................... 39
Oak (SOM)..................... 43
Oak (WES)..................... 93
Oak (N)........................ 92
Oak (SWY)..................... 90
Oak E (BRA)................... 84
Oak Ave (NQ).................. 71
Oak Ave (WNW)................ 65
Oak Rd (MED)................. 55
Oak Rd (WRX)................. 32
Oak Sq (BRI).................. 35
Oak Sq Ave (BRI)............. 35
Oak Sq Ter (SOM)............. 43
Oak St Pl (SOM).............. 43
Oak St & Ave (BEL).......... 78
Oak St & Pl (CHH)........... 67
Oak St & Pl (WAT)........... 72
Oak St & Pl (HP)............. 36
Oak St & Pl................... 11
Oak St & Rd (WAL)........... 54
Oak St & Rd (QUI)........... 69
Oak St & Rd (MIL)........... 87
Oak St & Ter (LEX).......... 73
Oak St & Ter (MAL).......... 48
Oak Ter (EV)................. 49
Oak Ter (NWH)................ 61
Oak Bluff (MED).............. 55
Oak Cliff Rd (NWV)........... 60
Oak Cliff Rd (WH)............ 81

Oak Cliff Rd (EWY)........... 89
Oak Grove Ct & Ter (MAL).... 48
Oak Grove Ter (QUI).......... 69
Oak Hill (NCE)................ 59
Oak Hill Ave (MAT)........... 26
Oak Hill Dr (ARL)............ 74
Oak Hill Rd (WAL)............ 54
Oak Hill Rd (EWY)............ 89
Oak Hill Rd (BRA)............ 85
Oak Hill Rd (N)............... 92
Oak Island St & Rd (REV)..... 51
Oak Knoll (ARL).............. 74
Oak Knoll Ter (N)............ 92
Oak Park Cir (LEX)........... 73
Oak Ridge Rd (MED).......... 55
Oak Vale Rd (WAB)........... 68
Oakburn Ave (RXC)........... 20
Oakcrest Rd (MAT)........... 26
Oakcrest Rd (N).............. 92
Oakcrest Rd (SWY)........... 90
Oakdale Ave (SWY).......... 90
Oakdale Ave (WES).......... 93
Oakdale Ave (WH)........... 81
Oakdale Ave (WR)........... 32
Oakdale Rd (MAL)........... 48
Oakdale Rd
  I-92 (NCE).................. 59
  93-OUT (NWH)............... 61
Oakdale St, Sq & Ter (JP).... 30
Oakden Ave (SWY)........... 90
Oakden Ave (BRA)........... 85
Oakencroft Rd (WEL)........ 81
Oakes (EV).................... 49
Oakhurst (DOR)............... 24
Oakhurst Cir (N)............. 92
Oakland (NEW)............... 58
Oakland (CAM)............... 39
Oakland (BRA)............... 84
Oakland (LEX)............... 73
Oakland (WAT)............... 72
Oakland (MEL)............... 76
Oakland Ave (AUB).......... 66
Oakland Ave (ARL).......... 74
Oakland Ave (WOL).......... 70
Oakland Ave (EV)............ 49
Oakland Ave (SOM).......... 45
Oakland Rd (N).............. 92
Oakland Rd (BRO)........... 46
Oakland Rd Ext (BRO)....... 46
Oakland St & Cir (WH)....... 81
Oakland St & Park (MED)..... 55
Oakland St & Park (ROX)..... 19
Oakland St & Pl (BRI)....... 35

Oakledge (ARL)............... 74
Oakledge Rd (WAL).......... 54
Oakleigh Rd (NEW).......... 58
Oakley (DOR)................ 24
Oakley Ln (WAL)............ 54
Oakley Rd (BEL)............. 78
Oakley Rd (WAT)............ 72
Oakman (DOR)............... 22
Oakmere (WRX).............. 32
Oakmont Rd (NCE)........... 59
Oakmount Cir (LEX)......... 73
Oakridge (MAT).............. 26
Oakridge Rd (NQ)........... 71
Oakridge Rd (WH)........... 81
Oakridge Rd (STO).......... 80
Oakridge St & Cir (WEY)..... 88
Oakton Ave (DOR)........... 22
Oakvale Ave (MAT).......... 26

Oakview Ave (ROX)........... 19
Oakview Tar (JP)............. 30
Oakville Ave (ROX).......... 19
Oakwood (DOR)............... 24
Oakwood (MAT).............. 26
Oakwood Ave (REV).......... 51
Oakwood Rd (NWV).......... 60
Oakwood Rd (QUI).......... 69
Oakwood Rd (AUB).......... 66
Oakwood Ter (NCE).......... 59
Ober Rd (NCE)............... 59
Obierne Pl (ROX)............ 19
Obrien Ct (CHA)............. 29
Obrien Msgr Hwy (CAM)..... 41
Ocallaghan Way (SB)........ 27
Ocean (DOR)................. 24
Ocean (NQ).................. 71
Ocean Ave (WIN)............ 52
Ocean Ave (REV)............ 51
Ocean Ave (NWY)........... 91
Ocean Pier Ave (REV)....... 51
Ocean Side Park (REV)...... 51
Ocean View Ave (REV)...... 51
Ocean View St & Way (WIN).. 52
Oconnell Ave (QUI)......... 69
Oconnell Rd (NCE).......... 59
Oconnell Rd (DOR).......... 24
October Ln (WES)........... 93
Ode (WAL)................... 54
Odom (DOR).................. 69
Odonnell Sq & Ter (DOR).... 22
Off Lake (EWY)............. 89
Off Park Ave (SWY)......... 90
Off Putnam (EWY)........... 89
Off River (NWY)............ 91
Off Station (EWY).......... 89
Off Summer (WY)........... 88
Ogden (DOR)................. 24
Ogden Rd (CHH)............. 67
Ohio......................... 16
Ohio Ave (NUF)............. 64
Okala Rd (EWY)............. 89
Olafson (BRA)............... 85
Olcutt (WAT)................ 72
Old Rd (WES)............... 93
Old Rd (DOR)............... 21
Old Brook Cir (MEL)........ 76
Old Carriage Ln & Way
  (BRA)..................... 84
Old Coach Rd (QUI)......... 69
Old Coach Rd (WES)........ 93
Old Coach Rd (BRA)........ 85
Old Colony Ave (SB)........ 27
Old Colony Ave & Ter (WOL).. 70
Old Colony Ln & Rd (ARL)... 74
Old Colony Rd (WH)........ 81
Old Colony Rd (CHH)....... 67
Old Colony Rd (WES)....... 93
Old Colony Ter (DOR)...... 25
Old Concord Rd (BEL)...... 78
Old Country Way (WY)...... 88
Old Country Way (BRA)..... 85
Old Dee Rd (CAM).......... 38
Old England Rd (CHH)...... 67
Old Farm Rd (WH).......... 81
Old Farm Rd (NCE)......... 59
Old Farm Rd (MIL)......... 86
Old Farm Rd (N)........... 92
Old Harbor (SB)............ 27
Old Heath (JP)............. 30
Old Ironsides Way (CHA)... 29
Old Landing Way (CHA)..... 29
Old Lexington Rd (WAL).... 54

313

Boston (Con.)	021	
Old Middlesex Path (ARL)	74	
Old Middlesex Rd (BEL)	78	
Old Morton (MAT)	26	
Old Mystic (ARL)	74	
Old North (BRA)	84	
Old Orchard Rd (CHH)	67	
Old Shade (LEX)	73	
Old Town Rd (WH)	81	
Old Winchester (NWH)	61	
Olde Field Rd (NCE)	59	
Oldfields Rd (DOR)	21	
Oldham Rd (WNW)	65	
Oldham Rd (ARL)	74	
Oleander (DOR)	25	
Oleary Way (JP)	30	
Oliva Rd (BRI)	35	
Olive (BRI)	35	
Olive (REV)	51	
Olive Ave (MAL)	48	
Olive Ave & Sq (SOM)	43	
Olive Pl (CAM)	40	
Oliver (SOM)	45	
Oliver (MAL)	48	
Oliver (NQ)	71	
Oliver		
1-OUT (ODD)	10	
2-10 (EVEN)	09	
12-OUT (EVEN)	10	
Oliver Pl	11	
Oliver Rd (EWY)	89	
Oliver Rd (WAB)	68	
Oliver Rd (BEL)	78	
Oliver St & Pl (EV)	49	
Oliver St & Rd (WAT)	72	
Oliver Ter (REV)	51	
Olmstead St & Park (JP)	30	
Olney (DOR)	21	
Olney (WAT)	72	
Omar Ter (NWV)	60	
Omeara Ct (CHA)	29	
Oneida (QUI)	69	
Oneil Pl (BRI)	35	
Onslow Ter (SB)	27	
Opera Pl	15	
Ophir (JP)	30	
Orange (CHE)	50	
Orange (WAL)	54	
Orange (ROS)	31	
Orange Ct (EV)	49	
Orchard (REV)	49	
Orchard (REV)	51	
Orchard (MAL)	48	
Orchard (NEW)	58	
Orchard (MED)	55	
Orchard (JP)	30	
Orchard (MAT)	26	
Orchard (NQ)	71	
Orchard (WAT)	72	
Orchard (BRA)	84	
Orchard (STO)	80	
Orchard (WH)	81	
Orchard (LEX)	73	
Orchard		
1-83 (CAM) (ODD)	40	
2-86 (CAM) (EVEN)	40	
85-OUT (WS) (ODD)	44	
88-OUT (WS) (EVEN)	44	
Orchard Ave (WES)	93	
Orchard Ave (WNW)	65	
Orchard Ave (WAB)	68	
Orchard Ave (WAL)	54	

Orchard Ln & Pl (MEL)	76	
Orchard Park (ROX)	19	
Orchard Pl & Ter (ARL)	74	
Orchard Rd (BRO)	46	
Orchard Rd (SWY)	90	
Orchard Rd (MIL)	86	
Orchard St & Cir (BEL)	78	
Orchardale (DOR)	24	
Orchardfield (DOR)	22	
Orchardhill Rd (JP)	30	
Ordway Rd (WH)	81	
Oregon Ave (BRA)	85	
Oregon Ct (RXC)	20	
Oreilley Way (CHA)	29	
Organ Park (ROS)	31	
Orient (STO)	80	
Oriole (WH)	81	
Oriole (WRX)	32	
Orkney Rd (BRO)	46	
Orlando (MAT)	26	
Orlando Ave (WIN)	52	
Orlando Ave (ARL)	74	
Orlando Ave (NWV)	91	
Orleans (QUI)	69	
Orleans (EB)	28	
Orleans Rd (WY)	88	
Ormond (MAT)	26	
Orne (DOR)	22	
Orono (MIL)	87	
Orourke Path (NCE)	58	
Orrin (CAM)	38	
Orris (AUB)	66	
Orris St & Pl (MEL)	76	
Ort (BRO)	46	
Orton Marotta Way (SB)	27	
Ortona (ARL)	74	
Orvis Cir & Rd (ARL)	74	
Orvis Rd (REV)	51	
Osborn Pl	16	
Osborne (CAM)	39	
Osborne Path (NCE)	59	
Osborne Rd (ARL)	74	
Osborne Rd (BRO)	46	
Osborne Rd (MED)	55	
Osborne Rd (MIL)	86	
Oscar (RXC)	20	
Osceola (MAT)	26	
Osceola Path (ARL)	74	
Osgood (MED)	55	
Osgood (SOM)	43	
Osgood Ct (ROX)	19	
Ossen (REV)	51	
Ossipee Rd (WS)	44	
Ossipee Rd (NUF)	64	
Oswald (RXC)	20	
Oswego (QUI)	69	
Otis (WAT)	72	
Otis	10	
Otis (SOM)	45	
Otis (CAM)	41	
Otis (WIN)	52	
Otis (MED)	55	
Otis (MAL)	48	
Otis (EV)	49	
Otis (MIL)	86	
Otis (SWY)	90	

Otis (N)	92	
Otis		
1-179 (NWV)	60	
180-OUT (WNW)	65	
Otis Park & Pl (NWV)	60	
Otis Pl (ROS)	31	
Otis Pl	08	
Otis St & Park (MEL)	76	
Otisfield (DOR)	21	
Ottawa (ROX)	19	
Ottawa Rd (ARL)	74	
Outlook Dr (LEX)	73	
Outlook Rd (MAT)	26	
Outlook Rd (WAL)	54	
Oval Rd (WOL)	70	
Overbrook Dr (WH)	81	
Overland	02215	
Overland Rd (WAL)	54	
Overlea Ave (CHE)	50	
Overlook (EB)	28	
Overlook Ave (REV)	51	
Overlook Dr & Rd (WES)	93	
Overlook Park (MAL)	48	
Overlook Park (NCE)	59	
Overlook Rd (QUI)	69	
Overlook Rd (ARL)	74	
Overlook Rd (MEL)	76	
Overlook Rd (WAL)	54	
Overlook Rd (WRX)	32	
Overlook Rd (EWY)	89	
Overlook Rd (N)	92	
Owaisa Rd (WAB)	68	
Owatonna (AUB)	66	
Owego Park (MEL)	76	
Owen (MAT)	26	
Owencroft Rd (DOR)	24	
Owens Pl (QUI)	69	
Oxbow Rd (LEX)	73	
Oxbow Rd (N)	92	
Oxbow Rd		
1-40 (WH)	81	
41-OUT (WES)	93	
Oxenbridge Rd (WOL)	70	
Oxford (LEX)	73	
Oxford (MEL)	76	
Oxford (ARL)	74	
Oxford (MAL)	48	
Oxford (SOM)	43	
Oxford		
1-110 (CAM)	38	
111-145 (CAM)	40	
146-146 (SOM)	43	
147-147 (CAM)	40	
148-148 (SOM)	43	
149-OUT (CAM)	40	
Oxford Ave		
1-69 (BEL) (ODD)	78	
2-72 (BEL) (EVEN)	78	
71-OUT (CAM) (ODD)	38	
74-OUT (CAM) (EVEN)	38	
Oxford Cir (BEL)	78	
Oxford Rd (NCE)	59	
Oxford Rd (WH)	81	
Oxford St & Park (REV)	51	
Oxford St & Pl	11	
Oxford Ter	16	
P (SB)	27	
Pacific (SB)	27	
Pacific (CAM)	39	
Packard Ave (DOR)	24	
Packard Ave		
1-107 (WS)	44	
108-OUT (MED)	55	

Boston (Con.)	021
Packard Dr (BRA)	84
Packard Ln (QUI)	69
Paddock Ln (LEX)	73
Padula Rd (WY)	88
Page (DOR)	21
Page (REV)	51
Page (MAL)	48
Page Rd (WES)	93
Page Rd (N)	92
Page Rd (LEX)	73
Page Rd (NWY)	60
Pages Ct (SB)	27
Pagoda St & Cir (MIL)	87
Pagum (MAL)	48
Paige Ave (SB)	27
Paine (WIN)	52
Paine (ROS)	31
Paine (WH)	81
Paisley Park (DOR)	24
Palace Rd	15
Palermo (EB)	28
Palermo (CAM)	41
Palfrey (ROS)	31
Palfrey (WAT)	72
Palfrey Rd (BEL)	78
Palmer (WAT)	72
Palmer (QUI)	69
Palmer (ARL)	74
Palmer (CAM)	38
Palmer (WAL)	54
Palmer (MED)	55
Palmer (ROX)	19
Palmer (SWY)	90
Palmer Ave (SOM)	45
Palmer Rd (WAB)	68
Palmer St & Ct (CHE)	50
Palmyra (WIN)	52
Pama Gdns (BRI)	35
Pamela Ct (AUB)	66
Pamela Dr (ARL)	74
Pantano (BRA)	84
Panteline Ter (WAT)	72
Paomet Rd (NWY)	91
Paradise Rd (MIL)	86
Paragon Rd (WRX)	32
Parallel (ARL)	74
Paris (MED)	55
Paris (EWY)	89
Paris St & Ct (EV)	49
Paris St, Ct & Pl (EB)	28
Parish (DOR)	22
Parish Rd (NH)	94
Park (MIL)	86
Park (CHA)	29
Park	08
Park (CHE)	50
Park (HP)	36
Park (BRO)	46
Park (BRA)	84
Park (STO)	80
Park (WOL)	70
Park (MEL)	76
Park	
1-199 (DOR)	22
200-OUT (DOR)	24
Park Ave (NH)	94
Park Ave (BRA)	85
Park Ave (SWY)	90
Park Ave (NQ)	71
Park Ave (CAM)	38
Park Ave (REV)	51
Park Ave (WS)	44
Park Ave W (SWY)	90
Park Ave Ext (ARL)	74
Park Ave, Cir, Dr, Pl & Ter (ARL)	74
Park Ave & Dr (WIN)	52
Park Ave & Pl (WH)	81
Park Ave & Rd (BEL)	78
Park Dr (NWH)	61
Park Dr	02215
Park Ln (NCE)	59
Park Ln, Pl & Rd (JP)	30
Park Pl (NWY)	60
Park Rd (WES)	93
Park Rd & Ter (EV)	49
Park Sq	16
Park St Ct (MED)	55
Park St Pl (ARL)	74
Park St & Ave (MED)	55
Park St & Ave (NEW)	58
Park St & Ave (MAL)	48
Park St & Dr (LEX)	73
Park St & Pl (SOM)	43
Park St & Pl (WAL)	54
Park St & Ter (WRX)	32
Park Ter Dr (MEL)	76
Park Front Rd (ROS)	31
Park Vale (BRO)	46
Park Vale Ave (ALL)	34
Park View (DOR)	21
Park View Rd (EV)	49
Park View Ter (MAL)	48
Parkdale (SOM)	43
Parker (MAL)	48
Parker (EV)	49
Parker (CHE)	50
Parker (CAM)	38
Parker (HP)	36
Parker (CHA)	29
Parker (MEL)	76
Parker (LEX)	73
Parker (WAT)	72
Parker (QUI)	69
Parker	
1-510	15
511-889 (RXC)	20
890-OUT (JP)	30
Parker Ave	
1-80 (NCE)	59
81-OUT (NWH)	61
Parker Rd (NH)	94
Parker Rd (NWY)	91
Parker Rd (WH)	81
Parker St & Pl (SOM)	43
Parker St & Rd (ARL)	74
Parker St, Rd & Ter (NCE)	59
Parker Chase Ln & Rd (STO)	80
Parker Hill Ave & Ter (RXC)	20
Parkers Ln (WAL)	54
Parkhurst (QUI)	69
Parking Way (QUI)	69
Parkinson (N)	92
Parkland (BRI)	35
Parkland Rd (NH)	94
Parklawn Rd (WRX)	32
Parkman (BRO)	46
Parkman (WOL)	70
Parkman	14
Parkman St & Pl (DOR)	22
Parkside Ave & Cir (BRA)	84
Parkson (HP)	36
Parkton Rd (JP)	30
Parkvale Rd (N)	92
Parkview Ave (NWY)	60
Parkview Rd (WAL)	54
Parkway (DOR)	24
Parkway Cres (MIL)	87
Parkway Ct (CHE)	50
Parkway Rd (BRO)	46
Parkway Rd (MED)	55
Parkway Rd (NWY)	60
Parkway Rd (STO)	80
Parkway Ter (CAM)	38
Parkwood Ter (JP)	30
Parkwood Dr (MIL)	86
Parley Ave (JP)	30
Parley Vale (JP)	30
Parlin (EV)	49
Parmelee	18
Parmenter	13
Parmenter Pl (QUI)	69
Parmenter Rd (WAL)	54
Parmenter Rd & Ter (WNW)	65
Parnell (NWY)	91
Parrott (HP)	36
Parsonage Rd (MAL)	48
Parsons (BRI)	35
Parsons (WNW)	65
Parsons (QUI)	69
Parsons Ave (WAL)	54
Parsons Ave (SWY)	90
Partridge (WRX)	32
Partridge (WAT)	72
Partridge Ave (SOM)	45
Partridge Cir (WAL)	54
Partridge Ln (WAV)	79
Partridge Pl (ROX)	19
Partridge Rd (WH)	81
Partridge Rd (LEX)	73
Partridge Rd (SWY)	90
Partridge Ter (EV)	49
Partridge Hill Rd (WES)	93
Partridge Hill Rd (BRA)	84
Pasadena Rd (DOR)	21
Pasteur (SWY)	90
Patricia Dr (BRA)	84
Patricia Dr & Ln (MIL)	86
Patricia Ln (SWY)	90
Patrick (ARL)	74
Patrick Rd (QUI)	69
Patriot Pky (REV)	51
Patriots Dr (LEX)	73
Patten (WOL)	70
Patten (WAT)	72
Patten (JP)	30
Patten Ave (BRA)	84
Patterson (DOR)	24
Patterson (EWY)	89
Patterson Rd (LEX)	73
Patterson Way (SB)	27
Patton Cir (NCE)	59
Patton Rd (WEL)	81
Paul (NCE)	59
Paul (WAT)	72
Paul (BRA)	85
Paul Rd (MED)	55
Paul St & Pl	18
Paul Gore St & Ter (JP)	30
Paul Revere Rd (NH)	94
Paul Revere Rd (LEX)	73
Paul Revere Rd (ARL)	74
Paula Ave (STO)	80
Paula Rd (MAT)	26
Paulding (ROX)	19
Paulina (WS)	44
Pauline (WIN)	52

Boston (Con.)	021	
Paulman Cir (WRX)	32	
Paulson Rd (WAB)	68	
Pawnee Cir (MIL)	86	
Pawnee Dr (ARL)	74	
Pawsey (QUI)	69	
Paxton (DOR)	24	
Payne (DOR)	22	
Payne (QUI)	69	
Payne Ave (SWY)	90	
Payne Rd (NWH)	61	
Payne Ter (MAL)	48	
Payson (WIN)	52	
Payson (REV)	51	
Payson (QUI)	69	
Payson (LEX)	73	
Payson Ave (DOR)	25	
Payson Pl (CHA)	29	
Payson Rd (CHH)	67	
Payson Rd & Ter (BEL)	78	
Peabody (NEW)	58	
Peabody	02215	
Peabody Pl (JP)	30	
Peabody Rd (ARL)	74	
Peabody Rd (STO)	80	
Peabody Sq (DOR)	24	
Peabody Ter (CAM)	38	
Peacedale Cir & Rd (N)	92	
Peacevale Rd (DOR)	24	
Peach (BRA)	85	
Peach Tree Ln (NCE)	59	
Peach Tree Rd (LEX)	73	
Peacock Ln (WRX)	32	
Peacock Farm Rd (LEX)	73	
Peak (BRA)	84	
Peak Hill Rd (ROS)	31	
Pear Tree Dr (LEX)	73	
Pearl (LEX)	73	
Pearl (SFO)	80	
Pearl (WAN)	79	
Pearl (MEL)	76	
Pearl (QUI)	69	
Pearl (WAT)	72	
Pearl (CAM)	39	
Pearl (MED)	55	
Pearl (MAL)	48	
Pearl (DOR)	46	
Pearl (EV)	49	
Pearl (CHE)	50	
Pearl (WAL)	54	
Pearl (NWY)	91	
Pearl (DOR)	25	
Pearl (CHA)	29	
Pearl	10	
Pearl Ave (REV)	51	
Pearl Ave (WIN)	52	
Pearl St Pl (CAM)	39	
Pearl St Pl (SOM)	45	
Pearl St Pl (CHA)	29	
Pearl St & Ct (NEW)	58	
Pearl St & Pl (BRA)	85	
Pearl St & Ter (SOM)	45	
Pearson Ave & Rd (WS)	44	
Pearson Rd (BEL)	78	
Pearson Ter (MAL)	48	
Pebble Ave (WIN)	52	
Pebble Rd (MEL)	76	
Peck Ave (WH)	81	
Peck Ave (ARL)	74	
Pecksuat Rd (NWY)	91	
Peddock Rd (NWY)	91	
Peirce (ARL)	74	
Pelham (NCE)	59	
Pelham (MAL)	48	
Pelham (CAM)	42	
Pelham Rd (WAL)	54	
Pelham Rd (LEX)	73	
Pelham Rd (WES)	93	
Pelham St & Ter	18	
Pelham Ter (ARL)	74	
Pelican Rd (QUI)	69	
Pelton (WRX)	32	
Pemberton (REV)	51	
Pemberton Sq	08	
Pemberton St & Ter (CAM)	40	
Pembroke (MED)	55	
Pembroke (NEW)	58	
Pembroke (CHE)	50	
Pembroke (QUI)	69	
Pembroke Rd (WEL)	81	
Pembroke Rd (WES)	93	
Pembroke St & Ct (SOM)	45	
Pembroke St & Ct	18	
Pender (WRX)	32	
Penfield (ROS)	31	
Penhallow (DOR)	24	
Penn (REV)	51	
Penn (QUI)	69	
Penney Rd (MEL)	76	
Penney Hill Rd (MEL)	76	
Penniman Rd (ALL)	34	
Penniman Rd (BRO)	46	
Penniman Ter (BRA)	84	
Penns-Hill Rd (QUI)	69	
Pennsylvania Ave (NUF)	64	
Pennsylvania Ave (SOM)	45	
Pennsylvania Ave (N)	92	
Penny Ln (STO)	80	
Penryth (ROX)	19	
Pepper (SWY)	90	
Pepper Mill Ln (MIL)	86	
Pequossette (WAT)	72	
Pequossette Rd (BEL)	78	
Pequot (RXC)	20	
Pequot Rd (DOR)	46	
Pequot Rd (NWY)	91	
Pera (REV)	51	
Perabo Ter (WRX)	32	
Perch (ROX)	19	
Percival (DOR)	22	
Percival Pl (EB)	28	
Percy Pl (CAM)	39	
Percy Rd (LEX)	73	
Peregrin Rd (BRA)	84	
Peregrine Rd (NCE)	59	
Perham (WRX)	32	
Perham Ave (MEL)	76	
Perkins (MEL)	76	
Perkins (WNW)	65	
Perkins (QUI)	69	
Perkins (ARL)	74	
Perkins (WIN)	52	
Perkins (CHA)	29	
Perkins Ave (HP)	36	
Perkins Ave (MAL)	48	
Perkins Rd (CHE)	50	
Perkins Rd (EWY)	89	
Perkins St & Pl (SOM)	45	
Perkins St & Sq (JP)	30	
Perley Pl (QUI)	69	
Permil Rd (NH)	94	
Perrin (ROX)	19	
Perrin Rd (BRO)	46	
Perry (BRO)	46	
Perry (SOM)	43	
Perry (CAM)	39	
Perry	18	
Perry (EWY)	89	
Perry (WAT)	72	
Perry Dr (N)	92	
Perry Ln (WES)	93	
Perry Pl (CHA)	29	
Perry Pl (EV)	49	
Perry Rd (WOL)	70	
Perry Rd (BRA)	84	
Perry Rd (AUB)	66	
Pershing Pl (STO)	80	
Pershing Rd (WNW)	65	
Pershing Rd (JP)	30	
Pershing Rd (NH)	94	
Perth (DOR)	21	
Perth Rd (ARL)	74	
Perthshire Rd (BRI)	35	
Peter Rd (NWY)	91	
Peter Parley Rd (JP)	30	
Peter Tufts Rd (ARL)	74	
Peterborough	02215	
Peters (SB)	27	
Peters (CAM)	39	
Peters (ROS)	31	
Peters Dr (STO)	80	
Peterson Rd (QUI)	69	
Peterson Rd (BRA)	85	
Peterson Ter (SOM)	43	
Petrel Park (WY)	88	
Petrel Rd (QUI)	69	
Petrini Cir (N)	92	
Pettee (NUF)	64	
Pevear Pl (ROX)	19	
Peverell (DOR)	25	
Pheasant (WRX)	32	
Pheasant Ave (ARL)	74	
Pheasant Rd (NWV)	60	
Pheasant Rd (WAL)	54	
Pheasant Rd (N)	92	
Pheasant Trl (WES)	93	
Philbrick (ROS)	31	
Philbrick Rd (BRO)	46	
Philbrick Rd (NCE)	59	
Philemon (ARL)	74	
Philip (DOR)	22	
Philip Rd (BEL)	78	
Philip Rd (LEX)	73	
Philips (ARL)	74	
Philips Rd (MEL)	76	
Phillips (WOL)	70	
Phillips (AUB)	66	
Phillips (WAT)	72	
Phillips	14	
Phillips (BRA)	85	
Phillips (WY)	88	
Phillips Ave (REV)	51	
Phillips Cir (WAL)	54	
Phillips Cir (MEL)	76	
Phillips Ln (NWV)	60	
Phillips Pl (SOM)	43	
Phillips Pl (CAM)	38	
Phillips St & Ct (MAL)	48	
Philmore Rd (NEW)	58	
Philpot Ter (MEL)	76	
Phinney Rd (LEX)	73	
Phipps (QUI)	69	
Phipps (CHA)	29	
Phyllis Ave (BRA)	85	
Phyllis Ln (MIL)	86	
Pickerel Rd & Ter (WH)	81	
Pickering Ave (ROX)	19	
Pickering St & Pl (N)	92	

Boston (Con.)   021

Pickwick Rd (WNW)............... 65
Pico Ave (WIN)..................... 52
Pie Aly................................. 08
Piedmont.............................. 16
Piedmont (ARL)..................... 74
Piedmont Ave (WAL)............... 54
Piedmont Rd (MED)................ 55
Pier View Ave (REV)............... 51
Pierce (REV).......................... 51
Pierce (WAL)......................... 54
Pierce (MAL)......................... 48
Pierce (BRO)......................... 46
Pierce (HP)........................... 36
Pierce (NQ).......................... 71
Pierce (MIL).......................... 86
Pierce Ave (EV)..................... 49
Pierce Ave (DOR).................. 22
Pierce Ct (NWY).................... 91
Pierce Rd (WY)...................... 88
Pierce Rd (WH)..................... 81
Pierce Rd (WAT).................... 72
Pierce Sq (DOR).................... 24
Piermont (WAT)..................... 72
Piermont (WOL)..................... 70
Pierpont Rd (WRX)................. 32
Pierrepont Rd (NLF)............... 62
Piety Cor Rd (WAL)................ 54
Pigeon Ln (WAL).................... 54
Pigeon Hill Rd (WES)............. 93
Piggott Rd (MED).................. 55
Pilgrim (CAM)....................... 39
Pilgrim Cir (WEL).................. 81
Pilgrim Pl (DOR)................... 25
Pilgrim Rd (BRA)................... 84
Pilgrim Rd (STO)................... 80
Pilgrim Rd (WH).................... 81
Pilgrim Rd (WAT).................. 72
Pilgrim Rd (BEL).................... 78
Pilgrim Rd (MEL)................... 76
Pilgrim Rd (ARL)................... 74
Pilgrim Rd (WAB).................. 68
Pilgrim Rd (MED).................. 55
Pilgrim Rd (WAL).................. 54
Pilgrim Rd.......................... 02215
Pilgrim Rd (NWY).................. 91
Pilgrim Rd (N)....................... 92
Pilgrim Rd
  1-37 (MIL) (ODD)................ 86
  2-22 (MIL) (EVEN)............... 86
  24-OUT (QUI) (EVEN).......... 69
  39-OUT (QUI) (ODD)............ 69
Pillion Ct (NWY)................... 60
Pillon Rd (MIL)..................... 86
Pilsudski Way (SB)................ 27
Pinckney............................. 14
Pinckney St & Pl (SOM)........ 45
Pine (WAL)........................... 54
Pine (CAM).......................... 39
Pice (CHE)........................... 50
Pine (MAL)........................... 48
Pine...................................... 11
Pine (BRA)........................... 84
Pine (WES)........................... 93
Pine (N)............................... 92
Pine (BEL)........................... 78
Pine (MEL)........................... 76
Pine (WAT)........................... 72
Pine (WH)............................ 81
Pine (STO)........................... 80
Pine (WOL).......................... 70

Pine
  1-84 (WNW).................... 65
  85-OUT (AUB)................. 66
Pine Ave (MIL).................... 86
Pine Rd (CHH).................... 67
Pine St, Ave & Ct (ARL)....... 74
Pine St, Ave & Ter (HP)....... 36
Pine St & Cir (SWY)............ 90
Pine Banks Rd (MAL)........... 48
Pine Banks Garden (MEL).... 76
Pine Cliff Rd (EWY).............. 89
Pine Crest Rd (BRA)............ 84
Pine Crest Rd (NCE)............ 59
Pine Croft Rd (WES)............ 33
Pine Grove (NH).................. 94
Pine Grove (MIL)................. 86
Pine Grove Ave (NLF)........... 62
Pine Grove Path (EWY)........ 89
Pine Hill Cir (WAL).............. 54
Pine Knoll Rd (LEX)............. 73
Pine Lodge Rd (WRX).......... 32
Pine Plain Rd (WH).............. 81
Pine Ridge Rd (WH)............. 81
Pine Ridge Rd (STO)............ 80
Pine Ridge Rd (ARL)............ 74
Pine Ridge Rd (WAB)........... 68
Pine Ridge Rd (MED)........... 55
Pine Ridge Rd (EWY)........... 89
Pine Ridge Rd (MAT)........... 26
Pine Tree Ave (MAL)............ 48
Pine Tree Rd (WEL)............. 81
Pine Vale Rd (WAL)............. 54
Pinecliff Rd (WRX).............. 32
Pinecrest (QUI)................... 69
Pinedale Rd (ROS)............... 31
Pinefield Ave, Rd & Ter (HP).. 36
Pinehurst (ROS).................. 31
Pinehurst Rd (BEL).............. 78
Pines Rd (REV)................... 51
Pinevale Ave (WH).............. 81
Pinewood (LEX)................... 73
Pinewood (MAT).................. 26
Pinewood Rd (MEL)............. 76
Pinewood Rd (N)................. 92
Ping On............................. 09
Pingree (HP)....................... 36
Pinkert (MED)..................... 55
Pinkham Rd (MED).............. 55
Pinkham Rd (MED).............. 74
Piper (QUI)......................... 69
Piper Rd (ARL).................... 74
Pitcairn (REV).................... 51
Pitcher Ave (MED).............. 55
Pitman (SOM)..................... 43
Pitsmoor Rd (ROS).............. 31
Pitts Ave (WOL).................. 70
Pittsburgh....................... 02210
Placid Rd (NCE).................. 59
Plain (QUI)......................... 69
Plain (DOR)......................... 22
Plain
  1-128 (BRA)..................... 85
  129-OUT (BRA)................ 84
Plain Rd (WES)................... 93
Plain Ter (SWY).................. 90
Plainfield (UP).................... 30
Plainfield (LEX).................. 73
Plainfield (WAB)................ 68
Plainfield Ave (MAL).......... 48
Plant Ct (UP)...................... 30
Plant Rd (WAL).................. 54
Platt Rd (BRI).................... 35
Playstead Rd (MAL)............ 48

Pleasant (WEL)................... 81
Pleasant (BRA)................... 84
Pleasant (LEX).................... 73
Pleasant (QUI).................... 69
Pleasant (WNW)................. 65
Pleasant (NCE)................... 59
Pleasant (MEL)................... 76
Pleasant (WAT).................. 72
Pleasant (DOR)................... 25
Pleasant (CHA)................... 29
Pleasant (MED).................. 55
Pleasant (BRO).................. 46
Pleasant (MAL).................. 48
Pleasant (HP)..................... 36
Pleasant (REV)................... 51
Pleasant (EV)..................... 49
Pleasant (N)....................... 92
Pleasant (MIL).................... 86
Pleasant
  1-273 (ARL) (ODD)........... 74
  1-599 (SWY)................... 90
  2-278 (ARL) (EVEN)......... 74
  275-727 (BEL) (ODD)....... 78
  280-728 (BEL) (EVEN)...... 78
  600-OUT (EWY)............... 89
  729-OUT (WAV)............... 79
Pleasant Ave (SOM)............ 43
Pleasant Park Rd (WIN)....... 52
Pleasant St Ct (MED).......... 55
Pleasant St Ct (CHA).......... 29
Pleasant St Park (MAL)....... 48
Pleasant St & Ave (WAL)..... 54
Pleasant St & Ct (WIN)....... 52
Pleasant St & Pl (CAM)...... 39
Pleasant St & Ter (STO)...... 80
Pleasant Hill Ave (MAT)...... 26
Pleasant Valley Cir (WRX)... 32
Pleasant View Ave (EV)....... 49
Pleasant View Ave (BRA)..... 84
Pleasant View Ave (WY)...... 68
Pleasant View Rd (WH)....... 81
Pleasant View Rd (ARL)...... 74
Pleasantdale Rd (WRX)....... 32
Pleasanton (DOR)............... 21
Pleasantview (ROS)............ 31
Plover (WRX)...................... 32
Plover Rd (QUI).................. 69
Plowgate Rd (CHH)............. 67
Plumer (EV)........................ 49
Plummer Ave (WIN)............ 52
Plummer Wharf (EB)........... 28
Plymouth (EV)..................... 49
Plymouth (CAM).................. 41
Plymouth (QUI)................... 69
Plymouth (ARL).................. 74
Plymouth....................... 02215
Plymouth Ave (BEL)............ 78
Plymouth Ave
  1-120 (BRA)..................... 86
  121-OUT (QUI)................. 69
Plymouth Ave & Dr (BRA).... 85
Plymouth Cir (MEL)............ 76
Plymouth Dr (WAL)............. 54
Plymouth Rd (MAL)............. 48
Plymouth Rd (WH).............. 81
Plymouth Rd (NWH)............ 61
Plymouth Rd (LEX)............. 73
Plymouth Rd (WES)............ 93
Plymouth Rd (N)................. 92
Plympton (CAM)................. 38
Plympton............................. 18
Plympton St Ext (WAL)........ 54
Plympton St, Ave & Cir

317

Boston (Con.)   021

(WAL)	54
Plymton Rd (WNW)	65
Poinsetta Ave (WY)	88
Polk (CHA)	29
Pollywog Ln (WES)	93
Pomeroy (ALL)	34
Pomeworth (STO)	80
Pomfret (WRX)	32
Pomona (REV)	51
Pomona Ave (WRX)	32
Pompeii (ROX)	19
Pond (DOR)	25
Pond (WIN)	52
Pond (WAL)	54
Pond (HP)	36
Pond (STO)	80
Pond (BEL)	78
Pond (MEL)	76
Pond (QUI)	69
Pond (WAT)	72
Pond (MIL)	86
Pond (BRA)	85
Pond (N)	92
Pond (SWY)	90
Pond Ave (BRO)	46
Pond Ave (NEW)	58
Pond Cir (MED)	55
Pond Ln & Ter (ARL)	74
Pond Pl (CAM)	39
Pond Rd (WH)	81
Pond St Ct (WAL)	54
Pond St Pl	13
Pond St & Cir (JP)	30
Pond Brook Cir (WES)	93
Pond Brook Rd (CHH)	67
Pond End Ln & Rd (WAL)	54
Pond View Ave (JP)	30
Ponderosa Dr (SWY)	90
Pondred (ROS)	31
Poadside Rd (WEL)	81
Pondview Rd (ARL)	74
Pontiac (RXC)	20
Pontiac Rd (WAB)	68
Pontiac Rd (QUI)	69
Poole (MED)	55
Pope (NQ)	71
Pope Hill Rd (MIL)	86
Popes Hill (DOR)	22
Poplar (BRA)	84
Poplar (STO)	80
Poplar (WAT)	72
Poplar (MEL)	76
Poplar (BEL)	78
Poplar (LEX)	73
Poplar (ROS)	31
Poplar (MAL)	48
Poplar (CHE)	50
Poplar Ave (QUI)	69
Poplar Rd (WH)	81
Poplar Rd (CAM)	38
Poplar St & Ct (SOM)	43
Port Norfolk (DOR)	22
Porter (JP)	30
Porter (EB)	28
Porter (CAM)	41
Porter (EV)	49
Porter (MEL)	76
Porter (WAT)	72
Porter Ave (REV)	51
Porter Ave (BRA)	85
Porter Cir, Park, Rd & Sq	

(CAM)	40
Porter Rd (MED)	55
Porter Rd (WAL)	54
Porter St & Ave (SOM)	43
Porter St & Ave (MAL)	48
Porter Ter (WRX)	32
Portino Rd (BRI)	35
Portland	14
Portland	
1-177 (CAM) (ODD)	39
2-170 (CAM) (EVEN)	39
172-OUT (CAM) (EVEN)	41
179-OUT (CAM) (ODD)	41
Portland Rd (BRA)	85
Portsmouth (BRI)	35
Portsmouth (MAL)	41
Possum Rd (WES)	93
Post Island Rd (QUI)	69
Post Office Sq	09
Potomac (WRX)	32
Potosi (DOR)	22
Potter (CAM)	42
Potter (MEL)	76
Potter Park (CAM)	38
Potter Rd (WAL)	54
Poulos Rd (BRA)	85
Powder House Blvd, Sq & Ter	
(WS)	44
Powder House Rd (N)	92
Powder House Rd Ext (MED)	55
Powder House Rd & Ter	
(MED)	55
Powell (WRX)	32
Powell (BRO)	46
Powellton Rd (DOR)	21
Power House (SB)	27
Powers (N)	92
Powers Ct	09
Poydras (MAT)	26
Prairie (MAT)	26
Prairie Ave (AUB)	66
Pratt (MEL)	76
Pratt (MAL)	48
Pratt (AL)	34
Pratt (WIN)	52
Pratt Ave (WAL)	54
Pratt Ave (NWY)	91
Pratt Ct (RXC)	20
Pratt Dr (WNW)	65
Pratt Rd (NQ)	71
Pratt St, Ct & Pl (REV)	51
Pray (QUI)	69
Preble (SB)	27
Preble Gardens Rd (BEL)	78
Prendergast Ave (BRO)	46
Prentice (WAL)	54
Prentice Rd (NCE)	59
Prentiss (WAT)	72
Prentiss (MAL)	48
Prentiss	
1-90 (CAM)	40
91-OUT (SOM)	43
Prentiss Ln (BEL)	78
Prentiss Rd (ARL)	74
Prentiss St & Pl (RXC)	20
Presby Pl (ROX)	19
Prescott (ROX)	19
Prescott (CHA)	29
Prescott (EB)	28
Prescott (ARL)	74
Prescott (MEL)	76
Prescott (WAT)	72
Prescott (NWV)	60

Prescott (WH)	81
Prescott (SWY)	90
Prescott (MAL)	48
Prescott (BRO)	46
Prescott (WIN)	52
Prescott (MED)	55
Prescott (SOM)	43
Prescott (CAM)	38
Prescott (HP)	36
Prescott Ave (CHE)	50
Prescott Ln (BRA)	84
Prescott Ln & Ter (QUI)	69
Prescott Pl (ALL)	34
Prescott St, Rd & Ter (EV)	49
Presentation Rd (BRI)	35
President Rd (ROS)	31
President Ter (ALL)	34
President Gardens Dr (QUI)	69
Presidents Ave & Ln (QUI)	69
Presidents Rd (BRA)	84
Presidents Rd (WY)	88
Presley (MAL)	48
Presley Rd (DOR)	22
Preston (MAL)	48
Preston (EV)	49
Preston Rd (WRX)	32
Preston Rd (SOM)	43
Preston Rd (LEX)	73
Price (NQ)	71
Price Rd (ALL)	34
Prichard Ave (WS)	44
Priesing (JP)	30
Priest Rd (WAT)	72
Primrose (ROS)	31
Primrose Ave (BRA)	84
Primrose Ln (EWY)	89
Primus Ave	14
Prince (JP)	30
Prince (EWY)	89
Prince (N)	92
Prince (MIL)	86
Prince (WNW)	65
Prince (WAV)	79
Prince (BRO)	46
Prince (CAM)	39
Prince (REV)	51
Prince	
1-164	13
165-165	09
166-OUT	13
Princess Rd (WNW)	65
Princess Eve Dr (WOL)	70
Princeton (WS)	44
Princeton (NEW)	58
Princeton (MED)	55
Princeton Ave (WAL)	54
Princeton Ave (NWY)	91
Princeton Rd (MAL)	48
Princeton Rd (BEL)	78
Princeton Rd (WH)	81
Princeton Rd (ARL)	74
Princeton Rd (CHH)	67
Princeton St & Pl (EB)	28
Priscilla Cir (WY)	88
Priscilla Cir & Rd (WH)	81
Priscilla Ln (QUI)	69
Priscilla Ln (MIL)	86
Priscilla Ln (WAL)	54
Priscilla Ln (MED)	55
Priscilla Rd (BRI)	35
Priscilla Rd (CHH)	67
Proctor (NWV)	60
Proctor (ROX)	19

Boston (Con.) 021

Proctor Ave (REV).................... 51
Proctor Rd (EV)........................ 49
Proctor Rd (BRA)...................... 85
Professors Row (MED)............. 55
Progress (WY)........................... 88
Proprietors Way (ARL)............. 74
Prospect (NQ).......................... 71
Prospect (WH).......................... 81
Prospect (BRA)........................ 84
Prospect (BEL)......................... 78
Prospect (STO)......................... 80
Prospect (MEL)........................ 76
Prospect (WAT)........................ 72
Prospect (N)............................. 92
Prospect (EV)........................... 49
Prospect (CAM)....................... 39
Prospect (WAL)........................ 51
Prospect (BRO)........................ 46
Prospect N (BRA)..................... 84
Prospect Ave (WOL)................. 70
Prospect Ave (ARL).................. 74
Prospect Ave (REV).................. 51
Prospect Ave (WIN).................. 52
Prospect Ave (ROS).................. 31
Prospect Ave, Park & Ter
  (NWV)................................... 65
Prospect Pl (WNW)................... 65
Prospect St Ave (WAL)............. 54
Prospect St & Ave (CHE).......... 50
Prospect St & Ave (CHA).......... 29
Prospect St & Ct (WY).............. 88
Prospect St & Pl (SOM)............ 43
Prospect St & Ter (MAL).......... 48
Prospect Hill (QUI).................. 69
Prospect Hill Ave (SOM).......... 43
Prospect Hill Ave, Ln, Park &
  Rd (WAL)............................. 54
Prospect Hill Dr (NWY)............ 91
Prospect Hill Rd (LEX)............. 73
Prosper (MAL)......................... 48
Prout (QUI).............................. 69
Providence (HP)....................... 36
Providence............................... 16
Province St & Ct....................... 08
Prudential Center..................... 99
Puddingstone Ln (NCE)............ 59
Puddingstone Rd (CHH)........... 67
Pulaski Ave (SB)...................... 27
Pulsifer (NWV)........................ 60
Purcell Rd (ARL)...................... 74
Purchase.................................. 10
Puritan Ave (DOR)................... 21
Puritan Dr (QUI)...................... 69
Puritan Rd (ARL)..................... 74
Puritan Rd (WAT).................... 72
Puritan Rd (EWY).................... 89
Puritan Rd (SOM).................... 45
Puritan Rd
  1-60 (NWH)........................... 61
  61-OUT (WAB)...................... 68
Purvis (WAT)........................... 72
Putnam (WAT).......................... 72
Putnam (QUI)........................... 69
Putnam (WNW)........................ 65
Putnam (NH)............................ 94
Putnam (EWY)......................... 89
Putnam (SOM)......................... 43
Putnam (WAL)......................... 54
Putnam (WIN).......................... 52

Putnam (EB)............................ 28
Putnam (CHA).......................... 29
Putnam Ave (BRA)................... 84
Putnam Ave. Ct & Gdns
  (CAM).................................. 39
Putnam Rd (SOM).................... 45
Putnam Rd (ARL)..................... 74
Putnam St & Pl (ROX).............. 19
Putnam St & Rd (REV).............. 51
Putney Ln (WAL)...................... 54
Putney Rd (WH)....................... 81
Quadrant Cir (QUI).................. 69
Quail (WRX)............................. 32
Quaker La................................ 09
Quarley Rd (ROS).................... 31
Quarry (QUI)............................ 69
Quarry Ave (EWY)................... 89
Quarry Ln (MIL)....................... 86
Quarter Deck Rd (QUI)............ 69
Queen (DOR)........................... 22
Queensberry............................ 02215
Queenwood Ter (MAL)............. 48
Quentin (MIL).......................... 86
Quidnic Rd (WAB)................... 68
Quimby (WAT).......................... 72
Quincefield (DOR)................... 25
Quincy (WAT)........................... 72
Quincy (ARL)........................... 74
Quincy (MAL).......................... 48
Quincy (SOM).......................... 43
Quincy (MED).......................... 55
Quincy
  1-269 (DOR) (ODD).............. 21
  2-262 (DOR) (EVEN)............ 21
  264-OUT (DOR) (EVEN)....... 25
  271-OUT (DOR) (ODD)......... 25
Quincy Ave (WIN).................... 52
Quincy Ave (BRA).................... 84
Quincy Ct................................. 13
Quincy Pl & Ter (DOR)............. 21
Quincy Rd (CHH)..................... 67
Quincy Row.............................. 09
Quincy St. Ave, Sq & Ter
  (QUI).................................... 69
Quincy St & Sq (CAM)............. 38
Quincy Mkt.............................. 09
Quincy Shore Dr
  1-593 (NQ)........................... 71
  594-1300 (WOL).................. 70
  1301-OUT (QUI).................. 69
Quinn Rd (ARL)....................... 74
Quinn Way (WRX).................... 32
Quinobequin Rd
  1-120 (NLF).......................... 62
  121-OUT (WAB).................... 68
Quint Ave (ALL)....................... 34
Quirk (WAT)............................. 72
Quirk Ct (NEW)........................ 58
Rachel Rd (NCE)...................... 59
Racine Ct (RXC)...................... 20
Radcliff (MED)......................... 55
Radcliffe (DOR)....................... 21
Radcliffe Rd (MAT).................. 26
Radcliffe Rd (ALL)................... 34
Radcliffe Rd (SOM).................. 45
Radcliffe Rd (ARL).................. 74
Radcliffe Rd (WAB).................. 68
Radcliffe Rd (WEL).................. 81
Radcliffe Rd (BEL).................. 78
Radcliffe Rd (WH).................... 76
Radcliffe Rd (WES).................. 93
Radford Ln (DOR).................... 24
Radford Pl (HP)....................... 36

Radnor Rd (BRI)...................... 35
Rae Ave (N)............................. 92
Raeburn Ter (NWH).................. 61
Rafferty Rd (STO).................... 80
Railroad (BRI)......................... 84
Railroad (LEX)......................... 73
Railroad Ave (ARL).................. 74
Railroad Ave (REV).................. 51
Railroad Ave (MAL)................. 48
Rainbow Ln (SWY).................. 90
Rainier Rd (MAT)..................... 26
Raldne Rd (HP)....................... 36
Raleigh (SWY)......................... 90
Raleigh................................... 02215
Raleigh (ARL).......................... 74
Raleigh Rd (BEL)..................... 78
Raleigh Rd (EWY).................... 89
Ralph (WAT)............................ 72
Ralph (MED)............................ 55
Ralph Talbot (SWY)................. 90
Ralston Rd (MAT).................... 26
Ralwood Rd (MAT).................. 26
Rambler Rd (JP)...................... 30
Rambler Rd (SWY).................. 90
Ramp....................................... 02210
Ramsdell (NWH)...................... 61
Ramsdell Ave (ROS)................ 31
Ramsdell Ct (ARL).................. 74
Ramsdell Rd (MAL)................. 48
Ramsey (STO).......................... 25
Ramshead Rd (MED)............... 55
Rand (MED)............................. 55
Rand (MAL)............................. 48
Rand (REV).............................. 51
Rand St & Pl (DOR)................. 25
Rand Ter (AUB)....................... 66
Randall (ROX)......................... 19
Randall (WAL)......................... 54
Randall Ave (EWY).................. 89
Randall Ave (BRA).................. 85
Randall Rd (REV)..................... 51
Randlett (WOL)....................... 70
Randlett Park (WNW).............. 65
Randlett Pl (DOR).................... 25
Rando Ln (WAL)...................... 54
Randolph................................. 18
Randolph (NWH)..................... 61
Randolph (ARL)....................... 74
Randolph (BEL)....................... 78
Randolph (SWY)...................... 90
Randolph Ave
  1-299 (MIL).......................... 87
  300-OUT (MIL)..................... 86
Randolph Rd (STO).................. 80
Randolph Rd (CHH)................. 67
Ranelegh Rd (BRI).................. 35
Range Rd (DOR)...................... 24
Rangeley (DOR)....................... 24
Rangeley Rd (WAL)................. 54
Rangeley Rd (CHH)................. 67
Rangeley Rd (ARL).................. 74
Rangeley Rd (WNW)................ 65
Rangeley Rd (WAT).................. 72
Ranger Cir (SWY).................... 90
Rangeway (LEX)....................... 73
Ranley Rd (MAT)..................... 26
Ransom Rd (NCE).................... 59
Ransom Rd (BRI)..................... 35
Rantoule (SWY)....................... 90
Ratchford (QUI)...................... 69
Raven (N)................................ 25
Ravena (REV).......................... 51
Ravenna Rd (ROS).................. 31

Boston (Con.)   021

Ravenswood Rd (WAL)	54
Ravine (ARL)	74
Ravine Rd (WH)	81
Ravine Rd (MEB)	55
Ravine Rd & Ter (MEL)	76
Rawson (DOR)	25
Rawson Ave (LEX)	73
Rawson Rd (ARL)	74
Rawson Rd (WOL)	70
Rawson Rd (BRO)	46
Rawston Rd (ROS)	31
Ray (ROX)	19
Ray Ln (BRA)	85
Rayburn Rd (WAV)	79
Raycroft (QUI)	69
Raycroft Ave (WY)	88
Raymond (EWY)	89
Raymond (QUI)	69
Raymond (LEX)	73
Raymond (ALL)	34
Raymond (MAL)	48
Raymond (MED)	55
Raymond (CAM)	40
Raymond (EV)	49
Raymond Ave (WS)	44
Raymond Pl (WNW)	65
Raymond Rd (STO)	80
Raymond St & Rd (REV)	51
Raynes Rd (HP)	36
Raynold Rd (HP)	36
Raynor Cir (STO)	88
Raynor Rd (WES)	93
Read (WIN)	52
Read Ave & Park (QUI)	69
Read Ct (NCE)	59
Reading (ROX)	19
Reading Hill Ave (MEL)	76
Readville (HP)	36
Realton Rd (WRX)	32
Reardon (QUI)	69
Reardon Rd (MEB)	55
Record Ct (SOM)	45
Rector Rd (MAT)	26
Red Coat Ln (LEX)	73
Red Bevil Ln (WAT)	72
Red Jacket Rd (SWY)	90
Red Pine Rd (HP)	36
Red Wing Rd (WH)	81
Reddington Rd (N)	92
Reddy Ave (HP)	36
Redfield (DOR)	22
Redford (ALL)	34
Redgate Rd (WRX)	32
Redlands Rd (WRX)	32
Redstone Shopping Center (STO)	80
Redwood (DOR)	22
Redwood Rd (NCE)	59
Reed (LEX)	73
Reed (ARL)	74
Reed	18
Reed (MIL)	86
Reed Ave (SWY)	90
Reed Ave (EV)	49
Reed St Ter (CAM)	40
Reed St & Ct (CAM)	40
Reed Hill Rd (BRA)	85
Reeds Ct (SOM)	45
Reedsdale (LEX)	34
Reedsdale Rd 1-125 (MIL)	87

126-OUT (MIL)	86
Regal (BRI)	35
Regan Rd (DOR)	24
Regatta Rd (NWY)	91
Regent (CAM)	40
Regent (WNW)	65
Regent Cir (BRO)	46
Regent Cir (JP)	30
Regent Rd (MAL)	48
Regent Rd (WAV)	79
Regent St, Ct, Pl & Sq (ROX)	19
Regina Rd (DOR)	24
Regina Rd (WEY)	88
Regina Rd & Ter (AUB)	66
Regis Rd (ARL)	74
Regis Rd (WEL)	81
Regis Rd (BRA)	85
Regis Rd (MAT)	26
Regis Rd (MED)	55
Reidy Rd (EWY)	89
Relda Rd (SWY)	90
Remick Ct (SOM)	45
Remick Ter (NEW)	58
Remington (CAM)	38
Remington (DOR)	24
Remington Ct (QUI)	69
Rena (ALL)	34
Rendall Pl (MEL)	76
Rendall Rd (WRX)	32
Renee Ter (NCE)	59
Renfrew (ARL)	74
Renfrew (MED)	55
Renfrew St & Ct (ROX)	19
Renwick Rd (MEL)	76
Reservation Rd (HP)	36
Reservation Rd (MIL)	86
Reserve (MAL)	48
Reservoir (CAM)	38
Reservoir Ave (REV)	51
Reservoir Ave, Dr, Ln & Rd (CHH)	67
Reservoir Ct (BRO)	46
Reservoir Rd (WAL)	54
Reservoir Rd (ARL)	74
Reservoir Rd (WOL)	70
Reservoir St, Ave & Ct (BRA)	84
Reservoir St, Ave, Ln & Park (NH)	94
Revere (MIL)	87
Revere (ARL)	74
Revere (LEX)	73
Revere (MAL)	48
Revere (REV)	51
Revere (WIN)	52
Revere (CAM)	38
Revere (EV)	49
Revere (JP)	30
Revere	14
Revere Ave	09
Revere Pl (MED)	55
Revere Rd (QUI)	69
Revere Rd (EWY)	89
Revere Beach Blvd Ct (REV)	51
Revere Beach Blvd & Pky (REV)	51
Revere Beach Pky (MED)	55
Revere Beach Pky (CHE)	50
Revere Beach Pky 1629-2385 (EV)	49
Revere Beach Pky Ct (CHE)	50
Reverend Nazareno Properzi Way (SOM)	43

Reverend Richard A Burke (SB)	27
Revolutionary Rd (LEX)	73
Rex Dr (BRA)	84
Rexford (MAT)	26
Rexhame (ROS)	31
Reyem (WAL)	54
Reynold Rd (HP)	36
Reynolds Ave (EV)	49
Reynolds Ave (CHE)	50
Rhinecliff (ARL)	74
Rhoades (DOR)	24
Rhoda (WRX)	69
Rhoda (WRX)	32
Rhode Island Ave (SOM)	45
Rhodes (LEX)	73
Rhude (QUI)	69
Rhuland Rd (STO)	80
Rice (WEL)	81
Rice (NCE)	59
Rice (BRO)	46
Rice (EB)	28
Rice (DOR)	22
Rice Ave (MED)	55
Rice Ave (REV)	51
Rice Rd (WOL)	70
Rice St & Cir (CAM)	40
Rich (WAL)	54
Rich (MAT)	26
Rich 1-OUT (EV) (ODD)	49
Rich 2-OUT (MAL) (EVEN)	48
Richard (REV)	51
Richard (MED)	55
Richard (MAL)	48
Richard (QUI)	69
Richard Rd (LEX)	73
Richard Rd (N)	92
Richard Rd (BRA)	85
Richard Ter (DOR)	24
Richardi La (BRA)	85
Richards	02218
Richards Ave (CAM)	40
Richards Cir (WNW)	65
Richards Rd (WAT)	72
Richards Rd (MIL)	86
Richards Rd (EWY)	89
Richardson (MAL)	48
Richardson (NEW)	58
Richardson (CAM)	39
Richardson (BRI)	35
Richardson Ave (ARL)	74
Richardson Dr (N)	92
Richardson Ln & Rd (STO)	80
Richardson Rd (BEL)	78
Richardson Rd (MEL)	76
Richardson Rd (NUF)	64
Richardson St & Ter (SOM)	45
Richdale Ave (SOM)	45
Richdale Ave (CAM)	40
Richdale Ave (EV)	49
Richdale Rd (NH)	94
Richfield (NQ)	71
Richfield Rd (WNW)	65
Richfield Rd (ARL)	74
Richfield St & Park (DOR)	25
Richgrain Ave (WAL)	54
Richie Rd (REV)	51
Richie Rd (QUI)	69
Richland Rd (WH)	81
Richmere Rd (MAT)	26
Richmond (DOR)	24
Richmond	09

Boston (Con.)   021

Richmond (WY) 88
Richmond Rd (BEL) 78
Richmond Rd (NEW) 58
Richview (DOR) 24
Richwood (WRX) 32
Ricker Rd (NEW) 58
Ricker St & Ct (MAL) 48
Ricker Ter
  1-3 (BRI) 35
  4-OUT (NEW) 58
Ricker Hill Rd (WRX) 32
Rider Ter (AUB) 66
Ridge (ARL) 74
Ridge (ROS) 31
Ridge Ave (NCE) 59
Ridge Rd (WAB) 68
Ridge Rd (WAV) 79
Ridge Rd (LEX) 73
Ridge Rd (REV) 51
Ridge Rd (MIL) 87
Ridge Hill Ave (MAL) 48
Ridge Hill Farm Rd (WH) 81
Ridgecrest Dr & Ter (WRX) 32
Ridgeley Ct (CAM) 38
Ridgemont (ALL) 34
Ridgeview Ave (MAT) 26
Ridgeway (WOL) 70
Ridgeway Ave & Ter (N) 92
Ridgeway Dr (QUI) 69
Ridgeway Ln 14
Ridgeway Rd (MED) 55
Ridgeway Rd
  1-3 (WH) 81
  4-OUT (WES) 93
Ridgewood Ter (NWH) 61
Ridgewood (DOR) 22
Ridgewood Rd (MEL) 76
Ridgewood Rd (MIL) 86
Ridgewood Rd (MAL) 48
Ridgewood Ter (WAL) 54
Ridgewood Ter (SWY) 90
Ridlon Rd (MAT) 26
Riedesel Ave (CAM) 38
Rifle Ct (WAT) 72
Riley Ave (EWY) 89
Riley Rd (HP) 36
Rill (DOR) 25
Rinaldo Rd (NWY) 91
Rindge (EWY) 89
Rindge Ave (LEX) 73
Rindge Ave Ext (CAM) 40
Rindge Ave & Ter (CAM) 40
Ridgefield (CAM) 40
Ring Ave (QUI) 69
Ringgold 18
Ripky (WAL) 54
Ripley (WAL) 48
Ripley Ln (WES) 93
Ripley Rd (MED) 55
Ripley Rd (DOR) 21
Ripley Rd (WAV) 79
Ripley St & Ter (NCE) 59
Risley Rd (WNW) 65
Risley Rd (CHH) 67
Rita Dr (MED) 55
Rita Rd (STO) 80
Rita Rd (BRA) 84
Rita Rd (DOR) 24
Ritchie (ROX) 19
Rivard Rd (N) 92
River (NWY) 91

River 08
River (WH) 81
River (BRA) 84
River (WNW) 65
River (QUI) 69
River (ARL) 74
River (CAM) 39
River
  1-855 (MAT) 26
  856-OUT (HP) 36
River Ave (REV) 51
River Ave (NUF) 64
River Park (NH) 94
River Rd (WES) 93
River Rd (WIN) 52
River Rd (BRO) 46
River Rd (SOM) 45
River St Pl 08
River St Ter (HP) 36
River St & Ave (WAL) 54
River Ridge Rd (WH) 81
River View Pl (NWY) 91
Riverbank Pl (MAT) 26
Riverbank Rd (NWY) 91
Riverbank Rd (QUI) 69
Riverdale (ALL) 34
Riverdale Ave (NEW) 58
Riverdale Rd (WH) 81
Riverdale Rd (MAT) 26
Riverglen Rd (WH) 81
Rivermoor (WRX) 32
Riverside (WAT) 72
Riverside (NH) 94
Riverside Ave (MIL) 86
Riverside Ave (QUI) 69
Riverside Ave (MED) 55
Riverside Dr (WAL) 54
Riverside Pl (CAM) 39
Riverside Rd (WES) 93
Riverside Sq (HP) 36
Riverview Ave (WAL) 54
Riverview Rd (BRI) 35
Riverview Rd (QUI) 69
Riverway (WRX) 32
Riverway
  1-339 02215
  340-OUT 15
Roach (DOR) 25
Road A (EV) 49
Road B (EV) 49
Roanoke (QUI) 69
Roanoke Ave (JP) 30
Roanoke Rd (MAT) 26
Roanoke Rd (WEL) 81
Roanoke Rd (ARL) 74
Robbart Ln (HP) 36
Robbie Rd (BRA) 84
Robbins (MAL) 48
Robbins (MIL) 86
Robbins Rd (ARL) 74
Robbins Rd (WAT) 72
Robbins Rd (LEX) 73
Robbins St & Pl (WAL) 54
Robert (ROS) 31
Robert Ter (MAL) 48
Robert E Kelley (CAM) 38
Robert Ford Rd (WAT) 72
Roberta Ln (WOL) 70
Roberta Rd (AUB) 66
Roberts (QUI) 69
Roberts (BRA) 84
Roberts (MAL) 48
Roberts (BRO) 46

Roberts (SOM) 45
Roberts Ave (NWY) 60
Roberts Dr (SWY) 90
Roberts Pl (HP) 36
Roberts Rd (CAM) 38
Roberts Rd (WAL) 54
Roberts Rd (MED) 55
Roberts Rd (WH) 81
Roberts Post Rd (SWY) 90
Robertson St & Ter (QUI) 69
Robeson (JP) 30
Robey
  1-79 (ROX) (ODD) 19
  2-74 (ROX) (EVEN) 19
  76-OUT (ROX) (EVEN) 25
  81-OUT (DOR) (ODD) 25
Robin (WRX) 32
Robin (EV) 49
Robin Rd (WES) 93
Robin Dell (AUB) 66
Robin Hood (DOR) 25
Robin Hood Rd (ARL) 74
Robin Hood Rd (STO) 80
Robinhood (AUB) 66
Robinson (DOR) 22
Robinson (CAM) 38
Robinson (SOM) 45
Robinson Ave (BRA) 84
Robinson Rd (LEX) 73
Robinson Rd (MED) 55
Robinson Rd (MAL) 48
Robinswood Rd (SWY) 90
Robinwood Ave (N) 92
Robinwood Ave (JP) 30
Robinwood Rd (WAV) 79
Robken Rd (ROS) 31
Rochdale (ROX) 19
Roche (QUI) 69
Rochester Rd (NEW) 58
Rock (ROX) 19
Rock Ave (DOR) 24
Rock Rd (MAT) 26
Rock Ter (DOR) 21
Rock Glen Cir & Rd (MED) 55
Rock Hill (MED) 55
Rock Island Rd (QUI) 69
Rock Ledge Rd (NWH) 61
Rock Ridge Rd (WH) 81
Rock Valley Ave (EV) 49
Rockaway Ln (ARL) 74
Rockcroft Rd (WY) 88
Rockdale (MAT) 26
Rockdale Rd (BRA) 84
Rockford (ROX) 19
Rockingham Ave (MAL) 48
Rockingham Ct (EB) 28
Rockingham Rd (MAT) 26
Rockingham St & Pl (CAM) 39
Rockland (NEV) 58
Rockland (WRX) 32
Rockland (WH) 81
Rockland (NWH) 61
Rockland (QUI) 69
Rockland (MEL) 76
Rockland Ave (ARL) 74
Rockland Ave, Park & Pl
  (MAL) 48
Rockland Pl (NUF) 64
Rockland St, Ave & Pl (ROX) .. 19
Rockledge (ROX) 19
Rockmere (DOR) 25
Rockmont Rd (ARL) 74
Rockmont Rd (BEL) 78

Boston (Con.)	021
Rockne Ave (DOR)	24
Rockport Rd (WES)	93
Rockridge Rd (WAL)	54
Rockvale Cir (JP)	30
Rockview Ave (MEL)	76
Rockview Rd (QUI)	69
Rockview Rd (MIL)	87
Rockview St, Pl & Ter (JP)	30
Rockville Ave (LEX)	73
Rockville Park (STO)	80
Rockville Park (ROX)	19
Rockway Ave (WEY)	88
Rockwell (DOR)	24
Rockwell (CAM)	39
Rockwell Ave (MED)	55
Rockwell Ave & Pl (MIL)	86
Rockwell St & Ter (MAL)	48
Rockwood (MEL)	76
Rockwood	
1-100 (JP)	30
101-OUT (BRO)	46
Rockwood Ln (N)	92
Rockwood Ter (AUB)	66
Rockwood Ter (MED)	55
Rockwood Ter (JP)	30
Rocky Nook Ter (JP)	30
Rocsam Park Rd (BRA)	85
Roddy Pl (BRI)	35
Rodgers Rd (STO)	80
Rodman (QUI)	69
Rodman (JP)	30
Rodney (BRI)	35
Rogers (NEW)	58
Rogers (CAM)	42
Rogers (SB)	27
Rogers (NWH)	61
Rogers (EWY)	89
Rogers Ave (WS)	44
Rogers Cir (BRA)	84
Rogers Park Ave (BRI)	35
Rogers Rd (LEX)	73
Rogers St & Ln (QUI)	69
Roine Rd (BRA)	84
Rokaby Rd (WAB)	68
Roland (NWH)	61
Roland (SOM)	43
Roland (SWY)	90
Roland (CHA)	29
Roland (MED)	55
Roland Rd (REV)	51
Rolfe Rd (LEX)	73
Rolling Ln (LEX)	73
Rolling Ln (CHH)	67
Rolling Ln (N)	92
Rolling Ln (WES)	93
Rollins	18
Rollins Ct (CAM)	39
Rollins Pl	14
Romar Ter (ROX)	19
Rome Dr (BRA)	84
Romsey (DOR)	25
Ronaele Rd (MED)	55
Ronald (DOR)	21
Ronald Rd (ARL)	74
Ronan (DOR)	25
Ronan Park (DOR)	22
Roosevelt Rd (LEX)	73
Roosevelt Rd (NCE)	59
Roosevelt Rd (MED)	55
Roosevelt Rd (WY)	88
Roosevelt St & Pl (REV)	51
Roosevelt Towers (CAM)	41
Rosa (HP)	36
Rosalie Rd (NH)	94
Rosalie Rd (NCE)	59
Rosalind Rd (NWY)	91
Rosaria (DOR)	22
Roscoe (NH)	94
Rose (MIL)	86
Rose (WY)	88
Rose (SOM)	43
Rose (REV)	51
Rose Ave (BRA)	85
Rose Ave (WAT)	72
Rose Dr (WRY)	65
Rose Ln (STO)	80
Rose Garden Cir (BRI)	35
Rose Hill Way (WAL)	54
Roseberry Rd (MAT)	26
Roseclair (DOR)	25
Rosecliff St & Ter (ROS)	31
Rosedale (DOR)	24
Rosedale Ave (EV)	49
Rosedale Ave (BRA)	85
Rosedale Rd (WAL)	72
Roseen Ave (WY)	88
Rosegate Rd (NH)	94
Roseglen Rd (MAT)	26
Roseland (DOR)	24
Roseland	
1-55 (CAM) (ODD)	40
2-64 (CAM) (EVEN)	40
57-OUT (SOM) (ODD)	43
66-OUT (SOM) (EVEN)	43
Roselin Ave (QUI)	69
Rosemary (NH)	94
Rosemary (JP)	30
Rosemary Ln (SWY)	90
Rosemary Ln (QUI)	69
Rosemere Ct (ROS)	31
Rosemont (MAL)	48
Rosemont (MAT)	26
Rosemont (DOR)	22
Rosemont Ave (WAL)	54
Rosemont Rd (NWY)	91
Roseway (JP)	30
Rosewood (MAT)	26
Rosewood Dr (WAL)	54
Rosina Rd (EWY)	89
Roslin (DOR)	24
Roslin Rd (ARL)	74
Roslindale Ave (ROS)	31
Roslyn Pl (JP)	30
Roslyn Rd (WAB)	68
Ross (MED)	55
Ross Pl (SB)	27
Ross Rd (BEL)	78
Ross Rd (LEX)	73
Rosselerin Rd (DOR)	22
Rosseter (DOR)	21
Rossetti (REV)	51
Rossmere (NWY)	60
Rossmore (SOM)	43
Rossmore Rd (JP)	30
Roswell (ROX)	19
Rotherwood Rd (NCE)	59
Rotterdam (ALL)	34
Roughan Rd & Ter (CHA)	29
Roughans (REV)	51
Roughans Point (REV)	51
Round Hill (JP)	30
Round Hill Rd (LEX)	73
Round Hill Rd (WES)	93
Roundwood Rd (NUF)	64
Rowe Pl	11
Rowe St & Pl (ROS)	31
Rowe Hill Rd (STO)	80
Rowell (DOR)	25
Rowen Ct (JP)	30
Rowena (DOR)	24
Rowena Rd (NCE)	59
Rowes Wharf	10
Rowland Ave (LEX)	73
Rowley (QUI)	69
Rowley (WY)	22
Roxana (HP)	36
Roxbury (WIN)	52
Roxbury St, Ct & Ter (ROX)	19
Roxton (DOR)	21
Royal (ALL)	34
Royal (WAL)	54
Royal (WOL)	70
Royal (STO)	80
Royal (WAT)	72
Royal Ave (CAM)	38
Royal Rd (BRO)	46
Royal Rd (BEL)	78
Royall (MED)	55
Royalston Rd (WH)	81
Royce Pl (SOM)	45
Royce Rd (ALL)	34
Royce Rd (NCE)	59
Roys (JP)	30
Rozella (DOR)	22
Ruane Cir & Rd (WRY)	65
Rublee (ARL)	74
Rucille Ave (WY)	88
Rudolph (MAL)	48
Ruffing (HP)	36
Rufo Rd (CAM)	41
Rugby Rd (MAT)	26
Rugdale Rd (DOR)	24
Rugg Rd (ALL)	34
Ruggiand Cir (WY)	88
Ruggles (MEL)	76
Ruggles (QUI)	69
Ruggles	
1-41 (ROX)	19
42-OUT (RXC) (EVEN)	20
43-239 (RXC) (ODD)	20
241-OUT (ODD)	15
Ruggles Ct (ROX)	19
Ruggles Ln (MIL)	87
Rumford Ave	
1-142 (WAL)	54
143-143 (AUB)	66
144-152 (WAL)	54
153-153 (AUB)	66
154-160 (WAL)	54
161-161 (AUB)	66
162-162 (WAL)	54
163-163 (AUB)	66
164-OUT (WAL)	54
Rumford Rd (LEX)	73
Rumford Rd (WRX)	32
Rumney Rd (REV)	51
Rundel Park (DOR)	24
Running Brook Rd (WRX)	32
Rural Ave (MED)	55
Rusfield (ROX)	32
Rush (SOM)	45
Rushmore (BRI)	35
Ruskin (WRX)	32
Ruskin Rd (HP)	36
Ruskindale Rd (MAT)	26
Russell (MED)	55
Russell (WIN)	52

Boston (Con.) 027

Russell (BRO) 46
Russell (WAL) 54
Russell (NQ) 71
Russell (MEL) 76
Russell (MIL) 87
Russell
1-15 (CAM) (ODD) 40
2-OUT (CAM) (EVEN) 40
17-OUT (WS) (ODD) 44
Russell Ct (NWV) 60
Russell Park (QUI) 69
Russell Rd (WNW) 65
Russell Rd (LEX) 73
Russell Rd (BRA) 84
Russell Rd (WH) 81
Russell Rd (SWY) 90
Russell Rd (N) 92
Russell Rd (NEW) 58
Russell Rd (WS) 44
Russell St & Ave (WAT) 72
Russell St, Ct & Park (MAL) 48
Russell St, Ct & Pl (CHA) 29
Russell St & Pl (EV) 40
Russell St & Ter (ARL) 74
Russell Ter (WAV) 79
Russett Ln (MEL) 76
Russett Rd
1-190 (WRX) 32
191-OUT (CHH) 67
Rustic (NEW) 58
Rustic Dr (SWY) 90
Rustic Pl (QUI) 69
Rustic Rd (WRX) 32
Rustic Rd & Ter (STO) 32
Rustlewood Rd (WRX) 32
Rustlewood Rd (MIL) 87
Rutgers Rd (WH) 81
Rutherford Ave (CHA) 29
Ruthven (NQ) 71
Ruthven Rd (NEW) 58
Ruthven St & Park (DOR) 21
Rutland (MAL) 48
Rutland (CAM) 38
Rutland (WAT) 72
Rutland St & Sq 18
Rutledge (WRX) 32
Rutledge Rd (BEL) 78
Rutledge Ter (WAL) 54
Ruxton Rd (MAT) 26
Ryan Ct (WNW) 65
Ryan Rd (BRI) 35
Ryan Rd (SOM) 45
Rybury Hillway (N) 92
Ryden (QUI) 69
Ryder (ARL) 74
Ryder Ave (MEL) 76
Ryder Rd (SWY) 90
Ryder Hill Rd (BRI) 35
Sabina Way (WAV) 79
Sables Ct (MED) 55
Sabrina (WH) 81
Sabrina Farm Rd (WH) 81
Sachem (RXC) 20
Sachem Ave (ARL) 74
Sachem Rd (NWY) 91
Sachem Rd (NH) 94
Sachem St & Ct (REV) 51
Sachem St & Park (WOL) 70
Sackville (CHA) 29
Saco (DOR) 22
Saco (NUF) 64

Sacramento
1-74 (CAM) 38
75-OUT (SOM) 43
Sacramento Pl (CAM) 38
Saddle Brook Dr (N) 92
Saddle Club Rd (LEX) 73
Saddle Hill Rd (WES) 93
Safford (BRA) 85
Safford (HP) 36
Safford
1-40 (NQ) 71
41-OUT (WOL) 70
Sagamore (BRA) 85
Sagamore (REV) 51
Sagamore (WIN) 25
Sagamore Ave (WIN) 52
Sagamore Ave (CHE) 50
Sagamore Ave & Park (MED) 55
Sagamore Rd (NWY) 91
Sagamore Rd (NWH) 61
Sagamore Rd (ARL) 74
Sagamore Rd (WH) 81
Sagamore St & Ave (NQ) 71
Sagamore Way (WAL) 54
Saginaw Ave (CAM) 40
Saint Agatha Rd (MIL) 86
Saint Albans Rd 15
Saint Alphonsus (RXC) 20
Saint Andrew Rd (EB) 28
Saint Ann (JP) 30
Saint Annes Rd (EWY) 89
Saint Anns Rd (WOL) 70
Saint Botolph
1-99 16
100-OUT 15
Saint Brendon Rd (DOR) 24
Saint Cecelia 15
Saint Charles 16
Saint Claire (BRA) 85
Saint Clare Rd (DOR) 22
Saint Clare Rd (MED) 55
Saint Clements Rd (WS) 44
Saint Cloud Ave (N) 92
Saint Denis Ave (MED) 55
Saint Edward Rd (EB) 28
Saint Francis (MED) 55
Saint Francis Desales (RXC) 20
Saint George 18
Saint Gerard Ter (CAM) 40
Saint Germain 15
Saint Germain (QUI) 69
Saint Gregory Ext (DOR) 24
Saint Gregory St & Ct (DOR) 24
Saint James Ave 16
Saint James Ave (WS) 44
Saint James Rd (MED) 55
Saint James St, Pl & Ter
(ROX) 19
Saint James St & Ter (NEW) 58
Saint John (JP) 30
Saint Johns Rd (CAM) 38
Saint Joseph (JP) 30
Saint Jude Ter (DOR) 22
Saint Lawrence (BRA) 85
Saint Lukes Rd (ALL) 34
Saint Margaret (EWY) 89
Saint Margaret (DOR) 25
Saint Mark (JP) 30
Saint Marks Rd (DOR) 24
Saint Martin (CHA) 29
Saint Mary
1-OUT (MED) (ODD) 55
2-OUT (MAL) (EVEN) 48

Saint Mary Rd (CAM) 39
Saint Marys 02215
Saint Marys (NH) 94
Saint Marys (NLF) 62
Saint Marys (WAT) 72
Saint Marys Ct (BRO) 46
Saint Marys Rd (MIL) 87
Saint Michael Rd (BRA) 85
Saint Paul (CAM) 39
Saint Paul St & Ter (BRO) 46
Saint Pauls Ave (JP) 30
Saint Peter (JP) 30
Saint Richard (ROX) 19
Saint Rose (JP) 30
Saint Sauveur Ct (CAM) 38
Saint Stephen 15
Saint Theresa Ave (WRX) 32
Saint Thomas More Dr (BRI) 35
Saint William (DOR) 25
Saipan Rd (CHE) 50
Salcombe (DOR) 25
Salem (CAM) 39
Salem (MED) 55
Salem (REV) 51
Salem (QUI) 69
Salem (WH) 81
Salem St Ave (CHA) 29
Salem St, Ct & Pl 13
Salem St & Pl (MAL) 48
Salem Hill Ct (CHA) 29
Sales (REV) 51
Salina Rd (DOR) 22
Salisbury Park (DOR) 22
Salisbury Rd (BRO) 46
Salisbury Rd (NEW) 58
Salisbury Rd (WAT) 72
Salman (WRX) 32
Salt Ln 09
Saltonstall Rd (MED) 55
Salutation 09
Sammet (EV) 49
Sammet Ave (ROS) 31
Sammett (MAL) 48
Samoset (DOR) 24
Samoset (SWY) 90
Samoset Ave (QUI) 69
Samoset Ln (WAL) 54
Samoset Rd (WAB) 68
Sampo Pl (QUI) 69
Sampson St, Ave & Pl (BRA) 84
Samson Rd (MED) 55
Samuel Morse Way (CHA) 29
San Jose Ter (STO) 80
Sanborn Ave (WRX) 32
Sanborn Ave & Ct (SOM) 43
Sanders Ln (WAL) 54
Sanderson Ave (EWY) 89
Sanderson Pl (BRI) 35
Sanderson Rd (WAL) 54
Sanderson Rd (LEX) 73
Sandra Ln (WY) 88
Sandrick Rd (BEL) 78
Sandy Way (NWY) 91
Sanford (MEL) 76
Sanford (HP) 36
Sanford (MAT) 26
Sanger (SB) 27
Sanger (MED) 55
Saning Rd (NWY) 91
Santilli Hwy (EV) 49
Santuit (DOR) 24
Saranac (DOR) 22
Saratoga (NQ) 71

Boston (Con.)   021

Saratoga Rd (ARL) 74
Saratoga St & Pl (EB) 28
Sargent (DOR) 25
Sargent (QUI) 69
Sargent (MEL) 76
Sargent (LEX) 73
Sargent (CAM) 40
Sargent (MAL) 48
Sargent (REV) 51
Sargent (N) 92
Sargent Ave (SOM) 45
Sargent Rd (BRO) 46
Sargent Rd (MED) 55
Sargent Rd (SWY) 90
Sargent Rd (BEL) 78
Sargent St & Park (NEW) 58
Sargent St & Ter (WIN) 52
Sargent Beechwood (BRO) 46
Sargent Crossways (BRO) 46
Sargents Wharf 09
Sarsfield (RXC) 20
Sartell Rd (WAL) 54
Sartwell Ave (WS) 44
Sassaman Ave (MIL) 86
Saunders (NWY) 91
Saunders (MED) 55
Saunders (ALL) 34
Saunders Ter (WH) 81
Savage (REV) 51
Savannah Ave (MAT) 26
Saville (WRX) 32
Saville (CAM) 38
Saville Ave (QUI) 69
Savin (MAL) 48
Savin (ROX) 19
Savin (MIL) 87
Savin Hill Ave, Ct & Ln
(DOR) 25
Savoy (DOR) 18
Savoy Rd (N) 92
Saw Mill Brook Pky (NCE) 59
Sawin (ARL) 74
Sawin (WAT) 72
Sawtelle (NWY) 91
Sawyer Ave (DOR) 25
Sawyer Rd (EWY) 89
Sawyer Rd (WH) 81
Sawyer Rd (MEL) 76
Sawyer Rd (WAL) 54
Sawyer St & Ave (MED) 55
Sawyer St & Ct (MAL) 48
Sawyer Ter (ALL) 34
Saxon Rd & Ter (NWH) 61
Saxton (DOR) 25
Saybrook St & Ter (BRI) 35
Sayward (DOR) 25
Sayward Pl (SB) 27
Scammell (QUI) 69
Scarsdale Rd (NWV) 60
Schaller (WH) 81
Schiller (JP) 30
Schiller Rd (WRX) 32
Schirmer Rd (WRX) 32
Schlager Ave (QUI) 69
Schofield Dr (NWV) 60
School (QUI) 69
School (BRA) 84
School (WEL) 81
School (BEL) 78
School (MEL) 76

School (STO) 80
School (ARL) 74
School (LEX) 73
School (CAM) 39
School (BRI) 35
School (BRO) 46
School (MAL) 48
School (NEW) 58
School (NWY) 51
School (CHE) 50
School (EV) 49
School (DOR) 24
School 08
School (ROX) 19
School (EWY) 89
School (N) 92
School (MIL) 87
School (WES) 93
School
1-163 (SOM) 43
164-OUT (SOM) 45
School St Pl (ROX) 19
School St Pl (CHA) 29
School St Pl (EV) 49
School St & Ave (WAL) 54
School St & Ln (WAT) 72
School House Rd (MED) 55
Schortmanns Ter (WRX) 32
Schouler Ct (ARL) 74
Schrepel Pl (SB) 27
Schubert (ROS) 31
Schuyler (DOR) 21
Sciarappa St & Pl (CAM) 41
Science Park 14
Scituate (ARL) 74
Scotch Pine Cir (WEL) 81
Scotch Pine Rd (WH) 81
Scotch Pine Rd (WES) 93
Scotch Pond Pl (QUI) 69
Scotia 15
Scotland Rd (LEX) 73
Scotney Rd (CHH) 67
Scott (MED) 55
Scott (CAM) 38
Scott Ln (BRA) 85
Scott Pl (SB) 27
Scott Rd (N) 92
Scott Rd (SWY) 90
Scott Rd (BEL) 78
Scottfield Rd (ALL) 34
Scribner Park (AUB) 66
Scribner Rd (HP) 36
Sea (EV) 49
Sea (MAL) 48
Sea (NWY) 91
Sea St & Ave (QUI) 69
Sea Foam Ave (WIN) 52
Sea View Ave (WIN) 52
Sea View Ave (MAL) 48
Sea View Ave (EB) 28
Sea View Ter (DOR) 25
Seaborn (DOR) 24
Seabury (NWY) 91
Seager Ct (BRI) 35
Seagrave Rd (CAM) 40
Seagull Rd (QUI) 69
Seal Rock Ln (NQ) 71
Sealund Rd (NQ) 71
Searle Ave (BRO) 46
Searle Rd (WRX) 32
Sears (REV) 51
Sears 10

Sears Ave (MEL) 76
Sears Rd (BRO) 46
Sears Rd (MIL) 86
Sears Rd (WES) 93
Seattle (ALL) 34
Seaver (BRO) 46
Seaver (WH) 81
Seaver (EB) 28
Seaver (DOR) 21
Seaver Pl 16
Seaver Rd (EWY) 89
Seeverns Ave (JP) 30
Seeverns Ln (WES) 93
Seaview Ave (REV) 51
Seaward Rd (WH) 81
Seaway Rd (NQ) 74
Seckle (CAM) 41
Second (MAL) 48
Second (WRX) 32
Second (CHE) 50
Second (EV) 49
Second (MED) 55
Second (LEX) 73
Second (WY) 88
Second (SB) 27
Second
1-159 (CAM) 41
160-OUT (CAM) 42
Second Ave (NH) 94
Second Ave (WAL) 54
Sedalia Rd (DOR) 24
Sedge Rd (LEX) 73
Sedgewick (JP) 30
Sedgewick Rd (WH) 38
Seery (MAL) 48
Sefton (MAT) 26
Segel (DOR) 21
Selden (DOR) 24
Selden (WAB) 68
Selkirk Rd (ARL) 74
Selkirk Rd (BRO) 46
Sellers (CAM) 39
Sellon Pl (SOM) 45
Selma (EB) 28
Selwyn (ROS) 31
Selwyn Rd (BEL) 78
Selwyn Rd (NWH) 61
Selwyn Rd (BRA) 85
Seminary (CHA) 29
Seminary Ave (AUB) 66
Seminole (MAT) 26
Seminole Ave (ARL) 74
Seminole Ave (WY) 88
Seminole Ave (WAL) 54
Semont Rd (DOR) 24
Senders Ct (HP) 36
Sentry Hill Pl 14
Service Dr & Rd (WH) 81
Sessions (WEL) 81
Seton Hill Rd (AUB) 66
Seven Pines Ave
1-23 (WS) (ODD) 44
2-OUT (CAM) (EVEN) 40
25-OUT (WS) (ODD) 40
Seventh (SB) 27
Seventh (CAM) 41
Seventh (MED) 55
Sever (CHA) 29
Sevland (NCE) 59
Sewall (WNY) 65
Sewall (MEL) 76
Sewall (WOL) 70
Sewall (RXC) 20

Boston (Con.)	021
Sewall (REV)	51
Sewall Ave (WIN)	52
Sewall Ave (BRO)	46
Sewall Cr (CT)	45
Sewall Woods Rd (MEL)	76
Seward Rd (STO)	80
Seward Rd (WH)	81
Sextant Cir (QUI)	69
Sexton (WAT)	72
Sexton Ct (DOR)	25
Seymour (QUI)	69
Seymour (WIN)	52
Seymour (ROS)	31
Seyon (WAL)	54
Shade (WAL)	54
Shade (LEX)	73
Shadow Ln (WH)	81
Shadow Rd (MEL)	76
Shady Ln (SWY)	90
Shady Ln (N)	92
Shady Brook Ln (BEL)	78
Shady Hill Rd (NWH)	61
Shady Hill Rd (WES)	93
Shady Hill Sq (CAM)	38
Shafter (DOR)	21
Shailer (BRO)	46
Shakespeare Rd (WAL)	54
Shaler Ln (CAM)	38
Shamrock (NEW)	58
Shanahan Pl (ROS)	31
Shandon Rd (DOR)	24
Shanley (BRI)	35
Shannon (BRI)	35
Shapley Ave (MED)	55
Sharon (MED)	55
Sharon (WAL)	54
Sharon (MAL)	48
Sharon Ave (AUB)	66
Sharon Rd (MEL)	76
Sharon Rd (NQ)	71
Sharp (DOR)	24
Sharpe Rd (BEL)	78
Sharpe Rd (NCE)	59
Shattuck	15
Shattuck Rd (WAT)	72
Shaw (WNW)	65
Shaw (QUI)	69
Shaw (WRX)	32
Shaw (NWY)	91
Shaw Pl (LEX)	73
Shaw Rd (BEL)	78
Shaw Rd (CHH)	67
Shaw Rd (WH)	81
Shaw St & Ave (BRA)	84
Shawmut (REV)	51
Shawmut (SOM)	43
Shawmut	16
Shawmut Ave	
1-99	16
100-652 (EVEN)	18
101-649 (ODD)	18
651-OUT (ROX) (ODD)	19
654-OUT (ROX) (EVEN)	19
Shawmut Park (NUF)	64
Shawmut Rd (WAL)	54
Shawmut St & Ave (EWY)	89
Shawmut St & Pl (CHE)	50
Shawmut St & Pl (QUI)	65
Shawmut St & Ter (MAL)	48
Shawnee Rd (ARL)	74
Shawsheen Rd (EB)	28
Shaylor La (WES)	93
Shea (QUI)	69
Shea Rd (CAM)	40
Sheafe (MAL)	48
Sheafe (CHA)	29
Sheafe	13
Sheafe Rd (CHH)	67
Shean Rd (BEL)	78
Shedd (QUI)	69
Sheffield Rd (MEL)	76
Sheffield Rd (NWV)	60
Sheffield Rd (WAL)	54
Sheffield Rd (ROS)	31
Sheila (LEX)	73
Shelburne Rd (WH)	81
Shelby (EB)	28
Sheldon (ROS)	31
Sheldon (MIL)	86
Sheldon Rd (NCE)	59
Sheldon Rd (WAT)	72
Shelley Rd (WH)	81
Shelley Rd (ARL)	74
Shelton Rd (QUI)	69
Shenandoah (DOR)	24
Shennen (QUI)	69
Shepard (NQ)	71
Shepard (CAM)	38
Shepard Ct (HP)	36
Shepard Rd (BRA)	85
Shepard St & Pl (BRI)	35
Shephard Way (BRI)	35
Shepherd Ave	15
Shepherd Park (WAB)	68
Shepherd Rd (MED)	55
Sheppard Ave (BRA)	84
Shepton (DOR)	24
Shepton Ter (SB)	27
Sheraton Ave (BRA)	85
Sheraton Park (ARL)	74
Sherborn (ARL)	74
Sherborn	02215
Sherborn Ct (SOM)	45
Sherbrook (WRX)	32
Sherbrook Ave (BRA)	85
Sherbrooke (NEW)	58
Sherburne Cir (WES)	93
Sherburne Cir (QUI)	69
Sherburne Rd (LEX)	73
Sheridan (LEX)	73
Sheridan (WNW)	65
Sheridan (MAL)	48
Sheridan Ave (MED)	56
Sheridan Cir & Rd (WH)	81
Sheridan Dr (MIL)	86
Sheridan Rd (STO)	80
Sheridan Rd (WAL)	54
Sheridan St & Pl (JP)	30
Sheridan St & Sq (CAM)	40
Sherman (ROS)	31
Sherman (EV)	49
Sherman (REV)	51
Sherman (ROX)	19
Sherman (BEL)	78
Sherman (LEX)	73
Sherman (WOL)	70
Sherman (NH)	94
Sherman	
1-43 (CAM) (ODD)	38
2-40 (CAM) (EVEN)	38
42-OUT (CAM) (EVEN)	40
45-OUT (CAM) (ODD)	40
Sherman Pl (AUB)	66
Sherman Rd (CHH)	67
Sherman Rd (STO)	80
Sherman Rd (MEL)	76
Sherman Rd (BRA)	85
Sherman St, Ct & Pl (MED)	55
Sherman St & Sq (CHA)	29
Sherrin (HP)	36
Sherrin Rd (CHH)	67
Sherrin Rd (NLF)	62
Sherwin	18
Sherwood (ROS)	31
Sherwood Ct (ROX)	18
Sherwood Ln (WAL)	54
Sherwood Rd (MED)	55
Sherwood Rd (MEL)	76
Sherwood Rd (STO)	80
Sherwood Rd (NWY)	91
Sheryl La (WIN)	52
Shetland (ROX)	19
Ship Ave (MED)	55
Shirley (EV)	49
Shirley (ROX)	19
Shirley (WNW)	65
Shirley (QUI)	69
Shirley (LEX)	73
Shirley Ave (REV)	51
Shirley Rd (MED)	55
Shirley Rd (WAL)	54
Shirley Rd (WH)	81
Shirley Rd (WH)	94
Shirley St & Ave (WIN)	52
Shore Ave (QUI)	69
Shore Dr (SOM)	45
Shore Dr (NWY)	91
Shore Rd (WAL)	54
Shore Rd (WH)	81
Shore Rd (ARL)	74
Shore Side (QUI)	69
Shoreham (NQ)	71
Shornecliffe Rd (NEW)	58
Short (MED)	55
Short (WIN)	52
Short (BRO)	46
Short (MAL)	48
Short (ARL)	74
Short (LEX)	73
Short (MEL)	76
Short (SWY)	90
Short	02215
Short (CHA)	29
Short (EB)	28
Short St Ct (CHA)	29
Short St Pl (CHA)	29
Shrewsbury Rd (ROS)	31
Shumaker Path (NCE)	59
Shuman Cir (NCE)	59
Shurland (JP)	30
Shurtleff (MAL)	48
Shurtleff (REV)	51
Shurtleff St & Pl (CHE)	50
Shute (EV)	49
Shute Path (NCE)	59
Siaz Ln (MIL)	86
Sibley Ct (CAM)	38
Sibley Ct & Pl (SOM)	45
Sibley Rd (WAL)	54
Sibley Rd (WES)	93
Sidlaw Rd (BRI)	35
Sidley Rd (WRX)	32
Sidney (CAM)	39
Sidney (WAT)	72
Sierra Rd (HP)	36
Signore Ter (REV)	51

Boston (Con.)   021

Sigourney (REV)	51
Sigourney (JP)	30
Silk (CHE)	50
Silk (ARL)	74
Silloway (DOR)	24
Silva Pl (ROX)	19
Silver (SB)	27
Silver (QUI)	69
Silver (MAL)	48
Silver Pl	14
Silver Rd (EV)	49
Silver Rd (BRA)	84
Silver Birch Rd (WAB)	68
Silver Brook Rd (MIL)	86
Silver Hill Ln (WAL)	54
Silver Hill Rd (WES)	93
Silver Lake Ave (NEW)	58
Silvey Pl (SOM)	43
Simmons (RXC)	20
Simmons Ave (BEL)	78
Simms Ave & Ct (WNW)	65
Simonds Ct (MED)	56
Simonds Rd (MEL)	76
Simonds Rd (LEX)	73
Simonelli Pl (EV)	49
Simpson (NEW)	58
Simpson Ave (WS)	44
Simpson Rd (WEL)	81
Simpson Ter (NWV)	60
Simpsons Ct (CHA)	29
Sims Rd (WOL)	70
Sinclair Rd (ALL)	34
Single Tree Ln (CHH)	67
Sioux Ave (WAL)	54
Siren (WIN)	52
Sixth (MED)	55
Sixth (CHE)	50
Sixth (MEL)	76
Sixth (SB)	27
Sixth	
1-113 (CAM) (ODD)	41
2-118 (CAM) (EVEN)	41
115-OUT (CAM) (ODD)	42
120-OUT (CAM) (EVEN)	42
Sixth Ave (QUI)	69
Skahon Rd (BEL)	78
Skating Pond Rd (WES)	93
Skehan (SOM)	43
Skelly Ave (EWY)	89
Skilton Ave (SOM)	45
Sky Line Dr (WH)	81
Sky View Rd (LEX)	73
Sky View Ter (NCE)	59
Skyline Dr (BRA)	84
Skyline Dr (ARL)	74
Skyline Rd (HP)	36
Skyview Cir (NCE)	59
Slade (BEL)	78
Slayton Rd (MEL)	76
Slayton Way (ROX)	19
Sleeper	02210
Sleepy Hollow Ln (ARL)	74
Slocum Rd (LEX)	73
Slocum Rd (JP)	30
Small (NQ)	71
Smart (CAM)	39
Smart (WAL)	54
Smith (WAL)	54
Smith (REV)	51
Smith (QUI)	69

Smith (ARL)	74
Smith (WEL)	81
Smith (RXC)	20
Smith (N)	92
Smith Ave (LEX)	73
Smith Ave (SOM)	43
Smith Ave & Ct (WNW)	65
Smith Ct	14
Smith Pl (CAM)	38
Smith Rd (MIL)	86
Smith St & Ln (MED)	55
Smith St & Ter (BRA)	85
Smyth (BRO)	46
Snake Hill Rd (BEL)	78
Snelling Pl	13
Snow (BRI)	35
Snow Ter (SOM)	45
Snow Hill	13
Snug Harbor Ct (QUI)	69
Sobin Park	02210
Soden St & Pi (CAM)	39
Solar Ave (BRA)	84
Solaris Rd (HP)	36
Soldiers Field Pl (BRI)	35
Soldiers Field Rd.	
1-399 (SF)	63
400-400 (ALL)	34
401-1000 (SF)	63
1001-1200 (ALL)	34
1201-OUT (BRI)	35
Soley (CHA)	29
Solon (WEL)	81
Solon (NWH)	61
Somerset (BEL)	78
Somerset	08
Somerset (EWY)	89
Somerset (EV)	49
Somerset Ave & Ter (WIN)	52
Somerset Rd (BRO)	46
Somerset Rd (WNW)	65
Somerset Rd (LEX)	73
Somerville Ave (BRA)	84
Somerville Ave	
1-811 (SOM)	43
812-OUT (CAM)	40
Songin Way (SB)	27
Sonoma (DOR)	21
Sonoma Rd (NQ)	71
Soper Ave (WY)	88
Soper House Ln (BRA)	84
Sorenson Ct (ARL)	74
Sorenti Cir (WEL)	81
Sorrento (ALL)	34
South (BRI)	35
South (CAM)	38
South (SOM)	43
South (MED)	55
South (WAL)	54
South (QUI)	69
South (STO)	80
South (CHH)	67
South (BRA)	85
South (N)	92
South	11
South	
1-400 (JP)	30
401-OUT (ROS)	31
South Ave (WES)	93
South Ave (EWY)	89
South Ave (MEL)	76
South Ave (WIN)	52
South Ave (REV)	51

South St Ct (MED)	55
South Bay Ave	18
South Bayfield Rd (NQ)	71
South Border Rd (MED)	55
South Cambridge (REV)	51
South Cedar Park (MEL)	76
South Cedar Pl	16
South Central Ave & Ter (WOL)	70
South Charlame Ct & Ter (ROX)	19
South Crescent Circuit (BRI)	35
South Eden (CHA)	29
South Fairview (ROS)	31
South Ferry (REV)	49
South Furness (REV)	51
South Gate Park (WNW)	65
South Genesee (REV)	51
South Hancock (REV)	51
South Hillside (STO)	90
South Hobart (BRI)	35
South Huntington Ave (JP)	30
South Irving (REV)	51
South Irving Park (WAT)	72
South Junior Ter (QUI)	69
South Main (WIN)	52
South Marble (STO)	80
South Market	09
South Munroe Ter (DOR)	22
South Normandy Ave (CAM)	38
South Park (WAT)	72
South Quincy Pl (CHA)	29
South Russell	14
South Shore Plz (BRA)	84
South Station	02210
South Sydney (DOR)	25
South Walnut (QUI)	69
South Walter (ROS)	31
South Washington (MAL)	48
South Waverly (BRI)	35
South Whitney (RXC)	20
Southampton	
1-443	18
444-OUT (SB)	27
Southbourne Rd (JP)	30
Souther Rd (DOR)	22
Southern Ave (DOR)	24
Southern Ave (WY)	88
Southern Artery	
1-226 (WOL)	70
227-OUT (QUI)	69
Southgate Rd (WEL)	81
Southmere Rd (MAT)	26
Southview (DOR)	25
Southwick (DOR)	22
Southwick Cir (WH)	81
Southwick Rd (WAB)	68
Southwood (ROX)	19
Spafford Rd (MIL)	86
Sparhawk (BRI)	35
Sparkill (WAL)	54
Sparkill (WAT)	72
Sparks St & Pi (CAM)	38
Sparrow (WRX)	32
Spaulding (EV)	49
Spaulding (QUI)	69
Spaulding (DOR)	22
Spaulding (JP)	30
Spaulding Ln (NCE)	59
Speakman (WOL)	70
Spear (QUI)	69
Spear (MEL)	76
Spear Pl	15

Boston (Con.)	021
Speedway Ave (ALL)	34
Speedwell (DOR)	22
Spence Ave (QUI)	69
Spencer (STO)	80
Spencer (WNW)	65
Spencer (BRA)	84
Spencer (LEX)	73
Spencer (DOR)	24
Spencer (WAL)	54
Spencer (MAL)	48
Spencer Ave (CHE)	50
Spencer Ave (WS)	44
Spencer Rd (MED)	55
Speridakis Ter (CAM)	39
Spevak Ter (MAL)	48
Spice (CHA)	29
Spiers Rd (NCE)	59
Spinney (WRX)	32
Spinney Ter (BEL)	78
Spofford Rd (ALL)	34
Spooner Rd (CHH)	67
Sprague (REV)	51
Sprague Ct (MED)	55
Sprague Rd (WH)	81
Sprague St & Ct (MAL)	48
Sprague St & Pl (HP)	36
Spray Ave (REV)	51
Spring (MAL)	48
Spring (SOM)	43
Spring (EV)	49
Spring (WAL)	54
Spring (WEL)	81
Spring (MEL)	76
Spring (NUF)	64
Spring (LEX)	73
Spring (WY)	88
Spring (BRA)	85
Spring Ct (ROX)	19
Spring Ln	09
Spring Rd (NH)	94
Spring Rd (WES)	93
Spring St Pl (CAM)	41
Spring St & Ave (REV)	51
Spring St, Ave & Rd (ARL)	74
Spring St & Ct (WAT)	72
Spring St & Ext (MED)	55
Spring St & Ln (STO)	80
Spring St & Pl (CAM)	41
Spring St & Rd (WRX)	32
Spring St & Ter (QUI)	69
Spring Garden (DOR)	25
Spring Glen Cir (BRA)	85
Spring Hill Rd (HP)	36
Spring Hill Ter (SOM)	43
Spring Park Ave (JP)	30
Spring Valley (ARL)	74
Spring Valley Rd (BEL)	78
Spring Valley Rd (WRX)	32
Springdale (MAL)	48
Springdale (DOR)	25
Springdale Ave (WH)	81
Springer (SB)	27
Springfield (BEL)	78
Springfield (QUI)	69
Springfield (WAT)	72
Springfield	
1-22 (CAM)	39
23-OUT (SOM)	43
Springvale Ave (NWY)	91
Springvale Ave (WRX)	32
Springvale Ave	
1-142 (CHE)	50
143-OUT (EV)	49
Spruce (MIL)	86
Spruce (MAL)	48
Spruce (WAL)	54
Spruce (EV)	49
Spruce (CHE)	50
Spruce (WAT)	72
Spruce (NQ)	71
Spruce (BEL)	78
Spruce (STO)	80
Spruce Ave (CAM)	38
Spruce Park (WH)	81
Spruce St, Ct & Pl	08
Spruce St & Ext (BRA)	84
Spruce Hill Rd (WES)	93
Spurr (ALL)	34
Spy Pond Ln & Pky (ARL)	74
Squanto Rd (QUI)	69
Squanto Rd (NWY)	91
Squantum (MIL)	86
Squire Rd (REV)	51
Squirrel Rd (WH)	81
Stacey (CHA)	29
Stadium Pl & Rd (ALL)	34
Stadium Rd (MAL)	48
Stafford (ROX)	19
Stafford Rd (NCE)	59
Stanbro (HP)	36
Standard (MAT)	26
Standish (DOR)	24
Standish (CAM)	38
Standish (NWH)	61
Standish (NWY)	91
Standish Ave (BRA)	85
Standish Ave (WOL)	70
Standish Cir & Rd (WH)	81
Standish Ct (WAL)	54
Standish Rd (REV)	51
Standish Rd (NQ)	71
Standish Rd (ARL)	74
Standish Rd (STO)	80
Standish Rd (WH)	76
Standish Rd (WAT)	72
Standish Rd (MIL)	87
Stanford Rd (SOM)	81
Stanford Ter (SOM)	43
Stanhope St & Ct	16
Staniford	14
Staniford (AUB)	66
Stanley (CAM)	25
Stanley (NWY)	91
Stanley Ave (WAT)	72
Stanley Ave (MED)	55
Stanley Cir (QUI)	69
Stanley Rd (WAB)	68
Stanley Rd (WAV)	79
Stanley Rd (WAL)	54
Stanmore Pl (ROX)	19
Stanton (MAL)	24
Stanton (MAL)	48
Stanton (WOL)	70
Stanton Ave (AUB)	66
Stanton Ave (REV)	51
Stanton Pl (ROX)	19
Stanton Rd (BRO)	46
Stanton Rd (STO)	80
Stanton Rd (MIL)	86
Stanwood St & Ter (DOR)	21
Staples (MEL)	76
Staples Ave (EV)	49
Star Rd (WNW)	65
Starbird (MEL)	76
Starbird (MAL)	48
Starbird Ave (ROS)	31
Stark (CHA)	29
Stark Ave (REV)	51
Starr Ln (JP)	30
Starr King Ct (CHA)	29
State	09
State (CAM)	39
State (QUI)	69
State (MIL)	86
State Rd (REV)	51
Staten Rd (BRA)	84
Station (QUI)	69
Station (BRO)	46
Station (EWY)	89
Station (RXC)	20
Station Ave (NWH)	61
Statler Pl (BEL)	78
Staunton (WOL)	76
Staunton Rd (BEL)	78
Stearns (NCE)	59
Stearns (MAL)	48
Stearns (CAM)	38
Stearns (WAL)	54
Stearns Ave (MED)	55
Stearns Rd (BRO)	46
Stearns Rd (WRX)	32
Stearns Rd (BEL)	78
Stearns Rd (WEL)	81
Stearns Rd (WAT)	72
Stearns Rd (LEX)	73
Stearns Ter (REV)	51
Stearns Hill Rd (WAL)	54
Stedman (BRO)	46
Stedman (QUI)	69
Stedman (JP)	30
Stedman Ave (BRA)	84
Stedman Rd (LEX)	73
Steele (STO)	80
Steep Rock Rd (ARL)	74
Steeple (REV)	51
Steeves Cir (WS)	44
Steeves Ct (MAL)	48
Stein Cir (NCE)	59
Stella Dr (WY)	88
Stella Rd (BEL)	78
Stella Rd (ROS)	31
Stellar Rd (BRA)	84
Stellman Rd (ROS)	31
Stephens Pl (NWH)	61
Sterling (WNW)	65
Sterling (NQ)	71
Sterling (MAL)	48
Sterling (WS)	44
Sterling (MED)	55
Sterling	
1-36 (WY)	88
1-50 (ROX)	19
37-OUT (BRA)	84
51-OUT (RXC)	20
Sterling Park (BRA)	84
Sterling Rd (WEL)	81
Sterling Rd (N)	92
Sterling Rd (WAL)	54
Sterling Sq (SB)	27
Stetson (BRO)	46
Stetson (WY)	88
Stetson (BRA)	84
Stetson (LEX)	73
Stetson Ct (CHA)	29
Stetson Way (WAB)	68
Stevens (QUI)	69
Stevens (STO)	80

Boston (Con.) 021

Stevens 18
Stevens (MAL) 48
Stevens (MED) 55
Stevens (REV) 51
Stevens Ave (BRA) 85
Stevens Pl & Rd (MEL) 76
Stevens Rd (LEX) 73
Stevens Rd (WEL) 81
Stevens Rd (N) 92
Stevens Ter (ARL) 74
Stevenson Ave (EV) 49
Stewart (QUI) 69
Stewart Rd (N) 92
Stewart Ter (BEL) 78
Stickney Ave (SOM) 45
Stickney Rd (MED) 55
Stiles Ter (NCE) 59
Still (BRO) 46
Stillings 02210
Stillman (EWY) 89
Stillman Rd (MEL) 76
Stillman St & Pl 13
Stillmeadow Ln (WES) 93
Stimson Ave (LEX) 73
Stimson St & Rd (WRX) 32
Stinson Ct (CAM) 39
Stock (DOR) 22
Stockdale Rd (N) 92
Stockton (DOR) 24
Stockton (CHE) 50
Stockwell (RXC) 20
Stoddard Ln (MIL) 86
Stone (REV) 51
Stone Ave (MAL) 76
Stone Ave (CHH) 67
Stone Ave & Pl (SOM) 43
Stone Rd (WAL) 54
Stone Rd (BEL) 78
Stone Rd (ARL) 74
Stone Ter (DOR) 24
Stone Hill Rd & Ter (HP) 36
Stonecleve Rd (WH) 81
Stonecroft Cir (WES) 93
Stonehill Dr (STO) 80
Stoneholm 15
Stonehurst (DOR) 22
Stonehurst Rd (N) 92
Stoneleigh Cir & Rd (WAT) 72
Stoneleigh Rd (WNW) 65
Stonely Rd (JP) 30
Stonewall Rd (LEX) 73
Stonewood Ave (MEL) 76
Stonewood Dr (NCE) 59
Stonewood Ln (BRA) 84
Stoney Brae Rd (NWH) 61
Stoney Brae Rd (WOL) 70
Stoney Brook Ln (WY) 88
Stony Brook Rd (WES) 93
Stony Brook Rd (BEL) 78
Stony Brook Rd (ARL) 74
Stony Brook Rd (JP) 30
Stony Brook Ter (HP) 36
Storer 10
Storey Pl (JP) 30
Storrs Ave (BRA) 84
Story (SB) 27
Story (CAM) 38
Stoughton (MED) 55
Stoughton 18
Stoughton (QUI) 69
Stoughton St Pl (DOR) 25

Stoughton St & Ter (DOR) 25
Stow (WAL) 54
Stow Rd (MAT) 26
Stowcroft Rd (MEL) 76
Stowe Croft Rd (ARL) 74
Stowers (REV) 51
Stowers Ave (MED) 55
Strandway (WIN) 52
Stratford (WRX) 32
Stratford Rd (MEL) 76
Stratford Rd (WNW) 65
Stratford Rd (N) 92
Stratford Rd (NWY) 91
Stratham Rd (LEX) 73
Strathcona Rd (DOR) 21
Strathmore Cir & Rd (BRA) 84
Strathmore Rd (WEL) 81
Strathmore Rd (MED) 55
Strathmore Rd
　1-130 (BRO) 46
　131-OUT (BRI) 35
Stratton (DOR) 24
Stratton Ter (WAL) 54
Strong Pl 14
Stuart 16
Stuart (EV) 49
Stuart (WAT) 72
Stuart Rd (WH) 81
Stuart Rd (NCE) 59
Studio Pl 16
Studio Rd (AUB) 66
Stultz Rd (BEL) 78
Sturbridge (MAT) 26
Sturbridge Rd (WH) 81
Sturges (MED) 55
Sturges Rd (WRX) 32
Sturgis (CHE) 50
Sturgis (WIN) 52
Sturtevant (DOR) 22
Sturtevant Rd (QUI) 69
Sturtevant Ter (MEB) 55
Suban Pl (NWH) 61
Sudan (DOR) 25
Sudbury Rd (WH) 81
Sudbury Rd (WES) 93
Suffolk (MED) 55
Suffolk (CHE) 50
Suffolk (CAM) 39
Suffolk (MAL) 48
Suffolk Ave (REV) 51
Suffolk Rd (WH) 81
Suffolk Rd (CHH) 67
Sullivan (LEX) 73
Sullivan (REV) 51
Sullivan Ave (NUF) 64
Sullivan Pl (CAM) 39
Sullivan Rd (QUI) 69
Sullivan Rd & Sq (CAM) 38
Sullivan St & Sq (CHA) 29
Sumac Rd (NQ) 71
Summe: (QUI) 69
Summer (NUF) 64
Summer (LEX) 73
Summer (STO) 80
Summer (MEL) 76
Summer (WAT) 72
Summer (ARL) 74
Summer (CHA) 29
Summer (HP) 36
Summer (REV) 51
Summer (CHE) 50
Summer (EV) 49
Summer (MED) 55

Summer (WRX) 32
Summer (WES) 93
Summer (BRA) 85
Summer (WY) 88
Summer
　1-192 10
　1-260 (SOM) (ODD) 43
　193-701 02210
　261-OUT (WS) 44
　792-OUT (SB) 27
Summer St Pl (HP) 36
Summer St Pl (ARL) 74
Summer St & Ave (MAL) 48
Summer St & Ave (WAL) 54
Summerhill (STO) 80
Summit (ARL) 74
Summit (ROS) 31
Summit (NEW) 58
Summit (WS) 44
Summit (WY) 88
Summit Ave (SOM) 43
Summit Ave (BRO) 46
Summit Ave (CHE) 50
Summit Ave (EV) 49
Summit Ave (REV) 51
Summit Ave (WIN) 52
Summit Ave (MEL) 76
Summit Ave (WOL) 70
Summit Ave (BRA) 84
Summit Ave & Rd (STO) 80
Summit Rd (WEL) 81
Summit Rd (WAT) 72
Summit Rd (LEX) 73
Summit Rd (MED) 55
Summit Rd (N) 92
Summit St & Ave (WAL) 54
Summit St & Cir (HP) 36
Summit St & Ter (MAL) 48
Summit Ridge Dr (BRA) 84
Sumner (QUI) 69
Sumner (NCE) 59
Sumner (REV) 51
Sumner (MIL) 86
Sumner Ave (BRA) 85
Sumner Ave (MED) 55
Sumner Ave (ROS) 31
Sumner Pl (RXC) 20
Sumner Rd (BRO) 46
Sumner Rd (CAM) 38
Sumner Rd (EWY) 89
Sumner Rd (WH) 81
Sumner St, Ct, Park, Rd, Sq
　& Ter (DOR) 25
Sumner St & Pl (EB) 28
Sun (WAL) 54
Sun Hill Ln (NCE) 59
Sun Valley Dr (BRA) 84
Sunapee Rd (ARL) 74
Suncrest Rd (MAT) 26
Sunderland (DOR) 21
Sundin Rd (WY) 88
Sunny Ct (JP) 30
Sunny Knoll Ave & Ter (LEX) 73
Sunny Plain Ave (WY) 88
Sunnybank Rd (WAT) 72
Sunnybank Rd (WRX) 32
Sunnyside (WAL) 54
Sunnyside (JP) 30
Sunnyside Ave (EV) 49
Sunnyside Ave (SOM) 45
Sunnyside Ave (ARL) 74
Sunnyside Ave (BRA) 84
Sunnyside Ave (WH) 81

Boston (Con.) 021

Sunnyside Ave & Park (WIN) 52
Sunnyside Pl (BEL) 78
Sunnyside Rd (NH) 94
Sunnyside Rd
  1-53 (QUI) (ODD) 69
  2-50 (QUI) (EVEN) 69
  52-OUT (MIL) (EVEN) 86
  55-OUT (MIL) (ODD) 86
Sunnyside St & Ave (HP) 36
Sunrise Ave (STO) 80
Sunrise Dr (NWY) 91
Sunrise Rd (NQ) 71
Sunset (LEX) 73
Sunset (RXC) 20
Sunset Ave (JP) 30
Sunset Ave (MED) 55
Sunset Ln (DOR) 24
Sunset Rd (NEW) 58
Sunset Rd (CAM) 38
Sunset Rd (WIN) 52
Sunset Rd (WS) 44
Sunset Rd (WAL) 54
Sunset Rd (STO) 80
Sunset Rd (MEL) 76
Sunset Rd (WEL) 81
Sunset Rd (ARL) 74
Sunset Rd (WAT) 72
Sunset Rd (WES) 93
Sunset Rd (EWY) 89
Sunset Rd (BRA) 85
Sunset Hill Path & Rd (ROS) 31
Suomi Rd (QUI) 69
Supple Rd (DOR) 21
Surfside Ave (WIN) 52
Surfside Ln (NQ) 71
Surrey (BRI) 35
Surrey (CAM) 38
Surrey (MED) 55
Surrey Ln (WES) 93
Surrey Rd (NEW) 58
Surrey Rd (ARL) 74
Surry Hill Ln (JP) 30
Susan Rd (SWY) 90
Susanna Ct (HP) 36
Sussex (RXC) 20
Sutcliffe Park (NWH) 61
Sutherland Rd (LEX) 73
Sutherland Rd (BRO) 46
Sutherland Rd & Ter (ARL) 74
Sutton (MAT) 26
Sutton (WY) 88
Sutton Rd (N) 92
Suwanee Rd (EWY) 89
Suzanne Rd (LEX) 73
Swains Pond Ave (MEL) 76
Swains Pond Ave (MAL) 48
Swallow (SB) 27
Swallow Dr (NLF) 62
Swan (MAL) 48
Swan (MED) 55
Swan (WRX) 32
Swan (EV) 49
Swan Ave (WNW) 65
Swan Ave (SWY) 90
Swan Ct (DOR) 24
Swan Ln (LEX) 73
Swan Rd (QUI) 69
Swan St & Pl (ARL) 74
Swarthmore Rd (WEL) 81
Sweet Fern Ter (DOR) 21

Swett Ct (WAT) 72
Swift St & Ter (EB) 16
Sycamore (EV) 49
Sycamore (ROS) 31
Sycamore (CAM) 40
Sycamore
  1-49 (SOM) 43
  1-147 (WAV) (ODD) 79
  2-138 (WAV) (EVEN) 79
  50-OUT (SOM) 45
  140-OUT (WAT) (EVEN) 72
  149-OUT (WAT) (ODD) 72
Sycamore Rd (SWY) 90
Sycamore Rd (BRA) 85
Sycamore Rd (NQ) 71
Sycamore Rd (NCE) 59
Sycamore Rd (MEL) 76
Sycamore Rd (STO) 80
Sycamore Ter (SOM) 45
Sydney (SOM) 43
Sydney (MED) 55
Sydney (MAL) 48
Sydney (DOR) 25
Sylvan (MAL) 48
Sylvan (MEL) 76
Sylvan Ave (WNW) 65
Sylvan Ln (WES) 93
Sylvan Rd (N) 92
Sylvan Rd (BEL) 78
Sylvan Rd (WH) 81
Sylvan Rd (WAL) 54
Sylvester Rd (WNW) 65
Sylvester Rd (DOR) 22
Sylvester Ter (WH) 81
Sylvia (ARL) 74
Sylvia (LEX) 73
Sylvia (JP) 30
Sylvia Ct (HP) 36
Sylvia Rd (MED) 55
Symmes (MED) 55
Symmes (ROS) 31
Symphony Rd 15
T Wharf 10
Tabe.. (OX) 19
Taber (QUI) 69
Tabor Ct (BRA) 84
Tabor Ct (WY) 88
Tabor Pl (BRO) 46
Tacoma (HP) 36
Taff Rd (MIL) 86
Taffrail Rd (QUI) 69
Taft (QUI) 69
Taft (MED) 55
Taft (REV) 51
Taft (DOR) 25
Taft Ave (LEX) 73
Taft Ave (WNW) 65
Taft Ct (ROS) 31
Taft Rd (WY) 88
Taft Hill Park & Ter (ROS) 31
Tafts Ave (WIN) 52
Tainter (MED) 55
Talbot (MAL) 48
Talbot (WNW) 65
Talbot Ave & Pl (DOR) 24
Talbot Rd (BRA) 85
Talbot St & Ave (MED) 55
Talmadge Ave (BRA) 85
Tamarac Ln (N) 92
Tamarac Rd (NUF) 64
Tamarack Rd (WES) 93
Tamarack Trl (SWY) 90
Tamerlane Ridge (SWY) 90

Tampa (MAT) 26
Tamworth 16
Tamworth Rd (WAB) 68
Tanager (ARL) 74
Tanglewood Rd (NCE) 59
Tanglewood Rd (WH) 81
Tanglewood Rd (DOR) 24
Tanglewood Rd (NH) 94
Tapley Ave & Pl (REV) 51
Tappan (WIN) 52
Tappan (BRO) 46
Tappan (ROS) 31
Tappan (EV) 49
Tappan (MEL) 76
Tappan Ave (WAT) 72
Tappan Rd (WEL) 81
Tara Dr (WY) 88
Tarbell Ave (LEX) 73
Tarleton Rd (NCE) 59
Tarleton Rd (WRX) 32
Taunton (SOM) 43
Taunton Ave (MAT) 26
Tavern Ln (LEX) 73
Tavern Rd 15
Tavern Rd & Sq (WAL) 54
Taylor (WAL) 54
Taylor (SOM) 45
Taylor (WIN) 52
Taylor (MED) 55
Taylor 18
Taylor (DOR) 22
Taylor (WAT) 72
Taylor (MEL) 76
Taylor (WOL) 70
Taylor (MIL) 86
Taylor (BRA) 85
Taylor (NH) 94
Taylor (NWY) 91
Taylor
  1-133 (MAL) 48
  134-134 (EV) 49
  135-OUT (MAL) 48
Taylor Rd (BEL) 78
Taylor Rd (WH) 81
Taylor Sq (CAM) 38
Taylor Ter (MAT) 26
Taylor Crossway (BRO) 46
Tchaptoulas (MAT) 26
Tebroc (DOR) 22
Technology Sq (CAM) 39
Teel (ARL) 74
Teel St Pl (ARL) 74
Teele Ave & Sq (WS) 44
Telegraph (SB) 27
Telford (BRI) 35
Temple (CAM) 39
Temple (MED) 55
Temple (REV) 51
Temple (MAT) 26
Temple 14
Temple (CHA) 29
Temple (ARL) 74
Temple (BEL) 78
Temple (MEL) 76
Temple (QUI) 69
Temple (WNW) 65
Temple Ave (WIN) 52
Temple Pl 11
Temple Rd (WAL) 54
Temple Rd (WEL) 81
Temple St & Rd (SOM) 45
Temple St & Sq (C/RX) 37
Templeton Pky (WAT) 72

Boston (Con.)   021

Templeton St & Way (DOR) 24
Ten Hills Rd (SOM) 45
Tenean (DOR) 22
Tenney (CAM) 40
Tenney Ct (SOM) 45
Tenney Rd (BRA) 85
Tennis Rd (MAT) 26
Tennyson (SOM) 45
Tennyson (WRX) 32
Tennyson Rd (WAL) 54
Tennyson Rd (WH) 81
Tennyson Rd (WNW) 65
Teregram (EB) 28
Teresa Cir (/.RL) 20
Terminal (CHA) 29
Terminal (EV) 49
Terminal Rd (EB) 28
Termine Ave (JP) 30
Terne Rd (QUI) 69
Terrace Ave (NWH) 61
Terrace Ave (WIN) 52
Terrace Rd (MED) 55
Terrace St & Pl (RXC) 20
Terrell Cres (CHH) 67
Terrier Rd (MED) 55
Terry (RXC) 20
Tesla (MAT) 26
Tesla Ave (MED) 55
Tetlow 15
Teton Ln (MED) 55
Tewksbury (WIH) 52
Tewksbury (LEX) 73
Texas (SWY) 90
Thacher
   1-190 (MIL) 87
   191-OUT (MIL) 86
Thacher St & Ct 13
Thackery Rd (WH) 81
Thane (DOR) 24
Thatcher (WOL) 70
Thatcher (MED) 55
Thatcher (HP) 36
Thatcher (BRO) 46
Thatcher (MAL) 48
Thaxter Rd (NWV) 60
Thayer (QUI) 69
Thayer 18
Thayer Ave (REV) 51
Thayer Ave (WY) 88
Thayer Ave & Pl (BRA) 85
Thayer Rd (WAL) 54
Thayer Rd (BRA) 84
Thayer St & Pl (BRO) 46
Thayer St & Rd (WAV) 79
The Ledgeway (MIL) 86
The Strand (WOL) 70
The Waterway (WH) 81
Thelma Rd (DOR) 22
Theodore (DOR) 24
Theodore Path & Rd (NCE) 59
Theodore A Glynn Way 18
Theodore Parker Rd (WRX) 32
Theresa Ave (MED) 55
Theresa Ave (LEX) 73
Theresa Ln (STO) 80
Theresa Rd (QUI) 69
Theriault Ct (CAM) 40
Thesda (ARL) 74
Thetford Ave (DOR) 24
Thetford Ave (BRA) 85
Theurer Park (WAT) 72

Thicket (SWY) 90
Thingvalla Ave
   1-73 (CAM) (ODD) 38
   2-OUT (CAM) (EVEN) 38
   75-81 (BEL) (ODD) 78
   83-OUT (CAM) (ODD) 38
Third (WY) 88
Third (ARL) 74
Third (LEX) 73
Third (SB) 27
Third (MED) 55
Third (BRI) 35
Third (MAL) 48
Third (EV) 49
Third (CHE) 50
Third
   1-245 (CAM) (ODD) 41
   2-220 (CAM) (EVEN) 41
   222-OUT (CAM) (EVEN) 42
   247-OUT (CAM) (ODD) 42
Third Ave (NH) 94
Third Ave (WAL) 54
Third Ave (SOM) 43
Third Pl (SB) 27
Third New Way (HP) 36
Thirteenth (MEL) 77
Thistle Ave (MIL) 86
Thistle Rd (BRA) 84
Thomas (BEL) 78
Thomas (ARL) 74
Thomas (QUI) 69
Thomas (MAL) 48
Thomas (MED) 55
Thomas (JP) 31
Thomas Park (SB) 27
Thomas Park (CAM) 38
Thomas Rd (WH) 81
Thomas Rd (SWY) 90
Thompson (QUI) 69
Thompson (HP) 36
Thompson Ln (MIL) 87
Thompson Pl (EV) 49
Thompson Pl (ARL) 74
Thompson Rd (BRA) 85
Thompson Rd (NWY) 91
Thompson St & Sq (CHA) 29
Thompsons Island (SB) 27
Thor Ter (ALL) 17
Thoreau Rd (NQ) 71
Thoreau Rd (LEX) 73
Thorn (MAT) 26
Thorn 18
Thorn Rd (ARL) 74
Thornberry Rd (LEX) 63
Thorndike (ARL) 74
Thorndike (BRA) 84
Thorndike 18
Thorndike (EV) 49
Thorndike (BRO) 46
Thorndike (CAM) 41
Thorndike (WS) 93
Thorndike (REV) 51
Thornley (DOR) 25
Thornton (REV) 51
Thornton (WOL) 70
Thornton Rd (CHH) 67
Thornton Rd (WAL) 54
Thornton Rd (N) 92
Thornton St & Park (WIN) 52
Thornton St & Pl (NEW) 58
Thornton St, Pl & Ter (ROX) 19
Thorpe (SOM) 43
Thorpe Rd (NH) 94

Thurlow (WRX) 32
Thurlow Ave (REV) 51
Thurman St & Park (EV) 49
Thurston (SOM) 45
Thurston (EB) 28
Thurston Ave (QUI) 69
Thurston Ln (N) 92
Thurston Rd (NUF) 64
Thurston Rd (MEL) 76
Thurston Rd (WAT) 72
Thwing (ROX) 19
Tibbetts Town Way (CHA) 29
Ticknor (SB) 27
Tierney (CAM) 38
Tilden Rd (SWY) 90
Tilesboro (DOR) 22
Tileston (MAT) 26
Tileston (EV) 49
Tileston Rd (WIN) 52
Tileston St & Pl. 13
Tillotson Rd (NH) 94
Tilman (DOR) 24
Timon Ave (CHH) 67
Timothy Ave (EV) 49
Timson Path (NCE) 59
Tina Ave (HP) 36
Tingley Cir & Rd (BRA) 84
Tinson Rd (QUI) 69
Tip Top (BRI) 35
Tip Top Ter (WAL) 54
Tirrell (NQ) 71
Tirrell (WY) 88
Tiverton Rd (MAT) 26
Tobey Rd (BEL) 78
Tobin Ave (REV) 51
Tobin Ct (RXC) 20
Tobin Rd (WRX) 32
Tocci Path (NCE) 59
Todd Rd (LEX) 73
Toland Ct (ROX) 19
Toledo Ter (DOR) 22
Tolman (DOR) 22
Tolman (WNW) 65
Tolman (WAL) 54
Tolman (N) 92
Tolman Pl (ROX) 19
Tomahawk Rd (ARL) 74
Tomlin (WAL) 54
Tonawanda (DOR) 24
Tonset (DOR) 24
Tontine (MED) 55
Topalian (MAT) 26
Topeka 18
Topliff (DOR) 22
Toppan Ave (ROS) 31
Torpie (RXC) 20
Torrey (DOR) 24
Torrey (SWY) 90
Torrey Rd (BRA) 85
Totman (QUI) 69
Totnes Rd (BRA) 84
Totten Cir & Ct (WAL) 54
Totten Pond Rd (WAL) 54
Touro Ave (MED) 55
Tovar (DOR) 22
Tower (EB) 28
Tower (JP) 30
Tower (NH) 94
Tower Ave (SWY) 90
Tower Rd (ARL) 74
Tower Rd (NUF) 64
Tower Rd (LEX) 73
Tower St & Ct (SOM) 43

Boston (Con.)　　　　　　　021

Tower Hill Rd (BRA) 84
Town (BRA) 85
Town Hill (QUI) 69
Town House Dr (NWV) 60
Town House Rd (WES) 93
Townley Rd (WAT) 72
Townsend (WAL) 54
Townsend (WIN) 52
Townsend (MAL) 48
Townsend
　1-86 (ROX) 19
　87-OUT (DOR) 21
Townsend Ave (BRA) 84
Townsend Pl 16
Townsend Rd (BEL) 78
Toxteth (BRO) 46
Tracton Ave (MAT) 26
Trafalgar Ct (SWY) 90
Trafford (QUI) 69
Traill (CAM) 38
Train (DOR) 22
Traincroft (MED) 55
Trainor Dr (BRA) 55
Transit (SB) 27
Trapelo (BRI) 35
Trapelo Rd (WAL) 54
Trapelo Rd
　1-232 (BEL) 78
　233-OUT (WAV) 79
Trask Ave (QUI) .... 69.
Traveler 18*
Traverse 14
Traverse (NEW) 34
Traverse (MAL) 48
Travis (ALL) 67
Travis Dr (CHH) 34
Trayes Ave (MAT) 48
Traymore (CAM) 40
Treadway Rd (DOR) 25
Treeland Cir (NEW) 58
Trefton Ave (WY) 88
Trefton Dr (BRA) 84
Tremlett (DOR) 24
Tremont (CHA) 29
Tremont (MEL) 76
Tremont (STO) 80
Tremont (WY) 94
Tremont (MAL) 48
Tremont (CHE) 50
Tremont
　1-129 08
　1-143 (BRI) (ODD) 35
　1-168 (CAM) 39
　1-255 (BRA) 85
　2-146 (BRI) (EVEN) 35
　130-186 11
　145-OUT (NEW) (ODD) 58
　148-OUT (NEW) (EVEN) 58
　169-OUT (SOM) 43
　187-555 (ODD) 16
　188-550 (EVEN) 16
　256-OUT (BRA) 84
　552-920 (EVEN) 18
　557-921 (ODD) 18
　922-OUT (RXC) 20
Tremont Pl (BRI) 35
Tremont Pl (SOM) 43
Tremont Pl & Row 08
Tremont St & Pl (EV) 49
Trent (DOR) 25

Trescott (DOR) 25
Tresland Way (QUI) 69
Trevalley Rd (REV) 51
Trevore (NQ) 71
Trewtawney (MAT) 26
Tricorne Rd (LEX) 73
Trident (EB) 28
Trident Ave (WIN) 52
Trifone (REV) 51
Trilling Way 02210
Trimont Ave (WAL) 54
Trimount Pl (SB) 27
Trinity Cir (WAL) 54
Trinity Ct (WI) 81
Trinity Ct & Pl 16
Trinity Ter (NCE) 59
Triton Ave (WIN) 52
Triton Pathway (WIN) 52
Trotter Ct 18
Trotting Horse Dr (LEX) 73
Trout Ave (MED) 55
Trout Brook Rd (MIL) 86
Trout Pond Ln (N) 92
Trowbridge (NCE) 59
Trowbridge (BEL) 78
Trowbridge (ARL) 74
Trowbridge Ave (NWV) 60
Trowbridge St, Pl & Ter
　(CAM) 38
Troy Ln (WAB) 68
Troy Rd (BEL) 78
True (REV) 51
True (EV) .... 49'
Trueman (MAT) 48
Trueman St & Pl (NH) 94
Trull (DOR) 25
Trull Ln (SOM) 43
Truman Hwy
　1-475 (MIL) 86
　476-1084 (HP) (EVEN) 36
　477-OUT (HP) (ODD) 36
　1086-OUT (MIL) (EVEN) 86
Truman Rd (NCE) 59
Trunfio Ln (EV) 49
Truro (QUI) 69
Truro Ln (MIL) 86
Trustman Ter (EB) 28
Tucker (DOR) 24
Tucker (MIL) 87
Tucker Ave (LEX) 73
Tucker St & Rd (MED) 55
Tuckerman (REV) 51
Tuckerman (SB) 27
Tudor (SB) 27
Tudor (REV) 51
Tudor (CHE) 50
Tudor (CAM) 39
Tudor (WAL) 54
Tudor Rd (CHH) 67
Tudor Rd (N) 92
Tudor Ter (AUB) 66
Tufts (ARL) 74
Tufts (CAM) 39
Tufts (SOM) 43
Tufts (MAL) 48
Tufts (CHA) 29
Tufts 11
Tufts Ave (EV) 49
Tufts Rd (LEX) 73
Tully (CHH) 67
Tupelo (ROX) 19
Turell Rd (MED) 55

Turner (WAL) 54
Turner (BRI) 35
Turner (QUI) 69
Turner Rd (WEL) 81
Turner St & Ter (NWV) 60
Turning Mill Rd (LEX) 73
Turtle Pond Pky & Ter (HP) .. 36
Tuscano Ave (REV) 51
Tuttle (REV) 51
Tuttle (DOR) 25
Tv Pl (NH) 94
Twilight Path (EWY) 89
Twin Cir Dr (ARL) 74
Twitchell (WEL) 81
Twomey Ct (SB) 27
Tyler 11
Tyler (HP) 36
Tyler
　1-54 (NQ) 71
　55-OUT (WOL) 70
Tyler Ave (MED) 55
Tyler Rd (WES) 93
Tyler Rd (LEX) 73
Tyler Rd (BEL) 78
Tyler St & Ct (MAL) 48
Tyler St, Ct & Pl (SOM) 43
Tyler Ter (NCE) 59
Tyndale (ROS) 31
Udine (ARL) 74
Ufford (DOR) 24
Ulene Ct (CHA) 29
Underhill (WIN) 52
Underwood (BEL) 78
Underwood Ave (WNW) 65
Underwood Ave (LEX) 73
Underwood Park
　1-33 (WAL) (ODD) 54
　2-42 (WAL) (EVEN) 54
　35-OUT (WNW) (ODD) 65
　44-OUT (WNW) (EVEN) 65
Undine Ave (WIN) 52
Undine Ave (REV) 51
Undine Rd (BRI) 35
Unicorn Ave (EWY) 89
Unicorn Ave (STO) 80
Union (MEL) 76
Union (STO) 80
Union (NCE) 59
Union (QUI) 69
Union (WAT) 72
Union (NH) 94
Union (SWY) 90
Union (BRI) 35
Union (REV) 51
Union (CHE) 50
Union
　1-15 (CAM) 39
　1-55 (ODD) 08
　1-240 (BRA) 85
　2-68 (EVEN) 08
　16-OUT (CAM) 41
　57-OUT (ODD) 14
　70-OUT (EVEN) 14
　241-OUT (BRA) 84
Union Ave (MIL) 87
Union Ave (JP) 30
Union Park 18
Union Park St. 18
Union Pl (BRA) 84
Union Pl & Ter (CAM) 41
Union Sq (SOM) 43
Union Sq (ALL) 34
Union St & Ave (EV) 49

Boston (Con.) 021

Union St & Ct (MED) 55
Union St & Ct (CHA) 29
Union St & Pl (MAL) 48
Union Wharf 09
Unity (QUI) 69
Unity Ave (BEL) 78
Unity Ave (REV) 51
Unity St & Ct 13
University Ave (MED) 55
University Hts (CHH) 67
University Park (WAL) 54
University Rd (BRO) 46
University Rd (CAM) 38
University Rd (ARL) 74
Unquity Rd (MIL) 86
Upcrest Rd (BRI) 35
Upham (REV) 51
Upham (WNW) 65
Upham Ave (DOR) 25
Upham St & Ter (MEL) 76
Upham St & Ter (MAL) 48
Upland (BRA) 84
Upland Ave (NWH) 61
Upland Ave (DOR) 24
Upland Park (SOM) 45
Upland Rd (WS) 44
Upland Rd (BRO) 46
Upland Rd (MAL) 48
Upland Rd (WIN) 52
Upland Rd (CAM) 54
Upland Rd (WAL) 40
Upland Rd (MED) 55
Upland Rd (EV) 49
Upland Rd (NWV) 60
Upland Rd (NWW) 81
Upland Rd (BEL) 78
Upland Rd (STO) 80
Upland Rd (MEL) 76
Upland Rd (ARL) 74
Upland Rd (WAB) 68
Upland Rd (QUI) 69
Upland Rd (WAT) 72
Upland Rd (LEX) 73
Upland Rd (WY) 88
Upland Rd W (ARL) 74
Upland Rd & Ter (N) 92
Upson Rd (WH) 81
Upton (QUI) 69
Upton (HP) 36
Upton (CAM) 39
Upton 18
Upton Rd (WAL) 54
Upton Ter (MED) 55
Upwey Rd (WH) 81
Usher Rd (MED) 55
Utica (QUI) 69
Utica (LEX) 73
Utica Rd (NH) 94
Utica St & Pl 11
Vail Ct (CAM) 39
Vaille Ave (LEX) 73
Vale (CHE) 50
Vale (ROX) 19
Valencia Rd (HP) 36
Valentine (CAM) 39
Valentine (ROX) 19
Valentine Rd (ARL) 74
Valentine Rd (MIL) 86
Valentine St & Park (WNW) .. 65
Vallar Rd (EB) 28
Vallero Rd (HP) 36

Valley (EV) 49
Valley (REV) 51
Valley (MAL) 48
Valley Ave (BRA) 85
Valley Park St (MED) 55
Valley Rd (WY) 88
Valley Rd (MIL) 87
Valley Rd (N) 92
Valley Rd (DOR) 24
Valley Rd (ARL) 74
Valley Rd (LEX) 73
Valley Rd (WH) 81
Valley Rd (CHH) 67
Valley Rd (STO) 80
Valley Rd Ext (MIL) 87
Valley St, Pl & Rd (MED) 26
Valley Spring Rd (NEW) 58
Valley View Rd (WAL) 54
Valley View Rd (WES) 93
Valleyfield (LEX) 73
Van Brunt (HP) 36
Van Ness 02215
Van Ness Rd (BEL) 78
Van Norden (CAM) 40
Van Roosen Rd (NCE) 59
Van Vechten (WAL) 54
Van Wart Path (NCE) 59
Van Winkle (DOR) 24
Vancouver
  1-24 15
  25-OUT (RXC) 20
Vanderbilt Ave (MAT) 26
Vandine (CAM) 41
Vane (REV) 51
Vane (WEL) 81
Vane (NQ) 71
Vanness Rd (NWY) 91
Vara Ln (NH) 94
Varick Rd (WAB) 68
Varick Rd (WRX) 32
Varick Hill Rd (WAB) 68
Varney (JP) 30
Varnum (ARL) 74
Varnum Park (WAL) 54
Vassall (WOL) 70
Vassall Ln (CAM) 38
Vassar (CAM) 39
Vassar (MED) 55
Vassar (DOR) 21
Vaughan (JP) 30
Vaughan Ave (DOR) 21
Vaughan Ave (NWH) 61
Veda Ct & Rd (SWY) 90
Vega (WY) 88
Vendon Pl (CHA) 29
Venice (EB) 28
Venner Rd (ARL) 74
Ventura (DOR) 24
Venus (WY) 88
Venus Rd (BRA) 84
Vera (DOR) 24
Vera (REV) 51
Vera Ln (STO) 80
Veranda Rd (BRA) 84
Verchild (QUI) 69
Verdun (CAM) 40
Verdun (DOR) 24
Vermont (WRX) 32
Vermont Ave (SOM) 45
Vernal (EV) 49
Verndale (MAT) 26
Verndale Rd (NWH) 61
Verndale Rd (MIL) 87

Verndale Rd (SWY) 90
Verndale St & Ter (BRO) 46
Vernon (BRO) 46
Vernon (MAL) 48
Vernon (CHE) 50
Vernon (SOM) 45
Vernon (HP) 36
Vernon (MED) 55
Vernon (NEW) 58
Vernon (WAL) 54
Vernon (BRA) 85
Vernon (QUI) 69
Vernon
  1-31 (ROX) 19
  32-OUT (RXC) 20
Vernon Ave (STO) 80
Vernon Ave (WIN) 52
Vernon Ct & Pl (RXC) 20
Vernon Rd (WAY) 79
Verona (JP) 30
Veronica Rd (EWY) 89
Verrill (MAT) 26
Vershire (NQ) 71
Vershire (WRX) 32
Vesper (WRX) 32
Vesta Rd (DOR) 24
Veterans Ave (EV) 49
Veterans Ln (STO) 80
Veterans Rd (WIN) 52
Veterans Of Foreign Wars
  Hwy (REV) 51
Veterans Of Foreign Wars Pky
  1-300 (ROS) 31
  301-683 (CHH) (ODD) 67
  302-500 (CHH) (EVEN) 67
  502-OUT (WRX) (EVEN) 32
  685-OUT (WRX) (ODD) 32
Vicki Rd (EWY) 89
Victor (MED) 55
Victor (MAL) 48
Victor (DOR) 25
Victoria (DOR) 25
Victoria (REV) 51
Victoria (EV) 49
Victoria (WS) 44
Victoria (MIL) 87
Victoria (BRA) 85
Victoria Cir (NCE) 59
Victoria Ln (STO) 80
Victoria Rd (QUI) 69
Victoria Rd (ARL) 74
Victory Ave
  1-29 (QUI) (ODD) 69
  2-OUT (MIL) (EVEN) 86
  31-OUT (MIL) (ODD) 86
Victory Rd (DOR) 22
Viden Rd (QUI) 69
Vienna (EB) 28
View (REV) 51
View (MAL) 48
View South Ave (JP) 30
Viking Ct & Way (ARL) 74
Viking Gdns (WIN) 52
Viking Pl (SB) 27
Viking Ter (MAT) 26
Vila (CHE) 50
Viles (WES) 93
Viles Ct (WAL) 54
Viles Rd (LEX) 73
Villa (WAL) 54
Villa Ave (EV) 49
Villa Ave (WIN) 52
Villa Ln (BRO) 46

Boston (Con.)   021

Village (CAM)	39
Village Ave (BRA)	84
Village Cir (NCE)	59
Village Ln (ARL)	74
Village Ln (N)	92
Village Ln & Sq (BRO)	46
Village Rd (EWY)	89
Village Rd (NWV)	60
Village St & Ct	18
Village St & Ter (SOM)	43
Village Hill Rd (BEL)	78
Vinal (SOM)	45
Vinal (BRO)	46
Vinal (REV)	51
Vinal Ave (SOM)	43
Vincent (CAM)	40
Vincent (WNW)	65
Vincent Ave (WAV)	79
Vincent Pl (NQ)	71
Vincent Rd (WH)	81
Vincent Rd (ROS)	31
Vine (EV)	49
Vine (MED)	55
Vine (BRA)	84
Vine (MEL)	76
Vine (LEX)	73
Vine (CHH)	67
Vine (CHA)	29
Vine (WY)	88
Vine Ave (QUI)	69
Vine Ave (WIN)	52
Vine Ct & Pl (SOM)	43
Vine St & Ave (ROX)	19
Vine Brook Rd (LEX)	73
Vinedale Rd (BRA)	84
Vineland (BRI)	35
Vinewood Rd (MIL)	86
Vineyard (CAM)	38
Vineyard Ave (LEX)	73
Vineyard Rd (NCE)	69
Vining (MAL)	48
Vining	15
Vinson (DOR)	24
Vinson Rd (SWY)	90
Vinton (SB)	27
Vinton (MEL)	76
Vinton Ave (BRA)	84
Vinton Ct (STO)	80
Viola (MIL)	87
Violante (MAT)	26
Violet (MAT)	26
Violet (WY)	88
Virgil Rd (WRX)	32
Virginia (SOM)	45
Virginia (MIL)	87
Virginia (DOR)	25
Virginia Rd (BRA)	85,
Virginia Rd (NH)	94
Virginia Rd (WAL)	54
Virginia Rd (MEL)	76
Virgie Rd (AUB)	66
Virginia Rd (QUI)	69
Virginia Rd (ARL)	74
Vista (MEL)	76
Vista (ROS)	31
Vista (MAL)	48
Vista Ave (MED)	55
Vista Ave (AUB)	66
Vista Cir (ARL)	74
Vista Rd (WH)	81
Vivian Dr (WAT)	72

Vivien (REV)	51
Vogel (WRX)	32
Vogel Ter (BRO)	46
Volunteer Way (LEX)	73
Volusia Rd (EWY)	89
Von Hillern (DOR)	25
Vose Ave (HP)	36
Vose Ter (NCE)	59
Vose Hill Rd (MIL)	86
Voses Ln (MIL)	87
Waban (WEL)	81
Waban Ave (WAB)	68
Waban Rd (QUI)	69
Waban St & Park (NEW)	58
Waban Hill Rd (CHH)	67
Waban Hill Rd N (CHH)	67
Wabash (MAT)	26
Wabasso Rd (WAL)	54
Wabeno (DOR)	21
Wabon (DOR)	21
Wachusett (MAT)	26
Wachusett (JP)	30
Wachusett Ave (ARL)	74
Wachusett Cir & Dr (LEX)	73
Wachusett Rd (CHH)	67
Wachusett Rd (WH)	81
Wachusett Rd (N)	92
Wachusett Rd (NWV)	91
Wadaga Rd (NWY)	60
Waddell (MED)	55
Wade (BRI)	35
Wade (NWH)	61
Wadleigh Ave (REV)	51
Wadleigh Pl (SB)	27
Wadman Cir (LEX)	73
Wadsworth (NQ)	71
Wadsworth (ALL)	34
Wadsworth (MAL)	48
Wadsworth (CAM)	42
Wadsworth (WY)	88
Wadsworth Ave (REV)	51
Wadsworth Ave (WIN)	52
Wadsworth Ave (WAL)	54
Wadsworth Rd (ARL)	74
Wagner (STO)	80
Wagner Rd (MED)	55
Wagon Rd (EWY)	99
Wainright Ave (SWY)	90
Wainwright (BRA)	84
Wainwright (DOR)	24
Wait (RXC)	20
Waite (REV)	51
Waite St Ext (MAL)	48
Waite St & Ct (MAL)	48
Waitt Ct & Park (REV)	51
Wakefield Rd (HP)	36
Wakullah (ROX)	19
Walbridge (ALL)	34
Walcott (WAT)	72
Waldeck (DOR)	24
Waldeck Rd (MIL)	86
Waldemar Ave (EB)	28
Waldemar Ave (WIN)	52
Walden (REV)	51
Walden (JP)	30
Walden (NWV)	60
Walden	
1-253 (CAM)	40
254-OUT (CAM)	38
Walden St & Pl (WIN)	52
Waldo (BRO)	46
Waldo Ct (WEL)	81
Waldo Rd (ARL)	74

Waldo Rd (MIL)	87
Waldo St & Ave (SOM)	43
Waldo Ter (BRI)	35
Waldorf (DOR)	24
Waldorf Rd	
1-50 (NWH)	61
51-OUT (NUF)	64
Waldren Rd (ROX)	19
Waldron Rd (BRA)	85
Wales (DOR)	24
Wales (NLF)	62
Watford Way (CHA)	29
Walk Hill	
1-171 (JP)	30
172-349 (ROS)	31
350-399 (MAT)	26
400-400 (DOR)	24
401-OUT (MAT)	26
Walker (WES)	93
Walker (WY)	88
Walker (NWV)	60
Walker (NQ)	71
Walker (WS)	44
Walker (MED)	55
Walker Ln (N)	92
Walker Rd (MEL)	76
Walker St Pl (CAM)	38
Walker St & Ave (CHA)	29
Walker St, Ct & Ter (CAM)	38
Walking Ct (MED)	55
Wall (WAL)	54
Wall (EV)	49
Wall (CHA)	29
Wall (QUI)	69
Wall (ARL)	74
Wall (WEL)	81
Wall's Ct (WAL)	54
Wallace (WS)	44
Wallace (MAL)	48
Wallace (NWH)	61
Wallace Ct (CHA)	29
Wallace Rd (JP)	30
Wallace Rd (QUI)	69
Walley (EB)	28
Wallingford Rd (BRI)	35
Wallis Ct (LEX)	73
Wallis Rd (CHH)	67
Wallis Pl (CHA)	29
Walmsley Ln (WEY)	88
Walnut (MIL)	86
Walnut	08
Walnut (LEX)	73
Walnut (NQ)	71
Walnut (BRA)	84
Walnut (MEL)	76
Walnut (WAV)	79
Walnut (STO)	80
Walnut (WAT)	72
Walnut (WAL)	54
Walnut (CHE)	58
Walnut (EV)	49
Walnut (MED)	55
Walnut	
1-97 (SOM)	43
1-649 (NWV)	60
98-OUT (SOM)	45
650-900 (NCE) (EVEN)	59
651-885 (NCE) (ODD)	59
887-OUT (NWH) (ODD)	61
902-OUT (NWH) (EVEN)	61
Walnut Ave (CAM)	40

Boston (Con.) 021

Walnut Ave
: 42 (WY) 88
1-452 (ROX) 19
43-OUT (BRA) 84
453-OUT (JP) 30
Walnut Ct & Park (ROX) 19
Walnut Park (NEW) 58
Walnut Pl (NWH) 61
Walnut Pl & Ter (NWV) 60
Walnut Rd (SOM) 45
Walnut Rd (WES) 93
Walnut St, Ave & Pl (REV) 51
Walnut St & Ct (DOR) 22
Walnut St, Ct & Pl (N) 92
Walnut St, Ct & Ter (ARL) 74
Walnut St, Path, Pl & Ter
(BRO) 46
Walnut St & Pl (HP) 36
Walnut St & Pl (WH) 81
Walnut St & Rd (WRX) 32
Walnut St & Ter (MAL) 48
Walnut Ter (QUI) 69
Walnut Hill Rd (CHH) 67
Walnut Hill Rd
1-70 (NCE) 59
71-OUT (NWH) 61
Walpole (QUI) 69
Walpole (RXC) 20
Walsh (MED) 55
Walsh Ave (STO) 80
Walsh Pl 09
Welsh Rd (NCE) 59
Walsingham (NLF) 62
Walter (NCE) 59
Walter (MED) 55
Walter (ROS) 31
Walter (HP) 36
Walter Ave (BRO) 46
Walter Ter (SOM) 45
Waltham (WNW) 65
Waltham (WAT) 72
Waltham (LEX) 73
Waltham 18
Walton (DOR) 24
Walton (WAL) 54
Walton Park (MEL) 76
Walworth (ROS) 31
Wamesit Rd (WAB) 68
Wampatuck Rd (QUI) 69
Wampatuck Rd (BRA) 85
Wampum (SWY) 90
Wampum Ave (WAL) 54
Wamsutta Ave (WAL) 54
Wapping (CHA) 29
Ward (RXC) 20
Ward (SOM) 43
Ward (LEX) 73
Ward
1-149 (CHH) 67
150-OUT (NCE) 59
Ward St & Ct (SB) 27
Wardman Rd (ROX) 19
Ware (DOR) 25
Ware (WES) 93
Ware (WS) 44
Ware (CAM) 38
Ware Rd (N) 92
Ware Rd (AUB) 66
Wareham (MED) 55
Wareham 18

Wareland Rd (WH) 81
Warner (DOR) 24
Warner (WS) 44
Warner Rd (MIL) 86
Warren (N) 92
Warren (MED) 55
Warren (BRI) 35
Warren (BRO) 46
Warren (REV) 51
Warren (EV) 49
Warren (LEX) 73
Warren (MEL) 76
Warren (STO) 80
Warren (WAT) 72
Warren (ARL) 74
Warren
1-49 (CAM) 41
1-443 (ROX) (ODD) 19
2-432 (ROX) (EVEN) 19
50-OUT (SOM) 43
434-OUT (DOR) (EVEN) 21
445-OUT (DOR) (ODD) 21
Warren Ave (MIL) 87
Warren Ave (BRA) 84
Warren Ave (WNW) 59
Warren Ave (CHE) 50
Warren Ave (MAL) 48
Warren Ave (SOM) 43
Warren Ave 16
Warren Ave, Ln & Pl (WES) 93
Warren Ave & Park (HP) 36
Warren Ave & Ter (WOL) 70
Warren Pl (ROX) 19
Warren Rd (WAB) 68
Warren Sq (JP) 30
Warren St & Ave (CHA) 29
Warren St & Ave (WAL) 54
Warren St & Ter (NCE) 59
Warren Bridge 14
Warrenton 16
Warwick (RXC) 20
Warwick (WOL) 70
Warwick (ARL) 74
Warwick Ave (WAL) 54
Warwick Park (CAM) 40
Warwick Rd (BRO) 46
Warwick Rd (WNW) 65
Warwick Rd (WAT) 72
Warwick Rd (MEL) 76
Warwick Rd (BEL) 78
Warwick St & Pl (SOM) 45
Washburn (EV) 49
Washburn (CHE) 50
Washburn (NEW) 58
Washburn (WAT) 72
Washburn (DOR) 25
Washburn (EWY) 89
Washburn Ave (N) 92
Washburn Ave (AUB) 66
Washburn Ave (WH) 81
Washburn Ave (REV) 51
Washburn Ave & Ter (CAM) 40
Washburn Pl & Ter (BRO) 46
Washington (MED) 55
Washington (EV) 49
Washington (BEL) 78
Washington (MEL) 76
Washington (LEX) 73
Washington
1-59 14
1-66 (BRO) 46
1-113 (MIL) 86
1-345 (DOR) 21

1-440 (WH) 81
1-621 (NEW) 58
1-646 (BRA) 84
1-805 (WY) (ODD) 88
60-192 (EVEN) 08
61-441 (ODD) 08
67-OUT (BRI) 35
114-OUT (WOL) 70
194-194 09
206-206 09
208-208 09
210-428 (EVEN) 08
346-OUT (DOR) 24
430-950 (EVEN) 11
441-OUT (WEL) 81
443-949 (ODD) 11
622-1050 (NWV) 60
647-OUT (BRA) 85
776-OUT (EWY) (EVEN) 89
807-OUT (EWY) (ODD) 89
951-1999 18
1051-1700 (WRW) 65
1701-1959 (AUB) 66
1960-OUT (NLF) 62
2000-3134 (ROX) (EVEN) 19
2001-3125 (ROX) (ODD) 19
3127-3799 (JP) (ODD) 30
3136-3798 (JP) (EVEN) 30
3800-4700 (ROS) (EVEN) 31
3801-4699 (ROS) (ODD) 31
4701-OUT (WRX) 32
Washington Ave (N) 92
Washington Ave (WNW) 65
Washington Ave (CHE) 50
Washington Ave (CAM) 40
Washington Ave (WAL) 54
Washington Ave (EB) 28
Washington Ave & Ter (WIN) 52
Washington Ct (WH) 81
Washington Park Rd (BRA) 85
Washington Park & Ter
(NWV) 60
Washington Pl (BRA) 84
Washington Pl (CHA) 55
Washington Sq (WY) 88
Washington St Pl (CHA) 36
Washington St & Ave (ARL) 74
Washington St, Ave & Ct
(STO) 80
Washington St, Ave & Sq
(REV) 51
Washington St, Ave & Ter
(SOM) 43
Washington St & Ct (CAM) 39
Washington St & Ct (QUI) 69
Washington St & Pl (HP) 36
Washington St & Pl (MAL) 48
Washington St, Pl, Sq & Ter
(CHA) 29
Washington Elms (CAM) 39
Washington Mall 08
Washington Park Blvd (ROX) ... 19
Wason (MED) 55
Water (MED) 55
Water (HP) 36
Water (CAM) 41
Water (SOM) 43
Water (WAL) 54
Water (DOR) 22
Water 09
Water (CHA) 29
Water (QUI) 69

Boston (Con.)   621

Water (MEL)	76
Water (ARL)	74
Water (NCE)	59
Water (WAT)	72
Water (EWY)	89
Water (BRA)	85
Water St Ct (MED)	55
Waterford	18
Waterhouse (WS)	44
Waterhouse (CAM)	38
Waterhouse Rd (STO)	80
Waterhouse Rd (BEL)	78
Waterloo (HP)	36
Waterlow (DOR)	21
Waterman Rd (CAM)	38
Waterman Rd (ROS)	31
Waters Ave (EV)	49
Waterston Ave (WOL)	70
Waterston Rd (NEW)	58
Watertown (LEX)	73
Watertown	
1-230 (WAT)	72
231-449 (NEW)	58
450-749 (NWV)	60
750-OUT (WNW)	65
Watertown Sq (WAT)	72
Watervale Rd (MED)	55
Watkins (WOL)	70
Watson (BRA)	84
Watson (CAM)	39
Watson (WS)	44
Watson	18
Watson Rd (QUI)	69
Watson Rd (LEX)	73
Watson Rd (BEL)	78
Watts (CHE)	50
Watts St & Pl (MAL)	48
Waumbeck (NQ)	71
Waumbeck (DOR)	21
Wauwinet Rd (WNW)	65
Wave Ave (DOR)	25
Wave Ave (REV)	51
Wave Way Ave (WIN)	52
Waverley (WAL)	54
Waverley	
1-163 (WAV)	79
164-OUT (BEL)	78
Waverley Ave (WAT)	72
Waverley Ave	
1-424 (NEW)	58
425-OUT (NCE)	59
Waverley Pl (NLF)	62
Waverley Ter (WAV)	79
Waverley Oaks Rd (WAL)	54
Waverly (BRO)	46
Waverly (MAL)	48
Waverly (CAM)	39
Waverly (BRI)	35
Waverly (STO)	80
Waverly (ARL)	74
Waverly (ROX)	19
Waverly Ave (REV)	51
Waverly Ave & Pl (MEL)	76
Waverly Rd (WRX)	32
Waverly St, Ave & Pl (EV)	49
Way (HP)	36
Way Pl (ROX)	19
Wayburn Rd (JP)	30
Wayland (DOR)	25
Wayland (WOL)	70
Waymount (RXC)	20

Wayne (DOR)	21
Wayne Ave (WAL)	54
Wayne Ave (BRA)	85
Wayne Rd (NH)	94
Wayne Rd (NCE)	59
Weaver Ct & Way (ROX)	19
Weaver Rd (EWY)	89
Webb (BRA)	85
Webb (WY)	88
Webb (LEX)	73
Webb Ave (WH)	81
Webb Park (SB)	27
Webber (MAL)	48
Webber (MED)	55
Webber St & Pl (ROX)	19
Webcowet Rd (ARL)	74
Weber Rd (BEL)	78
Webley Pl (ALL)	34
Webster (MED)	55
Webster (WAL)	54
Webster (EV)	49
Webster (REV)	51
Webster (SOM)	45
Webster (ARL)	74
Webster (NQ)	71
Webster (SWY)	90
Webster	
1-100 (WAT)	72
1-251 (WNW)	65
1-614 (NH)	94
.01-OUT (WAV)	79
252-OUT (AUB)	66
615-OUT (N)	92
Webster Ave (SOM)	43
Webster Ave (CAM)	41
Webster Ave & Ct (CHE)	50
Webster Ct (STO)	80
Webster Ct (NCE)	59
Webster Ct (CHA)	29
Webster Park (N)	92
Webster Park & Pl (WNW)	65
Webster Pl	13
Webster Rd (BRA)	84
Webster Rd (LEX)	73
Webster Rd (WES)	93
Webster Rd (MIL)	86
Webster St, Ave & Pl (EB)	28
Webster St, Ct & Pl (MAL)	48
Webster St & Pl (BRO)	46
Webster St & Sq (HP)	36
Wedgemere Rd (MAL)	48
Wedgemere Rd (MED)	55
Wedgemere Rd (WRX)	32
Wedgewood (EV)	49
Wedgewood (NQ)	71
Wedgewood (WH)	81
Wedgewood Rd (WNW)	65
Wedgewood Rd (ROS)	31
Wedmore (DOR)	25
Weeden Pl (QUI)	69
Weeks Ave (ROS)	31
Weir (AUB)	66
Weir Rd (WAL)	54
Weitz (ALL)	34
Welaka Rd (EWY)	89
Welch Rd (WRX)	32
Welch Rd (BRO)	46
Welch Rd (LEX)	73
Weld	
1-335 (ROS) (ODD)	31
2-378 (ROS) (EVEN)	31
337-OUT (WRX) (ODD)	32
340-OUT (WRX) (EVEN)	32

Weld Ave (ROX)	19
Weld Rd (STO)	80
Weld Hill (JP)	30
Weldon (DOR)	21
Weldon Rd (NEW)	58
Welgate Cir (WOL)	70
Welgate Rd (MED)	55
Well	41
Welland Cir & Rd (WY)	88
Welland Rd (BRO)	46
Welles (HP)	36
Welles Ave (DOR)	24
Welles Park (ROS)	31
Welleslev (MED)	55
Wellesley (WES)	93
Wellesley Ave (NH)	94
Wellesley Ave	
1-99 (WEL)	81
100-OUT (WH)	81
Wellesley Park (DOR)	24
Wellesley Rd (BEL)	78
Wellesley Rd (ARL)	74
Wellesley Sq (WEL)	81
Wellington (ARL)	74
Wellington (BRA)	84
Wellington	18
Wellington (MAL)	48
Wellington Ave (EV)	49
Wellington Ave (SOM)	45
Wellington Ct (DOR)	21
Wellingtn n Ln (CAM)	41
Wellington Ln (BEL)	78
Wellington Ln Ave (LEX)	73
Wellington Pl (CHA)	29
Wellington Rd (MED)	55
Wellington St Ext (ARL)	74
Wellington St, Ave & Grv (WAL)	54
Wellington Ter (BRO)	46
Wellington Hill (MAT)	26
Wellman (BRO)	46
Wells Ave (NCE)	59
Wells Ave (WAT)	72
Wellsmere Park, Rd & Ter (ROS)	31
Welsh (MAL)	48
Welton Rd (WRX)	32
Wendall (WAL)	54
Wendell (CAM)	38
Wendell	10
Wendell Ave (WOL)	70
Wendell Park E & W (MIL)	86
Wendell Rd (NCE)	59
Wendelier (SB)	27
Wendling Rd (N)	92
Wendover (DOR)	25
Wenham (N)	30
Wenham Rd (NWH)	61
Wenlock Rd (DOR)	22
Wenonah (DOR)	21
Wensley (RXC)	20
Wentworth Pl (BRO)	46
Wentworth Rd (REV)	51
Wentworth Rd (WOL)	70
Wentworth Rd (MEL)	76
Wentworth St, Ct & Ter (MAL)	48
Wentworth St & Ter (DOR)	24
Wescott (MAL)	48
Wesley (MAL)	48
Wesley (NEW)	58
Wesley (SOM)	45
Wesley (CHE)	50

Boston (Con.)   021

Wesley (CHA) ... 29
Wesley Park (SOM) ... 43
Wesley Pl ... 13
Wesmur Rd (MAL) ... 48
Wessagusett Rd (HWY) ... 91
Wessex (DOR) ... 24
Wessex Rd (NCE) ... 59
Wesson Ave (QUI) ... 69
West (QUI) ... 69
West (MEL) ... 76
West (ARL) ... 74
West (BEL) ... 78
West (STO) ... 80
West ... 11
West (CHA) ... 29
West (MIL) ... 87
West (NH) ... 94
West (MAL) ... 48
West (WS) ... 44
West (EV) ... 49
West (MED) ... 55
West (NEW) ... 58
West (HP) ... 36
West (WAL) ... 54
West
   1-88 (SWY) ... 90
   1-364 (BRA) ... 84
   89-OUT (SWY) ... 88
   365-OUT (BRA) ... 85
West Blvd Rd (NCE) ... 59
West Ct Ter (ARL) ... 74
West St & Pl (CAM) ... 39
West Adams (WS) ... 44
West Bellflower (DOR) ... 25
West Border Rd (MAL) ... 48
West Boundary Rd (WRO) ... 32
West Brookline ... 18
West Canton
   1-173 ... 18
   174-OUT ... 16
West Cedar
   1-31 (ODD) ... 08
   2-40 (EVEN) ... 08
   33-OUT (ODD) ... 14
   42-OUT (EVEN) ... 14
West Concord ... 18
West Cottage (DOR) ... 25
West Dedham ... 18
West Eagle (EB) ... 28
West Elm Ave (WOL) ... 70
West Foster (MEL) ... 76
West Fourth (SB) ... 27
West Hancock (STO) ... 80
West Hill Ave & Ter (MEL) ... 76
West Hill Pl ... 14
West Howard (QUI) ... 69
West Howell (DOR) ... 25
West Lake Dr (WY) ... 88
West Milton (HP) ... 36
West Newton
   1-183 (ODD) ... 18
   2-200 (EVEN) ... 18
   185-OUT (ODD) ... 16
   202-OUT (EVEN) ... 16
West Park (DOR) ... 24
West Pine (AUB) ... 66
West Quincy (WS) ... 44
West Riding (WEL) ... 81
West Roxbury Pky
   1-251 (CHH) ... 67
   252-400 (ROS) (EVEN) ... 31

253-765 (WRX) (ODD) ... 32
402-598 (WRX) (EVEN) ... 32
600-784 (ROS) (EVEN) ... 31
767-OUT (CHH) (ODD) ... 67
786-OUT (CHH) (EVEN) ... 67
West Rutland Sq ... 18
West Selden (MAT) ... 26
West Side Rd (MIL) ... 87
West Sorento (ALL) ... 34
West Springfield ... 18
West Squantum (MQ) ... 71
West Tremlett (DOR) ... 24
West Walnut Park (ROX) ... 19
West Wyoming Ave (MEL) ... 76
Westacott Ct (CAM) ... 39
Westbourne (ROS) ... 31
Westbourne (MIL) ... 86
Westbourne Rd (NCE) ... 59
Westbourne Ter (BRO) ... 46
Westbrook (EB) ... 28
Westbrook Cir (WAL) ... 54
Westchester Rd (NEW) ... 58
Westchester Rd (JP) ... 30
Westcliff Rd (WES) ... 93
Westcott (DOR) ... 24
Westcott Rd (STO) ... 80
Westerley (WEL) ... 81
Westerley (JP) ... 30
Westerly Rd (WES) ... 93
Western Ave (WY) ... 88
Western Ave (CAM) ... 39
Western Ave
   1-305 (ALL) (ODD) ... 34
   2-300 (ALL) (EVEN) ... 34
   302-OUT (BRI) (EVEN) ... 35
   307-OUT (BRI) ... 35
Westfield (N) ... 92
Westfield ... 18
Westfield Rd (WRW) ... 65
Westford (QUI) ... 69
Westford St & Pl (ALL) ... 34
Westgate (CAM) ... 39
Westgate Rd (WAL) ... 54
Westgate Rd (NCE) ... 59
Westgate Rd (WEL) ... 81
Westgate Rd (CHH) ... 67
Westglow (DOR) ... 22
Westland Ave ... 15
Westland Ave & Ter (WRW) ... 65
Westland Rd (WAT) ... 72
Westland Rd (WES) ... 93
Westley Ave (CAM) ... 40
Westlund Rd (BEL) ... 78
Westminster (HP) ... 36
Westminster (WS) ... 44
Westminster (RXC) ... 20
Westminster Ave (WAT) ... 72
Westminster Ave (ARL) ... 74
Westminster Ave (LEX) ... 73
Westminster Ave & Ter
   (ROX) ... 19
Westminster Rd (NCE) ... 59
Westminster Rd (EWY) ... 89
Westminster Ter (BRI) ... 35
Westmoor Cir, Rd & Ter
   (WRX) ... 32
Westmore Rd (MAT) ... 26
Westmoreland (DOR) ... 24
Westmoreland Ave (ARL) ... 74
Westmount Ave (WRX) ... 32
Weston (HP) ... 36
Weston (WAL) ... 54
Weston (LEX) ... 73

Weston (MIL) ... 87
Weston Ave (WOL) ... 70
Weston Ave (WS) ... 44
Weston Ave & Ct (BRA) ... 84
Weston Rd
   1-309 (WEL) ... 81
   310-OUT (WH) ... 81
Weston St & Pl (RXC) ... 20
Weston Ter (WEL) ... 81
Westover (WRX) ... 32
Westover (EV) ... 49
Westvale Rd (MED) ... 55
Westvale Rd (MIL) ... 86
Westview (LEX) ... 73
Westview St & Ter (DOR) ... 24
Westview Ter (WRW) ... 65
Westville
   1-130 (DOR) ... 24
   131-OUT (DOR) ... 22
Westville Ter (DOR) ... 24
Westwood (DOR) ... 21
Westwood (WRW) ... 65
Westwood Rd (LEX) ... 73
Westwood Rd (STO) ... 80
Westwood Rd (WEL) ... 81
Westwood Rd (MED) ... 55
Westwood Rd (SOM) ... 43
Wetherbee Rd (WAL) ... 54
Wetherell (NUF) ... 64
Wexford (NH) ... 94
Weyanoke (DOR) ... 24
Weybosset (MAT) ... 26
Weybosset (NWY) ... 91
Weybridge Rd (BRO) ... 46
Weyham Rd (HWY) ... 91
Weymouth (QUI) ... 69
Weymouth Ave (WRX) ... 32
Wharf (CHE) ... 50
Wharf (QUI) ... 69
Wharf (EWY) ... 89
Wharf (MIL) ... 87
Wharf ... 10
Wharf ... 09
Wharton Ct (HP) ... 36
Wheatland (SOM) ... 45
Wheatland Ave (DOR) ... 24
Wheaton (ARL) ... 74
Wheaton Sq (JP) ... 30
Wheeler (SOM) ... 45
Wheeler (CAM) ... 38
Wheeler (MAL) ... 48
Wheeler Ave (MED) ... 55
Wheeler Ave (MEL) ... 76
Wheeler Ct & Ln (WAT) ... 72
Wheeler Ln (ARL) ... 74
Wheeler Rd (NCE) ... 59
Wheeler Rd (LEX) ... 73
Wheelock (WIN) ... 52
Wheelock Ave (DOR) ... 25
Wheelock Rd & Ter (WAL) ... 54
Wheelwright Rd (MED) ... 55
Whip Hill Rd (MEL) ... 76
Whipple (MAL) ... 48
Whipple (WS) ... 44
Whipple ... 15
Whipple Ave (ROS) ... 31
Whipple Ave (STO) ... 80
Whipple Rd (LEX) ... 73
Whipple St & Cir (SWY) ... 90
Whitby (EB) ... 28
Whitby Ter (DOR) ... 25
Whitcomb (WAL) ... 54

Boston (Cen.)   021

Whitcomb
1-27 (WAV) (ODD)	79
2-24 (WAV) (EVEN)	79
26-OUT (WAT) (EVEN)	72
29-OUT (WAT) (ODD)	72
Whitcomb Ave (JP)	30
Whitcomb Ter (SWY)	90
White (SWY)	90
White (EB)	28
White (ARL)	74
White (QUI)	69

White
1-OUT (CAM) (ODD)	40
2-30 (CAM) (EVEN)	40
32-OUT (WS) (EVEN)	44
White Ave (NCE)	59
White Ave (CHH)	67
White Ln (WES)	93
White Pl (BRO)	46
White Rd (BRA)	84
White St Pl (EB)	28

White St Pl
1-OUT (CAM) (ODD)	40
2-12 (CAM) (EVEN)	40
14-22 (WS) (EVEN)	44
24-OUT (CAM) (EVEN)	40
White St & Ter (WAV)	79
White Ter (LEX)	73
White Oak Ln (EWY)	89
White Oak Rd (WH)	81
White Oak Rd (WAB)	68
White Oak Rd (WRX)	32
White Pine Ln (LEX)	64
White Pine Rd (NUF)	64
White Pine Rd (N)	92
Whitelawn Ave (MIL)	87
Whites Ave (WAT)	72
Whitfield (DOR)	24
Whitfield Rd (WS)	44
Whitford (ROS)	31
Whitford Ter (WAL)	54
Whitin Ave (REV)	51
Whitin Ave Ext (REV)	51
Whiting (ROX)	19
Whiting Rd (WH)	81
Whiting Way (N)	92
Whitlow Rd (WNW)	65
Whitman (EWY)	89
Whitman (DOR)	24
Whitman (WS)	44
Whitman (MAL)	48
Whitman Ave (MEL)	76
Whitman Cir (LEX)	73
Whitman Rd (QUI)	69
Whitman Rd (MED)	55
Whitman Rd (MIL)	86
Whitman Rd (N)	92

Whitman Rd
1-37 (WAT) (ODD)	72
2-OUT (WAL) (EVEN)	54
3S-OUT (WAL) (ODD)	54
Whitney (WAT)	72
Whitney (CHH)	67
Whitney Ave (CAM)	39
Whitney Rd (MED)	55
Whitney Rd (QUI)	69
Whitney Rd (NWV)	60
Whitney Tavern Rd (WES)	93
Whiton Ave (QUI)	69
Whitridge (DOR)	24

Whittemore (ARL)	74
Whittemore (MED)	55
Whittemore (WRX)	32
Whittemore Ave (CAM)	40
Whittemore Rd (NEW)	58
Whittemore Ter (DOR)	25
Whittemore Ter (WES)	93
Whitten (DOR)	22
Whittier (RXC)	20
Whittier (CAM)	40
Whittier (WIN)	52
Whittier (MEL)	76
Whittier Ave (WAL)	54
Whittier Dr (EV)	49
Whittier Pl	14
Whittier Rd (MED)	55
Whittier Rd (NWV)	60
Whittier Rd (LEX)	73
Whittier Rd (WH)	81
Whittier Rd (BRA)	84
Whittier Rd (N)	92
Whittier Rd (MIL)	86
Whittlesey Rd (NCE)	59
Whitwell (MEL)	76
Whitwell (QUI)	69
Whyte (MED)	55
Wichita Ter (MAT)	26
Wickfield Ct (EV)	49
Wicklow (MAL)	48
Wicklow Ave (MED)	55
Widett Cir	18
Wight (WAL)	54
Wigget	13
Wiggin	13
Wigglesworth (MAL)	48
Wigglesworth (SOM)	45

Wigglesworth
1-35 (RXC) (ODD)	20
2-22 (RXC) (EVEN)	20
24-OUT (EVEN)	15
37-OUT (ODD)	15
Wight (WAL)	54
Wigwam Cir (ARL)	74
Wilbur (WAL)	54
Wilbur (MAL)	48
Wilbur (EV)	49
Wilbur (SWY)	90
Wilbur (DOR)	25
Wilbur Ave (ARL)	74
Wilbur Ct (EB)	28
Wilcock (DOR)	24
Wilcox Rd (DOR)	24
Wilde (WH)	81
Wilde Rd (WAB)	68
Wilder (DOR)	21
Wildon Rd (WEL)	81

Wildwood
1-53 (DOR) (ODD)	24
2-64 (DOR) (EVEN)	24
55-OUT (MAT) (ODD)	26
66-OUT (MAT) (EVEN)	26
Wildwood Ave (BRA)	85
Wildwood Ave (ARL)	74
Wildwood Ave (NWV)	60
Wildwood Dr (N)	92
Wildwood Ln (WES)	93
Wildwood Ln (STO)	80
Wildwood Ln (WAL)	54
Wildwood Rd (MED)	55
Wildwood Rd (WEL)	81
Wildwood Rd (MEL)	76
Wildwood Rd (LEX)	73
Wildwood Rd (MIL)	86

Wildwood Rd (EWY)	89
Wiley (MAL)	48
Wiley Rd (WAV)	79
Wilgus Rd (QUI)	69
Wilkes	18
Wilkins Pl (ROS)	31
Wilkins Rd (BRA)	84
Wilkinson Park (DOR)	22
Willard (BRA)	84
Willard (MEL)	76
Willard (NWH)	61
Willard (MAL)	48
Willard (NEW)	58

Willard (WAL)	54
Willard (CHE)	50
Willard (CAM)	38
Willard Ave (MED)	55
Willard Pl	18
Willard Rd (BRO)	46
Willard Rd (WES)	93
Willard St Ct (CAM)	38
Willard St & Ter (QUI)	69
Willcut Rd (DOR)	21
Willers (WRX)	32
Willet (WOL)	70
William (WNW)	65
William (WH)	81
William (STO)	80
William (CAM)	39
William (WS)	44
William St & Pl (MED)	55
William F Mc Lellan Hwy
(EB)	28
William H Devine Way (SB)	27
William J Day Blvd (SB)	27
William Jackson Ave (BRI)	35
William Roger Greeley Vd
(LEX)	73

William T Morrissey Blvd
1-620 (DOR)	25
621-OUT (DOR)	22
Williams (NQ)	71
Williams (ARL)	74
Williams (WAT)	72
Williams (MAL)	48
Williams (BRO)	46
Williams (CHE)	50
Williams (EV)	49
Williams (WAL)	54
Williams (WIN)	52
Williams (JP)	30

Williams
1-50 (ROX)	19
51-OUT (RXC)	20
Williams Ave (SWY)	90

Williams Ave
1-174 (HP)	36
175-OUT (MIL)	86
Williams Ct (WY)	88
Williams Ct (SOM)	43
Williams Rd (LEX)	73
Williams Sq (RXC)	20
Williams St & Ct (BRA)	84
Williams St & Ct (NUF)	64
Willis (DOR)	25
Willis Ave (WIN)	52
Willis Ave (MED)	55
Willis Ter (ROX)	19
Williston Rd (BRO)	46
Williston Rd (AUB)	66
Williston Rd (BEL)	78
Willoughby (SOM)	43

Boston (Con.)   **021**

Willoughby (BRI) 35
Willoughby Pl (ROX) 19
Willoughby Rd (MIL) 87
Willow (N) 92
Willow 08
Willow (MAL) 48
Willow (WAL) 54
Willow (CHE) 50
Willow (BEL) 78
Willow (STO) 80
Willow (BRA) 84
Willow (WH) 81
Willow (LEX) 73
Willow
   1-174 (CAM) 41
   175-175 (SOM) 43
   176-OUT (CAM) 41
Willow Ave (NWY) 91
Willow Ave (WS) 44
Willow Ave (HP) 36
Willow Ave & Ter (WIN) 52
Willow Cres (BRO) 46
Willow Ct (ARL) 74
Willow Ct (DOR) 25
Willow Ln (EWY) 89
Willow Park (WAT) 72
Willow Park & Rd (WEL) ... 81
Willow Rd (WES) 93
Willow St & Ave (WOL) 70
Willow St & Park (MEL) 76
Willow St & Ter (NCE) 59
Willow St & Ter (WRX) 32
Willowdean Ave (WRX) 32
Willowwood (DOR) 24
Wilmarth Rd (BRA) 84
Wilmington Ave (DOR) 24
Wilmore (MAT) 26
Wilmot (WAT) 72
Wilmot (ROS) 31
Wilmot (WAL) 54

Wilna Ct (WRX) 32
Wilrose (DOR) 21
Wilshire (WIN) 52
Wilshire Park (N) 92
Wilson (REV) 51
Wilson (MED) 55
Wilson (DOR) 24
Wilson (WEL) 81
Wilson Ave (WAV) 79
Wilson Ave (WAT) 72
Wilson Ave (BRA) 84
Wilson Ave (ARL) 74
Wilson Ave (WOL) 70
Wilson Ave (MAL) 48
Wilson Ave (CAM) 40
Wilson Ave (SOM) 45
Wilson Ave (WY) 88
Wilson Ct (NQ) 71
Wilson Park (BRI) 35
Wilson Rd (WAL) 54
Wilson Rd (STO) 80
Wilson Rd (LEX) 73
Wilsons Ln (N) 92
Wilton (WAL) 54
Wilton (SOM) 45
Wilton (HP) 36
Wilton St & Ter (ALL) 34
Wiltshire Ct & Rd (NEW) ... 58
Wiltshire Rd (BRI) 35
Wimbledon Cir (WNW) 65
Winborough (MAT) 26

Winchester 16
Winchester (NWH) 61
Winchester (BRO) 46
Winchester (MAL) 48
Winchester Dr (LEX) 73
Winchester Rd (ARL) 74
Winchester Rd (NEW) 58
Winchester St, Ct & Pl
   (MED) 55
Winchester Ter (JP) 30
Windemere Cir (BRA) 84
Windemere Rd (WH) 81
Windemere Ave, Ln & Park
   (ARL) 74
Windermere Rd (AUB) 66
Windermere Rd (DOR) 25
Windham Rd (HP) 36
Winding River Cir (WH) 81
Winding River Rd
   1-157 (N) 92
   158-OUT (WH) 81
Windmill Ln (ARL) 74
Windom (ALL) 34
Windom (WS) 44
Windsor (SOM) 43
Windsor (EV) 49
Windsor (ARL) 74
Windsor (RXC) 20
Windsor
   1-300 (CAM) 39
   301-548 (CAM) 41
   549-OUT (SOM) 43
Windsor Rd (SWY) 90
Windsor Rd (N) 92
Windsor Rd (MIL) 87
Windsor Rd (WH) 81
Windsor Rd (NQ) 71
Windsor Rd (WAB) 68
Windsor Rd (WS) 44
Windsor Rd (MED) 55
Windsor Rd (BRO) 46
Windsor St & Rd (MEL) 76
Windsor Ter (WAL) 54
Winfield (N) 92
Winfield (SB) 27
Winford Way (MED) 55
Wingate Rd (WAL) 54
Wingate Rd (HP) 36
Wingate Rd (EWY) 89
Wingate Rd (WH) 81
Wingate Rd (LEX) 73
Winn (BEL) 78
Winn Ave (LEX) 73
Winn Ter (MAL) 48
Winnemere (MAL) 48
Winnetaska Rd (WAB) 68
Winnisimmet (CHE) 50
Winona (AUB) 66
Winona Way (NWY) 91
Winship (LEX) 73
Winship (MAL) 48
Winship St & Pl (BRI) 35
Winslow (EV) 49
Winslow (HP) 36
Winslow (CAM) 38
Winslow (ARL) 74
Winslow Ave (MED) 55
Winslow Ave (WS) 44
Winslow Rd (BRO) 46
Winslow Rd (WAB) 68
Winslow Rd (WAV) 79
Winslow Rd (BRA) 84
Winslow Rd (WH) 81

Winslow Rd (NQ) 71
Winslow St & Pl (ROX) 19
Winsom Ave (WAL) 54
Winsor Ave (WAT) 72
Winsor Way (WES) 93
Winstead Rd (EWY) 89
Winston Rd (LEX) 73
Winston Rd (NCE) 59
Winston Rd (DOR) 24
Winter (DOR) 22
Winter (NUF) 64
Winter (LEX) 73
Winter (WAT) 72
Winter (QUI) 69
Winter (BRA) 85
Winter (STO) 80
Winter (WAV) 79
Winter (ARL) 74
Winter (WY) 88
Winter (WES) 93
Winter (WAL) 54
Winter (WS) 44
Winter (MED) 55
Winter (CAM) 41
Winter (HP) 36
Winter (EV) 49
Winter St Pl (CAM) 41
Winter St & Ave (MAL) 48
Winter St & Pl (MEL) 76
Winter St & Pl 08
Winter Hill Cir (SOM) 45
Winter Hill Rd (MED) 55
Winthrop (HP) 36
Winthrop (CHE) 50
Winthrop (WAL) 54
Winthrop (WIN) 52
Winthrop (ROX) 19
Winthrop (EB) 28
Winthrop (CHA) 29
Winthrop (MEL) 76
Winthrop (STO) 80
Winthrop (WAT) 72
Winthrop (WNW) 65
Winthrop (MIL) 87
Winthrop Ave (WOL) 70
Winthrop Ave (NEW) 58
Winthrop Ave, Pky & Pl
   (REV) 51
Winthrop Ave & Rd (BRA) .. 85
Winthrop Rd (BEL) 78
Winthrop Rd (WEL) 81
Winthrop Rd (ARL) 74
Winthrop Rd (LEX) 73
Winthrop Rd (BRO) 46
Winthrop Sq 10
Winthrop St, Ct, Pl & Sq
   (MED) 55
Winthrop St & Park (MAL) .. 48
Winthrop St, Park & Pl (QUI) .. 69
Winthrop St & Rd (EV) 49
Winthrop St & Sq (CAM) ... 38
Winthrop Shore Dr (WIN) .. 52
Winton (ROS) 31
Wirt (BRI) 35
Wisconsin Ave (SOM) 45
Wise (JP) 30
Wistar Pl (CHA) 29
Wiswall (WNW) 65
Wiswall Cir (WEL) 81
Wiswall Rd (NCE) 59
Witherbee Ave (REV) 51
Withington (DOR) 24
Withington Rd (NWV) 60

Boston (Con.)   021

Wittawaumet Rd (NWY) 91
Woburn (LEX) 73
Woburn (MED) 55
Woburn (WAL) 54
Woerd Ave (WAL) 54
Wolcott (EV) 49
Wolcott (DOR) 21
Wolcott Rd (REV) 51
Wolcott Rd (STO) 80
Wolcott Rd (WAT) 72
Wolcott Rd (CHH) 67
Wolcott Rd (MIL) 86
Wolcott Rd Ext (CHH) 67
Wolcott St, Ct & Sq (HP) 36
Wolcott St & Park (MED) 55
Wolcott St & Park (AUB) 66
Wolcott St & Ter (MAL) 48
Wolfe (WRX) 32
Wollaston Ave (WOL) 70
Wollaston Ave (ARL) 74
Wollaston Ter (DOR) 24
Wollitzer Ln (WAT) 72
Wood (LEX) 73
Wood (CHA) 29
Wood (CAM) 40
Wood (MIL) 86
Wood Ave (EWY) 89
Wood Ave
 1-135 (MAT) (ODD) 26
 2-122 (MAT) (EVEN) 26
 124-OUT (HP) (EVEN) 36
 137-OUT (HP) (ODD) 36
Wood Rd (BRA) 84
Wood End Rd (WAB) 61
Wood Haven Rd (WAB) 68
Woodard Ave (WRX) 32
Woodberry Rd (LEX) 73
Woodbine (WOL) 70
Woodbine (WAL) 54
Woodbine (SOM) 43
Woodbine (ROX) 19
Woodbine Cir (NH) 94
Woodbine Rd (EWY) 89
Woodbine Rd (MED) 55
Woodbine Rd (WH) 81
Woodbine Rd (BEL) 78
Woodbine St & Ter (AUB) 66
Woodbole Ave (MAT) 26
Woodbourne Rd (JP) 30
Woodbriar Rd (MEL) 76
Woodbridge (CAM) 40
Woodbrier Rd (WRX) 32
Woodbrier Rd (NQ) 71
Woodbury (ARL) 74
Woodbury 18
Woodbury Dr (N) 92
Woodchester Cir & Rd (WAL) .. 54
Woodchester Dr (MIL) 86
Woodchester Dr (WES) 93
Woodchester Dr (CHH) 67
Woodchester Rd (WH) 81
Woodcliff (DOR) 25
Woodcliff Dr (WAL) 54
Woodcliff Rd (WH) 81
Woodcliff Rd (CHH) 67
Woodcliff Rd (QUI) 69
Woodcliff Rd (NWH) 61
Woodcliffe Rd (LEX) 73
Woodcrest Ct (SWY) 90
Woodcrest Dr E, N & W
 (MEL) 76

Woodale Ave (MAT) 26
Woodedge Ave, Cir & Ln
 (BRA) 85
Woodfall (BEL) 78
Woodfield (DOR) 22
Woodfield Rd (WH) 81
Woodford (DOR) 25
Woodgate (MAT) 26
Woodglen Rd (HP) 36
Woodhaven (MAT) 26
Woodland (EV) 49
Woodland (BEL) 78
Woodland (ARL) 74
Woodland Ave (MEL) 76
Woodland Ave (BRA) 85
Woodland Ave & Rd (MED) 55
Woodland Dr (SWY) 90
Woodland Pl (HP) 36
Woodland Rd (WAL) 54
Woodland Rd (REV) 51
Woodland Rd (WES) 93
Woodland Rd (MIL) 86
Woodland Rd (BRA) 84
Woodland Rd (WH) 81
Woodland Rd (STO) 80
Woodland Rd (LEX) 73
Woodland Rd (AUB) 66
Woodland Rd (CHH) 67
Woodland Rd (N) 30
Woodland St & Rd (MAL) 48
Woodland Hill (WH) 81
Woodlawn (JP) 30
Woodlawn Ave (WAL) 54
Woodlawn Ave (CHE) 50
Woodlawn Ave (N) 92
Woodlawn Ave & Oval (WH) 81
Woodlawn Dr (CHH) 67
Woodlawn St & Ave (EV) 49
Woodledge (DOR) 25
Woodledge Rd (N) 92
Woodleigh Rd (WAT) 72
Woodley Ave (WRX) 32
Woodman (QUI) 69
Woodman (JP) 30
Woodman Cir (SWY) 90
Woodman Rd (CHH) 67
Woodmont (BRI) 35
Woodridge Cir & Rd (WES) 93
Woodridge Rd (WEL) 81
Woodrock Rd (EWY) 89
Woodrow Ave (NWV) 60
Woodrow Ave (MAL) 48
Woodrow Ave (MED) 55
Woodrow Ave (DOR) 24
Woodrow Wilson Ct (ROX) 19
Woodrow Wilson Ct (CAM) 39
Woodruff Ave (MED) 55
Woodruff Ave (MEL) 76
Woodruff Way (MAT) 26
Woods Ave (REV) 51
Woods Ave (WS) 44
Woods Ln (MAL) 48
Woods Pl (CHA) 29
Woods Rd (MED) 55
Woods Rd (BEL) 78
Woods Edge Rd (MED) 55
Woodside Ave (EV) 49
Woodside Ave (BRA) 85
Woodside Ave (WH) 81
Woodside Ave (JP) 30
Woodside Ave & Park (MIL) 52
Woodside Dr (MIL) 86
Woodside Ln (ARL) 74

Woodside Path (EWY) 89
Woodside Rd (NWV) 60
Woodside Rd (MED) 55
Woodsom Dr (BRA) 85
Woodstock (WS) 44
Woodstock Ave (BRO) 46
Woodville (EV) 49
Woodville Ave (MIL) 86
Woodville St, Park & Ter
 (ROX) 19
Woodville Ter (MAL) 48
Woodward (EV) 49
Woodward
 1-186 (NWH) 51
 187-OUT (WAB) 68
Woodward Ave (ROX) 19
Woodward Ave (QUI) 69
Woodward Ct (MIL) 86
Woodward Ln (WES) 93
Woodward Park St (DOR) 25
Woodward St & Pl (SB) 27
Woodway Rd (WEL) 81
Woodworth (DOR) 22
Woolsey Sq (JP) 30
Woolson (MAT) 26
Worcester (WEL) 81
Worcester (BEL) 78
Worcester (WAT) 72
Worcester (CAM) 39
Worcester Ln (WAL) 54
Worcester St & Pl 18
Wordsworth St & Ter (EB) 28
Worley (WRX) 32
Wormwood 62210
Woronoco Rd (NWY) 91
Worster (MED) 55
Worster Ter (WY) 88
Worth (MEL) 76
Worth Cir (NEW) 58
Worthen Rd (LEX) 73
Worthern Ave (WY) 88
Worthington (CAM) 38
Worthington (RXC) 20
Worthington Cir (BRA) 84
Worthington Rd (BRO) 46
Wren (WRX) 32
Wren Ter (QUI) 69
Wrentham (DOR) 24
Wright (LEX) 73
Wright (ARL) 74
Wright (STO) 80
Wright (CAM) 38
Wright (SWY) 90
Wright Ave (MED) 55
Wright Rd (NCE) 45
Wyatt St & Cir (SOM) 43
Wycliff (WRX) 32
Wycliff Rd (EWY) 89
Wycoma Way (WAL) 54
Wyeth St & Ct (MAL) 48
Wykeham Rd (WMW) 65
Wyllis Ave
 1-OUT (MAL) (ODD) 48
 2-OUT (EV) (EVEN) 49
Wyman (WAB) 68
Wyman (MAL) 54
Wyman (MED) 55
Wyman (CAM) 40
Wyman (WIN) 52
Wyman Pl 16
Wyman Rd (LEX) 73
Wyman Rd (BRA) 84
Wyman Rd & Sq (CAM) 38

Boston (Con.)   021

Wyndmere Rd (MIL)	86
Wynnewood Rd (WEL)	81
Wynot Rd (BRA)	84
Wyola Pl (DOR)	21
Wyola Prospect (MAL)	54
Wyoming (DOR)	21
Wyoming Ave (N)	92
Wyoming Ave E & W (MEL)	76
Wyoming Ave & Pl (MAL)	48
Wyoming Hts & Ter (MEL)	76
Wyoming Rd (NWV)	60
Wyvern (ROS)	31
Yale (MED)	55
Yale Rd (ARL)	74
Yale Rd (NH)	94
Yale Ter (JP)	30
Yard Way (SB)	27
Yard Arm Ln (QUI)	69
Yarmouth	16
Yarmouth (EV)	49
Yarmouth Rd (WH)	81
Yarmouth Rd (CHH)	67
Yeamans (REV)	51
Yeoman St, Ct & Pl (ROX)	19
Yeomans Ave (MED)	55
Yerxa Rd (CAM)	40
Yerxa Rd (ARL)	74
Yetten Ter (WAL)	54
York (REV)	51
York (LEX)	73
York (DOR)	21
York Ave (WAT)	72
York Rd (WAB)	68
York Rd (BEL)	78
York St & Pl (CAM)	41
York Ter (BRO)	46
York Ter (MEL)	76
Yorktown (NQ)	71
Yorktown (WRX)	32
Yorktown (WS)	44
Youle (MEL)	76
Young (NQ)	71
Young (LEX)	73
Young Path (NCE)	59
Young Rd (WES)	93
Yuill Cir (HP)	36
Yukon Ave (WAT)	72
Yurich Rd (N)	92
Zamora St & Ct (JP)	30
Zeigler St & Pl (ROX)	19
Zeller (ROS)	31
Zoar Ave (LEX)	73

NUMBERED STREETS

1st (MEL)	76
1st (QUI)	69
1st	
1-140 (CAM)	41
141-OUT (CAM)	42
1st Ave (SOM)	43
1st thru 2nd St (WRX)	32
1st thru 3rd St (MAL)	48
1st thru 3rd St (SB)	27
1st thru 3rd St (WY)	88
1st thru 4th Ave (WAL)	54
1st thru 4th Ave (NH)	94
1st thru 4th St (LEX)	73
1st thru 9th St (MED)	55
2nd	
1-159 (CAM)	41

160-OUT (CAM)	42
2nd thru 3rd St (EV)	49
2nd thru 6th St (CHE)	50
3rd (ARL)	74
3rd	
1-245 (CAM) (ODD)	41
2-220 (CAM) (EVEN)	41
222-OUT (CAM) (EVEN)	42
247-OUT (CAM) (ODD)	42
3rd Ave (SOM)	43
3rd St Pl (SB)	27
4th (SB)	27
4th Ave (WY)	88
4th St Pl (SB)	27
5th	
1-199 (CAM)	41
200-OUT (CAM)	42
5th Ave (WAT)	72
5th thru 6th Ave (QUI)	69
5th thru 9th St (SB)	27
6th (MEL)	76
6th	
1-113 (CAM) (ODD)	41
2-118 (CAM) (EVEN)	41
115-OUT (CAM) (ODD)	42
120-OUT (CAM) (EVEN)	42
7th thru 8th St (CAM)	41
13th (MEL)	76

BROCKTON   024

POST OFFICE BOXES

Box Nos.		
1-128	Montello Sta	03
1-296	Campello Sta	03
1-972	Main Office	03

STATIONS, BRANCHES AND UNITS

Campello Sta	03
Center Street Sta	01
Montello Sta	03
General Delivery	03
Postmaster	03

APARTMENTS, HOTELS, MOTELS

Ardmore, 93 High	01
Bryant, 33 West Elm	01
Central 40 West Elm	01
Congress Inn, 1005 Belmont	01
Grayson, 32 High	01
Holiday Inn, Westgate Dr	01
West Elm, 56 West Elm	01

BUILDINGS

Ashland Heights Shopping Center, 466-72 E Ashland	02
Colonial Village, 626-32 Pleasant	01
Del'S Shopping Center, 459-465 Centre	02
East Shopping Plaza, 672-766 Crescent	02
East Side Shopping Center, 581-605 Center	02
Oak Village Shopping Center, 180-196 Oak	01

South Shopping Center 2071-2077 Main	01
Southgate Plaza 1640-1670 Main	01
West Shopping Center, 593-709 Belmont	01
Westgate Gardens Shopping Plaza, Westgate Drive	01

HOSPITALS

Brockton, 680 Center	02
Cardinal Cushing Gen Hospital, 235 No Pearl	01
Veterans Administration Hospital, 945 Belmont	01

CHICOPEE   010

POST OFFICE BOXES

Box Nos.		
A-V	Main Office	21
1-420	Chicopee Center Sta	14
1-680	Main Office	21

STATIONS, BRANCHES AND UNITS

Chicopee Center Sta	13
Westover A F B Sta	22
General Delivery	21
Postmaster	21

FALL RIVER   027

POST OFFICE BOXES

Box Nos.		
A-F	Somerset Br	26
A-O	South Sta	24
1-298	Flint Sta	23
1-326	Somerset Br	26
1-356	South Sta	24
1-2410	Main Office	22

STATIONS, BRANCHES AND UNITS

Flint Sta	23
Somerset Br	25
South Sta	24
General Delivery	22
Postmaster	22

HOSPITALS

Saint Anne's, 795 Middle St	22
Truesdale, 1820 Highland Ave	22
Union, Highland Ave	20

FALMOUTH   025

POST OFFICE BOXES

Box Nos.		
A-Z	Falmouth	41
1-736	Falmouth	41

Falmouth (Con.) 025

1-747	Woods Hole	
	Sta.	43
AA-JJ	Falmouth	41

STATIONS, BRANCHES AND UNITS

Woods Hole Sta	43
General Delivery	40
Postmaster	40

APARTMENTS, HOTELS, MOTELS

| Admiralty Apts. | 40 |
| Greengate Apts. | 40 |

BUILDINGS

Marine Biological Lab	43
Woods Hole Oceanographic	
Inst.	43

HOSPITALS

| Falmouth | 40 |

LAWRENCE 018

POST OFFICE BOXES

Box Nos.		
1-446	North Andover	
	Br	45
1-518	Methuen Br	44
1-1517	Main Office	42

RURAL ROUTES

| 1,2 | 44 |
| 3 | 45 |

STATIONS, BRANCHES AND UNITS

Merrimack College Br	45
Methuen Br	44
North Andover Br	45
General Delivery	42
Postmaster	42

UNIVERSITIES AND COLLEGES

| Merrimack College | 45 |

LOWELL 018

POST OFFICE BOXES

Box Nos.		
1-1600	Main Office	53
2001-2999	Highland Sta	51

STATIONS, BRANCHES AND UNITS

Highlands Sta	51
Kearney Square Sta	52
General Delivery	53
Postmaster	53

UNIVERSITIES AND COLLEGES

| Lowell State College | 54 |
| Lowell Technical Institute | 54 |

LYNN 019

POST OFFICE BOXES

Box Nos.		
1-74	East Lynn Sta	04
1-96	Nahant Br	08
1-219	West Lynn Sta.	05
1-294	Swampscott	
	Br	07
1-951	Main Office	05
1001-1231	Saugus Br	06

STATIONS, BRANCHES AND UNITS

East Lynn Sta	04
Nahant Br	08
Saugus Br	06
Swampscott Br	07
West Lynn Sta	05
General Delivery	01
Postmaster	01

NEW BEDFORD 027

POST OFFICE BOXES

Box Nos.		
A-A	Main Office	41
B-B	Main Office	41
C-C	Main Office	41
D-D	Main Office	42
E-E	Main Office	42
F-F	Main Office	42
G-G	Main Office	42
L-L	Lunds Corner	
	Sta	45
M-M	Division Sta	44
N-N	North Sta	46
P-P	Padanaram Br.	48
1-96	Nonquitt Br	48
1-118	Acushnet Br	43
1-237	North	
	Dartmouth Br	47
1-268	South	
	Dartmouth	48

RURAL ROUTES

1	43
2	48
3	47

STATIONS, BRANCHES AND UNITS

Acushnet Br	43
Division Street Sta	44
Lunds Corner Sta	45
Nonquitt Rural Br	48
North Sta	46
North Dartmouth Br	47
Padanaram Village Br	48
South Dartmouth Br	48
General Delivery	40
Postmaster	40

NORTH ATTLEBORO 027

POST OFFICE BOXES

Box Nos.		
1-1112	Main Office	61
1281-1349	Attleboro Falls	
	Sta.	63
1501-1828	Plainville Br	62

RURAL ROUTES

| 1,2 | 60 |
| 3 | 62 |

STATIONS, BRANCHES AND UNITS

Attleboro Falls Sta.	63
Plainville Br	62
General Delivery	60
Postmaster	60

PLYMOUTH 023

POST OFFICE BOXES

Box Nos.		
1-128	No Ply Sta	60
1-260	Kingston Br	64
1-537	Main Office	60

RURAL ROUTES

1	60
2	64
3,4	60

STATIONS, BRANCHES AND UNITS

Kingston Br	64
North Plymouth Sta	60
General Delivery	60
Postmaster	60

SPRINGFIELD 011

POST OFFICE BOXES

Box Nos.		
1-265	Brightwood	
	Sta	07
1-317	Forest Park	
	Sta	08
1-447	Highland Sta	09
1-3580	Main Office	01

STATIONS, BRANCHES AND UNITS

Brightwood Sta	07
Forest Park Sta.	08
Highland Sta	09
Longmeadow Br	06
Tapley Street Annex Sta	01
General Delivery	01
Postmaster	01

HOSPITALS

Mercy, 233 Carew	04
Municipal, 1414 State	09
Shriners, 516 Carew	04
Springfield Medical Center,	
759 Chestnut	07

Springfield (Con.)	011	1-295	Greendale Sta ..	06	Memorial, 119 Belmont	05
		1-1160	G P O		Saint Vincent, 25 Winthrop	10
Wesson Memorial, 140 High...	01		Worcester	13	Worcester City, 71 Jaques	
Wesson Womens, 735		1601-1728	C Sta	07	Ave	10
Chestnut	07				Worcester State, 305	
		0000149-			Belmont	04
		-0001591	Federal Sta	01		

UNIVERSITIES AND COLLEGES

American International, 170		**STATIONS, BRANCHES AND UNITS**			**UNIVERSITIES AND COLLEGES**	
Wilbraham Rd	09					
Junior Bay Path, 588		Assumption College Sta	09		Anna Maria	12
Longmeadow	06	Cherry Valley Br	11		Assumption, 500 Salisbury	09
Springfield, 263 Alden	09	Greendale Sta	06		Becker Junior, 61 Sever	09
Western New England, 1215		Mount Saint James Sta	10		Clark University, 950 Main	10
Wilbraham Rd	19	Parcel Post Sta	04		Holy Cross, College St	10
		Paxton Br	12		Notre Dame Academy,	
		Webster Square Sta	03		Salisbury	09
WORCESTER	**016**	West Side Sta	02		Quinsigamond Community	
		Postmaster	13		College 670 Boylston W	06
POST OFFICE BOXES					State Teachers, 486	
		HOSPITALS			Chandler	02
Box Nos.					Worcester Academy, 81	
1-240	West Side Sta .. 02	Doctors, 107 Lincoln	05		Providence	04
		Fairlawn, 189 May	02		Worcester Junior, 766 Main	08
		Hahnemann, 281 Lincoln	05		Worcester Polytechnic	
					Institute, Institute Rd	09

MICHIGAN   State List of Post Offices

MICHIGAN
(Abbreviation: MI)

Acme	49610	Athens	49011	Beach, Br. Detroit	48239
Ada (1st)	49301	Atlanta	49709	Beechwood	49909
Addison	49220	Atlantic Mine	49905	Belding (1st)	48809
Adrian (1st)	49221	Atlas	48411	Bellaire	49615
Afton	49705	Attica	48412	Belle River, R. Br. Saint	
Ahmeek	49901	Au Gres	48703	Cleir	48079
Airport, Br. Ypsilanti	48197	Au Train	49806	Belleville (1st)	48111
Akron	48701	Auburn	48611	Bellevue	49021
Alabaster, R. Br. Tawas City	48764	Auburn Heights, Br. Pontiac	48057	Belmont	49306
Alanson	49706	Augusta	49012	Bentley	48613
Alba	49611	Aura	49906	Benton Harbor (1st)	49022
Albion (1st)	49224	Avoca	48006	Benzonia	49616
Alden	49612	Azalia	48110	Bergland	49910
Alger	48610	Bach	48704	Berkley, Br. Royal Oak	48072
Algonac (1st)	48001	Bad Axe (1st)	48413	Berrien Center	49102
Allegan (1st)	49010	Bailey	49303	Berrien Springs (1st)	49103
Allen	49227	Baldwin	49304	Andrews, R. Br.	49104
Allen Park (1st)	48101	Baltic	49907	Berville, R. Br. Allenton	48062
Allendale	49401	Bancroft	48414	Bessemer	49911
Allenton	48002	Bangor (1st)	49013	Beulah	49617
Allouez	49805	Bannister	48807	Big Bay	49808
Alma (1st)	48801	Baraga	49908	Big Rapids (1st)	49307
Almont	48003	Barbeau	49710	Birch Run	48415
Alpena (1st)	49707	Bark River	49807		
Alpha	49902	Baroda	49101	BIRMINGHAM (1st) (see	
Alto ..	49302	Barron Lake, R. Br. Niles	49120	appendix)	
Amasa	49903	Barryton	49305	Bitely	49309
Anchorville	48004	Barton City	48705	Black River	48721
Andrews, R. Br. Berrien		Bath	48808	Blanchard	49310
Springs	49104	BATTLE CREEK (1st) (see		Blaney Park	49809
ANN ARBOR (1st) (see		appendix)		Blissfield (1st)	49228
appendix)		Bay City (1st)	48706	Bloomfield Hills (1st)	48013
Applegate	48401	A. Sta.	48706	Bloomingdale	49026
Arcadia	49613	University Center, R. Br.	48710	Boon	49618
Argyle	48410			Boyne City (1st)	49712
Armada	48005	Bay Port	48720	Boyne Falls	49713
Arnold, R. Br. Cornell	49819	Bay View, Br. Petoskey	49770	Bradley	49311
Ashley	48806	Bayshore, R. Br. Charlevoix	49711	Brampton	49810
		Bear Lake	49614	Branch	49402
		Beaverton	48612	Brant	48614
		Bedford	49020	Breckenridge	48615

Breedsville..................................49027
Brethren.....................................49619
Bridgeport (1st).........................48722
Bridgewater................................48115
Bridgman (1st)...........................49106
Brightmoor, Sta. Detroit............48223
Brighton (1st).............................48116
Brimley......................................49715
Britton..49229
Brohman.....................................49312
Bronson......................................49028
Brooklands, Br. Rochester..........48063
Brooklyn.....................................49230
Brown City.................................48416
Bruce Crossing...........................49912
Brunswick...................................49313
Brutus...49716
Buchanan (1st)...........................49107
  Glendora, R. Br....................49114
Buckley.......................................49620
Burlington...................................49029
Burnips.......................................49314
Burr Oak.....................................49030
Burt..48417
Burt Lake....................................49717
Byron..48418
Byron Center..............................49315
Cadillac (1st).............................49601
Cadmus.......................................49231
Caledonia....................................49316
Calumet (1st).............................49913
  Kearsarge, R. Br..................49942
  Laurium, Br..........................49913
Camden.......................................49232
Canal, Sta. Sault Sainte
  Marie......................................49783
Cannonsburg...............................49317
Capac..48014
Carland.......................................48810
Carleton......................................48117
Carlshend....................................49811
Carney...49812
Caro (1st)...................................48723
Carp Lake...................................49718
Carrollton....................................48724
Carson City.................................48811
Carsonville..................................48419
Caseville......................................48725
Casnovia.....................................49318
Caspian.......................................49915
Cass City (1st)...........................48726
Cassopolis (1st).........................49031
Castle, Sta. Saginaw...................48606
Castle Park, R. Br. Holland.........49422
Cedar..49621
Cedar Lake..................................48812
Cedar River.................................49813
Cedar Springs.............................49319
Cedarville....................................49719
  Coryell Islands, R. Br..........49719
  Les Cheneaux Club, R.
  Br..49754
Cement City................................49233
Center Line (1st)........................48015
Central Lake...............................49622
Centreville..................................49032
Ceresco.......................................49033
Champion....................................49814
Channing.....................................49815
Charlevoix (1st)..........................49720
  Bayshore, R. Br...................49711
Charlotte (1st)............................48813

Chase..49623
Chassell......................................49916
Chatham......................................49816
Cheboygan (1st).........................49721
Chelsea (1st)..............................48118
Chesaning (1st)..........................48616
Chief...49624
Chippewa Lake............................49320
Christmas, R. Br. Munising.........49862
Church Street, Sta. Flint.............48502
Clare (1st)...................................48617
Clarklake.....................................49234
Clarkston (1st)............................48016
Clarksville...................................48815
Clawson (1st).............................48017
Clayton..49235
Clifford..48727
Climax...49034
Clinton...49236
Clio (1st).....................................48420
Cloverdale....................................49035
Cody, Sta. Flint...........................48507
Cohoctah.....................................48816
Coldwater (1st)...........................49036
Coleman......................................48618
College Park, Sta. Detroit............48221
Coloma (1st)...............................49038
  Hagar Shores, R. Br.............49039
Colon...49040
Columbiaville...............................48421
Comins...48619
Commerce, R. Br. Union
  Lake.......................................48085
Comstock.....................................49041
Comstock Park (1st)....................49321
Concord.......................................49237
Conklin..49403
Constantine..................................49042
Conway..49722
Cooks..49817
Coopersville (1st)........................49404
Copemish.....................................49625
Copper City.................................49917
Copper Harbor............................49918
Coral..49322
Cornell...49818
  Arnold, R. Br........................49819
Corunna.......................................48817
Coryell Islands, R. Br.
  Cedarville..............................49719
Court, Sta. Kalamazoo (see
  appendix)
Covert..49043
  Palisades Park, R. Br...........49044
Covington.....................................49919
Cross Village...............................49723
Croswell.......................................48422
Crystal...48818
Crystal Falls................................49920
Curran..48728
Curtis...49820
Custer..49405
Dafter..49724
Daggett..49821
Dalton, R. Br. Muskegon.............49445
Dansville......................................48819
Davisburg.....................................48019
Davison (1st)..............................48423
De Tour Village...........................49725
De Witt...48820
DEARBORN (1st) (see
  appendix)

Dearborn Heights (1st)...............48127
Decatur..49045
Decker..48426
Deckerville..................................48427
Deerfield......................................49238
Deerton.......................................49822
Deford..48729
Delton, R. Br. Belleville..............49046
Denton, R. Br. Belleville..............48111
DETROIT (1st) (see
  appendix)
Detroit River, Sta. Detroit...........48222
Dexter (1st).................................48130
Dimondale....................................48821
Dodgeville....................................49921
Dollar Bay....................................49922
Dominican, Sta. Adrian...............49221
Donken...49923
Dorr...49323
Doster, R. Br. Plainwell..............49080
Douglas..49406
Dowagiac (1st)...........................49047
Dowling..49050
Downtown, Sta. Ann Arbor
  (see appendix)
Drayton Plains (1st)....................48020
Drummond Island.........................49726
Dryden...48428
Dundee...48131
Durand (1st)................................48429
Dutton, R. Br. Grand Rapids.......49511
Eagle..48822
Eagle Harbor, R. Br.
  Mohawk..................................49951
Eagle River..................................49924
East Detroit (1st)........................48021
East Jordan.................................49727
East Lansing (1st).......................48823
East Leroy....................................49051
East Side, Sta. Flint....................48508
East Tawas..................................48730
Eastlake.......................................49626
Eastland Center, Br. Detroit........48236
Eastport.......................................49627
Eaton Rapids (1st)......................48827
Eau Claire....................................49111
Eben Junction
  Rumely, R. Br.......................49826
Eckerman....................................49728
  Strongs, R. Br......................49790
Ecorse, Br. Detroit......................48229
Edenville......................................48620
Edmore..48829
Edwardsburg................................49112
  Union, R. Br.........................49130
Elberta...49628
Elk Rapids...................................49629
Elkton..48731
Ellsworth......................................49729
Elm Hall......................................48830
Elmira..49730
Eloise...48132
Elsie..48831
Elwell...48832
Emmett..48022
Empire..49630
Engadine......................................49827
Erie..48133
Escanaba (1st)............................49829
Essexville (1st)............................48732
Eureka...48833

343

Evart	49631
Ewen	49925
Fair Haven	48023
Fairgrove	48733
Fairplain Plaza, Br. Benton Harbor	49022
Fairview	48621
Falmouth	49632
Farmington (1st)	48024
Farwell	48622
Fayette	49830
Federal Station, Br. Pontiac (see appendix)	
Felch	49831
Fenkell, Sta. Detroit	48238
Fennville	49408
Fenton (1st)	48430
Fenwick	48834
Ferndale, Br. Detroit	48220
Ferry, R. Br. Shelby	49455
Ferrysburg	49409
Fibre	49732
Fife Lake	49633
Filer City	49634
Filion	48432
Fisher Building, Sta. Detroit	48202
Flat Rock (1st)	48134
FLINT (1st) (see appendix)	
Flushing (1st)	48433
Forest Lake	49832
Forestville	48434
Fort Dearborn, Sta. Dearborn (see appendix)	
Fort Shelby, Sta. Detroit (see appendix)	
Foster City	49834
Fostoria	48435
Fountain	49410
Fowler	48835
Fowlerville	48836
Frandor, Br. Lansing	48912
Frankenmuth (1st)	48734
Frankfort	49635
Franklin, Br. Birmingham	48025
Fraser (1st)	48026
Frederic	49733
Free Soil	49411
Freeland (1st)	48623
Freeport	49325
Fremont (1st)	49412
Frontier	49239
Fruitport	49415
Fulton	49052
Gaastra	49927
Gagetown	48735
Gaines	48436
Galesburg (1st)	49053
Galien	49113
Garden	49835
Garden City (1st)	48135
Garnet, R. Br. Naubinway	49734
Gay	49928
Gaylord (1st)	49735
General Post Office, Sta. Detroit	48232
Genesee	48437
Germfask	49836
Gibraltar, R. Br. Rockwood	48173
Gilford	48736
Gladstone (1st)	49837
Gladwin (1st)	48624
Glen Arbor	49636
Glendora, R. Br. Buchanan	49114
Glenn	49416
Glennie	48737
Glenside, Br. Muskegon	49441
Gobles	49055
Goetzville	49736
Good Hart	49737
Goodells	48027
Goodrich	48438
Gould City	49838
Gowen	49326
Grand Blanc (1st)	48439
Grand Circus Park, Sta. Detroit	48226
Grand Haven (1st)	49417
Grand Junction	49056
Grand Ledge (1st)	48837
Grand Marais	49839
GRAND RAPIDS (1st) (see appendix)	
Grand River, Sta. Detroit	48208
Grandville (1st)	49418
Grant	49327
Grass Lake	49240
Gratiot, Sta. Detroit	48207
Grawn	49637
Grayling (1st)	49738
Greenbush	48738
Greenfield Village, Sta. Dearborn	48120
Greenland	49929
Greenville (1st)	48838
Gregory	48137
Grind Stone City, R. Br. Port Austin	48467
Grosse Ile (1st)	48138
Grosse Pointe, Br. Detroit	48236
Gulliver	49840
Gwinn (1st)	49841
K I Sawyer A F B, Br. Princeton, R. Br.	49843
	49875
Hadley	48440
Hagar Shores, R. Br. Coloma	49039
Hale	48739
Hamburg	48139
Hamilton	49419
Hammond Bay, R. Br. Ocqueoc	49763
Hamtramck, Br. Detroit	48212
Hancock (1st)	49930
Hanover	49241
Harbert	49115
Harbor Beach	48441
Harbor Point, Br. Harbor Springs	49740
Harbor Springs	49740
Hardwood	49844
Harper, Sta. Detroit	48213
Harper Woods, Br. Detroit	48236
Harrietta	49638
Harris	49845
Harrison	48625
Harrisville	48740
Harsens Island	48028
Hart	49420
Hartford (1st)	49057
Hartland	48029
Harvey, Br. Marquette	49855
Haslett	48840
Hastings (1st)	49058
Hawks	49743
Hazel Park (1st)	48030
Hell, R. Br. Pinckney	48169
Hemlock	48626
Henderson	48841
Henry Street, Br. Muskegon	49441
Hermansville	49847
Herron	49744
Hersey	49639
Hesperia	49421
Hessel	49745
Hickory Corners	49060
Higgins Lake	48627
Highland	48031
Highland Park, Br. Detroit	48203
Hillman	49746
Hillsdale (1st)	49242
Holland (1st)	49423
Castle Park, R. Br.	49422
Windmill Island, Sta.	49423
Holly (1st)	48442
Holt	48842
Holton	49425
Homer	49245
Honor	49640
Hope	48628
Hopkins	49328
Horton	49246
Houghton (1st)	49931
Houghton Lake	48629
Houghton Lake Heights	48630
Howard City	49329
Howell (1st)	48843
Hoxeyville	49641
Hubbard Lake	49747
Hubbardston	48845
Hubbell	49934
Hudson	49247
Hudsonville	49426
Hulbert	49748
Huntington Woods, Br. Royal Oak	48070
Ida	48140
Idlewild	49642
Imlay City	48444
Indian River	49749
Ingalls	49848
Inkster (1st)	48141
Interlochen	49643
Ionia (1st)	48846
Iron Mountain (1st)	49801
Iron River (1st)	49935
Alvin, R. Br.	49936
Irons	49644
Ironwood (1st)	49938
Ishpeming (1st)	49849
Isle Royale National Park, R. Br. Grand Portage M N.	55617
Ithaca	48847
JACKSON (1st) (see appendix)	
Jamestown	49427
Jasper	49248
Jeddo	48032
Jefferson, Sta. Detroit	48214
Jenison (1st)	49428
Jeroma	49249
Johannesburg	49751
Jones	49061
Jonesville (1st)	49250
Joyfield, Sta. Detroit	48228
K I Sawyer A F B, Br. Gwinn	49843

KALAMAZOO (1st) (see appendix)
Kaleva 49645
Kalkaska 49646
Karlin 49647
Kawkawlin 48631
Kearsarge, R. Br. Calumet 49942
Keego Harbor (1st) 48033
Kendall 49062
Kensington, Sta. Detroit 48224
Nent City 49330
Kenton 49943
Kentwood, Br. Grand Rapids 49508
Kercheval, Sta. Detroit (see appendix)
Kewadin 49648
Keweenaw Bay 49944
Kincheloe A F B, Br. Sault Sainte Marie 49788
Kinde 48445
Kingsford, Br. Iron Mountain 49801
Kingsley 49649
Kingston 48741
Kinross 49752
L'Anse 49946
La Salle 48145
Lachine 49753
Lacota 49063
Laingsburg 48848
Lake 48632
Lake Ann 49650
Lake City 49651
Lake George 48633
Lake Leelanau 49653
Lake Linden 49945
Lake Odessa 48849
Lake Orion (1st) 48035
Lakeland 48143
Lakeport, R. Br. Port Huron 48060
Lakeside 49116
Lakeview 48850
Lakeville 48036
Lambertville 48144
Lamont 49430
LANSING (1st) (see appendix)
Lapeer (1st) 48446
    Lum, R. Br. 48452
Lathrup Village, Br. Southfield 48075
Laurium, Br. Calumet 49913
Lawrence 49064
Lawton 49065
Le Graph, Br. Dearborn 48125
Le Roy 49655
Leland 49654
Lennon 48449
Leonard 48038
Leonidas 49066
Les Cheneaux Club, R. Br. Cedarville 49754
Leslie 49251
Levering 49755
Lewiston 49756
Lexington 48450
Limestone 49851
Lincoln 48742
Lincoln Park (1st) 48146
Linden 48451
Linwood, Sta. Detroit 48206
Linwood 48634
Litchfield 49252
Little Lake 49833

Livernois, Sta. Detroit 48210
LIVONIA (1st) (see appendix)
Long Lake 48743
Loretto, R. Br. Vulcan 49852
Lowell (1st) 49331
Ludington (1st) 49431
Lum, R. Br. Lapeer 48452
Luna Pier 48157
Lupton 48635
Luther 49656
Luzerne 48636
Lyons 48851
M Fifty Nine Plaza, Br. Pontiac 48054
Macatawa 49434
Mackinac Island 49757
Mackinaw City 49701
Madison Heights, Br. Royal Oak ...48071
Mancelona 49659
Manchester 48158
Manistee (1st) 49660
Manistique (1st) 49854
    Thompson, R. Br. 49889
Manitou Beach 49253
Manton 49663
Maple, Sta. Dearborn 48120
Maple City 49664
Maple Rapids 48853
Marcellus 49067
Marenisco 49947
Marine City 48039
Marion 49665
Marlette (1st) 48453
Marne 49435
Marquette (1st) 49855
Marshall (1st) 49068
Martin 49070
Marysville (1st) 48040
Mason (1st) 48854
Mass 49948
Mattawan 49071
Maybee, Br. Monroe 48161
Mayfield 49666
Mayville 48744
Mc Bain 49657
Mc Brides 48852
Mc Gregor, R. Br. Deckerville 48427
Mc Millan 49853
Mears 49436
Mecosta 49332
Melvin 48454
Melvindale, Br. Dearborn 48122
Memphis 48041
Mendon 49072
Menominee (1st) 49858
Merrill 48637
Merritt 49667
Merriweather 49949
Mesick 49668
Metamora 48455
Metropolitan Airport, Br. Detroit ..48242
Metz, R. Br. Posen 49758
Michigamme 49861
Michigan Avenue, Sta. Lansing (see appendix)
Michigan Center 49254
Middlebelt, R. Br. Romulus 48174
Middleton 48856
Middleville 49333
Midland (1st) 48640

Milan (1st) 48160
Milburg, R. Br. Benton Harbor 49022
Milford (1st) 48042
Millbrook 49334
Millersburg 49759
Millington 48746
Milwaukee Junction, Sta. Detroit ..48211
Minden City 48456
Mio 48647
Mohawk Eagle Harbor, R. Br. 49951
Moline 49335
Monroe (1st) 48161
Montague (1st) 49437
Montgomery 49255
Montrose 48457
Moore Park, R. Br. Three Rivers ...49093
Moorestown, R. Br. Lake City 49651
Moran 49760
Morenci 49256
Morley 49336
Morrice 48857
Moscow 49257
Mosherville 49258
Mott Park, Sta. Flint 48504
Mount Clemens (1st) 48043
    Selfridge A F B, Br. 48045
Mount Elliott, Sta. Detroit 48234
Mount Morris (1st) 48458
Mount Pleasant (1st) 48858
Muir 48860
Mullett Lake 49761
Mulliken 48861
Munger 48747
Munising (1st) 49862
Munith 49259
Munson 49260
MUSKEGON (1st) (see appendix)
Muskegon Heights, Br. Muskegon ..49444
Nadeau 49863
Nahma 49864
Napoleon 49261
Nashville 49073
National City 48748
National Mine 49865
Naubinway 49762
Nazareth 49074
Negaunee (1st) 49866
Nestoria 49867
New Baltimore 48047
New Boston 48164
New Buffalo (1st) 49117
New Era 49446
New Haven 48048
New Hudson 48165
New Lothrop 48460
New Richmond 49447
New Troy 49119
Newaygo 49337
Newberry (1st) 49868
Newport 48166
Niles (1st) 49120
Nisula 49952
North Adams 49262
North Bradley 48648
North Branch 48461
North End, Sta. Detroit (see

appendix)
North Escanaba, Sta.
  Escanaba........................49829
North Lansing, Sta. Lansing
  (see appendix)
North Muskegon, Br.
  Muskegon.......................49445
North Side, Sta. Flint..........48505
North Star..........................48862
North Street........................48049
Northeast, Sta. Livonia........48152
Northgate, Br. Grand
  Rapids...........................49505
Northland...........................49869
Northland Center, Sta.
  Southfield......................48075
Northport...........................49670
Northville (1st)....................48167
Northwestern, Sta. Detroit....48204
Norvell..............................49263
Norway..............................49870
Nottawa.............................49075
Novi (1st)...........................48050
Nunica...............................49448
Oak Grove.........................48863
Oak Park, Br. Detroit..........48237
Oak Ridge, Sta. Royal Oak...48073
Oakley...............................48649
Ocqueoc............................49763
Oden.................................49764
Okemos (1st). 48864
Old Mission........................49673
Olivet................................49076
Omena...............................49674
Omer.................................48749
Onaway.............................49765
Onekama...........................49675
Onondaga...........................49264
Onsted...............................49265
Ontonagon.........................49953
Orchard Lake, Br. Keego
  Harbor............................48033
Orleans..............................48865
Ortonville...........................48462
Oscoda (1st)........................48750
  Wurtsmith A F B, Br. 48753
Oshtemo.............................49077
Osseo................................49266
Ossineke.............................49766
Otisville.............................48643
Otsego (1st)........................49078
Ottawa Lake.......................49267
Otter Lake..........................48464
Ovid..................................48866
Owasippe, R. Br. Twin Lake...49457
Owendale...........................48754
Owosso (1st).......................48867
Oxford (1st)........................48051
Painesdale..........................49955
Palisades Park, R. Br.
  Covert............................49044
Palmer...............................49871
Palms................................48465
Palmyra.............................49268
Palo..................................48870
Paradise.............................49768
Parchment, Br Kalamazoo....49004
Paris.................................49338
Park Grove, Sta. Detroit......48205
Park Plaza, Sta. Lincoln
  Park...............................48146
Parma...............................49269
Paulding, R. Br. Bruce

Crossing............................49956
Paw Paw (1st).....................49079
Pearl Beach........................48052
Peck..................................48466
Pelkie...............................49958
Pellston.............................49769
Penobscot, Sta. Detroit........48226
Pentwater...........................49449
Perkins..............................49872
Perrinton...........................48871
Perronville..........................49873
Perry.................................48872
Petersburg..........................49270
Petoskey (1st).....................49770
Pewamo.............................48873
Pickford.............................49774
Pierson..............................49339
Pigeon...............................48755
Pinckney............................48169
Pinconning (1st)...................48650
Pittsford.............................49271
Plainwell (1st)......................49080
Plaza, Br. Battle Creek........49015
Pleasant Lake......................49272
Pleasant Ridge, Br. Royal
  Oak...............................48069
Plymouth (1st).....................48170
Pointe Aux Barques, R. Br.
  Port Austin......................48467
Pointe Aux Pins...................49775
Pompeii.............................48874
PONTIAC (1st) (see
  appendix)
Port Austin.........................48467
Port Hope...........................48468
Port Huron (1st)...................48060
Port Sanilac........................48469
Portage (1st).......................49081
Portland (1st)......................48875
Posen................................49776
  Metz, R. Br.....................49758
Potterville..........................48876
Powers..............................49874
Prattville............................49273
Prescott.............................48756
Presque Isle........................49777
Princeton, R. Br. Gwinn.......49875
Prudenville.........................48651
Pullman..............................49450
Quincy...............................49082
Quinnesec..........................49876
Raco.................................49778
Raisinville, R. Br. Monroe.....48161
Ralph................................49877
Ramsay..............................49959
Rapid City..........................49676
Rapid River........................49878
Ravenna............................49451
Reading.............................49274
Redford, Sta. Detroit...........48219
Redford Heights, Br. Detroit...48240
Reed City (1st)....................49677
Reeds Lake, Br. Grand
  Rapids...........................49506
Reese................................48757
Remus...............................49340
Republic.............................49879
Rhodes..............................48652
Richland.............................49083
Richmond (1st)....................48062
Richville.............................48758
Ridgeway............................49275
Riga..................................49276

River Rouge, Br. Detroit.......48218
Riverdale............................48877
Riverside............................49084
Riverview, Br. Wyandotte.....48192
Rives Junction.....................49277
Rochester (1st)....................48063
Rock.................................49880
Rockford (1st)......................49341
Rockland............................49960
Rockwood...........................48173
Rodney..............................49342
Rogers City (1st)..................49779
Rollin................................49278
Romeo (1st)........................48065
Romulus (1st)......................48174
Roosevelt Park, Br.
  Muskegon.......................49444
Roscommon........................48653
Rose City...........................48654
Rosebush...........................48878
Roseville (1st)......................48066
Rothbury............................49452
ROYAL OAK (1st) (see
  appendix)
Ruby, R. Br. Goodells..........48027
Rudyard.............................49780
Rumely, R. Br. Eben
  Junction..........................49826
Ruth..................................48470
SAGINAW (1st) (see
  appendix)
Sagola...............................49881
Saint Charles.......................48655
Saint Clair (1st)....................48079
SAINT CLAIR SHORES (1st)
  (see appendix)
Saint Helen.........................48656
Saint Ignace........................49781
Saint James........................49782
Saint Johns (1st)..................48879
Saint Joseph (1st)................49085
Saint Louis (1st)...................48880
Salem................................48175
Saline (1st).........................48176
Samaria.............................48177
Sand Creek.........................49279
Sand Lake..........................49343
Sandusky (1st).....................48471
Sanford.............................48657
Saranac (1st).......................48881
Saugatuck..........................49453
Sault Sainte Marie (1st).......49783
  Canal, Sta......................49783
  Kincheloe A F B, Br........49788
Sawyer..............................49125
Schaffer.............................49882
Schoolcraft.........................49087
Scotts................................49088
Scottville............................49454
Sears................................49679
Sebewaing.........................48759
Selfridge A F B, Br Mount
  Clemens.........................48045
Seneca..............................49280
Seney................................49883
Seven Oaks, Sta Detroit......48235
Seymour Square, Sta Grand
  Rapids...........................49510
Shaftsburg..........................48882
Shelby...............................49455
Shelbyville..........................49344
Shepherd............................48883

Sheridan 48884
Sherwood 49089
Shingleton 49884
Shopping Center, Br.
  Monroe 48161
Sidnaw 49961
Sidney 48885
Silverwood 48760
Sister Lakes, R. Br.
  Dowagiac 49047
Six Lakes 48886
Skandia 49885
Skanee 49962
Skidway Lake, R. Br.
  Prescott 48756
Smiths Creek 48074
Smyrna 48887
Snover 48472
Sodus 49126
Somerset 49281
Somerset Center 49282
South, Sta. Warren (see
  appendix)
South Boardman 49680
South Branch 48761
South Cedar Street Annex,
  Sta. Lansing (see
  appendix)
South Haven (1st) 49090
South Lyon (1st) 48178
South Range 49963
South Rockwood 48179
Southfield (1st) 48075
Southgate, Br. Wyandotte 48192
Southkent, Br. Grand
  Rapids 49508
Southland Center, Sta.
  Taylor 48180
Spalding 49886
Sparta (1st) 49345
Spring Arbor 49283
Spring Lake (1st) 49456
Springfield, Br. Battle Creek 49015
Springport 49284
Springwells, Sta. Detroit 48209
Spruce 48762
Stalwart 49789
Stambaugh 49964
Standish 48658
Stanton 48888
Stanwood 49346
State Center, Br. Saginaw 48602
Stephenson 49887
Sterling 48659
STERLING HEIGHTS (see
  appendix)
Stevensville (1st) 49127
Stockbridge 49285
Stony Lake, R. Br. Shelby 49455
Strathmoor, Sta. Detroit 48227
Stronach 49681
Strongs, R. Br. Eckerman 49790
Sturgis (1st) 49091
Sumner 48889
Sunfield 48890
Suttons Bay 49682
Swartz Creek (1st) 48473

Tawas City (1st) 48763
  Alabaster, R. Br. 48764
Taylor (1st) 48180
Tecumseh (1st) 49286
Tekonsha 49092
Teleford, Sta. Dearborn 48128
Temperance (1st) 48182
Thompson, R. Br.
  Manistique 49889
Thompsonville 49683
Three Oaks 49128
Three Rivers (1st) 49093
Tipton 49287
Toivola 49965
Topinabee 49791
Tower 49792
Township, Br. Ypsilanti 48197
Traunik 49890
Traverse City (1st) 49684
Trenary 49891
Trenton (1st) 48183
Trimountain 49366
Trout Creek 49967
Trout Lake 49793
Troy (1st) 48084
Trufant 49347
Turner 48765
Tuscola, R. Br. Vassar 48769
Tustin 49688
Twin Lake 49457
Twining 48766
Ubly 48475
Union, R. Br. Edwardsburg 49130
Union City 49094
Union Lake (1st) 48085
  Commerce, R. Br. 48085
  White Lake, R. Br. 48086
Union Pier 49129
Unionville 48767
University Center, R. Br. Bay
  City 48710
Urbandale, Sta. Battle
  Creek 49017
Utica (1st) 48087
  Sterling Heights, Br. 48077
Vandalia 49095
Vanderbilt 49795
Vandercook Lake, Br.
  Jackson 49203
Vassar (1st) 48768
  Tuscola, R. Br. 48769
Vermontville 49096
Vernon 48476
Vestaburg 48891
Veterans Administration
  Hosp. Sta. Iron Mountain ...49801
Vicksburg (1st) 49097
Vulcan 49892
  Loretto, R. Br. 49852
Wabaningo, R. Br. Whitehall 49463
Wakefield 49968
Waldron 49288
Walhalla 49458
Walker, Br. Grand Rapids 49504
Walkerville 49459
Wallace 49893
Walled Lake (1st) 48088

WARREN (1st) (see
  appendix)
Washington 48094
Waterford (1st) 48095
Waters 49797
Watersmeet 49969
Watervliet 49098
Watton 49970
Waverly, Br. Lansing 48917
Wayland (1st) 49348
Wayne (1st) 48184
  Westland, Br. 48185
Webberville 48892
Weidman 48893
Wells 48894
Wellston 49689
Wequetonsing, Br. Harbor
  Springs 49740
West Bay, Br. Traverse City ...49684
West Branch (1st) 48661
West Main Street, Sta.
  Midland 48640
West Olive 49460
Westland, Br. Wayne 48185
Weston 49289

Westphalia 48894
Wetmore 49895
Wheeler 48662
White Cloud 49349
White Lake, R. Br. Union
  Lake 48085
White Pigeon 49099
White Pine 49971
Whitefish Point 49798
Whitehall (1st) 49461
  Wabaningo, R. Br. 49463
Whitmore Lake 48189
Whittaker 48190
Whittemore 48770
Williamsburg 49690
Williamston 48895
Willis 48191
Wilson 49895
Windmill Island, Sta.
  Holland 49423
Winn 48895
Winona 49972
Wixom (1st) 48096
Wolf Lake, Br. Muskegon 49442
Wolverine 49799
Woodhaven, Br. Trenton 48183
Woodland 48897
Wurtsmith A F B, Br.
  Oscoda 48753
Wyandotte (1st) 48192
Wyoming, Br. Grand Rapids ...49509
Wyoming Park, Br. Grand
  Rapids 49509
Yale 48097
Ypsilanti (1st) 48197
Zeeland (1st) 49464

ANN ARBOR   481

POST OFFICE BOXES

Box Nos.

A-D	Main Office	06
1-999	Downtown Sta	07
A-1-D-1	Main Office	06
1000-2199	Main Office Sta	06

RURAL ROUTES

1	03
2	05
3,4	03
5	04
6	05

STATIONS, BRANCHES AND UNITS

Downtown Sta	07
General Delivery	06
Postmaster	06

APARTMENTS, HOTELS, MOTELS

Alpine Manor, 1500 Pine Valley	04
Ann Arbor, Woods, 2167 Medford	04
Apartments Limited, 611 Church	04
Arbor Forest, 721 Forest Ave	04
Arbor Hills, 2000 Huron Pky	04
Arbor Lodge, 3245 Washtenaw Ave	04
Arbor Park, 2505 Ellsworth Rd E	04
Arbor Valley, 1500 Plymouth Rd	05
Bell Tower Motor Inn, 300 S Thayer	04
Brookside, 1513 Jones Dr	05
Campus Inn, 605 E Huron	08
Chapel Hill Townhouses, 300 Green Rd	05
Chatham Village, 2000 Pauline Blvd	03
Colonial Square, 3012 Williamsburg	04
Forest Plaza, 715 Forest Ave	04
Geddes Lakes Townhouses, Lakehaven Dr	05
Georgetown Manor, 2800 Page Ave	04
Glencoe Hills, 2236 Glencoe Hills Dr	04
Greenbrier, 3505 Greenbrier Dr	05
Hearth Stone, 1500 Pine Valley	04
Hillside Manor, 2000 Commerce	03
Holiday Inn-East, 3750 Washtenaw Ave	04
Holiday Inn-West, 2900 Jackson Ave	03
Howard Johnsons Motor Lodge, 2380 Carpenter Rd	04
Huron Towers, 2220 Fuller Rd	05
Imperial, 2315 Packard	04

Independence, 2407 Packard	04
Inn America, 3250 Washtenaw Ave	04
Island Drive, 1000 Island Dr	05
Lamp Post, 2424 E Stadium Blvd	04
Longshore Town Houses, 517 Kellogg	05
Maiden Lane, 1102 Maiden Ln Ct	05
Maple Ridge Manor, 2200 Dexter Ave	03
Maynard House, 400 Maynard	08
Michigan League, 227 S Ingalls	04
Michigan Union, 530 S State	04
Park Plaza, 1320 S University	04
Pontiac Hts Cooperative, 2319 Arrow Wood Trl	05
Ramada Inn, 126 E Huron	08
Ramada Inn, 2800 Jackson Ave	03
River House, 1200 Island Dr	05
Riverside Park Pl, 1050 Wall	05
Spruce Knob, 2960 Birch Hollow Dr	04
Statler Hilton-Inn, 610 Hilton Dr	04
Strawberry Hill, 2738 Golfside	04
Tiffany 1 & 2 731 & 736 Packard	04
Tower Plaza, 555 E. William	08
Town & Country, 2578 Carpenter Rd	04
Traver Knoll, 1023 Barton Dr	05
University Towers, 536 Forest Ave	04
University Towne Houses, 2505 Ellsworth Rd E	04
University, 1000 Broadway	05
Village Green, Village Green Ln	05
Village Green, 4800 Washtenaw Ave	04
Walden Hills, 2102-2120 Pauline Blvd	03
Weber'S Inn, 3050 Jackson Ave	03
Woodbury Gardens, 1865 Woodbury Ave	04
Woodland Hills, 4300 Packard	04
Ym-Ywca, 350 S 5th Ave	08

BUILDINGS

Ann Arbor Trust, 100 S Main	08
Brooks, 201 E Liberty	08
City Center, 220 E Huron	08
City Hall, 100 N 5th Ave	08
County, 101 E Huron	08
First National, 201 S Main	08
Fritz, 103 E Liberty	08
Gunn, 506 E Liberty	08
Huron Valley Bank, 125 S 5th Ave	08
Hutzel, 110 E Liberty	08
Kresge, 204 S Main	08
Michigan Theatre, 601 E Liberty	08

Municipal Court, 110 W Huron	08
National Bank & Trust, 125 S Main	08
National Sanitation Foundation, 3475 Plymouth Rd	06
Nickels Arcade, 300 Maynard	08
Professional, 425 E Washington	08
Trick, 725 N University	04
Wolverine, 202 E Washington	08

HOSPITALS

Mercywood, 4038 Jackson Rd Po Box 1127	06
Parkview Medical Center, 1000 Wall	05
St Joseph Mercy, 326 N Ingalls	04
University, 1405 E Ann	04
Veterans, 2215 Fuller	05

UNIVERSITIES AND COLLEGES

Concordia, 4090 Geddes Rd	05
University Of Michigan, Central Campus	04
University Of Michigan, North Campus	05
Washtenaw Community, 204 E Huron Po Box 345	07

BATTLE CREEK   490

RURAL ROUTES

| 1,2,3,4,5,6,7,8,9,10,11,12,13, 14 | 17 |

STATIONS, BRANCHES AND UNITS

Plaza Br	15
Springfield Br	15
Urbandale Sta	17
General Delivery	16
Postmaster	16

APARTMENTS, HOTELS, MOTELS

Cherry Hill Manor	17
Hart Hotel, 31 N Washington	14
Holiday Inn, Capital Ave & I 94	15
Howard Johnson'S Motor Lodge, 2590 Capital Ave SW	15
Kellogg Inn, 258 Champion	17
Williams House, 46 E Michigan Ave	14

BUILDINGS

Capital, 37 Capital Ave NE	14
City Hall, E Michigan Ave	14
Federal Bldg, 50 N Washington	17
Michigan Nat Bank Bldg, 1 W Michigan Ave	14

Battle Creek (Con.)   490

Post Bldg. 65 W Michigan Ave	14
Security Tower, 25 W Michigan Ave	14
Wolverine Tower, 70 W Michigan Ave	14

HOSPITALS

American Legion, Evergreen Rd	16
Battle Creek Sanitarium, 197 N Washington	16
Community, 200 Tompkins	16
Lakeview General, 80 N 20th	15
Leila Y Post, 9 Emmett	16
Veterans Administration	16

BIRMINGHAM   480

POST OFFICE BOXES

Box Nos.		
1-547	Main Office	12

STATIONS, BRANCHES AND UNITS

Franklin Br	25
General Delivery	12
Postmaster	12

DEARBORN   481

POST OFFICE BOXES

Box Nos.		
1-1999	Main Office	21
2001-2599	Fort Dearborn Sta	23
3001-3399	Melvindale Br	22
4001-4699	Maple St Sta	26
5001-5399	Teleford Sta	28

•STATIONS, BRANCHES AND UNITS

Fort Dearborn Sta	23
Greenfield Village Sta	20
Le Graph Sta	25
Maple Sta	20
Melvindale Br	22
Teleford Sta	28
General Delivery	20
Postmaster	20

APARTMENTS, HOTELS, MOTELS

Congress Inn 12000 Michigan Avenue	26
Dearborn Inn 20301 Oakwood Blvd	24
Dearborn Towers 22700 Garrison	24
Dearborn Towne House 2101 S Telegraph Rd	24

DETROIT   482

POST OFFICE BOXES

Box Nos.		
A-D	Kensington Sta	24
A-L	Grand River Sta	08
U-Z	North End Sta	02
1-86	Kensington Sta	24
1-87	Brightmoor Sta	23
1-120	Ferndale Br	20
1-121	River Rouge Br	18
1-149	Hamtramck Br	12
1-1130	College Park Sta	21
1-3199	Fort Shelby Sta	31
A 1/2 1-A-1599	General Post Office Sta	32
401-548	Northwestern Sta	04
601-746	Linwood Sta	06
1962-1968	Seven Oaks Sta	35
3201-3389	Jefferson Sta	14
3401-3671	Highland Park Br	03
3701-3786	Kercheval Sta	15
3701-3846	Oak Park Br	37
3801-3886	Park Grove Sta	05
3901-4016	Strathmoor Sta	27
4401-4486	Joyfield Sta	28
4501-4587	Ecorse Br	29
4601-6486	Mount Elliott Sta	34
4701-4949	Redford Sta	19
5001-5244	Grosse Pointe Br	36
5001-5399	Seven Oaks Sta	35
5301-5446	Milwaukee Junction Sta	11
5501-5616	Fenkell Sta	38
5701-5816	Beech Br	39
5901-6017	Livernois Sta	10
6501-6724	Redford Heights Br	40
6801-6884	Grosse Pointe Br	36
7001-7499	North End Sta	02
7501-7699	Springwells Sta	09
7701-7899	Gratiot Sta	07
7901-8017	Kercheval Sta	15
8100-8399	Harper Sta	13
8501-8699	Kensington Sta	24
8851-8938	Oak Park Br	37
9101-9154	Springwells Sta	09
9501-9590	North End Sta	02
03001-03999	Highland Park Br	03
05001-05999	Park Grove Sta	05
08001-08999	Grand River Sta	08
10001-10199	Livernois	18
14001-14999	Jefferson Sta	14
27001-27999	Strathmoor Sta	27
35001-35999	Seven Oaks Sta	35

STATIONS, BRANCHES AND UNITS

Beech Br	39
Brightmoor Sta	23
College Park Sta	21
Detroit River Sta	22
Eastland Center Br	36
Ecorse Br	29
Fenkell Sta	38
Ferndale Br	20
Fisher Building Sta	02
Fort Shelby Sta	26
General Post Office Sta	32
Grand Circus Park Sta	26
Grand River Sta	08
Gratiot Sta	07
Grosse Pointe Br	36
Hamtramck Br	12
Harper Sta	13
Harper Woods Br	36
Highland Park Br	03
Jefferson Sta	14
Joyfield Sta	28
Kensington Sta	24
Kercheval Sta	15
Linwood Sta	06
Livernois Sta	10
Metropolitan Airport Br	42
Milwaukee Junction Sta	11
Mount Elliott Sta	34
North End Sta	01
Northwestern Sta	04
Oak Park Br	37
Park Grove Sta	05
Penobscot Sta	26
Redford Sta	19
Redford Heights Br	40
River Rouge Br	18
Seven Oaks Sta	35
Springwells Sta	09
Strathmoor Sta	27
General Delivery	02
Postmaster	33

APARTMENTS, HOTELS, MOTELS

Abington, 700 Seward	02
Alden Park Manor, 8100 Jefferson E	14
American, 408 Temple	01
Chateau Frontenac, 10410 Jefferson E	14
Executive House, 114 Adams W	26
International Inn, 5440 Cass	02
Jeffersonian, 9000 Jefferson E	14
Lafayette Towers, 1321 Orleans	07
Lafayette Townhouses, 1321 Nicolet Pl	07
Leland House, 1701 Cass	26
Madison-Lenox, 230 Madison	26
Park Shelton, 15 Kirby E	02
Pavilion, 1 Lafayette Plaisance	07

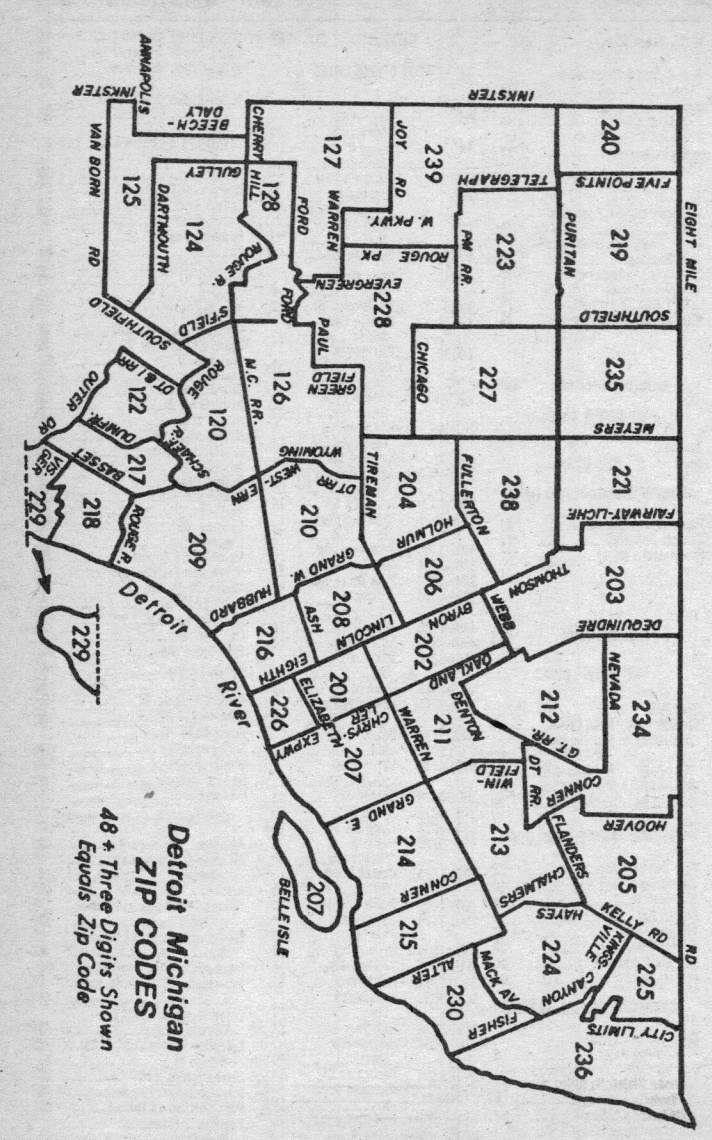

Detroit Michigan
ZIP CODES

48 + Three Digits Shown
Equals Zip Code

Detroit (Con.)　　　　482

Pick-Fort Shelby, 525
　Lafayette Blvd....................　31
Pontchartrain, 2 Washington
　Blvd..................................　26
River House Cooperative
　Incorporated, 8900
　Jefferson E........................　14
Saint Regis, 3017 Grand
　Blvd W.............................　02
Seventy West Apts, 70
　Alexandrine W...................　01
Seville, 3160 2nd Blvd.........　01
Sheraton-Cadillac, 1114
　Washington Blvd................　31
Statler Hilton, 1539
　Washington Blvd................　31
Town House, 1511 1st..........　26
Tuller, 521 Park Ave.............　26
Whittier, 415 Burns Dr.........　14

BUILDINGS

Book Or Tower, 1249
　Washington Blvd................　26
Boulevard Center, 6560
　Cass.................................　02
Boulevard, 7310 Woodward...　26
Broderick Tower, 10 Witherell.　26
Buhl, 535 Griswold...............　26
Cadillac Square Or Tower,
　Cadillac Sq & Bates...........　26
City-County, 2 Woodward.....　26
Club-Exchange, 150 Bagley....　26
Commonwealth, 719
　Griswold............................　26
David Stott, 1150 Griswold....　26
David Whitney, 1553
　Woodward.........................　26
Federal, 231 Lafayette Blvd...　26
First Federal, 1001
　Woodward.........................　26
First National, 660
　Woodward.........................　26
Fisher, 3011 Grand Blvd W....　02
Ford, 615 Griswold...............　26
Free Press, 321 Lafayette
　Blvd..................................　26
General Motors, 3044 Grand
　Blvd W.............................　02
Griswold Building, 1214
　Griswold............................　26
Guardian, 500 Griswold.........　26
Kales, 76 Adams W...............　26
Lafayette, 149 Michigan........　26
Metropolitan, 33 John R........　26
Michigan, 220 Bagley............　26
New Center, 7430 2nd Blvd....　02
Penobscot, 645 Griswold.......　26
Professional, 10 Peterboro ....　01
Water Board, 735 Randolph ...　26

HOSPITALS

Detroit General, Macomb &
　St Antoine.........................　26
Grace, 4160 John R...............　01
Harper, 3825 Brush...............　01
Henry Ford, 2799 Grand Blvd
　W.....................................　02
Herman Kiefer, Hamilton &
　Taylor................................　02
Highland Park General, 369

Glendale..............................　03
Hutzel, 432 Hancock E..........　01
Mt Carmel Mercy, 6071 Outer
　Dr W.................................　35
Saint John, 22101 Moross
　Rd....................................　36
Saint Joseph Mercy, 2200
　Grand Blvd E.....................　11
Sinai, 6767 Outer Dr W.........　35

UNIVERSITIES AND COLLEGES

Detroit College Of Law, 130
　Elizabeth E........................　01
Detroit Institute Of
　Technology, 2300 Park
　Ave...................................　01
Marygrove, 8425 Mc Nichols
　Rd W................................　21
Mercy College, 8200 Outer Dr
　W.....................................　19
University Of Detroit, 4001
　Mcnichols Rd W.................　21
Wayne State College Of
　Medicine, 540 Canfield E....　01
Wayne State University, 4841
　Cass.................................　02

NAMED STREETS

A Ct....................................　20
Aaron..................................　07
Abbott
　1-199................................　18
　400-1399...........................　26
　1400-OUT..........................　16
Abington Ave
　6300-9499..........................　28
　9500-OUT..........................　27
Abington Rd
　6300-9499..........................　28
　9500-OUT..........................　27
Acacia
　15500-18099.......................　27
　18100-23999.......................　23
　24000-25499.......................　39
Academy..............................　20
Ackley.................................　11
Adair...................................　07
Adams Ct.............................　07
Adams St E & W...................　26
Addison...............................　10
Adelaide
　1-899................................　01
　900-OUT............................　07
Adele...................................　11
Adeline................................　03
Afton Rd..............................　03
Agnes
　200-499.............................　29
　6800-7199..........................　07
　7200-OUT..........................　14
Akron..................................　12
Alameda..............................　03
Alaska.................................　04
Albany
　100-1799............................　20
　8200-15499.........................　37
　18000-20699.......................　34
Albert..................................　19
Alberta................................　20
Albion..................................　34

Alcoy...................................　05
Alden...................................　38
Alderton..............................　19
Alexander.............................　18
Alexander Ct.........................　29
Alexandrine E
　1-899................................　01
　900-OUT............................　07
Alexandrine W
　1-1399..............................　01
　1400-OUT..........................　08
Alexis St E & W....................　29
Alfred
　1-899................................　01
　900-OUT............................　07
Alger
　1-899................................　02
　900-OUT............................　11
Alger Pl
　1-99.................................　30
Algonac
　12000-17099.......................　05
　17100-OUT.........................　34
Algonquin.............................　15
Alice...................................　12
Aline Dr...............................　36
Allard Ave & Rd....................　36
Allen
　100-1799............................　20
　13600-OUT.........................　37
Allen Pl...............................　04
Allendale..............................　04
Allonby................................　27
Alma...................................　05
Almont
　1800-2199..........................　20
　8000-OUT..........................　34
Alpena................................　12
Alpha..................................　12
Alpine..................................　04
Alstead................................　36
Alter Rd
　1-4999..............................　15
　5000-OUT..........................　24
Alton...................................　39
Alwar...................................　05
Alwyne Ln............................　03
American
　7200-7999..........................　10
　8000-OUT..........................　04
Amherst...............................　09
Amity...................................　14
Amrad..................................　34
Amsterdam............................　02
Anatole................................　36
Anchor St E & W...................　18
Anderdon
　2100-4999..........................　15
　5000-OUT..........................　13
Anderson S............................　09
Andover................................　03
Andrus.................................　12
Anglin
　13400-17999.......................　12
　18000-OUT.........................　34
Anita
　500-2299...........................　36
　19600-OUT.........................　25
Ann Arbor Trl
　20000-20198 (EVEN)............　28
　22700-23299.......................　39
Anna Pl................................　11

Detroit (Con.) — 482

Annabelle
1200-2499 ... 26
Annabelle S
1000-3799 ... 17
Annapolis ... 04
Annchester Rd ... 19
Annin ... 13
Annland ... 03
Annott ... 04
Annsbury ... 85
9000-11499 ... 13
11500-OUT ... 05
Anson ... 09
Anstell ... 13
Anthon ... 09
Anthony Wayne Dr
4800-4999 ... 81
5000-OUT ... 82
Antietam Ave & Rd ... 67
Antoinette
1-1399 ... 62
1400-OUT ... 08
Antwerp ... 34
Anvil ... 05
Apple ... 28
Apolegrove ... 19
Appleton
8800-12599 ... 39
12600-16099 ... 23
16100-OUT ... 19
Appoline
8000-9499 ... 28
9500-16099 ... 27
16100-OUT ... 35
Arcadia ... 04
Archdale
6300-9499 ... 28
9500-16099 ... 27
16100-OUT ... 35
Archer ... 19
Arcola ... 34
Arden Park Blvd ... 02
Ardmore
12600-16099 ... 27
16100-OUT ... 35
Ardmore Dr ... 20
Argus ... 03
Argyle Cres ... 19
Arizona St E & W ... 03
Arlington ... 12
Armada ... 12
Armour ... 13
Army ... 09
Arndt ... 07
Arnold
8100-8599 ... 16
8800-OUT ... 39
Artesian
5600-12599 ... 28
12600-OUT ... 23
Arthur ... 25
Asa ... 04
Asbury Park
6300-9499 ... 28
9500-16099 ... 27
16100-OUT ... 35
Ash ... 08
Ashland ... 15
Ashley ... 36
Ashton Ave

5608-12599 ... 28
12600-16099 ... 23
16100-OUT ... 19
Ashton Rd
5600-12599 ... 28
12600-16099 ... 23
16100-OUT ... 19
Astor ... 13
Athens ... 13
Atkinson
1-1399 ... 62
1400-OUT ... 06
Atlants ... 13
Atlas ... 11
Atwater
1-899 ... 26
900-OUT ... 13
Aubrey ... 39
Auburn
5800-12599 ... 28
12600-OUT ... 23
Auburn St E & W ... 29
Auburndale ... 03
Audrey ... 35
Audubon Ave
1000-3399 ... 30
3400-OUT ... 24
Audubon Rd
1000-3399 ... 30
3400-OUT ... 24
August ... 05
Aurora ... 04
Austin ... 16
Avalon ... 03
Averhill Ct ... 15
Avery ... 09
Avis ... 30
Avon Ave
15400-16099 ... 23
16100-20699 ... 19
20700-OUT ... 37
Avon Ct
500-1199 ... 36
Avon Rd
15400-16099 ... 23
16100-20699 ... 19
20700-OUT ... 37
Avondale
12300-14999 ... 15
15000-OUT ... 30
B ... 16
B Ct ... 20
Bacon ... 09
Badger ... 13
Bagley
100-1399 ... 26
1400-3999 ... 16
4000-OUT ... 09
Baker ... 30
Baldwin
500-4999 ... 14
5000-OUT ... 13
Balfour Ave
600-3399 ... 38
3400-11999 ... 24
13600-14999 (OP) ... 37
19200-OUT ... 25
Balfour Rd
600-3399 ... 30
3400-11999 ... 24
13600-14999 (OP) ... 37
19200-OUT ... 25
Ballantyne Ct E & W ... 36

Ballantyne Rd ... 36
Balmoral Ave & Dr ... 03
Baltimore St E & W ... 02
Baltree Ct ... 36
Bangor Ave & Ct ... 10
Bank ... 09
Banmoor ... 28
Barbara
21400-22599 ... 23
26600-27399 ... 39
Barclay Rd ... 36
Barham ... 24
Barker ... 13
Barlow ... 05
Barium ... 10
Barnes ... 09
Barr ... 04
Barrett ... 13
Barrington Rd ... 30
Barron ... 09
Barry ... 14
Bartlett ... 03
Barton ... 10
Basil ... 35
Bassett S ... 17
Batavia ... 18
Bates ... 26
Baubee ... 10
Bauman ... 03
Baylis
15300-16099 ... 38
16100-OUT ... 21
Bayside S ... 17
Beach ... 29
Beacon ... 26
Beacon Hill Rd ... 36
Beaconsfield Ave
500-3399 ... 30
3400-19199 ... 24
19200-20699 ... 25
Beaconsfield Rd
500-3399 ... 30
3400-19199 ... 24
19200-20699 ... 25
Beals ... 14
Beaman ... 15
Beard ... 08
Beatrice S ... 17
Beaubien
200-2099 ... 26
2100-4999 ... 01
5000-OUT ... 02
Beaufait
400-4999 ... 07
5000-6199 ... 11
19800-21799 (HW) ... 25
Beaufait Dr
1700-2199 (GPW) ... 36
Beaufield ... 20
Beaumont ... 09
Beaupre Ln & Rd ... 36
Beaverland
7200-12599 ... 39
12600-16099 ... 23
16100-OUT ... 19
Bedford Ave
700-3399 ... 36
3400-OUT ... 24
Bedford Ln
600-699 ... 30
Bedford Rd
700-3399 ... 36

Detroit (Con.) 482

3400-OUT ....
Beech.................................. 26
Beech Ct 39
Beech Daly Rd
  8800-16099........................ 39
  16100-20699........................ 40
Beechdale............................ 04
Beechton.............................. 10
Beechwood
  200-599.............................. 18
  5700-7299........................... 10
  7300-OUT........................... 04
Begole................................. 10
Beland................................. 34
Belanger.............................. 36
Belden
  15400-16099........................ 38
  16100-OUT.......................... 21
Belfast................................ 10
Bell.................................... 29
Belle................................... 09
Belleterre............................. 04
Bellevue
  400-4999............................ 07
  5000-OUT........................... 11
Belmont
  1-899............................... 02
  1900-OUT........................... 12
Belton
  2100-12699.......................... 04
  12700-21959......................... 28
  22000-OUT.......................... 39
Belvid ...
  1200-4999........................... 14
  5000-OUT........................... 13
Benham............................... 11
Beniteau
  1-4999.............................. 14
  5000-OUT........................... 13
Bennett
  21300-24999......................... 19
  25000-27399......................... 40
Bennette St E & W................... 20
Benson................................ 07
Benson St E & W..................... 29
Bentler Ave
  12600-16099......................... 23
  16100-20699......................... 19
Bentler Ct............................ 19
Benton
  400-899............................. 01
  900-OUT............................ 07
Berden
  16500-18899......................... 24
  18900-19199......................... 36
  19200-OUT.......................... 25
Beresford............................. 03
Berg Rd............................... 19
Berkeley Rd........................... 21
Berkley............................... 37
Berkshire Ave
  700-3399............................ 30
  3400-OUT........................... 24
Berkshire Pl.......................... 36
Berkshire Rd
  700-3399............................ 30
  3400-OUT........................... 24
Bermuda.............................. 20
Bernard............................... 12
Berns Ct.............................. 36

Berres................................ 12
Berry................................. 34
Bertha................................ 20
Berwyn................................ 39
Bessemore............................ 13
Bethlawn.............................. 20
Bethune E............................ 02
Bethune W
  1-1399.............................. 02
  1400-OUT........................... 06
Bethune Pl N
  21000-21499......................... 20
Bethune Pl S
  21000-21499......................... 20
Beverly............................... 37
Beverly Ct............................ 04
Beverly Rd............................ 36
Bewick
  1400-4999........................... 14
  5000-OUT........................... 13
Biarritz Cir........................... 37
Biddle................................ 0f
Biltmore
  14800-16099......................... 27
  16100-OUT.......................... 3!
Binder
  17800-17999......................... 12
  18000-OUT.......................... 34
Bingham.............................. 28
Birch................................. 27
Birch Ln.............................. 36
Birchcrest Dr......................... 21
Birwood
  8000-12599.......................... 04
  12600-16099......................... 38
  16100-OUT.......................... 21
Bishop Ave
  1-3399.............................. 30
  3400-11099.......................... 24
  14400-OUT.......................... 37
Bishop Ln............................ 30
Bishop Rd
  1-3399.............................. 30
  3400-11099.......................... 24
  14400-OUT.......................... 37
Bivouac.............................. 09
Blackmoor........................... 34
Blackstone Ave
  12600-16099......................... 23
  16100-20699......................... 19
  21900-OUT.......................... 37
Blackstone Ct........................ 19
Blaine
  1-1399.............................. 02
  1400-3999........................... 06
  4000-OUT........................... 04
Blair................................. 13
Blairmoor Ave & Ct................... 36
Blake................................. 03
Bliss................................. 34
Bloom
  11800-17999......................... 12
  18000-OUT.......................... 34
Bloomfield Rd........................ 21
Bloomsburg Pl........................ 07
Blossom Ln........................... 37
Blowers.............................. 04
Bluehill.............................. 24
Blythe................................ 28
Boeing............................... 39
Boleyn............................... 24
Bondie............................... 29

Bonita................................ 24
Bonner............................... 20
Bonzanno............................ 29
Bordeau.............................. 04
Borgman............................. 37
Borman.............................. 28
Bortle................................ 14
Boston Blvd E........................ 02
Boston Blvd W
  1-1399.............................. 02
  1400-3999........................... 06
  4000-OUT........................... 04
Bostwick.............................. 09
Bosworth Ct.......................... 19
Botsford.............................. 12
Boulder............................... 05
Bourassa............................. 29
Bourke............................... 38
Bournemouth......................... 25
Bournemouth Cir & Rd............... 36
Boxwood.............................. 10
Boyd.................................. 09
Brace................................. 28
Braden............................... 10
Bradford
  11400-11499......................... 13
  11500-OUT.......................... 05
Bradley............................... 14
Brady Ave
  900-1399............................ 07
  8800-16099.......................... 39
  16100-OUT.......................... 40
Brady Ct.............................. 39
Braile
  7200-12599.......................... 28
  12600-16099......................... 23
  16100-OUT.......................... 19
Brainard
  400-1399............................ 01
  1400-OUT........................... 08
Bramell
  7200-12599.......................... 39
  12600-16099......................... 23
  16100-OUT.......................... 19
Bramford............................. 34
Brandon.............................. 09
Breakfast Dr.......................... 39
Breckenridge
  3200-3399........................... 08
  8100-OUT........................... 37
Breckenridge St E & W............... 20
Bremen............................... 24
Brennan.............................. 09
Brentwood E
  400-1899............................ 03
  1900-OUT........................... 34
Brentwood W......................... 03
Bretton Dr............................ 23
Brewster
  400-899............................. 01
  900-OUT............................ 07
Briar Dr.............................. 37
Briarcliff Dr
  1-1199 (GPS)........................ 36
Briarcliff Pl
  1-1199 (GPS)........................ 36
Briarcliff Rd
  19900-20499......................... 21
Brickley.............................. 20
Brierstone............................ 25
Brighton.............................. 03
Brimson.............................. 12

Detroit (Con.)   482

Bringard Dr	05
Brinker	34
Brinket	14
Bristol Pl	16
Bristow	12
Britain	24
Broadstone Ave	25
Broadstone Rd	36
Broadstreet Ave	
9200-12599	04
12600-OUT	38
Broadstreet Blvd	
9200-12599	04
12600-OUT	38
Broadway	
1-99	29
1200-OUT	26
Brock	05
Brockton	11
Brombach	12
Brooklyn	
1200-2099	26
2100-4999	01
5000-OUT	02
Brooks	15
Brown Pl	08
Browning	20
Brownlee	18
Bruce	14
Bruckner	10
Brunswick	24
Brush	
200-2099	26
2100-4999	01
5000-11699	02
11700-OUT	03
Bryanston Cres	07
Bryant	08
Bryden	
7200-7999	10
8000-OUT	04
Brys Dr N & S	35
Bryson	03
Buchanan	
2000-3999	08
4000-OUT	10
Buckingham Ave	
1000-3399	30
3400-OUT	24
Buckingham Rd	
1000-3399	30
3400-OUT	24
Buelow Ct	09
Buena Vis E	03
Buena Vis W	
1-1399	03
1400-12699	38
12700-OUT	27
Buffalo Ave	
5500-17999	12
18000-OUT	34
Buffalo Ct	12
Buhl	14
Buhr	12
Bulwer	10
Burchill Ct	13
Burdeno	09
Burdette	20
Burger	12
Burgess Ave	

13900-16099	23
16100-OUT	19
Burgess Ct	19
Burke	18
Burlage Pl	07
Burlingame	
1-1399	02
1400-3999	06
4000-OUT	04
Burlington Dr	03
Burnette	
7200-7999	10
8000-OUT	04
Burns Ave	
1-4999	14
5000-OUT	13
Burns Dr	14
Burnside	12
Burrell Pl	08
Burroughs	02
Burt Ct	
20900-20999	23
Burt Rd	
8000-12599	28
12600-16099	23
16100-20699	19
Burton	
4400-4799	10
10000-OUT	37
Burwell	10
Bushey	10
Butler	11
Butternut	16
Byron	
1-399	18
7300-11699	02
11700-OUT	03
C	16
Cabot	
1900-3599	09
3600-OUT	10
Cadet	09
Cadieux Rd	
300-3399	30
3400-OUT	24
Cadillac Ave	
1300-4999	14
5000-OUT	13
Cadillac Blvd	
1300-4999	14
5000-OUT	13
Cadillac Sq	26
Caely	12
Cahalan	09
Cairney	13
Caldwell	
12800-17999	12
18000-OUT	34
California	03
Calumet	
800-1399	01
1400-OUT	08
Calvert	
1-1399	02
1400-OUT	06
Calvin	36
Cambourne St E & W	20
Cambridge Ave	
1-199	36
2800-12699	21
12700-18099	35
18100-24999	19
25000-27399	40

Cambridge Rd	
1-199	36
2800-12699	21
12700-18099	35
18100-24999	19
25000-27399	40
Cambridge St N & S	21
Camden	
300-1899	20
11300-OUT	13
Cameron	
7300-11699	11
11700-OUT	03
Cameron Pl	30
Camille	15
Camley	24
Campbell	
1-599 (RR)	18
100-2699	09
Campbell S	
100-599	09
Campus Martius	26
Candler	03
Canfield E	
1-899	01
900-7199	07
7200-11999	14
12000-OUT	15
Canfield W	
1-1399	01
1400-OUT	08
Caniff	
900-1619	11
1620-OUT	12
Canonbury	05
Canterbury Rd	
400-1199	36
19100-OUT	21
Canton	
400-4999	07
5000-OUT	11
Canyon	36
Capital	37
Capitol	
12700-18099	27
18100-21999	28
22000-26599	39
Carbon	09
Carbondale	04
Cardoni	
8700-11699	11
11700-OUT	03
Carleton	14
Carlin	
8000-9499	28
9500-OUT	27
Carlisle	05
Carman	03
Carmel	
900-1199	03
Carmel Ln	
1-99	36
Carol	
16000-16099	39
20000-OUT	35
Caroline	
1-99	30
1900-OUT	08
Carpenter	12
Carrie	
6500-10499	11
10500-17999	12
18000-OUT	34

Detroit (Con.) 482	
Carson	09
Carten	14
Carter	
2600-3999	06
4000-OUT	04
Cartridge	09
Carver	36
Cascade	04
Casgrain	09
Casino	24
Casmere	12
Casper	
2300-3599	09
3600-OUT	10
Cass	
500-2099	26
2100-4999	01
5000-OUT	02
Castle	34
Castleton	27
Catalpa Ct	20
Cathedral	
15500-21999	28
22000-27399	39
Catherine	18
Cavalry	09
Cavalry S	10
Cecil	09
Cedar	09
Cedar Ct	25
Cedargrove	05
Cedarhurst Pl	03
Cedarlawn	04
Celeron	09
Celestine	05
Celia	08
Centerbrook	36
Central	
700-3599	09
900-2099 (FER)	20
3600-7999	10
8000-OUT	04
Centralia	
8800-16099	39
16100-20699	40
Centre	26
Chadwick	27
Chalfonte	
1-599	36
3100-12699	38
12700-18099	27
17500-17799 (GPC)	30
18100-OUT	23
Chalmers	
200-4999	15
5000-11499	13
11500-OUT	05
Chamberlain	09
Champine Pl	36
Chandler	02
Chandler Park Dr	
13000-14399	13
14400-18599	24
18600-OUT	36
Channing	20
Chapel	
12600-16099	23
16100-OUT	19
Chapin	13
Chapman	37
Charest	

9300-17999	12
18000-OUT	34
Charlemagne	13
Charles	
1-299	18
3800-6299	12
17500-OUT	30
Charleston	03
Charlevoix	
1-299	36
2600-7199	07
7200-11999	14
12000-14999	15
15000-17899	30
20700-OUT	36
Charlotte	20
Charlotte	
1-899	01
Charlotte E	
1-99	29
Charlotte W	
1-99	29
Chateaufort Pl	07
Chatfield	09
Chatham	
7200-12599	39
12600-16099	23
16100-OUT	19
Chatsworth	24
Chelsea	
10700-14999	13
15400-OUT	39
Chene	
200-4999	07
5000-OUT	11
Chenlot	04
Cherboneau Pl	07
Cherokee	19
Cherry	
600-1399	01
1400-OUT	16
Cherrygrove	29
Cherrylawn	
11200-12599	04
12600-16099	38
16100-OUT	21
Chesapeake	39
Cheshire	36
Chester	
2700-3399	20
17400-18899	24
18900-19199	36
19200-OUT	25
Chesterfield Rd	21
Chesterfield St E & W	20
Chestnut	
1-199	18
1400-3199	07
2100-2499 (FER)	20
Cheyenne	
8000-9499	28
9500-16099	27
16100-OUT	35
Chicago Blvd	
1-1399	02
1400-2599	06
Chipman	16
Chippewa	
3700-12699	21
12700-18099	35
18100-OUT	19
Chope Pl	08
Chopin	10

Christ Church Ln	36
Christiancy	09
Christine Ct & Dr	36
Christopher	11
Christy	05
Chrysler Fwy	
400-4998 (EVEN)	07
401-2099 (ODD)	26
2101-4999 (ODD)	01
5000-9799	11
9800-12899	12
12900-20699	03
Church Ave	
1-299	03
1400-1899	16
20700-OUT	37
Church Ct	25
Church Rd	
1-299	03
1400-1899	16
20700-OUT	37
Churchill	06
Cicotte	
1-499	29
3200-OUT	10
Cicotte E	
1-199	18
Cicotte W	
1-199	18
Cincinnati	24
Civic Pl	
10800-12699	04
12700-OUT	28
Civic Center Dr	26
Claireview Rd	36
Clairmount	
1-1399	02
1400-3999	06
4000-OUT	04
Clairpointe	15
Clairview	24
Clairview Ct E & W	36
Clarendon St N & S	04
Clarion	13
Clarita	
3100-12699	21
12700-18099	35
18100-24999	19
25000-27399	40
Clark	
100-2599	09
2600-OUT	10
Clark S	09
Clark Ct	09
Clarkdale	09
Clay	11
Clayburn	28
Clayton	10
Clements	38
Cliff	
17100-17999	12
18000-OUT	34
Clifford	
1-2099	26
2100-OUT	01
Clifton	10
Clinton	
400-899	26
900-OUT	07
Clippert	10
Clough	
11300-11599	34
11600-OUT	05

Detroit (Con.)   482

Cloverdale
8000-10899 (FER)........... 20
10600-12599.................... 04
12600-14999.................... 38
12700-15499 (OP)........... 37
Cloverlawn
8000-12599...................... 04
12600-16099.................... 38
20700-OUT...................... 37
Cloverly Rd...................... 36
Cobalt S........................... 09
Cobb Pl............................ 10
Cochrane
2200-3299....................... 16
3300-OUT........................ 08
Codding........................... 19
Cody................................ 12
Coe................................. 14
Colfax
5800-7299....................... 18
7300-OUT........................ 04
Colgate............................ 37
Colleen............................ 37
College
100-2099.......................... 20
11000-OUT...................... 05
Collingham Dr.................. 05
Collingwood
1-1399.............................. 02
1400-3999........................ 06
4000-OUT........................ 04
Colonial S......................... 17
Colonial Ct & Rd.............. 36
Colorado.......................... 03
Colton............................. 03
Columbia.......................... 39
Columbia E
1-899................................ 01
900-OUT.......................... 07
Columbia W...................... 01
Columbus
2600-3999........................ 06
4000-OUT........................ 04
Commercial....................... 09
Commonwealth.................. 08
Commor............................ 12
Compass........................... 27
Comstock
3300-5899........................ 12
5900-OUT........................ 11
Conant
7700-8899........................ 11
8900-17999...................... 12
18000-OUT...................... 34
Concord
400-4999.......................... 07
5000-10499...................... 11
10500-17999.................... 12
18000-OUT...................... 34
Condon............................ 37
Conger............................ 13
Congress E
1-899................................ 26
900-7199.......................... 07
7200-OUT........................ 14
Congress W...................... 26
Conley
13400-17999.................... 12
18000-OUT...................... 34
Connecticut...................... 03
Conner

400-4999.......................... 15
5000-11499...................... 13
11500-17099.................... 05
17100-OUT...................... 34
Conner Ln........................ 14
Conrad............................. 10
Constance
10600-12699.................... 37
16100-21999.................... 28
22000-OUT...................... 39
Continental....................... 15
Conway............................ 17
Cook................................ 10
Cook Rd........................... 36
Cooley............................. 19
Coolidge
1-1954............................. 18
20700-24999.................... 37
25001-26799 (ODD)......... 37
Coolidge Hwy
1-1954............................. 18
20700-24999.................... 37
25001-26799 (ODD)......... 37
Cooper
4500-4999........................ 14
5000-OUT........................ 13
Cope................................ 15
Copland........................... 09
Coplin
400-4999.......................... 15
5000-11499...................... 13
11500-OUT...................... 05
Cora................................ 18
Coram.............................. 05
Corbett............................ 13
Corbin............................. 17
Cordell............................ 05
Cordova........................... 34
Corey.............................. 15
Corning............................ 37
Cornwall.......................... 24
Cortland
1-1399.............................. 03
1400-3999........................ 06
4000-OUT........................ 04
Cottrell S.......................... 09
Council............................ 12
Country Club Dr
100-2199.......................... 36
19600-OUT...................... 25
Country Club Ln............... 36
Courtland......................... 37
Courville.......................... 24
Coventry
500-599............................ 36
19100-OUT...................... 03
Covert.............................. 12
Covington Dr.................... 63
Coy.................................. 20
Coyle
8000-9499........................ 28
9500-16099...................... 27
16100-19999.................... 35
23600-OUT...................... 37
Craft................................ 24
Craig............................... 11
Cranbrook Dr.................... 21
Crane
900-4999.......................... 14
5000-OUT........................ 13
Cranford Ln...................... 30
Cranshaw......................... 04
Crawford.......................... 09

Crawford S....................... 09
Crescent Dr...................... 23
Crescent Ln...................... 36
Cresswell.......................... 13
Crestwood Dr................... 36
Crocuslawn....................... 04
Cromwell.......................... 16
Crosley............................ 39
Cross............................... 26
Crossley S........................ 09
Crowley............................ 10
Crown.............................. 09
Crusade............................ 05
Cruse
14200-16099.................... 27
16100-OUT...................... 35
Culver.............................. 13
Cumberland Way.............. 03
Curt................................. 13
Curtis
3100-12699...................... 21
12700-18099.................... 35
18100-24999.................... 19
25000-27399.................... 40
Curwood........................... 03
Cushing........................... 05
Custer
1-899................................ 02
900-OUT.......................... 11
Cutler.............................. 14
Cymbal............................ 11
Cypress............................ 10
D..................................... 16
Dacosta
7200-12599...................... 39
12600-OUT...................... 23
Dailey Ave & Ct............... 04
Dakota St E & W.............. 03
Dalby
15900-16099.................... 39
16100-OUT...................... 40
Dale
8800-12599...................... 39
12600-16099.................... 23
16100-OUT...................... 19
Dallas.............................. 11
Dalrymple......................... 04
Dalzelle............................ 16
Damman........................... 25
Dan................................. 12
Danbury........................... 03
Danbury Ln...................... 25
Dane................................ 11
Danforth........................... 12
Daniels............................ 10
Dante.............................. 37
Darcy.............................. 23
Dartmouth........................ 37
Dartmouth S..................... 17
Darwin............................ 36
Davenport......................... 01
David............................... 14
Davis Pl........................... 11
Davison E
1-1899............................. 03
1900-OUT........................ 12
Davison W
1-1399.............................. 03
1400-12699...................... 38
12700-18099.................... 27
18100-23999.................... 23
24000-OUT...................... 39
Dawes.............................. 04

Detroit (Con.) 482

Dayton
  7600-8799 10
  18100-OUT 28
De Buel 11
De Soto 38
Deacon S 17
Dean
  13400-17999 12
  18000-20699 34
Dean Ln 36
Dearborn 09
Dearing 12
Deborah 39
Decatur
  8000-9499 28
  9500-OUT 27
Deeplands Ct 36
Deeplands Rd N & S 36
Defer Pl 14
Dehner 19
Delaware
  1-1399 02
  1400-2099 06
  14800-16099 39
  16100-20699 40
Delisle 18
Delmar 11
Delta 12
Deming 09
Deming Ln 36
Denby
  15300-16099 39
  16100-OUT 40
Denmark 17
Dennis 10
Dennison 10
Denton
  2100-2899 12
  2900-OUT 11
Denver 24
Dequindre
  100-4999 07
  5000-8399 11
  8400-17999 34
  18000-20699 34
Derby 03
Desmond 09
Desner 12
Detroit 24
Devereaux 10
Devine 13
Devon 05
Devonshire Ave
  1000-3399 30
  3400-OUT 24
Devonshire Rd
  1000-3399 30
  3400-OUT 24
Dewey 02
Dexter Ave
  7300-12599 06
  12600-16099 38
  16100-OUT 21
Dexter Blvd
  7300-12599 06
  12600-16099 38
  16100-OUT 21
Dey 09
Dey S 09
Dickerson

400-4999 15
5000-11499 13
11500-OUT 05
Bifl Pl 09
Distel 09
Diversey
  6300-7599 10
  15500-OUT 28
Division
  1-299 18
  400-899 01
  900-OUT 07
Dix 09
Dix S 17
Dixie 39
Dobel 34
Dodge 11
Dolphin
  7200-12599 39
  12600-16099 23
  16100-20599 19
Dolson 23
Domine 11
Donald Ave & Ct 39
Donald Pl 07
Dorchester 14
Doremus
  3300-5899 12
  5900-OUT 11
Doris
  1-1399 03
  1400-OUT 38
Doris Ct 39
Dorothy 11
Dorthen 36
Dover
  1500-1799 20
  6300-12699 04
  12700-21999 28
  22000-27399 39
Dow 39
Downing 17
Doyle 34
Doyle Ct 36
Doyle Pl E & W 36
Dragoon 09
Dragoon S 09
Drake 12
Drayton St E & W 20
Drennen 29
Dresden 05
Drexel
  300-4999 15
  5000-OUT 13
Drifton 05
Driggs 09
Duanc
  3700-3999 06
  4000-OUT 04
Dubay 34
Dubois
  100-4999 07
  5000-8399 11
  8400-OUT 12
Duchsrme Pl 07
Duchess 24
Dumbarton Rd 04
Dumfries S 17
Dundee 04
Dunedin 06
Dunkirk S 17

Dwyer
  8000-10499 11
  10500-17999 12
  18000-OUT 34
Dyar 12
Dyar Ln 36
Eagle 20
Earl Blvd 10
Earl Ct 36
Earle 08
Eason 03
Eastborne
  19200-19399 25
  19400-OUT 36
Eastbrook 36
Eastburn 05
Eastern Pl 08
Eastland Village Dr 25
Eastlawn
  100-4999 15
  5000-OUT 13
Eastwood
  21000-11599 34
  11600-16199 05
  21900-OUT 37
Eastwood Dr 25
Eaten
  500-599 18
  6300-12699 38
  12700-18099 27
  18100-OUT 23
Edgefield
  18900-19199 36
  19200-OUT 25
Edgemere Rd 36
Edgemont Park 38
Edgeton 12
Edgevale 03
Edgewood
  100-599 20
  8000-OUT 13
Edgewood Dr N & S 36
Edgeworth 29
Edinborough Rd 36
Edison
  1-1399 02
  1400-OUT 06
Edlie 14
Edmonton 04
Edmore Dr 05
Edmund Pl 01
Edmunton Dr 36
Edsel S 17
Edsel Ford Fwy E
  1-899 02
  900-7199 11
  7200-14399 13
  14400-19199 24
  19200-OUT 25
Edsel Ford Fwy W
  400-1399 02
  1400-3999 08
  4000-OUT 10
Edshire Ln 36
Edward
  6300-7699 10
  16000-OUT 03
Edwin
  1900-5899 12
  5900-OUT 11
Eileen 39
Elaine Ct 37

Detroit (Con.)   482

Elba
  3600-3799 07
  25500-OUT 39
Eldon 34
Eldred 09
Eldridge 12
Electric S. 07
Elford Ct. 36
Elgin
  8000-8599 34
  13600-OUT 37
Eliot
  1-899 01
  900-OUT 07
Eliza 29
Elizabeth
  1-99 (RR) 18
Elizabeth E
  1-999 01
  909-921 (ODD) 26
Elizabeth W
  1-1399 01
  1400-OUT 16
Elizabeth Ct. 36
Elkhart 25
Ellair Pl 38
Ellen 38
Ellery Ave
  2400-4999 07
  5000-8399 11
  8400-OUT 12
Ellery Pl 07
Elliott 18
Ellis
  10400-12699 04
  12700-OUT 28
Ellsworth
  6300-12699 38
  12700-OUT 27
Elm
  1-199 18
  1380-2099 16
  14400-OUT 37
Elm Ct
  1-99 36
  19800-OUT 25
Elmdale
  11100-15199 13
  15200-OUT 24
Elmer 10
Elmhurst
  1-1399 03
  1400-3999 06
  4000-OUT 04
Elmira
  8500-12699 04
  12700-18099 27
  18100-21999 28
  22000-27399 39
Elmo 05
Elmsleigh Pl 30
Elmwood
  400-4999 07
  5000-OUT 11
Elmwood Park Dr 07
Elsa 14
Elsinore 39
Elsmere 09
Elton 29
Emeline 12

Emerson 15
Emery
  1-1899 03
  1900-OUT 34
Emiline 18
Emily 34
Emmons 14
Emory Ct E & W 36
Emwill 20
Endicott 02
Engle 14
Engleside 05
Englewood 02
Epworth
  5900-7299 10
  7300-OUT 04
Erbie 13
Erie 09
Erle 03
Erskine
  1-899 01
  900-OUT 07
Erwin
  8800-9899 13
  9900-OUT 34
Esper 64
Essex Ave
  12300-14999 15
  15000-OUT 30
Essex Blvd
  12300-14999 15
  15000-OUT 30
Ethel S. 1
Euclid E
  1-899 02
  900-OUT 11
Euclid W
  1-1399 02
  1400-3999 06
  4000-OUT 04
Eugene 15
Eureka
  13400-17999 12
  18000-OUT 34
Evaline
  1900-5899 12
  5900-OUT 11
Evans 09
Evanston
  11200-14399 13
  14400-OUT 24
Evergreen Ave
  5600-6298 (EVEN) 28
  6300-12599 28
  12600-16099 23
  16100-20699 19
Evergreen Rd
  5600-6298 (EVEN) 28
  6300-12599 28
  12600-16099 23
  16100-20699 19
Evers Pl N & S. 20
Everts 24
Ewald Cir
  1800-3419 38
  3420-OUT 04
Ewers 10
Exeter 03
F 16
Faber 12
Fair 20
Fair Ct 36
Fairacres Dr 36

Fairchild S. 17
Faircrest 05
Fairfax
  14800-14999 15
  15000-OUT 30
Fairfield
  600-699 20
  14700-16099 38
  16100-OUT 21
Fairford Rd 36
Fairholme Rd 36
Fairlake Ln 36
Fairmont 18
Fairmount Dr 05
Fairport 05
Fairview
  1-4999 14
  5000-OUT 13
Fairway Dr
  17100-19099 21
  19800-OUT 36
Fairway Ln 36
Fairwood 20
Falcon
  8700-9299 09
  9800-OUT 12
Fargo
  15500-18099 35
  18100-24999 19
  25000-27399 40
Farley 39
Farmbrook 24
Farmdale 20
Farmer 26
Farnsworth
  1-899 02
  900-7199 11
  7200-OUT 13
Farr 11
Farrand Park 03
Farrow 20
Faust Ave
  5600-12599 28
  12600-16099 23
  16100-OUT 19
Faust Rd
  5600-12599 28
  12600-16099 23
  16100-OUT 19
Fayette 03
Federal 09
Felch 13
Fenelon
  11300-17999 12
  18000-OUT 34
Fenkell
  1800-12699 38
  12700-18099 27
  18100-OUT 23
Fenmore 35
Fenton
  8800-16099 39
  16100-OUT 19
Fenwick 09
Ferdinand 09
Ferdinand S. 09
Ferguson
  14700-16099 27
  16100-OUT 35
Fern
  6600-6799 18
  20700-OUT 37
Fernhill 03

Detroit (Con.)	482
Ferry W	02
Ferry Park	08
Field	
400-4999	14
5000-OUT	13
Fielding	
100-1499	20
7200-12599	28
12600-16099	23
16100-OUT	19
Filbert	05
Filer	
9100-10499	11
10500-17999	12
18000-OUT	34
Findlay	05
Finley	11
Firwood	
6300-7299	10
7300-OUT	04
Fischer	
900-4999	14
5000-OUT	13
Fisher Fwy E	
1-899	01
-900-2299	07
Fisher Fwy W	
1-1399	01
1400-3999	16
4000-9399	09
Fisher Rd	30
Fiske Dr	14
Fitzgerald Blvd	20
Fitzpatrick Ave & Ct	28
Five Points	40
Flanders	05
Fleet	38
Fleetwood Ave	
19600-OUT	25
Fleetwood Dr	36
Fleming	
11300-17999	12
18000-OUT	34
Flora	09
Florence	
1-99 (RR)	18
1-2199	03
2200-12699	21
3900-3999 (EC)	29
12700-18099	35
18100-24999	19
25000-OUT	40
Florian	12
Florida	10
Flower Ct	07
Flowerdale	20
Floyd	10
Foley	
10500-12699	04
12700-OUT	27
Fontaine Pl	37
Fontana Ln	36
Ford	
1-1399	03
1400-OUT	38
Ford Ct	36
Ford Rd	
18100-18954 (EVEN)	28
Fordale	17
Fordcroft	36

Fordham	05
Fordson S	17
Fordson Hwy	39
Fordyce	11
Forest	
1-99 (RR)	18
23000-OUT	37
Forest E	
1-899	01
900-7199	07
7200-11999	14
12000-OUT	15
Forest W	
1-1399	01
1400-OUT	08
Forest Ct	01
Forestlawn	34
Forman	09
Forman S	09
Forrer	
6300-9499	28
9500-16099	27
16100-OUT	35
Forsyth	02
Fort E	
300-899	26
900-OUT	07
Fort S	7
Fort W	
100-1399	26
1400-3999	16
4000-OUT	09
Fortune S	09
Foster	11
Fournier	05
Fox	
1300-1499	20
14500-16099	39
16100-OUT	40
Frances	29
Francis	17
Frank	01
Frankfort Ave	
12000-14399	13
14400-OUT	24
Frankfort Ct	
5200-5499	13
Franklin	
300-899	26
900-OUT	07
Frazer Pl	02
Frazier	18
Freda	04
Frederick	
200-899	02
900-7199	11
7200-OUT	13
Fredro	12
Freeland	
8000-9499	28
9500-16099	27
16100-OUT	35
Freer	10
Fremont Pl	07
French Rd	
3700-4999	14
5000-10099	13
10100-OUT	34
Freud	
10400-11999	14
12000-OUT	15
Frisbee	19

Frontenac	11
Fullerton	
1500-12699	38
12700-18099	27
18100-23999	23
24000-OUT	39
Fulton	09
G A R	10
Gable	
11300-17999	12
18000-OUT	34
Gainsboro	20
Gainsborough Rd	23
Galaxie	20
Gale	17
Gallagher	
8900-17999	12
18000-OUT	34
Galster	07
Garden	
6300-8099	64
25900-OUT	37
Garden Ln	20
Gardendale	
100-999	20
20100-OUT	21
Gardner	37
Garfield Ave	
1-899	01
900-7099	07
1200-2399 (FER)	20
8800-16099	39
16100-OUT	40
Garfield Ct	39
Garfield Pl	07
Garland	
1400-4999	14
5000-OUT	13
Garnet	05
Gartner	09
Garvin	12
Gary	03
Gates	09
Gates S	09
Gateshead	36
Gavel	27
Gaylord	
2900-3899	12
15000-16099	39
16100-OUT	40
Gaynor Ct	09
Geimer	12
Geitzen	
11300-11599	34
11600-OUT	05
Genessee	
1-499	18
9200-OUT	06
Geneva	
1-2099	03
23000-OUT	37
Genoa	13
Geoffrey Ct	37
George	03
Georgeland	04
Georgia	
4000-7199	11
7200-OUT	13
Gerald	03
Gerisch	09
Ghesquiere Ct	36
Gibbs	09
Gibson	01

Detroit (Con.) 482

Gilbert.................................... 10
Gilbo..................................... 34
Gilchrist
  15000-16099.................... 27
  16100-OUT...................... 35
Gillett................................... 11
Gilroy.................................... 17
Giltner Ct.............................. 20
Girardin
  7600-10499.................... 11
  10500-17999.................. 12
  18000-OUT..................... 34
Gitre..................................... 05
Gladstone
  1-1399.......................... 62
  1400-3999...................... 06
  4000-OUT...................... 04
Gladwin................................. 14
Gladys................................... 10
Glastonbury Ave
  11600-12599.................. 28
  12600-16099.................. 23
  16100-OUT..................... 19
Glastonbury Rd
  11600-12599.................. 28
  12600-16099.................. 23
  16100-OUT..................... 19
Gleason................................. 17
Glen Arbor Ln....................... 36
Glen Lodge........................... 20
Glenco................................... 19
Glendale
  1-1399.......................... 63
  1400-12699.................... 38
  12700-18099.................. 27
  18100-23999.................. 23
  24000-OUT.................... 39
Glenfield............................... 13
Glenhurst.............................. 19
Glenmore.............................. 40
Glenwood.............................. 05
Glenwood St E & W............. 29
Glinnan................................. 09
Globe.................................... 38
Gloucester Dr....................... 03
Glover................................... 14
Glynn Ct
  1-1399.......................... 02
  1400-OUT...................... 06
Goddard
  12200-17999.................. 12
  18000-OUT.................... 34
Goethe
  7200-11999.................... 14
  12000-14999.................. 15
  15000-17799.................. 30
  21400-OUT.................... 36
Golden Gate St E & W.......... 03
Goldner.................................. 10
Goldsmith............................... 09
Goodell.................................. 11
Goodell St E & W.................. 29
Goodrich............................... 20
Goodson................................ 12
Goodwin
  8900-11699.................... 11
  11700-OUT.................... 03
Gordon................................... 14
Gore...................................... 19
Goulburn............................... 05
Gould.................................... 09

Grand Blvd E
  1-1164.......................... 07
  1165-2851...................... 11
  2852-OUT...................... 02
Grand Blvd W
  1-887............................ 16
  888-2749....................... 08
  2750-OUT...................... 02
Grand Haven......................... 12
Grand Marais........................ 30
Grand River E....................... 26
Grand River W
  1-2099.......................... 26
  2100-3099...................... 01
  3100-7299...................... 08
  7300-12699.................... 04
  12700-18099.................. 27
  18100-19999.................. 23
  20000-24999.................. 19
  25000-27399.................. 40
Grandmont Ave
  6300-9499...................... 28
  9500-OUT...................... 27
Grandmont Rd
  6300-9499...................... 28
  9500-OUT...................... 27
Grandview.............................. 19
Grandville Ave
  5600-12599.................... 28
  12600-16099.................. 23
  16100-OUT..................... 19
Grandville Rd
  5600-12599.................... 28
  12600-16099.................. 23
  16100-OUT..................... 19
Grandy
  3400-4999...................... 07
  5000-OUT...................... 11
Granger................................. 13
Grant..................................... 12
Granzon................................. 37
Gratiot
  1-899............................ 26
  900-7199....................... 07
  7200-11999.................... 13
  12000-15599.................. 05
Graves................................... 14
Gravier.................................. 24
Gray
  1100-4999...................... 15
  5000-OUT...................... 13
Grayfield
  8800-12599.................... 39
  12600-16099.................. 23
  16100-OUT..................... 19
Grayling................................ 12
Grayson................................. 20
Grayton Ave
  1000-3399...................... 30
  3400-OUT...................... 24
Grayton Rd
  1000-3399...................... 30
  3400-OUT...................... 24
Great Lakes St E & W........... 18
Greeley
  8500-11699.................... 11
  11700-OUT.................... 03
Green S.................................. 09
Green St & Pl......................... 09
Greenbriar
  1-99.............................. 36
  13900-OUT.................... 37
Greendale St E & W.............. 03

Greenfield
  6301-7999 (ODD)........... 28
  8000-9499...................... 28
  9500-16099.................... 27
  16100-20699.................. 35
  20700-26700 (EVEN)..... 37
Greenlawn
  8000-12599.................... 04
  12600-16099.................. 38
  16100-OUT..................... 21
Greensboro............................ 24
Greenspan............................. 16
Greenview Ave
  5600-12599.................... 28
  12600-16099.................. 23
  16100-20699.................. 19
Greenview Rd
  5600-12599.................... 28
  12600-16099.................. 23
  16100-20699.................. 19
Greenway.............................. 04
Gregorie................................ 14
Greiner
  11000-11599.................. 34
  11600-OUT.................... 05
Greusel.................................. 10
Greydale Ave
  12600-16099.................. 23
  16100-OUT..................... 19
Greydale Ct........................... 19
Greyfriars S........................... 17
Griffin................................... 11
Griggs
  8600-12599.................... 04
  12600-16099.................. 38
  16100-OUT..................... 21
Grinnell................................. 13
Griswold................................ 26
Grixdale E
  1-1899.......................... 03
  1900-OUT...................... 34
Grixdale W............................ 03
Groesbeck Hwy..................... 05
Grosse Pointe Blvd............... 36
Grosse Pointe Ct................... 30
Grotto Ct............................... 05
Grove
  1-2199.......................... 03
  2200-12699.................... 21
  12700-18099.................. 35
  18100-24999.................. 19
  25000-27399.................. 40
Grover................................... 05
Grooveview........................... 20
Gruebner............................... 34
Guilford................................. 24
Gunston
  5800-11499.................... 13
  11500-OUT.................... 05
Guoin.................................... 07
Guthrie.................................. 13
Hackett................................. 27
Hafeli.................................... 13
Hague
  1-899............................ 02
  900-OUT....................... 11
Hale...................................... 07
Hall....................................... 13
Hall Pl.................................. 36
Halleck.................................. 12
Halley.................................... 23
Haltiner................................. 18
Hamata................................. 20

Detroit (Con.)   482

Hamilton Ave
| 9500-11699 | 02 |
| 11700-OUT | 03 |
Hamilton Ct | 36 |
Hamilton Rd
| 9500-11699 | 02 |
| 11700-OUT | 03 |
Hamlet | 34 |
Hammond
| 2300-2999 | 09 |
| 3000-OUT | 10 |
Hampshire | 13 |
Hampton
1-2299	36
14900-14999	15
15000-15199	30
20700-OUT	25
Hampton Rd
1-2299	36
14900-14999	15
15000-15199	30
20700-OUT	25
Hancock E
1-899	01
900-OUT	07
Hancock W
1-1399	01
1400-3999	08
4000-OUT	10
Hancock Ct	20
Handy Pl	36
Hanley	12
Hanna	03
Hanover	06
Hanson	10
Harbaugh	09
Harbaugh S	09
Harbor Ct	36
Harbor Hill Rd	36
Harbor Island	15
Harcourt Rd	30
Harding
400-4999	14
5000-8999	13
21600-OUT	37
Hardyke	13
Harlow	35
Harmon	02
Harned	34
Harnor Ct	06
Harold	12
Harper Ave
1-899	02
900-7199	11
7200-14399	13
14400-19199	24
19200-20999	25
19600-19698 (EVEN)	36
Harper Ct
1-899	02
900-7199	11
7200-14399	13
14400-19199	24
19200-20999	25
19600-19698 (EVEN)	36
Harrell | 13 |
Harriett Ct | 37 |
Harrington | 09 |
Harrington S | 09 |
Harris | 20 |
Harrison | |

2200-3299	16
3300-3999	08
6400-6499	09
Harry	13
Hart
600-3799	14
13600-OUT	37
Hart Pl N
21000-21499	20
Hart Pl S
21000-21499	20
Hartford	11
Hartwell
8000-9499	28
9500-16099	27
16100-OUT	11
Hartwick	35
Harvard Rd
1000-3399	30
3400-OUT	24
Harvey	09
Hasse
13400-17999	12
18000-OUT	34
Hastings	11
Hathon	13
Havana	03
Haverhill	24
Hawthorne
11300-11699	11
11700-20599	03
20600-OUT	25
Hawthorne Rd	36
Hayes
9000-11499	13
11500-20699	05
Hazel	08
Hazelhurst St E & W	05
Hazelridge	20
Hazelton
8800-12599	39
12600-16099	23
16100-OUT	19
Hazelwood
1-1399	02
1400-3999	66
4000-OUT	10
Hazlett	04
Healy
13400-17999	12
18000-OUT	34
Heather Ln	36
Heck Pl	07
Hecla	08
Hedge	11
Heidelberg	07
Heidt S	10
Heintz	11
Helen
400-4999	07
5000-10499	11
10500-17999	12
18000-20599	34
Helen Ave
19800-19999 (HW)	25
Helen Ct
19800-19999 (HW)	25
Hemingway	39
Hemlock	35
Henderson	67
Hendricks	67
Hendrie
1-899	02

| 900-7199 | 11 |
| 7200-OUT | 13 |
Hendrie Ln | 36 |
Henry
| 1-1399 | 01 |
Henry St E & W | 18 |
Herbert | 10 |
Hereford | 24 |
Herkimer | 09 |
Hern | 13 |
Hershey | 03 |
Hessel Ave
| 15600-18099 | 35 |
| 18100-OUT | 19 |
Hessel Ct | 19 |
Hewitt | 12 |
Heyden Ave
6300-7198 (EVEN)	28
7200-12599	28
12600-16099	23
16100-OUT	19
Heyden Ct	28
Hibbard	14
Hickory	05
Hidden Ln	36
Higbie Pl N & S	36
High	29
Highland
1-1399	03
1400-OUT	06
Hildale E
1-1899	03
1900-OUT	34
Hildale W	03
Hill
1-99 (RR)	18
1-2099	03
Hillcrest Ln & Rd	36
Hillger	14
Hillsboro	04
Hillview	27
Hilton Rd	20
Hindle	11
Hobart	02
Hobson	01
Hogarth
2600-3999	06
4000-OUT	04
Holborn	11
Holbrook
1-899	02
900-1799	11
1800-OUT	12
Holcomb
1100-4999	14
5000-OUT	13
Holden
800-1399	02
1400-OUT	08
Holford	18
Holiday Rd	36
Holly	09
Hollywood
500-2399	36
19500-OUT	25
Hollywood E
400-1899	03
1900-OUT	34
Hollywood W	03
Holmes
2300-2799	12
7000-OUT	10

Detroit (Con.)   482

Holmur
7500-12599	04
12600-16099	38
16100-OUT	21
Homedale	10
Homer	09
Homestead Pl	11
Honorah	09
Hooker	08
Hoover	05
Hope	39
Horatio	10

Horten
1-899	02
900-2499	11
2700-OUT	20
Hosmer	14
Houghton	19
House	34
Houston Whittier	05

Howard
400-1399	26
1400-3999	16
4000-OUT	09
Howe Ct	14

Howell
4700-7299	10
7300-9099	04
26900-27399	39
Hoyt	05

Hubbard
700-2599	09
2600-OUT	10

Hubbell
8000-9499	28
9500-16099	27
16100-20699	35
20700-OUT	37

Huber
5900-7199	11
7200-OUT	13
Hudson	08
Hughes	38
Hughes Ter	08
Hull	03

Humboldt
2600-3299	16
3300-OUT	08

Humphrey
3700-3999	06
4000-OUT	04
Hunt	07

Hunt Club Dr
1800-2199	36
19600-OUT	25

Huntington Ave
18500-21299 (HW)	25
Huntington Blvd	36

Huntington Rd
18500-21299 (HW)	25

Huntington (First Choice) Rd
16100-20699	19

Huribut
1400-4999	14
5000-OUT	13
Huron	16
Hussar	09
Hyacinthe	29
Hyde	11
Hyde Park Rd	07

Hyland	20
Ida	09
Ida La E & W	36
Idaho	38

Ikene
11600-12599	04
12600-16099	38
16100-OUT	21

Iliad
15300-16099	23
16100-16599	19

Iliad Ct
15700-16199	23

Illinois
900-OUT	67
Imperial Hwy	40

Indian
15700-16099	39
16100-20699	40

Indiana
8000-12599	04
12600-16099	38
16100-OUT	21
Indiandale	38
Infantry	09
Inglis	09

Inkster Rd
8800-16098 (EVEN)	39
16100-20698 (EVEN)	40
Inman	20

Intervale
6300-12699	38
12700-OUT	27

Inverness
15300-16099	38
16100-OUT	21
Iowa	12
Iris	27
Iron	07
Ironside	10

Ironwood
6000-7299	10
7300-OUT	04

Iroquois
700-4999	14
5000-OUT	13
Irvine Blvd	37
Irvine Ln	36

Irvington
19100-20599	03
26800-OUT	39
Isham	13

Ithaca
20700-22999	20
23000-OUT	37

Ivanhoe
4700-5699	04
25300-OUT	39
Jackson	10
Jacob	12

James
14000-15499	37
James Ct	13
James St E & W	18

James Couzens Fwy
15400-16099	38
16100-16774	21
16775-OUT	35
Jameson	14
Jan	39
Jane	05
Jarvis	20

Jason	23
Jay	07
Jean	20

Jefferson E
1-899	26
900-7199	07
7200-11999	14
12000-14999	15
15000-17899	30

Jefferson W
1-1399	26
1400-3999	16
4000-9999	09
10000-11453	18
Jefferson Ct	07

Jeffries Fwy
2600-3299	16
3300-7299	08
7300-12699	04
12700-18099	27
18100-19999	28
20000-23999	23
24000-27399	39
Jennie	10
Jennifer Ave & Ct	39
Jennings	27

Jerome
2000-3699	12
8800-9499	39
22000-OUT	37
Jewell	20
Joan	37
Joann	05
Joe	10

John C Lodge Fwy
100-2099	26
2100-4999	01
5000-11699	02
11700-12199	03
12200-OUT	38
John F Kennedy Pl	03
John Glenn Pl	03
John Kronk	10

John R
1-2099	26
2100-4999	01
5000-11699	02
11700-20599	03
Johnson	16
Joliet Pl	07
Jones	26
Jordan	34
Joseph	29

Joseph Campau
100-4999	07
5000-8399	11
8400-17999	12
18000-OUT	34
Josephine	02
Josephine St E & W	29
Joslyn	03

Joy Rd
2600-3999	06
4000-12699	04
12700-21999	28
22000-23226	39
23228-27398 (EVEN)	39
Julian	04

Junction
100-2999	09
3000-OUT	10
Junction S	09

Detroit (Con.)   482

Justine
  12200-17999 12
  18000-OUT 34
Kaier 09
Kalsh 34
Kane St N & S 23
Kanter 11
Karen 37
Karl 19
Kay 04
Keal 27
Keating 03
Keeler
  12700-18099 27
  18100-23999 23
  24000-OUT 39
Keelson Dr 15
Keibler 27
Keller 09
Kellogg Pl 11
Kelly Rd
  11300-19199 24
  19200-20699 25
Kempa 34
Kenberton Ave, Ct & Dr 37
Kendall Ave
  1-1399 03
  1400-12699 38
  12700-18099 27
  18100-23999 23
  24000-OUT 39
Kendall Ct 39
Kenilworth 02
Kenmoor 05
Kenmore Ave 25
Kenmore Dr 36
Kennebec 05
Kenneth
  20600-20699 03
  26200-OUT 39
Kenney 34
Kenosha
  18500-20899 (HW) ... 25
  20700-26799 (OP) ... 37
Kensington Ave
  100-999 20
  1000-3399 30
  3400-OUT 24
Kensington Rd
  100-999 20
  1000-3399 30
  3400-OUT 24
Kent 13
Kentfield
  12600-16099 23
  16100-OUT 19
Kentfurd 23
Kenton
  1500-1799 20
  14400-OUT 37
Kentucky
  8000-12599 04
  12600-16099 38
  16100-OUT 21
Kenwood
  1400-1651 11
  1652-1899 12
  3100-3399 20
  8100-OUT 37
Kenwood Ct & Rd 36
Kerby Ln & Rd 36

Kercheval Ave
  1-499 36
  6300-7199 07
  7200-11999 14
  12000-14999 15
  15000-OUT 30
Kercheval Pl 30
Kern 13
Kessler 19
Keystone
  13400-17999 12
  18000-OUT 34
Kilbourne 13
Kimberly Ct 04
Kimland Ct 39
King
  1-899 02
  900-OUT 11
King Pl, N
  21000-21499 20
King Pl, S
  21000-21499 20
King Richard 24
Kings Ct E & W 36
Kingsley Ct 02
Kingston 37
Kingston Rd 21
Kingsville
  18500-21899 25
  21900-OUT 36
Kingswood 21
Kinloch
  8800-16099 39
  16100-20699 40
Kinsman 10
Kipke 39
Kipling
  7300-7699 06
  20700-OUT 37
Kirby E
  1-899 02
  900-7199 11
  7200-OUT 13
Kirby W
  1-1399 02
  1400-OUT 08
Kirkwood
  6600-8799 10
  18100-OUT 28
Kitchener 11
Klein 11
Kleinow 18
Klenk 15
Klinger
  8200-8899 11
  8900-17999 12
  18000-OUT 34
Knight 39
Knodell 13
Knox
  1-99 29
  8900-OUT 11
Kolb 10
Konkel 10
Kopernick 10
Korte
  13100-14999 15
  15000-OUT 30
Krakow Pl 07
Kramer
  10200-12699 04
  12700-OUT 28
Kresge 13

Kress 19
Kulick 10
La Belle Ave
  1-1399 03
  400-499 (GPS) 36
  1400-2599 38
  13600-OUT 37
La Belle Rd
  1-1399 03
  400-499 (GPS) 36
  1400-2599 38
  13600-OUT 37
La Prairie 20
La Salle Blvd
  7300-12599 06
  12600-16099 38
  16100-OUT 21
La Salle Ct 38
La Salle Gdns N & S 06
La Salle Pl 36
Labadie Ave & Ct 29
Labrosse
  900-1399 26
  1400-OUT 16
Lafayette E
  300-899 26
  900-7199 07
  7200-OUT 14
Lafayette Blvd
  100-1399 26
  1400-3999 16
  4000-OUT 09
Lafayette Plaisance 07
Lafferty Pl 16
Lafontaine 36
Lahser Ave
  8800-12599 39
  12600-16099 23
  16100-20699 19
Lahser Rd
  8800-12599 39
  12600-16099 23
  16100-20699 19
Laing
  11400-19199 24
  19200-OUT 25
Lake Ct 30
Lake Shore Ln & Rd 36
Lakecrest Ln 36
Lakeland Ave & Ct 30
Lakepointe
  500-3399 30
  3400-OUT 24
Lakeview
  1-299 36
  1000-4999 15
  5000-OUT 13
Lakeview Ct 30
Lakewood
  1-4999 15
  5000-OUT 13
Lambert
  6300-7199 11
  7200-OUT 13
Lambie Pl 16
Lamont
  17100-17999 12
  18000-OUT 34
Lamothe 06
Lamphere
  7200-12599 39
  12600-16099 23
  16100-OUT 19

Detroit (Con.)   482

Lanark 24
Lancashire 23
Lancaster
  1800-2199 36
  19600-OUT 25
Lanco 04
Lane 09
Lang 17
Langholm 34
Lanman 08
Lannette 13
Lannoo 36
Lansdowne
  11100-19199 24
  19200-OUT 25
Lansing 09
Lantz E
  1-1899 03
  1900-OUT 34
Lantz W 03
Lappin
  11000-11599 34
  11600-OUT 05
Larchmont 04
Larchwood 03
Lark 13
Larkins 10
Larned E
  1-899 26
  900-OUT 07
Larned W 26
Latham 12
Lauder
  8000-9499 28
  9500-16099 27
  16100-OUT 35
Lauderdale 09
Laura 14
Laurel 05
Law 24
Lawley 12
Lawndale
  200-3599 09
  3600-OUT 10
Lawrence
  1-1399 02
  1400-3999 06
  4000-OUT 04
Lawton
  2600-3299 16
  3300-7299 08
  7300-12599 06
  12600-16099 38
  16100-OUT 21
Le Blanc
  1-99 (RR) 18
  1-99 (EC) 29
Le Grand 11
Le Roy
  1-199 (RR) 18
  100-1799 (FER) 20
  8200-9999 37
  11000-11499 13
  11500-OUT 05
Leach 14
Leander 34
Ledyard 01
Lee Ct 36
Lee Pl 06
Lee Gate Ln 36
Leewin 19

Lehman 12
Leib 07
Leicester Ct 02
Leidich 13
Leigh S 09
Leitch Rd 20
Leland
  900-3599 07
  1800-2199 (FER) 20
Lemay
  400-4999 14
  5000-OUT 13
Lennane
  14700-16099 39
  16100-OUT 40
Lennon
  1800-2199 36
  19600-OUT 25
Lennox
  (ODD) 20
Lenoir 18
Lenore
  8800-16099 39
  16100-OUT 19
Lenox
  1-4999 15
  5000-OUT 13
Leona Dr 39
Leonard 17
Leota 01
Lernoult 13
Leslie
  1-1399 03
  1400-4899 38
  14400-OUT 37
Lessing 14
Lesure
  13500-16099 27
  16100-OUT 35
Leverette
  1300-1399 26
  1400-OUT 16
Leverne 39
Lewerenz 36
Lewiston Rd 36
Lewiston St E & W 20
Lexington Ave
  400-499 36
  7000-7199 09
  13900-16099 39
  16100-OUT 40
Lexington Rd
  400-499 36
  7000-7199 09
  13900-16099 39
  16100-OUT 40
Liberal 65
Liberty 11
Library 26
Lichfield Rd 21
Liddesdale S 17
Liebold S 17
Lilac 21
Lillibridge
  400-4999 14
  5000-OUT 13
Lincoln Ave
  3400-6199 08
  6200-11699 02
  11700-14499 03
  13600-15499 02
Lincoln Blvd & Ter 37
Lincoln Rd 30

Lincolnshire Dr 03
Linden 18
Lindsay
  14800-16099 27
  16100-OUT 35
Linnhurst
  11000-11599 34
  11600-OUT 05
Linsdale 04
Linville
  12900-14399 13
  14400-18599 24
  18600-OUT 36
Linwood
  5200-7299 08
  7300-12599 06
  12600-16099 38
  16100-OUT 21
Linzee 10
Liptori 04
Lisbon 09
Littlefield
  8000-9499 28
  9500-16099 27
  16100-OUT 35
Littlestone Ave
  1600-2199 36
  19600-OUT 25
Littlestone Rd
  1600-2199 36
  19600-OUT 25
Livernois
  100-2699 (FER) 20
  100-2999 09
  3000-7999 10
  8000-12599 04
  12600-16099 38
  16100-OUT 21
Livernois S
  100-699 09
Livingstone 07
Lochmoor 25
Lochmoor Blvd 36
Lockwood 10
Lodewyck 24
Lodge Dr 14
Lodi 11
Log Cabin
  15300-16099 38
  16100-OUT 03
Logan 09
Lola Ave
  5900-5999 10
  15300-16099 39
  16100-OUT 40
Lola Dr
  5900-5999 10
  15300-16099 39
  16100-OUT 40
Lombard Ter 08
London 21
Longacre
  6300-5499 28
  9500-OUT 27
Longfellow
  1-1399 02
  1400-OUT 06
Longview 13
Longwood Ave E 03
Longwood Ave & Pl 03
Longwood Pl W 03
Longworth 09
Longyear 11

Detroit (Con.)   482

Lons ... 39
Lonyo
   2900-3599 ... 09
   3600-6226 ... 10
Loraine
   700-899 ... 30
   5000-OUT ... 08
Loretta Pl ... 37
Loretto ... 05
Lorman ... 14
Lorne ... 24
Lothrop Ave
   1-499 (GPS) ... 36
   1-1399 ... 02
   1400-OUT ... 06
Lothrop Rd
   1-499 (GPS) ... 36
   1-1399 ... 02
   1409-OUT ... 06
Louis
   1-99 ... 18
   8800-9299 ... 03
   9200-9499 ... 39
Louis First Choice
   8800-9299 ... 14
Louisiana ... 03
Lovett ... 10
Lowdell ... 17
Lowell Dr ... 03
Lozier
   13100-14899 ... 15
   14900-OUT ... 24
Luce ... 12
Lucerne Ave
   8800-14299 ... 39
   19000-OUT ... 03
Lucerne Dr
   8800-14299 ... 39
   19000-OUT ... 03
Lucky Pl ... 11
Ludden ... 07
Ludlow ... 37
Lumley ... 10
Lumpkin
   8400-17999 ... 12
   18000-OUT ... 34
Luther S. ... 17
Lycaste ... 14
Lyford ... 34
Lyle ... 09
Lyman Pl ... 11
Lynch Rd ... 34
Lyndon
   6300-12699 ... 38
   12700-18099 ... 27
   18100-23999 ... 23
   24000-27399 ... 39
Lynn ... 11
Lyon ... 09
Lyons ... 37
Lysander
   900-1399 ... 01
   1400-OUT ... 08
Mabel ... 03
Mac Arthur
   13900-16099 ... 39
   16100-OUT ... 40
Mac Crary ... 05
Mack Ave
   1-899 ... 01
   900-7199 ... 07

   7200-11999 ... 14
   12000-14899 ... 15
   14900-18199 ... 24
   18200-21401 ... 36
Mack Rd
   1-899 ... 01
   900-7199 ... 07
   7200-11999 ... 14
   12000-14899 ... 15
   14900-18199 ... 24
   18200-21401 ... 36
Mackay
   11300-17999 ... 12
   18000-OUT ... 34
Mackenzie
   6300-12699 ... 04
   12700-OUT ... 28
Mackinaw ... 04
Macomb
   300-899 ... 26
   900-OUT ... 07
Macon ... 13
Maddelein ... 05
Madeira ... 03
Madison
   1-899 ... 26
   400-499 (GPS) ... 36
   900-OUT ... 07
Madola ... 34
Magnolia
   1600-3999 ... 08
   4000-OUT ... 10
Mahan ... 20
Maiden ... 13
Maine
   12200-17999 ... 12
   18000-OUT ... 34
Maison Rd ... 36
Majestic
   6300-8099 ... 10
   15500-21999 ... 28
   20700-22999 (FER) ... 20
   22000-22799 ... 39
   23000-OUT ... 37
Major ... 17
Malcolm ... 13
Mallina ... 36
Malta ... 23
Malvern ... 13
Manatee ... 20
Manchester Ave
   1-299 ... 03
   1600-2199 ... 36
   20800-OUT ... 25
Manchester Blvd
   1-299 ... 03
   1600-2199 ... 36
   20800-OUT ... 25
Mandalay ... 04
Mandale ... 09
Manderson Rd ... 03
Manhattan
   8400-8599 ... 11
   13600-OUT ... 37
Manhattan Pl ... 37
Manila ... 14
Manistee ... 37
Manistique
   200-4999 ... 15
   5000-OUT ... 24
Manning
   11100-11599 ... 34
   11600-OUT ... 05

Manor
   400-499 ... 36
   8000-12599 ... 04
   12600-16099 ... 38
   16100-OUT ... 21
Mansfield
   6300-9499 ... 28
   9500-16099 ... 27
   16100-OUT ... 35
Manson ... 09
Mansur ... 11
Manuel ... 11
Maple
   1-199 ... 18
   900-OUT ... 07
Maple Ln ... 36
Mapledale ... 20
Maplehurst St E & W ... 20
Maplelawn ... 04
Mapleridge ... 05
Mapleton Rd ... 36
Mapleview ... 05
Maplewood ... 04
Marantette ... 16
Marbud ... 05
Marcus
   5900-7199 ... 11
   7200-OUT ... 13
Marene ... 19
Marford Ct ... 36
Margaret St E & W ... 03
Margareta
   3100-12699 ... 21
   12700-18099 ... 35
   18100-24999 ... 19
   25000-27399 ... 40
Marian Ct ... 36
Marian Pl ... 19
Marie
   1-99 ... 29
   1300-OUT ... 20
Marietta ... 14
Marion
   1-999 ... 18
   8000-8699 ... 13
   8800-OUT ... 39
Marion Cres ... 39
Marjorie ... 13
Mark ... 08
Mark Twain
   8000-9499 ... 28
   9500-16099 ... 27
   16100-OUT ... 35
Market ... 07
Marlborough
   200-4999 ... 15
   5000-OUT ... 24
Marlin Dr ... 39
Marlow St & Pl ... 37
Marlowe
   8000-9499 ... 28
   9500-16099 ... 27
   16100-OUT ... 35
Marne ... 24
Marquette ... 08
Marquette Dr ... 14
Marseilles ... 24
Marshall
   800-1099 ... 17
Marshall E
   100-1899 ... 20
Marshall W
   100-1799 ... 20

Detroit (Con.)   482

Marshfield	20
Marston	
1-899	02
900-OUT	11
Marter Rd	36
Martin	10
Martin Rd	20
Martindale St N & S	04
Marx	03
Mary	36
Marygrove Dr	21
Maryland	
1-3399	30
3400-OUT	24
Mason Pl	09
Massachusetts	03
Mather	10
Matthews	07
Maumee	30
Maxwell	
2100-4999	14
5000-OUT	13
May	13
Maybury Grand	
3300-OUT	08
Mayfield	05
Maynard	15
Maywood	13
Mc Bride Pl	27
Mc Clain Dr	37
Mc Clellan	
1200-4999	14
5000-OUT	13
Mc Cormick	
18500-20799	24
20800-OUT	36
Mc Donald	10
Mc Donald Pl	08
Mc Dougall	
1-4999	07
5000-8399	11
8400-17999	12
18000-OUT	34
Mc Dowell	20
Mc Graw	
1900-3999	08
4000-OUT	10
Mc Gregor	09
Mc Intyre	19
Mc Kinley	08
Mc Kinley Pl & Rd	36
Mc Kinney	24
Mc Kinstry	09
Mc Kinstry S	09
Mc Lean	
1-1899	03
1900-OUT	12
Mc Millan	
4600-OUT	09
Mc Millan Rd	
1-399	36
Mc Nichols Rd E	
1-1899	03
1900-7399	12
7400-11499	34
11500-OUT	05
Mc Nichols Rd W	
1-2199	03
2200-12699	21
12700-18099	35
18100-OUT	19

Mc Quade	06
Meade	12
Meadow Ln	36
Meadow Park	39
Meadow Lark	37
Meadowbrook Ave	
1-1399	14
14700-16099	39
16100-16199	40
25000-27399	39
Meadowbrook Rd	
1-1399	14
14700-16099	39
16100-16199	40
25000-27399	39
Meadowdale	
100-999	20
8200-OUT	28
Mecca	27
Mechanic	26
Medbury	
1300-7199	11
7200-OUT	13
Medina	09
Meige	09
Melbourne	
1-899	02
900-OUT	11
Meldrum Ave & Ct	07
Mellon	17
Melrose	11
Melville	09
Melvin	18
Memorial Ave	
6300-9499	28
9500-13699	27
17100-OUT	40
Memorial Dr	
6300-9499	28
9500-13699	27
17100-OUT	40
Mendota	
8000-12599	04
12600-16099	38
16100-20699	21
20700-OUT	20
Mercedes	39
Mercier	10
Merkel	13
Merlin	17
Merrick	
400-1399	02
1400-OUT	08
Merrill	02
Merrill Plaisance	03
Merritt	09
Merriweather Rd	36
Merton Rd	10
Merwin	10
Mettetal	
6300-9499	28
9500-OUT	27
Meuse	10
Meyers Rd	
8000-9499	28
9500-16099	27
16100-20699	35
20700-OUT	20
Miami	17
Michaux Ln	36
Michigan	
1-1399	26
1400-3999	16

4000-9999	10
Middle	26
Middlepoint	04
Middlesex Rd	30
Midfield	27
Midland	
1-1399	03
1400-12699	38
12700-18099	27
18100-23999	23
24000-OUT	39
Milbank	34
Miles	11
Milford	
3700-3999	08
4000-OUT	10
Military	
100-2999	09
3000-7999	10
8000-OUT	04
Military S	09
Mill	29
Miller	
2900-7199	11
7200-7999	13
14000-OUT	37
Miller Ct	07
Miller Rd	09
Milner	13
Milo	12
Milton	34
Milwaukee E	
1-899	02
900-OUT	11
Milwaukee W	02
Minden	05
Minerva	
3000-3399	20
17200-OUT	24
Minneapolis	24
Minnesota	
1-1899	03
1900-OUT	12
Minock	
5600-12599	28
12600-OUT	23
Minock Cir & Dr	39
Mint	09
Mirabeau Pl	36
Missouri	08
Mitcheldale	20
Mitchell	
3400-4999	07
5000-8399	11
8400-17999	12
18000-OUT	34
Modern	
1600-1899	03
1900-OUT	12
Mcenart	
11900-17999	12
18000-OUT	34
Moffat	13
Mogul	24
Mohawk	08
Mohican	05
Molena	34
Monarch	05
Monica	
8800-12599	04
12600-16099	38
16100-OUT	21

Detroit (Con.) 482

Monitor 34
Monroe
  1-899 26
  900-3799 07
  4200-OUT 29
Montana St E & W 03
Montcalm E
  1-899 01
  900-OUT 07
Montcalm W 01
Montclair
  300-4999 14
  5000-OUT 13
Monte Vis
  12600-16099 38
  16100-OUT 21
Monterey
  1-1399 03
  1400-3999 06
  4000-OUT 04
Montgomery
  2600-3999 06
  4000-OUT 04
Montlieu 34
Montmartre Ct 37
Montrose
  6300-9499 27
  9500-16099 28
  16100-OUT 35
Montville Pl 38
Moon 36
Moore Pl
  3500-3999 08
  4000-OUT 10
Moorhouse 20
Moorland Dr 36
Moran
  1-499 36
  3800-4999 07
  5000-8399 11
  8400-OUT 12
Moran Rd
  1-499 36
  3800-4999 07
  5000-8399 11
  8400-OUT 12
Morang Dr
  9000-18299 24
  18300-OUT 05
Morgan 34
Moritz 37
Morley 04
Morningside Dr 36
Moross Pl
  1-499 36
  16000-18799 05
  18500-20799 24
  20800-OUT 36
Moross Rd
  1-499 36
  16000-18499 05
  18500-20799 24
  20800-OUT 36
Morrell 09
Morrell S 09
Morrow
  300-399 18
  7800-OUT 11
Morrow Cir E
  8000-8399 04

Morse 10
Morton
  6300-6499 10
  21900-OUT 37
Moselle Pl 36
Moss 03
Motor Boat Ln 14
Mound
  11300-17999 12
  18000-20699 34
Mount Elliott Ave
  1-4999 07
  5000-10499 11
  10500-17999 34
  18000-OUT 34
Mount Elliott Ct 12
Mount Olivet 34
Mount Vernon
  1-899 02
  200-499 (GPS) 36
  900-OUT 11
Moyes 10
Muir Rd 36
Muirland
  14800-16099 38
  16100-OUT 21
Mulberry 08
Mullane 09
Mullet
  600-899 26
  900-OUT 07
Muncey 24
Munich 24
Murat 13
Murray 13
Murray Hill
  15300-16099 27
  16100-OUT 35
Musket 09
Muskoka Rd 36
Myrtle
  1-99 (RR) 18
  1-1399 01
  700-899 (FER) 20
  1400-OUT 08
Nadine 37
Nagel 12
Nagle 13
Nall
  3800-3999 08
  4000-OUT 10
Nancy 12
Naples 11
Napoleon
  400-899 01
  900-OUT 07
Nardin 04
Nashville 05
Nathaline 12
Naumann 15
Navahoe 14
Navarre 14
Navarre Pl 07
Navy 09
Neal 14
Nebraska 08
Neff La 30
Neff Rd
  300-3399 30
  3400-OUT 24
Negaunee
  15800-16099 39
  16100-20699 40

Neibel 12
Nelson 27
Nett 13
Netting 24
Nevada E
  1-1899 03
  1900-OUT 34
Nevada W 03
Neveux 24
New York 24
Newark 16
Newbern 12
Newberry 09
Newberry Pl 36
Newcastle Rd
  1500-1899 36
  21200-OUT 25
Newhall 11
Newport
  100-4999 15
  5000-11499 13
  11500-OUT 05
Newton 11
Nichols 13
Nicolet Pl 07
Nieman 18
Noble
  900-1399 01
Norborne
  8800-16099 39
  16100-20699 40
Norcross 13
Norfolk
  3100-12699 21
  12700-18099 35
  18100-24999 19
  25000-27399 40
Norfolk St N & S 35
Norman 09
Normandy
  15300-16099 38
  16100-OUT 21
Normile 04
North 03
North Campbell 10
North End
  1100-12699 29
  8500-9998 (EVEN) 37
  12700-OUT 37
North Oak Dr 20
Northampton 17
Northfield
  5800-7299 10
  7300-9599 04
  8400-15499 (OP) 37
Northgate 37
Northlawn
  8000-12599 04
  12600-16099 38
  16100-OUT 21
Northrop 19
Northway 20
Northwestern 06
Norton Ct 36
Norvell Ct 14
Norwalk
  1800-5899 12
  5900-OUT 11
Norway 17
Norwood
  1700-2199 (GPW) 36
  17800-17999 12
  18000-20599 34

Detroit (Con.)	482
19600-21299 (HW)	25
23000-OUT	37
Norwood Dr	
1700-2199 (GPW)	36
17800-17999	12
18000-20599	34
19600-21299 (HW)	25
23000-OUT	37
Notre Dame	30
Nottingham Rd	
800-3399	30
3400-OUT	24
Nevara	05
Nowak	10
Nuernberg	34
Oak	18
Oak Dr	21
Oak Park Blvd	37
Oak Crest Ave & Ct	37
Oakdale	09
Oakfield	
14800-16099	27
16100-OUT	35
Oakland	
6200-7299	02
7300-11699	11
11700-OUT	03
Oakman Blvd	
1-799	03
800-3419	38
3420-5969	04
5970-6799	28
Oakman Ct	
1-799	03
800-3419	38
3420-5969	04
5970-6799	28
Oakridge St E & W	20
Oakwood Dr	37
Ogden	
4800-5999	10
15400-OUT	39
Ohio	
8000-12599	04
12600-16099	38
16100-OUT	21
Oklahoma	12
Old Homestead Br	25
Old Mill Pl	38
Oldbrook Ln	24
Oldtown	36
Olga	13
Oliver	11
Olivet	09
Olympia	
8000-8399	13
17100-OUT	40
Omaha	17
Omara Ct	36
Omira	03
Oneida	37
Ontario	24
Opal	36
Orangelawn	
8500-12699	04
12700-18099	27
18100-21999	28
22000-27399	39
Orchard	
1-99	18

700-2499	20
21100-OUT	19
Oregon	04
Orion	34
Orleans	
100-4999	07
5000-11699	11
11700-OUT	03
Ormond	17
Otis	04
Otsego	10
Otto	04
Outer Dr E	
1400-6499	34
6500-9819	13
9820-OUT	24
Outer Dr W	
2900-4471	21
4472-8059	35
8060-9400	19
9401-13199	23
13200-14299	39
25691-26585 (ODD)	17
26600-27727	29
Owen	
1-899	02
900-OUT	11
Oxford Rd N & S	35
Oxley	11
Pacific	34
Packard	02
Page	09
Paget Ct	36
Pallister	
1-1399	02
1400-OUT	06
Palmer E	
1-899	02
900-7199	11
7200-OUT	03
Palmer W	02
Palmerston	18
Palmetto	34
Palms	09
Panama	10
Park Ave	
500-2099	26
2100-3199	01
9000-11499	13
11500-12699	05
14400-OUT	37
Park Dr	
500-2099	26
2100-3199	01
9000-11499	13
11500-12699	05
14400-OUT	37
Park Grv	
11000-11599	34
11600-OUT	05
Park Ln	30
Park Pl E	26
Park Ter	04
Park Lawn	37
Parkcrest Dr	25
Parkdale Ter	10
Parker	
500-4999	14
5000-OUT	13
Parkhurst Pl E & W	03
Parkinson	10
Parkland	39

Parkside	
14800-16099	38
16100-19599	21
20700-OUT	20
Parkview Ave & Dr	14
Parkway Dr	36
Parkwood	10
Parsons	01
Pasadena	
1-1399	03
1400-4399	38
8000-12699	20
12700-OUT	37
Patricia S	17
Patton	
7200-12599	28
12600-16099	23
16100-20699	19
Patton Ct	
20600-20699	28
Paul	
15500-18098 (EVEN)	28
18100-19999	28
Paxton	20
Payton	24
Peach Tree Ln	36
Pear	38
Pear Tree Ln	36
Pearl	09
Pearson	
100-1899	20
13600-OUT	37
Pease	11
Peerless	
10600-19199	24
19200-OUT	25
Pelham	09
Pelham S	09
Pelkey	05
Pelouze	10
Pemberton Rd	30
Pembridge Pl	07
Pembroke Ave	
3000-12699	21
12700-18099	35
18100-24999	19
25000-27399	40
Pembroke Rd	
3000-12699	21
12700-18099	35
18100-24999	19
25000-27399	40
Pennington Dr	21
Pennsylvania	
1200-4999	14
5000-OUT	13
Penrod	
5600-12599	28
12600-OUT	23
Penrose	09
Peoria	05
Pepper Rd	29
Perkins	10
Perrien	36
Perrin	18
Perry	
1000-1399	01
1400-OUT	16
Peter Hunt	13
Peterboro	01
Peters	17

Detroit (Con.) 482

Entry	Code
Pstoskey Ave	
8700-12599	04
12600-16099	38
16100-OUT	21
Petoskey Rd	
8700-12599	04
12600-16099	38
16100-OUT	21
Pfent	05
Phelps	13
Philadelphia E	
1-899	02
900-OUT	11
Philadelphia W	
1-1399	02
1400-3999	06
4000-OUT	04
Philip	
200-4999	15
5000-OUT	24
Phyllis	12
Picadilly Rd	21
Piche	36
Pickford	
3100-12699	21
12700-18099	35
18100-24999	19
25000-27399	40
Piedmont	
6000-12599	28
12600-OUT	23
Pierce	07
Pierson	
7200-12599	28
12600-16099	23
16100-OUT	19
Pierson Ct N & S	28
Pilgrim	
1-1399	03
1400-12699	38
1801-2899 (FER) (ODD)	20
12700-18099	27
18100-23999	23
24000-OUT	39
Pine	
1-199	18
900-1399	01
1400-OUT	16
Pine Ct	36
Pinecrest Dr	20
Pinehurst	
8000-12599	04
12600-16099	38
16100-OUT	21
Pinewood	05
Pingree	
1-1399	02
1400-3999	06
4000-OUT	04
Piper Blvd	15
Piquette	
1-899	02
900-OUT	11
Pitkin	03
Pitt	
4200-4299	29
7100-OUT	09
Pittsburg	10
Plainview Ave	
5600-12599	28
12600-16099	23
16100-OUT	19
Plainview Rd	
5600-12599	28
12600-16099	23
16100-OUT	19
Planavon	20
Platt	07
Pleasant	
500-699	20
11800-OUT	17
Pleasant St E & W	18
Plum	
600-1399	01
1400-OUT	16
Plumer	09
Plymouth Rd	
8300-12699	04
12700-18099	27
18100-21999	28
22000-27399	39
Poe	06
Poinciana	40
Pointer	34
Poland	12
Polk	18
Pomona Ave	
15300-16099	39
16100-16799	40
17400-OUT	24
Pomona Dr	
15300-16099	39
16100-16799	40
17400-OUT	24
Pontchartrain Blvd	03
Pontiac	08
Poplar	08
Port Dr	15
Portage	03
Porter	
600-1399	26
1400-3999	16
4000-OUT	05
Portlance	05
Portland	09
Posen	09
Post	09
Post S	09
Powell	17
Prairie	
7100-7999	18
8000-12599	04
12600-16099	38
16100-OUT	21
Prentis	01
Prescott	09
Pressler	13
Prest	
8000-9499	28
9500-16099	27
16100-OUT	35
Preston	
1-99	36
3000-7199	07
7200-OUT	14
Prestwick Ave	25
Prestwick Rd	36
Prevost	
8000-9499	28
9500-16099	27
16100-OUT	35
Princeton	
15300-16099	20
16100-OUT	21
Proctor	10
Promenade	
11000-15199	13
15200-OUT	24
Prospect	03
Provencal Rd	36
Pryor	14
Pulaski	
2100-2799	12
8600-9199	09
Pulford	07
Puritan	
1-2199	03
2200-12699	38
12700-18099	27
18100-23999	23
24000-27399	39
Putnam	
1-1399	02
1400-OUT	08
Putnam Pl	36
Queen	
9200-11499	13
11500-OUT	05
Queenston Pl	03
Quincy	
8400-12599	04
12600-16099	38
16100-OUT	21
Quinn	34
Racine	05
Radcliffe	
7500-8299	10
15500-OUT	28
Radclift St & Pl	37
Rademacher	
100-1999	09
Rademacher S	
100-799	09
Radford	04
Radio Pl	28
Radnor	24
Radnor Cir	36
Radom	12
Raine	37
Ralston	03
Randall	16
Randolph	26
Rangoon	
6500-7999	10
8000-OUT	04
Rankin	09
Ranspach	09
Rathbone	09
Rathbone Pl	30
Ravenswood	04
Ray	23
Raymond	
6600-9699	13
19200-OUT	36
Raynor	26
Redfern	19
Redford	19
Redmond	05
Reed Pl	02
Reeder	09
Regent Dr	05
Regular	09
Reid S	09
Reimanville	20
Reisener	09
Reissman	09
Remington E	
1-1899	03

Detroit (Con.)	482
1900-OUT	34
Remington W	03
Renaud Rd	36
Renaud Rd N & S	36
Renfrew Rd	21
Reno	
100-199	29
18400-OUT	05
Reno Ln	36
Rensselaer	37
Renville	10
Republic	
21600-22998 (EVEN)	20
21601-22999 (ODD)	37
23000-OUT	37
Reva	27
Revere	34
Rex	05
Reynolds	12
Rhode Island	03
Riad	
11600-19199	24
19200-OUT	25
Rich	10
Richard	09
Richardson	11
Richmond	11
Richter	
1-399	18
9300-OUT	14
Richton	
1-1399	03
1400-3999	06
4000-OUT	04
Ridge	
1-99	29
16200-OUT	19
Ridge Rd	
1-399	36
Ridgedale	37
Ridgemont Ave	
1-2299	36
19800-OUT	25
Ridgemont Rd	
1-2299	36
19800-OUT	25
Ridgewood	04
Rieden	09
Ries	17
Riopelle	
100-4999	07
5000-11699	11
11700-OUT	03
Risdon	16
Rivard	
100-4999	07
5000-OUT	11
Rivard Blvd	
200-999	30
River Cir	39
River Ct	14
River Rd	36
Riverdale Ave	
8800-12599	39
12600-16099	23
16100-OUT	19
Riverdale Dr N	
16100-OUT	19
Riverdale Dr S	
16100-OUT	19
Riverdale Dr W	
16100-OUT	19
Riverdale Rd	
8800-12599	39
12600-16099	23
16100-OUT	19
Riverpark	39
Riverside Blvd & Dr	15
Riverview	
8800-12599	39
12600-16099	23
16100-OUT	19
Riviera	04
Roanoke	37
Robert	13
Robert John Ave & Rd	36
Robindale	39
Robinwood E	
1-1899	03
1900-OUT	34
Robinwood W	03
Robson	
8000-9499	28
9500-16099	27
16100-OUT	35
Roby	11
Rochelle	05
Rochester	06
Rockcastle	
17800-18899	24
18900-19199	36
19200-OUT	25
Rockdale	
7200-12599	39
12600-16099	23
16100-OUT	19
Rockland	39
Rockwood	11
Rockwood St E & W	29
Rogers	09
Rogge	34
Rohns	
3400-4999	14
5000-OUT	13
Roland	13
Roland Ct & Rd	36
Rolandale	
18900-19199	36
19200-OUT	25
Rolf Pl	14
Rohyat	34
Romeo	20
Romeyn	09
Ronald Ct	37
Rondo	05
Roosevelt	
2400-3299	16
2900-3299 (HAM)	12
3300-OUT	08
Roosevelt Pl	30
Roscommon	25
Rose	16
Rose Ct	25
Roseberry	13
Rosedale Ct	
1-899	02
900-OUT	11
Rosedale Ct N & S	36
Roseland Ct	37
Roselawn	
8000-12599	04
12600-16099	38
16100-OUT	21
Rosemary	13
Rosemary Blvd	37
Rosemont Ave	
5600-12599	28
12600-16099	23
16100-OUT	19
Rosemont Rd	
5600-12599	28
12600-16099	23
16100-OUT	19
Rosewood	
100-1699	20
16300-17099	24
22000-OUT	37
Rosewood Ct	37
Roslyn Pl	
3300-3399	21
Roslyn Rd	
1-2299	36
21700-OUT	25
Roslyn (First Choice) Rd	
19500-19999	21
Ross Ct & Dr	39
Rossini Dr	05
Rossiter	
10900-19199	24
19200-OUT	25
Rouge S	17
Rouge Dr	17
Roulo Pl	09
Rowan	09
Rowe	05
Rowley	12
Roxbury	24
Roxford	19
Roy	10
Royal Grand	39
Rue Versailles	37
Ruedisale Ct	14
Rugg	11
Runyon	34
Rupert	12
Ruskin	16
Russell	
400-4999	07
5000-11699	11
11700-OUT	03
Ruth	
1-99	29
8600-OUT	13
Rutherford	
6300-9499	28
9500-16099	27
16100-OUT	35
Rutland	
6300-9499	28
9500-OUT	27
Ryan	
13400-17999	12
18000-20699	34
Ryland	
15500-16099	39
16100-OUT	40
Saddle Ln	36
Saginaw	11
Saint Albertus Pl	07
Saint Antoine	
400-2099	26
2100-4999	01
5000-OUT	02
Saint Aubin	
100-4999	07

Detroit (Con.)	**482**
5000-8399	11
8400-17999	12
18000-OUT	34
Saint Aubin Pl	
1100-1299	07
Saint Clair	
100-4999	14
300-999 (GPC)	30
5000-OUT	13
Saint Cyril	13
Saint Hedwig	10
Saint Ignace Pl	07
Saint James	10
Saint Jean	
1-4999	14
5000-OUT	13
Saint John	10
Saint Josafats Ct	
600-899	01
900-OUT	07
Saint Joseph	07
Saint Lawrence	10
Saint Louis	
100-999	20
11600-17999	12
18000-OUT	34
Saint Maron	07
Saint Martins Ave	
3600-12699	21
12700-18099	35
18100-24999	19
25000-27399	40
Saint Martins Rd	
3600-12699	21
12700-18099	35
18100-24999	19
25000-27399	40
Saint Martins St N & S	21
Saint Marys	
6300-9499	28
9500-16099	27
16100-OUT	35
Saint Patrick	05
Saint Paul	
6300-7199	07
7200-11999	14
12000-14999	15
15000-OUT	30
Saint Stephens	10
Saint Thomas	13
Sainte Anne	26
Salem	
8800-16099	39
16100-OUT	19
Salian	11
Salliotte	17
Salliotte Rd	29
Salter	05
Sampson	16
San Jose	39
San Juan Dr	
14000-16099	38
16100-OUT	21
Sanders	17
Sanford	05
Sanger	10
Sanilac	
9300-19199	24
19200-OUT	25
Santa Barbara Dr	21

Santa Clara	
3100-12699	21
12700-18099	35
18100-OUT	19
Santa Maria	
3100-12699	21
12700-18099	35
18100-24999	19
25000-OUT	40
Santa Rosa Dr	
12000-12599	04
12600-16099	38
16100-OUT	21
Sarasota Ave & Ct	39
Saratoga	
8200-12999	37
13600-OUT	05
Saratoga St E & W	20
Sarena	10
Sargent	11
Sarsfield	16
Sauer	
11300-11599	34
11600-OUT	05
Savage	34
Savannah St E & W	03
Savery	06
Savoy	16
Sawyer	
18100-21999	28
22000-OUT	39
Saxon	10
Scarsdale	23
Schaefer Hwy	
8000-9499	28
9500-16099	27
16100-OUT	35
Schaefer Hwy S	
101-1499 (ODD)	17
1500-2899	17
Scheffer Pl	11
Schiller	14
Schoenherr	05
School	12
Schoolcraft	
7400-12699	38
12700-18099	27
18100-23999	23
24000-27399	39
Schroeder S	09
Schuper	24
Schweizers Pl	26
Scotia	37
Scotia Ln	20
Scott	07
Scotten	
100-2599	09
2600-7299	10
7300-OUT	04
Scotten S	09
Scovel Pl	
3300-3999	08
4000-OUT	10
Scripps	15
Sears	03
Secor Pl	11
Seebaldt	04
Selden Ave	
1-1399	01
1400-OUT	08
Selden Ct	
1-1399	01
1400-OUT	08

Selfridge	12
Selkirk	11
Seminole	
700-4999	14
5000-6899	13
8800-16099	39
16100-20659	40
Senator	09
Seneca	
3700-4999	14
5000-6799	13
14800-15299	39
23000-OUT	37
Service	07
Severn Rd	
1500-2199	36
21200-OUT	25
Seward	
1-1399	02
1400-OUT	06
Seyburn	
500-4999	14
5000-OUT	13
Seymour	05
Shady Ln	16
Shaftsbury Ave & Rd.	19
Shakespeare	05
Sharon	
1900-3599	09
3600-OUT	10
Shasta Pl	20
Shaw	10
Shawcross Pl	03
Sheehan	13
Sheffield Rd	21
Shelbourne Rd	36
Shelby	26
Shelden Rd	36
Sherbourne Rd	21
Sheridan	
500-4999	14
5000-OUT	13
Sherman	
900-3199	07
22600-OUT	37
Sherwood	
6400-10499	11
10500-17999	12
13600-15099 (OP)	31
18000-20599	34
Shevlin	20
Shiawassee Dr	
18300-24999	19
Shiawassee Rd	
18300-24999	19
Shields	
13400-17999	12
18000-OUT	34
Shipherd Ave & Ct	14
Shirley	27
Shoemaker	13
Shorecrest Cir	36
Shoreham Rd	36
Short	19
Shrewsbury Rd	21
Sibley	01
Siebert	34
Signet	15
Silman	20
Simms	05
Simon K	12
Sioux	
8800-13899	39

Detroit (Con.)	482	Stahelin Rd		
		5600-12599	28	8000-9499 28
17100-OUT	24	12600-16099	23	9500-16099 27
Sire	09	16100-20699	19	16100-OUT 35
Sirron	34	Stair	09	Stratman 24
Sloan S	09	Standish	16	Stratton 09
Sloan Dr	25	Stanford	10	Stratton Pl 36
Sloman		Stanhope	36	Stringham Ct 13
1400-1499	11	Stanley		Strong
21900-OUT	37	900-1399	02	6300-7199 11
Smart	10	1400-OUT	08	7200-OUT 13
Smith		Stansbury		Stuart 07
1-899	02	13300-16099	35	Student 39
900-OUT	11	16100-OUT	37	Sturgis 34
Snowden Ave		Stanton	08	Sturtevant
14500-16099	27	Stanton Ln.	36	1-1399 03
16100-OUT	35	Starboard Dr	15	1400-3999 06
Snowden Ct		Stark	10	4000-OUT 04
14500-16099	27	State	26	Suburban 29
16100-OUT	35	State Fair E		Suffolk Dr 03
Sobieski	12	1-1899	03	Summit
Solvay	09	1900-11599	34	100-299 (RR) 18
Solvay S	09	11600-OUT	05	100-299 09
Somerset Ave		State Fair W	03	Summit S 09
1-3399	30	Stawell	04	Sumner
3400-OUT	24	Stearns	04	7700-8099 10
Somerset Rd		Steel		14900-16099 39
1-3399	30	8500-9499	28	16100-OUT 40
3400-OUT	24	9500-16099	27	Sunderland Rd 19
Sonoma	20	16100-OUT	35	Sunningdale Dr & Park 36
Sorrento		Steger Ct	38	Sunnyside
8000-9499	28	Stegner	23	1-99 29
9500-16099	27	Stender		23200-OUT 23
16100-OUT	35	1300-1899	03	Sunset
South	09	1900-OUT	12	13300-17999 12
South Cary	09	Stephens Rd	36	18000-20699 34
South Oakwood	17	Sterling	02	21900-OUT 37
Southampton		Sterling Ct	37	Sunset Blvd
12900-14399	13	Sterritt	13	13300-17999 12
14400-OUT	24	Stevens	03	18000-20699 34
Southfield Fwy		Stillmeadow Ln	36	21900-OUT 37
1-399	29	Stimson	01	Sunset Ln 36
5601-6299 (ODD)	28	Stocker	17	Superior
6300-12599	28	Stockton	34	400-599 (RR) 18
12600-16099	23	Stockwell	24	900-OUT 07
16100-20699	35	Stoepel		Sussex
Southwestern Hwy	39	8800-12599	04	8000-9499 28
Southwick	40	12600-16099	38	9500-16099 27
Sparling	12	16100-OUT	21	16100-19999 35
Sparta	10	Stoepel Pl	07	20700-24999 (OP) 37
Spaulding Ct	16	Stone	09	Sutherland 37
Spencer		Stonehurst Rd	36	Suzanne 34
100-1899	20	Stoner	18	Swain 09
19100-20599	34	Stotter	34	Swain S 09
Spinoza Dr	28	Stout		Swan 39
Spokane	04	7200-12599	28	Swift 03
Sprague	14	12600-16099	23	Sycamore 08
Springarden	05	16100-OUT	19	Sylbert Ct 39
Springfield	13	Stovell Pl	01	Sylbert St N & S 39
Springle	15	Strasburg	05	Sylvan 08
Springwells		Stratford		Sylvan Ct 37
500-3599	09	100-799	20	Sylvester
3600-OUT	10	19100-20699	21	3600-7199 87
Springwells S	09	20700-OUT	37	7200-OUT 14
Sproat	01	Stratford Pl		Symes Rd 20
Spruce		1-99	30	Syracuse
1000-1399	01	25900-OUT	37	12800-17999 12
1400-OUT	16	Stratford Rd		18000-20699 34
Stafford Pl	07	100-799	20	Tacoma 05
Stahelin Ave		19100-20699	21	Taft 08
5600-12599	28	20/00-OUT	37	Talbot
12600-16099	23	Strathcona Dr	03	3800-5899 12
16100-20699	19	Strathmoor		13600-OUT 37

Detroit (Con.)	482
Tappan	34
Ternow	10
Tate	39
Taylor	
1-1399	02
1400-3999	06
4000-OUT	04
Teaco	15
Tecumseh	
1-199	29
8800-OUT	39
Telegraph Rd	
8800-16099	39
16100-20699	19
Temple	
1-1399	01
1400-OUT	16
Tennessee	15
Tennyson	03
Teppert	34
Terminal	14
Ternes	10
Terrell	34
Terry	
8000-9499	28
9500-OUT	27
Thaddeus	09
Thatcher	
2900-12699	21
12700-18099	35
18100-OUT	19
Theodore	
200-899	02
900-7199	11
7200-OUT	13
Thole Ct	38
Thompson Ct	07
Thomson	03
Thorn Tree Rd	36
Thornhill Pl	07
Thornion	27
Tillman	
2800-3299	16
3300-OUT	08
Times Sq	26
Tireman	
4000-7499	04
8000-12698 (EVEN)	04
12700-15498 (EVEN)	28
15500-21999	28
22000-23199	39
Toledo	
3500-3999	16
4000-OUT	09
Toles Ln	36
Tonnancour Pl	36
Toronto	17
Torrey Ave & Ct	10
Torrey Rd	36
Touraine Rd	36
Tournier	27
Townsend	
400-4999	14
5000-OUT	13
Tracey	
14500-16099	27
16100-OUT	35
Tractor	17
Traverse	13
Treadway Pl	14
Trenton	10
Trevor Pl	07
Trinity	
8000-12599	28
12600-16099	23
16100-OUT	19
Troester	05
Trojan	
14600-18099	35
18100-OUT	19
Trombley Rd	30
Trombly	11
Trowbridge	
1-1899	02
1900-OUT	12
Troy	37
Troy Pl	03
Troy St E & W	20
Trumbull	
700-3299	16
3300-6199	08
6200-11699	02
11700-OUT	03
Tulare	37
Tuller	
12200-12599	04
12600-16099	38
1C100-OUT	21
Turney	34
Turner	
10500-12599	04
12600-16099	38
16100-OUT	21
Turner Pl	07
Tuscola	01
Tuxedo	
1-1399	03
1400-3999	06
4000-OUT	04
Tyler	
1-1399	03
1400-3999	38
12700-15499	27
25000-OUT	37
Tyrone	
18900-19199	36
19200-OUT	25
Ulster	19
Underwood	04
Union	
1-99	29
900-OUT	01
University	
100-1899	20
University Pl	
200-3399	30
3400-OUT	24
Uthes	09
Utica	04
Vale	37
Van Antwerp	
1800-2199	36
19900-OUT	25
Van Buren	
6300-12699	04
12700-21999	28
22000-23299	39
Van Dyke	
500-4999	14
5000-9899	13
9900-20561	34
Van Dyke Pl	
7800-7999	14
Van K Dr	36
Vancourt	10
Vancouver	04
Vanderbilt	09
Varjo	12
Varney	11
Vassar Ave	
13200-18099	35
18100-24999	19
25000-27399	40
Vassar Dr	
13200-18099	35
18100-24999	19
25000-27399	40
Vaughan	
6300-12599	28
12600-16099	23
16100-OUT	19
Veach	34
Vendome Ct & Rd	36
Venice	13
Verdun	19
Vermont	
500-3299	16
3300-OUT	08
Verne	
15500-18099	35
18100-OUT	19
Vernier Cir	36
Vernier Rd	
1-2299	36
17700-21599	25
Vernon	37
Vernor Hwy E	
1-899	01
900-7199	07
7200-11999	14
12000-14999	15
15000-OUT	30
Vernor Hwy W	
1-1399	01
1400-3999	16
4000-9399	09
Verona	05
Vester	20
Vicksburg	
2600-3999	06
4000-OUT	04
Victor	03
Victoria	
1-99	18
2000-3699	12
13600-OUT	37
Vigo	10
Village Ln	30
Vincennes Pl	36
Vincent	11
Vinewood	
100-3299	16
3300-OUT	08
Vinewood S	16
Vinton	13
Violetlawn	04
Virgil	
8800-12599	39
12600-16099	23
16100-OUT	19
Virginia Ct	29
Virginia Ln	36
Virginia Park	
1-1399	02
1400-3999	06
4000-OUT	04

Detroit (Con.)   482

Vasger
1-601 (ODD)	29
2-98 (EVEN)	29
100-598 (EVEN)	18
11700-OUT	17

Visger Rd
1-599 (ODD)	29
2-98 (EVEN)	29
100-598 (EVEN)	18
11700-OUT	17

Vista Ct	09
Voight	24
Voltaire Pl	36
Volte	27
Voss	09
Votrobeck Ct & Dr	19
Vulcan	11

Wabash
1400-3299	16
3300-7299	08
7300-12599	06
12600-OUT	38

Wade
11200-14499	13
14500-OUT	24

Wadsworth
10300-12699	04
12700-18099	27
18100-21999	28
22000-27399	39

Wager	06
Wagner	18
Wakefield Rd	21

Wakenden
15300-16099	39
16100-20699	40

Walbridge	13
Walden	13
Waldo	10
Wales	37
Walker	13
Wallace	07
Wallick Pl	03
Wallingford	24
Walnut	18

Walter P Chrysler Fwy
400-4998 (EVEN)	07
401-2099 (ODD)	26
2101-4999 (ODD)	01
5000-9799	11
9800-12899	12
12900-20699	03

Waltham	05
Walton	10
Wanamaker Pl	23

Wanda
100-1799	20
17100-OUT	03

Ward
8000-9499	28
9500-16099	27
16100-OUT	35

Waring S	17
Warner	14
Warner Rd	36

Warren E
1-899	01
900-7199	07
7200-11999	14
12000-14899	15
14900-18399	24

18400-OUT	36

Warren W
1-1399	01
1400-3999	08
4000-8099	10
15500-20200	28
20202-21998 (EVEN)	28
22000-22798 (EVEN)	39

Warren Ct	07
Warrington Dr	21
Warsaw Pl	07

Warwick
5600-12599	28
12600-16099	23
16100-OUT	19

Washburn
11600-12599	04
12600-16099	38
16100-OUT	21

Washington Blvd	26
Washington Rd	30
Washtenaw	25

Waterloo
1900-7199	07
7200-11999	14
12000-14999	15
15000-OUT	30

Waterman	09
Waterman S	09
Watko	12

Watson
1-899	01
900-OUT	07

Waveney
12500-14899	15
14900-OUT	24

Waverly
1-1399	03
1400-OUT	38

Waverly Ln	36

Wayburn
1000-3399	30
3400-OUT	24

Wayne	09
Weaver	07

Webb
1-1399	02
1400-3999	06
4000-OUT	04

Webber Dr	25
Webber Ln	36

Webster
4400-4699	24
23000-OUT	37

Webster Rd	36
Webster St E & W	20
Wedgewood Dr	36
Weitzel Ct	11
Wellesley Dr	03
Wellington	11
Wellington Pl	30
Welton	04
Wendell	09
Wendy Ln	36
Wesson	10

West Chicago
2600-3999	06
4000-12699	04
12700-21999	28
22000-27399	39

West End
100-299	09
101-1799 (FER) (ODD)	20

West End S	09
West Jefferson	29

West Parkway
7300-12599	39
12600-16099	23
16100-OUT	19

West Point	04
West Wind Ln	36

Westbrook
12600-16099	23
16100-20699	19
21600-OUT	36

Westchester Rd	30

Western
2800-3599	09
3600-OUT	10

Westfield
6300-12699	04
12700-21999	28
22000-27399	39

Westfield St E & W	29
Westgate Dr	39
Westhampton	37
Westland Rd	40

Westminster
1-899	02
900-OUT	11

Westmoreland Rd	19
Westover	04
Westphalia	05
Westridge Ct	20
Westview	20

Westwood
5800-12599	28
12600-OUT	23

Wetherby
7100-7999	10
8000-OUT	04

Wexford
17800-17999	12
18000-OUT	34

Weyher	14
Whalen	12
Wheeler	10
Wheelock	09
Whipple	13

Whitcomb
8000-9499	28
9500-16099	27
16100-OUT	35

Whitcomb Dr	36

White
1-399	29
8500-OUT	09

Whitehead	10
Whitehill	24
Whitewood	10
Whitfield	04
Whithorn	05
Whitlock	28

Whitmore
300-1099	03
21600-OUT	37

Whitmore Rd
300-1099	03
21600-OUT	37

Whitney
2600-3999	06
4000-OUT	04

Whittaker	09

Whittier Ave
700-3399	30
3400-11799	24

Detroit (Con.)   482

Whittier Rd
  700-3399 30
  3400-11799 24
Wicks Ln 36
Widman Pl 11
Wight 07
Wilbur 02
Wilbur Ct 39
Wilcox 28
Wilde 09
Wildemere
  7300-12599 06
  12600-16099 38
  16100-OUT 21
Wildwood
  900-1099 03
  20700-OUT 37
Wildwood Dr 25
Wilfred 13
Wilkie 09
Wilkins
  400-899 01
  900-OUT 07
Willard 14
Wilette 10
William Ct E & W 36
Williams
  1-399 36
  2700-3299 16
  3300-OUT 08
Williamsburg Ct 25
Willis E
  1-899 01
  900-OUT 07
Willis W -
  1-1399 01
  1400-OUT 08
Willison Rd 36
Willmarth 19
Willow Ln 36
Willow Tree Ln & Pl 36
Wilshire Dr 13
Winchester 37
Winchester E
  1-1899 03
  1900-OUT 34
Winchester W 03
Winder
  1-899 01
  900-OUT 07
Windmill Pointe Dr 30
Windsor 24
Winfield
  8500-9699 13
  9800-OUT 12
Wing Pl 16
Winger 12
Winkleman 11
Winona 03
Winslow 08
Winston
  8800-16099 39
  16100-OUT 19
Winter 07
Winthrop
  6300-9499 28
  9500-16099 27
  16100-OUT 35
Winthrop Pl 36
Wisconsin
  8000-12599 04

  12600-16099 38
  16100-OUT 21
Wisner 34
Witherell
  1-2099 26
  2100-OUT 01
Withington 20
Witt 09
Wolcott 20
Wolff 09
Wood 34
Woodbine
  8800-16099 39
  16100-OUT 19
Woodbridge
  100-899 26
  900-OUT 07
Woodcrest 25
Woodhall 24
Woodingham Dr
  15300-16099 38
  16100-OUT 21
Woodland
  1-899 02
  900-1499 11
  1500-1899 12
  18500-OUT 25
Woodland Ct 30
Woodland Pl 30
Woodland St E & W 20
Woodland Shores Dr 36
Woodlawn 13
Woodmere 09
Woodmont Ave
  6300-9499 28
  9500-15099 27
  18900-OUT 25
Woodmont Rd
  6300-9499 28
  9500-15099 27
  18900-OUT 25
Woodrow
  5600-6699 10
  26200-OUT 40
Woodrow Wilson
  7300-12599 06
  12600-OUT 38
Woods Ct & Ln 36
Woodside
  8200-8599 37
  9200-10099 04
  18500-20799 (HW) 25
  20700-21499 (FER) 20
Woodside Ct & Dr 04
Woodstock Dr
  2300-2999 03
  3000-OUT 21
Woodston Rd 03
Woodvale 37
Woodward
  1-2099 26
  2100-4999 01
  5000-11699 02
  11700-20699 03
  20700-23625 20
Woodward Hts 20
Woodward St E & W 29
Woodworth
  14800-16099 39
  16100-20699 40
Worcester Pl 03
Worden 24
Wordsworth 20

Wormer
  8800-16099 39
  16100-OUT 19
Wreford 08
Wrenson 20
Wyandotte 12
Wykes
  7200-7999 10
  8000-OUT 04
Wyman 19
Wyoming
  5202-6400 (EVEN) 10
  8000-12599 04
  12600-16099 38
  16100-20699 21
  20700-21799 20
  21600-21798 (EVEN) 37
  21800-21999 37
Yacama Rd 03
Yale 37
Yale S 09
Yates 14
Yellowstone 04
Yemans
  1900-5899 12
  5900-OUT 11
Yolanda 34
Yonka
  17800-17999 12
  18000-OUT 34
York 02
Yorkshire Ave
  1000-3399 30
  3400-OUT 24
Yorkshire Rd
  1000-3399 30
  3400-OUT 24
Yorktown 36
Yosemite 04
Young 05
Young Ln 36
Zender Pl 07
Zinow 12
Zug Island Rd 09

NUMBERED STREETS

1st
  500-1999 26
  4400-OUT 29
2nd Ave
  600-2099 26
  2100-4999 01
  4300-4599 (EC) 29
  5000-11699 02
  11700-OUT 03
2nd Blvd
  600-2099 26
  2100-4999 01
  4300-4599 (EC) 29
  5000-11699 02
  11700-OUT 03
3 Mile Dr
  800-3399 30
  3400-OUT 24
3rd
  500-2099 26
  2100-4999 01
  4300-4599 (EC) 29
  5000-11699 02
  11700-OUT 03
4th
  1200-2099 26

Detroit (Con.)   482

2100-4999...............	01
4400-4699 (EC).......	29
5000-OUT...............	02

5 Mile Rd............... 39

5th

1400-2099...............	26
2100-2799...............	01
4100-OUT...............	29

6 Mile Rd............... 49

6th

1200-2099...............	26
2100-4899...............	01
4100-4699 (EC).......	29

7 Mile Rd E

1-1899...............	63
1900-11599.............	34
11600-OUT.............	05

7 Mile Rd W

1-2199...............	63
2200-12699.............	21
12700-18099............	35
18100-24999............	19
25000-27399............	40

7th............... 29

8 Mile Rd E

2-1898 (EVEN).......	03
101-1899 (FER) (ODD)....	20
1701-2241 (GPW) (ODD)..	36
1900-9998 (EVEN).......	34
10000-17050 (EVEN).....	05
17052-OUT (EVEN).......	25

8 Mile Rd W

1-2999 (ODD).......	63
100-12698 (EVEN).......	20
3001-12699 (ODD).......	21
12700-15498 (EVEN).....	37
12701-18099 (ODD)......	35
18101-24999 (ODD)......	19
25001-27399 (ODD)......	40

8th

500-2299...............	16
3700-OUT.............	29

9 Mile Rd E

100-OUT...............	20

9 Mile Rd W

100-1699...............	29
8100-15499.............	37

9th............... 29

10 Mile Rd E

600-2498 (EVEN).......	20

10 Mile Rd W

8201-13599 (ODD)......	37
13600-15499............	37

10th

500-2099...............	16
3700-OUT.............	29

11 Mile Rd W

13601-15499 (ODD).....	37

11th

1900-2099...............	16
3700-OUT.............	29

12th

100-3299...............	16
3300-7299.............	08
3700-4399 (EC).......	29
7300-12599............	06
12600-16099...........	38
16100-OUT............	03

13th............... 29

14th

700-3299...............	16
3300-7299.............	08
3700-4099 (EC).......	29
7300-12599............	06
12600-OUT............	38

15th

300-3299...............	16
3300-6599.............	08
3700-4299 (EC).......	29

16th

500-3299...............	16
3300-6599.............	08
3700-4299 (EC).......	29

17th

500-3299...............	16
3300-5099.............	08
3700-4299 (EC).......	29

18th

500-3299...............	16
3300-4799.............	08
3700-4299 (EC).......	29

19th............... 16

20th thru 22nd St....... 16

23rd

1-3299...............	16
3300-OUT.............	08

24th

1-3299...............	16
3300-OUT.............	08

25th

1-3299...............	16
3300-OUT.............	08

28th thru 33rd St....... 10

35th............... 10

51st thru 52nd St....... 10

FLINT   485

POST OFFICE BOXES

Box Nos.

1-1999	Main Office......	01
3000-3999	Church Street Sta....	02
4000-4999	Mott Park Sta.	04
5000-5999	North Side Sta.	05
6000-6999	East Side Sta.	08
7000-7999	Cody Sta.	07

STATIONS, BRANCHES AND UNITS

Church Street Sta...............	02
Cody Sta...............	07
East Side Sta...............	08
Mott Park Sta...............	04
North Side Sta...............	05
General Deliver...............	02
Postmaster...............	02

APARTMENTS, HOTELS, MOTELS

Airport, 3040 W Bristol Rd	07
Ambassador Arms West, G 1/2 3348 Flushing Rd.......	04
Autorams, 2002 S Dort Hwy ..	03
Ballenger Manor, 810 S Ballenger Hwy...............	04
Beecher, G5326 N Saginaw....	05
Berridge, 421 Garland...........	01
Bervean, 318 W 2nd.............	02
Capitol, 139 E 2nd...............	01
Chase, 906 Garland...............	03

College Inn, 505 Detroit......	02
Colonial, G5661 S Saginaw...	07
Country Club Manor, 1902 Woodslea St...............	07
Dort, G3370 S Dort Hwy......	07
Durant, 607 E 2nd Ave.......	01
Ehrnst, 6550 N Dort Hwy.....	05
Elms, 2701 S Dort Hwy........	07
Flint, G5452 N Dort Hwy......	05
Forest Park Manor, 4060 Detroit...............	05
Hardy, 613 Clifford.............	02
Holiday Inn, 2207 W. Bristol Rd...............	07
Howard Johnson, G3129 Miller Rd...............	07
Hunters Ridge, 3020 Ridgecliffe St...............	04
Imperial 400, 902 Stevens....	03
Kearsley Lake Terrace, 3465 Benmarks Pl...............	06
Lawrence Manor, 5515 Detroit St...............	05
Mar-Jo, 1760 S Dort Hwy.....	03
Marvanette, 711 Mary........	03
Miller West Thirty 1/2 one Hundred, G 1/2 3100 Miller Rd...............	07
North West Manor, 5515 Detroit St...............	05
Oakview Manor, 125 W Gracelawn St...............	05
Orchard Lane, 2645 Orchard Lane...............	04
Parkview Manor, 915 E Court...............	03
Regency Park Cooperative, 2112 Trout Dr...............	07
River Forest, 3500 Riverforest St...............	04
Sheffield Manor, 328 Sheffield St...............	03
Stone, 222 E 1st...............	02
Sussex Arms, 1910 W Pierson Rd...............	04
Swayze, 224 E Court...........	02
Westgate Terrace, 3901 Hammerberg St...............	07
Westwood Manor, 4201 Clio Rd...............	04

BUILDINGS

A C Spark Plug...............	56
Atwood, 436 S Saginaw.......	02
Buick Motor Division........	50
Capitol, 134 E 2nd.............	02
Center, 201 N Saginaw........	02
Chevrolet Engine Plant......	52
Chevrolet Flint Assembly Division...............	51
Chevrolet Flint Manufacturing...............	55
Chevrolet Frame & Stamping Plant...............	53
Chevrolet National Parts.....	54
Chevrolet Zone Sales.........	01
Citizens Bank, 328 S Saginaw...............	02
College & Cultural Center, E Kearsley & Craps.......	02
Commerce, 242 S Saginaw St...............	02

Flint (Con.)	485

Community Service, 202 E.
Boulvard Dr 02
Dryden, 601 S Saginaw 02
Fisher Body Coldwater Rd
Plant 59
Fisher Body 1 57
Fisher Body 2 58
Genesee Bank, 346 S
Saginaw 02
Genesee Towers, 120 E 1st 02
Kresge, 108 E Kearsley 02
Metropolitan, 428 N Saginaw .. 02
Mott, 501 S Saginaw 02
National, 460 S Saginaw 02
North Flint Plaza, 102 W
Pierson Rd 05
Northwest Plaza, W Pierson &
Clio Rd 04
Palace Theatre Bldg, 201
Kearsley St 02
Paterson, 653 S Saginaw 02
Phoenix Bldg, 801 S Saginaw
St 02
Public Library, 1026 E
Kearsley 02
Sill, 257 S Saginaw 02
South Flint Plaza, Hemphill &
Fenton Rd 07
Walsh Bldg, 310 N Saginaw
St 02

GOVERNMENT OFFICES

City Hall, 1101 S Saginaw 02
Federal Building, 600
Church 02
State Police Headquarters,
G3478 Corunna Rd 04

HOSPITALS

Flint General, 765 E
Hamilton 05
Flint Osteopathic, 3921
Beecher Rd 02
Genesee Memorial, 702 S
Ballenger Hwy 02
Hurley, 6th Ave & Begole 02
Mc Laren General, 401 S
Ballenger Hwy 02
Saint Josephs, 302
Kensington 02
Walter Winchester, G4562
Flushing Rd 04

UNIVERSITIES AND COLLEGES

Baker Business
University,1110 Manitou 07
Flint Junior College, 1401 E
Ct 02
General Motors Institute, 3rd
Ave & Chevrolet. 02
University Of Michigan Flint
Branch, 1321 E Ct 02

GRAND RAPIDS	495

POST OFFICE BOXES

Box Nos.
A-T　　　　Main Office 01
1000-2999　　Main Office 01
6000-6999　　Station C 06
7000-7999　　Seymour
　　　　　　Square Sta 10
8000-8999　　South Kent Br 08
9000-9999　　Wyoming Br 09

RURAL ROUTES

1 08
2 04
3 06
4 05
5 09
6 09
7,8 08

STATIONS, BRANCHES AND UNITS

Dutton Rural Br 11
Kentwood Br 08
Northgate Br 04
Reeds Lake Br 06
Seymour Square Sta 10
Southkent Br 08
Walker Br 04
Wyoming Br 09
Wyoming Park Br 09
General Delivery 01
Postmaster 01

APARTMENTS, HOTELS, MOTELS

Fountain Hill, 301 Fountain
St NE 03
Herkimer, 323 Division Ave S . 02
Hillmount, 505 Cherry St SE... 03
Holland Home, 1450 Fulton,
East 03
Lakeshore, 2311 Wealthy St
SE 06
Milner, 74 Ionia Ave SW 02
Morton House, 72 Monroe Ave
NW 02
Oakway, 35 Oakes St SW 02
Oakwood Manor, 547 Cherry
St SE 02
Olds Manor, 201 Michigan St
NW 02
Pantlind, 187 Monroe Ave St
NW 02
Stuyvesant, 413 Cherry St
SE 03
Waters House, 500 Fulton St
E 03
Y M C A, 33 Library St NE 02
Y W C A, 25 Sheldon Ave SE... 02

BUILDINGS

A G Terminal, 900 Monroe
Ave NW 02
Castle,the, 455 Cherry SE..... 02
Commerce 5 Lyon NW 02
Exhibitors, 220 Lyon NW 02
Federal Square, 29 Pearl NW.. 02

G M A C, 345 State SE.......... 02
Goodspeed, 190 Monroe Ave
NW 02
Grand Rapids Mutual, 201
Monroe Ave, NW.......... 02
Grand Rapids Press, 155
Michigan St NW 02
Helmer, 21 Ottawa Ave NW.... 02
Keeler, 60 Division Ave N...... 02
Kendall, 16 Monroe Ave NE.... 02
Loraine, 124 Fulton St E....... 02
Luman, 45 Monroe Ave NW.... 02
Mckay Tower, 146 Monroe
Ave NW.......... 02
Medical Arts, 26 Sheldon
Ave, SE.......... 02
Michigan Consolidated Gas,
200 Monroe Ave NW.......... 02
Michigan National Bank, 77
Monroe Ave NW.......... 02
Old Kent Bank, 111 Lyon St
NW.......... 02
Peoples, 60 Monroe Ave NW ... 02
Prudential Insurance, 252
State St SE 02
Tanglefoot, 314 Straight Ave
SW.......... 02
Tower Medical, 21 Michigan
St., NE.......... 02
Trust, 40 Pearl St NW.......... 02
Union Bank, 200 Ottawa Ave
NW.......... 02
Waters, 161 Ottawa Ave NW... 02

GOVERNMENT OFFICES

City Hall, 300 Monroe Ave,
NW.......... 02
County Building, 300 Monroe
Ave, NW.......... 02
Federal Building, 150 Ionia
Ave, NW.......... 02
Hall Of Justice, 333 Monroe
Ave, NW.......... 02

HOSPITALS

Blodgett, 1840 Wealthy St
SE.......... 06
Butterworth, 100 Michigan St
NE.......... 03
Ferguson-Droste-Ferguson, 72
Sheldon Ave SE.......... 02
Grand Rapids Osteopathic,
1919 Boston St SE.......... 06
Kent Community, 750 Fuller
Ave, NE.......... 03
Michigan Veterans Facility.
3000 Monroe Ave NE.......... 05
Pine Rest Chr, 6850 Division
Ave S.......... 08
Saint Mary'S, 201 Lafayette
Ave SE.......... 03

UNIVERSITIES AND COLLEGES

Aquinas, 1607 Robinson Rd
SE.......... 06
Calvin Seminary, 3233
Burton St SE.......... 06
Calvin-Knollcrest Campus,
3215 Burton St SE.......... 06
Calvin, 1331 Franklin St SE.... 06

377

Grand Rapids (Con.)   495

Grace Bible, 1011 Aldon St
SW..................................... 09
Grand Rapids Baptist Bible
Col, 1001 E Beltline Ave
NE..................................... 05

JACKSON   492

POST OFFICE BOXES

Box Nos.
1-1324   Main Office 04

RURAL ROUTES

1,2,3,4,5,6,7,8,9,10,11,12,13,
14................................... 01

STATIONS, BRANCHES AND UNITS

Vandercook Lake Br 03
General Delivery 01
Postmaster 01

KALAMAZOO   490

POST OFFICE BOXES

Box Nos.
1-117   Parchment Br..... 04
1-1071   Court Sta........... 05
2001-2858   Main Office........ 03

RURAL ROUTES

1...................................... 09
2...................................... 04
3,4,5................................. 01
6...................................... 07
7...................................... 09
8...................................... 01
9...................................... 09
10.................................... 04
11,12................................ 09
14.................................... 01

STATIONS, BRANCHES AND UNITS

Court Sta. 06
Parchment Br 04
General Delivery 03
Postmaster 01

LANSING   489

POST OFFICE BOXES

Box Nos.
1-210   Lansing........... 01
211-510   Lansing........... 02
511-810   Lansing........... 03
811-1410   Lansing........... 04

2001-2364   Michigan
                  Avenue Sta..... 11
5001-5314   North Lansing
                  Sta................. 05
9001-9577   South Cedar
                  Annex Sta..... 09

RURAL ROUTES

1...................................... 06
2...................................... 17
3...................................... 10
4...................................... 06
5...................................... 17

STATIONS, BRANCHES AND UNITS

Frandor Br 12
Michigan Avenue Sta.............. 11
North Lansing Sta................... 05
South Cedar Street Annex Sta.. 09
Waverly Br 17
General Delivery 24
Postmaster 24

APARTMENTS, HOTELS, MOTELS

Capitol Club, 222 Seymour
Ave..................................... 33
Capitol Park Motor, 501
Townsend............................ 14
Central, 212 West
Kalamazoo........................... 33
Country Club Manor, 1815
Potomac Cir......................... 10
Dean, 727 North Capitol Ave.. 06
Embassy, 524-526 South
Chestnut.............................. 33
Ferris Park Towers, 323 N
Walnut................................ 33
Grand River Terrace, 2603-
2727 E Grand River.............. 12
Grand, 403 East Grand River
Ave..................................... 06
Heritage Arms, 3031 S
Washingto Ave..................... 10
Holiday Inn 3731 East Grand
Rive Ave.............................. 12
Holiday Inn, 1031 Pierpont..... 10
Home'S Motor Lodge, 6501 S
Cedar.................................. 10
Hospitality Motor Inn, I 496
At Dunckel........................... 10
Howard Johnson Motor Lodge,
6741 S Cedar....................... 10
Lansing Towers, 610 W
Ottawa................................ 33
Manor House, 920 S
Washington Ave................... 10
Motel 6, 112 E. Main............. 33
Olds Plaza, 125 W. Michigan
Ave..................................... 02
Ramada Inn, 1000 Ramada
Dr....................................... 10
Washington, 917 S
Washington Ave................... 10

BUILDINGS

American Bank And Trust
101 S Washington Sq............ 33
Bank Of Lansing, 101 N
Washington Sq..................... 33
Bauch, 115 West Allegan 33

Board Of Water & Light, 123
W Ottawa............................ 33
Builders & Traders, 1240 E
Saginaw.............................. 06
Capitol Savings & Loan, 112
East Allegan........................ 33
Civic Center, 505 West
Allegan................................ 33
Commerce Center, 300 S
Capitol Ave.......................... 33
County, 118 West Ottawa....... 33
Davenport, 144 West Ottawa.. 33
Federal, 315 West Allegan...... 33
Hollister, 108 West Allegan 33
Labor, 300 East Michigan
Ave..................................... 33
Lansing City Library, 401 S
Capitol Ave.......................... 14
Lansing Medical - Dental,
2909 E Grand River Ave........ 12
Leonard Plaza 309 N
Washington Sq..................... 33
Medical Arts, 1322 E
Michigan Ave....................... 12
Medical Center West, 701 N
Logan.................................. 15
Michigan Dental, 230 N.
Washington Sq..................... 33
Michigan National Tower,
124 West Allegan.................. 33
Michigan Theatre Arcade,
215 S Washington Ave.......... 33
State Employees Credit
Union, 501 S. Capitol
Ave..................................... 33
Stoddard, 125 West Allegan.... 33
Union Savings & Loan, 121
West Allegan........................ 33
Washington Sq Bldg. 109
West Michigan Ave............... 33
Ywca 217 Townsend............... 33

HOSPITALS

Edward W Sparrow, 1215
East Michigan Ave................ 02
Ingham Medical, 401 West
Greenlawn........................... 10
Lansing General, 2800
Devonshire Ave.................... 09
Saint Lawrence, 1210 West
Saginaw.............................. 14

UNIVERSITIES AND COLLEGES

Great Lakes Bible College,
6211 W Willow Hwy.............. 17
Lansing Business University,
200 North Capitol Ave.......... 33
Lansing Community College,
419 North Capitol Ave.......... 14

LIVONIA   481

POST OFFICE BOXES

Box Nos.
2001-2952   Main Office 51

STATIONS, BRANCHES AND UNITS

Northeast Sta 52
General Delivery 50

378

MUSKEGON 494

POST OFFICE BOXES

Box Nos.
1-1024	Main Office	43
4001-4432	Muskegon Heights Br	44
5001-5128	North Muskegon Br	45

RURAL ROUTES

1	44
2,3	45
4	42
5	45
6	42

STATIONS, BRANCHES AND UNITS

Dalton Rural Br	45
Glenside Br	41
Henry Street Br	41
Muskegon Heights Br	44
North Muskegon Br	45
Roosevelt Park Br	44
Wolf Lake Br	42
General Delivery	40
Postmaster	40

PONTIAC 480

POST OFFICE BOXES

Box Nos.
1-1072	Main Office	56
3001-3793	Federal Sta	59
4109-4700	Auburn Heights Br	57

RURAL ROUTES

1	57
2	54
3,4	55
5	54
6	55

STATIONS, BRANCHES AND UNITS

Auburn Heights Br	57
Federal Station Br	58
M Fifty Nine Plaza Br	54
General Delivery	56
Postmaster	53

APARTMENTS, HOTELS, MOTELS

Canterbury Apts., 900 East Blvd. S	53
Embassy East & West, 5367 Highland	54
Fountainbleau Apts., 995 N. Cass Lake	54
Grand Prix Apts., 311 S. Telegraph	53

BUILDINGS

Community National Bank Bldg., 30 N. Saginaw	58
County Court House, 1200 N. Telegraph	53
Federal Building, 35 E. Huron	58
Pontiac State Bank Bldg., 28 N. Saginaw	58
Riker Building, 35 E. Huron	58

HOSPITALS

Pontiac General Hospital, Seminole At W. Huron	53
Pontiac Osteopathic Hospital, 50 N. Perry	53
Pontiac State Hospital, 140 Elizabeth Lake	53
St. Joseph Mercy Hospital, 900 Woodward	53

ROYAL OAK 480

POST OFFICE BOXES

Box Nos.
A-H	Main Office	68
1-499	Main Office	68
1-699	Madison Heights Br	71
500	Oak Ridge Sta	73
701-947	Main Office	68
1000-1299	Berkley Br	72

STATIONS, BRANCHES AND UNITS

Berkley Br	72
Huntington Woods Br	70
Madison Heights Br	71
Oak Ridge Sta	73
Pleasant Ridge Br	69
General Delivery	67
Postmaster	67

SAGINAW 486

POST OFFICE BOXES

Box Nos.
501-1291	Castle Sta	06
1341-3306	Main Office	05

RURAL ROUTES

1	01
2	04
3,4	01
5,6,7,8	03
9	01

STATIONS, BRANCHES AND UNITS

Castle Sta	06

State Center Br	02
General Delivery	05
Postmaster	05

APARTMENTS, HOTELS, MOTELS

Amadore, 518 Thompson	07
Green Acres Village, 4545 Colonial	03
Hidden Hollow, 1800 Beacon Dr	02
Mac Arthur Square, 332 South Center Rd	03
Maplewood Manor, 535 S Warren	07
Poplar, 4440 State	03

BUILDINGS

Bearinger, 126 S Franklin	07
Chamber Of Commerce, Washington At Johnson	07
Eddy, 102 N Washington	07
First Savings & Loan, 124 S Jefferson	07
Second National Bank, 121 E Genesee	07
Wiechmann, 112 S Jefferson	07

GOVERNMENT OFFICES

Saginaw City Hall, 1315 S Washington	01
Saginaw County Court House, 111 S Michigan	02

HOSPITALS

Saginaw County, Hospital Rd.	05
Saginaw General, 1447 N Harrison	02
Saginaw Osteopathic, 515 N Michigan	02
Saint Lukes, 705 Cooper	02
Saint Marys, 830 S Jefferson	01

SOUTHFIELD 480

POST OFFICE BOXES

Box Nos.
1-200	Lathrup Village Branch	76
1-999	Main Office	75
1000-1399	Northland Center Station	75

STATIONS, BRANCHES AND UNITS

Lathrup Village Br	75
Northland Center Sta	75
General Delivery	75
Postmaster	75

SAINT CLAIR SHORES 480

POST OFFICE BOXES

Box Nos.
A-H	Main Office	83

| St. Clair Shores (Con.) | 480 | | **WARREN** | 480 | | **WYANDOTTE** | 481 |

STATIONS, BRANCHES AND UNITS

| General Delivery | 83 |
| Postmaster | 83 |

POST OFFICE BOXES

Box Nos.		
1-464	South Sta	90
501-1269	Main Office	
	Sta	90

POST OFFICE BOXES

Box Nos		
1-409	Main Office	92
AA-FF	Southgate Br	95
1001-1280	Southgate Br	92
2001-2154	Riverview Br	92

STERLING HEIGHTS 480

STATIONS, BRANCHES AND UNITS

| Sterling Heights Br | 77 |
| Postmaster | 77 |

STATIONS, BRANCHES AND UNITS

South Sta	92
General Delivery	89
Postmaster	89

STATIONS, BRANCHES AND UNITS

Riverview Br	92
Southgate Br	92
General Delivery	92
Postmaster	92

MINNESOTA

State List of Post Offices

MINNESOTA
(Abbreviation: MN)

Ada	56510
Adams	55909
Adolph	55701
Adrian	56110
Afton	55001
Ah-Gwah-Ching	56430
Aitkin (1st)	56431
Akeley	56433
Albany	56307
Albert Lea (1st)	56007
Alberta	56207
Albertville	55301
Alborn	55702
Alden	56009
Aldrich	56434
Alexandria (1st)	56308
Almelund	55002
Alpha	56111
Altura	55910
Alvarado	56710
Alvwood	56620
Amboy	56010
Amiret	56112
Angle Inlet	56711
Angora	55703
Angus	56712
Annandale	55302
Anoka (1st)	55303
Soderville, R. Br.	55304
Apache, Br. Minneapolis	55421
Appleton	56208
Arco	56113
Argyle	56713
Arlington	55307
Ashby	56309
Askov	55704
Atwater	56209
Audubon	56511
Aurora	55705
Austin (1st)	55912
Avoca	56114
Avon	56310
Babbitt	55706
Backus	56435
Badger	56714
Bagley	56621
Baker	56513
Balaton	56115

Ball Club, R. Br. Deer River	56622
Barnesville	56514
Barnum	55707
Barrett	56311
Barry	56210
Battle Lake	56515
Baudette (1st)	56623
Bayport (1st)	55003
Beardsley	56211
Beaver Bay	55601
Beaver Creek	56116
Becida	56625
Becker	55308
Bejou	56516
Belgrade	56312
Belle Plaine	56011
Bellingham	56212
Beltrami	56517
Belview	56214
Bemidji (1st)	56601
Bena	56626
Benedict	56436
Benson (1st)	56215
Beroun	55004
Bertha	56437
Bethel	55005
Bible College, R. Br. Saint	
Bonifacius	55375
Big Falls	56627
Big Lake	55309
Bigelow	56117
Bigfork	56628
Bingham Lake	56118
Birchdale	56629
Bird Island	55310
Biwabik	55708
Bixby	55916
Blackduck	56630
Blomkest	56216
Bloom Dale, Br. Minneapolis	55431
Blooming Prairie	55917
Bloomington, Br.	
Minneapolis (see	
appendix)	
Blue Earth (1st)	56013
Bluffton	56518
Bock	56313
Bongards	55311
Borup	56519
Bovey	55709
Bowlus	56314

Bowstring	56631
Boy River	56632
Boyd	56218
Braham	55006
Brainerd (1st)	56401
Brandon	56315
Breckenridge (1st)	56520
Brewster	56119
Bricelyn	56014
Brimson	55602
Britt	55710
Brook Park	55007
Quamba, R. Br.	55064
Brooklyn Center, Br.	
Minneapolis	55429
Brooks	56715
Brookston	55711
Brooten	56316
Browerville	56438
Browns Valley	56219
Brownsdale	55918
Brownsville	55919
Brownton	55312
Bruno	55712
Buckman	56317
Buffalo (1st)	55313
Buffalo Lake	55314
Buhl	55713
Burnett	55714
Burnsville, Br. Savage	55378
Burtrum	56318
Butterfield	56120
Buyck, R. Br. Orr	55771
Byron	55920
Caledonia	55921
Callaway	56521
Calumet	55716
Cambridge (1st)	55008
Camden, Sta. Minneapolis	
(see appendix)	
Campbell	56522
Canby	56220
Cannon Falls (1st)	55009
Canton	55922
Canyon	55717
Carlisle, R. Br. Fergus Falls	56538
Carlos	56319
Carlton	55718
Carver	55315
Cass Lake	56633
Castle Rock	55010

Cedar 55011
Cedar Mills, R. Br. Hutchinson 55391
Center City 55012
Central Avenue, Sta. Minneapolis 55418
Ceylon 56121
Champlin 55316
Chandler 56122
Chanhassen 55317
Chaska (1st) 55318
Chatfield 55923
Chester, R. Br. Rochester 55904
Chicago Lake, Sta. Minneapolis 55407
Chisago City 55013
Chisholm (1st) 55719
Chokio 56221
Circle Pines (1st) 55014
City, Sta. Rochester 55901
Civic Center, Sta. Duluth 55802
Clara City (1st) 56222
Claremont 55924
Clarissa 56440
Clarkfield 56223
Clarks Grove 56016
Clear Lake 55319
Clearbrook 56634
Clearwater 55320
Clements 56224
Clementson, R. Br. Baudette 56623
Cleveland 56017
Climax 56523
Eldred, R. Br. 56532
Clinton 56225
Clitherall 56524
Clontarf 56226
Cloquet (1st) 55720
Cloverton 55015
Cobden 56018
Cohasset 55721
Cokato 55321
Cold Spring 56320
Coleraine 55722
Collegeville (1st) 56321
Cologne 55322
Columbia Heights, Br. Minneapolis 55421
Comfrey 56019
Commerce, Sta. Minneapolis 55415
Como, Sta. Saint Paul 55108
Comstock 56525
Conger 56020
Cook 55723
Coon Rapids, Br. Minneapolis (see appendix)
Correll 56227
Cosmos 56228
Cottage Grove 55016
Cotton 55724
Cottonwood 56229
Courtland 56021
Crane Lake 55725
Cromwell 55726
Crookston (1st) 56716
Gentilly, R. Br. 56717
Crosby 56441
Crosslake 56442
Crystal, Br. Minneapolis (see appendix)
Crystal Bay 55323

Culver 55727
Currie 56123
Cushing 56443
Cyrus 56323
Dakota 55925
Dalbo 55017
Dalton 56324
Danube 56230
Danvers 56231
Darfur 56022
Darwin 55324
Dassel 55325
Kingston, R. Br. 55326
Dawson 56232
Dayton 55327
Daytons Bluff, Sta. Saint Paul 55106
De Graff 56233
Deephaven, Br. Wayzata 55391
Deer Creek 56527
Deer River 56636
Ball Club, R. Br. 56622
Talmoon, R. Br. 56637
Deerwood 56444
Delano 55328
Delavan 56023
Delft 56124
Delhi 56234
Denham 55728
Dennison 55018
Dent 56528
Detroit Lakes (1st) 56501
Dexter 55926
Diamond Lake, Sta. Minneapolis (see appendix)
Dilworth 56529
Dodge Center 55927
Donaldson 56720
Donnelly 56235
Doran 56530
Douglas, R. Br. Oronoco 55960
Dover 55929
Dovray 56125
Dresbach 55930
DULUTH (1st) (see appendix)
Dumont 56236
Dundas 55019
Dundee 56126
Dunnell 56127
Duquette 55729
Eagle Bend 56446
Eagle Lake 56024
East End, Sta. Duluth 55802
East Grand Forks (1st) 56721
Eastern Heights, Sta. Saint Paul 55119
Easton 56025
Ebro 56638
Echo 56237
Eden Prairie, Br. Hopkins 55343
Eden Valley 55329
Edgerton 56128
Edina, Br. Minneapolis (see appendix)
Effie 56639
Egan, Br. Saint Paul 55111
Eitzen 55931
Elbow Lake 56531
Eldred, R. Br. Climax 56532
Elgin 55932
Elizabeth 56533
Elk River (1st) 55330
Elko 55020

Elkton 55933
Ellendale 56026
Ellsworth 56129
Elmer 55730
Elmore 56027
Elmwood, Br. Minneapolis 55416
Elrosa 56325
Ely (1st) 55731
Elysian 56028
Embarrass 55732
Emily 56447
Emmons 56029
Erhard 56534
Ericksburg, R. Br. International Falls 56640
Erskine 56535
Esko 55733
Essig 56030
Euclid 56722
Evan 56238
Evansville 56326
Eveleth (1st) 55734
Excelsior (1st) 55331
Eyota 55934
Fairfax 55332
Fairhaven, R. Br. South Haven 55383
Fairmont (1st) 56031
Falcon Heights, Br. Saint Paul 55113
Faribault (1st) 55021
Farmington (1st) 55024
Farwell 56327
Federal Dam 56641
Felton 56536
Fergus Falls (1st) 56537
Carlisle, R. Br. 56538
Fertile 56540
Fifty Lakes 56448
Finland 55603
Isabella, R. Br. 55607
Finlayson 55735
Fisher 56723
Flensburg 56328
Flom 56541
Floodwood 55736
Florence 56130
Foley 56329
Forbes 55738
Forest Lake (1st) 55025
Foreston 56330
Fort Ripley 56449
Fosston 56542
Fountain 55935
Foxhome 56543
Franklin 55333
Franklin Avenue, Sta. Minneapolis 55404
Frazee 56544
Freeborn 56032
Freeport 56331
Fridley, Br. Minneapolis 55421
Frontenac 55026
Frost 56033
Fulda 56131
Garden City 56034
Garfield 56332
Garrison 56450
Garvin 56132
Gary 56545
Gatzke 56724
Gaylord (1st) 55334
Gemmell 56643
Geneva 56035

Genola, R. Br. Pierz	56365
Gentilly, R. Br. Crookston	56717
Georgetown	56546
Gheen	55740
Ghent	56239
Gibbon	55335
Gilbert	55741
Gilman	56333
Glencoe (1st)	55336
Glenville	56036
Glenwood (1st)	56334
Gluek, R. Br. Maynard	56261
Glyndon	56547
Golden Hills, Br. Minneapolis	55416
Golden Valley, Br. Minneapolis	55427
Gonvick	56644
Good Thunder	56037
Goodhue	55027
Goodland	55742
Goodridge	56725
Graceton	56645
Graceville	56240
Granada	56039
Grand Marais	55604
Grand Meadow	55936
Grand Portage	55605
Isle Royale National Park, R. Br.	55617
Grand Rapids (1st)	55744
Grandy	55029
Granger	55937
Granite Falls (1st)	56241
Grasston	55030
Henriette, R. Br.	55036
Green Isle	55338
Green Valley, R. Br. Marshall	56242
Greenbush	56726
Greenwald	56335
Grey Eagle	56336
Grove City	56243
Grygla	56727
Guckeen	56040
Guly	56646
Guthrie	56451
Hackensack	56452
Hadley	56133
Hallock	56728
Halma	56729
Halstad	56548
Hamburg	55339
Hamel	55340
Hammond, R. Br. Rochester	55938
Hampton	55031
Hancock	56244
Hanley Falls	56245
Hanover	55341
Hanska	56041
Harding, R. Br. Pierz	56364
Hardwick	56134
Harmony	55939
Harris	55032
Hartland	56042
Hastings (1st)	55033
Hatfield	56135
Hawick	56246
Hawley	56549
Hayfield	55940
Hayward	56043
Hazel Run	56247
Hector	55342
Henderson	56044
Hendricks	56136
Hendrum	56550
Henning	56551
Henriette, R. Br. Grasston	55036
Herman	56248
Heron Lake	56137
Hewitt	56453
Hibbing (1st)	55746
Highland, Sta. Minneapolis	55411
Highland Park, Sta. Saint Paul	55116
Hill City	55748
Hillman	56338
Hills	56138
Hillside, Sta. Duluth	55805
Hinckley	55037
Hines	56647
Hitterdal	56552
Hoffman	56339
Hokah	55941
Holdingford	56340
Holland	56139
Hollandale	56045
Holloway	56249
Holmes City	56341
Holyoke	55749
Homer, R. Br. Winona	55942
Hope	56046
Hopkins (1st)	55343
Houston	55943
Hovland	55606
Howard Lake	55349
Hoyt Lakes	55750
Hugo	55038
Humboldt	56731
Hunters Park, Sta. Duluth	55803
Huntley	56047
Hutchinson (1st)	55350
Cedar Mills, R. Br.	55351
Ihlen	56140
Indus	56648
Industrial, Sta. Saint Paul	55104
International Falls (1st)	56649
Ericksburg, R. Br.	56640
Inver Grove Heights, Br. South Saint Paul	55075
Iona	56141
Iron	55751
Ironton	56455
Isabella, R. Br. Finland	55607
Isanti	55040
Island Park, R. Sta. Mound	55364
Isle	56342
Ivanhoe	56142
Jackson (1st)	56143
Jacobson	55752
Janesville	56048
Jasper	56144
Jeffers	56145
Jenkins	56456
Johnson	56250
Jordan	55352
Judson	56049
Kanaranzi	56146
Kandiyohi	56251
Karlstad	56732
Kasota	56050
Kasson	55944
Keewatin	55753
Kelliher	56650
Kellogg	55945
Kelly Lake	55754
Kelsey	55755
Kennedy	56733
Kenneth	56147
Kensington	56343
Kent	56553
Kenwood, Sta. Duluth	55811
Kenyon	55946
Kerkhoven	56252
Kerrick	55756
Kettle River	55757
Kiester	56051
Kilkenny	56052
Kimball	55353
Kimberly	56457
Kingston, R. Br. Dassel	55326
Kinney	55758
Klossner	56053
Knife River	55609
La Crescent	55947
La Salle	56056
Lafayette	56054
Lake Benton	56149
Lake Bronson	56734
Lake City (1st)	55341
Lake Crystal	56055
Lake Elmo	55042
Lake George	56458
Lake Hubert	56459
Lake Itasca	56460
Lake Lillian	56253
Lake Park	56554
Lake Street, Sta. Minneapolis (see appendix)	
Lake Wilson	56151
Lakefield	56150
Lakeland	55043
Lakeside, Sta. Duluth	55804
Lakeville	55044
Lamberton	56152
Lamoille	55948
Lancaster	56735
Lanesboro	55949
Lansing	55950
Laporte	56461
Larsmont, R. Br. Two Harbors	55610
Lastrup	56344
Le Center (1st)	56057
Le Roy	55951
Le Sueur (1st)	56058
Leader, R. Br. Motley	56462
Lengby	56651
Leonard	56652
Leota	56153
Lester Prairie	55354
Lewiston	55952
Lewisville	56060
Linden Hills, Sta. Minneapolis	55410
Lindstrom	55045
Lismore	56155
Litchfield (1st)	55355
Little Falls (1st)	56345
Little Marais, R. Br. Silver Bay	55611
Little Sauk	56346
Littlefork	56653
Lockhart	56555
Loman	56654
London	56061
Long Lake	55356
Long Prairie (1st)	56347

382

Longville 56655
Lonsdale 55046
Loop, Sta. Minneapolis 55402
Loretto 55357
Loring, Sta. Minneapolis
  (see appendix)
Louisburg 56254
Lowry 56349
Lowry Hill, Sta. Minneapolis ... 55405
Lucan 56255
Lutsen 55612
Luverne (1st) 56156
Lyle 55953
Lynd 56157
Mabel 55954
Madelia (1st) 56062
Madison 56256
Madison Lake 56063
Magnolia 56158
Mahnomen 56557
Mahtomedi, Br. Saint Paul 55115
Mahtowa 55762
Makinen 55763
Manchester 56064
Manhattan Beach 56463
Manitou 56656
Mankato (1st) 56001
  North Mankato, Br. 56001
  Rapidan, R. Br. 56079
Mantorville 55955
Maple Lake 55358
Maple Plain (1st) 55359
Mapleton 56065
Maplewood, Br. Saint Paul 55109
Marble 55764
Marcell 56657
Margie 56658
Marietta 56257
Marine On Saint Croix 55047
Markville 55048
Marshall (1st) 56258
  Green Valley, R. Br. 56242
Matawan 56066
Max 56659
Mayer 55360
Maynard 56260
  Gluek, R. Br. 56261
Mazeppa 55956
Mc Grath 56350
Mc Gregor 55760
Mc Intosh 56556
Mc Kinley 55761
Meadowlands 55765
Medford 55049
Medicine Lake, Br.
  Minneapolis 55427
Melby 56351
Melrose 56352
Melrude 55766
Menahga 56464
Mendota, Br. Saint Paul 55050
Mentor 56736
Meriden 56067
Merrifield 56465
Middle River 56737
Midway, Sta. Saint Paul 55104
Milaca (1st) 56353
Milan 56262
Millville 55957
Milroy 56263
Miltona 56354
MINNEAPOLIS (1st) (see
  appendix)

Minnehaha, Sta.
  Minneapolis 55406
Minneiska 55958
Minneota 56264
Minnesota City 55959
Minnesota Lake 56068
Minnesota Transfer, Sta.
  Saint Paul 55114
Minnetonka, Br. Hopkins 55343
Minnetonka Beach 55361
Minnetonka Mills, Br.
  Hopkins 55343
Mizpah 56660
Montevideo (1st) 56265
Montgomery 56069
Monticello 55362
Montrose 55363
Moorhead (1st) 56560
Moose Lake 55767
Mora (1st) 55051
Morgan 56266
Morgan Park, Sta. Duluth 55808
Morris (1st) 56267
Morristown 55052
Morton 56270
Motley 56466
  Leader, R. Br. 56462
Mound (1st) 55364
Mountain Iron 55768
Mountain Lake 56159
Murdock 56271
Myrtle 56070
Nashua 56565
Nashwauk 55769
Nassau 56272
Navarre, R. Br. Wayzata 55392
Naytahwaush 56566
Nelson 56355
Nerstrand 55053
Nett Lake, R. Br. Orr 55772
Nevis 56467
New Auburn 55366
New Brighton, Br. Saint
  Paul 55112
New Germany 55367
New Hope, Br. Minneapolis 55428
New London 56273
New Market 55054
New Munich 56356
New Prague (1st) 56071
New Richland 56072
New Ulm (1st) 56073
New York Mills 56567
Newfolden 56738
Newport (1st) 55055
Nicollet 56074
Nielsville 56568
Nimrod, R. Br. Sebeka 56478
Nisswa 56468
Nokomis, Sta. Minneapolis 55417
Nopeming, R. Br. Duluth 55770
Norcross 56274
Normandale, Br. Minneapolis
  (see appendix)
North Branch 55056
North Douglas, Br.
  Minneapolis 55422
North Mankato, Br. Mankato ... 56001
North Redwood 56275
North Saint Paul, Br. Saint
  Paul 55109
Northcote 56739
Northfield (1st) 55057

Northome 56661
Northrop, Br. Fairmont 56075
Northside, Sta. Albert Lea 56007
Northwest Terminal, Sta.
  Minneapolis 55413
Norwood 55368
Noyes 56740
Number Five, Sta. Duluth 55802
Oak Island 56741
Oak Knoll, Br. Hopkins 55343
Oak Park 56357
Oak Street, Sta.
  Minneapolis 55414
Oakland 56076
Odessa 56276
Odin 56160
Ogema 56569
Ogilvie 56358
Okabena 56161
Oklee 56742
Olivia (1st) 56277
Onamia 56359
Orleans 56743
Ormsby 56162
Oronoco 55960
Orr 55771
  Buyck, R. Br. 55771
  Nett Lake, R. Br. 55772
Ortonville 56278
Osage 56570
Osakis 56360
Oslo 56744
Osseo (1st) 55369
Ostrander 55961
Otisco 56077
Ottertail 56571
Outing 56662
Owatonna (1st) 55060
Palisade 56469
Park Rapids (1st) 56470
Parkers Prairie 56361
Parkville 55773
Payne 55774
Payne Avenue, Sta. Saint
  Paul 55101
Paynesville 56362
Pease 56363
Pelican Rapids 56572
Pemberton 56378
Pencer 56746
Pengilly 55775
Pennington 56663
Pennock 56279
Pequaywan Lake, R. Br.
  Duluth 55803
Pequot Lakes 56472
Perham 56573
Perley 56574
Peterson 55962
Pierz 56364
  Genola, R. Br. 56365

  Harding, R. Br. 56364
Pike Lake, Br. Duluth 55811
Pillager 56473
Pine City 55063
Pine Island 55963
Pine River 56474
Pinecreek 56747
Pinewood 56664
Pioneer, Sta. Saint Paul 55101
Pipestone (1st) 56164
Pitt 56665
Plainview 55954

Plato	55370
Plummer	56748
Ponemah	56666
Ponsford	56575
Porter	56280
Powderhorn, Sta. Minneapolis	55407
Preston	55965
Princeton (1st)	55371
Prinsburg	56281
Prior Lake	55372
Procter, Br. Duluth	55810
Prosper	55966
Puposky	56667
Quamba, R. Br. Brook Park	55064
Racine	55967
Radium	56749
Randall	56475
Randolph	55065
Ranier	56668
Rapidan, R. Br. Mankato	56079
Ray	56669
Raymond	56282
Reading	56165
Reads Landing	55968
Red Lake Falls	56750
Red Wing (1st)	55066
Redby	56678
Redlake	56671
Redwood Falls (1st)	56283
Regal	56366
Remer	56672
Renville	56284
Revere	56166
Rice	56367
Rice Street, Sta. Saint Paul	55117
Richfield, Br. Minneapolis	55423
Richmond	56368
Richville	56576
Richwood	56577
Riverside, Sta. Minneapolis	55404
Riverview, Sta. Saint Paul	55107
Robbinsdale, Br. Minneapolis (see appendix)	
Rochert	56578
Rochester (1st)	55901
Chester, R. Br.	55904
City, Sta.	55901
Hammond, R. Br.	55938
Viola, R. Br.	55980
Rock Creek	55067
Rockford	55373
Rockville	56369
Rogers	55374
Rollingstone	55969
Ronneby	56370
Roosevelt	56673
Roscoe	56371
Rose Creek	55970
Roseau (1st)	56751
Rosemount (1st)	55068
Roseville, Br. Saint Paul	55113
Ross	56753
Rothsay	56579
Round Lake	56167
Royalton	56373
Rush City	55069
Rushford	55971
Rushmore	56168
Russell	56169
Ruthton	56170
Rutledge	55778

Sabin	56580
Sacred Heart	56285
Saginaw	55779
Saint Anthony Falls, Sta. Minneapolis	55424
Saint Bonifacius	55375
Saint Charles	55972
Saint Clair, Sta. Saint Paul	55105
Saint Clair	56080
Saint Cloud (1st)	56301
Saint Francis	55070
Saint Hilaire	56754
Saint James (1st)	56081
Saint Joseph	56374
Saint Stephen, R. Br.	56375
Saint Leo	56286
Saint Louis Park, Br. Minneapolis (see appendix)	
Saint Martin	56376
Saint Michael	55376
SAINT PAUL (1st) (see appendix)	
Saint Paul Park (1st)	55071
Saint Peter (1st)	56082
Saint Stephen, R. Br. Saint Joseph	56375
Saint Vincent	56755
Salol	56756
Sanborn	56083
Sandstone	55072
Santiago	55377
Sargeant	55973
Sartell	56377
Sauk Centre (1st)	56378
Sauk Rapids, Br. Saint Cloud	56379
Saum	56674
Savage (1st)	55378
Sawyer	55780
Scandia	55073
Schroeder	55613
Seaforth	56287
Searles	56084
Sebeka	56477
Nimrod, R. Br.	56478
Sedan	56380
Shafer	55074
Shakopee (1st)	55379
Shelly	56581
Sherburn	56171
Shevlin	56676
Side Lake	55781
Silver Bay	55614
Little Marais, R. Br.	55611
Silver Creek	55380
Silver Lake	55381
Slayton	56172
Sleepy Eye (1st)	56085
Soderville, R. Br. Anoka	55304
Solway	56678
Soudan	55782
South Haven	55382
Fairhaven, R. Br.	55383
South International Falls	56679
South Saint Paul (1st)	55075
Spicer	56288
Spring Grove	55974
Spring Lake	56680
Spring Lake Park, Br. Minneapolis	55432
Spring Park (1st)	55384
Spring Valley	55975

Springfield	56087
Squaw Lake	56681
Stacy	55079
Stanchfield	55080
Stanton	55081
Staples	56479
Starbuck	56381
Steen	56173
Stephen	56757
Stewart	55385
Stewartville	55976
Stillwater (1st)	55082
Stockton, R. Br. Winona	55988
Storden	56174
Strandquist	56758
Strathcona	56759
Sturgeon Lake	55783
Sunburg	56289
Svea	56290
Swan River	55784
Swanville	56382
Swatara	55785
Swift	56682
Taconite	55786
Talmoon, R. Br. Deer River	56637
Tamarack	55787
Taopi	55977
Taunton	56291
Taylors Falls	55084
Tenney	56582
Tenstrike	56683
Terrace	56383
Theilman	55978
Thief River Falls (1st)	56701
Thompson Park, Br. Minneapolis	55433
Tintah	56583
Tofte	55615
Togo	55788
Toivola	55789
Tower	55790
Tracy	56175
Traffic, Sta. Minneapolis	55403
Trail	56684
Trimont	56176
Trosky	56177
Truman	56088
Twig	55791
Twin Cities, Br. Saint Paul	55111
Twin Lakes	56089
Twin Valley	56584
Two Harbors (1st)	55616
Larsmont, R. Br.	55610
Tyler	56178
U S Air Force, Br. Duluth	55814
Ulen	56585
Underwood	56586
University, Sta. Minneapolis	55414
Upper Nicollet, Sta. Minneapolis	55403
Upsala	56384
Uptown, Sta. Minneapolis	55408
Uptown, Sta. Saint Paul (see appendix)	
Utica	55979
Valley Ridge, Br. Savage	55378
Verdi	56179
Vergas	56587
Vermillion	55085
Verndale	56481
Vernon Center	56090
Veseli	55086
Vesta	56292

Victoria	55386	Watson	56295	Willow River	55795
Viking	56760	Waubun	56589	Wilmont	56185
Villard	56385	Waverly	55390	Wilton	56687
Vining	56588	Wawina	55794	Windom (1st)	56101
Viola, R. Br. Rochester.	55980	Wayzata (1st)	55391	Winger	56592
Virginia (1st)	55792	Deephaven, Br.	55391	Winnebago	56098
Wabasha	55981	Navarre, R. Br.	55392	Winona (1st)	55987
Wabasso	56293	Webster	55088	Homer, R. Br.	55942
Waconia (1st)	55387	Welch	55089	Stockton, R. Br.	55988
Wadena (1st)	56482	Welcome	56181	Winsted	55395
Wahkon	56386	Wells	56097	Winthrop	55396
Waite Park, Br. Saint Cloud.	56387	Wendell	56590		
Waldorf	56091	West Concord	55985	Winton	55796
Walker	56484	West Duluth, Sta. Duluth	55807	Wirt	56688
Walnut Grove	56180	West End, Sta. Saint Paul	55102	Wolf Lake	56593
Walters	56092	West Saint Paul, Br. Saint		Wolverton	56594
Waltham	55982	Paul	55118	Wood Lake	56297
		West Union	56389	Woodland, Sta. Duluth	55803
Wanamingo	55983	Westbrook	56183	Woodstock	56186
Wanda	56294	Whalan	55986	Worthington (1st)	56187
Wannaska	56761	Wheaton	56296	Wrenshall	55791
Warba	55793	Whipholt	56485	Wright	55798
Warren	56762	White Bear Lake, Br. Saint		Wykoff	55990
Warroad	56763	Paul	55110	Wyoming	55092
Warsaw	55087	White Earth	56591	Young America	55397
Waseca (1st)	56093	Wilder	56184		
Waskish	56685	Wilernie	55090	Zim	55799
Watertown	55388	Williams	56686	Zimmerman	55398
Waterville	56096	Willmar (1st)	56201	Zumbro Falls	55991
Watkins	55389			Zumbrota	55992

DULUTH   558

POST OFFICE BOXES

Box Nos.

A-D	Proctor Br.	10
A-E	West Duluth Sta.	07
1-750	Civic Center Sta.	01
1001-1096	Proctor Br.	10
3000-3999	Mount Royal Sta.	03
6001-6999	Main Office	06
7001-7216	West Duluth Sta.	07
8001-8116	Morgan Park Sta.	08

RURAL ROUTES

1,2	11
3,4	03
5	10
6	04
7	10

STATIONS, BRANCHES AND UNITS

Civic Center Sta.	02
East End Sta.	02
Hillside Sta.	05
Hunters Park Sta.	03
Kenwood Sta.	11
Lakeside Sta.	04

Morgan Park Sta.	08
Nopeming Rural Br.	55770
Number Five Sta.	02
Pequaywan Lake Rural Br.	03
Pike Lake Br.	11
Procter Br.	10
U S Air Force Br.	14
West Duluth Sta.	07
Woodland Sta.	03
General Delivery	06
Postmaster	06

APARTMENTS, HOTELS, MOTELS

Arrowhead, 225 N 1st Ave W.	06
Buena Vista, 1144 Mesaba Ave.	11
Cascade, 103 W 3rd	05
Devonshire, 1321 E 1st	02
Downtown, 131 W 2nd	02
Duluth Hotel, 231 E Superior.	02
Duluth Motel, 4415 Grand Ave.	07
Edgewater, 2330 London Rd.	12
Fifth Avenue Apt, 501 E 3rd.	05
Grand View Manor, 301 E 2nd.	05
Grand, 4312 Grand Ave.	07
Hillcrest, 1721 E 3rd	02
Holiday Inn, 250 S 1st Ave E.	01
Lake Aire, 2416 London Rd.	12
Lakeview, 1703 E 3rd.	12
Lincoln, 317 W 2nd.	02
London Manor, 1801 London Rd.	12

London Road Court, 2521 London Rd.	12
Mount Royal Manor, 100 Elizabeth	03
Munger Terrace, 405 Mesaba Ave.	06
Radisson-Duluth 503 West Superior.	02
Saint Ann'S Home, 330 E 3rd.	05
Seaway, 2001 W Superior.	06
Select Homes, 801 E 2nd.	05
Skyline Court, 2930 Miller Trunk Hwy.	11
Yorkleigh, 1017 London Rd.	02

BUILDINGS

A M Clure Public Marine Terminal, 1200 Garfield Ave.	02
Aetna, 403 N Central Ave.	07
Alworth, 306 W Superior.	02
Armory, 1305 London Rd.	05
Beal, 3 N 3rd Ave W.	02
Board Of Trade, 301 W 1st.	02
Bradley, 10 E Superior.	02
Christie, 120 N 4th Ave W.	02
Duluth Clinic, 205 W 2nd.	02
Duluth International Airport.	11
Duluth National Bank, 2002 W Superior.	06
Engineers, 600 Lake Ave S.	02
Federal, 5th Ave W & 1st.	02
Fidelity, 14 W Superior.	02

385

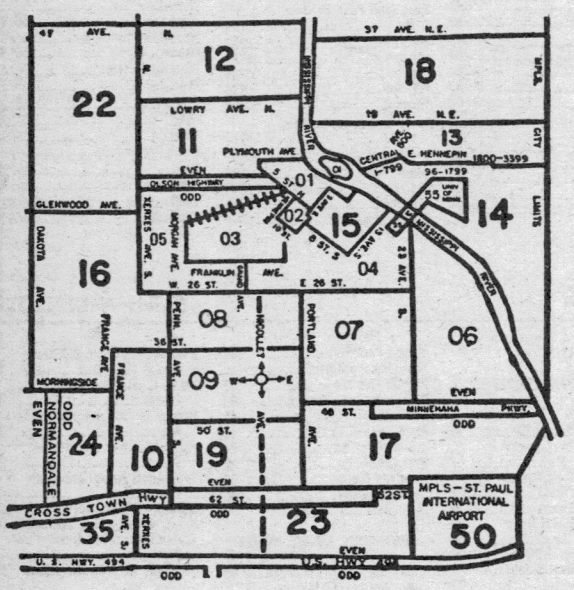

ZIP CODE

Minneapolis, Minn.

554 + Two Digits Shown = Zip Code

Duluth (Con.) 558

First American National
　Bank, 230 W Superior 02
Harbrace, 1 East 1st 02
Lonsdale, 302 W Superior 02
Medical Arts, 324 W
　Superior 02
Missabe 227 West 1st 02
New Garrick, 128 W 1st 02
Northland, 410 W Superior 02
Palladio, 5 North 4th Ave W ... 02
Phoenix, 333 W Superior 02
Providence, 334 W Superior 02
Public Library, 101 W 2nd 02
Sellwood, 200 W Superior 02
Terminal Public Marine, 1200
　Garfield Ave 02
Torrey, 314 W Superior 02
Winthrop, 325 W 1st 02
Y M C A, 302 W 1st 02
Y W C A, 202 West 2nd 02

GOVERNMENT OFFICES

City Hall, 4th Ave W & 1st .....
Courthouse County, 5th Ave
　W & 1st 02
Courthouse Federal, 5th Ave
　W & 1st 02
U S Engineers, 600 Lake Ave
　S 02

HOSPITALS

Miller Dwan, 504 E 2nd 05
Saint Lukes, 915 E 1st 05
Saint Marys, 407 E 3rd 05

UNIVERSITIES AND COLLEGES

Duluth Business University,
　418 W Superior 02
Saint Scholastica 11
University Of Minnesota
　Duluth, 2400 Oakland Ave. 12

MINNEAPOLIS 554

POST OFFICE BOXES

Box Nos.
1-1999　　Main Office 40
3101-3499　Traffic Sta 03
3501-3599　Upper Nicollet
　　　　　　Sta 03
3601-3999　Loring Sta 03
4201-4299　Saint Anthony
　　　　　　Falls Sta 14
4401-4499　Columbia
　　　　　　Heights Br 21
9501-9899　Main Office ... 40
02001-02999 Loop Sta 02
06001-06999 Minnehaha
　　　　　　Sta 06
07001-07999 Powderhorn
　　　　　　Sta 07
08001-08999 Lake Street
　　　　　　Sta 08
11001-11999 Highland Sta ... 11
12001-12999 Camden Sta ... 12

14001-14999 University Sta. .. 14
15001-15999 Commerce Sta.. 15
16001-16999 Elmwood Br. ... 16
17001-17999 Nokomis Sta... 17
18001-18999 Central Ave
　　　　　　Sta 18
19001-19999 Diamond Lake
　　　　　　Sta 19
20001-20999 Bloomington
　　　　　　Br 20
21001-21999 Columbia
　　　　　　Heights Br ... 21
22001-22999 Robbinsdale
　　　　　　Br 22
23001-23999 Richfield Br. ... 23
24001-24999 Edina Br. 24
26001-26999 Saint Louis
　　　　　　Park Br 26
27001-27299 Golden Valley
　　　　　　Br 27
32001-32999 Fridley Br. 32
33001-33999 Coon Rapids
　　　　　　Br 33
35501-35999 Normandale Br. 35

STATIONS, BRANCHES AND UNITS

Apache Br. 21
Bloom Dale Br. 31
Bloomington Br. 20
Brooklyn Center Br. 29
Camden Sta. 12
Central Avenue Sta. 18
Chicago Lake Sta. 07
Columbia Heights Br. 21
Commerce Sta. 15
Coon Rapids Br. 33
Crystal Br. 28
Diamond Lake Sta. 19
Edina Br. 24
Elmwood Br. 16
Franklin Avenue Sta. 04
Fridley Br. 21
Golden Hills Br. 16
Golden Valley Br. 27
Highland Sta. 11
Lake Street Sta. 04
Linden Hills Sta. 10
Loop Sta. 02
Loring Sta. 03
Lowry Hill Sta. 05
Medicine Lake Br. 27
Minnehaha Sta. 06
New Hope Br. 28
Nokomis Sta. 17
Normandale Br. 35
North Douglas Br. 22
Northwest Terminal Sta. 13
Oak Street Sta. 14
Powderhorn Sta. 07
Richfield Br. 23
Riverside Sta. 04
Robbinsdale Br. 22
Saint Anthony Falls Sta. 14
Saint Louis Park Br. 26
Spring Lake Park Br. 32
Thompson Park Br. 33
Traffic Sta. 03
University Sta. 14
Upper Nicollet Sta. 03
Uptown Sta. 08
General Delivery 01

Postmaster 01

APARTMENTS, HOTELS, MOTELS

Andrews, 5 S 4th 01
Curtis, 327 S 10th 04
Dyckman, 27 S 6th 02
Hampshire Arms, 900 4th
　Ave S. 04
Holiday Central, 1313
　Nicollet Ave 03
Leamington, 1014 3rd Ave S.. 04
Nicollet, 230 Nicollet Ave 01
Northstar Inn, 618 2nd Ave
　S. 02
Radisson, 45 S 7th 02
Sheraton-Ritz, 315 Nicollet
　Ave 01
Sheridan, 1112 Marquette
　Ave 03

BUILDINGS

American Hardware Mutual,
　3033 Excelsior Blvd. 16
Apache Plaza 21
Auditorium, 211 E Grant 03
Baker Arcade, 733 Marquette
　Ave 02
Baker, 706 2nd Ave S. 02
Builders Exchange, 609 2nd
　Ave S. 02
Cargill, 110 S 7th 02
Chamber Of Commerce 02
Citizens Aid, 404 S 8th 04
Dain Tower, 527 Marquette ... 02
Doctors, 90 S 9th. 02
Donaldson, 80 S 7th. 02
Farmers & Mechanics Bank,
　88 S 6th Street 02
First Federal Savings & Loan,
　634 Niequiet Mall 02
First National Bank Bldg,
　120 S 6th 02
First National Concourse, 515
　Marquette Ave 02
Flour Exchange, 310 4th Ave
　S. 15
Foshay Tower, 821 Marquette
　Ave 02
Gamble-Skogmo, 5100
　Gamble Dr 16
Grain Exchange, 400 S 4th ... 15
International Business
　Machines, 245 Marquette
　Ave 01
Investors, 733 Marquette
　Ave 02
Kresge, 628 Nicollet Ave 02
Loring Medical, 1409 Willow.. 03
Marquette Bank, 91 S 7th
　Street 02
Mc Knight, 415 2nd Ave S 01
Medical Arts, 825 Nicollet
　Ave 02
Merchandise Mart, 400 1st
　Ave N 01
Merchandise, 528 Hennepin
　Ave 03
Metropolitan Med Office Bldg
　825 S 8th 04
Midland Bank, 405 2nd Ave
　S. 01
Midwest Federal Savings &
　Loan, 801 Nicollet Mall 02

Minneapolis (Con.) 554

Midwest Plaza, 801 Nicollet
　Mall............................... 02
Minnesota Federal, 603
　Marquette Ave................ 02
National, 527 2nd Ave S..... 02
Northstar Center, 11u S 7th.. 02
Northwestern Bank, 620
　Marquette Ave................ 02
Northwestern Bell Telephone,
　224 S 5th........................ 02
Northwestern Federal, 730
　Hennepin Ave.................. 03
Northwestern Terminal, 600
　Stinson Blvd.................... 13
Physicians & Surgeons, 63 S
　9th................................ 02
Pillsbury, 608 2nd Ave S..... 02
Plymouth, 12 S 6th............ 02
Produce Bank, 100 N 7th..... 03
Public Library, 316 Nicollet
　Ave................................ 01
Roanoke, 109 S 7th............ 02
Sexton, 529 S 7th............. 15
Six-Hundred, 600 1st Ave N.. 03
Soo Line, 105 S 5th........... 02
Southdale........................ 35
Southdale Medical, 6545
　France Ave S................... 35
Southgate Plaza 5001 W
　78th............................... 37
Syndicate, 84 S 6th........... 02
Thorpe, 519 Marquette Ave.. 02
Title Insurance, 400 2nd Ave
　S................................... 01
Twin City Federal, 811
　Marquette Ave................ 02
Union Bus Depot, 29 N 9th... 03
Upper Midwest, 425
　Hennepin Ave.................. 0.
W C C θ, 625 2nd Ave S...... 02
Wesley Temple, 115 E Grant.. 03
Western Union, 317 2nd Ave
　................................... 01
Y M C A, 30 S 9th............. 02
Y W C A, 1130 Nicollet Ave.. 03

GOVERNMENT OFFICES

City Hall & Court House...... 15
Minneapolis St Paul Metro
　Center............................ 99
Public Health, 312 3rd Ave
　S................................... 15
United States Courthouse,
　110 S 4th........................ 01
United States Federal
　Building, 110 S 4th........... 01
United States Federal Office,
　200 Washington Ave S....... 01
United States Post Office,
　100 S 1st........................ 01

HOSPITALS

Abbott, 116 E 18th............ 03
Doctors Memorial, 1375
　Willow............................ 03
Eitel, 1375 Willow.............. 03
Elizabeth Kenny Institute,
　1800 Chicago Ave............. 04
Fairview, 2312 S 6th.......... 06
Glenwood Hills, 3901 Golden

Valley Rd......................... 22
Hennepin County General,
　619 S 5th........................ 15
Lutheran Deaconess, 2315
　14th Ave S...................... 04
Methodist, 6500 Excelsior
　Blvd............................... 26
Metropolitan Medical Center
　900 S 8th........................ 04
Mount Sinai, 2215 Park Ave.. 04
North Memorial, 3220 Lowry
　Ave N............................. 22
Northwestern, 810 E 27th.... 07
Saint Marys, 2414 S 7th...... 06
Sheltering Arms, 4330 W
　River Rd.......................... 06
Shriners, 2025 E River Rd.... 14
Southdale Fairview, 6401
　France Ave S................... 35
Unity, 550 Osborne Rd NE.... 32
University, 412 Union SE...... 55
Veterans, 4801 E 54th........ 17

UNIVERSITIES AND COLLEGES

Augsburg College, 707 21st
　Ave S............................. 04
Dunwoody Institute, 816
　Wayzata Blvd................... 03
University Of Minnesota...... 55

SAINT PAUL 551

POST OFFICE BOXES

Box Nos.		
1-1000	Uptown Sta	02
1001-1499	Saint Clair Sta.	05
1500-1999	Twin Cities Br.	11
2000-2499	North Saint Paul Br	09
2500-2999	New Brighton Br	12
3000-3999	Main Office	65
4000-4499	Highland Park Sta	16
4500-4999	Mahtomedi Br	15
5000-5999	Industrial Sta	04
6000-6499	West Saint Paul Br	18
6500-6999	Daytons Bluff Sta	06
7000-7499	Rice Street Sta	17
7500-7999	Eastern Heights Sta	19
8000-8499	Roseville Br	13
8500-8999	White Bear Lake Br	10
9000-9999	New Brighton Br	77
30000-30999	Main Office	75
80000-80499	Como Station	08

STATIONS, BRANCHES AND UNITS

Como Sta............................. 08
Daytons Bluff Sta.................. 06

Eastern Heights Sta........... 19
Egan Br.......................... 11
Falcon Heights Br.............. 13
Highland Park Sta............. 16
Industrial Sta................... 04
Mahtomedi Br.................. 15
Maplewood Br.................. 09
Mendota Br................. 55050
Midway Sta..................... 04
Minnesota Transfer Sta...... 14
New Brighton Br............... 12
North Saint Paul Br........... 09
Payne Avenue Sta............. 01
Pioneer Sta..................... 01
Rice Street Sta................. 17
Riverview Sta................... 07
Roseville Br..................... 13
Saint Clair Sta.................. 05
Twin Cities Br.................. 11
Uptown Sta..................... 02
West End Sta................... 01
West Saint Paul Br............ 18
White Bear Lake Br........... 10
General Delivery............... 01
Postmaster...................... 01

APARTMENTS, HOTELS, MOTELS

Capp Towers, 77 E 9th........ 01
Commodore, 79 N Western
　Ave............................... 02
Hilton, 11 E Kellogg Blvd.... 01
Holiday Inn, 161 St Anthony
　Ave............................... 03
Lowry, 339 N Wabasha........ 02
Midway Motor Lodge, 1964
　University Ave................. 04
Paul Bunyan, 2965 N
　Snelling Ave................... 13
Saint Paul Travelodge, 149. E
　University Ave................. 01
Saint Paul, 363 St Peter...... 02
Twins Motor Motel, 1975
　University Ave................. 04

BUILDINGS

Arts & Science Center, 30 E
　10th............................... 01
Bremer Arcade, 419 N
　Robert............................ 01
Burlington Northern, 176 E
　5th................................ 01
Centennial, 658 Cedar........ 01
Central Medical, 393 N
　Dunlap........................... 04
Commerce, 8 E 4th............ 01
Degree Of Honor, 325 Cedar.. 01
Dispatch, 55 E 4th............. 01
Endicott, 350 N Robert........ 01
Federal Land Bank, 375
　Jackson.......................... 01
Firm, 101 E 10th............... 01
First National Bank, 332
　Minnesota....................... 01
Griggs Midway, 1821
　University Ave W.............. 04
Guardian, 84 E 4th............ 01
Hamm, 408 St Peter........... 02
Lowry, 25 W 4th................ 02

St. Paul (Con.)   551

Lowry, 350 St Peter	02
Metro Square, 121 E 7th	01
Minnesota, 46 E 4th	01
Nalpac, 333 Sibley	01
Northwestern Bank, 55 E 5th	01
Osborn, 370 N Wabasha	02
Pioneer, 336 N Robert	01
Public Library, 90 W 4th	02
Public Safety, 101 E 10th	01
State Highway, John Ireland Blvd	01

GOVERNMENT OFFICES

Armory, 600 Cedar	01
Courthouse, 15 W Kellogg Blvd	02
Federal Bldg & U. S. Court House, 316 N Robert	01
Federal Bldg, Ft Snelling, Mn	11
Post Office & Custom House, 180 E Kellogg Blvd	01
State Capitol, Aurora Ave & Park	03

HOSPITALS

Bethesda, 559 Capitol Blvd	03
Childrens, 311 Pleasant Ave	02
Gillette State Hospital For Crippled Children, 1003 E Ivy	06
Midway, 1700 University Ave W	04
Miller, 125 W College Ave	02
Mounds Park, 200 Earl	06
Riverview Memorial, 225 Prescott	07
Saint Johns, 403 Maria	06
Saint Josephs, 69 W Exchange	02
Saint Lukes, 287 Smith Ave	02
Saint Paul Ramsey, 640 Jackson	01
Salvation Army Booth Memorial, 1471 Como Ave	08
Samaritan Hospital, 1515 Charles	04

MILITARY INSTALLATIONS

Armory, 600 Cedar	01

UNIVERSITIES AND COLLEGES

Bethel College & Seminary, 1480 N Snelling Ave	08
Concordia, 275 N Syndicate	04
Hamline University, 1536 Hewitt Ave	04
Luther Seminary, 2375 Como Ave	08
Macalester, 1600 Grand Ave	05
Saint Catherines, 2004 Randolph Ave	05
Saint Paul Bible, 1361 Englewood Ave	04
Saint Paul Seminary, 2200 Grand Ave	05
Saint Thomas, 2115 Summit Ave	05
U-Farm, 1444 N Cleveland Ave	08
William Mitchell College Of Law, 2100 Summit Ave	05

State List of Post Offices   MISSISSIPPI

MISSISSIPPI
(Abbreviation: MS)

Abbeville	38601
Aberdeen (1st)	39730
Ackerman	39735
Agricola, R. Br. Lucedale	39452
Alcorn College, R. Br. Lorman	39096
Algoma	38820
Alligator	38720
Amory (1st)	38821
Anguilla	38721
Apple Ridge, Sta. Jackson	39204
Arcola	38722
Arkabutla	38602
Artesia	39736
Ashland	38603
Askew	38604
Avalon	38912
Avon	38723
Bailey	39320
Baird	38724
Baldwyn	38824
Banner	38913
Bassfield	39421
Batesville (1st)	38606
Battlefield, Sta. Jackson	39204
Baxterville, R. Br. Lumberton	39455
Bay Saint Louis (1st)	39520
Bay Springs	39422
Beaumont	39423
Becker	38825
Belden	38826
Belen	38609
Bellefontaine	39737
Belmont	38827

Belzoni (1st)	39038
Benoit	38725
Stringtown, R. Br.	38777
Benton	39039
Bentonia	39040
Beulah	38726
Bexley, R. Br. Lucedale	39453
Big Creek	38914
Bigbee Valley	39738
BILOXI (1st) (see appendix)	
Black Hawk, R. Br. Carrollton	38918
Blaine, R. Br. Sunflower	38727
Blue Mountain	38610
Blue Springs	38828
Bobo, R. Br. Clarksdale	38728
Bogue Chitto	39629
Bolton	39041
Bond, R. Br. Wiggins	39550
Bonita	39321
Booneville (1st)	38829
Bourbon	38729
Boyle	38730
Brandon (1st)	39042
Johns, R. Br.	39042
Value, R. Br.	39178
Braxton	39044
Brazil	38956
Brookhaven (1st)	39601
Brooklyn	39425
Brooksville	39739
Bruce	38915
Buckatunna	39322
Bude	39630
Burns, R. Br. Raleigh	39153
Burnsville	38833
Byhalia	38611
Caledonia	39740

Calhoun City	38916
Slate Spring, R. Br.	38955
Camden	39045
Canaan	38612
Candlestick, Br. Jackson	39212
Canton (1st)	39046
Carlisle	39049
Carpenter	39050
Carriere	39426
Carrollton	38917
Black Hawk, R. Br.	38918
Carson	39427
Carthage (1st)	39051
Cary	39054
Cascilla	38920
Cedarbluff	39741
Centreville	39631
Chalybeate, R. Br. Walnut	38684
Charleston	38921
Chatawa	39632
Chatham	38731
Choctaw, Sta. Laurel	39440
Chunky	39323
Church Hill	39055
Clara	39324
Clarksdale (1st)	38614
Bobo, R. Br.	38728
Farrell, R. Br.	38630
Clermont Harbor	39551
Cleveland (1st)	38732
Cliftonville	39742
Clinton (1st)	39056
Clinton Plaza, Sta. Clinton	39056
Coahoma	38617
Cockrum, R. Br. Hernando	38632
Coffeeville	38922
Coila	38923
Coldwater	38618

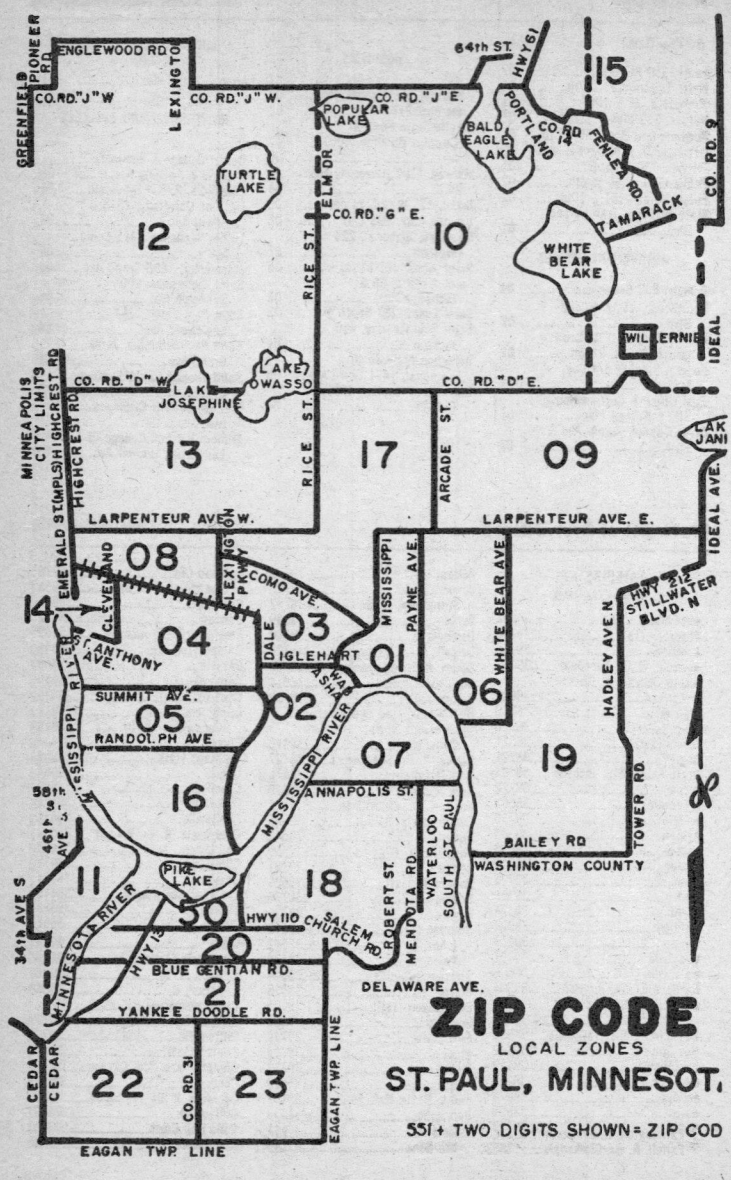

ZIP CODE
LOCAL ZONES
ST. PAUL, MINNESOT.

551 + TWO DIGITS SHOWN = ZIP COD

Coles, R. Br. Gloster	39639
College, Sta. Columbus	39701
Collins	39428
Collinsville	39325
Colonial, Sta. Jackson	39211
Columbia (1st)	39429
Columbus (1st)	39701
Columbus A F B, Br. Columbus	39701
Como	38619
Conehatta	39057
Corinth (1st)	38834
Courtland	38620
Crawford	39743
Crenshaw	38621
Crosby	39633
Crossroads, Sta. Greenville	38701
Crowder	38622
Cruger	38924
Crystal Springs (1st)	39059
Cuevas, R. Br. Pass Christian	39571
D'Iberville, Sta. Biloxi	39532
D'Lo	39062
Daleville	39326
Darling	38623
Darlove	38734
De Kalb	39328
De Lisle, R. Br. Pass Christian	39571
De Soto, R. Br. Shubuta	39360
Decatur	39327
Delta City	39061
Delta Drive, Sta. Jackson	39213
Delta State College, Sta. Cleveland	38732
Dennis	38838
Derma	38839
Doddsville	38736
Drew	38737
Parchman, R. Br.	38738
Dublin	38739
Duck Hill	38925
Dumas	38625
Duncan	38740
Dundee	38626
Durant	39063
Eastabuchie	39436
Eastlawn, Sta. Pascagoula	39567
Ebenezer	39064
Ecru	38841
Eddiceton, R. Br. Mc Call Creek	39634
Eden, R. Br. Yazoo City	39065
Edinburg, R. Br. Carthage	39051
Edwards	39066
Egypt, R. Br. Okolona	38842
Electric Mills	39329
Elizabeth	38742
Elliott, R. Br. Grenada	38926
Ellisville	39437
Enid	38927
Enterprise	39330
Escatawpa	39552
Ethel	39067
Etta	38627
Eupora	39744
Evergreen, Sta. Gulfport	39501
Fairlane, Sta. Columbus	39701
Falcon, R. Br. Sledge	38628
Falkner	38629
Farmington, R. Br. Corinth	38834
Farrell, R. Br. Clarksdale	38630

Fayette	39069
Fernwood	39635
Fitler	39070
Flora	39071
Pocahontas, R. Br.	39072
Florence	39073
Fondren, Sta. Jackson	39216
Forest (1st)	39074
Forkville	39076
Fort Adams	39636
Foxworth	39483
French Camp	39745
Friars Point	38631
Fruitland Park	39438
Fulton (1st)	38843
Gallman	39077
Gattman	38844
Gautier	39553
Georgetown	39078
Gholson	39331
Gibson, R. Br. Aberdeen	39730
Glen	38846
Glen Allan	38744
Glendora	38928
Gloster	39638
Coles, R. Br.	39639
Golden	38847
Goodman	39079
Gore Springs	38929
Grace	38745
Greenville (1st)	38701
Crossroads, Sta.	38701
Winterville, R. Br.	38782
Greenwood (1st)	38930
Greenwood Springs	38848
Grenada (1st)	38901
Elliott, R. Br.	38926
Gulfport (1st)	39501
Gunnison	38746
Guntown	38849
Hamburg, R. Br. Roxie	39661
Hamilton	39746
Handsboro, Sta. Gulfport	39501
Harperville	39080
Harriston	39081
Harrisville	39082
Hatley, R. Br. Amory	38821
Hattiesburg (1st)	39401
Hazlehurst (1st)	39083
Heidelberg	39439
Hermanville	39086
Hernando (1st)	38632
Hickory	39332
Hickory Flat	38633
Hillhouse	38747
Hillsboro	39087
Hiwannee	39333
Holcomb	38940
Hollandale	38748
Holly Bluff	39088
Holly Ridge	38749
Holly Springs (1st)	38635
Mount Pleasant, R. Br.	38649
Homewood	39089
Horn Lake	38637
Houlka	38850
Houston (1st)	38851
Hurley	39555
Independence	38638
Indianola (1st)	38751
Inverness	38753
Isola	38754
Itta Bena	38941

Iuka (1st)	38852
JACKSON (1st) (see appendix)	
Jayess	39641
Johns, R. Br. Brandon	39042
Johnstons Station	39642
Jonestown	38639
Keesler A F B, Sta. Biloxi	39534
Kilmichael	39747
Kiln	39556
Kokomo	39643
Kosciusko (1st)	39090
Kossuth, R. Br. Corinth	38834
Kreole, Sta. Moss Point	39563
Lafayette Springs	38640
Lake	39092
Lake Cormorant	38641
Lakeshore	39558
Lamar	38642
Lambert	38643
Lamont	38755
Lauderdale	39335
Laurel (1st)	39440
Lawrence	39336
Le Flore	38942
Le Tourneau, R. Br. Vicksburg	39180
Leaf	39450
Leakesville	39451
Learned	39093
Leavell Woods, Sta. Jackson	39212
Leland (1st)	38756
Tralake, R. Br.	38757
Lena	39094
Lexington	39095
Liberty	39645
Little Rock	39337
Long Beach (1st)	39560
Longview, R. Br. Starkville	39749
Lorman	39096
Louin	39338
Louise	39097
Louisville (1st)	39339
Lucedale (1st)	39452
Agricola, R. Br.	39452
Bexley, R. Br.	39453
Ludlow	39098
Lula	38644
Lumberton	39455
Lyman, R. Br. Gulfport	39501
Lyon	38645
Maben	39750
Macon (1st)	39341
Madden	39109
Madison	39110
Magee (1st)	39111
Sanitorium, Br.	39112
Magnolia	39652
Mantachie	38855
Mantee	39751
Marietta	38856
Marion	39342
Marks	38646
Mary Holmes, R. Br. West Point	39773
Matherville, R. Br. Shubuta	39360
Mathiston	39752
Mattson	38758
Mayersville	39113
Mayhew	39753
Mc Adams	39107
Mc Call Creek	39647
Eddiceton, R. Br.	39634

Mc Carley 38943
Mc Comb (1st) 39648
Mc Condy 38854
Mc Cool 39108
Mc Henry 39561
Mc Lain 39456
Mc Laurin, R. Br.
  Hattiesburg 39401
Mc Neill 39457
Mc Willie, Sta. Jackson 39206
Meadville 39653
Mendenhall 39114
Meridian (1st) 39301
Merigold 38759
Metcalfe 38760
Michigan City 38647
Midnight 39115
Mineral Wells 38648
Minter City 38944
Miss Valley State College, R.
  Br. Itta Bena 38941
Mississippi City, Sta.
  Gulfport 39501
Mississippi College, Br.
  Clinton 39058
Mize 39116
Money 38945
Monticello 39654
Montpelier 39754
Montrose 39343
Mooreville 38857
Moorhead 38761
Morgan City 38946
Morgantown 39484
Morton 39117
  Polkville, R. Br. 39118
Moselle 39459
Moss 39460
Moss Point (1st) 39563
Mound Bayou 38762
Mount Olive 39119
Mount Pleasant, R. Br. Holly
  Springs 38649
Myrtle 38650
Natchez (1st) 39120
Naval Air Station, Br.
  Meridian 39301
Neely 39461
Nesbit 38651
Neshoba 39344
Nettleton 38858
New Albany (1st) 38652
New Augusta 39462
New Site 38859
Newhebron 39140
Newton (1st) 39345
Nicholson 39463
Nitta Yuma 38763
North, Sta. Jackson 39206
North, Sta. Meridian 39301
North Carrollton 38947
Northwest Jr College, Sta.
  Senatobia 38668
Norwood Village, R. Br.
  Gulfport 39501
Noxapater 39346
Oak Vale 39656
Oakland 38948
Ocean Springs (1st) 39564
Ofahoma 39141
Okolona (1st) 38860
  Egypt, R. Br. 38842
Olive Branch 38654

Oma 39142
Onward 39143
Osyka 39657
Ovett 39464
Oxford (1st) 38655
Pace 38764
Pachuta 39347
Palmers Crossing, R. Br.
  Hattiesburg 39401
Panther Burn 38765
Parchman, R. Br. Drew 38738
Paris 38949
Pascagoula (1st) 39567
Pass Christian (1st) 39571
Pattison 39144
Paulding 39348
Paulette 39349
Pearl, Br. Jackson 39208
Pearlington 39572
Pelahatchie 39145
Percy, R. Br. Hollandale 38748
Perkinston 39573
Petal 39465
Pheba 39755
Philadelphia (1st) 39350
Philipp 38950
Picayune (1st) 39466
Pickens 39146
Pinckneyville 39658
Piney Woods 39148
Pinola 39149
Pittsboro 38951
Plain, R. Br. Jackson 39218
Plantersville 38862
Pocahontas, R. Br. Flora 39072
Polkville, R. Br. Morton 39118
Pontotoc (1st) 38863
Pope 38658
Poplarville (1st) 39470
Port Gibson 39150
Porterville 39352
Potts Camp 38659
Prairie 39756
Prairie Point 39353
Prentiss 39474
Preston 39354
Prichard, R. Br. Tunica 38660
Puckett 39151
Pulaski 39152
Purvis 39475
Quentin 39660
Quitman 39355
Raleigh 39153
Randolph 38864
Raymond 39154
Red Banks 38661
Redwood 39156
Reform 39757
Rena Lara 38767
Rich 38662
Richton 39476
Ridgeland 39157
Rienzi 38865
Ripley (1st) 38663
Robinsonville 38664
Rolling Fork 39159
Rome 38768
Rose Hill 39356
Rosedale 38769
Roxie 39661
Ruleville 38871
Russell 39357
Ruth 39662

Sallis 39160
Saltillo 38866
Sandersville 39477
Sandhill 39161
Sandy Hook 39478
Sanford, R. Br. Seminary ...39479
Sanitorium, Br. Magee 39112
Sarah 38665
Sardis 38666
Sarepta 38867
Satartia 39162
Saucier 39574
Savage 38667
Schlater 38952
Scobey 38953
Scooba 39358
Scott 38772
Sebastopol 39359
Seminary 39479
Senatobia (1st) 38668
Sessums 39758
Shannon 38868
Sharon 39163
Shaw 38773
Shelby 38774
Sherard 38669
Sherman 38869
Shivers 39164
Shubuta 39360
Shuqualak 39361
Sibley 39165
Sidon 38954
Silver City 39166
Silver Creek 39663
Skene 38775
Slate Spring, R. Br. Calhoun
  City 38955
Sledge 38670
  Falcon, R. Br. 38628
Smithdale 39664
Smithville 38870
Sontag 39665
Soso 39480
Southaven 39671
Southern, Sta. Hattiesburg 39401
Star 39164
Starkville (1st) 39759
  Longview, R. Br. 39749
State College (1st) 39762
State Line 39362
Steens 39766
Stewart 39767
Stoneville 38776
Stonewall 39363
Stovall 38672
Stringer 39481
Stringtown, R. Br. Benoit 38777
Sturgis 39769
Summit 39666
Sumner 38957
Sumrall 39482
Sunflower 38778
  Blaine, R. Br. 38727
Swan Lake 38958
Swiftown 38959
Sylvarena, R. Br. Raleigh 39153
Taylor 38673
Taylorsville (1st) 39168
Tchula 39169
Terry 39170
Thaxton 38871
The Mall, Sta. Vicksburg 39180
Thomastown 39171

Thornton 39172
Tie Plant 38960

Tillatoba 38961
Tinsley 39173
Tiplersville 38674
Tippo 38962
Tishomingo 38873
Toccopola 38874
Tomnolen 39770
Toomsuba 39364
Tougaloo 39174
Tralake, R. Br. Leland 38757
Trebloc 38875
Tremont 38876
Triangle Hospital, Sta.
  Biloxi 39530
Tribbett 38779
Tula 38675
Tunica 38676
  Prichard, R. Br. 38660
Tupelo (1st) 38801
Tutwiler 38963
Tylertown 39667
U S Naval Construction
  Batt. Sta. Gulfport 39501
Union 39365
Union Church 39668

Utica Junior College, R. Br.
  Utica 39175
Vaiden 39176
Valley Park 39177
Value, R. Br. Brandon 39178
Van Vleet 38877
Vance 38964
Vancleave, R. Br. Ocean
  Springs 39564
Vardaman 38878
Vaughan 39179
Verona 38879
Veterans Administration
  Cent. Sta. Biloxi 39531
Vicksburg (1st) 39180
Victoria 38879
Vossburg 39366
Wade, R. Br. Pascagoula 39575
Walls (1st) 38680
Walnut 38683
  Chalybeate, R. Br. 38684
Walnut Grove 39189
Walthall 39771
Washington 39190
Water Valley (1st) 38965
Waterford 38685
Waveland 39576

Waynesboro (1st) 39367
Wayside 38780
Webb 38966
Weir 39772
Wenasoga 38886
Wesson 39191
West 39192
West, Sta. Meridian 39301
West Biloxi, Sta. Biloxi 39531
West Jackson, Sta. Jackson
  (see appendx)
West Point (1st) 39773
West Union, R. Br. Myrtle 38650
Westland, Sta. Jackson 39209
Wheeler 38880
Whitfield 39193
Wiggins 39577
  Bond, R. Br. 39550
Willis Heights, Sta. Tupelo 38801
Winona (1st) 38967
Winstonville 38781
Winterville, R. Br. Greenville 38782
Woodland 39776
Woodville 39669
Woolmarket, R. Br. Biloxi 39532
Yazoo City (1st) 39194
  Eden, R. Br. 39065

BILOXI 395

POST OFFICE BOXES

Box Nos.
1-1209 .... Main Office 33
K65-K299 ...... Keesler Afb
                 Station 34
4001-4597 ..... West Biloxi
                 Sta. 31

RURAL ROUTES

1,2,3,4,5,6 32

STATIONS, BRANCHES AND UNITS

D'Iberville Sta. 32
Keesler A F B Sta. 34
Triangle Hospital Sta. 30
Veterans Administration
  CentSta 31
West Biloxi Sta. 31
Woolmarket Rural Br. 32
General Delivery 30
Postmaster 30

JACKSON 392

POST OFFICE BOXES

Box Nos.
1-2500 .... Main Office 05
2501-4198 ..... West Jackson
                 Sta. 07
4201-5047 ..... Fondren Sta. 16

5501-6127 ..... Pearl Br. 08
6501-7000 ..... Leavell Woods
                 Sta. 12
8001-8999 ..... Battlefield Sta. . 04
9561-10194 .... North 06
10201-10995 ... Westland Sta. 09
11001-11297 ... Delta Drive
                 Sta. 13
12001-13000 ... Colonial Sta 11
15001-16000 ... A Sta 10
16001-16500 ... Mc Willie 06
17001-19000 ... Station C 17

RURAL ROUTES

1,2 09
3 13
4 08
5 12
6 08

STATIONS, BRANCHES AND UNITS

Apple Ridge Sta. 04
Battlefield Sta. 04
Candlestick Br. 12
Colonial Sta. 11
Delta Drive Sta. 13
Fondren Sta. 16
Leavell Woods Sta. 12
Mc Willie Sta. 06
North Sta. 06
Pearl Br. 08
Plain Rural Br. 18
West Jackson Sta. 03
Westland Sta. 09
General Delivery 05
Postmaster 05

APARTMENTS, HOTELS, MOTELS

Camelot Apartments, 2840
  Robinson Road 09
Canton Road Manor, 4911
  Old Canton Rd 11
Capitol, 1315 W Capitol 03
Chateau, 1576 W Capitol 03
De Ville, 700 N Jefferson 02
Downtowner, 225 E Capitol 01
Hallmark, 987 E Northside
  Dr 06
Heidelberg, 131 E Capitol 01
Hylan Garden, 1297 Whitfield
  Mill Rd 03
Lakeland, 760 Lakeland Dr 16
Magnolia Towers Apts. 809 N
  State 01
Park Towne, 3895 Northview
  Dr 06
Park Villa, 624 Ellis Ave. 09
Raymond Garden, 386
  Raymond Rd 04
Sterling Towers Apts. 170 E
  Griffith 02
Sun N Sand, 401 N Lamar 01
University, 707 Lakeland Dr 16
Vieux Carre Apts. 3961 Hwy
  55, N 16

BUILDINGS

Bankers Trust-Plaza, 120 N
  Congress 01
Barnett, 200 S President 01
Court Square South, 429
  Tombigbee 01
Deposit Guaranty Bank, 200
  E Capitol 01

Jackson (Con.)   392

East Amite, 145 E Amite 01
Eight O Two, 802 N State...... 01
Electric, 126 S West 01
Federal, 245 E Capitol 01
First Federal Savings & Loan,
  525 E Capitol 01
First National Bank, 248 E
  Capitol 01
Gale, 126 S President............ 01
Hinds Professional, 1815
  Hospital Dr...................... 04
Lamar Life Insurance, 317 E
  Capitol 01
Magnolia State Savings &
  Loan, 202 N Congress........ 01
Medical Arts, 1151 N State 01
Medical Towers, 440 E
  Woodrow Wilson 16
Milner, 210 S Lamar.............. 01

Mississippi Farm Bureau,
  429 Mississippi 01
Morgan, 3100 Old Canton
  Rd 06
Petroleum, 200 E
  Pascagoula 01
Primos Fondren, 603 Duling.. 16
Primos, 414 N State 01
Six Fifty Six, 656 N State 01
Southern Farm Bureau, 501
  E Amite............................ 01
Standard Life, 127 S Roach.... 01
Three O One, 301 N Lamar.... 02
Two O Three 203 W Capitol.... 01
Two Thirty Six, 236 E Capitol. 01
University Plaza, 500 E
  Woodrow Wilson 16
Woolfolk State Office, 501 N
  West 01

HOSPITALS

Baptist, 1190 N State............ 01
Doctors, 2949 University Dr.... 16
Hinds General, 1850
  Chadwick Dr 04
Saint Dominic'S, 969
  Lakeland Dr 16
University Medical Center,
  2500 N State 16
Veterans Administration,
  1500 E Woodrow Wilson
  Ave 16

UNIVERSITIES AND COLLEGES

Belhaven, 1500 Peachtree 02
Jackson State, 1325 Lynch .. 03
Millsaps, 1701 N State.......... 02
University Medical Center,
  2500 N State 16

MISSOURI   State List of Post Offices

MISSOURI
(Abbreviation: MO)

Adrian 64720
Advance 63730
Affton, Br. Saint Louis............63123
Agency 64401
Alba 64830
Albany (1st) 64402
Aldrich 65601
Alexandria..............................63430
Allendale 64420
Allenton 63001
Allenville, R. Br. Chaffee 63741
Alley Spring 65431
Alma 64001
Altamont 64620
Altenburg 63732
Alton 65606
Amazonia 64421
Amity 64422
Amoret 64722
Amsterdam 64723
Anabel 63431
Anderson 64831
Annada 63330
Annapolis 63620
Anniston 63820
Antioch, Sta. Kansas City
  (see appendix)
Antonia, R. Br. Imperial 63052
Appleton City 64724
Arab 63733
Arbela 63432
Granger, R. Br. 63442
Arbyrd 63821
Arcadia 63621
Archie 64725
Arcola 65603
Argyle 65001
Armstrong 65230
Arnold (1st) 63010
Arrow Rock 65320
Asbury 64832
Ash Grove 65604

Ashburn 63433
Ashland 65010
Atherton, R. Br.
  Independence 64050
Atlanta 63530
Augusta 63332
Aurora (1st) 65605
  Jenkins, R. Br. 65677
Auxvasse 65231
Ava 65608
Avalon 64621
Avilla 64833
Avondale 64010
Baden, Sta. Saint Louis........63147
Bakersfield 65609
Ballwin (1st) 63011
Baring 63531
Barnard 64423
Barnett 65011
Barnhart 63012
Bates City 64011
Bay, R. Br. Hermann 65041
Beaufort 63013
Belgrade 63622
Bell City 63735
Belle 65013
Belleview 63623
Bellflower 63333
Belton (1st) 64012
Bendavis 65433
Benton 63736
Benton City............................65232
Benton Park, Sta. Saint
  Louis (see appendix)
Berger 63014
Berkeley, Br Saint Louis........63134
Bernie 63822
Berryman 65435
Bertrand 63823
Bethany (1st) 64424
Bethel 63434
Beulah 65436
Bevier 63532
Bigelow 64425
Billings 65610

Birch Tree 65438
  Thomasville, R. Br. 65578
Bismarck 63624
Bixby 65439
Black 63625
Blackburn 65321
Blackwater 65322
Blackwell 63626
Blairstown 64726
Bland 65014
  Mount Sterling, R. Br. 65062
Blodgett 63824
Bloomfield 63825
Bloomsdale 63627
Blue Eye 65611
Blue Springs (1st) 64015
Blythedale 64426
Bogard 64622
Bois D Arc 65612
Bolckow 64427
Bolivar (1st) 65613
Bonne Terre (1st) 63628
Bonnots Mill 65016
Boonville (1st) 65233
Boss 65440
Boston 64727
Bosworth 64623
Bourbon 65441
Bowling Green (1st) 63334
  Cyrene, R. Br. 63340
Bradleyville 65614
Bragg City 63827
Braggadocio 63826
Brandsville 65688
Branson (1st) 65616
Brashear 63533
Braymer 64624
Brazeau 63737
Breckenridge 64625
Bremen, Sta. Saint Louis......63160
Brentwood, Br Saint Louis......63144
Briar 63931
Bridgeton, Br. Hazelwood......63044
Brighton 65617
Brimson 64626

394

Brinktown 65443
Brixey 65618
Broadway, Sta. Saint Louis ...63147
Bronaugh 64728
Brookfield (1st) 64628
Brookline Station 65619
Broseley 63932
Brownbranch, R. Br. Ava 65608
Browning 64630
Brownington 64729
Brownwood 63738
Brumley 65017
Bruner 65620
Brunswick 65236
Bucklin 64631
Buckner 64016
Bucyrus 65444
Buell, R. Br. Montgomery
City 63361
Buffalo 65622
Bunceton 65237
Bunker 63629
Burfordville 63739
Burlington Junction 64428
Butler (1st) 64730
Butterfield, R. Br. Cassville ...65623
Bynumville, R. Br. Salisbury ...65238
Cabanne, Sta. Saint Louis 63161
Cabool 65689
Cadet 63630
Cainsville 64632
Cairo 65239
Caledonia 63631
Calhoun 65323
California (1st) 65018
Callao 63534
Camden 64017
Camden Point 64018
Camdenton (1st) 65020
Cameron (1st) 64429
Campbell 63933
Canalou 63828
Canton 63435
Cape Fair 65624
Cape Girardeau (1st) 63701
Caplinger Mills 65607
Cardwell 63829
Carl Junction 64834
Carondelet, Sta. Saint Louis ...63111
Carr, Sta. Florissant 63031
Carrollton (1st) 64633
Carterville 64835
Carthage (1st) 64836
Caruthersville (1st) 63830
Cascade 63632
Cassville (1st) 65625
Butterfield, R. Br. 65632
Catawissa 63015
Catron 63833
Caulfield 65626
Cedar City 65022
Cedar Hill 63016
Cedarcreek 65627
Center 63436
Centertown 65023
Centerview 64019
Centerville 63633
Corridon, R. Br. 63635
Central, Sta. Saint Louis
(see appendix)
Central, Sta. Kansas City
(see appendix)
Centralia (1st) 65240

Centropolis, Sta. Kansas
City 64126
Chadwick 65629
Chaffee 63740
Allenville, R. Br. 63741
Chamois 65024
Charles Nagel, Sta. Saint
Louis (see appendix)
Charleston (1st) 63834
Cherryville 65446
Chesterfield (1st) 63017
Chestnutridge 65630
Chilhowee 64733
Chillicothe (1st) 64601
Chouteau, Sta. Saint Louis ...63110
Christian Bechtold, Sta.
Saint Louis 63118
Chula 64635
Civic Center, Sta. Kansas
City 64106
Clara 65447
Clarence 63437
Clark 65243
Clarksburg 65025
Clarksdale 64430
Clarksville 63336
Clarkton 63837
Claycomo, Br. Kansas City 64119
Clayton, Br. Saint Louis 63105
Clearmont 64431
Clearwater 63634
Cleveland 64734
Clever 65631
Clifton Hill 65244
Climax Springs 65324
Clinton (1st) 64735
Clubb, R. Br. Piedmont 63934
Clyde 64432
Coatsville 63535
Coffey 64636
Coldwater, R. Br. Piedmont ...63934
Cole Camp 65325
College Mound, R. Br.
Excello 65245
Collins 64738
Columbia (1st) 65201
Commerce 63742
Commerce Tower, Sta.
Kansas City 64199
Commercial, Sta.
Springfield 65803
Conception 64433
Conception Junction 64434
Conclay, Br. Saint Louis 63124
Concordia 64020
Conran 63838
Conway 65632
Cook Station 65449
Cooter 63839
Corder 64021
Corning, R. Br. Craig 64435
Corridon, R. Br. Centerville ...63635
Corso 63337
Cosby 64436
Cottleville 63338
Couch 65690
Country Club, Sta. Kansas
City 64113
Courtois 65451
Cowgill 64637
Craig 64437
Corning, R. Br. 64435
Crane 65633

Creighton 64739
Crescent, R. Br. Eureka 63018
Creve Coeur, Br. Saint Louis ..63141
Crocker 65452
Cross Timbers 65634
Crystal City (1st) 63019
Cuba (1st) 65453
Curryville 63339
Cyrene, R. Br. Bowling
Green 63340
Dadeville 65635
Daisy 63743
Dalton 65246
Derlington 64438
Davisville 65456
Dawn 64638
De Kalb 64440
De Soto (1st) 63020
De Witt 64639
Dearborn 64439
Deepwater 64740
Deerfield 64741
Deering 63840
Defiance 63341
Delta 63744
Denver 64441
Des Arc 63636
Des Peres, Br. Saint Louis 63131
Desloge, Br. Flat River 63601
Devils Elbow 65457
Dexter (1st) 63841
Diamond 64840
Diehlstadt, R. Br.
Charleston 63834
Diggins 65636
Dillard 65458
Dittmer 63023
Dixon 65459
Doe Run 63637
Doniphan (1st) 63935
Dora 65637
Dorena 63844
Dover 64022
Downing 63536
Drexel 64742
Drury 65638
Dudley 63936
Duenweg 64841
Dugginsville 65639
Duke 65461
Dunnegan 65640
Durham 63438
Dutchtown 63745
Dutzow 63342
Eagle Rock 65641
Eagleville 64442
East Lynne 64743
East Prairie 63845
Easton 64443
Edgar Springs 65462
Edgerton 64444
Edina 63537
Edwards 65326
El Dorado Springs (1st) 64744
Eldon (1st) 65026
Eldridge 65463
Elijah 65642
Elk Creek 65464
Elkhead, R. Br. Sparta 65753
Elkland 65644
Ellington 63638
Sweetwater, R. Br 63680
Ellis Prairie 65465

Ellisville, Br. Ballwin............63011
Ellsinore...........................63937
Elmer..............................63538
Elmo...............................64445
Elsberry...........................63343
Elvins, Br. Flat River.............63639
Emden..............................63439
Eminence...........................65466
   Round Spring, R. Br.............65467
Emma...............................65327
Englewood, Sta.
   Independence....................64052
Eolia..............................63344
Essex..............................63846
Ethel..............................63539
Etterville.........................65031
Eudora, R. Br. Morrisville.........65645
Eugene.............................65032
Eunice.............................65468
Eureka (1st).......................63025
   Crescent, R. Br.................63018
Everton............................65646
Ewing..............................63440
Excello............................65247
   College Mound, R. Br............65245
Excelsior Springs (1st)............64024
Exeter.............................65647
Fagus..............................63938
Fair Grove.........................65648
Fair Play..........................65649
Fairdealing........................63939
Fairfax............................64446
Fairgrounds, Sta. Saint
   Louis...........................63107
Fairleigh, Sta. Saint Joseph.......64506
Fairmount, Sta.
   Independence....................64053
Fairport, R. Br. Maysville.........64447
Fairview...........................64842
Falcon.............................65470
   Nebo, R. Br.....................65471
Farber.............................63345
Farley.............................64028
Farmington (1st)...................63640
Farrar.............................63746
Faucett............................64448
Fayette............................65248
Federal Reserve, Sta.
   Kansas City.....................64198
Fenton (1st).......................63026
Ferguson, Br. Saint Louis..........63135
Ferrelview, R. Br. Kansas
   City............................64163
Festus (1st).......................63028
Field, Sta. Saint Louis............63108
Fillmore...........................64449
Fisk...............................63940
Flat River (1st)...................63601
   Desloge, Br.....................63601
   Elvins, Br......................63639
   Franklcay, R. Br................63644
   Leadwood, R. Br.................63653
Flemington.........................65650
Fletcher...........................63030
Flinthill..........................63346
Florence...........................65329
FLORISSANT (1st) (see
   appendix)
Foley..............................63347
Forbes.............................64450
Fordland...........................65652
Forest City........................64451
   Fortescue, R. Br................64452

Forest Green, R. Br.
   Salisbury.......................65249
Foristell..........................63348
Forsyth............................65653
   Hilda, R. Br....................65670
Fort Leonard Wood (1st)............65473
Fortescue, R. Br. Forest City......64452
Fortuna............................65034
Foster.............................64745
Franklcay, R. Br. Flat River.......63644
Frankford..........................63441
Franklin...........................65250
Fredericktown (1st)................63645
Freeburg...........................65035
Freeman............................64746
Fieistatt..........................65654
Fremont............................63941
French Village.....................63036
Friedheim..........................63747
Fristoe, R. Br. Warsaw.............65356
Frohna.............................63748
Fulton (1st).......................65251
Gainesville........................65655
   Howards Ridge, R. Br............65673
Galena.............................65656
Gallatin...........................64640
Galt...............................64641
Garden City........................64747
Gardner, Sta. Saint Louis..........63109
Garrison...........................65657
Gasconade..........................65036
Gashland, Sta. Kansas City.........64118
Gatewood...........................63942
Gentry.............................64453
Gerald.............................63037
Gibbs..............................63540
Gibson.............................63847
Gideon.............................63848
Gilliam............................65330
Gilman City........................64642
Gipsy..............................63750
Gladden............................65478
Gladstone, Br. Kansas City
   (see appendix)
Glasgow............................65254
Glenallen..........................63751
Glencoe............................63038
Glendale, Br. Saint Louis..........63122
Glenstone, Sta. Springfield........65804
Glenwood...........................63541
Glover.............................63646
Gobler.............................63849
Golden.............................65658
Golden City........................64748
Goldsberry.........................63542
Goodman............................64843
Goodson............................65659
Gordonville........................63752
Gorin..............................63543
Gower..............................64454
Graff..............................65660
Graham.............................64455
Grain Valley.......................64029
Granby.............................64844
Grand Pass.........................65331
Grandin............................63943
Grandview (1st)....................64030
Granger, R. Br. Arbela.............63442
Graniteville, R. Br. Ironton.......63650
Grant City.........................64456
Grassy.............................63753
Gravois, Sta. Saint Louis..........63116
Gravois Mills......................65037

Laurie, R. Br......................65038
Gray Summit........................63039
Grayridge..........................63850
Green Castle.......................63544
Green City.........................63545
Green Ridge........................65332
Greenfield.........................65661
Greentop...........................63546
Greenville.........................63944
Greenwood..........................64034
Grover.............................63040
Grovespring........................65662
Grubville..........................63041
Guilford...........................64457
Hale...............................64643
Half Way...........................65663
Hallsville.........................65255
Halltown...........................65664
Hamilton...........................64644
   Nettleton, R. Br................64666
Hammond............................65665
Hannibal (1st).....................63401
Hardenville........................65666
Hardin.............................64035
Harding, Sta. Kansas City..........64111
Harris.............................64645
Harrisburg.........................65256
Harrisonville (1st)................64701
Hartsburg..........................65039
Hartshorn..........................65479
Hartville..........................65667
Harvester, R. Br. Saint
   Charles.........................63303
Harviell...........................63945
Harwood............................64750
Hatfield...........................64458
Hawk Point.........................63349
Hayti..............................63851
HAZELWOOD (1st) (see
   appendix)
Helena.............................64459
Hematite...........................63047
Hemple, R. Br. Stewartsville.......64460
Hendrickson, R. Br. Poplar
   Bluff...........................63946
Henley.............................65040
Henrietta..........................64036
Herculaneum........................63048
Hermann (1st)......................65041
   Bay, R. Br......................65041
   Mc Kittrick, R. Br..............65056
Hermitage..........................65668
Hickman Mills, Sta. Kansas
   City (see appendix)
Higbee.............................65257
Higginsville (1st).................64037
High Hill..........................63350
High Point.........................65042
High Ridge.........................63049
Highlandville......................65669
Hilda, R. Br. Forsyth..............65670
Hillsboro (1st)....................63050
Hiram..............................63947
Hocomo.............................65691
Holcomb............................63852
Holden.............................64040
Holland............................63853
Holliday...........................65258
Hollister..........................65672
Hollywood..........................63854
Holt...............................64048
Holts Summit.......................65043

Hope, R. Br. Morrison...........65044
Hopewell, R. Br. Mineral
Point...............................63660
Hopkins..............................64461
Hornersville.......................63855
Horton...............................64751
House Springs.....................63051
Houston..............................65483
Houstonia...........................65333
Howards Ridge, R. Br.
Gainesville.......................65673
Howardville, R. Br. New
Madrid.............................63869
Huggins..............................65484
Hughesville.........................65334
Humansville.........................65574
Hume.................................64752
Humphreys...........................64646
Hunnewell...........................63443
Hunter...............................63948
Huntsville...........................65259
Hurdland.............................63547
Hurley...............................65675
Iantha...............................64753
Iberia...............................65486
Ilmo.................................63754
Imperial.............................63052
INDEPENDENCE (1st) (see
appendix)
Inza, Sta. Saint Joseph.........64508
Ionia.................................65335
Iron Mountain.......................63649
Irondale.............................63648
Ironton..............................63650
Irwin................................64754
Isabella.............................65676
Jackson (1st).......................63755
Jacksonville........................65260
Jadwin...............................65501
James Crews, Sta. Kansas
City.................................64108
Jameson..............................64647
Jamesport...........................64648
Jamestown...........................65046
Jane, R. Br. Pineville...........64846
Jasper...............................64755
Jefferson City (1st)..............65101
Jefferson Memorial, Sta.
Saint Louis.......................63102
Jenkins, R. Br. Aurora...........65677
Jennings, Br. Saint Louis........63136
Jerico Springs......................64756
Jerome...............................65529
Jesse James Territory, R. Br.
Sullivan...........................63080
Jonesburg...........................63351
Joplin (1st).........................64801
Jordan W Chambers, Sta.
Saint Louis.......................63106
Kahoka...............................63445
Medill, R. Br.....................63455
Kaiser...............................65047
KANSAS CITY (1st) (see
appendix)
Kearney..............................64060
Kelso................................63758
Keltner..............................65678
Kennett (1st).......................63857
Kenoma, R. Br. Lamar.............64759
Kersey Coates, Sta. Kansas
City.................................64105
Kewanee..............................63860

Keytesville.........................65261
Kidder...............................64649
Kimberling City, R. Br.
Reeds Spring......................65686
Kimmswick...........................63053
Kinder, R. Br. Puxico............63759
King City............................64463
Kingdom City........................65262
Kingston.............................64650
Kingsville...........................64061
Kinloch, Br. Saint Louis.........63140
Kirbyville...........................65679
Kirksville (1st)....................63501
Kirkwood, Br. Saint Louis
(see appendix)
Kissee Mills........................65680
Knob Lick............................63651
Knob Noster.........................65336
Knox City............................63446
Koch.................................63054
Koeltztown..........................65048
Koshkonong..........................65692
La Belle.............................63447
La Due...............................64758
La Grange............................63448
La Monte.............................65337
La Plata.............................63549
South Gifford, R. Br...........63564
La Russell...........................64848
Labadie..............................63055
Laclede..............................64651
Laddonia.............................63352
Lake Lotawana, R. Br. Lees
Summit..............................64063
Lake Ozark (1st)....................65049
Lake Sherwood, R. Br.
Marthasville......................63357
Lake Spring..........................65532
Lamar (1st)..........................64759
Lambert Airport, Br. Saint
Louis................................63145
Lampe................................65681
Lamagan..............................64847
Lancaster............................63548
Langdon, R. Br. Rock Port........64464
Lanton, R. Br. Thayer............65792
Laquey...............................65534
Laredo...............................64652
Latham...............................65050
Lathrop..............................64465
Latour...............................64760
Laurie, R. Br. Gravois Mills.....65038
Lawson...............................64062
Leadwood, R. Br. Flat River......63653
Leasburg.............................65535
Lebanon (1st).......................65536
Lecoma...............................65540
Leeds, Sta. Kansas City..........64129
Lees Summit (1st)..................64063
Leeton...............................64761
Lemay, Br. Saint Louis...........63125
Lemons...............................63550
Lenox................................65541
Lentner..............................63450
Leonard..............................63451
Leopold..............................63760
Leslie...............................63056
Lesterville..........................63654
Levasy...............................64066
Lewistown............................63452
Lexington (1st).....................64067
Liberal..............................64762

Liberty (1st).......................64068
Licking..............................65542
Liguori (1st).......................63057
Lilbourn.............................63862
Lincoln..............................65338
Linn.................................65051
Linn Creek...........................65052
Linneus..............................64653
Livonia..............................63551
Lock Springs........................64654
Lockwood.............................65682
Lodi.................................63950
Lohman...............................65053
Lone Jack............................64070
Lonedell.............................63060
Long Lane............................65590
Longrun, R. Br. Theodosia........65684
Longview, Sta. Kansas City
(see appendix)
Loose Creek.........................65054
Louisburg............................65685
Louisiana (1st).....................63353
Lowndes..............................63951
Lowry City...........................64763
Lucerne..............................64655
Ludlow...............................64656
Luebbering...........................63061
Luray................................63453
Lutesville...........................63762
Lynchburg............................65543
Macks Creek..........................65786
Macomb...............................65702
Macon (1st)..........................63552
Madison..............................65263
Maitland.............................64466
Malden (1st).........................63863
Malta Bend...........................65339
Manchester, Br. Ballwin..........63011
Manes, R. Br. Mountain
Grove...............................65703
Mansfield............................65704
Mapaville............................63065
Maplewood, Br. Saint Louis.......63143
Marble Hill..........................63764
Marceline (1st).....................64658
Marionville..........................65705
Marquand.............................63655
Marshall (1st)......................65340
Marshfield (1st)....................65706
Marston..............................63866
Marthasville.........................63357
Martinsburg..........................65264
Martinsville.........................64467
Maryland Heights, Br.
Hazelwood.........................63043
Maryville (1st).....................64468
Matthews.............................63867
Maysville............................64469
Fairport, R. Br...................64447
Mayview..............................64071
Maywood..............................63454
Mc Bride, R. Br. Perryville......63776
Mc Clurg.............................65701
Mc Fall..............................64657
Mc Gee...............................63763
Mc Girk..............................65055
Mc Kittrick, R. Br. Hermann......65056
Meadville............................64659
Medill, R. Br. Kahoka............63455
Mehlville, Br. Saint Louis.......63129
Memphis..............................63555
Mendon...............................64660
Mentor...............................63765

Mercer	64661
Meta	65058
Metz	64765
Mexico (1st)	65265
Miami	65344
Middle Brook	63656
Middletown	63359
Midway, R. Br. Columbia	65201
Milan	63556
Milford	64766
Mill Grove	64662
Mill Spring	63952
Millcreek	63658
Miller	65707
Millersville	63766
Milo	64767
Mindenmines	64769
Mine La Motte	63659
Mineola, R. Br. Montgomery City	63360
Mineral Point	63660
Missouri City	64072
Moberly (1st)	65270
Mokane	65059
Monett (1st)	65708
Monroe City	63456
Montauk	65545
Montgomery City	63361
Buell, R. Br.	63361
Mineola, R. Br.	63360
Monticello	63457
Montier	65546
Montreal	65591
Montrose	64770
Moody	65777
Mooresville	64664
Mora	65345
Morehouse	63868
Morgan	65709
Morley	63767
Morrison	65061
Hope, R. Br.	65044
Morrisville	65710
Eudora, R. Br.	65645
Morse Mill	63066
Mosby	64073
Moscow Mills	63362
Moselle, R. Br. Union	63067
Mound City	64470
Moundville	64771
Mount Moriah	64665
Mount Sterling, R. Br. Bland	65062
Mount Vernon (1st)	65712
Mountain Grove (1st)	65711
Manes, R. Br.	65703
Mountain View	65548
Myrtle	65778
Napoleon	64074
Napton	65346
Nashua, Sta. Kansas City	64155
Naylor	63953
Nebo, R. Br. Falcon	65471
Neck City	64849
Neelyville	63954
Nelson	65347
Neosho (1st)	64850
Nettleton, R. Br. Hamilton	64666
Nevada (1st)	64772
New Bloomfield	65063
New Boston	63557
New Cambria	63558
New Florence	63363
New Franklin	65274
New Hamburg, R. Br. Benton	63736
New Hampton	64471
New Hartford	63364
New Haven (1st)	63068
New London	63459
New Madrid	63869
New Melle	63365
New Offenburg	63661
New Point	64472
New Wells	63768
Newark	63458
Newburg	65550
Newtonia	64853
Newtown	64667
Niangua	65713
Nixa	65714
Noble	65715
Noel	64854
Norborne	64668
Normandy, Br. Saint Louis	63121
North County, Br. Saint Louis (see appendix)	
North Kansas City, Br. Kansas City (see appendix)	
Northeast, Sta. Kansas City	64123
Northview	65716
Northwest Plaza, Sta. Saint Ann	63074
Norwood	65717
Nottinghill	65718
Novelty	63460
Novinger	63559
O'Fallon (1st)	63366
Oak Grove	64075
Oak Ridge	63769
Oakwood, Sta. Hannibal	63401
Ocie, R. Br. Theodosia	65719
Odessa (1st)	64076
Old Appleton	63770
Old Monroe	63369
Old Town, Sta. Florissant	63031
Oldfield	65720
Olean	65064
Olive, Sta. Saint Louis	63101
Olivette, Br. Saint Louis (see appendix)	
Olney	63370
Oran	63771
Oregon	64473
Oronogo	64855
Orrick	64077
Osage Beach	65065
Osborn	64474
Osceola	64776
Otterville	65348
Otto, R. Br. Imperial	63052
Overland, Br. Saint Louis	63114
Owensville	65066
Oxly	63955
Ozark	65721
Pacific (1st)	63069
Painton	63772
Palmyra	63461
Paris	65275
Parkville, Br. Kansas City (see appendix)	
Parkway, Sta. Kansas City	64130
Parma	63870
Parnell	64475
Pascola	63871
Passaic	64777
Patterson	63956
Patton	63662
Pattonsburg	64670
Paynesville	63371
Peace Valley	65788
Peach Orchard	63872
Peculiar	64078
Perkins	63774
Perry	63462
Perryville (1st)	63775
Mc Bride, R. Br.	63776
Uniontown, R. Br.	63783
Peruque, R. Br. Saint Charles	63372
Pevely	63070
Philadelphia	63463
Phillipsburg	65722
Pickering	64476
Piedmont	63957
Clubb, R. Br.	63934
Coldwater, R. Br.	63934
Pierce City	65723
Pierre Laclede, Sta. Saint Louis	63108
Pilot Grove	65276
Pilot Knob	63663
Pine	63958
Pine Lawn, Br. Saint Louis	63120
Pineville	64856
Jane, R. Br.	64846
Pittsburg	65724
Plato	65552
Platte City	64079
Plattsburg	64477
Plaza, Sta. Kansas City	64112
Plaza, Sta. Saint Louis	63199
Pleasant Hill (1st)	64080
Pleasant Hope	65725
Plevna	63464
Pocahontas	63779
Point Lookout	65726
Point Pleasant, R. Br. Portageville	63873
Polk	65727
Pollock	63560
Polo	64671
Pomona	65789
Ponce De Leon	65728
Pontiac	65729
Poplar Bluff (1st)	63901
Hendrickson, R. Br.	63946
Portage Des Sioux	63373
Portageville	63873
Portland	65067
Potosi (1st)	63664
Pottersville	65790
Powell	65730
Powersite	65731
Powersville	64672
Poynor	63959
Prairie Home	65068
Preston	65732
Princeton	64673
Principia, Br. Saint Louis	63131
Progress, Sta. Saint Louis	63159
Protem	65733
Purcell	64857
Purdin	64674
Purdy	65734
Puxico	63960
Kinder, R. Br.	63759
Queen City	63561

Quincy	65735
Quitman	64478
Qulin	63961
Racine	64858
Ravenwood	64479
Raymondville	65555
Raymore	64083
Raytown, Br. Kansas City (see appendix)	
Rayville	64084
Rea	64480
Redford	63665
Reeds	64859
Reeds Spring	65737
Renick	65278
Republic	65738
Revere	63465
Reynolds	63666
Rhineland	65069
Rich Hill	64779
Richards	64778
Richards Gebaur A F B, Br.	
Grandview	64030
Richland	65556
Richmond (1st)	64085
Richmond Heights, Br. Saint Louis	63117
Richwoods	63071
Ridgedale	65739
Ridgeway	64481
Risco	63874
Ritchey	64860
River Roads, Br. Saint Louis	63136
Riverside, Br. Kansas City	64168
Riverton, R. Br. Alton	65606
Rives	63875
Roach	65787
Robert E Hannegan, Sta.	
Saint Louis	63139
Robertsville	63072
Roby	65557
Rocheport	65279
Rock Port	64482
Langdon, R. Br.	64464
Watson, R. Br.	64496
Rockaway Beach	65740
Rockbridge	65741
Rockville	64780
Taberville, R. Br.	64787
Rocky Comfort	64861
Rocky Mount	65072
Rocky Ridge, R. Br. Sainte Genevieve	63676
Rogersville	65742
Rolla (1st)	65401
Vida, R. Br.	65581
Rombauer	63962
Roscoe	64781
Rosebud	63091
Roselle, R Br. Ironton	63650
Rosendale	64483
Rothville	64676
Round Spring, R. Br. Eminence	65467
Rueter	65744
Rush Hill	65280
Rushville	64484
Russellville	65074
Rutledge	63563
Saco	63669
Saginaw	64854

Saint Albans	63073
Saint Ann (1st)	63074
Saint Catharine	64677
Saint Charles (1st)	63301
Harvester, R. Br.	63303
Peruque, R. Br.	63372
Saint Clair (1st)	63077
Saint Elizabeth	65075
Saint James	65559
Saint Johns, Br. Saint Louis	63114
SAINT JOSEPH (1st) (see appendix)	
SAINT LOUIS (1st) (see appendix)	
Saint Marys	63673
Saint Patrick	63466
Saint Paul. R. Br. O'Fallon	63366
Saint Peters	63376
Saint Robert, R. Br. Waynesville	65583
Saint Thomas	65076
Sainte Genevieve (1st)	63670
Rocky Ridge, R. Br.	63676
Weingarten, R. Br.	63676
Salem (1st)	65560
Salisbury	65281
Bynumville, R. Br.	65238
Forest Green, R. Br.	65249
Santa Fe	65282
Sappington, Br. Saint Louis (see appendix)	
Sarcoxie	64862
Savannah	64485
Saverton	63467
Schell City	64783
Scopus, R. Br. Lutesville	63762
Scott City	63780
Sedalia (1st)	65301
Sedgewickville	63781
Seligman	65745
Senath	63876
Seneca	64865
Seymour	65746
Shelbina	63468
Shelbyville	63469
Sheldon	64784
Shell Knob	65747
Viola, R. Br.	65748
Sheridan	64486
Sherman	63078
Shook	63963
Sibley	64088
Sikeston (1st)	63801
Silex	63377
Silva	63964
Silver Dollar City, R. Br. Branson	65616
Skidmore	64487
Slater	65349
Smithton	65350
Smithville	64089
Snyder	65288
Solo	65564
Souder	65751
Soulard, Sta. Saint Louis	63157
South Fork, R. Br. West Plains	65776
South Gifford, R. Br. La Plata	63564
South Greenfield	65752
South Mall, Sta.	

Warrensburg	64093
South Saint Joseph (1st)	64488
South Side, Sta. Springfield (see appendix)	
South Troost, Sta. Kansas City	64131
South West City	64863
Southeast, Sta. Kansas City	64132
Sparta	65753
Spickard	64679
Spokane	65754
SPRINGFIELD (1st) (see appendix)	
Squires	65755
Stanberry	64489
Stanton	63079
Stark City	64866
State Hospital, Br. Farmington	63640
Steedman	65077
Steele	63877
Steelville	65565
Viburnum, R. Br.	65566
Steffenville	63470
Stella	64867
Stet	64680
Stewartsville	64490
Hemple, R. Br.	64460
Stockton	65785
Stockyards, Sta. Kansas City	64102
Stotesbury	64786
Stotts City	65756
Stoutland	65567
Stoutsville	65283
Stover	65078
Strafford	65757
Strasburg	64090
Sturdivant	63782
Sturgeon	65284
Success	65570
Sugar Creek, Br. Independence	64054
Sullivan (1st)	63080
Sulphur Springs	63083
Summersville	65571
Sumner	64681
Sunny Slope, Sta. Kansas City	64110
Sunrise Beach	65079
Swedeborg	65572
Sweet Springs (1st)	65351
Sweetwater, R. Br. Ellington	63680
Sycamore	65758
Syracuse	65354
Taberville, R. Br. Rockville	64787
Tallapoosa	63878
Taneyville	65759
Tarkio	64491
Taylor	63471
Tebbetts	65080
Tecumseh	65766
Teresita	65573
Thayer	65791
Lanton, R. Br.	65792
Theodosia	65761
Longrun, R. Br.	65584
Ocie, R. Br.	65719
Thomasville, R. Br. Birch Tree	65578
Thompson	65285

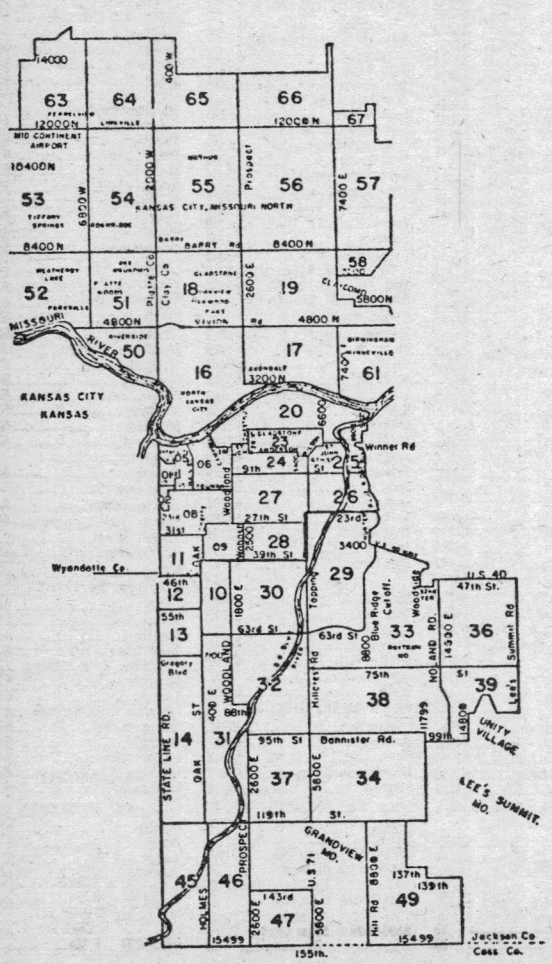

Thornfield	65762
Tiff	63674
Tiff City	64868
Tina	64682
Tipton	65081
Tower Grove, Sta. Saint	
Louis	63163
Tracy	64091
Treloar	63378
Trenton (1st)	64683
Trimble	64492
Triplett	65286
Troy (1st)	63379
Truesdail, R. Br. Warrenton	63380
Truxton	63381
Tunas	65764
Turners	65765
Turney	64493
Tuscumbia	65082
Udall	65766
Ulman	65083
Union (1st)	63084
Moselle, R. Br.	63067
Union Star	64494
Uniontown, R. Br. Perryville	63783
Unionville	63565
Unity Village, Br. Lees	
Summit	64063
University City, Br. Saint	
Louis	63130
Upton	65579
Urbana	65767
Urich	64788
Utica	64686
Valles Mines	63087
Valley Park	63088
Van Buren	63965
Vandalia	63382
Vanduser	63784
Vanzant	65768
Verona	65769
Versailles	65084
Veterans Hospital, Sta.	
Kansas City	64128

Viburnum, R. Br. Steelville	65566
Vichy	65580
Vida, R. Br. Rolla	65581
Vienna	65582
Villa Ridge	65089
Village Of St Francois, R.	
Br. Farmington	63640
Viola, R. Br. Shell Knob	65748
Vista	64789
Vulcan	63675
Waco	64869
Wakenda	64687
Waldron	64092
Walker	64790
Walnut Grove	65770
Walnut Shade	65771
Wappapello	63966
Wardell	63879
Warrensburg (1st)	64093
Warrenton	63383
Truesdail, R. Br.	63380
Warsaw (1st)	65355
Fristoe, R. Br.	63556
Washburn	65772
Washington (1st)	63090
Wasola	65773
Watson, R. Br. Rock Port	64496
Waverly	64096
Wayland	63472
Waynesville (1st)	65583
Weatherby	64497
Weaubleau	65774
Webb City (1st)	64870
Webster Groves, Br. Saint	
Louis	63119
Weingarten, R. Br. Sainte-	
Genevieve	63676
Wellington	64097
Wellston, Sta. Saint Louis	
(see appendix)	
Wellsville	63384
Wentworth	64873
Wentzville (1st)	63385
Wesco	65586
West Line	64791

West Plains (1st)	65775
South Fork, R. Br.	65776
Westalton	63386
Westboro	64498
Weston	64098
Westphalia	65085
Westport, Sta. Kansas City	64111
Wheatland	65779
Wheaton	64874
Wheeling	64688
Whiteman A F B, Br.	
Sedalia	65301
Whiteoak	63880
Whiteside	63387
Whitewater	63785
Willard	65781
Willhoit	65782
William M Chick, Sta.	
Kansas City	64124
Williamsburg	63388
Williamstown	63473
Williamsville	63967
Willow Springs (1st)	65793
Windsor (1st)	65360
Windyville	65783
Winfield	63389
Winigan	63566
Winona	65588
Winston	64689
Wittenberg	63786
Wolf Island	63881
Womack	63677
Wooldridge	65287
Wornall, Sta. Kansas City	
(see appendix)	
Worth	64499
Worthington	63567
Wright City	63390
Wyaconda	63474
Wyatt	63882
Wyatt Park, Sta. Saint	
Joseph	64507
Yukon	65589
Zalma	63787
Zanoni	65784

FLORISSANT   630

POST OFFICE BOXES

Box Nos.		
A-U	Carr Sta	31
1-399	Old Town	
	Station	32
AA-AB	Carr Sta	31
500-999	Florissant	33
1001-1499	Carr Sta	31

RURAL ROUTES

2		31

STATIONS, BRANCHES AND UNITS

Carr Sta		31
Old Town Sta		31
General Delivery		33
Postmaster		33

HAZELWOOD   630

STATIONS, BRANCHES AND UNITS

Bridgeton Br	44
Maryland Heights Br	43
General Delivery	42

INDEPENDENCE   640

POST OFFICE BOXES

Box Nos.		
A-C	Main Office	51
1-499	Main Office	51
600-900	Englewood Sta.	52
1001-1249	Main Office	51
7700-7899	Fairmount Sta.	53
8500-8699	Sugar Creek	
	Br	54

RURAL ROUTES

1,2,3		50

STATIONS, BRANCHES AND UNITS

Atherton Rural Br		50

KANSAS CITY   641

POST OFFICE BOXES

Box Nos.		
1-1999	Main Office	41
2000-3999	Central Sta.	42
4000-4299	A Sta	01
4300-4499	B Sta	27
4500-4599	William M	
	Chick Sta	24
4600-4899	E Sta	09

Kansas City (Con.)   641

4900-4999	F Sta	20
5000-5199	Southeast Sta	32
5200-5299	Plaza Sta	12
5300-5499	South Troost Sta	31
5500-5599	E Sta	09
5600-5799	Stockyards Sta	02
5800-5999	Westport Sta	11
6000-6199	Sunny Slope Sta	10
6200-6599	Centropolis Sta	26
6600-6799	Northeast Sta	23
6800-6999	Parkway Sta	30
7000-7299	Country Club Sta	13
7300-7599	North Kansas City Br	16
7600-7699	D Sta	28
7900-8099	Leeds Sta	29
8100-8199	Plaza Sta	12
8200-8399	Kersey Coates Sta	05
8400-8799	Wornall Sta	14
9000-9299	Riverside Br	68
9300-9599	Raytown Br	33
9600-9999	Hickman Mills Sta	34
10000-10499	Westport Sta	11
10500-10899	Gladstone Br	18
11000-11299	Antioch Sta	19
11300-11499	Plaza Sta	12
11500-11999	Longview Sta	38
12000-12299	Parkville Br	52
12300-12799	North Kansas City Br	16
12800-12999	William M Chick Sta	24
13000-13999	Commerce Tower Sta	99
15000-15999	Civic Center	06
16000-16499	Plaza	12
16500-16999	Raytown Br	33
17000-17299	Southeast	32
17300-17599	Parkway Sta	30
17700-17999	Hickman Mills Sta	34
9000-19999	Main Office	41

RURAL ROUTES

2,3		33
6		26
9		29
13		16
15		29
17		38
18,19		34
20		18
21		19
22,23,24,25,27		52
28,29		18
30		34
31		14

STATIONS, BRANCHES AND UNITS

Antioch Sta		19
Centropolis Sta		26
Civic Center Sta		06
Claycomo Br		19
Commerce Tower Sta		99
Country Club Sta		13
Federal Reserve Sta		98
Ferrelview Rural Br		63
Gashland Sta		18
Gladstone Br		18
Harding Sta		11
Hickman Mills Sta		34
James Crews Sta		08
Kersey Coates Sta		05
Leeds Sta		29
Longview Sta		38
Nashua Sta		55
North Kansas City Br		16
Northeast Sta		23
Parkville Br		50
Parkway Sta		30
Plaza Sta		12
Raytown Br		33
Riverside Br		68
South Troost Sta		31
Southeast Sta		32
Stockyards Sta		02
Sunny Slope Sta		10
Veterans Hospital Sta		28
Westport Sta		11
William M Chick Sta		24
Wornall Sta		14
General Delivery		08
Postmaster		08

APARTMENTS, HOTELS, MOTELS

Aladdin, 1215 Wyandotte		05
Ambassador, 3560 Broadway		11
Bellerive, 214 E Armour Blvd		11
Biarritz, 101 Ward Parkway		12
Boulevard Manor, 1115 E Armour Blvd		09
Casa Loma, 105 Ward Parkway		12
Cavalier, 1109 E Armour Blvd		09
Chatham, 3701 Broadway		11
Commodore, 1217 E Linwood Blvd		09
Continental, 106 W 11th		05
Dixon Inn, 1205 Baltimore		05
Downtowner, 1234 Central		05
Ellison, 300 W Armour Blvd		11
Executive, 509 W 13th		05
Georgian Court, 400 E Armour Blvd		09
Haven Hill, 700 W 47th		12
Hilton Inn, 610 Washington		05
Holiday Inn, At Municipal Airport		16
Howard Johnson0s, 1600 .e. Russell Rd		16
Hyde Park, 336 W 36th		11
Kansas Citian, 1216 Broadway		05
Locarno, 235 Ward Parkway		12
Mayfair, 1224 E Linwood Blvd		09
Montrose, 6 E 40th		11
Muehlebach, 107 W 12th		05
Netherlands, 3835 Main		11
New Yorker, 1114 Baltimore		05
Oak Hall, 4550 Warwick		11
Park Lane, 4600 J C Nichols Pkwy		12
Parkway Towers, 4545 Wornall		11
Plaza Inn, 1 E 45th		11
President, 1329 Baltimore		05
Prom, 5 E 6th Trafficway		06
Ramada Inn, 5100 E Linwood Blvd		28
Rasbach, 1116 Wyandotte		05
Riviera, 229 Ward Pkwy		12
Rodeway Inn, 1211 Armour Rd		16
Senate, 1015 E Armour Blvd		09
Southland, 3517 Main		11
Valentine On Broadway, 3724 Broadway		11
Villa Serena, 321 Ward Pkwy		12
Westport Arms, 301 W Armour Blvd		11

BUILDINGS

Altman, 103 E 11th		06
Argyle, 306 E 12th		06
B M A Tower, 700 Karnes		06
Balcony, 300 W 47th		12
Board Of Trade, 1005 Wyandotte		05
Bryant, 1102 Grand Ave		06
Centennial, 210 W 10th		05
City National Bank, 926 Grand Ave		06
Columbia Bank, 921 Walnut		06
Commerce Tower, 911 Main		06
Commerce, 922 Walnut		06
Congress, 3525 Broadway		11
Corrigan, 1828 Walnut		05
Davidson, 1627 Main		05
Doctor'S, 701-51 E 63rd		10
Dwight, 1004 Baltimore Ave		05
Fairfax, 101 W 11th		05
Farm & Home, 1021 Grand Ave		06
Federal Reserve, 925 Grand Ave		06
Finance, 1009 Baltimore Ave		05
First National Bank, 14 W 10th		05
Garden, 409 E 63rd		10
Grand Avenue Bank, 1805 Grand Ave		08
Graphic Arts, 934 Wyandotte		05
Hanover, 15 W 10th		05
Home Savings, 1006 Grand Ave		06
Insurance Exchange, 21 W 10th		05
Jason, 1211 Walnut		06
John Hancock, 800 W 47th		12
K C Board Of Trade, 4800 Main		12
K C Southern, 114 W 11th		05
Lathrop, 1005 Grand Ave		06
Law, 1207 Grand Ave		06
Lillis, 18 E 11th		06
Lincoln, 1605 E 18th		08
Live Stock Exchange, 1600 Genesee		02
Medical Plaza, 4320 Wornall Rd		11
Merchandise Mart, 2201 Grand Ave		08
Merchants Produce Bank, 531 Walnut		06

Kansas City (Con.)　641

Municipal Auditorium, 211 W
13th 05
National Fidelity Life, 1002
Walnut 06
Ozark National Life, 906
Grand Ave 06
Pershing, 215 W Pershing
Rd 08
Plaza Medical, 315 Nichols
Rd 12
Plaza Parkway, 4620 Nichols
Pkwy 12
Plaza Time, 411 Nichols Rd 12
Power & Light, 106 W 14th...... 05
Professional, 1103 Grand
Ave 06
Prudential, 427 W 12th 05
Public Library, 311 E 12th...... 06
Puritan, 405 E 13th............... 06
Scarritt Arcade, 817 Walnut 06
Scarritt, 818 Grand Ave.......... 06
Telephone, 324 E 11th............ 06
Temple, 903 Grand Ave 06
Tenmain Center, 920 Main 06
Title, 112 E 10th................... 06
Tower, 116 W 47th................. 12
Traders National Bank, 1125
Grand Ave 06
Union Carbide, 910 Baltimore
Ave 05
Union Station, 30 W Pershing
Rd 08
Uptown, 3706 Broadway.......... 11
V F W, 406 W 34th................. 11
Waldheim, 6 E 11th............... 06
Waltower, 823 Walnut 06
Wirthman, 3100 Troost Ave 09

GOVERNMENT OFFICES

City Hall, 414 E 12th.............. 06
Courthouse, 415 E 12th........... 06
Federal Office Bldg, 911
Walnut 06
Gsa Federal Office Bldg,
1500 E Bannister Rd.............. 31
Main Post Office, 315 W
Pershing Rd 08
Midwest Service Center, 2306
E Bannister Rd 70
Missouri State Employment
Security, 1411 Main 06
Missouri State Office, 615 E
13th 06
New Federal Office Bldg, 601
E 12th 06
US Marine Corps Finance
Center, 1500 E Bannister
Rd 97
United States Courthouse,
811 Grand Ave 06

HOSPITALS

Baptist Memorial, 6601
Rockhill Rd 31
Conley Maternity, 619
Garfield 24
Doctors, 2501 Gillham Rd 08
Downtown, 918 Oak............... 06
Florence Crittenton Home,

225 W 43rd......................... 11
General, 2400 Cherry............. 08
Lakeside, 8701 Troost Ave...... 31
Menorah Medical Center
4949 Rockhill Rd.................. 10
Mercy 2415 Locust................ 08
N K C Memorial, 2800
Hospital Dr......................... 16
Neurological, 2625 Paseo 08
Northeast Osteopathic, 620
Bennington Ave.................... 25
Osteopathic, 926 E 11th.......... 06
Psychiatric Receiving Center,
600 E 22nd.......................... 08
Ralph Clinic, 529 Highland
Ave 06
Research, 2316 E Meyer
Blvd 32
Saint Joseph's, 2510 Linwood
Blvd 28
Saint Luke's, 4401 Wornall
Rd 41
Saint Mary's, 101 Memorial
Dr 08
Trinity Lutheran, 3001
Wyandotte 08
Veterans Administration,
4801 Linwood Blvd............... 28
Wheatley Provident, 1826
Forest Ave.......................... 08

SAINT JOSEPH　645

POST OFFICE BOXES

Box Nos.
1-108 .... E Sta........... 05
1-114 .... A Sta........... 03
1-117 .... Inza Sta........ 08
1-189 .... D Sta........... 04
1-1105 .... Main Office 02
41-710 .... Fairleigh Sta... 06
301-356 .... A Sta........... 03
1601-1648 .... Wyatt Park Sta. 07
1701-1728 .... Wyatt Park Sta. 07

RURAL ROUTES

1 06
2 05
3 06
4,5 03
6,8 04

STATIONS, BRANCHES AND UNITS

Fairleigh Sta....................... 06
Inza Sta............................. 08
Wyatt Park Sta..................... 07
General Delivery 01
Postmaster 01

APARTMENTS, HOTELS, MOTELS

Ambassador, 30th & Parkway
A 07
Baxters Black Angus Motel,
1216 N Belt Hwy 06
Century, 627 N 25th.............. 06
Charleston, 615 Robidoux....... 01

Chateau 25, 702 N 25th.......... 06
Clay Hill, 1816 Clay.............. 01
Colonial, 2604 Frederick......... 06
Cook, 1025 Penn................... 03
Crestview Village, 2901
Frederick 06
Del Rosa, 312 Noyes Blvd....... 06
Eastern Gardens 3414 - 48
Messanie 01
Eastside 1401 N 36th............. 06
El Cid, 3515 Gene Field Rd...... 06
Field Eugene, 2124 Marion...... 05
Francis Street, 1307 Francis..... 01
Frederick Garden, 2602
Frederick 06
Georgian Court, 422 N 7th....... 01
Goff, 416 N 7th..................... 01
Gray, 2202 Duncan................ 07
Hall Manor, 801 Hall............. 01
Herman, 2522 Frederick.......... 06
Hillcrest, 2709 Frederick......... 06
Holiday Inn Motel, 4312
Frederick Ave 06
Jesse James Motel, 807 S
Belt Hwy 07
Lorraine, 521 N 7th............... 01
Mary Gale, 421 1/2 25 N
25th 01
Mertland, 210 N 8th............... 01
Northwood Pl 1100-1499
Maxwell Rd 05
Oakridge 1200-1299
Angelique 01
Park Lane, 128 Park Ln.......... 06
Parkview, 902 Seneca............. 03
Parkwood, 1202 N 22nd.......... 06
Pembroke Gardens, 2807 1/2
11 Pembroke Ln.................... 06
Plaza, 1821 Clay................... 01
Pony Express Motel, 1225 N
Belt Hwy 06
Ramada Inn 4016 Frederick
Ave 06
Ritchey, 801 N 25................. 06
Robidoux, 5th & Francis......... 01
Rose Lawn, 708 Hall.............. 01
San Regis, 1015 Faraon.......... 01
Senate, 2511 Mitchell Ave....... 07
Shamrock Motel, 3301 N Belt
Hwy 06
Shangri-La Motel, 2201 N
Belt Hwy 02
Summit Place, 516 N 10th....... 01
Tik-Tok Motel, 1414 S Belt
Hwy 07
Travelodge, 1320 N Belt Hwy ... 06
Victorian Court, 809 N 25th..... 06
Winston, 104 Winston Pl......... 06

BUILDINGS

American National Bank, 106
S 7th................................ 01
Arcade, 216 N 7th................. 01
Belt Professional Bldg, 908 N
Belt 06
Commerce Bank, 419
Edmond 01
Corby, 5th & Felix................. 01
Donnell Court, 507 Francis...... 01
East Hills Shopping Ctr.......... 06
Edmond Plaza, 708 Edmond..... 01
Empire Trust, 602 Edmond...... 01

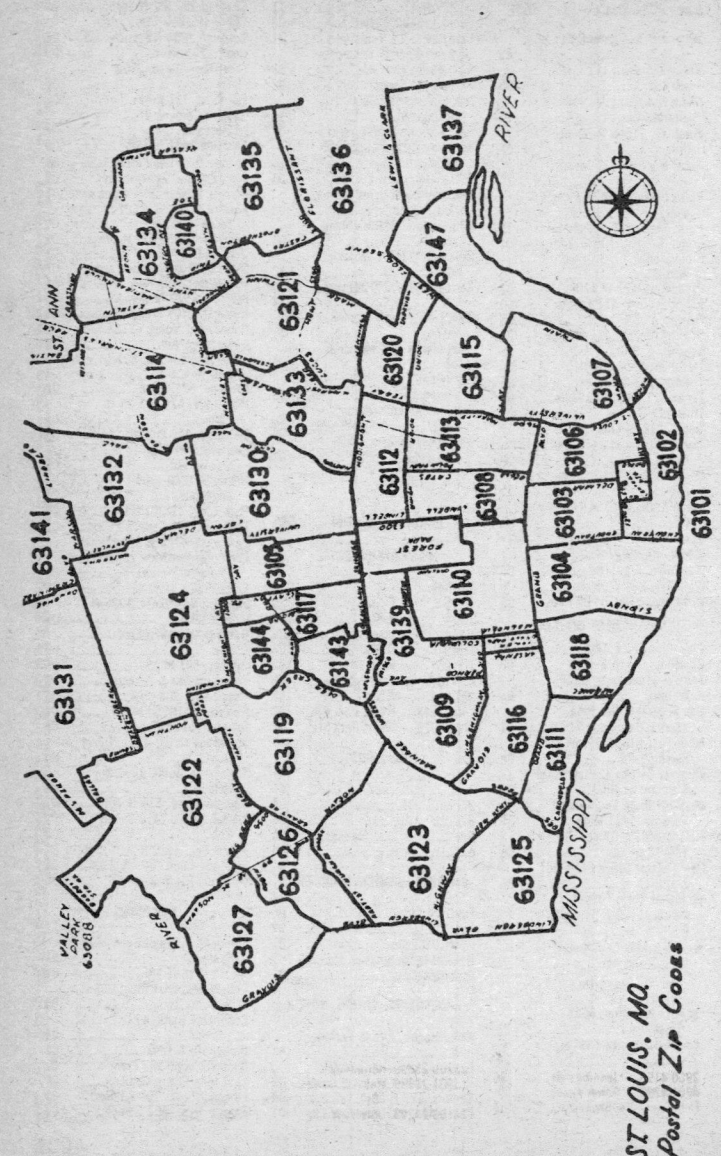

ST. LOUIS, MO.
Postal Zip Codes

Saint Joseph (Con.) 645

Federal, 8th & Edmond....	01
First National Bank, 4th & Felix................	01
Frederick Towers, 2400 Frederick	06
Herman, 622 Edmond......	01
King Hill, 819 1/2 Francis..	01
Kirkpatrick, 620 Francis...	01
Light & Power, 520 Francis.	01
Missouri Valley Trust, 400 Felix................	01
Physicians & Surgeons, 700 Francis...........	01

GOVERNMENT OFFICES

City Hall, 11th & Frederick Ave................	01
Court House, 302 N 5th....	01
U S Post Office & Court House, 8th & Edmond.	01

HOSPITALS

General Osteopathic, 117 & 15th...............	01
Methodist, 8th & Faraon..	01
Saint Josephs, 923 Powell..	01
State Hospital 2, Box 263..	02
Thompson-Brumm-Knepper Clinic, Box 8......	02

UNIVERSITIES AND COLLEGES

Gards Business University, 514 Francis......	01
Missouri Western College, Downs Dr.......	02
Platt College Of Commerce 8th & Felix........	01

SAINT LOUIS 631

POST OFFICE BOXES

Box Nos.

A-B	Normandy Br....	21
A-C	Carondelet Sta..	11
A-J	Webster Groves Br...........	19
1-530	Main Office	66
AA-AC	Clayton Br...	05
541-1626	Central Sta....	88
1801-1987	Christian Bechtold Sta..	18
2001-2199	Benton Park Sta...........	58
2201-2288	Gardner Sta....	09
2301-2599	Overland Br....	14
2601-2687	Gravois Sta....	16
2801-2889	Carondelet Sta.	11
2901-3199	University City Br...........	30
3401-3599	Maplewood Br..	43
3751-3898	Kirkwood Br....	22
3950-4196	Jennings Br....	36
4201-4290	Tower Grove Sta...........	63

4301-4399	Affton Br........	23
4701-4996	Field Sta........	08
5001-5114	Nagel Sta.......	15
5121-5194	Hannegan Sta...	39
5201-5234	Hannegan Sta...	39
5241-5394	Nagel Sta.......	15
5401-5599	Bremen Sta.....	60
5601-5799	Normandy Br....	21
5801-5999	Berkeley Sta....	34
6001-6116	Hannegan Sta...	39
6301-6479	Fairgrounds Sta.	07
6501-6699	Lemay Br........	25
6701-6877	Brentwood Br...	44
6900-6920	Affton Br........	23
7001-7499	Main Office	77
7501-7741	Progress Sta....	59
7801-7974	Jordan W Chambers Sta...	06
8001-8299	Pierre Laclede Sta...........	56
8301-8499	Olivette Br.....	32
8501-8646	Sappington Br...	26
8701-8999	Jefferson Memorial Sta...	02
9101-9399	Richmond Heights Br.....	17
9401-9599	Cabanne Sta....	61
9601-9699	Kirkwood Br....	22
9701-9899	Kinloch Br......	40
9901-9999	Kirkwood Br....	22
10001-10599	Lambert Airport Br...........	45
10601-10899	Mehlville Br....	29
10901-11100	Ferguson Sta...	35
11201-11899	Clayton Br.....	05
11901-12199	Wellston Sta...	12
12201-12399	Soulard Sta....	57
12401-12499	Olivette Br.....	32
12501-12599	Creve Coeur Br...........	41
13001-13199	Webster Groves Br...........	19
13201-13399	Soulard Sta....	57
13401-13699	North County Br...........	38
13800-13999	Baden Sta......	47
14001-14999	Main Office	78
15001-15599	Chouteau Sta...	10
15701-15799	Tower Grove Sta...........	63
15800-15999	Overland Br....	14
16501-16999	Clayton Br.....	05
20001-20099	Brentwood Br...	44
20101-20299	Affton Br........	23
20300-20499	Wellston Sta...	12
20501-20699	Hannegan Sta...	39
21100-21299	Baden Sta......	47
21301-21418	Nagel Sta.......	15
21501-21599	Olivette Br.....	32
21601-21999	Gardner Sta....	09
22001-22087	Sappington Br...	26
22100-22299	Gravois Sta....	16
22401-22449	Sappington Br...	26
22501-22899	Broadway Sta...	47
23001-23999	Pierre Laclede Sta...........	56
23501-23590	Wellston Sta...	12
23700-23899	Normandy Br...	21
23901-23999	Webster Groves Br...........	19
24100-24299	University City Br	

Br	30
24501-24699 Creve Coeur Br...........	41
24701-24899 Nagel Sta......	15
26001-26199 Jennings Br...	36

RURAL ROUTES

1................	41
9................	29
13................	41

STATIONS, BRANCHES AND UNITS

Affton Br........	23
Baden Br........	47
Benton Park Sta.	04
Berkeley Br.....	34
Bremen Sta.....	60
Brentwood Br...	44
Broadway Br....	47
Cabanne Br.....	61
Carondelet Sta..	11
Central Sta.....	81
Charles Nagel Sta.	13
Chouteau Sta...	10
Christian Bechtold Sta..	18
Clayton Br.....	05
Conclay Br.....	24
Creve Coeur Br..	41
Des Peres Br....	31
Fairgrounds Sta.	07
Ferguson Br....	35
Field Sta.......	08
Gardner Sta....	09
Glendale Br.....	22
Gravois Sta.....	16
Jefferson Memorial Sta.	02
Jennings Br.....	36
Jordan W. Chambers Sta.	06
Kinloch Br......	40
Kirkwood Br....	22
Lambert Airport Br..	45
Lemay Br.......	25
Maplewood Br..	43
Mehlville Br....	29
Normandy Br...	21
North County Br..	37
Olive Sta.......	01
Olivette Br.....	24
Overland Br....	14
Pierre Laclede Sta.	20
Pine Lawn Br...	20
Plaza Sta.......	99
Principia Br....	31
Progress Sta....	59
Richmond Heights Br..	17
River Roads Br..	36
Robert E. Hannegan Sta.	39
Saint Johns Sta.	14
Sappington Br...	26
Soulard Sta.....	57
Tower Grove Sta.	63
University City Br.	30
Webster Groves Br..	19
Wellston Sta....	12
General Delivery.	66
Postmaster......	55

APARTMENTS, HOTELS, MOTELS

A B C D, 4 N Kingshighway Blvd...........	08
Adlon, 3438 Russell Blvd	04

405

Saint Louis (Con.)   631

Adolphus, 5004 Delmar Blvd... 08
Airline Motel, 10124 Natural
    Brdge Rd.................................. 34
Alverne, 1014 Locust 01
Ambassador, 5340 Delmar
    Blvd.. 12
Baden, 8220 N Broadway......... 47
Baltimore, 205 N 9th................ 01
Bel Air Motel, 9745 Highway
    66.. 26
Biltmore, 3643 Washington
    Blvd.. 08
Blue Haven Motel, 10000
    Highway 66............................. 26
Branscome, 5370 Pershing
    Ave.. 12
Browning, 5536 Pershing
    Ave.. 12
Cambridge Ct, 4917
    Mcpherson Ave......................... 08
Canterbury Hall, 4132
    Washington Ave........................ 08
Carr Square, 1500 Carr Dr..... 06
Castle Point Auto Court
    Motel, 2468 Chambers Rd.... 36
Castlereagh, 6820 Delmar
    Blvd.. 30
Cathedral Court, 4362 Lindell
    Blvd.. 08
Catherine Springer Home,
    220 N Spring Ave.................... 03
Chase Park Plaza, 212 N
    Kingshighway Blvd.................... 08
Chase, 4931 Lindell Blvd 08
Chippewa Motel, 7880
    Watson Rd............................... 19
Claridge, 1800 Locust.............. 03
Clemens Hall, 3640 W Pine
    Blvd.. 08
Colonial Motel, 11777
    Highway 67.............................. 38
Congress, 275 Union Blvd...... 08
Convent Garden, 4497
    Pershing Ave............................ 08
Coral Court Motel, 7755
    Watson Rd............................... 19
Crystal Motel, 7746 Watson
    Rd... 19
Daniel Boone, 3733 Lindell
    Blvd.. 08
De Soto, 200 N 11th................. 01
Delmonte, 5622 Delmar Blvd... 12
Diplomat Motel, 433 N
    Kingshighway Blvd.................... 08
Ellington, 4961 Laclede Ave..... 08
Embassy, 530 Union Blvd......... 08
Eugene Field, 4339 Olive......... 08
Evangeline Residence 205 N
    18th....................................... 03
Evergreen Motel, 8715
    Watson Rd............................... 19
Fairmount, 7 Maryland Plaza... 08
Ford, 1405 Pine...................... 03
Forest Park, 4910 West Pine
    Blvd.. 08
Fremont, 4066 Lindell Blvd...... 08
Frontenac, 40 N
    Kingshighway Blvd.................... 08
Fusz Memorial, 3700 W Pine
    Blvd.. 08

Gatesworth, 245 Union Blvd.... 02
George Washington, 600 N
    Kingshighway Blvd.................... 08
Grand Towers 3520 Laclede
    Ave.. 03
Grays Cottage Camp, 7474
    St Charles Rock Rd.................. 33
Greater Saint Louis Trailer
    Park, 6825 St Charles Rck
    Rd.. 33
Gregorian, 5374 Delmar Blvd... 12
Harlan Court, 5455 Delmar
    Blvd.. 12
Hawthorne, 4475 W Pine
    Blvd.. 08
Holiday Inn Motel Downtown
    2211 Market............................ 03
Holiday Inn Motel Midtown
    4483 Lindell Blvd..................... 08
Holiday Inn Motel South,
    3660 S Lindbergh Blvd............. 27
Hollywood Tourist Court
    Motel, 10336 Manchester
    Rd.. 27
Howard Johnson Motor Lodge
    Motel, 6929 S Lindbergh
    Blvd.. 25
Hutchinson Arms, 2107 S
    Grand Blvd............................... 04
Ivy Motel, 10143 Olive Street
    Rd.. 41
Jefferson, 415 N 12th............... 01
John J Cochran, 1418 N 8th..... 06
Katherine, 4432 Washington
    Blvd.. 08
Kenrick Square, 3853 Lindell
    Blvd.. 08
King Bros Motel, 1335 S
    Lindbergh Blvd......................... 31
Kingsway, 108 N
    Kingshighway Blvd.................... 08
Knotty Pine Auto Court Motel,
    10130 Olive Street Rd.............. 41
Lennox 825 Washington Ave..... 01
Lindell Tower, 3745 Lindell
    Blvd.. 08
Lowell, 4140 Washington
    Blvd.. 08
Lucas & Hunt Village, 5303
    Lucas & Hunt Rd..................... 21
Mac Arthur, 100 N Broadway... 02
Manhasset Village, 8915
    Eager Rd................................. 44
Mansion House Ctr 400
    Mansion House Ctr................... 02
Mark Twain, 116 N 8th............. 01
Marlborough, 5696 Kingsbury
    Blvd.. 12
Mayfair, 806 St Charles............ 01
Mc Auley Hall, 325 N
    Newstead Ave.......................... 08
Mc Kinley, 806 N 12th.............. 01
Montclair, 18 S Kinshighway
    Blvd.. 08
Monticello, 4535 Lindell Blvd... 08
Neighborhood Gardens, 1201
    N 8th...................................... 06
Northwestern, 4919 Natural
    Bridge Av................................ 15
Ozark Plaza Motor Motel,
    10705 Highway 66................... 27
Park Manor, 5560 Pershing

Ave... 12
Park Plaza, 220 N
    Kingshighway Blvd.................... 08
Parkedge, 4907 W Pine............ 08
Parkhurst, 228 N Tayor Ave..... 08
Pierre Chouteau, 4440 Lindell
    Blvd.. 08
Plaza Square Apartments, 10
    Plaza Sq................................. 03
President, 4615 Lindell Blvd 08
Ranelagh, 5707 Mcpherson
    Ave.. 12
Roosevelt, 4903 Delmar Blvd . 08
Rose Bowl Motel, 9982
    Manchester Rd......................... 22
Royal Motel, 9282 Watson
    Rd.. 26
Saint Louis Gateway, 822
    Washington Av......................... 01
Saint Regis, 4950 Lindell
    Blvd.. 08
Sarah Belle, 4125 W Belle Pl.. 08
Saum, 1919 S Grand Blvd........ 04
Sherman, 6188 Mcpherson
    Ave.. 12
Sir Walter Raleigh, 3664
    Washington Blvd....................... 08
Sixty-Six Auto Court Motel,
    8730 Watson Rd....................... 19
Springdale Motel, 4121
    Springdale Ave......................... 34
Tower Motel, Highway 40 &
    Ballas Rd................................ 41
Town & Country, 8801 Eager
    Rd.. 44
Tramore Castle, 4525 Lindell
    Blvd.. 08
Twin-Six Auto Court Motel,
    10230 Highway 66................... 27
Ulysses S Grant Motel, 8498
    Watson Rd............................... 19
University, 3703 Washington
    Blvd.. 08
Versailles, 709 So Skinker
    Blvd.. 05
Walsh Hall, 3622 W Pine
    Blvd.. 08
Warwick, 1428 Locust.............. 03
Wayside Motel, 7800 Watson
    Rd.. 19
Wendell Pruitt 2407 Ofallon..... 06
Westgate, 706 N
    Kingshighway Blvd.................... 08
Westmoreland, 5330 Pershing
    Ave.. 12
Westward Motel, 1580 S
    Lindbergh Blvd......................... 27
Wiltshire, 725 S Skinker
    Blvd.. 05
Windsor, 4209 Lindell Blvd....... 08
Winston Churchill, 5475
    Cabanne Ave............................ 12

BUILDINGS

Ambassador, 411 N 7th............ 01
Arcade, 812 Olive.................... 01
Beaumont Medical, 3720
    Washington Blvd....................... 08
Bell Telephone, 1010 Pine....... 01
Beltmar, 5473 Delmar Blvd 12
Boatmens Bank, 314 N
    Broadway................................. 02

Saint Louis (Con.)　631

Boulevard, 508 N Grand
　Blvd..................................... 03
Brune, 806-808 Chestnut...... 01
Buder, 707 Market................ 01
Cambridge Medical, 150 N.
　Meramec Ave..................... 05
Centennial, 1139 Olive........ 01
Century, 313 N 9th.............. 01
Chemical, 721 Olive............ 01
Chouteau, 4030 Chouteau
　Ave.................................... 10
Clayton Central, 110 So
　Central Ave....................... 05
Columbia, 318 N 8th............ 01
Commerce, 418 Olive........... 02
Continental, 3615 Olive....... 08
Cotton Belt, 111 N 4th......... 02
Farm & Home, 411 N 10th..... 01
Fashion Square, 1307
　Washington Ave................. 03
Federal Commerce Trust 208
　N Broadway....................... 02
Fidelity, 820 N Grand Blvd.... 06
Field 4485 Olive................. 08
Frisco 906 Olive.................. 01
General American Life, 1505
　Locust............................... 03
General Van, 4908 Delmar
　Blvd................................... 08
Ghio, 506 N Vandeventer
　Ave.................................... 08
Globe Democrat, 710 N 12th.. 01
Goldman, 709 Pine.............. 01
Holland, 211 N 7th.............. 01
Imperial, 922 Pine.............. 01
International Office, 722
　Chestnut............................ 01
La Salle, 509 Olive.............. 01
Laclede Gas, 720 Olive........ 01
Leather Trades, 1602 Locust.. 03
Lindell Trust, 2739 N Grand
　Blvd................................... 06
Lister, 4500 Olive............... 08
Louderman, 317 N 11th........ 01
Martin, 923 Washington Ave.. 01
Mary Muffet, 1627 Locust..... 03
Merchants Exchange, 5100
　Oakland Ave...................... 10
Merchants Laclede, 408
　Olive.................................. 02
Mid City, 320 N Grand Blvd... 03
Mississippi Valley, 506 Olive.. 01
Missouri Pacific Annex, 1218
　Olive.................................. 03
Missouri Pacific, 210 N 13th.. 03
Monogram, 1718 Washington
　Ave.................................... 03
Musical Art, 459 N Boyle
　Ave.................................... 08
Nicholas, 1504 S Grand Blvd.. 04
Old Federal, 815 Olive......... 01
Olivia, 1023 N Grand Blvd.... 06
Paul Brown, 818 Olive......... 01
Pierce, 112 N 4th................ 02
Pineate, 804 Pine............... 01
Poe, 1492 Hodiamont Ave..... 12
Post-Dispatch, 1111 Olive..... 01
Railway Exchange, 611 Olive.. 01
Roosevelt, 4903 Delmar Blvd.. 08
Sacks, 803 Carondelet Ave.... 05
Saint Charles, 505 N 7th....... 01

Security, 319 N 4th............. 02
Seven-O-Five Olive, 705 Olive.. 01
Shell, 1221 Locust.............. 03
Silk Exchange, 503 N 12th..... 01
South Side National Bank,
　3606 Gravois Ave.............. 16
State National Life, 4 No 8th.. 01
Syndicate Trust, 915 Olive..... 01
Taylor-Olive, 4505 Olive....... 08
Title Guaranty, 706 Chestnut.. 01
Travelers, 522 Olive............ 01
University City, 6635 Delmar
　Blvd................................... 30
University Club 607 N Grand
　Blvd................................... 03
Victoria, 407 N 8th............. 01
Wainwright, 705 Chestnut..... 01
Wall, 3903 Olive................. 08
Western Union, 910
　Chestnut............................ 01

GOVERNMENT OFFICES

Chamber Of Commerce, 511
　Locust............................... 01
City Hall, 1206 Market......... 03
Civil Courts, 10 N 12th......... 01
Federal 1520 Market........... 03
Municipal Courts, 1320
　Market............................... 03
United States Courthouse,
　1114 Market...................... 01
United States Customhouse,
　1114 Market...................... 01

HOSPITALS

Alexian Bros., 3933 S.
　Broadway.......................... 18
Barnard Free Skin & Cancer,
　600 S Kingshighway Blvd... 10
Barnes, 600 S Kingshighway
　Blvd................................... 10
Bethesda, 3655 Vista Ave..... 10
Booth Memorial, 3740
　Marine.............................. 18
Cardinal Glennon Memorial,
　1465 S Grand Blvd............ 04
Christian, 4411 N Newstead
　Ave.................................... 15
City, 1515 Lafayette Ave....... 04
De Paul, 2415 N
　Kingshighway Blvd............ 13
Deaconess, 6150 Oakland
　Ave.................................... 39
Faith West 12634 Olive
　Street Rd........................... 41
Faith, 3300 N Kingshighway
　Blvd................................... 15
Firmin Desloge, 1325 S
　Grand Blvd........................ 04
Homer G Phillips, 2601
　Whittier............................. 13
Incarnate Word 3545
　Lafayette Ave..................... 04
Jewish, 216 S Kingshighway
　Blvd................................... 10
Lutheran, 2639 Miami......... 18
Malcolm A Bliss, 1420
　Grattan............................. 04
Masonic Home, 5351 Delmar
　Blvd................................... 12
Mc Millan, 640 S

Kingshighway Blvd.............. 10
Missouri Baptist, 3015
　Ballas Rd N....................... 31
Missouri Pacific, 1755 S
　Grand Blvd........................ 04
Mount Saint Rose, 9101 S
　Broadway.......................... 25
Normandy Osteopathic, 7840
　Natural Bridge Rd............. 21
Park Lane Memorial, 4930
　Lindell Blvd....................... 08
Public Health Service, 1520
　Market............................... 03
Saint Anne'S Home, 5351
　Page Ave........................... 12
Saint Anthonys, 3520
　Chippewa.......................... 18
Saint Johns Mercy, 615 New
　Ballas Rd S........................ 41
Saint Josephs, 525 Couch
　Ave.................................... 22
Saint Louis Childrens, 500 S
　Kingshighway Blvd............ 10
Saint Louis City, 1515
　Lafayette Ave..................... 04
Saint Louis County, 601 S
　Brentwood Blvd................. 05
Saint Louis Maternity, 630 S
　Kingshighway Blvd............ 10
Saint Lukes, 5535 Delmar
　Blvd................................... 12
Saint Marys Infirmary, 1536
　Papin................................ 03
Saint Marys, 6420 Clayton
　Rd..................................... 17
Saint Vincents, 7301 St
　Charles Rock Rd................ 33
Shriners Hospital For
　Crippled Chi, 2001 S
　Lindbergh Blvd.................. 31
State, 5400 Arsenal............. 39
Veterans Administration, 915
　N Grand Blvd..................... 06
Veterans, Jefferson Barracks.. 25
Washington University Nurses
　Res, 416 S Kingshighway
　Blv.................................... 10
Wohl Memorial, 4960
　Audubon Blvd.................... 10

UNIVERSITIES AND COLLEGES

Christian Brothers, 6501
　Clayton Rd........................ 17
Concordia Seminary, 801 De
　Mun Ave............................ 05
Covenant College &
　Theological Seminary,
　12330 Conway Rd.............. 41
David Ranken School, 4431
　Finney Ave........................ 13
Eden Seminary, 475 E
　Lockwood Ave.................... 19
Florissant Valley Community
　3400 Pershall Rd............... 35
Fontbonne, 6800 Wydown
　Blvd................................... 65
Forest Park Community
　College, 5600 Oakland
　Ave.................................... 10
Harris Teacher, 3026 Laclede
　Ave.................................... 03

Saint Louis (Con.) 631

Incarnate Word Convent,
2800 Normandy Ave 21

Junior College Dist Office St
Louis, 7508 Forsyth Blvd.... 05

Kenrick Seminary, 7800
Kenrick Rd 19

Marillac Seminary, 7800
Natural Bridge Rd. 21

Maryhurst Normal, 1101 S
Lindbergh Blvd 22

Maryville College Of The
Sacred Heart, 13550
Conway Rd......................... 41

Meramec Community, 11333
Big Bend Blvd 22

Missouri U. Stlouis Campus,
8001 Natural Bridge Rd...... 21

Principia, 13201 Clayton Rd... 31.

Saint Louis County
Vocational School, 5600
Countryday Ln .... 34.

Saint Louis Preparatory
Seminary, 5200
Shrewsbury Ave.................. 19

Saint Louis University, 221 N
Grand Blvd......................... 03

South Campus, 3230
Hartford............................ 18

Ursuline Convent & Academy,
800 E Monroe Ave 22

Visitation Academy, 3020 N
Ballas Rd........................... 31

Washington Univ Medical
School, 660 S
Kingshighway Blvd .... 10°

Washington University,
Lindell & Skinker Blvd........ 30

Webster, 470 E Lockwood
Ave................................... 19

SPRINGFIELD 858

POST OFFICE BOXES

Box Nos.

A-E	Glenstone Sta...	04
1-992	Harry S Jewell Sta...	01
901-1106	Commercial Sta...	03
1601-2004	South Side Sta..	05
2751-2894	Commercial Sta...	03

3001-3987	Glenstone Sta...	04
4281-4352	Glenstone Sta..	04

RURAL ROUTES

1	03
2	02
3	04
4	02
5,6	03
7	02
8	07
9	02
10,11	03
12	04

STATIONS, BRANCHES AND UNITS

Commercial Sta...	03
Glenstone Sta..	04
South Side Sta...	05
General Delivery	01
Postmaster	01

APARTMENTS, HOTELS, MOTELS

Arrowhead, 2501 N
Glenstone 03

Battlefield Inn, 2114 S
Glenstone 04

Beverly, 529 Cherry.............. 06

Camp Manor, 423 E Elm....... 06

Coach House Inn, 2535 N
Glenstone 03

Colonial Motor Lodge,
Highway 166...................... 07

Colonial, 330 St Louis.......... 05

Elms, 527 St Louis 06

Empire Inn North, 2555 N
Glenstone 03

Englenook, 700 E Walnut...... 06

Executive Arms, 2355 N
Glenstone 03

Hawks, 1839 E Sunshine....... 04

Hillcrest Ninety, 2444 N
Delaware........................... 03

Holiday Inn, 2700 N
Glenstone 03

Howard Johnsons, 2610 N
Glenstone 03

Imperial 400, 1001 St Louis... 06

Kelley Jane, 835 E Walnut..... 06

Kentwood Arms Motor, 700 St
Louis 05

Kingsbarde, 937 E Lombard ... 04

Lamplighter, 1839-E

Sunshine............................ 04

Lorraine, 527 E Walnut......... 06

Maple, 2233 N Glenstone...... 03

Missouri, 412 Commercial..... 03

North Terrace, 1646 E North.. 03

Queen Anne, 1750 Cherry..... 02

Rail Haven, 203 S Glenstone.. 02

Ramada Inn, 2715 N
Glenstone 03

Rock Castle, 401 Mt Vernon... 06

Sands, 1824 N Glenstone...... 03

Seville, 218 E Walnut 06

Ship & Anchor, 2137 N
Glenstone 03

Sir Robert, 1403 E Elm......... 02

State, 400 S Jefferson.......... 06

Sunvilla Tower, 833 E Elm..... 06

Travelodge, 503 St Louis....... 06

BUILDINGS

Empire, 430 South	06
Frisco, 3253 E Trafficway.....	02
Holland, 205 St Louis..........	06
Landers, 149 Public Sq	06
Landmark, 309 N Jefferson...	06
Mc Daniel, 318 St Louis.......	06
Professional, 609 Cherry......	06
Wilhoit, 300 E Pershing.......	06
Woodruff, 331 St Louis........	06

GOVERNMENT OFFICES

City Hall, 830 Boonville........ 02

Court House, 940 Boonville ... 02

Federal Building, 870
Boonville 01

HOSPITALS

Baptist, 440 S Market........... 06

Cox Lester E Medical Center,
1423 N Jefferson 02

Saint John'S, 1235 E
Cherokee........................... 02

Springfield Gen Osteopathic,
2828 N National 01

UNIVERSITIES AND COLLEGES

Baptist Bible, 628 E Kearney.. 02

Central Bible, 3000 N Grant... 02

Draughon'S Business, Wilhoit
Bldg 05

Drury, 900 N Benton 02

Evangel, 1111 N Glenstone... 02

Southwest Missouri State,
901 S National 02

MONTANA
(Abbreviation: MT)

Absarokee	59001
Nye, R. Br	59061
Acton	59002
Alberton	59820
Alder	59710
Alzada	59311
Anaconda (1st)	59711
Angela	59312
Antelope	59211
Arlee	59821
Ashland (1st)	59003
Augusta	59410
Avon	59713
Babb	59411
Bainville	59212
Baker	59313
Ballantine	59006
Basin	59631
Bearcreek	59007
Belfry	59008
Belgrade	59714
Belknap, R. Br. Trout Creek	59822
Belle Creek, Br. Broadus	59317
Belt	59412
Biddle	59314
Big Arm	59910
Big Sandy	59520
Big Timber	59011
Bigfork	59911
Bighorn	59010
BILLINGS (1st) (see appendix)	
Billings Heights, Br. Billings	59101
Birney	59012
Black Eagle	59414
Blackfoot	59415
Bloomfield	59315
Bonner	59823
Boulder	59632
Box Elder	59521
Boyd, R. Br. Roberts	59013
Boyes	59316
Bozeman (1st)	59715
Brady	59416
Bridger	59014
Broadus	59317
Belle Creek, Br.	59317
Sonnette, R. Br.	59348
Broadview	59015
Brockton	59213
Brockway	59214
Browning	59417
Brusett	59318
Buffalo	59418
Busby	59016
Butte (1st)	59701
Bynum	59419
Cameron	59720
Canyon Creek	59633
Capitol	59319
Cardwell	59721
Carlyle	59320
Carter	59420
Cascade	59421
Cat Creek, R. Br. Winnett	59017
Charlo	59824
Chester	59522
Chinook	59523
Choteau	59422
Christina	59423
Circle	59215
Clancy	59634
Clinton	59825
Clyde Park	59018
Coalridge	59216
Coalwood, R. Br. Miles City	59321
Coffee Creek	59424
Cohagen	59322
Colstrip	59323
Columbia Falls (1st)	59912
Columbus	59019
Condon	59826
Conner	59827
Conrad (1st)	59425
Cooke City	59020
Coram	59913
Corvallis	59828
Corwin Springs	59021
Crane	59217
Creston, R. Br. Kalispell	59902
Crow Agency	59022
Culbertson	59218
Cushman	59023
Custer	59024
Cut Bank (1st)	59427
Dagmar	59219
Danvers	59429
Darby	59829
Dayton	59914
De Borgia	59830
Decker	59025
Deer Lodge (1st)	59722
Dell	59724
Delphia, R. Br. Roundup	59073
Denton	59430
Devon	59431
Dillon (1st)	59725
Divide	59727
Dixon	59831
Dodson	59524
Drummond	59832
Dupuyer	59432
Dutton	59433
East Glacier Park	59434
East Helena	59635
Edgar	59026
Ekalaka	59324
Elliston	59728
Elmo	59915
Emigrant	59027
Enid	59220
Ennis	59729
Epsie	59325
Essex	59916
Ethridge	59435
Eureka	59917
Evergreen, Br. Kalispell	59901
Fairfield	59436
Fairview	59221
Fallon	59326
Ferdig	59437
Fergus	59438
Fishtail	59028
Flaxville	59222
Florence	59833
Floweree	59440
Forestgrove	59441
Forsyth	59327
Fort Benton	59442
Fort Harrison	59636
Fort Peck	59223
Fort Shaw	59443
Fortine	59918
Four Buttes	59224
Frazer	59225
Frenchtown	59834
Froid	59226
Fromberg	59029
Galata	59444
Gallatin Gateway	59730
Gardiner	59030
Garneill	59445
Garrison	59731
Garryowen	59031
Geraldine	59446
Geyser	59447
Gildford	59525
Glasgow (1st)	59230
Glasgow Air Base, R. Br.	59231
Glasgow Air Base, R. Br. Glasgow	59231
Glen	59732
Glendive (1st)	59330
Intake, R. Br.	59335
Glentana	59240
Goldcreek	59733
Grantsdale	59835
Grassrange	59032
GREAT FALLS (1st) (see appendix)	
Greenough	59836
Greycliff	59033
Hall	59837
Hamilton (1st)	59840
Hammond	59332
Hardin (1st)	59034
Yellowtail, R. Br.	59035
Harlem	59526
Harlowton	59036
Harrison	59735
Hathaway	59333
Haugan	59842
Havre (1st)	59501
Hays	59527
Heart Butte	59448
Helena (1st)	59601
Montana City, R. Br.	59602
State Capitol, Sta.	59601
Helmville	59843
Heron	59844
Highwood	59450
Hilger	59451
Hingham	59528
Hinsdale	59241
Hobson	59452
Hogeland	59529
Homestead	59242
Hot Springs	59845
Hungry Horse	59919
Huntley	59037
Huson	59846
Hysham	59038
Ingomar	59039
Intake, R. Br. Glendive	59335
Inverness	59530
Ismay	59336
Jackson	59736
Jeffers	59737
Jefferson City	59638
Joliet	59041
Joplin	59531
Jordan	59337
Judith Gap	59453
Kalispell (1st)	59901

Creston, R. Br.	59902	Oliva	59343	Shepherd	59079
Evergreen, Br.	59901	Olney	59927	Sheridan	59749
Nevin	59454	Opheim	59250	Shonkin	59476
Kila	59920	Otter	59062	Sidney (1st)	59270
Kinsey	59338	Outlook	59252	Silesia	59080
Kolin	59455	Ovando	59854	Silver Gate	59081
Kremlin	59532	Pablo	59855	Silver Star	59751
Lake Mc Donald, R. Br. West		Paradise	59856	Silverbow	59750
Glacier	59921	Park City	59063	Simms	59477
Lakeside	59922	Peerless	59253	Simpson	59541
Lambert	59243	Pendroy	59467	Somers	59932
Lame Deer	59043	Perma	59857	Sonnette, R. Br Broadus	59348
Landusky	59533	Philipsburg	59858	Springdale	59082
Larslan	59244	Pioneer, Sta. Billings	59102	Stanford	59479
Laurel (1st)	59044	Plains	59859	State Capitol, Sta. Helena	59601
Laurin	59738	Plentywood	59254	Stevensville	59870
Lavina	59046	Plevna	59344	Stockett	59480
Ledger	59456	Polaris	59746	Stryker	59933
Lewistown (1st)	59457	Polebridge	59928	Suffolk	59481
Libby (1st)	59923	Polson (1st)	59860	Sula	59871
Lima	59739	Pompeys Pillar	59064	Sumatra	59083
Lincoln	59639	Pony	59747	Sun River	59483
Lindsay	59339	Poplar	59255	Sunburst	59482
Livingston (1st)	59047	Potomac	59862	Superior	59872
Lloyd	59535	Powderville	59345	Swan Lake, R. Br Bigfork	59911
Locate	59340	Power	59468	Sweetgrass	59484
Lodge Grass	59050	Pray	59065	Tampico	59272
Lolo	59847	Proctor	59929	Teigen	59084
Loma	59460	Pryor	59066	Terminal Annex, Sta.	
Lonepine	59848	Radersburg, R. Br.		Billings	59101
Loring	59537	Townsend	59641	Terry	59349
Lothair	59461	Ramsay	59748	Thompson Falls	59873
Lustre, R. Br. Frazer.	59225	Rapelje	59067	Three Forks	59752
Luther	59051	Ravalli	59863	Toston	59643
Malmstrom A F B, Br. Great		Raymond	59256	Townsend	59644
Falls	59402	Raynesford	59469	Radersburg, R. Br	59641
Malta	59538	Red Lodge	59068	Trego	59934
Manhattan	59741	Redstone	59257	Trident	59753
Marion	59925	Reedpoint	59069	Trout Creek	59874
Martin City	59926	Regina	59539	Belknap, R. Br	59822
Martinsdale	59053	Reserve	59258	Troy	59935
Marysville	59640	Rexford	59930	Turner	59542
Maudlow	59742	Richey	59259	Twin Bridges	59754
Maxville	59850	Richland	59260	Twodot	59085
Mc Allister	59740	Ringling	59642	Ulm	59485
Mc Cabe	59245	Roberts	59070	Utica, R. Br Hobson	59452
Mc Leod	59052	Boyd, R. Br	59013	Valier	59486
Medicine Lake	59247	Rock Springs	59346	Vandalia	59273
Melrose	59743	Rollins	59931	Vaughn	59487
Melstone	59054	Ronan	59864	Victor	59875
Melville	59055	Roscoe	59071	Vida	59274
Mildred	59341	Rosebud	59347	Virginia City	59755
Miles City (1st)	59301	Roundup	59072	Volborg	59351
Coalwood, R. Br.	59321	Delphia, R. Br.	59073	Wagner	59543
Mill Iron	59342	Roy	59471	Walkerville, Br. Butte	59701
Milltown	59851	Rudyard	59540	Warmsprings	59756
Missoula (1st)	59801	Russell, Sta. Great Falls	59405	Waterloo	59757
Moccasin	59462	Ryegate	59074	West Glacier	59936
Moiese, R. Br. Charlo.	59824	Saco	59261	Lake Mc Donald, R. Br.	59921
Molt	59057	Saint Ignatius	59865	West Yellowstone	59758
Monarch	59463	Saint Mary, R. Br. Browning.	59417	Westby	59275
Montana City, R. Br. Helena.	59602	Saint Regis	59866	White Sulphur Springs	59645
Moore	59464	Saint Xavier	59075	Whitefish (1st)	59937
Mosby	59058	Saltese	59867	Whitehall	59759
Musselshell	59059	Sand Coulee	59472	Whitetail	59276
Myers	59060	Sand Springs	59077	Whitewater	59544
Nashua	59248	Sanders	59076	Whitlash	59545
Neihart	59465	Santa Rita	59473	Wibaux	59353
Niarada	59852	Savage	59262	Willard	59354
Norris	59745	Scobey	59263	Willow Creek	59760
Noxon	59853	Seeley Lake	59868	Wisdom	59086
Nye, R Br Absarokee	59061	Shawmut	59078	Winifred	59489
Oilmont	59466	Shelby (1st)	59474	Winnett	59087

Cat Creek, R Br	59017	Wise River	59762	Wyola	59089
Winston	59647	Wolf Creek	59648	Yellowtail, R Br Hardin	59035
Wisdom	59761	Wolf Point (1st)	59201	Zortman	59546
		Worden	59088	Zurich	59547

Appendix   Billings — Great Falls MONTANA

BILLINGS   591

POST OFFICE BOXES

Box Nos
1 2565	Main Office	03
20001 20869	Pioneer Sta	02

RURAL ROUTES

1	02
2;3	01
4	02
5	01

STATIONS, BRANCHES AND UNITS

Billings Heights Br	01
Pioneer Sta	02
Terminal Annex Sta	01
General Delivery	01
Postmaster	01

APARTMENTS, HOTELS, MOTELS

Acme, 109 1/2 N Broadway	01
Alexandra, 104 N 31st	01
Ardmore, 3010 N 2nd Ave	01
Arnatf, 3020 N 7th Ave	01
B & B, 524 N 23rd	01
Babcock, 118 1/2 N Broadway	01
Bede Apts, 1111 Main	01
Berger, 222 N 25th	01
Beta House, 2908 N 1st Ave	01
Carlin, 2501 Montana Ave	01
Colonial Courts Motel, 580 Main	01
Colonial, 223 S 27th	01
Darryl, 114 1/2 N 26th	01
Driftwood Court, 932 Ave B	02
Dude Rancher Lodge, 415 N 29th	01
Dupre Manor, 721 14th W	02
Executive, 445 Lordwith Dr	02
Gage, 2325 Montana Ave	01
General Custer, 106 N 27th	01
Grand, 16 S 27th	01
Hedgemere, 2803 N 7th Ave	01
Holiday Inn, Highway 10 E	01
James, 19 1/2 N 27th	01
Jean, 3405 N 1st Ave	01
Lee, 118 N 24th	01
Lincoln, 2520 1st Ave N	01
Lordwith Courts, 1601 Virginia Lane	02
Middleton Arms, 707 N 31	01
Mustang Motel, R 1/2 3	01
Northern, 19 N Broadway	01
Okerman, 23 Yellowstone Ave	01

Parkview, 420 Lordwith Dr	02
Ponderosa Acres Apartments, 1301 Industrial Ave	02
Ponderosa Inn, 2511 1st Ave N	01
Prior, 19 N 26th	01
Rex, 2401 Montana Ave	01
Reynolds, 224 S 30th	01
Ross, 1615 N 2nd Ave	01
Roxy, 15 1/2 N 29th	01
Santa Fe Arms, 2207 Central	02
Shaffer, 4 Lewis Ave	01
Sherton Arms, 1616 Ave E	02
Shield, 43 Broadwater Ave	02
Stratford, 2817 N 6th Ave	02
Terry Park, 421 W 5th	02
Thomas, 715 N 29th	01
Western Towers	01
Wreford, 3317 N 2nd Ave	01
Young Womens Apartment, 16 N 29th	01

BUILDINGS

Behner, 2822 N 3rd Ave	01
Doctors, 1231 N 29th	01
Electric, 113 N Broadway	01
Executive, 1925 Grand Ave	02
First National Bank, 2715 N 2nd Ave	01
Fratt, 2819 N 2nd Ave	01
Hart-Albin, 208 N Broadway	01
Hedden, 2911 N 2nd Ave	01
Kook, 3203 3rd Ave N	01
M & R, 1002 Division	01
Midland National Bank, 303 N Broadway	01
Petroleum, 2812 N 1st Ave	01
Professional, 1236 N Broadway	01
Securities, 2708 N 1st Ave	01
Security Bank, 2813 N 3rd Ave	01
Selvidge-Babcock, 2718 Montana Ave	01
Stapleton, 104 N Broadway	01
Transwestern Life Insurance, 404 N 31st	01
Treasure State, 2906 N 2nd Ave	01
West Professional, 17th W & Ave D	02
Wilcox, 3302 N 4th Ave	01

GOVERNMENT OFFICES

Chamber Of Commerce, 301 N 27th	01
City Hall, 220 N 27th	01
Court House, 2620 N 3rd Ave	01

Federal Building & U S Court House, 310 N 26th	01
United States Post Office, 2602 N 1st Ave	01

HOSPITALS

Billings Deaconess, 2813 N 9th Ave	01
New Western Manor, 2115 Central Ave	02
Saint Johns Lutheran Home, 3940 Rimrock Rd	02
Saint Vincents, 2915 N 12th Ave	01
Valley View Nursing Home, 1807 1/2 24 W	02
Yellowstone County, Yell River Blvd	01

UNIVERSITIES AND COLLEGES

Eastern Montana College Of Education, 1500 N 30th	01
Rocky Mountain, 1511 Poly Dr	02

GREAT FALLS   594

POST OFFICE BOXES

Box Nos.
1-3499	Main Office	03
1-5000	Malmstrom AFB	02

RURAL ROUTES

1,2	01

STATIONS, BRANCHES AND UNITS

Malmstrom A F B Br	02
Russell Sta	05
General Delivery	01
Postmaster	01

APARTMENTS, HOTELS, MOTELS

Adele Apts, 426 1st Ave SW	04
Bitterroot Apts, 400 5th St N	01
Blackstone Apts, 314 3rd St N	01
Cambridge Apts, 520 4th Ave N	01
Centaur Apts, 3345 11th Ave S	05
Country Club Motel, Country Club Addition	04

Great Falls (Con.)   594

Country Club Tower Apts,
   1536 Meadowlark Dr 04
Dearborn Apts, 121 5th St N .. 01
Devonshire Homes, 1200
   32nd St S 05
Don Plaza Motel, 1224 10th
   Ave S 05
Eagles Manor, 1421 9th St
   S 05
Elmore Hotel, 6 6th St S 01
Executive Apts, 3500 11th
   Ave S 05
Fergus Motel, 299 3rd St NW. 04

Geraldine Apts, 706 3rd Ave
   N 01
Glacier Apts, 505 3rd Ave N.... 01
Glendale Apts, 3161/2
   Central Ave 01
Harden Court Apts, 2525
   12th Ave S 05
Holiday Apts 3320 11th Ave
   S 05
Holiday Inn, 1411 10th Ave
   S 05
Imperial 400 Motel, 601 2nd
   Ave N 01
Jensen Apts, 801 4th Ave N.... 01
Leigland Apts, 11 9th St S 01
Leland Annex, 718 1st Ave N. 01

Leland Apts, 726 1st Ave N 01
Lexington Apts, 800 2nd Ave
   N 01
Marland Apts, 512 2nd Ave
   N 01
Midtown Motel, 525 2nd Ave
   N 01
New Villa Motel, 726 10th
   Ave S 05
O Haire Manor, 17 7th St S 01
Pennsylvania Apts, 116 3rd
   Ave N 01
Ponderosa Motel, 226
   Central 01
Racine Apts, 119 13th St N... 01
Rainbow Motel, 20 3rd St N... 01

NEBRASKA   State List of Post Offices

NEBRASKA
(Abbreviation: NE)

Abie, R. Br. Bruno 68001
Adams 68301
Agnew 68302
Ainsworth 69210
Albion (1st) 68620
Alda 68810
Alexandria 68303
Allen 68710
Alliance (1st) 69301
Alma 68920
Almeria 68811
Alvo 68304
Amelia 68711
Ames 68621
Ames Avenue, Sta. Omaha 68111
Amherst 68812
Angora 69331
Angus 68921
Anselmo 68813
Ansley 68814
Antioch 69332
Arapahoe 68922
Arcadia 68815
Archer 68816
Arlington 68002
Arnold 69120
Arthur 69121
Ashby 69333
Ashland 68003
Ashton 68817
Atkinson 68713
Atlanta 68923
Auburn (1st) 68305
Aurora (1st) 68818
Avoca 68307
Axtell 68924
Ayr 68925
Bancroft 68004
Barneston 68309
Bartlett 68622
Bartley 69020
Bassett 68714
Battle Creek 68715
Bayard 69334
Beatrice (1st) 68310
Beaver City 68926
Beaver Crossing 68313
Bee 68314

Beemer 68716
Belden 68717
Belgrade 68623
Bellevue (1st) 68005
Bellwood 68624
Belvidere 68315
Benedict 68316
Benkelman 69021
Bennet 68317
Bennington 68007
Benson, Sta. Omaha (see
   appendix)
Bertrand 68927
Berwyn 68819
Big Springs 69122
Bingham 69335
Bladen 68928
Blair (1st) 68008
Bloomfield 68718
Bloomington 68929
Blue Hill 68930
Blue Springs 68318
Boelus 68820
Boone 68625
Boys Town (1st) 68010
Bradshaw 68319
Brady 69123
Brainard 68626
Brandon, R. Br. Grant 69102
Brewster 68821
Bridgeport 69336
Bristow 68719
Broadwater 69125
Brock 68320
Broken Bow (1st) 68822
Brownlee 69126
Brownville 68321
Brule 69127
Bruning 68322
Bruno 68014
   Abie, R. Br. 68001
Brunswick 68720
Bucktail, R. Br. Paxton 69155
Burchard 68323
Burkett, Sta. Grand Island.... 68801
Burr 68324
Burton 68721
Burwell 68823
Bushnell 69128
Butte 68722
Byron 68325

Cairo 68824
Callaway 68825
Cambridge 69022
Campbell 68932
Carleton 68326
Carroll 68723
Cedar Bluffs 68015
Cedar Creek 68016
Cedar Rapids 68627
Center 68724
Central City 68826
Ceresco 68017
Chadron (1st) 69337
Chambers 68725
Champion 69023
Chapman 68827
Chappell 69129
Chester 68327
Clarks 68628
Clarkson 68629
Clatonia 68328
Clay Center 68933
Clearwater 68726
Cody 69211
   Eli, R. Br. 69213
Coleridge 68727
College View, Sta. Lincoln
   (see appendix)
Colon 68018
Columbus (1st) 68601
Comstock 68834
Concord 68728
Cook 68329
Cordova 68330
Cornlea 68630
Cortland 68331
Cotesfield 68829
Cozad (1st) 69130
Crab Orchard 68332
Craig 68019
Crawford 69339
Creighton 68729
Creston 68631
Crete (1st) 68333
Crofton 68730
Crookston 69212
Culbertson 69024
Curtis 69025
Dakota City 68731
Dalton 69131
Danbury 69026

Dannebrog	68831
Davenport	68335
Davey	68336
David City	68632
Garrison, R. Br.	68639
Dawson	68337
Daykin	68338
De Witt	68341
Decatur	68020
Denton	68339
Deshler	68340
Deweese	68934
Dickens	69132
Diller	68342
Dix	69133
Dixon	68732
Dodge	68633
Doniphan	68832
Dorchester	68343
Douglas	68344
Downtown, Sta. Omaha (see appendix)	
Du Bois	68346
Dunbar	68346
Duncan	68634
Dunning	68833
Dwight	68635
Eagle	68347
Eddyville	68834
Edgar	68935
Edison	68936
Elba	68835
Elgin	68636
Eli, R. Br. Cody	69213
Elk Creek	68348
Elkhorn	68022
Ellsworth	69340
Elm Creek	68836
Elmwood	68349
Elmwood Park, Sta. Omaha (see appendix)	
Elsie	69134
Elsmere	69135
Elwood	68937
Elyria	68837
Emerson	68733
Emmet	68734
Enders	69027
Endicott	68350
Ericson	68637
Eustis	69028
Ewing	68735
Exeter	68351
Fairbury (1st)	68352
Gladstone, R. Br.	68363
Powell, R. Br.	68425
Fairfield	68938
Fairmont	68354
Falls City (1st)	68355
Farnam	69029
Farwell	68838
Filley	68357
Firth	68358
Flats	69136
Florence, Sta. Omaha (see appendix)	
Fordyce	68736
Fort Calhoun	68023
Foster	68737
Franklin	68939
Fremont (1st)	68025
Friend	68359
Fullerton	68638

Funk	68940
Gandy	69137
Garland	68360
Garrison, R. Br. David City	68639
Gates	68839
Geneva	68361
Genoa	68640
Gering (1st)	69341
Gibbon	68840
Gilead	68362
Giltner	68841
Gladstone, R. Br. Fairbury	68363
Glenvil	68941
Goehner	68364
Gordon	69343
Gothenburg	69138
Grafton	68365
Grainton	69139
Grand Island (1st)	68801
Brandon, R. Br.	69102
Grant	69140
Greeley	68842
Greenwood	68366
Gresham	68367
Gretna	68028
Guide Rock	68942
Gurley	69141
Hadar, R. Br. Norfolk	68738
Hargier	69030
Hallam	68368
Halsey	69142
Hamlet	69031
Hampton	68843
Harbine, R. Br. Jansen	68369
Hardy	68943
Harrisburg	69345
Harrison	69346
Hartington	68739
Harvard	68944
Hastings (1st)	68901
Havelock, Sta. Lincoln	68529
Hay Springs	69347
Hayes Center	69032
Hazard	68844
Heartwell	68945
Hebron	68370
Hemingford	69348
Henderson	68371
Hendley	68946
Henry	69349
Herman	68029
Hershey	69143
Hickman	68372
Hildreth	68947
Holbrook	68948
Holdrege (1st)	68949
Holland	68373
Holmesville	68374
Holstein	68950
Homer	68030
Hooper	68031
Hordville	68846
Hoskins	68740
Howells	68641
Hubbard	68741
Hubbell	68375
Humboldt	68376
Humphrey	68642
Huntley	68951
Hyannis	69350
Imperial	69033
Inavale	68952
Indianola	69034

Inland	68954
Inman	68742
Ithaca	68033
Jackson	68743
Jamison	68744
Jansen	68377
Harbine, R. Br.	68369
Johnson	68378
Johnstown	69214
Julian	68379
Juniata	68955
Kearney (1st)	68847
Kenesaw	68956
Kennard	68034
Keystone	69144
Kilgore	69216
Kimball (1st)	69145
Lakeside	69351
Lamar	69035
Laurel	68745
Lawrence	68957
Lebanon	69036
Leigh	68643
Lemoyne	69146
Leshara, R. Br. Valley	68035
Lewellen	69147
Lewiston	68380
Lexington (1st)	68850
Liberty	68381
LINCOLN (1st) (see appendix)	
Lindsay	68644
Linwood	68036
Lisco	69148
Litchfield	68852
Lodgepole	69149
Long Pine	69217
Loomis	68958
Lorton	68382
Louisville	68037
Loup City	68853
Lushton, R. Br. Mc Cool Junction	68383
Lyman	69352
Lynch	68746
Lyons	68038
Macy	68039
Madison	68748
Madrid	69150
Magnet	68749
Malcolm	68402
Malmo	68040
Manley	68403
Marquette	68854
Marsland	69354
Martell	68404
Maskell	68751
Mason City	68855
Max	69037
Maxwell	69151
Maywood	69038
Mc Cook (1st)	69001
Mc Cool Junction	68401
Lushton, R. Br.	68383
Mc Grew	69353
Mc Lean	68747
Mead	68041
Meadow Grove	68752
Melbeta	69355
Memphis	68042
Merna	68856
Merriman	69218
Milburn	68857

413

Milford	68405
Millard, Br. Omaha	68137
Miller	68858
Milligan	68406
Mills	68753
Minatare	69356
Minden (1st)	68959
Mitchell	69357
Monroe	68647
Moorefield	69039
Morrill	69358
Morse Bluff	68648
Mount Michael, R. Br. Elkhorn	68022
Mullen	69152
Murdock	68407
Murray	68409
Naper	68755
Naponee	68960
Nebraska City (1st)	68410
Nehawka	68413
Neligh	68756
Nelson	68961
Nemaha	68414
Nenzel	69219
Newcastle	68757
Newman Grove	68758
Newport	68759
Nickerson	68044
Niobrara	68760
Nora	68962
Norden, R. Br. Springview	68778
Norfolk (1st)	68701
Hadar, R. Br.	68738
Norman	68963
North Bend	68649
North Loup	68859
North Platte (1st)	69101
Northport	69359
Northwest, Br. Omaha	68134
O'Neill (1st)	68763
Oak	68964
Oakdale	68761
Oakland	68045
Obert	68762
Oconto	68860
Octavia	68650
Odell	68415
Odessa	68861
Offutt A F B, Br. Omaha (see appendix)	
Ogallala (1st)	69153
Ohiowa	68416
OMAHA (1st) (see appendix)	
Ong, R. Br. Shickley	68452
Orchard	68764
Ord	68862
Orleans	68966
Osceola	68651
Oshkosh	69154
Osmond	68765
Otoe	68417
Overton	68863
Oxford	68967
Page	68766
Palisade	69040
Palmer	68864
Palmyra	68418
Panama	68419
Papillion (1st)	68046
Parks	69041
Pawnee City	68420
Paxton	69155

Pender	68047
Peru	68421
Petersburg	68652
Phillips	68865
Pickrell	68422
Pierce	68767
Pilger	68768
Plainview	68769
Platte Center	68653
Plattsmouth (1st)	68048
Pleasant Dale	68423
Pleasanton	68866
Plymouth	68424
Polk	68654
Ponca	68770
Poole	68867
Potter	69156
Powell, R. Br. Fairbury	68425
Prague	68050
Preston, R. Br. Falls City	68427
Primrose	68655
Prosser	68868
Purdum	69157
Raeville	68656
Ragan	68969
Ralston, Br. Omaha (see appendix)	
Randolph	68771
Ravenna	68869
Raymond	68428
Red Cloud	68970
Republican City	68971
Reynolds	68429
Richfield	68054
Richland	68657
Rising City	68658
Riverdale	68870
Riverton	68972
Roca	68430
Rockville	68871
Rogers	68659
Rosalie	68055
Roscoe	69159
Rose	68772
Roseland	68973
Royal	68773
Rulo	68431
Rushville	69360
Ruskin	68974
Saint Columbans (1st)	68056
Saint Edward	68660
Saint Helena	68774
Saint Libory	68872
Saint Mary	68432
Saint Paul	68873
Salem	68433
Sargent	68874
Saronville, R. Br. Sutton	68975
Schuyler (1st)	68661
Scotia	68875
Scottsbluff (1st)	69361
Scribner	68057
Seneca	69161
Seward (1st)	68434
Shelby	68662
Shelton	68876
Shickley	68436
Ong, R. Br.	68452
Shubert	68437
Sidney (1st)	69162
Silver Creek	68663
Smithfield	68976

Snyder	68664
South Bend	68058
South Omaha, Sta. Omaha (see appendix)	
South Sioux City (1st)	68776
Spalding	68665
Sparks	69220
Spencer	68777
Sprague	68438
Springfield	68059
Springview	68778
Stamford	68977
Stanton	68779
Staplehurst	68439
Stapleton	69163
State House, Sta. Lincoln	68509
Steele City	68440
Steinauer	68441
Stella	68442
Sterling	68443
Stock Yards, Sta. Omaha	68107
Stockham, R. Br. Aurora	68818
Stockville	69042
Streng	68444
Stratton	69043
Stromsburg	68666
Stuart	68780
Sumner	68878
Sunol	69164
Superior (1st)	68978
Surprise	68667
Sutherland	69165
Sutton	68979
Saronville, R. Br.	68975
Swanton	68445
Syracuse	68446
Table Rock	68447
Talmage	68448
Tarnov, R. Br. Humphrey	68642
Taylor	68879
Tecumseh	68450
Tekamah	68061
Thedford	69166
Thurston	68062
Tilden	68781
Tobias	68453
Trenton	69044
Trumbull	68980
Tryon	69167
Uehling	68063
Ulysses	68669
Unadilla	68454
Union	68455
University Place, Sta. Lincoln (see appendix)	
Upland	68981
Utica	68456
Valentine (1st)	69201
Valley	68064
Valparaiso	68065
Venango	69168
Verdel	68782
Verdigre	68783
Verdon	68457
Veterans Administration Hosp., Sta. Omaha	68105
Virginia	68458
Waco	68460
Wahoo (1st)	68066
Wakefield	68784
Wallace	69169

Dannebrog	68831	
Davenport	68335	
Davey	68336	
David City	68632	
Garrison, R. Br.	68639	
Dawson	68337	
Daykin	68338	
De Witt	68341	
Decatur	68020	
Denton	68339	
Deshler	68340	
Deweese	68934	
Dickens	69132	
Diller	68342	
Dix	69133	
Dixon	68732	
Dodge	68633	
Doniphan	68832	
Dorchester	68343	
Douglas	68344	
Downtown, Sta. Omaha (see appendix)		
Du Bois	68345	
Dunbar	68346	
Duncan	68634	
Dunning	68833	
Dwight	68635	
Eagle	68347	
Eddyville	68834	
Edgar	68935	
Edison	68936	
Elba	68835	
Elgin	68636	
Eli, R. Br. Cody	69213	
Elk Creek	68348	
Elkhorn	68022	
Ellsworth	69340	
Elm Creek	68836	
Elmwood	68349	
Elmwood Park, Sta. Omaha (see appendix)		
Elsie	69134	
Elsmere	69135	
Elwood	68937	
Elyria	68837	
Emerson	68733	
Emmet	68734	
Enders	69027	
Endicott	68350	
Ericson	68637	
Eustis	69028	
Ewing	68735	
Exeter	68351	
Fairbury (1st)	68352	
Gladstone, R. Br.	68363	
Powell, R. Br.	68425	
Fairfield	68938	
Fairmont	68354	
Falls City (1st)	68355	
Farnam	69029	
Farwell	68838	
Filley	68357	
Firth	68358	
Flats	69136	
Florence, Sta. Omaha (see appendix)		
Fordyce	68736	
Fort Calhoun	68023	
Foster	68737	
Franklin	68939	
Fremont (1st)	68025	
Friend	68359	
Fullerton	68638	

Funk	68940	
Gandy	69137	
Garland	68360	
Garrison, R. Br. David City	68639	
Gates	68839	
Geneva	68361	
Genoa	68640	
Gering (1st)	69341	
Gibbon	68840	
Gilead	68362	
Giltner	68841	
Gladstone, R. Br. Fairbury	68363	
Glenvil	68941	
Goehner	68364	
Gordon	69343	
Gothenburg	69138	
Grafton	68365	
Grainton	69139	
Grand Island (1st)	68801	
Brandon, R. Br.	69102	
Greeley	68842	
Greenwood	68366	
Gresham	68367	
Gretna	68028	
Guide Rock	68942	
Gurley	69141	
Hadar, R. Br. Norfolk	68738	
Haigler	69030	
Hallam	68368	
Halsey	69142	
Hamlet	69031	
Hampton	68843	
Harbine, R. Br. Jansen	68369	
Hardy	68943	
Harrisburg	69345	
Harrison	69346	
Hartington	68739	
Harvard	68944	
Hastings (1st)	68901	
Havelock, Sta. Lincoln	68529	
Hay Springs	69347	
Hayes Center	69032	
Hazard	68844	
Heartwell	68945	
Hebron	68370	
Hemingford	69348	
Henderson	68371	
Hendley	68946	
Henry	69349	
Herman	68029	
Hershey	69143	
Hickman	68372	
Hildreth	68947	
Holbrook	68948	
Holdrege (1st)	68949	
Holland	68373	
Holmesville	68374	
Holstein	68950	
Homer	68030	
Hooper	68031	
Hordville	68846	
Hoskins	68740	
Howells	68641	
Hubbard	68741	
Hubbell	68375	
Humboldt	68376	
Humphrey	68642	
Huntley	68951	
Hyannis	69350	
Imperial	69033	
Inavale	68952	
Indianola	69034	

Inland	68954	
Inman	68742	
Ithaca	68033	
Jackson	68743	
Jamison	68744	
Jansen	68377	
Harbine, R. Br.	68369	
Johnson	68378	
Johnstown	69214	
Julian	68379	
Juniata	68955	
Kearney (1st)	68847	
Kenesaw	68956	
Kennard	68034	
Keystone	69144	
Kilgore	69216	
Kimball (1st)	69145	
Lakeside	69351	
Lamar	69035	
Laurel	68745	
Lawrence	68957	
Lebanon	69036	
Leigh	68643	
Lemoyne	69146	
Leshara, R. Br. Valley	68035	
Lewellen	69147	
Lewiston	68380	
Lexington (1st)	68850	
Liberty	68381	
LINCOLN (1st) (see appendix)		
Lindsay	68644	
Linwood	68036	
Lisco	69148	
Litchfield	68852	
Lodgepole	69149	
Long Pine	69217	
Loomis	68958	
Lorton	68382	
Louisville	68037	
Loup City	68853	
Lushton, R. Br. Mc Cool Junction	68383	
Lyman	69352	
Lynch	68746	
Lyons	68038	
Macy	68039	
Madison	68748	
Madrid	69150	
Magnet	68749	
Malcolm	68402	
Malmo	68040	
Manley	68403	
Marquette	68854	
Marsland	69354	
Martell	68404	
Maskell	68751	
Mason City	68855	
Max	69037	
Maxwell	69151	
Maywood	69038	
Mc Cook (1st)	69001	
Mc Cool Junction	68401	
Lushton, R. Br.	68383	
Mc Grew	69353	
Mc Lean	68747	
Mead	68041	
Meadow Grove	68752	
Melbeta	69355	
Memphis	68042	
Merna	68856	
Merriman	69218	
Milburn	68857	

Walthill	68067		Wilsonville	69046
Walton	68461	(see appendix)	Winnebago	68071
Washington	68068	West Omaha, Sta. Omaha	Winnetoon	68789
Waterbury	68785	(see appendix)	Winside	68790
Waterloo	68069	West Point (1st)	68788	Winslow	68072
Wauneta	69045	Western	68464	Wisner	68791
Wausa	68786	Westerville	68881	Wolbach	68882
Waverly	68462	Weston	68070	Wood Lake	69221
Wayne (1st)	68787	Whitclay	69365	Wood River	68883
Weeping Water	68463	Whitman	69366	Wymore	68466
Weissert	68880	Whitney	69367	Wynot	68792
Wellfleet	69170	Wilber	68465	York (1st)	68467
		Wilcox	68982	Yutan	68073
West Dodge, Sta. Omaha		Willow Island	69171		

LINCOLN   685

POST OFFICE BOXES

Box Nos.

2300-2999	Sta B	02
4400-4699	University Place Sta	04
5000-5599	Sta C	05
6000-6399	College View Sta	06
29100-29399	Havelock Sta	29
30000-30399	Sta A	03
80001-83399	Main Office	01
94600-94899	State House Sta	09

RURAL ROUTES

1	02
2,3	05
5	08
6	03
8	06

STATIONS, BRANCHES AND UNITS

College View Sta	06
Havelock Sta	29
State House Sta	09
University Place Sta	04
General Delivery	01
Postmaster	01

APARTMENTS, HOTELS, MOTELS

Ambassador, 1330 J	08
Clayton House, 1020 O	08
Gateway Manor, 225 N 56	04
Lincoln, 147 N 9	01
Metropolitan, 502 S 12	08
Palisade, 1035 S 17	08
President, 1340 J	08
Radisson Cornhusker, 309 S 13	08
Regent, 1626 O	02
Sky Park Manor, 1301 J	08
Tower View, 1631-41 J	08
Trenridge Garden	05
University Park, 4300 Holdredge	03

BUILDINGS

Anderson, 116 N 12	08
First National Bank, 233 S 13	08
Gateway Shopping Area	05
Lincoln Benefit Life, 134 S 13	08
Lincoln, 1001 O	08
Rudge & Guenzel, 134 S 12	08
Sharp, 206 S 13	08
Stuart, 128 N 13	08
Terminal, 941 O	08

GOVERNMENT OFFICES

County-City, 555 S 10	08
Federal, 129 N 10	08
State Capitol, 1445 K	09

HOSPITALS

Bryan Memorial, 4848 Sumner	06
Lincoln General, 2300 S 16	02
Lincoln Regional Center, 2705 S Folsom	01
Providence, 4600 Valley Rd	10
Saint Elizabeth Community Health Center, 555 S 70th	10
Veterans Administration, 600 S 70th	01

UNIVERSITIES AND COLLEGES

Nebraska School Of Religion, 1237 R	08
Nebraska Wesleyan, 2630 N 50	04
Union, 3800 S 48	06
University Of Nebraska (City Campus)	08
University Of Nebraska (East Campus)	03
University Of Nebraska Agriculture College	03

OMAHA   681

POST OFFICE BOXES

Box Nos.

1-1999	Downtown Sta	01
2001-2999	A Sta	20
3001-3999	Main Office	03
4001-4999	Benson Sta	04
6001-6999	Elmwood Park Sta	06
7001-7999	South Omaha Sta	07
9001-9999	C Sta	09
11001-11999	Ames Avenue Sta	11
12001-12999	Florence Sta	12
13001-13999	Offutt Afb Br	13
14001-14999	West Omaha Sta	14
19001-19999	Air Mail Facility	19
27001-27999	Ralston	27
31001-31999	West Dodge Sta	31
34001-34299	Northwest Sta	34
37001-37999	Millard Br	37
55001-55999	B Sta	55

RURAL ROUTES

1	14
2	34
3	23
4	37
6	12

STATIONS, BRANCHES AND UNITS

Ames Avenue Sta	11
Benson Sta	04
Downtown Sta	01
Elmwood Park Sta	05
Florence Sta	02
Millard Br	37
Northwest Br	34
Offutt AFB Br	13
Ralston Br	27
South Omaha Sta	07
Stock Yards Sta	07
Veterans Administration Hosp. Sta	05

Walthill	68067
Walton	68461
Washington	68068
Waterbury	68785
Waterloo	68069
Wauneta	69045
Wausa	68786
Waverly	68462
Wayne (1st)	68787
Weeping Water	68463
Weissert	68880
Wellfleet	69170
West Dodge, Sta. Omaha	

(see appendix)	
West Omaha, Sta. Omaha	
(see appendix)	
West Point (1st)	68788
Western	68464
Westerville	68881
Weston	68070
Whiteclay	69365
Whitman	69366
Whitney	69367
Wilber	68465
Wilcox	68982
Willow Island	69171

Wilsonville	69045
Winnebago	68071
Winnetoon	68789
Winside	68790
Winslow	68072
Wisner	68791
Wolbach	68882
Wood Lake	69221
Wood River	68883
Wymore	68466
Wynot	68792
York (1st)	68467
Yutan	68073

Appendix   Lincoln — Omaha NEBRASKA

LINCOLN   685

POST OFFICE BOXES

Box Nos.		
2300-2999	Sta B	02
4400-4699	University Place Sta	04
5000-5599	Sta C	05
6000-6399	College View Sta	06
29100-29399	Havelock Sta	29
30000-30399	Sta A	03
80001-83399	Main Office	01
94600-94899	State House Sta	09

RURAL ROUTES

1	02
2,3	05
5	08
6	02
8	06

STATIONS, BRANCHES AND UNITS

College View Sta	06
Havelock Sta	29
State House Sta	09
University Place Sta	04
General Delivery	01
Postmaster	01

APARTMENTS, HOTELS, MOTELS

Ambassador, 1330 J	08
Clayton House, 1020 O	08
Gateway Manor, 225 N 56	04
Lincoln, 147 N 9	01
Metropolitan, 502 S 12	08
Palisade, 1035 S 17	08
President, 1340 J	08
Radisson Cornhusker, 309 S 13	08
Regent, 1626 D	02
Sky Park Manor, 1301 J	08
Tower View, 1631-41 J	08
Trenridge Garden	05
University Park, 4300 Holdredge	03

BUILDINGS

Anderson, 116 N 12	08
First National Bank, 233 S 13	08
Gateway Shopping Area	05
Lincoln Benefit Life, 134 S 13	08
Lincoln, 1001 O	08
Rudge & Guenzel, 134 S 12	08
Sharp, 206 S 13	08
Stuart, 128 N 13	08
Terminal, 941 O	08

GOVERNMENT OFFICES

County-City, 555 S 10	08
Federal, 129 N 10	08
State Capitol, 1445 K	09

HOSPITALS

Bryan Memorial, 4848 Sumner	06
Lincoln General, 2300 S 16	02
Lincoln Regional Center, 2705 S Folsom	01
Providence, 4600 Valley Rd	10
Saint Elizabeth Community Health Center, 555 S 70th	10
Veterans Administration, 600 S 70th	01

UNIVERSITIES AND COLLEGES

Nebraska School Of Religion, 1237 R	08
Nebraska Wesleyan, 2630 N 50	04
Union, 3800 S 48	06
University Of Nebraska (City Campus)	08
University Of Nebraska (East Campus)	03
University Of Nebraska Agriculture College	03

OMAHA   681

POST OFFICE BOXES

Box Nos.		
1-1999	Downtown Sta	01
2001-2999	A Sta	20
3001-3999	Main Office	03
4001-4999	Benson Sta	04
6001-6999	Elmwood Park Sta	06
7001-7999	South Omaha Sta	07
9001-9999	C Sta	09
11001-11999	Ames Avenue Sta	11
12001-12999	Florence Sta	12
13001-13999	Offutt Afb Br	13
14001-14999	West Omaha Sta	14
19001-19999	Air Mail Facility	19
27001-27999	Ralston	27
31001-31999	West Dodge Sta	31
34001-34299	Northwest Sta	34
37001-37999	Millard Br	37
55001-55999	B Sta	55

RURAL ROUTES

1	14
2	34
3	23
4	37
6	12

STATIONS, BRANCHES AND UNITS

Ames Avenue Sta	11
Benson Sta	04
Downtown Sta	01
Elmwood Park Sta	06
Florence Sta	02
Millard Br	37
Northwest Br	34
Offutt AFB Br	13
Ralston Br	27
South Omaha Sta	07
Stock Yards Sta	07
Veterans Administration Hosp. Sta	05

Omaha (Con.)   681

West Dodge Sts.   31
West Omaha   14
General Delivery   08
Postmaster   08

APARTMENTS, HOTELS, MOTELS

Adelphia, 836 Park Ave   05
Austin, 205 N 38   31
Austin, 206 N 37th   31
Austin, 3701 Davenport   31
Beverly Arms, 3420 Jones   05
Beverly Manor, 128 N 31st   31
Buckingham Manor, 4817
  Chicago   32
Carberry, 3910 Cass   31
Carberry, 501 N 40th   31
Castle, 632 S 16th   02
Cherry Garden Court, 813 S
  38th   05
Cherry Garden Court, 814 S
  37th Ave   05
Chula Vista, 1141 S 30th
  Ave   05
Chula Vista, 2968 Poppleton
  Ave   05
Colonial, 3804 Farnam   31
Commodore, 2410 Dodge   31
Conant, 1913 Farnam   02
Covert Ave 2235 St Marys
  Ave   02
Cox, 2235 St Marys Ave   02
Delmar, 219 S 24th   02
Diplomat, 1511 Farnam   02
Drake Court Annex, 2201
  Jones   02
Drake Court Office, 701 S
  22nd   02
Drake Court, 20th To 22nd &
  Jones   02
Dundee Court, 4728 Chicago   32
Dundee Manor, 106 N 49th   32
Dundee Towers, 110 S 49th   32
Dundee, 5019 Underwood
  Ave   32
Farnam, 3252 Farnam   31
Flatiron, 1722 St Marys   02
Hamilton, 2406 Farnam   02
Hill, 505 S 16th   02
Holiday Inn, 3321 S 72nd   24
Howard Johnsons 72nd & I-
  80   24
Imperial 400, 2211 Douglas   02
Knickerbocker, 3801 Jones   05
Knickerbocker, 702 S 38th   05
Landon Court, 519 S 24th   02
Logan, 1804 Dodge   02
Masonic Manor, 801 S 52   06
New Paxton 1405 Farnam   02
New Tower, 7764 Dodge   14
O E A Manor, 22nd &

Chicago   02
Omaha Hilton 1616 Dodge   02
Paxton Court, 25th Ave
  Douglas   31
Prom Town House, 7000
  Dodge   14
Radisson Blackstone, 302 S
  36th   31
Rorick, 604 S 22nd   02
Travelodge, 3902 Dodge   31
Tudor Arms, 131 S 39th   31
Twin Towers, 3000 Farnam   31
Windsor Arms, 544 S 25th
  Ave   05

BUILDINGS

Ames Plaza, 56th & Ames   04
Aquilla Court, 1615 Howard   02
Baird, 1704 Douglas   02
Barker, 306 S 15th   02
Beverly Hills, 79th & Dodge   14
Blondo Plaza, 80th & Blondo   34
Capitol Plaza, 1815 Capitol
  Ave   02
Center, 42nd & Center   05
City National Bank, 405 S
  16th   02
Continental, 209 So 19   02
Country Side Village, 87th &
  Pacific   14
Crossroads Shopping Center,
  72nd & Dodge   14
Doctors Building, 4239
  Farnam   31
Electric, 409 S 17th   02
Executive, 1624 Douglas   02
Faidley, 121 S 16th   02
Farm Credit, 206 S 19th   02
Farnam, 1613 Farnam   02
Federal Office, 106 S 15th   02
Federal, 215 N 17th   02
First National Bank, 1603
  Farnam   02
First National Center 16th
  And Dodge   02
Grain Exchange, 1905
  Harney   02
Karbach, 209 S 15th   02
Keeline, 319 S 17th   02
Kiewit Plaza, 3555 Farnam   31
Kilpatrick, 222 S 15th   02
Lawyers 3535 Harney   31
Live Stock Exchange, 29th O   07
Loveland Shopping Center,
  90th & Center   24
Lyric, 221 S 19th   02
Masonic Temple, 117 S 19th   02
Medical Arts Building, 105 S
  17th   02
Mid American Plaza, 71st &
  W Center Rd   06
Omaha, 1620 Farnam   02
Physicians Building, 3601

Dodge   31
Professional, 3510 Dodge   31

Redick Tower, 1504 Harney   02
Securities, 305 S 16th   02
Service Life, 1904 Farnam   02
South Omaha City Hall, 5002
  S 24th   07
Swanson, 8401 Dodge   14
Westgate Plaza, 84th &
  Hascall   24
Westroads Shopping Center,
  102nd West Dodge Rd   14
Woodmen Of The World, 1319
  Farnam   02
Woodmen Tower, 1700
  Farnam   02
Xerox, 7002 W Center Rd   06

GOVERNMENT OFFICES

City Hall, 108 So 18   02
County Court House, 1715
  Farnam   02

HOSPITALS

Archbishop Bergan-Mercy   24
Bishop Clarkson Memorial   05
Booth Memorial, 426 So.
  40th   31
Childrens Memorial, 502 S
  44th   05
Doctors, 501 Park Ave   05
Douglas County, 4102
  Woolworth   05
Eppley Care Center, 3612
  Cuming   31
Immanuel, 36th & Meredith   11
Lutheran, 515 S 26th   31
Nebraska Methodist, 8303 &
  Dodge   14
Richard A Young Memorial,
  402 S 24th Ave   31
Saint Catherines, 9th &
  Forest Ave   08
Saint Josephs, 2305 S 10th   05
Univ Of Nebraska College Of
  Medicine, 42nd Dewey
  Ave   05
Veterans Administration,
  42nd & Woolworth Ave   05

UNIVERSITIES AND COLLEGES

Ave   05
Creighton Medical School
  639 N 27th   31
Creighton University, 2500
  California   31
Saint Marys, 1901 S 72nd   24
University Of Nebr. At
  Omaha, 60th & Dodge   32
University Of Nebraska
  College Of Medicine 42nd
  & Dewey Ave   05

NEVADA
(Abbreviation: NV)

Airport, Br. Las Vegas........89111
Alamo 89001
Austin 89310
Babbitt, Br. Hawthorne......89416
Baker 89311
Battle Mountain 89820
Beatty 89003
Beowawe 89821
Black Spring, Br. Reno 89508
Blue Diamond 89004
Bonanza Annex, Sta. Las
  Vegas (see appendix)
Boulder City (1st)...............89005
Bunkerville 89007
Caliente 89008
Carlin 89822
Carp......................................89009
Carson City (1st)................89701
Cherry Creek 89312
Crescent Valley, R. Br.
  Beowawe 89821
Crystal Bay 89402
  Incline Village, Br. 89450
Currie 89313
Dayton 89403
Deeth 89823
Denio 89404
Downtown, Sta. Las Vegas..89101
Duckwater 89314
Dyer 89010
East Ely 89315
East Las Vegas, Br. Las
  Vegas 89112
Elko (1st) 89801
Ely (1st) 89301
Empire 89405
Eureka 89316
Fallon (1st) 89406
Federal, Sta. Las Vegas 89101
Fernley 89408
Gabbs 89409
Galena, Sta. Reno 89501

Gardnerville 89410
Garside, Sta. Las Vegas (see
  appendix)
Genoa 89411
Gerlach 89412
Glenbrook 89413
Golconda 89414
Goldfield 89013
Goodsprings, R. Sta. Jean..89019
Halleck 89824
Hawthorne (1st) 89415
  Babbitt, Br. 89416
Hazen 89417
Henderson (1st)..................89015
Hiko 89017
Huntridge, Sta. Las Vegas
  (see appendix)
Imlay 89418
Incline Village, Br. Crystal
  Bay 89450
Indian Springs 89018
Jackass Flats, Br. Mercury..89023
Jackpot 89825
Jarbidge 89826
Jean 89019
Jiggs 89827
Lake Mead Base, Br. Las
  Vegas 89110
Lamoille 89828
LAS VEGAS (1st) (see
  appendix)
Lathrop Wells 89020
Laughlin, R. Br. Searchlight..89046
Lee 89829
Logandale 89021
Lovelock 89419
Lund 89317
Luning 89420
Manhattan 89022
Mc Dermitt 89421
Mc Gill 89318
Mercury 89023
Mesquite 89024
Mina 89422
Minden 89423

Moapa 89025
Montello 89830
Mountain City 89831
Nellis A F B, Br. Las Vegas..89110
Nixon 89424
North Las Vegas (1st)........89030
Orovada 89425
Overton 89040
Owyhee 89832
Pahrump 89041
Panaca 89042
Paradise Valley 89426
Peavine, Sta. Reno 89502
Pioche 89043
Pittman 89044
RENO (1st) (see appendix)
Round Mountain 89045
Ruby Valley 89833
Ruth 89319
Schurz 89427
Searchlight 89046
Silver City 89428
Silver Springs 89429
Silverpeak 89047
Smith 89430
Sparks (1st) 89431
Stateline, Br. Zephyr Cove..89449
Steamboat 89436
Stewart 89437
Tonopah 89049
Tracy Clark, R. Sta. Sparks..89431
Tuscarora 89834
University, Sta. Reno 89507
Valmy 89438
Verdi 89439
Virginia City 89440
Wadsworth 89442
Washington, Sta. Reno 89503
Weed Heights 89443
Wellington 89444
Wells 89835
Winnemucca (1st) 89445
Yerington (1st) 89447
Zephyr Cove (1st) 89448
  Stateline, Br. 89449

Appendix   Las Vegas NEVADA

LAS VEGAS   891

POST OFFICE BOXES

Box Nos.
1-2196	Downtown Sta.	01
2201-2987	Huntridge Sta.	04
4001-4427	Bonanza Sta.	06
5301-5746	Garside Sta.	02
7331-7545	Downtown Sta.	01
9701-9789	Nellis A F B Br.	10
11001-11400	Airport Sta.	11
12051-12549	East Las Vegas Br.	12
14001-15555	Main Office	14
16000-16043	Federal Sta.	01

STATIONS, BRANCHES AND UNITS

Airport Br.....................................11
Bonanza Annex Sta........ 06

Downtown Sta 01
East Las Vegas Br........... 12
Federal Sta 01
Garside Sta. 02
Huntridge Sta. 04
Lake Mead Base Br 10
Nellis A F B Br. 10
General Delivery 14
Postmaster 14

APARTMENTS, HOTELS, MOTELS

Aladdin, 3667 Las Vegas
  Blvd S.......................... 09
Bonanza Hotel, 3645 Las
  Vegas Blvd S................ 09
Caesar'S Palace, 3570 Las
  Vegas Blvd S................ 09
Circus Circus, 2880 Las
  Vegas Blvd S................ 09
Desert Inn, 3145 Las Vegas
  Blvd S.......................... 09

El Cortez, 600 Fremont.......... 01
Flamingo, 3680 Las Vegas
  Blvd S.......................... 09
Four Queens, 202 E Fremont.. 01
Fremont, 200 Fremont........... 01
Frontier, 3120 Las Vegas
  Blvd S.......................... 09
International Hotel, 3000
  Paradise Rd.................. 09
Landmark Hotel, 364
  Convention Ctr Dr........ 09
Las Vegas Hacienda, 3950
  Las Vegas Blvd S......... 19
Riviera, 3200 Las Vegas Blvd
  S.................................. 89
Sahara, 2800 Las Vegas
  Blvd S.......................... 09
Showboat, 2800 E Fremont
  Ave............................. 04
Stardust, 3000 Las Vegas
  Blvd S.......................... 09
The Dunes, 3700 Las Vegas

Las Vegas (Con.) 891

Blvd S	09
The Mint, 110 Fremont	01
The Sands, 3317 Las Vegas	
Blvd S	09
Thunderbird, 2800 Las Vegas	
Blvd S	09
Tropicana, 3801 Las Vegas	
Blvd S	09
Union Plaza, 1 Main	01

HOSPITALS

Las Vegas, 201 N 8th	01
Southern Nevada Memorial	
Hospital, 1800 W	
Charleston Blvd	02
Sunrise, 3186 Maryland Pky	09
WomenÖs, 2025 E Sahara	
Ave	05

UNIVERSITIES AND COLLEGES

University Of Nevada Las	
Vegas, 4505 Maryland	
Pky	89

RENO 895

POST OFFICE BOXES

Box Nos.		
1-1399	Main Office	04

1400-4999	Main Office	05
5000-6999	Washington	
	Sta	03
7000-7999	Peavine Sta	02
8000-9999	University Of	
	Nevada Sta	07
10000-10999	Riverside	
	Annex	10
13001-14999	University Of	
	Nevada	
	Station	07

RURAL ROUTES

1,2	02
3	03
4	02
5	08

STATIONS, BRANCHES AND UNITS

Black Spring Br	08
Galena Sta	01
Peavine Sta	02
University Sta	07
Washington Sta	03
General Delivery	01
Postmaster	01

APARTMENTS, HOTELS, MOTELS

El Cortez, 239 West 2nd	01
Harrahs, 219 North Center	01
Holiday, 111 Mill	01
Mapes, 10 North Virginia	01
Overland, 246 North Center	01
Pioneer Inn, 221 S. Virginia	01
Ponderosa, 515 S Virginia	01
Riverside, 17 South Virginia	01

BUILDINGS

Arlington Towers, 100 N	
Arlington	01
First National Bank, 1 E 1st	01
Professional, 150 N Center	01

GOVERNMENT OFFICES

Court House, S Virginia	01
Federal Bldg, 300 Booth	02

HOSPITALS

Nevada State, Galletti Way	02
Saint Marys, 235 W 6th	03
Veterans, 1000 Locust	02
Washoe Medical Center, 90	
Kirman Ave	02

NEW HAMPSHIRE
(Abbreviation: NH)

Acworth	03601
Alstead	03602
South Acworth, R. Br.	03607
Alton	03809
Alton Bay	03810
Amherst	03031
Andover	03216
Antrim	03440
Ashland	03217
Ashuelot	03441
Atkinson	03811
Auburn	03032
Barnstead	03218
Barrington	03825
Bartlett	03812
Bath	03740
Bedford, R. Br. Manchester	03102
Beebe River, R. Br.	
Campton	03219
Belmont	03220
Bennington	03442
Berlin (1st)	03570
Bethlehem	03574
Blodgett Landing, Br.	
Newbury	02255
Boscawen, Br. Concord	03301
Bradford	03221

Bretton Woods, R. Br. Twin	
Mountain	03575
Bristol	03222
Brookline	03033
Burkehaven, Br. Sunapee	03782
Campton	03223
Beebe River, R. Br.	03219
Waterville Valley, R. Br.	03223
West Campton, R. Sta.	03228
West Thornton, R. Br.	03285
Canaan	03741
Candia	03034
Canterbury	03224
Center Barnstead	03225
Center Conway	03813
Center Harbor	03226
Center Ossipee	03814
Center Sandwich	03227
Center Strafford	03815
Center Tuftonboro, R. Br.	
Wolfeboro	03816
Charlestown	03603
Chester	03036
Chesterfield	03443
Chocorua	03817
Claremont (1st)	03743
Colebrook	03576
Concord (1st)	03301
Contoocook	03229

Conway	03818
Cornish Flat	03746
Crawford House, R. Br. Twin	
Mountain	03577
Danbury	03230
Danville	03819
Deerfield	03037
Derry (1st)	03038
Dover (1st)	03820
Drewsville	03604
Dublin (1st)	03444
Durham (1st)	03824
East Andover	03231
East Candia	03040
East Derry	03041
East Hampstead	03826
East Hebron	03232
East Kingston	03827
East Lempster	03605
East Madison	03828
East Rochester, Sta.	
Rochester	03867
East Sullivan	03445
East Swanzey	03446
East Wakefield	03830
Eaton Center, R. Br.	
Madison	03832
Elkins	03233

418

Enfield	03748
Enfield Center	03749
Epping	03042
Epsom	03234
Errol	03579
Etna	03750
Exeter (1st)	03833
Fabyan House, R. Sta. Twin Mountain	03595
Farmington	03835
Fitzwilliam	03447
Fitzwilliam Depot, R. Sta. Fitzwilliam	03447
Francestown	03043
Franconia	03580
Franklin (1st)	03235
Franklin Pierce College, R. Sta. Rindge	03461
Freedom	03836
Fremont	03044
Georges Mills	03751
Gilmanton	03237
Gilmanton Iron Works	03837
Gilsum	03448
Glen	03838
Glencliff	03238
Goffstown	03045
Gonic, Sta. Rochester	03867
Gorham	03581
Goshen	03752
Gossville	03239
Grafton	03240
Grantham	03753
Greenfield	03047
Greenland	03840
Greenville	03048
Groveton	03582
Guild	03754
Hampstead	03841
Hampton (1st)	03842
Hampton Beach, Sta. Hampton	03842
Hampton Falls	03844
Hancock	03449
Hanover (1st)	03755
Harrisville	03450
Haverhill	03765
Hebron	03241
Hedding, R. Sta. Epping	03042
Henniker	03242
Hill	03243
Hillsboro (1st)	03244
Hinsdale	03451
Holderness	03245
Hollis	03049
Hooksett, Br. Manchester	03106
Hopkinton, Br Concord	03301
Hudson (1st)	03051
Intervale	03845
Jackson	03846
Jaffrey (1st)	03452
Jaffrey Center, R. Sta.	03454
Jaffrey Center, R. Sta. Jaffrey	03454
Jefferson	03583
Kearsarge	03847
Keene (1st)	03431
Kingston	03848
Laconia (1st)	03246
Lakeport, Sta. Laconia	03246
Lancaster (1st)	03584
Lebanon (1st)	03766

Lempster	03606
Lincoln	03251
Lisbon	03585
Littleton (1st)	03561
Lochmere	03252
Londonderry	03053
Loudon, Br. Concord	03301
Lyme	03768
Lyme Center	03769
Madison	03849
Eaton Center, R. Br	03832
MANCHESTER (1st) (see appendix)	
Marlborough	03455
Marlow	03456
Meadows	03587
Melvin Village	03850
Meredith (1st)	03253
Meriden	03770
Merrimack	03054
Milan	03588
Milford (1st)	03055
Milton	03851
Milton Mills	03852
Mirror Lake	03853
Monroe	03771
Mont Vernon	03057
Moultonboro	03254
Mount Sunapee	03772
Mount Washington, R. Br. Twin Mountain	03589
Munsonville	03457
Nashua (1st)	03060
South Merrimack, R. Br.	03083
New Boston	03070
New Castle	03854
New Durham	03855
New Hampton	03256
New Ipswich	03071
New London (1st)	03257
Newbury	03255
Newfields	03856
Newmarket (1st)	03857
Newport (1st)	03773
Newton	03858
Newton Junction	03859
North Chichester	03258
North Conway (1st)	03860
North Hampton	03862
North Haverhill	03774
North Salem	03073
North Sandwich	03259
North Stratford	03590
North Sutton	03260
North Woodstock	03262
Woodstock, R. Sta.	03293
Northwood	03261
Nottingham	03290
Orford	03777
Orfordville	03778
Ossipee	03864
Pease A F B, Sta. Portsmouth	03801
Pelham	03076
Penacook, Sta Concord	03301
Percy	03591
Peterborough (1st)	03458
Piermont	03779
Pike	03780
Pittsburg	03592
Pittsfield	03263
Plainfield	03781
Plaistow (1st)	03865

Plymouth (1st)	03264
Portsmouth (1st)	03801
Potter Place	03265
Randolph	03593
Raymond	03077
Redstone (1st)	03866
Reeds Ferry, Sta. Merrimack	03054
Rindge	03461
Rochester (1st)	03867
Rollinsford	03869
Rumney	03266
Stinson Lake, R. Sta.	03274
Rye	03870
Rye Beach	03871
Salem (1st)	03079
Salisbury	03268
Sanbornton	03269
Sanbornville	03872
Sandown	03873
Sandwich	03270
Seabrook	03874
Silver Lake	03875
Snowville	03877
Somersworth (1st)	03878
South Acworth, R. Br. Alstead	03607
South Chatham, R. Br. Fryeburg, M E	04037
South Danville	03881
South Effingham	03882
South Lyndeboro	03082
South Merrimack, R. Br. Nashua	03083
South Newbury	03272
South Sutton	03273
South Tamworth	03883
Spofford	03462
Stinson Lake, R. Sta. Rumney	03274
Stoddard	03464
Strafford	03884
Stratham	03885
Strawbery Banke, Sta. Portsmouth	03801
Sugar Hill, Br. Lisbon	03585
Sunapee	03782
Suncook	03275
Surry, R. Br. Keene	03431
Tamworth	03886
Temple	03084
Tilton	03276
Troy	03465
Twin Mountain	03595
Bretton Woods, R. Br.	03575
Crawford House, R. Br.	03577
Fabyan House, R. Sta.	03595
Mount Washington, R. Br.	03589
Union	03887
Wakefield	03888
Walpole	03608
Warner	03278
Warren	03279
Washington	03280
Waterville Valley, R. Sta. Campton	03223
Weare	03281
Weirs Beach, Sta. Laconia	03246
Wendell	03783
Wentworth	03282
Wentworth By The Sea, Sta. New Castle	03854

West Campton, R. Sta. Campton	03228
West Canaan, R. Sta. Canaan	03741
West Chesterfield	03466
West Franklin, Sta. Franklin	03235
West Hampstead	03889
West Hopkinton	03283
West Lebanon	03784
West Nottingham	03291
West Ossipee	03890
West Peterborough	03468

West Rye	03891
West Springfield	03284
West Stewartstown	03597
West Swanzey	03469
West Thornton, R. Br. Campton	03285
Westmoreland	03467
Westville	03892
Whitefield	03598
Willey House	03893
Wilmot Flat	03287
Wilton	03086

Winchester	03470
Windham	03087
Winnisquam	03289
Wolfeboro (1st)	03894
Center Tuftonboro, R. Br.	03816
Wolfeboro Falls	03896
Wonalancet	03897
Woodstock, R. Sta. North Woodstock	03293
Woodsville	03785

MANCHESTER 031

POST OFFICE BOXES

Box Nos.

1-1080	Main Office	05
2001-2399	Hooksett Br	06

RURAL ROUTES

1	84
2	02
3	03
4,5	02

STATIONS, BRANCHES AND UNITS

Bedford Rural Br	02
Hooksett Br	06
General Delivery	01

Postmaster	01

APARTMENTS, HOTELS, MOTELS

Carpenter Motor, 323 Franklin	01
China Dragon, Hooksett	06
Holiday Inn, Amoskeag	02
Howard Johnson Motel Queen City Ave	02
Queen City Motel, Queen City Ave	01
Wayfarer Inn, S River Rd	02

GOVERNMENT OFFICES

City Hall, 908 Elm	01
County Court House, 300 Chestnut	01
Veterans Adminstration, 497 Silver	03

HOSPITALS

Elliot, 955 Auburn	03
Notre Dame, 337 Notre Dame Ave	02
Sacred Heart, 200 Hanover	04
United States Government Veterans Administration, Smyth	04

UNIVERSITIES AND COLLEGES

Mount Saint Marys College, Hooksett	06
N H College 2500 River Rd	04
Notre Dame College, 2321 Elm	04
Saint Anselms College, College Rd	02

NEW JERSEY
(Abbreviation: NJ)

Absecon (1st)	08201
Academy, Sta. Newark	07102
Adelphia	07710
Alfred Vail, Br. Eatontown	07724
Allaire, R. Br. Farmingdale	07727
Allamuchy	07820
Allendale (1st)	0740=
Allenhurst (1st)	07711
Allentown	08501
Allenwood	08720
Alloway	08001
Allwood, Sta. Clifton	07012
Alpha, Br. Phillipsburg	08865
Alpine	07620
Ampere, Sta. East Orange (see appendix)	
Ancora, Br. Hammonton	08037
Andover	07821
Annandale	08801
Arlington, Sta. Kearny	07032
Asbury	08802
Asbury Park (1st)	07712
Atco	08004
Athenia, Sta. Clifton	07013
ATLANTIC CITY (1st) (see appendix)	
Atlantic Highlands (1st)	07716
Audubon, Br. Camden	08106
Augusta	07822
Avalon	08202
Avenel (1st)	07001
Avon By The Sea (1st)	07717
Baptistown	08803
Barnegat	08005
Barnegat Light	08006
Barrington (1st)	08007
Basking Ridge (1st)	07920
Lyons, Br.	07939
Batsto, R. Br. Hammonton	08037
Bay Head, Br. Point Pleasant Beach	08742
Bayonne (1st)	07002
Bayville	08721
Bayway, Sta. Elizabeth	07202
Beach Haven (1st)	08008
Beachwood	08722
Bedminster	07921
Belford	07718
Belle Mead (1st)	08502
Belleville, Br. Newark	07109
Bellmawr, Br. Gloucester City	08030
Belmar (1st)	07719
Belvidere (1st)	07823
Bergen, Sta. Jersey City	07304
Bergen Mall, Sta. Paramus	07652
Bergen Point, Sta. Bayonne	07002
Bergenfield (1st)	07621
Bergenline, Sta. Union City	07087
Berkeley Heights (1st)	07922
Berlin (1st)	08009
Bernardsville (1st)	07924
Betsytown, Sta. Elizabeth	07201
Beverly (1st)	08010
Birmingham	08011
Blackwood (1st)	08012
Blackwood Terrace, Br. Woodbury	08096
Blairstown	07825
Blawenburg	08504
Bloomfield (1st)	07003
Bloomingdale (1st)	07403
Bloomsbury (1st)	08804
Bogota, Br. Hackensack	07603
Boonton (1st)	07005
Bordentown (1st)	08505
Bound Brook (1st)	08805
Bradley Beach (1st)	07720
Brainy Boro, Sta. Metuchen	08840
Branchville (1st)	07826
Breton Woods, Br. Brick	

Town..............................08723
Brick Church, Sta. East
  Orange (see appendix)
Brick Town (1st)................08723
Bridgeport.........................08014
Bridgeton (1st)...................08302
Brielle...............................08730
Brigantine..........................08203
Broadway...........................08808
Brookdale, Sta. Bloomfield...07003
Brooklawn, Br. Gloucester
  City..............................08030
Brookside...........................07926
Browns Mills (1st)...............08015
Browntown, Br. Old Bridge...08857
Budd Lake..........................0782R
Buena................................08310
Burlington (1st)...................08016
Butler (1st)........................07405
Buttzville...........................07829
Caldwell (1st).....................07006
Califon..............................07830
CAMDEN (1st) (see
  appendix)
Cape May (1st)....................08204
Cape May Court House (1st)..08210
Cape May Point...................08212
Carlstadt, Br. Rutherford......07072
Carneys Point, Br. Penns
  Grove............................08069
Carteret (1st).....................07008
Castle Point, Sta. Hoboken...07030
Cedar Brook........................08018
Cedar Grove (1st)................07009
Cedar Knolls (1st)...............07927
Cedarville..........................08311
Center, Sta. Trenton............08608
Central, Sta. East Orange
  (see appendix)
Chambersburg, Sta. Trenton..08611
Changewater.......................07831
Chatham (1st).....................07928
Chatsworth.........................08019
Cheesequake, Br. South
  Amboy...........................08879
Cherry Hill (1st)..................08002
Cherry Mall, Sta. Cherry Hill..08034
Chester (1st)......................07930
Chestnut, Sta. Union............07083
Cinnaminson, Br. Riverton.....08077
Circle, Br. Trenton...............08638
Circle City, Br. Phillipsburg...08865
Circle Plaza, Br.
  Manasquan......................08736
Clark, Br. Rahway................07066
Clarksboro.........................08020
Clarksburg.........................08510
Clayton.............................08312
Clementon (1st)..................08021
Cliffside Park (1st)...............07010
Cliffwood...........................07721
Cliffwood Beach, Br.
  Keyport.........................07735
CLIFTON (1st) (see
  appendix)
Clinton (1st).......................08809
Clinton Hill, Sta. Newark.......07108
Closter (1st).......................07624
Collingswood, Br. Camden.....08108
Cologne.............................08213
Colonia, Br. Rahway.............07067
Colts Neck.........................07722
Columbia............................07832

Columbus...........................08022
Convent Station, Br.
  Morristown......................07961
Cookstown..........................08511
Coytesville, Br. Fort Lee.......07024
Cranbury (1st).....................08512
Cranford (1st).....................07016
Creamridge........................08514
Cresskill (1st).....................07626
Crosswicks.........................08515
Dayton (1st).......................08810
Deal.................................07723
Deepwater (1st)..................08023
Deerfield Street...................08313
Delair, Br. Camden...............08110
Delanco, Br. Riverside..........08075
Delawanna, Sta. Clifton........07014
Delaware...........................07833
Delmont.............................08314
Delran, Br. Riverside............08075
Demarest (1st)....................07627
Dennisville.........................08214
Denville (1st)......................07834
Deptford, Br. Woodbury........08096
Dividing Creek.....................08315
Doddtown, Sta. East Orange..07017
Dorchester.........................08316
Dorothy.............................08317
Dover (1st).........................07801
Drew University, Br.
  Madison..........................07940
Dumont (1st)......................07628
Dundee, Br. Passaic.............07055
Dunellen (1st).....................08812
East, Sta. Paterson..............07514
East Brunswick (1st).............08816
East Camden, Sta. Camden....08105
East Hanover (1st)...............07936
East Keansburg, Br.
  Keansburg.......................07734
East Millstone, Br. Somerset..08873
EAST ORANGE (1st) (see
  appendix)
East Paterson (1st)..............07407
East Rutherford, Br.
  Rutherford......................07073
East Side, Sta. Bridgeton.....08302
East Windsor, Br.
  Hightstown.....................08520
Eatontown (1st)..................07724
Edgewater (1st)..................07020
Edison (1st)........................08817
Egg Harbor City (1st)...........08215
Elberon, Sta. Long Branch.....07740
ELIZABETH (1st) (see
  appendix)
Elizabethport, Sta. Elizabeth..07206
Elmer...............................08318
Elmora, Sta. Elizabeth.........07202
Elwood.............................08217
Emerson (1st).....................07630
ENGLEWOOD (1st) (see
  appendix)
Englewood Cliffs, Br.
  Englewood......................07632
Englishtown (1st).................07726
Ernston, Sta. Parlin.............08859
Essex Fells.........................07021
Estell Manor.......................08319
Ewan................................08025
Fair Haven, Br. Red Bank......07701
Fair Lawn (1st)....................07410
Fairfield, Br. Caldwell..........07006

Fairton..............................08320
Fairview (1st)......................07022
Fanwood (1st).....................07023
Far Hills............................07931
Farmingdale (1st)................07727
Five Corners, Sta. Jersey
  City..............................07308
Flagtown............................08821
Flanders............................07836
Flemington (1st)..................08822
Florence............................08518
Florham Park (1st)...............07932
Fords, Br. Perth Amboy........08863
Forked River.......................08731
Fort Dix, Br. Trenton............08640
Fort Lee (1st).....................07024
Fort Monmouth, Br. Red
  Bank.............................07703
Fortescue..........................08321
Forty Eighth Street, Br.
  Union City......................07087
Forty Third Street, Sta.
  Union City......................07087
Foster Village, Sta.
  Bergenfield......................07621
Franklin (1st)......................07416
Franklin Lakes (1st)..............07417
Franklin Park.......................08823
Franklinville.........................08322
Freehold (1st).....................07728
Frenchtown.........................08825
Garden State, Sta. Paramus..07652
Garfield (1st)......................07026
Garwood (1st).....................07027
General Lafayette, Sta.
  Jersey City......................07304
Gibbsboro...........................08026
Gibbstown...........................08027
Gillette..............................07933
Gladstone...........................07934
Glassboro (1st)....................08028
Glasser.............................07837
Glen Gardner......................08826
Glen Ridge (1st)..................07028
Glen Rock, Br. Ridgewood.....07452
Glendora............................08029
Glenwood...........................07418
Gloucester City (1st)............0803.)
Goshen.............................08218
Grantwood, Sta. Cliffside
  Park.............................07010
Grasselli, Sta. Linden............07036
Great Meadows....................07838
Green Brook, Br. Dunellen.....08812
Green Creek........................08219
Green Pond, R. Br.
  Newfoundland...................07435
Green Village.......................07935
Greendell...........................07839
Greenville, Sta. Jersey City...07305
Greenwich..........................08323
Grenloch............................08032
Greystone Park, Br. Morris
  Plains............................07950
Grove, Sta. Bloomfield.........07003
Groveville, Br. Trenton.........08620
Guttenberg, Br. West New
  York.............................07093
HACKENSACK (1st) (see
  appendix)
Hackettstown (1st)..............07840
Haddon Heights (1st)............08035
Haddonfield (1st)................08033

Mainesport	08036
Haledon-North Haledon, Br. Paterson	07508
Hamburg	07419
Hamilton Square, Br. Trenton	08690
Hammonton (1st)	08037
Hampton (1st)	08827
Hancocks Bridge	08038
Harrington Park	07640
Harrison (1st)	07029
Harrisonville	08039
Harvey Cedars, Br. Beach Haven	08008
Hasbrouck Heights, Br. Hackensack	07604
Haskell (1st)	07420
Haworth	07641
Hawthorne, Br. Paterson (see appendix)	
Hazlet (1st)	07730
Heislerville	08324
Helmetta	08828
Hewitt	07421
Hibernia	07842
High Bridge	08829
Highland Lakes	07422
Highland Park, Br. New Brunswick	08904
Highlands	07732
Hightstown (1st)	08520
Hillcrest, Sta. Paterson	07502
Hillsdale (1st)	07642
Hillside, Br. Elizabeth	07205
Ho Ho Kus (1st)	07423
Hoboken (1st)	07030
Holmdel (1st)	07733
Hopatcong (1st)	07843
Hope	07844
Hopewell (1st)	08525
Howell, Br. Farmingdale	07727
Hudson City, Sta. Jersey City	07307
Hudson Heights, Sta. North Bergen	07047
Imlaystown	08526
Industrial Hillside, Br. Elizabeth	07205
Ironbound, Sta. Newark	07105
Ironia	07845
Irvington, Br. Newark	07111
Iselin (1st)	08830
Island Heights	08732
Jackson (1st)	08527
Jackson Avenue, Sta. Jersey City	07305
Jamesburg (1st)	08831
JERSEY CITY (1st) (see appendix)	
Jobstown	08041
Johnsonburg	
Journal Square, Sta. Jersey City	07306
Juliustown	08042
Jutland, R. Br. Clinton	08809
Keansburg (1st)	07734
Kearny (1st)	07032
Keasbey	08832
Kendall Park (1st)	08824
Kenilworth (1st)	07033
Kenvil	07847
Keyport (1st)	07735
Kingston	08528

Kinnelon, Br. Butler	07405
Kirkwood	08043
Lafayette	07848
Lake Hiawatha (1st)	07034
Lake Hopatcong	07849
Lakehurst (1st)	08733
Lakehurst Naval Air Station, Br. Lakehurst	08733
Lakeland, R. Sta. Blackwood	08012
Lakewood (1st)	08701
Lambertville (1st)	08530
Landing	07850
Landisville	08326
Lanoka Harbor	08734
Laurel Springs, Br. Clementon	08021
Laurence Harbor, Br. South Amboy	08879
Lavallette	08735
Lawnside	08045
Lawrenceville, Br. Trenton	08648
Layton	07851
Lebanon (1st)	08833
Ledgewood	07852
Leeds Point	08220
Leesburg	08327
Leona, Jo.	07737
Leonia, Br. Hackensack	07605
Liberty Corner	07938
Lincoln Park	07035
Lincroft (1st)	07738
Linden (1st)	07036
Lindenwold, Br. Clementon	08021
Linwood (1st)	08221
Little Falls (1st)	07424
Little Ferry (1st)	07643
Little Silver (1st)	07739
Little York	08834
Livingston (1st)	07039
Locust, Br. Rumson	07760
Lodi (1st)	07644
Long Beach, Br. Beach Haven	08008
Long Branch (1st)	07740
Long Valley	07853
Longport, Br. Atlantic City	08403
Lopatcong, Br. Phillipsburg	08865
Lumberton	08048
Lyndhurst, Br. Rutherford	07071
Lyons, Br. Basking Ridge	07939
Madison (1st)	07940
Magnolia	08049
Mahwah (1st)	07430
Malaga	08328
Mall, Sta. Short Hills	07078
Manahawkin	08050
Manasquan (1st)	08736
Manor Park, Br. Brick Town	08723
Mantoloking	08738
Mantua (1st)	08051
Manville (1st)	08835
Maple Shade (1st)	08052
Maplecrest, Sta. Maplewood	07040
Maplewood (1st)	07040
Margate City, Br. Atlantic City	08402
Marlboro	07746
Marlton (1st)	08053
Marmora	08223
Martinsville	08836
Masonville	08054
Matawan (1st)	07747

Mauricetown	08329
Mays Landing (1st)	08330
Maywood, Br. Hackensack	07607
Mc Afee	07428
Mc Guire A F B, Br. Trenton	08641
Meadowview, Sta. North Bergen	07047
Medford (1st)	08055
Medford Lakes, Br. Medford	08055
Mendham (1st)	07945
Menlo Park, Sta. Edison	08817
Mercerville, Br. Trenton	08619
Merchantville, Br. Camden (see appendix)	
Metuchen (1st)	08840
Mickleton	08056
Middlebush, Br. Somerset	08873
Middlesex (1st)	08846
Middletown (1st)	07748
Middleville	07855
Midland Park (1st)	07432
Midtown, Sta. Newark	07102
Milford (1st)	08848
Military Ocean Terminal, Sta. Bayonne	07002
Millburn (1st)	07041
Millington	07946
Milltown (1st)	08850
Millville (1st)	08332
Milmay	08340
Milton, Sta. Oak Ridge	07438
Minotola	08341
Mizpah	08342
Monitor, Sta. West New York	07093
Monmouth Beach	07750
Monmouth Junction	08852
Monroe	07434
Monroeville	08343
MONTCLAIR (1st) (see appendix)	
Montvale (1st)	07645
Montville (1st)	07045
Moonachie, Br. Rutherford	07074
Moorestown (1st)	08057
Morganville	07751
Morris Plains (1st)	07950
Morris Street, Sta. Morristown	07960
Morristown (1st)	07960
Convent Station, Br.	07961
Morris Street, Sta.	07960
Mount Arlington	07856
Mount Ephraim (1st)	08059
Mount Freedom	07970
Mount Holly (1st)	08060
Mount Royal	08061
Mountain Lakes (1st)	07046
Mountainside, Br. Westfield	07092
Muhlenberg, Sta. Plainfield	07060
Mullica Hill	08062
Murray Hill, Br. New Providence	07974
National Park	08063
Navesink	07752
Neptune (1st)	07753
Neptune City, Br. Neptune	07753
Nesianic Station	08853
Netcong	07857
Netherwood, Sta. Plainfield	07062
NEW BRUNSWICK (1st) (see appendix)	
New Egypt	08533
New Gretna	08224
New Lisbon	08064

New Milford (1st) 07646
New Monmouth, Br.
   Middletown 07748
New Providence (1st) 07974
New Shrewsbury, Br.
   Eatontown 07724
New Vernon 07976
NEWARK (1st) (see
   appendix)
Newfield 08344
Newfoundland 07435
Newport 08345
Newton (1st) 07860
Newtonville 08346
Nixon, Sta. Edison 08817
Norma 08347
Normandy Beach 08739
North, Sta. Newark 07104
North Arlington, Br. Kearny 07032
North Bergen (1st) 07047
North Branch, Br.
   Somerville 08876
North Brunswick, Br. New
   Brunswick 08902
North Cape May, Br. Cape
   May 08204
North Center, Sta.
   Bloomfield 07003
North Elizabeth, Sta.
   Elizabeth 07208
North Hackensack, Sta.
   River Edge 07661
North Plainfield, Br.
   Plainfield 07060
North Wildwood, Br.
   Wildwood 08260
Northfield (1st) 08225
*Northvale (1st) 07647
Norwood (1st) 07648
Number Five, Sta. Asbury
   Park 07712
Number One, Sta. Ocean
   Grove 07756
Nutley, Br. Newark 07110
Oak Ridge (1st) 07438
Oakhurst (1st) 07755
Oakland (1st) 07436
Oaklyn, Br. Camden 08107
Ocean, Br. Asbury Park 07712
Ocean City (1st) 08226
Ocean Gate 08740
Ocean Grove (1st) 07756
Ocean View 08230
Oceanport 07757
Oceanville 08231
Ogdensburg 07439
Old Bridge (1st) 08857
Old Tappan, Br. Westwood ..07675
Oldwick 08858
Oradell (1st) 07649
ORANGE (1st) (see
   appendix)
Osbornsville, Br. Brick Town 08723
Outwater, Sta. Garfield 07026
Overbrook, Sta. Cedar Grove 07009
Oxford 07863
Packanack Lake, Sta.
   Wayne 07470
Palisade, Sta. Fort Lee 07024
Palisades Park (1st) 07650
Palmyra (1st) 08065
Pamrapo, Sta. Bayonne 07002
Paramus (1st) 07652

Park, Sta. Paterson 07513
Park Ridge (1st) 07656
Parlin (1st) 08859
Parsippany (1st) 07054
PASSAIC (1st) (see
   appendix)
Passaic Park, Sta. Passaic ..07055
PATERSON (1st) (see
   appendix)
Pattenburg 08860
Paulsboro (1st) 08066
Peapack 07977
Pedricktown 08067
Pemberton 08068
Pennington (1st) 08534
Penns Grove (1st) 08069
Pennsauken, Br. Camden 08110
Pennsville (1st) 08070
Pequannock (1st) 07440
Perrineville 08535
PERTH AMBOY (1st) (see
   appendix)
Phillipsburg (1st) 08865
Pine Beach 08741
Pine Brook (1st) 07058
Pine Hill, Br. Clementon 08021
Piscataway (1st) 08854
Pitman (1st) 08071
Pittstown 08867
PLAINFIELD (1st) (see
   appendix)
Plainsboro 08536
Plaza, Sta. Willingboro 08046
Pleasantville (1st) 08232
Pluckemin 07978
Point Pleasant, Br. Point
   Pleasant Beach 08742
Point Pleasant Beach (1st) ..08742
Pomona 08240
Pompton Lakes (1st) 07442
Pompton Plains (1st) 07444
Port Elizabeth 08348
Port Monmouth 07758
Port Murray 07865
Port Norris 08349
Port Reading 07064
Port Republic 08241
Pottersville 07979
Preakness, Sta. Wayne 07470
Presidential Lakes, R. Br.
   Browns Mills 08015
Princeton (1st) 08540
Princeton Junction 08550
Quakertown 08868
Quinton 08072
RAHWAY (1st) (see
   appendix)
Ramsey (1st) 07446
Rancocas 08073
Randolph, Sta. Dover 07801
Raritan (1st) 08869
Readington 08870
Red Bank (1st) 07701
   Fair Haven, Br. 07701
   Fort Monmouth, Br. 07703
   Shrewsbury, Br. 07701
   Suburban, Br. 07701
   Westboro, Sta. 07701
Richland 08350
Richwood 08074
Ridgefield (1st) 07657
Ridgefield Park (1st) 07660
RIDGEWOOD (1st) (see

appendix)
Ringoes 08551
Ringwood 07456
Rio Grande 08242
Ritz, Sta. Garfield 07026
River Edge (1st) 07661
River Road, Sta. Fair Lawn ..07410
River Street, Sta. Paterson ..07524
River Vale, Br. Westwood 07675
Riverdale (1st) 07457
Riverside (1st) 08075
Riverton (1st) 03077
Roadstown 08351
Robbinsville, Br. Trenton 08691
Rochelle Park (1st) 07662
Rockaway (1st) 07866
Rockleigh, Br. Northvale 07647
Rocky Hill 08553
Roebling 08554
Roosevelt 08555
Roseland (1st) 07068
Roselle, Br. Elizabeth 07203
Roselle Park, Br. Elizabeth ..07204
Rosemont 08556
Rosenhayn 08352
Roseville, Sta. Newark 07107
Rumson (1st) 07760
Runnemede (1st) 08078
RUTHERFORD (1st) (see,
   appendix)
Saddle Brook, Br. Rochelle
   Park 07662
Saddle River (1st) 07458
Salem (1st) 08079
Sayreville (1st) 08872
Schooleys Mountain 07870
Scobeyville, R. Br.
   Eatontown 07724
Scotch Plains (1st) 07076
Sea Bright, Br. Rumson 07760
Sea Girt 08750
Sea Isle City (1st) 08243
Seabrook, Br. Bridgeton 08302
Seaside Heights 08751
Seaside Park 08752
Secaucus (1st) 07094
Sergeantsville 08557
Sewaren 07077
Sewell 08080
Shiloh 08353
Ship Bottom, Br. Beach
   Haven 08008
Shore Acres, Br. Brick Town 08723
Short Hills (1st) 07078
Shrewsbury, Br. Red Bank ..07701
Sicklerville 08081
Skillman 08558
Smithville, Br. Absecon 08201
Somerdale (1st) 08083
Some's Point (1st) 08244
Somerset (1st) 08873
Somerville (1st) 08876
   North Branch, Br. 08876
South, Sta. Newark 07114
South Amboy (1st) 08879
South Bound Brook (1st) 08880
South Branch 08881
South Camden, Sta.
   Camden 08104
South Dennis 08245
South Hackensack, Br.
   Hackensack 07606
South Livingston, Sta.
   Livingston 07039

South Orange (1st)	07079
South Paterson, Sta. Paterson	07503
South Plainfield (1st)	07080
South River (1st)	08882
South Seaville	08246
South Toms River, Br. Toms River	08753
South Vineland, Sta. Vineland	08360
Sparta (1st)	07871
Spotswood (1st)	08884
Spring Lake (1st)	07762
Spring Lake Heights, Br. Spring Lake	07762
Springfield (1st)	07081
Stanhope	07874
Stanton	08885
State Hospital, Br. Trenton	08625
Stewartsville	08886
Stillwater	07875
Stirling (1st)	07980
Stockholm	07460
Stockton	08559
Stone Harbor	08247
Stratford (1st)	08084
Strathmere	08248
Suburban, Br. Red Bank	07701
Succasunna (1st)	07876
Summit (1st)	07901
Summit Avenue, Sta. Union City	07087
Surf City, Br. Beach Haven	08008
Sussex (1st)	07461
Swartswood	07877
Swedesboro	08085
Tabor	07878
Taurus, Sta. West New York	07093
Teaneck (1st)	07666
Tenafly (1st)	07670
Tennent	07763
Teterboro, Br. Hackensack	07608
Thorofare	08086
Three Bridges	08887
Titusville	08560
Toms River (1st)	08753
Totowa, Br. Paterson (see appendix)	
Towaco	07082
Town Center, Br. Orange	07051
Townley, Sta. Union	07083
Townsends Inlet, Sta. Sea Isle City	08243
Tranquility	07879
TRENTON (1st) (see appendix)	
Tuckahoe	08250
Tuckerton	08087
Turnersville, Br. Blackwood	08012
Tyler Park, Sta. North Bergen	07047
Union (1st)	07083
Union Beach, Br. Keyport	07735
Union Center, Sta. Union	07083
Union City (1st)	07087
Union Square, Sta. Elizabeth	07201
Upper Montclair, Sta. Montclair	07043
Uptown, Sta. Hoboken	07030
V A Hospital, Sta. East Orange	07018
Vailsburg, Sta. Newark	07106
Valley, Sta. Wayne	07470
Vauxhall (1st)	07088
Ventnor City, Br. Atlantic City	08406
Vernon	07462
Verona, Br. Montclair	07044
Vienna	07880
Villas	08251
Vincentown	08088
Vineland (1st)	08360
Voorhees, R. Br. Kirkwood	08043
Waldwick (1st)	07463
Wall, Br. Belmar	07719
Wallington, Br. Passaic	07057
Wallpack Center	07881
Wanaque	07465
Waretown	08758
Warren, Br. Plainfield	07060
Warren Point, Sta. Fair Lawn	07410
Washington (1st)	07882
Washington Park, Sta. Newark	07102
Washington Street, Sta. Hoboken	07030
Watchung, Br. Plainfield	07060
Waterford Works	08089
Watsessing, Sta. Bloomfield	07003
Wayne (1st)	07470
Weehawken, Br. Union City	07087
Weequahic, Sta. Newark	07112
Wenonah	08090
West, Sta. Newark	07103
West Berlin	08091
West Caldwell, Br. Caldwell	07006
West Carteret, Sta. Carteret	07008
West Collingswood, Br. Camden	08107
West Creek	08092
West End, Sta. Long Branch	07740
West Englewood, Sta. Teaneck	07666
West Hudson, Sta. Kearny	07032
West Keansburg, Br. Keansburg	07734
West Long Branch (1st)	07764
West Milford	07480
West New York (1st)	07093
West Orange, Br. Orange	07052
West Paterson, Br. Little Falls	07424
West Side, Sta. Jersey City	07304
West Side, Sta. Hoboken	07030
West Trenton, Br. Trenton	08628
Westboro, Sta. Red Bank	07701
WESTFIELD (1st) (see appendix)	
Westmont, Br. Camden	08108
Westville (1st)	08093
Westwood (1st)	07675
Wharton (1st)	07885
Whippany (1st)	07981
White House Station	08889
Whitehouse	08888
Whitesboro	08252
Whiting, Br. Lakehurst	08759
Wickatunk	07765
Wildwood (1st)	08260
Wildwood Crest, Br. Wildwood	08260
Williamstown (1st)	08094
Willingboro (1st)	08046
Windsor	08561
Winslow	08095
Wood-Ridge, Br. Rutherford (see appendix)	
Woodbine	08270
Woodbridge (1st)	07095
Woodbury (1st)	08096
Blackwood Terrace, Br.	08096
Deptford, Br.	08096
Woodbury Heights, Br.	08097
Woodbury Heights, Br. Woodbury	08097
Woodcliff, Sta. North Bergen	07047
Woodcliff Lake, Br. Westwood	07675
Woodcrest, Sta. Cherry Hill	08003
Woodlynne, Br. Camden	08107
Woodstown (1st)	08098
Wrightstown (1st)	08562
Wyckoff (1st)	07481
Yardville, Br. Trenton	08620
Zarephath	08890

Atlantic City NEW JERSEY   Appendix

ATLANTIC CITY   084

POST OFFICE BOXES

Box Nos.		
A-1	Main Office	04
1-1430	Main Office	04
421-597	Longport Br.	03
2000-2999	Ventnor Br.	06
3001-3246	Margate Br.	02

STATIONS, BRANCHES AND UNITS

Longport Br.	03
Margate City Br.	02
Ventnor City Br.	06
General Delivery	01
Postmaster	01

APARTMENTS, HOTELS, MOTELS

Admiral Apartments, 2 S Hartford Ave	01
Barclay Court Apartments, 9 S Penna Ave	01
Best Of Life Apartments, 129 S Va Ave	01
Biarritz Apartments, 37 S Iowa Ave	01

Atlantic City (Con.)   084

Chelsea Towers, 3817
   Ventnor Ave 01
Emmanuel Apartments, 1526
   Pacific Ave 01
Galbreath Apartments, 1500
   Pacific Ave 01
Grammercy Court
   Apartments, 14 Maine
   Ave 01
Haverford Apartments, 114 S
   Va Ave 01
Loumar Apartments, 1329
   Pacific Ave 01
Manhattan Apartments, 1106
   Atl Ave 01
Mayfair Apartments, S Albany
   Ave 01
Ocean Manor Apartments,
   101 Boardwalk 01
Park Lane Apartments, 117 S
   Illinois Ave 01
Plaza Apartments, Plaza And
   Boardwalk 01
Prestin Apartments, 3 N
   Penna Ave 01
Riviera Apartments, 116 S
   Raleigh Ave 01
Town House Apartments, 64
   S S Car Ave 01
Vermont Apartments, 245 S
   Vermont Ave 01

GOVERNMENT OFFICES

NAFEC 05

CAMDEN   081

POST OFFICE BOXES

Box Nos.
1-148   Audubon Br 06
1-218   Oaklyn Br 07
1-246   Pennsauken Br. 10
1-349   Collingswood
        Br 08
1-415   Delair Br 10
1-899   Main Office 01
1000-1099   Main Office 01
1001-1399   Merchantville
        Br 09
1201-1367   East Camden
        Sta 05
1900-1999   Main Office 01

STATIONS, BRANCHES AND UNITS

Audubon Br 06
Collingswood Br 08
Delair Br 10
East Camden Sta 05
Merchantville Br 09
Oaklyn Br 07
Pennsauken Br 10
South Camden Sta 04
West Collingswood Br 07

Westmont Br 08
Woodlynne Br 07
General Delivery 01
Postmaster 01

APARTMENTS, HOTELS, MOTELS

Ablett Village Housing Unit,
   E State & River Rd. 05
Audubon Park Housing Unit ... 06
Beacon Place, 1440
   Sheridan 04
Branch Village Housing Unit,
   9th & Van Hook 04
Canterbury, 9th & Morgan 04
Chelton Terr Housing Unit
   7th & Chelton 04
Cooper River Plaza, 5105
   North Park Drive 09
Crescent, 1624 Independence
   Rd 04
Crestfair, 8th & Morgan 04
Crestwood, 301 Champion
   Ave 07
Cuthbert Manor, East
   Cuthbert Rd 08
East State Village, East
   State & Harrison Ave 05
Eldridge Gardens, Eldridge &
   Taylor 07
Everett Gardens Housing
   Unit, 1507 S 7th St 04
Ferry Station, Ferry Ave : Old
   White Horse Pike 04
Franklin Place, Hull Rd 04
Haddon View, 1 Macarthur
   Blvd 04
Heather House, 201 Cuthbert
   Rd 07
Hillcrest, 215 E Garfield Ave ... 08
John F Kennedy Housing Unit,
   21st & Westminister 05
John Wesley Village, 805 N.
   Front 02
Marina Park, Cooper River
   Dr 68
Mc Guire Gardens Housing
   Unit, 21st & Westminister .. 04
Northgate, 7th & Linden 04
Parkview, White Hrs Pk &
   Collins Ave 07
Penn Gardens, 46th & Amon
   Ave 10
Penn Manor, Union &
   Stockton Ave 09
Plaza Motor, 5th & Cooper ... 02
Roosevelt Manor Housing
   Unit, 8th & Central Ave .. 04
Stockton Station, Dudley &
   Pleasant 05
Towne Park, 8th & Market 02
Walt Whitman, Broadway &
   Cooper 02
Washington Park, 342
   Marlton Ave 05
Westfield Acres, 31st &
   Westfield Ave 05
Westfield Gardens, 32nd &
   Westfield Ave 05
Westfield Towers 32nd And
   Westfield Ave 05

GOVERNMENT OFFICES

City Hall, 6th & Market 01
Post Office, 401 Market 01

HOSPITALS

Cooper, 6th & Stevens 03
Our Lady Of Lourdes, Haddon
   & Vesper Blvd 03
West Jersey, Mt Ephraim &
   Lansdowne 04

UNIVERSITIES AND COLLEGES

Rutgers College Of South
   Jersey, 406 Penn 02

CHERRY HILL   080

POST OFFICE BOXES

Box Nos.
A-D   Main Office 02
1-499   Main Office 02
500-899   Woodcrest
         Station 03

STATIONS, BRANCHES AND UNITS

Cherry Mall Sta 34
Woodcrest Sta 03
General Delivery 02
Postmaster 02

APARTMENTS, HOTELS, MOTELS

Chapel Manor 606 Cooper
   Landing Rd 34
Cherry Hill Apartments E &
   W Route 38 34
Cherry Hill Inn Route 38 34
Cherry Hill Lodge Route 38 .. 34
Colonial Apartments E & W
   836 Cooper Landing Rd ... 34
Colonial Motel Route 38 34
Country Squire Motel Route
   70 34
Hillside Motel Route 38 34
Holiday Inn Route 70 34
King George Motel Route 70 .. 34
Landmark Apartments Route
   70 & Interstate 295 34
Parkway Apartments Park
   Blvd & Kings Hwy 34
Plaza Towers 1200 Marlton
   Pk E 34
Provincial Apartments E & W
   Chestnut St 34
Rickshaw Inn Route 70 34
Sheraton Poste Inn Route 70 .. 34
Somerset House Apartments
   Cooper Landing Rd 34
Stuyvesant Terrace
   Apartments Cooper
   Landing 34
Sussex House Apartments
   Kings Hwy E 34
Towers Of Windsor
   Apartments Chapel Ave ... 34
Wallworth Park Apartments
   Park Blvd & Kings Hwy ... 34

Cherry Hill (Con.)   080

BUILDINGS

Barclay Pavilion Route 70 34
Barclay Shopping Center
  Route 70 34
Cherry Hill Mall Route 38 &
  Haddonfield Rd 34
Cherry Hill Plaza Route 70 34
Ellisburg Shopping Center
  Kings Hwy N 34
One Cherry Hill Mall Route
  38 & Haddonfield Rd 34
Provincial Executive Bldg
  Route 38 34
Woodcrest Shopping Center
  Berlin Rd & Browning Ln 03
523 Building Route 38 &
  Hollywood Ave 34

GOVERNMENT OFFICES

Cherry Hill Post Office 1588
  Kings Hwy N 02
Cherry Hill Township Bldg
  820 Mercer St 34
Woodcrest Station Cherry Hill
  Post Office Woodcrest 63

HOSPITALS

Cherry Hill Medical Center
  Chapel Ave & Cooper
  Landing Rd 34

CLIFTON   070

POST OFFICE BOXES

Box Nos.
1-417   Main Office 15
501-699   Allwood Sta 12
701-899   Athenia Sta 13
901-1125   Delawanna
           Sta............... 14

STATIONS, BRANCHES AND UNITS

Allwood Sta 12
Athenia Sta 13
Delawanna Sta 14
General Delivery 15
Postmaster 15

APARTMENTS, HOTELS, MOTELS

Colonial Gardens, 470 Piaget
  Ave 11
Country Club Towers, 100-
  140 Hepburn Rd 12
Franklin Gardens 11
Garret Village, 948 Valley Rd. 13
Jefferson Gardens 11
Maple Gardens, 765 Clifton
  Ave 13
Martha Washington, 1401
  Van Houten Ave 13
Middle Village, 24 Day 11

Richfield Village Gardens 12
Styertowne 12
Williamsburg N, 565 Grove...... 13
Williamsburg S, 605 Grove...... 13

EAST ORANGE   070

POST OFFICE BOXES

Box Nos.
1-1999   Main Office 19
2001-2999 Central Sta 19
3001-3999 Brick Church
           Sta............... 19
4001-4999 Ampere 19

STATIONS, BRANCHES AND UNITS

Ampere Sta 17
Brick Church Sta 18
Central Sta 18
Doddtown 17
V A Hospital Sta 18
General Delivery 19
Postmaster 19

HOSPITALS

East Orange General
  Hospital, 300 Central Ave ... 19
Veterans Administration
  Hospital, Tremont Ave 19

MILITARY INSTALLATIONS

National Guard Armory, 215
  N Graton Pkwy 17

UNIVERSITIES AND COLLEGES

Upsafa College, 345
  Prospect 19

ELIZABETH   072

POST OFFICE BOXES

Box Nos.
A-L   Industrial Br 05
A-Z   Main Office 07
1-85   Hillside Br 05
1-196   Roselle Park
           Sta............... 04
1-230   Elizabethtown
           Sta............... 06
1-264   Roselle Sta 03
1-697   Main Office 07
601-728   Industrial Br ... 05
901-954   North Elizabeth
           Sta............... 08

STATIONS, BRANCHES AND UNITS

Bayway Sta 02
Betsytown Sta 01
Elizabethport Sta 06
Elmora Sta 02
Hillside Br 05
Industrial Hillside Br 05
North Elizabeth Sta 08
Roselle Br 03
Roselle Park Br 04
Union Square Sta 01
General Delivery 07
Postmaster 07

APARTMENTS, HOTELS, MOTELS

Chilton Hall Apartments 02
Chilton Towers, 220 W Jersey .. 02
Elizabeth Carteret, 1155 E
  Jersey 07
Ford Leonard Towers, 71
  Division 01
Golden Age, 31 Cherry 02
Hancock House, 1380 North
  Ave 08
Hayes House, 330 W Jersey 02
John F Kennedy Arms, 70
  Westfield Ave 08
Park East, 1065 E Jersey 01
Pierce Manor Apartments,
  Irvington Ave 08
Queen Elizabeth, 801 N
  Broad 08
Queen Mary, 1341 North Ave.. 08
Salem Park Apartments,
  Salem Park 08
Templeton Arms, N Broad........ 08
Tudor Court Apartments, 800
  N Broad 08
Winfield Scott, 323 N Broad.. 07

BUILDINGS

Atbender, 1143 E Jersey 01
American Type, 200 Elmora
  Ave 07
Bayway Terminal, 666 S
  Front 02
Elizabethtown Plaza, 2
  Elizabethtown Plaza............. 02
Hersh Tower, 125 Broad 01
Industrial Park, 107
  Trumbull 06
Martin, 1139 E Jersey 01
Medical Arts, 230 W Jersey.... 02
New Jersey Employment
  Office, 1115 E Jersey.......... 01
Public Library, 1 S Broad 02
Social Security, 268 N Broad.. 01
Y M C A, 135 Madison Ave 01
Y W C A, 1131 E Jersey....... 01

GOVERNMENT OFFICES

City Hall, 50 W Scott Pl........ 07
Court House, 2 Broad 07

HOSPITALS

Alexian Brothers, 655 E
  Jersey 06

Elizabeth (Con.) 072

Elizabeth General. 925 E
Jersey 01
Saint Elizabeths, 204 S
Broad 07

ENGLEWOOD 076

POST OFFICE BOXES

Box Nos.
1-752   Englewood 31
900-1264   Englewood
      Cliffs Br 32

STATIONS, BRANCHES AND UNITS

Englewood Cliffs Br 32
General Delivery 31
Postmaster 31

HACKENSACK 076

POST OFFICE BOXES

Box Nos.
1-237   Leonia Br 05
1-347   Bogota 03
1-454   Hasbrouck
         Heights 04
1-970   Main Office 02
31-54   Maywood 07
801-947   Maywood 07
1501-2388   South
         Hackensack 06

STATIONS, BRANCHES AND UNITS

Bogota Br 03
Hasbrouck Heights Br 04
Leonia Br 05
Maywood Br 07
South Hackensack Br 06
Teterboro Br 08
General Delivery 01
Postmaster 02

HOSPITALS

Hackensack Hospital, 22
  Hospital Pl Hackensack 01
South Bergen Hospital, 214
  Terrace Ave Hasbrouck
  Heights 04

JERSEY CITY 073

POST OFFICE BOXES

Box Nos.
A-M   Bergen Sta 04

A-P   Hudson City
          Sta 07
A-Q   General
          Lafayette Sta 04
1-900   Main Office 03
7A-7DDD   Hudson City
          Sta 07
4001-4419   Bergen 04
5001-5148   Greenville Sta 05
6471-6950   Journal Square
          Sta 06
7001-7900   Hudson City
          Sta 07
8001-8207   Five Corners
          Sta 08
9001-9168   General
          Lafayette Sta 04

STATIONS, BRANCHES AND UNITS

Bergen Sta 04
Five Corners Sta 08
General Lafayette Sta 04
Greenville Sta 05
Hudson City Sta 07
Jackson Avenue Sta 05
Journal Square Sta 06
West Side Sta 04
General Delivery 03
Postmaster 03

APARTMENTS, HOTELS, MOTELS

Alban Court, 2540 Boulevard ... 04
Annabee, 28 Sherman Pl 07
Ariston, 63 Sherman Pl 07
Duncan, 2600 Boulevard 06
Embassy, 151 Sip Ave 06
Fairmount, 2595 Boulevard ... 06
Garrison Apartments, 121
  Garrison Ave 06
Gifford Court, 9 Gifford Ave ... 04
Gifford Gardens, 25 Gifford
  Ave 04
Gifford Hall, 17 Gifford Ave ... 04
Gifford Towers, 2465
  Boulevard 04
Glenwood, 2677 Boulevard 06
Gloria Gables, 131
  Kensington Ave 04
Gothic Towers, 50 Glenwood ... 06
Granada, 129 Magnolia Ave ... 06
Green Gables, 7 Tonnele Ave ... 06
Gregory Park, 280 Henderson . 02
Hampshire House, 20 Tonnele
  Ave 06
Holiday Inn, 180 12th 02
Holland, 9 Journal Sq 06
Jamid Court, 2520 Blvd 06
Lincoln, 137 Kensington Ave ... 04
Madeline Gardens, 40
  Glenwood Ave 05
Madrid, 821 Bergen Ave 06
Mayflower, 65 Tonnele Ave ... 06
Melbro Towers, 340
  Fairmount Ave 06
Melrita, 107 Kensington Ave ... 04
Mitchell, 31 Gifford Ave 04
Park Lane, 70 Danforth Ave ... 05
Plaza, 91 Sip Ave 06
Rosemont, 321 Fairmount
  Ave 06

Royal Park, 145 Kensington
  Ave 04
Saint Johns Apartment 2,
  225 St Pauls Ave 06
Saint Johns Apartments, 10
  Huron Ave 06
Stockadian, 88 Van Reypen ... 06
Sunny Towers, 2500
  Boulevard 04
The Bentley, 9 Bentley Ave ... 04
The Britton, 320 Fairmount
  Ave 06
The Dorian, 5 Bentley Ave ... 04
The Gifford, 11 Gifford Ave ... 04
The Netherlands, 2695 Blvd ... 04
The Sevilla, 2801 Blvd 06
The Shelbourne, 85 Van
  Reypen 06
The Summit, ... 06
The Washington, 2671 Blvd ... 06
Towne House, 57 Sip Ave 06
Windsor, 305 Academy 06

BUILDINGS

Administration, 595 Newark
  Ave 06
Catholic Youth Organization,
  380 Bergen Ave 04
Commercial Trust Company,
  15 Exchange Pl 02
First Jersey National Bank, 1
  Exchange Pl 02
Garden State National Bank ... 02
Harborside Terminal, 34
  Exchange Pl 02
Jersey Journal, 30 Journal Sq. 06
Labor Bank, 26 Journal Sq. ... 06
Lackawanna Terminal, 629
  Grove 02
Medical Arts, 8-12 Clifton Pl. . 04
New Jersey Employment
  Agency, 363 Summit Ave 06
Public Library, 472 Jersey
  Ave 02
Spingarn Arcade, 591
  Summit Ave 06
Trust Company Of New
  Jersey, 921 Bergen Ave 06
Ymca, 654 Bergen Ave 04
Ymca, 604 Bergen Ave 06
Ywca, 270 Fairmount Ave 06

GOVERNMENT OFFICES

Board Of Education, 2
  Harrison Ave 04
City Hall, 280 Grove 02
County Jail, 578 Pavonia Ave . 06
Court House, Newark Ave 06

HOSPITALS

Christ, 176 Palisade Ave 06
Door Of Hope Home &
  Hospital, 503 Garfield Ave ... 05
Elizabeth Kenny Institute,
  Baldwin Ave 04
Fairmount, 136 Summit Ave ... 04
Greenville, 1825 Boulevard 05
Hudson County Tuberculosis,

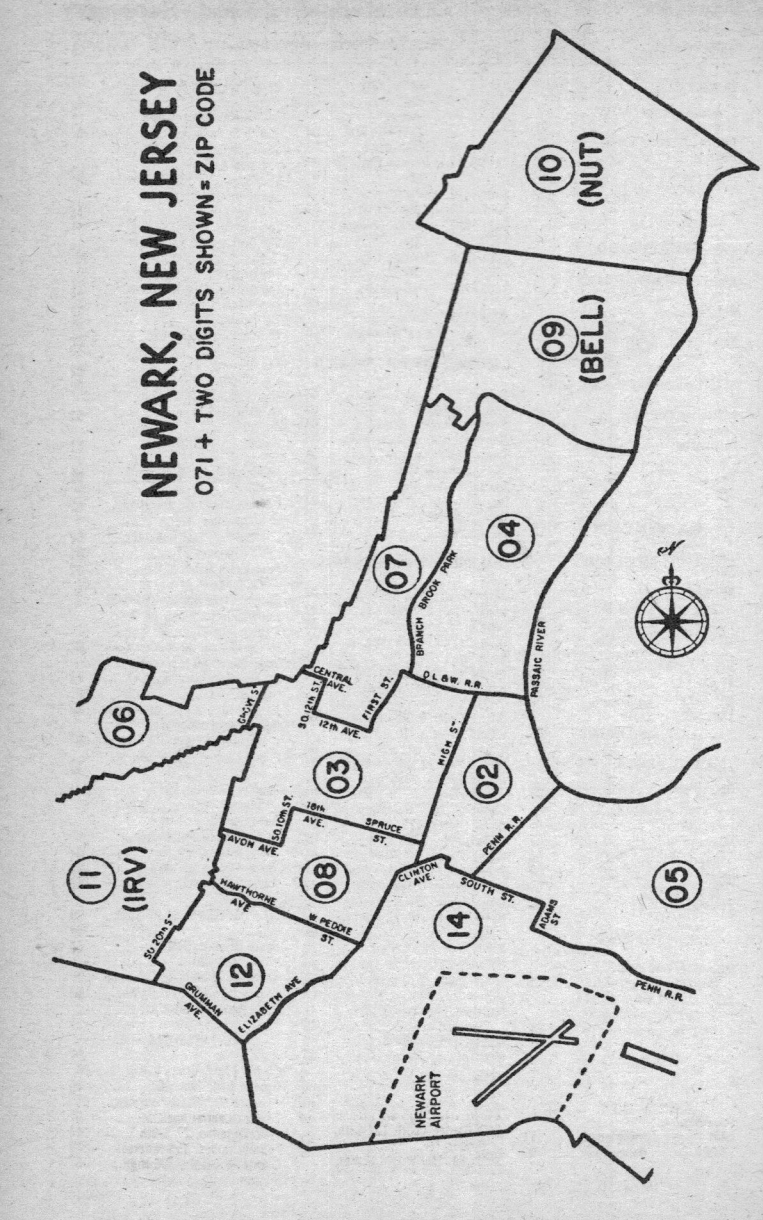

NEWARK, NEW JERSEY

071 + TWO DIGITS SHOWN = ZIP CODE

Jersey City (Con.)   073

100 Clifton Pl	04
Margaret Hague Maternity, Clifton Pl	04
Medical Center, Baldwin Ave	04
Mothers Institute, 400 3rd	02
Pollack, 100 Clifton Pl	04
Saint Francis, 25 Mc Williams Pl	02

UNIVERSITIES AND COLLEGES

College Of Medicine & Dentistry, 24 Baldwin Ave	04
Jersey City State College, 2039 Boulevard	05
Rutgers University, 168 Sip Ave	05
Saint Peters, 2641 Blvd	06

MONTCLAIR   070

POST OFFICE BOXES

Box Nos.

A-J	Verona	44
A-T	Main Office	42
A-Z	Main Office	42
1-341	Verona Br	44
AA-AK	Main Office	42
98-700	Main Office	42
701-937	Upper Montclair Sta	43

STATIONS, BRANCHES AND UNITS

Upper Montclair Sta	43
Verona Br	44
General Delivery	42
Postmaster	42

APARTMENTS, HOTELS, MOTELS

Clairidge House, Clairidge Dr	44
Rockcliffe	42

HOSPITALS

Community, 120 Harrison Ave	42
Mountainside, Bay Ave & Highland Ave	42
Saint Vincents, 45 Elm St	42

UNIVERSITIES AND COLLEGES

Montclair State, Normal Ave & Valley Rd	43

NEWARK   071

POST OFFICE BOXES

Box Nos.

A-N	Irvington	11
1-264	Belleville Br	09

1-268	Nutley Br	10
1-320	Irvington Br	11
1-2000	Main Office	01
2001-2999	South Sta	14
3001-3500	West Sta	03
4001-4400	Weequahic Sta	12
5001-5146	Ironbound Sta	05
6001-6144	Vailsburg Sta	06
7001-7209	Roseville Sta	07
8001-8236	Clinton Hill Sta	08
9001-9207	North Sta	04
10000-10187	Main Office	01

STATIONS, BRANCHES AND UNITS

Academy Sta	02
Belleville Br	09
Clinton Hill Sta	08
Ironbound Sta	05
Irvington Br	11
Midtown Sta	02
North Sta	04
Nutley Br	10
Roseville Sta	07
South Sta	14
Vailsburg Sta	06
Washington Park Sta	02
Weequahic Sta	12
West Sta	03
General Delivery	01
Postmaster	02

APARTMENTS, HOTELS, MOTELS

Archbishop Thomas J Walsh Homes, 1945 Mc Carter Hwy	04
Belmont, 1007 Broad	02
Christopher Columbus Homes, 112 8th Ave	04
Colonnade, 381 Broad	04
Devine Riviera, 169 Clinton Ave	08
Douglas, 15 Hill	01
Essex House, 1050 Broad	02
Felix Fuld Court, 80 Jelliff Ave	08
Franklin D Roosevelt Homes, 35 Riverview Ct	05
Holiday Inn, 430 Broad St	02
Ivy Hill Park, 5 Manor Dr	06
James M Baxter Terrace, 202 Orange	03
Joseph B Bradley Court, 46 N Munn Ave	06
Lincoln Park, 105 Lincoln Park	02
Mac Evoy Court, 140 Roseville Ave	07
Military Park, 16 Park Pl	01
New Tremont, 16 Fulton	01
Normandie, 103 Chancellor Ave	12
Otto Kretchmer Homes, 71 Ludlow	14
Park Lane, 79 Lincoln Park	02
Rev W P Hayes Homes, 71 Boyd	03
Robert Treat, 50 Park Pl	01
Seth Boyden Court, 124 Seth Boyden Ter	14
Stella Windsor Wright Homes,	

159 Spruce	08
Stephen Crane Village, 1 Stephen Crane Plaza	07
Weequahic Park Tower, 455 Elizabeth Ave	12

BUILDINGS

Academy, 17 Academy	02
American Insurance, 15 Washington	02
Broad & Market, 784 Broad	02
Chamber Of Commerce, 24 Branford Pl	02
Commerce Court, 10 Commerce Ct	02
Fatzler, 9 Hill	02
Federal Trust, 24 Commerce	02
Griffith, 605 Broad	02
Kinney, 790 Broad	02
Medical Tower, 31 Lincoln Park	02
Military Park, 60 Park Pl	02
Mutual Benefit Life Insurance, 520 Broad	02
National Newark & Essex, 744 Broad	02
National State Bank, 810 Broad	02
Prudential Insurance Company, 763 Broad	02
Raymond-Commerce, 1180 Raymond Blvd	02
Union, 9 Clinton	02
Wiss, 665 Broad	02

GOVERNMENT OFFICES

Federal Building, 970 Broad St	02
N J State Building, 1100 Raymond Blvd	02
United States Court House, Federal Square	02
United States Post Office, Federal Square	02
Veterans Administration, 20 Washington Pl	02

HOSPITALS

American Legion Memorial, 741 Broadway	04
Babies, 15 Roseville Ave	07
Beth Isreal, 201 Lyons Ave	12
Clara Maass, Franklin Ave. Belleville	09
Columbus, 495 N 13th	07
Doctors, 65 Avon Ave	08
Hospital & Home For Crippled Children, 89 Park Ave	04
Irvington General, 832 Chancellor Ave. Irvington	11
Martland Medical Center, 65 Bergen	07
Newark Convalescent, Ivy Hill	06
Newark Eye & Ear Infirmary, 77 Central Ave	02
Presbyterian, 27 S 9th	07
Saint James, 155 Jefferson	05
Saint Michaels, 306 High	02

Newark (Con.)   071

UNIVERSITIES AND COLLEGES

Essex County Community, 31 Clinton St	02
Newark College Of Engineering, 323 High	02
Rutgers University	02
Rutgers University College Of Pharmacy, 1 Lincoln Ave	04
Seton Hall University Law School, 40 Clinton St	02

NEW BRUNSWICK   085

POST OFFICE BOXES

Box Nos.		
1-1806	North Brunswick Br.	02
1-2020	Main Office	03
1200-1410	Highland Park Br	04

RURAL ROUTES

4	02

STATIONS, BRANCHES AND UNITS

Highland Park Br	04
North Brunswick Br	02
General Delivery	01
Postmaster	01

APARTMENTS, HOTELS, MOTELS

Bishop Towers	01
Colony House	01
Georgetown	02
Holiday Inn	02
Howard Johnson	01
Lionel Village	02
Park Lane	04
Park Town	04

BUILDINGS

National Bank Building	03

GOVERNMENT OFFICES

Highland Park Borough	04
Middlesex County Offices	01
New Brunswick City Hall	03
North Brunswick Township	02

HOSPITALS

Middlesex County Rehabilatation Center, Georges Rd	02
Middlesex General, 180 Somerset St	01
Saint Peters, Easton Ave	03

UNIVERSITIES AND COLLEGES

College Of Agriculture	03
Douglas College	03
Highland Park High	04
Livingston College	03
Middlesex County Vocational	01
New Brunswick Junior High	02
New Brunswick Senior High	02
New Brunswick Theological Seminary	01
Rutgers University	03
Saint Peters High	01

ORANGE   070

POST OFFICE BOXES

Box Nos.		
1-116	Town Center Br	52
1-717	Main Office	51

STATIONS, BRANCHES AND UNITS

Town Center Br	52
West Orange Br	52
General Delivery	50
Postmaster	50

PASSAIC   070

POST OFFICE BOXES

Box Nos.		
1-2999	Main Office	55
3101-3999	Wallington Br	57

STATIONS, BRANCHES AND UNITS

Dundee Sta	55
Passaic Park Sta	55
Wallington Br	57

HOSPITALS

Beth Israel Hospital, 70 Parker Ave	55
Passaic General Hospital, 350 Boulevard	55
Saint Mary Hospital, 211 Pennington Ave	55

PATERSON   075

POST OFFICE BOXES

Box Nos.		
1-296	Park Sta	13
1-352	Totowa Br	11
1-505	Hawthorne Br	07
1-600	Haledon No Haledon Br	08
AA-BM	Main Office	09

301-644	River Street Sta	24
701-1057	South Paterson	03
1101-3250	Main Office	09

STATIONS, BRANCHES AND UNITS

East Sta	14
Haledon-North Haledon Br	08
Hillcrest Sta	02
Park Sta	13
River Street Sta	24
South Paterson Sta	03
Totowa Br	12
General Delivery	10
Postmaster	10

APARTMENTS, HOTELS, MOTELS

Alexander Hamilton, 55 Church	05
Emperor Motel Lodge, US Highway 46	12
Kent Village, 769 11th Ave	14
Lido Arms Court, 154 Paterson	01
Mayfair, 185 E 33rd	04
Park East Terrace, E 43rd & 11th Ave	03
Riverview Towers, 85 Presidential Blvd	22
Stratford Motor Court, US Highway 46 Totowa	12
Thunderbird, 411 Broadway	01

BUILDINGS

Administration, 71 Hamilton	05
Colt 5, Colt	05
Fabian, 45 Church	05
First National Bank, 125 Ellison	05
Law, 64 Hamilton	05
Mainmark, 262 Main	05
Romaine, 136 Washington	05

GOVERNMENT OFFICES

City Hall Annex, 137 Ellison	05
Court House, 75 Hamilton	05

HOSPITALS

Barnert Memorial, 680 Broadway	14
Paterson General, 528 Market	01
Saint Josephs, 703 Main St	03
Valley View Or Preakness, Valley View Rd	09

PERTH AMBOY   088

POST OFFICE BOXES

Box Nos.		
1-299	Fords Br	63
1-1030	Perth Amboy	62

Perth Amboy (Con.) 088

STATIONS, BRANCHES AND UNITS

Fords Br	63
General Delivery	61
Postmaster	61

GOVERNMENT OFFICES

Internal Revenue	61
Social Security	61

HOSPITALS

Perth Amboy General Hosp	61

PLAINFIELD 070

POST OFFICE BOXES

Box Nos.

1-1474	Main Office	61
2500-2699	Muhlenberg Sta	60
2700-2974	Netherwood Sta	62
3000-3100	Station A	63
4001-4337	Warren Br	60

RURAL ROUTES

1,2	60

STATIONS, BRANCHES AND UNITS

Muhlenburg Sta	60
Netherwood Sta	62
North Plainfield Br	60
Warren Br	60
Watchung Br	60
General Delivery	61
Postmaster	61

APARTMENTS, HOTELS, MOTELS

Cyprus Gardens, 1165 Hgihway 22	60
Greenbrook Gardens, 1275 Rock Ave	60
Greenwood Gardens, 1300 Highway 22	60
Leland Gardens, 1227 E Front	62
Malcolm Gardens, 450 Little Pl	60
Meadowbrook Village, 1001 E Front	62
Pineview Gardens, 1000-1100 W 7th	63
Regency Village, 401 Highway 22	60
Terrace View, 300-301 Maple Ave	60
Windsor Terrace, 1300 Rock Ave	60

GOVERNMENT OFFICES

Selective Service Board 44, 325 E Front	60

HOSPITALS

Muhlenberg Hosipital, Randolph Rd	61

UNIVERSITIES AND COLLEGES

Mount Saint Mary'S Academy, Highway 22	61
Mount Saint Mary'S College, Highway 22	61

RAHWAY 070

POST OFFICE BOXES

Box Nos.

A-F	Main Office	65
AA-AK	Main Office	65
1-1274	Main Office	65
2-215	Colonia Br	67
701-978	Clark Br	66

STATIONS, BRANCHES AND UNITS

Clark Br	66
Colonia Br	67
General Delivery	65
Postmaster	65

RIDGEWOOD 074

POST OFFICE BOXES

Box Nos.

1-832	Main Office	51
1-1104	Glen Rock Br	52

STATIONS, BRANCHES AND UNITS

Glen Rock Br	52
General Delivery	51
Postmaster	51

BUILDINGS

C F Post Building, 20 Wilsey Sq	51
Glen Rock Professional, 66 Glen Ave	52
Glen Rock Public Library, 315 Rock Rd	52
Lincoln Building, 45 N Broad	50
Mallard Building, 1156 E Ridgewood Ave	51
Mcentegart-Melehan Bldg-139 Harrison Rd Glen Rock Nj	52
Medical Arts Building, 385 S Maple Ave	50
Reynolds, 125-127 E	

Ridgewood Ave	50
Ridgewood Public Library, 125 N Maple Ave	50
Teal, 1172 E Ridgewood Ave	51
Wilcox-Sithens, 75 N Maple Ave	51
Y M C A - Y W C A, 112 Oak St	51
Zecher Building, 1250 E Ridgewood Ave	51

HOSPITALS

Valley, Linwood & North Van Dien Ave	51

RUTHERFORD 070

POST OFFICE BOXES

Box Nos.

1-247	Wood Ridge Br	75
1-284	East Rutherford Br	73
1-317	Carlstadt Br	72
1-460	Rutherford Br	70
81-465	Lyndhurst Br	71

STATIONS, BRANCHES AND UNITS

Carlstadt Br	72
East Rutherford Br	73
Lyndhurst Br	71
Moonachie Br	74
Wood-Ridge Br	75
General Delivery	70
Postmaster	70

TRENTON 086

POST OFFICE BOXES

Box Nos.

1-181	Main Office	01
1-266	West Trenton Br	28
1-328	Yardville Br	20
1-428	Lawrenceville Br	48
1-514	Robbinsville Br	91
191-321	Main Office	02
331-511	Main Office	03
521-751	Main Office	04
761-970	Main Office	05
971-1201	Main Office	06
1211-2499	Main Office	07
2500-2699	Hamilton Square Br	90
2700-2768	Main Office	07
3001-3248	Mercerville Br	19
4000-4408	C Sta	10
4500-4599	Chambersburg Sta	11
5000-5999	Circle Fr	38

Trenton (Con.)   086

RURAL ROUTES

1	48
2	20
3,4	91

STATIONS, BRANCHES AND UNITS

Center Sta	08
Chambersburg Sta	11
Circle Br	38
Fort Dix Br	40
Greveville Br	20
Hamilton Square Br	90
Lawrenceville Br	48
Mc Guire A F B Br	41
Mercerville Br	19
Robbinsville Br	91
State Hospital Br	25
West Trenton Br	28
Yardville Br	20
General Delivery	08
Postmaster	08

APARTMENTS, HOTELS, MOTELS

Brookville, 1920 Riverside Dr.	18
Brookville, 321 Clearfield Ave	18
Cadwalader, 640 W State	18
Carteret Arms, 333 W State	18
Colonial Gardens, 455 W State	18
East Gate, 1501 Parkside Ave	38
Elmhurst, 879 Bellevue Ave	18
Hamilton Arms, Ward Ave Ext	19
Hamilton Arms, 1500 Nottingham Way	09
Hamilton Gardens, 2300 S Broad	10
Hamilton Park, 500 Arena Dr.	10
Hanover, 137 E Hanover	08

Hildebrecht, 27 W State	08
Holiday Inn Of Trenton, 240 W State	08
Hotel Fitchway, 200 S Broad	08
Imperial 400, 350 S Broad	08
Lalor Gardens, 700 Lalor	10
Leonard, 85 S Clinton Ave	09
Mayfair, 583 Bellevue Ave	18
Midtown Motel, 541 E State	09
Parkside Manor, 1400 Parkside Ave	38
Penn, 81 S Clinton Ave	09
Scudders Falls East, 325 W Upper Ferry Rd	28
West Gate, 550 Lawrenceville Rd	38
Woodbrook House, 865 lower Ferry Rd	28

BUILDINGS

Commonwealth, 150 E State	08
Federal, 402 E State	08
First-Mechanics Bank, 1 West State	08
Hamilton Township Municipal, 2090 Greenwood Ave	09
Mercer County Airport	28
N J National Bank	08
National State Bank	08
Professional, 1100 S Broad	11
Wallach, 86 E State	08
War Memorial, Memorial Dr	08

GOVERNMENT OFFICES

All Offices & Divisions, Trenton New Jersey	25
Div Of Motor Vehicles	66
Ewing Township Municipal 1872 Pennington Ave	18
Lawrence Township Municipal, 2207 Lawrenceville Rd	38
Mercer County Court House 209 S Broad	67
Trenton City Hall, E State	08

HOSPITALS

Donnelly Memorial, Hamilton Ave & Klockner Rd	19
Hamilton White Horse - Ham Sq Rd	90
Helene Fuld, Brunswick Ave At Fuld	38
Mercer, 446 Bellevue Ave	07
New Jersey State Hospital, Sullivan Way	25
Saint Francis, 601 Hamilton Ave	29

MILITARY INSTALLATIONS

Fort Dix New Jersey	40
Mc Guire Afb, New Jersey	41
U. S. Naval Air Propulsion Test Center	28

UNIVERSITIES AND COLLEGES

Board Of Education, 9 S Stockton	11
Mercer County Community College, 101 W State	08
Rider College, 2083 Lawrenceville Rd.	02
Trenton State College, Hillwood Lakes	25

WESTFIELD   070

POST OFFICE BOXES

Box Nos.		
A-H	Mountainside Branch	92
A-W	Main Office	91
1-880	Main Office	91
1001-1221	Mountainside Br	92

STATIONS, BRANCHES AND UNITS

Mountainside Br	92
General Delivery	91
Postmaster	91

NEW MEXICO   State List of Post Offices

NEW MEXICO
(Abbreviation: NM)

Abiquiu	87510
Alameda, Br. Albuquerque (see appendix)	
Alamo, R. Br. Magdalena	87825
Alamogordo (1st)	88310
Albert, R. Br. Mosquero	87733
ALBUQUERQUE (1st) (see appendix)	
Alcalde	87511
Algodones R. Br. Bernalillo	87001
Alto	88312
Amalia	87512
Ambrosia Lake, R. Br. Grants	87020
Amistad	88410

Ancho, R. Br. Carrizozo	88313
Animas	88020
Anthony	88021
Berino, R. Br.	88024
Anton Chico	87711
Apache Creek, R. Br. Reserve	87830
Aragon	87820
Arenas Valley	88022
Arrey	87930
Arroyo Hondo	87513
Arroyo Seco	87514
Artesia (1st)	88210
Aztec	87410
Bard	88411
Bayard	88023
Belen (1st)	87002

Bell Ranch, R. Br. Tucumcari	88441
Bellview	88111
Bent	88314
Berino, R. Br. Anthony	88024
Bernalillo	87004
Algodones, R. Br.	87001
Bingham	87815
Blanco	87412
Bloomfield	87413
Bluewater	87005
Boles, R. Br. Alamogordo	88310
Bosque	87006
Brimhall	87310
Broadmoor, Sta. Roswell	88201
Broadview	88112
Buckeye	88217

Buckhorn 88025
Buena Vista 87712
Bueyeros 88412
Caballo 87931
Campus, Sta. Socorro 87801
Canjilon 87515
Cannon A F B, Br. Clovis ... 88101
Canoncito, R. Br. Laguna ... 87026
Canones 87516
Capitan 88316
Caprock 88213
Capulin 88414
Carlsbad (1st) 88220
Carrizozo 88301
   Ancho, R. Br. 88313
Carson 87517
Casa Blanca 87007
Causey 88113
Cebolla 87518
Cedar Crest 87008
Cedarvale 87009
Central 88026
Cerrillos 87010
Cerro 87519
Chacon 87713
Chama 87520
Chamberino 88027
Chamisal 87521
Chimayo 87522
Church Rock 87311
Cimarron 87714
Claunch 87011
Clayton 88415
Cleveland 87715
Cliff 88028
Clines Corners, R. Br.
   Moriarty 87070
Cloudcroft 88317
Clovis (1st) 88101
Cochiti, R. Br. Penablanca ... 87041
Columbus 88029
Conchas Dam, R. Br.
   Tucumcari 88416
Continental Divide 87312
Cordova 87523
Corona 88318
Coronado, Sta. Santa Fe 87501
Corrales 87048
Costilla 87524
Counselor, R. Br. Cuba 87018
Coyote 87012
Crossroads 88114
Crownpoint 87313
Cuba 87013
   Counselor, R. Br. 87018
   Regina, R. Br. 87046
Cubero 87014
Cuchillo 87932
Cuervo 88417
Cundiyo, R. Br. Chimayo 87522
Datil 87821
Deming (1st) 88030
Derry 87933
Des Moines 88418
Dexter 88230
Dixon 87527
Dona Ana 88032
Dora 88115
Downtown, Sta. Albuquerque
   (see appendix)
Dulce 87528
Duran 88319
Dusty 87934

Eagle Nest 87718
East Vaughn 88320
Edgewood 87015
El Prado 87529
El Rito 87530
Elephant Butte 87935
Elida 88116
Elkins 88117
Embudo 87531
Encino 88321
Espanola (1st) 87532
   Fairview, Sta. 87532
   Hernandez, R. Br. 87537
   Truchas, R. Br. 87578
Estancia 87016
   Tajique, R. Br. 87057
Eunice 88231
Fairacres 88033
Fairview, Sta. Espanola 87532
Farley, R. Br. Springer 87720
Farmington (1st) 87401
Faywood 88034
Fence Lake 87315
Flora Vista 87415
Floyd 88118
Flying H 88322
Folsom 88419
Fort Bayard, R. Br. Silver
   City 88036
Fort Stanton 88323
Fort Sumner 88119
Fort Wingate 87316
Fruitland 87416
Gabaldon 87721
Gallina 87017
Gallup (1st) 87301
   Gamerco, R. Br. 87317
   Navajo, R. Br. 87328
   Vander Wagen, R. Br. 87326
Gamerco, R. Br. Gallup 87317
Garfield 87936
Garita 88421
Gila 88038
Gila Hot Springs, R. Br.
   Silver City 88061
Gladstone 88422
Glencoe 88324
Glenrio 88423
Glenwood 88039
Glorieta 87535
Gonzales Ranch 87536
Grady 88120
Grants (1st) 87020
Grenville 88424
Guadalupita 87722
Hachita 88040
Hagerman 88232
Hanover 88041
Hatch 87937
Hayden 88425
Hernandez, R. Br Espanola ... 87537
High Rolls Mountain Park 88325
Hillsboro 88042
Hobbs (1st) 88240
Holloman Air Force Base
   (1st) 88330
Holman 87723
Hondo 88336
Hope 88250
Horse Springs 87822
House 88121
Humble City 88251
Hurley 88043

Ilfeld, R. Br. Santa Fe 87538
Isleta 87022
Jal 88252
Jarales 87023
Jemez Pueblo 87024
Jemez Springs 87025
Kenna 88122
Kirtland 87417
Kirtland A F B, Br.
   Albuquerque (see
   appendix)
La Jara 87627
La Loma 88724
La Luz 88337
La Madera 87539
La Mesa 88044
   Vado, R. Br. 88072
La Plata 87418
Laguna 87026
Lajoya 87028
Lake Arthur 88253
Lakewood 88254
Lamy, R. Br. Santa Fe 87540
Las Cruces (1st) 88001
   University Park, Br. 88001
   White Sands Missile
   Range, Br 88002
Las Tablas 87541
Las Vegas (1st) 87701
Ledoux 87725
Lemitar 87823
Leyba 87542
Lincoln 88338
Linda Vista, Sta. Roswell ... 88201
Lindrith 87029
Lingo 88123
Llano, R. Br. Penasco 87543
Llaves 87030
Loco Hills 88255
Logan 88426
Lordsburg 88045
   Redrock, R. Br. 88055
Los Alamos (1st) 87544
Los Lunas 87031
Los Ranchos De
   Albuquerque, Br.
   Albuquerque (see
   appendix)
Loving 88256
Lovington (1st) 88260
Lumberton 87547
Luna 87824
Magdalena 87825
Malaga 88263
Maljamar 88264
Manuelito 87318
Maxwell 87728
Mayhill 88339
Mc Alister 88427
Mc Donald 88262
Mc Intosh 87032
Medanales 87548
Melrose 88124
Mentmore 87319
Mescalero 88340
Mesilla 88046
Mesilla Park 88047
Mesquite 88048
Mexican Springs 87320
Miami 87729
Milan, Br. Grants 87020
Mills 87730
Milnesand 88125

Mimbres	88049
Mogollon	88050
Montezuma	87731
Monticello	87939
Montoya	88428
Monument	88265
Mora	87732
Moriarty	87035
Clines Corners, R. Br.	87070
Stanley, R. Br.	87056
Mosquero	87733
Mount Dora	88429
Mountainair	87036
Mule Creek	88051
Nageezi	87037
Nara Visa	88430
Navajo, R. Br. Gallup	87328
Navajo Dam	87419
New Laguna	87038
Newkirk	88431
Nogal	88341
Ocate	87734
Oil Center	88266
Ojo Caliente	87549
Ojo Feliz	87735
Ojo Sarco	87550
Old Albuquerque, Sta. Albuquerque	87104
Organ	88052
Orogrande	88342
Paguate	87040
Paradise Hills, R. Br. Albuquerque	87114
Park View	87551
Pastura, R. Br. Santa Rosa	88435
Pecos	87552
Penablanca	87041
Penasco	87553
Llano, R. Br.	87543
Rodarte, R. Br.	87561
Pep	88126
Peñalta	87042
Petaca	87554
Picacho	88343
Pie Town	87827
Pinon	88344
Pinos Altos, R. Br. Silver City	88053
Placitas	87043
Pojoaque Valley, R. Br. Santa Fe	87501
Polvadera	87828
Ponderosa	87044
Portales (1st)	88130
Prewitt	87045
Puerto De Luna, R. Br. Santa Rosa	88432
Quay	88433
Quemado	87829
Questa	87556
Radium Springs	88054
Rainsville	87736
Ramah	87321
Ranches Of Taos	87557
Raton (1st)	87740
Red River	87558
Redrock, R. Br. Lordsburg	88055
Regina, R. Br. Cuba	87046
Rehoboth	87322
Rencona	87559

Reserve	87830
Ribera	87560
Rincon	87940
Rio Rancho Estates, Br. Albuquerque	87114
Rociada	87742
Rodarte, R. Br. Penasco	87561
Rodeo	88056
Rogers	88132
Roswell (1st)	88201
Rowe	87562
Roy	87743
Ruidoso (1st)	88345
Ruidoso Downs	88346
Rutheron	87563
Sabinoso	87744
Sacramento	88347
Saint Vrain	88133
Salem	87941
San Acacia	87831
San Antonio	87832
San Cristobal	87564
San Fidel	87049
San Jon	88434
San Jose	87565
San Juan Pueblo	87566
San Lorenzo, R. Br. Santa Rita	88057
San Mateo	87050
San Miguel	88058
San Patricio	88348
San Rafael	87051
San Ysidro	87053
Sandia Base, Br. Albuquerque (see appendix)	
Sandia Park	87047
Sanostee, R. Br. Shiprock	87420
Santa Cruz	87567
Santa Fe (1st)	87501
Coronado, Sta.	87501
Ilfeld, R. Br.	87538
Lamy, R. Br.	87540
Pojoaque Valley, R. Br.	87501
Santa Rita	88059
San Lorenzo, R. Br.	88057
Santa Rosa	88435
Pastura, R. Br.	88435
Puerto De Luna, R. Br.	88432
Santo Domingo Pueblo	87052
Sapello	87745
Scholle	87054
Seboyeta	87055
Sedan	88436
Sena	87568
Seneca	88437
Serafina	87569
Shiprock	87420
Silver City (1st)	88061
Fort Bayard, R. Br.	88036
Gila Hot Springs, R. Br.	88061
Pinos Altos, R. Br.	88053
Socorro (1st)	87801
Solano	87746
Springer	87747
Farley, R. Br.	87720
Stanley, R. Br. Moriarty	87056
Stead	88438
Sunland Park	88063

Sunspot	88349
Taiban	88134
Tajique, R. Br. Estancia	87057
Taos (1st)	87571
Taos Ski Valley, R. Br. Taos	87571
Tatum	88267
Tererro	87573
Tesuque	87574
Texico	88135
Thoreau	87323
Three Rivers, R. Br. Tularosa	88350
Tierra Amarilla	87575
Tijeras	87059
Tinnie	88351
Toadlena	87324
Tohatchi	87325
Tome	87060
Torreon	87061
Trampas	87576
Trementina	88439
Tres Piedras	87577
Truchas, R. Br. Espanola	87578
Trujillo	87748
Truth Or Consequences (1st)	87901
Tucumcari (1st)	88401
Bell Ranch, R. Br.	88441
Conchas Dam, R. Br.	88416
Tularosa	88352
Three Rivers, R. Br.	88350
Turnerville	88064
Tyrone	88065
University, Sta. Portales	88130
University Park, Br. Las Cruces	88001
Ute Park	87749
Vadito	87579
Vado, R. Br. La Mesa	88072
Valdez	87580
Vallecitos	87581
Valmora	87750
Vanadium	88073
Vander Wagen, R. Br. Gallup	87326
Vaughn	88353
Veguita	87062
Velarde	87582
Veterans Hospital, Br. Albuquerque	87108
Villanueva	87583
Wagon Mound	87752
Walker, Br. Roswell	88201
Waterflow	87421
Watrous	87753
Weed	88354
West Las Vegas, Br. Las Vegas	87701
White Rock, Sta. Los Alamos	87544
White Sands Missle Range, Br. Las Cruces	88002
Whites City	88268
Willard	87063
Williamsburg	87942
Winston	87943
Yeso	88136
Youngsville	87064
Zuni	87327

ALBUQUERQUE 871

POST OFFICE BOXES

Box Nos.
1-2999	Downtown Station	03
3000-3999	D Sta	10
4000-4999	A Sta	06
5001-5999	Sandia Base Br	15
6001-6999	B Sta	67
7000-7999	Old Albuquerque Sta	04
8001-8999	C Sta	08
9001-9999	Airport Mail Facility Sta	19
10001-10999	Alameda Br	14
11001-11999	E Sta	12
12001-12999	F	05
14000-14999	G	11
15000-15999	Rio Rancho Estates Br	24
18000-18999	Kirtland A F Base Br	18
25001-26999	Main Office	25

RURAL ROUTES

1	05
2	14
3	05
4	07
5	23
6	05
7	13
8,9	05
10	23
11,12	24
13	13
14,15	23

STATIONS, BRANCHES AND UNITS

Alameda Br	14
Downtown Sta	01
Kirtland AFB Br	17
Los Ranchos De Albuquerque Br	04
Old Albuquerque Sta	04
Paradise Hills Rural Br	14
Rio Rancho Estates Br	15
Sandia Base Br	08
Veterans Hospital Br	03
General Delivery	
Postmaster	

APARTMENTS, HOTELS, MOTELS

Albuquerque Lorlodge, 801 Central Ave NE	02
Alvarado, 110 1st SW	01
Ambassador East, 8911 Northeastrn Blvd NE	12
Broadmoor, 1115 Grand NE	06
Casa Del Norte, 900 Louisiana Blvd NE	10
Casa Grande Lodge, 2625 Central Ave NE	04
Chaparral, 521 Spruce SE	06
Cole, 123 5th NW	02
College Inn, 303 Ash NE	06
Continental Arms, 1200	
Continental East, 1101 Madeira Dr SE	08
Crossroads Motel, 1001 Central Ave NE	06
Desert Sands Motor, 5900 Central Ave SE	08
Downtowner Motor Inn, 717 Central Ave NW	01
El Camino Lodge, 6801 4th NW	07
Embassy House, 1330 Louisiana Blvd NE	10
Encino House, 601 Encino Pl NE	02
Gales, 6231 Gibson Blvd SE	08
Holiday Inn Of Albuquerque, 12901 Central Ave NE	23
Lanai, 1033 Madeira Dr SE	08
Landmark, 6303 Indian School Rd NE	10
Mitchell, 405 14th NW	04
Mountainview, 2323 Kathryn Ave SE	06
Nine-O-Nine, 909 Tijeras Ave NW	02
Ramada Inn, 4501 Central Ave NE	08
Sahara, 5915 Gibson Blvd SE	08
Six-Hundred Alcalde West, 1411 Coal Ave SW	04
Sundowner Motor, 6101 Central Ave NE	08
Trade Winds Motor, 5400 Central Ave NE	08
Virginian, 1400 Virginia NE	10
Western Gardens, 7310 Natalie Ave NE	10
Western Palasades, 1720 Atrisco Dr NW	05
Western Skies Motor, 13400 Central Av SE	23
White-Winrock, Winrock Center NE	10

BUILDINGS

Albuquerque National Bank, 123 Central Ave NW	01
Bank Of New Mexico, 222 Fourth SW	02
Civic Center, Cor Elm & Fruit NE	02
Del Castillo, 2933 Monte Vista Blvd NE	06
Federal, 517 Gold Ave SW	01
First National Bank East, 5301 Central Ave E	08
First National Bank, 219 Central Ave W	02
Fox, 120 Madeira Dr NE	08
Insurance, 610 Gold Ave SW	01
Korber, 208 2nd NW	02
Lawyers, 416 2nd NW	01
Mc Intosh, 220 Copper Ave NW	02
National, 505 Marquette Ave NW	01
Occidental Life, 3rd ' Gold SW	02
Oil Center, 3010 Monte Vista Blvd NE	06
Public Service, 414 Silver	

Ave SW	01
San Pedro Office, 525 San Pedro Dr NE	08
Scott, 114 Washington SE	08
Simms, 203 4th SW	02
Springer, 121 Tijeras Ave NE	02
Sunshine, 110 2nd SW	01
Tower Plaza, 510 2nd NW	02
Washington, 420 Washington SE	08
Western Insurance, 1015 Tijeras Ave NW	01

GOVERNMENT OFFICES

City Hall, 400 Marquette Ave NW	02
Old United States Courthouse, 421 Gold Ave SW	01

HOSPITALS

A T ' S F Association, 800 Central Ave SW	02
Albuquerque Medical Center, 109 Elm SE	01
Bataan Memorial Methodist, 5400 Gibson Blvd SE	08
Bernalillo County Medical Center, 2211 Lomas Blvd NE	06
Docotrs, 1010 Tijeras Ave NW	02
Encino Medical Plaza, 717 Encino Pl NE	06
La Mesa Medical Laboratory, 7000 Cutler Ave NE	
Lomas Medical, 718 Encino Pl NE	
Lovelace Clinic, 5200 Gibson Blvd SE	
Medical & Dental, 106 Girard Blvd NE	
Medical Arts Square, Lomas & Encino Pl NE	06
Nazareth, Alameda Road NE	13
Osteopathic, 1127 University NE	02
Presbyterian, 1012 Gold Ave SE	06
Saint Josephs, 715 Grand Ave NE	01
Sandia Ranch Sanitorium 6900 Edith Blvd NE	13
Southwest Dental, 123 Quincy NE	08

UNIVERSITIES AND COLLEGES

Albuquerque Business College, 221 San Pedro Dr NE	08
Browning Commercial School, 210 Yale Blvd SE	06
Draughns Business College, 110 Central Ave SW	02
Mc Caulley School Of Business, 115 Maple NE	06
University Of Albuquerque, Saint Joseph'S Pl NW	20
University Of New Mexico, University Hill NE	06
Western School For Secretaries, 805 Tieras Ave NW	01

435

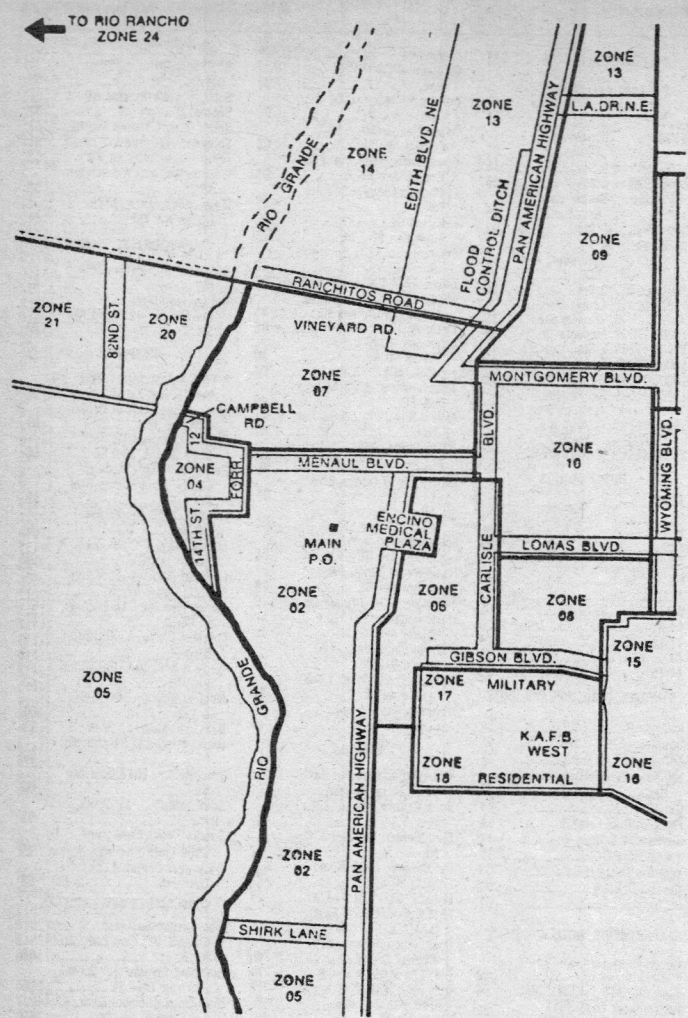

ZIP CODES
Albuquerque NM

871 + Two Digits Shown = ZIP Code

NEW YORK
(Abbreviation NY)

Academy, Sta. Albany 12208
Accord 12404
Acra 12405
Adams (1st) 13605
Adams Basin 14410
Adams Center 13606
Addison 14801
Adelphi, Sta. Brooklyn 11238
Adirondack............................12808
Afton 13730
Akron (1st) 14001
Alabama 14003
ALBANY (1st) (see appendix)
Albertson (1st) 11507
Albion (1st) 14411
Alcove 12007
Alden (1st) 14004
Alden Manor, Br Floral Park ..11003
Alder Creek...........................13301
Alexander 14005
Alexandria Bay 13607
Alfred (1st) 14802
Alfred Station 14803
Allegany................................14706
Allentown 14707
Allerton, Sta. Bronx 10467
Alma 14708
Almond 14804
Alpine 14805
Alplaus 12008
Altamont 12009
Altmar...................................13302
Alton 14413
Altona 12910
Amagansett 11930
Amawalk 10501
Amenia 12501
Ames, R. Br. Canajoharie 13317
Amherst, Br. Buffalo 14226
Amityville (1st) 11701
Amsterdam (1st) 12010
Ancram 12502
Ancramdale 12503
Andes 13731
Andover 14806
Angelica 14709
Angola (1st) 14006
Annandale-on-Hudson 12504
Ansonia, Sta. New York 10023
Antwerp 13608
    Oxbow, R. Sta. 13671

Apalachin 13732

Appleton 14008
Apulia Station 13020
Aquebogue 11931
Arcade (1st) 14005
Arden 10910
Ardonia 12505
Ardsley (1st) 10502
Ardsley-on-Hudson 10503
Argyle 12809
Arkport 14807
Arkville 12406
Arlington, Br. Poughkeepsie ..12603
Armonk (1st) 10504
Arverne, Sta. Far Rockaway ..11692
Ashland 12407
Ashville 14710

Astoria, Sta. Long Island
    City 11102

Athens 12015
Athol 12810
Athol Springs 14010
Atlanta 14808
Atlantic Beach 11509
Attica (1st) 14011
Au Sable Forks 12912
Auburn (1st) 13021
Audubon, Sta. New York 10032
Auriesville 12016
Aurora 13026
Ausable Chasm 12911
Austerlitz 12017
Ava 13303
Averill Park 12018
Avoca 14809
Avon (1st) 14414
BABYLON (1st) (see
    appendix)

Beinbridge (1st) 13733
Bakers Mills 12811
Baldwin (1st) 11510
Baldwin Place 10505
Baldwinsville (1st) 13027

Ballston Lake 12019
Ballston Spa (1st) 12020
Balmat 13609
Bangall 12506
Bangor, R. Br. North Bangor ..12966
Bank Plaza, Sta. Merrick 11566
Bardonia, Br. Nanuet 10954
Barker 14012
Barnes Corners 13610
Barneveld 13304
Barrytown 12507
Barryville 12719
Barton 13734
Basom 14013
Batavia (1st) 14020
Bath (1st) 14810
Bath Beach, Sta. Brooklyn 11214
Bay, Sta. Brooklyn 11235
Bay Ridge, Sta. Brooklyn 11220
Bay Shore (1st) 11706
    Fair Harbor, R. Br. 11734
    Kismet, R. Br. 11706
    Mall, Sta. 11706
    Penataquit, R. Br. 11707
    Saltaire, R. Br. 11706
Bay Terrace, Sta. Flushing 11360
Baychester, Sta. Bronx 10469
Bayport 11705
Bayside, Sta. Flushing (see
    appendix)

Bayville 11709
Beacon (1st) 12508
Bear Mountain 10911
Bearsville 12409
Beaver Dams 14812
Beaver Falls 13305
Beaver River, R. Br.
    Lowville 13306
Bedford (1st) 10506
Bedford Hills (1st) 10507
Beechwood, Sta. Rochester ...14609
Belfast 14711
Bellerose, Sta. Jamaica 11426

Belleville 13611
Bellevue, Sta. Schenectady ...12306
Bellmore (1st) 11710
Bellona 14415
Bellport (1st) 11713
Bellvale 10912
Belmont 14813
Bemus Point 14712
Bergen 14416
Berkshire 13736
Berlin 12022
Berne 12023
Bernhards Bay 13028
Bethel 12720
Bethpage (1st) 11714
Bible School Park 13737
Bidwell, Sta. Buffalo 14222
Big Flats 14814
Big Indian 12410
Big Moose 13307
Billings 12510

BINGHAMTON (1st) (see
    appendix)

Black Creek 14714
Black River 13612
Blasdell, Br. Buffalo 14219
Blauvelt (1st) 10913
Bliss 14024
Blodgett Mills 13738
Blooming Grove 10914
Bloomingburg 12721
Bloomingdale 12913
Bloomington 12411
Bloomville 13739
Blossvale 13306
Blue Mountain Lake 12812
Blue Point (1st) 11715
Bluff Point 14417
Blythebourne, Sta. Brooklyn ..11219
Boher's (1st) 11716
Boiceville 12412
Bolivar 14715
Bolton Landing 12814
Bombay 12914
Boonville (1st) 13309
Borough Hall, Sta. Jamaica ...11424
Boston 14025
Botanical, Sta. Bronx 10458
Bouckville 13310
Boulevard, Sta. Bronx (see
    appendix)

Bovina Center 13740
Bowling Green, Sta. New
    York 10004
Bowmansville 14026
Bradford 14815
Brainard 12024
Brainardsville 12915
Branchport 14418
Brandywine, Sta.
    Schenectady.....................12304
Brant 14027
Brant Lake 12815
Brantingham 13312
Brasher Falls 13613
Breesport 14816
Brentwood (1st) 11717
Brevoort, Sta. Brooklyn 11216
Brewerton 13029
Brewster (1st) 10509
Briarcliff Manor (1st) 10510
Bridge, Sta. Niagara Falls 14305

Bridgehampton	11932
Bridgeport	13030
Bridgewater	13313
Brier Hill	13614
Brighton, Sta. Brooklyn	11235
Brighton, Sta. Rochester	14610
Brightwaters (1st)	11718
Brisben	13741
Bristol Center	14419
Broad Channel, Sta. Far Rockaway	11693
Broadalbin	12025
Broadway, Sta. Long Island City	11106
Brockport (1st)	14420
Brocton	14716
BRONX (1st) (see appendix)	
Bronxville, Br. Yonkers	10708
Brookfield	13314
Brookhaven	11719
BROOKLYN (1st) (see appendix)	
Brooktondale	14817
Brookview	12026
Brownsville, Sta. Brooklyn	11212
Brownville	13615
Brushton	12916
Bryant, Sta. New York	10036
Buchanan	10511
BUFFALO (1st) (see appendix)	
Bulls Head, Sta. Rochester	14611
Bullville	10915
Burdett	14818
Burke	12917
Burlingham	12722
Burlington Flats	13315
Burnt Hills (1st)	12027
Burt	14028
Bush Terminal, Sta. Brooklyn	11232
Bushwick, Sta. Brooklyn	11221
Buskirk	12028
Butterfield, Br. Utica	13502
Byron	14422
Cadosia	13742
Cadyville	12918
Cairo	12413
Calcium	13616
Caledonia (1st)	14423
Callicoon	12723
Callicoon Center	12724
Calverton	11933
Cambria Heights, Sta. Jamaica	11411
Cambridge (1st)	12816
Camden (1st)	13316
Cameron	14819
Cameron Mills	14820
Camillus (1st)	13031
Camp Drum, MOU. Watertown	13601
Camp Smith, Br. Peekskill	10566
Campbell	14821
Campbell Hall	10916
Campus Plaza, Sta. Vestal	13850
Canaan	12029
Canada Lake, R. Br. Caroga Lake	12030
Canajoharie (1st)	13317
Canal Street, Sta. New York	10013
Canandaigua (1st)	14424
Canarsie, Sta. Brooklyn	11236
Canaseraga	14822
Canastota (1st)	13032
Candor	13743
Caneadea	14717
Canisteo	14823
Canton (1st)	13617
Cape Vincent	13618
Capitol, Sta. Albany (see appendix)	
Carle Place (1st)	11514
Carlisle	12031
Carmel (1st)	10512
Caroga Lake	12032
Canada Lake, R. Br	12030
Carthage (1st)	13619
Cass, Br Buffalo	14206
Cassadaga	14718
Cassville	13318
Castile	14427
Castle, Sta. New Rochelle	10801
Castle Creek	13744
Castle Hill, Sta. Bronx	10462
Castle Point	12511
Castleton on Hudson	12033
Castorland	13620
Cathedral, Sta. New York	10025
Cato	13033
Catskill (1st)	12414
Cattaraugus	14719
Cayuga	13034
Cayuta	14824
Cazenovia (1st)	13035
Cedarhurst (1st)	11516
Celoron	14720
Cementon	12415
Center Berlin, R. Sta. Berlin	12022
Cente Moriches (1st)	11934
Cen'ereach (1st)	11720
Centerport (1st)	11721
Centerville	14029
Central, Sta. Jamaica	11435
Central Bridge	12035
Central Islip (1st)	11722
Central Square	13036
Central Valley (1st)	10917
Central White Plains, Sta. White Plains (see appendix)	
Centuck, Sta. Yonkers	10710
Ceres	14721
Chadwicks	13319
Chaffee	14030
Champlain (1st)	12919
Chappaqua (1st)	10514
Charlotte, Sta. Rochester	14612
Charlotteville	12036
Chase Mills	13621
Chateaugay	12920
Chatham (1st)	12037
Chaumont	13622
Chautauqua	14722
Chazy	12921
Cheektowaga, Br. Buffalo	14225
Chelsea	12512
Chemung	14825
Chenango Bridge (1st)	13745
Chenango Forks	13746
Cherokee, Sta. New York	10028
Cherry Creek	14723
Cherry Grove, R. Br. Sayville	11782
Cherry Valley	13320
Cherryplain	12040
Chester (1st)	10918
Chestertown	12817
Chestnut Ridge, Br. Lockport	14094
Chichester	12416
Childwold	12922
Chinatown, Sta. New York	10013
Chippewa Bay	13623
Chittenango	13037
Church Street, Sta. New York (see appendix)	
Churchville	14428
Churubusco	12923
Cicero	13039
Cincinnatus	13040
Circleville	10919
City Island, Sta. Bronx	10464
Claremont Park, Sta. Bronx	10457
Clarence (1st)	14031
Clarence Center	14032
Clarendon	14429
Clark Mills	13321
Clarkson	14430
Clarksville	12041
Claryville	12725
Classon, Sta. Brooklyn	11238
Claverack	12513
Clay	13041
Clayton	13624
Clayville	13322
Clearfield, Br. Buffalo	14221
Clemons	12819
Cleveland	13042
Cleverdale	12820
Clifton	14431
Clifton Springs	14432
Climax	12042
Clinton (1st)	13323
Clinton Corners	12514
Clintondale	12515
Clintonville, R. Br Keeseville	12924
Clockville	13043
Clyde	14433
Clyme	14724
Cobleskill (1st)	12043
Hyndsville, R. Br	12044
Cochecton	12726
Cochecton Center	12727
Coeymans	12045
Coeymans Hollow	12046
Cohocton	14826
Cohoes (1st)	12047
Cold Brook	13324
Cold Spring	10516
Cold Spring Harbor (1st)	11724
Colden	14033
Colgate, Sta. Hamilton	13346
College, Sta. New York	10030
College Point, Sta. Flushing	11356
Colliersville	13747
Collins	14034
Collins Center	14035
Colonial Park, Sta. New York	10039
Colton	13625
Columbia University, Sta. New York	10025
Columbiaville	12050
Columbus, Sta. Mount Vernon	10553
Columbus Circle, Sta. New York	10023
Colvin, Sta. Syracuse	13205

Colvin Eggert, Br
  Tonawanda 14150
Commack (1st) 11725
Comstock 12821
Conesus 14435
Conewango Valley 14726
Coney Island, Sta. Brooklyn ... 11224
Congers 10920
Conklin 13748
Connelly 12417
Constable 12926
Constableville 13325
Constantia 13044
Cooks Falls 12728
Cooper, Sta. New York ... 10003
Coopers Plains 14827
Cooperstown (1st) 13326
  Middlefield, R. Br. ... 13405
Copake 12516
Copake Falls 12517
Copenhagen 13626
Copiague (1st) 11726
Coram 11727
Corbettsville 13749
Corfu 14036
Corinth 12822
Corners, Br. Ithaca 14850
Corning (1st) 14830
Cornwall 12518
Cornwall on the Hudson ... 12520
Cornwallville 12418
Corona-A, Sta. Flushing ... 11368
Corona-Elmhurst, Sta
  Flushing 11373
Cortland (1st) 13045
Cossayuna 12823
Cottekill 12419
Cowlesville 14037
Coxsackie 12051
Cragsmoor 12420
Cranberry Lake 12927
Crane Street, Sta.
  Schenectady 12303
Cranford, Sta. Bronx ... 10470
Craryville 12521
Crittenden 14038
Croghan 13327
Crompond 10517
Cropseyville 12052
Cross River 10518
Croton Falls 10519
Croton-on-Hudson (1st) ... 10520
  Crugers, Br. 10521
Crotona Park, Sta. Bronx ... 10460
Crown Point 12928
Crugers, Br.
  Croton-on-Hudson ... 10521
Cuba (1st) 14727
Cuddebackville 12729
Cutchogue (1st) 11935
Cuyler 13050
Cypress Hills, Sta. Brooklyn ... 11208
Dale 14039
Dalton 14836
Dannemora 12929
Dansville (1st) 14437
  Scottsburg, R. Br. ... 14545
Darien Center 14040
Davenport 13750
Davenport Center 13751
Davis Park, R. Br.
  Patchogue 11728
Dayton .... 14041•

De Kalb Junction 13630
De Lancey 13752
De Peyster 13633
De Ruyter 13052
De Witt, Br. Syracuse (see appendix)
Deansboro 13328
Deer Park (1st) 11729
Deer River 13627
Deferiet 13628
Degrasse 13629
Delanson 12053
Delaware, Sta. Albany ... 12209
Delevan 14042
Delhi (1st) 13753
Delmar (1st) 12054
Delphi Falls 13051
Delray, Br. Buffalo 14224
Denmark 13631
Denver 12421
Depauville 13632
Depew (1st) 14043
Deposit (1st) 13754
Derby 14047
Dewey, Sta. Rochester ... 14613•
Dewittville 14728
Dexter 13634
Diamond Point 12824
Dick Urban, Br. Depew ... 14043
Dickinson Center 12930
Dobbs Ferry (1st) 10522
Dolgeville (1st) 13329
Dorloo 12099
Dormansville 12055
Douglaston, Sta. Flushing ... 11363
Dover Plains 12522
Downsville 13755
Dresden 14441
Dryden 13053
Duanesburg 12056
Dundee 14837
Dunham, Sta. Utica 13502
Dunkirk (1st) 14048
  Van Buren Point, R. Br. ... 14166
Durham 12422
Durhamville 13054
Dyker Heights, Sta. Brooklyn... 11228
Eagle Bay 13331
Eagle Bridge 12057
Eagle Harbor 14442
Earlton 12058
Earlville 13332
East, Sta. Yonkers 10704
East Amherst 14051
East Aurora (1st) 14052
East Berne 12059
East Bethany 14054
East Bloomfield 14443
East Branch 13756
East Chatham 12060
East Concord 14055
East Durham 12423
East Elmhurst, Sta.
  Flushing 11369
East Freetown 13055
East Greenbush (1st) 12061
East Greenwich 12826
East Hampton (1st) 11937
East Homer 13056
East Islip (1st) 11730
East Jewett 12424
East Marion 11939
East Meadow, Br.

Hempstead 11554
East Meredith 13757
East Moriches 11940
East Nassau 12062
East New York, Sta.
  Brooklyn 11207
East Northport (1st) 11731
East Norwich (1st) 11732
East Otto 14729
East Palmyra 14444
East Patchogue, Br.
  Patchogue 11772
East Pembroke 14056
East Pharsalia 13758
East Quogue 11942
East Randolph 14730
East Rochester (1st) 14445
East Rockaway (1st) 11518
East Schodack 12063
East Setauket (1st) 11733
East Side, Sta. Binghamton ... 13904
East Springfield 13333
East Syracuse (1st) 13057
East White Plains, Br. White
  Plains 10604
East Williamson 14449
East Williston, Br. Williston
  Park 11596
East Windham 12425
East Worcester 12064
Eastchester, Br. Yonkers ... 10709
Eastport 11941
Eastwood, Sta. Syracuse ... 13206
Eaton 13334
Eddyville 12426
Eden (1st) 14057
Edinburg, R. Br. Northville... 12134
Edmeston 13335
Edwards 13635
Elba 14058
Elbridge 13060
Eldred 12732
Elizabethtown 12932
Elizaville 12523
Elka Park 12427
Ellenburg 12933
Ellenburg Center 12934
Ellenburg Depot 12935
Ellenville (1st) 12428
Ellicott, Sta. Buffalo 14205
Ellicottville 14731
Ellington 14732
Ellisburg 13636
Elma 14059
Elmhurst-A, Sta. Flushing ... 11373
ELMIRA (1st) (see appendix)
Elmira Heights, Br. Elmira... 14903
Elmont, Br. Floral Park ... 11003
Elmsford (1st) 10523
Elmwood, Sta. Syracuse... 13207
Elnora 12065
Elsmere, Br. Delmar 12054
Eltingville, Sta. Staten
  Island 10312
Elwood, Sta. East Northport... 11731
Embarkation, Sta. Brooklyn... 11250
Empire State, Sta. New York... 10001
Endicott (1st) 13760
Endwell, Br. Endicott 13760
Erieville 13061
Erin 14838
Esopus 12429
Esperance 12066

Esplanade, Sta. Bronx	10469
Essex	12936
Etna	13062
Evans Mills	13637
Fabius	13063
Fair Harbor, R. Br. Bay Shore	11734
Fair Haven	13064
Fairfield	13336
Fairport (1st)	14450
Falconer (1st)	14733
Falls, Sta. Niagara Falls	14303
Fallsburg	12733
Fancher	14452
FAR ROCKAWAY (1st) (see appendix)	
Farmersville Station	14060
Farmingdale (1st)	11735
Farmingville	11738
Farnham	14061
Farragut, Sta. Brooklyn	11203
Fayette	13065
Fayetteville (1st)	13066
Federal, Sta. Rochester (see appendix)	
Federal Reserve, Sta. New York	10045
Felts Mills	13638
Ferndale	12734
Feura Bush	12067
Fieldston, Sta. Bronx	10463
Fillmore	14735
Findley Lake	14736
Fine	13639
Fineview	13640
Fire Island Pines, Br. Sayville	11782
Fishers	14453
Fishers Island	06390
Fishers Landing	13641
Fishkill (1st)	12524
Fishs Eddy	13774
Flatbush, Sta. Brooklyn	11226
Fleetwood, Sta. Mount Vernon	10552
Fleischmanns	12430
FLORAL PARK (1st) (see appendix)	
Florida	10921
FLUSHING (1st) (see appendix)	
Fly Creek	13337
Fonda	12068
Fordham, Sta. Bronx	10458
Forest Hills, Sta. Flushing	11375
Forestport	13338
Otter Lake, R. Br.	13427
Forestville	14062
Fort Ann	12827
Fort Covington	12937
Fort Edward (1st)	12828
Fort George, Sta. New York	10040
Fort Hamilton, Sta. Brooklyn	11209
Fort Hunter	12069
Fort Jackson, R. Br. North Lawrence	12938
Fort Johnson	12070
Fort Montgomery	10922
Fort Plain (1st)	13339
Fort Tilden, Sta. Far Rockaway	11695
Fort Washington, Sta. New York	10032
Fosterdale	12735

Fpo (09517, Br. New York	09517
Frankfort	13340
Franklin	13775
Franklin D Roosevelt, Sta. New York	10022
Franklin Springs	13341
Franklin Square (1st)	11010
Franklinville	14737
Fraser, R. Br. Delhi	13753
Fredonia (1st)	14063
Freedom	14065
Freehold	12431
Freeport (1st)	11520
Freeville	13068
Fremont Center	12736
Fresh Meadows, Sta. Flushing	11365
Fresh Pond, Sta. Brooklyn	11227
Frewsburg	14738
Friendship	14739
Front Street, Br. Binghamton	13905
Frontenac, R. Br. Clayton	13624
Fulton (1st)	13069
Fultonham	12071
Fultonville	12072
Randall, R. Br.	12142
Gabriels	12939
Gainesville	14066
Gallupville	12073
Galway	12074
Gansevoort	12831
Garden City (1st)	11530
Gardiner	12525
Garnerville (1st)	10923
Garrattsville	13342
Garrison	10524
Gasport	14067
Gedney, Sta. White Plains	10605
Geneseo (1st)	14454
Geneva (1st)	14456
Genoa	13071
Georgetown	13072
Georgetown Square, Br. Buffalo	14221
Germantown	12526
Gerry	14740
Getzville	14068
Ghent	12075
Gilbertsville	13776
Gilboa	12076
Gimbels Number One, Sta. Valley Stream	11581
Glasco	12432
Glen Aubrey	13777
Glen Cove (1st)	11542
Glen Head (1st)	11545
Glen Island, R. Sta. Bolton Landing	12814
Glen Oaks, Br. Floral Park	11004
Glen Spey	12737
Glen Wild	12738
Glendale, Sta. Brooklyn	11227
Glenfield	13343
Glenford	12433
Glenham	12527
Glenmont	12077
Glens Falls (1st)	12801
Glenwood	14069
Glenwood Landing	11547
Gloversville (1st)	12078
Godeffroy	12739
Goldens Bridge	10526
Gorham	14461

Goshen (1st)	10924
Gouverneur (1st)	13642
Spragueville, R. Br.	13689
Governors Island, Br. New York	10004
Gowanda (1st)	14070
Gracie, Sta. New York	10028
Grafton	12082
Grahamsville	12740
Sundown, R. Br.	12782
Grand Central, Sta. New York	10017
Grand Gorge	12434
Grand Island (1st)	14072
Granite Springs	10527
Granville (1st)	12832
Gravesend, Sta. Brooklyn	11223
Great Bend	13643
Great Kills, Sta. Staten Island	10308
GREAT NECK (1st) (see appendix)	
Great River	11739
Great Valley	14741
Greece, Br. Rochester	14616
Greeley Square, Sta. New York	10001
Green Island, Br. Troy	12183
Greene (1st)	13778
Greenfield Center	12833
Greenfield Park	12435
Greenhurst	14742
Greenlawn (1st)	11740
Greenpoint, Sta. Brooklyn	11222
Greenport (1st)	11944
Greenvale (1st)	11548
Greenville	12083
Greenwich (1st)	12834
Greenwood	14839
Greenwood Lake	10925
Greig	13345
Grenell, R. Br. Clayton	13624
Griffiss A F B, Br. Rome	13440
Grindstone	13644
Grossinger, Br. Ferndale	12734
Groton (1st)	13073
Groveland	14462
Grover, Br. Buffalo	14226
Guilderland (1st)	12084
Guilderland Center	12085
Guilford	13780
Hadley	12835
Hagaman	12086
Hague	12836
Hailesboro	13645
Haines Falls	12436
Halcott Center	12437
Halcottsville	12438
Halesite, Br. Huntington	11743
Hall	14463
Halsey, Sta. Brooklyn	11233
Hamburg (1st)	14075
Hamden	13782
Hamilton (1st)	13346
Hamilton Grange, Sta. New York	10031
Hamlin	14464
Hammond	13646
Hammondsport (1st)	14840
Hampton	12837
Hampton Bays (1st)	11946
Hancock (1st)	13783
Hancock Field, MOU. Syracuse	13225

Hankins	12741
Hannacroix	12087
Hannawa Falls	13647
Hannibal	13074
Harford	13784
Harford Mills	13785
Harlem, Br. Buffalo	14226
Harpersfield	13786
Harpursville	13787
Harriman	10926
Harris	12742
Harrison (1st)	10528
Harrisville	13648
Hart Lot	13075
Hartford	12838
Hartsdale (1st)	10530
Hartwick	13348
Hartwick Seminary	13349
Hastings	13076
Hastings On Hudson, Br. Yonkers	10706
Hauppauge, Br. Smithtown	11787
Haverstraw (1st)	10927
Hawkeye, R. Br. Au Sable Forks	12912
Hawthorne (1st)	10532
Hayt Corners	14465
Heathcote, Br. Scarsdale	10583
Hector	14841
Helena	13649
Hell Gate, Sta. New York	10029
Helmuth	14079
Hemlock	14466
HEMPSTEAD (1st) (see appendix)	
Henderson	13650
Henderson Harbor	13651
Henrietta (1st)	14467
Hensonville	12439
Herkimer (1st)	13350
Hermon	13652
Herrings	13653
Hertel, Sta. Buffalo	14216
Heuvelton	13654
Hewlett (1st)	11557
HICKSVILLE (1st) (see appendix)	
Higgins Bay, R. Br. Lake Pleasant	12108
High Bridge, Sta. Bronx	10452
High Falls	12440
Highland (1st)	12528
Highland Falls (1st)	10928
Highland Lake	12743
Highland Mills	10930
Highlawn, Sta. Brooklyn	11223
Highmount	12441
Hiler, Br. Buffalo	14223
Hill, Sta. Middletown	10940
Hillburn	10931
Hillsdale	12529
Hillside, Sta. Bronx	10469
Hillside Manor, Br. New Hyde Park	11040
Hilton (1st)	14468
Himrod	14842
Hinckley	13352
Hinsdale	14743
Ischua, R. Br.	14746
Hobart	13788
Hoffmans	12088
Hoffmeister	13353
Hogansburg	13655

Holbrook (1st)	11741
Holcomb	14469
Holland	14080
Holland Patent	13354
Holley	14470
Hollis, Sta. Jamaica	11423
Hollowville	12530
Holmes	12531
Holmesville	13789
Holtsville	11742
Homecrest, Sta. Brooklyn	11229
Homer (1st)	13077
Homer Folks Hospital, R. Br. Oneonta	13820
Honeoye	14471
Honeoye Falls (1st)	14472
Hoosick	12089
Hoosick Falls (1st)	12090
Hope Farm, R. Br. Millbrook	12532
Hopewell Junction (1st)	12533
Hopkinton, R. Br. North Lawrence	12940
Horace Harding, Sta. Flushing	11362
Hornell (1st)	14843
Horseheads (1st)	14845
Hortonville	12745
Hospital, Sta. Binghamton	13904
Houghton	14744
Howard, Sta. New York	10013
Howard Beach, Sta. Jamaica	11414
Howells	10932
Howes Cave	12092
Hub, Sta. Bronx	10455
Hubbardsville	13355
Hudson (1st)	12534
Hudson Falls (1st)	12839
Hughsonville	12537
Huguenot	12746
Hulberton	14473
Huletts Landing	12841
Hume	14745
Hunt	14846
Hunter	12442
Huntington (1st)	11743
Huntington Station (1st)	11746
Hurley	12443
Hurleyville	12747
Hyde Park (1st)	12538
Hyndsville, R. Br. Cobleskill	12044
Ilion (1st)	13357
Indian Lake	12842
Industry	14474
Inlet	13360
Interlaken	14847
Inwood, Sta. New York	10034
Inwood L I, Br. Far Rockaway	11696
Ionia	14475
Irondequoit, Br. Rochester	14617
Irving	14081
Irvington (1st)	10533
Ischua, R. Br. Hinsdale	14746
Island Park (1st)	11558
Islip (1st)	11751
Islip Terrace (1st)	11752
Ithaca (1st)	14850
Ithaca College, Br. Ithaca	14850
Jackson Heights, Sta. Flushing	11372
Jacksonville	14854
JAMAICA (1st) (see appendix)	

Jamesport	11947
Jamestown (1st)	14701
Jamesville	13078
Jasper	14855
Java Center	14082
Java Village	14083
Jay	12941
Jefferson	12093
Jefferson Valley	10535
Jeffersonville	12748
Jericho (1st)	11753
Jerome Avenue, Sta. Bronx	10468
Jewett	12444
John F Kennedy Airport, Sta. Jamaica	11430
Johnsburg	12843
Johnson	10933
Johnson City (1st)	13790
Johnsonburg	14084
Johnsonville	12094
Johnstown (1st)	12095
Jonesville	12098
Jordan	13080
Jordanville	13361
Junction Boulevard, Sta. Flushing	11372
Kanona	14856
Katonah (1st)	10536
Kattskill Bay	12844
Kauneonga Lake	12749
Keene	12942
Keene Valley	12943
Keeseville	12944
Clintonville, R. Br.	12924
Kelly Corners	12445
Kelsey, R. Br. Hancock	13783
Kendall	14476
Kenmore, Br. Buffalo	14217
Kennedy	14747
Kenoza Lake	12750
Kensington, Sta. Brooklyn	11218
Kensington, Sta. Buffalo	14215
Kent	14477
Kenwood, Sta. Oneida	13421
Kerhonkson	12446
Kernan, Sta. Utica	13502
Keuka Park	14478
Kew Gardens, Sta. Jamaica	11415
Kiamesha Lake	12751
Kill Buck	14748
Killawog	13794
Kinderhook	12106
King Ferry	13081
Kings Bridge, Sta. Bronx	10463
Kings Park (1st)	11754
Kings Point, Br. Great Neck	11024
Kingston (1st)	12401
Kingsway, Sta. Brooklyn	11229
Kirkville	13082
Kirkwood	13795
Kismet, R. Br. Bay Shore	11706
Knapp Creek	14749
Knickerbocker, Sta. New York	10002
Knowlesville	14479
Knox	12107
Knoxboro	13362
Krumville	12447
Samsonville, R. Sta.	12476
La Fargeville	13656
La Fayette	13084
La Guarda Airport, Sta.	

Flushing	11371
La Salle, Sta. Niagara Falls	14304
Lackawanna, Br. Buffalo	14218
Laconia	12983
Lagrangeville	12540
Lake Carmel, Br. Carmel	10512
Lake Clear	12945
Lake George (1st)	12845
Lake Grove (1st)	11755
Lake Hill	12448
Lake Huntington	12752
Lake Katrine	12449
Lake Luzerne	12846
Lake Minnewaska, Br. New Paltz	12561
Lake Peekskill	10537
Lake Placid (1st)	12946
Lake Placid Club, Sta. Lake Placid	12946
Lake Pleasant	12108
Lake Ronkonkoma, Br. Ronkonkoma	11779
Lake Success, Sta. New Hyde Park	11040
Lake View	14085
Lakemont	14857
Lakeville	14480
Lakewood	14750
Lancaster (1st)	14086
Town Line, R. Br.	14165
Lanesville	12450
Lansingburg, Sta. Troy	12182
Larchmont (1st)	10538
Latham (1st)	12110
Laurel	11948
Laurens	13796
Lawrence (1st)	11559
Lawrenceville	12949
Lawtons	14091
Lawyersville	12113
Le Roy (1st)	14482
Lebanon	13085
Lebanon Springs	12114
Lee Center	13363
Leeds	12451
Lefferts, Sta. Brooklyn	11225
Leicester	14481
Lenox Hill, Sta. New York	10021
Leon	14751
Leonardsville	13364
Levittown (1st)	11756
Lewbeach	12753
Lewis	12950
Lewiston (1st)	14092
Lexington	12452
Liberty (1st)	12754
Lily Dale	14752
Lima	14485
Limerick	13657
Limestone	14753
Lincoln Park, Br. Buffalo	14223
Lincolndale	10540
Lincolnton, Sta. New York	10037
Linden Hill, Sta. Flushing	11354
Lindenhurst (1st)	11757
Lindley	14858
Linwood	14486
Lisbon	13658
Lisle	13797
Little Falls (1st)	13365
Little Genesee	14754
Little Neck, Sta Flushing (see appendix)	
Little Valley	14755
Little York	13087
Liverpool (1st)	13038
Livingston	12541
Livingston Manor	12758
Livonia	14487
Livonia Center	14488
Loch Sheldrake	12759
Locke	13092
Lockport (1st)	14094
Lockwood	14859
Locust Valley (1st)	11560
Lodi	14860
London Terrace, Sta. New York	10011
Long Beach (1st)	11561
Long Eddy	12760
LONG ISLAND CITY (1st) (see appendix)	
Long Lake	12847
Longwood, Sta. Bronx	10459
Loon Lake, R. Br. Onchiota	12951
Lorraine	13659
Loudonville, Br. Albany	12211
Lowman	14861
Lowville (1st)	13367
Beaver River, R. Br.	13306
Ludlowville	14862
Lycoming	13093
Lyell, Sta. Rochester	14606
Lynbrook (1st)	11563
Lyndonville	14098
Lyon Mountain	12952
Merrill, R. Br.	12955
Lyons (1st)	14489
Lyons Falls	13368
Lysander	13094
Mac Dougall	14501
Macedon (1st)	14502
Machias	14101
Madison	13402
Madison Square, Sta. New York	10010
Madrid	13660
Mahopac (1st)	10541
Mahopac Falls	10542
Main Mill, Br. Buffalo	14221
Maine	13802
Malden on Hudson	12453
Malden Bridge	12115
Mall, Sta. Bay Shore	11706
Mallory	13103
Malone (1st)	12953
Malverne (1st)	11565
Mamaroneck (1st)	10543
Manchester	14504
Manhasset (1st)	11030
Manhasset Hills, Sta. New Hyde Park	11040
Manhattanville, Sta. New York	10027
Manhattanville College, Sta. Purchase	10577
Manlius (1st)	13104
Mannsville	13661
Manorville	11949
Maple Springs	14756
Maple View	13107
Maplecrest	12454
Marathon	13803
Marcellus	13108
Marcy	13403
Margaretville	12455
Mariaville, R. Sta. Delanson	12053
Marietta	13110
Marilla	14102
Mariners Harbor, Sta. Staten Island	10303
Marion	14505
Market, Sta. Buffalo	14203
Marlboro	12542
Marquette, Br. Buffalo	14217
Martinsburg	13404
Martville	13111
Maryknoll (1st)	10545
Maryland	12116
Marymount, Sta. Tarrytown	10591
Masonville	13804
Maspeth, Sta. Flushing	11378
Massapequa (1st)	11758
Massapequa Park (1st)	11762
Massawepie, R. Br. Tupper Lake	12986
Massena (1st)	13662
Mastic	11950
Mastic Beach	11951
Mattituck	11952
Mattydale, Br. Syracuse	13211
Maybrook	12543
Mayfair, Br. Schenectady	12302
Mayfield	12117
Mayville (1st)	14757
Mc Connellsville	13401
Mc Donough	13801
Mc Graw (1st)	13101
Mc Kownville, Br. Albany	12203
Mc Lean	13102
Meacham, Br. Floral Park	11003
Mechanicville (1st)	12118
Mecklenburg	14863
Medford (1st)	11763
Medina (1st)	14103
Medusa	12120
Melcourt, Sta. Bronx	10451
Mellenville	12544
Melrose	12121
Melville, Br. Huntington Station	11746
Memphis	13112
Mendon	14506
Meredith	13805
Mendale	13206
Meridian	13113
Merrick (1st)	11566
Merrill, R. Br. Lyon Mountain	12955
Merriweather Campus, Br. Greenvale	11548
Metropolitan, Sta. Brooklyn	11206
Mexico	13114
Middle Falls	12848
Middle Granville	12849
Middle Grove	12850
Middle Hope, Br. Newburgh	12550
Middle Island	11953
Middle Village, Sta. Flushing	11379
Middleburg	12122
Middlefield, R. Br. Cooperstown	13405
Middleport (1st)	14105
Middlesex	14507
Middletown (1st)	10940
Middleville	13406
Midland Beach, Sta. Staten Island	10306

Midtown, Sta. New York	10018
Midtown Plaza, Sta. Rochester	14604
Midwood, Sta. Brooklyn	11230
Mileses	12761
Milford	13807
Mill Neck	11765
Millbrook (1st)	12545
Miller Place	11764
Millerton	12546
Millport	14864
Millwood	10546
Milton	12547
Mineola (1st)	11501
Minerva	12851
Minetto	13115
Mineville	12956
Minoa	13116
Model City	14107
Modena	12548
Mohawk (1st)	13407
Mohegan Lake	10547
Mohonk Lake, Br New Paltz	12561
Moira	12957
Mongaup Valley	12762
Monroe (1st)	10950
Monsey (1st)	10952
Montauk	11954
Montezuma	13117
Montgomery	12549
Monticello (1st)	12701
Montour Falls	14865
Montrose	10548
Mooers	12958
Mooers Forks	12959
Moravia (1st)	13118
Morgan, Sta New York	10001
Moriah	12960
Moriah Center	12961
Moriches	11955
Morley, R. Br. Canton	13617
Morningside, Sta New York	10026
Morris	13808
Morris Heights, Sta. Bronx	10453
Morris Park, Sta. Bronx	10461
Morrisania, Sta. Bronx	10456
Morrisonville	12962
Morristown	13664
Morrisville	13408
Morton	14508
Mosholu, Sta. Bronx	10467
Mott Haven, Sta. Bronx	10454
Mottville	13119
Mount Carmel, Sta. Bronx	10458
Mount Kisco (1st)	10549
Mount Marion	12456
Mount Morris	14510
Mount Pleasant, R. Br. Mount Tremper	12457
Mount Sinai	11766
Mount Tremper	12457
Mount Upton	13809
MOUNT VERNON (1st) (see appendix)	
Mount Vision	13810
Mountain Dale	12763
Mountain View, R. Br. Owls Head	12963
Mountainville	10953
Mumford	14511
Municipal Building, Sta Brooklyn	11201
Munnsville	13409

Murray Hill, Sta. New York	10016
Murray Isle, R. Br. Clayton	13624
Myers	14866
Nanuet (1st)	10954
Napanoch	12458
Naples	14512
Narrowsburg	12764
Nassau	12123
Natural Bridge	13665
Naval Hospital, Sta. Jamaica	11425
Nedrow	13120
Nelliston	13410
Nelsonville, Br. Cold Spring	10516
Nesconset	11767
Neversink	12765
New Baltimore	12124
New Berlin	13411
New Bremen	13412
New City (1st)	10956
New Dorp, Sta. Staten Island	10306
New Hamburg	12560
New Hampton	10958
New Hartford (1st)	13413
New Haven	13121
New Hyde Park (1st)	11040
New Kingston	12459
New Lebanon	12125
New Lebanon Center	12126
New Lisbon	13415
New Lots, Sta. Brooklyn	11208
New Market, Sta. Niagara Falls	14301
New Milford	10959
New Paltz (1st)	12561
NEW ROCHELLE (1st) (see appendix)	
New Russia	12964
New Scotland	12127
New Suffolk	11956
New Windsor, Br. Newburgh	12550
New Woodstock	13122
NEW YORK (1st) (see appendix)	
New York Mills	13417
Newark (1st)	14513
Newark Valley	13811
Newburgh (1st)	12550
Newcomb	1.852
Tahawus, R. Br	12879
Newfane	14108
Newfield	14867
Newkirk, Sta. Brooklyn	11226
Newport	13416
Newton Falls	13666
Newtonville	12128
NIAGARA FALLS (1st) (see appendix)	
Niagara Square, Sta. Buffalo (see appendix)	
Niagara University	14109
Nichols	13812
Nicholville	12965
Nineveh	13813
Niobe	14758
Niverville	12130
No One Hundred Thirty Eight, Sta New York	10001
Norfolk	13667
North, Sta Yonkers	10703
North Babylon, Br Babylon	11703
North Baldwin, Sta. Baldwin	11510

North Bangor	12906
Bangor, R. Br	12966
West Bangor, R. Br	12991
North Bay	13123
North Bellmore, Br. Bellmore	11710
North Blenheim	12131
North Boston	14110
North Branch	12766
North Brookfield	13418
North Chatham	12132
North Chili	14514
North Clymer	14759
North Cohocton	14868
North Collins	14111
North Creek	12853
North End, Br. Middletown	10940
North Evans	14112
North Granville	12854
North Greece	14515
North Hoosick	12133
North Hudson	12855
North Java	14113
North Lawrence	12967
Fort Jackson, R. Br	12938
Hopkinton, R. Br	12940
North Massapequa, Br. Massapequa	11758
North Merrick, Sta. Merrick	11566
North New Hyde Park, Br. New Hyde Park	11040
North Norwich	13814
North Pitcher	13124
North Pole, R. Br. Lake Placid	12946
North River	12856
North Rose	14516
North Salem	10560
North Syracuse, Br. Syracuse	13212
North Tarrytown, Br. Tarrytown	10591
North Tonawanda (1st)	14120
North Western	13419
North White Plains, Sta. White Plains (see appendix)	
Northport (1st)	11768
Northside, Sta. Corning	14830
Northtown, Br. Buffalo	14226
Northville	12134
Northwood, Br. Buffalo	14223
Norton Hill	12135
Norwich (1st)	13815
Norwood	13668
Nostrand, Sta. Brooklyn	11235
Number Eighteen, Sta. New York	10016
Number Eighty Two, Sta. New York	10022
Number Forty, Sta. New York	10001
Nunda	14517
Nyack (1st)	10960
Oak Beach, Br. Babylon	11702
Oak Hill	12460
Oak Point, Sta. Bronx	10455
Oakdale (1st)	11769
Oakfield	14125
Oakland Gardens, Sta. Flushing	11364
Oaks Corners	14518
Obernburg	12767

443

Ocean Beach 11770
Oceanside, Br. Rockville
  Centre 11572
Odessa 14869
Ogden, Sta. Bronx 10452
Ogdensburg (1st) 13669
Olcott 14126
Old Bethpage Branch, Br.
  Hicksville: 11804
Old Chatham 12136
Old Chelsea, Sta. New York 10011
Old Forge 13420
Old Village, Sta. Great Neck
  (see appendix)
Old Westbury, Br. Westbury 11568
Olean (1st) 14760
Olivebridge 12461
Oliverea 12462
Olmstedville 12857
Onchiota 12968
  Loon Lake, R. Br. 12951
Oneida (1st) 13421
Oneonta (1st) 13820
Onondaga, Br. Syracuse 13215
Ontario 14519
Ontario Center 14520
Oran 13125
Orangeburg (1st) 10962
Orchard Park (1st) 14127
Orient 11957
Oriskany 13424
Oriskany Falls 13425
Orwell 13426
Ossining (1st) 10562
Oswegatchie 13670
Oswego (1st) 13126
Otego 13825
Otisville 10963
Otselic 13129
Otter Lake, R. Br. Forestport 13427
Otto 14766
Ouaquaga 13826
Ovid 14521
Ovington, Sta. Brooklyn 11220
Owasco 13130
Owego (1st) 13827
Owls Head 12969
  Mountain View, R. Br. 12963
Oxbow, R. Sta. Antwerp 13671
Oxford 13830
Oyster Bay (1st) 11771
Ozone Park, Sta. Jamaica
  (see appendix)
Painted Post (1st) 14870
Palatine Bridge 13428
Palenville 12463
Palisades (1st) 10964
Palmer, Sta. Corinth 12822
Palmyra (1st) 14522
Panama 14767
Panorama, Br. Rochester 14625
Paradox 12858
Parcel Post, Sta. Far
  Rockaway 11691
Parcel Post, Sta. Long
  Island City 11101
Parcel Post, Sta.
  Hempstead 11550
Parcel Post, Sta. Jamaica 11418
Parcel Post, Sta. Brooklyn 11215
Paris 13429
Paris Station 13430

Parish 13131
Parishville 13672
Park Slope, Sta. Brooklyn 11215
Parkchester, Sta. Bronx 10462
Parkside, Sta. Flushing 11375
Parksville 12768
Parkville, Sta. Brooklyn 11204
Parkway, Sta. Bronx 10462
Patchin, Sta. New York 10011
Patchogue (1st) 11772
  Davis Park, R. Br. 11728
  East Patchogue, Br. 11772
Patroon, Sta. Albany 12204
Patterson 12563
Pattersonville 12137
Paul Smiths 12970
Pavilion 14525
Pawling (1st) 12564
Peakville 13831
Pearl River (1st) 10965
Peck Slip, Sta. New York 10038
Peconic 11958
Peekskill (1st) 10566
Pelham, Br. New Rochelle 10803
Penataquit, Sta. Bay Shore 11707
Penfield (1st) 14526
Penn Yan (1st) 14527
Pennellville 13132
Perkinsville 14529
Perry (1st) 14530
Perrysburg 14129
Perryville 13129
Peru 12972
Peter Stuyvesant, Sta. New
  York 10009
Peterboro 13134
Petersburg 12138
Phelps 14532
Philadelphia 13673
Phillipsport 12769
Philmont 12565
Phoenicia 12464
Phoenix 13135
Piercefield 12973
Piermont 10968
Pierrepont Manor 13674
Piffard 14533
Pike 14130
Pilgrim, Sta. Bronx 10461
Pilot Knob, R. Sta. Kattskill
  Bay 12844
Pine, Sta. Albany 12203
Pine Bush 12566
Pine City 14871
Pine Hill 12465
Pine Island 10969
Pine Plains 12567
Pine Valley 14872
Piseco 12139
Pitcher 13136
Pitt, Sta. New York 10002
Pittsford (1st) 14534
Plainview, Br. Hicksville 11803
Plainville 13137
Plandome, Br. Manhasset 11030
Planetarium, Sta. New York 10024
Plattekill 12568
Plattsburgh (1st) 12901
  Plattsburgh A F B, Br. 12903
Plattsburgh A F B, Br.
  Plattsburgh 12903
Plaza, Sta. Long Island City ... 11101
Pleasant Valley (1st) 12569

Pleasantville (1st) 10570
Plessis 13675
Plymouth 13832
Poestenkill 12140
Point Lookout 11569
Point Pleasant, Br.
  Rochester 14622
Point Vivian, R. Br.
  Alexandria Bay 13607
Poland 13431
Pomona 10970
Pomonok, Sta. Flushing 11365
Pompey 13138
Pond Eddy 12770
Poolville 13432
Poplar Ridge 13139
Port Authority, Sta. New
  York 10011
Port Byron 13140
Port Chester (1st) 10573
Port Crane 13833
Port Ewen 12466
Port Gibson 14537
Port Henry 12974
Port Jefferson Station (1st) 11776
Port Jervis (1st) 12771
  Westbrookville, R. Br. 12785
Port Kent 12975
Port Leyden 13433
Port Richmond, Sta. Staten
  Island 10302
Port Washington (1st) 11050
Portageville 14536
Porter Corners 12859
Portland 14769
Portlandville 13834
Portville 14770
Postal Concentration Center,
  Sta. New York 11101
Potsdam (1st) 13676
Pottersville 12860
POUGHKEEPSIE (1st) (see
  appendix)
Poughquag 12570
Pound Ridge (1st) 10576
Pratt, Sta. Brooklyn 11205
Pratts Hollow 13434
Prattsburg 14873
Prattsville 12468
Preble 13141
Preston Hollow 12469
Prince, Sta. New York 10012
Princes Bay, Sta. Staten
  Island 10309
Prospect 13435
Prospect Park West, Sta.
  Brooklyn 11215
Pulaski (1st) 13142
Pulteney 14874
Pultneyville 14538
Purchase (1st) 10577
Purdy Station 10578
Purling 12470
Putnam Station 12861
Putnam Valley 10579
Pyrites 13677
Quail, Sta. Albany 12206
Quaker Street 12141
Queens Village, Sta.
  Jamaica (see appendix)
Queensbury, Br. Glens Falls ... 12801
Quogue 11959
Radio City, Sta. New York 10019

Rainbow Lake	12976
Randall, R. Br. Fultonville	12142
Randolph	14772
Ransomville	14131
Raquette Lake	13436
Ravena	12143
Ravenwood, Br. Albany	12205
Ray Brook	12977
Raymondville	13678
Reading Center	14876
Red Creek	13143
Red Hook (1st)	12571
Red Hook, Sta. Brooklyn	11231
Redfield	13437
Redford	12978
Redwood	13679
Rego Park, Sta. Flushing	11374
Remsen	13438
Remsenburg	11960
Rensselaer (1st)	12144
Rensselaer Falls	13680
Rensselaerville	12147
Retsof	14539
Rexford	12148
Rexville	14877
Rhinebeck (1st)	12572
Rhinecliff	12574
Richburg	14774
Richfield Springs	13439
Richford	13835
Richland	13144
Richmond Hill, Sta. Jamaica	11418
Richmondville	12149
Richville	13681
Ridge	11961
Ridgemont Plaza, Br. Rochester	14626
Ridgewood, Sta. Brooklyn	11227
Rifton	12471
Riparius	12862
Ripley	14775
River Campus, Sta. Rochester	14627
Riverdale, Sta. Bronx	10471
Riverhead (1st)	11901
Rochdale Village, Sta. Jamaica (see appendix)	
ROCHESTER (1st) (see appendix)	
Rock City Falls	12863
Rock Glen	14540
Rock Hill	12775
Rock Stream	14878
Rock Tavern	12575
Rockaway Beach, Sta. Far Rockaway	11693
Rockaway Park, Sta. Far Rockaway	11694
Rockaway Point, Sta. Far Rockaway	11697
Rockefeller Center, Sta. New York	10020
ROCKVILLE CENTRE (1st) (see appendix)	
Rocky Point	11778
Rodman	13682
Roessleville, Br. Albany	12205
Rome (1st)	13440
Romulus	14541
Ronkonkoma (1st)	11779
Roosevelt (1st)	11575
Roosevelt Field, Sta. Garden City	11530

Rooseveltown	13683
Roscoe	12776
Rose	14542
Rosebank, Sta. Staten Island	10305
Roseboom	13450
Rosedale, Sta. Jamaica	11422
Rosendale	12472
Roseton	12576
Roslyn (1st)	11576
Roslyn Heights (1st)	11577
Rossburg	14776
Rossie, R. Br. Hammond	13646
Rotterdam, Br. Schenectady	12303
Rotterdam Junction	12150
Round Lake	12151
Round Top	12473
Rouses Point (1st)	12979
Roxbury	12474
Ruby	12475
Rugby, Sta. Brooklyn	11203
Rush	14543
Rushford	14777
Rushville	14544
Russell	13684
Ryder, Sta. Brooklyn	11234
Rye (1st)	10580
S U N Y, Sta. Albany	12203
Sabael	12864
Sackets Harbor	13685
Sag Harbor (1st)	11963
Sagaponack	11962
Saint Albans, Sta. Jamaica	11412
Saint Bonaventure	14778
Saint George, Sta. Staten Island	10301
Saint Huberts, R. Br. Keene Valley	12943
Saint James (1st)	11780
Saint Johns Place, Sta. Brooklyn	11213
Saint Johnsville	13452
Saint Josephs	12777
Saint Regis Falls	12980
Saint Remy, R. Br. Kingston	12401
Salamanca (1st)	14779
Salem	12865
Salina, Sta. Syracuse	13208
Salisbury Center	13454
Salisbury Mills	12577
Salt Point	12578
Saltaire, R. Br. Bay Shore	11706
Samsonville, R. Sta. Krumville	12476
Sanborn	14132
Sand Lake	12153
Sandusky	14133
Sandy Creek	13145
Sangerfield	13455
Sanitaria Springs	13836
Santapogue, Br. Babylon	11704
Saranac	12981
Saranac Inn, R. Br. Saranac Lake	12982
Saranac Lake (1st)	12983
Saranac Inn, R. Br.	12982
Saratoga Springs (1st)	12866
Sardinia	14134
Saugerties (1st)	12477
Sauquoit	13456
Savannah	13146
Savona	14879
Sayville (1st)	11782

Scarborough, Sta. Briarcliff Manor	10510
Scarsdale (1st)	10583
Schaghticoke	12154
SCHENECTADY (1st) (see appendix)	
Schenevus	12155
Schodack Landing	12156
Schoharie	12157
Schroon Lake	12870
Schuyler, R. Br. Utica	13502
Schuyler Falls	12985
Schuyler Lake	13457
Schuylerville	12871
Scio	14880
Scipio Center	13147
Scotia, Br. Schenectady	12302
Scottsburg, R. Br. Dansville	14545
Scottsville	14546
Sea Cliff (1st)	11579
Seaford (1st)	11783
Seamens Church Institute, Sta. New York	10004
Seaway Plaza, Br. Watertown	13601
Selden (1st)	11784
Selkirk	12158
Seneca Castle	14547
Seneca Falls (1st)	13148
Sennett	13150
Setauket, Br. East Setauket	11733
Severance	12872
Seward	12199
Shady	12479
Shandaken	12480
Sharon Springs	13459
Sheds	13151
Shelter Island	11964
Shelter Island Heights	11965
Shenorock	10587
Sherburne	13460
Sheridan	14135
Sherman	14781
Sherrill (1st)	13461
Shinhopple	13837
Shirley	11967
Shokan	12481
Shoreham	11786
Shortsville	14548
Shrub Oak	10588
Shushan	12873
Sidney (1st)	13838
Sidney Center	13839
Siena, Br. Albany	12211
Silver Bay	12874
Silver Creek (1st)	14136
Silver Lake	14549
Silver Springs	14550
Sinclairville	14782
Skaneateles (1st)	13152
Skaneateles Falls	13153
Slate Hill	10973
Slaterville Springs	14881
Slingerlands	12159
Sloansville	12160
Sloatsburg	10974
Smallwood	12778
Smithboro	13840
Smithtown (1st)	11787
Smithville	13686
Smithville Flats	13841
Smyrna	13464
Snyder, Br. Buffalo	14226

445

Sodus (1st)	14551
Sodus Center	14554
Sodus Point	14555
Solsville	13465
Solvay, Br. Syracuse	13209
Somers	10589
Sonyea	14556
Sound Beach	11789
Soundview, Sta. Bronx (see appendix)	
South, Sta. Yonkers	10705
South Bethlehem	12161
South Buffalo, Sta. Buffalo	14210
South Butler	13154
South Byron	14557
South Cairo	12482
South Colton	13687
South Corning, Br. Corning	14830
South Dayton	14138
South Edmeston	13466
South Fallsburg (1st)	12779
South Farmingdale, Br. Farmingdale	11735
South Jamesport	11970
South Kortright	13842
South Lansing	14882
South Lima	14558
South New Berlin	13843
South Otselic	13155
South Ozone Park, Sta. Jamaica	11420
South Park, Sta. Buffalo	14220
South Plymouth	13844
South Richmond Hill, Sta. Jamaica	11419
South Road, Br. Poughkeepsie	12601
South Rutland	13688
South Salem	10590
South Schodack	12162
South Schroon	12877
South Side, Sta. Elmira	14904
South Wales	14139
South Westerlo	12163
Southampton (1st)	11968
Southfields	10975
Southold (1st)	11971
Southtown, Br. Rochester	14623
Southview, Sta. Binghamton	13903
Sparkill	10976
Sparrow Bush	12780
Speculator	12164
Spencer	14883
Spencerport (1st)	14559
Spencertown	12165
Speonk	11972
Spragueville, R. Br. Gouverneur	13689
Sprakers	12166
Spring Brook	14140
Spring Glen	12483
Spring Valley (1st)	10977
Springfield Center	13468
Springfield Gardens, Sta. Jamaica	11413
Springville (1st)	14141
Springwater	14560
Staatsburg	12580
Stadium, Sta. Bronx	10452
Stafford	14143
Stamford (1st)	12167
Stanfordville	12581
Stanley	14561
Stanwix Heights, R. Br. Rome	13440
Stapleton, Sta. Staten Island	10304
Star Lake	13690
State University, Sta. Westbury	11568
STATEN ISLAND (1st) (see appendix)	
Steamburg	14783
Steel City, Br. Buffalo	14218
Steinway, Sta. Long Island City	11103
Stella Niagara	14144
Stephentown	12168
Stephentown Center	12169
Sterling	13156
Sterling Forest	10979
Stewart A F B, Br. Newburgh	12550
Stillwater	12170
Stittville	13469
Stockport	12171
Stockton	14784
Stone Ridge	12484
Stony Brook (1st)	11790
Stony Creek	12878
Stony Point (1st)	10980
Stormville	12582
Stottville	12172
Stow	14785
Stratford	13470
Strathmore, Sta. Manhasset	11030
Strykersville	14145
Stuyvesant	12173
Stuyvesant, Sta. Brooklyn	11233
Stuyvesant Falls	12174
Suffern (1st)	10901
Suffolk County A F B, MOU. Westhampton Beach	11978
Sugar Loaf	10981
Summit	12175
Summitville	12781
Sundown, R. Br. Grahamsville	12782
Sunmount, Br. Tupper Lake	12986
Sunnyside, Sta. Long Island City	11104
Sunset, Sta. Brooklyn	11220
Surprise	12176
Swain	14884
Swan Lake	12783
Swormville	14146
Sylvan Beach	13157
Syosset (1st)	11791
SYRACUSE (1st) (see appendix)	
Taberg	13471
Taconic Lake, R. Br. Petersburg	12138
Tahawus, R. Br. Newcomb	12879
Tallman	10982
Tannersville	12485
Tappan (1st)	10983
Tarrytown (1st)	10591
Ten Mile River, R. Br. Narrowsburg	12764
Terminal, Sta. Staten Island	10301
Thendara	13472
Theresa	13691
Thiells	10984
Thompson Ridge	10985
Thompsonville	12784
Thomson	12881
Thornwood (1st)	10594
Thousand Island Park	13692
Three Mile Bay	13693
Throggs Neck, Sta. Bronx	10465
Thurston Road, Sta. Rochester	14619
Ticonderoga (1st)	12883
Tillson	12486
Times Plaza, Sta. Brooklyn	11217
Times Square, Sta. New York	10036
Tioga Center	13845
Tivoli	12583
Tomkins Cove	10986
Tompkins Square, Sta. New York	10009
Tonawanda (1st)	14150
Tottenville, Sta. Staten Island	10307
Town Line, R. Br. Lancaster	14165
Trainsmeadow, Sta. Flushing	11370
Transitown, Br. Buffalo	14221
Treadwell	13846
Tremont, Sta. Bronx	10457
Tri Willow, Br. Rome	13440
Tribes Hill	12177
Triborough, Sta. New York	10035
Troupsburg	14885
Trout Creek	13847
TROY (1st) (see appendix)	
Trumansburg	14886
Truxton	13158
Tuckahoe, Br. Yonkers	10707
Tudor, Sta. New York	10017
Tully	13159
Tunnel	13848
Tupper Lake (1st)	12986
Massawepie, R. Br.	12986
Sunmount, Br.	12986
Turin	13473
Tuscarora	14562
Tuxedo Park	10987
Twelve Corners, Br. Rochester	14618
Tyrone	14887
U S C C, Sta. West Point	10996
U S Public Health Hosp, Sta. Staten Island	10304
Ulster Park	12487
Unadilla	13849
Union, Sta. Endicott	13760
Union Center, Br. Endicott	13760
Union Hill	14563
Union Springs	13160
Uniondale, Br. Hempstead	11553
Unionville	10988
United Nations New York, Sta. New York	10017
University, Sta. Syracuse	13210
University Heights, Sta. Bronx	10452
Upper Jay	12987
Upper Saint Regis, R. Br. Lake Clear	12945
Upper Union, Br. Schenectady	12309
Upton (1st)	11973
Uptown, Sta. Kingston	12401
UTICA (1st) (see appendix)	
Utopia, Sta. Flushing	11366
Vails Gate (1st)	12584

Valatie	12184	
Valhalla (1st)	10595	
Valley Cottage	10989	
Valley Falls	12185	
VALLEY STREAM (1st) (see appendix)		
Valois	14888	
Van Brunt, Sta. Brooklyn	11215	
Van Buren Point, R. Br. Dunkirk	14166	
Van Cott, Sta. Bronx	10467	
Van Del, Br. Buffalo	14217	
Van Etten	14889	
Van Hornesville	13475	
Van Nest, Sta. Bronx	10462	
Vandeveer, Sta. Brooklyn	11210	
Varna, Br. Ithaca	14850	
Varysburg	14167	
Venice Center	13161	
Verbank	12585	
Vermontville	12989	
Vernon	13476	
Vernon Center	13477	
Verona	13478	
Verona Beach	13162	
Verplanck	10596	
Versailles	14168	
Vestal (1st)	13850	
Veterans Administration, Br. Bath	14810	
Veterans Administration Faci. Sta. Batavia	14020	
Veterans Administration Hosp. Sta. Buffalo	14215	
Veterans Hospital, Sta. Syracuse	13210	
Victor	14564	
Victory Mills	12884	
Village, Sta. New York	10014	
Voorheesville	12186	
Waccabuc	10597	
Waddington	13694	
Wadhams	12990	
Wading River	11792	
Wadsworth	14565	
Wainscott	11975	
Wakefield, Sta. Bronx	10466	
Walden (1st)	12586	
Wales Center	14169	
Walker	14566	
Walker Valley	12588	
Wall Street, Sta. New York	10005	
Wallace	14890	
Wallkill	12589	
Walton (1st)	13856	
Walworth	14568	
Wampsville	13163	
Wanakena	13695	
Wantagh (1st)	11793	
Wappingers Falls (1st)	12590	
Warners	13164	
Warnerville	12187	
Warrensburg	12885	
Warsaw (1st)	14569	
Warwick (1st)	10990	
Washington Bridge, Sta. New York	10033	
Washington Mills	13479	
Washingtonville	10992	
Wassaic	12592	
Wassaic State School, R. Sta. Wassaic	12592	
Water Mill	11976	

Waterford (1st)	12188	
Waterloo (1st)	13165	
Waterport	14571	
Watertown (1st)	13601	
Waterville	13480	
Watervliet (1st)	12189	
Watkins Glen (1st)	14891	
Waverly (1st)	14892	
Wawarsing	12489	
Wayland	14572	
Wayne	14893	
Webster	14580	
Webster Crossing	14584	
Weedsport	13166	
Wells	12190	
Wells Bridge	13859	
Wellsburg	14894	
Wellsville (1st)	14895	
West Babylon, Br. Babylon	11704	
West Bangor, R. Br. North Bangor	12991	
West Berne	12191	
West Bloomfield	14585	
West Brentwood, Br. Brentwood	11717	
West Burlington	13482	
West Camp	12490	
West Chazy	12992	
West Clarksville	14786	
West Copake	12593	
West Corners, Br. Endicott	13760	
West Coxsackie	12192	
West Danby	14896	
West Davenport	13860	
West Eaton	13484	
West Edmeston	13485	
West Exeter	13487	
West Falls	14170	
West Farms, Sta. Bronx	10460	
West Fulton	12194	
West Gilgo Beach, Br. Babylon	11702	
West Haverstraw (1st)	10993	
West Hempstead, Br. Hempstead	11552	
West Henrietta	14586	
West Hurley	12491	
West Islip (1st)	11795	
West Kill	12492	
West Lebanon	12195	
West Leyden	13489	
West Monroe	13167	
West New Brighton, Sta. Staten Island	10310	
West Newburgh, Sta. Newburgh	12550	
West Nyack (1st)	10994	
West Oneonta	13861	
West Park	12493	
West Point (1st)	10996	
West Ridge, Sta. Rochester	14615	
West Rush	14587	
West Sand Lake	12196	
West Sayville	11796	
West Seneca, Br. Buffalo	14224	
West Shokan	12494	
West Side, Sta. Elmira	14905	
West Stockholm	13696	
West Valley	14171	
West Webster, Br. Webster	14580	
West Winfield	13491	
Westbrookville, R. Br. Port Jervis	12785	

Westbury (1st)	11590	
Old Westbury, Br.	11568	
State University, Sta.	11568	
Westchester, Sta. Bronx	10461	
Westdale	13483	
Westerlo	12193	
Westernville	13486	
Westfield (1st)	14787	
Westford	13488	
Westgate, Br. Rochester	14624	
Westhampton	11977	
Westhampton Beach (1st)	11978	
Westmoreland	13490	
Westons Mills	14788	
Westport	12993	
Westtown	10998	
Westview, Sta. Binghamton	13905	
Wevertown	12886	
Whallonsburg	12994	
Whippleville	12995	
White Creek, R. Br. Eagle Bridge	12057	
White Lake	12786	
WHITE PLAINS (1st) (see appendix)		
White Sulphur Springs	12787	
Whiteface, R. Br. Lake Placid	12946	
Whitehall	12887	
Whitesboro (1st)	13492	
Whitestone, Sta. Flushing	11357	
Whitesville	14897	
Whitney Point	13862	
Willard	14588	
Willet	13863	
Williams Bridge, Sta. Bronx	10467	
Williamsburg, Sta. Brooklyn	11211	
Williamson	14589	
Williamstown	13493	
Williamsville, Br. Buffalo	14221	
Williston Park (1st)	11596	
Willow	12495	
Willsboro	12996	
Willseyville	13864	
Wilmington	12997	
Wilson	14172	
Wilton, R. Br. Saratoga Springs	12866	
Windham	12496	
Windsor	13865	
Wingdale	12594	
Winthrop	13697	
Witherbee	12998	
Wolcott	14590	
Wood Haven, Sta. Jamaica	11421	
Woodbourne	12788	
Woodbury (1st)	11797	
Woodgate	13494	
Woodhull	14898	
Woodlawn, Sta. Bronx	10470	
Woodmere (1st)	11598	
Woodridge	12789	
Woodside, Sta. Flushing	11377	
Woodstock (1st)	12498	
Woodville	13698	
Woolsey, Sta. Long Island City	11105	
Worcester	12197	
Wurtsboro	12790	
Wyandanch (1st)	11798	
Wyckoff Heights, Sta. Brooklyn	11237	
Wykagyl, Sta. New Rochelle	10804	

Wynantskill (1st)	12198
Wyoming	14591
Yaphank	11980
YONKERS (1st) (see	
appendix)	
York	14592
Yorkshire	14173
Yorktown Heights (1st)	10598
Yorkville (1st)	13495
Youngstown	14174
Youngsville	12791
Yulan	12792

ALBANY 122

POST OFFICE BOXES

Box Nos.

1-2000	Main Office	01
4001-4200	Patroon Sta	04
5001-5200	Roessleville Br	05
6001-6200	Quail Sta	06
7001-7100	Capitol Annex Sta	25
7101-7400	Capitol Sta	24
8001-8200	Pine Sta	03
8501-8700	Academy Sta	08
9001-9100	Delaware Sta	09
11001-11790	Loudonville Br	11

RURAL ROUTES

1	03
2	05

STATIONS, BRANCHES AND UNITS

Academy Sta	08
Capitol Sta	24
Delaware Sta	09
Loudonville Br	11
Mc Kownville Br	03
Patroon Sta	04
Pine Sta	03
Quail Sta	06
Ravenwood Br	05
Roessleville Br	05
S U N Y Sta	03
Siena Br	11
General Delivery	01
Postmaster	07

APARTMENTS, HOTELS, MOTELS

Adams Park, 550 New Scotland Ave	08
Berkshire, 140 State	07
Cameo Apartments 12 California Ave	05
Banker Village, 129 Lincoln Ave	06
De Witt Clinton, 142 State	07
Dutch Village, Van Rensselaer Ave	04
Elouise, 11 South Lake Ave	03
Harmony Hill	03
Holiday Inn Of America, 1614 Central	05
Holiday Inn Of America, 575 Broadway, Menands	04
Howard Johnson Motor Lodge, Southern Blvd	09
Inn Towne Motel, 300 Broadway	07
Knickerbocker, 175 Jay	10
Lake, 47 South Lake Ave	03

Livingston Village, 421 Livingston Ave	06
Loudon Arms, 308 Northern Blvd	04
Maytlower, 6 South Lake Ave	03
Menands Garden	04
New Kenmore, 76 North Pearl	07
Park Lane	04
Philip Schuyler, 75 Willett	10
Riverhill, Van Rensselaer Blvd	04
Stonehenge, Circle Lane	03
Thruway, 1375 Washington Ave	06
Tom Sawyer Motor Inn, 1444 Western Ave	03
Towers Of Colonie Center, 420 Sandcreek Road	05
Town House Motor, Northern Blvd & Shaker Rd	04
Wellington, 136 State	07
Willett, 84 Willet	10

BUILDINGS

Albany County Airport, Albany Shaker Rd	11
Albany County Jail, Shaker Road	11
Albany Institute Of History & Art, 125 Washington Ave	10
Ann Lee Home	11
City & Country Savings Bank, 100 State	07
City Hall, Eagle Street	07
City Parks, Hoffman Ave	09
Colonie Center Central Ave At Wolf Road	05
County, Eagle	07
Delaware & Hudson, The Plaza	07
Executive Park, Western Ave Fuller Rd	03
Federal, Broadway	07
Harmanus Bleecker Library, Washington Ave & Dove	10
Home Savings Bank, 11 North Pearl	07
K-Mart 1860 Central Ave	05
National Savings Bank, 90 State	07
Nelson House, 5 Samaritan Rd	08
New York State Campus Site, Washington Ave	26
New York State Capitol, Eagle State & Washington Ave	24
New York State Education, Washington Ave	24
New York State Office, S Swan	25
New York Telephone	

Company, 158 State	07
Northway Mall 1440 Central Ave	05
Standard, 112 State	07
State Bank, 75 State	07
Stuyvesant Plaza, Western Ave & Fuller Rd	03
University Plaza, 1215 Western Ave	03
West Mall Plaza, Central Ave	06
Westgate, Central Ave & Colvin Ave	06

GOVERNMENT OFFICES

Court Of Appeals Hall, 20 Eagle	07
Internal Revenue Service, 161 Washington Ave	10
Old Post Office, Broadway & State	07

HOSPITALS

Albany Hospital For Incurables, Mc Carty Ave	02
Albany Palsy Center, 100 New Scotland Ave	08
Albany, 43 New Scotland Ave	08
Childs, University Heights	08
Memorial, Northern Blvd	04
Saint Margarets, 27 Hackett Blvd	08
Saint Peters, 632 New Scotland Ave	08
Veterans Administration, 113 Holland Ave	08

UNIVERSITIES AND COLLEGES

Albany Business, 130 Washington Ave	10
Albany College Of Pharmacy, 106 New Scotland Ave	08
Albany Law School, 80 New Scotland Ave	08
Albany Medical College, 47 New Scotland Ave	08
College Of St Rose, 979 Madison Ave	03
Maria College, 700 New Scotland Ave	08
Russell Sage	10
Siena College, Rt 9 Loudonville	11
State University Of New York At Alba, 1400 Washington Ave	03

BABYLON   117

POST OFFICE BOXES

Box Nos.

1-600	Main Office	02
1001-1128	West Babylon Br	04
2001-2310	North Babylon Br	03

STATIONS, BRANCHES AND UNITS

North Babylon Br	03
Oak Beach Br	02
Santapogue Br	04
West Babylon Br	04
West Gilgo Beach Br	02
General Delivery	02
Postmaster	02

BINGHAMTON   139

POST OFFICE BOXES

Box Nos.

1-117	East Side Sta	04
1-144	Southview Sta	03
1-235	Westview Sta	05
301-1895	Main Office	02

RURAL ROUTES

1,2	03
3	04
4	01
5	05
6	04

STATIONS, BRANCHES AND UNITS

East Side Sta	04
Front Street Br	05
Hospital Sta	04
Southview Sta	03
Westview Sta	05
General Delivery	02
Postmaster	02

APARTMENTS, HOTELS, MOTELS

Banner Motel, 1169 Front	05
Carlisle Apartments, 150 Moeller	04
Chenango Apartments, 100 Robert	01
Clayton Village Apartments, 412 Clubhouse Rd	03
Colonial Motor Inn, Vestal Pkwy	03
Country Towne, 100 Robert	01
Dixie, 106 Henry	04
Foothills Motel, Upper Court	04
Holiday Inn, Upper Court	04
Holiday Inn, Vestal Pkwy	03
Mayfair Motel, 1424 Front	01
Ramada Inn 65 Front	05
River House, 40 Front	05

Riverside Towers, 5 Riverside Dr	05
Saratoga Heights Apartments, Saratoga Hts	03
Saratoga Terrace Apartments, Saratoga Ter	03
Sheraton Inn, 50 Front	02
Terry Town Apartments, 414 Clubhouse Rd	03
Thruway Motel, 399 Court	04
Treadway Inn 2 4 Hawley St	02
Windermere, 260 Washington	01

BUILDINGS

Binghamton Plaza, West State	01
Chenango Plaza, Upper Front	01
Colonial Plaza 32 West State St	01
Fowler Dick & Walker, 19 Court	02
Marine Midland, 84 Court	01
Mc Leans Department Stores, 89 Court	02
Montgomery Ward Company, 38 Main	02
Oneil, 70 Court	01
Press, 19 Chenango	01
Public Library, 78 Exchange	01
Sears Roebuck & Company, 174 Court	02
Security Mutual, 84 Exchange	01
Vestal Plaza, Vestal Pkwy	03

GOVERNMENT OFFICES

Binghamton City School District, 98 Oak	05
City Hall, 95 Collier	01
County Welfare Dept, 901 Front	
Courthouse, Courthouse Square	01
Department Of Education, 98 Oak	05
Department Of Motor Vehicles District Office, 184 Court	01
Department Of Public Works, 71 Fredrick	01
Department Of Taxation & Finance, 184 Court	01
Fire Headquarters, 74 Carroll	01
General Services Administration, Hoyt Ave	01
Internal Revenue Service, 15 Henry	02
Labor, 221 Washington	01
Main Post Office, 115 Henry	02
Police Headquarters, 62 Water	01
Public Library, 78 Exchange	01
Social Security Administration, 107 Chenango	02
United States Courthouse, 15 Henry	02
Welfare Department, 251 Water	01

Workmans Compensation Board, 221 Washington	01

HOSPITALS

Binghamton General Hospital, 25 Park Ave	04
Binghamton State Hospital, 425 Robinson	01
County Home & Hospital Box 1704	02
Our Lady Of Lourdes Hospital, 169 Riverside Br	05

UNIVERSITIES AND COLLEGES

Broome Technical Community College, 907 Front	02
Harpur College State University Of New York, Vestal Pkwy	01

BRONX   164

POST OFFICE BOXES

Box Nos.

1-54	City Island Sta	64
1-90	Wakefield Sta	66
1-162	Morris Heights Sta	53
1-162	West Farms Sta	60
1-108	Baychester Sta	69
1-108	Fordham Sta	58
1-108	Parkchester Sta	62
1-108	Riverdale Sta	71
1-108	Throggs Neck Sta	65
1-108	Tremont Sta	57
1-108	Westchester Sta	61
1-108	Williams Bridge Sta	67
1-108	Woodlawn Sta	70
1-210	Boulevard Sta	59
1-216	High Bridge Sta	52
1-216	Hub Sta	55
1-216	Jerome Avenue Sta	68
1-216	Kings Bridge Sta	63
1-230	Mott Haven Sta	54
1-237	Morrisania Sta	56
1-243	Soundview Sta	72
1-252	Main Office	51

STATIONS, BRANCHES AND UNITS

Allerton Sta	67
Baychester Sta	69
Botanical Sta	58
Boulevard Sta	59
Castle Hill Sta	62
City Island Sta	64
Claremont Park Sta	57
Cranford Sta	70

Bronx (Con.)	104
Crotona Park Sta	60
Esplanade Sta	69
Fieldston Sta	63
Fordham Sta	58
High Bridge Sta	52
Hillside Sta	69
Hub Sta	55
Jerome Avenue Sta	68
Kings Bridge Sta	63
Longwood Sta	59
Melcourt Sta	51
Morris Heights Sta	53
Morris Park Sta	61
Morrisania Sta	56
Mosholu Sta	67
Mott Haven Sta	54
Mount Carmel Sta	58
Oak Point Sta	55
Ogden Sta	52
Parkchester Sta	62
Parkway Sta	62
Pilgrim Sta	61
Riverdale Sta	71
Soundview Sta	72
Stadium Sta	52
Throggs Neck Sta	65
Tremont Sta	57
University Heights Sta	52
Van Cott Sta	67
Van Nest Sta	62
Wakefield Sta	66
West Farms Sta	60
Westchester Sta	61
Williams Bridge Sta	67
Woodlawn Sta	70
General Delivery	51
Postmaster	51

BUILDINGS

Bronx Terminal Market, E.150th St & Cromwell Ave	51
N.Y.C. Terminal Market (Hunts P'T Mkt), Hunts Pt & E. Bay Av	74

HOSPITALS

Abraham Jacobi, Pelham Pkwy S & Eastchstr Rd	61
Albert Einstein, 1825 Eastchester Rd	61
Bronx Eye & Ear Infirmary, 321 E Tremont Ave	57
Bronx Municipal, Pelham Pkwy S & Eastchstr Rd	61
Bronx State Hospital, Haswell & Industrial	61
Bronx-Lebanon Concourse Div. Grand Concourse & E Mt Eden Av	57
Bronx-Lebanon Fulton Division, 1276 Fulton Ave	56
Fordham, Southern Blvd & E Fordham Rd	58
Frances Schervier, Independence Ave & W 227	63
Home Of Daughters Of Jacob, Findlay Ave & E 167th	56

House Of Calvary, 1600 Macombs Rd	52
Lincoln, Concord Ave & E 141st	54
Misericordia, 600 E 233rd	66
Montefiore, E Gunhill & Bainbridge Ave	67
Morrisania City, Walton Ave & E 168th	52
Mount Eden, 199 E Mt Eden Ave	57
Nathan B Van Etten, Morris Park Ave & Eastchstr Rd	61
Parkchester General, 1425 Zerega Ave	62
Pelham Bay General Hospital, 1870 Pelham Pkwy S	61
Prospect, 730 Kelly	55
Royal, 2021 Grand Concourse	53
Saint Barnabas Hosp For Chrodiseases, 4422 3rd Ave	57
Union, 260 E 188th	58
United States Veterans Administration,.130 W Kingsbridge Rd	68
University Heights, 76 W Tremont Ave	53
Westchester Square, 2475 Saint Raymonds Ave	61

UNIVERSITIES AND COLLEGES

Albert Einstein College Of Medicine, 1300 Morris Park Ave	61
Bronx Community College, 120 E 184th	68
Fordham, E Fordham Rd	58
Herbert H. Lehman, Bedford Park Blvd	68
Manhattan, Manhattan College Pkwy	71
Mount Saint Ursula, 330 Bedford Park Blvd	58
Mount Saint Vincent, Riverdale Av & W 261st	71
New York State Maritime College, Fort Schuyler	65
New York University, University Heights	53

BROOKLYN   112

POST OFFICE BOXES

Box Nos.		
1-89	New Lots Sta	68
1-89	Parkville Sta	04
1-100	Gravesend Sta	23
1-100	Stuyvesant Sta	33
1-108	Bushwick Sta	21
1-119	Canarsie Sta	36
1-119	Wyckoff Heights Sta	37
1-138	East New York Sta	07
1-140	Bush Terminal Sta	32

1-148	Bath Beach Sta	14
1-148	Blythebourne Sta	19
1-148	Dyker Heights Sta	28
1-148	Fort Hamilton Sta	09
1-148	Vanderveer Sta	10
1-149	Pratt Sta	05.
1-149	Red Hook Sta	31'
1-149	Ridgewood Sta	27
1-150	Kensington Sta	18
1-159	Bay Sta	35
1-179	Greenpoint Sta	22
1-179	Homecrest Sta	29
1-179	Saint Johns Place Sta	13
1-180	Metropolitan Sta	06
1-206	Flatbush Sta	26
1-208	Bay Ridge Sta	20
1-219	Coney Island Sta	24
1-227	Brevoort Sta	16
1-229	Rugby Sta	03
1-238	Brownsville Sta	12
1-239	Lefferts Sta	25
1-259	Midwood Sta	30
1-265	Ryder Sta	34
1-269	Van Brunt Sta	15
1-329	Adelphi Sta	38
1-359	Times Plaza Sta	17
1-374	Williamsburg Sta	11
1-1818	Main Office	02

STATIONS, BRANCHES AND UNITS

Adelphi Sta	38
Bath Beach Sta	14
Bay Sta	35
Bay Ridge Sta	20
Blythebourne Sta	19
Brevoort Sta	16
Brighton Sta	35
Brownsville Sta	12
Bush Terminal Sta	32
Bushwick Sta	21
Canarsie Sta	36
Classon St.	38
Coney Island Sta	24
Cypress Hills Sta	08
Dyker Heights Sta	28
East New York Sta	07
Embarkation Sta	50
Farragut Sta	03
Flatbush Sta	26
Fort Hamilton Sta	09
Fresh Pond Sta	27
Glendale Sta	27
Gravesend Sta	23
Greenpoint Sta	22
Halsey Sta	33
Highlawn Sta	23
Homecrest Sta	29
Kensington Sta	18
Kingsway Sta	29

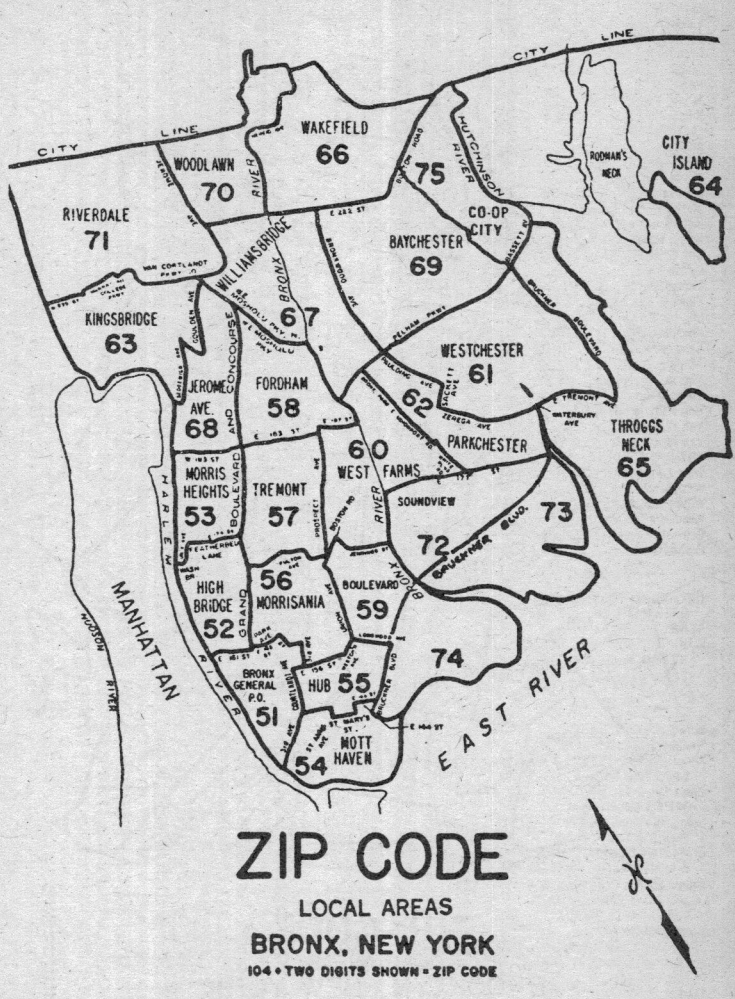

ZIP CODE

LOCAL AREAS

BRONX, NEW YORK

104 • TWO DIGITS SHOWN = ZIP CODE

ZIP CODE
LOCAL AREAS
BROOKLYN, NEW YORK

Brooklyn (Con.)   112

Lefferts Sta............................. 25
Metropolitan Sta...................... 06
Midwood Sta............................ 30
Municipal Building Sta.............. 01
New Lots Sta............................ 08
Newkirk Sta............................. 26
Nostrand Sta............................ 35
Ovington Sta............................ 20
Parcel Post Sta........................ 15
Park Slope Sta......................... 15
Parkville Sta............................ 04
Pratt Sta.................................. 05
Prospect Park West Sta............ 15
Red Hook Sta........................... 31
Ridgewood Sta......................... 27
Rugby Sta................................ 03
Ryder Sta................................. 34
Saint Johns Place Sta............... 13
Stuyvesant Sta......................... 33
Sunset Sta............................... 20
Times Plaza Sta....................... 17
Van Brunt Sta.......................... 15
Vanderveer Sta........................ 16
Williamsburg Sta...................... 11
Wyckoff Heights Sta................. 37
General Delivery...................... 01
Postmaster............................... 01

APARTMENTS, HOTELS, MOTELS

Albany Houses, 1229 Park Pl..   13
Atlantic Towers Plaza East,
    216 Rockaway Ave..............   33
Atlantic Towers Plaza West,
    249 Hopkinson Ave.............   33
Bay View Houses, 9800
    Seaview Ave......................   36
Beach Haven, 2611 West
    2nd..................................   23
Bossert, 98 Montague..............   01
Boulevard Houses, 812
    Ashford.............................   07
Breukelen Houses, 618 East
    108th.................................   36
Brevoort Houses, 296 Ralph
    Ave...................................   33
Brownsville Houses, 307
    Blake Ave...........................   12
Bushwick Houses, 372
    Bushwick Ave......................   06
Clinton Hill Apartments, 345
    Clinton Ave.........................   38
Concord Village, 215 Adams..   01
Coney Island Houses, 2793
    West 33rd...........................   24
Cooper Park, 40 Debevoise
    Ave...................................   11
Cypress Hills Houses, 600
    Euclid Ave..........................   08
Dayton Manor, 9315 Ft
    Hamilton Pkwy.....................   09
Ebbets Field Apartments,
    1720 Bedford Ave................   25
Eleanor Roosevelt Houses,
    314 Pulaski.........................   06
Farragut Houses, 251
    Nassau...............................   01
Flagg Court, 7200 Ridge
    Blvd...................................   09
Forest Crescent, 9060 Union

Turnpike.................................   27
Fort Hamilton Manor, 405
    Battery Ave.........................   09
Fort Hamilton Manor, 620
    Poly Pl...............................   09
Franklin Arms, 66 Orange........   01
Glenwood Houses, 1660
    Ralph Ave...........................   36
Golden Gate Inn, 3867 Shore
    Pkwy..................................   35
Gorman Apartments, 1371
    Linden Blvd.........................   12
Gowanus Houses, 211 Hoyt.....   17
Granada, Ashland Pl &
    Lafayette Ave......................   17
Gravesend Houses, 2793
    West 33rd...........................   24
Howard Houses, 1562 East
    New York Ave......................   12
Independence Houses, 80
    Taylor................................   11
Jimerson Houses, 1407
    Linden Blvd.........................   12
John F Hylan Houses, 372
    Bushwick Ave......................   06
Jonathan Williams Plaza, 227
    Division Ave........................   11
Kings Bay Houses, 2520
    Batchelder..........................   35
Kingsboro Houses, 1880
    Pacific...............................   33
Kingsview Homes, 115
    Ashland Pl..........................   01
Lafayette Garden, 387
    Lafayette Ave......................   38
Lafayette, 25 Lafayette Ave....   17
Linden Houses, 914 Van
    Siclen Ave..........................   07
Lindsay Park Co-Op, 555
    Broadway............................   06
Louis Heaton Pink House,
    2632 Linden Blvd.................   08
Luna Park Houses, 2880
    West 12th...........................   24
Majestic, 230 Duffield.............   01
Manhattan Beach, 156 West
    End Ave..............................   35
Marcy Houses, 648 Marcy
    Ave...................................   06
Margaret, 97 Columbia Hts.....   01
Marlboro Houses, 2740 86th...   23
Mohawk, 379 Washington
    Ave...................................   38
Nostrand Houses, 2955
    Avenue W...........................   29
Palm, 82 Pierrepont...............   01
Patio Gardens, 580 Flatbush
    Ave...................................   25
Philip Howard Apartments,
    1655 Flatbush Ave..............   18
Pierrepont, 55 Pierrepont.......   01
Raymond V Ingersoll, 120
    Navy Walk...........................   01
Red Hook Houses, 62 Mill......   31
Ryerson Towers, 309
    Lafayette Ave......................   38
Saint George, 51 Clark...........   01
Samuel J Tilden Houses, 282
    Dumont Ave.........................   12
Sheepshead Bay Houses,
    2955 Avenue W....................   29

Shorehaven, 2064 Cropsey
    Ave...................................   14
Standish Arms, 169
    Columbia Hts.......................   01
Sumner Houses, 20 Lewis
    Ave...................................   06
Times Plaza, 518 Atlantic
    Ave...................................   17
Tompkins Houses, 105
    Tompkins Ave.......................   06
Towers, 25 Clark.....................   01
Trump Village, 2942 West
    5th....................................   24
University Terrace, 21 St
    James Pl.............................   38
University Towers, 175
    Willoughby..........................   01
Van Dyke Houses, 378 Blake
    Ave...................................   12
Vanderveer Estates, 1352
    New York Ave......................   03
Walt Whitman Houses, 287
    Myrtle Ave...........................   95
Warbasse Houses, 425
    Neptune Ave........................   24
Williamsburg Houses, 176
    Maujer...............................   06
Willoughby Walk Apartments,
    195 Willoughby Ave.............   05
Zeckendorf Residence, 190
    Willoughby..........................   01

BUILDINGS

Albee, Albee Square...............   01
Board Of Education, 110
    Livingston...........................   01
Board Of Health, 295
    Flatbush Ave Ext..................   01
Borough Hall, 205 Joralemon..   01
Brooklyn Academy Of Music,
    30 Lafayette Ave.................   17
Brooklyn Botanic Garden,
    1000 Washington Ave...........   25
Brooklyn Eastern District
    Terminal, 86 Kent Ave..........   11
Brooklyn Museum, 178
    Eastern Pkwy......................   38
Brooklyn Savings Bank 211,
    Montague............................   01
Brooklyn Waterfront Terminal
    Dock, Foot Of Clinton...........   31
Chamber Of Commerce, 26
    Court..................................   42
Chanin, 105 Court...................   01
Civic Center Brooklyn War
    Memorial, Cadman Plaza
    West..................................   01
Clinton Wharf Dock.................   31
Commercial Wharf Dock...........   31
Department Of Welfare, 330
    Jay.....................................   01
Dime Savings Bank Of New
    York, 9 Dekalb Ave..............   01
Domestic Relations, 383
    Adams................................   01
Eighty Hanson Place
    Professional, 80 Hanson
    Pl......................................   17
Fox Medical, 1 Nevins.............   17
Fulton Savings Bank, 395
    Jay.....................................   01

453

Brooklyn (Con.) 112

Galen Hall, 184 Joralemon.... 01
Gowanus Lumber Terminal
Dock, Foot Of Columbia.... 31
Greenpoint Terminal Dock,
Foot Of Greenpoint Ave.... 22
Hall Of Records, 360 Adams.. 01
Kings Lafayette Bank, 200
Montague.................... 01
Lumber Exchange Terminal
Dock....................... 22
Manufacturers Trust, 177
Montague.................... 01
Medical Arts, 142 Joralemon.. 01
Montague Court, 16 Court..... 41
Municipal, Joralemon &
Court...................... 01
New York Docks Trade
Facilities, 360 Furman..... 01
North Pier Dock.............. 31
Pier A Dock.................. 31
Pier B Dock.................. 31
Red Cross, 1 Red Cross Pl.... 01
Supreme Court, 360 Adams..... 01
Temple Bar, 44 Court......... 01
Terminal, 50 Court........... 01
Transit Authority, 370 Jay... 01
U S Internal Revenue Bldg,
35 Tillary................. 01
U S Post Office & Federal
Bldg, 271 Cadman Plaza
East....................... 01
U.S. Courthouse, 225
Cadman Plaza East.......... 01
Williamsburg Savings Bank,
1 Hanson Pl................ 43

GOVERNMENT OFFICES

Immigration And
Naturalization Service, 250
Adams...................... 01

HOSPITALS

Adelphi, 50 Greene Ave....... 38
Bay Ridge, 437 Ovington
Ave........................ 09
Bethany Deaconess, 237 St
Nicholas Ave............... 37
Brookdale Hospital Center,
Linden Blvd & Rockaway
Pkwy....................... 12
Brooklyn Cancer Institute,
451 Clarkson Ave........... 03
Brooklyn Doctors, 4421 15th
Ave........................ 19
Brooklyn Eye & Ear, 29
Greene Ave................. 38
Brooklyn State Hospital For
Mentally Ill, 681 Clarkson. 03
Brooklyn Thoracic, 121 De
Kalb Ave................... 01
Brooklyn Womens, 1395
Eastern Pkwy............... 33
Brooklyn, De Kalb Ave &
Ashland.................... 01
Caledonian, Parkside Ave &
St Pauls................... 26
Carson C Peck Memorial,
Crown & Albany Ave......... 13

Community Hospital, 2525
Kings Hwy.................. 29
Coney Island, Ocean Pkwy &
Avenue Z................... 35
Cumberland, 39 Auburn Pl..... 05
Downstate Medical Center,
450 Clarkson Ave........... 03
Flatbush General Hospital,
719 Linden Blvd............ 03
Greenpoint, Kingsland Ave &
Jackson.................... 11
Holy Family, 155 Dean........ 17
House Of Saint Giles The
Cripple, 1346 President.... 13
Interboro General, 2749
Linden Blvd................ 08
Jewish Hospital Of Brooklyn,
555 Prospect Pl............ 38
Kings County, 451 Clarkson
Ave........................ 03
Kings Highway, 3201 Kings
Hwy........................ 34
Kingsbrook Jewish Med Ctr,
East 49th & Rutland Rd..... 03
Kingsway, 4422 Avenue J...... 34
Lefferts General Hospital,
460 Lefferts Ave........... 25
Linden General, 501 New
Lots Ave................... 07
Long Island College, Henry &
Pacific.................... 01
Lutheran Hospital Of
Brooklyn, E New York Ave
& Junius................... 12
Lutheran Medical Center
Maternity Division, 362 51
St......................... 20
Lutheran Medical Center,
4520 4th Ave............... 20
Maimonides Medical Center
4802 10th Avenue........... 19
Methodist Hospital Of
Brooklyn, 6th.............. 15
Metropolitan-Jewish Geriatric
Center-Parshelsky Pavilion,
2.......................... 24
Metropolitan-Jewish Geriatric
Center, 813 Howard Ave..... 12
Midwood, 19 Winthrop......... 25
Prospect Heights, 775
Washington Ave............. 38
Saint Charles, 277 Hicks..... 01
Saint Giles, 1346 President.. 13
Saint Johns Episcopal
Hospital Of Brooklyn, 480
Herkimer................... 13
Saint Marys, 1298 St. Marks
Ave........................ 13
Samaritan, 759 President..... 15
Shore Road, Shore Rd &
91st....................... 09
Sister Elizabeth Maternity,
362 51st................... 20
Swedish, 1350 Bedford Ave.... 16
Unity, 1545 St Johns Pl...... 13
Veterans Admin Hospital Of
Brooklyn, 800 Poly Pl...... 09
Victory Memorial, 9036 7th
Ave........................ 28
Williamsburg General, 757

Bushwick Ave................. 21
Wyckoff Heights Hospital Of
Brooklyn, 142 St Nicholas
Ave........................ 37

MILITARY INSTALLATIONS

Embarkation (Brooklyn Army
Terminal).................. 50
Fort Ham Military
Reservation................ 52
J.s. Naval Station, 136
Flushing Ave............... 51

UNIVERSITIES AND COLLEGES

Brooklyn College Of
Pharmacy, 600 Lafayette
Ave........................ 16
Brooklyn Law School, 250
Joralemon.................. 01
Brooklyn Polytechnic
Institute, 333 Jay St...... 01
Brooklyn, Bedford Ave &
Avenue H................... 10
Cathedral College Of
Immaculate Conception,
555 Washington............. 38
Long Island University, 385
Flatbush Ave Ext........... 01
New York City Community
College Arts & Science,
300 Pearl.................. 01
Packer Collegiate Institute,
170 Joralemon.............. 01
Pratt Institute, 215 Ryerson. 05
Saint Francis, 180 Remsen.... 01
Saint Johns University
Center, 96 Schermerhorn.... 01
Saint Josephs College For
Women, 245 Clinton Ave..... 05
State University Of N Y
College Of Med, 450
Clarkson Ave............... 03
Zeckendorf Campus, 385
Flatbush Ave Ext........... 01

BUFFALO 142

POST OFFICE BOXES

Box Nos.		
A-H	Kenmore Br	17
A-I	West Seneca	
	Br	24
A-J	B Sta	07
1-47	South Park	
	Sta	20
1-54	Cheektowaga	
	Br	25
1-67	Kensington	
	Sta	15
1-99	Lackawanna	
	Br	18
1-99	South	
	Cheektowaga	
	Br	27
1-117	Bidwell Sta	22
1-117	C Sta	09
1-117	J Sta	08

Buffalo (Con.)   142

1-119	G Sta	13
1-144	Market Sta	03
1-154	B Sta	07
1-177	Hiler Br	23
1-216	West Seneca Br	24
1-240	Kenmore Br	17
1-266	F Sta	12
1-267	Williamsville Br	21
1-270	Niagara Square Sta	01
1-1212	Main Office	40
1-3045	Ellicott Sta	05
900-999	C Sta	09
1000-1099	D Sta	10
1100-1199	E Sta	11
1400-1499	H Sta	14
1600-1699	Hertel Sta	16
1901-2047	Blasdell Br	19
2501-2599	Cheektowaga Br	25
2601-2747	Amherst Br	26

STATIONS, BRANCHES AND UNITS

Amherst Br	26
Bidwell Br	22
Blasdell Br	19
Cass Br	06
Cheektowaga Br	25
Clearfield Br	21
Delray Br	24
Ellicott Sta	05
Georgetown Square Br	25
Grover Br	26
Harlem Br	24
Hertel Sta	16
Hiler Br	23
Kenmore Br	17
Kensington Sta	15
Lackawanna Br	18
Lincoln Park Br	23
Main Mill Br	21
Market Sta	03
Marquette Br	17
Niagara Square Br	01
Northtown Br	26
Northwood Br	23
Snyder Br	26
South Buffalo Sta	10
South Park Sta	20
Steel City Br	18
Transitown Br	21
Van Del Br	17
Veterans Administration HospSta	15
West Seneca Br	24
Williamsville Br	21
General Delivery	40
Postmaster	40

APARTMENTS, HOTELS, MOTELS

Airways, Genesee & Airport Dr	25
Alfred D. Price Cts, 406 Jefferson Ave	04
Algonquin, 76 Johnson Pk	01
Ambassador, 175 North	01
Ashland, 712-718 Ashland Ave	22

Bennett, 2727 Main	14
Best, 4-16 Best	09
Boulevard Towers 90 Meyer Rd	26
Buffalo Travelodge, 984 Main	02
Campanile, 925 Delaware Ave	09
Canterbury Court, 2 Lexington Ave	22
Cathedral, 1022 Delaware Ave	02
Chapel Court, 71 Linda Dr	25
Chippewa, 47 W Chippewa	02
Clinton-Aire, 4237 Genesee	25
Colonial, 401 Delaware Ave	02
Commodore, 1240 Delaware Ave	09
Continental Inn, 3456 Delaware Ave	17
Delaware Park, 1995 Delaware Ave	16
Delaware Towers Apts, 1088 Delaware Ave	09
Elliott, 175 Linwood Ave	09
Elm-Nor, 209 Elmwood Ave	22
Executive Motor, 4243 Genesee	25
Executive Tower Apts, 849 Delaware Ave	09
Fairfax Motor Inn, 715 Delaware Ave	09
Gates Circle, 1306 Delaware Ave	09
Genesee, 308 Pearl	02
Graystone, 24 Johnson Park	01
High Street, 23 High	03
Holiday Inn - Airport, 4600 Genesee, E	25
Holiday Inn - Downtown, 620 Delaware Ave	02
Holiday Inn, Dingens & Rossler	06
Hyde Park, 196 North	01
Jewett, 4 Jewett Parkway	14
Kensington Heights, 32 Glenny Dr	14
La Salle, 186 W Chippewa	01
Lackawanna, 727 Ridge Rd	18
Lafayette, Washington & Clinton	05
Lenox, 140 North	01
Lin-Nor, 3 Linwood Ave	02
Lord Amherst Motor, 5000 Main	26
Mayflower, 66 Summer	09
Mohawk Motor Inn, Main & Michigan Ave	09
New Ashland, 7 Ashland Ave	22
North Court, 197 North	01
Park Lane, 33 Gates Cir	09
Pomeroy Lane, 3901 Main	26
Prince Edward, 490 Pearl	02
Princeton Court, 165 Princeton Ave	26
Regency Motor Hotel, 4408 Mile Strip Rd	19
Roosevelt, 12 Carlton	03
Sherwood, 140 Linwood Ave	02
Statler Hilton, Niagara Sq	02
Stratford Arms, 25 W Utica	09
Stuyvesant, 245 Elmwood	22

Towne House, 999 Main	03
Tudor Arms, 354 Franklin	02
Tudor Plaza, 731-751 West Ferry	22
Twelve Ninety Delaware Apts, 1290 Delaware Ave	09
Villa Nova, 234 Franklin	02
Virginia, 520 Virginia	02
Westbrook House, 675 Delaware Ave	02
Williamsville Motel & Inn, 5447 Main	21
Windsor, 703 W Ferry	22
Y M C A, 45 W Mohawk	02
Y W C A Residence, 245 North	01
400 Elmwood Avenue, 400 Elmwood Ave	22

BUILDINGS

Albright-Knox Art Gallery, 1285 Elmwood Ave	22
Andrews, 35 Court	02
Bank Of Buffalo, 17 Court	02
Blue Cross, 298 Main	02
Bowen, 36 W Huron	02
Brisbane, 403 Main	03
Buffalo & Erie County Historical Society, 25 Nottingham Ct	16
Buffalo & Erie County Public Library, 1 Broadway	03
Buffalo Catholic Institute, 836 Main	02
Buffalo Museum Of Science, Humboldt Parkway	11
Byers, 505 Pearl	02
Byers, 700 Main	02
Central Terminal, 495 Paderewski Dr	12
Corn Exchange, 100 South Elmwood Ave	02
Crosby, 170 Franklin	02
Delaware, 361 Delaware Ave	02
Dun, 110 Pearl	02
Edwards, 155 Franklin	02
Electric, 535 Washington	03
Ellicott Square, 295 Main	03
Erie County Savings Bank, Main Pl	02
Genesee, 1 W Genesee	02
Greater Buffalo Intl Airport, Genesee & Cayuga Rd	25
Henkel, 1377 Main	09
Hurst, 47 W Huron	02
Huyler, 374 Delaware Ave	02
Jackson, 220 Delaware Ave	02
Kleinhans Music Hall, Symphony Cir	01
Lafayette, 6 Broadway	03
Liberty Bank, 422 Main	02
Linwood Medical Ctr, 333 Linwood Ave	09
Lockwood, 80 W Genesee	02
M & T Plaza, 1 M & T Plaza	03
Main Place Tower	02
Marine Trust, 237 Main	03
Market Arcade, 617 Main	03
Memorial Auditorium, 140 Main	03
Merchants Mutual, 250 Main	02
Nellany, 485 Main	03
New York Telephone, 44	

Buffalo (Con.)   142

Church 02
Niagara Frontier Food
  Terminal, 1500 Clinton... 06
Niagara Frontier, 290 Main.. 02
Peace Bridge Plaza 13
Prudential, 28 Church 02
Rand, 14 Lafayette Sq...... 03
Roosevelt Apt. 921 Main 03
Root, 70 W Chippewa 02
Sidway, 775 Main 03
Statler-Hilton Hotel, Niagara
  Sq....................... 02
Thomas Industrial Center,
  1208 Niagara 13
Tishman, 10 Lafayette Sq.... 03
Two Ten Franklin, Two Ten
  Franklin 02
Vars, 344 Delaware Ave..... 02
Walbridge, 43 Court 02
Western, 15 Court 02
White, 292 Main 02
Ymca, 45 W.mohawk 02
Ywca, 190 Franklin 02

GOVERNMENT OFFICES

Buffalo City Hall, 65 Niagara
  Sq....................... 02
Chamber Of Commerce, 238
  Main 02
City Court, 42 Delaware Ave.. 02
County Court, 25 Delaware
  Ave...................... 02
County Hall, Franklin & W
  Eagle.................... 02
Donovan State Office, 125
  Main 03
Erie County, 134 West Eagle.. 02
Federal 111 West Huron..... 02
Federal, 121 Ellicott....... 03
Hud, Fha Office, 560 Main... 02
Rath County Office, 95
  Franklin 02
Social Security Office, 560
  Main 02
State Office, 65 Court...... 02
U S Court House, 64 Court... 02
U S Veterans Administration
  111 W Huron 02

HOSPITALS

Booth Memorial, 740
  Jefferson Ave............. 04
Buffalo Columbus, 300
  Niagara 01
Buffalo General, 100 High... 03
Buffalo State, 400 Forest
  Ave...................... 13
Childrens, 219 Bryant 22
Deaconess, 1001 Humboldt
  Parkway.................. 08
Emergency, 108 Pine 04
Kenmore Mercy, 2950
  Elmwood Ave............. 17
Lafayette General, 113
  Lafayette Ave............. 13
Mercy, 565 Abbott Rd 20
Meyer Memorial E I, 462
  Grider................... 15

Millard Fillmore, 3 Gates Cir.. 09
Our Lady Of Victory, 55
  Melroy................... 18
Roswell Park Memorial
  Institute, 666 Elm 03
Saint Francis, 2787 Main.... 14
Saint Josephs
  Intercommunity, 2605
  Harlem Rd................ 25
Sisters Of Charity, 2157
  Main 14
Veterans Administration,
  3495 Bailey Ave........... 15

UNIVERSITIES AND COLLEGES

Bryant & Stratton, 1028
  Main 02
Canisius 2001 Main 08
Dyouville, 320 Porter Ave... 01
Erie Community, (Ecti), Main
  & Youngs Rd.............. 21
Houghton College, Buffalo
  Campus, 910 Union Rd.... 24
Medaille College, 18 Agassiz
  Cir...................... 14
Rosary Hill, 4380 Main 26
State U Of N Y Interim
  Campus, 4224 - 4250
  Ridge Lea Rd............. 26
State University College At
  Buffalo, 1300 Elmwood
  Ave...................... 22
State University Of New York
  At Buffalo 14
State University Of New York
  Dentistry School, 3435
  Main 14
State University Of New York
  Law School, 77 W Eagle... 02
State University Of New York
  Medical School, 3435
  Main 14
Trocaire, 110 Red Jacket Pky.. 20
Villa Maria College, 240 Pine
  Ridge Rd................. 25

ELMIRA   149

POST OFFICE BOXES

Box Nos.
1-1999   Main Office 02
2001-2117   Elmira Heights
      Br 03
3001-3118   Westside Sta 05
4001-4119   Southside Sta.... 04

RURAL ROUTES

1 03
2 01

STATIONS, BRANCHES AND UNITS

Elmira Heights Br 03
South Side Sta 04
West Side Sta 05
General Delivery 02
Postmaster 01

APARTMENTS, HOTELS, MOTELS

Centennial, 511-519
  Westwater................ 05
Cherrywood Manor, Maple
  Ave...................... 04
Dades 03
Elms, 310 Walnut 01
Evans, 211 Walnut......... 05
Highland Terrace Ashland
  Ave & Mulberry 03
Holiday Inn, Box 64........ 02
Howard Johnson, Box 85.... 02
Mark Twain, Box 178....... 02
Newtown Towers, Dewitt Ave.. 01
Red Jacket, Box 489 02
Tom Sawyer, Box 1046...... 02
Woodland, 1849 West Water.. 05
Yorkshire, R D 01.......... 03

BUILDINGS

Hulett, 338 East Water..... 01
M C I, 212-214 College Ave.. 01
Perry, Box 345............. 02
Robinson, 155-167 Lake 01

HOSPITALS

Arnot Ogden, Grove St & Roe
  Ave...................... 01
Saint Josephs, Box 247..... 02

UNIVERSITIES AND COLLEGES

Elmira College, College Ave
  & Washington Ave........ 01

FAR ROCKAWAY   116

POST OFFICE BOXES

Box Nos.
1-21   Broad Channel
      Sta................. 93
1-116   Rockaway Park
      Sta................. 94
1-119   Arverne Sta 92
1-140   Fort Tilden Sta... 95
1-176   Inwood Long
      Island Br 96
1-205   Rockaway Point
      Sta................. 97
1-599   Far Rockaway 90
151-386   Rockaway
      Beach Sta 93

STATIONS, BRANCHES AND UNITS

Arverne Sta 92
Broad Channel Sta 93
Fort Tilden Sta 95
Inwood L I Br 96
Parcel Post Sta 91
Rockaway Beach Sta 93
Rockaway Park Sta 94
Rockaway Point Sta 97

Far Rockaway (Con.)   116

APARTMENTS, HOTELS, MOTELS

Allens, 163 Beach 98 94
Arlington, 430 Beach 20 91
Arverne Houses, 349 Beach
   54 92
Balfour Arms, 1170
   Nameoake 91
Barocrest, 121 Ocean
   Promenade 94
Bayswater Gardens, 2334
   Mott Ave 91
Beatrice Gardens, 2220
   Cornaga Ave 91
Belle Harbor Gardens, 128
   Newport Ave 94
Bermuda, 20 Elk Dr 91
Beyers, 179 Beach 129 94
Boulevard, 196 Beach 97 93
Catalina, 22 Brookhaven Ave 91
Commodore, 126 Rockaway
   Beach Blvd 94
Cornaga Apartments, 2311
   Cornaga Ave 91
Cornell Hall, 22 Brookhaven
   Ave 91
Crossway, 1502 Mott Ave 91
Crystal, 188 Beach 102 91
Dayton Beach Park 93
Daytona, 22 New Haven Ave 91
Dinsmore Towers, 10 Neilson
   Ave 91
Edgemere Houses, 434 Beach
   54 92
Fitzgeralds, 159 Beach 108 94
Garden House, 133 Rockaway
   Beach Blvd 94
Grand Apartments, 1001
   Nameoake St 91
Grassy Point, 18 Crossbay
   Blvd 93
Greenwood Gardens, 1430
   Greenport Rd 91
M.I.I., 1742 Seagirt Blvd 91
Hammel Houses, 85
   Rockaway Beach Blvd 93
Homestead Apartments, 1012
   Nameoke 91
Kay Rock Gardens, 1420
   Greenport Rd 91
Lawrence Arms, 1261 Central
   Ave 91
Lawrence T.a.i. 833 Central
   Ave 91
Lawrence, 158 Beach 116 94
Loyard, 122 Ocean
   Promenade 94
Manor, 259 Watjean Ct 91
Marguerita, 536 Beach 22 91
Marina Apartments, 2240
   Mott Ave 91
Martinique, 2204 Collier Ave 91
Mc Nultys Ocean, 108
   Rockaway Beach Blvd 94
Monte Carlo, 631 Beach 9 91
Muriel Arms, 22 Mott Ave 91
Nassau, 407 B 20 91
Neilson Apartments, 1011
   Neilson Ave 91
Neilson Gardens, 1014
   Neilson Ave 91

Neilson Imperial, 1040
   Neilson Ave 91
Newport Inn, 129 Newport
   Ave 94
Nordeck Houses, 349 Beach
   57 92
Ocean Country Apartments,
   705 Empire Ave 91
Ocean Park, 169 Beach 115 94
Oceancrest Apartments, 2944
   Beach Chl Dr 91
Oceanview Garden, 2316
   Mott Ave 91
Park Inn, 115 Ocean
   Promenade 94
Park Plaza, 170 Beach 121 94
Peninsula Apartments 91
Pickwiek Arms, 160 Beach
   117 94

Redfern Houses, 1456 Beach
   Channel Dr 91
Riviera, 707 Beach 9 91
Robert Arms, 2308 Mott Ave 91
Rogers, 116 Rockaway Beach
   Blvd 94
Rosoff Terrace, 123
   Rockaway Beach Blvd 94
See Isle, 133 Beach 120 94
Seagirt Apartments, 1430
   Seagirt Ave 91
Seville, 128 Rockaway Beach
   Blvd 94
Sheldon Terrace, 1007
   Hartman Lane 91
Shoreview Apartments, 2287
   Mott Ave 91
Shoreview Cooperative, 1141
   Mcbride 91
Surf House, 130 Beach 133 94
Surfside Park 94
The Leizabeth, 123 Ocean
   Promenade 94
Washington, 124 Rockaway
   Beach Blvd 94
Wavecrest Gardens, 20
   Seagirt Ave 91
White House, 109 Rockaway
   Beach Blvd 94
William, 1054 Beach 22 91

BUILDINGS

Chase Manhattan, 720
   Beach 20 91
Chase Manhattan, 84
   Rockaway Beach Blvd 93
Jamaica Saving Bank 1525
   Central Av 91
National Bank, 1624 Central
   Ave 91
Rockaway Savings Bank,
   1600 Central Ave 91
Smith, 19 Mott Ave 91
Telephone, 1311 Bayport Pl 91

HOSPITALS

Peninsula General Hospital,
   51 Beach Channel Dr 91
Saint Josephs, 327 Beach
   19 91

FLORAL PARK   110

POST OFFICE BOXES

Box Nos.
1-72   Meacham Br 03
1-234   Glen Oaks Br 04
1-448   Elmont Br 03
1-807   Main Office 02
301-389   Alden Manor
      Br 03

STATIONS, BRANCHES AND UNITS

Alden Manor Br 03
Elmont Br 03
Glen Oaks Br 04
Meacham Br 03
General Delivery 02
Postmaster 01

FLUSHING   113

POST OFFICE BOXES

Box Nos.
A-Z   Corona-
     Elmhurst Sta .. 73
1-72   Middle Village
     Sta 79
1-87   Rego Park Sta .. 74
1-146   Flushing A Sta . 58
1-146   Oakland
     Gardens Sta .. 64
1-147   Corona A Sta .. 68
1-163   Whitestone Sta . 57
1-171   College Point
     Sta 56
1-175   Elmhurst A
     Sta 73
1-176   Fresh Meadows
     Sta 85
1-194   Maspeth Sta .. 78
1-234   Little Neck 63
1-375   Bayside Sta 61
1-439   East Elmhurst
     Sta 69
1-574   Jackson
     Heights Sta ... 72
1-597   Forest Hills 75
1-619   Woodside Sta .. 77
1-832   Main Office 52
1-1039   La Guardia
     Airport Sta .. 71
AA-AG   Corona-
     Elmhurst Sta .. 73
400-440   Station C 67
501-1002   Corona-
     Elmhurst Sta .. 73
801-1197   Linden Hill Sta. 54

STATIONS, BRANCHES AND UNITS

Bayside Sta 60
Bay Terrace Sta 60
College Point Sta 56
Corona-A Sta 68
Corona-Elmhurst Sta 73
Douglaston Sta 63
East Elmhurst Sta 69
Elmhurst-A Sta 73

Flushing (Con.)   113

Forest Hills Sta. 75
Fresh Meadows Sta. 65
Horace Harding Sta. 62
Jackson Heights Sta. 72
Junction Boulevard Sta. 72
La Guarda Airport Sta. 71
Linden Hill Sta. 54
Little Neck Sta. 62
Maspeth Sta. 78
Middle Village Sta. 79
Oakland Gardens Sta. 64
Parkside Sta. 75
Pomonok Sta. 65
Rego Park Sta. 74
Trainsmeadow Sta. 70
Utopia Sta. 66
Whitestone Sta. 57
Woodside Sta. 52
General Delivery 52
Postmaster 51

APARTMENTS, HOTELS, MOTELS

Anchor Motor Inn, 204-10
    Northern Blvd. 61
Chateau Chapin, 35-14
    Parsons Blvd. 54
Crossway La Guardia Inn,
    100-30 Ditmars Blvd. 69
El Capitan Motel, 87-02 23rd
    Ave. 69
Fair Motor Inn, Long Island
    Exp & Gd Cent. 68
Forest Hills Inn, 1 Station
    Square. 75
Haven Motel, 68-05
    Woodhaven Blvd 74
Holiday Fair Apts, 97-11
    Horace Harding. 68
La Guardia Hotel, 99-11
    Ditmars Blvd. 69
Midway Motor, Long Island
    Exp & 108 St 68
New York Trades Council, 74-
    09 37th Ave. 72
Pan American Motor Inn, 79-
    00 Queens Blvd 73
Queens Motor Inn, 64-11
    Queens Blvd. 77
Sanford Motor, 140-40
    Sanford Ave 55
Sheraton Tenney Inn, 90-10
    Grand Central Pky 69
Skyway La Guardia, 102-10
    Ditmars Blvd. 69
Stadium View Inn, 37-10
    114th. 68
Sunchester, 37-52 80 St. 72
Travelers, 94-00 Ditmars
    Blvd. 69
Treadway Inn, 37-10 114th 68
Whitestone, 31st Ave &
    131st St 54

HOSPITALS

Booth Memorial, 56-45 Main. .. 55
Deepdale, 55-15 Little Neck
    Parkway. 62
Elmhurst General, 79th St &
    Broadway 73

Flushing, 44-14 Parsons
    Blvd. 55
Hillcrest General, 158-40
    79th Ave 66
Parkway, 70-35 113th. 75
Parsons, 35-06 Parsons Blvd... 54
Physicians, 34-01 73rd. 72
Saint Johns, 90-02 Queens
    Blvd. 73
Saint Marys Hospital For
    Children, 29-01 216th. 60
Salvation Army Maternity
    Home, 56-10 141st. 55
Whitestone, 166th St Corner
    12 Ave. 57
Wyckoff Heights, 102-01 66th
    Road. 75

UNIVERSITIES AND COLLEGES

Queens, 65-30 Kissena Blvd... 67
Queensboro Community, 56-X
    Springfield Blvd. 64

GREAT NECK   110

POST OFFICE BOXES

Box Nos.
261-1000   Great Neck 22
1000-OUT   Old Village
                 Sta. 23

STATIONS, BRANCHES AND UNITS

Kings Point Br. 24
Old Village Sta. 23
General Delivery 22
Postmaster 22

APARTMENTS, HOTELS, MOTELS

Bayberry, 75 No Station
    Plaza 21
Belgrave, 37 Brompton Rd 21
Clent, Clent Rd 21
Colony, 10 Bond 21
Kenwood, 160 Middle Neck
    Rd. 21
Knightsbridge, Knightsbridge
    Rd 21
Summit House. 21
Terrace, Terrace Circle. 21
Towers, 2-4 Spruce. 21
Town House, Cutter Mill Rd.... 21
Tuscan Court, 215 Middle
    Neck Rd 21
Windsor, 21 Barstow Rd 21
Wychwood Gardens, 28 So
    Station Plaza 21

BUILDINGS

Lake Success Industrial Park,
    Community Drive 21
Sperry Gyroscope, Marcus &
    Lakeville 20

HOSPITALS

Great Neck Medical Center,

Community Dr. 21
Great Neck Nursing Home,
    Community Dr 21

UNIVERSITIES AND COLLEGES

United States Merchant
    Marine Academy, Kings
    Point. 24

HEMPSTEAD   115

POST OFFICE BOXES

Box Nos.
1-147   Uniondale Br 53
1-175   East Meadow
              Br 54
1-528   West
              Hempstead
              Br. 52
1-642   Main Office 51

STATIONS, BRANCHES AND UNITS

East Meadow Br. 54
Parcel Post Sta. 50
Uniondale Br. 53
West Hempstead Br 52
General Delivery 51
Postmaster 51

UNIVERSITIES AND COLLEGES

Hofstra University-1000
    Fulton Ave. 50

HICKSVILLE   118

POST OFFICE BOXES

Box Nos.
A-F   Main Office 02
1-237   Plainview Br. 03
1-297   Old Bethpage
              Br 04
1-774   Main Office 02

STATIONS, BRANCHES AND UNITS

Old Bethpage Branch Br. 04
Plainview Br. 03
General Delivery 02
General Delivery Old
    Bethpag 04
General Delivery Plainview B... 03
Postmaster 02

APARTMENTS, HOTELS, MOTELS

Astro Motor-Inn, 828 S Oyster
    Bay Rd 01
Fairhaven Garden
    Apartments, Richard Ave... 01
Hicksville Motor Lodge, Old
    Country&wantagh Pky 01

Hicksville (Con.) 118

Holiday Inn, Sunnyside Blvd	03
Kings Grant Motor Inn, 150 Sunnyside Blvd	03
Pickwick Motor Inn, Roundswamp Rd	03

BUILDINGS

Gertz, Mid-Island Plaza	01
J C Penny, S Oyster Bay Rd	03
Mid Island Herald, 1 Jonathan Avenue	01
Mid-Island Times, 22 W Nicholai	01
Sears Roebuck, 185-195 N Broadway	02

GOVERNMENT OFFICES

Bureau Of Motor Vehicles	01
Department Of Agriculture	02
Hicksville Board Of Education	01
Hicksville Fire Department	01
Hicksville Water District	01
Office Of Civil Defense	01
Plainview Board Of Education	03
Plainview Fire Department	03
Plainview Water District	03
Post Office Department	02
Town Of Oyster Bay	01

HOSPITALS

Central General Of Plainview, 888 Old Country Rd	03
East Nassau Medical Center, 350 S Broadway	01

JAMAICA 114

POST OFFICE BOXES

Box Nos.

1-85	Rosedale Sta	22
1-87	Cambria Heights Sta	11
1-87	Springfield Gardens Sta	13
1-117	Bellerose Sta	26
1-146	Queens Village Sta	29
1-146	Saint Albans Sta	12
1-146	South Ozone Park Sta	20
1-158	South Richmond Hill Sta	19
1-176	Hollis Sta	23
1-186	Ozone Park Sta	17
1-227	Central Sta	35
1-384	Richmond Hill Sta	18
1-386	Kew Gardens Sta	15

1-589	Rochdale Village Sta	34
1-752	J F K Internatl Airport Sta	30
1-1080	Main Office	31
101-249	Howard Beach Sta	14
501-587	Borough Hall Sta	24
1101-1295	Woodhaven Sta	21

STATIONS, BRANCHES AND UNITS

Bellerose Sta	26
Borough Hall Sta	24
Cambria Heights Sta	11
Central Sta	35
Hollis Sta	23
Howard Beach Sta	14
John F Kennedy Airport Sta	30
Kew Gardens Sta	15
Naval Hospital Sta	25
Ozone Park Sta	16
Parcel Post Sta	18
Queens Village Sta	27
Richmond Hill Sta	18
Rochdale Village Sta	34
Rosedale Sta	22
Saint Albans Sta	12
South Ozone Park Sta	20
South Richmond Hill Sta	19
Springfield Gardens Sta	13
Wood Haven Sta	21
General Delivery	31
Postmaster	31

APARTMENTS, HOTELS, MOTELS

Air Host Inn 152-25 138 Ave	34
Bristol 161-01 89 Ave	32
Franklin, 89-05 163rd	32
Holiday Inn Of America, Inc., 175-15 Rockaway Blvd	34
International, Van Wyck Exp & S Cndt Av	30
Riviera Idlewild, 151-20 Baisley Blvd	34
Skyway, 132-10 S Conduit Av	30
Statler Hilton Inn, 138-10 135 Ave	36
Whitman, 160-11 89th Ave	32

BUILDINGS

Borough Hall, 120-55 Queens Blvd	24
Domestic Relations, 105-34 Union Hall	35

GOVERNMENT OFFICES

Board Of Health, 90-37 Parsons Blvd	32

HOSPITALS

Creedmoor State, Winchester Blvd & Hillside Ave	27
Interfaith Hospital Of Queens, 175-10 88 Ave	32
Jamaica, 89th Ave & Van	

Wyck Expway	18
Kew Gardens General, 80-02 Kew Gardens Rd	15
Mary Immaculate, 152-11 89th Ave	32
Queens General, 82-68 164th	32
Queens Village Sanatorium, 218-15 103 Rd Ave	29
Terrace Heights, 87-37 Palermo Ave	23
Triboro, Parsons Blvd & Goethals Dr	32
United States Naval Hospital, Linden Bd & 180th St	25

UNIVERSITIES AND COLLEGES

Saint Johns University, 81-10 Utopia Pkwy	32

LONG ISLAND CITY 111

POST OFFICE BOXES

Box Nos.

1001-1999	Main Office	01
2001-2999	Astoria Sta	02
3001-3999	Steinway Sta	03
4001-4999	Sunnyside Sta	04
5001-5999	Woolsey Sta	05
6001-6999	Broadway Sta	06

STATIONS, BRANCHES AND UNITS

Astoria Sta	02
Broadway Sta	06
Parcel Post Sta	01
Plaza Sta	01
Steinway Sta	03
Sunnyside Sta	04
Woolsey Sta	05
General Delivery	01
Postmaster	01

APARTMENTS, HOTELS, MOTELS

Astoria Housing Project	02
Crystal Gardens	04
Essex House, 42 43rd Ave	04
Golden Gate, 41 43rd Ave	04
Marine Terrace	05
Phipps Gardens, 51 39th Ave	04
Queensbridge Housing	01
Queensview Housing	06
Ravenswood Housing Project	06
Sunnyside Towers, 46 39th Ave	04

BUILDINGS

Boys Club Of Queens, 21-12 30th Road	02

GOVERNMENT OFFICES

Board Of Education, 28 Bridge Plaza N	01
City Prison, Court Square	01

Long Island City (Con.) 111

Criminal Court, 25 Court Sq..... 01
Fire College, 48 35th.......... 01
Health Center, 12 31st Ave..... 06
Labor Department, Bank
  Manhattan Bldg.......... 01
Magistrates Court, 25 Court
  Sq........... 01
Police Dep'T. 108 Pct.......... 01
Police Dep'T. 114 Pct.......... 02
Postal Concentration Center,
  48th & N Boulevard.......... 01
Salvation Army, 45
  Broadway.......... 03
Sanitation Department, 3
  Crescent.......... 01
Sanitation Department, 34
  21st.......... 06
Selective Service, 29 41st
  Ave.......... 01
Traffic Court, 25 Court Sq..... 01
United States Selective
  Service, 29 41st Ave.......... 01

HOSPITALS

Astoria General, 25 30th Ave. 02
Boulevard, 46 31st Ave.......... 03

MILITARY INSTALLATIONS

United States Army Pictorial
  Center, 35 35th Ave.......... 06

MOUNT VERNON 105

POST OFFICE BOXES

Box Nos.
1-147   Fleetwood Sta..... 52
1-1500   Main Office..... 51

STATIONS, BRANCHES AND UNITS

Columbus Sta.......... 53
Fleetwood Sta.......... 52
General Delivery.......... 51
Postmaster.......... 51

NEW ROCHELLE 108

POST OFFICE BOXES

Box Nos.
1-119   Wykagyl Sta..... 04
1-209   Pelham Br..... 03
1-1590   Main Office..... 02

STATIONS, BRANCHES AND UNITS

Castle Sta.......... 01
Pelham Br.......... 03
Wykagyl Sta.......... 04
General Delivery.......... 02
Postmaster.......... 02

UNIVERSITIES AND COLLEGES

Iona College.......... 01
New Rochelle College.......... 01

NEW YORK 100

POST OFFICE BOXES

Box Nos.
1-104   Prince Sta..... 12
1-154   Peck Slip Sta... 38
1-216   Fort George
          Sta..... 40
1-224   Inwood Sta..... 34
1-250   Knickerbocker
          Sta..... 02
1-300   Village Sta..... 14
1-324   Lincolnton Sta. 37
1-360   Audubon Sta.... 32
1-425   Bowling Green
          Sta..... 04
1-448   College Sta..... 30
1-456   Murray Hill
          Sta..... 16
1-475   Hell Gate Sta.. 29
1-503   Old Chelsea
          Sta..... 11
1-518   Hamilton
          Grange Sta..... 31
1-526   Washington
          Bridge Sta..... 33
1-539   Gracie Sta..... 28
1-554   Planetarium
          Sta..... 24
1-575   Canal Street
          Sta..... 13
1-575   Cooper Sta..... 03
1-600   Lenox Hill Sta.. 21
1-600   Midtown Sta..... 18
1-600   Triborough Sta. 35
1-615   Colonial Park
          Sta..... 39
1-650   Cathedral Sta... 25
1-670   Morningside
          Sta..... 26
1-756   Manhattanville
          Sta..... 27
1-779   Times Square
          Sta..... 36
1-927   Madison
          Square Sta..... 10
1-950   Wall Street
          Sta..... 05
1-1039   Peter
          Stuyvesant
          Sta..... 09
1-1175   Ansonia Sta..... 23
1-1200   Radio City Sta.. 19
1-1236   Seamens Ch
          Inst Sta..... 04
1-1299   Franklin D.
          Roosevelt
          Sta..... 22
1-3000   Main Office..... 01
1-3999   Church Street
          Sta..... 08

1-6000   Grand Central
          Sta..... 17
4000-15000 Church Street
          Sta..... 49

STATIONS, BRANCHES AND UNITS

Ansonia Sta.......... 23
Audubon Sta.......... 32
Bowling Green Sta.......... 04
Bryant Sta.......... 36
Canal Street Sta.......... 13
Cathedral Sta.......... 25
Cherokee Sta.......... 28
Chinatown Sta.......... 13
Church Street Sta.......... 07
College Sta.......... 30
Colonial Park Sta.......... 39
Columbia University Sta.......... 25
Columbus Circle Sta.......... 23
Cooper Sta.......... 03
Empire State Sta.......... 01
Federal Reserve Sta.......... 45
Fort George Sta.......... 40
Fort Washington Sta.......... 32
Franklin D Roosevelt Sta..... 22
Governors Island Br.......... 04
Gracie Sta.......... 28
Grand Central Sta.......... 17
Greeley Square Sta.......... 01
Hamilton Grange Sta.......... 31
Hell Gate Sta.......... 29
Howard Sta.......... 13
Inwood Sta.......... 34
Knickerbocker Sta.......... 02
Lenox Hill Sta.......... 21
Lincolnton Sta.......... 37
London Terrace Sta.......... 11
Madison Square Sta.......... 10
Manhattanville Sta.......... 27
Midtown Sta.......... 18
Morgan Sta.......... 01
Morningside Sta.......... 26
Murray Hill Sta.......... 16
No One Hundred Thirty Eight
  Sta.......... 01
Number Eighteen Sta.......... 16
Number Eighty Two Sta.......... 22
Number Forty Sta.......... 01
Old Chelsea Sta.......... 11
Patchin Sta.......... 11
Peck Slip Sta.......... 38
Peter Stuyvesant Sta.......... 09
Pitt Sta.......... 02
Planetarium Sta.......... 24
Port Authority Sta.......... 11
Postal Concentration Center
  Sta.......... 11101
Prince Sta.......... 12
Radio City Sta.......... 19
Rockefeller Center Sta.......... 20
Seamens Church Institute
  Sta.......... 04
Times Square Sta.......... 36
Tompkins Square Sta.......... 09
Triborough Sta.......... 35
Tudor Sta.......... 17
United Nations New York Sta 17
Village Sta.......... 14
Wall Street Sta.......... 05
Washington Bridge Sta.......... 33
General Delivery.......... 01

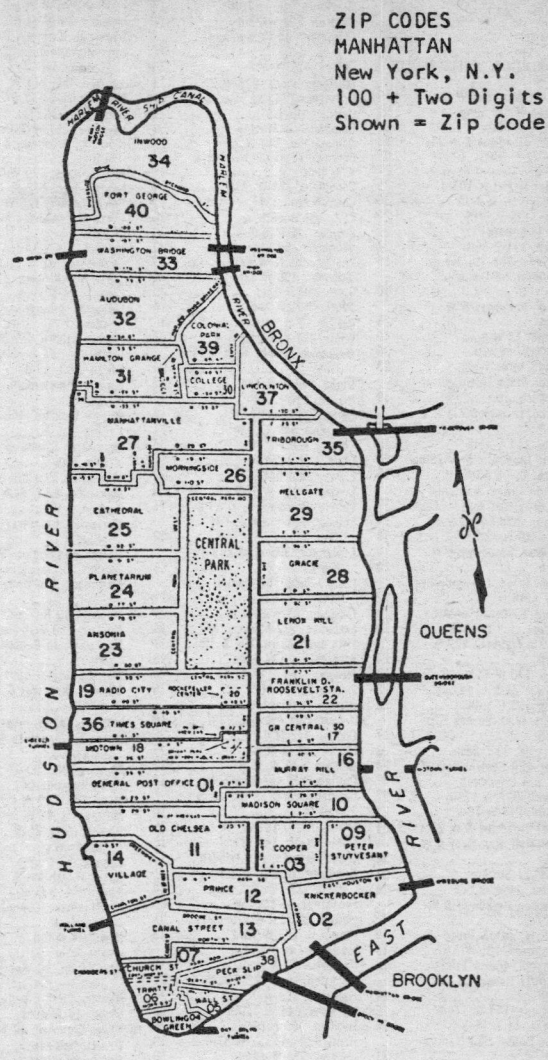

ZIP CODES
MANHATTAN
New York, N.Y.
100 + Two Digits
Shown = Zip Code

New York (Con.) 100

Postmaster 01

APARTMENTS, HOTELS, MOTELS

Abbey Victoria, 151 W 51st . 19
Aberdeen, 17 W 32nd 01
Adams, 2 E 86th 28
Alamac, Broadway & W 71st 23
Albert, 23 E 10th 03
Alden, 225 Central Pk W 24
Alexandria, 250 W 103rd..... 25
Algonquin, 59 W 44th........... 36
Allerton, 130 E 57th 22
Alrae, 37 E 64th 21
America, 331 E 86th............. 28
Americana, 801 7th Ave 19
Amsterdam, 57 Lexington
Ave 10
Ansonia, Broadway & W
73rd 23
Arlington, 18 W 25th............. 10
Ashley, 157 W 47th............... 36
Bancroft, 40 W 72nd............. 23
Barbizon Plaza, 106 Central
Pk S 19
Barbizon, Lexington Ave & E
63rd 21
Barclay, 111 E 48th.............. 17
Beacon, Broadway & W 75th.. 23
Bedford, 118 E 40th............. 16
Beekman Tower, 3 Mitchell
Pl 17
Beekman, 575 Park Ave....... 21
Belair, 349 W 48th................ 36
Belleclaire, Broadway & W
77th 24
Belmont Plaza, Lexington Ave
& E 49th............................. 22
Belmore, 61 Lexington Ave.. 10
Belvedere, 319 W 48th......... 36
Benjamin Franklin, 222 W
77th 24
Berkley, 170 W 74th............. 23
Berkshire, 21 E 52nd............ 22
Beverly, 125 E 50th.............. 22
Biltmore, Madison Ave & E
43rd 17
Blackstone, 50 E 58th.......... 22
Bolivar, 230 Central Park W.. 24
Bond, 125 Chambers............ 07
Braddock, 272 W 126th........ 27
Bradford, 210 W 70th........... 23
Breslin, Broadway & W 29th.. 01
Bretton Hall, Broadway & W
86th 24
Brevort, 11 5th Ave.............. 03
Brewster, 21 W 86th............. 24
Broadmoor, Broadway & W
102nd.................................. 25
Bryant, W 54th & Broadway.. 19
Buckingham, 101 W 57th...... 19
Butler Hall, 400 W 119........... 27
Cambridge House, 333 W
86th 24
Cambridge, 141 W 110th...... 26
Cameron, 41 W 86th............. 24
Carlton House, 680 Madison
Ave 21
Carlyle, 35 E 76th................. 21
Carriage House, 200 E 38th.. 16
Cecil, 208 W 118th................ 26

Chalfonte, 200 W 70th 23
Chelsea, 222 W 23rd 11
Claremont, 140 Claremont
Ave 27
Clifton, 127 W 79th............... 24
Coliseum House, 228 W 71st.. 23
Collingwood, 45 W 35th........ 01
Colony, 30 E 65 21
Columbia, 70 W 46th............ 36
Commander, 240 W 73rd...... 23
Commodore, Lexington Ave &
E 42nd 17
Consulate, 224 W 49th......... 19
Cornish Arms, 311 W 23rd ... 11
Cort, 301 W 48th 36
Croyden, 12 E 86th............... 28
Delmonico, 502 Park Ave..... 22
Des Artistes, 1 W 67th 23
Diplomat, 108 W 43rd........... 36
Dixie, 250 W 43rd 36
Doral, 70 Park Ave............... 16
Dorset, 30 W 54th................. 19
Dover, 687 Lexington Ave 22
Downtown Athletic Club, 19
West 04
Drake, 440 Park Ave 22
Dryden, 150 E 39th............... 16
Earle, 103 Waverly Pl........... 11
East End, 541 E 78th............ 21
Edison, 228 W 47th.............. 36
Elton, 101 E 26th.................. 10
Elysee, 60 E 54th................. 22
Embassy, 154 W 70th........... 23
Empire, Broadway & W 63rd.. 23
Endicott Apartment, 53 W
72nd.................................... 23
Esplanade, 305 West End
Ave 23
Essex House, 160 Central
Park S 19
Excelsior, 45 W 81st 24
Executive, 237 Madison Ave. 16
Fifth Avenue, 5th Ave & 9th.. 11
Franconia, 20 W 72nd 23
Franklin, 164 E 87th............. 28
Fulton, 266 W 46th................ 36
George Washington,
Lexington Ave & E 23rd 17
George, 112 W 47th.............. 36
Globe, 300 W 44th................ 36
Gorham, 136 W 55th............. 19
Gotham, 5th Ave & W 55th.... 19
Gramercy Park, 52 Gramercy
Park N 10
Grand Union, 1815 Park Ave. 35
Grand Union, 34 E 32nd....... 16
Great Northern, 118 W 57th.. 19
Greystone, Broadway & W
91st..................................... 24
Grosvenor, 35 5th Ave 03
Hadson, W 31st & Broadway.. 01
Hamilton, 143 W 73rd........... 23
Hampshire House, 150
Central Park S 19
Hampton House, 28 E 70th... 21
Hargrave, 112 W 72nd.......... 23
Harmony, 544 W 110th......... 25
Hatfield, 103 E 29th.............. 16
Henry Hudson, 353 W 57th... 19
Holland, 351 W 42nd............ 36
Hutton Hall, 304 W 92nd...... 25
Hyde Park, 25 E 77th........... 21
International House, 500

Riverside Dr 27
Iroquois, 49 W 44th............... 36
Irving, 26 Gramercy Pk. 03
John Murray House, 220
Madison Ave 16
Johnson Hall, 411 W 116th... 27
Kenmore Hall, 145 E 23rd..... 10
Kent, 31 West 71st 23
Keystone, 161 W 36th........... 18
Kimberly, Broadway & W
74th 23
King Edward, 120 W 44th...... 36
Kings Crown, 420 W 116th.... 27
Knickerbocker, 120 W 45th... 36
Lancaster, Madison Ave &
38th 16
Latham, 4 E 28th 16
Le Marquis, 12 E 31st........... 16
Lenox, 151 W 44th................. 36
Leonari, 26 E 63rd................. 21
Lexington, Lexington Ave & E
48th 17
Lincoln Square, 166 W 75th... 23
Lombardy, 111 E 56th............ 22
Lowell, 28 E 63rd................... 21
Lucerne, Amsterdam Ave & W
79th 24
Manger Windsor, 100 W
58th...................................... 19
Manhattan Towers, Broadway
& W 76th.............................. 24
Manhattan, 700 8th Ave........ 36
Mansfield, 12 W 44th............. 36
Marlton, 5 W 8th.................... 11
Marseilles, Broadway & W
103rd.................................... 25
Martha Washington, 29 E
29th...................................... 16
Martinique, Broadway & W
32nd..................................... 01
Master, 310 Riverside Dr....... 25
Mayfair, 610 Park Ave 21
Mayflower, 15 Central Park
West 23
Meurice, 145 W 58th.............. 19
Midway, Broadway & W
100th.................................... 25
Milburn, 242 W 76th.............. 23
Monterey, Broadway & W
94th...................................... 25
Morningside, 100
Morningside Dr 27
Motel City, 510 W 42nd......... 36
Murray Hill, 42 W 35th........... 01
Narragansett, 2510
Broadway 25
Nassau, 56 E 59th................. 22
National, 7th Ave & W 42nd... 36
Navarro, 112 Central Park S.. 19
New Endicott, Columbus Ave
& W 81st.............................. 24
New York Hilton, 1335 Ave Of
The Amer. 19
New Yorker, 8th Ave & W
34th...................................... 01
Newton, 2528 Broadway........ 25
Olcott, 27 W 72nd.................. 23
Oliver Cromwell, 12 W 72nd.. 23
One Fifth Avenue................... 03
One-Twenty-Three, 123 W
44th...................................... 36
Orleans 416 Columbus Ave... 24
Paramount, 235 W 46th......... 36

New York (Con.)　　100

Paris, West End Ave & W
97th.............................. 25
Park Plaza, 50 W 77th...... 24
Park Royal, 23 W 73rd....... 23
Park Sheraton, 7th Ave & W
56th.............................. 19
Park Wald, 117 W 58th...... 19
Peerless, 116 W 45th......... 36
Penn Garden, 391 7th Ave ... 01
Penn Post, 304 W 31st....... 01
Peter Cooper, 130 E 39th.... 16
Piccadilly, 227 W 45th........ 36
Pickwick Arms, 230 E 51st.... 22
Pierre, 5th Ave & E 61st..... 21
Plaza, 5th Ave & W 59th..... 19
President, 234 W 48th......... 36
Prince George, 14 E 28th.... 16
Regency, 540 Park Ave....... 22
Regent, Broadway & W
104th............................ 25
Remington, 129 W 46th....... 36
Rio, 132 W 47th................ 36
Ritz Tower, Park Ave & E
57th.............................. 22
Riverside Plaza, 253 W 73rd... 23
Roger Smith, Lexington Ave
& E 47th........................ 17
Roger Williams, 28 E 31st... 16
Roosevelt, Madison Ave & E
45th.............................. 17
Rosoff, 147 W 43rd............ 36
Roy, 535 W 112th.............. 25
Royalton, 44 W 44th........... 36
Rutledge, 161 Lexington Ave... 16
Ruxton, 50 W 72nd............. 23
Saint Agnes Residence, 237
W 74th........................... 23
Saint Francis, 124 W 47th.... 36
Saint George, Broadway & E
12th.............................. 03
Saint James, 109 W 45th..... 36
Saint Moritz, 50 Central Pk
S.................................. 19
Saint Regis, 5th Ave & E
55th.............................. 22
Salisbury, 123 W 57th......... 19
Salvation Army Retirement
Home West End Ave And
W 95th........................... 25
San Carlos, 150 E 50th....... 22
Scott, 132 W 45th.............. 36
Seamans Church Institute,
15 State......................... 04
Seville, Madison Ave & E
29th.............................. 16
Shelton, Lexington Ave & E
49th.............................. 17
Sheraton Motor Motel, 42nd
& 12th Ave...................... 36
Sheraton-Atlantic, Broadway
& W 34th......................... 01
Sheraton-Russell, Park Ave &
E 37th............................ 16
Sherry-Netherland, 5th Ave &
E 59th............................ 22
Simmons House, 350 W 88th... 24
Skyline Motel, 721 10th Ave.... 19
Somerset, 150 W 47th......... 36
Spencer Arms, Broadway & W
69th.............................. 23
Stanhope, 995 5th Ave........ 28

Strand, 206 W 43rd............ 36
Stratford Arms, 117 W 70th.... 23
Stratford, 11 E 32nd........... 16
Studio Club, 210 E 77th...... 21
Summit, Lexington Ave &
51st.............................. 22
Surrey, 20 E 76th.............. 21
Sutton Plaza, 116 E 58th..... 22
Sutton, 330 E 56th............. 22
Taft, 7th Ave & W 50th........ 19
Times Square, 8th Ave & W
43rd.............................. 36
Tudor, 304 E 42nd............. 17
Tuscany, 120 E 39th........... 16
University Broadway And W
3rd............................... 12
Van Rensselaer, 17 E 11th.... 03
Victoria, 7th Ave & W 51st.... 19
Volney, 23 E 74th.............. 21
Waldorf Astoria, Park Ave &
E 50th........................... 22
Wales, 1295 Madison Ave..... 28
Walton, 104 W 70th............ 23
Warrington, 161 Madison
Ave............................... 16
Warwick, 65 W 54th........... 22
Washington & Jefferson, 318
W 51 St.......................... 19
Wellington, 7th Ave & W
55th.............................. 19
Wentworth, 59 W 46th......... 36
Westbury, Madison Ave & E
69th.............................. 21
Westley, 126 W 73rd........... 23
Whitby, 325 W 45th............ 36
Whitehall, 250 W 100th........ 25
Willard, 330 West End Ave.... 28
Wilson, 308 W 58th............ 19
Windemere, 666 West End
Ave............................... 25
Winslow, Madison Ave &
E 55th............................ 22
Wolcott, 4 W 31st.............. 01
Woodstock, 127 W 43rd....... 36
Woodward, Broadway & W
55th.............................. 19
York, 7th Ave & W 36th........ 18

BUILDINGS

Associated Press, 50
Rockefeller Plaza.............. 20
Astor Plz........................ 36
Battery Park Plz................ 04
China Daily News, 20
Elizabeth........................ 13
China Tribune, 210 Canal..... 13
Daily News Record, 7 E 12.... 03
Daily News, 220 E 42........... 17
El Dario, 181 Hudson.......... 13
Forward, 175 E Broadway...... 02
Four Sherman Plz.............. 23
Gulf & Western Plz, 15
Columbus Cir................... 23
Hammarskjold Plz.............. 17
Il Progresso, 260 Audubon
Ave............................... 33
Journal Of Commerce, 99
Wall.............................. 05
La Prensa, 181 Hudson........ 13

Liberty Plz...................... 06
Lincoln Sq. Plz................. 23
Madison Sq. Plz................ 10
Morning Telegraph, 525 W
52................................ 19
New York Amsterdam News,
2340 8th Ave................... 27
New York Courier, 15 W
125th............................. 27
New York Plz.................... 04
New York Post 210 South..... 02
New York Times, 229 W 43 ... 36
One Pennsylvania Plz.......... 01
One Sherman Plz.............. 23
Pace Plz 41 Park Row......... 38
State Street Plz................. 04
Stevem Plz...................... 36
United Journal, 199 Canal..... 13
Wall Street Journal, 30
Broad............................ 04
Womens Wear, 7 E 12......... 03
World Trade Center............ 48
World Trade Center, New York
State Agencies................. 47
75 Rockefeller Plz.............. 19

GOVERNMENT OFFICES

Alcoholic Beverage Control
Board............................ 07
Athletic Commission, 226 W
47................................ 36
Banking Department, 100
Church........................... 07
Board Of Elections............ 13
Board Of Estimate............. 07
Bureau Of Motor Vehicles,
155 Worth....................... 13
Chief Medical Examiner....... 16
City Civil Service
Commission..................... 13
City Clerk........................ 07
City Collector................... 07
Commerce & Industrial
Development.................... 17
Customs House, Broadway &
Bowling Grn.................... 04
Depart. Of Consumer Affairs... 13
Department Of Buildings...... 07
Department Of Commerce,
230 Park Ave.................... 17
Department Of Correction..... 13
Department Of Finance........ 07
Department Of Health......... 13
Department Of Hospitals...... 13
Department Of Housing &
Building......................... 38
Department Of Insurance,
123 William...................... 38
Department Of License........ 13
Department Of Markets........ 13
Department Of Public Events... 22
Department Of Public Works... 07
Department Of Purchases..... 07
Department Of Sanitation..... 07
Department Of Taxation &
Finance, 80 Center............ 13
Department Of Water Supply
Gas & Electricity.............. 07
Department Of Welfare........ 13
District Attorney................ 13

New York (Con.) 100

Federal Building, 641
Washington 14
Federal Bureau Of
Investigation, 201 E 69th.. 21
Federal Communications
Commission, 641
Washington 14
Fire Department 07
Harness Racing Commission,
820 2nd Ave 17
Housing Authority 07
Human Rights Commission .. 13
Immigration & Naturalization
Service, 20 W Broadway.... 07
Interior Department Bureau
Of Commerce, 155 John.... 38
Internal Revenue Service,
120 Church 07
Marriage Licenses 07
Mayors Office 07
Office Of Civil Defense 22
Police Department 13
Police Hack Bureau 13
Port Of New York Authority,
111 8th Ave 11
Post Office Department, 419
8th Ave 01
Racing Commission, 598
Madison Ave 22
Railroad Retirement Board,
341 9th Ave 01
Reconstruction Finance
Corporation, 20 Exchange
Pl 05
Rent Commision Temporary
State Housing, 50 Park Pl.. 07
Selective Service System, 26
Federal Plz 07
Social Security
Adminstration, 39
Broadway 06
State Insurance Fund, 199
Church 07
Third Naval District, 90
Church 07
Veterans Administration, 252
7 Ave 81
Weather Bureau, 30
Rockefeller Center............. 20
Workmans Compensation, 50
Park Pl 07

HOSPITALS

Animal Medical Center, York
Ave & 62nd........................ 21
Babies, Broadway & 167th.... 32
Beekman Downtown, 178
William 38
Bellevue Medical, Foot Of E
26th 16
Bernstein Institute, 307 2nd
Ave 03
Beth Israel, Stuyvesant Sq &
E 17th 03
Bird S Coler, Welfare Island.. 17
Burke Foundation, 164 E
124th 35
College View Nursing Home,
421 W 144th...................... 31

Columbia Presbyterian, 622
W 168th 32
Columbus, 227 E 19th......... 03
Cornell Medical, 1300 York
Ave 21
Delafield Hospital, 99 Ft
Washington Ave 32
Doctors, East End Ave & E
87th 28
East Harlem Center, 2294
3rd Ave 35
Eye Institute, 635 W 165th.. 32
Flower & Fifth, 5th Ave & E
105th 29
French, 324 W 30th W......... 01
Goldwater Memorial, Welfare
Island 17
Gouverneur, Gouverneur Slip.. 02
Gracie Square, 420 E 76th.... 21
Guggenheim Hosp Mount
Sinai Hospital, 1176 5th
Ave 29
Harkness Pavilion, 180 Ft
Washington Ave 32
Harlem Health Center, 2238
5th Ave 37
Harlem Uptown Med., 2099
Lexington Ave 35
Harlem, Lenox Ave & W
136th 37
Home & Hospital Of The
Daughters Of Israel, 1260
5th Ave 29
Hospital For Joint Diseases,
1919 Madison Ave 35
Hospital For Special Surgery,
535 E 70th 21
Italian, 123 W 110th........... 26
James Ewing, 1250 1st Ave .. 21
Jewish Board Of Guardians,
120 W 57th......................... 19
Jewish Memorial, Broadway &
W 196th 40
Klingen Stein Pavilion Mount
Sinai, 1176 5th Ave 29
Knickerbocker, 70 Convent
Ave 27
Lenox Hill, 100 E 77th......... 21
Leroy, 40 E 61st................... 21
Madison, 30 E 76th.............. 21
Manhattan Eye Ear & Throat,
210 E 64th 21
Mayflower Nursing Home,
601 West End Ave 24
Medical Arts Center, 57 W
57th 19
Memorial Clinic, 1269 York
Ave 21
Memorial, 444 E 68th.......... 21
Metropolitan, 1901 1st Ave .. 29
Midtown, 309 E 49th........... 17
Mother Cabrini Memorial,
611 Edgecombe Ave 32
Mount Sinai, 5th Ave & E
100th 29
Neurological Institute, Ft
Wash Ave & W 168th......... 32
New York Eye & Ear
Infirmary, 310 E 14th......... 03
New York Foundling, 1175
3rd Ave 21

New York Hospital, 525 E
68th 21
New York Infirmary, 321 E
15th 03
New York University Bellevue
Medical, 550 1st Ave 16
Park East, 112 E 83rd.......... 28
Park West, 170 W 76th........ 23
Parkway, 123 W 110th......... 26
Physical Medicine &
Rehabilitation Institution,
400 E 34 16
Polyclinic, 345 W 50th......... 19
Regent, 115 E 61st.............. 21
Rockefeller Hospital, York Ave
& E 66th 21
Roosevelt, 9th Ave & W 59th.. 19
Saint Clares, 415 W 51st..... 19
Saint Elizabeths, 689 Ft
Washington Ave 48
Saint Lukes, 421 W 113th.... 25
Saint Vincents, 7th Ave & W
11th 11
Sanger Home, 500 W 57th... 19
Sloan Maternity, 622 W
168th 32
Sydenham, 565 Manhattan
Ave 27
Trafalgar, 161 E 90th........... 28
University, 560 1st Ave........ 16
Veterans Administration, 408
1st Ave 18
Wadsworth, 629 W 185th..... 33
Wickersham, 133 E 58th...... 22
Womans, 1111 Amsterdam
Ave 25

UNIVERSITIES AND COLLEGES

Barnard, Broadway & W
119th 27
Bellevue Medical, 550 1st
Ave 16
Borough Of Manhattan
Community College, 134 W
51st 20
Cathedral, 555 West End
Ave 24
City College Of New York, B.
Baruch Br, 17 Lexington
Ave 10
City University, Graduate
Center, 33 W 42nd............. 36
College Of Physicians &
Surgeons, 630 W 168th..... 32
College Of The City Of New
York, Convent Ave & W
139th 31
Columbia University College
Of Pharmacy, 121 W 68th.. 23
Columbia University New
York School Of Social, 2 E
91 St 28
Columbia University,
Broadway & W 116th......... 27
Convent Of The Sacred Heart,
1 E 91st.............................. 28
Cooper Union, 50 Astor
Place 03
Cornell University Medical,
1300 York Ave 21
Fordham Law School, 140 W
62nd.................................... 23

New York (Con.) 100

Fordham, 302 Broadway 07
General Theological
  Seminary, 175 9th Ave...... 11
Hebrew College, 40 W 68..... 23
Hunter, 695 Park Ave........... 21
Jewish Theological Seminary
  Of America, Broadway &
  122nd................................... 27
New School, 66 W 12th......... 11
New York College Of
  Dentistry, 421 First Ave..... 10
New York Medical College,
  1249 5th Ave...................... 29
New York Theological
  Seminary, 335 E 49th......... 17
New York Univ Courant Inst
  Of Math Sciences, 251
  Mercer................................ 12
New York University College
  Of Medicine, 550 1st Ave... 16
New York University,
  Washington Sq.................... 03
Pace, 41 Park Row................. 38
Rhodes School, 11 W 54th..... 19
Rockefeller University, York
  Ave & E 66th....................... 21
Teachers, 525 W 120th.......... 27
Union Theological Seminary,
  Broadway & W 120th.......... 27
Yeshiva Univ., Graduate
  Center, 55 5th Ave............. 03
Yeshiva Univ., Main Center,
  500 W 185th....................... 33
Yeshiva Univ., Midtown
  Center, 253 Lexington Ave. 16

NAMED STREETS

Abingdon Pl & Sq 14
Academy.................................. 34
Albany..................................... 06
Allen.. 02
Amsterdam Ave
  1-339................................... 23
  340-639................................ 24
  640-1098 (EVEN)................. 25
  641-1139 (ODD).................. 25
  1100-1478 (EVEN)............... 27
  1141-1479 (ODD)............... 27
  1480-1880............................ 31
  1881-2268............................ 32
  2269-2565............................ 33
  2566-OUT............................ 40
Ann... 38
Arden...................................... 40
Asser Levy Pl.......................... 10
Astor Pl.................................. 03
Astor Plz................................ 36
Attorney.................................. 02
Audubon Ave
  1-160................................... 32
  161-439................................ 33
  440-OUT.............................. 40
Avenue A................................ 09
Avenue B................................ 09
Avenue C................................ 09
Avenue D................................ 09
Avenue Of Americas
  1-204................................... 13
  205-415 (ODD).................... 14
  206-334 (EVEN).................. 14

336-650 (EVEN)..................... 11
417-649 (ODD)...................... 11
651-773................................. 10
774-960................................. 01
961-1080............................... 18
1081-1219............................. 36
1220-1279 (EVEN)................ 12
1280-OUT............................. 19
Bank...................................... 14
Barclay.................................. 07
Barrow................................... 14
Baruch Dr & Pl...................... 02
Battery Pl.............................. 04
Baxter
  25-OUT (ODD)................... 13
  28-OUT (EVEN).................. 13
Bayard
  1-38..................................... 02
  39-OUT................................ 13
Beach.................................... 13
Beak...................................... 34
Beaver
  1-53 (ODD)......................... 04
  2-74 (EVEN)....................... 04
  55-OUT (ODD).................... 05
  76-OUT (EVEN)................... 05
Bedford................................. 14
Beekman................................ 38
Beekman Pl............................ 22
Bennett Ave
  1-131................................... 33
  132-OUT.............................. 40
Benson.................................. 13
Bethune................................. 14
Birmingham........................... 02
Bishops Ln............................. 07
Bleecker
  1-226................................... 12
  227-OUT.............................. 13
Bloomfield............................. 14
Bogardus Pl.......................... 40
Bond...................................... 12
Bowery
  1-279 (ODD)....................... 02
  2-148 (EVEN)..................... 13
  150-364 (EVEN).................. 12
  281-OUT (ODD)................... 03
  366-OUT (EVEN).................. 04
Bowling Green....................... 03
Bradhurst Ave
  1-63..................................... 30
  64-OUT................................ 39
Bridge................................... 04
Broad
  1-23..................................... 05
  24-OUT................................ 04
Broadway
  1-27 (ODD)......................... 04
  2-70 (EVEN)....................... 04
  29-171 (ODD)..................... 06
  72-148 (EVEN).................... 05
  150-222 (EVEN).................. 38
  173-331 (ODD).................... 07
  224-334 (EVEN).................. 07
  333-487 (ODD).................... 13
  336-486 (EVEN).................. 13
  488-694 (EVEN).................. 12
  489-697 (ODD).................... 12
  696-900 (EVEN).................. 03
  699-901 (ODD).................... 03
  902-1139............................. 10
  1140-1330............................ 01
  1331-1450............................ 18

1451-1589 (ODD).................. 36
1452-1592 (EVEN)................ 36
1591-1809 (ODD).................. 19
1594-1810 (EVEN)................ 19
1811-2160............................. 23
2161-2459............................. 24
2460-2918 (EVEN)................ 25
2461-2959 (ODD).................. 25
2920-3298 (EVEN)................ 27
2961-3299 (ODD).................. 27
3300-3699............................. 31
3700-4100............................. 32
4101-4379............................. 33
4380-4759............................. 40
4760-5170............................. 34
Broadway Aly........................ 16
Broadway Ter........................ 40
Broome
  1-338................................... 02
  339-OUT.............................. 13
Burling Slip........................... 38
Cabrini Blvd
  1-250................................... 33
  251-OUT.............................. 40
Canal
  1-151 (ODD)....................... 02
  2-142 (EVEN)..................... 02
  144-OUT (EVEN).................. 13
  153-OUT (ODD)................... 13
Cannon.................................. 02
Cardinal Hayes Pl................. 07
Carl Schurz Park................... 28
Carlisle.................................. 06
Carmine................................. 14
Caroline................................. 13
Cathedral Cir......................... 26
Cathedral Hts........................ 25
Cathedral Pky
  1-399 (ODD)....................... 26
  2-348 (EVEN)..................... 26
  350-OUT (EVEN).................. 25
  401-OUT (ODD)................... 25
Catherine............................... 38
Catherine Ln.......................... 13
Catherine Slip....................... 38
Cedar
  1-1....................................... 05
  2-88 (EVEN)....................... 05
  3-27 (ODD)......................... 38
  29-87 (ODD)....................... 05
  89-OUT................................ 06
Central Park N....................... 26
Central Park S....................... 19
Central Park W
  1-160................................... 23
  161-310............................... 24
  311-OUT.............................. 25
Centre
  1-73 (ODD)......................... 07
  2 68 (EVEN)....................... 07
  70-OUT (EVEN).................... 13
  75-OUT (ODD)..................... 13
Centre Market Pl................... 14
Chambers.............................. 07
Charles St & Ln..................... 14
Charlton................................. 14
Chase Manhattan Plz............. 05
Chatham Sq........................... 38
Chelsea Sq............................ 11
Cherokee Pl........................... 21
Cherry................................... 02
Cherry Ln.............................. 14
Chisum Pl.............................. 27

Chittenden Ave & Pl	33
Christopher	14
Chrystie	02
Church	
1-18	06
19-225 (ODD)	07
20-168 (EVEN)	07
170-OUT (EVEN)	13
227-OUT (ODD)	13
City Hall	07
Claremont Ave	27
Clarkson	14
Cleveland Pl	12
Cliff	38
Clinton	02
Coenties Slip	04
Collister	13
Columbia	02
Columbus Ave	
1-339	23
340-639	24
640-OUT	25
Columbus Cir	
1-10	19
11-OUT	23
Commerce	14
Convent Ave	
1-116	27
117-OUT	31
Cooper	34
Cooper Sq	03
Cornelia	14
Cortlandt	07
Cortlandt Aly	13
Crosby	
1-40	13
41-OUT	12
Cumming	34
Delamater Sq	14
Delancey	02
Depeyster	05
Desbrosses	13
Dey	07
Division	02
Dominick	13
Dongan Pl	40
Dover	38
Downing	14
Doyers	13
Duane	
20-125	07
126-OUT	13
Duffy Sq	36
Dutch	38
Dyckman	
1-99	34
100-217	40
218-OUT	34
East Broadway	
1-15 (ODD)	38
2-10 (EVEN)	38
12-OUT (EVEN)	02
17-OUT (ODD)	02
East End Ave	
1-23 (ODD)	21
2-18 (EVEN)	21
20-OUT (EVEN)	28
25-OUT (ODD)	28
East Houston	
1-91 (ODD)	12
2-88 (EVEN)	12
90-OUT (EVEN)	02
93-OUT (ODD)	0.
East River Dr	
1-611	02
612-765	09
8-01-19-100	09
20-01-25-100	10
26-01-39-100	16
40-01-48-100	17
49-01-59-100	22
60-01-79-100	21
80-01-95-100	28
96-01-115-100	29
116-01-130-100	35
East River Piers	
1-9	04
10-14	05
15-26	38
27-54	02
55-68	09
69-73	10
Edgecombe Ave	
1-231	30
232-394	31
395-OUT	32
Edward M Morgan Pl	32
Eldridge	02
Elizabeth	
1-136	13
137-OUT	12
Elk	07
Ellis Island	04
Ellwood	40
Elm	07
Ericsson Pl	13
Esplanade Gdns Plz	39
Essex	02
Exchange Aly	06
Exchange Pl	
1-67 (ODD)	05
2-42 (EVEN)	05
44-OUT (EVEN)	04
69-OUT (ODD)	04
Fairview Ave	40
Federal Plz	07
Federal Reserve Bank	45
Fletcher	38
Foley Sq	07
Forsyth	02
Fort George Ave	40
Fort George Hill	40
Fort Jay	04
Fort Tryon Park	40
Fort Washington Ave	
1-300	32
301-599	33
600-OUT	40
Fort Washington Park	33
Frankfort	38
Franklin St & Pl	13
Franklin Ter	01
Franklin D Roosevelt Dr	
1-611	02
612-765	09
8-01-19-100	09
20-01-25-100	10
26-01-39-100	16
40-01-48-100	17
49-01-59-100	22
60-01-79-100	21
80-01-95-100	28
96-01-115-100	29
116-01-130-100	35
Frederick Douglas Cir	26
Front	
1-73 (ODD)	04
2-76 (EVEN)	04
75-151 (ODD)	05
78-154 (EVEN)	05
153-OUT (ODD)	38
156-OUT (EVEN)	38
Fulton	
1-167 (ODD)	38
2-158 (EVEN)	38
160-OUT (EVEN)	07
169-OUT (ODD)	07
Fulton Market	38
Gansevoort	14
Gansevoort Market	14
Gay	14
Gold	38
Gouverneur	02
Gouverneur Ln	05
Gouverneur Slip	02
Governors Island	04
Gracie Sq & Ter	28
Gramercy Park	
1-37	03
38-OUT	10
Grand	
1-235	13
236-OUT	02
Great Jones	12
Greene	
1-55	13
56-228	12
229-OUT	03
Greenwich	
1-40	04
41-169 (ODD)	06
42-164 (EVEN)	06
166-292 (EVEN)	07
171-301 (ODD)	07
294-552 (EVEN)	13
303-549 (ODD)	13
551-OUT (ODD)	14
554-OUT (EVEN)	14
Greenwich Ave	
1-OUT (ODD)	14
2-OUT (EVEN)	11
Grove St & Ct	14
Half Pl	03
Hamill Pl	07
Hamilton Pl & Ter	31
Hancock Pl & Sq	27
Hanover	
1-OUT (ODD)	05
2-6 (EVEN)	05
8-OUT (EVEN)	04
Hanover Sq	
1-5 (ODD)	04
2-2	04
4-OUT (EVEN)	05
7-OUT (ODD)	05
Harlem Market	29
Harlem River Dr	39
Harlem River Driveway	
155-01-160-100	39
161-01-172-100	32
173-01-186-100	33
187-01-192-100	40
193-01-OUT	34
Harrison	13
Harry Howard Sq	13
Haven Ave	
1-162	32
163-OUT	33

New York (Con.) 100

Haven Plz 09
Henderson Pl 28
Henry
  1-11 38
  12-OUT 02
Henry Hudson Pky 34
Henshaw 34
Herald Sq 01
Hester
  1-149 1/2 (ODD) 02
  2-134 (EVEN) 02
  136-OUT (EVEN) 13
  151-OUT (ODD) 13
High Bridge Park 33
Hillside Ave 40
Horatio 14
Howard 13
Hubert 13
Hudson
  1-339 (ODD) 13
  2-344 (EVEN) 13
  341-OUT (ODD) 14
  346-OUT (EVEN) 14
Indian Rd 34
Irving Pl 03
Isham St & Park 34
Jackson 02
James 38
Jane 14
Jay 13
Jefferson 02
Jersey 12
John 38
Jones 14
Jumel Pl & Ter 32
Kenmore 12
King
  1-5 12
  6-OUT 14
Knickerbocker Village 02
La Guardia Pl 12
La Salle 27
Lafayette
  1-39 (ODD) 07
  2-34 (EVEN) 07
  36-192 (EVEN) 13
  41-193 (ODD) 13
  194-372 12
  373-OUT 03
Laight 13
Laurel Hill Ter
  1-120 33
  121-OUT 40
Lenox Ave
  1-199 26
  200-402 (EVEN) 27
  201-399 (ODD) 27
  401-699 (ODD) 37
  404-698 (EVEN) 37
  700-OUT 37
Lenox Ter Pl 37
Leonard 13
Leroy 14
Lewis 02
Lexington Ave
  1-79 16
  80-353 16
  354-538 17
  539-765 (ODD) 22
  540-762 (EVEN) 22
  764-1162 (EVEN) 21

767-1171 (ODD) 21
1164-1486 (EVEN) 28
1173-1489 (ODD) 28
1488-1870 (EVEN) 29
1491-1869 (ODD) 29
1871-2169 35
2170-OUT 37
Liberty
  1-76 05
  77-OUT 06
Liberty Ct & Pl 38
Liberty Island 04
Lillian Wald Dr 09
Lincoln Sq Plz 23
Lispenard 13
Little West 12th 14
Ludlow 02
Mac Dougal
  1-7 (ODD) 13
  2-154 (EVEN) 12
  9-141 (ODD) 12
  143-OUT (ODD) 11
  156-OUT (EVEN) 11
Mac Dougal Aly 11
Macombs Pl 39
Madison
  1-67 (ODD) 38
  2-72 (EVEN) 38
  69-OUT (ODD) 02
  74-OUT (EVEN) 02
Madison Ave
  1-61 10
  62-280 (EVEN) 16
  63-277 (ODD) 16
  279-429 (ODD) 17
  282-430 (EVEN) 17
  431-651 22
  652-1056 (EVEN) 21
  653-1047 (ODD) 21
  1049-1379 (ODD) 28
  1058-1378 (EVEN) 28
  1380-1767 29
  1768-2059 35
  2060-OUT 37
Magaw Pl 33
Maiden Ln
  1-101 38
  102-134 (EVEN) 05
  103-133 (ODD) 38
  135-OUT 38
Mangin 02
Manhattan Ave
  1-239 25
  240-488 (EVEN) 26
  241-479 (ODD) 26
  481-OUT (ODD) 27
  490-OUT (EVEN) 27
Manhattan Pl 07
Marie Curie Ave 21
Market 02
Market Slip 02
Marketfield 04
Mercer
  1-63 13
  64-260 12
  261-OUT 03
Mill Ln 04
Milligan Pl 11
Minetta St, Ln & Pl 12
Mitchell Pl
  1-15 17
Mitchell Sq 32
Monroe 02

Montgomery 02
Moore 04
Morningside Ave
  1-58 26
  59-OUT 27
Morningside Dr
  1-59 25
  60-OUT 27
Morris
  1-9 (ODD) 04
  2-OUT (EVEN) 06
  11-OUT (ODD) 06
Morton 14
Mott
  1-173 (ODD) 13
  2-168 (EVEN) 13
  170-OUT (EVEN) 12
  175-OUT (ODD) 12
Mount Morris Park W 27
Mulberry
  10-176 (EVEN) 13
  13-177 (ODD) 13
  178-CJT 12
Murray 07
Nagle Ave
  1-169 40
  170-OUT 34
Nassau
  1-47 (ODD) 05
  2-40 (EVEN) 05
  42-OUT (EVEN) 38
  49-OUT (ODD) 38
Nathan D Perlman Pl 03
New
  1-11 (ODD) 05
  2-28 (EVEN) 05
  13-OUT (ODD) 04
  30-OUT (EVEN) 04
Norfolk 02
North Moore 13
North River Piers
  A-2 04
  3-11 06
  12-20 07
  21-36 13
  37-56 14
  57-64 11
  65-75 01
  76-80 18
  81-88 36
  89-99 19
Old Broadway 27
Old Slip 05
Oliver 38
Orchard 02
Overlook Ter
  1-65 33
  66-OUT 40
Paladino Ave 35
Park
  1-84 07
  85-OUT 13
Park Ave
  1-99 16
  100-299 17
  300-519 22
  520-914 (EVEN) 21
  521-923 (ODD) 21
  916-1240 (EVEN) 28
  925-1245 (ODD) 28
  1242-1636 (EVEN) 29
  1247-1637 (ODD) 29
  1638-1914 (EVEN) 35

New York (Con.)   100

1639-1919 (ODD)	35
1916-2298 (EVEN)	37
1921-2299 (ODD)	37
Park Ave S	
200-250	03
251-363 (ODD)	18
252-384 (EVEN)	18
365-OUT (ODD)	16
386-OUT (EVEN)	16
Park Pl	07
Park Row	
1-43	38
44-166 (EVEN)	07
45-165 (ODD)	38
167-OUT	38
Park Ter E & W	34
Patchin Pl	11
Payson Ave	34
Pearl	
1-117 (ODD)	04
2-100 (EVEN)	04
102-194 (EVEN)	05
119-197 (ODD)	05
196-462 (EVEN)	38
199-463 (ODD)	38
464-OUT	07
Peck Slip	36
Pell	13
Pennsylvania Plz	01
Perry	14
Peter Cooper Rd	10
Pike	02
Pike Slip	02
Pine	06
Pinehurst Ave	33
Pitt	02
Platt	38
Plaza Lafayette	33
Pleasant Ave	
1-299	29
300-OUT	35
Pomander Walk	25
Post Ave	34
Prince	12
Randalls Island	35
Reade	
1-83	07
84-OUT	13
Rector	06
Renwick	13
Ridge	02
Riverside Dr	
1-40	23
41-190	24
191-439	25
440-569	27
570-762	31
763-1150	32
1151-1599	33
1600-1780	40
1781-OUT	34
Riverside Dr W	
155-01-159-100	32
Riverview Ter	22
Rivington	02
Robert F Wagner Sr Pl	38
Rockefeller Plz	20
Roosevelt Sq	27
Rutgers	02
Rutgers Shp	02
Rutherford Pl	03

Saint Clair Pl	27
Saint James Pl	38
Saint Johns Ln	13
Saint Lukes Pl	14
Saint Marks Pl	
1-85 (ODD)	03
2-82 (EVEN)	03
84-OUT (EVEN)	09
87-OUT (ODD)	09
Saint Nicholas Ave	
1-201 (ODD)	26
2-198 (EVEN)	26
200-456 (EVEN)	27
203-455 (ODD)	27
457-699 (ODD)	30
458-690 (EVEN)	30
692-860 (EVEN)	31
701-861 (ODD)	31
862-1259	32
1260-1539	33
1540-OUT	40
Saint Nicholas Pl	
1-60	31
61-OUT	32
Saint Nicholas Ter	
1-55	27
56-OUT	31
Schiff Pky	62
Seaman Ave	34
Sheridan Sq	14
Sheriff	02
Sherman Ave	
1-84	40
85-801	34
Sherman Sq	23
Sickles	40
Sniffen Ct	16
South	
1-39	04
40-75	05
76-202	38
203-OUT	02
South Ferry	04
South Pinehurst Ave	33
South William	04
Spring	
1-220	12
221-OUT	13
Spruce	38
Staff	34
Stanton	02
Staple	13
State	04
Staten Island Ferry	04
Statue Of Liberty	04
Stone	04
Stuyvesant Oval	09
Stuyvesant St & Aly	09
Suffolk	02
Sullivan	12
Sutton Pl S	22
Sutton Pl & Sq	22
Sylvan Ct & Pl	35
Sylvan Ter	32
Szold Pl	09
Thames	06
Thayer	40
Thomas	
1-42	07
43-OUT	13
Thompson	
1-49	13
50-OUT	12

Treman Pl	27
Times Sq	36
Transverse Rd	24
Trimble Pl	07
Trinity Pl	06
Tudor City Pl	17
Union Sq	03
United Nations Plz	17
University Pl	03
Van Nest Pl	14
Vandam	13
Vanderbilt Ave	17
Vanderbilt Concourse	17
Varick	
1-169 (ODD)	13
2-172 (EVEN)	13
171-OUT (ODD)	14
174-OUT (EVEN)	14
Vermilyea Ave	34
Vesey	07
Vestry	13
Wadsworth Ave	
1-279	33
280-OUT	40
Wadsworth Ter	40
Walker	13
Wall	05
Wanamaker Pl	03
Wards Island	35
Warren	07
Washington	
1-39 (ODD)	04
2-32 (EVEN)	04
34-170 (EVEN)	06
41-169 (ODD)	06
171-286	07
287-531	13
532-OUT	18
Washington Pl	
1-60	03
61-90	11
91-OUT	14
Washington Sq E	
77-OUT	03
Washington Sq N	
1-13	03
14-27	11
Washington Sq S	
39 1/2-76	12
Washington Sq W	
28-39	11
Washington Ter	33
Washington Mews	03
Washington Sq Village	12
Water	
1-53 (ODD)	04
2-56 (EVEN)	04
55-55	41
57-69 (ODD)	05
58-152 (EVEN)	05
71-153 (ODD)	05
154-399	38
400-OUT	02
Watts	13
Waverly Pl	
1-99	03
100-130 (EVEN)	11
101-133 (ODD)	11
132-OUT (EVEN)	14
135-OUT (ODD)	14
Weehawken	14
Welfare Island	17

New York (Con.)   100

West
1-20................................. 04
21-114............................. 06
115-185........................... 07
186-324........................... 13
325-OUT........................... 14
West Broadway
1-95................................. 07
96-358 (EVEN).................. 13
97-373 (ODD)................... 13
370-OUT (EVEN)............... 12
375-OUT (ODD)................ 12
West End Ave
1-341............................... 23
342-640 (EVEN)................ 24
-343-637 (ODD)................ 24
639-OUT (ODD)................. 25
642-OUT (EVEN)............... 25
West Houston
1-177 (ODD).................... 12
2-170 (EVEN)................... 12
171-OUT (ODD)................ 14
179-OUT (ODD)................ 14
West Washington Market 14
White................................ 13
Whitehall........................... 04
Willett............................... 02
William
1-9 (ODD)........................ 04
2-6 (EVEN)...................... 04
8-78 (EVEN)..................... 05
11-83 (ODD).................... 05
80-OUT (EVEN)................ 38
85-OUT (ODD)................. 38
Wooster
1-55 (ODD)...................... 13
2-58 (EVEN)..................... 13
57-OUT (ODD).................. 12
60-OUT (EVEN)................ 12
World Trade Center.............. 48
World Trade Center (Hy St).... 47
Worth................................ 13
York................................. 13
York Ave
1-1509 (ODD)................... 21
2-1512 (EVEN).................. 2
1511-OUT (ODD)
1514-OUT (EVEN)

        NUMBERED STREETS

1st
1-73................................. 03
74-OUT............................. 09
1st Ave
1-343 (ODD)..................... 03
2-346 (EVEN).................... 09
345-443 (ODD)................. 10
348-444 (EVEN)................ 10
445-699............................ 16
700-876............................ 17
877-1095 (ODD)............... 22
878-1100 (EVEN).............. 22
1097-1531 (ODD)............. 21
1102-1538 (EVEN)........... 21
1533-1855 (ODD)............. 28
1540-1854 (EVEN)........... 28
1856-2254 (EVEN)........... 29
1857-2257 (ODD)............. 29
2256-OUT (EVEN)............ 35
2259-OUT (ODD)............. 35

2nd
1-87 (ODD)...................... 03
2-98 (EVEN)..................... 03
89-OUT (ODD).................. 09
100-OUT (EVEN).............. 09
2nd Ave
1-343............................... 03
344-459........................... 10
460-746........................... 16
747-922........................... 17
923-1141 (ODD)............... 22
924-1138 (EVEN).............. 22
1140-1536 (EVEN)........... 21
1143-1541 (ODD)............. 21
1538-1854 (EVEN)........... 28
1543-1863 (ODD)............. 28
1856-2258 (EVEN)........... 29
1865-2259 (ODD)............. 29
2260-OUT......................... 35
3rd E
1-99................................. 03
100-OUT........................... 09
3rd W................................ 12
3rd Ave
1-243............................... 03
244-356........................... 10
357-618........................... 16
619-796........................... 17
797-1009.......................... 22
1010-1409........................ 21
1410-1709........................ 28
1710-2120 (EVEN)........... 29
1711-2123 (ODD)............. 29
2122-2398 (EVEN)........... 35
2125-2399 (ODD)............. 35
4th E
1-133 (ODD).................... 03
2-20 (EVEN)..................... 12
22-130 (EVEN).................. 03
132-OUT (EVEN)............... 09
135-OUT (ODD)................ 09
4th W
1-151 (ODD).................... 12
2-154 (EVEN)................... 12
153-OUT (ODD)................ 14
156-OUT (EVEN).............. 14
4th Ave
1-OUT.............................. 03
4th Walk E......................... 09
5th
1-399............................... 03
400-OUT........................... 09
5th Ave
1-133 (ODD).................... 03
2-152 (EVEN)................... 11
135-231 (ODD)................. 10
154-216 (EVEN)............... 10
218-370 (EVEN)............... 01
233-459 (ODD)................. 16
372-498 (EVEN)............... 18
461-609 (ODD)................. 17
500-594 (EVEN)............... 36
596-638 (EVEN)............... 20
611-787 (ODD)................. 22
640-770 (EVEN)............... 19
772-786 (EVEN)............... 22
788-990........................... 21
991-1150.......................... 28
1151-1415 (ODD)............. 29
1152-1312 (EVEN)........... 29
1314-1416 (EVEN)........... 20
1417-2119 (ODD)............. 35

1418-2116 (EVEN)........... 35
2118-OUT (EVEN)............ 37
2121-OUT (ODD)............. 37
6th
1-399............................... 03
400-OUT........................... 09
7th
1-99................................. 03
90-OUT............................. 09
7th Ave
1-243 (ODD)..................... 11
2-240 (EVEN).................... 11
242-460 (EVEN)................ 01
245-461 (ODD)................. 01
462-576............................ 18
577-720............................ 36
721-941............................ 19
942-2000.......................... 26
2001-2259........................ 27
2260-2499........................ 30
2500-OUT......................... 39
7th Ave S.......................... 14
8th E
1-199............................... 03
200-OUT........................... 09
8th Ave
1-79 (ODD)...................... 14
2-66 (EVEN)..................... 14
68-278 (EVEN).................. 11
81-277 (ODD)................... 11
279-499............................ 01
500-637............................ 18
638-789............................ 36
790-996............................ 19
997-2223.......................... 26
998-2226 (EVEN).............. 26
2225-2481 (ODD)............. 27
2228-2488 (EVEN)........... 27
2483-2727 (ODD)............. 30
2490-2728 (EVEN)........... 30
2729-OUT......................... 39
8th thru 9th St W............... 11
9th E
1-399............................... 03
400-OUT........................... 09
9th Ave
1-43................................. 14
44-227............................. 11
228-449........................... 01
450-559........................... 18
560-700........................... 36
701-925........................... 19
926-OUT........................... 34
10th E
1-244............................... 03
245-OUT........................... 09
10th W
1-127............................... 11
128-OUT........................... 14
10th Ave
1-59................................. 14
60-240 (EVEN).................. 11
61-235 (ODD)................... 11
237-449 (ODD)................. 01
242-448 (EVEN)................ 01
450-555............................ 18
556-684 (EVEN)............... 36
557-703 (ODD)................. 36
686-906 (EVEN)............... 19
705-905 (ODD)................. 19
907-OUT........................... 34
11th E
1-399............................... 03

New York (Con.)   100

400-OUT	09

11th W
1-199	11
200-OUT	14

11th Ave
1-2	14
3-200	11
201-419 (ODD)	01
202-426 (EVEN)	01
421-533 (ODD)	18
428-538 (EVEN)	18
535-661 (ODD)	36
540-662 (EVEN)	36
663-OUT	19

12th E
1-399	03
400-OUT	09

12th W
1-229	11
230-OUT	14

12th Ave
1-99	14
100-164	11
165-360	01
361-499	18
500-639	36
640-874	19
875-2351	27
2352-OUT	31

13th E
1-399	03
400-OUT	09

13th W
1-299	11
300-OUT	14

14th E
1-399	03
400-OUT	09

14th W
1-299	11
300-OUT	14

15th E
1-399	03
400-OUT	09
15th thru 20th St W	11

16th E
1-399	03
400-OUT	09

17th E
1-399	03
400-OUT	09

18th E
1-399	03
400-OUT	09

19th E
1-399	03
400-OUT	09

20th E
1-399	03
400-OUT (EVEN)	09
401-OUT (ODD)	10

21st W
1-99	10
100-OUT	11
21st thru 25th St E	10

22nd W
1-99	10
100-OUT	11

23rd W
1-99	10
100-OUT	11.

24th W
1-99	10
100-OUT	11

25th W
1-99	10
100-OUT	01

26th E
1-399 (ODD)	10
2-OUT (EVEN)	10
401-OUT (ODD)	16

26th W
1-99	10
100-OUT	01
27th St & Dr W	01
27th thru 40th St E	16
28th thru 35th St W	01
36th thru 40th St W	18

41st W
1-99	18
100-OUT	36
41st thru 49th St E	17
42nd thru 47th St W	36

48th W
1-145 (ODD)	20
2-OUT (EVEN)	36

48th. W
147-OUT (ODD)	36

49th W
1-139 (ODD)	20
2-138 (EVEN)	20

49th. W
140-OUT	19

50th W
1-157 (ODD)	20
2-134 (EVEN)	20
136-OUT (EVEN)	19
159-OUT (ODD)	19
50th thru 60th St E	22

51st W
1-145 (ODD)	19
2-146 (EVEN)	20
147-OUT	19
52nd thru 59th St W	19
60th thru 61st St W	23
61st Dr W	23
61st thru 80th St E	21
62nd thru 76th St W	23
77th thru 91st St W	24
81st thru 96th St E	28
92nd thru 109th St W	29
97th thru 116th St E	25

110th W
1-399 (ODD)	26
2-348 (EVEN)	25
350-OUT (EVEN)	25
401-OUT (ODD)	25

111th W
1-399	26
400-OUT	25

112th W
1-399	26
400-OUT	25

113th W
1-399	26
400-OUT	25

114th W
1-399	26
400-500	25
501-599 (ODD)	27
600-OUT	25

115th W
1-399	26
400-499	25

500-599	27
600-OUT	25

116th W
1-399	26
400-OUT	27

117th W
1-399	26
400-OUT	27
117th thru 129th St E	35

118th W
1-399	26
400-OUT	27

119th W
1-399	26
400-OUT	27
120th thru 129th St W	27

130th W
1-99	37
100-OUT	27
130th thru 131st St E	37

131st W
1-99	37
100-OUT	27

132nd E
1-199	37

132nd W
1-99	37
100-OUT	27

133rd E
1-199	37

133rd W
1-99	37
100-349	30
350-OUT	27

134th E
1-199	37

134th W
1-99	37
100-399	30
400-699	31
700-OUT	27

135th E
1-99	37

135th W
1-99	37
100-399	30
400-699	31
700-OUT	27

136th E
1-99	37

136th W
1-99	37
100-399	30
400-699	31
700-OUT	27

137th E
1-99	37

137th W
1-99	37
100-399	30
400-OUT	31

138th E
1-99	37

138th W
1-97	37
98-399	30
400-OUT	31

139th E
1-99	37

139th W
1-99	37
100-399	30
403-OUT	31

New York (Con.)	100
140th E	
1-99	37
140th W	
1-99	37
100-399.	30
400-OUT	31
141st E	
1-99	37
141st W	
1-99	37
100-399.	30
400-OUT	31
142nd E	
1-99	37
142nd W	
1-99	37
100-399.	30
400-OUT	31
143rd W	
1-99	37
100-399.	30
400-OUT	31
144th W	
1-99	37
100-399	30
400-OUT	31
145th W	
1-399 (ODD)	39
2-356 (EVEN)	39
341-OUT (ODD)	31
358-OUT (EVEN)	31
146th W	
1-349	39
350-OUT	31
147th W	
1-349.	39
350-OUT	31
148th W	
1-349.	39
350-OUT	31
149th W	
1-349.	39
350-OUT	31
150th W	
1-349.	39
350-OUT	31
151st W	
1-349	39
350-OUT	31
152nd W	
1-349	39
350-OUT	31
153rd W	
1-349	39
350-OUT	31
154th W	
1-349	39
350-OUT	32
155th W	
1-349	39
350-OUT	32
156th W	
1-349	39
350-OUT	32
157th W	
1-349	39
350-OUT	32
158th W	
1-349	39
350-OUT	32

159th W	
1-349	39
350-OUT	32
160th W	
1-349	39
350-OUT	32
161st W	
300-399.	39
400-OUT	32
162nd thru 173rd St W	32
174th thru 187th St W	33
188th thru 199th St W	40
200th W	
1-99	34
100-217	40
218-OUT	34
201st thru 223rd St W	34

NIAGARA FALLS 143

POST OFFICE BOXES

Box Nos.		
1-286	La Salle Sta.	04
1-314	Bridge Sta.	05
1-1102	Main Office	02
651-1147	Falls Sta.	03
2001-2154	New Market Sta.	01

STATIONS, BRANCHES AND UNITS

Bridge Sta	05
Falls Sta	03
La Salle Sta	04
New Market Sta.	01
General Delivery	02
Postmaster	02

APARTMENTS, HOTELS, MOTELS

Beaton, 334 1st	03
Belmont, 411 2nd	01
Clifton, 18 W Falls	03
Converse, 325 1st	03
Eleanor, 702 8th	01
Estella, 942 Niagara Ave	05
Falls, 109 Falls	03
Hall, 552 3rd	01
Hennepin, 649 Jefferson Ave	03
Holiday Inn, 114 Buffalo Ave.	03
Jefferson, 250 Jefferson Ave	03
Lincoln, 1967 Niagara	03
Lochiel, 302 Buffalo Ave	03
Marquette, 505 Walnut Ave	01
Mathews, 918 Niagara Ave	05
Mc Kinstry, 308 Ferry Ave	01
Niagara, 1st St & Jefferson Ave	03
Park Place, 723 3rd	01
Parkway Inn, 401 Buffalo Ave	03
Parkway, 151 Buffalo Ave	03
Red Coach Inn, 2 Buffalo Ave	03
Sagamore, 528 Main	01
Sandra Court, 6627 Buffalo Ave	04
Schrafft'S Motor Inn, 443 Main	02
Simon, 230 1st	03
Spallino Towers, 720-10th	01
Stratford Arms, 555 7th	01

Stratford Arms, 703 Walnut Ave	01
Travelers Lodge, 200 Jefferson Ave	03
Treadway Inn, 7001 Buffalo Ave	04
Waldorf-Niagara, 130 Quay	03
Yorkshire, 630 9th	01

BUILDINGS

Federal, 615 Main	02
Hancock, 43 Falls	03
Lozina, 217 Falls	03
Medical Arts, 457 3rd	01
Neisner, 8 W Falls	03
Rieckhoff, 910 South Ave	05
United Office, 222 1st	03

GOVERNMENT OFFICES

City Hall, 745 Main	02
Niagara County, 775 3rd	02
Public Service, 520 Hyde Park Blvd	02

HOSPITALS

Niagara Falls Memorial Medical Ctr, 621-10th	02
Saint Marys Manor, 515 6th	01

UNIVERSITIES AND COLLEGES

Niagara County Community, 430 Buffalo Ave	03

POUGHKEEPSIE 126

POST OFFICE BOXES

Box Nos.		
1-1299	Main Office	02
1601-1799	South Road Br.	01
3000-3999	Arlington Br.	03
5001-5327	Main Office	02

RURAL ROUTES

1	01
2,3	03

STATIONS, BRANCHES AND UNITS

Arlington Br	03
South Road Br	01
General Delivery	01
Postmaster	01

APARTMENTS, HOTELS, MOTELS

Beechwood South, 363 South Rd	01
Binders Motel, 62 Haight Ave	03
Boulevard Knolls Court Apts	01
Camelot Inn, South Road	01
Canterbury Gardens, Janet Dr	03
Charles St Apts, Charles St.	01

Poughkeepsie (Con.)   126

Collegeview, 119-131 Fulton
Ave.. 03
Colonial Gardens, Corlies Ave
Ext... 01
Corlies Manor, Corlies Ave.... 01
Country Club Terrace,
Anthony Dr............................ 01
Delafield Ct Apt Delafield St.... 01
Dorchester Motor Lodge,
South Rd............................... 01
Dr Martin Luther King Apts
Washington St....................... 01
Dutch Garden Apts Hook
Road....................................... 01
Dutchess Motel, South Rd...... 03
Dutchess, Van Wagner Rd...... 03
Eden Roc, 166 Academy........ 01
Edison Motor Inn, Route 55..... 03
Envoy Plaza, 131 Beechwood
Ave... 01
Executive Towers Academy
St.. 01
Forbus Hill, 31 Forbus............ 01
Franklin Carroll, 55 Carroll... 01
Franklin-Carroll, 115 Franklin.. 01
Georgetown Square Apts 274
Hooker Ave............................ 03
Hamilton Garden, 94 S
Hamilton................................ 01
Hilbrae, Titusville Rd............... 03
Kings Court Hotel, 40
Cannon................................... 02
Manchester Gardens, 46
Manchester Rd....................... 03
Poughkeepsie Inn, 23
Cannon................................... 01
Poughkeepsie Motor Hotel,
418 South Rd......................... 01
Red Bull Motor Inn, 576
South Rd................................. 01
Ridge Field Apts Innis Ave...... 03
Rip Van Winkle House............. 01
River Terrace Apts Riverview
Blvd....................................... 01
Rivercrest Apts., Rivercrest
Court....................................... 01
Rochambeau Motel, South
Rd... 01
Rolling Hill Estates Maloney
Rd... 03
Rombout.................................... 01
St Simeon Apts 24
Beechwood Ave..................... 01
Vassar Garden, Lewis Ave...... 03

HOSPITALS

Hudson River State Hospital,
North Rd.................................
Saint Francis Hospital, North
Rd... 01
Vassar Brothers Hospital,
Reade Pl................................. 01

UNIVERSITIES AND COLLEGES

Dutchess Community College,
Pendell Rd............................. 01
Marist College, 82 North

Road.. 01
Vassar College, Raymond
Ave... 01

ROCHESTER   145

POST OFFICE BOXES

Box Nos.
1-335   Main Office 01
336-675   Main Office 02
676-2105   Main Office 03
2701-3000   Ridgemont
                Plaza 26
3001-3500   Federal 14
3501-3800   Beechwood
                Sta................. 09
3801-4100   Brighton Sta.... 10
4101-4400   Bulls Head
                Sta................. 11
4401-4700   Dewey Sta....... 13
4701-5000   Charlotte Sta.... 12
5001-7100   River Campus
                Sta................. 27
7101-7400   Greece Br 16
7401-7600   West Ridge
                Sta................. 15
7601-7800   Point Pleasant
                Br.................. 22
7801-8100   Lyell Sta.......... 06
8101-8300   Irondequoit Br... 17
8301-8500   Twelve Corners
                Br.................. 18
8501-8700   Thurston Rd
                Sta................. 19
8701-8999   Westgate Br..... 24
9101-9300   Panorama Br.... 25
9301-9697   Midtown Plaza
                Sta................. 04
9701-9980   Southtown Br.... 23
18001-18089 Twelve Corners
                Br.................. 18

STATIONS, BRANCHES AND UNITS

Beechwood Sta.......................... 09
Brighton Sta............................... 10
Bulls Head Sta........................... 11
Charlotte Sta.............................. 12
Dewey Sta.................................. 13
Federal Sta................................ 08
Greece Br.................................. 16
Irondequoit Br............................ 17
Lyell Sta..................................... 06
Midtown Plaza Sta..................... 04
Panorama Br.............................. 25
Point Pleasant Br....................... 22
Ridgemont Plaza Br.................. 26
River Campus Sta...................... 27
Southtown Br.............................. 23
Thurston Road Sta..................... 19
Twelve Corners Br..................... 18
West Ridge Sta.......................... 15
Westgate Br............................... 24
General Delivery........................ 03
Postmaster................................. 03

APARTMENTS, HOTELS, MOTELS

Ainslow, 56 Chestnut................ 07
Alexandrian, 300 Alexander..... 07

Algonquin, 34 S Goodman........ 07
Ambassador, 86 S Union.......... 07
Ardsley, 699 Main E.................. 05
Argyle, 154 Clinton Ave S........ 04
Barrington, 152 Barrington....... 07
Biltmore, 357 Alexander........... 07
Bretton Hall, 325 Alexander..... 07
Brown Stone, 241 Alexander.... 07
Buckingham, 713 Park Ave...... 07
Cadillac, 45 Chestnut................ 04
Campus, 1126 Dewey Ave....... 13
Claridge, 149 Clinton Ave N..... 04
Clintwood, Clintwood Dr........... 20
Clover East, 2410-2458 East
Ave... 16
Clover Garden, Clover Park
Dr.. 18
Colby Park, 1225 Park Ave...... 18
Colonial Manor, Cornelia Dr..... 06
Colonial, 28-30 Park Ave......... 07
Coolidge, 1650 East Ave.......... 10
Country Club Manor, 2405-
2415 East Ave........................ 16
East Avenue Court, 1625
East Ave................................. 16
East Avenue Towers, 2501
East Ave................................. 10
East Boulevard Manor, 76
East Blvd................................ 10
Eastman, 215 Chestnut............ 07
Ellison Park, Bobrich Dr........... 10
Elmwood Manor, 1308-1412
Elmwood Ave.......................... 20
Fairway, 4000 East River Rd.... 23
Falmouth, Falmouth.................. 15
Fernwood Park, 1000
Fernwood Pk.......................... 09
Five-Twenty East Avenue, 520
E Ave...................................... 07
Flagship Rochester, 70 State.... 03
Fredrick, 1640 East Ave........... 10
Gibbs, 53 Gibbs........................ 04
Glenora Gardens, Glenora
Gardens.................................. 15
Grecian Gardens, Grecian
Gardens.................................. 26
Haddon Hall, 505 University
Ave... 07
Highland Manor, 14 Manor
Pkwy....................................... 20
Highlander, 1307 South Ave..... 20
Hill Court, Hill Court Cir............ 21
Holiday Inn Downtown 120
Main E..................................... 04
Holleycroft, 400 Broad E.......... 04
Holyoke, 86 Holyoke................. 15
Imperial, 1693 Stone Rd........... 15
Landing Heights, 22
Knollbrook Rd......................... 10
Lee Garden, Lee Garden Pk.... 24
Lost Mountain, Lost Mountain
Trail.. 25
Manor Parkway, 90 Manor
Pkwy....................................... 20
Manor, 14 Manor Pkwy............. 20
Mariner Motor Inn 95 Main
W... 14
Mc Call Manor, 1131-1151
Stone Rd................................. 16
Midtown Towers, Midtown
Plaza....................................... 04
Milford, 86 Milford..................... 15

Rochester (Con.)   146

Mohawk Manor Motor Inn, 55
   Troup 08
Nathaniel Rochester Motor
   Inn 155 Broad E 04
Ninety Five Troup, 95 Troup.... 08
Normandie, 253 Alexander..... 07
Northgate Manor, Northgate
   Manor 16
Northside, 720-740 Carter...... 21
Norton Village, 1979 Norton 09
Parliament Arms, 2120 St
   Paul............................ 21
Plymouth Gardens, 1400
   Plymouth Ave S 11
Poplar Way, 1011 University
   Ave 07
Portland Manor, Portland Ct..... 21
Ramona Park, 800 Ramona..... 15
Ridgemont Park, Brambury
   Dr 21
Ridgeway, 1368 Ridgeway
   Ave 15
Roosevelt, 267 Oxford 07
Royal Manor, 75 East Blvd...... 10
Rushmore Estates, 68-138
   Floverton 10
Saegers Edison, 93 Elm......... 04
Saint Paul Court, 1564 St
   Paul............................ 21
Shelbourne, 517 University
   Ave 07
Sheraton, 111 East Ave.......... 04
Six-Eighty-Eight East Avenue,
   688 East Ave............... 07
Sixteen-Forty East Avenue,
   1640 East Ave............. 10
Sixteen-Hundred East Avenue,
   1600 East Ave............. 10
Spencerport Manor, Gates
   Manor Dr..................... 06
Stone Road, 1684-1746 Stone
   Rd 15
Strathmore, 970 Monroe Ave... 20
Suburban Court, Suburban
   Ct 20
Thirty S Goodman
   Incorporated, 30 S
   Goodman...................... 07
Thurston, 447 Thurston Rd...... 19
Town House Motel, 1325 Mt
   Hope Ave 02
Travelodge Motel, 390 South
   Ave 20
Treadway Inn, 384 East Ave.... 07
Two-Forty Goodman S, 240 S
   Goodman...................... 07
Valley Court, 1170 Genesee..... 11
Vassar, 593 Park Ave 07
Wedgewood West, 2001-2057
   E Henrietta Rd 23
Westmoor, 327 West Ave 11
Whittier, 270 S Goodman........ 07
Wilsonia, 62 Chestnut............ 07
Winslow, 565 Chili Ave........... 11

BUILDINGS

Abstract, 31 Exchange........... 14
Case, 82 St Paul.................. 04
Columbus, 50 Chestnut.......... 04
Commerce, 119 Main E........... 04

Community Savings, 235
   Main E......................... 04
Copeland, 133 Clinton Ave S.... 04
Cox, 36 St Paul................... 04
Crossroads, 2 State 14
Cutler, 42 East Ave............... 04
East Avenue, 49 East Ave....... 04
Educational, 13 Fitzhugh S...... 14
Eltwanger & Barry, 39 State..... 04
Engineering, 77 South Ave...... 04
Executive Office, 34 Main W..... 14
First Federal Savings, 328
   Main E......................... 04
Fitch, 315 Alexander............. 04
Gas & Electric, 89 East Ave..... 04
Granite, 130 Main E.............. 04
Hiram Sibley, 311 Alexander.... 04
I.B.M., 180 State................. 14
Kenning, 426 Main E............. 04
Lincoln, 10 Gibbs................. 04
Marine Midland, Marine
   Midland Plz................... 04
Midtown Tower, Midtown
   Plaza 04
Monroe County Office, 39
   Main W........................ 14
National, 32 South Ave........... 14
Powers, 16 Main W............... 14
Present, 27 Clinton Ave S........ 04
Professional, 35 Chestnut....... 04
Public Library, 115 South
   Ave 04
Reynolds Arcade, 16 Main E..... 14
Rochester Savings-Bank, 40
   Franklin 04
Rochester Savings Bank, 5
   Fitzhugh S.................... 14
Rundel Memorial, 115 South
   Ave 04
Searle, 183 St Paul............... 04
Security Towers, 1 East Ave 04
Sibley Tower, 25 North........... 04
Temple, 14 Franklin.............. 04
Terminal, 65 Broad 14
Times Square, 45 Exchange..... 14
Triangle, 335 Main E............. 04
Union Trust, 19 Main W.......... 14
War Memorial, 100 Exchange.... 14
Washington Square, 172 S
   Clinton 04
Washington, 155 W Main........ 14
Wilder, 8 Exchange 14
Xerox Square, Xerox Sq......... 03

GOVERNMENT OFFICES

City Hall, 20 Fitzhugh S.......... 14
City Public Safety Building,
   Civic Center Plaza 14
Federal, Church & N
   Fitzhugh 14
Hall of Justice, Civic Center
   Plaza 14

HOSPITALS

Community County Home,
   435 E. Henrietta Rd 20
Dale Sanitarium, 1040 Lake
   Ave 13
Eastman Dental Dispensary,
   800 Main E.................. 63
Field Sanitarium, 525 Lake

Ave 13
Genesee, 224 Alexander........ 07
Highland, Bellevue Dr 20
Knorr Sanitarium, 139 Troup ... 08
Lake Avenue, 179 Lake Ave..... 20
Municipal, Crittenden Blvd...... 20
Park Avenue, 789 Park Ave 07
Residential Treatment Center,
   2075 Scottsville Rd......... 23
Rochester General, 1425
   Portland Ave 21
Rochester State, 1600 South
   Ave 20
Saint Marys, 89 Genesee........ 11
State, 1600 South Ave........... 20
Strong Memorial, 260
   Crittenden Blvd 20

UNIVERSITIES AND COLLEGES

Colgate Rochester Divinity,
   1100 Goodman S............ 20
Monroe Community College,
   1000 East Henrietta Rd 23
Nazareth, 4245 East Ave........ 10
Roberts Wesleyan 2301 West
   Side Dr 24
Rochester Business Institute,
   172 Clinton Ave S 04
Rochester Institute Of
   Technology, 1 Lomb
   Memorial Dr 23
Saint Bernards Seminary,
   2260 Lake Ave.............. 12
Saint John Fisher, 3690 East
   Ave 18
Sch Of Medicine & Dentistry,
   U. Of R , 260 Crittenden
   Blvd............................ 20
University Of Rochester River
   Sta 27

ROCKVILLE CENTRE   115

POST OFFICE BOXES

Box Nos.
1-356   Oceanside Br..... 72
1-420   Main Office 71

STATIONS, BRANCHES AND UNITS

Oceanside Br...................... 72
General Delivery................... 71
General Delivery Oceanside..... 72
Postmaster......................... 70

SCHENECTADY   123

POST OFFICE BOXES

Box Nos.
1-87   Bellevue Sta..... 06
1-97   Crane Street
        Sta 63
1-147   Brandywine
        Sta 04
1-699   Main Office 01

Schenectady (Con.)   123

900-1090   Main Office   01
1101-1256   Scotia Br   02
2501-2697   Upper Union
                   Br   09

RURAL ROUTES

1,2   02
3   04
4   02
5   06

STATIONS, BRANCHES AND UNITS

Bellevue Sta   06
Brandywine Sta   04
Crane Street Sta   03
Mayfair Br   02
Rotterdam Br   03
Scotia Br   02
Upper Union Br   09
General Delivery   05
Postmaster   05

APARTMENTS, HOTELS, MOTELS

Colonial, 9 N Church   05
Douglas, 875 State   07
Foster, 508 State   05
Governor Yates, 206 Union ...   07
Griesmer   05
Hilliard, 243 Union   05
Jackson Avenue, Jackson Ave..   03
Jackson, 1100 Union   08
Lincoln, 114 Union   05
Mahoney, 133 S Brandywine
        Ave   07
Mohawk Gardens, Jackson
        Ave   05
Mohawk Manor, Duanesburg
        Rd   06
Netherlands Village, Mills 18
        Eyck Eyck Pky   08
Patroon, 223 Union   05
Queensbury, Queens Dr   04
Randi Gardens, Randi Rd   09
Roosevelt, 110 Union   05
Saint Regis, 602 Union   05
Schanowee Village, Hamilton
        & Millard   05
Schenectady, Broadway   05
Sheridan Village, Rosa Rd &
        Gerlino   08
Southgate, Watt   09
Steinmetz, Watt & Henry   04
Suellan, Suellan Rd   09
Ten Byck, Broadway   05
Van Antwerp, Van Antwerp
        Rd   09
Van Buren, Eastern Pkwy   09
Wade Lupe Towne Houses, 15
        Lafayette   05
Westinghouse, 244 Union   05

BUILDINGS

Education, 108 Union   05
Lorraine Block, 505 State   05

Phillips, 434 State   05
Picotte, 530 Franklin   05
Proctor Arcade, 434 State . , 05
Wedgeway, 277 State   05

GOVERNMENT OFFICES

City Hall, 105 Jay   05
Court House, 620 State   07

HOSPITALS

Bellevue Maternity, Troy Rd
        Stop 11   09
Eastern New York Orthopedic
        School, 124 Rosa Rd......   08
Ellis, Nott & Rosa Rd   08
Glenridge Tuberculosis,
        Glenridge Rd   02
Saint Clares, 514 Mcclellan ...   04
Schenectady County
        Tuberculosis, Glenridge
        Rd   02

UNIVERSITIES AND COLLEGES

Schenectady City Community
        College   05
Union, Union   08

STATEN ISLAND   103

POST OFFICE BOXES

Box Nos.
1-117   Rosebank Sta   05
1-119   Tottenville Sta ..   07
1-147   Mariners
                 Harbor Sta ...   03
1-149   Eltingville Sta ...   12
1-178   West New
                 Brighton Sta .   10
1-236   Princes Bay
                 Sta   09
1-239   Stapleton Sta ...   04
1-296   New Dorp Sta ...   06
1-391   Saint George   01
1-600   Gpo Sta   14
231-444   Great Kills Sta .   08
301-537   Port Richmond
                 Sta   02

STATIONS, BRANCHES AND UNITS

Eltingville Sta   12
Great Kills Sta   08
Mariners Harbor Sta   03
Midland Beach Sta   06
New Dorp Sta   06
Port Richmond Sta   02
Princes Bay Sta   09
Rosebank Sta   05
Saint George Sta   01
Stapleton Sta   04
Terminal Sta   07
Tottenville Sta   07
U S Public Health Hosp Sta ...   04
West New Brighton Sta   10
General Delivery   14
Postmaster   14

APARTMENTS, HOTELS, MOTELS

Adlon, 4 Chester Pl   04
Ambassador, 30 Daniel Low
        Ter   01
Avon Place, 29 Avon Pl   01
Bard Manor, 162 Bard Ave   10
Bayview, 299 St Marks Pl   01
Berry Homes, 1718 Richmond
        Rd   06
Beverly, 273 St Marks Pl   01
Bon-Aire, 15 Central Ave   01
Boulevard, 2071 Hylan Blvd ..   01
Carolina Gardens, 2862
        Hylan Blvd   06
Castleton Avenue, 585
        Castleton Ave   01
Castleton, 153 St Marks Pl   01
Century, 650 Victory Blvd   01
Christmas Tree Inn, 51
        Wilbur   09
Clifton, 630 Victory Blvd   01
Clove Lake Arms, 830 & 850
        Howard Ave   01
Columbia, 200 Victory Blvd ...   01
Court Plaza, 136 Stuyvesant
        Pl   01
Crestmort, 325 Westervelt
        Ave   01
Curtis Lodge, 261 Hamilton
        Ave   01
Fort Place Towers, Fort Place
        & Monroe Av   01
Golf Court, 215 Hart Blvd   01
Grey Court, 50 Wall   01
Grymes Hill Gardens, 6 Arlo
        Rd   01
Grymes Hill Manor Estates,
        25 Seth Ct   01
Heberton, 137 Heberton Ave ..   02
Hylan Motel, 481 Hylan Blvd ..   05
Imperial Towers, 55 Austin
        Pl   04
La Toja, 4408 Hylan Blvd   12
Lincoln, 630 Midland Ave   06
Mariners Harbor Housing,
        200 Lockman Ave   03
Markham Homes, 35
        Markham Rd   10
Mc Gregor Arms, 115
        Stuyvesant Pl   01
Motel Knickerbocker, 25
        Russell   08
Park Hills Gardens, 184
        Vanderbilt Ave   04
Park-View House, 700 Victory
        Blvd   01
Pentz, 33 Central Ave   01
Prospect Gables, 155
        Prospect Ave   01
Richmond, 71 Central Ave   01
Saint George Court, 100
        Stuyvesant Pl   01
Saint George Gardens, St
        Marks Pl & Hamilton   01
Saint Marks, 191 St Marks
        Pl   01
Silver Lake Arms, 800 Victory
        Blvd   01
Silver Lake Court, 459 Victory
        Blvd   01

Staten Island (Con.)   103

Skyline Terrace Co-Op, 350
　Richmond Ter.................... 01
South Beach Housing, 84
　Lamport Blvd.................... 05
Stapleton Housing, Broad &
　Tompkins Ave.................... 04
Staten, 610 Victory Blvd...... 01
The Castleton, 153 St Marks
　Pl................................. 01
The Sherman, 25 Sherman
　Ave............................... 01
Todt Hill Housing, 801 Manor
　Rd................................ 14
Walker Parks Apartments,
　102 Bard Ave.................... 10
Walker Parks Apartments, 91
　Davis Ave........................ 10
West Brighton Housing, 210
　Broadway......................... 10
Willowbrook, 125 Willowbrook
　Rd................................ 02
Wisteria, 141 St Marks Pl...... 01

BUILDINGS

Borough Hall, Hyatt &
　Stuyvesant Pl.................... 01
Crabtree, 42 Richmond Ter...... 01
Hugot, 36 Richmond Ter........ 01
New York Telephone, 130
　Stuyvesant Pl.................... 01
Pape, 15 Beach................... 04
Richmond, 350 St Marks Pl...... 01
S I Plaza Shopping Center,
　Barrett & Decker Aves.......... 02
Staten Island Medical Arts,
　100 Central Ave................. 01
Staten Island Museum, 75
　Stuyvesant Pl.................... 01
Staten Island Zoo, Broadway...... 10

GOVERNMENT OFFICES

Chamber Of Commerce, 130
　Bay.............................. 01
City Court House, 927
　Castleton Ave................... 10
County Court House, 10
　Richmond Terr................... 01
Court House, 71 Targee.......... 04
General Post Office, 550
　Manor Rd........................ 14
Motor Vehicle Bureau, 450
　Saint Marks Pl.................. 01
Police Precinct 0120, 58
　Richmond Ter.................... 01
Police Precinct 0122............ 06
Police Precinct 0123, 116
　Main............................. 07
Traffic, 71 Targee............... 04

HOSPITALS

Doctors Hospital, 1050
　Targee St....................... 04
Farm Colony, 460 Brielle Ave...... 14
Lakeview Home, 77 Chicago
　Ave.............................. 05

Richmond Boro, 460 Brielle
　Ave.............................. 14
Richmond Memorial, 375
　Seguine Ave..................... 09
Saint Vincents Medical Ctr O,
　Bard & Castleton Aves.......... 14
Sea View, 460 Brielle Ave....... 14
Staten Island Medical Center,
　307 Victory Blvd................ 01
Staten Island, 101 Castleton
　Ave.............................. 04
US Public Health Service
　Hosp, Bay St & Vanderbilt
　Ave.............................. 04
Willowbrook State, Victory
　Blvd............................. 14

MILITARY INSTALLATIONS

Fort Wadsworth.................. 05
Miller Field..................... 06

UNIVERSITIES AND COLLEGES

Notre Dame, 300 Howard
　Ave.............................. 01
Richmond, 130 Stuyvesant
　Pl................................ 01
Staten Island Community
　College, 715 Ocean Ter........ 01
Wagner, 631 Howard Ave........ 01

SYRACUSE   132

POST OFFICE BOXES

Box Nos.

1-89	Mattydale Br	11
1-116	Solvay Br	09
1-118	Elmwood Sta	07
1-157	Colvin Sta	05
1-177	Onondaga Br	15
1-207	Salina Sta	08
1-209	University Sta	10
1-278	Eastwood Sta	06
1-297	Dewitt Br	14
1-304	North Syracuse Br	12
1-1400	Main Office	01

RURAL ROUTES

1 09
2,3 15

STATIONS, BRANCHES AND UNITS

Colvin Sta...................... 05
Dewitt Br....................... 14
Eastwood Sta.................... 06
Elmwood Sta..................... 07
Hancock Field MOU............... 25
Mattydale Br.................... 11
North Syracuse Br............... 12
Onondaga Br..................... 15
Salina Sta...................... 08
Solvay Br....................... 09
University Sta.................. 10
Veterans Hospital Sta........... 10
General Delivery................ 01

Postmaster .... 0..

APARTMENTS, HOTELS, MOTELS

Alabama, 606 University Ave...... 10
Ambassador, 417 University
　Ave.............................. 10
Ambassador, 901 Madison........ 10
Belmore, 100 Wood Ave.......... 05
Berkeley, 735 W Onondaga...... 04
Castle, 124 W Castle............ 05
Chancellor, 2508 S Salina........ 05
Chatham, 644 W Onondaga...... 04
Commodore, 1505 E Genesee...... 10
Crown Arms, 307 Hawley
　Ave.............................. 03
Dewitt Arms, 401 Smith.......... 24
Edward, 1210 Bellevue Ave...... 04
Ellis Court, 101 Woodbine
　Ave.............................. 06
Frontenac, 1802 W Genesee...... 04
Genesee, 1804 W Genesee...... 04
Grant Village, 814 117 Edtim
　Rd................................ 06
Highland, 814 Bellevue Ave...... 04
Hillside, 1530 E Genesee........ 10
Huntley, 407 Stolp Ave.......... 07
Imperial Gardens, 989
　James............................ 03
James Plaza, 622 James........ 03
Kasson, 622 James.............. 03
Leavenworth, 828 SW............ 02
Leonard A, 828 SW.............. 02
Leonard B, 400 W Onondaga...... 02
Leonard C, 410 W Onondaga...... 02
Mayflower, 1030 E Genesee...... 10
Moore, 308 James................ 03
Parkwood, 140 Washington
　Sq............................... 08
Plaza, 1108 E Genesee.......... 10
Roosevelt, 1301 E Genesee...... 10
Sagamore, 666 W Onondaga...... 04
Schopfer Court, 708 James...... 03
Sherbrooke, 604 Walnut.......... 10
Sherbrooke, 920 Madison........ 10
Skyline, 753 James.............. 03
Snowden, 400 James............. 03
Swiss Village, Alpine Dr........ 14
Tower, 770 James................ 03
University Arms, 613
　University Ave.................. 10
Valley Court, 300 Mains Ave...... 07
Walnut Arms, 514 Walnut
　Ave.............................. 10
Washington Square, 1706
　Park............................. 08
Woodbine, 100 Woodbine Ave...... 06
111 & 121 Lafayette Rd.......... 05

BUILDINGS

Chimes, 109 W Onondaga...... 02
Daniel, 433 S Salina............ 02
Eckel, 214 E Fayette............ 02
Empire, 472 S Salina............ 02
Federal, Clinton Sq............. 02
First Trust & Deposit, 212 E
　Washington....................... 02
Gridley, 115 E Genesee.......... 02
Herald, 332 S Warren............ 02
Hills, 217 Montgomery........... 02
Jefferson, 204 E Jefferson...... 02
Lafayette, 210 E Fayette........ 02

Syracuse (Con.) 132

Larned, 114 S Warren 02
Lincoln Bank, 105 W Water 02
Marine Midland, 344 S
Warren 02
Mc Carthy, 113 E Onondaga .. 02
Merchants Bank, 214 S
Warren 02
Midtown Plaza, 700 E Water .. 10
Mony Plaza, 100 Madison
Street 02
Onondaga County Savings
Bank, 113 S Salina 02
Pickard, 5858 E Malloy Rd 11
Presidential Plaza, 600 E
Genesee St 02
Public Safety, 511 S State 02
Romax, 731 James 03
S A & K, 206 E Genesee 02
Seitz, 201 E Jefferson 02
State Office, 333 E
Washington 02
State Tower, 109 Swarren 02
Syracuse-Kemper, 224
Harnson 02

GOVERNMENT OFFICES

Chamber Of Commerce, 351
S Warren 02
City Hall, 233 E Washington .. 02
County Courthouse, 401
Montgomery 02

HOSPITALS

Community Hosp, Broad Rd.... 15
Crouse-Irving Memorial Hosp,
736 Irving Ave 10
Saint Josephs, 301 Prospect
Ave 03
Saint Marys, 1601 Court 08
Upstate Medical Center
Building, 766 Irving Ave 10
Van Duyn Hosp, W Seneca
Tpk 15
Veterans Hosp, 800 Irving
Ave 10
345 Renwick Ave 10

APARTMENTS, HOTELS, MOTELS

Ahern Apts, 127 Ferry 80
Corliss Park, Northern Dr...... 82
Fallon Arnold Apts Glen Ave .. 80
Griswold Hts, Madison Ave.... 80

STATIONS, BRANCHES AND UNITS

Green Island Br 83
Lansingburgh Sta 82
General Delivery 80
Postmaster 80
Hendrick Hudson Hotel, 200
Broadway 80
Holiday Inn, 1800 Sixth Ave . 80
Hotel Troy, 2 First 80
Kennedy Towers, 2100 Sixth
Ave 80
Martin Luther King Apts
Eddys Ln 80
Phelan Margaret Apts Phelan
Ct 80
Sweeney Catherine M Apts
4th St 80
Taylor Apts, 125 River 80
Trojan Hotel, 43 Third 80
Troy Garden Apts, 275
Hoosick 80
Troy Hills Apts, Marvin Ave .. 80
Troy Rose Garden Apts, 25th.. 80
Twin Towers Apts 1900 Sixth
Ave 80

HOSPITALS

Leonard New Turnpike Rd...... 82
Saint Mary'S, 1300
Massachusetts Ave 80
Samaritan, Peoples Ave 80

UNIVERSITIES AND COLLEGES

Emma Willard, Pawling Ave.. 80
Hudson Valley Community,
80 Vandenburgh Ave 80
Rensselaer Polytechnic, 110
Eighth 81
Russell Sage, 45 Ferry 80

TROY 121

POST OFFICE BOXES

Box Nos.
1-1079   Main Office 81
91-299   Lansingburgh
              Sta. 82
1501-1530   Green Island
              Br 83

RURAL ROUTES

1 80
2 82
3,4,5,6 80

UTICA 135

POST OFFICE BOXES

Box Nos.
1-874   Main Office 03

RURAL ROUTES

1,2 02

STATIONS, BRANCHES AND UNITS

Butterfield Br 02
Dunham Sta 02
Kernan Sta 02
Schuyler Rural Br 02

General Delivery 03
Postmaster 03

APARTMENTS, HOTELS, MOTELS

Algonquin, 1434 Genesee 02
Amlott, 1420 Genesee 02
Genesee Court, 1426
Genesee 02
Genesee Manor, 1400
Genesee 02
Georgian Courts, 2400
Oneida 01
Goldbas, 440 Whitesboro 02
Holland House Apts., 1629
Genesee 01
Kanatenah, 1504 Genesee 01
Olbiston, 1431 Genesee 01
Roosevelt, 1514 Genesee 02
Ropewalk, 1427 Oneida 01
Southwind Terrace, 141
Marlboro Rd 01
Utica Hotel, 102 Lafayette 03

BUILDINGS

Brock, 276 Genesee 02
Central N Y Power, 258
Genesee 02
Devereaux Block, 134
Genesee 02
First National Bank, 187
Genesee 01
Gardner, 190 Genesee 02
Genesee Corporation, 258
Genesee 02
Insurance, 110 Genesee 02
Kempf, 250 Genesee 02
Martin, 115 Genesee 01
Mayro, 239 Genesee 01
N.Y. State Office Bldg, 201
Genesee 01
Oneida County Office Bldg,
800 Park Ave 01
Paul, 209 Elizabeth 01
Security, 124 Bleecker 01

HOSPITALS

Childrens, 1675 Bennett 02
Faxton, 1675 Sunset Ave 02
Masonic Home, 2150
Bleecker 03
St Elizabeths, 2209 Genesee.. 01
St Lukes Memorial, Champlin
Rd 03
State Hospital, 1213 Court...... 02

UNIVERSITIES AND COLLEGES

M V C C, 1101 Sherman Dr.... 01
Utica College, Burrstone Rd ... 02

VALLEY STREAM 115

POST OFFICE BOXES

Box Nos.
A-L   Main Office 82

Valley Stream (Con.)   115

I-517   Main Office _____ 32

STATIONS, BRANCHES AND UNITS

Gimbels Number One Sta _____	81
General Delivery _____	80
Postmaster _____	80

HOSPITALS

Franklin General Hospital,
  900 Franklin Ave _____ 80

YONKERS   107

POST OFFICE BOXES

Box Nos.

I-128	Eastchester Br.	09
I-144	North	03
I-177	Centuck Sta	10
I-297	Hastings Br _____	06
I-338	South	05
I-386	East Sta	04
I-514	Bronxville	
	Branch _____	08
I-632	Yonkers	02
121-506	Tuckahoe Br _____	07

STATIONS, BRANCHES AND UNITS

Bronxville Br _____	08
Centuck Sta _____	10
East Sta _____	04
Eastchester Br _____	09
Hastings On Hudson Br _____	06
North Sta _____	03
South Sta _____	05
Tuckahoe Br _____	07
General Delivery _____	01
Postmaster _____	01

APARTMENTS, HOTELS, MOTELS

Dunwoodie Motor Court, Yonkers Ave _____	01
Gramatan, Pondfield Rd Bronxville _____	08
Holiday Inn Motel, Tuckahoe Rd _____	10
Rockledge Manor, 124 Bruce Ave _____	05
Trade Winds Motel, Yonkers Ave _____	04
Tuckahoe Motel, Tuckahoe Rd _____	10
Westchester Town House, Tuckahoe Rd _____	10
Windham, Hudson _____	01

HOSPITALS

Andrus Pavilion, North Broadway _____	01
Bates Memorial Hospital, Sprain Rd _____	10
Cross County Hospital, Cross County Center _____	04
Lawrence Hospital, Palmer Rd Bronxville _____	08
Professional Hospital, Ludlow _____	05
Saint Johns Riverside Hospital, North Broadway _____	01
Saint Josephs Hospital _____	01
Yonkers General Hospital, Ashburton Ave _____	01

UNIVERSITIES AND COLLEGES

Concordia College, White Plains Rd Bronxville _____	08
Saint Josephs Seminary, Seminary Avenue _____	04
Sarah Lawrence College, Kimball Av Bronxville _____	08
Seton College, North Broadway _____	01

WHITE PLAINS   106

POST OFFICE BOXES

Box Nos.

I-89	Gedney Sta _____	05
I-149	East White Plains Br _____	04
I-149	North White Plains Sta _____	03
I-1252	Main Office _____	02

STATIONS, BRANCHES AND UNITS

Central White Plains Sta _____	06
East White Plains Br _____	04
Gedney Sta _____	05
North White Plains Sta _____	03
General Delivery _____	02
Postmaster _____	02

APARTMENTS, HOTELS, MOTELS

Alton Gardens, 23 Mamaroneck Rd _____	05
Benjamin Franklin, 1 Broad Pkwy _____	01
Brentwood, 300 Main _____	01
Briarview Manor, 10 Nosband Ave _____	05

Broad Park Lodge, 292 Main _____	01
Bryant Gardens, 1 Bryant Cres _____	05
Edgebrook Estates, 1 Lawrence Dr _____	03
Fulton Park Apartments, Co Ctr Rd _____	07
Gedney House, 59 Mamaroneck Rd _____	05
Greenridge Court, 1 Greenridge Ave _____	05
Netherlands, 205 W Post Rd _____	06
River Park, 1 Virginia Rd _____	03
Surrey Strathmore, 90 Bryant Ave _____	05
Westview Gardens, 7 Westview Ave _____	03
White Swan, 1 S Broadway _____	01
Woodlands Hill _____	03

BUILDINGS

Bar, 199 Main _____	01
County Center, 198 Central Ave _____	07
Macys, 220 Main _____	01
Municipal, 279 Hamilton Ave _____	01
Northcourt, 175 Main _____	01
Peoples Bank, 31 Mamaroneck Ave _____	01
White Plains Plaza, 1 No. Broadway _____	01

GOVERNMENT OFFICES

City Hall 255 Main St _____	01
County Court House, 166 Main _____	01
County Office, 148 Martine Ave _____	01

HOSPITALS

Burke Foundation, 785 Mamaroneck Ave _____	05
Saint Agnes Hospital, North _____	05
White Plains Hospital, 41 E Post Rd _____	01

UNIVERSITIES AND COLLEGES

Battle Avenue, 155 Battle Ave _____	06
College Of White Plains, 76 No. Broadway _____	03
Dobbs Ferry Road, Dobbs Ferry Rd _____	07
Eastview, 25 Eastview Ave _____	01
George Washington, 100 Orchard _____	04
Greenburgh Junior High, 33 W Hillside Ave _____	07
Jewish Community Center, 252 Soundview Ave _____	06
Mamaroneck Avenue, 9 Nosband Ave _____	05

NORTH CAROLINA
(Abbreviation: NC)

Abbottsburg, R. Br.
  Bladenboro.................................28321
Aberdeen (1st)..............................28315
Advance.......................................27006
Ahoskie (1st)................................27910
Akers Center, Sta. Gastonia......28052
Alamance.....................................27201
Albemarle (1st).............................28001
Albertson.....................................28508
Alexander.....................................28701
Alexander Mills, R. Br.
  Forest City.................................28043
Alexis..28006
Alliance.......................................28509
Almond...28702
Altamahaw...................................27202
Anderson, R. Br. Kitty Hawk......27949
Andrews.......................................28901
Angier..27501
Ansonville....................................28007
Apex (1st)....................................27502
Apple Grove..................................28602
Aquone...28703
Arapahoe......................................28510
Ararat..27007
Archdale, Br. High Point............27263
Arcola, R. Br. Warrenton...........27589
Arden (1st)...................................28704
Ardmore, Sta. Winston-Salem
  (see appendix)
Ash..28420
  Freeland, R. Br. 28440
Asheboro (1st)..............................27203
ASHEVILLE (1st) (see
  appendix)
Ashford..28603
Assembly, R. Br. Lake
  Junaluska..................................28745
Atando, Sta. Charlotte................28206
Atkinson.......................................28421
Atlantic..28511
Atlantic Beach.............................28512
Atlantic Christian College,
  Sta. Wilson................................27893
Aulander......................................27805
Aurora..27806
Autryville.....................................28318
Avon...27915
Ayden...28513
Aydlett...27916
Azalea, Sta. Wilmington............28401
Badin..28009
Bahama..27503
Bailey...27807
Bakersville....................................28705
Bald Creek, R. Br.
  Burnsville..................................28714
Balfour...28706
Balsam...28707
Balsam Grove...............................28708
Banner Elk...................................28604
Barber..27008
Barco...27917
Barium Springs.............................28010
Barnardsville................................28709
Barnesville...................................28319
Bat Cave......................................28710
Bath...27808
Battleboro.....................................27809
Bayboro..28515

Bear Creek...................................27207
Bear Poplar, R. Br.
  Salisbury...................................28011
Beaufort (1st)...............................28516
Belcross.......................................27918
Belew Creek.................................27009
Belhaven......................................27810
Bellarthur.....................................27811
Belmont (1st)................................28012
Belvidere......................................27919
Bennett..27208
Benson...27504
Bessemer City..............................28016
Bethabara, Sta.
  Winston-Salem..........................27106
Bethania......................................27010
Bethel..27812
Bethlehem, R. Br. Hickory.........28601
Beulaville.....................................28518
Biggs Park, Sta. Lumberton.......28358
Biltmore, Sta. Asheville..............28803
Biscoe...27209
Black Creek..................................27813
Black Mountain (1st)....................28711
Black Mountain Sanatorium,
  R. Br. Black Mountain..............28711
Bladenboro..................................28320
  Abbottsburg, R. Br. 28321
Blanch...27212
Blounts Creek...............................27814
Blowing Rock................................28605
Blue Ridge, R. Br. Black
  Mountain..................................28711
Boger City, Br. Lincolnton...........28092
Boiling Spring Lakes, R. Br.
  Southport..................................28461
Boiling Springs.............................28017
Bolivia...28422
Bolton..28423
Bonlee...27213
Bonnie Doone, Br.
  Fayetteville...............................28303
Boomer..28606
Boone (1st)...................................28607
  Valle Crucis, R. Br. 28691
Boonville......................................27011
Bostic..28018
Boulevard, Sta. Eden..................27288
Bowdens.......................................28322
Brasstown....................................28902
Brevard (1st)................................28712
Bridgeton.....................................28519
Broadway.....................................27505
Brookford, R. Br. Hickory...........28601
Brookside, Br. Goldsboro............27530
Browns Summit............................27214
Brunswick....................................28424
Bryson City (1st)..........................28713
Buies Creek..................................27506
Bullock...27507
Bunn..27508
Bunnlevel.....................................28323
Burgaw (1st).................................28425
Burlington (1st)............................27215
Burnsville.....................................28714
Butner..27509
Butters...28324
Buxton...27920
Bynum, R. Br. Pittsboro.............27228
Ca Vel...27512
Calypso..28325
Camden..27921
Cameron.......................................28326

Cameron Village, Sta.
  Raleigh.....................................27605
Camp Lejeune, Br.
  Jacksonville..............................28542
Candler..28715
Candor...27229
Cane River, R. Br.
  Burnsville..................................28714
Canton (1st).................................28716
Cape Fear, Br. Wilmington.........28401
Caroleen.......................................28019
Carolina Beach.............................28428
Carolina Hills, R. Br.
  Fletcher....................................28732
Carrboro (1st)...............................27510
Carthage......................................28327
Cary (1st).....................................27511
Casar...28020
Cashiers.......................................28717
Castalia.......................................27816
Castle Hayne................................28429
Casville, R. Br. Ruffin................27326
Caswell, Br. Kinston...................28501
Catawba.......................................28609
Catawba Heights, Br.
  Belmont....................................28012
Cedar Falls...................................27230
Cedar Grove.................................27231
Cedar Island.................................28520
Cedar Mountain............................28718
Central Falls.................................27232
Century, Sta. Raleigh.................27602
Cerro Gordo.................................28430
Chadbourn....................................28431
Chadwick, Sta. Charlotte............28208
Chapel Hill (1st) (see
  appendix)....................................27514
CHARLOTTE (1st) (see
  appendix)
Charlottetown, Sta. Charlotte
  (see appendix)
Cherokee......................................28719
Cherry Point, Br. Havelock........28533
Cherryville (1st)............................28021
Chimney Rock...............................28720
China Grove..................................28023
Chinquapin...................................28521
Chocowinity..................................27817
Claremont.....................................28610
Clarendon.....................................28432
Clarkton..28433
Clayton...27520
Clemmons (1st).............................27012
Cleveland......................................27013
Cliffside.......................................28024
Climax...27233
Clinton (1st).................................28328
Clyde...28721
Coats...27521
Cofield...27922
Coinjock.......................................27923
Colerain..27924
Coleridge......................................27234
Colfax...27235
College, Sta. Durham.................27708
Collettsville..................................28611
Colon...27236
Columbia......................................27925
Columbus......................................28722
Comfort..28522
Como..27818
Concord (1st)................................28025
Conetoe..27819
Connellys Springs.........................28612

Conover (1st)............................28613
Conway...................................27820
Cooleemee..............................27014
Corapeake...............................27926
Cordova..................................28330
Cornelius.................................28031
Corolla...................................27927
Cottonade, Br. Fayetteville......28303
Council...................................28434
Court House, Sta. Asheville.....28807
Cove City.................................28523
Cramerton................................28032
Cranberry................................28614
Creedmoor...............................27522
Creston...................................28615
Creswell..................................27928
Crisp, R. Br. Macclesfield........27852
Crossnore................................28616
Crouse...................................28033
Crumpler.................................28617
Culberson................................28903
Cullowhee................................28723
Cumberland.............................28331
Cumnock, R. Br. Sanford........27237
Currie....................................28435
Currituck.................................27929
Dallas....................................28034
Dana.....................................28724
Danbury..................................27016
Davidson (1st)..........................28036
Davis.....................................28524
Deep Gap................................28618
Deep Run................................28525
Delco.....................................28436
Denton...................................27239
Denver...................................28037
Derita, Br. Charlotte.................28213
Dillsboro.................................28725
Dilworth, Sta. Charlotte...........28203
Dobson...................................27017
Dover.....................................28526
Downtown, Sta. Charlotte........28202
Draper, Sta. Eden.....................27288
Drexel (1st)..............................28619
Dublin....................................28332
Dudley....................................28333
Duke, Sta. Durham....................27706
Dunn (1st)...............................28334
Durants Neck, R. Br.
    Hertford..............................27930
DURHAM (1st) (see
    appendix)
Eagle Rock...............................27523
Eagle Springs............................27242
Earl.......................................2803?
East Bend................................270?
East Carolina University,
    Sta. Greenville......................278
East Durham, Sta. Durham......2770.
East Fayetteville, Br.
    Fayetteville..........................28301
East Flat Rock...........................29726
East Gastonia, R. Sta.
    Gastonia..............................28052
East Lake................................27931
East Laurinburg, R. Br.
    Laurinburg...........................28352
East Lumberton, Sta.
    Lumberton............................28358
East Rockingham, Br.
    Rockingham..........................28379
East Rocky Mount, Sta.
    Rocky Mount..........................27801

East Spencer............................28039
Eastgate, Sta. Chapel Hill.........27514
Eastway, Sta. Charlotte (see
    appendix)
Eden (1st)...............................27288
Edenton (1st)............................27932
Edgemont................................28620
Edneyville...............................28727
Edward...................................27821
Efland....................................27243
Elizabeth, Sta. Charlotte..........28204
Elizabeth City (1st)....................27909
Elizabethtown (1st)....................28337
Elk Park.................................28622
Elkin (1st)...............................28621
Ellenboro................................28040
Ellerbe...................................28338
Elm City (1st)...........................27822
Elon College (1st)......................27244
Emerson..................................28437
Emerywood, Sta. High Point.......27262
Encas, R. Br. Wilson..................27893
Enfield...................................27823
Engelhard................................27824
Englewood, Sta. Rocky
    Mount................................27801
Enka.....................................28728
Ennice...................................28623
Erlanger, Sta. Lexington............27292
Ernul....................................28527
Erwin.....................................28339
Ether.....................................27247
Etowah...................................28729
Eure......................................279?5
Eureka, R. Br. Fremont.............2783?
Eutaw, Sta. Fayetteville (see
    appendix)
Everetts..................................27825
Evergreen................................28438
Fair Bluff................................28439
Fairfield..................................27826
Fairmont.................................28340
Fairview..................................28730
Faison....................................28341
Faith.....................................28041
Falcon....................................28342
Falkland..................................27827
Fallston..................................28042
Farmer, R. Br. Asheboro...........27203
Farmville (1st)...........................27828
FAYETTEVILLE (1st) (see
    appendix)
Federal Building, Sta.
    Elizabeth City.......................27909
Ferguson.................................28624
Five Point, Sta. Raleigh.............27606
Flat Rock.................................28731
Fleetwood................................28626
Fletcher..................................28732
Fontana Dam.............................28733
Forest City (1st)........................28043
Forest Hills, Sta. Durham.........27707
Fort Bragg, Br. Fayetteville.......2830?
Fountain..................................27829
Four Oaks................................27524
Frank, R. Br. Newland...............28657
Franklin (1st)...........................28734
Franklin Street, Sta. Chapel
    Hill...................................27514
Franklinton..............................27525
Franklinville.............................27248
Freedom, Sta. Charlotte (see
    appendix)

Freeland, R. Br. Ash.................28440
Fremont...................................27830
Friendly, Sta. Greensboro.........27404
Frisco....................................27936
Fuquay-Varina (1st)...................27526
Gardner Webb College, R.
    Sta. Boiling Springs...............28017
Garland..................................28441
Garner (1st).............................27529
Garysburg...............................27831
Gaston...................................27832
Gastonia (1st)...........................28052
Gates.....................................27937
Gatesville................................27938
George...................................27833
Germanton...............................27019
Gerton...................................28735
Gibson...................................28343
Gibsonville..............................27249
Gilkey, R. Br. Rutherfordton......28141
Glade Valley............................28627
Glen Alpine..............................28628
Glen Lennox, Sta. Chapel
    Hill...................................27514
Glen Raven, Br. Burlington........27215
Glendale Springs.......................28629
Glendon..................................27251
Glenrock, Sta. Asheville...........28802
Glenville.................................28736
Glenwood................................28737
Gloucester...............................28528
Godwin...................................28344
Gold Hill.................................28071
Golden Gate, Sta.
    Greensboro..........................27405
Goldsboro (1st).........................27530
Goldston.................................27252
Grace, Sta. Asheville................28804
Graham (1st)............................27253
Grandy...................................27939
Granite Falls............................28630
Granite Quarry...........................28072
Grantham, R. Br. Goldsboro......27530
Grantsboro..............................28529
Grassy Creek............................28631
Grayson..................................28632
Greenmountain.........................28740
GREENSBORO (1st) (see
    appendix)
Greenville (1st)..........................27834
Gregory..................................27940
Grifton...................................28530
Grimesland..............................27837
Grover...................................28073
Guilford, Br. Greensboro...........27409
Guilford College, Br.
    Greensboro..........................27410
Gulf......................................27256
Gumberry................................27838
Half Moon, R. Br.
    Jacksonville.........................28540
Halifax...................................27839
Hallsboro................................28442
Hamilton.................................27840
Hamlet (1st).............................28345
Hampstead...............................28443
Hamptonville............................27020
Hanes, Sta. Winston-Salem.......27103
Harbinger................................27941
Harkers Island...........................28531
Harmony.................................28634
Harrells..................................28444
Harrellsville.............................27942

Harris	28074	
Harrisburg	28075	
Hassell	27841	
Hatteras	27943	
Havelock (1st)	28537	
Cherry Point, Br.	28531	
Haw River	27258	
Hayesville	28904	
Haymount, Sta. Fayetteville	28305	
Hays	28632	
Hayti, Sta. Durham	27701	
Haywood Road, Sta.		
Asheville	28806	
Hazelwood (1st)	28738	
Henderson (1st)	27536	
Hendersonville (1st)	28739	
Henrico	27842	
Henrietta	28076	
Henry River, R. Br. Hickory	28601	
Hertford	27944	
Durants Neck, R. Br.	27930	
Hickory (1st)	28601	
Hickory Grove, Br. Charlotte	28215	
Hiddenite	28636	
HIGH POINT (1st) (see		
appendix)		
High Rock, R. Br. Denton	27239	
High Shoals	28077	
Highfalls	27259	
Highlands	28741	
Hildebran	28637	
Hillsborough (1st)	27278	
Hilltop, Sta. Greensboro	27407	
Hobbsville	27946	
Hobgood	27843	
Hobucken	28537	
Hoffman	28347	
Holden Beach, R. Br. Supply	28462	
Hollister	27844	
Holly Ridge	28445	
Holly Springs	27540	
Hookerton	28538	
Hope Mills	28348	
Horse Shoe	28742	
Hot Springs	28743	
Hubert	28539	
Hudson	28638	
Huntersville	28078	
Hurdle Mills	27541	
Husk	28639	
Icard	28666	
Idlewild, Br. Charlotte	28212	
Indian Trail	28079	
Ingalls, R. Br. Newland	28657	
Ingold	28446	
Iron Station	28080	
Ivanhoe	28447	
Jackson	27845	
Jackson Hill	27280	
Jackson Park, Br.		
Kannapolis	28081	
Jackson Springs	27281	
Jacksonville (1st)	28540	
Camp Lejeune, Br.	28542	
Half Moon, R. Br.	28540	
M C A F New River, Br.	28540	
Midway Park, Br.	28544	
New River Plaza, Sta.	28540	
Northwoods, Sta.	28540	
Tarawa Terrace, Br.	28543	
Verona, R. Br.	28540	
James City, R. Br. New Bern	28560	
Jamestown	27282	

Jamesville	27846	
Jarvisburg	27947	
Jefferson	28640	
Jonas Ridge	28641	
Jonesboro Heights, Sta.		
Sanford	27330	
Jonesville	28642	
Julian	27283	
Kannapolis (1st)	28081	
Kelford	27847	
Kelly	28448	
Kenansville	28349	
Kenly	27542	
Kernersville (1st)	27284	
Kill Devil Hills	27948	
King	27021	
King Charles, Sta. Raleigh	27610	
Kings Mountain (1st)	28086	
Kinston (1st)	28501	
Kipling	27543	
Kittrell	27544	
Kitty Hawk	27949	
Knightdale	27545	
Knotts Island	27950	
Kure Beach	28449	
La Grange (1st)	28551	
Lafayette, Br. Fayetteville	28304	
Lake Junaluska	28745	
Lake Lure	28746	
Lake Toxaway	28747	
Lake Waccamaw	28450	
Lakedale, Sta. Fayetteville	28306	
Lakeview	28350	
Lakewood, Sta. Durham	27707	
Landis	28088	
Lansing	28643	
Lasker	27848	
Lattimore	28089	
Laurel Hill	28351	
Laurel Springs	28644	
Laurinburg (1st)	28352	
Lawndale	28090	
Lawsonville	27022	
Leasburg	27291	
Leicester	28748	
Leland	28451	
Lemon Springs	28355	
Lenoir (1st)	28645	
Lenoir Rhyne, Sta. Hickory	28601	
Lester, Sta. Kinston	28501	
Lewiston	27849	
Lewisville	27023	
Lexington (1st)	27292	
Liberty	27298	
Lilesville	28091	
Lillington	27546	
Lincolnton (1st)	28092	
Linden	28356	
Linville	28646	
Linville Falls	28647	
Linwood	27299	
Little Switzerland	28749	
Littleton	27850	
Locust	28097	
Long Beach, R. Br.		
Southport	28461	
Long View, Br. Hickory	28601	
Longhurst	27548	
Longisland	28648	
Longwood	28452	
Louisburg (1st)	27549	
Love Valley, R. Br.		
Statesville	28677	

Lowell	28098	
Lowgap	27024	
Lowland	28552	
Lucama	27851	
Lumber Bridge	28357	
Lumberton (1st)	28358	
Lynn	28750	
M C A F New River, Br.		
Jacksonville	28540	
Macclesfield	27852	
Macon	27551	
Madison (1st)	27025	
Maggie	28751	
Magnolia	28453	
Maiden	28650	
Main Street, Sta. Garner	27529	
Mamers	27552	
Manns Harbor	27953	
Manson	27553	
Manteo	27954	
Maple	27956	
Maple Hill	28454	
Marble	28905	
Margarettsville	27853	
Marietta	28362	
Marion (1st)	28752	
Mars Hill	28754	
Marshall	28753	
Marshallberg	28553	
Marshville	28103	
Marston	28363	
Matthews (1st)	28105	
Maury	28554	
Maxton	28364	
Mayodan	27027	
Maysville	28555	
Mc Adenville	28101	
Mc Cain	28361	
Mc Donalds, R. Br.		
Fairmont	28340	
Mc Farlan	28102	
Mc Grady	28649	
Mc Leansville	27301	
Mebane (1st)	27302	
Meredith College, R. Sta.		
Raleigh	27602	
Merritt	28556	
Merry Hill	27957	
Method (1st)	27554	
Methodist College, Br.		
Fayetteville	28301	
Micaville	28755	
Micro	27555	
Middleburg	27556	
Middlesex	27557	
Middletown, R. Br.		
Engelhard	27824	
Midland	28107	
Midway, Br. Kannapolis	28081	
Midway Park, Br.		
Jacksonville	28544	
Mill Spring	28756	
Millbrook	27558	
Millers Creek	28651	
Millside, R. Sta. Shelby	28150	
Milton	27305	
Milwaukee	27854	
Mineral Springs	28108	
Minneapolis	28652	
Minpro, R. Br. Spruce Pine	28777	
Mint Hill, R. Br. Charlotte	28212	
Misenheimer	28109	
Mocksville (1st)	27028	

Moncure....................................27559
Monroe (1st)...........................28110
Montezuma.............................28653
Montreat.................................28757
Mooresboro.............................28114
Mooresville (1st)...................28115
Moravian Falls........................28654
Mordecai, Sta. Raleigh...........27604
Morehead City (1st)..............28557
Morgans Corner, R. Br.
  Elizabeth City.....................27909
Morganton (1st).....................28655
Morrisville..............................27560
Morven...................................28119
Mount Airy (1st)....................27030
  White Plains, R. Br.............27031
Mount Gilead (1st)................27306
Mount Holly (1st)..................28120
Mount Mourne........................28123
Mount Olive (1st)..................28365
Mount Pleasant......................28124
Mount Tabor, Sta.
  Winston-Salem....................27106
Mount Ulla.............................28125
Mount Vernon Springs, R.
  Br. Siler City.......................27345
Mountain Home......................28758
Moyock...................................27958
Municipal Airport, Br.
  Charlotte..............................28208
Murfreesboro..........................27855
Murphy (1st)...........................28906
Myers Park, Sta. Charlotte....28207
Nags Head.............................27959
Nakina....................................28455
Naples....................................28760
Nashville.................................27856
Navassa, R. Br. Wilmington...28404
Nebo.......................................28761
Neuse.....................................27561
Neuse Forest, Br. New Bern...28560
New Bern (1st).......................28560
  James City, R. Br................28560
  Neuse Forest, Br................28560
  West New Bern, Sta...........28560
New Hill..................................27562
New Holland, R. Br.
  Swanquarter........................27885
New Hope, Br. Raleigh...........27604
New London............................28127
New River Plaza, Sta.
  Jacksonville.........................28540
Newbold, Sta. Fayetteville....28301
Newell.....................................28126
Newland...................................28657
Newport...................................28570
Newton (1st)............................28658
Newton Grove..........................28366
Niagara, R. Br. Southern
  Pines....................................28388
Norlina...................................27563
Norman...................................28367
North, Sta. Winston-Salem....27105
North Asheboro, Br.
  Asheboro.............................27203
North Belmont, Br. Belmont...28012
North Burlington, Sta.
  Burlington...........................27215
North Charlotte, Sta.
  Charlotte.............................28206
North Durham, Sta. Durham...27704
North Hills, Sta. Raleigh.......27609
North Wilkesboro (1st).........28659

Northgate, Sta. Durham........27701
Northside.................................27564
Northwoods, Sta.
  Jacksonville.........................28540
Norwood (1st).........................28128
Oak City..................................27857
Oak Ridge...............................27310
Oakboro..................................28129
Ocean Isle Beach, R. Br.
  Shallotte..............................28459
Ocracoke.................................27960
Old Fort (1st)...........................28762
Old Trap..................................27961
Olin..28660
Olivia......................................28368
Oriental...................................28571
Orrum.....................................28369
Oteen, Br. Asheville...............28805
Otto...28763
Overhills..................................28370
Oxford (1st)............................27565
Pactolus..................................27858
Palmyra..................................27859
Pantego...................................27860
Park Road, Sta. Charlotte.....28209
Park View, Sta. Kinston........28501
Parkton...................................28371
Parkwood, Br. Durham..........27707
Parmele..................................27861
Patterson.................................28661
Paw Creek (1st)......................28130
Peachland...............................28133
Pelham....................................27311
Pembroke................................28372
Pendleton................................27862
Penland...................................28765
Penrose...................................28766
Pensacola, R. Br. Burnsville...28714
Pfafftown................................27040
Pike Road, R. Br. Pantego....27860
Pikeville...................................27863
Pilot Mountain.......................27041
Pine Hall.................................27042
Pine Level...............................27568
Pinebluff.................................28373
Pinehurst (1st).........................28374
Pineola....................................28662
Pinetops..................................27864
Pinetown.................................27865
Pineville..................................28134
Piney Creek.............................28663
Pink Hill.................................28572
Pinkney, R. Br. Gastonia......28052
Pinnacle..................................27043
Pisgah Forest..........................28768
Pittsboro..................................27312
Plaza, Sta. Greensboro..........27408
Plaza, Sta. Charlotte (see
  appendix)
Pleasant Garden.....................27313
Pleasant Hill...........................27866
Plumtree.................................28664
Plymouth (1st)........................27962
Point Harbor...........................27964
Polkton...................................28135
Polkville..................................28136
Pollocksville............................28573
Pomona, Sta. Greensboro......27407
Pope A F B. MOU.
  Fayetteville.........................28308
Poplar Branch.........................27965
Potecasi..................................27867
Powells Point..........................27966

Powellsville.............................27967
Princeton.................................27569
Proctorville.............................28375
Prospect Hill...........................27314
Providence..............................27315
Purlear....................................28665
Raeford (1st)...........................28376
RALEIGH (1st) (see
  appendix)
Ramseur..................................27316
Randleman..............................27317
  Worthville, R. Br................27378
Randolph, Sta. Charlotte.......28211
Ranlo Smyre, Br. Gastonia....28052
Ransomville, R. Br.
  Belhaven.............................27810
Red Oak.................................27868
Red Springs (1st)....................28377
Reidsville (1st).........................27320
Relief.......................................28769
Research Triangle Park, Br.
  Durham...............................27709
Rex...28378
Reynolda, Sta.
  Winston-Salem....................27109
Rhodhiss.................................28667
Rich Square (1st)....................27869
Richfield.................................28137
Richlands................................28574
Ridgecrest..............................28770
Ridgeway................................27570
Riegelwood.............................28456
Rivermont, Br. Kinston.........28501
Roanoke Rapids (1st).............27870
Roaring Gap............................28668
Roaring River.........................28669
Robbins...................................27325
Robbinsville............................28771
Robersonville..........................27871
Rockford.................................27044
Rockingham (1st)...................28379
Rockwell.................................28138
Rocky Mount (1st)..................27801
Rocky Point............................28457
Rodanthe................................27968
Roduco...................................27969
Rolesville................................27571
Ronda.....................................28670
Roper......................................27970
Rose Hill.................................28458
Roseboro.................................28382
Rosman...................................28772
Rougemont..............................27572
Rowan Mill, R. Br. Salisbury...28144
Rowland..................................28383
Roxboro (1st)..........................27573
Roxobel...................................27872
Ruffin......................................27326
Rural Hall................................27045
Rutherford College.................28671
Rutherfordton (1st)................28139
  Gilkey, R. Br.......................28141
Saint Pauls..............................28384
Salem, Sta. Winston-Salem...27108
Salemburg...............................28385
Salisbury (1st).........................28144
  Bear Poplar, R. Br.............28011
  Rowan Mill, R. Br.............28144
Salter Path..............................28575
Saluda.....................................28773
Salvo.......................................27972
Sandy Ridge............................27046
Sanford (1st)...........................27330

Cumnock, R. Br.	27237
Jonesboro Heights, Sta.	27330
Sapphire	28774
Saratoga	27873
Saxapahaw	27340
Scaly Mountain	28775
Scotland Neck	27874
Scotts	28699
Scottville	28672
Scranton	27875
Seaboard	27876
Seagrove	27341
Sealevel	28577
Sedalia	27342
Sedgefield, Sta. Charlotte	28209
Selma	27576
Semora	27343
Seven Springs	28578
Severn	27877
Seymour Johnson A F B, Br.	
Goldsboro	27530
Shallotte (1st)	28459
Shamrock, Sta. Charlotte	28215
Shannon	28386
Sharon, Sta. Charlotte	28210
Sharpsburg	27878
Shawboro	27973
Shelby (1st)	28150
Shepard, Sta. Durham	27707
Sherrills Ford	28673
Shiloh	27974
Siler City (1st)	27344
Mount Vernon Springs, R.	
Br.	27345
Siloam	27047
Simpson	27879
Sims	27880
Skyland	28776
Smithfield (1st)	27577
Smyrna	28579
Sneads Ferry	28460
Snow Camp	27349
Snow Hill	28580
Sophia	27350
South Greensboro, Sta.	
Greensboro	27406
South Mills	27976
South Wilson, Sta. Wilson	27893
Southern Pines (1st)	28387
Niagara, R. Br.	28388
Southmont	27351
Southport	28461
Southside, Sta.	
Hendersonville	28739
Sparta	28675
Speed	27881
Spencer	28159
Spindale (1st)	28160
Spot	27977
Spray, Sta. Eden	27288
Spring Hope	27882
Spring Lake (1st)	28390
Spruce Pine (1st)	28777
Stacy	28581
Staley	27355
Stanfield	28163
Stanley	28164
Stantonsburg	27883
Star	27356
Starmount, Sta. Charlotte	
(see appendix)	
State Road	28676

State University, Sta.	
Raleigh	27607
Statesville (1st)	28677
Stedman	28391
Stella	28582
Stem	27581
Stokes	27884
Stokesdale	27357
Stoneville	27048
Stonewall	28583
Stony Point	28678
Stovall	27582
Stumpy Point	27978
Sugar Grove	28679
Suit, R. Br. Murphy	28906
Summerfield	27358
Summit, Sta. Greensboro	27405
Sunbury	27979
Sunrise, Sta. Goldsboro	27530
Sunset Beach, R. Br.	
Shallotte	28459
Supply	28462
Surf City, R. Br. Holly Ridge	28445
Swannanoa (1st)	28778
Swanquarter	27885
Swansboro	28584
Swepsonville	27359
Sylva (1st)	28779
Tabor City (1st)	28463
Tapoco	28780
Tar Heel	28392
Tarawa Terrace, Br.	
Jacksonville	28543
Tarboro (1st)	27886
Tate Street, Sta. Greensboro	27403
Taylorsville (1st)	28681
Teachey	28464
Terrell	28682
Thomasville (1st)	27360
Thurmond	28683
Tillery	27887
Timberlake	27583
Toast	27049
Tobaccoville	27050
Todd	28684
Tomahawk, R. Br. Harrells	28465
Topsail Beach, R. Br. Holly	
Ridge	28445
Topton	28781
Townsville	27584
Traphill	28685
Trenton	28585
Trinity	27370
Triplett	28686
Troutman	28166
Troy (1st)	27371
Tryon (1st)	28782
Tuckasegee	28783
Turkey	28393
Turnersburg	28688
Tuxedo	28784
Tyner	27980
U N C C, R. Br. Charlotte	28213
U S S North Carolina, R. Br	
Wilmington	28401
Unaka	28908
Union, R Br. Ahoskie	27910
Union Grove	28689
Union Mills	28167
University Park, Sta.	
Charlotte (see appendix)	
Valdese (1st)	28690
Vale	28168

Valle Crucis, R. Br. Boone	28691
Vanceboro	28586
Vandemere	28587
Vass	28394
Vaughan	27586
Verona, R. Br. Jacksonville	28540
Viewmont, Br. Hickory	28601
Vilas	28692
Waco	28169
Wade	28395
Wadesboro (1st)	28170
Wagram	28396
Wake Forest (1st)	27587
Wakulla	28397
Walkertown	27051
Wallace (1st)	28466
Walliburg	27373
Walnut, R. Br. Marshall	28753
Walnut Cove	27052
Walstonburg	27888
Wanchese	27981
Warne	28909
Warren Wilson College, R.	
Br. Swannanoa	28778
Warrensville	28693
Warrenton	27589
Warsaw	28398
Washington (1st)	27889
Watha	28471
Waughtown, Sta.	
Winston-Salem	27107
Waves	27982
Waxhaw	28173
Waynesville (1st)	28786
Weaverville (1st)	28787
Webster	28788
Weeksville, R. Br. Elizabeth	
City	27909
Welcome	27374
Weldon (1st)	27890
Wellons Village, Sta.	
Durham	27703
Wendell	27591
Wentworth	27375
Wesleyan College, R. Br.	
Rocky Mount	27801
West Asheville, Sta.	
Asheville	28806
West Concord, Br. Concord	28025
West Durham, Sta. Durham	27705
West End	27376
West Gastonia, Sta.	
Gastonia	28052
West Jefferson	28694
West Market Street, Sta.	
Greensboro	27402
West New Bern, Sta. New	
Bern	28560
West Rocky Mount, Sta.	
Rocky Mount	27801
West Statesville, Sta.	
Statesville	28677
Westfield	27053
Whispering Pines, R. Br.	
Carthage	28389
Whitakers	27891
White Lake, R. Br.	
Elizabethtown	28337
White Oak	28399
White Plains, R. Br. Mount	
Airy	27031
Whitehead	28695

Whiteville (1st)	28472	
Whitnel, Br. Lenoir	28645	
Whitsett	27377	
Whittier	28789	
Wil-Mar Park, Sta. Concord	28025	
Wilbar	28696	
Wildwood	28588	
Wilkesboro	28697	
Wilkinson Boulevard, Sta. Charlotte	28208	
Willard	28478	
Williamston (1st)	27892	
Williston	28589	
Willow Spring	27592	
Wilmington (1st)	28401	

Azalea, Sta.	28401
Cape Fear, Br.	28401
Navassa, R. Br.	28404
U S S North Carolina, R. Br.	28401
Wilson (1st)	27893
Wilsons Mills	27593
Windsor	27983
Winfall	27985
Wingate	28174
Winnabow	28479
WINSTON-SALEM (1st) (see appendix)	
Winterville	28590

Winton	27986
Wise	27594
Woodard, Sta. Wilson	27893
Woodland	27897
Woodlawn, Sta. Lowell	28098
Woodleaf	27054
Woodsdale	27595
Worthville, R. Br. Randleman	27378
Wrightsville Beach	28480
Yadkinville	27055
Yanceyville	27379
Youngsville	27596
Zebulon	27597
Zionville	28698
Zirconia	28790

ASHEVILLE   288

POST OFFICE BOXES

Box Nos.

1-3110	Asheville	02
4001-4296	Glenrock Sta.	02
5001-5977	Biltmore Sta.	03
6001-6964	West Asheville Sta.	06
7001-7667	Court House Sta.	07
8001-0008518	Grace Sta.	04
9001-9727	Oteen Br.	05
10501-10655	Biltmore Station	03

RURAL ROUTES

1	04
2	05
3,4	06
5,6,7	05
8	06

STATIONS, BRANCHES AND UNITS

Biltmore Sta.	03
Court House Sta.	07
Glenrock Sta.	02
Grace Sta.	04
Haywood Road Sta.	05
Oteen Br.	05
West Asheville Sta.	06
General Delivery	01
Postmaster	01

APARTMENTS, HOTELS, MOTELS

Alaine, 480 Tunnel Rd	05
Alamo Plaza, 90 Tunnel Rd	05
Alpine, 985 Patton Ave	06
Altamount 72 N. Market St	01

Amber Court, 850 Hendersonville Rd	03
American Court, 85 Merrimon Ave	01
Asheville Arms, 102 Furman Ave	01
Asheville Court, 130 Merrimon Ave	01
Aston Park Towers, 165 French Broad Ave S	01
Battery Park, Battle Sq.	02
Beaver Lake Court, 959 Merrimon Ave	04
Bennett'S, 107 Merrimon Ave.	01
Beverly, 615 Biltmore Ave.	03
Biltmore Gardens, 700 Biltmore Ave	03
Biltmore, R-5 Sweeten Cr Rd.	03
Blue Ridge Motor Lodge, 60 Tunnel Rd	05
Buena Vista, 1080 Hendersonville Rd	03
Carolinian Court, 929 Merrimon Ave	04
Cavalier, Hiawassee St	01
Cavalier, 2 Tunnel Rd	05
Central, 77 Central Ave	01
College Park	04
Deaverview 275 Deaverview Rd	06
Downtown, 65 Merrimon Ave	01
Downtowner Motor Inn 120 Patton Ave	01
Dunbar, 1 Conestee St	02
Edge-O-Town, 2 Weaverville Hi-Way	04
Edgewood Court, 1435 Merrimon Ave	04
Edgewood Knoll, 600 Merrimon Ave	04
Erskine Black	01
Evergreen, 612 Merrimon Ave	04
Farwood, 549 Merrimon Ave	04

Florida Court, 121 Tunnel Rd.	05
Forest Manor, 866 Hendersonville Rd	03
Gracelyn Garden, 30 Clairmont Ave	04
Grove Court, 55 Grove St	01
Grove Park Inn & Motor Lodge, 290 Macon Ave	02
Grove Park, 28-30 Edgemont Rd	01
Hamiltonian, 1526 Patton Ave	06
Hillcrest, Atkinson St	01
Holiday Inn Of America, 201 Tunnel Rd	05
Holiday Inn Of America, 275 Smoky Park Highway	06
Hollywood, 875 Tunnel Rd	05
Horne'S Motor Lodge, 166 Tunnel Rd	05
Host Of America Motor Lodge, 200 Tunnel Rd	05
Howard Johnson'S Motor Lodge, 190 Hendersonville Rd	03
Howard Johnson'S Motor Lodge, 29 Tunnel Rd	05
Lakeshore Gardens, 77 Lakeshore Dr	04
Laurel Terrace, 100 Tunnel Rd	05
Lee Walker Heights, 30 Wilbar Ave	01
Longchamps, 185 Macon Ave	04
Malvern Springs, 1616patton Ave	06
Manor, 265 Charlotte	01
Milestone Court, 380 Tunnel Rd	05
Mount-Vue, 15 Tunnel Rd	05
Mountaineer Court, 155 Tunnel Rd	05
Mountainside 56 Hunthill Pl	01

Parkway, 1060 Tunnel Rd	05
Pines, R-1weaverville Hi-Way	04
Pisgah View, Cordova, Granada, Hanover	06
Plaza Hotel Court, 111 Hendersonville Rd	03
Quality Court(Intown), 100 Tunnel Rd	05
Quality Court(Redmon), 501 Tunnel Rd	05
Ridge Town House, Wynne Way	05
Rock Haven Terrace, 1464 Patton Ave	06
Rockola Court & Trailer Park, 1655 Patton Ave	06
Royal Terrace 90 Tunnel Road	05
Shady Rest, 740 Hendersonville Rd	03
Shamrock Court, 140 Tunnel Rd	05
Sheraton Motor Inn 22 Woodfin	01
Singing Hills, 157 Smoky Park Hi-Way	06
Skyview, 37 Sunset Dr	04
Skyway, 135 Tunnel Rd	05
Sunset Court, 688 Merrimon Ave	04
Thunderbird, 835 Tunnel Rd	05
Tiara, 647 Town Mtn Rd	04
Tour-O-Tel, 640 Merrimon Ave	04
Town Motor Lodge, 820 Merrimon Ave	04
Vanderbilt 75 Haywood St	01
Walton	01
West Terrace, 1043 Haywood Rd	06
Whispering Pines, 140 Smoky Park Hi-Way	06

BUILDINGS

Biltmore Plaza, 3 Biltmore Plaza	03
Castanea, 55 1 1/2 2haywood St	01
Doctors, 50 Doctors Dr	01
First Union Bank, 82 Patton Ave	01
Flat Iron, 20 Battery Park Ave	01
Gennett, 29 N Market St	01
Haywood, 46 Haywood St	01
Jackson, 22 S Pack Sq	01
Legal, 10 S Pack Sq	01
Medical Center, 86 Victoria Rd	01
Medical Dental, 675 Biltmore Ave	03
Northwestern Bank, 1-11 Pack Sq NW	01
Parkway Office, 170-174 Woodfin St	01
Public Service, 91-93 Patton Ave	01
The Doctors Park, 400 Biltmore Ave	01
Wachovia Bank, 1 Haywood	01
York, 108 College	01

GOVERNMENT OFFICES

City Hall, 70 Court Plaza	01
County Court House, 60 Court Plaza	01
Eastern Aerial Photo Lab, 45 S French Broad Ave	01
Environmental Science Servs, 37 Battery Park Ave	01
Post Office, Post & Otis Streets	01

HOSPITALS

Asheville Orthopedic, 95 London Rd	03
Aston Park, 298 Hilliard Ave	02
Memorial Mission, 509 Biltmore Ave	01
Oteen-Va, Riceville & Tunnel Rds	05
Saint Josephs, 428 Biltmore Ave	01

UNIVERSITIES AND COLLEGES

Allen, 331 College	01
Asheville School For Boys, School Rd	06
Ben Lippen, Route 4 Box 100	06
Saint Genevieve-Of-The-Pines, 103 Victoria Rd	01
U N C At Asheville, College Hts	04

CHARLOTTE   282

POST OFFICE BOXES

Box Nos.		
1-720	Main Office	30
721-1300	Main Office	31
1301-1849	Main Office	32
1850-2190	Main Office 4	33
2331-2757	Main Office	34
3000-3999	Dilworth Sta	03
4000-4999	Charlottetown Sta	04
5000-5999	North Charlotte Sta	05
6000-6499	Myers Park Sta	07
8000-8999	Freedom Sta	08
9000-9999	Plaza Sta	05
10001-10628	Main Office	37
10631-10897	Main Office	34
11000-11999	Park Road Sta	09
12000-12999	Eastway Sta	05
15000-15999	Starmount Sta	10
16000-16999	University Park Sta	16
17001-17999	Randolph Sta	11
20001-20535	Downtown Sta	02
21000-21199	Atando Sta	06
23000-23199	Mint Hill R Br	12
24000-24199	Chadwick Sta	16
25000-25999	Idlewild Br	12
26001-26999	Derita Br	13
27000-27999	Municipal Airport Br	08

RURAL ROUTES

1	12
2,3	10
4,5,6	08
7	13
8	12
9	08
10,11	13

STATIONS, BRANCHES AND UNITS

Atando Sta	06
Chadwick Sta	08
Charlottetown Sta	04
Derita Br	13
Dilworth Sta	03
Downtown Sta	02
Eastway Sta	05
Elizabeth Sta	04
Freedom Sta	08
Hickory Grove Br	15
Idlewild Br	12
Mint Hill Rural Br	12
Municipal Airport Br	08
Myers Park Sta	07
North Charlotte Sta	06
Park Road Sta	09
Plaza Sta	05
Randolph Sta	11
Sedgefield Sta	09
Shamrock Sta	15
Sharon Sta	10
Starmount Sta	10
University Park Sta	08
UNCC Rural Br	13
Wilkinson Boulevard Sta	08
General Delivery	02
Postmaster	02

APARTMENTS, HOTELS, MOTELS

Aaloha 3770 Frew Rd	06
Alamo Plaza Courts, 2309 N Tryon	31
Alpine Lodge	10
Barcelona 3500 Sharon Amity Rd	05
Belvedere Homes 321 Judson Ave	08
Bordeaux 6600 Wisteria	10
Boulevard Homes West Boulevard	08
Briarcreek 3041 Karen Ct	05
Brookhill Village 606 Remount Rd	03
Camelot 1500 Eastcrest Dr	05
Canterbury Woods 2107 Canterwood Dr	13
Catalina Motor Lodge, 2403 Wilkinson Blvd	33
Cavalier Court 2800 Monroe Rd	05
Central Square 3101 Central Ave	05
Charlotte Woods 1116 Scalybark Rd	09
Chateau Villa 9700 University City Blvd	13
Claridge Nations Ford & Arrowhead Rd	10

Coliseum Motor Court, 3016
  E Independence Blvd 05
Cotswold 4425 Randolph Rd .. 11
Dalton Village West
  Boulevard 08
Darby Terrace, 4501 Central
  Ave 05
Double Oaks 2623 Double
  Oaks Rd 06
Dutch Village 1900 Eastway
  Dr 05
Earle Village 610 East 7th 02
East Forest Monroe &
  Idlewild Rds 12
East Lake Village
  Independence Blvd 12
Edwin Towers 210 West 10th . 02
Elmhurst Dorchester Pl 09
Fairview Homes 1026
  Oaklawn Ave 06
Forest Brook 5600
  Tuckaseegee Rd 08
Fountain Square 2400
  Eastway Dr 05
Four Seasons 5800 Albemarle
  Rd 12
Foxfire 6700 Idlewild Rd 12
Green Oaks, 1400-2831
  Eastcrest Dr 05
Guthrey, 508 N Tryon 02
Hope Valley 2609 Milton Rd.. 15
Idlewild 6507 Idlewild Rd 12
Italian Village 5600
  Providence Rd 11
Jackson Park 5509 Airport
  Dr 08
Jamestowne, 1201 Green
  Oaks Ln 05
Kings Creek 10
L Atriums North 1600 Tom
  Hunter Rd 13
Lake Hills 2326 Shade Valley
  Rd 05
Lake Plaza 15
Lemon Tree 5900 Monroe Rd . 12
Little Rock Homes West
  Boulevard 06
Manger Motor Inn, 631 N
  Tryon 32
Marlborough Homes
  Marlborough Rd 08
Milner Mecklenburg, 516 W
  Trade 32
Milton Road 1951 Milton Rd . 15
Morningside 2500 Mcclintock
  Rd 05
Oak Crest 217 Elmhurst Rd ... 05
Orvin Motor Court, 307 N
  Graham 31
Piedmont Courts 831 Seigle
  Ave 04
Pinehurst, 3910-4132
  Providence Rd 11
Plaza Terrace 3224 The
  Plaza 05
Providence Square 11
Quail Hill 5901 Quail Hollow
  Rd 10
Queens Tower, 1300 Queens
  Rd 07
Randolph Park 4516
  Randolph Rd 11
Roseland 1210 Pressley Rd ... 10

Sandhurst, 1701 W
  Boulevard 06
Selwyn Village 300
  Walkefield Dr 09
Shamrock Gardens 3779
  Michigan Ave 15
Sharon Lakes, Sharon Road
  West 10
Southgate, 3910-4300
  Conway Ave 09
Southside Homes 3400
  Griffith 03
Strawn 500 Butternut Ct 03
The Lake 5503 Albemarle Rd . 12
Tree Top Archdale Dr & I77 ... 10
Tryon Forest 300 Lambeth Dr . 13
Tryon Hill 200 W 26th 06
Versailles 2600 Park Rd 09
Vista Villa 6400 The Plaza 15
Westwood 1501 Evergreen Dr . 08
White House Inn, 237 W
  Trade 34
Williamsburg, 1210-1513
  Green Oaks Ln 05
Yorktown 254 Tyvola Rd 10

BUILDINGS

Albemarle Center 4822
  Albemarle Rd 05
American, 201 S Tryon 06
Attorneys, 806 E Trade 02
Bank Of N C Bldg 112 S
  Tryon 04
Builders, 312-14 W Trade 02
Charlotte Civic Center 101 S
  College 02
City National Bank, 237 S.
  Tryon 02
Cole 207 Hawthorne Ln 04
Colwick Towers 4401 Colwick
  Rd 11
Court Plaza 901 Elizabeth
  Ave 04
Doctors, 1012 S Kings Dr 83
Equity, 701 E Trade 02
Ervin 4037 E Independence
  Blvd 05
Executive Office Park 800
  Baxter 02
Executive, 623 E Trade 02
Home Federal, 139 S Tryon.... 02
Ina 4425 Randolph Rd 11
Independence, 102 W Trade ... 02
Jefferson First Union Plaza
  300 S College 82
Jefferson Standard 301 - 307
  S Tryon 02
Johnston, 212 S Tryon 81
Law, 730 E Trade 02
Merchandise Mart 2500 E
  Independence Blvd 05
North Carolina National
  Bank, 200 S Tryon 55
Professional, 403 N Tryon..... 02
Tryon Plaza 301-307 S Tryon.. 82
Wachovia Bank, 129 W
  Trade 02

GOVERNMENT OFFICES

City Hall, 600 E. Trade 02
Mecklenburg County Court
  House, 700 E. Trade 02
Mecklenburg County Office,
  720 E. 4th 02
United States Courthouse,
  401 W Trade 02
United States Post Office,
  401 W Trade 02

HOSPITALS

Charlotte Community, 801 S
  Graham 02
Charlotte Eye Ear Nose &
  Throat. 04
Charlotte Memorial, 1000
  Blythe Blvd 01
Mercy, 2000 E 5th 01
Presbyterian, 200 Hawthorne
  Ln 01

UNIVERSITIES AND COLLEGES

Central Piedmont Comm,
  1141 Elizabeth Ave 04
Johnson C Smith University,
  100 Beatties Ford Rd 18
Kings Business, 322 Lamar
  Ave 01
Queens, 1900 Selwyn Ave...... 74
U N C At Charlotte, Highway
  49 N 13

DURHAM   277

POST OFFICE BOXES

Box Nos.
1-2332   Main Office 02
2491-3205   West Durham
            Sta. 05
3801-3880   Burham 02
4001-5999   Duke Sta 06
6001-7699   College Sta...... 08
8001-8499   North Durham
            Sta. 04
8501-8999   Forest Hills
            Sta. 07
9001-9669   Duke Sta 06
11001-
0011637   East Durham
            Sta. 03
12001-12275 Research
            Triangle Park
            Br 09
18001-19919 Shepard Sta 07

RURAL ROUTES

1,2 05
3 07
4 03
5 02
6 03
7 07
8 04

STATIONS, BRANCHES AND UNITS

College Sta.	08
Duke Sta.	06
East Durham Sta.	03
Forest Hills Sta	07
Hayti Sta	01
Lakewood Sta	07
North Durham Sta.	04
Northgate Sta.	07
Parkwood Br.	07
Research Triangle Park Br.	09
Shepard Sta.	07
Wellons Village Sta.	03
West Durham Sta.	05
General Delivery	01
Postmaster	01

APARTMENTS, HOTELS, MOTELS

Alastair Court, 300 Swift.	05
Ambassador, 916 W Trinity Ave.	01
Anderson St, 1600 Anderson.	07
Atlas, 200 Atlas.	01
Bickett, 806 Gregson	05
Bristol, 1100 Douglas.	05
Campus, Elf	05
Capri	07
Carolee, 2200 Elder	05
Carriage House.	04
Carstelle, 1911 House Ave.	07
Carwin, 2213 Elder	05
Channing Court, Channing Ave.	04
Chesterfield Apts, 1808 Chapel Hill Rd.	07
Chesterfield Motel, 1900 N Roxboro	02
Churchill Court, 315 - 317 W Trinity.	01
College Plaza, 415 Pilot.	07
Colonial Terrace, 3022 Chapel Hill Rd.	07
Confederate, Hwy 70 West.	05
Damar Court, Morreene Rd.	05
Duke & Duchess, House Ave.	07
Duke Manor Morreene Rd.	05
Duke Motor Lodge, Durham - Chapel Hill Blvd	07
Dutch Village, 2306 Elder.	05
Eden Rock, Durham - Chapel Hill Blvd	07
El Rancho, Elf	05
Erwin, 312 Buchanan Blvd.	01
Executive, 900 W Trinity Ave.	01
Few Gardens.	03
Four Seasons, 2007 House Ave	07
General Joseph Johnston, Intersection Jct 70 W Inter 85.	05
Georgetown Manor, 1000 N Duke.	01
Glenn, 922 - 926 Dacian Ave.	01
Holiday Inn (Downtown), 605 W Chapel Hill.	02
Holiday Inn (West), 3460 Hillsborough Rd.	05
Holly Hills.	05
Homestead, Durham - Chapel Hill Blvd.	07

Howard Johnson, I - 85 & hillandale Rd.	05
Imperial, 301 W Trinity Ave.	01
Jack Tar, 207 N Corcoran.	02
Lincoln, Lakeland Ave.	01
Manor Court.	07
Mcdougald Terrace.	01
Morreene, 3600 Tremont.	05
Murchison, 809 Demerius.	01
Northwood Circle, 300 Northwood Cir.	01
Palomina Park, 1306 Leon.	05
Poplar, Erwin Rd.	05
Presidential, 1000 Ruby.	04
Princeton, Chapel Hill & Morehead.	07
Sedgefield Court, 1615 Sedgefield.	05
Seven Eleven, 711 N Duke.	01
Statler Hilton, 2424 Erwin Rd.	05
Town & Campus Of Durham, 4216 Garrett Rd.	07
Town & Campus, 910 W Trinity.	05
Town House, 301 Swift.	05
Triangle	05
Trinity North, 300 W Trinity.	01
University, Duke University Rd.	01
Valley Terrace, 2820 Chapel Hill Rd.	07
Vance, 922 - 926 Dacian Ave.	01
Voyager Inn, 15 - 501 By-Pass.	05
Weaver, 3000 Weaver.	07
Wellcraft Garden.	03
Westover Park, 2312 Pratt.	04
1100 Leon, 1100 Leon.	05
1200 Leon, 1200 Leon.	05

BUILDINGS

Central Carolina Bank, N Corcoran.	01
Environmental Protection Agency Davis Dr.	11
First Union Bank, 301 W Main.	01
North Carolina National Bank, 123 W Main.	01
Trust, 212 W Main.	01
Wachovia Bank, 130 W Main.	01

HOSPITALS

Duke West Campus.	10
Lincoln, 1301 Fayetteville.	07
Mc Pherson, 1110 W Main.	01
North Carolina Cerebral Palsy, 2910 Erwin Rd.	05
Veterans, 2500 Erwin Rd.	05
Watts, 2000 W Club Blvd.	05

UNIVERSITIES AND COLLEGES

Croft Business College, 111 Orange.	01
Duke University Mens Campus, Campus Dr.	06
Duke University Womens Campus, W Main.	08

Durham Business College, 3128 Fayetteville.	07
North Carolina College, 1805 Fayetteville.	07
Southeastern Business College, 603 S Alston Ave.	01

FAYETTEVILLE   283

POST OFFICE BOXES

Box Nos.

A-Z	Fayetteville	02
1-2000	Fayetteville	02
3000-3999	Haymount Sta	05
4000-4999	Lakedale Sta	06
5000-5999	Eutaw Sta	03

RURAL ROUTES

1,2	01
3	06
4	04
5,6	01
7	06
8	04
9,10	04
11	04

STATIONS, BRANCHES AND UNITS

Bonnie Doone Br.	03
Cottonade Br.	01
East Fayetteville Br.	01
Eutaw Sta.	03
Fort Bragg Br.	08
Haymount Sta	05
Lafayette Br.	04
Lakedale Sta.	06
Methodist College Br.	01
Newbold Sta.	01
Pope A F B Mou.	08
General Delivery	02
Postmaster	02

BUILDINGS

First Union National Bank, Donaldson St.	01
First-Citzens Bank, 109 Green St.	01
Grace Pittman, 431 Hay St.	01
Highland Office, 2504 Raeford Rd.	05
Huske, 417 Hay St.	01
Jessup, 2606 Raeford Rd.	03
Lawyers, Market Sq.	01
Professional, 155 Gillespie St.	01
Tolar, 1239 Fort Bragg Rd.	05
Wooten, 1220 Fort Bragg Rd.	05

GOVERNMENT OFFICES

Cumberland County Courthouse, Gillesepie St.	01
Federal, 301 Green St.	01

HOSPITALS

Cape Fear Valley, Owen Dr. ..   02
Highsmith-Rainey, Bradford
  Ave....   01
Veterans Administration,
  Ramsey St   01
Womack Army....   07

MILITARY INSTALLATIONS

Fort Bragg   07
Pope AFB   08

UNIVERSITIES AND COLLEGES

Fayetteville State, Murchison
  Rd..................   01
Fayetteville Technical
  Institue, Hull Rd   01
Methodist, Ramsey St   03

GREENSBORO   274

POST OFFICE BOXES

Box Nos.
A-ZI   West Market St
     Sta................   02
1-3999   West Market St
     Sta................   02
4001-4999   South
     Greensboro
     Sta................   06
5001-5999   Tate Street
     Sta................   03
6001-6999   Summit Sta.......   05
7001-7999   Hilltop Sta.......   07
8001-8999   Guilford
     College Br   10
9001-9999   Plaza Sta........   04
10001-10999   Friendly Sta.......   04
11001-11999   Guilford Br   09
13000-13999   Golden Gate   05
20001-22144   Main Office   20

RURAL ROUTES

1   06
2   05
3   10
4   06
5,6   05
7   08
8   06
9   09
10   06
11   10
12,13   08

STATIONS, BRANCHES AND UNITS

Friendly Sta................   04
Golden Gate Sta...........   05
Guilford Br   09
Guilford College Br.......   10
Hilltop Sta................   07
Plaza Sta.................   08
Pomona Sta...............   09
South Greensboro Sta.....   06
Summit Sta...............   05

Tate Street Sta....   03
West Market Street Sta..........   02
General Delivery   20
Postmaster   20

APARTMENTS, HOTELS, MOTELS

Alonzo Towers, 2314 Church.   05
Bob Pettys Court, 2228
  Osborne Rd.............   07
Bob Pettys, 3710 Oakwood
  Dr..................   07
Cabana Club, 2821 N
  O'Henry Blvd..........   05
Cannon Court, 828 N Elm   01
Carolina, 121 W Mc Gee   01
Churchill Arms, 301 N
  Mendenhall............   01
Cool Spring, 3200 Spring   05
Country Club Mobile Home,
  Rt 6 Box 188...........   05
Country Club, 1700 N Elm...   01
Diplomat 1/2 thunderbird, 29
  & 70 S................   06
Dixie, 336 Bellemeade   01
Dolly Madison, 1015 N Elm...   01
Donnells Lodge, 1112 W
  Market................   03
Fairfax, 203 E Bessemer Ave...   01
Francisco, 23 1/2 2499
  Patroit Way............   08
Frazier...................   10
Friendly Hills, Hunt Club Rd...   10
Gambles, Rt 1 Boxes 1-39.....   06
Garretts, 5704 High Point
  Rd..................   07
General Greene, US Highway
  29 S.................   02
Greensboro Travelodge, 225
  Church...............   01
Greenwich, 111 W
  Washington...........   01
Henry Louis Smith Homes,
  743 W Florida..........   06
Henrys, Rt 6 Box 509........   05
Hidden Valley, 6001 W
  Market...............   09
Holiday Inn N, US 29 at
  16th.................   05
Holiday Inn S, US 29 & 17.....   05
Howard Johnsons, U S Hwy
  855..................   02
Irving Park Manor, 1800 N
  Elm..................   08
Jamison, 2500 Hiatt........   03
Journeys End, 2310
  Battleground Ave........   08
Kent Court, Hwy 29 N........   01
Kings Arms, 1831 1/2 41
  Banking..............   08
Kings Inn, 1103 N Elm.......   01
Madison Woods, 5500
  Tomahawk............   10
Manor, 1045 W Market.......   02
Maplewood, 2500
  Battleground Ave........   08
Mark-Rand, 230 S Park Dr.....   01
Midtown, 817 Summit Ave.....   05
Morgan Court, 6706 W
  Market...............   09
Morningside Homes, 1843
  Everitt...............   01
O Henry, 101 Bellemeade   02

Oaks, 1118 Summit Ave........   05
Oakwood, 3701 High Point
  Rd..................   07
Palms The, 3100-3299
  Lawndale Dr...........   08
Piedmont, 209 N Cedar   01
Plantation, 3404 High Point
  Rd..................   04
Pleasant Acres, 814 Robs Ct..   06
Powhatan, 906 W Market......   01
Sands, 3114 O Henry Blvd   05
Sans Souci, 912 E Cone
  Blvd.................   05
Scott, 318 Asheboro.........   06
Sedgefield Inn, 5704 High
  Point Rd..............   07
Shady Lane, Rt 5 Box 30......   05
Shady Lawn, 1020 W Market...   01
Sheraton Motor Inn, 2838 S
  Elm..................   06
Shirley, 203 E Bessemer Ave...   01
Smith Ranch, 2210
  Randleman Rd.........   06
Stancils 421 No 1 & No 2,
  4309 Liberty Rd........   06
Three Fountains North
  Mcknight Mill Rd Rt Utah..   05
Towers, 1101 N Elm.........   01
Towne House Motor Lodge,
  1000 W Market.........   02
Travel Inn, Highway 29 S......   07
Troxlers, 1005 Alamance Rd...   06
Twin Maple, 4638 W Market...   07
Vance, 1104 Magnolia........   01
Victoria, 301 Mc Iver........   03
Victory, 1045 W Market......   01
Voyager Inn, 830 W Market ...   02
Whites, Rt 5 Box 39.........   05
Wildwood, 3521 Mc Cuistan
  Rd..................   07
Winburn Court, 203 Tate   03
Yesteroaks Pisgah Church Rd
  Rt Yesteroaks..........   05

BUILDINGS

Banner, 119 N Elm..........   01
Beaman, 2820 Lawndale Dr...   08
Brown, 438 W Market........   01
Butler, 430 W Gaston........   01
Dixie, 125 S Elm...........   01
Edgeworth, 232 N Edgeworth..   01
Federal, 324 W Market.......   02
Five-Hundred West Gaston,
  500 W Gaston..........   01
Freeman, 612 Pasteur Dr.....   03
Jefferson Standard, 101 N
  Elm..................   01
Piedmont, 114 N Elm........   01
Professional, 1030 Church....   01
Southeastern, 102 N Elm.....   01
Three Thirty-Eight North Elm,
  338 N Elm.............   01
Wachovia Bank, 201 N Elm....   01
Watson, 174 W Sycamore   01

GOVERNMENT OFFICES

City Offices, 210 N Greene....   02
Municipal Offices, 210 N
  Greene...............   02

HOSPITALS

Moses H. Cone Memorial, Po
Box 13227............................. 05
Richardson L Memorial, 2600
Southside Blvd..................... 06
Wesley Long Community, 501
N Elam Ave........................... 02

UNIVERSITIES AND COLLEGES

Agricultural & Technical Of
North Carolina, 312 N
Dudley................................... 11
Bennett College, Washington
& Macon................................ 20
Greensboro Division Of
Guilford College, 501 W
Washington............................ 02
Greensboro, W Market............ 20
Guilford, Friendly Rd.............. 16
Kings Business, 415 W
Friendly Ave.......................... 01
Womens College U Of N
Carolina, 1000 Spring
Garden................................... 12

HIGH POINT   272

POST OFFICE BOXES

Box Nos.
1-2152   Main Office....... 61
4001-4399   Archdale Br....... 63
5001-5619   Emerywood
                    Sta................ 62

RURAL ROUTES

1,2... 60
3,4,5...................................... 63

STATIONS, BRANCHES AND UNITS

Archdale Br............................. 63
Emerywood Sta........................ 62
General Delivery...................... 60
Postmaster............................. 60

RALEIGH   276

POST OFFICE BOXES

Box Nos.
1-3069   Century Sta....... 02
5001-5937   State College..... 07
6001-6527   Five Point Sta.... 08
7400-7599   B Sta................ 11
10001-10977   Cameron
                    Village Sta...... 05
11001-11524   Mordecai Sta..... 04
12000-12595   Cameron
                    Village Sta...... 05
14001-14467   King Charles
                    Sta................ 10
17001-17885   North Hills Sta... 09
25001-28272   Main Office........ 11

RURAL ROUTES

1... 09
2... 10

3... 03
4... 06
5... 04
6,7... 09
8... 07
10... 03

STATIONS, BRANCHES AND UNITS

Cameron Village Sta................ 05
Century Sta............................. 02
Five Point Sta.......................... 08
King Charles Sta...................... 10
Meredith College Rural Sta...... 02
Mordecai Sta.......................... 04
New Hope Br........................... 03
North Hills Sta........................ 09
State University Sta................. 07
General Delivery...................... 11
Postmaster............................. 11

APARTMENTS, HOTELS, MOTELS

Alamo Plaza, 1816 Louisburg
Rd... 02
Anclote Arms, 3609-21
Anclote Pl.............................. 07
Andrew Johnson, 100 W
Martin................................... 02
Baily Apartments, 200 E
Edenton................................. 01
Beckanna Apartments, 3939
Glenwood Ave........................ 09
Belvidere Motel, 2729 S
Wilmington............................ 03
Boylan Apartments, 753
Hillsboro................................ 03
Brookhill Townhouse, 5425
Dana Dr................................. 06
Cabanna Motel, 514 S
Salisbury.............................. 02
Cameron Courts Apartments,
783 Hillsboro......................... 03
Cameron Parks Apartments,
1213 Hillsboro....................... 03
Capital Apartments, 127 New
Bern Ave................................ 01
Carolina, 228 W Hargett.......... 02
College Inn, 2717 Western
Blvd...................................... 07
Country Club Homes,
Fairview & Oberlin Rd............ 06
Crabtree Manor Apartments,
200 E Six Forks Rd................. 09
Dods Motel, 1403 S
Wilmington............................ 03
Downtown Plaza, 531 N
Blount................................... 04
Downtowner, 309 Hillsboro...... 11
Fairfield, 1817 Louisburg Rd.... 04
Fincastle Apartments, 3109
Hillsboro................................ 07
Glenwood Arms Apartments,
2612 Glenwood Ave................ 08
Glenwood Gardens
Apartments, 2550
Glenwood Ave........................ 08
Golden Eagle Motor Inn, 525
Fayetteville........................... 01
Greystone Apartments, 701 N
Blount................................... 04

Grosvenor Garden
Apartments, 825 Hillsboro...... 03
Hillyer Apartments, 8 St
Marys.................................... 05
Holiday Inn 0 2, 306-18
Hillsboro................................ 02
Holiday Inn, 2813 North Blvd.... 04
Johnnys Motor Lodge, 1625
North Blvd............................. 04
Joslin Apartments, 705 W
Morgan.................................. 03
Mc Kimmon Village, Gorman
& Jackson.............................. 07
Montecito, 3939 Wake Forest
Rd... 09
North Carolina State College
Married Student Housing......... 07
Park Central, 130 W Martin...... 02
Parkview Apartments, 216 E
Jones.................................... 01
Penwood Apartments,
Penwood Rd........................... 06
Plantation Inn, US 1 North....... 04
Raleigh Apartments, 1020 W
Peace.................................... 01
Raleigh Towne House, 519-25
Wade Ave.............................. 05
Ranch Motel, 6129 Glenwood
Ave....................................... 09
Royal Hill Garden, 4315
Leesville Rd........................... 09
Simpson Apartments, 2402
Clark Ave.............................. 07
Sir Walter, 400 Fayetteville..... 02
Spanish Trace, 800 Dixie Trl.... 07
Swain Apartments, 121 N
Person.................................. 01
Tara Apartments, 109
Ramblewood Dr...................... 09
Town & Campus, 2700-2810
Conifer Dr.............................. 06
Travelodge, 300 N Dawson...... 11
Vance Apartments, 105 E
Edenton................................. 01
Velvet Cloak Inn, 1505
Hillsboro................................ 05
Voyager Motel Inn, Hillsboro
& Cox Ave.............................. 05
Webb Motel, 2718 S
Wilmington............................ 03
Wedgwood Apratments, 740
Smallwood Dr........................ 05
Western Manor Apartments,
2300 Avent Ferry Rd.............. 06
White Apartments, 217 E
North.................................... 01
Wilmont Apartments, 3200
Hillsboro................................ 07

BUILDINGS

Agriculture, Edenton &
Halifax.................................. 01
Alexander, 133 Fayetteville..... 01
Baptist Convention, 301
Hillsboro................................ 03
Branch Bank, 333
Fayetteville........................... 01
Brown-Rogers, 115 Hillsboro.... 03
Bryan, 2113 Cameron............. 05
C-E E, 333 Wade Ave.............. 05

Cameron-Brown, 900 Wade Ave	05
Cameron, 400 Oberlin Rd	05
Capital Club, 16 W Martin	01
Doctors, Wade Ave & St Mary'S	05
Education, W Edenton & Salisbury	03
First Citizens Bank, 14 E Martin	01
First Federal Savings & Loan, 300 S Salisbury	01
First Union National Bank, 234 Fayetteville	01
Glenwood Prof Village, Glenwood Ave Essex Cir	08
Insurance, 336 Fayetteville	01
Koger Executive Center	12
Lawyers, 320 S Salisbury	01
Ligon, 800 St Marys	05
Medical Arts, 1110 Wake Forest Rd	04
Methodists, Glenwood & Wade Ave	05
N C National Bank, 239 Fayetteville	01
Odd Fellows, 15 W Hargett	01
Phillips, 401 Oberlin Rd	05
Professional, 127 W Hargett	01
Raleigh Savings & Loan, 219 Fayetteville	01
Raleigh, 5 W Hargett	01
Wachovia Bank, 227 Fayetteville	01
Y M C A, 1601 Hillsboro	05
Y W C A, 217 W Jones	03
York, 2016 Cameron	05
1330, 1330 Saint Marys	05

HOSPITALS

Dorothea Dix State, S Boylan Ave	11
Mary Elizabeth, 1100 Wake Forest Rd	04
Medicenter, 616 Wade Ave	05
Rex Hospital, 1311 St Marys	03
Wake Memorial Hospital, 3000 New Bern Ave	10

UNIVERSITIES AND COLLEGES

Blind School, Ashe Ave & Park Ave	06
Governor Morehead School, Ashe Ave & Park Ave	06
Meredith, 3800 Hillsboro	11
Methodist Orphanage, 1001 Glenwood Ave	05
Nazareth Orphanage, Avent Ferry Rd & Price	11
North Carolina State College, 2205 Hillsboro	07
Peace College, 15 E Peace	04
Saint Augustine College, 1315 Oakwood Ave	11
Saint Marys College, 900 Hillsboro	11
Shaw University, 11 W South	02

WINSTON SALEM 271

POST OFFICE BOXES

Box Nos.

A-Z	Salem	08
1-3199	Main Office	02
N-1-99	North	05
4001-4499	North Sta	05
4501-4999	Waughtown Sta	07
5001-5999	Ardmore Sta	03
6001-9099	Reynolda Sta	09
10001-10999	Salem Sta	08
11001-11999	Bethabara	06
12001-12999	Waughtown	07
15001-15074	Ardmore	03

RURAL ROUTES

1	06
2	06
3	05
4,5,6	07
7	05
8	05
9,10	07
11	03

STATIONS, BRANCHES AND UNITS

Ardmore Sta	03
Bethabara Sta	06
Hanes Sta	03
Mount Tabor Sta	06
North Sta	05
Reynolda Sta	09
Salem Sta	08
Waughtown Sta	07
General Delivery	02
Postmaster	02

APARTMENTS, HOTELS, MOTELS

Ardmore Terrace Apts, 224 Melrose	03
Balcony Courts Apartments, 1606-1610 Northwest Blvd	04
Baptist Home Apts, Reynolds Park Rd	07
Carolina, 407 W 4th St	02
Chermar Apts, Bethania Sta Rd	06
Cloverdale Apts, 224 Melrose	03
College Village Apartments, 741 Avalon Rd	04
Colonial Village Apartments, 110 Martin St	03
Country Club Apts, N. Peace Haven Rd	04
Downtowner Motor Inn, 128 N Cherry St	01
Faculty Apartments, 2200 Faculty Dr	06
Georgetown Apts, Carriage Dr	06
Graycourt Apartments, 450 N Broad St	01
Greystone Downtown Motel, 650 W 4th St	01

Hawthorne Ct Apts, 1835 S Hawthorne Rd	03
Holiday Inn, Trentwest	03
Holiday Inn, 127 S Cherry St	01
Howard Johnson'S Motor Lodge, 150 S Stratford Rd	04
Johnsborough Town House Apts, 3629 Old Vineyard Rd	04
Lee Apts, Miller & Silas Creek Pky	03
Medical Foundation Apts, Hawthorne Rd	03
Miller Park Apartments, 2500-35 Miller Park Cir	03
Monticello Apartments, 755 Anson St	03
Parkland Apts, Hutton	03
Parkway Chalet Motor Lodge, 600 Peters Creek Pkwy	03
Plaza Apartments, 900 Thurmond St	05
Regency Apts, Old Vineyard Rd	03
Salem Square Apts, 3812 Country Club Rd	04
Sheraton Motor Inn, 380 Knollwood Ave	03
Spainhour Apts, Indiana Ave	06
Statler Hilton Inn, Marshall & High St	01
Students Apartments, 2300 Faculty Dr	06
Twin Castles Apartments, 2000 Beach St	03
Villas Apts, Old Vineyard Rd	04
Vineyard Garden Apts, Old Vineyard Rd	04
Wedgewood Apts, 1620 W 1st St	04
Westgate Luxury Apts, Westgate Cir	06
Winston Apartments, 654 W 4th St	01

BUILDINGS

Bolick Arcade, 119 W 2nd St	01
First Union 310 W 4th St	01
Forsyth Medical Park, 1900 S Hawthorne Rd	03
North Carolina National Bank, 240 N Liberty St	01
Northwestern Bank 235 Cherry NW	01
O Hanlon, 105 W 4th St	01
Pepper, 104 W 4th St	01
Professional, 2240 Cloverdale Ave	03
Public Library, 660 W 5th St	01
Reynolds, 401-405 N Main St	01
Stratford Medical Center, 107 S Stratford Rd	04
Wachovia, 301 N Main St	01

GOVERNMENT OFFICES

City Hall	01
County Court House	01
Government Center	01

HOSPITALS

Baptist Homes, Reynolds
   Park Rd 07
Casstevens Hospital, 514 S
   Stratford Rd 03
Forsyth County, Rt 7 05
Forsyth Memorial Hospital,
   3333 Silas Creek Pkwy 03
Graylyn Hospital, 2539
   Robinhood Rd 06

Kate Bitting Hospital, 1101 E
   7th St 01
North Carolina Baptist
   Hospital, 300 S Hawthorne
   Rd 03

UNIVERSITIES AND COLLEGES

Bowman Gray School Of Med
   Wake Forest, 300 S
   Hawthorne Rd 03

Salem College, Salem
   Square 08
Wake Forest Univ, Reynolda
   Rd 09
Winston-Salem State College,
   Columbia Hts 02

NORTH DAKOTA
(Abbreviation: ND)

Abercrombie	58001
Absaraka	58002
Adams	58210
Adrian	58410
Agate, R. Br. Bisbee	58310
Akra	58211
Alamo	58830
Alexander	58831
Alfred	58411
Alice	58003
Alkabo	58832
Almont	58520
Alsen	58311
Ambrose	58833
Amenia	58004
Amidon	58620
Anamoose	58710
Aneta	58212
Antler	58711
Appam	58834
Ardoch	58213
Arena	58412
Argusville	58005
Arnegard	58835
Arthur	58006
Arvilla	58214
Ashley	58413
Ayr	58007
Backoo	58215
Baker	58312
Baldwin	58521
Balfour	58712
Balta	58313
Bantry	58713
Barney	58008
Bartlett	58314
Barton, R Br. Rugby	58315
Bathgate	58216
Battleview	58714
Beach	58621
Belcourt	58316
Belden	58715
Belfield	58622
Benedict	58716
Bentley	58522
Bergen	58717
Berlin	58415
Berthold	58718
Beulah	58523
Binford	58416
Bisbee	58317
Agate, R. Br.	58310
Bismarck (1st)	58501
Livona, R. Br.	58501
Mc Kenzie, R. Br.	58553
Blaisdell	58720
Blanchard	58009
Bonetraill	58836
Bordulac	58417
Bottineau (1st)	58318
Bowbells	58721
Bowdon	58418
Bowesmont	58217
Bowman	58623
Braddock	58524
Brampton	58010
Brantford	58419
Breien	58525
Bremen	58319

Brinsmade	58320
Brocket	58321
Buchanan	58420
Bucyrus	58624
Buffalo	58011
Buford	58837
Burlington	58722
Foxholm, R. Br.	58738
Burnstad	58526
Burt	58527
Butte	58723
Buxton	58218
Caledonia	58219
Calio	58322
Calvin	58323
Cando	58324
Cannon Ball, R. Br. Fort	
Yates	58528
Carbury	58724
Carpio	58725
Carrington	58421
Carson	58529
Cartwright	58838
Casselton	58012
Cathay	58422
Cavalier	58220
Cayuga	58013
Center	58530
Chaffee, R. Br. Wheatland	58014
Charlson	58726
Chaseley	58423
Christine	58015
Churchs Ferry	58325
Cleveland	58424
Clifford	58016
Cogswell	58017
Coleharbor	58531
Colfax	58018
Colgan	58840
Colgate	58019
Columbus	58727
Concrete	58221
Conway, R. Br. Fordville	58232
Cooperstown	58425
Coteau	58728
Coulee	58729
Courtenay	58426
Crary	58327
Crete	58029
Crosby	58730
Crystal	58222
Crystal Springs	58427
Cummings	58223
Dahlen	58224
Davenport	58021
Dawson	58428
Dazey	58429
De Lamere, R. Br. Milnor	58022
Deering	58731
Denbigh	58732
Denhoff	58430
Des Lacs	58733
Devils Lake (1st)	58301
Dickey	58431
Dickinson (1st)	58601
Dodge	58625
Donnybrook	58734
Douglas	58735
Downtown, Sta. Minot	58701
Doyon	58328
Drake	58736
Drayton	58225

Dresden	58226
Driscoll	58532
Dunn Center	58626
Dunseith	58329
Durbin	58023
Dwight	58024
Eckelson, R. Br. Jamestown	58432
Edgeley	58433
Edinburg	58227
Edmore	58330
Edmunds	58434
Egeland	58331
Eldridge	58435
Elgin	58533
Ellendale	58436
Emerado	58228
Emmet	58534
Emrick	58437
Enderlin	58027
Englevale	58028
Epping	58843
Erie	58029
Esmond	58332
Fairdale	58229
Fairfield	58627
Fairmount	58030
Fargo (1st)	58102
Fessenden	58438
Fillmore	58333
Fingal	58031
Finley	58230
Flasher	58535
Raleigh, R. Br.	58564
Shields, R. Br.	58569
Flaxton	58737
Forbes	58439
Fordville	58231
Conway, R. Br.	58232
Forest River	58233
Forman	58032
Fort Ransom	58033
Fort Rice	58537
Fort Totten	58335
Fort Yates	58538
Cannon Ball, R. Br.	58528
Fortuna	58844
Foxholm, R. Br. Burlington	58738
Freda	58539
Fredonia	58440
Fullerton	58441
Gackle	58442
Galchutt	58034
Galesburg	58035
Gardar	58234
Gardena, R. Br. Kramer	58739
Gardner	58036
Garrison	58540
Gascoyne	58629
Geneseo	58037
Gilby	58235
Honeyford, R. Br.	58242
Johnstown, R. Br.	58245
Gladstone	58630
Glasston	58236
Glen Ullin	58631
Glenburn	58740
Glenfield	58443
Goldenvalley	58541
Golva	58632
Goodrich	58444
Gorham	58633
Grace City	58445

Grafton (1st) 58237
Grand Forks (1st) 58201
Grand Forks A F B, Br.
  Grand Forks 58201
Grand Rapids, R. Br. La
  Moure 58446
Grandin 58038
Granville 58741
Grassy Butte 58634
Great Bend 58039
Grenora 58845
Guelph 58447
Gwinner 58040
Hague 58542
Halliday 58636
Hamar 58336
Hamberg 58337
Hamilton 58238
Hamlet 58742
Hampden 58338
Hankinson 58041
Hannaford 58448
Hannah 58239
Hannover 58543
Hansboro, R. Br. Rocklake .. 58339
Harlow 58340
Harvey 58341
Harwood 58042
Hatton 58240
Havana 58043
Haynes 58637
Hazelton 58544
Hazen 58545
Heaton 58450
Hebron 58638
Heil 58546
Heimdal 58342
Hensel 58241
Hensler 58547
Hettinger 58639
Hickson 58044
Hillsboro 58045
Honeyford, R. Br. Gilby 58242
Hoople 58243
Hope 58046
Horace 58047
Huff, R. Br. Mandan 58555
Hunter 58048
Hurdsfield 58451
Inkster 58244
Jamestown (1st) 58401
  Eckelson, R. Br. 58432
  Nortonville, R. Br. 58473
Jessie 58452
Johnstown, R. Br. Gilby 58245
Joliette 58246
Juanita 58453
Jud 58454
Judson, R. Br. New Salem ... 58548
Karlsruhe 58744
Kathryn 58049
Keene 58847
Kenmare 58746
Kensal 58455
Kief 58747
Killdeer 58640
Kindred 58051
Kintyre 58549
Kloten 58248
Knox 58343
Kramer 58748
  Gardena, R. Br. 58739
Kulm 58456

La Moure 58458
  Grand Rapids, R. Br. 58446
Lakota 58344
Landa 58749
Langdon 58249
  Maida, R. Br. 58255
Lankin 58250
Lansford 58750
Larimore 58251
Lark 58550
Larson 58751
Lawton 58345
Leal 58459
Leeds 58346
Lefor 58641
Lehr 58460
Leith 58551
Leonard 58052
Leroy 58252
Lidgerwood 58053
Lignite 58752
Linton 58552
Lisbon 58054
Litchville 58461
Livona, R. Br. Bismarck 58501
Loraine 58753
Lostwood 58754
Ludden 58462
Luverne 58056
Maddock 58348
Maida, R. Br. Langdon 58255
Makoti 58756
Mandan (1st) 58554
  Huff, R. Br. 58555
Mandaree 58757
Manfred 58465
Manning 58642
Mantador 58058
Manvel 58256
Mapes 58349
Mapleton 58059
Marion 58466
Marmarth 58643
Marshall 58644
Martin 58758
Max 58759
Maxbass 58760
Mayville 58257
Mc Canna 58253
Mc Clusky 58463
Mc Gregor 58755
Mc Henry 58464
Mc Kenzie, R. Br. Bismarck .. 58553
Mc Leod 58057
Mc Ville 58254
Medina 58467
Medora 58645
Mekinock 58258
Menoken 58558
Mercer 58559
Merricourt 58469
Michigan 58259
Millarton 58470
Milnor 58060
  De Lamere, R. Br. 58022
Milton 58260
Minnewaukan 58351
Minot (1st) 58701
Minot A F B, Br. Minot 58701
Minto 58261
Moffit 58560
Mohall 58761
Monango 58471

Montpelier 58472
Mooreton 58061
Mott 58646
Mountain 58262
Munich 58352
Mylo 58353
Nanson 58354
Napoleon 58561
Nash 58264
Neche 58265
Nekoma 58355
New England 58647
New Hradec 58648
New Leipzig 58562
New Rockford 58356
New Salem 58563
  Judson, R. Br. 58548
New Town 58763
Newburg 58762
Niagara 58266
Niobe 58764
Nome 58062
Noonan 58765
Norma 58766
Northgate 58767
Northwood 58267
Nortonville, R. Br.
  Jamestown 58473
Norwich 58768
Oakes 58474
Oberon 58357
Oriska 58063
Orr 58268
Orrin 58359
Osnabrock 58269
Overly 58360
Page 58064
Palermo 58769
Park River 58270
Parshall 58770
Pekin 58361
Pembina (1st) 58271
Penn 58362
Perth 58363
Petersburg 58272
Pettibone 58475
Pillsbury 58065
Pingree 58476
Pisek 58273
Plaza 58771
Pleasant Lake 58364
Portal 58772
Portland 58274
Powers Lake 58773
Raleigh, R. Br. Flasher 58564
Raub 58774
Rawson 58848
Ray 58849
  Wheelock, R. Br. 58855
Reeder 58649
Regan 58477
Regent 58650
Reynolds 58275
Rhame 58651
Richardton 58652
Riverdale 58565
Robinson 58478
Rocklake 58365
  Hansboro, R. Br. 58339
Rogers 58479
Rolette 58366
Rolla 58367
Roseglen 58775

Ross	58776
Rugby (1st)	58368
Barton, R. Br.	58315
Ruso	58778
Rutland	58067
Ryder	58779
Saint Anthony	58566
Saint John	58369
Saint Michael	58370
Saint Thomas	58276
San Haven	58371
Sanborn	58480
Sanish	58780
Sarles	58372
Sawyer	58781
Scranton	58653
Selfridge	58568
Selz	58373
Sentinel Butte	58654
Sharon	58277
Sheldon	58068
Sherwood	58782
Sheyenne	58374
Shields, R. Br. Flasher	58569
Silva	58375
Silver Strip, Sta. Williston	58801
Solen	58570
Sours	58783
South Heart	58655
South Washington, Sta. Grand Forks	58201
Spiritwood	58481
Spring Brook	58850
Stanley	58784

Stanton	58571
Fort Clark, R. Br.	58536
Starkweather	58377
Steele	58482
Sterling	58572
Stirum	58069
Strasburg	58573
Straubville	58070
Streeter	58483
Surrey	58785
Sutton	58484
Sykeston	58486
Tappen	58487
Taylor	58656
Thompson	58278
Tioga	58852
Tokio	58379
Tolley	58787
Toina	58380
Tower City	58071
Towner	58788
Trenton	58853
Trotters	58657
Turtle Lake	58575
Tuttle	58488
Underwood	58576
Union	58279
University, Sta. Grand Forks	58202
Upham	58789
Valley City (1st)	58072
Velva	58790
Venturia	58489
Verona	58490
Voltaire	58792

Voss	58280
Wahpeton (1st)	58075
Walcott	58077
Wales	58281
Walhalla	58282
Warwick	58381
Washburn	58577
Watford City	58854
Webster	58382
West Fargo (1st)	58078
Westhope	58793
Wheatland	58079
Chatlee, R. Br.	58014
Wheelock, R. Br. Ray	58855
White Earth	58794
Whitman	58283
Wildrose	58795
Williston (1st)	58801
Willow City	58384
Wilton	58579
Wimbledon	58492
Wing	58494
Wishek	58495
Wolford	58385
Woodworth	58496
Wyndmere	58081
York	58386
Ypsilanti	58497
Zahl	58856
Zap	58580
Zeeland	58581

OHIO
(Abbreviation: OH)

(the) Delta Queen, Sta.
  Cincinnati 45202
Aberdeen 45101
Ada (1st) 45810
Adams Mills 43801
Adamsville 43802
Addison 45610
Addyston 45001
Adelphi 43101
Adena 43901
Adrian 44801
Air Materiel Command, Br.
  Dayton 45433
Airport, Sta. Columbus 43219
Airport, Br. Cleveland 44181
AKRON (1st) (see appendix)
Albany 45710
Alexandria 43001
Alger 45812
Alledonia 43902
Allensville 45611
Alliance (1st) 44601
Alpha 45301
Alvada 44802
Alvordton 43501
Amanda 43102
Amelia 45102
Amesville 45711
Amherst (1st) 44001
Amlin 43002
Amsden 44803
Amsterdam 43903
Andover 44003
Anna 45302
Ansonia 45303
Antioch 43710
Antwerp 45813
Apple Creek 44606
Arcadia 44804
Arcanum 45304
Archbold (1st) 43502
Arlington 45814
Armstrongs Mills 43904
Ashland (1st) 44805
Ashley 43003
Ashtabula (1st) 44004
Ashville 43103
Athens (1st) 45701
Atlanta 43104
Attica 44807
Atwater 44201
Augusta 44607
Aurora (1st) 44202
Austinburg 44010
Austintown, Br. Youngstown 44515
Ava 43711
Avon 44011
Avon Lake (1st) 44012
Bainbridge (1st) 45612
Bakersville 43803
Baltic 43804
Baltimore 43105
Bannock 43972
Barberton (1st) 44203
Barlow 45712
Barnesville (1st) 43713
Bartlett 45713
Barton 43905
Bascom 44809
Batavia (1st) 45103

Batesville 43715
Bath (1st) 44210
Bay Village, Br. Cleveland 44140
Beach City 44608
Beachland, Sta. Cleveland 44119
Beachwood, Br. Cleveland
  (see appendix)
Beallsville 43716
Beaver 45613
Beaverdam, R. Br. Lima 45808
Bedford, Br. Cleveland 44146
Beechwold, Sta. Columbus 43214
Bellaire (1st) 43906
Bellbrook 45305
Belle Center 43310
Belle Valley 43717
Bellefontaine (1st) 43311
Bellevue (1st) 44811
Bellville 44813
Belmont 43718
Belmore, R. Br. Leipsic 45815
Beloit 44609
Belpre (1st) 45714
Benton, R. Br. Millersburg 44654
Benton Ridge 45816
Bentonville 45105
Berea (1st) 44017
Bergholz 43908
Berkey 43504
Berlin 44610
Berlin Center 44401
Berlin Heights 44814
Bethel 45106
Bethesda 43719
Bettsville 44815
Beverly 45715
Bexley, Br. Columbus 43209
Bidwell 45614
Big Prairie 44611
Birmingham 44816
Blackfork 45615
Blacklick 43004
Bladensburg 43005
Blaine 43909
Blakeslee 43505
Blanchester (1st) 45107
Blissfield 43805
Bloomdale 44817
Bloomingburg 43106
Bloomingdale 43910
Bloomville 44818
Blue Creek 45616
Blue Rock 43720
Bluffton (1st) 45817
Boardman, Br. Youngstown 44512
Bolivar 44612
Bono 43401
Botkins 45306
Bourneville 45617
Bowerston 44695
Bowersville 45307
Bowling Green (1st) 43402
Bradford 45308
Bradner 43406
Brady Lake, R. Br. Kent 44211
Branch Hill 45108
Brecksville, Br. Cleveland 44141
Bremen (1st) 43107
Brewster 44613
Brice 43109
Bridgeport (1st) 43912
Briggs, Br. Cleveland 44134
Brilliant 43913

Brimfield, Br. Kent 44240
Brinkhaven 43006
Bristolville 44402
Broadway 43007
Brook Park, Br. Cleveland 44142
Brookfield 44403
Brooklyn, Br. Cleveland 44144
Brookville (1st) 45309
Brownsville 43721
Brunswick (1st) 44212
Bryan (1st) 43506
Buchtel 45716
Buckeye Lake 43008
Buckland, R. Br. Lima 45819
Bucyrus (1st) 44820
Buffalo 43722
Buford 45110
Burbank 44214
Burghill 44404
Burgoon 43407
Burkettsville 45310
Burnet Woods, Sta.
  Cincinnati 45220
Burton 44021
Butler 44822
Byesville 43723
Cable 43009
Cadiz (1st) 43907
Cairo 45820
Calcutta, Br. East Liverpool 43920
Caldwell 43724
Caledonia 43314
Cambridge (1st) 43725
Camden 45311
Cameron 43914
Camp Dennison 45111
Camp Ground, Br.
  Lancaster 43130
Campbell 44405
Campus, Sta. Cincinnati 45221
Canal Fulton 44614
Canal Winchester 43110
Canfield (1st) 44406
CANTON (1st) (see appendix)
Carbon Hill 43111
Carbondale, R. Br.
  Nelsonville 45717
Cardington 43315
Carey (1st) 43316
Carlisle, Br. Franklin 45005
Carroll 43112
Carrollton (1st) 44615
Carrothers 44823
Carthagena, R. Br. Celina 45822
Casstown 45312
Castalia 44824
Castine 45313
Catawba 43010
Cecil 45821
Cedarville 45314
Celina (1st) 45822
  Carthagena, R. Br. 45822
  Chickasaw, R. Br. 45826
Centerburg 43011
Centerville, Br. Dayton 45459
Central, Sta. Toledo (see
  appendix)
Chagrin Falls (1st) 44022
Chandlersville 43727
Chardon (1st) 44024
Charm 44617
Chatfield 44825
Chauncey 45719

Cherry Fork	45618	
Chesapeake	45619	
Cheshire	45620	
Chester	45720	
Chesterhill	43728	
Chesterland (1st)	44026	
Chesterville	43317	
Chickasaw, R. Br. Celina	45826	
Chillicothe (1st)	45601	
Chilo	45112	
Chippewa Lake	44215	
Christiansburg	45389	
CINCINNATI (1st) (see appendix)		
Circleville (1st)	43113	
Clarington	43915	
Clark	43810	
Clarksburg	43115	
Clarksville	45113	
Clay Center	43408	
Claysville	43729	
Clayton	45315	
CLEVELAND (1st) (see appendix)		
Cleveland Heights, Br. Cleveland (see appendix)		
Cleves	45002	
Clifton	45316	
Clinton	44216	
Cloverdale	45827	
Clyde (1st)	43410	
Coal Run	45721	
Coalton	45621	
Coldwater (1st)	45828	
Colerain	43916	
College Corner	45003	
College Hill, Sta. Cincinnati	45224	
College Springs, Br. Columbus	43219	
Collins	44826	
Collinsville	45004	
Collinwood, Sta. Cleveland	44110	
Colton	43510	
Columbia Station	44028	
Columbiana (1st)	44408	
COLUMBUS (1st) (see appendix)		
Columbus Grove	45830	
Commercial Point	43116	
Conesville	43811	
Conneaut (1st)	44030	
Conover	45317	
Constitution	45722	
Continental	45831	
Dupont, R. Br.	45837	
Convoy	45832	
Coolville (1st)	45723	
Copley, Br. Akron	44321	
Corning	43730	
Corryville, Sta. Cincinnati	45219	
Cortland (1st)	44410	
Coshocton (1st)	43812	
Covington (1st)	45318	
Cranwood, Sta. Cleveland	44128	
Creola	45622	
Crestline (1st)	44827	
Creston	44217	
Cridersville, Br. Lima	45806	
Crooksville	43731	
Croton	43013	
Crown City	45623	
Cuba	45114	
Cumberland	43732	

Cumminsville, Sta. Cincinnati	45223	
Curtice	43412	
Custar	43511	
Cutler	45724	
CUYAHOGA FALLS (1st) (see appendix)		
Cygnet	43413	
Cynthiana	45624	
Dabel, Sta. Dayton (see appendix)		
Dalton	44618	
Damascus	44619	
Danville	43014	
Darbydale, R. Br. Grove City	43123	
Dart	45725	
Day Heights, Br. Milford	45150	
DAYTON (1st) (see appendix)		
Dayton View, Sta. Dayton	45406	
De Graff	43318	
Decatur	45115	
Deer Park, Br. Cincinnati	45236	
Deerfield	44411	
Deersville	44693	
Defiance (1st)	43512	
Del Fair, Br. Cincinnati	45238	
Delaware (1st)	43015	
Dellroy	44620	
Delphos (1st)	45833	
Delta	43515	
Dennison	44621	
Derby	43117	
Derwent	43733	
Deshler	43516	
Devola, Br. Marietta	45750	
Dexter	45726	
Dexter City	45727	
Diamond	44412	
Dillonvale	43917	
Dunglen, R. Br.	43918	
Dola	45835	
Donnelsville	45319	
Dorset	44032	
Dover (1st)	44622	
Downtown, Sta. Akron	44302	
Downtown, Sta. Canton	44702	
Doylestown	44230	
Dresden	43821	
Dublin	43017	
Dunbridge	43414	
Duncan Falls	43734	
Dundas	45625	
Dundee	44624	
Dunglen, R. Br. Dillonvale	43918	
Dunkirk	45836	
Dupont, R. Br. Continental	45837	
East Akron, Sta. Akron	44305	
East Canton, Br. Canton	44730	
East Claridon	44033	
East Cleveland, B. Cleveland (see appendix)		
East End, Sta. Cincinnati	45226	
East Fultonham	43735	
East Liberty	43319	
East Liverpool (1st)	43920	
East Monroe	45116	
East Orwell	44034	
East Palestine (1st)	44413	
East Rochester	44625	
East Side, Sta. Youngstown	44506	
East Sparta	44626	
East Springfield	43925	
Eastlake, Br. Willoughby	44094	

Eaton (1st)	45320	
Edenton	45117	
Edgerton	43517	
Edgewater, Br. Cleveland	44107	
Edgewood, Br. Ashtabula	44004	
Edison	43320	
Edon	43518	
Elba	45728	
Eldorado	45321	
Elgin	45838	
Elida, Br. Lima	45807	
Elkton	44415	
Ellet, Sta. Akron	44312	
Elliston	43415	
Ellsworth	44416	
Elm Grove	45626	
Elmore	43416	
Elmwood Place, Br. Cincinnati	45216	
ELYRIA (1st) (see appendix)		
Empire	43926	
Englewood (1st)	45322	
Enon	45323	
Erieview, Sta. Cleveland (see appendix)		
Etna	43018	
Euclid, Br. Cleveland (see appendix)		
Evansport	43519	
Ewington	45627	
Excello, Br. Middletown	45042	
Fairborn (1st)	45324	
Fairfield, Br. Hamilton	45014	
Fairlawn, Br. Akron	44313	
Fairpoint	43927	
Fairport Harbor, Br. Painesville	44077	
Fairview	43736	
Fairview Park, Br. Cleveland	44126	
Far Hills, Br. Dayton	45419	
Farmdale	44417	
Farmer	43520	
Farmersville, Br. Germantown	45325	
Fayette	43521	
Fayetteville	45118	
Federal Reserve, Sta. Cincinnati	45201	
Federal Reserve, Sta. Cleveland	44101	
Feesburg	45119	
Felicity	45120	
Findlay (1st)	45840	
Jenera, R. Br.	45841	
Firebrick, R. Br. Oak Hill	45656	
Firestone Park, Sta. Akron (see appendix)		
Flat Rock	44828	
Fleming	45729	
Fletcher	45326	
Flushing	43977	
Fly	45730	
Forest	45843	
Forest Park, Br. Dayton (see appendix)		
Fort Jennings	45844	
Fort Loramie	45845	
Fort Recovery	45846	
Fort Scott Camps, R. Br. Harrison	45030	
Fort Seneca	44829	
Fosterville, Sta. Youngstown	44511	
Fostoria (1st)	44830	

Fountain Square, Sta.
  Cincinnati 45202
Fowler 44418
Frankfort 45628
Franklin (1st) 45005
Franklin Furnace 45629
Frazeysburg 43822
Fredericksburg 44627
Fredericktown 43019
Freeport 43973
Fremont (1st) 43420
Fresno 43824
Friendship 45630
Frost 45731
Fulton 43321
Fultonham 43738
Gahanna, Br. Columbus..43230
Galena 43021
Galion (1st) 44833
Gallipolis (1st) 45631
Galloway 43119
Gambier 43022
Garfield Heights, Br.
  Cleveland (see appendix)
Garrettsville (1st) 44231
Gates Mills 44040
Geneva (1st) 44041
  Geneva-on-the-Lake, R.
  Br. 44043
Geneva-on-the-Lake, R. Br.
  Geneva 44043
Genoa (1st) 43430
Georgetown 45121
Germano, R. Br. Jewett..43987
Germantown (1st) 45327
  Farmersville, Br. 45325
Gettysburg 45328
Gibsonburg 43431
Gilboa 45847
Girard (1st) 44420
Glandorf 45848
Glencoe 43928
Glendale, Br. Cincinnati..45246
Glenford 43739
Glenmary, Br. Cincinnati..45246
Glenmont 44628
Glouster 45732
Gnadenhutten 44629
Gomer, R. Br. Lima 45809
Good Hope, R. Br.
  Washington Court House..43121
Goodrich Street, Sta. Akron..44311
Gordon 45329
Gore 43122
Goshen 45122
Grafton 44044
Grand Rapids 43522
Grand River 44045
Granville (1st) 43023
Gratiot 43740
Gratis 45330
Graysville 45734
Graytown 43432
Green Camp 43322
Green Springs 44836
Greenfield (1st) 45123
  Rainsboro, R. Br. 45165
Greenford 44422
Greenhills, Br. Cincinnati..45218
Greensburg 44237
Greentown 44630
Greenville (1st) 45331
Greenwich 44837

Grelton, R. Br. Mc Clure..43523
Groesbeck, Br. Cincinnati..45239
Grove City (1st) 43123
Groveport 43125
Grover Hill 45849
Guernsey 43741
Guysville 45775
Gypsum 43433
Hallsville 45663
Hamden 45644
Hamersville 45130
HAMILTON (1st) (see
  appendix)
Hamler 43524
Hammondsville 43930
Hanging Rock 45635
Hannibal 43931
Hanoverton 44423
Harbor, Sta. Ashtabula..44004
Harbor View 43434
Harlem Springs 44631
Harpster 43323
Harrisburg 43126
Harrison (1st) 45030
Harrisonville, R. Br.
  Pomeroy 45737
Harrisville 43974
Harrod 45850
Hartford 44424
Hartville (1st) 44632
Harveysburg 45032
Haskins 43525
Haverhill 45636
Haviland 45851
Haydenville 43127
Hayesville 44838
Heath, Br. Newark 43055
Heathersdowns, Sta. Toledo..43614
Hebron 43025
Helena 43435
  Millersville, R. Br. 43448
Hemlock 43743
Hemlock Grove 45738
Hendrysburg 43744
Hicksville 43526
Hide-A-Way Hills, R. Br.
  Bremen 43107
Higginsport 45131
Highland 45132
Hilliard (1st) 43026
Hillsboro (1st) 45133
Hilltop, Sta. Columbus..43204
Hinckley 44233
Hiram 44234
Hocking, Sta. Lancaster..43130
Hockingport 45739
Holgate 43527
Holland 43528
Hollansburg 45332
Holloway 43985
Holmesville 44633
Homer 43027
Homerville 44235
Homeworth 44634
Hooven 45033
Hopedale 43976
Hopewell 43746
Houston 45333
Howard 43028
Hoytville 43529
Hubbard (1st) 44425
Huber Heights, Br. Dayton..45424
Hudson (1st) 44236

Huntsburg 44046
Huntsville 43324
Huron (1st) 44839
Hyde Park, Sta. Cincinnati..45208
Iberia 43325
Idaho, R. Br. Piketon..45661
Independence, Br. Cleveland..44131
Irondale 43932
Ironton (1st) 45638
Irwin 43029
Isle Saint George 43436
Ivorydale, Br. Cincinnati..45217
Jackson (1st) 45640
Jackson Center 45334
Jacksontown 43030
Jacksonville 45740
Jacobsburg 43933
Jamestown 45335
Jasper 45642
Jefferson (1st) 44047
Jeffersonville 43128
Jenera, R. Br. Findlay..45841
Jeromesville 44840
Jerry City 43437
Jerusalem 43747
Jewell 43530
Jewett 43986
  Germano, R. Br. 43987
Johnstown 43031
Junction City 43748
Kalida 45853
Kamms, Sta. Cleveland..44111
Kansas 44841
Keene 43828
Kelleys Island 43438
Kenmore, Sta. Akron..44314
Kensington 44427
Kent (1st) 44240
  Brady Lake, R. Br. 44211
  Brimfield, Br. 44240
  Streetsboro, Br. 44240
Kenton (1st) 43326
Kenwood, Sta. Toledo..43606
Kerr 45643
Kettering, Br. Dayton..45429
Kettlersville 45336
Kidron 44636
Kilbourne 43032
Killbuck 44637
Kimbolton 43749
Kings Mills 45034
Kingston 45644
Kingsville 44048
Kinsman 44428
Kipling 43758
Kipton 44049
Kirby 43330
Kirkersville 43033
Kirtland, Br. Willoughby..44094
Kitts Hill 45645
Kunkle 43531
La Rue 43332
Lacarne 43439
Lafayette, R. Br. Lima..45854
Lafferty 43951
Lagrange 44050
Laings 43752
Lake Milton 44429
Lakemore 44250
Lakeside-Marblehead..43440
Lakeview 43331
Lakeville 44638
Lakewood, Br. Cleveland..44107

Lancaster (1st)	43130	
Langsville	45741	
Lansing	43934	
Latham	45646	
Latty	45855	
Laura	45337	
Laurelville	43135	
Leavittsburg	44430	
Lebanon (1st)	45036	
Lee Road, Br. Cleveland	44129	
Lees Creek	45138	
Leesburg	45135	
Leesville	44639	
Leetonia	44431	
Leipsic	45856	
Belmore, R. Br.	45815	
Lemoyne	43441	
Leonardsburg	43034	
Lewis Center	43035	
Lewisburg	45338	
Lewistown	43333	
Lewisville	43754	
Lexington, Br Mansfield	44904	
Liberty, Br. Youngstown	44505	
Liberty Center	43532	
LIMA (1st) (see appendix)		
Limaville	44640	
Lincoln, Br. Mansfield	44905	
Lincoln Village, Br. Columbus	43228	
Lindenwald, Sta. Hamilton	45015	
Lindsey	43442	
Lisbon (1st)	44432	
Litchfield	44253	
Lithopolis	43136	
Little Hocking	45742	
Livingston, Sta. Columbus	43227	
Lockbourne	43137	
Lockbourne A F B, Br. Columbus	43217	
Lockland, Br. Cincinnati	45215	
Lodi	44254	
Logan (1st)	43138	
London (1st)	43140	
Londonderry	45647	
Long Bottom	45743	
LORAIN (1st) (see appendix)		
Lore City	43755	
Loudonville (1st)	44842	
Louisville (1st)	44641	
Loveland (1st)	45140	
Lowell	45744	
Lowellville	44436	
Lower Salem	45745	
Lucas	44843	
Lucasville	45648	
Luckey	43443	
Ludlow Falls	45339	
Lynchburg	45142	
Lyndhurst Mayfield, Br. Cleveland	44124	
Lyndon	45649	
Lynx	45650	
Lyons	43533	
Macedonia, Br. Northfield	44056	
Macksburg	45746	
Macon, R. Br. Sardinia	45143	
Madeira, Br. Cincinnati	45243	
Madison (1st)	44057	
Madison Avenue, Sta. Toledo	43624	
Madisonville, Sta. Cincinnati	45227	

Magnetic Springs	43036	
Magnolia	44643	
Maineville	45039	
Malaga	43757	
Malinta	43535	
Malta	43758	
Malvern	44644	
Manchester	45144	
MANSFIELD (1st) (see appendix)		
Mantua (1st)	44255	
Maple Heights, Br. Cleveland	44137	
Maple Valley, Sta. Akron	44320	
Maplewood	45340	
Marathon	45145	
Marengo	43334	
Maria Stein	45860	
Mariemont, Br. Cincinnati	45227	
Marietta (1st)	45750	
Marion (1st)	43302	
Marion Plaza, Br. Marion	43302	
Mark Center	43536	
Marshallville	44645	
Martel	43335	
Martin	43445	
Martins Ferry (1st)	43935	
Martinsburg	43037	
Martinsville	45146	
Marysville (1st)	43040	
Mason (1st)	45040	
Massillon (1st)	44646	
Masury	44438	
Maud, R. Br. West Chester	45069	
Maumee (1st)	43537	
Maximo	44650	
Maynard	43937	
Mc Arthur	45651	
Mc Clure	43534	
Grelton, R. Br.	43523	
Mc Comb	45858	
Mc Connelsville	43756	
Mc Cutchenville	44844	
Mc Dermott	45652	
Mc Donald	44437	
Mc Guffey	45859	
Mc Kinley Heights, Br. Niles	44446	
Mechanicsburg	43044	
Mechanicstown	44651	
Medina (1st)	44256	
Medway	45341	
Melmore	44845	
Melrose	45861	
Mendon	45862	
Mentor (1st)	44060	
Mentor-on-the-Lake, Br. Mentor	44060	
Mesopotamia	44439	
Metals Park, R. Br. Novelty	44073	
Metamora	43540	
Miami University, Sta. Oxford	45056	
Miamisburg (1st)	45342	
Miamitown	45041	
Miamiville	45147	
Mid City, Sta. Dayton	45402	
Middle Bass	43446	
Middle Point	45863	
Middlebranch	44652	
Middleburg	43336	
Middlefield (1st)	44062	
Middleport	45760	
Middletown (1st)	45042	

Midland	45148	
Midpark, Br. Cleveland	44130	
Midtown, Sta. Zanesville	43701	
Midvale	44653	
Milan	44846	
Milford (1st)	45150	
Day Heights, Br.	45150	
Mulberry, R Br	45150	
Perintown, R. Br.	45161	
Milford Center	43045	
Millbury	43447	
Milledgeville	43142	
Miller City	45864	
Millersburg (1st)	44654	
Millersport	43046	
Millersville, R. Br. Helena	43448	
Millfield	45761	
Millville, Br Hamilton	45013	
Milton Center	43541	
Mineral City	44656	
Mineral Ridge	44440	
Minersville	45763	
Minerva (1st)	44657	
Munford	45653	
Mingo	43047	
Mingo Junction	43938	
Minster	45865	
Mogadore (1st)	44260	
Monclova	43542	
Monroe	45050	
Monroeville	44847	
Montezuma	45866	
Montgomery, Br. Cincinnati	45242	
Montpelier (1st)	43543	
Montville	44064	
Moorefield	43979	
Moraine, Br. Dayton	45439	
Morral	43337	
Morristown	43759	
Morrow (1st)	45152	
Moscow	45153	
Moundbuilders, Sta. Newark	43055	
Mount Airy, Sta. Cincinnati	45239	
Mount Blanchard	45867	
Mount Carmel, Br. Cincinnati	45244	
Mount Cory	45868	
Mount Eaton	44659	
Mount Gilead (1st)	43338	
Mount Healthy, Br. Cincinnati	45231	
Mount Hope	44660	
Mount Liberty	43048	
Mount Orab	45154	
Mount Perry	43760	
Mount Pleasant	43939	
Mount Saint Joseph	45051	
Mount Sterling	43143	
Mount Union, Sta. Alliance	44601	
Mount Vernon (1st)	43050	
Mount Vernon Avenue, Sta. Columbus	43203	
Mount Victory	43340	
Mount Washington, Sta. Cincinnati (see appendix)		
Mowrystown	45155	
Moxahala	43761	
Mulberry, R. Br. Milford	45150	
Munroe Falls	44262	
Murray City	43144	
Nankin	44848	
Napoleon (1st)	43545	
Nashport	43830	

Nashville	44661	
Navarre	44662	
Neapolis	43547	
Neffs	43940	
Negley	44441	
Nelsonville	45764	
Carbondale, R. Br.	45717	
Nevada	44849	
Neville	45156	
New Albany	43054	
New Athens	43981	
New Bavaria	43548	
New Bloomington	43341	
New Boston, Br. Portsmouth	45662	
New Bremen (1st)	45869	
New Carlisle (1st)	45344	
New Concord (1st)	43762	
New Hampshire	45870	
New Haven	44850	
New Holland	43145	
New Knoxville	45871	
New Lebanon	45345	
New Lexington (1st)	43764	
New London (1st)	44851	
New Lyme	44066	
New Madison	45346	
New Marshfield	45766	
New Matamoras	45767	
New Miami, Br. Hamilton	45011	
New Middletown	44442	
New Paris	45347	
New Philadelphia (1st)	44663	
Wainwright, R. Br.	44686	
New Plymouth	45654	
New Richmond	45157	
New Riegel	44853	
New Rumley	43984	
New Springfield	44443	
New Straitsville	43766	
New Vienna	45159	
New Washington	44854	
New Waterford	44445	
New Weston, R. Br.		
Rossburg	45348	
Newark (1st)	43055	
Newburg, Sta. Cleveland	44105	
Newbury	44065	
Newcomerstown (1st)	43832	
Newport	45768	
Newton Falls (1st)	44444	
Newtonsville	45158	
Newtown, Br. Cincinnati	45244	
Ney	43549	
Niles (1st)	44446	
Nimisila, R. Br. Clinton	44216	
Noble, Br. Cleveland	44132	
North Baltimore	45872	
North Bend	45052	
North Benton	44449	
North Bloomfield	44450	
North Canton, Br. Canton		
(see appendix)		
North College Hill, Br.		
Cincinnati	45239	
North Dayton, St., Dayton		
(see appendix)		
North Fairfield	44855	
North Georgetown	44665	
North Hampton	45349	
North Hill, Sta. Akron	44310	
North Industry, Br. Canton	44707	
North Jackson	44451	
North Kingsville	44068	

North Lawrence	44666	
North Lewisburg	43060	
North Lima	44452	
North Madison, Br. Madison	44057	
North Olmsted (1st)	44070	
North Ridgeville, Br. Elyria	44035	
North Robinson	44856	
North Royalton, Br.		
Cleveland	44133	
North Side, Sta. Youngstown		
(see appendix)		
North Star	45350	
Northfield (1st)	44067	
Macedonia, Br.	44056	
Northridge, Br. Dayton	45414	
Northup	45655	
Northwest, Sta. Columbus	43220	
Norton, Br. Barberton	44203	
Norwalk (1st)	44857	
Norwich	43767	
Norwood, Br. Cincinnati (see		
appendix)		
Nova	44859	
Novelty (1st)	44072	
Metals Park, R. Br.	44073	
Oak Harbor (1st)	43449	
Oak Hill	45656	
Oakland Park, Br. Columbus	43224	
Oakley, Sta. Cincinnati	45209	
Oakwood	45873	
Oberlin (1st)	44074	
Obetz, Br. Columbus	43207	
Oceola	44860	
Ohio City	45874	
Okeana	45053	
Okolona	43550	
Old Fort	44861	
Old Washington	43768	
Old West End, Sta. Toledo		
(see appendix)		
Olmsted Falls, Br.		
Cleveland	44138	
Ontario	44862	
Orangeville	44453	
Oregon, Br. Toledo (see		
appendix)		
Oregonia	45054	
Orient	43146	
Orrville (1st)	44667	
Orwell	44076	
Osgood	45351	
Ostrander	43061	
Ottawa (1st)	45875	
Ottoville	45876	
Otway	45657	
Outville, R. Br. Pataskala	43062	
Overlook, Br. Dayton (see		
appendix)		
Overpeck	45055	
Owensville	45160	
Oxford (1st)	45056	
Painesville (1st)	44077	
Palestine	45352	
Pandora	45877	
Parcel Post, Sta.		
Steubenville	43952	
Parcel Post, Sta.		
Youngstown	44505	
Parcel Post Annex, Sta.		
Warren	44484	
Parcel Post Annex, Sta.		
Sandusky	44870	

Parcel Post Annex, Sta.		
Cleveland	44101	
Parcel Post Annex, Sta.		
Mansfield	44903	
Parcel Post Annex, Sta.		
Elyria	44035	
Paris	44669	
Parkdale, Br. Cincinnati (see		
appendix)		
Parkman	44080	
Parma, Br. Cleveland (see		
appendix)		
Pataskala	43062	
Patriot	45658	
Patterson	45878	
Paulding (1st)	45879	
Pavonia	44863	
Payne	45880	
Pearlbrook, Sta. Cleveland	44109	
Pedro	45659	
Peebles	45660	
Pemberton	45353	
Pemberville	43450	
Peninsula	44264	
Pennsville	43770	
Pepper Pike, Br. Cleveland	44124	
Perintown, R. Br. Milford	45161	
Perry	44081	
Perrysburg (1st)	43551	
Perrysville	44864	
Petersburg	44454	
Pettisville	43553	
Phillipsburg	45354	
Philo	43771	
Phoneton	45355	
Pickerington	43147	
Piedmont	43983	
Pierpont	44082	
Piketon	45661	
Piney Fork	43941	
Pioneer	43554	
Piqua (1st)	45356	
Pitsburg	45358	
Plain City	43064	
Plainfield	43836	
Plaza, Br. Youngstown	44512	
Pleasant City	43772	
Pleasant Hill	45359	
Pleasant Plain	45162	
Pleasantville	43148	
Plymouth	44865	
Point, Sta. Columbus (see		
appendix)		
Point Place, Sta. Toledo	43611	
Point Pleasant	45163	
Poland, Br. Youngstown	44514	
Polk	44866	
Pomeroy	45769	
Harrisonville, R. Br.	45737	
Port Clinton (1st)	43452	
Port Jefferson	45360	
Port Washington	43837	
Port William	45164	
Portage	43451	
Portland	45770	
Portsmouth (1st)	45662	
Post Office Annex, Sta.		
Cincinnati	45214	
Potsdam	45361	
Potter Village, Ste. Fremont	43420	
Powell	43065	

Powhatan Point	43942
Price Hill, Sta. Cincinnati	45205
Procter 'n	45669
Prospect	43342
Public Square, Sta. Cleveland	44114
Puritas Parks, Sta. Cleveland	44135
Put-in-Bay	43456
Quaker City	43773
Quincy	43343
Racine	45771
Radcliff	45670
Radnor	43066
Rainsboro, R. Br. Greenfield	45165
Randolph	44265
Rarden	45671
Ravenna (1st)	44266
Rawson	45881
Ray	45672
Rayland	43943
Raymond	43067
Reading, Br. Cincinnati	45215
Reedsville	45772
Reesville	45166
Reily, R. Br. Hamilton	45060
Reinersville	43774
Rendville	43775
Reno	45773
Republic	44867
Reynolds Corners, Sta. Toledo (see appendix)	
Reynoldsburg (1st)	43068
Richfield (1st)	44286
Richmond	43944
Richmond Dale	45673
Richmond Heights, Br. Cleveland	44143
Richwood	43344
Ridgeville Corners	43555
Ridgeway	43345
Rinard Mills	45774
Rio Grande	45674
Ripley	45167
Risingsun	43457
Rittman (1st)	44270
Robertsville	44670
Rock Camp	45675
Rock Creek	44084
Rockbridge	43149
Rockford	45882
Rockland, Sta. Belpre	45714
Rocky Ridge	43458
Rocky River, Br. Cleveland	44116
Rodney	45676
Rogers	44455
Rome	44085
Roosevelt, Sta. Dayton (see appendix)	
Rootstown	44272
Roselawn, Sta. Cincinnati	45237
Roseville	43777
Rosewood	43070
Ross	45061
Rossburg	45362
New Weston, R. Br.	45348
Rossford (1st)	43460
Rossmoyne, Br. Cincinnati	45236
Rossville, Sta. Hamilton	45013
Roundhead	43346
Rudolph	43462
Rushsylvania	43347

Rushville	43150
Russells Point	43346
Russellville	45168
Russia	45363
Rutland	45775
Sabina	45169
Saint Bernard, Br. Cincinnati	45217
Saint Clairsville (1st)	43950
Saint Henry	45883
Saint Johns	45884
Saint Louisville	43071
Saint Martin	45170
Saint Marys (1st)	45885
Saint Paris	43072
Salem (1st)	44460
Salesville	43778
Salineville	43945
Sandusky (1st)	44870
Sandyville	44671
Sarahsville	43779
Sardinia	45171
Macon, R. Br.	45143
Sardis	43946
Savannah	44874
Saylor Park, Sta. Cincinnati	45233
Scio	43988
Scioto Furnace	45677
Sciotoville, Sta. Portsmouth	45662
Scott	45886
Scottown	45678
Seaman	45679
Sebring (1st)	44672
Sedalia	43151
Selma, R. Br. South Charleston	45364
Senecaville	43780
Seven Mile	45062
Seville	44273
Shade	45776
Shadyside	43947
Shaker Heights, Sta. Cleveland	44120
Shandon	45063
Shanesville, Sta. Sugarcreek	44681
Sharon	43781
Sharon Center	44274
Sharonville, Br. Cincinnati	45241
Sharpsburg	45777
Shauck	43349
Shawnee	43782
Shawnee Hills, R. Br. Powell	43065
Sheffield Lake, Br. Lorain	44054
Shelby (1st)	44875
Shepard, Sta. Columbus	43219
Sherman, Sta. Mansfield	44906
Sherrodsville	44675
Sherwood	43556
Shiloh	44878
Shinrock	44879
Shore, Br. Cleveland	44123
Short Creek	43989
Shreve	44676
Sidney (1st)	45365
Sinking Spring	45172
Smithfield	43948
Smithville	44677
Solon, Br. Cleveland	44139
Somerdale	44678
Somerset	43783
Somerton	43784

Somerville	45064
Sonora	43785
South Arlington, Sta. Akron	44306
South Bloomingville	43152
South Charleston	45368
Selma, R. Br.	45364
South Euclid, Br. Cleveland (see appendix)	
South Lebanon	45065
South Lorain, Sta. Lorain	44055
South Olive, R. Br. Caldwell	43724
South Point	45680
South Salem	45681
South Side, Sta. Youngstown	44507
South Solon	43153
South Vienna	45369
South Webster	45682
South Zanesville, Br. Zanesville	43701
Southington	44470
Southwest, Sta. Mansfield	44907
Sparta	43350
Spencer	44275
Spencerville	45887
Spring Valley	45370
Springboro	45066
Springdale, Br. Cincinnati	45246
SPRINGFIELD (1st) (see appendix)	
Stafford	43786
State Road, Sta. Cuyahoga Falls	44223
State Street, Sta. Columbus	43215
Sterling	44276
Steubenville (1st)	43952
Stewart	45778
Stewartsville	43960
Stillwater	44679
Stock Yards, Sta. Cincinnati	45225
Stockdale	45683
Stockport	43787
Stone Creek	43840
Stony Ridge	43463
Stout	45684
Stoutsville	43154
Stow, Br. Cuyahoga Falls	44224
Strasburg	44680
Stratton	43961
Streetsboro, Br. Kent	44240
Strongsville, Br. Cleveland	44136
Struthers (1st)	44471
Stryker	43557
Sugar Grove	43155
Sugar Tree Ridge, R. Br. Hillsboro	45133
Sugarcreek	44681
Sullivan	44880
Sulphur Springs	44881
Summerfield	43788
Summit Station	43073
Summitville	43962
Sunbury	43074
Surfside, Br. Willoughby	44094
Swanton (1st)	43558
Sycamore	44882
Sycamore Valley	43789
Sylvania (1st)	43560
Syracuse	45779
Taft, Br. Cincinnati (see appendix)	

Tallmadge (1st)............44278
Tarlton............43156
Terrace Park............45174
The Avenue, R. Br. Masury....44438
The Delta Queen, Sta
　Cincinnati............45202
The Plains............45780
Thompson............44086
Thornville............43076
Thurman............45685
Thurston............43157
Tiffin (1st)............44883
Tiltonsville............43963
Tipp City (1st)............45371
Tippecanoe............44699
Tiro............44887
TOLEDO (1st) (see appendix)
Tontogany............43565
Torch............45781
Toronto (1st)............43964
Tremont City............45372
Trenton............45067
Tri Village, Sta. Columbus....43212
Trimble............45782
Trinway............43842
Trotwood, Br. Dayton (see
　appendix)
Troy (1st)............45373
Tuppers Plains............45783
Tuscarawas............44682
Twinsburg (1st)............44087
Uhrichsville (1st)............44683
Union, Br. Englewood............45322
Union Furnace............43158
Unionport............43966
Uniontown............44685
Unionville............44088
Urionville Center............43077
Uniopolis............45888
University, Sta. Columbus....43210
University Center, Sta.
　Cleveland............44106
University Heights, Br.
　Cleveland............44118
Upper Arlington, Br.
　Columbus............43221
Upper Sandusky (1st)............43351
Uptown, Sta. Cleveland............44114
Urbana (1st)............43078
Utica............43080
Valley City............44280
Van Buren............45889
Van Wert (1st)............45891
Vandalia (1st)............45377
Vanlue............45890
Vaughnsville............45893
Venedocia............45894
Venice, Sta. Sandusky............44870
Vermilion (1st)............44089
Verona............45378
Versailles............45380
Veterans Administration, Br.
　Dayton............45428
Vickery............43464
Vienna............44473
Vincent............45784
Vine Street, Br. Willoughby....44094
Vinton............45686
Wadsworth (1st)............44281
Wainwright, R. Br. New
　Philadelphia............44686
Wakefield............45687
Wakeman............44889

Walbridge............43465
Waldo............43356
Walhonding............43843
Walnut Creek............44687
Walnut Hills, Sta.
　Cincinnati............45206
Wapakoneta (1st)............45895
Warner............45785
Warnock............43967
WARREN (1st) (see
　appendix)
Warsaw............43844
Washington Court House
　(1st)............43160
　Good Hope, R. Br.............43121
Washingtonville............44490
Waterford............45786
Waterloo............45688
Watertown............45787
Waterville............43566
Wauseon (1st)............43567
Waverly (1st)............45690
Wayland............44285
Wayne............43466
Waynesburg............44688
Waynesfield............45896
Waynesville............45068
Wellington (1st)............44090
Wellston (1st)............45692
Wellsville (1st)............43968
Wernert, Sta. Toledo (see
　appendix)
West Akron, Sta. Akron....44307
West Alexandria............45381
West Carrollton, Br. Dayton
　(see appendix)
West Chester............45069
West Elkton............45070
West End, Sta. Ashtabula....44004
West Farmington............44491
West Jefferson............43162
West Lafayette............43845
West Liberty............43357
West Manchester............45382
West Mansfield............43358
West Middletown, R. Br.
　Middletown............45042
West Millgrove............43467
West Milton............45383
West Park, Sta. Cleveland....44111
West Point............44492
West Rushville............43163
West Salem............44287
West Side, Sta. Youngstown....44509
West Toledo, Sta. Toledo....43612
West Town, Sta. Marion....43302
West Union............45693
West Unity............43570
West Warren, Sta. Warren....44485
Western College, Br. Oxford....45056
Western Hills, Br. Cincinnati....45238
Westerville (1st)............43081
Westfield Center (1st)............44251
Westlake, Br. Cleveland....44145
Weston............43569
Westville............43083
Westwood, Br. Cincinnati....45211
Wharton............43359
Wheelersburg............45694
Whipple............45788
White Cottage............43791
Whitehall, Br. Columbus....43213

Whitehouse............43571
Wickliffe (1st)............44092
Wilberforce............45384
Wilkesville............45695
Willard (1st)............44890
Williamsburg............45176
Williamsfield............44093
Williamsport............43164
Williamstown............45897
Williston............43468
Willoughby (1st)............44094
Willow, Sta. Cleveland............44127
Willow Wood............45696
Willowick, Br. Willoughby....44094
Willshire............45898
Wilmington (1st)............45177
Wilmot............44689
Winchester............45697
Windham............44288
Windsor............44099
Winesburg............44690
Wingett Run............45789
Winona............44493
Wintersville, Br.
　Steubenville............43952
Winton Place, Sta.
　Cincinnati............45232
Withamsville, Br. Cincinnati....45245
Wolf Run............43970
Wonderland, R. Br.
　Columbus............43230
Woodsfield............43793
Woodstock............43084
Woodville............43469
Wooster (1st)............44691
Worthington, Br. Columbus....43085
Wren............45899
Wright Patterson A F B, Br.
　Dayton............45433
Wyoming, Br. Cincinnati....45215
Xavier Sta. Cincinnati............45207
Xenia (1st)............45385
Yellow Springs (1st)............45387
Yorkshire............45388
Yorkville............43971
YOUNGSTOWN (1st) (see appendix)
Zaleski............45698
Zanesfield............43360
Zanesville (1st)............43701
Zoar............44697
Zoarville............44698

AKRON 443

POST OFFICE BOXES

Box Nos.

A-P	East Akron	95
1-1590	Akron	09
2601-2794	Firestone Park Sta.	01
2999-2314	Goodrich Sta	11
3301-3499	West Akron Sta.	07
3500-3699	North Hill Sta.	10
3701-3864	Kenmore Sta.	14
4000-4499	Copley Br.	21
5108-5999	Fairlawn Br	13
6001-6389	Ellet Sta	12
7001-7999	South Arlington Sta.	06
8001-8184	Maple Valley Sta.	20
9001-9499	East Akron Sta.	05

RURAL ROUTES

7,14		13

STATIONS, BRANCHES AND UNITS

Copley Br	21
Downtown Sta	02
East Akron Sta	05
Ellet Sta	12
Fairlawn Br	13
Firestone Park Sta.	01
Goodrich Street Sta	11
Kenmore Sta	14
Maple Valley Sta	20
North Hill Sta	10
South Arlington Sta.	06
West Akron Sta.	07
General Delivery	09
Postmaster	09

APARTMENTS, HOTELS, MOTELS

Akron Tower Motor Inn, 50 W State	08
Alcazar, 627 W Market	03
Ambassador, 753 W Market	03
Arcadia, 322 W Market	03
Auldfarm, 345 Diagonal Rd	20
Avalon, 214 N Portage Path	03
Belvidere, 630 W Market	03
Blair House, 255 N Portage Path	03
Carlton House, 275 N Portage Path	03
Chesterfield, 1032 W Market	13
Crescent, 795 W Market	03
Diplomat House, 1350 N Howard	10
Highland Towers, 900 W Market	13
Hill Chateau, 26 E Tallmadge Ave	10
Holiday Inn, li Cascade Plaza	08
Mayfield, 222 Twin Oaks Rd	13
Midtown Motel, 219 E Market	08
New Portage, 10 N Main	08
Ontario, 264 W Market	03

Parkview, 1620 W Sunset View Dr		29
Pasadena, 218 Twin Oaks Rd		13
Plaza, 173 N Portage Path		03
Seville, 715 W Market		03
Twin Oaks, 202 Twin Oaks Rd		13
Westgate Manor, 64 Eastgay Dr		13
Y M C A, 80 W Center		08
Y W C A, 146 S High		08

BUILDINGS

A C & Y, 12 E Exchange	08
Akron Art Institute, 69 E Market	08
Akron Center, I Cascade Plaza	08
Akron Savings & Loan, 7 W Bowery	08
Cascade Plaza, S Main & W Bowery	08
City Bldg, 166 S High	08
Delaware, 137 S Main	08
Evans Savings, 333 S Main	08
Everett, 39 E Market	08
First Federal Savings, 326 S Main	08
First National Tower, 106 S Main	08
Metropolitan, 39 S Main	08
Ohio Bell Telephone, 50 W Bowery	08
Ohio, 175 S Main	08
Oneils, 226 S Main	08
Permanent Federal, 55 E Mill	08
Polskys, 225 S Main	08
Public Library, 55 S. Main	08
Ruhlin, li Cascade Plaza	08
Second National, 159 S Main	08
Union Depot, 220 Grant	08
United Rubber Workers, 87 S High	08
United, 9 S Main	08

GOVERNMENT OFFICES

City-County Safety Bldg, 217 S High	08
Courthouse, 209 S High	08
Municipal Bldg, 166 S High	08
Ohio Bureau Of Employment Services, 150 E Market	08

HOSPITALS

Akron City, 525 E Market	09
Akron General, 400 Wabash	07
Childrens, W Bowery & W Buchtel	08
Edwin Shaw Sanatorium, 2600 Sanatorium Rd	12
Saint Thomas, 444 N Main	10

MILITARY INSTALLATIONS

Akron Armory, 161 S High	08

Army Reserve Training Center, 1011 Gorge Blvd		10
Naval Reserve Training Center, 800 Dan		10

UNIVERSITIES AND COLLEGES

University Of Akron, 302 E Buchtel Ave	04

CANTON 447

POST OFFICE BOXES

Box Nos.

1-236	B Sta	06
1-327	North Industry Br	07
1-1031	Downtown Sta	01
1201-1430	C Sta	08
1401-1684	East Canton Br	30
1701-1900	A Sta	05
2101-2449	North Canton Br	20
8001-9200	Main Office	11

RURAL ROUTES

2,4		30

STATIONS, BRANCHES AND UNITS

Downtown Sta	02
East Canton Br	30
North Canton Br	20
North Industry Br	07
General Delivery	11
Postmaster	11

APARTMENTS, HOTELS, MOTELS

Ambassador, 2901 Tuscarawas E	07
Arcade, 133 4th NW	02
Belden, 103 6th NE	02
Canton Travelodge, 1031 Tuscarawas W	02
Downtowner Motor Inn, 621 Market Ave N	02
Harleigh Inn, 500 Main St N	20
Holiday Inn, 800 Tuscarawas W	02
Imperial House, 4343 Everhard Rd NW	18
Moon Mist, 4411 Tuscarawas E	30
Motel Quiet, 3205 Lincoln E	07
Onesto, 225 2nd NW	02
Stanley, 2801 Tuscarawas E	07
Top-O-The-Mark, 4135 Tuscarawas E	30
Towne Manor, 926 Tuscarawas W	02
Washington, 305 Mckinley Ave SW	01

BUILDINGS

Arcade Market, 135 3rd NW	C2
Citizens, 110 Central Plz S	02

Cleve-Tusc, 121 Cleveland Ave SW ... 02
Commercial, 205 Market Ave S... 02
Dime Bank, 307 Tuscarawas E... 02
First Federal Savings & Loan, 200 Tuscarawas W... 02
First National Bank, 120 Tuscarawas W... 02
Harter Bank, 138 2nd NE... 02
Home Savings And Loan, 315 Tuscarawas W... 02
Mellett, 115 Dewalt Ave NW... 02
Nationwide, 1020 Market Ave N... 02
Pepoles-Merchant Trust, 116 Cleveland Ave NW... 02
Professional, 816 Market Ave N... 02
Renkert, 306 Market Ave N... 02
Wells Professional, 515 3rd NW... 03

GOVERNMENT OFFICES

Chamber Of Commerce, 229 Wells Ave NW... 03
City Hall, 218 Cleveland Ave. S. W... 02
Stark County Court House Office, 209 Tuscarawas W... 02

HOSPITALS

Aultman, 2600 6th SW... 10
Shadyside, 932 Main N Onc... 20
Timken-Mercy, 2015 12th NW... 02

UNIVERSITIES AND COLLEGES

Kent State Univ, 6000 Frank Ave NW... 20
Malone College, 515 25th NW... 09
Walsh College, 2020 Easton NW... 20

CINCINNATI   452

POST OFFICE BOXES

Box Nos.

1-2550	Fountain Square Sta	01
5A-5E	Price Hill Sta	05
15A-15Q	Lockland Br	15
24A-24I	College Hill Sta	20
26A-26H	East End Sta	26
30A-30I	Mount Washington Sta	30
31A-31H	Mount Healthy Br	31
36A-36L	Taft Br	36
42A-42L	Montgomery Br	42
4001-4116	F Sta	04
5001-5149	Price Hill Sta	05
6001-6417	Walnut Hills Sta	06
8001-8959	Hyde Park Sta	08
9001-9143	Oakley Sta	09
10001-10214	V Sta	10
11001-11328	Westwood Br	11
12001-12480	Norwood Br	12
14001-14717	Annex Sta	14
15001-15460	Lockland Br	15
16001-16115	Elmwood Place Br	17
1700A-17001	Saint Bernard	17
17001-17134	Saint Bernard	17
18001-18116	Parkdale Br	40
19001-19297	Corryville Sta	19
20001-20138	Burnet Woods Sta	20
21001-21116	Campus Sta	21
23001-23205	Cumminsville Sta	23
24001-24199	College Hill Sta	24
25001-25146	Stock Yards Sta	25
26001-26116	East End Sta	26
27001-27155	Madisonville Sta	27
29001-29269	I Sta	29
30001-30279	Mount Washington Sta	30
31001-31158	Mount Healthy Br	31
32001-32115	Winton Place Br	17
33101-33157	Sayler Park Sta	33
36001-36280	Taft Br	36
37001-37908	Roselawn Sta	22
38001-38204	Western Hills Branch	38
39001-39518	Groesbeck Br	39
40101-40274	Parkdale Br	40
41001-41316	Sharonville Br	41
42001-42320	Montgomery Br	42
43001-43699	Madeira Br	43
44001-44147	Newtown Br	44
46001-46472	Parkdale Br	40
75000-75131	Airport Br	75

STATIONS, BRANCHES AND UNITS

Airport Br... 75
Burnet Woods Sta... 20
Campus Sta... 21
College Hill Sta... 24
Corryville Sta... 19
Cumminsville Sta... 23
Deer Park Br... 36
Del Fair Br... 38
East End Sta... 26
Elmwood Place Br... 16
Federal Reserve Sta... 01
Fountain Square Sta... 02
Glendale Br... 46
Glenmary Br... 46
Greenhills Br... 18
Groesbeck Br... 39
Hyde Park Sta... 08
Ivorydale Br... 17
Lockland Br... 15
Madeira Br... 43
Madisonville Sta... 27
Mariemont Br... 27
Montgomery Br... 42
Mount Airy Sta... 39
Mount Carmel Br... 44
Mount Healthy Br... 31
Mount Washington Sta... 30
Newtown Br... 44
North College Hill Br... 39
Norwood Br... 12
Oakley Sta... 09
Parkdale Br... 40
Post Office Annex Sta... 14
Price Hill Sta... 05
Reading Br... 15
Roselawn Sta... 37
Rossmoyne Br... 36
Saint Bernard Sta... 17
Saylor Park Sta... 33
Sharonville Br... 41
Springdale Br... 46
Stock Yards Sta... 25
Taft Br... 36
The Delta Queen Sta... 02
Walnut Hills Br... 06
Western Hills Br... 38
Westwood Br... 11
Winton Place Sta... 32
Withamsville Br... 45
Wyoming Br... 15
Xavier Sta... 07
General Delivery... 02
Postmaster... 02

APARTMENTS, HOTELS, MOTELS

Alms Motor Hotel, 2525 Victory Pkwy... 06
Anna Louise Inn, 300 Lytle... 02
Barkley House, Greater Cincinnati Airport... 75
Belvedere, 3851 Reading Rd... 29
Blue Fountain, 1673 Cedar Ave... 24
Boulevard Lawn, 2630 Victory Pkwy... 06
Carrousel Inn, 8001 Reading Rd... 37
Cincinnati Club, 30 Garfield Pl... 02
Cincinnati, 16 W 6th... 02
Clifton House, 2971 Deckebach Ave... 20
Clovernook Home For The Blind, 6990 Hamilton Ave... 31
Colonial Inn, 10200 Reading Rd... 41
Columbia Towers, 1815 Wm Howard Taft Rd... 06
Deupree House East, 3939 Erie Ave... 08
East Oak Manor, 310 Oak... 19
El Rancho Rankin, 5218 Beechmont Ave... 30
Essex House, 7610 Reading Rd... 37
Executive, 621 Mc Alpin Ave... 20
Fenwick, 423 Commercial Sq... 02
Fessel Garden, 3242 Whitfield Ave... 20
Fontbonne, 410 E 5th... 02

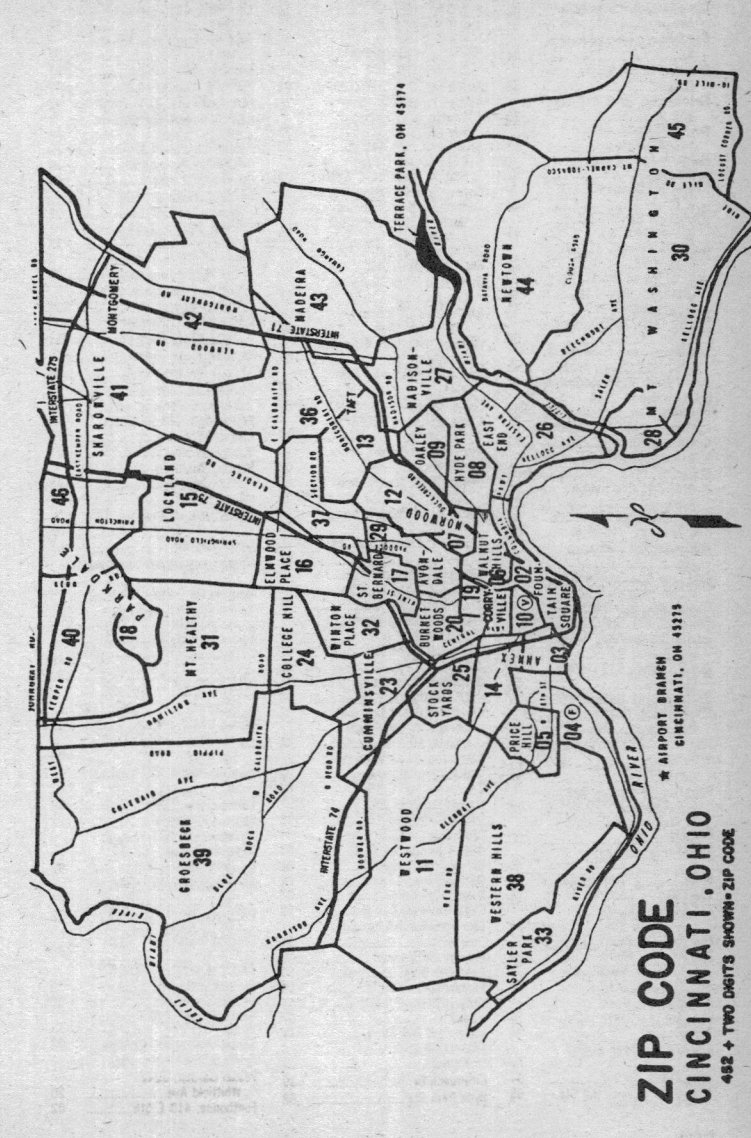

ZIP CODE
CINCINNATI, OHIO
452 + TWO DIGITS SHOWN = ZIP CODE

★ AIRPORT BRANCH
CINCINNATI, OH 45275

Fort Washington, 621 Main...... 02
Fountain Square, 420 Vine...... 01
Georgetown East 484 Batavia
  Rd... 44
Grasmoor House, 2370
  Madison Rd........................... 08
Haddon Hall, 3418 Reading
  Rd... 29
Hammond North, 5300
  Hamilton Ave....................... 24
Highland Towers, 380
  Oregon................................... 02
Holiday Inn Downtown, 802
  W 8th.................................... 03
Holiday Inn North, 2235 E
  Sharon Rd.............................. 41
Howard Johnson'S, 11440
  Chester Rd............................ 46
Imperial House Motel, 1717
  Glendale - Milford Rd......... 15
Interstate Motel, I-275......... 41
Kemper Lane, 2500 Kemper
  La... 06
Kensington Lane Town House,
  7752 Montgomery Road...... 36
Lytle Towers, 405 Broadway... 02
Madison House, 2324
  Madison Rd........................... 08
Mariemont Inn, 6839 Wooster
  Rd... 27
Milner Highlander, 108
  Garfield Pl............................ 02
Mont Michel, 688 Riddle
  Road...................................... 20
Netherland Hilton, 63 W 5th... 01
New Dennison, 716 Main........ 02
Panorama, 2375 Montana
  Ave... 11
Park-Lane Apartments, 4201
  Victory Pkwy........................ 29
Phelps Apts, 506 E 4th......... 02
Princeton, 431 Elm................. 02
Quality Courts Motel, 4747
  Montgomery Rd.................... 12
Queen'S Tower, 819 Matson
  Pl.. 04
Regency, 2444 Madison Rd..... 02
River Terrace, 2401
  Ingleside............................... 06
Riverview, 2538 Hackberry...... 06
Rowe Towers Stanley G, 1609
  Linn....................................... 14
Rowe Towers Stanley, 822
  Poplar Walk.......................... 14
Saint Margaret Hall, 1960
  Madison Rd........................... 06
Sheraton Gibson, 421
  Walnut................................... 01
Shullers Motel, 7759 Reading
  Rd... 37
Stouffer'S Cincinnati Inn,
  150 W 5 Th............................ 02
Summit View, 2701 Lehman
  Rd... 02
Terrace Hilton, 15 W 6th........ 01
Travelodge Motel, 3244
  Central Pkwy........................ 25
Vernon Manor, 2810 Burnet
  Ave... 19
Victory Lane, 2210 Victory
  Pkwy...................................... 06
Williamsburg Of Cincinnati,
  200 W Galbraith Rd............. 15

Y M C A, 1105 Elm................. 10
Y W C A, 898 Walnut.............. 02

BUILDINGS

American, 30 E Central Pkwy... 02
Ashtree Village Shopping
  Center, 4781 Hamilton
  Ave... 23
Atlas Bank, 524 Walnut.......... 02
B & O Railroad Freight
  Station, Nwc 2nd & Smith... 02
Becker, 705 Sycamore............ 02
Beechmont Mall Shopping
  Center, 7500 Beechmont
  Avenue................................... 30
Bell Telephone, 225 E 4th...... 02
Big Four Office, 517 W 3rd..... 02
Brentwood Plaza Shopping
  Center................................... 31
Brotherhood Of Railway
  Clerk, 1015 Vine.................. 02
Building Industries Bldg, 626
  Broadway.............................. 02
Carew Tower Arcade, 435
  Vine....................................... 02
Carew Tower, 441 Vine........... 02
Carrousel Towers, 8075
  Reading Rd............................ 37
Central Trust Towers Annex,
  309 Vine............................... 02
Central Trust Towers, 5 W
  4th.. 02
Cherry Grove Plaza Shopping
  Center................................... 30
Cincinnati Art Museum, Eden
  Park....................................... 02
Cincinnati Convention
  Exposition Center, 525
  Elm.. 02
Cincinnati Gas & Electric,
  319 Main................................ 02
Cincinnati Music Hall, 1245
  Elm.. 10
Cincinnati Observatory, 3489
  Observatory Pl..................... 08
Cincinnati Union Terminal
  Service, W Liberty At
  Mclean Av............................. 14
Cincinnati Union Terminal
  1301 Western Ave................ 03
Commerce 100 E 8th.............. 02
Daylight, 659 E 6th................. 02
Del-Fair Shopping Ctr............. 38
Dillonvale Shopping Ctr.......... 36
Dixie Terminal, 49 E 4th......... 02
Doctors, 19 Garfield Pl........... 02
Dubois Tower, 511 Walnut...... 02
Duttenhoefer, 299 E 6th........ 02
Eagle Savings, 914 Main......... 02
Elet Hall, Dana & Winding
  Way.. 29
Enquirer, 617 Vine.................. 02
Executive Bldg, 35 E 7th........ 02
Federal Office 550 Main......... 02
Federal Reserve Bank, 105 W
  4th.. 02
Federated, 707 Race.............. 02
Fifth Third Center, 511
  Walnut................................... 02
Film Center, 1632 Central
  Pkwy...................................... 10

Film Mart, 1635 Central
  Pkwy...................................... 14
First National Bank, 105 E
  4th.. 02
Formica 120 E 4th................... 02
Fourth & Walnut, 36 E 4th..... 02
Fruit Exchange, 27 W Front.... 02
Garfield Tower, 111 Garfield
  Pl.. 02
Greater Cincinnati Airport...... 75
Greenhills Shopping Ctr.......... 18
Gwynne, 602 Main................... 02
Hartford Insurance, 630
  Main...................................... 02
Hillcrest Square, 7162
  Reading Rd............................ 37
Hyde Park Plaza Shopping
  Ctr 3822 Paxton Ave........... 09
Inter-Ocean Insurance, 2600
  Victory Pkwy........................ 06
Kenwood Mall Shopping Ctr,
  7800 Montgomery Rd.......... 36
Kenwood Plaza Shopping Ctr
  7801 Montgomery Rd.......... 36
Kenwood Shopping Ctr 7565
  Kenwood Rd.......................... 36
Krippendorf, 628 Sycamore.... 02
Kroger, 1014 Vine................... 02
Masonic Temple, 317 E 5th.... 02
Mercantile Library, 414
  Walnut................................... 02
Merchants, 34 W 6th.............. 02
Methodist Book Concern, 429
  Plum....................................... 02
Mills, 31 E 4th......................... 02
Montgomery Square Shopping
  Ctr.. 42
Morgens Hall, 2930 Scioto..... 19
Northbrook Shopping Ctr........ 31
Northgate Mall,...................... 39
Northland Shopping Center..... 41
Norwood Plaza Shopping Ctr... 12
Palace, 12 E 6th..................... 02
Post-Times Star Tower, 800
  Broadway.............................. 02
Power, 224 E 8th.................... 02
Procter-Gamble, SE Cor 6th &
  Sycamore.............................. 02
Provident Bank, 632 Vine....... 02
Provident Towers, 1 E 4th...... 02
Public Library, 800 Vine......... 02
Pugh, 400 Pike........................ 02
Railway Express, Findlay At
  Mc Lean Ave......................... 14
Resor, 37 W 7th...................... 02
Riverfront Stadium 201 E
  2nd.. 02
Rookwood, 1077 Celestial...... 02
Roselawn Center, 1701
  Section Rd............................ 37
Salvation Army Citadel, 114
  E Central Pkwy.................... 10
Sawyer Hall, 2910 Scioto....... 19
Schwartz, 906 Main................ 02
Scioto Hall, 2920 Scioto......... 19
Second National, 830 Main..... 02
Seven-O-Seven Race, 707
  Race....................................... 02
Southern Ohio Bank, 519
  Main...................................... 02

Swift, 230 E 9th...... 02
Swifton Shopping Ctr. 37
Telephone 4th Street, 225 E 4th...... 02
Telephone 7th Street, 209 W 7th...... 02
Temple Bar, 138 E Court...... 02
Terrace-Hilton Bldg, 15 W 6th...... 02
Textile, 205 W 4th...... 02
Transit, 6 E 4th...... 02
Transportation, 307 E 4th...... 02
Tri County Shopping Ctr, 11700 Princeton Rd...... 46
Tri-State, 432 Walnut...... 02
Twenty Six East Sixth 26 E 6th...... 02
U S Post Office And Court House 100 E 5th...... 02
University Plaza Shopping Ctr, 1 Corry...... 19
Western Hills Plaza Shopping Ctr...... 11
Western Village Shopping Ctr...... 11
Western Woods Shopping Ctr...... 11
White Oak Shopping Ctr...... 39
Wiggins Block, 7 E 5th...... 02

GOVERNMENT OFFICES

Chamber Of Commerce, 309 Vine...... 02
Cincinnati Post Office Annex Bldg A, 1601 Dalton Ave.... 34
Cincinnati Post Office Annex Bldg B, 1589 Dalton Ave.... 34
Cincinnati Post Office Annex Office Tower, 1591 Dalton Ave...... 34
City Hall, 800 Central Ave...... 02
Environmental Protection Agency...... 68
Hamilton County Court House, 1000 Main...... 02
United States Courthouse, 100 E 5th...... 02
United States Post Office, 100 E 5th...... 02

HOSPITALS

Bethesda Suburban, 10500 Montgomery Rd...... 42
Bethesda, 619 Oak...... 06
Catherine Booth, 3595 Washington Ave...... 29
Childrens, 240 Bethesda...... 29
Christ, 2139 Auburn Ave...... 19
Cincinnati General, 234 Goodman...... 29
Deaconess, 311 Straight...... 19
Drake Memorial,151 W. Galbraith Rd...... 16
Dunham, Guerley Rd...... 05
Emerson A North, 5642 Hamilton Ave...... 24
Epp Memorial, 8000 Kenwood Rd...... 36

Good Samaritan, 3217 Clifton Ave...... 20
Holmes, Eden & Bethesda...... 19
Jewish, 3212 Burnet Ave...... 29
Longview, 6600 Paddock Rd.... 16
Maple Knoll, 11174 Springfield Rd...... 46
Our Lady Of Mercy, 7010 Rowan Hills Dr...... 27
Providence, 2366 Kipling Rd.. 39
Rollman Receiving, 3009 Burnet Ave...... 19
Saint Francis, 1860 Queen City Avenue...... 14
Saint George, 3156 Glenmore Ave...... 11
ShrinerOs Burns Institute 202 Goodman...... 19
Veterans, 3200 Vine...... 20

UNIVERSITIES AND COLLEGES

Cincinnati Bible Seminary, 2700 Glenway Ave...... 04
Cincinnati College Of Pharmacy, University Of Cincinnati...... 21
Cincinnati Law School, University Of Cincinnati 21
Cincinnati Technical Inst.,3520 Central Parkway...... 23
College Conservatory Of Music Of Cincinnati...... 21
College Of Medicine University Of Cincinnati 19
Edgecliff College, Edgecliff And Victory Parkway...... 06
Glenmary Seminary, 10295 Princeton Rd...... 45
Gods Bible School & College, 1810 Young...... 19
Hebrew Union College, 3101 Clifton Ave...... 20
Mount Saint Mary Seminary, 5440 Moeller Ave...... 12
Ohio College Of Applied Science, 100 E Central Parkway...... 10
Saint Gregory'S Seminary, 6616 Beechmont Ave...... 30
Salmon P Chase Law School, 1105 Elm...... 10
Teachers College Athenaeum Of Ohio, 5418 Moeller Ave. 12
Teachers College University Of Cincinnati, Clifton Ave.. 21
University Of Cincinnati, Clifton Ave...... 21
Xavier University, Dana & Victory Pkwy...... 07

CLEVELAND　441

POST OFFICE BOXES

Box Nos.
1-299　　Brecksville Br.... 41
1-299　　South Euclid Br...... 21
300-499　Willow Sta...... 27
500-699　Edgewater Br 07
700-899　Beachwood Br .. 22
1000-1099　A Sta...... 02
1100-1499　B Sta...... 03
1500-1699　C Sta...... 04
1700-1799　Newburg Sta 05
1800-2099　University Center Sta...... 06
2100-2199　H Sta...... 08
2200-2299　Pearlbrook Sta.. 09
2300-2399　Collinwood Sta. 10
2400-2599　East Cleveland Br...... 12
2600-2699　Lakewood Br.... 13
2700-2799　West Park Sta.. 11
2800-2999　Rocky River Br. 16
3000-3299　Euclid Br...... 17
3500-3599　Cleveland Heights Br...... 18
3600-3799　Beachland Sta. 19
3800-3899　Collinwood Sta. 10
3900-3999　Shaker Heights Sta...... 20
4000-4199　Shore Br...... 23
4200-4399　Noble Br...... 32
4400-4499　Garfield Heights Br...... 25
4500-4699　Lyndhurst-Mayfield Br.... 24
4700-4999　Fairview Park Br...... 26
5000-6999　Main Office 01
7000-7199　Cranwood Sta. 28
7200-7399　Parma Br...... 29
7400-7599　Midpark Br 30
7600-7899　Independence Br...... 31
8200-8399　North Royalton Br...... 33
8400-8599　Briggs Br...... 34
8600-8799　Puritas Park Sta...... 35
8800-8999　Strongsville Br. 36
9000-9199　Maple Heights Br...... 37
9200-9399　Olmsted Falls Br...... 38
9400-9599　Solon Br...... 39
9600-9799　Bay Village Br.. 40
9800-9999　Brook Park Br.. 42
02000-02999　A Sta...... 02
03000-03999　B Sta...... 03
05000-05999　Newburg Sta. 05
08000-08999　H Sta...... 08
09000-09999　Pearlbrook.... 09
10000-10999　Collingwood Sta...... 10
16000-16999　Rocky River Br. 16
18000-18999　Cleveland Heights Br...... 18
20000-20999　Shaker Heights Sta...... 20
22000-22999　Beachwood Br.. 22

24000-24999 Lyndhurst-Mayfield	24
29000-29999 Parma	29
30000-30999 Midpark Br.	30
33000-33999 North Royalton	33
36000-36999 Strongsville Br.	36
39000-39999 Solon	39
41000-41999 Brecksville	41
42000-42999 Brook Park	42
43000-43999 Richmond Heights	43
44000-44999 Brooklyn	44
45000-45999 Westlake	45
46000-46999 Bedford	46
81000-81999 Airport Mail Facility	81
91000-91999 Main Office	01

STATIONS, BRANCHES AND UNITS

Airport Br.	81
Bay Village Br.	40
Beachland Sta.	19
Beachwood Br.	22
Bedford Br.	46
Brecksville Br.	41
Briggs Br.	34
Brook Park Br.	42
Brooklyn Br.	44
Cleveland Heights Br.	18
Collinwood Sta.	10
Cranwood Sta.	28
East Cleveland Br.	12
Edgewater Br.	07
Erieview Sta.	99
Euclid Br.	17
Fairview Park Br.	26
Federal Reserve Sta.	01
Garfield Heights Br.	25
Independence Br.	31
Kamms Sta.	11
Lakewood Br.	07
Lee Road Br.	20
Lyndhurst-Mayfield Br.	24
Maple Heights Br.	37
Midpark Br.	30
Newburg Sta.	05
Noble Br.	32
North Royalton Br.	33
Olmsted Falls Br.	38
Parcel Post Annex Sta.	01
Parma Br.	29
Pearlbrook Sta.	09
Pepper Pike Br.	24
Public Square Sta.	14
Puritas Parks Sta.	35
Richmond Heights Br.	43
Rocky River Br.	16
Shaker Heights Sta.	20
Shore Br.	23
Solon Br.	39
South Euclid Br.	21
Strongsville Br.	36
University Center Sta.	06
University Heights Br.	18
Uptown Sta.	14
West Park Sta.	11
Westlake Br.	45
Willow Sta.	27
General Delivery	01
Postmaster	01

APARTMENTS, HOTELS, MOTELS

Alcazar, 2450 Derbyshire Rd	06
Belden, 1903 E 70th	03
Belmont, 3844 Euclid Ave	15
Bolton Square, 8907 Carnegie Ave	06
Commodore, 1990 Ford Dr	06
Fenway Motor Inn, 1986 E 107th	06
Graduate House, 10660 Carnegie Ave	06
Haddam, 10510 Euclid Ave	06
Knickerbocker, 8314 Euclid	03
Lake Shore, 12506 Edgewater Dr	07
Manger, 1802 E 13th	14
New Amsterdam, 2142 Euclid Ave	15
Park Lane Villa, 10510 Park Ln	06
Pick-Carter, 1012 Prospect Ave E	14
Regent, 10539 Euclid Ave	06
Sheraton-Cldeveland, 219 Superior Ave W	01
Statler-Hilton, 1127 Euclid Ave	01
Sterling, 3002 Prospect Ave E	15
University Towers, 1575 East Blvd	06
Wade Park Manor, 1890 E 107th	06
Westlake, 19030 Lake Rd	16

BUILDINGS

Airport Mail Facility, 19801 Five Points Rd	81
Arcade, 401 Euclid Ave	14
Bulkley Bldg Annex, 1501 Euclid Ave	15
Bulkley, 1501 Euclid	15
C T S, 1404 E 9th	14
Carnegie Medical Bldg, 10515 Carnegie Ave	06
Caxton, 812 Huron Rd E	15
Central National Bank Bldg, 800 Superior Ave	14
Chester-Twelfth, 1120 Chester Ave	14
Citizens, 850 Euclid Ave	14
Cleveland Athletic Club, 1118 Euclid Ave	15
Cleveland Stadium	14
Colonial Arcade, 530 Euclid Ave	15
Columbia, 112 Prospect Ave E	15
Continental Bank Bldg, 1255 Euclid Ave	15
Crown, 310 Lakeside Ave E	13
Cuyahoga, 216 Superior Ave E	14
East Ohio, 1717 E 9th	14
Engineers, 1365 Ontario	14
Euclid Arcade, 510 Euclid	15
Euclid Ninth Tower, 214 E 9th	15
Federal Reserve Bank, 1455 E 6th	01
Federal, 210 Superior Ave E	14
Fidelity, 1940 E 6th	14

Film Exchange, 2108 Payne Ave	14
Finance, 750 Prospect Ave E	15
Guildhall, 45 Prospect Ave W.	15
Hanna, 1422 Euclid Ave	15
Hippodrome Annex, 715 Prospect Ave	15
Hippodrome, 720 Euclid Ave	14
Illuminating, 55 Public Square	13
Investment Insurance, 601 Rockwell Ave	14
Investment Plaza, 1801 E 9th	14
Keith, 1621 Euclid	15
Leader, 526 Superior Ave East	14
Lincoln, 1367 E 6th	14
Livestock Exchange, 3200 W 65th	02
Mall, 118 St Clair Ave E	14
Marion, 1276 W 3rd	13
Merchandise Mart, 420 Prospect Ave	15
Midland, 101 Prospect Ave W.	15
Midwestern National, 75 Public Square	14
National City Bank, 629 Euclid Ave	14
National City East Sixth, 1953 E 6th	14
Nineteen-Hundred Euclid, 1900 Euclid Ave	15
Northern Ohio Food Terminal, 3800 Orange Ave	15
One Erieview Plaza, 1 Erieview Plaza	14
One Hundred Erieview Plaza, 100 Erieview Plaza	14
One Public Square Bldg, 1 Public Square	13
Osborne, 1020 Huron Rd E	15
Park-Chester Medical, 10605 Chester Ave	06
Park, 140 Public Square	14
Penton, 1213 E 3rd	13
Perry-Payne, 740 Superior Ave W	13
Plaza 9 Bldg	14
Post Office Bldg, 301 Prospect Ave W.	01
Prospect East Bldg, 1514 Prospect Ave	15
Prospect Fourth, 2077 E 4th	15
Public Auditorium Bldg, 1220 E 6th	14
Public Library, 325 Superior Ave E	14
Public Square, 33 Public Square	13
Republic, 25 Prospect Ave W.	15
Rockefeller Physics Bldg, 10900 Euclid Ave	06
Rockefeller, 614 Superior Ave W	13
Rose, 2060 E 9th	15
Schofield, 2014 E 9th	15
Severance Medical Arts Bldg, 5 Severance Cir	18
Six-Sixty-Six Bldg, 666 Euclid Ave	14

Society National Bank, 145
  Public Square 14
Standard, 1370 Ontario 13
Superior, 815 Superior Ave E... 14
Ten-Ten Euclid, 1010 Euclid
  Ave 15
Terminal Tower, 50 Public
  Sq. 13
Thirty Three Public Square,
  33 Public Square 13
Twelve-Twenty Huron, 1220
  Huron Rd E 15
Union Commerce Annex,
  1100 Chester Ave 14
Union Commerce Arcade,
  1030 Chester Ave 14
Union Commerce, 925 Euclid
  Ave 15
Union, 1836 Euclid Ave 15
United Office, 2012 W 25th..... 13
Western Reserve, 1468 W
  9th 13
Williamson, 215 Euclid........ 14

GOVERNMENT OFFICES

City Hall, 601 Lakeside Ave
  E.......................... 14
Courthouse, 1 Lakeside Ave.. 13
Federal Office Bldg, 1240 E
  9th St..................... 99
United States Post Office,
  301 Prospect Ave W 13

HOSPITALS

Babies & Children, 2103
  Adelbert Rd.............. 06
Bay View, 23200 Lake Rd..... 40
Bedford Municipal, 44 Blaine
  Ave....................... 46
Benjamin Rose, 2073
  Abington Rd.............. 06
Booth Memorial, 1881
  Torbenson Dr............ 12
Brecksville Veterans Admin,
  10000 Brecksville Rd..... 41
Brentwood, 4110 Warrensville
  Center Rd................ 22
Cleveland Clinic, 2050 E
  93rd St................... 06
Cleveland Metropolitan
  General, 3395 S Cranton
  Rd........................ 09
Cleveland State, 4455 Turney
  Rd........................ 05
Euclid-General, 101 E 185th... 19
Evangelical Deaconess, 4233
  Pearl Rd................. 09
Fairhill Psychiatric, 12200
  Fairhill Rd............... 20
Fairview General, 18101
  Lorain Ave............... 11
Forest City, 701 Parkwood Dr. 08
Grace, 2307 W 14th.......... 13
Hanna House, 2045 Adelbert
  Rd........................ 06
Highland View, 3901 Ireland
  Dr........................ 22
Hillcrest, 6760 Mayfield Rd.... 24
Huron Road, 13951 Terrace
  Rd........................ 12
Ingleside, 8811 Euclid Ave .. 06

Jewish Convalescent, 18810
  Harvard Ave.............. 22
Lakeside, 2065 Adelbert Rd.... 06
Lakewood, 14519 Detroit Ave. 07
Lutheran, 2609 Franklin Ave .. 13
Macdonald House, 2105
  Adelbert Rd.............. 06
Marymount, 12300 Mc
  Cracken Rd.............. 25
Mount Sinai, 1800 E 105th ... 06
Parma Community General,
  7007 Powers Blvd........ 29
Polyclinic, 6606 Carnegie
  Ave....................... 03
Rainbow, 1605 South Green
  Rd........................ 21
Richmond Heights General,
  27100 Chardon Rd....... 43
Saint Ann, 2475 East Blvd..... 20
Saint Johns, 7911 Detroit
  Ave....................... 02
Saint Lukes, 11311 Shaker
  Blvd...................... 04
Saint Vincent Charity, 2222
  Central Ave.............. 15
Saints Alexis, 5163
  Broadway................. 27
Suburban Community, 4180
  Warrensville Center Rd..... 22
Sunny Acres, 4310 Richmond
  Rd........................ 22
University, 2065 Adelbert Rd.. 06
Veterans Administration
  Hospital, 10701 East Blvd. 06
Womans, 1940 E 101th....... 06

UNIVERSITIES AND COLLEGES

Case Western Reserve
  University, 10900 Euclid
  Ave....................... 06
Cleveland Institute Of Art,
  11141 East Blvd.......... 06
Cleveland State University,
  1983 E 24th.............. 15
Cleveland-Marshall Law
  School, 1240 Ontario..... 13
Cuyahoga Community
  College, 2214 E 14th..... 15
Dyke & Spencerian College,
  1375 E 6th............... 14
Great Lakes College & Clinic,
  1900 Superior Ave....... 14
Griswold Institute, 2031
  Euclid Ave............... 15
John Carroll University,
  20700 North Park Blvd.... 18
Lincoln Extension Institute
  Incorporated, 1401 W
  75th...................... 02
Notre Dame College, 4545
  College Rd............... 21
Ohio College Of Podiatry,
  2057 Cornell Rd.......... 06
Saint John College, 1033
  Superior Ave E........... 14
Ursuline College, 2600
  Lander Rd................ 24

COLUMBUS   **432**

POST OFFICE BOXES

Box Nos.
A-E   Worthington
      Branch...........43085
A-H   Mount Vernon
      Avenue Sta..... 03
1-797   Worthington
      Branch...........43085
1-2519 Main Office........ 16
2731-2944 Hilltop Sta......... 04
3001-3179 University Sta..... 10
3451-3796 Beechwold Sta.... 14
4001-4089 H Sta............... 15
4391-4697 Tri-Village Sta 12
4701-4994 B Sta............... 02
5001-5254 Tri-Village Sta 12
5501-5874 Upper Arlington
      Br..................... 21
6301-6494 Oakland Park
      Br..................... 24
6501-6798 Bexley Br......... 09
6801-7124 E Sta............... 05
7301-7368 Bexley Br......... 09
7601-7892 G Sta............... 07
8001-8448 A Sta............... 01
8501-8799 State Street....... 15
9601-9807 F Sta............... 06
11301-11447 C Sta............ 11
13001-13500 Whitehall Br 13
14501-14774 Mount Vernon
      Avenue Sta..... 03
15001-15949 Civic Center.... 15
17000-17450 Lockbourne Air
      Force Br........ 17
19001-19244 Shepard Sta 19
19701-19999 Airport Sta...... 19
20001-20999 Northwest....... 20
23081-23424 Point Sta........ 23
27001-27990 Livingston Sta.. 27
28001-28999 Lincoln Village
      Br..................... 28
29001-29999 Northland....... 29
30100-30999 Gahanna....... 30

RURAL ROUTES

1 30
4 28

STATIONS, BRANCHES AND UNITS

Airport Sta...................... 19
Beechwold Sta.................. 14
Bexley Br....................... 09
College Springs Br............. 19
Gahanna Br..................... 30
Hilltop Sta...................... 04
Lincoln Village Br.............. 28
Livingston Sta.................. 27
Lockbourne A F B Br.......... 17
Mount Vernon Avenue Sta... 03
Northwest Sta.................. 20
Oakland Park Br............... 24
Obetz Br....................... 07
Point Sta....................... 23
Shepard Sta.................... 19
State Street Sta................ 15
Tri Village Sta.................. 12
University Sta.................. 10
Upper Arlington Br............ 21

Whitehall Br 13
Wonderland Rural Br............. 30
Worthington Br 43085
General Delivery 16
Postmaster 16

APARTMENTS, HOTELS, MOTELS

Arlington Arms, 1335 Dublin
   Rd 15
Beverly Manor, 374 N
   Virginia Lee 09
Bolivar Arms, Caldwell Pl 03
Broad Hampton, 42 N
   Hampton Rd...................... 13
Broad-Garfield, 775 E Broad... 05
Broad-Ohio, 1160 E Broad 05
Broadwin, 1312 E Broad........ 05
Cambridge Arms, 926 E
   Broad 05
Charminel, 342 E State........ 15
Christopher Inn, 300 E
   Broad 15
Clarmont Motor Inn, 650 S
   High 15
Clifton Court, 179 Clifton Ct.. 03
Clifton Park, 1761 Clifton
   Ave 03
Columbus Plaza, 50 N 3rd 15
Columbus Travelodge, 1070
   Dublin Rd........................ 15
Fairport Gardens, Fairway
   Blvd 13
First Community Village,
   1800 Riverside Dr............. 12
Fort Hayes, 31 W Spring........ 15
Frambes Hall, 47 E Frambes
   Ave 01
Greystone Court, 815 N High.. 15
Holiday Inn Of America
   Airport, 4300 E 17th Ave.... 19
Holiday Inn Of America
   Downtown, 175 E Town St.. 15
Holiday Inn Of America East,
   4801 E Broad 13
Holiday Inn Of America
   North, 1212 E Granville
   Rd 29
Holiday Inn Of America West,
   4601 W Broad................... 28
Howard Johnson East, 5000
   E Main 13
Howard Johnson North, 999 E
   Granville Rd..................... 29
Howard Johnson West, 3833
   W Broad........................... 28
Indianola Court, 1770 N
   High 01
International House-Men, 104
   15th Ave E 01
International House-Women,
   1875 Summit.................... 01
Jefferson, 17 E Spring........... 15
Leafy Dale, 789 Dennison
   Ave 15
Lincoln Lodge, 4950 W
   Broad 28
Lutheran Senior City, 977
   Parkview Blvd 19
Madonna, 79 Taylor Ave 03
Mayfair, 226 Mayfair Blvd 13
Mid-City, 950 E Broad........... 05
Nationwide Inn, 4101 W
   Broad 28

Neil Hall, 1634 Neil Ave 10
Neil House Motor Hotel, 41 S
   High 15
Neil-Wood Gables, 2090 Neil
   Ave 01
Northern, 493 1/2 N High....... 15
Norwick, State & 4th............. 15
Ohio Stater Inn, 2060 N
   High 01
Olentangy Inn, 1299
   Olentangy Rvr Rd 12
Park Tower, 1620 E Broad...... 03
Royal York, 1445 E Broad....... 05
Seneca, Broad & Grant.......... 15
Southern, Main & High.......... 15
Southgate Manor, 2207
   Winslow Dr 07
Stouffers University Inn,
   3025 Olentangy River Rd... 02
Thurber Towers, 645 Neil
   Ave 15
Town Terrace, 518 E Town..... 15
Townley Court, 580 E Town.... 15
University Arms, 505 Harley
   Dr 02
Virginia Lee Gardens, 3016
   Maryland Ave 09
Westgate Manor, 587
   Wedgewood Dr 28
Westminster Hall, 52 15th
   Ave E 01
Y M C A, 40 W Long St 15
Y W C A, 65 S 4th St............. 15

BUILDINGS

Atlas, 8 E Long 15
Beacon Mutual, 52 W Gay...... 15
Beggs, 21 E State................. 15
Blue Cross, 174 E Long 15
Brunson, 145 N High............. 15
Bryson, 156 Parsons Ave....... 15
Bryson, 700 Bryden Rd.......... 15
Buckeye & Loan, 36 E Gay..... 15
Catholic Center, 80 S 5th St... 15
City National Bank, 20 E
   Broad 15
Columbus Public Library, 96
   S Grant Ave 15
Continental, 11 E Gay............ 15
Curl, 1309 E Broad................ 05
Eighty-Eight East Broad, 88
   E Broad 15
Empire, 150 E Broad 15
First National, 33 N High........ 15
Franklin Federal Savings &
   Loan, 297 S High 15
Guarantee Title & Trust, 22
   W Gay 15
Hartman Theatre, 79 E State
   St 15
High-Long, 5 E Long 15
Huntington Bank, 17 S High.... 15
Lanman, 20 S 3rd.................. 15
Lincoln-Le Veque Tower, 50 W
   Broad 15
Masonic Temple, 34 N 4th
   St 15
Medical Arts, 327 E State St... 15
Medical Science, 9 Buttles
   Ave 15
Nationwide, 246 N High......... 16
Nitschke, 35 E Gay................ 15

Ohio State Federal Savings &
   Loan, 85 E Gay................. 15
Outlook, 44 E Broad.............. 15
Physicians & Surgeons, 350
   E Broad St 15
Physicians, 683 E Broad St..... 15
Spahr, 50 E Broad St 15
Stoneman, 335 S High........... 15
Three Ninety Five East Broad,
   395 E Broad St.................. 15
Trautman, 209 S High............ 15
University Club, 40 S 3rd....... 15

GOVERNMENT OFFICES

Chamber Of Commerce, 50 W
   Broad 15
City Hall, 90 W Broad............ 15
Court House, Mound & High.... 15
Federal Bldg, 85 Marconi
   Blvd 15
Main Post Office, 850 Twin
   Rivers Dr......................... 15
State House, Broad & High
   St 15
State Office Bldg, 65 S Front
   St 15

HOSPITALS

Benjamin Franklin, 1755
   Alum Creek Dr................. 07
Childrens, 561 S 17th............ 05
Columbus State School, 1601
   W Broad 23
Columbus State, 1960 W
   Broad 23
Doctors Lincoln Village, 5100
   W Broad 28
Doctors Main Hospital, 1087
   Denninson Ave 01
Grant, 309 E State................ 15
Harding, 445 E Granville Rd... 43085
Lincoln Memorial, 3341 E
   Livingston Ave 27
Mercy, 1430 S High............... 07
Mount Carmel, 793 W State.... 22
Ohio State University, 410 W
   10th Ave.......................... 10
Ohio Tuberculosis, 466 W
   10th Ave.......................... 10
Riverside Methodist, 3535
   Olentangy Rvr Rd 14
Saint Anns Maternity, 1555
   Bryden Rd........................ 05
Saint Anthony, 1450
   Hawthorne Ave 03

MILITARY INSTALLATIONS

Fort Hayes Military
   Reservation...................... 15
Lockbourne Air Force Base..... 17

UNIVERSITIES AND COLLEGES

Bliss Business, 131 E State.... 15
Capital University, 2199 E
   Main 09
Columbus Business
   University, 208 N High....... 15
Franklin University, 201 S.
   Grant 15

Ohio Dominican, 1216
  Sunbury Rd 19
Ohio State University, 1659 N
  High 10
Saint Charles, 2010 E Broad.. 09
Saint Mary Of The Springs,
  1616 Sunbury Rd. 19

CUYAHOGA FALLS 442

POST OFFICE BOXES

Box Nos.
1-600   Cuyahoga
     Falls 22
900-1200   State Road 23
1300-1900   Stow Br 24

STATIONS, BRANCHES AND UNITS

State Road Sta. 23
Stow Br. 24
General Delivery 22
Postmaster. 22

DAYTON 454

POST OFFICE BOXES

Box Nos.
1-176   Babel Br. 20
1-207   Centerville Br. 59
1-268   West Carrollton
     Br 49
1-297   Dayton View
     Sta. 06
1-297   Roosevelt Sta. 17
1-324   North Dayton
     Sta. 04
1-429   Forest Park Br. 05
1-597   Veterans
     Ad-
     ministration Br. 28
1-646   Far Hills Br. 19
1-1061   Mid City Sta. 02
1-1477   Main Office 01
1401-14229   Northridge-Br 14
2001-2384   Kettering Br. 29
3001-3175   Overlook Br. 31
3001-4077   Trotwood Br. 26
7001-7296   B Sta. 07
33001-33499   Wpafb Br. 33
33501-33619   Amc Br. 33

STATIONS, BRANCHES AND UNITS

Air Materiel Command Br. 33
Centerville Br. 59
Dabel Sta. 20
Dayton View Sta. 06
Far Hills Br. 19
Forest Park Br. 05
Huber Heights Br. 24
Kettering Br. 29
Mid City Sta. 02
Moraine Br. 39
North Dayton Sta. 04
Northridge Br. 14
Overlook Br. 31
Roosevelt Sta. 17

Trotwood Br. 26
Veterans Administration Br. 28
Wright Patterson AFB Br. 33
General Delivery 01
Postmaster. 01

APARTMENTS, HOTELS, MOTELS

Commodore, 522 Grand Ave .. 05
Gibbons Arcade, 26 W 3rd 02
Holden, 200 W 5th. 02
Holiday Inn, 2301 Wagoner
   Ford Rd 14
Howard Johnson'S, 2221
   Wagoner Ford Rd. 14
Imperial House North, 2401
   Needmore Rd. 14
Mall Motor Inn, 21 S
   Jefferson St. 02
Oakwood Manor, 1211 Far
   Hills Ave. 02
Red Horse Motor Inn, 4625 S
   Dixie Hgwy 39
Sheraton-Dayton, 210 N
   Main. 62
Statler-Hilton, 11 S Ludlow. 01
Stratford House, 330 W 1st. .. 02
Stratford Motel, 225 W 1st. .. 02
Travelodge North, 2833 N
   Dixie Dr 14
Travelodge South, 4530 S
   Dixie Hgwy 39
Travelodge, 222 E First St. 02

BUILDINGS

American, 4 S Main 02
Century 111 W 1st. 02
Commercial, 44 S Ludlow. 02
Dayco 333 W 1st. 02
Eleven West Monument, 11 W
   Monument Ave. 02
Fidelity 219 S Main. 02
Gas & Electric, 25 N Main 02
Gem City Savings, 4 N Main.. 02
Grant Denau Towers 40 W
   4th St. 02
Harries, 137 N Main 02
Hulman, 120 W 2nd. 02
I B M, 33 W 1st St 02
Municipal, 101 W 3rd 01
Reibold, 117 S Main 02
Safety, 325 W 3rd. 02
Talbott Towers, 118 W 1st 02
Talbott, 131 N Ludlow 02
Third National, 34 N Main 02
Twenty-Five South Main, 25 S
   Main. 02
Winters Bank, 40 N Main 02

GOVERNMENT OFFICES

Court House, 15 N Main 02
Federal Bureau Of
   Investigation 40 W 4th. 02
Internal Revenue Service 40
   W 4th. 02
Recruiting Offices, Centre
   City Bldg. 02
Selective Service Board,
   Knott Bldg. 02
Social Security Agency, 333
   W 1st. 02

Treasury Department
   Collector Of Customs 118
   W 3rd 02

HOSPITALS

Dayton Childrens Psychiatric,
   141 Firwood Dr. 19
Dayton State, 2335 Wayne
   Ave. 28
Good Samaritan, 1425 W
   Fairview Ave. 06
Grandview, 405 Grand Ave 05
Kettering Memorial, 3535
   Southern Blvd. 29
Miami Valley, 1 Wyoming 09
Saint Elizabeth, 49 Hopeland. 08
Stillwater Sanitarium, 8100
   N Main 15
Veterans Administration,
   4100 W 3rd. 28

MILITARY INSTALLATIONS

Defense Electronic Supply
   Center 44
Wright Patterson A F B. 33

UNIVERSITIES AND COLLEGES

University Of Dayton, 300
   College Park Ave. 69
Wright State University 7751
   Col Glenn Hwy. 31

ELYRIA 440

POST OFFICE BOXES

Box Nos.
A-M   Parcel Post
     Annex 35
1-145   North
     Ridgeville Br. 39
1-760   Main Office 35
901-1048   Parcel Post
     Annex. 35

RURAL ROUTES

1,2,3 35

STATIONS, BRANCHES AND UNITS

North Ridgeville Br. 35
Parcel Post Annex Sta. 35
General Delivery 35
Postmaster. 35

HAMILTON 450

POST OFFICE BOXES

Box Nos.
1-170   Fairfield Br. 14
1-958   Main Office 12
2001-2199   Lindenwald
     Sta. 15
3001-3090   Rossville Sta 13

RURAL ROUTES

1	11
2	13
3	15
4,5,6	13
7	11

STATIONS, BRANCHES AND UNITS

Fairfield Br	14
Lindenwald Sta	15
Millville Br	13
New Miami Br	11
Reily Rural Br	60
Rossville Sta	13
General Delivery	12
Postmaster	12

LIMA   458

POST OFFICE BOXES

Box Nos.		
1-162	Gomer R. Sta	09
1-170	Buckland R. Sta	19
1-197	Beaverdam R. Sta	08
1-1318	Main Office	02
2001-2086	Cridersville Br	06
3001-3116	Elida	07
7001-7250	Lafayette	54

RURAL ROUTES

1,2,3	07
4	06
5	01
6	06
7	54

STATIONS, BRANCHES AND UNITS

Beaverdam Rural Br	08
Buckland Rural Br	19
Cridersville Br	06
Elida Br	07
Gomer Rural Br	09
Lafayette Rural Br	54
General Delivery	01
Postmaster	02

LORAIN   440

POST OFFICE BOXES

Box Nos.		
1-570	Main Office	52
1001-1203	South Lorain Sta	55
2001-2095	Sheffield Lake Br	54

STATIONS, BRANCHES AND UNITS

Sheffield Lake Br	54
South Lorain Sta	55
General Delivery	52
Postmaster	52

MANSFIELD   449

POST OFFICE BOXES

Box Nos.		
1-790	Mansfield	01
1000-1499	Mansfield Annex Sta	08
1500-1999	Southwest Sta	07
2000-2499	Lincoln Br	05
2500-2999	Sherman Sta	06
3000-3499	Lexington Br	04

RURAL ROUTES

1,2,3,4,5,6	03
7,8	04

STATIONS, BRANCHES AND UNITS

Lexington Br	04
Lincoln Br	05
Parcel Post Annex Sta	03
Sherman Sta	06
Southwest Sta	07
General Delivery	01
Postmaster	01

APARTMENTS, HOTELS, MOTELS

Base Apartments, 270 N Main	02
Carriage Hill, 72 N Linden Rd	06
Charford Apts 74 Bowman St	02
Court, 115 N Main	02
Creamers, 304 N Main	02
Downtown Motor Lodge, 191 Park Ave W	02
Ebony, 831 Bowman	05
Forty-Two Motel, 2444 Lexington Ave	07
Gardner Apts 114 Park Avenue West	02
Holiday Inn Of America, Laver Rd	05
King Apts 616 King St	06
Leland Motor Hotel, 27 Park Ave W	02
Mansfield Apartments, 151 W 2nd	02
Newman, 316 N Main	02
Phoenix, 323 N Main	02
Ramada Inn, P.o. Box 2007	05
Southern, 2 S Park	02
Travel Lodge Of Mansfield, 137 Park Ave W	02
Zediker Apartments, 100 Blymer Ave	03
Zediker Apartments, 160 W 2nd	02
Zediker Apartments, 458 Woodward	03

BUILDINGS

City Bldg 27 West Second St	02
Courthouse 50 Park Avenue East	02
Farmers Bank, 28 Park Ave W	02

Richland Trust, 3 N Main	02
Stewart Towers, 13 Park Ave W	02

HOSPITALS

Beatty Clinic, 1695 Lucas Rd	03
Madison Hospital, 73 Madison Rd	05
Mansfield General Hospital, 335 Glessner Ave	03
Peoples Hospital, 597 Park Ave E	05

UNIVERSITIES AND COLLEGES

Mansfield Campus Ohio State U, 2275 Springmill Rd	06

SPRINGFIELD   455

POST OFFICE BOXES

Box Nos.		
1-1594	Springfield	01

RURAL ROUTES

1,2,3,4,5,6,7,8	02

STATIONS, BRANCHES AND UNITS

General Delivery	01
Postmaster	01

APARTMENTS, HOTELS, MOTELS

Allan Apartments, 1001 E High	05
Belmont Apartments, 1920 E High	05
Fairfax Motel, 2418 E Main	03
Governors Manor Apartments, 2100 E High	05
High Royal Apartments, 1590-1592 E High	05
Holiday Inn Motel, 1715 W North	04
Northridge Apartments, 4761-4953 Ridgewood Rd E	03
Ridgewood Apartments, 1009 E Home Rd	03
Scots Inn Motel 11 W Leffel Ln	06
Shawnee Apartments, 102 E Main	05
Southern Apartments, 501 S Limestone	05
Travelodge Motel, 325 W Columbia	04
Troy Plaza Apartments, 2107 Troy Rd	04
Williamsburg Apartments, 2650 E High	05

BUILDINGS

Arcade, 1 E High	02
Arcue, 6 W High	02

First National Bank, 4 W
  Main.................................... 02
Mc Adams, 31 E High............. 02
Mitchell, 42 S Limestone........ 02
New Merchants & Mechanics,
  20 S Limestone................... 02
Tecumseh, 34 W High............ 02
Winwood, 49 W High............. 02
Woolworth, 34 E High............ 02

HOSPITALS

Community Hospital, 2615 E
  High................................... 01
Ioof Home Hospital, 404 E
  Mccreight Ave..................... 01
Knights Of Pythian Home
  Hospital, 901 W High 01
Mercy Medical Center, 1343
  N Fountain Ave.................... 01
Rickley Memorial Hospital,
  West National Rd................. 01
Springview Hospital, 3130 E
  National Rd......................... 01

UNIVERSITIES AND COLLEGES

Wittenberg University.............. 01

TOLEDO   436

POST OFFICE BOXES

Box Nos.
1-357   A Sta........................ 05
1-1080   Main Office................ 01
1101-1290   Madison
           Avenue Sta............ 24
1501-2368   Central Sta................ 03
2501-2914   Sta Kenwood........... 06
3001-3499   C Sta....................... 07
3501-3678   D Sta....................... 08
4001-4317   E Sta....................... 09
4500-4716   Old West End
           Sta........................ 20
5001-5299   Point Place
           Sta........................ 11
5501-5897   Wernert Sta.............. 13
5001-6399   Heatherdowns
           Sta........................ 14
6401-6764   West Toledo
           Sta........................ 12
7001-7392   Reynolds
           Corners Sta............ 15
7501-7596   Oregon Br................ 16

RURAL ROUTES

5 18

STATIONS, BRANCHES AND UNITS

Central Sta............................ 04
Heatherdowns Sta.................. 14
Kenwood Sta.......................... 06
Madison Avenue Sta............... 24
Old West End Sta................... 20
Oregon Br.............................. 16
Point Place Sta....................... 11
Reynolds Corners Sta.............. 15
Wernert Sta........................... 13
West Toledo Sta..................... 12
General Delivery..................... 01
Postmaster............................ 01

APARTMENTS, HOTELS, MOTELS

Albertus Brown Homes, 300
  Avondale Ave...................... 02
Birmingham Terrace, 2100
  Consaul.............................. 05
Brand Whitlock Homes, 392
  Nebraska Ave...................... 02
Commodore Perry, 505
  Jefferson Ave...................... 03
Executive Towers, 1920
  Collingwood Blvd................. 24
Globe, 1001 Jefferson Ave....... 24
Hillcrest, 231 16th.................. 24
Holiday Inn N, 1821 E
  Manhattan Blvd................... 08
Hospitality Motor Inn, 1800
  Miami................................. 05
Lorraine, 1117 Jefferson Ave... 24
Mid City, 111 S Summit........... 24
Port Lawrence Homes, 200
  Indiana Ave........................ 02
Ravine Park Village, 2300
  Seaman.............................. 05
Secor, 425 Jefferson Ave......... 04
Southern, 5430 Telegraph
  Rd...................................... 12
Spieker Terrace, 385 Earl........ 05
Toledo Travel Lodge, 1919
  Collingwood Blvd................. 24
Town House, 1111 W
  Bancroft............................. 06
Waldorf, 310 Summit.............. 03
Weiler Homes, 601 Fassett...... 05
Willard Motor Lodge, 415 St
  Clair.................................. 03

BUILDINGS

Board Of Trade, 205 St Clair 04
Community Services, 1
  Stranahan Sq...................... 04
Edison, 420 Madison Ave......... 04
Federal Office, 234 Summit...... 04
Fiberglass Tower, 1 Levis Sq.... 04
Gardner, 506 Madison Ave....... 04
Great Eastern, 2500
  Woodville Rd....................... 16
Lamb, 406 Madison Ave.......... 04
Lof, 811 Madison Ave............. 24
Lucas County Bank, 515
  Madison Ave....................... 04
Lucas County, C H Adams At
  Erie.................................... 24
Miracle Mile, 4925 Jackman
  Rd...................................... 13
National Bank, 606 Madison
  Ave.................................... 04
Owens-Illinois, 405 Madison
  Ave.................................... 04
Professional, 1838 Parkwood
  Ave.................................... 24
Security, 243 Huron................ 04
Southland, 3300 Glendale........ 14
Spitzer, 520 Madison Ave........ 04
Toledo Trust, 241 Summit........ 04
United Savings, 240 Huron....... 04
Westgate, 3301 W Central
  Ave.................................... 06
Woodville Mall, 3725
  Williston Rd........................ 16

GOVERNMENT OFFICES

Chamber Of Commerce, 218
  Huron................................. 04
City Hall Safety, Erie &
  Jackson.............................. 24
United States Courthouse &
  Customs, 1710 Spielbush
  Blvd................................... 24

HOSPITALS

Flower, 3350 Collingwood
  Blvd................................... 10
Maumee Valley, 2025
  Arlington Ave...................... 09
Mercy, 2221 Madison Ave....... 24
Parkview 1920 Parkwood
  Ave.................................... 24
Riverside, 1609 Summit........... 04
Roche Memorial, 945 S
  Detroit............................... 14
Saint Charles, 2600 Navarre
  Ave.................................... 16
Saint Lukes, 2517 Robinwood
  Ave.................................... 10
Saint Vincents, 2213 Cherry..... 08
Toledo State, 930 S Detroit
  Ave.................................... 03
Toledo, 2142 N Cove Blvd 06

UNIVERSITIES AND COLLEGES

Davis Business, 701 Adams...... 24
Mary Manse, 2443
  Collingwood Blvd................. 20
Stautzenberger Business, 331
  1/2 St Clair......................... 04
University Of Toledo, 2801 W
  Bancroft............................. 06

WARREN   444

POST OFFICE BOXES

Box Nos.
100-1431   Main Office 82
2001-2999   Warren Annex
           Sta........................ 84
3000-3999   West Warren
           Sta........................ 85

RURAL ROUTES

1,2,3,4,6.............................. 81

STATIONS, BRANCHES AND UNITS

Parcel Post Annex Sta............. 84
West Warren Sta..................... 85
General Delivery..................... 82
Postmaster............................ 81

YOUNGSTOWN   445

POST OFFICE BOXES

Bex Nos.

1-1590	Main Office	01
1900-2099	East Side Sta	06
2100-2299	North Side Sta	04
2300-2499	West Side Sta	09
2500-2799	South Side Sta	07
2900-3099	Fosterville Sta	11
3100-3799	Boardman Br	12
3800-3999	Parcel Post Sta	05
4000-4199	Austintown Br	15
5000-5399	Poland Br	14

STATIONS, BRANCHES AND UNITS

Austintown Br	15
Boardman Br	12
East Side Sta	06
Fosterville Sta	11
Liberty Br	05
North Side Sta	04
Parcel Post Sta	05
Plaza Br	12
Poland Br	14
South Side Sta	07
West Side Sta	09
General Delivery	01
Postmaster	01

APARTMENTS, HOTELS, MOTELS

Alberta Terrace, 1918 Hillman	07
Belmont, 929 Belmont Ave	04
Buechner Hall, 620 Bryson	02
Canfield, 12-14 West Delason Ave	07
Caroline, 2116 Market	07
Colonial, 725 Bryson	02
Della, 2406 Market	07
Dora Terrace, 2145-55 Oak Hill Ave	07
Dorothy, 3325 Market	07
Edgewood, 55 E Dewey	07
Edna Terrace, 524-538 Belmont Ave	02
Elm Terrace, 200 West Scott	02
Elm, 1745 Elm	05
Evans Terrace, 204-214 Grant	02
Fifth Avenue, 804-812 Fifth Ave	04
Fithian, 145 East Midlothian Bd	07
Glenoir Terrace, 1501-15 Kennedy Ave	06
Home, 238 West Rayen Ave	02
Kalsander The, 374 E Boardman-Poland Rd	12
Kane, 511 West Indianola Ave	11
Kennedy Terrace, 1731-41 Hillman	07
Lillian Flats, 102 Benita Ave	05
Linberger Dwellings, 3820 Mahoning Ave	15
Lincoln Towers, 257 Lincoln Ave	03
La-Rayen, 143 W Rayen	03

Lora, 215-226 Lora Ave	04
Lorena Terrace, 1435-39 Wick Ave	05
Lustig, 802-812 5th Ave	04
Mar-Phil, 16 West Madison Ave	05
Mayfair, 5312 Glenwood Ave	12
Mc Vey Terrace, 108 W Madison Ave	05
Mellinger Terrace, 2201-09 Hillman	07
Merle Terrace, 240-48 Lincoln Park	06
Metro Plaza, 151 S Hazel	03
Newport, 3711 Glenwood Ave	11
Newport, 4000 Hillman Way	12
North Heights, 273-5 North Heights Ave	04
Ohio Hotel 121 West Boardman	01
Parkway Tower, 291 Park Ave	04
Pelton, 224 West Wood	02
Rayen, 305 Elm	03
Renner, 277 Park Ave	04
Ryder Terrace, 2129-39 Hillman	07
Shagrin, 204 West Madison Ave	04
Sunset, 369 East Midlothian Blvd	07
Valley, 31 Spring Common	03
Vindy, 32 E Front	03
Voyager Motor Inn, 129 Market	03
West, 308 Lincoln	02
Westlake Terrace, 976 W Federal St	10
Wickcliffe Manor, 28 Yorkshire Blvd	15
Williams Terrace, 2144 Oak Hill Ave	07
Youngstown, 311 W Boardman	03

BUILDINGS

American Legion Home, 34 West Spring	02
American Red Cross, 266 West Wood	02
Armory Ohio State, 325 West Rayen Ave	02
Binama Bldg, 112 W Commerce	03
Boardman Medical Arts, 7330 Market	12
Butler Art Institute, 524 Wick Ave	02
Central Tower, 11 Central Sq	03
Diocese Of Youngstown, 144 West Wood	03
Dollar Bank, 16 Wick Ave	03
Eagles, 272 West Rayen	03
Executive Bldg 123-25 W. Commerce	03
Federal, 18 N Phelps	03
Home Savings & Loan, 277 West Federal	03
Jewish Community Center, 505 Gypsy Lane	01
K Of C, 25 South Hazel	03

K Of P Hall, 247 West Federal	03
Lederer, 450 West Commerce.	03
Legal Arts, 101 Market	03
Mahoning Bank, 26 Market	03
Market Street Professional, 3718 Market	07
Masonic Temple, 233 Wick Ave	03
Medical Arts, 3031 Market	07
Ohio Edison, 25 East Boardman	03
Proffessional, 226 North Phelps	03
Public Library, 305 Wick Ave	03
Realty, 47 Central Sq	03
Renner Block, 33 North Hazel	03
Republic, 335 Market	03
South Side Bank, 1509 Market	07
Stambaugh Auditorium, 1000 Fifth Ave	04
Stambaugh, 44 Central Sq	03
Union Bank, 16 Central Sq	03
W F M J, 101 West Boardman	03
Wick, 30 W. Federal	03
Y W C A, 25 West Rayen Ave.	03
Ymca	01
Youngstown Catholic Action Center, 141 West Rayen Ave	03
Youngstown Symphony Center, 266 West Federal	03

GOVERNMENT OFFICES

City Hall, 106 W Boardman	03
City Jail, 116 West Boardman	03
County Jail, 21 West Boardman	03
Court House Mahoning County, 120 Market	03
U S Post Office And Court House, 9 West Front	03

HOSPITALS

Blackburn Home For Aged, 6 Botsford	14
Cafaro Memorial Hospital	01
Florence Crittendon Home, 1161 Mcguffey Rd	05
Mahoning County Tuberculosis Sanatorium, 4880 Kirk Rd	15
Saint Elizabeth, 1044 Belmont Ave	05
Stambaugh Nurses Home	01
Tod Nurses Home	01
Woodside Receiving, 800 E Indianola Ave	02
Youngstown North Side Unit	01
Youngstown Osteopathic	01
Youngstown South Side Unit	01

UNIVERSITIES AND COLLEGES

Penn Ohio, 3517 Market	07
Youngstown State University, 410 Wick Ave	03

OKLAHOMA
(Abbreviation: OK)

Achille....74720
Ada (1st)....74820
Adair....74330
Adams....73901
Adamson, R. Br. Hartshorne....74520
Addington....73520
Admiral, Sta. Tulsa (see appendix)
Afton....74331
Agra....74824
Airpark, Br. Ardmore....73401
Albany....74721
Albert....73001
Albion....74521
Alderson....74521
Alex....73002
Aline....73716
Allen....74821
Alluwe, R. Br. Nowata....74048
Alma....73003
Altus (1st)....73521
Altus A F B, Br. Altus....73521
Alva (1st)....73717
Amber....73004
Ames....73718
Amorita....73719
Anadarko (1st)....73005
Antlers....74523
Apache....73006
Arapaho....73620
Arcadia....73007
Ardmore (1st)....73401
Arkoma....74901
Arnett....73832
Asher....74826
  Pearson, R. Br.....74861
Ashland....74524
Atoka....74525
  Bentley, R. Br.....74527
  Farris, R. Br.....74542
Atwood....74827
Avant....74001
Bache....74526
Bacone....74420
Baker....73930
Balko....73931
Barnsdall....74002
Bartlesville (1st)....74003
  East Side, Sta.....74003
Battiest....74722
Bearden....74828
Beaver....73932
Beggs....74421
Bengal....74929
Bennington....74723
Bentley, R. Br. Atoka....74527
Bernice, R. Br. Afton....74331
Bessie....73622
Bethany (1st)....73008
Bethel....74724
Big Cabin....74332
Billings....74630
Binger....73009
Bison....73720
Bixby....74008
Blackburn, R. Cr. Pawnee....74058
Blackwell (1st)....74631
Blair....73526
Blanchard....73010
Blanco....74528

Blocker....74529
Blue....74725
Bluejacket....74333
Boise City....73933
  Wheeless, R. Br.....73952
Bokchito....74726
Bokoshe....74930
Boley....74829
Boswell....74727
Boulevard, Sta. Norman....73069
Bowlegs....74830
Bowring, R. Br. Pawhuska....74009
Boynton....74422
Bradley....73011
Braggs....74423
Braman....74632
Bray....73012
Breckinridge, R. Br. Enid....73721
Briartown, R. Br. Porum....74424
Bridgeport....73013
Bristow (1st)....74010
Britton, Sta. Oklahoma City....73114
Broken Arrow (1st)....74012
Broken Bow....74728
Bromide....74530
Buffalo....73834
Bunch....74931
Burbank....74633
Burlington....73722
Burneyville....73430
Burns Flat....73624
Butler....73625
Byars....74831
Byron....73723
Cache....73527
Caddo....74729
Calera....74730
Calumet....73014
Calvin....74531
  Gerty, R. Br.....74544
Camargo....73835
Cameron....74932
  Pocola, R. Br.....74902
Cameron College, Sta. Lawton....73501
Canadian....74425
Caney....74533
Canton....73724
Canute....73626
Capitol Hill, Sta. Oklahoma City (see appendix)
Capron....73725
Cardin....74335
Carmen....73726
Carnegie....73015
Carney....74832
Carrier....73727
Carter....73627
Cartersville....74934
Cartwright....74731
Cashion....73016
Castle....74833
Catoosa....74015
Cement....73017
Centrahoma....74534
Centralia....74336
Chandler....74834
Chattanooga....73528
Checotah....74426
Chelsea....74016
Cherokee....73728
Chester....73838
Cheyenne....73628

Chickasha (1st)....73018
Chilocco....74635
Choctaw....73020
Chouteau....74337
  Mazie, R. Br.....74353
Cimarron, Sta. Oklahoma City (see appendix)
Claremore (1st)....74017
Clarita....74535
Clayton....74536
Clearview....74835
Clebit....74732
Cleo Springs....73729
Cleveland....74020
Clinton (1st)....73601
Cloudy....74537
Coalgate....74538
Colbert....74733
Colcord....74338
Coleman....73432
College, Sta. Stillwater....74074
Collinsville (1st)....74021
Colony....73021
Comanche....73529
Commerce....74339
Concho....73022
Connerville....74836
Cookson....74427
Cooperton, R. Br. Gotebo....73023
Copan....74022
Cordell (1st)....73632
Corn....73024
Council Hill....74428
Countyline....73025
Covington....73730
Coweta....74429
Cox City, R. Br. Rush Springs....73082
Coyle....73027
Crawford....73638
Crescent....73028
Cromwell....74837
Crowder....74430
Cumberland....73433
Cushing (1st)....74023
Custer....73639
Cyril....73029
Dacoma....73731
Daisy....74540
Dale, R. Br. Shawnee....74838
Davenport....74026
Davidson....73530
Davis....73030
Dawson, Sta. Tulsa....74151
Deer Creek....74636
Del City, Br. Oklahoma City (see appendix)
Delaware....74027
Delhi....73640
Depew....74028
Depot, Br. Mc Alester....74501
Devol....73531
Dewar....74431
Dewey....74029
Dibble....73031
Drll City....73641
Disney....74340
Donaldson, Sta. Tulsa....74104
Dougherty....73032
Douglas....73733
Dover....73734
Dow, R Br Hartshorne....74541

Downtown, Sta. Oklahoma
  City (see appendix)
Drummond 73735
Drumright 74030
Duke 73532
Duncan (1st) 73533
Durant (1st) 74701
Durham 73642
Dustin 74839
Eagle City 73643
Eagletown 74734
Eakly 73033
Earlsboro 74840
East Side, Sta. Bartlesville 74003
Eastern, Sta. Oklahoma City ...73117
Eastern Okla A M College,
  Br. Wilburton............................74578
Edmond (1st) 73034
El Reno (1st) 73036
Eldorado 73537
Elgin 73538
Elk City (1st) 73644
Elmer 73539
Elmore City 73035
Elmwood 73935
Enid (1st) 73701
  Breckinridge, R. Br. 73721
  University, Sta. 73701
  Vance A F B. Br. 73701
  3, Sta. 73701
Erick 73645
Eucha 74342
Eufaula 74432
  Lenna, R. Br. 74443
Eva 73936
Fairfax 74637
Fairland 74343
Fairmont 73736
Fairview 73737
Fanshawe 74935
Fargo 73840
Farley, Sta. Oklahoma City
  (see appendix)
Farris, R. Br. Atoka 74542
Faxon 73540
Fay 73646
Felt 73937
Fillmore, R. Br. Milburn 73434
Finley 74543
Fittstown 74842
Fitzhugh 74843
Fletcher 73541
Foraker 74638
Forgan 73938
Fort Cobb 73038
Fort Gibson 74434
Fort Sill, Br. Lawton 73503
Fort Supply 73841
Fort Towson 74735
Foss 73647
Foster 73039
Fox 73435
Foyil 74031
Francis 74844
Frederick (1st) 73542
Freedom 73842
Gage 73843
Gans 74936
Garber 73738
Garvin 74736
Gate 73844
Geary 73040
Gene Autry 73436

Geronimo 73543
Gerty, R. Br. Calvin 74544
Glencoe 74032
Glenpool 74033
Glover, R. Br. Broken Bow 74728
Golden 74737
Goltry 73739
Goodwell 73939
Gore 74435
Gotebo 73041
  Cooperton, R. Br. 73023
Gould 73544
Gowen 74545
Gracemont 73042
Grady 73545
Graham 73437
Grainola 74639
Grandfield 73546
Granite 73547
Grant 74738
Greenfield 73043
Greenwood, Sta. Tulsa 74120
Griggs 73941
Grove 74344
Guthrie (1st) 73044
Guymon (1st) 73942
Haileyville 74546
Hallett 74034
Hammon 73650
Hanna 74845
Harden City 74846
Hardesty 73944
Harmon 73845
Harrah 73045
Harris, R. Br. Haworth 74739
Hartshorne 74547
  Adamson, R. Br. 74520
  Dow, R. Br. 74541
Haskell 74436
Hastings 73548
Haworth 74740
  Harris, R. Br. 74739
Haywood 74548
Headrick 73549
Healdton 73438
Heavener 74937
Helena 73741
Hendrix 74741
Hennepin 73046
Hennessey 73742
Henryetta (1st) 74437
Hillsdale 73743
Hinton 73047
Hitchcock 73744
Hitchita 74438
Hobart (1st) 73651
Hockerville, R. Br. Picher 74345
Hodgen 74939
Hoffman 74439
Holdenville (1st) 74848
Hollis 73550
Hollister 73551
Homestead 73745
Hominy 74035
Honobia 74549
Hooker 73945
Hopeton 73746
Howe 74940
Hoyt 74440
Hugo (1st) 74743
Hulbert 74441
Hunter 74640
Hydro 73048

Idabel (1st) 74745
Indiahoma 73552
Indianola 74442
  nola 74036
Isabella 73747
Jay 74346
Jefferson 73748
Jenks 74037
Jennings 74038
Jet 73749
Jones 73049
Jumbo 74551
Kansas 74347
Kaw 74641
Kellyville 74039
Kemp 74747
Kendrick 74040
Kenefic 74748
Kenton 73946
Kenwood 74348
Keota 74941
Ketchum 74349
Keyes 73947
Kiefer 74041
Kildare 74642
Kingfisher (1st) 73750
Kingston 73439
Kinta 74552
Kiowa 74553
Knowles 73847
Konawa 74849
Krebs 74554
Kremlin 73753
Lahoma 73754
Lakeside, Sta. Oklahoma
  City..73116
Lamar 74850
Lamont 74643
Lane 74555
Langley 74350
Langston 73050
Laverne 73848
Lawton (1st) 73501
  Cameron College, Sta. 73501
  Fort Sill, Br. 73503
  Meers, R. Br. 73558
  Sheridan, Sta. 73501
  Sullivan Village, R. Br. 73501
Leach 74351
Lebanon 73440
Leedey 73654
Leflore 74942
Lehigh 74556
Lenapah 74042
Lenna, R. Br. Eufaula 74443
Leon 73441
Leonard 74043
Lequire 74943
Lexington 73051
Lindsay (1st) 73052
Loco 73442
Locust Grove 74352
Logan 73849
Lone Grove 73443
Lone Wolf 73655
Longdale 73755
Lookeba 73053
Lookout 73850
Loveland 73553
Loyal 73756
Lucien 73757
Luther 73054
Macomb 74852

Madill 73446
Manchester......................73758
Mangum..........................73554
Manitou..........................73555
Mannford.........................74044
Mannsville.......................73447
Maramec.........................74045
Marble City......................74945
Marietta..........................73448
Marland...........................74644
Marlow............................73055
Marshall..........................73056
Martha............................73556
Mason.............................74853
Maud..............................74854
May.................................73851
Mayfield...........................73656
Maysville..........................73057
Mazie, R. Br. Chouteau......74353
Mc Alester (1st)................74501
Mc Curtain......................74944
Mc Loud..........................74851
Mc Millan.........................73445
Mead...............................73449
Medford............................73759
Medicine Park 73557
Meeker.............................74855
Meers, R. Br. Lawton.........73558
Memorial, Sta. Muskogee...74401
Meno................................73760
Meridian............................73058
Miami (1st).......................74354
Midwest City, Br. Oklahoma
  City (see appendix)
Milburn.............................73450
  Fillmore, R. Br................73434
Milfay...............................74046
Mill Creek.........................74856
Millerton...........................74750
Milo.................................73451
Minco...............................73059
Moffett..............................74946
Monroe.............................74947
Moodys.............................74401
Moore, Br. Oklahoma City...73160
Mooreland.........................73852
Morris...............................74445
Morrison...........................73061
Mounds............................74047
Mountain Park....................73559
Mountain View....................73062
Moyers.............................74557
Muldrow............................74948
Mulhall.............................73063
Muse................................74949
Muskogee (1st)..................74401
Mustang............................73064
Mutual..............................73853
Nardin...............................74646
Nash.................................73761
Nashoba............................74558
New Lima..........................74858
Newalla.............................74857
Newcastle..........................73065
Newkirk.............................74647
Nichols Hills, Br. Oklahoma
  City..............................73116
Nicoma Park.......................73066
Ninnekah...........................73067
Noble................................73068
Norman (1st)......................73069
North Mc Alester, Sta. Mc
  Alester..........................74501

North Miami.......................74358
Northside, Sta. Tulsa (see
  appendix)
Northwest, Sta. Oklahoma
  City..............................73106
Nowata (1st)......................74048
  Alluwe, R. Br.................74049
Oakhurst............................74050
Oakland.............................73452
Oaks.................................74359
Oakwood...........................73658
Ochelata............................74051
Octavia, R. Br. Smithville....74958
Oilton...............................74052
Okarche.............................73762
Okay................................74446
Okeene.............................73763
Okemah.............................74859
Okla College For Women,
  Sta. Chickasha...............73018
OKLAHOMA CITY (1st) (see
  appendix)
Okmulgee (1st)...................74447
Oktaha.............................74450
Oleta................................74751
Olustee.............................73560
Omega..............................73764
Oologah............................74053
Optima..............................73948
Orienta..............................73765
Orlando..............................73073
Osage................................74054
Oscar................................73561
Overbrook..........................73453
Owasso.............................74055
Paden................................74860
Page.................................74950
Panama.............................74951
Panola...............................74559
Paoli.................................73074
Park Hill............................74451
Pauls Valley (1st)...............73075
Pawhuska (1st)...................74056
  Bowring, R. Br...............74009
Pawnee.............................74058
  Blackburn, R. Br.............74058
Pearson, R. Br. Asher.........74861
Peckham...........................74648
Peggs................................74452
Perkins..............................74059
Pernell..............................73076
Perry (1st).........................73077
Pharoah.............................74862
Picher...............................74360
  Hockerville, R. Br............74345
Pickens..............................74752
Piedmont............................73078
Pittsburg............................74560
Platter...............................74753
Plunkettville........................74952
Pocasset............................73079
Pocola, R. Br. Cameron......74902
Ponca City (1st)..................74601
Pondcreek..........................73766
Pontotoc............................74863
Pooleville............................73454
Porter................................74454
Porum................................74455
  Briartown, R. Br.............74424
Poteau (1st).......................74953
Prague..............................74864
Preston..............................74456
Proctor..............................74457

Prue.................................74060
Pryor (1st).........................74361
Purcell (1st).......................73080
Putnam.............................73659
Quapaw.............................74363
Quinton.............................74561
Ralston..............................74650
Ramona.............................74061
Ranch Acres, Sta. Tulsa (see
  appendix)
Randlett............................73562
Ratliff City.........................73081
Rattan...............................74562
Ravia................................73455
Red Fork, Sta. Tulsa...........74153
Red Oak.............................74563
Redbird..............................74458
Redrock.............................74651
Reed.................................73563
Reeves, Sta. Muskogee.......74401
Renfrow.............................73767
Rentiesville.........................74459
Reydon..............................73660
Ringling.............................73456
Ringold..............................74754
Ringwood............................73768
Ripley................................74062
Rocky................................73661
Roff..................................74865
Roland...............................74954
Roosevelt...........................73564
Rose.................................74364
Rosedale, R. Br. Byars........74831
Rosston.............................73855
Rubottom...........................73457
Rufe.................................74755
Rush Springs......................73082
Ryan.................................73565
Saint Louis.........................74866
Salina...............................74365
Sallisaw (1st)......................74955
Sanatorium, R. Br. Talihina..74571
Sand Springs (1st)..............74063
Sapulpa (1st)......................74066
Sardis...............................74564
Sasakwa............................74867
Savanna............................74565
Sawyer.............................74756
Sayre................................73662
Schulter.............................74460
Scipio...............................74566
Seiling..............................73663
Selman..............................73856
Seminole (1st).....................74868
Sentinel.............................73664
Shady Point........................74956
Shamrock...........................74068
Sharon...............................73857
Shartel, Sta. Oklahoma City..73118
Shattuck.............................73858
Shawnee (1st)....................74801
  Dale, R. Br....................74838
  University, Sta................74801
Shepherd Mall, Sta.
  Oklahoma City................73107
Sheridan, Sta. Lawton........73501
Sherwood...........................74757
Shidler..............................74652
Skiatook.............................74070
Slick.................................74071
Smithville...........................74957
  Octavia, R. Br................74958
Snow................................74567

Snyder	73566	
Soper	74759	
South Coffeyville	74072	
Southard	73770	
Southeast, Sta. Tulsa (see appendix)		
Southside, Sta. Tulsa (see appendix)		
Southwest, Sta. Oklahoma City (see appendix)		
Sparks	74869	
Spavinaw	74366	
Spencer	73084	
Spencerville	74760	
Sperry	74073	
Spiro	74959	
Springer	73458	
State Capitol, Sta. Oklahoma City	73105	
Sterling	73567	
Stidham	74461	
Stigler	74462	
Stilwater (1st)	74074	
Stilwell	74960	
Stockyards, Sta. Oklahoma City (see appendix)		
Stonewall	74871	
Strang	74367	
Stratford	74872	
Stringtown	74569	
Strong City	73665	
Stroud	74079	
Stuart	74570	
Sullivan Village, R. Br. Lawton	73501	
Sulphur (1st)	73086	
Summerfield, R. Br. Wister	74966	
Sweetwater	73666	
Swink	74761	
Taft	74463	
Tahlequah (1st)	74464	
Talala	74080	
Talihina	74571	
Taloga	73667	
Tatums	73087	
Tecumseh	74873	
Temple	73568	
Teriton	74081	
Terral	73569	
Texhoma	73949	
Texola	73668	
Thackerville	73459	
Thirty Ninth Street, Sta. Oklahoma City (see appendix)		
Thomas	73669	
Tinker A F B, Br. Oklahoma City	73145	
Tipton	73570	
Tishomingo	73460	
Tom	74762	
Tonkawa	74653	
Tryon	74875	
Tullahassee	74466	
TULSA (1st) (see appendix)		
Tupelo	74572	
Turley, Br. Tulsa	74156	
Turpin	73950	
Tushka	74573	
Tuskahoma	74574	
Tussy	73088	
Tuttle	73089	
Twin Oaks	74368	
Tyrone	73951	
Uncas, R. Br. Ponca City	74601	
Union	73090	
University, Sta. Enid	73701	
University, Sta. Shawnee	74801	
Utica	74763	
Utica Square, Sta. Tulsa	74152	
Valliant	74764	
Vance A F B, Br. Enid	73701	
Vanoss	74876	
Velma	73091	
Vera	74082	
Verden	73092	
Vernon	74877	
Vian	74962	
Vici	73859	
Village, Br. Oklahoma City	73120	
Vinita (1st)	74301	
Vinson	73571	
Wagoner (1st)	74467	
Wainwright	74468	
Wakita	73771	
Walters	73572	
Wanette	74878	
Wann	74083	
Wapanucka	73461	
Wardville	74576	
Warner	74469	
Warr Acres, Br. Oklahoma City	73123	
Warwick	74879	
Washington	73093	
Washita	73094	
Watonga	73772	
Watson	74963	
Watts	74964	
Waukomis	73773	
Waurika	73573	
Wayne	73095	
Waynoka	73860	
Weatherford (1st)	73096	
Webb City	74654	
Webbers Falls	74470	
Welch	74369	
Weleetka	74880	
Welling	74471	
Wellston	74881	
Welty	74882	
West Tulsa, Sta. Tulsa (see appendix)		
Westville	74965	
Wetumka	74883	
Wewoka (1st)	74884	
Wheatland	73097	
Wheeless, R. Br. Boise City	73952	
Whitefield	74472	
Whitesboro	74577	
Whittier, Sta. Tulsa	74150	
Wilburton	74578	
Will Rogers, Sta. Oklahoma City	73159	
Willis	73462	
Willow	73673	
Wilson	73463	
Wirt	73464	
Wister	74966	
Woodford	73465	
Woodville	73466	
Woodward (1st)	73801	
Wright City	74766	
Wyandotte	74370	
Wynnewood	73098	
Wynona	74084	
Yale	74085	
Yeager	74885	
Yukon (1st)	73099	

OKLAHOMA CITY   731

POST OFFICE BOXES

Box Nos.

1-1999	Downtown Sta..	01
6001-6999	Moore Branch	60
10000-10999	Midwest City	
	Br	10
11000-11999	Cimarron Sta.	11
12000-12999	39th Street	
	Sta	12
14000-14999	Britton Sta	14
15000-15999	Del City Br	15
17000-17999	Eastern Sta.	17
18000-18999	Shartel Sta	18
19000-19999	Southwest Sta	19
20000-20999	Village Br	20
24000-24999	Main Office	24
25000-25999	Main Office	25
26000-26999	Main Office	26
32000-32999	Warr Acres Br.	32
52000-53999	State Capitol	05
59900-59999	Will Rogers	
	World Airport	
	Sta.	59
60000-69999	Northwest	06
75000-75999	Farley Sta.	07
82000-82999	Stockyards Sta.	08
94000-94999	Capitol Hill	
	Sta.	09

RURAL ROUTES

1	11
2	14
3	07
4	11
5	08
6	19
7,8	09
10,11	60
12	15

STATIONS, BRANCHES AND UNITS

Britton Sta.	14
Capitol Hill Sta.	09
Cimarron Sta.	11
Del City Br.	15
Downtown Sta.	01
Eastern Sta.	17
Farley Sta.	07
Lakeside Sta.	16
Midwest City Br.	10
Moore Br.	60
Nichols Hills Br.	16
Northwest Sta.	06
Shartel Sta.	18
Shepherd Mall Sta.	07
Southwest Mall Sta.	19
State Capitol Sta.	05
Stockyards Sta.	08
Thirty Ninth Street Sta.	12
Tinker AFB Br.	45
Village Br.	20
Warr Acres Br.	23
Will Rogers Sta.	59
General Delivery	25
Postmaster.	25

APARTMENTS, HOTELS, MOTELS

Aberdeen, 125 NW 15th	03
Black, 5 N Hudson	02
Downtowner Motor, 1305	
Classen Dr	03
Hotel Oklahoma Motor Inn,	
228 W Sheridan	02
Lakeview Towers, 6001 N	
Brookline	12
Leonhardt, 1125 N Lee	03
Regency Tower 333 NW 5th	02
Roberts, 15 N Broadway	02
Sieber, 1305 N Hudson	03
Skirvin Tower Park Ave And	
Bradway	02
Skirvin Tower, Park Ave. &	
Broadway	02
Tower, 125 NW 9th	02

BUILDINGS

American National 32 N	
Robinson	02
Citizens Bank Tower, 2200	
Classen Blvd	06
City National Bank, 101 W	
Main	02
Civic Center Music Hall, 201	
N Dewey	02
Colcord, 15 N Robinson	02
County Court House 321 Park	
Ave	02
Cravens, 119 N Robinson	02
Dan Lenniger, 3545 N W	
58th	12
Doctors Medical, 5700 NW	
Grand Blvd	12
Fidelity Bank Plaza 201	
Roberts Kerr Ave	02
Fidelity National Park O N	
Harvey	02
First National, 120 N	
Robinson	02
Hales, 109 N Robinson	02
Hightower, 105 N Hudson	02
Jim Thorpe, 2101 N Lincoln	
Blvd	05
Kermac, 134 Robert S Kerr	
Ave	02
Kerr Mc Gee, 133 NW Robert	
S Ave	02
Leonhardt, 228 NW Robert S	
Kerr	02
Lincoln Plaza, 4601 N	
Lincoln Blvd	05
Livestock Exchange, 2401	
Exchange Ave	08
Local Federal, 203 Park Ave	02
May-Ex, 3020 NW	
Expressway	12
Medical Tower, 3141 NW	
Expressway	12
Municipal, 200 N Walker	02
National Foundation Life,	
3521 N W 58th	12
Oklahoma Gas & Electric,	
321 N Harvey	02
Oklahoma Mortgage, 324 N	
Robinson	02
Oklahoma Natural Gas, 407	
N Harvey	02

Old Federal, 215 NW 3rd	02
Osler Bldg 1200 N Walker	03
Pasteur Bldg 1111 N Lee	03
Petroleum Club, 120 NW	
Robert S Kerr	02
Physicians &surgeons, 1211	
N Shartel	03
Security Federal Savings, 301	
N Harvey	02
Sequoyah Memorial, 2400 N	
Lincoln	05
South Community Medical	
Center, 4200 S Douglas	09
Southwestern Bell Telephone,	
405 N Broadway	02
Southwestern Bell Telephone,	
707 N Robinson	02
U S Court & Federal, 200 NW	
4th	02
United Founders Tower, 5900	
Mosteller Dr	12
Will Rogers Memorial, 2401	
N Lincoln	05
Y M C A, 125 NW 5th	02
Y W C A, 320 Park Ave	02

GOVERNMENT OFFICES

Post Office, 320 SW 5th	29
State Capitol, 2302 Lincoln	
Blvd	05
United States Court House,	
200 NW 4th	02
United States Federal	
Building, 200 NW 4th	02

HOSPITALS

Baptist Memorial, 5800 NW	
Grand Blvd	12
Bone& Joint 605 NW 10th	03
Crippled Childrens, 800 NE	
13th	04
Deaconess, 5401 N Portland	12
Doctors General 1407 N	
Robinson	03
Hillcrest Osteopathic, 2129	
SW 59th	19
Medicenter 700 N Lee	02
Mercy, 501 NW 12th	03
Midwest City, 2825 Park	
Lawn Dr	10
Moore Municipal Hosp 1500	
SE 4th	60
Presbyterian, 300 NW 12	03
Saint Anthony, 601 NW 9th	02
South Community, 1001 SW	
44th	09
University, 800 NE 13th	04
Veterans Administration, 921	
NE 13	04

UNIVERSITIES AND COLLEGES

Midwest Christian 6600 N	
Kelley	11
Oklahoma Christian, N	
Eastern&memorial Road	11
Oklahoma City University,	
2501 N Blackwelder	06
Southwestern 4700 NW 10th	27

TULSA 741

POST OFFICE BOXES

Box Nos.

A-Y	Admiral Sta......	15
1-3500	Main Office.........	01
AA-JJ	Admiral Sta......	15
3501-4099	Utica Square Sta.........	52
4100-4999	Donaldson Sta....	04
6001-6499	Northside Sta.....	06
6501-6999	Turley Br...........	56
7001-7795	Southside Sta.....	05
9001-9799	West Tulsa Sta.........	07
15001-15899	Admiral Sta......	15
45001-45999	Southeast.........	45
50000-50999	Whittier............	50
51000-51999	Dawson............	51

RURAL ROUTES

1..........	15
2..........	35
3..........	01
4..........	45
5..........	07
6..........	27
7..........	07
8..........	07
9..........	07
10..........	15
13..........	07

STATIONS, BRANCHES AND UNITS

Admiral Sta................	08
Dawson Sta................	51
Donaldson Sta............	04
Greenwood Sta...........	20
Northside Sta.............	06
Ranch Acres Sta.........	14
Red Fork Sta..............	53
Southeast Sta.............	45
Southside Sta.............	05
Turley Br...................	56
Utica Square Sta.........	52
West Tulsa Sta............	07
Whittier Sta................	50
General Delivery..........	01
Postmaster.................	01

APARTMENTS, HOTELS, MOTELS

Adams, 403 S Cheyenne Ave...	03
Albany, 518 S Cheyenne Ave...	01
Alvin Plaza, 631 S Main.....	01
Ambassador, 7 W 14th.......	19
Baltimore Arms, 24 E 17th....	01
Barcelona 5126 So. Yale.....	35
Boulder Park, 7 W 18th......	19
Center Plaza 100-200 401 W 11th...............	01
Chalet, 3903 Riverside Drive..	05
Cheyenne Arms, 1210 S Cheyenne Ave.........	19
City Gardens 3200 Hudson....	35
Country Club, 1120 N Osage Drive.................	06
Country Estates 1900-2100 East Skelly Dr.........	05
De Ville 1100 East 48th.....	05
French Villa 4700 So.	

Harvard...................	35
Gardens Of Cortez 100 No. Garnett..............	16
Georgetown 5500 East 47th Pl.................	35
Harbor 9700-9800 East 12th..	28
Hewgley Terrace 624 So. Lawton..............	27
Mansion House 1633 So. Carson..............	19
Marquis 1700 So. Memorial...	12
Mayo, 115 W 5th..........	01
Memorial Manor 1232 So. Memorial.............	12
Metro....................	03
Mingo Circle 300 So. Mingo..	28
Mingo Valley 1301 So. 107th East Ave..............	28
Mohawk Manor 3600 No. Birmingham...........	10
Monaco 5000 So. 72nd East Ave.................	45
Morning Star Village 2100 No. Hartford...........	06
Park Place 4901 So. Braden..	35
Pioneer Plaza 901 No. Elgin..	06
Place One 3200 Riverside Dr..................	05
Plaza Del Leon 8302 East 25th Pl..............	29
Pythian Manor 6568 East 21st Pl..............	29
Riverview Park 2300 So. Maybelle..............	07
Shamrock Lodge, 340 E 11th	20
Sophian Plaza, 1500 S Frisco Ave.................	19
Southern Hills Villa 6600 So. Lewis................	36
Spanish Gardens 2434 East 51st................	05
Spanish Villa 1050 East 61st................	36
Stratford House East 4300 East 51st............	35
Stratford House 4100 East 51st................	35
Trenton Terrace, 1607 E 12th................	01
Trimble, 215 S Boulder Ave...	01
Tulsa, 9 W 9th............	19
United Methodist Square 1600 East Young.......	06
University Club Towers 1720 So. Carson...........	19
Utica Square, 1724 E 22nd Pl................	14
Vernon Manor 500 East 32nd St. No.............	06
Versailles 4800 So. Sheridan..	45
Villa Fontana 7405 East 49th...............	45
Williamsburg Plaza 6801 So. Lewis................	36
Woodstock 3200 So. Lakewood..............	35
Yorktown Village 4900 So. Yorktown.............	05

BUILDINGS

Amoco....................	03

Atlas.....................	03
Beacon...................	03
Community Ins Center......	03
County Court House, 5th And Denver...............	03
Court Arcade..............	03
Enterprise................	03
Federal...................	03
First National Bank........	03
Fourth National Bank......	19
Home Federal.............	03
Mayo.....................	03
Mid-Continent.............	03
National Bank Of Commerce..	03
National Bank Of Tulsa.....	03
Oil Capital................	03
Palace....................	03
Petroleum................	03
Philtower.................	03
Plaza.....................	03
Resource Sciences.........	19
Shell.....................	19
Thompson................	03
Thurston NatOl............	03
Tri-State.................	19
Tulsa.....................	03
World....................	03
Wright...................	03

GOVERNMENT OFFICES

Corp. Of Engrs., 224 So. Boulder..............	03
Geol. Survey, 333 W. 4th....	03
Internal Revenue, 15 W. 6th..	19
Social Security, 333 W. 4th...	03

HOSPITALS

Childrens Medical Center, 4990 S Lewis Ave.....	05
Doctors Hospital, 2323 S Harvard.............	14
Glass Nelson Clinic, 2020 S Xanthus Ave..........	04
Hillcrest Medical Center, 1120 S Utica Ave........	04
Mercy-Sisler-Bone & Joint, 30/ So Elgin Ave......	20
Moton Memorial, 603 E Pine..	06
Oklahoma Osteopathic, 744 W 9th..............	27
Saint Francis, 61st & Yale Ave.................	35
Saint Johns, 1923 S Utica Ave.................	04
Springer Clinic, 6160 S Yale Ave.................	36
Tulsa Clinic, 915 S Cincinnati Ave.........	19
Utica Square Medical Center, 1980 Utica Square....	14

UNIVERSITIES AND COLLEGES

Oral Roberts University.....	02
University Of Tulsa, 600 S College Ave...........	04

518

OREGON
(Abbreviation: OR)

Adams	97810
Adel	97620
Adrian	97901
Agness	97406
Albany (1st)	97321
Alicel	97811
Allegany	97407
Aloha, Br. Beaverton	97006
Alpine, R. Br. Monroe	97408
Alsea	97324
Alvadore	97409
Amity	97101
Antelope	97001
Applegate, R. Br. Jacksonville	97530
Arago, R. Br. Myrtle Point	97458
Arch Cape	97102
Arlington	97812
Mikkalo, R. Br.	97861
Olex, R. Br.	97812
Arock	97902
Ashland (1st)	97520
Ashwood	97711
Astoria (1st)	97103
Athena	97813
Aumsville	97325
Aurora	97002
Azalea	97410
Baker (1st)	97814
Bridgeport, R. Br.	97819
Bandon	97411
Banks	97106
Barlow	97003
Bates	97817
Bay City, R. Br. Tillamook	97107
Beatty	97621
Beaver, R. Br. Cloverdale	97108
Beavercreek	97004
Beaverton (1st)	97005
Aloha, Br.	97006
Bend (1st)	97701
Birkenfeld, R. Br. Clatskanie	97016
Blachly	97412
Black Butte Ranch, R. Br. Sisters	97759
Blodgett	97326
Blue River	97413
Bly	97622
Boardman	97818
Bonanza	97623
Bonneville	97008
Boring (1st)	97009
Bridal Veil	97010
Bridgeport, R. Br. Baker	97819
Brightwood	97011
Broadbent	97414
Brogan	97903
Brookings (1st)	97415
Brooklyn, Sta. Portland	97242
Brooks, Br. Salem	97305
Brothers	97712
Brownsmead, R. Br. Clatskanie	97012
Brownsville	97327
Burns (1st)	97720
Diamond, R. Br.	97722
Fields, R. Br.	97710
Princeton, R. Br.	97721
Burnt Woods, R. Br.	

Eddyville	97328
Butte Falls	97522
Buxton	97109
Camas Valley	97416
Camp Sherman	97730
Campus, Sta. Corvallis	97331
Canby (1st)	97013
Cannon Beach	97110
Canyon City	97820
Canyonville	97417
Carlton	97111
Cascade Locks	97014
Cascade Summit	97418
Cascadia	97329
Cave Junction	97523
Kerby, R. Br.	97531
Oregon Caves, R. Br.	97523
Cayuse	97821
Cecil, R. Br. Ione	97822
Cedar Hills, Br. Portland	97225
Central, Sta. Portland (see appendix)	
Central Point, Br. Medford	97501
Charleston, R. Br. Coos Bay	97420
Chemawa, Br. Salem	97306
Chemult	97731
Cherry Grove, R. Br. Gaston	97119
Cheshire	97419
Chiloquin	97624
Crater Lake, R. Br.	97604
Sprague River, R. Br.	97639
Christmas Valley, R. Br. Silver Lake	97638
Clackamas	97015
Clatskanie	97016
Birkenfeld, R. Br.	97016
Brownsmead, R. Br.	97012
Mist, R. Br.	97016
Westport, R. Br.	97016
Cloverdale	97112
Beaver, R. Br.	97108
Neskowin, R. Br.	97149
Coburg, R. Br. Eugene	97401
Colton	97017
Columbia City	97018
Condon	97823
Coos Bay (1st)	97420
Coquille (1st)	97423
Corbett	97019
Cornelius	97113
Corvallis (1st)	97330
Campus, Sta.	97331
Cottage Grove (1st)	97424
Saginaw, R. Br.	97472
Cove	97824
Crabtree	97335
Crane	97732
Crater Lake, R. Br. Chiloquin	97604
Crawfordsville	97336
Crescent	97733
Crescent Lake	97425
Creston, Sta. Portland	97206
Creswell	97426
Culp Creek	97427
Culver	97734
Curtin	97428
Dairy, R. Br. Klamath Falls	97625
Dale, R. Br. Ukiah	97880
Dallas (1st)	97338
Days Creek	97429
Dayton	97114
Dayville	97825

Deadwood	97430
Deer Island, R. Br. Saint Helens	97054
Depoe Bay	97341
Detroit	97342
Dexter	97431
Diamond, R. Br. Burns	97722
Diamond Lake, R. Br. Chemult	97731
Dillard	97432
Disston	97433
Donald	97020
Dorena	97434
Drain	97435
Drewsey	97904
Dufur	97021
Dundee	97115
Durkee	97905
Eagle Creek	97022
Eagle Point	97524
East Portland, Sta. Portland (see appendix)	
Eastside, R. Br. Coos Bay	97420
Echo	97826
Eddyville	97343
Burnt Woods, R. Br.	97328
Elgin	97827
Elkton	97436
Elmira	97437
Empire, Sta. Coos Bay	97420
Enterprise	97828
Estacada	97023
EUGENE (1st) (see appendix)	
Fairview	97024
Fall Creek	97438
Falls City	97344
Federal, Sta. Portland (see appendix)	
Fields, R. Br. Burns	97710
Finn Rock, R. Br. Eugene	97401
Florence (1st)	97439
Forest Grove (1st)	97116
Gales Creek, R. Br.	97117
Forest Park, Sta. Portland	97210
Fort Klamath	97626
Fort Rock	97735
Fossil	97830
Foster	97345
Four Corners, Br. Salem	97301
Fox	97831
Frenchglen	97736
Friend	97025
Gales Creek, R. Br. Forest Grove	97117
Garden Home, Br. Portland (see appendix)	
Gardiner	97441
Garibaldi	97118
Gaston	97119
Gates, R. Br. Mill City	97346
Gaylord, R. Br. Myrtle Point	97458
Gearhart, Br. Seaside	97138
Gervais	97026
Gilchrist	97737
Gladstone (1st)	97027
Glendale	97442
Gleneden Beach, R. Br. Lincoln City	97388
Glenwood	97120
Glide	97443
Goble, R. Br. Rainier	97048
Gold Beach	97444
Gold Hill	97525

Goshen, R. Br. Eugene...........97401
Government Camp...............97028
Grand Ronde....................97347
Grants Pass (1st)................97526
　Wilderville, R. Br..............97543
Grass Valley.....................97029
Greenleaf........................97445
Gresham (1st)...................97030
Haines...........................97833
Halfway..........................97834
Halsey...........................97348
Hammond.........................97121
Harbor, R. Br. Brookings.........97415
Harper...........................979u6
Harrisburg.......................97446
Hebo.............................97122
Helix............................97835
Heppner..........................97836
　Lexington, R. Br...............97839
Hereford.........................97837
Hermiston (1st)..................97838
High School, Br. Saint
　Helens..........................97051
Highway, Sta. Woodburn...........97071
Hillsboro (1st)..................97123
　Manning, R. Br.................97125
Hines............................97738
Holladay Park, Sta. Portland
　(see appendix)
Hollywood, Sta. Salem............97303
Hood River (1st).................97031
Horton, R. Br. Junction City.....97448
Hubbard..........................97032
Huntington.......................97907
Idanha...........................97350
Idleyld Park.....................97447
Imbler...........................97841
Imnaha...........................97842
Independence.....................97351
Ione.............................97843
　Cecil, R. Br...................97822
Ironside.........................97908
Ir igon..........................97844
Island City, R. Br. La
　Grande..........................97851
Jacksonville.....................97530
Jamieson.........................97909
Jasper, R. Br. Eugene............97401
Jefferson........................97352
　Marion, R. Br..................97359
Jennings Lodge, R. Br.
　Portland........................97267
John Day.........................97845
Jordan Valley....................97910
Joseph...........................97846
Junction City (1st)..............97448
Juntura..........................97911
Keating..........................97847
Keizer, Br. Salem................97303
Keno.............................97627
Kent.............................97033
Kenton, Sta. Portland............97217
Kerby, R. Br. Cave Junction......97531
Kimberly.........................97848
Kings Valley.....................97353
Kingsley Field, Br. Klamath
　Falls...........................97601
Kingwood, Sta. Salem.............97304
Kinzua...........................97849
Klamath Falls (1st)..............97601
　Dairy, R. Br...................97625
　Kingsley Field, Br............97601

Lake Of The Woods, R.
　Br..............................97603
Oretech, Br......................97601
La Grande (1st)..................97850
　Island City, R. Br............97851
La Pine..........................97739
Lacomb, R. Br. Lebanon...........97354
Lafayette........................97127
Lake Grove, Sta. Lake
　Oswego..........................97034
Lake Of The Woods, R. Br.
　Klamath Falls..................97603
Lake Oswego (1st)................97034
Lakeside.........................97449
Lakeview (1st)...................97630
Langlois.........................57450
Lawen............................97740
Leaburg, R. Br. Eugene...........97401
Lebanon (1st)....................97355
　Lacomb, R. Br.................97354
Lees Camp, R. Br.
　Tillamook.......................97142
Lents, Sta. Portland (see
　appendix)
Lexington, R. Br. Heppner........97839
Lincoln City (1st)...............97367
　Gleneden Beach, R. Br.........97388
　Taft, Sta......................97367
Linnton, Sta. Portland...........97231
Logsden..........................97357
Long Creek.......................97856
Lorane...........................97451
Lostine..........................97857
Lowell...........................97452
Lyons............................97358
Madras (1st).....................97741
　Metolius, R. Br...............97742
Malin............................97632
Manhattan Beach, R. Br.
　Rockaway........................97136
Manning, R. Br. Hillsboro........97125
Manzanita........................97130
Mapleton.........................97453
Maplewood, Br. Portland
　(see appendix)
Marcola..........................97454
Marion, R. Br. Jefferson.........97359
Market, Br. Coos Bay.............97420
Marquam, R. Br. Mount
　Angel...........................97362
Maryhurst........................97036
Maupin...........................97037
　South Junction, R. Br.........97074
Mayville, R. Br. Fossil..........97830
Mc Kenzie Bridge, R. Br.
　Eugene..........................97401
Mc Minnville (1st)...............97128
Mc Nary..........................97858
Meacham, R. Br. Pendleton........97859
Medford (1st)....................97501
Medical Springs..................97860
Mehama, R. Br. Stayton...........97384
Merlin...........................97532
Merrill..........................97633
Metolius, R. Br. Madras..........97742
Midland..........................97634
Midway, Br. Portland (see
　appendix)
Mikkalo, R. Br. Arlington........97861
Mill City........................97360
　Gates, R. Br..................97346
Milo, R. Br. Canyonville.........97455

Milton-Freewater (1st)...........97862
　Umapine, R. Br................97881
Milwaukie, Br. Portland..........97222
Mist, R. Br. Clatskanie..........97016
Mitchell.........................97750
Molalla..........................97038
Monitor, R. Br. Woodburn.........97072
Monmouth (1st)...................97361
Monroe...........................97456
　Alpine, R. Br.................97408
Monument.........................97864
Moro.............................97039
Mosier...........................97040
Mount Angel......................97362
Mount Hood.......................97041
Mount Vernon.....................97865
Mulino...........................97042
Multnomah, Sta. Portland
　(see appendix)
Murphy...........................97533
Myrtle Creek.....................97457
Myrtle Point.....................97458
Nashville, R. Br. Philomath......97370
Nehalem..........................97131
Neotsu...........................97364
Neskowin, R. Br. Cloverdale......97149
Netarts, R. Br. Tillamook........97143
New Pine Creek...................97635
Newberg (1st)....................97132
Newport (1st)....................97365
　Otter Rock, R. Br.............97369
　Southbeach, R. Br.............97366
North Bend (1st).................97459
North Plains.....................97133
North Portland...................97043
North Powder.....................97867
North Roseburg, Br.
　Roseburg........................97470
Norway...........................97460
Noti.............................97461
Nyssa............................97913
O'Brien..........................97534
Oak Grove, Br. Portland..........97268
Oakland..........................97462
Oakridge.........................97463
Oceanside........................97134
Odell............................97044
Olex, R. Br. Arlington...........97812
Ontario (1st)....................97914
Ophir............................97464
Oregon Caves, R. Br. Cave
　Junction........................97523
Oregon City (1st)................97045
Oretech, Br. Klamath Falls.......97601
Otis.............................97368
　Rose Lodge, R. Br.............97372
Otter Rock, R. Br. Newport.......97369
Oxbow............................97840
Pacific City.....................97135
Paisley..........................97636
Parkdale.........................97047
Parkrose, Br. Portland (see
　appendix)
Paulina..........................97751
Pendleton (1st)..................97801
　Meacham, R. Br................97859
Perrydale, R. Br. Amity..........97101
Philomath........................97370
Phoenix..........................97535
Piedmont, Sta. Portland..........97211
Pilot Rock.......................97868
Pioneer, Sta. Portland (see
　appendix)

Pistol River, R. Br. Gold
  Beach..97444
Pleasant Hill, R. Br. Eugene...97401
Plush...97637
Port Orford..................................97465
PORTLAND (1st) (see
  appendix)
Portland Zoo Railway, Sta.
  Portland (see appendix)
Post...97752
Powell Butte.................................97753
Powers..97466
Prairie City.................................97869
Princeton, R. Br. Burns.............97721
Prineville (1st)...........................97754
Prospect.......................................97536
Rainier..97048
Raleigh Hills, Br. Portland.......97225
Redmond (1st)............................97756
Reedsport (1st)..........................97467
Remote..97468
Rhododendron..............................97049
  Zigzag, R. Br.............................97073
Richland..97870
Rickreall.......................................97371
Riddle...97469
Riley...97758
Ritter..97872
Riverside.......................................97917
Riverton, R. Br. Coquille...........97423
Rockaway.......................................97136
Rogue River..................................97537
Rose City Park, Sta.
  Portland (see appendix)
Rose Lodge, R. Br. Otis............97372
Roseburg (1st)............................97470
Rufus..97050
Saginaw, R. Br. Cottage
  Grove..97472
Saint Benedict..............................97373
Saint Helens (1st).......................97051
  Deer Island, R. Br...................97054
  High School, Br.........................97051
  Warren, R. Br............................97053
Saint Johns, Sta. Portland
  (see appendix)
Saint Paul....................................97137
SALEM (1st) (see appendix)
Sandy..97055
Scappoose.....................................97056
Scio..97374
Scotts Mills..................................97375
Scottsburg....................................97473
Seal Rock, R. Br. Waldport......97376
Seaside (1st)...............................97138
Selfwood Moreland, Sta.
  Portland...................................97202
Selma..97538
Seneca..97873
Shady Cove...................................97539
Shaniko..97057
Shedd..97377
Sheridan.......................................97378
Sherwood......................................97140
Siletz..97380
Silver Lake...................................97638
Silverton (1st)............................97381
Sisters..97759
Sixes..97476
South Junction, R. Br.
  Maupin......................................97074
Southbeach, R. Br. Newport.....97366
Southside, Sta. Eugene.............97405

Sprague River, R. Br.
  Chiloquin.................................97639
Spray..97874
Springfield (1st)........................97477
Stanfield.......................................97875
Stayton (1st)..............................97383
  Mehama, R. Br.........................97384
Sublimity.......................................97385
Summer Lake................................97640
Summerville..................................97876
Sumpter..97877
Sunny Valley, R Br. Wolf
  Creek.......................................97478
Sunriver, R. Br. Bend................97701
Sutherlin......................................97479
Sweet Home (1st).......................97386
Swisshome....................................97480
Taft, Sta. Lincoln City..............97367
Talent...97540
Tangent...97389
Telocaset......................................97878
Tenmile...97481
Terrebonne...................................97760
The Dalles (1st).........................97058
Thurston.......................................97482
Tidewater......................................97390
Tigard, Br. Portland (see
  appendix)
Tillamook (1st)...........................97141
  Bay City, R. Br........................97107
  Lees Camp, R. Br.....................97142
  Netarts, R. Br..........................97143
Tiller..97484
Timber..97144
Toledo..97391
Tolovana Park..............................97145
Trail...97541
Troutdale......................................97060
Tualatin..97062
Turner...97392
Twelve Mile, R. Br. Gresham...97030
Tygh Valley..................................97063
Ukiah..97880
Umapine, R. Br.
  Milton-Freewater......................97881
Umatilla..97882
Umpqua...97486
Union..97883
Unity...97884
University, Sta. Eugene.............97403
University Park, Sta.
  Portland (see appendix)
Vale..97918
Valsetz...97393
Veneta..97487
Vernonia.......................................97064
Vida..97488
Vista, Sta. Salem.......................97302
Waldport......................................97394
  Seal Rock, R. Br......................97376
Wallowa..97485
Walterville....................................97489
Walton...97490
Wamic, R. Br. Tygh Valley.......97063
Warm Springs...............................97761
Warren, R. Br. Saint Helens....97053
Warrenton.....................................97146
Wasco...97065
Waterloo.......................................97395
Wedderburn..................................97491
Wemme..97067

West Linn (1st)...........................97068
West Main, Br. Medford.............97501
West Oak, R. Sta. Oakridge.....97463
West Side, Sta. Eugene.............97402
West Slope, Br. Portland
  (see appendix)
West Stayton, R. Br.
  Aumsville................................97325
Westfall..97920
Westfir..97492
Westlake..97493
Weston..97886
Westport, R. Br. Clatskanie....97016
Wheeler...97147
White City, Br. Medford............97501
Wilbur...97494
Wilderville, R. Br. Grants
  Pass..97543
Willamette, Sta. West Linn......97068
Willamina.....................................97396
Williams..97544
Wilsonville...................................97070
Winchester....................................97495
Winchester Bay, R. Br.
  Reedsport................................97467
Winston...97496
Wolf Creek....................................97497
  Sunny Valley, R. Br...............97478
Woodburn (1st)...........................97071
  Highway, Sta...........................97071
  Monitor, R. Br.........................97072
Yachats...97498
Yamhill..97148
Yoncalla..97499
Zigzag, R. Br.
  Rhododendron..........................97073

EUGENE   974

POST OFFICE BOXES

Box Nos.

1-1999	Main Office	01
2000-2999	Westside Sta	02
3000-3999	University Sta	03
5000-5999	Southside	05
10000-10999	Main Office	01

RURAL ROUTES

1		02
2		01
3,4		05
5,6		02
7		05
8		01

STATIONS, BRANCHES AND UNITS

Coburg Rural Br	01
Finn Rock Rural Br	01
Goshen Rural Br	01
Jasper Rural Br	01
Leaburg Rural Br	01
Mc Kenzie Bridge Rural Br	01
Pleasant Hill Rural Br	01
Southside Sta	05
University Sta	03
West Side Sta	02
General Delivery	01
Postmaster	01

PORTLAND   972

POST OFFICE BOXES

Box Nos.

1-1799	Federal Sta	07
G-1-G-159	Garden Home Br	23
M-1-M-65	Maplewood Br	19
2700-4499	Main Office	08
6100-6299	Linnton Sta	31
8000-8599	Federal Sta	07
8700-9000	Main Office	08
02001-02999	Sellwood-Moreland	02
03001-03999	Saint Johns	03
06001-06999	Creston	06
10001-10999	Forest Park Sta	10
11001-11999	Piedmont Sta	11
12001-12999	Holladay Park Sta	12
13001-13999	Rose City Park	13
14000-14999	East Portland	14
16001-16999	Midway	16
17001-17999	Kenton Sta	17
19001-19999	Multnomah	19
20001-20999	Parkrose	20
22001-22999	Milwaukie Br	22
23001-23999	Tigard Br	23
25001-25999	West Slope Br	25
42001-42999	Brooklyn Sta	42
66001-66999	Lents Sta	66
67001-67999	Jennings Lodge Br	67

68001-68999	Oak Grove Br	68

RURAL ROUTES

1,2		31
3		23

STATIONS, BRANCHES AND UNITS

Brooklyn Sta	42
Cedar Hills Br	25
Central Sta	04
Creston Br	06
East Portland Sta	14
Federal Sta	05
Forest Park Sta	10
Garden Home Br	23
Holladay Park Sta	12
Jennings Lodge Br	67
Kenton Sta	17
Lents Sta	66
Linnton Sta	31
Maplewood Br	19
Midway Br	17
Milwaukie Br	22
Multnomah Sta	19
Oak Grove Br	68
Parkrose Br	20
Piedmont Sta	11
Pioneer Sta	04
Portland Zoo Railway Sta	21
Raleigh Hills Br	25
Rose City Park Sta	13
Saint Johns Sta	03
Sellwood Moreland Sta	02
Tigard Br	23
University Park Sta	03
West Slope Br	25
General Delivery	08
Postmaster	08

APARTMENTS, HOTELS, MOTELS

Benson	05
Congress	04
Cosmopolitan Portland Motor	32
Envoy	05
Fontaine	32
Heathman	05
Highlander Inn	07
Holiday Inn Of America	27
Hollywood Towne House	13
Hoyt	09
Imperial	05
Ione Plaza	01
King Tower	05
Mallory	05
Northwest Towers	09
Ongford	07
Panorama	05
Park Haviland	05
Park Plaza	01
Park Vista	07
Portland Hilton	05
Portland Towers	05
Riverside West Motor	04
Roosevelt	05
Sheraton Motor Inn	08
Terwilliger Plaza	01
Vista Saint Clair	05
Willamette View Manor	22

Attorneys, 1123 SW Yamhill	
Blue Cross 100 SW Market	01
Board Of Trade, 310 SW 4 Ave	04
Boise Cascade 1600 SW 4 Ave	01
Bullier, 420 SW Washington	04
California Towers 707 SW Washington	05
Cascade Plaza 2828 SW Corbett	01
Commerce, 225 SW Broadway	05
Crown Plaza, 1520 SW 1 Ave	01
Equitable, 1300 SW 6 Ave	01
Executive, 811 SW 6 Ave	04
Failing, 618 SW 5 Ave	04
First National Bank, 1300 SW 5 Ave	01
Franklin, 333 SW 5 Ave	04
Georgia Pacific 900 SW 5 Ave	04
Henry, 309 SW 4 Ave	04
Jackson Tower, 808 SW Broadway	05
Labor Center 201 SW Arthur	01
Lawyers, 521 SW Clay	05
Lewis, 333 SW Oak	04
Lincoln, 208 SW 5 Ave	04
Lloyd Center	32
Lloyd, 700 NE Multnomah	32
Mead, 421 SW 5 Ave	04
Mohawk, 222 SW Morrison	04
Morgan, 720 SW Washington	05
Oregon Bank, 319 SW Washington	04
Oregonian, 1320 SW Broadway	01
Pacific, 520 SW Yamhill	04
Pittock Block, 921 SW Washington	05
Portland, 425 SW Washington	04
Professional, 1033 SW Yamhill	05
Public Service, 920 SW 6 Ave	04
Riviera Plaza 1618 SW 1 Ave	01
Standard Plaza, 1100 SW 6 Ave	04
State Office, 1400 SW 5 Ave	01
Terminal Sales, 1220 SW Morrison	05
United States National Bank, 309 SW 6th Ave	04
Weatherly, 516 SE Morrison	14
Willamette, 534 SW 3 Ave	04
Yeon, 522 SW 5 Ave	04

GOVERNMENT OFFICES

United States Court House, 620 SW Main	05

HOSPITALS

Bess Kaiser, 5055 N Greeley Ave	17
City Of Roses Memorial, 1329 SE Harney	02

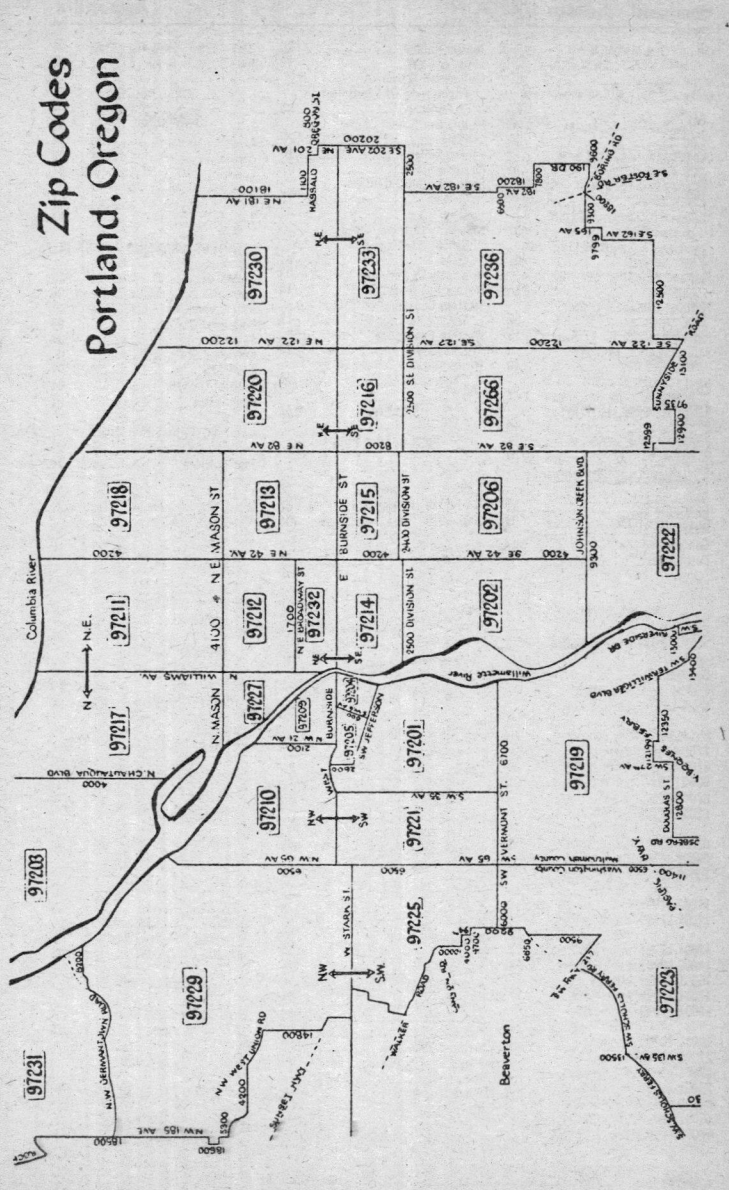

Zip Codes
Portland, Oregon

Doernbecher Memorial For Children, 3181 SW Sam Jackson Pk 61
Emanuel, 2801 N Gantenbein Ave 27
Fairlawn, 10404 SE Foster Rd 66
Good Samaritan, 1015 N W 22 Ave 10
Holladay Park, 220 N E Multnomah 32
Multnomah County, 3171 SW Jackson Pk Rd .... 0.
Physicians & Surgeons, 1927 NW Lovejoy 09
Portland Adventist, 6040 SE Belmont 15
Portland Osteopathic, 2900 SE Steele 02
Providence, 700 NE 47 Ave 13
Saint Vincents, 244/ NW Westover Rd 10
United States Veterans, SW U S Vets Hospital Rd 67
Wilcox Memorial, 1022 NW 22 Ave 10
Woodland Park, 10300 NE Hancock 20

UNIVERSITIES AND COLLEGES

Concordia 11
Conquerors Bible 03

Judson Baptist 20
Lewis & Clark 19
Multnomah School Of Engineering Of The Univer Of Portland 03
Multnomah School Of The Fible 20
Pacific Bible 16
Portland State 07
Portland State Extension Division 01
Reed 02
University Of Oregon Medical School, 3181 SW Sam Jackson 61
University Of Portland 03
Warner Pacific Bible 15
Western Conservative Baptist Theological 15
Western Evangelical Seminary 22
Western States College Of Chiropractic 06

SALEM   973

POST OFFICE BOXES

Box Nos.
1-2999   Salem 08
3001-3999   Vista Sta 02
5001-5999   Kingwood Sta ... 04

7001-7999   Hollywood Sta .. 03
9001-9999   Brooks Br 05

RURAL ROUTES

1 04
2 03
3,4 02
5 01
6 05
8 01
9 03

STATIONS, BRANCHES AND UNITS

Brooks Br 05
Chemawa Br 06
Four Corners Br 01
Hollywood Sta 03
Keizer Br 03
Kingwood Sta 04
Vista Sta 02
General Delivery 01
Postmaster 01

GOVERNMENT OFFICES

State Offices 16

PENNSYLVANIA
(Abbreviation: PA)

Aaronsburg................................16820
Abbottstown..............................17301
Abington (1st)...........................19001
Ackermanville, R. Br.
    Bangor..................................18010
Acme...15610
Acosta.......................................15520
Adah...15410
Adamsburg...............................15611
Adamstown...............................19501
Adamsville................................16110
Addison.....................................15411
Adrian.......................................16210
Airville......................................17302
Aitch..16610
Akron..17501
Aladdin, Br. Schenley.................15682
Alba..16910
Albion.......................................16401
Albrightsville.............................18210
Alburtis....................................18011
Aldan, Br. Clifton Heights...........19018
Alden, Br. Nanticoke..................18634
Aldenville, R. Br. Forest City.......18401
Aleppo......................................15310
Alexandria................................16611
Aliquippa (1st)..........................15001
Allegheny, Sta. Pittsburgh..........15212
Allen, R. Br. Boiling Springs........17001
Allenport...................................15412
Allensville.................................17002
ALLENTOWN (1st) (see
    appendix)
Allenwood.................................17810
Allison.......................................15413
Allison Park (1st)........................15101
Alport.......................................16821
ALTOONA (1st) (see
    appendix)
Alum Bank................................15521
Alverda.....................................15710
Alverton....................................15612
Amaranth, R. Br.
    Warfordsburg.......................17267
Amberson.................................17210
Ambler (1st).............................19002
Ambridge (1st)..........................15003
Amity..15311
Analomink.................................18320
Andalusia, Sta. Cornwells
    Heights.................................19020
Andreas....................................18211
Anita...15711
Annville (1st)............................17003
Ansonville.................................16612
Antes Fort.................................17720
Apollo (1st)...............................15613
Aquashicola..............................18012
Arcadia.....................................15712
Archbald (1st)...........................18403
Arcola......................................19420
Ardara.......................................15615
Ardmore (1st)...........................19003
Ardsley, Sta. Glenside................19038
Arendtsville...............................17303
Aristes.......................................17920
Armagh.....................................15920
Armbrust...................................15616
Arnold, Br. New Kensington.......15068

Arnot...16911
Arona..15617
Arsenal, Sta. Pittsburgh.............15201
Artemas....................................17211
Ashfield.....................................18212
Ashland (1st).............................17921
Ashley, Br. Wilkes-Barre.............18706
Ashville.....................................16613
    Coupon, R. Br. 16629
Aspers......................................17304
Aspinwall, Br. Pittsburgh............15215
Aston, Br. Chester.....................19014
Atglen.......................................19310
Athens (1st)..............................18810
Athol...19502
Atlantic.....................................16111
Atlas, Br. Mount Carmel............17851
Atlasburg...................................15004
Auburn......................................17922
Audubon, Br. Norristown............19407
Aultman.....................................15713
Austin..16720
    Keating Summit, R. Br. 16737
Avalon, Br. Pittsburgh................15202
Avella...15312
Avis...17721
Avoca, Br. Pittston.....................18641
Avon, Br. Lebanon.....................17042
Avondale....................................19311
Avonmore..................................15618
Baden (1st)...............................15005
Bainbridge.................................17502
Bair...17305
Bairdford....................................15006
Bakers Summit...........................16614
Bakerstown................................15007
Bala-Cynwyd (1st).....................19004
Bally..19503
Bangor (1st)..............................18013
    Ackermanville, R. Br. 18010
    East Bangor, R. Br. 18013
    Roseto, Br. 18013
Banning.....................................15414
Barking......................................15008
Barnesboro................................15714
Barnesville.................................18214
Barree.......................................16615
Bart...17503
Barto...19504
Bartonsville................................18321
Bath..18014
Bausman....................................17504
Beach Haven..............................18601
Beach Lake................................18405
Beallsville..................................15313
Bear Creek, R. Br.
    Wilkes-Barre.........................18602
Bear Lake..................................16402
Beaver (1st)..............................15009
Beaver Brook, R. Br.
    Hazleton...............................18215
Beaver Falls (1st).......................15010
Beaver Meadows.......................18216
Beaver Springs...........................17812
Beaverdale.................................15921
Beavertown................................17813
Beccaria....................................16616
Bechtelsville...............................19505
Bedford (1st).............................15522
Bedminster................................18910
Beech Creek...............................16822
    Orviston, R. Br. 16864

Bell Acres, R. Br. Sewickley........15143
Belle Vernon (1st)......................15012
Bellefonte (1st)..........................16823
    Pleasant Gap, Br. 16823
    Wingate, R. Br. 16880
Belleville....................................17004
Bellevue, Br. Pittsburgh..............15202
Bellwood...................................16617
Belsano......................................15922
Bendersville................................17306
Benezett.....................................15821
Benson East, Br. Jenkintown.......19046
Bentleyville................................15314
Benton.......................................17814
Berkeley Hills, Br.
    Pittsburgh.............................15237
Berlin...15530
Bernville....................................19506
Berrysburg..................................17005
Berwick (1st).............................18603
Berwyn (1st)..............................19312
Bessemer...................................16112
Bethel..19507
Bethel Park (1st)........................15102
BETHLEHEM (1st) (see
    appendix)
Bethton, Br. Souderton..............18964
Beulah, Br. Turtle Creek.............15145
Beyer...16211
Big Cove Tannery, R. Br.
    Needmore.............................17212
Big Run......................................15715
Bigler...16825
Biglerville...................................17307
Birchrunville...............................19421
Bird In Hand...............................17505
Birdsboro (1st)..........................19508
Black Lick..................................15716
Blain..17006
Blair, Sta. Clairton....................15025
Blairs Mills.................................17213
Blairsville (1st)...........................15717
Blakely, Br. Olyphant.................18447
Blakeslee...................................18610
Blanchard..................................16826
Blandburg..................................16619
Blandon.....................................19510
Blawnox, Br. Pittsburgh.............15238
Bloomfield, Sta. Pittsburgh.........15224
Blooming Glen............................18911
Bloomsburg (1st).......................17815
    Espy, Br. 17815
    Light Street, R. Br. 17839
Blossburg..................................16912
Blue Ball....................................17506
Blue Bell (1st)...........................19422
Blue Ridge Summit (1st).............17214
Boalsburg...................................16827
Bobtown....................................15315
Bodines, R. Br. Trout Run...........17722
Boiling Springs...........................17007
    Allen, R. Br. 17001
Bolivar.......................................15923
Bon Aire, Br. Butler....................16001
Boothwyn, Br. Marcus Hook.......19061
Boston, Br. Mc Keesport............15135
Boswell......................................15531
    Jenners, R. Br. 15546
Boulevard, Sta. Philadelphia.......19149
Bovard.......................................15619
Bowers.......................................19511
Bowmansdale.............................17008

Bowmanstown 18030
Bowmansville 17507
Boyds Mills 18406
Boyers 16020
Boyertown (1st) 19512
Boynton 15532
Brackenridge (1st) 15014
Brackney 18812
Braddock (1st) 15104
Bradenville 15620
Bradford (1st) 16701
Bradfordwoods 15015
Braeburn, R. Br. New
  Kensington 15016
Branch Dale 17923
Branchton 16021
Brandamore 19316
Brandy Camp 15822
Brave 15316
Breezewood 15533
Breinigsville 18031
Brentwood, Br. Pittsburgh 15227
Bridesburg, Sta.
  Philadelphia 19137
Bridgeport, Br. Norristown 19405
Bridgeville (1st) 15017
Brier Hill 15415
Brisbin 16620
Bristol (1st) 19007
Broad Street, Sta. Hazleton 18201
Broad Top 16621
Brockport 15823
Brockton 17925
Brockway (1st) 15824
Brodbecks 17308
Brodheadsville 18322
Brogue 17309
Brookhaven, Br. Chester 19015
Brookline, Sta. Pittsburgh 15226
Brooklyn 18813
Brookville (1st) 15825
Broomall (1st) 19008
Broughton, Br. Pittsburgh 15236
Brownfield 15416
Brownstown 17508
Brownsville (1st) 15417
Bruin 16022
Brunnerville, R. Br. Lititz 17543
Brush Valley 15720
Bryn Athyn 19009
Bryn Mawr (1st) 19010
Buck Hill Falls 18323
Buck Run 17926
Buckingham 18912
Buena Vista 15018
Buffalo Mills 15534
Buhl, Sta. Sharon 16146
Bulger 15019
Bunola 15020
Burgettstown (1st) 15021
  Florence, R. Br. 15040
  Paris, R. Br. 15021
Burlington 18814
Burnham 17009
Burnside 15721
Burnt Cabins 17215
Burtville 16721
Bushkill
  Tamiment, R. Br. 18371
  Unity House, R. Br. 18373
Bustleton, Sta. Philadelphia
  (see appendix)
Butler (1st) 16001

Butztown, Br. Bethlehem 18017
Byrnedale 15827
Cabot 16023
Cadogan 16212
Cairnbrook 15924
California (1st) 15419
Callensburg 16213
Callery 16024
Calumet 15621
Calvin 16622
Cambra 18611
Cambridge Springs 16403
Cammal. 17723
Camp Curtin, Sta.
  Harrisburg 17110
Camp Hill (1st) 17011
Campbelltown 17010
Camptown 18815
Canadensis 18325
Canonsburg (1st) 15317
Canton (1st) 17724
  Ellenton, R. Br. 17732
Carbondale (1st) 18407
Cardale 15420
Carlisle (1st) 17013
Carlisle Barracks, MOU.
  Carlisle 17013
Carlton 16311
Carmichaels 15320
Carnegie (1st) 15106
Carrolltown 15722
Carson, Sta. Pittsburgh 15203
Carversville 18913
Cascade, Br. New Castle 16101
Cashtown 17310
Cassandra 15925
Cassville 16623
Castanea 17726
Caste Village, Br.
  Pittsburgh 15236
Castle Shannon, Br.
  Pittsburgh 15234
Castor, Sta. Philadelphia 19149
Catasauqua (1st) 18032
Catawissa 17820
Cecil 15321
Cedar Run, R. Br. Jersey
  Shore 17727
Cedarhurst, Br. Pittsburgh 15243
Cedars 19423
Cementon, Sta. Whitehall 18052
Center Moreland, R. Br.
  Tunkhannock 18657
Center Square, R. Sta. Blue
  Bell 19422
Center Valley 18034
Centerport 19516
Centerville 16404
Central, Sta. Washington 15301
Central, Sta. Mc Keesport 15132
Central City 15926
Central Highlands, Br.
  Elizabeth 15037
Centralia 17927
Centre Hall 16828
Chadds Ford 19317
Chalfont (1st) 18914
Chalkhill 15421
Chambers Hill, Br.
  Harrisburg 17111
Chambersburg (1st) 17201
Chambersville 15723
Champion 15622

Chandlers Valley 16312
Chapman Lake, R. Br.
  Jermyn 18433
Charleroi (1st) 15022
Chatham 19318
Cheltenham (1st) 19012
Cherry Tree 15724
Cherryville 18035
Chest Springs 16624
CHESTER (1st) (see
  appendix)
Chester Heights 19017
Chester Springs 19425
Chestnut Hill, Sta.
  Philadelphia 19118
Chestnut Ridge 15422
Cheswick (1st) 15024
Cheyney 19319
Chicora 16025
  Kaylor, R. Br. 16042
Childs, Br. Carbondale 18407
Chinchilla 18410
Christiana 17509
Churchtown 17510
Churchville, Br.
  Southampton 18966
Clairton (1st) 15025
Clarence 16829
Clarendon 16313
Claridge 15623
Clarington 15828
Clarion (1st) 16214
Clark 16113
Clarks Mills 16114
Clarks Summit (1st) 18411
Clarksburg 15725
Clarksville 15322
Claysburg 16625
Claysville 15323
Clearfield (1st) 16830
Clearville 15535
Cleona, Br. Lebanon 17042
Clermont, R. Br. Mount
  Jewett 16722
Clifford 18413
Clifton Heights (1st) 19018
Climax 16216
Clinton 15026
Clintonville 16372
Clune 15727
Clymer 15728
Coal Center 15423
Coaldale 18218
Coalport 16627
Coatesville (1st) 19320
Coburn 16832
Cochranton (1st) 16314
Cochranville 19330
Cocolamus 17014
Codorus 17311
Cogan Station 17728
Cokeburg 15324
Colebrook 17015
College, Sta. Easton 18042
College Misericordia, Br.
  Dallas 18612
Collegeville (1st) 19426
Collingdale, Br. Darby 19023
Colmar (1st) 18915
Colonial Park, Br.
  Harrisburg 17109
Columbia (1st) 17512
Columbia Cross Roads 16914

Columbus....16405
Colver....15927
Commerce, Sta. Philadelphia....19108
Commodore....15729
Concord....17217
Concordville (1st)....19331
Conemaugh, Br. Johnstown....15909
Conestoga....17516
Confluence....15424
·Conneaut Lake....16316
Conneaut Lake Park, Br. Conneaut Lake....16316
Conneautville....16406
Connellsville (1st)....15425
Connoquenessing....16027
Conshohocken (1st)....19428
Continental, Sta. Philadelphia....19106
Conway....15027
Conyngham....18219
Cooksburg, R. Br. Punxsutawney....15730
Coopersburg....18036
Cooperstown....16317
Coplay....18037
Coral....15731
Coraopolis (1st)....15108
Corliss, Sta. Pittsburgh....15204
Cornwall....17016
Quentin, R. Br....17083
Cornwells Heights (1st)....19020
Corry (1st)....16407
Corsica....15829
Coryville, R. Br. Eldred....16723
Coudersport (1st)....16915
Coulters....15028
Coupon, R. Br. Ashville....16629
Courtney....15029
Covington....16917
Cowanesque....16918
Cowansville....16218
Crabtree....15624
Crafton, Br. Pittsburgh....15205
Craigsville....16219
Craley....17312
Cramer, R. Br. Seward....15954
Cranberry....16319
Cranesville....16410
Creamery....19430
Creekside....15732
Creighton....15030
Cresco....18326
Cresson (1st)....16630
Cressona....17929
Crooked Creek....16919
Crosby....16724
Cross Fork....17729
Crown....16220
Croydon, Br. Cornwells Heights....19020
Crucible....15325
Crum Lynne....19022
Crystal Spring....15536
Cuddy....15031
Cumbola....17930
Curllsville....16221
Curryville....16631
Curtisville....15032
Curwensville....16833
Custer City....16725
Cyclone....16726

Ormsby, R. Br....16741
Dagus Mines....15831
Daisytown....15427
Dallas (1st)....18612
Dallastown (1st)....17313
Dalmatia....17017
Dalton....18414
Damascus....18415
Galilee, R. Br....18423
Danboro....18916
Danielsville....18038
Danville (1st)....17821
Darby (1st)....19023
Darling, R. Br. Media....19063
Darlington....16115
Darragh....15625
Dauberville, R. Br. Leesport....19517
Dauphin....17018
Davidsville....15928
Davistown....15326
Dawson....15428
Dayton....16222
De Lancey....15733
De Young....16728
Deep Valley, R. Br. New Freeport....15352
Defiance....16633
Delano....18220
Delaware Water Gap (1st)....18327
Delmont....15626
Delta....17314
Denbo....15429
Denver (1st)....17517
Derrick City....16727
Derry....15627
Devault....19432
Devon (1st)....19333
Dewart....17730
Dickerson Run....15430
Dickinson....17218
Dickson City, Br. Scranton....18519
Dilliner....15327
Dillsburg (1st)....17019
Dilltown....15929
Dimock....18816
Dingmans Ferry....18328
Distant....16223
Dixonville....15734
Donaldson, Br. Tremont....17981
Donegal....15628
Donora (1st)....15033
Dora....15735
Dormont, Br. Pittsburgh....15216
Dornsife....17823
Douglassville....19518
Dover (1st)....17315
Downingtown (1st)....19335
Downtown, Sta. Uniontown....15401
Doylesburg, R. Br. Dry Run....17219
Doylestown (1st)....18901
Lumberville, R. Br....18933
New Britain, Br....18901
Dravosburg....15034
Dresher, Br. Fort Washington....19025
Drexel Hill (1st)....19026
Drifting....16834
Drifton....18221
Driftwood....15832
Drumore....17518
Drums....18222
Dry Run....17220
Doylesburg, R. Br....17219

Du Bois (1st)....15801
Dublin....18917
Dudley....16634
Duke Center....16729
Dunbar....15431
Duncannon....17020
Duncansville (1st)....16635
Dunlevy....15432
Dunlo....15930
Dunmore, Br. Scranton....18512
Dupont, Br. Pittston....18641
Duquesne (1st)....15110
Durham....18039
Duryea, Br. Pittston....18642
Dushore....18614
Dysart....16636
Eagles Mere....17731
Eagles Mere Park, R. Sta. Eagles Mere....17731
Eagleville, Br. Norristown....19408
Earlington....18918
Earlville....19519
East Bangor, R. Br. Bangor....18013
East Berlin....17316
East Brady....16028
East Butler....16029
East Earl....17519
East Falls, Sta. Philadelphia....19129
East Freedom....16637
East Germantown, Sta. Philadelphia....19138
East Greenville....18041
East Hickory....16321
East Hills, Br. Johnstown....15904
East Liberty, Sta. Pittsburgh....15206
East Mc Keesport (1st)....15035
East Millsboro....15433
East Petersburg (1st)....17520
East Pittsburgh (1st)....15112
East Prospect....17317
East Side, Sta. Nanticoke....18634
East Smethport....16730
East Smithfield....18817
East Springfield....16411
East Stroudsburg (1st)....18301
East Texas (1st)....18046
East Vandergrift....15629
East Waterford....17021
East York, Br. York....17402
Easton (1st)....18042
College, Sta.....18042
Raubsville, R. Br.....18075
Eau Claire....16030
Ebensburg (1st)....15931
Ebervale....18223
Eddington, Br. Cornwells Heights....19020
Eddystone, Br. Chester....19013
Edgemont....19028
Edinboro (1st)....16412
Edinburg....16116
Edison....18919
Edmon....15630
Edwardsville, Br. Wilkes-Barre....18704
Effort....18330
Egypt, Sta. Whitehall....18052
Eighty Four....15330
Elco....15434
Eldersville....15036
Elderton....15736
Eldred....16731

Coryville, R. Br.	16723
Elgin (1st)	16413
Elizabeth (1st)	15037
Elizabethtown (1st)	17022
Elizabethville	17023
Elkins Park, Br.	
Philadelphia	19117
Elkland	16920
Elienton, R. Br. Canton	17732
Elliottsburg	17024
Ellport, Br. Ellwood City	16117
Ellsworth	15331
Ellwood City (1st)	16117
Elm	17521
Elmhurst	18416
Elmora	15737
Elrama	15038
Elroy, Br. Souderton	18964
Elton	15934
Elverson	19520
Elwyn, Br. Media	19063
Elysburg	17824
Emeigh	15738
Emerald	18048
Emigsville	17318
Emlenton	16373
Emmaus (1st)	18049
Emporium (1st)	15834
Emsworth, Br. Pittsburgh	15202
Endeavor	16322
English Center	17733
Enola (1st)	17025
Enon Valley	16120
Entriken	16638
Ephrata (1st)	17522
Martindale, R. Br.	17549
Equinunk	18417
ERIE (1st) (see appendix)	
Ernest	15739
Erwinna	18920
Espy, Br. Bloomsburg	17815
Espyville Station, R. Br.	
Linesville	16414
Essington (1st)	19029
Etna, Br. Pittsburgh	15223
Etters	17319
Evans City	16033
Evansville	19521
Everett (1st)	15537
Everson	15631
Ewalt, Sta. Pittsburgh	15212
Excelsior	17825
Exeter, Br. Pittston	18643
Export	15632
Exton (1st)	19341
Lionville, R. Br.	19353
Eyers Grove, R. Br. Millville	17826
Eynon, Sta. Archbald	18403
Factoryville	18419
Fairbank	15435
Fairchance	15436
Fairfield	17320
Fairhill, Sta. Philadelphia	19133
Fairhope	15538
Fairless Hills (1st)	19030
Fairmount, Sta. Philadelphia	
(see appendix)	
Fairmount City	16224
Fairoaks, Br. Ambridge	15003
Fairview (1st)	16415
Fairview Village, Br.	
Norristown	19409
Fallentimber	16639

Falls	18615
Falls Creek	15840
Fallsington, Br. Levittown	19054
Fannettsburg	17221
Farmington	15437
Farrandsville	17734
Farrell (1st)	16121
Fawn Grove	17321
Fayette City	15438
Fayetteville	17222
Feasterville-Trevose, Br.	
Langhorne	19047
Federal Reserve, Sta.	
Pittsburgh	15230
Federal Reserve, Sta.	
Philadelphia	19107
Federal Square, Sta.	
Harrisburg	17108
Felton	17322
Fenelton	16034
Fern Glen, R. Br. Nuremberg	18241
Ferndale	18921
Fernway, Br. Zelienople	16063
Fernwood, Br. Lansdowne	19050
Fidelity, Sta. Philadelphia	19109
Finleyville	15332
Fisher	16225
Fishertown	15539
Fleetville	18420
Fleetwood	19522
Fleming	16835
Flemington, Br. Lock Haven	17745
Flicksville	18050
Flinton	16640
Floreffe	15039
Florence, R. Br.	
Burgettstown	15040
Flourtown (1st)	19031
Fogelsville	18051
Folcroft (1st)	19032
Folsom (1st)	19033
Fombell	16123
Forbes Road	15633
Force	15841
Ford City (1st)	16226
Ford Cliff	16228
Forest City (1st)	18421
Aldenville, R. Br.	18401
Vandling, Br.	18421
Forest Grove	18922
Forest Hills, Br. Pittsburgh	15221
Forestville	16035
Forksville	18616
Fort Hill	15540
Fort Littleton, R. Br. Mc	
Connellsburg	17223
Fort Loudon	17224
Fort Washington (1st)	19034
Fortieth Street, Sta.	
Philadelphia	19104
Forty Fort, Br. Wilkes-Barre	18704
Foster Brook, Br. Bradford	16701
Fountainville	18923
Fourth Avenue, Sta.	
Pittsburgh	15222
Fox Chapel, Br. Pittsburgh	15238
Fox Chase, Sta.	
Philadelphia	19111
Foxburg	16036
Frackville (1st)	17931
Franconia, R. Br. Souderton	18924
Frankford, Sta. Philadelphia	19124
Franklin (1st)	16323

Franklin Center, R. Br.	
Media	19063
Franklintown	17323
Frazer, Br. Malvern	19355
Frederick	19135
Fredericksburg	17026
Fredericktown	15333
Fredonia	16124
Freeburg	17827
Freedom	15042
Freeland (1st)	18224
Freemansburg, Br.	
Bethlehem	18017
Freeport	16229
Frenchville	16836
Lecontes Mills, R. Br.	16850
Friedens	15541
Friedensburg	17933
Friendsville	18818
Frostburg, R. Br.	
Punxsutawney	15740
Fryburg	16326
Fullerton, Sta. Whitehall	18052
Furlong	18925
Gaines	16921
Galeton	16922
Galilee, R. Br. Damascus	18423
Gallitzin	16641
Ganister	16642
Gans, R. Br. Lake Lynn	15439
Gap	17527
Gararcls Fort	15334
Garden Mart, Br. Pottstown	19464
Gardenville	18926
Gardners	17324
Garland	16416
Garrett	15542
Gastonville	15336
Gateway, Br. Wilkes-Barre	18704
Gateway Center, Sta.	
Pittsburgh	15222
Geigertown	19523
Geistown, Br. Johnstown	15904
Genesee	16923
Geneva, R. Br. Conneaut	
Lake	16316
George School, Br. Newtown	18940
Georgetown	15043
Germania, R. Br. Galeton	16922
Germansville	18053
Germantown, Sta.	
Philadelphia	19144
Gettysburg (1st)	17325
Gibbon Glade	15440
Gibraltar	19524
Gibson	18820
Gibsonia (1st)	15044
Gifford	16732
Gilbert	18331
Gilberton	17934
Gilbertsville	19525
Gillett	16925
Ginter	16643
Gipsy	15741
Girard (1st)	16417
Girard Avenue, Sta.	
Philadelphia	19122
Girardville	17935
Gladwyne (1st)	19035
Glasgow	16644
Glassport (1st)	15045
Glen Campbell	15742
Glen Lyon	18617

Glen Mills....................19342
Glen Richey..................16837
Glen Riddle..................19037
Glen Rock (1st)..............17327
Glencoe......................15543
Glenhope, R. Br. Irvona......16645
Glenmoore....................19343
Glenolden (1st)..............19036
Glenshaw (1st)...............15116
Glenside (1st)...............19038
Glenville....................17329
Glenwillard..................15046
  Wireton, R. Br...........15092
Goodville....................17528
Gordon.......................17936
Gordonville..................17529
Gouldsboro...................18424
Gowen City...................17828
Graceton.....................15743
Gradyville...................19039
Grampian.....................16838
Grand Valley.................16423
Grantham.....................17027
Grantville...................17028
Granville....................17029
Granville Summit.............16926
Grapeville...................15634
Grassflat....................16839
Gratz........................17030
Gray.........................15544
Grays Landing, R. Br.
  Masontown................15461
Graysville...................15337
Great Bend...................18821
Great Southern, Br.
  Bridgeville..............15017
Greater Pittsburgh Airport,
  Br. Pittsburgh...........15231
Greeley......................18425
Green Hills, Br. Sharon Hill.19079
Green Lane...................18054
Green Park...................17031
Greencastle (1st)............17225
Greene.......................17530
Greengate, Br. Greensburg....15601
Greenock.....................15047
Greensboro...................15338
Greensburg (1st).............15601
Greenstone...................17227
Greentown....................18426
Greenville (1st).............16125
Grindstone...................15442
Grove City (1st).............16127
Grover.......................17735
Guys Mills...................16327
Gwynedd......................19436
Gwynedd Valley...............19437
Hadley.......................16130
Halifax......................17032
Hallstead....................18822
Hallton......................15842
Hamburg (1st)................19526
Hamilton.....................15744
Hamlin.......................18427
Hammersley Fork..............17736
Hampden, Sta. Reading........19604
Hampton, R. Br. New Oxford...17330
Hannastown...................15635
Hanover (1st)................17331
Harborcreek..................16421
Harford......................18823
Harleigh.....................18225
Harleysville (1st)...........19438

Harmonsburg..................16422
Harmonville, Br.
  Conshohocken.............19428
Harmony......................16037
Harriman, Sta. Bristol.......19007
HARRISBURG (1st) (see
  appendix)
Harrison City................15636
Harrison Valley, R. Br.
  Westfield................16927
Harrisonville, R. Br.
  Hustontown...............17228
Harrisville..................16038
Hartleton....................17829
Hartstown....................16131
Harveys Lake.................18618
Harwick......................15049
Harwood Mines, R. Br.
  Hazleton.................18201
Hastings.....................16646
Hatboro (1st)................19040
Hatfield (1st)...............19440
Haverford (1st)..............19041
Havertown, Br. Upper Darby...19083
Hawk Run.....................16840
Hawley (1st).................18428
  Lakeville, R. Br.........18438
Hawthorn.....................16230
Hazel Hurst..................16733
Hazelwood, Sta. Pittsburgh...15207
Hazen........................15843
Hazleton (1st)...............18201
  Beaver Brook, R. Br......18215
  Broad Street, Sta........18201
  Harwood Mines, R. Br.....18201
  Jeanesville, R. Br.......18227
  West Hazleton, Br........18201
Heckscherville...............17937
Hegins.......................17938
Heidelberg, Br. Carnegie.....15106
Heilwood.....................15745
Helfenstein..................17939
Hellam, Br. York.............17406
Hellertown (1st).............18055
Hendersonville...............15339
Hendricks, R. Br. Woxall.....18979
Henryville...................18332
Hepburnville, R. Br. Cogan
  Station..................17728
Hereford.....................18056
Herman.......................16039
Herminie.....................15637
Hermitage, Br. Sharon........16146
Herndon......................17830
Herrick Center...............18430
Hershey (1st)................17033
Hessdale.....................17531
Hesston......................16647
Hibbs........................15443
Hickory......................15340
High Spire...................17034
Hill, Sta. Harrisburg (see
  appendix)
Hillcrest, Sta. Bethel Park..15102
Hiller.......................15444
Hilliards....................16040
Hillsdale....................15746
Hillsgrove...................18619
Hillsville...................16132
Hilltown.....................18927
Hoban Heights................18620
Hokendauqua, Sta
  Whitehall................18052

Holbrook.....................15341
Holicong.....................18928
Holiday Park, Br. Pittsburgh.15239
Hollidaysburg (1st)..........16648
Hollsopple...................15935
Holmes.......................19043
Holmesburg, Sta.
  Philadelphia.............19136
Holtwood.....................17532
Home.........................15747
Homer City (1st).............15748
Homestead (1st)..............15120
Hometown, R. Br. Tamaqua.....18252
Homewood, Sta. Pittsburgh....15208
Honesdale (1st)..............18431
Honey Brook..................19344
Honey Grove..................17035
Hookstown....................15050
Hooversville.................15936
Hop Bottom...................18824
Hopeland.....................17533
Hopewell.....................16650
Hopwood......................15445
Horsham (1st)................19044
Hospital, Sta. Norristown....19401
Hostetter....................15638
Houston......................15342
Houtzdale....................16651
Howard.......................16841
Hublersburg..................16842
Huey.........................16231
Hughesville..................17737
Hummels Wharf................17831
Hummelstown (1st)............17036
Hunker.......................15639
Hunlock Creek................18621
Hunting Park, Sta.
  Philadelphia.............19140
Huntingdon (1st).............16652
Huntingdon Valley (1st)......19006
Huntington Mills.............18622
Hustontown...................17229
  Harrisonville, R. Br.....17228
Hutchinson...................15640
Hyde.........................16843
Hyde Park....................15641
Hydetown.....................16328
Hyndman......................15545
  Wellersburg, R. Br.......15564
Hyner, R. Br. North Bend.....17738
Ickesburg....................17037
Idaville.....................17337
Imler........................16655
Immaculata...................19345
Imperial.....................15126
Independence.................15343
Indian Head..................15446
Indiana (1st)................15701
Indianola....................15051
Industry.....................15052
Ingomar......................15127
Ingram, Br. Pittsburgh.......15205
Intercourse..................17534
Irvine.......................16329
Irvona.......................16656
  Glenhope, R. Br..........16645
Irwin (1st)..................15642
Isabella.....................15447
Iselin, R. Br. Saltsburg.....15681
Ivyland, Br. Warminster......18974
Jackson......................18825
Jackson Center...............16133
Jacobs Creek.................15448

Jacobus, Br. York	17407	
James City	16734	
James Creek	16657	
Jamestown	16134	
Jamison	18929	
Jeanesville, R: Br. Hazleton	18227	
Jeannette (1st)	15644	
Jefferson	15344	
Jenkins, Br. Pittston	18640	
Jenkintown (1st)	19046	
Jenners; R. Br. Boswell	15546	
Jennerstown	15547	
Jermyn	18433	
Jerome	15937	
Jersey Mills	17739	
Jersey Shore (1st)	17740	
Cedar Run, R. Br.	17727	
Salladasburg, R. Br.	17740	
Jessup	18434	
Jim Thorpe	18229	
Joffre	15053	
John Wanamaker, Sta.		
Philadelphia	19107	
Johnsonburg	15845	
JOHNSTOWN (1st) (see		
appendix)		
Jones Mills	15646	
Jonestown	17038	
Josephine	15750	
Julian	16844	
Juneau	15751	
Junedale	18230	
Juniata, Sta. Altoona	16601	
Kane (1st)	16735	
Kantner	15548	
Karns City	16041	
Karthaus	16845	
Piper, R. Br.	16845	
Pottersdale, R. Br.	16871	
Kaska	17940	
Kaylor, R. Br. Chicora	16042	
Kaywin, Br. Bethlehem	18018	
Keating Summit, R. Br.		
Austin	16737	
Keisterville	15449	
Kelayres	18231	
Keliers Church, R· Br.		
Perkasie	18944	
Kelton	19346	
Kemblesville	19347	
Kempton	19529	
Kendall Creek, Sta.		
Bradford	16701	
Kennedy, Br. Mc Kees Rocks	15136	
Kennerdell	16374	
Kennett Square (1st)	19348	
Kensington, Sta.		
Philadelphia	19125	
Kent	15752	
Kersey	15846	
Keystone, Br. Chambersburg	17201	
Kilbuck, Sta. Pittsburgh	15233	
Kimberton	19442	
King Of Prussia, Br.		
Norristown	19406	
Kingsessing, Sta.		
Philadelphia	19143	
Kingsley	18826	
Kingston, Br. Wilkes-Barre	18704	
Kintnersville	18930	
Kinzers	17535	
Kirkwood	17536	
Kittanning (1st)	16201	

Kleinfeltersville	17039	
Klingerstown	17941	
Knox	16232	
Knox Dale	15847	
Knoxville	16928	
Koppel	16136	
Kossuth	16331	
Kreamer	17833	
Kresgeville	18333	
Kuipmont	17834	
Kulpsville	19443	
Kunkletown	18058	
Kutztown (1st)	19530	
Kylertown	16847	
La Belle	15450	
La Jose	15753	
La Plume	18440	
Laceyville	18623	
Lackawaxen	18435	
Lafayette Hill (1st)	19444	
Lahaska	18931	
Lairdsville	17742	
Lake Ariel	18436	
Lake City (1st)	16423	
Lake Como	18437	
Lake Harmony	18624	
Lake Lynn	15451	
Gans, R. Br.	15439	
Lake Winola	18625	
Lakemont, Br. Altoona	16602	
Lakeville, R. Br. Hawley	18438	
Lakewood	18439	
Lamar	16848	
Lamartine	16375	
Lamberton	15452	
Lampeter	17537	
LANCASTER (1st) (see		
appendix)		
Landenberg	19350	
Landingville	17942	
Landisburg	17040	
Landisville (1st)	17538	
Lanesboro	18827	
Langdondale	16658	
Langeloth	15054	
Langhorne (1st)	19047	
Lansdale (1st)	19446	
Lansdowne (1st)	19050	
Lanse	16849	
Lansford (1st)	18232	
Laporte	18626	
Large, Br. Clairton	15025	
Larimer	15647	
Latrobe (1st)	15650	
Lattimer Mines	18234	
Laughlintown	15655	
Laurel Gardens, Br.		
Pittsburgh	15229	
Laureldale, Br. Reading	19605	
Laureiton	17835	
Laurys Station	18059	
Lavelle	17943	
Lawn	17041	
Lawrence	15055	
Lawrenceville	16929	
Lawton	18828	
Layton	15453	
Le Raysville	18829	
Le Roy	17743	
Lebanon (1st)	17042	
Lebanon Church, Sta.		
Pittsburgh	15122	
Lerk Kill	17836	

Leckrone	15454	
Lecontes Mills, R. Br.		
Frenchville	16850	
Lederach	19450	
Leechburg (1st)	15656	
Leeper	16233	
Leesport (1st)	19533	
Dauberville, R. Br.	19517	
Leetsdale (1st)	15056	
Lehigh University, Sta.		
Bethlehem	18015	
Lehigh Valley, Br. Bethlehem		
(see appendix)		
Lehighton (1st)	18235	
Lehman	18627	
Leisenring	15455	
Lemasters	17231	
Lemont	16851	
Lemont Furnace	15456	
Lemoyne (1st)	17043	
Lenhartsville	19534	
Lenni	19052	
Lenoxville, R. Br. Nicholson	18441	
Leola (1st)	17540	
Lester, Br. Philadelphia	19113	
Level Green, R. Br. Trafford	15085	
LEVITTOWN (1st) (see		
appendix)		
Lewis Run	16738	
Lewisberry	17339	
Lewisburg (1st)	17837	
Lewistown (1st)	17044	
Lewisville	19351	
Liberty	16930	
Library	15129	
Lickingville	16332	
Light Street, R. Br.		
Bloomsburg	17839	
Ligonier (1st)	15658	
Lilly	15938	
Lima	19060	
Limekiln	19535	
Limeport	18060	
Limerick, Br. Royersford	19468	
Limestone	16234	
Lincoln Place, Sta.		
Pittsburgh	15207	
Lincoln University	19352	
Linden	17744	
Lindsey, Sta. Punxsutawney	15767	
Line Lexington	18932	
Linesville	16424	
Linfield, Br. Royersford	19468	
Linglestown, Br. Harrisburg		
(see appendix)		
Linwood, Br. Marcus Hook	19061	
Lionville, R. Br. Exton	19353	
Listie	15549	
Listonburg	15457	
Lititz (1st)	17543	
Brunnerville, R. Br.	17543	
Rothsville, R. Br.	17573	
Little Marsh	16931	
Little Meadows	18830	
Littlestown (1st)	17340	
Liverpool	17045	
Llewellyn	17944	
Lock Haven (1st)	17745	
Locust Gap	17840	
Locustdale	17945	
Logan, Sta Philadelphia	19141	
Loganton	17747	
Loganville	17342	

Long Pond 18334
Lopez 18628
Loretto (1st) 15940
Lost Creek 17946
Lowber 15660
Lower Burrell, Br. New
   Kensington 15068
Lower Paxton, Br.
   Harrisburg 17109
Loyalhanna 15661
Loysburg 16659
Loysville 17047
Lucernemines 15754
Lucinda 16235
Ludlow 16333
Lumberville, R. Br.
   Doylestown 18933
Lurgan 17232
Luthersburg 15848
Luxor 15662
Luzerne, Br. Wilkes-Barre 18709
Lykens (1st) 17048
Lyndell 19354
Lyndora 16045
Lynnewood, Br. Philadelphia 19150
Lynnport 18061
Lyon Station 19536
Mac Arthur, Sta. Aliquippa 15001
Macdonaldton, R. Br. Berlin 15530
Mackeyville 17750
Macungie 18062
Madera 16661
Madison 15663
Madisonburg 16852
Mahaffey 15757
Mahanoy City (1st) 17948
Mahanoy Plane 17949
Mahoningtown, Sta. New
   Castle 16102
Mainesburg 16932
Mainland 19451
Malvern (1st) 19355
Mammoth 15664
Manayunk, Sta.
   Philadelphia 19127
Manchester 17345
Manheim (1st) 17545
Manns Choice 15550
Manoa, Br. Upper Darby 19083
Manor 15665
Manor Oak, Br. Pittsburgh 15220
Manorville 16238
Mansfield (1st) 16933
Maple Glen, Br. Ambler 19002
Mapleton Depot 17052
Mar Lin 17951
Marble 16334
Marchand 15758
Marcus Hook (1st) 19061
Marianna 15345
Marienville 16239
Marietta (1st) 17547
Marion 17235
Marion Center 15759
Marion Heights 17832
Marion Hill, Br. New
   Brighton 15066
Market Street, Sta. West
   Chester 19380
Markleton 15551
Markleysburg 15459
Mars (1st) 16046
Marshalls Creek 18335

Marsteller 15760
Martin 15460
Martindale, R. Br. Ephrata 17549
Martins Creek 18063
Martinsburg 16662
Marwood 16047
Mary D 17952
Marysville 17053
Marywood College, Sta.
   Scranton 18509
Masontown 15461
Matamoras 18336
Mather 15346
Mattawana 17054
Maxatawny 19538
Mayfair, Sta. Philadelphia 19136
Mayfield, Br. Jermyn 18433
Mayport 16240
Maytown 17550
Mc Adoo (1st) 18237
Mc Alisterville 17049
Mc Clellandtown 15458
Mc Clure 17841
Mc Connellsburg 17233
   Fort Littleton, R. Br. 17223
Mc Connellstown 16660
Mc Coysville 17050
Mc Donald 15057
Mc Elhattan 17748
Mc Ewensville 17749
Mc Gees Mills 15755
Mc Grann 16236
Mc Intyre 17756
Mc Kean 16426
Mc Kees Rocks (1st) 15136
MC KEESPORT (1st) (see
   appendix)
Mc Knight, Br. Pittsburgh 15237
Mc Knightstown 17343
Mc Murray, Br. Canonsburg 15317
Mc Sherrystown 17344
Mc Veytown 17051
Meadow Lands 15347
Meadowbrook, Br.
   Jenkintown 19046
Meadville (1st) 16335
Mechanicsburg (1st) 17055
Mechanicsville 18934
MEDIA (1st) (see appendix)
Mehoopany 18629
Melcroft 15462
Mendenhall 19357
Menges Mills 17346
Mentcle 15761
Mercer (1st) 16137
Mercersburg (1st) 17236
Meridian, R. Br. Butler 16001
Merion Station (1st) 19066
Merrittstown 15463
Mertztown 19539
Meshoppen 18630
Mexico 17056
Meyersdale 15552
Middle City, Sta.
   Philadelphia (see
   appendix)
Middle Creek 17843
Middleburg (1st) 17842
Middlebury Center 16935
Middleport 17953
Middletown (1st) 17057
Midland (1st) 15059
Midway 15060

Mifflin 17058
Mifflinburg 17844
Mifflintown 17059
Mifflinville 18631
Milan 18831
Milanville 18443
Mildred 18632
Milesburg 16853
Milford (1st) 18337
Milford Square 18935
Mill Creek 17060
Mill Hall 17751
   Salona, R. Br. 17767
Mill Run 15464
Mill Village 16427
Millersburg (1st) 17061
Millerstown 17062
Millersville (1st) 17551
Millerton 16936
Millheim 16854
Millmont 17845
Millport, R. Br.
   Shinglehouse 16739
Millrift 18340
Mills 16937
Millsboro 15348
Millvale, Br. Pittsburgh 15209
Millville 17846
   Eyers Grove, R. Br. 17826
Milmont Park, Br. Folsom 19033
Milnesville 18239
Milroy 17063
Milton (1st) 17847
Mineral Point 15942
Mineral Springs 16855
Minersville (1st) 17954
Mingoville 16856
Minisink Hills 18341
Miquon 19452
Mocanaqua, R. Br.
   Shickshinny 18655
Modena 19358
Mohnton 19540
Mohrsville 19541
Monaca (1st) 15061
Monessen (1st) 15062
Monocacy Station 19542
Monongahela (1st) 15063
Monroeton 18832
Mont Alto 17237
Mont Clare 19453
Montandon 17850
Montgomery (1st) 17752
Montgomeryville (1st) 18936
Montour, Br. Pittsburgh 15244
Montoursville (1st) 17754
Montrose (1st) 18801
Moosic, Br. Scranton 18507
Morann 16663
Moravian, Sta. Bethlehem 18018
Morea Colliery 17955
Morgan 15064
Morgantown 19543
Morris 16938
Morris Run 16939
Morrisdale 16858
Morrisville (1st) 19067
Morton (1st) 19070
Morwood 18937
Moscow 18444
Moshannon 16859
Mount Aetna 19544
Mount Airy, Sta.

Philadelphia................19119
Mount Bethel...............18343
Mount Braddock............15465
Mount Carmel (1st)........17851
Mount Gretna..............17064
Mount Holly Springs.......17065
Mount Jewett..............16740
  Clermont, R. Br.......16722
Mount Joy (1st)...........17552
Mount Lebanon, Br.
  Pittsburgh............15228
Mount Morris..............15349
Mount Nebo, R. Br.
  Sewickley.............15143
Mount Oliver, Sta.
  Pittsburgh............15210
Mount Penn, Br. Reading...19606
Mount Pleasant (1st)......15666
Mount Pleasant Mills......17853
Mount Pocono (1st)........18344
Mount Union...............17066
Mount Washington, Sta.
  Pittsburgh............15211
Mount Wolf................17347
Mountain Top, Br.
  Wilkes-Barre..........18707
Mountainhome..............18342
Mountville................17554
Mowry.....................17956
Moylan, Br. Media.........19065
Muir......................17957
Muncy (1st)...............17756
  Pennsdale, R. Br......17761
Muncy Valley..............17758
  Sonestown, R. Br......17770
Munhall, Br. Homestead....15120
Munson....................16860
Murrysville (1st).........15668
Muse......................15350
Myerstown (1st)...........17067
Nagle Road, Br. Erie......16510
Nanticoke (1st)...........18634
Nanty Glo.................15943
Narberth (1st)............19072
Narrows, Br. Wilkes-Barre.18704
Narvon....................17555
Natalie...................17854
Natrona, Br. Natrona
  Heights...............15065
Natrona Heights (1st).....15065
Naval Hospital, Sta.
  Philadelphia..........19145
Nazareth (1st)............18064
Needmore..................17238
  Big Cove Tannery, R. Br.17212
Neelyton..................17239
Neffs.....................18065
Neffsville, Br. Lancaster.17601
Nelson....................16940
Nemacolin.................15351
Nescopeck.................18635
Neshannock, Br. New Castle.16105
Nesquehoning..............18240
Neville Island, Br.
  Pittsburgh............15225
New Albany................18833
New Alexandria............15670
New Baltimore.............15553
New Bedford...............16140
New Berlin................17855
New Berlinville...........19545
New Bethlehem.............16242
New Bloomfield............17068

New Brighton (1st)........15066
New Britain, Br. Doylestown.18901
New Buffalo...............17069
NEW CASTLE (1st) (see
  appendix)
New Columbia, R. Br. West
  Milton................17856
New Cumberland (1st)......17070
New Derry.................15671
New Eagle.................15067
New Enterprise............16664
New Florence..............15944
New Freedom...............17349
New Freeport..............15352
New Galilee...............16141
New Geneva................15467
New Germantown............17071
New Holland (1st).........17557
New Hope (1st)............18938
New Kensington (1st)......15068
  Arnold, Br............15068
  Braeburn, R. Br.......15016
  Lower Burrell, Br.....15068
  Parnassus, Sta........15068
New Kingstown.............17072
New London................19360
New Milford...............18834
New Millport..............16861
New Oxford................17350
  Hampton, R. Br........17330
New Paris.................15554
New Park..................17352
New Philadelphia..........17959
New Providence............17560
New Ringgold..............17960
New Salem.................15468
New Stanton...............15672
New Tripoli...............18066
New Wilmington............16142
Newberry, Sta. Williamsport.17701
Newburg...................17240
Newell....................15466
Newfield, Br. Verona......15147
Newfoundland..............18445
Newmanstown...............17073
Newport...................17074
Newportville, Br. Levittown.19056
Newry.....................16665
Newton Hamilton...........17075
Newtown (1st).............18940
Newtown Square (1st)......19073
Newville (1st)............17241
Niantic...................19546
Nicetown, Sta. Philadelphia.19140
Nicholson.................18446
  Lenoxville, R. Br.....18441
Nicktown..................15762
Ninepoints................17561
Nineveh...................15353
Nisbet....................17759
Nittany Mall, Br. State
  College...............16801
Nixon, Br. Butler.........16001
Noblestown, R. Br. Oakdale.15071
Normalville...............15469
NORRISTOWN (1st) (see
  appendix)
North Apollo..............15673
North Bend................17760
  Hyner, R. Br..........17738
North Bessemer, Br.
  Pittsburgh............15235
North Bingham.............16941

North Braddock, Br.
  Braddock..............15104
North Charleroi, Br.
  Charleroi.............15022
North East (1st)..........16428
North End, Sta. Wilkes-Barre.18705
North Hills, Sta. Glenside.19038
North Huntingdon, Br. Irwin.15642
North Philadelphia, Sta.
  Philadelphia..........19133
North Pine Grove..........16243
North Scranton, Sta.
  Scranton..............18508
North Springfield.........16430
North Versailles (1st)....15137
North Wales (1st).........19454
North Warren, Br. Warren..16365
North Washington..........16048
Northampton (1st).........18067
Northbrook................19361
Northpoint................15763
Northumberland (1st)......17857
Northwest, Br. State College.16801
Norvelt...................15674
Norwood (1st).............19074
Nottingham................19362
Noxen.....................18636
Nu Mine...................16244
Nuangola..................18637
Number Fifty Six, Sta.
  Philadelphia..........19107
Numidia...................17858
Nuremberg.................18241
Oak Hall..................16862
Oak Lane, Sta. Philadelphia.19126
Oak Ridge.................16245
Oakdale...................15071
Oakland, Sta. Pittsburgh..15213
Oakland Mills.............17076
Oakmont (1st).............15139
Oaks (1st)................19456
Obelisk, R. Br. Zieglerville.19492
Observatory, Sta. Pittsburgh.15214
Ogontz Campus, Br.
  Abington..............19001
Ohiopyle..................15470
Oil City (1st)............16301
Oil Creek, Sta. Oil City..16301
Olanta....................16863
Old Forge, Br. Scranton...18518
Old Zionsville............18068
Oley......................19547
Oliphant Furnace..........15471
Oliveburg.................15764
Oliver....................15472
Olney, Sta. Philadelphia..19120
Olyphant (1st)............18447
Oneida....................18242
Ono.......................17077
Orangeville...............17859
Orbisonia.................17243
Orefield..................18069
Oreland (1st).............19075
Ormsby, R. Br. Cyclone....16741
Orrstown..................17244
Orrtanna..................17353
Orson.....................18449
Orviston, R. Br. Beech
  Creek.................16864
Orwigsburg (1st)..........17961
Orwin, R. Br. Tower City..17980
Osceola...................16942
Osceola Mills.............16666

Sandy Ridge, R. Br.	16677
Osterburg	16667
Saint Clairsville, R. Br.	16676
Oswayo, R. Br. Coudersport	16915
Ottsville	18942
Overbrook, Sta. Philadelphia	19151
Oxford (1st)	19363
Palm	18070
Palmerton (1st)	18071
Palmyra (1st)	17078
Paoli (1st)	19301
Paradise	17562
Parcel Post. Sta. Reading	19603
Parcel Post. Sta. Pittsburgh	15233
Pardeesville	18243
Paris, R. Br. Burgettstown	15021
Park, Sta. Vandergrift	15690
Park Ridge, Br. Norristown	19401
Parker	16049
Parker Ford	19457
Parkesburg	19365
Parkhill	15945
Parkway Center, Br. Pittsburgh	15220
Parnassus, Sta. New Kensington	15068
Perryville	18244
Paschall, Sta. Philadelphia (see appendix)	
Patton	16668
Paupack	18451
Paxinos	17860
Paxtang, Br. Harrisburg	17111
Paxtonville	17861
Peach Bottom	17563
Peach Glen, R. Br. Bendersville	17306
Peckville	18452
Peely, Br. Wilkes-Barre	18706
Pen Argyl (1st)	18072
Penbrook, Br. Harrisburg	17103
Penfield	15849
Penllyn, Br. Blue Bell	19422
Penn	15675
Penn Center, Sta. Philadelphia	19103
Penn Hills, Br. Pittsburgh (see appendix)	
Penn Rose, Br. Verona	15147
Penn Run	15765
Penndel, Br. Langhorne	19047
Penns Creek	17862
Penns Park	18943
Pennsburg	18073
Pennsdale, R. Br. Muncy	17761
Pennsylvania Furnace	16865
Penryn	17564
Pequea	17565
Perkasie (1st)	18944
Perkiomenville	19074
Perry Square, Sta. Erie	16507
Perryopolis	15473
Perrysville, Br. Pittsburgh	15237
Perulack, R. Br. East Waterford	17021
Petersburg	16669
Petrolia	16050
PHILADELPHIA (1st) (see appendix)	
Philipsburg (1st)	16866
Phoenixville (1st)	19460
Picture Rocks	17762
Pilgrim Gardens, Sta. Drexel	

Hill	19026
Pillow	17080
Pine Avenue, Sta. Erie	16504
Pine Bank	15354
Pine Forge	19548
Pine Grove	17963
Pine Grove Mills	16868
Pineville	18946
Piper, R. Br. Karthaus	16845
Pipersville	18947
Pitman	17964
PITTSBURGH (1st) (see appendix)	
Pittsfield	16340
PITTSTON (1st) (see appendix)	
Plainfield	17081
Plains, Br. Wilkes-Barre	18705
Plainsville	18650
Plaza, Sta. Butler	16001
Pleasant Gap, Br. Bellefonte	16823
Pleasant Hall	17246
Pleasant Hills, Br. Pittsburgh	15236
Pleasant Mount	18453
Pleasant Unity	15676
Pleasant Valley	18948
Pleasantville	16341
Plum, Br. Pittsburgh	15239
Plumsteadville	18949
Plumville	16246
Plymouth (1st)	18651
Plymouth Meeting (1st)	19462
Pocono Lake	18347
Pocono Lake Preserve, R. Br.	18348
Pocono Lake Preserve, R. Br. Pocono Lake	18348
Pocono Manor	18349
Pocono Pines	18350
Pocono Summit	18346
Pocopson	19366
Point, Br. Butler	16001
Point Breeze, Sta. Philadelphia	19145
Point Marion	15474
Point Pleasant	18950
Polk	16342
Pomeroy	19367
Port Allegany (1st)	16743
Wrights, R. Br.	16752
Port Carbon	17965
Port Clinton	19549
Port Kennedy	19463
Port Matilda	16870
Port Royal	17082
Port Trevorton	17864
Port Vue, Br. Mc Keesport	15133
Portage	15946
Porter	15766
Porters Sideling, R. Br. Spring Grove	17354
Portersville	16051
Portland	18351
Portland Mills	15850
Pottersdale, R. R. Br. Karthaus	16871
Potts Grove	17865
Pottstown (1st)	19464
Pottsville (1st)	17901
Poyntelle	18454
Presque Isle, Br. Erie (see appendix)	
Presto	15142

Preston Park	18455
Pricedale	15072
Primos Secane, Br. Clifton Heights	19018
Prompton	18456
Prospect	16052
Prospect Park (1st)	19076
Prosperity	15329
Pulaski	16143
Punxsutawney (1st)	15767
Coolspring, R. Br	15730
Frostburg, R. Br.	15740
Lindsey, Sta.	15767
Puritan, R. Br. Portage	15946
Quakake	18245
Quakertown (1st)	18951
Quarryville (1st)	17566
Quecreek	15555
Queen	16670
Quentin, R. Br. Cornwall	17083
Quincy	17247
Racine, R. Br. Beaver Falls	15010
Radnor, Br. Wayne	19087
Railroad	17355
Ralston	17763
Ramey	16671
Ranshaw, R. Br. Shamokin	17866
Ransom	18653
Raubsville, R. Br. Easton	18075
Ravine	17966
Rea	15356
READING (1st) (see appendix)	
Reamstown	17567
Rebersburg	16872
Rebuck	17867
Rector	15677
Red Hill	18076
Red Lion (1st)	17356
Reeders	18352
Reedsville	17084
Refton	17576
Regency Mall, Br. Indiana	15767
Rehrersburg	19550
Reinerton, Br. Tower City	17980
Reinholds	17569
Renfrew	16053
Reno	16343
Renovo	17764
Renton, Br. Pittsburgh	15239
Republic	15475
Revere	18953
Revloc	15948
Rew	16744
Rexmont	17085
Reynoldsville	15851
Rheems	17570
Rhone, Sta. Nanticoke	18634
Rices Landing	15357
Riceville	16432
Richboro, Br. Southampton	18954
Richeyville	15358
Richfield	17086
Richland	17087
Richlandtown	18955
Richmond, Sta. Philadelphia	19134
Riddlesburg	16672
Ridgway (1st)	15853
Ridley Park (1st)	19078
Riegelsville	18077
Rillton	15678
Rimersburg	16248
Ringgold	15770

Ringtown	17967	
Riverside	17868	
Rixford	16745	
Roaring Branch	17765	
Roaring Spring (1st)	16673	
Robertsdale	16674	
Robesonia (1st)	19551	
Robinson	15949	
Rochester (1st)	15074	
Rochester Mills	15771	
Rock Glen	18246	
Rockledge, Br. Philadelphia	19111	
Rockton	15856	
Rockwood	15557	
Rogersville	15359	
Rohrerstown (1st)	17571	
Rome	18837	
Ronco	15476	
Ronks	17572	
Roscoe	15477	
Rosehill, Sta. Philadelphia	19140	
Rosemont, Br. Bryn Mawr	19010	
Roseto, Br. Bangor	18013	
Roslyn, Br. Abington	19001	
Rossiter	15772	
Rossville	17358	
Rostraver, Br. Belle Vernon	15012	
Rothsville, R. Br. Lititz	17573	
Roulette	16746	
Rouseville	16344	
Rouzerville	17250	
Rowland	18457	
Roxborough, Sta. Philadelphia	19128	
Roxbury	17251	
Royersford (1st)	19468	
Ruffs Dale	15679	
Rural Ridge	15075	
Rural Valley	16249	
Rushland	18956	
Rushville	18839	
Russell	16345	
Russellton	15076	
Rutherford Heights, Br. Harrisburg	17111	
Rutledge, Br. Morton	19070	
Rydal, Br. Jenkintown	19046	
Sabinsville	16943	
Sacramento	17968	
Sadsburyville	19369	
Saegertown	16433	
Sagamore	16250	
Saint Benedict	15773	
Saint Boniface	16675	
Saint Charles	16251	
Saint Clair	17970	
Saint Clairsville, R. Br. Osterburg	16676	
Saint Davids, Br. Wayne	19087	
Saint Johns	18247	
Saint Marys (1st)	15857	
Saint Michael	15951	
Saint Peters	19470	
Saint Petersburg	16054	
Saint Thomas	17252	
Salford	18957	
Salfordville	18958	
Salina	15680	
Salisbury	15558	
Salix	15952	
Salladasburg, R. Br. Jersey Shore	17740	

Salona, R. Br. Mill Hall	17767	
Saltillo	17253	
Saltsburg (1st)	15681	
Salunga, Br. Landisville	17538	
Sandy Lake	16145	
Sandy Ridge, R. Br. Osceola Mills	16677	
Sarver	16055	
Sassamansville	19472	
Saxonburg	16056	
Saxton	16678	
Saylorsburg	18353	
Sayre (1st)	18840	
Scalp Level, Br. Windber	15963	
Scenery Hill	15360	
Schaefferstown	17088	
Schellsburg	15559	
Schenley	15682	
Schnecksville	18078	
Schoeneck	17574	
Schuylkill, Sta. Philadelphia	19146	
Schuylkill Haven (1st)	17972	
Schwenksville	19473	
Sciota	18354	
Scotland	17254	
Scotrun	18355	
Scottdale (1st)	15683	
SCRANTON (1st) (see appendix)		
Seanor	15953	
Seelyville, Br. Honesdale	18431	
Selinsgrove (1st)	17870	
Sellersville (1st)	18960	
Seltzer	17974	
Seminole	16253	
Seneca	16346	
Sergeant	16747	
Seven Valleys	17360	
Seward	15954	
Sewickley (1st)	15143	
Shade Gap	17255	
Shady Grove	17256	
Shadyside, Sta. Pittsburgh	15232	
Shaft	17975	
Shamokin (1st)	17872	
Ranshaw, R. Br.	17866	
Shamokin Dam	17876	
Shamrock Station	15552	
Shanesville	15553	
Shanksville	15560	
Sharon (1st)	16146	
Sharon Hill (1st)	19079	
Sharpsburg, Br. Pittsburgh	15215	
Sharpsville	16150	
Shartlesville	19554	
Shavertown, Br. Wilkes-Barre	18708	
Shawanese	18654	
Shawnee On Delaware	18356	
Shawville	16873	
Sheakleyville	16151	
Sheffield	16347	
Shelocta	15774	
Shenandoah (1st)	17976	
Shenango	16152	
Sheppton	18248	
Shermans Dale	17090	
Shickshinny	18655	
Shillington, Br. Reading	19607	
Shinglehouse	16748	
Millport, R. Br.	16739	
Shippensburg (1st)	17257	
Shippenville	16254	

Shippingport	15077	
Shiremanstown, Br. Camp Hill	17011	
Shirleysburg	17260	
Shoemakersville	19555	
Shohola	18458	
Shrewsbury	17361	
Shunk	17768	
Sidman	15955	
Sigel	15860	
Silver Spring	17575	
Silverdale	18962	
Simpson, Br. Carbondale	18407	
Sinking Spring, Br. Reading	19608	
Sinnamahoning	15861	
Sipesville	15561	
Six Mile Run	16679	
Sixtieth Street, Sta. Philadelphia	19139	
Skippack	19474	
Skytop	18357	
Slate Run	17769	
Slatedale	18079	
Slatington (1st)	18080	
Slickville	15684	
Sligo	16255	
Slippery Rock (1st)	16057	
Slovan	15078	
Smethport	16749	
Smicksburg	16256	
Smithfield	15478	
Smithmill	16680	
Smithton	15479	
Smock	15480	
Smokerun	16681	
Smoketown	17576	
Snow Shoe	16874	
Snydersburg	16257	
Snydertown	17877	
Solebury	18963	
Somerset (1st)	15501	
Somerton, Sta Philadelphia	19116	
Sonestown, R Br. Muncy Valley	17770	
Soudersburg	17577	
Souderton (1st)	18964	
Bethton, Br.	18964	
Elroy, Br.	18964	
Franconia, R. Br.	18924	
South, Sta Butler	16001	
South Canaan	18455	
South Connellsville, Br. Connellsville	15425	
South Erie, Sta. Erie (see appendix)		
South Fork	15956	
South Gibson	18842	
South Heights	15081	
South Hills, Br. Pittsburgh	15216	
South Montrose	18843	
South Mountain	17261	
South New Castle, Sta. New Castle	16101	
South Plaza, Br. Indiana	15701	
South Side, Sta. Scranton	18505	
South Sterling	18460	
South Williamsport, Br. Williamsport	17701	
Southampton (1st)	18960	
Southview	15361	
Southwark, Sta. Philadelphia (see appendix)		
Southwest	15685	

Spangler 15775
Spartansburg 16434
Spinnerstown 18968
Spraggs 15362
Sprankle Mills 15776
Spring Church 15686
Spring City (1st) 19475
Spring Creek 16436
Spring Garden, Sta.
  Philadelphia (see
  appendix)
Spring Glen 17978
Spring Grove (1st) 17362

  Porters Sideling, R. Br. ...17354
Spring House (1st) 19477
Spring Mills 16875
Spring Mount 19478
Spring Run 17262
Springboro 16435
Springdale (1st) 15144
Springfield, Br. Media 19064
Springs 15562
Springtown 18081
Springville 18844
Sproul 16682
Spruce Creek 16683
Squirrel Hill, Sta. Pittsburgh ..15217
Stahlstown 15687
Star Junction 15482
Starford 15777
Starlight 18461
Starr 16348
Starrucca 18462
State College (1st) 16801
  Nittany Mall, Br. 16801
  Northwest, Br. 16801
  Toftrees, Br. 16801
  University Park, Sta. 16802
State Line 17263
Steelton, Br. Harrisburg ... 17113
Steelville 19370
Sterling 18463
Stevens 17578
Stevensville 18845
Stewartstown 17363
Stiles, Sta. Whitehall 18052
Stillwater 17878
Stockdale 15483
Stockertown 16083
Stoneboro 16153
Stony Run 19557
Stouchsburg, R. Br.
  Womelsdorf 19558
Stowe, Br. Pottstown 19464
Stoystown 15563
Strabane 15363
Strasburg 17579
Strattanville 16258
Strausstown 19559
Strong 17879
Strongstown, R. Br. Twin
  Rocks 15957
Stroudsburg (1st) 18360
Stump Creek 15863
Sturgeon 15082
Suburbia, Br. Pottstown ... 19464
Sugar Notch, Br.
  Wilkes-Barre 18706
Sugar Run 18846
Sugargrove 16350
Sugarloaf 18249
Summerdale 17093
Summerhill 15958

Summerville 15864
Summit Hill 18250
Summit Station 17979
Sumneytown 18084
Sunbury (1st) 17801
Suplee 19371
Susquehanna 18847
Sutersville 15083
Swarthmore (1st) 19081
Swedeland 19479
Sweet Valley 18656
Swengel 17880
Swiftwater 18370
Swissvale, Br. Pittsburgh ..15218
Swoyerville, Br. Wilkes-Barre ..18704
Sybertsville 18251
Sycamore 15364
Sykesville 15865
Sylvania 16945
Tacony, Sta. Philadelphia ...19135
Tafton 18464
Talmage 17580
Tamaqua (1st) 18252
Tamiment, R. Br. Bushkill ..18371
Tannersville 18372
Tarentum (1st) 15084
Tarrs 15688
Tatamy 18085
Taylor-Old Forge, Br.
  Scranton (see appendix)
Taylorstown 15365
Telford (1st) 18969
Temple (1st) 19560
Templeton 16259
Tenth Avenue, Sta.
  Bethlehem 18018
Terminal, Sta. Upper Darby ..19082
Terre Hill 17581
Thomasville 17364
Thompson 18465
Thompsontown 17094
Thorndale (1st) 19372
Thornton 19373
Three Springs 17264
Throop, Br. Scranton 18512
Tidioute 16351
Timblin 15778
Tioga 16946
Tiona 16352
Tionesta 16353
Tipton 16684
Tire Hill 15959
Titusville (1st) 16354
Tobyhanna (1st) 18466
Todd 16685
Toftrees, Br. State College ..16801
Topton (1st) 19562
Torrance 15779
Torresdale, Sta. Philadelphia
  (see appendix)
Toughkenamon 19374
Towanda (1st) 18848
Tower City 17980
Townville 16360
Trafford (1st) 15085
Transfer 16154
Treehaven, Sta. Bethel Park ..15102
Treichlers 18086
Tremont 17981
Trescow 18254
Trevorton 17881
Trevose, Br. Langhorne 19047
Trexlertown 18087

Trout Run 17771
  Bodines, R. Br. 17722
Troutville 15866
Troxelville 17882
Troy (1st) 16947
Trucksville, Br. Wilkes-Barre ..18708
Trumbauersville 18970
Tullytown, Br. Bristol 19007
Tunkhannock (1st) 18657
Turbotville 17772
Turkey City 16058
Turtle Creek (1st) 15145
Turtlepoint 16750
Tuscarora 17982
Twin Rocks 15960
  Strongstown, R. Br. 15957
Tyler Hill 18469
Tylersburg 16361
Tylersport 18971
Tylersville 17773
Tyre, R. Br. Imperial 15126
Tyrone (1st) 16686
U S Naval Base, Sta.
  Philadelphia 19112
Uledi 15484
Ulster 18850
Ulysses 16948
Union City (1st) 16438
Union Dale 18470
Union Trust, Sta. Pittsburgh ..15219
Uniontown (1st) 15401
Unionville 19375
United 15689
Unity House, R. Br. Bushkill ..18373
Unityville 17774
Universal, Br. Pittsburgh ..15235
University Park, Sta. State
  College 16802
Upper Black Eddy 18972
UPPER DARBY (1st) (see
  appendix)
Upper Saint Clair, Br.
  Pittsburgh 15241
Upper Strasburg 17265
Uptown, Sta. Pittsburgh ...15219
Ursina 15485
Utica 16362
Uwchland 19480
Valencia 16059
Valier 15780
Valley Forge (1st) 19481
Valley Forge Army Hospital,
  Br. Phoenixville 19460
Valley View 17983
Van 16363
Van Meter 15487
Van Voorhis 15366
Vanderbilt 15486
Vandergrift (1st) 15690
Vandling, Br. Forest City ...18421
Venango 16440
Venetia 15367
Venus 16364
Vera Cruz, R. Br. Emmaus ..18049
Vernfield 18973
Vernon Park, Sta.
  Philadelphia 19144
Verona (1st) 15147
Versailles, Br. Mc Keesport ..15132
Vestaburg 15368
Veterans Administration
  Hosp. Br. Butler 16001

Veterans Administration
  Hosp. Sta. Altoona 16603
Veterans Hospital, Sta.
  Wilkes-Barre 18703
Veterans Hospital, Br.
  Coatesville 19320
Veterans Hospital, Sta.
  Pittsburgh 15240
Vicksburg 17883
Villa Maria 16155
Village, Br. Pittsburgh 15241
Villanova (1st) 19085
Vintondale 15961
Virginville 19564
Volant 16156
Vowinckel 16260
Wabash Sta. Pittsburgh 15220
Wadsworth, Sta.
  Philadelphia 19150
Wagontown 19376
Wahnetah, Sta. Jim Thorpe ..18229
Wallaceton 16876
Wallingford, Br. Media 19086
Walnut Bottom 17266
Walnutport 18088
Walston 15781
Waltersburg 15488
Wampum 16157
Wapwallopen 18660
Ward 19377
Warfordsburg 17267
Warminster (1st) 18974
Warren (1st) 16365
Warren Center 18851
Warrendale 15086
Warrington (1st) 18976
Warriors Mark 16877
Washington (1st) 15301
Washington Boro 17582
Washington Crossing 18977
Washingtonville 17884
Waterfall 16689
Waterford 16441
Waterman, R. Br. Homer
  City 15748
Waterville 17776
Watsontown 17777
Wattsburg 16442
Waverly 18471
Wawa, R. Br. Media 19063
Waymart 18472
Wayne (1st) 19087
Waynesboro (1st) 17268
Waynesburg (1st) 15370
Weatherly 18255
Webster 15087
Weedville 15868
Weikert 17885
Weissport, Br. Lehighton 18235
Wellersburg, R. Br.
  Hyndman 15564
Wells Tannery 16691
Wellsboro (1st) 16901
Wellsville 17365
Wendel 15691
Wernersville 19565
Wescosville, Br. Allentown ..18106
Wesleyville, Br. Erie (see
  appendix)
West Alexander 15376
West Aliquippa, Sta.
  Aliquippa 15001

West Bridgewater, Br.
  Beaver 15009
West Bristol, Br. Bristol 19007
West Brownsville, Br.
  Brownsville 15417
West Chester (1st) 19380
West Conshohocken, Br.
  Conshohocken 19428
West Decatur 16878
West Elizabeth 15088
West End, Sta. Harrisburg ...17102
West Fairview, Br. Enola 17025
West Finley 15377
West Goshen, Br. West
  Chester 19380
West Grove (1st) 19390
West Hazleton, Br. Hazleton ..18201
West Hickory 16370
West Hills, Br. Coraopolis 15108
West Lawn, Br. Reading 19609
West Lebanon 15783
West Leisenring 15489
West Market Street, Sta.
  Philadelphia 19139
West Middlesex 16159
West Middletown 15379
West Milton 17886
  New Columbia, R. Br. 17856
West Monterey 16060
West Nanticoke, Br.
  Nanticoke 18634
West Newton (1st) 15089
West Park, Sta.
  Philadelphia 19131
West Pittsburg 16160
West Pittston, Br. Pittston ...18643
West Plaza, Br. Erie 16505
West Point (1st) 19486
West Reading, Br. Reading ...19602
West Ridge, Br. Erie 16506
West Salisbury 15565
West Scranton, Sta.
  Scranton 18504
West Side, Sta. Nanticoke 18634
West Springfield 16443
West Sunbury 16061
West View, Br. Pittsburgh 15229
West Willow 17583
West Winfield 16062
West Wyoming, Br. Pittston ..18644
Westfield 16950
  Harrison Valley, R. Br. 16927
Westford, R. Br. Jamestown ..16134
Westland 15378
Westline 16751
Westmoreland City 15692
Weston 18256
Westover 16692
Westport 17778
Westtown 19395
Westville 15869
Westwood, Br. Johnstown 15905
Wexford (1st) 15090
Wheatland 16161
Whitaker, Br. Homestead 15120
White 15490
White Deer 17887
White Haven 18661
White Mills 18473
White Oak, Br. Mc Keesport ..15131
Whitehall (1st) 18052
Whites Crossing, Br.
  Carbondale 18407

Whitney 15693
Whitsett 15491
Wickhaven 15492
Wiconisco 17097
Widener College, Sta.
  Chester 19013
Widnoon 16261
Wila, R. Br. Newport 17074
Wilburton 17888
Wilcox 15870
Wildwood 15091
WILKES-BARRE (1st) (see
  appendix)
Wilkinsburg, Br. Pittsburgh ..15221
William Penn Annex, Sta.
  Philadelphia (see
  appendix)
Williamsburg 16693
Williamson 17270
Williamsport (1st) 17701
Williamstown 17098
Willow Grove (1st) 19090
Willow Hill 17271
Willow Street 17584
Wilmerding (1st) 15148
Wilmore 15962
Wilson 15694
Wilson, Sta. Clairton 15025
Winburne 16879
Wind Ridge 15380
Windber (1st) 15963
Windgap (1st) 18091
Windsor 17366
Winfield 17889
Wingate, R. Br. Bellefonte ...16880
Wireton, R. Br. Glenwillard ..15092
Wissinoming, Sta.
  Philadelphia 19124
Witmer 17585
Womelsdorf 19567
  Stouchsburg, R. Br. 19558
Wood 16694
Woodbury 16695
Woodland 16881
Woodlyn (1st) 19094
Woodward 16882
Woolrich 17779
Worcester 19490
Wormleysburg, Br. Lemoyne ..17043
Worthington 16262
Worthville 15784
Woxall 18979
Wrights, R. Br. Port
  Allegany 16752
Wrightstown, Br. Newtown ...18940
Wrightsville (1st) 17368
Wyalusing 18853
Wyano 15695
Wycombe 18980
Wylie, Sta. Pittsburgh 15219
Wyncote (1st) 19095
Wynnewood (1st) 19096
Wyoming, Br. Pittston 18644
Wyomissing, Br. Reading 19610
Wysox 18854
Yardley, Br. Morrisville 19067
Yatesboro 16263
Yeadon, Br. Lansdowne 19050
Yeagertown 17099
Yellow House 19568
Yerkes 19491
Yoe, Br. Dallastown 17313

YORK (1st) (see appendix)
York Haven........................17370
York New Salem 17371
York Springs.....................17372
Youngstown.......................15696

Youngsville........................16371
Youngwood (1st) 15697
Yukon.................................15698
Zelienople (1st)..................16063
Zerbe, R. Br. Tremont 17981

Zieglerville........................19492
Zion Grove.........................17985
Zionhill..............................18981
Zionsville...........................18092
Zullinger............................17272

ALLENTOWN   181

POST OFFICE BOXES

Box Nos.
A-M	Main Office	05
1-1910	Main Office	05
3000-3999	Wescosville Branch	06

RURAL ROUTES

1		04
2		03
3		04
4		03

STATIONS, BRANCHES AND UNITS

Wescosville Br	06
General Delivery	05
Postmaster	01

APARTMENTS, HOTELS, MOTELS

Allen Gardens, 800 So 12th	03
Allen-Towne House Motel 647 Union Blvd	03
Americus Hotel 541 Hamilton	05
Colonial & Colonial Arms, 218 S 15th	02
Devonshire Apartments, 31st & Devonshire	03
Episcopal House, 1440 Walnut	02
Executive 901 So Jefferson	03
Hamilton Crest, 2122 Walnut	04
Hamilton Hotel 627 Hamilton	01
Hamilton Square 117 S 4th 350 Hickory Ln	02
Hampshire House, 15th 1/2 Hamilton	02
Highland Dwellings 2145 Livingston, 2144 Highland	04
Holiday Inn Of Allentown, Route 3	04
John Gross Towers, 1339 Allen	02
Livingston, 1411 Hamilton	02
Majestic, 127 N 8th	01
Regent, 923 Hamilton	01
Tourinns Motel Route 3	04
Traylor Hotel 1436 Hamilton	05
Tremont Apartments	04
Trexler Park 3616 Tilghman	04
Trout Hall Gardens	02
Valley View, S 15th & Elm	02

BUILDINGS

Administration, 31 S Penn	05
Allen Law, 133 N 5th	02
B & B, 546 Hamilton	01
Center Square, 11 N 7th	01
Colonial Theatre, 517 Hamilton	01
Commerce, 12 N 7th	01
Commonwealth, 514 Hamilton	01
Farr, 739 Hamilton	01
Federal, 442 Hamilton	01

Hamilton Law, 527 Hamilton	01
Hunsicker, 17 N 7th	01
Liberty Square Medical Center, 501 N 17th	04
Medical Arts, 941 Hamilton	01
Odd Fellows, 118 N 9th	02
Penn Trust, 801 Hamilton	01
Pennsylvania Power & Light Company, 901 Hamilton	01
Somach, 1132 Hamilton	01
Wetherhold & Metzger 719 Hamilton	01
Y M C A & W Y C A, 425 S 15th	02
Young, 714 Hamilton	05

GOVERNMENT OFFICES

City Hall, 435 Hamilton	01
Federal, 442 Hamilton	01
Lehigh County Court House, 455 Hamilton	05

HOSPITALS

Allentown Hospital, 1627 Chew	02
Allentown Osteopathic Hospital, 1736 Hamilton	04
Allentown State Hospital, 1700 Hanover Ave	03
Sacred Heart Hospital, 421 Chew W	02

UNIVERSITIES AND COLLEGES

Cedar Crest College, 30th & Walnut	04
Muhlenberg College, 2301 Chew	04
Penn Wesleyan College 1414 E Cedar St	03

ALTOONA   166

POST OFFICE BOXES

Box Nos
1 2032	Main Office	03

RURAL ROUTES

1,2,3,4	01

STATIONS, BRANCHES AND UNITS

Juniata Sta	01
Lakemont Br	02
Veterans Administration HospSta	03
General Delivery	03
Postmaster	03

BETHLEHEM   180

POST OFFICE BOXES

Box Nos.
1-800	Main Office	16
1001-1484	Moravian Sta	18

2001-2872	Lehigh Valley Br	01
3001-3178	Butztown Br	17
4001-4094	Tenth Ave Station Sta	18

RURAL ROUTES

1,2	17
3,4,5	15
6	17

STATIONS, BRANCHES AND UNITS

Butztown Br	17
Freemansburg Br	17
Kaywin Br	18
Lehigh University Sta	15
Lehigh Valley Br	01
Moravian Sta	18
Tenth Avenue Sta	18
General Delivery	15
Postmaster	16

CHESTER   190

POST OFFICE BOXES

Box Nos.
1-86	Aston	14
1-846	Main Office	16
1001-1159	Brookhaven	15

STATIONS, BRANCHES AND UNITS

Aston Br	14
Brookhaven Br	15
Eddystone Br	13
Widener College Sta	13
General Delivery	13
Postmaster	13

HOSPITALS

Crozer-Chester Medical Center, 15th & Upland Ave	13
Sacred Heart Hospital, 9th & Wilson St	13

UNIVERSITIES AND COLLEGES

Widener College 14th & Chestnut St	13

ERIE   165

POST OFFICE BOXES

Box Nos.
1-1440	Main Office	12
1501-1925	Perry Square Sta	07
2000-2999	Main Office	12
3001-3368	South Erie Sta	08
4000-6500	Main Office	12
7001-7999	Wesleyville Br	10
8000-8999	Presque Isle Br	05
9000-9500	Pine Avenue Sta	04

538

RURAL ROUTES

3,4,5	09
6,7	10
9,10	09

STATIONS, BRANCHES AND UNITS

Nagle Road Br	10
Perry Square Sta	07
Pine Avenue Sta	04
West Plaza Br	05
West Ridge Br	06
General Delivery	01
Postmaster	01

APARTMENTS, HOTELS, MOTELS

Audrey, 518 Holland	07
Boston, 516 E 6	01
Brownstone, 26 North Park Row	01
Center City 814 Sassafras	01
Downtowner, 205 W 10	01
El Patio, 2950 W Lake Rd	05
Fleming, 210 W 8	01
Glenwood Towers, 4601 Glenwood Park Ave	09
Hamel, 446-58 W 9	02
Harborview House, 210 W 6	07
Holiday Inn South, Rts 90 & 97	12
Holiday Inn, 18 W 18	02
Howard Johnson, 7575 Waterford Pike Rd	09
Kenilworth, 351-53 W 6	07
Keystone, 1206 E Lake Rd	07
Lininger, 425-31 Peach	01
Parade 701-03 Parade	03
Peach Hill, 2631 Peach	04
Pittsburgh, 2182 W 8	05
Plymouth, 604-08 Chestnut	02
Princeton, 238 W 6	01
Richford, 515 State	01
Schaaf, 10 E 34	04
Schaaf, 3004-16 State	08
Schaaf, 3309 State	08
Schaaf, 9 E 33	04
Scotts, 2930 W 6	05
Sharp, 727 French	01
Thirty-Five Thirty-Five, 3535 State	08
Town House 925 French	01

BUILDINGS

Baldwin, 1001 State	01
Commerce, 10 E 12	01
Marine Bank, 901-05 State	01
Masonic Temple, 24 W 8	01
Palace, 913 State	01
Professional, 1611 Peach	01
Rothrock, 121 W 10	01
Sumner Nichols 155 West 8th	01

HOSPITALS

Doctors 252 W 11	01
Erie Osteopathic, 5515 Peach	09
Grandview, 4728 Lake Pleasant Rd	04

Hamot, 4 E 2	12
Saint Vincents, 232 W 25	12
Veterans, 135 E 38	01
Zem Zem, 1645 W 8	05

UNIVERSITIES AND COLLEGES

Behrend Campus (Penn State U, Station Rd	10
Gannon, 10 9 W 6	01
Mercyhurst, 501 E 38	01
Villa Maria, 2551 W Lake Rd	05

HARRISBURG 171

POST OFFICE BOXES

Box Nos.

A-W	Federal Square Sta	08
1-1299	Federal Square Sta	08
1301-3999	Main Office	05
4000-4999	Paxtang Br	11
5000-5999	Camp Curtin Sta	10
6000-6999	Linglestown Br	12
7000-7999	Steelton Br	13

RURAL ROUTES

1	11
2	10
3,4	11

STATIONS, BRANCHES AND UNITS

Camp Curtin Sta	10
Chambers Hill Br	11
Colonial Park Br	09
Federal Square Sta	08
Hill Sta	12
Linglestown Br	12
Lower Paxton Br	09
Paxtang Br	11
Penbrook Br	03
Rutherford Heights Br	11
Steelton Br	13
West End Sta	02
General Delivery	05
Postmaster	05

APARTMENTS, HOTELS, MOTELS

Allen Hall	04
Beaufort Manor, 4100 Beechwood Ln	12
Bistline House 1291 S 28th	12
Blue Mountain, Rd 4	12
Brookridge Terrace	09
Brookwood Gardens, 2500 Brookwood	01
Capitol Hill 327 Market	01
Colonial Crest	09
Colonial, 420 Market	01
Donaldson, 204 N 2nd	01
East Park Garden, 200 N 40th	11
English Village, 3300 Paxton	11
Executive House, 101 S 2nd	01
Governor, Box 2101	05
Grayco, 115 North	01
Greene Hall	04
Harrisburg Park, 1400 S	

15th	04
Holiday East, Box 1855	05
Holiday Inn Town, Box 1855	05
Holiday West, Box 1855	05
Hoy Towers, 300 Mohn	13
Jackson Lick, 1300 N 6th	02
Locust Grove, Locust Grove Ct	09
Mitchell, 105 North	01
Mitchell, 611 N Front	01
Nationwide Inn, 900 Race	04
Packer House, 1700 State	03
Parkview, 2400 Market	03
Parkway, 925 N Front	02
Paxton Park, 600 Santanna Dr	09
Penn Harris Motor Inn, Box 2653	05
Penn Harris, Box 2651	05
Plaza, 423 Market	01
Presbyterian, 322 N 2nd	01
R D 4	12
Revere Hall	04
River House, 2311 N Front	10
Riverview Manor, 1519 N Front	02
Royal, 422 Market	01
Saint James, 405-A Market	01
Schuyler Hall	04
Scottsdale, 1021 S Progress Ave	11
Thornwood, 220 Thornwood Rd	04
Towne House, 660 Boas	02
Twin Lakes Manor 4401 Union Deposit Road	11
Warner, 17 N 2nd	01
Wayne Hall	04
Y M C A, 701 N Front	01
Y W C A, 4th & Walnut	01

BUILDINGS

Barto, 231 State	01
Bergner, 6 N 3rd	01
Blackstone, 112 Market	01
Brotherhood, 2107 N 6th	10
Calder, 16 N 2nd	01
Colonial Park Medical 4900 Constitution Avenue	09
Columbus, 229 Walnut	01
Commerce, 300 N 2nd	01
Dauphin, 203 Market	01
Farm Show, 1030 Maclay	20
Federal Office, 228 Walnut	08
Feller, 301 Market	01
Hall, 112 N 2nd	01
Kel-Front, 1801 N Front	02
Keystone, 20 S 3rd	01
Kline, 210 Walnut	01
Market Square, 2 N 2nd	01
Payne-Shoemaker, 240 N 3rd	01
Riverside Medical, 1919 N Front	02
Riverside Office Center, 2101 N Front	10
Scottish Rite Cathedral 2701 N 3rd	10
Shore Drive Office Center, 2001 N Front	02
State Street, 500 N 3rd	01
State Theatre, 212 Locust	01

Zembe Temple, 3rd &
  Division 10

GOVERNMENT OFFICES

All Other State Departments... 20
Bureau Of Motor Vehicles,
  Transp And Safety Bldg 22
City Hall, 423 Walnut 01
Department Of Revenue,
  Finance Building 27
Employment Security, Labor
  & Industry Bldg 21
Liquor Control, N W Office
  Bldg 24
Municipal, 423 Walnut 01
Personal Income Tax, Finance
  Bldg 29
Property & Supply, Main
  Capital 25
Public Instruction, Education
  Bldg 26
Taxes For Education, 1846
  Brookwood 28
Traffic Safety, Transp And
  Safety Bldg 23
United States Court House,
  Federal Office Bldg 08
United States Post Office,
  811 Market 05

HOSPITALS

Community General
  Osteopathic, 4300
  Londonderry Rd 09
Dauphin County, 1205 S
  28th 11
Harrisburg Polyclinic, Box
  3410 Gpo 05
Harrisburg, Front & Mulberry... 01
Mental 05
Pennsylvania State (Pouch
  A) 05

JOHNSTOWN   159

POST OFFICE BOXES

Box Nos.
1-184   Conemaugh Br 09
1-1017   Main Office 07

RURAL ROUTES

1 06
2,3 04
4,5 05
6 09

STATIONS, BRANCHES AND UNITS

Conemaugh Br 09
East Hills Br 04
Geistown Br 04
Westwood Br 05
General Delivery 01
Postmaster 01

APARTMENTS, HOTELS, MOTELS

Belmont Homes 04
Carriage Hill Apts 05
Center Town Apts 01
College Park Apts 04
Coopersdale Homes 06
Edwards Hill Apts 05
Norwood Gardens Apts 05
Oakhurst Homes 06
Soloman St Homes 02
Vine St Towers Apts 01

BUILDINGS

Carnegie 01
City Hall 01
Federal Bldg-U S Post Office... 01
First National Bank 01
Fisher 01
Johnstown Bank & Trust 01
Park 01
Savings Bank Plz 01
Swank 01
U S Bank 01

LANCASTER   176

POST OFFICE BOXES

Box Nos.
1-1799   Lancaster 04
5000-5500 Neffsville Br 01

RURAL ROUTES

2 03
4 02
6 03
7 02

STATIONS, BRANCHES AND UNITS

Neffsville Br 01
General Delivery 04
Postmaster 04

APARTMENTS, HOTELS, MOTELS

Barrcrest Manor, 1705
  Marietta Ave 03
Buchanan, 206 N Queen 04
Cedar Acres, Old
  Philadelphia Pk 02
Conestoga West, 200 Stone
  Mill Rd 03
Congress Inn, Lincoln Hwy E... 03
Devon House, 1527 Fruitville
  Pk 01
Essex House, 145 Maple
  Lane 01
Garden Spot Motel, Lincoln
  Hwy E 02
George Ross House, 114 E
  Lemon 02
Grand View Apts, Mcgrann
  Blvd 01
Hamilton Apts, Duke &
  Walnut 02

Hilton Inn N. Queen And
  Chestnut Sts 04
Holiday Inn East 1800
  Hempstead Rd 01
Holiday Inn, 1492 Lititz Pike... 01
Host Corral 2250 Lincoln
  Highway E 04
Host Farms, 2300 Lincoln
  Highway E 04
Host Motel, 30 Keller Ave 01
Howard Johnson'S Motor
  Lodge, 2100 Lincoln Hwy
  E 04
King Douglas, 105 E King 02
La Chateau De Eden Butter
  Rd 01
Lancaster Court, 1100
  Wabank Rd 03
Landis Vally Motor Inn, 2363
  Oregon Pike 01
Long Home Apts, Race &
  Marietta Aves 03
Manor House, 1400
  Millersville Pk 03
Mayfair, 800 Pleasure Rd 01
Oxford House, 146 Maple
  Lane 01
President Buchanan, 1400
  Passey Ln 03
Quality Court 500 Centerville
  Rd 01
River Park Gardens, 1125-
  1255 E Orange 02
Roseville House, 401 Eden
  Rd 01
Saint Charles Apartment,
  400 Euclid Ave 03
Spring Manor, 700
  Millersville Rd 03
Stevens House, Prince &
  King 03
Sweet Briar, Oregon Pike 01
Towne House, 742 N Duke 02
Travel Lodge, 2101 Columbia
  Ave 03
Treadway Inn 222 Eden Rd 01
Twin Towers, 403 W James 03
Wabank Country Club
  Estates, Michelle Dr 03
Wheatland Arms, 1115
  Marietta Ave 03
Willows The, Lincoln Hwy E 02
1722 Motor Lodge 1722 Old
  Philadelphia Pike 02

BUILDINGS

Agriculture, 45-47 N Duke 02
Appel, 33 N Duke 02
Coho, 53 N Duke 02
Conestoga Bank Bldg, 28
  Penn Square 03
Fulton Bank Bldg, 8 Penn
  Square 02
Greist Bldg, 2-8 N Queen 03
West End Medical Center,
  822 Marietta Ave 03
Y M C A, 572 N Queen 03
Y W C A, 149 E Orange 02

GOVERNMENT OFFICES

Federal Bldg. 48-50 W Chestnut	04
Lancaster County Court House, 51 E King	02
Lancaster County Health & Welfare, 630 Janet Ave	01
Lancaster School District Bldg. 225 W Orange	04
Lancaster Township Adm Bldg, 1240 Maple Ave	03
Manheim Township Muni Bldg, 1500 Lititz Pike	01
Manor Township Office, 1695 Temple Ave	03
Municipal Bldg. 120 N Duke	04
Public Safety Bldg, 208 N Duke	02

HOSPITALS

Conestoga View, 900 E King	02
Lancaster County Hospital, 900 E King	02
Lancaster General Hospital, 525 N Duke	04
Lancaster Osteopathic Hospital, 1100 E Orange	04
St Joseph Hospital, 250 College Ave	04

UNIVERSITIES AND COLLEGES

Franklin & Marshall, College Ave	04
Lancaster Country Day School, 725 Hamilton Rd	03
Lancaster Theological Seminary, James & College Ave	03
Stevens Trade School, 750 E King	02

LEVITTOWN   190

POST OFFICE BOXES

Box Nos.

1-269	A Sta	59
301-778	Main Office	58

STATIONS, BRANCHES AND UNITS

Fallsington Br	54
Newportville Br	56
General Delivery	58
Postmaster	58

APARTMENTS, HOTELS, MOTELS

Brittany Springs, Oxford Valley Rd	57
Camelot, Marion & Edgley Ave	55
Country Club Park, 1228 New Rodgers Rd	56
Country Manor, Lincoln Hwy	56
Fallingston Manor, 8590 Newportville-Fallsington Rd	54

Falls Creek 9161 Newportville Rd	54
Hamilton, 2130 New Rodgers Rd	56
Hidden Manor, 201 Woodburne Rd	56
Kenwood Court, Haines Rd	55
Madrid, 1338 New Rodgers Rd	56
Mill Creek Manor, 130 Tullytown-Fallsington Rd	54
Mill Creek, 7030 Mill Creek Rd	57
Orangewood, Orangewood Dr	57
Parkview, 2000 New Rodgers Rd	56
Queen Anne Court, 1550 Woodburne Rd	57
Racquet Club East, 1970 New Rodgers Rd	56
Valley Green, 3501 Oxford Valley Rd	57
Village Of Penbrook Apts 9071 Mill Creek Rd	54
Violetwood Garden Apts., 6750 Mill Creek Rd	57
Woodbourne Apts. 1350 Woodbourne Rd	57

MC KEESPORT   151

POST OFFICE BOXES

Box Nos.

1-96	Boston Br	35
1-805	Main Office	34

STATIONS, BRANCHES AND UNITS

Boston Br	35
Central Sta	32
Port Vue Br	33
Versailles Br	33
White Oak Br	31
General Delivery	34
Postmaster	34

APARTMENTS, HOTELS, MOTELS

Penn Mckee Hotel 130 5th Ave	32
Penn Sheratan Hotel 624 Lysle Blvd	32

HOSPITALS

Mckeesport Hospital 1500 5th Ave	32

MEDIA   190

POST OFFICE BOXES

Box Nos.

1-114	Elwyn Br	63
1-267	Springfield Br	64
1-319	Moylan Br	65
1-572	Main Office	63
37-389	Wallingford Br	86

STATIONS, BRANCHES AND UNITS

Darling Rural Br	63
Elwyn Br	63
Franklin Center Rural Br	63
Moylan Br	65
Springfield Br	64
Wallingford Br	86
Wawa Rural Br	63
General Delivery	63
Postmaster	63

NEW CASTLE   161

POST OFFICE BOXES

Box Nos.

1-1020	Main Office	03
1401-1552	Main Office	03
2201-2346	Mahoningtown Sta	02
4000-4999	South Side Office	01
5001-5999	Neshannock Br	05

RURAL ROUTES

2	01
3	05
4	01
5	05
6	01
7	02

STATIONS, BRANCHES AND UNITS

Cascade Br	01
Mahoningtown Sta	02
Neshannock Br	05
South New Castle Sta	01
General Delivery	01
Postmaster	01

APARTMENTS, HOTELS, MOTELS

Castle Arms, N. Mercer : Falls	01
Lawrence Manor 211 W Moody Ave	01
Mc Grath Manor 814 W Washington	01
New Penn Hotel 20 S Mercer	01
Skyview Towers 219 N Beaver	01

BUILDINGS

Centennial 7 S Mill	01
Central 101 S Mercer	01
First Federal Plaza 25 N Mill	01
First National Bank 101 E Washington	01
Lawrence Savings : Trust 223 E Washington	01

HOSPITALS

Jameson Memorial 222 W Leasure Ave	05

St Francis S Mercer At Phillips 01

UNIVERSITIES AND COLLEGES

New Castle Business College 316 Rhodes Pl 01

NORRISTOWN 194

POST OFFICE BOXES

Box Nos.

1-226	Eagleville Br	08
1-261	Bridgeport Br	05
1-292	Audubon Br	07
1-294	Fairview Village Br	09
1-389	King Of Prussia Br	06
1-999	Main Office	04

RURAL ROUTES

1,3 01

STATIONS, BRANCHES AND UNITS

Audubon Br	07
Bridgeport Br	05
Eagleville Br	08
Fairview Village Br	09
Hospital Sta	01
King Of Prussia Br	06
Park Ridge Sta	01
General Delivery	01
Postmaster	01

PHILADELPHIA 191

POST OFFICE BOXES

Box Nos.

A-H	William Penn Annex Sta	05
1-1999	William Penn Annex Sta	05
2000-2399	Middle City Sta	03
2400-2599	Southwark Sta	47
2600-2699	Fairmount Sta	21
2700-2799	Olney Sta	20
2800-2899	Spring Garden Sta	22
2900-2999	Oak Lane Sta	26
3000-3199	Wadsworth Sta	50
3200-3399	Fairmount Sta	21
3400-3599	Spring Garden Sta	22
3600-3799	Kensington Sta	25
3800-3999	Schuylkill Sta	46
4000-4099	Chestnut Hill Sta	18
4100-4299	Germantown Sta	44
4300-4399	Chestnut Hill Sta	18
4400-4499	Nicetown Sta	40
4500-4599	West Park Sta	31
4600-4699	Manayunk Sta	27
4700-4799	Richmond Sta	34
4800-4899	Frankford Sta	24
4900-1999	Mount Airy Sta	19
5000-5099	Fox Chase Sta	11
5100-5199	Logan Sta	41
5200-5299	Oak Lane Sta	26
5300-5399	Paschall Sta	42
5400-5599	Kingsessing Sta	43
5600-5699	East Falls Sta	29
5700-5799	Olney Sta	20
5800-5899	Roxborough Sta	28
5900-5999	Bridesburg Sta	37
6000-6099	Torresdale Sta	14
6100-6199	Bustleton Sta	15
6200-6299	Holmesburg Sta	36
6300-6399	West Market Sta	39
6400-6499	Point Breeze Sta	45
6500-6599	East Germantown Sta	38
6600-6699	Boulevard Sta	49
6700-6999	North Philadelphia Sta	32
7000-7099	Boulevard Sta	49
7100-7199	Elkins Park Br	17
7200-8799	General Post Office	01
8800-8899	Elkins Park Br	17
8900-8999	Tacony Sta	35
9001-9299	Lester Br	13
9300-9499	West Market Sta	39
9500-9599	Frankford Sta	24
9600-9699	West Park Sta	31
9700-9899.	Nicetown Sta	40
9900-9999	Chestnut Hill Sta	18
11000-11099	Logan Sta	41
11100-11199	Holmesburg Sta	36
11200-11299	Elkins Park Br	17
11300-11399	Bridesburg Sta	37
11400-11499	Fox Chase Sta	11
11500-11699	Somerton Sta	16
11700-11799	General Post Office	01
11800-11899	Roxborough Sta	28
11900-11999	Point Breeze Sta	45
12000-12199	William Penn Annex Sta	05
12200-12299	Germantown Sta	44
12300-12399	Mount Airy Sta	19
12400-12599	Overbrook Sta	51
12600-12699	East Falls Sta	29
12700-12799	Richmond Sta	34
12800-12999	Commerce Sta	08
13000-13999	General Post Office	01
14000-14099	Spring Garden Sta	22
14100-14299	East Germantown	38
14300-14599	Bustleton	15
14600-14999	Richmond	34
15000-15199	Fairmount Sta	21
15200-15299	Kensington	25
15300-15399	Fox Chase Sta	11
15400-15499	Boulevard	49
15500-15699	West Park	31
15700-15999	Middle City	03
16000-16399	Torresdale	14
16400-16499	Spring Garden	22
16600-16799	West Market	39
16800-16999	Paschall	42
17000-17599	Wm Penn Annex	05
17600-17999	Tacony	35
18000-18099	Southwark	47
18100-18299	Somerton	16
18300-18499	Olney	20
18500-18599	East Falls	29
18600-18799	North Philadelphia	32
18800-18999	Mount Airy	19
19500-19699	Frankford	24
19700-19899	Kingsessing	43
20000-20199	Pt Breeze	45
20200-20499	Wadsworth	50
20500-20799	East Germantown	38
20800-20999	Logan	41
21000-21299	Torresdale	14
21300-21499	Oak Lane	26
21500-21699	West Park	31
21700-21899	Schuylkill	46
22000-22999	Wm Penn Annex	05
24000-24299	West Market	39
24300-24599	Olney	20
24600-24799	Fox Chase	11
24800-24999	Fairmount	21
25000-25199	Southwark	47

STATIONS, BRANCHES AND UNITS

Boulevard Sta	49
Bridesburg Sta	37
Bustleton Sta	15
Castor Sta	49
Chestnut Hill Sta	18
Commerce Sta	08
Continental Sta	06
East Falls Sta	29
East Germantown Sta	38
Elkins Park Br	17
Fairhill Sta	33
Fairmount Sta	21
Federal Reserve Sta	07
Fidelity Sta	09
Forteith Street Sta	04
Fox Chase Sta	11
Frankford Sta	24
Germantown Sta	44
Girard Avenue Sta	22
Holmesburg Sta	36
Hunting Park Sta	40
John Wanamaker Sta	07
Kensington Sta	25
Lester Br	13
Logan Sta	41
Lynnewood Br	50
Manayunk Sta	27
Mayfair Sta	36
Middle City Sta	02
Mount Airy Sta	19
Naval Hospital Sta	45

ZIP CODES
PHILADELPHIA, Pennsylvania

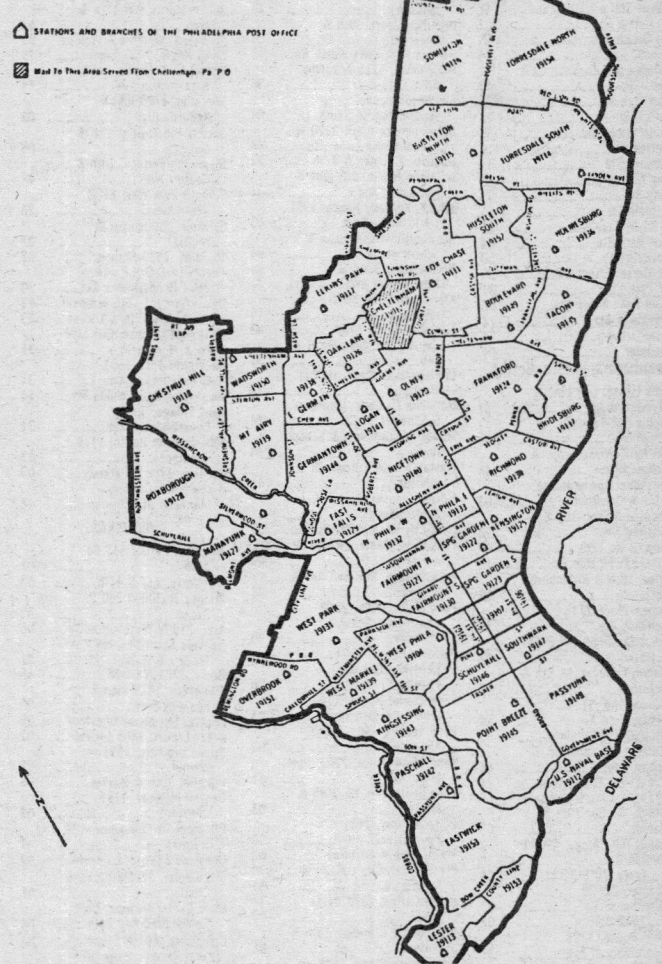

Nicetown Sta. 40
North Philadelphia Sta. 33
Number Fifty Six Sta. 07
Oak Lane Sta. 26
Olney Sta. 20
Overbrook Sta. 51
Paschall Sta. 42
Penn Center Sta. 03
Point Breeze Sta. 45
Richmond Sta. 34
Reckledge Br 11
Rosehill Sta. 40
Roxborough Sta. 28
Schuykill Sta. 46
Sixtieth Street Sta. 39
Somerton Sta. 16
Southwark Sta. 47
Spring Garden Sta. 22
Tacony Sta. 35
Torresdale Sta. 14
U.S. Naval Base Sta. 12
Vernon Sta. 44
Wadsworth Sta. 50
West Market Street Sta. 39
West Park Sta. 31
William Penn Annex Sta. 05
Wissinoming Sta. 24
General Delivery 04
Postmaster 04

APARTMENTS, HOTELS, MOTELS

Adams House, City Line &
  Monument Ave 31
Adelphia, NE 13th &
  Chestnut 07
Alden Park, Wissahickon &
  School House 44
Ambassador Towne House,
  21st & Chestnut 03
Ashbourne Manor, 155 E
  Godfrey Ave 20
Astoria, 2 No 12th 07
Atrium, 2555 Welsh Rd 14
Barclay, 18th & Rittenhouse
  Sq 03
Beekman Place 2746
  Belmont Ave 31
Bellevue-Stratford, SW Broad
  & Walnut 02
Benjamin Franklin, SE 9th &
  Chestnut 05
Birchwood Hill, 5115
  Wissahickon Ave 44
Brierhurst, 4527 Walnut 39
Cambridge, Wissahickon &
  School House 44
Carl Mackley, M & Bristol 24
Casa Fermi 13th & Lombard 47
Chatham, NE Cor 20th &
  Walnut 03
Chestnut Hill Village, 7900-B
  Stenton Ave 18
Divine Tracy, 20 S 36th 04
Dorchester, 226 W
  Rittenhouse Sq 03
Drake, 1512 Spruce 02
Duffield House, 3701
  Conshohocken Ave 31
Duval Manor, Johnson &
  Greene 44
Elkins Park House 7900 Old
  York Rd 17

Evergreen Park Manor,
  Woodward & Roosevelt
  Blvd 15
Evergreen Towers, 8900
  Roosevelt Blvd 15
Greene Manor 259 W
  Johnson 44
Hamilton Court, 39th &
  Chestnut 04
Holiday Park 2804 Welsh Rd 52
Holly Court, 9115 Academy
  Rd 36
Hopkinson House,
  Washington Sq South 06
Independence Plaza 3120 W
  School House Lane 44
Iroquois, City Ave & 47th 31
Jefferson House, City Line &
  Monument Ave 31
John F. Kennedy House, 1901
  J F Kennedy Blvd 03
Kenilworth, Wissahickon &
  School House 44
Kevon Arms, 52nd &
  Montgomery Ave 31
Krewstown Park, 8875
  Krewstown Rd 15
Latham 135 So 17th................... 03
Lebanon Arms, Bryn Mawr &
  Lebanon Av 31
Lynnewood Gardens, Mather
  Way 17
Manheim Gardens, Manheim
  & Schuyler 44
Manor, Wissahickon & School
  House 44
Mayfair House, Lincoln Dr &
  Johnson 44
Morgan House, Stenton Ave
  & Mermaid Ln 18
Park City West 3900 Ford Rd . 31
Park Drive Manor, Lincoln Dr
  & Harvey 44
Park Terrace, Rowland Ave &
  Rhawn 36
Park Towne Place, 2200
  Benjamin Franklin
  Parkway 30
Parkway House, 2201
  Benjamin Franklin
  Parkway 30
Penn Center House, 1900
  John F Kennedy Blvd 03
Penn Towers, 1801 John F
  Kennedy Blvd 03
Penn Wynn House, 2201 Bryn
  Mawr Ave 31
Penn-Center Inn, NE 20th &
  Market 03
Philadelphian, 2401
  Pennsylvania Ave 30
Plaza, 18th & Parkway 03
Presidential, City Line Av &
  Monument 31
Ridge Carlton 7373 Ridge
  Ave 28
Rittenhouse Claridge, 18th &
  Walnut 03
Rittenhouse Plaza, 1901
  Walnut 03
Rittenhouse Savoy, 1810
  Rittenhouse Sq 03

Rittenhouse Square, 1830
  Rittenhouse Sq 03
Rittenhouse Towers 222 W
  Rittenhouse Sq 03
River Park House, 3600
  Conshohocken Ave 31
Robert Morris, NW 17th &
  Arch 03
Roosevelt, SE 23rd & Walnut.. 03
Saint Regis, 2200 Tremont....... 15
School Lane House, 5450
  Wissahickon Ave 44
Sheraton, 1725 John F
  Kennedy Blvd 03
Society Hill Towers, 2nd &
  Locust 06
Stevenson Terrace, 10th &
  Godfrey Ave 41
Summit Park West 8200
  Henry Ave 28
Sylvania, SW Juniper &
  Locust 07
Touraine, 1520 Spruce 02
Twenty Six-O-One Parkway,
  2601 Pennsylvania Ave 30
Upsal Gardens, 246 W Upsal . 19
Warwick, NW 17th & Locust..... 03
Washington House, City Line
  Av & Monument 31
Watergate Apts, 3601
  Conshohocken Ave 31
Welshwood 2661 Willits Rd 14
West Village, 3901
  Conshohocken Ave 31
William Penn House, 1919
  Chestnut 03
Windsor, 17th & Parkway 03
Wissahickon Gardens,
  Manheim At Schuyler 44

BUILDINGS

American Patriot 112 So
  16th 02
Architects, 117 S 17th............... 03
Atlantic Richfield 260 S
  Broad 02
Ayer, 210 W Washington Sq ... 06
Bankers Securities, NW Cor
  Juniper & Walnut 07
Beury, 3701 N Broad 40
Boulevard, 1819 John F
  Kennedy Blvd 03
Bourse, 5th Above Chestnut ... 06
Broad-Locust, 1405 Locust 02
Brown Brothers, 1531
  Walnut 02
Bulletin, 30th & Market 04
Central Medical, 1737
  Chestnut 03
Chamber Of Commerce, 121
  S Broad 07
Chestnut East, 841 Chestnut. 07
City Center, SE Cor Broad &
  Cherry 04
Civic Center Museum Civic
  Center Blvd And 34th............ 04
Commerce, 401 N Broad 08
Federal Reserve Bank Of
  Philadelphia, 925
  Chestnut 01
Fidelity 123 S Broad 05
Fox, 1612 Market St................... 03

Fruit Produce, 330? S
  Galloway 48
Girard Stephen, 21 S 12th 07
Girard Trust, S Penn Sq &
  Broad 62
Guarantee Trust, 1420
  Walnut 62
I   B 1700 Market 63
In ependence, SE Cor 5th &
  Walnut 06
Inquirer 400 No Broad 30
Insurance Company Of North
  America, 16th & Arch.............. 03
Jefferson, 1015 Chestnut............ 87
Jewelry Trade, 740 Sansom 06
Keystone Auto Club, 2040
  Market 03
Lafayette 437 Chestnut 06
Land Title, SW Cor Broad &
  Chestnut 10
Lankenau Medical, Lancaster
  Ave & City Line 51
Lewis Tower, 15th & Locust 62
Liberty Trust, NE Cor Broad
  & Arch.. 07
Mall, NE Cor 4th & Chestnut.. 06
Medical Tower, 255 S 17th........ 03
One East Penn Square,
  Market & Juniper 87
Packard, SE Cor 15th &
  Chestnut 62
Penn Square, NE Cor Juniper
  & Filbert....................................... 87
Pennsylvania Lumbermens,
  SE Cor Broad & Walnut........ 07
Pennsylvania State Office,
  1400 Spring Garden 30
Pennsylvania 1500 Chestnut.... 02
Pennwalt 3 Benj Franklin
  Parkway.. 02
Phila Civic Center 34th And
  Civic Center Blvdh.................... 04
Philadelphia National Bank,
  NE Cor Broad & Chestnut 07
Philadelphia Saving Fund
  Society, 12th & Market............ 07
Professional, 1831 Chestnut...... 03
Provident Trust, SE Cor 17th
  & Chestnut 03
Public Ledger, 6th &
  Chestnut 06
Reading Terminal, 12th &
  Market 02
Robinson 42 So 15th.................... 02
Rohm & Haas, 28 So 6th........... 06
Schaff, 15th & Race.................... 02
Shubert, 250 S Broad 02
Stock Exchange, 120 S 17th.... 03
Suburban Station, 1617 John
  F Kennedy Blvd........................ 03
Sun Oil, 1608 Walnut 02
Terminal Commerce, 400 N
  13th 08
Terminal Commerce, 401 N
  Broad 08
U G I, NW Cor Broad & Arch.. 02
Western Saving SE Cor Broad
  & Chestnut 87
Widener, Chestnut & Juniper.... 04
Wilford, 33rd & Arch.................. 07
Witherspoon, 1321 Walnut........ 07

2 Penn Center Plaza, SW Cor
  15th & John F Kennedy
  Blvd... 02
3 Penn Center Plaza, NW Cor
  15th & Market............................ 02
4 Penn Center Plaza, SW
  16th & John F Kennedy 03
5 Penn Center Plaza 16th
  Market 03
6 Penn Center Plaza, 16 N
  17th 03
7 Penn Center Plaza, SE Cor
  17th & John F Kennedy......... 03

GOVERNMENT OFFICES

City Hall Annex Filbert &
  Juniper 07
City Hall Broad & Market 07
Internal Revenue Service
  Center, 11601 Roosevelt
  Blvd... 55
Municipal Services NE Cor
  15th & J F Kennedy Blvd ... 07
Naval Pub & Forms Ctr,
  5801 Tabor Rd........................... 11
State Office 1400 Spring
  Garden 30
United States Courthouse,
  9th & Chestnut.......................... 07
United States Custom House,
  2nd & Chestnut......................... 06
United States Mint
  Independence Mall 66

HOSPITALS

Albert Einstein Med Ctr, Nthn
  Div, Old York & Tabor
  Rds.. 41
Albert Einstein Medical Ctr
  Daroff Div 1425 S 5th............ 47
All Saints 8601 Stenton Ave.... 18
American Oncologic, Central
  & Shelmire Aves 11
Chestnut Hill, 8815
  Germantown Ave...................... 18
Childrens Heart Hospital Of
  Philadelphia,
  Conshohocken Av..................... 31
Childrens, 18th &
  Bainbridge................................... 46
Doctors 1700 Vine...................... 03
Eastern Penna Psychiatric
  Institute 29
Episcopal, Front & Lehigh
  Ave 25
Frankford, Frankford Ave &
  Wakeling 24
Friends Hospital For Mental
  & Nervous Disorders 24
Germantown, Penn & Chew.... 44
Graduate Hospital University
  Of Pennsylvania......................... 46
Hahnemann Medical, 230 N
  Broad 62
Institute, 111 N 49th St............ 39
Jeanes, Hasbrook Ave &
  Hartel 11
Jefferson, 11th & Walnut.......... 67
John F. Kennedy, Langdon &
  Cheltenham Ave 24
Juniata Park Medical Center,

Castor & Wyoming Ave...... 24
Kensington, 136 W Diamond .. 22
Lankenau Lancaster W Of
  City Line 51
Memorial, 5800 Ridge Ave...... 28
Mercy Douglass, 50th &
  Woodland Ave 43
Methodist Episcopal, Broad &
  Wolf 48
Metropolitan 201 No 8th........... 06
Misericordia, 54th & Cedar
  Ave 43
Moss Rehabilitation, 12th &
  Tabor Rd...................................... 41
Naval, 17th & Pattison Ave...... 45
Nazareth, 2601 Holme Ave 52
Northeastern, Allegheny Ave
  & Tulip.. 34
Olney, Palmetto & Devereaux.. 11
Oncologic, Central &
  Shelmire Aves 11
Osteopathic Hospital Of
  Philadelphia, 48th &
  Spruce.. 39
Parkview Castor And
  Wyoming Aves 24
Pennsylvania, 8th & Spruce 07
Philadelphia General, 34th &
  Civic Center Blvd..................... 04
Philadelphia State,
  Southampton Rd &
  Roosevelt Blvd 54
Presbyterian, 51 N 39th............ 04
Rolling Hill, 60 E Township
  Line Rd 17
Roxborough Memorial Ridge
  Ave & Rector. 28
Sacred Heart Home For
  Incurables, 1315 W
  Hunting Park Ave 40
Saint Agnes, 1900 S Broad 45
Saint Christophers, 2600 No
  Lawrence..................................... 33
Saint Josephs, 16th & Girard
  Ave 30
Saint Lukes & Childrens
  Medical, Franklin &
  Thompson.................................... 22
Saint Marys, Frankford Ave &
  Palmer.. 25
Saint Vincents, 70th &
  Woodland Ave 42
Shriners, 8400 Roosevelt
  Blvd... 52
Skin & Cancer, 3322 N
  Broad 40
Stetson, 1745 N 4th.................... 22
Temple University
  (Samaritan, 3401 N
  Broad 40
University, 34th & Spruce......... 04
Veterans Administration,
  University & Woodland
  Ave 64
West Park, 3905 Ford Rd......... 31
Wills, 16th & Spring Garden 30
Womans Medical, 3300 Henry
  Ave 29

UNIVERSITIES AND COLLEGES

Chestnut Hill College, Germantown & Northwestern Aves	18
Community College Of Philadelphia, 34 S 11th	07
Drexel Univ NE Corner 32nd & Chestnut	04
Dropsie, Broad Below York	32
Eastern Baptist Theological Seminary	51
Girard, Girard & Corinthian Av	21
Hahnemann Medical, 230 No Broad	02
Holy Family, NE Frankford & Grant Av	14
Jefferson Medical 11th & Walnut	07
La Salle, 20th & Olney Ave	41
Moore College Of Art 20th And Race St	03
Penna State College Of Optometry, 6100 N 12th	41
Philadelphia College Of Arts, NW Cor Broad & Pine	02
Philadelphia College Of Osteopathy, City Line & Monument	31
Philadelphia College Of Textiles & Science	44
Philadelphia College Pharmacy & Science, 43rd & Kingsessing	04
Saint Charles Seminary, City Line & Wynnewd Rd	51
Saint Josephs, 54th & City Line	31
Temple University, Broad & Montgomery Ave	22
University Of Pennsylvania, 34th & Spruce	04
Womans Medical Of Pennsylvania, 3300 Henry Ave	29

PITTSBURGH   152

POST OFFICE BOXES

Box Nos.		
1-3999	General Post Office	30
4000-4099	Arsenal Sta	01
4100-4224	Bellevue Br	02
4225-4299	Carson Sta	03
4300-4399	Corliss Sta	04
4400-4599	Crafton Br	05
4600-5574	East Liberty Sta	06
5575-5674	Hazelwood Sta	07
5675-5799	Homewood Sta	08
5800-5899	Millvale Br	09
5900-5999	Mount Oliver Sta	10
6000-6099	Mount Washington Sta	11
6100-7099	Allegheny Sta	12

7100-7599	Oakland Sta	13
7600-7699	Observatory Sta	14
7700-7899	Sharpsburg Br	15
7900-8099	South Hills Br	16
8100-8249	Squirrel Hill Sta	17
8250-8374	Swissvale Sta	18
8451-8599	Wabash Sta	20
8600-8999	Wilkinsburg Br	21
9000-9299	Bloomfield Sta	24
9300-9399	Neville Island Br	25
9500-9599	Etna Br	23
9600-9699	Brookline Sta	26
9700-9799	West View Br	29
9800-9899	Brentwood Br	27
9900-10099	Kilbuck Sta	33
10100-10299	Shadyside Sta	32
10300-10499	Castle Shannon Br	34
10500-10699	Penn Hills Br	35
10700-10799	Carson Sta	03
10800-10999	Pleasant Hills Br	36
11000-11199	Mcknight Br	37
11200-11599	Blawnox Br	38
11600-11900	Mount Lebanon Br	28
12000-12199	Veterans Hospital Sta	40
12300-12499	Greater Pittsburgh Airport Br	31
12500-12999	Upper St Clair Br	41
13000-13499	Cedarhurst Br	43
14000-14499	Plum Br	39
15000-15499	Mcknight Br	37
15500-15999	Montour Br	44
18000-18499	Pleasant Hills Br	36
34000-39999	General Post Office	30
40000-40999	Arsenal Sta	01
41000-41499	Bellevue Br	02
56751-56899	Homewood Sta	08
59000-59499	Mt Oliver Sta	10
71000-71499	Oakland Sta	13
86000-86499	Wilkinsburg Br	21
95000-95499	Etna Br	23
96000-96499	Brookline Sta	26
98000-98999	Brentwood Br	27

RURAL ROUTES

5	05

STATIONS, BRANCHES AND UNITS

Allegheny Sta	12
Arsenal Sta	01
Aspinwall Br	15
Avalon Br	02
Bellevue Br	02
Berkeley Hills Br	37
Blawnox Br	38
Bloomfield Sta	24
Brentwood Br	27
Brookline Sta	26
Broughton Br	36
Carson Sta	03

Castle Village Br	36
Castle Shannon Br	34
Cedarhurst Br	43
Corliss Sta	04
Crafton Br	05
Dormont Br	16
East Liberty Sta	06
Emsworth Br	02
Etna Br	23
Ewalt Sta	12
Federal Reserve Sta	30
Forest Hills Br	21
Fourth Avenue Sta	21
Fox Chapel Br	38
Gateway Center Sta	22
Greater Pittsburgh Airport Br	31
Hazelwood Sta	07
Holiday Park Br	39
Homewood Sta	08
Ingram Br	05
Kilbuck Sta	33
Laurel Gardens Br	29
Lebanon Church Sta	15172
Lincoln Place Sta	15
Manor Oak Br	20
Mc Knight Br	37
Millvale Br	09
Montour Br	44
Mount Lebanon Br	28
Mount Oliver Sta	10
Mount Washington Sta	11
Neville Island Br	25
North Bessemer Br	35
Oakland Sta	13
Observatory Sta	14
Parcel Post Sta	33
Parkway Center Br	20
Penn Hills Br	35
Perrysville Br	37
Pleasant Hills Br	36
Plum Br	39
Renton Br	39
Shadyside Sta	32
Sharpsburg Br	15
South Hills Br	16
Squirrel Hill Sta	17
Swissvale Br	18
Union Trust Sta	19
Universal Br	35
Upper Saint Clair Br	41
Uptown Sta	19
Veterans Hospital Sta	40
Village Br	41
Wabash Sta	20
West View Br	29
Wilkinsburg Br	21
Wylie Sta	19
General Delivery	30
Postmaster	19

APARTMENTS, HOTELS, MOTELS

Abbeyville, 115 Abbeyville Rd	28
Abigail, 2307 Brownsville Rd	10
Academy Mansion, 50 Academy Ave	28
Addison Hall, 131 Edgewood Ave	18
Admiral, 5615 Ellsworth	32
Admiral, 590 S Negley Ave	37
Akron 4514 Centre Ave	13
Akron, 275 N Craig	13
Alder Court, 6104 Alder	06

Alder Village, 5944 Alder....... 32
Alderdice, 640 Washington
  Rd........................... 28
Alderson, 5835 Alderson........ 17
Alexandria, 131 S Negley
  Ave.......................... 06
Alhambra, 209 S Mathilda...... 24
Alta Vista, 139 Lincoln Ave.... 02
Alvern Gardens, Vermont Av
  & Greenridge................. 34
Alvin Court, 1 Windsor Road.... 39
Ambassador East, 1601 Penn
  Ave.......................... 21
Ambassador West 1601 Penn
  Ave.......................... 21
Ambassador, 4733 Center
  Ave.......................... 13
Amberson Gardens, 1 Bayard
  Rd........................... 13
Amberson Towers 5 Bayard
  Road......................... 13
Andrea 201 E Swissvale 18
Ansonia, 5742 Holden.......... 32
Ansonia, 652 Maryland Ave..... 32
Ardmore Gardens, 1635-1645
  Ardmore Blvd................. 21
Arlington, 515 South Aiken
  Ave.......................... 32
Armada, 5620 Hobart........... 17
Atwood 1, 3609 Dawson......... 13
Atwood 2, 3609 Dawson......... 13
Atwood 3, 3609 Dawson......... 13
Auburn Towers 6290 Auburn
  St........................... 06
Aurora, 137 Bausman........... 10
Avalon Arms, 841 California
  Ave.......................... 02
Avon Court, 15 Bower Hill
  Rd........................... 28
Avon, 3436 Ward............... 13
Balboa 305 E Swissvale
  Ave.......................... 18
Baldwin Court Knoedler-
  Wolfe, Keeport & Macassar
  Dr........................... 36
Bard, 3444 Ward............... 13
Baum Grove, 5762 Baum
  Blvd......................... 06
Bayard Manor, 4600 Bayard..... 13
Bayard, 218 N Craig........... 13
Baywood Arms, 119 Baywood
  Ave.......................... 28
Baywood Manor, 125
  Baywood Ave.................. 28
Beacon, 5600 Munhall Rd....... 17
Bedford Dwelling, Bedford
  Ave.......................... 19
Beechview, 1500 Fallowfield
  Ave.......................... 16
Belcrest, 811 South Negley
  Ave.......................... 32
Bellcrest Mansionettes,
  Bellcrest Ave................ 27
Bellefield Dwellings, 4406
  Center Ave................... 13
Bellefonte, 5500 Elmer........ 32
Bellevue Courts, 50 Sumner
  Ave.......................... 02
Bellevue Gables, 25 Hawley
  Ave.......................... 02
Bellevue Gables, 30 Sprague
  Ave.......................... 02

Bellevue-Stratford, 215 South
  Millvale Ave................. 24
Belmar Towers, 245 Lincoln
  Ave.......................... 02
Belmont, 259 Beverly Rd....... 16
Belvedere Arms, 5914
  Walnut....................... 32
Belvedere, 5523 Ellsworth
  Ave.......................... 32
Berkeley, 405 Franklin Ave.... 21
Berkshire, 26 Academy Ave 28
Beverly Court, 221 Beverly
  Rd........................... 16
Beverly, 222 North Craig...... 13
Bigelow, Bigelow Sq........... 19
Blenheim, 4952 Friendship
  Ave.......................... 24
Bradberry, 1112 Reddour....... 12
Braeside Manor, 2135
  Wightman..................... 17
Breezwood, 560 Allenby Ave.... 18
Brentmor Junior, 3902
  Brownsville Rd............... 27
Brentmor, 3840 Brownsville
  Rd........................... 27
Brentshire Terrace, 2531
  Brownsville Rd............... 10
Brentshire Village, Pyramid
  Dr........................... 27
Brentwood Arms, 3820
  Brownsville Rd............... 27
Brittany, 3500 Brownsville Rd.. 27
Bryn Mawr, Bryn Mawr Ct....... 21
Bryn Mawr, 3301 Iowa.......... 19
Buchanan, 211 Buchanan Pl..... 28
Burkey, 37 Washington Ave..... 02
Burlington, 324 Mckee Pl...... 13
California, 5735 Ellsworth
  Ave.......................... 32
California, 909 California
  Ave.......................... 02
Cambridge Hall, 4630 5th
  Ave.......................... 13
Cambridge House, 1112 Mt
  Royal Blvd................... 23
Capon, 600 Rebecca Ave........ 21
Carlton House, 550 Grant...... 30
Carol 4909 Centre Ave......... 13
Carol, 72-76 S Freemont....... 13
Carriage House, 1515 Penn
  Ave.......................... 21
Carvel Hall, 436 Franklin
  Ave.......................... 21
Cary Hall, 305 East
  Swissvale Ave................ 18
Casablanca, 5731 Ellsworth
  Ave.......................... 32
Castle Stanton, 5652 Stanton
  Ave.......................... 06
Castleton, 5612 Hempstead
  Rd........................... 17
Castletone Shady Dr : Castle
  Shannon Blvd................. 28
Cathedral Mansions, 4716
  Ellsworth Ave................ 13
Cecil, 525 Brushton Ave....... 68
Center Court, 4716 Center
  Ave.......................... 13
Center-Negley, 5551 Center
  Ave.......................... 32
Central Arms, 101 Central
  Sq........................... 28

Central Square (A B C), 721
  Roselawn Ave................. 28
Central Square (E F G), 722
  Wisteria Ave................. 28
Centre Avenue 4750 Centre
  Ave.......................... 13
Centre Villa Court 5527
  Centre Ave................... 32
Charlemagne, 420 N
  Chestnut..................... 02
Chateaugay, 500 Hoodridge
  Dr........................... 34
Chatham Center Apt Towers..... 19
Chatham S, Chatham Park
  Dr........................... 20
Chatham Village............... 11
Chatham W, Oakville Dr........ 20
Chaucer Hall, 131 Edgewood
  Ave.......................... 18
Chestnut Manor, 415
  Chestnut St.................. 02
Chestnut Manor, 731
  California Ave............... 02
Cliffside Manor............... 02
Clover Leaf Towers, 10 Clover
  Dr........................... 36
Clover Leaf Village, 1
  Marhoefer Dr................. 36
College Gardens, 5820
  Elwood....................... 32
Colonial Arms, 253 Beverly
  Rd........................... 16
Colonial Terrace, 5440 5th
  Ave.......................... 32
Colonial, 717 Buchanan Pl..... 28
Columbian, 855 Rebecca
  Ave.......................... 21
Concord Plaza, 5532 Covode.... 17
Coronado 5260 Centre Ave...... 32
Craft, 3225 Joe Hammer Sq..... 13
Crafton Acres A, 102 W
  Steuben Ave.................. 05
Crafton Acres B, 102 W
  Steuben Ave.................. 05
Crafton Acres C, 102 W
  Steuben Ave.................. 05
Craig-Manor, 317 North
  Craig........................ 13
Craigwood Manor, 225 E
  Swissvale Ave................ 18
Cricklewood Hill 700 Forbes
  Ave.......................... 19
D'Arlington, 504 N Neville.... 13
Dagmar, 271 North Craig....... 13
Dana, 510 S Highland Ave...... 06
Delaware, 1139 N Highland
  Ave.......................... 06
Denholm, 202 Lincoln Ave...... 06
Denny, 1 St Johns Pl.......... 01
Denny, 3417 Liberty Ave....... 01
Denny, 3422 Denny............. 01
Denny, 3500 Howley............ 01
Denslow, 3622 California...... 12
Devon Towers, 4920 Centre
  Ave.......................... 13
Devonshire, 331 Devonshire.... 13
Devonshire, 4910 Center Ave... 13
Devonshire, 5871 Ellsworth
  Ave.......................... 32
Dietrich, 3301 Brighton Ave... 12
Dimling, 403 Oakland Ave...... 13
Dithridge, 144 North

Dithridge 13

Dover Gables, 555 S Negley
Ave. 32

Durban Hall, 4630 5th Ave. ... 13

East Liberty Gardens. 06

East Mall, 5805 Penn Mall,
W. 06

Edgemere Courts, 130 La
Crosse 18

Edgewater, 322 Mckee Pl ... 13

Edgewood Courts, 233-
Edgewood Ave 18

Edgewood, 100 West
Hutchinson Av 18

Elean Hall, 208 Darragh. 13

Ellison, 634 Washington Rd ... 28

Ellsworth, 5806 Ellsworth
Ave. 32

Elm, 100 Elm 18

Elmer, 5501 Elmer 32

Elsinore, 294 Craft Ave. 13

Elwood Gardens, 5819
Elwood. 32

Embassy, 230 Beverly Rd 16

Emerson, 270 Emerson 06

Emerson, 6111 Alder. 06

Englewood 5712 Forbes Ave .. 13

English Terrace Homes, 3200
5th Ave 13

English Terrace, 2720 Shady
Ave. 17

English Terrace, 5851
Morrowfield Ave 21

Etewanda, 224 East End Ave. . 02

Euclid, 16 South Euclid Ave. .. 13

Fairfax The, 4614 Fifth Ave ... 32

Fairview, 630 Maryland Ave .. 35

Fairway, 6703 Saltsburg Rd ...

Federal Dwellings, 11
Federal. 12

Fifth-Aiken, 5401 5th Ave. 32

Fifth-Maryland, 5800 5th Ave. . 32

Fifth-Morewood, 825
Morewood Ave 13

Fifth-Negley, 5700 5th Ave ... 32

Fifth-Neville, 4705 5th Ave ... 13

Fifty-One Hundred, 5100 5th
Ave. 32

Forbes Craig, 4531 Forbes
Ave. 13

Forbes Manor, 5624 Forbes
Ave. 17

Forest Acres, 588 Forest Ave. . 02

Forty-Seven-Fifty Centre
Avenue 4750 Centre
Avenue 13

Franklin, 200 Franklin Ave ... 21

Franklin, 305 Atwood. 13

Friendship, 4901 Friendship
Ave. 24

Front Royal, 6005 5th Ave. ... 32

Frontenac, 490 South
Highland Ave 06

Frontenac, 5931 Howe 06

Gable, 4800 Ellsworth Ave ... 13

Gable, 601 Clyde. 13

Garden Court, 416 Oakland
Ave. 13

Garden Courts, 2235
Braddock Ave. 18

Garden Villa, 3304
Brownsville Rd 27

Garfield Heights High Rise,

5330 Fern 24

Gateway Towers, 320 Fort
Duquesne Blvd 22

Gay Lebanon, 434 Cochran ... 28

General Forbes 5636 Forbes
Ave. 17

General Neville Mansionettes.. 25

General Neville, 1150
Bowerhill Rd 43

Georgian Junior, 255
Melwood Ave 13

Georgian, 5437 Ellsworth. 32

Gerber, 724 South Negley
Ave 32

Gilbert, 500 North Negley
Ave. 06

Glen Elm, Glen Elm Dr 36

Gordon Arms 128 Highland
Mall North. 06

Governor, 5935 Kirkwood ... 06

Graham Hall, 5525 Ellsworth
Ave 32

Greenlee Village, Victoria Dr .. 27

Greentree Gardens, 833
Greentree Rd 20

Hack, 116 Central Sq. 28

Haddon Hall 124 La Crosse.. 18

Haddon Hall 4730 Centre
Ave 13

Hamilton-Larimer, 6290
Auburn 06

Hampton Hall, 166 North
Dithridge. 13

Heatherstone, 5300 5th Ave .. 32

Heidelburg, 401 S Braddock
Ave 21

Hempstead, 5620 Hempstead
Rd 17

Herford, 816 Ivy 32

Heritage, 2522 Columbia
Ave 18

Herr, 1020 Wallace Ave 21

Hiawatha, 3833 Hiawatha ... 12

Highland Hall, 370 S.
Highland Ave 06

Highland House, 5700
Bunkerhill. 06

Highland Pines, Highland
Pines Dr 37

Highland Towers, 340 South
Highland Ave 06

Highland, 341 South
Highland Ave 06

Highwood, 372 South
Highland Ave 06

Hobart Court, 5555 Hobart.. 17

Hobart, 5703 Hobart 17

Holland, 3420 Louisa. 13

Holmes, 704 South Negley
Ave. 32

Homer, 5334 Jackson 06

Howard, 1137 North Highland
Ave. 06

Hunter 1328 Pocono Street... 18

Idaho, 5460 Penn Ave. 06

Iroquis 3604 Forbes Ave 13

Jacksonia, 110 Jacksonia. 12

Jamestown, Jamestown Ct ... 16

Jeanette, 732 South Millvale.. 13

Jefferson, 3440 Louisa. 13

Jefferson, 5660 Forward Ave .. 17

Kamins Cottages, 5552
Beacon 17

Kenmawr, 401 Shady Ave. 06

Kennilworth, 5700 Center
Ave. 06

Key Royale, 646 Grandview
Ave 02

Keystone, 813 Wood 21

King Edward Annex, 225
Melwood Ave. 13

King Edward, 4609 Bayard..... 13

Kings Arms, 800 S Negley
Ave 32

Kingston 301 So. Home
Avenue 02

Kingston, 5721 Elmer 32

Kirkpatrick, 4122 Butler. 01

Kirkwood, 5935 Kirkwood ... 06

Koch 5115 Centre Ave 32

La Belle, 5672 Hobart. 17

Laketon Garden, 3511
Laketon Rd. 35

Lancaster, 314 Mckee Pl 13

Lane, 228 Union 21

Lane, 701 Mifflin Ave 21

Larsen, 42 Academy Ave. 28

Laurel Ridge 100 102 104
106 15th. 29

Laurel Village, 700 Penn
Center Blvd. 35

Le Grand, 1411 Grandview
Av 11

Lebanon Hall, 318
Washington Rd 16

Lebanon Vue, 400 Cochran
Rd 28

Leland Park, Keeport Dr 36

Leland Park, Knoedler Dr 36

Leland Park, Youngridge Dr .. 36

Lennox 1, 223 South
Mathilda 24

Lennox 2, 223 South
Mathilda. 24

Lennox 3, 223 South
Mathilda. 24

Leonard, 5619 Hobart 17

Lexington House, 401 North
Lexington Ave. 08

Lexington, 7233 Penn Ave ... 08

Liberty Park 6209 Broad St ... 06

Lillian 2841 Centre Ave 19

Limbaugh, 1700 Crafton
Blvd. 05

Lincoln, 215 Lincoln Ave. 02

Lincoln, 374 South Mathilda .. 24

Linden, 3430 Bates. 13

Linwood, 6801 Mcpherson
Blvd. 08

Linwood, 75 North Linwood
Ave. 05

Lockhart 3200 Forbes Ave ... 13

Lois, 501 North Highland
Ave. 06

London Hall, 3100
Brownsville Rd 27

London Terrace, 135 North
Craig 13

Lorraine, 422 North Highland
Ave. 06

Louise, 87 Knox Ave. 10

Manor House 1726 Aurelius... 18

Manor House 425 N Neville .. 13

Manor, 111 Maple Ave...... 18
Manor, 5231 5th Ave...... 32
Maple, The Cambridge Ct...... 18
Maplewood 5716 Forbes Ave...... 17
Margaretta 5818 East Liberty Blvd...... 06
Mariana, 6780 Fifth Ave...... 08
Mark Twain, 406 North Neville...... 13
Markham, 60 Markham Dr...... 28
Marlin Arms, 5245 Center Ave...... 32
Marshall, 807 Wood...... 21
Martinque, 4746 Baum Blvd...... 13
Maryland Gardens, 5814 Elmer...... 32
Maryland, 510 Protectory Pl...... 19
Maxon Towers, 6315 Forbes Ave...... 17
Mayflower, 725 South Negley Ave...... 32
Mc Curdy, 201 California Ave...... 02
Mc Curdy, 223 Park Ave...... 02
Melvin Penn, Beulah Rd...... 35
Melwood, 334 Melwood...... 13
Midtown Towers 643 Liberty...... 22
Milton The, 3526 Forbes Ave...... 13
Model, 556 Dunfermline...... 08
Modercnest, 147 South Negley Av...... 06
Moderne Terrace 5219 Centre Ave...... 06
Montrose Manor, 5939 5th Ave...... 32
Montvue 5 Grandview Ave...... 11
Morewood Garden, 1060 Morewood Ave...... 13
Morewood 4924 Centre Ave...... 13
Morrison Court, 187 Morrison Dr...... 16
Morrow, 510 Mifflin Ave...... 21
Morrowfield, 2715 Murray Ave...... 17
Murray Beacon, 1914 Murray Ave...... 17
Navarre, 618 N Saint Clair...... 06
Negley Court, 5620 5th Ave...... 32
Negley Gardens, 400 N Negley Av...... 06
Negley Park, 1001 N Negley...... 06
Negley Park, 5545 Wellesley Av...... 06
Negley Park, 5570 Hampton...... 06
Negley, 300 N Negley Ave...... 06
Negley, 5607 Elmer...... 32
Nelda, 7522 Bennett...... 08
Netherlands The, 5721 Elwood...... 32
Neville A, 554 Neville...... 13
Neville B, 554 Neville...... 13
Neville C, 554 Neville...... 13
Neville Township Apartments...... 25
New Englander, 619 Center Ave...... 29
New President, 720 South Negley Ave...... 32
New Wendover, 5562 Hobart...... 17
New Yorker, 819 College Ave...... 32
Noble Manor, Brett St...... 05
Noble Manor, Chessland St...... 05

Noble Manor, Poplar St...... 05
Norfolk, 1131 North Highland Av...... 06
Normandy, 5520 5th Ave...... 32
North Windsor, 234 Melwood Ave...... 13
Northway, 411-481 Browns Lane...... 37
Oakland 3401 Forbes Ave...... 13
Oakmont The, 152 North Balph Ave...... 02
Ohara, 1 Ohara Pl...... 01
Ohara, 3625 Liberty Ave...... 01
Ohara, 510 37th...... 01
Olympia, 320 Mckee Pl...... 13
Ontario, 631 Maryland Ave...... 32
Overlook 4179 Centre Ave...... 13
Pacific, 329 South Pacific Ave...... 24
Palm Garden Village, 873 Boggs Ave...... 11
Panama, 5752 Ellsworth Ave...... 32
Park Mansions, 5023 Frew Ave...... 13
Park Place 1, 611 Alger...... 07
Park Place 2, 611 Alger...... 07
Park Plaza, 128 North Craig...... 13
Park View Arms, 336 Perry Highway...... 29
Park View, 1401 North Saint Clair...... 06
Parkline Court, Parkline Dr...... 27
Parkview, 45 N Balph Ave...... 02
Parkway, 2041 Wightman...... 17
Patterson, 906 Wood...... 21
Peacock Manor, 924 Farragut...... 06
Peerless, 624 Whitney Ave...... 21
Pendale Towers 460 Washington Rd...... 28
Penn Aiken, 5401 Penn Ave...... 06
Penn Brad 7508 Penn Ave...... 08
Penn Circle Towers, 6231 Penn Ave...... 06
Penn Dwellings, 7150 Penn Ave...... 08
Penn Lincoln, 789 Penn Ave...... 21
Penn Manor, 113 Enright Pl...... 06
Penn Plaza, 5600 Penn Ave...... 06
Penn Shady, 226 Shady Ave...... 06
Penn Towers 1100 Penn Center Blvd...... 35
Penn Towers, 11979 Frankstown Rd...... 35
Pennley Park, Penn Ave & North Negley Ave...... 06
Pennsylvania, 4403 Center Ave...... 13
Pennwood, 5722 Kentucky Ave...... 32
Pennwood, 623 Whitney Ave...... 21
Perry Manor, 810 Perry Hwy...... 29
Perrysville, 400 Perrysville Ave...... 29
Pershing, 758 Penn Ave...... 21
Phillips, 312 Mckee Pl...... 13
Pittsburgh Hilton-Commonwealth Pl...... 30
Plymouth Hall 131 Edgewood Ave...... 18
Point Breeze Manor, 6721 Thomas Blvd...... 08

Portland Manor, 5622 Stanton Ave...... 06
Potomac, 5722 Baum Blvd...... 06
President The, 306 Craft Ave...... 13
Princess Ann, 321 Beverly Rd...... 16
Princess, 7203 Idlewild...... 08
Prospect Mansions, 1685 Parkline Dr...... 27
Queensbury 220 S Home Ave...... 02
Ralston, 301 Warrington Ave...... 10
Rayette, 6712 Thomas Blvd...... 08
Revere, 309 Edgewood Ave...... 18
Ridgeview, Richland Ave...... 29
Ritz, 738 Brookline Blvd...... 26
Roberta, 1713 Termon Ave...... 12
Rockledge, 3201 Faronia...... 04
Roosevelt, 607 Penn Ave...... 30
Rosemont, 5504 Penn Ave...... 06
Rosmyl The, 900 Ross Ave...... 21
Royal Manor, 765 College Ave...... 32
Royal Plaza, 5506 5th Ave...... 32
Royal Windsor 1, 216 Melwood Ave...... 13
Royal Windsor 2, 216 Melwood Ave...... 13
Royal Windsor 3, 216 Melwood Ave...... 13
Royal Windsor 4, 216 Melwood Ave...... 13
Royal York, 3955 Bigelow Blvd...... 13
Royal, 500 Todd Ave...... 21
Ruskin Villa Annex 1104 Mulberry...... 21
Ruskin Villa, 735 Wallace Ave...... 21
Ruskin, 120 Ruskin Ave...... 13
Ruth Gardens, 5728 Beacon...... 17
Ruth, 2700 Broadway...... 16
Rutledge Hall, 600 South Negley Ave...... 32
Saint James, 5237 5th Ave...... 32
Saint Regis, 5806 Howe...... 32
Saint Regis, 905 Maryland Ave...... 32
Savoy, 571 Coal...... 21
Sceneridge, 3336 Brownsville Rd...... 27
Schenley Arms, 4041 Bigelow Blvd...... 13
Schenley House, 151 North Craig...... 13
Schenley Park, 4000 5th Ave...... 13
Seneca, 2039 5th Ave...... 19
Seton Hall, 120 North Homewood Ave...... 08
Seven Hundred Thirty 730 S Negley Ave...... 32
Shady East 607 Shady Ave...... 06
Shady Grove, 6300 Howe...... 06
Shamrock, 56 South Freemont...... 02
Sherwood Hall 131 Edgewood Ave...... 18
Shirley, 133 North Dithridge...... 13
Siebert Point, 3279 Babcock Blvd...... 37
Skyline, 1620 Skyline Dr...... 27
Skyview, 1550 Radford Rd...... 27
Smith, 815 Mill...... 21

Smith, 822 Ross Ave 21
South Aiken, 545 South Aiken
Ave 32
South Windsor, 216 Melwood
Ave 13
Stanford, 502 Jeanette 21
Stanton Arms, 5701 Stanton
Ave 06
Star, 740 Kelly Ave 21
Stephen Foster, 400 North
Neville 13
Stratford Arms, 5700
Munhall Rd 17
Stratford Hall 139 Edgewood
Ave 18
Summerlea, 5713 Elwood 32
Swissvale Apartments 1,
2103 S Braddock 18
Swissvale Apartments 2,
2103 S Braddock 18
Templeton, 753 Penn Ave 21
Ten Negley, 5700 Ellsworth
Ave 32
Terrace Court, 2123 Shady
Ave 17
Terrace Village 1 19
Terrace Village 2 13
Thames Manor, 585 South
Negley Ave 32
Thirty Five Hundred Fifth
Avenue, 3500 5th Ave 18
Thomas, 6716 Thomas Blvd.... 08
Tiffany, 925 California Ave 02
Town House, 6218 5th Ave 32
Townley Manor, 101 Lloyd
Ave 18
Triangle Hall, 5701 Munhall
Rd 17
Trinity The, Cambridge Ct 18
Tudor Hall 4825 Centre Ave ...
University Square No 1, 4625
5th Ave 13
University Square 2, 4601
5th Ave 13
Valley Vue, Keeport Dr 36
Valley Vue, Travis Dr 36
Valley Vue, Youngridge Dr 36
Valmar Gardens, 2648
Robinson Blvd 35
Venetian Garden, 100
Newburn Dr 16
Virginia Manor Greentree &
Cochran Rd 20
Virginia Manor, 5680
Munhall Rd 17
Virginia, 320 South Mathilda .. 24
Wabash, 318 Mckee Pl 13
Walden Court, 6349 Walnut ... 06
Waldorf Towers 100 Mcknight
Cir 37
Waldorf, 732 Roselawn Ave ... 28
Walker, 800 Ross Ave 21
Wallace, 2018 Noble 18
Wallace, 503 Lincoln Ave 02
Wallace, 512 Wallace Ave 21
Walnut Court, 5706 Walnut 32
Walnut Manor, 5920 Walnut ... 32
Walnut Terrace, 275 Walnut ... 38
Walnut, 5614 Walnut 32
Warwick Plaza, 5048 5th
Ave 32
Washington Arms, 769 Shady

Dr East 28
Washington Plaza, 1420
Centre Ave 19
Washingtonian, 1670
Washington Rd 28
Wayland, 6 South Fremont 02
Webster Hall, 4415 5th Ave.... 13
Webster Towers, 240
Melwood Ave 13
Wellesley Dwellings, 5517
Wellesley Ave 06
Wellington, 131 Sycamore 13
Wellington, 241 Melwood Ave . 13
Welton, 3 Mcdevitt Pl 13
Welton, 335 Melwood Ave 13
Wendover, 5557 Hobart 17
Westminster Manor, 5227 5th
Ave 32
Westminster, 800 South
Aiken Ave 32
White Oaks, 799 Stevens Dr ... 37
Wightman, 2130 Wightman 17
Wilburton, 235 South Millvale
Ave 24
William Penn, William Penn
Place 30
William Penn, 1805 Penn
Ave 21
William Pitt, 5610 Elmer 32
Williams, 125 Sycamore 11
Willmar 4524 Forbes Ave 13
Wilson Arms, 549 North
Neville 13
Wilson, 741 Rebecca Ave 21
Wiltshire, 225 South Millvale
Ave 24
Windcrest 7801 Lloyd 18
Windsor Hall, 131 Edgewood
Ave 18
Windsor, 221 South Millvale ... 24
Windsor, 3320 Ward 13
Windsor, 5630 Hobart 17
Winebiddle, 210 South
Winebiddle 24
Winslow, 525 Larimer Ave 06
Wisteria, Wisteria Ave 28
Wood Hill, 1309 Wood 21
Woodland Gardens, 5925 5th
Ave 32
Woodland Manor, 5826 5th
Ave 32
Woodland 735 Presque Isle
Dr ....
Woodland, 5176 Margaret
Morrison 13
Woodland, 5836 5th Ave 32
Woodward Court, 221
Buchanan Pl 28
Yale, 5700 Jackson 06
Yorkshire, 2145 Wightman 17

BUILDINGS

Abbott 100 Smithfield 22
Agricultural, 1730 Smallman ... 22
Alcoa, 425 6th Ave 19
Allegheny Center, Bldgs 1-10 .. 12
Allegheny County Court
House, 436 Grant 22
Allegheny County, 542 Forbes
Ave 22
Allegheny Towers, 625
Stanwix 22

Allegheny 429 Forbes Ave 19
Ardmore, 2300 Ardmore
Boulevard 21
Arrott, 401 Wood 22
Baum, 818 Liberty Ave 22
Beatty, 5907 Penn Ave 06
Bell Telephone Company 635
Grant 22
Benedum-Trees, 221 4th Ave .. 22
Berlin, 237 5th Ave 22
Bonn, 713 Penn Ave 22
Buhl, 204 5th Ave 22
Caldwell & Graham, 700
Penn Ave 21
Caldwell, 800 Wood 21
Carlton Center, 923 Penn
Ave 22
Catanzaro, 2018 Smallman 22
Centennial, 241 Fourth Ave 22
Central Warehouse, 222 W
Carson 19
Century, 130 7th 22
Chamber Of Commerce, 411
Seventh Ave 19
Chatham Center, Fifth Ave 19
City County, 414 Grant 19
Civic, 200 Ross 19
Clark, 717 Liberty Ave 22
Colonial, 205 Ross St 19
Commonwealth Annex, 317
3rd Ave 22
Commonwealth, 316 4th Ave ... 22
Conestoga, 7 Wood 22
Continental Insurance 200 S
Craig 13
Council Of Churches, 220
Grant 19
Duquesne Light Company
435 6th Ave 19
Educational Institute, 212
Ninth St 22
Empire, 501 Liberty Ave 22
Equitable Gas, 420
Boulevard Of The Allies 19
Ewart, 925 Liberty Ave 22
Federal Offices, 1000 Liberty
Ave 22
Federated Investors, 421 7th
Avenue 19
Fidelity, 341 4th Ave 22
Fifth-Grant, 508 Grant 19
Fifth-Wood, 256 5th Ave 22
First Federal, 600 Grant 19
Flannery, 3530 Forbes Ave 13
Forbes And Murray, 5800
Forbes Ave 13
Forbes, 3619 Forbes Ave 13
Fort Pitt Federal, 524 Penn
Ave 22
Freehold, 311 4th Ave 22
Frick, 437 Grant 19
Frick, 450 5th Ave 19
Fruit Exchange, 66 21st 22
Fulton, 101 6th 22
Gateway Polytechnic, 100 7th
St 22
Gateway Towers, 320 Fort
Duquesne Blvd 22
Gateway View Plaza, 1600 W.
Carson 19
Gateway 2, 603 Stanwix 22
Gateway 3, 401 Liberty Ave ... 22
Gateway 4, 444 Liberty Ave ... 22·

Gateway 5, 60 Boulevard Of
　The Allies 22
Golden Center, 300 Stanwix 22
Granite, 313 6th Ave 22
Grant, 310 Grant 19
Graphic Arts, 422 1st Ave 19
Greater Beneficial Union
　4254 Clairton Blvd 27
Gulf, 435 7th Ave 19
Heinz Hall Of Performing Arts
　600 Penn Ave 22
Highland 117 Highland Mall
　S 06
House, 4 Smithfield 22
International Business
　Machines, 60 Blvd Of The
　Allies 22
Investment, 237 4th Ave 22
Irish, 800 Penn Ave 22
Jenkins Arcade, 509 Liberty
　Ave 22
Jenkins, 504 Penn Ave 22
Jones Law Annex 530 Fourth
　Ave 19
Jones Law 311 Ross 19
Kern, 1136 Greenfield Ave 17
Keystone, 322 4th Ave 22
Kirkwood On The Mall 121
　Highland Mall N 06
Koppers, 436 7th Ave 19
Kossmann, 100 Forbes Ave 22
Lando, 907 Penn Ave 22
Law & Finance, 425 4th Ave 19
Lawyers, 428 Forbes Ave 22
Libbie, 245 4th Ave 22
Liberty 6101 Penn Mall E 06
Live Stock Exchange, Herrs
　Island 22
Loeffler, 121 Meyran Ave 13
Magee, 334 4th Ave 22
Maloney, 337 Boulevard Of
　The Allies 22
Manor Oak No 1 20
Manor Oak No 2 1910
　Cochran Rd 20
Manor, 564 Forbes Ave 19
Martin, 119 Federal 12
Masonic Temple, 4227 Fifth
　Ave 13
Masonic, 523 Lincoln Ave 02
May, 119 5th Ave 22
Mc Crady-Nicklos, 304 Ross 19
Mc Kay, 1005 Liberty Ave 22
Medical Arts 3700 Fifth Ave 13
Medical Center East 211 N
　Whitfield 06
Medical, 3401 Fifth Ave 13
Memorial Hall, 5th Ave &
　Bigelow Blvd 13
New Bell Telephone, 201
　Stanwix 22
Nine-Twenty-Four Penn
　Avenue, 924 Penn Ave 22
North American Rockwell,
　301-307 Fifth Ave 22
Oliver Henry W, 535
　Smithfield 22
One Hundred Fifth Ave, 100
　Fifth Ave 22
One Oliver Plaza, 210 Sixth
　Ave 22
Park, 351 5th Ave 22
Parkway Ctr 1 875 Greentree

Rd 20
Parkway Ctr 2, 875 Greentree
　Rd 20
Parkway Ctr 3, 875 Greentree
　Rd 20
Parkway Ctr 4, 875 Greentree
　Rd 20
Parkway Ctr 5, 875 Greentree
　Rd 20
Parkway Ctr 6, 875 Greentree
　Rd 20
Parkway Ctr 7, 875 Greentree
　Rd 20
Parkway Ctr 8 875 Greentree
　Rd 20
Penn Central Station 22
Penn Oak Professional, 77
　Universal Rd 35
Penn Rose, 1627 Penn Ave 22
Penn Wood, 620 Penn Ave 21
Penn, 721 Penn Ave 21
Penn, 810 Penn Ave 22
Pennsylvania Lines Produce,
　90 21st 22
Pennsylvania, 110 19th 22
Peoples Bank, 301 4th Ave 22
Pgh & Lerr, Smithfield And
　West Carson 19
Physicians, 121 University
　Place 13
Pitt-Penn Terminal, 1320
　Penn Ave 22
Pittsburgh Life, 219 6th 22
Pittsburgh National Bank
　128 5th Ave 22
Plaza, 535 5th Ave 19
Plumbers, 1901 5th Ave 19
Porter H K 601 Grant 19
Ppg Industries, 420 Fort
　Duquesne Blvd 22
Press, Boulevard Of The
　Allies 22
Professional, 722 Penn Ave 21
Public Safety, 100 Grant 19
Public School Administrative,
　341 Bellefield Ave 13
Publication, 209 9th 22
Rea, 704 2nd Ave 19
Remington-Rand, 312
　Stanwix 22
Renshaw, 217 9th 22
Ross, 4828 Liberty Ave 24
Rudd, 342 Boulevard Of The
　Allies 22
Saint Clair, 1725 Washington
　Rd 41
Second Federal, 335 5th Ave 22
Seven Eleven Penn Avenue,
　711 Penn Ave 22
Shields, 822 Wood 21
Smithfield Diamond, 415
　Smithfield 22
Smithfield Plaza 650
　Smithfield 22
Smithfield, 610 Smithfield 22
Standard Life, 345 4th Ave 22
State Office, 300 Liberty Ave 22
Stevenson, 666 Washington
　Rd 28
Syria Mosque, Bigelow Blvd 13
Templeton, 739 Penn Ave 22
Terminal 307 Carson E 19

Terrace Arcade, 107 Terrace
　Ct 27
Thirty Five Hundred Fifth
　Avenue, 3500 5th Ave 13
Three Hundred Sixth Ave, 300
　Sixth Ave 22
Three Rivers Stadium, 400
　Stadium Circle 12
Triangle 305 7th Ave 22
Try Street Terminal, 600 2nd
　Ave 19
Union Bank, 306 4th Ave 22
Union Title 210 Grant 19
Union Trust, 435 5th Ave 19
Union Trust, 523 Grant 19
United States Post Office &
　Court House, 700 Grant 19
United States Steel 600
　Grant 19
Wallace 6005 Penn Circle S 06
Westinghouse, 11 Stanwix 22
Whitehall Terrace 4120
　Brownsville Rd 27
Wilkinsburg Bank, 901 Wood 21
Y M C A (Central), 304 Wood
　St 22
Y M C A (E Liberty), 122
　South Whitfield 06
Y W C A (Central), 305 Wood
　St 22

GOVERNMENT OFFICES

Chamber Of Commerce, 411
　7th Ave 19
Federal Offices, 1000 Liberty
　Ave 22
United States Courthouse,
　700 Grant 19

HOSPITALS

Allegheny General, 320 E
　North Ave 12
C. Howard Marcy State
　Hospital, Leech Farm Rd 06
Childrens Hospital Of
　Pittsburgh, 125 De Sota
　St 13
Columbia, 312 Penn Ave 21
De Paul Institute, Dorchester
　Ave 26
Divine Providence Of
　Pittsburgh, 215 W
　Montgomery Ave 12
Doctors, 215 S Negley Ave 06
Eye & Ear, 230 Lothrop 13
Fairview Sanitarium 5601
　Forbes Ave 17
John J Kane, 201 Kane Blvd 43
Magee Womens Hosp 13
Mercy, 1400 Locust 19
Montefiore, 3459 5th Ave 13
North Hills Passavant, 9100
　Babcock Blvd 37
Pittsburgh, 6655 Frankstown
　Av 06
Presbyterian, 230 Lothrop 13
Saint Clair Memorial, 1000
　Bower Hill Rd 43
Saint Francis, 408 45th 01
Saint Johns General, 3331

Veterans Administration,
Leech Farm Rd 06
Veterans Administration,
University Dr 40
Veterans, Delafield Rd 40
West Penn, 4800 Friendship
Ave 24
Western State Psychiatric, De
Sota & Ohara 13
Womens Magee Hosp., Forbes
Ave & Halket 13

UNIVERSITIES AND COLLEGES

Allegheny Community, 808
Ridge Ave 12
Carlow College, 3333 5th
Ave 13
Carnegie-Mellon University,
Frew Ave & Margaret
Morrison 13
Chatham College, Woodland
Rd 32
Duquesne University, 801
Bluff 19
Point Park, Wood St & Blvd
Of Allies 22
Robert Morris, 610 Fifth Ave .. 19
University Of Pittsburgh,
4200 Fifth Ave 13
Mcclure Ave 12
Saint Josephs 2117 E
Carson 03
Saint Margaret Memorial,
265 46th 01
Shady Side, 5230 Center Ave. 32
South Hills Ear Nose &
Throat, 315 Mount
Lebanon Blvd 34
South Side, 111 South 20th.. 03
Suburban General, South
Jackson Ave 02
Tuberculosis League Of
Pittsburgh, 2851 Bedford
Ave 19

PITTSTON   186

POST OFFICE BOXES

Box Nos.
1-145   Duryea Br 42
1-177   Avoca Br 41
1-212   West Pittston
               Br 43
1-318   Wyoming Br 44
251-787   Main Office 40

RURAL ROUTES

1 43
2 41
3 44

STATIONS, BRANCHES AND UNITS

Avoca Br 41
Dupont Br 41
Duryea Br 42
Exeter Br 43
Jenkins Br 40
West Pittston Br 43
West Wyoming Br 44

READING   196

POST OFFICE BOXES

Box Nos.
1-227   Shillington Br .. 07
1-348   Wyomissing Br . 10
1-1702   Main Office 03
2000-2149   Sinking Spring
               Br 08
2501-2658   West Lawn Br.. 09
3000-3266   Hampden Sta .. 04
3500-3799   Laureldale Br .. 05
4001-4236   Mount Penn
               Sta 06

RURAL ROUTES

1 07
2 05
3,4 06
5,6 08

STATIONS, BRANCHES AND UNITS

Hampden Sta 04
Laureldale Br 05
Mount Penn Br 06
Parcel Post Ste 03
Shillington Br 07
Sinking Spring Br 08
West Lawn Br 09
West Reading Br 02
Wyomissing Br 10
General Delivery 03
Postmaster 03

APARTMENTS, HOTELS, MOTELS

Abraham Lincoln, 100 N 5th.. 03
Alden Terrace, 1401 Ridge
Ave 07
Antietam Arms, 850 Carsonia
Ave 06
Berkshire, 101 N 5th 03
Brighter, 205 Penn St 01
Brookline Manor, 1100 E
Wyoming Blvd 06
Carsonia Manor, 810 N 25th.. 06
Daniel Boone, 1022 Penn 02
Edgemont Terrace, 1515 Hill
Rd 02
Hampden House, 2001
Hampden Blvd 04
Hodges, 601 N 5th St 01
Hollywood Court, 2703
Hollywood Ct 06
Metropolitan, 920 N 4th St 01
Mifflin Park, 30 Mifflin Blvd... 07
Monahan, 125 S 4th St 03
Mt Penn Manor, 601 S 19th
St 06
Oak Forest, Pricetown &
Reservoir Rds 04
Pennhurst Mansion, 2252
Fairview Ave 06
Pennside Manor, 707 N 25th.. 06
Saylor, 1 N 9th St 01
Sherwood Terrace, 1400
Pershing Blvd 07
Springside Manor, 100-200
Springside Dr 07

Washington Towers 01
Woodland Plaza, Bern &
Woodland 10
Wynwood At Wyomissing, 855
N Park Rd 10
Wyomissing Park, 215 Alden
Ter 07

BUILDINGS

Administration, 8th &
Washington 01
Baer, 529 Court 01
Balis, 24 N 6th 01
Berks County Trust, 35 N
6th 01
Berks Title, 607 Washington .. 01
Caster, 434 Walnut 01
Colonial Trust, 447 Penn 01
Corbit, 147 N 5th 01
Medical Arts, 230 N 5th 01
Staufer, 62 S 6th 02
Y M C A, 631 Washington 01

GOVERNMENT OFFICES

City Hall, 8th & Washington.. 01
Courthouse, 33 N 6th 01

HOSPITALS

Community General, 135 N
6th 01
Reading, 6th & Spruce 03
Saint Josephs, 12th &
Walnut 03

UNIVERSITIES AND COLLEGES

Albright College, 13th &
Exeter 04
Mc Canns Business, 134 S
5th 02
Mount Alvernia, 464 St
Bernadine 07
Pennsylvania State
University, 814 Hill Ave.... 10
Reading Business Institute,
949 Penn 01

SCRANTON   185

POST OFFICE BOXES

Box Nos.
1-83   West Scranton
               Sta 04
1-118   Dickson City
               Br 19
1-135   Dunmore Br 12
1-238   Taylor-Old
               Forge Br 17
1-1355   Main Office 01

RURAL ROUTES

1 08

STATIONS, BRANCHES AND UNITS

Dickson City Br 19
Dunmore Br 12
Marywood College Sta 09

Moosic Br	07
North Scranton Sta	08
Old Forge Br	18
South Side Sta	05
Taylor-Old Forge Br	17
Throop Br	12
West Scranton Sta	04
General Delivery	01
Postmaster	03

APARTMENTS, HOTELS, MOTELS

Adams, 408 Adams Ave	10
Bellefonte Donny Dr	05
Carter, 801 Mulberry	10
Casey Inn, Adams & Lackawanna	03
Clay Avenue, 520 Clay Ave	10
Country Day, 1100 Quincy Ave	10
Duckworth, 711 Linden	10
Florence, 643 Adams	10
Greenwood Motel, 3505 Birney Ave	05
Hilton Inn 229 N Washington Ave	03
Holiday Inn Motel, Franklin Ave & Mulberry	03
Jackson Heights 1000 Jackson	04
Jermyn, Wyoming Ave & Spruce	03
Riverside Apartments	03
Rockledge Terrace 607 N Main Tay	17
Scranton, 500 Wyoming Ave	09
Taylor Village 600 Oak St Tay	17
Viewmont Village	08
Washington Ave West 537 N Washington Ave	09
Washington Plaza 600 N Washington Ave	09
Wyoming, 229 Wyoming Ave	03

BUILDINGS

Administration, 425 N Washington Ave	03
Brooks, 436 Spruce	03
Catholic Youth Center, 500 Jefferson Ave	10
Connell, 129 N Washington	03
Davidow, 411 Spruce	03
First Federal, 149 Adams	03
Glen Alden, 310 Jefferson	03
Jewish Community Center, 601 Jefferson Ave	10
Mears, 327 N Washington Ave	03
Medical Arts, 327 N Washington Ave	03
Miller, 422 Spruce	03
North Eastern National Bank, Wyoming Ave & Spruce St	03
Scranton Life, 538 Spruce	03
Scranton National Bank, 108 N Washington Ave	03
Scranton Real-Estate, 314 N Washington Ave	03
Scranton Times, 145 Penn	03

Y M C A, 419 Mulberry St	03
Y W C A, 638 Linden St	03

GOVERNMENT OFFICES

Chamber Of Commerce. 426 Mulberry	03
Court House Annex	03
Court House; 200 N Washington	03
Internal Revenue, Connell Bldg	14
Municipal Bldg, Washington & Mulberry	03

HOSPITALS

Community Medical Center E, 316 Colfax Ave	01
Mercy Heights, 930 Hickory	01
Mercy, 746 Jefferson Ave	01
Moses Taylor, 700 Quincy	10
Saint Josephs Maternity, 2010 Adams	09
State General, Mulberry & Franklin	01
West Mountain Sanitorium, Newton Rd	04

UNIVERSITIES AND COLLEGES

International Correspondence Schools, Keyser Ave & Oak St	15
Johnson School, 3427 N Main Ave	08
Marywood, 2300 Adams Ave	09
Pennsylvania State University, Keystone Industrial Park	12
Scranton Lackawanna Junior, 635 Linden	03
University Of Scranton, 4 Ridge Row	10

UPPER DARBY   190

POST OFFICE BOXES

Box Nos.

1-449	Main Office	84
501-899	Havertown Br	83

STATIONS, BRANCHES AND UNITS

Havertown Br	83
Manoa Br	83
Terminal Sta	82
General Delivery	82
Postmaster	82

GOVERNMENT OFFICES

Social Security Adm, 6801 Ludlow	82

WILKES BARRE   187

POST OFFICE BOXES

Box Nos.

A-H	North End Sta	05
1-117	Ashley Br	06
1-147	Mountaintop	07
1-184	Luzerne Br	09
1-1387	Main Office	03
1001-1508	Kingston Br	04
1601-1700	North End Sta	05
1701-1916	Shavertown Br	08
5006-5119	Sta A	10

RURAL ROUTES

1,2	02
3,4	07
5	08

STATIONS, BRANCHES AND UNITS

Ashley Br	06
Bear Creek Rural Br	18602
Edwardsville Br	04
Forty Fort Br	04
Gateway Br	04
Kingston Br	04
Luzerne Br	09
Mountain Top Br	07
Narrows Br	04
North End Sta	05
Peely Br	06
Plains Br	05
Shavertown Br	08
Sugar Notch Br	06
Swoyerville Br	04
Trucksville Br	08
Veterans Hospital Sta	03
General Delivery	03
Postmaster	01

APARTMENTS, HOTELS, MOTELS

Carousel Motel, 400 Kidder	02
Florence, 95 W Ross	02
Genettis, 77 E Market	01
Grand, 81 E Market	01
Holiday Inn	02
Host Motel, 500 Kidder	03
Irving, 307 S River	02
Ludwig, 273 S River	02
Margarida, 117 N Main	01
Margarida, 7 E Jackson	01
Margarida, 8 Bennett	01
Minrose, 267 S Franklin	02
Riverside, 120-130 W Ross	02
Riverside, 92-96 W River	02
Sandor, 110-116 W Ross	02
Sterling, Market & River	03
Wilkes, 45 N Main	01

BUILDINGS

Bennett, 2 N Main	01
Blue Cross, 15 S Franklin	01
First National Bank, 11 W Market	01
Golde, 2 E Northampton	01
I B E, 69 Public Square	01

Russian, 84 E Market............ 01
United Penn Bank, 8 W
  Market............................ 01
Veterans Administration, 19
  N Main.......................... 01

HOSPITALS

General, North River............ 02
Mercy, 196 Hanover.............. 03
Nesbitt Memorial, 562
  Wyoming Ave.................. 04
Valley Crest, East End Blvd.... 02
Veterans Administration
  Hosp, East End Blvd.......... 03
Wyoming Valley, 149 Dana..... 02

UNIVERSITIES AND COLLEGES

Kings, 133 N River................ 02
Luzerne County Community
  College, 19 N River.......... 02
Penna. State University
  Wilkes Barre Campus,
  Shavertown Br................ 08
Wilkes-Barre Business
  College, 69 Public Square.. 01
Wilkes, 184 S River.............. 03

YORK 174

POST OFFICE BOXES

Box Nos.
A-M	Jacobus Br	07
1-300	Jacobus Br	07
1-2356	Main Office	05
3001-3999	East York Br.	02
6121-6267	Hellam Br.	06

RURAL ROUTES

1	04
2	03
3	02
4	04
5	02
6	04
7	02
8	03
9	02
11,12	06

STATIONS, BRANCHES AND UNITS

East York Br....................... 02
Hellam Br.......................... 06
Jacobus Br......................... 07
General Delivery.................. 05
Postmaster........................ 05

APARTMENTS, HOTELS, MOTELS

Barnharts, 3021 E Market St. 02
Billy Bud Inn 334 Arsenal
  Rd................................ 02
Canterbury Court Apts, 199
  Silver Spur Dr................. 02
Carroll Apartments, 51 S
  Beaver St........................ 01
Cedar Village Apartments
  404 Cedar Village Rd........ 02

Char-Hill, R D 3................... 02
Chateau, R D 9.................... 02
Colonial Crest Apartments
  2160 D Maplewood Dr....... 03
Colonial, P O Box 547........... 05
Colony Park Apartments,
  1720 Devers Road............ 04
Congress Inn 2810 E Market
  Street............................ 02
Country Club Manor
  Apartments, Country Club
  Road............................. 03
Crestwood Arms Apartments,
  Suburban Road................ 03
Eastern Blvd Apartments,
  Eastern Blvd & Mill Rd...... 02
Elm Terrace Apartments, 450
  Madison Ave................... 04
Flamingo, 3600 E Market St.. 02
Holiday Inn, 2600 E Market
  St................................. 02
Howard Johnson, Arsenall
  Road Interchange............ 02
Lafayette Plaza Apartments,
  3201 E Market St............. 02
Leisureville Apts, Lark Cir...... 04
Milner, P O Box 547............. 05
Modernaire, 3311 E Market
  St................................. 02
North Hills Apartments, 1800
  North Hills Rd................. 02
Penn, 49 N George St............ 01
Playland Pool 2810 E Market
  Street............................ 02
Spheel Grund, 3522 E Market
  St................................. 02
Springetts Manor 16 Jamison
  Drive............................. 02
Suburban Park Apartments
  2685 Carnegie Road......... 02
Travelodge, 132-140 N
  George St....................... 01
Vern-Mar Apartments, 2101 E
  Market St....................... 02
Village East 3400 E Market
  Street............................ 02
York Hills Apartments, 1927
  Queenswood Drive........... 03
York Valley Inn (Quality
  Courts), 3883 E Market St. 02
Yorkshire Apartments, 3205
  Market St....................... 02
Yorktowne, P O Box 1106...... 05
Yost Apartments, 958 E
  Market St....................... 03

BUILDINGS

Crispus Attucks, 125 E
  Maple St........................ 03
Y M C A, 90 N Newberry St... 01
Y W C A, 320 E Market St...... 03

GOVERNMENT OFFICES

City Hall, P O Box 509.......... 05
County Home, R D 7............. 02
County Jail, 319 Chestnut St.. 03
Court House, 28 E Market St.. 01
United States Post Office,
  200 S George St............... 05

HOSPITALS

Memorial Osteopathic, 325 S
  Belmont St..................... 03
York Hospital, 1001 S George
  St................................. 05

UNIVERSITIES AND COLLEGES

Penn State Campus, 1031
  Edgecombe Ave.............. 03
School Administration, P O
  Box 1927....................... 05
Thompson School Of
  Business & Technology,
  1253 W Market............... 04
York College Of Pa, Country
  Club Road...................... 05

PUERTO RICO

(Abbreviation: PR)

Acueducto, Br. Cayey 00633
Adjuntas 00601
Aguada 00602
Aguadilla (1st) 00603
  Borinquen Road, Sta. 00603
  Coloso, R. Br. 00641
  Ramey A F B, Br. 00604
  Victoria Street, Sta. 00603
Aguas Buenas 00607
Aguirre 00608
Aibonito 00609
Almirante Norte, Br. Vega
  Baja 00763
Almirante Sur, Br. Vega
  Baja 00763
Altamesa, Sta. San Juan 00921
Alto Del Manzano, Br. Las
  Marias 00670
Anasco 00610
Angeles 00611
Arecibo (1st) 00612
Arroyo 00615
Asomante, Sta. Aibonito 00609
Atalaya, Sta. Aguada 00602
Bajadero 00616
Bajura, Br. Vega Alta 00762
Barceloneta 00617
Barinas, Br. Yauco 00768
Barranquitas 00618
Barriada Blondet, Br.
  Guayama 00654
Barriada Marin, Br.
  Guayama 00654
Barrio Cantito, Br. Manati 00701
Barrio Carmen, Br.
  Guayama 00654
Barrio Cortes, Br. Manati 00701
Barrio Espinar, Sta. Aguada 00602
Barrio-Obrero, Sta. San Juan
  (see appendix)
Bartolo, Br. Castaner 00631
Bitumul, Sta. San Juan 00917
Boca, Br. Guayanilla 00656
Boqueron 00622
Boquillas, Br. Manati 00701
Borinquen Road, Sta.
  Aguadilla 00603
Cabezas, Sta. Fajardo 00648
Cabo Rojo (1st) 00623
Caguas (1st) 00625
Camarones, Sta. Guaynabo 00657
Camino Nuevo, Br. Yabucoa 00767
Camuy 00627
Canovanas 00629
Caparra Heights, Br. San
  Juan (see appendix)
Carolina (1st) 00630
Carpenter Road, Sta. San
  Juan 00917
Carrasquillo, Sta. Cayey 00633
Caserio Roig, Sta. Humacao 00661
Casilla Gobernador, Br.
  Cayey 00653
Castaner 00631
Cayey (1st) 00633
Ceiba 00635
Central Eureka, Sta.
  Hormigueros 00660
Central Igualdad, Br.

Mayaguez 00708
Central San Vicente, Br.
  Vega Baja 00636
Cerrilios, Br. Cabo Rojo 00623
Cerro Gordo, Br. San
  Lorenzo 00754
Ciales 00638
Cidra 00639
Coamo 00640
Colegio Univ Decayey, Sta.
  Cayey 00653
College, Sta. Mayaguez 00708
Collores, Br. Juana Diaz 00665
Coloso, R. Br. Aguadilla 00641
Comerio 00642
Consumo, Br. Mayaguez 00708
Corazon, Br Guayama 00654
Corozal 00643
Corozo, Br. Boqueron 00622
Coto Laurel 00644
Country Club, Sta. San Juan 00924
Cuatro Calles, Br. Arroyo 00615
Cuatro Esquinas, Br. Cabo
  Rojo 00623
Cuesta Las Piedras, Br.
  Mayaguez 00708
Culebra 00645
Cuyon, Sta. Aibonito 00609
Delicias, Br. Cabo Rojo 00623
Descalabrado, Br. Santa
  Isabel 00757
Dorado 00646
Dorado Beach, Br. Dorado 00646
Duey, Br. Yauco 00768
Duque, Br. Naguabo 00718
El Albanico, Sta. Aibonito 00609
El Amendro, Br. San Juan 00632
El Bajo, Br. Patillas 00723
El Torito, Br. Cayey 00633
Emajaguas, Br. Maunabo 00707
Ensenada 00647
Esperanza, Sta. Vieques 00765
Fajardo (1st) 00648
Fernandez Juncos, Sta. San
  Juan (see appendix)
Fios, Sta. San Sebastian 00755
Florida 00650
Fort Buchanan, Br. San
  Juan 00934
Fortuna, Br. Juana Diaz 00651
Garrochales 00652
Grand Stand, Br. Guayama 00654
Guamani, Br. Guayama 00654
Guanica 00653
Guaniquilla Barrio, Br. Cabo
  Rojo 00623
Guaraquao, Sta. Guaynabo 00657
Guardarraya, Br. Patillas 00723
Guayama (1st) 00654
Guayanes, Br. Yabucoa 00767
Guayanilla 00656
Guaynabo 00657
Gurabo 00658
Hacienda Santa Rita, Br.
  Guanica 00653
Hatillo 00659
Hato Rey, Sta. San Juan
  (see appendix)
Hato Viejo, Br. Arecibo 00612
Hato Viejo Cumbre, Br.
  Ciales 00638
Hoconuco Alto, Br. San

German 00753
Honduras, Br. Barranquitas 00618
Hormigueros 00660
Hucares, Br. Naguabo 00718
Humacao (1st) 00661
Imbery, Br. Barceloneta 00617
International Airport, Br. San
  Juan 00913
Isabela (1st) 00662
Isla Verde, Br. Carolina 00630
Jagual, Br. San Lorenzo 00754
Jauca, Sta. Santa Isabel 00757
Jayuya 00664
Joyuda, Br. Cabo Rojo 00623
Juana Diaz 00665
Juana Matos, Br. San Juan 00632
Juncos 00666
Junquito, Br. Humacao 00661
Kofresi Sta Cabo Rojo 00623
La Garita, Br. Cabo Rojo 00623
La Placita, Sta. Cayey 00633
La Plata 00668
La Sierra, Br. Comerio 00642
La Trocha, Sta. Vega Baja 00763
La Tuna, Br. Cabo Rojo 00623
La Vega, Br. Barranquitas 00618
Laguna, Br. Vega Baja 00763
Lajas 00667
Lajas Arriba, Br. Lajas 00667
Lares 00669
Las Flores, Br. Coamo 00640
Las Granjas, Br. Vega Baja 00763
Las Marias 00670
Las Piedras 00671
Las Rocas, Sta. Guaynabo 00657
Lizas, Br. Maunabo 00707
Llanos, Br. Coamo 00640
Lluberas, Br. Yauco 00768
Loiza 00672
Loiza Street, Sta. San Juan
  (see appendix)
Luquillo 00673
Macana, Br. Guayanilla 00656
Magas Arriba, Br.
  Guayanilla 00656
Maguayo, Br. Lajas 00667
Magueyes, Br. Barceloneta 00617
Maizales, Br. Naguabo 00718
Mamey, Sta. Guaynabo 00657
Manati (1st) 00701
Mareas, Br. Guayama 00654
Maresua, Br. San German 00753
Maricao 00706
Marina, Sta. Mayaguez 00708
Maton, Br. Cayey 00633
Maunabo 00707
Mayaguez (1st) 00708
Mercedita 00715
Moca 00716
Monserrate, Sta. Vega Baja 00763
Monte Bello, Br. Manati 00701
Monte Grande, Br. Cabo
  Rojo 00623
Monte Santo, Sta. Vieques 00765
Montoso, Br. Mayaguez 00708
Morales Diaz, Br. Cabo Rojo 00623
Morovis 00717
Munoz Rivera, Sta.
  Guaynabo 00657
Naguabo 00718
Naranjito 00719
Naval Station, Sta. San
  Juan 00932

Nazario, Br. San Germán 00753
Nogueras, Br. Cidra 00639
Old San Juan, Sta. San
   Juan 00902
Olimpo, Br. Guayama.............00654
Orocovis 00720
Palmarejo, Br. Lajas 00667
Palmarillano, Sta. Lares 00669
Palmas Altas, Br.
   Barceloneta........................00617
Palmer 00721
Palo Hincado, Br.
   Barranquitas........................00618
Palomas, Br. Yauco...............00768
Parcelas Coqui, Br. Aguirre 00608
Parcelas Palmarejo, Br.
   Coamo 00640
Pastillo, Br. Juana Diaz 00665
Pasto, Br. Guayanilla............00656
Pasto Viejo, Br. Cayey..........00633
Patillas 00723
Peñuelas..............................00724
Pesa Cialitos, Br. Ciales 00638
Pitahaya, Br. Arroyo..............00615
Playa, Sta. Ponce 00731
Playa Cortada, Sta. Santa
   Isabel 00757
Polvora, Sta. Cayey...............00633
Polvorin Ward, Sta. Cayey......00633
Ponce (1st) 00731
Pozas, Br. Ciales 00638
Pueblito, Br. Manati..............00701
Puente Blanco, Br. Arroyo......00615
Puente De Jobos, Br.
   Guayama............................00654
Puerta De Tierra, Sta. San
   Juan 00906
Puerto Real...........................00740
Pugnado, Br. Manati..............00701

Pulguillas, Br. Aibonito...........00609
Punta Santiago......................00741
Quebrada Hondo, Br. San
   Lorenzo 00754
Quebrada Vueltas, Sta.
   Fajardo..............................00648
Quebradillas 00742
Quemado, Br. Mayaguez 00708
Ramey A F B, Br. Aguadilla....00604
Retiro Tea, Br. San German....00753
Rincon 00743
Rio Arriba, R. Sta. Arecibo.....00612
Rio Blanco 00744
Rio Grande 00745
Rio Piedras, Sta. San Juan
   (see appendix)
Rosario 00746
Rosario Alto, Br. San
   German 00753
Rubias, R. Br. Yauco 00768
Sabana Abajo, Br. Carolina....00630
Sabana Eneas, Br. San
   German 00753
Sabana Grande 00747
Sabana Hoyos.......................00748
Sabana Seca 00749
Saint Just.............................00750
Salinas 00751
Salud Ward, Sta. Mayaguez....00708
San Antonio..........................00752
San German (1st) 00753
San Ildefonso, Sta. Coamo.....00640
San Jose, Sta. San Juan 00930
SAN JUAN (1st) (see
   appendix)
San Lorenzo 00754
San Luis, Sta. Aibonito 00609
San Martin, Sta. San Juan 00924

San Sebastian (1st)...............00755
Santa Ana, Br. Mayaguez.......00708
Santa Catalina, Br. Coamo.....00640
Santa Isabel 00757
Santa Maria, Sta. Vieques......00765
Santiago, Br. San German......00753

Santurce, Sta. San Juan
   (see appendix)
Seco, Br. Maunabo................00707
Sierra Baja, Br. Guayanilla.....00656
Sitio Romero, Sta. Villalba.....00766
Toa Alta 00758
Toa Baja 00759
Toita, Br. Cayey...................00633
Tres Hermanos, Br. Anasco.....00610
Trujillo, Br. San Juan.............00760
Trujillo Alto..........................00760
University, Sta. San Juan........00931
Usabon, Sta. Aibonito 00609
Utuado (1st) 00761
Vega Alta 00762
Vega Baja (1st)....................00763
Victoria Street, Sta.
   Aguadilla............................00603
Vieques 00765
Villalba 00766
Walcott, Br. Arecibo..............00612
Yabucoa...............................00767
Yauco (1st).........................00768
Yaurel, Br. Arroyo.................00615
Yuquiyu...............................00769
Yuquiyu, Br. Luquillo.............00769

SAN JUAN 009

POST OFFICE BOXES

Box Nos.

A-Z	Caparra Heights Sta	22
A-Z	Hato Rey Sta	19
A-Z	Main Office	36
A-Z	Rio Piedras Sta	28
A-Z	University Of Puerto Rico Sta	31
1-1392	San Juan Sta	02
1-1924	Hato Rey Sta	19
1-5092	Main Office	36
AA-AK	Caparra Heights Sta	22
AA-AZ	Main Office	36
AA-AZ	Rio Piedras Sta	28
AA-AZ	University Of P. R. Sta	31
AA-XX	Hato Rey Sta	19
BA-BK	Caparra Heights Sta	22
BA-BN	University Of P. R. Sta	31
BA-BZ	Main Office	36
BA-BZ	Rio Piedras Sta	28
CA-CK	Caparra Heights Sta	22
CA-CN	Main Office	36
CA-CS	Rio Piedras Sta	28
DA-DQ	Caparra Heights Sta	22
EA-EK	Caparra Heights Sta	22
GA-GH	Caparra Heights Sta	22
SS-ZZ	Caparra Heights Sta	22
1401-3072	San Juan Sta	03
3081-3992	San Juan Sta	04
3751-4049	San Jose Sta	30
4001-5000	San Juan Sta	05
5001-5524	Puerta De Tierra Sta	06
5601-5760	San Juan Sta	05
5701-5917	Puerta De Tierra Sta	06
6001-6899	Loiza Street Sta	14
7001-7899	Barrio Obrero Sta	16
8001-8899	Fernandez Juncos Sta	10
9001-10249	Santurce Sta	08
10001-10998	Caparra Heights Sta	22
11001-11937	Fernandez Juncos Sta	10
12001-12386	Loiza Street Sta	14
13001-13962	Santurce Sta	08
14001-14594	Barrio Obrero Sta	16
20001-21337	Rio Piedras Sta	28
21301-23190	University Of	

	Puerto Rico Sta	31

RURAL ROUTES

1	14
2,3	28

STATIONS, BRANCHES AND UNITS

Altamesa Sta		21
Barrio Obrero Sta		16
Bitumul Sta		17
Caparra Heights Br		22
Carpenter Road Sta		17
Country Club Sta		24
El Amendro Br		00632
Fernandez Juncos Sta		10
Fort Buchanan Br		34
Hato Rey Sta		19
International Airport Br		13
Juana Matos Br		00632
Loiza Street Sta		11
Naval Station Sta		32
Old San Juan Sta		02
Puerta De Tierra Sta		06
Rio Piedras Sta		23
San Jose Sta		30
San Martin Sta		24
Santurce Sta		07
Trujillo Br		00632
University Sta		31
General Delivery		36
Postmaster		36

APARTMENTS, HOTELS, MOTELS

Altamesa Gardens, San Ignacio & San Alfonso	21
Americana, Boca De Cangrejos Rd, Isla Verde	13
Atlantic Beach, 1 Vendig	07
Borinquen Towers, Roosevelt & Ensenada	20
Capitol, 800 Ponce De Leon Ave	07
Caribbean Towers, 762 Ponce De Leon Ave (Stc)	07
Caribe Hilton, San Geronimo	07
Central, 202 San Jose (Sj)	01
Concordia Gardens, 65 Inf Ave	24
Condado Beach, 1071 Ashford Ave	07
Condado Del Mar, Ashford Ave	8
Condado Plaza, 1351 Magdalena Ave	8
Condado Towers, 30 Washington	07
Coral Beach, Isla Verde Rd	13
Darlington, Fdez Jcos Ave Stop 10 (Stc)	07
Darlington, Munoz Rivera Ave (Rp)	25
Del Mar, Delcasse & Marselle	07
El Convento, Cristo (Sj)	01
El Monte, 165 Hostos (Hr)	18
El Portal, 76 Condado	07
Gallardo, 1102 Magdalena Ave	07
Golden Beach, Isla Verde Rd	13
Iberia, 604 Ponce De Leon	

Ave	07
Isla Verde Towers, Isla Verde Rd	13
Jardines De Guayama, Guayama St	17
La Concha, Ashford Ave	07
La Rada, 1020 Ashford Ave	07
Laguna Gardens, Isla Verde Rd	13
Litheda, Cupey Bajo	26
Los Robles, Las Americas & Nevarez Ave	27
Mirabel, 606 Ponce De Leon Ave	07
Miramar Charterhouse, 600 Olimpo	07
Normandie, Escambron Ave	01
Olimpo Courts, 603 Miramar Ave	07
Palace, 157 Tetuan	01
Pierre, 105 De Diego Ave (Stc)	11
Pine Grove, Isla Verde Rd	14
San Cristobal, 450 Norzagaray	01
San Geronimo, Ashford Ave	07
San Juan Intercontinental, Isla Verde Rd	13
San Rafael,)miramar(	07
Sheraton, Ashford Ave	07
Town House, 65 Inf Ave	23

BUILDINGS

Alcazar, 562 Trigo	07
Ashford Medical, Ashford Ave	07
Banco De Ponce, Ponce De Leon Ave, Stop 18 1/2	07
Banco De San Juan, Tanca & Tetuan	01
Banco Popular Ctr, Ponce De Leon & Munoz Rivera Ave (Hr)	18
Banco Popular, 206 Tetuan	01
Capitol, Ponce De Leon Ave (Sj)	01
Center, De Diego Ave Stop 22 (Stc)	09
Chase Manhattan Bank, Ponce De Leon & Park St (Stc)	09
Chase Manhattan Bank, 1058 Munoz Rivera Ave (Rp)	27
Cobian Center, Ponce De Leon Ave & Park (Stc)	09
Eastern Airline, 155 De Diego Ave, Stop 22	11
El Imparcial, 450 Comercio	01
El Koury, Fernandez Juncos Ave & Villamil St	07
El Mundo, 383 F D Roosevelt Ave	18
Empire, De Diego Ave (Stc)	09
First Federal Savings, Munoz Rivera Ave (Rp)	27
First Federal Savings, Ponce De Leon Ave & Park St (Stc)	09
First National City Bank, Munoz Rivera Ave & Margarita	25
First National City Bank,	

Roberto H Todd Ave (Stc)...   07
First National City Bank, 252
  Ponce De Leon Ave (Hr).....   18
Las Americas Professional,
  Domenech Ave   18
New York Dept Store, Ponce
  De Leon Ave, Stop 16 1/2..   07
Ochoa, 300 Comercio (Sj).......   01
Padin, Fortaleza & Cruz.......   01
Pan Am, Ponce De Leon Ave
  & Bolivia (Hr)   17
Professional, De Diego Ave
  (Stc)...............................   09
Puerto Rico Development,
  Ponce De Leon Ave, Stop
  33 (Hr)   18
San Martin, Ponce De Leon
  Ave & Park St (Stc)........   09
San Rafael, Ponce De Leon
  Ave & Miramar Ave   07

HOSPITALS

Auxilio Mutuo, Ponce De Leon

Ave Stop 37 (Hr)..............   17
Centro Medico Universitario
  Centro Medico Grounds   35
Doctors Hospital, 1395 San
  Rafael (Stc)   09
Fernandez Garcia, 358 Ponce
  De Leon Ave(Hr)..............   18
Guadalupe, 435 Ponce De
  Leon Ave (Hr)   17
Instituto Oftalmico, 160
  Ponce De Leon Ave (Sj)   01
Julia, Ponce De Leon Ave
  Stop 31 (Hr)...................   17
Los Maestros, Domenech Ave
  (Hr)...............................   18
Mimiya, 303 De Diego Ave
  (Stc).............................   09
Pavia, Europa & Asia..............   09
Presbyterian, 1451 Ashford
  Ave................................   07
Professional, 310 De Diego
  Ave (Stc)........................   09
San Carlos, 1822 Ponce De
  Leon Ave (Stc)   09

San Jorge, 258 San Jorge
  (Stc).............................   12
Veterans, Puerto Nuevo...........   20
Woman'S, 450 Saldana (Stc)..   09

MILITARY INSTALLATIONS

U S Naval Base, Fern'Z
  Juncos Ave & Munoz
  Rivera Expy.....................   32
U S Navy Annex, Hwy 2   34

UNIVERSITIES AND COLLEGES

Immaculada, 1709 Ponce De .
  Leon Ave (Stc)   09
Puerto Rico Junior College,
  Cupey Bajo Rd Km 3.0......   26
Tropical School Of Medicine,
  Ponce De Leon Ave (Sj)......   01
University Of Puerto Rico,
  Ponce De Leon Ave (Rp).....   31

RHODE ISLAND
(Abbreviation RI)

Adamsville 02801
Albion ... .02802
Alton 02803
Annex, Sta Providence 02903
Anthony, Sta. Coventry 02816
Ashaway ... .02804
Ashton, Br Pawtucket 02864
Barrington (1st) 02806
Block Island 02807
Bradford 02808
Bristol (1st) 02809
Bristol Ferry, R. Sta.
  Portsmouth... 02811
Broadway, Sta Newport 02840
Brown, Sta. Providence..... ..C2912
Carolina 02812
Centerdale, Br Providence. ...02911
Central Falls, Br Pawtucket ..02863
Charlestown.. 02813
Chepachet.. 02814
Clayville.. 02815
Coddington Point, Br
  Newport ... .02840
Conimicut, Sta. Warwick ...02889
Coventry (1st)... 02816
Coventry Center, Sta.
  Coventry 02816
Cranston, Br Providence
  (see appendix)
Cumberland, Br Pawtucket ...02864
Cumberland Hill, Br
  Pawtucket 02864
Darlington, Sta. Pawtucket ...02860
Davisville, Sta. North
  Kingstown 02854
East Greenwich (1st) 02818
East Providence, Br.
  Providence (see appendix)
East Side, Sta. Providence.. . 02906
Edgewood, Sta Providence .02905
Elmwood, Sta Providence .02907
Escoheag 02821

Esmond, Br. Providence 02917
Exeter 02822
Fiskeville... 02823
Fleet, Br Newport 02840
Forestdale 02824
Foster 02825
Friar, Sta Providence... ...02918
Garden City, Br Providence...02920
Glendale 02826
Greene ... .02827
Greenville 02828
Harmony. 02829
Harrisville 02830
Hope ... .02831
Hope Valley... 02832
Hopkinton 02833
Howard 02834
Hoxsie, Sta. Warwick 02889
Jamestown 02835
Johnston, Br. Providence ...02919
Kenyon 02836
Kingston, Br. Wakefield... ...02881
Lincoln, Br Pawtucket ...02865
Little Compton 02837
  Acoaxet, R. Br... ...02701
Manville 02838
Mapleville 02839
Middletown, Br. Newport ...02840
Misquamicut, Sta Westerly ..02891
Narragansett, Br Wakefield ...02882
Naval Hospital, MOU.
  Newport 02840
Naval Training Station, Br.
  Newport 02840
Newport (1st) 02840
North, Sta Providence ...02908
North Kingstown (1st) ...02852
  Davisville, Sta... ...02854
  Quonset Point, Br. ...02819
North Scituate 02857
Oakland 02858
Olneyville, Sta Providence..02909
Parcel Post Annex, Sta.
  Westerly... 02891
Pascoag... 02859

PAWTUCKET (1st) (see
  appendix)
Peace Dale, Sta. Wakefield
  (see appendix)
Pilgrim, Sta. Warwick..........02888
Portsmouth (1st)... 02871
  Bristol Ferry, R. Sta.........02811
PROVIDENCE (1st) (see
  appendix)
Prudence Island ... .02872
Quonset Point, Br. North
  Kingstown 02819
Riverside, Br. Providence... ..02915
Rockville 02873
Rumford, Br. Providence...02916
Saunderstown... 02874
Scarborough Beach, R. Br.
  Wakefield 02882
Shannock 02875
Slatersville 02876
Slocum... 02877
Tiverton 02878
WAKEFIELD (1st) (see
  appendix)
Wallum Lake... 02884
Walnut Hill, Sta.
  Woonsocket 02895
Warren (1st) 02885
WARWICK (1st) (see
  appendix)
Warwick Neck, Sta. Warwick ..02889
Watch Hill, Sta. Westerly ...02891
Weekapaug, Sta. Westerly ...02891
West Barrington 02890
West Kingston 02892
West Warwick (1st) 02893
Westerly (1st) 02891
Weybosset Hill, Sta.
  Providence... 02903
Wildes Corner, Sta. Warwick ..02886
Wood River Junction ...02894
Woonsocket (1st) 02895
Wyoming 02898

PAWTUCKET 028

POST OFFICE BOXES

Box Nos.

A-D	Barrington Br	61
1-266	Central Falls	
	Br	63
1-237	Cumberland	
	Br	64
1-385	Lincoln Br	65
1-449	Ashton Br	64
1-1640	Main Office	62
2001-3032	Darlington Br	61

RURAL ROUTES

1	65
2,3	64
4	65
5	64

STATIONS, BRANCHES AND UNITS

Ashton Br	64
Central Falls Br	64
Cumberland Br	64
Cumberland Hill Br	64
Darlington Sta	60
Lincoln Br	65
General Delivery	60
Postmaster	60

PROVIDENCE 029

POST OFFICE BOXES

Box Nos.

1-2000	Annex Sta	01
2001-2300	Edgewood Sta	05
2301-2600	East Side Sta	06
2601-2900	Elmwood Sta	07
2901-3200	North Sta	08
3201-3500	Olneyville Sta	09
3501-3800	Cranston Br	10
3801-4100	Centerdale Br	11
4101-4400	East	
	Providence Br	14
4401-4700	Riverside Br	15
4701-5000	Rumford Br	16
5001-5300	Esmond Br	17
6000-7000	Main Office	04
7001-8000	Johnston Br	19
8001-9000	Garden City Br.	20

RURAL ROUTES

1,2	19
3,4	17
5	20

STATIONS, BRANCHES AND UNITS

Annex Sta	03
Brown Sta	12
Centerdale Br	11
Cranston Br	10
East Providence Br	14
East Side Sta	06
Edgewood Sta	05

Elmwood Sta	07
Esmond Br	17
Friar Sta	18
Garden City Br	20
Johnston Br	19
North Sta	08
Olneyville Sta	09
Riverside Br	15
Rumford Br	16
Weybosset Hill Sta	03
General Delivery	04
Postmaster	04

APARTMENTS, HOTELS, MOTELS

Colonial Hilton At Cranston, 1150 Narragansett Blvd	05
Dreyfus, 119 Washington	03
Holiday Inn, 21 Atwells Ave	03
Minden, 123 Waterman	06
Mohican, 344 Washington	03
Sheraton-Biltmore, 11 Dorrance	02
Wayland Manor, 500 Angell	06

BUILDINGS

Amica, 10 Weybosset	03
Blue Cross, 31 Canal	03
Hospital Trust, 15 Westminster	03
Howard, 10 Dorrance	03
Industrial Bank, 111 Westminster	03
Journal, 75 Fountain	02
Packet, 165 South Main	03
Physicians Office, 110 Lockwood	03
State House, 82 Smith	03
State Office, 101 Smith	03
Turks Head, 76 Westminster	03
Union Trust, 170 Westminster	03

GOVERNMENT OFFICES

City Hall, 25 Dorrance	03
Custom House, 24 Weybosset	03

HOSPITALS

Bradley 1011 Veterans Parkway	15
Charles V Chapin, 157 Eaton	08
Cranston General, 1763 Broad	05
Jane Brown, 44 Lockwood	02
Miriam, 164 Summit Ave	06
Our Lady Of Fatima, 200 High Service Ave N Providence	64
Providence Lying-In, 50 Maude	08
Rhode Island, 593 Eddy	02
Roger Williams General, 825 Chalkstone Ave	08
Saint Josephs, 21 Peace	07
Veterans Administration, Davis Park	08

UNIVERSITIES AND COLLEGES

Brown University, Prospect	12
Bryant College, Douglas Pike	17
Johnson & Wales Junior, Abbott Pk Pl	03
Pembroke, 172 Meeting	12
Providence College, River Ave	08
Rhode Island Junior, 199 Promenade	08
Rhode Island School Of Design, 14 College	03
Rhode Island, Mt Pleasant Ave	08
Roger Williams Junior, 160 Broad	03

WAKEFIELD 028

POST OFFICE BOXES

Box Nos.

1-209	Peace Dale	83
1-328	Kingston Br	81
1-552	Main Office	80
1-789	Narragansett Br	82

RURAL ROUTES

1	79
2	82
3	79
4	82
5	79
6,7	82

STATIONS, BRANCHES AND UNITS

Kingston Br	81
Narragansett Br	82
Peace Dale Sta	83
Scarborough Beach Rural Br	82
General Delivery	80
Postmaster	80

APARTMENTS, HOTELS, MOTELS

Faculty Apts	81
University Garden Apts	81

BUILDINGS

Narragansett Research Ctr	82

HOSPITALS

South County Hospital	79

UNIVERSITIES AND COLLEGES

Mount St Joseph College	80
University Of R I	81

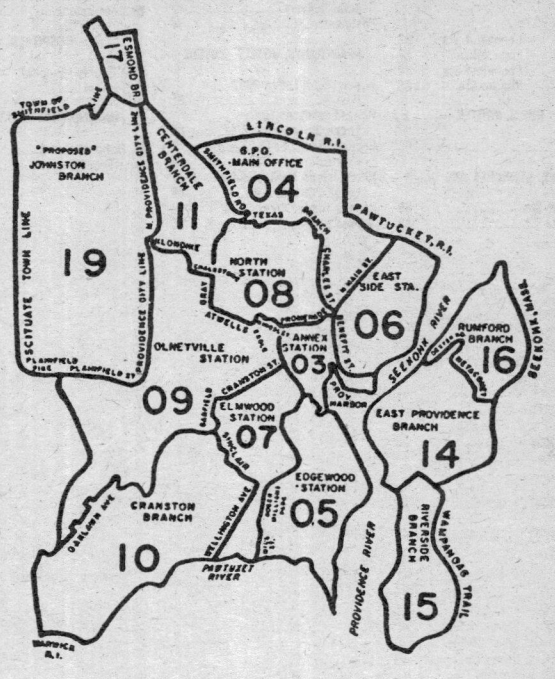

ZIP CODES
PROVIDENCE, Rhode Island
029 + Two Digits shown = Zip Code

WARWICK 028

POST OFFICE BOXES

Box Nos.
1-149	Conimicut Sta	89
1-392	Main Office	87
451-507	Conimicut Sta	89
701-909	Pilgrim Sta	88

RURAL ROUTES

1	86

STATIONS, BRANCHES AND UNITS

Conimicut Sta	89
Hoxsie Sta	89
Pilgrim Sta	88
Warwick Neck Sta	89
Wildes Corner Sta	86
General Delivery	87
Postmaster	87

APARTMENTS, HOTELS, MOTELS

Airport Motor Lodge 2082 Post Rd	86
Howard Johnsons Motor Lodge 24 Jefferson Blvd	88
Redwood Motor Lodge 2282 Post Rd	86
Rhode Island Yankee Motor Lodge 2081 Post Rd	86
Youngs Tourist Court 3880 Post Rd	86

GOVERNMENT OFFICES

Federal Aviation Adm.	86
Weather Bureau	86

HOSPITALS

Kent County Memorial Hospital	86

MILITARY INSTALLATIONS

Air National Guard	86
Army Reserve	86

SOUTH CAROLINA
(Abbreviation: SC)

Abbeville (1st)........................29620
Adams Run...............................29426
Adamsburg, R. Br. Union 29380
Aiken (1st)...............................29801
Alcolu......................................29001
Allendale (1st).........................29810
Alvin..29427
Anderson (1st).........................29621
Andrews..................................29510
Arcadia....................................29320
Ariail, R. Br. Easley.................29640
Arlington, R. Br. Greer 29651
Awendaw.................................29429
Aynor......................................29511
Baldwin Mills, R. Br.
    Chester................................29706
Ballentine.................................29002
Bamberg (1st)..........................29003
Baptist College, R. Br.
    Charleston............................29411
Barnwell (1st)...........................29812
    Hilda, R. Br..........................29813
    Kline, R. Br..........................29814
Batesburg................................29006
Bath..29816
Beaufort (1st)..........................29902
    Burton, Br............................29902
    Laurel Bay, R. Br................29902
    Marine Corps Air Station,
    Br..29902
    Naval Hospital, Br..............29902
    Parris Island, Br.................29905
Beech Island, R. Br. North
    Augusta...............................29842
Belton (1st)..............................29627
Belvedere, Br. North
    Augusta...............................29841
Bennettsville (1st)....................29512
Berea, Br. Greenville..............29601
Bethera....................................29430
Bethune....................................29009
Bishopville (1st).......................29010
Blacksburg..............................29702
Blackstock...............................29014
Blackville.................................29817
Blair...29015
Blenheim..................................29516
Bluffton....................................29910
Blythewood..............................29016
Bob Jones University, Sta.
    Greenville............................29614
Boiling Springs, R. Br.
    Spartanburg.........................29303
Bonneau...................................29431
Borden, R. Br. Rembert.........29017
Bowling Green.........................29703
Bowman....................................29018
Boykin.....................................29019
Bradley....................................29819
Branchville..............................29432
Branwood, Sta. Greenville
    (see appendix)
Broad Street, Sta. Sumter....29150
Brunson...................................29911
Bucksport, R. Br. Conway....29527
Buffalo.....................................29321
Burgess...................................29517
Burton, Br. Beaufort..............29902
Cades......................................29518
Calhoun Falls...........................29628

Callison....................................29820
Camden (1st)............................29020
Cameron...................................29030
    Lone Star, R. Br..................29077
Campobello...............................29322
Canadys...................................29433
Capitol, Sta. Columbia...........29211
Carlisle....................................29031
Carolina Mills, R. Br. Dillon...29537
Cassatt.....................................29032
Catawba...................................29704
Cateechee................................29629
Cayce (1st)...............................29033
Cedar Spring, Br. .
    Spartanburg.........................29303
Cedar Terrace, Sta.
    Columbia..............................29209
Centenary.................................29519
Central.....................................29630
Chapin......................................29036
Chappells.................................29037
CHARLESTON (1st) (see
    appendix)
Charleston A F B, Br.
    Charleston............................29404
Charleston Heights, Br.
    Charleston............................29405
Cheraw (1st)............................29520
Cherokee Falls.........................29705
Cherry Grove Beach, Br.
    North Myrtle Beach.............29582
Cherry Road, Sta. Rock Hill...29730
Chesnee....................................29323
Chester (1st)............................29706
    Baldwin Mills, R. Br............29706
    Hemlock, R. Br.....................29706
    Lowrys, R. Br.......................29725
Chesterfield..............................29709
Citadel, Sta. Charleston.........29409
City View, Br. Greenville.......29611
Clarks Hill................................29821
Clearwater................................29822
Clemson (1st)..........................29631
Clemson University, Sta.
    Clemson...............................29631
Cleveland.................................29635
Clifton......................................29324
Clinton (1st).............................29325
Clio..29525
Clover (1st) 29710
COLUMBIA (1st) (see
    appendix)
Conestee..................................29636
Converse..................................29329
Conway (1st)............................29526
    Bucksport, R. Br.................29527
Coosawhatchie, R. Br.
    Ridgeland.............................29912
Cope...29038
Cordesville...............................29434
Cordova...................................29039
Cottageville..............................29435
Coward.....................................29530
Cowpens...................................29330
Crescent Beach, Sta. North
    Myrtle Beach........................29582
Crocketville, R. Br. Hampton..29913
Cross.......................................29436
Cross Anchor...........................29331
Cross Hill.................................29332
Dale, R. Br. Seabrook............29914
Dalzell......................................29040
Darlington (1st)........................29532

Dovesville, R. Br.....................29540
Daufuskie Island 29915
Davis Station............................29041
Denmark...................................29042
Dentsville, Br. Columbia.........29204
Dillon (1st)...............................29536
    Carolina Mills, R. Br...........29537
Donalds....................................29638
Donaldson, Br. Greenville......29605
Dorchester................................29437
Dorchester-Waylyn, Br.
    Charleston............................29405
Dovesville, R. Br. Darlington...29540
Drayton....................................29333
Due West..................................29639
Duncan.....................................29334
Dunes, Sta. Myrtle Beach 29577
Dupont, Br. Charleston...........29407
Dutch Fork, Br. Columbia......29210
Early Branch............................29916
Easley (1st)..............................29640
Eastover...................................29044
Eau Claire, Sta. Columbia
    (see appendix)
Edgefield..................................29824
Edgemoor.................................29712
Edgewood, Sta. Columbia......29204
Edisto Island............................29438
Effingham.................................29541
Ehrhardt...................................29081
Elgin...29045
Elko..29826
Elliott.......................................29046
Elloree......................................29047
Enoree......................................29335
Estill...29918
    Scotia, R. Br........................29939
Eutawville.................................29048
Fair Play...................................29643
Fairfax......................................29827
Fairfield, Br. Hilton Head
    Island..................................29928
Fairforest..................................29336
Farrow Road, Br. Columbia....29203
Federal, Sta. Greenville..........29603
Fingerville................................29338
Five Points, Sta. Columbia....29205
Florence (1st)...........................29501
Floyd Dale................................29542
Folly Beach..............................29439
Forest Acres, Br. Columbia...29206
Foreston...................................29049
Fork...29543
Fort Jackson, Sta. Columbia...29207
Fort Lawn.................................29714
Fort Mill (1st)...........................29715
Fort Motte................................29050
Fountain Inn.............................29644
Fripp Island, R. Br.
    Frogmore.............................29920
Frogmore..................................29920
Furman.....................................29921
Furman University, Br.
    Greenville............................29613
Gable..29051
    Sardinia, R. Br....................29143
Gadsden...................................29052
Gaffney (1st)............................29340
Galivants Ferry........................29544
Garden City Beach, R. Br.
    Murrells Inlet.......................29576
Garnett.....................................29922
Gaston.....................................29053

Georgetown (1st)............29440
  Maryville, Br..............29440
  Plantersville, R. Br......29441
Gifford.............................29923
Gilbert.............................29054
Glendale...........................29346
Glenn Springs....................29347
Gloverville........................29828
Gooches, Br. Lancaster.......29720
Goose Creek......................29445
Gramling...........................29348
Graniteville......................29829
Gray Court........................29645
  Hickory Tavern, R. Br....29645
  Owings, R. Br.............29668
Great Falls........................29055
Greeleyville......................29056
Green Pond........................29446
Green Sea..........................29545
Greenview, Br. Columbia....29203
GREENVILLE (1st) (see
  appendix)
Greenwood (1st)................29646
Greer (1st)........................29651
Gresham............................29546
Grover.............................29447
Hamer.............................29547
Hampton (1st)....................29924
  Crocketville, R. Br.......29913
Hampton Park Terrace, Sta.
  Charleston................29403
Hanahan, Br. Charleston....29410
Hardeeville.......................29927
Harleyville........................29448
Harris, Br. Greenwood.......29646
Hartsville (1st)..................29550
Heath Springs....................29058
Hemingway........................29554
Hemlock, R. Br. Chester....29706
Hickory Grove....................29717
Hickory Tavern, R. Br. Gray
  Court.....................29645
Highway Four Forty One, R.
  Br. Sumter................29150
Hilda, R. Br. Barnwell.......29813
Hilton Head Island (1st).....29928
Hodges.............................29653
Holly Hill..........................29059
Hollywood..........................29449
Honea Path........................29654
  Princeton, R. Br..........29674
Hopkins.............................29061
Horatio.............................29062
Huger.............................29450
Inman.............................29349
Irmo.............................29063
Islandton..........................29929
Isle Of Palms....................29451
Iva.............................29655
Jackson.............................29831
Jacksonboro......................29452
James Island, Br.
  Charleston................29407
Jamestown..........................29453
Jefferson...........................29718
Jenkinsville......................29065
  Monticello, R. Br.........29106
  Parr, R. Br...............29066
Jericho.............................29454
Joanna.............................29351
Johns Island......................29455
Johnsonville......................29555
Johnston (1st)....................29832

Jonesville.........................29353
Kathwood, Br. West
  Columbia..................29169
Kennedy Street, Sta.
  Spartanburg...............29302
Kershaw............................29067
Kinards.............................29355
Kings Creek......................29719
Kingstree (1st)..................29556
Kline, R. Br. Barnwell.......29814
La France..........................29656
Ladson.............................29456
Lake City (1st)..................29560
Lake View..........................29563
Lamar.............................29069
Lancaster (1st)..................29720
Lando.............................29724
Landrum (1st)....................29356
Lane.............................29564
Langley.............................29834
Latta.............................29565
Laurel Bay, R. Br. Beaufort..29902
Laurens (1st)....................29360
Leesburg, Br. Columbia.......29201
Leesville..........................29070
Lena.............................29930
Lesslie, R. Br. Rock Hill....29734
Lexington (1st)..................29072
Liberty.............................29657
Liberty Hill......................29074
Little Mountain..................29075
Little River......................29566
Little Rock........................29567
Livingston........................29076
Lobeco.............................29931
Lockhart............................29364
Lodge.............................29082
Lone Star, R. Br. Cameron...29077
Longcreek..........................29658
Longs.............................29568
Loris (1st)........................29569
Lowndesville......................29659
Lowrys, R. Br. Chester......29725
Lugoff.............................29078
Luray.............................29932
Lydia.............................29079
Lydia Mills, R. Br. Clinton..29325
Lyman (1st)........................29365
Lynchburg..........................29080
Madison.............................29660
Manning (1st)....................29102
Marietta............................29661
Marine Corps Air Station, Br.
  Beaufort..................29902
Marion (1st)......................29571
Market Center, Br.
  Columbia..................29205
Martin.............................29836
Maryville, Br. Georgetown..29440
Mauldin (1st)....................29662
Mayesville..........................29104
Mayfair, Br. Taylors.........29687
Mayo.............................29368
Mc Bee.............................29101
Mc Clellanville..................29458
Mc Coll.............................29570
Mc Connells.......................29726
Mc Cormick........................29835
Meggett.............................29460
Miley.............................29933
Minturn.............................29573
Modoc.............................29838
Moncks Corner (1st)..........29461

Monetta............................29105
Monticello, R. Br.
  Jenkinsville..............29106
Montmorenci......................29839
Moore.............................29369
Mount Carmel....................29840
Mount Croghan....................29727
Mount Holly......................29463
Mount Pleasant (1st)..........29464
Mountain Rest....................29664
Mountville........................29370
Mullins (1st)....................29574
Murrells Inlet....................29576
Myers, Br. Charleston.......29405
Myrtle Beach (1st)..............29577
Myrtle Beach A F B, Br.
  Myrtle Beach..............29577
Naval Base, Br. Charleston..29408
Naval Hospital, Br. Beaufort..29902
Neeses.............................29107
Nesmith............................29580
New Easley Highway, Br.
  Greenville................29611
New Ellenton......................29809
New Zion..........................29111
Newberry (1st)..................29108
Newry.............................29665
Nichols.............................29581
Ninety Six........................29666
Norris.............................29667
North.............................29112
  Woodford, R. Br..........29184
North Anderson, Sta.
  Anderson..................29621
North Augusta (1st)..........29841
  Beech Island, R. Br......29842
  Belvedere, Br.............29841
North Charleston, Br.
  Charleston................29406
North Myrtle Beach (1st)....29582
Northbridge, Sta. Charleston..29407
Norway.............................29113
Oakley.............................29466
Oakway, R. Br. Westminster..29694
Olanta.............................29114
Olar.............................29843
Ora.............................29371
Orangeburg (1st)................29115
Osborn, R. Br. Adams Run...29426
Oswego.............................29121
Overbrook, Sta. Greenville..29601
Owings, R. Br. Gray Court..29668
Pacolet.............................29372
Pacolet Mills......................29373
Pageland............................29728
Palmetto Plaza, Sta. Sumter..29150
Pamplico............................29583
Paris, Br. Taylors...........29687
Park Place, Br. Greenville
  (see appendix)
Parksville..........................29844
Parr, R. Br. Jenkinsville....29066
Parris Island, Br. Beaufort..29905
Patrick.............................29584
Pauline.............................29374
Pawleys Island....................29585
Paxville, R. Br. Manning....29102
Peak.............................29122
Peedee.............................29586
Pelham, R Br. Greer.........29651
Pelion.............................29123
Pelzer.............................29669
Pendleton..........................29670

Perry 29124
Pickens (1st) 29671
Piedmont 29673
Pierpont, R. Br. Charleston ... 29407
Pineland 29934
Pineville 29468
Pinewood 29125
Pinopolis 29469
Plantersville, R. Br.
    Georgetown 29441
Plum Branch 29845
Pomaria 29126
Port Royal 29935
Poston 29588
Princeton, R. Br. Honea
    Path 29674
Prosperity 29127
Quinby, R. Br. Florence 29501
Rains 29589
Ravenel 29470
Reevesville 29471
Reidville 29375
Rembert 29128
    Borden, R. Br. 29017
Richburg 29729
Richland 29675
Ridge Spring 29129
Ridgeland (1st) 29936
    Coosawhatchie, R. Br. 29912
    Switzerland, R. Br. 29942
Ridgeville 29472
Ridgeway 29130
Rimini 29131
Rion 29132
Ritter 29473
Riverland Terrace, R. Br.
    Charleston 29407
Rivers Annex, Br.
    Charleston 29411
Rock Hill (1st) 29730
    Cherry Road, Sta. 29730
    Lesslie, R. Br. 29734
    Winthrop College, Sta. ... 29730
Rodman 29740
Roebuck 29376
Round O 29474
Rowesville 29133
Ruby 29741
Ruffin 29475
Russellville 29476
Saint Andrews, Br.
    Charleston 29407
Saint Charles 29134
Saint George (1st) 29477
Saint Matthews 29135
Saint Stephen 29479
Salem 29676
Salley 29137
Salters 29590
Saluda 29138
Saluda Gardens, Br. West
    Columbia 29169
Sandy Springs 29677
Sans Souci, Sta. Greenville ... 29609
Santee 29142
Sardinia, R. Br. Gable 29143
Scotia, R. Br. Estill 29939
Scranton 29591
Seabrook 29940
    Dale, R. Br. 29914
Sellers 29592
Seneca (1st) 29678
Shandon, Sta. Columbia 29205

Sharon 29742
Shaw A F B, Br. Sumter 29152
Sheldon 29941
Shelton 29144
Shoals Junction 29680
Shulerville 29480
Silverstreet 29145
Simpsonville (1st) 29681
Six Mile 29682
Slater 29683
Smoaks 29481
Smyrna 29743
Society Hill 29593
South, Br. Anderson 29621
South Greenwood, Sta.
    Greenwood 29646
South Of The Border, R. Br.
    Hamer 29547
South Windermere, Sta.
    Charleston 29407
Southern Shops, Br.
    Spartanburg 29303
SPARTANBURG (1st) (see
    appendix)
Springdale, Br. West
    Columbia 29169
Springfield 29146
Starr 29684
Startex 29377
State College, Sta.
    Orangeburg 29115
State Park 29147
Stuckey, R. Br. Hemingway ... 29554
Sullivans Island 29482
Summerton 29148
Summerville (1st) 29483
Sumter (1st) 29150
    Broad Street, Sta. 29150
    Highway Four Forty One,
        R. Br. 29150
    Palmetto Plaza, Sta. 29150
    Shaw A F B, Br. 29152
Sunset 29685
Surfside Beach, Br. Myrtle
    Beach 29577
Swansea 29160
Switzerland, R. Br.
    Ridgeland 29942
Sycamore 29846
Tamassee 29686
Tatum 29594
Taylors (1st) 29687
Tigerville 29688
Tillman 29943
Timmonsville 29161
Townville 29689
Travelers Rest 29690
Trenton 29847
Trio 29595
Troy 29848
Turbeville 29162
Ulmer 29849
Una 29378
Union (1st) 29379
    Adamsburg, R. Br. 29380
University, Sta. Columbia 29208
Valley Falls, R. Br.
    Spartanburg 29303
Van Wyck 29744
Vance 29163
Varnville 29944

Vaucluse 29850
Wade Hampton, Sta.
    Greenville 29607
Wadmalaw Island 29487
Wagener 29164
Walhalla (1st) 29691
Wallace 29596
Walterboro (1st) 29488
Wando 29492
Ward 29166
Ware Shoals (1st) 29692
Warrenville 29851
Waterloo 29384
Wedgefield 29168
Wellford 29385
Wesleyan, R. Br. Central 29630
West Columbia (1st) 29169
West Florence, Sta. Florence ... 29501
West Pelzer, Sta. Pelzer 29669
West Union 29696
Westminster (1st) 29693
    Oakway, R. Br. 29694
Westville 29175
Whipper Barony, Br.
    Charleston 29405
White Oak 29176
White Pond, R. Br. Williston ... 29854
White Rock 29177
White Stone 29386
Whitmire 29178
Whitney, Br. Spartanburg 29303
Williams 29493
Williamston 29697
Willington 29852
Williston 29853
    White Pond, R. Br. 29854
Wilson 29179
Windsor 29856
Windy Hill Beach, Sta. North
    Myrtle Beach 29582
Winnsboro (1st) 29180
Winthrop College, Sta. Rock
    Hill 29730
Wisacky 29183
Woodford, R. Br. North 29184
Woodruff (1st) 29388
Yemassee 29945
Yonges Island 29494
York (1st) 29745

CHARLESTON 294

POST OFFICE BOXES

Box Nos.

A-Z	Main Office	02
1-1137	Main Office	02
2000-2999	A Sta	03
3000-3999	St Andrews Br	07
4000-4999	Charleston Heights Br	05
5000-5999	North Charleston Br	06
6000-6999	Myers Br	05
7000-7999	Charleston Heights Br	05
9000-9999	Hanahan Br	10
10000-10999	Rivers Annex Br	11
12000-12999	James Island Br	12

RURAL ROUTES

1	12
2,3	05
4	07
5	12
6	06
7,8,9,10,11	12
12	12
13,14	05
15,16	05
17	18
18	05

STATIONS, BRANCHES AND UNITS

Baptist College Rural Br	11
Charleston A F B Br	04
Charleston Heights Br	05
Citadel Sta	09
Dorchester-Waylyn Br	05
Dupont Br	07
Hampton Park Terrace Sta	03
Hanahan Br	10
James Island Br	07
Myers Br	05
Naval Base Br	08
North Charleston Br	06
Northbridge Sta	07
Pierpont Rural Br	07
Riverland Terrace Rural Br	07
Rivers Annex Br	11
Saint Andrews Br	07
South Windermere Sta	07
Whipper Barony Br	05
General Delivery	01
Postmaster	01

APARTMENTS, HOTELS, MOTELS

Ashley Arms, 1551 Ashley River Rd	07
Ashley House, Lockwood Blvd.	01
Ashley Shores, Accabee Rd	05
Ben Tillman Homes, Charleston Hts	05
Berkeley, 63 Rutledge Ave	01
Carlton Arms, 59 Vanderhorst	03
Caroline, 148 Rutledge Ave	03

Charleston Arms, 1551 Hwy 7	07
Chicco Apts, 37 John St, 349 Meeting	03
Courtenay Doughty	03
Daniel Jenkins Homes, Charleston Hts	05
Darlington, 2106 Mount Pleasant	03
Dorchester Gardens, 5600 Dorchester Rd	05
Enston Homes, 900 King	03
Frewil, Vanderhorst & Smith	03
George Legare Homes, Charleston Hts	05
Governor Yeamans, Sedgefield Dr	06
John C Calhoun Homes, North Charleston	06
Kiawah Homes, Rutledge Ave & Mount Pleasant	03
Liberty Homes, North Charleston	06
Marlboro, 140 Queen	01
Murray, 20 Ehrhardt & 112 Doughty	03
Plantation, 1840 Carriage Ln.	07
Riverbend, 864 S Colony Dr	03
Rivercrest, 54 10th Ave	03
Riviera, Old Point Rd	06
Saint Angela, 173 Rutledge Ave	03
Saint Charles, 1085 King	03
Saint James, 193 Congress	03
Saint Regis, 17 8th Ave	03
Sergeant Jasper, West End Broad	01
The Palms, Royal Palm Blvd	07
Tomrad, 24 Thomas	03
Woodmere, 1735 Ashley Hall Rd	07

BUILDINGS

Federal, 334 Meeting	03
Fireproof, Meeting At Chalmers	01
Peoples Office, 18 Broad	01

GOVERNMENT OFFICES

City Hall, 80 Broad	01
Federal Building, 334 Meeting	03
Post Office, 81-83 Broad	01
U S Customs House, 200 E Bay	01

HOSPITALS

Alumni Memorial House, 45 Courtenay Dr	01
Baker Memorial, 55 Ashley Ave	01
Carolina Nursing Center, 341 Calhoun	01
Charles Webb Rehabilitation Center, 325 Calhoun	01
Charleston County Health Dept, 334 Calhoun	01
Easter Seal Orthopedic	

School, 325 Calhoun	01
Mc Clennon Banks, 25 Courtenay Dr	01
Medical Arts, 65 Gadsden	01
Medical College Nurses Home, 75 Doughty	01
Medical College, 55 Doughty	01
Riverside Geriatric & Convalescent Center, 295 Calhoun	01
Roper, 316 Calhoun	01
Saint Francis Nurses, 150 Ashley Ave	01
Saint Francis Xavier 135 Rutledge Ave	01
Veterans Administration, 109 Bee	03

MILITARY INSTALLATIONS

Atlantic Fleet, Naval Base	08
Charleston Air Force Base	04
Charleston Army Depot	06
Charleston Naval Shipyard	08
Commandant Sixth Naval District	08
M E N - R I V Park	08
Marine Barracks	08
Mineforce U S Atlantic Fleet	08
Naval Hospital	08
Naval Housing, Hunley Park	04
Naval Weapons Station	08
Polaris Missile Facilities Atlantic	08
U S Coast Guard Tradd	01
U S Naval Station	08

UNIVERSITIES AND COLLEGES

Ashley Hall School, 172 Rutledge Ave	03
Baptist College At Charleston, U S Hwy 78 At I-26	11
College Of Charleston, 66 George	01
Medical University Of S C 80 Barre St	01
Palmer College, 125 Bull	01
Porter-Gaud School, Albemarle Rd	07
Technical Education Center, 7000 Rivers Ave	05
The Citadel	09

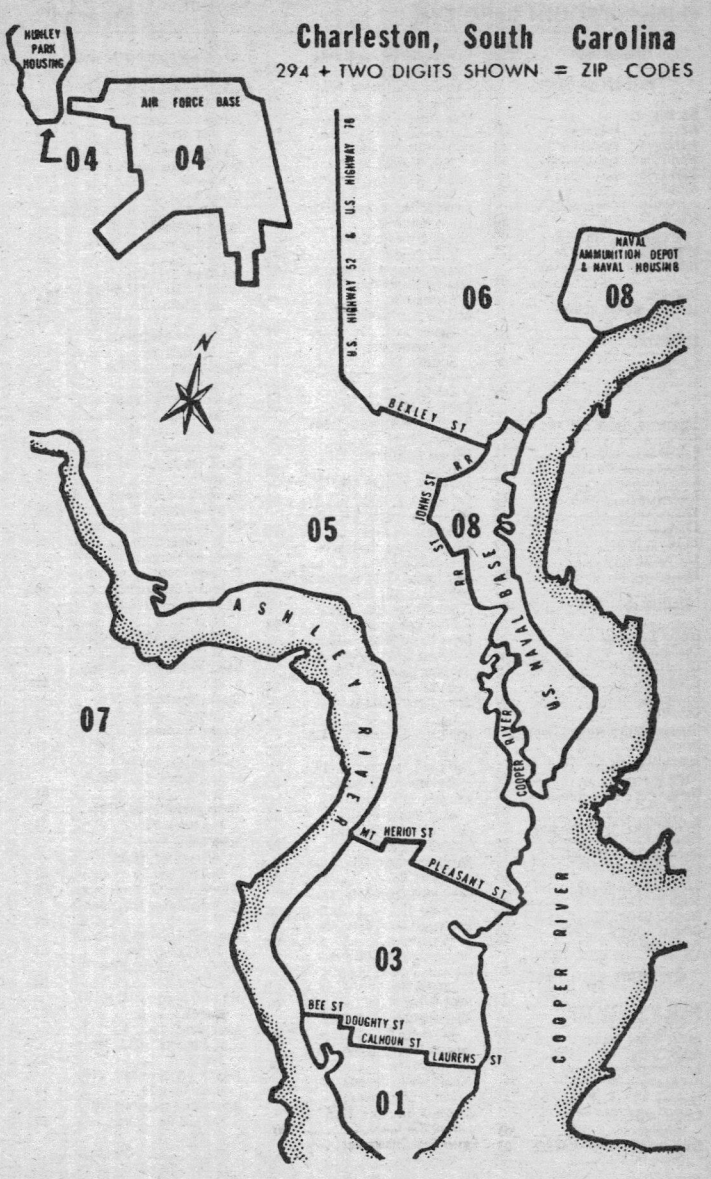

Charleston, South Carolina
294 + TWO DIGITS SHOWN = ZIP CODES

COLUMBIA   292

POST OFFICE BOXES

Box Nos.

1-1999	Columbia	02
3000-3999	Eau Claire Sta.	03
4000-4999	Edgewood Sta.	40
5000-5999	Five Points Sta.	05
6000-6999	Forest Acres Br.	60
9000-9999	Leesburg Br.	09
11000-12999	Capitol Sta.	11
13000-13999	Market Center Br.	01

RURAL ROUTES

1	03
2	10
3	06
4	09
5	03

STATIONS, BRANCHES AND UNITS

Capitol Sta	11
Cedar Terrace Sta	09
Dentsville Br	04
Dutch Fork Br	10
Eau Claire Sta	03
Edgewood Sta	40
Farrow Road Br	03
Five Points Sta	05
Forest Acres Br	06
Fort Jackson Sta	07
Greenview Br	03
Leesburg Br	09
Market Center Br	05
Shandon Sta	05
University Sta	08
General Delivery	01
Postmaster	01

APARTMENTS, HOTELS, MOTELS

Allen-Benedict Court, 1810 Court Plaza	04
Barkoot Apts, 2637 River Drive	01
Barkoot Apts, 3027 Belt Line Blvd	04
Becks Motor Court, 4345 Fort Jackson Blvd	05
Bloomwood Apts, 4426 Blossom Street	05
Camelot-In-The-Hills Apts, 3431 Covenant Rd	04
Capitol Terrace Motor, 1001 Assembly	02
Carnaby Square Apts Garner Ln	10
Carolina Gardens, 101 Pickens	05
Carolina Motel, 2709 Two Notch Rd	04
Carriage Hill Apartments, 5225 Clemson Ave	06
Charles Edwards Apartments, 2 Gibbes Ct	01
Chat N Rest Motel, 1608 Two Notch Rd	04

Chateau Deville Apartments, Chateau Dr	04
Christine Apartments, 927 Daly St	05
Claire Towers Apartments, 1041 Marion	01
Colony Forest Apartments, 3600 W Belt Line Blvd	03
Columbia Gardens, Plowden Road	05
Columbia Motor Court, 3315 Two Notch Rd	04
Cornell Arms Apartments, 1230 Pendleton	01
Coronet Motel, 6320 Main	03
Crescent Manor Apts 1700 Carnegie St	04
Davis & Apartments, 1728 Sumter	01
Davis Apartments, 1728 Sumter	01
Davis Apartments, 1728 Sumter	01
Davis, 1712 Sumter St	01
Downtowner Motor Inn, 1301 Main	02
Durham Apartments, 931 Daly	05
Edisto Apartments, 526 Edisto Ave	05
Edisto Apartments, 611 Waccamaw Ave	05
Elmtree Village, Elmtree Rd & Fairmont Dr	09
Forest Motel, 3111 Two Notch Rd	04
Forest Terrace Apartments, 2000 Belt Line Blvd	04
Glass Manor Motel, 5810 Wilson Blvd	03
Gonzales Gardens, 1505 Garden Plaza	04
Grand Motel, 3003 Two Notch Rd	04
Hall Court Apartments, 2318 Lee	05
Hall Court Apartments, 719 Meadow	05
Hampton Park Apartments, 4427 Blossom	05
Heart Of Columbia Motel, 1011 Assembly	02
Heathwood Court Apts, 4100 Stevens Rd	05
Heathwood Court Apts, 4103 Devine	05
Heathwood Court Apts, 700 Pointsettia	05
Hendley Homes, 501 S Bull	05
Highland Park Apartments, 3800 W Ave	03
Hotel Desoto, 1108 Lady St	01
Hunters Motor Court, 2322 Two Notch Rd	04
Jaggers Terrace, 2009 Jaggers Plaza	04
Jamestown Apartments, Bethel Church Road	06
Keenan Apartments, 1208 Elmwood Ave	01
King Cotton Motel, 3211 Two Notch Rd	04

King Court Apartments, 1460 King	05
Lakeshore Apartments, 5625 Percival Road	06
Lamplighter Apartments, 1730 Windover Rd	04
Latimer Manor	03
Matador Motor Inn, 922 Bush River Rd	10
Myron Manor Apartments, 4500 Fort Jackson Blvd	09
New York Avenue Apartments, 2400 Waites Rd	04
Oak-Read, 221, Read	04
Orleans Plaza, 1707 S Belt Line Blvd	05
Orvin Court, 821 Assembly	01
Paddington Apartments, 3700 West Ave	03
Palm Apartments, 5800 Percival Road	06
Palmetto Terrace Apartments, 2000 Sligh Ave	03
Plantation Oaks, 3206 Fernandina Rd	10
Quail Run Apts, 6101 Quail Run Dr	06
Ravenwood Apartments, 4200 Bethel Church Road	06
Regency Square Apartments, 2050 Beltline Blvd	04
Roosevelt Village	03
Rutledge Forest Apts, 3600 Falling Springs Rd	03
Saxon Homes, 2124 Saxon Plaza	04
Senate Plaza, 1520 Senate St	01
Sheraton Inn, 610 Assembly St	01
Singley Apartments, 1616 Green	01
Singley Apartments, 732 Pickens	01
The Hampton House Apartments, 1800 Senate St	01
Thoroughbred Motel, 3411 Two Notch Rd	04
Town House Motel Incorporated, 1619 Gervais	02
Villager Apts, Burnside Drive	09
Wade Hampton, 1201 Main St	02
Washington Carver Village, 3530 Colony Forest Dr	03
Willow Lakes Apts, 5315 Fairfield Rd	03
Wit-Mary Apartments, 1018 Marion	01
Woodland Terrace Apartments, 300 S Belt Line Blvd	05
Woodland Village Apts, 2400 Bush River Rd	10
Woodmere Apartments, 18 Berryhill Rd	10

BUILDINGS

Arcade, 1332 Main 01
Baker Bldg, 1616 Hampton
    St 01
Barringer, 1338 Main 01
City Schools Administration,
    1616 Richland 01
Columbia, 1203 Gerrais 01
County Agricultural, 1508
    Washington 01
Crawford, 1213 Lady St........ 01
Creason, 1247 Sumter.......... 01
Federal Land Bank, 1401
    Hampton 01
Federal Office, 901 Sumter..... 01
First National Bank, 1210
    Washington 01
Greystone Industrial Park...... 10
Insurance, 1300 Pickens....... 01
J. Marion Sims Bldg, 2600
    Bull St. 01
Jefferson Square, 1801 Main.... 02
John C Calhoun Office, 1228
    Senate 01
Klondike, 1813 Main St 01
Methodist, 1420 Lady 01
Middleburg Office Mall 04
Owens, 1321 Lady.............. 01
Palmetto State Life, 1310
    Lady 01
Palmetto, 1400 Main 01
Richland County Library,
    1400 Sumter 01
Ritz, 1325 Main 01
Rutledge Building 01
Security Federal, 1231
    Washington 01
Singley, 1215 Lady St.......... 01
South Carolina National Bank
    Center 1122 Lady............ 01
South Carolina National
    Bank, 1401 Main............. 01
South Carolina National
    Bank, 900 Assembly St...... 01
State House 01
Universal, 1725 Sumter........ 01
Varo, 1801 Assembly St........ 01
Wade Hampton Office Bldg 01
Y. M. C. A., 1420 Sumter St... 01

GOVERNMENT OFFICES

City Hall, 1737 Main........... 01
Richland County Court
    House, 1401 Sumter.......... 01
United States Courthouse,
    1100 Laurel 01

HOSPITALS

Baptist Hospital, 1330 Taylor
    St 01
Good Samaritan-Waverly
    Hospital, 2202 Hampton
    St 04
Providence Hospital, 2435
    Forest Dr 04
Richland Memorial Hospital.... 03
S. C. State Hospital 02
Veterans Hospital 01

Fonta Vis 04
Fontaine Rd.................... 04
Fontana Dr 09
Ford 03
Forest Dr
    2400-4199 04
    4200-5799 06
Forest Ridge La............... 06
Forestwood Dr................. 04
Formosa Dr 06
Forsyth........................ 01
Fort Jackson Blvd
    4300-4399 05
    4400-OUT 09
Foster 03

GREENVILLE   296

POST OFFICE BOXES

Box Nos		
A-V	Branwood Sta....	10
1-3135	Main Office......	02
3501-4387	Park Place Br....	08
5001-7015	B Sta.............	06
7051-7999	Branwood Sta....	10
8001-9044	A Sta.............	03
10001-10396	Federal Sta......	03

RURAL ROUTES

1 11
2 11
3 09
4 05
5 09
6 07
7 09
8 11
9 07
10 11
11 11

STATIONS, BRANCHES AND UNITS

Berea Br 01
Bob Jones University Sta 14
Branwood Sta.................. 10
City View Br 11
Donaldson Br.................. 05
Federal Sta.................... 03
Furman University Br 13
New Easley Highway Br 11
Overbrook Sta................. 09
Park Place Br.................. 08
Sans Souci Sta................ 09
Wade Hampton Sta 07
General Delivery 02
Postmaster.................... 02

APARTMENTS, HOTELS, MOTELS

Balfer Court Apts, Balfer Dr... 07
Botany Arms, 510 Edwards
    Rd 07
Calhoun Towers, 415 N Main.. 01
Carmil Court Apts, 38
    Southland Ave................ 01
Cedar Lane Apts. Columbia
    Ave 11
City Heights Apts. Off
    Furman Rd................... 09
Club Key East Apts.
    Cleveland Street 01

Colony House, Glenwood Rd... 07
Continental Apts, Glenwood
    Rd 07
Court Plaza Apts 01
Courtland, 504-92 E Faris
    Rd 05
Crestview Apts, Shaw 09
Davenport, 400 E
    Washington 01
East North Court Apts. East
    North St. Ext................. 07
Fieldcrest Village, Greenacre
    Rd 07
Franklin Court Apts. North
    Franklin Rd.................. 09
Fredricksburg Apts, Galphin
    Dr 09
Glenwood Terrace Apts.
    Glenwood Rd................. 07
Hampton Arms Apts, Wade
    Hampton Blvd................ 07
Hampton Trace Apts. Wade
    Hampton Blvd................ 07
Hillandale Apts................ 09
Kingston Court, Monroe &
    Huff........................... 01
Lakeshore Apts. Off Int. 85 ... 11
Lane Apts. Lane Ave........... 07
Lavista Villa Apts. Villa View
    Dr 09
Lewis Village, Lewis Village.... 05
Luitwater Apts. Kadena Pl..... 07
Maryland, 801 E North......... 01
Mc Daniel Heights, Mc Daniel
    Heights....................... 01
Mcdaniel Place Apts. 200
    Mcdaniel Ave................. 01
Middleton Apts, W Earl........ 09
Mountain View Homes, Perry
    Ave 11
Northway Apts. 3800 East
    North St. Ext................. 07
Oak Creek Court Apts 07
Orleans Court Apts, E. North
    St 07
Park Heights, 606 University
    Ridge 01
Pearce Homes. Hanson Pl..... 07
Pelham East, Pelham Rd...... 07
Piedmont Manor Shemwood
    Ln 05
Pinecrest Apts. Eugene St. 09
Plaza, 100 E Lewis Plaza 05
Poinsett, 400 Summit Dr 09
River Bend Apts. Cleveland.... 01
Roosevelt Heights, Roosevelt.. 07
Rutherford Court Apts.
    Greenbriar St................ 09
Sans Souci Apts. Buncombe
    Rd 09
Town Park Apts. E. North St.
    Ext 07
Trianon Village Apts........... 09
University Ridge, University
    Ridge 01
Villa Apts. Villa Rd............ 07
Virginia, 10 Manley............ 01
Westgate Motel Lilly........... 11
Wildaire Apts. Rushmore Dr... 09
Williamsburg Manor, Edwards
    Rd 07
Windsor, 3701 Buncombe Rd.. 09
Woodland Homes, Pearce

Ave	07
Yorktown, Pelham Rd..	07

BUILDINGS

Chamber Of Commerce, 19 S Irvine	01
County Court House, 309 E North	01
County Office, 130 S Main ..	01
Daniel, 301 N Main	02
Doctor'S, 12 S Calhoun	01
Federal, 300 E Washington..	03
Greenville City Hall, 214 S Main	02
Greenville Medical Ctr, 24 Vardry	01
I B M, 200 E Camperdown Way	01
Insurance, 135 S Main	01
Lawyers, 301 E North	01
Medical Court, 811 Pendleton	01
South Carolina National Bank, 13 S Main	01
Stokes, 314 E Coffee	01
Stone Avenue, 209 E Stone Ave	09
Two Fifty Two, 252 S Pleasanturg Dr	07
United, 217 E Stone Ave	09
Vardry Medical Court, 413 Vardry	01

HOSPITALS

Greenville General, 100 Mallard	02
Marshall I. Pickens Hospital, Grove Rd	05
Roger C Peace Hospital Grove Rd	05
Saint Francis, 40G Sumner	02
Shriners, 2100 N Pleasantburg Dr..	09
Wm G Sirrine Hospital, 1200 Pendleton	11

UNIVERSITIES AND COLLEGES

Bob Jones University Wade Hampton Blvd	14
Furman University Poinsett Hwy	13
Greenville Tech Educational Center S Pleasanturg Dr ..	06
Holmes Theological Seminary 115 Briggs Ave	01

SPARTANBURG   293

POST OFFICE BOXES

Box Nos.		
1-1999	Main Office	01
2000-3999	Kennedy Street Sta..	02
4000-4999	B Sta..	03
5000-6052	Main Office	01

RURAL ROUTES

1,2	02
3	01
4	02
5	01
6,7,8	03
9	11
11	02
110	03

STATIONS, BRANCHES AND UNITS

Boiling Springs Rural Br	03
Cedar Spring Br	03
Kennedy Street Sta	02
Southern Shops Br	03
Valley Falls Rural Br	03
Whitney Br	03
General Delivery	01
Postmaster	01

APARTMENTS, HOTELS, MOTELS

Abbie, Morningside Dr	01
Archibald Rutledge Apts, Centennial St	03
Brockwood Terrace Apts	01
Cabana Inn, 462 E Main	02
Cleveland, 178 W Main	01
Crystal Springs, Woodburn Rd	02
Franklin, 186 E Main	01
Georgetown Village Apts, 1421 Reidville Rd	01
Heart Of Spartanburg, 578 N Church	03
Highland Court, 144 W Henry	01
Highland Homes, 100 Highland	01
Holiday Inn, I-85	03
Howard Aden, 630 Howard	03
Howard Johnson, I-85	01
Hub City Courts, Vanderbilt Rd	01
Main Street Motel, 700 W Main	01
Morgan, 277 Magnolia	01
Northside Apts, Fremont & Howard Sts	03
Peach Blossom, I-85	03
Phyllis, Goins Court, Collins Ave	01
Pine Street, 150 Pine	02
Ramada Inn	03
Richmond, 225 E Main	01
Schuyler, 269 S Church	01
Travel-Lodge, 416 E Main	02
Woodworth Homes, Baltimore.	01

BUILDINGS

Andrews, 116 Morgan Sq	01
City Hall 145 W Broad	01
County, 188 Magnolia	01
Federal, 201 Magnolia	01
Medical, 711 N Church	03
Montgomery, 187 N Church	01
National Beta, 458 N Church.	01
News, Herald, 177 W Main	01
Schuyler Office, 296 S	

Church	01
U S District Court, 201 Magnolia	01

HOSPITALS

Mary Black, 1700 Skylyn Dr....	02
Spartanburg General 101 E Wood	03

UNIVERSITIES AND COLLEGES

Converse, 580 E Main	01
Spartanburg Junior, Textile Rd	01
Wofford, 429 N Church	01

SOUTH DAKOTA
(Abbreviation SD)

Aberdeen (1st)	57401
Putney, R. Br.	57402
Academy	57310
Agar	57520
Akaska	57420
Albee	57210
Alcester	57001
Alexandria	57311
Allen	57714
Alpena	57312
Altamont	57211
Amherst	57421
Andover	57422
Ardmore	57715
Arlington	57212
Armour	57313
Artas	57423
Artesian	57314
Ashton	57424
Astoria	57213
Athol	57425
Aurora	57002
Avon	57315
Badger	57214
Baltic	57003
Bancroft	57316
Barnard	57426
Batesland	57716
Bath	57427
Belle Fourche (1st)	57717
Belvidere	57521
Bemis	57215
Beresford	57004
Bethlehem, R. Br. Rapid City	57708
Big Stone City	57216
Bison	57620
Sorum, R. Br	57654
Black Hawk	57718
Blunt	57522
Bonesteel	57317
Bonilla	57318
Bowdle	57428
Box Elder	57719
Bradley	57217
Brandon	57005
Brandt	57218
Brentford	57429
Bridgewater	57319
Bristol	57219
Britton	57430
Brookings (1st)	57006
Bruce	57220
Bryant	57221
Buffalo	57720
Ladner, R. Br.	57753
Buffalo Gap	57722
Bullhead	57621
Burbank	57010
Burke	57523
Bushnell	57011
Butler	57222
Camp Crook	57724
Canistota	57012
Canning	57524
Canova	57321
Canton	57013
Capa	57525
Caputa	57725
Carpenter	57322

Carter	57526
Carthage	57323
Castle Rock	57726
Castlewood	57223
Cavour	57324
Cedarbutte	57727
Centerville	57014
Central City	57727
Chamberlain (1st)	57325
Chancellor	57015
Chelsea	57431
Cherry Creek, R. Br. Dupree	57622
Chester	57016
Claire City	57224
Claremont	57432
Clark	57225
Clear Lake	57226
Clearfield, R. Br. Winner	57581
Colman	57017
Colome	57528
Colton	57018
Columbia	57433
Commerce, Sta. Sioux Falls	57102
Conde	57434
Corona	57227
Corsica	57328
Corson	57019
Cottonwood	57728
Crandall	57228
Crazy Horse, R. Br. Custer	57730
Creighton	57729
Cresbard	57435
Crocker	57229
Crooks	57020
Custer	57730
Dallas	57529
Dante	57329
Davis	57021
De Smet	57231
Deadwood (1st)	57732
Dell Rapids	57022
Delmont	57330
Dempster	57230
Denby	57733
Dimock	57331
Dixon	57530
Doland	57436
Dolton	57023
Draper	57531
Dupree	57623
Cherry Creek, R. Br.	57622
Eagle Butte	57625
Eden	57232
Edgemont	57735
Egan	57024
Elk Point	57025
Elkton	57026
Ellsworth A F B, Br. Rapid City	57706
Elm Springs	57736
Emery	57332
Enning	57737
Erwin	57233
Esmond	57333
Estelline	57234
Ethan	57334
Eureka	57437
Fairburn	57738
Fairfax	57335
Fairpoint, R. Br. Sturgis	57739
Fairview	57027
Faith	57626
Maurine, R. Br.	57627

Farmer	57336
Farmingdale	57740
Faulkton	57438
Fedora	57337
Ferney	57439
Firesteel	57628
Flandreau	57028
Florence	57235
Forestburg	57338
Fort Meade	57741
Fort Pierre	57532
Fort Thompson	57339
Frankfort	57440
Frederick	57441
Freeman	57029
Fruitdale	57742
Fulton	57340
Gannvalley	57341
Garden City	57236
Garretson	57030
Gary	57237
Gayville	57031
Geddes	57342
Gettysburg	57442
Glad Valley	57629
Glencross	57630
Glenham	57631
Goodwin	57238
Greenway	57444
Gregory	57533
Granville	57239
Groton	57445
Hamill	57534
Hammer	57240
Harrington	57535
Harrisburg	57032
Harrison	57344
Harold	57536
Hartford	57033
Hayes	57537
Hayti	57241
Hazel	57242
Hecla	57446
Henry	57243
Hereford	57743
Hermosa	57744
Herreid	57632
Herrick	57538
Hetland	57244
Highmore	57345
Stephan, R. Br.	57346
Hill City	57745
Hisle	57539
Hitchcock	57348
Holabird	57540
Hoover	57746
Hosmer	57448
Hot Springs (1st)	57747
Houghton	57449
Hoven	57450
Howard	57349
Howes	57748
Hudson	57034
Humboldt	57035
Hurley	57036
Huron (1st)	57350
Ideal	57541
Interior	57750
Iona	57542
Ipswich	57451
Irene	57037
Iroquois	57353
Isabel	57633

Java	57452
Jefferson	57038
Kadoka	57543
Kaylor	57354
Keldron	57634
Kenel, R. Br. Mc Laughlin	57642
Kennebec	57544
Keyapaha	57545
Keystone	57751
Kidder	57457
Kimball	57355
Kirley	57546
Kranzburg	57245
Kyle	57752
La Bolt	57246
La Plant	57637
Ledner, R. Br. Buffalo	57753
Lake Andes	57356
Ravinia, R. Br.	57357
Lake City	57247
Lake Norden	57248
Lake Preston	57249
Lane	57358
Langford	57454
Lantry	57636
Lead (1st)	57754
Lebanon	57455
Lemmon	57638
Shadehill, R. Br.	57653
Thunder Hawk, R. Br.	57655
Lennox	57039
Leola	57456
Lesterville	57040
Letcher	57359
Lily	57250
Little Eagle	57639
Lodgepole	57640
Longlake	57457
Longvalley	57547
Loomis	57360
Lower Brule	57548
Lowry	57458
Loyalton	57459
Lucas	57549
Ludlow	57755
Lyons	57041
Madison (1st)	57042
Mahto, R. Br. Mc Laughlin	57643
Manderson	57756
Mansfield	57460
Marcus	57757
Marion	57043
Monroe, R. Br.	57047
Martin	57551
Vetal, R. Br.	57575
Marty	57361
Marvin	57251
Maurine, R. Br. Faith	57627
Mc Intosh	57641
Mc Laughlin	57642
Kenel, R. Br.	57642
Mahto, R. Br.	57643
Meadow	57644
Meckling	57044
Mellette	57461
Menno	57045
Midland	57552
Milbank (1st)	57252
Milesville	57553
Millboro	57554
Miller	57362
Mina	57451
Miranda	57463

Mission	57555
Mission Hill	57046
Mission Ridge	57557
Mitchell (1st)	57301
Mobridge (1st)	57601
Monroe, R. Br. Marion	57047
Montrose	57048
Morristown	57645
Mosher	57558
Mound City	57646
Mount Vernon	57363
Mud Butte	57758
Murdo	57559
Naples	57254
Nemo	57759
New Effington	57255
New Holland	57364
New Underwood	57761
Newell	57760
Nisland	57762
Norbeck	57464
Norris	57560
North Sioux City	57049
Northville	57465
Nunda	57050
Oacoma	57365
Oelrichs	57763
Oglala	57764
Okaton	57562
Okreek	57563
Oldham	57051
Olivet	57052
Onaka	57466
Onida	57564
Opal	57765
Oral	57766
Orient	57467
Ortley	57256
Ottumwa	57567
Owanka	57767
Parade	57647
Parker	57053
Parkston	57366
Parmelee	57566
Peever	57257
Philip	57567
Pickstown	57367
Piedmont	57769
Pierpont	57468
Pierre (1st)	57501
Pine Ridge	57770
Plainview	57771
Plankinton	57368
Flatte	57369
Pollock	57648
Porcupine	57772
Prairie City	57649
Presho	57568
Pringle	57773
Provo	57774
Pukwana	57370
Putney, R. Br. Aberdeen	57402
Quinn	57775
Ralph	57650
Ramona	57054
Rapid City (1st)	57701
Bethlehem, R. Br.	57708
Ellsworth A F B, Br.	57706
Rockerville, R. Br.	57701
Silver City, R. Br.	57781
Ravinia, R. Br. Lake Andes	57357
Raymond	57258
Redfield (1st)	57469

Redig	57776
Redowl	57777
Ree Heights	57371
Reliance	57569
Renner	57055
Reva	57651
Revillo	57259
Ridgeview	57652
Rochford	57778
Rockerville, R. Br. Rapid City	57701
Rockham	57470
Roscoe	57471
Rosebud	57570
Rosholt	57260
White Rock, R. Br.	57277
Roslyn	57261
Roswell	57372
Rowena, R. Br. Sioux Falls	57056
Rutland	57057
Saint Charles	57571
Saint Francis	57572
Saint Lawrence	57373
Saint Onge	57779
Salem	57058
Scenic	57780
Scotland	57059
Selby	57472
Seneca	57473
Shadehill, R. Br. Lemmon	57653
Sherman	57060
Silver City, R. Br. Rapid City	57781
Sinai	57061
SIOUX FALLS (1st) (see appendix)	
Sisseton (1st)	57262
Sky Ranch, R. Br. Camp Crook	57724
Smithwick	57782
Sorum, R. Br. Bison	57654
South Shore	57263
Spearfish (1st)	57783
Spencer	57374
Springfield	57062
Stephan, R. Br. Highmore	57346
Stickney	57375
Stockholm	57264
Stoneville, R. Br. Sturgis	57784
Strandburg	57265
Stratford	57474
Sturgis (1st)	57785
Fairpoint, R. Br.	57739
Stoneville, R. Br.	57784
Summit	57266
Tabor	57063
Tea	57064
Tekakwitha, R. Br. Sisseton	57262
Terraville	57786
Thunder Hawk, R. Br. Lemmon	57655
Timber Lake	57656
Tolstoy	57475
Toronto	57268
Trail City	57657
Trent	57065
Tripp	57376
Tulare	57476
Turton	57477
Tuthill	57574
Twin Brooks	57269
Tyndall	57066
Union Center	57787

University, Sta. Brookings	57006	Wanblee	57577
Utica	57067	Ward	57074
Vale	57788	Warner	57479
Valley Springs	57068	Wasta	57791
Vayland	57377	Watauga	57660
Veblen	57270	Watertown (1st)	57201
Verdon	57478	Waverly, R. Br.	57202
Vermillion (1st)	57069	Waubay	57273
Vetal, R. Br. Martin	57575	Waverly, R. Br. Watertown	57202
Viborg	57070	Webster	57274
Vienna	57271	Wecota	57480
Virgil	57379	Wentworth	57075
Vivian	57576	Wessington	57381
Volga	57071	Wessington Springs	57382
Volin	57072	Westport	57481
Wagner	57380	Wetonka	57482
Wakonda	57073	Wewela	57578
Wakpala	57658	White	57276
Walker	57659	White Lake	57383
Wall	57790	White Owl	57792
Wallace	57272	White River	57579

White Rock, R. Br. Rosholt	57277
Whitehorse	57661
Whitewood	57793
Willow Lake	57278
Wilmot	57279
Winfred	57076
Winner (1st)	57580
Cleafield, R. Br.	57581
Witten	57584
Wolsey	57384
Wood	57585
Woonsocket	57385
Worthing	57077
Wounded Knee	57794
Yale	57386
Yankton (1st)	57078
Zell	57483
Zeona	57795

SIOUX FALLS 571

POST OFFICE BOXES

Box Nos.		
	Main Office	01
A-Y	Main Office	01
1-1532	Main Office	01

RURAL ROUTES

1,2,3,4,5		01

STATIONS, BRANCHES AND UNITS

Commerce Sta.		02
Rowena Rural Br.	57056	
General Delivery		01
Postmaster		01

APARTMENTS, MOTELS, MOTELS

Ace Motel, 1903 E 10th St	03
Albert, 333 N Phillips Ave	02
Blackstone, 303 W 12th	02
Brown, 401 S Phillips Ave	02
Cambridge, 100 W 17th	04
Carriage Hill Garden, 205 W 18th	05
Colonial, 301 W 21st	05
Costello, 217 S Spring Ave	04
Country Club Estates, 2501 S Kiwanis Ave	05
Delux Motel, 1712 W 12th	04
Edgewood Motel, 4730 N Cliff Ave	04
Edwards, 430 W 10th	04
Harvey Motel, 2400 E 10th	03
Henderson, 115 W 12th	02
Holiday Inn Motel, 1301 W Russell	04
Holiday Inn, Downtown, 100 W 8th	02
Howard Johnson, 3308 W Russell	07

Kenwen, E25 S Phillips Ave	04
Kenwood Manor, 2420 W 18th	04
La Salle, 703 S Summit Ave	04
Laird Hall, 1001 S Phillips Ave	05
Lincoln, 104 N Main Ave	02
Lindendale Motel, 4201 S Minnesota Ave	05
Parkview, 500-600 S Kiwanis Ave	04
Pine Crest Motel, 3601 W 12th	06
Plaza Inn Motel, 2620 E 10th	03
Ramanda Inn Motel, 2400 N Louise Ave	07
Rushmore Motel, 2500 E 10th	03
Rushs Motel, 2401 W Russell	04
Sheraton-Cataract Motor Inn, 106 W 9th	02
Sioux Chief Train Motel, 3627 W 12th	06
Smiths Motel, 1223 W 12th	04
Suburban Motel, 3010 E 10th	03
Sunset Motel, 3921 W 12th	06
Tally Ho, 309 S Conklin Ave	03
Tartan Arms, 620 S 3rd	04
Town House Motel, 415 S Phillips	02
Travelodge Motel, 809 N West Ave	04
Westwick Motel, 5801 W 12th	06
Ymca, 236 S Minnesota Ave	02
Ywca, 300 W 11th	02

BUILDINGS

Boyce Greeley, 231 S Phillips.	02
First National Bank, 112 S Phillips.	02

Gas Company, 114 S Main	02
Home Federal Savings & Loan, 225 S. Main	02
K Mart, 3000 S Minnesota.	05
Kresge, 206 S Phillips	02
National Bank Of South Dakota, 141 N Main	02
National Reserve Bldg, 513 S Main Ave	02
Northwest Bank Bldg, 101 S Main Ave	02
Paulton, 304 S Phillips	02
Sioux Falls Stockyards	02
Western Mall, 2101 W 41st	05

GOVERNMENT OFFICES

City Hall, 230 W 9th	02
Costello Terminal	04
Federal Bldg, 400 S Phillips Ave	02
Joe Foss Field	04
Minnehaha County Courthouse, 415 N Dakota	02

HOSPITALS

Crippled Children, 2501 W 26th	05
Mc Kennan, 800 E 21st	01
Sioux Valley, 1123 S Euclid Ave	05
Veterans, 2501 W 22nd	01

UNIVERSITIES AND COLLEGES

Augustana, 29th & S Summit	02
Nettletons, 100 S. Spring Ave	01
North American Baptist Seminary, 1605 S. Euclid.	05
Sioux Falls, 1501 S Prairie Ave	01

TENNESSEE
(Abbreviation: TN)

Acklen, Sta. Nashville..........37212
Adams..................................37010
  Sadlersville, R. Br............37154
Adamsville (1st)...................38310
Afton..................................37616
Airport, Sta. Nashville..........37217
Airport Mail Facility, Sta.
  Memphis............................38130
Airport Road, Sta.
  Chattanooga.......................37421
Alamo.................................38001
Alcoa (1st)..........................37701
  Mentor, R. Br.....................37808
Alexandria...........................37012
Algood, Br. Cookeville...........38501
Allardt................................38504
Allons.................................38541
Allred.................................38542
Alpine................................38543
Altamont.............................37301
Alton Park, Sta.
  Chattanooga.......................37410
Andersonville.......................37705
Antioch...............................37013
Apison................................37302
Ardmore..............................38449
Arlington.............................38002
Armathwaite........................38506
Arnold A F B, Br. Tullahoma...37389
Arrington.............................37014
Arthur.................................37707
Ashland City (1st).................37015
Ashport..............................38003
Athens (1st).........................37303
Atoka..................................38004
Atwood...............................38220
Auburntown.........................37016
Baileyton, R. Br. Greeneville...37743
Bakewell, R. Br. Sale Creek...37304
Banner Springs, R. Br.
  Jamestown.........................38557
Baptist, Sta. Nashville..........37203
Bartlett...............................38005
Bath Springs........................38311
Baxter.................................38544
Bean Station........................37708
Beech Bluff..........................38313
Beechgrove..........................37018
Beersheba Springs................37305
Belfast................................37019
Bell Buckle..........................37020
Belle Meade, Br. Nashville
  (see appendix)
Bellevue..............................37021
Bells...................................38006
Belvidere.............................37306
Bemis..................................38314
Benton................................37307
Berclair, Sta. Memphis...........38117
Bethel Springs......................38315
Bethpage.............................37022
Big Rock..............................37023
Big Sandy............................38221
Big Spring, R. Br. Decatur......37323
Binghamton, Sta. Memphis....38112
Birchwood............................37308
Blaine.................................37709
Bloomingdale, Br. Kingsport...37660
Bloomington Springs..............38545
Blountville (1st)....................37617

Bluff City............................37618
Bogota................................38007
Bold Spring.........................37024
Bolivar (1st).........................38008
Bon Aqua............................37025
Bone Cave...........................38546
Bordeaux, Br. Nashville.........37218
Braden...............................38010
Bradford.............................38316
Bradyville............................37026
Brainerd, Sta. Chattanooga
  (see appendix)
Brentwood...........................37027
Briceville.............................37710
Brighton..............................38011
Bristol (1st)..........................37620
Brownsville (1st)...................38012
Bruceton (1st)......................38317
Brunswick...........................38014
Brush Creek.........................38547
Buchanan............................38222
Buena Vista.........................38318
Buffalo Valley.......................38548
Bulls Gap............................37711
Bumpus Mills.......................37028
Buntyn, Sta. Memphis...........38111
Burlington, Sta. Knoxville.......37914
Burlison..............................38015
Burns.................................37029
Burrville..............................37712
Butler.................................37640
Bybee.................................37713
Byrdstown...........................38549
Cades.................................38319
Calhoun..............................37309
Camden (1st).......................38320
Campaign............................38550
Capleville, R. Br. Memphis....38129
Carroll Reece, Sta. Johnson
  City..................................37601
Carthage (1st)......................37030
Caryville..............................37714
Castalian Springs..................37031
Cedar Grove........................38321
Cedar Hill............................37032
Celina.................................38551
Centerville...........................37033
Cerro Gordo.........................38322
Chapel Hill...........................37034
Chapmansboro......................37035
Charleston...........................37310
Charlotte.............................37036
CHATTANOOGA (1st) (see
  appendix)
Chesterfield..........................38823
Chestnut Mound....................38552
Chewalla.............................38393
Chickamauga, Sta.
  Chattanooga.......................37421
Christiana............................37037
Chuckey..............................37641
Church Hill...........................37642
Clairfield.............................37715
Clarkrange...........................38553
Clarksburg...........................38324
Clarksville (1st).....................37040
Cleveland (1st).....................37311
Clifton................................38425
Clinton (1st).........................37716
Coalfield..............................37719
Coalmont.............................37315
Cokercreek...........................37314
College, Sta. Maryville...........37801

College Grove.......................37046
Collegedale (1st)...................37315
Collierville (1st)....................38017
Collinwood...........................38450
Colonial Heights, Br.
  Kingsport...........................37663
Columbia (1st)......................38401
Como..................................38223
Conasauga...........................37316
Concord..............................37729
Cookeville (1st).....................38501
Copperhill............................37317
Cordova...............................38018
Cornersville..........................37047
Corryton..............................37721
Cosby.................................37722
Cottage Grove......................38224
Cottontown..........................37048
Counce...............................38326
Covington (1st).....................38019
Cowan.................................37318
Crab Orchard........................37723
Crawford.............................38554
Crockett Mills.......................38021
Cross Plains.........................37049
Crosstown, Sta. Memphis......38104
Crossville (1st).....................38555
Crump.................................38327
Culleoka..............................38451
Cumberland City...................37050
Cumberland Furnace..............37051
Cumberland Gap...................37724
Cunningham.........................37052
Cypress Inn..........................38452
Daisy..................................37319
Dandridge...........................37725
Darden................................38328
Daus...................................37320
Davis, Sta. Memphis.............38102
Davy Crockett, Sta.
  Greeneville........................37743
Dayton (1st).........................37321
De Soto, Sta. Memphis.........38102
Decatur...............................37322
  Big Spring, R. Br...............37323
Decaturville..........................38329
Decherd...............................37324
Deer Lodge..........................37726
Del Rio...............................37727
Delano................................37325
Dellrose...............................38453
Denmark..............................38391
Denver................................37054
Devonia...............................37728
Dickel, R. Br. Tullahoma.......37388
Dickson (1st)........................37055
Dixon Springs.......................37057
Donelson, Br. Nashville..........37214
Dover..................................37058
Dowelltown..........................37059
Downtown, Sta. Maryville......37801
Doyle..................................38559
Dresden...............................38225
Drummonds..........................38023
Duck River...........................38454
Ducktown............................37326
Duff....................................37729
Dukedom.............................38226
Dunlap................................37327
Dyer...................................38330
Dyersburg (1st).....................38024
Eads...................................38028
Eagan.................................37730

Eagleville.................................37060
East, Sta. Nashville (see
   appendix)
East Chattanooga, Sta.
   Chattanooga (see
   appendix)
East Lake, Sta.
   Chattanooga.................37407
East Memphis, Sta.
   Memphis.......................38111
East Ridge, Br.
   Chattanooga.................37412
Eastdale, Sta. Chattanooga..37411
Eastside, Sta. Kingsport......37664
Eaton.....................................38331
Eidson....................................37731
Elbridge.................................38227
Elgin......................................37732
   Rugby, R. Br................37733
Elizabethton (1st).................37643
Elk Valley..............................37734
Elkton...................................38455
Ellendale...............................38029
Elmwood................................38560
Elora.....................................37328
Emory Gap.............................37735
Englewood.............................37329
English Mountain, R. Br.
   Sevierville....................37862
Enville..................................38332
Erie......................................37736
Erin (1st)..............................37061
Erwin (1st)...........................37650
Estes Kefauver, Sta. Johnson
   City.............................37601
Estill Springs........................37330
Ethridge................................38456
Etowah..................................37331
Eva.......................................38333
Evensville.............................37332
Fairfield Glade, Br.
   Crossville....................38555
Fairview................................37062
Fall Branch............................37656
Farner...................................37333
Farragut, R. Br. Concord.....37720
Fayetteville (1st)...................37334
Federal Reserve, Sta.
   Nashville......................37203
Finger...................................38334
Finley....................................38030
Fisk University, Sta.
   Nashville......................37203
Five Points............................38457
Flag Pond..............................37657
Flat Woods.............................38458
Flintville................................37335
Forbus..................................38561
Forest Hill, R. Br.
   Germantown.................38031
Fort Pillow.............................38032
Fosterville..............................37063
Fountain City, Sta. Knoxville..37918
Fowlkes..................................38033
Frankewing.............................38459
Franklin (1st).........................37064
Frayser, Sta. Memphis...........38127
Friendship..............................38034
Friendsville............................37737
Fruitland................................38335
Fruitvale................................38336
Fulton, R. Br. Henning...........38035

Gadsden................................38337
Gainesboro............................38562
Gallatin (1st).........................37066
Gallaway................................38036
Gassaway..............................37070
Gates....................................38037
Gatlinburg (1st).....................37738
George W Lee, Sta.
   Memphis.......................38126
Georgetown...........................37336
Germantown...........................38038
   Forest Hill, R. Br.........38031
Gibson..................................38338
Gladeville..............................37071
Gleason.................................38229
Glenmary...............................37740
Goodlettsville (1st)................37072
Goodspring............................38460
Gordonsville...........................38563
Grand Junction.......................38039
Grandview..............................37337
Granville................................38564
Graysville...............................37338
Green Brier............................37073
Green Hills, Sta. Nashville.....37215
Greenback..............................37742
Greeneville (1st).....................37743
Greenfield..............................38230
Grimsley.................................38565
Gruetli...................................37339
Guild.....................................37340
Guys......................................38339
Halls......................................38040
Halls Crossroads, R. Br.
   Knoxville......................37918
Hampshire..............................38461
Hampton.................................37658
Harriman (1st)........................37748
Harrison.................................37341
Harrogate...............................37752
Hartford.................................37753
Hartsville...............................37074
Heiskell.................................37754
Helenwood.............................37755
Henderson (1st)......................38340
Hendersonville (1st)...............37075
Henning.................................38041
   Fulton, R. Br...............38035
Henry....................................38231
Henry Street, Sta.
   Morristown..................37814
Hermitage..............................37076
Hickman.................................38567
Hickory Valley.........................38042
Hickory Withe.........................38043
Highland Heights, Sta.
   Memphis.......................38122
Highland Park, Sta.
   Chattanooga.................37404
Highland Plaza, Br.
   Chattanooga.................37415
Highway One Hundred, Br.
   Nashville......................37205
Hilham..................................38568
Hilldale, Sta. Clarksville.......37040
Hillsboro................................37342
Hiwassee College, R. Br.
   Madisonville.................37354
Hixson (1st)...........................37343
Hohenwald.............................38462
Holiday City, Sta. Memphis...38118
Holladay.................................38341
Hollow Rock............................38342

Hollywood, Sta. Memphis......38108
Holtland.................................37077
Hornbeak................................38232
Hornsby.................................38044
Howell....................................37344
Humboldt (1st).......................38343
Huntingdon (1st).....................38344
Huntland................................37345
Huntsville...............................37756
   Norma, R. Br..............37827
Huron....................................38345
Hurricane Mills........................37078
Idlewild..................................38346
Indian Mound..........................37079
Iron City................................38463
Isabella..................................37346
Jacks Creek...........................38347
Jacksboro..............................37757
Jackson (1st).........................38301
Jackson Square, Sta. Oak
   Ridge.........................37830
Jamestown.............................38556
   Banner Springs, R. Br...38557
Jasper...................................37347
Jefferson City (1st)................37760
Jellico...................................37762
Jere Baxter, Br. Nashville.....37216
Joelton...................................37080
Johnson City (1st)..................37601
Jonesboro (1st)......................37659
Karns, R. Br. Knoxville..........37921
Kelso.....................................37348
Kenton...................................38233
Kepler, R. Br. Rogersville......37857
Kimberlin Heights, R. Br.
   Knoxville......................37920
Kimmins.................................37081
KINGSPORT (1st) (see
   appendix)
Kingston (1st)........................37763
Kingston Springs.....................37082
KNOXVILLE (1st) (see
   appendix)
Kodak....................................37764
Kyles Ford.............................37765
La Follette (1st)......................37766
La Grange..............................38046
La Vergne (1st).......................37086
Laager...................................37349
Laconia..................................38045
Lafayette................................37083
Lake City...............................37769
Lamar, Sta. Memphis.............38114
Lancaster...............................38569
Lancing..................................37770
Lane......................................38234
Lascassas..............................37085
Laurel Bloomery.....................37680
Lavinia...................................38348
Lawrenceburg (1st)................38464
Leach....................................38349
Lebanon (1st).........................37087
Lenoir City (1st).....................37771
Lenox....................................38047
Leoma...................................38468
Lewisburg (1st).......................37091
Lexington (1st).......................38351
Liberty...................................37095
Limestone..............................37681
Linden...................................37096
Livingston (1st)......................38570
Lobelville................................37097
Lone Mountain.......................37773

Lonsdale, Sta. Knoxville 37921
Lookout Mountain (1st) 37350
Lookout Valley, Br.
　Chattanooga 37419
Loretto 38469
Loudon (1st) 37774
Louisville 37777
Lowland 37778
Lupton City 37351
Luray 38352
Luttrell 37779
Lutts 38471
Lyles 37098
Lynchburg 37352
Lynn Garden, Br. Kingsport 37665
Lynnville 38472
Macon 38048
Madison (1st) 37115
Madison College, Br.
　Madison 37115
Madison Square, Br.
　Madison 37115
Madisonville 37354
Malesus 38354
Mallory, Sta. Memphis 38109
Manchester (1st) 37355
Mansfield 38236
Martin (1st) 38237
Maryville (1st) 37801
Mascot 37806
Mason 38049
Maury City 38050
Mayland 38572
Maynardville 37807
Mc Donald 37353
Mc Ewen 37101
Mc Kellar, Sta. Memphis 38106
Mc Kenzie (1st) 38201
Mc Lemoresville 38235
Mc Minnville (1st) 37110
Mc Nairy 38353
Medina 38355
Medon 38356
Melrose, Br. Nashville (see
　appendix)
MEMPHIS (1st) (see
　appendix)
Memphis State University,
　Sta. Memphis 38111
Mentor, R. Br. Alcoa 37808
Mercer 38392
Michie 38357
Middleton 38052
Midtown, R. Br. Harriman 37748
Midway 37809
Milan (1st) 38358
Milledgeville 38359
Milligan College 37682
Millington (1st) 38053
　Naval Air Station
　Memphis, Sta. 38054
　Naval Hospital, Sta. 38054
　Rosemark, R. Br. 38053
Milton 37118
Minor Hill 38473
Miston 38056
Mitchellville 37119
Mohawk 37810
Monoville 37121
Monroe 38573
Monteagle 37356
Monterey 38574
Montezuma 38360

Mooresburg 37811
Morley 37812
Morris Chapel 38361
Morrison 37357
Morristown (1st) 37814
Moscow 38057
Mosheim 37818
Moss 38575
Mount Carmel, Br. Church
　Hill 37642
Mount Juliet 37122
Mount Pleasant 38474
Mount Vernon 37358
Mountain City 37683
Mountain Home 37684
Mulberry 37359
Munford 38058
Murfreesboro (1st) 37130
Murray Lake Hills, Br.
　Chattanooga 37416
NASHVILLE (1st) (see
　appendix)
Naval Air Station Memphis,
　Sta. Millington 38054
Naval Hospital, Sta.
　Millington 38054
New Johnsonville 37134
New Market 37820
New Middleton, R. Br.
　Gordonsville 38563
New Providence, Sta.
　Clarksville 37040
New River 37824
New Tazewell 37825
Newbern 38059
Newcomb 37819
Newport (1st) 37821
Niota 37826
Nolensville 37135
Norene 37136
Norma, R. Br. Huntsville 37827
Normandy 37360
Norris 37828
North, Sta. Nashville (see
　appendix)
North, Sta Memphis 38107
North Chattanooga, Sta.
　Chattanooga 37405
North Knoxville, Sta.
　Knoxville 37917
Northeast, Sta. Nashville 37207
Norwood, Sta. Knoxville 37912
Nunnelly 37137
Oak Ridge (1st) 37830
Oakdale 37829
Oakfield 38362
Oakland 38060
Obion 38240
Ocoee 37361
Old Hickory (1st) 37138
Old Hometown, R. Br.
　Memphis 38116
Oldfort 37362
Olivehill 38475
Oliver Springs 37840
Oneida (1st) 37841
Only 37140
Ooltewah 37363
Orlinda 37141
Ozone 37842
Pall Mall 38577
Palmer 37365
Palmersville 38241

Palmyra 37142
Paris (1st) 38242
Parkway Village, Br.
　Memphis 38118
Parrotsville 37843
Parsons 38363
Pegram 37143
Pelham 37366
Persia, R. Br. Rogersville 37844
Petersburg 37144
Petros 37845
Philadelphia 37846
Pickwick Dam 38365
Pigeon Forge, Br. Sevierville 37863
Pikeville 37367
Piney Flats 37686
Pinson 38366
Pioneer 37847
Pleasant Hill 38578
Pleasant Shade 37145
Pleasant View 37146
Pleasantville 37147
Pocahontas 38061
Portland (1st) 37148
Postelle 37368
Powder Springs 37848
Powell 37849
Primm Springs 38476
Prospect 38477
Pruden 37851
Pulaski (1st) 38478
Puryear 38251
Quebeck 38579
Raleigh, Br. Memphis 38128
Ramer 38367
Readyville 37149
Reagan 38368
Red Bank, Br. Chattanooga 37415
Red Boiling Springs 37150
Reliance 37369
Reverie 38062
Riceville 37370
Richard City 37371
Rickman 38580
Riddleton 37151
Ridgely 38080
Ridgetop 37152
Ripley (1st) 38063
Riverside, Sta. Memphis 38113
Rives 38253
Roan Mountain 37687
Robbins 37852
Rock Island 38581
Rockford 37853
Rockvale 37153
Rockwood (1st) 37854
Rogersville (1st) 37857
　Kepler, R. Br. 37857
　Persia, R. Br. 37844
Rosemark, R. Br. Millington 38053
Rossville 38066
Royal, R. Br. Shelbyville 37160
Rugby, R. Br. Elgin 37733
Russellville 37860
Rutherford 38369
Rutledge 37861
Sadlersville, R. Br. Adams 37154
Saint Andrews 37372
Saint Bethlehem 37155
Saint Elmo, Sta.
　Chattanooga (see
　appendix)

576

Saint Joseph............................38481
Sale Creek..............................37373
   Bakewell, R. Br..............37304
Saltillo..................................38370
Samburg...............................38254
Santa Fe...............................38482
Sardis...................................38371
Saulsbury.............................38067
Savannah (1st)......................38372
Scotts Hill.............................38374
Selmer (1st)..........................38375
Sequatchie............................37374
Sevierville (1st).....................37862
Sewanee (1st).......................37375
Seymour...............................37865
Shady Valley.........................37688
Sharon..................................38255
Sharps Chapel.......................37866
Shawanee..............................37867
Shelby Center, R. Br.
   Memphis.........................38128
Shelbyville (1st)....................37160
Sherwood..............................37376
Shiloh....................................38376
Shop Spring...........................37164
Shouns..................................37689
Signal Mountain (1st)............37377
Silerton.................................38377
Silver Point...........................38582
Slayden.................................37165
Smartt...................................37378
Smithville..............................37166
Smoky Junction.....................37868
Smyrna (1st)..........................37167
Sneedville.............................37869
Soddy...................................37379
Somerville (1st).....................38068
South, Sta. Nashville.............37210
South Fulton, Br. Fulton, K
   Y...................................42041
South Harriman, R. Sta.
   Harriman........................37748
South Knoxville, Sta.
   Knoxville........................37920
South Pittsburg (1st)............37380
Southside..............................37171
Sparta (1st)..........................38583
Speedwell.............................37870
Spencer................................38585
Spring City............................37381
Spring Creek.........................38378
Spring Hill.............................37174
Springfield (1st)....................37172
Springville............................38256
Stahlman, Sta. Nashville......37201
Stanton.................................38069
Stantonville...........................38379
State University, Sta.
   Johnson City...................37601
Stephen Holston, Sta.
   Bristol............................37620
Stewart.................................37175
Strawberry Plains.................37871
Sugar Tree............................38380
Summertown.........................38483
Summitville...........................37382
Sunbright..............................37872
Surgoinsville.........................37873
Sweetwater (1st)..................37874
Taft......................................38488
Talbott..................................37877
Tallassee...............................37878
Tate Springs, R. Br. Bean

Station..................................37708
Tazewell...............................37879
Teachers College, Sta.
   Nashville.........................37203
Telford..................................37690
Tellico Plains.........................37385
Ten Mile...............................37880
Tennessee Ridge...................37178
Tennessee Tech, Sta.
   Cookeville.......................38501
Thompsons Station................37179
Thorn Hill.............................37881
Tigrett.................................38070
Tipton..................................38071
Tiptonville............................38079
Tom Murray, Sta. Jackson....38301
Toone...................................38381
Townsend..............................37882
Tracy City.............................37387
Trade...................................37691
Treadway..............................37883
Trenton (1st).........................38382
Trevecca College, Sta.
   Nashville.........................37210
Trezevant.............................38258
Trimble.................................38259
Troy.....................................38260
Tuckahoe, R. Br. Strawberry
   Plains..............................37871
Tullahoma (1st).....................37388
   Arnold A F B. Br.............37389
   Dickel, R. Br...................37388
Turtletown............................37391
Tusculum College, R. Br.
   Greeneville......................37743
Tyner...................................37392
Unicoi...................................37692
Union City (1st).....................38261
Unionville..............................37180
University, Sta. Knoxville......37916
University Of Tennessee,
   Sta. Martin......................38237
University Of The South, Br.
   Sewanee.........................37375
Uptown, Sta. Knoxville.........37901
Uptown Nashville, Sta.
   Nashville (see appendix)
Vale......................................38386
Vanleer.................................37181
Veterans Administration, Br.
   Murfreesboro...................37130
Victoria.................................37393
Viola.....................................37394
Vonore..................................37885
Wales....................................38484
Walker, Br. Memphis.............38109
Walland.................................37886
Walling..................................38587
Wartburg...............................37887
Wartrace...............................37183
Washburn...............................37888
Washington College, R. Br.
   Limestone.......................37681
Watauga...............................37694
Watertown.............................37184
Watts Bar Dam......................37395
Waverly.................................37185
Waynesboro..........................38485
West, Sta. Nashville..............37209
West Greene, Sta.
   Greeneville......................37743

West Knoxville, Sta.

Knoxville...............................37919
Westel...................................37889
Western State Hospital..........38074
Westmoreland........................37186
Westpoint..............................38486
Westport................................38387
Westwood, Br. Memphis.........38109
White, Sta. Memphis..............38117
White Bluff............................37187
White House..........................37188
White Pine.............................37890
Whitehaven, Sta. Memphis.....38116
Whites Creek.........................37189
Whitesburg............................37891
Whiteside...............................37396
Whiteville..............................38075
Whitleyville............................38588
Whitwell................................37397
Wilder...................................38589
Wildersville............................38388
Williamsport...........................38487
Williston................................38076
Winchester (1st)....................37398
Winfield.................................37892
Winona..................................37893
Woodbine, Sta. Nashville.......37211
Woodbury (1st).....................37190
Woodland Mills.......................38271
Woodlawn..............................37191
Wrigley, R. Br. Lyles.............37098
Wynnburg..............................38077
Yorkville................................38389
Yuma...................................38390

CHATTANOOGA 374

POST OFFICE BOXES

Box Nos.
1-1749	Main Office	01
1801-1999	East Lake Sta	07
2001-2294	St Elmo Sta	09
2501-2799	East Lake Sta	07
3001-3308	Highland Park Sta	64
4001-4299	North Chattanooga Sta	05
4300-4537	Red Bank Br	15
4801-4915	North Chattanooga Sta	05
5001-5395	East Chatt Sta	06
6001-6339	Main Office	01
6501-6598	B Sta	08
7001-7086	Alton Park Sta	10
8001-8568	Brainerd Sta	11
9001-9402	East Ridge Br	12
11001-11273	Main Office	01
15000-15700	Red Bank Br	15
21001-21300	Chickamauga Sta	21

RURAL ROUTES

2	16
3,4	09
5	05
6	21
8	11

STATIONS, BRANCHES AND UNITS

Airport Road Sta	21
Alton Park Sta	10
Brainerd Sta	11
Chickamauga Sta	21
East Chattanooga Sta	06
East Lake Sta	07
East Ridge Br	12
Eastdale Sta	11
Highland Park Sta	04
Highland Plaza Br	15
Lookout Valley Br	19
Murray Lake Hills Br	16
North Chattanooga Sta	05
Red Bank Br	15
Saint Elmo Sta	09
General Delivery	01
Postmaster	01

APARTMENTS, HOTELS, MOTELS

Alamo Plaza, 3000 Broad St S	08
Albemarle, 324 Mc Callie Ave	02
Albert Pick Motel, 3210 Broad S	09
Ayrshire, 418 Mc Callie Ave	02
Aztec, 2833 Dayton Blvd	15
Barbizon Terrace, 3945 Manor Dr	11
Battery Heights, 3401 Campbell St	06
Belmeade, 3725 Fountain Ave	12
Belvoir Hills, Bacon Tr	12

Bimini,	12
Bimini, 400 S Seminole	11
Boynton Ter, 953 Boynton Dr	03
Brainerd 3201 Brainerd Rd	11
Brainerd, 30 S Germantown	11
Brookwood, 621 Memorial Dr	15
Cardo, 1001 N Natchez Rd	05
Chateau Royale, 25 Germantown Rd., S	11
Colonial, 100 Joyce Ave	15
Continental, 1414 Continental Dr	05
Dallas Manor, 1103 E Dallas Rd	05
Dayton Manor, 101 Joyce Ave.	15
Dellwood 3205 Dellwood Pl	11
Downtowner, 901 Carter	02
El Cortijo, Pine St	16
El Matador, 3204 Redding Rd	15
Elks Golden Gateway, 1221 Grove St	03
Fort Wood, 870 Vine	03
Fountainbleau, 950 Spring Creek Rd	12
Glenwood Gardens, 2612 Gelnwood Pkwy	04
Grey Fox, 4105 Dayton Blvd	15
Hill Crest, Trenton St	15
Hogshead, 600 Georgia Ave	03
Holiday Inn East, 5505 Brainerd Rd	11
Holiday Inn Se, 6700 Ringgold Rd	21
Holiday Inn South, 2100 Market S	08
Holiday Inn, 401 9th W	02
Key, 831 Georgia Ave	01
Knox Manor, 2717 Folts Dr	15
Lakeshore Country Club, Lake Resort Dr	15
Laurel, 824 Dayton Blvd	15
Lomenacque, Ringgold Rd	12
Mary Walker Towers	68
Meadowbrook Manor, Meadowbrook Dr	15
Montview, 30 Tunnel Blvd	11
Mountain Creek, Mountain Creek Rd	05
Normandy, 3501 Dayton Blvd.	15
North River, Lyndon Ave	15
Patten, 1 E 11th	01
Read House, 2 W 9th	01
Renner, 656 Houston	03
Ridgeway, 1200 Poplar St Cts	03
Riviera River St	05
Robinson, 622 Georgia Ave	03
Royal Arms, 314 Mcbrien Rd.	11
Shepherd Hills, 404 Tunnel Blvd	11
Snooty Fox, Bacon Trl	12
St Barnabas, 6th St W	02
Stuart Manor, 2914 Haywood Ave	15
The Towers, 501 W 9th	02
Three Kings, Peace St	15
Thrippence, 3620 Fountain Ave	12
Twinam, 528 E 4th	03
Versailles, 3001 Dayton Blvd.	15
Virginia, 409 E 4th	03
Williamsburg Daytona Blvd	15

BUILDINGS

American National Bank, 736 Market	02
Blue Cross, 801 Pine St	02
Brainerd Professional, 314 Mcbrien Rd	11
Chattanooga Bank, 11 W 8th	02
Chattanooga Federal, 817 Broad	02
Doctors, 744 Mc Callie Ave	02
Dome, 738 Georgia Ave	02
Edney, 1100 Market	02
Emerson, 100 E 10th	02
Gateway Professional, 1001 Carter St	02
Hamilton National Bank, 701 Market	02
Interstate, 540 Mc Callie Ave	02
Jackson, 103 E 7th	02
James, 735 Broad	02
Mac Lellan, 721 Broad	02
Medical Arts, 546 Mc Callie Ave	02
Pioneer, 801 Broad	02
Professional, 301 Mc Callie Ave	02
Provident, Fountain Sq	02
Sisken Trans, 1478 Market	08
United Bank Bldg, 701 Chestnut St	02
Volunteer, 9th & Georgia Ave.	02
Whitehall, 960 E 3rd St.	03
Zayre W 9th	02
5700-6200	11

GOVERNMENT OFFICES

City Hall, 100 E 11th	02
Federal Building, 900 Georgia Ave.	02
Hamilton County Court House, E 7th	02

HOSPITALS

Bork Memorial, 2626 Walker Rd	21
Campbell 525 Mccallie	02
Childrens, 1001 Glenwood Dr.	06
Erlanger Hospital, 241 Wiehl.	04
Memorial, 2300 Citico Ave.	04
Moccasin Bend Psychiatric, Moccasin Bend Rd.	05
Parkridge, 2333 Mccallie Ave.	04
Tennessee Chest Disease, 2501 Milne Ave.	06
Tepper Pediatrics, 511 Mccallie Ave	02
Womans 863 Mccallie	03

UNIVERSITIES AND COLLEGES

Chattanooga State Tech, Amnicola Hwy	06
Tenn Temple, 1815 Union Ave	04
Univ Of Tenn At Chattanooga, 615 Mccallie Ave	01

KINGSPORT   376

POST OFFICE BOXES

Box Nos.

A-Y	Kingsport	62
1-1492	Kingsport	62
3000-3999	Eastside Sta	64
4000-4999	Lynn Garden Br	65
5001-5999	Colonial Heights Br	63

RURAL ROUTES

1,2	60
3	64
4,5,6,7	60
8	64
9	63
10	64
11,12	63
13	64

STATIONS, BRANCHES AND UNITS

Bloomingdale Br	60
Colonial Heights Br	63
Eastside Sta	64
Lynn Garden Br	65
General Delivery	62
Postmaster	62

KNOXVILLE   379

POST OFFICE BOXES

Box Nos.

1-2612	Main Office	01
3001-3467	North Knoxville Sta	17
4001-4999	Lonsdale Sta	21
5001-5500	Fountain City Sta	18
6001-6237	Burlington Sta	14
8001-8999	University Of Tennessee Sta	16
9001-9999	South Knoxville Sta	20
10001-10999	West Knoxville Sta	19
12000-12999	Norwood Sta	12

RURAL ROUTES

1	12
2	18
3	20
4,5,6	14
7	21
8	14
9,10	20
11,12,13	18
14	19
15	21
16	21
17,18	21
19	20
20	21

21	19
22	21
23	20
24,25	19

STATIONS, BRANCHES AND UNITS

Burlington Sta	14
Fountain City Sta	18
Halls Crossroads Rural Br	18
Karns Rural Br	21
Kimberlin Heights Rural Br	20
Lonsdale Sta	21
North Knoxville Sta	17
Norwood Sta	12
South Knoxville Sta	20
University Sta	16
Uptown Sta	01
West Knoxville Sta	19
General Delivery	01
Postmaster	01

APARTMENTS, HOTELS, MOTELS

Andrew Johnson, 914 Gay SW	02
Carlton Towers, 414 Forest Park Blvd	19
Dunbar, 105 Gay SW	02
Empire, 319 Depot Ave NW	17
Farragut, 530 Gay SW	02
Fort Sanders Manor, 400 17th SW	16
Hamilton House Apartments, 1400 Kenesaw Ave SW	19
Jackson, 432 Walnut SW	02
Knoxville, 408 Main Ave SW	02
Norris, 309 Depot Ave NW	17
Park, 510 Walnut SW	02
Parkway, 3701 Chapman Highway SW	20
Saint James, 311 Wall Ave SW	02
Shelbourne Towers, 840 20th SW	16
Southland, 409 Wall Ave SW	02
Taliwa Court, 120 Taliwa Ct SE	20
Y M C A, 605 Clinch Ave SW	02
Y W C A, 420 Clinch Ave SW	02

BUILDINGS

Amstein, 501 Market	02
Bank Of Knoxville, 623 Market SW	02
Blount Professional, Blount Ave SE	20
Burwell, 602 Gay SW	02
Cherokee, 402 Church Ave SW	02
Daylight, 503 Union Ave SW	02
Daylight, 517 Union Ave SW	02
Empire, 624 Market SW	02
Fidelity-Bankers Trust, 502 Gay SW	02
Flat-Iron, 705 Broadway NE	17
Greater Tennessee, Market & Cumberland SW	02
Hamilton National Bank, 531 Gay SW	02

Journal, 618 Gay SW	02
Mercantile, 623 Gay SW	02
Park National Bank, 312 Union SW	02
Seven-O-Six Walnut, 706 Walnut SW	02

GOVERNMENT OFFICES

Knox County Court House, Main Ave & Gay SW	02
Knox County Criminal Court & Jail, 913 Gay SW	02
Knox County Jail, 913 Gay SW	02
Tennessee State Offices, Cumberland & Locust SW	02
Tennessee Supreme Court, Cumberland & Locust SW	02
United States Post Office, Main & Walnut SW	02

HOSPITALS

Beverly Hills Sanitarium, Tazewell Pike NE	18
East Tennessee Baptist, Blount Ave SE	20
East Tennessee Crippled Children, 1912 Laurel Ave SW	16
East Tennessee Tuberculosis, Tazewell Pike NE	18
Eastern State, 5908 Lyons View Park SW	19
Fort Sanders Presbyterian, 1901 Clinch SW	16
Saint Marys, Oak Hill Ave NE	17
University Of Tennessee Clinic Infirmary, 820 Temple SW	16
University Of Tennessee Hospital, Alcoa Highway SW	20

UNIVERSITIES AND COLLEGES

Cooper Institute Of Business, 720 5th NE	17
Draughons Business College, 325 Clinch SW	02
Knoxville Business College, 209 Church SW	02
Knoxville College, 901 College NW	21
National Business College, 302 Gay SW	02
University Of Tennessee W, Cumberland Ave SW	16

MEMPHIS   381

POST OFFICE BOXES

Box Nos.

1-1999	Main Office	01
3000-3999	Front Street Sta	03
4000-4999	Crosstown Sta	04

6000-6999	Mc Kellar Sta... 05
7000-7999	North Sta.... 07
8000-8999	Hollywood Sta... 08
9000-9999	Mallory Sta 09
11000-11999	East Memphis Sta.... 11
12000-12999	Binghamton Sta.... 12
13000-13999	Riverside Sta... 13
14000-14999	Lamar Sta.... 14
16000-16999	Whitehaven Sta.... 16
17000-17999	White Sta.... 17
18000-18999	Holiday City Sta.... 18
22000-22999	Highland Heights Sta.... 22
26000-26999	Lee Sta.... 26
27000-27999	Frayser Sta.... 27
28000-28999	Raleigh Br.... 28
29001-29146	Buntyn Sta... 11
29201-29348	Station 7 27
30000-30999	Air Mail Facility Sta.... 30
38000-38999	Germantown Br.... 38
80000-0099999	Memphis State Univ.... 52
161000-161228	Whitehaven Sta.... 16

RURAL ROUTES

1	28
2	27
3	28
4	09
5,6,7,8	28
9	09
10	28
11	11
12	09
14,15	38

STATIONS, BRANCHES AND UNITS

Airport Mail Facility Sta.	30
Berclair Sta.	17
Binghamton Sta.	12
Buntyn Sta.	11
Capleville Rural Br.	29
Crosstown Sta	04
Davis Sta.	02
De Soto Sta	02
East Memphis Sta.	11
Frayser Sta.	27
George W Lee Sta.	26
Highland Heights Sta.	22
Holiday City Sta	18
Hollywood Sta.	08
Lamar Sta.	14
Mallory Sta.	09
Mc Kellar Sta.	06
Memphis State University Sta.	11
North Sta.	07
Old Hometown Rural Br.	16
Parkway Village Br.	18

Raleigh Br	28
Riverside Sta.	13
Shelby Center Rural Br.	08
Walker Br.	09
Westwood Br.	09
White Sta.	17
Whitehaven Sta.	16
General Delivery	01
Postmaster	01

APARTMENTS, HOTELS, MOTELS

Albert Pick 300 N 2nd St	05
Ambassador, 347 S Main St...	02
Americana Apartments, 2950 Winchester Pd.	16
Belvedere Apartments, 1733 Union Ave.	04
Cherokee Cabana Apartments, 2856 Kimball Ave.	14
Chisca Plaza, 272 S Main St.	01
Continental Luxury Apartments, 1422 Lamar Ave.	04
Embassy Apartments, 475 S Perkins	17
Gilmore Apartments, 6 S Mckan Blvd.	04
Goodman House, 777 Court Ave.	01
Holiday Tower, 383 Madison Ave.	03
Kimbrough Towers, 172 Kimbrough Pl.	04
Mayfair Apartments, 2277 Union Ave.	04
Oak Acres Apartments, 1128 Craft Rd.	16
Park Terrace Apartments, 2195 Poplar Ave.	04
Park Towers, 57 N Somerville St	04
Parkview Manor, 1914 Poplar Ave.	04
Parkway House, 1960 N Parkway.	12
Rosecrest Apartments, 45 S Idlewild	04
Sheraton-Peabody, 149 Union Ave.	01
Tennessee, 80 S 3rd St	03
The Tower Apartments, 91 N Main St	03
Town House Apartments, 1437 Central Ave.	04
University Towers Incorporated, 1380 Lamar Ave.	04
Viking 110 Monroe Ave	01
Woodmont Towers, 1550 N Parkway.	12
Yorktown Apartments, 4010 Jackson Ave	28

BUILDINGS

Century, 3294 Poplar	11
Clark Tower 5100 Poplar Ave .	37
Commerce Title, 12 S Main St	03

Cotton Exchange, 65 Union Ave.	03
Court Square, 128 S Court Ave.	03
Deluxe Arcade, 12 N 2nd St.	03
German, 46 N 3rd St	03
Du Pont, 22 S 2nd.	03
Emmons, 4745 Poplar Ave.	17
Exchange Building, 130 Madison Ave.	03
Falls, 22 N Front St.	03
Federal Securities, 81 Monroe Ave.	03
First American Bank, 147 Jefferson Ave.	03
First National Bank, 165 Madison Ave.	03
Goodwyn Institute 127 Madison Ave.	03
Hickman, 248 Madison Ave.	03
Joyner Rambert, 3340 Poplar Ave.	11
Lee, 114 Madison Ave.	03
Lincoln American Tower, 60 N Main St.	03
Mc Call, 79 Mccall Pl.	03
Mid South, 3181 Poplar Ave.	11
Nonconnah Corp. Center-Executive Park Plaza, 3003 Airways.	31
P & S, 899 Madison Ave.	03
Shrine, 66 Monroe Ave.	03
Sterick, 8 N 3rd St.	03
Tanehe 161 Jefferson Ave.	03
Union Planters National Bank, 67 Madison Ave.	03
White Station Tower, 5050 Poplar Ave.	17
100 North Main, 100 North Main St.	03
2600 Poplar, 2600 Poplar Ave.	12
3355 Poplar, 3355 Poplar Ave.	11
3373 Poplar, 3373 Poplar Ave.	11
63 South Main, 63 S Main St	03
81 Madison, 81 Madison Ave.	03

GOVERNMENT OFFICES

Chief Inspector Southern Region U S Postal Service.	01
City Hall, 125 N Main.	03
Defense Supply Agency 2163-65 Airways Blvd.	14
Federal Office, 167 N Main.	03
Internal Revenue Service Center, 3131 Democrat Rd.	16
State Office, 170 N Main.	03

HOSPITALS

Baptist Memorial 899 Madison	46
Bowld William F, 951 Court...	03
Campbell Clinic, 869 Madison	04
Crippled Adults, 1248 La Paloma	14

E H Crump Memorial, 853
　Jefferson.................... 03
Gailor Psychiatric, 42 N
　Dunlap...................... 03
Gartly-Ramsey, 696 Jackson... 05
John Gaston, 860 Madison.... 03
Le Bonheur Childrens, 848
　Adams....................... 03
Methodist, 1265 Union........ 04
Oakville Memorial
　Senatorium, Oakville....... 18
Saint Joseph, 220 Overton
　Ave......................... 01
Saint Jude, 332 N
　Lauderdale.................. 01
Shelby County, Route 8 Box
　500......................... 28
Tennessee Psychiatric
　Institute, 865 Poplar...... 04
Terrell Memorial, 698
　Williams.................... 26
Veterans Administration,
　1030 Jefferson............. 04
West Tennessee Tuberculosis,
　842 Jefferson.............. 03

UNIVERSITIES AND COLLEGES

Christian Brothers, 650 E
　Parkway S................... 04
Draughon'S Business, 253
　Madison..................... 01
Lausanne School For Girls,
　1381 Massey Rd............. 17
Le Moyne Owen, 807 Walker
　Ave......................... 26
Memphis Academy Of Arts,
　Overton Park............... 12
Memphis College Of Music,
　1822 Overton Park.......... 12
Memphis Hebrew Academy,
　390 S White Station Rd..... 17
Memphis State University,
　Southern Ave............... 52
Owen S A Junior College, 370
　S Orleans.................. 26
Saint Agnes Academy, 4830
　Walnut Grove............... 17
Siena, 4405 Poplar Ave...... 17
Southern College Of
　Optometry 1246 Union
　Ave......................... 04
Southwestern, 2000 N
　Parkway.................... 12
University Of Tennessee, 847
　Union....................... 03

NASHVILLE　　372

POST OFFICE BOXES

Box Nos.
A-0　　　Uptown Sta........ 19
1-1999　　Main Office........ 02
2001-2499　Donelson Br....... 14
2501-3299　Uptown Sta........ 19
3500-3999　Airport Sta....... 17
4501-4999　Jere Baxter....... 16
5001-5499　East Sta.......... 06
5500-5999　North Sta......... 08
6001-6499　Acklen Sta........ 12

6501-6999　Green Hills
　　　　　Sta............... 15
7001-7499　South Sta........ 10
7501-7999　West Sta......... 09
8001-8499　Northeast Sta.... 07
8501-8999　Woodbine Sta..... 11
9001-9699　Melrose Br....... 04
11000-11999 Woodbine Sta.... 11
12000-12600 Acklen Sta...... 12
15000-15999 Green Hills
　　　　　Sta............... 15
40000-40999 Melrose Sta..... 04
50001-50478 Belle Meade
　　　　　Sta............... 05
60000-60999 East Sta....... 06

RURAL ROUTES

1............................ 14
2............................ 09
3............................ 18
4............................ 11
5............................ 21

STATIONS, BRANCHES AND UNITS

Acklen Sta.................. 12
Airport Sta................. 17
Baptist Sta................. 03
Belle Meade Br............. 05
Bordeaux Br................ 18
Donelson Br................ 14
East Sta................... 06
Federal Reserve Sta........ 03
Fisk University Sta........ 03
Green Hills Sta............ 15
Highway One Hundred Br..... 05
Jere Baxter Br............. 16
Melrose Br................. 04
North Sta.................. 08
Northeast Sta.............. 07
South Sta.................. 10
Stahlman Sta............... 01
Teachers College Sta....... 03
Trevecca College Sta....... 10
Uptown Nashville Sta....... 19
West Sta................... 09
Woodbine Sta............... 11
General Delivery........... 02
Postmaster................. 02

APARTMENTS, HOTELS, MOTELS

Academy, Masonwood Dr...... 07
Alexandria, 3901 West End.. 05
Ambassador, 2418 Kirkland
　Ave......................... 12
Arlington, 1711 18th Avenue
　S........................... 12
Barbizon, 2006 Broadway.... 03
Belle Meade Terrace, 118
　Harding Pl................. 05
Belle Meade Towers, 105
　Leake...................... 05
Bellwood Terrace, 500
　Bowling.................... 12
Belmont Court, 1915 Belmont
　Blvd....................... 12
Blackstone, 3300 West End
　Ave......................... 03
Bow-Mar Apartments, 276
　White Bridge Rd........... 09
Cabana, 2020 Beech Ave..... 04

Caldwell Court, 550 Harding
　Pl.......................... 11
Capri, 261 White Bridge Rd.. 09
Carmichael Towers, 2321
　West End Ave.............. 03
Catalina, 111 Acklen Park
　Dr.......................... 03
Clarendon, 130 7th Ave S... 03
Continental Apartments,
　3415 West End Ave......... 03
Corvair, 2611 Belmont Blvd.. 12
Courtland, 3401 West End
　Ave......................... 03
Dville, 246 White Bridge Rd. 09
Elysian Gardens, Harding Pl. 11
Executive House, 860
　Murfreesboro Rd........... 17
Fairfax, 107 Fairfax........ 03
Fairmounte 107 Acklen Park
　Dr.......................... 03
Forest Hill, 2600 Hillsboro
　Rd.......................... 12
Fountains,the, 97 White
　Bridge..................... 05
Glencourt, 615 Belle Meade
　Blvd....................... 05
Graylyn, 913 20th Ave S.... 12
Green Hills Terrace, 1900
　Richard Jones Rd.......... 15
Grenada, 200 25th Ave N.... 03
Harding Court, 3101 West
　End Ave.................... 03
Harding House, 4200 West
　End Ave.................... 05
Heatherwood, 709 N 12th St.. 06
Hermitage, 231 6th Ave N.... 19
Hickory Hill, Stewart Ferry
　Pike....................... 14
Hillcrest, 236 Stewart Ferry
　Pike....................... 14
Hillsboro Court, 1405 21st
　Ave S...................... 12
Hillsboro Gardens, 3206
　Hillsboro Rd.............. 15
Imperial House, Bosley
　Springs Rd................ 05
Iroquois, 3301 Long Blvd.... 03
Jacksonian, 3010 West End
　Ave......................... 03
James Robertson, 118 7th
　Ave N....................... 03
Jefferson 2115 Portland Av).. 12
Kirkland, 2415 Kirkland Pl... 12
Lindsley, 15 Lindsley Ave.... 10
Marlborough, 200 8th Ave S.. 03
Mayflower, 1925 21st Ave S.. 12
Metro Manor Apartments,
　500 5th Ave N............. 19
Mikado, 3815 West End Ave... 05
Noel, 200 4th Ave N......... 19
Oxford House, 1313 21st Ave
　S........................... 12
Park Lawn, 2016 Terrace Pl... 03
Park Manor, 115 Woodmont
　Blvd....................... 05
Park Road, 3416 West End
　Ave......................... 03
Peabody Courts, 1411 21st
　Ave S...................... 12
Raleigh, 200 7th Ave S...... 03
Robert E Lee, 2108 Hayes.... 03
Royal Arms East, 2011
　Richard Jones Rd.......... 15

Royal Oaks, 4505 Harding Rd 05
Statler Hilton Airport Inn, International Plaza 17
Sun Valley, 256 Stewart Ferry Pike 14
Versailles, 3000 Hillsboro Rd. 15
Washington, 2001 21st Ave S... 12
Wellington Arms, 4225 Harding Rd 05
Windsor Towers, 4215 Harding Rd... 05
Woodmont Terrace, 910 Woodmont Blvd. 04

BUILDINGS

Albert, 146 7th Ave N 03
American Trust, 305 Union..... 01
Andrew Jackson State Office, 500 Deaderick 19
Arcade, 225 4th Ave N 19
Baker 110 21st Ave S.......... 03
Bennie Dillon, 700 Church 01
Broadway National Bank, 300 Broad 01
Capitol Boulevard, 226 Capitol Blvd 19
Capitol Towers 510 Gay.......... 19
Central Services, 503 5th Ave N 19
Commerce Union Bank, 400 Union.......... 19
Cordell Hull, 436 6th Ave N... 19
Court Square, 3rd & Jas Robt Pkwy.......... 01
Doctors, 702 Church.......... 03
Exchange, 311 Church.......... 01
Federal Office, 701 Broadway 03
First American National Bank, 326 Union.......... 19
First Federal, 236 4th Ave N... 19
Green Hills Shopping Center... 15
Greyhound Terminal, 517 Commerce 03

Hayes, 1710 Hayes.......... 03
Highway, 6th & Deaderick..... 19
International Business Machines, 450 James Robertson Pky.......... 19
J C Bradford, 170 4th Ave N... 19
Life & Casualty Tower, 4th & Church 19
Live Stock Exchange, 901 2nd Ave N.......... 01
Medical Arts, 1211 21st Ave S... 12
Mid-State Medical Center 2000 Church.......... 03
Morris Memorial, 4th & Cedar 01
Municipal Safety, 110 Public Square.......... 01
Nashville Trust, 315 Union..... 01
Parkway Towers, 404 James Robertson Pky.......... 19
Saint Catherine Hall, 2001 Church 03
Stahlman, 3rd & Union.......... 01
State Capitol 15
State Library & Archives, 411 7th Ave N.......... 19
Sudekum, 6th & Church 19
Supreme Court, 401 7th Ave.. 19
Third National Bank, 201 4th Ave N 19
Tuck, 1123 Church.......... 03
War Memorial, 300 Capitol Blvd.......... 19
Westmont, 201 22nd Ave N... 03

GOVERNMENT OFFICES

City Office, 2nd Ave S & Lindsley.......... 18
County Court House, Public Square.......... 01
Federal Office Bldg, 701 Broadway.......... 03
National Guard Center.......... 04
United States Courthouse, 801 Broadway.......... 03

HOSPITALS

Baptist, 2000 Church 36
Bordeaux, County Hospital Rd 18
Central State, Murfreesboro Rd 17
City General, 72 Hermitage Ave 18
Donelson, 3055 Lebanon Rd... 14
Hubbard, 1005 18th Ave N..... 08
Middle Tennessee Tuberculosis, Ben Allen Rd 16
Park View, 230 25th Ave N ... 03
Riverside Sanitarium & Hospital, 800 Youngs Lane.......... 07
Saint Thomas, 2000 Hayes.... 03
Vanderbilt, 21st Ave S.......... 03
Veterans Administration, 1310 24th Ave S.......... 03

MILITARY INSTALLATIONS

National Guard Center.......... 04

UNIVERSITIES AND COLLEGES

Aquinas Junior 4210 Harding Rd 05
Belmont College, 16th Ave S & Belcourt 03
David Lipscomb, Granny White Pike.......... 03
Fisk University, 17th Ave N ... 03
Meharry Medical, 1005 18th Ave N 08
Peabody, 21st Ave S.......... 03
Scarritt, 1008 19th Ave S...... 03
Trevecca Nazarene, 333 Murfreesboro Rd 10
University Of Tennessee, 810 Broadway.......... 03
Vanderbilt University, 21st Ave S.......... 03

TEXAS
(Abbreviation: TX)

Abbott 76621
Abernathy 79311
ABILENE (1st) (see
   appendix)
Abilene Christian College,
   Sta. Abilene 79601
Ace 77326
Ackerly 79713
Adamsville, R. Br.
   Lampasas 76510
Addicks, R. Br. Houston 77079
Addison 75001
Adkins 78101
Adrian 79001
Afton 79220
Agua Dulce 78330
Aiken 79221
Air Terminal, Sta. Midland..79701
Airlawn, Sta. Dallas 75235
Airport Mail Facility, Sta.
   Houston 77060
Alamo (1st) 78516
Alamo Heights, Br. San-
   Antonio (see appendix)
Alanreed 79002
Alba 75410
Albany 76430
Albert 78601
Albert Thomas, Br. Houston..77058
Aledo 76008
Algerita, R. Br. San Saba ...76877
Alice (1st) 78332
Alief 77411
Allen 75002
Alleyton, R. Br. Columbus...78935
Allison 79003
Alma, R. Br. Ennis 75119
Almeda, Sta. Houston (see
   appendix)
Alpine (1st) 79830
Alta Loma 77510
Altair 77412
Alto 75925
Alvarado 76009
Alvin (1st) 77511
Alvord 76225
AMARILLO (1st) (see
   appendix)
Amherst 79312
Anahuac 77514
Anderson 77830
Andice, R. Br. Georgetown..78626
Andrews (1st) 79714
   Florey, R. Br. 79732
Angelo State University, Sta.
   San Angelo 76901
Angleton (1st) 77515
Anna 75003
Annona 75550
Anson 79501
Anson Jones, Sta. Houston..77009
Antelope 76350
Anthony 88021
Anton 79313
Apple Springs 75926
Appleby, R. Br.
   Nacogdoches 75961
Aquilla 76622
Aransas Pass (1st) 78336
Arapaho, Sta. Richardson ...75080

Arcadia 77517
Archer City 76351
Argyle 76226
ARLINGTON (1st) (see
   appendix)
Arlington Heights, Sta. Fort
   Worth 76107
Armstrong 78338
Arp 75750
Art 76820
Artesia Wells 78001
Arthur City 75411
Asherton 78827
Aspermont 79502
Astrodome, Sta. Houston
   (see appendix)
Astroworld, Sta. Houston....77025
Atascosa 78002
Athens (1st) 75751
Atlanta (1si) 75551
Aubrey 76227
AUSTIN (1st) (see appendix)
Austwell 77950
Avalon 76623
Avery 75554
Avinger 75630
Avoca 79503
Avonbell, Sta. Amarillo 79106
Axtell 76624
Azle (1st) 76020
B U, Sta. Waco 76706
Baclift 77518
Bagwell 75412
Bailey 75413
Baird 79504
Bakersfield, R. Br. Mc
   Camey 79717
Balch Springs, Br. Mesquite..75149
Ballinger (1st) 76821
Balmorhea 79718
Bandera 78003
Bangs 76823
Banquete 78339
Bardwell 75101
Barker 77413
Barksdale 78828
Barnhart 76930
Barnum 75927
Barrett, R. Br. Crosby 77532
Barry 75102
Barstow 79719
Bartlett 76511
Basin, R. Br. Big Bend
   National Park 79834
Bastrop 78602
Batesville 78829
Batson 77519
Bay City (1st) 77414
Bayside 78340
Baytown (1st) 77520
Beacon Hill, Sta. San
   Antonio (see appendix)
Beasley 77417
BEAUMONT (1st) (see
   appendix)
Bebe 78603
Beckville 75631
Bedford 76021
Bedias 77831
Bee House 76512
Beeville (1st) 78102
Bellaire (1st) 77401
Bellevue 76228

Bellmead, Br. Waco (see
   appendix)
Bells 75414
Bellville 77418
Belmont 78604
Belton (1st) 76513
Ben Arnold 76517
Ben Bolt 78342
Ben Franklin 75415
Ben Wheeler 75754
Benavides 78341
Benbrook, Br. Fort Worth....76126
Bend 76824
Benjamin 79505
Berclair 78107
Berea, R. Br. Jefferson 75657
Bergheim, R. Br. Boerne.....78004
Bergstrom A F B, MOU.
   Austin 78743
Berry Street, Sta. Fort Worth
   (see appendix)
Bertram 78605
Best 76931
Bettie 75632
Beverly, Br. Waco 76711
Beverly Hills, Sta. Dallas
   (see appendix)
Big Bend National Park.......79834
Big Lake 76932
Big Sandy (1st) 75755
Big Spring (1st) 79720
Big Town, Sta. Mesquite.....75149
Big Wells 78830
Bigfoot 78005
Biggs Afb, Br. El Paso.........79908
Birome 76625
Bishop 78343
Bivins 75555
Black 79004
Blackwell 79506
Blanco 78606
Blanket 76432
Bledsoe 79314
Bleiblerville 78931
Blessing 77419
Bloomburg 75556
Blooming Grove 76626
Bloomington 77951
Blossom 75416
Blue Mound, Br. Fort Worth..76131
Blue Ridge 75004
Bluegrove 76352
Bluff Dale 76433
Bluffton 78607
Blum 76627
Bob Harris, Sta. Pasadena ..77502
Bob Lyons, Sta. Galveston ..77550
Boca Chica, R. Br.
   Brownsville 78520
Boerne (1st) 78006
   Bergheim, R. Br. 78004
   Sisterdale, R. Br. 78006
   Welfare, R. Br. 78036
Bogata 75417
Boling 77420
Bomarton 76353
Bon Wier 75928
Bonham (1st) 75418
Booker 79005
Booth 77421
Borger (1st) 79007
   Phillips, Br. 79071
   Phllrich, Sta. 79007

Yows Street Annex, Sta. 79007
Boston 75557
Bovina 79009
Bowie (1st) 76230
Boyd 76023
Boys Ranch 79010
Brackettville 78832
Brady (1st) 76825
Brandon 76628
Brashear 75420
Brazoria 77422
Breckenridge (1st) 76024
Bremond 76629
Brenham (1st) 77833
Bridge City (1st) 77611
Bridgeport 76026
Briggs 78608
Briscoe 79011
Bristol, R. Br. Ennis 75119
Broaddus 75929
Broadway, Sta. Mesquite ...75149
Bronco, R. Br. Plains 79315
Bronson 75930
Bronte 76933
Brook Hollow, Sta. Dallas ...75247
Brookeland 75931
Brookesmith 76827
Brooks A F B, Br. San
    Antonio 78235
Brookshire 77423
Brookside Village, R. Br.
    Pearland 77581
Brookston 75421
Brownfield (1st) 79316
Brownsboro 75756
Brownsville (1st) 78520
Brownwood (1st) 76801
Bruceville 76630
Bruni 78344
Bryan (1st) 77801
Bryson 76027
Buchanan Dam 78609
Buckeye 77424
Buckholts 76518
Buda 78610
Buffalo 75831
Buffalo Gap 79508
Bula 79320
Bullard 75757
Bulverde, R. Br. Wetmore ...78163
Buna 77612
Burkburnett (1st) 76354
Burke, R. Br. Diboll 75941
Burkett 76828
Burkeville 75932
Burleson (1st) 76028
Burlington 76519
Burnet (1st) 78611
Burton 77835
Bushland 79012
Byers 76357
Bynum 76631
Cactus 79013
Caddo 76029
Caddo Mills 75005
Caldwell 77836
Call 75933
Calliham 78007
Calvert 77837
Camden 75934
Cameron (1st) 76520
Camp Dale Robertson, R. Br.
    Avinger 75630

Camp San Saba 76829
Camp Verde, R. Br. Center
    Point 78010
Camp Wood 78833
Campbell 75422
Campbellton 78008
Canadian 79014
Canton 75103
Canutillo 79835
Canyon (1st) 79015
Canyon City, R. Br. New
    Braunfels 78130
Capitol, Sta. Austin 78711
Caradan 76830
Carbon 76435
Cardinal, Sta. Athens 75751
Carey 79222
Carl Range, Sta. Irving 75060
Carlsbad 76934
Carlton 76436
Carmine 78932
Carrizo Springs 78834
Carrollton (1st) 75006
Carswell A F B, Sta. Fort
    Worth 76127
Carta Valley 78835
Carthage (1st) 75633
Casa View, Sta. Dallas 75228
Cason 75636
Castell 76831
Castroville 78009
    Mico, R. Br. 78056
Cat Spring 78933
Catarina 78836
Cayuga 75832
Cedar Bayou, R. Sta.
    Baytown 77520
Cedar Creek 78612
Cedar Hill 75104
Cedar Lane 77415
Cedar Park 78613
Cedar Valley, R. Br. Austin ...78746
Cee Vee 79223
Celeste 75423
Celina 75009
Center (1st) 75935
Center Point 78010
Centerville 75833
Central, Sta. Fort Worth 76102
Central Park, Sta. Houston ...77011
Centralia 75834
Chalk 79224
Chandler 75758
Channelview (1st) 77530
Channing 79018
Chapman Ranch 78347
Chappell Hill 77426
Charleston, R. Br. Lake
    Creek 75424
Charlotte 78011
Chatfield 75105
Cheapside 77952
Cherokee 76832
Chester 75936
Chico 76030
Chicota 75425
Childress (1st) 79201
Chillicothe 79225
Chilton 76632
China 77613
China Spring 76633
Chireno 75937
Chriesman 77838

Christine 78012
Christoval 76935
Cibolo 78108
Cisco (1st) 76437
Civic Center, Sta. Houston ...77061
Clairemont 79509
Clairette 76441
Clarendon 79226
Clarksville (1st) 75426
Clarkwood, Sta. Corpus
    Christi 78406
Claude 79019
Clay, R. Br. Somerville 77839
Clayton 75637
Cleburne (1st) 76031
Clemville 77427
Cleo 76833
Cleveland (1st) 77327
Clifton (1st) 76634
Clint 79836
Clodine, R. Br. Richmond ...77469
Clute (1st) 77531
Clyde 79510
Coahoma 79511
Cocenter, Sta. Pampa 79065
Cockrell Hill, Br. Dallas 75211
Coldspring 77331
Coleman (1st) 76834
College Station (1st) 77840
    Redmond Terrace, Sta. ...77840
    South, Sta. 77840
Collegeport 77428
Colleyville 76034
Collinsville 76233
Colmesneil 75938
Colonial, Sta. Waco 76707
Colorado City (1st). 79512
Columbus (1st) 78934
    Alleyton, R. Br. 78935
    Glidden, R. Br. 78943
Comanche (1st) 76442
Combes 78535
Comfort 78013
Commerce (1st) 75428
Como 75431
Comstock 78837
Concan 78838
Concepcion 78349
Concord 77850
Cone 79321
Conroe (1st) 77301
Converse 78109
Conway 79020
Cookville 75558
Coolidge 76635
Cooper 75432
Copeville 75018
Coppell 75019
Copperas Cove (1st) 76522
Coronado, Sta. El Paso 79915
CORPUS CHRISTI (1st) (see
    appendix)
Corrigan 75939
Corsicana (1st) 75110
    Emhouse, R. Br. 75110
    Navarro, R. Br. 75151
Cost 78614
Cotton Center 79021
Cottonwood, R. Br. Baird ...79504
Cotulla 78014
Coupland 78615
Courtney 77851
Covington 76636

Coy City	78110
Coyanosa	79730
Crandall	75114
Crane	79731
Cranfills Gap	76637
Crawford	76638
Creedmoor, R. Br. Austin	78744
Cresson	76035
Cresthaven, Sta. San Antonio (see appendix)	
Crestwood, Sta. Odessa	79760
Crockett (1st)	75835
Crosby	77532
Crosbyton	79322
Cross Plains	76443
Crowell	79227
Crowley	76036
Crystal Beach, R. Br. Port Bolivar	77650
Crystal City (1st)	78839
Cuero (1st)	77954
Cumby	75433
Cuney	75759
Cunningham	75434
Cushing	75760
Cut And Shoot, R. Br. Conroe	77301
Cypress	77429
Cypress Mill, R. Br. Marble Falls	78654
D'Hanis	78850
Daingerfield	75638
Daisetta	77533
Dal Rich, Sta. Richardson	75080
Dale	78616
Dalhart (1st)	79022
Dallardsville	77332
DALLAS (1st) (see appendix)	
Damon	77430
Danbury	77534
Danciger	77431
Danevang	77432
Darrouzett	79024
Davilla	76523
Dawn	79025
Dawson	76639
Dayton	77535
De Berry	75639
De Kalb	75559
De Leon	76444
De Soto (1st)	75115
Deanville	77852
Decatur (1st)	76234
Deer Park (1st)	77536
Del Rio (1st)	78840
Del Valle	78617
Dell City	79837
Delmita	78536
Denison (1st)	75020
Dennis	76037
Denton (1st)	76201
North Texas, Sta.	76203
T W U, Sta.	76204
Denver City (1st)	79323
Denver Harbor, Sta. Houston	77020
Deport	75435
Dermott	79515
Desdemona	76445
Detroit	75436
Devers	77538
Devine	78016
Dewalt	77433
Deweyville	77614

Bial	79026
Diahville	75761
Diane	75640
Diboll	75941
Dickens	79229
Dickinson (1st)	77539
Dike	75437
Dilley	78017
Dime Box	77853
Dimmitt (1st)	79027
Dinero	78350
Dobbin	77333
Dodd City	75438
Dodge	77334
Dodson	79230
Dogwood, R. Br. Woodville	75979
Donie	75838
Donna (1st)	78537
Doole	76836
Dorchester	75030
Doss	78618
Doucette	75942
Dougherty	79231
Douglass	75943
Douglassville	75560
Downtown, Sta. Corpus Christi	78403
Downtown, Sta. Bryan	77801
Downtown, Sta. Amarillo	79101
Downtown, Sta. Freeport	77541
Driftwood	78619
Dripping Springs	78620
Driscoll	78351
Dryden	78851
Pumpville, R. Br.	78876
Dublin	76446
Duffau	76447
Dumas (1st)	79029
Dumont	79232
Duncanville (1st)	75116
Dundee, R. Br. Holliday	76358
Dunlay	78018
Dunn	79516
Dyess A F B, Br. Abilene	79607
Eagle Lake	77434
Eagle Pass (1st)	78852
Normandy, R. Br.	78875
Earth	79031
East Austin, Sta. Austin (see appendix)	
East Bernard	77435
East Grand, Sta. Dallas	75223
East Houston, Sta. Houston (see appendix)	
East Oak Cliff, Sta. Dallas	75203
East Side, Sta. Lamesa	79331
East Texas, Sta. Commerce	75428
Easter, R. Br. Hereford	79045
Easterly	77854
Eastland (1st)	76448
Easton	75641
Eastwood, Sta. Houston	77023
Ecleto	78111
Ector	75439
Edcouch	78538
Eddy	76524
Eden	76837
Edgewood	75117
Edinburg (1st)	78539
Edmonson	79032
Edna (1st)	77957
Edom, R. Br. Brownsboro	75756
Edroy	78352

Egypt	77436
El Campo (1st)	77437
El Indio	78860
EL PASO (1st) (see appendix)	
El Sauz	78544
Elbert	76359
Eldorado	76936
Electra	76360
Elgin	78621
Eliasville	76038
Elkhart	75839
Ellinger	78938
Ellington A F B, Br. Houston	77030
Ellwood, Sta. Lubbock (see appendix)	
Elm Mott	76640
Elmaton	77440
Elmendorf	78112
Elmo	75118
Elsa	78543
Elysian Fields	75642
Emhouse, R. Br. Corsicana	75110
Emory	75440
Encinal	78019
Encino	78353
Energy	76452
Enloe	75441
Ennis (1st)	75119
Enochs	79324
Eola	76937
Era	76238
Escobas	78354
Estelline	79233
Etoile	75944
Euless (1st)	76039
Eustace	75124
Evadale	77615
Evant	76525
Everman, Br. Fort Worth	76140
Exchange Park, Sta. Dallas	75235
Fabens	79838
Fair Park, Sta. Dallas (see appendix)	
Fairbanks, Sta. Houston (see appendix)	
Fairchilds, R. Br. Richmond	77469
Fairfield	75840
Fairview, Sta. Houston	77006
Falcon Heights	78545
Falfurrias (1st)	78355
Falls City	78113
Fannin	77960
Farmers Branch, Br. Dallas	75234
Farmersville	75031
Farnsworth	79033
Farwell	79325
Fashing	78020
Fate	75032
Fayetteville	78940
Fentress	78622
Ferris	75125
Field Creek	76838
Fieldton	79326
Fife	76839
Fischer	78623
Fisk	76840
Flat	76526
Flatonia	78941
Flint	75762
Flomot	79234
Florence	76527
Floresville	78114

585

Florey, R Br Andrews.	79732
Flour Bluff, R Sta Corpus Christi	78418
Floyd, R Br Greenville	75401
Floydada (1st)	79235
Fluvanna	79517
Flynn	77855
Follett	79034
Forest	75945
Forest Hills, Sta Tyler	75701
Forestburg	76239
Forney	75126
Forreston	76041
Forsan	79733
Fort Bliss, Br El Paso (see appendix)	
Fort Davis	79734
Fort Hancock	79839
Fort Hood, Br, Killeen	76544
Fort Mc Kavett	76841
Fort Sam Houston, Sta. San Antonio	78234
Fort Stockton (1st)	79735
Fort Wolters, Br Mineral Wells	76067
FORT WORTH (1st) (see appendix)	
Foster Place, Sta Houston (see appendix)	
Fowlerton	78021
Francitas	77961
Frankel City	79737
Franklin	77856
Franklin, Sta. Houston (see appendix)	
Frankston	75763
Fred	77616
Fredericksburg (1st)	78624
Fredonia	76842
Freeport (1st)	77541
Freer	78357
Freestone	75842
Fresno	77545
Friendswood	77546
Friona	79035
Frisco	75034
Fritch	79036
Fronton	78546
Frost	76641
Fruitvale	75127
Fulbright, R Br Detroit	75436
Fulshear	77441
Fulton	78358
Gail	79738
Gainesville (1st)	76240
Galena Park (1st)	77547
Gallatin	75764
Galveston (1st)	77550
Ganado	77962
Garciasville	78547
Garden City	79739
Garden Oaks, Sta Houston.	77018
GARLAND (1st) (see appendix)	
Garner, R Br Weatherford	76042
Garrett, R Br Ennis	75119
Garrison	75946
Garwood	77442
Gary	75643
Gatesville (1st)	76528
Ireland, R Br	76536
Pearl, R Br	76563
The Grove, R Br	76576
Gause	77857
Gay Hill	77858
Geneva	75947
Genoa, Sta. Houston (see appendix)	
George West	78022
Georgetown (1st)	78626
Geronimo	78115
Giddings (1st)	78942
Gilchrist	77617
Gillett	78116
Gilliland, R Br Truscott	79260
Gilmer (1st)	75644
Girard	79518
Girvin	79740
Gladewater (1st)	75647
Glazier	79037
Glen Cove	76843
Glen Flora	77443
Glen Rose	76043
Glencrest, Sta Fort Worth.	76119
Glendale	75843
Glidden, R Br Columbus	78943
Gober	75443
Godley	76044
Golden	75444
Golden Acres, Sta Pasadena	77503
Goldsboro	79519
Goldsmith	79741
Goldthwaite	76844
Goliad	77963
Gonzales (1st)	78629
Goodfellow A F B, Sta San Angelo	76901
Goodland	79327
Goodlett, R Br Quanah	79252
Goodrich	77335
Gordon	76453
Gordonville	76245
Goree	76363
Gorman	76454
Gouldbusk	76845
Graford	76045
Graham (1st)	76046
Granbury (1st)	76048
Grand Prairie (1st)	75050
Grand Saline	75140
Grandfalls	79742
Grandview	76050
Granger	76530
Grangerland, R Br Conroe.	77301
Grapeland	75844
Grapevine (1st)	76051
Gray A F B, MOU, Killeen	76544
Graybach, R Br Electra	76360
Grayburg	77618
Great S W Airport, Sta. Fort Worth	76125
Great Southwest, Sta. Arlington	76011
Green Acres, Sta Tyler	75701
Greens Bayou, Sta. Houston	77015
Greenville (1st)	75401
Greenville Avenue, Sta. Dallas (see appendix)	
Greenwood	76246
Greggton, Sta Longview	75601
Gregory	78359
Grit	76846
Groesbeck	76642
Groom	79039
Groves (1st)	77619
Groveton	75845
Gruila	78548
Gruver	79040
Guerra	78360
Guilbeau, Sta. San Antonio	78204
Gulfgate, Sta. Houston	77207
Gulfway, Sta. Corpus Christi (see appendix)	
Gunter	75058
Gustine	76455
Lamkin, R Br	76460
Guthrie	79236
Guy	77444
Hackberry, Sta San Antonio	78210
Hale Center	79041
Hallettsville (1st)	77964
Hallsville	75650
Haltom City, Br Fort Worth	76117
Hamilton (1st)	76531
Hamlin	79520
Hamshire	77622
Handley, Sta Fort Worth	76112
Hankamer	77560
Happy	79042
Hardin	77561
Hardin Simmons, Sta Abilene	79601
Hargill	78549
Harker Heights, Br Killeen	76541
Harlandale, Sta. San Antonio	78214
Harleton	75651
Harlingen (1st)	78550
Harper	78631
Harrisburg, Sta. Houston	77012
Harrold	76364
Hart	79043
Hartley	79044
Harwood	78632
Haskell	79521
Haslet	76052
Hasse	76456
Hawkins	75765
Hawley	79525
Hearne	77859
Hebbronville	78361
Hedley	79237
Heidenheimer	76533
Helotes	78023
Hemphill	75948
Hempstead (1st)	77445
Henderson (1st)	75652
Henrietta	76365
Hereford (1st)	79045
Hermleigh	79526
Herring, Sta. San Angelo	76901
Hewitt	76643
Hext	76848
Hico	76457
Hidalgo	78557
Higgins	79046
High Island	77623
Highland Hills, Sta San Antonio	78223
Highlands (1st)	77562
Hillister	77624
Hillsboro (1st)	76645
Hilltop Lakes, R Br Normangee	77871

Hitchcock ... 77563
Hobson ... 78117
Hochheim ... 77967
Hockley ... 77447
Holland ... 76534
Holliday ... 76366
  Dundee, R. Br. ... 76358
Hondo (1st) ... 78861
Honey Grove ... 75446
Hooks ... 75561
HOUSTON (1st) (see appendix)
Houston Heights, Sta. Houston ... 77008
Howe ... 75059
Hubbard ... 76648
Huffman ... 77336
Hufsmith, R Br. Tomball ... 77337
Hughes Springs ... 75656
Hull ... 77564
Humble (1st) ... 77338
Hungerford ... 77448
Hunt ... 78024
Huntington ... 75949
Huntsville (1st) ... 77340
  Sam Houston College. Sta ... 77340
Hurlwood ... 79328
Hurst (1st) ... 76053
Hutchins ... 75141
Hutto ... 78634
Hye ... 78635
Idalou ... 79329
Imperial ... 79743
Indian Gap ... 76535
Industrial, Sta Dallas (see appendix)
Industry ... 78944
Inez ... 77963
Ingleside ... 78362
Ingram ... 78025
Inwood, Sta. Dallas ... 75209
Iola ... 77861
Iowa Park (1st) ... 76367
Ira ... 79527
Iraan ... 79744
Iredell ... 76649
Ireland, R Br Gatesville ... 76536
Irene ... 76650
Irving (1st) ... 75060
Irvington, Sta Houston (see appendix)
Italy ... 76651
Itasca ... 76055
Ivanhoe ... 75447
Izoro, R Br Cupperas Cove ... 76522
I Frank Dobie, Sta San Antonio (see appendix)
Jacinto City, Br Houston ... 77029
Jacksboro ... 76056
Jacksonville (1st) ... 75766
James Moody, Sta Victoria ... 77901
Jarrell ... 76537
Jasper (1st) ... 75951
Jayton ... 79528
Jefferson (1st) ... 75657
Jensen Drive, Sta Houston ... 77026
Jermyn ... 76057
Jewett ... 75846
Joaquin ... 75954
Joe Pool, Sta Dallas ... 75224
John Allen, Sta Houston ... 77007

John Foster, Sta Pasadena ... 77502
Johnson City ... 78636
Johnsville ... 76459
Joinerville ... 75658
Jonesboro ... 76538
Jonestown, R Br Leander ... 78641
Jonesville ... 75659
Josephine ... 75064
Joshua ... 76058
Jourdanton ... 78076
Judson ... 75660
Junction ... 76849
Juno ... 76938
Justiceburg ... 79330
Justin ... 76247
Kamay ... 76369
Karnack ... 75661
Karnes City ... 78118
Katemcy ... 76810
Katy ... 77450
Kaufman (1st) ... 75112
Keene ... 76059
Keller ... 76248
Kellerville ... 79049
Kelly A F B, Br. San Antonio ... 78241
Keltys, Sta Lufkin ... 75901
Kemah ... 77565
Kemp ... 75143
Kempner ... 76539
Kendalia ... 78027
Kendleton ... 77451
Kenedy (1st) ... 78119
  Mineral, R. Br. ... 78125
Kennard ... 75847
Kennedale ... 76060
Kenney ... 77452
Kent, R. Br. Van Horn ... 79855
Kerens ... 75144
Kermit (1st) ... 79745
Kerrick ... 79051
Kerrville (1st) ... 78028
Kildare ... 75562
Kilgore (1st) ... 75662
Killeen (1st) ... 76541
  Fort Hood, Br. ... 76544
  Gray A F B, MOU. ... 76544
  Harker Heights, Br ... 76541
  Killeen Army Base, MOU. ... 76544
Killeen Army Base, MOU. Killeen ... 76544
Kingsbury ... 78638
Kingsland ... 78639
Kingsley, Sta. Garland ... 75041
Kingsville (1st) ... 78363
Kingsville Naval, Br. Kingsville ... 78363
Kirbyville (1st) ... 75956
Kirkland ... 79238
Kirvin ... 75848
Kleberg ... 75145
Kleberg, Sta. Corpus Christi ... 78404
Klondike ... 75448
Knickerbocker ... 76939
Knippa ... 78870
Knott ... 79748
Knox City ... 79529
Kopperl ... 76652
Kosse ... 76653
Kountze ... 77625
Kress ... 79052
Krum ... 76249
Kurten ... 77862
Kyle ... 78640

La Blanca ... 78558
La Coste ... 78039
La Feria ... 78559
La Grange (1st) ... 78945
La Joya ... 78560
La Marque (1st) ... 77568
La Porte (1st) ... 77571
La Pryor ... 78872
La Salle ... 77969
La Vernia ... 78121
La Villa ... 78562
La Ward ... 77970
Lackland A F B, Br. San Antonio (see appendix)
Ladonia ... 75449
Lago Vista, R. Br. Leander ... 78641
Laguna Park, R. Br. Clifton ... 76634
Laird Hill ... 75666
Lake Air, Sta Waco ... 76710
Lake Brownwood, R. Br. Brownwood ... 76801
Lake Creek ... 75450
  Charleston, R. Br. ... 75424
Lake Dallas ... 75065
Lake Jackson (1st) ... 77566
Lake Kiowa, R. Br. Gainesville ... 76240
Lake Worth, Br. Fort Worth ... 76135
Lakehills, R. Br. Pipe Creek ... 78063
Lakeview ... 79239
Lakewood, Sta. Dallas ... 75214
Lamar Park, Sta. Corpus Christi (see appendix)
Lamar Tech, Sta. Beaumont ... 77705
Lamesa (1st) ... 79331
Lamkin, R. Br. Gustine ... 76460
Lampasas (1st) ... 76550
  Adamsville, R. Br. ... 76510
Lancaster (1st) ... 75146
Lane City ... 77453
Laneville ... 75667
Langtry ... 78871
Lapham, Sta. San Antonio ... 78216
Laredo (1st) ... 78040
Laredo A F B, MOU. Laredo ... 78040
Lariat ... 79335
Larue ... 75770
Lasara ... 78561
Latexo ... 75849
Laughlin A F B, MOU. Del Rio ... 78840
Laurel Heights, Sta. San Antonio ... 78212
Lavon ... 75066
Lawn ... 79530
Lazbuddie ... 79053
Leaday ... 76851
League City (1st) ... 77573
Leakey ... 78873
Leander ... 78641
Leary, R. Br. Texarkana ... 75501
Ledbetter ... 78946
Leesburg ... 75451
Leesville ... 78122
Lefors ... 79054
Leggett ... 77350
Legion, Br. Kerrville ... 78028
Lela ... 79055
Lelia Lake ... 79240
Leming ... 78050
Lenorah ... 79749
Leon Junction ... 76552
Leona ... 75850

Leonard	75452
Leroy	76654
Levelland (1st)	79336
Lewisville (1st)	75067
Lexington	78947
Liberty (1st)	77575
Liberty Hill	78642
Lillian	76061
Lincoln	78948
Lindale (1st)	75771
Mount Sylvan, R. Br.	75777
Linden	75563
Lindsay	76250
Lingleville	76461
Linn	78563
Lipan	76462
Lipscomb	79056
Lissie	77454
Little Elm	75068
Little River	76554
Littlefield (1st)	79339
Liverpool	77577
Livingston (1st)	77351
Llano	78643
Lobo, R Br Van Horn	79855
Lockhart (1st)	78644
Lockney	79241
Lodi	75564
Lohn	76852
Lolita	77971
Lometa	76853
London	76854
Lone Grove	78646
Lone Oak	75453
Lone Star	75668
Long Branch	75669
Long Mott	77972
Long Point, Sta Houston	77055
Longview (1st)	75601
Longworth	79531
Loop	79342
Lopeno	78564
Loraine	79532
Lorena	76655
Lorenzo	79343
Los Angeles	78051
Los Ebanos	78565
Los Fresnos	78566
Los Indios	78567
Los Jardines, Sta San Antonio	78237
Los Saenz, Sta Roma	78584
Lott	76656
Louise	77455
Love Field Terminal, Sta Dallas	75235
Lovelady	75851
Loving	76062
Lowake	76855
Lozano	78568
LUBBOCK (1st) (see appendix)	
Luckenbach	78647
Lueders	79533
Lufkin (1st)	75901
Luling (1st)	78648
Lumberton, R. Br Silsbee	77656
Luther	79751
Lyford	78569
Lyons	77863
Lytle	78052
Mabank (1st)	75147
Macdona	78054
Madisonville (1st)	77864
Magnolia	77355
Magnolia Springs	75957
Main Place, Sta. Dallas	75250
Malakoff	75148
Malone	76660
Manchaca	78652
Manor	78653
Mansfield	76063
Manvel	77578
Maple	79344
Marathon	79842
Marble Falls (1st)	78654
Marfa	79843
Marietta	75566
Marion	78124
Markham	77456
Marlin (1st)	76661
Marquez	77865
Marshall (1st)	75670
Mart	76664
Martindale	78655
Martinsville	75958
Mary Hardin Baylor, Sta. Belton	76513
Maryneal	79535
Mason	76856
Masterson	79058
Matador	79244
Matagorda	77457
Mathis	78368
Maud	75567
Maurtceville	77626
Maverick, R. Br Ballinger	76821
Maxwell	78656
May	76857
Maydelle	75772
Maypearl	76064
Maysfield	76555
Mc Adoo	79243
Mc Allen (1st)	78501
Mc Camey	79752
Bakersfield, R. Br.	79717
Mc Caulley	79534
Mc Coy	78053
Mc Dade	78650
Mc Faddin	77973
Mc Gregor (1st)	76657
Mc Kinney (1st)	75069
Mc Lean	79057
Mc Leod	75565
Mc Murry, Sta Abilene	79605
Mc Nair, R. Br Baytown	77520
Mc Nary	79841
Mc Neil	78651
Mc Queeney	78123
Meadow	79345
Medical Center, Sta. Dallas	75219
Medina	78055
Medina Base, Br. San Antonio	78236
Megargel	76370
Melissa	75071
Melvin	76858
Memorial Park, Br Houston (see appendix)	
Memphis	79245
Menard	76859
Mentone	79754
Mercedes (1st)	78570
Merchandise Mart, Sta. Dallas	75201
Mercury	76860
Mereta	76940
Meridian	76665
Merit	75072
Merkel	79536
Mertens	76666
Mertzon	76941
Meskit, Sta Texas City	77590
Mesquite (1st)	75149
Mexia (1st)	76667
Meyersville	77974
Miami	79059
Mico, R. Br Castroville	78056
Middle Water	79060
Midfield	77458
Midkiff	79755
Midland (1st)	79701
Midlothian	76065
Midway	75852
Milam	75959
Milano	76556
Miles	76861
Milford	76670
Millersview	76862
Millican	77866
Millsap	76066
Minden	75680
Mineola (1st)	75773
Mineral, R. Br Kenedy	78125
Mineral Wells (1st)	76067
Minerva, R. Br Cameron	76520
Mingus	76463
Mirando City	78369
Mission (1st)	78572
Missouri City (1st)	77459
Mitchell Avenue, Sta. Waco (see appendix)	
Mobeetie	79061
Moline	76863
Monahans (1st)	79756
Monroe City	77579
Monroe Street, Sta. Wichita Falls	76309
Mont Belvieu	77580
Montague	76251
Montalba	75853
Monte Alto, Br. Edcouch	78538
Montgomery	77356
Moody	76557
Moore	78057
Moran	76464
Morgan	76671
Morgan Mill	76465
Morse	79062
Morton	79346
Moscow	75960
Mosheim	76672
Moss Hill, R. Br. Liberty	77575
Moulton	77975
Mound	76558
Mount Calm	76873
Mount Enterprise	75681
Mount Pleasant (1st)	75455
Mount Selman	75776
Mount Sylvan, R Br. Lindale	75777
Mount Vernon	75457
Mountain Home	78058
Muenster	76252
Muldoon	78949
Muleshoe (1st)	79347
Mullin	76864
Mumford	77867
Munday	76371

Murchison...................75778
Murryhill, Sta. Lubbock 79413
Myra........................76253
Nacogdoches (1st)........75961
Nada........................77460
Naples......................75568
Nash........................75569
Natalia......................78059
Natural Bridge Caverns, R.
  Br San Antonio..........78218
Naval Air, Sta Corpus
  Christi (see appendix)
Navarro, R. Br. Corsicana ...75151
Navasota (1st)............77258
Nazareth....................79063
Neches.....................75779
Nederland (1st)...........77627
Needville...................77461
Nemo.......................76070
Nevada.....................75073
New Baden..................77870
New Boston.................75570
New Braunfels (1st).......78130
New Caney..................77357
New Deal....................79350
New Home, R. Br. Wilson...79383
New London.................75682
New Summerfield..........75780
New Ulm....................78950
New Waverly................77358
Newark.....................76071
Newcastle..................76372
Newgulf....................77462
Newport....................76254
Newsome....................75459
Newton.....................75966
Nimitz, Sta San Antonio...78216
Nixon......................78140
Nocona (1st)..............76255
Nolan......................79537
Nolanville.................76559
Nome.......................77629
Nordheim...................78141
Normandy, R. Br Eagle
  Pass......................78875
Normangee..................77871
Normanna...................78142
North Amarillo, Sta. Amarillo
  (see appendix)
North Austin, Sta. Austin
  (see appendix)
North College, Sta. Lubbock
  (see appendix)
North Lake, Sta. Dallas.....75238
North Port Arthur, Sta. Port
  Arthur....................77640
North Texas, Sta. Denton ...76203
North Uvalde, Sta Uvalde...78801
North Zulch................77872
Northfield..................79246
Northgate, Sta El Paso....79924
Northpark, Sta. Dallas.....75225
Northwest, Sta Austin (see
  appendix)
Norton......................76865
Notrees....................79759
Novice.....................79538
Number Fourteen, Sta.
  Lubbock...................79412
Number Two, Sta Pans......75460
Nursery....................77976
O'Brien....................79539
O'Donnell..................79351

Oak Forest, Sta. Houston
  (see appendix)
Oak Hill, R. Br. Austin......78746
Oak Island, R. Br. Anahuac..77514
Oakalla....................76560
Oakhurst...................77359
Oakland....................78951
Oaks, Br. Fort Worth (see
  appendix)
Oakville, R. Br. Three Rivers...78060
Oakwood....................75855
Odell.......................79247
Odem.......................78370
Odessa (1st)..............79760
Oglesby....................76561
Oilton......................78371
Oklaunion...................76373
Old Glory..................79540
Old Ocean.................77463
Olden......................76466
Olmito.....................78575
Olmos Park, Br. San
  Antonio...................78212
Olney (1st)................76374
Olton......................79064
Omaha.....................75571
Onalaska..................77360
Orange (1st)..............77630
Orange Grove..............78372
Orangefield...............77639
Orchard....................77464
Ore City...................75683
Orient, R. Br. San Angelo...76942
Orla.......................79770
Osceola....................76674
Otey, R. Br Rosharon.....77583
Ottine......................78658
Otto.......................76675
Ovalo.....................79541
Overton....................75684
Ozona.....................76943
Paducah...................79248
Paige......................78659
Paint Rock.................76866
Paisano Annex, Sta. El Paso
  (see appendix)
Palacios...................77465
Palestine (1st)...........75801
Palm Village, Sta.
  Brownsville..............78520
Palmer.....................75152
Palo Pinto.................76072
Paluxy.....................76467
Pampa (1st)...............79065
Pandale....................76944
Pandora....................78143
Panhandle..................79068
Panna Maria...............78144
Panola.....................75685
Pantex, R. Br. Amarillo....79069
Paradise...................76073
Paris (1st)...............75460
Park Cities, Br. Dallas....75205
Park Place, Sta. Houston...77017
PASADENA (1st) (see
  appendix)
Patricia...................79352
Patroon...................75967
Pattison...................77466
Pattonville................75468
Pawnee....................78145
Peacock...................79542
Pear Ridge, Br. Port Arthur ..77640

Pear Valley................76867
Pearl, R. Br. Gatesville...76563
Pearland (1st)............77581
Pearsall..................78061
Peaster....................76074
Pecan Gap.................75469
Pecos (1st)...............79772
Peggy......................78062
Pendleton.................76564
Penelope..................76676
Penitas....................78576
Pennington................75856
Penwell....................79776
Pep........................79353
Perrin.....................76075
Perry......................76677
Perryton (1st)............79070
Petersburg................79250
Petrolia...................76377
Pettit......................79354
Pettus.....................78146
Petty......................75470
Pflugerville...............78660
Pharr (1st)...............78577
Phillips, Br. Borger......79071
Philrich, Sta. Borger.....79007
Pickton....................75471
Pierce.....................77467
Pilot Point................76258
Pinehurst..................77362
Pineland...................75968
Pioneer Town, R. Br.
  Wimberley...............78676
Pipe Creek.................78063
Pittsburg (1st)...........75686
Placedo....................77977
Placid, R. Br. Rochelle....76868
Plains.....................79355
  Bronco, R. Br...........79315
Plainview (1st)...........79072
Plano (1st)...............75074
Plantation, Sta. Lake
  Jackson..................77566
Plantersville..............77363
Pleasant Grove, Sta. Dallas
  (see appendix)
Pleasanton (1st)..........78064
Pledger....................77468
Plum.......................78952
Point......................75472
Point Comfort.............77978
Pointblank.................77364
Pollok.....................75969
Polytechnic, Sta. Fort Worth
  (see appendix)
Ponder.....................76259
Ponta......................75781
Pontotoc...................76869
Poolville..................76076
Port Acres, R. Br. Port
  Arthur....................77640
Port Aransas..............78373
Port Arthur (1st)........77640
Port Bolivar...............77650
Port Isabel................78578
Port Lavaca (1st).........77979
Port Mansfield, R. Br
  Raymondville...........78580
Port Neches (1st) 77651
Port O'Connor.............77982
Portairs, Sta. Corpus Christi
  (see appendix)
Porter.....................77365

Portland	78374	Ridge	77874	Saginaw, Br Fort Worth.	76179
Post	79356	Ridglea, Sta Fort Worth (see		Saint Hedwig	78152
Postoak.	76260	appendix)		Saint Jo	76265
Poteet	78065	Riesci.	76682	Salado	76571
Poth	78147	Ringgeld	76261	Salineno.	78585
Pottsboro	75076	Rio Frio	78879	Salt Flat	79847
Pottsville	76565	Ric Grande City	78582	Salt Gap	76876
Powderly	75473	Rio Hondo	78583	Saltillo	75478
Powel.	75153	Rio Vista	76683	Sam Houston, Sta. Houston	77052
Poynor	75782	Riomedina	78066	Sam Houston College, Sta.	
Prairie Hill	76678	Rising Star	76471	Huntsville.	77340
Prairie Lea	78661	River Oaks, Sta. Houston	77019	Sam Rayburn, R. Br. Jasper	75951
Prairie View, Br. Hempstead	77445	Riverside, Sta. Fort Worth	76111	Samnorwood	79077
Premont	78375	Riverside	77367	San Angelo (1st)	76901
Presidio.	79845	Riviera	78379	Angelo State University,	
Preston, Sta. Dallas	75225	Roanoke	76262	Sta.	76901
Price	75687	Roans Prairie	77875	Goodfellow A F B, Sta.	76901
Priddy	76870	Roaring Springs	79256	Herring, Sta.	76901
Primera, R. Br. Harlingen	78550	Robert Lee	76945	Orient, R. Br.	76942
Princeton	75077	Robinson, Br Waco	76706	SAN ANTONIO (1st) (see	
Proctor	76468	Robstown (1st)	78380	appendix)	
Progreso	78579	Roby.	79543	San Augustine (1st)	75972
Prosper	75078	Rochelle	76872	San Benito (1st).	78586
Pumpville, R. Br. Dryden.	78876	Placid, R Br	76868	San Carlos, R Br Edinburg	78539
Purdon	76679	Rochester	79544	San Diego	78384
Purmela	76566	Rock Island	77470	San Elizano	79849
Putnam	76469	Rockdale (1st)	76567	San Felipe	77473
Pyote.	79777	Rockland	75970	San Isidro	78588
Quail.	79251	Rockport (1st)	78382	San Jacinto, Sta Amarillo	79106
Quanah (1st)	79252	Rocksprings	78880	San Juan	78589
Queen City	75572	Rockwall	75087	San Leon, R Br Dickinson	77539
Quemado	78877	Rockwood	76873	San Marcos (1st)	78666
Quinlan	75474	Roganville.	75971	San Perlita	78590
Quitaque	79255	Rogers	76569	San Saba	76877
Quitman	75783	Roma	78584	San Ygnacio	78067
Rainbow.	76077	Romayor	77368	Sand, R Br Lamesa	79331
Ralls	79357	Roosevelt	76874	Sanderson.	79848
Ranchland, Sta. El Paso	79915	Ropesville	79358	Sandia	78383
Randolph	75475	Rosanky	78953	Sandy.	78665
Randolph A F B, Br.		Roscoe	79545	Sanford	79078
Universal City	78148	Rosebud	76570	Sanger	76266
Ranger	76470	Rosenberg (1st)	77471	Santa Anna	76878
Rankin	79778	Rosharon	77583	Santa Elena	78591
Ratcliff	75858	Ross	76684	Santa Maria	78592
Ravenna	75476	Rosser	75157	Santa Rosa	78593
Raymond A Stewart Jr, Sta.		Rosston	76263	Santo	76472
Galveston	77550	Rotan	79546	Saragosa	79780
Raymondville (1st)	78580	Round Mountain	78663	Saratoga	77585
Raywood	77582	Round Rock	78664	Sargent, Br Bay City	77414
Reagan	76680	Round Top	78954	Santa	78385
Highbank, R. Br.	76644	Rowena	76875	Saspamco	78153
Realitos	78376	Rowlett	75088	Satin	76685
Red Oak	75154	Roxton	75477	Savoy	75479
Red Rock	78662	Roy Miller, Sta Corpus		Schertz	78154
Red Springs.	76378	Christi (see appendix)		Schulenburg (1st)	78956
Redford	79846	Roy Royall, Sta Houston		Schwertner	76573
Redmond Terrace, Sta.		(see appendix)		Scotland	76379
College Station	77840	Royal Lane, Sta. Dallas (see		Scottsville	75688
Redwater	75573	appendix)		Scroggins	75480
Reese A F B, R. Br.		Royalty	79779	Scurry	75158
Lubbock	79401	Royse City	75089	Seabrook (1st)	77586
Refugio (1st)	78377	Rule	79547	Seadrift	77983
Reklaw	75784	Runge	78151	Seagoville (1st)	75159
Renner	75079	Rusk (1st)	75785	Seagraves	79359
Rhome	76078	Rye	77369	Sealy	77474
Rice	75155	S F A, Sta Nacogdoches	75961	Sebastian	78594
Richards	77873	S W B T S, Sta Fort Worth	76122	Segno	77370
Richardson (1st)	75080	Sabinal	78881	Seguin (1st)	78155
Richland	76681	Sabine Pass	77655	Selman City	75689
Richland Hills, Br. Fort		Sachse, R Br Garland	75040	Seminary Hill Sta Fort	
Worth	76118	Sacul	75788	Worth (see appendix)	
Richland Springs.	76875	Sadler	76264	Seminole (1st)	79360
Richmond (1st)	77469	Sagerton	79548	Serna, Sta San Antonio (see	

appendix)
Seymour (1st)............76380
Shady Oaks, Sta. Hurst.... . 76053
Shafter...............79850
Shallowater...........79363
Shamrock.............79079
Sharpstown, Sta. Houston
  (see appendix)
Sheffield..............79781
Shelbyville............75973
Shepherd..............77371
Sheppard A F B, Br. Wichita
  Falls................76311
Sheridan..............77475
Sherman (1st)..........75090
Sherwood.............76948
Sherwood Shores, R. Br.
  Marble Falls..........78654
Shiner................77984
Shiro.................77876
Sidney................76474
Sierra Blanca...........79851
Silsbee (1st)...........77656
Silver................76949
Silverton..............79257
Simms................75574
Simonton..............77476
Singleton..............77877
Sinton (1st)............78387
Sisterdale, R. Br. Boerne...78006
Sivells Bend, R. Br.
  Gainesville...........76240
Six Flags Over Texas, Sta.
  Arlington.............76010
Skellytown.............79080
Skidmore..............78389
Slaton (1st)............79364
  Southland, R. Br.........79368
Slidell................76267
Slocum, R. Br. Elkhart......75839
Smiley................78159
Smithfield.............76080
Smithland..............75690
Smithville.............78957
Smyer................79367
Snook................77878
Snyder (1st)...........79549
Somerset..............78069
Somerville.............77879
  Clay, R. Br 77839
Sonora...............76950
Sourlake..............77659
South, Sta College Station.. 77840
South Amarillo, Sta. Amarillo
  (see appendix)
South Austin, Sta. Austin
  (see appendix)
South Bend............76081
South Dallas, Sta. Dallas...75215
South End, Sta Beaumont...77705
South Fort Worth, Sta. Fort
  Worth...............76128
South Houston (1st).......77587
South Oak Cliff, Sta Dallas
  (see appendix)
South Padre Island, R. Br.
  Port Isabel...........78578
South Park, Sta Houston
  (see appendix)
South Plains...........79258
South Post Oak, Sta
  Houston (see appendix)
South San Antonio Sta San

Antonio (see appendix)
South Temple, Sta. Temple 76501
Southlake, R. Br. Grapevine 76051
Southland, R. Br. Slaton. . . 79368
Southmayd............76268
Southmore, Sta. Houston.. 77004
Spade 79369
Speaks 77985
Spearman (1st).........79081
Spicewood............78669
Splendora.............77372
Spofford..............78882
Spring................77373
Spring Branch..........78070
Spring Hill, Br. Longview....75601
Springlake............79082
Springtown............76082
Spur.................79370
Spurger..............77660
Stacy................76879
Stafford (1st)..........77477
Stamford (1st).........79553
Stanton..............79782
Staples...............78670
Star.................76880
Startzville, R Br New
  Braunfels............78130
Stephenville (1st) 76401
Sterling City...........76951
Stinnett..............79083
Stock Yard, Sta Fort Worth
  (see appendix)
Stockdale.............78160
Stonewall.............78671
Stonewall Mall, Sta. Corpus
  Christi..............78410
Stowell...............77661
Stratford..............79084
Strawn...............76475
Streetman.............75859
Sublime..............77986
Sudan................79371
Sugar Land (1st)........77478
Sul Ross, Sta. Alpine 79830
Sullivan City...........78595
Sulphur Bluff...........75481
Sulphur Springs (1st)......75482
Summerfield...........79085
Summit Heights, Sta. El
  Paso...............79930
Sumner...............75486
Sundown..............79372
Sunnyvale, R. Br. Mesquite.. 75149
Sunray...............79086
Sunset, Sta Lubbock......79407
Sunset 76270
Sutherland Springs.......78161
Sweeny...............77480
Sweet Home...........77987
Sweetwater (1st)........79556
Sylvester..............79560
T C U. Sta. Fort Worth....76129
T W U. Sta. Denton.......76204
Taft.................78390
Tahoka...............79373
Talco................75487
Talpa................76882
Tanglewood...........78958
Tarleton, Sta. Stephenville. . 76401
Tarpley...............78883
Tarzan...............79783
Tatum................75691
Taylor (1st)...........76574

Teague...............75860
Tech, Sta. Lubbock.......79405
Tehuacana............76686
Telegraph.............76883
Telephone.............75488
Telferner..............77988
Telico, R Br Ennis.......75119
Tell.................79259
Temple (1st)..........76501
Tenaha...............75974
Tennessee Colony.......75861
Tennyson.............76953
Terlingua.............79852
Terminal Annex, Sta. Dallas
  (see appendix)
Terrell (1st) 75160
Terrell Wells, Sta. San
  Antonio (see appendix)
Texarkana (1st).........75501
Texas City (1st) 77590
Texhoma.............73949
Texline...............79087
Texon................76954
Thalia, R. Br. Crowell......79227
The Grove, R Br Gatesville.. 76576
Thicket...............77374
Thomaston............77989
Thompsons............77481
Thorndale.............76577
Thornton..............76687
Thrall................76578
Three Rivers...........78071
  Oakville, R. Br.........78060
Throckmorton..........76083
Tigua, Sta El Paso.......79915
Tilden................78072
Timpson..............75975
Tioga................76271
Tivoli 77990
Tobe Hahn, Sta. Beaumont. 77706
Tokio................79376
Tolar................76476
Tom Bean............75489
Tomball (1st)..........77375
  Hufsmith, R. Br........77337
Tornillo..............79853
Tow.................78672
Town Hall, R. Br Mesquite. . 75149
Toyah................79785
Toyahvale.............79786
Trent................79561
Trenton..............75499
Trickham, R. Br. Santa
  Anna...............76878
Trinidad..............75163
Trinity...............75862
Troup................75789
Troy.................76579
Truscott..............79260
Tuleta...............78162
Tulia (1st).............79088
Turkey...............79261
Turnersville...........76580
Tuscola..............79562
Twitty................79090
Tye.................79563
Tyler (1st)............75701
Tynan................78391
Uhland, R. Br Kyle.......78640
Umbarger.............79091
Universal City (1st)......78148
University, Sta Austin 78712

University of Dallas, Sta. Irving 75060
University Park, Sta. Wichita Falls (see appendix)
University Park, Sta. San Antonio (see appendix)
Utopia 78884
Uvalde (1st) 78801
Valentine 79854
Valera 76884
Valley Hi, Br. San Antonio 78227
Valley Mills 76689
Valley Spring 76885
Valley View 76272
Van 75790
Van Alstyne 75095
Van Horn 79855
Van Vleck 77482
Vancourt 76955
Vanderbilt 77991
Vanderpool 78885
Vealmoor, R. Br. Big Spring 79720
Vega 79092
Venus 76084
Vera 76383
Verhalen, R. Br. Pecos 79772
Veribest 76886
Vernon (1st) 76384
Veterans Administration, Sta. Temple 76501
Veterans Administration, Br. Waco 76711

Viboras 78392
Vickery, Sta. Dallas 75231
Victoria (1st) 77901
Vidauri 77992
Vidor (1st) 77662
View 79564
Vigo Park, R. Br. Tulia 79088
Village, Sta. Midland 79701
Village, Br. Dallas 75205
Village Mills 77663
Vincent, R. Br. Coahoma 79511
Vineyard 76085
Voca 76887
Von Ormy 78073
Voss 76888
Votaw 77376
Voth, R. Sta. Beaumont 77709
WACO (1st) (see appendix)

Wadsworth 77483
Waelder 78959
Wainwright, Sta. San Antonio 78208
Waka 79093
Wake Village, Br. Texarkana 75501
Walburg 78673
Wall 76957
Waller 77484
Wallis 77485
Wallisville 77597
Walnut Hill, Sta. Dallas (see appendix)
Walnut Springs 76690
Warda 78960
Waring 78074
Warren 77664
Warrenton 78961
Washburn, R. Br. Claude 79019
Washington 77880
Waskom 75692

Wetauga, R. Br Keller 76248
Water Valley 76958
Waxahachie (1st) 75165
Wayside 79094
Weatherford (1st) 76086
Garner, R Br 76042
Webb A F B, Br. Big Spring 79720
Webster (1st) 77598
Wedgwood, Sta. Fort Worth (see appendix)
Weesatche 77993
Weimar 78962
Weinert 76388
Weir 78674
Welch 79377
Weldon 75863
Welfare, R. Br Boerne 78036
Wellborn 77881
Wellington 79095
Wellman 79378
Wells 75976
Weslaco (1st) 78596
West 76691
West Austin, Sta. Austin 78703
West Columbia 77486
West Galveston, R. Br. Galveston 77550
West Odessa, R. Br. Odessa 79760
West Orange, Br. Orange 77630
West Point 78963
West Port Arthur, Sta. Port Arthur 77640
West Side, Sta. Beaumont (see appendix)
West Texas, Sta. Canyon 79015
Westbrook 79565
Westfield, Br. Houston 77090
Westhoff 77994
Westminster 75096
Weston 75697
Westview, Sta Waco (see appendix)
Wetmore 78163
Wharton (1st) 77488
Wheeler 79096
Wheelock 77882
White Deer 79097
White Oak 75693
White Rock, Sta. Dallas 75218
White Settlement, Br. Fort Worth 76108
Whiteface 79379
Whitehouse 75791
Whitesboro 76273
Whitewright 75491
Whitharral 79380
Whitney 76692
Whitsett 78075
Whitt 76090
Whon 76889
WICHITA FALLS (1st) (see appendix)
Wickett 79788
Wiergate 75977
Wildorado 79098
Wildwood, R. Br. Village Mills 77663
Wilford Hall U S A F Hosp, Br. San Antonio 78236
William Beaumont Hospital, Br. El Paso 79920

William Rice, Sta. Houston 77005
Willis 77378
Willow City 78675
Wills Point (1st) 75169
Wilmer 75172
Wilson 79381
New Home, R. Br. 79383
Wimberley 78676
Winchester 78964
Windom 75492
Windthorst 76389
Winfield 75493
Wingate 79566
Wink 79789
Winkler 75864
Winnie 77665
Winnsboro (1st) 75494
Winona 75792
Winters 79567
Woden 75978
Wolfe City 75496
Wolfforth 79382
Woodlake 75865
Woodlawn 75694
Woodsboro 78393
Woodson 76091
Woodville (1st) 75979
Wortham 76693
Wrightsboro 78677
Wylie (1st) 75098
Yancey 78886
Yantis 75497
Yoakum (1st) 77995
Yorktown 78164
Yows Street Annex, Sta. Borger 79007
Ysleta, Sta. El Paso (see appendix)
Zapata 78076
Zavalla 75980
Zephyr 76890

ABILENE 796

POST OFFICE BOXES

Box Nos.
1-3282	Main Office	04
511-656	Dyess Afb Br	07
5091-5694	A Sta	05

RURAL ROUTES

1,2	01
3	05
4	01
5	05
6	01

STATIONS, BRANCHES AND UNITS

Abilene Christian College Sta	01
Dyess A F B Br	07
Hardin Simmons Sta	01
Mc Murry Sta	05
General Delivery	02
Postmaster	04

APARTMENTS, HOTELS, MOTELS

Abilene Manor, 609 Leggett Dr	05
Abilene Towers, 1102 N 3rd	01
Bowyer, 1705 S 3rd	02
Camelot, 5241 Alamo	05
Elmwood W Manor, 4025 S 7th	05
Fontaine, 2433 N 3rd	03
Le Martinique, 302 N Mockingbird	03
Maison Blanche, 2800 Sayles Blvd	05
Radford Hills, 765 E N 10th	01
Rio Vista, 4028 S 7th	05
Shoji House, 3201 N 3rd	03
Spanish Arms, 1717 N 6th	03
Twenty-One Twenty-One, 2121 N 6th	03
Villa Chateau, 2102 Beechwood	03
West Woods Terrace, 600 Westwood	03

BUILDINGS

Abilene Savings, 402 Cedar	01
Alexander, 102 Pine	01
C & T, 1333 N 2nd	01
Citizens National Bank, 402 Cypress	01
City Hall, 555 Walnut	01
Clinic, 598 Westwood	03
County Courthouse, S 3rd & Oak	02
Crescendo, 1052 N 5th	01
Duffy, 471 Cypress	01
Federal, 300 Pine	01
First National Bank, 401 Cypress	01
First State Bank, S 4th & Oak	02
Meadows Medical Center, 1325 Hickory	01

Mims, 1049 N 3rd	01
Oil & Gas, 1209 N 4th	01
Permian, 317 N Willis	03
Petroleum, 451 Pine	01
Professional, 1101 N 19th	01
Southwest Savings & Loan, 340 Hickory	01
West Texas Utilities, 1062 N 3rd	01

HOSPITALS

Cox Memorial, 618 Cedar	01
Hendrick Memorial, N 19th & Hickory	01
West Texas Medical Center, 650 E Hwy 80	01

MILITARY INSTALLATIONS

Dyess A F B	07

UNIVERSITIES AND COLLEGES

Abilene Christian College	01
Hardin Simmons University	01
Mc Murry College	05

AMARILLO 791

POST OFFICE BOXES

Box Nos.
1-2974	Downtown Sta	05
3000-3999	San Jacinto Sta	06
4000-4999	Main Office	05
5000-5999	North Amarillo Sta	07
6000-8999	South Amarillo Sta	09
9001-9278	Downtown Sta	05
10000-10999	Avonbell Sta	06
11000-11000	Main Office	05

RURAL ROUTES

1	06
2	01
3	07

STATIONS, BRANCHES AND UNITS

Avonbell Sta	06
Downtown Sta	05
North Amarillo Sta	07
Pantex Rural Br	79069
San Jacinto Sta	06
South Amarillo Sta	09
General Delivery	05
Postmaster	05

APARTMENTS, HOTELS, MOTELS

Amarillo, 2217 Polk	09
Ashby, 821 Evergreen	05
Astoria Park, 3116 W 15th	02
Badger, 1115 Jackson	01
Beverly Towers, 2706 Arcadia	09
Bon Vie 2815 W 27th	09
Carrolton, 1700 Jackson	02

Casa De Warren 4215 Western	09
Clifton, 920 Bryan	02
Continental, 1300 Jackson	01
Eden Roc, 2700 Westhaven Cir	09
El Dorado 4300 Prairie	09
Fairfax, 1218 W 10th	01
Fleetwood 3506 Janet	09
Green Acres, 3105 Plains Blvd	02
Greenhaven, 300 N Jefferson	07
Heritage 3320 Western	09
Imperial, 1501 W 9th	01
La Tour, 2028 Austin	09
Lantern Square 7208 W 34th	09
Lucerne, 1109 Polk	01
Mandalay, 3005 W 27th	09
Mark Twain, 500 W 10th	01
Medallion, 3001 W 27th	09
Modern Manor, 3404 Janet	09
Otis, 2306 W 6th	06
Palo Duro, 1601 Jackson	02
Paramount Terrace, 3809 Virginia	09
Parkview Manor, 121 Goliad	06
Resident, 1417 Harrison	01
Royal Palace, 1124 N Mirror	07
Talmage, 1401 Van Buren	01
Toscosa, 2118 Taylor	09
Villa, 2005 Austin	05
Vineyard Manor, 1205 Polk	01
West Hills Arms, 4218 W 2nd	06
Western Sky, 3007 W 27th	09
Westwood, 2008 Austin	09
Wolflin Village, 2301 Austin	09

BUILDINGS

Alta, 1500 Taylor	01
Amarillo National Bank	01
Amarillo Petroleum, 211 W 8th	01
Amarillo, 301 Polk	01
American National Bank, 116 W 7th	01
Bank Of The Southwest, 2201 Civic Cir	09
Barfield, 600 Polk	01
Bivins, 420 Polk	01
Brayboy, 2710 Civic Cir	09
Colonial Plaza, 1310 W 9th	01
Doctors, 1422 Tyler	01
First National Bank, 112 W 8th	01
Fisk, 724 Polk	01
Herring Plaza	01
Insurance, 212 East 6th	01
Mays, 908 Polk	01
Paramount, 811 Polk	01
Phoenix, 804 Rusk	06
Plaza One	01
Professional, 600 W 8th	01
Rule, 217 Polk	01
Santa Fe, 900 Polk	01
Springer, 1217 W 10th	01
Urban, 800 Bryan	06
Vaughn, 320 Polk	01
Western, 112 E 5th	01

GOVERNMENT OFFICES

County Court House Annex, 600 Taylor	(
County Court House, 511 Taylor	(
Old Post Office, 620 Taylor	0:
United States Post Office, 207 East 5th	01

HOSPITALS

Amarillo Hospital District, 2208 West 6th	06
Amarillo Osteopathic, 2828 W 27th	09
High Plains Baptist, 1600 Wallace	06
Hillhaven Convalescent, 2423 Line	06
Northwest Texas, 2103 W 6th	06
Saint Anthony, 735 N Polk	07
Veterans Administration, W 66th & Bell Ave	06

ARLINGTON 760

POST OFFICE BOXES

Box Nos.
1-1652	Main Office	10
3451-3629	Sta A	10
5001-6279	Great Southwest Sta	11

RURAL ROUTES

2,3,4,5	10

STATIONS, BRANCHES AND UNITS

Great Southwest Sta	11
Six Flags Over Texas Sta	10
General Delivery	10
Postmaster	10

APARTMENTS, HOTELS, MOTELS

Arlington Villa, 2601 W Randol Mill Rd	12
Cibola Inn, 1601 E Division	11
Six Flags Inn, Ave H & 107th	11

BUILDINGS

Forum 303 3000 E Pioneer Pkwy	10
Great Southwest Corp, 520 Ave H East	11
Six Flags Mall, 2801 E. Division	11
Six Flags Over Texas, 2201 Road To Six Flags	11

HOSPITALS

Arlington Community

Hospital, 711 W Randol Mill Rd	12
Arlington Memorial Hospital, 800 W Randol Mill Rd	12

UNIVERSITIES AND COLLEGES

University Of Texas At Arlington	10

AUSTIN 787

POST OFFICE BOXES

Box Nos.
A-Z	University Of Texas Sta	12
1-2999	Main Office	67
3000-3999	South Austin Sta	04
4000-4999	North Austin Sta	51
5000-5999	West Austin Sta	03
6000-6999	East Austin Sta	02
7000-8999	University Of Texas Sta	12
9000-9999	Northwest Sta	57
12000-13999	Capitol Sta	11
20001-23199	Bergstrom A F B	43

RURAL ROUTES

1	02
2	04
3	51
4	57
5	04
6	46
7,8,9	03
10	46

STATIONS, BRANCHES AND UNITS

Bergstrom AFB MOU	43
Capitol Sta	11
Cedar Valley Rural Br	46
Creedmoor Rural Br	44
East Austin Sta	02
North Austin Sta	23
Northwest Sta	56
South Austin Sta	04
University Sta	12
West Austin Sta	03
General Delivery	67
Postmaster	10
Star Route A	46

APARTMENTS, HOTELS, MOTELS

Alamo, 400 W 6th	01
Austin, 701 Congress Ave	01
Cambridge Tower, 1801 Lavaca	01
Castilian, 2323 San Antonio	05
Commodore Perry, 800 Brazos	01
Downtowner Motor Inn, 300 E 11th	01
Driskill, 117 E 7th	01
Gondolier-Ramada Motor,	

1001 S Interregional	41
Hardin House North, 801 W 24th	05
Holiday Inn Motor, 20 N Interregional	02
Holiday Inn Motor, 6901 Interregional Hwy	52
Jester Center Hall, 101 E 21st	05
Ramada Inn, 5650 Interregional Hwy	51
Sheraton-Crest Inn, 101-105 E 1st	01
Terrace Motor, 1201 S Congress Ave	04
Villa Capri Motor, 2360 Interregional Hwy	05
Westgate, 1122 Colorado	01

BUILDINGS

American National Bank Building, 111 W 6th	01
Austin National Bank, 501 Congress Ave	01
Austin Savings & Loan	01
Bolm	01
Brown	01
Bryan-Day	01
Capital National Bank	01
City National Building, 221 E 9th	01
Commodore Perry Hotel, 108 E 8th	01
Ernest O Thompson, 910 Colorado	01
Federal	01
First Austin	01
First Federal Savings & Loan Association	01
First National Life	01
Internal Revenue Service Center	40
International Life Insurance	01
John H Reagan State Office	01
Littlefield	01
Lowich	01
Medical Arts Sq	05
Medical Park Tower	05
Nash	01
Page	01
Perry-Brooks	01
Richmond Bldg 1411 West Ave	01
Sam Houston State Office	01
Scarbrough	01
State Capitol	11
State Dept Of Public Safety	51
State Finance	01
State Health	56
State Highway	01
State Insurance	01
State Library	01
Texas Employment Commission	01
Texas State Bank	01
Travis	01
Tribune	01
U S Treasury	41
V A Data Processing Center	41
V F W, 1011 San Jacinto	01
Vaughn	01
Westgate	01

GOVERNMENT OFFICES

County Court House 67
Supreme Court 11

HOSPITALS

Brackenridge, 1400 East Ave .. 01
Holy Cross, 2600 E 19th........ 02
Medical Arts Square.............. 05
Medical Park Tower, 1301 W
38th............................ 05
Saint Davids, 919 E 32nd........ 05
Seton, 600 W 26th............... 05
Shoalcreek Hospital, 3501
Mills Ave 31

UNIVERSITIES AND COLLEGES

Austin Presbyterian
Theological Seminary, 100
W 27th......................... 05
Episcopal Theological
Seminary, 606 Rathervue
Pl............................... 05
Huston-Tillotson, 1820 E 8th.. 02
Lutheran Concordia, 3400
East Ave....................... 05
Maryhill 3101 S Congress....... 04
Saint Edwards University,
3101 S Congress Ave.......... 04
The University Of Texas, 200
W 21st......................... 12

BEAUMONT 777

POST OFFICE BOXES

Box Nos.
1-4314   Main Office 04
500:-5599   West Side Sta .. 02
6001-6399   South End Sta.. 05
7001-7999   Tobe Hahn Sta. 06
10001-13999   Lamar Tech 10

RURAL ROUTES

1 06
2,4 05
5 06

STATIONS, BRANCHES AND UNITS

Lamar Tech Sta.................. 05
South End Sta 05
Tobe Hahn Sta 06
Voth Rural Sta 09
General Delivery 04
Postmaster 04

BUILDINGS

American Center................. 01
Beaumont Savings & Loans.... 01
Biscamp 02
Doctors 01
F & M 01
First Federal Savings & Loan.. 01
General Finance 01
Gilbert.......................... 01

Goodhue.......................... 01
Kaufman.......................... 01
Mc Faddin....................... 01
North............................ 02
Perlstein........................ 01
Petroleum........................ 01
Ridgewood Center................ 03
San Jacinto...................... 01

GOVERNMENT OFFICES

City Hall........................ 04
Court House...................... 01

HOSPITALS

Baptist.......................... 02
Saint Elizabeth.................. 01

UNIVERSITIES AND COLLEGES

Lamar Tech 10

CORPUS CHRISTI 784

POST OFFICE BOXES

Box Nos.
1-2831   Downtown Sta .. 03
3000-3999   Kleberg Sta 04
4000-4999   Main Office 08
5000-5999   Roy Miller Sta .. 05
6000-6999   Lamar Park
                Sta............. 11
7000-7999   Portairs Sta.... 15
8001-8669   Gulfway Sta..... 12
9000-9999   Main Office 08
10001-10260   Stonewall Mall . 10
60001-60296   Clarkwood....... 06

RURAL ROUTES

1 15
2 08
3 15

STATIONS, BRANCHES AND UNITS

Clarkwood Sta.................... 06
Downtown Sta.................... 03
Flour Bluff Rural Sta............ 18
Gulfway Sta...................... 12
Kleberg Sta...................... 04
Lamar Park Sta.................. 11
Naval Air Sta.................... 18
Portairs Sta..................... 15
Roy Miller Sta................... 05
Stonewall Mall Sta.............. 10
General Delivery 08
Postmaster 08

BUILDINGS

Atlantic-Mobil, 602
Winnebago 01
Bevly, 1220 S Staples........... 04
Center, 416 N Chaparral 01
Citizens Standard Insurance,
1305 N Shoreline.............. 01
Corpus Christi State National
Bank, 502 N Water............ 01
Cullen Mall 4800 S Alameda.. 12

Doctors, 3154 Reid Dr 04
Driscoll, 609 N Broadway...... 01
Federal, 521 Starr.............. 01
Guaranty National Tower, 711
N Carancahua 01
Gulf Security, 1806 S
Alameda 04
Hawn, 817 N Carancahua 01
International Business
Machines, 520 S
Chaparral...................... 01
Jones, 317 Peoples.............. 01
Kaffie, 205 N Chaparral........ 01
Klee Square, 505 S Water...... 01
La Ratama Library, 505
Mesquite 01
Lozano, 403 S Staples.......... 01
Medical Arts, 1001
Louisiana 04
Medical Center, 2482 Morgan
Ave 05
Medical Dental, 1807 S
Alameda 04
Medical Plaza, 1411-15 3rd
St 04
..il Industries, 723 N
Broadway...................... 01
Padre Staples Mall 53-5400
Padre Island 11
Palm Plaza, 1800 S Staples.... 04
Park Tower, 901 N
Carancahua 01
Parkdale Plaza 11
Petroleum Tower, 811 N
Carancahua 01
Smith, 425 Schatzel............ 01
Southern Bankers, 1630 S
Brownlee...................... 04
Stonewall Mall 10500
Leopard....................... 10
Sullivan, 3105 Leopard........ 08
Sun Texaco, 922 N
Carancahua 01
Swantner & Gordon............ 01
Tejas, 719 N Broadway......... 01
Town And Country, 4100 S
Alameda 11
United Savings, 3765 S
Alameda 11
Vaughn Plaza, 711 N
Carancahua 01
Weber 319 Mesquite........... 01
Wilson Tower, 606 N
Carancahua 01
Wilson, 545 N Broadway....... 01
Woodlawn Center................ 08
1800 S Staples Bldg, 1800 S
Staples........................ 04
600 Broadway, 601 N
Broadway...................... 01

GOVERNMENT OFFICES

City Hall, 302 S. Shoreline..... 01
County Court House, 1111 N
Mesquite 01

HOSPITALS

Corpus Christi Osteopathic,
1502 Tarlton 15
Doctors Hospital, 3160 Reid.. 04

Driscoll Foundation, 3533 S
  Alameda 11
Memorial Hospital, 2606
  Hospital 05
Physicians & Surgeons
  General, 4626 Weber 11
Spohn Hospital, 1436 3rd....... 04
Thoma-Spann, 1546 S
  Brownlee 04
U S Naval Hospital, Naval Air
  Station 19

MILITARY INSTALLATIONS

Army Aero Depot
  Maintenance Center 19
Naval Air Station, Naval
  Base.. 19

UNIVERSITIES AND COLLEGES

Del Mar College......................... 04
University Of Corpus Christi ... 11

DALLAS   752

POST OFFICE BOXES

Box Nos.
1-3699   Main Office 21
3701-4599   A Sta 08
5001-6499   Terminal Annex
               Sta 22
7001-7999   Inwood Sta 09
8001-8499   Park Cities Br 05
8501-8999   South Oak Cliff
               Sta 16
9501-9999   Lakewood Sta...... 14
10001-10999 Industrial Sta.... 07
11001-11499 East Grand
               Sta 23
12001-12999 Preston Sta 25
15001-15399 Merchandise
               Mart Sta 01
15401-15999 South Dallas
               Sta 15
17001-17999 Pleasant Grove
               Sta 17
18001-18999 White Rock
               Sta 18
19001-19999 Medical Center
               Sta 19
20001-20999 Walnut Hill
               Sta 20
21001-21999 Beverly Hills
               Sta 11
22001-22299 Terminal Annex
               Sta 22
23001-23999 East Oak Cliff
               Sta 03
24001-24999 Joe Pool Sta 24
26001-26999 Fair Park Sta 26
28001-28999 Casa View Sta . 28
29001-29999 Walnut Hill
               Sta 29
30001-30999 Royal Lane
               Sta 30
31001-31999 Vickery............ 31
34001-34999 Farmers
               Branch............... 34
35001-36259 Airlawn Sta 35
38001-38999 Northlake......... 38

45001-45999 Exchange Park .. 35
47001-47999 Brook Hollow
               Sta 47
50001-50999 Main Place
               Sta 50
57001-57999 Industrial 07
61001-61999 Dallas-Fort
               Worth Airport,
               Tx...................... 61
64001-64999 Greenville
               Avenue.............. 06

RURAL ROUTES

1 24
2 16
3 11

STATIONS, BRANCHES AND UNITS

Airlawn Sta............................... 35
Beverly Hills Sta...................... 11
Brook Hollow Sta...................... 47
Casa View Sta 28
Cockrell Hill Br........................ 11
East Grand Sta......................... 23
East Oak Cliff Sta.................... 03
Exchange Park Sta 35
Fair Park Sta............................ 16
Farmers Branch Br................... 34
Greenville Avenue Sta............. 06
Industrial Sta........................... 12
Inwood Sta................................ 09
Joe Pool Sta............................. 24
Lakewood Sta............................ 14
Love Field Terminal Sta.......... 35
Main Place Sta.......................... 50
Medical Center Sta 19
Merchandise Mart Sta.............. 01
North Lake Sta.......................... 38
Northpark Sta............................ 25
Park Cities Br........................... 05
Pleasant Grove Sta................... 17
Preston Sta............................... 25
Royal Lane Sta.......................... 30
South Dallas Sta....................... 15
South Oak Cliff Sta.................. 39
Terminal Annex Sta................. 02
Vickery Sta................................ 31
Village Br.................................. 05
White Rock Sta.......................... 18
General Delivery 21
Postmaster................................. 21

APARTMENTS, HOTELS, MOTELS

Adolphus, 1321 Commerce....... 21
Argyle, 3721 Hall 19
Athena, 6335 W Northwest
  Hwy 25
Baker, 1400 Commerce............ 21
Crest Park, 4242 Lomo Alto.... 19
Dallas, 312 S Houston............. 22
Fairmont, 1717 N Akard 01
Gold Crest, 3601 Turtle
  Creek 19
Highlander, 4217 Lomo Alto.... 19
Hockaday Village, 5615
  Belmont................................ 06
Manor House, 1222
  Commerce 02

Park Towers, 3318
  Fairmount............................. 01
Preston Tower, 6211 W
  Northwest Hwy 25
Sheraton-Dallas, Southland
  Center 21
Statler-Hilton, 1914
  Commerce 21
Towers, 3883 Turtle Creek..... 19
Turtle Creek North, 3701
  Turtle Creek 19
Turtle Creek, 3525 Turtle
  Creek 19
Wedgewood, 2511 Wedgles..... 11
White Plaza, 1933 Main 21
Whitmore, 1019 Commerce..... 02

BUILDINGS

Adolphus Tower, 1412 Main ... 02
Alford, 318 Cadiz 07
Apparel Mart, 2300 N
  Stemmons Fwy 07
Atlantic, 408 Bullington.......... 01
Baptist, 703 N Ervay 01
Blanton Towers, 3300 W
  Mockingbird 35
Blue Cross, 100 N Central
  Expressway............................ 01
Braniff, 400 N Exchange
  Park...................................... 35
Carter Towers, 351 W
  Jefferson.............................. 08
City Hall 2014 Main................. 01
Coke, 710 N St Paul................. 01
Collum, 318 N St Paul............. 01
Continental, 1500 Jackson...... 01
Corrigan Tower, 212 N St
  Paul...................................... 01
Cotton Exchange, 608 N St
  Paul...................................... 01
Dallas Athletic Club, 1805
  Elm....................................... 01
Dallas Federal Savings &
  Loan, 1505 Elm 01
Dallas Trade Mart, 2100 N
  Stemmons Fwy 07
Davis, 1309 Main...................... 02
Day, 425 S Field 02
Doctors, 3107 Gaston 46
Elm Place, 1015 Elm 02
Empire Bank, 1806 Main 01
Empire Central, 7701 N
  Stemmons Fwy 47
Empire Life, 1712 Commerce .. 01
Employers Insurance, 423 S
  Akard 02
Exchange Bank, 100 N
  Exchange Park 35
Expressway Tower, 6116 N
  Central Expwy 06
Fidelity Union Life, 1511
  Bryan.................................... 01
Fidelity Union Tower, 1507
  Pacific.................................. 01
First National Bank, 1401
  Elm....................................... 02
Five Eleven North Akard......... 01
Five Hundred South Ervay....... 01
Fourteen Sixteen Commerce.... 01
Frito-Lay, 300 N Exchange
  Park...................................... 35

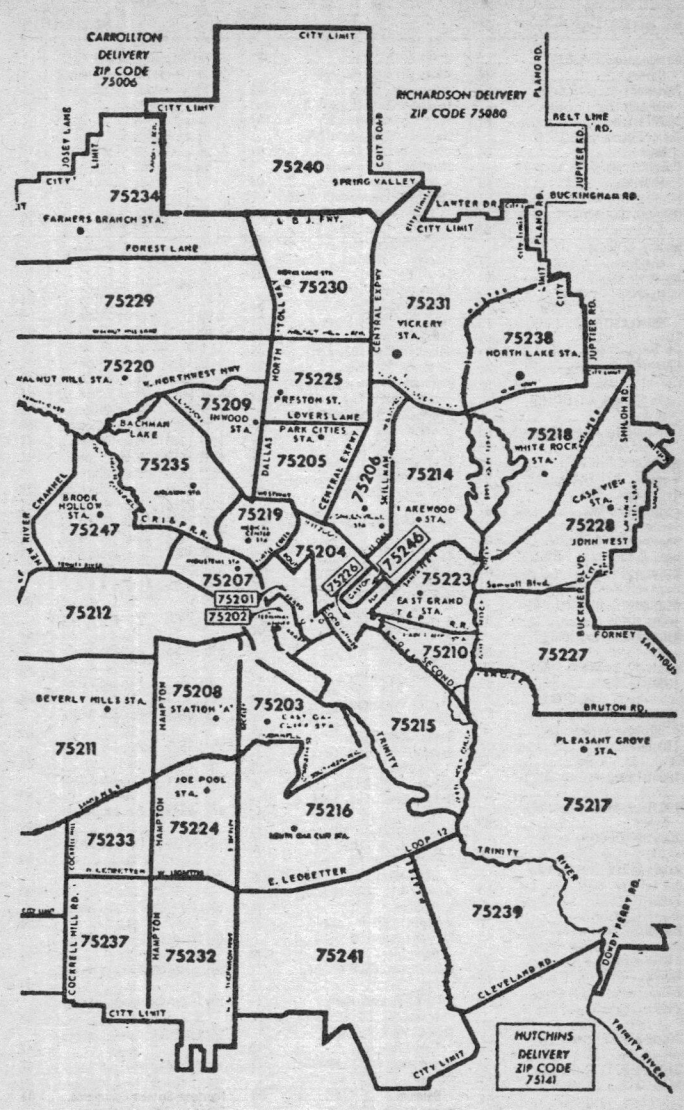

ZIP CODES
Dallas TX

Gaston Medical, 3607
Gaston.. 46
Gibraltar Life, 2006 Bryan...... 01
Great American Of Dallas,
2020 Live Oak..................... 01
Great National Life, 1604
Main...................................... 01
Guardian Savings & Loan,
1215 Main............................ 02
Hartford, 408 N St Paul........ 01
Home Furnishing Mart, 2000
N Stemmons Fwy.................. 07
Hudson & Hudson, 109 N
Akard..................................... 01
Insurance Plz., 411 N. Akard.. 01
International Business
Machines, 2911 Cedar
Springs.................................. 19
Kirby, 1509 Main.................... 01
L T V Tower, 1525 Elm.......... 01
Lacy, 1521 Commerce.............. 02
Life, 311 S Akard.................... 01
Locke Medical, 6011 Harry
Hines...................................... 35
Love Field Terminal, 8008
Cedar Springs...................... 35
Main Bank, 810 Main............ 02
Majestic, 1921 Elm................ 01
Market Hall, 2200 N
Stemmons Fwy...................... 07
Mayflower, 411 N Akard........ 01
Meadows, 5636 Milton.......... 06
Medical Arts, 1717 Pacific.... 01
Melba, 1313 Elm.................... 01
Mercantile Bank, 1700 Main.. 01
Mercantile Continental, 1810
Commerce.............................. 01
Mercantile Dallas, 1807
Commerce.............................. 01
Mercantile Securities, 1802
Main....................................... 01
Merchandise Mart, 500 S.
Ervay..................................... 01
Metropolitan Federal, 1401
Main....................................... 02
Mobil, 108 S Akard................ 02
National Bankers Life, 202 S
Ervay..................................... 01
Noel Page, 6440 N Central
Expwy.................................... 06
Oak Cliff Bank And Trust,
400 S Zang............................ 08
Oakwood Tower, 3626 Hall.... 19
One Lee Park West, 3303 Lee
Pky.. 19
One Main Place...................... 50
Praetorian, 1607 Main............ 01
Preston Forest Tower, 5925
Forest Ln............................... 30
Records, 509 Main.................. 02
Reliance Life, 505 N Ervay.... 01
Republic Bank Tower, 325 N
St Paul.................................. 01
Republic Bank, 300 N Ervay.. 01
Reserve Life, 403 S Akard...... 02
Santa Fe 2, 1118 Jackson...... 02
Santa Fe 3, 1104 Wood.......... 02
Santa Fe 4, 1033 Young........ 02
Simons, 1528 Main................ 01
Southland Center, 400 Olive.. 01
Southwest, 701 Elm................ 01
Southwestern Life, 1807

Ross.. 01
States General Life, 708
Jackson.................................. 02
Stemmons Empire, 8435 N.
Stemmons Fwy...................... 47
Stemmons Tower East 2700
N Stemmons Fwy.................. 07
Stemmons Tower North, 2710
N Stemmons Fwy.................. 07
Stemmons Tower South, 2726
N Stemmons Fwy.................. 07
Stemmons Tower West, 2730
N Stemmons Fwy.................. 07
Thomas, 1314 Wood.............. 02
Tower, 1907 Elm.................... 01
Trinity Universal, 820 N
Harwood................................ 01
Two Eleven North Ervay........ 01
Two-O-Nine Browder.............. 01
United Fidelity, 1025 Elm...... 02
Universal, 903 Ross................ 02
University Computing, 1949
N Stemmons Fwy.................. 07
Wholesale Merchants, 912
Commerce.............................. 01
Wilson, 1621 Main.................. 01
1516 Commerce...................... 01
1716 Commerce...................... 01
2001 Bryan Tower.................. 01

GOVERNMENT OFFICES

Dallas County Court House,
600 Commerce...................... 02
Dallas Water Utility................ 77
Federal U S Court House
1100 Commerce.................... 02
Federal, Bryan & Ervay........ 01
Old County Court House, 100
S. Houston............................ 02
Postal Data Center.................. 99

HOSPITALS

Baylor, 3500 Gaston.............. 46
Beverly Hills, 1353 N
Westmoreland........................ 11
Chester, 3330 S Lancaster.... 16
Dallas Osteopathic, 5003
Ross.. 06
East Dallas, 6003 Victor........ 14
Gaston, 3505 Gaston.............. 46
Granville C. Morton, 9000
Harry Hines.......................... 35
Medical Arts, Medical Arts
Building................................. 01
Methodist, 301 W Colorado.... 22
Parkland Memorial, 5201
Harry Hines.......................... 35
Presbyterian, 8200 Walnut
Hill.. 31
Saint Paul, 5909 Harry
Hines...................................... 35
Stevens Park, 2100 W.
Colorado................................ 11
Timberlawn, 4600 Samuell.... 21
Veterans, 4500 S Lancaster.... 16
Woodlawn, 3819 Maple.......... 19

UNIVERSITIES AND COLLEGES

Bishop, 3837 Simpson-Stuart
Rd.. 41

Dallas Baptist, 7501 W Kiest.. 11
Dallas Theological Seminary,
3901 Swiss............................ 04
Dallas, 500 N Akard.............. 01
El Centro, 801 Main.............. 02
Southern Methodist
University, Hillcrest &
University.............................. 22

EL PASO   799

POST OFFICE BOXES

Box Nos.		
A-N	Main Office	51
O-BB	Main Office	52
1-70	Main Office	40
71-140	Main Office	41
141-240	Main Office	42
241-512	Main Office	43
521-740	Main Office	44
741-920	Main Office	45
921-1112	Main Office	46
1121-1340	Main Office	47
1341-1612	Main Office	48
1621-1830	Main Office	49
1831-2040	Main Office	50
2041-2250	Main Office	51
2251-2460	Main Office	52
3001-3914	Station A	23
4001-4999	Northgate Sta.	14
6001-6636	Fort Bliss Br.	06
8001-8099	Biggs A F B Br	08
9000-9145	Paisano Annex Sta	82
9151-9295	Paisano Annex Sta	83
9301-9445	Paisano Annex Sta	84
9451-9566	Paisano Annex Sta	85
9571-9685	Paisano Annex Sta	86
9691-9764	Paisano Annex Sta	87
9771-9844	Paisano Annex Sta	88
9851-9924	Paisano Annex Sta	89
9931-10004	Paisano Annex Sta	90
10011-10102	Paisano Annex Sta	91
10111-10188	Paisano Annex Sta	92
10191-10268	Paisano Annex Sta	93
10271-10385	Paisano Annex Sta	94
10391-10545	Paisano Annex Sta	95
10551-10690	Paisano Annex Sta	96
10691-10762	Paisano Annex Sta	97
12000-12867	Coronado Sta	12
17001-17971	Ysleta Sta	17
20000-20999	Paisano Annex Sta	98
26001-26999	Ranchland Sta.	26

31001-31578 Summit
    Heights
    Station............ 31

RURAL ROUTES

1,2	27
3	35
4	34

STATIONS, BRANCHES AND UNITS

Biggs AFB Br.	08
Coronado Sta.	15
Fort Bliss Br.	06
Northgate Sta.	24
Paisano Annex Sta.	05
Ranchland Sta.	15
Summit Heights Sta.	30
Tigua Sta.	15
William Beaumont Hospital Br.	20
General Delivery	40
Postmaster	10
Principal Firms	99
Ysleta Sta.	07

APARTMENTS, HOTELS, MOTELS

Barbara Bassett, 6401 Gateway Blvd West	25
Caballero Motor, 6416 Montana Ave.	42
Chateau, 4510 Arlen Ave.	04
Chelsea Plaza Apartments 600 Chelsea	03
Cielo Vista, 6812 Cielo Vista Dr.	25
Colonial Motor, 8601 Dyer	04
Colonial Terrace Residential, 1413 Montana Ave.	02
Corinthian Plaza, 4155 Krupp Dr.	20
Del Camino Motor, 4910 Alameda Ave.	93
Desert Hills Motor, 4501 N Mesa	49
Desert Villa, 1630 Mescalero Dr.	25
Downtowner Motor Inn, 325 N Kansas	47
El Dorado, 303 Mesita Dr.	02
El Nido, 202 Alicia Dr.	05
Fairmount, 1800 N Stanton	02
Fountain Plaza, 4141 Westcity Dr.	02
Gardner, 311 E Franklin Ave.	40
Gateway, 104 S Stanton	49
Hallmark, 1620 Mescalero Dr.	25
Hillmark, 5000 Alabama	15
Hilton Inn, International Airport	49
Holiday Inn - Downtown, 113 W. Missouri Ave.	01
Holiday Inn-Midtown, 4800 Gateway Blvd East	05
Holiday Inn, 6655 Gateway Blvd West	90
Howard Johnson Motor Lodge, 8887 Gateway Blvd West	25
Iberville, 5216 Carousel Dr.	12
Imperial 400, 6363 Montana Ave.	25

La Posta Motor Lodge, 4111 N Mesa	02
La Quenta Motel, 6140 Gateway Blvd E.	05
Lakeside Village, 112 Little Flower Rd.	15
Mc Coy, Pioneer Plaza	41
Mountain Shadows, 2400 Morehead Ave.	30
Northgate, 5249 Wren Ave.	24
Paisano Annex Sta.	05
Paso Del Norte, 115 S El Paso	47
Plaza Motor, Corner Mills & Oregon.	49
Ramada Inn, 6099 Montana Ave.	84
Rodeway Inn, 6201 Gateway Blvd West	25
Royal Lodge Motel, 1401 N Mesa	02
Sagewood, 10000 Rushing Blvd.	24
Saint Regis, 323 N Oregon.	40
Sands Motel, 6941 Alameda Ave.	15
Starlite, 4651 Titanic Ave.	04
Sun Plaza, 1221 E San Antonio Ave.	01
Sunrise Arms, 4554 Hercules Ave.	04
Sunset Inn 4532 N Mesa.	12
Surrey Park, 351 Thunderbird Dr.	12
Sutton Place, 350 Thunderbird Dr.	12
The Diplomat, 601 W Yandell Dr.	02
The Executive House, 4501 Krupp Dr.	02
The Hawthorne House, 1700 Hawthorne.	02
The T W C Apts, 100 W Robinson Ave.	02
The Williamsburg, 300 W Schuster Ave.	02
Thunderbird Motor, 6405 N Mesa.	12
Travelodge Downtown, 1301 N Mesa.	02
Travelodge East, 6308 Montana Ave.	25
Travelodge El Paso Center 600 N Kansas.	01
Van Horne Park, Airport Rd.	06
Villa Del Norte, 6301 Delta Dr.	05
Villa Holiday, 9400 Montrose Ct.	25
Villa Riviera, 4165 Krupp Dr.	02
Villa Sierra, 2425 Mckinley Ave.	30

BUILDINGS

Abdou, 111 N Mesa	01
American Bank Of Commerce, 416 N Stanton.	01
Banner, 215 N Mesa.	01
Bassett Tower, 301 Texas	

Ave.	01
Blumenthal, 102 S El Paso	01
Caples, 300 E San Antonio Ave.	01
Coles, 202 1/2 E. San Antonio Ave.	01
Cotton Exchange, 104 1/2 N Stanton.	01
El Paso International, 119 N Stanton	01
El Paso National Bank, 201 E Main Dr	01
El Paso Natural Gas Company, 304 Texas Ave.	01
El Paso Professional Center, 1812 N Oregon	02
Electric, 215 N Stanton	01
First National, 109 N Oregon.	01
Fortune Coronado Tower, 6004 N Mesa	12
International Airport	25
Luther, 218 N Campbell	01
Medical Arts, 415 E Yandell Dr	02
Medical Center Of El Paso, 1501 Arizona Ave.	02
Mills, 303 N Oregon	01
Southwest National Bank, 300 E Main Dr.	01
State National Bank Plaza 221 N Kansas.	01
Sun Dancer, 6130 Montana Ave.	25
Surety Towers, 6281 Gila Rd.	05
University Towers, 1900 N Oregon.	02

GOVERNMENT OFFICES

El Paso Chamber Of Commerce, 820 N. Mesa St.	02
El Paso City-County, 500 E San Antonio Ave.	01
United States Courthouse, 511 E San Antonio Ave.	01

HOSPITALS

Campbell & 5th St Hospital Inc.	01
Delgado Green Cross, 118 N Harris.	07
El Paso Doctors Hospital 300 Waymore.	02
Four Seasons Nursing, 1600 Murchison Dr.	02
General R E Thomason, 4815 Alameda Ave.	05
Hotel Dieu, 1014 N Stanton.	02
Medi-Center Of America 2301 N Oregon.	02
Newark, 1109 E 5th Ave.	01
Providence Memorial, 2001 N Oregon.	02
Southwestern General 2001 Murchison Dr.	02
St Joseph Hospital The 1155 Idaho.	02
Suntowers, 1801 N Oregon.	02
Tigua General, 7722 North Loop Dr.	15
Valley Community, 7365	

Alameda Ave...... 15
William Beaumont General (Military Addresses Only)... 20

MILITARY INSTALLATIONS

Biggs A F B (Military Addresses Only)... 16
Fort Bliss Air Defense Center (Military Addresses Only)... 16

UNIVERSITIES AND COLLEGES

Administrative Mail U Of Texas At El Paso... 99
Hotel Dieu School Of Nursing, Arizona & Campbell... 02
Jesus & Mary Academy, 1501 Sun Bowl Dr... 02
Loretto Academy, 4600 Hueco Ave... 03
Lydia Patterson Institute, 517 S Florence... 01
Radford School For Girls, 2001 Radford... 03
Roger Bacon, 2400 Marr... 0?
Saint Anthonys Seminary, 4601 Hastings Dr... 03
University Of Texas At El Pa, College Campus... 02

FORT WORTH   761

POST OFFICE BOXES

Box Nos.		
1-2499	Main Office	01
2500-2599	Great Southwestern Airport Sta	25
3000-3999	Polytechnic Sta	05
4000-4999	Stock Yard Sta	06
5000-5999	White Settlement Br	08
6000-6999	Seminary Hill Sta	15
7000-7999	Riverside Sta	11
8000-8999	Handley Sta	12
9000-9999	Arlington Heights Sta	07
10000-10999	Oaks Br	14
11000-11999	Berry Street Sta	09
12000-12999	Ridglea Sta	16
13000-13999	Richland Hills Br	18
14000-14999	Haltom City Br	17
15000-15999	Glencrest Sta	19
16000-16999	Wedgwood Sta	33
17000-17999	Central Sta	02
21000-21999	Benbrook Br	26
22000-22299	S W Baptist Seminary	22
26000-26999	Ridglea Sta	16
27000-27999	Carswell Air Force Sta	27
28000-28999	South Fort Worth Sta	28
29000-30999	T C U Sta	29
40000-40999	Everman Br	40
48000-48999	Watagua Br	48
79000-79999	Saginaw Br	79

RURAL ROUTES
1... 79
2... 35
3... 34
4... 12
5... 16
7... 08
8... 09
9... 79
10... 35
12... 12
13... 19

STATIONS, BRANCHES AND UNITS
Arlington Heights Sta... 07
Benbrook Br... 26
Berry Street Sta... 09
Blue Mound Br... 31
Carswell AFB Sta... 27
Central Sta... 02
Everman Br... 40
Glencrest Sta... 19
Great S W Airport Sta... 25
Haltom City Br... 17
Handley Sta... 12
Lake Worth Br... 35
Oaks Br... 14
Polytechnic Sta... 03
Richland Hills Br... 18
Ridglea Sta... 16
Riverside Sta... 11
Saginaw Br... 79
Seminary Hill Sta... 15
South Fort Worth Sta... 28
Stock Yard Sta... 06
SWBTS Sta... 22
TCU Sta... 29
Wedgewood Sta... 32
White Settlement Br... 08
General Delivery... 01
Postmaster... 01

APARTMENTS, HOTELS, MOTELS
Commercial, 505 Main... 02
Crestwood Place, 3900 White Settlement Rd... 07
Downtowner, 1016 Houston... 02
Highland Park, 5302 Byers... 07
Loring, 3101 Camp Bowie Blvd... 07
Plaza, 303 Main... 02
Ridgeway Manor, 3901 Westridge... 16
Sheraton 815 Main... 02
Town House, 600 W 3rd... 02
Worth, 310 W 7th... 02

BUILDINGS
Bailey, 600 Bailey... 07
Baker, 110 W 7th... 02
Bewley, 212 W 7th... 02
Burk Burnett, 504 Main... 02
Century, 108 W 8th... 02
City Hall, 1000 Throckmorton... 02
Civil Courts, 100 N Houston... 02
Commerce, 307 W. 7th... 02
Continental Life, 714 Main... 02
Continental National Bank,
200 W 7th... 02
County Court House, 100 W Weatherford... 02
County Jail, 300 W. Belknap... 02
Criminal Courts, 300 W Belknap... 02
Dan Waggoner, 206 W 6th... 02
Doctor'S, 800 5th Ave... 04
Electric, 408 W 7th... 02
Ellison, 103 Main... 02
Equitab'e Savings, 811 Lamar... 02
Federal Courts, 501 W 10th... 02
First Life Insurance, 301 E 5th... 02
First National Bank, No. 1 Burnett Plaza... 02
Flat Iron, 1004 Houston... 02
Fort Worth Club - N. 307 W 6th... 02
Fort Worth Club - S, 306 W 7th... 02
Fort Worth Club-S, 304 W 7th... 02
Fort Worth National Bank, 115 W 7th... 02
Fort Worth Public Library, 210 W 9th... 02
Fritz G Lanahhafederal, 811 Taylor... 02
Fruit And Produce Terminal, 11101 11115 Jones... 02
Hughes, 411 W 7th... 02
James, 1/2 Houston... 02
Kirk-Mac, 600 Texas... 02
Lawyers, 503 1/2 Main... 02
Live Stock Exchange, 131 E. Exchange... 02
Lumbermens, 711 W. 7th... 02
Mallick Tower, 1 Summit Ave... 02
Mckeever, 2509 W. Berry... 09
Meacham, 110 W. 5th... 02
Medical Arts, 600 W 10th... 02
Medical Plaza & Office... 04
Mid-Continent, 106 W. 6th... 02
Mutual Savings, 815 Throckmorton... 02
Neil P Anderson, 411 W 7th... 02
Nine Ten Houston, 910 Houston... 02
Oil Gas Bldg, 309 W 7th... 02
Petroleum, 109 E. 9th... 02
Professional, 1216 Pennsylvania... 04
Rowan, 6000 Camp Bowie Blvd... 16
Schick, 208 W 6th... 02
Seminary South Office, Seminary South Shopping Center... 15
Service Life Center, 307 W 7th... 02
Shick, 208 W 6th... 02
Sinclair, 106 W 5th... 02
Stuart, 617 Texas... 02
Summit Center, 1330 Summit... 02
Summit, 1500 W 5th... 02
T & P Freight, 70 Jennings... 02
T & P Passenger, 221 W Lancaster... 02
Tarrant Savings, 600 Taylor... 02
Terminal, Meacham Field... 06

Trans-America Life, 103 E 7th	02
U. S. Courts, 501 W 10th	02
Union Bank, 100 Main	02
University Plaza, 100 N. University Dr.	07
W. T. Waggoner, 810 Houston	02
Western, 2525 Ridgmar Blvd.	16
Ymca, 512 Lamar	02
Ywca, 512 W 4th	02

HOSPITALS

All Saints Episcopal, 1400 Enderly Pl.	01
Boulevard, 3705 Camp Bowie Blvd.	07
Coffey Clinic, 306 W Broadway	04
Convalescent Center, 1000 6th Ave	04
Cook, 1212 W. Lancaster	02
Dorsey, 401 E 6th	02
Duncan Memorial, 2306 Hemphill	10
Elmwood Sanatorium, 2805 Kimbo Rd	11
Fifth Ave Clinic, 650 5th Ave.	04
Fort Worth Childrens, 1400 Cooper	04
Fort Worth Osteopathic, 1000 Montgomery	07
Glenview, 7501 Glenview	18
Harris Hospital, 1300 W Cannon	04
Howard Sanitorium, 921 W Cannon	04
John Peter Smith, 1500 S Main	04
Lake Worth Osteopathic, 6613 Jacksboro Highway	35
Medicenter, 815 8th Ave	04
Methodist, 1300 W Cannon	04
National Institute Of Mental Health, 3150 Horton	19
Northwest Hospital & Clinic, 2100 Highway 183	06
Saint Joseph, 1401 S Main	04
T And R Clinic, 2919 Markum Dr	17
Usaf Regional	27
Usphs, 3150 Horton	19
White Settlement Hospital, 701 S Cherry Ln	08

UNIVERSITIES AND COLLEGES

Brantley-Craughon, 1401 Henderson	02
Fort Worth Christian College, 7517 Bogart	18
South Campus	19
Southwestern Baptist Theological Seminary	15
Texas Christian University, Tcu Campus	29
Texas Wesleyan College, Twc Campus	05

GARLAND   750

POST OFFICE BOXES

Box Nos.		
1-1568	Main Office	40
2001-2795	Kingsley Sta	41

RURAL ROUTES

1,2,3	40

STATIONS, BRANCHES AND UNITS

Kingsley Sta	41
Sachse Rural Br.	40
General Delivery	40
Postmaster	40

HOUSTON   770

POST OFFICE BOXES

Box Nos.		
1-3399	Main Office	01
4001-4240	Franklin Sta	14
5001-5544	Harrisburg Sta	12
6501-6988	William Rice Sta	05
7001-7497	Houston Heights Sta	08
7501-7994	John Allen Sta	07
8001-8494	Southmore Sta	04
8501-8960	Anson Jones Sta	09
9001-9592	Central Park Sta	11
9601-9999	Greens Bayou Sta	15
10001-10379	Garden Oaks Sta	18
10501-10948	Oak Forest Sta	18
11001-11447	Roy Royall Sta	16
12001-12599	Park Place Sta	17
12601-12897	Park Place Hobby	17
13001-13592	River Oaks Sta	19
14001-14716	Foster Place Sta	21
15001-15669	Denver Harber Sta	20
16001-16380	Irvington Sta	22
17001-17239	Veterans Hospital Sta	31
18001-18755	Eastwood Sta	23
19001-19554	Memorial Park Br	24
20001-20629	Astrodome Sta	25
21001-21482	Jensen Drive Sta	26
22001-22822	Highland Village Sta	27
23001-23297	East Houston Br	28
24001-24444	Jacinto City Br	29
25001-25194	William Rice Sta	05
26001-26944	Gulfgate Sta	32
27001-27635	Julius Melcher Sta	27
33001-33630	South Park Sta	33
34001-34627	Genoa Br	34
35001-35999	South Post Oak Sta	35
36001-36880	Sharpstown Sta	36
39001-39262	Kinwood Br	39
40001-40552	Fairbanks Sta	40
45290-45924	Almeda Br	45
52001-53617	Sam Houston Sta	52
55001-55657	Long Point Sta	55
58001-58868	Albert Thomas Sta	58
60151-60774	Airport Mail Facility Sta	60
61001-61679	Civic Center Sta	61
66001-66916	Fairview Sta	06
70001-70358	John Allen Sta	07
88001-88094	Southmore Sta	04
90001-90665	Westfield	90
94001-94198	Oak Forest Sta	18
99001-99119	Central Park Sta	11

RURAL ROUTES

2	18
3	45
4	36
5	28
6	90
7	16
8	24
9,10	40
11	16
12,14	40
15	28
16	90
17	40
18	36
19,22,23	40
24	28
30	88
31	40

STATIONS, BRANCHES AND UNITS

Addicks Rural Br.	79
Airport Mail Facility Sta	60
Albert Thomas Br	58
Almeda Br	45
Anson Jones Sta	09
Astrodome Sta	25
Astroworld Sta	25
Central Park Sta	11
Civic Center Sta	61
Denver Harbor Sta	20
East Houston Sta	28
Eastwood Sta	23
Ellington AFB Br.	30
Fairbanks Sta	40
Fairview Sta	06
Foster Place Sta	21
Franklin Sta	02
Garden Oaks Sta	18
Genoa Sta	34
Greens Bayou Sta	15
Gulfgate Sta	32
Harrisburg Sta	12
Highland Village Sta	27
Houston Heights Sta	08
Irvington Sta	22
Jacinto City Br.	29

Jensen Drive Sta............ 26
John Allen Sta.............. 07
Long Point Sta............. 55
Memorial Park Br.......... 24
Oak Forest Sta............. 08
Park Place Sta............. 17
River Oaks Sta............. 19
Sam Houston Sta.......... 52
Sharpstown Sta............ 36
Southmore Sta............. 04
South Park Sta............. 33
South Post Oak Sta........ 35
Westfield Br................ 90
William Rice Sta........... 05
General Delivery............ 52
Postmaster................. 13

APARTMENTS, HOTELS, MOTELS

Ardmore, 5900 Ardmore.......... 21
Auditorium, 705 Texas........... 52
Bayou De Ville, 2500 Mac
    Gregor Way................... 04
Bayou Oaks, 8100 River Dr....... 17
Bellefontaine, 3203
    Bellefontaine................ 25
Ben Milam, 1521 Texas........... 52
Bissonett Plaza, 5202
    Buffalo Speedway............. 05
Braes-Field, 3822 Braeswood
    N............................ 25
Bryan, 1500 Capitol............. 02
Carrousel, 3499 Evergreen....... 17
Century National Bank
    Building, 2100 Travis........ 02
Continental Houston, 101
    Main......................... 02
Crosstimber Oaks, 2612
    Crosstimbers E............... 16
Dallas Avenue, 507 Dallas....... 02
De George, 1418 Preston......... 52
Downtowner Motel, 1015
    Texas........................ 02
Earle, 600 Preston.............. 02
El Tropical, 3501 Mac Gregor
    Way.......................... 04
Fleetwood, 2102 Telephone
    Rd........................... 23
Fourteen Hundred Hermann
    Drive, 1400 Hermann Dr....... 04
Garden Oaks Village, 3403 N
    Shepherd Dr.................. 18
Gilbert, 7925 Gulf Freeway...... 17
Glen Echo, 7939 Sarita.......... 12
Griggs Field, 3600 Griggs
    Rd........................... 21
Hermann, 1400 Hermann Dr....... 04
Hillcroft, 6203 Jessamine....... 36
Hillside, 5200 Memorial Dr...... 07
Judson, 711 La Branch........... 02
Kipling Plaza, 2203 Kipling..... 06
La Fonda West, 2827 Sage
    Rd........................... 27
La Fonda, 2227 Norfolk.......... 02
Lamar, Main & Lamar............. 52
Las Palmas, 3211 Las
    Palmas....................... 27
Lawndale Village, 1500
    Lawndale Plaza............... 23
Lazy Oaks, 1415 Wirt Rd......... 24
Lee, 1114 Polk.................. 02
Mayfair, 1600 Holcombe Blvd
    25

Mc Kinney, 916 Mc Kinney........ 52
Milby, 906 Texas................ 02
Montagu, 804 Fannin............. 52
Montclair, 5220 Weslayan........ 05
Montrose Boulevard, 1002
    Bissonnet.................... 02
Oak Lane, 2720 Revere........... 06
Park Lane....................... 04
Park Towers, 1700 Holcombe
    Blvd E....................... 25
Parkwood, 7331
    Staffordshire................ 25
Patricia Manor, 2522 Patricia
    Manor Pl..................... 12
Pickwick, 3102 Holcombe
    Blvd E....................... 21
Plaza, 5020 Montrose Blvd....... 01
Plum Creek Village, 314
    Winkler Dr................... 17
Post-Field, 1315 S Post Oak
    Ln........................... 27
Preston Villa, 2200 W
    Alabama...................... 06
Rice, Texas & Main.............. 52
River Oaks Gardens, 1601 S
    Shepherd Dr.................. 19
Royal Windsor, 5100
    Richmond Ave................. 27
Sam Houston, 1115 Prairie....... 52
Scarsdale, 1400 S Post Oak...... 27
Shamrock Hilton, South Main..... 01
Shamrock Plaza, 7006 Scott...... 21
Sheraton-Lincoln, 777 Polk...... 02
Sonesta 500 Jefferson........... 02
Stratford, 414 Fannin........... 52
Tall Timbers, 4040 San
    Felipe Rd.................... 27
Texas State, 720 Fannin......... 52
Town & Country, 2504 Mac
    Gregor Way S................. 21
Tudor City, 611 La Branch....... 02
Waldorf Arms, 5602 San
    Jacinto...................... 04
Warwick, 5701 Main.............. 01
William Penn, 1421 Texas........ 52
Wilshire Village, 1701 W
    Alabama...................... 06

BUILDINGS

Abstract & Title, 617
    Caroline..................... 02
Adams Petroleum Center,
    6910 Fannin.................. 25
American General Life, 2727
    Allen Pky.................... 19
Bank Of Commerce, 709
    Travis....................... 02
Bank Of The Southwest, 900
    Travis....................... 02
Bankers Mortgage, 708 Main..... 02
Bettes, 201 Main................ 02
C & I Life, 1006 Main........... 02
Capitol National Bank, 1300
    Main......................... 02
Century National Bank, 2120
    Travis....................... 02
Citizens State Bank, 400
    Main......................... 02
Columbia Life, 1007 Preston..... 02
Continental Bank, 220 Main...... 02
Cotton Exchange, 1300
    Prairie...................... 02
Cotton, 502 Caroline............ 02

County Civil Courts, 301
    Fannin....................... 02
De George, 3520 Montrose........ 06
Eastern Airlines 3700
    Greenway Plz................. 46
Electric, 611 Walker............ 02
Family Law Center, 1115
    Congress..................... 02
Fannin Bank, 1020 Holcombe
    Blvd E....................... 25
Federal Land Bank, 430
    Lamar........................ 02
Federal Office, 515 Rusk........ 02
Federal, 701 San Jacinto........ 02
First City National Bank,
    1021 Main.................... 02
Gibralter, 2302 Fannin.......... 02
Gid Neal, 5510 Greenbriar....... 05
Guaranty, 1302 Rusk............. 02
Gulf Annex, 717 Travis.......... 02
Gulf, 712 Main.................. 02
Hermann Professional, 6410
    Fannin....................... 25
Houston Bank & Trust, 1801
    Main......................... 02
Houston Bar Center, 723
    Main......................... 02
Houston Natural Gas, 1200
    Travis....................... 01
Houston Office Center, 6001
    Gulf Freeway................. 23
Houston Title, 1212 Dallas...... 02
Humble, 800 Bell................ 02
Jesse H. Jones Hall, 615
    Louisiana.................... 02
Kirby, 3801 Kirby Dr............ 06
Kress, 707 Main................. 02
Kurth, 5013 Fannin.............. 04
Legal Arts, 312 Fannin.......... 02
Lincoln Liberty Life, 711 Polk.. 02
Live Stock Exchange, 4904
    Calhoun Rd................... 04
M W Kellogg 3800 Greenway
    Plz.......................... 46
Main, 1216 Main................. 02
Mc Donald, 618 Prairie.......... 02
Medical Arts, 1215 Walker....... 02
Mellie Esperson, 815 Walker..... 02
Melrose, 1121 Walker............ 02
Memorial Professional, 1010
    Louisiana.................... 02
Merchants Exchange, 202
    Travis....................... 02
Niels Esperson, 804 Travis...... 02
Oil & Gas, 706 Lamar............ 02
Old National Life, 5619
    Fannin....................... 04
One Main Plaza 1 Main........... 02
One Shell Plz, 910 Louisiana.... 02
Petroleum, 1314 Texas........... 02
Post Oak Towers, 5045
    Westheimer Rd................ 27
Prudential, 1100 Holcombe
    Blvd E....................... 25
Republic, 1016 Preston.......... 02
Robert Neal, 1220 Polk.......... 02
Salvation Army, 204 Travis...... 02
San Jacinto Saving, 905 Or
    907 Main..................... 02
San Jacinto, 911 Walker......... 02
Scanlan, 405 Main............... 02
South Coast Life, 800 Main...... 02
Southern States Life, 3317

Montrose Blvd................... 06
Southwest Towers, 707 Mc
Kinney 02
State National Bank, 412
Main 02
Stewart, 403 Fannin........... 02
Tenneco, 1010 Milam.......... 02
Texaco, 1111 Rusk 02
Texas Gas, 2472 Bolsover... 05
Texas National Bank, 1300
Main 02
Two Shell Plz, 701 Walker...... 02
U. S. Custom House, 701
San Jacinto Or 702
Caroline.......................... 02
Union Carbide 3600
Greenway Plz Dr............ 46
United Gas, 1116 Texas...... 02
West, 817 Main.................. 02
Western Union, 914 Franklin.. 02
Wilson, 2601 Main 02
Womens Professional, 6436
Fannin............................ 25
World Trade Center, 1520
Texas.............................. 02
Zindler, 218 Fannin............ 02
1114 Texas Avenue, 1114
Texas.............................. 02
500 Jefferson, 500 Jefferson... 02
711 Main, 711 Main............ 02

GOVERNMENT OFFICES

Chamber Of Commerce, 914
Main 02
City Hall, 900 Brazos.......... 02
County Court House, 301 San
Jacinto............................ 02

HOSPITALS

Arabia Temple Crippled
Children Clinic, 1402
Outer Belt 25
Autrey Memorial, 3602 West
Dallas............................. 19
Community, 1405 Holland..... 29
Doctors, 5815 Airline.......... 22
General Ben Taub, 1502
Outer Belt Dr 25
Hedgecroft Hospital & Clinic,
5120 Montrose Blvd......... 06
Heights, 1917 Ashland........ 08
Hermann, 1203 Ross
Sterling.......................... 25
Homestead Road, 8214
Homestead Road.............. 28
Houston Eye Ear & Throat
Hospital, 1010 Louisiana ... 02
Houston General, 2715
Jensen Dr........................ 26
Jefferson Davis, 1801 Allen
Pkwy............................... 19
Little York, 2807 Little York
Rd................................... 16
Lockwood, 5001 Lockwood... 26
M D Anderson, 6723 Bertner.. 25
Medical-Arts 1215 Walker.... 02
Memorial Baptist Central
1100 Louisiana 02
Memorial Baptist Northwest
1635 North Loop W........... 08
Memorial Baptist Southeast

7655 Bellfort..................... 17
Memorial Baptist Southwest
6440 High Star................. 36
Memorial Baptist, 602
Lamar.............................. 02
Memorial City General 920
Frostwood........................ 24
Methodist, 6516 Bertner..... 25
North Houston, 8800
Arkansas......................... 16
Northshore, 1000 Federal Rd.. 15
Northwest General, 1615
Hillendahl........................ 24
Parkview, 7440 Harrisburg
Blvd................................ 11
Riverside General, 2900
Elgin............................... 04
Rockglen, 13131 Rockglen.... 15
Saint Elizabeths, 4500 Lyons
Ave................................. 20
Saint Josephs, 1910
Crawford.......................... 02
Saint Lukes Episcopal, 6621
Fannin............................. 25
Sam Houston Memorial, 1615
Hillendahl........................ 55
Spring Branch, 8846 Long
Point............................... 55
Texas Childrens, 6621
Fannin............................. 25
Veterans Administration,
2002 Holcombe Blvd......... 31
Wright Clinic & Hospital,
2407 Main N..................... 09
Yale, 510 W Tidwell........... 18

MILITARY INSTALLATIONS

Ellington A F B................... 30

UNIVERSITIES AND COLLEGES

Baylor University College Of
Medicine, 1200 M'D
Anderson......................... 25
Houston Baptist College,
7502 Fondren Rd.............. 36
Sacred Heart Dominican,
6501 Almeda Rd............... 21
South Texas One Main Plz.... 02
Texas Southern University,
3201 Wheeler................... 04
University Of Houston, 3801
Cullen.............................. 04
University Of Saint Thomas,
3812 Montrose.................. 06
University Of Texas Post
Graduate School, 1400
Outer Belt 25
University Of Texas School Of
Dentistry, 6515 Freeman.... 25
William Marsh Rice
University, 6100 Main 01

IRVING   **750**

POST OFFICE BOXES

Box Nos.
1-1658   Main Office...... 60
55000-5699   Carl Range
Station............. 62

RURAL ROUTES

1,2 62
3 60

STATIONS, BRANCHES AND UNITS

Carl Range Sta.................. 60
University Of Dallas Sta...... 60
General Delivery................ 60
Postmaster....................... 60

APARTMENTS, HOTELS, MOTELS

Holiday Inn-1930 East
Carpenter Fwy.................. 61
Lexington Apartments 909 W.
Carpenter Fwy. W............. 62
Ramada Hacienda Motor Inn
120 W. Carpenter Fwy.
W.................................... 62
Villa Inn West 215 E
Carpenter Fwy................. 62

BUILDINGS

Irving Bank Trust Tower
110 N. Main..................... 60
Professional Tower Bldg.
1711 W. Irving Blvd.......... 61
Southwest Bank Bldg. : 2520
W. Irving Blvd.................. 61

HOSPITALS

Gilbert Medical Surgical
101 S. O Connor Rd.......... 60
Irving Community Hospital-
1901 Macarthur Blvd......... 61
Medical Surgical Clinic
2120 Macarthur Blvd......... 61
Physicians Surgeons
Hospital 1735 W. Irving
Blvd................................ 61

UNIVERSITIES AND COLLEGES

University Of Dallas Station... 60

LUBBOCK   **794**

POST OFFICE BOXES

Box Nos.
1-2999   Main Office...... 08
3001-3357   Ellwood Sta.... 10
4001-4720   Tech Sta........ 09
5000-5834   North College
Sta 17
6000-6999   Murryhill Sta... 13
7000-7999   Lubbock
Christian
College 07
8000-9999   Reese Air Force
Base R. Sta... 01
10001-10436 Main Office...... 08
16000-16999 Sunset Sta....... 90

RURAL ROUTES

1 01
2 15
3 01

603

4	13
5	10
6,7	01
8	07

STATIONS, BRANCHES AND UNITS

Elwood Sta.	10
Murryhill Sta.	13
North College Sta.	10
Number Fourteen Sta.	12
Reese A F B Rural Br.	01
Sunset Sta.	07
Tech Sta.	09
General Delivery	06
Postmaster	06

APARTMENTS, HOTELS, MOTELS

Altura Towers, 1617 27th	05
Barcelona, 5416 50th	14
Bel-Aire, 1903 14th	01
Bosque, 1710 Main	01
Browns, 907 Idalou Highway	03
Camelot Mobile Homes, 6001 34th	07
Century House, 1625 16th	01
Circle V, 2103 33rd	11
Clark, 1701 Avenue L	01
Conquistadors, 5300 11th	16
Country Inn, 4021 21st	10
Cresthaven, 1700 E 22nd	04
Cresthaven, 1703 E 23rd	04
De Busk, 226 North Sherman	15
Desert Inn, 2800 43rd	13
Ebony Arms, 2800 Juniper	04
Ficas, 1602 Avenue K	01
Georgian Arms, 2405 8th	01
Greenbriar, 4303 19th	07
Hartford Park, 223 Indiana Ave	15
Heritage Arms, 5540 19th	07
Hub Homes, 4th & Avenue F	01
Indiana Terrace, 221 Indiana	15
Jackson, 1604 45th	12
K-C, 2422 15th	01
Kentwood, 1702 26th	11
Kobs, 1306 Avenue N	01
Lakeland Park, 2411 45th	12
Lakeview, 2102 38th	12
Lawdas Villa, 102 Avenue T	15
Lexington, 4521 Brownfield Hwy	07
Lindsey, 1604 Avenue W	01
Lindsey, 2302 17th	01
Lubbock, 2010 5th	01
Matador, 2301 7th	01
Midway, 1809 Broadway	01
Mimosa, 2410 14th	01
Montclair, 709 Avenue R	01
Nancy, 1621 16th	01
Olney, 116 Avenue X	15
Park Terrace, 2401 45th	12
Parr Place, 1202 23rd	05
Patio, 3300 Toledo	10
Plantation House, 2400 44th	12
Plaza, 2101-2102 34th	11
Plaza, 2102 & 2105 33rd	11
Raider Villa, 1612 Ave Y	01
Redwood, 2419 13th	01
Slater, 1922 5th	01
Stardust, 2301 50th	12
Stoneleigh, 2415 33rd	11

Studio, 1617 Avenue N	01
Summit, 1610 45th	12
Sycamore Park, 4300 E 4th	03
Tally Ho, 5105 Avenue W	12
Tech Arms, 1626 Avenue Y	01
Townhouse, 1801 Main	01
University Village, 3102 4th	15
Varsity Village, 3002 4th	15
Vickery, 2904 Texas	05
Villa West, 5401 4th	16
Villa, 2301 51st	12
Western Air, 2404 10th	01
Westwood Village, 2700 Fordham	15
Wilshire, 1922 5th	01
Wilshire, 722 Avenue T	01
Woody, 1608 Broadway	01

BUILDINGS

All American Security, 1401 19th	01
Briercroft Office Park	12
Carlock & Doughty, 1005 13th	01
Central American Life, 1202 Texas	01
Citizens Tower, 1210 14th	01
Commerce, 1603 Broadway	01
Cotton Exchange, 1320 Texas	01
Court Place Inc 916 Main	01
Federal 1205 Texas	01
Ferguson, 1412 Texas	01
Fields, 1946 Avenue Q	05
First National-Pioneer, 1500 Broadway	01
Gibson, 1414 Avenue J	01
Great Plains Life, 1107 Avenue L	01
Insurance, 2109 Avenue Q	05
Jones-Malone, 1203 University	01
Kerr-Easter, 1002 14th	01
Lubbock National, 916 Main	01
Medical Arts, 1318 Broadway	01
Medical Professional, 3801 19th	10
Myrick, 1215 Ave J	01
Owens, 1114 10th	01
Park Place, 1401 19th	01
Petroleum, 1802 Avenue Q	01
Rogers, 1515 Texas	01
Sanford, 1009 Texas	01
South Plains Mall 6000 Slide Rd	14
Sweetbriar, 1206 Avenue J	01
Wall, 1302 Texas	01
Watson, 1503 Avenue J	01
Weaver, 1106 Broadway	01
Whiteside, 1717 Avenue K	01

HOSPITALS

Highland, 2412 50th	12
Lubbock Osteopathic, 5301 University Ave	13
Methodist, 3615 19th	10
Porter, 2401 19th	01
St Marys Of The Plains, 4101 24th	10
University 6610 Quaker	13

West Texas, 1312 Main | 01 |

UNIVERSITIES AND COLLEGES

Lubbock Christian, 5601 19th	07
Texas Technological College Dormitories, University Ave	06
Texas Technological, University Ave	09

PASADENA 775

POST OFFICE BOXES

Box Nos.		
1-3488	Main Office	01
4001-4499	John Foster Sta.	02
5001-5499	Golden Acres Sta.	03
6001-7232	Bob Harris	02

STATIONS, BRANCHES AND UNITS

Bob Harris Sta.	02
Golden Acres Sta.	03
John Foster Sta.	02
General Delivery	01
Postmaster	01

SAN ANTONIO 782

POST OFFICE BOXES

Box Nos.		
1-300	Main Office	91
601-900	Main Office	93
901-1231	Main Office	94
1241-1540	Main Office	95
1541-1840	Main Office	96
1841-2171	Main Office	97
2181-2480	Main Office	98
2481-2780	Main Office	99
3001-3639	South San Antonio Sta.	11
5001-5528	Beacon Hill Sta.	01
6001-6999	Alamo Heights Br.	09
7001-7779	A Sta	07
8001-8695	Wainright Sta.	08
9001-9394	Guilbeau Sta	04
10001-10357	Hackberry Sta.	10
12001-12678	Laurel Heights Sta.	12
13001-13440	Cresthaven Sta.	13
14001-14535	Harlandale Sta.	14
16001-16299	Lapham Sta	46
18001-18428	Serna	18
20001-20399	J Frank Dobie	20
21001-21597	Terrell Wells Sta.	21
23001-23355	Highland Hills Sta.	23
27001-27391	Valley Hi Sta	27
28001-28529	University Park	

Sta......	28
30001-30199 Colonies North Contract Sta...	85
32001-32638 Nimitz Sta.....	16
37001-37392 Los Jardines	37

RURAL ROUTES

1.....	23
2.....	28
3.....	18
4.....	28
5.....	11
6.....	20
7.....	21
8.....	26
9.....	27
10.....	16
11.....	13
12.....	18
13.....	21
14.....	28
15.....	21
16.....	16
17.....	28

STATIONS, BRANCHES AND UNITS

Alamo Heights Br.....	09
Beacon Hill Sta.....	01
Brooks AFB Br.....	35
Cresthaven Sta.....	13
Fort Sam Houston Sta.....	34
Guilbeau Sta.....	04
Hackberry Sta.....	10
Harlandale Sta.....	14
Highland Hills Sta.....	23
J Frank Dobie Sta.....	20
Kelly AFB Br.....	41
Lackland AFB Br.....	36
Lapham Sta.....	16
Laurel Heights Sta.....	12
Los Jardines Br.....	37
Medina Base Br.....	36
Natural Bridge Caverns Rural Br.....	18
Nimitz Dta.....	16
Olmos Park Br.....	12
Serna Sta.....	18
South San Antonio Sta.....	11
Terrell Wells Sta.....	21
University Park Sta.....	27
Valley Hi Br.....	27
Wainwright Sta.....	08
Wilford Hall USAF Hosp Br.....	36
General Delivery.....	05
Postmaster.....	84

APARTMENTS, HOTELS, MOTELS

Aurora Apartment, 509 Howard.....	12
Bali Hai, 1234 E Mulberry.....	09
Bel-Air Motel, 511 S St Marys.....	85
Belmeade, 119 W Hathaway.....	09
Blue Bonnet, 426 N St Marys.....	05
Calvert, 136 Main Plaza.....	05
Capri, 211 Natalen.....	09
Casa Manana Motor, Highway 90 W.....	27
Crockett, 301 E Crockett.....	05
El Tropicano Motor, 110 Lexington.....	05
Flamingo, 1131 Austin Hwy.....	09
Granada Inn, 402 S St Marys.....	05
Grayson House, 819 E Grayson.....	08
Gunter, 205 E Houston.....	05
Highland Hills, 231 Burkedale.....	23
Hillcrest, 1243 Babcock.....	01
Hilton'S Palacio Del Rio, 203 S Alamo.....	05
Holiday, 3535 Broadway.....	09
La Mansion Motor Hotel 112 College.....	05
Le Chalet, 832 E Grayson.....	08
Menger, 204 Alamo Plaza.....	05
Morris, 128 Main Plaza.....	05
Navarro, 116 Navarro.....	05
Nueces, 513 N St Marys.....	05
Pan American, 5433 Broadway.....	09
Park Motel, 3617 Broadway.....	09
Park Plaza Motel, 2908 Broadway.....	09
Park Terrace, 201 Humphrey.....	09
Ramada Inn, 333 Military Dr NW.....	16
Rio Lado Motel, 1100 N St Marys.....	15
Robert E Lee, 111 W Travis.....	05
Saint Anthony, 300 E Travis.....	05
Sheraton San Antonio Motor Inn, 1400 Austin Hwy.....	09
South Saint Marys, 610 S St Marys.....	05
Sunset Ridge, 116 Vanderheck.....	09
Thunderbird, 211 W French.....	12
Travelers, 220 Broadway.....	05
Wayfarer Motor Hotel, 601 E Elmira.....	12
Westerner, 1116 Austin Hwy.....	09

BUILDINGS

Adams, 8622 Crownhill.....	09
Alamo National, 105 S St Marys.....	05
American Hospital & Life, 106 E Pecan.....	85
Architects & Engineers, 342 W Woodlawn.....	12
Aztec, 211 E Commerce.....	05
Brady, 202 E Houston.....	05
Calcasieu, 214 Broadway.....	04
Calvert, 535 S Main.....	05
Eighteen Hundred 1800 Loop 410 NW.....	17
Executive K, 1017 N Main.....	12
Farm & Home, 403 E Travis.....	05
Federal, 615 E Houston.....	05
Frost National Bank, Main Plaza W.....	85
Gibbs, 105 N Alamo.....	05
Glass, 4600 Broadway.....	09
Government Personnel Mutual, 800 N W Loop 410.....	16
Gpm 800 Loop 410 NW.....	16
Gunter, 159 E Houston.....	05
Hedrick, 603 N St Marys.....	05
International, 318 W Houston.....	05
James K, 419 S Main.....	04
Kallison Professional, 111 W Laurel.....	12
Kallison Tower, 1222 N Main.....	12
Kallison, 434 S Main.....	05
Lexington, 109 Lexington.....	05
M-S Tower, 730 N Main.....	05
Majestic, 212 E Houston.....	05
Maverick, 606 N Presa.....	05
Medical Professional, 1303 Mc Cullough.....	12
Mexican Consulate, 127 Navarro.....	05
Milam, 115 E Travis.....	05
Moore, 106 Broadway.....	05
Morris K, 214 Dwyer.....	04
National Bank Of Commerce, 430 Soledad.....	05
Nix Professional, 414 Navarro.....	05
Oppenheimer, 212 E Commerce.....	05
Petroleum Center, 900 N E Loop 410.....	09
Petroleum Commerce, 201 N St Marys.....	05
Plaza Professional, 6936 San Pedro.....	16
R L White, 116 E Travis.....	05
San Antonio Produce Terminal Market, 1500 S Zarzamora.....	87
San Antonio Savings, 111 Soledad.....	05
South Texas, 603 Navarro.....	05
Texas Continental, 406 W Market.....	05
Texas Theatre, 151 E Houston.....	05
Three A Life, 118 Broadway.....	05
Three O One, 301 Broadway.....	05
Tower Life, 310 S St Marys.....	05
Travis Park West 711 Navarro.....	05
Travis, 405 N St Marys.....	05
U S A A, 4119 Broadway.....	88
Western Union, 319 E Commerce.....	85
Y M C A 903 N St Marys.....	05

GOVERNMENT OFFICES

City Hall, Military Plaza.....	05
Court House, Main Plaza S.....	04
Federal, 615 E Houston.....	05

HOSPITALS

Baptist Memorial, 111 Dallas.....	05
Cypress Sanitorium, 300 W Cypress.....	12
Laurelwood Sanatorium, 2717 N Flores.....	12
Luthern General Hospital, 701 S Zarzamora.....	87
Medical & Convalescent, 323 W Cypress.....	12
Medical Arts, Medical Arts Bldg.....	05
Nix Memorial, 414 Navarro.....	05
Osteopathic Hospital, 210 W

Ashby 12
Robert B Green, 515 Morales 07
Saints, 501 S Hackberry 03
Salvation Army, 4019
    Broadway 09
San Antonio State
    Tuberculosis, Military Dr
    SE 23
San Antonio State, 5800
    Presa 23
Santa Rosa Medical Center,
    519 W Houston 07
Southwest Texas Methodist,
    Louis Pasteur & Wm Mayo
    Dr 29

MILITARY INSTALLATIONS

Brooks A F B 35
Ft Sam Houston 34
Kelly AFB 41
Lackland A F B 36
U S A F Security Service 43

UNIVERSITIES AND COLLEGES

Assumption Seminary, 3016
    W French 28
Draughons Business, 411 E
    Martin 05
Durhams Business, 105 San
    Pedro 05
Incarnate Word, 4301
    Broadway 09
International Bible, 2369
    Benrus 28
Nazarene Bible Institute, 700
    Lombrano 07
Oblate College Of The
    Southwest, 285 Oblate 16
Our Lady Of The Lake, 411
    SW 24th 07
Saint Johns Seminary, 222 E
    Mitchell 10
Saint Marys University, 2700
    Cincinnati 28
Saint Philips, 2111 Nevada 03
San Antonio, 1300 San
    Pedro 12
Trinity University, 715
    Stadium Dr 12
University Of Texas Medical
    School, 7703 Floyd Curl 29

WACO 767

POST OFFICE BOXES

Box Nos.
1-2451   Main Office 03
3001-3497   Colonial Sta 07
4001-4564   Bellmead Br 05
5001-5444   Mitchell
                 Avenue Sta 08
6001-6445   B U Station 06
7000-8389   Westview Sta 10

RURAL ROUTES

1,2 10
3 08
4,5 05
6 06

7,9 05
10 08

STATIONS, BRANCHES AND UNITS

B U Sta 06
Bellmead Br 04
Beverly Br 11
Colonial Sta 07
Lake Air Sta 10
Mitchell Ave Sta 08
Robinson Br 06
Veterans Administration Br 11
Westview Sta 10
General Delivery 03
Postmaster 01

BUILDINGS

Amicable, 425 Austin 01
Citizens Tower 501 Franklin ... 01
Federal, 800 Franklin 01
First National Bank, 811
    Washington 01
Lake Air National Bank Bldg,
    4901 Bosque 10
Liberty, 104 N 6th 01
Medical Arts, 900 Austin 01
Texas Center 900
    Washington 01

GOVERNMENT OFFICES

City Hall 01
County Jail, 219 N 6th 01
Court House Annex, 219 N
    6th 01
Court House, 501
    Washington 01
Vet Admin Regional Office,
    1400 N Valley Mills Dr 10

HOSPITALS

Hillcrest Memorial Hospital,
    3000 Herring 08
Providence Hospital, 1725
    Colcord 07
Veterans 11

UNIVERSITIES AND COLLEGES

Baylor University, 5th &
    Speight 06
Mclennan Community
    College, 1400 College 08
Paul Quinn College, 1020
    Elm 04
Texas State Technical Inst 05

WICHITA FALLS 763

POST OFFICE BOXES

Box Nos.
1-2611   Main Office 07
3000-3399   Monroe Street
                 Sta 09
4000-4399   University Park
                 Sta 08
5000-5399   Main Office 07
6000-6200   Sheppard A F
                 B Br 11

RURAL ROUTES

1,2 01
3 08
4 07

STATIONS, BRANCHES AND UNITS

Monroe Street Sta 09
Sheppard A F B Br 11
University Park Sta 08
General Delivery 07
Postmaster 07

APARTMENTS, HOTELS, MOTELS

Bel-Air, 918 E Scott 07
Brigadoon, 3220 Seymour Rd . 09
Camelot, 2202 Harrison 08
Catalina, Henrietta Rd 09
Chesterfield, 906 Grant 01
Flamingo, 3136 Seymour
    Hwy 01
Highlander, 2020 Santa Fe 09
Holiday Inn, 8th & Scott 07
Imperial 400, 306 Scott 01
Islands, 4709 Taft 08
Marchman, 10th & Lamar 07
Ramada Inn, 1211 Red River
    Expy 07
River Oaks, 1020 Red River
    Expy 07
Sands, 3153 Seymour Hwy 07
Sherwood Forest, 1717
    Hampstead 02
Southmoor, 3709 Southmoor .. 02
Spanish Trace, 4602 Spanish
    Trace 10
Timbers, 500 Fillmore 01
Town House, 1112 Sheppard
    Access Rd 07
Trade Winds, 1212 Broad 07
Triple D, Henrietta Rd 07
Villa, 4027 Eastside Dr 08
Wayfarer, Hwy 287 07
Wichita Manor, 2102-A
    Virginia Dr 09
William-Mary, 1000 - 10th 01

BUILDINGS

Brook Medical Center, 710
    Brook 01
Central Plaza, 211 Oil
    Center 02
City National Bank, 800
    Scott 01
County Court House, 6th &
    Lamar 01
Featherston, 922 - 8th 01
Federal, 1000 Lamar 01
First National, 708 - 8th 01
First-Wichita Nat'L, 719
    Scott 01
Hamilton, 900 - 8th 01
Medical & Surgical, 1518 -
    10th 01
Medical Arts, 500 Broad 01
Memorial Auditorium, 1300 -
    7th 01
Oil &gas, 813 - 8th 01
Parker Square Bank, Parker
    Square 08

UTAH
(Abbreviation: UT)

Alta, R. Br. Sandy..................84870
Altamont................................84001
Alton.....................................84710
Altonah..................................84002
American Fork (1st)...............84003
Aneth, R. Br. Montezuma
   Creek..............................84510
Annabella..............................84711
Antimony, R. Br. Junction.....84712
Arcadia..................................84005
Aurora....................................84620
Axtell.....................................84621
Bear River City.......................84301
Beaver...................................84713
Ben Lomond, Sta. Ogden.......84404
Beryl......................................84714
Bicknell.................................84715
   Torrey, R. Br......................84775
Bingham Canyon.....................84006
Blanding................................84511
Bluebell.................................84007
Bluff......................................84512
Bonanza.................................84008
Boulder..................................84716
Bountiful (1st).........................84010
Bridgeland.............................84012
Brigham City (1st)..................84302
   Collinston, R. Br.................84306
Bryce Canyon, R. Br.
   Panguitch..........................84717
Cache Junction.......................84304
Cannonville, R. Br. Tropic......84518
Castle Dale.............................84513
Castle Gate............................84514
Cedar City (1st)......................84720
   Kanarraville, R. Br.............84742
Cedar Valley..........................84013
Centerfield.............................84622
Centerville.............................84014
Central...................................84722 .
Chester, R. Br. Moroni...........84623
Circleville...............................84723
Cisco, R. Br. Green River.......84515
Clarkston................................84305
Clawson.................................84516
Clearfield (1st)........................84015
   Freeport Center, Sta...........84016
Cleveland...............................84518
Coalville.................................84017
Collinston, R. Br. Brigham
   City..................................84306
Columbia................................84519
Corinne..................................84307
Cornish, R. Br. Lewiston........84308
Cottonwood, Br. Salt Lake
   City..................................84121
Croydon..................................84018
Delta......................................84624
Deseret...................................84625
Deweyville..............................84309
Dragerton...............................84520
Draper....................................84020
Duchesne...............................84021
   Fruitland, R. Br..................84027
Dugway...................................84022
Dutch John.............................84023
Echo.......................................84024
Eden.......................................84310
Elberta...................................84626

Elmo.......................................84521
Elsinore..................................84724
Emery.....................................84522
Enterprise...............................84725
Ephraim..................................84627
Escalante................................84726
Eureka....................................84628
Fairgrounds, Sta. Salt Lake
   City..................................84116
Fairview..................................84629
Farmington.............................84025
Fayette, R. Br. Gunnison........84630
Ferron.....................................84523
Fielding..................................84311
Fillmore..................................84631
   Scipio, R. Br......................84656
Foothill, Sta. Salt Lake City...84108
Fort Duchesne.........................84026
   Gusher, R. Br.....................84030
   Ouray, R. Br......................84059
   Tridell, R. Br.....................84076
Fountain Green........................84632
Freeport Center, Sta.
   Clearfield...........................84016
Fremont..................................84727
Fruitland, R. Br. Duchesne.....84027
Fry Canyon.............................84524
Garden City............................84028
Garland...................................84312
Garrison..................................84728
Glen Canyon, R. Br. Kanab....84741
Glendale.................................84729
Glenwood................................84730
Gorder, Sta. Ogden.................84403
Goshen...................................84633
Granger-Hunter, Br. Salt
   Lake City (see appendix)
Grantsville..............................84029
Green River.............................84525
   Cisco, R. Br.......................84515
Greenville...............................84731
Greenwich...............................84732
Grouse Creek..........................84313
Gunlock..................................84733
Gunnison................................84634
   Fayette, R. Br....................84630
Gusher, R. Br. Fort
   Duchesne..........................84030
Hanksville..............................84734
Hanna.....................................84031
Hatch......................................84735
Heber City..............................84032
Helper.....................................84526
Henefer...................................84033
Henrieville..............................84736
Hiawatha................................84527
Hill A F B, Br. Ogden.............84406
Hinckley.................................84635
Holden....................................84636
Holladay, Br. Salt Lake City...84117
Honeyville..............................84314
Hooper....................................84315
Howell....................................84316
Huntington..............................84528
Huntsville...............................84317
Hurricane...............................84737
Hyde Park...............................84318
Hyrum.....................................84319
Ibapah....................................84034
Ivins......................................84738
Jensen....................................84035
Joseph....................................84739
Junction..................................84740

Antimony, R. Br......................84712
Kamas....................................84036
Kanab.....................................84741
Kanarraville, R. Br. Cedar
   City..................................84742
Kanosh....................................84637
Kaysville (1st)........................84037
Kearns, Br. Salt Lake City......84118
Kenilworth..............................84529
Kingston.................................84743
Koosharem..............................84744
La Sal.....................................84530
La Verkin................................84745
Laketown................................84038
Lapoint...................................84039
Lark..84040
Layton (1st)............................84041
Leamington.............................84638
Leeds, R. Br. Saint George.....84746
Lehi..84043
Levan......................................84639
Lewiston.................................84320
   Cornish, R. Br...................84308
Loa...84747
Logan (1st).............................84321
Lyman.....................................84749
Lynndyl..................................84640
Magna (1st)............................84044
Mammoth................................84641
Manila.....................................84046
Manti......................................84642
Marysvale...............................84750
Mayfield.................................84643
Meadow...................................84644
Mendon...................................84325
Mexican Hat............................84531
   Monument Valley, R. Br......84536
Midvale (1st)..........................84047
Midway....................................84049
Milford....................................84751
Millcreek, Br. Salt Lake City...84109
Millville..................................84326
Minersville.............................84752
Moab (1st)..............................84532
Modena...................................84753
Mona......................................84645
Monroe....................................84754
Montezuma Creek....................84534
   Aneth, R. Br......................84510
Monticello...............................84535
Monument Valley, R. Br.
   Mexican Hat.......................84536
Morgan (1st)...........................84050
Moroni....................................84646
   Chester, R. Br....................84623
Mount Carmel.........................84755
Mount Pleasant.......................84647
Mountain Home.......................84051
Murray, Br. Salt Lake City......84107
Myton.....................................84052
Neola......................................84053
Nephi......................................84648
New Harmony..........................84757
Newcastle...............................84756
Newton...................................84327
North Ogden, Br. Ogden (see
   appendix)
North Salt Lake (1st)...............84054
Oak City..................................84649
Oakley....................................84055
Oasis......................................84650
OGDEN (1st) (see appendix)

Orangeville 84537
Orderville 84758
Orem (1st) 84057
Ouray, R. Br. Fort Duchesne...84059
Panguitch 84759
   Bryce Canyon, R. Br. 84717
Paradise 84328
Paragonah, R. Br. Parowan...84760
Park City 84060
Park Valley 84329
Parowan 84761
   Paragonah, R. Br. 84760
   Summit, R. Br 84772
Payson 84651
Peoa 84061
Pintura 84762
Pioneer, Sta. Salt Lake City..84111
Pleasant Grove (1st) 84062
Plymouth 84330
Portage 84331
Price (1st) 84501
Providence 84332
Provo (1st) 84601
Randlett 84063
Randolph 84064
Redmond 84652
Richfield (1st) 84701
Richmond 84333
Riverside 84334
Riverton 84065
Rockville, R. Br. Springdale...84763
Roosevelt 84066
Roy (1st) 84067
Rubys Inn 84764
Saint George (1st) 84770
   Leeds. R. Br ... .84746

Saint John 84069
Salem 84653
Salina 84654
SALT LAKE CITY (1st) (see
   appendix)
Saltair, R. Br. Salt Lake
   City 84101
Sandy (1st) 84070
Santa Clara 84765
Santaquin 84655
Scipio, R. Br. Fillmore 84656
Scofield 84538
Sevier 84766
Sigurd 84657
Smithfield 84335
Snowville 84336
South Ogden, Br. Ogden
   (see appendix)
South Salt Lake, Br. Salt
   Lake City 84115
Spanish Fork (1st) 84660
Spring City 84662
Springdale 84767
   Rockville, R. Br. 84763
   Zion National Park, R.
     Br. 84767
Springville (1st) 84663
Sterling 84665
Stockton 84071
Sugar House, Sta. Salt Lake
   City (see appendix)
Summit, R. Br. Parowan 84772
Sunnyside 84539
Tabiona 84072
Talmage 84073
Teasdale 84773

Thistle 84666
Thompson 84540
Tooele (1st) 84074
Toquerville 84774
Torrey, R. Br. Bicknell 84775
Tremonton 84337
Trenton 84338
Tridell, R. Br. Fort Duchesne..84076
Tropic 84776
   Cannonville, R. Br. 84718
Trout Creek 84077
University, Sta. Provo 84601
Utah State University, Sta.
   Logan 84321
Venice 84777
Vernal (1st) 84078
Vernon 84080
Virgin 84779
Wales 84667
Wallsburg 84082
Washington 84780
Washington Terrace, Br.
   Ogden (see appendix)
Wellington 84542
Wellsville 84339
Wendover 84083
West Jordan 84084
Whiterocks 84085
Willard 84340
Woodruff 84086
Woods Cross 84087
Zion National Park, R. Br.
   Springdale 84767

OGDEN 844

POST OFFICE BOXES

Box Nos.
1-1640   Main Office 02
2001-2999   Ben Lomond
                    Sta. 04
3001-3999   Gorder Sta. 03

RURAL ROUTES

1 01
2,3 04
4,5,6 03
7 04

STATIONS, BRANCHES AND UNITS

Ben Lomond Sta. 04
Gorder Sta. 03
Hill A F B Br. 06
North Ogden Br. 04
South Ogden Br. 03
Washington Terrace Br. 03
General Delivery 01
Postmaster 01

APARTMENTS, HOTELS, MOTELS

Ben Lomond, 411 25th 01
Bigler Desert Inn, 1825
     Washington Blvd. 01
Harrisville Heights, 301
     Goodyear 04
Holiday Inn, 3306
     Washington Blvd. 01
Imperial 400, 1956
     Washington Blvd. 01
Ramada Inn, 2433 Adams
     Ave. 01
Resthaven, 1910 Washington
     Blvd. 01
Travelodge Inn, 2110
     Washington Blvd. 01
Western, 449 27th 01

BUILDINGS

Bank Of Utah Plaza, 2651
     Washington Blvd. 01
Bank Of Utah, 2641
     Washington Blvd. 01
Beatrice, 2954 Washington
     Blvd. 01
Citizens National Bank, 2168
     Washington Blvd. 01
Commercial Security Bank,
     2491 Washington Blvd. 01
Eccles, 385 24th 01
Exchange, 600 Exchange Rd .. 01
Federal Employees Credit
     Union, 3650 Wall Ave. 03
Federal, 340 25th 01
First Security Bank, 2404
     Washington Blvd. 01
Forest Service, 505 25th 01
Kiesel, 2411 Kiesel Ave. 01
Medical Dental Center 950
     25th 01
Municipal, 2549 Washington
     Blvd. 01
North Ogden Municipal, 400
     E 2600 N 04
Ogden Clinic 2955 Harrison

Blvd. 03
Virginia Professional, 441
     24th 01

GOVERNMENT OFFICES

United States Post Office,
     278 24th 01
Western Internal Revenue
     Service Center, 1160 W
     12th 05

HOSPITALS

McKay-Dee Hospital Center
     3939 Harrison Blvd 03
Saint Benedict, 3000 Polk
     Ave. 03

MILITARY INSTALLATIONS

Defense Depot Ogden 01
Hill Air Force Base 06

UNIVERSITIES AND COLLEGES

Stevens Henager, 2644
     Washington Blvd. 01
Weber State 3750 Harrison
     Blvd. 03

SALT LAKE CITY 841

POST OFFICE BOXES

Box Nos.
1-2610   Main Office 10
6001-6148   Sugar House
                    Sta. 06
7001-7416   Murray Br. 07
8001-8447   Foothill Sta. 08
11001-11999   Pioneer Sta. 11
15001-15490   South Salt
                    Lake Br. 15
16001-16194   Fairgrounds
                    Sta. 16
17001-17497   Holladay Br. 17
18451-18578   Kearns Br. 18
19001-19316   Granger Hunter
                    Br. 19
21101-21446   Cottonwood Br. 21

STATIONS, BRANCHES AND UNITS

Cottonwood Br. 21
Fairgrounds Sta. 16
Foothill Sta. 08
Granger-Hunter Br. 19
Holladay Br. 17
Kearns Br. 18
Millcreek Br. 09
Murray Br. 07
Pioneer Sta. 11
Saltair Rural Br. 01
South Salt Lake Br. 15
Sugar House Sta. 06
General Delivery 01
Postmaster 01

APARTMENTS, HOTELS, MOTELS

Alben, 1810 S Main 15

Ambassador, 149 South 5th
     East 02
Annie Laurie, 326 East 1st
     South 11
Barbara Worth, 326 East
     South Temple 11
Bel-Aire, 750 East 2nd South. 02
Ben Albert, 130 South 5th
     East 02
Castle Heights, 141 1st Ave. 03
Charleston, 470 South 13th
     East 02
Clarendon, 53 South 3rd
     East 11
Congress, 167 South State 11
Covey, 239 East South
     Temple 11
Crestholme, 336 East South
     Temple 11
Del Roya, 335 East 3rd
     South 11
Douglas Arms, 920 East 5th
     South 02
Eagle Gate, 105 East South
     Temple 11
Eastcliff, 425 East 2nd
     South 11
Fairmont, 50 East 5th South. 11
Gray Stone, 1170 East 27th
     South 06
Graylyn, 205 2nd Ave. 03
Hillcrest, 155 1st Ave. 03
Karen Lee, 4122 South 4000
     West 20
Kensington, 174 North Main. 03
Kimball, 150 North Main 03
Lafayette, 56 South 3rd East. 11
Lorna Doone, 320 East 1st
     South 11
Los Gables, 131 South 3rd
     East 11
Miles, 110 West 3rd South ... 01
Newhouse, 402 South Main ... 01
Oxford, 119 West North
     Temple 03
Panorama, 8 Hillside Ave 03
Ritz, 435 East South Temple.. 11
Roosevelt, 256 East 3rd
     South 11
Royal Arms, 70 West North
     Temple 03
Stratton, 49 South 4th East... 11
Temple Square, 75 West
     South Temple 01
University Heights, 130 South
     13th East 02
University Village, 2200
     Sunnyside Ave. 08
Waldorf, 553 East 1st South.. 02
Wells, 125 1st Ave. 03
Woodruff, 235 South 2nd
     East 11

BUILDINGS

American Oil, 10 West 3rd
     South 01
Atlas, 36 1/2 West 2nd
     South 01
Beneficial Life, 57 West
     South Temple 01
Boston, 1 Exchange Pl 11

Continental Bank, 200 South
  Main... 01
Crandall, 10 West 1st South.. 01
Deseret, 79 South Main........... 01
El Paso Natural Gas, 315
  East 2nd South...................... 11
Executive, 455 East 4th
  South..................................... 11
Federal, 125 South State........ 11
First Security Bank, 405
  South Main.............................. 11
Judge, 8 East Broadway......... 11
Kearns, 136 South Main.......... 01
Kennecott, 5 South Main........ 11
Ness, 28 West 2nd South........ 01
Newhouse, 10 Exchange Pl...... 11
Phillips Petroleum, 68 South
  Main..................................... 01
Salt Palace Complex, 100
  South West Temple.............. 01
Surety Life, 1935 South
  Main..................................... 15

Tribune, 143 South Main........ 11
Union Pacific Depot 3rd West
  And So Temple...................... 01
University Club, 136 E S
  Temple.................................. 11
Walker Bank, 175 South
  Main..................................... 11

HOSPITALS

Cottonwood, 5770 South 3rd
  East....................................... 07
Fort Douglas Veterans, 500
  Foothill Blvd......................... 13
Holy Cross, 1045 East 1st
  South..................................... 02
Latter-Day Saints, 325 8th
  Ave.. 03
Primary Childrens, 320 12th
  Ave.. 03
Saint Marks, 803 North 2nd
  West....................................... 03

Shriners Childrens, 1275
  Fairfax Ave............................ 03
University, 50 N Medical Dr.... 12
Valley West, 4160 West 3400
  South..................................... 20

UNIVERSITIES AND COLLEGES

B Y U Adult Education
  Center, 200 North Main....... 03
L D S Business, 411 E S
  Temple.................................. 11
Rowland Hall, 205 1st Ave..... 03
Saint Mary-Of-The-Wasatch,
  3000 East 13th South.......... 08
Stevens-Henager, 350 South
  7th East................................ 02
University Of Utah, 1400
  East 2nd South...................... 12
Westminister, 1800 South
  13th East................................ 05

VERMONT
(Abbreviation: VT)

Adamant 05640
Albany 05820
Alburg 05440
Arlington 05250
Ascutney 05030
Averill, R. Br. Canaan 05901
Bakersfield 05441
Barnard 05031
Barnet 05821
Barre (1st) 05641
Barton 05822
　Glover, R. Br. 05839
Bartonsville 05140
Beebe Plain 05823
Beecher Falls 05902
Bellows Falls (1st) 05101
Belmont 05730
Belvidere Center 05442
Bennington (1st) 05201
Bennington College, Sta.
　Bennington 05201
Benson, R. Br. Fair Haven ....057?1
Bethel 05032
Bolton Valley, R. Br.
　Richmond 05477
Bomoseen 05732
Bondville 05340
Bradford 05033
Brandon 05733
Brattleboro (1st) 05301
　South Newfane, R. Br. 05351
　West Brattleboro, Sta. 05301
Bread Loaf, R. Br.
　Middlebury 05753
Bridgewater 05034
Bridgewater Corners 05035
Bridport 05734
Bristol 05443
Brookfield 05036
Brownsville 05037
Burlington (1st) 05401
　North Burlington, Sta. 05401
　South Burlington, Br. 05401
　Winooski, Br. 05404
Cabot 05647
Calais 05648
Cambridge 05444
Cambridgeport 05141
Canaan 05903
　Averill, R. Br. 05901
Castleton 05735
Cavendish 05142
Center Rutland 05736
Charlotte 05445
Chelsea 05038
Chester 05143
Chester Depot 05144
Chittenden 05737
Colchester 05446
Concord 05824
　East Concord, R. Sta. 05834
Corinth 05039
Coventry 05825
Craftsbury 05826
Craftsbury Common 05827
Cuttingsville 05738
Danby 05739
Danville 05828
Derby 05829

Berby Line 05830
Dorset 05251
East Arlington 05252
East Barre 05649
East Berkshire 05447
East Burke 05832
East Calais 05650
East Charleston 05833
East Concord, R. Sta.
　Concord 05834
East Corinth 05040
East Dorset 05253
East Dover 05341
East Fairfield 05448
East Hardwick 05836
East Haven 05837
East Highgate, R. Sta.
　Highgate Center 05449
East Middlebury 05740
East Montpelier 05651
　North Montpelier, R. Br. 05666
East Poultney 05741
East Randolph 05041
East Ryegate 05042
East Saint Johnsbury 05838
East Thetford 05043
East Wallingford 05742
Eden 05652
　Eden Mills, R. Sta. 05653
Eden Mills, R. Sta. Eden 05653
Ely 05044
Enosburg Falls 05450
Essex 05451
Essex Junction (1st) 05452
Fair Haven 05743
　Benson, R. Br. 05731
Fairfax 05454
Fairfield 05455
Fairlee 05045
Ferrisburg 05456
Florence 05744
Forest Dale 05745
Franklin 05457
Gassetts 05145
Gaysville 05746
Gilman 05904
Glover, R. Br. Barton 05839
Grafton 05146
Granby 05840
Grand Isle 05458
Graniteville 05654
Granville 05747
Greensboro 05841
Greensboro Bend 05842
Groton 05046
Guildhall 05905
Hancock 05748
Hardwick 05843
Hartford 05047
Hartland 05048
Hartland Four Corners 05049
Healdville 05147
Highgate Center 05459
　East Highgate, R. Sta. 05449
Highgate Springs 05460
Hinesburg 05461
Hubbardton 05749
Huntington 05462
Huntington Center, R. Br.
　Huntington 05462
Hyde Park 05655
Hydeville 05750

Irasburg 05845
Island Pond 05846
Isle La Motte 05463
Jacksonville 05342
Jamaica 05343
Jay Peak, R. Br. North Troy 05859
Jeffersonville 05464
Jericho 05465
Jericho Center, R. Sta.
　Jericho 05465
Johnson 05656
Jonesville 05466
Killington 05751
Lake Elmore 05657
Leicester Junction 05752
Londonderry 05148
Lowell 05847
Lower Waterford 05848
Ludlow 05149
Lunenburg 05906
Lyman, Sta. White River
　Junction 05001
Lyndon 05849
Lyndon Center 05850
Lyndonville (1st) 05851
Mad River Glen, R. Br.
　Waitsfield 05673
Madonna, R. Br.
　Jeffersonville 05464
Manchester (1st) 05254
Manchester Center 05255
Manchester Depot, Sta.
　Manchester Center 05255
Marlboro 05344
Marshfield 05658
Mary Meyer, Sta. Townshend 05353
Mc Indoe Falls 05050
Middlebury (1st) 05753
Middletown Springs 05757
Milton 05468
Monkton 05469
Montgomery 05470
Montgomery Center 05471
Montpelier (1st) 05602
Moretown 05660
Morgan 05853
Morgan Center 05854
Morrisville 05661
Moscow 05662
Mount Holly 05758
Mount Snow, R. Br. West
　Dover 05356
New Haven 05472
Newbury 05051
Newfane 05345
Newport (1st) 05855
Newport Center 05857
North Bennington (1st) 05257
North Burlington, Sta.
　Burlington 05401
North Clarendon 05759
North Concord 05858
North Ferrisburg 05473
North Hartland 05052
North Hero 05474
North Hyde Park 05665
North Montpelier, R. Br. East
　Montpelier 05666
North Pomfret 05053
North Pownal 05260
North Springfield 05150
North Thetford 05054

North Troy.............05859
Northfield (1st).............05663
Northfield Falls.............05664
Norton.............05907
Norwich (1st).............05055
Orleans.............05860
Orwell.............05760
Passumpsic.............05861
Pawlet.............05761
Peacham.............05862
Perkinsville.............05151
Peru.............05152
Pittsfield.............05762
Pittsford.............05763
Plainfield.............05667
Plymouth.............05056
Plymouth Union.............05057
Post Mills.............05058
Poultney.............05764
Pownal.............05261
Proctor.............05765
Proctorsville.............05153
Putney (1st).............05346
Quechee.............05059
Randolph (1st).............05060
Randolph Center.............05061
Reading.............05062
Readsboro.............05350
Richford.............05476
Richmond.............05477
Ripton.............05766
Riverton.............05668
Rochester.............05767
Roxbury.............05669
Royalton.............05063
Rupert.............05768
Rutland (1st).............05701
Ryegate, R. Br. East
Ryegate.............05042
Saint Albans (1st).............05478
Saint Albans Bay.............05481
Saint Johnsbury (1st).............05819
Saint Johnsbury Center.............05863
Salisbury.............05769
Saxtons River.............05154
Shaftsbury.............05262
Sharon.............05065
Sheffield.............05866
Shelburne (1st).............05482

Sheldon.............05483
Sheldon Springs.............05485
Shoreham.............05770
South Barre.............05670
South Burlington, Br.
Burlington.............05401
South Dorset.............05263
South Hero.............05486
South Londonderry.............05155
South Lunenburg.............05908
South Newbury.............05066
South Newfane, R. Br.
Brattleboro.............05351
South Pomfret.............05067
South Royalton.............05068
South Ryegate.............05069
South Strafford.............05070
South Wallingford.............05771
South Woodbury.............05671
South Woodstock.............05071
Springfield (1st).............05156
Starksboro.............05487
Stockbridge.............05772
Stowe (1st).............05672
Strafford.............05072
Stratton Mountain, R. Br.
South Londonderry.............05155
Sutton.............05867
Swanton.............05488
Taftsville.............05073
Thetford.............05074
Thetford Center.............05075
Topsham.............05076
Townshend.............05353
Mary Meyer, Sta.............05353
West Townshend, R. Br. 05359
Troy.............05868
Tunbridge.............05077
Underhill.............05489
Underhill Center.............05490
Union Village.............05078
Vergennes (1st).............05491
Vernon.............05354
Vershire.............05079
Waitsfield.............05673
Wallingford.............05773
Wardsboro.............05355
Warren.............05674
Washington.............05675

Waterbury.............05676
Waterbury Center.............05677
Waterville.............05492
Websterville.............05678
Wells.............05774
Wells River.............05081
West Barnet.............05870
West Berkshire.............05493
West Brattleboro, Sta.
Brattleboro.............05301
West Burke.............05871
West Charleston.............05872
West Danville.............05873
West Dover.............05356
West Dummerston.............05357
West Fairlee.............05083
West Glover.............05875
West Halifax.............05358
West Hartford.............05084
West Newbury.............05085
West Pawlet.............05775
West Rupert.............05776
West Rutland.............05777
West Topsham.............05086
West Townshend, R. Br.
Townshend.............05359
West Wardsboro.............05360
Westfield.............05874
Westford.............05494
Westminster.............05158
Westminster Station.............05159
Weston.............05161
White River Junction (1st)....05001
Whiting.............05778
Whitingham.............05361
Wilder.............05088
Williamstown.............05679
Williamsville.............05362
Williston.............05495
Wilmington.............05363
Windsor (1st).............05089
Winooski, Br. Burlington.....05404
Wolcott.............05680
Woodbury.............05681
Woodstock (1st).............05091
Worcester.............05682

VIRGINIA
(Abbreviation: VA)

Abingdon (1st) 24210
Accomac 23301
Achilles 23001
Achsah, R. Br. Madison 22708
Afton 22920
Airlie, Br. Warrenton 22186
Alberte 23821
Aldie 22001
ALEXANDRIA (1st) (see appendix)
Affonso 22421
Allisonia 24310
Alps 22422
Altavista (1st) 24517
Alton 24520
Alum Ridge 24051
Amburg, R. Br. Deltaville 23044
Amelia Court House 23002
Amherst 24521
Amissville 22002
Ammon, R. Br. Ford 23822
Amonate 24601
Ampthill, Br. Richmond 23234
Andersonville 23911
Andover 24215
Annandale (1st) 22003
Appalachia 24216
Appomattox (1st) 24522
Ararat 24053
Accola 22010
Ark 23003
ARLINGTON (1st) (see appendix)
Arlington Hall, Sta.
Arlington 22212
Aroda 22709
Arrington 22922
Arvonia 23004
Ashburn 22011
Ashland (1st) 23005
Assawoman 23302
Atkins 24311
Atlantic 23303
Augusta Springs 24411
Austinville 24312
Axton 24054
Aylett 23009
Aylor 22710
Azalea, Br. Richmond 23227
Backbay, Sta. Virginia
Beach 23457
Bacova 24412
Baileys Crossroads, Br. Falls
Church 22041
Ballsville 23010
Banco 22711
Bandy 24602
Banner, R. Br. Coeburn 24231
Barboursville 22923
Barhamsville 23011
Barracks Road, Sta.
Charlottesville 22903
Barren Springs 24313
Baskerville 23915
Bassett (1st) 24055
Bastian 24314
Basye 22810
Batesville 22924
Battery Park 23304
Bavon 23013

Bay, Sta. Hampton 23363
Bayford 23305
Bayside, Sta. Virginia
Beach 23455
Bealeton 22712
Beaumont 23014
Beaverdam 23015
Beaverlett 23016
Bedford (1st) 24523
Bee 24217
Bellamy 23017
Belle Haven 23306
Belle View, Br. Alexandria 22307
Bellevue, Sta. Richmond 23227
Belmont, R. Br.
Spotsylvania 22553
Belspring 24058
Belt Boulevard, Br.
Richmond 23224
Ben Hur 24218
Bena 23018
Bennetts Creek, Br. Suffolk 23434
Bent Mountain 24059
Bentonville 22610
Bergton 22811
Berkley, Sta. Norfolk 23523
Berryville (1st) 22611
Beverlyville 22425
Big Island 24526
Big Rock 24603
Big Stone Gap 24219
Birchleaf 24220
Birdsnest 23307
Bishop 24604
Blackridge 23916
Blacksburg (1st) 24060
Blackstone (1st) 23824
Blackwater 24221
Blackwater Bridge, R. Sta.
Virginia Beach 23457
Blairs 24527
Blakes 23020
Bland 24315
Bloxom 23308
Blue Grass 24413
Blue Ridge 24064
Bluefield (1st) 24605
Bluemont 22012
Bohannon 23021
Boissevain 24606
Bolar 24414
Bon Air, Br. Richmond 23235
Bondtown, Sta. Coeburn 24230
Boones Mill 24065
Boonesville 22925
Boston 22713
Bowers Hill, R. Sta.
Chesapeake 23321
Bowlers Wharf, R. Br.
Tappahannock 22560
Bowling Green 22427
Boyce 22620
Boyd Tavern, R. Br. Keswick ...22947
Boydton 23917
Boykins 23827
Bracey 23919
Branchville 23828
Brandy Station 22714
Breaks 24607
Bremo Bluff 23022
Briarfield, Sta. Hampton 23369
Bridgewater 22812
Brightwood 22715

Bristol (1st) 24201
Bristow 22013
Broad Rock, Br. Richmond 23224
Broad Run 22014
Broadford 24316
Broadway 22815
Brodnax 23920
Brooke 22430
Brookneal 24528
Browns Store 22431
Brownsburg 24415
Browntown, R. Br.
Bentonville 22610
Brucetown 22622
Bruington 23023
Buchanan 24066
Buckingham 23921
Buckroe Beach, Sta.
Hampton 23364
Buena Vista (1st) 24416
Buffalo Junction 24529
Buford, Br. Richmond 23235
Bumpass 23024
Burgess 22432
Burke, Br. Springfield 22015
Burkes Garden, Br. Tazewell ...24608
Burkeville 23922
Burnsville 24420
Burr Hill 22433
Butyto 22434
Bybee 22926
Callands 24530
Callao 22435
Callaway 24067
Calverton 22016
Cambria, Sta.
Christiansburg 24073
Camden Mills, R. Sta.
Chesapeake 23320
Cana 24317
Cape Charles 23310
Cape Charles Air Force Sta.
Br. Cape Charles 23310
Capeville 23313
Capron 23829
Cardinal 23025
Caret 22436
Carousel, Br. Richmond 23225
Carrollton 23314
Carrsville 23315
Carson 23830
Cartersville 23027
Carterton, R. Br. Lebanon 24266
Carysbrook 22927
Casanova 22017
Cascade 24069
Cash 23028
Castleton 22716
Castlewood 24224
Catawba 24070
Catawba Sanatorium, R.
Br. 24071
Catawba Sanatorium, R. Br.
Catawba 24071
Catharpin 22018
Catlett 22019
Cauthornville 23029
Cedar Bluff 24609
Center Cross 22437
Central, Sta. Arlington 22203
Central, Sta. Richmond 23219
Central Martinsville, Sta.
Martinsville 24112

Centreville....................22020
Ceres...........................24318
Champlain....................22438
Chance.........................22439
Chancellor, R. Br.
  Fredericksburg...........22440
Chantilly......................22021
Charles City..................23030
Charlotte Court House.....23923
CHARLOTTESVILLE (1st) (see
  appendix)
Chase City (1st)............23924
Chatham (1st)...............24531
Check..........................24072
Cheriton......................23316
CHESAPEAKE (1st) (see
  appendix)
Chester (1st).................23831
Chester Gap..................22623
Chesterfield..................23832
Chilhowie.....................24319
Chincoteague.................23336
  Wallops Island, Br.......23337
Christchurch..................23031
Christiansburg (1st).........24073
Chuckatuck...................23339
Chula, R. Br. Amelia Court
  House........................23002
Church Road..................23833
Church View..................23032
Churchland, Br. Portsmouth...23703
Churchville...................24421
Cismont.......................22928
Civic Center, Sta. Richmond...23240
Claremont....................23899
Clarksville (1st)..............23927
Claudville.....................24076
Clayville.......................23034
Clear Brook..................22624
Cleveland.....................24225
Clifford........................24533
Clifton.........................22024
Clifton Forge (1st)...........24422
Clinchburg, R. Br.
  Meadowview..............24321
Clinchco......................24226
Clinchport....................24227
Clintwood....................24228
Clover.........................24534
Cloverdale....................24077
Cluster Springs..............24535
Cobbs Creek.................23035
Cobham, R. Br. Keswick....22929
Coeburn......................24230
  Banner, R. Br.............24231
  Bondtown, Sta............24230
  Tacoma, R. Br............24232
Coleman Falls................24536
Coles Point...................22442
College, Sta. Fredericksburg...22401
Collinsville (1st).............24078
Cologne, R. Br. West Point...23037
Colonial Beach...............22443
Colonial Heights (1st).......23834
Columbia......................23038
Community, Br. Alexandria...22306
Conaway......................24611
Concord.......................24538
Conicville.....................22819
Copper Hill...................24079
Copper Valley................24080
Corbin.........................22446
Council, R. Br. Honaker.....24260

Court House, Sta. Arlington
  (see appendix)
Courtland......................23837
Covesville.....................22931
Covington (1st)...............24426
Craddockville.................23341
Cradock, Sta. Portsmouth
  (see appendix)
Craigsville....................24430
Creeds, R. Sta. Virginia
  Beach........................23457
Crewe (1st)...................23930
Criders........................22820
Criglersville, R. Br. Madison...22727
Crimora.......................24431
Cripple Creek.................24322
Crittenden.....................23342
Critz...........................24082
Crockett.......................24323
Cross Junction...............22625
Crossroads, Br. Roanoke...24012
Crouch........................22447
Crozet (1st)...................22932
Crozier........................23039
Crystal Hill...................24539
Cullen.........................23934
Culpeper (1st)................22701
Cumberland...................23040
Cumnor.......................23041
Customhouse, Sta. Norfolk...23514
Dabneys.......................23042
Dahlgren......................22448
Daleville.......................24083
Dam Neck, Sta. Virginia
  Beach........................23461
Damascus.....................24236
Dante..........................24237
Danville (1st).................24541
Darlington Heights...........23935
Davenport.....................24239
Davis Wharf...................23345
Dayton........................22821
De Bree, Sta. Norfolk........23517
Deep Creek, Sta.
  Chesapeake...............23323
Deerfield......................24432
Defense General Supply Ctr,
  Br. Richmond.............23219
Delaplane......................22025
Deltaville......................23043
  Amburg, R. Br...........23044
Denbigh, Sta. Newport News...23602
Dendron.......................23839
Denniston.....................24548
Dewitt.........................23840
Diggs..........................23045
Dillwyn........................23936
Dinwiddie.....................23841
Disputanta....................23842
Doe Hill.......................24433
Dogue.........................22451
Dolphin........................23843
Doran..........................24612
Doswell........................23047
Downings......................24452
Downtown, Sta. Leesburg...22075
Dragonville....................23048
Drakes Branch................23937
Draper.........................24324
Drewryville....................23844
Driver..........................23346
Dry Fork......................24549
Dryden........................24243

Dublin.........................24084
Duffield........................24244
Dugspur.......................24325
Dulles International Airport,
  Br. Washington, D C.....20041
Dumfries......................22026
Dundalow, Sta. Suffolk.....23434
Dundas........................23938
Dungannon...................24245
Dunn Loring..................22027
Dunnsville....................22454
Dutton.........................23050
Dyke...........................22935
Eads, Sta. Arlington.........22202
Eagle Rock....................24085
Earlysville.....................22936
East End, Sta. Richmond...23223
East Stone Gap...............24246
Eastville.......................23347
Ebony.........................23845
Eclipse........................23349
Edinburg.......................22824
Edwardsville..................22456
Eggleston......................24086
Elberon........................23846
Elk Creek.....................24326
Elkton (1st)...................22827
Elkwood.......................22718
Elliston........................24087
Emory.........................24327
Emporia (1st).................23847
Engleside, Br. Alexandria...22309
Epworth.......................23052
Esmont........................22937
Esserville, R. Br. Norton....24274
Etlan, R. Br. Madison.......22719
Ettrick, Br. Petersburg......23803
Evergreen......................23939
Evington......................24550
Ewing..........................24248
Exeter.........................24249
Exmore........................23350
Faber..........................22938
Fairfax (1st)...................22030
Fairfax Station, Br. Fairfax...22039
Fairfield.......................24435
Fairlawn, Br. Radford........24141
Falling Creek, Br. Richmond...23234
FALLS CHURCH (1st) (see
  appendix)
Falls Mills.....................24613
Falmouth, Br.
  Fredericksburg...........22401
Fancy Gap.....................24328
Farmville (1st)................23901
Farnham.......................22460
Federal Reserve, Sta.
  Richmond.................23213
Fentress, R. Sta.
  Chesapeake...............23322
Ferncliff.......................23053
Ferrum........................24088
Fieldale........................24089
Fife............................23054
Fincastle.......................24090
First Street, Sta. Radford....24141
Fishers Hill....................22626
Fishersville....................22939
Fleet, Br. Norfolk............23511
Flint Hill......................22627
Floyd..........................24091
Foneswood....................22461
Ford...........................23850

Forest 24551
Forest Hill, Sta. Richmond 23225
Fork Union 23055
Forksville 23940
Fort Belvoir (1st) 22060
Fort Blackmore 24250
Fort Defiance 24437
Fort Eustis, Sta. Newport
   News 23604
Fort Hill, Sta. Lynchburg 24502
Fort Lee, Br. Petersburg 23801
Fort Mitchell 23941
Fort Monroe, R. Br.
   Hampton 23351
Fort Myer, Sta. Arlington 22211
Fort Story, Sta. Virginia
   Beach 23459
Foster 23056
Fosters Falls 24329
Foxwells, R. Br. White Stone ..22578
Franconia, Br. Alexandria 22310
Franklin (1st) 23851
Franktown 23354
Fredericks Hall, R. Br.
   Mineral 23057
Fredericksburg (1st) 22401
   Chancellor, R. Br. 22440
   College, Sta. 22401
   Falmouth, Br. 22401
Free Union 22940
Freeman 23856
Fries 24330
Front Royal (1st) 22630
Fulks Run 22830
Gainesboro, R. Br.
   Winchester 22636
Gainesville 22065
Galax (1st) 24333
Garrisonville 22463
Gasburg 23857
Gate City (1st) 24251
Geer 22941
George Washington, Sta.
   Alexandria 22305
Gether 22464
Glade Spring 24340
Gladehill 24092
Gladstone 24553
Gladys 24554
Glasgow 24555
Glass, R. Br. Hayes 23072
Glen Allen 23060
Glen Lea, Br. Richmond 23223
Glen Lyn 24093
Glen Wilton 24438
Glenns, R. Br. Saluda 23149
Gloucester 23061
Gloucester Point 23062
Goldbond 24094
Goldvein 22720
Gonyon 22467
Goochland 23063
Goode 24556
Goodview 24095
Gordonsville 22942
Gore 22637
Goshen 24439
Grafton, Br. Yorktown 23490
Grandin Road, Sta. Roanoke
   (see appendix)
Graves Mill 22721
Gray 23858
Great Bridge, Sta.

Chesapeake 23320
Great Falls 22066
Green Bay 23942
Greenbackville 23356
Greenbush 23357
Greenville 24440
Greenway, R. Br. Mc Lean 22067
Greenwood 22943
Gretna 24557
Grimstead 23064
Grottoes 24441
Grundy (1st) 24614
   Roseann, R. Br. 24645
   Royal City, Sta. 24614
   Stacy, R. Br. 24616
Gum Spring 23065
Gwynn 23066
Hacksneck 23358
Hadensville 23067
Hague 22469
Halifax 24558
Hallieford 23068
Hallwood 23359
Hamilton 22068
Hampden Sydney 23943
HAMPTON (1st) (see
   appendix)
Hampton Institute, Sta.
   Hampton 23368
Hampton Roads, Br. Norfolk ..23511
Handsom 23859
Hanover 23069
Harborton 23389
Hardy 24101
Hardyville 23070
Harman 24618
Harrisonburg (1st) 22801
Hartfield 23071
Hartwood 22471
Hatton 24560
Hayes 23072
   Glass, R. Br. 23072
Hayfield, R. Br. Winchester 22638
Haymarket 22069
Haynesville 22472
Haysi 24256
Haywood 22722
Head Waters 24442
Healing Springs 24443
Healys 23073
Heathsville 22473
Helmet 23074
Henry 24102
Herndon (1st) 22070
Hickory, R. Sta. Chesapeake ..23322
Hidenwood, Sta. Newport
   News 23606
Highland Springs 23075
Hightown 24444
Hillsboro, R. Br. Purcellville ..22132
Hillsville (1st) 24343
Hiltons 24258
Hinton 22831
Hiwassee 24347
Hobson 23390
Holland 23391
Hollins, Br. Roanoke 24019
Hollins College, Br. Roanoke ..24020
Honaker 24260
   Council, R. Br. 24260
   Venia, R. Br. 24260
Hood 22723
Hopeton, R. Br. Parksley 23392

Hopewell (1st) 23860
Horntown 23395
Horsepen 24619
Horsey 23396
Hot Springs 24445
Howardsville, R. Br.
   Scottsville 24562
Howertons 22475
Huddleston 24104
Hudgins 23076
Hume 22639
Huntly 22640
Hurley 24620
Hurt 24563
Hustle 22476
Hyacinth 22477
Independence 24348
Indian Neck 23077
Indian River, Sta.
   Chesapeake 23325
Indian Valley 24105
Ingram 24564
Inman 24262
Iron Gate 24448
Ironto, R. Br. Elliston 24087
Irvington 22480
Irwin 23078
Isle of Wight 23397
Ivanhoe 24350
Ivor 23866
Ivy 22945
Jamaica 23079
James Store 23080
Jamestown 23081
Jamesville 23398
Jarratt 23867
Java 24565
Jefferson Manor, Br.
   Alexandria 22303
Jeffersonton 22724
Jenkins Bridge 23399
Jersey 22481
Jetersville 23083
Jewell Ridge 24622
Jewell Valley 24623
Jonesville 24263
Jordan Mines 24449
Kable, Sta. Staunton 24401
Kathmoor, R. Br. Alexandria ..22310
Kecoughtan, Sta. Hampton 23367
Keeling 24566
Keen Mountain 24624
Keene 22946
Keezletown 22832
Keller 23401
Kenbridge 23944
Kents Store 23084
Keokee 24265
Keswick 22947
   Boyd Tavern, R. Br. 22947
   Cobham, R. Br. 22929
Keysville 23947
Kilmarnock 22482
Kimballton 24107
King And Queen Court
   House 23085
King George 22485
   Owens, R. Br. 22532
King William 23086
Kinsale 22488
L C Page, Sta. Norfolk 23518
La Crosse 23950
Laban 23087

Laburnum Manor, Br.
  Richmond 23222
Lacey Spring 22833
Lackey 23402
Ladysmith 22501
Lafayette 24108
Lafayette Boulevard, Sta.
  Norfolk 23509
Lahore 22502
Lakeside, Br. Richmond 23228
Lambsburg 24351
Lancaster 22503
Lanesville 23088
Laneview 22504
Lanexa 23089
Langley A F B, Sta.
  Hampton 23365
Laurel, R. Br. Glen Allen 23060
Laurel Fork 24352
Lawrenceville (1st) 23868
Lebanon (1st) 24266
Lebanon Church 22641
Lee Hall, Sta. Newport News ...23603
Lee Mont 23403
Leesburg (1st) 22075
Lennig 24568
Leon 22725
Lewisetta 22505
Lexington (1st) 24450
Lightfoot 23090
Lignum 22726
Lilian, R. Br. Reedville 22506
Lincoln, Br. Purcellville 22078
Lincolnia, Br. Alexandria 22312
Linden 22642
Linville 22834
Lithia 24110
Little Plymouth, R. Br. West
  Point 23091
Lively 22507
Locust Dale 22948
Locust Grove 22508
Locust Hill 23092
Locustville 23404
London Bridge, Sta. Virginia
  Beach 23454
Long Island 24569
Loretto 22509
Lorne 22510
Lorton 22079
Lottsburg 22511
Louisa (1st) 23093
  Trevilians, R. Br. 23170
Lovettsville 22080
Lovingston 22949
Lowesville 22951
Lowmoor 24457
Lowry 24570
Lunenburg 23952
Luray (1st) 22835
Lynch Station 24571
LYNCHBURG (1st) (see
  appendix)
Lyndhurst 22952
Lynnhaven, Sta. Virginia
  Beach 23452
Machipongo 23405
Macon 23101
Madison 22727
  Achsah, R. Br. 22708
  Criglersville, R. Br. 22727
  Etlan, R. Br. 22719
Madison Heights 24572

Madison Mills 22953
Madisonville, R. Br.
  Pamplin 23958
Maidens 23102
Manakin Sabot 23103
Manassas (1st) 22110
Manassas Park, Br.
  Manassas 22110
Mangohick 23104
Mannboro 23105
Manquin 23106
Mappsville 23407
Marine Corps Base, Br.
  Quantico 22134
Marion (1st) 24354
Marionville 23408
Markham 22643
Marshall 22115
Martinsville (1st) 24112
Maryus 23107
Mascot 23108
Massanetta Springs, Br.
  Harrisonburg 22801
Massies Mill 22954
Mathews 23109
Matoaca, R. Br. Petersburg 23803
Mattaponi 23110
Maurertown 22644
Mavisdale 24627
Max Meadows 24360
Maxie 24628
Mayo 24573
Mc Clure 24269
Mc Coy 24111
Mc Dowell 24458
Mc Gaheysville 22840
Mc Kenney 23872
Mc Lean (1st) 22101
  Greenway, R. Br. 22067
Meadows of Dan 24120
Meadowview 24361
  Clinchburg, R. Br. 24321
Mears 23409
Mechanicsville (1st) 23111
Medical College, Sta.
  Richmond 23219
Meherrin 23954
Melfa 23410
Melrose, Sta. Roanoke 24017
Mendota 24270
Meredithville 23871
Merrifield, Br. Fairfax 22030
Merry Point 22513
Messick, Br. Hampton 23362
Metro, Br. Richmond 23231
Mid Town, Sta. Portsmouth 23707
Middlebrook 24459
Middleburg 22117
Middletown 22645
Midland 22728
Midlothian 23113
Milan, Sta. Norfolk 23508
Miles 23114
Milford 22514
Mill Gap, R. Br. Monterey 24462
Millboro 24460
Millboro Springs, R. Br.
  Millboro 24460
Miller Park, Sta. Lynchburg 24501
Miller School, R. Br.
  Charlottesville 22901
Millers Tavern 23115

Millwood 22646
Mine Run, R. Br. Unionville 22568
Mineral 23117
  Fredericks Hall, R. Br. 23057
  Orchid, R. Br. 23117
  Pendletons, R. Br. 23117
Mint Spring 24463
Miskimon 22516
Mission Home 22956
Mitchells 22729
Mobjack 23118
Modern, Sta. Hampton 23366
Modest Town 23412
Mollusk 22517
Moneta 24121
Monroe 24574
Montebello 24464
Monterey 24465
  Mill Gap, R. Br. 24462
Monticello, R. Br.
  Charlottesville 22901
Montpelier 23192
Montpelier Station 22957
Montrose Heights, Sta.
  Richmond 23231
Montross 22520
  Templeman, R. Br. 22563
Montvale 24122
Moon 23119
Morattico 22523
Morrisville, R. Br.
  Remington 22734
Mosby, Br. Falls Church 22042
Moseley 23120
Mount Crawford 22841
Mount Hermon, Br. Danville 24511
Mount Holly 22524
Mount Jackson 22842
Mount Landing, R. Br.
  Tappahannock 22560
Mount Sidney 24467
Mount Solon 22843
Mount Vernon 22121
Mountain Lake, R. Br.
  Pembroke 24136
Mouth of Wilson 24363
Mustoe 24468
Narrows 24124
Naruna 24576
Nassawadox 23413
Nathalie 24577
Natural Bridge 24578
Natural Bridge Station 24579
Naval Air Station, Br.
  Norfolk 23511
Naval Amphibious Base, Br.
  Norfolk 23521
Naval Hospital, Sta.
  Portsmouth 23708
Naval Weapons Station, Br.
  Yorktown 23491
Navy Annex, Br. Washington,
  D C. 20370
Navy Yard, Sta. Portsmouth 23709
Naxera 23122
Nellysford 22958
Nelson 24580
Nelsonia 23414
New Canton 23123
New Castle 24127
New Church 23415
New Hope 24469

New Kent 23124
New Market 22844
New Point 23125
New River 24129
Newbern 24126
Newcomb Hall, Sta.
   Charlottesville 22901
Newington 22122
Newport 24128
NEWPORT NEWS (1st) (see
   appendix)
Newsoms 23874
Newtown 23126
Nickelsville 24271
Nimrod Hall 24470
Ninde 22526
Nokesville 22123
Nomini Grove 22527
Nora 24272
NORFOLK (1st) (see
   appendix)
Norge 23127
North 23128
North, Sta. Arlington 22207
North Garden 22959
North Springfield, Br.
   Springfield 22151
North Tazewell 24630
Northside, Sta. Richmond 23222
Northwest, R. Sta.
   Chesapeake 23322
Norton (1st) 24273
   Esserville, R. Br. 24274
Norview, Sta. Norfolk 23513
Norwood 24581
Nottoway 23955
Nuttsville 22528
Oak Grove, R. Br. Colonial
   Beach 22443
Oak Hall 23416
Oakpark 22730
Oakton 22124
Oakwood 24631
Occoquan 22125
Ocean View, Sta. Norfolk 23503
Oceana, Sta. Virginia Beach .. 23453
Oceana N A S, Sta. Virginia
   Beach 23460
Oilville 23129
Oldhams 22529
Olive, Sta. Portsmouth (see
   appendix)
Onancock 23417
Onemo 23130
Onley 23418
Ophelia 22530
Orange (1st) 22960
Orchid, R. Br. Mineral 23117
Ordinary 23131
Oriskany 24130
Orkney Springs 22845
Orlean 22128
Ottoman, R. Br. Lancaster 22503
Overall 22648
Owens, R. Br. King George 22532
Oyster 23419
Paces, R. Br. South Boston ... 24592
Paeonian Springs 22129
Paint Bank 24131
Painter 23420
Palmer Springs 23957
Palmyra 22963

Pamplin 23958
Parcel Post Annex, Sta.
   Norfolk 23516
Paris 22130
Park, Sta. Waynesboro 22980
Parkfairfax, Sta. Alexandria 22302
Parksley 23421
   Hopeton, R. Br. 23392
Parkview, Sta. Newport
   News 23605
Parrott 24132
Partlow 22534
Patrick Springs 24133
Patterson 24633
Pearisburg 24134
Peary 23133
Pemberton 23134
Pembroke 24136
Pendletons, R. Br. Mineral 23117
Penhook 24137
Penn Laird 22846
Pennington Gap 24277
   Woodway, R. Br. 24295
Pentagon, Br. Washington, D
   C 20301
Petersburg (1st) 23803
   Ettrick, Br 23803
   Fort Lee, Br. 23801
   Matoaca, R. Br. 23803
   Walnut Hill, Sta. 23803
   Western, Sta. 23803
Pettis, R. Br. Staunton 24401
Phenix 23959
Philomont 22131
Phoebus, Sta. Hampton 23363
Pilgrims Knob 24634
Pilot 24138
Pimmit, Br. Falls Church 22043
Pine Dell, Br. Richmond 23229
Pinero 23136
Piney River 22964
Pittsville 24139
Plain View 23137
Pleasant Valley 22848
Pocahontas 24635
Pocoshock, Br. Richmond 23235
Poquoson, Br. Hampton 23362
Port Haywood 23138
Port Republic 24471
Port Royal 22535
Portlock, Sta. Chesapeake 23324
PORTSMOUTH (1st) (see
   appendix)
Potomac, Sta. Alexandria 22301
Pound 24279
Pounding Mill 24637
Powhatan 23139
Prater, R. Br. Vansant 24638
Pratts 22731
Preston King, Sta. Arlington ... 22205
Prince George 23875
Princess Anne, Sta. Virginia
   Beach 23456
Prospect 23960
Providence Forge 23140
Pulaski (1st) 24301
Pungo, R. Sta. Virginia
   Beach 23456
Pungoteague 23422
Purcellville 22132
Purdy, R. Br. Emporia 23847
Quantico (1st) 22134

Quicksburg 22847
Quinby 23423
Quinque 22965
Quinton 23141
Radford (1st) 24141
Radford College, Sta.
   Radford 24141
Radiant 22732
Randolph 23962
Raphine 24472
Rapidan 22733
Rappahannock Academy 22538
Raven 24639
Rawlings 23876
Rectortown 22140
Red Ash 24640
   Shortt Gap, R. Br. 24647
Red House 23963
Red Oak 23964
Redart 23142
Redwood 24146
Reedville 22539
   Lilian, R. Br. 22506
Regina 22540
Rehoboth 23965
Reliance 22649
Remington 22734
Remlik, R. Br. Urbanna 23175
Republican Grove 24585
Rescue 23424
Reston, R. Br. Herndon 22070
Reva 22735
Rhoadesville 22542
Rice 23966
Rich Creek 24147
Richardsville 22736
Richlands (1st) 24641
RICHMOND (1st) (see
   appendix)
Ridge, Br. Richmond 23229
Ridgeway 24148
Rileyville 22650
Riner 24149
Ringgold 24586
Ripplemead 24150
Riverdale, Sta. Hampton 23366
Rivermont, Sta. Lynchburg 24503
Riverton 22651
Rixeyville 22737
ROANOKE (1st) (see
   appendix)
Robley 22543
Rochelle 22738
Rockbridge Baths 24473
Rockfish 22966
Rockville 23146
Rocky Gap 24366
Rocky Mount (1st) 24151
Roda, R. Br. Appalachia 24216
Rollins Fork 22544
Rose Hill 24281
Roseann, R. Br. Grundy 24645
Rosedale 24280
Roseland 22967
Rosslyn, Sta. Arlington 22209
Round Hill 22141
Rowe 24646
Royal City, Sta. Grundy 24614
Ruby 22545
Ruckersville 22968
Rural Retreat 24368
Rushmere 23425

Rustburg........................24588
Ruther Glen....................22546
Ruthville.......................23147
Saint Brides, R. Sta.
  Chesapeake..................23322
Saint Charles..................24282
Saint Davids Church.......22652
Saint Paul.....................24283
Saint Stephens Church....23148
Salem (1st)....................24153
Saltville........................24370
Saluda..........................23149
Samos, R. Br. Urbanna....23175
Sanatorium, R. Br.
  Charlottesville.............22901
Sandston (1st)...............23150
Sandy Hook...................23153
Sandy Level...................24161
Sanford........................23426
Saunders, Sta. Richmond...23220
Saxe............................23567
Saxis...........................23427
Schley..........................23154
Schoolfield, Sta. Danville...24541
Schuyler........................22969
Scottsburg.....................24589
Scottsville.....................24590
  Howardsville, R. Br........24562
Seaford.........................23428
Sealston........................22547
Seapines, Sta. Virginia
  Beach..........................23451
Seaview........................23878
Sedley..........................23878
Selma...........................24474
Seven Corners, Br. Falls
  Church........................22044
Seven Fountains.............22653
Seven Mile Ford..............24373
Severn..........................23155
Shacklefords...................23156
Shadow.........................23157
Shanghai.......................23158
Sharps..........................22548
Shawsville.....................24162
Shenandoah...................22849
Shenandoah Caverns, R. Br.
  Quicksburg..................22847
Shiloh..........................22549
Shipman........................22971
Shirley Duke, Sta.
  Alexandria...................22304
Shirlington, Sta. Arlington...22206
Short Gap, R. Br. Red Ash...24647
Shumansville..................22550
Simonsdale, Sta.
  Portsmouth..................23701
Simpsons.......................24163
Singers Glen...................22850
Skippers........................23879
Skipwith........................23968
Smithfield (1st)...............23430
Snell, R. Br. Spotsylvania...22553
Snowden........................24591
Snowflake, R. Br. Gate City...24251
Somerset........................22972
Somerville......................22739
South, Sta. Arlington........22204
South Boston (1st)...........24592
South Covington, Sta.
  Covington....................24426
South Hill (1st)...............23970

South Martinsville, Sta.
  Martinsville..................24112
South Norfolk, Sta.
  Chesapeake..................23324
South Roanoke, Sta.
  Roanoke......................24014
Southampton, Sta. Hampton...23369
Southside, Sta. Richmond...23224
Sparta..........................22552
Speedwell.......................24374
Spencer.........................24165
Sperryville......................22740
  Woodville, R. Br.............22749
Spotsylvania...................22553
Spottswood....................24475
Spout Spring..................24593
Spring Grove...................23881
SPRINGFIELD (1st) (see
  appendix)
Springwood, R. Br.
  Buchanan....................24066
Sprouses Corner, R. Br.
  Dillwyn........................23936
Stacy, R. Br. Grundy........24616
Stafford.........................22554
Staffordsville...................24167
Stage Junction................23159
Stanardsville..................22973
Stanley..........................22851
Stanleytown (1st)............24168
Star Tannery...................22654
State Farm.....................23160
Staunton (1st)................24401
Steeles Tavern.................24476
Stephens City..................22655
Stephenson....................22656
Sterling.........................22170
Stevensburg...................22741
Stevensville....................23161
Stewart, Sta. Richmond...23221
Stewartsville, R. Br. Vinton...24179
Stonega.........................24285
Stony Creek....................23882
Stormont, R. Br. Saluda...23149
Strasburg (1st)................22657
Stratford........................22558
Stratford Hills, Br.
  Richmond....................23225
Stuart..........................24171
Stuarts Draft...................24477
Studley.........................23162
Suffolk (1st)....................23434
Sugar Grove....................24375
Sugar Loaf, Br. Roanoke...24018
Sumerduck.....................22742
Sunnyside, R. Br.
  Winchester...................22601
Sunset Hills, R. Br. Herndon...22070
Supply..........................22559
Surry...........................23883
Susan..........................23163
Sussex.........................23884
Sutherland.....................23885
Sutherlin.......................24594
Sweet Briar....................24595
Swoope........................24479
Swords Creek..................24649
Syria...........................22743
Syringa.........................23165
Tabb, R. Br. Newport News...23602
Tacoma, R. Br. Coeburn...24232
Tamworth.....................23166
Tangier........................23440

Tannersville....................24377
Tappahannock (1st).........22560
Tasley..........................23441
Tazewell (1st).................24651
Temperanceville...............23442
Temple Trailer, Sta.
  Alexandria...................22314
Tempieman, R. Br. Montross...22563
Tetotum........................22564
Thaxton........................24174
The Plains......................22171
Theological Seminary, Sta.
  Alexandria...................22304
Thomas Corner, Sta. Norfolk...23502
Thornburg......................22565
Timberlake, Br. Lynchburg...24502
Timberville.....................22853
Tiptop..........................24655
Toano...........................23168
Toms Brook....................22660
Topping........................23169
Townsend......................23443
Trammel........................24289
Trevilians, R. Br. Louisa...23170
Triangle........................22172
Triplet..........................23886
Trout Dale.....................24378
Troutville.......................24175
Troy............................22974
Tuckahoe, Br. Richmond...23229
Tucker Hill, R. Br. Kinsale...22488
Tunstall........................23172
Turbeville......................24596
Twymans Mill..................22744
Tye River.......................22975
Tyro............................22976
Union Hall......................24176
Union Level....................23973
Unionville.......................22567
  Mine Run, R. Br.............22568
University, Sta.
  Charlottesville.............22903
University of Richmond......23173
Upperville.......................22176
Upright.........................22569
Urbanna.......................23175
Valentines......................23887
Vansant........................24656
  Prater, R. Br...............24638
Venia, R. Br. Honaker.......24260
Vernon Hill.....................24597
Verona (1st)...................24482
Vesta..........................24177
Vesuvius.......................24483
Veterans Administration
  Hosp. Br. Richmond......23219
Victoria........................23974
Vienna (1st)...................22180
Viewtown......................22746
Village.........................22570
Villamont.......................24178
Vint Hill Farms, Br.
  Warrenton..................22186
Vinton (1st)....................24179
Virgilina........................24598
VIRGINIA BEACH (1st) (see
  appendix)
Virginia Union University,
  Sta. Richmond..............23220
Volney..........................24379
Wachapreague................25480
Wake...........................23176
Wakefield......................23888

Walkerton.................................23177
Wallops Island, Br.
  Chincoteague.....................23337
Walmsley.................................22571
Walnut Hill, Sta. Petersburg...23803
Walters, R. Br. Windsor.......23481
Wardtown.................................23482
Ware Neck.............................23178
Warfield..................................23889
Warm Springs.......................24484
Warner...................................23179
Warrenton (1st).....................22186
Warsaw (1st)..........................22572
Warwick, Sta. Newport News..23601
Washington.............................22747
Washingtons Birthplace.........22575
Water View............................23180
Waterford...............................22190
Waterlick...............................22661
Wattsville..............................23483
Waverly..................................23890
Waynesboro (1st)....................22980
Weber City, R. Br. Gate City...24251
Weems.....................................22576
Weirwood................................23484
Wellington, Br. Alexandria.....22308
West Annex, MOU. Norfolk....23520
West Augusta..........................24485
West End, Br. Richmond.........23230
West Norfolk, Br.
  Portsmouth.....................23703
West Point (1st).....................23181
  Cologne, R. Br..................23037
  Little Plymouth, R. Br........23091
West Springfield, Br.
  Springfield......................22152

Western, Sta. Petersburg......23803
Westhampton, Sta.
  Richmond.........................23226
Westmoreland.........................22577
Westwood, Br. Richmond.......23230
Weyers Cave..........................24486
Whaleyville............................23485
Whitacre................................22662
White Hall..............................22987
White Marsh...........................23183
White Plains............................23893
White Post..............................22663
White Stone............................22578
Whitethorne...........................24183
Whitetop................................24292
Whitewood..............................24657
Wicomico...............................23184
Wicomico Church....................22579
Williamsburg (1st)..................23185
Williamson Road, Sta.
  Roanoke..........................24012
Williamsville..........................24487
Willis....................................24380
Willis Wharf...........................23486
Wilmington.............................22988
Wilsons..................................23894
Winchester (1st)......................22601
  Gainesboro, R. Br.............22636
  Hayfield, R. Br.................22638
  Sunnyside, R. Br...............22601
Windmill Point, R. Br. White
  Stone...............................22578
Windsor..................................23487
  Walters, R. Br..................23481
Wingina..................................24599
Winterpock, R. Br.

Chesterfield...........................23832
Wirtz.....................................24184
Wise......................................24293
Witch Duck, Sta. Virginia
  Beach..............................23462
Withams.................................23488
Wolford..................................24658
Wolftown...............................22748
Woodberry Forest...................22989
Woodbridge (1st)....................22191
Woodford................................22580
Woodlawn...............................24381
Woodrow Wilson, R. Br.
  Fishersville.....................22939
Woodrum, Sta. Staunton........24401
Woods Cross Roads.................23190
Woodstock (1st)......................22664
Woodville, R. Br. Sperryville...22749
Woodway, R. Br. Pennington
  Gap.................................24295
Woolwine...............................24185
Wright, Sta. Norfolk...............23505
Wylliesburg............................23976
Wythe, Sta. Hampton.............23361
Wytheville (1st)......................24382
Yale......................................23897
Yards....................................24659
Yorkshire, Br. Manassas.........22110
Yorktown (1st)........................23490
  Grafton, Br.......................23490
  Naval Weapons Station,
  Br.................................23491
Zacata...................................22581
Zanoni...................................23191
Zuni......................................23898

ALEXANDRIA   223

POST OFFICE BOXES

Box Nos.

1-1359	Main Office	13
2001-2297	Potomac Sta.	01
3001-3348	Parkfairfax Sta.	02
4001-4148	Jefferson Manor Br.	03
5001-5127	George Washington Sta.	05
6001-6358	Community Br.	06
7001-7900	Belle View	07
9001-9645	Shirley Duke Sta.	04
10001-10424	Franconia	10
15001-15160	Engleside Br.	09

RURAL ROUTES

5		10

STATIONS, BRANCHES AND UNITS

Belle View Br.	07
Community Br.	06
Engleside Br.	09
Franconia Br.	10
George Washington Sta.	05
Jefferson Manor Br.	03
Kathmoor Rural Br.	10
Lincolnia Br.	12
Parkfairfax Sta.	02
Potomac Sta.	01
Shirley Duke Sta.	04
Temple Trailer Sta.	14
Theological Seminary Sta.	04
Wellington Br.	08
General Delivery	13
Postmaster	13

APARTMENTS, HOTELS, MOTELS

Americana Landmark Apartments, 16 Van Dorn S.	04
Auburn Gardens, 101 Glebe Rd E.	05
Belle Haven Towers, 6038 Richmond Hwy.	03
Beverly Park Gardens, 527 Four Mile Rd.	05
Bradlee Apartments, 3810 King.	02
Calvert Apartments, 3110 Mt Vernon Ave.	05
Chadwick Towers Apartments, 100 Reynolds S.	04
Charter House Motel, Edsall Rd & Shirley Hwy.	12
Dominion Gardens, 3800 Milan Dr.	05
Duchess Gardens, 4309 Duke.	04
George Mason Hotel, Prince & Washington.	13
Glebe House, 25 Glebe Rd W.	05
Goldengate Apartments, 3529 Leesburg Pike	02

Holiday Inn, 6100 Richmond Hwy.	03
Holmes Run Apartments, 5465 Morgan N.	12
Hunting Terrace Apartments, 1205 Washington S.	14
Hunting Towers Apartments, 1200 Washington S.	14
Jamestown Village, 1523 Van Dorn N.	04
Kent Towers, 5851 Quantrell Ave.	12
Landmark Towers, 101 Whiting S.	04
Landover House, 3201 Landover.	05
Mayfair Mall Apartments, 5335-5405 Duke.	04
Mayfair Towers Apartments, 5340 Duke.	04
Monticello, 805 King.	14
Mount Vernon Apartments, 8259 Russell Rd.	09
Mount Vernon Motor Lodge, 7226 Richmond Hwy.	06
Normandy Hills, 145 Normandy Hill Dr.	04
Olde Colony Motor Lodge, N Washington & 1st.	13
Park Alexandria Apartments, 5340 Holmes Run Pky.	04
Parkwood Terrace Apartments, 107 Ripley N.	04
Port Royal Apartments, 801 Pitt N.	14
Presidential Garden Apartments, Mt Vernon Ave & Russel.	05
Presidential Gardens Motor, Mt Vernon & Russell Rd.	05
River Towers, 6631 River Towers Dr.	07
Riverview Apartments, 1116 Pitt N.	14
Seminary Hill Apartments, 4700 Kenmore Ave.	04
Seminary Towers East, 4701 Kenmore Ave.	04
Seminary Towers West, 4801 Kenmore Ave.	04
Shirley Duke Apartments, 4447 Duke.	04
Southern Towers Apartments, 4901-5055 Seminary Rd.	11
Stones Motel, 4256 King.	02
Towne Motel, 808 Washington N.	14
Travelers Motel, 5916 Richmond Hwy.	03
Van Duke Apartments, 420 Van Dorn N.	04
Virginia Lodge, 6027 Richmond Hwy.	03
Virginia Motel, 700 Washington N.	14
Wagon Wheel Motel, 7212 Richmond Hwy.	06
Wapleton Mansion Apartments, 5250 Valley Forge Dr.	04
Warwick Village, 1 Kennedy.	05

BUILDINGS

Alexandria Medical, 312 Washington S.	14
American Red Cross, 615 St Asaph N.	14
Bradlee Medical, 3541 King.	02
Doniphan, 101 Columbus N.	14
Fruit Growers Express, 16 Roth.	14
George Washington Masonic Temple.	01
Hoffman, 2461 Eisenhower Ave.	14

HOSPITALS

Alexandria Hospital, 4320 Seminary Rd.	14
Circle Terrace Hospital, 904 Circle Terrace Dr.	02
Jefferson Memorial Hospital, 4600 King.	02

MILITARY INSTALLATIONS

Cameron Station, 5010 Duke.	14
Defense Documentation Center, 5010 Duke.	14
Defense Supply Agency, 5010 Duke.	14

ARLINGTON   222

POST OFFICE BOXES

Box Nos.

1-499	Main Office	10
501-999	Courthouse Sta.	16
1100-1199	Fort Myer Sta.	11
2000-2999	Eads Sta.	02
3000-3999	Central Sta.	03
4000-4999	South Sta.	04
5000-5999	Preston King Sta.	05
6000-6999	Shirlington Sta.	06
7000-7999	North Sta.	07
9000-9999	Rosslyn Sta.	09

STATIONS, BRANCHES AND UNITS

Arlington Hall Sta.	12
Central Sta.	03
Court House Sta.	01
Eads Sta.	02
Fort Myer Sta.	11
North Sta.	07
Preston King Sta.	05
Rosslyn Sta.	09
Shirlington Sta.	06
South Sta.	04
General Delivery	10
Postmaster	10

APARTMENTS, HOTELS, MOTELS

Arva Motor Hotel, 2201 Arlington Blvd.	01
Cardinal House, 3000 Spout Run Parkway.	01

Cherry Blossom Motor Inn,
3030 Columbia Pike............ 04
Clarendon Hotel Court, 3824
Wilson Blvd........................ 03
Crystal House, 1900 S Eads... 02
Diplomat, 5565 Columbia
Pike.................................. 04
Dominion Arms, 333 S Glebe
Rd.................................... 04
Dominion Plaza, 1200 S
Court House Rd.................. 04
Dominion Towers, 1201 S
Court House Rd.................. 04
Dorchester Towers, 2001
Columbia Pike.................... 04
Executive Central, 1201
South Scott........................ 04
Executive North, 1850
Columbia Pike.................... 04
Executive South, 1301 South
Scott................................. 04
Holiday Inn, Shirley Hwy & S
Glebe Rd........................... 06
Holiday Inn, 1499 Jefferson
Davis Highway................... 02
Holiday Inn, 1850 N Fort
Myer Dr............................ 09
Hospitality House Motor Inn
2000 Jefferson Davis Hwy.. 02
Iwo Jima Motor Hotel, 1501
Arlington Blvd................... 09
Marriott Motor Hotel, Crystal
City.................................. 02
Marriott Motor Hotel, Key
Bridge.............................. 09
Marriott Motor Hotel, Twin
Bridges............................ 02
Motel Fifty, 1601 Arlington
Blvd................................. 09
Park Adams, 2000 North
Adams............................... 01
Park Arlington, Arlington Blvd
& N Court House............... 01
Pentagon Motel, 901 S Clark.. 02
Potomac Towers, 2001 N
Adams............................... 01
River House South, 1600
South Joyce...................... 02
River House West, 1400
South Joyce...................... 02
River House, 1111 S Army
Navy Dr............................ 02
Shirlington House, 4201
South 31st........................ 06
South Gate Motor Hotel,
Shirley Hwy & S Glebe Rd.. 06
Virginian, 1500 Arlington
Blvd................................. 09
Wildwood Park, 5555
Columbia Pike.................... 04
Windsor Towers, 5535
Columbia Pike.................... 04

BUILDINGS

Jefferson, 1021 Arlington
Blvd................................. 09
Madison, 1111 Arlington
Blvd................................. 09
Tyler, 1121 Arlington Blvd.... 09
Washington, 1011 Arlington
Blvd................................. 09

622

GOVERNMENT OFFICES

Office Of Naval Research...... 17

MILITARY INSTALLATIONS

Arlington Hall...................... 12
Fort Myer........................... 11
Henderson Hall.................... 14
Office Of Naval Research...... 17

CHARLOTTESVILLE 229

POST OFFICE BOXES

Box Nos.
1-1608   Main Office...... 02
1841-4008   University Sta... 03
5001-5738   Barracks Road
Sta... 03

RURAL ROUTES

1,2,3,4,5,6,7,8...................... 01

STATIONS, BRANCHES AND UNITS

Barracks Road Sta................ 03
Miller School Rural Br.......... 01
Monticello Rural Br.............. 01
Newcomb Hall Sta................ 01
Sanatorium Rural Br............ 01
University Sta...................... 03
General Delivery.................. 01
Postmaster......................... 02

UNIVERSITIES AND COLLEGES

University Of Virginia........... 04

CHESAPEAKE 233

POST OFFICE BOXES

Box Nos.
1-299   Bowers Hill
Rural Sta... 21
301-499   Northwest
Rural Sta... 22
501-599   Fentress Rural
Sta... 22
601-999   Money Order
Unit 01... 22
1001-2099   Main Office...... 20
5001-5299   So Norfolk Sta... 24
6001-6999   Deep Creek
Sta... 23
7501-7999   Portlock Sta..... 24
13001-13999 Indian River
Sta... 25
15001-15299 Great Bridge
Sta... 20

STATIONS, BRANCHES AND UNITS

Bowers Hill Rural Sta........... 21
Camden Mills Rural Sta........ 20
Deep Creek Sta.................... 23

Fentress Rural Sta................ 22
Great Bridge Sta.................. 20
Hickory Rural Sta................. 22
Indian River Sta................... 25
Northwest Rural Sta............. 22
Portlock Sta........................ 24
Saint Brides Rural Sta.......... 22
South Norfolk Sta................ 24
General Delivery.................. 20
Postmaster......................... 20

APARTMENTS, HOTELS, MOTELS

Cavalier, 1125 S Military
Hwy................................. 20
Colonial Motor Court, 5109
Geo Washington Hwy......... 23
Ellis, Military Hwy............... 23
Greenbriar, 2412 S Military
Hwy................................. 20
Holiday Inn, Military Hwy...... 23
Howard Johnson Motor Lodge,
Military Hwy...................... 23
Portsmouth, Military Hwy...... 23
Scotties, 4330 Bainbridge
Blvd................................. 24
Sunset Manor, Military Hwy... 23
Travelers, 2109 Bainbridge
Blvd................................. 24
Virginia Reel, Military Hwy.... 20

FALLS CHURCH 220

POST OFFICE BOXES

Box Nos.
1-699   Main Office...... 46
1000-1299   Bailey
Crossroads
Br... 41
2001-2372   Mosby............ 42
3001-3099   Pimmit........... 43
4001-5066   Seven Corners
Br... 44

STATIONS, BRANCHES AND UNITS

Baileys Crossroads Br.......... 41
Mosby Br............................ 42
Pimmit Br........................... 43
Seven Corners Br................. 44
General Delivery.................. 46
Postmaster......................... 46

BUILDINGS

Anderson, 450 W Broad St..... 46
City Hall, 300 Park Ave......... 46
Dominian, 311 Park Ave........ 46
Donovan, 106 Little Falls...... 46
Falls Church Medical Center,
6060 Arlington Blvd........... 44
Fink Professional, 200 Little
Falls................................. 46
Luria, 6269 Leesburg Pike..... 44
Medical Arts, 2946 Sleepy
Hollow Rd......................... 44
Melpar Inc, 7700 Arlington
Blvd................................. 46

Nasiff, 5611 Columbia Pike.... 41
Nationwide Insurance, 6506
  Arlington Blvd................... 42
Park Ave Professional, 313
  Park Ave.............................. 46
Professional Bldg. 5600
  Columbia Pike................... 41
Providence, 6521 Arlington
  Blvd.................................... 42
Robertson, 100 N
  Washington........................ 46
Seven Corners Medical, 6305
  Castle Place........................ 44
Seven Corners Professional,
  6319 Castle Place............... 44
The Lee, 5881 Leesburg Pike... 41
The Williamsburg, 108 N
  Virginia Ave....................... 46
Virginia, 210 Little Falls......... 46

HOSPITALS

Fairfax Hospital, 3300
  Gallows Rd........................ 46
Northern Va Mental Health,
  3302 Gallows Rd............... 42
Powhatan Nursing Home,
  2100 Powhatan................. 43
Whitehall Sanitarium 335
  Little Falls......................... 46

UNIVERSITIES AND COLLEGES

Northern Virginia Community,
  3443 S Carlyn Spring Rd... 41

HAMPTON   233

POST OFFICE BOXES

Box Nos.		
1-657	Main Office	69
600-899	Langley Air	
	Force Base	
	Sta.	65
1200-1999	Wythe Sta.	61
2000-2999	Poquoson Br.	62
3000-3999	Phoebus Sta.	63
4000-4999	Buckroe Beach	
	Sta.	64
5100-5999	Kecoughtan	
	Sta.	67
6000-6999	Hampton	
	Institute Sta.	68
7000-7999	Riverdale	69
9000-9999	Briarfield	69

STATIONS, BRANCHES AND UNITS

Bay Sta.	63
Briarfield Sta.	69
Buckroe Beach Sta.	64
Fort Monroe Rural Br.	51
Hampton Institute Sta.	68
Kecoughtan Sta.	67
Langley A F B Sta.	65
Messick Sta.	67
Modern Sta.	66
Phoebus Sta.	63
Poquoson Br.	62

Riverdale Sta................. 66
Southampton Sta.......... 69
Wythe Sta..................... 61
General Delivery........... 69
Postmaster................... 69

HOSPITALS

Bayberry........................ 69
Dixie............................. 69

LYNCHBURG   245

POST OFFICE BOXES

Box Nos.		
1-1540	Main Office	05
2001-2999	Miller Park Sta.	01
3001-3999	Rivermont Sta.	03
4001-4999	Fort Hill Sta	02

RURAL ROUTES

1	01
2	01
3	04
4	03

STATIONS, BRANCHES AND UNITS

Fort Hill Sta.	02
Miller Park Sta.	01
Rivermont Sta.	03
Timberlake Br.	02
General Delivery	05
Postmaster	05

HOSPITALS

Guggenheimer Memorial
  Hospital 1902 Grace
  Street............................... 04
Lynchburg General, 1901
  Tate Springs Rd................ 04
Lynchburg Training School &
  Hospital, Lynchburg, Va... 05
Virginia Baptist, 3300
  Rivermont Ave................. 04

UNIVERSITIES AND COLLEGES

Lynchburg College, 500
  Vernon.............................. 04
Randolph Macon Woman'S
  College, 2500 Rivermont
  Ave.................................. 04
Virginia Community College... 02
Virginia Seminary & College,
  2058 Garfield Ave............ 01

NEWPORT NEWS   236

POST OFFICE BOXES

Box Nos.		
1-980	Main Office	07
621-1378	Fort Eustis Sta.	04
1001-1899	Warwick Sta.	01
2001-2447	Denbigh Sta.	02
3001-3368	Lee Hall	03

5001-5798	Parkview Sta.	05
6001-6500	Hidenwood Sta.	06

STATIONS, BRANCHES AND UNITS

Denbigh Sta.	02
Fort Eustis Sta.	04
Hidenwood Sta.	06
Lee Hall Sta	03
Parkview Sta.	05
Tabb Rural Br.	02
Warwick Sta.	01
General Delivery	07
Postmaster	07

APARTMENTS, HOTELS, MOTELS

Beechmont, 204 Beechmont
  Dr..................................... 02
Beechmont, 335-391
  Beechmont Drive.............. 02
Boulevard, 100 Impala Dr..... 06
Cambridge, 5100 - 5134
  Goldsboro Dr.................... 05
Carriage Park, 11100
  Jefferson Ave.................... 01
Chantilly, 5500 Marshall Ave.. 05
Christopher Newport, 409
  Logan Pl............................ 01
Clover Leaf Village, 1 - 99
  Traverse Rd...................... 06
College Court, 12373
  Warwick Blvd................... 06
Colony Hilton, 500 Bulkely Pl. 01
Colony, 13441 Warwick Blvd.. 02
Criston, 2100 2138 Criston
  Dr..................................... 02
Deer Park East, 11430
  Jefferson Ave.................... 01
Deer Park, 11425 Jefferson
  Ave................................... 01
Denbigh 14262 - 14272 Old
  Courthouse Way............... 02
Dresden Arms, 624 Dresden
  Dr..................................... 01
Dresden Drive, 684 Dresden
  Dr..................................... 01
Dutch Village, 500 Logan Pl... 01
Eastwood, 5 Eastwood Dr,
  420 Shawn Cir.................. 02
Glen Garden, 1300 79th St 05
Ivy The, 501 Adams Dr.......... 01
Jamestown, 100 Yeardley Dr.. 01
Jefferson East, 711 J Clyde
  Morris Blvd...................... 01
Mariners Park, 410 Logan Pl... 01
Newsome Townhouses,4100-
  4351 Newsome Dr,4100-
  4547 Orcutt Av................ 07
Orlean Court, 817 Woods Rd.. 06
Pavilion, 11700 Jefferson
  Ave................................... 06
Presidential, 731 Adams Dr.... 01
Randolph Court, 500
  Bellwood Rd..................... 01
Saint James Terrace, 80
  30th.................................. 07
Saint James Terrace, 80
  51st.................................. 07
Saint James Terrace, 85
  29th.................................. 07
Sherwood, 3752 - 3778
  Sherwood Pl..................... 02

Tabb Lane, 25 Tabbs Lane..... 02
Tarrytown, 11112 Jefferson
  Ave.................................. 01
Winston Townhouse, 11310-
  11411 Winston Pl.............. 01

UNIVERSITIES AND COLLEGES

Christopher Newport, Shoe
  Lane................................ 06

NORFOLK 235

POST OFFICE BOXES

Box Nos.
1-2999   Main Office......... 01
3000-3999   Customhouse
              Sta............... 14
4001-4999   Berkley Sta........ 23
5501-5999   Parcel Post
              Annex Sta........ 16
6001-6999   Milan Sta.......... 08
7001-7499   Lafayette
              Boulevard
              Sta............... 09
8001-8999   Ocean View
              Sta............... 68
9501-9999   Wright Sta......... 05
10001-10999   Norview Sta........ 13
11001-11999   Debree Sta......... 17
12001-12999   Thomas Corner
              Sta............... 02
14001-14999   L C Page Sta....... 18

STATIONS, BRANCHES AND UNITS

Berkley Sta.......................... 23
Customhouse Sta..................... 14
Le Bree Sta......................... 17
Fleet Br............................ 11
Hampton Roads Br.................... 11
L C Page Sta........................ 18
Lafayette Boulevard Sta............. 09
Milan Sta........................... 08
Naval Air Station Br................ 11
Naval Amphibious Base Br............ 11
Norview Sta......................... 13
Ocean View Sta...................... 63
Parcel Post Annex Sta............... 16
Thomas Corner Sta................... 02
West Annex Mou...................... 20
Wright Sta.......................... 05
General Delivery.................... 01
Postmaster.......................... 01

APARTMENTS, HOTELS, MOTELS

Admiralty, 1170 N Military
  Hwy................................ 02
Airport, Municipal Airport......... 18
Algonquin House, 7320
  Glenroie Ave...................... 05
Atlantic, 111 Granby................ 01
Bel-Aire, 1001 N Military
  Hwy................................ 02
Commodore Maury, 345
  Granby............................ 10
Bel Mar, 5578 Virginia Beach
  Blvd.............................. 02

Fairfax, 117 W City Hall Ave....... 01
Gilbert, 225 Granby................ 10
Golden Triangle, 201 E Olney
  Rd................................ 01
Hague Park, 408 Dundaff........... 07
Hague Towers East, 330 W.
  Brambleton Ave................... 10
Holiday Towers, 1850 E Little
  Creek Rd......................... 18
Interstate, 525 N Military
  Hwy............................... 02
Jefferson, 232 W Bute.............. 10
Lafayette Motor Hotel, 4233
  Granby............................ 04
Lafayette Tower, 4601
  Mayflower Rd..................... 06
Monticello, 108 E City Hall
  Ave............................... 01
Nansemond, 236 W Ocean
  View Ave......................... 03
New Virginia, 108 E Plume.......... 10
Pembroke Towers, 601
  Pembroke Ave..................... 07
Pine Crest, 9650 Norfolk Ave....... 93
Plaza, 1787 Church St.............. 04
Sea Isle, 315 E Ocean View
  Ave............................... 03
Sheraton Hotel : Motor Inn......... 02
Surf, 2918 E Ocean View
  Ave............................... 18
Thomas Nelson, 245 Granby
  St................................ 01
Vanns, 3022 E Ocean View
  Ave............................... 03
Voyager, 719 E Ocean View
  Ave............................... 02
Warm Sands, 9635 Shore Dr..........

BUILDINGS

Allard, 106 W Olney Rd............. 01
Atlantic National Bank 415
  St Paul's Blvd................... 10
Attucks, 1008 Church St............ 10
Bank Of Virginia 500 E
  Plume............................ 10
Bankers Trust, 109 W City
  Hall Ave......................... 10
Batleman, 300 Boush................ 10
Bel-Aire, 1600 E Little Creek
  Rd................................ 18
Board Of Trade, 304 E
  Plume............................ 10
Citizens Bank, 109 E Main.......... 15
City Hall, 810 Union............... 10
Civic Center, 100 Saint
  Paul's Blvd...................... 10
Customhouse, 101 E Main
  St................................ 10
Dean, 201 E Plume St............... 10
Depaul Medical, 110 Kingsley
  Lane............................. 05
Downtown Plaza Shopping
  Center X 200-500 St.
  Paul's Blvd...................... 10
Driver, 339 Boush.................. 10
Duke-Grace, 740 Duke St............ 10
Elray, 7460 Tidewater Dr........... 05
Essex, 315 E Plume................. 10
Executive Medical, 463 N
  Military Hwy..................... 02
Executive Office, 2 Janaf
  Shopping Center.................. 02

Federal, 600 Granby................ 10
First & Merchants National
  Bank 300 E Main.................. 10
First National Bank, 200
  Monticello....................... 10
Flatiron, 110 W Charlotte.......... 10
Franklin, 700 Duke................. 10
Golden Triangle, 201 E Olney
  Road............................. 10
Granby Professional, 7314
  Granby........................... 05
Helena, 161 N Plume................ 10
I B M, 225 W Virginia Beach
  Blvd............................. 10
Janaf, 112 Janaf Shopping
  Center........................... 02
Juvenile Court 800 E City
  Hall Ave......................... 10
Kresge, 232 Granby................. 10
Larrymore Lawns Medical
  Center, 7709 Wildwood
  Drive............................ 18
Law, 147 Granby.................... 10
Lonsdale, 207 Granby............... 10
Maritime Tower, 234
  Monticello Ave................... 10
Medical Tower, 400 Gresham
  Drive............................ 07
Metropolitan Bank & Trust,
  700 Church....................... 10
Midtown, 112 E Little Creek
  Rd................................ 05
Monticello Arcade, 208 E
  Plume............................ 10
Municipal Air Terminal,
  Municipal Airport................ 18
Municipal Auditorium, 900
  Granby........................... 10
National Maritime Union Hall,
  523 E Bute....................... 10
Navy Y M C A 500 Dunmore
  St................................ 18
New Monroe, 254 Granby............. 10
Norfolk Medical Center, 401
  Colley Ave....................... 07
Pinewood Professional, 1516
  Harmon........................... 18
Plaza 1 1 Main Plaza E............. 10
Professional Arts, 142 W
  York............................. 10
Professional Associates, 549
  E Brambleton Ave................. 10
Public Safety, 811 E City
  Hall Ave......................... 10
Rotunda, 415 Saint Paul'S
  Blvd............................. 10
Reyster, 203 Granby................ 10
Scope, 201 E. Brambleton
  Avenue........................... 10
Selden Arcade, 205 E Plume......... 10
Social Service Bureau, 235 E
  Plume............................ 10
Southern Bank, 101 Granby.......... 10
Southern Office, 1 Southern
  Shopping Center.................. 05
Southgate Terminal, Foot Of
  W Tazewell....................... 18
Suburban Professional, 119 E
  Little Creek Rd.................. 05
Telephone, 120 W Bute.............. 10
Tidewater Executive Center,
  Center Drive..................... 02

Time, 1701 Colley Ave	17
Town Point, 111 W Main	10
Twin Towers, 900 Park Ave	04
United Va Bank, 5 Main Plaza E	10
Virginia National Bank, 1 Commercial Place	10
Wainwright, 229 W Bute	10
Wheat J C 3 Main Plaza E	10
Y M C A Central Branch, 312 W Bute	10
Y M C A Hunton Branch, 512 Wood	04
Y W C A Phyllis Wheatly Branch, 927 Park Ave	04
Y W C A, 249 W Freemason	10
Youth Center, 1300 Kempsville Rd	02
4100, 4101 Granby	04
64-West, 586 Virginian Dr	05

HOSPITALS

Depaul, 120 Kingsley Lane	05
Kings Daughters (Childrens), 609 Colley Ave	07
Lake Taylor City, 1300 Kempsville Rd	02
Leigh Memorial, 358 Mowbray Arch	07
Mc Coy-Stokes, 1400 Colonial Ave	17
Norfolk Community, 2539 Corprew Ave	04
Norfolk General, 600 Gresham Dr	07
Rhodes Dental, 501 E Brambleton Ave	10
U S Public Health Service, 6500 Hampton Blvd	08

MILITARY INSTALLATIONS

Armed Forces Staff College	11
Naval Air Station	11
Naval Amphibious Base	21
Naval Supply Center	12
United States Naval Station	11

UNIVERSITIES AND COLLEGES

Norfolk State, 2401 Corprew Ave	04
Old Dominion, 5201 Hampton Blvd	08
Virginia Wesleyan, 1584 Wesleyan Drive	02

PORTSMOUTH   237

POST OFFICE BOXES

Box Nos.

A-K	Main Office	05
1-1426	Main Office	05
2000-2599	Cradock Sta	02
3000-3317	Olive Sta	01
6000-6647	Churchland	03
7000-7250	Mid-Town Sta	07

RURAL ROUTES

1	63

STATIONS, BRANCHES AND UNITS

Churchland Br	03
Mid Town Sta	07
Naval Hospital Sta	08
Navy Yard Sta	09
Simonsdale Sta	01
West Norfolk Br	03
General Delivery	05
Postmaster	05

APARTMENTS, HOTELS, MOTELS

Carver Home, 2500 Queen	07
Cherokee Park, 700 Cherokee Rd	01
Colonial Manor, 3622 Princeton Pl	07
Crawford House, 1 Crawford Parkway	04
Dale Homes,, 240 Dale Homes	04
Edinburg, 344 Court	04
Ft Nelson Towers 333 Green	04
Fulton, 340 Hatton	04
Gates, 200 Effingham	04
Glensheliah, 3610 Hartford	07
Gloucester, 359 Middle	04
Governor Dinwiddie, 506 Dinwiddie	05
Hampton Crest, 320 Dinwiddie	04
Hampton, 528 Hampton Pl	04
Herbor Court, 310 Court	04
Harbor View, 230 Swimming Point	04
Holiday Inn, 10 Crawford Parkway	04
Howard Homes, 102 Howard	07
Ida B Barbour, 1104 Barbour Dr	04
Imperial 400, 333 Effingham	04
Kellys, 817 County	04
Lee Hall, 900 Suburban Parkway	02
Lincoln Park, 4 Lexington Dr	04
Malvern Hill, 426 King	04
Malvern Hill, 511 Dinwiddle	04
Midtown, 700 Frederick Blvd	07
Moore, 501 Hampton Pl	04
Patio Plaza, 700 Crawford Parkway	04
Philgrador, 1015 Blair	04
Portsmouth Gardens, 1 Lawrence Cir	07
Sussex, 422 King	04
Town & Country, 300 Ansell Ave	02
Waterview, 3650 Western Br Blvd	07
Westhampton, 538 Hampton Pl	04
Westhaven, 4708 County	07
Williams Court, 98 Jameson	04
Wilson Jeffery Homes	07
Wilson Manor, 3501	

Commerce	07

BUILDINGS

American Bank, 234 High	04
Building & Loan Bldg, 435 Court St	04
Citizens Trust Bldg, 355 Crawford Parkway	04
Civic Center	04
Federal, 431 Crawford	04
Kirn (New), 339 High	04
Medic-Home Health Center, 320 Effingham	04
Merchants & Farmers Bank Bldg., 430 Crawford St.	04
Municipal, 1 High	04
Portsmouth Medical, 1100 Hamilton	07
Professional, 505 Washington	04
Star, 101 High	04

HOSPITALS

Maryview, 3636 High	07
Portsmouth General, 900 Lockie	04

MILITARY INSTALLATIONS

Base Coast Guard District, Wythe	04
Coast Guard Commander 5th Coast Guard District	05
Naval Ammunition Depot	02
Naval Hospital	08
Naval Shipyard	09

UNIVERSITIES AND COLLEGES

Frederick Academy, 1801 Portsmouth Blvd	07
Frederick Community College	03

RICHMOND   232

POST OFFICE BOXES

Box Nos.

1-180	Capitol	01
1A-1M	Capitol	01
1N-1Y	Capitol	02
2A-2K	Capitol	03
2L-2U	Capitol	04
2V-2Z	Capitol	05
3A-3M	Capitol	06
3N-3Y	Capitol	07
5A-5Z	Capitol	13
6B-6G	Capitol	14
6H-6N	Capitol	15
60-6Q	Capitol	16
6R-6T	Capitol	17
181-360	Capitol	02
2AB-2AF	Capitol	05
3AB-3AJ	Capitol	08
361-468	Capitol	03
471-568	Capitol	04
571-668	Capitol	05
671-800	Capitol	06

801-980	Capitol	07
981-1140	Capitol	08
1141-1240	Capitol	09
1241-1340	Capitol	10
1341-1440	Capitol	11
1441-1560	Capitol	12
1561-1690	Capitol	13
1651-1818	Capitol	14
1831-1969	Capitol	15
1971-2149	Capitol	16
2151-2309	Capitol	17
2331-2450	Capitol	18
2881-3387	Bon Air Br	35
3401-3998	Ampthill Br	34
4001-4434	Southside Sta	24
4501-4997	Ridge Br	29
5001-5897	Saunders Sta	20
6001-6199	Northside Sta	22
6201-6996	West End Br	30
7001-7475	Stewart Sta	21
7501-7744	Montrose Heights Sta	31
7901-8191	East End Sta	23
8201-8767	Westhampton Sta	26
8801-9097	Forest Hill Sta	25
9101-9247	Bellevue Sta	27
9401-9899	Lakeside Br	28
10001-10510	Civic Center Sta	40
11001-11293	West End	30
12000-12999	Central Sta	41
16000-16999	Northside	22
25001-26432	Richmond	60
26441-27632	Richmond	61

RURAL ROUTES

2		29
5,6,14		31
15		34

STATIONS, BRANCHES AND UNITS

Ampthill Br	34
Azalea Br	27
Bellevue Sta	27
Belt Boulevard Br	24
Bon Air Br	35
Broad Rock Br	24
Buford Br	35
Carousel Br	25
Central Sta	19
Civic Center Sta	40
Defense General Supply Ctr Br	19
East End Sta	23
Falling Creek Br	34
Federal Reserve Sta	13
Forest Hill Sta	25
Glen Lea Br	23
Laburnum Manor Br	22
Lakeside Br	28
Medical College Sta	19
Metro Br	31
Montrose Heights Sta	31
Northside Sta	22
Pine Dell Br	29
Pocoshock Br	35
Ridge Br	29
Saunders Sta	20
Southside Sta	24
Stewart Sta	21

Stratford Hills Br		25
Tuckahoe Br		29
Veterans Administration HospBr		19
Virginia Union University Sta		20
West End Br		30
Westhampton Sta		26
Westwood Br		30
General Delivery		32
Postmaster		32

APARTMENTS, HOTELS, MOTELS

Berkshire Apartments, 300 W Franklin	20
Bon Haven, 2506 Atwell Dr	34
Capitol, 8th & Grace	19
Chesterfield, 900 W Franklin	20
Gresham Court, 1030 W Franklin	20
Imperial Plaza, 1717 Bellevue	27
Jefferson, Franklin & Jefferson	11
John Marshall, 5th & Franklin	11
Keswick Gardens, 5200 Wythe Ave	26
Lexington Tower Apartments, 104 W Franklin	20
Lock Lane, 35 Lock Lane	26
Prestwould, 612 W Franklin	20
Raleigh, 9th & Bank	03
Richmond West, 801 E Broad	19
Sevilla Apartments, 115 N Jefferson	11
Stuart Courts, 1600 Monument Ave	20
The 5100, 5100 Monument Ave	38
Tuckahoe, 5621 Cary St Rd	26
William Byrd, 2501 W Broad	20

BUILDINGS

Blanton, 1220 Bank	19
Broad Grace Arcade, 215 E Broad	19
Broad Grace Arcade, 216 E Grace	19
Builders Exchange, 3701 W Broad	30
Central National Bank, 217 E Broad	19
Consolidated Bank & Trust Company, 328 N 1st	40
Electric, 700 E Franklin	19
Eskimo, 530 E Main	19
Federal, 400 N 8th	40
Fidelity, 9th & Main	19
First & Merchants National Bank, 827 E Main	19
Hermitage	19
James Madison, 109 Governor	19
Life Insurance Company Of Virginia, 914 Capitol	19
Mosque, Laurel & Main	20
Presbyterian, 6 N 6th	19
Professional, 501 E Franklin	19
Richmond Federal, 728 E	

Main	19
Ross, 801 E Main	19
Safety & Welfare, 501 N 9th	19
Sauer, 1900 W Broad	20
Seaboard, 3600 W Broad	30
Southern Bank & Trust Company, 1442 E Main	19
Southern States, 627 E Main	19
State Capitol, Capitol Square	19
State Finance, Capitol Square	19
State Library, 1101 Capitol	19
State Office Building, 9th 1/2 grace	19
State Office, Capitol Square	19
State Planters, 904 E Main	19
Travelers, 1108 E Main	19
Virginia, 500 E Main	19
W R N L Radio Center, 111 N 4th	19
700, 7th & Main	19

GOVERNMENT OFFICES

City Hall 900 E Broad	19
Henrico County Court House, 21st & Main	07

HOSPITALS

Grace, 401 W Grace	20
Johnston-Willis, 2908 Kensington Ave	21
Mcguires 1201 Broad Rock Rd	24
Medical College Of Virginia, 1200 E Broad	19
Retreat For The Sick, 2621 Grove Ave	20
Richmond Community, 1210 Overbrook Rd	20
Richmond Eye Ear Nose & Throat, 408 N 12th	19
Richmond Memorial, 1300 Westwood Ave	27
Saint Elizabeths, 617 W Grace	20
Saint Lukes, 1000 W Grace	20
Saint Mary, 5801 Bremo	26
Sheltering Arms, 1311 Palmyra Ave	27
Stuart Circle, 413 Stuart Cir	20
Tuckers, 212 W Franklin	20
Vet Admin 1201 Broad Rock Rd	24
Westbrook Sanatorium, 1500 Westbrook Ave	27

UNIVERSITIES AND COLLEGES

Medical College Of Virginia, 1200 E Broad	19
Presbyterian School Of Christian Education, 1205 Palmyra	27
Smithdeal-Massey Business College, 300 W Grace	01
Union Theological Seminary, 3401 Brook Rd	27
University Of Richmond	

School Of Business Administration		20
Virginia Commonwealth Univ (M C V), 1200 E Broad		11
Virginia Commonwealth Univ (R p.i.), 901 W Franklin		20
Virginia Union University, 1500 N Lombardy		20

ROANOKE 240

POST OFFICE BOXES

Box Nos.

1-40	Main Office	01
41-301	Main Office	02
311-571	Main Office	03
581-841	Main Office	04
851-1111	Main Office	05
1121-1300	Main Office	06
1301-1600	Main Office	07
1601-1951	Main Office	08
1961-2281	Main Office	09
2291-2611	Main Office	10
2701-2912	Main Office	01
4000-4999	Grandin Road Sta	15
5000-5999	Williamson Road Sta	12
6000-6999	Melrose Sta	17
7000-7999	Hollins Br	19
8000-8999	South Roanoke	14
9000-10999	Hollinscollege Br	20

RURAL ROUTES

1	12
2	19
5,6	14
7	18

8	14
11	19

STATIONS, BRANCHES AND UNITS

Crossroads Br	12
Grandin Road Sta	15
Hollins Br	19
Hollins College Br	20
Melrose Sta	17
South Roanoke Sta	14
Sugar Loaf Br	18
Williamson Road Sta	12
General Delivery	01
Postmaster	01

SPRINGFIELD 221

POST OFFICE BOXES

Box Nos.

1-999	Main Office	50
1000-1999	N Springfield Br	51

RURAL ROUTES

27	50

STATIONS, BRANCHES AND UNITS

Burke Br	22015
North Springfield Br	51
West Springfield Br	52
General Delivery	50
Postmaster	50

BUILDINGS

Executive Building 6901 Old Keene Mill Rd	5.

VIRGINIA BEACH 234

POST OFFICE BOXES

Box Nos.

1-340	Main Office	58
501-1099	Seapines Sta	51
2001-2999	Lynn Haven Sta	52
3001-3999	Oceana Sta	53
4001-4999	London Bridge Sta	54
5001-5999	Bayside Sta	55
6001-6999	Princess Anne Sta	56
7001-7199	Back Bay Sta	57
62001-62999	Witch Duck	62

RURAL ROUTES

1,2	56
3,4,SR5	57

STATIONS, BRANCHES AND UNITS

Backbay Sta	57
Bayside Sta	55
Blackwater Bridge Rural Sta	57
Creeds Rural Sta	57
Dam Neck Sta	61
Fort Story Sta	59
London Bridge Sta	54
Lynnhaven Sta	52
Oceana Sta	53
Oceana N A S Sta	60
Princess Anne Sta	56
Pungo Rural Sta	56
Seapines Sta	51
Witch Duck Sta	62
General Delivery	58
Postmaster	58

WASHINGTON
(Abbreviation- WA)

Aberdeen (1st)	98520
Acme	98220
Addy	99101
Adna	98522
Aeneas	98810
Airway Heights	99001
Albion	99102
Alder	98301
Alderwood Manor, Sta. Lynnwood	98036
Algona, Br. Auburn	98002
Allen, R. Br. Bow	98232
Allyn	98524
Almira	99103
Aloha	98525
Amanda Park	98526
Amber	99002
Amboy	98601
American Lake, Br. Tacoma	98493
Anacortes (1st)	98221
Anatone	99401
Appleton	98602
Ardenvoir	98811
Ariel	98603
Arlington (1st)	98223
Arnada Park Annex, Sta. Vancouver (see appendix)	
Ashford	98304
Asotin	99402
Auburn (1st)	98002
Algona, Br.	98002
Federal Way, Br.	98002
Pacific, R. Br.	98047
Redondo, R. Br.	98054
Westfair, Br.	98002
Azwell, R. Br. Chelan	98816
B and G, Br. Everett	98201
B And M, R. Br. Lake Stevens	98258
Bainbridge Island Winslow, Br. Seattle	98110
Ballard, Sta. Seattle	98107
Baring	98224
Battle Ground	98604
Bay Center	98527
Beaver	98305
Belfair	98528
BELLEVUE (1st) (see appendix)	
Bellingham (1st)	98225
Belmont, R. Br. Farmington	99104
Benge	99105
Benton City	99320
Beverly	99321
Bickleton	99322
Bingen	98605
Bitter Lake, Sta. Seattle (see appendix)	
Black Diamond	98010
Blaine (1st)	98230
Blakely Island, R. Br. Friday Harbor	98222
Blanchard	98231
Bluecreek	99106
Bothell (1st)	98011
Bow	98233
Boyds	99107
Bremerton (1st)	98310
Gorst, R. Br.	98337
Manette, Sta.	98310

Naval Base, Sta.	98314
Sheridan Park, Sta.	98310
Wycoff, Sta.	98310
Brewster	98812
Bridgeport	98813
Brier, Br. Lynnwood	98036
Brinnon	98320
Broadway, Sta. Seattle	98102
Brownstown	98920
Brush Prairie	98606
Buckley	98321
Bucoda	98530
Buena	98921
Burbank	99323
Burien, Br. Seattle (see appendix)	
Burley	98322
Burlington (1st)	98233
Burton	98013
Camas (1st)	98607
Campus, Sta. Bellingham	98225
Capitol Hill, Sta. Seattle	98102
Carbonado	98323
Carlsborg	98324
Carlton	98814
Carnation	98014
Carrolls	98609
Carson	98610
Cascade, Br. Renton	98055
Cashmere (1st)	98815
Castle Rock	98611
Cathlamet	98612
Cedonia	98108
Centerville	98613
Central Park, Br. Aberdeen	98520
Centralia (1st)	98531
Chattaroy	99003
Chehalis (1st)	98532
Chelan (1st)	98816
Chelan Falls	98817
Cheney (1st)	99004
Chesaw	98818
Chewelah	99109
Chimacum	98325
Chinook	98614
Cinebar	98533
Clallam Bay	98326
Claremont, Sta. Everett	98203
Clarkston (1st)	99403
Clayton	99110
Cle Elum	98922
Clearlake	98235
Clearview, R. Br. Snohomish	98290
Clearwater, R. Br. Forks	98399
Clinton	98236
Clipper, R. Br. Deming	98244
Colbert	99005
Colfax (1st)	99111
College, Sta. Pullman	99163
College Place (1st)	99324
Colton	99113
Columbia, Sta. Seattle	98118
Colville (1st)	99114
Conconully	98819
Concrete	98237
Connell	99326
Conway	98238
Cook, R. Br. Bingen	98605
Copalis Beach	98535
Copalis Crossing	98536
Cosmopolis	98537
Cougar	98616
Coulee City	99115

Coulee Dam	99116
Country Homes, Br. Spokane	99218
Coupeville	98239
Cowiche	98923
Creston	99117
Crossroads, Sta. Bellevue	98008
Crystal Mountain, R. Br. Enumclaw	98022
Cumberland, R. Br. Enumclaw	98015
Cunningham	99327
Curlew	99118
Curtis	98538
Cusick	99119
Custer	98240
Dallesport	98617
Danville	99121
Darrington	98241
Dash Point, R. Br. Tacoma	98422
Davenport	99122
Dayton	99328
Deep River	98618
Deer Harbor	98243
Deer Park	99006
Deming	98244
Des Moines, Br. Seattle (see appendix)	
Dishman, Br. Spokane	99213
Dixie	99329
Dockton	98018
Doty	98539
Dryden	98821
Du Pont	98327
Duvall	98019
East Hill, Br. Kent	98031
East Olympia	98540
East Union, Sta. Seattle	98122
East Wenatchee, Br. Wenatchee	98801
Eastgate, Sta. Bellevue	98007
Easton	98925
Eastsound	98245
Eatonville	98328
Edison	98246
Edmonds (1st)	98020
Edwall	99008
Elbe	98330
Electric City	99123
Elk	99009
Ellensburg (1st)	98926
Vantage, R. Br.	98950
Elma	98541
Elmer City	99124
Eltopia	99330
Endicott	99125
Entiat	98822
Enumclaw (1st)	98022
Crystal Mountain, R. Br.	98022
Cumberland, R. Br.	98015
Ephrata (1st)	98823
Espanola	99010
Ethel	98542
Evans	99126
EVERETT (1st) (see appendix)	
Everson	98247
Ewan	99127
Fairchild Air Force Base (1st)	99011
Fairfield	99012
Fall City	98024
Farmington	99128
Federal, Sta. Seattle	98104

Federal Way. Br. Auburn 98002
Fern Hill, Sta. Tacoma 98412
Ferndale (1st).............98248
Fife, R. Br. Tacoma 98424
Finley, R. Br. Kennewick 99336
Fircrest, Br. Tacoma 98466
Ford 99013
Forest Park, Br. Seattle 98155
Forks 98331
  Clearwater. R. Br. 98399
Fort Lewis, Br. Tacoma 98433
Fort Steilacoom, Br. Tacoma 98494
Four Lakes 99014
Fourth Plain, Sta. Vancouver
  (see appendix)
Fox Island 98333
Fpo 98777, Br. Seattle 98777
Frances 98543
Freeland 98249
Freeman 99015
Friday Harbor 98250
  Blakely Island, R. Br. 98222
  Roche Harbor, R. Br. 98250
Fruitland, R. Br. Hunters 99129
Galvin 98544
Gardiner, R. Br. Sequim 98334
Garfield 99130
Garland, Sta. Spokane 99209
George, R. Br. Quincy 98824
Georgetown, Sta. Seattle 98108
Gifford 99131
Gig Harbor (1st) 98335
Glacier, R. Br. Deming 98244
Gleed, R. Br. Yakima 98904
Glenoma 98336
Glenwood 98619
Gold Bar 98251
Goldendale (1st) 98620
Gooseprairie, R. Br. Naches 98929
Gorst, R. Br. Bremerton 98337
Graham 98338
Grand Coulee 99133
Grandview (1st) 98930
Granger 98932
Granite Falls 98252
Grapeview 98546
Grayland 98547
Grays River 98621
Greenacres 99016
Greenbank 98253
Greenwood, Sta. Seattle 98103
Grotto 98254
Hadlock 98339
  Port Ludlow, R. Br. 98365
Hamilton 98255
Hansville 98340
Harper 98341
Harrah 98933
Harrington 99134
  Mohler, R. Br. 99154
Hartline 99135
Hatton 99332
Hay, R. Br. Lacrosse 99136
Hayes Park, Sta. Spokane 99207
Hazel Dell, Br. Vancouver 98660
Heisson 98622
Highlands, Sta. Renton 98055
Hillyard, Sta. Spokane 99207
Hobart 98025
Holden Village, R. Br.
  Chelan 98816
Hoodsport 98548
Hooper 99333

Hoquiam (1st) 98550
  Ocean Shores, P. Br. 98551
Humptulips 98552
Hunters 99137
  Fruitland, R. Br. 53129
Husum 98623
Hyak 98026
Ilwaco 98624
Inchelium 99138
Index 98256
Indianola 98342
Inglewood, Br. Bothell 98011
International, Sta. Seattle
  (see appendix)
Ione 99139
Irby, R. Br. Odessa 99159
Issaquah (1st) 98027
Joyce 98343
Juanita, Br. Kirkland 98033
K Street, Sta. Tacoma 98405
Kahlotus 99335
Kalama 98625
Kapowsin 98344
Keller 99140
Kelso (1st) 98626
Kenmore (1st) 98028
Kennewick (1st) 99336
Kent (1st) 98031
Kettle Falls 99141
  Orient, R. Br. 99160
Kewa 99142
Keyport 98345
Kingston 98346
Kiona 99340
Kirkland (1st) 98033
Kittitas 98934
Klickitat 98628
La Center 98629
La Conner 98257
La Grande 98348
La Push 98350
Lacey, Br. Olympia 98503
Lacrosse 99143
  Hay, R. Br. 99136
Lake City, Sta. Seattle (see
  appendix)
Lake Hill, Br. Everett 98203
Lake Hills, Sta. Bellevue 98007
Lake Stevens 98258
Lakebay 98349
  Longbranch, R. Br. 98351
Lakeview, Br. Tacoma 98491
Lakewood 98259
Lakewood Center, Br.
  Tacoma (see appendix)
Lamona 99144
Lamont 99017
Langley 98260
Latah 99018
Laurel 98630
Laurier 99146
Leavenworth 98826
Lebam 98554
Lester, Br. Seattle 98035
Liberty Lake 99019
Lilliwaup 98555
Lincoln 99147
Lind 99341
Littlerock 98556
Long Beach 98631
  Nahcotta, R. Br. 98637
Longbranch, R. Br. Lakebay 98351
Longmire, R. Br. Tacoma 98397

Longview (1st) 98632
Loomis 98827
Loon Lake 99148
Lopez 98261
Lowden 99342
Lowell, Sta. Everett 98203
Lummi Island 98262
Lyle 98635
Lyman 98263
Lynden (1st) 98264
Lynnwood (1st) 98036
Mabton 98935
Magnolia, Sta. Seattle 98199
Malaga 98828
Malden 99149
Malo 99150
Malone 98559
Malott 98829
Manchester 98353
Manette, Sta. Bremerton 98310
Manhattan, Br. Seattle 98148
Manito, Sta. Spokane 99203
Mansfield 98830
Manson 98831
Maple Falls 98266
Maple Valley 98038
Marblemount 98267
Marcus 99151
Marietta 98268
Marlin 98832
Marshall 99200
Marysville (1st) 98270
Matlock 98560
Mattawa, R. Br. Othello 99344
Mazama 98833
Mc Chord A F B, Br.
  Tacoma 98438
Mc Cleary 98557
Mc Kenna 98558
Mc Micken Heights, Br.
  Seattle 98188
Mc Millin 98352
Mead 99021
Medical Lake 99022
Medina 98039
Menlo 98561
Mercer Island (1st) 98040
Mesa 99343
Metaline 99152
Metaline Falls 99153
Methow 98834
Mica 99023
Midway, Sta. Kent 98031
Milan 99024
Millwood, Br. Spokane 99212
Milton 98354
Mineral 98355
Minnehaha, Br. Vancouver 98661
Moclips 98562
Mohler, R. Br. Harrington 99154
Monitor 98836
Monroe (1st) 98272
Monta Vista, Br. Tacoma 98499
Montesano (1st) 98563
Morton 98356
Moses Lake (1st) 98837
Mossyrock 98564
Mount Vernon (1st) 98273
Mountlake Terrace (1st) 98043
Moxee City 98936
Mukilteo 98275
Naches 98937
  Gooseprairie, R. Br. 98929

629

White Pass, R. Br. 98937
Nahcotta, R. Br. Long
  Beach 98637
Napavine 98565
Naselle 98638
Naval Air Station, Sta.
  Seattle 98115
Naval Base, Sta. Bremerton ...98314
Neah Bay 98357
Neilton 98566
Nespelem 99155
Newman Lake 99025
Newport 99156
Newport Hills, Br. Bellevue ...98006
Nine Mile Falls 99026
  Tumtum, R. Br. 99034
Nooksack 98276
Nordland 98358
North Bend 98045
North Bonneville 98639
North Central, Sta. Spokane ...99205
North City, Br. Seattle 98155
North Fort Lewis, Br.
  Tacoma 98433
North Lynnwood, Br.
  Lynnwood 98036
Northgate, Sta. Seattle 98125
Northport 99157
Oak Harbor (1st) 98277
Oakesdale 99158
Oakville 98568
Ocean City 98569
Ocean Park 98640
Ocean Shores, R. Br
  Hoquiam 98551
Odessa 99159
Okanogan (1st) 98840
Otalla 98359
Olga 98279
OLYMPIA (1st) (see
  appendix)
Omak (1st) 98841
Onalaska 98570
Opportunity, Br. Spokane 99214
Orcas 98280
Orchards, Br. Vancouver 98662
Orient, R. Br. Kettle Falls 99140
Orondo 98843
Oroville 98844
Orting 98360
Oso, R. Br. Arlington 98223
Othello (1st) 99344
Otis Orchards 99027
Outlook 98938
Oysterville 98641
Pacific, R. Br. Auburn 98047
Pacific Beach 98571
Packwood 98361
Palisades 98845
Palmer 98048
Palouse 99161
Paradise Inn, R. Br. Tacoma ...98398
Parker 98939
Parkland, Br. Tacoma (see
  appendix)
Parkwater, Sta. Spokane 99211
Pasco (1st) 99301
  Tri Cities, Sta. 99302
Pateros 98846
Paterson 99345
Pe Ell 98572
Peshastin 98847
Pinehurst, Sta. Everett 98203

Plaza 99028
Plymouth 99346
Point Roberts 98281
Pomeroy 99347
Port Angeles (1st) 98362
Port Blakely, Br. Seattle 98110
Port Gamble 98364
Port Ludlow, R. Br. Hadlock ...98365
Port Orchard (1st) 98366
  Retsil, R. Br. 98378
  South Park Village, Br. 9x366
Port Townsend (1st) 98368
Potlatch 98574
Poulsbo (1st) 98370
Prescott 99348
Preston 98050
Proctor, Sta. Tacoma (see
  appendix)
Prosser (1st) 99350
Pullman (1st) 99163
Puyallup (1st) 98371
Queen Anne, Sta. Seattle
  (see appendix)
Quilcene 98376
Quinault 98575
Quincy (1st) 98848
  George, R. Br. 98824
Rainier 98576
Ralston 99165
Randle 98377
Ravensdale 98051
Raymond (1st) 98577
Reardan 99029
Redmond (1st) 98052
Redondo, R. Br. Auburn 98054
Renton (1st) 98055
Republic 99166
Retsil, R. Br. Port Orchard 98378
Rice 99167
Richland (1st) 99352
Richmond Beach, Br.
  Seattle 98160
Ridgefield 98642
Ritzville 99169
Riverside 98849
Riverton Heights, Br. Seattle
  (see appendix)
Roche Harbor, R. Br. Friday
  Harbor 98250
Rochester 98579
Rock Island 98850
Rockford 99030
Rockport 98283
Rollingbay 98061
Ronald 98940
Roosevelt 99356
Rosalia 99170
Rosburg 98643
Rose Hill, Br. Kirkland 98033
Rosewood, Br. Spokane (see
  appendix)
Roslyn 98941
Roy 98580
Royal City 99357
Ryderwood 98581
Saint John 99171
Salkum 98582
Sappho 98379
Satsop 98583
Schwarder, R. Br. Yakima 98905
Sea First, Sta. Seattle 98104
Seabeck 98380

Seahurst 98062
SEATTLE (1st) (see
  appendix)
Seattle Heights (1st) 98063
Seaview 98644
Sedro Woolley (1st) 98284
  Wickersham, R. Br. 98285
Sekiu 98381
Selah 98942
Selleck 98064
Sequim (1st) 98382
  Gardiner, R. Br. 98334
Shaw Island 98286
Shelton (1st) 98584
Sheridan Park, Sta.
  Bremerton 98310
Silvana 98287
Silver Creek 98585
Silverdale 98383
Silverlake 98645
Sixth Avenue, Sta. Tacoma ...98406
Skamania 98646
Skamokawa 98647
Skykomish 98288
Skyway, Br. Seattle 98178
Snohomish (1st) 98290
Snoqualmie 98065
Snoqualmie Falls 98066
Snoqualmie Pass, R. Br.
  Seattle 98068
Soap Lake 98851
South Bellingham, Sta.
  Bellingham 98225
South Bend 98586
South Cle Elum 98943
South Colby 98384
South Park Village, Br. Port
  Orchard 98366
South Prairie 98385
South Tacoma, Sta. Tacoma ...98409
Southgate, Br. Olympia 98501
Southworth 98386
Spanaway 98387
Spangle 99031
SPOKANE (1st) (see
  appendix)
Spokane International Airprt,
  Br. Spokane 99219
Sprague 99032
Springdale 99173
Stanwood (1st) 98292
Starbuck 99359
Startup 98293
Stehekin 98852
Steilacoom, Br. Tacoma 98388
Steptoe 99174
Stevenson 98648
Stratford 98853
Sultan 98294
Sumas 98295
Sumner (1st) 98390
Sunnyside (1st) 98944
Suquamish 98392
TACOMA (1st) (see
  appendix)
Taholah 98587
Tahuya 98588
Tanglewild, Br. Olympia 98501
Tekoa 99033
Tenino 98589
Terminal, Sta. Tacoma (see
  appendix)

Terminal Annex, Sta. Seattle
  (see appendix)
Terminal Annex, Sta.
  Spokane 99220
Terrace Heights, Br. Yakima...98901
Thornton 99176
Thorp 98946
Tieton 98947
Tiger 99177
Tillicum, Br. Tacoma 98492
Times Square, Sta. Seattle.....98101
Tokeland 98590
Toledo 98591
Tonasket 98855
Toppenish (1st).............................98948
Touchet 99360
Toutle 98649
Tracyton 98393
Trentwood, Br. Spokane...............99215
Tri Cities, Sta. Pasco.................99302
Trout Lake 98650
Tukwila, Br. Seattle.....................98188
Tumtum, R. Br. Nine Mile
  Falls 99034
Tumwater, Br. Olympia 98502
Twisp 98856
Tyler 99035
Underwood 98651
Union 98592
Union Gap, Br. Yakime 98903
Uniontown 99179
University, Sta. Seattle.............98105
Usk 99180

Vader 98593
Valley 99181
Valleyford 99036
VANCOUVER (1st) (see
  appendix)
Vantage, R. Br. Ellensburg.....98950
Vashon (1st).....................................98070
Vaughn 98394
Veradale 99037
Veterans Administration
  Hosp., Sta. Vancouver.........98661
Wahkiacus 98670
Waitsburg 99361
Waldron 98297
Walla Walla (1st)...........................99362
Wallingford, Sta. Seattle.........98103
Wallula 99363
Wapato (1st) 98951
Warden 98857
Washougal 98671
Washtucna 99371
Waterville 98858
  Withrow, R. Br..............................98863
Wauconda 98859
Waukon 99038
Wauna 98395
Waverly 99039
Wedgwood, Sta. Seattle.............98115
Weir Park, Br. Camas 98607
Wellpinit 99040
Wenatchee (1st)..............................98801
West Richland, R. Br.
  Richland 99352

West Seattle, Sta. Seattle
  (see appendix)
West Side, Sta. Yakima 98902
Westfair, Br. Auburn 98002
Westport 98595
Whidbey Island Naval Air
  Sta., Br. Oak Harbor...........98277
White Center, Br. Seattle
  (see appendix)
White Pass, R. Br. Naches.....98937
White Salmon 98672
White Swan 98952
Wickersham, R. Br. Sedro
  Woolley 98285
Wilbur 99185
Wiley, R. Br. Yakima 98906
Wilkeson 98396
Wilson Creek 98860
Winlock 98596
Winona 99186
Winthrop 98862
Wishram 98673
Withrow, R. Br. Waterville.....98863
Woodinville 98072
Woodland 98674
Wycoff, Sta. Bremerton 98310
Yacolt 98675
YAKIMA (1st) (see appendix)
Yelm 98597
Zenith, Br. Seattle.......................98188
Zillah 98953

BELLEVUE 980

POST OFFICE BOXES

Box Nos.
A-H	Main Office Sta	09
1-2034	Main Office Sta	09

STATIONS, BRANCHES AND UNITS

Crossroads Sta	08
Eastgate Sta	07
Lake Hills Sta	07
Newport Hills Br	06
General Delivery	09
Postmaster	09

APARTMENTS, HOTELS, MOTELS

Bellevue Motel, 1647-104 Ave. NE	04
Eastgate Motel, 14632 Sunset Hwy	07
Fortnighter, 475-100 Ave NE	04
Holiday Inn, 11211 Main	04
Newporter Apts, 5900-119 Ave SE	06
Thunderbird Inn, 818-112 Ave NE	04
Travelodge, 11011 NE 8	04
Villa La Paz, 15200-20 NE 16 Pl	07

BUILDINGS

Bellevue Business Center, 777-106 Ave NE	04
Bellevue Square	04
Benaroya Business Park, 300 120 Ave N)	05
Carlson, 808-106 Ave NE	04
Cascade, 855-106 Ave NE	04
City Hall, 111-116 Ave SE	04
Commons, 1200-112 Ave NE	04
Crossroads Shopping Center, NE 8 & 156 Ave NE	08
Ditty, 612-104 Ave NE	04
Drave, 225-108 Ave NE	04
Four Hundred, 400-108 Ave NE	04
K-Mart Plaza, 15015 Main	07
Northwest, 700-112 Ave NE	04
Prudential, 700-108 Ave NE	04
Redwood, 845-106 Ave NE	04
Sunset Village, 3080-148 Ave SE	07
Surrey, 10777 Main	04
Tally, 200-112 Ave NE	04

HOSPITALS

Overlake Memorial, 1035-116 Ave NE	04

UNIVERSITIES AND COLLEGES

Bellevue Community College, 3000-145 Pl SE	07

EVERETT 982

POST OFFICE BOXES

Box Nos.
1-1999	Main Office Boxes	06
2000-2999	Claremont Station Boxes	03
3000-3999	Lowell Station Boxes	03
4000-4999	Pinehurst Station Boxes	03

RURAL ROUTES

1,2	05
4	04
6,7	05

STATIONS, BRANCHES AND UNITS

B And G Br	01
Claremont Sta	03
Lake Hill Br	03
Lowell Sta	03
Pinehurst Sta	03
General Delivery	01
Postmaster	01

GOVERNMENT OFFICES

City Hall	01
Federal Bldg	01
Snohomish County Court House	01

HOSPITALS

General Hospital (P.O. Box 1147)	06
Providence Hospital	01

UNIVERSITIES AND COLLEGES

Everett Community College (P.O. Box 478	06

OLYMPIA 985

POST OFFICE BOXES

Box Nos.
A-D	Lacey Branch	03
1-2999	Main Office	07
3001-3999	Lacey Branch	03
4001-4999	Tumwater Branch	02

RURAL ROUTES

1	02
2	03
3	06
4,5	02
6	06
7	02
8	02
9	06
10	03
11	02
12	03
13,14,15	02
16	06
17	03
18	01

STATIONS, BRANCHES AND UNITS

Lacey Br	03
Southgate Br	01
Tanglewild Br	01
Tumwater Br	02
General Delivery	01
Postmaster	07

APARTMENTS, HOTELS, MOTELS

Angelus Apt Hotel 204 W 4th	01
Aquarian Trace 301 W. T	02
Capitol Club Apt 3800 Elizabeth	03
Diamond Head Apt 1510 SE 46th	03
El Rio Vista Apt 1275 S 2nd	02
Fir Grove Motel 2307 Pacific	01
Firs Apt 100 NE 68th	06
Fourth Ave Apt 5061/2 E 4th	01
Franklin Hotel Apt 2181/2 E 4th	01
Maple Vista Apt 1517 S Cap W	01
Martin Apt 5th : Wash	01
Olympian Hotel Apt Leg : Wash	01
Tourovilla Apt 7304 M.w	06
Trails End Motel 5300 Cap Blvd	01
Turf Apt Rt 2	03
Villa Capri Apt 600 Black Lake Blvd	02

BUILDINGS

Capital Theatre Bldg 416 S Wash	01
Employment Security Bldg Cap Campus	04
Federal Bldg 800 S Cap W	01
Gen Admin Bldg Cap Campus	04
Health Bldg Cap Campus	04
Highway Admin Bldg Cap Campus	04
Institutions Bldg Cap Campus	04
Insurance Bldg Cap Campus	04
Legislative Bldv Cap Campus	04
License Bldg Cap Campus	04
Natnumhank Of Commerce Bldg 402 S Cap W	01
Old Capital Bldg Cap Campus	04
Professional Arts Bldg 208 E 11 Th	01
Security Bldg 203 E 4th	01
Union Ave Bldg	04
Union Ave Bldg 120 Union Ave	01

GOVERNMENT OFFICES

City Hall 8th - Plum	01
County Court House 1100 S Cap Way	04
Employment Security Employment Security Bldg	04
Governor Legislative Bldg	04
Highway Highway Admin Bldg	04
Internal Revenue 1007 S Wash	04
Labor And Industry Cap Campus	04
Motor Vehicles License Bldg	04
Public Assistance Cap Campus	04
Revenue Cap Campus	04
Selective Service 800 S Cap Way	01
Supreme Court Temple Of Justice	04
U.S. Post Office 900 S Jefferson	01
Washington State Agencies	04

HOSPITALS

St Peters Hosp 413 N Lilly Rd	06

MILITARY INSTALLATIONS

National Guard 515 S Eastside	01

UNIVERSITIES AND COLLEGES

Evergreen State College R-15.	05
St Martins College 700 College Way	03

SEATTLE   981

POST OFFICE BOXES

Box Nos.

A-D	Columbia Sta	18
A-H	Queen Anne Sta	09
A-J	Burien Br	66
1-267	University Sta	05
1-298	Richmond Beach Br	60
1-299	Port Blakely Br.	10
1-747	Bainbridge Island - Winslow Br	10
1-1316	Main Office	11
1301-1399	Capitol Hill Sta	12
1401	Greenwood Sta.	03
1501	Wallingford Sta.	03
1700-2156	Main Office	11
3001	International Sta	14
3501-3999	Terminal Sta	24
5001-5499	Ballard Sta.	07
6001-6288	Riverton	

	Heights Br	88
6501-6914	West Seattle Sta	16
7001	Richmond Highlands Contract Br	33
7301-7599	Bitter Lake Sta	33
8801-8999	Skyway Br	78
9000	Queen Anne Sta	09
12301-12939	Main Office	11
15001-15480	Wedgwood Sta	15
18001-18214	Columbia Sta	18
22001-22156	East Union Sta	22
24001-24672	Terminal Station	24
25001	Northgate Sta.	25
25501-25746	Lake City Sta	25
46001	White Center Br	46
55001-55199	North City Br	55
66001-66597	Burien Br	66
70101-70672	Ballard Sta.	07
80001-80816	Georgetown Sta	08
88501-88952	Tukwila Br	88
89001-89548	Zenith Br	88
98001-98872	Des Moines Br.	88
99001-99274	Magnolia Sta.	99

RURAL ROUTES

4,5,6,7,8	10

STATIONS, BRANCHES AND UNITS

Bainbridge Island Winslow Br	10
Ballard Sta.	07
Bitter Lake Sta.	33
Broadway Sta.	02
Burien Br	48
Capitol Hill Sta.	02
Columbia Sta.	18
Des Moines Br.	88
East Union Sta.	22
Federal Sta.	04
Forest Park Br	55
Gerogetown Br	08
Greenwood Sta.	03
Internat nal Sta.	04
Lake City Sta.	25
Lester Rural Br	98035
Magnolia Sta.	99
Manhattan Br	48
McMicken Heights Br	88
Naval Air Station Sta.	15
North City Br	55
Northgate Sta.	25
Port Blakely Br.	10
Queen Anne Sta	09
Richmond Beach Br	60
Rivertown Heights Br.	88
Sea First Sta.	04
Skyway Br.	78
Snoqualmie Pass Rural Br	98068
Terminal Annex Sta.	34
Times Square Sta.	01
Tukwila Br	88
University Sta.	05

Wallingford Sta.	03
Wedgwood Sta.	15
West Seattle Sta.	16
White Center Br.	46
Zenith Br.	88
General Delivery.	01
Postmaster.	09

APARTMENTS, HOTELS, MOTELS

Camlin, 1619 9th Ave.	01
Edgewater Inn, 2500 Alaskan Way	21
Frye Drive-In, 223 Yesler Way	04
Heart Of Seattle, 315 Seneca	01
Hilton Inn, 17620 Pacific Hwy S.	88
Hungerford, 1100 4th Ave	01
Mayflower, 405 Olive Way.	01
Moore, 1926 2nd Ave.	01
Olympic, 416 Seneca	11
Seattle Hilton, 1301 6th Ave.	11
Sherwood Motor Inn, 400 N E 45th	05
Sorrento, 1001 Terry Ave.	04
Stratford, 1121 3rd Ave.	01
Swept Wing Inn Motor, 18601 Pacific Hwy S.	88
Vance, 620 Ster art.	01
Washington Park Towers, 1620 43rd Ave E.	02
Washington Plaza, 1900 5th Ave.	01
Windsor, 1405 6th Ave.	01

BUILDINGS

Alaska, 618 2nd Ave.	04
Arcade Plaza, 1321 2nd Ave.	01
Arcade, 1319 2nd Ave	01
Arctic, 704 3rd Ave.	04
Areis, 2366 Eastlake Ave E	02
Central, 810 3rd Ave	04
Chamber Of Commerce, 215 Columbia	04
Cobb Medical Center, 1305 4th Ave	01
Colman, 811 1st Ave.	04
County Administration, 500 4th Ave	04
Denny, 2200 6th Ave	21
Dexter Horton, 710 2nd Ave.	04
Exchange, 821 2nd Ave	04
Federal Office, 909 1st Ave.	04
Fischer Studio, 1519 3rd Ave.	01
General Insurance, 4347 Brooklyn Ave NE	05
Green.joshua, 1425 4th Ave.	01
Hoge, 701 2nd Ave.	04
I B M, 1200 5th Ave.	01
Jones, 1331 3rd Ave	01
King County Court House, 516 3rd Ave	04
Labor Temple, 2800 1st Ave.	21
Lander St Annex, 2460 4th Ave S.	34
Lloyd, 603 Stewart	01
Logan, 500 Union	01
Lowman, 107 Cherry	04
Lyon, 607 3rd Ave.	04
Maritime, 911 Western Ave.	04
Medical Dental, 509 Olive Way	01

Metropole, 423 2nd Ave...... 04
Northern Life, 1100 3rd Ave... 01
Northwestern Life, 120 6th
  Ave N 09
Norton, 801 2nd Ave........... 04
Olympic National Life, 920
  2nd Ave...................... 04
Pacific, 720 3rd Ave............ 04
Park Place, 1200 6th Ave...... 01
Plaza 600, 600 Stewart........ 01
Polson, 71 Columbia............ 01
Public Safety, 610 3rd Ave.... 04
Republic, 1511 3rd Ave........ 01
Sage, 1305 3rd Ave............. 01
Seaboard, 1506 Westlake
  Ave 01
Seattle District Office, 415
  1st Ave N..................... 09
Seattle Municipal, 600 4th
  Ave 04
Seattle Public Library, 1000
  4th Ave....................... 04
Seattle Tower, 1218 3rd Ave.. 01
Seattle-First National Bank,
  1001 4th Ave................. 54
Securities, 1904 3rd Ave...... 01
Sixth & Pine, 523 Pine......... 01
Skinner, 1326 5th Ave......... 01
Smith Tower, 506 2nd Ave..... 01
Teamsters Hall, 552 Denny
  Way 09
Terminal Annex, 2445 3rd
  Ave S.......................... 34
Terminal Sales, 1932 1st
  Ave 01
Times Square, 414 Olive
  Way 01
Tower, 1807 7th Ave............ 01
U S Court House, 1010 5th
  Ave 04
Union Federal Savings, 1505
  4th Ave....................... 01
United Pacific, 1000 2nd
  Ave 04
University District, 1107 NE
  45th 05
Vance, Joseph, 1402 3rd Ave.. 01
Washington, 1325 4th Ave..... 01
White Henry Stuart, 1318 4th
  Ave 01

HOSPITALS

Ballard General, 5409 Barnes
  Ave NW........................ 07
Burien General, 16200 8th
  Ave SW........................ 66
Children'S Orthopedic, 4800
  Sand Point Way N E.......... 05
Doctors, 909 University........ 01
Firland Sanatorium, 1704 NE
  150th 55
Group Health, 201 16th Ave
  E............................... 12
Harborview, 325 9th Ave...... 04
King County Central Blood
  Bank, 921 Terry Ave......... 04
King County 1, 325 9th Ave.... 04
King County 2, 100 Crockett... 09
King County 3, 1704 NE
  150th 55
Northgate General, 120
  Northgate Plaza.............. 25
Northwest, 1551 N 120th...... 33

Providence, 530 17th Ave...... 22
Riverton General, 12844
  Military Rd S................. 68
Saint Frances Cabrini, 918
  Terry Ave..................... 04
Seattle General, 1309
  Summit Ave................... 01
Seneca Summit Surgery,
  1305 Seneca.................. 01
Standring Memorial, 12845
  12th Ave SW.................. 46
Swedish, 1212 Columbia....... 04
U S Public Health Service,
  1131 14th Ave S............. 14
United States Veterans
  Administration, 4435
  Beacon Ave S................. 08
University Of Washington,
  1959 NE Pacific.............. 95
Virginia Mason, 1111 Terry
  Ave 01
West Seattle General, 2601
  SW Webster................... 26

UNIVERSITIES AND COLLEGES

Seattle Community College,
  Central Campus Admin
  1718 Bdwy.................... 22
Seattle Community College,
  Dist 5, 401 Queen Anne
  Ave N......................... 09
Seattle Pacific, 3307 3rd Ave
  W.............................. 19
Seattle University, 900
  Broadway..................... 22
Univ Of Washington, Adm
  Bldg, 4000 15th Ave N E.... 05

SPOKANE   992

POST OFFICE BOXES

Box Nos.
1-999   Millwood Br...... 12
1-999   Parkwater Sta... 11
1-999   Trentwood Br.... 15
1-2299   Main Office...... 10
2500-3999   Terminal Annex
             Sta............. 20
4000-4999   B Sta........... 02
5000-5999   North Central
             Sta............. 05
6000-6999   Hillyard Sta.... 07
7200-7499   Hays Park Sta... 07
7500-7999   Rosewood Br.... 08
8000-8999   Manito Sta...... 03
9000-9999   Garland Sta..... 09
13000-13999 Dishman Br...... 13
14000-14999 Opportunity Br... 14
19000-19999 Spokane Intl
             Airport Br..... 19

RURAL ROUTES

1 04
2 07
3 03
4 08
5 08
7 04
10 04

11 08

STATIONS, BRANCHES AND UNITS

Country Homes Br.............. 18
Dishman Br..................... 13
Garland Sta..................... 09
Hayes Park Sta................. 07
Hillyard Sta..................... 07
Manito Sta...................... 03
Millwood Br..................... 12
North Central Sta............... 05
Opportunity Br.................. 14
Parkwater Sta.................. 11
Rosewood Br.................... 08
Spokane International
  AirprtBr....................... 19
Terminal Annex Sta............ 20
Trentwood Br................... 15
General Delivery............... 10
Postmaster..................... 10

APARTMENTS, NOTELS, MOTELS

Adlon, 526 1/2 W Main Ave... 01
Alberta, 172 1/2 S Madison... 04
Alberts, 152 S Pine............ 02
Alexander, 423 1/2 W Main
  Ave 01
Alexandria, 623 S Howard..... 04
Altadena, 608 Stevens S...... 04
Argonne, 101 N Argonne....... 06
Arlington, 302 W Sprague
  Ave 04
Avalon, 507 W 5th Ave........ 04
Avenida, 2009 W Pacific Ave.. 04
Blackstone, 803 W 3rd Ave... 04
Breslin, 729 S Bernard........ 04
Briggs, 225 S Wall............. 04
Brownstone, 223 S Browne.... 04
Brunot Hall, 2209 W Pacific
  Ave 04
Cambridge Court, 206 W 8th
  Ave 04
Carlyle, 206 S Post............ 04
Coeur D Alene, 228 N
  Howard........................ 18
Colonial, 124 1/2 N Post...... 01
Como, 403 W 1st Ave.......... 04
Cooper-George, 707 W 5th
  Ave 04
Culmstock Arms, 328 W 8th
  Ave 04
Daniel, 529 W Sinto Ave...... 01
Davenport, 807 W Sprague
  Ave 18
Del Cardo, 726 W 1st Ave..... 04
Dresden, 707 N Monroe........ 01
Dunsmuir, 21 E 2nd Ave....... 02
Earl, 224 S Lincoln............ 04
Elizabethan, 1429 W 9th Ave.. 04
Espanola, 155 S Oak........... 04
Fairmont, 315 W Riverside
  Ave 01
Felix, 1108 W 1st Ave.......... 04
Franklin Hall, 704 W 6th Ave.. 04
Granby Court, 28 N Madison... 01
Grand Coulee, 1401 W 1st
  Ave 04
Hosea, 1821 E Sprague Ave... 02
Jefferson, 618 S Jefferson.... 04
Kempis, 523 S Washington.... 04
Knickerbocker, 507 S Howard. 04
Kozy, 303 S Adams............. 04

Lloyd, 1006 W Mansfield Ave . 05
Marlboro, 180 S Cannon........ 04
Monrovia, 508 S Monroe....... 04
Montvale, 108 S Monroe........ 04
Mount Vernon, 1303 W 10th
   Ave.............................. 04
New Madison, 1029 W 1st
   Ave.............................. 04
Norland, 235 W Trent Ave..... 01
Otis, 110 S Madison............. 04
Oxford, 319 1/2 W Sprague
   Ave.............................. 04
Oxford, 702 S Bernard.......... 04
Parkwater, 1916 N Airport..... 06
Parsons, 108 S Jefferson....... 04
Pedicord, 213 W Riverside
   Ave.............................. 01
Pine Court, 27 E 8th Ave....... 02
Ridpath, 515 W Sprague....... 10
Roosevelt, 524 W 7th Ave..... 04
Saint Regis, 109 N Bernard.... 04
San Marco, 1230 W Sprague
   Ave.............................. 04
Seymour, 125 W 6th Ave....... 04
Sunshine, 5 S Cedar............. 04
Victoria, 618 W 1st Ave........ 04
Villa Nova, 1418 W Riverside
   Ave.............................. 01
Vista Court, 627 S Bernard.... 04
Washington, 1417 N
   Washington...................... 01
Washington, 327 1/2 W 2nd
   Ave.............................. 04
Wellington, 605 S Stevens..... 04
Westminster, 2301 W Pacific
   Ave.............................. 04

BUILDINGS

Bank Of Washington, 9 N
   Post............................... 01
Bon Marche, 214 N Wall........ 01
Chancery, 1023 W Riverside
   Ave.............................. 10
Chronicle, 926 W Sprague
   Ave.............................. 04
Civic, 1020 W Riverside Ave... 01
Columbia, 107 S Howard....... 01
Fidelity Plaza..................... 01
Fidelity, 522 W Riverside Ave. 01
First National, 502 W
   Riverside Ave................... 01
Great Western, 905 W
   Riverside........................ 01
Hillyard Branch, Spokane &
   Eastern Bank, 3009 E
   Olympic Ave.................... 07
Hutton, 9 S Washington........ 04
Hyde, 611 1/2 W Riverside
   Av................................. 01
Lincoln, 818 W Riverside Ave. 01
Masonic Temple, 1108 W
   Riverside Ave................... 01
Medical Center, 820 S Mc
   Clellan.......................... 04
Mohawk, 515 W Riverside
   Ave.............................. 01
Monroe, 1821 N Monroe........ 05
North Spokane Professional,
   5901 N Lidgerwood............ 07
Northtown Office, 4407 N
   Division......................... 07

Old National, 422 W
   Riverside Ave................... 01
Parkade Plaza.................... 01
Paulsen Medical & Dental,
   407 W Riverside Ave.......... 01
Paulsen, 421 W Riverside...... 01
Peyton, 10 N Post............... 01
Review, 927 W Riverside Ave. 01
Rookery, 14 N Howard.......... 01
Sherwood, 510 W Riverside
   Ave.............................. 01
Sixth Avenue Medical, 508 W
   6th Ave......................... 04
Spokane & Eastern, 601 W
   Riverside Ave................... 01
Spokane Coliseum, 1101 N
   Howard.......................... 01
State Theatre, 903 W
   Sprague Ave.................... 04
Symons, 7 S Howard............ 04
Telephone, 501 W 2nd Ave.... 04
Washington Trust, 713 W
   Sprague Ave.................... 04
Zukor, 705 W Riverside Ave... 01

GOVERNMENT OFFICES

Chamber Of Commerce, 1020
   W Riverside Ave................ 01
City Hall, 221 N Wall........... 01
County-City Public Safety
   Bldg., 1100 W Mallon Ave.... 01
Farm Credit Banks Of
   Spokane Bldg, 705 W 1st
   Ave.............................. 04
Spokane County Court House,
   1116 W Broadway Ave......... 01
U S Court House, 920 W
   Riverside Ave................... 01
U S Federal Bldg & Post
   Office, 904 W Riverside
   Ave.............................. 01
United States Post Office
   Terminal Annex, 703 E
   Trent Ave....................... 02

HOSPITALS

Deaconess, 800 W 5th Ave.... 10
Holy Family, 5633 N
   Lidgerwood...................... 20
Sacred Heart, 101 W 8th
   Ave.............................. 04
Saint Luke'S Memorial, 711 S
   Cowley........................... 10
Shriners Hospital For
   Crippled Children, 820 W
   Summit Blvd.................... 01
Valley General Hospital
   12606 E Mission Ave.......... 20
Veterans Administration
   Hospital, 4815 N
   Assembly........................ 08

UNIVERSITIES AND COLLEGES

Fort Wright College Of Holy
   Names, W 4000 Randolph
   Rd................................ 04
Gonzaga University, 502 E
   Boone Ave....................... 02

Spokane Community (East
   Miss Campus) 3403 E
   Mission Ave.................... 02
Spokane Falls Community, Ft
   Wright Campus, W 3410
   Ft Wright........................ 04
Whitworth College, Country
   Homes Estate................... 18

TACOMA   984

POST OFFICE BOXES

Box Nos.
1-350   Fern Hill Sta..... 12
1-447   Lakeview Br...... 91
1-570   Tillicum Br 92
1-2277   Main Office...... 01
1-448S   South Tacoma
                   Sta............ 09
3001-3470   Lakewood
                   Center Br..... 99
4000-4299   Mc Chord Air
                   Force Base
                   Br............. 38
5001-5294   Kay Street Sta... 05
7001-7358   Proctor.......... 07
9901-9480   South Tacoma
                   Sta............ 09
11001-11397   Terminal Annex
                   Sta............ 11
33001-33208   Fort Lewis...... 33
44001-44669   Parkland Br..... 44
94001-94999   Fort
                   Steilacoom.... 94

RURAL ROUTES

2.................................... 24
6.................................... 22
12................................... 24

STATIONS, BRANCHES AND UNITS

American Lake Br................. 93
Dash Point Rural Br............. 22
Fern Hill Sta...................... 12
Fife Br............................. 24
Fircrest Br........................ 66
Fort Lewis Br..................... 33
Fort Steilacoom Br.............. 94
K Street Sta....................... 05
Lakeview Br....................... 91
Lakewood Center Br............. 99
Longmire Rural Br...........98397
McChord AFB Br.................. 38
Monta Vista Br.................... 99
North Fort Lewis Br............. 33
Paradise Inn Rural Br.......98398
Parkland Br....................... 44
Proctor Sta........................ 07
Sixth Avenue Sta................. 06
South Tacoma Sta................ 09
Steilacoom Br.................98388
Terminal Sta...................... 04
Tillicum Br........................ 92
General Delivery.................. 02
Postmaster......................... 02

APARTMENTS, HOTELS, MOTELS

Ambassador House, 3502
   92nd S............................ 09

Americana, 242 St Helens S... 02
Ansonia, 219 Tacoma Ave N... 03
Broadmoor, 431 Broadway S.. 02
Buckingham, 1001 Yakima
N.. 03
Cambridge, 415 6th Ave....... 02
Capri, 4910 108th St SW....... 99
Carlton, 1552 Jefferson Ave
S.. 02
Finnisterre, 601 Jackson Ave
N.. 06
Holiday Inn, 3518 Pacific
Hwy E................................. 01
Ingleside, 205 Tacoma Ave
.... 03
Manor House, 5800 100th
SW...................................... 99
Miramar, 7320 6th Ave......... 06
Olympic Manor, 7301 6th
Ave..................................... 06
Olympic, 304 Tacoma Ave S.. 02
Olympus, 815 Pacific Ave S.. 02
Park Towers 220 Tacoma Ave
S.. 02
Rainier Village, 9206 Pacific
Ave S................................. 44
Saint James, 821 Yakima
Ave S................................. 05
Sky Terrace, 235 Broadway .. 02
Thunderbird, 8210
Steilacoom Blvd SW............ 98
Town House, 117 Tacoma
Ave N................................. 03
Vista Manor, 319 Tacoma
Ave N................................. 03
Walker, 405 6th Ave............. 02
Washington, 518 7th S.......... 02
Winthrop, 773 Broadway S... 02

BUILDINGS

County-City, 930 Tacoma Ave
S.. 02
Federal, 1102 A.................... 02
Labor Temple, 950 Fawcett
Ave S................................. 02
Medical Arts, 740 St. Helens
Ave S................................. 02
Perkins, 1103 A.................... 02
Public Service, 1301 Tacoma
Ave S................................. 02
Puget Sound Bank, 1117
Pacific Ave S...................... 02
Rust, 950 Pacific Ave S........ 02
Tacoma, 1015 A.................... 02
Washington Plaza, 1201
Pacific Ave S...................... 02
Washington, 1019 Pacific
Ave S................................. 02

HOSPITALS

Allenmore, 1901 Union Ave
.... 05
Doctors, 737 Fawcett S......... 02
Lakewood General, 5702
100th SW............................ 99
Madigan General, Fort Lewis. 31
Mary Bridge Childrens, 311 L
S.. 05
Puget Sound General, 215 36
.... 08

Saint Josephs, 1812 Eye S.... 01
Tacoma General, 315 K S..... 05
United States Veterans,
American Lake.................. 93
Western State, Fort
Steilacoom........................ 94

UNIVERSITIES AND COLLEGES

Pacific Lutheran University,
Parkland............................ 47
Tacoma Community College,
5900 12th S........................ 65
University Of Puget Sound,
1500 Warner N................... 16

VANCOUVER 986

POST OFFICE BOXES

Box Nos.
1-1500   Main Office 60
1501-2000   Arnada Park
             Annex Sta...... 63
2001-2500   Fourth Plain
             Sta............. 61
2501-3000   Orchards Br.... 62

RURAL ROUTES

1,2,5 62
6,7 65

STATIONS, BRANCHES AND UNITS

Arnada Park Annex Sta........ 63
Fourth Plain Sta.................. 61
Hazel Dell Br...................... 60
Minnehaha Br...................... 61
Orchards Br........................ 62
Veterans Administration
Hosp Sta............................ 61
General Delivery................. 60
Postmaster........................ 60

APARTMENTS, HOTELS, MOTELS

Aloha, 708 NE 78................. 65
Fort Motel, 500 E 13th......... 60
Franklin Court, 1013
Franklin............................ 60
Mid Columbia Manor, 515
Washington........................ 60
Normandy, 316 E 7th............ 60
Riviera, 105 E 5th................ 60
Travelodge, 601 Broadway... 60
Valley, 1800 Simpson Ave 60
Van Vista Plaza 410 W 13th
St...................................... 60

BUILDINGS

Adams, 1105 Broadway......... 60
American Legion, 301 E 7th... 60
Carpenters Union Hall, 612 E
Mc Laughlin Blvd................ 63
Central, 1206 1/2 Main......... 60
Clark County Court House,
1200 Franklin..................... 60
Clark County P U D, 1200
Fort Vancouver Way............ 63
Elks Club, 105 W Evergreen

Blvd.................................. 60
Federal, 500 W 12th.............. 60
Ford, 601 Main..................... 60
Fort Vancouver Regional Libr,
1007 E Mill Plain Blvd......... 63
Freeway, 1401 C................... 63
Labor Temple, 205 11th........ 60
Masonic Temple, 2500 NE
78...................................... 65
Medical Arts, 1104 Main....... 60
Municipal, 210 E 13th........... 60
Pacific Tel N W, 112 11th...... 60
Patio, 108 W Evergreen Blvd.. 60
State-Federal Office, 1408
Franklin............................ 60
Vancouver School Dist 37,
605 N Devine Rd................. 61

HOSPITALS

U S Veterans, 1603 Fourth
Plain Blvd.......................... 61
Vancouver Memorial, 3400
Main.................................. 63
600 NE 92 Ave P O Box
1687................................... 61

UNIVERSITIES AND COLLEGES

Clark, 1925 Ft Vancouver
Way.................................... 63

YAKIMA 989

POST OFFICE BOXES

Box Nos.
1-1999   Main Office 01
2000-2999   West Side Sta .. 02
3000-3999   Union Gap Br... 03

RURAL ROUTES

1 01
2 01
3 02
4 05
5 03
6 02
7 03
8 02

STATIONS, BRANCHES AND UNITS

Gleed Rural Br..................... 04
Schwarder Rural Br.............. 05
Terrace Heights Br............... 01
Union Gap Br....................... 03
West Side Sta....................... 02
Wiley Rural Br...................... 06
General Delivery................. 01
Postmaster........................ 01

APARTMENTS, HOTELS, MOTELS

Chieftain, 17 S 2nd............... 01
Chinook, Box 821................. 01
Yakima, P O Box 22.............. 01

BUILDINGS

City Hall, 129 N 2nd............... 01
Federal, 25 S 3rd.................. 01
Larson, 6 S 2nd.................... 01
Miller, 205 E. Yakima Ave....... 01
Yakima County Courthouse, N
  2nd & E B...................... 01

HOSPITALS

Saint Elizabeth, 110 So 9th
  Ave............................. 02
Vally Osteopathic, 3003
  Tieton Dr...................... 02
Yakima Valley Memorial,
  2811 Tieton Dr................ 02

MILITARY INSTALLATIONS

Yakima Firing Center.............. 01

UNIVERSITIES AND COLLEGES

Yakima Valley College, 16th
  Ave & W Nob Hill.............. 02

WEST VIRGINIA
(Abbreviation: WV)

Abraham...............................25955
Accoville.............................25606
Adolph................................26247
Adrian................................26210
Advent................................25231
Albright..............................26519
Alderson..............................24910
Alexander.............................26211
Algoma................................24807
Alkol.................................25501
Allen Junction........................25810
Alloy.................................25002
Alma..................................26320
Alpoca................................24710
Alta..................................26655
Alton.................................26212
Alum Bridge...........................26321
Alum Creek............................25003
Alvy..................................26322
Amboy.................................26701
Ameagle...............................25004
Amherstdale...........................25607
Amigo.................................25811
Amma..................................25005
Anawalt...............................24808
Anmoore...............................26323
Annamoriah............................26130
Ansted................................25812
Anthony...............................24914
Antioch...............................26702
Apple Grove...........................25502
Arbovale..............................24915
Arbuckle..............................25006
Arden, R. Br. Moatsville..............26324
Arnett................................25007
Arnoldsburg...........................25234
Arthur................................26816
Arthurdale............................26520
Artie.................................25008
Asbury................................24916
Asco..................................24809
Ashford...............................25009
Ashland...............................24810
Ashton................................25503
Athens................................24712
Auburn................................26325
Augusta...............................26704
Aurora................................26705
    Horse Shoe Run, R. Br. 26769
Auto..................................24917
Avondale..............................24811
Baileysville..........................24812
Baisden...............................25608
Baker.................................26801
Bakerton, R. Br. Harpers
    Ferry.............................25410
Bald Knob.............................25010
Baldwin...............................26326
Ballard...............................24918
Ballengee.............................24919
Bancroft..............................25011
Bandytown.............................25012
Barboursville (1st)...................25504
Barnabus..............................25609
Barnum................................26706
Barrackville..........................26559
Barrett...............................25013
Bartley...............................24813
Bartow................................24920
Basin, R. Br. Herndon.................24727

Baxter, R. Br. Rivesville.............26560
Bayard................................26707
Beard.................................24921
Beards Fork...........................25014
Beartown, R. Br. Bradshaw.............24814
Beaver................................25813
Beckley (1st).........................25801
Beckwith..............................25814
Beech Bottom..........................26030
Beeson................................24714
Belington.............................26250
Belle.................................25015
    Diamond, R. Br. 25015
    Quincy, R. Br. 25016
    Shrewsbury, R. Br. 25184
Bellepoint, Sta. Hinton...............25951
Belleville............................26133
Bellview, Sta. Fairmont...............26554
Belmont...............................26134
Belva.................................26656
Bens Run..............................26135
Bentree...............................25018
Benwood...............................26031
Berea.................................26327
Bergoo................................26298
Berkeley Springs......................25411
Berwind...............................24815
Besoco, R. Br. Rhodell................25815
Bethany...............................26032
Beverly...............................26253
Beverly Hills, Sta.
    Huntington.......................25705
Bickmore..............................25019
Big Chimney, R. Br.
    Charleston.......................25302
Big Creek.............................25505
Big Otter.............................25020
Big Run...............................26561
Big Sandy.............................24816
Big Springs...........................26137
Bigbend...............................26136
Bim...................................25021
Birch River...........................26610
Blackberry City.......................25664
Blacksville...........................26521
Blair.................................25022
Blandville............................26328
Bloomery..............................26817
Bloomingrose..........................25024
Blount................................25025
Blue Creek............................25026
Blue Jay..............................25816
Bluefield (1st).......................24701
Bluewell, R. Br. Bluefield............24701
Bob White.............................25028
Boggs.................................26299
Bolair, R. Br. Webster
    Springs..........................26288
Bolivar, R. Br. Harpers Ferry.........25426
Bolt..................................25817
Bomont................................25030
Boomer................................25031
Booth.................................26522
Borderland............................25665
Bowden................................26254
Bozoo.................................24923
Bradley...............................25818
Bradshaw..............................24817
    Beartown, R. Br. 24814
Braeholm..............................25610
Bramwell..............................24715
Branchland............................25506
Brandonville..........................26523

Brandywine............................26802
Breeden...............................25666
Brenton...............................24818
Bretz.................................26524
Bridgeport (1st)......................26330
Bristol...............................26332
Broaddus, Br. Philippi................26416
Brohard...............................26138
Brooks................................25957
Brownton..............................26334
Bruceton Mills........................26525
Bruno.................................25611
Buckeye...............................24924
Buckhannon (1st)......................26201
    Queens, R. Br. 26231
Bud...................................24716
Buffalo...............................25033
Bunker Hill...........................25413
Burlington............................26710
Burning Springs.......................26139
Burnsville............................26335
    Copen, R. Br. 26615
Burnt House...........................26336
Burnwell..............................25034
Burton................................26562
Cabin Creek...........................25035
    Chelyan, R. Br. 25041
Cabins................................26855
Cairo.................................26337
Caldwell..............................24925
Calvin................................26660
Camden................................26338
Camden On Gauley......................26208
Cameron...............................26033
Camp Creek............................25820
Canebrake.............................24819
Cannelton.............................25036
Canvas................................26662
Capels................................24820
Capitol, Sta. Charleston..............25311
Capon Bridge..........................26711
Capon Springs.........................26823
Carbon................................25037
Caretta...............................24821
Carlisle..............................25821
Carolina..............................26563
Cascade...............................26526
Cashmere..............................24926
Cass..................................24927
Cassville.............................26527
Catawba, R. Br. Fairmont..............26564
Cedar Grove...........................25039
Cedarville............................26611
Center Point..........................26339
Central Station.......................26340
Centralia.............................26612
Century...............................26214
Ceredo................................25507
Chapmanville..........................25508
Charles Town (1st)....................25414
CHARLESTON (1st) (see
    appendix)
Charlton Heights......................25040
Charmco...............................25958
Chattaroy.............................25667
Chauncey..............................25612
Chelyan, R. Br. Cabin Creek...........25041
Cherry Grove..........................26803
Cherry Run............................25418
Chesapeake, Br. Charleston............25315
Chester (1st).........................26034
Chloe.................................25235
Cinco, R. Br. Charleston..............25306

Circleville	26804
Clarksburg (1st)	26301
Nutter Fort Stonewood, Br.	26302
Wilsonburg, R. Br.	26461
Clay	25043
Clear Creek	25044
Clear Fork	24822
Clem	26626
Clendenin	25045
Cleveland	26215
Clifftop	25831
Clifton	25237
Clintonville	24928
Clio	25046
Clothier	25047
Coal City	25823
Coal Fork, R Br. Charleston	25306
Coal Mountain	24823
Coaldale	24717
Coalton	26257
Coalwood	24824
Coburn	26562
Colcord	25048
Colfax	26566
Colliers	26035
Comfort	25049
Cool Ridge	25825
Copen, R. Br. Burnsville	26615
Cora	25614
Core	26529
Corinne	25826
Corinth	26713
Corley	26616
Cornstalk	24930
Corton	25050
Costa	25051
Cottageville	25239
Cottle	26207
Cove, Sta. Weirton	26062
Cove Gap	25509
Covel	24719
Cowen	26206
Coxs Mills	26342
Crab Orchard	25827
Craigsville	26205
Cranberry	25828
Crawford	26343
Crawley	24931
Creston	26141
Crichton	25961
Cross Lanes, Br. Charleston	25313
Crown	25616
Crown Hill	25052
Crum	25669
Crumpler	24825
Cucumber	24826
Culloden	25510
Cunard	25830
Curtin	26204
Cuzzart	26530
Cyclone	24827
Dailey	26259
Dallas	26036
Danese	25831
Daniels	25832
Danville	25053
Davin	25617
Davis	26260
Davisville	26142
Davy	24828
Dawes	25054
Dawmont	26344
Dawson	24932
Deep Water	25057
Dehue	25618
Delbarton	25670
Dellslow	26531
Delray	26714
Diamond, R. Br. Belle	25015
Diana	26217
Dille	26617
Dingess	25671
Dink	25058
Dixie	25059
Dorcas	26835
Dorothy	25060
Dothan	25833
Dott	24721
Downtown, Sta. Wheeling	26003
Drennen	26667
Droop	24933
Dry Creek	25062
Drybranch	25061
Dryfork	26263
Duck	25063
Duhring	24722
Dunbar (1st)	25064
Duncan	25240
Dunlow	25511
Dunmore	24934
Durbin	26264
Earling	25619
East Bank	25067
East Beckley, Sta. Beckley	25801
East Lynn	25512
Eastgulf	25835
Eastside, Sta. Fairmont	26554
Eccles	25836
Eckman	24829
Edgarton	25672
Edmond	25837
Egion	26716
Elbert	24830
Eleanor	25070
Elgood	24723
Elizabeth	26143
Elk Garden	26717
Elkhorn	24831
Elkins (1st)	26241
Elkview	25071
Ellamore	26267
Ellenboro	26346
Elm Grove, Sta. Wheeling	26003
Elmira	26618
Elton	25965
Emmett	25620
Emoryville, R. Br. Elk Garden	26717
English	24832
Enterprise	26568
Erbacon	26203
Eskdale	25075
Ethel	25076
Eureka	26144
Evans	25241
Everettville	26533
Excelsior, R. Sta. War	24833
Exchange	26619
Fairdale	25839
Fairlea, R. Br. Lewisburg	24902
Fairmont (1st)	26554
Bellview, Sta.	26554
Catawba, R. Br.	26554
Eastside. Sta.	26554
Monongah, Br.	26554
Watson, Sta.	26554
Fairview	26570
Falling Rock	25079
Falling Waters	25419
Falls Mill	26620
Fanrock	24834
Farmington	26571
Fayetteville	25840
Federal, Sta. Bluefield	24701
Fenwick	26202
Ferrellsburg	25513
Filbert	24835
Fireco, R. Br. Coal City	25823
Fisher	26818
Five Forks	26145
Flat Top	25841
Flatwoods	26621
Flemington	26347
Floe	25242
Flower	26622
Fola	25080
Follansbee	26037
Folsom	26348
Forest Hill	24935
Fort Ashby	26719
Fort Gay	25514
Fort Neal, Sta. Parkersburg	26101
Fort Seybert	26806
Fort Spring	24936
Foster	25081
Four States	26572
Frame, R. Br. Elkview	25071
Frametown	26623
Servia, R. Br.	26637
Frank	24937
Frankford	24938
Franklin	26807
Fraziers Bottom	25082
Freeman	24724
French Creek	26218
Frenchton, R. Br.	26219
Frenchton, R. Br. French Creek	26219
Friars Hill	24939
Friendly	26146
Gaines	26220
Gallagher	25083
Gallipolis Ferry	25515
Galloway	26349
Gandeeville	25243
Gap Mills	24941
Garrison	25084
Garten	25842
Gary	24836
Gassaway	26624
Gauley Bridge	25085
Gauley Mills	26240
Gay	25244
Gem	26625
Genoa	25517
Gerrardstown	25420
Ghent	25843
Gilbert	25621
Gilboa	26671

Gilkam	24837
Gilmer	26350
Given	25245
Glace	24942
Glady	26268
Glasgow	25086
Glen	25088
Glen Dale	26038
Glen Daniel	25844
Glen Easton	26039
Glen Ferris	25090
Glen Fork	25845
Glen Jean	25846
Glen Morgan	25847
Glen Rogers	25848
Glen White	25849
Glendon	26626
Glengary	25421
Glenhayes	25519
Glenville	26351
Glenwood	25520
Goffs	26353
Gordon	25093
Gormania	26720
Grafton (1st)	26354
Grant Town	26574
Grantsville	26147
Granville	26534
Grassy Meadows	24943
Great Cacapon	25422
Green Bank	24944
Green Spring	26722
Green Sulphur Springs	25966
Greenville	24945
Greenwood	26360
Griffithsville	25521
Grimms Landing	25095
Guardian	26221
Guyandotte, Sta. Huntington	25702
Gypsy	26361
Hacker Valley	26222
Hager	25522
Hallburg	25101
Halltown	25423
Hambleton	26269
Hamlin	25523
Hampden	25623
Hancock	25424
Handley	25102
Hanover	24839
Hansford	25103
Harman	26270
Harmony	25246
Harper	25851
Harpers Ferry	25425
Bakerton, R. Br.	25410
Bolivar, R. Br.	25426
Harrison	25105
Harrisville	26362
Hartford	25247
Harts	25524
Harvey	25852
Hastings	26365
Havaco	24841
Hawwood	26366
Hazelgreen	26367
Hazelton	26535
Heaters	26627
Hebron	26368
Hedgesville	25427
Helen	25853
Helvetia	26224
Hemphill	24842

Henderson	25106
Hendricks	26271
Henlawson	25624
Hensley	24843
Hepzibah	26369
Herndon	24726
Basin, R. Br.	24727
Hernshaw	25107
Herold	26628
Hewett	25108
Hiawatha	24729
Hico	25854
High View	26808
Highland	26371
Hillsboro	24946
Hilltop	25855
Hines	25967
Hinton (1st)	25951
Hix	25968
Holcomb, R. Br. Richwood	26262
Holden	25625
Hollywood	24947
Hometown	25109
Hominy Falls, R. Br.	
Summersville	26673
Hopemont	26723
Horner	26372
Horse Shoe Run, R. Br.	
Aurora	26769
Hugheston	25110
Hundred	26575
Hunt, R. Br. Man	25635
HUNTINGTON (1st) (see appendix)	
Hurricane (1st)	25526
Hurst	26373
Hutchinson	25627
Huttonsville	26273
Iaeger	24844
Idamay	26576
Ikes Fork	24845
Independence	26374
Indian Mills	24949
Indore	25111
Industrial	26375
Institute	25112
Inwood	25428
Ireland	26376
Isaban	24846
Itmann	24847
Ivanhoe	26227
Ivydale	25113
Jacksonburg	26377
Jane Lew	26378
Jeffrey	25114
Jenkinjones	24848
Jere	26536
Jesse	24849
Job	26274
Jodie	26674
Jolo	24850
Jonben	25856
Jones Springs	25429
Jordan	26577
Josephine	25857
Josephs Mills	26379
Julian	25529
Jumping Branch	25969
Junction	26824
Junior	26275
Justice	24851
Kanawha City, Sta.	
Charleston	25384

Kanawha Falls	25115
Kanawha Head	26228
Kasson	26380
Kayford	25116
Kearneysville	25430
Kegley	24731
Kellysville	24732
Kenna	25248
Kenova	25530
Kentuck	25249
Kerens	26276
Kermit	25674
Keslers Cross Lanes	26675
Kessler	25970
Keyser (1st)	26726
Keystone	24852
Kiahsville	25534
Kieffer	24950
Kilsyth	25859
Kimball	24853
Kimberly	25118
Kincaid	25119
Kingmont	26578
Kingston	25120
Kingwood (1st)	26537
Kirby	26729
Kistler	25628
Knob Fork	26579
Kopperston	24854
Kyle	24855
Lahmansville	26731
Lake	25121
Lakin	25250
Lanark	25860
Landes, R. Br. Petersburg	26832
Landville	26629
Lanham, R. Br. Poca	25159
Lansing	25862
Lashmeet	24733
Lavalette	25535
Lawton	25863
Layland	25864
Le Roy	25252
Leckie	24856
Leet	25536
Leewood	25122
Left Hand	25251
Lehew	26843
Leivasy	26676
Lenore	25676
Leon	25123
Leopold	26382
Lerona	25971
Lesage	25537
Leslie	25972
Lester	25865
Letart	25253
Letter Gap	25255
Levels	25431
Lewisburg (1st)	24901
Fairlea, R. Br.	24902
Liberty	25124
Lima	26383
Linden	25256
Lindside	24951
Rock Camp, R. Br.	24967
Linn	26384
Little Birch	26629
Little Falls	26540
Littleton	26581
Liverpool	25257
Lizemores	25125
Lobata	25677

Lochgelly	25866
Lockbridge	25973
Lockney	25258
Lockwood, R. Br.	
Summersville	26677
Logan (1st)	25601
London	25126
Long Branch	25867
Longacre	25127
Lookout	25868
Looneyville	25259
Lorado	25630
Lorentz	26229
Lost City	26810
Lost Creek	26385
Lost River	26811
Lumberport	26386
Lundale	25631
Lyburn	25632
Lynco	24857
Maben	25870
Mabie	26278
Mabscott	25871
Mac Arthur	25873
Mace	26279
Macfarlan	26148
Madison	25130
Mahan	25131
Mahone	26402
Maidsville	26541
Malden, R. Br. Charleston	25306
Mallory	25634
Mammoth	25132
Man	25635
Manheim	26403
Mannington	26582
Maplewood	25874
Marfrance	25975
Marianna, R. Br. Pineville	24859
Marlinton	24954
Marmet, Br. Charleston	25315
Marshall University, Sta.	
Huntington	25703
Martinsburg (1st)	25401
Mason	25260
Masontown	26542
Matewan	25678
Matheny	24860
Mathias	26812
Matoaka	24736
Maxwelton	24957
Maybeury	24861
Maysel	25133
Maysville	26833
Mc Alpin	25869
Mc Comas	24735
Mc Connell	25633
Mc Dowell	24858
Mc Graws	25875
Saulsville, R. Br.	25876
Mc Mechen	26040
Mc Whorter	26401
Mead	25877
Meador	25682
Meadow Bluff	24958
Meadow Bridge	25976
Meadow Creek	25977
Meadowbrook	26404
Medley	26734
Merrimac, R. Br. Williamson	25661
Metz	26585
Miami	25134
Middlebourne	26149

Midkiff	25540
Midway	25878
Milam	26838
Mill Creek	26280
Mill Point	24959
Millstone	25261
Millville	25432
Millwood	25262
Milton	25541
Minden	25879
Mineralwells	26150
Mingo	26281
Minnehaha Springs	24960
Minnora	25263
Moatsville	26405
Arden, R. Br.	26324
Mohawk	24862
Monaville	25636
Monongah, Br. Fairmont	26554
Montana Mines	26586
Montcalm	24737
Montcoal	25135
Monterville	26282
Montgomery (1st)	25136
Montrose	26283
Moorefield	26836
Morgantown (1st)	26505
Sabraton, Sta.	26505
Star City, Br.	26505
Westover, Br.	26505
Morrisvale	25542
Moundsville (1st)	26041
Mount Alto	25264
Mount Carbon	25139
Mount Clare	26408
Mount Gay	25637
Mount Hope	25880
Mount Lookout	26678
Mount Nebo	26679
Mount Storm	26739
Mount Zion	26151
Mountain	26407
Mouth of Seneca	26884
Moyers	26813
Mud	25543
Mullens	25882
Munday	26152
Murraysville	26153
Myra	25544
Myrtle	25684
Nallen	26680
Naoma	25140
Napier	26631
Naugatuck	25685
Nebo	25141
Nellis	25142
Nemours	24738
Neola, R. Br. White Sulphur	
Springs	24961
Nettie	26681
Neville, Sta. Beckley	25801
New Creek	26743
New Cumberland	26047
New England	26154
New Haven	25265
New Manchester	26056
New Martinsville (1st)	26155
New Milton	26411
New Richmond	24867
Newberne	26409
Newburg	26410
Newell	26050
Newhall	24866

Newton	25266
Newton D Baker V A Center,	
Br. Martinsburg	25401
Newtown	25686
Newville	26632
Nicut	26633
Nimitz	25978
Nitro (1st)	25143
Nobe	26158
Nolan	25687
Normantown	25267
North Matewan	25688
North Parkersburg, Sta.	
Parkersburg	26101
North Spring	24869
Northfork	24868
Northriver Mills	26744
Norton	26285
Nutter Fort Stonewood, Br.	
Clarksburg	26301
Oak Hill (1st)	25901
Oakvale, R. Br. Princeton	24739
Oceana	24870
Odd	25902
Ohley	25147
Old Fields	26845
Omar	25638
Omps	25433
Ona	25545
Onego	26886
Orgas	25148
Orient Hill, R. Br. Charmco	25958
Orlando	26412
Orma	25268
Osage	26543
Ottawa	25149
Ovapa	25150
Owings	26413
Oxford, R. Br. West Union	26414
Packsville, R. Br.	
Whitesville	25151
Paden City	26159
Page	25152
Pageton	24871
Palermo	25546
Palestine	26160
Panther	24872
Parcoal	26265
Parkersburg (1st)	26105
Parsons	26287
Patterson Creek	26746
Paw Paw	25434
Pax	25904
Paynesville	24873
Peach Creek	25639
Pecks Mill	25547
Pemberton	25905
Pence Springs	24962
Pennsboro	26415
Pentress	26544
Perkins	26634
Perry	26844
Petersburg	26847
Landes, R. Br.	26832
Peterstown	24963
Petroleum	26161
Pettus, R. Br. Whitesville	25153
Peytona	25154
Philippi (1st)	26416
Pickaway	24964
Pickens	26230
Pie	25689
Piedmont	26750

Pigeon	25155
Pinch	25156
Pine Grove	26419
Pineville	24874
Marianna, R. Br.	24859
Piney View	25906
Pipestem	25979
Pisgah	26545
Pliny	25158
Poca	25159
Poe	26683
Point Pleasant (1st)	25550
Points	25437
Pond Gap	25160
Pool	26684
Port Amherst, R. Br. Charleston	25306
Porters Falls	26162
Powellton	25161
Power	26054
Powhatan	24877
Pratt	25162
Premier	24878
Prenter	25163
Prichard	25555
Prince	25907
Princeton (1st)	24740
Oakvale, R. Br.	24739
Princewick	25908
Procious	25164
Proctor	26055
Prosperity	25909
Pullman	26421
Purgitsville	26852
Pursglove	26546
Queens, R. Br. Buckhannon	26231
Quick, R. Br. Clendenin	25045
Quincy, R. Br. Belle	25016
Quinnimont	25910
Quinwood	25981
Rachel	26587
Racine	25165
Radnor	25556
Ragland	25690
Rainelle	25962
Raleigh	25911
Ramage	25166
Ramsey	25912
Rand, Br. Charleston	25306
Ranger	25557
Rangoon	26232
Ranson	25438
Ravencliff	25913
Ravenswood (1st)	26164
Rawl	25691
Raysal	24875
Reader	26167
Red Creek	26289
Red House	25168
Red Jacket	25692
Redstar	25914
Reedsville	26547
Reedy	25270
Renick	24966
Replete	26233
Reynoldsville	26422
Rhodell	25915
Besoco, R. Br.	25815
Richwood	26261
Holcomb, R. Br.	26262
Ridgeley	26753
Ridgeview	25169
Ridgeway	25440

Riffle	26635
Rig	26854
Rio	26755
Ripley	25271
Rippon	25441
Riverton	26814
Rivesville	26588
Baxter, R. Br.	26560
Roanoke	26423
Robertsburg	25172
Robinette	25642
Robson	25173
Rock	24747
Rock Camp, R. Br. Lindside	24957
Rock Castle	25272
Rock Cave	26234
Rock Creek	25174
Rock View	24880
Rockport	26169
Roderfield	24881
Romance	25175
Romney	26757
Ronceverte	24970
Rosedale	26636
Rosemont	26424
Rossmore	25643
Rough Run	26860
Rowlesburg	26425
Runa	26688
Rupert	25984
Russellville	26689
Sabine	25916
Sabraton, Sta. Morgantown	26505
Saint Albans (1st)	25177
Saint George	26290
Saint Marys	26170
Salem	26426
Salt Rock	25559
Saltpetre	25558
Sand Fork	26430
Sand Ridge	25274
Sandstone	25985
Sandyville	25275
Sarah Ann	25644
Sarton	24973
Saulsville, R. Br. Mc Graws	25876
Saxon	25180
Scarbro	25917
Scherr, R. Br. Keyser	26726
Scott Depot	25560
Secondcreek	24974
Seebert	24975
Selbyville	26236
Servia, R. Br. Frametown	26637
Seth	25181
Shady Spring	25918
Shanks	26761
Sharon	25182
Sharples	25183
Shaw	26762
Shenandoah Junction	25442
Shepherdstown	25443
Sherman	26173
Sherrard	26057
Shinnston	26431
Shirley	26434
Shively	25561
Shoals	25562
Shock	26638
Short Creek	26058
Shrewsbury, R. Br. Belle	25184
Sias	25563
Simon	24882

Simpson	26435
Sinks Grove	24976
Sissonville, Br. Charleston	25320
Sistersville	26175
Skelton	25919
Skygusty	24883
Slab Fork	25920
Slanesville	25444
Slatyfork	26291
Sleepy Creek	25445
Smithburg	26436
Smithers	25186
Smithfield	26437
Smithville	26178
Smoot	24977
Sod	25564
Sophia	25921
Stotesbury, R. Br.	25929
South Charleston, Br. Charleston	25303
South Williamson Ky. Br. Williamson	25661
Southside	25187
Spanishburg	25922
Spelter	26438
Spencer (1st)	25276
Sprague	25926
Sprigg	25693
Spring	25986
Spring Dale	25986
Spring Hill, Br. Charleston	25309
Springfield	26763
Springton	24748
Spurlockville	25565
Squire	24884
Stanaford	25927
Star City, Br. Morgantown	26505
Statts Mills	25279
Steeles, R. Br. Iaeger	24844
Stephenson	25928
Stickney	25188
Stirrat	25645
Stollings	25646
Stonewall, Sta. Charleston	25302
Stony Bottom	24979
Stotesbury, R. Br. Sophia	25929
Stouts Mills	26439
Strange Creek	26639
Streeter	25987
Stumptown	25280
Sugar Grove	26815
Sullivan	25930
Sumerco	25567
Summerlee	25931
Summersville (1st)	26651
Hominy Falls, R. Br.	26673
Lockwood, R. Br.	26677
Summit Point	25446
Sundial	25189
Superior	24886
Surveyor	25932
Sutton	26601
Sweet Springs	24980
Sweetland	25568
Swiss	26690
Switchback	24887
Switzer	25647
Sylvester	25193
Tad	25201
Talcott	24981
Telimansville	26237
Tams	25933
Tanner	26179
Taplin	25648

Tariff	25281
Teays	25569
Terra Alta	26764
Terry	25934
Tesla	26640
Thacker	25694
Thomas	26292
Thornton	26440
Thorpe	24888
Three Churches	26765
Thurmond	25936
Tioga	26691
Toll Gate	26442
Tornado	25202
Triadelphia	26059
Trout	24982
Troy	26443
True	25988
Tunnelton	26444
Turtle Creek	25203
Twilight	25204
Twin Branch	24889
Tyler Heights, Br. Charleston	25312
Uler	25282
Uneeda	25205
Unger	25447
Union	24983
Upper Tract	26866
Upperglade	26266
Vadis	26445
Valley Bend	26293
Valley Chapel	26446
Valley Fork	25283
Valley Grove	26060
Valley Head	26294
Vallscreek	24890
Van	25206
Varney	25696
Verdunville	25649
Verner	25650
Vicars	25284
Victor	25938
Vienna, Br. Parkersburg	26101
Virginville	26061
Vivian	24891

Volga	26238
Vulcan	25697
Wadestown	26589
Waiteville	24984
Walker	26180
Walkersville	26447
Wallace	26448
Wallback	25285
Walton	25286
Wana	26590
Waneta	26295
War	24892
Excelsior, R. Sta.	24833
Wardensville	26851
Warriormine	24894
Warwood, Sta. Wheeling	26003
Washington (1st)	26181
Watson, Sta. Fairmont	26555
Waverly	26184
Wayne (1st)	25570
Wayside	24985
Webster Springs	26288
Weirton (1st)	26062
Welch (1st)	24801
Wellsburg (1st)	26070
Wendel	26450
West Columbia	25287
West Hamlin	25571
West Huntington, Sta. Huntington	25704
West Liberty	26074
West Logan, R. Br. Logan	25601
West Milford	26451
West Union	26456
Oxford, R. Br.	26414
Weston (1st)	26452
Westover, Br. Morgantown	26505
Wharncliffe	25651
Wharton	25208
Wheeling (1st)	26003
Whitby	25939
White Oak	25989
White Sulphur Springs (1st)	24986
Neola, R. Br.	24961
Whitesville	25209
Packsville, R. Br.	25151

Pettus, R. Br.	25153
Whitman	25652
Whitmer	26296
Whittaker	25210
Wick	26185
Widen	25211
Wikel	24990
Wilbur	26459
Wilcoe	24895
Wildcat	26460
Wiley Ford	26767
Wileyville	26186
Wilkinson	25653
Williams Mountain	25212
Williamsburg	24991
Williamson (1st)	25661
Williamstown	26187
Willis Branch, R. Br. Mount Hope	25880
Willow Bend	24992
Willow Island	26190
Wilsie	26641
Wilson	26768
Wilsonburg, R. Br. Clarksburg	26461
Wilsondale	25699
Winding Gulf	25941
Windsor Heights	26075
Winfield	25213
Winifrede	25214
Winona	25942
Wolf Pen	24896
Wolf Summit	26462
Wolfcreek	24993
Wolfe	24751
Woodville	25572
Worth	24897
Worthington	26591
Wyatt	26463
Wyco	25943
Wymer	26297
Wyoming	24898
Yawkey	25573
Yellow Spring	26865
Yolyn	25654
Yukon	24899

643

CHARLESTON　253

POST OFFICE BOXES

Box Nos.

1-54	Malden R Br	06
1-210	Sissonville Br	20
1-307	Port Amherst R. Sta	06
1-313	Main Office	21
20-77	Coal Fork R. Sta	06
42-1045	Rand Br	06
131-274	Tyler Heights Br	12
181-324	Chesapeake R Br	15
321-633	Main Office	22
401-888	Big Chimney R. Sta	02
621-953	Main Office	23
961-1233	Main Office	24
1241-1513	Main Office	25
1521-1793	Main Office	26
1801-2073	Main Office	27
2081-2393	Main Office	28
2401-2633	Main Office	29
2641-2993	Main Office	30
3001-3112	Main Office	31
3121-3232	Main Office	32
4001-4444	Kanawha City Sta	04
5001-5356	Capitol Sta	11
6001-6812	Stonewall Sta	02
8001-8767	South Charleston Br	03
9001-9457	Spring Hill Br	09
10001-10194	C Sta	12
15001-15216	Marmet Br	15

RURAL ROUTES

1	12
2	14
4,5	12
6	11
7	09

STATIONS, BRANCHES AND UNITS

Big Chimney Rural Br	02
Capitol Sta	11
Chesapeake Br	15
Cinco Rural Br	06
Coal Fork Rural Br	06
Kanawha City Sta	04
Malden Rural Br	06
Marmet Br	15
Port Amherst Rural Br	06
Rand Br	06
Sissonville Br	20
South Charleston Br	03
Spring Hill Br	09
Stonewall Br	02
Tyler Heights Br	12
General Delivery	01
Postmaster	01

APARTMENTS, HOTELS, MOTELS

Ambassador, 19 Bradford St	01
Argonne, 27 Ruffner Ave	11
Broadmoor, 1545 Lewis	11
Cavalier, 1316 Virginia St E	01
Charleston & Holiday Inn 02, 600 Kanawha Blvd E	01
Chateau, 24 Bradford	01
Daniel Boone, Capitol At Washington	28
Dupont, 170 Summers	01
Edgewater, 1330 Kanawha Blvd E	01
Fairfax Hall, 1317 Lee	01
Grant, 1012 Quarrier	01
Greenbrier Garden, 714 Canterbury Dr	14
Harding, 1201 Lee	01
Heart O'Town, Broad & Washington Sts	24
Holiday Inn 01, 2 Kanawha Blvd E	01
Holley, 1006 Quarrier	30
Imperial Towers, Round Hill Road	14
Kanawha Village, 3900 Mccorkle Ave	04
Lee Terrace, 1319 Lee St E	01
Madison Hall, 1317 Lee	01
Midtown Motel, 1316 Kanawha Blvd E	01
One Morris, 1 Morris	01
Regal, 1424 Kanawha Blvd E	01
Richmond, 105 Bradford	01
Riverview Terrace, 1108 Kanawha Blvd E	01
Sherwood, 1134 Lee	01
Town House, 1202 Kan Blvd E	01
Washington, 129 Summers	22
Worthy, 1018 Quarrier	01

BUILDINGS

Arcade, 710 Virginia St E	01
Atlas, 1031 Quarrier	01
Berman, 612 Virginia St E	01
Capitol City, 807 Quarrier	01
Charleston National Plaza	01
City Of Charleston, 501 Virginia St E	01
Commerce Square	
Courthouse, 407-09 Virginia St E	01
Davidson, 910 Quarrier	01
Day & Night, 710 Lee	01
Dominion, 804 Quarrier	01
Embleton, 922 Quarrier	01
Federal, 500 Quarrier	01
Kanawha Banking & Trust, 111 Capitol	
Kanawha County Library, 123 Capitol	01
Kanawha Valley, 300 Capitol	01
Knight, 901 Quarrier	01
L & S, 812 Quarrier	01
Masonic Temple, 820 Virginia E	01
May, 818 1/2 Quarrier	01
Medical Arts, 1021-25 Quarrier	01
Morrison, 815 Quarrier	01
National Bank Commerce Bldg	01
Nelson, 1018 Kanawha Blvd	

E	01
Noyes, 200 Broad	01
Odd Fellows, 717 Lee	01
Ott, Corner Dunbar & Quarr	01
Payne, 811 Lee	01
Peoples, 179 Summers	01
Professional, 1036 Quarrier	01
Security, 100 Capitol	01
Smallridge, 1013 Quarrier	01
State Capitol, 1800 Kanawha Blvd E	05
Terminal, 20 Capitol	01
Union, 723 Kanawha Blvd E	01
Y M C A, 311 Capitol	01
Y W C A, 1114 Quarrier	01

HOSPITALS

Charleston General, 1201 Elmwood Ave	25
Charleston Memorial, 3300 Noyes Ave SE	04
Ear & Eye Clinic, 1306 Kanawha Blvd	01
Herbert J Thomas Memorial, 4605 Mccorkle Ave SW	09
Highland, 56th & Noyes Ave SE	04
Kanawha Valley, 1014 Virginia St E	32
Mc Millan, Morris At Lee	32
Mountain State, 1301 Virginia St E	27
Saint Francis, 333 Laidley	01
Southern Hills, 30 Mc Corkle SW	03
Staats, 123 Washington St W	02

UNIVERSITIES AND COLLEGES

Morris Harvey College, 2300 Mccorkle Avenue, S.e	04

HUNTINGTON　257

POST OFFICE BOXES

Box Nos.

1-147	Huntington	06
151-299	Huntington	07
301-410	Huntington	08
411-510	Huntington	09
511-610	Huntington	10
611-760	Huntington	11
761-940	Huntington	12
941-1090	Huntington	13
1091-1270	Huntington	14
1271-1420	Huntington	15
1421-1600	Huntington	16
1601-1700	Huntington	17
1701-1800	Huntington	18
1801-1897	Huntington	19
1901-2070	Huntington	20
2081-2127	Huntington	21
2131-2187	Huntington	22
2201-2236	Huntington	23
2261-2396	Huntington	24
2401-2536	Huntington	25
3001-3199	Guyandotte Sta	02

5401-5587	Marshall University Sta.	03
8001-8158	Beverly Hills Sta.	05
9001-9519	West Huntington Sta.	04

RURAL ROUTES

1	01
2	02
3	01
4,5	04

STATIONS, BRANCHES AND UNITS

Beverly Hills Sta.	05
Guyandotte Sta.	02
Marshall University Sta.	03
West Huntington Sta.	04
General Delivery	01
Postmaster	01

APARTMENTS, HOTELS, MOTELS

Appollo, 749. 3rd	01
Arlington, 639 9th.	01
Ashworth, 1801 3rd Ave	03
Belford Village, 612 11th Ave	01
Bertram, 612 9th Ave. ..	01
Biggs, 1030 9th.	01
Biggs, 902 11th Ave.	01
Biltmore, 936 7th Ave.	07
Burgess, 1143 9th Ave.	01
Bush, 1011 6th Ave.	01
Cabell, 333 14th.	01
Clark, 912 6th.	01
College, 329 15th.	01
Conley, 1026 12th Ave.	01
Del-Mar, 1018 12th Ave.	01
Denning, 819 10th Ave.	01
Emmons Junior, 1209 3rd Ave	01
Emmons Senior, 1201 3rd Ave	01
Executive, 1020 9th Ave.	01
Fifth Ave, 901 5th Ave.	08
Frederick, 940 4th Ave.	16
Golden, 1300 Kanawha Ter.	01
Grace, 1029 10th.	01
Grace, 940 11th Ave.	01
Guthrie, 541 6th Ave.	01
Hamil, 815 10th Ave.	01
Harlan, 1134 9th Ave.	01
Holiday Inn, 3325 Route 60.	24
Holiday, 419 6th.	01
Huff, 535 4th Ave.	01
Huntington, 901 6th Ave.	01
Keister, 603 Trenton Pl.	01
Kenmore, 410 12th.	01
La Salle, 1024 8th.	01
Malone, 625 6th Ave.	01
Marcum Terrace Housing Development, Olive St & St Louis.	05
Milner, 4th Ave & 7th.	01
Morgan, 640 9th Ave.	01
Mossman, 1239 Charleston Ave.	01

Northcott Court Housing Development, Doulton Ave & 16th.	01
Pack, 932 9th Ave.	01
Park Lane, 1028 8th.	01
Park Terrace, 1320 12th.	01
Parkview, 726 13th Ave.	01
Patrician, 839 9th Ave.	01
Powell, 930 11th Ave.	01
Price, 2823 Collis Ave.	02
Prichard, 9th St & 6th Ave.	22
Ritter Park, 938 13th Ave.	01
Roxen, 1001 11th Ave.	01
Southworth, 928 9th Ave.	01
Stone Lodge, 5600 Route 60.	13
Summers, 1112 9th.	01
Summers, 901 11th Ave.	01
Tomkies, 1231 10th Ave.	01
Tourist, 343 Washington Ave.	01
Traymore, 339 6th Ave.	01
Traymore, 612 Trenton Pl.	01
University, 329 16th.	01
Uptowne Arms, 1342-44 4th Ave	01
Uptowner Motel, 1415 4th Ave.	22
Virginia, 427 7th.	01
Vison, 1122 13th.	01
Washington Arms, 963 Washington Ave.	04
Washington Square Housing Development, 8th Ave & 16th.	03
Wheeler, 1145 9th Ave.	01

BUILDINGS

C & O, 407 11th.	01
Chafin, 517 9th.	01
Federal, 502 8th.	01
Fifth Ave, 824 5th Ave.	01
First Huntington National Bank, 10th St & 4th Ave.	01
Guaranty National Bank, 919 5th Ave.	10
Huntington State Hospital, 1530 Norway Ave.	09
Huntington Trust & Savings Bank, 1050 4th Ave.	21
Twentieth Street Bank, 1956 3rd Ave.	03
West Virginia, 912 4th Ave.	01

GOVERNMENT OFFICES

Cabell County Court House, 5th Ave & 8th.	01
City Hall, 802 5th Ave.	17
United States Courthouse, 5th Ave & 9th.	01
United States Post Office, 5th Ave & 9th.	01

HOSPITALS

Cabell-Huntington, 1340 16th.	01
Guthrie, 6th Ave & 6th.	01
Huntington Hospital Inc, 1230 6th Ave.	19

Ave.	01
Saint Marys, 2900 1st Ave.	01
Veterans Administration, 1540 Spring Valty Dr.	01

UNIVERSITIES AND COLLEGES

Marshall University, 4th Ave & 16th.	01

WISCONSIN
(Abbreviation: WI)

Abbotsford 54405
Abrams 54101
Adams 53910
Adell 53001
Afton 53501
Albany 53502
Algoma (1st) 54201
Allenton 53002
Alma 54610
Alma Center 54611
Almena 54805
Almond 54909
Altoona 54720
Alvin, R. Br. Iron River, M I...49936
Amberg 54102
Amery (1st) 54001
Amherst 54406
Amherst Junction 54407
Aniwa 54408
Antigo (1st) 54409
   Phlox, R. Br. 54464
Appleton (1st) 54911
Arbor Vitae 54510
Arcadia 54612
Arena 53503
Argonne 54511
   Hiles, R. Br. 54533
Argyle 53504
Arkansaw 54721
Arkdale 54613
Arlington 53911
Armstrong Creek 54103
Arpin 54410
Ashippun 53003
Ashland (1st) 54806
Ashwaubenon, Br. Green
   Bay 54304
Astico 53912
Athelstane 54104
Athens 54411
Auburndale 54412
Augusta 54722
Auroraville 54920
Avalon 53505
Avoca 53506
Babcock 54413
Bagley 53801
Baileys Harbor 54202
Baldwin 54002
Balsam Lake 54810
Bancroft 54921
Bangor 54614
Baraboo (1st) 53913
Barneveld 53507
Barron (1st) 54812
Barronett 54813
Barton, Sta. West Bend ...53095
Bassett 53101
Bay City 54723
Bay View, Sta. Milwaukee ...53207
Bayfield 54814
Bear Creek 54922
Beaver 54105
Beaver Dam (1st) 53916
Beetown 53802
Beldenville 54003
Belgium (1st) 53004
Belleville 53508
Belmont 53510
Beloit (1st) 53511

Benet Lake, R. Br. Trevor ...53102
Bennett 54815
Benoit 54816
Benton 53803
Berlin (1st) 54923
Big Bend 53103
Bug Falls 54926
Billings Park, Sta. Superior ...54880
Birchwood 54817
Birnamwood 54414
Black Creek 54106
Black Earth 53515
Black River Falls (1st) ...54615
Blair 54616
Blanchardville 53516
Blenker 54415
Bloom City 54617
Bloomer 54724
Bloomington 53804
Blue Mounds 53517
Blue River 53518
Bonduel 54107
   Navarino, R. Br. 54108
Boscobel 53805
Boulder Junction 54512
Bowler 54416
Boyceville 54725
Boyd 54726
Bradley, Sta. Milwaukee (see
   appendix)
Branch 54203
Brandon 53919
Brantwood 54513
Briggsville 53920
Brill 54818
Brillion (1st) 54110
Bristol 53104
Brodhead (1st) 53520
Brokaw 54417
Brookfield (1st) 53005
Brooklyn 53521
Brooks 53921
Brookwood, Sta. Madison
   (see appendix)
Brown Deer, Br. Milwaukee
   (see appendix)
Brownsville 53006
Browntown 53522
Bruce 54819
Brule 54820
Brussels 54204
Bryant 54418
Burkhardt, R. Br. Hudson ...54016
Burlington (1st) 53105
Burnett 53922
Butler (1st) 53007
Butte Des Morts 54927
Butternut 54514
Byron 53009
Cable 54821
Cadott 54727
Caledonia 53108
Cambria 53923
Cambridge 53523
Cameron 54822
Camp Douglas 54618
Camp Lake 53109
Campbellsport 53010
Canton 54823
Caroline 54928
Carrollville, Sta. Oak Creek...53154
Cascade 53011
Casco 54205

Cashton 54619
Cassville 53806
Cataract 54620
Catawba 54515
Cato 54206
Cavour 54516
Cazenovia 53924
Cecil 54111
Cedar Grove 53013
Cedarburg (1st) 53012
Center Valley, R. Br. Black
   Creek 54106
Centuria 54824
Chaseburg 54621
Chelsea 54419
Chetek 54728
Chili 54420
Chilton (1st) 53014
Chippewa Falls (1st) 54729
City Point, R. Br. Pittsville ...54466
Clam Falls, R. Br. Frederic ...54825
Clam Lake 54517
Clayton 54004
Clear Lake 54005
Clearwater Lake 54518
Cleveland 53015
Clinton 53525
Clintonville (1st) 54929
Clyman 53016
Cobb 53526
Cochrane 54622
Colby 54421
Coleman 54112
Colfax 54730
Colgate 53017
Collins 54207
Coloma 54930
Columbus (1st) 53925
Combined Locks 54113
Comstock 54826
Conover 54519
Conrath 54731
Coon Valley 54623
Cornell 54732
Cornucopia 54827
Cottage Grove 53527
Couderay 54828
Crandon 54520
Crivitz 54114
Cross Plains 53528
Cuba City 53807
Cudahy (1st) 53110
Cumberland 54829
Curtiss 54422
Cushing 54006
Custer 54423
Dairyland, R. Br. Danbury ...54830
Dale 54931
Dallas 54733
Dalton 53926
Danbury 54830
   Dairyland, R. Br. 54830
   Webb Lake, R. Br. 54892
Dane 53529
Darien 53114
Darlington 53530
De Forest (1st) 53532
De Pere (1st) 54115
De Soto 54624
Deer Park 54007
Deerbrook 54424
Deerfield 53531
Delafield 53018

Delavan (1st) 53115
Dellwood, R. Br. Friendship ... 53927
Denmark 54208
Deronda 54008
Dickeyville 53808
Dodge 54625
Dodgeville (1st) 53533
Dorchester 54425
Dousman 53118
Downing 54734
Downsville 54735
Doylestown 53928
Dresser 54009
Drummond 54832
Dunbar 54119
Durand 54736
Eagle 53119
Eagle River (1st) 54521
Earl 54833
East Ellsworth, Br.
  Ellsworth 54011
East End, Sta. Superior 54880
East Side, Sta. Madison (see
  appendix)
East Troy (1st) 53120
Eastman 54626
Eau Claire (1st) 54701
Eau Galle 54737
Eden 53019
Edgar 54426
Edgerton (1st) 53534
Edgewater 54834
Edmund 53535
Egg Harbor 54209
Eland 54427
Elcho 54428
Elderon 54429
Eldorado 54932
Eleva 54738
Elk Mound 54739
Elkhart Lake 53020
Elkhorn (1st) 53121
Ellison Bay 54210
Ellsworth 54011
Elm Grove (1st) 53122
Elmwood 54740
Elroy 53929
Elton 54430
Embarrass 54933
Emerald 54012
Endeavor 53930
Ephraim 54211
Ettrick 54627
Eureka 54934
Evansville (1st) 53536
Exeland 54835
Fair Water 53931
Fairchild 54741
Fairview, Br. Milwaukee (see
  appendix)
Fall Creek 54742
Fall River 53932
Federal, Sta. Milwaukee 53202
Fence 54120
Fennimore 53809
Fenwood 54431
Ferryville 54628
Fifield 54524
Fish Creek 54212
Florence 54121
Fond du Lac (1st) 54935
Fontana 53125
Footville 53537

Forest Junction 54123
Forestville 54213
Fort Atkinson (1st) 53538
Fountain City 54629
Fox Lake 53933
Fox Point, Br. Milwaukee 53217
Foxboro 54836
Francis Creek 54214
Franklin, R. Br. Hales
  Corners 53132
Franksville 53126
Fred John, Sta. Milwaukee
  (see appendix)
Frederic 54837
  Clam Falls, R. Br. 54825
Fredonia 53021
Freedom, R. Br. Kaukauna 54131
Fremont 54940
French Island, Br. La
  Crosse 54601
Friendship 53934
  Dellwood, R. Br. 53927
Friesland 53935
Galesville 54630
Galloway 54432
Gays Mills 54631
Genesee Depot 53127
Genoa 54632
Genoa City 53128
Germantown 53022
Gile 54525
Gillett 54124
Gillingham 54633
Gilman 54433
  Jump River, R. Br. 54434
Gilmanton 54743
Gleason 54435
Glen Flora 54526
Glen Haven 53810
Glenbeulah 53023
Glenwood City 54013
Glidden 54527
Goodman 54125
Gordon 54838
Gotham 53540
Grafton (1st) 53024
Grand Marsh 53936
Grand View 54839
Granton 54436
Grantsburg 54840
Gratiot 53541
GREEN BAY (1st) (see
  appendix)
Greer Lake (1st) 54941
Green Valley 54127
Greenbush 53026
Greendale (1st) 53129
Greenfield, Br. Milwaukee
  (see appendix)
Greenleaf 54126
Greenville 54942
Greenwood 54437
Gresham 54128
Gurney 54528
Hager City 54014
Hales Corners (1st) 53130
  Franklin, R. Br. 53132
Hamburg 54438
Hammond 54015
Hampton, Sta. Milwaukee
  (see appendix)
Hancock 54943
Hannibal 54439

Hanover 53542
Harbor, Sta. Milwaukee 53204
Harshaw 54529
Hartford (1st) 53027
Hartland (1st) 53029
Hatley 54440
Haugen 54841
Haven 53030
Hawkins 54530
Hawthorne 54842
Hayward (1st) 54843
Hazel Green 53811
Hazelhurst 54531
Heafford Junction 54532
Helenville 53137
Herbster 54844
Hertel 54845
Hewitt 54441
High Bridge 54846
Highland 53543
Hilbert 54129
Hiles, R. Br. Argonne 54533
Hilldale, Sta. Madison (see
  appendix)
Hillpoint 53937
Hillsboro 54634
Hillsdale 54744
Hilltop, Sta. Milwaukee (see
  appendix)
Hingham 53031
Hixton 54635
Holcombe 54745
Hollandale 53544
Holmen 54636
Honey Creek 53138
Horicon (1st) 53032
Hortonville 54944
Howard, Br. Green Bay 54303
Howards Grove - Millersville,
  R. Br. Sheboygan 53081
Hubertus 53033
Hudson (1st) 54016
Humbird 54746
Hurley 54534
Hustisford 53034
Hustler 54637
Independence 54747
Ingram 54535
Iola 54945
Irma 54442
Iron Belt 54536
Iron Ridge 53035
Iron River 54847
Ironton 53938
Itasca, Sta. Superior 54880
Ixonia 53036
Jackson 53037
Janesville (1st) 53545
Jefferson (1st) 53549
Jim Falls 54748
Johnson Creek 53038
Juda 53550
Jump River, R. Br. Gilman 54434
Junction City 54443
Juneau 53039
Kansasville 53139
Kaukauna (1st) 54130
  Freedom, R. Br. 54131
Kellnersville 54215
Kempster 54444
Kendall 54638
Kennan 54537
Kenosha (1st) 53140

Keshena	54135
Kewaskum (1st)	53040
Kewaunee (1st)	54216
Kiel (1st)	53042
Kieler	53812
Kimberly	54136
King	54946
Kingston	53939
Knapp	54749
Knowles	53043
Kohler (1st)	53044
Krakow	54137
La Crosse (1st)	54601
La Farge	54639
La Pointe	54850
La Valle	53941
La Verne Dilweg, Sta. Green Bay	54303
Lac Du Flambeau	54538
Ladysmith (1st)	54848
Lake Delton	53940
Lake Geneva (1st)	53147
Lake Mills (1st)	53551
Lake Nebagamon	54849
Lake Tomahawk	54539
Lakewood	54138
Lancaster (1st)	53813
Land O Lakes	54540
Lannon	53046
Laona	54541
Larsen	54947
Layton Park, Sta. Milwaukee (see appendix)	
Lebanon	53047
Lena	54139
Leopolis	54948
Lewis	54851
Lily	54445
Limeridge	53942
Linden	53553
Little Chute	54140
Little Suamico	54141
Livingston	53554
Lodi	53555
Loganville	53943
Lomira	53048
Lone Rock	53556
Long Lake	54542
Loomis, R. Br. Peshtigo	54158
Loretta	54852
Lowell	53557
Loyal	54446
Lublin	54447
Luck	54853
Luxemburg	54217
Lyndon Station	53944
Lynxville	54640
Lyons	53148
MADISON (1st) (see appendix)	
Maiden Rock	54750
Malone	53049
Manawa	54949
Manchester	53945
Manitowish Waters Winchester, R. Br.	54545 54567
Manitowoc (1st)	54220
Maple	54854
Maplewood	54226
Marathon	54448
Marengo	54855
Maribel	54227
Marinette (1st)	54143

Marion	54950
Markesan	53946
Marquette	53947
Marshall	53559
Marshfield (1st)	54449
Mason	54856
Mather	54641
Mattoon	54450
Mauston (1st)	53948
Mayfair, Br. Milwaukee	53226
Mayville (1st)	53050
Mazomanie	53560
Mc Farland	53558
Mc Naughton	54543
Medford (1st)	54451
Mellen	54546
Melrose	54642
Melvina, R. Br. Cashton	54619
Menasha (1st)	54952
Menekaunee, Sta. Marinette	54143
Menomonee Falls (1st)	53051
Menomonie (1st)	54751
Mequon, Br. Thiensville	53092
Mercer	54547
Merrill (1st)	54452
Merrillan	54754
Merrimac	53561
Merton	53056
Mid City, Sta. Milwaukee	53208
Middle Inlet	54148
Middleton, Br. Madison	53562
Midway, Br. Green Bay	54301
Mikana	54857
Milan	54453
Milladore	54454
Millston	54643
Milltown	54858
Milton	53563
Milton Junction	53564
MILWAUKEE (1st) (see appendix)	
Mindoro	54644
Mineral Point	53565
Minocqua (1st)	54548
Minong	54859
Mishicot	54228
Mondovi	54755
Monico	54549
Monona, Br. Madison	53716
Monroe (1st)	53566
Montello	53949
Montfort	53569
Monticello	53570
Montreal	54550
Morrisonville	53571
Mosinee	54455
Mount Calvary	53057
Mount Hope	53816
Mount Horeb	53572
Mount Sterling	54645
Mountain	54149
Mukwonago	53149
Muscoda	53573
Muskego	53150
Nashotah	53058
Navarino, R. Br. Bonduel	54108
Necedah	54646
Neenah (1st)	54956
Neillsville (1st)	54456
Nekoosa	54457
Nelson	54756
Nelsonville	54458
Neopit	54150

Neosho	53059
Neshkoro	54960
New Auburn	54757
New Franken	54229
New Glarus	53574
New Holstein (1st)	53061
New Lisbon	53950
New London (1st)	54961
New Munster	53152
New Richmond (1st)	54017
Newald	54551
Newburg	53060
Newton	53063
Niagara	54151
Nichols	54152
North Fond Du Lac, Br. Fond du Lac	54935
North Freedom	53951
North Lake	53064
North Prairie	53153
Northfield, R. Br. Hixton	54635
Northside, Sta. La Crosse	54601
Norwalk	54648
Oak Creek (1st)	53154
Oakdale	54649
Oakfield	53065
Oconomowoc (1st)	53066
Oconto (1st)	54153
Oconto Falls	54154
Odanah	54861
Ogdensburg	54962
Ogema	54459
Ojibwa	54862
Okauchee	53069
Omro	54963
Onalaska (1st)	54650
Oneida	54155
Ontario	54651
Oostburg	53070
Oregon	53575
Orfordville	53576
Osceola	54020
Oshkosh (1st)	54901
Osseo	54758
Owen	54460
Oxford	53952
Packwaukee	53953
Palmyra	53156
Pardeeville	53954
Park Falls (1st)	54552
Parklawn, Sta. Milwaukee	53216
Patch Grove	53817
Pearson	54462
Peebles	53071
Pelican Lake	54463
Pell Lake	53157
Pembine	54156
Pence	54553
Pepin	54759
Peshtigo, Loomis, R. Br.	54157 54158
Pewaukee (1st)	53072
Phelps	54554
Phillips	54555
Phlox, R. Br. Antigo	54464
Pickerel	54465
Pickett	54364
Pigeon Falls	54760
Pine River	54965
Pittsville	54466
Plain	53577
Plainfield	54966
Platteville (1st)	53818

Pleasant Prairie.................53158
Plover...............................54467
Plum City..........................54761
Plymouth (1st)...................53073
Polar, R. Br. Bryant..........54418
Poplar..............................54864
Port Edwards (1st)............54469
Port Washington (1st)........53074
Port Wing..........................54865
Portage (1st).....................53901
Porterfield........................54159
Poskin..............................54866
Potosi...............................53820
Potter...............................54160
Pound...............................54161
Powers Lake.....................53159
Poy Sippi..........................54967
Poynette...........................53955
Prairie Du Chien (1st)........53821
Prairie Du Sac...................53578
Prairie Farm......................54762
Preble, Sta. Green Bay......54302
Prentice............................54556
Prescott............................54021
Presque Isle......................54557
Princeton..........................54968
Pulaski (1st)......................54162
Pulcifer.............................54164
RACINE (1st) (see appendix)
Radisson...........................54867
Randolph (1st)...................53956
Random Lake....................53075
Readfield..........................54969
Readstown........................54652
Redgranite.........................54970
Reedsburg (1st).................53959
Reedsville.........................54230
Reeseville..........................53579
Rewey..............................53580
Rhinelander (1st)...............54501
Rib Lake...........................54470
Rice Lake (1st)..................54868
Richfield...........................53076
Richland Center (1st).........53581
Ridgeland..........................54763
Ridgeway..........................53582
Ringle...............................54471
Rio...................................53960
Rio Creek.........................54231
Riplinger, R. Br. Spencer....54472
Ripon (1st)........................54971
River Falls (1st).................54022
Roberts.............................54023
Rochester..........................53167
Rock Falls.........................54764
Rock Springs.....................53961
Rockfield...........................53077
Rockland...........................54653
Rosendale.........................54974
Rosholt.............................54473
Rothschild.........................54474
Royalton...........................54975
Rubicon............................53078
Rudolph............................54475
Saint Cloud.......................53079
Saint Croix Falls................54024
Saint Germain....................54558
Saint Nazianz....................54232
Salem...............................53168
Salvatorian Center, Sta. New
  Holstein........................53061
Sand Creek........................54765
Sarona..............................54870

Sauk City..........................53583
Saukville...........................53080
Saxeville...........................54976
Saxon...............................54559
Sayner..............................54560
Scandinavia.......................54977
Schofield (1st)....................54476
Seneca..............................54654
Sextonville........................53584
Seymour............................54165
Sharon..............................53585
Shawano (1st)....................54166
Sheboygan (1st).................53081
Sheboygan Falls (1st)..........53085
Sheldon.............................54766
Shell Lake.........................54871
Sheridan............................54477
Sherwood..........................54169
Shiocton............................54170
Shorewood, Br. Milwaukee..53211
Shullsburg.........................53586
Silver Lake........................53170
Sinsinawa..........................53824
Siren................................54872
Sister Bay..........................54234
Slinger.............................53086
Sobieski............................54171
Soldiers Grove....................54655
Solon Springs.....................54873
Somers..............................53171
Somerset............................54025
South Byron.......................53087
South Milwaukee (1st).........53172
South Range.......................54874
South Wayne......................53587
Sparta (1st).......................54656
Spencer.............................54479
  Riplinger, R. Br............54472
Spooner (1st).....................54801
Spring Green......................53588
Spring Valley......................54767
Springbrook........................54875
Springfield.........................53176
Stanley..............................54768
Star Prairie........................54026
Starlake.............................54561
State Street, Sta. Racine.....53404
Stetsonville........................54480
Steuben.............................54657
Stevens Point (1st).............54481
Stiles................................54172
Stitzer..............................53825
Stockbridge........................53088
Stockholm..........................54769
Stoddard............................54658
Stone Lake........................54876
Stoughton (1st)..................53589
Stratford............................54484
Strum...............................54770
Sturgeon Bay (1st).............54235
Sturtevant..........................53177
Suamico............................54173
Sullivan.............................53178
Summit Lake......................54485
Sun Prairie (1st)................53590
Superior (1st).....................54880
Suring...............................54174
Sussex..............................53089
Taycheedah........................53090
Taylor...............................54659
Teutonia, Sta. Milwaukee....53206
Theresa.............................53091
Thiensville (1st)..................53092

Thorp (1st)........................54771
Three Lakes.......................54562
Tiffany..............................53592
Tigerton............................54486
Tilleda..............................54978
Tisch Mills.........................54240
Tomah (1st).......................54660
Tomahawk (1st)..................54487
Tony.................................54563
Townsend...........................54175
Trego................................54888
Trempealeau.......................54651
Trevor...............................53179
  Benet Lake, R. Br.........53102
Tri City, Sta. Oak Creek......53154
Tripoli..............................54564
Troy Center........................53180
Tunnel City.........................54662
Turtle Lake.........................54889
Twin Lakes.........................53181
Two Rivers (1st).................54241
Underhill............................54176
Union Center......................53962
Union Grove (1st)...............53182
Unity................................54488
University, Sta. Madison.......53715
Upper Third Street, Sta.
  Milwaukee.....................53212
Upson...............................54565
Uptown, Sta. Racine...........53403
Valders..............................54245
Valley Fair, Br. Appleton.....54911
Vandyne............................54979
Verona, Br. Madison...........53593
Vesper..............................54489
Veterans Administration
  Hosp. Sta. Madison.......53705
Victory, R. Br. De Soto........54663
Villard, Sta. Milwaukee........53209
Viola.................................54664
Viroqua (1st)......................54665
Wabeno.............................54566
Waldo...............................53093
Wales................................53183
Walworth (1st)....................53184
Warrens.............................54666
Wascott.............................54890
Washburn...........................54891
Washington Island..............54246
Waterford...........................53185
Waterloo (1st).....................53594
Watertown (1st)..................53094
Waubeka, R. Br. Fredonia...53021
Waukau.............................54980
Waukesha (1st)...................53186
Waumandee, R. Br.
  Cochrane.......................54622
Waunakee..........................53597
Waupaca (1st)....................54981
Waupun (1st).....................53963
Wausau (1st)......................54401
Wausaukee.........................54177
Wautoma...........................54982
Wauwatosa, Br. Milwaukee
  (see appendix)
Wauzeka.............................53826
Wayside, R. Br. Greenleaf...54126
Webb Lake, R. Br. Danbury..54892
Webster.............................54893
Wentworth..........................54894
West Allis, Br. Milwaukee.....53214
West Bend (1st)..................53095
West De Pere, Sta. De Pere..54115

West Lima	54668
West Racine, Sta. Racine (see appendix)	
West Salem	54669
Westboro	54490
Westby	54667
Western, Sta. Milwaukee	53210
Westfield	53964
Weyauwega	54983
Weyerhauser	54895
Wheeler	54772
White Lake	54491
Whitefish Bay, Br. Milwaukee	53217
Whitehall	54773
Whitelaw	54247
Whitewater (1st)	53190
Whittlesey	54492
Wild Rose	54984
Willard	54493
Williams Bay	53191
Wilmot (1st)	53192
Wilson	54027
Wilton	54670
Winchester, R. Br. Manitowish Waters	54567
Wind Lake, Br. Waterford	53185
Windsor	53598
Winnebago	54985
Winneconne	54986
Winter	54896
Wisconsin Dells (1st)	53965
Wisconsin Rapids (1st)	54494
Withee	54498
Wittenberg	54499
Wonewoc	53968
Wood	53193
Woodford	53599
Woodland	53099
Woodman	53827
Woodruff	54568
Woodville	54028
Woodworth	53194
Wrightstown	54180
Wyeville	54671
Wyocena	53969
Yuba	54672
Zachow	54182
Zenda	53195

GREEN BAY   543

POST OFFICE BOXES

Box Nos.

1-1572	Main Office	05
2001-2524	A Sta	06
3001-3999	Dilweg	03

RURAL ROUTES

1,2,3	01
4,5	03
6	01
7	03
8	01
9,10	03

STATIONS, BRANCHES AND UNITS

Ashwaubenon Br	04
Howard Br	03
La Verne Dilweg Sta	03
Midway Br	01
Preble Sta	05
General Delivery	02
Postmaster	05

APARTMENTS, HOTELS, MOTELS

Arena Motel, 871 Highland Ave	04
Bay Motel, Military Ave	04
Beaumont Inn, 406 N Washington	05
Downtowner Motel, 321 S Washington	01
Gladstone, 1529 W Mason	03
Hi-Way 141 Motel, 217 N Main Blvd	02
Holiday Inn Of Green Bay, Route 7	05
Imperial 400, 119 N Monroe	01
Midway Motor Lodge, 780 Packer Dr	04
North Star Motel, 1111 N Military	03
Northland, 304 N Adams	05
Packer City Motel, R 3	03
Skylit Motel, 565 W Morris	04
Valley Motel, 116 N Military	0

BUILDINGS

Bellin, 130 E Walnut	01
Columbus, 414 E Walnut	01
Federal, 325 E Walnut	01
Minahan, 205 E Walnut	01
Nicolet, 225 N Adams	01
Northern, 305 E Walnut	01
Sheridan, 226 N Washington	01

GOVERNMENT OFFICES

Brown County Courthouse Annex, 306 E Walnut	01
Brown County Courthouse, 100 S Jefferson	01

HOSPITALS

Bellin Hospital, 744 S	

Webster Ave	01
Brown County Hospital, Route 6	01
Saint Marys Hospital, 1726 Shawano Ave	03
Saint Vincents Hospital, 835 S Van Buren	05

MADISON   537

POST OFFICE BOXES

Box Nos.

1-2999	Main Office	01
3000-3999	East Side Sta	04
4000-4999	Brookwood Sta	11
5000-5999	Hilldale Sta	05
6000-6999	Monona Br	16

RURAL ROUTES

1	04
2,3,4	11
5	04

STATIONS, BRANCHES AND UNITS

Brookwood Sta	11
East Side Sta	04
Hilldale Sta	05
Monona Br	16
Middleton Br	53562
University Sta	15
Verona Br	53593
Veterans Administration Hosp Sta	05
General Delivery	03
Postmaster	01

APARTMENTS, HOTELS, MOTELS

Aloha Inn, 3177 E Washington Ave	04
Ambassador, 522 N Pinckney	03
Bel Aire, 3351 W Beltine Hwy	13
Bellevue, 29 E Wilson	03
Capitol, 208 King St	01
Cardinal, 416 E Wilson	03
Carpenter, 222 S Carroll	03
Clarendon, 1620 Monroe	11
Claridge, 333 W Washington Ave	03
Eagle Heights	05
Edgewater, 666 Wisconsin Ave	01
Fess, 123 E Doty	01
Hamacher, 5101 University Ave	05
Holiday Inn No 1, 4402 E Washington Ave	04
Holiday Inn No 2, 6301 E Broadway	04
Howard Johnsons, 4838 E Washington Ave	04
Ivy Inn, 2355 University Ave	05
Kennedy Manor, 1 Langdon	03
Lake Shore, 122 E Gilman	03
Loraine, 123 W Washington Ave	01
Madison Inn, 601 Langdon	03
Madison Travelodge, 909 W Beltine Hwy	13

Madison, 4402 E Broadway	16
Mayflower, 2500 Perry St	13
Motel Royal, 705 Redland Dr	14
Park Tower, 4801 Sheboygan Ave	05
Park, 22 S Carroll	03
Quisling Towers, 1 E Gilman	03
Sands Motel, 2800 W Broadway	13
Sherman Terrace, 1601 Sherman Ave	04
Spences, 3575 E Washington Ave	04
Sterling, 901 W Beltine Hwy	13
Town Campus, 441 N Frances	03
Trails End, 99 W Beltine Hwy	13
Vikingtown, 4353 W Beltine Hwy	11
Washington, 636 W Washington Ave	03
Wilson, 522 E Wilson	03

BUILDINGS

Anchor, 25 W Main	03
Bank Of Madison, 1 W Main	03
City-County, 210 Monona Ave	09
Commercial State Bank, 102 State	03
First National Bank, 1 S Pinckney	03
Gay, 16 N Carroll	03
Hilldale State Bank, 401 N Segoe Rd	05
Insurance, 119 Monona Ave	03
Lake City Bank, 1202 N Sherman Ave	04
Memorial Union, 770 Langdon	06
Park Bank, 2401 S Park	13
State Capitol, Capitol Square	02
State Office, 1 W Wilson	02
State Office, 4802 Sheboygan Ave	02
Tenney, 110 E Main	03
United Bank & Trust	03
Westgate Bank, 670 S Whitney Way	11

HOSPITALS

Central Colony & Training School, 317 Knutson Dr	04
Madison General, 202 S Park	15
Mendota State Hospital, 301 Troy Dr	04
Methodist, 309 W Washington Ave	03
Morningside Sanatorium, 300 Femrite Dr	16
Saint Marys Hospital, 720 South Brooks	15
University Hospitals, 1300 University Ave	06
Veterans Administration Hospital, 2500 Overlook Ter	05
Wisconsin Neurological Foundation, 1954 E Washington Ave	04

UNIVERSITIES AND COLLEGES

Edgewood, 855 Woodrow	11
Madison Area Technical College, 211 N Carroll	03
Madison Business, 215 W Washington Ave	03
University Of Wisconsin	06

MILWAUKEE   532

POST OFFICE BOXES

Box Nos.

1-2199	Main Office	01
2200-2399	Upper Third Street Sta	12
2400-2699	West Allis Br	14
2700-2899	Fairview Br	19
2900-3199	Hampton Sta	18
3200-3399	Mid-City Sta	08
3400-3599	Teutonia Sta	06
3600-3799	Whitefish Bay Br	17
3800-4099	Hilltop Sta	05
4100-4399	Western Sta	10
4400-4599	Bay View Sta	07
4600-4999	Layton Park Sta	15
5000-5399	Harbor Sta	04
5400-5699	Shorewood Br	11
5700-5999	Greenfield Br	20
6000-6499	Villard Sta	09
6500-6799	Parklawn Sta	16
6800-6999	Tuckaway Sta	21
7000-7499	Wauwatosa Br	13
7500-7699	Swan Sta	22
8000-8199	Bradley Sta	23
8200-8399	Fred John	25
8400-8599	Wauwatosa Br	26
8600-8799	Root River Br	27
23000-23999	Bradley Sta	23
90000-92199	Federal	02

RURAL ROUTES

1	23

STATIONS, BRANCHES AND UNITS

Bay View Sta	07
Bradley Sta	23
Brown Deer Br	09
Fairview Br	19
Federal Sta	02
Fox Point Br	17
Fred John Sta	25
Greenfield Br	20
Hampton Sta	18
Harbor Sta	04
Hilltop Sta	05
Layton Park Sta	15
Mayfair Br	26
Mid City Sta	08
Parklawn Sta	16
Shorewood Br	11
Teutonia Sta	06
Upper Third Street Sta	12
Villard Sta	09
Wauwatosa Br	13
West Allis Br	14
Western Sta	10

Whitefish Bay Br	17
General Delivery	01
Postmaster	03

APARTMENTS, HOTELS, MOTELS

Abbot Crest, 1226 W Wisconsin Ave	33
Ambassador, 2308 W Wisconsin Ave	33
Antlers, 616 N 2nd	03
Astor, 924 E Juneau Ave	02
Belmont, 751 N 4th	03
Biltmore Grand, 1343 W Wisconsin Ave	33
Continental Motel, 3001 W Wisconsin Ave	08
Cudahy Tower, 925 E Wells	02
Holiday Inn Of America Central, 1926 W. Wisconsin Ave	33
Holiday Inn Of America- Midtown, 2611 W. Wisconsin Ave	33
Milwaukee Inn, 916 E State	02
Pan American Motel, 3808 W Wisconsin Ave	08
Pfister, 424 E Wisconsin Ave	02
Plankinton, 609 N Plankinton Ave	03
Plaza, 1007 N Cass	02
Ramada Inn,633 W. Michigan St	03
Red Carpet Inn, 4747 S Howell Ave	07
Sheraton Schroeder, 509 W Wisconsin Ave	02
Shorecrest, 1962 N Prospect Ave	02
Stratford, 1404 W Wisconsin Ave	33
Towne, 723 N 3rd	03
Tyrolean Town House, 1673 S 108th	14
Wisconsin, 720 N 3rd	03
1028 Juneau	02

BUILDINGS

Badger Bus Depot, 635 N 7th	33
Greyhound Bus Depot, 606 N 7th	33
Marine Plaza, 111 E Wisconsin Ave	02
Union Depot, 433 W Saint Paul Ave	03
War Memorial, 730 N Lincoln Memorial Dr	02
1st Wisconsin National Bank, 735 N Water	02

GOVERNMENT OFFICES

City Hall, 200 E Wells	02
County Court House, 901 N 9th	33
Milwaukee County Airport, 5300 S Howell	07
Milwaukee Muncipal, 841 N Broadway	02
Milwaukee Safety, 822 W Kilbourn Ave	33

Post Office, 345 W. St. Paul Ave	03
Public Library, 814 W Wisconsin Ave	33

HOSPITALS

Columbia, 3321 N Maryland Ave	11
Deaconess, 620 N 19th	33
Doctors, 2711 W Wells	08
Emergency City, 1230 W Grant	15
Johnston Municipal, 1230 W Grant	15
Lakeview, 10010 W Blue Mound Rd	26
Lutheran Hospital Milwaukee, 2200 W Kilbourn Ave	33
Milwaukee Childrens, 1700 W Wisconsin Ave	33
Milwaukee County General, 8700 W Wisconsin Ave	26
Milwaukee Sanitarium, 1220 Dewey Ave	13
Mount Sinai, 948 N 12th	33
Nicolet, 1971 W. Capitol Dr	06
Northwest General, 5310 W Capitol Dr	16
Sacred Heart Rehabilitation, 1545 S Layton Blvd	15
Saint Anthonys, 1004 N 10th	33
Saint Camillus, 10100 W Bluemound Rd	26
Saint Francis, 3237 S 16th	15
Saint Josephs, 5000 W Chambers	10
Saint Lukes, 2900 W Oklahoma Ave	15
Saint Mary'S Hill, 1445 S 32nd	15
Saint Marys, 2320 N Lake Dr	11
Saint Michaels, 2400 W Villard Ave	09
West Allis Memorial, 8901 W Lincoln Ave	27

UNIVERSITIES AND COLLEGES

Alverno, 3401 S 39th	15
Cardinal Stritch, 6801 N Yates Rd	17
Concordia, 3126 W Kilborn Ave	08
Layton Art School, 1362 N Prospect Ave	02
Marquette University, 615 N 11th	33
Milwaukee School Of Engineering, 1025 N. Milwaukee	01
Mount Mary, 2900 N Menomonee River Pkwy	22
Saint Francis Seminary, 3257 S Lake Dr	07
University Of Wisconsin In Milwaukee, 3203 N Downer	01

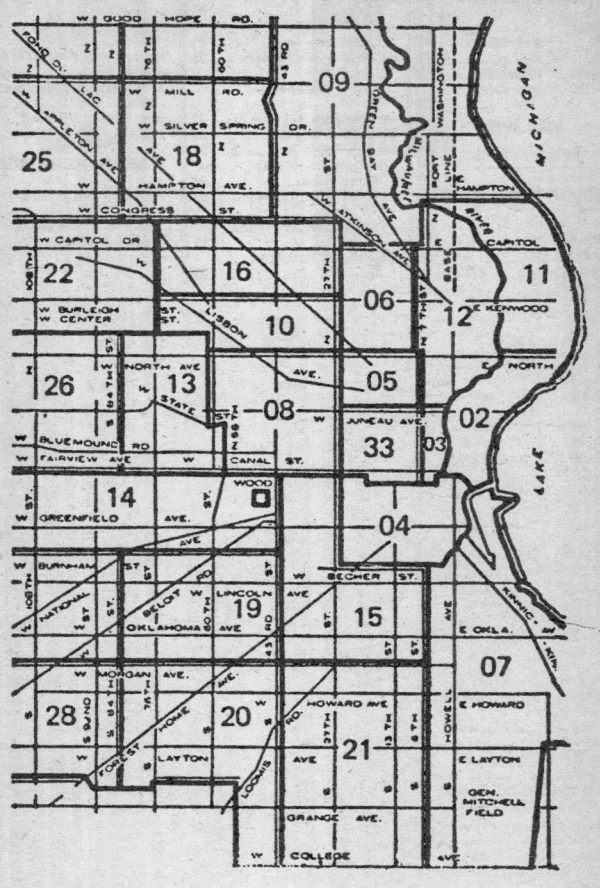

ZIP CODES
MILWAUKEE, Wisconsin
532 + two digits shown = zip code

RACINE   534

POST OFFICE BOXES

Box Nos.

1-799	Main Office	01
1-799	Racine	01
801-899	Uptown Sta	03
901-1199	West Racine Sta	05

RURAL ROUTES

1	02
2	03

STATIONS, BRANCHES AND UNITS

State Street Sta	04
Uptown Sta	03
West Racine Sta	05
General Delivery	01
Postmaster	01

APARTMENTS, HOTELS, MOTELS

Clayton House, 5005 Washington	06
Holiday Inn, 3700 Northwestern Ave	05
Racine Motor Inn, 535 Main	03

BUILDINGS

American Bank, 441 Main St.	03
Badger, 610 Main St	03
Baker, 523 Main St	03
First National Bank, 500 Wisconsin Ave	03
Main 1/2 Lake, 423 Main	03

GOVERNMENT OFFICES

City Hall, 730 Washington Ave	03

Court House, 730 Wisconsin Ave	03
Safety Bldg, 730 Center	03

HOSPITALS

Racine County Home, 2433 S Green Bay	06
Saint Lukes, 1320 Wisconsin Ave	03
Saint Marys, 1526 Grand Ave	03

UNIVERSITIES AND COLLEGES

Dominican College, 5915 Erie	02
Vocational & Adult School, 800 Center	03

WYOMING
(Abbreviation: WY)

Acme	82830
Afton	83110
Airport, Sta. Cheyenne	82001
Aladdin, R. Br. Sundance	82710
Albin	82050
Alcova	82620
Alpine, R. Br. Thayne	83127
Alva	82711
Arapahoe, R. Br. Riverton	82510
Arminto, R. Br. Casper	82630
Arvada	82831
Auburn	83111
Baggs	82321
Bairoil	82322
Banner	82832
Basin	82410
Bear Lodge, R. Br. Dayton	82836
Bedford, R. Br. Thayne	83112
Beulah	82712
Big Horn	82833
Big Piney	83113
Bill	82631
Bondurant	82922
Bosler	82051
Boulder	82923
Buffalo (1st)	82834
Saddlestring, R. Br.	82840
Buford	82052
Burlington	82411
Burns	82053
Burris	82511
Byron	82412
Canyon, Sta. Yellowstone National Park	82190
Carlile, R. Br. Moorcroft	82713
Carpenter	82054
Casper (1st)	82601
Arminto, R. Br.	82630
Hilltop, Sta.	82601
Shirley Basin, R. Br.	82601
Sunside, Sta.	82601
Centennial	82055
Cheyenne (1st)	82001
Chugwater	82210
Clearmont	82835
Cody (1st)	82414
Cokeville	83114
Colter Bay, R. Br. Jackson	83001
Cora	82925
Cowley	82420
Crowheart	82512
Daniel	83115
Dayton	82836
Deaver	82421
Devils Tower	82714
Diamondville	83116
Dixon	82323
Douglas	82633
Orin, R. Br.	82652
Dubois	82513
Dwyer	82211
Eden, R. Br. Rock Springs	82926
Edgerton	82635
Elk Mountain	82324
Emblem	82422
Encampment	82325
Ethete, R. Br. Lander	82520
Etna, R. Br. Thayne	83118
Evanston (1st)	82930

Evansville	82636
Fairview	83119
Farson	82932
Fishing Bridge, Sta. Yellowstone National Park	82190
Fort Bridger	82933
Fort Laramie	82212
Fort Washakie	82514
Four Corners, R. Br. Newcastle	82715
Foxpark, R. Br. Laramie	82057
Francis E Warren A F B, Br. Cheyenne	82001
Frannie	82423
Freedom	83120
Frontier	83121
Garland	82424
Garrett	82058
Gas Hills, R. Br. Riverton	82501
Gillette (1st)	82716
Glendo	82213
Glenrock	82637
Granger	82934
Granite Canon	82059
Grass Creek	82425
Green River (1st)	82935
Greybull	82426
Grover	83122
Guernsey	82214
Hamilton Dome	82427
Hanna	82327
Hartville	82215
Hawk Springs	82217
Hiland	82638
Hillsdale	82060
Hilltop, Sta. Casper	82601
Horse Creek	82061
Hudson	82515
Hulett	82720
Huntley	82218
Hyattville	82428
Iron Mountain	82062
Jackson (1st)	83001
Colter Bay, R. Br.	83001
Teton Village, R. Br.	83025
Jay Em	82219
Jeffrey City, R. Br. Rawlins	82310
Jelm, R. Br. Laramie	82063
Kaycee	82639
Keeline	82220
Kelly	83011
Kemmerer	83101
Kinnear	82516
Kirby, R. Br. Worland	82430
La Barge	83123
Lagrange	82221
Lamont	82328
Lance Creek	82222
Lander (1st)	82520
Laramie (1st)	82070
Foxpark, R. Br.	82057
Jelm, R. Br.	82063
University, Sta.	82075
Leiter	82837
Linch	82640
Lingle	82223
Little America	82929
Lonetree	82936
Lost Springs	82224
Lovell	82431

Lusk	82225
Lyman	82937
Lysite	82642
Manderson	82432
Manville	82227
Mc Fadden	82080
Mc Kinnon	82938
Medicine Bow	82329
Meeteetse	82433
Meriden	82081
Midwest	82643
Mills (1st)	82644
Moneta	82645
Moorcroft	82721
Carlile, R. Br.	82713
Moose	83012
Moran	83013
Morton	82522
Mountain View	82939
Natrona	82646
New Haven	82722
Newcastle (1st)	82701
Four Corners, R. Br.	82715
Node	82228
Number One, Sta. Cheyenne	82001
Old Faithful, Sta. Yellowstone National Park	82190
Opal	83124
Orin, R. Br. Douglas	82652
Osage	82723
Oshoto	82724
Otto	82434
Pahaska, R. Br. Cody	82414
Parkman	82838
Pavillion	82523
Pine Bluffs	82082
Pinedale	82941
Point of Rocks, R. Br. Rock Springs	82942
Powder River	82648
Powell (1st)	82435
Ralston	82440
Ranchester	82839
Rawlins (1st)	82301
Jeffrey City, R. Br.	82310
Recluse	82725
Reliance	82943
Riverton (1st)	82501
Arapahoe, R. Br.	82510
Gas Hills, R. Br.	82501
Sand Draw, R. Br.	82501
Robertson	82944
Rock River	82083
Rock Springs (1st)	82901
Eden, R. Br.	82926
Point of Rocks, R. Br.	82942
Rockypoint	82726
Rozet	82727
Ryan Park	82330
Saddlestring, R. Br. Buffalo	82840
Sage	83125
Saint Stephens	82524
Sand Draw, R. Br. Riverton	82501
Saratoga	82331
Savery	82332
Seminoe Dam	82333
Shawnee	82229
Shell	82441
Sheridan (1st)	82801
Shirley Basin, R. Br. Casper	82601
Shoshoni	82649

655

Sinclair	82334
Slater	82230
Smoot	83126
South Pass City, R. Br.	
Lander	82520
Story	82842
Sundance	82729
Aladdin, R. Br.	82710
Sunside, Sta. Casper	82601
Superior	82945
Ten Sleep	82442
Teton Village, R. Br.	
Jackson	83025
Thayne	83127
Alpine, R. Br.	83127

Bedford, R. Br.	83112
Etna, R. Br.	83118
Thermopolis (1st)	82443
Thumb, Sta. Yellowstone	
National Park	82190
Tie Siding	82084
Torrington (1st)	82240
Ulm, R. Br. Clearmont	82835
University, Sta. Laramie	82070
Upton	82730
Valley, R. Br. Cody	82414
Van Tassell	82242
Veteran	82243
Walcott	82335
Wamsutter	82336

Wapiti	82450
Weston	82731
Wheatland (1st)	82201
Wilson	83014
Wolf	82844
Worland (1st)	82401
Kirby, R. Br.	82430
Wyarno	82845
Yellowstone National Park	
(1st)	82190
Yoder	82244

CAROLINE ISLANDS

Post Office ZIP Code

Kanifay, R. Br. Yap, Caroline
　Islands..............................96943
Koror, Caroline Islands..........96940
Kusaie, Caroline Islands.........96944
Map, R. Br. Yap, Caroline
　Islands..............................96943
Metelanim, R. Br. Ponape,
　Caroline Islands..................96941
Ponape, Caroline Islands.......96941
Rumung, R. Br. Yap,
　Caroline Islands..................96943
Truk, Caroline Islands............96942
Uh, R. Br. Ponape, Caroline
　Islands..............................96941
Yap, Caroline Islands............96943

GUAM

Post Office ZIP Code

Agana, Guam (1st)................96910
Agat, Sta. Agana, Guam.........96910
Anderson A F B, Br. Agana,
　Guam................................96910
Barrigada, Sta. Agana,
　Guam................................96910
Inarjan, R. Sta. Agana,
　Guam................................96910
Merizo, R. Sta. Agana,
　Guam................................96910
Naval Air Station, Br.
　Agana, Guam.....................96910

Naval Station, Br. Agana,
　Guam................................96910
Santa Rita, Sta. Agana,
　Guam................................96910
Sinajana, Sta. Agana,
　Guam................................96910
Talofofo, R. Sta. Agana,
　Guam................................96910
Tamuning, Sta. Agana,
　Guam................................96910
Umatac, R. Sta. Agana,
　Guam................................96910
Yona, R. Sta. Agana, Guam ...96910

MARIANA ISLANDS

Post Office ZIP Code

Capitol Hill, R. Br. Saipan,
　Mariana Islands..................96950
Rota, Mariana Islands............96951
Saipan, Mariana Islands
　(1st).................................96950
San Jose Village, R. Br.
　Saipan, Mariana Islands......96950

MARSHALL ISLANDS

Eyebe, Marshall Islands.........96970
Majuro, Marshall Islands........96960

SAMOA

Post Office ZIP Code

Eastern District Samoa, Br.
　Pago Pago Samoa...............96920
Fitiuta, Br. Pago Pago
　Samoa...............................96799
Ofu-Manua Samoa, Br. Pago
　Pago Samoa........................96920
Ofosega Maua Samoa, Br.
　Pago Pago Samoa...............96920
Pago Pago Samoa (1st).........96799
Ta'U Manu'A, Br. Pago Pago
　Samoa...............................96799

VIRGIN ISLANDS

Post Office ZIP Code

Charlotte Amalie (1st)............00801
Christiansted (1st).................00820
Cruz Bay..............................00830
Downtown, Sta.
　Christiansted......................00820
Frederiksted (1st)..................00840
Kingshill..............................00850
Kronprindsens Gade, Sta.
　Kingshill............................00850
Kronprindsens Gade, Sta.
　Charlotte Amalie.................00801

WAKE

Wake, Wake Island................96798

Zip Codes Frequently Used

ADDRESS	ZIP CODE